WEBSTER'S

ENGLISH

LANGUAGE

DESK REFERENCE

WEBSTER'S
ENGLISH
LANGUAGE
DESK REFERENCE

THE ALL-IN-ONE DICTIONARY,
THESAURUS, VOCABULARY
BUILDER, AND GRAMMAR GUIDE

Second Edition
Revised and Expanded

GRAMERCY BOOKS
NEW YORK

This 2005 edition is published by Gramercy Books, an imprint of Random House Value Publishing, by arrangement with Random House Information Group, divisions of Random House, Inc., New York.

The Random House Living Dictionary Database™ is a trademark of Random House, Inc.

Trademarks
A number of entered words that we have reason to believe constitute trademarks have been designated as such. However, no attempt has been made to designate as trademarks or service marks all terms or words in which proprietary rights might exist. The inclusion, exclusion, or definition of a word or term is not intended to affect, or to express a judgment on, the validity of legal status of the word or term as a trademark, service mark, or other proprietary term.

Gramercy is a registered trademark and the colophon is a trademark of Random House, Inc.

Random House
New York • Toronto • London • Sydney • Auckland
www.randomhouse.com

Printed and bound in the United States

Previously published as *Random House Webster's English Language Desk Reference, Second Edition*.

Library of Congress Cataloging-in-Publication Data

[Random House Webster's English language desk reference]
Webster's English language desk reference : the all-in-one dictionary, thesaurus, vocabulary builder, and grammar guide.—2nd ed., rev. and expanded
p. cm.
Originally published: Random House Webster's English language desk reference. 2nd ed. New York : Random House, 1999.
Includes index.
ISBN 0-517-22434-8
1. English language—Grammar—Handbooks, manuals, etc. 2. English language—Synonyms and antonyms. 3. English language—Dictionaries. 4. Vocabulary. 5. Spellers.
PE1112.R28 2005
428—dc22
2004053921

10 9 8 7 6 5 4 3 2 1

Contents in Brief

Staff

Project Editor: Georgia S. Maas
Copyeditor: Robin Perlow
Proofreaders: Nancy Armstrong, Amy Touchette
Support staff: Geraldine Albert, Annette Apitz, Joel Levine, Amy Warner
Editorial Production Services: Jennifer Dowling, Seaside Press
Design: Leon Bolognese & Associates, Inc.
Database Associate: Diane M. João
Database Manager: Constance A. Baboukis
Production Editor: Joseph W. Sora
Director of Production: Patricia W. Ehresmann
Managing Editor: Andrew Ambraziejus
Editorial Director: Wendalyn Nichols
Associate Publisher: Page Edmunds
Publisher: Charles M. Levine

Contents

Part Three
Ready-Reference Guide   727

PART ONE

Guide
for
Writers

1

Mastering Grammar, Usage, and Punctuation

Grammar

One's ability to communicate ideas clearly and effectively depends on one's understanding of and familiarity with English grammar. Grammatical rules and terms help define the construction of our language and show us how to use words correctly in both written and spoken English.

Parts of Speech

The English language consists of nine basic classes of words, or parts of speech: **nouns, pronouns, verbs, adjectives, determiners, adverbs, prepositions, conjunctions,** and **interjections.**

Words often serve more than one grammatical function, depending on their position, meaning, and use in a sentence. Therefore, the same word can be a different part of speech in different sentences. For example, the word "help" can function as both a noun and a verb.

"Help" as a noun:
The offer of help *was greatly appreciated.*
(Here "help" is the name of something.)

"Help" as a verb:
They help *the community by volunteering their time to tutor illiterate adults.*
(Here "help" expresses an action.)

Since words can work in different ways, you must determine how the word is functioning within a sentence before you can label it as a specific part of speech. You cannot assume that any word will always be the same part of speech and fulfill the same grammatical function.

Words and phrases from different parts of speech often modify other words and phrases. For instance, an adjective modifies a noun by describing the noun (a *blue* hat). An adverb modifies an adjective, a verb, or another adverb by giving more specific information about it (a *light* blue hat; He spoke *quickly;* He spoke *very* quickly.)

Nouns

A *noun* is a word used to name a person, place, thing, idea, state, or quality.

Person	Place	Thing
Mary	library	flowers
Edward	Ontario	mutiny
American	coastline	computer
cousin	Paris	house
Mr. Jones	city	rabbit

Idea	State	Quality
democracy	hunger	integrity
equality	poverty	courage
Hinduism	happiness	sincerity
justice	rage	decency
evil	joy	bravery

Some of the nouns listed above can be further classified into specific types.

Common nouns name any of a class of people, places, or things:

girl
city
river
road

Proper nouns name specific people, places, and things:

Lisa
Vienna

Ohio River
Main Street

Collective nouns name groups of people or things:

team
clan
flock
tribe
pack
committee

Mass nouns name qualities or things that cannot be counted and do not have plural forms:

laughter
sand
valor
exhaustion
anger
wheat

Compound nouns are made up of two or more words. The words may be separate, hyphenated, or combined:

boarding pass
mother-in-law
housework
runaway
airport
schoolroom

Pronouns

A *pronoun* is a word that takes the place of a noun.

Ellen has been working on the project for a long time. She spends eight hours a day on it. Her time is well spent, however, as she herself recognizes.

Antecedents

An **antecedent** is the noun, phrase, clause, or sentence to which a pronoun refers. Use a singular pronoun to refer to a singular antecedent and a plural pronoun to refer to a plural antecedent. In the above example, the antecedent of the pronoun *she* is *Ellen;* the antecedent of the pronoun *it* is *project.*

Types of Pronouns

***Personal pronouns* refer to the one speaking, the one spoken to, or the one spoken about.** Personal pronouns that refer to the speaker are known as first-person pronouns; those that refer to the person spoken to are known as second-person pronouns; those that refer to the person, place, or thing spoken about are known as third-person pronouns.

Singular

First person	I	me	my, mine
Second person	you	you	your, yours
	he	him	his
Third person	she	her	her, hers
	it	it	its

Plural

First person	we	us	our, ours
Second person	you	you	your, yours
Third person	they	them	their, theirs

Both **intensive** and **reflexive** pronouns end in -*self* or -*selves.*

myself	ourselves
yourself	yourselves
himself	themselves
herself	
itself	

***Intensive pronouns* add emphasis to a noun or pronoun:**

I myself *have never given much thought to the matter.*
Mary hung the striped wallpaper herself.

***Reflexive pronouns* show that the subject of the sentence also receives the action of the verb:**

I treated myself *to a new pair of shoes.*
Michael kept telling himself *that it was not his fault.*

***Interrogative pronouns* are used to ask questions.** These pronouns do not have to have a specific antecedent.

which   what   who   whom   whose

What *did you call me for in the first place?*
Whom *have you called about this matter?*
Whose *is that?*

Relative pronouns are used to tie together or relate groups of words. Relative pronouns begin subordinate clauses (see page 49).

which   that   who   whom   whose

Debbie enrolled in the class that *her employer recommended.*
Charles has a friend who *lives in Toronto.*

Demonstrative pronouns are used to point out nouns, phrases, or clauses. They can be placed before or after their antecedents.

this   that   these   those

This *is the book I told you about last week.*
That *is a perfect place to sit down and have lunch.*
Is that *the house with the Japanese garden in the back yard?*

Indefinite pronouns take the place of a noun but do not have to have a specific antecedent. Following is a list of some common indefinite pronouns.

all	everything	none
another	few	nothing
any	little	one
anybody	many	other
anyone	more	others
anything	most	several
both	much	some
each	neither	somebody
either	no one	someone
everybody	nobody	something

Indefinite pronouns can have a specific antecedent, or no specific antecedent.

Specific antecedent
The casserole was so delicious that none was left by the end of the meal.
A few of the relatives usually lend a hand when my husband undertakes one of his home repair projects.

No specific antecedent:
> *Someone arrived at the party early, much to the embarrassment of the unprepared host and hostess.*
> *Everyone stayed late, too.*

Case

The majority of English words rely on their position within a sentence rather than their form to show their function. In most instances, the placement of a word determines whether it is a subject or object. Certain nouns and pronouns, however, change their form to indicate their use.

Case is the form of a noun or pronoun that shows how it is used and how it relates to other words in a sentence.

English has three cases: **nominative, objective,** and **possessive.** In general, pronouns take the nominative case when they function as the subject of a sentence or clause and the objective case when they function as the object of a verb or a preposition. Pronouns and nouns take the possessive case to indicate ownership.

Nouns change form only in the possessive case: for example, *a dog's book, Maria's hair.* Some pronouns, in contrast, change form in the nominative, objective, and possessive cases. The following table shows how personal pronouns change form in the three different cases.

Nominative	Objective	Possessive
I	*me*	*my, mine*
you	*you*	*your, yours*
he	*him*	*his*
she	*her*	*her, hers*
it	*it*	*its*
we	*us*	*our, ours*
you	*you*	*your, yours*
they	*them*	*their, theirs*

Nominative Case

The *nominative case* is sometimes called the "subjective case" because it is used when pronouns function as subjects. The following examples illustrate how personal pronouns are used in the nominative case.

Subject of a Verb

> *We understand that they will be late.*
> *Neither she nor I will be attending.*

Appositive Identifying a Subject

An **appositive** is a word or a phrase appearing next to a noun or pronoun that explains or identifies it and is equivalent to it:

Both physicists, Marie Curie and he, *worked on isolating radium*

Mr. Brown, our English teacher, *went on the class trip with us.*

Predicate Nominative

The *predicate nominative* is the noun or pronoun after a linking verb that renames the subject. The linking verb *to be* functions as an equals sign: the words on either side must be in the same case.

It is I.
The primary supervisor is she.
The fastest runners are Lenore *and* he.

Since the predicate nominative can sound overly formal in speech, many people use the colloquial: It's me. It's her. In formal speech and edited writing, however, the nominative forms are used: It must be he. The person at the door was she, not her husband. This is she. In some instances, revising the sentence can produce a less artificial sound.

Predicate nominative
The delegates who represented the community at last evening's town board meeting were he and I.

Revision
He and I *represented the community at last evening's town board meeting.*

Objective Case

The *objective case* is used when a personal pronoun is a direct object, indirect object, or object of a preposition.

Direct Object

Bob's jokes embarrassed me.
When you reach the station, call either him *or* me.

Indirect Object

The glaring sun gave my friends and me *a headache.*
My aunt brought us *pottery from Mexico.*
Please give him *some money.*

Object of a Preposition

The cat leaped onto the bed *and curled up beside* me.
They fully understood why she had come with us *rather than with* him.
Let's keep the understanding between you *and* me.

Case after *than* or *as*

If the word following *than* or *as* begins a clause, the pronoun takes the nominative case. If the word following *than* or *as* does not begin a clause, the pronoun takes the objective case. In some instances, the case depends on the meaning of the sentence. To help decide whether the sentence requires a pronoun in the nominative or objective case, complete the clause.

She has been working at Smithson longer than he *(has).*
Kevin is more proficient at marketing than I *(am).*
They are going to be informed as quickly as we *(are).*
I have stayed with Julia as long as she *(has stayed with her).*
I have stayed with Julia as long as her *(as I have stayed with her).*

Uses of *Who* and *Whom*

The form of the pronoun *who* depends on its function within a clause.

Subordinate Clauses and *who/whom*

In subordinate clauses, use *who* and *whoever* for all subjects, *whom* and *whomever* for all objects, regardless of whether the clause itself acts as a subject or object:

Distribute the food to whoever *needs it.*
(Since *whoever* is the subject of "needs," it is in the nominative case. The entire clause *whoever needs it* is the object of the preposition "to.")
We did not realize whom *the specialist had called.*
(Since *whom* is the object of "called," it is in the objective case.

The entire clause *whom the specialist had called* is the object of the verb "realize.")

Frederick is the lawyer whom *most people hire for this type of work.*

(Since *whom* is the object of "hire," it is in the objective case. The clause *whom most people hire for this type of work* modifies the noun "lawyer.")

She is the candidate who *everyone thinks will win.*

(Since *who* is the subject of "will win," it is in the nominative case. The clause *who everyone thinks will win* modifies the noun "candidate.")

There is only one doctor who *I know makes house calls.*

(Since *who* is the subject of "makes," it is in the nominative case. The clause *who makes house calls* modifies the noun "doctor.")

He will speak to whoever *will listen.*

(Since *whoever* is the subject of "will listen," it is in the nominative case. The clause *whoever will listen* is the object of the preposition "to.")

Questions and who/whom

Use *who* at the beginning of a question about a subject; use *whom* at the beginning of a question about an object.

In informal speech, the distinction is not always made, and *who* is used for the first word of a question, regardless of whether the question is about a subject or an object.

To determine whether to use *who* or *whom*, use a personal pronoun to construct an answer to the question. The case of the personal pronoun determines whether *who* (nominative) or *whom* (objective) is required:

Who left the car doors open?

(Possible answer to the question: "He left the car doors open." Since *he* is in the nominative case, the question is about a subject and thus requires *who*.)

Whom should I see about this invoice?

(Possible answer to the question: "You should see him." Since *him* is in the objective case, the question is about an object and thus requires *whom*.)

Possessive Case

Use the *possessive case* of a pronoun to show ownership.

The possessives *my, mine; your, yours; her, hers; our, ours;* and *their, theirs* have two different forms. Which one is used depends on whether the possessive comes before a noun or takes the place of a noun. *His* and *its* are used in either position.

Use the possessive pronouns *my, her, your, our, their* before a noun:

> My *cat sleeps all day.*
> *Where is* your *umbrella?*
> *Joan left* her *coat in the theater.*
> Our *son is graduating from high school this year.*

Use the possessive pronouns *mine, hers, yours, ours, theirs* alone to indicate possession:

> *This idea was* mine, *not* yours.
> *Is this article really* hers?
> *Do you believe that it's* theirs?
> *The red one is* ours.

Use the possessive case before gerunds in most instances.

A **gerund** is the *-ing* form of the verb *(swimming, snoring)* used as a noun. Possessive pronouns and nouns often precede gerunds, as in *The landlord objected to my* (not *me*) *having guests late at night.*

> My *shoveling the snow saved the mail carrier a nasty fall.*
> *Do you mind* my *eating the rest of the cake?*
> *She wholeheartedly supported* his *exercising.*
> My *colleagues were annoyed by* my *coughing.*

A possessive is not used before a gerund when it would create a clumsy sentence. In these instances, rewrite the sentence to eliminate the awkward construction.

Awkward
> *The neighbors spread the news about somebody's wanting to organize a block party.*

Revision
> *We heard from the neighbors that somebody wants to organize a block party.*

Note: Never use an apostrophe with a possessive pronoun. The following personal pronouns are already possessive and have no need for an apostrophe: *my, mine, your, yours, her, hers, its, our, ours, their,* and *theirs.* **Do not confuse the contraction** *it's* **(for** *it is***) with the possessive pronoun** *its.*

Ambiguous References

Make sure that the reference is clear when two pronouns could logically refer to either of two antecedents. The following examples demonstrate how ambiguities can occur.

Unclear
The manager told Mrs. Greenberger that she will have to train her new people by June.

As the sentence is written, it is unclear whether the manager or Mrs. Greenberger will have to train the new people and whose new people have to be trained.

Clearer
Since Mrs. Greenberger will have to train her new people by June, she decided to take her vacation in the spring.

If the reference to an antecedent is not specific, confusion can arise. An unclear pronoun reference can usually be clarified by rearranging the sentence or by using the noun rather than the pronoun, as the following examples show.

Unclear
When you have finished with the stamp and bound the report, please return it to the storeroom.

Clearer
When you have finished with the stamp and bound the report, please return the stamp to the storeroom.

Sometimes, using *it, they,* and *you* incorrectly will result in a sentence that is vague or wordy. Removing the pronoun, eliminating excess words, or revising the sentence helps produce a clearer and more vigorous style.

Wordy
In the cookbook it says that wooden chopping blocks should be disinfected with bleach.

Better
> The cookbook says that wooden chopping blocks should be
> disinfected with bleach.

Wordy
> They say you should use a cold steam vaporizer instead of the
> traditional hot steam one.

Better
> The doctor recommends using a cold steam vaporizer instead of
> the traditional hot steam one.

Verbs: Types of Verbs

**A *verb* is a word that expresses an action, an occurrence, or a
state of being.**

Action	*Occurrence*	*State of being*
jump	become	be
swim	happen	seem
throw		
speak		

Action verbs can describe mental as well as physical actions. The
verb *think,* for example, describes a mental action, one that cannot be seen. Additional examples of action verbs that describe unseen mental actions include *understand, welcome, enjoy, relish,
ponder, consider,* and *deliberate.* Action verbs are divided into two
groups, **transitive** and **intransitive,** depending on how they function within a sentence.

**A *transitive verb* is a verb that requires a direct object to
complete its meaning. The direct object receives the action of
the verb:**

> My son ate the last piece of chocolate cake.
> My sister baked another cake.
> Please call your mother.
> Sally read twenty-five books during the summer.

**An *intransitive verb* is a verb that does not need a direct object
to complete its meaning:**

> When they heard about it, my friends laughed.
> Even the baby giggled.

Please sit *down.*
I worked *hard all winter.*

Many verbs can be either transitive or intransitive.

Transitive
Carlos eats *breakfast at 7:30, lunch at 12:30, and dinner at*
*   6:30. (What does Carlos eat? He eats breakfast, lunch, and*
*   dinner.)*
My daughter teaches *math. (What does my daughter teach? She*
*   teaches math.)*

Intransitive
Carlos eats *at regular times.*
My daughter has been teaching *for four years.*

Some verbs that can be both transitive and intransitive are ergatives. An *ergative* is a verb in which the subject of the intransitive form is also the object of the transitive form:

The boat capsized.
They capsized *the boat.*

The dress buttons *down the front.*
She buttoned *her dress.*

Marie sat.
He sat *the baby in her highchair.*

The boat sank *to the bottom of the lake.*
They deliberately sank *the boat.*

The doorbell rang.
They rang *the doorbell.*

A *linking verb,* or *copula,* describes an occurrence or a state of being. It connects parts of a sentence.
    The most common linking verb is the verb *to be.* Following are some other linking verbs.

appear	seem
become	smell
feel	sound
grow	stay
look	taste
remain	

> *The supports* looked *fragile.*
> *The actor* seemed *nervous when the play began.*
> *It* sounds *like a fire alarm.*
> *I* became *increasingly certain that he was lying.*

The verbs on the list do not always function as linking verbs. To determine whether the word is functioning as a linking verb or as an action verb, examine its role in the sentence.

Linking verb
> *The child* grew *tired by the end of the evening.*
> *The milk* smells *sour.*
> *The lemonade* tastes *too sweet.*

Action verb
> *My mother* grows *the best tomatoes I have ever eaten.*
> *Can you* smell *those roses?*
> *Have you* tasted *the lemonade?*

A *predicate nominative* (noun, pronoun, or adjective) follows a linking verb and describes or identifies the subject. Predicate nominatives are also called subject complements.

> *My sister* is *a pediatrician.*
> *The lemonade* tastes *sour.*
> Is *that you?*
> *I* feel *sick.*

Since the linking verb serves as an "equals sign," the words on both sides of it must be in the same case, i.e., the nominative case.

> *We all assumed that it was* he.
> *I am waiting for mother to call. Is that* she?

An *auxiliary verb,* or *helping verb,* is used with a main verb to form a verb phrase. The three helping verbs are *be, have,* and *do.*

> Are *you enjoying the play?*
> Did *you complete the project on time?*
> Have *you ever eaten at the Chinese restaurant on 12th Street?*

There is another class of auxiliary verbs called "modals." These verbs express ability, possibility, obligation, permission, intention, and probability. The modal auxiliaries are *can, could, may, might, shall, should, will, would,* and *must. Dare, had better, have to, need, ought to,* and *used to* are also used as modals.

I might *work late tonight.*
Can *you help me?*
Could *you please help me?*
You really should *not do that.*
May *I please have a cup of coffee?*
I must *go to the office early tomorrow morning.*
You had better *do your homework before you go out.*
You ought to *try it.*

Phrasal Verbs

A *phrasal verb* is a combination of a verb and one or more adverbs or prepositions. The meaning of the phrase is often idiomatic and is not predictable from the individual parts. Examples of phrasal verbs are: *call off, catch on, get along with, put up with, send for, show up, stand up to, take off, throw away.*

It won't take you long to catch on to *the new routine.*
She has trouble getting along with *her coworkers.*
What time did they finally show up?
You ought to stand up to *him.*
Did your flight take off *on time?*
She has thrown away *several opportunities.*

Verbs: Forms, Tense, Mood, Voice

Forms

All English verbs have four basic *forms,* or *principal parts:* the *infinitive,* the *past,* the *past participle,* and the *present participle.*
   The *infinitive* is the basic form of a verb:

to grin
to talk
to snore
to walk
to drop

The *bare infinitive* is the form found in dictionaries, without *to:*

grin
talk
snore
walk
drop

The infinitive (*to* + the bare form of a verb) can begin a clause that acts as the object of the main verb. Main verbs that take this pattern include *ask, beg, expect, help, intend, like, mean, prefer, want, wish, would hate,* and *would like:*

> *We* would like *to go to Paris in June.*
> *They* had not expected *to go to Italy last winter.*
> *I* would have liked to *hear at least one of Mozart's operas during my trip to Vienna last year. (But I was not able to.)*
> *She* wanted *to win that award.*

The perfect infinitive (*to have* + the past participle) is used:
With a main verb in the present tense to express action that will be completed by a future date:

> *They* expect to have seen *three plays by the time they return.*
> *We* hope to have moved *into our new house before Christmas.*

With *would like/love* to express a wish that did not in fact happen:

> *She* would like to have won *that award.*
> *He* would love to have bought *a new car.*

The *past* form is used to form the past tense. It indicates that the verb's action took place in the past. The past form of regular verbs is formed by adding -*d* or -*ed* to the infinitive, sometimes requiring the doubling of a final consonant. (See below for irregular verbs.)

> *grinned*
> *talked*
> *snored*
> *walked*
> *dropped*

The *past participle* is used with at least one helping verb and/or modal verb to form the perfect tenses. (See page 24.) The past participle of regular verbs is the same as the past form. See below for irregular verbs.

> *grinned*
> *talked*
> *snored*
> *walked*
> *dropped*

The past participle can also be used as an adjective:

Where is the finished *product?*
My nephew refuses to eat cooked *vegetables.*

The *present participle* is used with the verb *to be* to create progressive forms, which show continuing action. (See page 26.) The present participle is formed by adding -*ing* to the infinitive, sometimes requiring the doubling of a final consonant.

grinning
talking
snoring
walking
dropping

The present participle can also be used as an adjective:

Stand clear of the closing *doors.*
She picked up the crying *child.*

Regular and Irregular Verbs
The majority of English verbs are regular and change their form by adding -*ing*, -*ed*, or -*d* to the infinitive. However, many verbs do not follow this pattern. These irregular verbs form their past tense and past participle in a number of different ways: some change an internal vowel and add -*n* to the past participle; some retain the same spelling in all three forms or in the past tense and past participle; some follow no discernible pattern.

The following list includes the most common irregular verbs. For information about verbs not included below, consult a dictionary. If a verb is regular, the dictionary will usually give only the infinitive. If the verb is irregular, the dictionary will include the past tense and past participle along with the infinitive; if only two forms are given, the past tense and the past participle are identical.

Common Irregular Verbs

Present Tense	Past Tense	Past Participle
arise	arose	arisen
be	was/were	been
bear	bore	borne, born
beat	beat	beaten
become	became	become
begin	began	begun
bend	bent	bent
bet	bet, betted	bet
bid	bid, bade	bid, bidden
bind	bound	bound
bite	bit	bitten
blow	blew	blown
break	broke	broken
bring	brought	brought
burn	burned, burnt	burned, burnt
burst	burst	burst
buy	bought	bought
catch	caught	caught
choose	chose	chosen
cling	clung	clung
come	came	come
creep	crept	crept
cut	cut	cut
deal	dealt	dealt
dig	dug	dug
dive	dived, dove	dived
do	did	done
draw	drew	drawn
dream	dreamed, dreamt	dreamed, dreamt
drink	drank	drunk
drive	drove	driven
eat	ate	eaten
fall	fell	fallen
fight	fought	fought
find	found	found
flee	fled	fled
fling	flung	flung
fly	flew	flown
forbid	forbade, forbad	forbidden, forbid

Present Tense	Past Tense	Past Participle
forget	*forgot*	*forgotten, forgot*
forgive	*forgave*	*forgiven*
freeze	*froze*	*frozen*
get	*got*	*got, gotten*
give	*gave*	*given*
go	*went*	*gone*
grow	*grew*	*grown*
hang (suspend)	*hung*	*hung*
hang (execute someone)	*hanged*	*hanged*
hear	*heard*	*heard*
hide	*hid*	*hidden*
hold	*held*	*held*
keep	*kept*	*kept*
kneel	*knelt*	*knelt*
know	*knew*	*known*
lay (put down)	*laid*	*laid*
lead	*led*	*led*
lie (rest; recline)	*lay*	*lay*
lose	*lost*	*lost*
mistake	*mistook*	*mistaken*
pay	*paid*	*paid*
ride	*rode*	*ridden*
ring	*rang*	*rung*
rise	*rose*	*risen*
run	*ran*	*run*
see	*saw*	*seen*
set	*set*	*set*
sew	*sewed*	*sewed, sewn*
shake	*shook*	*shaken*
shrink	*shrank*	*shrunk*
sing	*sang, sung*	*sung*
sit	*sat*	*sat*
slay	*slew*	*slain*
speak	*spoke*	*spoken*
spend	*spent*	*spent*
spring	*sprang*	*sprung*
stand	*stood*	*stood*
steal	*stole*	*stolen*
strike	*struck*	*struck*
swear	*swore*	*sworn*
sweep	*swept*	*swept*
swim	*swam*	*swum*

Present Tense	Past Tense	Past Participle
take	took	taken
teach	taught	taught
tear	tore	torn
throw	threw	thrown
wake	woke, waked	woken, waked
wear	wore	worn
weep	wept	wept
win	won	won
wind	wound	wound
wring	wrung	wrung
write	wrote	written

Tense

Tense refers to the form of a verb that indicates the time of the action, occurrence, or state of being expressed by the verb.

Tense is different from time. The present tense, for instance, shows present time, but it can also indicate future time or a generally accepted belief.

English has two groups of tenses: the simple tenses (present, past, and future) and the perfect tenses (present perfect, past perfect, and future perfect).

The Simple Tenses

The *simple tenses* generally show that an action or state of being is taking place now, in the future, or in the past relative to the speaker or writer. The simple tenses indicate a finished, momentary, or habitual action or condition.

Present:	smile (smiles)	go (goes)
Past:	smiled	went
Future:	will (shall) smile	will (shall) go

Note: "Shall" is rarely used except in formal speaking and writing, to express determination, and in laws and directives.

> I shall *call the governor myself.*
> We shall *overcome.*
> You shall *not go!*
> All new students shall *report to the dean upon arrival.*

The Present Tense

Except when the subjects are singular nouns or third-person singular pronouns, the **present tense** is the same as the infinitive form of the verb *(I walk, you skip, we jump, they catch)*. With singular nouns or third-person singular pronouns, *-s* or *-es* is added to the infinitive *(Robert walks, she skips, he jumps, it catches)*.

The present tense is used:

To state present action

Nick prepares *the walls for painting.*

To show present condition

The secretary is efficient.

To show that an action occurs regularly

Louise prepares *a report for her supervisor every week.*

To show a condition that occurs regularly

The traffic is usually backed up at the bridge in the evening.

To indicate future time, as an alternative to the future tense when a specific time is indicated

The income tax refund arrives tomorrow.

To state a generally held belief

Haste makes waste.

To state a scientific truth

A body in motion tends to stay in motion.

To discuss literary works, films, etc.

In Hamlet, Claudius poisons *his brother,* marries *his former sister-in-law, and* seizes *the throne.*

To narrate historical events as if they were happening in the present time (the "historical present")

In 1781 Cornwallis surrenders to Washington at Yorktown.

The Past Tense

The **past tense** of regular verbs is formed by adding *-d* or *-ed* to the infinitive. The past tense of irregular verbs is formed in a variety of ways. Consult the table on pages 20–22 for forms of irregular verbs.

The past tense is used:

To show actions and conditions that began and ended in the past, or were true at a particular time in the past

Johnny walked *the dog last night.*
Joan was *very happy.*

To show recurring past actions that do not extend to the present

During World War II, Eric saw *the fighting through the lens of a camera.*

The Future Tense
The **future tense** is formed by using the modal verbs *will* or *shall* plus the bare infinitive form of the verb.
     The future tense is used:
To show a future action

Tomorrow the sun will set *at 6:45 P.M.*

To show a future condition

They will be excited *when they see the presents.*

To indicate intention

The Board of Education has announced that it will begin *repairs on the town pool as soon as possible.*

To show probability

The decrease in land values in the Northeast will *most likely* continue *into next year.*

The Perfect Tenses
The *perfect tenses* **indicate that one action was or will be finished before an indicated time.**

Present:	have (has) smiled	have (has) gone
Past:	had smiled	had gone
Future:	will (shall) have smiled	will (shall) have gone

The Present Perfect Tense
The **present perfect tense** is formed by using the present tense of the auxiliary verb *have* plus the past participle of the main verb.
     The present perfect tense is used:

To show completed action

Martin has finished *talking to his clients.*

To show past action or condition continuing into the present

We have been waiting *for a week.*

To show action that occurred at an unspecified past time

I have reviewed *all the new procedures.*

The Past Perfect Tense

The **past perfect tense** is formed by using the past tense of the auxiliary verb *have* plus the past participle of the main verb.

The past perfect tense is used

To show one action or condition completed before another

By the time her employer returned, Linda had completed *all her assigned tasks.*

To show an action that occurred before a specific past time

By 1930, insulin had been isolated, refined, *and* distributed.

To show that something that was assumed or expected did not in fact happen

We had hoped *to have the new cabin ready by the first of June.*

The Future Perfect Tense

The **future perfect tense** is formed by using the auxiliary verbs *will* and *have* plus the past participle of the main verb.
The future perfect tense is used:
To show a future action or condition completed before another

By the time you read this letter, Bill will have left *California for Mexico.*

To show that an action will be completed by a specific future time

By tomorrow, the bonds will have lost *over fifty percent of their face value.*

Progressive Forms

Progressive forms are verb phrases that show continuing action. They are created by using the present participle of the main verb with forms of the verbs *to be* and *to have.*

The **present progressive** is used to show continuing action or condition. It is formed with the present from of the verb *to be* plus the present participle:

I am finishing *the painting while the children are at camp.*
Medicine is becoming *increasingly specialized.*

The **past progressive** is used to show an action or condition continuing in the past and to show two past actions occurring simultaneously. It is formed with the past form of the verb *to be* plus the present participle:

She was becoming *disenchanted with the radical diet.*
Mike fell off his bike while he was watching *a cat climb a tree.*

The **future progressive** is used to show continuing future action and to show continuing action at a specific future time. It is formed with *will* plus *be* plus the present participle:

She will be studying *all night.*
Will *you* be traveling *to Japan again in the spring?*

The **present perfect progressive** is used to show that an action or condition is continuing from the past into the present and/or the future. It is formed with the present form of the verb *to have* plus *been* plus the present participle:

The amount of pollution has been increasing *sharply.*
I have been waiting *for a train for fifteen minutes.*

The **past perfect progressive** is used to show that a continuing past action has been interrupted by another. It is formed with *had* plus *been* plus the present participle:

Alice had been taking *a detour through town until the new bridge was finished.*
The workers had been planning *a strike when the management made a new offer.*

The **future perfect progressive** is used to show that an action or condition will continue until a specific time in the future. It is formed with *will* plus *have* plus *been* plus the present participle.

By Monday, I will have been working *on that project for a month.*

Next September, they will have been traveling *for nearly a year.*

Using Tenses

The **sequence of tenses** refers to the relationship among the verbs within a sentence or in sentences that follow each other. Illogical shifts in verb tenses confuse readers and muddle meaning. For clarity and sense, all the verbs must accurately reflect changes in time. Using tenses correctly allows you to express the desired sequence of events correctly.

Simultaneous Actions

If the actions described occur at approximately the same time, the tenses of all the verbs must be the same.

The audience applauded *when the conductor* mounted *the podium.*

Although we have analyzed *the data, we* have *not* been able *to come to a firm conclusion.*

William Carlos Williams was a *pediatrician in Paterson, New Jersey, who* wrote *some of the most distinctive verse of the twentieth century.*

Actions Occurring at Different Times

If the verbs within a sentence describe actions that have occurred, are occurring, or will occur at different times, the tenses of the verbs must be different to express the different time sequence.

The conference had been *over for an hour by the time I* arrived.

I asked *if he* had consulted *his attorney last week.*

Joe was *worried that his dog* had bitten *the mail carrier.*

Conditional Sentences

When the situation described in the main clause depends on another situation, a **conditional clause** is used. Conditional clauses usually begin with *if* or *unless.*

We'll stay home if it rains.
We'll go unless it rains.

If the situation described is likely to occur, use the present tense in the conditional clause and *will* (or *won't*) in the main clause:

If you take *the train, you* will *be in the center of the city by*
    3:00.
If you wear *boots, your feet* won't *get cold.*

If the situation described is imaginary or unlikely to occur, use the past tense form in the conditional clause and *would, might,* or *could* in the main clause.

If I had *her address, I* could send *her flowers.*
if wishes were *horses, beggars* would ride.
If he called *me, I* might go.

If you want to describe a conditional situation that occurred in the past, use the past perfect form in the conditional clause and would have in the main clause.

If they had arrived *on time, we* would have been *able to go to a*
    movie.
The curtains would not have gotten *wet if I* had remembered *to*
    close the windows.

Using Participles Logically
The **present participle** expresses action occurring at the same time as that of the main verb.

Chewing *his pencil absently, Dick* stared *out the window at the*
    mountains in the distance.

The **present perfect participle** expresses action occurring before that of the main verb.

Having operated *the terminal for a month, the assistant* knew
    how to repair the malfunction.

Mood

The *mood* of a verb shows how the writer or speaker regards what he or she is saying. The form of the verb changes to indicate the mood. In English, there are three moods: the *indicative,* the *imperative,* and the *subjunctive.*

The *indicative mood* is used to state a fact or to ask a question:

Henry James wrote *"The Turn of the Screw."*
We hold *soccer games only on Saturdays.*
Did *T.S. Eliot* have *a great impact on twentieth-century
    literature?*
Do *you* hold *soccer games only on Saturdays?*

The *imperative mood* is used to give directions or express commands. Frequently, the subject (usually *you*) is understood rather than stated. *Let's* or *let us* can be used before the basic form of the verb in a command:

Get up!
Let's go *to Mario's for dinner.*
Turn *left at the convenience store.*

The *subjunctive mood* has traditionally been used to state wishes or desires, requirements, suggestions, or conditions that are contrary to fact. It has distinctive forms only in the present and past tenses of the verb *to be* and in the third-person singular present tense of other verbs.

Although it has largely disappeared from English, the subjunctive survives in sentences with conditional clauses that are contrary to fact and in subordinate clauses after verbs like *wish*. In these cases, the subjunctive requires the form "were":

He acted as if he were the owner.
If I were you, I would write them a letter.
I wish I were more organized.

The subjunctive is required in clauses expressing resolution, demand, recommendation, or motion. In these cases, the subjunctive requires the bare infinitive form of the verb:

I move that the minutes be accepted.
He recommended that she hire an attorney.
They demanded that he come immediately.

The subjunctive is also used in certain idioms and set phrases:

Far be it from me . . .
If need be . . .
Be that as it may.
The people be damned.
Come rain or come shine.
As it were . . .

Suffice *it to say* . . .
Come *what may* . . .

Voice

Voice shows whether the subject of a verb acts or is acted upon. There are two voices, *active* and *passive*. Only transitive verbs (those that take objects) can show voice.

Active Voice

When the subject of the verb does the action, the verb is in the active voice:

I hit *the ball across the field.*

The subject, *I,* does the action, *hit.*

Passive Voice

When the subject of the verb receives the action, the verb is in the passive voice:

The ball was hit *by me.*

The subject, *the ball,* receives the action, *was hit.*

To convert an active verb to a passive verb, a form of *to be* is used with the past participle.

Active
The storms damaged *many homes.*
Mary's dog bit *Christopher.*
Keats wrote *"The Eve of St. Agnes."*
Sean will make *dinner.*

Passive
Many homes were damaged *by the storms.*
Christopher was bitten *by Mary's dog.*
"The Eve of St. Agnes" was written *by Keats.*
Dinner will be made *by Sean.*

When to Use the Active Voice

In general, use the active voice to emphasize the performer of the action. Except for a small number of specific situations, which are described below, the active voice is usually clearer and more powerful than the passive voice.

When to Use the Passive Voice

The passive voice is preferable to the active voice:

When you do not wish to mention the performer of the action

A mistake has been made.
A check has been returned *marked "insufficient funds."*

When it is necessary to avoid vagueness

Furniture is manufactured *in Hickory, North Carolina.*
(Recasting this sentence in the active voice—"They manufacture furniture in Hickory, North Carolina"—results in the vague "they.")

When the performer of the action is not known

Plans for fifty units of low-income housing were unveiled *at today's county meeting.*
The computer was stolen.

When the result of the action is more important than the person performing the action

The driver was arrested *for speeding.*
The chief suspect was freed *on bail pending trial.*

Verbals

A verbal is a verb form—a *participle,* a *gerund,* or an *infinitive*—used as another part of speech. Verbals can function as nouns, adjectives, or adverbs.

Verbals can be modified by adverbs and adverbial phrases. They can also take objects and complements, but they cannot function as the only verb form in a sentence. The verbal phrase includes the verbal and the words related to it.

Signs hung on this wall *will be removed.*
(*Hung on this wall* is a participial phrase functioning as an adjective and modifying "signs.")
Eating a low-fat diet reduces the risk of many diseases.
(*Eating a low-fat diet* is a gerund phrase functioning as a noun. It is the subject of the verb "reduces.")
She likes to read science fiction novels.
(*To read science fiction novels* is an infinitive phrase functioning as a noun. It is the object of the verb "likes.")

Determiners

A *determiner,* sometimes also called a *noun marker,* is a word that determines the use of a noun without actually modifying it. Determiners are placed before nouns or noun phrases.

Examples of determiners are the articles *a, an,* and *the;* the demonstrative pronouns *this, that, these,* and *those;* the possessive pronouns *my, your, her, his, our, their;* and indefinite pronouns such as *some* and *each.*

Adjectives

An *adjective* is a word that modifies (describes) a noun or a pronoun.

The illness has affected twelve people in the apartment complex.
We could give you additional reasons why that would not be a wise decision, but we believe these will suffice.
You have had enough cookies for one day.
The gold earrings go with that outfit much better than the silver ones do.
The eerie noise seems to come from the basement.
This is the third time I've asked you to clean your room!
The red, white, and blue eye shadow proclaimed her patriotism but did little for her appearance.

Nouns and Pronouns as Adjectives

Nouns and pronouns can also function as adjectives.

The produce stand is open all night.
He has always enjoyed piano concertos.
We look forward to our coffee break.

Some common phrases in which nouns are used as adjectives

amusement park
apple pie
art history
beach towel
child care
dance class
flood control
flower bed

horse trailer
Star Wars
truth serum
water cooler

The demonstrative pronouns *this, that, these, those;* the interrogative pronouns *which* and *what;* and the indefinite pronouns *some, another, both, few, many, most, more,* etc., can all function as adjectives as well.

Are those *socks yours or his?*
This *bus is rarely on time in the winter.*
Which chores do you dislike the least?
What hobbies and sports do you enjoy the most?
Some people have managed to get tickets for the concert.
Any fan who wanted tickets had to be at the stadium at 4:00
  A.M.

Special Adjectives

There are also two special kinds of adjectives: **proper adjectives** and **compound adjectives**.

An adjective derived from a proper noun is called a **proper adjective**. Many of these adjectives are forms of people's names, as in *Emersonian,* from the nineteenth-century writer Ralph Waldo Emerson.

Kafkaesque situation
Shavian wit (Shaw)
Italian food
Chinese silk
March wind

An adjective made up of two or more words is called a **compound adjective.** The words in a compound adjective may be combined or hyphenated.

nearsighted
soft-shelled
open-and-shut
hardworking
close-by

Note: A compound that is not hyphenated when it is another part of speech becomes hyphenated when it acts as an adjective. Compare:

Is there a grocery store close by?
a close-by *grocery store*

Adverbs

An *adverb* is a word that modifies (describes) a verb, an adjective, or another adverb.

Adverbs add description and detail to writing by more closely focusing the meaning of a verb, an adjective, or another adverb. They can sometimes provide a wider range of description than adjectives alone. They describe by telling "where," "when," "how," or "to what extent."

> *The pot boiled* over.
> *The rain came* down.
> Yesterday *it snowed;* today *it all melted.*
> *The children* often *talk about going to Disneyland.*
> *I* quickly *changed the topic.*
> *The days are* slowly *getting longer.*
> *Wash your hands* thoroughly, *please.*
> *The child has* fully *recovered from her illness.*

Sentence Adverbs

Sentence adverbs are adverbs that modify or comment on the sentence as a whole or on the conditions under which the sentence is spoken.

> Frankly, *I don't believe him.*
> Really, *you are too clever for me.*

Compare:

> *"Things will be all right,"* she said hopefully. *(The adverb "hopefully" modifies "said."*
> "Hopefully, *things will be all right," she said. (The sentence adverb "hopefully" modifies the full statement.)*

Distinguishing Adjectives from Adverbs

Many adverbs end in *-ly,* but this is not a reliable way to distinguish adverbs from adjectives. Not all adverbs end in *-ly (far, fast, little, well).* There are some adjectives that end in *-ly (curly, surly, lovely)* and some adverbs that have two different forms. The part of speech is determined by the word's function in the sentence, not by its ending.

Examples of Adverbs that Have Two Forms:

He *aims* high *in his political ambitions.*
I don't care for highly *seasoned food.*

Look sharp!
The car swerved sharply *to the left.*

Don't arrive too late.
He has been sick a lot lately.

Don't talk so loud.
"I want to go home," my daughter said loudly.

Winter is drawing near.
He nearly *fell into the ditch.*

You did it wrong *again.*
You were blamed wrongly.

In some instances, the choice of form depends on the idiomatic use of the word. *Nearly,* for example, is used to mean "almost," while *near* is used to mean "close in time." *Slow* is used in spoken commands with short verbs that express motion, such as "drive" and "run" *(Drive slow)* and combined with present participles to form adjectives *(a slow-moving vehicle). Slowly* is commonly found in writing, and is used in both speech and writing before a verb *(He slowly swam across the cove)* as well as after a verb *(He swam slowly through the waves).*

In general, the short forms are used more often in informal speech and writing; the long forms are found more often in formal discourse.

Using Adjectives after Linking Verbs

A **linking verb** connects a subject with its complement, a noun, pronoun, or adjective that completes the meaning of the verb. Do not use an adverb after a linking verb.

The words that follow linking verbs are called **subject complements** or **predicate nominatives.** The most common linking verbs include forms of *to be;* verbs such as *appear, seem, believe, become, grow, turn, prove,* and *remain;* and sensory verbs such as *sound, look, hear, smell, feel,* and *taste.*

The dog smelled bad.
The girl appeared content.
The cold milk tasted good.

That sounds wonderful.
She grew thoughtful.

Using Adjectives or Adverbs after Direct Objects

If the verb's **direct object** is followed by a word that describes the verb, the word must be an adverb.

He muttered the words angrily.
(The adverb *angrily* modifies the verb "muttered.")

On the other hand, if the direct object is followed by a word that describes the object, the word must be an adjective.

The red pepper made the soup spicy.
(The adjective *spicy* modifies the noun "soup.")

Compare the following pairs of sentences:

His mother called him quiet.
(The adjective *quiet* modifies the pronoun "him.")
His mother called him quietly.
(The adverb *quietly* modifies the verb "called.")

The evaluation committee considered the firm's work complete.
(The adjective *complete* modifies the noun "work.")
The evaluation committee considered the firm's work completely.
(The adverb *completely* modifies the verb "considered.")

Words That Can Be Either Adjectives or Adverbs

Depending on how they are used, some words can function as either adjectives or adverbs.

Adverb
I think you ought to go to bed early *tonight.*
Janine is fortunate that she lives close *to public transportation.*

Adjective
I had an early *appointment this morning.*
That certainly was a close *call!*

Using Adjectives and Adverbs to Make Comparisons

Many adjectives and adverbs take different forms when they are used to make comparisons. The three forms are the positive degree, the comparative degree, and the superlative degree.

Positive degree

The positive degree is the basic form of the adjective or the adverb, the form listed in the dictionary. Since the positive degree does not indicate any comparison, the adjective or adverb does not change form.

Comparative degree

The comparative form indicates a greater degree by comparing two things. In the comparative form, adjectives and adverbs add -er or *more*.

Superlative degree

The superlative form indicates the greatest degree of difference or similarity by comparing three or more things. In this form, adjectives and adverbs add -est or *most*.

Using less/least/more/most or -er/-est

A number of one- or two-syllable adjectives and adverbs use -er to form the comparative degree and -est to form the superlative degree. In some instances, these words use *more* and *most* when necessary to avoid awkwardness:

Positive	Comparative	Superlative
clear	clearer	clearest
poor '	poorer	poorest
rich	richer	richest
pretty	prettier	prettiest
heavy	heavier	heaviest
steady	steadier	steadiest
childlike	more childlike	most childlike
youthful	more youthful	most youthful
golden	more golden	most golden

Most adjectives and adverbs of three or more syllables and nearly all adverbs ending in -ly use *more/less* and *most/least* to form the comparative and superlative degrees:

Positive	Comparative	Superlative
customary	more/less customary	most/least customary
regular	more/less regular	most/least regular
admiring	more/less admiring	most/least admiring
slowly	more/less slowly	most/least slowly
harshly	more/less harshly	most/least harshly
rudely	more/less rudely	most/least rudely

Irregular Adjectives and Adverbs

Some adverbs and adjectives are irregular in the comparative and superlative degrees, as shown in the table below:

Adjectives

Positive	Comparative	Superlative
good	better	best
bad	worse	worst
little	littler, less, lesser	littlest, least
many, some, much	more	most

Adverbs

Positive	Comparative	Superlative
well	better	best
badly	worse	worst

Comparative Versus Superlative

In general, use the comparative form to compare two things; use the superlative form to compare three or more things.

Twiskers was the smarter of the two hamsters.
Marc was the taller of the two second-graders.
Louisa is the quicker of the two runners.

Of the six hamsters, Twiddles is the smartest.
Among the six of you, Robert is the tallest.
Of all the runners, Louisa is the quickest.

Double Comparisons

Do not use double comparatives or double superlatives.

Amanda gets a bigger allowance because she is older (not "more older") than I am.
She is the nicest (not "most nicest") girl in the class.

Completing Comparisons

Be careful not to omit words needed to complete comparisons.

Incomplete
    Steve's salary is less than his wife.

Complete:
Steve's salary is less than that of his wife.

or

Steve's salary is less than his wife's.

Incomplete:
Cooking with herbs is more healthful than fat.

Complete:
Cooking with herbs is more healthful than cooking with fat.

Incomplete:
Rainy days in Tucson are as rare as Santa Fe.

Complete:
Rainy days in Tucson are as rare as they are in Santa Fe.

Incomplete:
Denver is farther from Pueblo than Boulder.

Complete:
Denver is farther from Pueblo than it is from Boulder.

Incomplete:
New York City has more movie theaters.

Complete:
New York City has more movie theaters than any other city in the state.

Note: There are a number of words whose positive degree describes their only form. Words such as *central, dead, empty, excellent, impossible, infinite, perfect, straight,* and *unique* cannot have a greater or lesser degree. Therefore, something cannot be "more unique" or "most infinite."

In general, avoid using comparative or superlative forms for adjectives and adverbs that cannot be compared.

Prepositions

A *preposition* is a word used to connect and relate a noun or pronoun to some other word in the sentence.

Common Prepositions

about	by	outside
above	concerning	over
across	despite	past
after	down	regarding
against	during	round
along	except	since
amid	excepting	through
among	for	throughout
around	from	till
as of	in	to
at	inside	toward
before	into	under
behind	like	underneath
below	near	until
beneath	of	up
beside	off	upon
besides	on	with
between	onto	within
beyond	opposite	without
but	out	

Phrasal Prepositions (Two or More Words)

according to	by reason of	in spite of
along with	by way of	instead of
apart from	except for	on account of
as for	in addition to	out of
as of	in case of	up to
as regards	in front of	with reference to
aside from	in lieu of	with regard to
because of	in place of	with respect to
by means of	in regard to	with the exception of

Prepositional Phrases

A preposition always has an object, which is a noun or pronoun. The preposition with its object and any modifiers is called a **prepositional phrase**. A prepositional phrase can be made up of any number of words:

> *toward the mountain*
> *away from the ocean*
> *by the side of the cliff*
> *in front of the bushes*
> *on account of his gross negligence*
> *with the exception of three players*

Placement of Prepositions

A preposition usually precedes its object, but it may also follow its object. A preposition may also come at the end of the sentence:

> *What did Allison do that* for?
> *Josh and Kate had many things to talk* about.
> *For a week, she couldn't get the horrible scene* out of *her mind.*
> In addition to *having a superb academic record, he was an outstanding athlete and humanitarian.*
> *We know which chair you are hiding* behind.

Prepositional Phrases as Adverbs and Adjectives

Prepositional phrases can function as adverbs or adjectives.

Prepositional phrases as adverbs
> *He hammered rapidly* underneath the overhang.
> *The children flew their new dragon kite* on the beach.
> *Charles drove* through the night.

Prepositional phrases as adjectives
> *Melinda is the girl* with the missing front tooth.
> *The reporter* in the red dress *asked the first question.*
> *New York is a city that has something* for everyone.
> *She was carrying a bag* of groceries.

Prepositions and Adverbs

To distinguish between prepositions and adverbs, remember that prepositions, unlike adverbs, can never function alone within a sentence. A preposition must always have an object.

Prepositions
  The children went into the house.
  Crowds of people were skiing down the icy slopes.

Adverbs
  They went in.
  After the fifth book fell down, we decided it was time to
    rearrange the bookshelves.

Conjunctions

A *conjunction* is a word used to connect words, phrases, or clauses.

The three kinds of conjunctions are **coordinating, correlative,** and **subordinating.** Adverbs can also be used to link related ideas. When adverbs are used in this way, they are called **conjunctive adverbs.**

Coordinating Conjunctions

A **coordinating conjunction** connects sentence parts (individual words, phrases, or clauses) of equal rank. Following are the most common coordinating conjunctions:

and	or
but	so
for	yet
nor	

And shows connections

  The children cleaned up quickly and quietly.
  We went to a concert, and the children went to a movie.

But, nor, and *yet* show contrast

The living room was extremely elegant but *surprisingly comfortable.*

My supervisor will never give us half days on Friday, nor *will she agree to our other demands.*

She took good care of the houseplant, yet *it wilted and lost its leaves anyway.*

Or shows choice

You can have the spaghetti and meatballs or *the veal and peppers.*

We can have a picnic in the park, or *we can drive out to the lake.*

So shows result

All the stores were closed, so *we ended up eating peanut butter and jelly sandwiches.*

For shows causality

Laura stayed in the office late all week, for *she had to finish the project by Friday.*

Correlative Conjunctions

Correlative conjunctions also link sentence parts of equal grammatical rank. These conjunctions always work in pairs to connect words, phrases, or clauses.

both . . . and
either . . . or
neither . . . nor
not only . . . but also
not . . . but
whether . . . or

Both *the bank* and *the post office are closed on national holidays.*

Either *you agree to ratify our contract now,* or *we will have to return to the bargaining table.*

The envelopes are neither *in the drawer* nor *in the cabinet.*

Not only *the children* but also *the adults were captivated by the dancing bears at the circus.*

Not *the renters* but *the homeowners were most deeply affected by the recent change in the tax laws.*
Whether you agree to implement my plan or not, *you have to concede that it has merit.*

Note: The two elements connected by correlative conjunctions must be in parallel form. (See page 78 for further information on parallel structure.)

Incorrect:
Neither the dripping cat nor the dog that was muddy was welcome in my foyer.
The hosts paid attention not only to the refreshments, but they also were paying attention to the music.

Correct:
Neither the dripping cat nor the muddy dog was welcome in my foyer.
The hosts paid attention not only to the refreshments but also to the music.

Subordinating Conjunctions

A **subordinating conjunction** is a word that connects two thoughts by making one subordinate to, or dependent on, the other. (See page 49 on subordinate, or dependent, clauses.)

To "subordinate" suggests making one statement less important than the other:

Although some people tried to repair the tennis courts, they were unable to gain sufficient public backing.

The main idea, "they were unable to gain sufficient public backing," is an independent clause (complete sentence); the subordinate idea, "Although some people tried to repair the tennis courts," is a dependent clause that functions here as an adverb. Either clause may come first in the sentence.

Common Subordinating Conjunctions

after	even though	though
although	if	till
as	if only	unless
as of	in order that	until
as long as	now that	when
as soon as	once	whenever
as though	rather than	where
because	since	whereas
before	so that	wherever
even if	than	while
	that	

Although *traffic was light every morning,* he was unable to arrive at work on time.

The little girl overheard her parents arguing in the next room even though *they were whispering.*

We ordered pizza so that *we wouldn't have to go out in the rain.*

Don't forget that *your taxes are due on the fifteenth of the month.*

Until *you make up your mind,* we won't be able to leave.

Please retype this letter after *you return from lunch.*

Do you know where *he lives?*

That is more than *I can afford.*

Subordinating Conjunctions Versus Prepositions

A word such as *until, before, since, till,* or *after* can function as either a preposition or a subordinating conjunction. Remember that subordinating conjunctions, unlike prepositions, connect two complete ideas.

Subordinating conjunctions

Please drop this tape off at the video store since *you are driving in that direction anyway.*

After *you finish reading that book,* may I borrow it?

Prepositions

I have had a headache since *this morning.*

After *lunch I am going shopping for a new pair of shoes.*

Conjunctive Adverbs and Transitional Phrases

A **conjunctive adverb** is an adverb that connects two clauses or sentences by describing their relationship to each other.

Common Conjunctive Adverbs

also	however	next
anyway	incidentally	nonetheless
besides	indeed	otherwise
consequently	instead	still
finally	likewise	then
furthermore	meanwhile	therefore
hence	moreover	thus
	nevertheless	

The electric company promised that power would be restored by tomorrow; meanwhile, we are using a generator.

The memo required an immediate response; consequently, we sent a fax.

You should not be angry at them for arriving early; undoubtedly, they were nervous and overestimated the time that the drive would take.

Expressions that are used to link complete ideas are called **transitional phrases.**

Common Transitional Phrases

after all	for example
as a result	in addition
at any rate	in fact
at the same time	in other words
by the way	on the contrary
even so	on the other hand

The school building is in great disrepair; for example, the roof is leaking, the paint is peeling, and the heating system works erratically.

The voters rejected an increase in the school tax; as a result, the repairs will not be done this year.

There is a great public clamor for better schools; at the same time, no one wants to spend the necessary money.

Note: A semicolon is used before a conjunctive adverb or a transitional phrase that is placed between main clauses. The adverb or phrase itself is set off by a comma.

Conjunctive adverbs and transitional phrases can be moved within a sentence; coordinating conjunctions cannot:

> The taxi was late; however, we arrived in time to catch the entire first act.
> The taxi was late; we arrived, however, in time to catch the entire first act.
> The taxi was late; we arrived in time to catch the entire first act, however.

Interjections

An *interjection* is a word used to express strong emotion. It functions independently within a sentence.

In Latin, the word *interjection* means "something thrown in." In a sense, interjections are "thrown in" to add strong feeling. For maximum effect, interjections should be used sparingly in your writing. Since they are independent from the rest of the sentence, they can be set off by commas or followed by an exclamation point.

Common Interjections

ah	darn	ouch
alas	hey	shh
bah	nonsense	well
bravo	oh	wow

Darn! The cat got out again.
Oh, I didn't expect you so early.
Hey! Do you know what you're doing?

Phrases and Clauses

Phrases

A *phrase* is a group of related words that does not contain both a subject and a verb. Phrases are classified as *verb phrases, noun phrases, prepositional phrases,* and *verbal phrases* (*participial phrases, gerund phrases,* and *infinitive phrases*).

Verb Phrases

A **verb phrase** contains a main verb and an auxiliary verb.

The cat has eaten *the carnations.*
Let's go *to the movies.*
Can you read *his handwriting?*

Noun Phrases

A **noun phrase** contains a noun and one or more modifiers.

The brilliant sunshine *only made the old house look more dilapidated.*
I have heard that she is a very interesting speaker.
A tall blue heron *stood motionless on the shore.*

Prepositional Phrases

A **prepositional phrase** is a group of words that opens with a preposition and ends with a noun or pronoun.

Prepositional phrases can function as adjectives, as adverbs, or, occasionally, as nouns.

Prepositional phrases used as adjectives
The price of the dinner *was exorbitant.*
My house is the one between the twisted oak tree and the graceful weeping willow.

Prepositional phrases used as adverbs
The joggers ran with determination.
My flight is scheduled to leave at 6 p.m.

Prepositional phrases used as nouns
After lunch *is too late.*
Beyond the oak tree *is out of bounds.*

Verbal Phrases

A **verbal** is a verb form used as another part of speech. Participles, infinitives, and gerunds are verbals. The verbal and all the words related to it are called a **verbal phrase.**

Participial phrases function as adjectives. They can be placed before or after the word they describe.

Shaking with fear, *the defendant stood before the jury.* [present participle]
She got a hot dog drenched in mustard. [past participle]

Gerund phrases function as nouns. Gerunds always end in -*ing*:

Swimming laps *three times a week helps her stay in shape.*
Hiking in the Rockies *is my idea of a great vacation.*

Infinitive phrases can function as nouns, adjective, or adverbs. An infinitive phrase always begins with the word *to*:

To shop in that store *is a nightmare.* [noun]
We plan to fly to Houston on Monday. [noun]
He gave us a lot of homework to do. [adjective]
She struggled to overcome her disability. [adverb]

Clauses

A *clause* **is a group of related words that contains both a subject and a verb. There are two types of clauses:** *independent* **(***main***) and** *dependent* **(***subordinate***).**

An **independent (main)** clause can stand alone as a complete sentence.

Swimming is suitable for people of all ages.
He missed his train.
Marcia plans to open a catering business.

A **dependent (subordinate)** clause functions as a part of speech that relates to an element in the main clause.

Swimming, which is very good exercise, *is suitable for people of all ages.*
Because he overslept, *he missed his train.*
Marcia, who won the blue ribbon in the cooking contest, *plans to open a catering business.*

Functions of Dependent Clauses

A dependent clause functions as a part of speech—as an adjective, an adverb, or a noun.

Adjective Clauses

An **adjective clause** is a subordinate clause that modifies a noun or pronoun. It usually begins with a relative pronoun: *which, what, whatever, who, whose, whom, whoever, whomever,* or *that.* It may also begin with words such as *when, where, before, since,* or *why.* An adjective clause almost always follows the word it modifies:

We hired the candidates who came with the strongest recommendations.

The child whom you saw in the magazine *is my niece.*

Did Fred tell you the reason why he was late for work this morning?

Good restaurants where one can eat cheaply *are very rare in this town.*

Adverb Clauses

An **adverb clause** is a subordinate clause that modifies a verb, an adjective, an adverb, or a verbal. Adverb clauses usually begin with subordinating conjunctions (See page 45 for a list of subordinating conjunctions). Unlike adjective clauses, adverb clauses can be separated from the word they modify and can be placed anywhere in the sentence. If the clause is placed at the beginning or in the middle of a sentence, if is often set off by commas.

Since the guests were so convivial, *I soon forgot my troubles.*

Did you visit the Metropolitan Museum when you were in New York?

I decided, after I lost an important document, *to make backup copies of all my files.*

Noun Clauses

A **noun clause** is a subordinate clause that acts as a noun. Noun clauses can function as subjects, objects, and predicate nouns within sentences. They begin either with a relative pronoun or with a word such as *how, why, where, when, if,* or *whether.*

Noun clauses can be difficult to identify. Since so many different words can be used to begin a noun clause, the opening word itself cannot be used as a determinant. You must discover the function of the clause within the sentence to identify it as a noun clause.

Whoever washes the dishes *will be allowed to choose which program to watch.* [subject]

Do you know where they went on vacation? [direct object]

They talked about whether they could take the time off from work. [object of a preposition]

That is what I meant. [predicate nominative]

Elliptical Clauses

An **elliptical clause** is a subordinate clause that is grammatically incomplete but nonetheless clear because the missing element can be understood from the rest of the sentence.

The word *elliptical* comes from *ellipsis,* which means "omission." The verb from the second part of the comparison may be missing, or the relative pronouns *that, which,* and *whom* may be omitted from adjectival clauses. Often, elliptical clauses begin with *as* or *than,* although any subordinating conjunction that makes logical sense can be used. In the following examples, the omitted words are supplied in parentheses:

Chad's younger cousin is as tall as he *(is).*
Aruba is among the islands (that) they visited on their recent cruise.
When *(he was)* only a child, *Barry was taken on a tour around the world.*
Although *(they were)* common fifty years ago, *passenger pigeons are extinct today.*

Sentences

A *sentence* is the expression of a complete thought.

Subjects and Predicates

There are two basic parts to every sentence: the subject and the predicate. The simple subject is the noun or pronoun that identifies the person, place, or thing the sentence is about. The complete subject is the simple subject and all the words that modify it. The predicate contains the verb that explains what the subject is doing. The simple predicate contains only the verb; the complete predicate contains the verb and any complements and modifiers.

Subject:	Predicate:
The motorcycle	veered away from the boulder.

Subject:	Predicate:
Calico cats	are always female.

Subject:	Predicate:
One of Hawthorne's direct blood relatives	was the famous "hanging judge" of the Salem witchcraft trials.

Subject:
   Farmingdale, in the town
      of Oyster Bay,

Predicate:
   has recently begun a
      massive recycling project.

Hard-to-Locate Subjects

Commands or Directions

In some instances, the subject can be difficult to locate. In commands or directions, for instance, the subject is often not stated because it is understood to be *you*.

Subject:
   (you)

Predicate:
   Please unload the dishwasher and
      tidy the kitchen.

Subject:
   (you)

Predicate:
   Just tell me what happened that
      evening.

Questions

In questions, too, subjects can be difficult to locate because they often follow the verb rather than come before it. Rewriting the question as a statement will make it easier to find the subject.

Question:
Are you planning to go to Oregon this weekend or next?

Rewritten as a statement:
You are planning to go to Oregon this weekend or next.

Sentences Beginning with there or here

If you are having trouble locating the subject of a sentence beginning with *there* or *here,* try rephrasing the sentence:

There is your wallet on the table.
Here are the peaches from the farm market.

Rewritten:
Your wallet is there on the table.
The peaches from the farm market are here.

Inverted Sentences

Inverted sentences place the subject after the verb for emphasis.

High on the cliff above the ocean stood the diver.
On a rack behind the door hung a dripping raincoat.
Even more significant was the lack of a firm objective.

Sentence Complements

Along with a verb, complete predicates often contain a complement. A **complement** is a word or word group that completes the meaning of the verb.

There are four primary kinds of sentence complements: **direct objects, indirect objects, object complements,** and **predicate nominatives** (nouns, pronouns, and adjectives). Predicate nominatives are also called **subject complements.**

Direct Objects

A *direct object* is the noun, pronoun, or word acting as a noun that completes the meaning of a transitive verb.

A direct object completes the meaning of the transitive verb by receiving the action. (Intransitive verbs do not have direct objects.) To help decide if a word is a direct object, ask *What?* or *Whom?* after an action verb:

Martha won the stuffed dog.
(What *did she win?* The stuffed dog.)

The hurricane destroyed the beach and the boardwalk.
(What *did the hurricane destroy?* The beach and the boardwalk.)

The waiter served Jack.
(Whom *did the waiter serve?* Jack.)

Indirect Objects

An *indirect object* is a noun or pronoun that names the person or thing that something is done to or given to:

Indirect objects are located after the verb and before the direct object. Obviously, they are found only in sentences that have direct objects. Indirect objects answer the questions "To whom?" "For whom?" "To what?" or "For what?"

My aunt lent me her motorcycle.
(To whom *did my aunt lend her motorcycle?* To me.)

I gave my daughter a computer for her birthday.
(To whom *did I give a computer.* To my daughter.)

Maria sent Serge an invitation.
(To whom *did Maria send an invitation?* To Serge.)

Object Complements
An *object complement* **is a noun or adjective immediately following a direct object. It either renames or describes the direct object.**

She called him a fool.
We made the platypus our mascot.
They named the kitten Ivan the Terrible.

Subject Complements or Predicate Nominatives
Subject complements, like object complements, are found in the predicate of a sentence.

A subject complement is a noun, pronoun, or adjective that follows a linking verb and gives further information about the subject of a sentence.

A predicate noun or pronoun follows a linking verb to identify the subject of a sentence:

The new head of the division will be Henry Williams.
Which of those two phones is the newer one?

A predicate adjective follows a linking verb to describe the subject of a sentence:

The vegetable soup smells delicious.
My daughter's stamp collection grows larger and more valuable
   every day.

Forming Sentences
Independent and dependent clauses can be combined in various ways to create four basic types of sentences: *simple, compound, complex,* and *compound-complex.*

Simple Sentences
A **simple sentence** is one independent clause, a group of words containing a subject and a predicate. This does not mean, however, that a simple sentence must be short. Both the subject and the verb may be compounded. In addition, a simple sentence may contain describing phrases. By definition, though, a simple

sentence cannot have a subordinate clause or another independent clause.

Heather shopped.
The carpenter and the electrician arrived simultaneously.
The shingle flapped, folded, and broke off.
Either my mother or my great-aunt bought and wrapped this lovely crystal decanter.
Freezing unexpectedly, the water in the copper lines burst the gaskets.

Compound Sentences

A *compound sentence* is two or more independent clauses joined together. Since the clauses in a compound sentence are independent, each can be written as an individual sentence. A compound sentence does not have dependent clauses. The independent clauses can be connected by a comma and a coordinating conjunction *(and, but, or, for, so, yet)* or by a semicolon. If the clauses are very short, the comma before the coordinating conjunction may be omitted.

Mary went to the concert, but Bill stayed home with the baby.
You may mail the enclosed form back to our central office, or you may call our customer service representative at the number listed above.
Eddie typed the report in three hours; Fran spent five hours editing it.
I ate lunch and then I took a nap.

Complex Sentences

A **complex sentence** contains one independent clause and one or more subordinate clauses. To distinguish it from the other clauses, the independent clause in a complex sentence is called the main clause. In a complex sentence, each clause has its own subject and verb. The subject in the main clause is called the subject of the sentence; the verb is the main clause is called the main verb. An independent clause can stand alone as a complete sentence; a dependent clause cannot.

In the following examples, the main clauses are in roman.

As we were looking over your sign-in sheets for May and June, we noticed a number of minor problems.

While Mary went to the concert, Bill stayed home with the
baby.
No one responded *when she rang the front doorbell.*
The owners of the small mountain inns rejoiced *when the snow
fell.*

Compound-Complex Sentences

A **compound-complex sentence** has at least two independent
clauses and at least one dependent clause. The compound-
complex sentence is so named because it shares the characteristics of both compound and complex sentences. Like the
compound sentence, the compound-complex has at least two
main clauses. Like the complex sentence, it has at least one subordinate clause. The subordinate clause can be part of an independent clause.

In the following examples, the main clauses are in roman.

Since my memo seems to outline our requirements fully, we are
circulating it to all the departments; please notify us *if we can
be of any further assistance.*
When the heat comes, the lakes dry up, *and* farmers know that
their crops will fail.

Review of Sentence Forms

The following five sentence forms are the basic templates on
which all sentences are built.

1. Subject + intransitive verb
   Bond prices fell.

2. Subject + transitive verb + direct object
   Bob hummed the song.

3. Subject + transitive verb + direct object + object complement
   The committee appointed Eric secretary.

4. Subject + linking verb + subject complement
   The procedure was tedious.
   The gift was a silk scarf.

5. Subject + transitive verb + indirect object + direct object
   The clerk gave us the receipt.

Sentence Functions

In addition to the form they take, sentences can also be classified according to function. There are four main types of sentences: *declarative, interrogative, imperative,* and *exclamatory.*

Declarative Sentences
A **declarative sentence** makes a statement and always ends with a period:

On Thursday we are going to see a movie.
We have been waiting for two weeks for the movie to open here.
The reviews were excellent.

Interrogative Sentences
An **interrogative sentence** asks a question and always ends with a question mark:

Are we going to see the movie on Tuesday?
How long have you been waiting for the movie to open?
What did the reviewers say about it?

Imperative Sentences
An **imperative sentence** makes a command. In many instances, the subject of an imperative sentence is understood to be you and is thus not stated. In other instances, the sentence may be phrased as a question but does not end with a question mark.

Take this money in case you change your mind.
Clean up that mess!
Will you please reply at your earliest convenience.
Would someone please move those books to the top shelf.

Exclamatory Sentences
An **exclamatory sentence** conveys strong feeling and always ends with an exclamation point. Many exclamatory sentences are very strongly stated declarative sentences. Since the exclamatory sentence conveys strong emotions, it is not found much in formal writing.

They still haven't called!
The dress is ruined!

Sentence Errors

Sentence errors **fall into three main divisions: parts of sentences set off as though they were complete** (*fragments*), **two or more sentences incorrectly joined** (*run-ons*), **and sentence parts misplaced or poorly connected to the rest of the sentence** (*misplaced, dangling,* **or** *squinting modifiers*).

Fragments

A *fragment* **is part of a sentence presented as though it were a complete sentence.** The fragment may lack a subject or verb or both, or it may be a subordinate clause not connected to a complete sentence. Since fragments are not complete sentences, they do not express complete thoughts.

No subject:
Ran to catch the bus.
Ate all the chocolate hidden in the drawer.

No main verb:
The box sitting in the trunk.
The man in the room.

No subject or main verb:
Feeling happy.
Acting poorly.

Subordinate clause:
When I woke him up early this morning.
If it is as pleasant as you expect today.

Correcting Fragments

Fragments are often created when phrases and subordinate clauses are punctuated as though they were complete sentences. Recall that phrases can never stand alone because they are groups of words that do not have subjects or verbs. To correct phrase fragments, add the information they need to be complete.

Subordinate clauses, on the other hand, do contain subjects and verbs. Like phrases, however, they do not convey complete thoughts. They can be completed by connecting them to main clauses. They can also be completed by dropping the subordinating conjunction. Correct each fragment in the way that makes the most logical sense within the context of the passage.

Phrase fragment
   a big house

Corrected
   A big house at the end of the block burned down last night.
   (Fragment becomes subject; predicate is added.)

   My sister recently bought a big house.
   (Fragment becomes direct object; subject and verb are added.)

   She earned enough money for a big house.
   (Fragment becomes object of the preposition; subject, verb, and direct object are added.)

   Did you hear about his newest acquisition, the big house on Maple Street?
   (Fragment becomes appositive; subject, verb, and prepositional phrase are added.)

Subordinating clause fragment
   If it is as pleasant as you expected today.

Corrected
   It is as pleasant as you expected today.
   (Subordinating conjunction dropped.)

   If it is as pleasant as you expected today, we will be able to go to the beach.
   (Fragment connected to a main clause.)

Run-ons

A *run-on* is two complete ideas incorrectly joined. Run-ons are generally classified as either *comma splices* or *fused sentences*.

A *comma splice* incorrectly joins two independent clauses with a comma.

Mary walked into the room, she found a mouse on her desk.
The vest was beautiful, it had intricate embroidery.
My daughter loves the X-Files, she watches it every week.

A *fused sentence* runs two independent clauses together without an appropriate conjunction or mark of punctuation:

Many people are afraid of computers they do not realize how easy it is to learn basic tasks.

All the word processing programs come with built-in lessons you can learn to do basic word processing in an afternoon or less.

The on-line spell check and thesaurus are especially handy they do not take the place of a good dictionary.

Correcting Run-on Sentences

There are four ways to correct both comma splices and fused sentences.

1. Separate the clauses into two sentences.

    Mary walked into the room. She found a mouse on her desk.

    Many people are afraid of computers. They do not realize how easy it is to learn basic tasks.

2. Insert a comma and coordinating conjunction between clauses to create a compound sentence.

    Mary walked into the room, and she found a mouse on her desk.

    Many people are afraid of computers, for they do not realize how easy it is to learn basic tasks.

3. Insert a semicolon between the clauses.

    Mary walked into the room; she found a mouse on her desk.

    Many people are afraid of computers; they do not realize how easy it is to learn basic tasks.

4. Subordinate one clause to the other to create a complex sentence.

    When Mary walked into the room, she found a mouse on her desk.

    Many people are afraid of computers because they do not realize how easy it is to learn basic tasks.

Misplaced Modifiers

A *misplaced modifier* occurs when the modifier appears to describe the wrong word in the sentence.

As a general rule, a modifier should be placed as close as possible to the word it modifies. When a clause, phrase, or word is placed too far from the word it modifies, the sentence may fail

to convey the intended meaning and therefore produce ambiguity or amusement. When this occurs, the modifier is called
"misplaced."

Words misplaced:
  To get to the ski slope we nearly drove five hours.
  I almost drank a whole quart of water.

Revised:
  To get to the ski slope we drove nearly five hours.
  I drank almost a whole quart of water.

Phrases misplaced:
  We all stared at the woman who was talking to the governor
    with green spiked hair.
  Tom served champagne to his guests in antique crystal.
  The professor explained how her grading system worked on
    Monday.

Revised:
  We all stared at the woman with green spiked hair who was
    talking to the governor.
  Tom served champagne in antique crystal to his guests.
  On Monday the professor explained how her grading system
    worked.

Clauses misplaced:
  I bought Brie in the new shop on North Road that cost $8.00 a
    pound.
  We saved the balloons for the children that had been left on the
    table.

Revised:
  I bought Brie that cost $8.00 a pound in the new shop on North
    Road.
  We saved the balloons that had been left on the table for the
    children.

Dangling Modifiers
A *dangling*—or *unattached*—*modifier* occurs when a modifier does not logically or grammatically describe anything in
the sentence because the noun or pronoun to which a phrase
or clause refers is either in the wrong place or missing. Like
misplaced modifiers, dangling modifiers cause confusion.

Examples of dangling modifiers:
While reading the paper, the birds on the railing caught my eye.
Biking up the hill, a Jaguar went roaring past.
Drinking a cup of coffee, the cat leaped on the table.
The evening passed contentedly, reading and listening to music.
Sitting on the riverbank, the sun glinted on the rippling waves.
After closing the door, the room got very warm.
In planning a European trip, consideration of the amount of luggage is needed.
To graduate with honors, exceptional ability and hard work are needed.
When travelling, my passport is in my inside pocket.
When at the age of five, my Aunt Rose gave me a black kitten.

Revised:
While I was reading the paper, the birds on the railing caught my eye.
As I was biking up the hill, a Jaguar went roaring past.
While I was drinking a cup of coffee, the cat leaped on the table.
We passed the evening contentedly, reading and listening to music.
Sitting on the riverbank, I watched the sun glinting on the rippling waves.
After I had closed the door, the room got very warm.
In planning a European trip, one needs to consider the amount of luggage one can carry.
To graduate with honors, one needs exceptional ability and hard work.
When travelling, I carry my passport in my inside pocket.
   Or
When I am travelling, my passport is in my inside pocket.
When I was at the age of five, my Aunt Rose gave me a black kitten.

Squinting Modifiers

A *"squinting"* modifier is one that may refer to either a preceding or following word and therefore causes ambiguity and confusion.

Examples of squinting modifiers:
We said when we were coming back from the Cape that we
   would like to buy some local produce.
Exercising often gives me energy.
The case that the prosecution had prepared quickly forced it to
   declare the defendant's sister a hostile witness.

Revised:
We said we would like to buy some local produce when we were
   coming back from the Cape.
Or
When we were coming back from the Cape, we said we would
   like to buy some local produce.

Often, exercising gives me energy.
Or
It gives me energy to exercise often.

The case that the prosecution had quickly prepared forced it to
   declare the defendant's sister a hostile witness.
Or
The case that the prosecution had prepared forced it quickly to
   declare the defendant's sister a hostile witness.

Agreement of Sentence Parts

Agreement is what it sounds like—matching. Specifically, agreement refers to the matching of number, person, and gender within a sentence. Subjects and verbs must match in number (singular or plural) and person (first, second, or third). Pronouns and their antecedents (the words to which they refer) must also match in gender (masculine, feminine, or neuter).

Sentences that do not maintain agreement among all their elements sound clumsy and can be ambiguous.

Subject-Verb Agreement

A subject must agree with its verb in number. A singular subject takes a singular verb. A plural subject takes a plural verb.

First, find the subject; then determine whether it is singular or plural. The subject is the noun or pronoun that is doing the action. Often, it will be located at the beginning of the sentence, as in the following example:

I recommend that company highly.

Here, the subject "I" is doing the action "recommend."

Sometimes the subject will follow the verb, as in questions and in sentences beginning with *here* and *there*. In the following example, the verb "are" comes before the subject "roads":

There are two roads you can take.

The same is true of the placement of the subject and verb in the following question, as the verb "is" comes before the subject "briefcase":

Where is your briefcase?

After you have located the subject, decide whether it is singular or plural. In English, confusion can arise because most present-tense verbs add *-s* or *-es* when their subject is third-person singular *(He runs fast. She studies a lot.),* whereas nouns ending in *-s* or *-es* are plural *(potatoes, computers).* The following table shows how regular English verbs are conjugated in the present tense:

Singular	Plural
I dream	*we dream*
you dream	*you dream*
he, she, it dreams	*they dream*

There are a number of plural nouns that are regarded as singular in meaning, as well as other nouns that can be both singular and plural, depending on the context of the sentence. *Acoustics, athletics, economics, gymnastics, mathematics, physics, politics,* and *statistics,* for example, are often treated as singular nouns.

Acoustics is *the branch of physics that deals with sound.*
The acoustics *in the new hall* are *excellent.*

Gymnastics is *an Olympic sport.*
Verbal gymnastics are *his forte.*

Statistics is *the science that deals with the collection and analysis of numerical data.*
The statistics show *that the town's population has increased by 22 percent in the past decade.*

Often, a phrase or clause will intervene between a subject and a verb. These intervening words do not affect subject-verb agreement, as illustrated in the following examples.

The supervisor of the department, together with her sales force,
  is taking *the 8:30 shuttle to Washington.*
The deputies to the mayor are exploring *alternate methods of*
  disposing of newspapers.
A display of luscious foods sometimes encourages *impulse*
  buying.
The profits earned this quarter are *much higher than we had*
  expected.

Singular subjects connected by *or, nor, either . . . or,* or *nei-*
ther . . . nor take a singular verb if both subjects are singular, a
plural verb if both subjects are plural.

Either your supervisor or your colleague has *to take*
  responsibility for the error.
Either supervisors or colleagues have *to take responsibility for*
  the error.
Neither the sled nor the snow shovel has *been put*
  away.
Either the clown or the magician is scheduled *to appear at the*
  library on Sunday afternoon.
Neither boots nor shoes are included *in the one-day*
  sale.

If a subject consists of both singular and plural nouns or pronouns connected by *or* or *nor,* the verb usually agrees with the
nearer noun or pronoun.

In the following sentence, the plural verb "want" agrees with
the plural noun "students":

Neither the teacher nor the students want *to be here.*

Notice that the verb becomes singular when "teacher" and
"students" are reversed:

Neither the students nor the teacher wants *to be here.*

Practice in this matter varies, however, and often the presence
of one plural subject, no matter what its position, results in the
use of a plural verb. Sometimes writers place the plural subject
closer to the verb to avoid awkwardness:

Neither we nor she has distributed *the memo yet.*
Neither she nor we have distributed *the memo yet.*
Either Martha, Ruth, or the Champney girls are planning *to*
  organize the graduation party.

Two or more subjects, phrases, or clauses connected by *and* take a plural verb. Whether the individual subjects are singular or plural, together they form a compound subject, which is plural:

The president and her advisers were behind schedule.
The faculty and staff have planned a joint professional retreat.
Richard and his dog jog before work every morning.
Sleeping late Sunday morning and reading the paper help me relax after a long week at work.

Traditionally, when the subjects joined by *and* refer to the same object or person or stand for a single idea, the entire subject is treated as a unit. Most often, the personal pronoun or article before the parts of the compound subject indicates whether the subject is indeed seen as a unit. As with other matters of agreement, this varies widely in actual use:

Unit as singular:
   Ham and Swiss is my favorite sandwich.
("Ham and Swiss" is treated as a type of sandwich.)
   My mentor and friend guides me through difficult career decisions.
(Mentor and friend are the same person.)

Unit as plural:
   Ham and Swiss make a great sandwich.
(Each ingredient is treated as separate.)
   My mentor and my friend guide me through difficult career decisions.
(Mentor and friend are two different people.)

Mixed units:
   Ham and eggs was once considered a nutritious and healthful breakfast; now, cereal and fresh fruit are considered preferable.

Nouns that refer to weight, extent, time, fractions, portions, or amount considered as one unit usually take a singular verb; those that indicate separate units usually take a plural verb.

In the first two examples below, the subjects are considered as single units and therefore take a singular verb. In the last two, the subjects are considered as individual items and therefore take a plural verb.

Seventy-five cents is *more than enough to buy what you want at the penny carnival.*

Three-fourths of the harvest was saved *through their heroic efforts.*

Half of the nails were rusted.

Fifty pounds of homegrown tomatoes are being divided *among the eager shoppers.*

Collective Nouns

Collective nouns **(nouns that are singular in form but denote a group of persons or objects) may be either singular or plural, depending on the meaning of the sentence.**

Common Collective Nouns

assembly	couple	minority
association	crowd	number
audience	family	pair
board	flock	part
class	group	percent
commission	half	press
committee	herd	public
company	jury	series
corporation	legion	staff
council	majority	

Determine agreement for each collective noun on a sentence-by-sentence basis. If the sentence implies that the group named by the collective noun acts as a single unit, use a singular verb. If the sentence implies that the group named by the collective noun acts individually, use a plural verb.

The budget committee is voting *on a new accountant this week.*

The budget committee are *in complete disagreement about the choice of a new accountant.*

The team has *eight games scheduled for September.*

The jury, not the judge, makes *the final decision.*

Gotthelf & Company is hosting *its annual holiday party this Friday evening.*

The phrases *the number* and *the total* are usually singular, but the phrases *a number* and *a total* are usually plural:

> *The number of new members* is *astonishing.*
> *A number of new members* were *at the meeting.*

When the collective nouns *couple* and *pair* refer to people, they are usually treated as plurals:

> *The pair* are hosting *a New Year's open house.*
> *The couple* have bought *a large apartment with a view of the river.*

Note: In British English, a collective noun naming an organization regarded as a unit is usually treated as plural:

> *Gotthelf & Company* are hosting *their annual holiday party this Friday evening.*
> *The team* have *eight games scheduled for September.*

Pronouns

A *pronoun* must agree with its antecedent—the word to which the pronoun refers—in number and gender.

Traditionally, certain indefinite pronouns were always considered singular, some were always considered plural, and some could be both singular and plural. As language changes, however, many of these rules are changing. *None,* for example, was always treated as a singular pronoun even though it has been used with both singular and plural verbs since the ninth century. When the sense is "not any persons or things," the plural is more commonly used:

> *The rescue party searched for survivors, but none* were *found.*

When none is clearly intended to mean "not one" or "not any," it is followed by a singular verb:

> *Of all my court cases, none* has been *more stressful than yours.*
> *None of us* is going *to the concert.*

The following lists, therefore, are presented as general guidelines, not hard-and-fast rules. In general, use singular verbs with indefinite pronouns.

Indefinite Pronouns That Are Most Often Considered Singular

anybody	everybody	nothing
anyone	everyone	one
anything	everything	somebody
each	many a	someone
either	neither	
every	nobody	

Indefinite Pronouns That Are Always Considered Plural

both
few
many
others
several

Indefinite Pronouns That Can Be Considered Singular or Plural

all
any
more
most
none
some

Each of the people observes *all the safety regulations.*
Few are comfortable during a job interview.
Some of the water is seeping *into the wall, but most of the files*
    remain dry.
All the food has been donated *to charity.*
All the children have had *cake and ice cream.*

The effort to avoid the sexist implications of *he* has led to the general acceptance, at least in informal speech and writing, of *they, their,* and *them* to refer to indefinite pronouns:

Everyone began putting on their *coats.*
If anybody calls, tell them *I'll call back after 10:00.*

Shifts

A *shift* is an unnecessary or illogical change of tense, voice, mood, person, number, tone or style, viewpoint, or direct and indirect quotations within a sentence, paragraph, or essay. Shifts confuse your reader and distort the meaning of your writing.

Shifts in Tense

A **shift in tense** occurs when the tenses of verbs within a sentence or paragraph do not logically match.

Confusing:
> Throughout the eighties the junk-bond market rose *steadily;* as a result, small investors invest *heavily from 1985 to 1989.*

Revised:
> Throughout the eighties the junk-bond market rose *steadily;* as a result, small investors invested *heavily from 1985 to 1989.*

Confusing:
> Last night I was watching *my favorite television show. Suddenly the show* is interrupted *for a special news bulletin.* I lean *forward and* will *eagerly* watch *the screen for information.*

Revised:
> Last night I was watching *my favorite television show. Suddenly the show* was interrupted *for a special news bulletin.* I leaned *forward and eagerly* watched *the screen for information.*

Note: If you are using the present tense to narrate the events in a literary work, be careful not to slip into the past tense.

Shifts in Voice

Voice shows whether the subject of the verb acts or is acted upon. When the subject of the verb does the action, the sentence is said to be in the active voice:

Dave hit *a home run.*

When the subject of the verb receives the action, the sentence is said to be in the passive voice:

The home run was hit *by Dave.*

Confusing:
> As we finished *our coffee, the servers* were seen *clearing the adjacent tables.*

Revised:
> As we finished *our coffee, we* saw *the servers clearing the adjacent tables.*

Confusing:
> The cook mixed *the bread dough until it was blended and then it* was set *in the warm oven to rise.*

Revised:
> The cook mixed *the bread dough until it was blended and then* set *it in the warm oven to rise.*

Or
> The bread dough was mixed *until it was blended, and then it* was set *in the warm oven to rise.*

Shifts in Mood

The **mood** of a verb indicates the manner in which it is used. English has three moods: indicative, subjunctive, and imperative. (See page 28.)

Confusing:
> Stroke *the paint on evenly, but* you should not *dab it on corners and edges.* [Shift from imperative to indicative]

Revised:
> Stroke *the paint on evenly, but* don't *dab it on corners and edges.*

Or

> You should *stroke the paint on evenly, but* you shouldn't *dab it on corners and edges.*

Confusing:

> The cleaning service asked that they get *better hours and they* want *to work fewer weekends as well.* [Shift from subjunctive to indicative]

Revised:

> The cleaning service asked that they get *better hours and that they* work *fewer weekends as well.*

Or

> The cleaning service asked to work *better hours and fewer weekends.*

Or

> The cleaning service wants to work *better hours and fewer weekends.*

Confusing:

> If the rain stopped *and the sun* comes out, *we could have a* picnic. [Shift from subjunctive to indicative]

Revised:

> If the rain stopped *and the sun* came out, *we could have a* picnic.

Or

> If the rain stops *and the sun* comes out, *we can have a picnic.*

Shifts in Person

Person means the form a pronoun or verb takes to show the person or persons speaking: the first person *(I, we)*, the second person *(you)*, or the third person *(he, she, it, they)*. As the pronouns indicate, the first person is the person speaking, the second person is the person spoken to, and the third person is the person, concept, or thing spoken about.

Shifts between second- and third-person pronouns cause the most confusion. The following examples illustrate common shfits in person and different ways to revise such shifts.

Confusing:
When one *shops for an automobile,* you *should research various models in consumer magazines and read all the advertisements as well as speak to salespeople.* [Shift from the third to the second person]

Revised:
When you *shop for an automobile,* you *should research various models in consumer magazines and read all the advertisements as well as speak to salespeople.*

Or
When one *shops for an automobile,* one *should research various models in consumer magazines and read all the advertisements as well as speak to salespeople.*

Or
When people *shop for an automobile,* they *should research various models in consumer magazines and read all the advertisements as well as speak to salespeople.*

Confusing:
When a person *applies themselves diligently,* you *can accomplish a surprising amount.*

Revised:
When people *apply themselves diligently,* they *can accomplish a surprising amount.*

Or
When you *apply yourself diligently,* you *can accomplish a surprising amount.*

Or
When a person *applies himself or herself diligently,* he or she *can accomplish a surprising amount.*

Shifts in Perspective

Shifts in perspective are related to shifts in person in that both change the vantage point from which a story is told. As with other shifts, there will be occasions when it is desirable to shift perspective, but unnecessary shifts confuse readers. In the following example, the perspective shifts from above the water to below without adequate transition.

Confusing:
> The frothy surface of the ocean danced with bursts of light, and the fish swam lazily through the clear water and waving plants.

Revised:
> The frothy surface of the ocean danced with bursts of light; below, the fish swam lazily through the clear water and waving plants.

Shifts in Number

Number indicates one (singular) or more than one (plural). Shifts in number occur with nouns and personal pronouns because both change form to show differences in number. Confusion with number occurs especially often between a pronoun and its antecedent and between words whose meanings relate to each other. Remember to use singular pronouns to refer to singular antecedents and plural pronouns to refer to plural antecedents.

Confusing:
> If a person *does not keep up with household chores,* they *will find that things pile up with alarming speed.*

Revised:
> If a person *does not keep up with household chores,* he or she *will find that things pile up with alarming speed.*

Or
> If people *do not keep up with household chores,* they *will find that things pile up with alarming speed.*

Confusing:
> *All the* repair stations *have a good* reputation.

Revised:
> All the repair stations *have good* reputations.

Person and Number with Collective Nouns

Maintaining consistency of person and number is especially tricky with collective nouns since many can be either singular or plural, depending on the context. Once you establish a collective noun as singular or plural within a sentence, maintain consistency throughout.

Confusing:
> Because my company bases their *bonus on amount of income generated yearly, we must all do our share to enable* it *to give a generous bonus.*

Revised:
> Because my company bases its *bonus on amount of income generated yearly, we must all do our share to enable* it *to give a generous bonus.*

Or
> Because my company bases their *bonus on amount of income generated yearly, we must all do our share to enable* them *to give a generous bonus.*

Confusing:
> The jury is *divided on whether or not* they *should demand additional evidence.*

Revised:
> The jury are *divided on whether or not* they *should demand additional evidence. [Jury functioning as separate individuals]*

Shifts in Tone and Style

Tone is the writer's attitude toward his or her readers and subject. As pitch and volume convey tone in speaking, so word choice and sentence structure help convey tone in writing. Tone can be formal or informal, humorous or earnest, distant or friendly, pompous or personal. Obviously, different tones are appropriate for different audiences.

Style is a writer's way of writing. Style comprises every way a writer uses language. Elements of style include tone, word choice, figurative language, grammatical structure, rhythm, and sentence length and organization.

A piece of writing is more powerful and effective if consistent tone and style are maintained throughout.

Shift:
> Reporters who assert that freedom of the press can be maintained without judicial intervention are out of their minds. [Shift from elevated diction to colloquial]

Revised:
> Reporters who assert that freedom of the press can be maintained without judicial intervention are greatly mistaken.

Shift:
> Their leavetaking was marked by the same affability that had characterized their entire visit with us. Later, we discussed what cool dudes they were. [Shift from standard English to colloquial]

Revised:
> Their leavetaking was marked by the same affability that had characterized their entire visit with us. Later, we discussed their good humor, consideration, and generosity.

Shifts in Direct and Indirect Quotations

Direct quotations use quotation marks to report a speaker's exact words. *"I'll be the referee for today's game,"* Ms. Kinsella said. Usually, direct quotations are also marked by a phrase such as *she said* or *he remarked*, which indicates the speaker.

Indirect quotations report what was said, but not necessarily in the speaker's own words: *Ms. Kinsella said that she would be the referee for today's game.* Since the remarks do not have to be reproduced exactly, indirect quotations do not use quotation marks. Often, a reported statement will be introduced by *that, who, how, if, what, when,* or *whether.*

Illogical shifts between direct and indirect quotations can become wordy and confuse readers. As the following examples show, these errors can usually be eliminated by recording a speaker's remarks with logic and consistency regardless of whether direct or indirect quotations or a combination of the two are used.

Wordy:
> Poet and critic T.S. Eliot said that he feels that the progress of an artist was like a long process of sacrifice of self, "a continual extinction of personality."

Revised:
> Poet and critic T.S. Eliot said that the progress of an artist was like a long process of self-sacrifice, "a continual extinction of personality."

Or
> Poet and critic T.S. Eliot said that to progress, artists must sacrifice and extinguish the self.

Confusing:
> Jill asked whether we had cut down the storm-damaged tree and was there any further damage.

Revised:
> Jill asked whether we had cut down the storm-damaged tree and if there was any further damage.

Or
> Jill asked, "Did you cut down the tree damaged by the storm? Was there any further damage?"

Confusing:
> My son said he was very busy and would I please take the cat to the vet.

Revised:
   My son said he was very busy and asked if I would take the cat
   to the vet.

Parallel Structure

Parallel structure, or *parallelism,* means that grammatical elements that share the same function will share the same form.
Parallel structure ensures that ideas of equal rank are expressed in similar ways and that separate word groups appear
in the same grammatical forms.

   Individual words, phrases, clauses, or sentences can be paral-
leled. For example, adjectives are paired with adjectives, and verbs
correspond with matching verbs in tense, mood, voice, and number. Parallel structure helps coordinate ideas and strengthen logic
and symmetry.

   Study the following pairs of examples. Note how much more
smoothly the sentences flow when the constructions are parallel.

Not parallel:
   Allison was hot, cranky, and needed food.

Parallel:
   Allsion was hot, cranky, and hungry.

Not parallel:
   Sam is organized, efficient, and works hard.

Parallel:
   Sam is organized, efficient, and industrious.

Not parallel:
   Knowing how to win is important, but it is even more important
   to know how to lose.

Parallel:
   Knowing how to win is important, but knowing how to lose is
   even more important.

Not parallel:
   We can go out to eat, or ordering a pizza would do as well.

Parallel:
   We can go *out to eat, or* we can order a *pizza.*

Not parallel:
   He has plundered *our seas, ravaged our coasts, and was burning our towns.*

Parallel:
   He has plundered *our seas,* ravaged *our coasts, and* burnt *our towns.*

Not parallel:
   The only good *is knowledge, and evil is the only ignorant thing.*

Parallel:
   The only good *is knowledge, and* the only evil *is ignorance.*

Not parallel:
   Cursed be the social wants that sin against the strength of youth!
   Cursed be the social ties that warp us from the living truth!
   Cursed be the sickly forms that err from honest nature's rule!
   The gold that gilds the straighten'd forehead of the fool is also cursed.

Parallel:
   Cursed *be the social wants that sin against the strength of youth!*
   Cursed be *the social ties that warp us from the living truth!*
   Cursed be *the sickly forms that err from honest nature's rule!*
   Cursed be *the gold that gilds the straighten'd forehead of the fool.*

Parallel Items in Series

Items in a series have greater impact when arranged in parallel order. The items can be words, phrases, or clauses:

> *Passions, prejudices, fears, and neuroses spring from ignorance, and take the form of myth and illusions.—Sir Isaiah Berlin*
>
> *When any of the four pillars of the government, religion, justice, counsel, and treasure, are mainly shaken or weakened, men have need to pray for fair weather.—Francis Bacon*

In the opening of *A Tale of Two Cities*, Charles Dickens arranged paired items in a series for a powerful effect:

> *It was the best of times, it was the worst of times,*
> *it was the age of wisdom, it was the age of foolishness,*
> *it was the epoch of belief, it was the epoch of incredulity,*
> *it was the season of Light, it was the season of Darkness,*
> *it was the spring of hope, it was the winter of despair . . .*

Parallel Outlines and Lists

Arranging outlined ideas and lists in parallel structure helps solidify thinking. Maintaining one format (for example, complete sentences, clauses, or phrases) throughout serves to order ideas, as the following sentence outline shows:

I. Cigarette smoke harms the health of the general public.
  A. Cigarette smoke may lead to serious diseases in nonsmokers.
    1. It leads to lung cancer.
      a. It causes emphysema.
      b. It causes mouth cancer.
    2. It leads to circulatory disease.
      a. It causes strokes.
      b. It causes heart disease.
  B. Cigarette smoke worsens less serious health conditions in nonsmokers.
    1. It aggravates allergies.
    2. It intensifies pulmonary infections.

Usage

Spelling Rules

Correct spelling is an important part of correct usage. English spellings present some difficulties because so many words are not spelled the way they sound. The following rules can serve as general guidelines. Remember that no spelling rule should be followed blindly because every rule has its exceptions.

1. Silent *E* Dropped. Silent *e* at the end of a word is usually dropped before a suffix beginning with a vowel: *abide, abiding; recite, recital.*

   Exceptions: Words ending in *ce* or *ge* retain the *e* before a suffix beginning with *a* or *o* to keep the soft sound of the consonant: *notice, noticeable; courage, courageous.*

2. Silent *E* Kept. A silent *e* following a consonant (or another *e*) is usually retained before a suffix beginning with a consonant: *late, lateness; spite, spiteful.*

   Exceptions: *fledgling, acknowledgment, judgment, wholly,* and a few similar words.

3. Final Consonant Doubled. A final consonant following a single vowel in one-syllable words, or in a syllable that will take the main accent when combined with a suffix, is doubled before a suffix beginning with a vowel: *begin, beginning; occur, occurred; bat, batted.*

   Exceptions: *h* and *x* in final position; *transferable, gaseous,* and a few others.

4. Final Consonant Single. A final consonant following another consonant, a double vowel or diphthong, or that is not in a stressed syllable, is not doubled before a suffix beginning with a vowel: *part, parting; remark, remarkable.*

   Exceptions: an unaccented syllable does not prevent doubling of the final consonant, especially in British usage: *traveller* for *traveler.*

5. Double Consonants Remain. Double consonants are usually retained before a suffix except when a final *l* is to be followed by *ly* or *less.* To avoid a triple *lll,* one *l* is usually dropped: *full, fully.*

   Exceptions: Usage is divided, with some preferring *skilful* over *skillful, instalment* over *installment,* etc.

6. Final *Y.* If the *y* follows a consonant, change *y* to *i* before all end-

ings except *ing*. Do not change it before *ing* or if it follows a vowel: *bury, buried, burying; try, tries;* but *attorney, attorneys*. Exceptions: *day, daily; gay, gaily; lay, laid; say, said*.

7. Final *ıE* to *Y*. Words ending in *ie* change to *y* before *ing: die, dying; lie, lying*

8. Double and Triple *E* Reduced. Words ending in double *e* drop one *e* before an ending beginning in *e*, to avoid a triple *e*. Words ending in silent *e* usually drop the *e* before endings beginning in *e* to avoid forming a syllable. Other words ending in a vowel sound commonly retain the letters indicating the sound. *Free + ed = freed*.

9. *EI* or *IE*. Words having the sound of *ē* are commonly spelled *ie* following all letters but *c*; with a preceding *c*, the common spelling is *ei*. Examples: *believe, achieve, besiege;* but *conceit, ceiling, receive, conceive*. When the sound is *ā* the common spelling is *ei* regardless of the preceding letter. Examples: *eight, weight, deign*.

   Exceptions: *either, neither, seize, financier;* some words in which *e* and *i* are pronounced separately, such as *notoriety*.

10. Words Ending in *C*. Before an ending beginning with *e*, *i*, or *y*, words ending in *c* commonly add *k* to keep the *c* hard: *panic, panicky*.

11. Compounds. Some compounds written as a unit bring together unusual combinations of letters. They are seldom changed on this account: *bookkeeper, roommate*.

   Exceptions: A few words are regularly clipped when compounded, such as *full* in *awful, cupful*, etc.

Words Most Often Misspelled

We have listed here some of the words that have traditionally proved difficult to spell. The list includes not only exceptions, words that defy common spelling rules, but some that pose problems even while adhering to these conventions.

aberrant	accordion	across	against
abscess	accumulate	address	aggravate
absence	accustom	adequate	aggression
absorption	achievement	adherent	aging
abundance	acknowledge	adjourn	aisle
accede	acknowledgment	admittance	alien
acceptance	acoustics	adolescence	all right
accessible	acquaintance	adolescent	allegiance
accidentally	acquiesce	advantageous	almost
accommodate	acquire	advertisement	already
according	acquittal	affidavit	although

always
amateur
analysis
analytical
analyze
anesthetic
annual
anoint
anonymous
answer
antarctic
antecedent
anticipation
antihistamine
anxiety
aperitif
apocryphal
apostasy
apparent
appearance
appetite
appreciate
appropriate
approximate
apropos
arctic
arguing
argument
arouse
arrangement
arthritis
article
artificial
asinine
asked
assassin
assess
asthma
athlete
athletic
attorneys
author
authoritative
auxiliary

bachelor
balance
bankruptcy
barbiturate
barrette
basically

basis
beggar
beginning
belief
believable
believe
beneficial
beneficiary
benefit
benefited
blizzard
bludgeon
bologna
bookkeeping
bouillon
boundaries
braggadocio
breathe
brief
brilliant
broccoli
bronchial
brutality
bulletin
buoy
buoyant
bureau
bureaucracy
burglary
business

cafeteria
caffeine
calisthenics
camaraderie
camouflage
campaign
cancel
cancellation
candidate
cantaloupe
capacity
cappuccino
carburetor
career
careful
carriage
carrying
casserole
category
caterpillar

cavalry
ceiling
cellar
cemetery
census
certain
challenge
chandelier
changeable
changing
characteristic
chief
choir
choose
cinnamon
circuit
civilized
clothes
codeine
collateral
colloquial
colonel
colossal
column
coming
commemorate
commission
commitment
committed
committee
comparative
comparison
competition
competitive
complaint
concede
conceivable
conceive
condemn
condescend
conferred
confidential
congratulate
conscience
conscientious
conscious
consensus
consequently
consistent
consummate
continuous

control
controlled
controversy
convalesce
convenience
coolly
copyright
cornucopia
corollary
corporation
correlate
correspondence
correspondent
counselor
counterfeit
courageous
courteous
crisis
criticism
criticize
culinary
curiosity
curriculum
cylinder

debt
debtor
deceive
decide
decision
decisive
defendant
definite
definitely
dependent
de rigueur
descend
descendant
description
desiccate
desirable
despair
desperate
destroy
develop
development
diabetes
diaphragm
different
dilemma
dining

diocese
diphtheria
disappear
disappearance
disappoint
disastrous
discipline
disease
dissatisfied
dissident
dissipate
distinguish
divide
divine
doesn't
dormitory
duly
dumbbell
during

easier
easily
ecstasy
effervescent
efficacy
efficiency
efficient
eighth
eightieth
electrician
eligibility
eligible
eliminate
ellipsis
embarrass
encouraging
endurance
energetic
enforceable
enthusiasm
environment
equipped
erroneous
especially
esteemed
exacerbate
exaggerate
exceed
excel
excellent
except

exceptionally
excessive
executive
exercise
exhibition
exh..arate
existence
expense
experience
experiment
explanation
exquisite
extemporaneous
extraordinary
extremely

facilities
fallacy
familiar
fascinate
fascism
feasible
February
fictitious
fiend
fierce
fiftieth
finagle
finally
financial
fluorine
foliage
forcible
forehead
foreign
forfeit
formally
forte
fortieth
fortunately
forty
fourth
friend
frieze
fundamental
furniture

galoshes
gauge
genealogy

generally
gnash
government
governor
graffiti
grammar
grateful
grievance
grievous
guarantee
guard
guidance

handkerchief
haphazard
harass
harebrained
hazard
height
hemorrhage
hemorrhoid
hereditary
heroes
hierarchy
hindrance
hoping
hors d'oeuvres
huge
humorous
hundredth
hurrying
hydraulic
hygiene
hygienist
hypocrisy

icicle
identification
idiosyncrasy
imaginary
immediately
immense
impostor
impresario
inalienable
incident
incidentally
inconvenience
incredible
indelible

independent
indestructible
indictment
indigestible
indispensable
inevitable
inferred
influential
initial
initiative
innocuous
innuendo
inoculation
inscrutable
installation
instantaneous
intellectual
intelligence
intercede
interest
interfere
intermittent
intimate
inveigle
irrelevant
irresistible
island

jealous
jeopardize
journal
judgment
judicial

khaki
kindergarten
knowledge

laboratory
laid
larynx
leery
leisure
length
liable
liaison
libel
library
license
lieutenant

lightning
likelihood
liquefy
liqueur
literature
livelihood
loneliness
losing
lovable

magazine
maintenance
manageable
management
maneuver
manufacturer
maraschino
marital
marriage
marriageable
mathematics
mayonnaise
meant
medicine
medieval
memento
mileage
millennium
miniature
minuet
miscellaneous
mischievous
misspell
mistletoe
moccasin
molasses
molecule
monotonous
mortgage
murmur
muscle
mutual
mysterious

naive
naturally
necessarily
necessary
necessity
neighbor
neither

nickel
niece
ninetieth
ninety
ninth
noticeable
notoriety
nuptial

obbligato
occasion
occasionally
occurred
occurrence
offense
official
omission
omit
omitted
oneself
ophthalmology
opinion
opportunity
optimism
optimist
ordinarily
origin
original
outrageous

paean
pageant
paid
pamphlet
paradise
parakeet
parallel
paralysis
paralyze
paraphernalia
parimutuel
parliament
partial
participate
particularly
pasteurize
pastime
pavilion
peaceable
peasant

peculiar
penicillin
perceive
perform
performance
peril
permanent
permissible
perpendicular
perseverance
persistent
personnel
perspiration
persuade
persuasion
persuasive
petition
philosophy
physician
piccolo
plaited
plateau
plausible
playwright
pleasant
plebeian
pneumonia
poinsettia
politician
pomegranate
possess
possession
possibility
possible
practically
practice
precede
precedence
precisely
predecessor
preference
preferred
prejudice
preparatory
prescription
prevalent
primitive
prior
privilege
probability
probably

procedure
proceed
professor
proffer
pronounce
pronunciation
propagate
protégé(e)
psychiatry
psychology
pursuant
pursue
pursuit
putrefy

quantity
questionnaire
queue

rarefy
recede
receipt
receivable
receive
recipe
reciprocal
recognize
recommend
reference
referred
reign
relegate
relevant
relieve
religious
remembrance
reminisce
remiss
remittance
rendezvous
repetition
replaceable
representative
requisition
resistance
responsibility
restaurant
restaurateur
resuscitate
reticence

reveille
rhyme
rhythm
riddance
ridiculous
rococo
roommate

sacrifice
sacrilegious
safety
salary
sandwich
sarsaparilla
sassafras
satisfaction
scarcity
scene
scenery
schedule
scheme
scholarly
scissors
secede
secrecy
secretary
seize
seizure
separate
separately
sergeant
serviceable
seventieth
several
sheik
shepherd
sheriff
shining
shoulder
shrapnel
siege
sieve
significance
silhouette
similar

simultaneity
simultaneous
sincerely
sixtieth
skiing
soci ;lly
society
solemn
soliloquy
sophomore
sorority
sovereign
spaghetti
spatial
special
specifically
specimen
speech
sponsor
spontaneous
statistics
statute
stevedore
stiletto
stopped
stopping
strength
strictly
studying
stupefy
submitted
substantial
subtle
subtly
succeed
successful
succession
successive
sufficient
superintendent
supersede
supplement
suppress
surprise
surveillance
susceptible

suspicion
sustenance
syllable
symmetrical
sympathize
sympathy
synchronous
synonym
syphilis
systematically

tariff
temperament
temperature
temporarily
tendency
tentative
terrestrial
therefore
thirtieth
thorough
thought
thousandth
through
till
titillate
together
tonight
tournament
tourniquet
tragedy
tragically
transferred
transient
tries
truly
twelfth
twentieth
typical
tyranny

unanimous
undoubtedly
unique
unison
unmanageable

unnecessary
until
upholsterer
usable
usage
using
usually
utilize

vacancy
vacuum
vague
valuable
variety
vegetable
veil
vengeance
vermilion
veterinarian
vichyssoise
village
villain

warrant
Wednesday
weird
wherever
whim
wholly
whose
wield
woolen
wretched
writing
written
wrote
wrought

xylophone

yacht
yield

zealous
zucchini

Using a Spell Checker

A spell checker is a computer program that checks or verifies the spelling of words in an electronic document. While it can be a valuable tool for writers, it cannot be relied upon to catch all types of spelling errors. It is most useful in finding misspellings that produce "nonwords"—words with transposed, wrong, or missing letters. For example, it will reject *ther* (for *there*) and *teh* (for *the*). However, it cannot distinguish between words that sound or look alike but differ in meaning. It will accept *to* or *too* regardless of whether the context is correct, and it will accept typos such as *on* (for *of*) or *form* (for *from*). It is important, therefore, not to rely too heavily on spell checkers and to go over your writing carefully to avoid such mistakes.

Rules of Word Division

It is often necessary to divide a word at the end of a line. Words must always be divided between syllables. Consult a dictionary if you are not sure where the syllable division occurs. The following rules should be followed to avoid confusing the reader.

1. Do not divide a one-syllable word. This includes past tenses like *walked* and *dreamed,* which should never be split before the *-ed* ending.
2. Do not divide a word so that a single letter is left at the end of a line, as in *a·bout,* or so that a single letter starts the following line, as in *cit·y.*
3. Hyphenated compounds should preferably be divided only after the hyphen. If the first portion of the compound is a single letter, however, as in *D-day,* the word should not be divided.
4. Word segments like *-ceous, -scious, -sial, -tion, -tious* should not be divided.
5. The portion of a word left at the end of a line should not encourage a misleading pronunciation, as would be the case if *acetate,* a three-syllable word, were divided after the first *e.*

Words Often Confused

Words are often confused if they have similar or identical forms or sounds. You may have the correct meaning in mind, but choosing the wrong word will change your intended meaning. An *ingenuous* person is not the same as an *ingenious* person. Similarly, you may be using a word that is correct in a different context but does not express your intended meaning. To *infer* something is not the same as to *imply* it.

Use of the wrong word is often the result of confusing words that are identical or very similar in pronunciation but different in spelling. An example of a pair of words with the same pronunciation is "compliment, complement." The confusion may arise from a small difference in spelling, as the pair "canvas, canvass"; or the soundalikes may be spelled quite differently, as the pairs "manor, manner" and "brake, break." An example of a pair of words with similar but not identical pronunciation is "accept, except"; they are very different in usage and grammatical function.

Words may also be confused if they are spelled the same way but differ in meaning or in meaning and pronunciation, as the soundalikes *bear* "animal" and *bear* "carry, support" or the lookalikes *row* (rō) "line" and *row* (rou) "fight."

Errors in word choice may also result if word groups overlap in meaning or usage. In informal contexts, *aggravate* may be used to mean "annoy" and *mad* may be used to mean "angry." *Leave* and *let* are interchangeable when followed by the word "alone" in the sense "to stop annoying or interfering with someone."

The following glossary lists words that are commonly confused and discusses their meanings and proper usage.

accept/except *Accept* is a verb meaning "to receive": *Please accept a gift. Except* is usually a preposition or a conjunction meaning "other than" or "but for": *He was willing to accept an apology from everyone except me.* When *except* is used as a verb, it means "to leave out": *He was excepted from the new regulations.*

accidentally/accidently The correct adverb is *accidentally*, from the root word *accidental*, not *accident* (*Russell accidentally slipped on the icy sidewalk*). *Accidently* is a misspelling.

adoptive/adopted *Adoptive* refers to the parent: *He resembles his adoptive father. Adopted* refers to the child: *Their adopted daughter wants to adopt a child herself.*

adverse/averse Both words are adjectives, and both mean "opposed" or "hostile." *Averse*, however, is used to describe a subject's opposition to something (*The minister was averse to the new trends developing in the* *country),* whereas *adverse* describes something opposed to the subject *(The adverse comments affected his self-esteem).*

advice/advise *Advice,* a noun, means "suggestion or suggestions": *Here's some good advice. Advise,* a verb, means "to offer ideas or suggestions": *Act as we advise you.*

affect/effect Most often, *affect* is a verb, meaning "to influence," and *effect* is a noun meaning "the result of an action": *His speech affected my mother very deeply, but had no effect on my sister at all. Affect* is also used as a noun in psychology and psychiatry to mean "emotion": *We can learn much about affect from performance.* In this usage, it is pronounced with the stress on the first syllable. *Effect* is also used as a verb meaning "to bring about": *His letter effected a change in their relationship.*

aggravate/annoy In informal speech and writing, *aggravate* can be used as a synonym for *annoy.* However, in formal discourse the words mean different things and should be used in this way: *Her back condition was aggravated by lifting the child, but the child's crying annoyed her more than the pain did.*

agree to/agree with *Agree to* means "to consent to, to accept" (usually a plan or idea). *Agree with* means "to be in accord with" (usually a person or group): *I can't believe they will agree to your proposal when they don't agree with each other on anything.*

aisle/isle *Aisle* means "a passageway between sections of seats": *It was impossible to pass through the airplane aisle during the meal service. Isle* means "island": *I would like to be on a desert isle on such a dreary morning.*

all ready/already *All ready,* a pronoun and an adjective, means "entirely prepared"; *already,* an adverb, means "so soon" or "previously": *I was all ready to leave when I noticed that it was already dinnertime.*

allusion/illusion An *allusion* is a reference or hint: *He made an allusion to the past.* An *illusion* is a deceptive appearance: *The canals on Mars are an illusion.*

a lot/allot/alot *A lot* is always written as two words. It is used informally to mean "many": *The unrelenting heat frustrated a lot of people. Allot* is a verb meaning "to divide" or "to set aside": *We alloted a portion of the yard for a garden. Alot* is not a word.

altogether/all together *Altogether* means "completely" or "totally"; *all together* means "all at one time" or "gathered together": *It is altogether proper that we recite the Pledge all together.*

allude/elude Both words are verbs. *Allude* means "to mention briefly or accidentally": *During our conversation, he alluded to his vacation plans. Elude* means "to avoid or escape": *The thief has successfully eluded capture for six months.*

altar/alter *Altar* is a noun meaning "a sacred place or platform": *The couple approached the altar for the wedding ceremony. Alter* is a verb meaning "to make different; to change": *He altered his appearance by losing fifty pounds, growing a beard, and getting a new wardrobe.*

amend/emend *Amend* means to make improvements or corrections in: *The U.S. Constitution was first amended in 1791.* The verb *emend* has a more technical use and usually applies to the correction of a text in the process of editing; it implies improvement in the sense of greater accuracy: *The original texts of his stories have been collected and emended.*

amount/number *Amount* refers to quantity that cannot be counted: *The amount of work accomplished before a major holiday is always negligible. Number,* in contrast, refers to things that can be counted: *He has held a number of jobs in the past five months.* But some concepts, like time, can use either *amount* or *number,* depending on how the elements are identified in the specific sentence: *We were surprised by the amount of time it took us to settle into our new surroundings. The number of hours it took to repair the sink pleased us.*

ante-/anti- The prefix *ante-* means "before" *(antecedent, antechamber, antediluvian);* the prefix *anti-* means against *(antigravity, antifreeze). Anti-* takes a hyphen before an *i* or a capital letter: *anti-inflationary, anti-Marxist.*

anxious/eager Traditionally, *anxious* means "nervous" or "worried" and consequently describes negative feelings. In addition, it is usually followed by the word "about": *I'm anxious about my exam. Eager* means "looking forward" or "anticipating enthusiastically" and consequently describes positive feelings. It is usually followed by "to": *I'm eager to get it over with.* Today, however, it is standard usage for *anxious* to mean "eager": *They are anxious to see their new home.*

any more/anymore *Any more* means "no more"; *anymore,* an adverb, means "nowadays" or "any longer": *We don't want any more trouble. We won't go there anymore.*

anybody, any body/anyone, any one *Anybody* and *anyone* are pronouns; *any body* is a noun modified by "any" and *any one* is a pronoun or adjective modified by "any." They are used as follows: *Was anybody able to find any body in the debris? Will anyone help me? I have more cleaning than any one person can ever do.*

apt/likely *Apt* is standard in all speech and writing as a synonym for "likely" in suggesting chance without inclination: *They are apt to call any moment now. Likely,* meaning "probably," is frequently preceded by a qualifying word: *The new school budget will very likely raise taxes.* However, *likely* without the qualifying word is standard in all varieties of English: *The new school budget will likely raise taxes.*

ascent/assent *Ascent* is a noun that means "a move upward or a climb": *Their ascent up Mount Rainier was especially dangerous because of the recent rock slides. Assent* can be a noun or a verb. As a verb, *assent* means "to concur, to express agreement": *The union representative assented to the agreement.* As a noun, *assent* means "an agreement": *The assent was not reached peacefully.*

assistance/assistants *Assistance* is a noun that means "help, support": *Please give us your assistance here for a moment. Assistants* is a plural noun that means "helpers": *Since the assistants were late, we found ourselves running behind schedule.*

assure, ensure, insure *Assure* is a verb that means "to promise": *The plumber assured us that the sink would not clog again.* *Ensure* and *insure* are both verbs that mean "to make certain," although some writers use *insure* solely for legal and financial writing and *ensure* for more widespread usage: *Since it is hard to insure yourself against mudslide, we did not buy the house on the hill. We left late to ensure that we would not get caught in traffic.*

bare/bear *Bare* is an adjective or a verb. As an adjective, *bare* means "naked, unadorned": *The wall looked bare without the picture.* As a verb, *bare* means "to reveal": *He bared his soul.* *Bear* is a noun or a verb. As a noun, *bear* refers to the animal: *The teddy bear was named after Theodore Roosevelt.* As a verb, *bear* means to carry: *He bears a heavy burden.*

before/prior to *Prior to* is used most often in a legal sense: *Prior to settling the claim, the Smiths spent a week calling the attorney general's office.* Use *before* in almost all other cases: *Before we go grocery shopping, we sort the coupons we have clipped from the newspaper.*

beside/besides Although both words can function as prepositions, they have different shades of meaning: *beside* means "next to"; *besides* means "in addition to" or "except": *Besides, Richard would prefer not to sit beside the dog. There is no one here besides John and me.* *Besides* is also an adverb meaning "in addition to": *Other people besides you feel the same way about the dog.*

bias/prejudice Generally, a distinction is made between *bias* and *prejudice.* Although both words imply "a preconceived opinion" or a "subjective point of view" in favor of something or against it, *prejudice* is generally used to express unfavorable feelings.

blonde/blond A *blonde* indicates a woman or girl with fair hair and skin. *Blond*, as an adjective, refers to either sex *(I have three blond children. He is a cute blond boy)*, but *blonde,* as an adjective, still applies to women: *The blonde actress and her companion made the front page of the tabloid.*

borrow/lend *Borrow* means "to take with the intention of returning": *The book you borrow from the library today is due back in seven days.* *Lend* means "to give with the intention of getting back": *I will lend you the rake, but I need it back by Saturday.* The two terms are not interchangeable.

brake/break The most common meaning of *brake* as a noun is a device for slowing a vehicle: *The car's new brakes held on the steep incline.* *Brake* can also mean "a thicket" or "a species of fern." *Break,* a verb, means "to crack or make useless": *Please be especially careful that you don't break that vase.*

breath/breathe *Breath,* a noun, is the air taken in during respiration: *Her breath looked like fog in the frosty morning air.* *Breathe,* a verb, refers to the process of inhaling and exhaling air: *"Please breathe deeply," the doctor said to the patient.*

bring/take *Bring* is to carry toward the speaker: *She brings it to me.* *Take* is to carry away from the speaker: *She takes it away.*

buy/by *Buy,* a verb, means "to acquire goods at a price": *We have to buy a* *new dresser. By* can be a preposition, an adverb, or an adjective. As a preposition, *by* means "next to": *I pass by the office building every day.* As an adverb, *by* means "near, at hand": *The office is close by.* As an adjective, *by* means "situated to one side": *They came down on a by passage.*

canvas/canvass *Canvas,* a noun, refers to a heavy cloth: *The boat's sails are made of canvas. Canvass,* a verb, means "to solicit votes": *The candidate's representatives canvass the neighborhood seeking support.*

capital/Capitol *Capital* is the city or town that is the seat of government: *Paris is the capital of France. Capitol* refers to the building in Washington, D.C., in which the U.S. Congress meets: *When I was a child, we went for a visit to the Capitol.* When used with a lowercase letter, *capitol* is the building of a state legislature. *Capital* also means "a sum of money": *After the sale of their home, they had a great deal of capital.* As an adjective, *capital* means "foremost" or "first-rate": *He was a capital fellow.*

censor/censure Although both words are verbs, they have different meanings. To *censor* is to remove something from public view on moral or other grounds, and to *censure* is to give a formal reprimand: *The committee censored the offending passages from the book and censured the librarian for placing it on the shelves.*

cite/sight/site To *cite* means to "quote a passage": *The scholar often cited passages from noted authorities to back up his opinions. Sight* is a noun that means "vision": *With her new glasses, her sight was once again perfect. Site* is a noun that means "place or location": *They picked out a beautiful site overlooking a lake for their new home.*

climatic/climactic The word *climatic* comes from the word "climate" and refers to weather: *This summer's brutal heat may indicate a climatic change. Climactic,* in contrast, comes from the word "climax" and refers to a point of high drama: *In the climactic last scene the hideous creature takes over the world.*

clothes/cloths *Clothes* are garments: *For his birthday, John got some handsome new clothes. Cloths* are pieces of fabric: *Use these cloths to clean the car.*

coarse/course *Coarse,* an adjective, means "rough or common": *The horsehair fabric was too coarse to be made into a pillow. Although he's a little coarse around the edges, he has a heart of gold. Course,* a noun, means "a path" or "a prescribed number of classes": *They followed the bicycle course through the woods. My courses include English, math, and science.*

complement/compliment Both words can function as either a noun or a verb. The noun *complement* means "that which completes or makes perfect": *The rich chocolate mousse was a perfect complement to the light meal.* The verb *complement* means "to complete": *The oak door complemented the new siding and windows.* The noun *compliment* means "an expression of praise or admiration": *The mayor paid the visiting officials the compliment of escorting them around town personally.* The verb *compliment* means "to pay a compliment to": *Everyone complimented her after the presentation.*

complementary/complimentary *Complementary* is an adjective that means "forming a complement, completing": *The complementary colors suited the mood of the room. Complimentary* is an adjective that means "expressing a compliment": *The complimentary reviews ensured the play a long run. Complimentary* also means "free": *We thanked them for the complimentary tickets.*

compose/comprise *Compose* means "to make up" or "to constitute": *Twelve former Soviet republics compose the Commonwealth of Independent States.* "*Composed of*" means "made up of" or "consisting of": *The Commonwealth of Independent States is composed of twelve former Soviet republics. Comprise* means "to include," "to contain," or "to consist of": *The Commonwealth of Independent States comprises twelve former Soviet republics.* The expression *comprised of*, which is increasingly common, is still considered by many to be incorrect.

continual/continuous Use *continual* to mean "intermittent, repeated often" and *continuous* to mean "uninterrupted, without stopping": *We suffered continual losses of electricity during the hurricane. They had continuous phone service during the hurricane. Continuous* and *continual* are never interchangeable with regard to spatial relationships, *a continuous series of passages.*

corps/corpse Both words are nouns. A *corps* is a group of people acting together; the word is often used in a military context: *The officers' corps assembled before dawn for the drill.* A *corpse* is a dead body: *The corpse was in the morgue.*

counsel/council *Counsel* is a verb meaning "to give advice": *They counsel recovering gamblers. Council* is a noun meaning "a group of advisers": *The trade union council meets in Ward Hall every Thursday.*

credible/creditable/credulous These three adjectives are often confused. *Credible* means "believable": *The tale is unusual, but seems credible to us. Creditable* means "worthy": *Sandra sang a creditable version of the song. Credulous* means "gullible": *The credulous Marsha believed that the movie was true.*

demur/demure *Demur* is a verb meaning "to object": *The board wanted her to be treasurer, but she demurred. Demure* is an adjective meaning "modest" or "reserved": *Her response to their compliments was a demure smile.*

descent/dissent *Descent*, a noun, means "downward movement": *Much to their surprise, their descent down the mountain was harder than their ascent had been. Dissent*, a verb, means "to disagree": *The town council strongly dissented with the proposed measure. Dissent* as a noun means "difference in sentiment or opinion": *Dissent over the new proposal caused a rift between colleagues.*

desert/dessert *Desert* as a verb means "to abandon"; as a noun, "an arid region": *People deserted in the desert rarely survive. Dessert*, a noun, refers to the sweet served as the final course of a meal: *My sister's favorite dessert is strawberry shortcake.*

device/devise *Device* is a noun meaning "invention or contrivance": *Do you think that device will really save us time? Devise* is a verb meaning "to contrive or plan": *Did he devise some device for repairing the ancient pump assembly?*

die/dye *Die*, as a verb, means "to cease to live": *The frog will die if released from the aquarium into the pond. Dye* as a verb means "to color or stain something": *I dye the drapes to cover the stains.*

discreet/discrete *Discreet* means "tactful"; *discrete*, "separate." For example: *Do you have a discreet way of refusing the invitation? The mosaic is made of hundreds of discrete pieces of tile.*

disinterested/uninterested *Disinterested* is used to mean "without prejudice, impartial" *(He is a disinterested judge)* and *uninterested* to mean "bored" or "lacking interest." *(They are completely uninterested in sports.)*

dominant/dominate *Dominant*, an adjective, means "ruling, controlling": *Social scientists have long argued over the dominant motives for human behavior. Dominate*, a verb, means "to control": *Advice columnists often preach that no one can dominate you unless you allow them to.*

elicit/illicit *Elicit*, a verb, means "call forth"; *illicit*, an adjective, means "against the law": *The assault elicited a protest against illicit handguns.*

emigrate/immigrate *Emigrate* means "to leave one's own country to settle in another": *She emigrated from France. Immigrate* means "to enter a different country and settle there": *My father immigrated to America when he was nine years old.*

eminent/imminent *Eminent* means "distinguished": *Marie Curie was an eminent scientist in the final years of her life. Imminent* means "about to happen": *The thundershower seemed imminent.*

envelop/envelope *Envelop* is a verb that means "to surround": *The music envelops him in a soothing atmosphere. Envelope*, a noun, is a flat paper container, usually for a letter: *Be sure to put a stamp on the envelope before you mail that letter.*

especially/specially The two words are not interchangeable: *especially* means "particularly," *specially* means "for a specific reason." For example: *I especially value my wedding ring; it was made specially for me.*

ever so often/every so often *Ever so often* means happening very often and *every so often* means happening occasionally.

everybody, every body/everyone, every one *Everybody* and *everyone* are indefinite pronouns: *Everybody likes William, and everyone enjoys his company. Every body* is a noun modified by "every" and *every one* is a pronoun modified by "every": both refer to a part of a specific group and are usually followed by "of": *Every body of water in our area is polluted; every one of our ponds is covered in debris.*

everyday/every day *Everyday* is an adjective that means "used daily, typical, ordinary"; *every day* is made up of a noun modified by the adjective "every" and means "each day": *Every day they had to deal with the everyday business of life.*

exam/examination *Exam* should be reserved for everyday speech and *ex-*

amination for formal writing: *The College Board examinations are scheduled for this Saturday morning at 9:00.*

explicit/implicit *Explicit* means "stated plainly"; *implicit* means "understood, implied": *You know we have an implicit understanding that you are not allowed to watch any television shows that contain explicit sex.*

fair/fare *Fair* as an adjective means "free from bias," "ample," "unblemished," "of light hue," or "attractive." As an adverb, it means "favorably." It is used informally to mean "honest." *Fare* as a noun means "the price charged for transporting a person" or "food."

farther/further Traditionally, *farther* is used to indicate physical distance *(Is it much farther to the hotel?)* and *further* is used to refer to additional time, amount, or abstract ideas *(Your mother does not want to talk about this any further).*

flaunt/flout *Flaunt* means "to show off"; *flout*, "to ignore or treat with disdain." For example: *They flouted convention when they flaunted their wealth.*

flounder/founder *Flounder* means "to struggle with clumsy movements": *We floundered in the mud. Founder* means "to sink": *The ship foundered.*

formally/formerly Both words are adverbs. *Formally* means "in a formal manner": *The minister addressed the king and queen formally. Formerly* means "previously": *Formerly, he worked as a chauffeur; now, he is employed as a guard.*

forth/fourth *Forth* is an adverb meaning "going forward or away": *From that day forth, they lived happily ever after. Fourth* is most often used as an adjective that means "next after the third": *Mitchell was the fourth in line.*

gibe/jibe/jive The word *gibe* means "to taunt, deride, jeer." The word *jibe* means "to be in agreement with, accord, correspond": *The facts of the case didn't jibe.* The word *jive* is slang, and means "to tease, fool, kid."

healthy/healthful *Healthy* means "possessing health"; *healthful* means "bringing about health": *They believed that they were healthy people because they ate healthful food.*

historic/historical The word *historic* means "important in history": *a historic speech; a historic battlefield.* The word *historical* means "being a part of, or inspired by, history": *historical records; a historical novel.*

home in/hone in The expression *home in* means "to approach or focus on (an objective)." It comes from the language of guided missiles, where *homing in* refers to locking onto a target. The expression *hone in* is an error.

human/humane Both words are adjectives. *Human* means "pertaining to humanity": *The subject of the documentary is the human race. Humane* means "tender, compassionate, or sympathetic": *Many of her patients believed that her humane care speeded their recovery.*

idea/ideal *Idea* means "thought," while *ideal* means "a model of perfection" or "goal." The two words are not interchangeable. They should be used as follows: *The idea behind the blood drive is that our ideals often move us to help others.*

imply/infer *Imply* means "to suggest without stating": *The message on Karen's postcard implies that her vacation has not turned out as she wished.* *Infer* means "to reach a conclusion based on understood evidence": *From her message I infer that she wishes she had stayed home.* When used in this manner, the two words describe two sides of the same process.

incredible/incredulous *Incredible* means "cannot be believed"; *incredulous* means "unbelieving": *The teacher was incredulous when she heard the pupil's incredible story about the fate of his term project.*

individual/person/party *Individual* should be used to stress uniqueness or to refer to a single human being as contrasted to a group of people: *The rights of the individual should not supersede the rights of a group.* *Person* is the preferred word in other contexts. *What person wouldn't want to have a chance to sail around the world? Party* is used to refer to a group: *Send the party of five this way, please. Party* is also used to refer to an individual mentioned in a legal document.

ingenious/ingenuous *Ingenious* means "resourceful, clever": *My sister is ingenious when it comes to turning leftovers into something delicious. Ingenuous* means "frank, artless": *The child's ingenuous manner is surprising considering her fame.*

later/latter *Later* is used to refer to time; *latter,* the second of two items named: *It is later than you think. I prefer the latter offer to the former one.*

lay/lie *Lay* is a transitive verb that means "to put down" or "to place." It takes a direct object: *Please lay the soup spoon next to the teaspoon. Lie* is an intransitive verb that means "to be in a horizontal position" or "be situated." It does not take a direct object: *The puppy lies down where the old dog had always lain. The hotel lies on the outskirts of town. I just want to lie down and go to sleep.* The confusion arises over *lay,* which is the present tense of the verb *lay* and the past tense of the verb *lie.*

To lay (put down)
Present: *He lays (is laying) his dice down.*
Future: *He will lay his dice down.*
Past: *He laid his dice down.*
Perfect: *He has (had, will have) laid his dice down.*

To lie (recline)
Present: *Spot lies (is lying) down.*
Future: *Spot will lie down.*
Past: *Spot lay down.*
Perfect: *Spot has (had, will have) lain down.*

Although *lie* and *lay* tend to be used interchangeably in informal speech, the following phrases are generally considered nonstandard and are avoided in standard English: *Lay down, dears. The dog laid in the sun. Abandoned cars were laying in the junkyard. The reports have laid in the mailbox for a week.*

lead/led *Lead* as a verb means "to take or conduct on the way": *I plan to lead a quiet afternoon. Led* is the past tense: *He led his followers through the dangerous underbrush. Lead,* as a noun, means "a type of metal": *Pipes are made of lead.*

learn/teach *Learn* is to acquire knowledge: *He learned fast. Teach* is to impart knowledge: *She taught well.*

leave/let *Leave* and *let* are interchangeable only when followed by the word "alone": *Leave him alone. Let him alone.* In other instances, *leave* means "to depart" or "permit to remain in the same place": *If you leave, please turn off the copier. Leave the extra paper on the shelf. Let* means "to allow": *Let him work with the assistant, if he wants.*

lessen/lesson *Lessen* is a verb meaning "to decrease": *To lessen the pain of a burn, apply ice to the injured area. Lesson* is most often used as a noun meaning "material assigned for study": *Today, the lesson will be on electricity.*

lightening/lightning *Lightening* is a form of the verb that means "to brighten": *The cheerful new drapes and bunches of flowers went a long way in lightening the room's somber mood. Lightning* is a noun that means "flashes of light generated during a storm": *The thunder and lightning frightened the child.*

loose/lose *Loose* is an adjective meaning "free and unattached": *The dog was loose again. Loose* can also be a verb meaning "let loose": *The hunters loose the dogs as soon as the ducks fall. Lose* is a verb meaning "to part with unintentionally": *He will lose his keys if he leaves them on the countertop.*

luxuriant/luxurious *Luxuriant* means "abundant, lush, or profuse": *luxuriant auburn hair; luxuriant vegetation. Luxurious* means "characterized by or loving luxury": *a luxurious hotel suite; luxurious tastes.*

mad/angry Traditionally, *mad* has been used to mean "insane"; *angry* has been used to mean "full of ire." While *mad* can be used to mean "enraged, angry," in informal usage, you should replace *mad* with *angry* in formal discourse: *The president is angry at Congress for overriding his veto.*

maybe/may be *Maybe,* an adverb, means "perhaps": *Maybe the newspapers can be recycled with the plastic and glass. May be,* a verb, means "could be": *It may be too difficult, however.*

moral/morale As a noun, *moral* means "ethical lesson": *Each of Aesop's fables has a clear moral. Morale* means "state of mind" or "spirit": *Her morale was lifted by her colleague's good wishes.*

orient/orientate The two words both mean "to adjust to or familiarize with new surroundings; place in a particular position." There is no reason to prefer or reject either word, although sometimes people object to *orientate.*

passed/past *Passed* is a form of the verb meaning "to go by": *Bernie passed the same buildings on his way to work each day. Past* can function as a noun, adjective, adverb, or preposition. As a noun, *past* means "the history of a nation, person, etc.": *The lessons of the past should not be forgotten.* As an adjective, *past* means "gone by or elapsed in time": *John is worried about his past deeds.* As an adverb, *past* means "so as to pass by": *The fire engine raced past the parked cars.* As a preposition, *past* means "beyond in time": *It's past noon already.*

patience/patients *Patience,* a noun, means "endurance": *Chrissy's patience makes her an ideal baby-sitter. Patients* are people under medical treatment: *The patients must remain in the hospital for another week.*

peace/piece *Peace* is "freedom from discord": *The negotiators hoped that the new treaty would bring about lasting peace. Piece* is "a portion of a whole" or "a musical or literary arrangement": *I would like just a small piece of cake, please. The piece in E flat is especially beautiful.*

percent/percentage *Percent* is used with a number, *percentage* with a modifier. *Percentage* is used most often after an adjective: *A high percentage of your earnings this year is tax deductible.*

perquisite/prerequisite *Perquisite* is a noun meaning "an accidental payment, benefit, or privilege over and above regular income": *Among the perquisites of the job were a generous expense account and use of a company jet.* It can also mean "something due as a particular privilege": *the perquisites of royalty.* A *prerequisite* is "something required beforehand": *French 101 is a prerequisite for all other French courses. Prerequisite* is also an adjective meaning "required beforehand": *prerequisite knowledge.*

personal/personnel *Personal* means "private": *The lock on her journal showed that it was clearly personal. Personnel* refers to employees: *Attention all personnel!* The use of *personnel* as a plural has become standard in business and government: *The personnel were dispatched to the Chicago office.*

plain/plane *Plain* as an adjective means "easily understood," "undistinguished," or "unadorned": *His meaning was plain to all. The plain dress suited the gravity of the occasion.* As an adverb, *plain* means "clearly and simply": *She's just plain foolish.* As a noun, *plain* is a flat area of land: *The vast plain seemed to go on forever.* As a noun, *plane* has a number of different meanings. It most commonly refers to an airplane, but is also used in mathematics and fine arts and to refer to a tool used to shave wood.

practicable/practical *Practicable* means "capable of being done": *My decorating plans were too difficult to be practicable. Practical* means "pertaining to practice or action": *It was just not practical to paint the floor white.*

precede/proceed Both words are verbs, but they have different meanings. *Precede* means "to go before": *Morning precedes afternoon. Proceed* means "to move forward": *Proceed to the exit in an orderly fashion.*

presence/presents *Presence* is used chiefly to mean "attendance, close proximity": *Your presence at the ceremony will be greatly appreciated. Presents* are gifts. *Thank you for giving us such generous presents.*

principal/principle *Principal* can be a noun or an adjective. As a noun, *principal* means "chief or head official" *(The principal decided to close school early on Tuesday)* or "sum of capital" *(Invest only the interest, never the principal).* As an adjective, *principal* means "first or highest": *The principal ingredient is sugar. Principle* is a noun only, meaning "rule" or "general truth": *Regardless of what others said, she stood by her principles.*

quiet/quite *Quiet,* as an adjective, means "free from noise": *When the master of ceremonies spoke, the room became quiet. Quite,* an adverb, means "completely, wholly": *By the late afternoon, the children were quite exhausted.*

quotation/quote *Quotation,* a noun, means "a passage quoted from a speech or book": *The speaker read a quotation of twenty-five lines to the audience. Quote,* a verb, means "to repeat a passage from a speech, etc.": *Marci often quotes from popular novels. Quote* and *quotation* are often used interchangeably in speech; in formal writing, however, a distinction is still observed between the two words.

rain/reign/rein As a noun, *rain* means "water that falls from the atmosphere to earth." As a verb, *rain* means "to send down, to give abundantly": *The crushed piñata rained candy on the eager children.* As a noun, *reign* means "royal rule," as a verb, "to have supreme control": *The monarch's reign was marked by social unrest.* As a noun, *rein* means "a leather strap used to guide an animal," as a verb, "to control or guide": *He used the rein to control the frisky colt.*

raise/rise/raze *Raise,* a transitive verb, means "to elevate": *How can I raise the value of my house? Rise,* an intransitive verb, means "to go up, to get up": *Will housing costs rise this year? Raze* is a transitive verb meaning "to tear down, demolish": *The wrecking crew was ready to raze the condemned building.*

respectful/respective *Respectful* means "showing (or full of) respect": *If you are respectful toward others, they will treat you with consideration as well. Respective* means "in the order given": *The respective remarks were made by executive board members Joshua Whittles, Kevin McCarthy, and Warren Richmond.*

reverend/reverent As an adjective (usually capitalized), *Reverend* is an epithet of respect given to a member of the clergy: *The Reverend Mr. Jones gave the sermon.* As a noun, a *reverend* is "a member of the clergy": *In our church, the reverend opens the service with a prayer. Reverent* is an adjective meaning "showing deep respect": *The speaker began his remarks with a reverent greeting.*

right/rite/write *Right* as an adjective means "proper, correct" and "as opposed to left"; as a noun it means "claims or titles"; as an adverb it means "in a straight line, directly"; as a verb it means "to restore to an upright position." *Rite* is a noun meaning "a solemn ritual": *The religious leader performed the necessary rites. Write* is a verb meaning "to form characters on a surface": *The child liked to write her name over and over.*

sensual/sensuous *Sensual* carries sexual overtones: *The massage was a sensual experience. Sensuous* means "pertaining to the senses": *The sensuous aroma of freshly baked bread wafted through the house.*

set/sit *Set,* a transitive verb, describes something a person does to an object: *She set the book down on the table. Sit,* an intransitive verb, describes a person resting: *Marvin sits on the straight-backed chair.*

somebody/some body *Somebody* is an indefinite pronoun: *Somebody recommended this restaurant. Some body* is a noun modified by an adjective: *I have a new spray that will give my limp hair some body.*

someone/some one *Someone* is an indefinite pronoun: *Someone who ate here said the pasta was delicious. Some one* is a pronoun or adjective modified by "some": *Please pick some one magazine that you would like to read.*

sometime/sometimes/some time Traditionally, these three words have carried different meanings. *Sometime* means "at an unspecified time in the future": *Why not plan to visit Niagara Falls sometime? Sometimes* means "occasionally": *I visit my former college roommate sometimes. Some time* means "a span of time": *I need some time to make up my mind about what you have said.*

stationary/stationery Although these two words sound alike, they have very different meanings. *Stationary* means "staying in one place": *From this distance, the satellite appeared to be stationary. Stationery* means "writing paper": *A hotel often provides stationery with its name preprinted.*

straight/strait *Straight* is most often used as an adjective meaning "unbending": *The path cut straight through the woods. Strait,* a noun, is "a narrow passage of water connecting two large bodies of water" or "distress, dilemma": *He was in dire financial straits. Strait* is also found in older literature as an adjective meaning either "strict" or "narrow": *Strait is the gate.*

subsequently/consequently *Subsequently* means "occurring later, afterward": *We went to a new French restaurant for dinner; subsequently, we heard that everyone who had eaten the Caesar salad became ill. Consequently* means "therefore, as a result": *The temperature was above 90 degrees for a week; consequently all the tomatoes burst on the vine.*

taught/taut *Taught* is the past tense of "to teach": *My English teachers taught especially well. Taut* is "tightly drawn": *Pull the knot taut or it will not hold.*

than/then *Than,* a conjunction, is used in comparisons: *Robert is taller than Michael. Then,* an adverb, is used to indicate time: *We knew then that there was little to be gained by further discussion.*

their/there/they're These three words sound alike, but they have very different meanings. *Their,* the possessive form of "they," means "belonging to them": *Their house is new. There* can point out place *(There is the picture I was telling you about)* or call attention to someone or something *(There is a mouse behind you!). They're* is a contraction for "they are": *They're not at home right now.*

threw/through/thru *Threw,* the past tense of the verb "throw," means "to hurl an object": *He threw the ball at the batter. Through* means "from one end to the other" or "by way of": *They walked through the museum all af-*

ternoon. *Through* should be used in formal writing in place of *thru,* an informal spelling.

to/too/two These words sound alike, but they are different parts of speech and have different meanings. *To* is a preposition indicating direction or part of an infinitive; *too* is an adverb meaning "also" or "in extreme"; and *two* is a number: *I have to go to the store to buy two items. Do you want to come too?*

tortuous/torturous These two adjectives sound similar, but they have different meanings. *Tortuous* means "full of twists and turns" and "convoluted": *a tortuous road; tortuous logic. Torturous* comes from *torture* and means "involving or causing pain or suffering": *torturous heat; torturous memories.*

track/tract *Track,* as a noun, is a path or course: *The railroad track in the Omaha station has recently been electrified. Track,* as a verb, is "to follow": *Sophisticated guidance control systems are used to track the space shuttles. Tract* is "an expanse of land" or "a brief treatise": *Jonathan Swift wrote many tracts on the political problems of his day.*

unexceptional/unexceptionable Both *unexceptional* and *unexceptionable* are adjectives, but they have different meanings and are not interchangeable. *Unexceptional* means "commonplace, ordinary": *Despite the glowing reviews the new restaurant had received, we found it offered unexceptional meals and service. Unexceptionable* means "not offering any basis for exception or objection, beyond criticism": *We could not dispute his argument because it was unexceptionable.*

usage/use *Usage* is a noun that refers to the generally accepted way of doing something. The word refers especially to the conventions of language: *"Most unique" is considered incorrect usage. Use* can be either a noun or a verb. As a noun, *use* means "the act of employing or putting into service": *In the adult education course, I learned the correct use of tools. Usage* is often misused in place of the noun *use: Effective use (not "usage") of your time results in greater personal satisfaction.*

use/utilize/utilization *Utilize* means "to make use of": *They should utilize the new profit-sharing plan to decrease taxable income. Utilization* is the noun form of *utilize.* In most instances, however, *use* is preferred to either *utilize* or *utilization* as less overly formal and stilted: *They should use the new profit-sharing plan to decrease taxable income.*

which/witch *Which* is a pronoun meaning "what one": *Which desk is yours? Witch* is a noun meaning "a person who practices magic": *The superstitious villagers accused her of being a witch.*

who's/whose *Who's* is the contraction for "who is" or "who has": *Who's the person in charge here? Who's got the money? Whose* is the possessive form of "who": *Whose book is this?*

your/you're *Your* is the possessive form of "you": *Your book is overdue at the library. You're* is the contraction of "you are": *You're just the person we need for this job.*

Usage Basics

Language and the way it is used change constantly. This glossary provides a concise guide to contemporary English usage. It will show you how certain words and phrases are used and why certain usage is unacceptable.

"Informal" indicates that a word or phrase is often used in everyday speech but should generally be avoided in formal discourse. "Nonstandard" means that the word or phrase is not suitable for everyday speech and writing or in formal discourse.

a/an In both spoken and written English, *an* is used before words beginning with a vowel sound *(He carried an umbrella. The Nobel is an honor)* and when the consonants *f, h, l, m, n, r, s,* and *x* are pronounced by name *(The renovations created an L-shaped room. Miles received an F in physics)*. Use *a* before words beginning with a consonant sound *(What a fish! I bought a computer)* and words that start with vowels but are pronounced as consonants. *(A union can be dissolved. They live in a one-room apartment)*. Also use *a* with words that start with consonant letters not listed above and with the vowel *u (She earned a C in French. He made a U-turn)*.

For words that begin with *h,* if the initial *h* is not pronounced, the word is preceded by *an (It will take an hour)*. Adjectives such as *historic, historical, heroic,* and *habitual* are commonly preceded by *an,* especially in British English, but the use of *a* is common in both writing and speech *(She read a historical novel)*. When the *h* is strongly pronounced, as in a stressed first syllable, the word is preceded by *a (I bought a history of Long Island)*.

a number/the number As a subject, *a number* is most often plural and *the number* is singular. *A number of choices are available. The number of choices is limited.* As with many agreement questions, this guideline is followed more often in formal discourse than in speech and informal writing.

above *Above* is most commonly a preposition *(They live on the floor above us),* but it can also be used as an adjective *(The above entry is incomplete)* or as a noun *(First, please read the above)* in referring to what has been previously mentioned in a passage. Both uses are standard in formal writing.

ain't The term is nonstandard for "am not," "isn't," or "aren't." It is used in informal speech and writing for humorous effect or for emphasis, usually in dialogue.

all right/alright *All right* is always written as two words: *alright* is a misspelling: *Betsy said that it was all right to use her car that afternoon.*

almost/most *Almost,* an adverb, means "nearly"; *most,* an adjective, means "the greatest part of" something. *Most* is not synonymous with *almost,* as the following example shows: *During our vacation we shop at that store almost every day and buy most of the available snack foods.*

In informal speech, *most* (as a shortened form of *almost*) is used as an adverb. It occurs before such pronouns as *all, anyone, anybody, everyone,* and *everybody;* the adjectives *all, any,* and *every;* and the adverbs *anywhere* and *everywhere.* For example: *Most everyone around here is related.* The use of *most* as an adverb is nonstandard and is uncommon in formal writing except when used to represent speech.

A.M., P.M./a.m., p.m. These abbreviations for time are most frequently restricted to use with figures: *The ceremony begins at 10:00 a.m. (*not *"ten thirty a.m.")*

among/between *Among* is used to indicate relationships involving more than two people or things, while *between* is used to show relationships involving two people or things, or to compare one thing to a group to which it belongs: *The three quarreled among themselves because she had to choose between two of them. Between* is also used to express relationships of persons or things considered individually, no matter how many: *Between holding public office, teaching, and raising a family, she has little free time.*

and etc. Since *etc.* means "and all the rest," *and etc.* is redundant; the "and" is not needed. Many prefer to use "and so forth" or "and the like" as a substitute for the abbreviation.

and/or The combination *and/or* is used mainly in legal and business writing. Its use should be avoided in general writing, as in *He spends his weekends watching television and/or snacking.* In such writing, either one or the other word is sufficient. If you mean "either," use *or;* if you mean "both," use *and.* To make a greater distinction, revise the phrasing: *He spends his weekends watching television, snacking, or both.*

and which/and who "And" is unnecessary when "which" or "who" is used to open a relative clause. Use *and which* or *and who* only to open a second clause starting with the same relative pronoun: *Elizabeth is my neighbor who goes shopping every morning and who calls me every afternoon to tell me about the sales.*

anyplace *Anyplace* is an informal expression for "anywhere." It occurs in speech and informal writing but is best avoided in formal prose.

anyways/anyway; anywheres/anywhere *Anyways* is nonstandard for *anyway; anywheres* is nonstandard for *anywhere.*

as Do not use *as* in place of *whether: We're not sure whether* (not *"as")* *you should do that.* Also avoid using *as* as a substitute for *because, since, while, whether,* or *who,* where its use may create confusion. In the following sentence, for example, *as* may mean "while" or "because": *As they were driving to California they decided to see the Grand Canyon.*

as/because/since While all three words can function as subordinating conjunctions, they carry slightly different shades of meaning. *As* establishes a time relationship and can be used interchangeably with "when" or "while." *Because* and *since,* in contrast, describe causes and effects: *As we brought out the food, it began to drizzle. Because (since) Nancy goes skiing infrequently, she prefers to rent skis.*

as/like When *as* functions as a preposition, the distinction between *as* and *like* depends on meaning. *As* suggests that the subject is equivalent to the description: *He was employed as a teacher. Like,* in contrast, suggests similarity but not equivalence: *Speakers like her excel in front of large groups.*

at Avoid using *at* after "where": *Where are you seeing her* (not *"at"*)? Whether used as an adverb or as a preposition, "where" contains the preposition "at" in its definition.

at this point in time Although the term *at this point in time* is widely used (especially in politics), many consider it verbose and stuffy. Instead, use "now" or "at this time": *We are not now ready to discuss the new budget.*

awful/awfully Avoid using *awful* or *awfully* to mean "very" in formal discourse: *We had an awfully busy time at the amusement park.* Although the use of *awful* to mean "terrible" (rather than "inspiring awe") has permeated all levels of writing and speech, consider using in its place a word that more closely matches your intended meaning: *We had an unpleasant* (not *"awful"*) *time because the park was hot, noisy, and crowded.*

awhile/a while *Awhile* is an adverb and is always spelled as one word: *We visited awhile. A while* is a noun phrase (an article and a noun) and is used after a preposition: *We rested for a while.*

backward/backwards In formal discourse, *backward* is preferred: *This stroke is easier if you use a backward motion* (adjective). *Counting backward from 100 can be an effective way to induce sleep* (adverb).

bad/badly *Bad,* an adjective, is used to describe a noun or pronoun. *Badly,* an adverb, is used to describe a verb, adjective, or another adverb. Thus: *She felt bad because her broken leg throbbed badly.*

because/due to the fact that/since *Because* or *since* is preferred over the wordy phrase *due to the fact that: He wrote the report longhand because* (not *"due to the fact that"*) *his computer was broken.*

being as/being that Avoid both *being as* and *being that* in formal writing. Instead, use "since" or "because." For example: *Since you asked, I'll be glad to help.*

better/had better The verb "had" is necessary in the phrase *had better* and should be retained. *She had better return the lawn mower today.*

between you and I Pronouns that function as objects of prepositions are traditionally used in the objective case. *Please keep this between you and me. I would appreciate it if you could keep this between her and them.*

bi- Many words that refer to periods of time through the prefix *bi-* are potentially confusing. Ambiguity is avoided by using the prefix *semi-,* meaning "twice each" *(semiweekly, semimonthly, semiannual)* or by using the appropriate phrases *(twice a week, twice each month, every two months, every two years).*

borrow off/borrow from *Borrow off,* considered informal, is not used in formal speech and writing; *borrow from* is the preferred expression.

bottom line This overworked term is frequently used as a synonym for "outcome" or "the final result": *The bottom line is that we have to reduce inventory to maintain profits.* Careful writers and speakers avoid it for less shopworn descriptions.

bunch Use the noun *bunch* in formal writing only to refer to clusters of things grouped together, such as grapes or bananas: *That bunch of grapes looks better than the other one.* In formal writing, use *group* or *crowd* to refer to gatherings of people; *bunch* is used to refer to groups of people or items only in speech and informal writing.

burst, bursted/bust, busted *Burst* is a verb meaning "to come apart suddenly." Both the past tense and the past participle are *burst.* The word *bursted* is not acceptable in either speech or writing. The verb *bust* and adjective *busted* are both informal or slang terms; as such, they should not be used in formal writing.

but however/but yet There is no reason to combine *but* with another conjunction: *She said she was leaving, yet (*not *"but yet") she poured another cup of coffee.*

but that/but what As with the previous example, there is no reason to add the word *but* to either *that* or *what: We don't doubt that (*not *"but that") you will win this hand.*

calculate/figure/reckon None of these words is an acceptable substitute for *expect* or *imagine* in formal writing, although they are used in speech and informal prose.

can/may Traditionally, *may* is used in formal writing to convey permission; *can,* ability or capacity. In speech, however, the terms are used interchangeably to mean permission: *Can (May) I borrow your hedge clippers? Can* and *may* are frequently but not always interchangeable when used to mean possibility: *A blizzard can (*or *may) occur any time during February.* In negative constructions, *can't* is more common than *mayn't,* the latter being rare. *You can't eat that taco in the den.*

cannot/can not *Cannot* is occasionally spelled *can not.* The one-word spelling is by far the more common. The contraction *can't* is used mainly in speech and informal writing.

can't help but *Can't help but,* as in: *You can't help but like her,* is a double negative. This idiom can be replaced by the informal *can't help* or the formal *cannot but* where each is appropriate: *She can't help wishing that it were spring. I cannot but wish things had turned out differently.* While *can't help but* is common in all types of speech, avoid using it in formal writing.

cause of . . . on account of/due to The phrases *on account of* and *due to* are unnecessary with *cause of.* Omit the phrases or revise the entire sentence: *One cause of physical and psychological problems is due to too much stress.* Change the sentence to: *Too much stress causes physical and psychological problems.*

center around/center on Although both phrases are often criticized for being illogical, they have been used in writing for more than a hundred years to express the notion of collecting or gathering as if around a center point. The phrase *revolve around* is often suggested as an alternative, and the prepositions *at, in,* and *on* are considered acceptable with *center* in the following sense: *Their problems centered on their lack of expertise.*

chair/chairperson *Chairperson* is used widely in academic and governmental circles as an alternative to "chairman" or "chairwoman." While some reject the term *chairperson* as clumsy and unnecessary and use the term *chair* for any presiding officer, regardless of sex, *chairperson* is still standard in all types of writing and speech.

choose/chose *Choose* is a verb that means "to select one thing in preference to another": *Why choose tomatoes when they are out of season? Chose* is the past tense of "to choose": *I chose tomatoes over cucumbers at the salad bar.*

conformity to/conformity with Although the word *conformity* can be followed by either "to" or "with," *conformity to* is generally used when the idea of obedience is implied. *The new commissioner issued a demand for conformity to health regulations. Conformity with* is used to imply agreement or correspondence: *This is an idea in conformity with previous planning.*

consensus/consensus of The expression *consensus of (consensus of opinion)* is considered redundant, and the preferred usage is the single noun *consensus,* meaning "general agreement or concord": *Since the consensus was overwhelming, the city planners moved ahead with the proposal.* The phrase *general consensus* is also considered redundant. Increasingly, the word *consensus* is widely used attributively, as in the phrase *consensus politics.*

contact The word is both a verb and a noun. As a verb, it is frequently used imprecisely to mean "to communicate" when a more exact word *(telephone, write to, consult)* would better communicate the idea. *Contact* as a noun meaning "a person through whom one can obtain information" is now standard usage: *He is my contact in the state department.*

couple/couple of Both phrases are informally used to mean "two" or "several": *I need a couple more cans of paint. I took a couple of aspirins for my headache.* The expression *a couple of* is used in standard English, especially in referring to distance, money, or time: *He is a couple of feet away. I have a couple of thousand dollars in the bank. The store will open in a couple of weeks. Couple* may be treated as either a singular or plural noun.

criteria/criterion *Criteria* is the plural of *criterion* (a standard for judgment). For example: *Of all their criteria for evaluating job performance, customer satisfaction was the most important criterion.*

data/datum *Data* is the plural of *datum* (fact). Although *data* is often used as a singular, it should still be treated as plural in formal speech and writing: *The data pertain* (not *"pertains"*) *to the first half of the experiment.* To avoid awkward constructions, most writers prefer to use a more commonplace term such as "fact" or "figure" in place of *datum.*

decimate The word *decimate* comes from a Latin term that meant "to select by lot and kill one person in ten of (a rebellious military unit)." The usual use of the word in English is "to destroy a large amount or proportion of": *Disease decimated the population.* Some people claim that *decimate* should be used only to mean "to destroy a tenth of," but in fact the word has never been used this way in English. There is nothing wrong with the sense "to destroy a large amount or proportion of."

differ from/differ with *Differ from* means "to be unlike"; *differ with* means "to disagree with": *The sisters differ from each other in appearance. We differ with you on this matter.*

different from/different than Although *different from* is the preferred usage *(His attitude is different from mine)*, *different than* is widely accepted when a clause follows, especially when the word "from" would create an awkward sentence. Example: *The stream followed a different course than the map showed.*

don't/does not *Don't* is the contraction for "do not," not for *does not,* as in *I don't care, she doesn't* (not *don't) care.*

done Using *done* as an adjective to mean "through, finished" is standard. Originally, *done* was used attributively *(The pact between them was a done thing),* but it has become more common as a complement: *Are your pictures done yet? When we were done with the power saw, we removed the blade.*

double negatives Although the use of double negatives *(They never paid no dues)* was standard for many years in English, today certain uses of the double negative are universally considered unacceptable: *He didn't have nothing to do,* for example. In educated speech and writing, "anything" would be used in place of "nothing."

doubt that/doubt whether/doubt if *Doubt that* is used to express conviction *(I doubt that they intended to hurt your feelings); doubt whether* and *doubt if* are used to indicate uncertainty: *I doubt whether (or if) anyone really listened to the speaker.*

due to In formal discourse, *due to* is acceptable only after a form of the verb "to be": *Her aching back was due to poor posture. Due to* is not acceptable as a preposition meaning "because of" or "owing to": *Because of (not "due to") the poor weather, the bus was late.*

each When *each* is used as a pronoun, it takes a singular verb *(Each was born in Europe),* although plurals are increasingly used in formal speech and writing in an attempt to avoid using "he" or "his" for sentences that include females or do not specify sex *(Each of them had their (rather than "his") own agenda).* More and more, the same pattern of pronoun agreement is being used with the singular pronouns *anyone, anybody, everyone, everybody, no one, someone,* and *somebody.* When the pronoun *each* is followed by an "of" phrase containing a plural noun or pronoun, usage guides suggest that the verb be singular, but the plural is used often even in formal writing: *Each of the children has (or "have") had a school physical.*

When the adjective *each* follows a plural subject, the verb agrees with the subject: *The rooms each have separate thermostats.*

each and every Use "each" or "every" in place of the phrase *each and every,* generally considered wordy: *Each of us enjoyed the concert. Every one of us stayed until the end of the performance.*

each other/one another *Each other* is traditionally used to indicate two members; *one another* for three or more: *The two children trade lunches with each other. The guests greeted one another fondly.* In standard practice, though, these distinctions are not observed in either speech or writing.

enormity The word *enormity* means "outrageousness, atrociousness, monstrousness": *the enormity of his crime.* It is often used to mean "great size, enormousness": *The enormity of the task overwhelmed her.* Though this use is common, many people consider it to be an error.

enthused/enthusiastic The word *enthused* is used informally to mean "showing enthusiasm." For formal writing and speech, use the adjective *enthusiastic: The team was enthusiastic about the quarterback's winning play.*

-ess/-or/-er The suffix *-ess* has often been used to denote feminine nouns. While many such words are still in use, English is moving increasingly toward nouns that do not denote sex differences. The most widely observed guideline today is that if the sex of the performer is not relevant to the performance of the task or function, the neutral ending *-or* or *-er* should be used in place of *-ess.* Thus, words such as *ambassadress, ancestress, authoress, poetess, proprietress,* and *sculptress* are no longer used, and the airlines, for example, have replaced both *steward* and *stewardess* with *flight attendant.*

et al. *Et al.,* the Latin abbreviation for "and other people," is fully standard for use in a citation to refer to works with more than three authors: *Harris et al.*

etc. Since *etc. (et cetera)* is the Latin abbreviation for "and other things," it should not be used to refer to people. In general, it should be avoided in formal writing as imprecise. In its place, provide the entire list of items or use "and so on."

-ette English nouns whose *-ette* ending signifies a feminine role or identity are passing out of usage. *Suffragette* and *usherette,* for example, have been replaced by *suffragist* and *usher,* respectively.

everywheres/everywhere *Everywheres* is a nonstandard term for *everywhere* and should be avoided in speech and writing.

except for the fact that/except that Use *except that* in place of the verbose phrase *except for the fact that: Except that* (not *"except for the fact that"* the button is missing, this is a lovely skirt.*

fewer/less Traditionally, *fewer,* a plural noun, has most often been used to refer to individual units that can be counted: *There are fewer buttons on this shirt. No fewer than forty of the fifty voters supported the measure. Less,* a singular noun, is used to refer to uncountable quantities: *She eats less every day. I have less patience than I used to.*

Standard English does not always reflect these distinctions, however. When followed by "than," *less* is used as often as *fewer* to indicate plural nouns that refer to items that can be counted. *There were no less than eight million people. No less than forty of the fifty voters supported the measure.*

figuratively/literally *Figuratively,* meaning "involving a figure of speech," usually implies that the statement is not true. *Literally,* meaning "actually, without exaggeration," implies that the statement is true: *The poet Robert Frost once figuratively described writing poetry without regular meter and rhyme as playing tennis with the net down. My sister literally passed out when she saw what had happened to her new car.*

   Literally is commonly used as an intensifier meaning "in effect, virtually": *The state representative was literally buried alive in the caucus.* This usage should be avoided in formal discourse.

fix The verb *fix,* meaning "to repair," is fully accepted in all areas of speech and writing. The noun *fix,* meaning "repair" or "adjustment," is used informally.

fixing to/intend to Use *intend to* in place of the informal or dialectal term *fixing to: The community intends to* (not *"is fixing to") raise money to help the victims of the recent fire.*

flunk/fail Use the standard term *fail* in speech and writing; *flunk* is an informal substitute.

former/latter *Former* is used to refer to the first of two items; *latter,* the second: *We enjoy both gardening and painting, the former during the summer and the latter during the winter.* When dealing with three or more items, use "first" and "last" rather than *former* and *latter: We enjoy gardening, painting, and skiing, but the last is very costly.*

fortuitous *Fortuitous* means "happening accidentally": *A fortuitous meeting with a former acquaintance led to a change in plans.* It is also used sometimes as a synonym for "lucky" or "fortunate."

from whence Although the phrase *from whence* is sometimes criticized on the grounds that "from" is redundant because it is included in the meaning of "whence," the idiom is nonetheless standard in both speech and writing: *She finally moved to Kansas, from whence she began to build a new life.*

fulsome Originally, *fulsome* meant "abundant," but for hundreds of years the word has been used to mean "offensive, disgusting, or excessively lavish." While the word still maintains the connotations of "excessive" or "offensive," it has also come to be used in the original sense as well: *Compare the severe furniture of the living room to the fulsome decorations in the den.*

fun *Fun* should not be used as an adjective in formal writing. Instead, substitute a word such as "happy," "pleasant," or "entertaining": *They had a pleasant* (not *"fun") afternoon at the park.*

gentleman Once used only to refer to men of high social rank, the term *gentleman* now also specifies a man of courtesy and consideration: *He behaves like a gentleman.* It is also used as a term of polite reference and address in the singular and plural: *This gentleman is waiting to be served. Are we ready to begin, gentlemen?*

get The verb *get* is used in many slang and informal phrases as a substitute for forms of "to be." For example: *They won't get accepted with that attitude.* In American English, an alternative past participle is *gotten,* especially in the sense of "received" and "acquired": *I have gotten (or "got") all I ever wanted.*

Both *have* and *has got* (meaning "must") are occasionally criticized as being redundant, but are nonetheless fully standard in all varieties of speech and writing: *You have got to carry your driver's license at all times.*

good/well *Good,* an adjective, should be used to describe someone or something: *Joe is a good student. Well,* when used as an adverb, should describe an action: *She and Laura play well together on the swing set. Well,* when used as an adjective after "look," "feel," or other linking verbs, often refers to good health: *You're looking well.*

good and/very Avoid using *good and* as a substitute for *very: I was very (*not *"good and") hungry.*

graduate The passive form, once considered the only correct usage, is seldom used today: *I was graduated from the Merchant Marine Academy last May.* Although some critics condemn the use of *graduate* as a verb meaning "to receive a degree or diploma (from)" its use is common in both speech and writing: *She graduated from elementary school in Cleveland.*

great The word *great* has been overused in informal writing and speech as a synonym for "enthusiastic," "good," or "clever": *She was really great at making people feel at home.*

had drank/had drunk According to some authorities, *had drank* is acceptable usage: *I had drank a gallon of milk. Had drunk,* though, is fully standard and the preferred usage.

had ought/ought *Had ought* is considered wordy; the preferred usage is *ought: She ought (*not *"had ought") to heed her mother's advice.*

has/have; has got/have got The word "got" is unnecessary; simply use *has* or *have: Jessica has a mild case of chicken pox.*

half/a half a/a half Use either *half* or *a half; a half a* is considered wordy: *Please give me a half (*not *"a half a") piece. I'd like half that slice, please.*

hanged/hung Although both words are past-tense forms of "to hang," *hanged* is used to refer to executions: *(Billy Budd was hanged)* and *hung* is used for all other meanings: *The stockings were hung by the chimney with care.*

have/of Use *have* rather than *of* after helping verbs like "could," "should," "would," "may," and "might": *They should have (*not *"of") let me know of their decision earlier.*

he, she; he/she The pronouns *he* and *she* refer to male and female antecedents, respectively. Traditionally, when an antecedent in singular form could be either female or male, "he" was always used to refer to either sex: *A child is often apprehensive when he first begins school.* Today, however, various approaches have been developed to avoid the all-purpose "he." Many people find the construction *he/she* (or *he or she*) awkward: *A child is often apprehensive when he/she first begins school.* The blended form *s/he* has not been widely adopted, probably because of confusion over pronunciation. Most people now favor either rephrasing the sentence entirely to omit the pronoun or reconstructing the sentence in the third-person plural: *Children are often apprehensive when they first begin school.*

hopefully *Hopefully* originally meant "in a hopeful manner": *The beggar looked up hopefully.* It is now often used to mean "it is to be hoped; I hope; let us hope": *Hopefully, we'll get there on time.* Although this sense is common and standard, many people consider it incorrect.

how come/why *How come* is used informally in speech to substitute for *why.*

if/whether Use *whether* rather than *if* to begin a subordinate clause when the clause states a choice: *I don't know whether (not "if") I should stay until the end or leave right after the opening ceremony.*

impact Both the noun and verb *impact* are used to indicate forceful contact: *I cannot overstate the impact of the new policy on productivity.* Some speakers and writers avoid using *impact* as a verb to mean "to have an effect," as in *Our work here impacts on every division in the firm.*

in Several phrases beginning with *in* are verbose and should be avoided in formal writing. Refer to the following list.

Replace the phrase
in this day and age
With
now

Replace the phrase
in spite of the fact that
With
although or even though

Replace the phrase
in the neighborhood of
With
approximately or about

Replace the phrase
in the event that
With
if

The following phrases can be omitted entirely: *in a very real sense, in number, in nature, in reality, in terms of,* and *in the case of.*

in/into *In* is used to indicate condition or location, "positioned within": *She was in labor. The raccoon was in the woodpile. Into,* in contrast, indicates movement or a change in condition "from the outside to the inside": *The raccoon went into the shed. He went into cardiac arrest. Into* is also used as a slang expression for "involved with" or "interested in": *They are really into health foods.*

in regards to/with regards to Both terms are considered nonstandard terms for "regarding," "in regard to," "with regard to," and "as regards:" *As regards* (not *"in regards to"*) *your request of April 1, we have traced your shipment and it will be delivered tomorrow.*

inferior than *Inferior to* and *worse than* are the generally preferred forms: *This wine is inferior to* (not *"inferior than"*) *the burgundy we had last night.*

inside/outside; inside of/outside of When the words *inside* and *outside* are used as prepositions, the word *of* is not included: *Stay inside the house. The authorization is outside my department. Inside of* is used informally to refer to time *(I'll be there inside of an hour)* but in formal speech or writing *within* is the preferred usage: *The dump was cleaned up within a month.*

insignia *Insignia* was originally the plural of the Latin word "insigne." The plural term *insignias* has been standard usage since the eighteenth century.

irregardless/regardless *Regardless* is the standard term; avoid *irregardless* in both speech and writing.

its/it's/its' *Its* is the possessive form of *it: The shrub is losing its blossoms. It's* is the contraction for *it is: It's a nice day.* The two are often confused because possessives are most frequently formed with -'s. *Its'* is nonstandard usage.

It's me/It's I The traditional rule is that personal pronouns after the verb "to be" take the nominative case *(I, she, he, we, they).* Today, however, such usage as *it's me, that's him, it must be them* is almost universal in informal speech. The objective forms have also replaced the nominative forms in informal speech in such constructions as *me neither* and *who, them?* In formal discourse, however, the nominative forms are still used: *it's I, that is he.*

-ize/-wise Use the suffix -*ize* to change a noun or adjective into a verb: *categorize.* Use the suffix -*wise* to change a noun or adjective into an adverb: *otherwise.*

kind of/sort of/type of Avoid using either *kind of, sort of,* or *type of* as synonyms for "somewhat" in formal speech and writing. Instead, use "rather": *She was rather* (not *"kind of"*) *slender.* It is acceptable to use the three terms only when the word *kind, sort,* or *type* is stressed: *This kind of cheese is hard to digest.* Do not add "a": *I don't know what kind of* (not *"kind of a"*) *cheese that is.* When the word *kind, sort,* or *type* is not stressed, omit the phrase entirely: *That's an unusual* (not *"unusual kind of"*) *car. She's a pleasant* (not *"pleasant sort of a"*) *person.*

let's *Let's* is often used as a word in its own right rather than as the contraction of "let us." As such, it is often used in informal speech and writing with redundant or appositional pronouns: *Let's us take in a movie. Let's you and me go for a walk.* Usage guides suggest avoiding *let's us* in formal speech and writing, although both *let's you and me* and *let's you and I* occur in the everyday speech of educated speakers. While the former conforms to the traditional rules of grammar, the latter, nevertheless, occurs more frequently.

like/such as Use *like* to compare an example to the thing mentioned and *such as* to show that the example is representative of the thing mentioned: *Judy wants to be a famous clothing designer like John Weitz, Liz Claiborne, and Yves St. Laurent. Judy has samples of many fine articles such as evening dresses, suits, and jackets.*

Many writers favor not separating *such* and *as* with an intervening word: *samples of many fine articles such as* rather than *samples of such fine articles as.*

lots/lots of Both terms are used in informal speech and writing as a substitute for "a great many," "very many," or "much."

man The use of the term *man* as a synonym for "human being," both by itself and in compounds *(mankind)*, is declining. Terms such as *human being(s), human race, humankind, humanity, people,* and, when necessary, *men and women* or *women and men* are widely accepted in formal usage.

-man/-person The use of the term *man* as the last element in compound words referring to a person of either sex who performs some function *(anchorman, chairman, spokesman)* has declined in recent years. Now such compound words are widely used only if the word refers to a male. The sex-neutral word *person* is otherwise substituted for *man (anchorperson, chairperson, spokesperson)*. In other instances, a form without a suffix *(anchor, chair)*, or a word that does not denote gender *(speaker)*, is used.

The compound words *freshman, lowerclassmen, underclassmen* are still generally used in schools, and *freshman* is used in the U.S. Congress as well. These terms are applied to members of both sexes. As a modifier, *freshman* is used with both singular and plural nouns: *freshman athlete, freshman legislators.* See also *chair/chairperson.*

me and *Me and* is considered nonstandard usage when part of a compound subject: *Bob and I* (not *"Me and Bob") decided to fly to Boston.*

media *Media*, the plural of *medium*, is used with a plural verb: *Increasingly, the radio and television media seem to be stressing sensational news.*

mighty *Mighty* is used informally for "very" or "extremely": *He is a mighty big fighter.*

more important/more importantly Both phrases are acceptable in standard English: *My donations of clothing were tax deductible; more important(ly), the clothes were given to homeless people.*

Ms. (or Ms) The title *Ms.* is widely used in business and professional circles as an alternative to "Mrs." and "Miss," both of which reveal a woman's marital status. Some women prefer "Mrs.," where appropriate, or the traditional "Miss," which is still fully standard for an unmarried woman or a woman whose marital status is unknown. Since *Ms.* is not an abbreviation, some sources spell it without a period; others use a period to parallel "Mr." It is correctly used before a woman's name but not before her husband's name: *Ms. Leslie Taubman* or *Ms. Taubman* (not *"Ms. Steven Taubman")*.

much/many Use *many* rather than *much* to modify plural nouns: *They had many* (not *"much") dogs. There were too many* (not *"much") facts to absorb.*

Muslim/Moslem *Muslim* is now the preferred form for an adherent of Islam, though *Moslem,* the traditional form, is still in use.

mutual One current meaning of *mutual* is "reciprocal": *Employers and employees sometimes suffer from a mutual misunderstanding. Mutual* can also mean "held in common, shared": *Their mutual goal is clearly understood.*

myself; herself; himself; yourself The -*self* pronouns are intensive or reflexive, intensifying or referring to an antecedent: *Kerri herself said so. Mike and I did it ourselves.* Questions are raised when the -*self* forms are used instead of personal pronouns ("I," "me," etc.) as subjects, objects, or complements. This use of the -*self* forms is especially common in informal speech and writing: *Many came to welcome my wife and myself back from China.* All these forms are also used, alone or with other nouns or pronouns, after "as," "than," or "but" in all varieties of speech and writing: *Letters have arrived for everyone but the counselors and yourselves.* Although there is ample precedent in both British and American usage for the expanded uses of the -*self* constructions, the -*self* pronouns should be used in formal speech and writing only with the nouns and pronouns to which they refer: *No one except me* (not *"myself") saw the movie.*

nauseous/nauseated *Nauseated* is generally preferred in formal writing over *nauseous: The wild ride on the roller coaster made Wanda feel nauseated.*

neither . . . nor When used as a correlative, *neither* is almost always followed by *nor: neither Caitlyn nor her father. . . .* The subjects connected by *neither . . . nor* take a singular verb when both subjects are singular *(Neither Caitlyn nor her father is going to watch the program)* and a plural verb when both are plural *(Neither the rabbits nor the sheep have been fed yet today).* When a singular and a plural subject are joined by these correlatives, the verb should agree with the nearer noun or pronoun: *Neither the mayor nor the council members have yielded. Neither the council members nor the mayor has yielded.*

no . . . nor/no . . . or Use *no . . . or* in compound phrases: *We had no milk or eggs in the house.*

nohow The word *nohow,* nonstandard usage for "in no way" or "in any way," should be avoided in speech and writing.

none *None* can be treated as either singular or plural depending on its meaning in a sentence. When the sense is "not any persons or things," the plural is more common: *The rescue party searched for survivors, but none were found.* When *none* is clearly intended to mean "not one" or "not any," it is followed by a singular verb: *Of all the ailments I have diagnosed during my career, none has been stranger than yours.*

nothing like, nowhere near Both phrases are used in informal speech and writing, but they should be avoided in formal discourse. Instead, use "not nearly": *The congealed pudding found in the back of the refrigerator is not nearly as old as the stale bread on the second shelf.*

nowheres/nowhere The word *nowheres,* nonstandard usage for *nowhere,* should be avoided in speech and writing.

of Avoid using *of* with descriptive adjectives after the adverbs "how" or "too" in formal speech and writing. This usage is largely restricted to informal discourse: *How long of a ride will it be? It's too cold of a day for swimming.*

off of/off *Off of* is redundant and awkward; use *off: The cat jumped off the sofa.*

OK/O.K./okay All three spellings are considered acceptable, but the phrases are generally reserved for informal speech and writing.

on account of/because of Since it is less wordy, *because of* is the preferred phrase: *Because of her headache they decided to go straight home.*

on the one hand/on the other hand These two transitions should be used together: *On the one hand, we hoped for fair weather. On the other hand, we knew the rain was needed for the crops.* This usage, though, can be wordy. Effective substitutes include "in contrast," "but," "however," and "yet": *We hoped for fair weather, yet we knew the rain was needed for the crops.*

only The placement of *only* as a modifier is more a matter of style and clarity than of grammatical rule. In strict formal usage, *only* should be placed as close as possible **before** the word it modifies. In the following sentence, for example, the placement of the word *only* suggests that no one but the children was examined: *The doctor examined only the children.* In the next sentence, the placement of *only* says that no one but the doctor did the examining: *Only the doctor examined the children.* Nonetheless, in all types of speech and writing, people often place *only* before the verb regardless of what it modifies. In spoken discourse, speakers may convey their intended meaning by stressing the word or construction to which *only* applies.

owing to the fact that "Because" is generally accepted as a less wordy substitute for *owing to the fact that.*

pair/pairs When modified by a number, the plural of *pair* is commonly *pairs,* especially when referring to persons: *The three pairs of costumed children led off the Halloween parade.* The plural *pair* is used mainly in reference to inanimate objects or nonhumans: *There are four pair (or "pairs") of shoelaces. We have two pair (or "pairs") of rabbits.*

people/persons In formal usage, *people* is most often used to refer to a general group, emphasizing anonymity: *We the people of the United States. . . .* Use *persons* to indicate any unnamed individuals within the group: *Will the persons who left their folders on the table please pick them up at their earliest convenience?* Except when individuals are being emphasized, *people* is generally used rather than *persons.*

per; a/an *Per,* meaning "for each," occurs mainly in technical or statistical contexts: *This new engine averages fifty miles per hour. Americans eat fifty* *pounds of chicken per person per year.* It is also frequently used in sports commentary: *He scored an average of two runs per game.* A or *an* is often considered more suitable in nontechnical use: *The silk costs ten dollars a yard. How many miles an hour can you walk?*

percent/per cent *Percent* comes from the English *per cent.*, an abbreviation of the Latin *per centum.* It almost always follows a number: *I made 12 percent interest by investing my money in that new account.* In formal writing, use the word rather than the symbol (%). The use of the two-word form *per cent* is diminishing.

phenomena Like words such as *criteria* and *media, phenomena* is a plural form (of "phenomenon"), meaning "an observable fact, occurrence, or circumstance": *The official explained that the disturbing phenomena we had seen for the past three evenings were nothing more than routine aircraft maneuvers.*

plenty As a noun, *plenty* is acceptable in standard usage: *I have plenty of money.* In informal speech and writing *plenty* is often a substitute for "very": *She was traveling plenty fast down the freeway.*

plus *Plus* is a preposition meaning "in addition to": *My salary plus overtime is enough to allow us a gracious lifestyle.* Recently, *plus* has been used as a conjunctive adverb in informal speech and writing: *It's safe, plus it's economical.* Many object to this use.

practically Use *practically* as a synonym for "in effect," or "virtually." It is also considered correct to use it in place of "nearly" in all varieties of speech and writing.

previous to/prior to "Before" is generally preferred in place of either expression: *Before (not "previous to" or "prior to") repairing the tire, you should check to see if there are any other leaks.*

providing/provided Both forms can serve as subordinating conjunctions meaning "on the condition that": *Provided (Providing) that we get the contract in time, we will be able to begin work by the first of the month.* While some critics feel that *provided* is more acceptable in formal discourse, both are correct.

rarely ever/rarely/hardly The term *rarely ever* is used informally in speech and writing. For formal discourse, use either *rarely* or *hardly* in place of *rarely ever: She rarely calls her mother. She hardly calls her mother.*

real/really In formal usage, *real* (an adjective meaning "genuine") should not be used in place of *really* (an adverb meaning "actually"): *The platypus hardly looked real. How did it really happen?*

reason is because/reason is since Although both expressions are commonly used in informal speech and writing, formal usage requires a clause beginning with "that" after "reason is": *The reason the pool is empty is that (not "because" or "since") the town recently imposed a water restriction.* Another alternative is to recast the sentence: *The pool is empty because the town recently imposed a water restriction.*

regarding/in regard to/with regard to/relating to/relative to/with respect to/respecting All the above expressions are wordy substitutes for "about," "concerning," or "on": *Janet spoke about (not "relative to," etc.) the PTA's plans for the September fund drive.*

relate to The phrase *relate to* is used informally to mean "understand" or "respond in a favorable manner": *I don't relate to chemistry.* It is rarely used in formal writing or speech.

repeat it/repeat it again *Repeat it* is the expression to use to indicate that someone should say something for a second time: *I did not hear your name; please repeat it. Repeat it again* indicates the answer is to be said a third time. In the majority of instances, *repeat it* is the desired phrase; *again,* an unnecessary addition.

says/said Use *said* rather than *says* after a verb in the past tense: *At the public meeting, he stood up and said (not "says") "The bond issue cannot pass."*

seldom ever/seldom *Seldom* is the preferred form in formal discourse: *They seldom (not "seldom ever") visit the beach.*

shall/will Today, *shall* is used for first-person questions requesting consent or opinion. *Shall we go for a drive? Shall I buy this dress or that? Shall* can also be used in the first person to create an elevated tone: *We shall call on you at six o'clock.* It is sometimes used with the second or third person to state a speaker's resolution: *You shall obey me.*

Traditionally, *will* was used for the second and third persons: *Will you attend the party? Will he and she go as well?* It is now widely used in speech and writing as the future-tense helping verb for all three persons: *I will drive, you will drive, they will drive.*

should/would Rules similar to those for choosing between "shall" and "will" have long been advanced for *should* and *would.* In current American usage, use of *would* far outweighs that of *should. Should* is chiefly used to state obligation: *I should repair the faucet. You should get the parts we need. Would,* in contrast, is used to express a hypothetical situation or a wish: *I would like to go. Would you?*

since *Since* is an adverb meaning "from then until now": *She was appointed in May and has been supervisor ever since.* It is also used as an adverb meaning "between a particular past time and the present, subsequently": *They had at first refused to cooperate, but have since agreed to volunteer.* As a preposition, *since* means "continuously from": *It has been rainy since June.* It is also used as a preposition meaning "between a past time or event and the present": *There have been many changes since the merger.* As a conjunction, *since* means "in the period following the time when": *He has called since he changed jobs. Since* is also used as a synonym for "because": *Since you're here early, let's begin.*

situation The word *situation* is often added unnecessarily to a sentence: *The situation is that we must get the painting done by the weekend.* In such instances, consider revisiting the sentence to pare excess words: *We must get the painting done by the weekend.*

slow/slowly Today *slow* is used chiefly in spoken imperative constructions with short verbs that express motion, such as "drive," "walk," "swim," and "run." For example: *Drive slow. Don't walk so slow. Slow* is also combined with present participles to form adjectives: *He was slow-moving. It was a slow-burning fire. Slowly* is used in both speech and writing before a verb *(H? slowly walked through the hills)* as well as after a verb *(He walked slowly through the hills).*

so Many writers object to *so* being used as an intensifier, noting that in such usage it is often vague: *They were so happy. So* followed by "that" and a clause usually eliminates the vagueness: *They were so happy that they had been invited to the exclusive party.*

so/so that *So that,* rather than *so,* is most often used in formal writing to avoid the possibility of ambiguity: *He visited Aunt Lucia so that he could help her clear the basement.*

some *Some* is often used in informal speech and writing as an adjective meaning "exceptional, unusual" and as an adverb meaning "somewhat." In more formal instances, use "somewhat" in place of *some* as an adverb or a more precise word such as "remarkable" in place of *some* as an adjective: *Those are unusual* (not *"some"*) *shoes. My sister and brother-in-law are going to have to rush somewhat* (not *"some"*) *to get here in time for dinner.*

someplace/somewhere *Someplace* should be used only in informal writing and speech; use *somewhere* for formal discourse.

somewheres *Somewheres* is not accepted in formal writing or speech; use the standard "somewhere": *She would like to go somewhere* (not *"somewheres"*) *special to celebrate New Year's Eve.*

split infinitive There is a longstanding convention that prohibits placing a word between "to" and the verb: *To understand fully another culture, you have to live among its people for many years.* This convention is based on an analogy with Latin, in which an infinitive is only one word and therefore cannot be divided. Criticism of the split infinitive was especially strong when the modeling of English on Latin was popular, as it was in the nineteenth century. Today many note that a split infinitive sometimes creates a less awkward sentence: *Many American companies expect to more than double their overseas investments in the next decade.*

suppose to/supposed to; use to/used to Both *suppose to* and *use to* are incorrect. The preferred usage is *supposed to* or *used to: I was supposed to* (not *"suppose to"*) *get up early this morning to go hiking in the mountains. I used to* (not *"use to"*) *enjoy the seashore but now I prefer the mountains.*

sure/surely When used as an adverb meaning *surely, sure* is considered inappropriate for formal discourse. A qualifier like "certainly" should be used instead of *sure: My neighbors were certainly right about it.* It is widely used, however, in speech and informal writing: *They were sure right about that car.*

sure and/sure to; try and/try to *Sure to* and *try to* are the preferred forms for formal discourse: *Be sure to* (not *"sure and"*) *come home early tonight. Try to* (not *"try and"*) *avoid the traffic on the interstate.*

that The conjunction *that* is occasionally omitted, especially after verbs of thinking, saying, believing, and so forth: *She said (that) they would come by train.* The omission of the conjunction almost always occurs when the dependent clause begins with a personal pronoun or a proper name. The omission is most frequent in informal speech and writing.

that/which Traditionally, *that* is used to introduce a restrictive clause: *They should buy the cookies that the neighbor's child is selling. Which,* in contrast, is used to introduce nonrestrictive clauses: *The cookies, which are covered in chocolate, would make a nice evening snack.* This distinction is maintained far more often in formal writing than in everyday speech, where voice can often distinguish restrictive from nonrestrictive clauses.

that/which/who The relative pronoun *that* is used to refer to animals, things, and people. It can substitute in most cases for either *which* or *who(m): The computer that* (or *which) I bought last year is already outdated. The cat that* (or *which) appeared on our porch during the winter is now sleeping on my bed every night. The hitchhiker that* (or *whom) we picked up was a student at the state university.* In accepted usage, *who* is used only to refer to people. *Which* is used to refer to animals and to inanimate objects: *The puppy, which my son gave me for Christmas, now weighs forty pounds. My best pen, which I had left on my desk, disappeared during the meeting.*

them/those *Them* is nonstandard when used as an adjective: *I enjoyed those* (not *"them") apples a great deal.*

they/their/them Although the word *they* is traditionally a third-person plural pronoun, many people now use it as a singular pronoun, in place of "he" or "she": *If anyone comes to the door, tell them I'm not at home.* Some people disapprove of this use, but it is becoming very common, especially in informal use. This is partly because there is no gender-neutral pronoun in English.

this here/these here/that there/them there Each of these phrases is nonstandard: *this here* for "this," *these here* for "these," *that there* for "that," *them there* for "those."

thusly/thus *Thusly* is a pointless synonym for *thus.* Speakers and writers often use *thusly* only for a deliberately humorous effect.

till/until/'til *Till* and *until* are used interchangeably in speech and writing; *'til,* a shortened form of *until,* is rarely used.

time period The expression *time period* is redundant, since "period" is a period of time: *The local ambulance squad reported three emergency calls in a one-week period* (not *"time period").*

too Be careful when using *too* as an intensifier in speech and writing: *The dog is too mean.* Adding an explanation of the excessive quality makes the sentence more logical: *The dog is too mean to trust alone with children.*

toward/towards The two words are used interchangeably in both formal and informal speech and writing.

try and/try to While *try to* is the preferred form for formal speech and writing, both phrases occur in all types of speech and writing.

type/type of In written English, *type of* is the preferred construction: *This is an unusual type of flower.* In informal speech and writing, it is acceptable to use *type* immediately before a noun: *I like this type car.*

used to could/used to be able to The phrase *used to could* is nonstandard for *used to be able to: I used to be able to* (not *"used to could") touch my toes.*

very The adverb *very* is sometimes used unnecessarily, especially in modifying an absolute adjective: *It was a very unique experience.* In such instances, it clearly should be omitted. Further, *very* has become overworked and has lost much of its power. Use more precise modifiers such as "extremely" and "especially."

want in/want out Both phrases are informal: *want in* for "want to enter," *want out* for "want to leave": *The dog wants to enter* (not *"wants in"*). *The cat wants to leave* (not *"wants out"*).

way/ways *Way* is the preferred usage for formal speech and writing; *ways* is used informally: *They have a little way* (not *"ways"*) *to go before they reach the campground.*

when/where *Where* and *when* are not interchangeable: *Weekends are occasions when* (not *"where"*) *we have a chance to spend time with the family.*

where/that *Where* and *that* are not interchangeable: *We see by the memo that* (not *"where"*) *overtime has been discontinued.*

where at/where to Both phrases are generally considered to be too informal to be acceptable in good writing and speech: *Where is John?* (not *"Where is John at?"*) *Where is Mike going?* (not *"Where is Mike going to?"*)

who/whoever; whom/whomever Traditionally, *who/whoever* is used as a subject (the nominative case) and *whom/whomever* as an object (the objective case). In informal speech and writing, however, since *who* and *whom* often occur at the beginning of a sentence, people usually select *who*, regardless of grammatical function.

with regards to/with regard to/as regards/regarding Use *with regard to, regarding,* or *as regards* in place of *with regards to* in formal speech and writing: *As regards your inquiry, we have asked our shipping department to hold the merchandise until Monday.*

without/unless *Without* as a conjunction is a dialectical or regional use of *unless.*

would have Do not use the phrase *would have* in place of *had* in clauses that begin with "if" and express a state contrary to fact: *If the driver had* (not *"would have"*) *been wearing his seat belt, he would have escaped without injury.*

would of/could of There is no such expression as *would of* or *could of: He would have* (not *"would of"*) *gone.* Also, "of" is not a substitute for " 've": *She would've* (not *"would of"*) *left earlier.*

you was *You was* is nonstandard for *you were: You were* (not *"you was"*) *late on Thursday.*

Avoiding Insensitive and Offensive Language

This essay is intended as a general guide to language that can, intentionally or not, cause offense or perpetuate discriminatory values and practices by emphasizing the differences between people or implying that one group is superior to another.

Several factors complicate the issue. A group may disagree within itself as to what is acceptable and what is not. Many seemingly inoffensive terms develop negative connotations over time and become dated or go out of style as awareness changes. A "within the group" rule often applies, which allows a member of a group to use terms freely that would be considered offensive if used by an outsider.

While it is true that some of the more extreme attempts to avoid offending language have resulted in ludicrous obfuscation, it is also true that heightened sensitivity in language indicates a precision of thought and is a positive move toward rectifying the unequal social status between one group and another.

Suggestions for avoiding insensitive or offensive language are given in the following pages. The suggested terms are given on the right. While these suggestions can reflect trends, they cannot dictate or predict the preferences of each individual.

Sexism

Sexism is the most difficult bias to avoid, in part because of the convention of using *man* or *men* and *he* or *his* to refer to people of either sex. Other, more disrespectful, conventions include giving descriptions of women in terms of age and appearance while describing men in terms of accomplishment.

Replacing man *or* men

Man traditionally referred to a male or to a human in general. Using *man* to refer to a human is often thought to be slighting of women.

Avoid this	Use this instead
mankind, man	human beings, humans, humankind, humanity, people, society, men & women
man-made	synthetic, artificial

man in the street	average person, ordinary person

Using Gender-Neutral Terms for Occupations, Positions, Roles, Etc.

Terms that specify a particular sex can unnecessarily perpetuate certain stereotypes when used generically.

Avoid this	Use this instead
anchorman	anchor
bellman, bellboy	bellhop
businessman	businessperson, executive, manager, business owner, retailer, etc.
chairman	chair, chairperson
cleaning lady, girl, maid	housecleaner, housekeeper, cleaning person, office cleaner
clergyman	member of the clergy, rabbi, priest, etc.
clergymen	the clergy

congressman	representative, member of Congress, legislator
fireman	firefighter
forefather	ancestor
girl/gal Friday	assistant
housewife	homemaker
insurance man	insurance agent
layman	layperson, nonspecialist, nonprofessional
mailman, postman	mail or letter carrier
policeman	police officer, law enforcement officer
salesman, saleswoman, saleslady, salesgirl	salesperson, sales representative, sales associate, clerk
spokesman	spokesperson, representative
stewardess, steward	flight attendant
weatherman	weather reporter, weathercaster, meteorologist
workman	worker
actress	actor

Replacing the Pronoun he

The generic use of *he* can also be seen to exclude women.

Avoid this	Use this instead
When a driver approaches a red light, he must prepare to stop.	When drivers approach a red light, they must prepare to stop.
	When a driver approaches a red light, he or she must prepare to stop.
	When approaching a red light, a driver must prepare to stop.

Referring to Members of Both Sexes with Parallel Names, Titles, or Descriptions

Don't be inconsistent unless you are trying to make a specific point.

Avoid this	Use this instead
men and ladies	men and women, ladies and gentlemen
Betty Schmidt, an attractive 49-year-old physician, and her husband, Alan Schmidt, a noted editor	Betty Schmidt, a physician, and her husband, Alan Schmidt, an editor
Mr. David Kim and Mrs. Betty Harrow	Mr. David Kim and Ms. Betty Harrow (unless *Mrs.* is her known preference)
man and wife	husband and wife
Dear Sir:	Dear Sir/Madam: Dear Madam or Sir: To whom it may concern:
Mrs. Smith and President Jones	Governor Smith and President Jones

Race, Ethnicity, and National Origin

Some words and phrases that refer to racial and ethnic groups are clearly offensive. Other words (e.g., *Oriental, colored*) are outdated or inaccurate. *Hispanic* is generally accepted as a broad term for Spanish-speaking people of the Western Hemisphere, but more specific terms *(Latino, Mexican American)* are also acceptable and in some cases preferred.

Avoid this	Use this instead
Negro, colored, Afro-American	black, African-American (generally preferred to Afro-American)
Oriental, Asiatic	Asian, or more specific designations such as Pacific Islander, Chinese American, Korean

Indian	*Indian* properly refers to people who live in or come from India.
	American Indian, Native American, or more specific designations (Chinook, Hopi), are usually preferred when referring to the native peoples of the Western Hemisphere.
Eskimo	Inuit, Alaska Natives
native (n.)	native peoples, early inhabitants, aboriginal peoples (but not aborigines)

Age

The concept of aging is changing as people are living longer and more active lives. Be aware of word choices that reinforce stereotypes *(decrepit, senile)* and avoid mentioning age unless it is relevant.

Avoid this	Use this instead
elderly, aged, old, geriatric, the elderly, the aged	older person, senior citizen(s), older people, seniors

Sexual Orientation

The term *homosexual* to describe a man or woman is increasingly replaced by the terms *gay* for men and *lesbian* for women. *Homosexual* as a noun is sometimes used only in reference to a male. Among homosexuals, certain terms (such as *queer* and *dyke*) that are usually considered offensive have been gaining currency in recent years. However, it is still prudent to avoid these terms in standard contexts.

Avoiding Depersonalization of Persons with Disabilities or Illnesses

Terminology that emphasizes the person rather than the disability is generally preferred. *Handicap* is used to refer to the environmental barrier that affects the person. (Stairs handicap a person who uses a wheelchair.) While words such as *crazy, demented,* and *insane* are used in facetious or informal contexts, these terms are not used to describe people with clinical diagnoses of mental illness. The euphemisms *challenged, differently abled,* and *special* are preferred by some people, but are often ridiculed and are best avoided.

Avoid this	Use this instead
Mongoloid	person with Down syndrome
wheelchair-bound	person who uses a wheelchair
AIDS sufferer, person afflicted with AIDS, AIDS victim	person living with AIDS, P.W.A., HIV+, (one who tests positive for HIV but does not show symptoms of AIDS)
polio victim	has/had polio
the handicapped the disabled, or cripple	persons with disabilities, person with a disability, person who uses crutches, *or* more specific description
deaf-mute, deaf and dumb	deaf person

Avoiding Patronizing or Demeaning Expressions

Avoid this	Use this instead
girls (when referring to adult women), the fair sex	women
sweetie, dear, dearie, honey	(usually not appropriate with strangers or in public situations)
old maid, bachelorette, spinster	single woman, woman, divorced woman (but only if one would specify "divorced man" in the same context)

Avoid this	Use this instead	Avoid this	Use this instead
the little woman, old lady, ball and chain	wife	lawyers and their wives	lawyers and their spouses
boy (when referring to or addressing an adult man)	man, sir	a secretary and her boss	a secretary and boss, a secretary and his or her boss
		the male nurse	the nurse
		Arab man denies assault charge	Man denies assault charge
		the articulate black student	the articulate student
		Marie Curie was a great woman scientist	Marie Curie was a great scientist. (unless the intent is to compare her only with other women in the sciences)

Avoiding Language that Excludes or Unnecessarily Emphasizes Differences

References to age, sex, religion, race, and the like should be included only if they are relevant.

Punctuation

Period

Rule	Example
A period is used: after a statement,	Some of us still support the mayor. Others think he should retire.
after an indirect question,	She asked what time the train leaves.
after a mild command,	Would you close the door, please. Read the next two chapters by Tuesday.
and after a question used as a statement.	It's hot today, isn't it.
A period is used after many abbreviations.	i.e., e.g., etc., Mr., Mrs., Ms., Dr., Inc., U.S., M.D., Sept., Pa., D.C.
A period is *not* used in acronyms, in U.S. Postal Service state abbreviations, with initials used in place of personal names, or after metric abbreviations.	UNICEF, UNESCO, NASA, NATO, IRA, AIDS, OPEC, NAFTA NY, PA, CA, ME, MD FDR, JFK, LBJ 50 km, 3 kg, 100 mm
A period is used within decimal numbers and amounts of money.	A sales tax of 7.5 percent is leveled on all clothing in this state. He spent $44.50 on the shirt, $36.09 on the pants, and $22.00 on the tie.

Rule	Example

Question Mark

Sentences that ask a question should be followed by a question mark.	Who invited him to the party? "Is something the matter?" she asked. What constitutional principle did John Marshall establish in *Marbury v. Madison?* in *McCullough v. Maryland?* in *Fletcher v. Peck?* You can get us in free?
A question mark is also used to indicate doubt about information.	Socrates was born in 470 (?) B.C. The codes dates back to A.D. 500 (?)
A question mark is not used after an indirect question or after a polite command phrased as a question.	I wonder why. She asked if the application had been mailed. Won't you sit down. Why don't you take off your coat.

Exclamation Point

| An exclamation point is used to end a sentence, clause, phrase, or single word that expresses strong emotion, such as surprise, command, or admiration. | Go away!
What a week this has been! |

Note: Avoid overusing exclamation points in writing. They are effective only when used sparingly.

Comma

The comma is the most frequently used mark of punctuation within a sentence. The main use of a comma is to clarify the structure and meaning of a sentence. The secondary use of a comma is to indicate emphasis, pauses, and stress. Adding unnecessary commas or omitting necessary ones can confuse a reader and obscure the meaning of a sentence.

Rule	Example
Independent clauses may be grouped into sentences by using the coordinating conjunctions *and, but, yet, for, or, nor,* and *so.* The first clause is usually followed by a comma. If the subject of both clauses is the same, the comma is generally omitted.	We tried to reason with him, but he had already made up his mind. Joe is finishing high school this year, and Jennifer is a junior at Harvard. Take six cooking apples and put them into a flameproof dish.
Introductory words, phrases, clauses, and transitional expressions are set off by a comma.	Your honor, I object. Theoretically, she will have to get the permission of the chairman. Thoroughly chilled, he decided to set out for home. Yes, we are prepared for any motion that the prosecution may make. However, it is important to understand everyone's point of view. Born to wealthy parents, he was able to pursue his career without financial worries. After the first few years of marriage, most couples realize that there are certain matters upon which they will never agree.

Rule	Example
	Since the team was in last place, it was not surprising that only fifteen hundred fans showed up for the final game of the season.
When the introductory phrase is short, the comma is often omitted, but be certain that the sentence is clear as it stands.	In this article I will demonstrate that we have chosen the wrong policy. At the present time the number of cigarette smokers is declining.
Conjunctive adverbs, transitional expressions, and parenthetical expressions that occur in the middle of the sentence require two commas to set them off.	It is important, however, to understand everyone's point of view. Most new employees, after the first month, settle easily into the company's routine. We can, I hope, agree on a budget for next year. You may, if you insist, demand a retraction.
If a sentence can be read without pauses before and after the modifier, the commas may be omitted.	We can therefore conclude that the defendant is innocent of the charges. The applicant must understand before sending in the forms that the deposit fee is not refundable.
A phrase or clause is called "restrictive" if omitting it would change the meaning of the sentence. Such a phrase or clause "restricts" or limits the meaning of the word or words it applies to and therefore cannot be omitted. Restrictive phrases and clauses are not set off by commas.	The Elizabethan composers Byrd, Gibbons, and Dowland influenced her greatly. The novel that she wrote in 1996 won a literary award. The only state that is in the Hawaii-Aleutian time zone is Hawaii. The city where I live is Seattle.

Rule	Example
When a phrase or clause is not essential to the meaning of the sentence, it is called "nonrestrictive." Such phrases and clauses are set off by commas.	She was much influenced by Elizabethan composers, especially Byrd, Gibbons, and Dowland. Her most recent novel, written in 1996, won a literary award. Hawaii, which is the fiftieth state, is in the Hawaii-Aleutian time zone. Seattle, the city where I live, is close to both the sea and the mountains.
Conjunctive adverbs can be placed anywhere in a sentence depending on where you want the emphasis. They are always set off by commas.	However, it is important to understand everyone's point of view. It is important, however, to understand everyone's point of view. It is important to understand everyone's point of view, however.
Appositives are words that give additional information about the preceding or following word or expression. Many appositives are nonrestrictive and are thus set off from the rest of the sentence with commas. Be careful not to set off restrictive appositives, which are necessary for the meaning of the sentence.	March, the month of crocuses, can still bring snow and ice. Mr. Case, a member of the committee, refused to comment. His favorite author, Stephen King, entered the auditorium. My friend Mary spoke at the convention. The crowd fell silent as the author Stephen King entered the auditorium.
A comma is used to separate words, phrases, and clauses that are part of a series of three or more items, with a word like *and* or *or* usually occurring between the last two items.	The chief agricultural products of Denmark are butter, eggs, potatoes, beets, wheat, barley, and oats. England, Scotland, and Wales share the island of Great Britain.

Rule	Example
	Cabbage is especially good with corned beef, game, or smoked meats.
	Environmentally conscious businesses used recycled paper, photocopy on both sides of a sheet, and use ceramic cups.

Note: Some writers omit the final comma when punctuating a series, and newspapers and magazines sometimes follow this practice. Book publishers and educators, however, usually follow the practice recommended above.

Rule	Example
In a series of adjectives, commas must be used when each adjective is considered separately, not as a modifier of other adjectives.	the beautiful, expensive dress the happy, smiling children the hungry, meowing cat
Do not use commas to separate adjectives that are so closely related that they appear to form a single element with the noun they modify. Adjectives that refer to the number, age, size, color, or location of the noun often fall within this category. To determine whether or not to use the comma in these instances, insert the word *and*. If *and* cannot replace the comma without creating an awkward sentence, it is safe to conclude that a comma is not necessary.	twenty happy little children several dingy old Western mining towns beautiful tall golden aspens a dozen long white dresses
When dates and addresses are used in sentences, they are followed by a comma. When only the month and year are given, the comma is usually omitted.	All contributions should be sent to the recording secretary at 4232 Grand Boulevard, Silver Spring, MD 70042, as soon as possible.

Rule	Example
	She was born on Tuesday, December 20, 1901, in a log cabin near Casey Creek, Kentucky.
	We took our first trip to Alaska in August 1988.
Use a comma when it is necessary to prevent misreading. The comma tells the reader to stop briefly before reading on. Words may run together in confusing ways unless you use a comma to separate them. Use a comma in such sentences even though no rule requires one.	Soon after, she quit the job for good.
	The people who can, usually contribute some money to the local holiday drive.
	After she ate, the cat washed herself and went to sleep.

Semicolon

A semicolon is used to separate parts of a sentence—such as independent clauses, items in a series, and explanations or summaries—from the main clause. It makes a stronger break in the sentence than a comma does. In choosing among the three punctuation marks that separate main clauses—the comma, the semicolon, and the colon—a writer needs to decide on the relationship between ideas.

Rule	Example
Separate independent clauses not joined by a coordinating conjunction are separated by a semicolon.	The house burned down; it was the last shattering blow.
	We have made several attempts to reach you by telephone; not a single call has been returned.
When separate independent clauses are joined by a conjunctive adverb such as *however, nevertheless, otherwise, therefore, besides, hence, indeed, instead, nonetheless, still, then,* or *thus,* a semicolon is used after the first clause.	The funds are inadequate; therefore, the project will close down.
	Enrollments exceed all expectations; however, there is a teacher shortage.
	He knew the tickets for the performance would be scarce;

Rule	Example
	therefore, he arrived at the concert hall two hours early.
Long or possibly ambiguous items in a series, especially when those items already include commas, are separated by a semicolon.	In the next year, they plan to open stores in Sewickley, Pennsylvania; Belleville, Illinois; Breckenridge, Colorado; and Martinez, California. Academically talented students were selected on the basis of grades; tests of vocabulary, memory, reading, inductive reasoning, math, and perceptual speed and accuracy; and teacher recommendations.
A semicolon is used before *i.e., e.g., that is, for example,* etc., when the next part of the sentence is a complete clause.	On the advice of his broker, he chose to invest in major industries; i.e., he invested in steel, automobiles, and oil. She organizes her work well; for example, she puts correspondence in folders of different colors to indicate degrees of urgency.

Colon

As a mark of introduction, the colon tells the reader that the first statement is going to be explained by the second or that a quotation or series will follow.

A colon is used to introduce a long formal statement or a quotation.	This I believe: All people are created equal and must enjoy equally the rights that are inalienably theirs. Fagles's translation of the *Iliad* begins: "Rage—Goddess, sing the rage of Peleus' son Achilles, murderous, doomed, that cost the Achaeans countless losses, . . ."

Rule	Example
When one independent clause is followed by another that explains or exemplifies it, they can be separated by a colon. The second clause may or may not begin with a capital letter.	They cannot pay their monthly bills because their money is tied up in their stocks and bonds: they are paper-rich and cash-poor. There's only one solution: we must reduce next year's budget. The negotiators finally agreed on a basic principle: neither side would seek to resupply the troops during the cease-fire. The conference addresses a basic question: How can we take the steps needed to protect the environment without stalling economic growth?
A colon is used to introduce a series or list.	There were originally five Marx brothers: Groucho, Chico, Harpo, Zeppo, and Gummo. The senior citizens demanded the following: better police protection, more convenient medical facilities, and a new recreational center.
A colon is used to follow the salutation in a formal letter.	Dear Mr. Czerny: Dear Ms. McFadden: Dear Valued Customer:
The parts of a citation are separated by a colon.	Genesis 3:2 *Journal of Astrophysics* 43:2
A colon is placed between the title and the subtitle of a book.	In 1988, Brooks published *Gilded Twilight: The Later Years of Melville and Twain.*
A colon is used to separate hours from minutes in indicating time.	1:30 P.M. 12:30 A.M.

Rule	Example
In a bibliographical citation, a colon may separate the place of publication from the name of the publisher.	New York: Random House, Inc.
Do not use a colon to introduce a list that is the object of the verb.	The senior citizens' demands included better police protection, more convenient medical facilities, and a new recreational center.
Do not used a colon to introduce a list after the verb "to be" or to introduce a list following a preposition:	The courses she is taking are French, medieval history, Greek, and the nineteenth-century novel. I have had enough of mosquitoes, leaking tents, wet blankets, and whining children. The committee consisted of nine teachers, twelve parents, and six business leaders.

Dash

A dash is used to show sudden changes in thought or to set off certain sentence elements. Like the exclamation point, dashes are dramatic and thus should be used sparingly in formal writing. Do not confuse the dash with the hyphen (see page 144 on the hyphen).

The dash may be used to mark an abrupt change in thought or shift in tone.	He won the game—but I'm getting ahead of the story. She told me—does she really mean it?—that she will inform us of any changes in advance.
Where commas might cause confusion, a dash may be used to set off appositives.	The premier's promise of changes—land reform and higher wages—was not easily fulfilled.

Rule	Example
	The qualities Renoir valued in his painting—rich shadows, muted colors, graceful figures—were abundant in the ballet dancers he used as subjects.
A dash may be used to add emphasis to parenthetical material or to mark an emphatic separation between that material and the rest of the sentence.	Her influence—she was a powerful figure in the community—was a deterrent to effective opposition. The car he was driving—a gleaming red convertible—was the most impressive thing about him.
Halting or hesitant speech may be indicated by a dash.	"Well—er—it's hard to explain," he faltered. Madame de Vionnett instantly rallied. "And you know—though it might occur to one—it isn't in the least that he's ashamed of her. She's really—in a way—extremely good looking." —Henry James
Interrupted speech may also be indicated by a dash.	"Harvey, don't climb up that—." It was too late. If they discovered the truth—he did not want to think of the consequences.
A dash may replace an offensive word or part of one.	Where's that son of a b—? "You're full of —!" he shouted.

Rule	Example

Ellipsis

The ellipsis mark consists of three spaced periods (. . .).

It is sometimes convenient to omit part of a quotation. When this is done, the omission must be marked with points of ellipsis, usually with spaces between them. When the omission comes in the middle of a sentence, three points are used. When the omission includes the end of one or more sentences, four points are used.	Lewis Thomas offers the following advice: If something is to be quoted, the exact words must be used. If part of it must be left out . . . insert three dots to indicate the omission, but it is unethical to do this if it means connecting two thoughts which the original author did not intend to have tied together.
Ellipsis may also be used to indicate breaks in thought in quoted speech (compare with dash).	"I don't know where he is. . . ." "If only she hadn't died so soon. . . ."

Note: If the sentence is complete, the period is added, resulting in four spaced periods. If the sentence is incomplete, use only three dots for the ellipsis.

Parentheses

Parentheses are used to enclose nonessential material within a sentence. This can include facts, explanations, digressions, and examples that may be helpful but are not necessary for the sentence. Do not put a comma before a parenthesis.	Faulkner's stories (but not his novels) were required reading for the course. The community didn't feel (and why should they?) that there was adequate police protection. Many workers (including those in the mail room) distrust the new shipping regulations.
Parentheses are also used to enclose part of a sentence that would be confusing if enclosed by commas.	The authors he advised (none other than Hemingway, Lewis, and Cather) would have been delighted to honor him today.

Rule	Example
An explanatory item that is not part of the statement is enclosed in parentheses.	He wrote to *The Paris* (Illinois) *News.*
Parentheses are used to enclose numbers or letters that designate each item in a series.	The project is (1) too time-consuming, (2) too expensive, and (3) poorly staffed.
Parentheses are used to indicate an abbreviation that will be used in the remainder of the paragraph.	The Federal Trade Commission (FTC) has issued regulations on the advertising of many products.
If a full sentence is enclosed within the parentheses, the period comes before the closing parenthesis.	Seven U.S. presidents were born in Virginia. (The other southern states were the birthplaces of only one or two presidents each.) Ohio also produced seven, and Massachusetts and New York, four each.
If the parenthetical element is a fragment of a sentence, the period goes outside the closing parenthesis.	Two U.S. presidents were born in Vermont (Chester Alan Arthur and Calvin Coolidge), and one was born in New Hampshire (Franklin Pierce).

Brackets

When writers insert something within a quoted passage, the insertion should be set off with brackets. Insertions are sometimes used to supply words that explain, clarify, or correct the contents of a direct quotation.	According to the *Globe* critic, "This [*Man and Superman*] is one of Shaw's greatest plays." "Young as they are," he writes, "these students are afflicted with cynicism, world-weariness, and *a total disregard for tradition and authority.*" [Emphasis is mine.] "As a result of the Gemini V

Rule	Example
	mission [the flight by astronauts Cooper and Conrad in August 1965], we have proof that human beings can withstand the eight days in space required for a round trip to the moon." Lewis Thomas warns that it is "unethical to [omit words in a quotation] . . . if it means connecting two thoughts which the original author did not intend to have tied together."
Writers can make clear that an error in the quotation has been carried over from the original by using the Latin word *"sic,"* meaning "thus."	"George Washington lived during the seventeenth [*sic*] century." "The governor of Missisipi [*sic*] addressed the student body."
Brackets are used to enclose comments made in a verbatim transcript.	Sen. Eaton: The steady rise in taxes must be halted. [Applause]
Brackets are used to substitute for parentheses with material already enclosed in parentheses.	[1]See "Rene Descartes" (M.C. Beardsley, *The European Philosophers from Descartes to Nietzsche* [New York, 1960]).
The publication date, inserted by the editor, of an item appearing in an earlier issue of a periodical is enclosed in brackets.	Dear Sir: Your excellent article on China [April 15] brings to mind my recent experience . . . When traveling in India [*Travel Monthly,* March 1997], one should recall the words of . . .

Rule	Example

Quotation Marks

The main function of quotation marks is to enclose a direct quotation. Quotation marks are always used in pairs to mark the beginning and end of the quotation.	"They've come back!" she exclaimed.
Words or groups of words that are quoted from the original are enclosed in quotation marks.	Portia's speech on "the quality of mercy" is one of the most quoted passages from Shakespeare. It was Shaw who wrote: "All great truths begin as blasphemies."
Titles of essays, short stories, poems, chapters of books, songs, and radio and television programs are usually enclosed in quotation marks. (See the section on the use of italics below.)	Our anthology contains such widely assorted pieces as Bacon's essay "Of Studies," Shelley's "Ode to the West Wind," Gilman's "The Yellow Wallpaper," and an article on criticism from the *New Yorker*. My daughter watches "Sesame Street" every morning. "Summertime" is from *Porgy and Bess*.
Quotation marks are used to emphasize a word or phrase that is the subject of discussion or to suggest that a word or phrase is being used ironically.	The words "imply" and "infer" are not synonymous. Such Freudian terms as "ego," "superego," "id," and "libido" have now entered popular usage and are familiar to most Americans. The radio blasting Kim's favorite "music" is to his parents an instrument of torture. Bob's skiing "vacation" consisted of three weeks with his leg in a cast.

Rule	Example
A quotation within a quotation is enclosed in single quotation marks.	Reading Jill's letter, Pat said, "Listen to this! 'I've just received notice that I made the dean's list.' Isn't that great?"
Final quotation marks follow other punctuation marks, except for semicolons and colons.	After dinner Ed began looking up all the unfamiliar allusions in Milton's "L'Allegro"; then, shortly after midnight, he turned to "Il Penseroso."
Question marks and exclamation marks precede final quotation marks when they refer to the quoted words. They follow when they refer to the sentence as a whole.	Once more she asked, "What do you think we should do about this?" What do you suppose Carla meant when she said, "I'm going to do something about this"? "Be off with you!" he yelled.

Note: Use a comma between the quotation and phrases such as *according to the speaker, he said,* and *she replied* that introduce or conclude a quotation.

If a quotation consists of two or more consecutive paragraphs, use quotation marks at the beginning of each paragraph, but place them at the end of the last paragraph only.

Italics/Underlining

Italics are used to emphasize or set apart specific words and phrases. In handwritten papers, underlining indicates italics.

The titles of newspapers, magazines, and books are italicized.	Her job requires her to read the *New York Times,* the *Wall Street Journal,* and the *Washington Post* every day. "Song of Myself" is the first poem in Whitman's *Leaves of Grass.* Every year *Consumer Reports* runs "Best Buy Gifts" in the November issue.

Rule	Example
Italics are used for the titles of plays and movies and for the titles of works of art and long musical works.	Shakespeare's *Hamlet* *The Playboy of the Western World* the movie *High Noon* Huston's *The Maltese Falcon* Leonardo da Vinci's *Last Supper* Georgia O'Keeffe's *Black Iris* Handel's *Messiah* *Don Giovanni* by Mozart *Porgy and Bess*
Italics are used for the names of ships and planes	the aircraft carrier *Intrepid* Lindbergh's *The Spirit of St. Louis*
Words and phrases from a foreign language are italicized. Accompanying translations are often enclosed in quotation marks. Words of foreign origin that have become familiar in an English context should not be italicized.	As a group, these artists appear to be in the avant-garde. They are not, however, to be thought of as *enfants terribles,* or "terrible children," people whose work is so outrageous as to shock or embarrass.
Italics are used for words used as words and letters used as letters.	I can never remember how to spell *broccoli.* Be sure to pronounce the final *e* in *Nike.*
Italics are used to show that words are to be emphasized.	The boss is *very* hard to get along with today. Joan loaned the tape to Robert, and *he* gave it to Sally.

Rule	Example
Forward Slash (Also Called "Solidus" or "Virgule")	
A forward slash is used to separate lines of poetry within the text.	William Blake's stanza on anger in "A Poison Tree" seems as appropriate today as when it was first written: "I was angry with my friend:/I told my wrath, my wrath did end./I was angry with my foe:/I told it not, my wrath did grow."
A forward slash is used in dates and fractions.	winter 1998/99 the fiscal year 1997/98 3/4 + 2/3 x/y − y/x
Options and alternatives are separated by a forward slash.	I have never seen the advantage of pass/fail courses.
Apostrophe	
An apostrophe is used in contractions to show where letters or numerals have been omitted.	I'm he's didn't won't let's Ma'am four o'clock readin', 'ritin', an' 'rithmetic the class of '99
An apostrophe is used when making letters or numbers plural.	GI's V.I.P.'s figure 8's The handwriting is very hard to read: the *n*'s and *u*'s look alike.

Rule	Example
	The number of Ph.D.'s awarded to U.S. citizens declined in the 1980's.

Note: The apostrophe may be omitted in dates: 1980s.

Rule	Example
The apostrophe is used with nouns to show possession.	The company's management resisted the union's demands.
An apostrophe plus *s* is added to all words—singular or plural—that do not end in *-s*.	the little boy's hat the front office's idea children's literature a week's vacation somebody else's fault the mice's tails
Just an apostrophe is added at the end of plural words that end in *-s*.	the little boys' hats the farmers' demands the Joneses' yard two weeks' vacation the oil companies' profits for old times' sake
Style guides disagree on how to treat singular nouns that end in *-s*. Perhaps the best practice is to follow one's own pronunciation. If the possessive form has an extra syllable, then add an apostrophe and *s;* otherwise just add an apostrophe.	Tess's bad luck Socrates' wordview for goodness' sake Williams's poems Dickens' (*or* Dickens's) novels the class's attitude Ulysses' voyage Marx' (*or* Marx's) philosophy
The possessive of compound words or two or more proper names is formed by adding an apostrophe plus *s* to the last word of the compound.	sister-in-law's job editor-in-chief's pen Japan and Germany's agreement Lewis and Clark's expedition the University of South Carolina's mascot one another's books anyone else's property

Note: Never use an apostrophe with a possessive personal pronoun. These personal pronouns are already possessive and therefore have no need for an apostrophe: *my, mine, your, yours, her, hers, its, our, ours, their,* and *theirs.*

Hyphen

Although a hyphen and a dash may appear to be the same at first glance, they are two very different marks of punctuation. The dash is more than twice as long as the hyphen. The hyphen is used to group words and parts of words together, while the dash is used to clarify sentence structure. A dash is formed by typing two successive hyphens (--) on a word processor that does not have a dash character.

Rule	Example
A hyphen is used at the end of a line of text when part of a word must be carried over to the next line. (See page 87 in the Usage section for rules of word division.)	. . . insta- bility
Hyphens are sometimes used to form compound words.	twenty-five three-fourths forty-one sixty-fourths mother-in-law president-elect double-breasted self-confidence ex-wife hands-on the nineteen-eighties
In certain situation, hyphens are used between prefixes and root words to prevent confusion in pronunciation or to avoid confusing a word with another whose spelling is identical. If you are uncertain about a particular word, consult a dictionary.	catlike but bull-like antibiotic but anti-intellectual semiliterate but semi-invalid recover vs. re-cover coop vs. co-op recreation vs. re-creation

Rule	Example
When the root word of a compound is a proper noun or proper adjective, a hyphen is used to separate the prefix.	anti-American neo-Nazi non-European pro-French
Hyphens are used to combine the elements of a compound modifier when used before the noun it modifies.	hand-to-hand combat a well-dressed woman a double-parked car an out-of-work actor
These modifiers are usually not hyphenated when they follow the noun.	They fought hand to hand. She is always very well dressed. The car was double parked. She is out of work.
When two modifiers are joined together, common elements are often not repeated.	This textbook covers both macro- and microeconomics. The study included fourth-, eighth-, and twelfth-grade students.

Note: Consult a dictionary if you don't know whether or not a compound noun is hyphenated.

Rule	Example
The hyphen can be used as a substitute for *to*, with the meaning "up to and including." It should not, however, be used in conjunction with *from*.	The text of the Constitution can be found on pages 679-87. The period 1890-1914 was a particularly tranquil time in Europe. The Civil War lasted from 1861 to 1865. (*not* from 1861-1865) The San Francisco-Vancouver flight has been cancelled.

Capitalization

The important words in titles are capitalized. This includes the first and last words and all other words except articles, prepositions, and coordinating	*Gone with the Wind* *With Malice toward None* *The Universe Within* *Sports-related Injuries* *The Brain: A User's Manual*

Rule	Example
conjunctions, such as *and, but,* and *or.*	*A World to Lose* *The Great War, 1914–1918* *Twentieth-Century Views*
Proper nouns—names of specific people, places, organizations, groups, events, etc.—are capitalized, as are the proper adjectives derived from them.	Martin Luther King, Jr. United States Coast Guard New Orleans Jeremy Canada Latinos Spanish Civil War Canadian Jeffersonian
When proper nouns and adjectives have taken on a specialized meaning, they are often no longer capitalized.	My brother ordered a turkey sandwich with russian dressing. The shop specializes in china and plaster of paris ornaments. The address was written in india ink on a manila envelope.
Titles of people are capitalized when they are used before a name or when they are used in place of a name to refer to the specific person who holds the title. They are not capitalized when they refer to the office rather than to the person.	Queen Victoria reigned from 1837 to 1901. The Queen's husband, Prince Albert, died in 1861. Some of England's greatest novels were written while she was queen. President Lincoln was assassinated in 1865. The President and his wife were attending a performance at Ford's Theater. During the years he was president, the South seceded from the Union, and the Civil War began.

Rule	Example
Kinship terms are capitalized when they are used before a name or alone in place of a name. They are not capitalized when they are preceded by modifiers.	I'm expecting Aunt Alice to drop by this weekend. I forgot to call Mother on her birthday. I forgot to call my mother on her birthday.
Geographical features are capitalized when they are part of the official name. In the plural, they are capitalized when they precede names, but not when they follow.	The Sonoran Desert is in southern Arizona. The Arizona desert is beautiful in the spring. In recent years, Lakes Erie and Ontario have been cleaned up. The Hudson and Mohawk rivers are both in New York State.
Points of the compass are capitalized only when they are used as the name of a section of the country.	We've been driving east for over two hours. We visited the South last summer and the Southwest the year before. He was born in southwestern Nebraska.

2

Preparing and Marking up a Manuscript

Manuscript Preparation

Manuscripts should be printed or typed on standard-size paper— 8 1/2 by 11 inches. If the paper is being submitted for publication and will be edited and set into type, everything should be double-spaced—including block quotations, footnotes, and references— since it is difficult to edit material that has less than a full line of space between lines of text. Many instructors also prefer that papers be double-spaced. While covers may be attractive for certain purposes, most editors and instructors find that they make manuscripts more difficult to handle efficiently. Pages must be numbered, preferably in the upper right-hand corner and far enough from the edge so that the numbers are not accidentally left off when the manuscript is photocopied. Every manuscript should be copied as a safeguard against loss of the original.

Word processing makes available several features that are not available on the conventional typewriter—italics, boldface, various typefaces, and different possibilities for spacing. If a manuscript is being prepared for its final readership, then it makes sense to use these capabilities to make it as attractive and readable as possible. On the other hand, if the manuscript will be edited and set into type, it will be easier to deal with if a single typeface is used.

If you are submitting a manuscript to a publisher, ask if there are guidelines for writers. Knowing the required format in advance can save you a great deal of time.

Proofread your work carefully before submitting it. A manuscript that has mistakes in spelling and grammar will not be taken seriously by an editor and may be rejected by an instructor.

Footnotes

Footnotes can be used for additional material that does not fit conveniently into the text. They may be placed at the bottom of the page or at the end of the text, in which case they are often referred to as endnotes. Traditionally, footnotes have also been used to cite the sources of information, ideas, and quotations included in a text. This is no longer a recommended practice. It is now more common to include brief identifications of sources in parentheses within a text and give full information in a reference list at the end. In-text citations and reference lists are discussed in the next two sections.

In-Text Citations

There are two main ways of citing sources within a text: (1) the author-page system, which is widely used in the humanities; and (2) the author-date system, which has been adopted by the social sciences and some of the natural sciences. Each of these systems has several variations. The recognized standard for the author-page system is *The MLA Style Manual,* which is published by the Modern Language Association. The most widely used version of the author-date system can be found in the *Publication Manual of the American Psychological Association* (APA), 3rd ed. The brief descriptions of each system that follow are based on these two sources.

The basic technique in both systems is to include just enough information in the text to enable the reader to find the relevant item in the reference list. In the author-page system, this information includes the author of the work referred to and the relevant page number.

> *American novelists have always had a difficult relationship with their public (Brooks 247).*

If the author is mentioned in the text, then just the page number is needed in parentheses.

> *As Brooks has observed, American novelists have always had a difficult relationship with their public (247).*

If the reference is to a work as a whole rather than to a specific part, then no additional citation is needed.

> *In* Gilded Twilight, *Brooks establishes himself as the most thoughtful of poststructuralist critics.*

When there is more than one item in the reference list by the same author, the title of the work referred to is included in the parentheses, usually in a shortened form.

> *Brooks' comments on Melville are surprisingly negative* (Gilded *83).*

When works by different authors are referred to, all the references are included in the same parentheses.

> *Recently critics have had surprisingly negative things to say about Melville (Brooks,* Gilded *83; Adams and Rubens 432; Leibniz 239).*

In the author-date system, the in-text citations include the author's name and the date of publication. As with the author-page system, material that already appears in the text is not repeated within the parentheses.

> *A recent study carried out at McGill came to the opposite conclusion (McBain, 1991).*
>
> *McBain (1991) demonstrates that there is at least one alternative to the accepted view.*
>
> *In a 1991 study, McBain showed that there is at least one alternative to the accepted view.*

When the reference list contains more than one work published by a particular author in the same year, letters are used to distinguish among them.

> *Several innovative studies in the last few years have demonstrated that this matter is not as settled as was once thought (Brewer, 1989; Fischer & Rivera, 1988; McBain, 1989a, 1989b, 1991; Silvano, Blomstedt & Meigs, 1987).*

Ordinarily, page numbers are included only when there is a direct quotation.

> *One respected researcher notes that little notice has been taken of "the substantial number of counterexamples that have not been either questioned or explained" (McBain, 1991, p. 238).*

Notice how the two systems differ in details: for example, one uses *and*, the other *&;* one follows the author's name with a comma, while the other does not.

In some publications in the sciences, the items in the reference list are numbered and these numbers are used in citations in the text.

> *One group of experiments has led researchers to believe that despite the enormous difficulties, a vaccine will eventually be produced (3,22,39). Much depends on the availability of funds and staff to carry out the work (14). Motley observes, however, that "whether the administration has the will to make the painful choices necessary is highly doubtful" (19, p. 687).*

With a number system, the items in the reference list may be put in either alphabetical order or the order in which they occur in the text.

Reference Lists

The following table shows how items in the reference list would be treated in the author-page and author-date systems. It is important to realize that in following a particular style, the writer must be consistent in every detail of wording, abbreviation, spacing, and punctuation. There is space here for only a limited variety of items. Those who are preparing texts for publication will probably need to consult the relevant manual.

Sample Reference Lists

Type of Document	Author-Page System (MLA) Works Cited	Author-Date (APA) References
Journal article	Stewart, Donald C. "What Is an English Major, and What Should It Be?" *College Composition and Communication* 40 (1989): 188–202.	Roediger, H. L. (1990). Implicit memory: A commentary. *Bulletin of the Psychonomic Society, 28,* 373–380.

Type of Document	Author-Page System (MLA) Works Cited	Author-Date (APA) References
Journal article two authors	Brownell, Hiram H., and Heather H. Potter. "Inference Deficits in Right-Brain Damaged Patients." *Brain and Language* 27 (1986): 310–21.	Tulving, E., & Schacter, D. L. (1990). Priming and human memory systems. *Science, 247,* 301–305.
Journal article more than two authors	Mascia-Lees, Frances E., Pat Sharpe, and Colleen B. Cohen. "Double Liminality and the Black Woman Writer." *American Behavioral Scientist* 31 (1987): 101–14.	Barringer, H. R., Takeuchi, D. T., & Xenos, P. C. (1990). Education, occupational prestige and income of Asian Americans: Evidence from the 1980 Census. *Sociology of Education, 63,* 27–43.
Book	Hammond, Nicholas G. *The Genius of Alexander the Great.* Chapel Hill: U of North Carolina P, 1997.	Rossi, P. H. (1989). *Down and out in America: The origins of homelessness.* Chicago: University of Chicago Press.
Book revised edition	Eagleton, Terry. *Literary Theory: An Introduction.* 2nd ed. Minneapolis: U of Minnesota P, 1996.	Kail, R. (1990). *Memory development in children* (3rd ed.). New York: Freeman.
Book corporate author	College Board. *College-bound Seniors: 1989 SAT Profile.* New York: College Entrance Examination Board, 1989.	American Psychiatric Association. (1987). *Diagnostic and statistical manual of mental disorders* (3rd ed., rev.). Washington, DC: Author.
Book no author	*Guidelines for the Workload of the College English Teacher.* Urbana: National Council of Teachers of English, 1987.	*Standards for educational and psychological tests.* (1985). Washington, DC: American Psychological Association.
Edited book	Kerckhove, Derrick de, and Charles J. Lumsden, eds. *The Alphabet and the Brain: The Lateralization of Writing.* Berlin: Springer-Verlag, 1988.	Campbell, J. P., Campbell, R. J., & Associates. (Eds.). (1988). *Productivity in organizations.* San Francisco, CA: Jossey-Bass.
Selection from edited book	Glover, David. "The Stuff That Dreams Are Made Of: Masculinity, Femininity, and the Thriller." *Gender, Genre and Narrative Pleasure.* Ed. Derek Longhurst. London: Unwin Hyman, 1989. 67–83.	Wilson, S. F. (1990). Community support and integration: New directions for outcome research. In S. Rose (Ed.), *Case management: An overview and assessment.* White Plains, NY: Longman.

Type of Document	Author-Page System (MLA) Works Cited	Author-Date (APA) References
Translated book	Mann, Thomas. *Buddenbrooks: The Decline of a Family.* Trans. John E. Woods. New York: Knopf, 1993.	Michotte, A. E. (1963). The perception of causality (T. R. Miles & E. Miles, Trans.). London: Methuen. (Original work published 1946)
Republished book	Hurston, Zora Neale. *Their Eyes Were Watching God.* 1937. Urbana: U of Illinois P, 1978.	Ebbinghaus, H. (1964). *Memory: A contribution to experimental psychology.* New York: Dover. (Original work published 1885; translated 1913)
Magazine article	Miller, Mark Crispen. "Massa, Come Home." *New Republic* 16 Sept. 1981: 29–32.	Gibbs, N. (1989, April 24). How America has run out of time. *Time,* pp. 58–67.
Newspaper article	"Literacy on the Job." *USA Today* 27 Dec. 1988: 6B.	Freudenheim, M. (1987, December 29). Rehabilitation in head injuries in business and health. *New York Times,* p. D2.
Review	Kidd, John. "The Scandal of *Ulysses.*" Rev. of *Ulysses: The Corrected Text,* by Hans Walter Gabler. *New York Review of Books* 30 June 1988: 32–39.	Falk, J. S. (1990). [Review of *Narratives from the crib*]. *Language, 66,* 558–562.
Report available from ERIC	Baurer, Barbara A. *A Study of the Reliabilities and Cost Efficiencies of Three Methods of Assessment for Writing Ability.* ERIC, 1981. ED 216 357.	Hill, C., & Larsen, E. (1984). *What reading tests call for and what children do.* Washington, DC: National Institute of Education. (ERIC Document Reproduction Service No. ED 238 904)
University report	Flower, Linda. The Role of Task Representation in Reading to Write. Technical Report No. 6. Berkeley: Center for the Study of Writing at U of California, Berkeley and Carnegie Mellon U, 1987.	Elman, J., & Zipser, D. (1987). *Learning the hidden structure of speech* (Report No. 8701). Institute for Cognitive Science, University of California, San Diego.
Dissertation	Hubert, Henry Allan. "The Development of English Studies in Nineteenth-Century Anglo-Canadian Colleges." Diss. U of British Columbia, 1988.	Thompson, I., (1988). *Social perception in negotiation.* Unpublished doctoral dissertation, Northwestern University, Evanston, IL.

Type of Document	Author-Page System (MLA) Works Cited	Author-Date (APA) References
Conference paper	Moffett, James. "Censorship and Spiritual Education." The Right to Literacy Conference. Columbus, Ohio, September 1988.	Hogan, R., Raskin, R., & Fazzini, D. (1988, October). *The dark side of charisma.* Paper presented at the Conference on Psychological Measures and Leadership, San Antonio, TX.

Proofreaders' Marks

The marks shown below are used in proofreading and revising printed material. The mark should be written in the margin, directly in line with the part of the text in which the change is being made, and the line of text should show the change. When more than one change is being made in the same line, slash marks are used in the margin to separate the respective marks. A slash may also be used after a single correction.

Mark in margin	Indication in text	Meaning of instruction
a / r	Peter left town in hurfy.	Insert at carets (∧)
ℐ or ℽ	Joan sent me the the book.	Delete
⌒	ma ke	Close up; no space
ℐ	I haven't seen them in years.	Delete and close up
stet	They phoned both Al and Jack.	Let it stand; disregard indicated deletion or change
ℋ	up the river. Two years	Start new paragraph
no ℋ or *run in*	many unnecessary additives. The most dangerous one	No new paragraph
tr	Put the book on the table. Put the table on the book.	Transpose
tr up or *tr* ↑	to Eva Barr, who was traveling abroad. Ms. Barr, an actress,	Transpose to place indicated above
tr down or *tr* ↓	in the clutch. The final score was 6-5. He pitched the last two innings.	Transpose to place indicated below
sp	He owes me 6 dollars.	Spell out
fig	There were eighteen members present.	Set in figures
#	It was a smallvillage.	Insert one letter space
##	too late.After the dance	Insert two letter spaces

Mark in margin	Indication in text	Meaning of instruction
hr #	jeroboam	Insert hair space (very thin space)
line #	Oscar Picks ——— # This year's Academy Awards nomination.	Insert line space
eq #	Ron ✓ got rid ✓ of the dog.	Equalize spacing between words
=	three days later	Align horizontally
‖	‖ the earth's surface, bounded by lines parallel to the equator	Align vertically
run over	enhance production⌡ 2. It will	Start new line
▢	▢ Rose asked the price.	Insert one em space
▢▢	▢▢ The Use of the Comma	Insert two em spaces
⊏	⊏ What's his last name?	Move left
⊐	April 2, 1945 ⊐	Move right
⌐⌐	⌐ Please go now. ⌐	Move up
⌐_⌐	⌐ Well, that's that! ⌐	Move down
⊐ ⊏	⊐ ATOMIC ENERGY ⊏	Center (heading, title, etc.)
fl	⊏ 2. Three (3) skirts	Flush left
fr	Total: $89.50 ⊐	Flush right
sint /?	He the copy.	Insert missing word?
(OK?) or (?)	by Francis Gray. (She) wrote	Query or verify; is this correct?
(out: see copy)	the discovery of but near the hull	Something missing
⊙	Anna teaches music	Insert period
⸴	We expect Eileen Tom, and Ken.	Insert comma
;	I came; I saw I conquered.	Insert semicolon
(:)	Ben got up at 630 a.m.	Insert colon

Mark in margin	Indication in text	Meaning of instruction
=	Douglas got a two thirds majority.	Insert hyphen
$\frac{1}{m}$	Mike then left very reluctantly.	Insert em dash
$\frac{1}{n}$	See pages 96 124.	Insert en dash
ᶜ	Don't mark the authors copy. Don't mark the authors copy.	Insert apostrophe
!	Watch out	Insert exclamation point
?	Did she write to you	Insert question mark
⟨⟨/⟩⟩	Ode on a Grecian Urn, by Keats	Insert quotation marks
⟨/⟩	She said, "Read The Raven tonight."	Insert single quotation marks
(/) or ⊱/⊰	The Nile is 3473 miles 5592 km long.	Insert parentheses
[/] or ⊱/⊰	"He Dickson finished first."	Insert brackets
ital	I've seen <u>Casablanca</u> six times.	Set in *italics*
rom	Gregory drove to Winnipeg.	Set in roman
bf	See the definition of peace.	Set in **boldface**
lf	She repaired the motor easily.	Set in lightface
Cap or u/c	the italian role in Nato	Set in CAPITAL letter(s)
sc	He lived about 350 B.C.	Set in SMALL CAPITAL letter(s)
lc or l/c	Of Mice And Men	Set in lowercase
u+lc or c+lc or uc+lc	STOP! STOP!	Set in uppercase and lowercase
$\hat{}$ 2	H2O	Set as subscript
2	$A^2 + B2$	Set as superscript
×	They drove to Miami	Broken (damaged) type
wf	Turn Right	Wrong font

Enhancing Vocabulary

Introduction

This section of the *Random House Webster's English Language Desk Reference* is designed to help you increase the range of your vocabulary and use words more accurately and concisely. English has been influenced by languages from all over the world, but thousands of English words are built on Latin and Greek prefixes, suffixes, and roots. The first two chapters of this section focus on these building blocks of English. The next chapters deal with the histories of a number of English words and with some specialized vocabularies. Finally, there are comprehensive alphabetical lists of prefixes, suffixes, and roots with their meanings and examples of their use.

Words Built with Prefixes and Suffixes

Prefixes

A prefix is a letter or group of letters placed at the beginning of a word to change its meaning and make a new word. In the following chapter, we will show you how a knowledge of Latin and Greek roots can help you figure out the meanings of many English words. The following, for example, is a sampling of words that derive from the Latin prefix "circum-," meaning around.

Circum- Words

circumambulate	to walk around
circumference	the outer boundary of something
circumfluent	flowing around; encompassing
circumfuse	to surround, as with fluid
circumjacent	lying around; surrounding
circumlocution	a roundabout way of speaking
circumlunar	rotating about the moon
circumnavigate	to sail around
circumpolar	around or near one of the earth's poles
circumrotate	to rotate like a wheel
circumscribe	to encircle; mark off or delimit; restrict

Lesson 1. Common Latin Prefixes

Below are ten common Latin prefixes and their variations. Study the chart and examples. Then, to help you remember them, complete the quizzes that follow.

Prefix	Meaning	Variations	Examples
1. ad-	to, toward		adjoin, adverb
		a-	ascribe
		ac-	accede
		af-	affix
		ag-	aggregate
		at-	attempt
2. com-	with, together		commotion
		co-	cohabit, coworker
		col-	collaborate
		con-	concede, conduct
		cor-	correlate, correspond
3. de-	down		depress, deform
4. dis-	away, apart, opposite of		disagree, dishonest
		di-	divert
		dif-	diffuse
5. ex-	out		exchange, excavate
		e-	elongate, evaporate
		ec-	eccentric
		ef-	effluent, effuse
6. in-	in, into		inscribe, inhabit
		il-	illuminate
		im-	import, impart
		ir-	irradiate

7. in-	not	inflexible, indecent
	ig-	ignoble
	il-	illiterate, illegal
	im-	immodest, impatient
	ir-	irregular
8. pre-	before	premature
9. pro-	forward	proclaim
10. re-	again, back	recover, return

Quiz 1: Synonyms

Each of the following phrases contains an italicized word. Based on the meaning of its prefix, select the closest synonym.

1. *adjudicate* the matter
   a. sit in judgment on   b. throw out   c. argue   d. adjust
2. an *illicit* affair
   a. public   b. external   c. unlawful   d. renewed
3. an important *confederation*
   a. visit   b. return   c. church   d. alliance
4. *prolong* a speech
   a. shorten   b. dictate   c. extend   d. preserve
5. an *accredited* school
   a. second-rate   b. authorized   c. undesirable   d. separated
6. valuable *collateral*
   a. security   b. comments   c. opinions   d. animals
7. *ascribe* the phrase to
   a. write   b. scrawl   c. scribble   d. credit
8. *imbibe* too freely
   a. speak   b. drink   c. travel   d. laugh
9. *precursor* of greater things
   a. banner   b. detractor   c. forerunner   d. hope
10. *compress* metal
    a. help   b. coat   c. squeeze   d. buff

Quiz 2: Defining Words

Based on the meaning of its prefix, define each of the following words.

1. accord _____

2. irradiate _____

3. predestination _____

4. reincarnation _____

5. convolution _____

6. invoke _____

7. cohabit _____

8. irrelevant _____

9. irreducible _____

10. excommunicate _____

Suggested Answers: 1. agreement 2. illuminate 3. fate; destiny 4. rebirth; resurrection 5. a rolled up or coiled condition 6. to request or call forth 7. to live together as husband and wife 8. not relevant 9. incapable of being reduced 10. to exclude from communion

Lesson 2. Common Greek Prefixes

Below are five common Greek prefixes and their variations. Study the chart and examples. Then, to help you remember the prefixes, complete the quizzes that follow.

Prefix	Meaning	Variations	Examples
1. a-	not, without		atypical, asexual
		an-	anarchy
2. apo-	off, away		apology, apostrophe
3. epi-	beside, upon		epigraph, epidermis
		ep-	epoch
4. para-	beside		paragraph, paraphrase
5. syn-	together, with		synthesis, synonym
		syl-	syllable, syllogism
		sym-	symbiosis, symphony

Quiz 3: Synonyms

Each of the following phrases contains an italicized word. Based on the meaning of its prefix, select the closest synonym.

Formed from:

1. a new *synagogue*
   a. combination   b. sentence
   c. house of worship   d. building

   Greek "syn-"
   + "agogos,"
   bringer, gatherer

2. the true *apogee*
   a. limit of endurance   b. insult
   c. closest point of an   d. farthest point of an
      orbit   orbit

   Greek "apo-" +
   "ge," *earth*

3. the fifth annual *synod*
   a. church council   b. religious holiday   Greek "syn-" +
   c. house-cleaning   d. painting   "hodos," *way*

4. the sad *episode*
   a. incident   b. anecdote   Greek "epi-" +
   c. death   d. accident   "hodos," *way*

5. the witty *epigram*
   a. television show   b. radio broadcast   Greek "epi-" +
   c. saying   d. song   "gramma," *something written*

6. guilty of *apostasy*
   a. murder   b. desertion   Greek "apo-" +
   c. an unnamed crime   d. abandonment of   "stasis," *standing*
            religious faith

7. *aseptic* ointment
   a. free from germs   b. effective   Greek "a-" +
   c. expensive   d. greasy   "septos," *rotted*

8. clear and effective *syntax*
   a. treatment   b. word arrangement   Greek "syn-" +
   c. speech   d. magazine article   "taxis," *order*

9. injured *epidermis*
   a. leg ligament   b. elbow   Greek "epi-" +
   c. skin   d. shinbone   "dermis," *skin*

10. a cutting *epithet*
    a. weapon   b. funeral oration   Greek "epi-" +
    c. knife   d. descriptive word   "theton," *placed*

Quiz 4: Matching

Based on your knowledge of Greek prefixes, match each of the numbered words with the closest synonym. Write your answer in the space provided.

1. syllogism	a. running beside	_____
2. paralegal	b. climax; highest point	_____
3. anonymous	c. bottomless hole	_____
4. anesthetic	d. one sent out; messenger	_____
5. apostle	e. logical argument	_____
6. parallel	f. doubting God's existence	_____
7. apocryphal	g. attorney's assistant	_____
8. apogee	h. false; spurious	_____
9. agnostic	i. causing loss of feeling	_____
10. abyss	j. nameless	_____

Lesson 3. Old English Prefixes

Below are the five most common Old English prefixes and their variations. Study the chart and examples. Then, to help you remember the prefixes, complete the quizzes that follow.

Prefix	Meaning	Examples
a-	on, to, at, by	ablaze, afoot
be-	over, around	bespeak, besiege
mis-	wrong, badly	mistake, misspell
over-	beyond, above	overreach, overawe
un-	not	unwilling, unethical

Quiz 5: Synonyms

Each of the following phrases contains an italicized word. Based on the meaning of its prefix, select the closest synonym.

1. a *miscarriage* of justice
   a. instance b. hero c. failure d. example
2. *beseech* movingly
   a. implore b. search c. evoke d. refuse
3. walking two *abreast*
   a. together b. side by side c. back to back d. in tandem
4. *bestowed* on us
   a. hurled b. smashed c. dependent d. presented
5. an unfortunate *misalliance*
   a. treaty b. conversation c. bad deal d. improper marriage
6. an *overwrought* patient
   a. highly emotional b. extremely ill c. very restrained
   d. overmedicated
7. an *unkempt* look
   a. funny b. messy c. ugly d. pretty
8. an embarrassing *miscue*
   a. joke b. anecdote c. step d. error
9. *bedaub* with clay
   a. sculpt b. present c. smear d. create
10. *bemoan* his situation
    a. celebrate b. share c. lament d. hide

Quiz 6: Matching

Based on your knowledge of Old English prefixes, match each of the numbered words with the closest synonym. Write your answer in the space provided.

1. unfeigned	a. conquer	_____
2. misbegotten	b. right on the mark	_____
3. beguile	c. too fervent	_____
4. miscarriage	d. envy, resent	_____
5. bemuse	e. sincere, genuine	_____
6. mishap	f. accident	_____
7. overcome	g. illegitimate	_____
8. begrudge	h. mislead	_____
9. unerring	i. bewilder	_____
10. overzealous	j. spontaneous abortion	_____

Suffixes

A suffix is a letter or group of letters placed at the end of a word to change its grammatical function, tense, or meaning. Suffixes can be used to create a verb from a noun or adjective or an adjective from a verb, for example. They can change a word's tense as well; "-ed" can make a present-tense verb into a past participle, for instance. They can even change a word's meaning; the suffix "-ette," for example, can make a word into its diminutive: "kitchen" becomes "kitchenette."

Just as recognizing a small number of prefixes can help you figure out many unfamiliar words, so knowing a few common suffixes can help you build a more powerful vocabulary.

Lesson 4. Ten Powerful Suffixes

Below are ten useful suffixes. Read through the chart and examples. To reinforce your study, complete the quizzes that follow.

Suffix	Meaning	Variations	Examples
1. -ate	to make		alienate, regulate
	marked by		passionate, affectionate
2. -en	to make		weaken, moisten
3. -ism	the quality or practice of		absolutism, baptism
4. -ation	the act or condition of		allegation, affirmation
		-ition	recognition
		-tion	commotion
5. -ty	the state of		modesty
		-ity	security

6. -er	one that does or deals with		worker, teacher
		-ar	scholar
		-ier	furrier
		-or	bettor
7. -an	one that does or deals with		comedian, historian
8. -al	resembling or pertaining to		natural, accidental
9. -ous	full of		perilous
		-ious	gracious, vicious
10. -able	capable of being		lovable, affordable
		-ible	reversible

Quiz 7: Synonyms

Each of the following phrases contains an italicized word. Based on the meaning of its suffix, select the closest synonym.

1. *combustible* rubbish
   a. unbreakable   b. able to burst   c. affordable   d. flammable
2. *pastoral* scenes
   a. clerical   b. attractive   c. rural   d. homely
3. a *partisan* of the rebellion
   a. flag   b. supporter   c. sign   d. result
4. a *palatial* home
   a. magnificent   b. modest   c. formal   d. enjoyable
5. the *collegiate* atmosphere
   a. churchlike   b. friendly   c. cooperative   d. academic
6. *assiduity* in studies
   a. alacrity   b. cleverness   c. diligence   d. laziness
7. a number of *pedestrians*
   a. scholars   b. walkers   c. shopkeepers   d. students
8. an *abstemious* eater
   a. aloof   b. idle   c. absent-minded   d. sparing
9. *perilous* practices
   a. commonplace   b. rare   c. dangerous   d. useless
10. *deleterious* effects
    a. good   b. neutral   c. bad   d. delightful

Quiz 8: Matching

Based on your knowledge of suffixes, match each of the numbered words with the closest synonym. If in doubt, refer to the root word that follows each numbered word. Write your answer in the space provided.

1. **culpable**
   (Root word: Latin "culpa," *blame*)

   a. blameworthy _____

2. **parity**
   (Root word: Latin "par," *equal*)

   b. injurious _____

3. **amenable**
   (Root word: French "amener," *to lead to*)

   c. everlasting _____

4. **mendacious**
   (Root word: Latin "mendax," *dishonest*)

   d. reversion to type _____

5. **sempiternal**
   (Root word: Latin "semper," *always*)

   e. equality _____

6. **nihilism**
   (Root word: Latin "nihil," *nothing*)

   f. to chastise; censure _____

7. **atavism**
   (Root word: Latin "atavus," *remote*)

   g. willing _____

8. **fealty**
   (Root word: French "fealté," *fidelity*)

   h. total rejection of law _____

9. **castigate**
   (Root word: Latin "castus," *chaste*)

   i. lying; false _____

10. **noxious**
    (Root word: Latin "noxa," *harm*)

    j. faithfulness _____

Lesson 5. Ten Additional Powerful Suffixes

The following ten suffixes will help you understand countless additional words. After you read through the suffixes and their definitions, complete the two quizzes at the end of the lesson.

Suffix	Meaning	Examples
1. -esque	in the manner of; like	Lincolnesque
2. -aceous	resembling or having	carbonaceous
3. -ic	associated with	democratic
4. -age	act or process of; quantity or measure	marriage, coverage; footage
5. -itis	inflammation	tonsillitis
6. -ish	similar to; like a	foolish; babyish
7. -less	without	guiltless; helpless
8. -ship	occupation or skill; condition of being	authorship, penmanship; friendship
9. -ian	a person who is, does, or participates in	comedian
10. -ferous	bearing or conveying	odoriferous

Quiz 9: Matching

Based on your knowledge of suffixes, match each of the numbered words with its closest synonym. Write your answer in the space provided.

1. waspish	a. inattentive, sloppy	_____
2. fellowship	b. egotistic	_____
3. angelic	c. distance	_____
4. mileage	d. huge	_____
5. picturesque	e. eternal	_____
6. curvaceous	f. irritable	_____
7. titanic	g. voluptuous	_____
8. careless	h. companionship	_____
9. selfish	i. innocent	_____
10. timeless	j. colorful	_____

Quiz 10: Synonyms

Each of the following phrases contains an italicized word. Based on the meaning of its suffix, select the closest synonym. If in doubt, refer to the root word listed in the right-hand column.

Root Word

1. *auriferous* mineral
   a. containing gold   b. extremely hard   Latin "aurum," *gold*
   c. having an odor   d. very common

Root Word

2. *conical* shape
   a. humorous; amusing b. like a cone   Greek "konos," *cone*
   c. spherical d. rigid
3. suffering from *carditis*
   a. eye infection b. a tin ear   Greek "kardia," *heart*
   c. inflammation of the heart d. stiff joints
4. graceful *Romanesque*
   a. architectural style b. departure
   c. essay d. apology
5. *olivaceous* color
   a. oily b. deep green
   c. faded d. attractive
6. frightful *carnage*
   a. journey b. slaughter   Latin "carnis," *flesh*
   c. scened. d. sensuality
7. *satanic* nature
   a. evil b. cheerful
   c. shiny d. generous
8. admirable *craftsmanship*
   a. display b. individual
   c. shop d. artfulness
9. *veracious* remarks
   a. vivid b. vicious   Latin "verus," *true*
   c. windy d. truthful
10. painful *appendicitis*
    a. news b. surgery
    c. inflammation of the appendix d. removal of the appendix

Answers to Quizzes on Prefixes and Suffixes

Answers to Quiz 1
1. a 2. c 3. d 4. c 5. b 6. a 7. d 8. b 9. c 10. c

Answers to Quiz 3
1. c 2. d 3. a 4. a 5. c 6. d 7. a 8. b 9. c 10. d

Answers to Quiz 4
1. e 2. g 3. j 4. i 5. d 6. a 7. h 8. b 9. f 10. c

Answers to Quiz 5
1. c 2. a 3. b 4. d 5. d 6. a 7. b 8. d 9. c 10. c

Answers to Quiz 6
1. e 2. g 3. h 4. j 5. i 6. f 7. a 8. d 9. b 10. c

Answers to Quiz 7
1. d 2. c 3. b 4. a 5. d 6. c 7. b 8. d 9. c 10. c

Answers to Quiz 8
1. a 2. e 3. g 4. i 5. c 6. h 7. d 8. j 9. f 10. b

Answers to Quiz 9
1. f 2. h 3. i 4. c 5. j 6. g 7. d 8. a 9. b 10. e

Answers to Quiz 10
1. a 2. b 3. c 4. a 5. b 6. b 7. a 8. d 9. d 10. c

Recognizing Latin and Greek Roots

One of the quickest and most effective ways to improve your vocabulary is by learning to recognize the most common Latin and Greek roots, since any one of them can help you define a number of English words. Whenever you come upon an unfamiliar word, first check to see if it has a recognizable root. Even if you cannot define a word exactly, recognizing the root will still give you a general idea of the word's meaning.

Lesson 1. Common Latin Roots

Root	Meaning	Example	Definition
ag	act	agent	representative
cad, cas	fall	cadence	rhythmic flow
cap, cept	take, hold	receptacle	container
ced, cess	go	recessive	tending to go back
cid, cis	kill, cut	incision	cut, gash
clud, clus	shut	seclusion	separation from others
cred	believe	credible	believable
cur(r), curs	run	concur	agree (i.e., run together)
fer	bear	odoriferous	yielding an odor
her, hes	cling	adhere	cling, stick
ject	throw	projection	jutting out, protrusion

leg, lect	read	legible	easily readable
pel(l), puls	drive	repulse	repel (i.e., drive back)
pon, posit	put	postpone	defer
port	carry	portable	movable
rupt	break	abrupt	sudden, quick
scrib, script	write	inscription	engraving, writing
sect	cut	dissect	cut apart
sent, sens	feel	sensitive	tender
sequ, secut	follow	sequel	result
spect	look	prospect	outlook, expectation
sta, stat	stand	stable	fixed, firm
tang, tact	touch	tactile	tangible
termin	end	terminate	abolish, end
tract	pull, draw	tractor	vehicle that pulls
ven, vent	come	convene	assemble (i.e., come together)
vert, vers	turn	invert	overturn
vid, vis	see	provident	having foresight
vinc, vict	conquer	invincible	unconquerable
volv, volut	roll, turn	evolve	develop

Quiz 1: Synonyms

Each of the following phrases contains an italicized word. Based on the meaning of the root, select the closest synonym.

1. a *captive* animal
   a. confined   b. wild   c. charming   d. domestic
2. an *inverted* glass
   a. broken   b. upside-down   c. returned   d. drunk from
3. an *abrupt* stop
   a. slow   b. bad   c. sudden   d. harmful
4. a disappointing *sequel*
   a. television show   b. beginning   c. movie   d. follow-up
5. *terminate* the relationship
   a. doubt   b. intensify   c. begin   d. finish
6. an *incredible* story
   a. outlandish   b. unbelievable   c. foolish   d. upsetting
7. a *recessive* trait
   a. dominant   b. receding   c. hurtful   d. missing
8. *illegible* writing
   a. unreadable   b. graceful   c. distinct   d. large

9. a thorough *dissection*
   a. cutting apart   b. conference   c. discussion   d. putting together

10. an *unstable* relationship
    a. new   b. unsteady   c. one-sided   d. unreliable

11. an *odoriferous* cheese
    a. commonplace   b. brightly colored   c. malodorous   d. faded

12. an *invincible* warrior
    a. huge   b. foreign   c. defeated   d. unbeatable

13. the *advent* of summer
    a. departure   b. middle   c. arrival   d. complaint

14. a *provident* move
    a. prosperous   b. injudicious   c. prudent   d. hurtful

15. the top-secret *projectile*
    a. missile   b. project   c. plan   d. meeting

Quiz 2: True/False

In the space provided, write T if the definition of the numbered word is true or F if it is false.

		T or F
1. adhere	cling	_____
2. cadaver	cavort	_____
3. evolve	develop	_____
4. incision	cut	_____
5. concurrent	disjointed	_____
6. recluse	vivacious person	_____
7. inscription	story	_____
8. agent	deputy	_____
9. tactile	tangible	_____
10. repulse	repel	_____

Lesson 2. Common Greek Roots

Root	Meaning	Example	Definition
aster, astro	star	asterisk	star-shaped mark
chrom	color	chromatic	pertaining to color
chron, chrono	time	synchronize	occur simultaneously
cosmo	world	cosmopolitan	citizen of the world
dem	people	democracy	government by the people

meter	measure	thermometer	instrument that measures temperature
onym	name, word	pseudonym	a fictitious name
path	feeling	apathy	absence of feeling
phob	fear	claustrophobia	fear of enclosed places
phon	sound	cacophony	harsh, discordant sound
psycho	mind	psychology	science of the mind
soph	wisdom	sophistry	subtle, tricky reasoning

Quiz 3: True/False

In the space provided, write T if the definition of the numbered word is true or F if it is false.

		T or F
1. epidemic	plague	_____
2. homonym	same-sounding name	_____
3. claustrophobia	fear of dogs	_____
4. cacophony	dissonance	_____
5. apathy	enthusiasm	_____
6. accelerometer	instrument for measuring acceleration	_____
7. synchronize	squabble	_____
8. cosmopolitan	international	_____
9. sophism	specious argument	_____
10. chromatic	crisp	_____

Quiz 4: Defining Words

Based on the meaning of its root, define each of the following words. If in doubt, check the suggested answers.

1. asteroid _____

2. chromatics _____

3. cosmos _____

4. anonymous _____

5. Anglophobia _____

6. cosmography _____

7. synchronous _____

8. pathetic _____

9. pedometer _____

10. democracy _____

11. phonograph _____

12. demographics _____

13. psychotic _____

14. sophisticated _____

15. cognition _____

Suggested Answers   1. a small mass that orbits the sun 2. the science of colors 3. universe 4. without any name acknowledged 5. fear of things English 6. the study of the structure of the universe 7. coinciding in time 8. evoking feelings of pity 9. an instrument that measures distance covered in walking 10. government by the people 11. a sound-reproducing machine. 12. the statistical data of a population 13. a person who is mentally ill 14. worldly-wise 15. act or fact of knowing

Lesson 3. "Other Places, Other Faces": *al, all, alter*

An "alibi" is a defense by an accused person who claims to have been elsewhere at the time the offense was committed. The word comes from the Latin root "al," meaning *other*. Outside of law, an alibi often means an excuse, especially to avoid blame.

The Latin roots "al" and "alter," as well as the related Greek root "all" or "allo," all mean *other* or *another,* and form the basis of a number of English words. Below are ten such words. After you study the definitions and practice the pronunciations, complete the quizzes.

1. **alien** (āl′yən, ā′lē ən) a person born in and owing allegiance to a country other than the one in which he or she lives; a nonterrestrial being; foreign or strange.

    Although my neighbor is not an American citizen, he has lived in this country so long he no longer thinks of himself as an alien.

2. **allegory** (al′ə gôr′ē) a representation of an abstract meaning through concrete or material forms; figurative treatment of one subject under the guise of another.

    Nathaniel Hawthorne's short story "Young Goodman Brown." can be read as an allegory of an average person's encounter with sin and temptation.

3. **alias** (ā'lē əs) a false or assumed name, especially as used by a criminal. From the Latin word meaning *otherwise*.

    Many criminals use an alias with the same initials as their real name. Clyde Griffith, for example, took as his alias "Chester Gillett."

4. **alienate** (āl'yə nāt', ā'lē ə-) to make indifferent or hostile. From Latin "alienare," *to make another*.

    Unkempt yards alienate prospective home buyers.

5. **altruism** (al'trōōiz'əm) unselfish concern for the welfare of others.

    Devotion to the poor, sick, and unfortunate of the world shows a person's altruism.

6. **altercation** (ôl'tər kā'shən) a heated or angry dispute; noisy argument or controversy. From Latin "altercari," *to quarrel with another*.

    The collision resulted in an altercation between the two drivers.

7. **inalienable** (in āl'yə nə bəl, -ā'lē ə-) not transferable to another; incapable of being repudiated.

    Freedom of speech is the inalienable right of every American citizen.

8. **allograft** (al'ə graft') tissue grafted or transplanted to another member of the same species.

    Allografts of vital organs have saved many lives.

9. **allogamy** (ə log'ə mē) cross-fertilization in plants. From "allo-," *other* + "-gamy," *pollination*.

    To ensure allogamy, the farmer set out many different plants close together.

10. **alter** ego (ôl'tər ē'gō) another self; an inseparable friend.

    Superman's alter ego, the mild-mannered Clark Kent, is a reporter for the *Daily Planet*.

Quiz 5: Matching

Match each of the numbered words with its closest synonym. Write your answer in the space provided.

1. alien	a. absolute	_____
2. alias	b. cross-fertilization	_____
3. alter ego	c. selflessness, kindness	_____
4. allogamy	d. best friend	_____
5. allegory	e. another name	_____
6. inalienable	f. transplant	_____

7. altruism   g. contention, quarrel   _____
8. alienate   h. symbolic narrative   _____
9. allograft   i. stranger, outcast   _____
10. altercation   j. turn away, estrange   _____

Quiz 6: True/False

In the space provided, write T if the definition of the numbered word is true or F if it is false.

			T or F
1.	alien	foreign	_____
2.	alias	excuse	_____
3.	alter ego	egotist	_____
4.	allogamy	multiple marriage	_____
5.	allegory	moral story	_____
6.	inalienable	without basis in fact	_____
7.	altruism	unselfishness	_____
8.	alienate	estrange	_____
9.	allograft	illegal money	_____
10.	altercation	dispute	_____

Lesson 4. "The Breath of Life": *anima*

Ancient peoples connected the soul with the breath. They saw that when people died they stopped breathing, and they believed that the soul left the body at the same time. They also believed that when people sneezed, the soul left the body for a moment, so they muttered a hasty blessing to ensure that the soul would return quickly to its rightful place. The Latin root for air or breath, "anima," also means *soul, spirit,* or *mind,* reflecting this belief in a connection between life and breathing. Many English words come from this root.

Below are ten words linked to "anima." After you study the definitions and practice the pronunciations, complete the quizzes.

1. **animation** (an'ə mā'shən) liveliness or vivacity; the act or an instance of animating or enlivening. From Latin "animare," *to give life to.*

    In speech class we learned how to talk with animation to make our presentations more interesting.

2. **animadversion** (an'ə mad vûr'zhən, -shən) criticism; censure. From Latin "animus," *mind, spirit* + "adversio," *attention, warning.*

The critic's animadversion on the subject of TV shows revealed his bias against popular culture.

3. **animus** (an'ə məs) hostile feeling or attitude.

The jury's animus toward the defendant was obvious from the jurors' stony faces and stiff posture.

4. **pusillanimous** (pyo͞o'sə lan'ə məs) lacking courage or resolution; cowardly. From Latin "pusillus," *very small* + "animus," *spirit.*

He was so pusillanimous that he wouldn't even run away from a bully.

5. **unanimity** (yo͞o' nə nim'i tē) the state or quality of being in complete agreement; undivided opinion or a consensus. From Latin "unus," *one* + "animus," *mind, spirit.*

The school board's unanimity on the controversial issue of sex education was all the more surprising in light of their well-known individual differences.

6. **animate** (an'ə māt') to give life or liveliness to; alive.

Her presence animated the otherwise dull party.

7. **animalcule** (an'ə mal'kyo͞ol) a minute or microscopic organism. From Latin "animalis," *living, animal* + "-culum," *tiny thing.*

The animalcule could not be seen with the naked eye.

8. **magnanimous** (mag nan'ə məs) generous in forgiving an insult or injury; free from petty resentfulness. From Latin "magnus," *large, great* + "animus," *soul.*

The governor's magnanimous pardon of the offender showed his liberal nature.

9. **inanimate** (in an'ə mit) not alive or lively; lifeless.

Pinocchio was inanimate, a puppet carved from a block of wood.

10. **animism** (an'ə miz'əm) the belief that natural objects, natural phenomena, and the universe itself possess souls or consciousness.

Their belief in animism drew them to the woods, where they felt more in touch with nature's spirit.

Quiz 7: Matching

Match each of the numbered words with the closest synonym. Write your answer in the space provided.

1. animadversion	a. enliven	_____
2. animus	b. harmony	_____
3. pusillanimous	c. generous	

4. unanimity   d. cowardly   _____
5. animate   e. hostility   _____
6. animalcule   f. spirit, zest   _____
7. magnanimous   g. a censorious remark _____
8. inanimate   h. a belief in spirits _____
9. animation   i. a minute organism _____
10. animism   j. insert   _____

Quiz 8: True/False

In the space provided, write T if the definition of the numbered word is true or F if it is false.

		T or F
1. animadversion	praise	_____
2. animus	hostility	_____
3. pusillanimous	cowardly	_____
4. unanimity	total agreement	_____
5. animate	deaden	_____
6. animalcule	small soul	_____
7. magnanimous	generous	_____
8. inanimate	living	_____
9. animation	liveliness	_____
10. animism	love of animals	_____

Lesson 5. "The Year of Wonders": *ann, enn*

While certain years are celebrated for great wonders, the first year that was actually designated "The Year of Wonders," *Annus Mirabilis,* was 1666. The English poet, dramatist, and critic John Dryden (1631–1700) enshrined that year as "Annus Mirabilis" in his poem of the same name, which commemorated the English victory over the Dutch and the Great Fire of London. "Annus," meaning *year* comes from the Latin root "ann," a source of many useful English words. The same root is also written "enn" in the middle of a word.

Below are ten words drawn from this root. After you look over the definitions and practice the pronunciations, complete the quizzes that follow.

1. **per annum** (pər an'əm) by the year; yearly.
   The firm promised to bill the additional interest charges per annum, the invoice to arrive every January.

2. **annual** (an′yo͞o əl) of, for, or pertaining to a year; yearly.

   The annual enrollment in the high school has increased sharply since the new housing was built.

3. **anniversary** (an′ə vûr′sə rē) the yearly recurrence of the date of a past event, especially the date of a wedding. From Latin "ann(i)," *year* + "vers(us)," *turned* + adjectival suffix "-ary."

   For their twenty-fifth wedding anniversary, the happy couple decided to have dinner at the restaurant where they first met.

4. **biennial** (bī en′ē əl) happening every two years; lasting for two years. From Latin "bi-," *two* + root "enn" + adjectival suffix "-ial."

   My flowering fig tree has a biennial cycle; it blooms every two years.

5. **triennial** (trī en′ē əl) occurring every three years; lasting three years. From Latin "tri-," *three* + root "enn" + adjectival suffix "-ial."

   The university has set up a triennial cycle of promotions to review candidates for advancement.

6. **decennial** (di sen′ē əl) of or for ten years; occurring every ten years. From Latin "dec(em)," *ten* + root "enn" + adjectival suffix "-ial."

   Every ten years, the PTA holds its decennial meeting in the state capital.

7. **centennial** (sen ten′ē əl) of or pertaining to a period of one hundred years; recurring once every hundred years. From Latin "cent(um)," *hundred* + root "enn" + adjectival suffix "-ial."

   To celebrate the railroad's centennial anniversary, the town's historical society restored the run-down station so it looked exactly as it did when it was built a hundred years ago.

8. **bicentennial** (bī′sen ten′ē əl) pertaining to or in honor of a two-hundredth anniversary; consisting of or lasting two hundred years.

   To advertise its bicentennial festivities next year, the town has adopted the slogan "Celebrating Two Hundred Years of Progress."

9. **millennium** (mi len′ē əm) a period of one thousand years. From Latin "mille," *thousand* + root "enn" + noun suffix "-ium."

   Technology advances so rapidly now that we can scarcely imagine what life will be like in the next millennium.

10. **annuity** (ə no͞o′ i tē, ə nyo͞o′-) a specified income payable each

year or at stated intervals in consideration of a premium paid. From Latin "ann(uus)," *yearly* + noun suffix "-ity."

The annuity from her late husband's life-insurance policy was barely adequate for the poor widow's needs.

Quiz 9: Matching

Select the best definition for each numbered word. Write your answer in the space provided.

1. bicentennial	a. every ten years	_____
2. anniversary	b. every two years	_____
3. decennial	c. every two hundred years	_____
4. millennium	d. every three years	_____
5. per annum	e. one thousand years	_____
6. centennial	f. fixed payment	_____
7. annuity	g. yearly recurrence of a date	_____
8. triennial	h. every hundred years	_____
9. biennial	i. by the year	_____
10. annual	j. yearly	_____

Quiz 10: True/False

In the space provided, write T if the definition of the numbered word is true or F if it is false.

		T or F
1. annuity	every two hundred years	_____
2. bicentennial	every other year	_____
3. millennium	one thousand years	_____
4. annual	fixed amount of money	_____
5. centennial	every hundred years	_____
6. triennial	every three years	_____
7. per annum	by order	_____
8. biennial	every third year	_____
9. decennial	every thousand years	_____
10. anniversary	yearly event	_____

Lesson 6. "Man of the World": *anthropo*

In the early twentieth century, Rudolph Steiner developed an esoteric system of knowledge he called "anthroposophy." Steiner developed the word from the Greek roots "anthropo," meaning *man* or *human,* and "soph," meaning *wisdom.* He defined his philosophy as "the knowledge of the spiritual human being . . . and of everything which the spirit man can perceive in the spiritual world."

We've taken several more words from "anthropo"; below are six of them. After you look over the definitions and practice the pronunciations, complete the quizzes that follow.

1. **anthropoid** (an'thrə poid') resembling humans.
   The child was fascinated by the anthropoid ape on display in the natural history museum.

2. **anthropomorphism** (an'thrə pə môr'fiz əm) the ascription of human form or attributes to a being or thing not human, such as a deity.
   To speak of the "cruel, crawling foam" is an example of anthropomorphism, for the sea is not cruel.

3. **misanthrope** (mis'ən thrōp', miz'-) a hater of humankind. From Greek "mis(o)," *hate* + "anthropos," *man*.
   In *Gulliver's Travels,* the great misanthrope Jonathan Swift depicts human beings as monstrous savages.

4. **philanthropy** (fi lan'thrə pē) good works; affection for humankind, especially as manifested in donations, as of money, to needy persons or to socially useful purposes. From Greek "phil(o)," *loving* + "anthropos," *man*.
   Thanks to the philanthropy of a wealthy patron, the new hospital wing was fully stocked with the latest equipment.

5. **anthropology** (an'thrə pol'ə jē) the science that deals with the origins, physical and cultural development, racial characteristics, and social customs and beliefs of humankind.
   After the student completed the anthropology course, she visited some of the exotic cultures she had read about.

6. **anthropocentric** (an'thrə pō sen'trik) regarding humans as the central fact of the universe.
   Philosophy that views and interprets the universe in terms of human experience and values is anthropocentric.

Quiz 11: Matching

Select the best definition for each numbered word. Write your answer in the space provided

1. anthropology   a. believing that humans are the center of the universe _____
2. philanthropy   b. one who dislikes people   _____

3. anthropocentric   c. science of humankind's origins, beliefs, and customs _____
4. anthropoid   d. personification of inanimate things _____
5. anthropomorphism   e. doing good for people _____
6. misanthrope   f. humanlike _____

Quiz 12: True/False

In the space provided, write T if the definition of the numbered word is true or F if it is false.

			T or F
1.	misanthrope	cynic	_____
2.	philanthropy	goodwill to humankind	_____
3.	anthropomorphism	insecurity	_____
4.	anthropocentric	unselfish	_____
5.	anthropology	science of flowers	_____
6.	anthropoid	resembling humans	_____

Lesson 7. "Know Thyself": *gno*

One of the fascinating things about the study of words is the discovery of close relationships between seemingly unrelated words. Because English draws its vocabulary from many sources, it often appropriates foreign words that ultimately derive from the same source as a native English word. A good example is our word "know," which has its exact equivalent in the Latin and Greek root "gno." Here are eight words from this root. First read through the pronunciations, definitions, and examples. Then complete the quizzes that follow.

1. **cognizant** (kog′nə zənt, kon′ə-) aware. From Latin "cognoscere," *to come to know* ("co-," *together* + "gnoscere," *to know*).
   He was fully cognizant of the difficulty of the mission.
2. **incognito** (in′kog nē′tō, in kog′ni tō′) with one's identity concealed, as under an assumed name. From Latin "incognitus," *not known* ("in-," *not* + "cognitus," *known*).
   The officer from naval intelligence always traveled incognito to avoid any problems with security.
3. **prognosticate** (prog nos′ti kāt′) to forecast from present indi-

cations. From Greek "prognostikos," *knowing beforehand* ("pro-," *before* + "(gi)gno(skein)," *to know*).

The fortuneteller was able to prognosticate with the help of her tea leaves, crystal ball, and a good deal of inside information about her client.

4. **diagnostician** (di'əg no stish'ən) an expert in determining the nature of diseases. From Greek "diagnosis," *determination* (of a disease) ("dia-," *through* + "(gi)gno(skein)," *to know*).

The diagnostician was able to allay her patient's fears after the x-ray showed that he had suffered only a sprain, not a break.

5. **cognoscenti** (kon'yə shen'tē, kog'nə-) well-informed persons, especially in a particular field, as in the arts. From Italian, ultimately derived from Latin "co-," *together* + "gnoscere," *to know.*

Although the exhibit had only been open one week, the cognoscenti were already proclaiming it the show of the decade.

6. **gnostic** (nos'tik) pertaining to knowledge, especially to the esoteric knowledge taught by an early Christian mystical sect. From Greek "gnostikos," *knowing,* from the root of "(gi)gno(skein)," *to know.*

The gnostic view that everything is knowable is opposed by the agnostic view.

7. **ignoramus** (ig'nə rā'məs, -ram'əs) an extremely uninformed person. From the Latin word meaning *we don't know,* derived from "ignorare," *to not know* ("i(-n-)," *not* + the root of "gno(scere)," *to come to know*).

Only an ignoramus would insist that the earth is flat.

8. **cognition** (kog nish'ən) the act or process of knowing; perception. From Latin "cognitio," derived from "cognoscere," *to come to know* ("co-," *together* + "gnoscere," *to know*).

Cognition is impaired by narcotic drugs.

Quiz 13: True/False

In the space provided, write T if the definition of the numbered word is true or F if it is false.

			T or F
1.	gnostic	knowing	_____
2.	incognito	disguised	_____
3.	prognosticate	curse	_____
4.	ignoramus	ignorant person	_____
5.	cognoscenti	aromatic herb	_____
6.	cognition	perception	_____

7. diagnostician   expert mechanic   _____
8. cognizant   conscious   _____

Quiz 14: Defining Words

Define each of the following words.

1. ignoramus _____

2. cognoscenti _____

3. cognition _____

4. incognito _____

5. gnostic _____

6. prognosticate _____

7. diagnostician _____

8. cognizant _____

Suggested Answers 1. unschooled person 2. those who have a superior knowledge 3. the act or process of knowing; perception 4. with one's identity concealed 5. pertaining to knowledge 6. to forecast 7. an expert in making diagnoses 8. aware

Lesson 8. "Rulers and Leaders": *arch*

In Christian theology, Michael is given the title of "archangel," principal angel and primary opponent of Satan and his horde. The Greek root "arch," meaning *chief, first, rule* or *ruler,* is the basis of a number of important and useful words.

Below are ten words drawn from this root. Read the definitions and practice the pronunciations. Then study the sample sentences and see if you can use the words in sentences of your own.

1. **archenemy** (arch′en′ə mē) a chief enemy; Satan.
   In Christian theology, Satan is the archenemy.

2. **patriarch** (pā′trē ärk′) the male head of a family or tribe. From Greek "patria," *family* + "-arches," *head, chief.*
   When we gathered for Thanksgiving dinner, our great-grand-father, the family patriarch, always sat at the head of the table.

3. **anarchy** (an′ər kē) society without rule or government; law-lessness; disorder; confusion; chaos. From Greek "an-," *not* + "arch(os)," *rule, ruler.*
   The king's assassination led to anarchy throughout the country.

4. **hierarchy** (hī′ə rär′kē, hī′rär-) any system of persons or things ranked one above another; formerly, rule by church leaders, especially a high priest. From Greek "hieros," *sacred* + "arch(os)," *rule, ruler.*

 The new office hierarchy ranks assistant vice presidents over directors.

5. **monarchy** (mon′ər kē) rule or government by a king, queen, emperor, or empress. From Greek "mon(o)-," *one* + "arch(os)," *rule, ruler.*

 The French Revolution ended with the overthrow of the monarchy.

6. **oligarchy** (ol′i gär′kē) rule or government by a few persons. From Greek "oligos," *few* + "arch(os)," *rule, ruler.*

 After the revolution, an oligarchy of army officers ruled the newly liberated country.

7. **archbishop** (ärch′bish′əp) a bishop of the highest rank; chief bishop.

 The archbishop meets with the bishops from his area once a month to discuss their concerns.

8. **matriarch** (mā′trē ärk′) the female head of a family or tribe. From Greek "matri-," *mother* + "-arches," *head, chief.*

 The younger members of the clan usually seek out Grandma Josie, the family matriarch, for advice.

9. **archetype** (är′ki tīp′) the original pattern or model after which a thing is made; prototype. From Greek "arch(e)-," *first, original* + "typos," *mold, type.*

 Odysseus is the archetype for James Joyce's Leopold Bloom in his novel *Ulysses.*

10. **archaic** (är kā′ik) marked by the characteristics of an earlier period, antiquated. From Greek "arch(aios)," *old, early, first.*

 With the advent of the pocket calculator, the slide rule has become archaic.

Quiz 15: Synonyms

Select the best synonym for each of the italicized words.

1. the ***archbishop*** of Canterbury
 a. oldest bishop   b. youngest bishop   c. highest-ranking bishop
 d. recently appointed bishop

2. a strong ***monarchy***
 a. government by a president   b. government by a consortium

c. government by the proletariat   d. government by a king or queen

3. an *archaic* device
   a. old-fashioned   b. complicated   c. expensive   d. useful

4. a wise *patriarch*
   a. old woman   b. general   c. revolutionary
   d. male family head

5. the literary and social *archetype*
   a. concern   b. exhibition   c. prototype   d. major problem

6. a state of *anarchy*
   a. hopefulness   b. lawlessness   c. strict order
   d. female control

7. a brutal *archenemy*
   a. less powerful enemy   b. chief enemy   c. strict enemy
   d. Gabriel

8. the iron-handed *oligarchy*
   a. government by few   b. communist state   c. democracy
   d. unstable government

9. a highly respected *matriarch*
   a. confidant   b. duke   c. male leader   d. female family head

10. the strict governmental *hierarchy*
    a. leadership   b. promotions   c. system of ranking
    d. discipline

Quiz 16: True/False

In the space provided, write T if the synonym or definition of the numbered word is true or F if it is false.

			T or F
1.	patriarch	male family head	_____
2.	archetype	model	_____
3.	archenemy	chief enemy	_____
4.	monarchy	royal government	_____
5.	oligarchy	chaos	_____
6.	archbishop	church deacon	_____
7.	matriarch	wife and mother	_____
8.	anarchy	political lawlessness	_____
9.	hierarchy	higher orders	_____
10.	archaic	old-fashioned	_____

Lesson 9. "To Life!": *bio*

In 1763 the Scottish writer James Boswell was first introduced to the acclaimed English poet, literary critic, and dictionary-maker Samuel Johnson, setting the stage for the birth of modern biography. From 1772 until Johnson's death in 1784, the two men were closely associated, and Boswell devoted much of his time to compiling detailed records of Johnson's activities and conversations. Seven years after Johnson's death, Boswell published his masterpiece, the *Life of Samuel Johnson*. The word "biography," *a written account of another person's life,* comes from the Greek root "bio," meaning *life,* and "graphy," meaning *writing.* Besides *life,* "bio" can also mean *living, living thing,* or *biological.*

A number of other important words come from "bio." Here's a list of eight of them. Read through the definitions and practice the pronunciations, then go on to the quizzes.

1. **biodegradable** (bī´ō di grā´də bəl) capable of being decomposed by living organisms, as paper and kitchen scraps are, as opposed to metals, glass, and plastics, which do not decay.

   After a long campaign, the local residents persuaded the supermarkets to use biodegradable paper bags rather than nondegradable plastic.

2. **biofeedback** (bī´ō fēd´bak´) a method of learning to modify one's own bodily or physiological functions with the aid of a visual or auditory display of one's brain waves, blood pressure, or muscle tension.

   Desperate to quit smoking, she made an appointment to try biofeedback.

3. **bioengineering** (bī´ō en´jə nēr´ing) the application of engineering principles and techniques to problems in medicine and biology.

   In the last few decades, bioengineering has made important progress in the design of artificial limbs.

4. **biological clock** (bī´ə loj´i kəl klok´) an innate system in people, animals, and organisms that causes regular cycles of function or behavior.

   Recently the term "biological clock" has been used in reference to women in their late thirties and early forties who are concerned about having children before they are no longer able to reproduce.

5. **bionic** (bī on'ik) utilizing electronic devices and mechanical parts to assist humans in performing tasks, as by supplementing or duplicating parts of the body. Formed from "bio-" + "(electr)onic."

   The scientist used a bionic arm to examine the radioactive material.

6. **biopsy** (bī'op sē) the excision for diagnostic study of a piece of tissue from a living body. From "bio-" + Greek "opsis," *sight, view.*

   The doctor took a biopsy from the patient's lung to determine the nature of the infection.

7. **biota** (bī ō'tə) the plant and animal life of a region or period. From Greek "biote," *life,* from the root "bio."

   The biota from the cliffside proved more useful for conservation than the biologists had initially suspected.

8. **biohazard** (bī'ō haz'ərd) a disease-causing agent or organism, especially one produced by biological research; the health risk caused by such an agent or organism.

   Will new technology like gene splicing produce heretofore unknown biohazards to threaten the world's population?

Quiz 17: Definitions

Select the word that best fits the definition. Write your answer in the space provided.

_____ 1. the excision for diagnostic study of a piece of tissue from a living body
   a. biopsy   b. bioengineering   c. incision

_____ 2. utilizing electronic devices and mechanical parts to assist humans in performing tasks
   a. biota   b. bioengineering   c. bionic

_____ 3. capable of decaying and being absorbed by the environment
   a. biogenic   b. biodegradable   c. bionic

_____ 4. a method of learning to modify one's own bodily or physiological functions
   a. autobiography   b. biofeedback   c. biota

_____ 5. the application of engineering principles and techniques to problems in medicine and biology
   a. bioengineering   b. autobiography   c. biometry

_____ 6. an innate system in people, animals, and organisms that causes regular cycles of function
   a. biota   b. bionic   c. biological clock

_____ 7. the plant and animal life of a region
       a. biota   b. autobiography   c. biometry
_____ 8. an agent or organism that causes a health risk
       a. biopsy   b. biohazard   c. biota

Quiz 18: True/False

In the space provided, write T if the definition of the numbered word is true or F if it is false.

		T or F
1. **biopsy**	tissue sample	_____
2. **biota**	plants and animals	_____
3. **biological clock**	perpetual clock	_____
4. **biohazard**	health risk	_____
5. **biodegradable**	capable of decomposing	_____
6. **bionic**	superhero	_____
7. **biofeedback**	culinary expertise	_____
8. **bioengineering**	railroad supervision	_____

Lesson 10. "Speak!": *dict, dic*

The earliest known dictionaries were found in the library of the Assyrian king at Nineveh. These clay tablets, inscribed with cuneiform writing dating from the seventh century B.C., provide important clues to our understanding of Mesopotamian culture. The first English dictionary did not appear until 1440. Compiled by the Dominican monk Galfridus Grammaticus, the *Storehouse for Children or Clerics*, as the title translates, consists of Latin definitions of 10,000 English words. The word "dictionary" was first used in English in 1526, in reference to a Latin dictionary by Peter Berchorius. This was followed by a Latin-English dictionary published by Sir Thomas Elyot in 1538. The first monolingual English dictionary was published by Thomas Cawdrey in 1604. All these early efforts confined themselves to uncommon words and phrases not generally known or understood, because the daily language was not supposed to require explanation.

Today we understand the word "dictionary" to mean *a book containing a selection of the words of a language, usually arranged alphabetically, giving information about their meanings, pronunciations, etymologies, etc.; a lexicon.* The word comes from the Latin root "dictio," taken from "dicere," meaning *to say, state, declare, speak.* This root has given us scores of important English words.

Below are eight for you to examine. After you read through their pronunciations and definitions, complete the quizzes.

1. **malediction** (mal′i dik′shən) a curse or the utterance of a curse. From Latin "male-," *evil* + "dictio," *speech, word.*
   After the witch delivered her malediction, the princess fell into a swoon.
2. **abdication** (ab′di kā′shən) the renunciation or relinquishment of something such as a throne, right, power, or claim, especially when formal.
   Following the abdication of Edward VIII for the woman he loved, his brother George VI assumed the throne of England.
3. **benediction** (ben′i dik′shən) the invocation of a blessing. From Latin "bene-," *well, good* + "dictio," *speech, word.*
   The chaplain delivered a benediction at the end of the service.
4. **edict** (ē′dikt) a decree issued by a sovereign or other authority; an authoritative proclamation or command.
   Herod's edict ordered the massacre of male infants throughout his realm.
5. **predicate** (pred′i kāt′) to proclaim, declare, or affirm; base or found.
   Your acceptance into the training program is predicated upon a successful personal interview.
6. **jurisdiction** (jŏŏr′is dik′shən) the right, power, or authority to administer justice.
   The mayor's jurisdiction extends only to the area of the village itself, outside its limits, the jurisdiction passes to the town board.
7. **dictum** (dik′təm) an authoritative pronouncement; saying or maxim.
   The firm issued a dictum stating that smoking was forbidden on the premises.
8. **predictive** (pri dik′tiv) indicating the future or future conditions; predicting.
   Although the day was clear and balmy, the brisk wind was predictive of the approaching cold snap.

Quiz 19: Matching

Match each of the following numbered words with its closest synonym. Write your answer in the space provided.

1. predictive	a. assert	_____
2. edict	b. maxim	_____

3. predicate c. indicating the future _____
4. benediction d. authority _____
5. abdication e. decree _____
6. malediction f. imprecation, curse _____
7. dictum g. blessing _____
8. jurisdiction h. renunciation _____

Quiz 20: True/False

In the space provided, write T if the definition of the numbered word is true or F if it is false.

		T or F
1. predictive	indicative of the future	_____
2. predicate	declare	_____
3. edict	decree	_____
4. jurisdiction	authority	_____
5. dictum	blessing	_____
6. abdication	assumption	_____
7. malediction	machismo	_____
8. benediction	opening services	_____

Lesson 11. "Lead On, Macduff!": *duc, duct*

Aqueducts, artificial channels built to transport water, were used in ancient Mesopotamia, but the ones used to supply water to ancient Rome are the most famous. Nine aqueducts were built in all; eventually they provided Rome with about thirty-eight million gallons of water daily. Parts of several are still in use, supplying water to fountains in Rome. The word "aqueduct" comes from the Latin "aqua," meaning *water*, and "ductus," meaning *a leading* or *drawing off*.

A great number of powerful words are derived from the "duc, duct" root. Here are nine such words. Read through the definitions and practice the pronunciations. Try to use each word in a sentence of your own. Finally, work through the two quizzes at the end of the lesson to help fix the words in your memory.

1. **induce** (in dōōs′, -dyōōs′) to influence or persuade, as to some action.
    Try to induce her to stay at least a few hours longer.
2. **misconduct** (mis kon′dukt) improper conduct or behavior.
    Such repeated misconduct will result in a reprimand, if not an outright dismissal.

3. **abduct** (ab dukt') to carry (a person) off or lead (a person) away illegally; kidnap.

   Jason's mother was so fearful that he might be abducted by a stranger that she refused even to let him walk to school alone.

4. **deduce** (di d$\overline{oo}$s', -dy$\overline{oo}$s') to derive as a conclusion from something known or assumed.

   The detective was able to deduce from the facts gathered thus far that the murder took place in the early hours of the morning.

5. **viaduct** (vī'ə dukt') a bridge for carrying a road or railroad over a valley, gorge, or the like, consisting of a number of short spans; overpass.

   The city government commissioned a firm of civil engineers to explore the possibility of building a viaduct over the river.

6. **reductive** (ri duk'tiv) pertaining to or producing reduction or abridgment. From Latin "reduct-, reducere," *to lead back*.

   There was an urgent need for reductive measures.

7. **seduce** (si d$\overline{oo}$s', -dy$\overline{oo}$s') to lead astray, as from duty or principles.

   He was seduced by the prospect of gain.

8. **traduce** (trə d$\overline{oo}$s', -dy$\overline{oo}$s') to speak maliciously and falsely of; slander. From Latin "traducere," *to transfer, lead across.*

   To traduce someone's character can do permanent harm to his or her reputation.

9. **ductile** (duk'tl) pliable or yielding.

   The new plastic is very ductile and can be molded into many forms.

Quiz 21: Matching

Match each of the numbered words with the closest synonym. Write your answer in the space provided.

1. seduce	a. overpass	_____
2. viaduct	b. minimizing	_____
3. induce	c. kidnap	_____
4. reductive	d. bad behavior	_____
5. traduce	e. infer	_____
6. abduct	f. entice	_____
7. misconduct	g. pliable	_____
8. deduce	h. defame	_____
9. ductile	i. persuade	_____

Quiz 22: True/False

In the space provided, write T if the definition of the numbered word is true or F if it is false.

			T or F
1.	deduce	infer	_____
2.	ductile	pliable	_____
3.	seduce	lead astray	_____
4.	reductive	magnifying	_____
5.	traduce	malign	_____
6.	viaduct	overpass	_____
7.	abduct	restore	_____
8.	misconduct	improper behavior	_____
9.	induce	persuade	_____

Lesson 12. "Just the Facts, Ma'am": *fac, fact, fect*

We have formed a great many important and useful words from the Latin "facere," *to make* or *do*. A "facsimile," for example, derives from the Latin phrase "fac simile," meaning *to make similar,* and has come to mean *an exact copy.* Since facsimile copiers and transmitters have become very common, "facsimile" is now generally shortened and changed in spelling to "fax."

Many potent words are derived from the "fac, fact, fect" root. Eight such words follow. Learn them by completing this lesson; then try to use the root to help you figure out other "fac, fact" words you encounter.

1. **factious** (fak′shəs) given to or marked by discord; dissenting. From Latin "factio," *act of doing or of making connections; group* or *clique,* derived from "facere," *to do* or *make.*
    Factious groups threatened to break up the alliance.

2. **factotum** (fak tō′təm) a person employed to do all kinds of work, as a personal secretary or the chief servant of a household.
    Jeeves was the model of a gentleman's gentleman—the indispensable factotum of the frivolous Bertie Wooster.

3. **factitious** (fak tish′əs) made artificially; contrived.
    The report was merely a factitious account, not factual at all.

4. **facile** (fas′il) moving or acting with ease; fluent. From Latin "facilis," *easy to do,* derived from "facere," *to do.*

With his facile mind, he often thought of startlingly original solutions to old problems.

5. **artifact** (är'tə fakt') any object made by human skill or art. From the Latin phrase "arte factum," *(something) made with skill.*

   The archaeologists dug up many artifacts from the ancient Indian culture.

6. **facsimile** (fak sim'ə lē) an exact copy, as of a book, painting, or manuscript; a method of transmitting typed or printed material by means of radio or telegraph.

   If they could not obtain a facsimile of the document by noon, the deal would fall through.

7. **putrefaction** (pyoo'trə fak'shən) the decomposition of organic matter by bacteria and fungi. From Latin "putrere," *to rot* + "factio," *act of doing.*

   Once the putrefaction of the compost pile was complete, the gardener used the rotted material to enrich the soil.

8. **prefect** (prē'fekt) a person appointed to any of various positions of command, authority, or superintendence. From Latin "praefectus," formed from "prae," *ahead, surpassing* + "fectus," *doing* (from "facere," *to do*).

   The prefect was appointed to a term of three years.

Quiz 23: Definitions

Select the word that best fits the definition. Write your answer in the space provided.

_____ 1. the decomposition of organic matter by bacteria and fungi
   a. chemical analysis   b. hypothermia
   c. putrefaction

_____ 2. not natural; artificial
   a. factious   b. facile   c. factitious

_____ 3. an exact copy, as of a book, painting, or manuscript
   a. factoid   b. facsimile   c. putrefaction

_____ 4. given to dissension or strife
   a. facile   b. factious   c. obsequious

_____ 5. an object made by humans
   a. artifact   b. factotum   c. factious

_____ 6. a person employed to do all kinds of work
   a. facile   b. factotum   c. faculty

_____ 7. moving or acting easily
    a. putrefaction   b. prefect   c. facile

_____ 8. someone appointed to any of various positions of command, authority, or superintendence
    a. prefect   b. facile   c. factotum

Quiz 24: True/False

In the space provided, write T if the definition of the numbered word is true or F if it is false.

		T or F
1. factitious	contrived	_____
2. factotum	carrier	_____
3. putrefaction	rotting	_____
4. artifact	machinery	_____
5. facsimile	instant transmission	_____
6. prefect	administrator	_____
7. factious	dissenting	_____
8. facile	fluent	_____

Lesson 13. "Always Faithful": *feder, fid, fide*

"Semper fidelis" is Latin for *always faithful.* The phrase is the motto of the United States Marine Corps and the title of an 1888 march by John Philip Sousa. This phrase, as with a number of useful words, comes from the Latin root "fid, fide," meaning *trust, faith.*

Below are seven words derived from this root. Read through the meanings, practice the pronunciations, and complete the quizzes that follow to help fix the words in your memory.

1. **fidelity** (fi del′i tē) faithfulness; loyalty.
    Dogs are legendary for their fidelity to their masters.

2. **fiduciary** (fi doo′shē er′ē, -dyoo′-) a person to whom property or power is entrusted for the benefit of another; trustee. From Latin "fiducia," *trust,* related to "fidere," *to trust.*
    The bank's fiduciary administers the children's trust funds.

3. **infidel** (in′fi dl, -del′) a person who does not accept a particular religious faith. From Latin "in," *not* + "fidelis," *faithful* (from "fide," *faith*).
    The ayatollah condemned Salman Rushdie as an infidel.

4. **perfidious** (pər fid′ē əs) deliberately faithless; treacherous. From Latin "perfidia" ("per-," *through* + "fide," *faith*).

   The perfidious lover missed no opportunity to be unfaithful.

5. **confide** (kən fīd′) to entrust one's secrets to another. From Latin "confidere" ("con-," *with* + "fidere," *to trust*).

   The two sisters confided in each other.

6. **bona fide** (bō′nə fīd′, bon′ə) genuine; real; in good faith.

   To their great astonishment, the offer of a free vacation was bona fide.

7. **affidavit** (af′i dā′vit) a written declaration upon oath made before an authorized official. From a Medieval Latin word meaning *(he) has declared on oath,* from Latin "affidare," *to pledge on faith.*

   In the affidavit, they swore they had not been involved in the accident.

Quiz 25: Matching

Match each of the following numbered words with its closest synonym. Write your answer in the space provided.

1. confide	a. faithfulness	_____
2. fidelity	b. heathen	_____
3. bona fide	c. declaration	_____
4. infidel	d. entrust	_____
5. affidavit	e. trustee	_____
6. perfidious	f. genuine	_____
7. fiduciary	g. faithless	_____

Quiz 26: Definitions

Select the best definition for each numbered word. Write your answer in the space provided.

_____ 1. bona fide
   a. unauthorized   b. deboned   c. real
   d. well-trained

_____ 2. perfidious
   a. irreligious   b. content   c. loyal
   d. treacherous

_____ 3. fidelity
   a. loyalty   b. alliance   c. great affection
   d. random motion

_____ 4. fiduciary
      a. bank teller   b. trustee   c. insurance
      d. default

_____ 5. infidel
      a. warrior   b. intransigent   c. heathen
      d. outsider

_____ 6. affidavit
      a. affright   b. declaration   c. loyalty
      d. betrothal

_____ 7. confide
      a. combine   b. recline   c. entrust   d. convert

Lesson 14. "Flow Gently, Sweet Afton": *flu*

In 1998, the upper fifth of working Americans took home more money than the other four-fifths put together—the highest proportion of wealthy people since the end of World War II. One word to describe such wealthy people is "affluent," *prosperous.* The word comes from the Latin root "fluere," meaning *to flow.* As a river would flow freely, so the money of the affluent flows easily.

Seven of the most useful and important words formed from the "flu" root follow. Study the definitions and read through the pronunciations. Then do the quizzes.

1. **flume** (floom) a deep, narrow channel containing a mountain stream or torrent; an amusement-park ride through a water-filled chute or slide.
   The adults steadfastly refused to try the log flume ride, but the children enjoyed it thoroughly.

2. **confluence** (kon'floo əns) a flowing together of two or more streams; their place of junction.
   The confluence of the rivers is marked by a strong current.

3. **fluent** (floo'ənt) spoken or written effortlessly; easy; graceful; flowing.
   Jennifer was such a fluent speaker that she was in great demand as a lecturer.

4. **fluctuation** (fluk'choo ā'shən) continual change from one course, condition, etc., to another.
   The fluctuation in temperature was astonishing, considering it was still only February.

5. **fluvial** (floo′vē əl) of or pertaining to a river; produced by or found in a river.

   The contours of the riverbank were altered over the years by fluvial deposits.

6. **influx** (in′fluks′) a flowing in.

   The unexpected influx of refugees severely strained the community's resources.

7. **flux** (fluks) a flowing or flow; continuous change.

   His political views are in constant flux.

Quiz 27: True/False

In the space provided, write T if the definition of the numbered word is true or F if it is false.

			T or F
1.	fluctuation	change	_____
2.	fluvial	deep crevasse	_____
3.	fluent	flowing	_____
4.	flux	flow	_____
5.	influx	egress	_____
6.	confluence	diversion	_____
7.	flume	feather	_____

Quiz 28: Matching

Select the best definition for each numbered word. Write your answer in the space provided.

1.	flux	a.	gorge	_____
2.	confluence	b.	flowing easily	_____
3.	flume	c.	continual shift	_____
4.	fluctuation	d.	an inflow	_____
5.	fluent	e.	a flow	_____
6.	influx	f.	riverine	_____
7.	fluvial	g.	convergence	_____

Lesson 15. "In The Beginning": *gen*

Genesis, the first book of the Old Testament, is an account of the beginning of the world. The English word "genesis" is taken from the Greek word for *origin* or *source*. From the root "gen," meaning *beget, bear, kind,* or *race,* a number of powerful vocabulary builders has evolved.

Here are ten "gen" words. Study the definitions and practice the pronunciations to help you learn the words. To accustom yourself to using these new terms in your daily speech and writing, work through the two quizzes at the end of the lesson.

1. **gene** (jēn) the unit of heredity in the chromosomes that controls the development of inherited traits. From Greek "-genes," *born, begotten.*
   The gene for color blindness is linked to the Y chromosome.

2. **engender** (en jen′dər) to produce, cause, or give rise to.
   Hatred engenders violence.

3. **gentility** (jen til′i tē) good breeding or refinement.
   Her obvious gentility marked her as a member of polite society.

4. **gentry** (jen′trē) wellborn and well-bred people; in England, the class under the nobility.
   In former times, the gentry lived on large estates with grand houses, lush grounds, and many servants.

5. **genus** (jē′nəs) the major subdivision of a family or subfamily in the classification of plants and animals, usually consisting of more than one species.
   The biologist assigned the newly discovered plant to the appropriate genus.

6. **genial** (jēn′yəl, jē′nē əl) cordial; warmly and pleasantly cheerful; favorable for life, growth, or comfort.
   Under the genial conditions in the greenhouse, the plants grew and flourished.

7. **congenital** (kən jen′i tl) existing at or from one's birth.
   The child's congenital defect was easily corrected by surgery.

8. **eugenics** (yo͞o jen′iks) the science of improving the qualities of a breed or species, especially the human race, by the careful selection of parents.
   Through eugenics, scientists hope to engineer a superior race of human beings.

9. **genealogy** (jē′nē ol′ə jē) a record or account of the ancestry and descent of a person, family, group, etc.; the study of family ancestries.
   Genealogy shows that Franklin Delano Roosevelt was a cousin of Winston Churchill.

10. **congenial** (kən jēn′yəl) agreeable or pleasant; suited or adapted in disposition; compatible.
    The student enjoyed the congenial atmosphere of the library.

Quiz 29: Definitions

Select the word that best fits the definition. Write your answer in the space provided.

_____ 1. the major subdivision of a family or subfamily in the classification of plants and animals
a. gene   b. genus   c. genial   d. gentry

_____ 2. suited or adapted in disposition; agreeable
a. genial   b. congenial   c. genealogy
d. congenial

_____ 3. wellborn and well-bred people
a. gene   b. gentry   c. nobility   d. gentility

_____ 4. the science of improving the qualities of a breed or species
a. genetics   b. gentry   c. genealogy
d. eugenics

_____ 5. the unit of heredity transmitted in the chromosome
a. ancestry   b. DNA   c. gene   d. genus

_____ 6. cordial; favorable for life, growth, or comfort
a. genial   b. gentry   c. eugenics
d. hospitality

_____ 7. to produce, cause, or give rise to
a. gentility   b. engender   c. genealogy
d. genial

_____ 8. a record or account of the ancestry of a person, family, group, etc
a. gene   b. genealogy   c. glibness   d. gentry

_____ 9. good breeding or refinement
a. reductive   b. genus   c. gentility
d. eugenics

_____ 10. existing at or from one's birth
a. congenital   b. genus   c. congenial
d. gene

Quiz 30: True/False

In the space provided, write T if the definition of the numbered word is true or F if it is false.

		T or F
1. gentry	peasants	_____
2. congenital	incurable	_____
3. genial	debased	_____
4. gene	genetic material	_____

5.	eugenics	matricide	_____
6.	gentility	viciousness	_____
7.	genealogy	family history	_____
8.	congenial	pleasant	_____
9.	genus	subdivision	_____
10.	engender	cease	_____

Lesson 16. "This Way to the Egress": *grad, gres, gress*

P.T. Barnum was a nineteenth-century American showman whose greatest undertaking was the circus he called "The Greatest Show on Earth." The circus, which included a menagerie featuring Jumbo the elephant and a museum of freaks, was famous all over the country. After its merger in 1881 with James Anthony Bailey's circus, the enterprise gained international renown. When Barnum's customers took too long to leave his famous exhibits, he posted a sign: "This way to the egress." Following the arrow in eager anticipation of a new oddity, the visitors were ushered through the egress—the exit.

Knowing that the root "grad, gres, gress" means *step, degree,* or *walk* might have given these suckers a few more minutes to enjoy the exhibits, and it can certainly help you figure out a number of powerful words. Here are nine words that use this Latin root. Study the definitions, practice the pronunciations, and work through the two quizzes.

1. **digress** (di gres′, dī-) to wander away from the main topic. From Latin "digressus, digredi," *to walk away* ("di-," *away, apart* + "gressus, gredi," *to walk, step*)

   The manager cautioned her salespeople that they would fare better if they did not digress from their prepared sales talks.

2. **transgress** (trans gres′, tranz-) to break or violate a law, command, moral code, etc. From Latin "transgressus, transgredi," *to step across.*

   Those who transgress the laws of their ancestors often feel guilty.

3. **retrograde** (re′trə grād′) moving backward; having backward motion.

   Most of the townspeople regarded the new ordinance as a prime example of retrograde legislation.

4. **regression** (ri gresh′ən) the act of going or fact of having gone back to an earlier place or state.
   The child's regression could be seen in his thumbsucking.

5. **degrade** (di grād′) to reduce the dignity of (someone); deprive (someone) of office, rank, or title; lower (someone or something) in quality or character.
   He felt they were degrading him by making him wash the dishes.

6. **Congress** (kong′gris) the national legislative body of the United States, consisting of the Senate and the House of Representatives; *(lower case)* a formal meeting of representatives.
   Congress held a special session to discuss the situation in the Middle East.

7. **gradation** (grā dā′shən) any process or change taking place through a series of stages, by degrees, or gradually. From Latin "gradatio," *series of steps,* derived from "gradus," *step, degree.*
   He decided to change his hair color by gradation rather than all at once.

8. **gradient** (grā′dē ənt) the degree of inclination, or the rate of ascent or descent, in a highway, railroad, etc.
   Although they liked the house very much, they were afraid that the driveway's steep gradient would make it hard to park a car there in the winter.

9. **progressive** (prə gres′iv) characterized by progress or reform; innovative; going forward, gradually increasing.
   The progressive legislation wiped out years of social inequity.

Quiz 31: Matching

Match each of the following numbered words with its closest synonym. Write your answer in the space provided.

1. congress	a. backward moving	_____
2. regression	b. depart from a subject	_____
3. gradient	c. disobey	_____
4. progressive	d. meeting	_____
5. digress	e. stage, degree	_____
6. gradation	f. reversion	_____
7. retrograde	g. humiliate	_____
8. degrade	h. innovative	_____
9. transgress	i. incline	_____

Quiz 32: Defining Words

Define each of the following words.

1. gradient _____

2. Congress _____

3. progressive _____

4. regression _____

5. retrograde _____

6. degrade _____

7. digress _____

8. gradation _____

9. transgress _____

Suggested Answers 1. the degree of inclination, or the rate of ascent or descent, in a highway, etc. 2. the national legislative body of the United States; a meeting or assembly 3. characterized by re-form; increasing gradually 4. the act of going back to an earlier place or state 5. moving backward; having backward motion 6. to reduce (someone) to a lower rank; deprive of office, rank, or title, to lower in quality or character 7. to wander away from the main topic 8. any process or change taking place through a series of stages, by degrees, or gradually 9. to break or violate a law, command, moral code, etc.

Lesson 17. "Splish, Splash, I Was Taking a Bath": *hydro, hydr*

According to mythology, the ancient Greeks were menaced by a monstrous nine-headed serpent with fatally poisonous breath. Killing it was no easy matter. When you lopped off one head, it grew two in its place, and the central head was immortal. Hercules, sent to destroy the serpent as the second of his twelve labors, was triumphant when he burned off the eight peripheral heads and buried the ninth under a huge rock. From its residence, the watery marsh, came the monster's name, "Hydra," from the Greek root "hydr(o)," meaning *water*.

Quite a few words are formed from the "hydro" or "hydr" root. Here are ten of them. Read through the definitions, practice the pronunciations, and then work through the two quizzes that follow.

1. **hydrostat** (hī′drə stat′) an electrical device for detecting the presence of water, as from an overflow or a leak.
    The plumber used a hydrostat to locate the source of the leak in the bathroom.

2. **dehydrate** (dē hī′drāt) to deprive of water; dry out.
   Aside from being tasty and nutritious, dehydrated fruits and vegetables are easy to store and carry.

3. **hydrophobia** (hī′drə fō′bē ə) rabies; fear of water.
   Sufferers from hydrophobia are unable to swallow water.

4. **hydroplane** (hī′drə plān′) a light, high-powered boat, especially one with hydrofoils or a stepped bottom, designed to travel at very high speeds.
   The shore police acquired a new hydroplane to help them apprehend boaters who misuse the waterways.

5. **hydroponics** (hī′drə pon′iks) the cultivation of plants by placing the roots in liquid nutrients rather than soil.
   Some scientists predict that in the future, as arable land becomes increasingly more scarce, most of our vegetables will be grown through hydroponics.

6. **hydropower** (hī′drə pou′ər) electricity generated by falling water or another hydraulic source.
   Hydropower is efficient, clean, and economical.

7. **hydrate** (hī′drāt) to combine with water.
   Lime is hydrated for use in plaster, mortar, and cement.

8. **hydrangea** (hī drān′jə) a showy shrub, cultivated for its large white, pink, or blue flower clusters, that typically requires deep watering. From Greek "hydr-," *water* + "angeion," *vessel.*
   Hydrangeas require a great deal of water to flourish.

9. **hydrotherapy** (hī′drə ther′əpē) the treatment of disease by the scientific application of water both internally and externally.
   To alleviate strained muscles, physical therapists often prescribe hydrotherapy.

10. **hydrosphere** (hī′drə sfēr′) the water on or surrounding the surface of the planet Earth, including the water of the oceans and the water in the atmosphere.
    Scientists are investigating whether the greenhouse effect is influencing the hydrosphere.

Quiz 33: Definitions

Select the word that best fits the definition. Write your answer in the space provided.

_____   1. electricity generated by water
     a. hydropower   b. hydrangea   c. hydrotherapy
     d. electrolysis

_____ 2. the treatment of disease by the scientific application of water both internally and externally
a. hydrate   b. electrolysis   c. hydrotherapy
d. hydroponics

_____ 3. a light, high-powered boat, especially one with hydrofoils or a stepped bottom
a. hydropower   b. hydroplane   c. hydroelectric
d. hydroship

_____ 4. rabies; fear of water
a. hydrate   b. hydrotherapy   c. hydroponics
d. hydrophobia

_____ 5. the water on or surrounding the surface of the globe, including the water of the oceans and the water in the atmosphere
a. hydrosphere   b. hydrate   c. hydrofoil
d. hydrangea

_____ 6. to deprive of water
a. hydrate   b. dehydrate   c. hydrolyze
d. hydrotherapy

_____ 7. a showy shrub with large white, pink, or blue flower clusters
a. hydrate   b. hydrangea   c. hydroponics
d. hydrofoil

_____ 8. the cultivation of plants by placing the roots in liquid nutrient solutions rather than soil
a. hydrotherapy   b. hydrangea   c. hydroponics
d. hydrolyze

_____ 9. to combine with water
a. hydrostat   b. hydrosphere   c. hydrangea
d. hydrate

_____ 10. an electrical device for detecting the presence of water, as from an overflow or a leak
a. hydrosphere   b. hydrangea   c. hydroponics
d. hydrostat

Quiz 34: True/False

In the space provided, write T if the definition of the numbered word is true or F if it is false.

		T or F
1. **hydropower**	hydroelectric power	_____
2. **hydroplane**	boat	_____
3. **hydroponics**	gardening in water	_____

4. hydrostat	water power	_____
5. hydrangea	flowering plant	_____
6. hydrotherapy	water cure	_____
7. hydrate	lose water	_____
8. hydrosphere	bubble	_____
9. dehydrate	wash thoroughly	_____
10. hydrophobia	pneumonia	_____

Lesson 18. "After Me, The Deluge": *lav, lu*

The failure of Louis XV (1710–74) to provide strong leadership and badly needed reforms contributed to the crisis that brought about the French Revolution. Louis took only nominal interest in ruling his country and was frequently influenced by his mistresses. In the last years of his reign, he did cooperate with his chancellor to try to reform the government's unequal and inefficient system of taxation, but it was too late. His reported death-bed prophecy, "After me, the deluge," was fulfilled in the overthrow of the monarchy less than twenty years later. The word "deluge," meaning *flood*, comes from the Latin root "lu," *to wash*. As a flood, a deluge would indeed wash things clean.

A number of words were formed from the "lav, lu" root. Here are several examples. Study the definitions and practice the pronunciations. To help you remember the words, complete the two quizzes at the end of the lesson.

1. **dilute** (di lo͞ot′, dī-) to make thinner or weaker by adding water; to reduce the strength or effectiveness of (something). From Latin "dilutus, diluere," *to wash away.*
   The wine was too strong and had to be diluted.

2. **lavabo** (lə vä′bō, -vä′-) the ritual washing of the celebrant's hands after the offertory in the Mass; the passage recited with the ritual. From the Latin word meaning *I shall wash*, with which the passage begins.
   The priest intoned the Latin words of the lavabo.

3. **lavage** (lə väzh′) a washing, especially the cleansing of an organ, as the stomach, by irrigation.
   Lavage is a preferred method of preventing infection.

4. **diluvial** (di lo͞o′vē əl) pertaining to or caused by a flood or deluge.

The diluvial aftermath was a bitter harvest of smashed gardens, stained siding, and missing yard furniture.

5. **alluvium** (ə l$\overline{oo}$′vē əm) a deposit of sand, mud, etc., formed by flowing water.
   Geologists study alluvium for clues to the earth's history.
6. **ablution** (ə bl$\overline{oo}$′shən) a cleansing with water or other liquid, especially as a religious ritual; a washing of the hands, body, etc.
   He performed his morning ablutions with vigor.

Quiz 35: Matching

Select the best or closest synonym for each numbered word. Write your answer in the space provided.

_____   1. lavage
            a. molten rock   b. sewage   c. washing
            d. religious ritual
_____   2. alluvium
            a. great heat   b. rain   c. flood   d. deposit of sand
_____   3. lavabo
            a. religious cleansing   b. volcano   c. flooding
            d. lavatory
_____   4. ablution
            a. cleansing with water   b. absence   c. sacrifice
            d. small font
_____   5. dilute
            a. wash   b. weaken   c. cleanse   d. liquefy
_____   6. diluvial
            a. before the flood   b. antedate   c. monarchy
            d. of a flood

Quiz 36: True/False

In the space provided, write T if the definition of the numbered word is true or F if it is false.

		T or F
1. **dilute**	reduce strength	_____
2. **diluvial**	two-lipped	_____
3. **lavage**	security	_____
4. **alluvium**	molten rock	_____

5. ablution   washing   _____
6. lavabo   religious ritual _____

Lesson 19. "Silver Tongue": *loqui, loqu, locu*

For many years, the ventriloquist Edgar Bergen amused audiences as he tried to outwit his monocled wooden dummy, Charlie McCarthy. Among the most popular entertainers of his age, Bergen astonished audiences with his mastery of ventriloquism, the art of speaking so that projected sound seems to originate elsewhere, as from a hand-manipulated dummy. This ancient skill sounds easier than it is, since it requires modifying the voice through slow exhalation, minimizing movement of the tongue and lips, and maintaining an impassive expression to help shift viewers' attention to the illusory source of the voice.

The word "ventriloquism" comes from Latin "ventri-," *abdomen, stomach,* and the root "loqui," *to speak* (because it was believed that the ventriloquist produced sounds from his stomach). Many useful and important words were formed from the "loqui, loqu" root. Below are seven you should find especially helpful. Study the definitions and practice the pronunciations. To reinforce your learning, work through the two quizzes.

1. **obloquy** (ob′lə kwē) blame, censure, or abusive language.
   The vicious obloquy surprised even those who knew of the enmity between the political rivals.

2. **colloquial** (kə lō′kwē əl) characteristic of or appropriate to ordinary or familiar conversation rather than formal speech or writing.
   In standard American English, "He hasn't got any" is colloquial, while "He has none" is formal.

3. **soliloquy** (sə lil′ə kwē) the act of talking while or as if alone.
   A soliloquy is often used as a device in a drama to disclose a character's innermost thoughts.

4. **eloquent** (el′ə kwənt) having or exercising the power of fluent, forceful, and appropriate speech; movingly expressive.
   William Jennings Bryan was an eloquent orator famous for his "Cross of Gold" speech.

5. **interlocution** (in′tər lō kyōō′shən) conversation; dialogue.
   The interlocutions disclosed at the Watergate hearings riveted the American public to their TV sets.

6. **loquacious** (lō kwā'shəs) talking much or freely; talkative; wordy.

 After the sherry, the dinner guests became loquacious.

7. **elocution** (el'ə kyo͞o'shən) a person's manner of speaking or reading aloud; the study and practice of public speaking.

 After completing the course in public speaking, the pupils were skilled at elocution.

Quiz 37: Matching

Match each of the numbered words with its closest synonym. Write your answer in the space provided.

1. loquacious	a. censure	_____
2. interlocution	b. informal	_____
3. elocution	c. monologue	_____
4. colloquial	d. talkative	_____
5. soliloquy	e. conversation	_____
6. obloquy	f. fluent	_____
7. eloquent	g. public speaking	_____

Quiz 38: Definitions

Select the word that best fits the definition. Write your answer in the space provided.

_____ 1. a person's manner of speaking or reading aloud; the study and practice of public speaking
  a. obloquy b. soliloquy c. prologue
  d. elocution

_____ 2. conversation; dialogue
  a. colloquial b. interlocution c. monologue
  d. elocution

_____ 3. tending to talk; garrulous
  a. eloquent b. colloquial c. loquacious
  d. elocutionary

_____ 4. characteristic of or appropriate to ordinary or familiar conversation rather than formal speech or writing
  a. colloquial b. eloquent c. prologue
  d. dialogue

_____ 5. the act of talking while or as if alone
  a. circumlocution b. dialogue c. soliloquy
  d. obloquy

_____ 6. having or exercising the power of fluent, forceful, and appropriate speech; movingly expressive
   a. interlocution   b. eloquent   c. colloquial
   d. loquacious

_____ 7. censure; abusive language
   a. interlocution   b. soliloquy   c. obloquy
   d. dialogue

Lesson 20. "Star Light, Star Bright": *luc, lux, lum*

Before he was driven out of heaven for the sin of pride, Satan was called "Lucifer," which translates as *bringer of light.* In his epic retelling of the Bible, *Paradise Lost,* John Milton used the name "Lucifer" for the demon of sinful pride, and we call the planet Venus "Lucifer" when it appears as the morning star. "Lucifer" comes from the root "luc, lux" meaning *light.*

A number of powerful words derive from "luc" and its variations. We trust that you'll find the following seven *light* words "enlightening"! Study the definitions and practice the pronunciations. Then complete the two quizzes at the end of the lesson.

1. **pellucid** (pə lo͞o'sid) allowing the maximum passage of light; clear.
   The pellucid waters of the Caribbean allowed us to see the tropical fish clearly.

2. **lucid** (lo͞o'sid) shining or bright; clearly understood.
   Stephen Hawking's lucid explanation of astrophysics became a bestseller.

3. **translucent** (trans lo͞o'sənt, tranz-) permitting light to pass through but diffusing it so that persons, objects, etc., on the opposite side are not clearly visible.
   Frosted window glass is translucent.

4. **elucidate** (i lo͞o'si dāt') to make light or clear; explain.
   Once my math teacher elucidated the mysteries of geometry, I had no further difficulty solving the problems.

5. **lucubrate** (lo͞o'kyo͞o brāt') to work, write, or study laboriously, especially at night. From Latin "lucubrare," *to work by artificial light.*
   The scholar lucubrated for many long nights in an attempt to complete his thesis.

6. **luminary** (lo͞o'mə ner'ē) an eminent person; an object that gives light.

Certain that the elegant woman emerging from the limousine had to be a theatrical luminary, the crowd surged forward to get a closer look.

7. **luminous** (lōō'mə nəs) radiating or emitting light; brilliant.
   The luminous paint emitted an eerie glow—not at all what the designer had envisioned.

Quiz 39: True/False

In the space provided, write T if the definition of the numbered word is true or F if it is false.

		T or F
1. lucid	comprehensible	_____
2. elucidate	explain	_____
3. lucubrate	lubricate	_____
4. pellucid	limpid, clear	_____
5. luminous	reflective	_____
6. luminary	lightning	_____
7. translucent	opaque	_____

Quiz 40: Matching

Select the best definition for each numbered word. Write your answer in the space provided.

1. luminous	a. study hard	_____
2. elucidate	b. prominent person	_____
3. pellucid	c. brilliant	_____
4. lucubrate	d. permitting but diffusing	_____
	light	
5. lucid	e. clearly understood	_____
6. luminary	f. allowing the passage of	_____
	maximum light	
7. translucent	g. clarify	_____

Lesson 21. "Evil Be to Him Who Does Evil": *male, mal*

"Malnutrition" is defined as *a lack of the proper type and amount of nutrients required for good health.* It is estimated that more than ten million American children suffer from malnutrition; the World Health Organization reports that over 600 million people suffer from malnutrition in the emerging countries alone. Malnourished people endure a variety of side effects, including a failure to grow; increased susceptibility to infection; anemia; diarrhea; and lethargy.

The root "mal" in the word "malnourished" means *bad, evil,* and words formed around this root invariably carry negative overtones. In Latin, the root is spelled "male"; in French, it's "mal," but regardless of the spelling, the root means *evil.* Study the definitions and pronunciations of the following "mal" words until you become comfortable with them. Then work through the two quizzes.

1. **maladjusted** (mal'ə jus'tid) badly adjusted.
   Despite attempts by the psychologist to ease him into his environment, the child remained maladjusted.

2. **malefactor** (mal'ə fak'tər) a person who violates the law; a criminal.
   The police issued an all-points bulletin for the apprehension of the malefactor.

3. **maladroit** (mal'ə droit') unskillful; awkward; clumsy.
   With his large hands and thick fingers, the young man was maladroit at fine needlework.

4. **malevolent** (mə lev'ə lənt) wishing evil to another or others; showing ill will.
   Her malevolent uncle robbed the heiress of her estate and made her a virtual prisoner.

5. **malapropism** (mal'ə prop iz'əm) a confused use of words, especially one in which one word is replaced by another of similar sound but ludicrously inappropriate meaning: an instance of such a use. The word comes from Mrs. Malaprop, a character in Sheridan's comedy *The Rivals* (1775), noted for her misapplication of words. Sheridan coined the character's name from the English word "malapropos," meaning *inappropriate,* derived from the French phrase "mal à propos," *badly (suited) to the purpose.*
   "Lead the way and we'll precede" is a malapropism.

6. **malicious** (mə lish'əs) full of or characterized by evil intention.
   The malicious gossip hurt the young couple's reputation.

7. **malfeasance** (mal fē'zəns) the performance by a public official of an act that is legally unjustified, harmful, or contrary to law.
   Convicted of malfeasance, the mayor was sentenced to six months in jail.

8. **malignant** (mə lig'nənt) disposed to cause harm, suffering, or distress; tending to produce death, as a disease or tumor.
   The patient was greatly relieved when the pathologist reported that the tumor was not malignant.
9. **malign** (mə līn') to speak harmful untruths about; slander.
   "If you malign me again," the actor threatened the tabloid reporter, "I will not hesitate to sue."

Quiz 41: Matching

Match each of the numbered words with its closest synonym. Write your answer in the space provided.

1. maladroit	a. wishing others evil	_____
2. malicious	b. harmful; fatal	_____
3. malapropism	c. official misconduct	_____
4. malfeasance	d. bungling, tactless	_____
5. malign	e. badly adjusted	_____
6. malignant	f. spiteful	_____
7. malefactor	g. criminal	_____
8. malevolent	h. revile, defame	_____
9. maladjusted	i. confused use of words	_____

Quiz 42: True/False

In the space provided, write T if the definition of the numbered word is true or F if it is false.

		T or F
1. malefactor	ranger	_____
2. malapropism	faulty stage equipment	_____
3. malfeasance	food poisoning	_____
4. malicious	spiteful	_____
5. maladjusted	poorly adjusted	_____
6. malignant	benign	_____
7. maladroit	clumsy	_____
8. malevolent	bad winds	_____
9. malign	defame	_____

Lesson 22. "I Do!": mater, matr

The word "matrimony," meaning *marriage*, derives from the Latin root "mater," *mother*, because the union of a couple was established through motherhood. Most of us accept without question the idea of matrimony based on romantic love, but this is a relatively new belief. Only recently, following the rise of the middle class and the growth of democracy, has there been a tolerance of romantic marriages based on the free choice of the partners involved. Arranged marriages, accepted almost everywhere throughout history, eventually ceased to prevail in the West, although they persist in aristocratic circles to the present. The most extreme application of the custom of arranged marriages occurred in prerevolutionary China, where the bride and groom often met for the first time only on their wedding day.

We've inherited and created a number of significant words from the "mater, matr" root. Below are eight such words to help make your vocabulary more powerful and precise. Study the definitions and pronunciations; then complete the two quizzes.

1. **maternal** (mə tûr′nl) having the qualities of a mother; related through a mother.

    On his maternal side, he is related to Abigail and John Adams.

2. **matron** (mā′trən) a married woman, especially one with children, or one who has an established social position.

    The matrons got together every Thursday to play bridge or mahjong.

3. **mater** (mā′tər) informal or humorous British usage for "mother."

    "Mater is off to London again," said Giles snidely.

4. **matrix** (mā′triks) that which gives origin or form to a thing, or which serves to enclose it.

    Rome was the matrix of Western civilization.

5. **alma mater** (äl′mə mä′tər, al′-) a school, college, or university where a person has studied, and, usually, from which he or she has graduated. From the Latin phrase meaning *nourishing mother*.

    Ellen's alma mater is Queens College.

6. **matrilineal** (ma′trə lin′ē əl, mā′-) inheriting or determining descent through the female line.

    In a matrilineal culture, the children are usually part of the mother's family.

7. **matronymic** (ma′trə nim′ik) derived from the name of the mother or another female ancestor; named after one's mother. The word is also spelled "metronymic" (mē′trə nim′ik, me′-).

    Some men have matronymic middle names.

8. **matriculate** (mə trik′yə lāt′) to enroll or cause to enroll as a student, especially in a college or university.
She intends to matriculate at City College in the fall.

Quiz 43: Definitions

Select the word that best fits the definition. Write your answer in the space provided.

_____ 1. that which gives origin or form to a thing, or which serves to enclose it
a. matrix   b. matrimonial   c. mater
d. alma mater

_____ 2. a school, college, or university at which a person has studied, and, usually, from which he or she has graduated
a. maternal   b. alma mater   c. maternity
d. matrimony

_____ 3. inheriting or determining descent through the female line
a. femaleness   b. matrix   c. matrilineal
d. lineage

_____ 4. derived from the name of the mother or another female ancestor; named after one's mother
a. matriarch   b. matrilocal   c. alma mater
d. matronymic

_____ 5. having the qualities of a mother
a. alma mater   b. matrilineal   c. maternal
d. matrix

_____ 6. a married woman, especially one with children, or one who has an established social position
a. matrix   b. matron   c. alma mater
d. homemaker

_____ 7. to enroll or cause to enroll as a student, especially in a college or university
a. matriculate   b. graduate   c. matrix
d. alma mater

_____ 8. informal British usage for "mother"
a. mater   b. matriarch   c. matron   d. ma

Quiz 44: True/False

In the space provided, write T if the definition of the numbered word is true or F if it is false.

		T or F
1. matrix	outer edges	_____
2. alma mater	stepmother	_____
3. matrilineal	grandmotherly	_____
4. matriculate	study for a degree	_____
5. mater	mother	_____
6. maternal	motherly	_____
7. matronymic	from the mother's name	_____
8. matron	single woman	_____

Lesson 23. "Birth and Rebirth": *nasc, nat*

The Renaissance (also spelled Renascence) occurred between 1300 and 1600, when the feudal society of the Middle Ages became an increasingly urban, commercial economy with a central political institution. The term "Renaissance," or *rebirth*, was first applied in the mid-nineteenth century by a French historian to what has been characterized as nothing less than the birth of modern humanity and consciousness. The word goes back to Latin "renasci," *to be reborn*, from "re-," *again* + "nasci," *to be born*.

Many significant words evolved from the "nasc, nat" root. Here are eight such words for your consideration. First, read through the pronunciations, definitions, and sentences. Then, to reinforce your reading, complete the two quizzes.

1. **natal** (nāt′l) of or pertaining to one's birth.
   The astrologer cast a natal chart for his client.
2. **nativity** (nə tiv′i tē, nā-) birth; the birth of Christ.
   The wanderer returned to the place of his nativity.
3. **nativism** (nā′ti viz′əm) the policy of protecting the interests of native inhabitants against those of immigrants.
   The supporters of nativism staged a protest to draw attention to their demands for protection against the newcomers.
4. **innate** (i nāt′) existing from birth; inborn.
   The art lessons brought out her innate talent.
5. **nascent** (nas′ənt, nā′sənt) beginning to exist or develop.
   The nascent republic petitioned for membership in the United Nations.
6. **nationalism** (nash′ə nl iz′əm, nash′nə liz′-) national spirit or aspirations; devotion to the interests of one's own nation.

From Latin "natio," *nation, race,* derived from "nasci," *to be born.*

Many Americans feel a stirring of nationalism when they see the flag or hear the national anthem.

7. **naturalize** (nach'ər ə līz', nach'rə-) to invest (an alien) with the rights and privileges of a citizen. From Latin "natura," *birth, nature,* derived from "nasci," *to be born.*

To become naturalized American citizens, immigrants have to study the Constitution of their adopted country.

8. **nee** (nā) born. The word is placed after the name of a married woman to introduce her maiden name. From French "nee," going back to Latin "nata," *born,* from "nasci," *to be born.*

Madame de Staël, nee Necker, was the central figure in a brilliant salon.

Quiz 45: True/False

In the space provided, write T if the definition of the numbered word is true or F if it is false.

		T or F
1. nativism	protectionism	_____
2. naturalize	admit to citizenship	_____
3. nee	foreign wife	_____
4. natal	pertaining to birth	_____
5. nationalism	immigration	_____
6. nativity	rebirth	_____
7. nascent	native-born	_____
8. innate	inborn	_____

Quiz 46: Matching

Select the best definition for each numbered word. Write your answer in the space provided.

1. innate	a. admit to citizenship	_____
2. nationalism	b. relating to birth	_____
3. naturalize	c. beginning to exist	_____
4. nee	d. birth	_____
5. natal	e. protection of native inhabitants	_____
6. nascent	f. inborn	_____
7. nativism	g. indicating maiden name	_____
8. nativity	h. patriotism	_____

Lesson 24. "A Rose by Any Other Name": *nomin, nomen*

The differences between the nominative and objective cases have baffled countless generations of English-speaking students. Is it I or me? Who or whom? The nominative case is so named because it *names* the subject, the doer of the action, whereas the objective case refers to the object, as of a verb or preposition. Here are eight words formed from the Latin root "nomin, nomen," *name.*

1. **nominee** (nom′ə nē′) a person named, as to run for elective office or to fill a particular post.
   In order to qualify for consideration, the nominee was required to present a petition with three hundred verifiable signatures.

2. **misnomer** (mis nō′mər) a misapplied name or designation; an error in naming a person or thing.
   "Expert" was a misnomer; "genius" was a far more accurate description of the young chess player.

3. **nomenclature** (nō′mən klā′chər) a set or system of names or terms, as those used in a particular science or art.
   The scientific nomenclature devised by Linnaeus was a great innovation.

4. **ignominious** (ig′nə min′ē əs) disgracing one's name; humiliating; discreditable; contemptible.
   The army suffered an ignominious defeat.

5. **nominal** (nom′ə nl) being such in name only; so-called.
   The silent partner is the nominal head of the firm.

6. **nominate** (nom′ə nāt′) to name (someone) for appointment or election to office.
   The delegate from Vermont was pleased to nominate a favorite son for President at the Democratic convention.

Quiz 47: True/False

In the space provided, write T if the definition of the numbered word is true or F if it is false.

		T or F
1. **ignominious**	foolish, ignorant	_____
2. **nominate**	name as a candidate	_____
3. **nomenclature**	clamp	_____
4. **nominee**	candidate	_____

5. nominal	so-called	_____
6. misnomer	faux pas	_____

Quiz 48: Synonyms

Select the best synonym for each numbered word. Write your answer in the space provided.

_____ 1. ignominious
         a. ignorant   b. enormous   c. disgraceful
         d. successful

_____ 2. nomenclature
         a. biology   b. classification   c. torture device
         d. international transport

_____ 3. nominee
         a. elected official   b. hereditary title
         c. candidate   d. assumed name

_____ 4. misnomer
         a. misapplied name   b. married name
         c. wrong road   d. misapplied remedy

_____ 5. nominal
         a. a lot   b. allot   c. so-called   d. summons

_____ 6. nominate
         a. apply   b. designate   c. reject   d. elect

Lesson 25. "Oh My Papa": *pater, patr*

To sociologists and anthropologists, patriarchy is a system of social organization in which descent is traced through the male line and all offspring have the father's name or belong to his people. Often, the system is connected to inheritance and social prerogatives, as in primogeniture, in which the eldest son is the sole heir. The ancient Greeks and Hebrews were a patriarchal society, as were the Europeans during the Middle Ages. While many aspects of patriarchy, such as the inheritance of the family name through the male line, persist in Western society, the exclusive male inheritance of property and other patriarchal customs are dying out.

From the Latin root "pater, patr," meaning *father,* we have formed many useful words. Eight of them follow. Go through the pronunciations, definitions, and sentences to help you make the words part of your daily speech and writing. Then complete the two quizzes.

1. **patrician** (pə trish′ən) a member of the original senatorial aristocracy in ancient Rome; any person of noble or high rank.

   You could tell she was a patrician from her elegant manner.

2. **expatriate** (*v.* eks pā′trē āt′; *n.* eks pā′trē it) to banish (a person) from his or her native country; one who has left his or her native country.

   Among the most famous American expatriates in the 1920s were the writers F. Scott Fitzgerald, Ernest Hemingway, and Gertrude Stein.

3. **patronage** (pā′trə nij, pa′-) the financial support or business afforded to a store, hotel, or the like, by customers, clients, or paying guests; the encouragement or support of an artist by a patron; the control of appointments to government jobs, especially on a basis other than merit alone. From Latin "patronus," *patron, protector, advocate,* derived from "pater," father.

   To show its appreciation for its clients' patronage, the beauty shop offered a half-price haircut to all regular customers for the month of January.

4. **paternalism** (pə tûr′nl iz′əm) the system, principle, or practice of managing or governing individuals, businesses, nations, etc., in the manner of a father dealing benevolently and often intrusively with his children.

   The employees chafed under their manager's paternalism.

5. **paternoster** (pā′tər nos′tər, pä′-, pat′ər-) the Lord's Prayer, especially in the Latin form. The term is often capitalized.

   The term "paternoster" is a translation of the first two words of the prayer in the Vulgate version, "our Father."

6. **paterfamilias** (pā′tər fə mil′ē əs, pä′-, pat′ər-) the male head of a household or family.

   The paterfamilias gathered his children about him.

7. **patronymic** (pa′trə nim′ik) (a name) derived from the name of a father or ancestor, especially by the addition of a suffix or prefix indicating descent; family name or surname.

   Their patronymic was Williamson, meaning "son of William."

8. **patrimony** (pa′trə mō′nē) an estate inherited from one's father or ancestors; heritage.

   For his share of the patrimony, John inherited the family mansion at Newport.

Quiz 49: Definitions

Select the word that best fits the definition. Write your answer in the space provided.

_____ 1. the Lord's Prayer
    a. patrician   b. paternoster   c. paternalism
    d. expatriate

_____ 2. derived from the name of a father or ancestor; family name or surname
    a. paterfamilias   b. patronage   c. pater
    d. patronymic

_____ 3. the male head of a household or family
    a. paterfamilias   b. patronymic   c. patrician
    d. patrimony

_____ 4. any person of noble or high rank
    a. patricide   b. patrician   c. expatriate
    d. patriot

_____ 5. the system, principle, or practice of managing or governing in the manner of a father dealing with his children
    a. paterfamilias   b. expatriate   c. paternalism
    d. patronymic

_____ 6. to banish someone from his or her native country; one who has left his or her native country
    a. repatriate   b. patronize   c. paternalize
    d. expatriate

_____ 7. an estate inherited from one's father or ancestors; heritage
    a. patrimony   b. patricide   c. paternoster
    d. patronage

_____ 8. the financial support or business afforded to a store by its clients; the support of a patron; control of appointments to government jobs
    a. patronymic   b. pater   c. patronage
    d. paterfamilias

Quiz 50: Matching

Match each of the numbered words with its closest synonym. Write your answer in the space provided.

1. paternoster   a. financial backing   _____
2. patronymic   b. exile   _____
3. paterfamilias   c. male head of a family   _____

4. patrimony   d. fatherly management   _____
5. patronage   e. the Lord's Prayer   _____
6. paternalism   f. aristocrat   _____
7. patrician   g. surname   _____
8. expatriate   h. inheritance   _____

Lesson 26. "Keep On Truckin' ": *ped, pod*

From the Latin root "ped" and the related Greek root "pod," both meaning *foot,* we have derived many words relating to movement by foot. The English word "foot" is itself a Germanic cousin of the Latin and Greek forms. One curious aberration is "peddler" (also spelled "pedlar," "pedler"), for it is *not* from the root "ped," as we would expect. The word may be derived from "pedde," a Middle English word for a lidless hamper or basket in which fish and other items were carried as they were sold in the streets, though it is generally thought to be of unknown origin.

The following eight words, however, all come from the "ped, pod" roots. Practice the pronunciations, study the definitions, and read the sentences. Then, to help set the words in your mind, complete the two quizzes that follow.

1. **quadruped** (kwod'roŏ ped') any animal, especially a mammal, having four feet.
   Horses, dogs, and cats are all classified as quadrupeds.

2. **podiatrist** (pə dī'ə trist') a person who treats foot disorders. From Greek "pod-," *foot* + "-iatros," *physician.*
   Podiatrists were formerly known as chiropodists.

3. **chiropodist** (ki rop'ə dist', kī-) a podiatrist. From Greek "cheir," *hand* + "podos," *foot.*
   A chiropodist treats minor problems of the feet, including corns and bunions.

4. **biped** (bī'ped) a two-footed animal.
   Humans are bipeds.

5. **expedient** (ik spē'dē ənt) tending to promote some desired object; fit or suitable under the circumstances. From Latin "expedire," *to make ready,* literally *to free the feet.*
   It was expedient for them to prepare all the envelopes at the same time.

6. **pseudopod** (soō'də pod') an organ of propulsion on a protozoan.

Amebas use pseudopods, literally "false feet," as a means of locomotion.

7. **pedigree** (ped'i grē') an ancestral line; lineage. From the French phrase "pied de grue," *foot of a crane* (from the claw-shaped mark used in family trees to show lineage); "pied," *foot,* going back to the Latin root "ped."

The dog's pedigree could be traced six generations.

8. **pedometer** (pə dom'i tər) an instrument that measures distance covered in walking by recording the number of steps taken.

The race walker used a pedometer to keep track of how much distance she could cover in an hour.

Quiz 51: Definitions

Select the best definition for each numbered word. Write your answer in the space provided.

_____ 1. pedigree
   a. dog training   b. lineage   c. horse racing
   d. nature walking

_____ 2. biped
   a. false feet   b. horses   c. two-footed animal
   d. winged creature

_____ 3. pedometer
   a. race walking   b. jogger's injury   c. foot care
   d. measuring device

_____ 4. expedient
   a. advantageous   b. extra careful   c. unnecessary
   d. walking swiftly

_____ 5. quadruped
   a. four-footed animal   b. four-wheeled vehicle
   c. racehorse   d. four animals

_____ 6. chiropodist
   a. orthopedic surgeon   b. chiropractor
   c. podiatrist   d. physician's assistant

_____ 7. podiatrist
   a. children's doctor   b. foot doctor
   c. chiropractor   d. skin doctor

_____ 8. pseudopod
   a. false seed pod   b. widow's peak   c. bad seed
   d. organ of propulsion

Quiz 52: True/False

In the space provided, write T if the definition of the numbered word is true or F if it is false.

			T or F
1.	chiropodist	foot doctor	_____
2.	pedigree	lineage	_____
3.	expedient	advantageous	_____
4.	podiatrist	foot doctor	_____
5.	quadruped	four-footed animal	_____
6.	pedometer	scale	_____
7.	pseudopod	cocoon	_____
8.	biped	stereo	_____

Lesson 27: "It's My Pleasure": *plac*

"S'il vous plait" is what the French say to be polite. "Plait" derives from "plaire," *to please* which goes back to the Latin "placere." Thus the "plac" root, meaning *please,* forms the basis of the French expression for *if you please.* Many other words, including adjectives, nouns, and verbs, also derive from this root. Below are six "pleasing" words to add to your vocabulary. Look over the pronunciations, definitions, and sentences. Then to reinforce your memory, complete the two quizzes.

1. **placid** (plas′id) pleasantly peaceful or calm.
   The placid lake shimmered in the early morning sun.
2. **complacent** (kəm plā′sənt) pleased, especially with oneself or one's merits, advantages, situation, etc., often without awareness of some potential danger, defect, or the like.
   She stopped being so complacent after she lost her job.
3. **placebo** (plə sē′bō) a substance having no pharmacological effect but given to a patient or subject of an experiment who supposes it to be a medicine. From the Latin word meaning *I shall please.*
   In the pharmaceutical company's latest study, one group was given the medicine; the other, a placebo.
4. **placate** (plā′kāt) to appease or pacify.
   To placate an outraged citizenry, the Board of Education decided to schedule a special meeting.

5. **implacable** (im plak′ə bəl, -plā′kə-) incapable of being appeased or pacified; inexorable.

Despite concessions made by the allies, the dictator was implacable.

6. **complaisant** (kəm plā′sənt, -zənt, kom′plə zant′) inclined or disposed to please; obliging; gracious. From "plaisant," the French word for *pleasing,* derived ultimately from Latin "complacere," *to be very pleasing.*

Jill's complaisant manner belied her reputation as a martinet.

Quiz 53: Synonyms

Select the best synonym for each numbered word. Write your answer in the space provided.

_____ 1. complaisant
   a. self-satisfied   b. fake   c. agreeable
   d. successful
_____ 2. implacable
   a. obliging   b. foolish   c. calm   d. inexorable
_____ 3. placid
   a. lake   b. tranquil   c. wintery
   d. nature-loving
_____ 4. complacent
   a. smug   b. wretched   c. contemplative
   d. obsessively neat
_____ 5. placebo
   a. strong medicine   b. harmless drug
   c. sugar cube   d. cure
_____ 6. placate
   a. offend   b. advertise   c. cause   d. appease

Quiz 54: Matching

Match each of the numbered words with its closest synonym. Write your answer in the space provided.

1. **placebo**   a. self-satisfied   _____
2. **complaisant**   b. serene   _____
3. **implacable**   c. harmless substance   _____
4. **complacent**   d. incapable of being   _____
                         appeased
5. **placate**   e. pacify   _____
6. **placid**   f. obliging   _____

Lesson 28. "The City of Brotherly Love": *phil, philo*

The site of the future city of Philadelphia was settled in the mid-seventeenth century by Swedish immigrants. Later the prominent English Quaker William Penn (1644–1718) determined to establish a New World colony where religious and political freedom would be guaranteed. He first obtained from Charles II a charter for Pennsylvania (which was actually named by the king). In 1682 he surveyed the land and laid out the plan for the "City of Brotherly Love," Philadelphia. The settlement flourished from the time of its foundation, growing into a thriving center of trade and manufacturing.

The Greek root "phil, philo," meaning *love*, has given us many other words besides "Philadelphia." Here are ten of them to add to your vocabulary.

1. **philanthropy** (fi lan'thrə pē) affection for humankind, especially as manifested in donations of money, property, or work to needy persons or for socially useful purposes. From Greek "philanthropia," *love of humanity*.

    Millions of people have benefited from Andrew Carnegie's works of philanthropy.

2. **philanderer** (fi lan'dər ər) a man who makes love without serious intentions, especially one who carries on flirtations.

    When she discovered that her husband was a philanderer, she sued for divorce.

3. **bibliophile** (bib'lē ə fīl', -fil) a person who loves or collects books, especially as examples of fine or unusual printing, binding, or the like. From Greek "biblion," *book* + "philos," *loving*.

    The bibliophile was excited by the prospect of acquiring a first edition of Mark Twain's *Life on the Mississippi*.

4. **philharmonic** (fil'här mon'ik) a symphony orchestra.

    The philharmonic is presenting a concert this week.

5. **philately** (fi lat'l ē) the collection and study of postage stamps. From Greek "phil-," *loving* + "ateleia," *exemption from charges* (due to a sender's prepayment shown by a postage stamp).

    To pursue his hobby of philately, the collector attended stamp exhibitions as often as possible.

6. **philhellene** (fil hel′ēn) a friend and supporter of the Greeks.
   George was a philhellene whose greatest passion was ancient Greek sculpture.

7. **philter** (fil′tər) a potion or drug that is supposed to induce a person to fall in love with someone.
   He so desperately wanted her love that he resorted to dropping a philter into her drink.

8. **Anglophile** (ang′glə fīl′, -fil) a person who greatly admires England or anything English.
   A devoted Anglophile, Barry visits England at least twice a year.

9. **philodendron** (fil′ə den′drən) an ornamental tropical plant.
   The word "philodendron," meaning *fond of trees,* refers to the plant's climbing habit.

10. **philology** (fi lol′ə jē) the study of written records, their authenticity and original form, and the determination of their meaning; in earlier use, linguistics. From Greek "philo-," *loving* + "logos," *word, speech, reason.*
    The subject of philology, in its broadest sense, is culture and literature.

Quiz 55: Definitions

Select the word that best fits the definition. Write your answer in the space provided.

_____ 1. a person who greatly admires England or anything English
   a. Anglophile   b. philhellene   c. bibliophile
   d. philanderer

_____ 2. an ornamental tropical plant
   a. philanthropy   b. philodendron   c. philately
   d. Anglophile

_____ 3. a love potion
   a. philhellene   b. philology   c. philter
   d. bibliophile

_____ 4. the collection and study of stamps
   a. philanthropy   b. philology   c. philharmonic
   d. philately

_____ 5. a symphony orchestra
   a. philodendron   b. philter   c. philharmonic
   d. philately

_____   6. a friend and supporter of the Greeks
              a. philanderer   b. philhellene   c. Anglophile
              d. bibliophile

_____   7. linguistics
              a. philter   b. philately   c. philosophy
              d. philology

_____   8. a person who loves books
              a. philanderer   b. philter   c. Anglophile
              d. bibliophile

_____   9. concern for humanity
              a. philanthropy   b. philodendron   c. philology
              d. philter

_____ 10. a man who makes love without serious intentions,
              especially one who carries on flirtations
              a. bibliographer   b. philanderer   c. bibliophile
              d. Anglophile

Quiz 56: True/False

In the space provided, write T if the definition of the numbered word is true or F if it is false.

			T or F
1.	philately	fondness for stamps	_____
2.	philhellene	supporter of Greek culture	_____
3.	bibliophile	lover of books	_____
4.	philanderer	womanizer	_____
5.	philodendron	plant	_____
6.	philology	study of geography	_____
7.	philter	filtration	_____
8.	philanthropy	stinginess	_____
9.	philharmonic	fond of books	_____
10.	Anglophile	stamp collector	_____

Lesson 29. "Hang In There, Baby!": *pend*

The word "appendix" has two meanings. First, it is an organ located in the lower right side of the abdomen. It is believed to be a vestigial organ that has no function in humans. Second, it refers to the supplementary material found at the back of a book. The two meanings can be surmised from their root, "pendere," *to hang or weigh.* The appendix (vermiform appendix, strictly speaking) "hangs" in the abdomen, as the appendix "hangs" at the end of a text.

Awareness of the "pend" root can help you figure out the meanings of other words as well. Below are eight such words to help you hone your language skills.

1. **append** (ə pend′) to add as a supplement or accessory.
   My supervisor asked me to append this material to the report we completed yesterday.
2. **appendage** (ə pen′dij) a subordinate part attached to something; a person in a subordinate or dependent position.
   The little boy had been hanging on his mother's leg for so long that she felt he was a permanent appendage.
3. **compendium** (kəm pen′dē əm) a brief treatment or account of a subject, especially an extensive subject.
   The medical editors put together a compendium of modern medicine.
4. **stipend** (stī′pend) fixed or regular pay; any periodic payment, especially a scholarship allowance. From Latin "stips," *a coin* + "pendere," *to weigh, pay out*.
   The graduate students found their stipends inadequate to cover the cost of living in a big city.
5. **pendulous** (pen′jə ləs, pend′yə-) hanging down loosely; swinging freely.
   She had pendulous jowls.
6. **pendant** (pen′dənt) a hanging ornament.
   She wore a gold necklace with a ruby pendant.
7. **impending** (im pen′ding) about to happen; imminent.
   The impending storm filled them with dread.
8. **perpendicular** (pûr′pən dik′yə lər) vertical; upright.
   They set the posts perpendicular to the ground.

Quiz 57: Matching

Match each of the numbered words with its closest synonym. Write your answer in the space provided.

1. appendage	a. upright	_____
2. compendium	b. salary	_____
3. impending	c. hanging	_____
4. pendulous	d. adjunct	_____
5. perpendicular	e. ornament	_____
6. append	f. summary	_____
7. pendant	g. attach	_____
8. stipend	h. imminently menacing	_____

Quiz 58: True/False

In the space provided, write T if the definition of the numbered word is true or F if it is false.

		T or F
1. pendulous	swinging freely	_____
2. perpendicular	curved	_____
3. pendant	hanging ornament	_____
4. stipend	fasten	_____
5. append	add	_____
6. compendium	excised section	_____
7. appendage	adjunct	_____
8. impending	imminent	_____

Lesson 30. "Oh God!": *the, theo*

Atheism is the doctrine that denies the existence of a supreme deity. Many people have been incorrectly labeled atheists because they rejected some popular belief in divinity. The Romans, for example, felt the early Christians were atheists because they did not worship the pagan gods. Buddhists and Jains have been called atheistic because they deny a personal God. The word "atheism" comes from the Greek prefix "a-," *without,* and the root "the, theo," meaning *god.*

Many words derive from this root. The following section provides just a few useful examples.

1. **theology** (thē ol′ə jē) the field of study that deals with God or a deity.
   Modern theology is chiefly concerned with the relationship between humanity and God.
2. **theism** (thē′iz′ əm) the belief in the existence of a God or deity as the creator and ruler of the universe.
   The religious seminary taught its students the philosophy of theism.
3. **monotheism** (mon′ə thē iz′əm) the doctrine or belief that there is only one God.
   Judaism and Christianity preach monotheism.
4. **theocracy** (thē ok′rə sē) a form of government in which God or a deity is recognized as the supreme ruler.
   Puritan New England was a theocracy, with ministers as governors and the Bible as its constitution.

5. **pantheism** (pan'thē iz'əm) the doctrine that God is the transcendent reality of which the material universe and human beings are only manifestations.

    The New England philosophy of Transcendentalism that flourished in the mid-nineteenth century included elements of pantheism.

6. **apotheosis** (ə poth'ē ō'sis, ap'ə thē'ə sis) the exaltation of a person to the rank of a god; ideal example; epitome.

    This poem is the apotheosis of the Romantic spirit.

7. **theogony** (thē og'ə nē) an account of the origin of the gods.

    Hesiod wrote a theogony of the Greek gods.

Quiz 59: Defining Words

Define each of the following words.

1. pantheism _____

2. theology _____

3. theogony _____

4. theism _____

5. apotheosis _____

6. theocracy _____

7. monotheism _____

Suggested Answers   1. the doctrine that God is the transcendent reality of which the material universe and human beings are only manifestations 2. the field of study that treats of the deity, its attributes, and its relation to the universe 3. an account of the origin of the gods. 4. the belief in one God as the creator and ruler of the universe 5. the exaltation of a person to the rank of a god; the glorification of a person, act, principle, etc., as an ideal 6. a form of government in which God or a deity is recognized as the supreme civil ruler 7. the doctrine or belief that there is only one God

Quiz 60: True/False

In the space provided, write T if the definition of the numbered word is true or F if it is false.

		T or F
1. **apotheosis**	epitome	_____
2. **theogony**	account of the origin of the gods	_____
3. **theocracy**	religious government	_____
4. **theism**	belief in rebirth	_____
5. **monotheism**	viral illness	_____

6. pantheism   rejected beliefs   _____
7. theology   study of divine things   _____

Lesson 31. "Call Out!": *voc*

The voice box (more properly called the "larynx") is the muscular and cartilaginous structure in which the vocal cords are located. The vibration of the vocal cords by air passing out of the lungs causes the formation of sounds that are then amplified by the resonating nature of the oral and nasal cavities. The root "voc," meaning *call* or *voice,* is the basis of words like "vocal," as well as a host of other powerful words. Now study the following ten "vocal" words.

1. **avocation** (av′ə kā′shən) a minor or occasional occupation; hobby. From Latin "avocatio," *distraction,* derived from "avocare," *to call away.*
   His avocation is bird-watching.

2. **vocable** (vō′kə bəl) a word, especially one considered without regard to meaning. From Latin "vocabulum," derived from "vocare," *to call,* from "voc-, vox," *voice.*
   Lewis Carroll coined many nonsense vocables, such as *jabberwocky* and *bandersnatch.*

3. **vociferous** (vō sif′ər əs) crying out noisily; clamorous; characterized by noise or vehemence.
   She was vociferous in her support of reform legislation.

4. **advocate** (ad′və kāt′) to plead in favor of; support.
   The citizens' committee advocated a return to the previous plan.

5. **convoke** (kən vōk′) to summon to meet. From Latin "convocare" ("con-," *with together* + "vocare," *to call*).
   They will convoke the members for a noon meeting.

6. **evoke** (i vōk′) to call up, as memories or feelings. From Latin "evocare."
   The music evoked the mood of spring.

7. **revoke** (ri vōk′) to take back or withdraw; cancel. From Latin "revocare," *to call again, recall.*
   The king revoked his earlier decree.

8. **invoke** (in vōk′) to call forth or pray for; appeal to or petition; declare to be in effect. From Latin "invocare."
   The defendant invoked the Fifth Amendment so as not to incriminate himself.

9. **equivocal** (i kwiv′ə kəl) of uncertain significance; not determined; dubious. From Latin "aequivocus" ("aequus," *equal* + "vox," *voice*).

Despite his demands for a clear-cut decision, she would give only an equivocal response.

10. **irrevocable** (i rev′ə kə bəl) incapable of being revoked or recalled; unable to be repealed or annulled.

Once Caesar crossed the Rubicon, his decision to begin the civil war against Pompey was irrevocable.

Quiz 61: Matching

Match each of the numbered words with its closest synonym. Write your answer in the space provided.

1. convoke	a. word	_____
2. advocate	b. hobby	_____
3. revoke	c. uncertain	_____
4. equivocal	d. permanent	_____
5. invoke	e. summon	_____
6. vocable	f. pray for	_____
7. evoke	g. support	_____
8. vociferous	h. loud	_____
9. irrevocable	i. cancel	_____
10. avocation	j. call up; produce	_____

Quiz 62: True/False

In the space provided, write T if the definition of the numbered word is true or F if it is false.

		T or F
1. revoke	restore	_____
2. avocation	profession	_____
3. vociferous	quiet	_____
4. advocate	oppose	_____
5. evoke	stifle	_____
6. equivocal	unambiguous	_____
7. invoke	suppress	_____
8. irrevocable	changeable	_____
9. convoke	summon	_____
10. vocable	word	_____

Answers to Quizzes on Greek and Latin Roots

Answers to Quiz 1

1. a 2. b 3. c 4. d 5. d 6. b 7. b 8. a 9. a 10. b 11. c 12. d 13. c 14. c 15. a

Answers to Quiz 2

1. T 2. F 3. T 4. T 5. F 6. F 7. F 8. T 9. T 10. T

Answers to Quiz 3

1. T 2. T 3. F 4. T 5. F 6. T 7. F 8. T 9. T 10. F

Answers to Quiz 5

1. i 2. e 3. d 4. b 5. h 6. a 7. c 8. j 9. f 10. g

Answers to Quiz 6

1. T 2. F 3. F 4. F 5. T 6. F 7. T 8. T 9. F 10. T

Answers to Quiz 7

1. g 2. e 3. d 4. b 5. a 6. i 7. c 8. j 9. f 10. h

Answers to Quiz 8

1. F 2. T 3. T 4. T 5. F 6. F 7. T 8. F 9. T 10. F

Answers to Quiz 9

1. c 2. g 3. a 4. c 5. i 6. h 7. f 8. d 9. b 10. j

Answers to Quiz 10

1. F 2. F 3. T 4. F 5. T 6. T 7. F 8. F 9. F 10. T

Answers to Quiz 11

1. c 2. e 3. a 4. f 5. d 6. b

Answers to Quiz 12

1. F 2. T 3. F 4. F 5. F 6. T

Answers to Quiz 13

1. F 2. T 3. F 4. T 5. F 6. T 7. F 8. T

Answers to Quiz 15
1. c 2. d 3. a 4. d 5. c 6. b 7. b 8. a 9. d 10. c

Answers to Quiz 16
1. T 2. T 3. T 4. T 5. F 6. F 7. F 8. T 9. F 10. T

Answers to Quiz 17
1. a 2. c 3. b 4. b 5. a 6. c 7. a 8. b

Answers to Quiz 18
1. T 2. T 3. F 4. T 5. T 6. F 7. F 8. F

Answers to Quiz 19
1. c 2. e 3. a 4. g 5. h 6. f 7. b 8. d

Answers to Quiz 20
1. T 2. T 3. T 4. T 5. F 6. F 7. F 8. F

Answers to Quiz 21
1. f 2. a 3. i 4. b 5. h 6. c 7. d 8. e 9. g

Answers to Quiz 22
1. T 2. T 3. T 4. F 5. T 6. T 7. F 8. T 9. T

Answers to Quiz 23
1. c 2. c 3. b 4. b 5. a 6. b 7. c 8. a

Answers to Quiz 24
1. T 2. F 3. T 4. F 5. F 6. T 7. T 8. T

Answers to Quiz 25
1. d 2. a 3. f 4. b 5. c 6. g 7. e

Answers to Quiz 26
1. c 2. d 3. a 4. b 5. c 6. b 7. c

Answers to Quiz 27
1. T 2. F 3. T 4. T 5. F 6. F 7. F

Answers to Quiz 28
1. e 2. g 3. a 4. c 5. b 6. d 7. f

Answers to Quiz 29
1. b 2. d 3. b 4. d 5. c 6. a 7. b 8. b 9. c 10. a

Answers to Quiz 30
1. F 2. F 3. F 4. T 5. F 6. F 7. T 8. T 9. T 10. F

Answers to Quiz 31
1. d 2. f 3. i 4. h 5. b 6. e 7. a 8. g 9. c

Answers to Quiz 33
1. a 2. c 3. b 4. d 5. a 6. b 7. b 8. c 9. d 10. d

Answers to Quiz 34
1. T 2. T 3. T 4. F 5. T 6. T 7. F 8. F 9. F 10. F

Answers to Quiz 35
1. c 2. d 3. a 4. a 5. b 6. d

Answers to Quiz 36
1. T 2. F 3. F 4. F 5. T 6. T

Answers to Quiz 37
1. d 2. e 3. g 4. b 5. c 6. a 7. f

Answers to Quiz 38
1. d 2. b 3. c 4. a 5. c 6. b 7. c

Answers to Quiz 39
1. T 2. T 3. F 4. T 5. F 6. F 7. F

Answers to Quiz 40
1. c 2. g 3. f 4. a 5. e 6. b 7. d

Answers to Quiz 41
1. d 2. f 3. i 4. c 5. h 6. b 7. g 8. a 9. e

Answers to Quiz 42

1. F 2. F 3. F 4. T 5. T 6. F 7. T 8. F 9. T

Answers to Quiz 43

1. a 2. b 3. c 4. d 5. c 6. b 7. a 8. a

Answers to Quiz 44

1. F 2. F 3. F 4. T 5. T 6. T 7. T 8. F

Answers to Quiz 45

1. T 2. T 3. F 4. T 5. F 6. F 7. F 8. T

Answers to Quiz 46

1. f 2. h 3. a 4. g 5. b 6. c 7. e 8. d

Answers to Quiz 47

1. F 2. T 3. F 4. T 5. T 6. F

Answers to Quiz 48

1. c 2. b 3. c 4. a 5. c 6. b

Answers to Quiz 49

1. b 2. d 3. a 4. b 5. c 6. d 7. a 8. c

Answers to Quiz 50

1. e 2. g 3. c 4. h 5. a 6. d 7. f 8. b

Answers to Quiz 51

1. b 2. c 3. d 4. a 5. a 6. c 7. b 8. d

Answers to Quiz 52

1. T 2. T 3. T 4. T 5. T 6. F 7. F 8. F

Answers to Quiz 53

1. c 2. d 3. b 4. a 5. b 6. d

Answers to Quiz 54

1. c 2. f 3. d 4. a 5. c 6. b

Answers to Quiz 55

1. a 2. b 3. c 4. d 5. c 6. b 7. d 8. d 9. a 10. b

Answers to Quiz 56

1. T 2. T 3. T 4. T 5. T 6. F 7. F 8. F 9. F 10. F

Answers to Quiz 57

1. d 2. f 3. h 4. c 5. a 6. g 7. e 8. b

Answers to Quiz 58

1. T 2. F 3. T 4. F 5. T 6. F 7. T 8. T

Answers to Quiz 60

1. T 2. T 3. F 4. F 5. F 6. F 7. T

Answers to Quiz 61

1. e 2. g 3. i 4. c 5. f 6. a 7. j 8. h 9. d 10. b

Answers to Quiz 62

1. F 2. F 3. F 4. F 5. F 6. F 7. F 8. F 9. T 10. T

Word Histories

However helpful it is to learn how to figure out the meanings of words from their prefixes, suffixes, and roots, you may sometimes encounter an unusual or exotic word that resists the universal formula. Some words can only be understood by puzzling through their histories. Often the most powerful words come to us through mythology or biblical stories, historical events or literary works, obscure languages or twisted etymologies.

Lesson 1

Words, like people, have a past, and as with people, some words have more interesting stories than others. Knowing a word's history can help you remember it and incorporate it into your daily speech. The following ten words have especially intriguing backgrounds. Read through their histories, then complete the quizzes that follow.

1. **bootlegger** (boot'leg'ər) Originally, a "bootlegger" was a person who smuggled outlawed alcoholic liquor in the tops of his tall boots. The term was more common during the Prohibition era of the early twentieth century, but it is still used to mean *someone who unlawfully makes, sells, or transports alcoholic beverages without registration or payment of taxes.*

2. **bugbear** (bug'bâr') The word refers to *a source of fears, often groundless.* It comes from a Welsh legend about a goblin in the shape of a bear that ate up naughty children.

3. **fiasco** (fē as'kō) "Fiasco" is the Italian word for *flask* or *bottle.* How it came to mean *a complete and ignominious failure* is obscure. One theory suggests that Venetian glassblowers set aside fine glass with flaws to make into common bottles.

4. **jackanapes** (jak'ə nāps') Today the word is used to describe *an impertinent, presumptuous young man; a whippersnapper.* Although its precise origin is uncertain, we know that the term was first used as an uncomplimentary nickname for William de la Pole, Duke of Suffolk, who was murdered in 1450. His badge was an ape's clog and chain. In a poem of the time, Suffolk was called "the Apeclogge," and later referred to as an ape called "Jack Napes."

5. **jeroboam** (jer'ə bō'əm) We now use the term "jeroboam" to refer to *a wine bottle having a capacity of about three liters.* Historically, Jeroboam was the first king of the Biblical kingdom of Israel, described in I Kings 11:28 as "a mighty man of valor," who, three verses later, "made Israel to sin." Some authorities trace the origin of today's usage to the king, reasoning that since an oversized bottle of wine can cause sin, it too is a jeroboam.

6. **nonplus** (non plus', non'plus') The word "nonplus" means *to make utterly perplexed; to puzzle completely.* The original Latin phrase was "non plus ultra," meaning *no more beyond,* allegedly inscribed on the Pillars of Hercules, beyond which no ship could safely sail.

7. **quisling** (kwiz'ling) This term refers to *a traitor,* a person who betrays his or her own country by aiding an enemy and often serving later in a puppet government. It is directly derived from the name of Vidkun Quisling (1887–1945), a Norwegian army officer turned fascist who collaborated with the Nazis early in World War II.

8. **bowdlerize** (bōd'lə rīz', boud'-) In 1818, Scottish physician

Dr. Thomas Bowdler published a new edition of Shakespeare's works. The value of his edition, he stated, lay in the fact that he had edited it so that all "words and expressions are omitted which cannot with propriety be read aloud to the family." Good intentions aside, he found himself being held up to ridicule. From his name is derived the word "bowdlerize," meaning *to expurgate a literary text in a prudish manner.*

9. **boycott** (boi′kot) In an attempt to break the stranglehold of Ireland's absentee landlords, Charles Stewart Parnell advocated in 1880 that anyone who took over land from which a tenant had been evicted for nonpayment of rent should be punished "by isolating him from his kind as if he was a leper of old." The most famous application of Parnell's words occurred soon after on the estate of the Earl of Erne. Unable to pay their rents, the earl's tenants suggested a lower scale, but the manager of the estate, Captain Charles Cunningham Boycott, would not accept the reduction. In retaliation, the tenants applied the measures proposed by Parnell, not only refusing to gather crops and run the estate, but also intercepting Boycott's mail and food, humiliating him in the street, and threatening his life. Their treatment of Boycott became so famous that within a few months the newspapers were using his name to identify any such nonviolent coercive practices. Today "boycott" means *to join together in abstaining from, or preventing dealings with, as a protest.*

10. **chauvinism** (shō′və niz′əm) One of Napoleon's most dedicated soldiers, Nicolas Chauvin, was wounded seventeen times fighting for his emperor. After he retired from the army, he spoke so incessantly of the majestic glory of his leader and the greatness of France that he became a laughingstock. In 1831, his name was used for a character in a play who was an almost idolatrous worshiper of Napoleon. The word "chauvin" became associated with this type of extreme hero worship and exaggerated patriotism. Today we use the term "chauvinism" to refer to *zealous and belligerent nationalism.*

Quiz 1: Matching

Match each of the numbered words with its closest synonym. Write your answer in the space provided.

1. **bootlegger**	a. fanatical patriotism	_____
2. **bugbear**	b. total failure	_____

3. fiasco	c. expurgate	_____
4. jackanapes	d. groundless fear	_____
5. jeroboam	e. oversized wine bottle	_____
6. nonplus	f. unlawful producer of alcohol	_____
7. quisling	g. rude fellow	_____
8. bowdlerize	h. perplex	_____
9. boycott	i. traitor	_____
10. chauvinism	j. strike	_____

Quiz 2: True/False

In the space provided, write T if the definition of the numbered word is true or F if it is false.

		T or F
1. bowdlerize	expurgate	_____
2. boycott	male child	_____
3. bootlegger	petty thief	_____
4. fiasco	celebration	_____
5. chauvinism	fanatical patriotism	_____
6. jackanapes	jack-of-all-trades	_____
7. quisling	turncoat	_____
8. bugbear	baseless fear	_____
9. jeroboam	ancient queen	_____
10. nonplus	certain	_____

Lesson 2

The origins of the following words can be traced to Latin. Read through the histories, then complete the quizzes.

1. **aberration** (ab′ə rā′shən) This word comes from the Latin verb "aberrare," *to wander away from.* A person with a psychological "aberration" exhibits behavior that strays from the accepted path; hence the word means *deviation from what is common, normal, or right.*

2. **abominate** (ə bom′ə nāt′) "Abominate" is from the Latin "abominor," meaning *I pray that the event predicted by the omen may be averted.* The Romans murmured the word to keep away the evil spirits whenever anyone said something unlucky. Today we use it to mean *to regard with intense aversion or loathing; abhor.*

3. **impeccable** (im pek′ə bəl) The word comes from the Latin

"impeccabilis," *without sin.* The religious meaning has been only slightly extended over the years. Today an "impeccable" reputation is *faultless, flawless, irreproachable.*

4. **recalcitrant** (ri kal′si trənt) The word was formed from the Latin prefix "re-," *back,* and "calcitrare," *to kick.* Thus, a "recalcitrant" person is one who kicks back, resisting authority or control.

5. **ebullient** (i bul′yənt, i bool′-) This word derives from the Latin "ebullire," *to boil over.* A person who is "ebullient" is *overflowing with fervor, enthusiasm, or excitement.*

6. **enclave** (en′klāv, än′-) The word "enclave" refers to *a country or territory entirely or mostly surrounded by another country.* More generally, it means *a group enclosed or isolated within a larger one.* The word comes ultimately from Latin "inclavare," *to lock in.*

7. **expedite** (ek′spi dīt′) The word "expedite" means *to speed up the progress of something.* It comes from the Latin "expedire," *to set the feet free.*

8. **expunge** (ik spunj′) To indicate that a soldier had retired from service, the ancient Romans wrote a series of dots or points beneath his name on the service lists. The Latin "expungere" thus meant both *to prick through* and *to mark off on a list.* Similarly, the English word "expunge" means *to strike or blot out; to erase.*

9. **inchoate** (in kō′it, -āt) "Inchoate" comes from the Latin "inchoare," *to begin.* Thus, an "inchoate" plan is *not yet fully developed,* or *rudimentary.*

10. **prevaricate** (pri var′i kāt′) Today "prevaricate" means *to speak falsely or misleadingly with deliberate intent; to lie.* It has its origin in a physical act. The Latin verb "praevaricare" means *to spread apart.* The plowman who "prevaricated," then, made crooked ridges, deviating from straight furrows in the field.

Quiz 3: True/False

In the space provided, write T if the definition of the numbered word is true or F if it is false.

			T or F
1.	enclave	rendezvous	_____
2.	abominate	detest	_____
3.	recalcitrant	easygoing	_____
4.	expunge	erase	_____

5. prevaricate	preplan	_____
6. inchoate	illogical	_____
7. aberration	fidelity	_____
8. expedite	slow down	_____
9. impeccable	perfect	_____
10. ebullient	enthusiastic	_____

Quiz 4: Matching

Match each of the following numbered words with its closest synonym. Write your answer in the space provided.

1. recalcitrant	a. dispatch	_____
2. enclave	b. divergence	_____
3. inchoate	c. balky	_____
4. abominate	d. obliterate	_____
5. aberration	e. misstate	_____
6. impeccable	f. enclosure	_____
7. expunge	g. detest	_____
8. expedite	h. without fault	_____
9. ebullient	i. incipient	_____
10. prevaricate	j. high-spirited	_____

Lesson 3

Some of the most disarming words have their beginnings in historical events, myths and legends, and special terminology. Here are ten more powerful words with interesting or unusual histories. Read through their backgrounds, then complete the quizzes that follow.

1. **abracadabra** (ab′rə kə dab′rə) This intriguing-sounding word was first used as a charm in the second century. The Romans believed that the word had the ability to cure toothaches and other illnesses. Patients seeking relief wrote the letters in the form of a triangle on a piece of parchment and wore it around their necks on a length of thread. Today "abracadabra" is used as a pretend conjuring word. It also means *meaningless talk, nonsense.*

2. **ambrosia** (am brō′zhə) Originally, "ambrosia" was the food of the Olympian gods (as "nectar" was their drink). The word comes from the Greek "a," *not,* and "brostos," *mortal,* hence, eating ambrosia conferred immortality. Today the word means *an especially delicious food,* with the implication that the con-

coction is savory enough to be fit for the gods. A popular dessert by this name contains shredded coconut, sliced fruits, and cream.

3. **gerrymander** (jer′i man′dər, ger′-) In 1812, Massachusetts governor Elbridge Gerry conspired with party members in order to change the boundaries of voting districts to enhance their own political clout. Noticing that one such district resembled a salamander, a newspaper editor coined the term "gerrymander" to describe *the practice of dividing a state, county, etc., into election districts so as to give one political party a majority while concentrating the voting strength of the other party into as few districts as possible.*

4. **mesmerize** (mez′mə rīz′, mes′-) The Austrian doctor Friedrich Anton Mesmer first publicly demonstrated the technique of hypnotism in 1775. Today the term "mesmerize" is still used as a synonym for *hypnotize,* but it has broadened to also mean *spellbind* or *fascinate.*

5. **quintessence** (kwin tes′əns) The word comes from the medieval Latin term "quinta essentia," *the fifth essence.* This fifth primary element was thought to be ether, supposedly the constituent matter of the heavenly bodies, the other four elements being air, fire, earth, and water. The medieval alchemists tried to isolate ether through distillation. These experiments gave us the contemporary meaning of "quintessence": *the pure and concentrated essence of a substance; the most perfect embodiment of something.*

6. **desultory** (des′əl tôr′ē) Some Roman soldiers went into battle with two horses, so that when one steed wearied, the soldier could vault onto the second horse striding along parallel to the first without losing any time. The same skill was employed by circus performers, especially charioteers, who could leap between two chariots riding abreast. Such a skilled horseman was called a "desultor," *a leaper.* Perhaps because these equestrians stayed only briefly on their mounts, the word "desultory" acquired its present meaning: *lacking in consistency, constancy, or visible order.*

7. **aegis** (ē′jis) When Zeus emerged victorious from his rebellion against the Titans, he attributed his success in part to his shield, which bore at its center the head of one of the Gorgons. The shield was reputedly made of goatskin, and hence its name, "aigis," was said to derive from the Greek "aig-," the stem of "aix," *goat.* Our present use of the word to mean

protection or *sponsorship* evolved from the notion of eighteenth-century English writers who assumed that the "egis" of Zeus or Athena—or their Roman counterparts Jove and Minerva—protected all those who came under its influence. Today the preferred spelling of the word is "aegis."

8. **utopia** (yōo tō'pē ə) Sir Thomas More (1478–1535) was one of the great humanists of the Renaissance era in England. More held important government offices under Henry VIII, but as a devout Roman Catholic, he refused to accept the Act of Supremacy, which made the king the head of the English Church. He was imprisoned in the Tower of London and ultimately beheaded under a charge of treason. His *Utopia* (1516) is an account of an ideal state founded entirely on reason. More derived the title of his masterpiece from the Greek for "not a place." The popularity of this specific work has transformed the word "utopia" into a generic term meaning *any ideal place or state; a visionary system of social or political perfection.*

9. **aloof** (ə lōōf') This was originally a sailor's term, "a loof," *to the luff or windward direction,* perhaps from the Dutch "te loef," *to windward.* Etymologists believe that our use of the word to mean *at a distance, especially in feeling or interest,* comes from the idea of keeping a ship's head to the wind, and thus clear of the lee shore toward which it might drift.

10. **bluestocking** (blōo'stok'ing) A "bluestocking" is *a woman with considerable scholarly, literary, or intellectual ability or interest.* The word originated in connection with intellectual gatherings held in London about 1750 in the homes of women bored by the more frivolous pastimes of their age. Lavish evening dress was not required at these affairs; in fact, to put at ease visitors who could not afford expensive clothing, the women themselves dressed simply. One of the male guests went so far as to wear his everyday blue worsted stockings rather than the black silk ones usually worn at evening social gatherings. In response to their interests and dress, the English naval officer Admiral Edward Boscawen (1711–61) is said to have sarcastically called these gatherings "the Blue Stocking Society."

Quiz 5: Definitions

Select the best definition for each numbered word. Write your answer in the space provided.

1. mesmerize   _____
   a. attack   b. burst forth   c. fascinate
2. desultory   _____
   a. aggressive   b. fitful   c. nasty
3. aloof   _____
   a. remote   b. sailing   c. windy
4. aegis   _____
   a. intense interest   b. goat   c. sponsorship
5. gerrymander   _____
   a. medieval gargoyle   b. combine for historical sense
   c. redistrict for political advantage
6. abracadabra   _____
   a. beauty   b. hocus pocus   c. boredom
7. utopia   _____
   a. paradise   b. hell   c. delicious food
8. ambrosia   _____
   a. suppository   b. flower   c. delicious food
9. quintessence   _____
   a. pith   b. fruit   c. oil
10. bluestocking   _____
   a. chic woman   b. intellectual woman   c. poor man

Quiz 6: Matching

Select the best synonym for each numbered word. Write your answer in the space provided.

1. **utopia**	a. delicious food	_____
2. **aloof**	b. inconsistent; random	_____
3. **gerrymander**	c. distant; remote	_____
4. **ambrosia**	d. ideal state	_____
5. **abracadabra**	e. sponsorship	_____
6. **bluestocking**	f. enthrall	_____
7. **desultory**	g. mumbo-jumbo	_____
8. **aegis**	h. concentrated essence	_____
9. **mesmerize**	i. divide a political district	_____
10. **quintessence**	j. a well-read woman	_____

Lesson 4

The following words are all based on Greek myths and legends. Read through their histories, then complete the quizzes.

1. **amazon** (am′ə zon′) The word comes ultimately from the Greek, but the origin of the Greek word is uncertain. "Amazon" refers to *a tall, powerful, aggressive woman.* The Amazons of legend were female warriors who were allied with the Trojans against the Greeks.

2. **herculean** (hûr′ kyə lē′ ən) Hercules, who was by far the most popular of all Greek heroes, is often portrayed as a muscular he-man wearing a lion skin and bearing a huge club. As an infant, he strangled two serpents in his cradle. Later, he performed the prodigious twelve labors, slaying one monster after another and cleansing the Augean stables to gain immortality among the gods. Sophocles, Euripides, and Seneca all celebrated his exploits in their plays. We use the word "herculean" to mean *of enormous power, size, or courage,* or to describe a task *requiring extraordinary strength or exertion.*

3. **cornucopia** (kôr′nə kō′pē ə, -nyə-) According to Greek mythology, to save the infant Zeus from being swallowed by his father Cronus, his mother, Rhea, hid her son in a cave and tricked Cronus into swallowing a stone wrapped in a cloth. The infant was then entrusted to the care of the nymph Amaltheia, who fed him on goat's milk. One day she filled a goat's horn with fresh fruit and herbs. The horn was thereafter magically refilled, no matter how much the child ate. To the Greeks, this boundless source was the horn of Amaltheia; to the Romans, it was the "cornu copiae," from "cornu," *horn,* and "copia," *plenty.* We know a "cornucopia" as *a horn containing food or drink in endless supply* or *horn of plenty.* It is often used as a symbol of abundance.

4. **diadem** (dī′ə dem′) In his quest to create a vast, unified empire with Babylon as its capital, the Macedonian hero Alexander the Great adopted a number of Persian and Oriental customs. He began to wear a blue-edged white headband with two ends trailing to the shoulders, a Persian symbol of royalty. The Greeks called this headpiece a "diadema," literally *a binding over.* The headpiece was adopted by other monarchs down through the ages and further embellished with gold and gems, eventually evolving into a rich crown. Today a "diadem" is *a crown* or *a headband worn as a symbol of royalty.*

5. **epicure** (ep′i kyo͞or′) Epicurus was a Greek philosopher who lived from 342 to 270 B.C. He believed that pleasure, attained

mainly through pure and noble thoughts, constituted the highest happiness. After his death, his disciples spread his views. Their critics argued that Epicurus's theory was little more than an excuse for debauchery. From this argument we derive the present-day meaning of "epicure," *a person with luxurious tastes or habits, especially in eating or drinking.*

6. **esoteric** (es′ə ter′ik) From the Greek "esoterikos," *inner,* the word was used to describe the secret doctrines taught by the philosopher Pythagoras to a select few of his disciples. Hence "esoteric" means *understood by or meant only for those who have special knowledge or interest: recondite.*

7. **labyrinth** (lab′ə rinth′) According to the Greek myth, King Minos of Crete ordered Daedalus to build a prison for the Minotaur, a half-bull, half-human monster. Daedalus succeeded by creating a series of twisting passageways that kept the monster imprisoned. Today a "labyrinth" is *a devious arrangement of linear patterns forming a design; a maze.*

8. **lethargy** (leth′ər jē) The Greeks believed in an afterlife. In their mythology, the dead crossed the river Lethe, which flowed through Hades, the underground realm. Anyone who drank its water forgot the past. The Greek word "lethargia" derives from "lethe," *forgetfulness.* Hence our English word "lethargy," *drowsiness* or *sluggishness.*

9. **mentor** (men′tôr, -tər) In the *Odyssey* of Homer, Mentor is Odysseus's friend and tutor to his son Telemachus. Today the word "mentor" means *trusted teacher or guide.*

10. **nemesis** (nem′ə sis) Nemesis was the Greek goddess of vengeance, whose task it was to punish the proud and the insolent. Today a "nemesis" is *an agent or act of retribution or punishment,* or *something that a person cannot conquer or achieve.*

Quiz 7: True/False

In the space provided, write T if the definition of the numbered word is true or F if it is false.

			T or F
1.	**diadem**	crown	_____
2.	**labyrinth**	lazy	_____
3.	**mentor**	mendacious	_____
4.	**amazon**	female warrior	_____
5.	**herculean**	puny	_____

6. esoteric	arcane	_____
7. lethargy	lassitude	_____
8. nemesis	downfall	_____
9. cornucopia	foot ailment	_____
10. epicure	hidden	_____

Quiz 8: Defining Words

Define each of the following words.

1. diadem _____

2. esoteric _____

3. mentor _____

4. nemesis _____

5. amazon _____

6. epicure _____

7. herculean _____

8. cornucopia _____

9. labyrinth _____

10. lethargy _____

Suggested Answers 1. crown 2. meant only for the select few with special knowledge or interest 3. trusted teacher or guide 4. act of retribution, or that which a person cannot conquer or achieve 5. female warrior 6. a person with luxurious tastes or habits, especially in eating or drinking 7. strong; powerful; courageous; mighty; difficult 8. boundless source 9. maze 10. sluggishness; weariness

Lesson 5

Now study the curious origins of these ten words and work through the two quizzes that follow.

1. **ostracize** (os'trə sīz') The word "ostracize" comes originally from the Greek "ostrakon," *tile, potsherd, shell.* It refers to the ancient Greek practice of banishing a man by writing his name on a shell or a bit of earthen tile. Anyone considered dangerous to the state was sent into exile for ten years. The judges cast their votes by writing on the shells or pottery shards and dropping them into an urn. The word "ostracize" still retains the same sense, *to exclude, by general consent, from society.*

2. **sycophant** (sik′ə fənt, -fant′) The word "sycophant" now means *a self-seeking, servile flatterer.* Originally, it was used to refer to an informer or slanderer. Curiously, it comes from Greek "sykon," *fig,* and "-phantes," *one who shows;* thus, *a fig-shower.* One explanation for this odd coinage is that in ancient Greece a sycophant was an informer against merchants engaged in the unlawful exportation of figs.

3. **cynosure** (sī′nə sho͞or′, sin′ə-) According to the myth, Zeus chose to honor the nymph who cared for him in his infancy by placing her in the sky as a constellation. One of her stars was so brilliant and stationary that all the other stars seemed to revolve around it. To the practical-minded ancient mariners, however, the bottom three stars of the constellation looked like a dog's tail. They named the entire constellation "Cynosura," *dog's tail.* From its name we get our word "cynosure," *something that attracts attention by its brilliance or interest.* By the way, we now call the constellation "Ursa Minor," *Little Bear,* and the bright star "Polaris," *Pole Star* or *North Star.*

4. **Hobson's choice** (hob′sənz) Thomas Hobson (1544–1631) was a stable owner in Cambridge, England, who gave his name to this very useful, pithy phrase meaning *the choice of taking that which is offered or nothing at all; the lack of a real alternative.* Hobson gave his customers only one choice of a mount: that of the horse nearest the stable door. In a charming 1954 film of this title directed by David Lean, Charles Laughton hams it up as a prosperous but dipsomaniacal bootmaker hoist by his own petard when he banishes his oldest spinster daughter after she marries his best cobbler. When Hobson (the bootmaker) refuses to deal fairly with their demands for more equitable treatment as the mainstays of the business, the young couple set up in a nearby shop of their own that steals away his former customers. In the end, Hobson's choice is unavoidable and nonnegotiable: he is forced to turn over his shop to the clever couple and retire from business.

5. **tantalize** (tan′tl īz′) For his transgressions against the Greek god Zeus, Tantalus was condemned to Tartarus, where he stood in a pool with his chin level with the water, eternally parched with thirst. When he bowed his head to drink, the water ebbed away. Above his head were trees laden with juicy fruits, but when he tried to seize them, the wind swept

them out of his reach. From this hellish dilemma, we derive the word "tantalize," *to torment with the sight of something desired but out of reach; tease by arousing expectations.*

6. **eldorado** (el'də rä'dō, -rä'-) The word comes from Spanish legends of an incredibly wealthy city in South America, so rich that its streets were paved with gold. Many adventurers set off to find this elusive city; in 1595 Sir Walter Raleigh ventured into Guiana in a vain attempt to locate it. Among the Spaniards, the king of this fabulous land came to be called "El Dorado," *the Golden One.* Today "eldorado" is used generally to mean *any fabulously wealthy place.*

7. **mercurial** (mər kyo͞or'ē əl) Even schoolchildren are familiar with the character of the Mad Hatter from Lewis Carroll's account of *Alice's Adventures in Wonderland* and the concomitant phrase "as mad as a hatter," but few people are aware that the phrase had a basis in reality: many hatmakers indeed were known to go mad as a result of the use of mercury, a poisonous substance, in their work. The celebrated English physicist and mathematician Sir Isaac Newton (1642–1727) was also known to behave somewhat strangely at times following his scientific experiments with mercury. Today we use the word "mercurial" to mean *changeable; fickle; flighty; erratic* or sometimes *animated; lively.*

8. **filibuster** (fil'ə bus'tər) In the seventeenth century, English seamen who attacked Spanish ships and brought back wealth from New Spain were called "buccaneers." In Holland, they were known as "vrijbuiters," *free robbers.* In French, the word became first "fribustier" and then "flibuster." In Spain, the term was "filibustero." Then, when the nineteenth-century American soldier of fortune William Walker tried to capture Sonora, Mexico, the Mexicans promptly dubbed him a "filibuster." Today the term refers to *the use of irregular or disruptive tactics, such as exceptionally long speeches, by a member of a legislative assembly.* The current use of the word may have arisen through a comparison of a legislator's determination to block a bill with the tactics used by William Walker to evade the law.

9. **sophistry** (sof'ə strē) In the fifth century B.C.E., the Sophists were peripatetic Greek teachers paid to instruct the sons of the upper class who sought political and legal careers in pragmatic rhetorical skills. They sought knowledge primar-

ily as a source of intellectual amusement, power, and social prominence. Thus, they were noted more for their ingenuity and speciousness in argumentation than their desire to discover the truth or establish moral principles. Some of them even boasted that they could "make the worst appear the better reason." Gorgias, one of the leading lights of the Sophist school, argued that nothing exists and nothing is knowable, since reality is entirely relative to the subjective experience of the individual. Not surprisingly, Socrates, who would accept no payment for his teaching, regarded their influence as pernicious. The current meaning of "sophistry," therefore, is *a subtle, tricky, superficially plausible but generally fallacious method of reasoning; a false argument or fallacy.*

10. **galvanize** (gal′və nīz′) In the mid-eighteenth century, Luigi Galvani, a professor of anatomy at the University of Bologna, concluded that the nerves are a source of electricity. Although Volta later proved his theory incorrect, Galvani's pioneering work inspired other scientists to produce electricity by chemical means. From the old-fashioned term "galvanism," *electricity,* which honors Galvani, we have derived the word "galvanize," *to stimulate; startle into activity.*

Quiz 9: Definitions

Each of the following phrases contains an italicized word. See how many you can define correctly. Write your answer in the space provided.

_____ 1. accept a *Hobson's choice*
a. firm offer   b. victory   c. nonnegotiable demand   d. hobbled horse

_____ 2. *ostracized* from society
a. banished   b. beaten   c. walked
d. welcomed

_____ 3. a shameless *sycophant*
a. dreamer   b. alcoholic   c. romantic
d. toady

_____ 4. clever *sophistry*
a. embroidery   b. truth   c. teaching
d. fallacy

_____ 5. seek *eldorado*
a. physical comfort   b. delicious food
c. wealthy place   d. death

_____ 6. a *mercurial* disposition
 a. erratic   b. happy   c. sour   d. steady
_____ 7. *tantalize* with promises
 a. frighten   b. tease   c. emboldon
 d. discourage
_____ 8. a lengthy *filibuster*
 a. entertainment   b. obstructive tactics
 c. childhood   d. voyage
_____ 9. *galvanize* the crowd
 a. stir up   b. silence   c. insult   d. bore
_____ 10. the *cynosure* of all eyes
 a. defect   b. attraction   c. sky-blue color
 d. cynicism

Quiz 10: True/False

In the space provided, write T if the definition of the numbered word is true or F if it is false.

		T or F
1. Hobson's choice	lack of alternative	_____
2. tantalize	tempt	_____
3. mercurial	unpredictable	_____
4. ostracize	exclude	_____
5. filibuster	obstruction	_____
6. sophistry	specious reasoning	_____
7. cynosure	sarcasm	_____
8. eldorado	Spain	_____
9. galvanize	pulverize	_____
10. sycophant	flatterer	_____

Lesson 6

Exotic words not only impress your listeners and readers; they also help to stretch your own imagination. Here are ten new ones to add to your growing vocabulary. Read through the etymologies and complete the two quizzes that follow.

1. **juggernaut** (jug′ər nôt′, -not′) Our modern word "juggernaut" comes from the Hindi name for a huge image of the god Vishnu, "Jagannath," at Puri, a city in Orissa, India. Each summer, the statue is moved to a new location a little less than a mile away from the old one. Early tourists to India brought back strange stories of worshipers throwing them-

selves under the wheels of the wagon carrying the idol. Since any shedding of blood in the presence of the god is sacrilege, what these travelers probably witnessed was a weary pilgrim being accidentally crushed to death. Thus, thanks to exaggeration and ignorance, "juggernaut" came to mean *blind and relentless self-sacrifice.* More often it is used to mean *any large, overpowering, or destructive force.*

2. **iconoclast** (ī kon'ə klast') An "iconoclast" is *a person who attacks cherished beliefs or traditional institutions.* It is from the Greek "eikon," *image,* and "klastes," *breaker.* Although the contemporary usage is figurative, the word was originally used in a literal sense to describe the great controversy within the Christian church in the eighth century over religious images. One camp held that all visual representations should be destroyed because they encouraged idol worship; the other, that such artworks simply inspired the viewers to feel more religious. By the mid-eighth century, untold numbers of relics and images had been destroyed. The issue was not settled for nearly a century, when the images were restored to the church in Constantinople.

3. **laconic** (lə kon'ik) In Sparta, the capital of the ancient Greek region of Laconia, the children were trained in endurance, cunning, modesty, and self-restraint. From the terse style of speech and writing of the Laconians we derive the English word "laconic." Today the word retains this meaning, *expressing much in few words.*

4. **gamut** (gam'ət) Guido of Arezzo, one of the greatest musicians of medieval times, is credited with being first to use the lines of the staff and the spaces between them. He used the Greek letter "gamma" for the lowest tone in the scale. This note was called "gamma ut." Contracted to "gamut," it then designated the entire scale. The word quickly took on a figurative as well as a literal sense. Today "gamut" is defined as *the entire scale or range,* as in the phrase "to run the gamut."

5. **guillotine** (gil'ə tēn', gē'ə-) After the outbreak of the French Revolution, Dr. Joseph Ignace Guillotin became a member of the National Assembly. During an early debate, he proposed that future executions in France be conducted by a humane beheading machine that he had seen in operation in another country. His suggestion was received favorably; in 1791, after Dr. Guillotin had retired from public service, the machine that bears his name was designed by Antoine Louis

and built by a German named Schmidt. The guillotine was first used in 1792 to behead a thief. At that time, the device was called a "Louisette" after its designer; but the public began calling it after Dr. Guillotin, the man who had first advocated its use. The device proved so popular among the masses, it seemed to demand more victims to satisfy their blood lust. During the subsequent Reign of Terror, more than 17,000 people were guillotined, including Robespierre, the author of the Terror.

6. **horde** (hôrd) Upon the death of Genghis Khan, his grandson Batu Khan led the Mongol invasion of Europe, cutting a merciless swath from Moscow to Hungary. At each post, Batu erected a sumptuous tent made of silk and leather. His followers called it the "sira ordu," *the silken camp.* In Czech and Polish the Turkic "ordu" was changed to "horda." The name came to be applied not only to Batu's tent but also to his entire Mongol army. Because of the terror they inspired across the land, "horde" eventually referred to any Tartar tribe. Today, it means *any large crowd; swarm.*

7. **lyceum** (lī sē′əm) The Lyceum was the shrine dedicated to Apollo by the Athenians. The name came from the Greek "Lykeion," meaning *Wolf Slayer,* a nickname of Apollo. The shrine was a favorite haunt of the Athenian philosophers, especially Aristotle, who taught his disciples while walking along its paths. Thus, the word "lyceum" came to mean *an institute for popular education, providing discussions, lectures, concerts, and so forth.* The term is most popular in New England, and is often used as a proper name for theaters.

8. **macabre** (mə kä′brə, -kä′bər) In modern usage, "macabre" means *gruesome and horrible; pertaining to death.* Its history is uncertain. However, most etymologists believe that the word's use in the French phrase "Danse Macabre," *dance of Macabre,* a translation of Medieval Latin "chorea Macchabeorum," connects the word with the Maccabees, the leaders of the Jewish rebellion against Syria about 165 B.C., whose death as martyrs is vividly described in the Book of Maccabees (a part of the Apocrypha).

9. **gargantuan** (gär gan′chōō ən) The sixteenth-century French writer François Rabelais created a giant he named "Gargantua" after a legendary giant of the Middle Ages. To fuel his enormous bulk—Gargantua rode on a horse as large as six

elephants—he had to consume prodigious amounts of food and drink. Today we use the word "gargantuan" to mean *gigantic, enormous.*

10. **libertine** (lib'ər tēn') In ancient Rome, "libertinus" referred to a freed slave. Since those freed from slavery were unlikely to be strict observers of the laws that had enslaved them in the first place, "libertine" came to designate *a person who is morally or sexually unrestrained.*

Quiz 11: Matching

Match each of the numbered words with its closest synonym. Write your answer in the space provided.

1. lyceum	a. skeptic	_____
2. libertine	b. academy	_____
3. iconoclast	c. overpowering force	_____
4. horde	d. terse	_____
5. gargantuan	e. gruesome	_____
6. laconic	f. dissolute person	_____
7. guillotine	g. beheading machine	_____
8. juggernaut	h. entire range	_____
9. gamut	i. huge	_____
10. macabre	j. crowd	_____

Quiz 12: Defining Words

Define each of the following words

1. iconoclast _____

2. libertine _____

3. gamut _____

4. macabre _____

5. guillotine _____

6. laconic _____

7. gargantuan _____

8. lyceum _____

9. horde _____

10. juggernaut _____

Suggested Answers 1. a person who attacks cherished beliefs or traditional institutions 2. a rake 3. the entire scale or range 4. horrible, gruesome 5. a machine used to behead criminals 6. terse 7. enormous, colossal 8. institute for popular education 9. large group 10. an overpowering force

Lesson 7

The English language has adopted a prodigious number of words from unexpected sources, including literary works. Read through the histories of the ten unusual words that follow and then complete the quizzes.

1. **imp** (imp) In Old English, an "imp" was originally a young plant or seedling. Eventually, the term came to be used figuratively to indicate a descendant of a royal house, usually a male. Probably because of the behavior of such children, the word became synonymous with a young demon. Since the sixteenth century, the original meaning of "imp" as *scion* has been completely dropped, and the word is now used exclusively to mean *a little devil or demon, an evil spirit,* or *an urchin.*

2. **kaleidoscope** (kə lī′də skōp′) Invented in 1816 by Scottish physicist Sir David Brewster, the "kaleidoscope" is a scientific toy constructed of a series of mirrors within a tube. When the tube is turned by hand, symmetrical, ever-changing patterns can be viewed through the eyepiece. Brewster named his toy from the Greek "kalos," *beautiful;* "eidos," *form;* and "skopos," *watcher.* In general, we use the term to mean *a continually shifting pattern or scene.*

3. **knave** (nāv) In Old English, the word "knave" (then spelled "cnafa") referred to *a male child, a boy.* It was later applied to *a boy or man employed as a servant.* Many of these boys had to be wily to survive their hard lot; thus the word gradually evolved to mean *a rogue* or *rascal.*

4. **Machiavellian** (mak′ē ə vel′ē ən) The Florentine political philosopher Nicolò Machiavelli (1469–1527) was a fervent supporter of a united Italy. Unfortunately, his methods for achieving his goals placed political expediency over morality. His masterpiece, *The Prince* (1513), advocated deception and hypocrisy on the grounds that the end justifies the means. Therefore, the adjective "Machiavellian" means *unscrupulous, cunning,* and *deceptive in the pursuit of power.*

5. **indolence** (in′dl əns) Originally, "indolence" meant *indifference.* The word was used in that sense until the sixteenth century. Probably because indifference is frequently accompanied by an unwillingness to bestir oneself, the term has now come to mean *lazy* or *slothful.*

6. **incubus/succubus** (in′kyə bəs, ing′-; suk′yə bəs) In the Middle Ages, women were thought to give birth to witches after being visited in their sleep by an "incubus," or *evil male spirit.* The female version of this spirit, said to be the cause of nightmares, was a "succubus." Because the evil spirit pressed upon the sleeper's body and soul, the term "incubus" also means *something that oppresses like a nightmare.*

7. **hoyden** (hoid′n) A "hoyden" is *a boisterous, ill-bred girl; a tomboy.* The word is usually linked to the Dutch "heyden," meaning *a rustic person* or *rude peasant,* originally *a heathen* or *pagan,* and is related to the English word "heathen." At first in English the word meant *a rude, boorish man,* but beginning in the 1600s it was applied to girls in the sense of *a tomboy.* How the change came about is uncertain.

8. **Faustian** (fou′stē ən) The story of Dr. Faustus, a medieval alchemist or magician who sold his soul to the devil in exchange for knowledge and power, has its roots in German legend. Its most famous interpretations are to be found in the works of the English dramatist Christopher Marlowe (c. 1558) and the German poet Goethe (1770 and 1831), but the theme has proved so enduring that it found a new popularity in the mid-twentieth-century Broadway musical *Damn Yankees,* about a ballplayer willing to trade his soul for a pennant win over the then-indomitable New York Yankees. A "Faustian" bargain, therefore, is one *sacrificing spiritual values for power, knowledge, or material gain.* The word may also mean *characterized by spiritual dissatisfaction or torment,* or *obsessed with a hunger for knowledge or mastery.*

9. **macadam** (mə kad′əm) While experimenting with methods of improving road construction, John McAdam, a Scotsman, concluded that the prevailing practice of placing a base of large stones under a layer of small stones was unnecessary. As surveyor-general for the roads of Bristol, England, in the early nineteenth century, McAdam built roads using only six to ten inches of small crushed stones, thereby eliminating the cost of constructing the base. Not only were the results impressive, the savings were so remarkable that his idea soon spread to other countries. McAdam's experiments led to our use of the term "macadam" for *a road or pavement* of compacted crushed stones, usually bound with asphalt or tar.

10. **albatross** (al′bə trôs′) Generations of students have enjoyed "The Rime of the Ancient Mariner" by Samuel Taylor Coleridge (1772–1834). One of the seminal works of the Romantic movement in England, this haunting, dreamlike poem tells the tale of a sailor forced by his shipmates to wear suspended from his neck the corpse of the albatross, or frigate bird, that he carelessly shot down with his cross-bow. Since seamen traditionally regarded the bird as a lucky omen, they attributed the many disasters that befell the ship thereafter to the man who killed it. The poem is so famous and beloved that the word "albatross" has come to mean *a seemingly inescapable moral or emotional burden, as of guilt or responsibility; a burden that impedes action or progress.*

Quiz 13: True/False

In the space provided, write T if the definition of the numbered word is true or F if it is false.

			T or F
1.	incubus	evil spirit	_____
2.	hoyden	howl	_____
3.	Faustian	swift	_____
4.	macadam	raincoat	_____
5.	albatross	reward	_____
6.	imp	male servant	_____
7.	Machiavellian	principled	_____
8.	kaleidoscope	optical toy	_____
9.	indolence	laziness	_____
10.	knave	dishonest fellow	_____

Quiz 14: Matching

Select the best definition for each numbered word. Write your answer in the space provided.

1. macadam	a. burden	_____
2. hoyden	b. little mischiefmaker	_____
3. Faustian	c. laziness	_____
4. albatross	d. optical toy	_____
5. Machiavellian	e. pavement	_____
6. imp	f. rogue	_____
7. kaleidoscope	g. evil spirit	_____
8. knave	h. materialistic	_____
9. indolence	i. sly and crafty	_____
10. incubus	j. tomboy	_____

Lesson 8

Our language is not only a record of our past; it is also a living organism that morphs over time to accommodate new usages. Follow the evolution of these ten words by studying their histories; then complete the quizzes that follow.

1. **maelstrom** (mâl'strəm) The word's figurative meaning, *a restless, disordered state of affairs,* is derived from its literal one. Today's meaning comes from "Maelstrom," the name of a strong tidal current off the coast of Norway. The current creates a powerful whirlpool because of its configuration. According to legend, the current was once so strong that it could sink any vessel that ventured near it.

2. **insolent** (in'sə lənt) The word comes from the Latin "insolentem," which literally meant *not according to custom.* Since those who violate custom are likely to offend, "insolent" evolved to imply that the person was also vain and conceited. From this meaning we derive our present usage, *contemptuously rude or impertinent in speech or behavior.*

3. **interloper** (in'tər lō'pər) The word "interloper" was used in the late sixteenth century to describe Spanish traders who carved out for themselves a piece of the successful trade the British had established with the Russians. The word was formed on the analogy of "landloper," meaning *one who trespasses on another's land,* from a Dutch word literally meaning *land runner.* Although the dispute over the Spanish intrusion was settled within a few years, the word remained in use to mean *a person who intrudes into some region or field of trade without a proper license; one who thrusts himself or herself into the affairs of others.*

4. **halcyon** (hal'sē ən) According to classical mythology, the demigod Halcyone threw herself into the sea when she saw the drowned body of her beloved mortal husband. After her tragic death, the gods changed Halcyone and her husband into birds, which they called "halcyons," our present-day kingfishers. The Greeks believed the sea calmed as the birds built their nests and hatched their eggs upon its waves during the seven days before and after the winter solstice. This period came to be known as "halcyon days." The adjective is now used to mean *calm, peaceful, prosperous,* or *joyful.*

5. **hector** (hek'tər) Hector was a great Trojan hero, son of King

Priam. As Homer recounts in the *Iliad*, Hector took advantage of his enemy Achilles's departure from the Greek camp to drive the Greeks back to their ships and slay Achilles's dearest friend, Patroclus. To the Romans, who regarded themselves as descendants of the Trojans, Hector was a symbol of courage. But in the seventeenth century, the name was applied to the gangs of bullies who terrorized anyone who ventured into the back streets of London. It is to their transgressions that we owe the present use of "hector," *to harass or persecute.*

6. **helpmeet** (help'mēt') This synonym for *helpmate, companion, wife,* or *husband* is the result of a misunderstanding. The word comes from Genesis 2:18, "And the Lord God said, It is not good that the man should be alone; I will make him an help meet for him." In this passage, "meet" means *proper* or *appropriate,* but the two words came to be read as one, resulting in the word's current spelling.

7. **hermetic** (hûr met'ik) The Greeks linked the Egyptian god Thoth with Hermes, calling him "Hermes Trismegistus," Hermes Three-Times Greatest. He was accepted as the author of the books that made up the sum of Egyptian learning, called the "Hermetic Books." Since these forty-two works largely concerned the occult sciences, "hermetic" came to mean *secret,* and in a later usage, *made airtight by fusion or sealing.*

8. **intransigent** (in tran'si jənt) When Amadeus, the son of Victor Emmanuel II of Italy, was forced to abdicate the throne of Spain in 1873, those favoring a republic attempted to establish a political party. This group was called in Spanish "los intransigentes" (from "in," *not* and "transigente," *compromising*) because they could not come to terms with the other political parties. The term passed into English as "intransigent." Today the word retains the same meaning: *uncompromising* or *inflexible.*

9. **jitney** (jit'nē) The origin of this term has long baffled etymologists. The word first appeared in American usage in the first decade of the twentieth century as a slang term for a nickel. It then became associated with the public motor vehicles whose fare was five cents. Some authorities have theorized that the term is a corruption of "jeton," the French word for *token.* Today a "jitney" is *a small passenger bus following a regular route at varying hours.*

10. **junket** (jung′kit) At first, the word referred to a basket of woven reeds used for carrying fish; it is ultimately derived from Latin "juncus," *reed*. Then the basket was used to prepare cheese, which in turn came to be called "junket." Since the basket also suggested the food it could carry, "junket" later evolved to mean *a great feast*. Today we use the term in closely related meanings: *a sweet custard-like food* or *flavored milk curdled with rennet* or *a pleasure excursion*.

Quiz 15: Matching

Match each numbered word with its closest synonym. Write your answer in the space provided.

1. halcyon	a. tightly sealed	_____
2. intransigent	b. intruder	_____
3. jitney	c. impertinent	_____
4. maelstrom	d. peaceful	_____
5. junket	e. inflexible	_____
6. hector	f. small bus	_____
7. insolent	g. companion	_____
8. hermetic	h. pleasure trip	_____
9. interloper	i. harass	_____
10. helpmeet	j. disorder	_____

Quiz 16: True/False

In the space provided, write T if the definition of the numbered word is true or F if it is false.

		T or F
1. halcyon	calm	_____
2. jitney	juggler	_____
3. maelstrom	masculine	_____
4. intransigent	uncompromising	_____
5. insolent	rude	_____
6. interloper	welcome guest	_____
7. junket	refuse	_____
8. hector	helper	_____
9. hermetic	airtight	_____
10. helpmeet	newcomer	_____

Lesson 9

Once you know the origins of these ten words, it should be easier to remember their current meanings. Complete the quizzes to reinforce your memory.

1. **Olympian** (ə lim′pē ən) In Greek mythology, the snow-topped summit of Olympus, a mountain range in northern Greece, eclipsed from the sight of mortal humans by a perpetual cloud cover, was the dwelling place of the gods. The divine family of twelve deities was headed by the all-powerful Zeus and his queen Hera. Poseidon ruled the sea and Pluto the underworld. Ares, Hermes, Apollo, Hephaestus, Athena, Aphrodite, Artemis, and Dionysus occupied the lower echelons of the pantheon. Our word "Olympian," meaning *majestic; aloof; disdainful; haughty,* reflects the remote grandeur of the far-removed mountain abode of these immortal beings.

2. **Pollyanna** (pol′ē an′ə) Pollyanna, the child heroine created by the U.S. writer Eleanor Porter (1868–1920), was immortalized on the silver screen in 1960 by the young Hayley Mills. An orphan who comes to live with her strict, dour, but very rich and influential aunt, the high-spirited girl gradually wins over the unhappy townspeople and even her mean old aunt with her ingenuous charm and cheerful outlook. Since many adult readers tend to find the story somewhat treacly, a "Pollyanna" now means *an excessively or blindly optimistic person.*

3. **garret** (gar′it) Originally, the French word "garite" referred to a watchtower from which a sentry could look out for approaching enemies. Among the linguistic innovations the Normans brought when they conquered England was the word "garite." In England the word came to mean a *loft* or *attic,* and its spelling was altered to "garret."

4. **lilliputian** (lil′i pyōō′shən) *Gulliver's Travels,* the enduring masterpiece by Jonathan Swift (1667–1745), is a scathing satire on politics and society that purports to be an account of the voyages of a naive traveler named Lemuel Gulliver to Brobdinag, a land of giants, and Lilliput, a country inhabited by people who measure around six inches tall. In honor of this Swiftian work, we use the word "lilliputian" to refer first of all to a person or thing that is *extremely small* but also one that is *narrow; petty; trivial.*

5. **gazette** (gə zet′) In the beginning of the sixteenth century, Venetians circulated a small tin coin of little value they called a "gazzetta," a diminutive of the word "gaza," magpie. Soon after, the government began to print official bulletins with news of battles, elections, and so forth. Because the cost of the newspaper was one gazzetta, the leaflet itself eventually came to be called a "gazzetta." By the end of the century, the term was used in England as well. The present spelling is the result of French influence. Today a "gazette" refers to *a newspaper* or *official government journal.*

6. **martinet** (mär′tn et′, mär′tn et′) In a move to improve his army, in 1660 Louis XIV hired Colonel Jean Martinet, a successful infantry leader, to devise a drill for France's soldiers. Martinet drilled his soldiers to such exacting standards that his name came to be applied to any officer intent on maintaining military discipline or precision. Thus, in English, a "martinet" is *a strict disciplinarian, especially a military one.* Interestingly, in France, Martinet's name acquired no such negative connotation.

7. **gorgon** (gôr′gən) The name comes from the Greek myth of the three monstrous sisters who inhabited the region of Night. Together they were known as the Gorgons; their individual names were Stheno, Euryale, and Medusa. Little has been written about the first two. Medusa was the most hideous and dangerous; her appearance, with her head of writhing serpents, was so ghastly that anyone who looked directly at her was turned to stone. Therefore, the current meaning of "gorgon" is *a mean or repulsive woman.*

8. **maudlin** (môd′lin) This word, meaning *tearfully or weakly emotional,* comes from the miracle plays of the Middle Ages. Although these plays depicted many of the Biblical miracles, the most popular theme was the life of Mary Magdalene. The English pronounced her name "maudlin," and since most of the scenes in which she appeared were tearful, this pronunciation of her name became associated with mawkish sentimentality.

9. **meander** (mē an′dər) In ancient times, the Menderes River in western Turkey was so remarkable for its twisting path that its Greek name, "Maiandros," came to mean *a winding.* In Latin this word was spelled "maeander," hence English "meander," used mainly as a verb and meaning *to proceed by a winding or indirect course.*

10. **gossamer** (gos′ə mər) In early times, November was a time of feasting and merrymaking in Germany. The time-honored meal was roast goose. So many geese were eaten that the month came to be called "Gänsemonat," *goose month.* The term traveled to England but in the course of migration, it became associated with the period of unseasonably warm autumn weather we now call "Indian summer." During the warm spell, large cobwebs are found draped in the grass or suspended in the air. These delicate, airy webs, which we call "gossamer," are generally believed to have taken their name from "goose summer," when their appearance was most noticeable. We now define "gossamer" as *something fine, filmy, or light.* It also means *thin and light.*

Quiz 17: Sentence Completion

Complete each sentence with the appropriate word from the following list.

gossamer	gorgon	maudlin
Pollyanna	garret	meander
lilliputian	Olympian	gazette
martinet		

1. It is pleasant to _____ slowly down picturesque country roads on crisp autumn afternoons.

2. The movie was so _____ that I was still crying when the closing credits began to roll.

3. The teacher was such a _____ that his students soon rebelled fiercely against his strict regulations.

4. She was charmed by the _____ furnishings of the dollhouse.

5. Even in the worst of times, he remained a _____.

6. Many budding artists have romantic fantasies about living in a wretched _____ and starving for the sake of their art.

7. His _____ manner intimidated the other actors.

8. The _____ cobwebs shredded at the slightest touch.

9. Since the daily _____ has excellent coverage of local sports, cultural events, and regional news, we tend to overlook its weak coverage of international events.

10. The gossip columnist was so mean and ugly that her victims referred to her as a _____.

Quiz 18: Definitions

Select the correct definition for each numbered word. Write your answer in the space provided.

_____   1. Olympian
                a. majestic   b. athletic   c. mountainous
                d. abject
_____   2. meander
                a. moan   b. ramble   c. strike back   d. starve
_____   3. gorgon
                a. misunderstood person   b. foregone conclusion
                c. hideous monster   d. midget
_____   4. Pollyanna
                a. doll   b. traitor   c. pessimist   d. optimist
_____   5. lilliputian
                a. flowering plant   b. giant   c. great thinker
                d. pygmy
_____   6. garret
                a. basement   b. attic   c. garage
                d. unsuccessful artist
_____   7. maudlin
                a. warlike   b. married   c. mawkish
                d. intense
_____   8. martinet
                a. strict disciplinarian   b. facile problem
                c. hawk   d. musical instrument
_____   9. gazette
                a. journal   b. gazebo   c. silver coin
                d. book of maps
_____   10. gossamer
                a. variety of goose   b. grasp   c. flimsy material
                d. idle talk

Lesson 10

Learning the backgrounds of the following ten words will give you an edge in recalling their meanings and using them in your conversation or writing. When you are finished reading, complete the two quizzes that follow.

1. **meerschaum** (mēr'shəm, -shôm) Since it is white and soft and often found along seashores, ancient people believed

this white claylike mineral was foam from the ocean turned into stone. As a result, in all languages it was called "sea foam." It was of little use until German artisans began to carve it into pipes. As it absorbs the nicotine from the tobacco, it acquires a deep honey color. Because the Germans were the first to find a use for it, the German name stuck: "meer," *sea;* "schaum," *foam.* In English "meerschaum" often means *a tobacco pipe with a bowl made of meerschaum* (the mineral).

2. **toady** (tō′dē) In the seventeenth century, people believed that toads were poisonous, and anyone who mistakenly ate a toad's leg instead of a frog's leg would die. Rather than swear off frogs' legs, people sought a cure for the fatal food poisoning. Charlatans would sometimes hire an accomplice who would pretend to eat a toad, at which point his employer would whip out his instant remedy and "save" his helper's life. For his duties, the helper came to be called a "toad-eater." Since anyone who would consume anything as disgusting as a toad must be completely under his master's thumb, "toad-eater" or "toady" became the term for *an obsequious sycophant; a fawning flatterer.*

3. **gregarious** (gri gâr′ē əs) The Latin term for a herd of animals is "grex." Because a group of people banded together in military formation resembles a herd of animals, the word "grex" was applied to people as well as animals. The way the people grouped together was called "gregarius," *like a herd.* The word has come down to us as "gregarious," meaning *friendly* or *fond of the company of others.*

4. **miscreant** (mis′krē ənt) The word's source, the Old French "mes," *wrongly,* and "creant," *believing,* tells us that "miscreant" was originally used to describe a heretic. The word has evolved over the centuries, however, to refer to *a base, villainous, or depraved person.*

5. **sinecure** (sī′ni kyŏor′, sin′i-) "Sinecure," a word meaning *an office or position requiring little or no work, especially one yielding profitable returns,* originally began as a church term, from the Latin "beneficium sine cura," *a benefice without care.* It referred to the practice of rewarding a church rector by giving him a parish for which he had no actual responsibilities. The real work was carried on by a vicar, but his absent superior received the higher recompense. Al-

though the church practice was abolished in the mid-nineteenth century, the term is often used today in a political context.

6. **mecca** (mek′ə) The prophet Muhammad (570?–632), the founder and great lawgiver of Islam, was born to a wealthy family in the city of Mecca, in Saudi Arabia, long a center of pagan religious sects. At the age of forty, he was selected by Allah to be the Arabian prophet of true religion and the successor of Jesus Christ; many of his revelations were later collected in the Koran. The prophet's flight, or *hegira,* from Mecca under the threat of a murder plot in the year 622 is now considered the beginning of the Muslim era, the date from which the calendar is calculated. Muhammad spent the rest of his life in Medina, but captured Mecca in a bloodless battle in 630, to complete his conquest of Arabia. Each of the 1.1 billion Muslims in the world is required to pray five times a day while facing Mecca, regarded as the holiest city of Islam. No non-Muslims are permitted to enter the city, and every one of the faithful who is financially able is required to make the annual *hajj,* or pilgrimage, to Mecca at least once.

7. **namby-pamby** (nam′bē pam′bē) The term "namby-pamby," used to describe anything *weakly sentimental, pretentious, or affected,* comes from Henry Carey's parody of Ambrose Philips's sentimental children's poems. Carey titled his parody "Namby Pamby," taking the "namby" from the diminutive of "Ambrose" and using the first letter of his surname, "P," for the alliteration. Following a bitter quarrel with Philips, Alexander Pope seized upon Carey's parody in the second edition of his *Dunciad* in 1733. Through the popularity of Pope's poem, the term "namby-pamby" passed into general usage.

8. **mountebank** (moun′tə bangk′) During the Middle Ages, Italians conducted their banking in the streets, setting up business on convenient benches. In fact, the Italian word "banca" has given us our word "bank." People with less honest intentions realized that it would be relatively easy to cheat the people who assembled around these benches. To attract a crowd, these con men often worked with jugglers, clowns, rope dancers, or singers. Since they always worked around a bench, they were known as "montimbancos." Although the word was Anglicized to "mountebank," it still refers to *a huckster or charlatan who sells quack medicines*

*from a platform in a public place, appealing to his audience
by using tricks, storytelling, and so forth.*

9. **Svengali** (sven gä´lē) In one of his most memorable film roles,
the great matinee idol John Barrymore steals the show as the evil
hypnotist Svengali, a mad genius whose intense, piercing gaze is
irresistible to the innocent artist's model Trilby, the heroine of the
novel published in 1894 by George Du Maurier. Under his tutelage, Trilby is transformed into a great singer. Barrymore appears
as a ghoulish, bearded creature dressed in disheveled clothing
like a sort of dissolute monk. The 1931 film, of course, was called
Svengali, not (like the original novel) *Trilby.* His is the image we
summon up when we think of a "Svengali," *a person who completely dominates another, usually with evil or selfish motives.*

10. **mugwump** (mug´wump´) This word entered the English language in a most curious fashion. In the mid-1600s, the clergyman John Eliot, known as the Apostle to the Indians,
translated the Bible into the Algonquian language. When he
came to the thirty-sixth chapter of Genesis, he had no word
for "duke," so he used "mugquomp," an Algonquian term
for *chief* or *great man.* Historians of the language theorize
that the term might already have been in circulation at that
time, but they know for certain that by 1884 it was in fairly
general use. In the presidential election that year, a group of
Republicans threw their support to Grover Cleveland rather
than to the party's nominee, James G. Blaine. The newspapers scorned the renegade Republicans as "mugwumps,"
those who thought themselves too good to vote for Blaine.
The scorned Republicans got the last word when they
adopted the same term to describe themselves, saying they
were independent men proud to call themselves "mugwumps," or *great men.* Today we use the term "mugwump"
to describe *a person who takes an independent position* or
one who is neutral on a controversial issue.

Quiz 19: True/False

In the space provided, write T if the definition of the numbered
word is true or F if it is false.

			T or F
1.	toady	sycophant	_____
2.	miscreant	sociable person	_____
3.	mugwump	political ally	_____
4.	namby-pamby	cereal	_____

5. gregarious	affable	_____
6. Svengali	politician	_____
7. mountebank	impostor	_____
8. meerschaum	mixup	_____
9. mecca	shrine	_____
10. sinecure	sincere	_____

Quiz 20: Matching

Match each of the following numbered words with its closest synonym. Write your answer in the space provided.

1. mountebank	a. easy job	_____
2. gregarious	b. knave	_____
3. mecca	c. charlatan	_____
4. toady	d. master	_____
5. miscreant	e. sociable	_____
6. mugwump	f. independent	_____
7. namby-pamby	g. sycophant	_____
8. sinecure	h. pipe	_____
9. Svengali	i. place of pilgrimage	_____
10. meerschaum	j. sentimental	_____

Lesson 11

Here are ten new words to enhance your word power. When you have finished reading the history of each word, complete the quizzes.

1. **oscillate** (os′ə lāt′) In ancient Rome, the grape growers hung little images with the face of Bacchus, the god of wine, on their vines. Since the Latin word for face is "os," a little face would be called an "oscillum." Because the images swung in the wind, some students of language concluded that the Latin verb "oscillare" came from a description of this motion. Most scholars have declined to make this connection, saying only that our present word "oscillate," *to swing to and fro*, is derived from Latin "oscillare," *to swing,* which in turn comes from "oscillum," *a swing.*

2. **nabob** (nā′bob) The Mogul emperors, who ruled India from the sixteenth until the middle of the nineteenth century, delegated authority to men who acted as governors of various parts of India. To the native Indians, such a ruler was known as a "nawwab," *deputy.* The word was changed by the Euro-

peans into "nabob." The nabobs were supposed to tithe money to the central government, but some of the nabobs withheld the money, and thereby became enormously wealthy. From their fortunes came the European custom of using the word "nabob" to refer to a person, especially a European, who had attained great wealth in India or another country of the East. The usage spread to England, and today we use the term to describe *any very wealthy or powerful person.*

3. **pander** (pan′dər) "Pander," *to act as a go-between in amorous intrigues* or *to act as a pimp* or *procurer* or *to cater basely,* comes from the medieval story of Troilus and Cressida. In his retelling, Chaucer describes how the love-stricken Troilus calls upon his friend Pandarus, kin to Cressida, to aid him in his quest for her love. Much of Chaucer's tale is devoted to the different means used by Pandarus to help Troilus win his love. Shakespeare later recycled the same legend. As the story gained in popularity the name "Pandarus" was changed in English to "pandare" and then to "pander." The noun now has the negative connotation of *pimp* or *procurer for illicit sexual intercourse.*

4. **pedagogue** (ped′ə gog′, -gôg′) Wealthy Greek families kept a special slave to supervise their sons. The slave's responsibilities included accompanying the boys as they traveled to and from school and walked in the public streets. To describe a slave's chores, the Greeks coined the term "paidagogos," *a leader of boys.* Occasionally, when the slave was an educated man captured in warfare and sold into slavery, the slave also tutored his charges. From the Greek word we derived the English "pedagogue," *teacher* or *educator.*

5. **quack** (kwak) Noticing how the raucous shouts of the charlatans selling useless concoctions sounded like the strident quacks of ducks, the sixteenth-century Dutch called these charlatans "quacksalvers"—literally, *ducks quacking over their salves.* The term quickly spread through Europe. The English shortened it to "quack," and used it to describe *any fraudulent or ignorant pretender to medical skills,* the meaning we retain today.

6. **nepotism** (nep′ə tiz′əm) This word for *patronage bestowed or favoritism shown on the basis of family relationships,* as in business or politics, can be traced to the popes of the fifteenth and sixteenth centuries. To increase their power, these men surrounded themselves with people they knew

would be loyal—members of their own family. Among the most popular candidates were the popes' own illegitimate sons, called "nephews," from the Latin "nepos," *a descendant,* as a mark of respect. Eventually the term "nepotism" came to mean favoritism to all family members, not just nephews.

7. **pompadour** (pom′pə dôr′, -door′) Sheltered by a wealthy family and educated as though she were their own daughter, at twenty the exquisite Jeanne Antoinette Poisson Le Normant d'Étioles married her protector's nephew and began her reign over the world of Parisian fashion. Soon after, King Louis XV took her as his mistress, established her at the court of Versailles, and gave her the estate of Pompadour. The Marquise de Pompadour created a large and high-swept hairstyle memorialized by her name. The upswept style is still known by her name whether it is used to describe a man's or women's hairdo.

8. **nostrum** (nos′trəm) The word "nostrum," *a patent or quack medicine,* became current around the time of the Great Plague in the mid-seventeenth century. Doctors were helpless to combat the disease, so charlatans and quacks flooded the market with their own "secret"—and useless—concoctions. To make their medicines seem more effective, they labeled them with the Latin word "nostrum." The term came to be used as a general word for any quack medicine. Ironically, "nostrum" means *our own,* as in "nostrum remedium," *our own remedy;* thus it makes no claims at all for the remedy's effectiveness.

9. **narcissism** (när′sə siz′əm) The word "narcissism," *inordinate fascination with oneself,* comes from the Greek myth of Narcissus. According to one version of the legend, an exceptionally handsome young man fell in love with his own image reflected in a pool. When he tried to embrace his image, he drowned. According to another version, Narcissus fell in love with his identical twin sister. After her death, he sat and stared at his own reflection in the pool until he died from grief.

10. **nepenthe** (ni pen′thē) According to Greek legend, when Paris kidnapped Helen and took her to Troy, he wanted her to forget her previous life. In Homer's version of the tale, Paris gave Helen a drug thought to cause loss of memory. The drug was called "nepenthes." The word has come down to us with its meaning intact: *anything inducing a pleasurable sensation of forgetfulness.*

Quiz 21: True/False

In the space provided, write T if the definition of the numbered word is true or F if it is false.

			T or F
1.	nepenthe	remembrance	_____
2.	nepotism	impartiality	_____
3.	pander	procurer	_____
4.	pompadour	crewcut	_____
5.	oscillate	swing	_____
6.	pedagogue	teacher	_____
7.	narcissism	self-love	_____
8.	nabob	pauper	_____
9.	nostrum	patent medicine	_____
10.	quack	expert	_____

Quiz 22: Defining Words

Define each of the following words.

1. pompadour _____

2. nepenthe _____

3. oscillate _____

4. nostrum _____

5. quack _____

6. nabob _____

7. pander _____

8. nepotism _____

9. pedagogue _____

10. narcissism _____

Suggested Answers 1. upswept hairstyle 2. something inducing forgetfulness 3. to swing back and forth 4. patent or useless remedy 5. medical charlatan 6. wealthy, powerful person 7. pimp or procurer 8. patronage given to family members 9. teacher 10. excessive self-love

Lesson 12

Each of these ten words beginning with the letter "p" has a particularly captivating tale behind it. Read the stories, then complete the two quizzes at the end of the lesson.

1. **palaver** (pə lav′ər, -lä′vər) The word "palaver" derives ultimately from the Greek word "parabola," *comparison*, liter-

ally *a placing beside.* From this came English "parable," *a story that makes comparisons.* In Latin the word came to mean *speech, talk, word.* Later, Portuguese traders carried the term to Africa in the form "palavra" and used it to refer to the long talk with native chiefs required by local custom. English traders picked up the word in the eighteenth century, spelling it as we do today. The word retains its last meaning, *a long parley, especially one with people indigenous to a region* or *profuse, idle talk.*

2. **pharisaic** (far′ə sā′ik) The Pharisees were one of the two great Jewish sects of the Old Testament; their opponents were known as Sadducees. The Pharisees placed great emphasis on the strict observance of religious law, rites, and ceremonies. By the time of Jesus, many of the common people had become alienated from the Pharisees, who, according to the Gospels, "preach but do not practice." The word "pharisaic" reflects this New Testament view of the Pharisees and now means *practicing external ceremonies without regard to the spirit; hypocritical.*

3. **pariah** (pə rī′ə) The term "pariah," *an outcast,* comes from the name of one of the lowest castes in India. Composed of agricultural laborers and household servants, it is not the lowest caste, but its members are still considered untouchable by the Brahmans. The British used the term "pariah" for anyone of low social standing. The term "pariah" now is used for *any outcast among his or her own people.*

4. **pecuniary** (pi kyōō′nē er′ē) The Romans measured a man's worth by the number of animals he kept on his farm. They adapted the Latin word for a farm animal, "pecu," to refer to individual wealth. But as people acquired new ways of measuring wealth, such as money and land, the Roman word evolved into "pecunia," which referred most specifically to money. From this came the adjective "pecuniary," *pertaining to or consisting of money.*

5. **phantasmagoria** (fan taz′mə gôr′ē ə) In the early years of the nineteenth century, an inventor named Philipstal created a wondrous device for producing optical illusions. By projecting colored slides onto a thin silk screen, Philipstal made his spectral images appear to move. Today, of course, we take such motion-picture illusions for granted, but in the age of the magic lantern, such visions were marvelous indeed. Philipstal named his invention "phantasmagoria," which we

now apply to *a shifting series of phantasms or deceptive appearances, as in a dream.*

6. **pooh-bah** (po͞o′bä′) *The Mikado* (1885) is probably the most popular light opera written by the collaborative team of Gilbert and Sullivan. Ostensibly the story of the thwarted love of Nanki-Poo for the beauteous Yum-Yum, set at the imperial court of Japan, it is actually an incisive satire on the society of the Victorian era. The absurd character of the overbearing high official known as Pooh-Bah has given us this generic term meaning *a person who holds several positions at once* or—more pungently—*any pompous, self-important person.*

7. **precipitate** (pri sip′i tāt′) The word "precipitate" is based on the Latin root "caput," meaning *head.* In fact, the word was first used to apply to those who had been executed or killed themselves by being hurled or jumping headlong from a "precipice" or high place. Later, the word came to mean *to rush headlong.* From this has come today's meaning, *to hasten the occurrence of; to bring about prematurely.*

8. **precocious** (pri kō′shəs) To the Romans, the Latin word "praecox," the source of English "precocious," was a culinary term meaning *precooked.* In time, however, its meaning was extended to *acting prematurely.* It is this later meaning of "precocious" that we use today, *unusually advanced in development, especially mental development.*

9. **pretext** (prē′tekst) "Pretext" comes from the Latin word "praetexta," meaning *an ornament,* such as the purple markings on a toga denoting rank. In addition to its literal sense, however, the word carried the connotation of something to cloak one's true identity. We have retained only the word's figurative meaning, *something that is put forward to conceal a true purpose or object, an ostensible reason.*

10. **procrustean** (prō krus′tē ən) According to one version of the Greek myth, Procrustes was a bandit who made his living waylaying unsuspecting travelers. He tied everyone who fell into his grasp to an iron bed. If they were longer than the bed, he cut short their legs to make their bodies fit; if they were shorter, he stretched their bodies until they fit tightly. Hence, "procrustean" means *tending to produce conformity through violent or arbitrary means.*

Quiz 23: True/False

In the space provided, write T if the definition of the numbered word is true or F if it is false.

			T or F
1. procrustean	marine life		_____
2. pecuniary	picayune		_____
3. precipitate	play		_____
4. pretext	falsification		_____
5. pariah	outcast		_____
6. pooh-bah	denunciation		_____
7. palaver	serving tray		_____
8. precocious	advanced		_____
9. pharisaic	hypocritical		_____
10. phantasmagoria	illusions		_____

Quiz 24: Matching

Match each of the following numbered words with its closest synonym. Write your answer in the space provided.

1. pooh-bah	a. excuse	_____
2. palaver	b. producing conformity by violent means	_____
3. pecuniary	c. pompous fool	_____
4. phantasmagoria	d. fantasy	_____
5. pretext	e. expedite	_____
6. precocious	f. idle chatter	_____
7. precipitate	g. advanced	_____
8. pariah	h. outcast	_____
9. procrustean	i. hypocritical	_____
10. pharisaic	j. monetary	_____

Lesson 13

Here is a *potpourri* or *ollo* or *gallimaufry* (all meaning "mixed bag") of ten more fascinating words. Read through the interesting stories behind them. Then work through the two quizzes to see how many of the words you can use correctly.

1. **proletariat** (prō′li târ′ē ət) "Proletariat" derives from the Latin "proletarius," *a Roman freeman who lacked property and money*. The word came from "proles," *offspring, children*. Although the freemen had the vote, many wealthy Romans de-

spised them, saying they were useful only to have children. They called them "proletarii," *producers of children.* Karl Marx picked up the word in the mid-nineteenth century as a label for the lower-class working people of his age. "Proletariat" retains the same meaning today: *members of the working class, especially those who do not possess capital and must sell their labor to survive.*

2. **Arcadian** (är kā′dē ən) The residents of landlocked Arcadia, in ancient Greece, did not venture to other lands. As a result, they maintained traditional ways and lived what others imagined to be a simpler life. Ancient classical poets made "Arcadia" a symbol for a land of pastoral happiness. In the sixteenth century, English poet Sir Philip Sidney imagined a bucolic land he called "Arcadia." The word has retained this meaning, and today we consider residents of an "Arcadian" place to be *rustic, simple, and innocent.*

3. **rake** (rāk) "Rake," meaning *a dissolute person, especially a man,* was originally "rakehell." In the sixteenth century, this colorful term was used to describe a person so dissipated that he would "rake hell" to find his pleasures. "Rakehell" is now considered a somewhat archaic term to describe such roués; "rake" is the more common word.

4. **pygmy** (pig′mē) The ancient Greeks were entranced by stories of a tribe of dwarfs in the Upper Nile who were so small that they could be swallowed by cranes. To describe these tiny people, the Greeks used the word "pygmaios," which also referred to the distance on a person's arm from the elbow to the knuckles. The word became English "pygmy," *a tiny person or thing; a person or thing of small importance.*

5. **sardonic** (sär don′ik) The ancient Greeks described a plant on the island of Sardinia whose flesh, if eaten, caused the victim's face to become grotesquely convulsed, as if in scornful laughter. The Greek name for Sardinia was "Sardos"; therefore, "sardonios" came to refer to any mocking laughter. The English word eventually became "sardonic," *characterized by bitter irony or scornful derision.*

6. **tartar** (tär′tər) The fierce Genghis Khan and his successors led an army of bloodthirsty warriors, including the Ta-ta Mongols, in a series of conquests throughout Asia and into Europe. Their name, "Tartar" or "Tatar," became closely associated with brutal massacres. Today the word "tartar" refers to *a savage, ill-tempered, or intractable person.*

7. **argosy** (är′gə sē) In the Middle Ages, cities on the Mediterranean coast maintained large fleets to ship goods around the known world. Ragusa was a Sicilian city well known for its large ships, called "ragusea." In English, the initial two letters became ⁀witched, creating "argusea." From there it was a short step to "argosy," *a large merchant ship, especially one with a rich cargo.* Because of Ragusa's wealth, the word "argosy" also came to mean *an opulent supply or collection.*

8. **Balkanize** (bôl′kə nīz′) After centuries of war, in 1912 the Balkan nations united to conquer the Turks and divide the spoils among themselves. The following year, however, the Balkan nations quarreled over how to divide their booty and began to fight among themselves. From this experience comes the verb "Balkanize," *to divide a country or territory into small, quarrelsome, ineffectual states.* The term has taken on new pungency since the breakup of the former Yugoslavia in the 1990s.

9. **Rabelaisian** (rab′ə lā′zē ən, -zhən) A classic old *New Yorker* cartoon shows two laughing men in Renaissance dress, one of whom is saying, "Ho ho ho! Monsieur Rabelais, there is just no word to describe that earthy humor of yours!" The joke is that there *is* one and only one such word, and that word is "Rabelaisian." The masterpiece of François Rabelais, *Gargantua and Pantagruel,* contains serious discussions of education, politics, and philosophy, but it is most remarkable for its broad, ribald, often scatalogical humor—a humor unique in world literature for its daring and immodest hilarity that has given birth to the word "Rabelaisian," meaning *coarsely humorous.*

10. **hegira** (hi jī′rə, hej′ər ə) Around the year 600, the prophet Muhammad began to preach the new faith of Islam. To escape persecution, he was forced to flee his home in Mecca. Eventually, his followers increased, and by his death in 632, he controlled Arabia. Within a century, the empire of Islam had spread throughout western Asia and northern Africa. The turning point, Muhammad's flight from Mecca, came to be called the "Hegira," after the Arabic word for *flight* or *emigration.* The "Hegira" is the starting point on the Muslim calendar, and we now apply the word to *any flight or journey to a desirable or congenial place.*

Quiz 25: True/False

In the space provided, write T if the definition of the numbered word is true or F if it is false.

			T or F
1.	rake	roué	_____
2.	proletariat	wealthy persons	_____
3.	hegira	flight	_____
4.	Rabelaisian	modest	_____
5.	tartar	disciple	_____
6.	arcadian	rustic	_____
7.	sardonic	derisive	_____
8.	pygmy	monkey	_____
9.	argosy	rich supply	_____
10.	Balkanize	vulcanize	_____

Quiz 26: Matching

Select the best definition for each numbered word. Write your answer in the space provided.

1.	rake	a.	bucolic	_____
2.	pygmy	b.	merchant ship	_____
3.	Rabelaisian	c.	midget	_____
4.	arcadian	d.	break up into antagonistic units	_____
5.	argosy	e.	the working class	_____
6.	hegira	f.	scornful; mocking	_____
7.	Balkanize	g.	ribald	_____
8.	proletariat	h.	bad-tempered person	_____
9.	sardonic	i.	journey or flight	_____
10.	tartar	j.	roué	_____

Lesson 14

The following ten words have peculiar backgrounds that might make them hard to decipher without a little help from a word historian. First review the stories behind them. Then complete the two quizzes to help you add them to your vocabulary.

1. **ballyhoo** (bal′ē hoō′) The word "ballyhoo" is of uncertain origin. Some, however, have connected it with the Irish town of Ballyhooy, known for the rowdy and often uncontrolled quarrels of its inhabitants. Today "ballyhoo" is an Ameri-

canism with a specific meaning: *a clamorous attempt to win customers or advance a cause; blatant advertising or publicity.*

2. **tawdry** (tô'drē) In the seventh century, an Englishwoman named Etheldreda fled her husband to establish an abbey. When the Venerable Bede recounted her story in the early eighth century, he claimed that her death had been caused by a tumor in her throat, which she believed was a punishment for her early vanity of wearing jewelry about her neck. Her abbey eventually became the Cathedral of Ely; her name, Audrey. In her honor, the cathedral town held an annual fair where "trifling objects" were hawked. One theory as to the development of the word "tawdry" relates to the hawkers' cry, "Saint Audrey's lace!" This became "Sin t'Audrey lace" and then "tawdry lace." By association with these cheap trinkets, the word "tawdry" has come to mean *gaudy, showy,* or *cheap.*

3. **phoenix** (fē'niks) According to legend, the phoenix was a fabulous Arabian bird that ignited itself on a pyre of flames after its allotted life span of 500 years; a new phoenix then arose from its ashes. Thus, the symbol of the phoenix has often been used to designate the cycle of death and resurrection. We use the word to describe *a person or thing that has been restored after suffering calamity or apparent annihilation.*

4. **wiseacre** (wīz'ā'kər) Although the word "acre" in "wiseacre" makes it appear that the term refers to a unit of measurement, "wiseacre" is actually used contemptuously to mean a *wise guy* or a *smart aleck.* The term comes from the Dutch "wijssegger," which means *soothsayer.* Since soooth-sayers were considered learned, it was logical to call them "wise," which is what "wijs" means. The word "acre" is a mispronunciation of the Dutch "segger," *sayer.* There is a famous story in which the word was used in its present sense. In reponse to the bragging of a wealthy landowner, the English playwright Ben Jonson is said to have replied, "What care we for your dirt and clods? Where you have an acre of land, I have ten acres of wit." The chastened landowner is reported to have muttered: "He's Mr. Wiseacre."

5. **carpetbagger** (kär'pit bag'ər) After the Civil War, many unscrupulous Northern adventurers flocked to the South to become profiteers and to seize political power during the

chaotic Reconstruction period. The epithet "carpetbagger" referred to the unstable future symbolized by the flimsy carpetbags in which they carried their possessions. We still use this vivid term to describe *any person, especially a politician, who takes up residence in a new place for opportunistic reasons.*

6. **silhouette** (sil′o͞o et′) At the urging of his mistress, Madame de Pompadour, the French king Louis XV appointed Etienne de Silhouette as his finance minister. His mission was to enact strict economy measures to rescue the government from near-bankruptcy. At the same time, there was a revival of the practice of tracing profiles created by shadows. Since they replaced more costly paintings, these outlines came to be derided as "à la Silhouette"—another of his money-saving measures. Although Silhouette lasted in office less than a year, he achieved a sort of immortality when his name became permanently associated with *a two-dimensional representation of the outline of an object, as a person's profile, generally filled in with black.*

7. **philistine** (fil′ə stēn′,-stīn′) The Philistines were a non-Semitic people who settled in ancient Palestine after their migration from the Aegean area in the twelfth century B.C.E. As rivals of the Israelites for many centuries, they have long suffered from an undeserved bad reputation: there is no real historical proof to indicate that they were as rough and uncivilized as the modern word "philistine" suggests. The word is used to refer to *a person who is lacking in or smugly indifferent to culture and aesthetic refinement; one who is contentedly commonplace in ideas and tastes.*

8. **caprice** (kə prēs′) "Caprice," *a sudden, unpredictable change of mind, a whim,* doesn't remind us of hedgehogs, yet these animals probably played a role in this word's past. "Caprice" comes ultimately from the Italian word "capriccio," which originally meant *fright, horror.* The word is thought to be a compound of "capo," *head,* and "riccio," *hedgehog,* because when people are very frightened, their hair stands on end, like a hedgehog's spines.

9. **treacle** (trē′kəl) Originally, "treacle" was an ointment used by the ancient Romans and Greeks against the bite of wild animals. But in the eighteenth and nineteenth centuries, competing quack medicine hawkers added sweetening to make their bitter potions more palatable. After a while, the

sweetening agent itself, usually molasses, came to be called "treacle." We retain this meaning and have extended it to refer figuratively to *contrived or unrestrained sentimentality* as well.

10. **billingsgate** (bil'ingz gāt') In the 1500s, Belin's gate, a walled town within London, was primarily a fish market. The name was soon distorted to "billingsgate," and since many fish-wives and seamen were known for their salty tongues, the word "billingsgate" came to mean *coarse or vulgar abusive language.*

Quiz 27: True/False

In the space provided, write T if the definition of the numbered word is true or F if it is false.

			T or F
1.	wiseacre	large ranch	_____
2.	caprice	capable	_____
3.	philistine	lover	_____
4.	carpetbagger	skinflint	_____
5.	ballyhoo	dance	_____
6.	tawdry	gaudy	_____
7.	billingsgate	profane language	_____
8.	phoenix	reborn person	_____
9.	treacle	sugar	_____
10.	silhouette	outline	_____

Quiz 28: Matching

Match each of the following numbered words with its closest synonym. Write your answer in the space provided.

1.	phoenix	a. whim	_____
2.	ballyhoo	b. cheap	_____
3.	treacle	c. verbal abuse	_____
4.	tawdry	d. comeback kid	_____
5.	carpetbagger	e. outline	_____
6.	wiseacre	f. clamor	_____
7.	silhouette	g. smarty-pants	_____
8.	caprice	h. mawkish sentimentality	_____
9.	philistine	i. boor	_____
10.	billingsgate	j. opportunist	_____

Lesson 15

The stories behind these ten words provide intriguing reading and can add muscle to your vocabulary. After you study the words, complete the two quizzes to see how many of them you can use correctly.

1. **apartheid** (ə pärt′hāt, -hīt) "Apartheid," the term for *a policy of racial segregation and discrimination against non-whites,* entered English from Afrikaans, the language of South Africa's Dutch settlers, the Boers. They created the word from the Dutch word for "apart" and the suffix "-heid," related to our suffix "-hood." Thus, the word literally means *apartness* or *separateness.* It was first used in 1947, in a South African newspaper. Apartheid is no longer practiced in South Africa, but the term has passed into general use to describe *extreme racism.*

2. **quixotic** (kwik sot′ik) The word "quixotic," meaning *extravagantly chivalrous or romantic,* is based on the character of Don Quixote, the chivalrous knight in Cervantes' 1605 masterpiece *Don Quixote de la Mancha.* The impractical, visionary knight was ludicrously blind to the false nature of his dreams.

3. **bromide** (brō′mīd) "Bromides" are chemicals, several of which can be used as sedatives. In 1906, the American humorist Gelett Burgess first used the word to mean *a boring person,* one who is likely to serve the same purpose as a sedative. The term was then extended to mean *a platitude,* the kind of remark one could expect from a tiresome person.

4. **profane** (prə fān′, prō-) Only fully initiated men were allowed to participate in Greek and Roman religious rites; those not admitted were called "profane," from "pro," *outside,* and "fanum," *temple.* When the word came into English, it was applied to persons or things not part of Christianity. Probably in reference to the contempt of nonbelievers, "profane" now means *characterized by irreverence for God or sacred things.*

5. **rialto** (rē al′tō) In the late sixteenth century, the Venetians erected a bridge across the Grand Canal. Since the bridge spanned deep waters, it was called the "Rialto," *deep stream.* The bridge led to the creation of a busy shopping area in the center of the city. From this shopping center we derive our present meaning of "rialto," *an exchange or mart.* The word

is also used to refer to a theater district, especially Broadway, in New York City.

6. **thespian** (thes′pē ən) A Greek poet named Thespis, who flourished circa 534 B.C., enlarged the traditional celebrations at the festival of Dionysus by writing verses to be chanted alternately by individuals and the chorus. This opportunity to be a solo performer was a first. From the poet's name we derive the word "thespian," *an actor or actress.*

7. **siren** (sī′rən) The Sirens of Greek legend were three sea nymphs with the head of a woman and the body of a bird who inhabited an island surrounded by rocky shoals and lured passing mariners to their death with their enchanting songs. Jason and the Argonauts were saved from them by the lyre-playing of Orpheus, which was even sweeter than the Sirens' song. Odysseus, who could not resist the temptation of listening to them, instructed his shipmates to tie him to the mast and plug up their own ears to avoid a shipwreck. Today a "siren" is *a seductively beautiful or charming woman, especially one who beguiles men; an enchantress.*

8. **chagrin** (shə grin′) The word "chagrin," meaning *a feeling of vexation due to disappointment,* does not derive from "sha-green," *a piece of hard, abrasive leather used to polish metal,* even though both words are spelled identically in French. French scholars connect "chagrin," *vexation, grief,* with an Old French verb, "chagreiner," *to turn melancholy or gloomy,* which evolved in part from a Germanic word related to English "grim."

9. **shibboleth** (shib′ə lith, -leth′) In the twelfth chapter of Judges, Jephthah and his men gained a victory over the warriors of Ephraim. After the battle, Jephthah gave his guards the password "shibboleth" to distinguish friends from foes; he picked the word because the Ephraimites could not pronounce the "sh" sound. His choice was shrewd, and many of his enemies were captured and killed. Thus, "shibboleth" has come to mean *a peculiarity of pronunciation, usage, or behavior that distinguishes a particular class or set of persons.* It also can mean *slogan; catchword.*

10. **vie** (vī) The word "vie," *to strive in competition or rivalry with another, to contend for superiority,* was originally a shortened version of "envien," a sixteenth-century gaming term meaning *to raise the stake.* The contraction, "vie," came to mean *to contend, compete.*

Quiz 29: True/False

In the space provided, write T if the definition of the numbered word is true or F if it is false.

			T or F
1.	chagrin	chafe	_____
2.	vie	accede	_____
3.	profane	irreverent	_____
4.	siren	seductress	_____
5.	quixotic	ill-tempered	_____
6.	rialto	marketplace	_____
7.	apartheid	foreigner	_____
8.	shibboleth	platitude	_____
9.	thespian	actor	_____
10.	bromide	explosive	_____

Quiz 30: Definitions

Select the best definition for each numbered word. Write your answer in the space provided.

_____ 1. bromide
   a. cliché   b. effervescence   c. angst

_____ 2. vie
   a. treat   b. contend   c. despise

_____ 3. quixotic
   a. alien   b. romantic   c. fictional

_____ 4. siren
   a. frump   b. noisemaker   c. enchantress

_____ 5. shibboleth
   a. peculiarity   b. forbidden   c. murdered

_____ 6. profane
   a. pious   b. irreverent   c. exploding

_____ 7. thespian
   a. actress   b. speech impairment   c. playwright

_____ 8. apartheid
   a. discrimination   b. unity   c. hopelessness

_____ 9. rialto
   a. shipyard   b. reality   c. exchange

_____ 10. chagrin
   a. stiff   b. vexation   c. smirk

Lesson 16

The following ten words are derived from earlier terms that can provide a window on the past, as well as suggesting the ways in which the genius of the English language borrows and adapts words for its own purposes. Study the words, then work through the two quizzes that follow.

1. **Promethean** (prə mē′thē ən) According to Greek myth, as punishment for stealing fire from the gods and giving it to mortal humans, Prometheus was bound to the side of a mountain, where he was attacked daily by a fierce bird that feasted upon his liver. At night his wounds healed; the next day he was attacked anew. Because of his extraordinary boldness in stealing the divine fire, the word "Promethean" has come to mean *creative, boldly original.*

2. **sarcophagus** (sär kof′ə gəs) Although the majority of ancient Greeks favored burial or cremation, some obtained limestone coffins that could dissolve a body in little over a month. The coffin was called a "sarcophagus," from the Greek "sarx," *flesh,* and "phagos," *eating.* Today we use the term to refer to *a stone coffin, especially one bearing sculpture, an inscription, etc., often displayed as a monument.*

3. **quorum** (kwôr′əm) The word "quorum" was first used as part of a Latin phrase meaning *to select people for official court business.* Ultimately, it came to mean *the number of members of a group or organization required to be present to transact business; legally, usually a majority.*

4. **antimacassar** (an′ti mə kas′ər) In the 1800s, macassar oil was imported from Indonesia to England as a popular remedy for baldness. Based on its reputation, men began to apply it liberally to their scalps, but the oil stained the backs of sofas and chairs where they rested their oily heads. Therefore, homemakers began to place pieces of fabric over sofa and chair backs, since these scraps could be washed more easily than stained upholstery. These fabric pieces came to be called "antimacassars"—*against macassar oil.* These *little doilies* are now regarded as highly collectible relics of the Victorian era because of their elaborate designs and fine handiwork—now a lost art.

5. **lackey** (lak′ē) After their invasion of Spain in 711, the Moors conquered nearly the entire country and established a glit-

tering civilization. But it was not to last. By 1100, Christians had already wrested half of Spain from the Moors. Two hundred years later, the Moors retained only a small toehold; and a hundred years after that, they were driven out of Europe entirely. As the Moors suffered repeated defeats, their captured soldiers became servants to their Spanish conquerors. They were called "alacayo." The initial "a" was later dropped, and the word was rendered in English as "lackey," *a servile follower.*

6. **Sisyphean** (sis′ə f ē′ən) In Greek mythology, Sisyphus was the founder and king of Corinth who was condemned to Tartarus for his disrespect to Zeus. There he performed the eternal task of rolling a heavy stone to the top of a steep hill, where it inevitably slipped away from him and rolled back down again. His punishment has given us the term "Sisyphean," meaning *futile* or *hopeless,* especially in relation to an impossible task. In a 1942 essay, the existentialist writer Albert Camus (1913–60) popularized the myth as a metaphor for modern life.

7. **paladin** (pal′ə din) The original paladins were Charlemagne's twelve knights. According to legend, the famous paladin Roland was caught in an ambush and fought valiantly with his small band of followers to the last man. Because of his actions, "paladin" has come down to us as *any champion of noble causes.*

8. **hobnob** (hob′nob′) Those who "hobnob" with their buddies *associate on very friendly terms* or *drink together.* The word comes from the Anglo-Saxon "haebbe" and "naebbe," *to have* and *to have not.* In the 1700s, "hobnob" meant *to toast friends and host alternate rounds of drinks.* Each person thus had the pleasure of treating, creating a sense of familiarity. Today this usage survives, even if those hobnobbing are teetotalers.

9. **helot** (hel′ət, hē′lət) Around the eighth century B.C., the Spartans conquered and enslaved the people of the southern half of the Peloponnesus. They called these slaves "helots," perhaps from the Greek word meaning *to enslave.* Today "helot" still means *serf or slave; bondsman.* Fans of the 1941 movie *Meet John Doe* may recall that this is the favorite epithet of Gary Cooper's hobo sidekick, played by Walter Brennan, which he applies to anyone who threatens his freewheeling lifestyle.

10. **kowtow** (kow′tou′) The Chinese people, who were largely iso-

lated from the West until Portuguese traders established a post outside Canton, regarded their emperor as a representation of God on earth. Those approaching the emperor had to fall to the ground and strike their heads against the floor as a sign of humility. This was called a "kowtow," from the Chinese word that meant *knock-head*. As a verb, the English word follows the original meaning, *to touch the forehead to the ground while kneeling, as an act of worship;* but from this meaning we have derived a figurative use as well: *to act in an obsequious manner; show servile deference.*

Quiz 31: Defining Words

Define each of the following words.

1. Sisyphean _____
2. Promethean _____
3. helot _____
4. sarcophagus _____
5. kowtow _____
6. lackey _____
7. antimacassar _____
8. hobnob _____
9. quorum _____
10. paladin _____

Suggested Answers 1. impossible; hopeless 2. creative, boldly original 3. serf, slave 4. coffin 5. deference 6. a servile follower 7. doily 8. associate on friendly terms; drink together 9. majority 10. champion

Quiz 32: True/False

In the space provided, write T if the definition of the numbered word is true or F if it is false.

		T or F
1. lackey	servant	_____
2. quorum	majority	_____
3. Sisyphean	futile	_____
4. hobnob	twisted logic	_____
5. promethean	creative	_____
6. sarcophagus	cremation	_____

7. **helot**	hell-on-wheels	_____
8. **antimacassar**	against travel	_____
9. **kowtow**	bow low	_____
10. **paladin**	villain	_____

Lesson 17

The quirky stories behind the following ten words can help you understand and remember them better. Read through the histories and complete the two quizzes to add to your mastery of language.

1. **quahog** (kwô′hôg, -hog̩) Despite the "hog" at the end of the word, a "quahog" has nothing to do with a pig. Rather, it is a clam; the word comes from the Algonquian (Narragansett) word "poquauhock." It is one of many terms the European settlers adopted from the Native Americans to describe the local wildlife. Other such borrowings include *raccoon, opossum, moose, skunk, woodchuck, squash, maize, tomato, chocolate,* and *cocoa.*

2. **protean** (prō′tē ən) According to Greek legend, Proteus was a sea god who possessed the power to change his shape at will. He also had the ability to foretell the future, but those wishing to avail themselves of his power first had to steal up on him at noon when he checked his herds of sea calves, catch him, and bind him securely. Thus bound, Proteus would change shape furiously, but the petitioner who could keep him restrained until he returned to his original shape would receive the answer to his question—if he still remembered what he wanted to know. From Proteus, then, we get the word "protean," *readily assuming different forms or characters; variable.*

3. **noisome** (noi′səm) Although the words appear to have the same root, "noisome" bears no relation to "noise." "Noisome" means *offensive* or *disgusting,* as an odor, and comes from the Middle English word "noy," meaning *harm.* The root is related, however, to the word "annoy," *to molest or bother.*

4. **chimerical** (ki mer′i kəl, -mēr′-) The Chimera was originally a fire-breathing monster of classical myth that was represented as having a lion's head, a goat's body, and a serpent's tail. According to Greek myth, it was slain by the gallant warrior Bellerophon, who attacked it astride the winged horse Pega-

sus. Later the word meant *any horrible or grotesque imaginary creature;* then, *a fancy or dream.* Today we use "chimerical" to mean *unreal or imaginary; wildly fanciful or unrealistic.*

5. **simony** (sī′mə nē, sim′ə-) Simon the sorcerer offered to pay the Apostle Peter to teach him the wondrous cures he had seen Peter perform, not understanding that his feats were miracles rather than magic tricks. From Simon's name comes the term "simony," *the sin of buying or selling ecclesiastical preferments.*

6. **rigmarole** (rig′mə rōl′) In fourteenth-century England, a register of names was called a "rageman." Later it became a "ragman," then "ragman roll." As it changed, the term evolved to refer to a series of unconnected statements. By the 1700s, the word had become "rigmarole," with its present meaning, *an elaborate or complicated procedure.*

7. **bolshevik** (bōl′shə vik) At a rally of Communist leaders in 1903, Lenin garnered a majority of the votes. He cleverly dubbed his supporters "Bolsheviks," meaning *the majority.* His move was effective propaganda. Even though his supporters actually comprised only a minority, the name stuck and came to be associated with *a member of the Russian Communist party.* The word is also used in a derogatory sense to denote *an extreme political radical; a revolutionary.*

8. **jingoism** (jing′gō iz′əm) This word, meaning *belligerent patriotism and the advocacy of an aggressive foreign policy,* has a rather obscure source. It was extrapolated from the phrase "by jingo" in a political song written by George Ward Hunt supporting the entrance of England and the use of British forces in the Russo-Turkish War of 1877–78 on the side of the Turks. Fortunately, cooler heads prevailed, but the term has been current ever since to describe such hotheaded, opportunistic aggression.

9. **Tweedledum and Tweedledee** (twēd′l dum′ ən twēd′l dē′) The chubby schoolboy characters of Tweedledum and Tweedledee famous for their recitation in Lewis Carroll's *Through the Looking Glass* of "The Walrus and the Carpenter" actually have an earlier historical counterpart. This humorous coinage, devised in imitation of the sounds of their musical compositions, was apparently first applied to Italian composer Giovanni Bononcini (1670–1747) and his German-born rival Georg Friedrich Handel (1685–1759). Whichever

reference you prefer, the term "Tweedledum and Twee-dledee" still means *two persons nominally different but practically the same; a nearly identical pair.*

10. **sylph** (silf) A German alchemist of the 1700s coined the term "Sylphis" to describe the spirits of the air. He envisioned them as looking like humans but able to move more swiftly and gracefully. Over the years, the word evolved to mean *a slender, graceful girl or woman.*

Quiz 33: True/False

In the space provided, write T if the definition of the numbered word is true or F if it is false.

		T or F
1. jingoism	happiness	_____
2. chimerical	unreal	_____
3. simony	slickness	_____
4. bolshevik	sheik	_____
5. protean	changeable	_____
6. noisome	clamorous	_____
7. sylph	svelte female	_____
8. quahog	bivalve	_____
9. rigmarole	simplification	_____
10. Tweedledum and Tweedledee	identical couple	_____

Quiz 34: Matching

Match each of the numbered words with its closest synonym from the list of lettered words in the second column. Write your answer in the space provided.

1. sylph	a. indistinguishable pair	_____
2. quahog	b. bellicose patriotism	_____
3. Tweedledum and Tweedledee	c. ecclesiastical favors	_____
4. bolshevik	d. slender girl	_____
5. chimerical	e. Communist	_____
6. jingoism	f. involved process	_____
7. noisome	g. variable	_____
8. protean	h. clam	_____
9. rigmarole	i. foul	_____
10. simony	j. fanciful	_____

Lesson 18

Now read the histories of these ten unique words. Fix them in your memory by completing the two quizzes that follow and devising some new sentences of your own. The words can make your speech and writing more colorful, interesting, and effective.

1. **solomonic** (sol′ə mon′ik) Solomon, the tenth-century B.C.E. Hebrew king who was the son and successor of David, was renowned for his wisdom. Probably most famous was his decision in the case of the two women who claimed to be the mother of the same infant. When Solomon announced his decision to resolve the bitter dispute by severing the child in two and awarding one half to each of the disputants, one woman enthusiastically agreed to comply with his judgment while the other offered to give up the child rather than seeing it murdered before her eyes. Solomon handed over the child to the second woman, whom he deemed to be its true mother. Thus, we say that a "solomonic" decision or person is one that is *wise or reasonable in character; sagacious.*

2. **sybarite** (sib′ə rīt′) The ancient Greek colony of Sybaris in southern Italy was known for its luxurious life style. The residents were so famous for their opulent ways that the word "sybarite" came to be used for *any person devoted to luxury and pleasure.*

3. **rostrum** (ros′trəm) Today a "rostrum" is *any platform, stage, or the like for public speaking.* The word comes from the victory in 338 B.C. of the Romans over the pirates of Antium (Anzio), off the Italian coast. The victorious consul took back to Rome the prows of the six ships he had captured. These were attached to the lecterns used by Roman speakers. They came to be called "rostra," or *beaks.* We use the singular, "rostrum."

4. **draconian** (drā kō′nē ən, drə-) Draco (fl. 621 B.C.E.) was a Greek politician who is most famous for his codification of Athenian customary law. Though little of his code is extant, later commentators on his work indicated that the death penalty was prescribed for the most trivial offenses. Therefore, his name has come down to us to refer to punishment or rule that is *unusually cruel or severe.*

5. **spoonerism** (spoo′nə riz′əm) The English clergyman W. A. Spooner (1844–1930) was notorious for his habit of transposing the initial letters or other sounds of words, as in "a blushing crow" for "a crushing blow." Since the good rev-

erend was not unique in his affliction, we use the word "spoonerism" to describe these *unintentional transpositions of sounds.*

6. **Pyrrhic victory** (pir′ik) Pyrrhus (c. 318–272 B.C.E.) was a Greek warrior-king whose incessant warfare against the Romans as well as fellow Greeks ultimately brought ruin on his own kingdom. Though he defeated the Romans at Aesculum in 279, his losses were so heavy that he was later said by the Greek historian and biographer Plutarch to have declared, "One more such victory and I am undone." Thus a "Pyrrhic victory" is *a victory or attainment achieved at too great a cost to be worthwhile.*

7. **pundit** (pun′dit) Today we use the word "pundit" to mean *an expert or authority;* but in the nineteenth century, the word was usually applied to a learned person in India. It comes from the Hindi word "pandit," meaning *learned man,* a Brahman with profound knowledge of Sanskrit, Hindu law, and so forth.

8. **yahoo** (yä′hōō) This word for a *coarse, uncouth person* was coined by Jonathan Swift in his 1726 novel *Gulliver's Travels.* In Swift's satire, the Yahoos were a race of humanoid brutes ruled by the Houyhnhnms, civilized horses.

9. **stoic** (stō′ik) The Stoics were philosophers of ancient Greece who believed in self-restraint. Their name comes from Greek *stoa,* "porch," where they habitually walked. Hence the word "stoic," which describes a person who is *impassive, calm, and austere.*

10. **wormwood** (wûrm′wŏŏd′) "Wormwood" is the active narcotic ingredient of absinthe, a bitter green liqueur now banned in most Western countries. Originally, however, the herb was used as a folk remedy for worms in the body. Because of the herb's bitter qualities, we also use it figuratively to mean *something bitter, grievous, or extremely unpleasant.*

Quiz 35: True/False

In the space provided, write T if the definition of the numbered word is true or F if it is false.

		T or F
1. spoonerism	Midwesterner	_____
2. yahoo	oaf	_____
3. wormwood	bitterness	_____
4. solomonic	love-struck	_____

5. pundit	bad kick	_____
6. draconian	harsh	_____
7. sybarite	slender	_____
8. stoic	austere	_____
9. Pyrrhic victory	enslavement	_____
10. rostrum	register	_____

Quiz 36: Matching

Select the best definition for each numbered word. Write your answer in the space provided.

1. rostrum	a. wise	_____
2. yahoo	b. something bitter	_____
3. solomonic	c. cruel	_____
4. spoonerism	d. victory at too great a cost	_____
5. wormwood	e. impassive	_____
6. sybarite	f. stage or platform	_____
7. draconian	g. authority	_____
8. pundit	h. lover of luxury	_____
9. Pyrric victory	i. transposition of sounds in words	_____
10. stoic	j. boor	_____

Lesson 19

Here are ten more words with intriguing pasts. Read through the histories, then complete the quizzes that follow. Spend a few minutes devising sentences for each of the words to help you make them part of your regular speech and writing.

1. **termagant** (tûr′mə gənt) The word "termagant," meaning *a violent, turbulent, or brawling woman,* comes from a mythical deity that many Europeans of the Middle Ages believed was worshiped by the Muslims. It often appeared in morality plays as a violent, overbearing personage in a long robe. In modern usage, "termagant" is applied only to women.

2. **blarney** (blär′nē) According to Irish legend, anyone who kisses a magical stone set twenty feet beneath the ground of a castle near the village of Blarney, in Ireland, will henceforth possess the gift of eloquence. One story claims the Blarney stone got its powers from the eloquence of the seventeenth-century Irish patriot Cormac McCarthy, whose soft speech won favorable terms from Elizabeth I after an

Irish uprising. From this stone-kissing custom, "blarney" has come to mean *flattering or wheedling talk; cajolery.*

3. **charlatan** (shär′lə tn) During the Renaissance, the village of Cerreto, in Umbria, Italy, was noted for its medical quacks, who became known as "cerretanos," after the town's name. The combination of "cerretano" with "ciartatore," an imitative word meaning *chatterer,* created the Italian term "cialatano." When the word was transplanted to the shores of England, it remained nearly intact as "charlatan," *a person who pretends to special knowledge or skill; fraud.*

4. **eunuch** (yōō′nək) A "eunuch" is *a castrated man,* especially formerly, one employed by Oriental rulers as a harem attendant. The word is based on the Greek "eunouchos," from "eune," *bed,* and "echein," *to keep,* since a eunuch is perfectly suited for guarding a woman's bed. The word is used figuratively to refer to *a weak, powerless person.*

5. **tartuffe** (tär tōōf′, -tōōf′) The French actor and playwright Molière (1622–73) is famed for his farces and comedies of manners, which ridicule human foibles and excesses in the person of a main character that epitomizes such vices as hypocrisy, misanthropy, affected intellectualism, and social snobbery. The title character of *Le Tartuffe,* first performed in 1664, is the source for this word meaning *a hypocritical pretender to piety; a religious hypocrite.*

6. **shrew** (shrōō) In Old English, the word "shrew" described *a small, fierce rodent.* The word was later applied to *a person with a violent temper and tenacious personality* similar to the rodent's. Although "shrew" has retained this meaning, it is usually applied only to a woman.

7. **kudos** (kōō′dōz, kyōō′-) Although "kudos" has come down to us from the Greek intact in both form and meaning— *praise, glory*—in the process it has come to be regarded as a plural word, although it is singular. As a result, another new word has been formed, "kudo." Although purists still prefer "kudos is" to "kudos are," only time will tell if the transformation to kudo/kudos becomes permanent.

8. **bohemian** (bō hē′mē ən) In the early fifteenth century, a band of vagabond peasants took up residence in Paris. Knowing that they had come from somewhere in central Europe, the French dubbed the gypsies "Bohemians," in the belief that they were natives of Bohemia. Working from the stereotyped view of gypsies as free spirits, the French then

applied the term "bohemian" to *a person, typically one with artistic or intellectual aspirations, who lives an unconventional life.*

9. **rhubarb** (rōō′bärb) In conventional usage, the word refers to *a long-stalked plant, used in tart conserves and pie fillings;* it is also a slang term for *quarrel* or *squabble.* The ancient Greeks gave the plant its name. Since it grew in an area outside of Greece, they called it "rha barbaron." "Rha" was the name of the plant and "barbaron" meant *foreign.*

10. **lacuna** (lə kyōō′nə) "Lacuna," *a gap or missing part; hiatus,* comes from the identical Latin word, "lacuna," meaning *a hollow.* It first entered English to refer to a missing part in a manuscript. It is also the root of "lagoon."

Quiz 37: True/False

In the space provided, write T if the definition of the numbered word is true or F if it is false.

			T or F
1.	kudos	compliment	_____
2.	blarney	cajolery	_____
3.	shrew	cleverness	_____
4.	tartuffe	pious hypocrite	_____
5.	lacuna	hiatus	_____
6.	termagant	intermediate	_____
7.	bohemian	businesslike	_____
8.	charlatan	quack	_____
9.	rhubarb	sweet	_____
10.	eunuch	castrated man	_____

Quiz 38: Definitions

Select the best definition for each numbered word. Write your answer in the space provided.

_____ 1. kudos
      a. enclave   b. martial arts   c. acclaim
      d. humiliation
_____ 2. eunuch
      a. hero   b. warrior   c. castle   d. castrated
      man
_____ 3. bohemian
      a. free spirit   b. butcher   c. foreigner
      d. master chef

_____ 4. shrew
        a. virago   b. sly   c. bibliophile   d. hearty

_____ 5. lacuna
        a. hot tub   b. gap   c. lake   d. cool water

_____ 6. termagant
        a. lease   b. eternal   c. possessive
        d. brawling woman

_____ 7. charlatan
        a. expert   b. aristocrat   c. doctor   d. fraud

_____ 8. rhubarb
        a. root   b. ridicule   c. squabble   d. arrow

_____ 9. blarney
        a. mountain climbing   b. sweet talk
        c. sightseeing   d. luncheon meats

_____ 10. tartuffe
        a. religious hypocrite   b. renegade   c. saint
        d. ruthless fighter

Lesson 20

Familiarizing yourself with the history of these ten words can help you retain their meanings and make them part of your stock of words. Go through the following word histories and complete the quizzes that follow. Then review the histories to help you remember the words.

1. **solecism** (sol′ə siz′əm, sō′lə-) To the ancient Greeks, the people of the colony of Soloi spoke inexcusably poor Greek. The Greeks were perhaps most offended by the Solois' errors in grammar and usage. They called such barbarous speech "soloikismos," _the language of Soloi._ Through Latin, the word became "solecism," _a substandard or ungrammatical usage, a breach of good manners or etiquette._

2. **requiem** (rek′wē əm) A "requiem" is _a mass celebrated for the repose of the souls of the dead._ It comes from the opening line of the Roman Catholic mass for the dead. "Requiem aeternam dona ers, Domine," meaning _Give them eternal rest, Lord._ It can refer more loosely to _any memorial for the dead,_ or _a tribute,_ as in the title of the film _Requiem for a Heavyweight,_ about a washed-up prizefighter.

3. **tariff** (tar′if) "Tariff," _an official schedule of duties or customs imposed by a government on imports and exports,_ comes

from the Arabic term for *inventory,* "ta‿rif." Perhaps because this story is so unexciting, a false etymology claims that the word instead comes from the name of a Moorish town near the straits of Gibraltar formerly used as a base for daring pirate raids. Colorful, but not true. The word is also used more loosely to mean *cost* or *price of admission.*

4. **blitzkrieg** (blits′krēg′) The German word "Blitzkrieg," literally *a lightning war,* describes the overwhelming Nazi attacks on Poland in 1940. In two weeks, Germany pounded Poland into submission; in six weeks, it crushed the French army. Although ultimately the Germans met defeat, their method of attack has found a place in our language, and "blitzkrieg" has come to denote *an overwhelming, all-out attack.*

5. **spartan** (spär′tn) Sparta was the rival city-state of ancient Greece that ultimately destroyed the high civilization of Athens in the petty squabbles of the Peloponnesian War (431–404 B.C.E.). Though both empires were equally ruthless, the Spartans were renowned for their superior military discipline, which began in early childhood. A famous story tells of the proud stoicism of a boy who allowed a fox smuggled into school under his clothing to slowly disembowel him rather than cry out and admit his transgression. So extreme was their emphasis on the virtues of self-denial and toughness that the word "spartan" came to be synonymous with *a person who is sternly disciplined and rigorously simple, frugal, or austere.*

6. **pecksniffian** (pek snif′ē ən) The often lovable, sometimes villainous, but always memorable eccentrics that populate the literary universe of Charles Dickens made him one of the most popular and enduring English novelists of the nineteenth century. Indeed we often speak of peculiar characters with notable quirks as being "Dickensian." Everyone knows that a "scrooge" is a miser, thanks to the numerous versions of *A Christmas Carol* that are performed every year at Christmas time. Far fewer people are familiar with Seth Pecksniff, a minor character in *Martin Chuzzlewit* (1843), one of Dickens' lesser-known works. But he so thoroughly embodies the trait of *hypocritically affecting benevolence or high moral principles* that we can find no better word to describe such pious frauds than "pecksniffian."

7. **bacchanalia** (bak′ə nā′lē ə, -nāl′yə) In Greek times, a Bacchanalia was originally a religious festival in honor of Bac-

chus, the god of wine and protector of the vineyards. Bacchus was also a god of vegetation and fertility, and his religious ceremonies ultimately degenerated into occasions for drunkenness, lewd behavior, and other excesses. Therefore, the word "bacchanalia" (or "bacchanal") has come to mean *drunken revelry; orgy.*

8. **kibitzer** (kib'it sər) A "kibitzer" is *a spectator, especially at a card game, who gives unwanted advice to a player; a meddler.* This word came from Yiddish, which derived it from the German verb "kiebitzen," *to be a busybody, give unwanted advice to card players.* The verb, in turn, came from "Kiebitz," the German word for a lapwing, an inquisitive little bird given to shrill cries.

9. **lampoon** (lam poon') "Lampoon," *a sharp, often virulent satire* comes from the French word "lampon," which is thought to come from "lampons," *let's drink,* a common ending to seventeenth-century French satirical drinking songs. We also use the word as a verb meaning *to mock or ridicule.*

10. **scapegoat** (skāp'gōt') The term "scapegoat," *a person made to bear the blame for others or to suffer in their place,* comes from the sixteenth chapter of Leviticus, which describes how the high priest Aaron was directed to select two goats. One goat was to be a burnt offering to the Lord; the other, an "escape goat" for atonement, was presented alive to the Lord and sent away into the wilderness to carry away the sins of the people. The word "scape" was a shortening of "escape."

Quiz 39: True/False

In the space provided, write T if the definition of the numbered word is true or F if it is false.

			T or F
1.	kibitzer	busybody	_____
2.	bacchanalia	tea party	_____
3.	blitzkrieg	negotiations	_____
4.	solecism	bad grammar	_____
5.	tariff	price of admission	_____
6.	pecksniffian	villainous	_____
7.	requiem	revival	_____
8.	lampoon	enlighten	_____
9.	scapegoat	substitute victim	_____
10.	spartan	austere	_____

Quiz 40: Matching

Match each of the following numbered words with its closest synonym. Write your answer in the space provided.

1. tariff	a. feigning kindness	_____
2. lampoon	b. mock	_____
3. kibitzer	c. funeral mass	_____
4. scapegoat	d. drunken orgy	_____
5. bacchanalia	e. customs duties	_____
6. requiem	f. disciplined person	_____
7. solecism	g. busybody	_____
8. blitzkrieg	h. grammatical error	_____
9. pecksniffian	i. victim	_____
10. spartan	j. all-out attack	_____

Answers to Quizzes on Word Histories

Answers to Quiz 1
1. f 2. d 3. b 4. g 5. e 6. h 7. i 8. c 9. j 10. a

Answers to Quiz 2
1. T 2. F 3. F 4. F 5. T 6. F 7. T 8. T 9. F 10. F

Answers to Quiz 3
1. F 2. T 3. F 4. T 5. F 6. F 7. F 8. F 9. T 10. T

Answers to Quiz 4
1. c 2. f 3. i 4. g 5. b 6. h 7. d 8. a 9. j 10. e

Answers to Quiz 5
1. c 2. b 3. a 4. c 5. c 6. b 7. a 8. c 9. a 10. b

Answers to Quiz 6
1. d 2. c 3. i 4. a 5. g 6. j 7. b 8. e 9. f 10. h

Answers to Quiz 7
1. T 2. F 3. F 4. T 5. F 6. T 7. T 8. T 9. F 10. F

Answers to Quiz 9
1. c 2. a 3. d 4. d 5. c 6. a 7. b 8. b 9. a 10. b

Answers to Quiz 10

1. T 2. T 3. T 4. T 5. T 6. T 7. F 8. F 9. F 10. T

Answers to Quiz 11

1. b 2. f 3. a 4. j 5. i 6. d 7. g 8. c 9. h 10. e

Answers to Quiz 13

1. T 2. F 3. F 4. F 5. F 6. F 7. F 8. T 9. T 10. T

Answers to Quiz 14

1. e 2. j 3. h 4. a 5. i 6. b 7. d 8. f 9. c 10. g

Answers to Quiz 15

1. d 2. e 3. f 4. j 5. h 6. i 7. c 8. a 9. b 10. g

Answers to Quiz 16

1. T 2. F 3. F 4. T 5. T 6. F 7. F 8. F 9. T 10. F

Answers to Quiz 17

1. meander 2. maudlin 3. martinet 4. lilliputian 5. Pollyanna 6. garret   7. Olympian 8. gossamer 9. gazette 10. gorgon

Answers to Quiz 18

1. a 2. b 3. c 4. d 5. d 6. b 7. c 8. a 9. a 10. c

Answers to Quiz 19

1. T 2. F 3. F 4. F 5. T 6. F 7. T 8. F 9. T 10. F

Answers to Quiz 20

1. c 2. e 3. i 4. g 5. b 6. f 7. j 8. a 9. d 10. h

Answers to Quiz 21

1. F 2. F 3. T 4. F 5. T 6. T 7. T 8. F 9. T 10. F

Answers to Quiz 23

1. F 2. F 3. F 4. T 5. T 6. F 7. F 8. T 9. T 10. T

Answers to Quiz 24

1. c 2. f 3. j 4. d 5. a 6. g 7. e 8. h 9. b 10. i

Answers to Quiz 25

1. T 2. F 3. T 4. F 5. F 6. T 7. T 8. F 9. T 10. F

Answers to Quiz 26

1. j 2. c 3. g 4. a 5. b 6. i 7. d 8. e 9. f 10. h

Answers to Quiz 27

1. F 2. F 3. F 4. F 5. F 6. T 7. T 8. T 9. F 10. T

Answers to Quiz 28

1. d 2. f 3. h 4. b 5. j 6. g 7. e 8. a 9. i 10. c

Answers to Quiz 29

1. F 2. F 3. T 4. T 5. F 6. T 7. F 8. F 9. T 10. F

Answers to Quiz 30

1. a 2. b 3. b 4. c 5. a 6. b 7. a 8. a 9. c 10. b

Answers to Quiz 32

1. T 2. T 3. T 4. F 5. T 6. F 7. F 8. F 9. T 10. F

Answers to Quiz 33

1. F 2. T 3. F 4. F 5. T 6. F 7. T 8. T 9. F 10. T

Answers to Quiz 34

1. d 2. h 3. a 4. e 5. j 6. b 7. i 8. g 9. f 10. c

Answers to Quiz 35

1. F 2. T 3. T 4. F 5. F 6. T 7. F 8. T 9. F 10. F

Answers to Quiz 36

1. f 2. j 3. a 4. i 5. b 6. h 7. c 8. g 9. d 10. e

Answers to Quiz 37

1. T 2. T 3. F 4. T 5. T 6. F 7. F 8. T 9. F 10. T

Answers to Quiz 38

1. c 2. d 3. a 4. a 5. b 6. d 7. d 8. c 9. b 10. a

Answers to Quiz 39

1. T 2. F 3. F 4. T 5. T 6. F 7. F 8. F 9. T 10. T

Answers to Quiz 40

1. e 2. b 3. g 4. i 5. d 6. c 7. h 8. j 9. a 10. f

Borrowed Words

The roots of English are Anglo-Saxon, but there have been so many other influences over the centuries that we can hardly recognize ourselves as speaking a Germanic language. Nevertheless, though only around one-fifth of our vocabulary stems from those Germanic roots, these basic words comprise the vast majority of the ones we use to communicate with each other every day. It is estimated that around three-fifths of our vocabulary derives from French, Latin, and Greek; the remaining one-fifth has been borrowed from languages all around the globe.

French

Nearly half of our French borrowings came into English before the fifteenth century; thereafter, the adaptations tended to be of a more literary nature.

Lesson 1

avant-garde (ə vänt′gärd′, ə vant′-, av′änt-, ä′vänt-) the advance group in any field, especially in the visual, literary, or musical arts, whose works are unorthodox and experimental.

bon vivant (bon′vē vänt′, bôn′vē vän′) a person who lives luxuriously and enjoys good food and drink.

cause célèbre (kôz′sə leb′, -leb′rə) any controversy that attracts great public attention.

coup d'état (ko̅o̅′ dā tä′) a sudden and decisive action in politics, especially one effecting a change of government, illegally or by force.

cul-de-sac (kul′də sak′) a street, lane, etc., closed at one end; blind alley.

demimonde (dem′ ē mond′) a group that has lost status or lacks respectability.

envoy (en′voi, än′-) a diplomatic agent; an accredited messenger or representative.

esprit de corps (e sprē′ də kôr′) a sense of union and of common interests and responsibilities, as developed among a group of persons associated together.

idée fixe (ē′dā fēks′) a fixed idea; obsession.

joie de vivre (zhwä′də vēv′, vē′vrə) a delight in being alive.

laissez-faire (les′ā fâr′) the theory that government should intervene as little as possible in economic affairs.

milieu (mil yoo′, mēl-) an environment; medium.

rapport (ra pôr′, rə-) a harmonious or sympathetic relationship or connection.

rendezvous (rän′də voo′, -dä-) an agreement between two or more people to meet at a certain time and place.

repartee (rep′ər tē′, -tä′, -är-) witty conversation; a quick reply.

Quiz 1: Matching

Match each of the following numbered words with its closest synonym. Write your answer in the space provided.

1. rendezvous	a. team spirit	_____
2. rapport	b. experimental artists	_____
3. cul-de-sac	c. hands-off policy	_____
4. bon vivant	d. love of life	_____
5. idée fixe	e. meeting	_____
6. joie de vivre	f. environment	_____
7. repartee	g. diplomatic agent	_____
8. milieu	h. harmony	_____
9. avant-garde	i. controversy	_____
10. coup d'état	j. government overthrow	_____
11. demimonde	k. dead end	_____
12. esprit de corps	l. disreputable group	_____
13. envoy	m. big spender	_____
14. cause célèbre	n. clever banter	_____
15. laissez-faire	o. obsession	_____

Quiz 2: True/False

In the space provided, write T if the definition of the numbered word is true or F if it is false.

		T or F
1. laissez-faire	a policy of leaving alone	_____
2. esprit de corps	harmony and union	_____
3. milieu	setting	_____
4. rendezvous	meeting	_____
5. idée fixe	obsession	_____
6. repartee	departure	_____
7. envoy	letter	_____
8. rapport	announcement	_____
9. joie de vivre	good vintage	_____
10. coup d'état	headache	_____
11. cause célèbre	controversy	_____
12. cul-de-sac	dead end	_____

13. bon vivant   high liver   _____
14. demimonde   underworld   _____
15. avant-garde   front-runners   _____

Lesson 2

agent provocateur (ā′jənt prə vok′ə tûr′, tŏŏr′) outside agitator.
chic (shēk) attractive and fashionable in style; stylish.
connoisseur (kon′ə sûr′, -sŏŏr′) a person who is especially competent to pass critical judgments in art or in matters of taste.
decolletage (dā′kol täzh′) the neckline of a dress cut low in the front or back and often across the shoulders.
éminence grise (ā mē näns grēz′) a person who exercises power unofficially and surreptitiously.
en masse (än mas′) as a group.
mêlée (mā′lā, mā lā′) a confused, general hand-to-hand fight.
pièce de résistance (pyes də Rā zē stäns′) showpiece; principal object or event.
poseur (pôzûr′) a person who attempts to impress others by assuming or affecting a manner, degree of elegance, etc.
protégé (prō′tə zhā′, prō′tə zhā′) a person under the patronage or care of someone influential who can further his or her career.
raconteur (rak′on tûr′, -tŏŏr′) a person who is skilled in relating anecdotes.
riposte (ri pōst′) a quick, sharp retort; retaliation.
saboteur (sab′ə tûr′) a person who deliberately destroys property, obstructs services, or undermines a cause.
tour de force (tŏŏr′də fôrs′) an exceptional achievement using the full skill, ingenuity, and resources of a person, country, or group.
vis-à-vis (vē′zə vē′) face to face; opposite; in relation to.

Quiz 3: Defining Words

Define each of the following words.

1. pièce de résistance _____

2. riposte _____

3. éminence grise _____

4. vis-à-vis _____

5. décolletage _____

6. en masse _____

7. tour de force _____

8. chic _____

9. protégé _____

10. connoisseur _____

11. raconteur _____

12. mêlée _____

13. saboteur _____

14. poseur _____

15. agent provocateur _____

Suggested Answers 1. showpiece 2. retort 3. an unofficial power 4. in relation to everybody 5. a low-cut neckline or backless dress 6. as a group 7. an exceptional achievement using the full skill, ingenuity, and resources of a person, country or group 8. attractive and fashionable in style 9. a person under the patronage or care of someone influential who can further his or her career 10. a person who is especially competent to pass critical judgments in art, especially one of the fine arts, or in matters of taste 11. a person who is skilled in relating anecdotes 12. a confused, general hand-to-hand fight 13. a person who destroys property, obstructs services, or subverts a cause 14. a person who attempts to impress others by assuming or affecting a manner, degree of elegance, etc. 15. outside agitator

Quiz 4: Synonyms

Each of the following phrases contains an italicized word. Select the best synonym for each word from the choices provided.

1. a daring *décolletage*
   a. low-cut neckline   b. dance   c. acrobatics   d. behavior

2. a *chic* hat
   a. French   b. imported   c. expensive   d. stylish

3. a daring *agent provocateur*
   a. actor   b. secret agent   c. talent scout   d. striptease artist

4. sitting *vis-à vis* an opponent
   a. next to   b. astride   c. facing   d. below

5. the entertaining *raconteur*
   a. comedian   b. storyteller   c. singer   d. poet

6. an amazing *tour de force*
   a. voyage   b. war victory   c. humiliation   d. achievement

7. to act *en masse*
   a. all together   b. religiously   c. stupidly   d. separately

8. a transparent *poseur*
   a. model   b. prank   c. fraud   d. gag

9. a captured *saboteur*
   a. spy   b. weapon   c. turncoat   d. revolutionary

10. my *protegé*
    a. mentor   b. tutor   c. proponent   d. dependent

11. a mighty *éminence grise*
    a. old man   b. battleship   c. soldier   d. secret power
12. a violent *mêlée*
    a. free-for-all   b. storm   c. criminal   d. sea
13. a noted *connoisseur*
    a. expert   b. politician   c. hostess   d. professor
14. a magnificent *pièce de résistance*
    a. argument   b. rebellion   c. centerpiece   d. fortress
15. a disarming *riposte*
    a. letter   b. artwork   c. weapon   d. swift reply

Lesson 3

arriviste (arʹē vēstʹ) a person who has recently acquired wealth or status; upstart.
au courant (ōʹ kōō ränʹ) up-to-date; fully aware; cognizant.
au fait (ō feʹ) well-versed; expert; experienced.
beau monde (bōʹ mondʹ, -môndʹ) the fashionable world; high society.
bête noir (bātʹ nwärʹ) pet peeve; annoyance.
bonhomie (bonʹə mēʹ, bōʹnə-) good nature; geniality.
bon mot (bôN mōʹ) clever turn of phrase; witticism.
cachet (ka shāʹ) superior status; prestige; a distinguishing feature.
canaille (kə nīʹ, -nālʹ) the common people; rabble.
carte blanche (kärtʹ blänchʹ, bläNshʹ) full authority or access; unconditional authority.
causerie (kōʹzə rēʹ) informal conversation; chat.
comme il faut (kô mēl f ōʹ) as it should be; proper; appropriate.
contretemps (konʹtrə täNʹ) mishap; inconvenience.
coterie (kōʹtə rē) a group of close associates; exclusive group or clique.
coup de grâce (kōōʹ də gräsʹ) final blow; a finishing or decisive stroke.

Quiz 5: True/False

In the space provided, write T if the definition of the numbered word or phrase is true or F if it is false.

			T or F
1.	coterie	close associates	_____
2.	bête noir	annoyance	_____
3.	au courant	out of sync	_____
4.	contretemps	tempo	_____
5.	coup de grâce	final stroke	_____
6.	arriviste	newly rich person	_____
7.	comme il faut	proper	_____
8.	beau monde	high society	_____

9.	bon mot	good taste	_____
10.	causerie	chat	_____
11.	cachet	notebook	_____
12.	bonhomie	old friend	_____
13.	canaille	rabble	_____
14.	au fait	accomplished	_____
15.	carte blanche	unconditional authority	_____

Quiz 6: Synonyms

Each of the following sentences contains an italicized word or phrase. From the selection provided, pick the closest definition.

1. She aspired to be a member of the **beau monde.**
   a. athletic team   b. acting profession   c. underworld
   d. fashionable society

2. His **bon mot** brought a smile to everyone's lips.
   a. witticism   b. social blunder   c. somersault   d. fine cooking

3. She considered herself superior to the **canaille.**
   a. neighbors   b. common people   c. snobs   d. artistocrats

4. Reading the newspaper will keep you **au courant.**
   a. nervous   b. busy   c. ignorant   d. in the know

5. Her boss gave her **carte blanche** to negotiate the contract.
   a. a piece of paper   b. confidence   c. full authority   d. a high salary

6. His **bonhomie** won him many friends.
   a. good nature   b. stylishness   c. wealth   d. humility

7. His opponent administered the **coup de grâce** with enthusiasm.
   a. first strike   b. gracious bow   c. illegal hit   d. death blow

8. No one takes that **arriviste** seriously.
   a. tourist   b. clown   c. upstart   d. amateur

9. She is **au fait** in the ways of the world.
   a. awkward   b. experienced   c. old-fashioned   d. ignorant

10. His elegant wardrobe gave him a certain **cachet.**
    a. prestige   b. arrogance   c. contempt   d. debt

11. Slangy speech was his **bête noir.**
    a. specialty   b. worst fault   c. pet peeve   d. source of amusement

12. It was difficult to gain admission to their **coterie.**
    a. clique   b. nightclub   c. confidence   d. estate

13. They were engaged in a private **causerie.**

a. love affair   b. argument   c. conversation   d. political movement

14. The unfortunate *contretemps* created a great deal of confusion.
a. bad timing   b. mishap   c. counterstrike   d. rebuttal

15. She was hired to ensure that everything would be done *comme il faut*.
a. as it should be   b. rapidly   c. on time   d. at great expense

Lesson 4

déclassé (dā′kla sā′, -klä-) reduced to or having low status.
denouement (dā′no͞o mäN′) resolution or outcome, especially of a story.
de rigueur (də ri gûr′, -rē) strictly according to the rules; required.
dernier cri (dern′yā krē′) the last word; the ultimate; latest fashion.
detritus (di trī′təs) debris; rubbish.
de trop (də trō′) too much or too many; unwanted; in the way.
divertissement (di vûr′tis mənt; dē veR tēs -mäN′) a diversion or entertainment.
doyen (doi en′; dwA yaN′) the senior member of a group or profession; a leader or ultimate authority in a field.
echelon (esh′ə lon′) a level of authority, rank, or command.
éclat (ā klä′) flair, dash; brilliance; showy or elaborate display; acclaim or acclamation.
élan (ā län′, ā läN′) vivacity; verve.
enfant terrible (äN fäN te Rē′bl³) irresponsible person; unconventional or shocking person; incorrigible child.
engagé (äN gA zhā′) politically committed; involved in a cause.
ennui (än wē′) boredom; a sense of weariness and discontent.
en passant (äN′ pa säN′, äN′) in passing; by the way.

Quiz 7: Matching

Match each of the following numbered words and phrases with their closest synonyms. Write your answer in the space provided.

1. dernier cri   a. acclamation   _____
2. enfant terrible   b. by the way   _____
3. divertissement   c. too many   _____
4. déclassé   d. by the rules   _____
5. éclat   e. the ultimate   _____
6. de rigeur   f. vivacity   _____
7. echelon   g. boredom   _____
8. ennui   h. incorrigible person   _____
9. de trop   i. involved in a cause   _____

10. engagé   j. amusement   _____
11. denouement   k. having low status   _____
12. doyen   l. level of authority   _____
13. élaт.   m. debris   _____
14. detritus   n. outcome   _____
15. en passant   o. senior member   _____

Quiz 8: Synonyms

Each of the following sentences contains an italicized word or phrase. Choose the best synonym from the selection provided.

1. She rose to the highest *echelon* of her profession.
   a. rank   b. demands   c. challenge   d. temptation
2. The affair ultimately had a satisfactory *denouement.*
   a. division   b. prosecution   c. resolution   d. marriage
3. Their presence was regarded as *de trop* by the event's organizers.
   a. desirable   b. essential   c. awkward   d. unwanted
4. I mentioned it to her *en passant.*
   a. secretly   b. in the hallway   c. in passing   d. in a low voice
5. Her new book is the *dernier cri.*
   a. latest thing   b. laughingstock   c. mistaken notion
   d. critical success
6. He is the *doyen* of art criticism.
   a. opponent   b. student   c. amateur   d. leading authority
7. His performance was marked by great *éclat.*
   a. brilliance   b. awkwardness   c. noisiness   d. mediocrity
8. Formal dress is *de rigeur* for this event.
   a. too much   b. optional   c. required   d. inappropriate
9. Even the thought of visiting them fills me with *ennui.*
   a. elation   b. weariness   c. fear   d. excitement
10. Playing cards provided a *divertissement* for their guests.
    a. hardship   b. expense   c. entertainment   d. boring pastime
11. The *engagé* students mounted a protest in support of the striking workers.
    a. married   b. busy   c. politically committed   d. immature
12. Somebody has to deal with the *detritus* after the party.
    a. rubbish   b. stragglers   c. bills   d. complaints
13. That *enfant terrible* tries our patience at times.
    a. political activist   b. irresponsible person   c. bore
    d. Neanderthal

14. Loud, pushy people are so *déclassé.*
    a. annoying   b. inconsiderate   c. low-status   d. exhilarating
15. The *élan* she brings to her work is infectious.
    a. high spirits   b. bad temper   c. meticulousness   d. boredom

Lesson 5

fait accompli (fe tA kôN plē′) accomplished act; done deal.
fracas (frā′kəs, frak′əs) noisy disturbance; disorderly fight.
gaffe (gaf) blunder; faux pas.
gaucherie (gō′shə rē′) awkwardness; vulgarity.
Grand Guignol (grän̈ gē nyôl′) a drama emphasizing horror or sensationalism.
habitué (hə bich′o͞o ā′) a frequent visitor to a place; regular client; devotee.
hauteur (hō tûr′, ō tûr′) snobbishness; aloofness; superior air; haughtiness; arrogance.
ingénue (an′zhə no͞o′, aN ′-) a naive or innocent young woman.
lèse majesty (lēz′ maj′ə stē) an attack on a ruler or established authority; an affront to dignity.
maladroit (mal′ə droit′) lacking in adroitness; awkward.
mélange (mā läNzh′, -länj′) mixture; medley.
métier (mā′tyā, mā tyā′) vocation or calling; forte.
motif (mō tēf′) a recurring theme; a repeated element of design.
mot juste (mō zhy̆st′) precise word; pithy phrase.
mystique (mi stēk′) an aura of mystery; a framework of beliefs lending enhanced value or meaning to a person or thing.

Quiz 9: True/False

In the space provided, write T if the definition of the numbered word is true or F if it is false.

			T or F
1.	métier	rhythm	_____
2.	Grand Guignol	sensationalistic drama	_____
3.	fracas	breakage	_____
4.	habitué	devotee	_____
5.	gaffe	long pole	_____
6.	mot juste	pithy phrase	_____
7.	ingénue	naive girl	_____
8.	fait accompli	accomplished act	_____
9.	gaucherie	awkwardness	_____
10.	mystique	secret plot	_____
11.	maladroit	clumsy	_____

12. mélange	medley	_____
13. motif	intention	_____
14. hauteur	arrogance	_____
15. lèse-majesty	affront to dignity	_____

Quiz 10: Synonyms

Each of the following sentences contains an italicized word or phrase. Choose the best definition from the selection provided.

1. Her *hauteur* made her unpopular.
   a. height   b. low status   c. awkwardness   d. haughtiness
2. He had a certain gift for the *mot juste.*
   a. bargain   b. most clues   c. precise word   d. right answer
3. Garbo's *mystique* lingered long after her retirement from the movies.
   a. mysterious aura   b. popularity   c. income   d. illness
4. Their *fracas* broke up the party.
   a. complaints   b. embarrassment   c. noisy fight   d. boring speeches
5. The artist was a *habitué* of the small café.
   a. critic   b. regular   c. debtor   d. employee
6. His *gaucherie* embarrassed everyone in the room.
   a. shabby clothing   b. lies   c. snobbishness   d. vulgarity
7. The publication was an act of *lèse-majesty.*
   a. groveling   b. courage   c. noninterference in policy
   d. attack on authority
8. Her performance as an aging movie queen turned psychotic was pure *Grand Guignol.*
   a. comedy   b. sensational horror   c. ham acting
   d. sentimentality
9. His *maladroit* behavior marked him as an ill-bred person.
   a. evil   b. inconsiderate   c. awkward   d. snobbish
10. The wallpaper had a floral *motif.*
    a. repeated design   b. centerpiece   c. border   d. hint
11. The alliance was by then a *fait accompli.*
    a. failure   b. fated   c. old news   d. done deal
12. His *gaffe* cost him his job.
    a. laughter   b. error   c. insubordination   d. arrogance
13. She chose her *métier* after years of indecision.
    a. spouse   b. vocation   c. favorite poem   d. major subject
14. The *ingénue* was dressed in a demure fashion.

a. unworldly girl   b. infant   c. sophisticate   d. engineer
15. His art was a *mélange* of different elements.
a. satire   b. mixture   c. denial   d. derivation

Lesson 6

nom de guerre (nom′ də gâr′) an assumed name; pseudonym; stage name; alias.
nouveau riche (no͞o′vō rēsh′) a newly rich person, especially one who is ostentatious or uncultivated.
parvenu (pär′və no͞o′, -nyo͞o′) newcomer; upstart.
penchant (pen′chənt) a strong inclination, taste, or liking for something.
pied-à-terre (pē ā′də târ′) a part-time or temporary residence.
précis (prā sē′, prā′sē) a short, concise summary.
rapprochement (rap′rōsh mäN′) an establishment or renewal of friendly relations.
recherché (rə shâr′shā) esoteric or obscure; select or rare; mannered or affected.
risqué (ri skā′) racy, indelicate, or suggestive.
sang-froid (säN fRwA′) self-possession; composure; calmness or equanimity.
savoir-faire (sav′wär fâr′) know-how; tact; social polish.
soigné (swän yā′) well-groomed; carefully or elegantly done.
succès d'estime (sYk se des tēm′) critical success; success achieved by merit rather than popularity.
tête-à-tête (tāt′ə tāt′, tet′ə tet′) intimate, private conversation.
volte-face (volt fäs′, vōlt-) reversal; turnabout; about-face.

Quiz 11: Matching

Match each of the following numbered words or phrases with its closest synonym. Write your answer in the space provided.

1. rapprochement
2. sang-froid
3. nom de guerre
4. penchant
5. savoir-faire
6. volte-face
7. recherché
8. nouveau riche
9. pied-à-terre
10. tête-à-tête
11. risqué
12. succès d'estime

a. private conversation
b. about-face
c. elegantly done
d. indelicate
e. renewal of relations
f. self-possession
g. temporary residence
h. affected
i. critical success
j. assumed name
k. inclination
l. know-how

13. précis   m. concise summary   _____
14. parvenu   n. newly rich person   _____
15. soigné   o. upstart   _____

Quiz 12: Synonyms

Each of the following sentences contains an italicized word or phrase. From the selection provided, choose the best definition.

1. The assignment was to write a **précis** of the essay.
   a. criticism   b. summary   c. outline   d. fictionalization
2. *Lady Chatterley's Lover* is **risqué.**
   a. risky   b. scholarly   c. racy   d. sentimental
3. A **soigné** escort is every woman's best accessory.
   a. well-groomed   b. wealthy   c. polite   d. helpful
4. The foreign film was a **succès d'estime** but it lost money at the box office.
   a. critical favorite   b. diatribe   c. successful remake
   d. tearjerker
5. The divorced couple reached a **rapprochement.**
   a. impasse   b. disagreement   c. state of friendly relations
   d. boiling point
6. We maintain a **pied-à-terre** in the city.
   a. part-time residence   b. small garden   c. business office
   d. old friend
7. The text is too **recherché** to appeal to a wide audience.
   a. pornographic   b. well-researched   c. obscure   d. expensive
8. She maintained her **sang-froid** in the face of criticism.
   a. composure   b. options   c. combativeness   d. ability to
   speak well
9. When he was confronted with the evidence, he did a **volte-face.**
   a. special plea   b. impersonation   c. admission of guilt
   d. reversal
10. The **nouveau riche** businessman tried to buy social acceptance.
    a. newly rich   b. impoverished   c. avant-garde   d. haughty
11. He is more well known by his **nom de guerre.**
    a. war exploits   b. bad reputation   c. alias   d. birth name
12. He asked her to join him at the café for a **tête-à-tête.**
    a. light meal   b. intimate chat   c. debate   d. love affair
13. His **savoir-faire** helped him to smooth over a difficult situation.
    a. manservant   b. physical attractiveness   c. impersonation
    d. social tact

14. She's only a *parvenu* in that field.
    a. newcomer b. part-time worker c. dabbler d. outsider
15. His home reflects a *penchant* for Oriental art.
    a. expertise b. distaste c. misunderstanding d. strong liking

Greek

Though we have already seen the influence of Ancient Greek on the English language in some earlier chapters, there are still a number of terms that are so pungent and precise that they survive in our vocabulary to this day. In many cases, Greek terms embody abstract concepts that are otherwise hard to describe in English.

Lesson 7

acedia (ə sē′dē ə) listlessness, sloth; indifference; apathy.
alpha and omega (al′fə and ō mā′gə, ō mē′gə) the beginning and the end; the basic or essential elements.
anathema (ə nath′ə mə) detested or loathed thing or person; curse.
anomie (an′ə mē′) a sense of dislocation; alienation; despair.
catharsis (kə thär′sis) a purging of emotion or release of emotional tensions.
charisma (kə riz′mə) personal magnetism; the capacity to lead or inspire others.
despot (des′pət, -pot) absolute ruler; tyrant or oppressor.
diatribe (dī′ə trīb′) a bitter denunciation; abusive criticism.
enigma (ə nig′mə) puzzle, riddle; a person or thing of a confusing and contradictory nature.
ephemera (i fem′ər ə) short-lived or transitory things.
epiphany (i pif′ə nē) revelation; sudden, intuitive insight into reality.
epitome (i pit′ə mē) embodiment; a person or thing that is typical of a whole class.

Quiz 13: True/False

In the space provided, write T if the definition of the numbered word is true or F if it is false.

		T or F
1. **enigma**	distinctive feature	_____
2. **catharsis**	release of tension	_____
3. **alpha and omega**	married couple	_____
4. **despot**	absolute ruler	_____
5. **ephemera**	short poem	_____
6. **anathema**	curse	_____

7. diatribe	sharp criticism	_____
8. epitome	large book	_____
9. acedia	apathy	_____
10. charisma	attractive aura	_____
11. anomie	despair	_____
12. epiphany	sudden insight	_____

Quiz 14: Synonyms

Each of the following sentences contains an italicized word or phrase. Select the best synonym from the choices provided.

1. After the fall of the republic, the empire was ruled by a succession of *despots*.
   a. madmen   b. drunkards   c. tyrants   d. illiterates

2. Rock and roll was *anathema* to the classical musician.
   a. revolutionary   b. loathsome   c. inspiring   d. noisy

3. The candidate's *charisma* ensured his election to national office.
   a. personal magnetism   b. credit   c. following   d. cheerfulness

4. All of Samuel Beckett's characters are afflicted with *anomie*.
   a. hunger   b. halitosis   c. alienation   d. poverty

5. She wastes all her time with *ephemera*.
   a. jewels   b. insignificant things   c. false friends   d. magic

6. Her changeable moods made her something of an *enigma* to her friends.
   a. puzzle   b. annoyance   c. delight   d. bore

7. Food and wine are the *alpha and omega* of the gourmet's existence.
   a. pitfalls   b. end-all and be-all   c. expenses   d. amusements

8. A severe attack of *acedia* kept him from meeting his deadline.
   a. indigestion   b. anxiety   c. insects   d. listlessness

9. The solution to the math problem came to him in an *epiphany*.
   a. envelope   b. sudden revelation   c. graveyard   d. pithy saying

10. The dramatic events of the play caused a general *catharsis* among the members of the audience.
    a. riot   b. exodus   c. emotional purging   d. noisy complaint

11. Jackie was the *epitome* of style and elegance.
    a. embodiment   b. sworn enemy   c. proponent   d. antithesis

12. He had few friends left after his outspoken *diatribe*.
    a. commendation   b. filibuster   c. gibberish   d. denunciation

Lesson 8

ethos (ē′thos, ē′thōs) the fundamental character or spirit of a culture; distinguishing character or disposition of a group.

euphoria (yo͞o fôr′ē ə) elation; strong feeling of happiness, confidence, or well-being.

exegesis (ek′si jē′sis) a critical explanation or interpretation, especially of a text.

halcyon (hal′sē ən) happy, joyful, or carefree; prosperous; calm, peaceful, or tranquil.

hedonist (hēd′n ist) a person who is devoted to self-gratification as a way of life; pleasure-seeker.

hoi polloi (hoi′ pə loi′) the common people; the masses.

hubris (hyo͞o′bris, ho͞o′-) excessive pride or self-confidence; arrogance.

iota (ī ō′tə) a very small quantity; jot; whit.

metamorphosis (met′ə môr′fə sis) transformation; profound or complete change.

miasma (mī az′mə) noxious fumes; poisonous effluvia; a dangerous, foreboding, or deathlike influence or atmosphere.

myriad (mir′ē əd) of an indefinitely great number; innumerable.

omphalos (om′fə ləs) navel; central point.

Quiz 15: Matching

Match each of the following numbered words or phrases with its closest synonym. Write your answer in the space provided.

1. **myriad**   a. interpretation   _____
2. **omphalos**   b. elation   _____
3. **exegesis**   c. prosperous   _____
4. **hubris**   d. the masses   _____
5. **miasma**   e. cultural spirit   _____
6. **euphoria**   f. whit   _____
7. **hoi polloi**   g. uncountable   _____
8. **ethos**   h. navel   _____
9. **halcyon**   i. transformation   _____
10. **iota**   j. arrogance   _____
11. **metamorphosis**   k. poisonous atmosphere _____
12. **hedonist**   l. pleasure-seeker   _____

Quiz 16: Synonyms

For each of the italicized words or phrases in the following sentences, select the best synonym from the choices provided.

1. He expressed his contempt for the ***hoi polloi.***
   a. tasteless food   b. cheap gifts   c. common people
   d. baseless accusations

2. His newfound love filled him with *euphoria.*
   a. fear b. happiness c. arrogance d. suspicion

3. The ancient people built their temple at the *omphalos* of the kingdom.
   a. center b. end c. highest point d. beginning

4. She longed for the *halcyon* days of her youth.
   a. carefree b. bohemian c. expatriate d. studious

5. When they donned their costumes, the *metamorphosis* was complete.
   a. deception b. party c. examination d. transformation

6. She was trapped in the *miasma* of her own sins.
   a. dangerous atmosphere b. outcome c. awkwardness
   d. pride

7. The anthropologist studied the *ethos* of the tribe.
   a. anatomy b. underlying beliefs c. love life d. military practices

8. Don Juan was a *hedonist.*
   a. pleasure-seeker b. Spaniard c. courtier d. ruffian

9. Leonardo da Vinci had *myriad* talents.
   a. artistic b. limited c. innumerable d. diplomatic

10. The scholar spent many years refining his *exegesis.*
    a. library b. prose style c. rejection d. interpretation

11. Not one *iota* of your argument is acceptable to me.
    a. little bit b. idea c. excuse d. interpretation

12. Tragic heroes are destroyed by their own *hubris.*
    a. armies b. language c. pride d. followers

Lesson 9

panacea (pan′ə sē′ə) cure-all; a solution for all difficulties.

pantheon (pan′thē on′) the realm of the heroes or idols of any group; illustrious leaders.

paradigm (par′ə dīm′) an example serving as a model; pattern.

pathos (pā′thos, -thōs) pity; compassion; suffering.

pedagogue (ped′ə gog′, -gôg′) a teacher; a person who is pedantic, dogmatic, and formal.

plethora (pleth′ər ə) overabundance; excess; a great number.

protagonist (prō tag′ə nist) an actor who plays the main role; the chief proponent or leader of a movement or cause.

psyche (sī′kē) the human soul, spirit, or mind.

stasis (stā′sis) equilibrium or inactivity; stagnation.

stigma (stig′mə) a stain or reproach on one's reputation; a mark or defect of a disease.

trauma (trou'mə, trô'-) wound or shock; a wrenching or distressing experience.

troglodyte (trog'lə dīt') cave dweller or Neanderthal; brutal or degraded person; reactionary.

Quiz 17: True/False

In the space provided, write T if the definition of the word is true or F if it is false.

			T or F
1.	pedagogue	teacher	_____
2.	troglodyte	reactionary	_____
3.	panacea	poison	_____
4.	plethora	plea	_____
5.	stigma	stain	_____
6.	trauma	wound	_____
7.	paradigm	nonsense	_____
8.	psyche	spirit	_____
9.	stasis	equilibrium	_____
10.	pantheon	wild animal	_____
11.	pathos	pity	_____
12.	protagonist	enemy	_____

Quiz 18: Synonyms

Each of the following sentences contains an italicized word. From the selection provided, find the best synonym for that word.

1. Her dilemma evoked great *pathos* in the onlookers.
   a. contempt   b. amusement   c. compassion   d. contributions
2. He could never escape the *stigma* associated with his criminal conviction.
   a. misery   b. puzzle   c. victim   d. bad reputation
3. That professor has a reputation as a *pedagogue.*
   a. tyrant   b. sex fiend   c. athlete   d. pedant
4. The *trauma* of her childhood led her to seek therapy.
   a. distress   b. grandparents   c. poverty   d. dreams
5. The resilience of the human *psyche* is an amazing thing.
   a. body   b. spirit   c. love life   d. family
6. She was elevated into the *pantheon.*
   a. stratosphere   b. attic   c. realm of heroes   d. executive ranks
7. Booze and drugs reduced him to the status of a *troglodyte.*
   a. brute   b. outcast   c. bankrupt   d. academic dropout
8. *Stasis* is the enemy of progress in society.

a. moral turpitude   b. criminality   c. national pride
d. stagnation

9. She is the *paradigm* of what a woman should be.
a. opposite   b. model   c. teacher   d. failure

10. There is always a *plethora* of junk mail on my desk.
a. excess   b. pleasing amount   c. variety   d. lack

11. Che is remembered as the *protagonist* of the revolution.
a. destroyer   b. loser   c. dead hero   d. proponent

12. She thought her divorce from her first husband would work as a *panacea.*
a. cure for all problems   b. inspiration   c. example   d. source of wealth

Latin

The Latin influence on the English language comes primarily through the Romance languages, particularly French and to a lesser degree Italian, as well as through the borrowings associated with the renewed interest in classical sources during the Renaissance. Note how many Latin legal terms have been carried over into English.

Lesson 10

ad hoc (ad hok′, hōk′) for a specific or particular purpose.
antebellum (an′tē bel′əm) prewar.
caveat (kav′ē ät′) a warning or caution; admonition.
decorum (di kôr′əm) dignity; proper behavior, manners, or appearance.
de facto (dē fak′tō, dā) in fact; in reality; actually existing.
de profundis (dā prō fōōn′dis) out of the depths of sorrow or despair.
dementia (di men′shə) madness; insanity; severely impaired mental function.
desideratum (di sid′ə rā′təm, -rä′-) something wanted or needed.
dolor (dō′lər) sorrow; grief.
ex cathedra (eks′ kə thē′drə) from the seat of authority; by virtue of one's office.
exemplar (ig zem′plər, -plär) model or pattern; example or instance; original or archetype.
exigent (ek′si jənt) urgent; pressing.

Quiz 19: Matching

Match each of the following numbered words or phrases with its closest synonym. Write your answer in the space provided.

1. desideratum   a. grief   _____
2. exigent   b. madness   _____
3. caveat   c. prewar   _____
4. dementia   d. from the depths   _____
5. decorum   e. in fact   _____
6. antebellum   f. urgent   _____
7. exemplar   g. with special purpose   _____
8. dolor   h. caution   _____
9. ad hoc   i. necessary thing   _____
10. ex cathedra   j. archetype   _____
11. de facto   k. dignity   _____
12. de profundis   l. official   _____

Quiz 20: Synonyms

Each of the following sentences contains an italicized word or phrase. Choose the best synonym from the selection provided.

1. Nothing could assuage his *dolor.*
   a. courage b. sadness c. anger d. impatience
2. The *antebellum* plantation fell into disrepair.
   a. southern b. magnificent c. enemy d. prewar
3. She ignored his *caveat.*
   a. tie b. small dog c. warning d. example
4. Their leader made an *ex cathedra* pronouncement.
   a. authoritative b. religious c. profane d. revolutionary
5. They formed an *ad hoc* committee to address the problem.
   a. warlike b. finance c. permanent d. limited-purpose
6. An *exigent* matter requires immediate action.
   a. dangerous b. pressing c. confusing d. scandalous
7. Her *decorum* at the ball convinced everyone that Eliza was a lady.
   a. proper behavior b. fancy dress c. conversation
   d. arrogance
8. The prince was given to fits of *dementia.*
   a. laughter b. laziness c. insanity d. indecision
9. Having a comfortable home was her main *desideratum.*
   a. expense b. wish c. failure d. occupation
10. The leader served as an *exemplar* for the rest of the group.
    a. model b. tyrant c. encouragement d. warning
11. The tortured soul gave a cry *de profundis.*
    a. of exultation b. suddenly c. out of the depths d. of relief

12. The *de facto* government operated without a constitution.
    a. lawful   b. efficient   c. unfair   d. actually existing

Lesson 11

ex nihilo (eks nī′hi lō′, nē′-) out of nothing.
ex post facto (eks′ pōst′ fak′tō) after the fact; subsequently; retroactively.
factotum (fak tō′təm) assistant or aide; deputy.
imprimatur (im′pri mä′tər) sanction; approval.
in toto (in tō′tō) in all; completely, entirely; wholly.
literati (lit′ə rä′tē) intellectuals or scholars; highly educated persons.
mea culpa (mā′ə kul′pə) my fault; an admission of guilt.
modus operandi (mō′dəs op′ə ran′dē, -dī) way of operating; method of working.
non compos mentis (non′ kom′pəs men′tis) of unsound mind; mentally incompetent.
nonsequitur (non sek′wi tər) something that does not follow from the preceding series; illogical conclusion.
odium (ō′dē əm) intense hatred or dislike; reproach or discredit.
pro forma (prō fôr′mə) done perfunctorily; done as a formality.

Quiz 21: True/False

In the space provided, write T if the definition of the numbered word or phrase is true or F if it is false.

		T or F
1. in toto	completely	_____
2. ex post facto	after the fact	_____
3. nonsequitur	logical series	_____
4. ex nihilo	from the top	_____
5. modus operandi	dishonest tactics	_____
6. pro forma	as a formality	_____
7. imprimatur	blessing	_____
8. mea culpa	mean person	_____
9. odium	bad debt	_____
10. literati	educated persons	_____
11. factotum	fact sheet	_____
12. non compos mentis	mentally incompetent	_____

Quiz 22: Synonyms

Each of the following sentences contains an italicized word or phrase. From the choices provided, choose the best definition.

1. The plan has the *imprimatur* of the highest authority.
    a. contempt b. approval b. semblance c. arrogance

2. He inspired intense **odium** in everyone who knew him.
   a. admiration   b. excitement   c. hatred   d. curiosity

3. The defendant was acquitted on grounds of **non compos mentis.**
   a. innocence   b. extenuating circumstances   c. youth
   d. insanity

4. He built an empire **ex nihilo.**
   a. out of nothing   b. illegally   c. rapidly   d. extravagantly

5. All the **literati** were in attendance at the ceremony.
   a. litterbugs   b. students   c. movie stars   d. intellectuals

6. His speech was filled with **nonsequiturs.**
   a. nonsense words   b. faulty logic   c. sound arguments
   d. condemnations

7. She offered a **pro forma** apology for her lapse in manners.
   a. lengthy   b. informal   c. perfect   d. perfunctory

8. All the details were handled by her **factotum.**
   a. father   b. accountant   c. deputy   d. factory

9. The posse was composed of twelve members **in toto.**
   a. in all   b. in disguise   c. as a rule   d. on foot

10. Her **modus operandi** is slow but efficient.
    a. means of conveyance   b. argument   c. way of working
    d. dressmaker

11. An **ex post facto** law is unfair.
    a. strict   b. arbitrary   c. foreign   d. retroactive

12. All his **mea culpas** did not soften her anger.
    a. confessions of guilt   b. gifts   c. poor excuses   d. entreaties

Lesson 12

prolix (prō liks′, prō′liks) wordy; talkative; tediously long.

quidnunc (kwid′nungk′) busybody; a person eager to know the latest gossip.

quid pro quo (kwid′ prō kwō′) equal exchange; substitute; something given or taken in return for something else.

rara avis (râr′ə ā′vis) a rare person or thing; anything unusual; rarity.

sanctum sanctorum (sangk′təm sangk tôr′əm) sacred place; the holiest of places.

sine qua non (sin′ā kwä nōn′) an indispensable condition; prerequisite.

status quo (stā′təs kwō, stat′əs) conditions as they are now; the existing state.

sub rosa (sub rō′zə) confidentially; secretly; privately; undercover.

sui generis (sōō′ē jen′ər is) of its own kind; unique; one of a kind; unparalleled.

terra incognita (ter′ə in kog′ni tə) unknown territory; an unexplored region; uncharted ground.

viva voce (vī′və vō′sē) aloud, orally; by word of mouth.

vox populi (voks′ pop′yə lī′) popular opinion; the voice of the people.

Quiz 23: Matching

Match each of the following numbered words or phrases with its closest definition. Write your answer in the space provided.

1. sui generis	a. unusual thing		_____
2. rara avis	b. substitute		_____
3. quidnunc	c. unparalleled		_____
4. terra incognita	d. existing state		_____
5. sine qua non	e. privately		_____
6. prolix	f. uncharted ground		_____
7. sub rosa	g. by word of mouth		_____
8. viva voce	h. wordy		_____
9. status quo	i. voice of the people		_____
10. vox populi	j. gossip		_____
11. sanctum sanctorum	k. necessary condition		_____
12. quid pro quo	l. holy place		_____

Quiz 24: Synonyms

Each of the following sentences contains an italicized word or phrase. Choose the best definition from the selection of synonyms provided.

1. The students took their exams *viva voce.*
   a. secretly   b. orally   c. outdoors   d. with lively enthusiasm

2. He retreated to the *sanctum sanctorum* of his den.
   a. sacred place   b. chaotic mess   c. workshop   d. worldly comforts

3. A true friend is a *rara avis.*
   a. temporary thing   b. necessity   c. rarity   d. phantasm

4. The revolutionary is never satisfied with the *status quo.*
   a. corrupt government   b. common people   c. agenda
   d. things as they are

5. Outer space remains *terra incognita.*
   a. unknown territory   b. terrifying   c. fascinating   d. an object of study

6. If you offer them a *quid pro quo,* it will settle the dispute once and for all.
   a. apology   b. ultimatum   c. small bonus   d. equal exchange

7. The *vox populi* called for his acquittal.
   a. popular opinion   b. rabble   c. senate   d. loudmouths
8. The conspirators met *sub rosa.*
   a. in the garden   b. secretly   c. as a group   d. in the open air
9. None of the students wanted to attend his *prolix* lectures.
   a. scholarly   b. informal   c. frequent   d. tediously long
10. Her *sui generis* prose style attracted the attention of the critics.
    a. unique   b. flamboyant   c. formal   d. simple
11. None of the neighbors welcomed the presence of that *quidnunc.*
    a. unruly child   b. glutton   c. meddlesome person   d. liar
12. Mutual trust is the *sine qua non* of a lasting relationship.
    a. secret ingredient   b. embodiment   c. outcome
    d. prerequisite

Italian

Many of the Italian words that survive intact in the English vocabulary are musical, artistic, and architectural terms that reflect the Italian emphasis on refinement and good living. In addition, many French-appearing terms are barely disguised versions of the original Italian *(caricature, burlesque, carnival, buffoon, façade).*

Lesson 13

al fresco (al fres′kō) out-of-doors; in the open air.
bravura (brə vyŏŏr′ə, -vŏŏr′ə) a florid, brilliant style; a display of daring.
dolce far niente (dōl′chä fär nyen′tā) sweet inactivity.
focaccia (fō kä′chə) a round, flat Italian bread, sprinkled with oil and herbs before baking.
imbroglio (im brōl′yō) a confused state of affairs; a complicated or difficult situation; bitter misunderstanding.
inamorata (in am′ə rä′tə, in′am-) a female sweetheart or lover.
incognito (in′kog nē′tō) with one's identity hidden or unknown; in disguise.
la dolce vita (lä dōl′chä vē′tä) the good life.
manifesto (man′ə fes′tō) a public declaration of intentions, opinions, or objectives, as issued by an organization.
panache (pə nash′, -näsh′) a grand or flamboyant manner; flair; verve; stylishness.
punctilio (pungk til′ē ō′) strict or exact observance of formalities; fine point or detail of conduct or procedure.
vendetta (ven det′ə) a prolonged or bitter feud or rivalry; the pursuit of vengeance.

Quiz 25: True/False

In the space provided, write T if the definition of the numbered word or phrase is true or F if it is false.

			T or F
1.	vendetta	saleswoman	_____
2.	incognito	hidden identity	_____
3.	la dolce vita	easy living	_____
4.	bravura	acclamation	_____
5.	punctilio	proper procedure	_____
6.	focaccia	thin pancake	_____
7.	dolce far niente	leisure time	_____
8.	panache	flamboyant manner	_____
9.	imbroglio	embroidery	_____
10.	al fresco	in the open air	_____
11.	inamorata	unloving	_____
12.	manifesto	open apology	_____

Quiz 26: Synonyms

Each of the following sentences contains an italicized word or phrase. Select the best synonym from the choices provided.

1. Cut the *focaccia* into eight pieces.
   a. pie b. cake c. bread d. pizza
2. He wrote poetry for his *inamorata.*
   a. patron b. teacher c. self-satisfaction d. sweetheart
3. The family liked to dine *al fresco.*
   a. outdoors b. at restaurants c. in formal dress d. late at night
4. The revolutionaries issued a *manifesto.*
   a. barrage of gunfire b. apology c. map
   d. statement of purpose
5. The soprano's *bravura* performance brought down the house.
   a. off-key b. brilliant c. unexpected d. improvised
6. The royal family was traveling *incognito.*
   a. at night b. at great expense c. in disguise d. forcibly
7. The ambassador performed his duties with *punctilio.*
   a. speed b. arrogance c. timeliness d. strict formality
8. They looked forward to living *la dolce vita* after their retirement.
   a. the good life b. inexpensively c. quietly d. in seclusion

9. Their longstanding **vendetta** led to ruin for both parties.
   a. debts   b. feud   c. business deal   d. love affair
10. Coco always dressed with **panache.**
    a. carelessness   b. great speed   c. stylishness   d. bad taste
11. His scandalous behavior created an **imbroglio** for his government.
    a. difficult situation   b. diversion   c. opportunity   d. expense
12. The playboy lived a life of **dolce far niente.**
    a. erotic pleasure   b. ambition   c. artistic pursuits   d. sweet inactivity

Lesson 14

chiaroscuro (kē är′ə skyōōr′ō, -skōōr′ō) the distribution of light and dark areas, as in a picture.

cognoscenti (kon′yə shen′tē, kog′nə-) those in the know; intellectuals; well-informed persons.

crescendo (kri shen′dō, -sen′dō) a steady increase in force or loudness; a climactic point or peak.

dilettante (dil′i tänt′, dil′i tän′tā) dabbler; amateur; devotee.

diva (dē′və) an exalted female singer; any goddess-like woman.

impresario (im′prə sär′ ē ō′) a person who organizes public entertainment; an entrepreneur, promoter, or director.

pentimento (pen′tə men′tō) the reappearance of an earlier stage, as in a painting.

prima donna (prē′mə don′ə) the principal singer in an opera company; any vain, temperamental person who expects privileged treatment.

sotto voce (sot′ō vō′chē) in a soft, low voice, so as not to be overheard.

staccato (stə kä′tō) abruptly disconnected; disjointed; herky-jerky.

tempo (tem′pō) rate of speed; rhythm or pattern.

virtuoso (vûr′chōō ō′sō) highly skilled performer; a person who has special knowledge or skill in a field; highly cultivated person.

Quiz 27: Matching

Match each of the following numbered words or phrases with its closest synonym. Write your answer in the space provided.

1. **diva**   a. in a low voice   _____
2. **virtuoso**   b. amateur   _____
3. **pentimento**   c. goddess   _____
4. **crescendo**   d. rate of speed   _____
5. **chiaroscuro**   e. skilled performer   _____
6. **sotto voce**   f. emergence of an earlier
                              stage   _____

7. cognoscenti   g. temperamental person   _____
8. impresario   h. climactic point   _____
9. tempo   i. pattern of light and
                            shadow   _____
10. staccato   j. intellectuals   _____
11. dilettante   k. entrepreneur   _____
12. prima donna   l. disjointed   _____

Quiz 28: Synonyms

Each of the following sentences contains an italicized word or phrase. Select the best synonym from the choices provided.

1. She is a *virtuoso* in her field.
    a. skilled person   b. moral person   c. failure   d. celebrity
2. Diaghilev was the most famous *impresario* of his age.
    a. emperor   b. performer   c. artistic promoter   d. statesman
3. The *prima donna* always got her way.
    a. consort   b. president's wife   c. temperamental woman
    d. saint
4. Lillian Hellman's memoir of her youth was aptly entitled *Pentimento.*
    a. regrets   b. sentiments   c. reemergence of an earlier stage
    d. souvenirs
5. The parade proceeded at a *staccato* pace.
    a. smooth   b. rapid   c. staggering   d. stop-and-go
6. Rock and roll has as many *divas* as the world of opera.
    a. goddesses   b. hangouts   c. devotees   d. flops
7. A *dilettante* has passion but no real talent.
    a. watercolorist   b. lawyer   c. accompanist   d. dabbler
8. The *cognoscenti* are flocking to this new play.
    a. ignoramuses   b. well-informed people   c. rich people
    d. tourists
9. The conspirators conversed *sotto voce.*
    a. loudly   b. seductively   c. in a low voice   d. under the stairs
10. The candlelight bathed the room in *chiaroscuro.*
    a. romance   b. brilliance   c. sweet smells   d. areas of light
    and shadow
11. His anger reached a *crescendo.*
    a. peak   b. credibility   c. turning point   d. decrease
12. He never quite adjusted to the *tempo* of city life.
    a. cruelty   b. sophistication   c. anonymity   d. rhythms

Spanish

Spanish has had a less pervasive influence on the English language than some other European sources, but we have borrowed a substantial number of useful words from the Spanish culture of the Southwest. A number of unique American terms are actually mispronunciations of the original Spanish words: *vamoose, mustang, calaboose, lariat, buckaroo,* and *hoosegow* are all coinages that evoke the bygone world of the American cowboy.

Lesson 15

aficionado (ə fish′yə nä′dō) fan; enthusiast; ardent devotee.
bonanza (bə nan′zə) stroke of luck; sudden source of wealth; spectacular windfall.
bravado (brə vä′dō) swaggering display of courage.
desperado (des′pə rä′dō) a bold, reckless criminal; outlaw.
duenna (do͞o en′ə, dyo͞o-) chaperone; an older woman who serves as an escort for young ladies.
embargo (em bär′gō) a government order restricting commerce; any restraint or prohibition.
fiesta (fē es′tə) a festival or feast; any joyous or merry celebration.
incommunicado (in′kə myo͞o′ni kä′dō) in solitary confinement; without any means of communicating with others.
lagniappe (lan yap′, lan′yap) bonus; gratuity or tip.
machismo (mä chēz′mō) an exaggerated sense of masculinity; boastful or swaggering virility.
peccadillo (pek′ə dil′ō) a minor offense; venial sin.
siesta (sē es′tə) a midafternoon rest; nap.

Quiz 29: Matching

Match each of the following numbered words with its closest synonym. Write your answer in the space provided.

1. machismo	a. official restraint	_____
2. bravado	b. chaperone	_____
3. desperado	c. gratuity	_____
4. aficionado	d. exaggerated masculinity	_____
5. lagniappe	e. venial sin	_____
6. duenna	f. celebration	_____
7. peccadillo	g. midafternoon rest	_____
8. bonanza	h. enthusiast	_____
9. siesta	i. stroke of luck	_____
10. embargo	j. pretense of courage	_____

11. incommunicado   k. in seclusion   _____
12. fiesta   l. bold criminal   _____

Quiz 30: Synonyms

Each of the following sentences contains an italicized word. From the choices provided, select the closest definition.

1. She never went anywhere without her *duenna*.
   a. best friend b. chaperone c. handbag d. identification card
2. They kept the prisoner *incommunicado*.
   a. under guard b. in a public place c. in solitary d. in disguise
3. There is an *embargo* on new shipments.
   a. tax b. watchman c. prohibition d. quota
4. She was given a small *lagniappe* for her services.
   a. punishment b. bonus c. checklist d. salary
5. She is a sports *aficionado*.
   a. fan b. competitor c. commentator d. hater
6. He forgave her for her *peccadillo*.
   a. serious violation b. bad taste c. minor sin d. breach of trust
7. A little *siesta* will make you feel refreshed.
   a. bath b. nap c. snack d. encouragement
8. The posse captured the *desperado*.
   a. outlaw b. public imagination c. wild horse d. runaway child
9. The villagers held an annual *fiesta*.
   a. potluck supper b. bonfire c. election d. festival
10. The unexpected inheritance proved to be a genuine *bonanza*.
    a. disappointment b. windfall c. fraud d. burden
11. An exaggerated sense of *machismo* turned him into a bully.
    a. virility b. justice c. fear d. vengeance
12. His *bravado* masked the genuine terror he felt on the battlefield.
    a. bravery b. laughter c. swaggering manner d. self-mockery

Lesson 16

bodega (bō dä′gə) small grocery store; wineshop.
campesino (kam′pə sē′nō) a farmer or peasant.

caudillo (kou dē′lyō, -dē′yō) a head of state, especially a military dictator.

compañero (kom′pən yâr′ō) companion; partner; bosom buddy.

embarcadero (em bär′kə dâr′ō) a pier, wharf, or jetty.

garrote (gə rot′, -rōt′) to strangle or throttle.

guerrilla (gə ril′ə) a member of a small, independent band of soldiers that harass the enemy by surprise raids, sabotage, etc.

junta (hōōn′tə, jun′tə) a small group ruling a country, especially after a revolutionary seizure of power.

peon (pē′ən, pē′on) a farm worker or unskilled laborer; a person of low social status who does menial work; drudge.

presidio (pri sid′ē ō′) fort or garrison; military post.

ramada (rə mä′də) an open shelter with a thatched roof.

vigilante (vij′ə lan′tē) an unauthorized volunteer who takes the law into his or her own hands; a self-appointed avenger of injustice.

Quiz 31: True/False

In the space provided, write T if the definition of the numbered word is true or F if it is false.

			T or F
1.	compañero	companion	_____
2.	junta	joint rulers	_____
3.	vigilante	watchman	_____
4.	bodega	lottery	_____
5.	peon	drudge	_____
6.	guerrilla	reactionary	_____
7.	campesino	peasant	_____
8.	presidio	judge	_____
9.	garrote	strangle	_____
10.	ramada	lean-to	_____
11.	embarcadero	pier	_____
12.	caudillo	head of state	_____

Quiz 32: Synonyms

Each of the following sentences contains an italicized word. From the choices provided, select the best definition.

1. The enemy attacked the *presidio*.
   a. president   b. occupying forces   c. military post   d. seaport
2. The rule of the *junta* was harsh.
   a. king   b. enemy   c. conservatives   d. ruling coalition
3. I relied on the support of my *compañero*.
   a. spouse   b. partner   c. political party   d. employer

4. *Vigilante* law was tolerated in the Old West.
   a. immediate vengeance   b. inefficient   c. unpopular   d. harsh
5. Menial tasks were done by the *peons.*
   a. immigrants   b. unskilled laborers   c. victims of prejudice
   d. young people
6. The *guerrillas* hid in the mountainous areas of the country.
   a. shepherds   b. great apes   c. escaped criminals
   d. revolutionary soldiers
7. We strolled along the *embarcadero.*
   a. wharf   b. highway   c. mountain ridge   d. shopping district
8. Everyone dreaded the *caudillo.*
   a. hot weather   b. revolutionaries   c. military dictator
   d. monster
9. The *ramada* offered very little protection.
   a. band of soldiers   b. military fort   c. thatched lean-to
   d. naval forces
10. The owners of the *bodega* were well-respected in the
    community.
    a. ranch   b. small grocery   c. restaurant   d. pier
11. They enlisted the aid of the *campesinos.*
    a. small farmers   b. clergy   c. cowboys   d. outdoor campers
12. He *garroted* his victim.
    a. throttled   b. mocked   c. stabbed   d. threatened

German

English is a Germanic language, but it diverged from the language
that is the ancestor of Modern German about 1,500 years ago.
Most English words that come from German are relatively recent
borrowings. German borrowings are especially common in intellectual fields, including science, philosophy, and psychology.

Lesson 17

angst (ängkst) a feeling of dread, anxiety, or anguish.
ersatz (er′zäts, -säts) fake; synthetic; artificial.
festschrift (fest′shrift′) a volume of scholarly articles contributed by
   many authors to commemorate a senior scholar or teacher.
gemütlichkeit (gə mʏt′likн kīt′) comfortable friendliness; cordiality; congeniality.
gestalt (gə shtält′) a form having properties that cannot be derived by the
   summation of its component parts.

götterdämmerung (got′ər dam′ə rōōng′) total destruction or downfall, as in a great final battle.

kitsch (kich) something of tawdry design, appearance, or content created to appeal to people having popular or undiscriminating taste.

lebensraum (lā′bəns roum′) additional space needed to function.

realpolitik (rā äl′pō′ lē tēk′) political realism; specifically, a policy based on power rather than ideals.

schadenfreude (shäd′n froi′də) pleasure felt at another's misfortune.

weltanschauung (vel′tän shou′ōong) world-view; a comprehensive conception of the universe and humanity's relation to it.

weltschmerz (velt′shmerts′) sorrow that one feels is one's necessary portion in life; sentimental pessimism.

Quiz 33: True/False

In the space provided, write T if the definition of the numbered word is true or F if it is false.

T or F

1. gestalt — guesswork _____
2. schadenfreude — despair _____
3. götterdämmerung — apocalypse _____
4. weltanschauung — overview _____
5. angst — anxiety _____
6. realpolitik — political idealism _____
7. festschrift — forbidden act _____
8. kitsch — bad taste _____
9. weltschmerz — sorrow _____
10. ersatz — phony _____
11. lebensraum — abandonment _____
12. gemütlichkeit — friendliness _____

Quiz 34: Synonyms

Each of the following sentences contains an italicized word. Select the closest synonym from the choices provided.

1. The *festschrift* was timed to coincide with the professor's retirement.
   a. festival   b. conference   c. debate   d. commemorative volume
2. Her sympathy for her rival was *ersatz.*
   a. genuine   b. fake   c. powerful   d. well known
3. The Romantic poet was afflicted with *weltschmerz.*
   a. sentimental pessimism   b. negative criticism   c. an artificial style   d. a desire to travel

4. The country inn was known for its *gemütlichkeit.*
   a. fine cooking   b. remoteness   c. homey atmosphere   d. bad taste

5. The prophet predicted *götterdämmerung.*
   a. victory   b. total devastation   c. drought   d. prosperity

6. The prospect of meeting her at last filled him with *angst.*
   a. dread   b. anticipation   c. elation   d. lust

7. Her whole house is decorated in *kitsch.*
   a. country style   b. tawdry objects   c. elegant taste   d. bright colors

8. The dictator's excuse for the invasion was a need for *lebensraum.*
   a. slave labor   b. power   c. food   d. more space

9. The president's closest adviser was an advocate of *realpolitik.*
   a. political realism   b. liberalism   c. war games   d. peace

10. She felt a twinge of *schadenfreude* at his bad luck.
    a. guilt   b. sympathy   c. anguish   d. pleasure in another's misfortune

11. His novels reflect a pessimistic *weltanschauung.*
    a. world-view   b. political realism   c. sorrow   d. bias

12. She finally grasped the *gestalt* of the matter through an intuitive insight.
    a. hopelessness   b. falsity   c. whole sense   d. peculiarity

Lesson 18

doppelgänger (dop′əl gang′ər) phantom double; a ghostly counterpart of a living person; alter ego; dead ringer.

echt (екнt) real; authentic; genuine.

kaput (kä pŏŏt′, -pŏŏt′) finished, ruined; broken.

leitmotif (līt′mō tēf′) a recurring theme; a motif in a dramatic work that is associated with a particular person, idea, or situation.

lumpenproletariat (lum′pən prō′li târ′ē ət) a crude and uneducated underclass comprising unskilled laborers, vagrants, and criminals.

poltergeist (pōl′tər gīst′) a ghost that makes loud knocking or rapping noises.

sturm and drang (shtŏŏrm′ ŏŏnt dräng′) turmoil; tumult; upheaval; extreme emotionalism.

übermensch (ŏŏ′bər mensh′) superman; an ideal superior being.

verboten (fər bōt′n, vər-) forbidden; prohibited.

wanderlust (won′dər lust′) a strong desire to travel.

wunderkind (vŏŏn′dər kind′, wun′-) prodigy; gifted child; a person who succeeds at an early age.

zeitgeist (tsīt′gīst′, zīt′-) the spirit of the time; the general trend of thought and feeling that is characteristic of the era.

Quiz 35: Matching

Match each of the following numbered words or phrases with its closest definition. Write your answer in the space provided.

1. verboten	a. turmoil	_____
2. echt	b. gifted child	_____
3. kaput	c. riffraff	_____
4. wunderkind	d. superior being	_____
5. lumpenproletariat	e. spirit of the age	_____
6. wanderlust	f. recurrent theme	_____
7. doppelgänger	g. prohibited	_____
8. leitmotif	h. ruined	_____
9. sturm und drang	i. desire to travel	_____
10. poltergeist	j. genuine	_____
11. zeitgeist	k. phantom double	_____
12. übermensch	l. noisy ghost	_____

Quiz 36: Synonyms

Each of the following sentences contains an italicized word or phrase. Choose the closest synonym from the selection provided.

1. After graduation, she was seized with **wanderlust.**
   a. sexual desire   b. intense boredom   c. a desire to travel
   d. joyfulness

2. My TV set is **kaput.**
   a. broken   b. first-rate   c. secondhand   d. repaired

3. Mozart was a world-renowned **wunderkind.**
   a. wonderful friend   b. prodigy   c. late bloomer   d. unique
   person

4. Adolescence is a period of **sturm und drang.**
   a. rapid growth   b. great freedom   c. emotional upheaval
   d. romantic affairs

5. Smoking is **verboten.**
   a. forbidden   b. unhealthful   c. permitted   d. very bad

6. The **übermensch** is not subject to the same laws as ordinary
   people.
   a. aristocrat   b. ghost   c. criminal   d. superman

7. She was an **echt** genius.
   a. self-described   b. authentic   c. arrogant   d. child

8. The support of the *lumpenproletariat* brought the fascists to power.
   a. unions b. artistocrats c. liberals d. rabble

9. If it wasn't you, it must have been your *doppelgänger.*
   a. accomplice b. factotum c. distant relative d. phantom double

10. The townspeople were prejudiced against the *gastarbeiters.*
    a. migrant workers b. local artisans c. bohemians d. young people

11. All great artists are tuned in to the *zeitgeist.*
    a. sense of sorrow b. godhead c. spirit of the age
    d. romantic feelings

12. The loss of innocence is a *leitmotif* of the novel.
    a. motive b. recurring theme c. flawed conception d. false lead

Yiddish

Yiddish, the language spoken by the Jews of Eastern Europe, derives from the German of the Middle Ages, with the addition of many Hebrew and Aramaic words, but it has absorbed many other words and expressions from the native cultures of the countries where the Jews have settled. Since Hebrew is the traditional means of expression of learned Jews, Yiddish tends to be a folksy, colorful language that expresses the day-to-day concerns of the common people.

Lesson 19

chutzpah (кнōōt′spə, hōōt′-) gall; nerve; brashness.
golem (gō′ləm) robot; lifelike creature.
gonif (gon′əf) a thief, swindler, crook, or rascal.
haimish (hā′mish) homey; cozy.
klutz (kluts) clumsy or awkward person.
kvell (kvel) be delighted; take pleasure.
kvetch (kvech) complain, whine, nag; crotchety person.
macher (mä′кнər) wheeler-dealer; big shot.
maven (mā′vən) expert; connoisseur.
megillah (mə gil′ə) tediously long story; rigmarole; complicated matter.
mensch (mensh) admirable person; decent human being.
meshuga (mə shōōg′ə) crazy; mad; nutty.
nebbish (neb′ish) nobody; loser; hapless person.

nosh (nosh) snack; nibble.

nudge (nŏŏj) nag; annoy or pester; a pest or annoying person.

Quiz 37: Matching

Match each of the following numbered words with its closest synonym. Write your answer in the space provided.

1. maven	a. nibble	_____
2. klutz	b. be pleased	_____
3. mensch	c. pester	_____
4. kvell	d. nutty	_____
5. nosh	e. robot	_____
6. chutzpah	f. admirable person	_____
7. kvetch	g. expert	_____
8. macher	h. thief	_____
9. meshuga	i. big shot	_____
10. golem	j. clumsy person	_____
11. nebbish	k. loser	_____
12. haimish	l. brashness	_____
13. gonif	m. rigmarole	_____
14. nudge	n. homey	_____
15. megillah	o. complain	_____

Quiz 38: Synonyms

Each of the following sentences contains an italicized word. From the selection provided, choose the closest definition.

1. He's a big *macher* out in Hollywood.
   a. moocher   b. engineer   c. troublemaker   d. wheeler-dealer

2. She *kvelled* over the news about her son.
   a. wept   b. complained   c. took pleasure   d. fainted

3. His apartment is very *haimish*.
   a. cozy   b. cluttered   c. expensive   d. uncomfortable

4. He got the job through sheer *chutzpah*.
   a. hard work   b. nerve   c. good humor   d. pull

5. She liked to have a little *nosh* in the midafternoon.
   a. nap   b. drink   c. snack   d. chat

6. Give me the facts, not a whole *megillah*.
   a. document   b. testimony   c. excuse   d. lengthy explanation

7. Walter Mitty was a *nebbish* who lived in his daydreams.
   a. nobody   b. liar   c. psychotic   d. visionary

8. Her dance instructor told her she was a *klutz.*
   a. beginner   b. graceful person   c. clumsy person   d. failure
9. I should never have trusted that *gonif.*
   a. gossip   b. swindler   c. incompetent   d. amateur
10. He's like an unth..nking *golem.*
    a. boxer   b. scientist   c. servant   d. robot
11. Everyone who attended the funeral service said he was a *mensch.*
    a. decent person   b. crook   c. wheeler-dealer   d. connoisseur
12. Her continual *kvetching* gets on my nerves.
    a. pushiness   b. gossiping   c. whining   d. bragging
13. Pay no attention to his *meshuga* ideas.
    a. crazy   b. old-fashioned   c. immature   d. ambitious
14. The opera *maven* had a vast collection of old records.
    a. performer   b. impresario   c. connoisseur   d. amateur
15. His mother *nudged* him to get married.
    a. helped   b. forbade   c. discouraged   d. needled

Lesson 20

schlemiel (shlə mēl′) unlucky person; misfit; failure; awkward person.
schlep (shlep) drag or lug around; trudge; a slow, awkward person; a tedious journey.
schlock (shlok) shoddy merchandise; junk.
schmaltz (shmälts) mawkishness; sentimentality; mush.
schmatte (shmä′tə) rag; article of cheap clothing.
schmooze (shmo͞oz) chitchat; gab; gossip.
schmutz (shmo͞ots) dirt; garbage.
schnook (shno͞ok) pathetic person; sucker, easy mark; lovable fool.
schnorrer (shnôr′ər) sponger; parasite.
shtick (shtik) comic routine; special interest or talent.
tchotchkes (choch′kəz) knickknacks; baubles or trinkets.
tsuris (tso͞or′is, tsûr′-) worries; woes; afflictions.
tzimmes (tsim′əs) fuss, to-do; uproar, disturbance.
yenta (yen′tə) busybody; gossip; nosy old woman.
zaftig (zäf′tik, -tig) juicy; plump; voluptuous; curvy.

Quiz 39: True/False

In the space provided, write T if the definition of the numbered word is true or F if it is false.

			T or F
1.	tsuris	uproar	_____
2.	schmatte	rag	_____

3.	schmutz	garbage	_____
4.	yenta	busybody	_____
5.	schlock	crazy person	_____
6.	tchotchkes	bric-a-brac	_____
7.	schlemiel	big shot	_____
8.	tzimmes	to-do	_____
9.	schlep	awkward person	_____
10.	zaftig	magic	_____
11.	schmaltz	snack	_____
12.	schnorrer	tedious person	_____
13.	schmooze	chitchat	_____
14.	shtick	sadness	_____
15.	schnook	easy mark	_____

Quiz 40: Synonyms

Each of the following sentences contains an italicized word. Choose the nearest definition from the selection provided.

1. She says her kids give her nothing but *tsuris.*
   a. joy   b. troubles   c. knickknacks   d. junk
2. She wiped the *schmutz* off her face.
   a. smile   b. sorrow   c. dirt   d. makeup
3. The women in the paintings of Rubens are *zaftig.*
   a. plump   b. skinny   c. magnificent   d. cheap-looking
4. They like to *schmooze* after work.
   a. nap   b. stroll   c. snack   d. gab
5. All the merchandise at that store is *schlock.*
   a. discount   b. junk   c. first-rate   d. expensive
6. She came to the door in her *schmatte.*
   a. bad temper   b. designer dress   c. cheap dress
   d. underwear
7. They had a collection of *tchotchkes* from their trips abroad.
   a. knickknacks   b. memories   c. fine art   d. tedious stories
8. That new movie is pure *schmaltz.*
   a. comedy   b. junk   c. genius   d. mush
9. Don't ever invite that *schnorrer* to my house again.
   a. noisy person   b. gossip   c. sponger   d. bore
10. She *schlepped* all over town.
    a. celebrated   b. trudged   c. shopped   d. gossiped
11. Chaplin's signal character was a *schnook.*
    a. lovable fool   b. parasite   c. big shot   d. clumsy person

12. Her closest confidante turned out to be a *yenta.*
    a. fool   b. parasite   c. gossip   d. liar
13. The *schlemiel* frittered away his inheritance.
    a. playboy   b. wheeler-dealer   c. idealist   d. unlucky person
14. Doing impersonations of celebrities is his *shtick.*
    a. special talent   b. worst fault   c. tedious habit   d. aspiration
15. They made a *tzimmes* out of nothing.
    a. fuss   b. snack   c. fortune   d. pack of lies

Japanese

Though the first European contact with Japan was made by Portuguese sailors in the sixteenth century, it was not until the middle of the nineteenth century that the United States forced the opening of trade with the West. Many of our more recent borrowings from the Japanese are business terms; others are artistic or religious. The growing popularity of the martial arts has given us still other new words and concepts.

Lesson 21

futon (f o͞o′ton) a thick, quiltlike mattress placed on the floor for sleeping and folded up for seating or storage.

geisha (gā′shə, gē′-) a young woman trained as a gracious companion for men; hostess.

haiku (hī′ko͞o) a short, pithy verse in three lines of five, seven, and five syllables.

kabuki (kə bo͞o′kē) a popular entertainment characterized by stylized acting, elaborate costumes, and exaggerated makeup.

karaoke (kar′ē ō′kē) an act of singing along to a music video, especially one that has had the original vocals electronically eliminated.

koan (kō′än) a nonsensical proposition or paradoxical question presented to a student of Zen as an object of meditation; unsolvable riddle.

noh (nō) classical lyric drama characterized by chants, the wearing of wooden masks, and highly stylized movements drawn from religious rites.

origami (ôr′i gä′mē) the art of folding paper into representational forms.

roshi (rō′shē) a Zen master; a teacher in a monastery.

satori (sə tôr′ē) enlightenment; ultimate insight into the nature of reality.

Shinto (shin′tō) the traditional Japanese system of nature and ancestor worship.

shoji (shō′jē) a room divider or sliding screen made of translucent paper.

tanka (täng′kə) traditional verse form having five-line stanzas with alternate lines of five and seven syllables.

tatami (tə tä′mē) a woven straw mat used as a floor covering.

tsunami (tso͞o nä′mē) a huge sea wave produced by an undersea earthquake or volcanic eruption.

Zen (zen) a sect of Buddhism that emphasizes enlightenment through meditation.

Quiz 41: Matching

Match each of the following numbered words with its closest synonym. Write your answer in the space provided.

1. tatami	a. riddle	_____
2. karaoke	b. classical drama	_____
3. geisha	c. enlightenment	_____
4. noh	d. ancestor worship	_____
5. shoji	e. short poem	_____
6. Zen	f. paper folding	_____
7. kabuki	g. singalong	_____
8. origami	h. paper screen	_____
9. tsunami	i. straw mat	_____
10. futon	j. popular entertainment	_____
11. satori	k. Buddhist school	_____
12. haiku	l. long poem	_____
13. koan	m. tidal wave	_____
14. Shinto	n. mattress	_____
15. tanka	o. female companion	_____
16. roshi	p. Buddhist priest	_____

Quiz 42: Synonyms

Each of the following sentences contains an italicized word. From the selection provided, choose the best definition.

1. After work, the businessmen enjoy *karaoke* bars.
   a. underworld   b. singalong   c. health food   d. sex

2. The small island community was threatened by a *tsunami*.
   a. war lord   b. tornado   c. epidemic   d. tidal wave

3. She was trained to be a *geisha*.
   a. hostess   b. ballerina   c. businessperson   d. teacher

4. *Origami* requires great skill and dexterity.
   a. traditional drama   b. painting   c. calligraphy   d. paper folding

5. She meditated on the **koan** her teacher set before her.
   a. straw mat   b. poem   c. sofa   d. riddle

6. **Noh** is a very ancient art that requires many years of training.
   a. classical drama   b. paper folding   c. scroll painting
   d. meditation

7. **Kabuki** is an entertainment enjoyed by all social classes.
   a. the art of self-defense   b. singing   c. telling riddles
   d. popular drama

8. He sat cross-legged on the **tatami**.
   a. mattress   b. straw mat   c. low table   d. sofa

9. She was admitted through the **shoji**.
   a. solution to a riddle   b. poetry competition   c. sliding screen
   d. school

10. He achieved **satori** after many years of study.
    a. enlightenment   b. an acting role   c. a poetry prize   d. honor

11. Put the **futon** on the floor.
    a. mattress   b. straw mat   c. rice paper   d. sandals

12. He was the acknowledged master of the **tanka**.
    a. classical drama   b. art of paper folding   c. traditional poem
    d. Zen student

13. **Shinto** is the ancient religion of Japan.
    a. Confucianism   b. ancestor worship   c. meditation
    d. monotheism

14. They competed to see who could produce the best **haiku**.
    a. woodblock   b. lyric drama   c. scroll painting   d. short,
    pithy verse

15. His **Zen** teacher slapped him hard across the face to provoke
    him.
    a. martial arts   b. Buddhism   c. poetry   d. acting

16. She bowed before the **roshi**.
    a. emperor   b. Zen master   c. business executive   d. poet

Lesson 22

aikido (ī kē′dō) a form of self-defense using wrist, joint, and elbow grips
to immobilize or throw one's opponent.

bushido (bōō′shē dō′) the code of honor of the samurai, stressing loyalty and obedience.

dojo (dō′jō) a school or practice hall where martial arts are taught.

hara-kiri (här′ə kēr′ē, har′ə-) ritual suicide by disembowelment; any
self-destructive act.

judo (jōō′dō) a martial art based on jujitsu that bans dangerous blows or throws, stressing the athletic or sport element.

jujitsu (jōō jit′sōō) a method of self-defense that uses the strength and weight of one's opponent to disable him or her.

kamikaze (kä′mi kä′zē) person on a suicide mission; a wild or reckless act.

karate (kə rä′tē) self-defense using fast, hard blows with the hands, elbows, knees, or feet.

keiretsu (kā ret′sōō) a loose coalition of business groups.

ninja (nin′jə) a mercenary trained in martial arts and stealth.

samurai (sam′ōō rī′) a noble warrior; warrior class.

shogun (shō′gən, -gun) a military commander; war lord.

sumo (sōō′mō) a form of wrestling aimed at forcing one's opponent out of the ring or causing him to touch the ground with any body part other than the soles of the feet.

tycoon (tī kōōn′) a businessperson of great wealth or power; magnate.

yakuza (yä′kōō zä′) a member of a crime syndicate; racketeer; gangster.

zaibatsu (zī bät′ sōō) a great industrial or financial conglomerate.

Quiz 43: True/False

In the space provided, write T if the definition of the numbered word is true or F if it is false.

			T or F
1.	sumo	wrestling	_____
2.	kamikaze	reckless act	_____
3.	jujitsu	chewy candies	_____
4.	dojo	priest	_____
5.	aikido	artwork	_____
6.	zaibatsu	poetry competition	_____
7.	yakuza	racketeer	_____
8.	bushido	code of ethics	_____
9.	judo	martial sport	_____
10.	keiretsu	business coalition	_____
11.	shogun	war lord	_____
12.	hara-kiri	ritual suicide	_____
13.	tycoon	whirlwind	_____
14.	samurai	warrior	_____
15.	karate	fit for consumption	_____
16.	ninja	soldier for hire	_____

Quiz 44: Synonyms

Each of the following sentences contains an italicized word. Choose the best definition from the selection provided.

1. She was honored to be accepted by the *dojo.*
   a. financial conglomerate   b. Zen master   c. school of martial arts   d. acting company

2. The *ninja* offered his services for hire.
   a. noble warrior   b. suicidal pilot   c. martial artist   d. mercenary soldier

3. An act of *hara-kiri* will redeem his honor.
   a. ceremonial suicide   b. self-defense   c. war   d. meditation

4. She practiced her *aikido* moves.
   a. calligraphy   b. business   c. self-defense   d. paper folding

5. Practitioners of *judo* never intentionally hurt each other.
   a. big business   b. meditation   c. poetry   d. a martial art that bans dangerous blows

6. He adhered strictly to the principles of the *bushido.*
   a. self-defense   b. crime syndicate   c. code of honor   d. suicide mission

7. The *zaibatsu* wielded enormous economic power.
   a. war lord   b. crime syndicate   c. priest   d. financial conglomerate

8. They agreed to join the *keiretsu.*
   a. coalition of business groups   b. crime syndicate   c. school of martial arts   d. suicide mission

9. The *yakuza* swore a bloody vengeance.
   a. person on a suicide mission   b. crime syndicate   c. business magnate   d. military commander

10. Women who practice *jujitsu* may have an advantage over their male attackers.
    a. self-defense that focuses on an opponent's size   b. wrestling   c. meditation   d. unfair business practices

11. The *kamikaze* acts out of a sense of honor and duty.
    a. mercenary   b. person on a suicide mission   c. guerrilla   d. female companion

12. The *tycoon* expected absolute loyalty from his underlings.
    a. war lord   b. gangster   c. business magnate   d. Zen teacher

13. The *samurai* are a hereditary class in Japan.
    a. gangsters   b. noble warriors   c. Zen masters   d. classical actors

14. The *shogun* was the real power behind the emperor.

a. military commander   b. business coalition   c. crime syndicate   d. female companion

15. **Sumo** requires superior height and weight.
a. kick boxing   b. Japanese-style wrestling   c. success in business   d. arm wrestling

16. **Karate** requires speed, concentration, and the intimidation of one's opponent.
a. wrestling   b. self-defense based on fast, hard blows   c. chess d. success in business

Answers to Quizzes on Borrowed Words

Answers to Quiz 1
1. e 2. h 3. k 4. m 5. o 6. d 7. n 8. f 9. b 10. j 11. l 12. a 13. g 14. i 15. c

Answers to Quiz 2
1. T 2. T 3. T 4. T 5. T 6. F 7. F 8. F 9. F 10. F 11. T 12. T 13. T 14. T 15. T

Answers to Quiz 4
1. a 2. d 3. b 4. c 5. b 6. d 7. a 8. c 9. a 10. d 11. d 12. a 13. a 14. c 15. d

Answers to Quiz 5
1. T 2. T 3. F 4. F 5. T 6. T 7. T 8. T 9. F 10. T 11. F 12. F 13. T 14. T 15. T

Answers to Quiz 6
1. d 2. a 3. b 4. d 5. c 6. a 7. d 8. c 9. b 10. a 11. c 12. a 13. c 14. b 15. a

Answers to Quiz 7
1. e 2. h 3. j 4. k 5. a 6. d 7. l 8. g 9. c 10. i 11. n 12. o 13. f 14. m 15. b

Answers to Quiz 8
1. a 2. c 3. d 4. c 5. a 6. d 7. a 8. c 9. b 10. c 11. c 12. a 13. b 14. c 15. a

Answers to Quiz 9
1. F 2. T 3. F 4. T 5. F 6. T 7. T 8. T 9. T 10. F 11. T 12. T 13. F 14. T 15. T

Answers to Quiz 10
1. d 2. c 3. a 4. c 5. b 6. d 7. d 8. b 9. c 10. a 11. d 12. b 13. b 14. a 15. b

Answers to Quiz 11

1. e 2. f 3. j 4. k 5. l 6. b 7. h 8. n 9. g 10. a 11. d 12. i 13. m 14. o 15. c

Answers to Quiz 12

1. b 2. c 3. a 4. a 5. c 6. a 7. c 8. a 9. d 10. a 11. c 12. b 13. d 14. a 15. d

Answers to Quiz 13

1. F 2. T 3. F 4. T 5. F 6. T 7. T 8. F 9. T 10. T 11. T 12. T

Answers to Quiz 14

1. c 2. b 3. a 4. c 5. b 6. a 7. b 8. d 9. b 10. c 11. a 12. d

Answers to Quiz 15

1. g 2. h 3. a 4. j 5. k 6. b 7. d 8. e 9. c 10. f 11. i 12. d

Answers to Quiz 16

1. c 2. b 3. a 4. a 5. d 6. a 7. b 8. a 9. c 10. d 11. a 12. c

Answers to Quiz 17

1. T 2. T 3. F 4. F 5. T 6. T 7. F 8. T 9. T 10. F 11. T 12. F

Answers to Quiz 18

1. c 2. d 3. d 4. a 5. b 6. c 7. a 8. d 9. b 10. a 11. d 12. a

Answers to Quiz 19

1. i 2. f 3. h 4. b 5. k 6. c 7. j 8. a 9. g 10. l 11. e 12. d

Answers to Quiz 20

1. b 2. d 3. c 4. a 5. d 6. b 7. a 8. c 9. b 10. a 11. c 12. d

Answers to Quiz 21

1. T 2. T 3. F 4. F 5. F 6. T 7. T 8. F 9. F 10. T 11. F 12. T

Answers to Quiz 22

1. b 2. e 3. d 4. a 5. d 6. b 7. d 8. c 9. a 10. c 11. d 12. a

Answers to Quiz 23

1. c 2. a 3. j 4. f 5. k 6. h 7. e 8. g 9. d 10. i 11. l 12. b

Answers to Quiz 24

1. b 2. a 3. c 4. d 5. a 6. d 7. a 8. b 9. d 10. a 11. c 12. d

Answers to Quiz 25

1. F 2. T 3. T 4. F 5. T 6. F 7. T 8. T 9. F 10. T 11. F 12. F

Answers to Quiz 26

1. c 2. d 3. a 4. d 5. b 6. c 7. d 8. a 9. b 10. c 11. a 12. d

Answers to Quiz 27

1. c 2. e 3. f 4. h 5. i 6. a 7. j 8. k 9. d 10. l 11. b 12. g

Answers to Quiz 28

1. a 2. c 3. c 4. c 5. d 6. a 7. d 8. b 9. c 10. d 11. a 12. d

Answers to Quiz 29

1. d 2. j 3. l 4. h 5. c 6. b 7. e 8. i 9. g 10. a 11. k 12. f

Answers to Quiz 30

1. b 2. c 3. c 4. b 5. a 6. c 7. b 8. a 9. d 10. b 11. a 12. e

Answers to Quiz 31

1. T 2. T 3. F 4. F 5. T 6. F 7. T 8. F 9. T 10. T 11. T 12. T

Answers to Quiz 32

1. c 2. d 3. b 4. a 5. b 6. d 7. a 8. c 9. c 10. b 11. a 12. a

Answers to Quiz 33

1. F 2. F 3. T 4. T 5. T 6. F 7. F 8. T 9. T 10. T 11. F 12. T

Answers to Quiz 34

1. d 2. b 3. a 4. c 5. b 6. a 7. b 8. d 9. a 10. d 11. a 12. c

Answers to Quiz 35

1. g 2. j 3. h 4. b 5. c 6. i 7. k 8. f 9. a 10. l 11. e 12. d

Answers to Quiz 36

1. e 2. a 3. b 4. c 5. a 6. d 7. b 8. d 9. d 10. a 11. c 12. b

Answers to Quiz 37

1. g 2. j 3. f 4. b 5. a 6. l 7. o 8. i 9. d 10. e 11. k 12. n 13. h 14. c 15. m

Answers to Quiz 38

1. d 2. c 3. a 4. b 5. c 6. d 7. a 8. c 9. b 10. d 11. a 12. c 13. a 14. c 15. d

Answers to Quiz 39

1. F 2. T 3. T 4. T 5. F 6. T 7. F 8. T 9. T 10. F 11. F 12. F 13. T 14. F 15. T

Answers to Quiz 40

1. b 2. c 3. a 4. d 5. b 6. c 7. a 8. d 9. c 10. b 11. a 12. c 13. d 14. a 15. a

Answers to Quiz 41

1. i 2. g 3. o 4. b 5. h 6. k 7. j 8. f 9. m 10. n 11. c 12. e 13. a 14. d 15. l 16. p

Answers to Quiz 42

1. b 2. d 3. a 4. d 5. d 6. a 7. d 8. b 9. c 10. a 11. a 12. c 13. b 14. d 15. b 16. b

Answers to Quiz 43

1. T 2. T 3. F 4. F 5. F 6. F 7. T 8. T 9. T 10. T 11. T 12. T 13. F 14. T 15. F 16. T

Answers to Quiz 44

1. c 2. d 3. a 4. c 5. d 6. c 7. d 8. a 9. b 10. a 11. b 12. c 13. b 14. a 15. b 16. b

Specialized Vocabularies

Even after you have acquired a more powerful general vocabulary, you may still encounter terms that are unfamiliar to you because they are part of the special vocabulary of a discipline you have not studied. Many of these fields are central to modern life. Computer literacy, for example, is fast becoming a necessity for people in virtually all trades and professions, and everyone is bound to have some dealings with the legal profession at some time.

Here is a brief selection of current and basic terminology drawn from seven important spheres of American life—business, science, computers, law, fashion, and sports. These terms will provide an introduction and orientation to the current status of each of these professions.

A. Business

The vocabulary of business has grown at an astonishing rate. The executive, the student, the investor, the job seeker, the consumer are all affected by the world of business, and all of them need to be familiar with its specialized terminology. Even an experienced business professional may need to learn terminology that is outside his or her particular field. The common thread that runs through the world of business is the making, marketing, and management of a product or service. The catchall term "business" encompasses fields as diverse as personal finance, economics, insurance, manufacturing, retailing, marketing, and much more.

Specialized/Technical Terms

bear a person who believes that stock prices will decline.

bull a person who believes that stock prices will rise.

proxy a written authorization for one person to act for another, as at a meeting of stockholders.

securities stocks and bonds.

contrarian a person who rejects the majority opinion, especially an investor who buys when others are selling, and vice versa.

drive time the rush hour, when commuters listen to car radios: perceived as a time for generating advertising revenue.

emerging market a market in a less developed country whose economy is just beginning to grow.

mutual fund an investment company that invests its pooled funds in a diversified list of securities.

golden parachute an employment agreement guaranteeing an executive substantial compensation in the event of dismissal.

small-cap referring to a stock with a market capitalization of under $500 million, and considered to have more growth potential.

large-cap referring to a stock with a market capitalization of $1 billion or more.

superstore a very large store that stocks a great variety of merchandise.

hedge fund an investment company that uses high-risk speculative methods to obtain large profits.

flexdollars money given by an employer that an employee can apply to any of various benefits.

outsourcing the purchase of goods or contracting of services from an outside company.

short selling borrowing shares from a broker and selling them, then buying back the same shares at a lower price.

capital gains income from the sale of assets, such as bonds or real estate.

Informal or Slang

bean counter a person who makes judgments based primarily on numerical calculations.

dead-cat bounce a temporary recovery in stock prices after a steep decline, often resulting from the purchase of securities that have been sold short.

road warrior a person who travels extensively on business.

comp time compensatory time off from work, granted to an employee in lieu of overtime pay.

Acronyms

COBRA Consolidated Omnibus Budget Reconciliation Act: a federal law guaranteeing the right to continue participation in an employee health plan after coverage has been terminated due to layoff, divorce, etc.

SKU stockkeeping unit: a retailer-defined coding system used to distinguish individual items within a retailer's accounting and warehousing systems.

REIT real estate investment trust: a mutual fund that invests in real estate and must distribute at least 90% of its income as dividends.

Abbreviations

IPO initial public offering: a company's first stock offering to the public.

NAV net asset value: the price of a share in a mutual fund, equal to the total value of the fund's securities divided by the number of shares outstanding.

UGMA Uniform Gifts to Minors Act: a law that provides a means to transfer securities or money to a minor without establishing a formal trust, the assets being managed by a custodian.

APR annual percentage rate: the annual rate of interest, or the total interest to be paid in a year divided by the balance due.

Usage Issues

Journalese, bureaucratese, computerese, and legalese all afflict the uninitiated. As with other specialized industries, occupations, and academic disciplines, the language of business has been criticized and ridiculed for its overuse of jargon. The following is a discussion of usage issues that relate to the business field.

impact The figurative use of this verb, in the sense "to have an influence or effect (on)," has been criticized in recent years. However, this use is fully standard and fairly well established in the language. There are many examples in business and financial contexts: *to impact sales; to impact profits; to impact on the bottom line.*

proactive This adjective means "serving to prepare for, intervene in, or control an expected occurrence or situation." It has been criticized for overuse and stigmatized as jargon: *proactive measures against corruption; a proactive approach to fighting crime.*

price point This noun means "the price for which something is sold on the retail market." Some usage experts point out that it is redundant, since the word "price" has almost the same meaning. However, the term "price point" emphasizes the price of something in contrast to competitive prices for the same item: *The price point of this paperback is too high for the student market.*

incentivize This verb means "to give incentives to": *The government should incentivize the private sector to create jobs.* Many verbs ending in *-ize* have been disapproved of in recent years, particularly "finalize" and "prioritize." Although fully standard, such words are most often criticized when they become vogue terms, heard and seen everywhere. They are especially used in the contexts of advertising, commerce, and government—forces claimed to have a corrupting influence on the language.

B. Science

Vocabulary in the world of science has undergone a virtual explosion during the past few decades. This growth of new terms is the result not only of the accelerated progress of scientific discovery but also a number of crucial changes in emerging scientific theory.

antigravity a hypothesized force that behaves in ways opposite to gravity and repels matter.

antimatter matter composed only of antiparticles, which have attributes that are the reverse of those of matter. The basic difference between matter and antimatter is in the electric charge (negative vs. positive); for each particle of matter, there is a particle of antimatter.

antiparticle a particle whose properties, as mass, spin, or electric charge, have the same magnitude as, but the opposite algabraic sign of, a specific elementary particle. Where one is positive, the other is negative.

astronomy the science that deals with the universe beyond the earth's atmosphere, including the other planets in Earth's solar system, the stars, galaxies other than our own, and various other phenomena, such as quarks and black holes.

atom the basic component of an element, consisting of a nucleus containing combinations of neutrons and protons and one or more electrons bound to the nucleus by electrical attraction.

atomic weight the average weight of an atom of an element.

baryon a proton, neutron, or any elementary particle that decays into a set of particles that includes a proton.

Big Bang theory a theory that holds that our universe had its origins in an explosive cataclysm. Before that, the entire substance of the universe existed in a dense, compact kind of "cosmic soup"; since then, it has been expanding.

black hole a massive object in space, formed by the collapse of a star at the end of its life, whose gravitational field is so intense that no electromagnetic radiation can escape, not even light.

cosmology the branch of astronomy that deals with the general structure and evolution of the universe.

coulomb the basic unit of quantity of electricity, equal to the quantity of electric charge transferred in one second across a conductor.

cyclotron an accelerator in which particles are propelled in spiral paths by the use of a constant magnetic field. It is used to initiate nuclear transformations.

dark matter a hypothetical form of matter, probably making up over ninety percent of the mass of the universe, that is invisible to electromagnetic radiation and therefore undetectable. It is thought to account for the gravitational forces that are observable in the universe.

electric charge one of the basic properties of the elementary particles of matter giving rise to all electric and magnetic forces and interactions. The two kinds of charge are given negative and positive algebraic signs.

element one of a class of substances that cannot be separated into simpler substances by chemical means.

galaxy a large system of stars, such as our own Milky Way, held together by mutual gravitation and isolated from similar systems by vast regions of space.

gluon an unobserved massless particle that is believed to transmit the strong force between quarks, binding them together into baryons and mesons.

gravity the force of attraction by which terrestrial bodies tend to fall toward the center of the earth. It is also the similar attractive effect, considered as extending throughout space, of matter on other matter, including light.

MACHOs Massive Astrophysical Compact Halo Objects; brown dwarfs (small, cold stars), planets, or other objects hypothesized as constituting part of the dark matter in the halo of the Milky Way.

mass the quantity of matter in a body as determined from its weight or measured by its motion.

matter the substance or substances of which any physical object consists or is composed. Matter is made up of atoms; it has mass and can be measured.

meson any strongly interacting, unstable subatomic particle, other than a baryon, made up of two quarks.

Milky Way the spiral galaxy containing our solar system. With the naked eye it is observed as a faint luminous band stretching across the heavens, composed of at least 100 billion stars, including the sun, most of which are too distant to be seen individually.

neutrino any of three uncharged elementary particles or antiparticles having virtually no mass.

neutron an elementary particle having no electric charge, and having mass slightly greater than that of a proton.

neutron star an extremely dense, compact star composed primarily of neutrons, especially the collapsed core of a supernova.

nova a star that suddenly becomes thousands of times brighter and then gradually fades to its original intensity.

nuclear fission the splitting of the nucleus of an atom into nuclei of lighter atoms, accompanied by the release of great amounts of energy.

nuclear fusion a thermonuclear reaction in which nuclei of light atoms are fused, joining to form nuclei of heavier atoms, and releasing large amounts of energy.

nucleus the positively charged mass within an atom, composed of neutrons and protons, and possessing most of the mass but occupying only a small fraction of the volume of the atom.

particle 1. one of the extremely small constituents of matter, as an atom or nucleus. **2.** an elementary particle, quark, or gluon.

periodic table a table illustrating the periodic system, in which the chemical elements, formerly arranged in the order of their atomic weights and now according to their atomic numbers, are shown in related groups.

physics the science that deals with matter, energy, motion, and force.

planet 1. any of the nine large heavenly bodies revolving about the sun and shining by reflected light. In the order of their proximity to the sun, they are: Mercury, Venus, Earth, Mars, Jupiter, Saturn, Uranus, Neptune, and Pluto. **2.** a similar body revolving about a star other than the sun.

proton a positively charged elementary particle that is a fundamental constituent of all atomic nuclei. It is the lightest and most stable baryon, having an electric charge equal in magnitude to that of the electron.

pulsar one of several hundred known celestial objects, generally believed to be rapidly rotating neutron stars, that emit pulses of radiation, especially radio waves, with a high degree of regularity.

quark any of the hypothetical particles that, together with their antiparticles, are believed to constitute all the elementary particles classed as baryons and mesons; they are distinguished by their flavors, designated as up (u), down (d), strange (s), charm (c), bottom or beauty (b), and top or truth (t), and their colors, red, green, and blue.

radio astronomy the branch of astronomy that uses extraterrestrial radiation in radio wavelengths for the study of the universe, rather than using visible light.

SETI Search for Extraterrestrial Intelligence; any of several research projects designed to explore the universe for signs of patterned signals that would indicate the presence of intelligent life in outer space.

solar system the sun together with all the planets and other bodies that revolve around it.

space-time the four-dimensional continuum, a combination of space and time, having three spatial coordinates and one temporal coordinate, in which all physical quantities may be located. The implication is that space and time are one thing, not separate.

spin the intrinsic angular momentum characterizing each kind of elementary particle, which exists even when the particle is at rest.

steady-state theory a theory in which the universe is assumed to have average properties that are constant in space and time so that new matter must be continuously and spontaneously created to maintain average densities as the universe expands. This theory is now largely discredited in its original form. See Big Bang theory.

supernova the explosion of a star, possibly caused by gravitational collapse, during which the star's luminosity increases by as much as twenty magnitudes and most of the star's mass is blown away at very high velocity, sometimes leaving behind an extremely dense core.

Theory of Everything a theory, sought by scientists, that would show that the weak, strong, and gravitational forces of the universe are components of a single force. This theory would unify all the forces of nature.

universe the totality of known or supposed objects and phenomena throughout space; the cosmos; macrocosm. Originally thought to include only the solar system, then expanded to admit our Milky Way galaxy, the concept of the universe now encompasses everything known or not yet known in space.

C. Computers

Computer literacy is normally defined as familiarity with computers and how they work. But the term means more than that. Computer literacy is not just the ability to sit at a computer and use it to perform a few practical tasks, such as word processing or calculating interest payments with a spreadsheet program; it requires an understanding of the basic vocabulary of computer hardware and software.

alpha test an early test of new or updated computer software conducted by the developers of the program prior to beta testing by potential users.

American Standard Code for Information Interchange See ASCII.

applet a small application program that can be called up for use while working in another application. A typical example would be an on-screen calculator that you can use while working in a word processor.

application a specific kind of task, as database management or word processing, that can be done using an application program.

application program a computer program created for use in accomplishing a specific kind of task, as word processing or desktop publishing.

ASCII American Standard Code for Information Interchange: a standardized code in which characters are represented for computer storage and transmission by the numbers 0 through 127. See also UNICODE.

backup a copy or duplicate version, especially of a data file or program, retained for use in the event that the original becomes unusable or unavailable.

bay an open compartment in the console housing a computer's CPU in which a disk drive, tape drive, etc., may be installed. Also called **drive bay.**

beta test a test of new or updated computer software or hardware conducted at select user sites just prior to release of the product. Experienced beta testers try to push a new program to its limits, to see what kinds of behavior will make it break. This helps the programmers to eliminate bugs.

boot to start (a computer) by loading the operating system.

bug a defect, error, or imperfection, as in computer software.

byte a group of adjacent bits, usually eight, processed by a computer as a unit.

cache (pronounced like cash, not catch) a piece of computer hardware or a section of RAM dedicated to selectively storing and speeding access to frequently used program commands or data.

central processing unit See CPU.

CD-ROM a compact disc on which a large amount of digitized read-only data can be stored.

chat to engage in dialogue by exchanging electronic messages, usually in real time.

click to depress and release a mouse button rapidly, as to select an icon. Some functions in a program require a single click, some a double click.

compression reduction of the size of computer data by efficient storage. Compressed data can be stored in fewer bits than uncompressed data, and therefore takes up less space. This is useful not only for saving space on a hard disk, for example, but also for communicating data through a modem more rapidly.

copy protection a method of preventing users of a computer program from making unauthorized copies, usually through hidden instructions contained in the program code.

CPU Central Processing Unit: the key component of a computer. It houses the essential electronic circuitry that allows the computer to interpret and execute program instructions.

crash (of a computer) to suffer a major failure because of a malfunction of hardware or software. A crash is usually not the user's fault.

cursor a movable, sometimes blinking, symbol used to indicate where data (as text, commands, etc.) may be input on a computer screen.

cyber- a combining form representing "computer" *(cybertalk; cyberart)*.

cyberspace the realm of electronic communication, as exemplified by the Internet.

database a collection of ordered, related data in electronic form that can be accessed and manipulated by specialized computer software. Commonly, database information is organized by RECORDS, which are in turn divided into FIELDS.

desktop publishing the design and production of publications by means of specialized software enabling a personal computer to generate typeset-quality text and graphics. The kinds of publications that can be produced by means of desktop publishing now range from something as small as a business card to large books.

directory See FOLDER.

drive bay a compartment in the console that houses a computer's CPU in which a storage device, like a disk drive or tape drive, may be installed. Internal bays hold mass storage devices, like hard disks, while external, or open, bays house devices that give the user access to removable disks, tape, compact discs, etc.

documentation instructional materials for computer software or hardware. Some of these materials still come in print, in books or brochures, but increasingly, documentation is available primarily on line, as through a program's Help files.

dot pitch a measure of the distance between each pixel on a computer screen. A lower number indicates a sharper image.

download to transfer (software or data) from a computer or network to a smaller computer or a peripheral device.

export to save (documents, data, etc.) in a format usable by another application program.

fax modem a modem that can fax electronic data, as documents or pictures, directly from a computer. Many fax modems can also receive faxes, in electronic form, which can then be printed out.

field a unit of information, as a person's name, that combines with related fields, as an official title, an address, or a company name, to form one complete record in a computerized database.

file a collection of related computer data or program records stored by name, as on a disk.

flame *Slang.* (esp. on a computer network) **1.** an act or instance of angry criticism or disparagement. **2.** to behave in an offensive manner; rant. **3.** to insult or criticize angrily.

floppy disk a thin, portable, flexible plastic disk coated with magnetic material, for storing computer data and programs. Currently, the 3 1/2–inch disk, housed in a square rigid envelope, is the common size used with personal computers.

folder a place on a disk for holding multiple files. Using folders, disks can be organized in a hierarchical structure, with folders contained within other folders. The designation folder is used in environments with a graphical user interface. The equivalent term in operating systems like DOS and

Unix, known as command-line systems, and in early versions of Windows, was directory.

font a set of characters that have a given shape or design. The characters in a scalable font can be enlarged or reduced. A given font is a combination of the typeface, size, pitch, weight, and spacing.

freeware computer software distributed without charge. Compare SHAREWARE.

FTP File Transfer Protocol: a software protocol for exchanging information between computers over a network. Files are commonly downloaded from the Internet using FTP.

gigabyte a measure of data storage capacity equal to a little over one billion (10^9) BYTES, or 1,024 MEGABYTES. Hard disk drives with a capacity of several gigabytes are no longer uncommon.

graphical user interface a software interface designed to standardize and simplify the use of computer programs, as by using a mouse to manipulate text and images on a display screen featuring icons, windows, and menus. Also called **GUI.**

hard copy computer output printed on paper; printout.

hard disk a rigid disk coated with magnetic material. Hard disks are used for storing programs and relatively large amounts of data. Such storage is permanent, in that a disk's contents remain on the disk when the computer is shut off and can be accessed again when the computer is turned on.

hardware all the physical devices included in a computer system, as the CPU, keyboard, monitor, internal and external disk drives, and separate peripherals, like a printer or scanner.

HTML HyperText Markup Language: a set of standards, a variety of SGML, used to tag the elements of a hypertext document; the standard for documents on the World Wide Web.

hypertext data, as electronic text, graphics, or sound, linked to one another in paths determined by the creator of the material. Hypertext is usually stored with the links overtly marked, so that a computer user can move nonsequentially through a link from one object or document to another.

icon a small graphic image on a computer screen representing a disk drive, a file, or a software command, as a picture of a wastebasket to which a file one wishes to delete can be dragged with a mouse, or a picture of a printer that can be pointed at and clicked on to print a file.

inkjet printer a computer printer that prints text or graphics by spraying jets of ink onto paper to form a high-quality image approaching that of a laser printer.

install to put in place or connect for service or use: to install software on a computer; to install a scanner in one's computer system.

interface computer hardware or software designed to communicate information between hardware devices, between software programs, between devices and programs, or between a computer and a user.

Internet a large computer network linking smaller computer networks worldwide.

laptop a portable personal computer that is small, light, and thin enough to rest on the lap while in use. The screen is usually on the inside of the hinged top cover, becoming visible when when one opens the computer. Most laptops can be operated either through an electrical connection or batteries.

laser printer a high-speed, high-resolution computer printer that uses a laser to form dot-matrix patterns and an electrostatic process to print a page at a time.

macro a single instruction, for use in a computer program, that represents a sequence of instructions or keystrokes.

megabyte a measure of data storage capacity equal to approximately one million bytes.

memory the capacity of a computer to store information, especially internally in RAM, while electrical power is on. Do not confuse memory with storage.

menu a list, displayed on a computer screen, from which one can choose options or commands.

modem an electronic device that allows the transmission of data to or from a computer via telephone or other communication lines.

monitor a component part of a computer system that includes a display screen for viewing computer data.

multimedia the combined use of several media, such as sound, text, graphics, animation, and video, in computer applications. Multimedia is featured, for example, in games and in reference works on CD-ROMs.

newsgroup a discussion group maintained on a computer network, usually focused on a specific topic.

notebook a small, lightweight laptop computer.

OCR Optical Character Recognition: the reading of printed or typed text by electronic means, as by using a scanner and OCR software. In this process, the text is converted to digital data, which can then be manipulated and edited on the computer by using an application program, such as a word processor, spreadsheet, or database.

peripheral an external hardware device connected to a computer's CPU. Examples are printers, keyboards, and scanners.

printout computer output produced by a printer; hard copy.

RAM Random Access Memory: volatile computer memory that can store information while the electrical power is on. The information disappears when the computer is shut off. The amount of RAM a computer has is determined by the number and capacity of the RAM chips in the computer.

record a group of related FIELDS treated as a unit in a DATABASE.

resolution the degree of sharpness of a computer-generated image, as on a display screen or printout. Resolution is measured by the number of pixels across and down on a screen and by the number of dots per linear inch on hard copy.

SGML Standard Generalized Markup Language: a set of standards enabling a user to create an appropriate scheme for tagging the elements of an electronic document.

shareware computer software distributed without initial charge but for which the user is encouraged to pay a nominal registration fee after trying the program out. Such fees cover support for continued use and often entitle the user to inexpensive updates.

software programs for directing the operation of a computer or for processing electronic data. Software is, roughly, divided into utility programs and application programs.

spreadsheet a large electronic ledger sheet that can be used for financial planning. Electronic spreadsheets provide "what if" calculations, enabling the user to change estimated figures and see immediately what effect that change will have on the rest of the calculations in the spreadsheet.

storage the capacity of a device, such as a hard disk or a CD-ROM, to hold programs or data permanently. In the case of hard disks, one can remove such programs or data deliberately. Do not confuse storage with memory.

surge protector a device to protect computer circuitry from electrical spikes and surges by diverting the excess voltage through an alternate pathway.

typeface a design for a set of characters, especially numbers and letters, devised to provide the group of symbols with a unified look. Some popular typefaces often found on computer systems include Courier, Times Roman, and Helvetica, but the number of available typefaces has reached the thousands.

Unicode a standard for coding alphanumeric characters using sixteen bits for each character. Unlike ASCII, which uses eight-bit characters, Unicode can represent 65,000 unique characters. This allows a user of software that is Unicode-compatible to access the characters of most European and Asian languages.

URL Uniform Resource Locater: a protocol for specifying addresses on the Internet.

utility program a system program used to simplify standard computer operations, as sorting, copying, or deleting files.

virtual temporarily simulated by software. You can have *virtual memory* on a hard disk or *virtual storage* in RAM. *Virtual reality* simulates a real-world environment.

Web site a connected group of pages on the World Wide Web regarded as a single entity, usually maintained by one person or organization and devoted to one single topic or several closely related topics.

word processing the automated production and storage of documents using computers, electronic printers, and text-editing software.

World Wide Web a system of extensively linked hypertext documents; a branch of the Internet.

WYSIWYG What You See Is What You Get: of, pertaining to, or being a screen display that shows text as it will appear when printed, as by using display-screen versions of the printer's typefaces.

D. Politics

For as long as America has existed as a country, its people have been obsessed with politics. The speeches of politicians are learned in history classes, our important documents are still debated in the newspapers every day, and political campaigns are constantly claiming the interest of the public. The words used to discuss politics have likewise generated great interest. Sometimes politicians speak so as to evade issues, other times they create memorable words or expressions to memorialize their efforts.

Beltway, the the Washington, D.C., area; the U.S. government (used with *inside* or *outside*).

bloviate to speak pompously.

bork to systematically attack (a candidate or the like), especially in the media.

curve the forefront of any issue: *ahead of the curve; behind the curve.*

dirty tricks unethical or illegal activities directed against a political opponent.

dove a person who advocates peace or a conciliatory military position.

full-court press an all-out effort.

-gate (used to indicate political scandals, especially ones resulting from a cover-up): *Watergate; Irangate.*

goo-goo an idealistic supporter of political reform.

gridlock a complete stoppage of normal activity: *legislative gridlock.*

hawk a person who advocates war or a belligerent military position.

Hill, the the United States Congress; Capitol Hill.

hot-button arousing passionate emotions: *hot-button issues.*

policy wonk a person obsessively devoted to the most intricate details of policy.

pork political appropriations or appointments made solely for political reasons.

pork barrel a government bill, policy, or appropriation that supplies funds for local improvements, designed to ingratiate legislators with their constituents.

smoking gun indisputable evidence or proof, as of a crime or misdeed.

sound bite a brief, striking remark taken from a speech for use in a news story.

spin a particular viewpoint or bias, as on a news issue; *(as a verb)* to put a spin on: *The press secretary spun the debate to make it look like his candidate won.*

spin doctor an expert in spinning.

Teflon impervious to blame or criticism: *the Teflon president.*

wedge issue an issue that divides an otherwise united group or political party.

E. Law

Rarely has a profession captivated the public imagination more thoroughly than law. Whether your goal is to enrich your understanding of these events and stories or to deal with the mundane, practical legal matters in your personal and professional life, exposure to legal terminology is a necessity. Much of the vocabulary encountered in legal contexts is common enough to require little interpretation, but some legal language is unfamiliar or just plain difficult.

abet to encourage, instigate, or support some criminal activity. Used almost exclusively in the phrase *aid and abet.*

abscond to leave a jurisdiction in order to avoid arrest, service of a summons, or other imposition of justice.

abuse mistreatment of someone, such as physical abuse, psychological abuse, or sexual abuse. Abusive actions subject to legal intervention include (but are not limited to) child abuse and spousal abuse.

accessory a person who assists a criminal in committing a crime without being present when the crime is committed. An accessory is considered as culpable as someone who actually commits the crime.

adjourn to suspend or postpone a legal proceeding, either temporarily or indefinitely.

adjudication the hearing and disposition of a case in a proper court or agency. Adjudication includes a decision, as by a judge or jury, and, when appropriate, sentencing.

affidavit a formal written statement swearing to the truth of the facts stated and signed before a notary public. Dishonesty in an affidavit is either FALSE SWEARING or PERJURY.

amicus curiae, *pl.* **amici curiae** (literally, "friend of the court") someone who, although not a party to the litigation, volunteers or is invited by the court to submit views on the issues in the case.

arraignment the proceeding in which a criminal defendant is brought before the court, formally advised of charges, and required to enter a plea.

attachment the seizing or freezing of property by court order, either to resolve a dispute over ownership or to make the property available to satisfy a judgment against the owner.

certiorari a writ issuing from a superior court calling up the record of a proceeding in an inferior court for review. Also called **writ of certiorari.**

charge 1. a judge's instruction to the jury on a particular point of law. **2.** a formal allegation that a person has violated a criminal law. **3.** to make or deliver a charge.

conflict of interest the circumstance of a public officeholder, business executive, or the like, whose personal interests might benefit from his or her official actions or influence, especially when those personal interests conflict with one's duty.

contract an agreement between two or more parties for one to do or not do something specified in exchange for something done or promised by the other(s).

counterclaim a claim made to offset another claim, especially one made by the defendant against the plaintiff in a legal action.

cross examination an examination, usually by a lawyer, of a witness for the opposing side, especially for the purpose of discrediting the witness's testimony.

due process fair administration of the law in accordance with established procedures and with due regard for the fundamental rights and liberties of people in a free society.

escheat the reverting of property to the state when there are no persons that can be found who are legally qualified to inherit or to claim.

exclusionary rule a rule that forbids the introduction of illegally obtained evidence in a criminal trial.

extradition the surrender of a suspect by one state, nation, or authority to another.

false swearing the crime of making a false statement, as under oath (for example, in a civil case), knowing that the statement is not true. *False swearing* is not considered as serious a crime as PERJURY.

garnishment the attachment of money or property so they can be used to satisfy a debt.

grand jury a group of citizens assembled to hear evidence presented by a prosecutor against a particular person for a particular crime. A *grand jury* is convened in order to determine whether or not there is sufficient evidence to issue an indictment. The standards for indictment are considerably less than those for conviction at trial.

gravamen the fundamental part of an accusation; the essence of a complaint or charge.

hearsay evidence testimony based on what a witness has heard from another person rather than on direct personal knowledge or experience.

hostile witness a witness called by one side in a case who is known to be friendly to the other side or who turns out to be evasive in answering questions.

impeachment the institution of formal misconduct charges against a government official as a basis for removal from office.

in flagrante delicto in the very act of committing the offense: *They were caught in flagrante delicto.*

judicial district a geographic division established for the purpose of organizing a court system.

jurisdiction the geographic area throughout which the authority of a court, legislative body, law enforcement agency, or other governmental unit extends.

kangaroo court a mock court convened to reach a predetermined verdict of guilty, such as one set up by vigilantes.

litigant a party to a lawsuit.

litigation the process of making something the subject of a lawsuit; contesting an issue in a judicial proceeding.

litigator a lawyer who specializes in litigation.

malfeasance the performance by a public official of an act that is legally unjustified, harmful, or contrary to law.

mandamus a writ from a superior court to an inferior court or to an officer, corporation, etc., commanding that a specified thing be done; usually issued only in rare cases, to remedy an injustice.

monopoly the intentional acquisition or retention of exclusive control of a commodity or service in a particular market, especially so as to exclude competition and make possible the manipulation of prices.

nolo contendere (in a criminal case) a defendant's pleading that does not admit guilt but subjects him or her to punishment as though a guilty plea had been entered. Unlike a guilty plea, however, a plea of *nolo contendere* cannot be used as proof of guilt in a subsequent civil proceeding.

perjury the willful giving of false testimony under oath or affirmation, in a judicial or administrative proceeding, upon a point material to a legal inquiry. Compare FALSE SWEARING.

plaintiff the person who starts a lawsuit by serving or filing a complaint.

plea a criminal defendant's formal response to charges. The defendant may plead *guilty, not guilty,* or *nolo contendere.*

prima facie (of a case, evidence, or proof) sufficient to support a contending party's claim and to warrant a verdict in favor of that party regarding that issue.

pro bono (of legal services) performed without fee, for the sake of the public good.

replevin an action for the recovery of tangible personal property wrongfully taken or detained by another.

special prosecutor an outside person appointed to investigate and, if warranted, prosecute a case in which the prosecutor who would normally handle the case has a conflict of interest.

statute of limitations a statute defining the period of time after an event within which legal action arising from that event may be taken.

subornation of perjury the crime of inducing another person to commit perjury.

surrogate court (in some states) a court having jurisdiction over the probate of wills, the administration of estates, etc.

venue the county or judicial district where the courts have jurisdiction to consider a case.

voir dire an examination of a proposed witness or juror to determine if there are possible sources of bias that would militate against his or her objectivity in serving on a jury; an oath administered to a prospective witness or juror by which he or she is sworn to speak the truth so that the examiner can ascertain his or her competence.

writ a court order by which a court commands a certain official or body to carry out a certain action.

F. Fashion

Dressing stylishly is an important means of self-expression for many people, and the fashion industry is one of the biggest businesses in America, with its own customs, its own newspapers, and its own language. Here is a selection of recent words referring to clothing and fashion, along with definitions of some enduring classics.

fashionista an influential person in the fashion world; a devotee of fashion.

fashion victim a person whose attempts to follow the dictates of fashion have backfired ludicrously; one whose obsession with fashion is excessive.

fashion police a jocular imaginary force invoked as criticism of a person who is badly or unstylishly dressed.

supermodel a prominent fashion model who commands the highest fees and can usually be recognized by first name only.

haute couture high fashion; the most fashionable, exclusive, and expensive designer clothing, made to measure of luxurious fabrics after extensive fittings.

atelier a workshop or studio of a high-fashion designer.

ready-to-wear ready-made clothing. Also **prêt-à-porter; off-the-peg; off-the-rack.**

vintage referring to clothing purchased at resale shops that evokes the style of an earlier era in fashion.

casual day a day (usually Friday) on which office workers are permitted to dress in sportswear. Also **dress-down day.**

Gothic look a style marked by bizarre or outré makeup (for men as well as women), dress, and hairstyle in a Romantic vein reminiscent of classic horror films. Also **Goth.**

grunge a style marked by dirty, unkempt, often torn, secondhand clothing.

gangsta a style derived from the inner-city ghetto emphasizing baggy clothing, designer sportswear, cutting-edge athletic shoes, and sometimes gold jewelry. Also **hip-hop.**

Saville Row an area of London specializing in elegant and classic hand-tailored menswear.

bespoke (of menswear) referring to hand-tailored suits, custom-fitted shirts, bench-made shoes, etc.

bias-cut referring to fabric cut on the bias to drape gracefully on the body.

asymmetrical-cut referring to necklines or hemlines that are not symmetrical.

thigh-cut referring to bathing suits cut high on the thigh to expose the hip.

kente a colorful striped fabric of Ghanaian origin often worn as a symbol of African-American pride.

Gore-Tex™ a breathable, water-repellent fabric laminate originally used for outdoor sportswear, often produced in bright colors.

microfiber an extremely fine polyester fiber used in clothing.

spandex a polyurethane fabric with elastic properties.

bandage dress a dress of spandex that totally conforms to the wearer's body; originated by Hervé Leger.

wrap dress a patterned polyester or cotton knit dress that ties on the side to drape naturally over the wearer's body; originated by Diane Von Furstenburg in the 1970s and revived in the 1990s.

sheath a close-fitting, simple, unbelted dress with a straight drape, usually sleeveless with a plain neckline.

slip dress a loose-fitting unadorned dress with skinny straps, modeled on women's undergarments of the earlier twentieth century.

little black dress a basic, unadorned black dress popularized by Coco Chanel in the early twentieth century for its flexibility and utility as a wardrobe mainstay, especially as a cocktail dress.

caftan a full, long robe with loose sleeves, worn for lounging; based on similar Middle Eastern garments.

pareo a length of fabric tied at the side to drape over the hips, usually worn over a matching bathing suit. Also **sarong.**

pedal pushers casual slacks reaching to mid-calf. Also **capri pants; clam diggers.**

palazzo pants women's wide-legged trousers cut to resemble a long skirt.

skort a women's garment for the lower body that resembles a skirt but has separate openings for the legs.

cargo pants loose-cut trousers with a number of deep pockets on the legs to accommodate extra baggage; originally a military style.

leggings tight-fitting elasticized pants for women; modeled on dancer's tights.

ski pants snug-fitting pants of a stretch fabric, usually having straps for the feet to keep them from bunching at the boot line.

bell-bottoms trousers with wide, flaring legs, modeled on sailor's pants.

khakis loose-fitting trousers made of a stout beige fabric, worn as casual sportswear.

pantsuit a softened version for women of the classic menswear suit, having a jacket with lapels and tailored trousers.

power suit a tailored women's suit with jacket and skirt designed in imitation of a man's business suit and usually including shoulder pads; popular among businesswomen of the 1980s.

Chanel suit a women's suit usually with a cropped jacket having a round neck, several buttons, and often braid trim, worn with a skirt.

catsuit a one-piece garment for women with long sleeves and leggings, often made of a polyester fabric to cling tightly to the shape of the wearer.

bodysuit a short, one-piece garment for women with a snap closure at the crotch, designed to eliminate bunching at the waist and create a smooth line under a skirt or pants; adapted from a dancer's leotard.

thong a skimpy garment for the lower body that exposes the buttocks, usually having a strip of fabric passing between the legs attached to a waistband.

tank top a low-cut, sleeveless pullover with shoulder straps, often made of a lightweight knit.

racer back a tank top with the back cut out to expose the shoulder blades; modeled on similar designs in bathing suits designed to cut friction in speed-swimming contests.

crop top a casual pullover sport shirt cut short to expose the midriff.

shell a short, sleeveless, usually round-necked blouse for women, often worn under a jacket.

camisole a women's waist-length top with skinny shoulder straps, usually worn under a sheer bodice.

bustier a women's tight-fitting, sleeveless, strapless top worn as a blouse and usually exposing decolletage; modeled on the corset.

sweater set a short-sleeved, round-necked sweater for women accompanied by a matching cardigan. Also **twin set.**

cowlneck sweater a sweater with a neckline made of softly draped fabric.

blouson a full-cut shirt or jacket tied at the waist for a balloon effect.

Rugby shirt a full-cut, usually broad-striped cotton pullover with a contrasting white turnover collar and three-button placket; modeled on shirts worn by English Rugby or soccer players.

polo shirt a cotton pullover sport shirt with a round neck or turnover collar, usually with short sleeves.

Hawaiian shirt a loose-fitting, button-front, short-sleeved cotton shirt with a turnover collar, made in bright colors and loud patterns with a tropical theme, such as palm trees or parrots.

button-down (of a collar) having buttonholes at the ends with which it can be buttoned to the front of the garment.

French cuffs generous foldover shirt cuffs that require cufflinks or studs.

fisherman's sweater an elaborately designed, solid-color, hand-knit and cable-stitched sweater of heavy wool; originally made by the wives of sailors in the Aran Islands of Ireland.

pea jacket a heavy, double-breasted, short wool jacket; originally worn by seamen. Also **peacoat.**

bomber jacket a short jacket with a fitted or elasticized waist, often made of leather and lined with fleece; originally worn by fliers.

motorcycle jacket a short leather jacket resembling a bomber jacket, but usually embellished with zippers, buckles, studs, etc.

duffel coat a hooded overcoat of sturdy wool, usually fastened with toggle buttons.

polo coat a tailored overcoat of camel's hair or a similar fabric, single- or double-breasted and often belted or half-belted.

maxi coat a full-length overcoat extending to the ankles.

chesterfield a single- or double-breasted overcoat with a velvet collar, often made of herringbone wool.

parka a hooded, straight-cut jacket made of materials that provide warmth against very cold temperatures; often a down- or polyester-filled nylon shell, sometimes quilted for extra warmth.

faux fur artificial fleece dyed and styled to resemble animal fur.

fun fur a fur jacket or coat dyed and cut in an outré style to be worn as sportswear.

thigh-highs stockings that come to mid-thigh, often worn under a short skirt so that the stocking tops are visible.

Birkenstocks™ open leather sandals.

boat shoes rubber-soled mocassins worn to provide a firm grip on a boat's deck.

driving shoes soft, semi-flexible leather or suede loafers with a rubber sole designed to grip the pedals of a car.

stilettos very high, narrow heels that taper to a point, used on women's shoes. Also **spike heels.**

slides backless women's shoes of varying heights. Also **mules.**

platforms shoes with a thick insert of leather, cork, plastic, or other sturdy material between the upper and the sole.

wedgies women's shoes with a heel formed by a roughly triangular or wedge-like piece that extends from the front or middle to the back of the sole.

slingbacks open-backed women's shoes with a strap to secure the heel.

jellies transparent polyurethane shoes with a cross-strap and very low heels.

cross-trainers athletic shoes designed to be used for more than one sport.

high tops sneakers with fabric extending to the ankles.

ballerina flats low-heeled women's shoes modeled on the soft exercise slippers worn by dancers.

espadrilles flat shoes with a cloth upper, a rope sole, and sometimes lacing around the ankles.

cowboy boots chunky-heeled boots with a pointed toe and highly decorative stitching and embossing.

weave false hair woven into the natural hair.

hair extensions false hair woven into a person's natural hair to give the illusion of greater length and fullness.

dreadlocks a hairstyle of many long, ropelike braids.

cornrows narrow braids of hair plaited tightly against the scalp.

Kelly bag a squarish or slightly trapezoidal women's handbag first made by Hermès for Princess Grace of Monaco.

Chanel bag a women's handbag of quilted leather suspended from the shoulder on a gold chain.

backpack a pack or knapsack carried on one's back to keep the hands free; first popularized by campers and students, later made in leather and adopted by fashionable women in lieu of a handbag.

G. Sports

The American devotion to sports is almost religious in its fervor. Every sport has its own complicated rules and language; there are entire books devoted to sports terminology. Here is a short list of some recent sports-related words and expressions.

beach volleyball competitive volleyball played outdoors on sand.

bungee jumping jumping from a high surface to which one is attached by elasticized cords, so that the body bounces back before hitting the ground.

extreme sports sports that are viewed as being very dangerous, such as bungee-jumping or sky surfing.

full-court press a defensive strategy in basketball in which the defensive team pressures the offensive team the entire length of the court.

Hacky Sack™ a small leather beanbag juggled with the feet as a game.

Hail Mary a long football pass thrown in desperation, with a low chance of being caught.

high five a gesture of greeting or congratulation where one person slaps the open palm of another as it is held at head level.

in-line skate a roller skate having typically four hard-rubber wheels in a line resembling the blade of an ice skate.
in-your-face (in basketball) confrontational; provocative.

Jet Ski™ a small jet-propelled boat ridden like a motorcycle.

Rollerblade™ a brand of in-line skates.

sky surfing jumping from a plane with a parachute while wearing a board resembling a snowboard, so that one can "skate" on the air currents.
snowboard a board for gliding on the snow, resembling a wide ski, that one rides in an upright, standing position resembling the motion of surfing.

triathlon an athletic contest consisting of swimming, running, and cycling.
trash-talking (in basketball) the use of aggressive, boastful, or insulting language.

Zamboni™ a machine for smoothing the ice at a rink.

Shortened Forms in English

Though some language experts regard the modern predilection for abbreviations and shortened forms as a kind of barbarism, it is a trend that reflects the pressures of modern life, as we attempt to compress long utterances into more compact expressive forms. Abbreviations are also a natural outgrowth of the underlying preference of English speakers for monosyllabic forms.

Here is an overview of shortened forms in English, along with some notes on their formation and use.

An *abbreviation* is a shortened or contracted form created from the initial or first few letters, or any group of letters, of a word or series of words. The series of words in the full form can be a title, name, or set phrase. Examples: *E* (for East); *Dr.* (for Doctor); *lb.* (for Latin "libra," pound); *etc.* (for et cetera).

An *initialism* is a shortened form created from the initial letters of a series of words, with each letter pronounced separately. Examples: *FDR* (for Franklin Delano Roosevelt); *CIA* (for Central Intelligence Agency).

An *acronym* is a pronounceable word created from the initial or first few letters of a series of words. Sometimes a vowel is inserted in the acronym to aid pronunciation. Very often the full or expanded form of an acronym is not widely known; few people know what the letters in *laser* stand for. The acronym may be a word that already exists in the language, such as *CARE* and *SHAPE*. Examples: *NASA* (for National Aeronautics and Space Administration); *scuba* (for self-contained underwater breathing apparatus).

A *hybrid* is a shortened form that cannot be neatly classified as an abbreviation, initialism, or acronym. One type of hybrid can be pronounced as the word it spells or as a series of letters, as *AWOL*. Another type of hybrid is an initialism that is pronounced as a word, as *SCSI* (skuz′ē). There are also shortened forms composed of a short form and a word, as *D-day* and *CAT scan*. Sometimes a shortened form can be considered both an abbreviation and a word, as *math* (for mathematics) and *prof* (for professor).

A *symbol* is a letter, figure, or other conventional mark, or a combination of letters, used to designate an object, quality, process, etc. Symbols are used in specialized fields, such as physics and music. Examples: *Au* (for gold, the chemical element); *X* (for ten, the Roman numeral).

The Formation and Use of Short Forms

Short forms are commonly encountered in newspapers, magazines, advertising, and daily conversation. In addition to the forms in general, everyday use, each specialized field has its own set of technical short forms.

Abbreviations, acronyms, and symbols are created for several reasons. They are easy to pronounce or remember, and they save time in speaking and writing. Many are catchy, such as *GUI* (Graphical User Interface) and *WYSIWYG* (What You See Is What You Get), or useful in advertising slogans and newspaper headlines. Some serve as euphemisms, such as *B.O.* for body odor.

A full form may have several different short forms in common use. Not all are equally correct, acceptable, or widespread. For example, *acct.* is more common than *acc.* as an abbreviation for "account."

Many short forms are informal or slang, as *P.D.Q.* (for pretty damn quick) and *OK*. Others are formal or fully standard in the language. In fact, some short forms are used instead of their corresponding full forms. We commonly speak of *VCRs, TVs,* and *HMOs,* but rarely of *videocassette recorders, televisions,* and *health maintenance organizations.*

Although short forms are acceptable and widely used, some are not immediately recognizable. They may be derived from foreign words or phrases, such as *no.* from Latin "numero." Some short forms stand for more than one full form and are therefore ambiguous. These forms should be defined the first time they are mentioned, and the short form can be used thereafter. Example: *The Central Intelligence Agency (CIA) was established in 1947. The CIA is a federal agency that conducts intelligence activities outside the United States.*

For abbreviations and initialisms, the trend is to leave out the periods, especially in scientific and technical notation and in capitalized forms, such as *F* (for Fahrenheit) and *RNA.* However, some short forms always take periods to avoid confusion, as *B.A.* (for Bachelor of Arts), *art.* (for article), *D.C.* (District of Columbia), and *no.* (for number).

The great majority of abbreviations are written with capital letters regardless of whether the constituent words are usually capitalized, as *LCD* (for liquid-crystal display). Acronyms are usually capitalized, as *NATO,* but common ones often appear in lowercase, as *radar.* Short forms standing for proper nouns or important words in names or titles are usually capitalized, as *UFT* (for United Federation of Teachers) and *Span.* (for Spanish). Short forms standing for common nouns, adjectives, or adverbs are usually lowercased, as *spec.* (for special). Units of weight and measure, such as *kg* and *hr,* are written in lowercase. Symbols for chemical elements have only the first letter capitalized, as *Fe* (for iron).

The plural of a short form is often the same as the singular; in fact, there is a trend toward abolishing all pluralized forms. Short forms may be pluralized by adding "s" or "es," as *lbs.* (pounds), *nos.* (numbers), *HMOs* (health maintenance organizations), and *PCs* (personal computers). Sometimes apostrophes are used in plural forms, as *pj's.* There is a small group of abbreviations that form the plural by doubling a consonant, as *mss* (manuscripts), *ll* (lines), and *pp.* (pages).

Short forms can function as more than one part of speech. For example, *OK* is used as a noun, interjection, verb, adjective, and adverb. In these cases, the form is inflected in a predictable manner: *OK'ed* (or *OK'd*), *OK'ing*.

List of Prefixes

a-[1] from Old English, used **1.** before some nouns to make them into adverbs showing "place where": *a- + shore → ashore = on (or into) the shore.* **2.** before some verbs to make them into words showing a state or process: *a- + sleep → asleep (= sleeping); a- + blaze → ablaze (= blazing).*

a-[2] a variant spelling of **an-**. It comes from Latin and is used before some adjectives to mean "not"; *a- + moral → amoral (= without morals); a- + tonal → atonal (= without tone).*

ab- from Latin, used before some words and roots to mean "off, away": *abnormal (= away from what is normal).* Compare A-[2].

ad- from Latin, meaning "toward" and indicating direction or tendency: *ad- + join → adjoin* (= join toward, attack).

ambi- from Latin, meaning "both" and "around." These meanings are found in such words as: *ambiguous, ambivalence, ambiance.*

amphi- from Greek, meaning "both; on two sides." This meaning is found in such words as: *amphibian, amphibious, amphitheater.*

an- from Greek, used before roots or stems beginning with a vowel or *h*, meaning "not; without; lacking": *anaerobic (= without oxygen); anonymous (= without name).* Compare A-[2].

ante- from Latin, used before roots, meaning **1.** "happening before": *antebellum (= before the war).* **2.** "located in front of": *anteroom (= room located in front of another).*

anti- from Greek, used before nouns and adjectives, meaning **1.** against, opposed to: *anti-Semitic, antislavery.* **2.** preventing, counteracting, or working against: *anticoagulant, antifreeze.* **3.** destroying or disabling: *antiaircraft, antipersonnel.* **4.** identical to in form or function, but lacking in some important ways: *anticlimax, antihero, antiparticle.* **5.** an antagonist or rival of: *Antichrist, antipope.* **6.** situated opposite: *Anti-Lebanon.* Also, before a vowel, **ant-**.

apo- from Greek, meaning "away, off, apart": *apo- + strophe → apostrophe* (= a turn away, digression).

aqua- from Latin, meaning "water." This meaning is found in such words as: *aquaculture, aqualung, aquarium, aquatic, aqueduct, aqueous, aquifer.*

auto- from Greek, meaning "self." This meaning is found in such words as: *autocrat, autograph, autonomous, autonomy, autopsy.* Also, esp. before a vowel, **aut-**.

baro- from Greek, meaning "weight." This meaning is found in such words as: *barograph, barometer, baroreceptor.*

be- from Old English, used **1.** to make verbs meaning "to make, become, treat as": *be- + cloud → becloud (= make like a cloud, hard to see); be- + friend → befriend (= treat someone as a friend).* **2.** before adjectives and verbs ending in -*ed* to mean "covered all over; completely; all around": *be-* + *decked* → *bedecked* (= *decked or covered all over*); *be-* + *jeweled* → *bejeweled* (= *covered with jewels*).

bi- from Latin, meaning "twice, two." This meaning is found in such words as: *biennial, bisect, bicentennial, bigamy, biped, binoculars, bilateral, bipartisan, biweekly.* —**Usage.** In some words, especially words referring to time periods, the prefix *bi-* has two meanings: "twice a + ~" and "every two + ~ -s". Thus, *biannual* means both "twice a year" and "every two years." Be careful; check many of these words.

bio- from Greek, meaning "life." This meaning is found in such words as: *biodegradable, biology, biosphere.*

centi- from Latin, used before roots to mean "hundredth" or "hundred": *centiliter* (= *one hundredth of a liter*); *centipede* (= *(creature having) one hundred feet*).

chiro- from Greek, meaning "hand." This meaning is found in such words as: *chirography, chiropodist, chiropractor, chiromancy.*

circum- from Latin, meaning "round, around." This meaning is found in such words as *circuit, circuitous, circumcise, circumference, circumnavigate, circumstance, circumvent, circumlocution, circus.*

co- from Latin, meaning **1.** "joint, jointly, together." This meaning is found in such words as: *cochair, costar, coworker.* **2.** "auxiliary, helping." This meaning is found in such words as: *copilot.*

col-[1], var. of COM- before *l: collateral.*

col-[2], var. of COLO- before a vowel: *colectomy.*

com- from Latin, meaning "with, together with." This meaning is found in such words as: *combine, compare, commingle.* For variants before other sounds, see CO-, COL-[1], CON-, COR-.

con- a variant spelling of COM-. It comes from Latin, meaning "together, with." This meaning is found in such words as: *convene, condone, connection.*

contra- from Latin, meaning "against, opposite, opposing." This meaning is found in such words as: *contraband, contraception, contradict, contrary.*

cor- another form of COM- that is used before roots beginning with *r: correlate.*

counter- from Middle English, meaning "against, counter to, opposed to." This meaning is found in such words as: *counterattack, counteroffer, counterclockwise.*

de- from Latin, used to form verbs and some adjectives meaning **1.** motion or being carried down from, away, or off: *deplane* (= *move down or off an airplane*); *descend* (= *move or go down*); **2.** reversing or undoing the effects of an action: *deflate* (= *reverse the flow of air out of something*); *dehumanize* (= *reverse the positive, humanizing effects of something*); **3.** taking out or removal of a thing: *decaffeinate* (= *take out the caffeine from something*); *declaw* (= *remove the claws of an animal*); **4.** finishing or completeness of an action: *defunct* (= *completely non-functioning*); *despoil* (= *completely spoil*).

deci- from Latin, meaning "ten." This meaning now appears in the names of units of measurement that are one tenth the size of the unit named by the second element of the compound: *decibel (= one tenth of a bel); deciliter (= one-tenth of a liter)*. See the root -DEC-.

dem- from Greek, meaning "people." This meaning is found in such words as: *demagogue, democracy, demography*.

demi- from French, meaning "half." This meaning is found in such words as: *demigod, demitasse*.

demo- like DEM-, from Greek, meaning "people, population." This meaning is found in such words as: *democracy, demography*.

di- from Greek, meaning "two, double." This meaning is found in such words as: *diptych, dioxide*.

dia- from Greek, meaning "through, across, from point to point; completely." These meanings are found in such words as: *diachronic, diagnosis, dialogue, dialysis, diameter, diaphanous, diarrhea, diathermy*.

dis- from Latin, meaning "apart." It now has the following meanings: **1.** opposite of: *disagreement (= opposite of agreement)*. **2.** not: *disapprove: (= not to approve); dishonest (= not honest); disobey (= not obey)*. **3.** reverse; remove: *disconnect (= to remove the connection of); discontinue (= to stop continuing); dissolve (= remove the solidness of; make liquid)*.

dys- from Greek, meaning "ill, bad." This meaning is found in such words as: *dysentery, dyslexia, dyspepsia*.

electro- from New Latin, meaning "electric" or "electricity": *electro- + magnetic → electromagnetic*.

em- a form of EN- used before roots beginning with *b, p,* and sometimes *m: embalm*. Compare IM-[1].

en- ultimately from Latin, used before adjectives or nouns to form verbs meaning **1.** to cause (a person or thing) to be in (the place, condition, or state mentioned); to keep in or place in: *en- + rich → enrich (= to cause to be rich); en- + tomb → entomb (= to cause to be in a tomb)*; **2.** to restrict on all sides, completely: *en- + circle → encircle (= to restrict on all sides within a circle)*.

epi- from Greek, meaning "on, upon, at" (*epicenter*), "outer, exterior" (*epidermis*), "accompanying, additional" (*epiphenomenon*).

eu- from Greek, meaning "good, well"; it now sometimes means "true, genuine." This meaning is found in such words as: *eugenics, eulogize, eulogy, euphemism, euphoria, euthanasia*.

Euro- contraction of "Europe," used with roots and means "Europe," "Western Europe," or "the European Community": *Euro- + -centric → Eurocentric (= centered on Europe); Euro- + -crat → Eurocrat (= bureaucrat in the European Community)*. Also, *esp. before a vowel,* **Eur-**.

ex- from Latin, meaning **1.** "out, out of, away, forth." It is found in such words as: *exclude, exhale, exit, export, extract*. **2.** "former; formerly having been": *ex-member (= former member)*.

exo- from Greek, meaning "outside, outer, external": *exocentric*. Also, *before a vowel,* **ex-**.

extra- from Latin, meaning "outside of; beyond": *extra- + galactic → extragalactic (= outside the galaxy); extra- + sensory → extrasensory (= beyond the senses).*

fore- from Old English, used before nouns, meaning **1.** before (in space, time, condition, etc.): *fore- + -cast → forecast (= prediction before weather comes); fore- + taste → foretaste (= a taste before the event takes place); fore- + warn → forewarn (= to warn ahead of time).* **2.** front: *fore- + head → forehead (= front of the head).* **3.** preceding: *fore- + father → forefather (= father that came before).* **4.** superior: *fore- + man → foreman (= superior to the other workers).*

hemo- (or **hema-**) from Greek, meaning "blood." This meaning is found in such words as: *hemoglobin, hemophilia, hemorrhage, hemorrhoid.* Also, esp. before a vowel, **hem-**.

hyper- from Greek, used **1.** before nouns and adjectives meaning "excessive; overly; too much; unusual": *hyper- + critical → hypercritical (= overly critical); hyper- + inflation → hyperinflation (= inflation that is unusual or too high).* Compare SUPER-. **2.** in computer words to refer to anything not rigidly connected in a step-by-step manner: *hyper- + text → hypertext (= text or information that the user can gain access to in the order he or she chooses).*

hypo- from Greek, used before roots, meaning "under, below": *hypo- + dermic → hypodermic (= under the skin); hypo- + thermia → hypothermia (= heat or temperature below what it should be).* Also, esp. before a vowel, **hyp-**.

il-[1] another form of IN-[2] that is used before roots beginning with *l;* it means "not": *il- + legible → illegible (= that cannot be easily read).*

il-[2] another form of IN-[1] that is used before roots beginning with *l;* it means "in, into": *il- + -luminate (= light) → illuminate (= shine on or into).*

im-[1] another form of IN-[2] that is used before roots beginning with *p, b,* and *m;* it means "not": *im- + possible → impossible (= that is not possible).*

im-[2] another form of IN-[1] that is used before roots beginning with *p, b,* and *m;* it means "in, into": *im- + -migrate → immigrate (= travel in or into).*

in-[1] from Old English, used before verbs and nouns and means "in; into; on": *in- + come → income (= money coming in); in- + corporate (= body) → incorporate (= make into one body); in- + land → inland (= in the land).*

in-[2] from Latin, used before adjectives, meaning "not": *in- + accurate → inaccurate (= not accurate); in- + capable → incapable (= not capable); in- + direct → indirect (= not direct).* For variants before other sounds, see IM-, IL-, IR-.

inter- from Latin, meaning "between, among": *intercity (= between cities); interdepartmental (= between or among departments).*

intra- from Latin, meaning "within": *intraspecies (= within species).* Compare INTRO-, INTER-.

intro- from Latin, meaning "inside, within": *intro- + duce (= lead) → intro-*

duce (= bring inside or within to meet someone); intro- + version (= a turn-ing) → introversion (= a turning inside or within). Compare INTRA-.

ir-¹ another form of IN-¹ that is used before roots beginning with r: ir- + radi-ate → irradiate.

ir-² another form of IN-² that is used before roots beginning with r: ir- + re-ducible → irreducible.

iso- from Greek, meaning "equal." This meaning is found in such scientific and chemical words as: *isochromatic*.

kilo- from Greek, used before quantities, meaning "thousand": *kilo- + liter → kiloliter (= one thousand liters); kilo- + watt → kilowatt (= one thousand watts)*.

mal- from Latin, meaning "bad; wrongful; ill." This meaning is found in such words as: *maladroit, malcontent, malfunction*.

maxi- contraction of the word *maximum,* meaning "very large or long in comparison with others of its kind." This meaning is found in such words as: *maxiskirt*.

mega- from Greek, meaning **1.** extremely large, huge: *megalith (= extremely large stone or rock); meagstructure (= a huge structure)*. **2.** one million of the units of (the base root or word): *megahertz (= one million hertz); megaton (= one million tons)*. **3.** very large quantities or amounts: *megabucks (= a great deal of money); megadose (= a large dose of medi-cine)* **4.** things that are extraordinary examples of their kind: *megahit (= a smash movie or stage hit); megatrend (= important, very popular trend)*.

meta- from Greek, meaning "after, along with, beyond, among, behind." These meanings are found in such words as: *metabolism, metamorphosis, metaphor, metaphysics*.

micro- from Latin, meaning **1.** small or very small in comparison with others of its kind: *micro- + organism → microorganism (= very small living crea-ture)*. **2.** restricted in scope: *micro- + habitat → microhabitat; micro- + eco-nomics → microeconomics*. **3.** containing or dealing with texts that require enlargement to be read: *micro- + film → microfilm*. **4.** one millionth: *micro- + gram → microgram*. Also, esp. before a vowel, **micr-**.

mid- from Old English, meaning "being at or near the middle point of": *mid-day; mid-Victorian; mid-twentieth century*.

milli- from Latin, meaning **1.** one thousand: *milli- + -pede (= foot) → milli-pede (= a small creature with very many legs)*. **2.** (in the metric system) equal to 1/1000 of the unit mentioned: *milli- + meter → millimeter (= 1/1000 of a meter)*.

mini- contraction of the word *minimum,* meaning **1.** of a small or reduced size in comparison with others of its kind: *mini- + car → minicar; mini- + gun → minigun*. **2.** limited in scope, intensity, or duration: *mini- + boom (= economic upturn) → miniboom (= short-lived economic boom); mini- + course → minicourse (= short course of study)*. **3.** (of clothing) short; not reaching the knee: *mini- + dress → minidress; mini- + skirt → miniskirt*. See -MIN-, -MICRO-.

mis- from Old English, used before nouns, verbs, and adjectives meaning **1.** mistaken; wrong; wrongly; incorrectly: *mis- + trial → mistrial (= a trial conducted improperly); mis- + print → misprint (= something incorrectly printed); misfire: (= fail to fire properly).* **2.** the opposite of: *mis- + trust → mistrust (= the opposite of trust).*

mono- from Greek, meaning "one, single, lone." This meaning is found in such words as: *monarch, monastery, monochrome, monocle, monogamy, monogram, monograph, monolingual, monolith, monologue, mononucleosis, monopoly, monopterous, monorail, monosyllable, monotonous.*

multi- from Latin, meaning "many, much, multiple, many times, more than one, composed of many like parts, in many respects": *multi- + colored → multicolored (= having many colors); multi- + vitamin → multivitamin (= composed of many vitamins).*

neo- from Greek, meaning "new." It has come to mean "new, recent, revived, changed": *neo- + colonialism → neocolonialism (= colonialism that has been revived); neo- + -lithic → neolithic (= of a recent Stone Age).* Also, esp. before a vowel, **ne-**.

neuro- from Greek, meaning "nerve, nerves." Its meaning now includes "nervous system," and this meaning is found in such words as: *neurology, neurosurgery.*

non- from Latin, usually meaning "not," used **1.** before adjectives and adverbs and means a simple negative or absence of something: *non- + violent → nonviolent.* **2.** before a noun of action and means the failure of such action: *non- + payment → nonpayment (= failure to pay).* **3.** before a noun to suggest that the thing mentioned is not true, real, or worthy of the name, as in *nonbook, noncandidate, non-event.*

ob- from Latin, used before roots, meaning "toward," "to," "on," "over," "against": *ob- + -jec- → object.*

octa- from Greek, meaning "eight": *octa- + -gon → octagon (= eight-sided figure).*

omni- from Latin, meaning "all": *omni- + directional → omnidirectional (= in all directions).*

ortho- from Greek, meaning "straight, upright, right, correct": *ortho- + graph → orthography (= correct writing); ortho- + dontics → orthodontics (= dentistry dealing with straightening teeth); ortho- + pedic → orthopedic (= correction of improper bone structure from childhood).*

out- from Old English, used **1.** before verbs, meaning "going beyond, surpassing, or outdoing (the action of the verb)": *out- + bid → outbid; out- + do → outdo; out- + last → outlast.* **2.** before nouns to form certain compounds meaning "outside; out": *out- + cast → outcast; out- + come → outcome; out- + side → outside.*

over- from Old English, meaning **1.** the same as the adverb or adjective OVER, as in: *overboard; overcoat; overhang; overlord; overthrow.* **2.** "over the limit; to excess; too much; too": *overact (= to act too much); overcrowd (= to crowd too many people or things into); overaggressive (= too aggressive);*

overfull; overweight. **3.** "outer," as when referring to an outer covering: *overskirt (= a skirt worn over something, such as a gown).*

pan- from Greek, meaning "all." This meaning is found in such words as: *panorama; pantheism.* It is also used esp. in terms that imply or suggest the union of all branches of a group: *Pan-American; Pan- + hellenic (Greek)* → *Panhellenic (= all Greeks united in one group); Pan-Slavism (= all the people of Slavic background united).*

para-¹ from Greek, meaning 1. "at or to one side of, beside, side by side." This meaning is found in such words as: *parabola; paragraph.* 2. "beyond, past, by": *paradox.* 3. "abnormal, defective": *paranoia.* 4. (before names of jobs or occupations) "ancilliary, subsidiary, assisting." This meaning is found in such words as: *paralegal; paraprofessional.* Also, esp. before a vowel, **par-**.

para-² taken from PARACHUTE, and is used to form compounds that refer to persons or things that use parachutes or that are landed by parachute: *paratrooper.*

penta- from Greek, meaning "five": *penta- + -gon* → *pentagon (= five-sided figure).*

per- from Latin, used before roots, meaning "through, thoroughly, completely, very": *per- + -vert* → *pervert (= a person completely turned away from the normal); per- + -fect* → *perfect (= thoroughly or completely done).*

peri- from Greek, used before roots, meaning **1.** "about, around": *peri- + meter* → *perimeter (= distance around an area); peri- + -scope* → *periscope (= instrument for looking around oneself).* **2.** "enclosing, surrounding": *peri- + cardium* → *pericardium (= a sac surrounding the heart).* **3.** "near": *peri- + helion* → *perihelion (= point of an orbit nearest to the sun).*

petro-¹ from Greek, meaning "rock, stone": *petro- + -ology* → *petrology (= the study of rocks or stone).*

petro-² taken from PETROLEUM and used to form compounds: *petro- + chemistry* → *petrochemistry; petro- + power* → *petropower (= power derived from petroleum).*

photo- from Greek, meaning "light": *photo- + biology* → *photobiology; photo- + -on* → *photon (= elementary "particle" of light).* Also means "photographic" or "photograph": *photo- + copy* → *photocopy.*

poly- from Greek, meaning "much, many": *polyandry (= the custom of having many husbands); polyglot (= speaking many languages).*

post- from Latin, meaning "after (in time), following (some event)"; "behind, at the rear or end of": *post- + industrial* → *postindustrial (= after the industrial age); post- + war* → *postwar (= after the war).*

pre- from Latin, **1.** meaning "before, in front of," "prior to, in advance of," "being more than, surpassing": *pre- + -dict* → *predict (= say in advance of something); pre- + eminent* → *preeminent (= surpassing or being more than eminent); pre- + face* → *preface (= something written in front of a book, etc.)* **2.** used before verbs to form new verbs that refer to an activity taking place before or instead of the usual occurrence of the same activity: *pre- + board* → *preboard (= to board an airplane before the*

other passengers); pre- + cook → precook (= cook before regular cooking).
3. used in forming adjectives that refer to a period of time before the event, period, person, etc., mentioned in the root: *pre- + school → preschool (= before the age of starting school); pre- + war → prewar (= before the war started).*

pro-[1] from Latin, **1.** meaning "forward, forward movement or location; advancement": *proceed; progress; prominent; promote; propose.* **2.** used before roots and words, meaning "bringing into existence": *procreate; produce.* **3.** used before roots and words, meaning "in place of": *pronoun.* **4.** used to form adjectives, meaning "favoring the group, interests, course of action, etc., named by the noun; calling for the interests named by the noun": *pro- + choice → pro-choice (= in favor of allowing a choice to be made regarding abortions); pro- + war → prowar (= in favor of fighting a war).*

pro-[2] from Greek, meaning **1.** "before, beforehand, in front of": *prognosis; prophylactic; prothesis; proboscis.* **2.** "primitive or early form": *prodrug; prosimian.*

proto- from Greek, meaning "first, foremost, earliest form of": *proto- + lithic → protolithic; protoplasm.* Also, esp. before a vowel, **prot-.**

pseudo- from Greek, meaning **1.** "false; pretended; unreal": *pseudo- + intellectual → pseudointellectual (= a person pretending to be an intellectual).* **2.** "closely or deceptively resembling": *pseudo- + carp → pseudocarp (= a fish closely resembling a carp); pseudo- + -pod- → pseudopod (= a part of an animal that closely resembles a foot).* Also, *esp. before a vowel,* **pseud-.**

psycho- from Greek, meaning "soul; mind." This meaning is found in such words as: *parapsychology, psychedelic, psychiatry, psychic, psychological, psychology, psychopath, psychosis, psychotic.*

pyro- from Greek, meaning "fire, heat, high temperature": *pyromaniac, pyrotechnics.*

quasi- from Latin, meaning "as if, as though." It is used before adjectives and nouns and means "having some of the features but not all; resembling; almost the same as": *quasi-scientific, quasiparticle, quasi-stellar.*

radio- ultimately from Latin *radius,* meaning "beam, ray." It is used before roots and nouns and means "radiant energy": *radiometer.* It is also used to mean "radio waves": *radiolocation; radiotelephone.* Other meanings are: **1.** the giving off of rays as a result of the breakup of atomic nuclei: *radioactivity; radiocarbon.* **2.** x-rays: *radiograph; radiotherapy.*

re- from Latin, used **1.** before roots and sometimes words to form verbs and nouns meaning or referring to action in a backward direction: *re- + -cede- → recede (= fall back); re- + -vert- → revert (= turn back).* **2.** to form verbs or nouns showing action in answer to or intended to undo or reverse a situation: *rebel; remove; respond; restore; revoke.* **3.** to form verbs or nouns showing action that is done over, often with the meaning that the outcome of the original action was in some way not enough or not long lasting, or that the performance of the new action brings back an earlier state of affairs: *recapture; reoccur; repossess; resole (= put another sole on a shoe); re-type.*

retro- from Latin, meaning "back, backward": *retro-* + *-gress* → *retrogress (= proceed backward); retro-* + *rocket* → *retrorocket.*

self- from Old English, used **1.** before nouns to refer to something that one does by oneself or to oneself: *self-control (= control of oneself); self-government; self-help; self-portrait.* **2.** before adjectives and nouns to refer to an action that is done without assistance: *self-adhesive; a self-loading gun; self-study.*

semi- from Latin, meaning **1.** "half": *semiannual; semicircle.* **2.** "partially; partly; somewhat": *semiautomatic; semidetached; semiformal.* **3.** "happening or occurring twice in (a certain length of time)": *semiannual.*

sex- from Latin, meaning "six": *sexpartite (= having six parts or divisions).*

socio- from Latin, used before roots and sometimes words, meaning "social; sociological; society": *socio-* + *economic* → *socioeconomic; socio-* + *-metry* → *sociometry (= social statistics).*

step- from Old English, used before words to name a member of a family related by the remarriage of a parent and not by blood: *When my father married his second wife, she already had a son who became my stepbrother.*

sub- from Latin, meaning **1.** "under, below, beneath": *subsoil; subway.* **2.** "just outside of, near": *subalpine; subtropical.* **3.** "less than, not quite": *subhuman; subteen.* **4.** "secondary, at a lower point in a hierarchy": *subcommittee; subplot.* Sometimes this prefix is spelled as **su-, suc-, suf-, sug-, sum-, sup-, sur-, sus-.**

super- from Latin, meaning **1.** "above, beyond; above or over (another); situated or located over": *superimpose, superstructure, superficial.* **2.** "an individual, thing, or property that surpasses customary or normal amounts or levels, as being larger, more powerful, or having something to a great degree or to too great a degree": *superconductivity, superman, supercomputer, superhighway, superhuman, supercritical, supercool.*

supra- from Latin, meaning "above, over; beyond the limits of": *supraorbital; supranational.* Compare SUPER-.

sur- from French, meaning "over, above, in addition": *surcharge; surname; surrender.*

sym- another form of the prefix SYN-. It appears before roots beginning with *b, p, m: symbol; symphony; symmetry.*

syn- from Greek, meaning "with; together." This meaning is found in such words as: *synchronous, idiosyncrasy, photosynthesis, synagogue, synchronize, synonym, synthesis.* See SYM-.

tele- **1.** from Greek, meaning "far." It is used before roots and sometimes words and means "reaching over a distance, carried out between two remote points, performed or operating through electronic transmissions": *telegraph; telekinesis; teletypewriter.* **2.** *tele-* is also used to mean "television:" *telegenic; telethon.* Also, esp. before a vowel, **tel-.**

trans- from Latin, used **1.** before verb roots that refer to movement or carrying from one place to another; it means "across; through": *transfer; transmit; transplant.* **2.** to mean "complete change": *transform; transmute.* **3.** before roots to form adjectives that mean "crossing, going beyond, on the other side of (the place or thing named)": *transnational; trans-Siberian.*

tri- from Latin, meaning "three": *triatomic; trilateral.*

ultra- from Latin, meaning **1.** "located beyond, on the far side of": *ultraviolet.* **2.** "carrying to the furthest degree possible, on the fringe of": *ultraleft; ultramodern.* **3.** "extremely": *ultralight.* **4.** "going beyond normal or customary bounds or limits": *ultramicroscope; ultrasound; ultrastructure.*

un-¹ from Old English, used very freely to form adjectives and the adverbs and nouns formed from these adjectives. It means "not," and it brings negative or opposite force: *unfair, unfairly, unfairness; unfelt; unseen; unfitting; unformed; unheard-of; unrest; unemployment.*

un-² from Old English, used **1.** before verbs, meaning "a reversal of some action or state, or a removal, a taking away, or a release": *unbend; uncork; unfasten.* **2.** before some verbs to intensify the meaning: *unloose (= let loose with force).*

under- from Old English, meaning **1.** "a place or situation below or beneath": *underbrush; undertow.* **2.** "lower in grade, rank or dignity": *undersheriff; understudy.* **3.** before adjectives to mean "of lesser degree, extent, or amount": *undersized.* **4.** "not showing enough; too little": *underfed.*

vice- from Latin, meaning "in place of, instead of." It is used before roots and sometimes words and means "deputy"; it is used esp. in the titles of officials who serve in the absence of the official named by the base word: *viceroy (→ vice- + roy, "king"); vice-chancellor; vice-chairman.*

List of Suffixes

-ability ultimately from Latin, a combination of -ABLE and -ITY, used to form nouns from adjectives that end in *-able: capable (adjective)* → *capability (noun); reliable (adjective)* → *reliability (noun).*

-able ultimately from Latin, added to verbs to form adjectives meaning "capable of, fit for, tending to": *teach + -able* → *teachable (= capable of being taught); photograph + -able* → *photographable = (fit for photographing).* Compare -IBLE.

-aceous from Latin, meaning "having the nature of, made of." This meaning is found in such words as *herbaceous, cretaceous.*

-acious from Latin, used after some roots to form adjectives meaning "tending to; abounding in": *tenacious (from ten- "hold on" + -acious) = tending to hold on; loquacious (from loq(u)- "talk" + -acious) = tending to talk.* Compare -OUS.

-acity from Middle English, used after some roots to form nouns with the meaning "tendency toward; abundance in": *tenacity (from- ten- "hold on" + -acity) = tendency toward holding on.*

-age ultimately from Latin, used to form noncount mass or abstract nouns **1.**

from other nouns, with meanings such as "collection" (*coinage = a collection or group of coins*) and "quantity or measure" (*footage = quantity of feet in measurement*). **2.** from verbs, with meanings such as "process" (*coverage = the act or process of covering*), "the outcome of, the fact of" or "the physical effect or remains of" (*spoilage = the result of spoiling; wreckage = the remains of wrecking*), and "amount charged" (*towage = charge for towing; postage = amount charged for posting, that is, sending through the mail*).

-aholic (originally taken from the word ALCOHOLIC) used to form new words with the general meaning "a person who is addicted to or strongly desires" the activity being shown by the initial part of the word. Thus, a *chargeaholic* is someone who uses a charge card a lot; a *foodaholic* is someone who always wants food. Compare -HOLIC.

-al[1] from Latin, added to nouns to form adjectives meaning "relating to, of the kind of, having the form or character of": *autumn + -al → autumnal (= relating to the season autumn); nature + -al → natural (= having the character of nature)*.

-al[2] from Latin, added to verbs to form nouns meaning "the act of": *deny + -al → denial (= the act of denying); refuse + -al → refusal (= the act of refusing)*.

-ally form from **-al**[1] + **-ly,** used to form adverbs from certain adjectives ending in -IC: *terrific (adj.) + -ally → terrifically (adverb)*.

-an from Latin, meaning "of, pertaining to, having qualities of," **1.** added to names of places or people to form adjectives and nouns meaning **a.** being connected with a place: *Chicago + -an → Chicagoan;* **b.** having membership in a group of: *Episcopal + -(i)an → Episcopalian;* **2.** used to form adjectives meaning "of or like (someone); supporter or believer of": *Christ + -(i)an → Christian; Freud + -(i)an → Freudian (= supporter of or believer in the theories of Sigmund Freud)*. **3.** used to form nouns from words ending in -*ic* or -*y* meaning "one who works with": *electric + -(i)an → electrician; comedy + -an → comedian*.

-ance ultimately from Latin, used **1.** after some adjectives ending in -ANT to form nouns meaning "quality or state of": *brilliant + -ance → brilliance.* **2.** *after some verb roots to form nouns: appear + -ance → appearance; resemble + -ance → resemblance. See* -ANT, -ENCE.

-ant from Latin, used **1.** after some verbs to form adjectives meaning "doing or performing (the action of the verb)": *please + -ant → pleasant (= doing the pleasing).* **2.** after some verbs to form nouns meaning "one who does or performs (the action of the verb, often a formal action)": *serve + -ant → servant (= one who serves); apply (+ ic) + -ant → applicant (= one who formally applies, as for a job).* **3.** after some verbs to form nouns meaning: "substance that does or performs (the action of the verb)": cool *(verb = "to make cool") + -ant → coolant (= substance to keep engines cool). See* -ENT.

-ar from Latin, used **1.** after some nouns (many of which have an *l* before the end) to form adjectives: *circle + -ar → circular; single + -ar → singular.* **2.** after some verbs to form nouns meaning "one who does or performs an act of": *beg + -ar → beggar; lie + -ar → liar*.

ard from French, used after some verbs and nouns to form nouns that refer to persons who regularly do an activity, or who are characterized in a certain way, as indicated by the stem: *dullard (= one who is dull); drunkard (= one who is drunk)*.

arian from Latin, used **1.** after some nouns and adjectives that end in -ARY to form personal nouns: *library + -arian → librarian; seminary + -arian → seminarian; veterinary + -arian → veterinarian.* **2.** after some roots to form nouns meaning "a person who supports, calls for, or practices the principles of (the root noun)": *authority + -arian → authoritarian (= one who believes in central authority); totality + -arian → totalitarian (= one who believes in total governmental rule)*.

art variant form of -ARD, found in such words as: *braggart.*

ary from Latin, used **1.** after some nouns to form adjectives meaning: "relating to, connected with": *element + -ary → elementary; honor + -ary → honorary.* **2.** after some roots to form personal nouns, or nouns that refer to objects that hold or contain things: *secretary; -libr- (= root meaning "book") + -ary → library (= place for holding books); glossary (= place containing specialized words and their meanings).* **3.** after some nouns to form adjectives meaning "contributing to; for the purpose of": *inflation + -ary → inflationary (= contributing to inflation); compliment + -ary → complimentary (= for the purpose of complimenting)*.

ate 1. from Latin, used to form adjectives meaning "showing; full of": *passion + -ate → passionate (= showing passion); consider + -ate → considerate (= showing the action of considering); literate.* **2.** used to form verbs meaning "cause to become (like); act as": *regular + -ate → regulate (= make regular, act by rule); active + -ate → activate (= cause to become active); hyphenate; calibrate.* **3.** used to form nouns meaning **a.** a group of people: *elector + -ate → electorate (= group who elect).* **b.** an area ruled by: *caliph (a kind of ruler) + -ate → caliphate (= area ruled by a caliph); protector + -ate → protectorate (= area ruled by a protecting nation).* **c.** the office, institution, or function of: *consul + -ate → consulate; magistrate; potentate.*

ation from Latin, used after some verbs or adjectives (some of which end in -ATE) to form nouns meaning "state or process of": *starve + -ation → starvation (= condition of starving); separate + -ation → separation (= state of being separate)*.

ative from Latin, used after some verbs (some of which end in -ATE) and nouns to form adjectives: *regulate + -ative → regulative (= with the power to regulate); norm (= rule) + -ative → normative (= having rules)*.

ator from Latin, used after verbs ending in -ATE to form nouns meaning "person or thing that does or performs (the action of the verb": *agitate + -ator → agitator (= person who agitates; machine that agitates); vibrate + -ator → vibrator (= thing that vibrates); narrator; generator; mediator; incubator.*

based from the word *base,* used **1.** after nouns to form adjectives. **2.** after nouns of place to form adjectives meaning "operating or working from":

ground + -based → ground-based (= operating from the ground); New York + -based → New York-based (= working from New York). **3.** after nouns to form adjectives meaning "making use of": computer + based → computer-based (= making use of computers; "as in "computer-based instruction"); logic + -based → logic-based (= making use of logic).

-burger (originally taken from the word hamburger) used after roots and some words to form nouns that mean "the food added to, or substituted for, a basic hamburger": cheese + -burger → cheeseburger (= a hamburger with cheese added on top); fish + -burger → fishburger (= fish substituted for the meat of a hamburger).

-cracy ultimately from Greek, meaning "power; rule; government," used after roots to form nouns meaning "rule; government": auto- + -cracy → autocracy (-government by one ruler); theo- ("God") + -cracy → theocracy (-a country governed by the rule of God or a god). Compare -CRAT.

-crat ultimately from Greek, meaning "ruler; person having power," used after roots to form nouns meaning "ruler; member of a ruling body": auto- + -crat → autocrat (= a ruler governing alone). Compare -CRACY.

-cy from French and Latin, used **1.** to form nouns from adjectives that have stems that end in -t, -te, -tic, and esp. -nt **a.** to form abstract nouns: democrat + -cy → democracy; accurate + -cy → accuracy; expedient + -cy → expediency; lunatic + -cy → lunacy. **b.** to form action nouns: vacant + -cy → vacancy; occupant + -cy → occupancy. **2.** to form nouns meaning "rank or office of": captain + -cy → captaincy (= rank or office of a captain); magistra(te) + -cy → magistracy (= office of a magistrate).

-dom from Old English, used after some nouns and adjectives to form nouns meaning **1.** domain or area ruled: king + -dom → kingdom (= area a king rules). **2.** collection of persons: official + -dom → officialdom (= a collection of officials). **3.** rank: earl + -dom → earldom (= the rank or position of an earl). **4.** general condition: free + -dom → freedom (= general condition of being free).

-ed from Old English, **1.** added to words with the following rules of form: **a.** For most regular verbs that end in a consonant, -ed is added directly afterwards: cross + -ed → crossed. When the verb ends in -y, the -y changes to -i and -ed is added: ready + -ed → readied. If the root ends in -e, an e is dropped: save + -ed → saved. **b.** The pronunciation of the suffix -ed depends on the sound that appears before it. After the sounds (p, k, f, th, s, sh, and ch) the suffix is pronounced (t): cross + -ed → crossed (krôst); after the sounds (t, d) it is pronounced (id): edit + -ed → edited (ed'i tid); after all other sounds it is pronounced (d): budge + -ed → budged (bujd). **2.** carries a number of different meanings. It is used **a.** to form the past tense and past participle of regular verbs: He crossed the river. He had crossed the river when we got there. **b.** to form an adjective indicating a condition or quality due to action of the verb: inflated balloons (= balloons that have been inflated). **c.** after nouns to form adjectives meaning "possessing, having, or characterized by (what-ever the noun base is)": *beard + -ed → bearded (= possessing or hav-ing a beard)*.

ee from French, used **1.** after verbs that take an object to form nouns mean-ing "the person who is the object of the action of the verb": *address + -ee → addressee (= the person whom someone else addresses)*. **2.** after verbs that do not take an object to form nouns meaning "the one doing or performing the act of the verb": *escape + -ee → escapee (= one performing the act of escaping)*. **3.** after other words to form nouns meaning "the one who is or does": *absent + -ee → absentee (= one who is absent)*.

eer from French, used to form nouns meaning "the person who produces, handles, or is associated with" the base word: *engine + -eer → engineer (= person handling an engine)*.

en from Old English, used **1. a.** after some adjectives to form verbs meaning "to be or make": *hard + -en → harden (= to be or make hard)*. **b.** after some nouns to form verbs meaning "to add to, cause to be, or have": *length + -en → lengthen (= to add length to; make long)*. **2.** after some nouns that are materials or sources of something to form adjectives that describe the source or material: *gold + -en → golden (= like gold)*.

ence from Latin, used **1.** after some adjectives ending in -ENT to form nouns meaning "quality or state of": *abstin(ent) + -ence → abstinence*. **2.** after some verb roots to form nouns: *depend + -ence → dependence*. See -ANCE, -ENT.

ent from Latin, used **1.** after some verbs to form adjectives meaning "doing or performing (the action of the verb)": *differ + -ent → different*. **2.** after some verbs to form nouns meaning "one who does or performs (the ac-tion)": *stud(y) + -ent → student (= one who studies)*. See -ANT, -ENCE.

er[1] from Old English, used **1.** after verbs to form nouns meaning "a person, animal or thing that performs the action of the verb" or "the person, ani-mal or thing used in performing the action of the verb": *bake + -er → baker (= a person who bakes); teach + -er → teacher (= a person who teaches); fertilize + -er → fertilizer (= a thing that is used to fertilize)* **2.** after nouns to form new nouns that refer to the occupation, work, or labor of the root noun: *hat + -er → hatter (= one whose work is making hats); roof + -er → roofer (= one whose occupation is repairing roofs)*. **3.** after nouns to form new nouns that refer to the place of origin, or the dwelling place, of the root noun: *Iceland + -er → Icelander (= person who originally comes from Iceland); southern + -er → southerner (= a person who originally comes from, or lives in, the south)*. Compare -IER, -OR.

er[2] from Middle English, regularly used to form the comparative form of short adjectives and adverbs: *hard + -er → harder; small + -er → smaller; fast + -er → faster*.

ery (or **-ry**) from French, used **1.** to form nouns that refer to **a.** things in a collection: *green + -ery → greenery (= green plants as a group); machine + -ery → machinery (= a group or collection of machines)* **b.** people in a col-lection: *Jew + -ry → Jewry (= Jews as a group); peasant + -ry → peasantry (= peasants as a group)* **c.** an occupation, activity, or condition: *dentist +*

-ry → dentistry (= occupation of a dentist); rival + -ry → rivalry (= condition of being a rival); rob + -ery → robbery (= activity of robbing or being robbed). **2.** to form nouns that refer to a place where the activity of the root is done: bake + -ery → bakery (= place where baking is done); wine + -ery → winery (= place where wine is made).

-ese ultimately from Latin, used **1.** after nouns that refer to place names: **a.** to form adjectives to describe things made in or relating to the place: Japan + -ese → Japanese (= of or relating to Japan or its people); Vienna + -ese → Viennese (= of or relating to Vienna or its people) **b.** to form nouns with the meanings "the people living in (the place)" or "the language of (the place)": Vietnam + -ese → Vietnamese (= the people living in/the language spoken in Vietnam). **2.** to form nouns that describe in an insulting or humorous way the language characteristic of or typical of the base word: Brooklyn + -ese → Brooklynese (= the language characteristic of Brooklyn); journal + -ese → journalese (= the language typical of journalists).

-esque from French, used after nouns and proper names to form adjectives meaning "resembling," "in the style or manner of," "suggesting the work of" the person or thing denoted by the base word: Kafka + -esque → Kafkaesque (= in the style or manner of Franz Kafka); Lincoln + -esque → Lincolnesque (= in the style of Abraham Lincoln); picture + -esque → picturesque (= resembling or suggesting a picture).

-ess from French, used to form a feminine noun: count + -ess → countess; god + -ess → goddess; lion + -ess → lioness. **—Usage.** The use of words ending in -ESS has declined sharply in the latter half of the 20th century, but some are still current: actress (but some women prefer actor); adventuress; enchantress; governess (only in its child-care sense); heiress (largely in journalistic writing); hostess (but women who conduct radio and television programs are hosts); seamstress; seductress; temptress; and waitress.

-est from Old English, regularly used to form the superlative form of short adjectives and adverbs: fast + -est → fastest; soon + -est → soonest; warm + -est → warmest.

-ette from French, used **1.** after nouns to form nouns that refer to a smaller version of the original noun or root: kitchen + -ette → kitchenette (= small kitchen); novel + -ette → novelette (= smaller novel). **2.** after nouns to form nouns that refer specifically to a female: major + -ette → majorette (= female leader of a band, or baton twirler); usher + -ette → usherette (= female usher in a movie theater). **3.** after nouns to form nouns that refer to a name that is an imitation product of the root: leather + -ette → leatherette (= imitation leather product). **—Usage.** English nouns in which -ETTE signifies a feminine role or identity have been thought of as implying inferiority or unimportance and are now generally avoided. Only (drum) majorette is still widely used, usually indicating a young woman who twirls a baton with a marching band.

-ferous from the root -fer + the suffix -ous. This suffix is found in such words as: coniferous, pestiferous.

fest from German, added to nouns to form nouns meaning "an assembly of people engaged in a common activity" named by the first element of the compound: *gab* + *-fest* → *gabfest* (= *group of people gabbing or talking a lot*); *song* + *-fest* → *songfest* (= *assembly of people singing together*).

fold from Old English, used after words that refer to a number or quantity to form adjectives meaning "having the number of kinds or parts" or "multiplied the number of times": *four* + *-fold* → *fourfold* (= *multiplied four times*); *many* + *-fold* → *manyfold* (= *having many parts or kinds*).

footed from the word *foot,* added to nouns to form adjectives meaning "having (the kind of, number of, etc.) a foot or feet indicated": *a four-footed animal* (= *an animal having four feet*).

free from Old English, used after nouns to form adjectives meaning "not containing (the noun mentioned); without": *sugar* + *-free* → *sugar-free* (= *not containing sugar*); *trouble* + *-free* → *trouble-free* (= *without trouble*).

ful from Old English, used **1.** after nouns to form adjectives meaning "full of; characterized by": *beauty* + *-ful* → *beautiful* (= *full of beauty*); *care* + *-ful* → *careful* (= *characterized by care*). **2.** after verbs to form adjectives meaning "tending to; able to": *harm* + *-ful* → *harmful* (= *tending to harm*); *wake* + *-ful* → *wakeful* (= *tending to stay awake*). **3.** after nouns to form nouns meaning "as much as will fill": *spoon* + *-ful* → *spoonful* (= *as much as will fill a spoon*); *cup* + *-ful* → *cupful* (= *as much as will fill a cup*).

fy ultimately from Latin, used **1.** after roots to form verbs meaning "to make; cause to be; render": *pure* + *-fy* → *purify* (= *to make pure*); *simple* + *-fy* → *simplify* (= *make simple*); *liquid* + *-fy* → *liquefy* (= *to make into a liquid*). **2.** to mean "cause to conform to": *citify* (= *cause to conform to city ways*). Compare -IFY.

gate derived from *Watergate,* originally the name of a hotel complex where officials of the Republican party were caught trying to burglarize Democratic party headquarters. *Watergate* then came to be associated with "a political cover-up and scandal." The suffix is used after some nouns to form nouns that refer to scandals resulting from concealed crime in government or business: *Iran* + *-gate* → *Irangate* (= *a scandal involving arms sales to Iran*).

gon from Greek, meaning "side; angle." This suffix is used after roots to form nouns that refer to plane figures having the number of sides mentioned: *poly-* (= *many*) + *-gon* → *polygon* (= *a many-sided figure*).

gram from Greek, meaning "what is written." It is used after roots to form nouns that refer to something written or drawn, either by hand or machine: *cardio-* (= *of or relating to the heart*) + *-gram* → *cardiogram* (= *a recording and diagram of a heartbeat, drawn by a machine*). Compare -GRAPH-.

hearted from Middle English, used after adjectives to form adjectives meaning "having the character or personality of (the adjective mentioned)": *cold* + *-hearted* → *coldhearted* (= *having a cold heart; unkind or mean*); *light* + *-hearted* → *lighthearted* (= *feeling light and happy*).

-holic another form of -AHOLIC: *choco(late)* + *-holic* → *chocoholic* (= *person addicted to chocolate*).

-hood from Old English, used to form nouns meaning **1.** "the state or condition of": *likely* + *-hood* → *likelihood* (= *the state or condition of being likely*); *child* + *-hood* → *childhood* (= *the state or period of time of being a child*). **2.** "a body or group of persons of a particular character or class": *priest* + *-hood* → *priesthood* (= *a body of priests*).

-ian from Latin, used to form nouns and adjectives with the meanings of -AN: *Orwell* + *-ian* → *Orwellian* (= *interested in, or relating to, the writing of George Orwell*); *Washington* + *-ian* → *Washingtonian* (= *a person who lives in Washington*).

-iatrics from Greek, used after some roots to form nouns meaning "healing; the medical practice of": *ger-* (= *old people*) + *-iatrics* → *geriatrics* (= *the healing of older people*); *ped-* (= *child*) + *-iatrics* → *pediatrics* (= *medical practice involving children*).

-iatry from Greek, used after some roots to form nouns meaning "healing; the medical practice of": *pod-* (= *foot*) + *-iatry* → *podiatry* (= *the healing of the foot*); *psych-* (= *the mind*) + *-iatry* → *psychiatry* (= *the medical practice dealing with the mind*).

-ibility from Latin, used to form nouns from adjectives that end in *-ible*: *reducible (adjective)* → *reducibility* (= *the state or condition of being reducible, of being able to be reduced*); *flexible (adjective)* → *flexibility* (= *the state or condition of being able to move smoothly*) See -ABILITY, -ABLE, -IBLE.

-ible a variant form of -ABLE, used after roots, mostly of verbs, to form adjectives meaning "capable of, fit for, tending to": *cred-* (= *believe*) + *-ible* → *credible* (= *that can be believed*); *vis-* (= *see*) + *-ible* → *visible* (= *that can be seen*); *reduce* + *-ible* → *reducible* (= *that can be reduced*). See -ABILITY, -ABLE, -IBILITY.

-ic from Middle English, used after nouns to form adjectives meaning "of or relating to": *metal* + *-ic* → *metallic*; *poet* + *-ic* → *poetic*. This suffix is also used after nouns to form adjectives meaning "having some characteristics of; in the style of": *ballet* + *-ic* → *balletic*; *sophomore* + *-ic* → *sophomoric*; *Byron* + *-ic* → *Byronic* (= *in the style of the writer Byron*).

-ical a combination of -IC and -AL[1], used after roots to form adjectives meaning "of or relating to": *rhetor-* + *-ical* → *rhetorical*. This suffix originally provided synonyms to adjectives that ended in -IC: *poet* + *-ic* → *poetic*; *poet* + *-ical* → *poetical*. But some of these pairs of words or formations are now different in meaning: *econom-* + *-ic* → *economic* (= *of or relating to economics*); *econom-* + *-ical* → *economical* (= *being careful in spending money*); *histor-* + *-ic* → *historic* (= *having a long history; important*); *histor-* + *-ical* → *historical* (= *happening in the past*).

-ician extracted from *physician*, *musician*, etc., used after nouns or roots to form nouns meaning "the person having the occupation or work of": *beauty* + *-ician* → *beautician* (= *person who works in a beauty shop*); *mort-*

(= *death*) + *-ician* → *mortician* (= *person working to prepare dead people for burial*).

ics from Latin, used after roots to form nouns meaning "a body of facts, knowledge, or principles." Such nouns usually correspond to adjectives ending in IC or-ICAL: *eth-* (= *custom; character*) + *-ics* → *ethics* (= *the principles of good character*); *phys-* (= *body*) + *-ics* → *physics* (= *the principles of bodies in motion and at rest*).

ier from French, used after nouns or roots to form nouns meaning "person or thing that does (the action of the word mentioned); person or thing in charge of (the word mentioned)": *finance* + *-ier* → *financier* (= *person doing finance*); *cour-* (= *run*) + *-ier* → *courier* (= *messenger*); *hotel* + *-ier* → *hotelier* (= *person in charge of hotels*). Compare -ER[1].

ify from French, used to form verbs meaning "cause to be in (a stated condition); to make or cause to become (a certain condition)": *intense* + *-ify* → *intensify* (= *cause to be intense*); *speechify* (= *make speeches*). See -FY.

in extracted from *sit-in*, used after some verbs to form nouns that refer to organized protests through, using, or in support of the named activity: *pray* + *-in* → *pray-in* (= *a protest in which participants engage in passive resistance and prayer*).

ine[1] from Latin, used after some roots or nouns to form adjectives meaning "of, relating to, or characteristic of; of the nature of; made of": *crystal* + *-ine* → *crystalline* (= *of, like, or made of crystal*); *equ-* (= *horse*) + *-ine* → *equine* (= *of or relating to horses*).

ine[2] from French, used after some roots to form nouns that name chemical substances and elements: *caffe-* (= *coffee*) + *-ine* → *caffeine* (= *a chemical substance found in coffee*); *chlor-* + *-ine* → *chlorine*.

ing[1] 1. from Old English, used after verbs to form nouns that express the action of the verb or its result, product, material, etc.: *build* + *-ing* → *building: the art of building; a new building.* 2. after roots (other than verb roots) to form nouns: *off* + *-ing* → *offing*.

ing[2] from Middle English, used after verbs to form the present participle of verbs: *walk* + *-ing* → *walking: Is the baby walking yet?* These participles are often used as adjectives: *war* + *-ing* → *warring: warring factions.* Some adjectives ending in *-ing* are formed by combining a prefix with a verb. Thus *outgoing* is formed from *out-* + the present participle form of the verb *go* (= *going*). Other examples: *uplifting, outstanding, incoming.*

ion ultimately from Latin, used after some roots to form nouns that refer to action or condition: *uni-* (= *one*) + *-ion* → *union* (= *condition of being one*). Compare -TION.

ious from Latin, a variant form of -OUS, used after roots to form adjectives: *hilar-* (= *cheerful*) + *-ious* → *hilarious* (= *very funny*).

ise *Chiefly British.* See -IZE.

ish from Old English, used 1. after nouns or roots to form adjectives meaning **a.** relating to; in the same manner of; having the characteristics of: *brute* + *-ish* → *brutish*. **b.** of or relating to the people or language of: *Brit-* + *-ish* → *British; Swede* + *-ish* → *Swedish*. **c.** like; similar to: *baby* + *-ish*

→ *babyish; mule* + *-ish* → *mulish; girl* + *-ish* → *girlish.* **d.** addicted to; inclined or tending to: *book* + *-ish* → *bookish* (= *tending to read books a great deal*). **e.** near or about: *fifty* + *-ish* → *fiftyish* (*nearly fifty years old*). **2.** after adjectives to form adjectives meaning "somewhat, rather": *old* + *-ish* → *oldish* (= *somewhat old*); *red* + *-ish* → *reddish* (= *somewhat red*); *sweet* + *-ish* → *sweetish.*

-ism from Greek, used **1.** after verb roots to form action nouns: *baptize* → *bapt-* + *-ism* → *baptism.* **2.** to form nouns showing action or practice: *adventure* + *-ism* → *adventurism* (= *the action or practice of taking risks in intervening in international affairs*). **3.** used to form nouns showing state or condition: *alcoholism* (= *disease or condition in which alcohol is involved*). **4.** after roots to form nouns showing the names of principles or doctrines: *Darwinism* (= *principles of Darwin's theory of evolution*); *despotism.* **5.** to form nouns showing an example of a use: *witticism* (= *example of something witty*); *Africanism* (= *word from Africa or from an African language*). Compare -IST, -IZE.

-ist from French and Latin, forms nouns usually corresponding to verbs ending in *-ize* and nouns ending in *-ism,* and referring to a person who practices or is concerned with something: *novel* + *-ist* → *novelist* (= *someone writing a novel*); *terrorist* (= *one who practices terrorism, one who terrorizes*).

-ite from Latin, used after nouns and roots to form nouns meaning: **1.** a person associated with or living in a place; a person connected with a tribe, leader, set of beliefs, system, etc.: *Manhattan* + *-ite* → *Manhattanite; Israel* + *-ite* → *Israelite; Labor* + *-ite* → *Laborite* (= *someone following the Labor Party*). **2.** mineral or fossil; explosive; chemical compound or drug product: *anthracite; cordite; dynamite; sulfite.*

-itis ultimately from Greek, used **1.** after roots that refer to an inflammation or disease affecting a certain part of the body: *appendix* + *-itis* → *appendicitis; bronchi* (= *part of the lungs*) + *-itis* → *bronchitis.* **2.** to form nouns made up for a particular occasion to refer to something comparable in a funny way to a disease: *The teenagers seem to be suffering from telephonitis* (= *excessive use of the telephone, as if using it were a disease*).

-ive from French and Latin, used after roots or nouns to form adjectives meaning "having a tendency or connection with; like": *act(ion)* + *-ive* → *active* (= *tending to be full of action or activity*); *sport* + *-ive* → *sportive* (= *like sports*).

-ize ultimately from Greek, used to form verbs meaning **1.** "to make; cause to become": *fossil* + *-ize* → *fossilize* (= *to make something into a fossil*); *sterile* + *-ize* → *sterilize* (= *to make something sterile*). **2.** "to convert into, give a specified character or form to; change to a state of": *computer* + *-ize* → *computerize* (= *make an office use computers*); *dramat-* + *-ize* → *dramatize* (= *give the form of a drama to some other piece of work*); *American* + *-ize* → *Americanize* (= *convert to an American character*). **3.** "to subject to; cause to undergo or suffer from (an emotion or a process, sometimes named after its originator)": *hospital* + *-ize* → *hospitalize* (= *cause to un-*

dergo treatment in a hospital); terror + -ize → terrorize (= cause to suffer terror); galvan- + -ize → galvanize (= to coat metal or stimulate electrically, as by the experiments of L. Galvani, Italian physicist). Also, chiefly British, **-ise.**

less from Old English, used **1.** after nouns to form adjectives meaning "without, not having (the thing or quality named by the noun)": care + -less → careless; shame + -less → shameless **2.** after verbs to form adjectives meaning "that cannot be" plus the -ed/en form of the verb; or "that never" plus the -s form of the verb: tire + -less → tireless (= that never tires); count + -less → countless (= that cannot be counted).

let from Middle English, used **1.** after a noun to form a noun that is a smaller version of the original noun or root: book + -let → booklet (= a smaller book); pig + -let → piglet (= a smaller pig). **2.** after a noun to form a noun that is a band, ornament, or article of clothing worn on the part of the body mentioned: ankle + -let → anklet (= piece of clothing like a sock worn on the ankle); wrist + -let → wristlet (= ornament like a bracelet worn on the wrist).

like from Middle English, used after nouns to form adjectives meaning "of or resembling (the noun base)": child + -like → childlike; life + -like → life-like.

ling from Old English, used **1.** to form a noun that indicates a feeling of distaste or disgust for the person or thing named: hire + -ling → hireling (= someone hired to do menial or distasteful tasks); under + -ling → underling. **2.** to form a noun that is a smaller version or example of the base word: prince + -ling; duck + -ling → duckling.

logy from Greek, meaning "word." It is used after roots to form nouns meaning "field of study, discipline; list of": astro- (= star) + -logy → astrology (= study of the influence of stars or events); bio- (= life) + -logy → biology (= study of living things).

ly from Middle English, used **1.** after adjectives to form adverbs: glad + -ly → gladly; gradual + -ly → gradually. **2.** after nouns that refer to units of time, to form adjectives and adverbs meaning "at or for every (such unit of time)": hour + -ly → hourly (= at every hour); day + -ly → daily (= on or for every day). **3.** after nouns to form adjectives meaning "like (the noun mentioned):" saint + -ly → saintly; coward + -ly → cowardly.

man from Old English, used to form nouns meaning "person, or man, who is or does (something connected with the noun base)": mail + -man → mailman (= person who delivers mail).

mania from Greek, used after roots to form nouns meaning "great or strong enthusiasm for (the element of the root)": biblio- (= book) + -mania → bibliomania (= excessive or strong interest or enthusiasm for books).

ment from French and Latin, used **1.** after verbs to form nouns that refer to the action of the verb: govern + -ment → government. **2.** after verbs to form nouns that refer to a state or condition resulting from the action of a verb:

refresh + -ment → refreshment. **3.** after verbs to form nouns that refer to a product resulting from the action of a verb: *frag- + -ment → fragment (= a piece resulting from the breaking off of something).*

-ness from Old English, used after adjectives and verbs ending in *-ing* or *-ed/ -en* to form nouns that refer to the quality or state of the adjective or verb: *dark + -ness → darkness; prepared + -ness → preparedness (= a state of being prepared).*

-o derived from Romance nouns ending in -o, used **1.** as the final element in certain nouns that are shortened from longer nouns: *ammo* (from "ammunition"); *combo* (from "combination"); *promo* (from "promotion"). **2.** after certain adjectives and nouns to form nouns that have an unfavorable or insulting meaning: *weird + -o → weirdo (= a very weird person); wine + -o → wino (= someone who drinks too much wine).* **3.** after certain nouns and adjectives to form informal nouns or adjectives; these are often used when speaking directly to another: *kid + -o → kiddo (= a kid or person); neat + -o → neato (= an informal use of "neat"); right + -o → righto (= an informal use of "right").*

-off from Old English, used to form nouns that name or refer to a competition or contest, esp. between finalists or to break a tie: *cook + -off → cookoff (= a cooking contest); runoff (= a deciding final contest).*

-oid from Greek, used to form adjectives and nouns meaning "resembling, like," with the suggestion of an incomplete or imperfect similarity to the root element: *human + -oid → humanoid (= resembling a human, but not quite the same).*

-onym from Greek, meaning "word, name." This meaning is found in such words as: *pseudonym, homonym.*

-or from French, used to form nouns that are agents, or that do or perform a function: *debtor; tailor; traitor; projector; repressor; sensor; tractor.*

-ory[1] **1.** from Middle English, used after nouns and verbs that end in *-e* to form adjectives meaning "of or relating to (the noun or verb mentioned)": *excrete + -ory → excretory (= of or relating to excreting); sense + -ory → sensory (= of or relating to the senses).* **2.** after certain roots to form adjectives meaning "providing or giving": *satisfact- + -ory → satisfactory (= giving satisfaction).*

-ory[2] from Latin, used after roots to form nouns that refer to places or things that hold (the root), or places that are used for (the root): *cremat- + -ory → crematory (= a place where bodies are cremated); observat(ion) + -ory → observatory (= place where observations of the heavens are made).*

-ose[1] from Latin, used after roots to form adjectives meaning "full of, abounding in, given to, or like (the root)": *verb- (= word) + -ose → verbose (= full of words); bellic- (= war) + -ose → bellicose (= eager for fighting or war).*

-ose[2] extracted from *glucose,* used after roots to form nouns that name sugars, carbohydrates, and substances that are formed from proteins: *fruct- + -ose → fructose (= a fruit sugar); lact- + -ose → lactose (= a milk sugar); prote- + ose → proteose (= a compound made from protein).*

ous from French, used **1.** after roots to form adjectives meaning "possessing, full of (a given quality)": *glory + -ous → glorious; wonder + ous → wondrous; covet + -ous → covetous; nerve + -ous → nervous.* **2.** after roots to form adjectives referring to the names of chemical elements: *stannous chloride,* $SnCl^2$.

person from Latin, used to replace some paired, sex-specific suffixes such as -MAN and -WOMAN or -ER[1] and -ESS: *salesman/saleswoman* are replaced by *sales + -person → salesperson; waiter/waitress* are replaced by *wait + -person → waitperson.*

phile from Greek, used **1.** after roots and sometimes words to form nouns meaning "lover of, enthusiast for (a given object)": *biblio- + -phile → bibliophile (= lover of books); Franco- + -phile → Francophile (= lover of France or French things).* **2.** after roots to form nouns meaning "a person sexually attracted to or overly interested in (a given object)": *pedo- + -phile → pedophile (= someone with a sexual attraction for children).*

phobe from Greek, used after roots and sometimes words to form nouns that refer to persons who have a fear of something named by the root or preceding word: *Anglo- + phobe → Anglophobe (= fear of English-speakers or of England).*

phobia from Greek, used after roots and sometimes words to form nouns with the meaning "dread of, unreasonable hatred toward (a given object)": *agora- (= open space) + phobia → agoraphobia (= fear of open spaces); xeno- (= foreign) + -phobia → xenophobia (= hatred toward foreigners).*

phobic from Greek, used after roots and words to form adjectives or nouns meaning "(a person) having a continuous, irrational fear or hatred toward" the object named in the root or preceding word: *xeno- (= foreign) + -phobic → xenophobic (= (a person) having a fear or hatred of foreigners).*

proof ultimately from Latin, used to form adjectives meaning "resistant; not allowing through" the word mentioned: *child + -proof → childproof (= resistant to a child's opening it); water + proof → waterproof (= not allowing water through).*

ry See -ERY.

s[1] (or **-es**), (s, z, iz) from Old English, used after the root form of verbs and marks the third person singular present indicative form, agreeing with a subject that is singular: *He walks. She runs. The wind rushes through the trees.*

s[2] (or **-es**) from Old English, used after count nouns and marks the plural form: *weeks; days; bushes; taxes; ladies; pianos; potatoes.*

ship from Old English, used to form nouns meaning **1.** "state or condition of": *friend + -ship → friendship; kin + -ship → kinship.* **2.** "the skill or ability of": *statesman + -ship → statesmanship; apprentice + -ship → apprenticeship.* **3.** "the relation of": *fellow + -ship → fellowship.*

sick from Old English, used to form adjectives meaning "sick or ill of or from (the noun of the root)": *car + -sick → carsick (= sick from traveling in a car); air + -sick → airsick (= sick from flying in a plane).*

-some¹ from Old English, used to form adjectives meaning "like; tending to": *burden + -some → burdensome (= like a burden); quarrel + -some → quarrelsome (= tending to quarrel).*

-some² from Old English, used to form nouns meaning "a collection (of the number mentioned) of objects": *threesome (= a group of three).*

-speak from Old English, used after the ends of words and sometimes roots to form compound nouns that name the style or vocabulary of a certain field of work, interest, time period, etc., that is mentioned in the first word or root: *ad(vertising) + -speak → adspeak (= the jargon of advertising); art + -speak → artspeak (= the language used in discussing art); future + -speak → futurespeak.*

-ster from Old English, used at the ends of words to form nouns, often implying a bad or negative sense, and referring esp. to one's occupation, habit, or association: *game + ster → gamester (= one greatly interested in games); trick + -ster → trickster (= one who uses or enjoys dishonest tricks).*

-th ultimately from Greek, used after words that refer to numbers to form adjectives referring to the number mentioned: *four + -th → fourth; tenth.*

-tion from Latin, used after verbs to form nouns that refer to actions or states of the verb: *relate + -tion → relation; sect- + -tion → section; abbreviate + -tion → abbreviation.* Compare -ION.

-tious from Latin, used after roots to form adjectives, some of which are related to nouns: *fiction: fictitious; ambition: ambitious; caution: cautious; rambunctious, propitious.*

-tude from Latin, used after roots, especially adjectives, to form nouns that refer to abstract ideas: *exact + -tude → exactitude; apt + -tude → aptitude; gratitude; altitude.*

-ty from French, used after adjectives to form nouns that name or refer to a state or condition: *able + -ty → ability; certain + -ty → certainty; chaste + -ty → chastity.*

-ure from French, used after roots and verbs to form abstract nouns that refer to action, result, and instrument or use: *press- + -ure → pressure; legislate + -ure → legislature; fract- + ure → fracture.*

-ville from French, used **1.** in place names, where it meant "city, town": *Charlottesville.* **2.** after roots or words to form informal words, not all of them long-lasting, that characterize a condition, place, person, group, or situation: *dulls + -ville (= a dull, boring situation); gloomsville.*

-ward from Old English, used to form adjectives or adverbs meaning "in or toward a certain direction in space or time": *backward.* Also, **-wards.**

-ways from Middle English, used to form adjectives or adverbs meaning "in a certain direction, manner, or position": *sideways.*

-wide from Old English, used to form adjectives meaning "extending or applying throughout a certain, given space," as mentioned by the noun: *community + -wide → communitywide (= applying to or throughout the community); countrywide; worldwide.*

-wise from Old English, used **1.** to form adjectives and adverbs meaning "in a particular manner, position, or direction": *clockwise (= moving in a direction like the hands of a clock).* **2.** to form adverbs meaning "with reference to": *Timewise we can finish the work, but qualitywise, I'm not so sure.*

-woman from Middle English, used to form nouns meaning "involving a woman; a woman in the role of": *chairwoman; spokeswoman.*

-worthy from Old English, used to form adjectives meaning **1.** "deserving of, fit for": *news + -worthy → newsworthy (= fit for the news); trust + -worthy → trustworthy.* **2.** "capable of travel in or on": *road + -worthy → roadworthy (= capable of traveling on the road); seaworthy.*

-y[1] from Old English, used to form adjectives meaning "having, showing, or similar to (the substance or action of the word or stem)": *blood + -y → bloody; cloud + -y → cloudy; sexy; squeaky.*

-y[2] (or **-ie**) from Middle English, used **1.a.** to form nouns that bring or add a meaning of dearness or familiarity to the noun or adjective root, such as proper names, names of pets, or in baby talk: *Bill + -y → Billy; Susan + -ie → Susie; bird + -ie → birdie; sweetie.* **b.** to form nouns that are informal, new, or intended to be new; sometimes these have slightly unpleasant meanings or associations: *boondocks → boon- + -ies → boonies; group + -ie → groupie; Okie (a person from Oklahoma); preemie (= a premature baby); rookie.* **2.** after adjectives to form nouns, often with the meaning that the noun is an extreme (good or bad) example of the adjective or quality: *bad + -ie → baddie; big + -ie → biggie; toughie; sharpie; sickie; whitey.* Compare -o.

-y,[3] *suffix.* from Latin, used after verbs to form nouns of action, and certain other abstract nouns: *inquire + -y → inquiry; in + fame + -y → infamy.*

List of Roots

-acr- from Latin, meaning "sharp." This meaning is found in such words as: *acerbic, acrid, acrimonious, exacerbate.*

-acro- from Greek, meaning "high." This meaning is found in such words as: *acrobat, acronym, acrophobia.*

-act- from Latin, meaning "to do; move." It is related to the root -AG-. This meaning is found in such words as: *act, action, exact, transact.*

-ag- from Latin and Greek, meaning "to move, go, do." This meaning is found in such words as: *agent, agenda, agile, agitate.*

-agon- from Greek, meaning "struggle, fight." This meaning is found in such words as: *agony, antagonist, protagonist.*

-agr- from Latin, meaning "farming; field." This meaning is found in such words as: *agriculture, agronomy.*

-alesc- from Latin, meaning "grow, develop." This meaning is found in such words as: *adolescence, adolescent, coalesce.*

-alg- from Greek, meaning "pain." This meaning is found in such words as: *analgesic, neuralgia, nostalgia.*

-ali- from Latin, meaning "other, different." This meaning is found in such words as: *alias, alibi, alien, alienate.*

-alte- from Latin, meaning "other, different." This meaning is found in such words as: *alter, alternate, alternative, alternator, altruism, altruist.*

-alti- from Latin, meaning "high; height." This meaning is found in such words as: *altimeter, altitude, alto, exalt.*

-am-[1] from Latin, meaning "love, like." This meaning is found in such words as: *amiable, amorous, amour, paramour.*

-am-[2] from Latin, meaning "take out; come out." This meaning is found in such words as: *example, sample.*

-ambl- from Latin, meaning "walk." This meaning is found in such words as: *amble, ambulance, ambulate, perambulator, circumambulate.*

-ampl- from Latin, meaning "enough; enlarge." This meaning is found in such words as: *ample, amplify, amplitude.*

-andro- from Greek, meaning "male; man." This meaning is found in such words as: *androgynous, android, polyandry.*

-anima- from Latin, meaning "spirit, soul." This meaning is found in such words as: *animate, animosity, animus, equanimity, inanimate.*

-ann- from Latin, meaning "year." This meaning is found in such words as: *annals, anniversary, annual, annuity, biannual, semiannual, superannuated.*

-anthro- from Greek, meaning "man; human." This meaning is found in such words as: *anthropocentric, anthropoid, anthropology, anthropomorphism, misanthrope.* See -ANDRO-.

-apt- from Latin, meaning "fit, proper." This meaning is found in such words as: *adapt, apt, aptitude, inept.*

-arch- 1. from Greek, meaning "chief; leader, ruler." This meaning is found in such words as: *archbishop, archdiocese, archpriest, monarch, matriarch, patriarch, anarchy, hierarchy, monarchy.* **2.** also used to form nouns that refer to persons who are the most important, most notable, or the most extreme examples of (the following noun): *archenemy (= the most important enemy); archconservative (= the most extreme example of a conservative).* **3.** also appears with the meaning "first, earliest, original, oldest in time." This meaning is found in such words as: *archaeology, archaism, archaic, archetype.*

-arm- from Latin, meaning "weapon." This meaning is found in such words as: *armada, armament, arms, disarmament.*

-astro- (or **-aster-**) from Greek, meaning "star; heavenly body; outer space." These meanings are found in such words as: *aster, asterisk, asteroid, astrology, astronomy, astronaut, disaster.*

-athl- from Greek, meaning "contest, prize." This meaning is found in such words as: *athlete, athletics, pentathlon.*

aud- from Latin, meaning "hear." This meaning is found in such words as: *audible, audience, audio, audit, audition, auditorium.*

bat- from Latin, meaning "beat, fight." This meaning is found in such words as: *battalion, batten, batter, battle, combat.*

bell- from Latin, meaning "war." This meaning is found in such words as: *antebellum, bellicose, belligerence, belligerent.*

bene- from Latin, meaning "well." This meaning is found in such words as: *benediction, benefactor, beneficial, benefit, benevolent, beneficent.*

biblio- from Greek, meaning "book." This meaning is found in such words as: *bible, bibliography, bibliophile.*

botan- from Greek, meaning "plant, herb." This meaning is found in such words as: *botanical, botany.*

brev- from Latin, meaning "short." This meaning is found in such words as: *abbreviate, abridge, brevity, brief.*

cad- (or -**cas**-) from Latin, meaning "fall." This meaning is found in such words as: *cadence, cadenza, decadent.* See -CIDE-[2].

cap- from Latin, meaning "take, hold." This meaning is found in such words as: *capacious, captures, caption.*

caut- from Latin, meaning "care; careful." This meaning is found in such words as: *caution, cautious, caveat, precaution.*

cede- from Latin, meaning "go away from; withdraw; yield." This meaning is found in such words as: *accede, antecedent, cede, concede, precede, precedent, recede, secede.* See -CEED-, -CESS-.

ceed- from Latin, meaning "go; move; yield." It is related to -CEDE-. This meaning is found in such words as: *proceed, succeed.*

ceive- from Latin, meaning "get, receive." This meaning is found in such words as: *conceive, deceive, misconceive, perceive, receive, transceiver.*

celer- from Latin, meaning "swift, quick." This meaning is found in such words as: *accelerate, celerity, decelerate.*

cent- from Latin, meaning "one hundred." This meaning is found in such words as: *cent, centavo, centigrade, centimeter, centennial, centipede, century, percent.*

cep- from Latin, meaning "get, receive, take." This meaning is found in such words as: *accept, anticipate, perception, reception.* See -CEIVE-.

cern- from Latin, meaning "separate; decide." These meanings are found in such words as: *concern, discern.*

cert- from Latin, meaning "certain; sure; true." This meaning is found in such words as: *ascertain, certain, certificate, certify, concert, disconcerted.*

cess- from Latin, meaning "move, yield." It is related to -CEDE-. This meaning is found in such words as: *access, accessible, accessory, cession, process, procession, recess, recession, success, succession.*

chor- from Greek, meaning "sing; dance." This meaning is found in such words as: *choir, choral, chord, chorus, choreograph, chorister.*

-chrom- from Greek, meaning "color." This meaning is found in such words as: *chromatic, chromosome, lipochrome, monochrome, polychromatic.*

-chron- from Greek, meaning "time." This meaning is found in such words as: *anachronism, chronic, chronicle, chronology, synchronize.*

-cide-[1] from Latin, meaning "kill; cut down." This meaning is found in such words as: *biocide, genocide, germicide, herbicide, homicide, insecticide, matricide, patricide, suicide.*

-cide-[2] from Latin, meaning "fall; happen." It is related to -CAD-. This meaning is found in such words as: *accident, incident.*

-cise- from Latin, meaning "cut (down)." It is related to -CIDE-[2]. This meaning is found in such words as: *circumcise, decisive, incision, incisor, incisive, precise, scissors.*

-claim- from Latin, meaning "call out; talk; shout." This meaning is found in such words as: *acclaim, claim, clamor, exclaim, proclaim.*

-clos- from Latin, meaning "close." This meaning is found in such words as: *cloister, close, closet, disclose, enclose.*

-clud- (or **-clus-**) from Latin, meaning "to close, shut." This meaning is found in such words as: *include, seclude, inclusion, seclusion.*

-cord- from Latin, meaning "heart." This meaning is found in such words as: *accord, concord, concordance, cordial, discord.*

-corp- from Latin, meaning "body." This meaning is found in such words as: *corpora, corporal, corporation, corps, corpse, corpus, corpuscle, incorporate.*

-cosm- from Greek, meaning "world, universe; order, arrangement." This meaning is found in such words as: *cosmetic, cosmic, cosmopolitan, cosmos, microcosm.*

-cour- ultimately from Latin where it has the meaning "run; happen." It is related to -CUR-. This meaning is found in such words as: *concourse, courier, course, discourse, recourse.*

-cred- from Latin, meaning "believe." This meaning is found in such words as: *credence, credential, credible, credit, credo, credulous, creed, incredible.*

-cres- from Latin, meaning "grow." This meaning is found in such words as: *crescendo, crescent, decrease, increase.*

-culp- from Latin, meaning "blame." This meaning is found in such words as: *culpable, culprit, exculpate.*

-cum- from Latin, meaning "with." It is used between two words to mean "with; combined with; along with": *a garage-cum-workshop (= a garage that is combined with a workshop).*

-cur- from Latin, meanings "run; happen." These meanings are found in such words as: *concur, concurrent, currency, current, curriculum, cursive, cursor, cursory, occur, occurrence, recur, recurrence.* See -COUR-.

-cura- from Latin, meaning "help; care." This meaning is found in such words as: *accurate, curable, curate, curator, curative, cure, manicure, pedicure, secure, sinecure.*

-cycle- from Greek, meaning "cycle; circle; wheel." This meaning is found in such words as: *bicycle, cycle, cyclo, cyclone, cyclotron, recycle, tricycle.*

dece- from Latin, meaning "correct, proper." This meaning is found in such words as: *decent, indecent.*

dent- from Latin, meaning "tooth." This meaning is found in such words as: *dental, dentifrice, dentist, dentistry, denture.*

derm- from Greek, meaning "skin." This meaning is found in such words as: *dermatitis, dermatology, dermis, epidermis, hypodermic, pachyderm, taxidermy.*

dict- from Latin, meaning "say, speak." This meaning is found in such words as: *benediction, contradict, Dictaphone, dictate, dictator, diction, dictionary, dictum, edict, predict.*

doc- from Latin, meaning "to teach." This meaning is found in such words as: *docile, doctor, doctrine, document.*

dox- from Greek, meaning "opinion, idea, belief." This meaning is found in such words as: *doxology, orthodox.*

drom- from Greek, meaning "run; a course for running." This meaning is found in such words as: *aerodrome, dromedary, hippodrome, palindrome, syndrome, velodrome.*

du- from Latin, meaning "two." This meaning is found in such words as: *dual, duel, duet, duo, duplex, duplicity.*

duc- from Latin, meaning "to lead." This meaning is found in such words as: *abduct, abduction, adduce, aqueduct, conducive, conduct, deduce, deduct, ducal, duct, duke, educate, induce, induction, introduce, oviduct, produce, production, reduce, reduction, seduce, seduction, viaduct.*

dur- from Latin, meaning "hard; strong; lasting." These meanings are found in such words as: *durable, duration, duress, during, endure.*

dyn- from Greek, meaning "power." This meaning is found in such words as: *dynamic, dynamism, dynamite, dynamo, dynasty.*

equa- (or **-equi-**) from Latin, meaning "equal; the same." This meaning is found in such words as: *equable, equal, equanimity, equilibrium, equity, equivocal, inequality, inequity, unequal.*

fac- from Latin, meaning "do; make." This meaning is found in such words as: *benefactor, de facto, facsimile, fact, faction, faculty, manufacture.* See -FEC-, -FIC-.

face- from Latin, meaning "form; face; make." It is related to -FAC-. This meaning is found in such words as: *deface, efface, facade, face, facet, facial, surface.*

fec- from Latin, meaning "do; make." It is related to the root -FAC-. This meaning is found in such words as: *affect, defecate, defect, effect, infect.*

fed- from Latin, meaning "group; league; trust." This meaning is found in such words as: *confederate, federal, federalize, federation.*

fend- from Latin, meaning "strike." This meaning is found in such words as: *defend, defense, defensive, fend, forfend, indefensible, offend, offense, offensive.*

fer- from Latin, meaning "carry." This meaning is found in such words as:

confer, defer, differ, efferent, ferrous, ferry, infer, pestiferous, prefer, transfer.

-fess- from Latin, meaning "declare; acknowledge." This meaning is found in such words as: *confess, confession, confessional, profess, profession, professional, professor.*

-fic- from Latin, meaning "make, do." It is related to -FAC- and -FEC-. This meaning is found in such words as: *beneficial, certificate, efficacy, fiction, honorific, horrific, pacific, prolific, simplification.*

-fid- Latin, meaning "faith; trust." This meaning is found in such words as: *confide, confidence, fidelity, fiduciary.*

-fin- from Latin, meaning "end; complete; limit." This meaning is found in such words as: *confine, define, definite, definition, final, finale, finance, fine, finish, finite.*

-fix- from Latin, meaning "fastened; put; placed." This meaning is found in such words as: *affix, fixation, infix, prefix, suffix.*

-flat- from Latin, meaning "blow; wind." This meaning is found in such words as: *conflate, deflate, flatulence, inflate.*

-flect- from Latin, meaning "bend." It is related to -FLEX-. This meaning is found in such words as: *deflect, inflect, genuflect, reflect.*

-flex- from Latin, meaning "bend." It is related to -FLECT-. This meaning is found in such words as: *circumflex, flex, flexible, reflex, reflexive.*

-flor- from Latin, meaning "flower." This meaning is found in such words as: *efflorescence, flora, floral, florescence, florid, florist, flour, flourish, flower.*

-flu- from Latin, meaning "flow." This meaning is found in such words as: *affluence, affluent, confluence, effluence, effluent, flu, flue, fluctuate, fluent, fluid, flume, fluoride, flux, influence, influenza.*

-foli- from Latin, meaning "leaf." This meaning is found in such words as: *defoliate, foil, foliage, folio, portfolio.*

-form- from Latin, meaning "form, shape." This meaning is found in such words as: *conform, deform, formalize, format, formula, malformed, multiform, nonconformist, perform, platform, reform, transform, uniform.*

-fort- from Latin, meaning "strong; strength." This meaning is found in such words as: *comfort, discomfort, effort, fort, forte, fortify, fortitude, fortress, uncomfortable.*

-fortun- from Latin, meaning "by chance; luck." This meaning is found in such words as: *fortuitous, fortunate, fortune, misfortune, unfortunate.*

-frac- Latin, meaning "break; broken." This meaning is found in such words as: *fractious, fracture, fragile, fragment, frail, infraction, refraction.*

-frat- from Latin, meaning "brother." This meaning is found in such words as: *fraternal, fraternity, fratricide.*

-fug- from Latin, meaning "flee; move; run." This meaning is found in such words as: *centrifugal, centrifuge, fugitive, fugue, refuge, subterfuge.*

-funct- from Latin, meaning "perform, execute; purpose, use." This meaning is found in such words as: *defunct, disfunction, function, functional, malfunction, perfunctory.*

-fus- from Latin, meaning "pour, cast; join; blend." This meaning is found in such words as: *confuse, defuse, diffuse, effusive, fuse, fusion, infuse, profuse, suffuse, transfusion.*

gam- from Greek, meaning "marriage." This meaning is found in such words as: *bigamy, bigamist, gamete, misogamist, polygamy.*

gen- from Greek and Latin, meaning "race; birth; born; produced." These meanings are found in such words as: *antigen, carcinogen, congenital, degenerate, engender, erogenous, eugenics, gender, gene, generate, genus, homogenize.*

geo- from Greek, meaning "the earth; ground." This meaning is found in such words as: *apogee, geography, geology, geopolitics, perigee.*

gest- from Latin, meaning "carry; bear." This meaning is found in such words as: *congestion, digest, gestation, gesticulate, gesture, ingest, suggest.*

glot- from Greek, meaning "tongue." This meaning is found in such words as: *diglossia, epiglottis, gloss, glossary, glossolalia, glottis, isogloss, polyglot.*

gnos- from Greek and Latin, meaning "knowledge." This meaning is found in such words as: *agnostic, cognition, cognizant, diagnosis, diagnostic, incognito, precognition, prognosis, recognize.*

grad- from Latin, meaning "step; degree; rank." This meaning is found in such words as: *biodegradable, centrigrade, degrade, grad, gradation, gradient, gradual, graduate, retrograde, undergraduate, upgrade.* See -GRESS-.

graph- from Greek, meaning "written down, printed, drawn." This meaning is found in such words as: *autograph, bibliography, biography, calligraphy, cartography, choreography, cinematography, cryptography, demographic, digraph, epigraph, ethnography, geography, graph, graphic, graphite, hagiography, holography, homograph, ideograph, lexicography, lithography, mimeograph, monograph, oceanography, orthography, paragraph, phonograph, photograph, pictograph, polygraph, pornography, seismograph, telegraph, typography.* See -GRAM.

grat- from Latin, meaning "pleasing; thankful; favorable." This meaning is found in such words as: *congratulate, grateful, gratify, gratis, gratitude, gratuitous, gratuity, ingrate, ingratiate, ingratitude.*

greg- from Latin, meaning "group; flock." This meaning is found in such words as: *aggregate, congregate, desegregate, egregious, gregarious, segregate.*

gress- from Latin, meaning "step; move." It is related to -GRAD-. This meaning is found in such words as: *aggression, congress, digress, egress, ingress, progress, regress, transgress.*

gyn- from Greek, meaning "wife; woman." This meaning is found in such words as: *androgyny, gynecology, misogyny.*

hab- from Latin, meaning "live, reside." This meaning is found in such words as: *cohabit, habitant, habitable, habitat, habitation, inhabit.*

habil- from Latin, meaning "handy; apt; able." These meanings are found in such words as: *ability, able, habilitate, rehabilitate.*

-hale- from Latin, meaning "breathe." This meaning is found in such words as: *exhale, halitosis, inhale.*

-hap- from Old Norse, meaning "luck; chance." This meaning is found in such words as: *haphazard, hapless, happen, mishap, perhaps.*

-helio- from Greek, meaning "sun." This meaning is found in such words as: *aphelion, heliocentric, helium, perihelion.*

-here- from Latin, meaning "cling, stick tight." It is related to -HES-. This meaning is found in such words as: *adhere, adherent, cohere, coherence, coherent.* See -HES-.

-hes- Latin, meaning "cling, stick to." It is related to -HERE-. This meaning is found in such words as: *adhesive, cohesive, hesitate.*

-hetero- from Greek, meaning "the other of two; different." This meaning is found in such words as: *heterogeneous, heterosexual.*

-hexa- from Greek, meaning "six." This meaning is found in such words as: *hexagon, hexameter.*

-homo- from Greek, meaning "same, identical." This meaning is found in such words as: *homogeneous, homogenize, homonym.*

-horr- from Latin, meaning "shake, tremble." This meaning is found in such words as: *abhor, abhorrent, horrendous, horrible, horrify, horror.*

-hum- from Latin, meaning "ground." This meaning is found in such words as: *exhume, humble, humiliate, humility, humus, posthumous.*

-hydr- from Greek, meaning "water." This meaning is found in such words as: *anhydrous, carbohydrate, dehydration, hydrant, hydrate, hydraulic, hydrocarbon, hydroelectric, hydrofoil, hydrogen, hydrophobia, hydroplane, hydroponics, hydrotherapy.*

-jec- from Latin, meaning "throw; be near; place." This meaning is found in such words as: *eject, adjacent, adjective, ejaculate, abject, dejection, conjecture, object, reject, inject, project, interject, trajectory, subject.*

-jour- from French and ultimately from Latin, meaning "daily; of or relating to one day." This meaning is found in such words as: *adjourn, journal, journey, sojourn.*

-jud- from Latin, meaning "judge." It is related to -JUR- and -JUS-. This meaning is found in such words as: *adjudge, adjudicate, injudicious, judge, judicial, misjudge, nonjudgmental, prejudgment, prejudice.*

-junc- from Latin, meaning "join; connect." This meaning is found in such words as: *adjoin, adjunct, conjunction, disjointed, disjunctive, enjoin, injunction, join(t), rejoinder, subjunctive.*

-jur- from Latin, meaning "swear." It is related to the root -JUS-, meaning "law; rule." This meaning is found in such words as: *abjure, conjure, injure, juridical, jurisdiction, jury, perjure.*

-jus- from Latin, meaning "law; rule; fair; just." It is related to the root -JUR-. This meaning is found in such words as: *adjust, just, justice, maladjusted, readjust, unjust.*

-lab- from Latin, meaning "work." This meaning is found in such words as: *belabor, collaborate, elaborate, labor, laborious.*

laps- from Latin, meaning "slip; slide; fall; make an error." This meaning is found in such words as: *collapse, elapse, lapse, prolapse, relapse.*

lat-[1] from Latin, meaning "carried." This meaning is found in such words as: *ablative, collate, correlate, dilatory, elated, oblate, prelate, prolate, relate, relative.*

lat-[2] from Latin, meaning "line; side." This meaning is found in such words as: *bilateral, collateral, dilate, equilateral, lateral, latitude, unilateral, vasodilator.*

lax- from Latin, meaning "loose, slack." This meaning is found in such words as: *lax, laxative, relax.*

lec- from Latin (and sometimes Greek), meaning "gather; choose" and also "read." This meaning is found in such words as: *collect, eclectic, eligible, elite, ineligible, election, lectern, lector, lecture, recollect, select.* See -LEG-.

leg- from Latin, meaning "law" and "to gather," also "to read." It is related to -LEC-. These meanings are found in such words as: *delegate, eclectic, illegal, illegible, intellect, intelligent, legacy, legal, legate, legend, legible, legion, legitimate, legislate, paralegal, privilege, relegate, sacrilege.*

lev- from Latin, meaning "lift; be light." This meaning is found in such words as: *alleviate, cantilever, elevate, elevator, levee, lever, leverage, levitate, levity, levy, relevant, relieve.*

liber- from Latin, meaning "free." This meaning is found in such words as: *deliver, liberal, liberate, libertine, liberty, livery.*

libr- from Latin, meaning "book." This meaning is found in such words as: *libel, library, libretto.*

libra- from Latin, where it has the meaning "balance; weigh." This meaning is found in such words as: *deliberate, equilibrium, librate.*

lig- from Latin, meaning "to tie; bind." This meaning is found in such words as: *ligament, ligature, obligate, oblige, religion.*

lim- from Latin, meaning "line; boundary; edge; threshold." This meaning is found in such words as: *eliminate, illimitable, limbic, limbo, liminal, limit, preliminary, sublime, subliminal.* See -LIN-.

lin- from Latin, meaning "string; line." This meaning is found in such words as: *crinoline, colinear, curvilinear, delineate, line, lineage, lineal, lineament, linear, linen, lingerie, matrilinear, patrilineal, rectilinear.* The meaning is also found in many compound words with *line* as the last part, such as *baseline, guideline, hairline, pipeline, sideline, underline.* See -LIM-.

ling- from Latin, meaning "tongue." This meaning is found in such words as: *bilingual, interlingual, language, lingo, linguine, linguistic, monolingual.*

lit- from Latin, meaning "letter; read; word." This meaning is found in such words as: *alliteration, illiterate, letter, literacy, literal, literary, obliterate, transliteration.*

lith- from Greek, meaning "stone." This meaning is found in such words as: *lithium, lithography, megalith, microlith, monolith, neolithic, paleolithic.*

loc- from Latin, meaning "location; place." This meaning is found in such words as: *allocate, collocation, dislocate, echolocation, local, locale, locate, locative, locomotive, locus, relocate.*

-log- from Greek, meaning "speak; word; speech." This meaning is found in such words as: *analog, apology, chronology, decalogue, dialogue, doxology, epilogue, eulogy, ideology, homologous, illogical, logarithm, logic, logo, monologue, neologism, philology, syllogism, tautology, terminology.*

-loq- (or **-loc-**) from Latin, meaning "speak; say." This meaning is found in such words as: *circumlocution, elocution, eloquent, grandiloquent, interlocutor, locution, loquacious, magniloquent, soliloquy, ventriloquist.*

-lu- (or **-lav-**) from Latin, meaning "wash." This meaning is found in such words as: *dilute, lavatory, ablution.*

-luc- from Latin, meaning "light." This meaning is found in such words as: *elucidate, lucid, Lucite, lucubrate, pellucid, relucent, translucent.*

-lud- (or **-lus-**) from Latin, meaning "to play." This meaning is found in such words as: *allude, allusion, collusion, delude, elusive, illusion, illusory, interlude, ludicrous, prelude.*

-lys- from Greek and Latin, meaning "to break down, loosen, dissolve." This meaning is found in such words as: *analysis, catalyst, dialysis, electrolysis, electrolyte, hydrolysis, paralysis, paralytic, palsy, urinalysis.*

-man-[1] from Latin, meaning "hand." This meaning is found in such words as: *amanuensis, legerdemain, maintain, manacle, manage, manual, maneuver, manufacture, manure, manuscript.*

-man-[2] *-man-* comes from Latin, meaning "stay; to last or remain." This meaning is found in such words as: *immanent, impermanent, permanent, remain.*

-mand- from Latin, meaning "order." This meaning is found in such words as: *command, countermand, demand, mandate, mandatory, remand.*

-mater- from Latin, meaning "mother." This meaning is found in such words as: *maternal, maternity, matriarch, matricide, matrimony, matrix, matron.*

-mech- from Greek (but for some words comes through Latin), meaning "machine," and therefore "instrument or tool." This meaning is found in such words as: *machination, machine, machinery, mechanic, mechanical, mechanize.*

-medi- from Latin, meaning "middle." This meaning is found in such words as: *immediate, intermediate, media, medial, median, mediate, mediator, medieval, mediocre, medium, multimedia.*

-mem- from Latin, meaning "mind; memory." This meaning is found in such words as: *commemorate, immemorial, memento, memo, memorandum, memoir, memorabilia, memorial, memory, remember, remembrance.*

-men- from Latin, meaning "mind." This meaning is found in such words as: *commentary, mental, mentality, mention, reminiscent.*

-merc- from Latin, meaning "trade." This meaning is found in such words as: *commerce, commercial, infomercial, mercantile, mercenary, merchant.*

-merg- from Latin, meaning "plunge; dip; mix." This meaning is found in such words as: *emerge, emergency, immerse, immersion, merge, merger, submerge.*

-meter- from Greek, where it has the meaning "measure." This meaning is found in such words as: *anemometer, barometer, centimeter, chronometer,* *diameter, geometry, kilometer, meter, metric, metronome, nanometer, odometer, parameter, pedometer, perimeter, symmetry.*

migr- from Latin, meaning "move to a new place; migrate." This meaning is found in such words as: *emigrant, emigrate, immigrate, migrant, migrate, transmigration.*

min- from Latin, meaning "least; smallest." This meaning is found in such words as: *diminish, diminution, diminutive, miniature, minimal, minimum, minor, minority, minuend, minus, minute.*

mir- from Latin, meaning "look at." This meaning is found in such words as: *admirable, admire, admiration, miracle, miraculous, mirage, mirror.*

mis- from Latin, meaning "send." It is related to -MIT-. This meaning is found in such words as: *admission, commissar, commissary, commission, compromise, demise, dismiss, emissary, impermissible, intermission, missal, missile, mission, missionary, missive, omission, permission, permissive, promise, promissory, remiss, submission, surmise, transmission.*

misc- from Latin, meaning "mix." This meaning is found in such words as: *miscegenation, miscellaneous, miscellany, miscible, promiscuous.*

miser- from Latin, meaning "wretched." This meaning is found in such words as: *commiserate, miser, miserable, miserly, misery.*

mit- from Latin, meaning "send." It is related to -MIS-. This meaning is found in such words as: *admit, commit, committee, emit, intermittent, noncommittal, omit, permit, remit, remittance, submit, transmit.*

mne- from Greek, meaning "mind; remembering." This meaning is found in such words as: *amnesia, amnesty, mnemonic.*

mob- from Latin, meaning "move." It is related to -MOT- and -MOV-. This meaning is found in such words as: *automobile, mobile, mobility, mobilize.*

mod- from Latin, meaning "manner; kind; measured amount." This meaning is found in such words as: *accommodate, commodious, immoderate, immodest, modal, mode, model, modern, modicum, module, mood, outmoded, remodel.*

mon- from Latin, meaning "warn." This meaning is found in such words as: *admonish, admonitory, admonition, monitor, monitory, monition, monster, monstrous, monument, premonition, summon.*

monstr- from Latin, meaning "show; display." This meaning is found in such words as: *demonstrate, monstrance, muster, remonstrate.*

mor- from Latin, meaning "custom; proper." This meaning is found in such words as: *amoral, demoralize, immoral, moral, morale, morality, mores.*

morph- from Greek, meaning "form; shape." This meaning is found in such words as: *allomorph, amorphous, anthropomorphism, metamorphic, metamorphosis, morph, morpheme, morphine.*

mort- from Latin, meaning "death." This meaning is found in such words as: *amortize, immortal, immortality, immortalize, morgue, mortal, mortality, mortgage.*

mot- from Latin, meaning "move." It is related to -MOV-. This meaning is found in such words as: *automotive, commotion, demote, emote, emotion, immotile, locomotive, motif, motion, motive, motivate, motor, promote, remote.*

-mov- from Latin, meaning "move." It is related to -MOT-. This meaning is found in such words as: *movable, move, movement, removal, remove, unmoving.*

-mut- from Latin, meaning "change." This meaning is found in such words as: *commute, commutation, immutable, mutate, mutation, mutual, parimutuel, permutation, permute, transmute.*

-nat- (or **-nasc-**) from Latin, meaning "born; birth." This meaning is found in such words as: *cognate, denatured, innate, naive, nascent, natal, nativity, nation, national, native, nature, naturalize, supernatural.*

-naut- from Greek, meaning "sailor." It has become generalized to mean "traveler." These meanings are found in such words as: *aeronautic, astronaut, cosmonaut, nautical, nautilus.*

-nav- from Latin, meaning "boat, ship." It is related to -NAUT-. This meaning is found in such words as: *circumnavigate, naval, nave, navicular, navigable, navigate, navy.*

-nec- (or **-nex-**) from Latin, meaning "tie; weave; bind together." This meaning is found in such words as: *annex, connect, disconnect, interconnect, nexus, unconnected.*

-neg- from Latin, meaning "deny; nothing." This meaning is found in such words as: *abnegate, negate, negation, negative, neglect, negligee, negligence, negligible, renegade, renege.*

-noc- (or **-nox-**) from Latin, meaning "harm; kill." This meaning is found in such words as: *innocent, innocuous, nocuous, noxious, obnoxious.*

-noct- from Latin, meaning "night." This meaning is found in such words as: *equinoctial, noctambulism, nocturnal, nocturne.*

-nom-[1] from Greek, meaning "custom; law; manage; control." This meaning is found in such words as: *agronomy, anomalous, anomaly, anomie, astronomy, autonomic, autonomous, autonomy, economy, gastronome, gastronomy, taxonomy.*

-nom-[2] from Latin and from Greek, meaning "name." This meaning is found in such words as: *binomial, cognomen, denomination, ignominious, ignominy, monomial, nomen, nomenclature, misnomer, nominal, nominate, nominative, noun, onomastic, onomatopoeia, polynomial, pronominal.*

-norm- from Latin, meaning "a carpenter's square; a rule or pattern." This meaning is found in such words as: *abnormal, enormous, enormity, norm, normal, normalcy, normalize, paranormal, subnormal.*

-nota- from Latin, meaning "note." This meaning is found in such words as: *annotate, connotation, denote, notable, notary, notarize, notation, note, notorious, notoriety.*

-nounce- from Latin, meaning "call; say." It is related to -NUNC-. This meaning is found in such words as: *announce, denounce, mispronounce, pronounce, renounce.*

-nov- from Latin, meaning "new." This meaning is found in such words as: *innovate, innovation, nova, novel, novella, novelette, novelist, novelty, novice, novitiate, renovate, renovation.*

null- from Latin, meaning "none; not one." This meaning is found in such words as: *annul, null, nullify.*

num- from Latin, meaning "number." This meaning is found in such words as: *enumerate, innumerable, number, numeral, numerator, numerous, outnumber, supernumerary.*

nunc- from Latin, meaning "call; say." It is related to -NOUNCE-. This meaning is found in such words as: *annunciation, denunciation, enunciate, mispronunciation, nuncio, renunciation.*

ocul- from Latin, meaning "eye." This meaning is found in such words as: *binocular, monocle, ocular, oculist.*

oper- from Latin, meaning "work." This meaning is found in such words as: *cooperate, inoperative, opera, operate, opus.*

opt- from Latin, meaning "choose; choice." This meaning is found in such words as: *adopt, co-opt, opt, option, optional.*

opti- from Greek, meaning "light; sight." This meaning is found in such words as: *autopsy, biopsy, myopia, myopic, ophthalmology, optic, optical, optician, optometrist, optometry, synoptic.*

ord- from Latin, meaning "order; fit." This meaning is found in such words as: *coordinate, extraordinary, inordinate, insubordinate, ordain, order, ordinance, ordinal, ordinary, ordination, subordinate.*

orga- from Greek, meanings "tool; body organ; musical instrument." These meanings are found in such words as: *disorganize, homorganic, inorganic, microorganism, organ, organize, reorganize.*

ori- from Latin, meaning "rise; begin; appear." This meaning is found in such words as: *aboriginal, aborigine, abort, abortion, disorient, orient, orientation, origin, original.*

pac- from Latin, meaning "peace." This meaning is found in such words as: *pacific, pacify, pact.*

pact- from Latin, meaning "fasten." This meaning is found in such words as: *compact, impact, impacted, subcompact.*

pand- from Latin, meaning "spread; get larger." This meaning is found in such words as: *expand, expansion, expanse, expansive, spandrel.*

par- from Latin, meaning "equal; a piece." This meaning is found in such words as: *apart, apartheid, bipartisan, comparable, compare, compartment, counterpart, depart, department, departure, disparage, impart, incomparable, pair, par, parenthesis, part, partial, participle, particle, particular, partisan, partition, party, repartee.*

pare-[1] from Latin, meaning "prepare." This meaning is found in such words as: *apparatus, disparate, pare, prepare, preparation, rampart, repair, separate.*

pare-[2] from Latin, meaning "to bring forth; breed." This meaning is found in such words as: *multiparous, parent, postpartum, parturition, vivaparous.*

pass-[1] from Latin, meaning "step; pace." This meaning is found in such words as: *bypass, compass, encompass, impasse, pass, passable, passage, passageway, passport, surpass, trespass, underpass.*

-pass-[2] from Latin, meaning "suffer; experience." It is related to -PAT-. This meaning is found in such words as: *compassion, compassionate, dispassionate, impassioned, impassive, passion, passive.*

-pat- from Latin, meaning "suffer; experience." It is related to -PASS-[2] This meaning is found in such words as: *compatible, impatience, impatient, incompatible, patience, patient, simpatico.*

-path- from Greek, meaning "suffering; disease; feeling." This meaning is found in such words as: *antipathy, apathetic, apathy, empathy, homeopathy, osteopath, pathetic, pathology, pathos, psychopath, sympathetic, sympathize, sympathy, telepathy.*

-patr- from Latin, meaning "father." This meaning is found in such words as: *compatriot, expatriate, paterfamilias, paternal, paternity, patriarch, patrician, patricide, patriot, patron, patroon, patronymic.*

-ped-[1] from Latin, meaning "foot." This meaning is found in such words as: *biped, centipede, expedient, expedite, expedition, impede, impediment, millipede, moped, pedal, pedicure, pedestal, pedestrian, pedometer, quadruped.*

-ped-[2] from Greek, meaning "child." This meaning is found in such words as: *encyclopedia, orthopedic, pedagogue, pedagogy, pederasty, pediatrics, pediatrician, pedophile.*

-pel- from Latin, meaning "drive; push." It is related to the root -PULS-. This meaning is found in such words as: *compel, dispel, expel, impel, propel, propeller, repel, repellant.*

-pen- from Latin and Greek, meaning "penalty; wrong," and hence "repent." These meanings are found in such words as: *impenitent, penal, penalize, penitence, penology, repent, repentance, subpoena.*

-pend- from Latin, meaning "hang; be suspended or weighed." This meaning is found in such words as: *append, appendage, appendix, compendium, depend, expend, impending, independent, pending, pendant, pendulum, pendulous, spend, stipend, suspend.*

-pet- from Latin, meaning "seek; strive for." This meaning is found in such words as: *appetite, centripetal, compete, competition, competence, competent, impetigo, impetuous, impetus, perpetual, petition, petulant, repeat, repetition.*

-phil- from Greek, meaning "love; loving." This meaning is found in such words as: *hemophilia, necrophilia, philander, philanthropic, philanthropy, philharmonic, philodendron, philology, philosophy.*

-phon- from Greek, meaning "sound; voice." This meaning is found in such words as: *cacophony, euphony, homophone, microphone, megaphone, phoneme, phonetic, phonics, phonograph, phonology, polyphony, saxophone, stereophonic, symphony, telephone, xylophone.*

-phys- from Greek, meaning "origin; form; nature; natural order." This meaning is found in such words as: *geophysics, metaphysics, physic, physician, physics, physiognomy, physiology, physique.*

-plac- from Latin, meaning "to please." This meaning is found in such words as: *complacent, implacable, placate, placebo, placid.*

plaud- from Latin, meaning "clap; noise." It is related to the root -PLOD-. This meaning is found in such words as: *applaud, plaudit, plausible.*

plen- from Latin, meaning "full." It is related to the root -PLET-. This meaning is found in such words as: *plenary, plenipotentiary, plenitude, plenteous, plenty, plenum, replenish.*

plet- from Latin and Greek, meaning "full." This meaning is found in such words as: *complete, deplete, plethora, replete.* See -PLEN-.

plex- from Latin, meaning "fold." It is related to the root -PLIC-. This meaning is found in such words as: *complex, duplex, multiplex, perplex, Plexiglas, plexus.*

plic- from Latin, meaning "fold, bend." This meaning is found in such words as: *accomplice, application, complicate, complicity, duplicate, duplicity, explicable, explicate, explicit, implicate, implicit, inexplicable, multiplication, replica, replicate, supplicant.* See -PLEX-.

plod- from Latin, meaning "noise." This meaning is found in such words as: *explode, implode.* See -PLAUD-.

ploy- from French and ultimately from Latin, meaning "bend; fold; use; involve." It is related to -PLIC-. This meaning is found in such words as: *deploy, employ, employee, employer, employment, ploy.*

pod- from Greek, meaning "foot." This meaning is found in such words as: *antipode, arthropod, chiropodist, podiatrist, podiatry, podium, pseudopod, tripod.*

point- from French and ultimately from Latin, meaning "point, prick, pierce." It is related to the root -PUNCT-. This meaning is found in such words as: *appoint, disappoint, midpoint, pinpoint, point, pointless, viewpoint.*

poli- from Latin, meaning "polish, smooth." This meaning is found in such words as: *impolite, polish, polite.*

polis- from Greek, meaning "city." This meaning is found in such words as: *cosmopolitan, geopolitical, impolitic, megalopolis, metropolis, metropolitan, necropolis, police, policy, politicize, political, politico, politics, polity.*

pon- from Latin, meaning "put, place." It is related to the root -POSIT-. This meaning is found in such words as: *component, deponent, exponent, opponent, postpone, proponent.*

pop- from Latin, meaning "people." This meaning is found in such words as: *populace, popular, popularity, popularize, populate, populous.*

port- from Latin, meaning "carry; bring." This meaning is found in such words as: *comport, comportment, deport, export, import, importance, important, opportune, opportunity, portable, portage, portfolio, porter, portmanteau, purport, rapport, report, support, transport, transportation.*

posit- from Latin, meaning "to put, place." It is related to the root -PON-. This meaning is found in such words as *deposit, position, postpone.*

pot- from Latin, meaning "power; ability." This meaning is found in such words as: *impotence, impotent, omnipotent, plenipotentiary, potent, potential, potency.*

pound- from French and ultimately from Latin, meaning "put; place." It is related to the root -PON-. This meaning is found in such words as: *compound, expound, impound, propound.*

-preci- from Latin, meaning "value; worth; price." This meaning is found in such words as: *appreciate, depreciate, precious, price, semiprecious.*

-prehend- from Latin, meaning "seize; grasp hold of; hold on to." This meaning is found in such words as: *apprehend, comprehend, misapprehend, prehensile.* See -PRIS-.

-press- from Latin, meaning "squeeze; press (down)." This meaning is found in such words as: *acupressure, compress, compression, decompress, decompression, depress, depression, express, impress, impressive, irrepressible, oppress, press, pressure, repress, suppress.*

-prim- from Latin, meaning "first." This meaning is found in such words as: *primacy, primary, primal, primeval, primate, prime, primitive, primo, primogeniture, primordial, prince, principal, principle, unprincipled.*

-pris- from French and ultimately from Latin, meaning "grasp; take hold; seize." It is related to the root -PREHEND-. This meaning is found in such words as: *apprise, comprise, enterprise, prison, prize, reprisal, reprise, surprise.*

-priv- from Latin, meaning "separated; apart; restricted." This meaning is found in such words as: *deprivation, deprive, privacy, private, privation, privatize, privilege, privy, underprivileged.*

-prob- from Latin, meaning "prove." This meaning is found in such words as: *approbation, improbable, opprobrious, opprobrium, probable, probability, probate, probation, probe, probity, reprobate.* See -PROV-.

-propr- from Latin, meaning "one's own." This meaning is found in such words as: *appropriate, expropriate, improper, impropriety, misappropriate, proper, property, proprietary, proprietor, propriety.*

-prov- from French and ultimately from Latin, meaning "prove." It is related to the root -PROB-. This meaning is found in such words as: *approve, approval, disapprove, disprove, improve, proof, prove, proven.*

-prox- from Latin, meaning "close; near." This meaning is found in such words as: *approximate, approximation, proximity.*

-pter- from Greek, meaning "wing; feather." This meaning is found in such words as: *archaeopteryx, dipterous, helicopter, monopterous, pterodactyl.*

-pugn- from Latin, meaning "fight; fist." This meaning is found in such words as: *impugn, pugilism, pugnacious, repugnant.*

-puls- from Latin, meaning "push; drive." This meaning is found in such words as: *compulsion, expulsion, impulse, impulsive, propulsion, pulsar, pulsation, pulse, repulse, repulsive.* See -PEL-.

-punct- from Latin, meaning "point; prick; pierce." This meaning is found in such words as: *acupuncture, compunction, expunge, punctilious, punctual, punctuality, punctuation, puncture, pungent.* See -POINT-.

-pur- from Latin, meaning "pure." This meaning is found in such words as: *expurgate, impure, impurity, pure, purée, purgative, purgatory, purge, purify, puritan, purity.*

-pute- from Latin, meaning "to clean, prune; consider; think." This meaning is found in such words as: *amputate, compute, computation, deputy,* *dispute, disreputable, impute, indisputable, putative, reputable, reputation.*

quad- from Latin, meaning "four, fourth." This meaning is found in such words as: *quad, quadrangle, quadrant, quadriplegic, quadruped, quadruplet.*

quer- from Latin, meaning "seek; look for; ask." This meaning is found in such words as: *conquer, query.* See -QUIR-, -QUES-, -QUIS-.

ques- from Latin, meaning "seek; look for; ask." This meaning is found in such words as: *conquest, inquest, quest, question, request.*

quie- from Latin, meaning "quiet, still." This meaning is found in such words as: *acquiesce, acquiescent, disquieting, quiescent, quiet, quietude.*

quir- from Latin, meaning "seek; look for." This meaning is found in such words as: *acquire, enquiry, inquire, inquiry, require, requirement.* See -QUIS-, -QUER-.

quis- from Latin, meaning "seek; look for." This meaning is found in such words as: *acquisition, exquisite, inquisitive, inquisition, perquisite, prerequisite, requisite.* See -QUIR-.

quit- from Latin, meaning "release; discharge; let go." This meaning is found in such words as: *acquit, quit, quite, requite, unrequited.*

quot- from Latin, meaning "how many; divided." This meaning is found in such words as: *quota, quotation, quote, quotidian, quotient.*

rape- from Latin, meaning "carry off by force." This meaning is found in such words as: *enrapture, rape, rapid, rapine, rapt, rapture.*

rase- from Latin, meaning "rub; scrape." This meaning is found in such words as: *abrasion, erase, raze, razor.*

ratio- from Latin, meaning "logic; reason; judgment." This meaning is found in such words as: *irrational, overrated, rate, ratify, ratio, ration, rational.*

real- from Latin, meaning "in fact; in reality." This meaning is found in such words as: *real, reality, realistic, realize, really, surreal.*

rect- from Latin, meaning "guide; rule; right; straight." This meaning is found in such words as: *correct, direct, erect, indirect, insurrection, misdirect, resurrection, rectangle, rectify, rectitude, rector, rectum.*

reg- from Latin, meaning "rule; direct; control." This meaning is found in such words as: *deregulate, interregnum, irregular, regal, regalia, regency, regular, regicide, regime, regimen, regiment, region, regional.*

rend- from Latin, meaning "give." This meaning is found in such words as: *render, rendition, surrender.*

roga- from Latin, meaning "ask; demand." This meaning is found in such words as: *abrogate, arrogant, derogatory, interrogate, prerogative, surrogate.*

rota- from Latin, meaning "round." This meaning is found in such words as: *orotund, rotary, rotate, rotation, rotogravure, rotor, rotund, rotunda.*

rupt- from Latin, meaning "break." This meaning is found in such words as: *abrupt, corrupt, disrupt, erupt, eruption, incorruptible, interrupt, rupture.*

-salv- from Latin, meaning "save." This meaning is found in such words as: *salvation, salvage, salver, salvo.*

-san- from Latin, meaning "health." This meaning is found in such words as: *insane, insanitary, sanatorium, sane, sanitary, sanitize.*

-sanct- from Latin, meaning "holy." This meaning is found in such words as: *sacrosanct, sanctify, sanction, sanctity, sanctuary.*

-sat- from Latin, meaning "full, enough, sufficient." This meaning is found in such words as: *dissatisfy, dissatisfaction, insatiable, sate, satiated, satire, satisfy, satisfaction, saturate, unsatisfied.*

-scend- from Latin, meaning "climb." This meaning is found in such words as: *ascend, condescend, descend, transcend, transcendent.*

-schol- from Latin, meaning "school." This meaning is found in such words as: *scholar, scholastic, school, unschooled.*

-sci- from Latin, meaning "to know." This meaning is found in such words as: *conscience, conscious, omniscient, omniscience, prescient, prescience, science, scientific.*

-scope- from Greek, meaning "see." This meaning is found in such words as: *fluoroscope, gyroscope, horoscope, microscope, microscopic, oscilloscope, periscope, radioscopy, spectroscope, stethoscope, telescope, telescopic.*

-scrib- from Latin, meaning "write." This meaning is found in such words as: *ascribe, circumscribe, conscribe, describe, indescribable, inscribe, prescribe, proscribe, scribble, scribe, subscribe, transcribe.*

-script- from Latin, meaning "writing." This meaning is found in such words as: *description, inscription, scripture.*

-sect- from Latin, meaning "cut." This meaning is found in such words as: *bisect, dissect, intersect, resection, section, sector, vivisection.*

-semble- from Latin, meaning "seem; appear(ance)." This meaning is found in such words as: *assemble, assembly, dissemble, ensemble, resemblance, resemble, semblance.*

-sene- from Latin, meaning "old." This meaning is found in such words as: *senate, senescence, senescent, senile, senior.*

-sens- from Latin, meaning "sense; feel." This meaning is found in such words as: *consensus, dissension, extrasensory, insensible, insensitive, nonsense, sensation, sensational, sense, senseless, sensitive, sensor, sensory, sensual, sensuous.* See -SENT-.

-sent- from Latin, meaning "feel." It is related to the root -SENS-. This meaning is found in such words as: *assent, consent, dissent, presentiment, resent, resentful, resentment, scent, sentence, sentient, sentiment.*

-seq- from Latin, meaning "follow." This meaning is found in such words as: *consequence, consequent, consequential, inconsequential, obsequious, sequel, sequence, sequential, subsequent.*

-serv-[1] from Latin, meaning "slave." This meaning is found in such words as: *deserve, disservice, servant, serve, service, servile, servitude, subservient.*

-serv-[2] from Latin, meaning "save." This meaning is found in such words as: *conserve, conservation, observe, observation, preserve, preservation, reserve, reservation, reservoir, unreserved.*

-sess- from Latin, meaning "sit; stay." It is related to the root -SID-. This meaning is found in such words as: *assess, assessor, dispossess, intersession, obsession, possession, repossession, session.*

sid- from Latin, meaning "sit; stay; live in a place." This meaning is found in such words as: *assiduous, dissident, insidious, preside, president, presidium, presidio, reside, residual, residue, siege, subside, subsidiary, subsidy, subsidize.* See -SESS-.

sign- from Latin, meaning "sign; have meaning." This meaning is found in such words as: *assign, assignation, consign, cosign, design, designate, ensign, insignia, insignificant, resign, signal, signature, signet, significant, signify.*

simil- from Latin, meaning "alike, similar." This meaning is found in such words as: *assimilate, assimilation, dissimilar, dissimulate, facsimile, similar, simile, simulcast, simulate, simultaneous, verisimilitude.*

sist- from Latin, meaning "remain; stand; stay." This meaning is found in such words as: *assist, consist, desist, inconsistent, insist, irresistible, persist, resist, subsist, subsistence.*

soc- from Latin, meaning "partner; comrade." This meaning is found in such words as: *associate, association, disassociate, disassociation, social, socialize, society, socio-, unsociable.*

sola- from Latin, meaning "soothe." This meaning is found in such words as: *console, consolation, disconsolate, inconsolable, solace.*

sole- from Latin, meaning "only; alone." This meaning is found in such words as: *desolate, desolation, sole, soliloquy, solipsism, solitaire, solitary, solitude, solo.*

solv- from Latin, meaning "loosen; release; dissolve." This meaning is found in such words as: *absolve, dissolve, insolvent, resolve, solve.*

som- from Greek, meaning "body." This meaning is found in such words as: *chromosome, psychosomatic, ribosome, somatic.*

son- from Latin, meaning "sound." This meaning is found in such words as: *consonant, dissonant, dissonance, resonant, resonance, resonate, resound, sonar, sonata, sonic, sonnet, sonogram, sound, supersonic, ultrasonic, unison.*

soph- from Greek, meaning "wise." This meaning is found in such words as: *philosopher, philosophy, sophism, sophistry, sophisticated, sophomore, theosophical, theosophy, unsophisticated.*

sort- from Latin, meaning "kind; type; part." This meaning is found in such words as: *assorted, consort, consortium, resort, sort.*

spec- from Latin, meaning "look at; examine." This meaning is found in such words as: *aspect, expect, inspect, inspector, inspection, introspection, irrespective, perspective, prospect, prospective, prospectus, respect, respectable, retrospect, special, specialty, specialize, specie, species, specific, specify, specimen, specious, spectacle, spectacular, spectrum, speculate, suspect.*

sper- from Latin, meaning "hope; hope for; expect." This meaning is found in such words as: *desperado, desperate, prosper, prosperity, prosperous.*

spir- from Latin, meaning "breathe; have a longing for." This meaning is found in such words as: *aspire, conspire, expire, inspire, perspire, respiration, respiratory, respire, spiracle, spirit, transpire.*

-spond- from Latin, meaning "pledge; promise." This meaning is found in such words as: *correspond, correspondent, correspondence, despondent, respond, transponder.*

-stab- from Latin, meaning "stand." This meaning is found in such words as: *establish, instability, stabilize, stable, unstable.*

-stan- from Latin, meaning "stand; remain." This meaning is found in such words as: *constant, circumstance, distance, distant, happenstance, inconstant, inconstancy, insubstantial, stance, stanch, stanchion, stand, stanza, stanch, substance, substantial, substantive, transubstantiation.*

-stat- from Latin (and in some cases from Greek), meaning "stand; remain." This meaning is found in such words as: *hemostat, instate, interstate, misstate, overstate, photostat, prostate, reinstate, rheostat, state, static, station, statistics, stative, statute, status, statutory, thermostat, understate.*

-stin- from Latin, meaning "separate; mark by pricking." This meaning is found in such words as: *distinct, distinguish, indistinct, indistinguishable, instinct.*

-stit- from Latin, meaning "remain; stand." This meaning is found in such words as: *constitute, constitution, destitute, institute, prostitute, prostitution, reconstitute, restitution, substitute, superstition, unconstitutional.*

-strain- from French and ultimately from Latin, meaning "stretch; tighten; bind." It is related to the root -STRICT-. This meaning is found in such words as: *constrain, restrain, strain, strait, straiten, unrestrained.*

-strat- from Latin, meaning "cover; throw over" and "level." These meanings are found in such words as: *prostrate, strata, stratify, stratosphere, stratum, substrate.*

-strict- from Latin, meaning "draw tight; bind; tighten." This meaning is found in such words as: *constrict, district, redistrict, restrict, strict, stricture, vasoconstrictor.*

-stroph- from Greek, meaning "turn; twist." This meaning is found in such words as: *apostrophe, catastrophe, strophe.*

-stru- from Latin, meaning "build, as by making layers; spread." This meaning is found in such words as: *construct, construction, construe, destruct, destruction, indestructible, infrastructure, instruct, instruction, instrument, instrumentation, misconstrue, obstruct, reconstruct, structure.*

-stud- from Latin, meaning "be busy with; devote oneself to." This meaning is found in such words as: *student, studio, study, understudy.*

-suade- from Latin, meaning "recommend; urge as being agreeable or sweet." This meaning is found in such words as: *dissuade, persuade.*

-sum- from Latin, meaning "take up; pick up." This meaning is found in such words as: *assume, assumption, consume, consumption, presume, presumption, presumptuous, resume, resumé, resumption, subsume, sumptuous.*

-tact- (or **-tang-**) from Latin, meaning "touch." This meaning is found in such words as: *contact, intact, tact, tactile, tangent, tangible.*

-tail- from French and ultimately from Latin, meaning "cut." This meaning is found in such words as: *curtail, detail, entail, retail, tailor.*

tain- from French and ultimately from Latin, meaning "hold." It is related to the root -TEN-. This meaning is found in such words as: *abstain, attain, contain, detain, entertain, maintain, obtain, pertain, rein, retain, retinue, sustain.*

tech- from Greek, meaning "skill; ability." This meaning is found in such words as: *polytechnic, pyrotechnic, tech, technical, technician, technique, technology.*

temp- from Latin, meaning "time." This meaning is found in such words as: *contemporary, contretemps, extemporaneous, tempo, temporary, temporize.*

ten- from Latin, meaning "hold." This meaning is found in such words as: *abstinence, content, continent, countenance, incontinent, impertinent, incontinence, lieutenant, pertinent, retentive, sustenance, tenable, tenacious, tenant, untenable.* See -TAIN-.

tend- from Latin, meaning "stretch; stretch out; extend; proceed." This meaning is found in such words as: *attend, contend, distend, extend, intend, portend, pretend, superintend, tend, tender, tendency, tendon.*

term- from Latin, meaning "end; boundary; limit." This meaning is found in such words as: *determine, exterminate, indeterminate, interminable, predetermine, term, terminal, terminate, terminology, terminus.*

terr- from Latin, meaning "earth; land." This meaning is found in such words as: *extraterrestrial, extraterritorial, subterranean, terrace, terrain, terrarium, terrestrial, terrier, territory.*

test- from Latin, meaning "witness." This meaning is found in such words as: *attest, contest, detest, incontestable, intestate, pretest, protest, protestation, Protestant, test, testament, testate, testify, testimonial, testimony.*

theo- from Greek, meaning "god." This meaning is found in such words as: *atheism, atheist, monotheism, pantheon, polytheism, theocracy, theology, theosophy.*

therm- from Greek, meaning "heat." This meaning is found in such words as: *hypothermia, thermal, thermodynamics, thermometer, thermostat.*

thes- from Greek, meaning "put together; set down." This meaning is found in such words as: *antithesis, epenthesis, hypothesis, parenthesis, photosynthesis, prosthesis, synthesis, synthetic, thesis.*

tom- from Greek, meaning "cut." This meaning is found in such words as: *anatomy, appendectomy, atom, diatom, dichotomy, hysterectomy, lobotomy, mastectomy, tome, tomography, tonsilectomy, vasectomy.*

ton- from Greek, meaning "sound." This meaning is found in such words as: *atonal, baritone, detonate, intonation, intone, monotone, monotonous, overtone, semitone, tonal, tone, tonic, undertone.*

tort- from Latin, meaning "twist." This meaning is found in such words as: *contort, distort, extort, retort, tort, torte, tortilla, tortuous, torture.*

tox- from Latin, meaning "poison." This meaning is found in such words as: *antitoxin, detoxify, intoxicated, intoxication, toxic, toxin.*

trac- from Latin, meaning "pull." This meaning is found in such words as: *abstract, attract, attraction, contract, contraction, detract, distract, extract, extractor, intractable, protracted, protractor, retract, subcontract, subtract, tract, tractable, traction, tractor.*

-troph- from Greek, meaning "food, nourishment." This meaning is found in such words as: *atrophy, isotrophy, phototrophic, trophic.*

-trude- from Latin, meaning "thrust, push." This meaning is found in such words as: *extrude, intrude, obtrude, protrude.*

-turb- from Latin, meaning "stir up." This meaning is found in such words as: *disturb, disturbance, imperturbable, masturbate, perturb, perturbation, turbid, turbine, turbo, turbulent.*

-type- from Greek, meaning "impression." This meaning is found in such words as: *archetype, atypical, prototype, stereotype, type, typical, typify, typography.*

-ult- from Latin, meaning "beyond; farther." This meaning is found in such words as: *antepenultimate, penultimate, ulterior, ultimatum, ultimate, ultra-.*

-uni- from Latin, meaning "one." This meaning is found in such words as: *reunion, reunite, unicameral, unicorn, unicycle, uniform, unify, unilateral, union, unique, unisex, unit, unitary, unite, university.*

-urb- from Latin, meaning "city." This meaning is found in such words as: *conurbation, suburb, suburban, suburbanite, suburbia, urb, urban, urbane.*

-vac- from Latin, meaning "empty." This meaning is found in such words as: *evacuate, vacancy, vacant, vacate, vacation, vacuous, vacuum.*

-vade- from Latin, meaning "go." This meaning is found in such words as: *evade, invade, pervade.*

-val- from Latin, meaning "value; worth; health; be strong." This meaning is found in such words as: *devalue, equivalent, evaluate, prevalent, undervalue, value, valiant, valid, validate, valor.*

-var- from Latin, meaning "change." This meaning is found in such words as: *invariable, variable, variance, variant, variation, varied, variegate, variety, variform, various, vary.*

-vec- from Latin, meaning "drive; convey." This meaning is found in such words as: *convection, invective, vector.*

-ven- from Latin, meaning "come." This meaning is found in such words as: *advent, adventure, avenue, circumvent, contravene, convene, convention, convenience, convent, covenant, event, eventual, inconvenience, inconvenient, intervene, invent, invention, inventory, misadventure, prevent, provenance, revenue, souvenir, unconventional, uneventful, venture, venturesome, venue.*

-venge- from Latin, meaning "protect, avenge, punish." This meaning is found in such words as: *avenge, revenge, vengeance.*

-ver- from Latin, meaning "true; truth." This meaning is found in such words as: *veracious, veracity, verily, verify, verisimilitude, veritably, verity.*

-verb- from Latin, meaning "word." This meaning is found in such words as: *adverb, adverbial, proverb, proverbial, verb, verbal, verbalize, verbatim, verbiage, verbose.*

verg- from Latin, meaning "turn; bend." This meaning is found in such words as: *converge, diverge, verge*. See -VERT-.

vert- (or **-vers-**) from Latin, meaning "turn; change." This meaning is found in such words as: *adversary, adverse, advertise, advertisement, aversion, avert, controversial, controversy, conversation, conversant, converse, conversion, convert, diverse, diversion, divert, extrovert, extroversion, inadvertent, incontrovertible, introvert, invert, inversion, irreversible, obverse, perverse, perversion, pervert, reversal, reverse, revert, subversive, subversion, subvert, transverse, traverse, universal, universe, versatile, verse, versed, version, versus, vertebra, vertebrate, vertex, vertical, vertiginous, vertigo.*

via- from Latin, meaning "way; route; a going." This meaning is found in such words as: *deviant, devious, obviate, trivial, via, viaduct.*

vict- from Latin, meaning "conquer." It is related to the root -VINC-. This meaning is found in such words as: *convict, evict, victor, victorious, victory.*

vide- from Latin, meaning "see." It is related to the root -VIS-. This meaning is found in such words as: *evidence, evident, provide, providence, providential, video, videodisc, videocassette, videotape.*

vinc- from Latin, meaning "conquer; defeat." This meaning is found in such words as: *convince, evince, invincible, vincible. See -VICT-.*

vis- from Latin, meaning "see." This meaning is found in such words as: *advice, advisable, advise, envisage, envision, inadvisable, invisible, provision, proviso, revise, revision, supervise, supervision, supervisor, television, visa, visage, vis-à-vis, visible, vision, visit, visor, vista, visual.* See -VIDE-.

vit- from Latin, meaning "life; living." It is related to the root -VIV-. This meaning is found in such words as: *aqua vitae, curriculum vitae, revitalize, vita, vital, vitalize, vitamin.*

viv- from Latin, meaning "life; alive; lively." This meaning is found in such words as: *convivial, revival, revive, survival, survive, survivor, viva, vivacious, vivid, viviparous, vivisection.*

voc- from Latin, meaning "call." This meaning is found in such words as: *advocate, avocation, convocation, convoke, equivocal, evocative, evoke, invocation, invoke, irrevocable, provocation, provocative, provoke, revocation, revoke, unequivocal, unprovoked, vocabulary, vocal, vocation, vociferous.*

vol- from Latin, meaning "wish; will." This meaning is found in such words as: *benevolent, involuntary, malevolent, volition, voluntary, volunteer.*

volv- (or **-volut-**) from Latin, meaning "turn, roll." This meaning is found in words such as: *evolve, revolve, evolution, revolution.*

vor- from Latin, meaning "eat." This meaning is found in such words as: *carnivore, carnivorous, devour, herbivore, omnivore, omnivorous, voracious.*

vot- from Latin, meaning "vow." This meaning is found in such words as: *devote, devotee, devout, vote.*

voy- from French, ultimately from Latin VIA, meaning "way; send." This meaning is found in such words as: *envoy, invoice, voyage.*

Concise Dictionary and Thesaurus

ABBREVIATIONS USED

adj.	adjective	*colloq.*	colloquial	*interj.*	interjection	*pron.*	pronoun
adv.	adverb	*conj.*	conjunction	*l.c.*	lower case	*pt.*	past tense
art.	article	*def.*	definition	*n.*	noun	*sing.*	singular
aux.	auxiliary	*esp.*	especially	*pl.*	plural	*usu.*	usually
cap.	capital	*fem.*	feminine	*prep.*	preposition	*v.*	verb

PRONUNCIATION KEY

a	act, bat	ī	ice, bite	ou	out, loud	z	zeal, lazy, those
ā	able, cape	j	just, edge	p	page, stop	zh	vision, measure
â	air, dare	k	kept, make	r	read, cry	ə	occurs only in un-
ä	art, calm	l	low, all	s	see, miss		accented syllables
b	back, rub	m	my, him	sh	shoe, push		and indicates the
ch	chief, beach	n	now, on	t	ten, bit		sound of
d	do, bed	ng	sing, England	ŧh	thin, path		a *in* alone
e	ebb, set	o	box, hot	th	that, other		e *in* system
ē	equal, bee	ō	over, no	u	up, love		i *in* easily
f	fit, puff	ô	order, bail	û	urge, burn		o *in* gallop
g	give, beg	oi	oil, joy	v	voice, live		u *in* circus
h	hit, hear	o͝o	book, put	w	west, away		
i	if, big	o͞o	ooze, rule	y	yes, young		

A

A, a (ā) *n.* first letter of English alphabet.

a (ə; *when stressed* ā) *adj. or indef. art. before initial consonant sounds.* **1.** some. **2.** one. **3.** any.

a-, prefix indicating: **1.** not, as *atypical.* **2.** without, as *amorality.*

AA, 1. administrative assistant. **2.** Alcoholics Anonymous. **3.** anti-aircraft.

A.A., Associate in Arts.

aard/vark/ (ärd/värk/) *n.* African anteating mammal.

A.B., Bachelor of Arts.

A.B.A., American Bar Association.

a·back/ (ə bak/) *adv.* by surprise.

ab/a·cus (ab/ə kəs) *n.* calculating device using rows of sliding beads.

ab/a·lo/ne (ab/ə lō/nē) *n.* edible mollusk with mother-of-pearl shell.

a·ban/don (ə ban/dən) *v.* **1.** leave completely; forsake. **2.** give up. —*n.* **3.** surrender to natural impulses. —**a·ban/don·ment,** *n.*

a·ban/doned, *adj.* **1.** forsaken or deserted. **2.** lacking in moral restraint.

a·base/ (ə bās/) *v.,* **abased, abasing.** lower; degrade.

a·bash/ (ə bash/) *v.* embarrass or shame.

a·bate/ (ə bāt/) *v.,* **abated, abating.** lessen or subside.

abatement, *n.* **1.** alleviation, mitigation, lessening, let-up, diminution, decrease, slackening. **2.** suppression, termination, ending, end, cessation. **3.** subsidence, decline, sinking, ebb, slack, fade-out, fading. —**Ant.** intensification, increase.

ab/at·toir/ (ab/ə twär/, ab/ə twär/) *n.* slaughterhouse.

ab/bé (a bā/, ab/ā) *n.* abbot; priest.

ab/bess (ab/is) *n.* convent head.

ab/bey (ab/ē) *n.* monastery or convent.

ab/bot (ab/ət) *n.* monastery head.

abbr., abbreviation.

ab·bre/vi·ate/ (ə brē/vē āt/) *v.,* **-ated, -ating.** shorten. —**ab·bre/vi·a/tion,** *n.*

abbreviation, *n.* shortening, abridgment, reduction, curtailment, cut, contraction, compression; truncation; condensation, digest, epitome, brief, essence, heart, core, soul. —**Ant.** lengthening, expansion.

ABC, *n., pl.* **ABC's, ABCs. 1.** alphabet. **2.** (*pl.*) basics.

ABC's, *n.* essentials, rudiments, basics, fundamentals, principles, grammar, elements.

ab/di·cate/ (ab/di kāt/) *v.,* **-cated, -cating.** give up (power or office). —**ab/di·ca/tion,** *n.*

abdication, *n.* renunciation, disclaimer, disavowal, repudiation, resignation, retirement, quittance; abandonment, surrender, cession, waiver. —**Ant.** commitment.

ab/do·men (ab/də mən) *n.* part of body between thorax and pelvis; belly. —**ab·dom/i·nal** (ab dom/ə nl) *adj.*

ab·dom/i·nals, *n.pl.* muscles of abdomen. Also, **abs.**

ab·duct/ (ab dukt/) *v.* kidnap. —**ab·duc/tion,** *n.* —**ab·duc/tor,** *n.*

abduction, *n.* kidnapping, capture, ravishment, seizure.

a·bed/ (ə bed/) *adv.* in bed.

aberrant, *adj.* **1.** straying, stray, deviating, deviate, wandering, errant, erring, devious, erratic, rambling, diverging, divergent. **2.** abnormal, irregular, unusual, odd, eccentric, peculiar, exceptional, weird, queer, curious, singular, strange; unconforming, nonconforming, anomalous. —**Ant.** direct; normal.

ab/er·ra/tion (ab/ə rā/shən), *n.* **1.** deviation from what is usual, normal, or right. **2.** mental unsoundness or disorder. —**ab·er/rant** (ə ber/ənt, ab/ər-), *adj.*

a·bet/ (ə bet/) *v.,* **abetted, abetting.** encourage in wrongdoing.

a·bey/ance (ə bā/əns) *n.* temporary inactivity.

ab·hor/ (ab hôr/) *v.,* **-horred, -horring.** loathe; find repugnant. —**ab·hor/rence,** *n.* —**ab·hor/rent,** *adj.*

abhorrence, *n.* hate, hatred, loathing, execration, odium, abomination, aversion, repugnance, revulsion, disgust, horror, antipathy, detestation, animosity, enmity. —**Ant.** love, attraction.

abhorrent, *adj.* **1.** hating, loathing, loathsome, execrating, execratory, antipathetic, detesting, detestable. **2.** horrible, horrifying, shocking, disgusting, revolting, sickening, nauseating, obnoxious, repellant, offensive, repugnant, repulsive, odious; hateful, detestable, abominable, invidious, contemptible, loathsome, horrid, heinous, execrable. **3.** remote, far, distant, removed. —**Ant.** amiable, lovable.

a·bide/ (ə bīd/) *v.,* **abode** (ə bōd/) *or* **abided, abiding. 1.** remain; stay. **2.** reside. **3.** wait for. **4.** agree; conform. **5.** *Informal.* tolerate; bear.

a·bid/ing, *adj.* steadfast; lasting.

a·bil/i·ty (ə bil/i tē) *n., pl.* **-ties. 1.** power or talent. **2.** competence.

ab/ject (ab/jekt, ab jekt/) *adj.* **1.** humiliating. **2.** despicable.

ab·jure/ (ab jŏŏr/) *v.,* **-jured, -juring.** renounce or abstain from.

ab/la·tive (ab/lə tiv) *adj. Gram.* denoting origin, means, etc.

a·blaze/ (ə blāz/) *adj.* **1.** on fire. **2.** gleaming. **3.** excited.

a/ble (ā/bəl) *adj.,* **abler, ablest. 1.** having sufficient power or qualification. **2.** competent. —**a/bly,** *adv.*

-able, suffix indicating: **1.** able to be, as *readable.* **2.** tending to, as *changeable.* **3.** worthy of, as *loveable.*

a/ble-bod/ied, *adj.* physically fit.

ab·lu/tion (ə blōō/shən) *n.* ritual washing.

ab/ne·gate/ (ab/ni gāt/) *v.,* **-gated, -gating.** deny to oneself.

ab·nor/mal (ab nôr/məl) *adj.* not normal; not usual or typical. —**ab/nor·mal/i·ty** (-mal/i tē) *n.* —**ab·nor/mal·ly,** *adv.*

abnormality, *n.* unusualness, eccentricity, abnormity, irregularity, unconformity, anomaly, peculiarity, aberrance, aberration, deviation, idiosyncrasy, singularity, curiosity; malformation, monstrosity, freakishness, deformity, distortion, defect. —**Ant.** regularity, normality.

a·board/ (ə bôrd/) *adv.* **1.** on a ship, train, etc. —*prep.* **2.** on.

a·bode/ (ə bōd/) *n.* **1.** home. **2.** stay.

a·bol/ish (ə bol/ish) *v.* do away with; annul.

ab/o·li/tion (ab/ə lish/ən) *n.* **1.** act of abolishing. **2.** end of slavery in the U.S. —**ab/o·li/tion·ist,** *n.*

A/-bomb/ (ā/bom/) *n.* atomic bomb.

a·bom/i·na·ble (ə bom/ə nə bəl) *adj.* hateful; loathsome.

a·bom/i·nate/ (-nāt/) *v.,* **-nated, -nating.** abhor or hate.

abomination, *n.* **1.** hatred, loathing, abhorrence, detestation, revulsion, loathsomeness, odiousness, odium; aversion. **2.** vice, sin, impurity, corruption, wickedness, evil, viciousness, depravity, immorality, amorality, profligacy, defilement, pollution, filth.

ab/o·rig/i·nal (ab/ə rij/ə nl) *adj.* **1.** original. —*n.* **2.** aborigine.

ab/o·rig/i·ne (-rij/ə nē) *n.* original inhabitant of a land.

a·bort/ (ə bôrt/) *v.* **1.** have or cause abortion. **2.** terminate prematurely. —**a·bor/tive,** *adj.*

a·bor/tion, *n.* end of pregnancy by expulsion of fetus before it is viable. —**a·bor/tion·ist,** *n.*

abortive, *adj.* **1.** failing, unsuccessful, miscarrying, immature, premature. **2.** undeveloped, underdeveloped, rudimentary, primitive. —**Ant.** consummate, complete, successful.

a·bound/ (ə bound/) *v.* be or have a lot of.

a·bout/ (ə bout/) *prep.* **1.** concerning. **2.** near, in, on, or around. **3.** ready. —*adv.* **4.** approximately. **5.** almost. **6.** on all sides. **7.** oppositely. —*adj.* **8.** astir. —**Usage.** Both ON and ABOUT mean "concerning"; ABOUT is used when the information given is general and not too technical: *a novel* ABOUT *the Civil War.* ON is used when the information is particular, as by being scholarly or technical: *an important article* ON *the Civil War.*

about-face, *n.* **1.** 180° turn, reversal, turnabout, reverse, changeabout, reversion, volte-face.

a·bove/ (ə buv/) *adv.* **1.** higher. **2.** previously. **3.** in or to heaven. —*prep.* **4.** higher or greater than. —*adj.* **5.** foregoing.

a·bove/board/, *adv., adj.* honest; fair.

ab/ra·ca·dab/ra (ab/rə kə dab/rə) *n.* word used in magic.

abrade, *v.* wear off, wear down, scrape off; erode, wear away, rub off.

a·bra/sion (ə brā/zhən), *n.* **1.** wearing or rubbing away. **2.** scraped area on skin. —**a·brade/,** *v.*

a·bra/sive (ə brā/siv, -ziv) *adj.* **1.** abrading. **2.** annoying. —*n.* **3.** material used to grind or smooth. —**a·bra/sive·ly,** *adv.*

a·breast/ (ə brest/) *adv., adj.* **1.** side by side. **2.** informed; aware.

a·bridge/ (ə brij/) *v.,* **abridged, abridging.** shorten.

abridgment, *n.* **1.** condensation, shortening, digest, epitome, curtailment, reduction, abbreviation, contraction, retrenchment, compression; compendium, synopsis, abstract, abstraction, summary, syllabus, brief, outline, précis. **2.** dispossession, limitation. —**Ant.** expansion, extension, enlargement.

a·broad/ (ə brôd/) *adv., adj.* **1.** out of one's own country. **2.** in circulation.

ab/ro·gate/ (ab/rə gāt/) *v.,* **-gated, -gating.** annul or repeal.

abrogation, *n.* abolition, cancellation, annulment, repeal, disannulment, revocation, rescission, nullification, invalidation. —**Ant.** establishment.

ab·rupt/ (ə brupt/) *adj.* **1.** sudden; unexpected. **2.** steep. —**ab·rupt/ly,** *adv.* —**ab·rupt/ness,** *n.*

ab/scess (ab/ses) *n.* infected, pus-filled place on the body.

ab·scond/ (ab skond/) *v.* leave suddenly and secretly.

absence, *n.* **1.** want, lack, need, deficiency, defect. **2.** nonappearance. —**Ant.** presence.

ab/sent *adj.* (ab/sənt) **1.** not present.

2. lacking. —*v.* (ab sent´) **3.** keep away. —**ab´sence,** *n.*

ab´sen·tee´ (ab´sən tē´) *n.* absent person.

ab´sent-mind´ed, *adj.* forgetful or preoccupied. —**ab´sent-mind´ed·ly,** *adv.* —**ab´sent-mind´ed·ness,** *n.*

ab´so·lute´ (ab´sə lōōt´) *adj.* **1.** complete; perfect. **2.** pure. **3.** unrestricted. **4.** despotic. **5.** definite. —**ab´so·lute·ly,** *adv.*

absolutely, *adv.* **1.** completely, wholly, entirely, unqualifiedly, definitely, unconditionally. **2.** positively, affirmatively, unquestionably, definitely, unequivocally, indubitably, really, without doubt, beyond doubt.

absolute zero, temperature (−273.16° C or −459.69° F) at which molecular activity ceases.

ab·solve´ (ab zolv´) *v.,* -solved, -solving. pardon sins of. —**ab´so·lu´tion** (ab´sə lōō´shan) *n.*

ab·sorb´ (ab sôrb´, -zôrb´) *v.* **1.** take in. **2.** occupy completely; fascinate. —**ab·sorb´ent,** *adj., n.* —**ab·sorb´ing,** *adj.* —**ab·sorp´tion,** *n.*

ab·stain´ (ab stān´) *v.* refrain (from). —**ab·sten´tion** (-sten´shan) *n.*

ab·ste´mi·ous (ab stē´mē əs) *adj.* moderate in eating, drinking, etc.

ab·sti´nence (ab´stə nəns) *n.* forbearance; self-restraint.

ab´stract *adj.* (ab strakt´, ab´strakt) **1.** apart from specific objects. **2.** theoretical. **3.** hard to understand. **4.** (of art) not representing natural objects or forms. —*n.* (ab´strakt) **5.** summary. **6.** essence. —*v.* (ab strakt´) **7.** remove or steal. **8.** summarize. —**ab·strac´tion,** *n.*

ab·stract´ed, *adj.* preoccupied; absentminded.

ab·struse´ (ab strōōs´) *adj.* hard to understand.

ab·surd´ (ab sûrd´, -zûrd´) *adj.* ridiculous. —**ab·surd´ly,** *adv.* —**ab·surd´i·ty,** *n.*

a·bun´dance (ə bun´dəns) *n.* plentiful supply. —**a·bun´dant,** *adj.* —**a·bun´dant·ly,** *adv.*

abundant, *adj.* abounding, teeming, thick, plentiful, plenteous, flowing, copious, profuse, overflowing, rich, replete, ample, oversufficient, superabundant, excess, excessive, inexhaustible, bountiful, bounteous, abounding in, rich in, luxuriant, lavish. —**Ant.** sparse, scarce, poor.

a·buse´ *v.,* abused, abusing, *n.* —*v.* (ə byōōz´) **1.** use wrongly. **2.** treat badly. —*n.* (ə byōōs´) **3.** wrong use or treatment. **4.** insult. —**a·bu´sive,** *adj.*

a·but´ (ə but´) *v.,* abutted, abutting. touch at the edge.

a·bys´mal (ə biz´məl) *adj.* **1.** very deep. **2.** dreadful.

a·byss´ (ə bis´) *n.* **1.** very deep chasm. **2.** hell.

Ab´ys·sin´i·an (ab´ə sin´ē ən) *adj.* **1.** from ancient Ethiopia. —*n.* **2.** type of cat.

AC, 1. air conditioning. **2.** Also, **ac., a.c., A.C.** alternating current.

a·ca´cia (ə kā´shə) *n.* small tree or shrub.

ac´a·dem´ic (ak´ə dem´ik) *adj.* **1.** of a school, college, etc. **2.** theoretical. —*n.* **3.** college student or teacher. —**ac´a·dem´i·cal·ly,** *adv.*

a·cad´e·my (ə kad´ə mē) *n., pl.* -mies Also. **1.** school. **2.** cultural society.

a´ cap·pel´la (ä´ kə pel´ə) *adv., adj. Music.* without instrumental accompaniment.

ac·cede´ (ak sēd´) *v.,* -ceded, -ceding. **1.** consent. **2.** assume.

ac·cel´er·ate´ (ak sel´ə rāt´) *v.,* -ated, -ating. speed up; hasten. —**ac·cel´er·a´tion,** *n.*

ac·cel´er·a´tor, *n.* pedal that controls vehicle's speed.

ac´cent *n.* (ak´sent) **1.** emphasis. **2.** characteristic pronunciation. **3.** mark showing stress, etc. —*v.* (ak´sent) **4.** emphasize.

ac·cen´tu·ate´ (ak sen´chōō āt´) *v.,* -ated, -ating. stress or emphasize.

ac·cept´ (ak sept´) *v.* **1.** receive willingly. **2.** agree to. **3.** believe. —**ac·cept´a·ble,** *adj.* —**ac·cept´ed,** *adj.* —**ac·cept´a·bil´i·ty,** *n.* —**ac·cept´a·bly,** *adv.* —**ac·cept´ance,** *n.*
—**Usage.** Because of similarity in pronunciation, ACCEPT and EXCEPT are sometimes confused in writing. ACCEPT is a verb meaning "to receive willingly": *Please accept my gift.* EXCEPT is usually a preposition meaning "other than": *Everybody came except you.* When EXCEPT is used as a verb, it means "to leave out": *Some students were excepted from taking the exam.*

ac´cess (ak´ses) *n.* **1.** right to enter or use. —*v.* **2.** gain access to. **3.** find in a computer.

ac·ces´si·ble, *adj.* easy to reach or influence. —**ac·ces´si·bil´i·ty,** *n.*

ac·ces´sion (-sesh´ən) *n.* **1.** attainment of an office, etc. **2.** increase.

ac·ces´so·ry (-ses´ə rē) *n., pl.* -ries. **1.** something added for convenience, decoration, etc. **2.** one who helps another commit a felony.

ac´ci·dent (ak´si dənt) *n.* unexpected event, usually unfortunate. —**ac´ci·den´tal,** *adj.* —**ac´ci·den´tal·ly,** *adv.*

accidental, *adj.* **1.** casual, fortuitous, chance, lucky, unlucky, unfortunate, serendipitous, unpremeditated, unintentional, unwitting, inadvertent, unexpected, unanticipated, random, unforeseen, undesigned, unplanned, contingent. **2.** nonessential, incidental, subsidiary, secondary, dispensable, expendable, adventitious. —**Ant.** planned, designed, essential.

ac´ci·dent-prone´, *adj.* inclined to have accidents.

ac·claim´ (ə klām´) *v.* **1.** salute with applause, cheers, etc. —*n.* **2.** applause, cheers, etc.

acclaimed, *adj.* notable, distinguished, great, major, famous, honored, famed, renowned, celebrated, prominent, world-renowned, worldfamous, stellar, world-class, outstanding, preeminent, premier.

ac´cli·mate´ (ak´lə māt´, ə klī´mit) *v.,* -ated, -ating. accustom to new conditions. Also, **ac·cli´ma·tize´.**

ac·co·lade´ (ak´ə lād´, -läd´) *n.* award, honor, or applause.

ac·com´mo·date´ (ə kom´ə dāt´) *v.,* -dated, -dating. **1.** do a favor for. **2.** supply. **3.** provide with room, food, etc. **4.** adjust.

ac·com´mo·dat´ing, *adj.* helpful; obliging.

ac·com´mo·da´tion, *n.* **1.** act of accommodating. **2.** (*pl.*) space for lodging or travel.

ac·com´pa·ni·ment (ə kum´pə ni·mənt, ə kump´ni-) *n.* **1.** something added as decoration, etc. **2.** subsidiary music for performer.

ac·com´pa·ny, *v.,* -nied, -nying. **1.** go or be with. **2.** provide musical accompaniment for. —**ac·com´pa·nist,** *n.*

ac·com´plice (ə kom´plis) *n.* partner in crime.

ac·com´plish (ə kom´plish) *v.* do or finish.

ac·com´plished, *adj.* expert.

ac·com´plish·ment, *n.* **1.** completion. **2.** skill or learning.

ac·cord´ (ə kôrd´) *v.* **1.** agree; be in harmony. **2.** cause to agree. **3.** grant; allow. —*n.* **4.** agreement; harmony. —**ac·cord´ance,** *n.*

ac·cord´ing·ly, *adv.* therefore.

according to, 1. in keeping with or proportion to. **2.** on authority of.

ac·cor´di·on (ə kôr´dē ən) *n.* musical instrument with keyboard and bellows.

ac·cost´ (ə kôst´) *v.* approach or confront.

ac·count´ (ə kount´) *n.* **1.** report. **2.** reason. **3.** importance. **4.** money in bank. **5.** record of business transactions. —*v.* **6.** explain. **7.** consider.

ac·count´a·ble, *adj.* **1.** responsible. **2.** explainable. —**ac·count´a·bly,** *adv.*

ac·count´ant, *n.* person whose profession is accounting. —**ac·count´an·cy,** *n.*

ac·count´ing, *n.* organization and maintenance of financial records.

ac·cred´it (ə kred´it) *v.* **1.** attribute. **2.** authorize or approve. —**ac·cred´i·ta´tion,** *n.*

ac·crue´ (ə krōō´) *v.,* -crued, -cruing. be added (to). —**ac·cru´al,** *n.*

ac·cul´tur·ate´ (ə kul´chə rāt´) *v.,* -ated, -ating. adopt cultural traits of another group.

ac·cu´mu·late´ (ə kyōō´myə lāt´) *v.,* -lated, -lating. gather; collect. —**ac·cu´mu·la´tion,** *n.* —**ac·cu´mu·la·tive** (-lə tiv) *adj.* —**ac·cu´mu·la´tor,** *n.*

ac·cu·rate (ak´yər it) *adj.* exact; correct. —**ac´cu·rate·ly,** *adv.* —**ac´cu·ra·cy,** *n.*

ac·curs´ed (ə kûr´sid, ə kûrst´) *adj.* **1.** cursed. **2.** hateful.

ac·cu´sa·tive (ə kyōō´zə tiv) *adj. Gram.* denoting verb's direct object.

ac·cuse´ (ə kyōōz´) *v.,* -cused, -cusing. blame; charge. —**ac´cu·sa´tion** (ak´yōō zā´shən) *n.* —**ac·cus´er,** *n.*

ac·cused´, *n.* person tried in court.

ac·cus´tom (ə kus´təm) *v.* make used to.

ac·cus´tomed, *adj.* **1.** usual; habitual. **2.** habituated.

ace (ās) *n., v.* aced, acing. —*n.* **1.** playing card with single spot. **2.** expert who excels at something. **3.** *Tennis.* serve opponent cannot touch. —*v.* **4.** score ace against. **5.** do very well on.

a·cer´bic (ə sûr´bik) *adj.* **1.** sour. **2.** sharp or severe. —**a·cer´bi·ty,** *n.*

a·ce´ta·min´o·phen (ə sē´tə min´ə·fən) *n.* substance used to reduce pain or fever.

ac´e·tate´ (as´i tāt´) *n.* salt or ester of acetic acid.

a·ce´tic (ə sē´tik) *adj.* of or producing vinegar.

acetic acid, sharp-tasting acid found in vinegar.

ac´e·tone´ (as´i tōn´) *n.* flammable liquid used as a solvent.

a·cet´y·lene´ (ə set´l ēn´) *n.* gas used in welding, etc.

ache (āk) *v.,* ached, aching, *n.* —*v.* **1.** suffer dull pain. —*n.* **2.** dull pain.

a·chieve´ (ə chēv´) *v.,* achieved, achieving. accomplish; bring about. —**a·chieve´ment,** *n.*

achievement, *n.* **1.** exploit, feat, deed, victory, triumph. **2.** accomplishment, realization, attainment, consummation, acquisition, acquirement, fulfillment, completion. —**Ant.** failure.

A·chil´les heel (ə kil´ēz) vulnerable spot.

ac′id (as′id) *n.* **1.** chemical compound containing hydrogen replaceable by a metal to form a salt. **2.** sour substance. —*adj.* **3.** of acids. **4.** sour or sharp. —a•cid′ic, *adj.* —a•cid′i•ty, *n.*

acid rain, rain containing chemicals from industrial pollution.

ac•knowl′edge (ak nol′ij) *v.,* -edged, -edging. **1.** recognize; admit. **2.** show appreciation for. —ac•knowl′edg•ment, *n.*

ac′me (ak′mē) *n.* highest point.

ac′ne (ak′nē) *n.* skin disorder.

ac′o•lyte′ (ak′ə līt′) *n.* **1.** altar attendant. **2.** follower.

a′corn (ā′kôrn, ā′kərn) *n.* fruit or nut of the oak.

a•cous′tic (ə kōō′stik) *adj.* of sound or hearing. —a•cous′ti•cal•ly, *adv.*

a•cous′tics, *n.* **1.** science of sound. **2.** sound qualities.

ac•quaint′ (ə kwānt′) *v.* make known or familiar.

ac•quaint′ance, *n.* **1.** someone personally known. **2.** personal knowledge.

ac′qui•esce′ (ak′wē es′) *v.,* -esced, -escing. agree or comply. —ac′qui•es′cence. *n.* —ac′qui•es′cent, *adj.*

ac•quire′ (ə kwī′r′) *v.,* -quired, -quiring. get; obtain. —ac•quire′ment, *n.*

ac′qui•si′tion (ak′wə zish′ən) *n.* **1.** acquiring. **2.** something acquired.

ac•quis′i•tive (ə kwiz′i tiv) *adj.* eager to acquire.

ac•quit′ (ə kwit′) *v.,* -quitted, -quitting. **1.** free of blame or guilt. **2.** behave or conduct. —ac•quit′tal, *n.*

a′cre (ā′kər) *n.* unit of land area (1/640 sq. mi. or 43,560 sq. ft.). —a′cre•age, *n.*

ac′rid (ak′rid) *adj.* sharp; biting.

acrimonious, *adj.* harsh, bitter, biting, sharp, rancorous, angry, contentious, disputatious, antagonistic, hostile, vitriolic. —**Ant.** peaceful, pacific, irenic, tactful, diplomatic.

ac′ri•mo′ny (ak′rə mō′nē) *n.* harshness or bitterness of manner or speech. —ac′ri•mo′ni•ous, *adj.*

ac′ro•bat′ (ak′rə bat′) *n.* performer on trapeze, tightrope, etc. —ac′ro•bat′ic, *adj.*

ac′ro•bat′ics, *n.* (*used with a pl. v.*) **1.** acrobat's feats. **2.** any feats requiring skill.

ac′ro•nym (ak′rə nim) *n.* word formed from successive initials or groups of letters, as NATO, UNICEF.

ac′ro•pho′bi•a (ak′rə fō′bē ə) *n.* fear of heights.

a•cross′ (ə krôs′) *prep.* **1.** from side to side of. **2.** on the other side of. —*adv.* **3.** from one side to another.

across-the-board, *adj.* applying to all members or categories.

a•cryl′ic (ə kril′ik) *n.* chemical used to make textile fibers and paints.

act (akt) *n.* **1.** something done. **2.** law or decree. **3.** part of a play or opera. —*v.* **4.** do something. **5.** behave. **6.** pretend. **7.** perform in play, movie, etc.

act′ing, *adj.* substitute.

ac•tin′i•um (ak tin′ē əm) *n.* radioactive metallic element.

ac′tion (ak′shən) *n.* **1.** state of being active. **2.** something done. **3.** behavior. **4.** combat. **5.** lawsuit.

ac′tion•a•ble, *adj.* providing grounds for a lawsuit.

ac′ti•vate′ (ak′tə vāt′) *v.,* -vated, -vating. make active; start. —ac′ti•va′tion, *n.*

ac′tive (ak′tiv) *adj.* **1.** in action; busy, nimble, or lively. **2.** indicating that the subject performs the action of the verb. —ac′tive•ly, *adv.*

ac′tiv•ism, *n.* vigorous action toward social or political goals. —ac′tiv•ist, *n.*

ac•tiv′i•ty (ak tiv′i tē) *n., pl.* -ties. **1.** being active. **2.** busy action. **3.** specific occupation or pursuit.

ac′tor (ak′tər) *n.* performer in play or movie. —ac′tress, *n.fem.*

ac′tu•al (ak′chōō əl) *adj.* real. —ac′tu•al•ly, *adv.* —ac′tu•al′i•ty (-al′i tē) *n.*

ac′tu•ar′y (ak′chōō er′ē) *n., pl.* -aries. calculator of insurance rates and risks. —ac′tu•ar′i•al, *adj.*

ac′tu•ate′ (ak′chōō āt′) *v.,* -ated, -ating. cause to act; effect.

a•cu′i•ty (ə kyōō′i tē) *n.* sharpness of perception.

a•cu′men (ə kyōō′mən) *n.* mental keenness.

ac′u•punc′ture (ak′yōō pungk′chər) *n.* Chinese art of healing by inserting needles into the skin. —ac′u•punc′tur•ist, *n.*

a•cute′ (ə kyōōt′) *adj.* **1.** sharp; pointed. **2.** severe. **3.** crucial. **4.** keen, clever. **5.** high-pitched. **6.** (of an angle) less than 90 degrees. —a•cute′ly, *adv.* —a•cute′ness, *n.*

ad (ad) *n. Informal.* advertisement.

A.D., anno Domini: in the year of our Lord.

ad′age (ad′ij) *n.* proverb.

a•da′gio (ə dä′jō, -zhē ō′) *adj., adv. Music.* slow.

ad′a•mant (ad′ə mənt) *adj.* insistent.

Ad′am's ap′ple (ad′əmz) projection of thyroid cartilage in front of neck.

a•dapt′ (ə dapt′) *v.* adjust to new requirements. —a•dapt′a•ble, *adj.* —a•dapt′a•bil′i•ty, *n.* —ad′ap•ta′tion (ad′ap tā′shən) *n.* —a•dapt′er, a•dap′tor, *n.*

add (ad) *v.* **1.** unite or join. **2.** find the sum (of). **3.** increase. **4.** say more.

ad•den′dum (ə den′dəm) *n., pl.* -da (-də). something to be added.

ad′der (ad′ər) *n.* small venomous snake.

ad′dict, (ad′ikt) **1.** person dependent on a drug, etc. —*v.* (ə dikt′) **2.** make dependent on. —ad•dic′tion, *n.* —ad•dic′tive, *adj.*

addiction, *n.* dependency, compulsive need, obsession, fixation, habit, craving, appetite, itch, lust, passion, monkey on one's back, jones, substance abuse.

ad•di′tion (ə dish′ən) *n.* **1.** adding. **2.** anything added. **3.** in addition to, besides. —ad•di′tion•al, *adj.* —ad•di′tion•al•ly, *adv.*

ad′di•tive (ad′i tiv) *n.* added ingredient.

ad′dle (ad′l) *v.,* -dled, -dling. confuse.

ad•dress′ (ə dres′) *n.* **1.** formal speech. **2.** place of residence. —*v.* **3.** speak or write (to). **4.** send. **5.** apply (oneself). —ad′dress•ee′ (ə dre sē′) *n.*

ad•duce′ (ə dōōs′, ə dyōōs′) *v.,* -duced, -ducing. present; cite.

ad′e•noid′ (ad′n oid′) *n.* mass of tissue between back of nose and throat.

a•dept′, *adj.* (ə dept′) **1.** skilled. —*n.* (ad′ept, ə dept′) **2.** expert.

ad′e•quate (ad′i kwit) *adj.* sufficient; fit. —ad′e•quate•ly, *adv.* —ad′e•qua•cy, *n.*

ad•here′ (ad hēr′) *v.,* -hered, -hering. **1.** stick or cling. **2.** be faithful or loyal. —ad•her′ence, *n.* —ad•her′ent, *n., adj.* —ad•he′sion (-hē′zhən) *n.*

adherent, *n.* **1.** supporter, follower, partisan, disciple; devotee, enthusiast,

maven, groupie, fan, aficionado. —*adj.* **2.** clinging, adhering, sticking, cleaving. —**Ant.** recreant, deserter.

ad•he′sive (ad hē′siv, -ziv) *adj.* **1.** coated with a sticky substance. **2.** sticky. —*n.* **3.** adhesive substance.

ad hoc (ad hok′, hōk′) for a specified purpose.

a•dieu′ (ə dōō′, ə dyōō′) *interj., n. French.* good-by; farewell.

ad in′fi•ni′tum (ad in′fə nī′təm) to infinity; endlessly.

adj., 1. adjective. **2.** adjustment. **3.** adjutant.

ad•ja′cent (ə jā′sənt) *adj.* near; adjoining.

ad′jec•tive (aj′ik tiv) *n.* word describing a noun. —ad′jec•ti′val (-tī′val) *adj.*

ad•join′ (ə join′) *v.* be next to.

adjoining, *adj.* bordering, neighboring, abutting, contiguous, adjacent, near or close or next to, touching.

ad•journ′ (ə jûrn′) *v.* suspend (meeting) till another time. —ad•journ′ment, *n.*

ad•judge′ (ə juj′) *v.,* -judged, -judging. **1.** decree or decide. **2.** award.

ad•ju′di•cate′ (ə jōō′di kāt′) *v.,* -cated, -cating. decide on as a judge. —ad•ju′di•ca′tion, *n.*

ad′junct (aj′ungkt) *n.* something added.

ad•just′ (ə just′) *v.* **1.** fit; adapt. **2.** regulate. **3.** settle. —ad•just′a•ble, *adj.* —ad•just′er, ad•jus′tor, *n.* —ad•just′ment, *n.*

ad′ju•tant (aj′ə tənt) *n.* military assistant to commandant.

ad-lib′ (ad lib′) *v.,* -libbed, -libbing. improvise (speech, music, etc.). —ad-lib′, *adv.*

Adm., admiral.

adm. or admn., 1. administration. **2.** administrative. **3.** administrator.

ad′man′ (ad′man′, -mən) *n.* advertising professional.

ad•min′is•ter (ad min′ə stər) *v.* **1.** manage; direct. **2.** dispense or give.

ad•min′is•tra′tion (-ə strā′shən) *n.* **1.** management. **2.** dispensing. **3.** executive officials. —ad•min′is•tra′tive, *adj.*

ad•min′is•tra′tor, *n.* manager.

ad′mi•ra•ble (ad′mar ə bəl), *adj.* worthy of admiration.

ad′mi•ral (ad′mər əl) *n.* **1.** high-ranking navy officer. **2.** brightly colored type of butterfly.

ad′mi•ral•ty, *n., pl.* -ties. navy department.

admiration, *n.* wonder, awe, pleasure, approbation, delight, esteem, appreciation, reverence, veneration; liking, affection, regard. —**Ant.** abhorrence, disgust, hatred.

ad•mire′ (ad mīr′) *v.,* -mired, -miring. regard highly. —ad•mir′er, *n.* —ad′mi•ra′tion (ad′mə rā′shən) *n.*

ad•mis′si•ble (ad mis′ə bəl) *adj.* allowable.

ad•mis′sion (-mish′ən) *n.* **1.** act of admitting. **2.** entrance price. **3.** confession or acknowledgment.

ad•mit′ (-mit′) *v.,* -mitted, -mitting. **1.** allow to enter. **2.** permit. **3.** confess or acknowledge. —ad•mit′tance, *n.* —ad•mit′ted•ly, *adv.* without doubt.

ad•mon′ish (ad mon′ish) *v.* **1.** warn. **2.** reprove. —ad•mon′i•to′ry (ad mə-nish′ən) *n.* —ad•mon′i•to′ry, *adj.*

ad nau′se•am (ad nô′zē əm) to a sickening degree.

a•do′ (ə dōō′) *n.* activity; fuss.

a•do′be (ə dō′bē) *n.* sun-dried brick.

ad′o•les′cence (ad′l es′əns) *n.* period between childhood and adult-hood. —**ad•o•les′cent**, *adj.*, *n.*

adolescent, *adj.* **1.** immature, puerile, juvenile; maturing, pubescent, teen-aged, youthful, young. —*n.* **2.** youth, teenager, teen, teenybopper, juvenile, minor. —**Ant.** adult.

a•dopt′ (ə dopt′) *v.* take or accept as one's own. —**a•dop′tion**, *n.* —**a•dopt′ive,** *adj.*

a•dore′ (ə dôr′) *v.*, **adored, adoring.** love; worship. —**a•dor′a•ble,** *adj.* —**ad′o•ra′tion** (ad′ə rā′shən) *n.*

a•dorn′ (ə dôrn′) *v.* decorate. —**a•dorn′ment,** *n.*

ad•re′nal (ə drēn′l) *adj.* of a pair of glands near the kidneys.

ad•ren′al•in (ə dren′l in) *n.* glandular secretion that speeds heart, etc.

a•drift′ (ə drift′) *adv.*, *adj.* floating about, esp. helplessly.

a•droit′ (ə droit′) *adj.* expert; deft. —**a•droit′ly,** *adv.*

ad′u•la′tion (aj′ə lā′shən) *n.* excessive praise. —**ad′u•late′,** *v.*

a•dult′ (ə dult′) *adj.* **1.** full-grown; mature. —*n.* **2.** full-grown person. —**a•dult′hood,** *n.*

a•dul′ter•ate′, *v.*, **-ated, -ating.** make impure.

a•dul′ter•y, *n.*, *pl.* **-teries.** marital infidelity. —**a•dul′ter•er,** *n.* —**a•dul′ter•ess,** *n.* —**a•dul′ter•ous,** *adj.*

adv., **1.** advance. **2.** adverb. **3.** adverbial. **4.** advertisement.

ad•vance′ (ad vans′) *v.*, **-vanced, -vancing. 1.** move forward. **2.** propose. **3.** raise in rank, price, etc. **4.** supply beforehand. —*n.* **5.** forward move. **6.** promotion. **7.** increase. **8.** loan. **9.** friendly gesture. —*adj.* **10.** early. —**ad•vance′ment,** *n.*

ad•vanced′, *adj.* **1.** progressive. **2.** relatively learned, old, etc.

ad•van′tage (ad van′tij) *n.* **1.** more favorable condition. **2.** benefit. —**ad′van•ta′geous,** *adj.*

ad′vent (ad′vent) *n.* **1.** arrival. **2.** coming of Christ. **3.** (*cap.*) month before Christmas.

ad′ven•ti′tious (ad′vən tish′əs) *adj.* accidentally added.

ad•ven′ture (ad ven′chər) *n.*, *v.*, **-tured, -turing.** —*n.* **1.** risky undertaking. **2.** exciting event. —*v.* **3.** risk or dare. —**ad•ven′tur•er,** *n.* —**ad•ven′tur•ous,** *adj.*

adventurous, *adj.* daring, bold, intrepid, brave, temerarious, heroic, fearless, audacious, courageous, venturous, venturesome, enterprising, dashing, risk-taking, cutting-edge, daredevil, brash, rash, foolhardy, reckless, devil-may-care, hazardous, risky, dangerous, perilous. —**Ant.** timid, tame, docile, cautious, unadventurous.

ad′verb (ad′vûrb) *n.* word modifying a verb, verbal noun, or other adverb. —**ad•ver′bi•al,** *adj.*

ad′ver•sar•y (ad′vər ser′ē) *n.*, *pl.* **-saries.** opponent.

ad•verse′ (ad vûrs′) *adj.* opposing; antagonistic. —**ad•verse′ly,** *adv.*

ad•ver′si•ty (-vûr′si tē) *n.*, *pl.* **-ties.** misfortune.

ad′ver•tise′ (ad′vər tīz′) *v.*, **-tised, -tising.** bring to public notice. —**ad′ver•tis′er,** *n.* —**ad′ver•tise′ment,** *n.* —**ad′ver•tis′ing,** *n.*

ad•vice′ (ad vīs′) *n.* **1.** opinion offered. **2.** news.

ad•vis′a•ble (ad vī′zə bəl) *adj.* wise or desirable. —**ad•vis′a•bil′i•ty,** *n.*

ad•vise′ (ad vīz′) *v.* **-vised, -vising. 1.** offer an opinion. **2.** recommend. **3.** consult (with). **4.** give news. —**ad•vis′er, ad•vi′sor,** *n.*

---

ad•vis′ed•ly, *adv.* deliberately.

ad•vi′so•ry, *adj.* giving advice.

ad′vo•cate′, *v.*, **-cated, -cating.** —*v.* (ad′və kāt′) **1.** urge; recommend. —*n.* (-kit) **2.** supporter of cause. **3.** lawyer. —**ad′vo•ca•cy,** *n.*

adz (adz) *n.* axlike tool.

ae′gis (ē′jis) *n.* sponsorship or protection.

ae′on (ē′ən, ē′on) *n.* eon.

aer′ate (âr′āt) *v.*, **-ated, -ating.** expose to air.

aer′i•al (âr′ē əl) *adj.* **1.** of or in air. **2.** lofty. —*n.* **3.** antenna.

aer′ie (âr′ē, ēr′ē) *n*, *pl.* **-ies.** eagle's nest.

aero-, prefix indicating: **1.** air. **2.** aircraft. Also, **aer-.**

aer•o′bic (â rō′bik) *adj.* **1.** needing oxygen to live. **2.** of aerobics.

aer•o′bics, *n.pl.* exercises designed to strengthen the heart and lungs.

aer′o•dy•nam′ics (âr′ō dī nam′iks) *n.* science of action of air against solids. —**aer′o•dy•nam′ic,** *adj.*

aer′o•naut′ (âr′ə n.ôt′) *n.* pilot.

aer′o•nau′tics, *n.* science of flight in aircraft. —**aer′o•naut′i•cal,** *adj.*

aer′o•plane′ (âr′ə plān′) *n.* Brit. airplane.

aer′o•sol′ (âr′ə sôl′) *n.* **1.** liquid distributed through a gas. **2.** spray of such liquid.

aer′o•space′ (âr′ō spās′) *n.* **1.** earth's atmosphere and the space beyond. —*adj.* **2.** of missiles, aircraft, and spacecraft.

aes•thete′, *n.* art lover, dilettante, connoisseur, virtuoso, expert, collector, tastemaker, maven.

aes•thet′ic (es thet′ik) *adj.* **1.** of beauty. **2.** appreciating beauty.

aes•thet′ics, *n.* study of beauty.

a•far′ (ə fär′) *adv.* at a distance.

af′fa•ble (af′ə bəl) *adj.* friendly; cordial. —**af′fa•bil′i•ty,** *n.*

af•fair′ (ə fâr′) *n.* **1.** matter of business. **2.** event. **3.** amorous relationship.

af•fect′ (ə fekt′) *v.* **1.** produce an effect; act on. **2.** impress the feelings of; move. **3.** pretend to possess or feel. —**Usage.** Because of similarity in pronunciation, AFFECT and EFFECT are sometimes confused in writing. The verb AFFECT means "to act on" or "to move": *His words affected the crowd so deeply that many wept.* The verb EFFECT means "to bring about, accomplish": *The new taxes effected many changes in people's lives.* The noun EFFECT means "result, consequence": *the tragic effect of the hurricane.*

af′fec•ta′tion (af′ek tā′shən) *n.* pretense.

af•fect′ed (ə fek′tid) *adj.* **1.** vain; haughty. **2.** pretended.

affecting, *adj.* touching, pathetic, piteous, moving, impressive.

af•fec′tion (ə fek′shən) *n.* love.

af•fec′tion•ate, *adj.* fondly tender; loving. —**af•fec′tion•ate•ly,** *adv.*

affectless, *adj.* unemotional, unfeeling, remote, numb, dead, distant, passionless, dispassionate, detached, disinterested, indifferent, lukewarm, impersonal, cold, cool, cold-blooded, self-absorbed, impassive, untouchable. —**Ant.** emotional, animated, passionate, excitable.

af•fi•da•vit (af′i dā′vit) *n.* written statement under oath.

af•fil′i•ate′, *v.*, **-ated, -ating,** *n.* —*v.* (ə fil′ē āt′) **1.** join; connect. —*n.* (-ē it) **2.** associate.

af•fin′i•ty (ə fin′i tē) *n.*, *pl.* **-ties. 1.** attraction. **2.** similarity.

---

af•firm′ (ə fûrm′) *v.* **1.** state; assert. **2.** ratify. —**af′fir•ma′tion** (af′ər mā′shən) *n.*

af•firm′a•tive, *adj.* saying yes; affirming.

affirmative action, policy to increase employment opportunities for women and minorities.

af•fix′ *v.* (ə fiks′) **1.** attach. —*n.* (af′iks) **2.** added part.

af•flict′ (ə flikt′) *v.* distress; trouble. —**af•flic′tion,** *n.*

affliction, *n.* **1.** pain, distress, grief, adversity, misfortune, hardship, ordeal, torment, trial, mishap, trouble, tribulation, calamity, catastrophe, disaster. **2.** sickness, loss, calamity, persecution, suffering, misery, woe, depression, wretchedness, heartbreak; curse, disease, plague, scourge, epidemic. —**Ant.** relief.

af′flu•ent (af′lōō ənt) *adj.* rich; abundant. —**af′flu•ence,** *n.*

af•ford′ (ə fôrd′) *v.* **1.** have resources enough. **2.** provide.

af•fray′ (ə frā′) *n.* fight.

af•front′ (ə frunt′) *n.*, *v.* insult.

af′ghan (af′gan) *n.* knitted blanket.

a•field′ (ə fēld′) *adv.* astray.

a•fire′ (ə fīᵊr′) *adv.*, *adj.* on fire.

a•flame′ (ə flām′) *adv.*, *adj.* in flames.

AFL-CIO, American Federation of Labor and Congress of Industrial Organizations.

a•float′ (ə flōt′) *adv.*, *adj.* **1.** floating. **2.** in circulation. **3.** out of debt.

a•foot′ (ə fōōt′) *adv.*, *adj.* **1.** on foot. **2.** in existence.

a•fore′said′ (ə fôr′sed′) *adj.* said before. Also, **a•fore′men′tioned** (-men′-shənd).

a•fraid′ (ə frād′) *adj.* feeling fear.

a•fresh′ (ə fresh′) *adj.* anew.

Af′ri•can (af′ri kən) *n.* native of Africa. —**Af′ri•can,** *adj.*

Af′ri•can-A•mer′i•can, *n.*, *adj.* black American.

Af′ri•kaans′ (af′ri käns′, -känz′) *n.* language of South Africa, derived from Dutch.

Af•ri•ka′ner (-kä′nər, -kan′ər) *n.* white South African who speaks Afrikaans.

Af′ro (af′rō) *n.* full, bushy hairstyle.

Af′ro-A•mer′i•can, *n.*, *adj.* African-American.

aft (aft) *adv.* Naut. at or toward the stern.

af′ter (af′tər) *prep.* **1.** behind. **2.** about. **3.** later than. **4.** in imitation of. —*adv.* **5.** behind. **6.** later.

af′ter•birth′, *n.* placenta and other matter expelled from uterus after childbirth.

af′ter•care′, *n.* care of recovering patient.

af′ter•ef•fect′, *n.* reaction.

af′ter•glow′, *n.* **1.** glow after sunset. **2.** pleasant memory.

af′ter•life′, *n.* life after death.

af′ter•math′ (-math′) *n.* results.

af′ter•noon′, *n.* period between noon and evening.

af′ter•thought′, *n.* later thought.

af′ter•ward (-wərd) *adv.* later. Also, **af′ter•wards.**

a•gain′ (ə gen′) *adv.* **1.** once more. **2.** besides.

a•gainst′ (ə genst′) *prep.* **1.** opposed to. **2.** in or into contact with.

a•gape′ (ə gāp′) *adv.*, *adj.* wide open.

ag′ate (ag′it) *n.* kind of quartz.

agcy., agency.

age (āj) *n.*, *v.*, **aged, aging.** —*n.* **1.** length of time in existence. **2.** stage;

period. **3.** legal maturity. —*v.* **4.** make or become older.

ag′ed (ā′jid *for 1;* ājd *for 1–3*) *adj.* **1.** having lived long. **2.** matured. —*n.pl.* **3.** elderly persons.

age′ism, *n.* discrimination against elderly persons. —**age′ist,** *n.*

age′less, *adj.* **1.** apparently not aging. **2.** not outdated.

a′gen·cy (ā′jən sē) *n., pl.* **-cies. 1.** office. **2.** action. **3.** means.

a·gen′da (ə jen′də) *n.* matters to be dealt with.

a′gent (ā′jənt) *n.* **1.** person acting for another. **2.** means. **3.** official.

ag·glom′er·ate′, *v.,* **-ated, -ating,** *adj., n.* —*v.* (ə gläm′ə rāt′) **1.** collect into a mass. —*adj.* (-ər it) **2.** collected in a mass. —*n.* (-ər it) **3.** such a mass.

ag·gran′dize (ə gran′dīz, ag′rən-dīz′) *v.,* **-dized, -dizing.** increase in size, rank, etc. —**ag·gran′dize·ment** (-diz mənt) *n.*

ag′gra·vate′ (ag′rə vāt′) *v.,* **-vated, -vating. 1.** make worse. **2.** annoy. —**ag′gra·va′tion,** *n.* ——**Usage.** In formal speech and writing, the meaning "to annoy" (*Stop aggravating me!*) is sometimes criticized and is used less often than the meaning "to make worse" (*His insulting words aggravated the tense situation*).

ag′gre·gate, *adj., n., v.,* **-gated, -gating.** —*adj.* (ag′ri git) **1.** combined. —*n.* (-git) **2.** whole amount. —*v.* (-gāt′) **3.** collect; gather.

ag·gres′sion (ə gresh′ən) *n.* hostile act; attack. —**ag·gres′sor,** *n.*

ag·gres′sive (ə gres′iv) *adj.* **1.** boldly energetic. **2.** hostile.

ag·grieve′ (ə grēv′) *v.,* **-grieved, -grieving.** wrong severely.

a·ghast′ (ə gast′) *adj.* shocked or horrified.

ag′ile (aj′əl) *adj.* quick; nimble. —**a·gil′i·ty** (ə jil′i tē) *n.*

ag′i·tate′ (aj′i tāt′) *v.,* **-tated, -tating. 1.** shake. **2.** disturb; excite. —**ag′i·ta′tion,** *n.* —**ag′i·ta′tor,** *n.*

agitation, *n.* **1.** agitating, shaking, jarring, disturbing, churning, stirring. **2.** turbulence, arousal, commotion, ferment, stimulation, overstimulation, provocation, incitement, rabble-rousing, disturbance, excitement, turmoil, tumult, storm; unrest, disquiet; struggle, conflict; perturbation, flurry, ado, to-do. **3.** urging, persistence; debate, discussion, dispute, argument, campaign. ——**Ant.** serenity, calm, tranquility.

ag·nos′tic (ag nos′tik) *n.* one who believes God is beyond human knowledge. —**ag·nos′ti·cism** (-tə siz′əm) *n.*

a·go′ (ə gō′) *adj., adv.* in the past.

a·gog′ (ə gog′) *adj.* eagerly excited.

ag′o·nize′ (ag′ə nīz′) *v.,* **-nized, -nizing.** suffer anxiety.

ag′o·ny (-nē) *n., pl.* **-nies.** intense pain or suffering.

ag′o·ra·pho′bi·a (ag′ər ə fō′bē ə) *n.* fear of open spaces.

a·grar′i·an (ə grâr′ē ən) *adj.* of the land.

a·gree′ (ə grē′) *v.,* **agreed, agreeing. 1.** consent or promise. **2.** be in harmony. **3.** be similar.

a·gree′a·ble, *adj.* **1.** pleasant. **2.** willing. —**a·gree′a·bly,** *adv.*

a·gree′ment *n.* **1.** harmony. **2.** arrangement.

ag′ri·busi′ness (ag′rə biz′nis) large-scale business of growing, processing, and distributing farm products.

ag′ri·cul′ture, *n.* science of farming. —**ag′ri·cul′tur·al,** *adj.*

a·gron′o·my (ə gron′ə mē) *n.* science of farm management.

a·ground′ (ə ground′) *adv., adj. Naut.* onto the bottom or shore.

ah (ä) *interj.* (exclamation of pain, surprise, or satisfaction)

a·head′ (ə hed′) *adv.* **1.** in front; forward. **2.** winning.

a·hoy′ (ə hoi′) *interj. Naut.* (hey there!)

aid (ād) *v., n.* help.

aide (ād) *n.* assistant.

aide-de-camp (ād′də kamp′) *n., pl.* **aides-de-camp.** military assistant.

AIDS (ādz) *n.* acquired immunity deficiency syndrome, a disease making one increasingly susceptible to infections and other diseases.

ai′ler·on′ (ā′lə ron′) *n.* flap on airplane wing.

ailing, *adj.* sickly, sick, ill, unwell, not well, failing, weak, flagging, languishing, abed, indisposed, infirm, diseased, queasy, unhealthy, troubled, afflicted, suffering, in distress, distressed, in pain, hurting, bothered, disabled, under the weather, feeling poorly, in poor health, prostrate, infected, laid up, bedridden, confined to one's bed, hospitalized, on the sick list, out of commission, out of sorts, laid low, listless. ——**Ant.** healthy, well.

ail′ment, *n.* illness.

aim (ām) *v.* **1.** point or direct. **2.** intend. —*n.* **3.** act of aiming. **4.** target. **5.** purpose. —**aim′less,** *adj.*

ain′t (ānt) *v. Nonstandard or Dial.* am not; are not; is not. ——**Usage.** AIN'T is more common in uneducated speech, though it occurs with some frequency in the informal speech of the educated: *I ain't going. He ain't so young anymore.* The question form "Ain't I...?" is sometimes substituted for "Aren't I...?", which is usually considered to be ungrammatical. AIN'T also occurs in some humorous or set phrases, and it is sometimes used to give emphasis: *Ain't it the truth! It just ain't so!*

air (âr) *n.* **1.** mixture of gases forming atmosphere of earth. **2.** appearance; manner. **3.** tune. —*v.* **4.** expose to air. **5.** broadcast.

air bag, bag that inflates automatically to protect passengers in a car collision.

air′borne′, *adj.* carried by air; flying.

air′brush′, *n.* **1.** atomizer for spraying paint. —*v.* **2.** paint with an air-brush.

air conditioning, control of interior air for temperature, humidity, etc. —**air-conditioned,** *adj.*

air′craft′, *n.* vehicle or vehicles for flight.

air′field′, *n.* ground area for airplanes to land on and take off from.

air′ force′, military branch for air operations.

air′head′, *n. Slang.* scatterbrained or stupid person.

air′lift′, *n.* **1.** major transport by air. —*v.* **2.** move by airlift.

air′line′, *n.* air transport company.

air′lin′er, *n.* large passenger airplane operated by airline.

air′mail′, *n.* **1.** system of sending mail by airplane. **2.** mail sent by airmail. —**air′mail′,** *v.*

air′man, *n., pl.* **-men.** aviator.

air′plane′, *n.* powered heavier-than-air craft with wings.

air′port′, *n.* place where aircraft pick up passengers and cargo.

air raid, attack by aircraft.

air′ship′, *n.* lighter-than-air aircraft.

air′sick′ness, *n.* nausea from motion in air travel. —**air′sick′,** *adj.*

air′space′, *n.* space above a nation, city, etc., over which it has control.

air′tight′, *adj.* **1.** impermeable to air. **2.** perfect; free of error.

air′waves′, *n.pl.* medium of radio and television broadcasting.

air′y, -ier, -iest. 1. of or like air. **2.** delicate. **3.** well ventilated. **4.** light; lively. —**air′i·ly,** *adv.*

aisle (īl) *n.* passageway.

a·jar′ (ə jär′) *adj., adv.* partly open.

AK, Alaska.

a.k.a., also known as.

a·kim′bo (ə kim′bō) *adj., adv.* with hands at hips.

a·kin′ (ə kin′) *adj.* alike.

-al, **1.** adjective suffix meaning: of or pertaining to, as *tribal;* characterized by, as *typical.* **2.** noun suffix meaning: act or process, as *refusal.*

AL, Alabama.

à la or **a la** (ä′ lä, ä′ lə) *prep.* in the manner or style of.

Ala., Alabama.

al′a·bas′ter (al′ə bas′tər) *n.* white gypsum.

à la carte (ä′ lə kärt′) with each dish separately priced.

a·lac′ri·ty (ə lak′ri tē) *n.* quickness; readiness.

à la mode (ä′ lə mōd′) **1.** in the fashion. **2.** with ice cream.

a·larm′ (ə lärm′) *n.* **1.** fear of danger. **2.** sudden warning. **3.** call to arms. —*v.* **4.** fill with fear.

alarm clock, clock with device to awaken sleeper.

a·las′ (ə las′) *interj.* (cry of sorrow.)

al′ba·tross′ (al′bə trôs′) *n.* large white sea bird.

al·be′it (ôl bē′it) *conj.* though.

al·bi′no (al bī′nō) *n., pl.* **-nos.** one lacking in pigmentation.

al′bum (al′bəm) *n.* **1.** blank book for pictures, stamps, etc. **2.** collection of recordings.

al·bu′men (al byoo′mən) *n.* egg white.

al·bu′min (-mən) *n.* water-soluble protein found in egg white, milk, blood, etc.

al′che·my (al′kə mē) *n.* medieval chemistry. —**al′che·mist,** *n.*

al′co·hol′ (al′kə hôl′) *n.* colorless intoxicating liquid.

al′co·hol′ic, *adj.* **1.** of alcohol. —*n.* **2.** one addicted to alcohol.

al′co·hol·ism, *n.* addiction to alcohol.

al′cove (al′kōv) *n.* recessed space.

al′der (ôl′dər) *n.* small tree, usually growing in moist places.

al′der·man (ôl′dər mən) *n., pl.* **-men.** city official.

ale (āl) *n.* dark, bitter beer.

a·lert′ (ə lûrt′) *adj.* **1.** vigilant. —*n.* **2.** air-raid alarm. —*v.* **3.** warn.

al·fal′fa (al fal′fə) *n.* forage plant also grown as food.

al·fres′co (al fres′kō) *adv., adj.* in the open air. Also, **al fres′co.**

al′ga (al′gə) *n., pl.* **-gae** (-jē). water plant; seaweed.

al′ge·bra (al′jə brə) *n.* branch of mathematics using symbols rather than specific numbers. —**al′ge·bra′ic** (-jə-brā′ik) *adj.*

Al·gon′qui·an (al gong′kē ən, -kwē-ən) *n.* member of a North American Indian people. Also, **Al·gon′ki·an.**

al′go·rithm (al′gə rith′əm) *n.* set of rules or steps to solve mathematical problem, program computer, etc. —**al′go·rith′mic,** *adj.*

a′li•as (ā′lē əs) *adv.* **1.** otherwise known as. —*n.* **2.** assumed name.

al′i•bi′ (al′ə bī′) *n.* **1.** defense by accused person of being elsewhere. **2.** excuse.

al′ien (āl′yən) *n.* **1.** foreigner. **2.** creature from outer space. —*adj.* **3.** foreign.

al′ien•ate′ (-yə nāt′) *v.*, **-ated, -ating.** lose friendship of; repel. —**al′ien•a′tion,** *n.*

a•light′ (ə līt′) *v.* **1.** dismount after travel. **2.** descend to perch or sit. —*adv., adj.* **3.** lighted up.

a•lign′ (ə līn′) *v.* bring into line. —**a•lign′ment,** *n.*

a•like′ (ə līk′) *adv.* **1.** similarly. —*adj.* **2.** similar.

al′i•men′ta•ry (al′ə men′tə rē) *adj.* of or for food.

alimentary canal, tube in body for digestion of food.

al′i•mo′ny (al′ə mō′nē) *n.* money for support of a spouse after separation or divorce.

a•live′ (ə līv′) *adj.* **1.** living. **2.** active. **3.** lively. **4.** teeming.

al′ka•li′ (al′kə lī′) *n.* chemical that neutralizes acids to form salts. —**al′ka•line′,** *adj.*

al′ka•loid′ (-loid′) *n.* organic compound in plants, as morphine.

all (ôl) *adj.* **1.** the whole of. **2.** every. —*n., pron.* **3.** the whole; everything. —*adv.* **4.** entirely.

Al′lah (al′ə, ä′lə) *n.* Muslim name for God.

All′-Amer′ican, *adj.* **1.** best in the U.S., as in a sport. **2.** typically American. —*n.* **3.** all-American player or team.

all′-around′, *adj.* **1.** versatile. **2.** having many uses.

al•lay′ (ə lā′) *v.* quiet or lessen.

al•lege′ (ə lej′) *v.*, **-leged, -leging.** state, often without proof. —**al′le•ga′tion** (al′i gā′shən) *n.* —**al•leg′ed•ly** (-lej′id-) *adv.*

al•le′giance (ə lē′jəns) *n.* loyalty.

al′le•go′ry (al′ə gôr′ē) *n., pl.* **-ries.** symbolic story. —**al′le•gor′i•cal,** *adj.*

al•le′gro (ə lā′grō, ə leg′rō) *adv.* Music. fast.

al•le•lu′ia (al′ə loō′yə) *interj.* (halle- lujah.)

al′ler•gen (al′ər jən) *n.* substance that causes allergic reaction. —**al′ler•gen′ic** (-jen′ik) *adj.*

al′ler•gy (-jē) *n., pl.* **-gies.** bodily sensitiveness to certain substances. —**al•ler′gic** (ə lûr′jik) *adj.*

al•le′vi•ate′ (ə lē′vē āt′) *v.*, **-ated, -ating.** lessen; relieve.

al′ley (al′ē) *n.* narrow street.

alley cat, stray cat.

al•li′ance (ə lī′əns) *n.* **1.** union. **2.** treaty. **3.** parties to treaty.

al•lied′ (ə līd′, al′īd) *adj.* **1.** joined by treaty. **2.** related.

al′li•ga′tor (al′i gā′tər) *n.* broad- snouted type of crocodile.

all′-in•clu′sive, *adj.* comprehensive.

al•lit′er•a′tion (ə lit′ə rā′shən) *n.* series of words starting with the same sound.

al′lo•cate′ (al′ə kāt′) *v.*, **-cated, -cating.** allot. —**al′lo•ca′tion,** *n.*

al•lot′ (ə lot′) *v.*, **-lotted, -lotting.** **1.** divide; distribute. **2.** assign.

all′-out′, *adj.* total; unrestricted.

al•low′ (ə lou′) *v.* **1.** permit. **2.** give. **3.** admit. —**al•low′a•ble,** *adj.* —**al•low′ance,** *n.*

allowance, *n.* **1.** allotment, stipend, pin *or* pocket money, ration, allocation, dole, quota. **2.** deduction, dis-

count, rebate, reduction, credit. **3.** acceptance, admission, concession, acknowledgment. **4.** sanction, tolerance, leave, permission, license, permit, authorization, authority, approval, approbation, imprimatur, sufferance.

al′loy, *n.* (al′oi) **1.** mixture of metals. —*v.* (ə loi′) **2.** mix (metals). **3.** adulterate.

all right, 1. yes; I agree. **2.** in a satisfactory way. **3.** safe; sound. **4.** acceptable; satisfactory. —**Usage.** The one-word spelling ALRIGHT is used in informal writing, probably by analogy with such words as *altogether* and *already*. However, the phrase ALL RIGHT is preferred in formal, edited writing.

All Saints′ Day, church festival Nov. 1 in honor of saints.

all′spice′, *n.* sharp, fragrant spice.

all′-star′, *adj.* consisting of star performers.

all′-time′, *adj.* never equaled or surpassed.

al•lude′ (ə loōd′) *v.*, **-luded, -luding.** refer (to) in words. —**al•lu′sion,** *n.*

al•lure′ (ə loōr′) *v.*, **-lured, -luring.** attract; tempt. —**al•lure′ment,** *n.*

al•lu′vi•um (ə loō′vē əm) *n.* earth deposited by rivers, etc.

al•ly′, *v.*, **-lied, -lying,** *n., pl.* **-lies.** —*v.* (ə lī′) **1.** unite in an alliance. —*n.* (al′ī) **2.** person, nation, etc., bound to another, as by treaty.

al′ma ma′ter (äl′mə mä′tər; al′mə mä′tər) one's school.

al′ma•nac′ (ôl′mə nak′) *n.* calendar showing special events, etc.

al•might′y (ôl mī′tē) *adj.* **1.** having all power. —*n.* **2.** (*cap.*) God.

al′mond (ä′mənd) *n.* edible nut of the almond tree.

al′most (ôl′mōst, ôl mōst′) *adv.* nearly.

alms (ämz) *n.pl.* charity.

a•loft′ (ə lôft′) *adv., adj.* high up.

a•lo′ha (ə lō′ə, ä lō′hä) *n., interj.* **1.** (hello). **2.** (farewell.)

a•lone′ (ə lōn′) *adj., adv.* **1.** apart. **2.** by oneself.

a•long′ (ə lông′) *prep.* **1.** through length of. —*adv.* **2.** onward. **3.** together; with one.

a•long′side′, *adv.* **1.** to one's side. —*prep.* **2.** beside.

a•loof′ (ə loōf′) *adv.* **1.** at a distance. —*adj.* **2.** reserved; indifferent.

a•lot′ (ə lot′) *n.* LOT (def. 4). —**Usage.** The spelling ALOT, though fairly common in informal writing such as memos and personal letters, is usually considered an error. The two-word spelling A LOT is the accepted form: *He has a lot of money. I like her a lot.* A LOT is itself considered informal; in formal speech or writing, the phrases "a great number," "a great amount," or "a great deal" are usually substituted for A LOT.

a•loud′ (ə loud′) *adv.* loudly.

al•pac′a (al pak′ə) *n.* South American sheep with soft, silky wool.

al′pha (al′fə) *n.* first letter of Greek alphabet.

al′pha•bet′ (al′fə bet′, -bit) *n.* letters of a language in order. —**al′pha•bet′i•cal,** *adj.* —**al′pha•bet•ize′,** *v.*

al′pha•nu•mer′ic, *adj.* using both letters and numbers.

al′pine (al′pīn, -pin) *adj.* growing or found in high mountains.

al•read′y (ôl red′ē) *adv.* previously.

al•right′ (ôl rīt′) *adv., adj.* ALL RIGHT. —**Usage.** See ALL RIGHT.

al′so (ôl′sō) *adv.* in addition.

alt., 1. alteration. **2.** alternate. **3.** altitude. **4.** alto.

al′tar (ôl′tər) *n.* **1.** platform for religious rites. **2.** communion table.

al′ter (ôl′tər) *v.* change.

al′ter•ca′tion (ôl′tər kā′shən) *n.* dispute.

alter ego, other side of one's personality.

al′ter•nate′, *v.*, **-nated, -nating,** *adj.*, *n.* —*v.* (-nāt′) **1.** occur or do in turns. —*adj.* (-nit) **2.** being by turns. —*n.* (-nit) **3.** substitute.

alternating current, electric current that regularly reverses its direction.

al•ter′na•tive (-tûr′nə tiv) *n.* **1.** other choice. —*adj.* **2.** offering a choice.

al′ter•na′tor (-tər nā′tər) *n.* generator of alternating current.

al•though′ (ôl t͟hō′) *conj.* even though.

al•tim′e•ter (al tim′i tər, al′tə mē′tər) *n.* device for measuring altitude.

al′ti•tude′ (al′ti toōd′, -tyoōd′) *n.* height.

al′to (al′tō) *n., pl.* **-tos.** lowest female voice.

al′to•geth′er (ôl′tə geth′ər) *adv.* entirely.

al′tru•ism′ (al′troō iz′əm) *n.* devotion to others. —**al′tru•is′tic,** *adj.*

al′um (al′əm) *n.* astringent substance, used in medicine, etc.

a•lu′mi•num (ə loō′mə nəm) *n.* light, silvery metal. Also, *Brit.,* **al•u•min′i•um** (al′yə min′ē əm).

a•lum′na (ə lum′nə) *n., pl.* **-nae** (-nē). female graduate.

a•lum′nus (-nəs) *n., pl.* **-ni** (-nī). graduate.

al′ways (ôl′wāz, -wēz) *adv.* **1.** all the time. **2.** every time.

Alz•hei′mer's disease (älts′hī mərz, ôlts′-) disease marked by increasing memory loss and mental deterioration, usually in old age.

am (*am; unstressed* əm, m) *v.* 1st pers. sing. pres. indic. of **be.**

Am., 1. America. **2.** American.

a.m., the period before noon. Also, **A.M.**

A.M.A., American Medical Association.

a•mal′gam (ə mal′gəm) *n.* mixture, esp. one with mercury.

a•mal′ga•mate′ (-gə māt′) *v.*, **-mated, -mating.** combine.

am′a•ret′to (am′ə ret′ō, ä′mə-) almond-flavored liqueur.

am′a•ryl′lis (am′ə ril′is) *n.* plant with large, lilylike flowers.

a•mass′ (ə mas′) *v.* collect.

am′a•teur′ (am′ə choōr′, -chər) *n.* nonprofessional artist, athlete, etc. —**am′a•teur′ish,** *adj.*

am′a•to′ry (am′ə tôr′ē) *adj.* of love.

a•maze′ (ə māz′) *v.*, **amazed, amazing.** astonish. —**a•maze′ment,** *n.*

Am′a•zon′ (am′ə zon′, -zən) *n.* tall, powerful woman.

am•bas′sa•dor (am bas′ə dər, -dôr′) *n.* diplomat of highest rank.

am′ber (am′bər) *n.* **1.** yellowish fossil resin. —*adj.* **2.** yellowish.

am′ber•gris′ (-grēs′) *n.* secretion of sperm whale, used in perfumes.

am′bi•dex′trous (am′bi dek′strəs) *adj.* using both hands equally well.

am′bi•ence (am′bē əns) *n.* surroundings; atmosphere. Also, **am′bi•ance.** —**am′bi•ent,** *adj.*

am•big′u•ous (am big′yoō əs) *adj.* unclear in meaning. —**am′bi•gu′i•ty,** *n.*

am•bi′tion (-bish′ən) *n.* **1.** desire for success, power, etc. **2.** object so desired. —**am•bi′tious,** *adj.*

ambitious, *adj.* **1.** aspiring, enterprising, hopeful, enthusiastic, energetic, vigorous, zealous, eager, desirous. **2.** showy, pretentious, ostentatious, overweening, pushy. —**Ant.** apathetic; humble.

am·biv′a·lent (-biv′ə lənt) *adj.* with conflicting emotions. —**am·biv′a·lence,** *n.*

am′ble (am′bəl) *v.,* -**bled,** -**bling,** *n.* —*v.* **1.** to go at an easy pace. —*n.* **2.** easy pace.

am·bro′sia (am brō′zhə) *n.* food of Greek and Roman gods.

am′bu·lance (am′byə ləns) *n.* vehicle for sick or wounded.

am′bu·la·to′ry (-lə tôr′ē) *adj.* able to walk.

am′bush (-boŏsh) *n.* **1.** concealment for a surprise attack. **2.** surprise attack. **3.** place of such concealment. —*v.* **4.** attack thus.

a·me′ba (ə mē′bə) *n., pl.* -**bas** or -**bae** (-bē). microscopic one-celled animal. Also, **a·moe′ba.**

a·mel/io·rate′ (ə mēl′yə rāt′) *v.,* -**rated,** -**rating.** improve.

a′men′ (ā′men′, ä′men′) *interj.* (so be it!)

a·me′na·ble (ə mē′nə bəl, ə men′ə-) *adj.* willing; agreeable.

a·mend′ (ə mend′) *v.* **1.** change or correct. **2.** improve.

a·mend′ment, *n.* change in a law.

a·mends′, *n.pl.* reparation.

a·men′i·ty (ə men′i tē) *n., pl.* -**ties.** pleasant feature, etc.

Am′er·a·sian (am′ə rā′zhən) *n.* person of mixed American and Asian descent.

A·mer′i·can (ə mer′i kən) *n.* **1.** citizen of the U.S. **2.** native of N. or S. America. —*adj.* **3.** of the U.S. or its inhabitants. **4.** of N. or S. America.

American Indian, member of the indigenous peoples of N. or S. America.

A·mer′i·can·ism (-kə niz′əm) *n.* **1.** devotion to the U.S. **2.** custom, etc., of the U.S.

A·mer′i·can·ize′ (-kə nīz′) *v.,* make or become American in character.

American plan, payment of fixed hotel rate for room, service, and meals.

am′e·thyst (am′ə thist) *n.* violet quartz used in jewelry.

a′mi·a·ble (ā′mē ə bəl) *adj.* pleasantly kind or friendly.

am′i·ca·ble (am′i kə bəl) *adj.* not hostile. —**am′i·ca·bly,** *adv.*

a·mid′ (ə mid′) *prep.* among. Also, **a·midst′.**

a·mi′go (ə mē′gō, ä mē′-) *n., pl.* -**gos.** *Spanish.* friend.

a·mi′no ac′id (ə mē′nō, am′ə nō) type of organic compound from which proteins are made.

a·miss′ (ə mis′) *adv.* **1.** wrongly. —*adj.* **2.** wrong.

am′i·ty (am′i tē) *n.* friendship.

am′me·ter (am′mē′tər) *n.* instrument for measuring current in amperes.

am·mo (am′ō) *n. Slang.* ammunition.

am·mo′nia (ə mōn′yə) *n.* colorless, pungent, water-soluble gas.

am′mu·ni′tion (am′yə nish′ən) *n.* bullets, shot, etc., for weapons.

am·ne′sia (am nē′zhə) *n.* loss of memory. —**am·ne′si·ac′** (-zhē ak′, -zē-), **am·ne′sic,** *adj., n.*

am′nes·ty (am′nə stē) *n.* pardon for political crimes.

am′ni·o·cen·te′sis (am′nē ō sen tē′sis) *n., pl.* -**ses** (-sēz). surgical procedure of withdrawing fluid from pregnant woman for genetic diagnosis of fetus.

a·mok′ (ə muk′, ə mok′) *adv.* amuck.

a·mong′ (ə mung′) *prep.* **1.** in the midst of. **2.** in the group of. Also, **a·mongst′.** —**Usage.** See BETWEEN.

a·mor′al (ā môr′əl) *adj.* indifferent to moral standards.

am′o·rous (am′ər əs) *adj.* inclined to, or showing, love.

a·mor′phous (ə môr′fəs) *adj.* formless.

am′or·tize′ (am′ər tīz′, ə môr′tīz′) *v.,* -**tized,** -**tizing.** pay off.

a·mount′ (ə mount′) *n.* **1.** sum total. **2.** quantity. —*v.* **3.** add up (to); equal. —**Usage.** AMOUNT refers to quantity that cannot be counted (*the amount of paperwork; the amount of energy*), while NUMBER refers to things that can be counted (*a number of songs; a number of days*).

a·mour′ (ə moŏr′) *n.* love affair.

am′per·age (am′pər ij, am pēr′-) *n.* strength of an electric current.

am′pere (am′pēr) *n.* unit measuring electric current.

am′per·sand′ (am′pər sand′) *n.* sign (&) meaning "and."

am·phet′a·mine (am fet′ə mēn′, -min) *n.* stimulating drug.

am·phib′i·an (-fib′ē ən) *n.* **1.** animal living both in water and on land. —*adj.* **2.** Also, **am·phib′i·ous.** operating on land or water.

am′phi·the′a·ter (am′fə thē′ə tər, -thē⁰′-) *n.* theater with seats tiered around its center.

am′ple (am′pəl) *adj.,* -**pler,** -**plest.** **1.** sufficient. **2.** abundant.

am′pli·fy′ (am′plə fī′) *v.,* -**fied,** -**fying.** make larger or louder. —**am′pli·fi′er** *n.* —**am′pli·fi·ca′tion,** *n.*

am′pli·tude′ (-toŏd′, -tyoŏd′) *n.* **1.** extent. **2.** abundance.

am′pu·tate′ (am′pyŏŏ tāt′) *v.,* -**tated,** -**tating.** cut off (limb). —**am′pu·ta′tion,** *n.* —**am′pu·tee′,** *n.*

a·muck′ (ə muk′) *adv.* violently; in an uncontrolled way.

am′u·let (am′yə lit) *n.* magical charm.

a·muse′ (ə myoŏz′) *v.,* amused, amusing. **1.** entertain. **2.** cause to laugh. —**a·muse′ment,** *n.*

amusement park, park with roller coasters or other recreational rides.

amusing, *adj.* **1.** entertaining, diverting, pleasing, charming, cheering, lively. **2.** comical, comic, droll, risible, laughable, delightful, mirth-provoking, funny, farcical, ludicrous, ridiculous, absurd. —**Ant.** boring, tedious.

an (ən; *when stressed* an) *adj. or indef. art. before initial vowel sounds.* See **a.**

a·nach′ro·nism (ə nak′rə niz′əm) *n.* chronological discrepancy.

an′a·con′da (an′ə kon′də) *n.* large South American snake.

an′a·gram′ (an′ə gram′) *n.* word formed from letters of another.

a′nal (ān′l) *adj.* of the anus.

an′al·ge′sic (an′əl jē′zik) *n.* drug for relieving pain.

a·nal′o·gy (ə nal′ə jē) *n., pl.* -**gies.** similarity in some respects. —**a·nal′o·gous** (-gəs) *adj.*

a·nal′y·sis (-sis) *n., pl.* -**ses** (-sēz′). **1.** separation into constituent parts. **2.** summary. **3.** psychoanalysis. —**an′a·lyst** (an′l ist) *n.* —**an′a·lyt′ic, an′a·lyt′i·cal,** *adj.* —**an′a·lyze′,** *v.,* -**lyzed,** -**lyzing.**

an′ar·chy (an′ər kē) *n.* lawless society. —**an′ar·chism,** *n.* —**an′ar·chist,** *n.*

a·nath′e·ma (ə nath′ə mə) *n.* **1.** solemn curse. **2.** thing or person detested.

a·nat′o·my (ə nat′ə mē) *n., pl.* anat-omies. **1.** structure of an animal or

plant. **2.** science dealing with such structure. —**an′a·tom′i·cal** (an′ə-tom′i kəl) *adj.*

-ance, suffix meaning: action, as *appearance;* state or quality, as *brilliance;* thing or object, as *contrivance.*

an′ces·tor (an′ses tər) *n.* person from whom one is descended. —**an′ces·try,** *n.* —**an·ces′tral,** *adj.*

ancestral, *adj.* hereditary, inherited, patrimonial.

ancestry, *n.* **1.** pedigree, descent, stock, genealogy, heritage. **2.** family, house, race, line, lineage, forebears, forefathers. —**Ant.** posterity, descendants.

an′chor (ang′kər) *n.* **1.** heavy device for keeping boats, etc., in place. **2.** main broadcaster who introduces TV or radio newscast. —*v.* **3.** fasten by an anchor. **4.** serve as anchor for (newscast).

an′chor·man, *n., pl.* -**men.** person who anchors a newscast. Also, *fem.,* **an′chor·wom′an;** *masc.* or *fem.*

an′cho·vy (an′chō vē) *n., pl.* -**vies.** small herringlike fish.

an′cient (ān′shənt) *adj.* **1.** of long ago. **2.** very old. —*n.* **3.** person who lived long ago.

an′cil·lar′y (an′sə ler′ē) *adj.* subordinate; auxiliary.

and (and; *unstressed* ənd, ən, n) *conj.* **1.** with; also. **2.** *Informal.* (used in place of **to** in infinitive): *Try and stop me.*

an·dan′te (än dän′tā) *adv. Music.* at moderate speed.

and′i′rons (and′ī′ərnz) *n.pl.* metal supports for logs in fireplace.

an′dro·gen (an′drə jən) *n.* male sex hormone, as testosterone.

an·drog′y·nous (an droj′ə nəs) *adj.* having both masculine and feminine characteristics.

an′droid (an′droid) *n.* automaton in human form.

an′ec·dote′ (an′ik dōt′) *n.* short story.

a·ne′mi·a (ə nē′mē ə) *n.* inadequate supply of hemoglobin and red blood cells. —**a·ne′mic,** *adj.*

a·nem′o·ne′ (ə nem′ə nē′) *n.* buttercuplike plant with colorful flowers.

an′es·the′sia (an′əs thē′zhə) *n.* insensibility to pain, usually induced by a drug **(an′es·thet′ic)** (-thet′ik). —**an·es′the·tize′** (ə nes′thə tīz′) *v.,* -**tized,** -**tizing.**

a·new′ (ə noŏ′, ə nyoŏ′) *adv.* again.

an′gel (ān′jəl) *n.* **1.** spiritual being who is messenger of God. **2.** very kind and helpful person.

angel food cake, light, spongy cake made with egg whites.

an′ger (ang′gər) *n.* **1.** strong displeasure; outrage. —*v.* **2.** cause anger in.

an·gi′na pec′to·ris (an jī′nə pek′tə-ris) coronary attack.

an′gle (ang′gəl) *n., v.,* -**gled,** -**gling.** —*n.* **1.** spread between converging lines or surfaces. —*v.* **2.** fish with a hook on a line. **3.** try for something by artful means. **4.** bend in angles. —**an′gler,** *n.*

An′gli·can (ang′gli kən) *adj.* **1.** of the Church of England. —*n.* **2.** member of this church.

An′gli·cize′ (-sīz′) *v.,* -**cized,** -**cizing.** make or become English in form or character.

An′glo-Sax′on (ang′glō sak′sən) *n.* **1.** person of English descent. **2.** inhabitant of England before 1066. —*adj.* **3.** of Anglo-Saxons.

An·go′ra (ang gôr′ə) *n.* **1.** cat, goat, or rabbit with long, silky hair. **2.** (*l.c.*)

yarn or fabric from Angora goat or rabbit.

an'gry (ang'grē) *adj.*, **-grier**, **-griest**. **1.** full of anger. **2.** inflamed. —**an'gri•ly**, *adv.*

angst (ängkst) *n.* feeling of dread, anxiety, or anguish.

an'guish (ang'gwish) *n.* intense pain or grief.

an'gu•lar (ang'gyə lər) *adj.* having angles. —**an•gu•lar'i•ty**, *n.*

an'i•mad•vert' (an'ə mad vûrt') *v.* criticize. —**an'i•mad•ver'sion** (-vûr'zhən) *n.*

an'i•mal (an'ə məl) *n.* **1.** living thing that is not a plant. **2.** beast. —*adj.* **3.** of animals.

an'i•mate, *v.*, **-mated**, **-mating**, *adj.* —*v.* (-māt') **1.** make alive or lively. **2.** make move. —*adj.* (-mit) **3.** alive.

an'i•ma'tion, *n.* **1.** liveliness. **2.** animated cartoon.

an'i•mism (-miz'əm) *n.* belief that animals and natural objects have souls. —**an'i•mist**, *n.*, *adj.*

an'i•mos'i•ty (an'ə mos'i tē) *n.*, *pl.* **-ties.** strong dislike or enmity.

an'i•mus (-məs) *n.* strong dislike; animosity.

an'ise (an'is) *n.* plant yielding aromatic seed (**an'i•seed'**).

an'kle (ang'kəl) *n.* joint between foot and leg.

an'klet (-klit) *n.* **1.** short, ankle-length sock. **2.** ornament for ankle.

an'nals (an'lz) *n.pl.* historical record of events.

an•neal' (ə nēl') *v.* to toughen or temper.

an•nex', *v.* (ə neks') **1.** add; join. —*n.* (an' eks) **2.** attached building. —**an'nex•a'tion**, *n.*

an•ni'hi•late' (ə nī'ə lāt') *v.*, **-lated**, **-lating.** destroy completely. —**an•ni'hi•la'tion**, *n.*

an'ni•ver'sa•ry (an'ə vûr'sə rē) *n.*, *pl.* **-ries.** annual recurrence of the date of a past event.

an'no•tate' (an'ə tāt') *v.*, **-tated**, **-tating.** supply with notes.

an•nounce' (ə nouns') *v.*, **-nounced**, **-nouncing.** make known. —**an•nounce'ment**, *n.*

an•noy' (ə noi') *v.* irritate or trouble. —**an•noy'ance**, *n.*

an'nu•al (an'yōō əl) *adj.* **1.** yearly. **2.** living only one season. —*n.* **3.** annual plant. **4.** yearbook. —**an'nu•al•ly**, *adv.*

an•nu'i•ty, *n.*, *pl.* **-ties.** income in annual payments.

an•nul' (ə nul') *v.*, **-nulled**, **-nulling.** make void. —**an•nul'ment**, *n.*

An•nun'ci•a'tion (ə nun'sē ā'shən) *n.* announcement to Virgin Mary of incarnation of Christ (March 25).

an'ode (an'ōd) *n.* **1.** electrode with positive charge. **2.** negative terminal of a battery.

a•noint' (ə noint') *v.* to put oil on, as in consecration.

a•nom'a•ly (ə nom'ə lē) *n.*, *pl.* **-lies.** something irregular or abnormal. —**a•nom'a•lous**, *adj.*

a•non' (ə non') *adv. Archaic.* soon.

anon., anonymous.

a•non'y•mous (ə non'ə məs) *adj.* by someone unnamed. —**an'o•nym'i•ty** (an'ə nim'i tē) *n.* —**a•non'y•mous•ly**, *adv.*

an'o•rak' (an'ə rak') *n.* hooded jacket; parka.

an'o•rex'i•a (an'ə rek'sē ə) *n.* Also, anorexia ner•vo'sa (nûr vō'sə). eating disorder marked by excessive dieting. —**an'o•rex'ic**, *adj.*, *n.*

an•oth'er (ə nuth'ər) *adj.* **1.** additional. **2.** different. —*n.* **3.** one more. **4.** different one.

an'swer (an'sər) *n.* **1.** reply. **2.** solution. —*v.* **3.** reply to. **4.** suit. **5.** be responsible. **6.** correspond.

an'swer•a•ble, *adj.* **1.** able to be answered. **2.** responsible.

answering machine, device that answers telephone calls with recorded message and records messages from callers.

ant (ant) *n.* common small insect.

-ant, suffix meaning: one that performs or promotes, as *pollutant*; performing, promoting, or being, as *pleasant*.

ant•ac'id (ant as'id) *n.* medicine to counteract acids.

an•tag'o•nism (an tag'ə niz'əm) *n.* hostility. —**an•tag'o•nize'**, *v.*, **-nized**, **-nizing.**

antagonist, *n.* opponent, adversary, rival, competitor, contestant, contender, competition, opposition, enemy, foe. —**Ant.** ally, friend.

ant•arc'tic (ant ärk'tik, -är'tik) *adj.* (*often cap.*) of or at the South Pole.

an'te (an'tē) *n.* **1.** (in poker) stake put in pot before cards are dealt. **2.** price or cost of something.

ante- prefix indicating: **1.** happening before, as *antediluvian*. **2.** in front of, as *anteroom*.

ant'eat'er, *n.* tropical American mammal having long snout and feeding on ants and termites.

an'te•bel'lum (an'tē bel'əm) *adj.* before a war, esp. the American Civil War.

an'te•ced'ent (an'tə sēd'nt) *adj.* **1.** prior. —*n.* **2.** anything that precedes.

an'te•di•lu'vi•an (an'tē di lōō'vē-ən) *adj.* before the Flood.

an'te•lope' (an'tl ōp') *n.* deerlike animal.

an•ten'na (an ten'ə) *n.*, *pl.* **antennae** (-nē), *for 1.* **1.** feeler on the head of an insect, etc. **2.** wires for transmitting radio waves, TV pictures, etc.

an•te'ri•or (an tēr'ē ər) *adj.* **1.** earlier. **2.** frontward.

an'te•room' (an'tē rōōm', -rŏŏm') *n.* room before the main room.

an'them (an'thəm) *n.* patriotic or sacred hymn.

an'ther (an'thər) *n.* pollen-bearing part of stamen.

an•thol'o•gy (an thol'ə jē) *n.*, *pl.* **-gies.** collection of writings.

an'thra•cite' (an'thrə sīt') *n.* hard coal.

an'thrax (an'thraks) *n.* cattle disease.

an'thro•poid' (an'thrə poid') *adj.* resembling a human or an ape.

an'thro•pol'o•gy (-pol'ə jē) *n.* science of humankind. —**an'thro•pol'o•gist**, *n.*

an'thro•po•mor'phic (-pə môr'fik) *adj.* ascribing human qualities to a nonhuman thing or being. —**an'thro•po•mor'phism** (-fiz əm) *n.*

anti-, prefix indicating: **1.** against or opposed to, as *antisocial*. **2.** acting against, as *antihistamine*.

an'ti•bi•ot'ic (an'ti bī ot'ik) *n.* substance used to destroy microorganisms.

an'ti•bod'y, *n.*, *pl.* **-bodies.** substance in the blood that destroys bacteria.

an'tic (an'tik) *n.* **1.** odd behavior. —*adj.* **2.** playful.

an•tic'i•pate' (an tis'ə pāt') *v.*, **-pated**, **-pating.** **1.** expect and prepare for. **2.** foresee.

an'ti•cli'max (an'tē klī'maks, an'tī-) *n.* disappointing or undramatic outcome.

an'ti•de•pres'sant (an'tē di pres'ənt, an'tī-) *n.* drug for relieving depression.

an'ti•dote' (an'ti dōt') *n.* medicine counteracting poison, etc.

an'ti•freeze' (an'ti frēz', an'tē-) *n.* liquid used in engine's radiator to prevent freezing of cooling fluid.

an'ti•his'ta•mine' (an'tē his'tə-mēn', -min) *n.* substance used esp. against allergic reactions.

an'ti•mat'ter (an'tē mat'ər, an'tī-) *n.* matter with charges opposite to those of common particles.

an'ti•mo'ny (an'tə mō'nē) *n.* brittle white metallic element.

an'ti•pas'to (an'tē pä'stō) *n.*, *pl.* **-pastos**, **-pasti** (-pä'stē). Italian appetizer.

an•tip'a•thy (an tip'ə thē) *n.*, *pl.* **-thies.** dislike; aversion.

an'ti•per'spi•rant (an'ti pûr'spər-ənt) *n.* astringent product for reducing perspiration.

an•tip'o•des (an tip'ə dēz') *n.pl.* places opposite each other on the globe.

an'ti•quar'i•an (an'ti kwâr'ē ən) *adj.* **1.** of the study of antiquities. —*n.* **2.** antiquary.

an'ti•quar'y (-kwer'ē) *n.*, *pl.* **-ries.** collector of antiquities.

an'ti•quat'ed (-kwā'tid) *adj.* old or obsolete.

an•tique' (an tēk') *adj.* **1.** old or old-fashioned. —*n.* **2.** valuable old object.

an•tiq'ui•ty (-tik'wi tē) *n.*, *pl.* **-ties.** **1.** ancient times. **2.** something ancient.

an'ti-Sem'ite (an'tē sem'īt, an'tī-) *n.* person hostile to Jews. —**an'ti-Se•mit'ic** (-sə mit'ik) *adj.* —**an'ti-Sem'i•tism** (-sem'i tiz'əm) *n.*

an'ti•sep'tic (an'tə sep'tik) *adj.* **1.** destroying certain germs. —*n.* **2.** antiseptic substance.

an'ti•so'cial (an'tē sō'shəl, an'tī-) *adj.* **1.** hostile to society. **2.** not sociable.

an•tith'e•sis (an tith'ə sis) *n.*, *pl.* **-ses.** direct opposite.

an'ti•tox'in (an'ti tok'sin) *n.* substance counteracting germ-produced poisons in the body.

ant'ler (ant'lər) *n.* horn on deer, etc.

an'to•nym (an'tə nim) *n.* word of opposite meaning.

a'nus (ā'nəs) *n.* opening at lower end of alimentary canal.

an'vil (an'vil) *n.* iron block on which hot metals are hammered into shape.

anx•i'e•ty (ang zī'i tē) *n.*, *pl.* **-ties.** worried distress. —**anx'ious** (angk'shəs) *adj.* —**anx'ious•ly**, *adv.*

anxious, *adj.* concerned, worried, apprehensive, uneasy, troubled, disquieted, uncertain, apprehensive, tense, distressed, disturbed, nervous, fretful, edgy, on edge, perturbed, restless, upset, wary, cautious, watchful. —**Ant.** secure, certain, sure, confident.

an'y (en'ē) *adj.* **1.** one; some. **2.** every. —*pron.* **3.** any person, etc. —**an'y•bod'y**, **an'y•one'**, *pron.* —**an'y•thing'**, *pron.* —**Usage.** See SOME.

an'y•how', *adv.* in any way, case, etc. Also, **an'y•way'**.

an'y•place', *adv.* anywhere.

an'y•time', *adv.* at any time.

an'y•where', *adv.* in, at, or to any place.

A' one' (ā' wun') *adj.* excellent. Also, **A' 1'**, **A'-1'**.

a•or'ta (ā ôr'tə) *n.*, *pl.* **-tas**, **-tae** (-tē). main blood vessel from heart.

a•pace' (ə pās') *adv.* quickly.

A•pach'e (ə pach'ē) *n.*, *pl.* **Apache**,

Apaches. member of a group of American Indian peoples of the U.S. Southwest.

a·part′ (ə pärt′) *adv.* **1.** into pieces. **2.** separately.

a·part′heid (-hāt, -hīt) *n.* (formerly, in South Africa) separation of and discrimination against blacks.

a·part′ment (-mənt) *n.* set of rooms to live in in a building.

apathetic, *adj.* unfeeling, passionless, emotionless, indifferent, unconcerned, impassive, stoical, cool, cold, uninterested, phlegmatic, dull, lifeless, flaccid, obtuse, sluggish, torpid, callous, coldblooded, insensible, soulless. —**Ant.** alert, emotional, passionate, ardent, animated.

ap′a·thy (ap′ə thē) *n., pl.* **-thies.** lack of emotion or interest. —**ap′a·thet′ic** (-thet′ik) *adj.*

ape (āp) *n., v.,* **aped, aping.** —*n.* **1.** large, tailless monkeylike animal. —*v.* **2.** imitate stupidly.

a·pé·ri·tif (ə per′i tēf′) *n.* liquor served before meal.

ap′er·ture (ap′ər chər) *n.* opening.

a′phid (ā′fid, af′id) *n.* plant-sucking insect.

aph′o·rism′ (af′ə riz′əm) *n.* brief maxim.

aph′ro·dis′i·ac′ (af′rə dē′ze ak′, -diz′ē ak′) *adj.* **1.** sexually exciting. —*n.* **2.** aphrodisiac food, drug, etc.

a·pi′ar·y (ā′pē er′ē) *n., pl.* **-ries.** place where bees are kept.

a·piece′ (ə pēs′) *adv.* for each.

a·plen′ty (ə plen′tē) *adv., adv.* in generous amounts.

a·plomb′ (ə plom′, ə plum′) *n.* poise; self-possession.

A·poc′a·lypse (ə pok′ə lips) *n.* **1.** revelation of the apostle John. **2.** (*l.c.*) prophetic revelation. —**a·poc′a·lyp′tic,** *adj.*

A·poc′ry·pha (ə pok′rə fə) *n.* uncanonical parts of the Bible.

a·poc′ry·phal, *adj.* not verified; dubious.

ap′o·gee′ (ap′ə jē′) *n.* remotest point of satellite orbit.

a′po·lit′i·cal (ā′pə lit′i kəl) *adj.* not interested in politics.

a·pol′o·gist (ə pol′ə jist) *n.* advocate; defender.

a·pol′o·gize′ *v.,* **-gized, -gizing.** offer apology.

a·pol′o·gy, *n., pl.* **-gies. 1.** statement of regret for one's act. **2.** stated defense. —**a·pol′o·get′ic** (-jet′ik) *adj.*

ap′o·plex′y (ap′ə plek′sē) *n.* sudden loss of bodily function due to bursting of blood vessel.

a·pos′tate (ə pos′tāt, -tit) *n.* deserter of one's faith, cause, etc.

a′ pos·te·ri·o′ri (ā′ po stēr′ē ôr′ī, -ôr′ē) *adj.* **1.** from particular instances to a general principle. **2.** based on observation or experiment.

a·pos′tle (ə pos′əl) *n.* **1.** disciple sent by Jesus to preach gospel. **2.** moral reformer.

a·pos′tro·phe (ə pos′trə fē) *n.* **1.** sign (') indicating an omitted letter, the possessive, or certain plurals. **2.** words in passing to one person or group.

a·poth′e·car′y (ə poth′ə ker′ē) *n., pl.* **-ries.** druggist.

a·poth′e·o′sis (ə poth′ē ō′sis, ə poth′ē·ə′ sis) *n., pl.* **-ses** (-sēz). **1.** elevation to the rank of a god. **2.** ideal example; epitome.

ap·pall′ (ə pôl′) *v.* fill with horror. Also, **ap·pal′.** —**ap·pall′ing,** *adj.*

ap′pa·ra′tus (ap′ə rat′əs, -rā′təs) *n.*

1. instruments and machines for some task. **2.** organization.

ap·par′el (ə par′əl) *n.* clothes.

ap·par′ent (ə par′ənt, ə pâr′-) *adj.* **1.** obvious. **2.** seeming. —**ap·par′ent·ly,** *adv.*

ap′pa·ri′tion (ap′ə rish′ən) *n.* specter.

ap·peal′ (ə pēl′) *n.* **1.** call for aid, mercy, etc. **2.** request for corroboration or review. **3.** attractiveness. —*v.* **4.** make an appeal. **5.** be attractive.

ap·pear′ (ə pēr′) *v.* **1.** come into sight. **2.** seem.

ap·pear′ance (-əns) *n.* **1.** act of appearing. **2.** outward look.

ap·pease′ (ə pēz′) *v.,* **-peased, -peasing. 1.** placate. **2.** satisfy.

ap·pel′late (ə pel′it) *adj.* dealing with appeals.

ap·pend′ (ə pend′) *v.* add; join.

ap·pend′age (ə pen′dij) *n.* subordinate attached part.

ap·pen·dec′to·my (ap′ən dek′tə mē) *n., pl.* **-mies.** removal of the appendix.

ap·pen′di·ci′tis (ə pen′də sī′tis) *n.* inflammation of appendix.

ap·pen′dix (ə pen′diks) *n., pl.* **-dixes, -dices** (-də sēz′). **1.** supplement. **2.** closed tube from the large intestine.

ap′per·tain′ (ap′ər tān′) *v.* belong or pertain.

ap′pe·tite′ (ap′i tīt′) *n.* desire, esp. for food.

ap′pe·tiz′er (-tī′zər) *n.* portion of food or drink served before meal to stimulate appetite.

ap·plaud′ (ə plôd′) *v.* praise by clapping, cheers, etc. —**ap·plause′** (ə plôz′) *n.*

applause, *n.* hand-clapping, cheering, cheers, shouting; approval, acclamation, approbation, acclaim, plaudits; laurels, éclat, commendation, praise, kudos. —**Ant.** disapproval, condemnation.

ap′ple (ap′əl) *n.* round fruit with firm, white flesh.

ap′ple·jack′, *n.* brandy made from fermented cider.

apple-polish, *v.* fawn, toady, flatter, kowtow, truckle, blandish, cajole, honey, sweet-talk, butter up, bootlick, suck up to, brown-nose.

ap′ple·sauce′, *n.* apples stewed to a pulp.

ap·pli′ance (ə plī′əns) *n.* special device or instrument.

ap′pli·ca·ble (ap′li kə bəl) *adj.* that can be applied.

ap′pli·cant (-kənt) *n.* one who applies.

ap′pli·ca′tion (-kā′shən) *n.* **1.** act of applying. **2.** use to which something is put. **3.** relevance. **4.** persistent attention.

ap′pli·ca′tor, *n.* device for applying a substance, as medication.

ap′pli·qué′ (ap′li kā′) *n., v.,* **-quéd, -quéing.** —*n.* **1.** cutout design of one material applied to another. —*v.* **2.** decorate with appliqué.

ap·ply′ (ə plī′) *v.* **-plied, -plying. 1.** put on. **2.** put into practice. **3.** use or devote. **4.** be relevant. **5.** make request.

ap·point′ (ə point′) *v.* **1.** choose; name. **2.** furnish.

ap·point′ment, *n.* **1.** act of choosing. **2.** prearranged meeting.

ap·por′tion (ə pôr′shən) *v.* divide into shares. —**ap·por′tion·ment,** *n.*

ap′po·site (ap′ə zit) *adj.* suitable.

ap·praise′ (ə prāz′) *v.,* **-praised,**

-praising. estimate the value of. —**ap·prais′al,** *n.* —**ap·prais′er,** *n.*

ap·pre′ci·a·ble (ə prē′shē ə bəl) *adj.* noticeable; significant.

ap·pre′ci·ate′ (-shē āt′) *v.,* **-ated, -ating. 1.** value at true worth. **2.** increase in value.

ap′pre·hend′ (ap′ri hend′) *v.* **1.** take into custody. **2.** understand.

ap′pre·hen′sion (-hen′shən) *n.* **1.** anxiety. **2.** comprehension. **3.** arrest.

ap′pre·hen′sive (-siv) *adj.* worried.

ap·pren′tice (ə pren′tis) *n., v.,* **-ticed, -ticing.** —*n.* **1.** assistant learning a trade. —*v.* **2.** bind as such an assistant.

ap·prise′ (ə prīz′) *v.,* **-prised, -prising.** notify. Also, **ap·prize′.**

ap·proach′ (ə prōch′) *v.* **1.** come near to. **2.** make a proposal to. —*n.* **3.** coming near. **4.** access. **5.** method.

ap′pro·ba′tion (ap′rə bā′shən) *n.* approval.

ap·pro′pri·ate′, *adj., v.,* **-ated, -ating.** —*adj.* (ə prō′prē it) **1.** suitable; proper. —*v.* (-prē āt′) **2.** designate for a use. **3.** take possession of. —**ap·pro′pri·ate·ly,** *adv.* —**ap·pro′pri·ate·ness,** *n.* —**ap·pro′pri·a′tion,** *n.*

ap·prove′ (ə prōōv′) *v.,* **-proved, -proving. 1.** think or speak well of. **2.** confirm. —**ap·prov′al,** *n.*

approx., approximate.

ap·prox′i·mate, *adj., v.,* **-mated, -mating.** —*adj.* (ə prok′sə mit) **1.** near; similar. —*v.* (-māt′) **2.** come near to. —**ap·prox′i·mate′ly,** *adv.* —**ap·prox′i·ma′tion,** *n.*

ap·pur′te·nance (ə pûr′tn əns) *n.* accessory.

Apr., April.

a′pri·cot′ (ap′ri kot′, ā′pri-) *n.* small peachlike fruit.

A′pril (ā′prəl) *n.* fourth month of year.

a′ pri·o′ri (ā′ prē ôr′ī, -ôr′ē) *adj.* from a general law to a particular instance.

a′pron (ā′prən) *n.* protective garment for the front of one's clothes.

ap′ro·pos′ (ap′rə pō′) *adv.* **1.** opportunely. **2.** with reference. —*adj.* **3.** timely.

apse (aps) *n.* vaulted recess in a church.

apt (apt) *adj.* **1.** prone. **2.** likely. **3.** skilled; able. —**apt′ly,** *adv.*

apt., apartment.

ap′ti·tude′ (ap′ti tōōd′, -tyōōd′) *n.* skill; talent.

Aq′ua·lung′, Trademark. underwater breathing device.

aq′ua·ma·rine′, *n.* **1.** light greenish blue. **2.** gemstone of this color.

a·quar′i·um (ə kwâr′ē əm) *n., pl.* **-iums, -ia** (-ē ə). place for exhibiting aquatic animals and plants.

a·quat′ic (ə kwat′ik, ə kwot′-) *adj.* of or living in water.

aq′ue·duct′ (ak′wi dukt′) *n.* artificial channel for conducting water.

a′que·ous (ā′kwē əs, ak′wē-) *adj.* of or like water.

aq′ui·line′ (ak′wə līn′, -lin) *adj.* (of a nose) curved like a beak.

AR, Arkansas.

Ar′ab (ar′əb) *n.* **1.** member of a people living or originating in Arabia, a peninsula in SW Asia. —*adj.* **2.** of Arabs. Also, **A·ra′bi·an** (ə rā′bē ən).

Ar′a·bic (ar′ə bik) *n.* **1.** Semitic language spoken chiefly in S.W. Asia and N. Africa. —*adj.* **2.** of Arabic, Arabia, or Arabs.

Arabic numeral, any of the numerals 0, 1, 2, 3, 4, 5, 6, 7, 8, or 9.

ar′a·ble (ar′ə bəl) *adj.* plowable.

a·rach′nid (ə rak′nid) *n.* small eight-legged arthropod, as the spider.

A·rap′a·ho′ or **-hoe′** (ə rap′ə hō′) *n.*, *pl.* **-hos** or **-hoes** or **-hoe.** member of a North American Indian people.

ar′bit·er (är′bi tər) *n.* judge.

ar′bi·trage′ (-träzh′) *n.* simultaneous sale of security or commodity in different markets to profit from unequal prices. —**ar′bi·trag′er** *n.*

ar′bi·trar′y (är′bi trer′ē) *adj.* **1.** subject to personal judgment. **2.** capricious. **3.** abusing powers. —**ar′bi·trar′i·ly,** *adv.*

ar′bi·trate′ (-trāt′) *v.,* **-trated, -trating.** adjudicate as, or submit to, an arbiter. —**ar′bi·tra′tion,** *n.* —**ar′bi·tra′tor,** *n.*

ar′bor (är′bər) *n.* tree-shaded walk or garden.

ar·bo′re·al (-bôr′ē əl) *adj.* of or living in trees.

ar·bo·re′tum (är′bə rē′təm) *n., pl.* **-tums, -ta** (-tə). parklike area with trees or shrubs for study or display.

arc (ärk) *n.* **1.** part of circle. **2.** luminous current between two electric conductors.

ar·cade′ (är kād′) *n.* **1.** row of archways. **2.** covered passage with stores.

ar·cane′ (är kān′) *adj.* known only to those with special knowledge.

arch (ärch) *n.* **1.** upwardly curved structure. —*v.* **2.** cover with an arch. —*adj.* **3.** chief. **4.** roguish. —**arch′ly,** *adv.*

ar′chae·ol′o·gy (är′kē ol′ə jē) *n.* study of past cultures from artifacts. Also, **ar′che·ol′o·gy.** —**ar′chae·o·log′i·cal** (-ə loj′i kəl) *adj.* —**ar′chae·ol′o·gist,** *n.*

ar·cha′ic (är kā′ik) *adj.* **1.** no longer used. **2.** ancient.

arch′an′gel (ärk′ān′jəl) *n.* chief angel.

arch′bish′op (ärch′bish′əp) *n.* bishop of highest rank.

arch′di′o·cese (ärch dī′ə sis, -sēz′, -sēs′) *n.* diocese of archbishop.

arch′duke′, *n.* royal prince.

arch′en′e·my, *n., pl.* **-mies.** chief enemy.

arch′er (är′chər) *n.* one who shoots a bow and arrow. —**arch′er·y,** *n.*

ar′che·type′ (är′ki tīp′) *n.* original pattern or model.

ar′chi·pel′a·go′ (är′kə pel′ə gō′) *n., pl.* **-gos, -goes. 1.** body of water with many islands. **2.** the islands.

ar′chi·tect′ (är′ki tekt′) *n.* designer of buildings. —**ar′chi·tec′ture,** *n.* —**ar′chi·tec′tur·al,** *adj.*

ar′chives (är′kīvz) *n.pl.* **1.** documents. **2.** place for documents.

arch′way′ (ärch′wā′) *n.* entrance covered by arch.

arc′tic (ärk′tik, är′tik) *adj.* (*often cap.*) of or at the North Pole.

ar′dent (är′dnt) *adj.* earnest; zealous. —**ar′dent·ly,** *adv.*

ar′dor (är′dər) *n.* zeal.

ar′du·ous (är′jŏŏ əs) *adj.* **1.** difficult. **2.** steep. **3.** severe.

are (är; *unstressed* ər) *v.* pres. indic. pl. of **be.**

ar′e·a (âr′ē ə) *n.* **1.** extent of surface; region. **2.** scope.

area code, three-digit number used in long-distance telephone dialing.

a·re′na (ə rē′nə) *n.* open space for contests, shows, etc.

aren′t (ärnt, är′ənt) contraction of **are not.**

ar′got (är′gət, -gō) *n.* special vocabulary used by particular group of people.

ar′gue (är′gyōō) *v.,* **-gued, -guing. 1.** present reasons for or against something. **2.** dispute. **3.** persuade. —**ar′gu·ment,** *n.*

argument, *n.* **1.** controversy, dispute, debate, discussion, disagreement, quarrel, polemic, altercation, conflict. **2.** reasoning, reason, proof, point, position, logic, plea, claim, assertion, contention, defense, ground, evidence. **3.** fact, statement; theme, thesis, topic, subject, matter. —**Ant.** agreement.

ar′gu·men′ta·tive (-men′tə tiv) *adj.* tending to dispute.

ar′gyle (är′gīl) *n.* (*often cap.*) diamond-shaped knitting pattern, as of socks.

a′ri·a (är′ē ə) *n.* operatic solo.

-arian, suffix indicating: **1.** one connected with, as *librarian.* **2.** one supporting or practicing, as *vegetarian.*

ar′id (ar′id) *adj.* dry.

a·right′ (ə rīt′) *adv.* rightly.

a·rise′ (ə rīz′) *v.,* **arose** (ə rōz′), **arisen** (ə riz′ən), **arising. 1.** move or get up. **2.** occur.

ar·is·toc′ra·cy (ar′ə stok′rə sē) *n., pl.* **-cies. 1.** state governed by nobility. **2.** nobility. —**a·ris′to·crat′** (ə ris′tə krat′) *n.* —**a·ris′to·crat′ic,** *adj.*

a·rith′me·tic (ə rith′mə tik) *n.* computation with figures. —**ar′ith·met′i·cal** (ar′ith met′i kəl) *adj.* —**ar′ith·met′i·cal·ly,** *adv.*

Ar·iz′, Arizona.

ark (ärk) *n. Archaic.* large ship.

Ark. Arkansas.

arm (ärm) *n.* **1.** upper limb from hand to shoulder. **2.** weapon. **3.** combat branch. **4.** armlike part. —*v.* **5.** equip with weapons; outfit.

ar·ma′da (är mä′də) *n.* fleet of warships.

ar′ma·dil′lo (är′mə dil′ō) *n.* burrowing mammal covered with plates of bone and horn.

ar′ma·ged′don (är′mə ged′n) *n.* crucial or final conflict.

ar′ma·ment (är′mə mənt) *n.* military weapons.

arm′chair′, *n.* chair with supports for the arms.

armed forces, military, naval, and air forces.

ar′mi·stice (är′mə stis) *n.* truce.

ar′mor (är′mər) *n.* protective covering against weapons.

ar′mor·y (-mə rē) *n., pl.* **-ries.** storage place for weapons.

arm′pit′, *n.* hollow part under arm at shoulder.

ar′my (är′mē) *n., pl.* **-mies. 1.** military force for land combat. **2.** large group.

a·ro′ma (ə rō′mə) *n.* odor. —**ar′o·mat′ic** (ar′ə mat′ik) *adj.*

a·ro′ma·ther′a·py, *n.* use of fragrances to alter a person's mood and make them feel healthy.

a·round′ (ə round′) *adv., prep.* **1.** on every side of. **2.** somewhere in or near. **3.** about.

a·rouse′ (ə rouz′) *v.,* **aroused, arousing. 1.** awaken. **2.** stir to act. —**a·rous′al,** *n.*

ar·raign′ (ə rān′) *v.* **1.** call to court. **2.** accuse. —**ar·raign′ment,** *n.*

ar·range′ (ə rānj′) *v.,* **-ranged, -ranging. 1.** place in order. **2.** plan or prepare. —**ar·range′ment,** *n.*

ar·ray′ (ə rā′) *v.* **1.** arrange. **2.** clothe. —*n.* **3.** arrangement, as for battle. **4.** clothes.

ar·rears′ (ə rērz′) *n.pl.* overdue debt.

ar·rest′ (ə rest′) *v.* **1.** seize (person) by law. **2.** stop. —*n.* **3.** seizure. **4.** stoppage.

ar·rest′ing, *adj.* attracting attention; engaging.

arrival, *n.* **1.** advent, coming, appearance. **2.** reaching, attainment, success. **3.** newcomer; passenger, traveler, tourist. —**Ant.** departure.

ar·rive′ (ə rīv′) *v.,* **-rived, -riving.** reach a place. —**ar·riv′al,** *n.*

arrogance, *n.* haughtiness, pride, insolence, disdain, effrontery, superciliousness, scorn, contumely, self-confidence, self-importance, self-aggrandizement, self-glorification, self-applause, self-assertion, impertinence, presumption, presumptuousness, nerve, gall, loftiness, hubris, pomposity, pompousness, pretension, pretentiousness, braggadocio, bluster, swagger, snobbery, snobbishness, snobbism, brazenness, overbearing manner, imperiousness, highhandedness, contemptuousness, uppitiness, superiority, airs, vainglory, ostentation, bombast, bumptiousness, cheek, impudence, audacity, immodesty, conceit, egotism, hauteur. —**Ant.** humility.

ar′ro·gant (ar′ə gənt) *adj.* insolently proud. —**ar′ro·gance,** *n.* —**ar′ro·gant·ly,** *adv.*

ar′ro·gate′ (-gāt′) *v.,* **-gated, -gating.** claim presumptuously; appropriate. —**ar′ro·ga′tion,** *n.*

ar′row (ar′ō) *n.* pointed stick shot by a bow.

ar′row·head′, *n.* pointed tip of arrow.

ar′row·root′, *n.* edible starch from tropical plant root.

ar·roy′o (ə roi′ō) *n., pl.* **-os.** steep, dry gulch.

ar′se·nal (är′sə nl) *n.* military storehouse or factory.

ar′se·nic (är′sə nik) *n.* **1.** metallic element. **2.** poisonous powder.

ar′son (är′sən) *n.* malicious burning of a building.

art (ärt) *n.* **1.** production of something beautiful or extraordinary. **2.** skill; ability. **3.** cunning. —**art′ful,** *adj.*

art dec′o (dek′ō) *n.* (*often caps.*) 1920s decorative art with geometric designs.

ar·te′ri·o·scle·ro′sis (är tēr′ē ō-sklə rō′sis) *n.* hardening of arteries.

ar′ter·y (är′tə rē) *n., pl.* **-ries. 1.** blood vessel from the heart. **2.** main channel. —**ar·te′ri·al** (-tēr′ē əl) *adj.*

ar·thri′tis (är thrī′tis) *n.* inflammation of a joint.

ar′thro·pod′ (är′thrə pod′) *n.* invertebrate with segmented body and jointed legs, as the lobster.

ar′ti·choke′ (är′ti chōk′) *n.* plant with an edible flower head.

ar′ti·cle (är′ti kəl) *n.* **1.** literary composition. **2.** thing; item. **3.** the words *a, an,* or *the.*

ar·tic′u·late, *adj., v.,* **-lated, -lating.** —*adj.* (är tik′yə lit) **1.** clear. **2.** able to speak. **3.** jointed. —*v.* (-lāt′) **4.** speak, esp. distinctly. **5.** joint. —**ar·tic′u·la′tion,** *n.*

ar′ti·fact′ (är′tə fakt′) *n.* object made by human being or beings.

ar′ti·fice (är′tə fis) *n.* trick.

ar′ti·fi′cial (-tə fish′əl) *adj.* **1.** manufactured, esp. as an imitation. **2.** affected. —**ar′ti·fi′cial·ly,** *adv.* —**ar′ti·fi′ci·al′i·ty** (-fish·ē al′i tē) *n.*

artificial respiration, forcing of air into and out of lungs of a nonbreathing person.

ar·til′ler·y (är til′ə rē) *n.* large guns.

ar′ti·san (är′tə zən) *n.* person skilled in a practical art.

art′ist (är′tist) *n.* practitioner of fine art. —**ar·tis′tic,** *adj.* —**art′ist·ry,** *n.*

art′less, *adj.* natural.

art′y, *adj.,* **artier, artiest.** *Informal.* self-consciously artistic.

as (az; *unstressed* əz) *adv.* **1.** to such an extent. —*conj.* **2.** in the manner, etc., that. **3.** while. **4.** because. —*pron.* **5.** that.

ASAP (ā′es′ā′pē′, ā′sap) **1.** as soon as possible. **2.** without delay. Also, **A.S. A.P., a.s.a.p.**

as·bes′tos (as bes′təs, az-) *n.* fibrous material formerly used in fireproofing.

as·cend′ (ə send′) *v.* climb. —**as· cent′,** *n.*

as·cend′an·cy, *n.* domination; power. —**as·cend′ant,** *adj., n.*

As·cen′sion (ə sen′shən) *n.* bodily passing of Christ to heaven.

as′cer·tain′ (as′ər tān′) *v.* find out.

as·cet′ic (ə set′ik) *n.* **1.** one who lives austerely. —*adj.* **2.** austere or abstemious.

ASCII (as′kē) *n.* standardized code for computer storage and transmission.

as·cor′bic ac′id (ə skôr′bik) vitamin C.

as′cot (as′kət, -kot) *n.* tie or scarf with broad ends.

as·cribe′ (ə skrīb′) *v.,* **-cribed, -crib-ing.** attribute.

a·sep′sis (ā sep′sis, ā sep′-) *n:* absence of certain harmful bacteria.

a·sex′u·al (ā sek′shōō əl) *adj.* **1.** without sex; sexless. **2.** having no sex organs.

ash (ash) *n.* **1.** (*pl.* **ashes**) residue of burned matter. **2.** a common tree. —**ash′y,** *adj.*

a·shamed′ (ə shāmd′) *adj.* feeling shame.

ash′en (ash′ən) *adj.* pale gray.

a·shore′ (ə shôr′) *adv., adj.* on or to shore.

ash′tray, *n.* small dish for tobacco ashes.

A′sian (ā′zhən) *n.* native of Asia. —**Asian,** *adj.*

A′si·at′ic (ā′zhē at′ik) *adj., n. Offensive.* Asian.

a·side′ (ə sīd′) *adv.* **1.** on or to one side. **2.** separate.

as′i·nine′ (as′ə nīn′) *adj.* stupid.

ask (ask) *v.* **1.** put a question to. **2.** request. **3.** invite. **4.** inquire.

a·skance′ (ə skans′) *adv.* with doubt or disapproval.

a·skew′ (ə skyōō′) *adv., adj.* twisted.

a·sleep′ (ə slēp′) *adj., adv.* sleeping.

a·so′cial (ā sō′shəl) *adj.* **1.** not sociable. **2.** selfish.

asp (asp) *n.* poisonous snake.

as·par′a·gus (ə spar′ə gəs) *n.* plant with edible shoots.

as′pect (as′pekt) *n.* **1.** appearance. **2.** phase. **3.** direction faced.

as′pen (as′pən) *n.* variety of poplar.

as·per′i·ty (ə sper′i tē) *n., pl.* **-ties.** roughness.

as·per′sion (ə spûr′zhən, -shən) *n.* derogatory remark.

as′phalt (as′fôlt) *n.* hard, black material used for pavements.

as·phyx′i·ate′ (as fik′sē āt′) *v.,* **-ated, -ating.** affect by a lack of oxygen; choke or smother. —**as·phyx′i· a′tion,** *n.*

as·pire′ (ə spīr′) *v.,* **-pired, -piring.** long, aim, or seek for. —**as′pi·ra′tion** (as′pə rā′shən) *n.*

as′pi·rin (as′pər in, -prin) *n.* crystalline derivative of salicylic acid, used to reduce pain and fever.

ass (as) *n.* **1.** donkey. **2.** fool.

as·sail′ (ə sāl′) *v.* attack. —**as·sail′-ant,** *n.*

as·sas′sin (ə sas′in) *n.* murderer, esp.

of an important person. —**as·sas′si-nate′,** *v.,* **-nated, -nating.** —**as·sas′si-na′tion,** *n.*

assassinate, *v.* murder, kill, slay, destroy, dispatch, do in, immolate, butcher, slaughter, bring *or* take down, do away with, put to death, execute, take *or* put out a contract on, put a hit on, hit, deliver the coup de grace, massacre, make a martyr of, martyr, commit homocide, deal a mortal *or* fatal *or* lethal blow, take out, hire a hit man, extinguish, take *or* end someone's life, shed someone's blood, mark for death, shoot down, finish off, put an end to, eliminate, rub out, conspire against, attack, make an attempt on someone's life; waste.

as·sault′ (ə sôlt′) *n., v.* attack.

as·say′ (ə sā′) *v.* analyze or evaluate. —*as′say, n.* —**as·say′er,** *n.*

as·sem′blage (ə sem′blij) *n.* **1.** group; assembly. **2.** act of assembling.

as·sem′ble (ə sem′bəl) *v.,* **-bled, -bling.** come or bring together.

as·sem′bly, *n., pl.* **-blies. 1.** group gathered together. **2.** legislative body. **3.** putting together of parts.

as·sem′bly·man, *n., pl.* **-men.** member of legislative assembly. Also, *fem.,* **as·sem′bly·wom′an.**

as·sent′ (ə sent′) *v.* **1.** agree. —*n.* **2.** agreement.

as·sert′ (ə sûrt′) *v.* **1.** state; declare. **2.** claim. **3.** present (oneself) boldly. —**as·ser′tion,** *n.* —**as·ser′tive,** *adj.*

assertion, *n.* allegation, statement, contention, pronouncement, pronunciamento, insistence, proclamation, avowal, declaration, claim, affirmation, predication, vindication, defense. —Ant. denial, contradiction.

as·sess′ (ə ses′) *v.* evaluate, as for taxes. —**as·sess′ment,** *n.* —**as·ses′-sor,** *n.*

as′set (as′et) *n.* **1.** item of property. **2.** quality.

as·sid′u·ous (ə sij′ōō əs) *adj.* persistent; devoted. —**as·sid′u·ous·ly,** *adv.* —**as′si·du′i·ty,** *n.*

as·sign′ (ə sīn′) *v.* **1.** give. **2.** appoint. **3.** transfer. —**as·sign′a·ble,** *adj.* —**as·sign′ment,** *n.*

as′sig·na′tion (as′ig nā′shən) *n.* appointment; rendezvous.

as·sim′i·late′ (ə sim′ə lāt′) *v.,* **-lated, -lating.** absorb or become absorbed.

as·sist′ (ə sist′) *v., n.* help; aid. —**as·sist′ant,** *n., adj.* —**as·sist′ance,** *n.*

assn., association.

as·so′ci·ate′, *v.,* **-ated, -ating,** *n., adj.* —*v.* (ə sō′shē āt′) **1.** connect or join. **2.** keep company. —*n.* (-it) **3.** partner; colleague. —*adj.* (-it) **4.** allied. —**as·so′ci·a′tion,** *n.*

association, *n.* organization, alliance, union, guild, group, confraternity, sodality, sisterhood, brotherhood, team, society, club, fraternity, sorority, lodge; company, corporation, firm, partnership; set, coterie, clique, band. **2.** companionship, relationship, camraderie, intimacy, fellowship, friendship. **3.** connection, combination, link, affiliation, conjunction, bond, tie, pairing, relationship, linkage.

as′so·nance (as′ə nəns) *n.* similarity of sound in words or syllables.

as·sort′ed (ə sôr′tid) *adj.* of various kinds.

as·sort′ment a mixed collection.

asst., assistant.

as·suage′ (ə swāj′) *v.,* **-suaged, -suaging.** lessen (pain, grief, etc.).

as·sume′ (ə sōōm′) *v.,* **-sumed, -suming. 1.** take without proof. **2.** un-

dertake. **3.** pretend. **4.** take upon oneself.

as·sump′tion (ə sump′shən) *n.* **1.** unverified belief. **2.** undertaking. **3.** (*cap.*) ascent to heaven of Virgin Mary.

assurance, *n.* **1.** declaration, avowal, averment, deposition. **2.** pledge, promise, guarantee, commitment, vow, word of honor, warranty, surety, guaranty, oath. **3.** certainty, certitude, security, confidence, firmness, trust. **4.** courage, bravery, self-reliance, self-confidence, intrepidity, sang-froid. **5.** boldness, impudence, presumption, arrogance, effrontery, rudeness, impertinence, nerve, cheek, audacity, insolence, brazenness. —**Ant.** denial; distrust, uncertainty; cowardice, diffidence.

as·sure′ (ə shōōr′) *v.,* **-sured, -suring. 1.** affirm to. **2.** guarantee. **3.** encourage. **4.** insure. —**as·sur′ance,** *n.* —**as·sured′,** *adj., n.*

as′ter (as′tər) *n.* plant with many petals around a center disk.

as′ter·isk (as′tə risk) *n.* star (*) symbol used in writing as a reference mark. —**Pronunciation.** The word ASTERISK is pronounced (as′tə risk). Note that the final syllable is pronounced (-risk), with the (s) before the (k). Both (as′tə riks) and (as′tə risk), although occasionally heard among educated speakers, are considered nonstandard pronunciations.

a·stern′ (ə stûrn′) *adv., adj. Naut.* toward or at the rear.

as′ter·oid (as′tə roid′) *n.* planetlike body beyond Mars.

asth′ma (az′mə) *n.* painful respiratory disorder. —**asth·mat′ic** (az mat′-ik) *adj., n.*

a·stig′ma·tism (ə stig′mə tiz′əm) *n.* eye defect resulting in imperfect images.

a·stir′ (ə stûr′) *adj., adv.* active.

as·ton′ish (ə ston′ish) *v.* surprise greatly; amaze. —**as·ton′ish·ing,** *adj.* —**as·ton′ish·ing·ly,** *adv.* —**as·ton′-ish·ment,** *n.*

as·tound′ (ə stound′) *v.* amaze greatly.

as′tral (as′trəl) *adj.* of the stars.

a·stray′ (ə strā′) *adj., adv.* straying.

a·stride′ (ə strīd′) *adv., adj., prep.* straddling.

as·trin′gent (ə strin′jənt) *adj.* causing constriction of skin tissue.

as·trol′o·gy (ə strol′ə jē) *n.* study of stars to determine their influence on human affairs. —**as′tro·log′i·cal** (as′-trə loj′i kəl) *adj.* —**as·trol′o·ger,** *n.*

as′tro·naut (as′trə nôt′) *n.* traveler outside earth's atmosphere.

as′tro·nau′tics, *n.* science and technology of space travel.

as′tro·nom′i·cal (-nom′i kəl) *adj.* **1.** of astronomy. **2.** extremely great, etc. —**as′tro·nom′i·cal·ly,** *adv.*

as·tron′o·my (ə stron′ə mē) *n.* science of all the celestial bodies. —**as′-tron′o·mer,** *n.*

as′tro·phys′ics (as′trō fiz′iks) *n.* branch of astronomy dealing with physical properties of celestial bodies. —**as′tro·phys′i·cist** (-ə sist) *n.*

as·tute′ (ə stōōt′, ə styōōt′) *adj.* shrewd; clever. —**as·tute′ly,** *adv.*

a·sun′der (ə sun′dər) *adv., adj.* apart.

a·sy′lum (ə sī′ləm) *n.* **1.** institution for care of ill or needy persons. **2.** place of refuge; sanctuary.

a·sym′me·try (ā sim′i trē) *n.* lack of symmetry. —**a′sym·met′ric** (ā′sə me′-trik), **a′sym·met′ri·cal,** *adj.*

at (at; *unstressed* ət, it) *prep.* (word used in indicating place, time, etc.)

at·a·vism (at′ə viz′əm) *n.* reappearance of ancestral traits.

ate (āt; *Brit.* et) *v.* pt. of **eat.**

at·el·ier (at′l yā′) *n.* studio, esp. of an artist.

a·the·ism (ā′thē iz′əm) *n.* belief that there is no God. —**a′the·ist,** *n.*

atheist, *n.* agnostic, disbeliever, nonbeliever, infidel, skeptic, doubter, heathen, pagan, gentile. —**Ant.** believer.

ath·lete (ath′lēt) *n.* one who participates in sports or physical exercises. —**ath·let·ic** (-let′ik) **—ath·let′ics,** *n.* **—Pronunciation.** The word ATHLETE is normally pronounced as a two-syllable word: (ath′lēt). Similarly, ATHLETIC has only three syllables: (athlet′ik). Pronunciations of these words that add an extra syllable, with a weak vowel sound inserted between the (th) and the (l), are not considered standard.

athlete's foot, ringworm of the feet.

at·las (at′ləs) *n.* book of maps.

ATM, automated-teller machine, which provides certain bank services when an electronic card is inserted.

at·mos·phere (at′məs fēr′) *n.* **1.** air surrounding earth. **2.** pervading mood. —**at′mos·pher′ic** (-fer′ik) *adj.*

at·oll (at′ôl) *n.* ring-shaped coral island.

at·om (at′əm) *n.* smallest unit making up chemical element. —**a·tom′ic** (ə-tom′ik) *adj.* —**a·tom′i·cal·ly,** *adv.*

atomic bomb, bomb whose force is derived from nuclear fission of certain atoms, causing the conversion of some mass to energy (**atomic energy**). Also, **atom bomb.**

at′om·iz′er (at′ə mī′zər) *n.* device for making a fine spray.

a·ton·al (ā tōn′l) *adj.* lacking tonality. —**a′to·nal′i·ty** (-nal′i tē) *n.*

a·tone′ (ə tōn′) *v.,* **atoned, atoning.** make amends (for). —**a·tone′ment,** *n.*

a·top′ (ə top′) *adj., adv., prep.* on or at the top of.

a′tri·um (ā′trē əm) *n., pl.* **atria, atriums. 1.** enclosed court in building. **2.** either of two upper chambers of the heart.

a·tro′cious (ə trō′shəs) *adj.* **1.** wicked. **2.** very bad. —**a·troc′i·ty** (ə-tros′i tē) *n.*

at·ro·phy (a′trə fē) *n., v.,* **-phied, -phying.** —*n.* **1.** wasting away of the body. —*v.* **2.** cause or undergo atrophy.

at·tach′ (ə tach′) *v.* **1.** fasten or join. **2.** take by legal authority.

at·ta·ché (at′ə shā′) *n.* embassy official.

at·tach′ment (ə tach′mənt) *n.* **1.** an attaching. **2.** something fastened on. **3.** emotional tie.

at·tack′ (ə tak′) *v.* **1.** act against with sudden force **2.** do vigorously. —*n.* **3.** an attacking; onset.

at·tain′ (ə tān′) *v.* **1.** reach; arrive at. **2.** accomplish; fulfill. —**at·tain′a·ble,** *adj.* —**at·tain′ment,** *n.*

at·tempt′ (ə tempt′) *v., n.* try.

at·tend′ (ə tend′) *v.* **1.** be present at. **2.** go with. **3.** take care of. **4.** give heed to. —**at·tend′ance,** *n.* —**at·tend′ant,** *n., adj.*

attendant, *n.* **1.** escort, companion, comrade, follower; servant, waiter, valet, footman, lackey, flunky, menial, slave. **2.** attender, frequenter. **3.** concomitant, accompaniment, consequence. —*adj.* **4.** present, in attend-

ance, accompanying, concomitant, consequent.

at·ten′tion (ə ten′shən) *n.* **1.** act of attending. **2.** careful notice. —**at·ten′tive,** *adj.* —**at·ten′tive·ly,** *adv.*

attentive, *adj.* **1.** observant, intent, regardful, mindful, heedful, thoughtful, alive, alert, awake, on the qui vive; wary, circumspect, watchful, careful. **2.** polite, courteous, gallant, gracious, accommodating, considerate, solicitous, civil, respectful, deferential, assiduous. —**Ant.** inattentive, unwary; discourteous.

at·ten′u·ate′ (-yōō āt′) *v.,* **-ated, -ating. 1.** make thin. **2.** lessen.

at·test′ (ə test′) *v.* declare or certify as true, genuine, etc.

at′tic (at′ik) *n.* room under the roof.

at·tire′ (ə tīr′) *v.,* **-tired, -tiring.** —*v.* **1.** dress; adorn. —*n.* **2.** clothes.

at′ti·tude′ (at′i tōōd′, -tyōōd′) *n.* **1.** feeling or opinion, esp. as expressed. **2.** posture.

attn., attention.

at·tor′ney (ə tûr′nē) *n.* lawyer.

attorney general, *pl.* **attorneys general, attorney generals.** chief law officer of a country or state.

at·tract′ (ə trakt′) *v.* **1.** draw toward. **2.** invite; allure. —**at·trac′tion,** *n.* —**at·trac′tive,** *adj.* —**at·trac′tive·ly,** *adv.* —**at·trac′tive·ness,** *n.*

at·trib·ute, *v.,* **-uted, -uting,** *n.* —*v.* (ə trib′yōōt) **1.** ascribe; credit; impute. —*n.* (at′rə byōot′) **2.** special quality, aspect, etc.

at·tri′tion (ə trish′ən) *n.* wearing down.

at·tune′ (ə tōōn′, ə tyōōn′) *v.,* **-tuned, -tuning.** harmonize.

atty., attorney.

ATV, *n.* all-terrain vehicle: small motor vehicle with treads or wheels for non-road travel.

a·typ′i·cal (ā tip′i kəl) *adj.* not typical; irregular. —**a·typ′i·cal·ly,** *adv.*

au′burn (ô′bərn) *adj.* reddish brown.

auc′tion (ôk′shən) *n.* **1.** sale of goods to highest bidders. —*v.* **2.** sell by auction. —**auc′tion·eer′,** *n., v.*

au·da′cious (ô dā′shəs) *adj.* bold; daring. —**au·dac′i·ty** (-das′i tē) *n.*

au′di·ble (ô′də bəl) *adj.* that can be heard. —**au′di·bly,** *adv.*

au′di·ence (ô′dē əns) *n.* **1.** group of hearers or spectators. **2.** formal hearing or interview.

au′di·o′ (ô′dē ō′) *adj.* **1.** of sound reception or reproduction. —*n.* **2.** audible part of TV.

au′di·ol′o·gy (-ol′ə jē) *n.* study and treatment of hearing disorders.

au′di·om′e·ter (-om′i tar) *n.* instrument for testing hearing.

au′di·o·tape′ (ô′dē ō-) *n.* magnetic tape for recording sound.

au′di·o·vis·u·al, *adj.* using films, TV, and recordings, as for education.

au′dit (ô′dit) *n.* official examination of accounts. —**au′dit,** *v.* —**au′di·tor,** *n.*

au·di′tion (ô dish′ən) *n.* **1.** trial performance. —*v.* **2.** give an audition.

au′di·to′ri·um (-tôr′ē əm) *n.* large meeting room.

au′di·to′ry, *adj.* of hearing.

Aug., August.

au′ger (ô′gər) *n.* drill.

aught (ôt) *n.* **1.** anything. **2.** zero (0). —*adv.* **3.** at all.

aug·ment′ (ôg ment′) *v.* increase. —**aug′men·ta′tion,** *n.*

au′gur (ô′gər) *v.* predict; bode.

Au′gust (ô′gəst) *n.* eighth month of year.

au·gust′ (ô gust′) *adj.* majestic.

auk (ôk) *n.* northern diving bird.

auld lang syne (ôld′ lang zīn′) fondly remembered times.

aunt (ant, änt) *n.* **1.** sister of a parent. **2.** wife of an uncle.

au pair (ō pâr′) person, usu. young foreign visitor, who does household tasks in exchange for room and board.

au′ra (ôr′ə) *n.* **1.** atmosphere, quality, etc. **2.** radiance coming from the body.

au′ral (ôr′əl) *adj.* of or by hearing.

au′re·ole′ (ôr′ē ōl′) *n.* halo.

au′ re·voir′ (ō′ rə vwär′) *French.* good-by.

au′ri·cle (ôr′i kəl) *n.* **1.** outer part of ear. **2.** chamber in heart.

au·ror′a (ə rôr′ə) *n.* display of bands of light in the night sky.

aus′pice (ô′spis) *n.* (*usually pl.*) patronage.

aus·pi′cious (ô spish′əs) *adj.* favorable. —**aus·pi′cious·ly,** *adv.*

aus·tere′ (ô stēr′) *adj.* **1.** harsh; stern. **2.** severely simple. —**aus·ter′i·ty** (ô stēr′i tē) *n.*

austerity, *n.* severity, harshness, strictness, asceticism, rigor, rigidity, rigorousness, stiffness, inflexibility. —**Ant.** lenience, flexibility.

Aus·tral′ian (ô strāl′yən) *n.* native or citizen of Australia. —**Australian,** *adj.*

Aus′tri·an (ô′strē ən) *n.* native of Austria. —**Austrian,** *adj.*

au·then′tic (ô then′tik) *adj.* reliable; genuine. —**au·then·tic′i·ty** (-tis′i tē) *n.* —**au·then′ti·cate′,** *v.*

au′thor (ô′thər) *n.* writer or creator. —**au′thor·ship′,** *n.*

au·thor′i·tar′i·an (ə thôr′i târ′ē ən) *adj.* requiring total obedience.

au·thor′i·ta′tive (-tā′tiv) *adj.* to be accepted as true.

au·thor′i·ty, *n., pl.* **-ties. 1.** right to order or decide. **2.** one with such right. **3.** respected source of information.

au′thor·ize′ (ô′thə rīz′) *v.,* **-ized, -izing.** permit officially.

au′tism (ô′tiz əm) *n.* disorder characterized by extreme self-absorption and detachment from reality. —**au·tis′tic** (ô tis′tik) *adj.*

au′to (ô′tō) *n.* automobile.

auto-, prefix meaning self or same, as *autograph.*

au′to·bi·og′ra·phy, *n., pl.* **-phies.** story of one's own life.

au·toc′ra·cy (ô tok′rə sē) *n., pl.* **-cies.** dictatorial political power.

au′to·di′dact (ô′tō dī′dakt) *n.* self-taught person.

au′to·graph′ (ô′tə graf′) *n.* **1.** signature. —*v.* **2.** sign.

au′to·im·mune′ (ô′tō i myōōn′) *adj.* of or relating to the body's immune response to its own components.

au′to·mat′ (ô′tə mat′) *n.* restaurant with coin-operated service.

au′to·mate′ (-māt′) *v.,* **-mated, -mating.** make or become automatic.

au′to·mat′ic (-mat′ik) *adj.* **1.** self-acting. **2.** inevitably following. —**au′to·mat′i·cal·ly,** *adv.*

automatic pilot, automatic electronic control system for piloting aircraft.

au′to·ma′tion (-mā′shən) *n.* system of controlling a mechanical process automatically, as by electronic devices.

au·tom′a·ton (ô tom′ə ton′) *n.* mechanical device or figure; robot.

au′to·mo·bile′ (ô′tə mə bēl′) *n.* motorized passenger vehicle.

au·ton′o·my (ô ton′ə mē) *n.* self-government. —**au·ton′o·mous,** *adj.*

au′top•sy (ô′top sē) *n., pl.* **-sies.** examination of body for causes of death.

au′tumn (ô′təm) *n.* season before winter; fall. —**au•tum′nal** (ô tum′nl) *adj.*

aux•il′ia•ry (ôg zil′yə rē) *adj., n., pl.* **-ries.** —*adj.* **1.** assisting. **2.** subsidiary. —*n.* **3.** verb preceding other verbs to express tense, etc.

a•vail′ (ə vāl′) *v.* **1.** be of use, value, etc. **2.** take to (oneself) advantageously. —*n.* **3.** benefit; advantage.

a•vail′a•ble, *adj.* present for use. —a•vail•a•bil′i•ty, *n.*

av′a•lanche′ (av′ə lanch′) *n.* mass of falling snow, ice, etc.

a•vant′-garde′ (ə vänt′gärd′, av′änt-) *adj.* progressive, esp. in art.

av′a•rice (av′ər is) *n.* greed. —**av′a•ri′cious** (-rish′əs) *adj.*

ave., avenue.

a•venge′ (ə venj′) *v.,* **avenged, avenging.** take vengeance for.

av′e•nue′ (av′ə nyōō′) *n.* **1.** broad street. **2.** approach.

a•ver′ (ə vûr′) *v.,* **averred, averring.** affirm; declare.

av′er•age (av′ər ij) *n., adj., v.,* **-aged, -aging.** —*n.* **1.** sum of a series of numbers divided by the number of terms in the series. —*adj.* **2.** of or like an average. **3.** typical. —*v.* **4.** find average of.

a•verse′ (ə vûrs′) *adj.* unwilling.

a•ver′sion (ə vûr′zhən) *n.* dislike.

a•vert′ (ə vûrt′) *v.* **1.** turn away. **2.** prevent.

avg., average.

a′vi•ar′y (ā′vē er′ē) *n., pl.* **-aries.** place in which birds are kept.

a′vi•a′tion (ā′vē ā′shən) *n.* science of flying aircraft. —**a′vi•a′tor,** *n.* —**a′vi•a′trix,** *n.fem.*

av′id (av′id) *adj.* eager. —**a•vid′i•ty,** *n.* —**av′id•ly,** *adv.*

av′o•ca′do (av′ə kä′dō, ä′və-) *n., pl.* **-dos.** tropical pear-shaped fruit.

av′o•ca′tion (av′ə kā′shən) *n.* hobby.

a•void′ (ə void′) *v.* shun; evade. —**a•void′a•ble,** *adj.* —**a•void′ance,** *n.*

av′oir•du•pois′ (av′ər də poiz′) *n.* system of weights with 16-ounce pounds.

a•vow′ (ə vou′) *v.* declare; confess. —**a•vow′al,** *n.* —**a•vowed′,** *adj.*

a•wait′ (ə wāt′) *v.* wait for.

a•wake′ (ə wāk′) *v.,* **awoke** (ə wōk′) or **awaked, awaking,** *adj.* —*v.* **1.** Also, **a•wak′en.** rouse from sleep. —*adj.* **2.** not asleep.

a•wak′en (ə wā′kən) *v.* awake. —**a•wak′en•ing,** *n., adj.*

a•ward′ (ə wôrd′) *v.* **1.** bestow; grant. —*n.* **2.** thing bestowed.

a•ware′ (ə wâr′) *adj.* conscious (of). —**a•ware′ness,** *n.*

a•wash′ (ə wosh′) *adj.* flooded.

a•way′ (ə wā′) *adv.* **1.** from this or that place. **2.** apart. **3.** aside. —*adj.* **4.** absent. **5.** distant.

awe (ô) *n., v.,* **awed, awing.** —*n.* **1.** respectful fear. —*v.* **2.** fill with awe.

awe′some (ô′səm) *adj.* **1.** inspiring or characterized by awe. **2.** *Slang.* very impressive.

awe′struck′, *adj.* filled with awe.

aw′ful (ô′fəl) *adj.* **1.** fearful. **2.** very bad. **3.** *Informal.* very.

aw′ful•ly, *adv.* **1.** very badly. **2.** *Informal.* very.

a•while′ (ə hwīl′) *adv.* for a short time. —**Usage.** AWHILE is always spelled as one word: *We rested awhile.* A WHILE is a noun phrase (an article and a noun) and is used af-

ter a preposition: *We rested for a while.*

awk′ward (ôk′wərd) *adj.* **1.** clumsy. **2.** embarrassing. **3.** difficult; risky. —**awk′ward•ly,** *adv.*

awl (ôl) *n.* tool for making holes.

awn′ing (ô′ning) *n.* canvas overhang.

AWOL (*pronounced as initials or* ā′wôl) *adj., adv.* absent without leave.

a•wry′ (ə rī′) *adv., adj.* **1.** twisted. **2.** wrong.

ax (aks) *n.* small chopping tool. Also, **axe.**

ax′i•om (ak′sē əm) *n.* accepted truth. —**ax′i•o•mat′ic** (-ə mat′ik) *adj.*

ax′is (ak′sis) *n., pl.* **axes** (ak′sēz). line about which something turns.

ax′le (ak′səl) *n.* bar on which a wheel turns.

a′ya•tol′lah (ä′yə tō′lə) *n.* chief Muslim leader.

aye (ī) *adv., n.* yes.

a•zal′ea (ə zāl′yə) *n.* flowering shrub.

AZT, *n. Trademark.* drug used in AIDS treatment.

Az′tec (az′tek) *n.* American Indian people whose Mexican empire was conquered by Spaniards in 1521. —**Az′tec•an,** *adj.*

az′ure (azh′ər) *adj., n.* sky-blue.

B

B, b (bē) *n.* second letter of English alphabet.

B.A., Bachelor of Arts.

bab′ble (bab′əl) *v.,* **-bled, -bling. 1.** talk indistinctly or foolishly. **2.** murmur. —**bab′ble,** *n.*

babe (bāb) *n.* **1.** baby. **2.** innocent person.

ba•boon′ (ba bōōn′, bə-) *n.* large monkey of Africa and Arabia.

ba′by (bā′bē) *n., pl.* **-bies,** *v.,* **-bied, -bying.** —*n.* **1.** infant. **2.** childish person. —*v.* **3.** pamper. —**ba′by•ish,** *adj.*

baby boom, period of increase in the rate of births. —**baby boomer.**

ba′by-sit′, *v.,* **baby-sat** (-sat′), **baby-sitting.** tend another's child for a few hours. —**ba′by-sit′ter,** *n.*

bac•ca•lau′re•ate (bak′ə lôr′ē it) *n.* bachelor's degree.

bac′cha•nal′ (bak′ə nal′) *n.* drunken revelry.

bach′e•lor (bach′ə lər) *n.* **1.** unmarried man. **2.** person holding first degree at a college.

ba•cil′lus (bə sil′əs) *n., pl.* **-cilli** (-sil′ī). type of bacteria.

back (bak) *n.* **1.** rear part of human and animal body. **2.** rear. **3.** spine. —*v.* **4.** sponsor. **5.** move backward. **6.** bet in favor of. **7.** furnish or form a back. —*adj.* **8.** being behind. **9.** in the past. **10.** overdue. —*adv.* **11.** at or toward the rear. **12.** toward original point or condition. **13.** in return. —**back′er,** *n.* —**back′ing,** *n.*

back′bite′, *v.,* **-bit** (-bit′), **-bitten, -biting.** discuss (someone) maliciously.

back′board′, *n.* in basketball, vertical board behind basket.

back′bone′, *n.* **1.** spine. **2.** strength of character. —**back′boned′,** *adj.*

back′break′ing, *adj.* fatiguing.

back′drop′, *n.* **1.** curtain at the back of a stage. **2.** background of an event; setting.

back′field′, *n.* football players behind the line.

back′fire′, *v.,* **-fired, -firing. 1.** (of an engine) ignite prematurely. **2.** bring

results opposite to those planned. —**back′fire′,** *n.*

back′gam′mon (-gam′ən) *n.* board game for two persons.

back′ground′, *n.* **1.** parts in the rear. **2.** distant portions in a picture. **3.** origins; antecedents.

back′hand′, *n.* **1.** in tennis and other sports, stroke made with back of hand facing direction of movement. —*adj.* **2.** backhanded. —*v.* **3.** hit with a backhand.

back′hand′ed, *adj.* **1.** with upper part of hand forward. **2.** ambiguous.

back′lash′, *n.* retaliatory reaction.

back′log′, *n.* reserve or accumulation, as of work.

back′pack′, *n.* **1.** knapsack. —*v.* **2.** hike using backpack.

back′-ped′al, *v.,* **back-pedaled, back-pedaling. 1.** slow a bicycle by pressing backward on pedals. **2.** retreat from or reverse a previous stand or opinion.

back′side′, *n.* **1.** rear. **2.** rump.

back′slide′, *v.,* **-slid** (-slid′), **-slidden** or **-slid, -sliding.** relapse into bad habits. —**back′slid′er,** *n.*

back′stage′, *adv.* in theater wings or dressing rooms.

back′stroke′, *n.* swimming stroke performed while lying on back.

back talk, impertinent talk.

back′track′, *v.* retreat slowly.

back′up′, *n.* **1.** person or thing that supports or reinforces another. **2.** accumulation caused by a stopping, as of traffic. **3.** alternate kept in reserve.

back′ward (-wərd) *adv.* Also, **back′wards. 1.** toward the back or rear. **2.** back foremost. **3.** toward or in the past. —*adj.* **4.** toward the back or past. **5.** behind in time or progress. **6.** bashful.

back′wa′ter, *n.* place that is backward or stagnant.

back′woods′, *n.pl.* wooded or unsettled districts.

ba′con (bā′kən) *n.* cured back and sides of a hog.

bac•te′ri•a (bak tēr′ē ə) *n.pl., sing.* **-um** (-əm). group of one-celled organisms, involved in fermentation, infectious disease, etc. —**bac•te′ri•al,** *adj.* —**bac•te′ri•al•ly,** *adv.*

bac•te′ri•ol′o•gy (-ol′ə jē) *n.* science dealing with bacteria. —**bac•te′ri•o•log′i•cal** (-ə loj′i kəl) *adj.* —**bac•te′ri•ol′o•gist,** *n.*

bad (bad) *adj.,* **worse** (wûrs), **worst** (wûrst), *n.* —*adj.* **1.** not good. —*n.* **2.** bad thing, condition, or quality. —**bad′ly,** *adv.* ———**Usage.** The adjective BAD, meaning "unpleasant, unattractive, unfavorable, spoiled, etc.," is the usual form after such verbs as *sound, smell, look,* and *taste: The music sounds bad. The locker room smells bad. You look pretty bad; are you sick? The water tasted bad.* After the verb *feel,* the adjective BADLY may also be used (*She was feeling badly that day*), although BAD is more common in formal writing. BAD as an adverb appears mainly in informal situations: *He wanted to win pretty bad.*

bad blood, hostility.

badge (baj) *n.* emblem or insignia.

badg′er (baj′ər) *n.* **1.** burrowing mammal. —*v.* **2.** harass.

bad′min•ton (bad′min tn) *n.* game similar to lawn tennis.

bad′-mouth′ (-mouth′, -mouth′) *v.* criticize. Also, **bad′mouth′.**

baf′fle (baf′əl) *v.,* **-fled, -fling,** *n.* —*v.* **1.** thwart; confuse. —*n.* **2.** obstacle; obstruction.

bag (bag) *n.*, *v.*, **bagged, bagging.** —*n.* **1.** sack or receptacle of flexible material. **2.** purse. —*v.* **3.** bulge. **4.** put into a bag. **5.** kill or catch. —**bag′gy,** *adj.* —**bag′gi•ness,** *n.*

bag′a•telle′ (bag′ə tel′) *n.* article of small value.

ba′gel (bā′gəl) *n.* hard ringlike roll.

bag′gage (bag′ij) *n.* trunks, suitcases, etc., for travel.

bag′pipe′, *n.* (*often pl.*) musical instrument with windbag and two or more pipes. —**bag′pip′er,** *n.*

bah (bä, ba) *interj.* (exclamation of contempt or annoyance).

bail (bāl) *n.* **1.** security for the return of a prisoner to custody. **2.** person giving bail. **3.** release following payment of security. —*v.* **4.** give or obtain liberty by bail. **5.** dip water out of boat. **6. bail out,** make a parachute jump. —**bail′a•ble,** *adj.*

bail′iff (bā′lif) *n.* public officer similar to sheriff or deputy.

bail′i•wick (bā′lə wik′) *n.* person's area of authority, skill, etc.

bail′out′, *n.* rescue from financial problems.

bait (bāt) *n.* **1.** food used as lure in fishing or hunting. —*v.* **2.** prepare with bait. **3.** set dogs upon for sport.

bake (bāk) *v.*, **baked, baking. 1.** cook by dry heat, as in oven. **2.** harden by heat. —**bak′er,** *n.*

baker's dozen, a dozen plus one; 13.

bak′er•y, *n.*, *pl.* **-eries.** place for baking; baker's shop.

baking powder, white powder used as leavening agent in baking.

baking soda, sodium bicarbonate, white powder used as an antacid and in baking.

bal′ance (bal′əns) *n.*, *v.*, **-anced, -ancing.** —*n.* **1.** instrument for weighing. **2.** equilibrium. **3.** harmonious arrangement. **4.** act of balancing. **5.** remainder, as of money due. —*v.* **6.** weigh. **7.** set or hold in equilibrium. **8.** be equivalent to. **9.** reckon or adjust accounts.

bal′co•ny (bal′kə nē) *n.*, *pl.* **-nies. 1.** platform projecting from wall of building. **2.** theater gallery.

bald (bôld) *adj.* **1.** lacking hair on scalp. **2.** plain; undisguised.

bal′der•dash′ (bôl′dər dash′) *n.* nonsense.

bale (bāl) *n.*, *v.*, **baled, baling.** —*n.* **1.** large bundle or package. —*v.* **2.** make into bales. —**bale′ful,** *adj.* evil; menacing.

balk (bôk) *v.* **1.** stop or stop short. **2.** hinder; thwart. —*n.* **3.** hindrance. **4.** in baseball, illegal stop in pitcher's motion. —**balk′y,** *adj.*

ball (bôl) *n.* **1.** round or roundish object. **2.** game played with ball. **3.** social assembly for dancing. **4.** *Informal.* good time. —*v.* **5.** make or form into ball.

bal′lad (bal′əd) *n.* **1.** narrative folk song or poem. **2.** sentimental song.

bal′last (bal′əst) *n.* **1.** heavy material carried to ensure stability. —*v.* **2.** furnish with ballast.

ball bearing, bearing in which a moving part turns on steel balls.

bal′le•ri′na (bal′ə rē′nə) *n.* woman ballet dancer.

bal′let′ (ba lā′) *n.* theatrical entertainment by dancers.

ballistic missile (bə lis′tik) guided missile completing its trajectory in free fall.

bal•lis′tics, *n.* study of the motion of projectiles. —**bal•lis′tic,** *adj.*

bal•loon′ (bə lōōn′) *n.* **1.** bag filled with a gas lighter than air, designed to float in atmosphere. —*v.* **2.** go up in balloon. **3.** increase rapidly. —**bal•loon′ist,** *n.*

bal′lot (bal′ət) *n.*, *v.*, **-loted, -loting.** —*n.* **1.** paper used in voting. **2.** vote. —*v.* **3.** vote by ballot.

ball′park′, *n.* baseball arena.

ball′point′ pen, pen laying down ink with small ball bearing.

ball′room′, *n.* room for dancing.

bal′ly•hoo′ (bal′ē hōō′) *n. Informal.* exaggerated publicity.

balm (bäm) *n.* **1.** fragrant, oily substance obtained from tropical trees. **2.** aromatic ointment or fragrance.

balm′y, *adj.*, **balmier, balmiest. 1.** mild; refreshing. **2.** fragrant.

ba•lo′ney (bə lō′nē) *n. Informal.* **1.** bologna. **2.** false or foolish talk.

bal′sa (bôl′sə, bäl′-) *n.* tropical tree with light wood.

bal′sam (bôl′səm) *n.* **1.** fragrant substance exuded from certain trees. **2.** any of these trees. —**bal•sam′ic** (bôl-sam′ik) *adj.*

bal′us•ter (bal′ə stər) *n.* pillarlike support for railing.

bal′us•trade′ (-ə strād′) *n.* series of balusters supporting a railing.

bam•boo′ (bam bōō′) *n.*, *pl.* **-boos.** treelike tropical grass having a hollow woody stem.

bam•boo′zle (bam bōō′zəl) *v.*, **-zled, -zling.** *Informal.* trick.

ban (ban) *v.*, **banned, banning.** *n.* —*v.* **1.** prohibit. —*n.* **2.** prohibition.

ba•nal′ (bə nal′, -näl′, bān′l) *adj.* trite. —**ba•nal′i•ty,** *n.*

ba•nan′a (bə nan′ə) *n.* **1.** tropical plant. **2.** yellow fruit of this plant.

band (band) *n.* **1.** strip of material for binding. **2.** stripe. **3.** company of persons. **4.** group of musicians. —*v.* **5.** mark with bands. **6.** unite.

band′age (ban′dij) *n.*, *v.*, **-aged, -aging.** —*n.* **1.** strip of cloth for binding wound. —*v.* **2.** bind with bandage. —**band′ag•er,** *n.*

Band′-Aid′, *n. Trademark.* small adhesive bandage with gauze center.

ban•dan′na (ban dan′ə) *n.* colored handkerchief worn on head. Also, **ban•dan′a.**

ban′dit (ban′dit) *n.* robber; outlaw.

band′stand′, *n.* platform on which band performs.

band′wag′on, *n.* cause or movement that appears popular and successful.

ban′dy (ban′dē) *v.*, **-died, -dying.** *adj.* —*v.* **1.** exchange (words) back and forth. —*adj.* **2.** bent outward. —**ban′dy-leg′ged** (-leg′id, -legd′) *adj.*

bane (bān) *n.* thing causing death or destruction.

bane′ful, *adj.* destructive.

bang (bang) *n.* **1.** loud, sudden noise. **2.** (*often pl.*) fringe of hair across forehead. —*v.* **3.** make loud noise. **4.** strike noisily.

ban′gle (bang′gəl) *n.* bracelet.

bang′-up′, *adj. Informal.* excellent.

ban′ish (ban′ish) *v.* **1.** exile. **2.** drive or put away. —**ban′ish•ment,** *n.*

ban′is•ter (ban′ə stər) *n.* **1.** baluster. **2.** (*pl.*) balustrade.

ban′jo (ban′jō) *n.*, *pl.* **-jos, -joes.** musical instrument similar to guitar, with circular body. —**ban′jo•ist,** *n.*

bank (bangk) *n.* **1.** pile; heap. **2.** slope bordering stream. **3.** place or institution for receiving and lending money. **4.** store of something, such as blood, for future use. —*v.* **5.** border with or make into bank. **6.** cover fire to make burn slowly. **7.** slope upward. **8.** de-posit or keep money in bank. **9.** rely (on). —**bank′er,** *n.* —**bank′ing,** *n.*

bank′roll′, *n.* **1.** money possessed. —*v.* **2.** pay for; fund.

bank′rupt (-rupt) *n.* **1.** insolvent person. —*adj.* **2.** insolvent. **3.** lacking. —*v.* **4.** make bankrupt. —**bank′rupt•cy,** *n.*

ban′ner (ban′ər) *n.* flag.

banns (banz) *n.pl.* notice of intended marriage. Also, **bans.**

ban′quet (bang′kwit) *n.* **1.** feast. —*v.* **2.** dine or entertain at banquet.

ban′shee (ban′shē) *n.* female spirit of Irish folklore whose wailing means a loved one is about to die.

ban′tam (ban′təm) *n.* **1.** breed of small domestic fowl. —*adj.* **2.** tiny.

ban′ter (ban′tər) *n.* **1.** good-natured teasing. —*v.* **2.** use banter.

ban′yan (ban′yən) *n.* East Indian fig tree.

bap′tism (bap′tiz əm) *n.* immersion in or application of water, esp. as initiatory rite in Christian church. —**bap•tis′mal,** *adj.*

Bap′tist (-tist) *n.* Christian who undergoes baptism only after profession of faith.

bap•tize′ (bap tīz′, bap′tīz) *v.*, **-tized, -tizing. 1.** administer baptism. **2.** christen. —**bap•tiz′er,** *n.*

bar (bär) *n.*, *v.*, **barred, barring,** *prep.* —*n.* **1.** long, evenly shaped piece, esp. of wood or metal. **2.** band; stripe. **3.** long ridge in shallow waters. **4.** obstruction; hindrance. **5.** line marking division between two measures of music. **6.** place where liquors are served. **7.** legal profession or its members. **8.** railing in courtroom between public and court officers. **9.** place in courtroom where prisoners are stationed. —*v.* **10.** provide or fasten with a bar. **11.** block; hinder. —*prep.* **12.** except for. —**barred,** *adj.*

barb (bärb) *n.* **1.** point projecting backward. —*v.* **2.** furnish with barb. —**bar•bar′i•an** (bär bâr′ē ən) *n.* **1.** savage or uncivilized person. —*adj.* **2.** uncivilized. —**bar•bar′ic,** *adj.* —**bar•bar′i•cal•ly,** *adv.*

bar′ba•rism (-bə riz′əm) *n.* barbarian state or act.

bar•bar′i•ty (-bar′i tē) *n.*, *pl.* **-ties. 1.** cruelty. **2.** crudity.

bar′ba•rous (-bər əs) *adj.* **1.** barbarian. **2.** harsh; heavily accented.

bar′be•cue′ (bär′bi kyōō′) *n.*, *v.*, **-cued, -cuing.** —*n.* **1.** outdoor meal at which foods are roasted over an open fire. —*v.* **2.** broil over an open fire. Also, **bar′be•que′.**

bar′ber (bär′bər) *n.* **1.** one who gives haircuts, shaves, etc. —*v.* **2.** shave or cut the hair.

bar•bi′tu•rate (bär bich′ər it, bär′bi tōōr′it, -tyōōr′-) *n.* sedative drug.

bar code, series of lines of different widths placed on item for identification by computer scanner.

bard (bärd) *n.* poet.

bare (bâr) *adj.*, **barer, barest,** *v.*, **bared, baring.** —*adj.* **1.** uncovered; unclothed. **2.** unfurnished. **3.** unconcealed. **4.** mere. —*v.* **5.** make bare. —**bare′foot′,** *adj.*, *adv.*

bare′back′, *adv.*, *adj.* without a saddle.

bare′faced′, *adj.* **1.** undisguised. **2.** impudent.

bare′ly, *adv.* no more than; only.

bar′gain (bär′gən) *n.* **1.** agreement. **2.** advantageous purchase. —*v.* **3.** discuss or arrive at agreement.

barge (bärj) *n.*, *v.*, **barged, barging.** —*n.* **1.** unpowered vessel for freight.

—*v.* **2.** carry by barge. **3.** move clumsily. **4.** *Informal.* intrude.

bar′i•tone′ (bar′i tōn′) *n.* male voice or part between tenor and bass.

bar′i•um (bâr′ē əm, bar′-) *n.* metallic element.

bark (bärk) *n.* **1.** cry of a dog. **2.** external covering of woody plants. **3.** Also, **barque.** three-masted sailing ship. —*v.* **4.** sound a bark. **5.** utter with barking sound. **6.** strip from bark. **7.** scrape the skin of.

bark′er (bär′kər) *n.* person who stands at the entrance to a show, shouting out its attractions.

bar′ley (bär′lē) *n.* edible cereal plant.

bar mitz′vah (bär mits′və) Jewish religious ceremony recognizing manhood.

barn (bärn) *n.* farm building for storage and stabling. —**barn′yard′,** *n.*

bar′na•cle (bär′nə kəl) *n.* type of shellfish that clings to ship bottoms, etc. —**bar′na•cled,** *adj.*

barn′storm′, *v.* tour rural areas giving speeches or performing plays.

ba•rom′e•ter (bə rom′i tər) *n.* instrument for measuring atmospheric pressure.

bar′on (bar′ən) *n.* member of lowest nobility. Also, *n.fem.* **bar′on•ess.** —**bar′on•age,** *n.* —**ba•ro′ni•al** (bə-rō′ nē əl) *adj.*

bar′on•et (-ə nit, -net′) *n.* member of nobility ranking below baron. —**bar′on•et•cy,** *n.*

Ba•roque′ (bə rōk′) *n.* artistic style marked by exuberant decoration and grotesque effects.

bar′rack (bar′ək) *n.* (*usually pl.*) building for lodging soldiers.

bar′ra•cu′da (bar′ə kōō′də) *n.* edible eellike fish.

bar•rage′ (bə räzh′) *n.* concentrated artillery fire.

bar′rel (bar′əl) *n., v.,* **-reled, -reling.** —*n.* **1.** wooden cylindrical vessel with bulging sides. **2.** quantity held in such vessel. —*v.* **3.** put in barrel or barrels.

bar′ren (bar′ən) *adj.* **1.** sterile; unfruitful. **2.** dull. —**bar′ren•ness,** *n.*

bar•rette′ (bə ret′) *n.* clasp for hair.

bar′ri•cade′ (bar′i kād′, bar′i kād′) *n., v.,* **-caded, -cading.** —*n.* **1.** defensive barrier. —*v.* **2.** block or defend with barricade.

bar′ri•er (bar′ē ər) *n.* obstacle; obstruction.

bar′ring (bär′ing) *prep.* excepting.

bar′ris•ter (bar′ə stər) *n.* in England, lawyer in higher courts.

bar′row (bar′ō) *n.* **1.** flat frame for carrying load. **2.** artificial mound, as over a grave.

bar′tend′er (bär′-) *n.* person mixing and serving drinks at a bar.

bar′ter (bär′tər) *v.* **1.** trade by exchange. —*n.* **2.** act of bartering.

ba•salt′ (bə sôlt′, bā′sôlt) *n.* dark, hard rock. —**ba•sal′tic,** *adj.*

base (bās) *n., v.,* **based, basing,** *adj.,* **baser, basest.** —*n.* **1.** bottom or foundation of something. **2.** fundamental principle. **3.** starting point. **4.** *Mil.* **a.** protected place from which operations proceed. **b.** supply installation. **5.** chemical compound which unites with an acid to form a salt. —*v.* **6.** make foundation for. —*adj.* **7.** despicable. **8.** inferior.

base′ball′, *n.* **1.** ball game played by two teams of nine players on diamond-shaped field. **2.** ball used.

base′board′, *n.* board or molding at the base of a room's walls.

base′less, *adj.* unfounded.

base′line′, *n.* **1.** line between bases

on baseball diamond. **2.** line at each end of tennis court. **3.** basic standard or level; guideline.

base′ment, *n.* story of building below the ground floor.

base on balls, *pl.* **bases on balls.** awarding of first base to a batter after four pitches not strikes.

bash (bash) *v.* **1.** hit hard. —*n.* **2.** hard blow. **3.** big, lively party.

bash′ful, *adj.* shy; timid.

ba′sic (bā′sik) *adj.* **1.** rudimentary. **2.** essential. —*n.* **3.** (*pl.*) rudiments. —**ba′si•cal•ly,** *adv.*

BASIC (bā′sik) *n.* computer programming language using English words, punctuation, and algebraic notation.

bas′il (baz′əl, bā′zəl) *n.* aromatic mintlike herb.

ba•sil′i•ca (bə sil′i kə) *n.* **1.** ancient church. **2.** Roman Catholic church.

ba′sin (bā′sən) *n.* **1.** circular vessel for liquids. **2.** area drained by river.

ba′sis (bā′sis) *n., pl.* **-ses** (-sēz). **1.** base (defs. 1, 2). **2.** principal ingredient.

bask (bask) *v.* expose to warmth.

bas′ket (bas′kit) *n.* receptacle woven of twigs, strips of wood, etc.

bas′ket•ball′, *n.* **1.** ball game played by two teams of five players on rectangular court. **2.** ball used.

bas′-re•lief′ (bä′ri lēf′) *n.* sculpture in which figures are raised slightly.

bass *adj., n., pl.* (for 3) **basses, bass.** —*adj.* (bās) **1.** of the lowest musical part or range. —*n.* **2.** (bās) bass part, voice, instrument, etc. **3.** (bas) any of various edible, spiny fishes.

basset hound (bas′it) short-legged hound with drooping ears.

bas′si•net′ (bas′ə net′) *n.* basket with hood, used as cradle.

bas•soon′ (ba sōōn′, bə-) *n.* baritone woodwind instrument.

bas′tard (bas′tərd) *n.* **1.** illegitimate child. **2.** *Slang.* mean person. —*adj.* **3.** illegitimate in birth. **4.** not pure or authentic.

baste (bāst) *v.,* **basted, basting. 1.** sew with temporary stitches. **2.** moisten (meat, etc.) while cooking.

bas′tion (bas′chən) *n.* **1.** fortified place. **2.** something that preserves or protects.

bat (bat) *n., v.,* **batted, batting.** —*n.* **1.** stick or club, esp. as used in ball games. **2.** nocturnal flying mammal. —*v.* **3.** strike with bat. **4.** take turn in batting. **5.** blink; flutter.

batch (bach) *n.* material, esp. bread, prepared in one operation.

bat′ed (bā′tid) *adj.* (of breath) held back in suspense.

bath (bath) *n., pl.* **baths. 1.** washing of entire body. **2.** water used. —**bath′room′,** *n.* —**bath′tub′,** *n.*

bathe (bāth) *v.,* **bathed, bathing. 1.** take a bath. **2.** immerse in liquid; moisten. —**bath′er,** *n.*

bathing suit, garment worn for swimming; swimsuit.

ba′thos (bā′thos, -thōs) *n.* **1.** ludicrous change in tone from lofty to commonplace. **2.** false pathos; trite sentiment.

bath′robe′, *n.* robe worn going to and from bath.

ba•tik′ (bə tēk′) *n.* cloth partly waxed to resist dye.

bat mitz′vah (bät mits′və) Jewish religious ceremony for a girl, paralleling the bar mitzvah.

ba•ton′ (bə ton′, ba-) *n.* staff used by orchestral conductor.

bat•tal′ion (bə tal′yən) *n.* military unit of three or more companies.

bat′ten (bat′n) *n.* **1.** strip of wood. —*v.* **2.** fasten with battens.

bat′ter (bat′ər) *v.* **1.** beat persistently. **2.** damage by hard usage. —*n.* **3.** semiliquid cooking mixture. **4.** one who bats.

bat′ter•y, *n., pl.* **-teries. 1.** device for producing electricity. **2.** combination of artillery pieces. **3.** illegal attack by beating or wounding.

bat′tle (bat′l) *n., v.,* **-tled, -tling.** —*n.* **1.** hostile encounter. —*v.* **2.** fight. —**bat′tle•field′,** *n.*

bat′tle•ment, *n.* indented parapet.

bat′tle•ship′, *n.* heavily armed warship.

bat′ty (bat′ē) *adj.,* **-tier, -tiest.** *Slang.* crazy or eccentric.

bau′ble (bô′bəl) *n.* trinket.

baud (bôd) *n.* unit used to measure speed of a signal or data transfer, as in computers.

baux′ite (bôk′sīt, bō′zīt) *n.* principal ore of aluminum.

bawd′y (bô′dē) *adj.,* **bawdier, bawdiest.** obscene.

bawl (bôl) *v.* **1.** shout out. —*n.* **2.** shout.

bay (bā) *n.* **1.** inlet of sea or lake. **2.** vertical section of window. **3.** compartment or recess in a building. **4.** deep, prolonged bark. **5.** stand made by hunted animal or person. **6.** reddish brown. **7.** laurel tree. —*v.* **8.** bark. **9.** bring to bay (def. 5). —*adj.* **10.** of the color bay.

bay′ber•ry, *n., pl.* **-ries.** fragrant shrub with berries.

bay leaf, dried leaf of the laurel, used in cooking.

bay′o•net (bā′ə net′, bā′ə nit) *n., v.,* **-neted, -neting.** —*n.* **1.** dagger attached to rifle muzzle. —*v.* **2.** kill or wound with bayonet.

bay′ou (bī′ōō) *n., pl.* **bayous.** arm of river, etc.

ba•zaar′ (bə zär′) *n.* **1.** marketplace. **2.** charity sale.

ba•zoo′ka (bə zōō′kə) *n.* hand-held rocket launcher.

BB (bē′bē′) *n., pl.* **BB's.** small metal shot fired from an air rifle (**BB gun**).

B.C., before Christ.

B.C.E., before the Common (or Christian) Era.

be (bē; *unstressed* bē, bi) *v.* **1.** exist. **2.** occur.

beach (bēch) *n.* **1.** sand or pebbles of seashore. —*v.* **2.** run or pull a ship onto beach.

beach′comb′er, *n.* **1.** person who gathers salable jetsam or refuse on a beach. **2.** vagrant living on a beach.

beach′head′, *n.* part of beach landed on and seized by military force.

bea′con (bē′kən) *n.* signal, esp. a fire.

bead (bēd) *n.* **1.** small ball of glass, pearl, etc., designed to be strung. **2.** (*pl.*) necklace. —*v.* **3.** ornament with beads. —**bead′ing,** *n.*

bea′gle (bē′gəl) *n.* short-legged hunting dog.

beak (bēk) *n.* **1.** bill of bird. **2.** beaklike object.

beak′er, *n.* large glass.

beam (bēm) *n.* **1.** horizontal support secured at both ends. **2.** ray of light or other radiation. —*v.* **3.** emit beams. **4.** smile radiantly.

bean (bēn) *n.* **1.** edible seed of certain plants. **2.** plant producing such seed.

bear (bâr) *v.,* **bore** (bôr), **borne** (bôrn), **bearing,** *n., adj.* —*v.* **1.** support. **2.** carry. **3.** undergo; endure. **4.** move; go. **5.** give birth to. —*n.* **6.** large shaggy mammal. **7.** clumsy or rude person. **8.** speculator who counts on falling prices. —*adj.* **9.** marked by falling prices.

beard (bērd) *n.* **1.** hair on face of man. **2.** similar growth or part. —*v.* **3.** defy. —**beard'ed,** *adj.*

bear hug, tight embrace.

bear'ing *n.* **1.** manner. **2.** reference; relation. **3.** *Mach.* part in which another part moves. **4.** (*often pl.*) position; direction.

beast (bēst) *n.* **1.** animal. **2.** coarse or inhuman person.

beast'ly, *adj.,* **-lier, -liest. 1.** brutish. **2.** nasty. —**beast'li·ness,** *n.*

beat (bēt) *v.,* **beat, beaten** or **beat, beating,** *n.* —*v.* **1.** strike repeatedly. **2.** dash against. **3.** mark time in music. **4.** defeat. **5.** throb. —*n.* **6.** blow. **7.** sound of a blow. **8.** habitual rounds. **9.** musical time.

be·a·tif'ic (bē'ə tif'ik) *adj.* blissful.

be·at'i·tude' (bē at'i tōōd', -tyōōd') *n.* **1.** blessedness. **2.** (*often cap.*) declaration of blessedness made by Christ (Matthew 5).

beat'nik (bēt'nik) *n.* disillusioned, unconventional person, esp. of the 1950s.

beau (bō) *n., pl.* **beaus, beaux. 1.** lover. **2.** fop.

beau'te·ous (byōō'tē əs) *adj.* beautiful.

beau·ti'cian (-tish'ən) *n.* person who works in beauty parlor.

beau'ti·ful (-tə fəl) *adj.* having beauty. —**beau'ti·ful·ly,** *adv.*

beau'ti·fy' (-fī') *v.,* **-fied, -fying.** make beautiful.

beau'ty, *n., pl.* **-ties. 1.** quality that excites admiration. **2.** beautiful thing or person.

beauty parlor, salon for women's haircuts and styling.

bea'ver (bē'vər) *n.* **1.** amphibious rodent. **2.** its fur.

be·cause' (bi kôz', -koz', -kuz') *conj.* **1.** for the reason that. —*adv.* **2.** by reason (of).

beck (bek) *n.* beckoning gesture.

beck'on (-ən) *v.* signal by gesture.

be·cloud' (bi kloud') *v.* **1.** obscure with clouds. **2.** confuse.

be·come' (bi kum') *v.,* **became** (-kām'), **become, becoming. 1.** come to be. **2.** suit. —**be·com'ing,** *adj.*

bed (bed) *n.* **1.** piece of furniture on or in which a person sleeps. **2.** sleep. **3.** piece of ground for planting. **4.** foundation. —**bed'time',** *n.*

bed'bug', *n.* bloodsucking insect.

bed'ding, *n.* blankets, sheets, etc., for a bed.

be·dev'il (bi dev'əl) *v.,* **-iled, -iling. 1.** torment maliciously. **2.** confuse; confound.

bed'lam (bed'ləm) *n.* **1.** scene of loud confusion. **2.** lunatic asylum.

Bed'ou·in (bed'ōō in) *n.* **1.** desert Arab. **2.** nomad.

bed'pan', *n.* shallow pan used as toilet for bedridden person.

be·drag'gled (bi drag'əld) *adj.* soiled and wet.

bed'rid·den, *adj.* confined to bed.

bed'rock', *n.* **1.** continuous solid rock under soil. **2.** firm foundation.

bed'room', *n.* sleeping room.

bed'sore', *n.* skin ulcer caused by long confinement in bed.

bed'spread', *n.* cover for bed.

bed'stead' (-sted', -stid) *n.* frame for bed.

bee (bē) *n.* **1.** four-winged, nectar-

gathering insect. **2.** local gathering. —**bee'hive',** *n.* —**bee'keep'er,** *n.*

beech (bēch) *n.* tree bearing small edible nuts (**beech'nuts'**).

beef (bēf) *n., pl.* **beeves. 1.** bull, cow, or steer. **2.** edible flesh of such an animal. **3.** brawn. —**beef'steak',** *n.*

bee'line', *n.* direct course.

beep (bēp) *n.* **1.** short tone, usu. high in pitch, as from electronic device. —*v.* **2.** make a beep.

beep'er, *n.* small electronic device whose signal notifies person carrying it of telephone message.

beer (bēr) *n.* beverage brewed and fermented from cereals.

beet (bēt) *n.* plant with edible root.

bee'tle (bēt'l) *n., v.,* **-tled, -tling,** —*v.* **1.** project. —*n.* **2.** insect with hard, horny forewings.

be·fall' (bi fôl') *v.,* **-fell, -fallen, -falling.** happen; happen to.

be·fit' (bi fit') *v.,* **-fitted, -fitting.** be fitting for. —**be·fit'ting,** *adj.*

be·fore' (bi fôr') *adv.* **1.** in front. **2.** earlier. —*prep.* **3.** in front of. **4.** previously to. **5.** in preference to. **6.** in precedence of. **7.** in presence of. —*conj.* **8.** previously to time when.

be·fore'hand', *adv.* in advance; ahead of time.

be·friend' (bi frend') *v.* act as friend toward.

be·fud'dle (bi fud'l) *v.,* **-dled, -dling.** confuse thoroughly.

beg (beg) *v.,* **begged, begging. 1.** ask for charity. **2.** ask humbly.

be·get' (bi get') *v.,* **begot** (bi got'), **begotten** or **begot, begetting.** procreate. —**be·get'ter,** *n.*

beg'gar (beg'ər) *n.* **1.** one who begs alms. **2.** penniless person. —*v.* **3.** reduce to poverty.

beg'gar·ly, *adj.* very poor.

be·gin' (bi gin') *v.,* **-gan** (-gan'), **-gun** (-gun'), **beginning. 1.** start. **2.** originate. —**be·gin'ner,** *n.* —**be·gin'ning,** *n.*

be·gone' (bi gôn') *interj.* (depart!)

be·gon'ia (bi gōn'yə) *n.* tropical flowering plant.

be·grudge' (bi gruj') *v.,* **-grudged, begrudging. 1.** envy the good fortune or pleasure of. **2.** give or allow reluctantly.

be·guile' (bi gīl') *v.,* **-guiled, -guiling. 1.** delude. **2.** charm; divert.

be·half' (bi haf') *n.* **1.** side; part. **2.** interest; favor.

be·have' (bi hāv') *v.,* **-haved, -having. 1.** conduct oneself. **2.** act properly.

be·hav'ior (-yər) *n.* manner of behaving.

be·head' (bi hed') *v.* cut off the head of.

be·hest' (bi hest') *n.* urgent request.

be·hind' (bi hīnd') *prep.* **1.** at the back of. **2.** later than. —*adv.* **3.** at the back. **4.** in arrears. —*n.* **5.** *Informal.* buttocks.

be·hold' (bi hōld') *v.,* **beheld, beholding,** *interj.* —*v.* **1.** look at; see. —*interj.* **2.** look! —**be·hold'er,** *n.*

be·hold'en, *adj.* obliged.

be·hoove' (bi hōōv') *v.,* **-hooved, -hooving.** be necessary for (someone).

beige (bāzh) *n.* light brown.

be'ing (bē'ing) *n.* **1.** existence. **2.** something that exists.

be·la'bor (bi lā'bər) *v.* **1.** discuss, etc., excessively. **2.** beat.

be·lat'ed (bi lā'tid) *adj.* late.

belch (belch) *v.* **1.** eject gas from stomach. **2.** emit violently. —*n.* **3.** act of belching.

be·lea'guer (bi lē'gər) *v.* beset with difficulties.

bel'fry (bel'frē) *n., pl.* **-fries.** bell tower.

be·lie' (bi lī') *v.,* **-lied, belying. 1.** misrepresent. **2.** show to be false.

be·lief' (bi lēf') *n.* **1.** thing believed. **2.** conviction. **3.** faith.

be·lieve' (bi lēv') *v.,* **-lieved, -lieving. 1.** trust. **2.** accept as true. **3.** regard as likely. —**be·liev'a·ble,** *adj.* —**be·liev'er,** *n.*

be·lit'tle (bi lit'l) *v.,* **-littled, -littling.** disparage.

bell (bel) *n.* **1.** metal instrument producing ringing sound. —*v.* **2.** put bell on. **3.** flare outward.

bel'la·don'na (bel'ə don'ə) *n.* poisonous plant yielding medicinal drug.

belle (bel) *n.* beautiful woman.

bell'hop', *n.* person who carries luggage and runs errands in a hotel. Also, **bell'boy'.**

bel'li·cose (bel'i kōs') *adj.* warlike.

bel·lig'er·ent (bə lij'ər ənt) *adj.* **1.** warlike. **2.** engaged in war. —*n.* **3.** nation at war. —**bel·lig'er·ence.** *n.* —**bel·lig'er·ent·ly,** *adv.*

bel'low (bel'ō) *v.* **1.** roar, as a bull. **2.** utter in deep, loud voice. —*n.* **3.** act or sound of bellowing.

bel'lows (bel'ōz, -əz) *n.sing. and pl.* collapsing device producing strong current of air.

bell pepper, plant yielding a mild, bell-shaped pepper.

bell'weth'er (bel'weth'ər) *n.* one that leads or marks a trend.

bel'ly (bel'ē) *n., pl.* **-lies,** *v.,* **-lied, -lying.** —*n.* **1.** abdomen. —*v.* **2.** swell out.

bel'ly·ache', *n., v.,* **-ached, -aching.** —*n.* **1.** pain in the abdomen. —*v.* **2.** *Informal.* complain.

be·long' (bi lông') *v.* **1.** be a member of. **2.** belong to, be the property of.

be·long'ings, *n.pl.* possessions; effects.

be·lov'ed (bi luv'id, -luvd') *adj.* **1.** greatly loved. —*n.* **2.** object of love.

be·low' (bi lō') *adv.* **1.** beneath. **2.** in lower rank. —*prep.* **3.** lower than.

belt (belt) *n.* **1.** band for encircling waist. **2.** any flexible band. —*v.* **3.** put a belt around. **4.** hit hard.

belt'way', *n.* highway around perimeter of urban area.

be·moan' (bi mōn') *v.* lament.

be·mused' (bi myōōzd') *adj.* lost in thought; preoccupied.

bench (bench) *n.* **1.** long seat. **2.** judge's seat. **3.** body of judges. **4.** work table.

bench'mark', *n.* standard against which others can be measured.

bend (bend) *v.,* **bent, bending,** *n.* —*v.* **1.** curve. **2.** become curved. **3.** turn or incline. —*n.* **4.** a bending. **5.** something bent.

be·neath' (bi nēth') *adj.* **1.** in a lower place, state, etc. —*prep.* **2.** under. **3.** lower than. **4.** unworthy of.

ben·e·dic'tion (ben'i dik'shən) *n.* blessing.

ben'e·fac'tor (-fak'tər) *n.* one who gives financial help. —**ben'e·fac'tress,** *n.fem.*

be·nef'i·cent (bə nef'ə sənt) *adj.* doing good. —**be·nef'i·cence,** *n.*

ben·e·fi'cial (ben'ə fish'əl) *adj.* helpful. —**ben'e·fi'cial·ly,** *adv.*

ben'e·fi'ci·ar·y (-fish'ē er'ē, -fish'ə rē) *n., pl.* **-aries.** recipient of benefits or funds.

ben'e·fit (-fit) *n., v.,* **-fited, -fiting.** —*n.* **1.** advantage. **2.** money from insurance, etc. **3.** entertainment for worthy cause. —*v.* **4.** do good to. **5.** gain advantage.

be·nev·o·lent (bə nev′ə lənt) *adj.* kind and charitable. —**be·nev′o·lence,** *n.*

be·night′ed (bi nī′tid) *adj.* ignorant.

be·nign′ (bi nīn′) *adj.* **1.** kind. **2.** favorable. —**be·nign′ly,** *adv.*

be·nig′nant (-nig′nənt) *adj.* **1.** kind. **2.** beneficial.

bent (bent) *adj.* **1.** curved. **2.** determined. —*n.* **3.** inclination.

be·numb′ (bi num′) *v.* **1.** make numb. **2.** make inactive; stupefy.

ben′zene (ben′zēn, ben zēn′) *n.* inflammable liquid, used as solvent.

be·queath′ (bi kwēth′, -kwēth′) *v.* dispose of by will.

be·quest′ (bi kwest′) *n.* legacy.

be·rate′ (bi rāt′) *v.*, **-rated, -rating.** scold.

be·reaved′ (bi revd′) *adj.* suffering a loved one's death. —**be·reave′,** *v.* —**be·reave′ment,** *n.*

be·reft′ (-reft′) *adj.* deprived of something.

be·ret′ (bə rā′) *n.* cloth cap.

ber′i·ber′i (ber′ē ber′ē) *n.* disease caused by vitamin deficiency.

ber′ry (ber′ē) *n.*, *pl.* **-ries,** *v.*, **-ried, -rying.** —*n.* **1.** small juicy fruit. —*v.* **2.** produce or gather berries.

ber·serk′ (bər sûrk′, -zûrk′) *adj.* wild; frenzied.

berth (bûrth) *n.* **1.** sleeping space for traveler. **2.** mooring space for vessel. —*v.* **3.** provide with a berth.

ber′yl (ber′əl) *n.* green mineral.

be·seech′ (bi sēch′) *v.*, **-sought, -seeching.** implore; beg.

be·set′ (bi set′) *v.*, **-set, -setting. 1.** attack on all sides. **2.** surround.

be·side′ (bi sīd′) *prep.* **1.** at the side of. **2.** compared with. **3.** in addition to. —*adv.* **4.** in addition.

be·sides′, *adv.* **1.** moreover. **2.** otherwise. —*prep.* **3.** in addition to. **4.** other than.

be·siege′ (bi sēj′) *v.*, **-sieged, -sieging.** lay siege to.

be·smirch′ (bi smûrch′) *v.* defile.

be·sot′ted (bi sot′id) *adj.* **1.** drunk. **2.** infatuated.

be·speak′ (bi spēk′) *v.*, **-spoke** (-spōk), **-spoken** or **-spoke, -speaking. 1.** ask for in advance. **2.** imply.

best (best) *adj.* **1.** of highest quality. **2.** most suitable. —*adv.* **3.** most excellently. **4.** most fully. —*n.* **5.** best person or thing. —*v.* **6.** defeat.

bes′tial (bes′chəl, bēs′-) *adj.* **1.** beastlike. **2.** brutal.

be·stir′ (bi stûr′) *v.*, **-stirred, -stirring.** stir up.

best man, chief attendant of the bridegroom at a wedding.

be·stow′ (bi stō′) *v.* present.

be·strew′ (bi strōō′) *v.*, **-strewed, -strewed** or **-strewn, -strewing. 1.** cover. **2.** scatter.

bet (bet) *v.*, **bet** or **betted, betting,** *n.* —*v.* **1.** risk on a chance result. —*n.* **2.** thing or amount bet.

be·take′ (bi tāk′) *v.*, **-took** (-tōōk′), **-taken, -taking.** betake oneself, go.

bête′ noire′ (bāt′ nwär′, bet′) most dreaded person or thing.

be·tide′ (bi tīd′) *v.*, **-tided, -tiding.** happen to.

be·tray′ (bi trā′) *v.* **1.** expose by treachery. **2.** be unfaithful to. **3.** reveal. **4.** deceive. **5.** seduce. —**be·tray′al,** *n.* —**be·tray′er,** *n.*

be·troth′ (bi trōth′, -trôth′) *v.* promise to marry. —**be·troth′al,** *n.*

bet′ter (bet′ər) *adj.* **1.** of superior quality. **2.** healthier. —*adv.* **3.** in a more excellent way. **4.** more. —*n.* **5.** something or someone better. **6.** one's superior. —*v.* **7.** improve on.

be·tween′ (bi twēn′) *prep.* **1.** in the space separating. **2.** intermediate to. **3.** connecting. **4.** one or the other of. **5.** by the combined effect of. —*adv.* **6.** in the intervening space or time.
—**Usage.** Traditionally, BETWEEN is used to show relationship involving two people or things (*to decide between tea and coffee*), while AMONG expresses more than two (*The four brothers quarrelled among themselves*). BETWEEN, however, is also used to express relationship of persons or things considered individually, no matter how many: *Between holding public office, teaching, and raising a family, she has little free time.*

be·twixt′ (bi twikst′) *prep.*, *adv.* between.

bev′el (bev′əl) *n.*, *v.*, **-eled, -eling.** —*n.* **1.** surface cutting off a corner. —*v.* **2.** cut or slant at a bevel.

bev′er·age (bev′ər ij) *n.* drink.

bev′y (bev′ē) *n.*, *pl.* **bevies.** group.

be·wail′ (bi wāl′) *v.* lament.

be·ware′ (bi wâr′) *v.*, **-wared, -waring.** be wary (of).

be·wil′der (bi wil′dər) *v.* confuse or puzzle. —**be·wil′der·ment,** *n.*

be·witch′ (bi wich′) *v.* enchant. —**be·witch′ing,** *adj.*

be·yond′ (bē ond′) *prep.* **1.** on the farther side of. **2.** farther, more, or later on. —*adv.* **3.** farther on.

bi-, prefix meaning twice or two, as *bisect.*

bi·an′nu·al (bī an′yōō əl) *adj.* occurring twice a year. —**bi·an′nu·al·ly,** *adv.*

bi′as (bī′əs) *n.* **1.** slant. **2.** prejudice. **3.** prejudice.

bi·ath′lon (bī ath′lon) *n.* athletic contest comprising two consecutive events.

bib (bib) *n.* cloth to protect clothing while eating.

Bi′ble (bī′bəl) *n.* Old and New Testaments. —**Bib′li·cal** (bib′li kəl) *adj.* —**Bib′li·cal·ly,** *adv.*

bib′li·og′ra·phy (bib′lē og′rə fē) *n.*, *pl.* **-phies.** list of sources.

bi·cam′er·al (bī kam′ər əl) *adj.* composed of two legislative bodies.

bi·car′bo·nate of soda (bī kär′bə-nit, -nāt′) baking soda.

bi·cen·ten′ni·al, *n.* two-hundredth anniversary. Also, **bi·cen·ten′a·ry.**

bi′ceps (-seps) *n.* muscle of upper arm.

bick′er (bik′ər) *v.* squabble.

bi·cus′pid, *n.* tooth having two cusps or points.

bi′cy·cle (bī′si kəl) *n.*, *v.*, **-cled, -cling.** —*n.* **1.** two-wheeled vehicle. —*v.* **2.** ride a bicycle. —**bi′cy·clist,** *n.*

bid (bid) *v.*, **bade** (bad, bād) or **bid** (for **3**), **bidden** or **bid, bidding,** *n.* —*v.* **1.** command. **2.** say. **3.** offer. —*n.* **4.** offer. —**bid′der,** *n.*

bide (bīd) *v.*, **bided, biding. bide** one's time, await opportunity.

bi·det′ (bē dā′) *n.* tub for bathing genital areas.

bi·en′ni·al (bī en′ē əl) *adj.* occurring every two years. —**bi·en′ni·al·ly,** *adv.*

bier (bēr) *n.* stand for a coffin.

bi·fo′cal (bī fō′kəl, bī′fō′-) *adj.* **1.** having two focuses. **2.** (of eyeglass lens) having separate areas for near and far vision. —*n.* **3.** (*pl.*) eyeglasses with bifocal lenses.

big (big) *adj.*, **bigger, biggest. 1.** large. **2.** important. —**big′ness,** *n.*

big′a·my (big′ə mē) *n.*, *pl.* **-mies.** crime of marrying again while legally married. —**big′a·mist,** *n.*

big bang theory, theory that universe began with explosion of dense mass of matter and is still expanding.

big′horn′ (big′hôrn′) *n.* wild sheep of western U.S.

bight (bīt) *n.* **1.** loop of rope. **2.** deep bend in seashore.

big′ot (big′ət) *n.* bigoted person. —**big′ot·ry,** *n.*

big′ot·ed, *adj.* intolerant of another's creed, belief, or opinion.

big shot, *Informal.* important person.

bike (bīk) *n.* **1.** bicycle or motorcycle. —*v.* **2.** ride a bike. —**bik′er,** *n.*

bi·ki′ni (bi kē′nē) *n.* woman's brief two-piece bathing suit.

bi·lat′er·al (bī lat′ər əl) *adj.* on or affecting two sides.

bile (bīl) *n.* **1.** digestive secretion of the liver. **2.** ill nature.

bilge (bilj) *n.* lowest inner part of ship bottom.

bi·lin′gual (bī ling′gwəl) speaking or expressed in two languages.

bil′ious (bil′yəs) *adj.* **1.** pertaining to bile or excess bile. **2.** peevish.

bilk (bilk) *v.* cheat; defraud.

bill (bil) *n.* **1.** account of money owed. **2.** piece of paper money. **3.** draft of proposed statute. **4.** written list. **5.** horny part of bird's jaw. **6.** poster. —*v.* **7.** charge.

bill′board′, *n.* large outdoor advertising display panel.

bil′let (bil′it) *n.*, *v.*, **-leted, -leting.** —*n.* **1.** lodging for a soldier. —*v.* **2.** provide with lodging.

bil′let-doux′ (bil′ā dōō′) *n.*, *pl.* **billets-doux** (-dōōz′). love letter.

bill′fold′, *n.* wallet.

bil′liards (bil′yərdz) *n.* game played with hard balls on a table.

bil′lion (bil′yən) *n.* thousand million. —**bil′lionth,** *adj.*, *n.*

bil′lion·aire′ (-âr′) *n.* owner of a billion dollars or more.

bill of sale, document transferring personal property from seller to buyer.

bil′low (bil′ō) *n.* **1.** great wave. —*v.* **2.** surge. —**bil′low·y,** *adj.*

billy goat, male goat.

bim′bo (bim′bō) *n.*, *pl.* **-bos, -boes.** *Slang.* unintelligent young woman with loose morals.

bi·month′ly (bī munth′lē) *adv.*, *adj.* every two months.

bin (bin) *n.*, *v.*, **binned, binning.** —*n.* **1.** box for storing grain, coal, etc. —*v.* **2.** store in bin.

bi′na·ry (bī′nə rē) *adj.* **1.** involving two parts, choices, etc. **2.** of a numerical system in which each place of a number is expressed as 0 or 1.

bind (bīnd) *v.*, **bound, binding. 1.** tie or encircle with band. **2.** unite. **3.** oblige. **4.** attach cover to book.

bind′ing, *n.* **1.** something that binds. —*adj.* **2.** obligatory.

binge (binj) *n.*, *v.*, **binged, binging.** —*n.* **1.** bout of excessive indulgence, as in eating. —*v.* **2.** go on binge.

bin′go (bing′gō) *n.* game of chance using cards with numbered squares.

bin′na·cle (bin′ə kəl) *n.* stand for ship's compass.

bin·oc′u·lars (bə nok′yə lərz, bī-) *n.pl.* field glasses.

bio-, prefix meaning life or living organisms, as *biodegradable.*

bi·o·chem·is·try (bī′ō kem′ə strē) *n.*

chemistry of living matter. —**bi′o·chem′ist,** n.

bi·o·de·grad′a·ble, adj. decaying and being absorbed into environment.

bi′o·en′gi·neer′ing, n. 1. application of engineering principles to problems in biology and medicine. 2. application of biological principles to manufacturing or engineering processes.

bi′o·eth′ics, n. study of ethical implications of medical or biological procedures.

bi′o·feed′back′, n. method for achieving self-control through observation of one's brain waves, blood pressure, etc.

bi·og′ra·phy (bī og′rə fē) n., pl. **-phies.** written account of person's life. —**bi·og′ra·pher,** n. —**bi′o·graph′i·cal** (-ə graf′i kəl) adj.

bi′o·haz′ard, n. anything used in or produced in biological research that poses a health hazard.

biol., biology.

biological clock, 1. natural mechanism regulating bodily cycles. 2. this mechanism seen as the passage of one's child-bearing ability.

biological warfare, use of toxic organisms as weapons.

bi·ol′o·gy (bī ol′ə jē) n. science of living matter. —**bi′o·log′i·cal** (-ə loj′i-kəl) adj.—**bi·ol′o·gist,** n.

bi·on′ics (bī on′iks) n. use of electronic devices to increase human strength or ability. —**bi·on′ic,** adj.

bi′op·sy (bī′op sē) n., pl. **-sies.** examination of specimen of living tissue.

bi′o·rhythm (bī′ō-) n. natural, periodic bodily cycle, as sleeping and waking.

bi′o·sphere′ (bī′ə-) n. the part of the earth's surface and atmosphere that supports life.

bi′o·tech·nol′o·gy (bī′ō-) n. use of living organisms in making products or to manage the environment.

bi·par′ti·san (bī pär′tə zən) adj. representing two parties.

bi·par′tite (-pär′tīt) adj. 1. having two parts. 2. shared by two; joint.

bi′ped (-ped) n. 1. two-footed animal. —adj. 2. having two feet.

birch (bûrch) n. tree with light bark.

bird (bûrd) n. vertebrate with feathers and wings.

bird′ie, n. score of one under par on a golf hole.

bird′s′-eye′ (bûrdz′ī′) adj. seen from above.

birth (bûrth) n. 1. fact of being born. 2. lineage. 3. origin. —**birth′day′,** n. —**birth′place′,** n.

birth control, contraception.

birth′mark′, n. blemish on the skin at birth.

birth′rate′, n. number of births in given time and place.

birth′right′, n. hereditary right.

bis′cuit (bis′kit) n. small, soft, raised bread.

bi·sect′ (bī sekt′) v. cut into two parts. —**bi·sec′tion,** n.

bi·sex′u·al, adj. 1. being both heterosexual and homosexual. —n. 2. bisexual person. —**bi·sex′u·al′i·ty,** n.

bish′op (bish′əp) n. 1. overseer of a diocese. 2. piece in chess.

bish′op·ric (-rik) n. diocese or office of bishop.

bi′son (bī′sən) n., pl. **bisons, bison.** oxlike mammal.

bis′tro (bis′trō, bē′strō) n. French café.

bit (bit) n., v., **bitted, bitting.** —n. 1. mouthpiece of bridle. 2. small amount.

3. drill. 4. unit of computer information. —v. 5. restrain with a bit.

bitch (bich) n. 1. female dog. 2. Slang. mean woman. —v. 3. Slang. complain.

bite (bīt) v., **bit, bitten** or **bit, biting,** n. —v. 1. cut or grip with teeth. 2. sting. 3. corrode. —n. 4. act of biting. 5. wound made by biting. 6. sting. 7. piece bitten off.

bit′ing, adj. 1. harsh to the senses. 2. severely critical. —**bit′ing·ly,** adv.

bit′ter (bit′ər) adj. 1. of harsh taste. 2. hard to bear. 3. intensely hostile. —n. 4. something bitter. —**bit′ter·ly,** adv. —**bit′ter·ness,** n.

bit′tern (bit′ərn) n. type of heron.

bit′ter·sweet′, adj. 1. tasting both bitter and sweet. 2. being both painful and pleasant.

bi·tu′men (bi tōō′mən, -tyōō′-) n. asphalt or asphaltlike substance.

bituminous coal, soft coal that burns with a yellow, smoky flame.

bi′valve′, n. mollusk with two shells hinged together.

biv·ou·ac′ (biv′ōō ak′) n., v., **-acked, -acking.** —n. 1. temporary resting or assembly place for troops. —v. 2. dispose or meet in bivouac.

bi·week′ly (bī-) adv., adj. 1. every two weeks. 2. twice a week.

bi·zarre′ (bi zär′) adj. strange.

blab (blab) v., **blabbed, blabbing.** 1. talk idly. 2. reveal secrets.

black (blak) adj. 1. without brightness or color. 2. having dark skin color. 3. without light. 4. gloomy. 5. wicked. —n. 6. member of a dark-skinned people, esp. of Africa or African ancestry. 7. black clothing. 8. something black. —v. 9. make or become black.

black′-and-blue′, adj. discolored, as by bruising.

black′ball′, n. 1. adverse vote. —v. 2. ostracize.

black′ber′ry, n., pl. **-ries.** 1. dark-purple fruit. 2. plant bearing it.

black′bird′, n. black-feathered American bird.

black′board′, n. dark board for writing on with chalk.

black′en, v. 1. black (def. 9). 2. defame.

black′guard (blag′ärd, -ərd) n. despicable person.

black′head′, n. (blak′-) n. small dark fatty mass in a skin follicle.

black hole, area in outer space whose great density prevents radiation of light.

black′jack′, n. 1. short flexible club. 2. game of cards; twenty-one. —v. 3. strike with a blackjack.

black′list′, n. list of persons in disfavor. —**black′list′,** v.

black magic, sorcery.

black′mail′, n. 1. extortion by intimidation. —v. 2. extort by blackmail. —**black′mail′·er,** n.

black market, illegal buying and selling of goods in violation of laws.

black′out′, n. 1. extinction of lights. 2. loss of consciousness.

black sheep, person who causes embarrassment or shame to his or her family.

black′smith′, n. person who shoes horses or forges iron objects.

black′thorn′, n. thorny shrub with plumlike fruit.

black′top′, n., v., **-topped, -topping.** —n. 1. bituminous paving substance, as asphalt. —v. 2. pave with blacktop.

black widow, poisonous spider.

blad′der (blad′ər) n. sac in body holding urine.

blade (blād) n. 1. cutting part of knife,

sword, etc. 2. leaf. 3. thin, flat part. 4. dashing young man.

blame (blām) v., **blamed, blaming,** n. —v. 1. hold responsible for fault. 2. find fault with. —n. 3. censure. —**blame′less,** adj.

blanch (blanch) v. whiten.

bland (bland) adj. 1. not harsh. 2. not flavorful. —**bland′ly,** adv.

blan′dish·ment (blan′dish mənt) n. coaxing.

blank (blangk) adj. 1. not written on. 2. without interest or emotion. 3. white. 4. unrhymed. —n. 5. place lacking something. 6. space to be filled in. 7. paper with such space. —v. 8. make blank. —**blank′ly,** adv. —**blank′ness,** n.

blan′ket (blang′kit) n. 1. warm bed covering. —v. 2. cover.

blare (blâr) v., **blared, blaring,** n. —v. 1. sound loudly. —n. 2. loud, raucous noise.

blar′ney (blär′nē) n. 1. flattery. —v. 2. flatter.

bla·sé′ (blä zā′) adj. bored; unimpressed.

blas·pheme′ (blas fēm′) v. speak impiously or evilly. —**blas′phe·mous** (blas′fə məs) adj. —**blas′phe·my,** n.

blast (blast) n. 1. gust of wind. 2. loud trumpet tone. 3. explosion. 4. charge of explosive. —v. 5. blow. 6. blight; destroy. 7. explode.

blast furnace, forced-air furnace for smelting iron ore.

blast′off′, n. rocket launching.

bla′tant (blāt′nt) adj. brazenly obvious. —**bla′tan·cy,** n.

blaze (blāz) n., v., **blazed, blazing.** —n. 1. bright flame. 2. bright glow. 3. brightness. 4. mark cut on tree. 5. white spot on animal's face. —v. 6. burn or shine brightly. 7. mark with blazes (def. 4).

blaz′er, n. sports jacket.

bldg., building.

bleach (blēch) v. 1. whiten. —n. 2. bleaching agent.

bleach′ers, n.pl. tiers of spectators' seats.

bleak (blēk) adj. 1. bare. 2. cold. 3. dreary; depressing. —**bleak′ly,** adv. —**bleak′ness,** n.

blear′y (blēr′ē) adj. unclear.

bleat (blēt) v. 1. cry, as sheep, goat, etc. —n. 2. such a cry.

bleed (blēd) v., **bled** (bled), **bleeding.** lose or cause to lose blood.

bleep (blēp) v. delete (sound, esp. speech) from a broadcast.

blem′ish (blem′ish) v. 1. mar. —n. 2. defect.

blend (blend) v. 1. mix. —n. 2. mixture.

blend′er, n. electric appliance that purées or mixes food.

bless (bles) v., **blessed** or **blest, blessing.** 1. consecrate. 2. request divine favor on. 3. extol as holy. —**bless′ing,** n.

blight (blīt) n. 1. plant disease. 2. ruin. —v. 3. wither. 4. ruin.

blimp (blimp) n. small nonrigid airship.

blind (blīnd) adj. 1. sightless. 2. uncomprehending. 3. hidden. 4. without an outlet. 5. without advance knowledge. —v. 6. make blind. —n. 7. window covering. 8. ruse or disguise. —**blind′ly,** adv.

blind date, arranged date between two strangers.

blind′fold′, v. 1. cover eyes. —n. 2. covering over eyes. —adj. 3. with covered eyes.

blind′side′, *v.,* **-sided, -siding.** hit someone unawares.

blink (blingk) *v.* **1.** wink. —*n.* **2.** act of blinking. **3.** gleam.

blip (blip) *n.* **1.** point of light on radar screen, indicating an object. **2.** brief interruption or upward turn in a continuity.

bliss (blis) *n.* **1.** gladness. **2.** supreme happiness. —**bliss′ful,** *adj.*

blis′ter (blis′tər) *n.* **1.** swelling on the skin containing watery liquid. —*v.* **2.** raise blisters on.

blithe (blīth, blīth) *adj.* joyous; cheerful. —**blithe′ly,** *adv.*

blitz (blits) *n.* Also, **blitz′krieg′** (-krēg′). **1.** swift, violent war, waged by surprise. **2.** attack by blitz.

bliz′zard (bliz′ərd) *n.* severe snowstorm.

bloat (blōt) *v.* swell.

blob (blob) *n.* **1.** small lump or drop. **2.** shapeless mass.

bloc (blok) *n.* political or economic confederation.

block (blok) *n.* **1.** solid mass. **2.** platform. **3.** obstacle. **4.** single quantity. **5.** unit of city street pattern. —*v.* **6.** obstruct. **7.** outline roughly. —**block′er,** *n.*

block•ade′ (blo kād′) *n., v.,* **-aded, -ading.** —*n.* **1.** shutting-up of place by armed force. **2.** obstruction. —*v.* **3.** subject to blockade.

block′age, *n.* obstruction.

block′bust′er, *n.* highly successful movie, novel, etc.

block′head′, *n.* stupid person.

blond (blond) *adj.* **1.** light-colored. **2.** having light-colored hair, skin, etc. —*n.* **3.** blond person. —**blonde,** *adj., n.fem.*

blood (blud) *n.* **1.** red fluid in arteries and veins. **2.** bloodshed. **3.** extraction. —**blood′y,** *adj.*

blood count, number of red and white blood cells in specific volume of blood.

blood′cur′dling, *adj.* causing terror or horror.

blood′hound′, *n.* large dog with acute sense of smell.

blood′mo•bile′ (-mə bēl′) *n.* truck for receiving blood donations.

blood pressure, pressure of blood against inner walls of blood vessels.

blood′shed′, *n.* slaughter.

blood′shot′, *adj.* with eye veins conspicuous.

blood′stream′, *n.* blood flowing through the body's circulatory system.

blood′suck′er, *n.* **1.** leech. **2.** extortionist.

blood′thirst′y, *adj.* murderous.

blood vessel, artery, vein, or capillary.

bloom (blōōm) *n.* **1.** flower. **2.** healthy glow. —*v.* **3.** blossom. **4.** flourish. —**bloom′ing,** *adj.*

bloom′ers (blōō′mərz) *n.pl.* short loose trousers formerly worn as underwear by women.

bloop′er (blōō′pər) *n.* embarrassing mistake.

blos′som (blos′əm) *n.* **1.** flower. —*v.* **2.** produce blossoms. **3.** develop.

blot (blot) *n., v.,* **blotted, blotting.** —*n.* **1.** stain. —*v.* **2.** spot. **3.** dry with absorbent material.

blotch (bloch) *n.* **1.** large spot. —*v.* **2.** stain; spot. —**blotch′y,** *adj.*

blot′ter, *n.* piece of paper for blotting.

blouse (blous, blouz) *n.* women's upper garment.

blow (blō) *v.,* **blew** (blōō), **blown,**

blowing, *n.* —*v.* **1.** (of air) move. **2.** drive by current of air. **3.** sound a wind instrument. **4.** shape by blowing. **5.** explode. **6.** *Informal.* bungle. —*n.* **7.** blast of air. **8.** sudden stroke. **9.** sudden shock, calamity, etc.

blow′-by-blow′, *adj.* detailed.

blow′out′, *n.* rupture of tire.

blow′torch′, *n.* device producing hot flame.

blow′up′, *n.* **1.** explosion. **2.** *Informal.* emotional outbreak. **3.** photographic enlargement.

blub′ber (blub′ər) *n.* **1.** fat of whales. —*v.* **2.** weep.

bludg′eon (bluj′ən) *n.* **1.** heavy club. —*v.* **2.** strike with a bludgeon.

blue (blōō) *n., adj.,* **bluer, bluest,** *v.,* **blued, bluing** or **blueing.** —*n.* **1.** color of sky. —*adj.* **2.** (of skin) discolored by cold, etc. **3.** melancholy. —*v.* **4.** make blue.

blue′ber′ry, *n., pl.* **-ries.** edible berry, usually bluish.

blue′bird′, *n.* small, blue North American bird.

blue blood, aristocrat.

blue chip′, high-priced stock yielding regular dividends.

blue′-col′lar, *adj.* of or designating manual laborers.

blue′jay′, *n.* crested North American jay.

blue jeans, trousers of blue denim.

blue law, law against certain practices, as business, on Sunday.

blue′print′, *n.* **1.** white-on-blue photocopy of line drawing. **2.** plan of action.

blue ribbon, highest award.

blues, *n.pl.* **1.** melancholy. **2.** melancholy genre of jazz.

bluff (bluf) *v.* **1.** mislead by show of boldness. —*n.* **2.** act of bluffing. **3.** steep cliff or hill. —*adj.* **4.** vigorously frank. —**bluff′er,** *n.*

blu′ing, *n.* bleaching agent. Also, **blue′ing.**

blun′der (blun′dər) *n.* **1.** mistake. —*v.* **2.** err. **3.** move blindly.

blunt (blunt) *adj.* **1.** having a dull edge or point. **2.** abrupt in manner. —*v.* **3.** make blunt. —**blunt′ly,** *adv.*

blur (blûr) *v.,* **blurred, blurring.** —*v.* **1.** obscure. **2.** make or become indistinct. —*n.* **3.** smudge. —**blur′ry,** *adj.*

blurb (blûrb) *n.* brief advertisement.

blurt (blûrt) *v.* utter suddenly.

blush (blush) *v.* **1.** redden. **2.** feel shame. **3.** reddening. **4.** reddish tinge.

blush′er, *n.* cosmetic used to color cheeks.

blus′ter (blus′tər) *v.* **1.** blow violently. **2.** be noisy or swaggering. —*n.* **3.** tumult. **4.** noisy talk.

blvd., boulevard.

bo′a (bō′ə) *n.* **1.** large snake. **2.** long scarf of silk or feathers.

boar (bôr) *n.* male of swine.

board (bôrd) *n.* **1.** thin flat piece of timber. **2.** daily meals. **3.** official controlling body. **4.** cover with boards. **5.** furnish with food. **6.** take meals. **7.** enter (a ship, train, etc.). —**board′er,** *n.*

board′ing•house′, *n.* house where one can get room and board for payment.

board′walk′, *n.* wooden walk along beach.

boast (bōst) *v.* **1.** speak with pride; be proud of. —*n.* **2.** thing boasted.

boat (bōt) *n.* **1.** vessel. —*v.* **2.** go or move in boat. —**boat′house′,** *n.* —**boat′man,** *n.* —**boat′ing,** *n.*

boat′swain (bō′sən) *n.* petty officer on ship.

bob (bob) *n., v.,* **bobbed, bobbing.** —*n.* **1.** short jerky motion. **2.** short haircut. —*v.* **3.** move jerkily. **4.** cut short. —**bob′ber,** *n.*

bob′bin (bob′in) *n.* reel; spool.

bob′by pin, flat metal hairpin.

bob′cat′, *n., pl.* **-cats, -cat.** North American lynx.

bob′o•link′ (-ə lingk′) *n.* meadowdwelling songbird.

bob′sled′, *n., v.,* **-sledded, -sledding.** —*n.* **1.** long sled with two pairs of runners and a steering mechanism. —*v.* **2.** ride on a bobsled.

bob′tail′, *n.* **1.** short tail. —*v.* **2.** cut short.

bob′white′, *n.* North American quail.

bode (bōd) *v.,* **boded, boding.** portend.

bod′ice (bod′is) *n.* top part of dress.

bod′y (bod′ē) *n., pl.* **bodies. 1.** animal's physical structure. **2.** corpse. **3.** main mass. **4.** collective group.

bod′y•guard′, *n.* guard for personal safety.

body language, communication through gestures or attitudes.

body piercing, piercing of a body part, as the navel, to insert ornamental ring or stud.

bog (bog) *n., v.,* **bogged, bogging.** —*n.* **1.** swampy ground. —*v.* **2.** sink or catch in a bog. —**bog′gy,** *adj.*

bog′gle (bog′əl) *v.,* **-gled, -gling.** overwhelm or bewilder.

bo′gus (bō′gəs) *adj.* fake.

bo′gy (bō′gē, bōōg′ē, bōō′gē) *n., pl.* **-gies.** hobgoblin. Also, **bo′gey, bo′gie.**

bo•he′mi•an (bō hē′mē ən) *n.* **1.** person who leads an unconventional life. —*adj.* **2.** unconventional.

boil (boil) *v.* **1.** heat to bubbling point. **2.** be agitated. **3.** cook by boiling. —*n.* **4.** act or state of boiling. **5.** inflamed sore. —**boil′er,** *n.*

bois′ter•ous (boi′stər əs) *adj.* rough; noisy.

bok′ choy′ (bok′ choy′) Asian plant whose leaves are used as a vegetable. Also, **bok′-choy′.**

bold (bōld) *adj.* **1.** fearless. **2.** conspicuous. —**bold′ly,** *adv.*

bo•le′ro (bə lâr′ō, bō-) *n., pl.* **-ros. 1.** lively Spanish dance. **2.** waist-length, open vest.

boll (bōl) *n.* rounded seed pod.

boll weevil, beetle that attacks bolls of cotton.

bo•lo′gna (bə lō′nē) *n.* beef and pork sausage.

Bol′she•vik (bōl′shə vik) *n., pl.* **-viks, -viki.** Russian communist. Also, **Bol′she•vist** (-vi₊t).

bol′ster (bōl′stər) *n.* **1.** long pillow. —*v.* **2.** support.

bolt (bōlt) *n.* **1.** bar fastening a door. **2.** similar part in a lock. **3.** threaded metal pin. **4.** sudden flight. **5.** roll of cloth. **6.** thunderbolt. —*v.* **7.** fasten. **8.** swallow hurriedly. **9.** move or leave suddenly. **10.** sift.

bomb (bom) *n.* **1.** projectile with explosive charge. **2.** *Slang.* total failure. —*v.* **3.** attack with bombs. **4.** *Slang.* fail totally. —**bomb′proof′,** *adj.*

bom•bard′ (bom bärd′) *v.* **1.** attack with artillery or bombs. **2.** assail vigorously. —**bom′bar•dier′** (-bər dēr′) *n.* —**bom•bard′ment,** *n.*

bom′bast (bom′bast) *n.* pompous words. —**bom•bas′tic, bom•bas′ti•cal,** *adj.*

bomb′er (bom′ər) *n.* **1.** airplane that

drops bombs. **2.** one who plants bombs.

bomb/shell/, *n.* something or someone having a sensational effect.

bo/na fide/ (bō′nə fīd′) real.

bo·nan/za (bə nan′zə) *n.* **1.** rich mass of ore. **2.** good luck.

bon/bon/ (bon′bon′) *n.* piece of candy.

bond (bond) *n.* **1.** something that binds or unites. **2.** bondsman. **3.** written contractual obligation. **4.** certificate held by creditor. —*v.* **5.** put on or under bond. **6.** mortgage.

bond/age (bon′dij) *n.* slavery.

bond/man, *n., pl.* **-men.** male slave. Also, **bond/wom/an,** *n.fem.*

bonds/man, *n., pl.* **-men.** person who gives surety for another.

bone (bōn) *n., v.,* **boned, boning.** —*n.* **1.** piece of the skeleton. **2.** hard substance composing it. —*v.* **3.** remove bones of. —**bon/y,** *adj.*

bon/er (bō′nər) *n. Slang.* stupid mistake.

bon/fire/ (bon′-) *n.* outdoor fire.

bon/go (bong′gō) *n., pl.* **-gos, -goes.** small hand drum.

bon/kers (bong′kərz) *adj. Slang.* crazy.

bon/net (bon′it) *n.* hat formerly worn by women or children.

bo/nus (bō′nəs) *n.* extra payment.

boo (bōō) *interj.* (exclamation used to frighten or express contempt.)

boo/-boo/, *n. Slang.* **1.** stupid mistake. **2.** minor injury.

boo/by (bōō′bē) *n., pl.* **-bies.** *Informal.* fool. Also, **boob.**

booby prize, prize given to worst player in contest.

booby trap, trap set for unsuspecting person.

book (bōōk) *n.* **1.** printed or blank sheets bound together. **2.** *(pl.)* accounts. **3.** division of literary work. —*v.* **4.** enter in book. **5.** engage beforehand. —**book/bind/er,** *n.* —**book/case/,** *n.* —**book/keep/er,** *n.* —**book/let,** *n.* —**book/sell/er,** *n.* —**book/store/, book/shop/,** *n.*

book/end/, *n.* prop for books.

book/ie, *n.* bookmaker.

book/ing, *n.* engagement of professional entertainer.

book/ish, *adj.* fond of reading.

book/mak/er, *n.* one who takes bets.

book/mark/, *n.* something for marking one's place in a book.

book/worm/, *n.* person who likes reading.

boom (bōōm) *v.* **1.** make a loud hollow sound. **2.** flourish vigorously. —*n.* **3.** loud hollow sound. **4.** rapid development. **5.** spar extending sail. **6.** beam on derrick.

boom/er·ang/ (bōō′mə rang′) *n.* **1.** Australian stick that returns when thrown. —*v.* **2.** cause harm to the originator; backfire.

boon (bōōn) *n.* benefit.

boon/docks/, *n.pl.* **1.** backwoods. **2.** remote rural area.

boon/dog/gle (-dog′əl) *n. Informal.* useless work paid for with public money.

boor (bōōr) *n.* unmannerly, rude person. —**boor/ish,** *adj.*

boost (bōōst) *v.* **1.** lift by pushing. **2.** praise; advocate. **3.** increase. —*n.* **4.** upward push. **5.** assistance.

boot (bōōt) *n.* **1.** covering for foot and leg. **2.** kick. —*v.* **3.** kick.

booth (bōōth) *n.* **1.** light structure for exhibiting goods, etc. **2.** small compartment.

boot/leg/, *n., v.,* **-legged, -legging,** *adj.* —*n.* **1.** illicit liquor. —*v.* **2.** deal in illicit goods. —*adj.* **3.** illicit. —**boot/leg/ger,** *n.*

boot/less, *adj.* futile; useless.

boo/ty (bōō′tē) *n., pl.* **-ties.** plunder.

booze (bōōz) *n., v.,* **boozed, boozing.** *Informal.* —*n.* **1.** liquor. —*v.* **2.** drink liquor excessively.

bop (bop) *v.,* **bopped, bopping,** *n. Slang.* —*v.* **1.** hit. —*n.* **2.** a blow.

bo/rax (bôr′aks) *n.* white crystalline substance used as cleanser, in glassmaking, etc.

bor·del/lo (bôr del′ō) *n.* brothel.

bor/der (bôr′dər) *n.* **1.** edge; margin. **2.** frontier. —*v.* **3.** make a border. **4.** adjoin. —**bor/der·line/,** *n.*

bore (bôr) *v.,* **bored, boring,** *n.* —*v.* **1.** drill into. **2.** be uninteresting to. —*n.* **3.** bored hole. **4.** inside diameter. **5.** dull person. —**bore/dom,** *n.*

born (bôrn) *adj.* brought forth from the womb by birth.

born/-a·gain/, *adj.* recommitted to faith through an intensely religious experience.

bor/ough (bûr′ō, bur′ō) *n.* **1.** small incorporated municipality. **2.** division of city.

bor/row (bor′ō) *v.* **1.** take or obtain on loan. **2.** adopt. —**Usage.** Do not confuse BORROW and LEND. One way to keep the meanings distinct is to think of BORROW as "take," while LEND is "give." So you can *borrow* something you don't have, and you can *lend* something you do have.

bos/om (bōōz′əm, bōō′zəm) *n.* **1.** breast. —*adj.* **2.** intimate. —**bos/om·y,** *adj.*

boss (bôs) *n.* **1.** employer. **2.** powerful politician. —*v.* **3.** control; manage. **4.** be domineering. —**boss/y,** *adj.*

bot/a·ny (bot′n ē) *n.* science of plant life. —**bo·tan/i·cal** (bə tan′i kəl) *adj.* —**bot/a·nist,** *n.*

botch (boch) *v.* **1.** bungle. **2.** do clumsily. —*n.* **3.** botched work.

both (bōth) *adj., pron.* **1.** the two. —*conj., adv.* **2.** alike.

both/er (both′ər) *v.* **1.** annoy. **2.** trouble or inconvenience (oneself). —*n.* **3.** annoying or troublesome thing. —**both/er·some,** *adj.*

bot/tle (bot′l) *n., v.,* **-tled, -tling.** —*n.* **1.** sealed container for liquids. —*v.* **2.** put into bottle.

bot/tle·neck/, *n.* **1.** narrow passage. **2.** place of impeded progress.

bot/tom (bot′əm) *n.* **1.** lowest or deepest part. **2.** underside. **3.** lowest rank. —*v.* **4.** reach the lowest level.

bot/tom·less, *adj.* **1.** without bottom. **2.** without limit.

bottom line, basic or decisive point.

bot/u·lism/ (boch′ə liz′əm) *n.* disease caused by eating spoiled foods.

bou/doir (bōō′dwär, -dwôr) *n.* woman's bedroom.

bouf·fant/ (bōō fänt′) *adj.* puffed out, as a hairdo.

bough (bou) *n.* branch of tree.

bouil/lon (bōōl′yon, -yən, bōō′-) *n.* clear broth.

boul/der (bōl′dər) *n.* large rock.

boul/e·vard/ (bōōl′ə värd′) *n.* broad avenue.

bounce (bouns) *v.,* **bounced, bouncing,** *n.* —*v.* **1.** spring back. —*n.* **2.** act of bouncing. —**boun/ci·ness,** *n.* —**bounc/y,** *adj.*

bounc/ing, *adj.* healthy.

bound (bound) *adj.* **1.** in bonds. **2.** made into book. **3.** obligated. **4.** going toward. **5.** jump. **6.** limit. **7.** ad-

join. —*n.* **8.** jump. **9.** *(usually pl.)* boundary.

bound/a·ry (boun′də rē, -drē) *n., pl.* **-ries.** borderline; limit.

bound/less, *adj.* unlimited.

boun/te·ous (boun′tē əs) *adj.* generous. Also, **boun/ti·ful.**

boun/ty (boun′tē) *n., pl.* **-ties.** **1.** generosity. **2.** gift.

bou·quet/ (bō kā′, bōō-) *n.* **1.** bunch of flowers. **2.** aroma.

bour/bon (bûr′bən) *n.* corn whiskey.

bour·geois/ (bōōr zhwä′) *n., pl.* **-geois.** **1.** one of the middle class. —*adj.* **2.** of the middle class.

bour/geoi·sie/ (-zē′) *n.* middle class.

bout (bout) *n.* **1.** contest. **2.** attack.

bou·tique/ (bōō tēk′) *n.* small shop with fashionable items.

bo/vine (bō′vīn, -vēn) *adj.* oxlike or cowlike.

bow (bou, *for 1, 2, 3, 5, 9;* bō, *for 4, 6, 7, 8),* *v.* **1.** bend down. **2.** bend in worship, respect, etc. **3.** subdue. **4.** curve. —*n.* **5.** inclination of head or body. **6.** strip of bent wood for shooting arrow. **7.** looped knot. **8.** rod for playing violin. **9.** front of ship. —**bow/man,** *n.*

bow/el (bou′əl, boul) *n.* intestine. Also, **bow/els.**

bow/er (bou′ər) *n.* leafy shelter.

bowl (bōl) *n.* **1.** deep round dish. **2.** rounded hollow part. **3.** ball rolled at pins in various games. —*v.* **4.** roll a ball underhand. **5.** play bowling games. —**bowl/ing,** *n.*

bow/leg/ged (bō′leg′id) *adj.* having legs curved outward.

box (boks) *n.* **1.** receptacle of wood, metal, etc. **2.** compartment. **3.** blow with fist. **4.** Also, **box/wood/.** evergreen tree or shrub. —*v.* **5.** put into box. **6.** fight with fists. —**box/er,** *n.* —**box/ing,** *n.*

box/car/, *n.* completely enclosed railroad freight car.

box office, office at which tickets are sold.

boy (boi) *n.* male child. —**boy/hood,** *n.* —**boy/ish,** *adj.*

boy/cott/ (-kot) *v.* **1.** abstain from dealing with or using. —*n.* **2.** instance of boycotting.

boy/friend/, *n.* **1.** male sweetheart or lover. **2.** male friend.

Boy Scout, member of organization for boys **(Boy Scouts)** promoting self-reliance and service.

bra (brä) *n.* brassiere.

brace (brās) *n., v.,* **braced, bracing.** —*n.* **1.** stiffening device. **2.** pair. **3.** character, {or}, used to connect words or lines to be considered together. **4.** *(pl.)* device to straighten teeth. —*v.* **5.** fasten with brace. **6.** make steady. **7.** stimulate.

brace/let (brās′lit) *n.* ornamental band for the wrist.

brack/et (brak′it) *n.* **1.** armlike support for ledge. **2.** mark, [or], for enclosing parenthetical words. —*v.* **3.** place within brackets.

brack/ish (brak′ish) *adj.* salty.

brad (brad) *n.* small wire nail.

brag (brag) *v.,* **bragged, bragging,** *n.* boast. —**brag/gart** (-ərt) *n.*

braid (brād) *v.* **1.** weave together. —*n.* **2.** something braided.

braille (brāl) *n.* *(often cap.)* alphabet for the blind.

brain (brān) *n.* **1.** soft mass of nerves in cranium. **2.** intelligence. —*v.* **3.** dash out the brains.

brain death, complete ending of brain function, used as legal definition of death. —**brain/-dead,** *adj.*

brain drain, loss of trained professional personnel to another company, nation, etc.

brain′storm′, n. sudden idea.

brain′wash′, v. indoctrinate under stress. —**brain′wash′ing,** n.

braise (brāz) v., **braised, braising.** cook slowly in moisture.

brake (brāk) n., v., **braked, braking.** —n. **1.** device for stopping a vehicle. —v. **2.** slow or stop with a brake.

bram′ble (bram′bəl) n. prickly shrub. —**bram′bly,** adj.

bran (bran) n. husk of grain.

branch (branch) n. **1.** division of plant's stem. **2.** local office, store, etc. **3.** division of body, system, family, etc. —v. **4.** put forth or divide into branches.

brand (brand) n. **1.** kind; make. **2.** burned mark. **3.** burning piece of wood. —v. **4.** mark with a brand.

brand′ish (bran′dish) v. wave.

brand′-new′ (bran′-, brand′-) adj. extremely new.

bran′dy (bran′dē) n., pl. **-dies.** spirit from fermented grapes.

brash (brash) adj. **1.** impudent; tactless. **2.** rash; impetuous.

brass (bras) n. **1.** alloy of copper and zinc. **2.** musical instrument such as trumpet or horn. **3.** Informal. high-ranking officials. **4.** impudence. —**brass′y,** adj.

bras·siere′ (brə zēr′) n. undergarment supporting the breasts.

brass tacks, n.pl. basics.

brat (brat) n. spoiled or rude child.

brat′wurst′ (brat′wûrst, -vŏorst′, brät′-) n. pork sausage.

bra·va′do (brə vä′dō) n., pl. **-does, -dos.** boasting; swaggering.

brave (brāv) adj., **braver, bravest,** n., v., **braved, braving.** —adj. **1.** courageous. —n. **2.** North American Indian warrior. —v. **3.** meet courageously. **4.** defy. —**brave′ly,** adv. —**brave′ness, brav′er·y,** n.

bra′vo (brä′vō, brä vō′) interj. well done!

brawl (brôl) n. **1.** quarrel. —v. **2.** quarrel noisily. —**brawl′er,** n.

brawn (brôn) n. **1.** muscles. **2.** muscular strength. —**brawn′y,** adj.

bray (brā) n. **1.** cry of a donkey. —v. **2.** sound a bray.

bra′zen (brā′zən) adj. **1.** of or like brass. **2.** shameless; impudent. —v. **3.** face boldly. —**bra′zen·ness,** n.

bra′zier (brā′zhər) n. receptacle for burning charcoal.

Bra·zil′ nut (brə zil′) three-sided edible seed of South American tree.

breach (brēch) n. **1.** a breaking. **2.** gap. **3.** infraction; violation. **4.** break. —v. **5.** make breach.

bread (bred) n. **1.** food of baked dough. **2.** Slang. money. —v. **3.** cover with breadcrumbs.

bread′crumb′, n. (usually pl.) a crumb of bread.

breadth (bredth, bretth) n. width.

bread′win′ner, n. main money earner in family.

break (brāk) v., **broke** (brōk), **broken, breaking,** n. —v. **1.** separate into parts. **2.** violate; dissolve. **3.** fracture. **4.** interrupt. **5.** disclose. **6.** fail; disable. **7.** (pp. **broke**) ruin financially. **8.** tame. —n. **9.** forcible disruption or separation. **10.** gap. **11.** attempt to escape. **12.** brief rest. **13.** Informal. opportunity. —**break′a·ble,** adj.

break′down′, n. **1.** failure to operate. **2.** nervous crisis. **3.** analysis of figures.

break′er, n. wave breaking on land.

break′fast (brek′fəst) n. **1.** first meal of day. —v. **2.** eat breakfast.

break′-in′ (brāk′-) n. illegal forcible entry into home, office, etc.

break′neck′, adj. reckless or dangerous, esp. because of excessive speed.

break′through′, n. important discovery.

break′up′, n. **1.** dispersal or disintegration. **2.** ending of a personal relationship.

break′wa′ter, n. barrier against the force of waves.

breast (brest) n. **1.** chest. **2.** milk gland.

breast′bone′, n. sternum.

breast′stroke′, n. swimming stroke in which the arms move forward, outward, and rearward while the legs kick outward.

breath (breth) n. **1.** air inhaled and exhaled. **2.** ability to breathe. **3.** light breeze. —**breath′less,** adj.

breathe (brēth) v., **breathed, breathing. 1.** inhale and exhale. **2.** blow lightly. **3.** live. **4.** whisper.

breath′er (brē′thər) n. Informal. short rest.

breath′tak′ing (breth′-) adj. awesome or exciting.

breech′es (brich′iz) n.pl. trousers.

breed (brēd) v., **bred** (bred), **breeding,** n. —v. **1.** produce. **2.** raise. —n. **3.** related animals. **4.** lineage.

breed′ing, n. **1.** ancestry. **2.** training. **3.** manners.

breeze (brēz) n. light current of air. —**breez′y,** adj.

breeze′way′, n. open-sided roofed passageway joining two buildings.

breth′ren (breth′rin) n. a pl. of brother.

bre·vi·ar·y (brē′vē er′ē, brev′ē-) n., pl. **-aries.** book of daily prayers and readings.

brev′i·ty (brev′i tē) n. shortness.

brew (brōō) v. **1.** prepare beverage such as beer or ale. **2.** concoct. —n. **3.** quantity brewed. **4.** act or instance of brewing. —**brew′er,** n. —**brew′er·y,** n.

bri′ar (brī′ər) n. brier.

bribe (brīb) n., v., **bribed, bribing.** —n. **1.** gift made for corrupt performance of duty. —v. **2.** give or influence by bribe. —**brib′er·y,** n.

bric′-a-brac′ (brik′ə brak′) n. trinkets.

brick (brik) n. **1.** building block of baked clay. —v. **2.** fill or build with brick. —**brick′lay′er,** n. —**brick′lay′ing,** n.

brick′bat′, n. **1.** fragment of brick. **2.** caustic criticism.

bride (brīd) n. woman newly married or about to be married. —**brid′al,** adj.

bride′groom′, n. man newly married or about to be married.

brides′maid′, n. bride's wedding attendant.

bridge (brij) n., v., **bridged, bridging.** —n. **1.** structure spanning river, road, etc. **2.** card game for four players. **3.** artificial replacement for teeth. —v. **4.** span.

bridge′work′, n. dental bridges.

bri′dle (brīd′l) n., v., **-dled, -dling.** —n. **1.** harness at horse's head. **2.** anything that restrains. —v. **3.** put bridle on. **4.** restrain.

brief (brēf) adj. **1.** short. **2.** concise. —n. **3.** concise statement. **4.** outline of arguments and facts. —v. **5.** instruct in advance. —**brief′ly,** adv.

brief′case′, n. flat carrier for business papers, etc.

bri′er (brī′ər) n. **1.** prickly plant. **2.** plant with woody root.

brig (brig) n. **1.** two-masted square-rigged ship. **2.** ship's jail.

bri·gade′ (bri gād′) n. large military unit or body of troops.

brig·a·dier′ (brig′ə dēr′) n. military officer between colonel and major general. Also, **brigadier general.**

brig′and (brig′ənd) n. bandit.

bright (brīt) adj. **1.** shining. **2.** filled with light. **3.** brilliant. **4.** clever. —**bright′en,** v. —**bright′ly,** adv. —**bright′ness,** n.

bril′liant (bril′yənt) adj. **1.** sparkling. **2.** illustrious. **3.** highly intelligent. —n. **4.** brilliant diamond. —**bril′liant·ly,** adv. —**bril′liance,** n.

brim (brim) n., v., **brimmed, brimming.** —n. **1.** upper edge; rim. —v. **2.** fill or be full to brim. —**brim′ful,** adj.

brim′stone′, n. sulfur.

brin′dle (brin′dl) n. brindled coloring or animal.

brin′dled, adj. having dark streaks or spots.

brine (brīn) n., v., **brined, brining.** —n. **1.** salt water. **2.** sea. —v. **3.** treat with brine. —**brin′y,** adj.

bring (bring) v., **brought** (brôt), **bringing. 1.** fetch. **2.** cause to come. **3.** lead.

brink (bringk) n. edge.

bri·quette′ (bri ket′) n. small block of compressed coal dust or charcoal used as fuel. Also, **bri·quet′.**

brisk (brisk) adj. **1.** lively. **2.** stimulating. —**brisk′ly,** adv.

bris′ket (bris′kit) n. animal's breast.

bris′tle (bris′əl) n., v., **-tled, -tling.** —n. **1.** short, stiff, coarse hair. —v. **2.** rise stiffly. **3.** show indignation.

britch′es (brich′iz) n. (used with a pl. v.) breeches.

Brit′ish (brit′ish) adj. of Great Britain or its inhabitants.

British thermal unit, amount of heat needed to raise temperature of 1 lb. (0.4 kg) water 1°F. Abbr.: Btu, BTU

Brit′on (brit′n) n. native of Great Britain.

brit′tle (brit′l) adj. breaking readily.

broach (brōch) v. **1.** pierce. **2.** mention for first time.

broad (brôd) adj. **1.** wide. **2.** main. **3.** liberal. —**broad′ly,** adv.

broad′cast′, v., **-cast** or **-casted, -casting,** n. —v. **1.** send by radio or television. **2.** scatter widely. —n. **3.** something broadcasted. **4.** radio or television program. —**broad′cast′er,** n.

broad′cloth′, n. fine cotton material.

broad′en, v. widen.

broad jump, long jump.

broad′loom′, n. carpet woven on wide loom.

broad′-mind′ed, adj. tolerant.

broad′side′, n. **1.** simultaneous firing of all guns on one side of warship. **2.** verbal attack.

broad′-spec′trum, adj. (of antibiotics) effective against wide range of organisms.

bro·cade′ (brō kād′) n. woven fabric with raised design.

broc′co·li (brok′ə lē) n. green plant with edible flower heads.

bro·chure′ (brō shŏor′) n. pamphlet; booklet.

brogue (brōg) n. Irish accent.

broil (broil) v. cook by direct heat. —**broil′er,** n.

broke (brōk) adj. without money.

bro′ken (brō′kən) v. **1.** pp. of **break.** —adj. **2.** in fragments. **3.** fractured. **4.**

incomplete. **5.** weakened. **6.** imperfectly spoken.

bro′ken·heart′ed, *adj.* sorrowing deeply.

bro′ker, *n.* commercial agent.

bro′mide (brō′mīd, -mid) *n.* soothing compound.

bro′mine (brō′mēn, -min) *n.* reddish, toxic liquid element.

bron′chi·al (brong′kē əl) *adj.* of the bronchi, two branches of the trachea.

bron·chi′tis (-kī′tis) *n.* inflammation in windpipe and chest.

bron′co (brong′kō) *n., pl.* **-cos.** pony or small horse of western U.S.

bronze (bronz) *n., v.,* **bronzed, bronzing.** —*n.* **1.** alloy of copper and tin. **2.** brownish color. —*v.* **3.** make bronze in color.

brooch (brōch) *n.* clasp or ornament.

brood (brōod) *n.* **1.** group of animals born at one time. —*v.* **2.** hatch. **3.** think moodily.

brook (brŏŏk) *n.* **1.** small stream. —*v.* **2.** tolerate.

broom (brōom, brŏŏm) *n.* **1.** sweeping implement. **2.** shrubby plant.

broom′stick, *n.* handle of a broom.

bros., brothers.

broth (brôth) *n.* thin soup.

broth′el (broth′əl) *n.* house of prostitution.

broth′er (bruth′ər) *n., pl.* **brothers, brethren. 1.** male child of same parents. **2.** member of same group. —**broth′er·hood′,** *n.*

broth′er-in-law′, *n., pl.* **brothers-in-law. 1.** husband's or wife's brother. **2.** sister's husband.

brou/ha·ha′ (brōo′hä hä′) *n., pl.* **-has.** uproar.

brow (brou) *n.* **1.** eyebrow. **2.** forehead. **3.** edge of a height.

brow′beat′, *v.,* **-beat, -beaten, -beating.** bully.

brown (broun) *n.* **1.** dark reddish or yellowish color. —*adj.* **2.** of this color. —*v.* **3.** make or become brown.

brown′-bag′, *v.,* **brown-bagged, brown-bagging.** bring (one's lunch) to work or school. —**brown′-bag′ger,** *n.*

brown′ie (brou′nē) *n.* **1.** small, chewy chocolate cake. **2.** *(cap.)* Girl Scout aged 6 to 8.

brown′out′, *n.* reduction of electric power to prevent a blackout.

browse (brouz) *v.,* **browsed, browsing. 1.** graze; feed. **2.** examine books, etc., at leisure.

bruise (brōoz) *v.,* **bruised, bruising,** *n.* —*v.* **1.** injure without breaking. —*n.* **2.** bruised injury.

bruis′er *n. Informal.* strong, tough man.

brunch (brunch) *n.* **1.** meal that serves as both breakfast and lunch. —*v.* **2.** eat brunch.

bru·net′ (brōo net′) *adj.* dark brown, esp. of skin or hair.

bru·nette′ (brōo net′) *n.* woman with dark hair and usu. dark skin.

brunt (brunt) *n.* main force.

brush (brush) *n.* **1.** instrument with bristles. **2.** bushy tail. **3.** brief encounter. **4.** dense bushes, shrubs, etc. —*v.* **5.** use brush. **6.** touch lightly.

brush′-off′, *n.* abrupt rebuff.

brusque (brusk) *adj.* abrupt; blunt. Also, **brusk.** —**brusque′ly,** *adv.*

Brus′sels sprouts (brus′əlz) plant with small, edible heads.

bru′tal (brōot′l) *adj.* **1.** cruel. **2.** severe. —**bru·tal′i·ty,** *n.*

bru′tal·ize′ *v.,* **-ized, -izing. 1.** make brutal. **2.** treat brutally.

brute (brōot) *n.* **1.** beast. **2.** beastlike person. —*adj.* **3.** not human. **4.** irrational. **5.** like animals. **6.** savage. —**bru′tal,** *adj.* —**brut′ish,** *adj.*

B.S., Bachelor of Science.

Btu, British thermal unit. Also, **BTU**

bu., bushel.

bub′ble (bub′əl) *n., v.,* **-bled, -bling.** —*n.* **1.** globule of gas, esp. in liquid. —*v.* **2.** make or give off bubbles. —**bub′bly,** *adj.*

buc′ca·neer′ (buk′ə nēr′) *n.* pirate.

buck (buk) *v.* **1.** leap to unseat a rider. **2.** resist. —*n.* **3.** male of the deer, rabbit, goat, etc.

buck′et (buk′it) *n.* deep, open-topped container; pail.

buck′le (buk′əl) *n., v.,* **-led, -ling.** —*n.* **1.** clasp for two loose ends. —*v.* **2.** fasten with buckle. **3.** bend. **4.** set to work.

buck′ler, *n.* shield.

buck′ram (buk′rəm) *n.* stiff cotton fabric.

buck′shot′, *n.* large lead shot.

buck′skin′, *n.* skin of buck.

buck′tooth′, *n., pl.* **-teeth.** projecting tooth.

buck′wheat′, *n.* plant with edible triangular seeds.

bu·col′ic (byōo kol′ik) *adj.* rustic.

bud (bud) *n., v.,* **budded, budding.** —*n.* **1.** small bulge on plant stem, from which leaves or flowers develop. **2.** small rounded part. —*v.* **3.** produce buds. **4.** begin to grow.

Bud′dhism (bōo′diz əm, bŏŏd′iz-) *n.* Eastern religion based on teachings of Buddha. —**Bud′dhist,** *n.*

bud′dy (bud′ē) *n., pl.* **-dies.** *Informal.* friend; comrade.

budge (buj) *v.,* **budged, budging.** move slightly.

budg′et (buj′it) *n.* **1.** estimate of income and expense. —*v.* **2.** plan allotment of. **3.** allot.

buff (buf) *n.* **1.** thick light-yellow leather. **2.** yellowish brown. **3.** enthusiast. —*adj.* **4.** made or colored like buff. —*v.* **5.** polish brightly.

buf′fa·lo′ (buf′ə lō′) *n., pl.* **-loes, -los, -lo.** large bovine mammal.

buff′er, *n.* **1.** cushioning device. **2.** polishing device.

buf′fet *n.* **1.** (buf′it) blow. **2.** (bə fā′) cabinet. **3.** (bə fā′) food counter. **4.** (bə fā′) meal where guests serve themselves. —*v.* (buf′it) **5.** strike.

buf·foon′ (bə fōon′) *n.* clown.

bug (bug) *n., v.,* **bugged, bugging.** —*n.* **1.** insect. **2.** microorganism. **3.** defect or imperfection. **4.** hidden microphone. —*v.* **5.** install secret listening device in. **6.** *Informal.* pester.

bug′bear′, *n.* any source, real or imaginary, of fright or fear. Also, **bug′a·boo′** (bug′ə bōo′).

bug′gy (bug′ē) *n., pl.* **-gies.** carriage.

bu′gle (byōo′gəl) *n., v.,* **-gled, -gling.** —*n.* **1.** cornetlike wind instrument. —*v.* **2.** sound a bugle.

build (bild) *v.,* **built, building,** *n.* —*v.* **1.** construct. **2.** form. **3.** develop. —*n.* **4.** manner or form of construction. —**build′er,** *n.*

build′ing, *n.* **1.** structure with roof and walls. **2.** construction business.

build′up′, *n. Informal.* **1.** steady increase. **2.** publicity.

built′-in′, *adj.* built as part of a structure.

built′-up′, *adj.* **1.** made bigger or higher by addition. **2.** filled in with buildings.

bulb (bulb) *n.* **1.** underground bud. **2.** rounded part. **3.** electric lamp.

—*n.* **1.** rounded projection. —*v.* **2.** swell out. —**bulg′y,** *adj.*

bu·lim′i·a (byōo lim′ē ə, -lē′mē ə, bōo-) *n.* disorder marked by eating binges followed by self-induced vomiting.

bulk (bulk) *n.* **1.** magnitude. **2.** main mass. —*v.* **3.** increase in size.

bulk′head′, *n.* wall-like partition in a ship.

bulk′y, *adj.,* **bulkier, bulkiest.** of great bulk. —**bulk′i·ness,** *n.*

bull (bŏŏl) *n.* **1.** male bovine. **2.** bull-like person. **3.** speculator who depends on rise in prices. **4.** papal document. **5.** *Slang.* lying talk. —*adj.* **6.** male. **7.** marked by rise in prices. —**bull′ish,** *adj.*

bull′dog′, *n.* breed of heavily built dog.

bull′doz′er, *n.* powerful earth-moving tractor.

bul′let (bŏŏl′it) *n.* projectile for firing from small guns.

bul′le·tin (bŏŏl′i tn, -tin) *n.* brief public statement, esp. late news.

bull′fight′, *n.* combat between man and a bull. —**bull′fight′er,** *n.*

bull′frog′, *n.* large frog.

bull′head′ed, *adj.* stubborn.

bul′lion (bŏŏl′yən) *n.* uncoined gold or silver.

bull′ock (bŏŏl′ək) *n.* castrated bull.

bull′pen′, *n.* place where relief pitchers warm up.

bull′s′-eye′, *n.* center of target.

bul′ly (bŏŏl′ē) *n., pl.* **-lies,** *v.,* **-lied, -lying.** —*n.* **1.** overbearing person who hurts smaller or weaker people. —*v.* **2.** intimidate.

bul′rush′ (bŏŏl′rush′) *n.* rushlike plant.

bul′wark (bŏŏl′wərk, -wôrk) *n.* **1.** rampart. **2.** protection.

bum (bum) *n. Informal.* **1.** tramp or hobo. **2.** loafer; idler. —*v.* **3.** *Informal.* beg. —*adj.* **4.** of poor quality.

bum′ble (bum′bəl) *v.,* **-bled, -bling. 1.** blunder. **2.** bungle; botch.

bum′ble·bee′, *n.* large bee.

bum′mer (bum′ər) *n. Slang.* frustrating or bad experience.

bump (bump) *v.* **1.** strike; collide. —*n.* **2.** act or shock of bumping. **3.** swelling. —**bump′y,** *adj.*

bump′er, *n.* **1.** device for protection in collisions. **2.** glass filled to brim. —*adj.* **3.** abundant.

bump′kin (bump′kin) *n.* awkward, simple person from rural area.

bun (bun) *n.* kind of bread roll.

bunch (bunch) *n.* **1.** cluster. **2.** group. **3.** group; gather.

bun′dle (bun′dl) *n., v.,* **-dled, -dling.** —*n.* **1.** group bound together. **2.** package. —*v.* **3.** wrap in bundle. **4.** dress warmly.

bun′ga·low′ (bung′gə lō′) *n.* cottage.

bun′gle (bung′gəl) *v.,* **-gled, -gling,** *n.* —*v.* **1.** fail to do properly. —*n.* **2.** something bungled.

bun′ion (bun′yən) *n.* swelling on foot.

bunk (bungk) *n.* **1.** built-in bed. **2.** bunkum.

bunk′er (bung′kər) *n.* **1.** bin. **2.** underground refuge.

bun′kum (bung′kəm) *n.* nonsense. Also, **bunk.**

bun′ny (bun′ē) *n., pl.* **-nies.** *Informal.* rabbit.

bunt (bunt) *v.* push or tap forward.

bun′ting (bun′ting) *n.* **1.** fabric for flags, etc. **2.** flags. **3.** finchlike bird.

buoy (bŏŏ′ē, boi) *n.* **1.** floating

marker. —v. 2. support. 3. mark with buoy. 4. raise the spirits of.

buoy′ant (boi′ənt, bōō′yənt) adj. 1. tending to float. 2. cheerful. —**buoy′an•cy,** n.

bur (bûr) n. prickly seed case.

bur′den (bûr′dn) n. 1. load. —v. 2. load heavily. —**bur′den•some,** adj.

bur′dock (bûr′dok) n. prickly plant.

bu′reau (byŏŏr′ō) n., pl. **-eaux.** 1. chest of drawers. 2. government department.

bu•reauc′ra•cy (byŏŏ rok′rə sē) n., pl. **-cies.** 1. government by bureaus. 2. bureau officials.

bu′reau•crat′ (byŏŏr′ə krat′) n. official of a bureaucracy. —**bu′reau•crat′ic,** adj.

bur′geon (bûr′jən) v. 1. grow quickly. 2. begin to grow.

burg′er (bûr′gər) n. hamburger.

bur′glar (bûr′glər) n. thief who breaks and enters. —**bur′glar•ize′,** v. —**bur′gla•ry,** n.

Bur′gun•dy (bûr′gən dē) n., pl. **-dies.** dry red wine.

bur′i•al (ber′ē əl) n. act of burying.

bur′lap (bûr′lap) n. coarse fabric of jute, etc.

bur•lesque′ (bər lesk′) n., v., **-lesqued, -lesquing.** —n. 1. artistic travesty. 2. sexually suggestive entertainment. —v. 3. make a burlesque of.

bur′ly (bûr′lē) adj., **-lier, burliest.** 1. of great size. 2. brusque

burn (bûrn) v., **burned** or **burnt, burning,** n. —v. 1. be on fire. 2. consume with fire. 3. heat. 4. glow. 5. feel passion. —n. 6. burned place.

bur′nish (bûr′nish) v. polish.

burn′out′, n. 1. point at which rocket engine stops because it runs out of fuel. 2. fatigue and frustration from too much work and stress.

burp (bûrp) n. belch. —**burp,** v.

burr (bûr) n. bur.

bur′ro (bûr′ō, bŏŏr′ō, bur′ō) n., pl. **-ros.** donkey.

bur′row (bûr′ō, bur′ō) n. 1. animal's hole in ground. —v. 2. make or lodge in burrow.

bur′sar (bûr′sər, -sär) n. treasurer, esp. of a college.

bur•si′tis (bər sī′tis) n. inflammation of a bursa (sac containing fluid) in a joint.

burst (bûrst) v., **burst, bursting,** n. —v. 1. break open or issue forth violently. 2. rupture. —n. 3. act or result of bursting. 4. sudden display.

bur′y (ber′ē) v., **buried, burying.** 1. put into ground and cover. 2. conceal.

bus (bus) n., pl. **buses, busses, busing** or **bussed, busing** or **bussing.** —n. 1. large passenger motor vehicle. —v. 2. move by bus.

bus′boy′, n. helper of waiter.

bush (bŏŏsh) n. 1. shrubby plant. 2. land covered by bushes.

bushed, adj. Informal. exhausted.

bush′el (bŏŏsh′əl) n. unit of 4 pecks.

bush league, secondary baseball league. —**bush leaguer,** n.

busi′ness (biz′nis) n. 1. occupation; profession. 2. trade. 3. trading enterprise. 4. affair; matter. —**busi′ness•man′,** **busi′ness•wom•an,** n.

busi′ness•like′, adj. practical and efficient.

bus′ing (bus′ing) n. moving of pupils by bus to achieve racially balanced classes. Also, **bus′sing.**

bust (bust) n. 1. sculpture of head and shoulders. 2. bosom. —v. Informal. 3. burst or break. 4. become or make bankrupt. 5. arrest. 6. hit.

bus′tle (bus′əl) v., **-tled, -tling.** 1. move or act energetically. —n. 2. energetic activity.

bus′y (biz′ē) adj., **busier, busiest,** v., **busied, busying.** —adj. 1. actively employed. 2. full of activity. —v. 3. make or keep busy.

bus′y•bod′y, n., pl. **-bodies.** meddler.

but (but; unstressed bət) conj. 1. on the contrary. 2. except. 3. except that. —prep. 4. except. —adv. 5. only.

bu′tane (byōō′tān) n. colorless gas used as fuel.

butch (bŏŏch) adj. Slang. 1. (of a woman) having traits usu. associated with men. 2. (of a man) having exaggerated masculine traits.

butch′er (bŏŏch′ər) n. 1. dealer in meat. 2. slaughterer. —v. 3. kill for food. 4. bungle. —**butch′er•y,** n.

but′ler (but′lər) n. chief male servant.

butt (but) n. 1. thick or blunt end. 2. object of ridicule. 3. large cask. 4. cigarette end. 5. Slang. buttocks. —v. 6. be adjacent; join. 7. strike with head or horns.

but′ter (but′ər) n. 1. solid fatty part of milk. —v. 2. put butter on.

but′ter•cup′, n. plant with yellow cup-shaped flowers.

but′ter•fin′gers, n., pl. **-gers.** clumsy person.

but′ter•fly′, n., pl. **-flies.** insect with colorful wings.

but′ter•milk′, n. sour liquid remaining after butter is made.

but′ter•nut′, n. nut of walnutlike tree.

but′ter•scotch′, n. kind of taffy.

but′tock (but′ək) n. (usually pl.) one of two protuberances forming lower back part of human body.

but′ton (but′n) n. 1. disk or knob for fastening. 2. buttonlike object. —v. 3. fasten with button.

but′ton•down′, adj. 1. (of a collar) having buttonholes for attachment to shirt. 2. conventional.

but′ton•hole′, n., v., **-holed, -holing.** —n. 1. slit through which a button is passed. —v. 2. accost and detain in conversation.

but′tress (bu′tris) n. 1. structure steadying wall. —v. 2. support.

bux′om (buk′səm) adj. (of a woman) attractively plump.

buy (bī) v., **bought** (bôt) **buying.** 1. acquire by payment. 2. bribe.

buy′back′, n. repurchase by a company of its own stock.

buy′out′, n. purchase of a majority of shares in a company.

buzz (buz) n. 1. low humming sound. —v. 2. make buzz.

buz′zard (buz′ərd) n. carnivorous bird.

buzz′word′, n. Informal. fashionable cliché used to give specious weight to argument.

by (bī) prep. 1. near to. 2. through. 3. not later than. 4. past. 5. using as means or method. —adv. 6. near. 7. past.

bye (bī) n. (in a tournament) automatic advancement to the next round.

by′-elec′tion, n. special election to fill vacancy.

by′gone′, adj. 1. past. —n. 2. something past.

by′law′, n. rule within corporation.

by′line′, n. line, as in a newspaper, giving the writer or reporter's name.

by′pass′, n. 1. detour. 2. surgical procedure in which diseased or blocked organ is circumvented. —v. 3. avoid through bypass.

by′-prod′uct, n. secondary product.

by′road′, n. side road; byway.

by′stand′er, n. chance looker-on.

byte (bīt) n. unit of computer information, larger than bit.

by′way′, n. little-used road.

by′word′, n. proverb.

Byz•an′tine (biz′ən tēn′, -tīn′) adj. (sometimes l.c.) 1. complex; intricate. 2. marked by intrigue.

C

C, c (sē) n. third letter of English alphabet.

C, Celsius, Centigrade.

c., 1. centimeter. 2. century. 3. copyright.

CA, California.

ca., circa.

cab (kab) n. 1. taxicab. 2. one-horse carriage. 3. part of locomotive, truck, etc., where driver sits.

ca•bal′ (kə bal′) n. group of plotters.

ca•ban′a (kə ban′ə, -ban′yə) n. small structure at beach or pool.

cab′a•ret′ (kab′ə rā′) n. restaurant providing entertainment.

cab′bage (kab′ij) n. plant with edible head of leaves.

cab′in (kab′in) n. 1. small house. 2. room in a ship or plane.

cab′i•net (kab′ə nit) n. 1. advisory council. 2. cupboard.

ca′ble (kā′bəl) n., v., **-bled, -bling.** —n. 1. thick, strong rope. 2. cablegram. 3. bundle of electrical wires. —v. 4. send cablegram (to).

ca′ble•gram′, n. telegram sent by underwater wires.

cable TV, system of distributing television programs to subscribers over coaxial cables.

ca•boose′ (kə bōōs′) n. car for the crew at the end of a train.

ca•ca′o (kə kā′ō) n., pl. **-caos.** tropical tree whose seeds yield cocoa.

cache (kash) n., v., **cached, caching.** —n. 1. hiding place for treasure, etc. —v. 2. hide.

ca•chet′ (ka shā′) n. 1. official seal or sign. 2. superior status; prestige.

cack′le (kak′əl) v., **-led, -ling,** n. —v. 1. utter shrill, broken cry. —n. 2. act or sound of cackling.

ca•coph′o•ny (kə kof′ə nē) n., pl. **-nies.** harsh, discordant sound.

cac′tus (kak′təs) n., pl. **-tuses, -ti** (-tī). leafless, spiny plant.

cad (kad) n. ungentlemanly person.

ca•dav′er (kə dav′ər) n. corpse.

CAD/CAM (kad′kam′) n. computer-aided design and computer-aided manufacturing.

cad′die (kad′ē) n., v., **-died, -dying.** —n. 1. person who carries one's golf clubs. —v. 2. work as caddie. Also, **cad′dy.**

ca′dence (kād′ns) n. rhythmic flow or beat.

ca•det′ (kə det′) n. military student.

cadge (kaj) v., **cadged, cadging.** obtain by begging.

cad′mi•um (kad′mē əm) n. white metallic element used in plating.

ca′dre (kä′drä, kad′rē) n. highly trained group within organization.

Cae•sar′e•an (si zâr′ē ən) n. Cesarean.

ca•fé′ (ka fā′) n. restaurant.

caf′e•te′ri•a (kaf′i tēr′ē ə) n. self-service restaurant.

caf′feine (ka fēn′) n. chemical in coffee, etc., used as stimulant. Also, **caf′-fein**.

caf′tan (kaf′tan) *n.* long wide-sleeved garment.

cage (kāj) *n., v.,* **caged, caging.** —*n.* **1.** barred box or room. —*v.* **2.** put in cage.

cag′ey, *adj.* **-ier, -iest.** shrewd; cautious. Also, **cag′y.** —**cag′i•ly,** *adv.*

cais′son (kā′son, -sən) *n.* **1.** ammunition wagon. **2.** airtight underwater chamber.

ca•jole′ (kə jōl′) *v.,* **-joled, -joling.** coax; wheedle. —**ca•jol′er•y,** *n.*

Ca′jun (kā′jən) *n.* Louisianan of Nova Scotia-French origin.

cake (kāk) *n., v.,* **caked, caking.** —*n.* **1.** sweet baked dough. **2.** compact mass. —*v.* **3.** form into compact mass.

Cal., California. Also, **Calif.**

cal., **1.** caliber. **2.** calorie.

cal′a•bash′ (kal′ə bash′) *n.* kind of gourd.

ca•la•ma′ri (kal′ə mär′ē, kä′lə-) *n.* cooked squid.

cal′a•mine′ (kal′ə mīn′) *n.* powder used in skin lotions.

ca•lam′i•ty (kə lam′i tē) *n., pl.* **-ties.** disaster. —**ca•lam′i•tous,** *adj.*

cal′ci•fy′ (kal′sə fī′) *v.* **-fied, -fying.** harden.

cal′ci•um (kal′sē əm) *n.* white metallic chemical element.

cal′cu•late′ (kal′kyə lāt′) *v.,* **-lated, -lating.** compute or estimate by mathematics. —**cal′cu•la′tion,** *n.*

cal′cu•lat′ing, *adj.* shrewd.

cal′cu•la′tor, *n.* small electronic or mechanical device that performs mathematical calculations.

cal′cu•lus (kal′kyə ləs) *n.* a method of calculation by a system of algebraic notations.

cal′dron (kôl′drən) *n.* cauldron.

cal′en•dar (kal′ən dər) *n.* **1.** list of days, weeks, and months of year. **2.** list of events.

calf (kaf) *n., pl.* **calves.** **1.** young of cow, etc. **2.** fleshy part of leg below knee.

cal′i•ber (kal′ə bər) *n.* **1.** diameter of bullet or gun bore. **2.** quality. Also **cal′i•bre.**

cal′i•brate′ (-brāt′) *v.,* **-brated, -brating.** mark for measuring purposes. —**cal′i•bra′tion,** *n.*

cal′i•co′ (kal′i kō′) *n., pl.* **-coes, -cos.** printed cotton cloth.

cal′i•per (kal′ə pər) *n.* (*usu. pl.*) compass for measuring.

ca′liph (kā′lif) *n.* former title of Islamic religious and civil ruler.

cal′is•then′ics (kal′əs then′iks) *n.pl.* physical exercises.

calk (kôk) *v.* caulk.

call (kôl) *v.* **1.** cry out loudly. **2.** announce. **3.** summon. **4.** telephone. **5.** name. **6.** visit briefly. —*n.* **7.** cry or shout. **8.** summons. **9.** brief visit. **10.** need; demand. —**call′er,** *n.*

call girl, female prostitute who is called for services.

cal•lig′ra•phy (kə lig′rə fē) *n.* fancy penmanship; art of beautiful writing.

call′ing, *n.* **1.** trade. **2.** summons.

cal′lous (kal′əs) *adj.* unsympathetic. —*v.* **2.** harden.

cal′low (kal′ō) *adj.* immature.

cal′lus (kal′əs) *n.* hardened part of the skin.

calm (käm) *adj.* **1.** undisturbed. **2.** not windy. —*n.* **3.** calm state. —*v.* **4.** make calm. —**calm′ly,** *adv.*

ca•lor′ic (kə lôr′ik) *adj.* **1.** of heat or calories. **2.** high in calories.

cal′o•rie (kal′ə rē) *n.* measured unit

of heat, esp. of fuel or energy value of food.

ca•lum′ni•ate′ (kə lum′nē āt′) *v.,* **-ated, -ating.** slander. —**cal′um•ny** (kal′əm nē) *n.*

calve (kav, käv) *v.* give birth to calf.

ca•lyp′so (kə lip′sō) *n.* musical style of the West Indies.

ca′lyx (kā′liks) *n.* small leaflets around flower petals.

cam (kam) *n.* device for changing circular movement to straight.

ca′ma•ra•de•rie (kä′mə rä′də rē) *n.* comradeship; fellowship.

cam′ber (kam′bər) *n.* slight upward curve; convexity.

cam′bric (kām′brik) *n.* close-woven fabric.

cam′cord′er (kam′kôr′dər) *n.* handheld television camera with an incorporated VCR.

came (kām) *v.* pt. of **come.**

cam′el (kam′əl) *n.* large humped quadruped.

ca•mel′lia (kə mēl′yə) *n.* shrub with glossy leaves and roselike flowers.

cam′e•o′ (kam′ē ō′) *n., pl.* **-eos.** gem with head carved in relief.

cam′er•a (kam′ər ə) *n.* device for making photographs.

cam′i•sole′ (kam′ə sōl′) *n.* woman's sleeveless undershirt.

cam′o•mile′ (kam′ə mīl′) *n.* chamomile.

cam′ou•flage′ (kam′ə fläzh′) *n., v.,* **-flaged, -flaging.** —*n.* **1.** deceptive covering. —*v.* **2.** hide by camouflage.

camp (kamp) *n.* **1.** place of temporary lodging, esp. in tents. **2.** faction. **3.** something that amuses by being overdone or tasteless. —*adj.* **4.** Also, **camp′y.** amusing as camp. —*v.* **5.** form or live in camp. —**camp′er,** *n.* —**camp′site′,** *n.*

cam•paign′ (kam pān′) *n.* **1.** military operation. **2.** competition for political office, sales, etc. —*v.* **3.** engage in campaign.

cam′phor (kam′fər) *n.* white crystalline substance used as moth repellent, medicine, etc.

cam′pus (kam′pəs) *n.* school grounds.

cam′shaft′, *n.* engine shaft fitted with cams.

can, *v.,* **canned** (**could** for def. 1), **canning** (for def. 2), *n.* —*v.* **1.** (kan; *unstressed* kən) be able or qualified to. **2.** (kan) put in airtight container. —*n.* **3.** (kan) cylindrical metal container. —**can′ner,** *n.*

Ca•na′di•an (kə nā′dē ən) *n.* citizen of Canada. —**Canadian,** *adj.*

ca•nal′ (kə nal′) *n.* **1.** artificial waterway. **2.** tube in animal or plant.

can′a•pé (kan′ə pē, -pā′) *n.* morsel of food served as appetizer.

ca•nar′y (kə nâr′ē) *n., pl.* **-ries.** yellow cage bird.

can′cel (kan′səl) *v.,* **-celed, -celing.** **1.** cross out. **2.** make void. —**can′cel•la′-tion,** *n.*

can′cer (kan′sər) *n.* malignant growth. —**can′cer•ous,** *adj.*

can′de•la′brum (kan′dl ä′brəm) *n., pl.* **-bra** (-brə). branched candlestick. Also, **can′de•la′bra,** *pl.* **candela-bras.**

can′did (kan′did) *adj.* frank or honest. —**can′did•ly,** *adv.*

can′di•da (kan′di də) *n.* disease-causing fungus.

can′di•date′ (kan′di dāt′, -dit) *n.* one seeking to be elected or chosen. —**can′di•da•cy,** *n.*

can′dle (kan′dl) *n.* waxy cylinder with wick for burning.

can′dor (kan′dər) *n.* frankness.

can′dy (kan′dē) *n., pl.* **-dies,** *v.,* **-died, -dying.** —*n.* **1.** sweet confection. —*v.* **2.** cover with sugar.

cane (kān) *n., v.,* **caned, caning.** —*n.* **1.** stick used in walking. **2.** long, woody stem. —*v.* **3.** beat with a cane.

ca′nine (kā′nīn) *adj.* **1.** of dogs. —*n.* **2.** animal of dog family.

canine tooth, one of the four pointed teeth next to the incisors.

can′is•ter (kan′ə stər) *n.* small box.

can′ker (kang′kər) *n.* ulcerous sore. —**can′ker•ous,** *adj.*

can′na•bis (kan′ə bis) *n.* hemp plant; marijuana, used as drug.

canned, *adj.* **1.** put into cans or sealed jars. **2.** *Informal.* recorded.

can′ner•y, *n., pl.* **-ies.** factory where foods are canned.

can′ni•bal (kan′ə bəl) *n.* person who eats human flesh.

can′ni•bal•ize′, *v.,* **-ized, -izing.** strip of reusable parts.

can′non (kan′ən) *n.* large mounted gun. —**can′non•eer′,** *n.*

can′non•ade′ (-ə nād′) *n.* long burst of cannon fire.

can′not (kan′ot, ka not′, kə-) *v.* am, are, or is unable to.

can′ny (kan′ē) *adj.* **-nier, -niest. 1.** careful. **2.** shrewd.

ca•noe′ (kə nōō′) *n.* light boat propelled by paddles.

can′on (kan′ən) *n.* **1.** rule or law. **2.** recognized books of Bible. **3.** church official.

can′on•ize′, *v.,* **-ized, -izing.** declare as saint.

can′o•py (kan′ə pē) *n., pl.* **-pies.** overhead covering.

cant (kant) *n.* **1.** insincerely virtuous talk. **2.** special jargon.

can′t (kant) contraction of **cannot.**

can′ta•loupe′ (kan′tl ōp′) *n.* small melon with orange flesh.

can•tan′ker•ous (kan tang′kər əs) *adj.* ill-natured.

can•ta′ta (kən tä′tə) *n.* dramatic choral composition.

can•teen′ (kan tēn′) *n.* **1.** container for water, etc. **2.** cafeteria or entertainment place for soldiers, etc.

can′ter (kan′tər) *n.* **1.** easy gallop. —*v.* **2.** go at easy gallop.

can′ti•cle (kan′ti kəl) *n.* hymn.

can′ti•le′ver (kan′tl ē′vər) *n.* structure secured at one end only.

can′to (kan′tō) *n., pl.* **-tos.** section of a long poem.

can′ton (kan′tn, kan ton′) *n.* small territorial district in Switzerland.

can′tor (kan′tər) *n.* synagogue official who sings certain prayers.

can′vas (kan′vəs) *n.* **1.** cloth used for sails, tents, etc. **2.** sails.

can′vas•back′, *n., pl.* **-backs, -back.** wild duck with a whitish or grayish back.

can′vass (kan′vəs) *v.* **1.** investigate. **2.** solicit votes, etc. —**can′vass•er,** *n.*

can′yon (kan′yən) *n.* narrow valley.

cap (kap) *n., v.,* **capped, capping.** —*n.* **1.** brimless hat with visor. **2.** cover. —*v.* **3.** cover. **4.** surpass.

cap., **1.** capacity. **2.** capital(ize). **3.** capital letter.

ca′pa•ble (kā′pə bəl) *adj.* able; qualified. —**ca′pa•bil′i•ty,** *n.*

ca•pa′cious (kə pā′shəs) *adj.* roomy.

ca•pac′i•tor (kə pas′i tər) *n.* device for collecting and holding an electrical charge.

ca•pac′i•ty, *n., pl.* **-ties. 1.** volume. **2.** capability. **3.** role.

cape (kāp) *n.* **1.** sleeveless coat. **2.** projecting point of land.

ca′per (kā′pər) *v.* **1.** leap playfully. —*n.* **2.** playful leap. **3.** bud of shrub, used as seasoning.

cap′il·lar·y (kap′ə ler′ē) *adj.*, *n.*, *pl.* **-laries.** —*adj.* **1.** of or in a thin tube. —*n.* **2.** tiny blood vessel.

cap′i·tal (kap′i tl) *n.* **1.** city in which government is located. **2.** letter different from and larger than its corresponding lowercase letter. **3.** money available for business use. —*adj.* **4.** important or chief. **5.** excellent. **6.** uppercase. **7.** punishable by death.

capital gain, profit from the sale of an asset.

capital goods, *n.pl.* machines for production of goods.

cap′i·tal·ism, *n.* system of private investment in and ownership of business. —**cap′i·tal·ist,** *n.*

cap′i·tal·ize′, *v.*, **-ized, -izing. 1.** put in capital letters. **2.** use as capital. **3.** take advantage.

cap′i·tal·ly, *adv.* well.

cap′i·tol (kap′i tl) *n.* building used by legislature.

ca·pit′u·late′ (kə pich′ə lāt′) *v.*, **-lated, -lating.** surrender.

cap′let (kap′lit) *n.* oval medicinal tablet, coated for easy swallowing.

ca′pon (kā′pon, -pən) *n.* castrated rooster.

cap·puc·ci·no (kap′ə chē′nō) *n.* espresso coffee with steamed milk.

ca·price′ (kə prēs′) *n.* whim. —**ca·pri′cious** (-prish′əs, -prē′shəs) *adj.*

cap′size (kap′sīz) *v.*, **-sized, -sizing.** overturn; upset.

cap′stan (kap′stən, -stan) *n.* device turned to pull cables.

cap′sule (kap′səl) *n.* small sealed container. —**cap′su·lar,** *adj.*

capt., captain.

cap′tain (kap′tən) *n.* **1.** officer below major or rear admiral. **2.** ship master. **3.** leader of sports team. —**cap′tain·cy,** *n.*

cap′tion (kap′shən) *n.* heading. —**cap′tious·ly,** *adv.*

cap′tious (kap′shəs) *adj.* noting trivial faults. —**cap′tious·ly,** *adv.*

cap′ti·vate′ (kap′tə vāt′) *v.*, **-vated, -vating.** charm.

cap′tive (-tiv) *n.* prisoner. —**cap·tiv′i·ty,** *n.*

cap′ture (-chər) *v.*, **-tured, -turing,** *n.* —*v.* **1.** take prisoner. —*n.* **2.** act of capturing. —**cap′tor,** *n.*

car (kär) *n.* **1.** vehicle, esp. automobile. **2.** cage of elevator.

ca·rafe′ (kə raf′) *n.* broad-mouthed bottle for wine, water, etc.

car′a·mel (kar′ə məl, kär′məl) *n.* confection made of burnt sugar.

car′at (kar′ət) *n.* **1.** unit of weight for gems. **2.** karat.

car′a·van′ (kar′ə van′) *n.* group traveling together, esp. over deserts.

car′a·way′ (kar′ə wā′) *n.* herb bearing aromatic seeds.

car′bide (kär′bīd) *n.* carbon compound.

car′bine (kär′bēn, -bīn) *n.* short rifle.

car′bo·hy′drate (kär′bō hī′drāt, -bə-) *n.* organic compound group including starches and sugars.

car·bol′ic acid (kär bol′ik) brown germicidal liquid.

car′bon (kär′bən) *n.* chemical element occurring as diamonds, charcoal, etc. —**car·bon·if′er·ous,** *adj.*

car′bon·ate′ (kär′bə nāt′) *v.*, **-ated, -ating.** charge with carbon dioxide.

carbon dioxide, chemical compound of carbon and oxygen: a gas produced esp. by animal respiration.

carbon monoxide, chemical compound of carbon and oxygen: a poisonous gas produced esp. by automobile engines.

carbon paper, paper coated with a carbon pigment, used to make copies.

car·bun·cle (kär′bung kəl) *n.* painful inflammation under skin.

car′bu·re′tor (kär′bə rā′tər, -byə-) *n.* mechanism that mixes gasoline and air in motor.

car′cass (kär′kəs) *n.* dead body of an animal.

car·cin′o·gen (kär sin′ə jən) *n.* cancer-producing substance. —**car′cin·o·gen′ic** (-sə nə jen′ik) *adj.*

car·ci·no·ma (kär′sə nō′mə) *n.*, *pl.* **-mas, -mata.** malignant tumor.

card (kärd) *n.* **1.** piece of stiff paper, with one's name **(calling card)**, marks for game purposes **(playing card)**, etc. **2.** comb for wool, flax, etc. —*v.* **3.** dress (wool, etc.) with card. **4.** ask for proof of age.

card′board′, *n.* **1.** thin, stiff pasteboard. —*adj.* **2.** flimsy. **3.** seeming fake.

car′di·ac′ (kär′dē ak′) *adj.* of the heart.

cardiac arrest, abrupt stopping of the heartbeat.

car′di·gan (kär′di gən) *n.* sweater that buttons down the front.

car′di·nal (kär′dn l) *adj.* **1.** main; chief. **2.** (of numbers) used to express quantities or positions in series, e.g., 3, 15, 45. **3.** deep red. —*n.* **4.** red bird. **5.** high official of Roman Catholic Church.

cardio-, prefix meaning heart, as *cardiology.*

car′di·o·graph′ (kär′dē ə graf′) *n.* instrument for recording movements of heart. —**car′di·o·gram′,** *n.*

car′di·ol′o·gy (-ol′ə jē) *n.* study of the heart and its functions.

car′di·o·pul′mo·nar′y (kär′dē ō-) *adj.* of the heart and lungs.

car′di·o·vas′cu·lar, *adj.* of the heart and blood vessels.

card′sharp′, *n.* person who cheats at card games. Also, **card shark.**

care (kâr) *n.*, *v.*, **cared, caring.** —*n.* **1.** worry. **2.** caution. —*v.* **3.** be concerned. —**care′free′,** *adj.*

ca·reen′ (kə rēn′) *v.* tip; sway.

ca·reer′ (kə rēr′) *n.* **1.** profession followed as one's lifework. **2.** course through life. **3.** speed. —*v.* **4.** speed.

care′ful, *adj.* **1.** cautious. **2.** exact. —**care′ful·ly,** *adv.*

care′giv′er, *n.* person who cares for a child or an invalid.

care′less, *adj.* **1.** not paying attention. **2.** not accurate.

ca·ress′ (kə res′) *v.*, *n.* touch in expressing affection.

car′et (kar′it) *n.* insertion mark (^).

care′tak′er (kâr′-) *n.* **1.** maintenance person. **2.** caregiver.

car′fare′ (kär′fâr′) *n.* cost of ride.

car′go (kär′gō) *n.*, *pl.* **-goes, -gos.** goods carried by vessel.

car′i·bou′ (kar′ə bōō′) *n.* North American reindeer.

car′i·ca·ture (kar′i kə chər) *n.* mocking portrait. —**car′i·ca·ture,** *v.*, **-tured, -turing.**

car′ies (kâr′ēz) *n.*, *pl.* **-ies.** tooth decay.

car′il·lon′ (kar′ə lon′, -lən) *n.* musical bells.

car′jack′ing (kär′jak′ing) *n.* theft of car by force. —**car′jack′er,** *n.*

car′mine (-min) *n.*, *adj.* crimson or purplish red.

car′nage (-nij) *n.* massacre.

car′nal (-nl) *adj.* of the body.

car·na′tion (kär nā′shən) *n.* common fragrant flower.

car′ni·val (kär′nə vəl) *n.* **1.** amusement fair. **2.** festival before Lent.

car′ni·vore′ (-vôr′) *n.* flesh-eating mammal. —**car·niv′o·rous** (-niv′ə-rəs) *adj.*

car′ob (kar′əb) *n.* **1.** tree bearing long pods. **2.** pulp from the pods, used as chocolate substitute.

car′ol (kar′əl) *n.*, *v.*, **-oled, -oling.** —*n.* **1.** Christmas song. —*v.* **2.** sing joyously. —**car′ol·er,** *n.*

car′om (kar′əm) *v.* **1.** hit and rebound. —*n.* **2.** rebound.

ca·rot′id (kə rot′id) *n.* either of two large arteries in the neck.

ca·rouse′ (kə rouz′) *n.*, *v.*, **-roused, -rousing.** —*n.* **1.** noisy or drunken feast. —*v.* **2.** engage in a carouse.

carp (kärp) *v.* **1.** find fault. —*n.* **2.** large fresh-water fish.

car′pal (kär′pəl) *adj.* **1.** of the carpus. —*n.* **2.** wrist bone.

carpal tunnel syndrome, chronic wrist pain associated esp. with repetitive movements, as at a keyboard.

car′pel (kär′pəl) *n.* seed-bearing leaf.

car′pen·ter (-pən tər) *n.* builder in wood. —**car′pen·try,** *n.*

car′pet (-pit) *n.* **1.** fabric covering for floors. —*v.* **2.** cover with carpet.

car′pool′, *n.* **1.** group of automobile owners who take turns to drive, for example, to work. —*v.* **2.** participate in a carpool.

car′port′, *n.* roof that provides shelter for a car.

car′pus (kär′pəs) *n.*, *pl.* **-pi** (pī). **1.** wrist. **2.** wrist bones as a group.

car′rel (kar′əl) *n.* small study space in a library. Also, **car′rell.**

car′riage (-ij) *n.* **1.** wheeled vehicle. **2.** posture. **3.** conveyance.

car′ri·on (-ē ən) *n.* dead flesh.

car′rot (-ət) *n.* orange root vegetable.

car′rou·sel′ (kar′ə sel′) *n.* merry-go-round.

car′ry (kar′ē) *v.*, **car-ried, car-rying. 1.** transport. **2.** support; bear. **3.** behave. **4.** win. **5.** extend. **6.** have in stock. **7.** carry out, accomplish.

car′ry-out′, *adj.*, *n.* takeout.

car′sick′ (kär′-) *adj.* nauseated and dizzy from car travel.

cart (kärt) *n.* small wagon.

carte blanche (kärt′ blänch′, blänsh′) unconditional authority.

car·tel′ (kär tel′) *n.* syndicate controlling prices and production.

car′ti·lage (kär′tl ij) *n.* flexible connective body tissue.

car·tog′ra·phy (kär tog′rə fē) *n.* map production.

car′ton (kär′tn) *n.* cardboard box.

car·toon′ (kär tōōn′) *n.* **1.** comic drawing. **2.** design for large art work. —**car·toon′ist,** *n.*

car′tridge (kär′trij) *n.* **1.** case containing bullet and explosive. **2.** container with frequently replaced machine parts.

cart′wheel′, *n.* **1.** sideways handspring. —*v.* **2.** roll forward end over end.

carve (kärv) *v.*, **carved, carving.** cut into shape. —**carv′er,** *n.*

cas·cade′ (kas kād′) *n.* waterfall.

case (kās) *n.*, *v.*, **cased, casing.** —*n.* **1.** example. **2.** situation. **3.** event. **4.** statement of arguments. **5.** medical patient. **6.** lawsuit. **7.** category in inflection of nouns, adjectives, and pronouns. **8. in case,** if. **9.** container. —*v.* **10.** put in case.

ca′sein (kā′sēn) *n.* protein derived from milk, used in making cheese.

case′ment (kās′mənt) *n.* hinged window.

cash (kash) *n.* **1.** money. —*v.* **2.** give or get cash for.

cash′ew (kash′ōō, kə shōō′) *n.* small curved nut.

cash·ier′ (ka shēr′) *n.* **1.** person in charge of money. —*v.* **2.** dismiss in disgrace.

cash′mere (kazh′mēr, kash′-) *n.* soft wool fabric.

cas′ing (kā′sing) *n.* **1.** outer covering. **2.** framework, as of a door.

ca·si′no (kə sē′nō) *n., pl.* **-nos.** amusement or gambling hall.

cask (kask) *n.* barrel for liquids.

cas′ket (kas′kit) *n.* coffin.

cas·sa′va (kə sä′və) *n.* tropical plant with starchy roots.

cas′se·role′ (kas′ə rōl′) *n.* covered baking dish.

cas·sette′ (kə set′) *n.* compact case that holds film or recording tape.

cas′sock (kas′ək) *n.* long ecclesiastical vestment.

cast (kast) *v.*, **cast, casting,** *n.* —*v.* **1.** throw. **2.** deposit (vote). **3.** pour and mold. —*n.* **4.** act of casting. **5.** actors in play. **6.** form; mold. **7.** rigid surgical dressing. **8.** tinge.

cas′ta·net′ (kas′tə net′) *n.* pieces of shell, etc., held in the palm and struck together.

cast′a·way′, *n.* shipwrecked person.

caste (kast) *n.* hereditary social division of Hindu society.

cast′er, *n.* small swivel-mounted wheel. Also, **cast′or.**

cas′ti·gate′ (kas′ti gāt′) *v.*, **-gated, -gating.** scold severely.

cast iron, hard, brittle alloy of carbon, iron, and silicon.

cas′tle (kas′əl) *n., v.*, **-tled, -tling.** —*n.* **1.** royal or noble residence, usually fortified. **2.** chess piece; rook. —*v.* **3.** *Chess.* transpose rook and king.

cas′tor oil (kas′tər) cathartic oil.

cas′trate (kas′trāt) *v.*, **-trated, -trating.** remove testicles of.

cas′u·al (kazh′ōō əl) *adj.* **1.** accidental; not planned. **2.** not caring.

cas′u·al·ty, *n., pl.* **-ties. 1.** accident injurious to person. **2.** soldier missing in action, killed, wounded, or captured.

cas′u·ist·ry, *n., pl.* **-ries.** adroit, specious argument. —**cas′u·ist,** *n.*

cat (kat) *n.* common domestic animal. —**cat′like′,** *adj.*

cat′a·clysm′ (kat′ə kliz′əm) *n.* upheaval. —**cat′a·clys′mic,** *adj.*

cat′a·comb′ (-kōm′) *n.* underground cemetery.

cat′a·logue′ (kat′l ôg′) *n., v.*, **-logued, -loguing.** —*n.* **1.** organized list. —*v.* **2.** enter in catalogue. Also, **cat′a·log′.**

ca·tal′pa (kə tal′pə) *n.* tree with bell-shaped white flowers.

cat′a·lyst (kat′l ist) *n.* **1.** substance that causes a chemical reaction without itself being affected. **2.** anything that precipitates an event.

cat′a·ma·ran′ (kat′ə mə ran′) *n.* two-hulled boat.

cat′a·mount′, *n.* cougar.

cat′a·pult′ (-pult′, -pŏōlt′) *n.* **1.** device for hurling or launching. —*v.* **2.** hurl.

cat′a·ract′ (-rakt′) *n.* **1.** waterfall. **2.** opacity of eye lens.

ca·tarrh′ (kə tär′) *n.* inflammation of respiratory mucous membranes.

ca·tas′tro·phe (kə tas′trə fē) *n.*

great disaster. —**cat′a·stroph′ic** (kat′-ə strof′ik) *adj.*

cat′bird′, *n.* songbird with catlike call.

cat′call′, *n.* jeer.

catch (kach) *v.*, **caught** (kôt), **catching,** *n.* —*v.* **1.** capture. **2.** trap or surprise. **3.** hit. **4.** seize and hold. **5.** be in time for. **6.** get or contract. **7.** be entangled. —*n.* **8.** act of catching. **9.** thing that catches. **10.** thing caught. **11.** snag.

Catch-22 (katch′twen′tē tōō′) *n.* frustrating situation involving contradictions.

catch′ing, *adj.* contagious.

catch′up, *n.* ketchup.

catch′word′, *n.* slogan.

catch′y, *adj.*, **-ier, -iest.** memorable and pleasing.

cat′e·chism (kat′i kiz′əm) *n.* set of questions and answers on religious principles.

cat′e·gor′i·cal (-gôr′i kəl) *adj.* unconditional.

cat′e·go′ry (-gôr′ē) *n., pl.* **-ries.** division; class. —**cat′e·go·rize′** (-gə rīz′) *v.*, **-rized, -rizing.**

ca′ter (kā′tər) *v.* **1.** provide food, etc. **2.** make special effort to provide what is needed. —**ca′ter·er,** *n.*

cat′er-cor′nered (kat′i-, kat′ē-, kat′-ər-) *adj.* **1.** diagonal. —*adv.* **2.** diagonally.

cat′er·pil′lar (kat′ə pil′ər) *n.* **1.** wormlike larva of butterfly. **2.** type of tractor.

cat′er·waul′ (kat′ər wôl′) *v.* **1.** utter long wails, as cats in rut. —*n.* **2.** such a wail.

cat′fish′, *n.* fresh-water fish.

cat′gut′, *n.* string made from animal intestine.

ca·thar′sis (kə thär′sis) *n.* **1.** purging of emotions, as through art. **2.** evacuation of bowels.

ca·thar′tic, *adj.* **1.** effecting a catharsis. **2.** evacuating the bowels. —*n.* **3.** medicine doing this.

ca·the′dral (kə thē′drəl) *n.* main church of diocese.

cath′e·ter (kath′i tar) *n.* tube inserted into a body passage.

cath′ode (kath′ōd) *n.* **1.** electrode with negative charge. **2.** positive terminal of a battery.

cathode ray, beam of electrons coming from a cathode.

cathode-ray tube, vacuum tube generating cathode rays directed at screen, used to display images on receiver or monitor. *Abbr.:* CRT.

Cath′o·lic (kath′ə lik) *adj.* **1.** of Roman Catholic Church. **2.** (*l.c.*) universal. —*n.* **3.** member of Roman Catholic Church. —**Ca·thol′i·cism** (kə thol′ə-siz′əm) *n.*

cat′kin (kat′kin) *n.* spike of bunched small flowers.

cat′nap′, *n.* **1.** short, light sleep. —*v.* **2.** sleep briefly.

cat′nip, *n.* plant with scented leaves.

CAT scan (kat) **1.** examination using x-rays at various angles to show cross section of body. **2.** image produced by CAT scan. —**CAT scanner**

cat′s′-paw′, *n.* person exploited by another.

cat′sup (kat′səp, kech′əp, kach′-) *n.* ketchup.

cat′tail′, *n.* tall spiky marsh plant.

cat′tle (kat′l) *n.* livestock.

cat′ty (kat′ē) *adj.*, **-tier, -tiest.** maliciously gossiping.

cat′walk′, *n.* narrow walkway.

Cau·ca′sian (kô kā′zhən) *adj.* **1.** of or characteristic of one of the racial di-

visions of humankind, marked by minimum skin pigmentation. —*n.* **2.** Caucasian person.

cau′cus (kô′kəs) *n.* political meeting.

caul′dron (kôl′drən) *n.* large kettle.

cau′li·flow′er (kô′lə flou′ər) *n.* plant with an edible head.

caulk (kôk) *v.* **1.** close seams of to keep water or air out. —*n.* **2.** Also, **caulk′ing.** material used to caulk.

cause (kôz) *n., v.*, **caused, causing.** —*n.* **1.** person or thing producing an effect. **2.** reason. **3.** aim; purpose. —*v.* **4.** bring about; produce. —**caus′al,** *adj.* —**cau·sa′tion,** *n.*

cause cé·lè·bre (kôz′ sə leb′) *n., pl.* **causes cé·lè·bres** (kôz′ sə leb′). controversy attracting attention.

cause′way′, *n.* raised road.

caus′tic (kô′stik) *adj.* **1.** corroding. **2.** sharply critical.

cau′ter·ize′ (kô′tə rīz′) *v.*, **-ized, -izing.** burn. —**cau′ter·y,** *n.*

cau′tion (kô′shən) *n.* **1.** carefulness. **2.** warning. —*v.* **3.** warn. —**cau′tious,** *adj.*

cav′al·cade′ (kav′əl kād′) *n.* procession, esp. on horseback.

cav′a·lier′ (kav′ə lēr′) *n.* **1.** knight or horseman. **2.** courtly gentleman. —*adj.* **3.** haughty; indifferent. **4.** offhand.

cav′al·ry (kav′əl rē) *n., pl.* **-ries.** troops on horseback or in armored vehicles. —**cav′al·ry·man,** *n.*

cave (kāv) *n., v.*, **caved, caving.** —*n.* **1.** hollow space in the earth. —*v.* **2.** fall or sink.

ca′ve·at′ (kav′ē ät′) *n.* warning.

cave man, 1. Stone Age cave dweller. **2.** rough, brutal man.

cav′ern (kav′ərn) *n.* large cave.

cav′i·ar′ (-ē är′) *n.* roe of sturgeon, etc., eaten as a delicacy.

cav′il (-əl) *v.*, **-iled, -iling,** *n.* —*v.* **1.** find trivial faults. —*n.* **2.** trivial objection.

cav′i·ty (-i tē) *n., pl.* **-ties.** hollow.

ca·vort′ (kə vôrt′) *v.* prance about.

caw (kô) *n.* **1.** harsh call of a crow. —*v.* **2.** make a caw.

cay·enne′ (kī en′) *n.* hot pepper.

CB, citizens band: private two-way radio.

cc, 1. carbon copy. **2.** cubic centimeter.

CCU, coronary-care unit.

CD, 1. certificate of deposit. **2.** Civil Defense. **3.** compact disc.

CD-ROM (sē′dē′rom′) *n.* compact disc for storing digitized read-only data.

cease (sēs) *v.*, **ceased, ceasing,** *n.* stop; end. —**cease′less,** *adj.*

cease′-fire′, *n.* truce.

ce′dar (sē′dər) *n.* coniferous tree.

cede (sēd) *v.*, **ceded, ceding.** yield or give up.

ceil′ing (sē′ling) *n.* **1.** upper surface of room. **2.** maximum altitude.

cel′e·brate′ (sel′ə brāt′) *v.*, **-brated, -brating. 1.** commemorate. **2.** act rejoicingly. **3.** perform ritually. **4.** extol. —**cel′e·bra′tion,** *n.*

ce·leb′ri·ty (sə leb′ri tē) *n., pl.* **-ties. 1.** famous person. **2.** fame.

ce·ler′i·ty (sə ler′i tē) *n.* speed.

cel′er·y (sel′ə rē) *n.* plant with edible leaf stalks.

ce·les′tial (sə les′chəl) *adj.* of heaven or the sky.

cel′i·ba·cy (sel′ə bə sē) *n.* **1.** unmarried state. **2.** sexual abstinence.

cell (sel) *n.* **1.** a small room. **2.** microscopic biological structure. **3.** electric battery. **4.** organizational unit. —**cel′lu·lar,** *adj.*

cel′lar (sel′ər) *n.* basement.

cel′lo (chel′ō) *n.*, *pl.* **-los.** large violin-like instrument. —**cel′list,** *n.*

cel′lo·phane′ (sel′ə fān′) *n.* transparent wrapping material.

cellular phone, mobile telephone. Also, **cell phone.**

cel′lu·lite′ (sel′yə līt′, -lēt′) *n.* lumpy fat deposits, esp. in thighs.

cel′lu·loid′ (-loid′) *n.* hard, flammable substance.

cel′lu·lose′ (-lōs′) *n.* carbohydrate of plant origin.

Cel′si·us (sel′sē əs) *n.* temperature scale in which water freezes at 0° and boils at 100°.

ce·ment′ (si ment′) *n.* **1.** clay-lime mixture that hardens into stonelike mass. **2.** binding material. —*v.* **3.** treat with cement. **4.** unite.

cem′e·ter′y (sem′i ter′ē) *n.*, *pl.* **-ter-ies.** burial ground.

cen′o·taph′ (sen′ə taf′) *n.* monument for one buried elsewhere.

Ce′no·zo′ic (sē′nə zō′ik) *adj.* of the present geologic era.

cen′ser (sen′sər) *n.* incense burner.

cen′sor (sen′sər) *n.* **1.** person eliminating undesirable words, pictures, etc. —*v.* **2.** deal with as a censor. —**cen′sor·ship′,** *n.*

cen·so′ri·ous (-sôr′ē əs) *adj.* severely critical.

cen′sure (-shər) *n.*, *v.*, **-sured, -suring.** —*n.* **1.** disapproval. —*v.* **2.** rebuke.

cen′sus (sen′səs) *n.* count of inhabitants.

cent (sent) *n.* $\frac{1}{100}$ of a dollar; penny.

cent., century.

cen′taur (sen′tôr) *n.* mythological creature, half horse and half man.

cen·ten′ar·y (sen ten′ə rē, sen′tn-er′ē) *n.*, *pl.* **-aries.** 100th anniversary.

cen·ten′ni·al (-ten′ē əl) *n.* **1.** 100th anniversary. —*adj.* **2.** of 100 years.

cen′ter (sen′tər) *n.* **1.** middle point, part, or person. —*v.* **2.** place or gather at center. **3.** concentrate. Also, **cen′tre.**

cen′ter·fold′, *n.* page that folds out from magazine center.

cen′ter·piece′, *n.* decoration for center of table.

cen′ti·grade′ (sen′ti grād′) *adj.* Celsius.

cen′ti·gram′, *n.* $\frac{1}{100}$ of gram.

cen′ti·li·ter (-lē′tər) *n.* $\frac{1}{100}$ of liter.

cen′ti·me′ter, *n.* $\frac{1}{100}$ of meter.

cen′ti·pede′ (-pēd′) *n.* insect with many legs.

cen′tral (sen′trəl) *adj.* **1.** of or at center. **2.** main. —**cen′tral·ly,** *adv.*

cen′tral·ize′, *v.*, **-ized, -izing. 1.** gather at a center. **2.** concentrate control of. —**cen′tral·i·za′tion,** *n.*

cen·trif′u·gal (-trif′yə gəl, -ə gəl) *adj.* moving away from center.

cen′tri·fuge′ (-fyooj′) *n.* high-speed rotating apparatus for separating substances of different densities.

cen′trist (sen′trist) *n.* **1.** person with political views that are not extreme. —*adj.* **2.** of views that are not extreme.

cen′tu·ry (sen′chə rē) *n.*, *pl.* **-ries.** period of one hundred years.

CEO, chief executive officer.

ce·ram′ic (sə ram′ik) *adj.* of clay and similar materials. —**ce·ram′ics,** *n.*

ce′re·al (sēr′ē əl) *n.* **1.** plant yielding edible grain. **2.** food from such grain.

cer′e·bel′lum (ser′ə bel′əm) *n.* rear part of brain.

cer′e·bral (ser′ə brəl, sə rē′-) *adj.* **1.** of brain. **2.** intellectual.

cerebral palsy, paralysis due to brain injury.

cer′e·brum (sə rē′brəm, ser′ə-) *n.*, *pl.* **-brums, -bra** (-brə). front, upper part of brain.

cer′e·mo′ny (ser′ə mō′nē) *n.*, *pl.* **-nies.** formal act or ritual.

ce·rise′ (sə rēs′, -rēz′) *adj.*, *n.* medium to deep red.

cer′tain (sûr′tn) *adj.* **1.** without doubt; sure. **2.** agreed upon. **3.** definite but unspecified. —**cer′tain·ly,** *adv.* —**cer′tain·ty,** *n.*

cer·tif′i·cate (sər tif′i kit) *n.* document of proof.

cer′ti·fy′ (sûr′tə fī′) *v.*, **-fied, -fying. 1.** guarantee as certain. **2.** vouch for in writing. —**cer′ti·fi·ca′tion,** *n.*

cer′ti·tude′ (-tōōd′, -tyōōd′) *n.* sureness.

ce·ru′le·an (sə rōō′lē ən) *adj.* deep blue.

cer′vix (sûr′viks) *n.*, *pl.* **cervixes, cervices** (sûr′və sēz′, sər vī′sēz). necklike part, esp. lower end of uterus. —**cer′vi·cal** (-vi kəl) *adj.*

Ce·sar′e·an (si zârē ən) *n.* delivery of baby by cutting through abdomen and uterus. Also, **Cesare·an section, C-section, Cae·sar′e·an.**

ces·sa′tion (se sā′shən) *n.* stop.

ces′sion (sesh′ən) *n.* ceding.

cess′pool′ (ses′pōōl′) *n.* receptacle for waste, etc., from house.

cf., compare.

cg., centigram.

ch., **1.** chapter. **2.** church.

Cha·blis′ (sha blē′) *n.* dry white wine. Also, **cha·blis′.**

chafe (chāf) *v.*, **chafed, chafing.** make sore by rubbing.

chaff (chaf) *n.* **1.** grain husks. **2.** worthless matter. —*v.* **3.** tease.

chafing dish (chā′fing) device for warming food at table.

cha·grin′ (shə grin′) *n.* **1.** shame or disappointment. —*v.* **2.** cause chagrin to.

chain (chān) *n.* **1.** connected series of links. **2.** any series. **3.** mountain range. —*v.* **4.** fasten with chain.

chain reaction, process which automatically continues and spreads.

chain saw, power saw with teeth set on endless chain.

chair (châr) *n.* **1.** seat with a back and legs. **2.** position of authority. **3.** chairperson. —*v.* **4.** preside over.

chair′man, *n.*, *pl.* **-men.** presiding officer. Also, *fem.*, **chair′wom′an;** *masc. or fem.*, **chair′per′son.**

chaise longue (shāz′ lông′) type of couch.

cha·let′ (sha lā′) *n.* mountain house.

chal′ice (chal′is) *n.* cup for ritual wine.

chalk (chôk) *n.* **1.** soft limestone used to write on chalkboards. —*v.* **2.** mark with chalk. —**chalk′board′,** *n.*

chal′lenge (chal′inj) *n.*, *v.*, **-lenged, -lenging.** —*n.* **1.** call to fight, contest, etc. **2.** demand for identification. **3.** objection to juror. —*v.* **4.** make challenge to.

cham′ber (chām′bər) *n.* **1.** room, esp. bedroom. **2.** assembly hall. **3.** legislative body. **4.** space in gun for ammunition.

cham′ber·maid′, *n.* maid who cleans bedrooms.

chamber music, music for performance by a small ensemble in a room or parlor.

cha·me′le·on (kə mē′lē ən) *n.* lizard able to change color.

cham′ois (sham′ē) *n.* **1.** European antelope. **2.** soft leather from its skin.

cham′o·mile (kam′ə mīl′, -mēl′) *n.* plant whose flowers are used as a tea. Also, **cam′o·mile.**

champ, *n.* (champ). **1.** *Informal.* champion. —*v.* (chomp, champ). **2.** bite.

cham·pagne′ (sham pān′) *n.* sparkling white wine.

cham′pi·on (cham′pē ən) *n.* **1.** best competitor. **2.** supporter. —*v.* **3.** advocate. —*adj.* **4.** best. —**cham′pi·on·ship′,** *n.*

chance (chans) *n.*, *v.*, **chanced, chancing,** *adj.* —*n.* **1.** fate; luck. **2.** possibility. **3.** opportunity. **4.** risk. —*v.* **5.** occur by chance. **6.** risk. —*adj.* **7.** accidental.

chan′cel (chan′səl) *n.* space around church altar.

chan′cel·ler·y (-sə lə rē, -səl rē) *n.*, *pl.* **-leries.** offices of chancellor.

chan′cel·lor (-sə lər) *n.* **1.** high government official. **2.** university head.

chan′cre (shang′kər) *n.*, lesion, as of syphilis.

chanc′y (chan′sē) *adj.*, **-cier, -ciest.** risky; uncertain.

chan·de·lier′ (shan′dl ēr′) *n.* hanging lighting fixture.

change (chānj) *v.*, **changed, changing,** *n.* —*v.* **1.** alter in condition, etc. **2.** substitute for. **3.** put on other clothes. —*n.* **4.** alteration. **5.** substitution. **6.** novelty. **7.** coins of low value. —**change′a·ble,** *adj.*

change of life, menopause.

change′o′ver, *n.* change from one system to another.

chan′nel (chan′l) *n.*, *v.*, **-neled, -neling.** —*n.* **1.** bed of stream. **2.** wide strait. **3.** access; route. **4.** broadcast frequency band. —*v.* **5.** convey or direct in channel.

chant (chant) *n.* **1.** song; psalm. —*v.* **2.** sing, esp. slowly.

chant′ey (shan′tē) *n.*, *pl.* **-eys, -ies.** sailors' song. Also, **chant′y.**

Cha′nu·kah (кнä′nə kə, hä′-) *n.* Hanukkah.

cha′os (kā′os) *n.* utter disorder. —**cha·ot′ic** (-ot′ik) *adj.*

chap (chap) *v.*, **chapped, chapping,** *n.* **1.** roughen and redden. —*n.* **2.** *Informal.* fellow.

chap., chapter.

chap′el (chap′əl) *n.* small church.

chap′er·on′ (shap′ə rōn′) *n.*, *v.*, **-oned, -oning.** —*n.* **1.** escort of young unmarried woman for propriety. —*v.* **2.** be a chaperon to or for. Also, **chap′er·one′.**

chap′lain (chap′lin) *n.* institutional clergyman.

chaps (chaps, shaps) *n.pl.* leather leg protectors worn by cowboys.

chap′ter (chap′tər) *n.* **1.** division of book. **2.** branch of society.

char (chär) *v.*, **charred, charring.** burn slightly.

char′ac·ter (kar′ik tər) *n.* **1.** personal nature. **2.** reputation. **3.** person in fiction. **4.** written or printed symbol.

char′ac·ter·is′tic (-tə ris′tik) *adj.* **1.** typical. —*n.* **2.** special feature; trait.

char′ac·ter·ize′, *v.*, **-ized, -izing. 1.** distinguish. **2.** describe. —**char′ac·ter·i·za′tion,** *n.*

cha·rades′ (shə rādz′) *n.pl.* miming game.

char′broil′ (chär′-) *v.* broil over charcoal fire.

char′coal′, *n.* carbonized wood.

chard (chärd) *n.* plant with edible green leafy stalks.

Char′don·nay′ (shär′dn ā′) *n.* dry white wine.

charge (chärj) *v.*, **charged, charging,** *n.* —*v.* **1.** load or fill. **2.** put electricity through or into. **3.** command. **4.** accuse. **5.** ask payment of. **6.** attack. —*n.* **7.** load. **8.** unit of explosive. **9.** care. **10.** command. **11.** accusation. **12.** expense. **13.** price. **14.** attack. —**charge′a•ble,** *adj.*

charg′er, *n.* battle horse.

char′i•ot (char′ē ət) *n.* ancient two-wheeled carriage. —**char′i•ot•eer′,** *n.*

cha•ris′ma (kə riz′mə) *n.* power to charm and inspire people. —**char′is•mat′ic** (kar′iz mat′ik) *adj.*

char′i•ty (char′i tē) *n.*, *pl.* **-ties. 1.** aid to needy persons. **2.** benevolent institution. —**char′i•ta•ble,** *adj.*

char′la•tan (shär′lə tn) *n.* fraud.

charm (chärm) *n.* **1.** power to attract and please. **2.** magical object, verse, etc. —*v.* **3.** attract; enchant. —**charm′er,** *n.* —**charm′ing,** *adj.*

char′nel house (chär′nl) place for dead bodies.

chart (chärt) *n.* **1.** map. —*v.* **2.** make a chart of.

char′ter, *n.* **1.** document authorizing new corporation. —*v.* **2.** establish by charter. **3.** hire; lease.

char•treuse′ (shär trōōz′) *adj.*, *n.* yellowish green.

char′wom′an (chär′-) *n.* woman who cleans offices, houses, etc.

char′y (châr′ē) *adj.*, **charier, chariest.** careful.

chase (chās) *v.*, **chased, chasing,** *n.* —*v.* **1.** go after. **2.** drive away. —*n.* **3.** instance of chasing.

chasm (kaz′əm) *n.* deep cleft in earth.

chas′sis (chas′ē, shas′ē) *n.* frame, wheels, and motor of vehicle.

chaste (chāst) *adj.*, **chaster, chastest. 1.** virtuous. **2.** simple. —**chas′ti•ty** (chas′ti tē) *n.*

chas′ten (chā′sən) *v.* discipline.

chas•tise′ (chas tīz′, chas′tīz) *v.*, **-tised, -tising.** punish; beat.

chat (chat) *v.*, **chatted, chatting,** *n.* —*v.* **1.** talk informally. —*n.* **2.** informal talk.

cha•teau′ (sha tō′) *n.*, *pl.* **-teaux** (-tōz′). stately residence, esp. in France.

chat′tel (chat′l) *n.* article of property other than real estate.

chat′ter (chat′ər) *v.* **1.** talk rapidly or foolishly. **2.** click or rattle rapidly. —*n.* **3.** rapid or foolish talk.

chat′ter•box′, *n.* talkative person.

chat′ty (chat′ē) *adj.*, **-tier, -tiest.** loquacious.

chauf′feur (shō′fər, shō fûr′) *n.* hired driver.

chau•vin•ism′ (shō′və niz′əm) *n.* **1.** blind patriotism. **2.** fanatic devotion to one's race, gender, etc. —**chau′vin•ist** (-və nist) *n.*, *adj.*

cheap (chēp) *adj.* of low price or value. —**cheap′en,** *v.*

cheap′skate′, *n.* stingy person.

cheat (chēt) *v.* **1.** defraud; deceive. —*n.* **2.** fraud. **3.** one who defrauds.

check (chek) *v.* **1.** stop or restrain. **2.** investigate; verify. **3.** note with a mark. **4.** leave or receive for temporary custody. —*n.* **5.** stop; restraint. **6.** written order for bank to pay money. **7.** bill. **8.** identification tag. **9.** square pattern. **10.** *Chess.* direct attack on king.

check′er, *n.* **1.** piece used in checkers. **2.** (*pl.*) game played by two persons, each with 12 pieces.

check′er•board′, *n.* board with 64 squares on which checkers is played.

check′ered, *adj.* **1.** marked with squares. **2.** varied. **3.** dubious.

check′list′, *n.* list of items for comparison, verification, etc.

check′mate′ (-māt′) *n.*, *v.*, **-mated, -mating.** *Chess.* —*n.* **1.** inescapable check. —*v.* **2.** put into inescapable check.

check′out′, *n.* **1.** act of leaving and paying for hotel room. **2.** counter where customers pay for purchases.

check′point′, *n.* place, as at a border, where travelers are checked.

check′up′, *n.* physical examination.

ched′dar (ched′ər) *n.* sharp cheese.

cheek (chēk) *n.* **1.** soft side of face. **2.** *Informal.* impudence. —**cheek′•i•ly,** *adv.* —**cheek′y,** *adj.*

cheer (chēr) *n.* **1.** shout of support. **2.** gladness. —*v.* **3.** shout encouragement to. **4.** gladden. —**cheer′ful,** *adj.* —**cheer′less,** *adj.* —**cheer′y,** *adj.*

cheese (chēz) *n.* solid, edible product from milk.

cheese′burg′er, *n.* hamburger with melted cheese.

cheese′cloth′, *n.* open cotton fabric.

chee′tah (chē′tə) *n.* wild cat resembling leopard.

chef (shef) *n.* professional cook.

chem′i•cal (kem′i kəl) *adj.* **1.** of chemistry. —*n.* **2.** substance in chemistry. —**chem′i•cal•ly,** *adv.*

chemical warfare, warfare with the use of chemicals.

che•mise′ (shə mēz′) *n.* woman's undershirt.

chem′is•try (kem′ə strē) *n.* science of composition of substances. —**chem′ist,** *n.*

che•mo•ther′a•py (kē′mō ther′ə pē) *n.* treatment of disease, esp. cancer, with chemicals.

cheque (chek) *n.* *Brit.* bank check.

cher′ish (cher′ish) *v.* treat as dear.

Cher′o•kee′ (cher′ə kē′) *n.*, *pl.* **-kee, -kees.** member of an American Indian people.

cher′ry (cher′ē) *n.*, *pl.* **-ries.** small red fruit of certain trees.

cher′ub (cher′əb) *n.* **1.** *pl.* **cherubim** (-ə bim). celestial being. **2.** *pl.* **cherubs.** angelic child.

chess (ches) *n.* board game for two, each using 16 pieces.

chest (chest) *n.* **1.** part of body between neck and abdomen. **2.** large box.

chest′nut′ (ches′nut′) *n.* **1.** edible nut. **2.** reddish brown.

chev′i•ot (shev′ē ət) *n.* sturdy worsted fabric.

chev′ron (shev′rən) *n.* set of stripes indicating military rank.

chew (chōō) *v.* crush with teeth.

chew′y, *adj.*, **-ier, -iest,** not easily chewed.

Chey•enne′ (shī en′, -an′) *n.*, *pl.* **-enne, -ennes.** member of an American Indian people.

Chi•an′ti (kē än′tē) *n.* dry red wine.

chic (shēk) *adj.* stylish.
—**Pronunciation.** The pronunciation (chik) for the word chic is considered nonstandard except when used jokingly.

chi•can′er•y (shi kā′nə rē, chi-) *n.*, *pl.* **-ies.** deception; trick.

Chi•ca′no (chi kä′nō) *n.*, *pl.* **-nos.** Mexican-American. Also, *n.fem.*, **Chica′na.**

chick (chik) *n.* **1.** young chicken. **2.** *Slang.* young woman.

chick′a•dee′ (chik′ə dē′) *n.* small gray North American bird.

Chick′a•saw′ (chik′ə sô′) *n.*, *pl.* **-saw, -saws.** member of an American Indian people.

chick′en (chik′ən) *n.* common domestic fowl.

chicken pox, viral disease marked by eruption of blisters.

chick′pea′, *n.* **1.** legume with pealike seeds. **2.** its seed.

chic′o•ry (-ə rē) *n.*, *pl.* **-ries.** plant with edible leaves and root.

chide (chīd) *v.*, **chided, chiding.** scold. —**chid′er,** *n.*

chief (chēf) *n.* **1.** leader. —*adj.* **2.** main; principal. —**chief′ly,** *adv.*

chief′tain (-tən) *n.* leader.

chif•fon′ (shi fon′) *n.* sheer silk or rayon fabric.

chif′fo•nier′ (shif′ə nēr′) *n.* tall chest of drawers.

chig′ger (chig′ər) *n.* larva of certain mites.

chil′blains′ (chil′blānz′) *n.pl.* inflammation caused by overexposure to cold, etc.

child (chīld) *n.*, *pl.* **children** (chil′drən). **1.** baby. **2.** son or daughter. —**child′bear′ing,** *n.*, *adj.* —**child′birth,** *n.* —**child′hood,** *n.* —**child′ish,** *adj.* —**child′less,** *adj.* —**child′like′,** *adj.*

child′proof′, *adj.* designed to prevent child from being hurt.

chil′i (chil′ē) *n.*, *pl.* **-ies. 1.** pungent pod of a red pepper. **2.** dish made with these peppers. Also, **chil′e.**

chill (chil) *n.* **1.** coldness. —*adj.* **2.** cold. **3.** not cordial. —*v.* **4.** make or become cool. —**chill′y,** *adv.*

chime (chīm) *n.*, *v.*, **chimed, chiming.** —*n.* **1.** set of musical tubes, bells, etc. —*v.* **2.** sound harmoniously.

chi•me′ra (ki mēr′ə, kī-) *n.* **1.** (*often cap.*) mythical monster with lion's head, goat's body, and serpent's tail. **2.** dream.

chim′ney (chim′nē) *n.* passage for smoke.

chim•pan•zee′ (chim′pan zē′, chim-pan′zē) *n.* large, intelligent African ape.

chin (chin) *n.* part of face below mouth.

chi′na (chī′nə) *n.* ceramic ware.

chin•chil′la (chin chil′ə) *n.* small rodent valued for its fur.

Chi•nese′ (chī nēz′, -nēs′) *n.*, *pl.* **-nese.** native or language of China.

chink (chingk) *n.* **1.** crack. **2.** short ringing sound. —*v.* **3.** make such a sound.

Chi•nook′ (shi nōōk′, -nŏōk′, chi-) *n.*, *pl.* **-nook** or **-nooks.** member of an American Indian people.

chintz (chints) *n.* printed fabric.

chintz′y, *adj.*, **-ier, -iest.** cheap-looking.

chip (chip) *n.*, *v.*, **chipped, chipping.** —*n.* **1.** small flat piece. **2.** broken place. **3.** small plate carrying electric circuit. —*v.* **4.** cut or break off (bits). **5.** chip in, contribute.

chip′munk (-mungk) *n.* small striped rodent resembling squirrel.

chip′per, *adj. Informal.* lively.

chi•rop′o•dy (ki rop′ə dē, kī-) *n.* treatment of foot ailments.

chi′ro•prac′tor (kī′rə prak′tər) *n.* one who practices therapy based upon adjusting body structures.

chirp (chûrp) *n.* **1.** short, sharp sound of birds, etc. —*v.* **2.** make such sound. Also, **chir′rup** (chêr′əp, chûr′-).

chis′el (chiz′əl) *n.* **1.** tool with broad cutting tip. —*v.* **2.** cut with such tool. **3.** *Informal.* cheat.

chit′chat′ (chit′chat′) *n.* light talk.

chiv′al•ry (shiv′əl rē) *n.*, *pl.* **-ries. 1.** qualities such as courtesy and courage. **2.** knightly way of life. —**chiv′al•ric, chiv′al•rous,** *adj.*

chive (chīv) *n.* (*usually pl.*) onionlike plant with slender leaves.

chlo•rine (klôr′ēn, -in) *n.* green gaseous element. **—chlor′in•ate′** (-i nāt′) *v.*, **-ated, -ating.**

chlo′ro•form′ (klôr′ə fôrm′) *n.* **1.** liquid used as anesthetic. **—v. 2.** administer chloroform to.

chlo′ro•phyll (-fil) *n.* green coloring matter of plants.

chock (chok) *n.* wedge; block.

choc′o•late (chô′kə lit) *n.* **1.** product made from cacao seeds. **2.** dark brown.

Choc′taw (chok′tô) *n.*, *pl.* **-taw, -taws.** member of an American Indian people.

choice (chois) *n.* **1.** act or right of choosing. **2.** person or thing chosen. **—adj. 3.** excellent.

choir (kwīr) *n.* group of singers.

choke (chōk) *v.*, **choked, choking, —v. 1.** stop breath of. **2.** obstruct. **3.** be unable to breathe. **—n. 4.** act of choking.

chol′er•a (kol′ər ə) *n.* acute, often deadly, disease.

cho•les′te•rol′ (kə les′tə rôl′) *n.* fatty, crystalline substance in animal tissues.

chomp (chomp) *v.* chew noisily.

choose (chōōz) *v.*, **chose** (chōz), **chosen, choosing.** take as one thinks best. **—choos′er,** *n.*

choos′y, *adj.*, **-ier, -iest.** hard to please; particular.

chop (chop) *v.*, **chopped, chopping,** *n.* **—v. 1.** cut with blows. **2.** cut in pieces. **—n. 3.** sharp blow. **4.** slice of meat with rib. **5.** jaw.

chop′per, *n.* **1.** thing that chops. *Informal.* helicopter.

chop′py, *adj.*, **-pier, -piest.** forming short waves.

chop′sticks′, *n.pl.* sticks used in eating, esp. in some Asian countries.

chop su′ey (sōō′ē) Chinese-style vegetable dish.

cho′ral (kôr′əl) *adj.* for chorus.

cho•rale′ (kə ral′, -räl′) *n.* **1.** type of hymn. **2.** choir.

chord (kôrd) *n.* **1.** combination of harmonious tones. **2.** straight line across circle.

chore (chôr) *n.* routine job.

cho′re•og′ra•phy (kôr′ē og′rə fē) *n.* art of composing dances. **—cho′re•o• graph′** (-ə graf′) *v.* **—cho′re•og′ra• pher,** *n.*

chor′is•ter (kôr′ə stər) *n.* choir singer.

chor′tle (chôr′tl) *v.*, **-tled, -tling,** *n.* chuckle.

cho′rus (kôr′əs) *n.* **1.** group of singers. **2.** recurring melody.

chow (chou) *n. Slang.* food.

chow′der (chou′dər) *n.* vegetable soup usu. containing clams or fish.

chow mein (mān) Chinese-style dish served on fried noodles.

Christ (krīst) *n.* Jesus Christ; (in Christian belief) the Messiah.

chris′ten (kris′ən) *v.* baptize; name.

Chris′ten•dom (kris′ən dəm) *n.* all Christians.

Chris′tian (kris′chən) *adj.* **1.** of Jesus Christ, his teachings, etc. **—n. 2.** believer in Christianity.

Chris′ti•an′i•ty (-chē an′i tē) *n.* religion based on teachings of Christ.

Christ′mas (kris′məs) *n.* festival in honor of birth of Christ.

chro•mat′ic (krō mat′ik, krə-) *adj.* **1.** of color. **2.** *Music.* progressing by semitones.

chro′mi•um (krō′mē əm) *n.* lustrous metallic element. Also, **chrome.**

chro′mo•some′ (krō′mə sōm′) *n.* part of cell carrying genes.

chron′ic (kron′ik) *adj.* constant; longlasting; habitual.

chron′i•cle (kron′i kəl) *n.*, *v.*, **-cled, -cling. —n. 1.** record of events in order. **—v. 2.** record in chronicle.

chrono-, prefix meaning time, as *chronometer.*

chro•nol′o•gy (krə nol′ə jē) *n.*, *pl.* **-gies.** historical order of events. **—chron′o•log′i•cal** (kron′l· oj′i kəl) *adj.*

chro•nom′e•ter (krə nom′i tər) *n.* very exact clock.

chrys′a•lis (kris′ə lis) *n.* pupa.

chry•san′the•mum (kri san′thə məm) *n.* large, colorful flower.

chub′by, *adj.*, **-bier, -biest.** plump.

chuck (chuk) *v.* **1.** pat lightly. **—n. 2.** light pat. **3.** cut of beef.

chuck′le (chuk′əl) *v.*, **-led, -ling,** *n.* **—v. 1.** laugh softly. **—n. 2.** soft laugh.

chum (chum) *n.* close friend. **—chum′my,** *adj.*, **-mier, -miest.**

chump (chump) *n. Informal.* fool.

chunk (chungk) *n.* big lump.

chunk′y, *adj.*, **-ier, -iest. 1.** thick or stout; stocky. **2.** full of chunks.

church (chûrch) *n.* **1.** place of Christian worship. **2.** sect.

churl′ish (chûr′lish) *adj.* boorish.

churn (chûrn) *n.* **1.** agitator for making butter. **—v. 2.** agitate.

chute (shōōt) *n.* sloping slide.

chut′ney (chut′nē) *n.* East Indian relish.

chutz′pah (кнооt′spə, hoot′-) *n. Slang.* nerve; gall. Also, **chutz′pa.**

CIA, Central Intelligence Agency.

ci•ca′da (si kā′də) *n.* large insect with shrill call.

-cide, suffix indicating: **1.** killer, as *pesticide.* **2.** killing, as *homicide.*

ci′der (sī′dər) *n.* apple juice.

ci•gar′ (si gär′) *n.* roll of tobacco for smoking.

cig′a•rette′ (sig′ə ret′) *n.* roll of smoking tobacco in paper.

cinch (sinch) *n.* **1.** firm hold. **2.** *Informal.* sure or easy thing.

cin′der (sin′dər) *n.* burned piece; ash.

cin′e•ma (sin′ə mə) *n.* **1.** motion pictures. **2.** movie theater.

cin′e•ma•tog′ra•phy (-tog′rə fē) *n.* art or technique of motion-picture photography.

cin′na•mon (sin′ə mən) *n.* brown spice from bark of Asian tree.

ci′pher (sī′fər) *n.* **1.** the symbol (0) for zero. **2.** secret writing, using code. **—v. 3.** calculate.

cir′ca (sûr′kə) *prep.* approximately.

cir′cle (sûr′kəl) *n.*, *v.*, **-cled, -cling. —n. 1.** closed curve of uniform distance from its center. **2.** range; scope. **3.** group of friends or associates. **—v. 4.** enclose or go in circle.

cir′cuit (-kit) *n.* **1.** tour, esp. in connection with duties. **2.** electrical path or arrangement. **—cir′cuit•ry,** *n.*

circuit breaker, device that interrupts electrical circuit to prevent excessive current.

cir•cu′i•tous (sər kyōō′i təs) *adj.* roundabout. **—cir•cu′i•tous•ly,** *adv.*

cir′cu•lar (-kyə lər) *adj.* **1.** of or in circle. **—n. 2.** advertisement distributed widely.

cir′cu•late′ (-lāt′) *v.*, **-lated, -lating.** move or pass around. **—cir′cu•la′tion,** *n.* **—cir′cu•la•to′ry** (-lə tôr′ē) *adj.*

circum-, prefix indicating around or about, as *circumnavigate.*

cir′cum•cise′ (sûr′kəm sīz′) *v.*, **-cised, -cising.** remove foreskin of. **—cir′cum•ci′sion** (-sizh′ən) *n.*

cir•cum′fer•ence (sər kum′fər əns) *n.* outer boundary of a circle.

cir′cum•flex′ (sûr′kəm fleks′) *n.* diacritical mark (ˆ).

cir′cum•lo•cu′tion (-lō kyōō′shən) *n.* roundabout expression.

cir′cum•nav′i•gate′ (-nav′i gāt′) *v.*, **-gated, -gating.** sail around.

cir′cum•scribe′ (-skrīb′) *v.*, **-scribed, -scribing. 1.** encircle. **2.** confine.

cir′cum•spect′ (-spekt′) *adj.* cautious. **—cir′cum•spec′tion** (-spek′- shən) *n.*

cir′cum•stance′ (-stans′) *n.* **1.** condition accompanying or affecting event. **2.** existing condition, esp. with regard to finances. **3.** ceremony.

cir′cum•stan′tial (-stan′shəl) *adj.* of or from circumstances.

cir′cum•vent′ (-vent′) *v.* outwit or evade. **—cir′cum•ven′tion,** *n.*

cir′cus (sûr′kəs) *n.* show with animals, acrobats, etc.

cir•rho′sis (si rō′sis) *n.* chronic liver disease.

cir′rus (sir′əs) *n.* fleecy cloud.

cis′tern (sis′tərn) *n.* reservoir.

cit′a•del (sit′ə dl, -ə del′) *n.* fortress.

cite (sīt) *v.*, **cited, citing. 1.** mention in proof, etc. **2.** summon. **3.** commend. **—ci•ta′tion,** *n.*

cit′i•zen (sit′ə zən, -sən) *n.* subject of a country. **—cit′i•zen•ship′,** *n.*

citric acid (si′trik) white powder in citrus fruits.

cit′ron (si′trən) *n.* lemonlike fruit.

cit′ro•nel′la (si′trə nel′ə) *n.* pungent oil used esp. as insect repellent.

cit′rus (si′trəs) *adj.* of the genus including the orange, lemon, etc.

cit′y (sit′ē) *n.*, *pl.* **-ies.** large town.

civ′ic (siv′ik) *adj.* **1.** of cities. **2.** of citizens.

civ′ics, *n.* study of citizenship.

civ′il (-əl) *adj.* **1.** of citizens. **2.** civilized. **3.** polite. **—ci•vil′i•ty** (-vil′i tē) *n.*

ci•vil′ian (si vil′yən) *n.* **1.** nonmilitary or nonpolice person. **—adj. 2.** of such persons.

civ′i•li•za′tion (siv′ə lə zā′shən) *n.* **1.** process of civilizing. **2.** culture of a people or period.

civ′i•lize (-līz′) *v.*, **-lized, -lizing.** bring out of savage state.

civil liberty, fundamental right guaranteed by law.

civil rights, rights of all people to freedom and equality.

civil servant, employee of civil service.

civil service, branches of governmental administration outside the armed services.

civil war, war between parts of same country.

cl., centiliter.

claim (klām) *v.* **1.** demand as one's right, property, etc. **2.** assert. **—n. 3.** demand. **4.** assertion. **5.** something claimed. **—claim′ant,** *n.*

clair•voy′ant (klâr voi′ənt) *adj.* seeing beyond physical vision. **—clair• voy′ant,** *n.* **—clair•voy′ance,** *n.*

clam (klam) *n.* common mollusk.

clam′ber (klam′bər, klam′ər) *v.* climb awkwardly.

clam′my, *adj.*, **-mier, -miest.** cold and moist. **—clam′mi•ness,** *n.*

clam′or (klam′ər) *n.* **1.** loud outcry or noise. **—v. 2.** raise clamor. **—clam′or• ous,** *adj.*

clamp (klamp) *n.* **1.** clasping device. —*v.* **2.** fasten with clamp.

clan (klan) *n.* related families.

clan•des/tine (klan des/tin) *adj.* done in secret.

clang (klang) *v.* **1.** ring harshly. —*n.* **2.** Also, **clang/or.** harsh ring.

clank (klangk) *v.* **1.** ring dully. —*n.* **2.** dull ringing.

clap (klap) *v.,* **clapped, clapping,** *n.* —*v.* **1.** hit together, as hands in applause. —*n.* **2.** act of clapping.

clap/board (klab/ərd) *n.* overlapping boards on exterior walls.

clap/trap/ (klap/-) *n.* empty speech.

clar/et (klar/it) *n.* dry red wine.

clar/i•fy/ (klar/ə fī/) *v.,* **-fied, -fying.** make or become clear. —**clar/i•fi•ca/tion,** *n.*

clar/i•net/ (-ə net/) *n.* musical wind instrument.

clar/i•on (-ē ən) *adj.* clear and loud.

clar/i•ty (-i tē) *n.* clearness.

clash (klash) *v.* **1.** conflict. **2.** collide. —*n.* **3.** collision. **4.** conflict.

clasp (klasp) *n.* **1.** fastening device. **2.** hug. —*v.* **3.** fasten. **4.** hug.

class (klas) *n.* **1.** group of similar persons or things. **2.** social rank. **3.** group of students. **4.** division. **5.** *Informal.* elegance, grace, or dignity. —*v.* **6.** place in classes. —**class/mate/,** *n.* —**class/room/,** *n.*

class action, lawsuit on behalf of persons with complaint in common.

clas/sic (klas/ik) *adj.* Also, **clas/si•cal.** **1.** of finest or fundamental type. **2.** in Greek or Roman manner. —*n.* **3.** author, book, etc., of acknowledged superiority. —**clas/si•cism/** (klas/ə siz/əm) *n.*

clas/si•fied/ (klas/ə fīd/) *adj.* limited to authorized persons.

clas/si•fy/, *v.,* **-fied, -fying.** arrange in classes. —**clas/si•fi•ca/tion,** *n.*

class•y, *adj.,* **-ier, -iest.** *Informal.* stylish; elegant. —**class/i•ness,** *n.*

clat/ter (klat/ər) *v., n.* rattle.

clause (klôz) *n.* part of sentence with its own subject and predicate.

claus/tro•pho/bi•a (klô/strə fō/bē ə) *n.* dread of closed places. —**claus/tro•pho/bic,** *adj.,*

clav/i•chord/ (klav/i kôrd/) *n.* early keyboard instrument.

clav/i•cle (klav/i kəl) *n.* collarbone.

claw (klô) *n.* **1.** sharp, curved nail on animal's paw. —*v.* **2.** dig or scratch roughly.

clay (klā) *n.* soft earth, used in making bricks, pottery, etc.

clean (klēn) *adj.* **1.** free from dirt. **2.** complete. —*adv.* **3.** completely. —*v.* **4.** make clean. —**clean/er,** *n.*

clean•ly (klen/lē) *adj.* keeping or kept clean. —**clean/li•ness,** *n.*

cleanse (klenz) *v.,* **cleansed, cleansing.** make clean. —**cleans/er,** *n.*

clear (klēr) *adj.* **1.** bright. **2.** easily perceived. **3.** evident. **4.** unobstructed. **5.** free of obligations. **6.** blameless. —*adv.* **7.** in a clear manner. —*v.* **8.** make or become clear. **9.** pay in full. **10.** pass beyond. —**clear/ly,** *adv.*

clear/ance, *n.* **1.** space between objects. **2.** authorization.

clear/-cut/, *adj.* apparent; obvious.

clear/ing, *n.* treeless space.

cleat (klēt) *n.* metal piece to which ropes, etc., are fastened.

cleav/age (klē/vij) *n.* space between woman's breasts.

cleave (klēv) *v.,* **cleft** (kleft) or **cleaved, cleaving.** split.

cleave (klēv) *v.,* **cleaved, cleaving. 1.** cling **2.** remain faithful.

cleav/er, *n.* heavy knife.

clef (klef) *n.* musical symbol indicating pitch.

cleft (kleft) *n.* split.

cleft palate, birth defect involving fissure in the roof of the mouth.

clem•a•tis (klem/ə tis) *n.* flowering vine.

clem/ent (klem/ənt) *adj.* **1.** lenient. **2.** mild. —**clem/en•cy,** *n.*

clench (klench) *v.* close tightly.

cler/gy (klûr/jē) *n., pl.* **-gies.** religious officials. —**cler/gy•man,** *n.* —**cler/gy•wom•an,** *n.fem.*

cler/ic (kler/ik) *n.* member of the clergy.

cler/i•cal, *adj.* **1.** of clerks. **2.** of clergy.

clerk (klûrk) *n.* **1.** employee who keeps records, etc. **2.** sales person in store.

clev/er (klev/ər) *adj.* bright, witty, or creative. —**clev/er•ly,** *adv.*

CLI or **cli,** cost-of-living index.

cli•ché/ (klē shā/) *n.* trite expression.

click (klik) *n.* **1.** slight, sharp noise. —*v.* **2.** make a click. **3.** *Slang.* succeed.

cli/ent (klī/ənt) *n.* customer.

cli/en•tele/ (-ən tel/) *n.* patrons.

cliff (klif) *n.* steep bank.

cliff/-hang/er, *n.* suspenseful situation.

cli/mate (klī/mit) *n.* weather conditions. —**cli•mat/ic** (-mat/ik) *adj.*

cli/max (klī/maks) *n.* high point. —**cli•mac/tic** (-mak/tik) *adj.*

climb (klīm) *v.* **1.** ascend. **2.** climb down, **a.** descend. **b.** *Informal.* compromise. —*n.* **3.** ascent.

clinch (klinch) *v.* **1.** fasten (a nail) by bending the point. **2.** hold tightly. **3.** settle decisively. —*n.* **4.** act of clinching. —**clinch/er,** *n.*

cling (kling) *v.,* **clung** (klung), **clinging.** hold firmly to.

clin/ic (klin/ik) *n.* hospital for nonresident or charity patients. —**clin/i•cal,** *adj.*

clink (klingk) *v.* **1.** make light, ringing sound. —*n.* **2.** such a sound.

clink/er (kling/kər) *n.* fused mass of incombustible residue.

clip (klip) *v.,* **clipped, clipping,** *n.* —*v.* **1.** cut with short snips. **2.** hit sharply. —*n.* **3.** act of clipping. **4.** clasp. **5.** cartridge holder.

clip/per (klip/ər) *n.* **1.** cutting device. **2.** fast sailing vessel.

clique (klēk) *n.* elitist group.

clit/o•ris (klit/ər is) *n., pl.* **clitorises** or **clitorides** (kli tôr/i dēz/). erectile organ of vulva.

cloak (klōk) *n.* **1.** loose outer garment. —*v.* **2.** cover with cloak. **3.** hide.

cloak/-and-dag/ger, *adj.* of espionage or intrigue.

clob/ber (klob/ər) *v. Informal.* batter or defeat.

clock (klok) *n.* device for telling time.

clock/wise/, *adv., adj.* in direction that clock hands turn.

clock/work/, *n.* **1.** mechanism of a clock. **2.** perfectly regular function, like that of a clock.

clod (klod) *n.* piece of earth.

clog (klog) *v.,* **clogged, clogging,** *n.* —*v.* **1.** hamper; obstruct. —*n.* **2.** obstruction, etc. **3.** heavy wooden shoe.

clois/ter (kloi/stər) *n.* **1.** covered walk. **2.** monastery or nunnery.

clone (klōn) *n., v.,* **cloned, cloning.** —*n.* **1.** organism created by asexual reproduction. **2.** *Informal.* duplicate. —*v.* **3.** grow as clone.

close, *v.,* **closed, closing,** *adj., n.,* **closest,** *adv., n.* —*v.* (klōz) **1.** shut,

obstruct, or end. **2.** come to terms. —*adj.* (klōs) **3.** shut. **4.** confined. **5.** lacking fresh air. **6.** secretive. **7.** compact. **8.** near. **9.** intimate. —*adv.* (klōs) **10.** in a close manner. —*n.* (klōz) **11.** end. —**close/ly,** *adv.* —**clo/sure** (klō/zhər) *n.*

close call (klōs) narrow escape.

closed/-cap/tioned, *adj.* broadcast with captions visible only with decoding device.

closed shop, place where workers must belong to union.

close/out/ (klōz/-) *n.* sale at greatly reduced prices.

clos/et (kloz/it) *n.* **1.** cabinet for clothes, etc. —*adj.* **2.** clandestine.

close/up/ (klōs/-) *n.* photograph taken at close range.

clot (klot) *n., v.,* **clotted, clotting.** —*n.* **1.** mass, esp. of dried blood. —*v.* **2.** form clot.

cloth (klôth) *n.* fabric of threads.

clothe (klōth) *v.,* **clothed** or **clad** (klad), **clothing.** dress.

clothes (klōz, klōthz) *n.pl.* garments; apparel. Also, **cloth/ing.**

cloud (kloud) *n.* **1.** mass of water particles, etc., in the air. —*v.* **2.** grow dark or gloomy. **3.** lose or deprive of transparency. —**cloud/y,** *adj.*

clout (klout) *n.* **1.** blow from hand. **2.** influence. —*v.* **3.** hit with hand.

clove (klōv) *n.* **1.** tropical spice. **2.** section of plant bulb.

clo/ver (klō/vər) *n.* three-leaved plant.

clown (kloun) *n.* **1.** comic performer. **2.** prankster. **3.** fool. —*v.* **4.** act like a clown. —**clown/ish,** *adj.*

cloy (kloi) *v.* weary by excess, as of sweetness.

club (klub) *n., v.,* **clubbed, clubbing.** —*n.* **1.** bat. **2.** organized group. **3.** (*pl.*) suit of playing cards. —*v.* **4.** beat with club.

club/foot/, *n.* deformed foot.

club soda, soda water.

cluck (kluk) *n.* **1.** call of hen. —*v.* **2.** utter such call.

clue (klōō) *n.* hint in solving mystery, etc.

clump (klump) *n.* cluster.

clum/sy (klum/zē) *adj.,* **-sier, -siest.** awkward. —**clum/si•ly,** *adv.*

clus/ter (klus/tər) *n.* **1.** group; bunch. —*v.* **2.** gather into cluster.

clutch (kluch) *v.* **1.** grasp. —*n.* **2.** grasp. **3.** (*pl.*) control. **4.** device for engaging or disengaging machinery.

clut/ter (klut/ər) *v.* **1.** litter untidily. —*n.* **2.** disorderly heap.

cm., centimeter.

CO, 1. Colorado. **2.** Commanding Officer.

co-, prefix indicating: **1.** together, as *cooperate.* **2.** joint or jointly, as *coauthor.*

Co., 1. Company. **2.** County.

c/o, care of.

coach (kōch) *n.* **1.** enclosed carriage, bus, etc. **2.** trainer. —*v.* **3.** instruct.

co•ag/u•late/ (kō ag/yə lāt/) *v.,* **-lated, -lating.** thicken or clot.

coal (kōl) *n.* black mineral burned as fuel.

co•a•lesce/ (kō/ə les/) *v.,* **-lesced, -lescing.** unite or ally.

co/a•li/tion (-lish/ən) *n.* alliance.

coarse (kôrs) *adj.,* **coarser, coarsest. 1.** rough or harsh. **2.** vulgar. —**coarse/ly,** *adv.* —**coars/en,** *v.*

coast (kōst) *n.* **1.** seashore. —*v.* **2.** drift easily. —**coast/al,** *adj.*

coast/er, *n.* object protecting surfaces from moisture.

coast guard, military service that enforces maritime laws, saves lives at sea, etc.

coat (kōt) *n.* **1.** outer garment. **2.** covering, as fur or bark. —*v.* **3.** cover or enclose.

coat′ing, *n.* outer layer.

coat of arms, emblems, motto, etc., of one's family.

co•au′thor (kō ô′thər, kō′ô′-) *n.* one of two or more joint authors. —**co•au′thor,** *v.*

coax (kōks) *v.* influence by persuasion, flattery, etc. —**coax′er,** *n.*

co•ax′i•al (kō ak′sē əl) *adj.* having a common axis, as **coaxial cables** for simultaneous long-distance transmission of radio or television signals.

cob (kob) *n.* corncob.

co′balt (kō′bôlt) *n.* silvery metallic element.

cob′ble (kob′əl) *v.,* **-bled, -bling,** *n.* —*v.* **1.** mend (shoes). —*n.* **2.** Also, **cob′ble•stone′.** round stone for paving, etc. —**cob′bler,** *n.*

COBOL (kō′bôl) *n.* computer language for writing programs to process large files.

co′bra (kō′brə) *n.* venomous snake.

cob′web′ (kob′-) *n.* spider web.

co•caine′ (kō kān′, kō′kān) *n.* narcotic drug.

cock (kok) *n.* **1.** male bird. **2.** valve. **3.** hammer in gun. **4.** pile of hay. —*v.* **5.** set cock of (a gun). **6.** set aslant.

cock•ade′ (ko kād′) *n.* hat ornament.

cock′a•too′ (kok′ə tōō′, kok′ə tōō′) *n.* colorful crested parrot.

cock′eyed′, *adj.* **1.** tilted to one side. **2.** absurd. **3.** drunk.

cock′le (kok′əl) *n.* **1.** mollusk with radially ribbed valves. **2.** inmost part.

cock′ney (-nē) *n.* **1.** resident of London, esp. East End. **2.** pronunciation of such persons.

cock′pit′, *n.* space for pilot.

cock′roach′, *n.* common crawling insect.

cock′tail′, *n.* **1.** drink containing mixture of liquors. **2.** mixed appetizer.

cock′y, *adj.,* **-ier, -iest.** too sure of oneself. —**cock′i•ness,** *n.*

co′coa (kō′kō) *n.* **1.** powdered seeds of cacao, used esp. in making a beverage. —*adj.* **2.** brown.

co′co•nut′ (kō′kə nut′, -nət) *n.* large, hard-shelled seed of the **co′co palm.**

co•coon′ (kə kōōn′) *n.* silky larval covering.

cod (kod) *n.* edible Atlantic fish.

C.O.D., cash, or collect, on delivery.

co′da (kō′də) *n.* final passage of a musical movement.

cod′dle (kod′l) *v.,* **-dled, -dling. 1.** pamper. **2.** cook in boiling water.

code (kōd) *n., v.,* **coded, coding.** —*n.* **1.** collection of laws or rules. **2.** system of signals or secret words. —*v.* **3.** put in code.

co′deine (kō′dēn) *n.* drug derived from opium.

codg′er (koj′ər) *n.* eccentric man.

cod′i•cil (kod′ə səl) *n.* supplement, esp. to a will.

cod′i•fy′ (kod′ə fī′, kō′də-) *v.,* **-fied, -fying.** organize into legal or formal code. —**cod′i•fi•ca′tion,** *n.*

co′ed′ (kō′ed′, -ed′) *n.* female student, esp. in coeducational school.

co′ed•u•ca′tion, *n.* education of both sexes in the same classes.

co′ef•fi′cient (kō′ə fish′ənt) *n.* number by which another is multiplied.

co•erce′ (kō ûrs′) *v.,* **-erced, -ercing.** force; compel. —**co•er′cive,** *adj.* —**co•er′cion** (-ûr′shən) *n.*

co′ex•ist′ (kō′ig zist′) *v.* **1.** exist simultaneously. **2.** exist together peacefully. —**co′ex•ist′ence,** *n.*

cof′fee (kô′fē) *n.* **1.** brown seeds of tropical tree. **2.** beverage made by roasting and grinding these seeds.

cof′fer (kô′fər) *n.* chest.

cof′fin (kô′fin) *n.* box for a corpse.

cog (kog) *n.* tooth on wheel (**cog′wheel′**), connecting with another such wheel.

co′gent (kō′jənt) *adj.* convincing. —**co′gen•cy,** *n.* —**co′gent•ly,** *adv.*

cog′i•tate′ (koj′i tāt′) *v.,* **-tated, -tating.** ponder. —**cog′i•ta′tion,** *n.*

co′gnac (kōn′yak) *n.* brandy.

cog′nate (kog′nāt) *adj.* related.

cog•ni′tion (-nish′ən) *n.* knowing.

cog′ni•zance (-nə zəns) *n.* notice, esp. official. —**cog′ni•zant,** *adj.*

cog•no•scen′ti (kon′yə shen′tē, kog′-nə-), *n.pl., sing.* **-te** (-tā; -tē). those having superior knowledge.

co•hab′it (kō hab′it) *v.* live together, esp. as husband and wife without being married. —**co•hab′i•ta′tion,** *n.*

co•here′ (kō hēr′) *v.,* **-hered, -hering.** stick together. —**co•he′sion** (-hē′-zhən) *n.* —**co•he′sive** (-siv) *adj.*

co•her′ent (-hēr′ənt, -her′-) *adj.* making sense. —**co•her′ence,** *n.*

co′hort (kō′hôrt) *n.* **1.** companion. **2.** group, esp. of soldiers.

coif•fure′ (kwä fyōōr′) *n.* arrangement of hair.

coil (koil) *v.* **1.** wind spirally or in rings. —*n.* **2.** ring. **3.** series of spirals.

coin (koin) *n.* **1.** piece of metal used as money. —*v.* **2.** make metal into money. **3.** invent. —**coin′age,** *n.*

co′in•cide′ (kō′in sīd′) *v.,* **-cided, -ciding. 1.** occur at same time, place, etc. **2.** match. —**co•in′ci•dence** (-si-dəns) *n.* —**co•in′ci•den′tal** (-den′tl) *adj.* —**co•in′ci•den′tal•ly,** *adv.*

co′i•tus (kō′i təs) *n.* sexual intercourse. —**co′i•tal,** *adj.*

coke (kōk) *n.* —*n.* **1.** solid carbon produced from coal. **2.** *Slang.* cocaine.

Col., 1. Colonel. **2.** Colorado.

co′la (kō′lə) *n.* soft drink containing extract from kola nuts.

col′an•der (kul′ən dər, kol′-) *n.* large strainer.

cold (kōld) *adj.* **1.** without warmth. **2.** not cordial. —*n.* **3.** absence of heat. **4.** common illness marked by runny nose. —**cold′ly,** *adv.*

cold′-blood′ed, *adj.* **1.** callous; unemotional. **2.** with blood at same temperature as environment.

cold cream, preparation for cleansing or soothing the skin.

cold feet, *Informal.* lack of courage.

cold shoulder, deliberate show of indifference.

cold turkey, *Informal.* —*n.* **1.** abrupt withdrawal from addictive substance. —*adv.* **2.** impromptu.

cold war, rivalry between nations just short of armed conflict.

cole′slaw′ (kōl′slô′) *n.* sliced raw cabbage.

col′ic (kol′ik) *n.* pain in bowels.

col′i•se′um (kol′i sē′əm) *n.* large stadium.

co•li′tis (kə lī′tis, kō-) *n.* inflammation of the colon.

col•lab′o•rate′ (kə lab′ə rāt′) *v.,* **-rated, -rating.** work together. —**col•lab′o•ra′tion,** *n.* —**col•lab′o•ra′tor,** *n.*

col•lage′ (kə läzh′) *n.* work of art made with various materials pasted on a surface.

col•lapse′ (kə laps′) *v.,* **-lapsed, -lapsing,** *n.* —*v.* **1.** fall in or together.

2. fail abruptly. —*n.* **3.** a falling-in. **4.** sudden failure. —**col•laps′i•ble,** *adj.*

col′lar (kol′ər) *n.* **1.** part of garment around neck. —*v.* **2.** seize by collar.

col′lar•bone′, *n.* slender bone connecting sternum and scapula; clavicle.

col•lat′er•al (kə lat′ər əl) *n.* **1.** security pledged on loan. —*adj.* **2.** additional. **3.** on side.

col′league (kol′ēg) *n.* associate in work, etc.

col•lect′ (kə lekt′) *v.* **1.** gather together. **2.** take payment of. —*adj., adv.* **3.** payable on delivery. —**col•lec′tion,** *n.* —**col•lec′tor,** *n.*

col•lect′i•ble, *n.* **1.** object collected. —*adj.* **2.** able to be collected.

col•lec′tive, *adj.* **1.** by a group. —*n.* **2.** socialist productive group.

collective bargaining, negotiation between union and employer.

col•lec′tiv•ism, *n.* principle of communal control. —**col•lec′tiv•ist,** *n.*

col′lege (kol′ij) *n.* school of higher learning. —**col•le′giate** (kə lē′jit) *adj.*

col•lide′ (kə līd′) *v.,* **-lided, -liding.** strike together violently.

col′lie (kol′ē) *n.* kind of large, long-haired dog.

col′lier (kol′yər) *n.* **1.** ship for carrying coal. **2.** coal miner.

col•li′sion (kə lizh′ən) *n.* **1.** crash. **2.** conflict.

col•lo′qui•al (kə lō′kwē əl) *adj.* appropriate to casual rather than formal speech or writing.

col•lo′qui•um (-kwē əm) *n., pl.* **-quiums, -quia** (-kwē ə). conference of experts.

col′lo•quy (kol′ə kwē) *n., pl.* **-quies.** conversation.

col•lu′sion (kə lōō′zhən) *n.* illicit agreement.

Colo., Colorado.

co•logne′ (kə lōn′) *n.* perfumed toilet water.

co′lon (kō′lən) *n.* **1.** mark of punctuation (:). **2.** part of large intestine. —**co•lon′ic** (kə lon′ik) *adj.*

colo′nel (kûr′nl) *n.* military officer below general. —**colo′nel•cy,** *n.*

co•lo′ni•al•ism (kə lō′nē ə liz′əm) *n.* policy of extending national authority over foreign territories.

col′on•nade′ (kol′ə nād′) *n.* series of columns.

col′o•ny (kol′ə nē) *n., pl.* **-nies. 1.** group of people settling in another land. **2.** territory subject to outside ruling power. **3.** community. —**co•lo′ni•al** (kə lō′nē əl) *adj., n.* —**col′o•nist,** *n.* —**col′o•nize′,** *v.,* **-nized, -nizing.**

col′or (kul′ər) *n.* **1.** quality of light perceived by human eye. **2.** pigment. **3.** complexion. **4.** vivid description. **5.** (*pl.*) flag. **6.** race. —*v.* **7.** apply color to. Also, *Brit.,* **col′our.** —**col′or•ing,** *n.*

col′o•ra•tu′ra (kul′ər ə tōōr′ə, -tyōōr′ə, kol′-) *n.* soprano specializing in music containing ornamental trills.

col′or-blind′, *adj.* **1.** unable to distinguish certain colors. **2.** without racial bias.

col′ored, *adj. Often Offensive.* belonging to a race other than Caucasian.

col′or•ful, *adj.* **1.** full of color. **2.** vivid; interesting.

col′or•less, *adj.* **1.** without color. **2.** uninteresting. —**col′or•less•ly,** *adv.*

co•los′sal (kə los′əl) *adj.* huge.

co•los′sus (-los′əs) *n.* anything colossal.

colt (kōlt) *n.* young male horse.

col′umn (kol′əm) *n.* **1.** upright shaft or support. **2.** long area of print. **3.** regular journalistic piece. **4.** long group of troops, ships, etc. —**col′um‑nist** (-əm nist) *n.*

com-, prefix indicating: **1.** with or together, as *commingle.* **2.** completely, as *commit.*

co′ma (kō′mə) *n.* unconscious state. —**com′a·tose′** (-tōs′) *adj.*

Co·man′che (kə man′chē) *n., pl.* **-che, -ches.** member of an American Indian people.

comb (kōm) *n.* **1.** toothed object, for straightening hair or fiber. **2.** growth on a cock's head. —*v.* **3.** tidy with comb. **4.** search.

com·bat′, *v.*, -bated, -bating, *n.* —*v.* (kəm bat′, kom′bat) **1.** fight. —*n.* (kom′bat) **2.** battle. —**com·bat′ant**, *n.* —**com·bat′ive,** *adj.*

com′bi·na′tion (kom′bə nā′shən) *n.* **1.** act of combining. **2.** mixture. **3.** alliance. **4.** sets of figures dialed to operate a lock.

com·bine′, *v.*, -bined, -bining, *n.* —*v.* (kəm bīn′) **1.** unite; join. —*n.* (kom′bīn) **2.** combination. **3.** machine that cuts and threshes grain.

com′bo (kom′bō) *n., pl.* -bos. *Informal.* small jazz band.

com·bus′ti·ble (kəm bus′tə bəl) *adj.* **1.** inflammable. —*n.* **2.** inflammable substance.

com·bus′tion (-chən) *n.* burning.

come (kum) *v.*, came, come, coming. **1.** approach or arrive. **2.** happen. **3.** emerge.

come′back′, *n.* **1.** return to former status. **2.** retort.

co·me′di·an (kə mē′dē ən) *n.* humorous actor or performer. —**co·me′di·enne′,** *n.fem.*

com′e·dy (kom′i dē) *n., pl.* -dies. humorous drama.

come′ly (kum′lē) *adj.*, -lier, -liest. attractive. —**come′li·ness,** *n.*

com′er (kum′ər) *n. Informal.* one likely to have great success.

com′et (kom′it) *n.* celestial body orbiting around and lighted by sun, often with misty tail.

com′fort (kum′fərt) *v.* **1.** console or cheer. —*n.* **2.** consolation. **3.** ease. —**com′fort·a·ble,** *adj.* —**com′fort·a·bly,** *adv.*

com′fort·er, *n.* **1.** one who comforts. **2.** warm quilt.

com′ic (kom′ik) *adj.* **1.** of comedy. **2.** Also, **com′i·cal.** funny. —*n.* **3.** comedian. **4.** (*pl.*) comic strips.

comic strip, sequence of drawings relating comic incident or story.

com′ma (kom′ə) *n.* punctuation mark (,).

com·mand′ (kə mand′) *v.* **1.** order. **2.** control. —*n.* **3.** order. **4.** control. **5.** troops, etc., under commander.

com′man·dant′ (kom′ən dant′, -dänt′) *n.* commanding officer.

com′man·deer′ (-dēr′) *v.* seize for official use.

com·mand′er, *n.* **1.** chief officer. **2.** *Navy.* officer below captain.

com·mand′ment, *n.* **1.** command. **2.** precept of God.

com·man′do (kə man′dō) *n., pl.* -dos, -does. soldier making brief raids against enemy.

com·mem′o·rate′ (kə mem′ə rāt′) *v.*, -rated, -rating. honor memory of. —**com·mem′o·ra′tion,** *n.* —**com·mem′o·ra·tive** (-rə tiv) *adj.*

com·mence′ (kə mens′) *v.*, -menced, -mencing. start.

com·mence′ment, *n.* **1.** beginning. **2.** graduation day or ceremonies.

com·mend′ (kə mend′) *v.* **1.** praise. **2.** entrust. —**com·mend′a·ble,** *adj.*

—**com′men·da′tion** (kom′ən dā′shən) *n.* —**com·mend′a·to′ry,** *adj.*

com·men′su·rate (-men′shə rit, -sə-) *adj.* equal or corresponding.

com′ment (kom′ent) *n.* **1.** remark or criticism. —*v.* **2.** make remarks.

com′men·tar′y (-ə ter′ē) *n., pl.* -ta·ries. explanatory comments.

com′men·ta′tor (-tā′tər) *n.* one who discusses news events, etc.

com′merce (kom′ərs) *n.* trade.

com·mer′cial (kə mûr′shəl) *adj.* **1.** of or in commerce. —*n.* **2.** radio or television advertisement.

com·mer′cial·ize′, *v.*, -ized, -izing. treat as a business.

com·min′gle (kə ming′gəl) *v.*, -gled, -gling. blend.

com·mis′er·ate′ (kə miz′ə rāt′) *v.*, -ated, -ating. sympathize.

com′mis·sar′y (kom′ə ser′ē) *n., pl.* -ies. store selling food, etc.

com·mis′sion (kə mish′ən) *n.* **1.** act of committing. **2.** document giving authority. **3.** group of persons with special task. **4.** usable condition. **5.** fee for agent's services. —*v.* **6.** give commission to. **7.** authorize. **8.** put into service.

com·mis′sion·er, *n.* government official.

com·mit′ (kə mit′) *v.*, -mitted, -mitting. **1.** give in trust or custody. **2.** refer to committee. **3.** do. **4.** obligate. —**com·mit′ment,** *n.*

com·mit′tee (kə mit′ē) *n.* group assigned to special duties.

com·mode′ (kə mōd′) *n.* **1.** chest of drawers. **2.** stand with washbasin. **3.** toilet.

com·mo′di·ous (kə mō′dē əs) *adj.* roomy.

com·mod′i·ty (kə mod′i tē) *n., pl.* -ties. article of commerce.

com′mo·dore′ (kom′ə dôr′) *n.* officer below rear admiral.

com′mon (kom′ən) *adj.* **1.** joint. **2.** ordinary. **3.** vulgar. —*n.* **4.** area of public land. —**com′mon·ly,** *adv.*

com′mon·er, *n.* one of common people.

common law, system of law based on custom and court decisions.

com′mon·place′, *adj.* **1.** ordinary; trite. —*n.* **2.** commonplace remark.

com′mons, *n.* **1.** (*cap.*) elective house of certain legislatures. **2.** large dining room.

common sense, sound practical judgment. —**com′mon·sense′,** *adj.*

com′mon·weal′ (-wēl′) *n.* public welfare.

com′mon·wealth′ (-welth′) *n.* **1.** democratic state. **2.** people of a state.

com·mo′tion (kə mō′shən) *n.* disturbance.

com·mu′nal (kə myoon′l, kom′yə nl) *adj.* of or belonging to a community.

com·mune′, *v.*, -muned, -muning, *n.* —*v.* (kə myoon′) **1.** talk together. —*n.* (kom′yoon) **2.** small community with shared property.

com·mu′ni·cate′ (kə myoo′ni kāt′) *v.*, -cated, -cating. **1.** make known. **2.** transmit. **3.** exchange news, etc. —**com·mu′ni·ca·ble** (-ni kə bəl) *adj.* —**com·mu′ni·ca·tion,** *n.* —**com·mu′ni·ca·tive** (-kā′tiv, -kə-) *adj.*

com·mun′ion (kə myoon′yən) *n.* **1.** act of sharing. **2.** sacrament commemorating Jesus' last supper.

com·mu′ni·qué′ (kə myoo′ni kā′) *n.* official bulletin.

com′mu·nism (kom′yə niz′əm) *n.* **1.** social system based on collective ownership of property. **2.** (*cap.*) political

doctrine advocating this. —**com′mu·nist** (-nist) *n., adj.*

com·mu′ni·ty (kə myoo′ni tē) *n., pl.* -ties. people with common culture living in one locality.

com·mute′ (kə myoot′) *v.*, -muted, -muting. **1.** reduce (punishment). **2.** travel between home and work. —**com·mut′er,** *n.*

com·pact′, *adj.* (kəm pakt′, kom′pakt) **1.** packed together. **2.** pithy. —*v.* (kəm pakt′) **3.** pack together. —*n.* (kom′pakt) **4.** small cosmetic case. **5.** agreement.

compact disc, optical disc on which music, data, or images are digitally recorded. Also, **CD.**

com·pac′tor (kəm pak′tər, kom′pak-) *n.* appliance that compresses trash into small bundles.

com·pan′ion (kəm pan′yən) *n.* **1.** associate. **2.** mate. —**com·pan′ion·a·ble,** *adj.* —**com·pan′ion·ship′,** *n.*

com′pa·ny (kum′pə nē) *n., pl.* -nies. **1.** business organization. **2.** companionship. **3.** guests. **4.** military unit.

com·par′a·tive (kəm par′ə tiv) *adj.* **1.** of or based on comparison. —*n.* **2.** *Gram.* intermediate degree of comparison. —**com·par′a·tive·ly,** *adv.*

com·pare′ (kəm pâr′) *v.*, -pared, -paring. consider for similarities. —**com′pa·ra·ble** (kom′pər ə bəl) *adj.* —**com·par′i·son** (kəm par′ə sən) *n.*

com·part′ment (kəm pärt′mənt) *n.* separate room, space, etc. —**com·part·men′tal·ize′,** *v.*, -ized, -izing.

com′pass (kum′pəs) *n.* **1.** instrument for finding direction. **2.** extent. **3.** tool for making circles.

com·pas′sion (kəm pash′ən) *n.* pity or sympathy. —**com·pas′sion·ate,** *adj.* —**com·pas′sion·ate·ly,** *adv.*

com·pat′i·ble (kəm pat′ə bəl) *adj.* congenial. —**com·pat′i·bil′i·ty,** *n.*

com·pa′tri·ot (kəm pā′trē ət) *n.* person from one's own country.

com·pel′ (kəm pel′) *v.*, -pelled, -pelling. force.

com·pel′ling, *adj.* **1.** forceful. **2.** demanding attention.

com·pen′di·ous (kəm pen′dē əs) *adj.* concise.

com·pen′di·um (-dē əm) *n., pl.*, -di·ums, -dia (-dē ə). summary.

com′pen·sate′ (kom′pən sāt′) *v.*, -sated, -sating. **1.** make up for. **2.** pay. —**com′pen·sa′tion,** *n.*

com·pete′ (kəm pēt′) *v.*, -peted, -peting. contend; rival.

com′pe·tent (kom′pi tənt) *adj.* **1.** able enough. **2.** legally qualified. —**com′pe·tence, com′pe·ten·cy,** *n.* —**com′pe·tent·ly,** *adv.*

com′pe·ti′tion (kom′pi tish′ən) *n.* **1.** contest. **2.** rivalry. —**com·pet′i·tive** (kəm pet′i tiv) *adj.* —**com·pet′i·tor,** *n.*

com·pile′ (kəm pīl′) *v.*, -piled, -piling. put together; assemble. —**com·pil′er,** *n.* —**com′pi·la′tion** (kom′pə lā′shən) *n.*

com·pla′cen·cy (kəm plā′sən sē) *n., pl.* -cies. satisfaction, esp. with self. Also, **com·pla′cence.** —**compla′cent,** *adj.* —**com·pla′cent·ly,** *adv.*

com·plain′ (kəm plān′) *v.* **1.** express pain, dissatisfaction, etc. **2.** accuse. —**com·plain′er, com·plain′ant,** *n.* —**com·plaint′,** *n.*

com·plai′sant (kəm plā′sənt) *adj.* obliging.

com′ple·ment *n.* (kom′plə mənt) **1.** that which completes. **2.** full amount. —*v.* (-ment′) **3.** complete. —**com′ple·men′ta·ry,** *adj.*

com·plete′ (kəm plēt′) *adj.*, *v.,*

-pleted, -pleting. —*adj.* **1.** entire. —*v.* **2.** make complete. —**com•plete′ly,** *adv.* —**com•ple′tion,** *n.*

com•plex′ *adj.* (kəm pleks′, kom′-pleks) **1.** having many parts; intricate. —*n.* (kom′pleks) **2.** obsession. —**com•plex′i•ty,** *n.*

com•plex′ion (kəm plek′shən) *n.* color of skin.

com′pli•ca′ted (kom′pli kā′tid), *adj.* complex or difficult. —**com′pli•cate′,** *v.*

com•plic′i•ty (kəm plis′i tē) *n.*, *pl.* -ties. partnership in crime.

com′pli•ment *n.* (kom′plə mənt) **1.** expression of praise. —*v.* (-ment′) **2.** express praise.

com′pli•men′ta•ry, *adj.* **1.** of or being a compliment; praising. **2.** free.

com•ply′ (kəm plī′) *v.*, -plied, -ply-ing. act in accordance. —**com•pli′ance,** *n.* —**com•pli′ant,** *adj.*

com•po′nent (kəm pō′nənt) *adj.* **1.** composing. —*n.* **2.** part of whole.

com•port′ (kəm pôrt′) *v.* **1.** conduct (oneself). **2.** suit.

com•pose′ (kəm pōz′) *v.*, -posed, -posing. **1.** make by uniting parts. **2.** constitute. **3.** calm. **4.** create and write. **5.** set type. —**com′po•si′tion** (kom′pə zish′ən) *n.*

com•posed′, *adj.* calm.

com•pos′er, *n.* writer, esp. of music.

com•pos′ite (kəm poz′it) *adj.* made of many parts.

com′post (kom′pōst) *n.* decaying mixture of leaves, etc.

com•po′sure (kəm pō′zhər) *n.* calm.

com′pote (kom′pōt) *n.* stewed fruit.

com′pound *adj.* (kom′pound) **1.** having two or more parts, functions, etc. —*n.* (kom′pound) **2.** something made by combining parts. **3.** enclosure with buildings. —*v.* (kəm pound′) **4.** combine. **5.** make worse.

com′pre•hend′ (kom′pri hend′) *v.* **1.** understand. **2.** include. —**com′pre•hen′si•ble,** *adj.* —**com′pre•hen′sion,** *n.*

com′pre•hen′sive (-hen′siv) *adj.* inclusive.

com•press′, *v.* (kəm pres′) **1.** press together. —*n.* (kom′pres) **2.** pad applied to affected part of body. —**com•pres′sion,** *n.* —**com•pres′sor,** *n.*

com•prise′ (kəm prīz′) *v.*, -prised, -prising. consist of.

com′pro•mise′ (kom′prə mīz′) *n.*, *v.*, -mised, -mising. —*n.* **1.** agreement to mutual concessions. **2.** something intermediate. —*v.* **3.** settle by compromise. **4.** endanger.

comp•trol′ler (kən trō′lər) *n.* controller.

com•pul′sion (kəm pul′shən) *n.* compelling force. —**com•pul′so•ry** (-sə rē) *adj.*

com•pul′sive, *adj.* due to or acting on inner compulsion.

com•punc′tion (kəm pungk′shən) *n.* remorse.

com•pute′ (kəm pyōōt′) *v.*, -puted, -puting. calculate; figure. —**com′pu•ta′tion** (kom′-) *n.*

com•put′er, *n.* electronic apparatus for processing data.

com•pu′ter•ize′, *v.*, -ized, -izing. **1.** do by computer. **2.** automate by computer, as a business.

com′rade (kom′rad) *n.* companion. —**com′rade•ship′,** *n.*

con (kon) *adv.*, *v.*, conned, conning. —*adv.* **1.** opposed to a plan, etc. —*n.* **2.** argument against. —*v.* **3.** *Informal.* deceive; swindle.

con•cave′ (kon kāv′) *adj.* curved inward. —**con•cave′ly,** *adv.* —**con•cav′i•ty** (-kav′i tē) *n.*

con•ceal′ (kən sēl′) *v.* hide. —**con-ceal′ment,** *n.*

con•cede′ (kən sēd′) *v.*, -ceded, -ceding. **1.** admit. **2.** yield.

con•ceit′ (kən sēt′) *n.* **1.** excess self-esteem. **2.** fanciful idea. —**con•ceit′ed,** *adj.*

con•ceive′ (kən sēv′) *v.*, -ceived, -ceiving. **1.** form (plan or idea). **2.** understand. **3.** become pregnant. —**con-ceiv′a•ble,** *adj.*

con′cen•trate′ (kon′sən trāt′) *v.*, -trated, -trating, *n.* —*v.* **1.** bring to one point. **2.** intensify. **3.** give full attention. —*n.* **4.** product of concentration. —**con′cen•tra′tion,** *n.*

concentration camp, guarded compound where political prisoners, minorities, etc., are confined.

con•cen′tric (kən sen′trik) *adj.* having common center.

con′cept (kon′sept) *n.* notion.

con•cep′tion (kən sep′shən) *n.* **1.** act of conceiving. **2.** idea.

con•cep′tu•a•lize′ (-chōō ə līz′) *v.*, -lized, -lizing. **1.** form a concept of. **2.** think in concepts.

con•cern′ (kən sûrn′) *v.* **1.** relate to. **2.** involve. **3.** worry. —*n.* **4.** worry. **5.** business firm.

con•cerned′, *adj.* **1.** interested or affected. **2.** troubled; anxious.

con•cern′ing, *prep.* about.

con′cert (kon′sûrt) *n.* **1.** musical performance. **2.** accord.

con•cert′ed (kən sûr′tid) *adj.* **1.** planned together. **2.** performed together or in cooperation.

con′cer•ti′na (kon′sər tē′nə) *n.* small accordion.

con•cer′to (kən cher′tō) *n.*, *pl.* -tos or -ti (-tē). musical piece for principal instruments and orchestra.

con•ces′sion (kən sesh′ən) *n.* **1.** act of conceding. **2.** what is conceded. **3.** grant conceded by authority.

conch (kongk, konch) *n.* spiral shell.

con•cil′i•ate′ (kən sil′ē āt′) *v.*, -ated, -ating. win over; reconcile. —**con•cil′i•a′tion,** *n.* —**con•cil′i•a•to′ry** (-ə-tôr′ē) *adj.*

con•cise′ (kən sīs′) *adj.* brief; succinct. —**con•cise′ly,** *adv.*

con′clave (kon′klāv) *n.* private meeting.

con•clude′ (kən klōōd′) *v.*, -cluded, -cluding. **1.** finish; settle. **2.** infer. —**con•clu′sion** (-klōō′zhən) *n.* —**con•clu′sive,** *adj.*

con•coct′ (kon kokt′, kən-) *v.* make by combining. —**con•coc′tion,** *n.*

con•com′i•tant (kon kom′i tant, kən-) *adj.* **1.** accompanying. —*n.* **2.** anything concomitant.

con′cord (kon′kôrd, kong′-) *n.* agreement.

con•cord′ance (kon kôr′dns, kən-) *n.* **1.** concord. **2.** index of key words of book.

con•cor′dat (kon kôr′dat) *n.* agreement, esp. between Pope and a government.

con′course (kon′kôrs, kong′-) *n.* place for crowds in motion.

con′crete, *adj.*, *n.*, *v.*, -creted, -creting. —*adj.* (kon′krēt, kon krēt′) **1.** real; objective. **2.** made of concrete. —*n.* (kon′krēt) **3.** material of cement and hard matter. —*v.* **4.** become solid. —**con•crete′ly,** *adv.* —**con•crete′ness,** *n.*

con•cu′bine′ (kong′kyə bīn′) *n.* woman living with but not married to a man.

con•cur′ (kən kûr′) *v.*, -curred, -curr-ing. **1.** agree. **2.** coincide. —**con•cur′rence,** *n.* —**con•cur′rent,** *adj.* —**con•cur′rent•ly,** *adv.*

con•cus′sion (kən kush′ən) *n.* injury to brain from blow, etc.

con•demn′ (kən dem′) *v.* **1.** denounce. **2.** pronounce guilty. **3.** judge unfit. —**con′dem•na′tion** (kon′dem-nā′shən, -dəm-) *n.*

con•dense′ (kən dens′) *v.*, -densed, -densing. **1.** reduce to denser form. **2.** make or become compact. —**con′den-sa′tion** (kon′den sā′shən) *n.* —**con•dens′er,** *n.*

condensed milk, thick, sweetened milk.

con′de•scend′ (kon′də send′) *v.* **1.** pretend equality with an inferior. **2.** deign. —**con′de•scen′sion,** *n.*

con′di•ment (kon′də mənt) *n.* seasoning.

con•di′tion (kən dish′ən) *n.* **1.** state of being or health. **2.** fit state. **3.** requirement. —*v.* **4.** put in condition. —**con•di′tion•al,** *adj.* —**con•di′tion-er,** *n.*

con•dole′ (kən dōl′) *v.*, -doled, -doling. sympathize in sorrow. —**con•do′lence,** *n.*

con′dom (kon′dəm, kun′-) *n.* contraceptive device worn over penis.

con′do•min′i•um (kon′də min′ē-əm) *n.* apartment house in which units are individually owned. Also, *Informal.* **con′do** (-dō).

con•done′ (kən dōn′) *v.*, -doned, -doning. excuse.

con′dor (kon′dər, -dôr) *n.* vulture.

con•du′cive (kən dōō′siv, -dyōō′–) *adj.* tending (to).

con′duct, (kon′dukt) *n.* **1.** behavior. **2.** management. —*v.* (kən dukt′) **3.** behave. **4.** manage. **5.** lead or carry. **6.** transmit, as electric current. —**con•duc′tion,** *n.*

con•duc′tor (kən duk′tər) *n.* **1.** guide. **2.** director of an orchestra. **3.** official on trains. **4.** substance that conveys electricity, heat, etc.

con′duit (kon′dwit) *n.* pipe for water, etc.

cone (kōn) *n.* **1.** form tapering from round base to single point. **2.** fruit of fir, pine, etc.

con′fab (kon′fab) *n.* conversation.

con•fec′tion (kən fek′shən) *n.* candy or other sweet preparation. —**con•fec′tion•er,** *n.* —**con•fec′tion•er′y,** *n.*

con•fed′er•a•cy (kən fed′ər ə sē) *n.*, *pl.* -cies. **1.** league. **2.** (*cap.*) Confederate States of America.

con•fed′er•ate, *adj.*, *n.*, *v.*, -ated, -ating. —*adj.* (kən fed′ər it) **1.** in league. **2.** (*cap.*) of **Confederate States of America,** separated from U.S. during Civil War. —*n.* (-ər it) **3.** ally. **4.** accomplice. **5.** (*cap.*) citizen of Confederate States of America. —*v.* (-ə rāt′) **6.** be allied. —**con•fed′er•a′tion,** *n.*

con•fer′ (kən fûr′) *v.*, -ferred, -fer-ring. **1.** bestow. **2.** consult. —**con•fer′ment,** *n.*

con′fer•ence (kon′fər əns) *n.* **1.** meeting. **2.** discussion.

con•fess′ (kən fes′) *v.* **1.** admit. **2.** declare one's sins, as to priest. —**con-fes′sion,** *n.*

con•fess′ed•ly (-id lē) *adv.* by confession; admittedly.

con•fes′sion•al, *adj.* **1.** characteristic of confession. —*n.* **2.** place in church set apart for confession.

con•fes′sor, *n.* **1.** one who confesses. **2.** one who hears confessions.

con·fet'ti (kən fet'ē) n. bits of colored paper thrown at festive events.

con'fi·dant' (kon'fi dant', -dänt') n. one to whom secrets are told. —**con'fi·dante'**, n.fem.

con·fide' (kən fīd') v., -fided, -fiding. 1. trust with secret. 2. entrust.

con'fi·dence (kon'fi dəns) n. 1. full trust. 2. assurance. —**con'fi·dent**, adj. —**con'fi·dent·ly**, adv.

con'fi·den'tial (-den'shəl) adj. 1. entrusted as secret. 2. private. —**con'fi·den'tial·ly**, adv.

con·fig'u·ra'tion (kən fig'yə rā'shən) n. external form.

con·fine' v., -fined, -fining, n. —v. (kən fīn') 1. keep within bounds. 2. shut or lock up. —n. (pl.) (kon'fīnz) 3. boundary.

con·fined', adj. restricted.

con·fine'ment, n. 1. imprisonment. 2. childbirth.

con·firm' (kən fûrm') v. 1. make sure. 2. make valid. 3. admit into church. —**con·fir·ma'tion** (kon'fər-) n.

con·firmed', adj. habitual.

con'fis·cate' (kon'fə skāt') v., -cated, -cating. seize by public authority. —**con'fis·ca'tion**, n.

con'fla·gra'tion (kon'flə grā'shən) n. fierce fire.

con·flict', v. (kən flikt') 1. oppose; clash. —n. (kon'flikt) 2. battle. 3. antagonism.

con'flu·ence (kon'flōō əns) n. act or place of flowing together. —**con'flu·ent**, adj.

con·form' (kən fôrm') v. 1. adapt. 2. make similar. —**con·form'ist**, n. —**con·form'i·ty**, n.

con·found' (kon found') v. 1. confuse. 2. perplex.

con·found'ed, adj. 1. bewildered. 2. damned.

con·front' (kən frunt') v. 1. meet or set facing. 2. challenge openly. —**con'fron·ta'tion** (kon'frən tā'shən) n. —**con·fron·ta'tion·al**, adj.

con·fuse' (kən fyōōz') v., -fused, -fusing. 1. throw into disorder. 2. associate wrongly. 3. disconcert. —**con·fu'sion**, n.

con·fute' (-fyōōt') v., -futed, -futing. prove to be wrong.

Cong., 1. Congregational. 2. Congress. 3. Congressional.

con·geal' (kən jēl') v. make solid or thick. —**con·geal'ment**, n.

con·gen'ial (kən jēn'yəl) adj. agreeable; suited. —**con·ge'ni·al'i·ty** (-jē'nē al'i tē) n.

con·gen'i·tal (kən jen'i tl) adj. innate. —**con·gen'i·tal·ly**, adv.

con·gest' (kən jest') v. fill to excess. —**con·ges'tion**, n.

con·glom'er·ate', n., adj., v., -ated, -ating. —n. (kən glom'ər it) 1. mixture. 2. rock formed of pebbles, etc. 3. company owning variety of other companies. —adj. (-ər it) 4. mixed. —v. (-ə rāt') 5. gather into mass. —**con·glom'er·a'tion**, n.

con·grat'u·late' (kən grach'ə lāt') v., -lated, -lating. express sympathetic joy. —**con·grat'u·la'tion**, n.

con'gre·gate' (kong'gri gāt') v., -gated, -gating. assemble. —**con'gre·ga'tion**, n.

con'gre·ga'tion·al, adj. 1. of congregations. 2. (cap.) denoting church denomination wherein each church acts independently. —**con'gre·ga'tion·al·ism**, n.

con'gress (kong'gris) n. 1. national legislative body, esp. (cap.) of the U.S. 2. formal meeting. —**con·gres'sion·al**

(kəng gresh'ə nl) adj. —**con'gress·man**, n. —**con'gress·per'son**, n. —**con'gress·wom'an**, n.fem.

con'gru·ent (kong'grōō ənt) adj. 1. agreeing. 2. (of geometric figures) coinciding at all points when superimposed. —**con·gru·ence**, n.

con·gru'i·ty (kən grōō'i tē) n., adj. -ties. agreement. —**con'gru·ous** (kong'grōō əs) adj.

con'ic (kon'ik) adj. of or like cone. Also, **con'i·cal**.

co'ni·fer (kō'nə fər, kon'ə-) n. tree bearing cones. —**co·nif'er·ous** (-nif'ər əs) adj.

con·jec'ture (kən jek'chər) n., v., -tured, -turing. guess.

con·join' (kən join') v. join together.

con'ju·gal (kon'jə gəl) adj. of marriage. —**con'ju·gal·ly**, adv.

con'ju·gate' (kon'jə gāt') v., -gated, -gating. give inflected forms of (verb). —**con'ju·ga'tion**, n.

con·junc'tion (kən jungk'shən) n. 1. union; combination. 2. Gram. word that joins words, phrases, clauses, or sentences. —**con·junc'tive**, adj.

con·junc'ti·vi'tis (kən jungk'tə vī'tis) n. inflammation of mucous membrane of the eye.

con·jure (kon'jər, kun'-) v., -jured, -juring. invoke or produce by magic. —**con·jur·er**, n.

conk (kongk) v. Slang. 1. strike on the head. 2. **conk out. a.** break down. **b.** go to sleep. —n. 3. blow on the head.

Conn. Connecticut.

con·nect' (kə nekt') v. join; link. —**con·nec'tion;** Brit. **con·nex'ion**, n. —**con·nec'tive**, adj., n.

con·nive' (kə nīv') v., -nived, -niving. conspire. —**con·niv'ance**, n.

con·nois·seur (kon'ə sûr') n. skilled judge.

con·note' (kə nōt') v., -noted, -noting. signify in addition; imply. —**con'no·ta'tion** (kon'ə tā'shən) n.

con·nu'bi·al (kə nōō'bē əl, -nyōō'-) adj. matrimonial.

con'quer (kong'kər) v. 1. acquire by force. 2. defeat. —**con'quer·or**, n. —**con'quest**, n.

con·quis'ta·dor' (kong kwis'tə dôr', -kēs'-) n., pl. **conquis'ta·dors, conquis'ta·do'res** (-kēs'tə dôr'ēz, -äz). 16th-century Spanish conqueror of the Americas.

con'science (kon'shəns) n. recognition of right or wrong in oneself.

con'sci·en'tious (-shē en'shəs), adj. hardworking.

conscientious objector, person who refuses to serve in military for moral reasons.

con'scious (kon'shəs) adj. 1. in possession of one's senses. 2. aware. 3. deliberate. —**con'scious·ly**, adv. —**con'scious·ness**, n.

con'script, adj. (kon'skript) 1. drafted. —n. (kon'skript) 2. one drafted. —v. (kən skript') 3. draft for military service. —**con·scrip'tion**, n.

con'se·crate' (kon'si krāt') v., -crated, -crating. 1. make sacred. 2. devote. —**con'se·cra'tion**, n.

con·sec'u·tive (kən sek'yə tiv) adj. successive.

con·sen'sus (kən sen'səs) n. agreement.

con·sent' (kən sent') v. 1. agree; comply. —n. 2. assent.

con'se·quence (kon'si kwens', -kwəns) n. 1. effect. 2. importance.

con'se·quent', adj. following; resulting. —**con'se·quent·ly**, adv.

con'ser·va'tion (kon'sər vā'shən) n.

preservation of resources. —**con'ser·va'tion·ist**, n.

con·serv'a·tive (kən sûr'və tiv) adj. 1. favoring status quo. 2. cautious. —n. 3. conservative person. —**con·serv'a·tive·ly**, adv. —**con·serv'a·tism**, n.

con·serv'a·to'ry (-tôr'ē) n., pl. -ries. 1. school of music or drama. 2. hothouse.

con·serve', v., -served, -serving, n. —v. (kən sûrv') 1. keep intact. —n. (kon'sûrv) 2. preserves.

con·sid'er (kən sid'ər) v. 1. think over. 2. deem. 3. respect. —**con·sid'er·ate**, adj. —**con·sid'er·ate·ly**, adv.

con·sid'er·a·ble, adj. important or sizable. —**con·sid'er·a·bly**, adv.

con·sid'er·a'tion (-ə rā'shən) n. 1. thought. 2. regard. 3. fee.

con·sid'er·ing, prep. in view of.

con·sign' (kən sīn') v. 1. deliver. 2. entrust. —**con·sign'ment**, n.

con·sist' (kən sist') v. be composed.

con·sist'en·cy (-sis'tən sē) n., pl. -cies. 1. firmness. 2. density. 3. adherence to principles, behavior, etc. —**con·sist'ent**, adj.

con·sole', v., -soled, -soling, n. —v. (kən sōl') 1. comfort. —n. (kon'sōl) 2. control panel. —**con'so·la'tion**, n. —**con·sol'a·ble**, adj.

con·sol'i·date' (kən sol'i dāt') v., -dated, -dating. 1. make or become firm. 2. unite. —**con·sol'i·da'tion**, n.

con·som·mé' (kon'sə mā') n. clear soup.

con'so·nant (kon'sə nənt) n. 1. letter for sound made by obstruction of breath. —adj. 2. in agreement.

con'sort, n. (kon'sôrt) 1. spouse. —v. (kən sôrt') 2. associate.

con·sor'ti·um (kən sôr'shē əm, -tē-) n., pl. -tia (-shē ə, -tē ə). 1. combination for business purposes. 2. association.

con·spic'u·ous (kən spik'yōō əs) adj. 1. easily seen. 2. notable. —**con·spic'u·ous·ly**, adv.

con·spire' (kən spīr') v., -spired, -spiring. plot together. —**con·spir'a·cy** (-spir'ə sē) n. —**con·spir'a·tor**, n.

con'sta·ble (kon'stə bəl) n. police officer.

con·stab'u·lar'y (kən stab'yə ler'ē) n., pl. -ies. police.

con'stant (kon'stənt) adj. 1. uniform. 2. uninterrupted. 3. faithful. —n. 4. something unchanging. —**con'stan·cy**, n. —**con'stant·ly**, adv.

con'stel·la'tion (kon'stə lā'shən) n. group of stars.

con'ster·na'tion (kon'stər nā'shən) n. utter dismay.

con'sti·pate' (kon'stə pāt') v., -pated, -pating. cause difficult evacuation of bowels. —**con'sti·pa'tion**, n.

con·stit'u·ent (kən stich'ōō ənt) adj. 1. being part; composing. —n. 2. ingredient. 3. represented voter. —**con·stit'u·en·cy**, n.

con'sti·tute' (kon'sti tōōt', -tyōōt') v., -tuted, -tuting. 1. compose. 2. make.

con'sti·tu'tion (kon'sti tōō'shən) n. 1. make-up. 2. physical condition. 3. system of governmental principles. —**con'sti·tu'tion·al**, adj.

con·strain' (kən strān') v. 1. force or oblige. 2. confine. —**con·strained'**, adj. —**con·straint'**, n.

con·strict' (kən strikt') v. draw together; shrink. —**con·stric'tion**, n.

con·struct' (kən strukt') v. build or devise. —**con·struc'tion**, n.

con·struc'tive, adj. 1. of construction. 2. helpful.

con•strue′ (kən strōō′) *v.*, **-strued, -struing.** interpret.

con′sul (kon′səl) *n.* local diplomatic official. **—con′su•lar,** *adj.* **—con′su•late** (-sə lit) *n.*

con•sult′ (kən sult′) *v.* **1.** ask advice of. **2.** refer to. **3.** confer. **—con•sult′ant,** *n.* **—con′sul•ta′tion,** *n.*

con•sume′ (kən sōōm′) *v.*, **-sumed, -suming. 1.** use up. **2.** devour.

con•sum′er, *n.* **1.** one that consumes. **2.** purchaser of goods.

con•sum′er•ism, *n.* policies protecting consumers.

con′sum•mate′, *v.*, **-mated, -mating,** *adj.* **—v.** (kon′sə māt′), *adj.* (kən-sum′it, kon′sə mit). complete or perfect. **—con′sum•ma′tion,** *n.*

con•sump′tion (kən sump′shən) *n.* **1.** act of consuming. **2.** amount consumed. **3.** wasting disease, esp. tuberculosis of lungs. **—con•sump′tive,** *adj.*, *n.*

cont., continued.

con′tact (kon′takt) *n.* **1.** a touching. **2.** association. **3.** business acquaintance. **—v. 4.** put or bring into contact. **5.** communicate with.

contact lens, corrective lens put directly on eye.

con•ta′gion (kən tā′jən) *n.* spread of disease by contact. **—con•ta′gious,** *adj.*

con•tain′ (kən tān′) *v.* **1.** have within itself. **2.** have space for. **—con•tain′er,** *n.*

con•tam′i•nate′ (kən tam′ə nāt′) *v.*, **-nated, -nating.** make impure.

contd., continued.

con′tem•plate′ (kon′təm plāt′, -tem-) *v.*, **-plated, -plating. 1.** consider. **2.** observe. **—con′tem•pla′tion,** *n.*

con•tem′po•rar′y (kən tem′pə rer′ē) *adj.*, *n.*, *pl.* **-raries. —adj. 1.** Also, **con•tem′po•ra′ne•ous** (-rā′nē əs). of same age or period. **—n. 2.** contemporary person.

con•tempt′ (kən tempt′) *n.* **1.** scorn. **2.** disgrace. **3.** disrespect of court. **—con•tempt′i•ble,** *adj.* **—con•temp′tu•ous,** *adj.*

con•tend′ (kən tend′) *v.* **1.** be in struggle. **2.** assert.

con•tent′, *adj.* (kən tent′) **1.** Also, **con•tent′ed.** satisfied. **—v.** (kən tent′) **2.** make content. **—n.** (kən tent′) **3.** Also, **con•tent′ment.** ease of mind. **4.** (kon′tent) *(often pl.).* what is contained. **5.** (kon′tent) capacity. **—content′ed•ly,** *adv.*

con•ten′tion (-shən) *n.* controversy. **—con•ten′tious,** *adj.*

con′test, *n.* (kon′test) **1.** struggle; competition. **—v.** (kən test′) **2.** fight for. **3.** dispute. **—con•test′ant,** *n.*

con′text (kon′tekst) *n.* surrounding words or circumstances.

con•tig′u•ous (kən tig′yōō əs) *adj.* **1.** touching. **2.** near.

con′ti•nent (kon′tn ənt) *n.* **1.** major land mass. **—adj. 2.** self-restrained. **—con′ti•nen′tal** (-nen′tl) *adj.*

con•tin′gen•cy (kən tin′jən sē) *n.*, *pl.* **-cies.** chance; event.

con•tin′gent, *adj.* **1.** conditional; possible. **—n. 2.** group. **3.** contingency.

con•tin′u•al (kən tin′yōō əl) *adj.* **1.** happening regularly or frequently. **2.** happening without interruption.
—Usage. Use CONTINUAL for actions that occur over and over again (especially actions that are annoying): *The dog's continual barking was driving me crazy.* The word CONTINUOUS is used for actions that keep going and do not

stop: *We had continuous electricity during the big storm.*

con•tin′ue, *v.*, **-tinued, -tinuing. 1.** go or carry on. **2.** stay. **3.** extend. **4.** carry over. **—con•tin′u•al•ly,** *adv.*

con′ti•nu′i•ty (kon′tn ōō′i tē, -tn-yōō′-) *n.*, *pl.* **-ties. 1.** continuous whole. **2.** script.

con•tin′u•ous (kən tin′yōō əs) *adj.* going on without stop; uninterrupted. **—con•tin′u•ous•ly,** *adv.* **—Usage.** See CONTINUAL.

con•tin′u•um (-yōō əm) *n.*, *pl.* **-tinua.** continuous extent, series, or whole.

con•tort′ (kən tôrt′) *v.* twist; distort. **—con•tor′tion,** *n.*

con•tor′tion•ist, *n.* person who can twist into unusual positions.

con′tour (kon′tōōr) *n.* outline.

contra-, prefix meaning against, opposite, or opposing, as *contradict*.

con′tra•band′ (kon′trə band′) *n.* goods prohibited from shipment. **—con′tra•band′,** *adj.*

con′tra•cep′tion (-sep′shən) *n.* deliberate prevention of pregnancy. **—con′tra•cep′tive,** *adj.*, *n.*

con•tract′, *n.* (kon′trakt) **1.** agreement. **—v.** (kən trakt′) **2.** shorten. **3.** become ill. **4.** agree. **—con•trac′tion,** *n.*

con′trac•tor (kon′trak tər) *n.* one who supplies work by contract.

con′tra•dict′ (kon′trə dikt′) *v.* deny as being correct. **—con′tra•dic′tion,** *n.* **—con′tra•dic′to•ry,** *adj.*

con•tral′to (kən tral′tō) *n.*, *pl.* **-tos.** lowest female voice.

con•trap′tion (kən trap′shən) *n.* strange machine; gadget.

con′tra•ry (kon′trer ē) *adj.*, *n.*, *pl.* **-ries. —adj. 1.** opposite. **2.** *(also* kən-trâr′ē) perverse. **—n. 3.** something contrary. **—con′tra•ri•ly,** **—con′tra•ri•wise′,** *adv.*

con•trast′, *v.* (kən trast′) **1.** show unlikeness. **2.** compare. **—n.** (kon′trast) **3.** show of unlikeness. **4.** something unlike.

con′tra•vene′ (kon′trə vēn′) *v.*, **-vened, -vening. 1.** oppose. **2.** violate. **—con′tra•ven′tion** (-ven′shən) *n.*

con•trib′ute (kən trib′yōōt) *v.*, **-uted, -uting.** give with others; donate. **—con′tri•bu′tion** (kon′trə byōō′shən) *n.* **—con•trib′u•tor,** *n.* **—con•trib′u•to′ry,** *adj.*

con•trite′ (kən trīt′) *adj.* penitent. **—con•tri′tion** (-trish′ən) *n.*

con•trive′ (kən trīv′) *v.*, **-trived, -triving. 1.** plan; devise. **2.** plot.

con•trol′ (kən trōl′) *v.*, **-trolled, -trolling,** *n.* **—v. 1.** have direction over. **2.** restrain. **—n. 3.** power of controlling. **4.** restraint. **5.** regulating device. **—con•trol′la•ble,** *adj.*

con•trol′ler, *n.* **1.** officer who superintends finances. **2.** regulator.

con′tro•ver′sy (kon′trə vûr′sē) *n.*, *pl.* **-sies.** dispute or debate. **—con′tro•ver′sial** (-vûr′shəl) *adj.* **—con′tro•ver′sial•ly,** *adv.*

con′tro•vert′ (kon′trə vûrt′, kon′trə-vûrt′) *v.* dispute.

con′tu•ma′cious (kon′tōō mā′shəs, -tyōō-) *adj.* stubbornly disobedient.

con′tu•me•ly (kon′tōō mə lē, -tyōō-) *n.*, *pl.* **-lies.** contemptuous treatment.

con•tu′sion (kən tōō′zhən, -tyōō′-) *n.* bruise.

co•nun′drum (kə nun′drəm) *n.* riddle involving pun.

con′ur•ba′tion (kon′ər bā′shən) *n.* continuous mass of urban settlements.

con′va•lesce′ (kon′və les′) *v.*, **-lesced, -lescing.** recover from illness.

—con′va•les′cence, *n.* **—con′va•les′cent,** *adj.*, *n.*

con•vec′tion (kən vek′shən) *n.* transference of heat by movement of heated matter.

con•vene′ (kən vēn′) *v.*, **-vened, -vening.** assemble.

con•ven′ient (-vēn′yənt) *adj.* handy or favorable. **—con•ven′ience,** *n.* **—con•ven′ient•ly,** *adv.*

con′vent (kon′vent, -vənt) *n.* community of nuns.

con•ven′tion (kən ven′shən) *n.* **1.** meeting. **2.** accepted usage. **—con•ven′tion•al,** *adj.*

con•verge′ (kən vûrj′) *v.*, **-verged, -verging.** meet in a point.

con•ver′sant (kən vûr′sənt) *adj.* acquainted.

con′ver•sa′tion (kon′vər sā′shən) *n.* informal discussion. **—con′ver•sa′tion•al,** *adj.*

con•verse′, *v.*, **-versed, -versing,** *adj.*, *n.* **—v.** (kən vûrs′) **1.** talk informally. **—adj.**, *n.* (adj. kən vûrs′; n. kon′vûrs) **2.** opposite. **—con•verse′ly,** *adv.*

con•vert′, *v.* (kən vûrt′) **1.** change. **2.** persuade to different beliefs. **—n.** (kon′vûrt) **3.** converted person. **—con•ver′sion,** *n.* **—con•vert′er,** *n.*

con•vert′i•ble, *adj.* **1.** able to be converted. **—n. 2.** automobile with folding top.

con•vex′ (kon veks′) *adj.* curved outward. **—con•vex′i•ty,** *n.*

con•vey′ (kən vā′) *v.* **1.** transport. **2.** transmit.

con•vey′ance, *n.* **1.** act of conveying. **2.** vehicle. **3.** transfer of property.

con•vict′, *v.* (kən vikt′) **1.** find guilty. **—n.** (kon′vikt) **2.** convicted person.

con•vic′tion, *n.* **1.** a convicting. **2.** firm belief.

con•vince′ (kən vins′) *v.*, **-vinced, -vincing.** cause to believe. **—con•vinc′ing,** *adj.*

con•viv′i•al (kən viv′ē əl) *adj.* sociable. **—con•viv′i•al′i•ty** (-al′i tē) *n.*

con•voke′ (kən vōk′) *v.*, **-voked, -voking.** call together. **—con′vo•ca′tion** (kon′vō kā′shən) *n.*

con′vo•lu′tion (kon′və lōō′shən) *n.* coil. **—con′vo•lut′ed,** *adj.*

con′voy (kon′voi) *v.* **1.** escort for protection. **—n. 2.** group of ships.

con•vulse′ (kən vuls′) *v.*, **-vulsed, -vulsing.** shake violently. **—con•vul′sion,** *n.* **—con•vul′sive,** *adj.*

co′ny (kō′nē, kun′ē) *n.*, *pl.* **-nies.** rabbit fur.

coo (kōō) *v.*, **cooed, cooing.** murmur softly. **—coo,** *n.*

cook (kōōk) *v.* **1.** prepare by heating. **—n. 2.** person who cooks. **—cook′-book′,** *n.* **—cook′er•y,** *n.*

cook′ie, *n.* small sweet cake.

cook′out′, *n.* outdoor gathering at which food is cooked and eaten.

cool (kōōl) *adj.* **1.** moderately cold. **2.** calm. **3.** not enthusiastic. **4.** *Slang.* great; excellent. **—v. 5.** make or become cool. **—cool′ant,** *n.* **—cool′er,** *n.* **—cool′ly,** *adv.*

coo′lie (kōō′lē) *n.* unskilled laborer, esp. formerly in Far East.

coop (kōōp, kōōp) *n.* **1.** cage for fowls. **—v. 2.** keep in coop.

coop′er, *n.* barrel maker.

co-op′er•ate′ (kō op′ə rāt′) *v.*, **-ated, -ating.** work or act together. **—co-op′er•a′tion,** *n.*

co-op′er•a•tive (-ər ə tiv) *adj.* **1.** involving cooperation. **2.** willing to act with others. **—n. 3.** Also, **co-op** (kō′op′). jointly owned apartment house or business.

co-opt' (kō opt') v. 1. choose as fellow member. 2. win over into larger group.

co·or'di·nate', v., -nated, -nating, adj., n. —v. (kō ôr'dn āt') 1. put in order. 2. adjust. —adj., n. (-dn it) 3. equal. —co·or'di·na'tion, n.

coot (kōōt) n. aquatic bird.

cop (kop) n. Slang. police officer.

co'pay' (kō'pā') n. percentage of fee, or fixed amount, paid by patient to health-care provider. Also, **co'pay'-ment.**

cope (kōp) v., coped, coping, n. —v. 1. deal with problems or duties. —n. 2. cloak worn by priests.

cop'i·er (kop'ē ər) n. machine for making copies.

co'pi'lot (kō'pī'lət) n. aircraft pilot second in command.

cop'ing (kō'ping) n. top layer of wall.

co'pi·ous (kō'pē əs) adj. abundant.

cop'per (kop'ər) n. soft reddish metallic element.

cop'per·head', n. venomous snake.

copse (kops) n. thicket. Also, **cop'pice.**

cop'u·late' (kop'yə lāt') v., -lated, -lating. have sexual intercourse. —**cop'u·la'tion**, n.

cop'y (kop'ē) n., pl. **copies**, v., copied, copying. —n. 1. reproduction or imitation. 2. material to be copied. —v. 3. make copy of.

cop'y·cat', n. imitator.

cop'y·right', n. 1. exclusive control of book, picture, etc. —v. 2. secure copyright on. —adj. 3. covered by copyright.

co·quette' (kō ket') n. female flirt. —**co·quet'tish,** adj.

cor'al (kôr'əl) n. 1. substance formed of skeletons of certain marine animals. 2. yellowish pink.

cord (kôrd) n. 1. small rope. 2. Elect. small insulated cable.

cor'dial (kôr'jəl) adj. 1. hearty; friendly. —n. 2. liqueur. —**cor·dial'i·ty** (-jal'i tē, jē al'-) n.

cord'less, adj. (of electrical appliance) having self-contained power supply.

cor'don (kôr'dn) n. line of police.

cor'do·van (kôr'də vən) n. soft leather.

cor'du·roy' (kôr'də roi') n. ribbed fabric.

core (kôr) n., v., cored, coring. —n. 1. central part. —v. 2. remove core of.

co'ri·an'der (kôr'ē an'dər) n. herb with pungent leaves and seeds.

cork (kôrk) n. 1. bark of an oak tree. 2. stopper of cork, rubber, etc. —v. 3. close with a cork.

cork'screw', n. 1. spiral, pointed instrument for pulling corks.

cor'mo·rant (kôr'mər ənt) n. water bird.

corn (kôrn) n. 1. maize. 2. any edible grain. 3. horny callus, esp. on toe. —v. 4. preserve in brine.

corn bread, n. bread made with cornmeal.

corn'cob', n. core of an ear of corn which holds grains.

cor'ne·a (kôr'nē ə) n. transparent part of coat of the eye.

cor'ner (kôr'nər) n. 1. place or point where two lines or streets meet. 2. exclusive control. —v. 3. put in corner. 4. gain exclusive control of (stock or commodity).

cor'ner·stone', n. 1. stone representing start of building construction. 2. something basic.

cor·net' (kôr net') n. wind instrument resembling trumpet.

cor'nice (kôr'nis) n. horizontal projection at top of a wall.

corn'meal', n. meal made from corn.

corn'starch', n. starchy flour made from corn.

cor·nu·co·pi·a (kôr'nə kō pē ə, -nyə-) n. horn-shaped container of food, etc.; horn of plenty.

corn'y, adj., -ier, -iest. trite, sentimental, or old-fashioned.

co·rol'la (kə rol'ə, -rō'lə) n. petals of a flower.

cor'ol·lar'y (kôr'ə ler'ē) n., pl. -ies. logical deduction.

co·ro'na (kə rō'nə) n., pl. -nas, -nae (-nē) circle of light, esp. around sun or moon.

cor'o·nar'y (kôr'ə ner'ē) adj., n., pl. -naries. —adj. 1. of arteries supplying heart. —n. 2. heart attack.

cor'o·na'tion (kôr'ə nā'shən) n. crowning.

cor'o·ner (kôr'ə nər) n. official who investigates suspicious deaths.

cor'o·net (kôr'ə net') n. small crown.

corp., corporation.

cor'po·ral (kôr'pər əl) adj. 1. physical. 2. Mil. officer below sergeant.

cor'po·ra'tion (-rā'shən) n. legally formed association for business, etc. —**cor'po·rate** (-pər it, -prit) adj.

cor·po're·al (kôr pôr'ē əl) adj. tangible.

corps (kôr) n., pl. **corps.** 1. military unit. 2. any group.

corpse (kôrps) n. dead body.

cor'pu·lent (kôr'pyə lənt) adj. fat.

cor'pus (kôr'pəs) n., pl. -pora (-pər ə). 1. comprehensive collection of writings. 2. body, esp. when dead.

cor'pus·cle (kôr'pə səl) n. blood cell.

cor·ral' (kə ral') n., v., -ralled, -ralling. —n. 1. pen for stock. —v. 2. keep in corral. 3. corner or capture.

cor·rect' (kə rekt') v. 1. mark or remove errors. 2. rebuke or punish. —adj. 3. right. —**cor·rec'tion,** n. —**cor·rec'tive,** adj., n.

cor're·late' (kôr'ə lāt') v., -lated, -lating. bring into mutual relation. —**cor're·la'tion,** n.

cor're·spond' (kôr'ə spond') v. 1. conform or be similar. 2. communicate by letters. —**cor're·spond'ence,** n.

cor're·spond'ent, n. 1. letter writer. 2. reporter. —adj. 3. corresponding.

cor'ri·dor (kôr'i dər) n. passageway.

cor·rob'o·rate' (kə rob'ə rāt') v., -rated, -rating. confirm. —**cor·rob'o·ra'tion,** n. —**cor·rob'o·ra'tive** (-ə rā'tiv, -ər ə tiv) adj.

cor·rode' (kə rōd') v., -roded, -roding. eat away gradually. —**cor·ro'sion** (-rō'zhən) n. —**cor·ro'sive,** adj., n.

cor'ru·gate' (kôr'ə gāt') v., -gated, -gating. bend into folds.

cor·rupt' (kə rupt') adj. 1. dishonest. 2. tainted. —v. 3. make or become corrupt. —**cor·rup'tion,** n.

cor·sage' (kôr säzh') n. small bouquet to be worn.

cor'sair (kôr'sâr) n. pirate.

cor'set (kôr'sit) n. undergarment for shaping the body.

cor·tege' (kôr tezh') n. procession.

cor'tex (kôr'teks) n. 1. bark. 2. outer covering of brain or organ.

cor'ti·sone' (kôr'tə zōn', -sōn') n. hormone used esp. in treating inflammatory diseases.

cor·vette' (kôr vet') n. small fast vessel.

cos·met'ic (koz met'ik) n. 1. beauti-

fying product. —adj. 2. of cosmetics. 3. superficial.

cos'mic (koz'mik) adj. 1. of the cosmos. 2. vast.

cos·mol'o·gy (-mol'ə jē) n. study of the origin and structure of the universe.

cos'mo·pol'i·tan (koz'mə pol'i tn) adj. worldly.

cos'mos (-məs, -mōs) n. ordered universe.

cost (kôst) n. 1. price paid. 2. loss or penalty. —v. 3. require as payment. —**cost'ly,** adj.

cost'-ef·fec'tive, adj. producing optimum results for the expenditure.

cost of living, average amount paid for basic necessities.

cos'tume (kos'tōōm, -tyōōm) n. historical or theatrical dress.

co'sy (kō'zē) adj., -sier, -siest. cozy.

cot (kot) n. light bed.

cote (kōt) n. shelter for pigeons, sheep, etc.

co'te·rie (kō'tə rē) n. group of social acquaintances.

co·til'lion (kə til'yən) n. 1. elaborate dance. 2. formal ball.

cot'tage (kot'ij) n. small house.

cottage cheese, soft, mild cheese made from skim milk.

cot'ton (kot'n) n. downy plant substance made into fabric.

cot'ton·mouth' (-mouth') n. venomous snake. Also, **water moccasin.**

cot'ton·seed', n. seed of cotton plant, yielding an oil (**cottonseed oil**) used in cooking and medicine.

couch (kouch) n. 1. bed. —v. 2. express.

couch potato, Informal. person who watches a lot of television.

cou'gar (kōō'gər) n. large American wildcat.

cough (kôf) v. 1. expel air from lungs suddenly and loudly. —n. 2. act or sound of coughing.

cough drop, lozenge for relieving sore throat, etc.

could (kōōd; unstressed kəd) v. pt. of can.

coun'cil (koun'səl) n. deliberative or advisory body. —**coun'ci·lor, coun'cil·lor,** n.

coun'sel (koun'səl) n., v., -seled, -seling. —n. 1. advice. 2. consultation. 3. lawyer. —v. 4. advise. —**coun'se·lor, coun'sel·lor,** n.

count (kount) v. 1. find total number. 2. name numbers to. 3. esteem. 4. rely. 5. be noticed. —n. 6. a counting. 7. total number. 8. item in indictment. 9. nobleman.

count'down', n. backward counting in time units to scheduled event.

coun'te·nance (koun'tn əns) n., v., -nanced, -nancing. 1. appearance. —v. 2. tolerate.

count'er (koun'tər) n. 1. table or display case in store. 2. one that counts. 3. anything opposite. —v. 4. oppose. 5. return (blow). —adv., adj. 6. contrary.

counter-, prefix indicating: 1. against, as counterintelligence. 2. in response to, as counterattack. 3. opposite, as counterclockwise. 4. complementary, as counterbalance.

coun'ter·act', v. neutralize.

coun'ter·at·tack', n., v. attack in response.

coun'ter·bal'ance, n., v., -anced, -ancing. —n. (koun'tər bal'əns) 1. anything that balances another. —v. (koun'tər bal'əns) 2. offset.

coun'ter·clock'wise', adv., adj. opposite to direction of turning clock hands.

coun′ter•cul′ture, *n.* culture of those opposed to prevailing culture.

coun′ter•feit (-fit) *adj.* **1.** fake. —*n.* **2.** fraudulent imitation. —*v.* **3.** make counterfeits. **4.** feign.

coun′ter•in•tel′li•gence, *n.* thwarting of espionage of a foreign power.

coun′ter•mand′ (-mand′) *v.* revoke (command).

coun′ter•part′, *n.* match or complement.

coun′ter•point′, *n.* combining of melodies.

coun′ter•pro•duc′tive, *adj.* giving contrary results.

coun′ter•sign′, *n.* **1.** secret signal. —*v.* **2.** sign to confirm another signature.

count′ess (koun′tis) *n.* **1.** wife of count or earl. **2.** woman equal in rank to count or earl.

count′less, *adj.* innumerable.

coun′try (kun′trē) *n., pl.* **-tries. 1.** nation. **2.** rural districts. —**coun′try•side′,** *n.*

coun′ty (koun′tē) *n., pl.* **-ties.** political unit within state.

coup (kōō) *n., pl.* **coups.** daring and successful stroke.

coup d′é•tat′ (kōō′ dä täz′) *pl.* **coups d′état** (-dä täz′, -tä′). overthrow of a government.

coupe (kōōp) *n.* small, two-door car. Also, **cou•pé′** (kōō pā′).

cou′ple (kup′əl) *n., v.,* **-pled, -pling.** —*n.* **1.** pair. —*v.* **2.** fasten or unite. —**cou′pling,** *n.* —**Usage.** Do not confuse PAIR and COUPLE. Both words have the meaning "a group of two" but are used differently. PAIR is used when two things come as a set, with one not usually used without the other: *a pair of socks, a pair of gloves* or when there is one item that has two parts, as in *a pair of shorts, a pair of scissors*. COUPLE is used for things of the same kind that happen to be two in number: *a couple of books, a couple of chairs*.

cou′plet (kup′lit) *n.* pair of rhyming lines.

cou′pon (kōō′pon, kyōō′-) *n.* certificate entitling holder to a gift or discount.

cour′age (kûr′ij, kur′-) *n.* bravery. —**cou•ra′geous** (kə rā′jəs) *adj.* —**cou•ra′geous•ly,** *adv.*

cour′i•er (kûr′ē ər) *n.* messenger.

course (kôrs) *n., v.,* **coursed, coursing.** —*n.* **1.** continuous passage. **2.** route. **3.** series of lessons. **4.** one part of meal. —*v.* **5.** run.

court (kôrt) *n.* **1.** enclosed space. **2.** level area for certain games. **3.** palace. **4.** assembly held by sovereign. **5.** homage or attention. **6.** place where justice is dealt. **7.** judge or judges. —*v.* **8.** woo. —**court′house,** *n.* —**court′room,** *n.* —**court′ship,** *n.* —**court′yard′,** *n.*

cour′te•san (kôr′tə zən) *n.* prostitute with noble or wealthy clients.

cour′te•sy (kûr′tə sē) *n., pl.* **-sies. 1.** good manners. **2.** indulgence. —**cour′te•ous** (-tē əs) *adj.*

cour′ti•er (kôr′tē ər) *n.* person in attendance at court.

court′ly, *adj.* elegant.

court′-mar′tial, *n., pl.* **courts-martial,** *v.,* **court-martialed, court-martialing.** —*n.* **1.** military court. —*v.* **2.** try by court-martial.

cous′in (kuz′ən) *n.* child of uncle or aunt.

cou•tu′ri•er (kōō tōōr′ē ər, -ē ā′) *n.* designer of stylish clothes.

cove (kōv) *n.* recess in shoreline.

cov′en (kuv′ən, kō′vən) *n.* assembly of witches.

cov′e•nant (kuv′ə nənt) *n.* solemn agreement; oath or pact.

cov′er (kuv′ər) *v.* **1.** be or put something over. **2.** include. **3.** have in range. **4.** meet or offset. —*n.* **5.** thing that covers.

cov′er•age (-ij) *n.* **1.** protection by insurance. **2.** reporting of news.

cov′er•let (-lit) *n.* quilt.

cov′ert (kō′vərt) *adj.* secret. —**cov′ert•ly,** *adv.*

cov′er-up′, *n.* concealing of illegal activity, a blunder, etc.

cov′et (kuv′it) *v.* desire greatly or wrongfully. —**cov′et•ous,** *adj.*

cov′ey (kuv′ē) *n., pl.* **-eys.** small flock.

cow (kou) *n.* **1.** female of bovine or other large animal. —*v.* **2.** intimidate.

cow′ard (kou′ərd) *n.* person who lacks courage. —**cow′ard•ice** (-ər dis) *n.* —**cow′ard•ly,** *adj., adv.*

cow′boy′, *n.* cattle herder. Also, **cow′hand′; cow′girl′,** *n. fem.*

cow′er (kou′ər) *v.* crouch in fear.

cowl (koul) *n.* hoodlike part.

cow′lick′, *n.* tuft of hair growing in a different direction.

cow′slip′, *n.* plant with yellow flowers.

cox′swain (kok′sən) *n.* person who steers boat or racing shell. Also, **cox.**

coy (koi) *adj.* affectedly shy. —**coy′ly,** *adv.* —**coy′ness,** *n.*

coy•o′te (kī ō′tē) *n.* wild animal related to wolf.

coz′en (kuz′ən) *v.* cheat or deceive.

co′zy (kō′zē) *adj.,* **-zier, -ziest.** comfortable; snug. —**co′zi•ly,** *adv.* —**co′zi•ness,** *n.*

CPA, certified public accountant.

CPI, consumer price index.

CPR, cardiopulmonary resuscitation: a form of lifesaving.

CPU, central processing unit, the key component of a computer system.

crab (krab) *n.* crustacean with broad flat body.

crab apple, small tart apple.

crab′by, *adj.,* **-bier, -biest.** grouchy.

crack (krak) *v.* **1.** make sudden, sharp sound. **2.** break without separating. —*n.* **3.** sudden, sharp sound. **4.** break without separation. **5.** smokable form of cocaine.

crack′down′, *n.* stern enforcement of regulations.

crack′er, *n.* **1.** crisp biscuit. **2.** firecracker.

crack′le (krak′əl) *v.,* **-led, -ling,** *n.* —*v.* **1.** crack repeatedly. —*n.* **2.** crackling sound.

crack′pot′, *n.* person with irrational theories.

crack′up′, *n.* breakdown.

cra′dle (krād′l) *n., v.,* **-dled, -dling.** —*n.* **1.** bed for baby. —*v.* **2.** place in cradle. **3.** hold protectively.

craft (kraft) *n.* **1.** skill; skilled trade. **2.** cunning. **3.** vessels or aircraft. —**crafts′man,** *n.* —**crafts′wom•an,** *n. fem.* —**crafts′man•ship′,** *n.*

craft′y, *adj.,* **-ier, -iest.** cunning.

crag (krag) *n.* steep rough rock.

cram (kram) *v.,* **crammed, cramming. 1.** fill tightly. **2.** study hard.

cramp (kramp) *n.* **1.** involuntary muscular contraction. —*v.* **2.** affect with a cramp. **3.** hamper.

cramped (krampt) *adj.* confined or limited.

cran′ber′ry (kran′ber′ē) *n., pl.* **-ries.** red acid edible berry.

crane (krān) *n.* **1.** tall wading bird. **2.** lifting device or machine.

cra′ni•um (krā′nē əm) *n., pl.* **-niums, -nia** (-nē ə). skull.

crank (krangk) *n.* **1.** right-angled lever to operate machine. **2.** *Informal.* grouchy person. —*v.* **3.** turn with a crank.

crank′y (krang′kē) *adj.,* **-ier, -iest.** ill-tempered. —**crank′i•ness,** *n.*

cran′ny (kran′ē) *n., pl.* **-nies.** cleft.

crap (krap) *n. Slang.* **1.** worthless material. **2.** false or meaningless statements.

crape (krāp) *n.* crepe (defs. 1, 2).

craps (kraps) *n.* dice game.

crash (krash) *v.* **1.** strike or collide noisily. **2.** land or fall with damage. —*n.* **3.** noise or act of crashing. **4.** collapse. **5.** act of crashing.

crass (kras) *adj.* insensitive; crude.

crate (krāt) *n., v.,* **crated, crating.** —*n.* **1.** box or frame for packing. —*v.* **2.** put in crate.

cra′ter, *n.* cup-shaped hole, as in volcano or on moon.

cra•vat′ (krə vat′) *n.* necktie.

crave (krāv) *v.,* **craved, craving.** yearn or beg for.

cra′ven (krā′vən) *adj.* **1.** cowardly. —*n.* **2.** coward.

crav′ing, *n.* intense yearning.

crawl (krôl) *v.* **1.** move slowly, as on stomach. —*n.* **2.** act of crawling. **3.** swimming stroke. —**crawl′er,** *n.*

cray′fish′ (krā′fish′) *n.* crustacean resembling a lobster. Also, **craw′fish′** (krô′-).

cray′on (krā′on) *n.* stick of colored wax or chalk for drawing.

craze (krāz) *v.,* **crazed, crazing,** *n.* —*v.* **1.** make insane. **2.** mark with fine cracks, as glaze. —*n.* **3.** mania.

cra′zy (krā′zē) *adj.,* **-zier, -ziest. 1.** insane. **2.** impractical.

creak (krēk) *v.* **1.** squeak sharply. —*n.* **2.** creaking sound.

cream (krēm) *n.* **1.** fatty part of milk. **2.** best part of anything. —*v.* **3.** thick, smooth substance to put on skin. **4.** make with cream. **5.** mix until creamy. **6.** *Informal.* defeat utterly. —**cream′y,** *adj.*

cream′er•y, *n., pl.* **-ies.** place where dairy goods are produced.

crease (krēs) *n., v.,* **creased, creasing.** —*n.* **1.** mark from folding. —*v.* **2.** make creases in.

cre•ate′ (krē āt′) *v.,* **-ated, -ating.** cause to exist. —**cre•a′tion,** *n.* —**cre•a′tive,** *adj.* —**cre•a′tor,** *n.*

crea′ture (krē′chər) *n.* **1.** animate being. **2.** anything created.

cre′dence (krēd′ns) *n.* belief.

cre•den′tial (kri den′shəl) *n.* (*usually pl.*) verifying document.

cre•den′za (kri den′zə) *n.* sideboard, esp. one without legs.

cred′i•ble (kred′ə bəl) *adj.* believable. —**cred′i•bil′i•ty,** *n.*

cred′it (kred′it) *n.* **1.** belief. **2.** honor. **3.** time allowed for payment. **4.** balance in person's favor. —*v.* **5.** believe. **6.** ascribe to.

cred′it•a•ble, *adj.* worthy.

credit card, card entitling holder to charge purchases.

cred′i•tor, *n.* person owed.

credit union, cooperative group that makes loans to its members at low interest rates.

cred′u•lous (krej′ə ləs) *adj.* too trusting. —**cre•du′li•ty** (krə dōō′li tē, -dyōō′-) *n.*

creed (krēd) *n.* formula of belief.

creek (krēk, krik) *n.* brook.

creep (krēp) *v.*, **crept** (krept) or **creeped, creeping,** *n.* —*v.* **1.** move stealthily; crawl. —*n.* **2.** *Slang.* disagreeable person.

creep′y, *adj.*, **-ier, -iest.** causing uneasiness.

cre′mate (krē′māt) *v.*, **-mated, -mating.** burn (corpse) to ashes. —**cre•ma′tion,** *n.* —**cre′ma•to′ry,** *n.*

Cre′ole (krē′ōl) *n.* **1.** one of French and Spanish blood born in Louisiana. **2.** (*l.c.*) pidgin that has become native language of a group.

cre′o•sote′ (krē′ə sōt′) *n.* oily liquid from tar.

crepe (krāp; *for 3 also* krep) *n.* **1.** light crinkled fabric. **2.** Also, **crepe paper.** thin, wrinkled paper used for decorating. **3.** thin, light pancake.

cre•scen′do (kri shen′dō) *n.*, *pl.* **-dos.** *Music.* gradual increase in loudness.

cres′cent (kres′ənt) *n.* **1.** moon in its first or last quarter. **2.** object having this shape.

cress (kres) *n.* plant with pungent leaves, eaten in salads.

crest (krest) *n.* **1.** tuft or plume. **2.** figure above coat of arms.

crest′fal′len, *adj.* abruptly discouraged or depressed.

cre′tin (krēt′n) *n.* boorish person.

cre•tonne′ (kri ton′) *n.* heavily printed cotton.

cre•vasse′ (krə vas′) *n.* fissure, esp. in glacier.

crev′ice (krev′is) *n.* fissure.

crew (krōō) *n.* **1.** group of persons working together, as on ship. —*v.* **2.** form crew of.

crew cut, haircut in which the hair is cut close to the head.

crib (krib) *n.*, *v.*, **cribbed, cribbing.** —*n.* **1.** child's bed. **2.** rack or bin. —*v.* **3.** put in a crib. **4.** plagiarize.

crib′bage (krib′ij) *n.* card game using score-board with pegs.

crick (krik) *n.* muscular spasm.

crick′et (krik′it) *n.* **1.** leaping, noisy insect. **2.** British outdoor ballgame with bats and wickets.

cri′er (krī′ər) *n.* one who announces.

crime (krīm) *n.* **1.** unlawful act. **2.** sin. —**crim′i•nal** (krim′ə nl) *adj.*, *n.* —**crim′i•nal•ly,** *adv.*

crimp (krimp) *v.* **1.** make wavy. —*n.* **2.** crimped form.

crim′son (krim′zən) *n.*, *adj.* deep red.

cringe (krinj) *v.*, **cringed, cringing.** shrink in fear or embarrassment.

crin′kle (kring′kəl) *v.*, **-kled, -kling,** *n.* wrinkle. —**crin′kly,** *adj.*

crin′o•line (krin′l in) *n.* **1.** stiff, coarse fabric. **2.** petticoat.

crip′ple (krip′əl) *n.*, *v.*, **-pled, -pling.** —*n.* **1.** *Sometimes Offensive.* lame or disabled person or animal. —*v.* **2.** make lame; disable.

cri′sis (krī′sis) *n.*, *pl.* **-ses** (-sēz). decisive stage or point.

crisp (krisp) *adj.* **1.** brittle. **2.** firm and fresh. **3.** brisk. **4.** cold and dry. —*v.* **5.** make or become crisp. —**crisp′ly,** *adv.* —**crisp′ness,** *n.*

criss′cross′ (kris′krôs′) *adj.* **1.** marked with crossed lines. —*v.* **2.** crisscross pattern. —*v.* **3.** mark with crossed lines.

cri•te′ri•on (krī tēr′ē ən) *n.*, *pl.* **-teria** (-tēr′ē ə). standard for judgment.

crit′ic (krit′ik) *n.* **1.** judge of art or literature. **2.** faultfinding person.

crit′i•cal, *adj.* **1.** severe in judgment. **2.** involving criticism. **3.** crucial.

crit′i•cize′ (-sīz′) *v.*, **-cized, -cizing. 1.** discuss as a critic. **2.** find fault with. —**crit′i•cism** (-siz′əm) *n.*

cri•tique′ (kri tēk′) *n.* critical article.

crit′ter (krit′ər) *n.* *Dial.* creature.

croak (krōk) *v.* utter a hoarse cry.

cro•chet′ (krō shā′) *v.* form thread into designs with hooked needle.

crock (krok) *n.* earthen jar. —**crock′er•y,** *n.*

croc′o•dile′ (krok′ə dīl′) *n.* large aquatic legged reptile with long, powerful jaws and tail.

cro′cus (krō′kəs) *n.* small bulbous plant blooming in early spring.

crois•sant′ (*Fr.* krwa sän′; *Eng.* krə-sänt′) *n.* crescent-shaped pastry.

crone (krōn) *n.* witchlike old woman.

cro′ny (krō′nē) *n.*, *pl.* **-nies.** close friend.

crook (krōōk) *n.* **1.** curved tool. **2.** dishonest person. —**crook′ed,** *adj.*

croon (krōōn) *v.* sing softly.

crop (krop) *n.*, *v.*, **cropped, cropping.** —*n.* **1.** produce from the soil. **2.** short whip. **3.** pouch in gullet of bird. —*v.* **4.** remove ends. **5.** cut short. **6.** reap. **7. crop up,** appear.

cro•quet′ (krō kā′) *n.* game with wooden balls and mallets.

cro•quette′ (krō ket′) *n.* fried or baked piece of chopped food.

cro′sier (krō′zhər) *n.* staff of bishop.

cross (krôs) *n.* **1.** structure whose basic form has an upright with transverse piece. **2.** emblem of Christianity. **3.** figure resembling cross. **4.** mixture of breeds. —*v.* **5.** make sign of cross over. **6.** put, lie, or pass across. **7.** oppose or frustrate. **8.** mark (out). **9.** mix (breeds). —*adj.* **10.** transverse. **11.** ill-humored. —**cross′ly,** *adv.*

cross′bow′ (-bō′) *n.* weapon consisting of a bow fixed on a stock like that of a rifle.

cross′ breed′, **cross bred, cross breeding.** —*v.* **1.** hybridize. —*n.* **2.** hybrid.

cross′-coun′try, *adj.* **1.** proceeding over fields, through woods, etc., rather than on a road or track. **2.** from one end of a country to the other. —*n.* **3.** sport of cross-country racing.

cross′-ex•am′ine, *v.*, **cross-examined, cross-examining.** examine closely, as opposing witness. —**cross′-ex•am′in•a′tion,** *n.*

cross′-eye′, *n.* visual disorder. —**cross′-eyed′,** *adj.*

cross reference, reference to another part of book.

cross′roads′, *n.* **1.** intersection. **2.** decisive point.

cross section, 1. section made by cutting across something. **2.** representative sample of a whole.

cross′walk′, *n.* place where people can cross the street.

cross′word puz′zle, puzzle in which words determined from numbered clues are fitted into pattern of horizontal and vertical squares.

crotch (kroch) *n.* place where something divides, as the human body between the legs.

crotch′et (kroch′it) *n.* whim.

crotch′et•y, *adj.* grumpy.

crouch (krouch) *v.* **1.** stoop or bend low. —*n.* **2.** act of crouching.

croup (krōōp) *n.* inflammation of throat.

crou•pi•er (krōō′pē ər, -pē ā′) *n.* attendant who handles bets and money at gambling table.

crou′ton (krōō′ton) *n.* small cube of toasted bread.

crow (krō) *v.* **1.** cry, as cock. **2.** boast.

—*n.* **3.** cry of cock. **4.** black, harsh-voiced bird. **5.** (*cap.*) member of an American Indian people.

crow′bar′, *n.* iron bar for prying.

crowd (kroud) *n.* **1.** large group of people. —*v.* **2.** throng.

crown (kroun) *n.* **1.** ornate headgear for sovereign. **2.** power of a sovereign. **3.** top. —*v.* **4.** put crown on. **5.** reward or complete.

crow′s-foot′, *n.*, *pl.* **crow′s-feet.** (*usually pl.*) tiny wrinkle at outer corner of the eye.

CRT, cathode-ray tube.

cru′cial (krōō′shəl) *adj.* decisive.

cru′ci•ble (krōō′sə bəl) *n.* vessel for melting metals, etc.

cru′ci•fix (krōō′sə fiks) *n.* cross with figure of Jesus crucified.

cru′ci•fy′ (-fī′) *v.*, **-fied, -fying. 1.** put to death on cross. **2.** persecute. —**cru′ci•fix′ion,** *n.*

crude (krōōd) *adj.*, **cruder, crudest,** *n.* —*adj.* **1.** unrefined. **2.** unfinished. —*n.* **3.** *Informal.* unrefined petroleum. —**crude′ly,** *adv.*

cru•di•tés′ (krōō′di tā′) *n.pl.* cut-up raw vegetables served with a dip.

cru′el (krōō′əl) *adj.* disposed to inflict pain. **2.** causing pain. —**cru′el•ly,** *adv.* —**cru′el•ty,** *n.*

cru′et (krōō′it) *n.* stoppered bottle for vinegar, etc.

cruise (krōōz) *v.*, **cruised, cruising,** *n.* —*v.* **1.** sail or fly at moderate speed. **2.** travel for pleasure. —*n.* **3.** cruising trip.

cruis′er, *n.* **1.** kind of warship. **2.** small pleasure boat.

crumb (krum) *n.* small bit of bread, cookie, etc.

crum′ble (krum′bəl) *v.*, **-bled, -bling.** break into fragments; decay.

crum′my (krum′ē) *adj.*, **-mier, -miest.** *Informal.* **1.** shabby. **2.** cheap. **3.** miserable.

crum′ple (krum′pəl) *v.*, **-pled, -pling,** *n.* wrinkle; rumple.

crunch (krunch) *v.* **1.** chew or crush noisily. —*n.* **2.** crunching sound.

cru•sade′ (krōō sād′) *n.*, *v.*, **-saded, -sading.** —*n.* **1.** Christian expedition to recover Holy Land from Muslims. **2.** campaign for good cause. —*v.* **3.** engage in crusade. —**cru•sad′er,** *n.*

crush (krush) *v.* **1.** bruise or break by pressing. **2.** subdue. —*n.* **3.** dense crowd. **4.** infatuation.

crust (krust) *n.* **1.** hard outer part or covering. —*v.* **2.** cover with crust. —**crust′y,** *adj.*

crus•ta′cean (kru stā′shən) *n.* sea animal having hard shell.

crutch (kruch) *n.* **1.** stick fitting under the armpit for support in walking. **2.** *Informal.* temporary aid or prop.

crux (kruks) *n.*, *pl.* **cruxes, cruces** (krōō′sēz). vital point.

cry (krī) *v.*, **cried, crying,** *n.*, *pl.* **cries.** —*v.* **1.** make sounds of grief, etc. **2.** utter characteristic sounds. **3.** shout. —*n.* **4.** act or sound of crying.

cry′o•gen′ics (krī′ə jen′iks) *n.* study or use of extremely low temperatures. —**cry′o•gen′ic,** *adj.*

crypt (kript) *n.* underground chamber.

cryp′tic, *adj.* mysterious.

crys′tal (kris′tl) *n.* **1.** clear transparent mineral. **2.** body with symmetrical plane faces. **3.** fine glass. —**crys′tal•line** (-tl in, -īn′) *adj.*

crys′tal•lize′, *v.*, **-lized, -lizing. 1.** form or cause to form into crystals. **2.** assume or cause to assume definite form. —**crys′tal•li•za′tion,** *n.*

C′-sec′tion, *n.* Cesarean.

CST, Central Standard Time.

CT, Connecticut.

Ct., 1. Connecticut. **2.** Count.

ct., 1. carat. **2.** cent. **3.** court.

cu., cubic.

cub (kub) *n.* young fox, bear, etc.

cub′by•hole′ (kub′ē-) *n.* small enclosed space.

cube (kyōob) *n., v.,* **cubed, cubing.** —*n.* **1.** solid bounded by six squares. **2.** *Math.* third power of a quantity. —*v.* **3.** make into cubes. **4.** *Math.* raise to third power. —**cu′bic,** *adj.*

cu′bi•cle (kyōo′bi kəl) *n.* small room.

cub′ism, *n.* artistic style marked by reduction of natural forms to geometric shapes. —**cub′ist,** *adj., n.*

Cub Scout, Boy Scout aged 8 to 10.

cuck′old (kuk′əld) *n.* husband of unfaithful wife.

cuck′oo (kōo′kōo, kōok′ōo) *n.* small bird.

cu′cum•ber (kyōo′kum bər) *n.* green-skinned cylindrical fruit.

cud (kud) *n.* food that cow returns to mouth for further chewing.

cud′dle (kud′l) *v.,* **-dled, -dling.** hold tenderly. —**cud′dly,** *adj.*

cudg′el (kuj′əl) *n.,* **-eled, -eling.** —*n.* **1.** short thick stick. —*v.* **2.** beat with cudgel.

cue (kyōo) *n.* **1.** (esp. on stage) something that signals speech or action. **2.** rod for billiards.

cuff (kuf) *n.* **1.** fold or band at end of sleeve or trouser leg. **2.** slap. —*v.* **3.** slap.

cui•sine′ (kwi zēn′) *n.* cookery.

cu′li•nar′y (kyōo′lə ner′ē, kul′ə-) *adj.* of cooking.

cull (kul) *v.* select best parts of.

cul′mi•nate′ (kul′mə nāt′) *v.,* **-nated, -nating.** reach highest point. —**cul′mi•na′tion,** *n.*

cul′pa•ble (kul′pə bəl) *adj.* deserving blame. —**cul′pa•bil′i•ty,** *n.*

cul′prit (kul′prit) *n.* person arraigned for or guilty of an offense.

cult (kult) *n.* **1.** religious sect or system. —*adj.* **2.** popular with some people.

cul′ti•vate′ (kul′tə vāt′) *v.,* **-vated, -vating. 1.** prepare and care for (land). **2.** develop possibilities of. —**cul′ti•va′tion,** *n.*

cul′ti•vat′ed, *adj.* educated.

cul′ture (kul′chər) *n.* **1.** raising of plants or animals. **2.** development of mind. **3.** state or form of civilization. —**cul′tur•al,** *adj.*

culture shock, distress of person exposed to new culture.

cul′vert (kul′vərt) *n.* channel under road, etc.

cum′ber•some (kum′bər səm) *adj.* clumsy or bulky.

cu′mu•la•tive (kyōo′myə lə tiv) *adj.* increasing by accumulation.

cu′mu•lus (kyōo′myə ləs) *n., pl.* **-li.** rounded cloud.

cu•ne′i•form′ (kyōo nē′ə fôrm′) *adj.* composed of wedge-shaped elements, as some ancient writing.

cun′ning (kun′ing) *adj.* **1.** clever. **2.** sly. —*n.* **3.** skill. **4.** guile.

cup (kup) *n., v.,* **cupped, cupping.** —*n.* **1.** small open drinking vessel. —*v.* **2.** shape like a cup.

cup′board (kub′ərd) *n.* closet for dishes, etc.

Cu′pid (kyōo′pid) *n.* Roman god of carnal love.

cu•pid′i•ty (-pid′i tē) *n.* greed.

cu′po•la (kyōo′pə lə) *n.* rounded dome.

cur (kûr) *n.* worthless dog.

cu′rate (kyōōr′it) *n.* clergyman assisting rector or vicar.

cu•ra′tor (kyōo rā′tər, kyōōr′ā-) *n.* person in charge of museum.

curb (kûrb) *n.* **1.** strap for restraining horse. **2.** restraint. **3.** edge of sidewalk. —*v.* **4.** control.

curd (kûrd) *n.* **1.** substance formed when milk coagulates. —*v.* **2.** change into curd.

cur′dle (kûr′dl) *v.,* **-dled, -dling.** congeal, turn into curd.

cure (kyōor) *n., v.,* **cured, curing.** —*n.* **1.** treatment of disease. **2.** restoration to health. —*v.* **3.** restore to health. **4.** preserve.

cur′few (kûr′fyōo) *n.* order to be home or off the streets by a certain time.

cu′ri•o′ (kyōor′ē ō′) *n., pl.* **-rios.** unusual valuable article.

cu′ri•os′i•ty (kyōor′ē os′i tē) *n., pl.* **-ties. 1.** desire to know. **2.** odd thing.

cu′ri•ous (-əs) *adj.* **1.** wanting to know. **2.** prying. **3.** strange.

curl (kûrl) *v.* **1.** form in ringlets. **2.** coil. —*n.* **3.** ringlet. —**curl′er,** *n.* —**curl′y,** *adj.*

cur′lew (kûr′lōo) *n.* shore bird.

curl′i•cue (kûr′li kyōo′) *n.* fancy curl.

cur•mudg′eon (kər muj′ən) *n.* bad-tempered, difficult person.

cur′rant (kûr′ənt) *n.* **1.** small seedless raisin. **2.** edible acid berry.

cur′ren•cy (kûr′ən sē) *n., pl.* **-cies. 1.** money in use in a country. **2.** prevalence. **3.** circulation.

cur′rent (kûr′ənt) *adj.* **1.** present. **2.** generally known or believed. —*n.* **3.** stream; flow. **4.** water, air, etc., moving in one direction. **5.** movement of electricity.

cur•ric′u•lum (kə rik′yə ləm) *n., pl.* **-lums, -la** (-lə). course of study.

cur′ry (kûr′ē, kur′ē) *n., pl.* **-ries,** *v.,* **-ried, -rying.** —*n.* **1.** East Indian hot dish or powder **(curry powder).** —*v.* **2.** prepare with curry. **3.** rub and comb (horse, etc.). **4.** seek (favor) with servility.

cur′ry•comb′, *n.* wire brush for horse.

curse (kûrs) *n., v.,* **cursed** or **curst, cursing.** —*n.* **1.** wish that evil befall someone. **2.** evil so invoked. **3.** profane oath. **4.** cause of evil. —*v.* **5.** wish evil upon. **6.** swear. **7.** afflict.

cur′sive (kûr′siv) *adj.* (of handwriting) in flowing strokes with letters joined together.

cur′sor (-sər) *n.* movable symbol on computer screen to indicate where data may be input.

cur′so•ry, *adj.* superficial.

curt (kûrt) *adj.* brief, esp. rudely so.

cur•tail′ (kər tāl′) *v.* cut short. —**cur•tail′ment,** *n.*

cur′tain (kûr′tn) *n.* **1.** piece of fabric hung to adorn, conceal, etc. —*v.* **2.** cover with curtains.

curt′sy (kûrt′sē) *n., pl.* **-sies,** *v.,* **-sied, -sying.** —*n.* **1.** bow by women. —*v.* **2.** make curtsy.

cur′va•ture (kûr′və chər) *n.* **1.** a curving. **2.** degree of curving.

curve (kûrv) *n., v.,* **curved, curving.** —*n.* **1.** bending line. —*v.* **2.** bend or move in a curve.

cush′ion (kōosh′ən) *n.* **1.** soft bag of feathers, air, etc. —*v.* **2.** lessen the effects of.

cush′y (kōosh′ē) *adj. Informal.* easy and profitable.

cusp (kusp) *n.* pointed end.

cus′pid (kus′pid) *n.* canine tooth.

cuss (kus) *v. Informal.* curse.

cus′tard (kus′tərd) *n.* cooked dish of eggs and milk.

cus′to•dy (-tə dē) *n., pl.* **-dies. 1.** keeping; care. **2.** imprisonment. —**cus•to′di•al** (kə stō′dē əl) *adj.* —**cus•to′di•an,** *n.*

cus′tom (kus′təm) *n.* **1.** usual practice. **2.** set of such practices. **3.** (*pl.*) **a.** duties on imports. **b.** agency collecting these. —*adj.* **4.** made for the individual. —**cus′tom•ar′y,** *adj.*

cus′tom•er, *n.* **1.** purchaser or prospective purchaser. **2.** *Informal.* person.

cus′tom•ize′, *v.,* **-ized, -izing.** make to individual specifications.

cut (kut) *v.,* **cut, cutting,** *n.* —*v.* **1.** sever or penetrate as with knife. **2.** wound feelings of. **3.** reap or trim. **4.** shorten by omitting part. **5.** dilute. **6.** move or cross. **7.** be absent from. —*n.* **8.** a cutting. **9.** result of cutting. **10.** straight passage.

cu•ta′ne•ous (kyōo tā′nē əs) *adj.* of the skin.

cut′back′, *n.* reduction in rate, quantity, etc.

cute (kyōot) *adj.,* **cuter, cutest.** pretty or pleasing.

cu′ti•cle (kyōo′ti kəl) *n.* epidermis, esp. around nails.

cut′lass (kut′ləs) *n.* short curved sword.

cut′ler•y (-lə rē) *n.* knives collectively.

cut′let (-lit) *n.* slice of meat for frying or broiling.

cut′off′, *n.* **1.** point beyond which something is no longer effective or possible. **2.** road that leaves another to make a shortcut.

cut′-rate′, *adj.* offered at reduced prices.

cut′ter, *n.* **1.** one that cuts. **2.** small fast vessel. **3.** sleigh.

cut′throat′, *n.* **1.** murderer. —*adj.* **2.** ruthless.

cut′tle•fish′ (kut′l fish′) *n., pl.* **-fish, -fishes.** mollusk with ten arms and hard internal shell **(cut′tle•bone′).**

cy′a•nide′ (sī′ə nīd′) *n.* poisonous salt of hydrocyanic acid.

cyber-, prefix meaning computer, as *cyberspace.*

cy′ber•net′ics (sī′bər net′iks) *n.* study of control and communications systems.

cy′ber•space′, *n.* **1.** realm of electronic communication. **2.** virtual reality.

cy′cle (sī′kəl) *n., v.,* **-cled, -cling.** —*n.* **1.** recurring time or process. **2.** complete set. **3.** bicycle, etc. —*v.* **4.** ride bicycle.

cy′clone (sī′klōn) *n.* tornado. —**cy•clon′ic** (-klon′ik) *adj.*

cy′clo•pe′di•a (sī′klə pē′dē ə) *n.* encyclopedia.

cy′clo•tron′ (-tron′) *n.* device used in splitting atoms.

cyg′net (sig′nit) *n.* young swan.

cyl′in•der (sil′in dər) *n.* **1.** round elongated solid with ends that are equal parallel circles. **2.** machine part or opening in this form. —**cy•lin′dri•cal,** *adj.*

cym′bal (sim′bəl) *n.* brass plate used in orchestras.

cyn′ic (sin′ik) *n.* person who doubts or lacks goodness of motive. —**cyn′i•cal,** *adj.* —**cyn′i•cism** (-ə siz′əm) *n.*

cy′no•sure′ (sī′nə shōor′) *n.* object that attracts by its brilliance.

cy′press (sī′prəs) *n.* evergreen tree of pine family.

cyst (sist) *n.* abnormal sac containing

matter formed in live tissue. —**cys'tic**, *adj.*

cys'tic fi•bro'sis (sis'tik fī brō'sis) hereditary disease marked by breathing difficulties and growth of excess fibrous tissue.

czar (zär) *n.* former emperor of Russia. Also, **tsar.**

cza•ri'na (zä rē'nə) *n.* wife of a czar.

Czech (chek) *n.* native or language of Czech Republic.

D

D, d (dē) *n.* fourth letter of English alphabet.

d. 1. date. **2.** deceased. **3.** degree. **4.** diameter. **5.** dose.

D.A. District Attorney.

dab (dab) *v.*, **dabbed, dabbing. 1.** apply lightly. —*n.* **2.** small quantity.

dab'ble (dab'əl) *v.*, **-bled, -bling. 1.** splatter. **2.** be interested superficially. —**dab'bler,** *n.*

dachs'hund' (däks'hŏŏnt', -hŏŏnd') *n.* kind of long, short-legged dog.

Da'•cron (dā'kron, dak'ron) *n. Trademark.* strong synthetic fabric.

dad (dad) *n. Informal.* father.

dad'dy (dad'ē) *n.*, *pl.* **-dies.** *Informal.* father.

dad'dy-long'legs', *n.*, *pl.* **daddy-longlegs.** spiderlike arachnid with long, slender legs. Also, **dad'dy long'-legs', *n., pl.* daddy longlegs.**

daf'fo•dil (daf'ə dil) *n.* plant with yellow trumpet-shaped flowers.

daft (daft) *adj.* **1.** insane. **2.** foolish.

dag'ger (dag'ər) *n.* short knifelike weapon.

dahl'ia (dal'yə, däl'-) *n.* showy cultivated flowering plant.

dai'ly (dā'lē) *adj.* **1.** of or occurring each day. —*n.* **2.** daily newspaper.

dain'ty (dān'tē) *adj.*, **-tier, -tiest,** *n.*, *pl.* **-ties.** —*adj.* **1.** delicate. **2.** delicacy. —**dain'ti•ly,** *adv.*

dair'y (dâr'ē) *n.*, *pl.* **-ies.** place for making or selling milk, butter, etc.

da'is (dā'is) *n.* raised platform.

dai'sy (dā'zē) *n.*, *pl.* **-sies.** flower with yellow center and white petals.

Da•ko'ta (də kō'tə) *n.*, *pl.* **-ta, -tas.** member of a North American Indian people.

dale (dāl) *n.* valley.

dal'ly (dal'ē) *v.*, Also **dallied, -lying. 1.** flirt. **2.** delay. —**dal'li•ance,** *n.*

Dal•ma'tian (dal mā'shən) *n.* large white-and-black dog.

dam (dam) *n.*, *v.*, **dammed, damming.** —*n.* **1.** barrier to obstruct water. **2.** female quadruped parent. —*v.* **3.** obstruct flow.

dam'age (dam'ij) *n.*, *v.*, **-aged, -aging.** —*n.* **1.** injury. **2.** (*pl.*) payment for injury. —*v.* **3.** injure.

dam'ask (dam'əsk) *n.* **1.** woven figured fabric. —*adj.* **2.** pink.

dame (dām) *n.* **1.** woman of rank. **2.** *Slang (sometimes offensive).* any woman.

damn (dam) *v.* **1.** declare bad. **2.** condemn to hell. —**dam'na•ble** (-nə bəl) *adj.* —**dam•na'tion,** *n.*

damp (damp) *adj.* **1.** moist. —*n.* **2.** moisture. —*v.* Also, **dampen. 3.** moisten. **4.** discourage. **5.** deaden. —**damp'ness,** *n.*

damp'er, *n.* **1.** control for air or smoke currents. **2.** discouraging influence.

dam'sel (dam'zəl) *n.* maiden.

dam'son (dam'zən, -sən) *n.* small plum.

dance (dans) *v.*, **danced, dancing,** —*v.* **1.** move rhythmically. —*n.* **2.** act of dancing. **3.** gathering or music for dancing. —**danc'er,** *n.*

dan'de•li'on (dan'dl ī'ən) *n.* plant with yellow flowers.

dan'der (-dər) *n. Informal.* temper.

dan'dle (dan'dl) *v.*, **-dled, -dling.** move (a child) lightly up and down.

dan'druff (-drəf) *n.* scales of dry skin on scalp.

dan'dy (-dē) *n.*, *pl.* **-dies,** *adj.*, **-dier, -diest.** —*n.* **1.** fashionable dresser. —*adj.* **2.** fine.

Dane (dān) *n.* native of Denmark.

dan'ger (dān'jər) *n.* exposure to harm. —**dan'ger•ous,** *adj.* —**dan'ger•ous•ly,** *adv.*

dan'gle (dang'gəl) *v.*, **-gled, -gling.** hang loosely.

Dan'ish (dā'nish) *adj.* **1.** of Denmark, the Danes, or their language. —*n.* **2.** the language of the Danes. **3.** (*sometimes l.c.*) filled pastry.

dank (dangk) *adj.* unpleasantly damp. —**dank'ness,** *n.*

dap'per (dap'ər) *adj.* neat and well-dressed.

dap'ple (dap'əl) *adj.*, *v.*, **-pled, -pling.** —*adj.* **1.** mottled. Also, **dap'pled.** —*v.* **2.** mottle.

dare (dâr) *v.*, **dared** or **durst** (dûrst), **dared, daring.** —*v.* **1.** be bold enough. **2.** challenge. —*n.* **3.** challenge. —**dar'ing,** *adj.*, *n.*

dare'dev'il, *n.* **1.** recklessly daring person. —*adj.* **2.** recklessly daring.

dark (därk) *adj.* **1.** lacking light. **2.** blackish. **3.** gloomy. —*n.* **4.** absence of light. —**dark'en,** *v.* —**dark'ly,** *adv.* —**dark'ness,** *n.*

Dark Ages, Middle Ages, esp. from A.D. 476 to about 1000.

dark horse, unexpected winner.

dark'room', *n.* place for developing and printing films.

dar'ling (där'ling) *n.* **1.** loved one. **2.** favorite. **3.** cherished. **4.** charming.

darn (därn) *v.* mend with rows of stitches. —**darn'er,** *n.*

dart (därt) *n.* **1.** slender pointed missile. **2.** (*pl.*) game of throwing darts at target. **3.** tapered seam. —*v.* **4.** move swiftly.

dash (dash) *v.* **1.** strike or throw violently. **2.** frustrate. **3.** do something quickly. **4.** hurry. —*n.* **5.** violent blow. **6.** small quantity. **7.** punctuation mark (—) noting abrupt break. **8.** rush.

dash'board', *n.* instrument board on motor vehicle.

dash'ing, *adj.* **1.** lively. **2.** stylish.

das'tard (das'tərd) *n.* coward. —**das'tard•ly,** *adj.*

da'ta (dā'tə, dat'ə) *n.pl., sing.* **datum** (dā'təm, dat'əm). facts or other information.

da'ta•base', *n.* collection of data, esp. one accessible by computer.

data processing, high-speed handling of information by computer.

date (dāt) *n.*, *v.*, **dated, dating.** —*n.* **1.** particular month, day, and year. **2.** fleshy, edible fruit of **date palm. 3.** social engagement arranged beforehand, esp. one of a romantic nature. **4.** person with whom one has a date. —*v.* **5.** exist from particular time. **6.** fix date with.

dat'ed, *adj.* **1.** having or showing a date. **2.** out-of-date.

da'tive (dā'tiv) *adj.* denoting verb's indirect object.

daub (dôb) *v.* **1.** paint clumsily. —*n.* **2.** something daubed on.

daugh'ter (dô'tər) *n.* female child.

daugh'ter-in-law', *n.*, *pl.* **daughters-in-law.** son's wife.

daunt (dônt, dänt) *v.* dishearten.

daunt'less, *adj.* bold; fearless.

dav'en•port' (dav'ən pôrt') *n.* large sofa.

daw'dle (dôd'l) *v.*, **-dled, -dling.** waste time. —**daw'dler,** *n.*

dawn (dôn) *n.* **1.** break of day. —*v.* **2.** begin to grow light. **3.** become apparent.

day (dā) *n.* **1.** period between two nights. **2.** period (24 hours) of earth's rotation on its axis.

day'break', *n.* first appearance of light; dawn.

day care, supervised care for young children or the elderly, usu. in daytime and at a center outside the home. —**day'-care',** *adj.*

day'dream', *n.* **1.** reverie; fancy. —*v.* **2.** indulge in reveries. —**day'dream'er,** *n.*

day'light', *n.* **1.** light of day. **2.** openness. **3.** (*pl.*) wits; sanity.

daylight-saving time, time one hour later than standard time. Also, **daylight-savings time.**

day'time', *n.* time from sunrise to sunset.

day'-to-day', *adj.* routine.

daze (dāz) *v.*, **dazed, dazing.** —*v.* **1.** stun. —*n.* **2.** dazed state.

daz'zle (daz'əl) *v.*, **-zled, -zling.** overwhelm with light.

dba, doing business as.

dbl. 1. decibel. **2.** double.

DC, 1. direct current. **2.** District of Columbia.

D.D., Doctor of Divinity.

D.D.S., **1.** Doctor of Dental Science. **2.** Doctor of Dental Surgery.

DDT, strong insecticide, now banned from use.

de-, prefix indicating: **1.** reverse, as *deactivate.* **2.** remove, as *decaffeinate.* **3.** reduce, as *degrade.*

dea'con (dē'kən) *n.* **1.** cleric inferior to priest. **2.** lay church officer. —**dea'con•ess,** *n.fem.*

de•ac'ti•vate' (dē ak'tə vāt') *v.*, **-vated, -vating.** make inactive.

dead (ded) *adj.* **1.** no longer alive or active. **2.** exhausted. **3.** absolute. —*n.* **4.** dead persons. **5.** darkest, coldest time. —*adv.* **6.** completely. **7.** directly. —**dead'en,** *v.*

dead'beat', *n.* **1.** person who avoids paying. **2.** sponger.

dead end, 1. street, corridor, etc., with no exit. **2.** position with no hope of progress. —**dead'-end',** *adj.*

dead heat, race that finishes in a tie.

dead'line', *n.* last allowable time.

dead'lock', *n.* standstill.

dead'ly, *adj.*, **-lier, -liest. 1.** fatal. **2.** dreary. **3.** extremely accurate. —*adv.* **4.** extremely.

dead'pan', *adj.* without expression.

dead'wood', *n.* useless or extraneous persons or things.

deaf (def) *adj.* unable to hear. —**deaf'en,** *v.* —**deaf'ness,** *n.*

deaf'-mute', *n. Often Offensive.* person unable to hear or speak.

deal (dēl) *v.*, **dealt** (delt), **dealing,** *n.* —*v.* **1.** be concerned with. **2.** do business. **3.** distribute. —*n.* **4.** transaction. **5.** quantity. —**deal'er,** *n.*

deal'ing, *n.* (*usually pl.*) transactions or interactions with others.

dean (dēn) *n.* **1.** head of academic faculty. **2.** head of cathedral organization.

dear (dĕr) *adj.* **1.** loved. **2.** expensive. **—n. 3.** dear one. **—dear′ly,** *adv.*

dearth (dûrth) *n.* scarcity.

death (deth) *n.* end of life. **—death′-ly,** *adj.*, *adv.* **—death′bed′,** *n.*

death′less, *adj.* enduring.

de•ba′cle (də bä′kəl, -bak′əl, dā-) *n.* **1.** breakup; rout. **2.** utter failure.

de•bar′ (di bär′) *v.*, **-barred, -barring.** exclude. **—de•bar′ment,** *n.*

de•bark′ (di bärk′) *v.* disembark. **—de′bar•ka′tion,** *n.*

de•base′ (di bās′) *v.*, **-based, -basing.** reduce in quality.

de•bate′ (di bāt′) *n.*, *v.*, **-bated, -bating.** **—n.** **1.** controversial discussion. **—v. 2.** argue; discuss. **—de•bat′a•ble,** *adj.*

de•bauch′ (di bôch′) *v.* corrupt; pervert. **—de•bauch′er•y,** *n.*

de•bil′i•tate′ (di bil′i tāt′) *v.*, **-tated, -tating.** weaken.

de•bil′i•ty, *n.*, *pl.* **-ties.** weakness.

debt (det) *n.* **1.** recorded debt. **2.** account of debts. **—v. 3.** charge as debt.

deb′o•nair′ (deb′ə når′) *adj.* **1.** suave; urbane. **2.** relaxed; calm.

de•brief′ (dē brēf′) *v.* gather information from someone about a completed mission.

de•bris′ (də brē′, dā′brē) *n.* rubbish; ruins.

debt (det) *n.* **1.** something owed. **2.** obligation to pay. **—debt′or,** *n.*

de•bug′ (dē bug′) *v.*, **-bugged, -bugging.** **1.** remove defects or errors from (computer program). **2.** remove electronic bugs from (room or building).

de•bunk′ (di bungk′) *v.* expose as false.

de•but′ (dā byoo′, di-, dā′byoo) *n.* first public appearance. **—deb′u•tante′,** *n.fem.*

Dec., December.

dec′ade (dek′ād) *n.* 10-year period.

dec′a•dence (dek′ə dəns, di kād′ns) *n.* decline in morality; corruption. **—dec′a•dent,** *adj.*

de•caf′fein•at′ed (dē kaf′ə nā′tad), *adj.* having the caffeine removed.

dec′a•he′dron (dek′ə hē′drən) *n.*, *pl.* **-drons, -dra** (-drə). solid figure with 10 faces.

de′cal (dē′kal, di kal′) *n.* picture or design on specially prepared paper for transfer to wood, metal, etc.

Dec′a•logue′ (dek′ə lôg′) *n.* Ten Commandments.

de•camp′ (di kamp′) *v.* depart, esp. secretly.

de•cant′ (di kant′) *v.* pour off.

de•cant′er, *n.* ornamental bottle.

de•cap′i•tate′ (di kap′i tāt′) *v.*, **-tated, -tating.** behead.

de•cath′lon (di kath′lon) *n.* contest of 10 events.

de•cay′ (di kā′) *v.*, *n.* decline in quality, health, etc.

de•cease′ (di sēs′) *n.*, *v.*, **-ceased, -ceasing.** **—n. 1.** death. **—v. 2.** die. **—de•ceased′,** *adj.*, *n.*

de•ceit′ (di sēt′) *n.* **1.** fraud. **2.** trick. **—de•ceit′ful,** *adj.*

de•ceive′ (di sēv′) *v.*, **-ceived, -ceiving.** lead into error; mislead.

De•cem′ber (di sem′bər) *n.* 12th month of year.

de′cen•cy (dē′sən sē) *n.*, *pl.* **-cies. 1.** conformity to moral standards. **2.** respectability. **3.** adequacy. **4.** kindness or willingness to help. **—de′cent,** *adj.* **—de′cent•ly,** *adv.*

de•cen′tral•ize′ (dē sen′trə līz′) *v.*, **-ized, -izing.** end central control of.

de•cep′tion (di sep′shən) *n.* **1.** act of deceiving. **2.** fraud. **—de•cep′tive,** *adj.*

dec′i•bel′ (des′ə bel′, -bəl) *n.* unit of intensity of sound.

de•cide′ (di sīd′) *v.*, **-cided, -ciding.** settle; resolve.

de•cid′ed, *adj.* unambiguous; emphatic. **—de•cid′ed•ly,** *adv.*

de•cid′u•ous (di sij′ōō əs) *adj.* shedding leaves annually.

dec′i•mal (des′ə məl) *adj.* **1.** of tenths. **2.** proceeding by tens. **—n. 3.** fraction in tenths, hundredths, etc., indicated by dot (**decimal point**) before numerator.

dec′i•mate′ (des′ə māt′) *v.* **-mated, -mating.** kill or destroy much of.

de•ci′pher (di sī′fər) *v.* find meaning of. **—de•ci′pher•a•ble,** *adj.*

de•ci′sion (di sizh′ən) *n.* **1.** something decided. **2.** firmness of mind.

de•ci′sive (-sī′siv) *adj.* **1.** determining. **2.** resolute. **—de•ci′sive•ly,** *adv.* **—de•ci′sive•ness,** *n.*

deck (dek) *n.* **1.** level on ship. **2.** pack of playing cards. **—v. 3.** array.

de•claim′ (di klām′) *v.* speak rhetorically. **—de•claim′er,** *n.*

dec′la•ma′tion (dek′lə mā′shən) *n.* oratorical speech.

de•clare′ (di klâr′) *v.*, **-clared, -claring. 1.** make known. **2.** affirm. **—dec′la•ra′tion** (dek′lə rā′shən) *n.* **—de•clar′a•tive,** *adj.*

de•clen′sion (di klen′shən) *n.* grammatical inflection or set of inflections.

de•cline′ (di klīn′) *v.*, **-clined, -clining,** *n.* **—v. 1.** refuse. **2.** slant down. **3.** give grammatical inflections. **4.** fail; diminish. **—n. 5.** downward slope. **6.** deterioration.

de•code′ (dē kōd′) *v.*, **-coded, -coding.** decipher from code.

de′com•mis′sion, *v.* retire (vessel) from active service.

de′com•pose′ (-kəm pōz′) *v.*, **-posed, -posing. 1.** separate into constituent parts. **2.** rot. **—de′com•po•si′tion,** *n.*

de′con•ges′tant (dē′kən jes′tənt) *adj.* **1.** relieving congestion of the upper respiratory tract. **—n. 2.** decongestant agent.

de′con•tam′i•nate (-nāt′) *v.*, **-nated, -nating.** make safe by removing or neutralizing harmful contaminants.

dé•cor′ (dā kôr′, di-) *n.* style of decoration, as of a room. Also, **de•cor′.**

dec′o•rate′ (dek′ə rāt′) *v.*, **-rated, -rating. 1.** add something attractive to. **2.** honor. **—dec′o•ra′tion,** *n.* **—dec′o•ra•tive** (-ər ə tiv) **—dec′o•ra′tor,** *n.*

dec′o•rous, *adj.* proper; dignified.

de•co′rum (di kôr′əm) *n.* propriety.

de•coy′ (n. dē′koi, di koi′; v. di koi′, dē′koi) *n.*, *v.* lure.

de•crease′ *v.* **-creased, -creasing,** *n.* **—v.** (di krēs′) **1.** lessen. **—n.** (dē′krēs, di krēs′) **2.** lessening.

de•cree′ (di krē′) *n.*, *v.*, **-creed, -creeing.** **—n. 1.** published command. **—v. 2.** proclaim or command.

de•crep′it (di krep′it) *adj.* old and feeble. **—de•crep′i•tude′,** *n.*

de•cre•scen′do (dē′kri shen′dō, dā′-) *adj.*, *adv. Music.* gradually decreasing in loudness.

de•crim′i•nal•ize′ (dē krim′ə nl īz′) *v.*, **-ized, -izing.** cease to treat as a crime. **—de•crim′i•nal•i•za′tion,** *n.*

de•cry′ (di krī′) *v.*, **-cried, -crying.** publicly disapprove of.

ded′i•cate′ (ded′i kāt′) *v.*, **-cated, -cating. 1.** set apart. **2.** devote. **3.** inscribe in honor of. **—ded′i•ca′tion,** *n.*

de•duce′ (di dōōs′, -dyōōs′) *v.*, **-duced, -ducing.** derive logically.

de•duct′ (di dukt′) *v.* subtract. **—de•duct′i•ble,** *adj.*

de•duc′tion, *n.* **1.** subtraction. **2.** conclusion. **—de•duc′tive,** *adj.*

deed (dēd) *n.* **1.** act. **2.** written conveyance of property. **—v. 3.** transfer by deed.

dee′jay′ (dē′jā′) *n.* disc jockey.

deem (dēm) *v.* think; estimate.

deep (dēp) *adj.* **1.** extending far down or in. **2.** difficult to understand. **3.** intense. **4.** low in pitch. **—n. 5.** deep part or space. **—adv. 6.** at great depth. **—deep′en,** *v.* **—deep′ly,** *adv.*

deep′-freeze′, *v.*, **deep-froze, deep-frozen, deep-freezing.** —*v.* **1.** freeze rapidly for preservation. **—n. 2.** refrigerator that deep-freezes.

deep′-fry′, *v.*, **deep-fried, deep-frying.** cook in boiling fat. **—deep′-fry′er,** *n.*

deep′-seat′ed, *adj.* firmly fixed. Also, **deep′-root′ed.**

deep space, space beyond the solar system.

deer (dēr) *n.*, *pl.* **deer.** hoofed, ruminant animal, the male of which usually has antlers.

de•face′ (di fās′) *v.*, **-faced, -facing.** spoil appearance of.

de fac′to (dē fak′tō, dā) **1.** in fact; in reality. **2.** actually existing, esp. without legal authority.

de•fame′ (di fām′) *v.*, **-famed, -faming.** attack the reputation of. **—def′a•ma′tion** (def′ə mā′shan) *n.* **—de•fam′a•to′ry** (-fam′ə tôr′ē) *adj.*

de•fault′ (di fôlt′) *n.* **1.** failure; neglect. **—v. 2.** fail to meet obligation.

de•feat′ (di fēt′) *v.*, *n.* overthrow.

de•feat′ist *n.* one who accepts defeat too easily. **—de•feat′ism,** *n.*

def′e•cate′ (def′i kāt′) *v.*, **-cated, -cating.** void feces from bowels. **—def′e•ca′tion,** *n.*

de′fect *n.* (dē′fekt, di fekt′) **1.** fault; imperfection. **—v.** (di fekt′) **2.** desert a cause, country, etc. **—de•fec′tive,** *adj.*

de•fec′tion, *n.* desertion of a cause, country, etc.

de•fend′ (di fend′) *v.* **1.** protect against attack. **2.** uphold. **—de•fend′er,** *n.*

de•fend′ant, *n.* person accused of a crime or sued in court.

de•fense′ (di fens′) *n.* **1.** resistance to attack. **2.** defending argument. **—de•fense′less,** *adj.* **—de•fen′sive,** *adj.*, *n.*

de•fer′ (di fûr′) *v.*, **-ferred, -ferring. 1.** postpone. **2.** yield to someone's opinion. **—de•fer′ment,** *n.*

def′er•ence (def′ər əns) *n.* act of showing respect. **—def′er•en′tial** (-ə•ren′shəl) *adj.*

de•fi′ance (di fī′əns) *n.* **1.** bold resistance. **2.** disregard. **—de•fi′ant,** *adj.* **—de•fi′ant•ly,** *adv.*

de•fi′cien•cy (di fish′ən sē) *n.*, *pl.* **-cies.** lack. **—de•fi′cient,** *adj.*

def′i•cit (def′ə sit) *n.* lack of funds.

de•file′ (di fīl′) *v.*, **-filed, -filing,** *n.* **—v. 1.** dirty. **2.** desecrate. **—n. 3.** narrow pass.

de•fine′ (di fīn′) *v.*, **-fined, -fining. 1.** state meaning of. **2.** determine precisely. **—def′i•ni′tion,** *n.*

def′i•nite (def′ə nit) *adj.* **1.** exact. **2.** with fixed limits. **—def′i•nite•ly,** *adv.*

de•fin′i•tive (di fin′i tiv) *adj.* conclusive. **—de•fin′i•tive•ly,** *adv.*

de•flate′ (di flāt′) *v.*, **-flated, -flating.** release gas from.

de•fla′tion, *n.* sharp fall in prices.

de·flect′ (di flekt′) v. turn from true course. **—de·flec′tion,** n.

de·fo′li·ate′ (dē fō′lē āt′) v., **-ated, -ating. 1.** strip of leaves. **2.** clear of vegetation, as to expose hidden enemy forces. **—de·fo′li·a′tion,** n. **—de·fo′li·ant** (-ənt) n.

de·for′est (di fôr′ist) v. clear of trees. **—de·for′es·ta′tion,** n.

de·form′, v. distort. **—de·form′i·ty,** n.

de·fraud′, v. cheat. **—de·fraud′er,** n.

de·fray′, v. pay (expenses).

de·frost′, v. **1.** remove frost or ice from. **2.** thaw.

deft (deft) adj. quick and skillful.

de·funct′ (di fungkt′) adj. no longer in existence.

de·fuse′ (dē fyooz′) v. **1.** remove detonating fuse from. **2.** make less dangerous or tense.

de·fy′ (di fī′) v., **-fied, -fying.** challenge; resist.

de·gen′er·ate′, v., **-ated, -ating.** adj., n. **—v.** (di jen′ə rāt′) **1.** decline; deteriorate. **—adj.** (-ər it) **2.** having declined **3.** corrupt. **—n.** (-ər it) **4.** degenerate person.

de·grade′ (di grād′) v., **-graded, -grading.** reduce in status. **—deg′ra·da′tion** (deg′ri dā′shən) n.

de·gree′ (di grē′) n. **1.** stage or extent. **2.** 360th part of a circle. **3.** unit of temperature. **4.** title conferred by college.

de·hu′man·ize′ (dē hyoo′mə nīz′; often -yoo′-) v., **-ized, -izing.** treat as lacking human qualities or requirements.

de·hu·mid′i·fi′er, n. device for removing moisture from air. **—de·hu·mid′i·fy,** v.

de·hy′drate′, v., **-drated, -drating.** deprive of moisture. **—de·hy·dra′tion,** n.

de·i′fy′ (dē′ə fī′) v., **-fied, -fying.** make a god of. **—de·i·fi·ca′tion,** n.

deign (dān) v. condescend.

de·in·sti·tu′tion·al·ize′, v., **-ized, -izing.** release from an institution to community care.

de′ism (dē′iz əm) n. belief in the existence of a God based on reason and evidence in nature, rather than on divine revelation. **—de′ist,** n.

de′i·ty (dē′i tē) n., pl. **-ties.** god or goddess.

dé′jà vu′ (dā′zhä voo′) feeling of having lived through same moment before.

de·ject′ed (di jek′tid) adj. disheartened. **—de·jec′tion,** n.

de ju′re (di joor′ē, dā joor′ā) by right or according to law.

Del. Delaware.

de·lay′ (di lā′) v. **1.** postpone. **2.** hinder. **—n. 3.** act of delaying. **4.** instance of being delayed.

de·lec′ta·ble (di lek′tə bəl) adj. delightful or delicious.

del′e·gate n., v., **-gated, -gating. —n.** (del′i git, -gāt′) **1.** deputy. **2.** legislator. **—v.** (-gāt′) **3.** send as deputy. **4.** give (powers) to another. **—del′e·ga′tion,** n.

de·lete′ (di lēt′) v., **-leted, -leting.** cancel; erase. **—de·le′tion,** n.

del′e·te′ri·ous (del′i tēr′ē əs) adj. harmful.

del′i (del′ē) n. delicatessen.

de·lib′er·ate adj., v., **-ated, -ating. —adj.** (di lib′ər it) **1.** intentional. **2.** unhurried. **—v.** (-ə rāt′) **3.** consider. **4.** confer. **—de·lib′er·a′tion,** n. **—de·lib′er·ate·ly,** adv.

del′i·ca·cy (del′i kə sē) n., pl. **-cies. 1.** fineness. **2.** frailty. **3.** choice food.

del′i·cate (-kit) adj. **1.** fine. **2.** fragile. **3.** tactful. **—del′i·cate·ly,** adv.

del′i·ca·tes′sen (del′i kə tes′ən) n. store that sells prepared food.

de·li′cious (di lish′əs) adj. pleasing, esp. to taste. **—de·li′cious·ly,** adv.

de·light′ (di līt′) n. **1.** joy. **—v. 2.** please highly. **3.** take joy. **—de·light′ed,** adj. **—de·light′ful,** adj.

de·lim′it (di lim′it) v. fix or mark limits of. **—de·lim′i·ta′tion,** n.

de·lin′e·ate′ (di lin′ē āt′) v., **-ated, -ating.** sketch; outline.

de·lin′quent (di ling′kwənt) adj. **1.** neglectful; guilty. **—n. 2.** delinquent one. **—de·lin′quen·cy,** n.

de·lir′i·um (di lēr′ē əm) n. mental disorder marked by excitement, visions, etc. **—de·lir′i·ous,** adj.

de·liv′er (di liv′ər) v. **1.** give up. **2.** hand over. **3.** utter. **4.** direct. **5.** give birth. **6.** assist at birth. **—de·liv′er·ance,** n. **—de·liv′er·y,** n.

dell (del) n. small, wooded valley.

del·phin′i·um (del fin′ē əm) n., pl. **-iums, -ia** (-ē ə). tall blue garden flower.

del′ta (del′tə) n. **1.** 4th letter of Greek alphabet. **2.** triangular area between branches of river mouth.

de·lude′ (di lood′) v., **-luded, -luding.** mislead or deceive.

del′uge (del′yooj) n., v., **-uged, -uging. —n. 1.** great flood. **—v. 2.** flood. **3.** overwhelm.

de·lu′sion (di loo′zhən) n. false opinion or conception.

de·luxe′ (də luks′) adj. of finest quality.

delve (delv) v., **delved, delving.** search carefully for information.

Dem. 1. Democrat. **2.** Democratic.

dem′a·gogue′ (dem′ə gog′) n. unscrupulous popular leader. **—dem′a·gogu′er·y,** n.

de·mand′ (di mand′) v. **1.** claim. **2.** require. **3.** ask for in urgent or peremptory manner. **—n. 4.** claim. **5.** requirement. **6.** desire for a product.

de·mar′cate (di mär′kāt, dē′mär·kāt′) v., **-cated, -cating.** set limits of. **—de·mar·ca′tion,** n.

de·mean′ (di mēn′) v. **1.** conduct (oneself). **2.** lower in dignity.

de·mean′or, n. conduct; behavior.

de·ment′ed (di men′tid) adj. crazed.

de·men′tia (-shə, -shē ə) n. severe mental impairment.

de·mer′it (di mer′it) n. **1.** fault. **2.** rating for misconduct.

demi-, prefix indicating half or lesser, as *demigod*.

dem′i·god′ (dem′ē god′) n. one partly divine and partly human.

de·mil′i·ta·rize′ (dē mil′i tə rīz′) v., **-rized, -rizing.** free from military influence. **—de·mil′i·ta·ri·za′tion,** n.

de·mise′ (di mīz′) n., v., **-mised, -mising. —n. 1.** death. **2.** transfer of estate. **—v. 3.** transfer.

dem′i·tasse′ (dem′i tas′, -täs′) n. small coffee cup.

dem′o (dem′ō) n. product displayed or offered for trial.

de·mo′bi·lize′ (dē mō′bə līz′) v., **-lized, -lizing.** disband (army).

de·moc′ra·cy (di mok′rə sē) n., pl. **-cies. 1.** government in which the people hold supreme power. **2.** social equality. **—dem′o·crat′** (dem′ə krat′) n. **—dem′o·crat′ic,** adj.

Democratic Party, a major political party in the U.S.

dem′o·graph′ic (dem′ə graf′ik) adj. of statistics on population. **—dem′o·**

graph′i·cal·ly, adv. **—dem′o·graph′ics,** n.pl.

de·mol′ish (di mol′ish) v. destroy. **—dem′o·li′tion** (dem′ə lish′ən) n.

de′mon (dē′mən) n. evil spirit.

de·mon′ic (di mon′ik) adj. **1.** inspired. **2.** like a demon.

dem′on·strate′ (dem′ən strāt′) v., **-strated, -strating. 1.** prove. **2.** describe and explain. **3.** display. **4.** parade in support or opposition. **—de·mon′stra·ble** (di mon′strə bəl) adj. **—dem′on·stra′tion,** n. **—dem′on·stra′tor,** n.

de·mon′stra·tive (də mon′strə tiv) adj. expressive.

de·mor′al·ize′ (di môr′ə līz′) v., **-ized, -izing.** destroy confidence of.

de·mote′ (di mōt′) v., **-moted, -moting.** reduce in rank. **—de·mo′tion,** n.

de·mur′ (di mûr′) v., **-murred, -murring,** n. **—v. 1.** object. **—n. 2.** objection. **—de·mur′ral,** n.

de·mure′ (di myoor′) adj. modest. **—de·mure′ly,** adv.

den (den) n. **1.** cave of wild beast. **2.** room at home for relaxing.

de·na′ture (dē nā′chər) v., **-tured, -turing.** make (alcohol) unfit to drink.

de·ni′al (di nī′əl) n. **1.** contradiction. **2.** refusal to agree or give.

den′i·grate′ (den′i grāt′) v., **-grated, -grating.** speak badly of.

den′im (den′əm) n. **1.** heavy cotton fabric. **2.** (pl.) trousers of this.

den′i·zen (den′ə zən) n. inhabitant.

de·nom′i·nate′ (di nom′ə nāt′) v., **-nated, -nating.** name specifically.

de·nom′i·na′tion, n. **1.** name or designation. **2.** religious group. **3.** value of piece of money.

de·nom′i·na′tor, n. lower term in fraction.

de·note′ (di nōt′) v., **-noted, -noting. 1.** indicate. **2.** mean.

de′noue·ment′ (dā′noo män′) n. **1.** final resolution of plot or story. **2.** outcome of series of events. Also, **dé′noue·ment′.**

de·nounce′ (di nouns′) v., **-nounced, -nouncing. 1.** condemn. **2.** inform against.

dense (dens) adj., **denser, densest. 1.** compact. **2.** stupid. **—den′si·ty,** n. **—dense′ly,** adv.

dent (dent) n. **1.** hollow. **—v. 2.** make a dent.

den′tal (den′tl) adj. of teeth.

den′ti·frice (-tə fris) n. teeth-cleaning substance.

den′tin (-tn, -tin) n. hard tissue that forms most of a tooth. Also, **den′tine** (-tēn).

den′tist (-tist) n. person who prevents and treats tooth disease. **—den′tist·ry,** n.

den′ture (-chər, -choŏr) n. artificial tooth.

de·nude′ (di nood′, -nyood′) v., **-nuded, -nuding.** make bare; strip.

de·nun′ci·a′tion (di nun′sē ā′shən) n. **1.** condemnation. **2.** accusation.

de·ny′ (di nī′) v., **-nied, -nying. 1.** declare not to be true. **2.** refuse to agree or give.

de·o′dor·ant (dē ō′dər ənt) n. agent for destroying odors.

de·o′dor·ize′, v., **-ized, -izing.** rid of odors. **—de·o′dor·iz′er,** n.

de·part′ (di pärt′) v. **1.** go away. **2.** die. **—de·par′ture,** n.

de·part′ment, n. **1.** part; section. **2.** area. **—de·part·men′tal,** adj.

de·pend′ (di pend′) v. **1.** rely. **2.** be contingent. **—de·pend′ence,** n. **—de·pend′ent,** adj., n.

de•pend′a•ble, adj. reliable. **—de•pend′a•bil′i•ty,** n.

de•pict′ (di pikt′) v. **1.** portray. **2.** describe. **—de•pic′tion,** n.

de•pil′a•to′ry (di pil′ə tôr′ē) adj., n., pl. **-ries.** —adj. **1.** cap₌ble of removing hair. **—**n. **2.** depilatory agent.

de•plete′ (di plēt′) v., **-pleted, -pleting.** reduce in amount.

de•plore′, v. (di plôr′ -plôr′) **-plored, -ploring.** lament. **—de•plor′a•ble,** adj.

de•ploy′ (-ploi′) v. place strategically. **—de•ploy′ment,** n.

de′po•lit′i•cize′ (dē′pə lit′ə sīz′) v., **-cized, -cizing.** remove from realm of politics.

de•pop′u•late′ (dē pop′yə lāt′) v., **-lated, -lating.** reduce population of. **—de•pop′u•la′tion,** n.

de•port′ (di pôrt′) v. **1.** expel from country. **2.** conduct (oneself).

de′por•ta′tion (dē′pôr tā′shən) n. expulsion from country.

de•port′ment, n. conduct.

de•pose′ (di pōz′) v., **-posed, -posing. 1.** remove from office. **2.** testify. **—dep′o•si′tion** (dep′ə zish′ən) n.

de•pos′it (di poz′it) v. **1.** place. **2.** place for safekeeping. **—**n. **3.** sediment. **4.** something deposited.

de•pos′i•to′ry (di poz′i tôr′ē) n., pl. **-ries.** place for safekeeping.

de′pot (dē′pō; Mil. or Brit. dep′ō) n. **1.** station. **2.** storage base.

de•prave′ (di prāv′) v., **-praved, -praving.** corrupt morally. **—de•praved′,** adj. **—de•prav′i•ty** (-prav′i-tē) n.

dep′re•cate′ (dep′ri kāt′) v., **-cated, -cating. 1.** disapprove of. **2.** belittle. **—dep′re•ca•to′ry,** adj.

de•pre′ci•ate′ (di prē′shē āt′) v., **-ated, -ating. 1.** reduce or decline in value. **2.** belittle.

dep′re•da′tion (dep′ri dā′shən) n. plunder.

de•press′ (di pres′) v. **1.** deject. **2.** weaken. **3.** press down. **—de•pressed′,** adj.

de•pres′sion (di presh′ən) n. **1.** act of depressing. **2.** depressed state. **3.** depressed place. **4.** decline in business. **—de•pres′sive,** adj.

de•prive′ (-prīv′) v., **-prived, -priving.** withhold from. **—dep′ri•va′tion,** n.

dept., 1. department. **2.** deputy.

depth (depth) n. **1.** distance down. **2.** intensity. **3.** lowness of pitch. **4.** deep part.

dep′u•ta′tion (dep′yə tā′shən) n. delegation.

dep′u•ty (-tē) n., pl. **-ties.** agent; substitute. **—dep′u•tize′** (-tīz′) v., **-tized, -tizing.**

de•rail′ (dē rāl′) v. cause to run off rails. **—de•rail′ment,** n.

de•range′ (di rānj′) v., **-ranged, -ranging.** make insane.

der′by (dûr′bē; Brit. där′-) n., pl. **-bies. 1.** stiff, rounded hat. **2.** race.

de•reg′u•late′ (dē reg′yə lāt′) v., **-lated, -lating.** free of regulation.

der′e•lict (der′ə likt) adj. **1.** abandoned. **2.** neglectful. **—**n. **3.** something abandoned. **4.** vagrant.

der′e•lic′tion, n. neglect.

de•ride′ (di rīd′) v., **-rided, -riding.** mock. **—de•ri′sion** (-rizh′ən) n. **—de•ri′sive** (-rī′siv) adj.

de•rive′ (di rīv′) v., **-rived, -riving. 1.** get from source. **2.** trace. **3.** deduce. **4.** originate. **—der′i•va′tion** (der′ə-vā′shən) n. **—de•riv′a•tive** (di riv′ə-tiv) n., adj.

der′ma•ti′tis (dûr′mə tī′tis) n. inflammation of the skin.

der′ma•tol′o•gy (-tol′ə jē) n. medical study and treatment of the skin.

der′o•gate′ (der′ə gāt′) v., **-gated, -gating.** detract.

de•rog′a•to′ry (di rog′ə tôr′ē) adj. disparaging.

der′rick (der′ik) n. crane with boom pivoted at one end.

der′ri•ère′ (der′ē är′) n. buttocks.

de•scend′ (di send′) v. **1.** move down. **2.** have as relative in the past. **—de•scent′,** n.

de•scend′ant, n. person descended from specific ancestor; offspring.

de•scribe′ (di skrīb′) v., **-scribed, -scribing. 1.** put down in words. **2.** trace. **—de•scrip′tion** (-skrip′shən) n. **—de•scrip′tive,** adj.

de•scry′ (di skrī′) v., **-scried, -scrying.** happen to see.

des′e•crate′ (des′i krāt′) v., **-crated, -crating.** divest of sacredness; profane. **—des′e•cra′tion,** n.

de•seg′re•gate′ (dē seg′ri gāt′) v., **-gated, -gating.** eliminate racial segregation in.

de•sen′si•tize′ (dē sen′si tīz′) v., **-tized, -tizing.** make less sensitive.

des′ert n. **1.** (dez′ərt) arid region. **2.** (di zûrt′) (often pl.) due reward or punishment. **—**v. **3.** (di zûrt′) abandon. **—de•sert′er,** n. **—de•ser′tion,** n.

de•serve′ (di zûrv′) v., **-served, -serving.** be worthy of; merit.

des′ic•cate′ (des′i kāt′) v., **-cated, -cating.** dry up.

de•sid′er•a′tum (di sid′ə rā′təm, -rä′-, -zid′-) n., pl. **-ta** (-tə). something wanted.

de•sign′ (di zīn′) v. **1.** plan. **2.** conceive form of. **—**n. **3.** sketch or plan. **4.** art of designing. **5.** pattern. **6.** purpose. **—de•sign′er,** n.

des′ig•nate′ (dez′ig nāt′) v., **-nated, -nating. 1.** indicate. **2.** name. **—des′ig•na′tion,** n.

designated driver, person who does not drink alcohol at a gathering in order to drive companions home safely.

de•sign′ing, adj. scheming.

de•sire′ (di zī°r′) v., **-sired, -siring,** n. **—**v. **1.** wish for. **2.** request. **—**n. **3.** longing. **4.** request. **5.** thing desired. **6.** lust. **—de•sir′a•ble,** adj.

de•sist′ (di zist′, -sist′) v. stop.

desk (desk) n. **1.** table for writing. **2.** specialized section of organization, esp. in newspaper office.

desk′top′ publishing, design and production of publications using a microcomputer.

des′o•late adj., v., **-lated, -lating.** —adj. (des′ə lit) **1.** barren. **2.** lonely. **3.** dismal. **—**v. (-ə lāt′) **4.** lay waste. **5.** make hopeless. **—des′o•la′tion,** n.

de•spair′ (di spâr′) n. **1.** hopelessness. **—**v. **2.** lose hope.

des′per•a′do (des′pə rä′dō, -rā′-) n., pl. **-does, -dos.** wild outlaw.

des′per•ate (des′pər it) adj. **1.** reckless from despair. **2.** despairing. **—des′per•a′tion,** n.

des′pi•ca•ble (des′pi kə bəl, di spik′-ə-) adj. contemptible.

de•spise′ (di spīz′) v., **-spised, -spising.** scorn or hate.

de•spite′ (di spīt′) prep. in spite of.

de•spoil′ (di spoil′) v. plunder.

de•spond′ent (di spon′dənt) adj. in low spirits; dejected. **—de•spond′en•cy** n.

des′pot (des′pət, -pot) n. tyrant. **—des•pot′ic,** adj.

des•sert′ (di zûrt′) n. final course of meal, usually sweet.

des′ti•na′tion (des′tə nā′shən) n. goal of journey.

des′tine (-tin) v., **-tined, -tining. 1.** set apart. **2.** predetermine by fate.

des′ti•ny, n., pl. **-nies. 1.** predetermined future. **2.** fate.

des′ti•tute′ (-tōōt′, -tyōōt′) adj. **1.** very poor. **2.** deprived.

de•stroy′ (di stroi′) v. **1.** ruin. **2.** end. **3.** kill.

de•stroy′er, n. **1.** one that destroys. **2.** naval vessel.

de•struct′ (di strukt′) v. be destroyed automatically.

de•struc′tion, n. **1.** act or means of destroying. **2.** fact of being destroyed. **—de•struc′tive,** adj.

des′ul•to′ry (des′əl tôr′ē) adj. not methodical. **—des′ul•to′ri•ly,** adv.

de•tach′ (di tach′) v. take off or away. **—de•tach′a•ble,** adj.

de•tached′, adj. **1.** separate. **2.** uninterested.

de•tach′ment, n. **1.** act of detaching. **2.** unconcern. **3.** impartiality. **4.** troops for special duty.

de•tail′ (di tāl′, dē′tāl) n. **1.** individual or minute part. **2. in detail,** with all details specified. **3.** troops or group selected for special duty. **—**v. **4.** relate in detail. **5.** assign.

de•tain′ (di tān′) v. **1.** delay. **2.** keep in custody. **—de•ten′tion,** n.

de•tect′ (di tekt′) v. **1.** discover. **2.** perceive. **—de•tec′tion,** n. **—de•tec′tor,** n.

de•tec′tive, n. professional investigator of crimes, etc.

dé•tente (dā tänt′) n. lessening of international hostility.

de•ter′ (di tûr′) v., **-terred, -terring.** discourage or restrain.

de•ter′gent (di tûr′jənt) adj. **1.** cleansing. **—**n. **2.** cleansing agent.

de•te′ri•o•rate′ (di tēr′ē ə rāt′) v., **-rated, -rating.** make or become worse. **—de•te′ri•o•ra′tion,** n.

de•ter′mi•na′tion (-nā′shən) n. **1.** act of determining. **2.** firmness of purpose.

de•ter′mine (-min) v., **-mined, -mining. 1.** settle; decide. **2.** ascertain. **3.** limit.

de•ter′mined adj. resolved.

de•ter′rence (di tûr′əns) n. discouragement, as of crime or military aggression. **—de•ter′rent,** adj., n.

de•test′ (di test′) v. hate or despise. **—de•test′a•ble,** adj.

de•throne′ (di thrōn′) v., **-throned, -throning.** remove from a throne.

det′o•nate′ (det′n āt′) v., **-nated, -nating.** explode. **—det′o•na′tion,** n.

de′tour (dē′tōōr, di tōōr′) n. **1.** roundabout course. **—**v. **2.** make detour.

de′tox n., v., **-toxed, -toxing.** Informal. **—**n. **1.** (dē′toks) **1.** detoxification. **2.** hospital unit for patients undergoing detoxification. **—**v. (dē toks′) **3.** detoxify.

de•tox′i•fy, v., **-fied, -fying.** rid of effects of alcohol or drug use. **—de•tox′i•fi•ca′tion,** n.

de•tract′ (di trakt′) v. take away quality or reputation.

det′ri•ment (de′trə mənt) n. damage or loss. **—det′ri•men′tal** (-men′tl) adj.

de•tri′tus (di trī′təs) n. rock particles worn away from a mass; debris.

deuce (dōōs, dyōōs) n. **1.** card or die with two pips. **2.** tie score as in tennis.

de•val′u•ate′ (dē val′yōō āt′) v., **-ated, -ating.** reduce in value; depreciate. **—de•val′u•a′tion,** n.

dev·as·tate (dev′ə stāt′) v., -tated, -tating. lay waste. —**dev′as·ta′tion**, n.

de·vel·op (di vel′əp) v. **1.** mature. **2.** elaborate. **3.** bring into being. **4.** make (images on film) visible. **5.** acquire. —**de·vel′op·ment**, n. —**de·vel′op·er**, n.

de·vi·ate (dē′vē āt′) v., -ated, -ating. **1.** digress. **2.** depart from normal. —**de′vi·a′tion**, n. —**de′vi·ant**, adj., n.

de·vice′ (di vīs′) n. **1.** contrivance. **2.** plan. **3.** slogan or emblem.

dev′il (dev′əl) n. **1.** Satan. **2.** evil spirit or person. —**dev′il·ish**, adj. —**dev′il·try**, n.

dev·il-may-care′, adj. reckless.

devil's advocate, person who takes opposing view for the sake of argument.

devil's food cake, rich chocolate cake.

de·vi·ous (dē′vē əs) adj. **1.** circuitous. **2.** not sincere.

de·vise′ (di vīz′) v., -vised, -vising. **1.** plan; contrive. **2.** bequeath.

de·vi′tal·ize′ (dē vīt′l īz′) v., -ized, -izing. remove vitality of.

de·void′ (di void′) adj. destitute.

de·volve′ (di volv′) v., -volved, -volving. **1.** transfer or delegate. **2.** fall as a duty.

de·vote′ (di vōt′) v., -voted, -voting. **1.** give up or apply to a certain pursuit, cause, etc. **2.** dedicate.

de·vot′ed, adj. **1.** zealous. **2.** dedicated.

dev·o·tee′ (dev′ə tē′) n. devoted one.

de·vo′tion (di vō′shən) n. **1.** consecration. **2.** attachment or dedication. **3.** (pl.) worship.

de·vour′ (di vour′) v. consume ravenously.

de·vout′ (di vout′) adj. pious.

dew (dōō, dyōō) n. atmospheric moisture condensed in droplets at night. —**dew′y**, adj.

dex·ter·i·ty (dek ster′i tē) n. **1.** physical skill. **2.** cleverness. —**dex′ter·ous** (dek′stər əs, -strəs) adj.

dex′trose (dek′strōs) n. type of sugar.

di·a·be·tes (dī′ə bē′tis, -tēz) n. disease characterized by high levels of glucose in the blood. —**di′a·bet′ic** (-bet′ik) adj., n.

di·a·bol′ic (dī′ə bol′ik) adj. fiendish. Also, **di′a·bol′i·cal.**

di·a·crit′ic (dī′ə krit′ik) n. mark added to a letter to give it a particular phonetic value.

di·a·dem′ (dī′ə dem′) n. crown.

di·ag·nose′ (dī′əg nōs′, -nōz′) v., -nosed, -nosing. determine nature of (disease). —**di′ag·no′sis**, n. —**di′ag·nos′tic** (-nos′tik) adj.

di·ag·o·nal (dī ag′ə nl) adj. **1.** connecting two non-adjacent angles. **2.** oblique. —**di·ag·o·nal·ly**, adv.

di′a·gram′ (dī′ə gram′) n., v., -gramed, -graming. chart or plan.

di′al (dī′əl, dīl) n., v., dialed, dialing. —n. **1.** numbered face, as on a watch. —v. **2.** select or contact by using a dial.

di′a·lect′ (dī′ə lekt′) n. language of district or class.

di′a·lec′tic, n. art or practice of debate or conversation by which truth of theory or opinion is arrived at logically. Also, **di′a·lec′tics.** —**di′a·lec′ti·cal**, adj.

di′a·logue′ (dī′ə lôg′) n. conversation between two or more people. Also, **di′a·log′.**

di·al′y·sis (dī al′ə sis) n. process of removing waste products from blood of someone with kidney disease.

di·am′e·ter (dī am′i tər) n. straight line through center of a circle.

di′a·met′ri·cal (-ə me′tri kəl) adj. **1.** of diameters. **2.** completely in contrast. —**di′a·met′ri·cal·ly**, adv.

dia′mond (dī′mənd, dī′ə-) n. **1.** hard, brilliant precious stone. **2.** rhombus or square. **3.** (pl.) suit of playing cards. **4.** baseball field.

dia′mond·back′, n. venomous rattlesnake.

di·a·per (dī′pər, dī′ə pər) n. **1.** infant's underpants. —v. **2.** put diaper on.

di·aph·a·nous (dī af′ə nəs) adj. very sheer and light.

di′a·phragm′ (dī′ə fram′) n. **1.** muscle between chest and abdomen. **2.** vibrating membrane. **3.** contraceptive device.

di·ar·rhe·a (dī′ə rē′ə) n. intestinal disorder. Also, **di′ar·rhoe′a.**

di′a·ry (dī′ə rē) n., pl. -ries. personal daily record. —**di′a·rist**, n.

di′a·tribe′ (-trīb′) n. denunciation.

dib′ble (dib′əl) n. pointed instrument for planting.

dice (dīs) n.pl., sing. die, v., diced, dicing. —n. **1.** small cubes, used in games. —v. **2.** cut into small cubes.

dic′ey (dī′sē) adj. -ier, -iest. risky.

di·chot′o·my (dī kot′ə mē) n., pl. -mies. division into two irreconcilable groups.

dick′er (dik′ər) v. bargain.

di·cot′y·le′don (dī kot′l ēd′n, dī′kot l-) n. plant having two embryonic seed leaves.

Dic′ta·phone′ (dik′tə fōn′) n. Trademark. brand name for machine that records and plays back dictated speech.

dic′tate (dik′tāt) v., -tated, -tating, n. —v. **1.** say something to be written down. **2.** command. —n. **3.** command. —**dic·ta′tion**, n.

dic′ta·tor, n. absolute ruler. —**dic′ta·to′ri·al** (-tə tôr′ē əl) adj. —**dic·ta′tor·ship′**, n.

dic′tion (dik′shən) n. style of speaking.

dic′tion·ar′y (dik′shə ner′ē) n., pl. -aries. book on meaning, spelling, pronunciation, etc., of words.

dic′tum (dik′təm) n., pl. -ta, -tums. authoritative declaration.

di·dac′tic (dī dak′tik) adj. instructive.

didn′t (did′nt) contraction of **did not.**

die (dī) v., died, dying, n., pl. (for 3) **dies.** —v. **1.** cease to be. **2.** lose force; fade. —n. **3.** shaping device. **4.** sing. of **dice.**

die′hard′, n. defender of lost cause.

di·er·e·sis (dī er′ə sis) n., pl. -ses. sign (¨) over a vowel indicating separate pronunciation, as in Noël.

die′sel (dē′zəl, -səl) n. **1.** engine using air compression for ignition. **2.** machine powered by diesel engine. **3.** fuel used by diesel engine.

di′et (dī′it) n. **1.** food one eats. **2.** food specially chosen for health or weight control. **3.** formal assembly. —v. **4.** adhere to diet. —**di′e·tar′y** (-i ter′ē) adj. —**di′e·tet′ic** (-tet′ik) adj.

di′e·ti·tian (dī′i tish′ən) n. expert in nutrition and dietary requirements. Also, **di′e·ti′cian.**

dif′fer (dif′ər) v. **1.** be unlike. **2.** disagree.

dif′fer·ence (dif′ər əns, dif′rəns) n. **1.** unlikeness. **2.** disagreement. **3.** amount separating two quantities.

—**dif′fer·ent**, adj. —**dif′fer·ent·ly**, adv. —**Usage.** DIFFERENT FROM is more common today in introducing a phrase, but DIFFERENT THAN is also used: New York speech is different from/than that of Chicago. DIFFERENT THAN is usually used when a clause follows, especially when the word "from" would create an awkward sentence: The stream followed a different course than the map showed.

dif′fer·en′ti·ate′ (-en′shē āt′) v., -ated, -ating. **1.** alter. **2.** distinguish. —**dif′fer·en′ti·a′tion**, n.

dif′fi·cult′ (dif′i kult′, -kəlt) adj. **1.** hard to do or understand. **2.** unmanageable.

dif′fi·cul′ty, n., pl. -ties. **1.** condition of being difficult. **2.** difficult situation. **3.** trouble. **4.** disagreement.

dif′fi·dent (-dənt) adj. timid; shy.

dif·frac′tion (di frak′shən) n. breaking up of rays of light to produce spectrum.

dif·fuse′ v., -fused, -fusing, adj. —v. (di fyōōz′) **1.** spread or scatter. —adj. (-fyōōs′) **2.** not to the point. **3.** spread or scattered.

dig (dig) v., dug (dug) or digged, digging, n. —v. **1.** remove earth. **2.** uncover by removing earth. **3.** form by removing earth. **4.** Slang. understand or appreciate. —n. **5.** sarcastic remark. —**dig′ger**, n.

di·gest′ v. (di jest′) **1.** prepare (food) for assimilation. **2.** assimilate mentally. —n. (dī′jest) **3.** collection or summary, esp. of laws. —**di·ges′tion**, n. —**di·ges′tive**, adj.

dig′it (dij′it) n. **1.** finger or toe. **2.** any Arabic numeral.

dig′it·al (-i tl) adj. of, using, or expressing data in numerals.

dig′i·tize′ (-tīz′) v., -tized, -tizing. convert (data) to digital form.

dig′ni·fied′ (dig′nə fīd′) adj. marked by dignity; stately.

dig′ni·fy′, v., -fied, -fying. **1.** honor. **2.** honor more than is deserved.

dig′ni·tar′y (-ter′ē) n., pl. -ries. high-ranking person.

dig′ni·ty, n., pl. -ties. **1.** nobility. **2.** worthiness. **3.** high rank, office, or title.

di·gress′ (di gres′, dī-) v. wander from main purpose, theme, etc. —**di·gres′sion**, n.

dike (dīk) n. **1.** bank for restraining waters. **2.** ditch.

di·lap′i·dat′ed (di lap′i dā′tid) adj. decayed.

di·lap′i·da′tion, n. ruin; decay.

di·late′ (dī lāt′) v., -lated, -lating. expand. —**di·la′tion**, n.

dil′a·to′ry (dil′ə tôr′ē) adj. delaying; tardy. —**dil′a·to′ri·ness**, n.

di·lem′ma (di lem′ə) n. predicament.

dil′et·tante′ (dil′i tänt′, dil′i tänt′) n. superficial practitioner.

dil′i·gence (dil′i jəns) n. earnest effort. —**dil′i·gent**, n.

dill (dil) n. herb with aromatic seeds and leaves.

dil′ly·dal′ly (dil′ē dal′ē) v., dilly-dallied, dilly-dallying. waste time, esp. by indecision.

di·lute′ (di lōōt′, dī-) v., -luted, -luting. thin, as with water; weaken. —**di·lu′tion**, n.

dim (dim) adj., dimmer, dimmest, v., dimmed, dimming. —adj. **1.** not bright. **2.** indistinct. —v. **3.** make or become dim. —**dim′ly**, adv.

dime (dīm) n. coin worth 10 cents.

di·men′sion (di men′shən, dī-) n. **1.** extension in a given direction. **2.** magnitude. —**di·men′sion·al**, adj.

di·min'ish (di min'ish) v. lessen; reduce.

di·min'u·en'do (di min'yōō en'dō) adj., adv. Music. gradually reducing in loudness.

di·min'u·tive (di min'yə tiv) adj. **1.** small. —n. **2.** diminutive form, as of a word.

dim'i·ty (dim'i tē) n., pl. **-ties.** thin cotton fabric.

dim'ple (dim'pəl) n. small hollow, esp. in cheek.

dim'wit', n. Slang. stupid person. —dim'wit'ted, adj.

din (din) n., v., **dinned, dinning.** —n. **1.** confused noise. —v. **2.** assail with din.

dine (dīn) v., **dined, dining.** eat dinner or another meal.

din'er, n. **1.** person who dines. **2.** railroad dining car. **3.** restaurant.

di·nette' (-net') n. small area or alcove for dining.

din'ghy (ding'gē) n., pl. **-ghies.** small boat.

din'gy (din'jē) adj., **-gier, -giest.** dark; dirty.

din'ner (din'ər) n. main meal.

di'no·saur' (dī'nə sôr') n. any of various extinct reptiles.

dint (dint) n. **1.** force. **2.** dent.

di'o·cese' (dī'ə sis, -sēz', -sēs') n. district under a bishop. —**di·oc'e·san** (-os'ə sən) adj., n.

di'o·ram'a (dī'ə ram'ə, -rä'mə) n. miniature three-dimensional scene against painted background.

di·ox'ide (dī ok'sīd, -sid) n. oxide with two atoms of oxygen.

di·ox'in (-ok'sin) n. toxic by-product of pesticide.

dip (dip) v., **dipped, dipping**, n. —v. **1.** plunge temporarily in liquid. **2.** bail or scoop. **3.** slope down. —n. **4.** act of dipping. **5.** downward slope. **6.** substance into which something is dipped.

diph·the'ri·a (dif thēr'ē ə, dip-) n. infectious disease of air passages, esp. throat.

diph'thong (dif'thông, dip'-) n. sound containing two vowels.

di·plo'ma (di plō'mə) n. document of academic qualifications.

di·plo'ma·cy (-sē) n., pl. **-cies. 1.** conduct of international relations. **2.** skill in negotiation. —**dip'lo·mat'** (dip'lə mat') n.

dip'lo·mat'ic, adj. **1.** of diplomacy. **2.** tactful.

dip'so·ma'ni·a (dip'sə mā'nē ə, -sō-) n. morbid craving for alcohol. —**dip'so·ma'ni·ac,** n.

dir., director.

dire (dīr) adj., **direr, direst.** dreadful.

di·rect' (di rekt', dī-) v. **1.** guide. **2.** command. **3.** manage. **4.** address. —adj. **5.** straight. **6.** straightforward. —**di·rect'ly,** adv. —**di·rect'ness,** n. —**di·rec'tor,** n.

direct current, electric current flowing continuously in one direction.

di·rec'tion, n. **1.** act of directing. **2.** line along which a thing lies or moves. —**di·rec'tion·al,** adj.

di·rec'tive, n. order or instruction from authority.

di·rec'to·ry, n., pl. **-ries.** list of locations, telephone numbers, etc.

dirge (dûrj) n. funeral song.

dir'i·gi·ble (dir'i jə bəl, di rij'ə-) n. airship.

dirk (dûrk) n. dagger.

dirt (dûrt) n. **1.** filth. **2.** earth.

dirt'y, adj., **-ier, -iest,** v., **-ied, -ying.** —adj. **1.** soiled. **2.** indecent. —v. **3.** soil. —**dirt'i·ness,** n.

dis (dis) v., **dissed, dissing,** n. Slang. —v. **1.** show disrespect for. **2.** disparage. —n. **3.** disparagement or criticism.

dis- prefix indicating: **1.** reversal, as disconnect. **2.** negation or lack, as distrust. **3.** removal, as disbar.

dis·a'ble (-ā'bəl) v., **-bled, -bling.** damage capability of. —**dis'a·bil'i·ty,** n.

dis·a'bled, adj. handicapped; incapacitated.

dis·a·buse' (-byōōz') v., **-bused, -busing.** free from deception.

dis'ad·van'tage, n. **1.** drawback; handicap. **2.** injury.

dis'ad·van'taged, adj. lacking economic and social opportunity.

dis·af·fect', v. alienate.

dis'a·gree', v., **-greed, -greeing.** differ in opinion. —**dis'a·gree'ment,** n.

dis'a·gree·a·ble, adj. unpleasant.

dis·al·low', v. refuse to allow.

dis'ap·pear', v. **1.** cease to be seen. **2.** cease to exist. —**dis'ap·pear'ance,** n.

dis'ap·point', v. fail to fulfill hopes of. —**dis'ap·point'ment,** n.

dis'ap·pro·ba'tion, n. disapproval.

dis'ap·prove', v., **-proved, -proving.** condemn; censure. —**dis'ap·prov'al,** n.

dis·arm', v. **1.** deprive of arms. **2.** reduce one's own armed power.

dis'ar·range', v., **-ranged, -ranging.** disorder.

dis'ar·ray', n. lack of order.

dis·as·so'ci·ate' (-āt') v., **-ated, -ating.** dissociate.

dis·as'ter (di zas'tər) n. extreme misfortune. —**dis·as'trous,** adj.

dis'a·vow', v. deny responsibility for. —**dis'a·vow'al,** n.

dis·band', v. break up (an organization). —**dis·band'ment,** n.

dis·bar', v., **-barred, -barring.** expel from law practice.

dis'be·lieve', v., **-lieved, -lieving.** reject as untrue. —**dis·be·lief',** n.

dis·burse' (dis bûrs') v., **-bursed, -bursing.** pay out.

disc (disk) n. **1.** disk. **2.** phonograph record.

dis·card' v. (di skärd') **1.** reject. —n. (dis'kärd) **2.** something discarded. **3.** discarded state.

dis·cern' (di sûrn', -zûrn') v. **1.** see. **2.** distinguish. —**dis·cern'i·ble,** adj. —**dis·cern'ing,** adj. —**dis·cern'ment,** n.

dis·charge' v., **-charged, -charging,** n. —v. (dis chärj') **1.** rid of load. **2.** send forth. **3.** shoot. **4.** end employment of. **5.** fulfill. —n. (dis'chärj) **6.** act of discharging. **7.** something discharged.

dis·ci'ple (di sī'pəl) n. follower.

dis'ci·pline (dis'ə plin) n., v., **-plined, -plining.** —n. **1.** training in rules. **2.** punishment. **3.** subjection to rules. **4.** branch of instruction or learning. —v. **5.** train. **6.** punish. —**dis'ci·pli·nar'y,** adj.

disc jockey, person who plays and comments on recorded music on a radio program. Also, **disk jockey.**

dis·claim' (dis klām') v. disown.

dis·close' (di sklōz') v., **-closed, -closing.** reveal. —**dis·clo'sure,** n.

dis'co (dis'kō) n., pl. **-cos. 1.** discotheque. **2.** rhythmic style of dance music.

dis·col'or (dis kul'ər) v. change in color. —**dis·col'or·a'tion,** n.

dis'com·bob'u·late' (dis'kəm bob'yə lāt') v., **-lated, -lating.** confuse or perturb.

dis·com'fit (dis kum'fit) v. defeat; thwart. —**dis·com'fi·ture,** n.

dis·com'fort (dis kum'fərt) n. lack of comfort.

dis'com·mode' (dis'kə mōd') v., **-moded, -moding.** cause inconvenience to.

dis'com·pose', v., **-posed, -posing. 1.** upset the order of. **2.** disturb the composure of.

dis'con·cert' (dis'kən sûrt') v. perturb.

dis'con·nect', v. break connection of.

dis·con'so·late (dis kon'sə lit) adj. sad. —**dis·con'so·late·ly,** adv.

dis'con·tent' (-kən tent') adj. Also **dis'con·tent'ed. 1.** not contented. —n. **2.** lack of contentment.

dis'con·tin'ue, v., **-tinued, -tinuing.** end; stop.

dis'cord (dis'kôrd) n. **1.** lack of harmony. **2.** strife. —**dis·cord'ance,** n. —**dis·cord'ant,** adj.

dis'co·theque' (dis'kə tek', dis'kə tek') n. nightclub where recorded dance music is played.

dis'count v. (dis'kount, dis kount') **1.** deduct. **2.** advance money after deduction of interest. **3.** disregard. —n. (dis'kount) **4.** deduction.

dis·coun'te·nance, v., **-nanced, -nancing. 1.** disconcert regularly. **2.** show disapproval of.

dis·cour'age (di skûr'ij, -skur'-) v., **-aged, -aging. 1.** deprive of resolution. **2.** hinder.

dis'course, n., v., **-coursed, -coursing.** —n. (dis'kôrs) **1.** talk. **2.** formal discussion. —v. (dis kôrs') **3.** talk.

dis·cour'te·sy, n., pl. **-sies. 1.** lack of courtesy. **2.** impolite act. —**dis·cour'te·ous,** adj.

dis·cov'er (di skuv'ər) v. learn or see for first time. —**dis·cov'er·y,** n. —**dis·cov'er·er,** n. —**Usage.** Do not confuse DISCOVER and INVENT, two words that deal with something new. DISCOVER is used when the object is an idea or place that existed before, but few people or no one knew about it. In the sentence Columbus discovered the New World, the New World clearly existed and was known to the people living there, but not to Columbus and the people of his time. INVENT is used when the object is a device or thing built. In the sentence Edison invented the light bulb, the light bulb did not exist before Edison invented it, and it was not known by anyone.

dis·cred'it, v. **1.** defame. **2.** disbelieve. —n. **3.** lack of belief. **4.** disrepute.

dis·creet' (di skrēt') adj. wise; prudent. —**dis·creet'ly,** adv.

dis·crep'an·cy (di skrep'ən sē) n., pl. **-cies.** difference; inconsistency.

dis·crete' (di skrēt') adj. separate.

dis·cre'tion (di skresh'ən) n. **1.** freedom of choice. **2.** prudence.

dis·crim'i·nate' (di skrim'ə nāt') adj. —v. (di skrim'ə nāt') **1.** distinguish accurately. **2.** show bias. —adj. (-ə nit) **3.** making distinctions. —**dis·crim'i·na'tion,** n.

dis·cur'sive (di skûr'siv) adj. rambling.

dis'cus (dis'kəs) n. disk for throwing in athletic competition.

dis·cuss' (di skus') v. talk about. —**dis·cus'sion,** n.

dis·dain' (dis dān', di stān') v., n. scorn. —**dis·dain'ful,** adj.

dis·ease' (di zēz') n., v., **-eased, -easing.** —n. **1.** ailment. —v. **2.** affect with disease. —**dis·eased',** adj.

dis·em·bark′ (dis′em bärk′) v. leave airplane or ship. —**dis·em·bar·ka′·tion,** n.

dis·em·bod′y, v., -bodied, -bodying. free from the body.

dis·en·chant′, v. free from enchantment or illusion.

dis·en·gage′, v., -gaged, -gaging. separate; disconnect.

dis·fa′vor, n. 1. displeasure. 2. disregard. —v. 3. regard or treat with disfavor.

dis·fig′ure, v., -ured, -uring. spoil appearance of. —**dis·fig′ure·ment′,** n.

dis·fran′chise, v., -chised, -chising. deprive of franchise.

dis·gorge′ (dis gôrj′) v., -gorged, -gorging. vomit forth.

dis·grace′ (dis grās′) n., v., -graced, -gracing. —n. 1. state or cause of dishonor. —v. 2. bring shame upon. —**dis·grace′ful,** adj. —**dis·grace′ful·ly,** adv.

dis·grun′tle (dis grun′tl) v., -tled, -tling. make discontented.

dis·guise′ (dis gīz′, di skīz′) v., -guised, -guising. n. —v. 1. conceal true identity of. —n. 2. something that disguises.

dis·gust′ (dis gust′, di skust′) v. 1. cause loathing in. —n. 2. loathing. —**dis·gust′ed,** adj. —**dis·gust′ing,** adj.

dish (dish) n. 1. open shallow container. 2. article of food.

dis·ha·bille′ (dis′ə bēl′, -bē′) n. state of being partially dressed.

dis·heart′en, v. discourage.

di·shev′el (di shev′əl) v., -eled, -eling. let (hair, clothes) look messy.

dis·hon′est, adj. not honest.

dis·hon′or, n. 1. lack of honor. 2. disgrace. —v. 3. disgrace. 4. fail to honor. —**dis·hon′or·a·ble,** adj.

dish′wash′er, n. person or machine that washes dishes.

dis·il·lu′sion, v. free from illusion.

dis·in·cline′, v., -clined, -clining. make or be averse.

dis·in·fect′, v. destroy disease germs in. —**dis·in·fect′ant,** n., adj.

dis·in·for·ma′tion, n. false information released by a government to mislead rivals.

dis·in·gen′u·ous, adj. lacking frankness.

dis·in·her′it, v. exclude from inheritance.

dis·in′te·grate′, v., -grated, -grating. break into parts. —**dis·in′te·gra′·tion,** n.

dis·in′ter′, v., -terred, -terring. take out of the place of interment.

dis·in′ter·est, n. indifference.

dis·in′ter·est′ed, adj. 1. not partial or biased. 2. not interested. —**Usage.** Do not confuse DISINTERESTED and UNINTERESTED. DISINTERESTED usually means "able to act fairly; not partial or biased," while UNINTERESTED means "not taking an interest." But the second meaning of DISINTERESTED listed here means the same as UNINTERESTED and many users of English consider this use of DISINTEREST incorrect.

dis·joint′ed, adj. 1. separated at joints. 2. incoherent.

disk (disk) n. 1. flat circular plate. 2. phonograph record. 3. plate for storing electronic data. 4. roundish, flat anatomical part, as in the spine.

disk·ette′ (di sket′) n. floppy disk.

disk jockey, disc jockey.

dis·like′, v., -liked, -liking. n. —v. 1. regard with displeasure. —n. 2. distaste.

dis·lo·cate′ (dis′lō kāt′, dis lō′kāt) v., -cated, -cating. 1. displace. 2. put out of order.

dis·lodge′, v., -lodged, -lodging. force from place.

dis·loy′al, adj. not loyal; traitorous.

dis′mal (diz′məl) adj. 1. gloomy. 2. terrible. —**dis′mal·ly,** adv.

dis·man′tle (dis man′tl) v., -tled, -tling. 1. deprive of equipment. 2. take apart. —**dis·man′tle·ment,** n.

dis·may′ (dis mā′) v. 1. dishearten. —n. 2. consternation.

dis·mem′ber (dis mem′bər) v. remove limbs of.

dis·miss′ (dis mis′) v. 1. direct or allow to go. 2. remove from service. 3. reject. —**dis·mis′sal,** n.

dis·mount′, v. 1. get or throw down from saddle. 2. take apart.

dis·o·be′di·ent, adj. not obedient. —**dis·o·be′di·ence,** n. —**dis·o·bey′,** v.

dis·or′der, n. 1. lack of order. 2. illness or disease. —v. 3. create disorder in. —**dis·or′der·ly,** adj.

dis·or′gan·ize′, v., -ized, -izing. throw into disorder. —**dis·or′gan·i·za′tion,** n.

dis·o′ri·ent′, v. 1. cause to lose one's way. 2. confuse.

dis·own′, v. repudiate.

dis·par′age (di spar′ij) v., -aged, -aging. speak badly of; belittle.

dis′par·ate (dis′pər it, di spar′-) adj. distinct in kind; dissimilar. —**dis·par′i·ty,** n.

dis·pas′sion·ate, adj. impartial; calm. —**dis·pas′sion·ate·ly,** adv.

dis·patch′ (di spach′) v. 1. send off. 2. transact quickly. 3. kill. —n. 4. act of sending off. 5. killing. 6. speed. 7. message or report.

dis·pel′ (di spel′) v., -pelled, -pelling. drive off; scatter.

dis·pen′sa·ry (di spen′sə rē) n., pl. -ries. place for dispensing medicines.

dis·pen·sa′tion (dis′pən sā′shən, -pen-) n. 1. act of dispensing. 2. divine order. 3. relaxation of law.

dis·pense′ (di spens′) v., -pensed, -pensing. 1. distribute. 2. make up (medicines). 3. forgo. 4. do away. —**dis·pens′er,** n.

dis·perse′ (di spûrs′) v., -persed, -persing. scatter. —**dis·per′sal,** n.

dis·pir′it·ed, adj. downhearted.

dis·place′, v., -placed, -placing. 1. put out of place. 2. replace. —**dis·place′ment,** n.

dis·play′ (di splā′) v., n. exhibit.

dis·please′, v., -pleased, -pleasing. offend. —**dis·pleas′ure** (-plezh′ər) n.

dis·pose′, v., -posed, -posing. 1. arrange. 2. incline. 3. decide. 4. get rid. —**dis·pos′a·ble,** adj., n. —**dis·pos′al,** n.

dis′po·si′tion (dis′pə zish′ən) n. 1. mood. 2. tendency. 3. disposal.

dis′pos·sess′, v. deprive of possession. —**dis′pos·ses′sion,** n.

dis′pro·por′tion, n. lack of proportion. —**dis′pro·por′tion·ate,** adj.

dis·prove′, v., -proved, -proving. prove false.

dis·pute′ (di spyoot′) v., -puted, -puting. n. —v. 1. argue or quarrel. —n. 2. argument; quarrel. —**dis·put′a·ble,** adj. —**dis′pu·ta′tion,** n.

dis·qual′i·fy, v., -fied, -fying. make ineligible. —**dis·qual′i·fi·ca′tion,** n.

dis·qui′et, v. 1. disturb. —n. 2. lack of peace.

dis′re·gard′, v. 1. ignore. —n. 2. neglect.

dis′re·pair′, n. bad condition.

dis′re·pute′, n. ill repute. —**dis′rep′u·ta·ble,** adj.

dis′re·spect′, n. lack of respect. —**dis′re·spect′ful,** adj.

dis·robe′, v., -robed, -robing. undress.

dis·rupt′ (dis rupt′) v. break up or interrupt. —**dis·rup′tion,** n. —**dis·rup′tive,** adj.

dis·sat′is·fy′, v., -fied, -fying. make discontented. —**dis′sat·is·fac′tion** (-fak′shən) n.

dis·sect′ (di sekt′, dī-) v. cut apart for examination; analyze in detail. —**dis·sec′tion,** n.

dis·sem′ble (di sem′bəl) v., -bled, -bling. feign. —**dis·sem′bler,** n.

dis·sem′i·nate′ (di sem′ə nāt′) v., -nated, -nating. spread widely.

dis·sen′sion (di sen′shən) n. 1. disagreement. 2. discord.

dis·sent′ (di sent′) v. 1. disagree. —n. 2. difference of opinion.

dis′ser·ta′tion (dis′ər tā′shən) n. formal essay or thesis.

dis·serv′ice, n. harm or injury.

dis′si·dent (dis′i dənt) adj. 1. refusing to agree or conform. —n. 2. dissident person. —**dis′si·dence,** n.

dis·sim′i·lar, adj. not similar. —**dis·sim′i·lar′i·ty** (-lar′i tē) n.

dis·sim′u·late′ (di sim′yə lāt′) v., -lated, -lating. disguise; dissemble.

dis′si·pate′ (dis′ə pāt′) v., -pated, -pating. 1. scatter. 2. squander. 3. live dissolutely. —**dis′si·pa′tion,** n.

dis·so′ci·ate′ (di sō′shē āt′, -sē-) v., -ated, -ating. separate.

dis′so·lute′ (dis′ə loot′) adj. immoral; licentious.

dis·solve′ (di zolv′) v., -solved, -solving. 1. make solution of. 2. terminate. —**dis′so·lu′tion** (dis′ə loo′shən) n.

dis′so·nance (dis′ə nəns) n. inharmonious or harsh sound.

dis·suade′ (di swād′) v., -suaded, -suading. persuade against.

dist., 1. distance. 2. district.

dis′taff (dis′taf) n. 1. staff for holding wool, flax, etc., in spinning. —adj. 2. of women.

dis′tance (dis′təns) n. 1. space between. 2. remoteness. 3. aloofness.

dis′tant (dis′tənt) adj. 1. remote. 2. reserved. —**dis′tant·ly,** adv.

dis·taste′, n. dislike; aversion. —**dis·taste′ful,** adj.

dis·tem′per (dis tem′pər) n. infectious disease of dogs and cats.

dis·tend′ (di stend′) v. expand abnormally. —**dis·ten′tion,** n.

dis·till′ (di stil′) v. 1. obtain by evaporation and condensation. 2. purify. 3. fall in drops. —**dis·till′er,** n. —**dis·till′er·y,** n.

dis·tinct′ (di stingkt′) adj. 1. clear. 2. separate. —**dis·tinct′ly,** adv.

dis·tinc′tion, n. 1. act or instance of distinguishing. 2. discrimination. 3. difference. 4. special honor. —**dis·tinc′tive,** adj.

dis·tin′guish (di sting′gwish) v. 1. identify as different. 2. perceive. 3. make eminent.

dis·tin′guished, adj. dignified or elegant.

dis·tort′ (di stôrt′) v. 1. twist out of shape. 2. hide true meaning of.

dis·tract′ (di strakt′) v. divert attention of. —**dis·trac′tion,** n.

dis·traught′ (di strôt′) adj. crazed with anxiety; agitated.

dis·tress′ (di stres′) n. 1. pain or sorrow. 2. state of emergency. —v. 3. afflict with pain or sorrow.

dis·trib·ute (di strib′yōōt) v., **-uted**, **-uting**. **1.** divide in shares. **2.** spread. **3.** sort. —**dis·tri·bu′tion**, n. —**dis·trib′u·tor**, n.

dis′trict (dis′trikt) n. **1.** political division. **2.** region.

district attorney, attorney for the government within a given district, whose job is primarily prosecuting.

dis·trust′, v. **1.** suspect. —n. **2.** suspicion; doubt.

dis·turb′ (di stûrb′) v. **1.** interrupt peace of. **2.** unsettle. —**dis·turb′ance**, n.

dis·use′ (dis yōōs′) n. lack of use.

ditch (dich) n. **1.** trench; channel. —v. **2.** Slang. get rid of.

dith′er (dith′ər) n. **1.** flustered excitement or fear. —v. **2.** vacillate.

dit′to (dit′ō) n., pl. **-tos**, adv. —n. **1.** the same. —adv. **2.** as stated before.

ditto mark, mark (″) indicating repetition.

dit′ty (dit′ē) n., pl. **-ties**. simple song.

di·u·ret′ic (dī′ə ret′ik) adj. promoting urination. —**di·u·ret′ic**, n.

di·ur′nal (dī ûr′nl) adj. daily.

div., **1.** dividend. **2.** division. **3.** divorced.

di′va (dē′və, -vä) n. prima donna (def. 1).

di′van (dī van′) n. sofa.

dive (dīv) v., **dived** or **dove** (dōv), **dived**, **diving**, n. —v. **1.** plunge into water. **2.** plunge deeply. —n. **3.** act of diving. —**div′er**, n.

di·verge′ (di vûrj′, dī-) v., **-verged**, **-verging**. **1.** move or lie in different directions. **2.** differ. —**di·ver′gence**, n. —**di·ver′gent**, adj.

di′vers (dī′vərz) adj. various.

di·verse′ (di vûrs′, dī-) adj. of different kinds. —**di·ver′si·fy′**, v., **-fied**, **-fying**. —**di·ver′si·ty**, n.

di·vert′ (di vûrt′, dī-) v. **1.** turn aside. **2.** amuse. —**di·ver′sion**, n.

di·vest′ (di vest′, dī-) v. deprive; dispossess.

di·vide′ (di vīd′) v., **-vided**, **-viding**, n. —v. **1.** separate into parts. **2.** apportion. —n. **3.** zone separating drainage basins. —**di·vid′er**, n.

div′i·dend (div′i dend′) n. **1.** number to be divided. **2.** share in profits.

di·vine′ (di vīn′) adj., n., v., **-vined**, **-vining**. —adj. **1.** of or from God or a god. **2.** religious. **3.** godlike. —n. **4.** theologian or clergyman. —v. **5.** prophesy. **6.** perceive. —**di·vine′ly**, adv.

divining rod, forked stick for finding water deposits.

di·vin′i·ty (-vin′i tē) n., pl. **-ties**. **1.** divine nature. **2.** god.

di·vi′sion (di vizh′ən) n. **1.** act or result of dividing. **2.** thing that divides. **3.** section. **4.** military unit under major general. —**di·vis′i·ble**, adj. —**di·vi′sive** (-vī′siv) adj.

di·vi′sor (-vī′zər) n. number dividing dividend.

di·vorce′ (di vôrs′) n., v., **-vorced**, **-vorcing**. —n. **1.** legal dissolution of marriage. **2.** separation. —v. **3.** separate by divorce. —**di·vor′cee′** (-sē′) n.fem.

div′ot (div′ət) n. turf gouged out by a golf club stroke.

di·vulge′ (di vulj′, dī-) v., **-vulged**, **-vulging**. disclose.

Dix′ie (dik′sē) n. southern states of the U.S., esp. those that joined Confederacy.

Dix′ie·land′, n. style of jazz marked by accented four-four rhythm and improvisation.

diz′zy (diz′ē) adj., **-zier**, **-ziest**. **1.**

giddy. **2.** confused. **3.** Informal. foolish; silly. —**diz′zi·ly**, adv.

D.J. (dē′jā′) disc jockey. Also, **DJ**, **deejay**.

DNA, deoxyribonucleic acid, substance that carries genes along its strands.

do (dōō; unstressed dōō, də) v., **did**, **done**, **doing**, n. —v. **1.** perform; execute. **2.** behave. **3.** fare. **4.** finish. **5.** effect. **6.** render. **7.** suffice. —n. **8.** Informal. social gathering. **9.** (dō). first note of musical scale.

DOA, dead on arrival.

doc′ile (dos′əl) adj. **1.** readily taught. **2.** submissive.

dock (dok) n. **1.** wharf. **2.** place for ship. **3.** prisoner's place in courtroom. —v. **4.** put into dock. **5.** cut off end of. **6.** deduct from (pay).

dock′et (dok′it) n. **1.** list of court cases. **2.** label.

doc′tor (dok′tər) n. **1.** medical practitioner. **2.** holder of highest academic degree. —v. **3.** treat medicinally. **4.** tamper with.

doc′tor·ate (-it) n. doctor's degree.

doctor's degree, degree of the highest rank awarded by universities.

doc′trine (-trin) n. **1.** principle. **2.** teachings. —**doc′tri·nal**, adj.

doc′u·dra′ma (dok′yə drä′mə, -dram′ə) n. fictionalized TV drama depicting actual events.

doc′u·ment, n. (-mənt) **1.** paper with information or evidence. —v. (-ment′) **2.** support by documents.

doc′u·men′ta·ry (-men′tə rē) adj., n., pl. **-ries**. —adj. **1.** of or derived from documents. —n. **2.** film on factual subject.

dod′der (dod′ər) v. shake; totter.

dodge (doj) v., **dodged**, **dodging**, n. —v. **1.** elude. —n. **2.** act of dodging. **3.** trick. —**dodg′er**, n.

do′do (dō′dō) n., pl. **-dos**, **-does**. extinct bird.

doe (dō) n. female deer, etc.

does (duz) v. third pers. sing. pres. indic. of **do**.

does′n′t (duz′ənt) contraction of does not.

doff (dof) v. remove.

dog (dôg) n., v., **dogged**, **dogging**. —n. **1.** domesticated carnivore. —v. **2.** follow closely.

dog′-ear′, n. folded-down corner of book page. —**dog′-eared′**, adj.

dog′ged (dô′gid) adj. persistent.

dog′house′, n. shelter for dog. **2.** place of disfavor.

dog′ma (-ma) n. system of beliefs.

dog·mat′ic (-mat′ik) adj. **1.** of dogma. **2.** opinionated.

dog′ma·tism′, n. aggressive assertion of opinions.

dog′wood′, n. flowering tree.

doi′ly (doi′lē) n., pl. **-lies**. small napkin.

dol′drums (dōl′drəmz, dol′-) n.pl. **1.** flat calms at sea. **2.** listless mood.

dole (dōl) n., v., **doled**, **doling**. —n. **1.** portion of charitable gift. —v. **2.** give out sparingly.

dole′ful, adj. sorrowful; gloomy.

doll (dol) n. **1.** toy representing baby or other human being. **2.** attractive or nice person.

dol′lar (dol′ər) n. monetary unit equal to 100 cents.

dol′lop (dol′əp) n. lump or blob of soft substance, as whipped cream.

dol′ly (dol′ē) n., pl. **-lies**. **1.** low cart for moving heavy loads. **2.** movable platform for movie or TV camera.

dol′or·ous (dō′lər əs, dol′ər-) adj. grievous.

dol′phin (dol′fin) n. whalelike animal.

dolt (dōlt) n. fool. —**dolt′ish**, adj.

-dom, suffix indicating: **1.** domain, as kingdom. **2.** rank or station, as dukedom. **3.** general condition, as freedom.

do·main′ (dō mān′) n. **1.** ownership of land. **2.** realm.

dome (dōm) n. hemispherical roof.

do·mes′tic (də mes′tik) adj. **1.** of the home. **2.** not foreign. —n. **3.** household servant. —**do′mes·tic′i·ty** (dō′me stis′i tē) n.

do·mes′ti·cate′ (-kāt′) v., **-cated**, **-cating**. tame.

domestic partner, unmarried person who cohabits with another.

dom′i·cile (dom′ə sīl′, -səl, dō′mə-) n. home.

dom′i·nate′ (dom′ə nāt′) v., **-nated**, **-nating**. **1.** rule. **2.** tower above. —**dom′i·na′tion**, **dom′i·nance**, n. —**dom′i·nant**, adj.

dom′i·neer′ (dom′ə nēr′) v. rule oppressively.

do·min′ion (də min′yən) n. **1.** power of governing. **2.** territory governed.

dom′i·no′ (dom′ə nō′) n., pl. **-noes**. oblong dotted piece used in game of dominoes.

don (don) v., **donned**, **donning**. put on.

do′nate (dō′nāt, dō nāt′) v., **-nated**, **-nating**. give.

don′key (dong′kē, dông′-, dung′-) n. **1.** ass. **2.** fool.

do′nor (dō′nər) n. giver.

doo′dle (dōōd′l) v., **-dled**, **-dling**. scribble. —**doo′dler**, n.

doom (dōōm) n. **1.** fate. **2.** ruin. **3.** judgment. —v. **4.** condemn.

dooms′day′, n. day the world ends; Judgment Day.

door (dôr) n. **1.** movable barrier at entrance. **2.** Also, **door′way′**. entrance. —**door′step′**, n.

door′yard′, n. yard near front door of house.

dope (dōp) n., v., **doped**, **doping**. —n. **1.** Informal. narcotic. **2.** Slang. information; news. **3.** Informal. stupid person. —v. **4.** drug.

dop′ey, adj., **-ier**, **-iest**. Informal. **1.** stupid. **2.** sluggish or confused, as from drug use. Also, **dop′y**.

dor′mant (dôr′mənt) adj. **1.** asleep. **2.** inactive. —**dor′man·cy**, n.

dor′mer (dôr′mər) n. vertical window projecting from sloping roof.

dor′mi·to′ry (dôr′mi tôr′ē) n., pl. **-ries**. group sleeping place. Also, **dorm.**

dor′mouse′ (dôr′mous′) n., pl. **-mice**. small rodent.

dor′sal (dôr′səl) adj. of or on the back.

do′ry (dôr′ē) n., pl. **-ries**. flat-bottomed rowboat.

DOS (dôs) n. disk operating system for microcomputers.

dose (dōs) n., v., **dosed**, **dosing**. —n. **1.** amount of medicine taken at one time. —v. **2.** give doses to.

dos′si·er′ (dos′ē ā′) n. file of documents.

dot (dot) n., v., **dotted**, **dotting**. —n. **1.** small spot. —v. **2.** mark with or make dots.

do′tard (dō′tərd) n. senile person.

dote (dōt) v., **doted**, **doting**. **1.** be overfond. **2.** be senile. —**dot′age**, n.

dou′ble (dub′əl) adj., n., v., **-bled**, **-bling**. —adj. **1.** twice as great, etc. **2.** of two parts. **3.** deceitful. —n. **4.** double quantity. **5.** duplicate. —v. **6.** make or become double. **7.** bend or fold. **8.** turn back.

double bass (bās) lowest-pitched instrument of violin family.

doub′le-cross′, v. cheat or betray.

dou′ble en•ten′dre (än tän′drə, -tänd′) n., pl. **dou′ble en•ten′dres** (än tän′drəz, -tändz′). saying with two meanings.

dou′ble•head′er, n. two games played on the same day in rapid succession.

double play, baseball play in which two players are put out.

double standard, standard that differs for different persons or groups.

double take, delayed response, as to something not immediately recognized.

doub′le-talk′, n. evasive talk.

doubt (dout) v. **1.** be uncertain about. —n. **2.** uncertainty.

doubt′ful, adj. **1.** having doubts. **2.** causing doubts or suspicion.

douche (dōōsh) n., v., **douched, douching.** —n. **1.** jet of liquid applied to a body part or cavity. —v. **2.** apply a douche.

dough (dō) n. mixture of flour, liquid, etc., for baking.

dough′nut (dō′nət, -nut′) n. ringlike cake of fried, sweet dough.

dour (dōōr, dou′ər, dou′ər) adj. sullen.

douse (dous) v., **doused, dousing. 1.** plunge; dip. **2.** extinguish.

dove (duv) n. pigeon.

dove′cote′, n. structure for tame pigeons. Also, **dove′cot′.**

dove′tail′, n. **1.** tenon-and-mortise joint. —v. **2.** join by dovetail. **3.** fit together harmoniously.

dow′a•ger (dou′ə jər) n. **1.** titled or wealthy widow. **2.** dignified elderly woman.

dow′dy (dou′dē) adj., **-dier, -diest.** not stylish or attractive.

dow′el (dou′əl) n. wooden pin fitting into hole.

dow′er (dou′ər) n. widow's share of husband's property.

down (doun) adv. **1.** to, at, or in lower place or state. **2.** on or to ground. **3.** on paper. —prep. **4.** in descending direction. —n. Also **5.** soft feathers. —v. **6.** subdue. —down′wards, adv. —down′ward, adv., adj.

down′cast′, adj. dejected.

down′er, n. Informal. **1.** depressing experience or person. **2.** sedative drug.

down′fall′, n. **1.** ruin. **2.** fall.

down′grade′, v., **-graded, -grading,** n. —v. **1.** reduce in rank. —n. **2.** downward slope.

down′heart′ed, adj. dejected.

down′hill′ (adv. -hil′; adj. -hil′) adv., adj. in downward direction.

down′play′, v. minimize.

down′pour′, n. heavy rain.

down′right′, adj. **1.** thorough. —adv. **2.** completely.

down′scale′, adj. of or for people at lower end of economic scale.

down′size′, v., **-sized, -sizing.** reduce in size or number.

down′stage′ adv. at or toward front of stage.

down′stairs′ (adv. -stârz′; adj. -stârz′) adv., adj. to or on lower floor.

down′stream′, adv., adj. with current of stream.

Down syndrome, genetic disorder characterized by mental retardation, a wide, flattened skull, and slanting eyes. Also, **Down's syndrome.**

down′-to-earth′, adj. practical.

down′town′, n. **1.** central part of town. —adj. **2.** of this part. —adv. **3.** to or in this part.

down′trod′den, adj. oppressed.

down′turn′, n. downward trend.

down′y, adj. like soft feathers.

dow′ry (dou′rē) n., pl. **-ries.** bride's property given to husband.

dowse (dous) v., **dowsed, dowsing.** use divining rod.

doz., dozen.

doze (dōz) v., **dozed, dozing,** n. —v. **1.** sleep lightly. —n. **2.** light sleep.

doz′en (duz′ən) n., pl. **dozen, dozens.** group of 12.

Dr., 1. Doctor. **2.** Drive.

drab (drab) n., adj., **drabber, drabbest.** —n. **1.** dull brownish gray. —adj. **2.** uninteresting.

draft (draft) n. **1.** sketch. **2.** rough version. **3.** current of air. **4.** haul. **5.** swallow of liquid. **6.** selection for military service. **7.** written request for payment. —v. **8.** plan. **9.** write. **10.** enlist by draft. —draft′y, adj. —draft•ee′, n.

drafts′man, n. person who draws plans, etc.

drag (drag) v., **dragged, dragging,** n. —v. **1.** draw heavily; haul. **2.** dredge. **3.** trail on ground. **4.** pass slowly. —n. **5.** thing used in dragging. **6.** hindrance.

drag′net′, n. **1.** net for dragging in water. **2.** system for catching criminal.

drag′on (drag′ən) n. fabled reptile.

drag′on•fly′, n., pl. **-flies.** large four-winged insect.

dra•goon′ (drə gōōn′) n. **1.** heavily armed mounted soldier, formerly common in European armies. —v. **2.** force; coerce.

drag race, race with cars accelerating from a standstill.

drain (drān) v. **1.** draw or flow off gradually. **2.** empty; dry. **3.** exhaust. —n. **4.** channel or pipe for draining. —drain′age, n.

drake (drāk) n. male duck.

dram (dram) n. **1.** apothecaries' weight, equal to $\frac{1}{8}$ ounce. **2.** small drink of liquor.

dra′ma (drä′mə, dram′ə) n. **1.** story acted on stage. **2.** vivid series of events.

dra•mat′ic (drə mat′ik) adj. **1.** of plays or theater. **2.** highly vivid.

dra•mat′ics, n. **1.** theatrical art. **2.** exaggerated conduct or emotion.

dram′a•tist (dram′ə tist, drä′mə-) n. playwright.

dram′a•tize′, v., **-tized, -tizing.** put in dramatic form.

drape (drāp) v., **draped, draping.** —v. **1.** cover with fabric. **2.** arrange in folds. —n. **3.** draped hanging. —dra′per•y, n.

dras′tic (dras′tik) adj. extreme.

draught (draft) n. Brit. draft.

draw (drô) v., **drew** (drōō), **drawn, drawing,** —v. **1.** pull; lead. **2.** take out. **3.** attract. **4.** sketch. **5.** take in. **6.** deduce. **7.** stretch. **8.** make or have as draft. —n. **9.** act of drawing. **10.** equal score. **11.** Informal. attraction to public.

draw′back′, n. disadvantage.

draw′bridge′, n. bridge that can be drawn up.

draw′er (drôr for 1, 2; drô′ər for 3) n. **1.** sliding compartment. **2.** (pl.) trouserlike undergarment. **3.** person who draws.

draw′ing, n. drawn picture.

drawl (drôl) v. **1.** speak slowly. —n. **2.** drawled utterance.

drawn (drôn) adj. tense; haggard.

dray (drā) n. low, strong cart.

dread (dred) v. **1.** fear. —n. **2.** fear. **3.** awe. —adj. **4.** feared. **5.** revered.

dread′ful, adj. **1.** very bad. **2.** inspiring dread.

dread′ful•ly, adv. Informal. very.

dread′locks′, n. hairstyle with many long, ropelike pieces.

dream (drēm) n. **1.** ideas imagined during sleep. **2.** reverie. —v. **3.** have dream (about). **4.** imagine.

drear′y, adj., **drearier, dreariest.** gloomy or boring. —drear′i•ly, adv.

dredge (drej) n., v., **dredged, dredging.** —n. **1.** machine for moving earth at the bottom of river, etc. —v. **2.** move with dredge. **3.** sprinkle with flour.

dregs (dregz) n.pl. sediment.

drench (drench) v. soak.

dress (dres) n. **1.** woman's garment. **2.** clothing. —v. **3.** clothe. **4.** ornament. **5.** prepare. **6.** treat (wounds).

dres•sage′ (drə säzh′, dre-) n. art of training a horse in obedience and precision of movement.

dress circle, semicircular division of seats in a theater.

dress′er, n. **1.** chest of drawers. **2.** person who dresses another.

dress′ing, n. **1.** sauce or stuffing. **2.** application for wound.

dress rehearsal, final rehearsal with costumes.

dress′y, adj., **-ier, -iest.** fancy; formal.

drib′ble (drib′əl) v., **-bled, -bling,** n. —v. **1.** fall in drops. **2.** bounce repeatedly. —n. **3.** trickle.

dri′er (drī′ər) n. dryer.

drift (drift) n. **1.** deviation from set course. **2.** tendency. **3.** something driven, esp. into heap. —v. **4.** carry or be carried by currents.

drift′er, n. person who moves frequently.

drill (dril) n. **1.** boring tool. **2.** methodical training. **3.** furrow for seeds. **4.** sowing machine. **5.** strong twilled cotton. —v. **6.** pierce with drill. **7.** train methodically.

drink (dringk) v., **drank** (drangk), **drunk** (drungk), **drinking,** n. —v. **1.** swallow liquid. **2.** swallow alcoholic liquids. —n. **3.** liquid for quenching thirst. **4.** alcoholic drink.

drip (drip) v., **dripped, dripping. 1.** fall or let fall in drops. —n. **2.** act or sound of dripping.

drive (drīv) v., **drove** (drōv), **driven, driving,** n. —v. **1.** send by force. **2.** control. **3.** convey or travel in vehicle. **4.** impel. —n. **5.** military offensive. **6.** strong effort. **7.** trip in vehicle. **8.** road for driving.

drive′-by′, n., pl. **drive-bys. 1.** action of driving by something specified. **2.** shooting that occurs from vehicle driving by. —drive′-by′, adj.

drive′-in′, adj. **1.** designed for persons in automobiles. —n. **2.** a drive-in bank, movie theater, etc.

driv′el (driv′əl) v., **-eled, -eling,** n. —v. **1.** drool. **2.** talk foolishly. —n. **3.** foolish talk.

drive′way′, n. road on private property.

driz′zle (driz′əl) v., **-zled, -zling,** n. rain in fine drops.

droll (drōl) adj. amusingly odd.

drom′e•dar′y (drom′i der′ē, drum′-) n., pl. **-daries.** one-humped camel.

drone (drōn) v., **droned, droning,** n. —v. **1.** make humming sound. **2.** speak dully. —n. **3.** monotonous tone. **4.** male of honeybee.

drool (drōōl) v. **1.** salivate. —n. **2.** saliva dripping from the mouth.

droop (drōōp) v. **1.** sink or hang

down. **2.** lose spirit. —*n.* **3.** act of drooping. —**droop′y,** *adj.*

drop (drop) *n., v.,* **dropped, dropping.** —*n.* **1.** small mass of liquid. **2.** small quantity. **3.** fall. **4.** steep slope. —*v.* **5.** fall or let fall. **6.** cease. **7.** visit. —**drop′per,** *n.*

drop kick, kick made by dropping ball to the ground and kicking it as it starts to bounce up.

drop′out′, *n.* student who quits before graduation.

dross (drôs) *n.* refuse.

drought (drout) *n.* dry weather.

drove (drōv) *n.* **1.** group of driven cattle. **2.** crowd.

drown (droun) *v.* suffocate by immersion in liquid.

drow′sy (drou′zē) *adj.* sleepy.

drub (drub) *v.,* **drubbed, drubbing. 1.** beat. **2.** defeat.

drudge (druj) *n., v.,* **drudged, drudging.** —*n.* person doing tedious work. —**drudg′er•y,** *n.*

drug (drug) *n., v.,* **drugged, drugging.** —*n.* **1.** therapeutic chemical. **2.** narcotic. —*v.* **3.** mix or affect with drug. —**drug′store′,** *n.*

drug′gist, *n.* **1.** pharmacist. **2.** person who operates drugstore.

dru′id (drōō′id) *n.* (*often cap.*) member of a pre-Christian religious order in Europe. —**dru′id•ism,** *n.*

drum (drum) *n., v.,* **drummed, drumming.** —*n.* **1.** percussion musical instrument. **2.** eardrum. —*v.* **3.** beat on or as on drum.

drum major, leader of marching band.

drum majorette, majorette.

drum′stick′, *n.* **1.** stick for beating a drum. **2.** leg of a cooked fowl.

drunk (drungk) *adj.* intoxicated.

drunk′ard (drung′kərd) *n.* habitually drunk person.

dry (drī) *adj.,* **drier, driest,** *v.,* **dried, drying.** —*adj.* **1.** not wet. **2.** rainless. **3.** not yielding liquid. **4.** thirsty. **5.** boring. **6.** not expressing emotion. **7.** not sweet. —*v.* **8.** make or become dry. —**dry′ly,** *adv.*

dry′ad (drī′əd, -ad) *n.* (*often cap.*) nymph of the woods.

dry′-clean′, *v.* clean with solvents. —**dry′-clean′er,** *n.*

dry′er, *n.* machine for drying.

dry ice, solid carbon dioxide, used esp. as a refrigerant.

dry run, rehearsal or trial.

DST, daylight-saving time.

du′al (dōō′əl, dyōō′-) *adj.* twofold.

dub (dub) *v.,* **dubbed, dubbing. 1.** name formally. **2.** furnish with new sound track.

du′bi•ous (dōō′bē əs) *adj.* doubtful.

du′cal (dōō′kəl, dyōō′-) *adj.* of dukes.

duch′ess (duch′is) *n.* **1.** duke's wife. **2.** woman equal in rank to duke.

duch′y (duch′ē) *n., pl.* **duchies. 1.** territory of duke. **2.** small state.

duck (duk) *v.* **1.** plunge under water. **2.** stoop quickly. **3.** avoid. —*n.* **4.** act of ducking. **5.** type of swimming bird. **6.** heavy cotton fabric. —**duck′ling,** *n.*

duck′bill′, *n.* small, egg-laying mammal.

duct (dukt) *n.* tube or canal in body. —**duct′less,** *adj.*

duc′tile (duk′til, -til) *adj.* **1.** readily drawn out; malleable. **2.** compliant.

duct tape (duk, dukt) strongly adhesive cloth tape, used in plumbing, household repairs, etc.

dud (dud) *n. Informal.* failure.

dude (dōōd, dyōōd) *n.* **1.** man exces-

sively concerned with his clothes. **2.** *Slang.* fellow; guy.

dudg′eon (duj′ən) *n.* indignation.

due (dōō, dyōō) *adj.* **1.** payable. **2.** proper. **3.** attributable. **4.** expected. —*n.* **5.** something due. **6.** (*sometimes pl.*) regularly payable fee for membership. —*adv.* **7.** in a straight line.

du′el (dōō′əl, dyōō′-) *n., v.* **-eled, -eling.** —*n.* **1.** prearranged combat between two persons. —*v.* **2.** fight in duel. —**du′el•er, du′el•ist,** *n.*

du•et′ (dōō et′, dyōō-) *n.* music for two performers.

duf′fel bag′ (duf′əl) cylindrical bag for carrying belongings.

duff′er (duf′ər) *n.* **1.** *Informal.* incompetent person. **2.** person inept at a specific sport, as golf.

dug′out′, *n.* **1.** boat made by hollowing a log. **2.** roofed structure where baseball players sit when not on the field. **3.** rough shelter dug in the ground, as by soldiers.

duke (dōōk, dyōōk) *n.* nobleman below prince. —**duke′dom,** *n.*

dul′ci•mer (dul′sə mər) *n.* musical instrument with metal strings.

dull (dul) *adj.* **1.** stupid. **2.** not brisk. **3.** tedious. **4.** not sharp. **5.** dim. —*v.* **6.** make or become dull.

du′ly (dōō′lē, dyōō′-) *adv.* **1.** properly. **2.** punctually.

dumb (dum) *adj.* **1.** temporarily unable to speak. **2.** *Often Offensive.* lacking the power of speech. **3.** *Informal.* stupid.

dumb′bell′, *n.* **1.** weighted bar for exercising. **2.** *Informal.* stupid person.

dumb′found′ (dum found′, dum′found′) *v.* astonish. Also, **dum•found′.**

dumb′wait′er, *n.* small elevator for moving food, etc.

dum′my, *n., pl.* **-mies,** *adj.* —*n.* **1.** model or copy. **2.** *Informal.* **a.** *Offensive.* mute. **b.** stupid person. —*adj.* **3.** counterfeit.

dump (dump) *v.* **1.** drop heavily. **2.** empty. —*n.* **3.** place for dumping. **4.** *Informal.* dilapidated, dirty place.

dump′ling (-ling) *n.* mass of steamed dough.

dump′y, *adj.,* **-ier, -iest.** short and stout. —**dump′i•ness,** *n.*

dun (dun) *v.,* **dunned, dunning,** *n.* —*v.* **1.** demand payment of. —*n.* **2.** demand for payment. **3.** dull brown.

dunce (duns) *n.* stupid person.

dune (dōōn, dyōōn) *n.* sand hill formed by wind.

dung (dung) *n.* manure; excrement.

dun′ga•ree′ (dung′gə rē′) *n.* coarse cotton fabric for work clothes **(dungarees).**

dun′geon (dun′jən) *n.* underground cell.

dunk (dungk) *v.* **1.** dip in beverage before eating. **2.** submerge briefly in liquid. **3.** thrust (basketball) downward through basket.

du′o (dōō′ō, dyōō′ō) *n.* **1.** duet. **2.** couple or pair.

du′o•de′num (dōō′ə dē′nəm, dyōō′-; dōō od′n əm, dyōō-) *n.* uppermost part of small intestine.

dupe (dōōp, dyōōp) *n., v.,* **duped, duping.** —*n.* **1.** deceived person. —*v.* **2.** deceive.

du′plex (dōō′pleks, dyōō′-) *n.* **1.** apartment with two floors. **2.** house for two families.

du′pli•cate, *adj., n., v.,* **-cated, -cating.** —*adj.* (dōō′pli kit) **1.** exactly like. **2.** double. —*n.* (-kit) **3.** copy. —*v.* (-kāt′) **4.** copy. **5.** double.

du•plic′i•ty (dōō plis′i tē, dyōō-) *n., pl.* **-ties.** deceitfulness.

du′ra•ble (dōōr′ə bəl, dyōōr′-) *adj.* enduring. —**du′ra•bil′i•ty,** *n.*

du•ra′tion (dōō rā′shən, dyōō-) *n.* continuance in time.

du•ress′ (dōō res′, dyōō-, dōōr′is, dyōōr′-) *n.* compulsion.

dur′ing (dōōr′ing, dyōōr′-) *prep.* in the course of.

du′rum (dōōr′əm, dyōōr′-) *n.* kind of wheat flour used in pasta.

dusk (dusk) *n.* twilight.

dust (dust) *n.* **1.** fine particles of earth, etc. —*v.* **2.** free from dust. **3.** sprinkle. —**dust′y,** *adj.*

Dutch (duch) *n.* people or language of the Netherlands.

Dutch uncle, mentor who criticizes very frankly.

du′ti•ful (dōō′tə fəl, dyōō′-) *adj.* doing one's duties.

du′ty (dōō′tē, dyōō′-) *n., pl.* **-ties. 1.** moral or legal obligation. **2.** function. **3.** tax, esp. on imports.

dwarf (dwôrf) *n.* **1.** abnormally small person, etc. —*v.* **2.** make or make to seem small.

dwell (dwel) *v.,* **dwelt** or **dwelled, dwelling. 1.** reside. **2.** linger, esp. in words. —**dwell′ing,** *n.*

dwin′dle (dwin′dl) *v.,* **-dled, -dling.** shrink; lessen.

dye (dī) *n., v.,* **dyed, dyeing.** —*n.* **1.** coloring material. —*v.* **2.** color with dye. —**dye′ing,** *n.* —**dy′er,** *n.*

dyed′-in-the-wool′, *adj.* uncompromising.

dyke (dīk) *n.* **1.** dike. **2.** *Slang* (*often offensive*). female homosexual.

dy•nam′ic (dī nam′ik) *adj.* **1.** of force. **2.** energetic. —**dy′na•mism** (dī′nə miz′əm) *n.*

dy′na•mite′ (dī′nə mīt′) *n., v.,* **-mited, -miting.** —*n.* **1.** explosive. —*v.* **2.** blow up with dynamite.

dy′na•mo′ (-mō′) *n., pl.* **-mos. 1.** machine for generating electricity. **2.** energetic, forceful person.

dy′nas•ty (dī′nə stē) *n., pl.* **-ties.** rulers of same family.

dys-, prefix meaning ill or bad, as *dysfunction.*

dys′en•ter′y (dis′ən ter′ē) *n.* infectious disease of bowels.

dys•func′tion (dis fungk′shən) *n.* ineffective functioning.

dys•lex′i•a (dis lek′sē ə) *n.* impairment of ability to read. —**dys•lex′ic,** *adj., n.*

dys•pep′sia (dis pep′shə, -sē ə) *n.* indigestion.

dz., dozen.

E

E, e (ē) *n.* fifth letter of English alphabet.

E, 1. east, eastern. **2.** English.

ea., each.

each (ēch) *adj., pron.* **1.** every one. —*adv.* **2.** apiece.

ea′ger (ē′gər) *adj.* ardent.

ea′gle (ē′gəl) *n.* large bird of prey.

ea′gle-eyed′, *adj.* having unusually sharp vision.

ear (ēr) *n.* **1.** organ of hearing. **2.** grain-containing part of cereal plant.

ear′drum′, *n.* sensitive membrane in ear.

earl (ûrl) *n.* nobleman ranking below marquis. —**earl′dom,** *n.*

ear′ly (ûr′lē) *adv.,* **-lier, -liest,** *adj.* **1.** in first part of. **2.** before usual time.

ear/mark/ (ēr/märk/) n. **1.** identifying mark. —v. **2.** designate.

ear/muffs/, n.pl. warm connected coverings for the ears.

earn (ûrn) v. gain by labor or merit.

ear/nest (ûr/nist) adj. very serious.

earn/ings, n.pl. profits.

ear/phone/ (ēr/fōn/) n. sound receiver held to the ear.

ear/ring/ (ēr/ring/, ēr/ing) n. ornament worn on ear lobe.

ear/shot/, n. hearing range.

ear/split/ting, adj. extremely loud or shrill.

earth (ûrth) n. **1.** planet we inhabit. **2.** dry land. **3.** soil.

earth/en, adj. made of clay or earth. —earth/en•ware/, n.

earth/ly, adj., **-lier, -liest.** of or in this world.

earth/quake/, n. vibration of earth's surface.

earth/work/, n. **1.** fortification formed of moved earth. **2.** work of art involving large land area.

earth/worm/, n. burrowing worm.

earth/y, adj., **-ier, -iest. 1.** practical; realistic. **2.** coarse; unrefined.

ease (ēz) n., v., **eased, easing.** —n. **1.** freedom from work, pain, etc. **2.** facility. —v. **3.** relieve.

ea/sel (ē/zəl) n. support stand, as for picture.

east (ēst) n. **1.** direction from which sun rises. **2.** (sometimes cap.) region in this direction. —adj., adv. **3.** toward, in, or from east. —east/er•ly, adj., adv. —east/ern, adj. —east/ward, adv., adj. —East/ern•er, n.

East/er (ē/stər) n. anniversary of resurrection of Christ.

eas/y (ē/zē) adj., **easier, easiest. 1.** not difficult. **2.** at ease. **3.** moderate. —eas/i•ly, adv.

eas/y-go/ing, adj. **1.** casual; relaxed. **2.** lenient.

eat (ēt) v., **ate** (āt), **eating, eaten. 1.** take into the mouth and swallow. **2.** wear away or dissolve.

eat/er•y, n., pl. **-eries.** Informal. restaurant.

eaves (ēvz) n.pl. overhanging edge of roof.

eaves/drop/, v., **-dropped, -dropping.** listen secretly.

ebb (eb) n. **1.** fall of tide. **2.** decline. —v. **3.** flow back. **4.** decline.

eb/on•y (eb/ə nē) n. **1.** hard black wood. —adj. **2.** very dark.

e•bul/lient (i bul/yənt, i bōōl/-) adj. full of enthusiasm.

ec•cen/tric (ik sen/trik) adj. **1.** odd. **2.** off center. —n. **3.** odd person. —ec/cen•tric/i•ty (-tris/i tē) n.

ec•cle/si•as/tic (i klē/zē as/tik) n. **1.** member of the clergy. —adj. **2.** Also, **ec•cle/si•as/ti•cal.** of church or clergy.

ech/e•lon (esh/ə lon/) n. level of command.

ech/o (ek/ō) n., pl. **echoes, v., echoed, echoing.** —n. **1.** repetition of sound, esp. by reflection. —v. **2.** emit or repeat as echo.

é•clair/ (ā klâr/) n. cream- or custard-filled pastry.

é•clat/ (ā klä/) n. **1.** brilliance, as of success. **2.** acclaim.

ec•lec/tic (i klek/tik) adj. chosen from various sources.

e•clipse/ (i klips/) n., v., **eclipsed, eclipsing.** —n. **1.** obscuring of light of sun or moon by passage of body in front of it. —v. **2.** obscure.

e•clip/tic (i klip/tik) n. apparent annual path of sun.

eco-, prefix meaning ecology, environment or natural habitat, as ecocide.

e/co•cide/ (ek/ə sīd/, ē/kə-) n. widespread destruction of natural environment.

e•col/o•gy (i kol/ə jē) n. science of relationship between organisms and environment. —e•col/o•gist, n.

e/co•nom/i•cal (ek/ə nom/i kəl, ē/kə-) adj. thrifty.

ec/o•nom/ics, n. production, distribution, and use of wealth. —e•co•nom/ic, adj. —e•con/o•mist (i kon/ə-mist) n.

e•con/o•mize/ (i kon/ə mīz/) v., **-mized, -mizing.** save; be thrifty.

e•con/o•my, n., pl. **-mies. 1.** thrifty management. **2.** system of producing and distributing wealth.

ec/o•sys/tem (ek/ō sis/təm, ē/kō-) n. distinct ecological system.

ec/ru (ek/rōō) n., adj. light brown; beige. Also, **éc•ru** (ā/krōō).

ec/sta•sy (ek/stə sē) n., pl. **-sies. 1.** overpowering emotion. **2.** rapture. —ec•stat/ic (ek stat/ik) adj.

-ectomy, suffix meaning surgical removal of, as tonsillectomy.

ec/u•men/i•cal (ek/yōō men/i kal) adj. **1.** universal. **2.** pertaining to movement for universal Christian unity.

ec/ze•ma (ek/sə mə, eg/zə-, ig zē/-) n. disease of skin.

E/dam (ē/dəm) n. mild yellow cheese.

ed/dy (ed/ē) n., pl. **-dies, v., -died, -dying.** —n. **1.** current at variance with main current. —v. **2.** whirl in eddies.

e/del•weiss/ (ād/l vīs/, -wīs/) n. small, flowering Alpine plant.

e•de/ma (i dē/mə) n. abnormal accumulation of fluid in body tissue.

E/den (ēd/n) n. garden where Adam and Eve first lived; paradise.

edge (ej) n., v., **edged, edging.** —n. **1.** border; brink. **2.** cutting side. —v. **3.** border. **4.** move sidewise. —edge/wise/, adv.

edg/y, adj., **edgier, edgiest.** nervous or tense.

ed/i•ble (ed/ə bəl) adj. fit to be eaten. —ed/i•bil/i•ty, n.

e/dict (ē/dikt) n. official decree.

ed/i•fice (ed/ə fis) n. building.

ed/i•fy/, v., **-fied, -fying.** instruct.

ed/it (ed/it) v. prepare for or direct publication of. —ed/i•tor, n.

e•di/tion (i dish/ən) n. one of various printings of a book.

ed/i•to/ri•al (ed/i tôr/ē əl) n. **1.** article in periodical presenting its point of view. —adj. **2.** of or written by editor. —ed/i•to/ri•al•ize/, v., **-ized, -izing.**

EDP, electronic data processing.

ed/u•cate/ (ej/ōō kāt/) v., **-cated, -cating.** provide with knowledge or instruction. —ed/u•ca/tion, n. —ed/u•ca/tion•al, adj.

-ee, suffix denoting person who is the object, beneficiary, or performer of an act, as addressee; grantee; escapee.

EEG, electroencephalogram.

eel (ēl) n. snakelike fish.

e'er (âr) adv. Poetic. ever.

ee/rie (ēr/ē) adj., **-rier, -riest.** weird; unsettling. —ee/ri•ly, adv.

ef•face/ (i fās/) v., **-faced, -facing.** wipe out. —ef•face/ment, n.

ef•fect/ (i fekt/) n. **1.** result; consequence. **2.** power to produce results. **3.** operation. **4.** (pl.) personal property. —v. **5.** bring about. —Usage. See AFFECT.

ef•fec/tive, adj. **1.** producing intended results. **2.** in force.

ef•fec/tive•ly, adv. **1.** in an effective way. **2.** for all practical purposes.

ef•fec/tu•al (-chōō əl) adj. **1.** capable; adequate. **2.** valid or binding.

ef•fem/i•nate (i fem/ə nit) adj. (of a man) having feminine traits.

ef/fer•vesce/ (ef/ər ves/) v., **-vesced, -vescing.** give off bubbles of gas. —ef/fer•ves/cence, n. —ef/fer•ves/cent, adj.

ef•fete/ (i fēt/) adj. worn out.

ef/fi•ca/cious (ef/i kā/shəs) adj. effective. —ef/fi•ca•cy (-kə sē) n.

ef•fi/cient (i fish/ənt) adj. acting effectively. —ef•fi/cien•cy, n.

ef/fi•gy (ef/i jē) n., pl. **-gies.** visual representation of person.

ef/flu•ent (ef/lōō ənt) n. something that flows out.

ef/fort (ef/ərt) n. **1.** exertion of power. **2.** attempt.

ef•fron/ter•y (i frun/tə rē) n., pl. **-te-ries.** impudence.

ef•fu/sion (i fyōō/zhən) n. free expression of feelings. —ef•fu/sive, adj.

e.g., for example.

e•gal/i•tar/i•an (i gal/i târ/ē ən) adj. having all persons equal in status.

egg (eg) n. **1.** reproductive body produced by animals. —v. **2.** encourage.

egg/head/, n. Slang. impractical intellectual.

egg/nog/ (-nog/) n. drink containing eggs, milk, etc.

egg/plant/, n. purple, egg-shaped fruit, eaten as a vegetable.

e/go (ē/gō) n. self.

e/go•cen/tric (-sen/trik) adj. self-centered.

e/go•ism, n. thinking only in terms of oneself. —e/go•ist, n.

e/go•tism (ē/gə tiz/əm) n. vanity. —e/go•tist, n. —e/go•tis/tic, e/go•tis/ti•cal, adj.

e•gre/gious (i grē/jəs) adj. flagrant.

e/gress (ē/gres) n. exit.

e/gret (ē/grit) n. kind of heron.

E•gyp/tian (i jip/shən) n. native or citizen of Egypt. —E•gyp/tian, adj.

eh (ā, e) interj. (exclamation of surprise or doubt).

ei/der duck (ī/dər) northern sea duck yielding eiderdown.

eight (āt) n., adj. seven plus one. —eighth, adj., n.

eight•een/ (ā/tēn/) n., adj. ten plus eight. —eight•eenth/, adj., n.

eight/y, n., adj. ten times eight. —eight/i•eth, adj., n.

ei/ther (ē/thər, ī/thər) adj., pron. **1.** one or the other of two. —conj. **2.** (introducing an alternative) —adv. **3.** (after negative clauses joined by and, or, nor.) —Pronunciation. The pronunciations (ē/thər) for the word EITHER and (nē/thər) for the word NEITHER, with the vowel of see, are the usual ones in American English. The pronunciations (ī/thər) and (nī/thər), with the vowel of sigh, occur occasionally in the U.S., chiefly in the speech of the educated and in the standard English of radio and television. Since the 19th century, the (ī) has been the more common pronunciation in standard British speech.

e•jac/u•late/ (i jak/yə lāt/) v., **-lated, -lating. 1.** exclaim. **2.** eject; discharge. —e•jac/u•la/tion, n.

e•ject/ (i jekt/) v. force out.

eke (ēk) v., **eked, eking. eke out, 1.** supplement. **2.** make (livelihood) with difficulty.

EKG, 1. electrocardiogram. **2.** electrocardiograph.

e•lab/o•rate, adj., v., **-rated, -rating.** —adj. (i lab/ər it) **1.** done with care and detail. —v. (-ə rāt′) **2.** supply details; work out.

é·lan′ (ā län′, ā län′) n. dashing spirit.

e·lapse′ (i laps′) v., **elapsed, elapsing.** (of time) pass; slip by.

e·las′tic (i las′tik) adj. **1.** springy. —n. **2.** material containing rubber.

e·late′ (i lāt′) v., **elated, elating.** put in high spirits. —e·la′tion, n.

el′bow (el′bō) n. **1.** joint where arm bends. —v. **2.** jostle.

elbow grease, hard work.

el′bow·room′, n. space to move or work freely.

eld′er (el′dər) adj. **1.** older. —n. **2.** older person. **3.** small tree bearing clusters of **el′der·ber′ries.**

eld′er·ly, adj. rather old.

eld′est (el′dist) adj. oldest.

e·lect′ (i lekt′) v. **1.** select by vote. —adj. **2.** selected. —n. **3.** (pl.) persons chosen. —e·lec′tion, n.

e·lec′tion·eer′, v. work for candidate in an election.

e·lec′tor·al college (-tər əl) body of special voters (**electors**) chosen to elect president and vice-president of U.S.

e·lec′tor·ate (-tər it) n. voters.

e·lec′tri′cian (i lek trish′ən, ē′lek-) n. one who installs or repairs electrical systems.

e·lec·tric′i·ty (-tris′i tē) n. **1.** agency producing certain phenomena as light, heat, attraction, etc. **2.** electric current. —e·lec′tric, e·lec′tri·cal, adj. —e·lec′tri·cal·ly, adv. —e·lec′tri·fy′, v., -fied, -fying.

e·lec′tro·car′di·o·gram′ (i lek′trō-kär′dē ə gram′) n. graphic record of heart action.

e·lec′tro·car′di·o·graph′, n. instrument for making electrocardiograms.

e·lec′tro·cute′ (i lek′trə kyōōt′) v., -cuted, -cuting. kill by electricity.

e·lec′trode (i lek′trōd) n. conductor through which current enters or leaves electric device.

e·lec′tro·en·ceph′a·lo·gram′ (i lek′trō en sef′ə lə gram′) n. graphic record of brain action.

e·lec′tro·en·ceph′a·lo·graph′, instrument for making electro-encephalograms.

e·lec·trol′o·gist (i lek trol′ə jist) n. person trained in electrolysis for removing unwanted hair, moles, etc.

e·lec·trol′y·sis (-ə sis) n. **1.** decomposition by electric current. **2.** destruction by electric current.

e·lec′tro·lyte′ (-trə līt′) n. substance that conducts electricity when melted or dissolved.

e·lec′tro·mag′net (i lek′trō-) n. device with iron or steel core made magnetic by electric current in surrounding coil. —e·lec′tro·mag·net′ic, adj.

e·lec′tron (i lek′tron) n. minute particle containing a unit of negative electricity.

electronic mail, e-mail.

e·lec·tron′ics, n. science dealing with development of devices involving flow of electrons. —e·lec·tron′ic, adj. —e·lec·tron′i·cal·ly, adv.

el′e·gant (el′i gənt) adj. luxurious or refined. —el′e·gance, n.

el′e·gy (el′i jē) n., pl. -gies. poem of mourning. —el′e·gi′ac (-jī′ak), adj.

el′e·ment (el′ə mənt) n. **1.** part of whole. **2.** rudiment. **3.** suitable environment. **4.** (pl.) atmospheric forces. **5.** substance that cannot be broken down chemically. **6.** (pl.) bread and wine of the Eucharist.

el′e·men′ta·ry (-tə rē) adj. of or dealing with elements or rudiments.

elementary school, school giving elementary instruction in six or eight grades.

el′e·phant (el′ə fənt) n. large mammal with long trunk and tusks.

el′e·phan′tine (el′ə fan′tēn, -tīn) adj. **1.** huge. **2.** clumsy.

el′e·vate′ (el′ə vāt′) v., -vated, -vating. **1.** raise higher. **2.** exalt.

el′e·va′tion, n. **1.** high place. **2.** height. **3.** drawing of vertical face.

el′e·va′tor, n. **1.** platform for lifting. **2.** grain storage place.

e·lev′en (i lev′ən) n., adj. ten plus one. —e·lev′enth, adj., n.

elf (elf) n., pl. **elves.** tiny mischievous sprite. —elf′in, adj.

e·lic′it (i lis′it) v. draw forth; evoke.

e·lide′ (i līd′) v., -lided, -liding. omit in pronunciation.

el′i·gi·ble (el′i jə bəl) adj. fit to be chosen. —el′i·gi·bil′i·ty, n.

e·lim′i·nate′ (i lim′ə nāt′) v., -nated, -nating. get rid of.

e·lite′ (i lēt′, ā lēt′) adj. **1.** chosen or regarded as finest. —n. **2.** (sing. or pl.) elite group of persons.

e·lit′ism, n. rule by an elite. —e·lit′ist, n., adj.

e·lix′ir (i lik′sər) n. preparation supposed to prolong life.

elk (elk) n. large deer.

el·lipse′ (i lips′) n. closed plane curve forming regular oblong figure.

el·lip′sis (i lip′sis) n., pl. -ses. omission of word or words.

elm (elm) n. large shade tree.

el′o·cu′tion (el′ə kyōō′shən) n. art of speaking in public.

e·lon′gate (i lông′gāt) v., -gated, -gating. lengthen. —e·lon·ga′tion, n.

e·lope′ (i lōp′) v., eloped, eloping. run off with lover to be married. —e·lope′ment, n.

el′o·quent (el′ə kwənt) adj. fluent and forcible. —el′o·quence, n.

else (els) adv. **1.** instead. **2.** in addition. **3.** otherwise.

else′where, adv. somewhere else.

e·lu′ci·date′ (i lōō′si dāt′) v., -dated, -dating. explain. —e·lu′ci·da′tion, n. —e·lu′ci·da′tor, n.

e·lude′ (i lōōd′) v., eluded, eluding. **1.** avoid cleverly. **2.** baffle. —e·lu′sive, adj. —Usage. See ESCAPE.

e·ma′ci·ate′ (i mā′shē āt′) v., -ated, -ating. make thin. —e·ma′ci·a′tion, n.

e′·mail′ (ē′māl′) n. **1.** system for sending messages between computers. **2.** message sent by e-mail. —v. **3.** send message to by e-mail. Also, **E-mail.**

em′a·nate′ (em′ə nāt′) v., -nated, -nating. come forth.

e·man′ci·pate′ (i man′sə pāt′) v., -pated, -pating. liberate. —e·man′ci·pa′tion, n.

e·mas′cu·late′ (i mas′kyə lāt′) v., -lated, -lating. **1.** castrate. **2.** weaken. —e·mas′cu·la′tion, n.

em·balm′ (em bäm′) v. treat (dead body) to prevent decay. —em·balm′er, n.

em·bank′ment (em bank′mənt) n. long earthen mound.

em·bar′go (em bär′gō) n., pl. -goes. government restriction of movement of ships or goods.

em·bark′ (em bärk′) v. **1.** put or go on board ship. **2.** start. —em′bar·ka′tion, n.

em·bar′rass (em bar′əs) v. **1.** make self-conscious or ashamed. **2.** complicate. —em·bar′rass·ment, n.

em·bas′sy (em′bə sē) n., pl. -sies. **1.** ambassador and staff. **2.** headquarters of ambassador.

em·bat′tled (em bat′ld) adj. prepared for or engaged in conflict.

em·bed′ (em bed′) v., -bedded, -bedding. fix in surrounding mass.

em·bel′lish (em bel′ish) v. decorate. —em·bel′lish·ment, n.

em′ber (em′bər) n. live coal.

em·bez′zle (em bez′əl) v., -zled, -zling. steal (money entrusted). —em·bez′zle·ment, n.

em·bit′ter (em bit′ər) v. make bitter.

em·bla′zon (em blā′zən) v. decorate, as with heraldic devices.

em′blem (em′bləm) n. symbol.

em·bod′y, v., -bodied, -bodying. **1.** put in concrete form. **2.** comprise. —em·bod′i·ment, n.

em′bo·lism (em′bə liz′əm) n. closing off of blood vessel, as by gas bubble or fat globule.

em·boss′ (em bôs′) v. ornament with raised design.

em·brace′ (em brās′) v., -braced, -bracing. —v. **1.** clasp in arms. **2.** accept willingly. **3.** include. —n. **4.** act of embracing.

em·broi′der (em broi′dər) v. decorate with needlework. —em·broi′der·y, n.

em·broil′, v. involve in strife.

em′bry·o′ (em′brē ō′) n., pl. -bryos. organism in first stages of development. —em′bry·on′ic, adj.

em·cee′ (em′sē′) n., v. -ceed, -ceeing. —n. **1.** master of ceremonies; person who conducts an event, as a banquet. —v. **2.** act as emcee.

e·mend′ (i mend′) v. correct.

em′er·ald (em′ər əld) n. **1.** green gem. **2.** of a clear, deep green.

e·merge′ (i mûrj′) v., emerged, emerging. come forth or into notice. —e·mer′gence, n.

e·mer′gen·cy (i mûr′jən sē) n., pl. -cies. urgent situation requiring action.

em′er·y (em′ə rē) n. mineral used for grinding, etc.

e·met′ic (i met′ik) n. medicine that induces vomiting.

em′i·grate′ (em′i grāt′) v., -grated, -grating. leave one's country to settle in another. —em′i·gra′tion, n.

é′mi·gré′ (em′i grā′) n. emigrant who flees esp. for political reasons.

em′i·nence (em′ə nəns) n. high repute. —em′i·nent, adj.

em′is·sar′y (em′ə ser′ē) n., pl. -saries. agent on mission.

e·mit′ (i mit′) v., emitted, emitting. send forth. —e·mis′sion, n.

e·mol′lient (i mol′yənt) adj. **1.** softening; soothing. —n. **2.** emollient substance.

e·mol′u·ment (i mol′yə mənt) n. salary.

e·mote′ (i mōt′) v., emoted, emoting. show emotion in or as if in acting. —e·mot′er, n.

e·mo′tion (i mō′shən) n. state of feeling. —e·mo′tion·al, adj.

em′pa·thy (em′pə thē) n. sensitive awareness of another's feelings. —em′pa·thize′, v.

em′per·or (em′pər ər) n. ruler of empire. —em′press, n.fem.

em′pha·sis (em′fə sis) n., pl. -ses. greater importance; stress. —em·phat′ic (-fat′ik) adj. —em·phat′i·cal·ly, adv. —em′pha·size′, v.

em′phy·se′ma (em′fə sē′mə) n. chronic lung disease.

em′pire (em′pīr) n. nations under one ruler.

em·pir′i·cal (em pir′i kəl) *adj.* drawing on experience or observation only.

em·ploy′ (em ploi′) *v.* **1.** use or hire. —*n.* **2.** employment. —**em·ploy′ee,** *n.* —**em·ploy′er,** *n.* —**em·ploy′ment,** *n.*

em·po′ri·um (em pôr′ē əm) *n.* large store.

em·pow′er, *v.* **1.** authorize to act for one. **2.** enable. —**em·pow′er·ment,** *n.*

emp′ty (emp′tē) *adj.,* **-tier, -tiest,** *v.,* **-tied, -tying.** —*adj.* **1.** containing nothing. —*v.* **2.** deprive of contents. **3.** become empty.

empty nest syndrome, depressed state felt by some parents after their children have grown up and left home.

EMT, emergency medical technician.

e′mu (ē′myōō) *n.* large flightless Australian bird.

em′u·late′ (em′yə lāt′) *v.,* **-lated, -lating.** try to equal or surpass.

e·mul′si·fy′ (i mul′sə fī′) *v.,* **-fied, -fying.** make into emulsion.

e·mul′sion (-shən) *n.* **1.** milklike mixture of liquids. **2.** light-sensitive layer on film.

en-, prefix meaning: **1.** put into or on, as *enthrone.* **2.** cover or surround with, as *encircle.* **3.** make or cause to be, as *enlarge.*

en·a′ble (en ā′bəl) *v.,* **-bled, -bling.** give power, means, etc., to.

en·act′, *v.* **1.** make into law. **2.** act the part of. —**en·act′ment,** *n.*

en·am′el (i nam′əl) *n., v.,* **-eled, -eling.** —*n.* **1.** glassy coating fused to metal, etc. **2.** paint giving a glossy surface. **3.** surface of teeth. —*v.* **4.** apply enamel to.

en·am′or (i nam′ər) *v.* fill with love.

en·camp′, *v.,* settle in camp. —**en·camp′ment,** *n.*

en·cap′su·late′ (en kap′sə lāt′) *v.,* **-lated, -lating.** summarize; condense.

en·case′ (en kās′) *v.,* **-cased, -casing.** enclose in or as if in a case.

-ence, suffix meaning: act or fact (*abhorrence*); state or quality (*absence*).

en·ceph′a·li′tis (en sef′ə lī′tis) *n.* inflammation of the brain.

en·chant′ (en chant′) *v.* bewitch; charm. —**en·chant′ment,** *n.*

en′chi·la′da (en′chə lä′də) *n.* food consisting of a tortilla rolled around a filling, usu. with a chili-flavored sauce.

en·cir′cle, *v.,* **-cled, -cling.** surround.

encl., **1.** enclosed. **2.** enclosure.

en′clave (en′klāv, än′-) *n.* country, etc., surrounded by alien territory.

en·close′ (en klōz′) *v.,* **-closed, -closing.** **1.** close in on all sides. **2.** put in envelope. —**en·clo′sure,** *n.*

en·code′, *v.,* **-coded, -coding.** convert into code.

en·co′mi·um (en kō′mē əm) *n., pl.* **-miums, -mia.** praise; eulogy.

en·com′pass (en kum′pəs) *v.* **1.** encircle. **2.** contain.

en′core (äng′kôr, än′-) *interj.* **1.** again! bravo! —*n.* **2.** additional song, etc.

en·coun′ter (en koun′tər) *v.* **1.** meet, esp. unexpectedly. —*n.* **2.** casual meeting. **3.** combat.

en·cour′age (en kûr′ij, -kur′-) *v.,* **-aged, -aging.** inspire or help. —**en·cour′age·ment,** *n.*

en·croach′ (en krōch′) *v.* trespass.

en·cum′ber (en kum′bər) *v.* impede; burden. —**en·cum′brance,** *n.*

en·cyc′li·cal (en sik′li kəl) *n.* letter from Pope to bishops.

en·cy′clo·pe′di·a (en sī′klə pē′dē ə) *n.* reference book giving information on many topics. —**en·cy′clo·pe′dic,** *adj.*

end (end) *n.* **1.** extreme or concluding part. **2.** close. **3.** purpose. **4.** result. —*v.* **5.** bring or come to an end. **6.** result. —**end′less,** *adj.*

en·dan′ger (en dān′jər) *v.* expose to danger.

en·dear′ (en dēr′) *v.* make beloved.

en·deav′or (en dev′ər) *v., n.* attempt.

en·dem′ic (en dem′ik) *adj.* belonging to a particular people or place.

end′ing (en′ding) *n.* close.

en′dive (en′dīv, än dēv′) *n.* plant for salad.

en′do·crine (en′də krin, -krīn′) *adj.* secreting internally into the blood or lymph.

en·dorse′ (en dôrs′) *v.,* **-dorsed, -dorsing.** **1.** approve or support. **2.** sign on back of (a check, etc.).

en·dow′ (en dou′) *v.* **1.** give permanent fund to. **2.** equip.

en·dure′ (en dōōr′, -dyōōr′) *v.,* **-dured, -during.** **1.** tolerate. **2.** last. —**en·dur′ance,** *n.*

en′e·ma (en′ə mə) *n.* liquid injection into rectum.

en′em·y (en′ə mē) *n., pl.* **-mies.** adversary; opponent.

en′er·gize′ (en′ər jīz′) *v.,* **-gized, -gizing.** give energy to.

en′er·gy (-jē) *n., pl.* **-gies.** capacity for activity; vigor. —**en·er·get′ic** (-jet′ik) *adj.*

en′er·vate′ (en′ər vāt′) *v.,* **-vated, -vating.** weaken.

en·fee′ble (en fē′bəl) *v.,* **-bled, -bling.** weaken.

en·fold′ (en fōld′) *v.* wrap around.

en·force′ (en fôrs′) *v.,* **-forced, -forcing.** compel obedience to. —**en·force′ment,** *n.* —**en·forc′er,** *n.*

en·fran′chise (en fran′chīz) *v.,* **-chised, -chising.** grant citizenship to.

en·gage′ (en gāj′) *v.,* **-gaged, -gaging.** **1.** occupy. **2.** hire. **3.** please. **4.** betroth. **5.** interlock with. **6.** enter into conflict with. —**en·gaged′,** *adj.* —**en·gage′ment,** *n.*

en·gag′ing, *adj.* attractive.

en·gen′der (en jen′dər) *v.* cause.

en′gine (en′jən) *n.* **1.** machine for converting energy into mechanical work. **2.** locomotive.

en′gi·neer′ (en′jə nēr′) *n.* **1.** expert in engineering. **2.** engine operator. —*v.* **3.** contrive.

en′gi·neer′ing, *n.* practical application of physics, chemistry, etc.

Eng′lish (ing′glish; *often* -lish) *n.* language of the people of Great Britain, Australia, the U.S., etc. —**Eng′lish,** *adj.*

en·gorge′ (en gôrj′) *v.,* **-gorged, -gorging.** fill or congest, esp. with blood. —**en·gorge′ment,** *n.*

en·grave′ (en grāv′) *v.,* **-graved, -graving.** cut into hard surface. —**en·grav′er,** *n.* —**en·grav′ing,** *n.*

en·gross′ (en grōs′) *v.* occupy wholly.

en·gulf′ (en gulf′) *v.* swallow up.

en·hance′ (en hans′) *v.,* **-hanced, -hancing.** improve.

e·nig′ma (ə nig′mə) *n.* something puzzling. —**en·ig·mat′ic,** *adj.*

en·join′ (en join′) *v.* command or prohibit. —**en·join′der,** *n.*

en·joy′ (en joi′) *v.* find pleasure in or for. —**en·joy′a·ble,** *adj.* —**en·joy′ment,** *n.*

en·large′ (en lärj′) *v.,* **-larged, -larging.** make or grow larger. —**en·large′ment,** *n.*

en·light′en (en līt′n) *v.* impart knowledge to.

en·list′ (en list′) *v.* enroll for service. —**en·list′ment,** *n.*

en·liv′en (en līv′vən) *v.* make active.

en masse′ (än mas′, äN) in a mass; all together.

en·mesh′ (en mesh′) *v.* entangle.

en′mi·ty (en′mi tē) *n., pl.* **-ties.** hatred.

en·nui′ (än wē′) *n.* boredom.

e·nor′mi·ty (i nôr′mi tē) *n., pl.* **-ties.** **1.** extreme wickedness. **2.** grievous crime; atrocity.

e·nor′mous (-məs) *adj.* huge.

e·nough′ (i nuf′) *adj.* **1.** adequate. —*n.* **2.** adequate amount. —*adv.* **3.** sufficiently.

en·quire′ (en kwīr′) *v.,* **-quired, -quiring.** inquire. —**en·quir′y,** *n.*

en·rage′ (en rāj′) *v.,* **-raged, -raging.** make furious.

en·rap′ture (en rap′chər) *v.,* **-tured, -turing.** delight.

en·rich′ (en rich′) *v.* make rich or better. —**en·rich′ment,** *n.*

en·roll′ (en rōl′) *v.* take into group or organization. —**en·roll′ment,** *n.*

en route (än rōōt′) on the way.

en·sconce′ (en skons′) *v.,* **-sconced, -sconcing.** settle securely or snugly.

en·sem′ble (än säm′bəl) *n.* assembled whole.

en·shrine′ (en shrīn′) *v.,* **-shrined, -shrining.** cherish.

en·shroud′ (en shroud′) *v.* conceal.

en·sign′ (en′sīn; *Mil.* -sən) *n.* **1.** flag. **2.** lowest commissioned naval officer.

en·slave′ (en slāv′) *v.,* **-slaved, -slaving.** make slave of.

en·snare′ (en snär′) *v.,* **-snared, -snaring.** entrap.

en·sue′ (en sōō′) *v.,* **-sued, -suing.** follow.

en·sure′ (en shōōr′) *v.,* **-sured, -suring.** make certain; secure.

-ent, suffix equivalent to *-ant,* as *president, insistent.*

en·tail′ (en tāl′) *v.* involve.

en·tan′gle (en tang′gəl) *v.,* **-gled, -gling.** involve; entrap.

en·tente′ (än tänt′) *n.* international agreement on policy.

en′ter (en′tər) *v.* **1.** come or go in. **2.** begin. **3.** record.

en′ter·i′tis (en′tə rī′tis) *n.* inflammation of the intestines.

en′ter·prise′ (en′tər prīz′) *n.* **1.** project. **2.** initiative.

en′ter·pris′ing, *adj.* showing initiative.

en′ter·tain′ (en′tər tān′) *v.* **1.** amuse. **2.** treat as guest. **3.** hold in mind. —**en′ter·tain′er,** *n.* —**en′ter·tain′ment,** *n.*

en·thrall′ (en thrôl′) *v.* **1.** hold by fascination; captivate. **2.** enslave.

en·throne′ (en thrōn′) *v.,* **-throned, -throning.** place on or as if on a throne. —**en·throne′ment,** *n.*

en·thuse′ (en thōōz′) *v.,* **-thused, -thusing.** show enthusiasm.

en·thu′si·asm (-thōō′zē az′əm) *n.* lively interest. —**en·thu′si·ast′,** *n.* —**en·thu′si·as′tic,** *adj.*

en·tice′ (en tīs′) *v.,* **-ticed, -ticing.** lure. —**en·tice′ment,** *n.*

en·tire′ (en tī′ər) *adj.* whole. —**en·tire′ly,** *adv.* —**en·tire′ty,** *n.*

en·ti′tle, *v.,* **-tled, -tling.** permit (one) to claim something.

en′ti·ty (en′ti tē) *n., pl.* **-ties.** real or whole thing.

en·tomb′, *v.* bury.

en′to·mol′o·gy (en′tə mol′ə jē) *n.* study of insects.

en′tou·rage′ (än′tōō räzh′) *n.* group of personal attendants.

en·trails (en′trālz, -trəlz) *n.pl.* internal parts of body, esp. intestines.

en·trance, *n.*, *v.*, **-tranced, -trancing.** —*n.* (en′trans) **1.** act of entering. **2.** place for entering. **3.** admission. —*v.* (en trans′) **4.** charm.

en·trant (en′trənt) *n.* person who enters competition or contest.

en·trap′ (en trap′) *v.*, **-trapped, -trapping. 1.** catch in a trap. **2.** entice into guilty situation.

en·treat′ (en trēt′) *v.* implore.

en·treat′y, *n.*, *pl.* **-ies.** earnest request.

en·tree (än′trā) *n.* **1.** main dish of meal. **2.** access.

en·trench′ (en trench′) *v.* fix in strong position.

en·tre·pre·neur′ (än′trə prə nûr′) *n.* independent business manager. —**en′·tre·pre·neur′i·al**, *adj.*

en·tro·py (en′trə pē) *n.* **1.** measure of the amount of energy unavailable for useful work in a thermo-

dynamic process. **2.** tendency toward disorder in any system.

en·trust′ (en trust′) *v.* give in trust.

en·try (en′trē) *n.*, *pl.* **-tries. 1.** entrance. **2.** recorded statement, etc. **3.** contestant.

en·twine′ (en twīn′) *v.*, **-twined, -twining.** twine around or together.

e·nu′mer·ate′ (i nōō′mə rāt′, i nyōō′-) *v.*, **-ated, -ating.** list; count. —**e·nu′mer·a′tion,** *n.*

e·nun′ci·ate′ (i nun′sē āt′) *v.*, **-ated, -ating.** say distinctly.

en·vel′op (en vel′əp) *v.* surround.

en′ve·lope′ (en′və lōp′, än′-) *n.* covering for letter.

en·vi′ron·ment (en vī′rən mənt, -vī′ərn-) *n.* surrounding things, conditions, etc. —**en·vi′ron·men′tal** (-men′tl) *adj.*

en·vi′ron·men′tal·ist (-men′tl ist) *n.* person working to protect environment from pollution, etc.

en·vi′rons, *n.pl.* outskirts.

en·vis·age (en viz′ij) *v.*, **-aged, -aging.** form mental picture of. Also, **en·vi′sion.**

en′voy (en′voi, än′-) *n.* **1.** diplomatic agent. **2.** messenger.

en′vy (en′vē) *n.*, *pl.* **-vies,** *v.*, **-vied, -vying.** —*n.* **1.** discontent at another's good fortune. **2.** thing coveted. —*v.* **3.** regard with envy. —**en′vi·ous,** *adj.* —**en′vi·ous·ly,** *adv.*

en′zyme (en′zīm) *n.* bodily substance capable of producing chemical change in other substances.

e′on (ē′ən, ē′on) *n.* long period of time.

EPA, Environmental Protection Agency.

ep′au·let′ (ep′ə let′, -lit) *n.* shoulder piece worn on uniform. Also, **ep′au·lette′.**

e·phem′er·al (i fem′ər əl) *adj.* brief; transitory.

ep′ic (ep′ik) *adj.* **1.** describing heroic deeds. —*n.* **2.** epic poem.

ep′i·cen′ter (ep′ə sen′tər) *n.* point directly above center of earthquake.

ep′i·cure′ (ep′i kyŏŏr′) *n.* connoisseur of food and drink.

ep′i·dem′ic (ep′i dem′ik) *adj.* **1.** affecting many persons at once. —*n.* **2.** epidemic disease.

ep′i·der′mis, *n.* outer layer of skin.

ep′i·glot′tis (-glot′is) *n.*, *pl.* **-glottises, -glottides** (-glot′i dēz′). thin structure that covers larynx during swallowing.

ep′i·gram′ (ep′i gram′) *n.* witty statement.

ep′i·lep′sy (ep′ə lep′sē) *n.* nervous

disease often marked by convulsions. —**ep′i·lep′tic,** *adj.*, *n.*

ep′i·logue′ (ep′ə lôg′) *n.* concluding part or speech.

e·piph′a·ny (i pif′ə nē) *n.* **1.** appearance. **2.** sudden realization. **3.** (*cap.*) festival, Jan. 6, commemorating the Wise Men's visit to Christ.

e·pis′co·pal (-pal) *adj.* **1.** governed by bishops. **2.** (*cap.*) designating Anglican Church. —**E·pis′co·pa′lian** (-pā′lē ən) *n.*, *adj.*

ep′i·sode′ (ep′ə sōd′) *n.* incident. —**ep′i·sod′ic,** (-sod′ik) *adj.*

e·pis′tle (i pis′əl) *n.* letter.

ep′i·taph′ (ep′i taf′) *n.* inscription on tomb.

ep′i·thet′ (ep′ə thet′) *n.* descriptive term for person or things.

ep′i·tome (i pit′ə mē) *n.* **1.** summary. **2.** typical specimen. —**e·pit′o·mize′,** *v.*, **-mized, -mizing.**

e plu′ri·bus u′num (e plōō′ri bŏōs/ ōō′nŏōm; *Eng.* ē′ plōōr′ə bəs yōō′nəm) *Latin.* out of many, one (motto of the U.S.).

ep′och (ep′ək) *n.* distinctive period of time. —**ep′och·al,** *adj.*

ep·ox′y (i pok′sē) *n.*, *pl.* **-ies.** tough synthetic resin used in glues.

Ep′som salts (ep′səm) salt used esp. as a cathartic.

eq′ua·ble (ek′wə bəl) *adj.* even.

e′qual (ē′kwəl) *adj.*, *n.*, *v.*, **equaled, equaling.** —*adj.* **1.** alike in quantity, rank, size, etc. **2.** uniform. **3.** adequate. —*n.* **4.** one that is equal to. —*v.* **5.** be equal to. —**e·qual′i·ty,** *n.* —**e′qual·ize′,** *v.*

equal sign, symbol (=) indicating equality between terms. Also, **equals sign.**

e′qua·nim′i·ty (ē′kwə nim′i tē) *n.* calmness.

e·quate′ (i kwāt′) *v.*, **equated, equating.** make or consider as equal.

e·qua′tion (i kwā′zhən) *n.* expression of equality of two quantities.

e·qua′tor (-tər) *n.* imaginary circle around earth midway between poles. —**e′qua·to′ri·al,** *adj.*

e·ques′tri·an (i kwes′trē ən) *adj.* **1.** of horse riders or horsemanship. —*n.* **2.** Also, *for a woman,* **e·ques′tri·enne′.** horse rider.

e′qui·dis′tant (ē′kwi dis′tənt) *adj.* equally distant.

e′qui·lat′er·al, *adj.* having all sides equal.

e′qui·lib′ri·um (-lib′rē əm) *n.*, *pl.* **-riums, -ria.** balance.

e′quine (ē′kwīn) *adj.* of horses.

e′qui·nox′ (ē′kwə noks′) *n.* time when night and day are of equal length.

e·quip′ (i kwip′) *v.*, **equipped, equipping.** furnish. —**e·quip′ment,** *n.*

eq′ui·ta·ble (ek′wi tə bəl) *adj.* fair.

eq′ui·ty, *n.*, *pl.* **-ties. 1.** fairness. **2.** share.

e·quiv′a·lent (i kwiv′ə lənt) *adj.*, *n.* equal. —**e·quiv′a·lence,** *n.*

e·quiv′o·cal (i kwiv′ə kəl) *adj.* **1.** ambiguous. **2.** questionable.

e·quiv′o·cate′ (-kāt′) *v.*, **-cated, -cating.** express oneself ambiguously or indecisively. —**e·quiv′o·ca′tion,** *n.*

ER, emergency room.

-er, suffix meaning: person occupied with or working at something, as *roofer;* resident, as *southerner;* person or thing associated with particular characteristic or circumstance, as *teenager;* one that performs or is used in performing action, as *fertilizer.*

e′ra (ēr′ə, er′ə) *n.* period of time.

ERA, 1. Also, **era.** earned run average. **2.** Equal Rights Amendment.

e·rad′i·cate′ (i rad′i kāt′) *v.*, **-cated, -cating.** remove completely.

e·rase′ (i rās′) *v.*, **erased, erasing.** rub out. —**e·ras′a·ble,** *adj.* —**e·ras′er,** *n.* —**e·ra′sure,** *n.*

ere (âr) *prep., conj. Archaic.* before.

e·rect′ (i rekt′) *adj.* **1.** upright. —*v.* **2.** build.

e·rec′tion (-shən) *n.* **1.** something erected. **2.** erect state of an organ, as the penis.

erg (ûrg) *n.* unit of work or energy.

er′go (ûr′gō, er′gō) *conj., adv.* therefore.

er′go·nom′ics (ûr′gə nom′iks) *n.* applied science that coordinates workplace design and equipment with workers' needs.

er′mine (ûr′min) *n.* kind of weasel.

e·rode′ (i rōd′) *v.*, **eroded, eroding.** wear away. —**e·ro′sion,** *n.*

e·rog′e·nous (i roj′ə nəs) *adj.* sensitive to sexual stimulation.

e·rot′ic (i rot′ik) *adj.* **1.** of sexual love. **2.** arousing sexual desire. —**e·rot′i·cism** (-ə siz′əm) *n.*

e·rot′i·ca (-i kə) *n.pl.* erotic literature and art.

err (ûr, er) *v.* **1.** be mistaken. **2.** sin.

er′rand (er′ənd) *n.* trip for special purpose.

er′rant (er′ənt) *adj.* roving.

er·rat′ic (i rat′ik) *adj.* uncontrolled or irregular.

er·ra′tum (i rä′təm, i rat′əm) *n.*, *pl.* **-ta.** (*usually pl.*) error in printing.

er·ro′ne·ous (ə rō′nē əs, e rō′-) *adj.* incorrect.

er′ror (er′ər) *n.* **1.** mistake. **2.** sin.

er·satz′ (er zäts′) *adj.* artificial.

erst′while′, *adj.* former.

ERT, estrogen replacement therapy.

er′u·dite′ (er′yōō dīt′) *adj.* learned.

e·rupt′ (i rupt′) *v.* burst forth. —**e·rup′tion,** *n.*

-ery, suffix meaning: things or people collectively (*machinery; peasantry*); occupation, activity, or condition (*archery*); place for (*winery*); characteristic conduct (*prudery*).

es′ca·late′ (es′kə lāt′) *v.*, **-lated, -lating.** increase in intensity or size.

es′ca·la·tor, *n.* moving stairway.

es·cal′lop (e skol′əp, e skal′-) *v.* **1.** finish with scallops (def. 2) **2.** bake in breadcrumb-topped sauce. —*n.* **3.** scallop.

es′ca·pade′ (es′kə pād′) *n.* wild prank.

es·cape′ (i skāp′) *v.*, **-caped, -caping.** —*v.* **1.** get away. **2.** avoid; elude. —*n.* **3.** act or means of escaping. —**es·cap′ee,** *n.* —**Usage.** ESCAPE, ELUDE, EVADE mean to keep away from something. To ESCAPE is to manage to keep away from danger, pursuit, observation, etc.: *to escape punishment.* To ELUDE is to slip through an apparently tight net, and implies using skill or cleverness: *The fox eluded the hounds.* To EVADE is to turn aside from or go out of reach of a person or thing, usually by moving or directing attention elsewhere: *We evaded the traffic jam by taking an alternate route.*

es·cape′ment (i skāp′mənt) *n.* part of clock that controls speed.

es·cap′ism (i skāp′iz′əm) *n.* attempt to forget reality through fantasy. —**es·cap′ist,** *n.*, *adj.*

es′ca·role′ (es′kə rōl′) *n.* broadleaved endive.

es·carp′ment (i skärp′mənt) *n,* long clifflike ridge.

es·chew′ (es chōō′) *v.* avoid.

es·cort, *n.* (es′kôrt) **1.** accompanying person or persons. —*v.* (i skôrt′) **2.** accompany as escort.

es·cutch′eon (i skuch′ən) *n.* coat of arms.

Es′ki·mo′ (es′kə mō′) *n.* Arctic North American people or language.

ESL, English as a second language.

e·soph′a·gus (i sof′ə gəs) *n.*, *pl.* **-gi** (-jī′). tube connecting mouth and stomach.

es′o·ter′ic (es′ə ter′ik) *adj.* understood by a select few.

ESP, extrasensory perception.

esp., especially.

es′pa·drille′ (es′pə dril′) *n.* flat shoe with cloth upper and rope sole.

es·pe′cial (i spesh′əl) *adj.* special.

Es′pe·ran′to (es′pə rän′tō, -ran′-) *n.* artificial language based on major European languages.

es′pi·o·nage′ (es′pē ə näzh′, -nij) *n.* work or use of spies.

es′pla·nade′ (es′plə näd′, -nād′) *n.* open level space for public walks.

es·pouse′ (i spouz′, i spous′) *v.*, **-poused, -pousing. 1.** advocate. **2.** marry. —**es·pous′al,** *n.*

es·pres′so (e spres′ō) *n.* strong coffee made with steam.

es·prit′ de corps′ (e sprē′ də kôr′) sense of common purpose.

es·py′ (i spī′) *v.*, **-pied, -pying.** catch sight of.

Es·quire′ (es′kwīr′) *n. Brit.* title of respect after man's name, in the U.S. chiefly applied to lawyers. *Abbr.:* Esq.

es′say (n. (es′ā) **1.** literary composition. **2.** attempt. —*v.* (e sā′) **3.** try.

es′say·ist, *n.* writer of essays.

es′sence (es′əns) *n.* **1.** intrinsic nature. **2.** concentrated form of substance or thought.

es·sen′tial (ə sen′shəl) *adj.* **1.** necessary. —*n.* **2.** necessary thing.

es·sen′tial·ly, *adv.* basically; necessarily.

EST, Eastern Standard Time.

est., 1. established. **2.** estimate. **3.** estimated.

es·tab′lish (i stab′lish) *v.* **1.** set up permanently. **2.** prove.

es·tab′lish·ment, *n.* **1.** act of establishing. **2.** institution or business. **3.** (often cap.) group controlling government and social institutions.

es·tate′ (i stāt′) *n.* **1.** landed property. **2.** one's possessions.

es·teem′ (i stēm′) *v.* **1.** regard. —*n.* **2.** opinion.

es′ter (es′tər) *n.* chemical compound produced by reaction between an acid and an alcohol.

es′thete, *n.* aesthete.

es′ti·ma·ble (es′tə mə bəl) *adj.* worthy of high esteem.

es′ti·mate′ *v.*, **-mated, -mating,** *n.* —*v.* (es′tə māt′) **1.** calculate roughly. —*n.* (-mit) **2.** rough calculation. **3.** opinion. —**es′ti·ma′tion,** *n.*

es·trange′ (i strānj′) *v.*, **-tranged, -tranging.** alienate.

es′tro·gen (es′trə jən) *n.* any of several female sex hormones.

es′tu·ar′y (es′chōō er′ē) *n.*, *pl.* **-aries.** part of river affected by sea tides.

ETA, estimated time of arrival.

et al. (et al′, äl′, ôl′) and others.

et cet′er·a (et set′ər ə, se′trə) and so on. *Abbr.:* etc.

etch (ech) *v.* cut design into (metal, etc.) with acid. —**etch′ing,** *n.*

e·ter′nal (i tûr′nl) *adj.* **1.** without beginning or end. —*n.* **2.** (cap.) God. —**e·ter′ni·ty,** *n.*

eth′ane (eth′ān) *n.* flammable gas used chiefly as a fuel.

e′ther (ē′thər) *n.* **1.** colorless liquid used as an anesthetic. **2.** upper part of space.

e·the′re·al (i thēr′ē əl) *adj.* **1.** delicate. **2.** heavenly.

eth′ics (eth′ə sist) *n.pl.* principles of conduct. —**eth′i·cal,** *adj.*

eth′nic (eth′nik) *adj.* **1.** sharing a common culture. —*n.* **2.** member of minority group.

eth·nic′i·ty (-nis′i tē) *n.* ethnic traits or association.

eth·nol′o·gy (eth nol′ə jē) *n.* branch of anthropology dealing with cultural comparisons.

e·thol′o·gy (ē thol′ə jē) *n.* scientific study of animal behavior.

e′thos (ē′thos, eth′ōs) *n.* distinguishing characteristics of person, group, or culture.

eth′yl (eth′əl) *n.* fluid containing lead, added to gasoline.

et′i·quette (et′i kit, -ket′) *n.* conventions of social behavior.

et seq., and the following.

e′tude (ā′tōōd, ā′tyōōd) *n.* musical composition played to improve technique but also for its artistic merit.

et′y·mol′o·gy (et′ə mol′ə jē) *n.*, *pl.* **-gies.** history of word or words.

eu-, prefix meaning good, as *eugenics*.

eu′ca·lyp′tus (yōō′kə lip′təs) *n.*, *pl.* **-ti.** Australian tree.

Eu′cha·rist (yōō′kə rist) *n.* Holy Communion.

eu·gen′ics (yōō jen′iks) *n.* science of improving human race.

eu′lo·gy (yōō′lə jē) *n.*, *pl.* **-gies.** formal praise. —**eu′lo·gize′,** *v.*

eu′nuch (yōō′nək) *n.* castrated man.

eu′phe·mism (yōō′fə miz′əm) *n.* substitution of mild expression for blunt one. —**eu′phe·mis′tic,** *adj.*

eu′pho·ny (yōō′fə nē) *n.*, *pl.* **-nies.** pleasant sound. —**eu·pho′ni·ous** (-fō′nē əs) *adj.*

eu·pho′ri·a (yōō fôr′ē ə) *n.* strong feeling of happiness or well-being. —**eu·phor′ic,** *adj.*

Eur·a′sian (yōō rā′zhən) *adj.* of or originating in both Europe and Asia, or in the two considered as one continent.

eu·re′ka (yōō rē′kə) *interj.* (exclamation of triumph at a discovery.)

Eu′ro·pe′an (yōōr′ə pē′ən) *n.* native of Europe. —**Eu′ro·pe′an,** *adj.*

European plan, system of paying a fixed hotel rate that covers lodging only.

Eus·ta′chian tube (yōō stā′shən) (often l.c.) canal between middle ear and pharynx.

eu′tha·na′sia (yōō′thə nā′zhə) *n.* mercy killing.

e·vac′u·ate′ (i vak′yōō āt′) *v.*, **-ated, -ating. 1.** vacate; empty. **2.** remove. —**e·vac′u·a′tion,** *n.*

e·vade′ (i vād′) *v.*, **-vaded, -vading.** avoid or escape from by cleverness. —**e·va′sion,** *n.* —**e·va′sive,** *adj.* —**Usage.** See ESCAPE.

e·val′u·ate′ (i val′yōō āt′) *v.*, **-ated, -ating.** appraise.

ev′a·nes′cent (ev′ə nes′ənt) *adj.* fading away.

e′van·gel′i·cal (ē′van jel′i kəl, ev′ən-) *adj.* **1.** of or in keeping with Gospel. **2.** of those Protestant churches that stress personal conversion through faith.

e·van′ge·list (i van′jə list) *n.* **1.** preacher. **2.** One of the writers of Gospel. —**e·van′ge·lism,** *n.* —**e·van′ge·lize′,** *v.*

e·vap′o·rate′ (i vap′ə rāt′) *v.*, **-rated, -rating.** change into vapor.

eve (ēv) *n.* evening before.

e′ven (ē′vən) *adj.* **1.** smooth. **2.** uniform. **3.** equal. **4.** divisible by 2. **5.** calm. —*adv.* **6.** still; yet. **7.** indeed. —*v.* **8.** make even.

e′ven·hand′ed, *adj.* impartial; fair.

eve′ning (ēv′ning) *n.* early part of night; end of day.

evening star, bright planet, esp. Venus, visible around sunset.

e·vent′ (i vent′) *n.* anything that happens. —**e·vent′ful,** *adj.*

e·ven′tu·al (i ven′chōō əl) *adj.* final. —**e·ven′tu·al·ly,** *adv.*

e·ven′tu·al′i·ty, *n.*, *pl.* **-ties.** possible event.

ev′er (ev′ər) *adv.* at all times.

ev′er·glade′, *n.* tract of low, swampy ground.

ev′er·green′, *adj.* **1.** having its leaves always green. —*n.* **2.** evergreen plant.

ev′er·last′ing, *adj.* lasting forever or indefinitely.

eve′ry (ev′rē) *adj.* **1.** each. **2.** all possible. —**eve′ry·bod′y** (-bod′ē, -bud′ē), **eve′ry·one′,** *pron.* —**eve′ry·thing′,** *pron.* —**eve′ry·where′,** *adv.* —**eve′ry·day′,** *adj.*

e·vict′ (i vikt′) *v.* legally remove from property. —**e·vic′tion,** *n.*

ev′i·dence (ev′i dəns) *n.*, *v.*, **-denced, -dencing.** —*n.* **1.** grounds for belief. —*v.* **2.** prove.

ev′i·dent, *adj.* clearly so. —**ev′i·dent·ly** (ev′i dənt lē, ev′i dent′) *adv.*

e′vil (ē′vəl) *adj.* **1.** wicked. **2.** unfortunate. —**e′vil·do′er,** *n.*

evil eye, look thought capable of doing harm.

e·vince′ (i vins′) *v.*, **evinced, evincing.** show.

e·vis′cer·ate′ (i vis′ə rāt′) *v.*, **-ated, -ating. 1.** remove entrails of. **2.** deprive of vital or essential parts.

e·voke′ (i vōk′) *v.*, **evoked, evoking.** call forth. —**ev′o·ca′tion** (ev′ə kā′shən) *n.* —**e·voc′a·tive** (i vok′-) *adj.*

e·volve′ (i volv′) *v.*, **evolved, evolving.** develop gradually. —**ev′o·lu′tion,** *n.*

ewe (yōō) *n.* female sheep.

ew′er (yōō′ər) *n.* wide-mouthed pitcher.

ex-, prefix meaning: **1.** out of or from, as *export*. **2.** utterly or thoroughly, as *exacerbate*. **3.** former, as *ex-governor*.

ex., 1. example. **2.** except. **3.** exception. **4.** exchange.

ex·ac′er·bate′ (ig zas′ər bāt′, eksas′-) *v.*, **-bated, -bating.** make more severe or violent.

ex·act′ (ig zakt′) *adj.* **1.** precise; accurate. —*v.* **2.** demand; compel. —**ex·act′ing,** *adv.* severe.

ex·ag′ger·ate′ (ig zaj′ə rāt′) *v.*, **-ated, -ating.** magnify beyond truth.

ex·alt′ (ig zôlt′) *v.* **1.** elevate. **2.** extol. —**ex′al·ta′tion,** *n.*

ex·am′ (ig zam′) *n. Informal.* examination.

ex·am′ine (-in) *v.*, **-ined, -ining. 1.** investigate. **2.** test. **3.** interrogate. —**ex·am′i·na′tion,** *n.* —**ex·am′in·er,** *n.*

ex·am′ple (ig zam′pəl) *n.* **1.** typical one. **2.** model. **3.** illustration.

ex·as′per·ate′ (ig zas′pə rāt′) *v.*, **-ated, -ating.** make angry.

ex′ca·vate′ (eks′kə vāt′) *v.*, **-vated, -vating. 1.** dig out. **2.** unearth. —**ex′ca·va′tion,** *n.* —**ex′ca·va′tor,** *n.*

ex·ceed′ (ik sēd′) *v.* go beyond; surpass.

ex·ceed′ing·ly, adv. very.

ex·cel′ (ik sel′) v., **-celled, -celling.** do very well; be superior (to).

ex′cel·len·cy (ek′sə lən sē) n., pl. **-cies. 1.** (cap.) title of honor. **2.** excellence.

ex′cel·lent, adj. remarkably good. —**ex′cel·lence,** n.

ex·cept′ (ik sept′) prep. **1.** Also, **except′ing.** other than; excluding. —v. **2.** leave out; exclude. **3.** object. —**Usage.** See ACCEPT.

ex·cep′tion·a·ble, adj. causing objections.

ex·cep′tion·al, adj. unusual.

ex′cerpt, n. (ek′sûrpt) **1.** passage from longer writing. —v. (ik sûrpt′, ek′sûrpt) **2.** take (passage) from a book, film, etc.

ex·cess′, n. (ik ses′) **1.** amount over that required. —adj. (ek′ses) **2.** more than necessary, usual, or desirable.

ex·ces′sive, adj. more than desirable. —**ex·ces′sive·ly,** adv.

ex·change′ (iks chānj′) v., **-changed, -changing.** —v. **1.** change for something else. —n. **2.** act of exchanging. **3.** thing exchanged. **4.** trading place.

ex·cheq′uer (iks chek′ər) n. Brit. treasury.

ex′cise, n., v., **-cised, -cising.** —n. (ek′sīz) **1.** tax on certain goods. —v. (ik sīz′) **2.** cut out.

ex·cite′ (ik sīt′) v., **-cited, -citing. 1.** stir up. (emotions, etc.). **2.** cause. —**ex·cit′a·ble,** adj. —**ex·cite′ment,** n.

ex·claim′ (ik sklām′) v. cry out. —**ex′cla·ma′tion,** n.

ex·clude′ (ik sklōōd′) v., **-cluded, -cluding.** shut out. —**ex·clu′sion,** n.

ex·clu′sive (ik sklōō′siv) adj. **1.** belonging or pertaining to one. **2.** excluding others. **3.** stylish; chic.

ex′com·mu′ni·cate′ (eks′kə myōō′ ni kāt′) v., **-cated, -cating.** cut off from membership of church. —**ex′com·mu′ni·ca′tion,** n.

ex·co′ri·ate′ (ik skôr′ē āt′) v., **-ated, -ating.** denounce.

ex′cre·ment (ek′skrə mənt) n. bodily waste.

ex·cres′cence (ik skres′əns) n. abnormal growth. —**ex·cres′cent,** adj.

ex·crete′ (ik skrēt′) v., **-creted, -creting.** eliminate from body. —**ex·cre′tion,** n.

ex·cru′ci·at′·ing (ik skrōō′shē ā′ ting) adj. **1.** causing intense suffering. **2.** intense or extreme.

ex′cul·pate′ (ek′skul pāt′, ik skul′ pāt) v., **-pated, -pating.** free of blame. —**ex′cul·pa′tion,** n.

ex·cur′sion (ik skûr′zhən) n. short trip.

ex·cuse′, v., **-cused, -cusing.** —v. (ik skyōoz′) **1.** pardon. **2.** apologize for. **3.** justify. **4.** seek or grant release. —n. (ik skyōos′) **5.** reason for being excused.

ex′e·crate′ (ek′si krāt′) v., **-crated, -crating. 1.** abominate. **2.** curse. —**ex′e·cra·ble,** adj.

ex′e·cute′ (ek′si kyōōt′) v., **-cuted, -cuting. 1.** do. **2.** kill legally. —**ex′e·cu′tion,** n. —**ex′e·cu′tion·er,** n.

ex·ec′u·tive (ig zek′yə tiv) adj. **1.** responsible for directing affairs. —n. **2.** administrator.

ex·ec′u·tor (-tər) n. person named to carry out provisions of a will. —**ex·ec′u·trix′,** n.fem.

ex·em′plar (ig zem′plər, -plär) n. model or pattern.

ex·em′pla·ry (-plə rē) adj. worthy of imitation.

ex·em′pli·fy′ (-plə fī′) v., **-fied, -fying.** show or serve as example.

ex·empt′ (ig zempt′) v., adj. free from obligation. —**ex·emp′tion,** n.

ex′er·cise′ (ek′sər sīz′) n., v., **-cised, -cising.** —n. **1.** action to increase skill or strength. **2.** performance. **3.** (pl.) ceremony. —v. **4.** put through exercises. **5.** use.

ex·ert′ (ig zûrt′) v. put into action. —**ex·er′tion,** n.

ex·hale′ (eks hāl′) v., **-haled, -haling.** breathe out; emit breath.

ex·haust′ (ig zôst′) v. **1.** use up. **2.** fatigue greatly. —n. **3.** used gases from engine. —**ex·haus′tion,** n.

ex·haus′tive, adj. thorough.

ex·hib′it (ig zib′it) v., n. show; display. —**ex·hi·bi′tion** (ek′sə bish′ən) n. —**ex·hib′i·tor,** n.

ex′hi·bi′tion·ism (-bish′ə niz′əm) n. **1.** desire or tendency to display oneself. —**ex′hi·bi′tion·ist,** n.

ex·hil′a·rate′ (ig zil′ə rāt′) v., **-rated, -rating.** cheer; stimulate. —**ex·hil′a·ra′tion,** n.

ex·hort′ (ig zôrt′) v. advise earnestly. —**ex′hor·ta′tion** (eg′zôr tā′shən) n.

ex·hume′ (ig zōōm′, -zyōōm′) v., **-humed, -huming.** dig up a dead body, etc.

ex′i·gen·cy (ek′si jən sē) n., pl. **-cies.** urgent requirement. —**ex′i·gent,** adj.

ex′ile (eg′zīl, ek′sīl) n., v., **-iled, -iling.** —n. **1.** enforced absence from one's country or home. **2.** one so absent. —v. **3.** send into exile.

ex·ist′ (ig zist′) v. be; live. —**ex·ist′ ence,** n. —**ex·ist′ent,** adj.

ex′is·ten′tial (eg′zi sten′shəl, ek′si-) adj. of human life; based on experience.

ex′is·ten′tial·ism, n. philosophy that stresses personal liberty and responsibility. —**ex′is·ten′tial·ist,** n., adj.

ex′it (eg′zit, ek′sit) n. **1.** way out. **2.** departure. —v. **3.** leave.

exo-, prefix meaning outside or outer, as exosphere.

ex′o·crine (ek′sə krin, -krīn′) adj. secreting externally through a duct.

ex′o·dus (ek′sə dəs) n. departure.

ex′ of·fi′ci·o (eks′ ə fish′ē ō′) because of one's office.

ex·on′er·ate′ (ig zon′ə rāt′) v., **-ated, -ating.** free of blame.

ex·or′bi·tant (ig zôr′bi tənt) adj. excessive, esp. in cost.

ex′or·cise′ (ek′sôr sīz′, -sər-) v., **-cised, -cising.** expel (evil spirit). —**ex′or·cism,** n. —**ex′or·cist,** n.

ex′o·sphere′ (ek′sō sfēr′) n. highest region of the atmosphere.

ex·ot′ic (ig zot′ik) adj. **1.** foreign; alien. **2.** strikingly unusual.

ex·pand′ (ik spand′) v. increase; spread out. —**ex·pan′sion,** n.

ex·panse′ (ik spans′) n. wide extent.

ex·pan′sive (ik span′siv) adj. warm and benevolent.

ex·pa′ti·ate′ (ik spā′shē āt′) v., **-ated, -ating.** talk or write at length.

ex·pa′tri·ate′, v., **-ated, -ating,** n., adj. —v. (eks pā′trē āt′) **1.** exile. **2.** remove (oneself) from homeland. —n. (-it) **3.** expatriated person. —adj. (-it) **4.** exiled; banished.

ex·pect′ (ik spekt′) v. look forward to. —**ex·pect′an·cy,** n. —**ex·pect′ ant,** adj. —**ex′pec·ta′tion,** n.

ex·pec′to·rate′ (-rāt′) v., **-rated, -rating.** spit. —**ex·pec′to·rant,** n.

ex·pe′di·ent, adj. **1.** desirable in given circumstances. **2.** conducive to

advantage. —n. **3.** expedient means.

ex′pe·dite′ (ek′spi dīt′) v., **-dited, -diting.** speed up.

ex′pe·di′tion (ek′spi dish′ən) n. **1.** journey to explore or fight. **2.** promptness.

ex′pe·di′tious, adj. prompt.

ex·pel′ (ik spel′) v., **-pelled, -pelling.** force out.

ex·pend′ (ik spend′) v. **1.** use up. **2.** spend. —**ex·pend′i·ture,** n.

ex·pend′a·ble, adj. **1.** available for spending. **2.** that can be sacrificed if necessary.

ex·pense′ (ik spens′) n. **1.** cost. **2.** cause of spending.

ex·pen′sive, adj. costing much.

ex·pe′ri·ence (ik spēr′ē əns) n., v., **-enced, -encing.** —n. **1.** something lived through. **2.** knowledge from such things. —v. **3.** have experience of.

ex·pe′ri·enced, adj. wise or skillful through experience.

ex·per′i·ment, n. (ik sper′ə mənt) **1.** test to discover or check something. —v. (-ment′) **2.** perform experiment. —**ex·per′i·men′tal** (-men′tl) adj. —**ex·per′i·men·ta′tion,** n. —**ex· per′i·ment′er,** n.

ex′pert, n. (ek′spûrt) **1.** skilled person. —adj. (ek′spûrt; also ik spûrt′) **2.** skilled. —**ex·pert′ly,** adv.

ex′per·tise′ (ek′spər tēz′) n. expert skill.

ex′pi·ate′ (ek′spē āt′) v., **-ated, -ating.** atone for. —**ex′pi·a′tion,** n.

ex·pire′ (ik spīr′) v., **-pired, -piring. 1.** end. **2.** die. **3.** breathe out.

ex·plain′ (ik splān′) v. **1.** make clear. **2.** account for. —**ex′pla·na′tion,** n. —**ex·plan′a·to′ry** (ik splan′-) adj.

ex′ple·tive (ek′spli tiv) n. exclamatory oath, usu. profane.

ex·pli·cate′ (-kāt′) v., **-cated, -cating.** explain in detail.

ex·plic′it (ik splis′it) adj. **1.** clearly stated. **2.** outspoken. **3.** having sexual acts or nudity clearly depicted.

ex·plode′ (ik splōd′) v., **-ploded, -ploding. 1.** burst violently. **2.** disprove; discredit. —**ex·plo′sion,** n. —**ex·plo′sive,** n., adj.

ex·ploit′, n. (eks′ploit) **1.** notable act. —v. (ik sploit′) **2.** use, esp. selfishly. —**ex′ploi·ta′tion,** n. —**ex·ploit′a· tive,** adj.

ex·plore′ (ik splôr′) v., **-plored, -ploring.** examine from end to end. —**ex′plo·ra′tion** (ek′splə rā′shən) n. —**ex·plor′er,** n. —**ex·plor′a·to′ry,** adj.

ex·po′nent (ik spō′nənt or, esp. for 3, ek′spō nənt) n. **1.** person who explains. **2.** symbol. **3.** Math. symbol placed to the upper right of another to indicate the power to which the latter is to be raised.

ex·port′, v. (ik spôrt′) **1.** send to other countries. —n. (ek′spôrt) **2.** what is sent. —**ex′por·ta′tion,** n.

ex·pose′ (ik spōz′) v., **-posed, -posing. 1.** lay open to harm, etc. **2.** reveal. **3.** allow light to reach (film). —**ex·po′sure,** n.

ex′po·sé′ (ek′spō zā′) n. exposure of wrongdoing.

ex′po·si′tion (ek′spə zish′ən) n. **1.** public show. **2.** explanation.

ex·pos′i·to′ry (ik spoz′i tôr′ē) adj. serving to expound or explain.

ex post facto (eks′ pōst′ fak′tō) adj. made or done after the fact; retroactive.

ex·pos′tu·late′ (ik spos′chə lāt′) v., **-lated, -lating.** protest.

ex·pound/ (ik spound/) v. state in detail.

ex·press/ (ik spres/) v. **1.** convey in words, art, etc. **2.** press out. —*adj.* **3.** definite. —*n.* **4.** fast or direct train, etc. **5.** delivery system. —**ex·pres/sion**, n. —**ex·pres/sive**, adj.

ex·press/way/, n. road for high-speed traffic.

ex·pro/pri·ate/ (eks prō/prē āt/) v., -ated, -ating. take for public use.

ex·pul/sion (ik spul/shən) n. act of driving out.

ex·punge/ (ik spunj/) v., -punged, -punging. obliterate.

ex/pur·gate/ (ek/spər gāt/) v., -gated, -gating. remove objectionable parts from.

ex/qui·site (ik skwiz/it, ek/skwi zit) adj. delicately beautiful.

ex/tant (ek/stənt, ik stant/) adj. still existing.

ex·tem/po·ra/ne·ous (ik stem/pə-rā/nē əs) adj. impromptu. —**ex·tem/po·re** (ik stem/pə rē) adv.

ex·tend/ (ik stend/) v. **1.** stretch out. **2.** offer. **3.** reach. **4.** increase. —**ex·ten/sion**, n.

extended family, family comprising a married couple, their children, and close relatives.

ex·ten/sive (-siv) adj. far-reaching.

ex·tent/ (ik stent/) n. degree; breadth.

ex·ten/u·ate/ (ik sten/yōō āt/) v., -ated, -ating. lessen seriousness of (fault).

ex·te/ri·or (ik stēr/ē ər) adj. **1.** outer. —*n.* **2.** outside.

ex·ter/mi·nate/ (ik stûr/mə nāt/) v., -nated, -nating. get rid of by destroying. —**ex·ter/mi·na/tion**, n. —**ex·ter/mi·na/tor**, n.

ex·ter/nal (ik stûr/nl) adj. outer.

ex·tinct/ (ik stingkt/) adj. no longer existing. —**ex·tinc/tion**, n.

ex·tin/guish (ik sting/gwish) v. put out; end. —**ex·tin/guish·er**, n.

ex/tir·pate/ (ek/stər pāt/) v., -pated, -pating. destroy totally.

ex·tol/ (ik stōl/) v., -tolled, -tolling. praise highly.

ex·tort/ (ik stôrt/) v. get by force, threat, etc. —**ex·tor/tion**, n.

ex·tor/tion·ate (ik stôr/shə nit) adj. excessive.

ex/tra (ek/strə) adj. additional.

extra-, prefix meaning outside or beyond, as *extrasensory.*

ex·tract/, v. **1.** draw out. —*n.* (ek/strakt) **2.** something extracted. —**ex·trac/tion**, n.

ex/tra·cur·ric/u·lar (ek/strə kə rik/-yə lər) adj. outside the regular curriculum, as of a school.

ex/tra·dite/ (ek/strə dīt/) v., -dited, -diting. deliver (fugitive) to another state. —**ex/tra·di/tion** (-dish/ən) n.

ex/tra·le/gal, adj. beyond the authority of law.

ex/tra·mu/ral (-myŏŏr/əl) adj. involving members of more than one school.

ex·tra/ne·ous (ik strā/nē əs) adj. irrelevant. —**ex·tra/ne·ous·ly**, adv.

ex·traor/di·nar/y (ik strôr/dn er/ē, ek/strə ôr/-) adj. unusual or remarkable. —**ex·traor/di·nar/i·ly**, adv.

ex/trap·o·late/ (ik strap/ə lāt/) v., -lated, -lating. infer from known data. —**ex·trap/o·la/tion**, n.

ex/tra·sen/so·ry (ek/strə sen/sə rē) adj. beyond one's physical senses.

ex/tra·ter·res/tri·al, adj. **1.** being or from outside the earth's limits. —*n.* **2.** extraterrestrial being.

ex·trav/a·gant (ik strav/ə gənt) adj.

1. spending imprudently. **2.** immoderate. —**ex·trav/a·gance**, n.

ex·trav/a·gan/za (-gan/zə) n. lavish production.

ex·treme/ (ik strēm/) adj. **1.** not moderate or ordinary. **2.** very great. **3.** outermost. —*n.* **4.** utmost degree.

ex·trem/ism, n. tendency to take extreme measures, esp. in politics.

ex·trem/i·ty (ik strem/i tē) n., pl. -ties. **1.** farthest point. **2.** arm or leg. **3.** distress.

ex/tri·cate/ (ek/stri kāt/) v., -cated, -cating. disentangle.

ex·trin/sic (ik strin/sik, -zik) adj. **1.** not inherent or essential. **2.** being or coming from without; external.

ex/tro·vert/ (ek/strə vûrt/) n. outgoing person. —**ex/tro·ver/sion**, n. —**ex/tro·vert/ed,** adj.

ex·trude/ (ik strōōd/) v., -truded, -truding. force or press out.

ex·u/ber·ant (ig zōō/bər ənt) adj. **1.** joyful; vigorous. **2.** abundant. —**ex·u/ber·ance**, n.

ex·ude/ (ig zōōd/, ik sōōd/) v., -uded, -uding. **1.** ooze out. **2.** radiate. —**ex/u·da/tion,** n.

ex·ult/ (ig zult/) v. rejoice. —**ex·ult/ant,** adj. —**ex/ul·ta/tion,** n.

eye (ī) n., v., **eyed, eying** or **eyeing.** —*n.* **1.** organ of sight. **2.** power of seeing. **3.** close watch. —*v.* **4.** watch closely. —**eye/ball/,** n., v. —**eye/sight/,** n.

eye/brow/, n. ridge and line of short hairs over eye.

eye/ful (ī/fŏŏl) n., pl. -fuls. **1.** thorough view. **2.** Informal. attractive person.

eye/glass/es, n.pl. pair of corrective lenses in a frame.

eye/lash/, n. short hair at edge of eyelid.

eye/let (ī/lit) n. small hole.

eye/lid/, n. movable skin covering the eye.

eye/o/pen·er, n. something that causes sudden enlightenment.

eye/sore/, n. something unpleasant to look at.

eye/tooth/, n. canine tooth in upper jaw.

eye/wash/, n. **1.** soothing solution for eyes. **2.** nonsense.

eye/wit/ness, n. person who sees event.

ey/rie (âr/ē, ēr/ē) n., pl. -ies. aerie.

F

F, f (ef) n. sixth letter of English alphabet.

F, 1. Fahrenheit. **2.** female.

f., 1. feet. **2.** female. **3.** folio. **4.** foot. **5.** franc.

FAA, Federal Aviation Administration.

fa/ble (fā/bəl) n. **1.** short tale with moral. **2.** untrue story.

fab/ric (fab/rik) n. cloth.

fab/ri·cate/ (-ri kāt/) v., -cated, -cating. **1.** construct. **2.** invent (lie).

fab/u·lous (fab/yə ləs) adj. **1.** marvelous. **2.** suggesting fables.

fa·çade/ (fə säd/) **1.** building front. **2.** superficial appearance.

face (fās) n., v., **faced, facing.** —*n.* **1.** front part of head. **2.** surface. **3.** appearance. **4.** dignity. —*v.* **5.** look toward. **6.** confront. —**fa/cial** (fā/shəl) adj.

face/less, adj. lacking identity.

face/-lift/, n. **1.** surgery to eliminate

facial sagging. **2.** renovation to improve appearance of building.

face/-sav/ing, adj. saving one's prestige or dignity.

fac/et (fas/it) n. **1.** surface of cut gem. **2.** aspect.

fa·ce/tious (fə sē/shəs) adj. joking, esp. annoyingly so.

face value (fās/ val/yōō for 1; fās/ val/yōō for 2) **1.** value printed on the face of a stock, bond, etc. **2.** apparent value.

fac/ile (fas/il) adj. easy; effortless.

fa·cil/i·tate/ (fə sil/i tāt/) v., -tated, -tating. make easier. —**fa·cil/i·ta/tion,** n. —**fa·cil/i·ta/tor,** n.

fa·cil/i·ty (-i tē) n., pl. -ties. **1.** something designed or installed for a purpose. **2.** ease.

fac/ing (fā/sing) n. **1.** decorative or protective outer material. **2.** lining.

fac·sim/i·le (fak sim/ə lē) n. exact copy.

fact (fakt) n. truth. —**fac/tu·al,** adj.

fac/tion (fak/shən) n. competing internal group. —**fac/tion·al,** adj.

fac/tious, adj. causing strife.

fac/tor (fak/tər) n. **1.** element. **2.** one of two numbers multiplied.

fac/to·ry (fak/tə rē) n., pl. -ries. place where goods are made.

fac/ul·ty (fak/əl tē) n., pl. -ties. **1.** special ability. **2.** power. **3.** body of teachers.

fad (fad) n. temporary fashion.

fade (fād) v., **faded, fading. 1.** lose freshness, color, or vitality. **2.** disappear gradually.

fag (fag) v., **fagged, fagging,** n. —*v.* **1.** exhaust. —*n.* **2.** Also, **fag/got.** Offensive. homosexual.

fag/ot (fag/ət) n. bundle of firewood.

Fahr/en·heit/ (far/ən hīt/) adj. measuring temperature so that water freezes at 32° and boils at 212°.

fail (fāl) v. **1.** be unsuccessful or lacking (in). **2.** become weaker. **3.** cease functioning. —**fail/ure,** n.

fail/ing, n. **1.** weak point of character. —*prep.* **2.** in the absence of.

faille (fīl, fāl) n. ribbed fabric.

fail/-safe/, adj. ensured against failure of a mechanical system, etc. or against consequences of its failure.

faint (fānt) adj. **1.** lacking strength. —*v.* **2.** lose consciousness briefly.

faint/heart/ed, adj. lacking courage.

fair (fâr) adj. **1.** behaving justly. **2.** moderately good. **3.** sunny. **4.** lighthued. **5.** attractive. —*n.* **6.** exhibition. —**fair/ly,** adv. —**fair/ness,** n.

fair shake, just and equal opportunity or treatment.

fair/y (fâr/ē) n., pl. **fairies. 1.** tiny supernatural being. **2.** Offensive. homosexual. —**fair/y·land/,** n.

fairy tale, story, usu. for children, about magical creatures. **2.** misleading account.

faith (fāth) n. **1.** confidence. **2.** religious belief. **3.** loyalty.

faith/ful, adj. **1.** loyal. **2.** having religious belief. **3.** copying accurately.

fake (fāk) v., **faked, faking,** n., adj. Informal. —*v.* **1.** counterfeit. —*n.* **2.** thing faked. —*adj.* **3.** deceptive.

fa·kir/ (fə kēr/) n. Muslim or Hindu monk.

fa·la/fel (fə lä/fəl), n. fried ball of ground chickpeas.

fal/con (fôl/kən, fal/-) n. bird of prey. —**fal/con·ry,** n.

fall (fôl) v., **fell** (fel), **fallen, falling,** n. —*v.* **1.** drop. **2.** happen. —*n.* **3.** descent. **4.** autumn.

fal/la·cy (fal/ə sē) n., pl. -cies.

false belief. **2.** unsound argument. —**fal•la′cious** (fə lā′shəs) *adj.*

fall guy, *Slang.* **1.** easy victim. **2.** scapegoat.

fal′li•ble (fal′ə bəl) *adj.* liable to error. —**fal′li•bil′i•ty,** *n.*

fall′ing-out′, *n., pl.* **fallings-out, falling-outs.** quarrel.

fal•lo′pian tube (fə lō′pē ən) either of pair of ducts in female abdomen that transport ova from ovary to uterus. Also, **Fallopian tube.**

fall′out′, *n.* **1.** radioactive particles carried by air. **2.** incidental outcome or product.

fal′low (fal′ō) *adj.* plowed and not seeded.

fallow deer, Eurasian deer with yellowish coat that is white-spotted in summer.

false (fôls) *adj.,* **falser, falsest. 1.** not true. **2.** faithless. **3.** deceptive. —**false′hood,** *n.* —**false′ly,** *adv.* —**fal′si•fy,** *v.,* **-fied, -fying.**

fal•set′to (fôl set′ō) *n., pl.* **-tos.** unnaturally high voice.

fal′ter (fôl′tər) *v.* hesitate; waver.

fame (fām) *n.* widespread reputation; renown. —**famed,** *adj.*

fa•mil′iar (fə mil′yər) *adj.* **1.** commonly known. **2.** intimate. —**fa•mil′i•ar′i•ty** (-ē ar′i tē, -yar′-) *n.* —**fa•mil′iar•ize′,** *v.,* **-ized, -izing.**

fam′i•ly (fam′ə lē, fam′lē) *n., pl.* **-lies. 1.** parents and their children. **2.** relatives. —**fa•mil′ial** (fə mil′yəl) *adj.*

family tree, genealogical chart of a family.

fam′ine (fam′in) *n.* scarcity of food.

fam′ish (fam′ish) *v.* starve.

fa′mous (fā′məs) *adj.* widely known; renowned.

fa′mous•ly, *adv.* very well.

fan (fan) *n., v.,* **fanned, fanning. —**n. **1.** device for causing current of air. **2.** *Informal.* devotee. —*v.* **3.** blow upon with fan. **4.** stir up.

fa•nat′ic (fə nat′ik) *n.* person excessively devoted to cause. —**fa•nat′i•cal,** *adj.* —**fa•nat′i•cism** (-ə siz′əm) *n.*

fan′ci•er (fan′sē ər) *n.* person interested in something, as dogs.

fan′cy (fan′sē) *n., pl.* **-cies,** *adj.,* **-cier, -ciest,** *v.,* **-cied, -cying. —**n. **1.** imagination. **2.** thing imagined. **3.** whim. **4.** taste. —*adj.* **5.** ornamental. —*v.* **6.** imagine. **7.** crave.

fan′cy-free′, *adj.* free from emotional ties, esp. from love.

fan′cy•work′, *n.* ornamental needlework.

fan′fare′, *n.* **1.** chorus of trumpets. **2.** showy flourish.

fang (fang) *n.* long, sharp tooth.

fan′ny, *n., pl.* **-nies.** *Informal.* buttocks.

fan•ta′sia (fan tā′zhə) *n.* fanciful musical work.

fan′ta•size′ (-tə sīz′) *v.,* **-sized, -sizing.** have fantasies.

fan•tas′tic (-tas′tik) *adj.* **1.** wonderful and strange. **2.** fanciful.

fan′ta•sy (-tə sē, -zē) *n., pl.* **-sies. 1.** imagination. **2.** imagined thing.

far (fär) *adv., adj.,* **farther, farthest.** at or to great distance.

far′a•way′ (-ə wā′) *adj.* **1.** distant. **2.** preoccupied; dreamy.

farce (färs) *n.* light comedy. —**far′ci•cal,** *adj.*

fare (fâr) *n., v.,* **fared, faring. —**n. **1.** price of travel. **2.** food. —*v.* **3.** get along.

Far East, countries of east and southeast Asia.

fare′well′ (fâr′wel′) *interj., n., adj.* good-by.

far′-fetched′, *adj.* not reasonable or probable.

far′-flung′, *adj.* **1.** extending over a great distance or wide area. **2.** widely distributed.

fa•ri′na (fə rē′nə) *n.* flour or grain cooked as a cereal.

farm (färm) *n.* **1.** tract of land for agriculture. —*v.* **2.** cultivate land. —**farm′er,** *n.* —**farm′house′,** *n.* —**farm′ing,** *n.* —**farm′yard′,** *n.*

far′o (fâr′ō) *n.* gambling game in which players bet on cards.

far′-off′, *adj.* distant.

far′-out′, *adj. Slang.* extremely unconventional.

far′-reach′ing, *adj.* of widespread influence.

far′row (far′ō) *n.* **1.** litter of pigs. —*v.* **2.** (of swine) bear.

far′-sight′ed (-sī′tid, -sī′-) *adj.* **1.** seeing distant objects best. **2.** planning for future.

far′ther (fär′thər) *compar. of* **far.** *adv.* **1.** at or to a greater distance. —*adj.* **2.** more distant. **3.** additional. —**Usage.** FARTHER is used to indicate physical distance: *Is it much farther to the hotel?* FURTHER is used to refer to additional time, amount, or abstract ideas: *I would rather not talk about this further.* But both FARTHER and FURTHER are often used for distance of any kind: *Here is the solution; look no farther/further. His story of the novel reaches farther/further than any earlier one.*

far′thest (-thist) *superl. of* **far.** *adv.* **1.** at or to the greatest distance. —*adj.* **2.** most distant.

fas′ci•nate′ (fas′ə nāt′) *v.,* **-nated, -nating.** attract irresistibly. —**fas′ci•na′tion,** *n.*

fas′cism (fash′iz əm) *n.* principle of strong undemocratic government. —**fas′cist,** *n., adj.* —**fa•scis′tic,** *adj.*

fash′ion (fash′ən) *n.* **1.** prevailing style. **2.** manner. —*v.* **3.** make.

fash′ion•a•ble, *adj.* of the latest style. —**fash′ion•a•bly,** *adv.*

fast (fast) *adj.* **1.** quick; swift. **2.** secure. —*adv.* **3.** tightly. **4.** swiftly. —*v.* **5.** abstain from food. —*n.* **6.** such abstinence.

fas′ten (fas′ən) *v.* fix or attach securely. —**fas′ten•er,** *n.*

fast′-food′, *adj.* specializing in food that is prepared and served quickly.

fas•tid′i•ous (fa stid′ē əs, fə-) *adj.* highly critical and demanding.

fast′ness, *n.* fortified place.

fat (fat) *n., adj.,* **fatter, fattest. —**n. **1.** greasy substance. —*adj.* **2.** fleshy. —**fat′ty,** *adj.*

fa′tal (fāt′l) *adj.* causing death or ruin. —**fa′tal•ly,** *adv.*

fa′tal•ism, *n.* belief in unchangeable fate. —**fa′tal•ist,** *n.*

fa•tal′i•ty (fā tal′i tē, fə-) *n., pl.* **-ties. 1.** death by a disaster. **2.** fate.

fate (fāt) *n., v.,* **fated, fating.** —*n.* **1.** destiny. **2.** death or ruin. —*v.* **3.** destine.

fat′ed, *adj.* subject to fate; destined.

fate′ful, *adj.* involving important or disastrous events.

fa′ther (fä′thər) *n.* **1.** male parent. **2.** (*cap.*) God. **3.** priest. —**fa′ther•hood′,** *n.* —**fa′ther•ly,** *adv.*

fa′ther-in-law′, *n., pl.* **fathers-in-law.** spouse's father.

fa′ther•land′, *n.* **1.** one's native country. **2.** land of one's ancestors.

fath′om (fath′əm) *n.* **1.** nautical measure equal to six feet. —*v.* **2.** understand.

fa•tigue′ (fə tēg′) *n., v.,* **-tigued, -tiguing.** —*n.* **1.** weariness. **2.** (*pl.*) military work clothes. —*v.* **3.** weary.

fat′ten, *v.* grow fat or wealthy.

fatty acid, organic acid found in animal and vegetable fats.

fat′u•ous (fach′ō̄ əs) *adj.* foolish or stupid.

fau′cet (fô′sit) *n.* valve for controlling flow of liquids.

fault (fôlt) *n.* defect. —**faul′ty,** *adj.*

faun (fôn) *n.* Roman deity, part man and part goat.

fau′na (fô′nə) *n., pl.* **-nas, -nae** (-nē). animals or animal life of particular region or period.

faux pas′ (fō pä′) social error.

fa′vor (fā′vər) *n.* **1.** kind act. **2.** high regard. —*v.* **3.** prefer. **4.** resemble. —**fa′vor•a•ble,** *adj.*

fa′vor•ite, *n.* **1.** one preferred. **2.** one most likely to win. —*adj.* **3.** preferred.

fa′vor•it•ism (fā′vər ə tiz′əm) *n.* preference shown toward certain persons.

fawn (fôn) *n.* **1.** young deer. —*v.* **2.** seek favor by servility.

fax (faks) *n.* **1.** method of sending documents by telephone. **2.** item sent in this way. —*v.* **3.** send by fax. **4.** communicate with by fax.

faze (fāz) *v.,* **fazed, fazing.** *Informal.* daunt.

FBI, Federal Bureau of Investigation.

FCC, Federal Communications Commis- ˙sion.

FDA, Food and Drug Administration.

FDIC, Federal Deposit Insurance Corporation.

fear (fēr) *n.* **1.** feeling of impending harm. **2.** awe. —*v.* **3.** be afraid of. **4.** hold in awe. —**fear′ful,** *adj.*

fea′si•ble (fē′zə bəl) *adj.* able to be done. —**fea′si•bil′i•ty,** *n.*

feast (fēst) *n.* **1.** sumptuous meal. **2.** religious celebration. —*v.* **3.** provide with or have feast.

feat (fēt) *n.* remarkable deed.

feath′er (feth′ər) *n.* one of the growths forming bird's plumage.

fea′ture (fē′chər) *n., v.,* **-tured, -turing.** —*n.* **1.** part of face. **2.** special part, article, etc. —*v.* **3.** give prominence to.

Feb., February.

Feb′ru•ar′y (feb′rōō er′ē, feb′yōō-) *n., pl.* **-aries.** second month of year. —**Pronunciation.** The second pronunciation for FEBRUARY shown above, with the first (r) replaced by (y), occurs because neighboring sounds that are alike tend to become different. This word also conforms to the pattern (-yōō er′ē) by analogy with the pronunciation of the first month of the year, *January.* Although the pronunciation of FEBRUARY with (y) is often criticized, both pronunciations are used by educated speakers and are considered standard.

fe′ces (fē′sēz) *n.pl.* excrement.

feck′less (fek′lis) *adj.* **1.** incompetent. **2.** irresponsible and lazy.

fe′cund (fē′kund) *adj.* productive.

fed., **1.** federal. **2.** federated. **3.** federation.

fed′er•al (fed′ər əl) *adj.* **1.** of states in permanent union. **2.** (*sometimes cap.*) of U.S. government.

fed′er•ate′ (fed′ə rāt′) *v.,* **-ated, -ating.** unite in league.

fe•do′ra (fi dôr′ə) *n.* soft felt hat.

fee (fē) *n.* payment for services, etc.

fee′ble (fē′bəl) *adj.,* **-bler, -blest.** weak. —**fee′bly,** *adv.*

feed (fēd) v., **fed** (fed), **feeding,** n. —v. **1.** give food to. **2.** eat. —n. **3.** food for livestock. —**feed′er,** n.

feed′back′, n. **1.** return of part of output of a process to its input. **2.** informative response.

feel (fēl) v., **felt** (felt), **feeling,** n. —v. **1.** perceive or examine by touch. **2.** be conscious of. **3.** have emotions. —n. **4.** touch.

feel′er, n. **1.** proposal or remark designed to elicit opinion or reaction. **2.** organ of touch, as an antenna.

feign (fān) v. pretend.

feint (fānt) n. **1.** deceptive move. —v. **2.** make feint.

feist′y (fī′stē) adj. **1.** full of energy; spirited. **2.** ready to argue or fight; pugnacious.

fe•lic′i•tate′ (fə lis′i tāt′) v., **-tated, -tating.** congratulate.

fe•lic′i•tous (-təs) adj. suitable.

fe•lic′i•ty, n., pl. **-ties.** happiness.

fe′line (fē′līn) adj. **1.** of or like cats. —n. **2.** animal of the cat family.

fell (fel) v. cut or strike down.

fel′low (fel′ō) n. **1.** man. **2.** companion. **3.** peer. **4.** member of learned or professional group. —**fel′low•ship′,** n.

fel′on (fel′ən) n. criminal.

fel′o•ny (fə lō′nē əs) n., pl. **-nies.** serious crime. —**fe•lo′ni•ous,** adj.

felt (felt) n. **1.** matted fabric. —adj. **2.** of felt.

fem., **1.** female. **2.** feminine.

fe′male (fē′māl) adj. **1.** belonging to sex that bears babies. —n. **2.** female person or animal.

fem′i•nine (fem′ə nin) adj. of women. —**fem′i•nin′i•ty,** n.

fem′i•nism (-i niz′əm) n. support of equal rights for women. —**fem′i•nist,** adj., n.

fe′mur (fē′mər) n. thigh bone.

fen (fen) n. swampy ground; marsh.

fence (fens) n., v., **fenced, fencing.** —n. **1.** wall-like enclosure around open area. **2.** person who receives and disposes of stolen goods. —v. **3.** fight with sword for sport. **4.** sell to a fence.

fend (fend) v. ward off.

fend′er, n. metal part over automobile wheel.

fen′nel (fen′l) n. plant with seeds used for flavoring.

fe′ral (fēr′əl, fer′-) adj. in a wild state; not tamed.

fer′ment, n. (fûr′ment) **1.** substance causing fermentation. **2.** agitation. —v. (fər ment′) **3.** cause or undergo fermentation.

fer′men•ta′tion, n. chemical change involving effervescence or decomposition.

fern (fûrn) n. nonflowering plant with feathery leaves.

fe•ro′cious (fə rō′shəs) adj. savagely fierce. —**fe•roc′i•ty** (fə ros′i tē) n.

fer′ret (fer′it) n. **1.** kind of weasel. —v. **2.** search intensively.

Fer′ris wheel (fer′is) amusement ride consisting of large upright wheel with suspended seats.

fer′rous (fer′əs) adj. of or containing iron. Also, **fer′ric** (ik).

fer′ry (fer′ē) n., pl. **-ries,** v., **-ried, -rying.** —n. **1.** Also, **fer′ry•boat′.** boat making short crossings. **2.** place where ferries operate. —v. **3.** carry or pass in ferry.

fer′tile (fûr′tl) adj. **1.** producing abundantly. **2.** able to bear young.

fer′ti•lize′ v. **1.** make new life begin. **2.** make fertile. —**fer′ti•li•za′tion,** n. —**fer′ti•liz′er,** n.

fer′vent (fûr′vənt) adj. ardent; passionate. —**fer′ven•cy, fer′vor,** n.

fer′vid (-vid) adj. vehement.

fes′ter (fes′tər) v. **1.** generate pus. **2.** rankle.

fes′ti•val (fes′tə vəl) n. celebration. Also, **fes•tiv′i•ty** (-tiv′i tē). —**fes′tive•ly,** adv.

fes•toon′ (fe stōōn′) n. **1.** garland hung between two points. —v. **2.** adorn with festoons.

fet′a (fet′ə) n. Greek cheese usu. from sheep's or goat's milk.

fetch (fech) v. go and bring.

fetch′ing, adj. attractive.

fete (fāt, fet) n., v., **feted, feting.** —n. **1.** festival. **2.** party. —v. **3.** honor with a fete.

fet′id (fet′id, fē′tid) adj. stinking.

fe′tish (fet′ish, fē′tish) n. object worshiped. —**fet′ish•ism,** n.

fet′lock (fet′lok′) n. **1.** part of horse's leg behind hoof. **2.** tuft of hair on this part.

fet′ter (fet′ər) n. **1.** shackle for feet. **2.** (pl.) anything that restrains. —v. **3.** put fetters on. **4.** restrain.

fet′tle (fet′l) n. condition.

fe′tus (fē′təs) n. unborn offspring. —**fe′tal,** adj.

feud (fyōōd) n. **1.** lasting hostility. —v. **2.** engage in feud.

feu′dal•ism (fyōōd′l iz′əm) n. system by which land is held in return for service. —**feu′dal,** adj.

fe′ver (fē′vər) n. **1.** high body temperature. **2.** intense nervous excitement. —**fe′ver•ish,** adj.

few (fyōō) adj., n. not many. —**Usage.** See LESS.

fey (fā) adj. **1.** strange; whimsical. **2.** supernatural; enchanted.

fez (fez) n., pl. **fezzes.** cone-shaped felt hat.

ff, **1.** folios. **2.** (and the) following (pages, verses, etc.).

FG, field goal(s).

fi′an•cé′ (fē′än sā′, fē än′sā) n. betrothed man. —**fi′an•cée′,** n.fem.

fi•as′co (fē as′kō) n., pl. **-cos, -coes.** failure.

fi′at (fē′ät, fī′ət) n. decree.

fib (fib) n., v., **fibbed, fibbing.** —n. **1.** mild lie. —v. **2.** tell a fib.

fi′ber (fī′bər) n. **1.** threadlike piece, esp. one that can be worn. **2.** any of the threadlike structures that form plant or animal tissue. **3.** roughage. Also, **fi′bre.** —**fi′brous,** adj. —**fi′broid,** adj.

fi′ber•glass′, n. material composed of fine glass fibers.

fiber optics, technology of sending light and images through glass or plastic fibers. —**fi′ber•op′tic,** adj.

fib′ril•la′tion (fib′rə lā′shən, fī′brə-) n. abnormally fast and irregular heartbeat. —**fib′ril•late,** v.

fib′u•la (fib′yə lə) n., pl. **-lae** (-lē), **-las.** outer thinner bone from knee to ankle.

FICA (fī′kə, fē′-) Federal Insurance Contributions Act.

fiche (fēsh) n. microfiche.

fick′le (fik′əl) adj. inconstant.

fic′tion (fik′shən) n. **1.** narrative of imaginary events. **2.** something made up. —**fic′tion•al,** adj.

fic•ti′tious (-tish′əs) adj. false.

fid′dle (fid′l) n., v., **-dled, -dling.** —n. **1.** violin. —v. **2.** play tunes on violin. **3.** move hands nervously.

fid′dle•sticks′, interj. (exclamation of impatience, disbelief, etc.).

fi•del′i•ty (fi del′i tē, fī-) n., pl. **-ties.** faithfulness.

fidg′et (fij′it) v. **1.** move restlessly. —n. **2.** (pl.) restlessness.

fi•du′ci•ar′y (-shē er′ē) adj., n., pl. **-ies.** —adj. **1.** being a trustee. **2.** held in trust. —n. **3.** trustee.

field (fēld) n. **1.** open ground. **2.** area of interest.

field day, 1. day for outdoor sports or contests. **2.** chance for unlimited enjoyment.

fiend (fēnd) n. **1.** devil. **2.** cruel person. **3.** Informal. addict; fan. —**fiend′ish,** adj.

fierce (fērs) adj., **fiercer, fiercest.** wild; violent. —**fierce′ly,** adv.

fier′y (fīr′rē, fī′ə rē) adj., **-ier, -iest.** **1.** of or like fire. **2.** ardent.

fi•es′ta (fē es′tə) n. festival.

fife (fīf) n. high-pitched flute.

fif′teen′ (fif′tēn′) n., adj. ten plus five. —**fif•teenth′,** adj., n.

fifth (fifth) adj. **1.** next after fourth. **2.** fifth part.

fifth column, traitorous group within a country.

fifth wheel, one that is unnecessary or unwanted.

fif′ty (fif′tē) n., adj. ten times five. —**fif′ti•eth,** adj., n.

fig (fig) n. fruit of semitropical tree.

fig. (fig) **1.** figurative. **2.** figuratively. **3.** figure.

fight (fīt) n., v., **fought, fighting.** battle or argue. —**fight′er,** n.

fig′ment (fig′mənt) n. something imagined.

fig′ur•a•tive (-yər ə tiv) adj. not literal. —**fig′ur•a•tive•ly,** adv.

fig′ure, n., v., **-ured, -uring.** —n. **1.** written symbol, esp. numerical. **2.** amount. **3.** shape. —v. **4.** calculate. **5.** be prominent.

fig′ure•head′, n. powerless leader.

figure of speech, use of words in nonliteral sense.

fig′ur•ine′ (-yə rēn′) n. miniature statue.

fil′a•ment (fil′ə mənt) n. fine fiber.

fil′bert (fil′bərt) n. kind of hazelnut.

filch (filch) v. steal.

file (fīl) n., v., **filed, filing.** —n. **1.** storage place for documents. **2.** line of persons, etc. **3.** metal rubbing tool. —v. **4.** arrange or keep in file. **5.** march in file. **6.** rub with file.

fil′i•al (fil′ē əl) adj. befitting sons and daughters.

fil′i•bus′ter (fil′ə bus′tər) n. **1.** delay of legislation by long speeches. —v. **2.** use filibuster to impede legislation.

fil′i•gree′ (-i grē′) n. ornamental work of fine wires.

Fil′i•pi′no (fil′ə pē′nō) n. native of t'e Philippines.

fill (fil) v. **1.** make full. **2.** pervade. **3.** supply. —n. **4.** full supply.

fil•let′ (fi lā′) n. narrow strip, esp. of meat or fish. Also, **fi′let.**

fil′lip (fil′əp) n. thing that excites.

fil′ly (fil′ē) n., pl. **-lies.** young female horse.

film (film) n. **1.** thin coating. **2.** roll or sheet with photographically sensitive coating. **3.** motion picture. —v. **4.** make motion picture of.

film′strip′, n. length of film containing still pictures for projecting on screen.

film′y, adj., **-ier, -iest. 1.** partly transparent. **2.** blurred.

fil′ter (fil′tər) n. **1.** device for straining substances. —v. **2.** remove by or pass through filter. —**fil•tra′tion,** n.

filth (filth) n. **1.** dirt. **2.** obscenity; offensive indecency. —**filth′y,** adj.

fin (fin) n. winglike organ on fishes.

fi·na′gle (fi nā′gəl) v., **-gled, -gling.** practice or obtain by trickery.

fi′nal (fīn′l) adj. last. —**fi′nal·ist,** n. —**fi·nal′i·ty** (fī nal′i tē) n. —**fi′nal·ize′,** v. **-ized, -izing.**

fi·na′le (fi nä′lē) n. last part.

fi·nance′ (fi nans′, fī′nans) n., v., **-nanced, -nancing.** —n. **1.** money matters. **2.** (pl.) funds. —v. **3.** supply with money. —**fi·nan′cial,** adj.

fin·an·cier′ (fin′ən sēr′, fī′nən-) n. professional money handler.

finch (finch) n. small songbird.

find (fīnd) v., **found** (found), **finding,** n. —v. **1.** come upon. **2.** learn. —n. **3.** discovery.

fine (fīn) adj., **finer, finest,** n., v., **fined, fining.** —adj. **1.** excellent. **2.** delicate; thin. —n. **3.** money exacted as penalty. —v. **4.** subject to fine.

fine art, (usually pl.) painting, sculpture, etc., created primarily for beauty.

fin′er·y, n. showy dress.

fi·nesse′ (fi ness′) n. delicacy of performance or skill.

fin′ger (fing′gər) n. **1.** one of five parts on end of hand. **2.** touch with fingers. —**fin′ger·nail′,** n. —**fin′ger·tip,** n.

fin′ger·print′, n. **1.** impression of markings of surface of finger, used for identification. —v. **2.** take or record fingerprints of.

fin′ick·y (fin′i kē) adj., **-ier, -iest.** fussy. Also, **fin′ic·al.**

fi′nis (fin′is, fē nē′, fī′nis) n. end.

fin′ish (fin′ish) v. **1.** end. **2.** perfect. **3.** give desired surface to. —n. **4.** completion. **5.** surface coating or treatment.

fi′nite (fī′nīt) adj. having bounds or limits. —**fi′nite·ly,** adv.

Finn (fin) n. native of Finland.

Finn′ish (fin′ish) n. **1.** language of Finland. —adj. **2.** of Finland, the Finns, or Finnish.

fiord (fyôrd, fē ôrd′) n. narrow arm of sea. Also, **fjord.**

fir (fûr) n. cone-bearing evergreen tree.

fire (fīr) n., v., **fired, firing.** —n. **1.** burning. **2.** ardor. **3.** discharge of firearms. —v. **4.** set on fire. **5.** discharge. **6.** Informal. dismiss.

fire′arm′, n. gun.

fire′bomb′, n. **1.** incendiary bomb. —v. **2.** attack with firebombs.

fire′crack′er, n. small firework that makes a noise.

fire′fight′er, n. person who fights destructive fires.

fire′fly′, n., pl. **-flies.** nocturnal beetle that produces light.

fire′man (fīr′mən) n., pl. **-men. 1.** firefighter. **2.** stoker.

fire′place′, n. semiopen place for fire.

fire′plug′, n. hydrant with water for fighting fires.

fire′proof′, adj. safe against fire.

fire′side′, n. area close to fireplace.

fire′trap′, n. dilapidated building.

fire′works′, n.pl. devices ignited for display of light.

firm (fûrm) adj. **1.** hard or stiff. **2.** fixed. **3.** resolute. —v. **4.** make or become firm. —n. **5.** business organization.

fir′ma·ment (fûr′mə mənt) n. sky.

first (fûrst) adj., adv. **1.** before all others. —n. **2.** first thing, etc.

first aid, emergency treatment.

first class, 1. highest class or grade. **2.** most expensive class in travel. **3.** class of mail sealed against inspection. —**first′-class′,** adj.

first′hand′, adj., adv. from the first or original source.

first′-rate′, adj. **1.** of the highest quality. —adv. **2.** very well.

fis′cal (fis′kəl) adj. financial.

fish (fish) n., pl. **fish, fishes,** v. —n. **1.** cold-blooded aquatic vertebrate. —v. **2.** try to catch fish. —**fish′er·man,** n. —**fish′er·y,** n.

fish′y, adj., **-ier, -iest. 1.** like a fish, esp. in taste or smell. **2.** questionable; dubious. —**fish′i·ness,** n.

fis′sion (fish′ən) n. division into parts. —**fis′sion·a·ble,** adj.

fis′sure (fish′ər) n. narrow opening caused by break; crack.

fist (fist) n. closed hand.

fist′ful (-fŏol) n., pl. **-fuls.** handful.

fist′i·cuffs′ (-i kufs′) n.pl. fight with the fists.

fit (fit) adj., **fitter, fittest,** v., **fitted, fitting,** n. —adj. **1.** suitable. **2.** healthy. —v. **3.** be or make suitable. **4.** equip. —n. **5.** manner of fitting. **6.** sudden attack of illness or emotion. —**fit′ness,** n.

fit′ful, adj. irregular.

fit′ting, adj. **1.** appropriate. —n. **2.** attached part. **3.** trial of new clothes, etc., for fit.

five (fīv) n., adj. four plus one.

fix (fiks) v. **1.** make fast or steady. **2.** repair. **3.** prepare.

fix·a′tion (fik sā′shən) n. obsession.

fixed, adj. not changing.

fix′ings, n.pl. Informal. things accompanying main item.

fix′ture (-chər) n. thing fixed in place.

fizz (fiz) v., n. hiss.

fiz′zle (fiz′əl) v., **-zled, -zling,** n. —v. **1.** hiss weakly. **2.** Informal. fail. —n. **3.** act of fizzling.

fjord (fyôrd, fē ôrd′) n. fiord.

FL, Florida.

fl., 1. (he or she) flourished. **2.** fluid.

Fla., Florida.

flab (flab) n. loose, excessive flesh.

flab′ber·gast′ (flab′ər gast′) v. Informal. astound.

flab′by (flab′ē) adj., **-bier, -biest.** not firm. —**flab′bi·ness,** n.

flac′cid (flak′sid, flas′id) adj. flabby.

flag (flag) n., v., **flagged, flagging.** —n. **1.** cloth with symbolic colors or design. **2.** plant with long narrow leaves. **3.** Also, **flag′stone′.** paving stone. —v. **4.** signal with flags (def. 1). **5.** lose vigor, energy, etc.

flag′el·late′ (flaj′ə lāt′) v., **-lated, -lating.** whip; flog.

flag′on (flag′ən) n. large bottle.

fla′grant (flā′grənt) adj. glaring.

flag′ship′, n. ship of commander.

flail (flāl) n. **1.** hand instrument for threshing grain. —v. **2.** strike or strike at as with flail.

flair (flâr) n. aptitude; talent.

flak (flak) n. **1.** antiaircraft fire. **2.** critical or hostile reaction.

flake (flāk) n., v., **flaked, flaking.** —n. **1.** small thin piece. —v. **2.** separate into flakes.

flak′y, adj., **-ier, -iest. 1.** of or like flakes. **2.** lying or coming off in flakes. **3.** Slang. eccentric; odd.

flam·blé (fläm bā′), adj. served in flaming liquor.

flam·boy′ant (flam boi′ənt) adj. showy; colorful.

flame (flām) n., v., **flamed, flaming.** blaze.

fla·men′co (flə meng′kō) n. Spanish gypsy dance and music style.

fla·min′go (flə ming′gō) n., pl. **-gos, -goes.** tall, red, aquatic bird.

flam′ma·ble (flam′ə bəl) easily set on fire. —**flam′ma·bil′i·ty,** n.

flange (flanj) n. projecting rim.

flank (flangk) n. **1.** side. —v. **2.** be at side of. **3.** pass around side of.

flan′nel (flan′l) n. soft wool fabric.

flap (flap) v., **flapped, flapping,** n. —v. **1.** swing loosely and noisily. **2.** move up and down. —n. **3.** flapping movement. **4.** something that hangs loosely. **5.** Informal. emotionally agitated state.

flare (flâr) v., **flared, flaring,** n. —v. **1.** suddenly become brighter or excited. **2.** spread outward. —n. **3.** signal fire.

flare′up′, n. sudden outburst or outbreak.

flash (flash) n. **1.** brief light. **2.** instant. **3.** news dispatch. —v. **4.** gleam suddenly.

flash′back′, n. **1.** earlier event inserted out of order in a story. **2.** sudden recollection of a past event.

flash′bulb′, n. bulb giving burst of light for photography.

flash′light′, n. portable battery-powered light.

flash′y, adj., **-ier, -iest.** showy.

flask (flask) n. kind of bottle.

flat (flat) adj., **flatter, flattest,** n. —adj. **1.** level. **2.** horizontal. **3.** not thick. **4.** absolute. **5.** dull. **6.** below musical pitch. —n. **7.** something flat. **8.** apartment. —**flat′ten,** v.

flat′bed′, n. truck with trailer platform open on all sides.

flat′car′, n. railroad car without sides or top.

flat′fish′, n. fish with broad, flat body, as flounder.

flat′foot′, n., pl. **-feet** for 1, **-foots** for 2. **1.** flattened condition of arch of foot. **2.** Slang. police officer.

flat′-out′, adj. Informal. **1.** using full speed, resources, etc. **2.** downright.

flat′ter (flat′ər) v. praise insincerely. —**flat′ter·y,** n.

flat′u·lent (flach′ə lənt) adj. **1.** having an accumulation of gas in the intestines. **2.** inflated and empty; pompous. —**flat′u·lence,** n.

flat′ware′, n. table utensils.

flaunt (flônt) v. display boldly.

fla′vor (flā′vər) n. **1.** taste. —v. **2.** give flavor to. —**fla′vor·ing,** n.

flaw (flô) n. defect. —**flawed,** adj.

flax (flaks) n. linen plant. —**flax′en,** adj.

flay (flā) v. strip skin from.

flea (flē) n. small, bloodsucking insect.

flea market, market, often outdoors, where used articles, antiques, etc., are sold.

fleck (flek) n. **1.** speck. —v. **2.** spot.

fledg′ling (flej′ling) n. young bird.

flee (flē) v., **fled** (fled), **fleeing.** run away from.

fleece (flēs) n., v., **fleeced, fleecing.** —n. **1.** wool of sheep. —v. **2.** swindle. —**fleec′y,** adj.

fleet (flēt) n. **1.** organized group of ships, aircraft, or road vehicles. —adj. **2.** swift.

fleet′ing, adj. temporary.

flesh (flesh) n. **1.** muscle and fat of animal body. **2.** body. **3.** soft part of fruit or vegetable. —**flesh′y,** adj.

flesh′pot′, n. place of unrestrained pleasure.

flex (fleks) v. bend.

flex′i·ble, adj. **1.** capable of bending. **2.** adaptable.

flick (flik) n. **1.** light stroke. —v. **2.** strike lightly.

flick′er, *v.* **1.** glow unsteadily. —*n.* **2.** unsteady light.

fli′er (flī′ər) *n.* aviator.

flight (flīt) *n.* **1.** act or power of flying. **2.** trip through air. **3.** series of steps. **4.** hasty departure.

flight′less, *adj.* incapable of flying.

flight′y, *adj.,* **-ier, -iest.** frivolous.

flim′sy (flim′zē) *adj.,* **-sier, -siest.** weak or thin. —**flim′si·ness,** *n.*

flinch (flinch) *v.* shrink; wince.

fling (fling) *v.,* **flung** (flung), **flinging,** *n.* —*v.* **1.** throw violently. —*n.* **2.** act of flinging.

flint (flint) *n.* hard stone that strikes sparks. —**flint′y,** *adj.*

flip (flip) *v.,* **flipped, flipping,** *n., adj.,* **flipper, flippest.** —*v.* **1.** move with sudden stroke. **2.** turn over with sudden stroke. —*n.* **3.** such movement. —*adj.* **4.** flippant.

flip′-flop′, *n.* **1.** sudden reversal, as of opinion. **2.** backward somersault.

flip′pant (flip′ənt) *adj.* pert; disrespectful. —**flip′pan·cy,** *n.*

flip′per, *n.* broad flat limb for swimming.

flirt (flûrt) *v.* **1.** act amorously without serious intentions. —*n.* **2.** person who flirts. —**flir·ta′tion,** *n.* —**flir·ta′tious,** *adj.*

flit (flit) *v.,* **flitted, flitting.** move swiftly and lightly.

float (flōt) *v.* **1.** rest or move on or in liquid, air, etc. —*n.* **2.** something that floats. **3.** decorated parade wagon. —**flo·ta′tion,** *n.*

flock (flok) *n.* **1.** group of animals. —*v.* **2.** gather in flock.

floe (flō) *n.* field of floating ice.

flog (flog) *v.,* **flogged, flogging.** beat; whip.

flood (flud) *n.* **1.** overflowing of water. —*v.* **2.** overflow or cover with water, etc.

flood′light′, *n.* artificial light for large area.

floor (flôr) *n.* **1.** bottom surface of room, etc. **2.** level in building. **3.** right to speak. —*v.* **4.** furnish with floor. **5.** knock down.

floor′ing, *n.* floor covering.

flop (flop) *v.,* **flopped, flopping,** *n. Informal.* —*v.* **1.** fall flatly. **2.** fail. **3.** flap. —*n.* **4.** act of flopping.

flop′py, *adj.* **-pier, -piest.** limp.

floppy disk, thin plastic disk for storing computer data.

flo′ra (flôr′ə) *n., pl.* **floras, florae** (flôr′ē). plants or plant life of a particular region or period.

flo′ral, *adj.* of flowers.

flor′id (flôr′id) *adj.* ruddy.

flo′rist, *n.* dealer in flowers.

floss (flôs) *n.* **1.** silky fiber from certain plants. **2.** thread used to clean between teeth. —*v.* **3.** use dental floss. —**floss′y,** *adj.*

flo·til′la (flō til′ə) *n.* small fleet.

flot′sam (flot′səm) *n.* floating wreckage.

flounce (flouns) *v.,* **flounced, flouncing,** *n.* —*v.* **1.** go with exaggerated movements. —*n.* **2.** flouncing movement. **3.** ruffle.

floun′der (floun′dər) *v.* **1.** struggle clumsily. —*n.* **2.** flat edible fish.

flour (flou^ər, flou′ər) *n.* finely ground grain.

flour′ish (flûr′ish) *v.* **1.** thrive. **2.** brandish. —*n.* **3.** act of brandishing. **4.** decoration.

flout (flout) *v.* mock; scorn.

flow (flō) *v.* **1.** move in stream. —*n.* **2.** act or rate of flowing.

flow chart, chart showing steps in procedure or system.

flow′er (flou′ər) *n., v.* blossom.

flu (flōō) *n.* influenza.

flub (flub) *v.,* **flubbed, flubbing.** botch; bungle.

fluc′tu·ate′ (fluk′chōō āt′) *v.,* **-ated, -ating.** vary irregularly.

flue (flōō) *n.* duct for smoke, etc.

flu′ent (flōō′ənt) *adj.* writing and speaking with ease. —**flu′en·cy,** *n.*

fluff (fluf) *n.* downy particles.

flu′id (flōō′id) *n.* **1.** substance that flows. —*adj.* **2.** liquid or gaseous.

fluke (flōōk) *n.* **1.** lucky chance. **2.** flounder (def. 2).

flume (flōōm) *n.* channel; trough.

flunk (flungk) *v. Informal.* fail, esp. in a course or examination.

flun′ky, *n., pl.* **-kies.** servant or follower.

fluo·res′cence (flōō res′əns, flō) *n.* emission of light upon exposure to radiation, etc. —**fluo·res′cent,** *adj.*

fluorescent lamp, tubular lamp using phosphors to produce radiation of light.

fluor′i·da′tion (flōōr′ə dā′shən, flôr′-) *n.* addition of fluorides to drinking water to reduce tooth decay.

fluor·ide′ (-īd) *n.* chemical compound containing fluorine.

fluor′ine (-ēn) *n.* yellowish toxic gaseous element.

flur′ry (flûr′ē) *n., pl.* **-ries. 1.** light snowfall. **2.** agitated state.

flush (flush) *n.* **1.** rosy glow. —*v.* **2.** redden. **3.** wash out with water. —*adj.* **4.** even with surrounding surface. **5.** well supplied.

flus′ter (flus′tər) *v.* confuse.

flute (flōōt) *n., v.,* **fluted, fluting.** —*n.* **1.** musical wind instrument. **2.** groove. —*v.* **3.** form grooves in.

flut′ist, *n.* flute player. Also, **flau′tist** (flô′tist, flou′-).

flut′ter (flut′ər) *v.* **1.** wave in air. —*n.* **2.** agitation. —**flut′tery,** *adj.*

flux (fluks) *n.* **1.** a flowing. **2.** continuous change. **3.** substance that promotes fusion of metals.

fly (flī) *v.,* **flew** (flōō), **flown** (flōn), **flying,** *n., pl.* **flies.** —*v.* **1.** move or direct through air. **2.** move swiftly. —*n.* **3.** winged insect. —**fly′er,** *n.*

fly′-blown′, *adj.* tainted; spoiled.

fly′-by-night′, *adj.* unreliable.

flying saucer, disk-shaped missile or plane, thought to come from outer space.

fly′leaf′, *n., pl.* **-leaves.** blank page in front or back of a book.

fly′wheel′, *n.* wheel for equalizing speed of machinery.

foal (fōl) *n.* young horse.

foam (fōm) *n.* **1.** mass of tiny bubbles. —*v.* **2.** form foam.

foam rubber, spongy rubber used esp. in cushions.

fob (fob) *n.* watch chain.

fo′cus (fō′kəs) *n., pl.* **-cuses, -ci** (-sī), *v.,* **-cused, -cusing.** —*n.* **1.** point at which refracted rays meet. **2.** state of sharpness for image from optical device. **3.** central point. —*v.* **4.** bring into focus. —**fo′cal,** *adj.*

fod′der (fod′ər) *n.* livestock food.

foe (fō) *n.* enemy.

fog (fog) *n., v.,* **fogged, fogging.** —*n.* **1.** thick mist. **2.** mental confusion. —*v.* **3.** make or become enveloped with fog. —**fog′gy,** *adj.*

fo′gy (fō′gē) *n., pl.* **-gies.** old-fashioned person.

foi′ble (foi′bəl) *n.* weak point.

foil (foil) *v.* **1.** frustrate. —*n.* **2.** thin metallic sheet. **3.** thing that sets off another by contrast. **4.** thin sword.

foist (foist) *v.* impose unjustifiably.

fold (fōld) *v.* **1.** bend over upon itself. **2.** wrap. **3.** collapse. —*n.* **4.** folded part. **5.** enclosure for sheep.

-fold, suffix meaning: **1.** having so many parts, as *a fourfold plan.* **2.** times as many, as *to increase tenfold.*

fold′er, *n.* **1.** folded printed sheet. **2.** outer cover.

fo′li·age (fō′lē ij) *n.* leaves.

folic acid (fō′lik, fol′ik) vitamin used in treating anemia.

fo′li·o′ (fō′lē ō′) *n., pl.* **-ios.** sheet of paper folded once.

folk (fōk) *n., pl.* **folk** or **folks. 1.** people. —*adj.* **2.** of or from the common people.

folk′lore′, *n.* customs and beliefs of people.

folk′lor′ist, *n.* expert on folklore.

folk song, song originating among the common people.

folk′sy, *adj.,* **-sier, -siest.** *Informal.* suggesting genial simplicity.

fol′li·cle (fol′i kəl) *n.* **1.** seed vessel. **2.** small cavity, sac, or gland.

fol′low (fol′ō) *v.* **1.** come or go after. **2.** pursue. **3.** conform to. **4.** move along. **5.** watch or understand. **6.** result.

fol′low·er, *n.* **1.** person who follows. **2.** disciple.

fol′low·ing, *n.* group of admirers or disciples.

fol′low-through′, *n.* **1.** last part of a motion, as after a ball has been struck. **2.** act of continuing a plan, program, etc., to completion.

fol′ly (fol′ē) *n., pl.* **-lies.** foolishness.

fo·ment′ (fō ment′) *v.* foster.

fond (fond) *adj.* **1.** having affection. **2.** foolish. —**fond′ly,** *adv.*

fon′dle (fon′dl) *v.,* **-dled, -dling.** caress.

fon·due′ (fon dōō′, -dyōō′) *n.* dip of melted cheese, liquor, and seasonings.

font (font) *n.* **1.** receptacle for baptismal water. **2.** printing type style.

food (fōōd) *n.* what is taken in for nourishment.

food processor, appliance for chopping, shredding or otherwise processing food.

fool (fōōl) *n.* **1.** person acting stupidly. —*v.* **2.** trick. **3.** act frivolously. —**fool′ish,** *adj.*

fool′har′dy, *adj.,* **-dier, -diest.** rash.

fool′proof′, *adj.* proof against misuse or mistake.

foot (fōōt) *n., pl.* **feet** (fēt), *v.* —*n.* **1.** part of leg on which body stands. **2.** unit of length equal to 12 inches. **3.** lowest part. **4.** group of syllables. —*v.* **5.** pay. —**foot′print′,** *n.*

foot′ball′, *n.* game played with pointed leather ball.

foot′hill′, *n.* hill at foot of mountains.

foot′hold′, *n.* secure place for foot to rest.

foot′ing, *n.* **1.** secure position. **2.** basis for relationship.

foot′less, *adj.* having no basis.

foot′lights′, *n.pl.* **1.** lights at the front of a stage floor. **2.** acting.

foot′lock′er, *n.* small trunk.

foot′loose′, *adj.* free to go or travel about.

foot′man, *n.* male servant.

foot′note′, *n.* note at foot of page.

foot′-pound′, *n.* work done by force

of one pound moving through distance of one foot.

foot′step′, *n.* sound of walking.

foot′stool′, *n.* low stool for resting the feet.

fop (fop) *n.* overdressed man.

for (fôr; *unstressed* fər) *prep.* **1.** with the purpose of. **2.** in the interest of. **3.** in place of. **4.** in favor of. **5.** during. —*conj.* **6.** because.

for′age (fôr′ij) *n.*, *v.*, **-aged, -aging.** —*n.* **1.** food for animals. —*v.* **2.** search for supplies.

for′ay (fôr′ā) *n.* **1.** raid. **2.** venture.

for·bear′ (fôr bâr′) *v.*, **-bore** (-bôr′), **forborne** (-bôrn′), **forbearing. 1.** refrain from. **2.** be patient.

for·bid′ (fər bid′, fôr-) *v.*, **-bade** (-bad′, -bād′) or **-bad, -bidden** or **-bid, -bidding.** give order against.

for·bid′ding, *adj.* intimidating or discouraging.

force (fôrs) *n.*, *v.*, **forced, forcing.** —*n.* **1.** strength. **2.** coercion. **3.** armed group. **4.** influence. —*v.* **5.** compel. **6.** make yield.

for′ceps (fôr′saps, -seps) *n.* medical tool for seizing and holding.

for′ci·ble (fôr′sə bəl) *adj.* by means of force. —**for′ci·bly,** *adv.*

ford (fôrd) *n.* **1.** place for crossing water by wading. —*v.* **2.** cross at ford. —**ford′a·ble,** *adj.*

fore (fôr) *adj.*, *adv.* **1.** at the front. **2.** earlier. —*n.* **3.** front.

fore-, prefix meaning: **1.** before, as *forewarn.* **2.** front, as *forehead.* **3.** preceding, as *forefather.* **4.** chief, as *foreman.*

fore′arm′, *n.* arm between elbow and wrist.

fore′bear′, *n.* ancestor.

fore·bode′, *v.*, **-boded, -boding.** portend.

fore′cast′, *v.*, **-cast, -casting,** *n.* —*v.* **1.** predict. —*n.* **2.** prediction.

fore′cas·tle (fōk′səl, fôr′kas′əl) *n.* forward part of vessel's upper deck.

fore·close′ (-klōz′) *v.*, **-closed, -closing.** deprive of the right to redeem (mortgage, etc.).

fore′fa′ther, *n.* ancestor. —**fore′moth′er,** *n.fem.*

fore′fin′ger, *n.* finger next to thumb.

fore′front′, *n.* foremost place.

fore·go′ing, *adj.* previous.

fore′gone′ conclusion, inevitable result.

fore′ground′, *n.* nearest area.

fore′hand′, *n.* in sports, stroke made with palm of hand facing direction of movement. —**fore′hand′,** *adj.*

fore′head (fôr′id, fôr′hed′) *n.* part of face above eyes.

for′eign (fôr′in) *adj.* **1.** of or from another country. **2.** from outside.

fore′man or **-wom′an** or **-per′son** *n.*, *pl.* **-men** or **-women** or **-persons.** person in charge of work crew or jury.

fore′most′, *adj.*, *adv.* first.

fore′noon′, *n.* daylight time before noon.

fo·ren′sic (fə ren′sik) *adj.* of or for public discussion or courtroom procedure.

fore′play′, *n.* sexual stimulation leading to intercourse.

fore′run′ner, *n.* predecessor.

fore·see′, *v.*, **-saw, -seen, -seeing.** see beforehand. —**fore′sight′,** *n.*

fore·shad′ow, *v.* indicate beforehand.

fore′skin′, *n.* skin on end of penis.

for′est (fôr′ist) *n.* land covered with trees. —**for′est·ry,** *n.*

fore·stall′, *v.* thwart by earlier action.

for′est·a′tion (fôr′ə stā′shan) *n.* planting of forests.

forest ranger, officer who supervises care of forests.

fore·tell′, *v.*, **-told, -telling.** predict.

fore′thought′, *n.* prudence.

for·ev′er (fôr ev′ər, fər-) *adv.* always.

fore·warn′, *v.* warn in good time.

fore′word′, *n.* introduction.

for′feit (fôr′fit) *n.* **1.** penalty. —*v.* **2.** lose as forfeit. —*adj.* **3.** forfeited.

for·gath′er, *v.* assemble.

forge (fôrj) *n.*, *v.*, **forged, forging.** —*n.* **1.** place for heating and shaping metal. —*v.* **2.** form by heating and hammering. **3.** imitate fraudulently. **4.** press ahead. —**forg′er·y,** *n.*

for·get′ (fər get′) *v.*, **-got** (-got′), **-gotten, -getting.** fail to remember. —**for·get′ful,** *adj.*

for·get′-me-not′, *n.* small plant with blue flowers.

for·give′ (fər giv′) *v.*, **-gave** (-gāv′), **-given, -giving.** grant pardon.

for·go′ (fôr gō′) *v.*, **-went** (-went′), **-gone** (-gon′), **-going.** do without.

fork (fôrk) *n.* **1.** pronged instrument. **2.** point of division. —*v.* **3.** branch.

fork′lift′, *n.* vehicle with two power-operated prongs for lifting heavy weights.

for·lorn′ (fôr lôrn′) *adj.* abandoned.

form (fôrm) *n.* **1.** shape. **2.** mold. **3.** custom; standard practice. **4.** document to be filled in. —*v.* **5.** shape.

for′mal (fôr′məl) *adj.* **1.** according to custom or standard practice. **2.** ceremonious. **3.** precisely stated. —**for′mal·ize′,** *v.*

form·al′de·hyde′ (fôr mal′də hīd′, far-) *n.* solution used as disinfectant and preservative.

for·mal′i·ty (-mal′i tē) *n.*, *pl.* **-ties. 1.** accordance with custom. **2.** act done as matter of standard practice.

for′mat (fôr′mat) *n.*, *v.*, **-matted, -matting.** —*n.* **1.** general arrangement. —*v.* **2.** prepare (a computer disk) for writing and reading.

for·ma′tion (fôr mā′shan) *n.* **1.** act of forming. **2.** material that forms. **3.** pattern of ships, aircraft, etc., moving together.

form′a·tive (fôr′mə tiv) *adj.* **1.** giving or acquiring form. **2.** relating to formation and development.

for′mer (fôr′mər) *adj.* **1.** earlier. **2.** first-mentioned. —**for′mer·ly,** *adv.*

for′mi·da·ble (fôr′mi də bəl) *adj.* awesome. —**for′mi·da·bly,** *adv.*

form letter, standardized letter that can be sent to many people.

for′mu·la (fôr′mya lə) *n.*, *pl.* **-las, -lae** (-lē′). **1.** scientific description in figures and symbols. **2.** set form of words. **3.** milk mixture for baby.

for′mu·late′ (fôr′mya lāt′) *v.*, **-lated, -lating. 1.** state systematically. **2.** devise.

for′ni·cate′ (fôr′ni kāt′) *v.*, **-cated, -cating.** have illicit sexual relations.

for·sake′ (fôr sāk′) *v.*, **-sook** (-sŏŏk′), **-saken, -saking.** desert.

for·swear′, *v.*, **-swore, -sworn, -swearing. 1.** renounce. **2.** perjure.

for·syth′i·a (fôr sith′ē ə, far-) *n.* shrub bearing yellow flowers.

fort (fôrt) *n.* fortified place.

forte (fôrt, fôr′tā) *n.* **1.** one's strong point. —*adv.* (fôr′tā). **2.** *Music.* loudly. ——**Pronunciation.** In the noun sense (*She draws pretty well, but sculpture is really her forte*), the established, traditional pronunciation of FORTE is with one syllable: (fôrt). How-

ever, the two-syllable pronunciation (fôr′tā), which is correct for the adverb (a musical term borrowed from Italian), is increasingly heard for the noun as well, and is now also considered standard.

forth (fôrth) *adv.* onward.

forth′com′ing, *adj.* about to appear.

forth′right′, *adj.* direct in manner or speech.

forth′with′, *adv.* at once.

for′ti·fi·ca′tion (fôr′tə fi kā′shən) *n.* defensive military construction.

for′ti·fy′ (fôr′tə fī′) *v.*, **-fied, -fying.** strengthen.

for·tis′si·mo′ (fôr tis′ə mō′) *adj.*, *adv. Music.* very loud.

for′ti·tude′ (fôr′ti tōōd′, -tyōōd′) *n.* patient courage.

fort′night′, *n.* two weeks.

FORTRAN (fôr′tran) *n.* computer programming language used esp. for solving problems in science and engineering.

for′tress (fôr′tris) *n.* fortified place.

for·tu′i·tous (fôr tōō′i təs, -tyōō′-) *adj.* **1.** accidental. **2.** lucky.

for′tu·nate (fôr′chə nit) *adj.* lucky.

for′tune, *n.* **1.** wealth. **2.** luck.

for′tune-tell′er, *n.* person who claims to read the future.

for′ty (fôr′tē) *n.*, *adj.* ten times four. —**for′ti·eth,** *adj.*, *n.*

fo′rum (fôr′əm) *n.* assembly for public discussion.

for′ward (fôr′wərd) *adv.* **1.** onward. —*adj.* **2.** advanced. **3.** bold. —*v.* **4.** send on. —**for′ward·er,** *n.*

fos′sil (fos′əl) *n.* petrified remains of animal or plant. —**fos′sil·i·za′tion,** *n.* —**fos′sil·ize′,** *v.*

fos′ter (fô′stər) *v.* **1.** promote growth. —*adj.* **2.** reared in a family but not related.

foul (foul) *adj.* **1.** filthy; dirty. **2.** abominable. **3.** unfair. —*n.* **4.** violation of rules in game. —*v.* **5.** make or become foul. **6.** entangle.

foul′-up′, *n.* mix-up caused esp. by bungling.

found (found) *v.* establish.

foun·da′tion, *n.* **1.** base for building, etc. **2.** organization endowed for public benefit. **3.** act of founding.

foun′der (foun′dər) *v.* **1.** sink. —*n.* **2.** person who founds.

found′ling, *n.* abandoned child.

found′ry (foun′drē) *n.*, *pl.* **-ries.** place where molten metal is cast.

foun′tain (foun′tn) *n.* **1.** spring of water. **2.** source. Also, **fount.**

foun′tain·head′, *n.* source.

four (fôr) *n.*, *adj.* three plus one. —**fourth,** *n.*, *adj.*

four′-flush′, *v.* bluff.

four′-score′, *adj.* eighty.

four′some (-səm) *n.* **1.** group of four. **2.** golf match between two pairs.

four′square′, *adj.* **1.** firm; forthright. —*adv.* **2.** firmly; frankly.

four′teen′, *n.*, *adj.* ten plus four. —**four′teenth′,** *adj.*, *n.*

fowl (foul) *n.* bird, esp. hen or rooster.

fox (foks) *n.* **1.** carnivorous animal of dog family. **2.** crafty person. —*v.* **3.** trick.

fox′glove′, *n.* tall plant with bell-shaped flowers.

fox′hole′, *n.* small pit used for cover in battle.

fox trot, dance for couples.

fox′y, *adj.*, **-ier, -iest. 1.** cunning. **2.** *Slang.* attractive.

foy′er (foi′ər, foi′ā) *n.* lobby.

FPO, 1. field post office. **2.** fleet post office.

Fr., 1. Father. **2.** French. **3.** Friar. **4.** Friday.

fra/cas (frā/kəs, frak/əs) *n.* tumult.

frac/tion (frak/shən) *n.* part of whole. —**frac/tion•al,** *adj.*

frac/tious (frak/shəs) *adj.* unruly.

frac/ture (frak/chər) *n., v.,* **-tured, -turing.** break or crack.

frag/ile (fraj/əl) *adj.* easily damaged. —**fra•gil/i•ty** (frə jil/i tē) *n.*

frag/ment, *n.* (frag/mənt) **1.** broken part. **2.** bit. —*v.* (frag/ment, frag/ment/) **3.** break into fragments.

fra/grance (frā/grəns) *n.* pleasant smell. —**fra/grant,** *adj.*

frail (frāl) *adj.* weak; fragile.

frame (frām) *n., v.,* **framed, framing.** —*n.* **1.** enclosing border. **2.** skeleton. —*v.* **3.** devise. **4.** put in frame. —**frame/work/,** *n.*

frame/-up/, *n.* fraudulent incrimination.

franc (frangk) *n.* French coin.

fran/chise (fran/chīz) *n.* **1.** right to vote. **2.** right to do business.

frank (frangk) *adj.* **1.** candid. —*v.* **2.** mail without charge.

frank/furt•er (frangk/fər tər) *n.* cooked sausage.

frank/in•cense/ (frang/kin sens/) *n.* aromatic resin.

fran/tic (fran/tik) *adj.* wildly emotional. —**fran/ti•cal•ly,** *adv.*

fra•ter/nal (frə tûr/nl) *adj.* brotherly. —**fra•ter/nal•ly,** *adv.*

fra•ter/ni•ty, *n., pl.* **-ties.** male society.

frat/er•nize/ (frat/ər nīz/) *v.,* **-nized, -nizing.** associate fraternally or intimately.

frat/ri•cide/ (fra/tri sīd/, frā/-) *n.* **1.** act of killing one's brother. **2.** person who kills his or brother.

fraud (frôd) *n.* trickery. —**fraud/u•lent,** *adj.* —**fraud/u•lent•ly,** *adv.*

fraught (frôt) *adj.* full; charged.

fray (frā) *n.* **1.** brawl. —*v.* **2.** ravel.

fraz/zle (fraz/əl) *v.,* **-zled, -zling,** *n. Informal.* —*v.* **1.** fray. **2.** fatigue. —*n.* **3.** state of fatigue.

freak (frēk) *n.* abnormal phenomenon, person, or animal.

freck/le (frek/əl) *n.* small brownish spot on skin. —**freck/led,** *adj.*

free (frē) *adj., v.,* **freer, freest,** *adv., v.,* **freed, freeing.** —*adj.* **1.** having personal rights or liberty. **2.** independent. **3.** open. **4.** without charge. —*adv.* **5.** without charge. —*v.* **6.** make free. —**free/dom,** *n.*

free/boot/er, *n.* pirate.

free/-for-all/, *n. Informal.* brawl; melee.

free/lance/ (-lans/) *adj., n., v.,* **-lanced, -lancing.** *adj.* **1.** hiring out one's work job by job. —*n.* **2.** Also, **free/lanc/er.** freelance worker. —*v.* **3.** work as freelance.

free/load/, *v. Informal.* take advantage of the generosity of others.

Free/ma/son, *n.* member of secret fraternal association for mutual assistance. —**Free/ma/son•ry,** *n.*

free radical, molecule capable of multiplying rapidly and harming the immune system.

free/think/er, *n.* person with original religious opinions.

free/way/, *n.* major highway.

freeze (frēz) *v.,* **froze** (frōz), **frozen, freezing,** *n.* —*v.* **1.** harden into ice. **2.** fix (prices, etc.) at a specific level. **3.** make unnegotiable. —*n.* **4.** act of freezing.

freight (frāt) *n.* **1.** conveyance of goods. **2.** goods conveyed. **3.** price paid.

freight/er, *n.* ship carrying mainly freight.

French (french) *n.* language or people of France. —**French,** *adj.*

French dressing, 1. salad dressing of oil and vinegar. **2.** creamy orange salad dressing.

French fries, strips of potato that have been deep-fried.

French horn, coiled brass wind instrument.

fre•net/ic (frə net/ik) *adj.* frantic.

fren/zy (fren/zē) *n., pl.* **-zies.** wild excitement. —**fren/zied,** *adj.*

fre/quen•cy (frē/kwən sē) *n., pl.* **-cies. 1.** state of being frequent. **2.** rate of recurrence. **3.** *Physics.* number of cycles in a unit of time.

fre/quent *adj.* (frē/kwənt) **1.** occurring often. —*v.* (fri kwent/) **2.** visit often.

fres/co (fres/kō) *n., pl.* **-coes, -cos.** painting on damp plaster.

fresh (fresh) *adj.* **1.** new. **2.** not salty, as water. **3.** not preserved. **4.** *Informal.* impudent. —**fresh/en,** *v.*

fresh/et (fresh/it) *n.* sudden flooding of a stream.

fresh/man, *n., pl.* **-men.** first-year student.

fresh/wa/ter, *adj.* of or living in water that is not salty.

fret (fret) *n., v.,* **fretted, fretting.** —*n.* **1.** vexation. **2.** interlaced design. **3.** metal or wood ridge across strings of an instrument, as a guitar. —*v.* **4.** or-nament with fret. **5.** worry. —**fret/ful,** *adj.*

Freud/i•an (froi/dē ən) *adj.* **1.** relating to psychoanalytic theories of Sigmund Freud. —*n.* **2.** person who follows Freud's theories.

fri/a•ble (frī/ə bəl) *adj.* crumbly.

fri/ar (frī/ər) *n.* member of Roman Catholic order. —**fri/ar•y,** *n.*

fric/as•see/ (frik/ə sē/) *n.* stewed meat or fowl.

fric/tion (frik/shən) *n.* **1.** act or effect of rubbing together. **2.** conflict.

Fri/day (frī/dā, -dē) *n.* sixth day of week.

friend (frend) *n.* **1.** person one likes. **2.** *cap.*) Quaker; member of **Society of Friends,** a Christian sect. —**friend/-ly,** *adj.* —**friend/ship,** *n.*

frieze (frēz) *n.* decorative, often carved band, as around a room.

frig/ate (frig/it) *n.* **1.** fast sailing warship. **2.** destroyerlike warship.

fright (frīt) *n.* **1.** sudden fear. **2.** shocking thing. —**fright/en,** *v.*

fright/ful, *adj.* **1.** causing fright. **2.** *Informal.* ugly; tasteless.

fright/ful•ly, *adv. Informal.* very.

frig/id (frij/id) *adj.* **1.** very cold. **2.** coldly disapproving. **3.** lacking sexual appetite. —**fri•gid/i•ty,** *n.*

frill (fril) *n.* **1.** ruffle. **2.** unnecessary feature. —*v.* **3.** ruffle. —**frill/y,** *adj.*

fringe (frinj) *n.* border of lengths of thread, etc.

frip/per•y (frip/ə rē) *n., pl.* **-peries.** cheap finery.

frisk (frisk) *v.* **1.** frolic. **2.** search (person) for concealed weapon, drugs, etc.

frisk/y, *adj.* playful.

frit/ter (frit/ər) *v.* **1.** squander little by little. —*n.* **2.** fried batter cake.

friv/o•lous (friv/ə ləs) *adj.* not serious or appropriate. —**fri•vol/i•ty** (fri vol/i tē) *n.*

frizz (friz) *v., n.,* curl. —**friz/zy,** *adj.*

fro (frō) *adv.* from; back.

frock (frok) *n.* **1.** dress. **2.** loose robe.

frog (frog) *n.* **1.** small, tailless amphibian. **2.** hoarseness.

frol/ic (frol/ik) *n., v.,* **-icked, -icking.** —*n.* **1.** fun; gaiety. —*v.* **2.** play merrily. —**frol/ic•some,** *adj.*

from (frum, from; *unstressed* frəm) *prep.* **1.** out of. **2.** because of. **3.** starting at.

frond (frond) *n.* divided leaf.

front (frunt) *n.* **1.** foremost part. **2.** area of battle. **3.** appearance; pretense. **4.** false operation concealing illegal activity. —*adj.* **5.** of or at the front. —*v.* **6.** face. —**fron/tal,** *adj.*

front/age (frun/tij) *n.* front extent of property.

front burner, condition of top priority.

fron•tier/ (frun tēr/) *n.* **1.** border of a country. **2.** outer edge of civilization. —**fron•tiers/man,** *n.*

fron/tis•piece/ (frun/tis pēs/, fron/-) *n.* picture preceding title page.

front/-run/ner, *n.* person who leads in a competition.

frost (frôst) *n.* **1.** state of freezing. **2.** cover of ice particles. —*v.* **3.** cover with frost or frosting.

frost/bite/, *n.* gangrenous condition caused by extreme cold.

frost/ing, *n.* sweet preparation for covering cakes.

froth (frôth) *n., v.* foam.

fro/ward (frō/wərd, frō/ərd) *adj.* perverse.

frown (froun) *v.* **1.** show concentration or displeasure on face. —*n.* **2.** frowning look.

frowz/y (frou/zē) *adj.* **-ier, -iest.** slovenly.

fruc/ti•fy (fruk/tə fī/, frōōk/-) *v.,* **-fied, -fying. 1.** bear fruit. **2.** make productive. —**fruc/ti•fi•ca/tion,** *n.*

fruc/tose (-tōs) *n.* sweet sugar in honey and many fruits.

fru/gal (frōō/gəl) *adj.* thrifty.

fruit (frōōt) *n.* **1.** edible product of a plant. **2.** result.

fruit/ful, *adj.* productive; successful.

fru•i/tion (frōō ish/ən) *n.* attainment.

fruit/less, *adj.* unsuccessful.

frump (frump) *n.* dowdy, unattractive woman. —**frump/y,** *adj.*

frus/trate (frus/trāt) *v.,* **-trated, -trating.** thwart. —**frus•tra/tion,** *n.*

fry (frī) *v.,* **fried, frying,** *n., pl.* **fries,** (for 4) **fry.** —*v.* **1.** cook in fat over direct heat. —*n.* **2.** something fried. **3.** feast of fried things. **4.** young fish.

ft., **1.** feet. **2.** foot. **3.** fort.

FTC, Federal Trade Commission.

fuch/sia (fyōō/shə) *n.* **1.** plant with drooping flowers. **2.** bright purplish red color.

fudge (fuj) *n.* kind of soft candy.

fuel (fyōō/əl) *n., v.,* **fueled, fueling.** —*n.* **1.** substance that maintains fire. —*v.* **2.** supply with or take in fuel.

fu/gi•tive (fyōō/ji tiv) *n.* **1.** fleeing person. —*adj.* **2.** fleeing. **3.** impermanent.

-ful, suffix meaning: **1.** full of or characterized by, as *beautiful.* **2.** tending to or able to, as *harmful.* **3.** as much as will fill, as *spoonful.*

ful/crum (fōōl/krəm, ful/-) *n., pl.* **-crums, -cra.** support on which lever rests.

ful•fill/ (fōōl fil/) *v.* **1.** carry out. **2.** satisfy. —**ful•fill/ment,** *n.*

full (fōōl) *adj.* **1.** filled. **2.** complete. **3.** abundant. —*adv.* **4.** completely. **5.** very. —**ful/ly,** *adv.*

full/back/, *n.* (in football) running

back positioned behind the quarter-back.

full′-bod′ied, *adj.* of full strength, flavor, or richness.

full′-fledged′, *adj.* fully developed.

full′-scale′, *adj.* **1.** of exact size as an original. **2.** all-out.

ful′mi·nate′ (ful′mə nāt′) *v.,* **-nated, -nating. 1.** explode loudly. **2.** issue de-nunciations.

ful′some (fŏŏl′səm, ful′-) *adj.* exces-sive.

fum′ble (fum′bəl) *v.,* **-bled, -bling,** *n.* —*v.* **1.** grope clumsily. **2.** drop. —*n.* **3.** act of fumbling.

fume (fyŏŏm) *n., v.,* **fumed, fuming.** —*n.* **1.** vapor. —*v.* **2.** emit fumes. **3.** show anger.

fu′mi·gate′ (fyŏŏ′mi gāt′) *v.,* **-gated, -gating.** disinfect with fumes. —**fu′mi·ga′tion,** *n.*

fun (fun) *n.* play; joking.

func′tion (fungk′shən) *n.* **1.** proper activity. **2.** formal social gathering. —*v.* **3.** act; operate.

func′tion·ar′y (-shə ner′ē) *n., pl.* **-aries.** official.

fund (fund) *n.* **1.** stock of money. —*v.* **2.** pay for.

fun′da·men′tal (fun′də men′tl) *adj.* **1.** basic. —*n.* **2.** basic principle.

fun′da·men′tal·ist, *n.* believer in literal interpretation of a religious text, as the Bible.

fu′ner·al (fyŏŏ′nər əl) *n.* burial rite.

fu·ne′re·al (-nēr′ē əl) *adj.* **1.** mourn-ful. **2.** of funerals.

fun′gus (fung′gəs) *n., pl.* **fungi** (fun′-jī). plant of group including mush-rooms and molds.

funk (fungk) *n. Informal.* depression.

funk′y (fung′kē) *adj.,* **-ier, -iest. 1.** earthy, as blues-based jazz. *Slang.* offbeat.

fun′nel (fun′l) *n., v.,* **-neled, -neling.** —*n.* **1.** cone-shaped tube. **2.** smoke-stack of vessel. —*v.* **3.** channel or fo-cus.

fun′ny (fun′ē) *adj.,* **-nier, -niest. 1.** amusing. **2.** strange.

funny bone, part of elbow that tin-gles when the nerve is hit.

fur (fûr) *n., v.,* **furred, furring.** —*n.* **1.** thick hairy skin of animal. **2.** garment made of fur. —*v.* **3.** trim with fur. —**fur′ry,** *adj.*

fur′bish (fûr′bish) *v.* polish; renew.

fu′ri·ous (fyŏŏr′ē əs) *adj.* very angry.

furl (fûrl) *v.* roll tightly.

fur′long (fûr′lông) *n.* ⅛ of mile; 220 yards.

fur′lough (fûr′lō) *n.* **1.** leave of ab-sence. —*v.* **2.** give a furlough to.

fur′nace (fûr′nis) *n.* structure in which to generate heat.

fur′nish (fûr′nish) *v.* **1.** provide. **2.** fit out with furniture.

fur′nish·ing, *n.* **1.** article of furni-ture, etc. **2.** clothing accessory.

fur′ni·ture (-ni chər) *n.* tables, chairs, beds, etc.

fu′ror (fyŏŏr′ôr, -ər) *n.* general excite-ment.

fur′ri·er (fûr′ē ər) *n.* dealer in furs.

fur′row (fûr′ō) *n.* **1.** trench made by plow. **2.** wrinkle. —*v.* **3.** make furrows in.

fur′ther (fûr′thər) *adv.* **1.** to a greater distance or extent. **2.** moreover. —*adj.* **3.** more. —*v.* **4.** promote. —**fur′ther·ance,** *n.* —**Usage.** See FARTHER.

fur′ther·more′, *adv.* in addition.

fur′ther·most′, *adj.* most distant.

fur′thest (-thist) *adj.* **1.** most distant or remote. —*adv.* **2.** to greatest dis-tance.

fur′tive (-tiv) *adj.* stealthy.

fu′ry (fyŏŏr′ē) *n., pl.* **-ries. 1.** violent passion, esp. anger. **2.** violence.

fuse (fyŏŏz) *n., v.,* **fused, fusing.** —*n.* **1.** safety device that breaks an electri-cal connection under excessive cur-rent. **2.** Also, **fuze.** device for igniting explosive. —*v.* **3.** blend, esp. by melt-ing together. —**fu′si·ble,** *adj.* —**fu′sion** (fyŏŏ′zhən) *n.*

fu′se·lage′ (fyŏŏ′sə läzh′, -lij) *n.* framework of an airplane.

fu′sil·lade′ (fyŏŏ′sə läd′, -läd′) *n.* si-multaneous gunfire.

fuss (fus) *n.* **1.** needless concern or ac-tivity. —*v.* **2.** make a fuss.

fus′ty (fus′tē) *adj.,* **-tier, -tiest. 1.** moldy; musty. **2.** old fashioned; out-of-date.

fu′tile (fyŏŏt′l, fyŏŏ′tīl) *adj.* useless; unsuccessful. —**fu·til′i·ty** (-til′i tē) *n.*

fu′ton (fŏŏ′ton) *n.* thin, quiltlike mat-tress.

fu′ture (fyŏŏ′chər) *n.* **1.** time to come. —*adj.* **2.** that is to come. —**fu′tur·is′tic,** *adj.*

fuzz (fuz) *n.* fluff.

fuzz′y, *adj.,* **-ier, -iest. 1.** covered with fuzz. **2.** blurred. —**fuzz′i·ly,** *adv.* —**fuzz′i·ness,** *n.*

FYI, for your information.

G

G, g (jē) *n.* seventh letter of English alphabet.

G, motion picture rating: general; suita-ble for all ages.

g, 1. good. **2.** gram. **3.** gravity.

GA, 1. Gamblers Anonymous. **2.** gen-eral of the army. **3.** Georgia.

Ga., Georgia.

gab (gab) *n., v.,* **gabbed, gabbing.** *In-formal.* chatter. —**gab′by,** *adj.*

gab′ar·dine′ (gab′ər dēn′) *n.* twill fabric.

gab′ble (gab′əl) *n., v.,* **-bled, -bling.** —*n.* **1.** rapid, unintelligible talk. —*v.* **2.** talk gabble.

ga′ble (gā′bəl) *n.* triangular wall from eaves to roof ridge.

gad (gad) *v.,* **gadded, gadding.** wan-der restlessly.

gad′a·bout′, *n.* person who flits from one social activity to another.

gad′fly′, *n., pl.* **-flies.** annoyingly crit-ical person.

gadg′et (gaj′it) *n.* any ingenious de-vice. —**gad′get·ry,** *n.*

gaff (gaf) *n.* hook for landing fish.

gaffe (gaf) *n.* social blunder.

gaf′fer, *n.* **1.** chief electrician on a film or TV show. **2.** *Informal.* old man.

gag (gag) *v.,* **gagged, gagging,** *n.* —*v.* **1.** stop up mouth to keep (person) silent. **2.** suppress statements of. **3.** retch. —*n.* **4.** something that gags. **5.** *Informal.* joke.

gage (gāj) *n., v.,* **gaged, gaging.** —*n.* **1.** token of challenge. **2.** pledge. **3.** gauge. —*v.* **4.** gauge.

gag′gle (gag′əl) *n.* flock of geese.

gai′e·ty (gā′i tē) *n., pl.* **-ties.** merri-ment.

gai′ly (gā′lē) *adv.* merrily.

gain (gān) *v.* **1.** obtain. **2.** earn. **3.** im-prove. **4.** move faster than another. —*n.* **5.** profit.

gain′say′ (gān′sā′, gān sā′) *v.,* **-said, -saying.** contradict.

gait (gāt) *n.* manner of walking.

gal (gal) *n. Informal.* girl.

gal., gallon.

ga′la (gā′lə, gal′ə; *esp. Brit.* gä′lə) *adj.* **1.** festive. —*n.* **2.** festive occasion.

gal′ax·y (gal′ak sē) *n., pl.* **-axies. 1.** (*often cap.*) Milky Way. **2.** brilliant as-semblage. —**ga·lac′tic** (gə lak′tik) *adj.*

gale (gāl) *n.* **1.** strong wind. **2.** noisy outburst, as of laughter.

gall (gôl) *v.* **1.** chafe. **2.** irritate. —*n.* **3.** sore due to rubbing. **4.** bile. **5.** *In-formal.* impudence. **6.** abnormal growth on plants.

gal′lant (gal′ənt; gə lant′, -länt′) *adj.* chivalrous.

gall bladder, sac on liver in which bile is stored.

gal′le·on (gal′ē ən, gal′yən) *n.* large sailing vessel.

gal′ler·y (gal′ə rē) *n.* **1.** corridor. **2.** balcony. **3.** place for art exhibits.

gal′ley (gal′ē) *n.* **1.** vessel propelled by many oars. **2.** kitchen of ship.

gal′li·vant′ (gal′ə vant′) *v.* travel about, seeking pleasure.

gal′lon (gal′ən) *n.* unit of capacity equal to 4 quarts.

gal′lop (gal′əp) *v.* **1.** run at full speed. —*n.* **2.** fast gait.

gal′lows (gal′ōz, -əz) *n.* wooden frame for execution by hanging.

gall′stone′, *n.* stone formed in bile passages.

ga·lore′ (gə lôr′) *adj.* in abundance.

ga·losh′es (gə losh′iz) *n.pl.* over-shoes.

gal′va·nize′ (gal′və nīz′) *v.,* **-nized, -nizing. 1.** stimulate by or as by elec-tric current. **2.** coat with zinc.

gam′bit (gam′bit) *n.* **1.** sacrificial move in chess. **2.** clever tactic.

gam′ble (gam′bəl) *v.,* **-bled, -bling,** *n.* —*v.* **1.** play for stakes at game of chance. **2.** wager; risk. —*n.* **3.** uncer-tain venture. —**gam′bler,** *n.*

gam′bol (gam′bəl) *v.,* **-boled, -bol-ing,** *n.* frolic.

game (gām) *n.* **1.** pastime or contest. **2.** wild animals, hunted for sport. —*adj.* **3.** brave and willing. **4.** lame. —**game′ly,** *adv.*

game plan, carefully planned strategy or course of action.

gam′ete (gam′ēt) *n.* mature sexual reproductive cell that unites with an-other to form a new organism.

gam′ut (gam′ət) *n.* full range.

gam′y (gā′mē) *adj.,* **-ier, -iest.** having the strong flavor of game.

gan′der (gan′dər) *n.* male goose.

gang (gang) *n.* **1.** group; band. **2.** work crew. **3.** band of criminals.

gan′gling (gang′gling) *adj.* awk-wardly tall and thin.

gan′gli·on (gang′glē ən) *n., pl.* **-glia, -glions.** nerve center.

gang′plank′ (gang′plangk′) *n.* tem-porary bridge to docked vessel.

gan′grene (gang′grēn, gang grēn′) *n.* death of body tissue. —**gan′gre·nous,** *adj.*

gang′ster, *n.* member of a criminal gang.

gang′way′ *n.* (gang′wā′) **1.** entrance to ship. **2.** narrow passage. —*interj.* (gang′wā′) **3.** (make way!)

gan′try (gan′trē) *n., pl.* **-tries.** frame-work for traveling crane or rocket.

gaol (jāl) *n., v. Brit.* jail.

gap (gap) *n.* **1.** opening; vacant space. **2.** ravine.

gape (gāp, gap) *v.,* **gaped, gaping. 1.** open mouth as in wonder. **2.** open wide.

ga·rage′ (gə räzh′, -räj′) *n.* place where motor vehicles are kept or re-paired.

garb (gärb) *n.* **1.** clothes. —*v.* **2.** clothe.

gar′bage (gär′bij) *n.* refuse; trash.

gar′ble (gär′bəl) *v.*, **-bled, -bling.** misquote or mix up.

gar′den (gär′dn) *n.* **1.** area for growing plants. —*v.* **2.** make or tend garden. —**gar′den•er,** *n.*

gar•de′nia (gär dē′nyə, -nē ə) *n.* flowering evergreen shrub.

gar′den-vari′ety, *adj.* common.

gar•gan′tu•an (gär gan′chōō ən) *adj.* gigantic; colossal.

gar′gle (gär′gəl) *v.*, **-gled, -gling,** *n.* —*v.* **1.** rinse throat. —*n.* **2.** liquid for gargling.

gar′goyle (gär′goil) *n.* grotesquely carved figure.

gar′ish (gâr′ish, gar′-) *adj.* glaring; showy. —**gar′ish•ly,** *adv.*

gar′land (gär′lənd) *n.* **1.** wreath of flowers, etc. —*v.* **2.** deck with garland.

gar′lic (gär′lik) *n.* plant with edible, pungent bulb. —**gar′lick•y,** *adj.*

gar′ment (gär′mənt) *n.* article of clothing.

gar′ner (gär′nər) *v.* gather; acquire.

gar′net (gär′nit) *n.* deep-red gem.

gar′nish (gär′nish) *v.* **1.** adorn. **2.** decorate (food). —*n.* **3.** decoration for food.

gar′nish•ee′ (gär′ni shē′) *v.*, **-nisheed, -nisheeing.** attach (money or property of defendant).

gar′ret (gar′it) *n.* attic.

gar′ri•son (gar′ə sən) *n.* **1.** body of defending troops. **2.** military post. —*v.* **3.** provide with garrison.

gar•rote′ (gə rot′, -rōt′) *n.*, *v.*, **-roted, -roting.** —*n.* **1.** strangulation. —*v.* **2.** strangle.

gar′ru•lous (gar′ə ləs, gar′yə-) *adj.* talkative. —**gar•ru′li•ty,** *n.*

gar′ter (gär′tər) *n.* fastening to hold up stocking.

garter snake, common, harmless striped snake.

gas (gas) *n.*, *pl.* **gases,** *v.*, **gassed, gassing.** —*n.* **1.** fluid substance, often burned for light or heat. **2.** gasoline. —*v.* **3.** overcome with gas.

gash (gash) *n.* **1.** long deep cut. —*v.* **2.** make gash in.

gas′ket (gas′kit) *n.* ring or strip used to make joint watertight.

gas′o•line′ (gas′ə lēn′, gas′ə lēn′) *n.* inflammable liquid from petroleum, used esp. as motor fuel.

gasp (gasp) *n.* **1.** sudden short breath. —*v.* **2.** breathe in gasps.

gas′tric (gas′trik) *adj.* of stomach.

gas′tro•nom′i•cal (gas′trə nom′i kəl) *adj.* of good eating. —**gas•tron′o•my** (gə stron′ə mē) *n.*

gate (gāt) *n.* movable hinged barrier.

gate′way′, *n.* passage or entrance.

gath′er (gath′ər) *v.* **1.** bring or come together. **2.** infer. **3.** harvest. —*n.* **4.** pucker. —**gath′er•ing,** *n.*

gauche (gōsh) *adj.* unsophisticated; socially clumsy.

gaud′y (gô′dē) *adj.*, **-ier, -iest.** vulgarly showy. —**gaud′i•ly,** *adv.*

gauge (gāj) *v.*, **gauged, gauging,** *n.* —*v.* **1.** estimate. **2.** measure. —*n.* **3.** standard of measure. **4.** device for measuring. **5.** distance between railroad rails.

gaunt (gônt) *adj.* haggard; bleak.

gaunt′let (gônt′lit, gänt′-) *n.* **1.** large-cuffed glove. **2.** Also, **gant′let** (gant′-). ordeal.

gauze (gôz) *n.* transparent fabric.

gav′el (gav′əl) *n.* chairperson's mallet.

gawk (gôk) *v.* stare stupidly.

gawk′y, *adj.*, **-ier, -iest.** clumsy.

gay (gā) *adj.*, **gayer, gayest,** *n.* —*adj.* **1.** joyous. **2.** bright. **3.** *Slang.* homosexual. —*n.* **4.** *Slang.* homosexual. —**gay′ly,** *adv.*

gaze (gāz) *v.*, **gazed, gazing,** *n.* —*v.* **1.** look steadily. —*n.* **2.** steady look.

ga•ze′bo (gə zā′bō, -zē′-) *n.*, *pl.* **-bos, -boes.** open structure on a site with a pleasant view in a garden.

ga•zelle′ (gə zel′) *n.* small antelope.

ga•zette′ (gə zet′) *n.* newspaper.

gaz′et•teer′ (gaz′i tēr′) *n.* geographical dictionary.

gaz•pa′cho (gäz pä′chō) *n.* Spanish chilled vegetable soup.

gear (gēr) *n.* **1.** toothed wheel that engages with another. **2.** equipment. —*v.* **3.** connect by gears. **4.** adjust.

gear′shift′, *n.* gear-changing lever in automotive transmission system.

geck′o (gek′ō) *n.*, *pl.* **-os** or **-oes.** small tropical lizard.

GED, general equivalency diploma.

gee (jē) *interj.* (exclamation of surprise or disappointment.)

gee′zer (gē′zər) *n.* odd or eccentric man, esp. an older one.

Gei′ger counter (gī′gər) instrument for measuring radioactivity.

gei′sha (gā′shə, gē′-) *n.* Japanese woman trained to provide entertainment and companionship for men.

gel (jel) *n.*, *v.*, **gelled, gelling.** —*n.* **1.** jellylike or gluelike substance. —*v.* **2.** become gel.

gel′a•tin (jel′ə tn) *n.* substance from animal skins, etc., used in jellies, glue, etc. —**ge•lat′i•nous** (jə lat′n əs) *adj.*

geld′ing (gel′ding) *n.* castrated male horse. —**geld,** *v.*

gel′id (jel′id) *adj.* icy.

gem (jem) *n.* precious stone.

Gen., General.

gen′darme (zhän′därm) *n.* French police officer.

gen′der (jen′dər) *n.* **1.** *Gram.* set of classes including all nouns, distinguished as masculine, feminine, neuter. **2.** character of being male or female; sex.

gene (jēn) *n.* biological unit that carries inherited traits.

ge′ne•al′o•gy (jē′nē ol′ə jē, -al′-, jen′ē-) *n.*, *pl.* **-gies.** study or account of ancestry.

gen′er•al (jen′ər əl) *adj.* **1.** of or including all. **2.** usual. **3.** undetailed. —*n.* **4.** highest-ranking army officer. —**gen′er•al•ly,** *adv.*

gen′er•al′i•ty (-al′i tē) *n.*, *pl.* **-ties.** general statement.

gen′er•al•ize′, *v.*, **-ized, -izing.** make generalities.

general practitioner, doctor whose practice is not limited to any specific branch of medicine.

gen′er•ate′ (jen′ə rāt′) *v.*, **-ated, -ating.** produce.

gen′er•a′tion, *n.* **1.** all individuals born in one period. **2.** such period (about 30 years). **3.** production.

Generation X (eks) the generation born in the U.S. after 1965.

gen′er•a′tor, *n.* device for producing electricity, gas, etc.

ge•ner′ic (jə ner′ik) *adj.* **1.** of entire categories. **2.** (of merchandise) unbranded. —**ge•ner′i•cal•ly,** *adv.*

gen′er•ous (jen′ər əs) *adj.* **1.** giving freely. **2.** abundant. —**gen′er•os′i•ty** (-ə ros′i tē) *n.*

gen′e•sis (-ə sis) *n.* birth or origin.

ge•net′ics (jə net′iks) *n.* science of heredity. —**ge•net′ic,** *adj.*

gen., genl., general.

gen′ial (jēn′yəl, jē′nē əl) *adj.* openly friendly.

ge′nie (jē′nē) *n.* spirit, often appearing in human form.

gen′i•ta′li•a (jen′i tā′lē ə, -tāl′yə) *n.pl.* genitals.

gen′i•tals (-tlz) *n.pl.* sexual organs.

gen′i•tive (jen′i tiv) *n.* **1.** grammatical case usu. indicating possession. —*adj.* **2.** of or relating to this case.

gen′ius (jēn′yəs) *n.* **1.** exceptional natural ability. **2.** person having such ability.

gen′o•cide′ (jen′ə sīd′) *n.* planned extermination of national or racial group.

gen′re (zhän′rə) *n.* class or category of artistic work.

gen•teel′ (jen tēl′) *adj.* well-bred; refined. —**gen•til′i•ty** (-til′i tē) *n.*

gen′tian (jen′shən) *n.* plant with blue flowers.

gen′tile (jen′tīl) *adj.* (sometimes cap.) not Jewish or Mormon.

gen′tle (jen′tl) *adj.*, **-tler, -tlest. 1.** mild; kindly. **2.** respectable. **3.** careful in handling things.

gen′tle•man, *n.*, *pl.* **-men. 1.** man of good breeding and manners. **2.** (used as polite term) any man.

gen′tri•fi•ca′tion (jen′trə fi kā′shən) *n.* replacement of existing population by others with more wealth or status. —**gen′tri•fy,** *v.*, **-fied, -fying.**

gen′try, *n.* wellborn people.

gen•u•flect′ (-yōō flekt′) *v.* kneel partway in reverence.

gen′u•ine (-yōō in or, sometimes, -īn′) *adj.* real. —**gen′u•ine•ly,** *adv.*

ge′nus (jē′nəs) *n.*, *pl.* **genera, genuses.** biological group including one or several species.

Gen X (jen′ eks′) Generation X. Also, **GenX.**

geo-, prefix meaning the earth or ground, as *geography.*

ge′ode (jē′ōd) *n.* hollow nodular stone often lined with crystals.

ge′o•des′ic dome (jē′ə des′ik, -dē′sik) dome with framework of straight members that form grid.

ge•og′ra•phy (jē og′rə fē) *n.* study of earth's surface, climate, etc. —**ge•og′ra•pher,** *n.* —**ge′o•graph′i•cal** (-ə graf′i kəl) *adj.*

ge•ol′o•gy (jē ol′ə jē) *n.* science of earth's structure. —**ge•ol′o•gist,** *n.*

ge′o•mag•net′ic (jē′ō mag net′ik) *adj.* of the earth's magnetism.

ge•om′e•try (jē om′i trē) *n.* branch of mathematics dealing with shapes. —**ge′o•met′ric** (-ə me′trik) *adj.*

ge′o•phys′ics (jē′ō fiz′iks) *n.* science of the physics of the earth and its atmosphere.

ge′o•pol′i•tics, *n.* study of politics in relation to geography.

ge′o•sta′tion•ar′y, *adj.* of an orbiting satellite remaining in same spot over the earth.

ge′o•ther′mal, *adj.* of the earth's internal heat.

ge•ra′ni•um (ji rā′nē əm) *n.* small plant with showy flowers.

ger′bil (jûr′bəl) *n.* small burrowing rodent, popular as a pet.

ger′i•at′rics (jer′ē a′triks, jēr′-) *n.* branch of medicine dealing with aged persons. —**ger′i•at′ric,** *adj.*

germ (jûrm) *n.* **1.** microscopic disease-producing organism. **2.** seed or origin.

Ger′man (jûr′mən) *n.* native or language of Germany. —**German,** *adj.*

ger•mane′ (jər mān′) *adj.* pertinent.

German measles, rubella.

German shepherd, large dog with thick, usually gray or black-and-tan coat.

ger′mi·cide′ (jûr′mə sīd′) *n.* agent that kills germs. —**ger′mi·cid′al,** *adj.*

ger′mi·nate′, *v.,* -nated, -nating. begin to grow. —**ger′mi·na′tion,** *n.*

ger′on·tol′o·gy (jer′ən tol′ə jē, jēr′-) *n.* study of aging and problems and care of old people.

ger′ry·man′der (jer′ē man′dər) *v.* divide into voting districts so as to give one group or area an unequal advantage.

ger′und (jer′ənd) *n.* noun form of a verb.

ges·ta′tion (je stā′shən) *n.* period of being carried in womb.

ges·tic′u·late′ (je stik′yə lāt′) *v.,* -lated, -lating. make gestures.

ges′ture (jes′chər) *n., v.,* -tured, -turing. —*n.* **1.** expressive movement of body, head, etc. **2.** act demonstrating attitude or emotion. —*v.* **3.** make expressive movements.

get (get) *v.,* **got** (got), **got** or **gotten, getting. 1.** obtain. **2.** cause to be or do. **3.** be obliged to. **4.** arrive. **5.** become.

get′a·way′, *n.* **1.** escape. **2.** start of race. **3.** place for relaxing, etc.

get′-up, *n. Informal.* outfit.

gey′ser (gī′zər, -sər) *n.* hot spring that emits jets of water.

ghast′ly (gast′lē) *adj.,* -lier, -liest. **1.** frightful. **2.** deathly pale.

gher′kin (gûr′kin) *n.* **1.** small cucumber. **2.** small pickle.

ghet′to (get′ō) *n., pl.* -tos, -toes. **1.** (formerly) Jewish part of city. **2.** city area in which mostly poor minorities live. —**ghet′to·ize,** *v.,* -ized, -izing.

ghost (gōst) *n.* disembodied soul of dead person. —**ghost′ly,** *adj.*

ghost′writ′er, *n.* person who writes for another who is presumed to be the author. —**ghost′write′,** *v.*

ghoul (gool) *n.* **1.** spirit that preys on dead. **2.** person morbidly interested in misfortunes.

G.I. (jē′ī′) enlisted soldier.

gi′ant (jī′ənt) *n.* **1.** being of superhuman size. **2.** person of great accomplishments. —**gi′ant·ess,** *n.fem.*

gib′ber (jib′ər) *v.* speak unintelligibly. —**gib′ber·ish,** *n.*

gib′bet (jib′it) *n.* gallows with projecting arm.

gib′bon (gib′ən) *n.* small, long-armed ape.

gibe (jīb) *v.,* **gibed, gibing,** *n.* jeer.

gib′lets (jib′lits) *n.pl.* heart, liver, and gizzard of a fowl.

gid′dy (gid′ē) *adj.,* -dier, -diest. **1.** frivolous. **2.** dizzy.

gift (gift) *n.* **1.** present. **2.** act of giving. **3.** talent.

gift′ed, *adj.* **1.** talented. **2.** highly intelligent.

gig (gig) *n.* **1.** carriage drawn by one horse. **2.** light boat. **3.** *Slang.* engagement, as of musician.

gi·gan′tic (jī gan′tik, ji-) *adj.* befitting a giant. —**gi·gan′ti·cal·ly,** *adv.*

gig′gle (gig′əl) *v.,* -gled, -gling, *n.* —*v.* **1.** laugh lightly in a silly way. —*n.* **2.** silly laugh.

GIGO (gī′gō) *n.* axiom that faulty data input to a computer will result in faulty output.

gig′o·lo′ (jig′ə lō′) *n., pl.* -los. man supported by his female lover.

Gi′la monster (hē′lə) large, venomous lizard.

gild (gild) *v.,* **gilded** or **gilt, gilding.** coat with gold.

gill *n.* **1.** (gil) breathing organ on fish.

2. (jil) unit of liquid measure, $\frac{1}{4}$ pint (4 fluid ounces).

gilt (gilt) *n.* gold used for gilding.

gilt′-edged′, *adj.* of the highest quality. Also, **gilt′-edge′.**

gim′let (gim′lit) *n.* small tool for boring holes.

gim′mick (gim′ik) *n.* device or trick.

gimp′y (gim′pē) *adj.,* gimpier, gimpiest. *Slang.* limping or lame.

gin (jin) *n., v.,* **ginned, ginning.** —*n.* **1.** flavored alcoholic drink. **2.** machine for separating cotton from its seeds. **3.** trap. **4.** card game. —*v.* **5.** put (cotton) through gin.

gin′ger (jin′jər) *n.* plant with spicy root used in cookery.

ginger ale, carbonated soft drink flavored with ginger.

gin′ger·bread′, *n.* cake flavored with ginger and molasses.

gin′ger·ly, *adj.* **1.** wary. —*adv.* **2.** warily.

gin′ger·snap′, *n.* crisp cookie flavored with ginger.

ging′ham (ging′əm) *n.* checked cotton fabric.

gin·gi·vi′tis (jin′jə vī′tis) *n.* inflammation of the gums.

gink′go (ging′kō, jing′-) *n., pl.* -goes. shade tree native to China, with fan-shaped leaves.

gin′seng (jin′seng) *n.* plant with a medicinal root.

gi·raffe′ (jə raf′) *n.* tall, long-necked animal of Africa.

gird (gûrd) *v.,* **girt** or **girded, girding. 1.** encircle with or as with belt. **2.** prepare.

gird′er, *n.* horizontal structural beam.

gir′dle, *n., v.,* -dled, -dling. —*n.* **1.** encircling band. **2.** light corset. —*v.* **3.** encircle.

girl (gûrl) *n.* female child. —**girl′hood′,** *n.* —**girl′ish,** *adj.*

girl′friend′, *n.* frequent or favorite female companion.

Girl Scout, member of organization for girls (**Girl Scouts**).

girth (gûrth) *n.* **1.** distance around. —*v.* **2.** gird.

gis′mo (giz′mō) *n.* gadget.

gist (jist) *n.* essential meaning.

give (giv) *v.,* **gave** (gāv), **given, giving,** *n.* —*v.* **1.** bestow. **2.** emit. **3.** present. **4.** yield. —*n.* **5.** elasticity.

give′a·way′, *n.* **1.** revealing act, remark, etc. **2.** TV show in which contestants compete for prizes.

giv′en, *adj.* **1.** stated. **2.** inclined. —*n.* **3.** established fact or condition.

giz′zard (giz′ərd) *n.* muscular stomach of birds.

gla′cial (glā′shəl) *adj.* **1.** of glaciers or ice sheets. **2.** bitterly cold.

gla′cier, *n.* mass of ice moving slowly down slope.

glad (glad) *adj.,* **gladder, gladdest. 1.** pleased; happy. **2.** causing joy. —**glad′den,** *v.* —**glad′ness,** *n.*

glade (glād) *n.* open space in forest.

glad′i·a′tor (glad′ē ā′tər) *n.* Roman swordsman fighting for public entertainment.

glad′i·o′lus (-ō′ləs) *n., pl.* -lus, -li (-lī), -luses. plant bearing tall spikes of flowers. Also, **glad′i·o′la.**

glad′ly, *adv.* **1.** with pleasure. **2.** willingly.

glam′or·ize′ (glam′ə rī′) *v.,* -ized, -izing. make glamorous.

glam′our (glam′ər) *n.* alluring charm. —**glam′or·ous,** *adj.*

glance (glans) *v.,* **glanced, glancing,** *n.* —*v.* **1.** look briefly. **2.** strike obliquely. —*n.* **3.** brief look.

gland (gland) *n.* body organ that secretes some substance.

glans (glanz) *n.* head of penis or clitoris.

glare (glâr) *n., v.,* **glared, glaring.** —*n.* **1.** strong light. **2.** fierce look. —*v.* **3.** shine with strong light. **4.** stare fiercely.

glar′ing, *adj.* very obvious.

glass (glas) *n.* **1.** hard, brittle, transparent substance. **2.** (*pl.*) eyeglasses. **3.** drinking vessel of glass. **4.** anything made of glass. —*adj.* **5.** of glass. —*v.* **6.** cover with glass. —**glass′ware′,** *n.*

glass ceiling, not generally acknowledged upper limit to professional advancement, esp. for women or minorities.

glass′y, *adj.,* -ier, -iest. **1.** like glass. **2.** without expression; dull.

glau·co′ma (glô kō′mə, glou-) *n.* condition of elevated fluid pressure within the eyeball, ^ausing increasing loss of vision.

glaze (glāz) *v.,* **glazed, glazing,** *n.* —*v.* **1.** fit with glass. **2.** put glossy surface on. **3.** make (eyes) expressionless. —*n.* **4.** glossy coating.

gla′zier (glā′zhər) *n.* person who installs glass.

gleam (glēm) *n.* **1.** flash of light. —*v.* **2.** emit gleams.

glean (glēn) *v.* gather laboriously, as grain left by reapers.

glee (glē) *n.* mirth. —**glee′ful,** *adj.*

glen (glen) *n.* narrow valley.

glib (glib) *adj.* suspiciously fluent.

glide (glīd) *v.,* **glided, gliding,** *n.* —*v.* **1.** move smoothly and effortlessly. —*n.* **2.** gliding movement.

glid′er, *n.* motorless aircraft.

glim′mer (glim′ər) *n.* **1.** faint unsteady light. **2.** small amount. —*v.* **3.** shine faintly. —**glim′mer·ing,** *n.*

glimpse (glimps) *n., v.,* **glimpsed, glimpsing.** —*n.* **1.** brief view. —*v.* **2.** catch glimpse of.

glint (glint) *n., v.* gleam.

glis′ten (glis′ən) *v., n.* sparkle.

glitch (glich) *n. Informal.* defect or error.

glit′ter (glit′ər) *v.* **1.** reflect light with a brilliant sparkle. **2.** make a brilliant show. —*n.* **3.** sparkling light or luster. **4.** showy brilliance. **5.** small glittering ornaments.

glitz′y (glit′sē) *adj.,* -ier, -iest. *Informal.* tastelessly showy; flashy and pretentious.

gloam′ing (glō′ming) *n.* dusk.

gloat (glōt) *v.* gaze or speak with unconcealed triumph.

glob (glob) *n.* rounded lump or mass.

global warming (glō′bəl) increase in the average temperature of the earth's atmosphere, causing changes in climate.

globe (glōb) *n.* **1.** earth; world. **2.** sphere depicting the earth. **3.** any sphere. —**glob′al,** *adj.*

globe′trot′ter, *n.* one who travels regularly all over the world.

glob′ule (glob′yool) *n.* small sphere. —**glob′u·lar,** *adj.*

gloom (gloom) *n.* **1.** low spirits. **2.** darkness.

gloom′y, *adj.,* -ier, -iest. **1.** dejected; low-spirited. **2.** depressing. **3.** dark; dismal. —**gloom′i·ly,** *adv.*

glop (glop) *n.* messy mixture.

glo′ri·fy′ (glôr′ə fī′) *v.,* -fied, -fying. **1.** extol. **2.** make glorious.

glo′ry, *n., pl.* -ries, *v.,* -ried, -rying. —*n.* **1.** great praise or honor. **2.** magnificence. **3.** heavenly bliss. —*v.* **4.** exult. —**glor′i·ous,** *adj.*

gloss (glos) *n.* **1.** external show. **2.**

shine. **3.** explanation of text. —v. **4.** put gloss on. **5.** annotate. **6.** explain away. —**glos′sy,** adj.

glos′sa·ry (glos′ə rē) n., pl. **-ries.** list of key words with definitions.

glot′tis (glot′is) n. opening at upper part of larynx. —**glot′tal,** adj.

glove (gluv) n., v., **gloved, gloving.** —n. **1.** hand covering with piece for each finger. —v. **2.** cover with glove. —**gloved,** adj.

glow (glō) n. **1.** light emitted by substance. **2.** brightness or warmth. —v. **3.** shine.

glow′er (glou′ər) v. **1.** frown sullenly. —n. **2.** frown.

glow′worm′ (glō′wûrm′) n. kind of firefly.

glu′cose (glōō′kōs) n. sugar found in fruits and animal tissues.

glue (glōō) n., v., **glued, gluing.** —n. **1.** adhesive substance, esp. from gelatin. —v. **2.** join with glue.

glum (glum) adj., **glummer, glummest.** gloomily sullen.

glut (glut) v., **glutted, glutting,** n. —v. **1.** feed or fill to excess. —n. **2.** full supply. **3.** surfeit.

glu′ten (glōōt′n) n. substance left in flour after starch is removed.

glu′tin·ous, adj. gluelike.

glut′ton (glut′n) n. greedy person. —**glut′ton·ous,** adj. —**glut′ton·y,** n.

glyc′er·in (glis′ər in) n. thick liquid used as a sweetener, lotion, etc. Also, **glyc′er·ine.**

gnarl (närl) n. knot on a tree.

gnarled (närld) adj. bent and distorted.

gnash (nash) v. grind (the teeth) together, as in rage.

gnat (nat) n. small fly.

gnaw (nô) v. **1.** wear away by biting. **2.** distress. —**gnaw′ing,** adj.

gnome (nōm) n. dwarf in fairy tales.

GNP, gross national product.

gnu (nōō, nyōō) n., pl. **gnus, gnu.** African antelope.

go (gō) v., n. **went** (went), **gone** (gôn), **going,** pl. **goes.** —v. **1.** move; depart. **2.** act. **3.** become. **4.** harmonize. —n. **5.** energy. **6.** attempt.

goad (gōd) n. **1.** stimulus. —v. **2.** tease; taunt.

goal (gōl) n. **1.** aim. **2.** terminal or target in race or game. **3.** single score in various games.

goal′keep′er, n. in sports, player whose chief duty is to prevent opposition from scoring a goal. Also, **goal′tend′er;** Informal. **goal′ie.**

goat (gōt) n. horned mammal related to sheep.

goat·ee′ (gō tē′) n. pointed beard.

gob (gob) n. mass.

gob′ble (gob′əl) v., **-bled, -bling,** n. —v. **1.** eat greedily. **2.** make cry of male turkey. —n. **3.** this cry.

gob′ble·de·gook′ (-dē gōōk′) n. nonsense.

gob′bler, n. male turkey.

go′-be·tween′, n. intermediary.

gob′let (gob′lit) n. stemmed glass.

gob′lin (gob′lin) n. elf.

God (god) n. **1.** Supreme Being. **2.** (l.c.) deity. —**god′dess,** n.fem.

god′ly, adj., **-lier, -liest. 1.** of God or gods. **2.** conforming to religion.

god′par′ent, n. sponsor of child at baptism. —**god′child′,** n. —**god′daugh′ter,** n. —**god′fath′er,** n. —**god′moth′er,** n. —**god′son′,** n.

god′send′, n. anything unexpected but welcome.

goes (gōz) third pers. sing. pres. indic. of **go.**

go′fer (gō′fər) n. Slang. employee who mainly runs errands.

gog′gle (gog′əl) n., v., **-gled, -gling.** —n. **1.** (pl.) protective eyeglasses. —v. **2.** stare with wide-open eyes.

goi′ter (goi′tər) n. enlargement of thyroid gland.

gold (gōld) n. **1.** precious yellow metal. **2.** bright yellow. —**gold, gold′en,** adj.

gold′brick′, Slang. —n. **1.** Also, **gold′brick′er.** person who shirks work. —v. **2.** shirk work.

gold′en·rod′, n. plant bearing clusters of yellow flowers.

gold′finch′, n. yellow-feathered American finch.

gold′fish′, n. small, gold-colored fish.

golf (golf) n. game played on outdoor course with special clubs and small ball. —**golf′er,** n.

go′nad (gō′nad, gon′ad) n. ovary or testis. —**go·nad′al,** adj.

gon′do·la (gon′dl ə or, esp. for 0, gon dō′lə) n. narrow canal boat used in Venice. —**gon′do·lier′** (-lēr′) n.

gon′er (gô′nər) n. Informal. person or thing that is dying or past help.

gong (gông) n. brass or bronze disk sounded with hammer.

gon′or·rhe′a (gon′ə rē′ə) n. contagious venereal disease.

goo (gōō) n., pl. **goos. 1.** thick or sticky substance. **2.** sentimentality.

good (gŏŏd) adj. **1.** morally excellent. **2.** of high or adequate quality. **3.** kind. **4.** skillful. —n. **5.** benefit. **6.** excellence. **7.** (pl.) possessions.

good′-by′, interj., n., pl. **good-bys.** farewell. Also, **good′-bye′** pl., **good-byes.**

Good Friday, Friday before Easter.

good′ly, adj., **-lier, -liest.** numerous; abundant.

good Sa·mar′i·tan (sə mar′i tn) person who helps those in need.

good′will′, n. friendly feelings or intentions.

good′y (gŏŏd′ē) n., pl. **-ies.** food pleasing to eat, as candy.

goof (gōōf) Informal. —n. **1.** fool. **2.** blunder. —v. **3.** blunder. —**goof′y,** adj.

goon (gōōn) n. Slang. **1.** hoodlum hired to threaten or commit violence. **2.** stupid, foolish, or awkward person.

goose (gōōs) n., pl. **geese.** web-footed water bird.

goose′ber′ry, n., pl. **-ries.** tart edible fruit.

goose flesh, bristling of hair on the skin, as from cold or fear. Also, **goose pimples, goose bumps.**

G.O.P., Grand Old Party (epithet of the Republican Party).

go′pher (gō′fər) n. burrowing rodent.

gore (gōr) n., v., **gored, goring.** —n. **1.** clotted blood. **2.** triangular insert of cloth. —v. **3.** pierce with horn or tusk. —**gor′y,** adj.

gorge (gôrj) n., v., **gorged, gorging.** —n. **1.** narrow rocky cleft. —v. **2.** stuff with food.

gor′geous (gôr′jəs) adj. **1.** splendid. **2.** very beautiful.

go·ril′la (gə ril′ə) n. large African ape.

gos′ling (goz′ling) n. young goose.

gos′pel (gos′pəl) n. **1.** teachings of Christ and apostles. **2.** absolute truth.

gos′sa·mer (gos′ə mər) n. **1.** filmy cobweb. —adj. **2.** like gossamer.

gos′sip (gos′əp) n., v., **-siped, -siping.** —n. **1.** idle talk, esp. about others. **2.** person who spreads gossip. —v. **3.** talk idly about others.

Goth′ic (goth′ik) adj. **1.** noting a style of European architecture from the 12th to 16th centuries. **2.** (often l.c.) noting a style of literature marked by gloomy settings and sinister events.

Gou′da (gou′də, gōō′-) n. mild, yellowish Dutch cheese.

gouge (gouj) n., v., **gouged, gouging.** —n. **1.** chisel with hollow blade. —v. **2.** dig out with gouge. **3.** extract by coercion.

gou′lash (gōō′läsh, -lash) n. seasoned stew.

gourd (gôrd, gōōrd) n. dried shell of squash.

gour′mand (gŏŏr mänd′, gŏŏr′mənd) n. enthusiastic eater.

gour′met (gŏŏr mā′, gŏŏr′mā) n. lover of fine food.

gout (gout) n. painful disease of joints. —**gout′y,** adj.

gov., 1. government. **2.** governor.

gov′ern (guv′ərn) v. **1.** rule. **2.** influence. **3.** regulate.

gov′ern·ess, n. woman who teaches children in their home.

gov′ern·ment (-ərn mənt, -ər mənt) n. **1.** system of rule. **2.** political governing body.

gov′er·nor (-ər nər, -ə nər) n. **1.** person who governs, esp. head of a state in the U.S. **2.** device that controls speed.

govt., government.

gown (goun) n. **1.** woman's dress. **2.** loose robe.

G.P., General Practitioner.

grab (grab) v., **grabbed, grabbing.** —v. **1.** seize eagerly. —n. **2.** act of grabbing.

grace (grās) n., v., **graced, gracing.** —n. **1.** beauty of form, movement, etc. **2.** goodwill. **3.** God's love. **4.** prayer said at table. —v. **5.** lend grace to; favor. —**grace′ful,** adj.

gra′cious (grā′shəs) adj. kind.

grack′le (grak′əl) n. blackbird with iridescent black plumage.

gra·da′tion (grā dā′shən) n. step in series of stages.

grade (grād) n., v., **graded, grading.** —n. **1.** degree in a scale. **2.** scholastic division. **3.** Also, **gra′di·ent.** slope. —v. **4.** arrange in grades. **5.** level.

grade crossing, intersection of a railroad track and a road.

grade school, elementary school.

grad′u·al (graj′ōō əl) adj. changing, moving, etc., by degrees.

grad′u·ate, n. (-it) **1.** recipient of diploma. —adj. (-it) **2.** graduated. **3.** of or in academic study beyond the baccalaureate level. —v. (-āt′) **4.** receive or confer diploma or degree. **5.** mark in measuring degrees.

graf·fi′ti (grə fē′tē) n.pl., sing. **graffito** (-tō). markings written on public walls, etc.

graft (graft) n. **1.** twig, etc., inserted in another plant to unite with it. **2.** profit through dishonest use of one's position. —v. **3.** make graft. **4.** make dishonest profits.

gra′ham (grā′əm, gram) adj. made of unsifted whole-wheat flour.

Grail (grāl) n. in medieval legend, the cup or chalice used at the last supper of Christ with the apostles.

grain (grān) n. **1.** seed of cereal plant. **2.** particle. **3.** pattern of wood fibers. —**grain′y,** adj.

gram (gram) n. metric unit of weight.

-gram, suffix meaning something written or drawn, as diagram.

gram′mar (gram′ər) n. **1.** features of a language as a whole. **2.** knowledge or usage of the preferred forms in

grope

speaking or writing. —**gram·mar′i·an** (grə mar′ē ən) *n.* —**gram·mat′i·cal** (-mat′i kəl) *adj.*

gran′a·ry (grā′nə rē, gran′ə-) *n., pl.* **-ries.** storehouse for grain.

grand (grand) *adj.* **1.** large; major. **2.** impressive. —*n.* **3.** grand piano. **4.** *Informal.* a thousand dollars.

grand′child′ (gran′chīld′) *n.* child of one's son or daughter. —**grand′son′,** *n.* —**grand′daugh′ter,** *n.fem.*

gran·dee′ (gran dē′) *n.* nobleman.

gran′deur (gran′jər, -jŏŏr) *n.* imposing greatness.

gran·dil′o·quence (gran dil′ə-kwəns) *n.* lofty, often pompous speech. —**gran·dil′o·quent,** *adj.*

gran·di·ose′ (gran′dē ōs′) *adj.* grand or pompous.

grand jury, jury designated to determine if a law has been violated and whether the evidence warrants prosecution.

grand′par′ent, *n.* parent of parent. —**grand′fa′ther,** *n.* —**grand′moth′er,** *n.fem.*

grand piano, large piano with a horizontal case on three legs.

grand slam, home run with three runners on base.

grand′stand′ (gran′-, grand′-) *n.* **1.** sloped open-air place for spectators. —*v.* **2.** conduct oneself or perform to impress onlookers.

grange (grānj) *n.* farmers' organization.

gran′ite (gran′it) *n.* granular rock.

gra·no′la (grə nō′lə) *n.* cereal of dried fruit, grains, nuts, etc.

grant (grant) *v.* **1.** bestow. **2.** admit. —*n.* **3.** thing granted.

grants′man·ship′, *n.* skill in securing grants, as for research.

gran′u·late′ (gran′yə lāt′) *v.,* **-lated, -lating.** form into granules.

gran′ule (-yōōl) *n.* small grain.

grape (grāp) *n.* smooth-skinned fruit that grows in clusters.

grape′fruit′, *n.* large yellow citrus fruit.

grape′vine′, *n.* **1.** vine on which grapes grow. **2.** person-to-person route by which gossip spreads.

graph (graf) *n.* diagram showing relations by lines, etc.

-graph, suffix meaning: **1.** something written or drawn, as *autograph.* **2.** instrument that writes or records, as *seismograph.*

graph′ic, *adj.* **1.** vivid. **2.** of writing, drawing, engraving, etc.

graph′ics, *n.pl.* **1.** the arts of drawing, engraving, etc. **2.** drawings, charts, etc.

graph′ite (-īt) *n.* soft, dark mineral.

graph·ol′o·gy (gra fol′ə jē) *n.* study of handwriting.

-graphy, suffix meaning: **1.** process or form of writing, printing, recording, or describing, as *biography.* **2.** art or science concerned with these, as *geography.*

grap′nel (grap′nl) *n.* hooked device for grasping.

grap′ple (grap′əl) *n., v.,* **-pled, -pling.** —*n.* **1.** hook for grasping. —*v.* **2.** try to grasp. **3.** try to cope.

grasp (grasp) *v.* **1.** seize and hold. **2.** understand. —*n.* **3.** act of gripping. **4.** mastery.

grasp′ing, *adj.* greedy.

grass (gras) *n.* ground-covering plant. —**grass′y,** *adj.*

grass′hop′per, *n.* leaping insect.

grass′land′, *n.* open grass-covered land; prairie.

grass roots, ordinary citizens, as contrasted with leadership or elite. —**grass′-roots′,** *adj.*

grass widow, woman who is separated or divorced.

grate (grāt) *v.,* **grated, grating,** *n.* —*v.* **1.** irritate. **2.** make harsh sound. **3.** rub into small bits. —*n.* **4.** Also, **grat′ing.** metal framework.

grate′ful, *adj.* **1.** thankful. **2.** welcome as news. —**grate′ful·ly,** *adv.*

grat′i·fy′ (grat′ə fī′) *v.,* **-fied, -fying.** please. —**grat′i·fi·ca′tion,** *n.*

gra′tis (grat′is, grā′tis) *adv., adj.* free of charge.

grat′i·tude′ (grat′i tōōd′, -tyōōd′) *n.* thankfulness.

gra·tu′i·tous (grə tōō′i təs, -tyōō′-) *adj.* **1.** free of charge. **2.** without reasonable cause.

gra·tu′i·ty, *n., pl.* **-ties.** tip.

grave (grāv) *n., adj.* **graver, gravest.** —*n.* **1.** place of or excavation for burial. —*adj.* **2.** solemn. **3.** important. —**grave′yard′,** *n.*

grav′el (grav′əl) *n.* small stones.

grav′el·ly, *adj.* **1.** made up of or like gravel. **2.** harsh-sounding.

graveyard shift, work shift usu. beginning about midnight.

grav′i·ta′tion (grav′i tā′shən) *n.* force of attraction between bodies. —**grav′i·tate′,** *v.,* **-tated, -tating.**

grav′i·ty, *n., pl.* **-ties. 1.** force attracting bodies to the earth's center. **2.** seriousness.

gra′vy (grā′vē) *n., pl.* **-vies.** juices from cooking meat.

gray (grā) *n.* **1.** color between black and white. —*adj.* **2.** of this color. **3.** ambiguous. **4.** vaguely depressing.

gray matter, *Informal.* brains.

graze (grāz) *v.,* **grazed, grazing. 1.** feed on grass. **2.** brush in passing.

grease *n., v.,* **greased, greasing.** —*n.* (grēs) **1.** animal fat. **2.** fatty or oily matter. —*v.* (grēs, grēz) **3.** put grease on or in. —**greas′y,** *adj.*

great (grāt) *adj.* **1.** very large. **2.** important. —**great′ly,** *adv.*

Great Dane, kind of very large dog.

grebe (grēb) *n.* diving bird.

greed (grēd) *n.* excessive desire. —**greed′i·ly,** *adv.* —**greed′y,** *adj.*

Greek (grēk) *n.* native or language of Greece. —**Greek,** *adj.*

green (grēn) *adj.* **1.** of color of vegetation. **2.** unripe. **3.** inexperienced. —*n.* **4.** green color. **5.** grassy land.

green′back′, *n.* U.S. legal-tender note.

green′belt′, *n.* area of open land surrounding a community.

green′er·y, *n., pl.* **-eries.** plants.

green′gro′cer, *n.* retailer of fresh fruit and vegetables.

green′horn′, *n.* **1.** novice. **2.** naive or gullible person.

green′house′, *n.* building where plants are grown.

greenhouse effect, heating of atmosphere resulting from absorption by certain gases of solar radiation.

green′room′, *n.* lounge in theater for use by performers.

green thumb, exceptional skill for growing plants.

greet (grēt) *n.* **1.** address on meeting. **2.** react to. —**greet′ing,** *n.*

gre·gar′i·ous (gri gâr′ē əs) *adj.* fond of company.

grem′lin (grem′lin) *n.* mischievous elf.

gre·nade′ (gri nād′) *n.* hurled explosive.

gren′a·dier′ (gren′ə dēr′) *n. Brit.* member of special infantry regiment.

grey (grā) *n., adj.* gray.

grey′hound′, *n.* slender swift dog.

grid (grid) *n.* **1.** covering of crossed bars. **2.** system of crossed lines.

grid′dle (grid′l) *n.* shallow frying pan.

grid′i′ron, *n.* **1.** grill. **2.** football field.

grid′lock′, *n.* **1.** complete stoppage of movement in all directions due to traffic. **2.** stoppage of a process, as legislation.

grief (grēf) *n.* keen sorrow.

griev′ance (grē′vəns) *n.* **1.** wrong. **2.** complaint against wrong.

grieve (grēv) *v.,* **grieved, grieving.** feel sorrow; inflict sorrow on.

griev′ous, *adj.* causing grief.

grif′fin (grif′in) *n.* monster of fable with head and wings of eagle and body of lion. Also, **gryph′on.**

grill (gril) *n.* **1.** barred utensil for broiling. —*v.* **2.** broil on grill. **3.** question persistently.

grille (gril) *n.* ornamental metal barrier.

grim (grim) *adj.,* **grimmer, grimmest. 1.** stern. **2.** harshly threatening. —**grim′ly,** *adv.*

grim′ace (grim′əs, gri mās′) *n., v.,* **-maced, -macing.** —*n.* **1.** twisted expression. —*v.* **2.** twist the face.

grime (grīm) *n.* dirt. —**grim′y,** *adj.*

grin (grin) *v.,* **grinned, grinning,** *n.* —*v.* **1.** smile openly and broadly. —*n.* **2.** broad smile.

grind (grīnd) *v.,* **ground** (ground), **grinding,** *n.* —*v.* **1.** wear, crush, or sharpen by friction. **2.** operate by turning crank. —*n.* **3.** *Informal.* dreary routine. —**grind′stone,** *n.*

grip (grip) *n., v.,* **gripped, gripping.** —*n.* **1.** grasp. **2.** small suitcase. **3.** handle. —*v.* **4.** grasp.

gripe (grīp) *v.,* **griped, griping,** *n.* —*v.* **1.** produce pain in bowels. **2.** *Informal.* complain. —*n.* **3.** *Informal.* complaint. —**grip′er,** *n.*

grippe (grip) *n.* influenza.

gris′ly (griz′lē) *adj.,* **-lier, -liest.** gruesome.

grist (grist) *n.* grain to be ground.

gris′tle (gris′əl) *n.* cartilage.

grit (grit) *n., v.,* **gritted, gritting.** —*n.* **1.** fine particles. **2.** courage. —*v.* **3.** cause to grind together.

grits (grits) *n.pl.* ground grain.

griz′zly (griz′lē) *adj.,* **-zlier, -zliest.** gray, as hair or fur. Also, **griz′zled.**

grizzly bear, large bear of western U.S. and Canada.

groan (grōn) *n.* **1.** moan of pain, derision, etc. —*v.* **2.** utter groans.

gro′cer (grō′sər) *n.* dealer in foods, etc.

gro′cer·y, *n., pl.* **-ies. 1.** store selling food. **2.** (*usually pl.*) food bought at such a store.

grog (grog) *n.* **1.** mixture of rum and water. **2.** any alcoholic drink.

grog′gy, *adj.,* **-gier, -giest.** dizzy.

groin (groin) *n.* hollow where thigh joins abdomen.

grom′met (grom′it, grum′-) *n.* eyelet.

groom (grōōm, grŏŏm) *n.* **1.** person who takes care of horses. **2.** bridegroom. —*v.* **3.** make neat.

grooms′man, *n., pl.* **-men.** attendant of bridegroom.

groove (grōōv) *n., v.,* **grooved, grooving.** —*n.* **1.** furrow. —*v.* **2.** form groove in.

grope (grōp) *v.,* **groped, groping.** feel blindly.

grosbeak 490

gros'beak/ (grōs'bēk/) *n.* finch with a thick, conical bill.

gross (grōs) *adj.* **1.** before deductions. **2.** disgusting. **3.** very fat. **4.** flagrant. —*n.* **5.** amount before deductions. **6.** twelve dozen.

gross national product, total monetary value of all goods produced in a country during one year.

gro·tesque/ (grō tesk/) *adj.* fantastically ugly or absurd.

grot'to (grot'ō) *n., pl.* **-tos, -toes.** cave.

grouch (grouch) *v.* **1.** sulk. —*n.* **2.** sulky person. **3.** sullen mood. —**grouch'y,** *adj.*

ground (ground) *n.* **1.** earth's solid surface. **2.** tract of land. **3.** motive. **4.** (*pl.*) dregs. **5.** rational basis. —*adj.* **6.** of or on ground. —*v.* **7.** teach the basics to. **8.** run aground.

ground ball, batted baseball that rolls or bounces along the ground.

ground'hog/, *n.* woodchuck.

ground'less, *adj.* without rational basis.

ground rules, basic rule of conduct in a situation.

ground'swell/, *n.* surge of feelings, esp. among the general public.

ground'work/, *n.* basic work.

group (grōōp) *n.* **1.** number of persons or things considered together. —*v.* **2.** place in or form group.

group'er (grōō'pər) *n., pl.* **-ers, -er.** large sea bass of warm waters.

group'ie, *n., pl.* **-ies.** young fan of rock group or celebrity.

grouse (grous) *n.* game bird of America and Britain.

grout (grout) *n.* thin, coarse mortar, used between tiles.

grove (grōv) *n.* small wood.

grov'el (grov'əl, gruv'-) *v.,* **-eled, -eling.** humble oneself.

grow (grō) *v.,* **grew** (grōō), **grown,** **growing.** **1.** increase in size; develop. **2.** cultivate. —**grow'er,** *n.*

growl (groul) *n.* **1.** guttural, angry sound. —*v.* **2.** utter growls.

grown'up/, *n.* adult. —**grown'-up/,** *adj.*

growth (grōth) *n.* **1.** act of growing. **2.** something that has grown.

grub (grub) *n., v.,* **grubbed, grubbing.** —*n.* **1.** larva. **2.** *Informal.* food. —*v.* **3.** dig.

grub'by, *adj.,* **-bier, -biest.** dirty.

grudge (gruj) *n. v.,* **grudged, grudging.** —*n.* **1.** lasting malice. —*v.* **2.** begrudge.

gru'el (grōō'əl) *n.* thin cereal.

gru·el·ing (grōō'ə ling, grōō'ling) *adj.* exhausting; arduous.

grue'some (grōō'səm) *adj.* causing horror and repugnance.

gruff (gruf) *adj.* surly.

grum'ble (grum'bəl) *v.,* **-bled, -bling.** murmur in discontent.

grump'y (grum'pē) *adj.,* **grumpier, grumpiest.** surly.

grun'gy (grun'jē) *adj.,* **-gier, -giest.** *Slang.* dirty or run down.

grunt (grunt) *n.* **1.** guttural sound. —*v.* **2.** utter grunts.

gryph'on (grif'ən) *n.* griffin.

gua'no (gwä'nō) *n.* manure; excrement of sea birds.

guar., guarantee(d).

guar'an·tee/ (gar'ən tē/) *n., v.,* **-teed, -teeing.** —*n.* **1.** pledge given as security. —*v.* **2.** pledge. **3.** assure. Also, **guar'an·ty/.** —**guar'an·tor/** (-tôr/) *n.*

guard (gärd) *v.* **1.** watch over. —*n.* **2.** person who guards. **3.** body of guards. **4.** close watch.

guard'ed, *adj.* **1.** cautious; prudent. **2.** protected or restrained.

guard'i·an, *n.* **1.** person who guards. **2.** person entrusted with care of another.

gua'va (gwä'və) *n.* large yellow fruit of tropical tree.

gu'ber·na·to'ri·al (gōō'bər nə tôr'ē-əl, gyōō'-) *adj.* of governors.

guer·ril'la (gə ril'ə) *n.* member of band of soldiers that harasses the enemy.

guess (ges) *v.* **1.** form opinion on incomplete evidence. **2.** be right in such opinion. —*n.* **3.** act of guessing.

guess'work/, *n.* **1.** act of guessing. **2.** conclusions from guesses.

guest (gest) *n.* **1.** visitor. **2.** customer at hotel, restaurant, etc.

guf·faw/ (gu fô/, gə-) *n.* **1.** loud laughter. —*v.* **2.** laugh loudly.

guid'ance (gīd'ns) *n.* **1.** act or instance of guiding. **2.** advice over period of time.

guide (gīd) *v.,* **guided, guiding,** *n.* —*v.* **1.** show the way. —*n.* **2.** one that guides.

guide'book/, *n.* book of directions, advice, and information, as for tourists.

guided missile, radio-controlled aerial missile.

guide'line/, *n.* guide or indication of future course of action.

guild (gild) *n.* commercial organization for common interest.

guile (gīl) *n.* cunning.

guil'lo·tine/ (gil'ə tēn/, gē'ə-) *n.* machine for beheading.

guilt (gilt) *n.* fact or feeling of having committed a wrong. —**guilt'i·ly,** *adv.* —**guilt'y,** *adj.*

guin'ea (gin'ē) *n., pl.* **-eas.** former British coin, worth 21 shillings.

guinea fowl, domesticated fowl. Also, **guinea hen.**

guinea pig, **1.** South American rodent. **2.** subject of experiment.

guise (gīz) *n.* outward appearance.

gui·tar/ (gi tär/) *n.* stringed musical instrument. —**gui·tar'ist,** *n.*

gulch (gulch) *n.* ravine.

gulf (gulf) *n.* **1.** arm of sea. **2.** abyss.

gull (gul) *n.* **1.** web-footed sea bird. **2.** dupe. —*v.* **3.** cheat; trick.

gul'let (gul'it) *n.* throat.

gul'li·ble (gul'ə bəl) *adj.* easily deceived. —**gul/li·bil/i·ty,** *n.*

gul'ly (gul'ē) *n., pl.* **-lies.** deep channel cut by running water.

gulp (gulp) *v.* **1.** swallow in large mouthfuls. —*n.* **2.** act of gulping.

gum (gum) *n., v.,* **gummed, gumming.** —*n.* **1.** sticky substance. **2.** chewing gum. **3.** tissue around teeth. —*v.* **4.** smear with gum.

gum'bo (gum'bō) *n., pl.* **-bos.** soup made with okra.

gum'drop/, *n.* small chewy candy.

gump'tion (gump'shən) *n.* **1.** initiative; resourcefulness. **2.** courage.

gum'shoe/, *n., pl.* **-shoes. 1.** *Slang.* detective. **2.** rubber overshoe.

gun (gun) *n., v.,* **gunned, gunning.** —*n.* **1.** tubular weapon that shoots missiles with explosives. —*v.* **2.** hunt with gun. **3.** cause (an engine) to speed up quickly.

gun'fire/, *n.* the firing of guns.

gung'-ho/ (gung'hō/) *adj. Informal.* thoroughly enthusiastic and loyal.

gunk (gungk) *n. Slang.* sticky or greasy matter.

gun'man, *n., pl.* **-men.** armed criminal.

gun'ny, *n., pl.* **-nies.** coarse material used for sacks.

gun'pow'der, *n.* explosive mixture.

gun'shot/, *n.* shot fired from gun.

gun'smith/, *n.* person who makes or repairs firearms.

gun'wale (gun'l) *n.* upper edge of vessel's side.

gup'py (gup'ē) *n., pl.* **-pies.** tiny tropical fish.

gur'gle (gûr'gəl) *v.,* **-gled, -gling,** *n.* —*v.* **1.** flow noisily. —*n.* **2.** sound of gurgling.

gur'ney (gûr'nē) *n.* wheeled table or stretcher for transporting patients.

gu'ru (gōōr'ōō, gōō rōō/) *n.* **1.** Hindu spiritual teacher. **2.** any respected leader.

gush (gush) *v.* **1.** flow or emit suddenly. **2.** talk effusively. —*n.* **3.** sudden flow. —**gush'y,** *adj.*

gush'er, *n.* jet of petroleum from underground.

gus'set (gus'it) *n.* angular insertion, as in clothing.

gus'sy (gus'ē) *v.,* **-sied, -sying.** dress up or decorate showily.

gust (gust) *n.* **1.** blast of wind. **2.** outburst. —**gust'y,** *adj.*

gus'ta·to'ry (gus'tə tôr'ē) *adj.* of taste.

gus'to (gus'tō) *n., pl.* **-toes.** keen enjoyment.

gut (gut) *n., v.,* **gutted, gutting.** —*n.* **1.** intestine. **2.** (*pl.*) *Informal.* courage. —*v.* **3.** destroy interior of.

guts'y, *adj.,* **gutsier, gutsiest.** daring or courageous. —**guts'i·ness,** *n.*

gut'ter (gut'ər) *n.* channel for leading off rainwater.

gut'tur·al (gut'ər əl) *adj.* **1.** of or in throat. —*n.* **2.** guttural sound.

guy (gī) *n.* **1.** rope used to steady object. **2.** *Informal.* fellow.

guz'zle (guz'əl) *v.,* **-zled, -zling.** eat or drink greedily. —**guz'zler,** *n.*

gym·na'si·um (jim nā'zē əm) *n., pl.* **-siums, -sia.** place for physical exercise. *Informal.* **gym.**

gym'nast (jim'nəst, -nast) *n.* performer of gymnastics.

gym·nas'tics (-nas'tiks) *n.pl.* physical exercises that demonstrate strength, balance, or agility.

gy'ne·col·o·gy (gī'ni kol'ə jē, jin'i-) *n.* branch of medicine dealing with care of women.

gyp (jip) *v.,* **gypped, gypping.** *Informal.* cheat.

gyp'sum (jip'səm) *n.* soft common mineral.

Gyp'sy (jip'sē) *n., pl.* **-sies.** member of wandering people.

gy'rate (jī'rāt, jī rāt/) *v.,* **-rated, -rating.** whirl. —**gy·ra'tion,** *n.*

gy'ro·scope/ (jī'rə skōp/) *n.* rotating wheel mounted to maintain equilibrium and determine direction.

H

H, h (āch) *n.* eighth letter of English alphabet.

ha (hä) *interj.* (exclamation of surprise, suspicion, etc.)

ha'be·as cor'pus (hā'bē əs kôr'pəs) writ requiring that arrested person be brought before court to determine whether he or she is being detained.

hab'er·dash·er·y (hab'ər dash'ə rē) *n., pl.* **-eries.** shop selling men's items. —**hab'er·dash'er,** *n.*

hab/it (hab/it) *n.* **1.** customary practice or act. **2.** monk's or nun's clothing. **3.** addiction. —**ha·bit/u·al** (hə-bich/ōō əl) *adj.*

hab/it·a·ble (hab/i tə bəl) *adj.* able to be inhabited.

hab/i·tat/ (-tat/) *n.* natural dwelling.

hab/i·ta/tion, *n.* abode.

ha·bit/u·ate/ (hə bich/ōō āt/) *v.,* **-ated, -ating.** accustom.

ha·bit/u·é/ (-ōō ā/) *n.* habitual visitor.

hack (hak) *v.* **1.** cut. **2.** cough sharply. —*n.* **3.** cut or notch. **4.** artistic drudge. **5.** vehicle for hire. —*adj.* **6.** routine.

hack/er, *n. Slang.* **1.** skilled computer enthusiast. **2.** computer user who tries to gain unauthorized access to systems.

hack/les (hak/əlz) *n.pl.* **1.** hair that can bristle on the back of an animal's neck. **2.** anger.

hack/ney (-nē) *n., pl.* **-neys.** horse or carriage for hire.

hack/neyed, *adj.* trite; common.

hack/saw/, *n.* saw for cutting metal.

had/dock (had/ək) *n.* food fish of northern Atlantic.

Ha/des (hā/dēz) *n.* hell.

haft (haft) *n.* handle.

hag (hag) *n.* repulsive old woman.

hag/gard (hag/ərd) *adj.* gaunt with fatigue.

hag/gle (hag/əl) *v.,* **-gled, -gling.** argue over price.

hail (hāl) *n.* **1.** ice pellets (**hail/stones/**). **2.** shower. **3.** call or greeting. —*v.* **4.** pour down hail. **5.** greet. **6.** call out to.

hair (hâr) *n.* **1.** filament on human head, animal body, etc. **2.** hairs collectively. —**hair/y,** *adj.* —**hair/dres/ser,** *n.* —**hair/pin/,** *n.*

hair/breadth/, *n.* narrow margin of safety. Also, **hairs/breadth/.**

hair/cut/, *n.* **1.** act of cutting hair. **2.** hair style.

hair/do/ (-dōō/) *n., pl.* **-dos.** hair arrangement.

hair/piece/, *n.* toupee or wig.

hair/-rais/ing, *adj.* terrifying.

hair/spray/, *n.* liquid spray for holding the hair in place.

hair/style/, *n.* way of cutting or arranging hair. —**hair/styl/ist,** *n.*

hair/-trig/ger, *adj.* easily set off.

hake (hāk) *n.* codlike marine food fish.

hal/cy·on (hal/sē ən) *adj.* peaceful; happy; carefree.

hale (hāl) *v.,* **haled, haling,** —*v.* **1.** compel to go. —*adj.* **2.** healthy.

half (haf) *n., pl.* **halves,** *adj., adv.* —*n.* **1.** one of two equal parts. —*adj.* **2.** being half. **3.** incomplete. —*adv.* **4.** partly.

half/back/, *n.* (in football) one of two backs who line up on each side of the fullback.

half/-baked/, *adj.* **1.** not sufficiently planned or prepared. **2.** foolish.

half/-breed/, *n. Offensive.* offspring of parents of two races.

half brother, brother related through one parent only.

half/-cocked/, *adj.* ill-prepared.

half/-heart/ed, *adj.* unenthusiastic.

half sister, sister related through one parent only.

half/-truth/, *n.* deceptive statement that is only partly true.

half/way/ (-wā/, -wā/) *adv.* **1.** to the midpoint. **2.** partially or almost. —*adj.* **3.** midway. **4.** partial or inadequate.

halfway house, residence for persons

released from hospital, prison, etc., to ease their return to society.

half/-wit/, *n.* foolish person.

hal/i·but (hal/ə bət, hol/-) *n.* large edible fish.

hal/i·to/sis (hal/i tō/sis) *n.* bad breath.

hall (hôl) *n.* **1.** corridor. **2.** large public room.

hal/le·lu/jah (hal/ə lōō/yə) *interj.* Praise ye the Lord!

hall/mark/ (hôl/-) *n.* **1.** mark or indication of genuineness or quality. **2.** distinguishing characteristic.

hal/low (hal/ō) *v.* consecrate.

Hal/low·een/ (hal/ə wēn/, -ō ēn/, hol/-) *n.* the evening of October 31, observed by dressing in costumes. Also, **Hal/low·e/en/.**

hal·lu/ci·na/tion (hə lōō/sə nā/shən) *n.* perception of something that is not real. —**hal·luc/i·nate/,** *v.*

hal·lu/ci·no·gen (-nə jən) *n.* substance that produces hallucinations.

hall/way/, *n.* corridor.

ha/lo (hā/lō) *n., pl.* **-los, -loes.** radiance surrounding a head.

halt (hôlt) *v.* **1.** falter; limp. **2.** stop. —*adj.* **3.** lame. —*n.* **4.** stop.

hal/ter (hôl/tər) *n.* **1.** strap for horse. **2.** noose. **3.** woman's top tied behind the neck and back.

halve (hav) *v.,* **halved, halving.** divide in half.

ham (ham) *n., v.* **hammed, hamming.** —*n.* **1.** meat from rear thigh of hog. **2.** amateur radio operator. **3.** performer who overacts. —*v.* **4.** overact. —**ham/my,** *adj.*

ham/burg/er (ham/bûr/gər) *n.* sandwich of ground beef in bun.

ham/let (ham/lit) *n.* small village.

ham/mer (ham/ər) *n.* **1.** tool for pounding. —*v.* **2.** pound with hammer.

ham/mock (ham/ək) *n.* hanging bed of canvas, etc.

ham/per (ham/pər) *v.* **1.** impede. —*n.* **2.** large basket.

ham/ster (ham/stər) *n.* small burrowing rodent kept as a pet.

ham/string/, *n., v.,* **-strung, hamstringing.** —*n.* **1.** tendon behind the knee. —*v.* **2.** disable by cutting hamstring. **3.** make powerless or ineffective.

hand (hand) *n.* **1.** terminal part of arm. **2.** worker. **3.** side or direction. **4.** style of handwriting. **5.** pledge of marriage. **6.** cards held by player. —*v.* **7.** pass by hand.

hand/bag/, *n.* woman's purse.

hand/ball/, *n.* ball game played against a wall.

hand/bill/, *n.* small printed notice usu. distributed by hand.

hand/book/, *n.* small manual.

hand/cuff/, *n.* **1.** metal ring for prisoner's wrist. —*v.* **2.** put handcuff on.

hand/ful (-fōōl) *n., pl.* **-fuls.** **1.** amount hand can hold. **2.** difficult person or thing.

hand/gun/, *n.* pistol.

hand/i·cap/ (han/dē kap/) *n., v.,* **-capped, -capping.** —*n.* **1.** disadvantage. —*v.* **2.** subject to disadvantage.

hand/i·craft/, *n.* **1.** manual skill. **2.** work or products requiring such skill. Also, **hand/craft/.**

hand/i·work/, *n.* **1.** work done by hand. **2.** personal work or accomplishment.

hand/ker·chief (hang/kər chif, -chēf/) *n.* small cloth for wiping nose.

han/dle (han/dl) *n., v.,* **-dled, -dling.** —*n.* **1.** part to be grasped. —*v.* **2.** feel or grasp. **3.** manage. **4.** *Informal.* endure. **5.** deal in.

hand/made/, *adj.* made individually by worker.

hand/out/, *n.* **1.** something given to a beggar. **2.** item of publicity.

hand/shake/, *n.* clasping of hands in greeting or agreement.

hands/-off/, *adj.* characterized by nonintervention.

hand/some (han/səm) *adj.* **1.** good-looking. **2.** generous.

hands/-on/, *adj.* involving active personal participation.

hand/spring/, *n.* complete flipping of body, landing first on hands, then on feet.

hand/-to-mouth/, *adj.* providing bare existence; precarious.

hand/writ/ing, *n.* writing done by hand. —**hand/writ/ten** (-rit/n) *adj.*

hand/y (han/dē) *adj.,* **-ier, -iest.** **1.** convenient. **2.** dexterous. **3.** useful.

han/dy·man/, *n., pl.* **-men.** worker at miscellaneous physical chores.

hang (hang) *v.,* **hung** (hung), or **hanged, hanging,** *n.* —*v.* **1.** suspend. **2.** suspend by neck until dead. —*n.* **3.** manner of hanging. —**hang/man,** *n.*

hang/ar (hang/ər) *n.* shed, esp. for aircraft.

hang/dog/, *adj.* shamefaced or cowed.

hang glider, kitelike glider for soaring through the air from hilltops, etc. (**hang gliding**).

hang/nail/, *n.* small piece of loose skin around fingernail.

hang/o/ver, *n.* ill feeling from too much alcohol.

hang/up/, *n. Informal.* obsessive problem.

hank (hangk) *n.* skein of yarn.

han/ker (hang/kər) *v.* yearn.

hank/y-pank/y (hang/kē pang/kē) *n. Informal.* **1.** mischief. **2.** illicit sexual relations.

han/som (han/səm) *n.* two-wheeled covered cab.

Ha·nuk·kah (кнä/nə kə, hä/-) *n.* annual Jewish festival.

hap/haz/ard (hap haz/ərd) *adj.* **1.** accidental. —*adv.* **2.** by chance.

hap/less, *adj.* unlucky.

hap/pen (hap/ən) *v.* occur. —**hap/pen·ing,** *n.*

hap/pen·stance/ (-stans/) *n.* chance happening or event.

hap/py (hap/ē) *adj.,* **-pier, -piest.** **1.** pleased; glad. **2.** pleasurable. **3.** bringing good luck.

ha·rangue/ (hə rang/) *n., v.,* **-rangued, -ranguing.** —*n.* **1.** vehement speech. —*v.* **2.** address in harangue.

ha·rass/ (hə ras/, har/əs) *v.* annoy; disturb. —**har·ass/ment,** *n.* —**Pronunciation.** HARASS has traditionally been pronounced (har/əs). A newer pronunciation, (hə ras/), which has developed in North American but not British English, is sometimes criticized. However, it is now the more common pronunciation among younger educated U.S. speakers, some of whom are barely familiar with the older form.

har/bin·ger (här/bin jər) *n., v.* herald.

har/bor (här/bər) *n.* **1.** sheltered water for ships. **2.** shelter. —*v.* **3.** give shelter.

hard (härd) *adj.* **1.** firm; not soft. **2.** difficult. **3.** severe. **4.** indisputable. —**hard/en,** *v.* —**hard/ness,** *n.*

hard/-bit/ten, *adj.* tough; stubborn.

hard/-boiled/, *adj.* **1.** boiled long enough for yolk and white to solidify. **2.** not sentimental; tough.

hard cider, fermented cider.

hard′-core′, *adj.* graphic; explicit.

hard′hat′, *n.* **1.** worker's helmet. **2.** working-class conservative.

hard′head′ed, *adj.* **1.** practical; realistic; shrewd. **2.** obstinate; willful.

hard′heart′ed, *adj.* unfeeling.

hard′-line′, *adj.* uncompromising, as in politics. Also, **hard′line′.**

hard′ly, *adv.* barely.

hard′-nosed′, *adj. Informal.* **1.** practical and shrewd. **2.** tough; stubborn. —**hard′nose′,** *n.*

hard′ship, *n.* suffering or need.

hard′tack′, *n.* hard biscuit.

hard′ware′, *n.* **1.** metalware. **2.** the machinery of a computer.

hard′wood′, *n.* hard, compact wood of various trees.

har′dy (här′dē) *adj.,* **-di·er, -di·est.** able to endure hardship.

hare (hâr) *n.* mammal resembling rabbit.

hare′brained′, *adj.* foolish.

hare′lip′, *n.* split upper lip.

har′em (hâr′əm, har′-) *n.* **1.** women's section of Muslim palace. **2.** the women there.

hark (härk) *v.* listen. Also, **hark′en.**

har′le·quin (här′lə kwin, -kin) *n.* masked clown in theater.

har′lot (här′lət) *n.* prostitute.

harm (härm) *n.* **1.** injury. **2.** evil. —*v.* **3.** injure. —**harm′ful,** *adj.*

harm′less, *adj.* **1.** causing no harm. **2.** immune from legal action.

har·mon′i·ca (här mon′i kə) *n.* small wind instrument with metal reeds.

har′mo·ny (här′mə nē) *n., pl.* **-nies. 1.** agreement. **2.** combination of agreeable musical sounds. —**har′mo·nize′,** *v.,* **-nized, -nizing.** —**har·mon′i·ous** (-mō′nē əs) *adj.*

har′ness (här′nis) *n.* **1.** horse's working gear. —*v.* **2.** put harness on. **3.** make use of.

harp (härp) *n.* **1.** plucked musical string instrument. —*v.* **2.** repeat tediously. —**harp′ist, harp′er,** *n.*

har·poon′ (här pōōn′) *n.* **1.** spear used against whales. —*v.* **2.** strike with harpoon.

harp′si·chord′ (härp′si kôrd′) *n.* keyboard instrument with plucked strings. —**harp′si·chord′ist,** *n.*

har′ri·dan (har′i dn) *n.* scolding, vicious woman.

har′ri·er (har′ē ər) *n.* hunting dog.

har′row (har′ō) *n.* **1.** implement for leveling or breaking up plowed land. —*v.* **2.** draw a harrow over. **3.** distress. —**har′row·ing,** *adj.*

har′ry (har′ē) *v.,* **-ried, -rying.** harass.

harsh (härsh) *adj.* **1.** rough. **2.** unpleasant. **3.** highly severe.

har′vest (här′vist) *n.* **1.** gathering of crops. **2.** season for this. **3.** crop. —*v.* **4.** reap. —**har′vest·er,** *n.*

has (haz; *unstressed* həz, əz) *v.* third pers. sing. pres. indic. of **have.**

has′-been′, *n.* one that is no longer effective, successful, etc.

hash (hash) *n.* **1.** chopped meat and potatoes. **2.** *Slang.* hashish. —*v.* **3.** chop.

hash′ish (hash′ēsh, hä shēsh′) *n.* narcotic of Indian hemp.

hasn′t (haz′ənt) contraction of **has not.**

hasp (hasp) *n.* clasp for door or lid.

has′sle (has′əl) *n., v.,* **-sled, -sling.** *Informal.* —*n.* **1.** disorderly dispute. **2.** troublesome situation. —*v.* **3.** bother; harass.

has′sock (has′ək) *n.* cushion used as footstool, etc.

haste (hāst) *n.* **1.** swiftness of motion. **2.** rash action. —**hast′y,** *adj.* —**hast′i·ness,** *n.*

has′ten (hā′sən) *v.* hurry.

hat (hat) *n.* covering for head.

hatch (hach) *v.* **1.** oring forth young from egg. **2.** be hatched. —*n.* **3.** cover for opening. —**hatch′er·y,** *n.*

hatch′et (hach′it) *n.* small ax.

hatchet job, maliciously destructive critique.

hatch′way′, *n.* opening in ship's deck.

hate (hāt) *v.,* **hated, hating,** *n.* —*v.* **1.** feel enmity. —*n.* **2.** Also, **hat′red.** strong dislike.

hate′ful, *adj.* **1.** full of hate. **2.** arousing hate. —**hate′ful·ly,** *adv.*

haugh′ty (hô′tē) *adj.* **-tier, -tiest.** disdainfully proud.

haul (hôl) *v.* **1.** pull; drag. —*n.* **2.** pull. **3.** distance of carrying. **4.** thing hauled. **5.** amount collected.

haunch (hônch, hänch) *n.* hip.

haunt (hônt, hänt) *v.* **1.** visit or inhabit as ghost. **2.** visit often. —*n.* **3.** place of frequent visits. —**haunt′ed,** *adj.*

haunt′ing, *adj.* lingering in the mind.

haute cou·ture′ (ōt′ kōō tōōr′) high fashion.

haute cui·sine′ (ōt′ kwi zēn′) gourmet cooking.

have (hav; *unstressed* həv, əv;) *v.,* **had, having.** **1.** possess; contain. **2.** get. **3.** be forced or obligated. **4.** be affected by. **5.** give birth to. —**Usage.** See OF.

ha·ven (hā′vən) *n.* **1.** harbor. **2.** place of shelter.

have′-not′, *n.* (*usually pl.*) individual or group without wealth.

haven′t (hav′ənt) contraction of **have not.**

hav′er·sack′ (hav′ər sak′) *n.* bag for carrying supplies.

hav′oc (hav′ək) *n.* devastation.

Haw. (hô) Hawaii.

hawk (hôk) *n.* **1.** bird of prey. —*v.* **2.** hunt with hawks. **3.** peddle.

hawk′er, *n.* peddler.

haw′thorn′ (hô′thôrn′) *n.* small tree with thorns and red berries.

hay (hā) *n.* grass cut and dried for fodder. —**hay′stack′,** *n.*

hay fever, disorder of eyes and respiratory tract, caused by pollen.

hay′wire′, *adj. Informal.* amiss.

haz′ard (haz′ərd) *n., v.* risk.

haze (hāz) *v.,* **hazed, hazing,** *n.* —*v.* **1.** play abusive tricks on. —*n.* **2.** fine mist. —**ha′zy,** *adj.*

ha′zel (hā′zəl) *n.* **1.** tree bearing edible nut (**ha′zel·nut′**). **2.** light reddish brown.

H′-bomb′, *n.* hydrogen bomb.

hdqrs., headquarters.

HDTV, high-definition television.

he (hē; *unstressed* ē) *pron.* **1.** male last mentioned. —*n.* **2.** male.

head (hed) *n.* **1.** part of body joined to trunk by neck. **2.** leader. **3.** top or foremost part. —*adj.* **4.** at the head. **5.** leading or main. —*v.* **6.** lead. **7.** move in certain direction.

head′ache′, *n.* **1.** pain in upper part of head. **2.** worrying problem.

head′dress′, *n.* covering or decoration for the head.

head′first′, *adv.* headlong.

head′ing, *n.* caption.

head′light′, *n.* light with reflector at front of vehicle.

head′line′, *n.* title of news story.

head′long′, *adj., adv.* **1.** with the

head foremost. **2.** in impulsive manner.

head′-on′, *adj., adv.* with the head or front foremost.

head′phone′, *n.* (*usually pl.*) device worn over the ears for listening to an audiotape, etc.

head′quar′ters, *n.* center of command or operations.

head′stone′, *n.* stone marker at head of grave.

head′strong′, *adj.* willful.

head′way′, *n.* progress.

head′y, *adj.,* **headier, headiest. 1.** impetuous. **2.** intoxicating.

heal (hēl) *v.* **1.** restore to health. **2.** get well.

health (helth) *n.* **1.** soundness of body or mind. **2.** physical condition. —**health′ful,** —**health′y,** *adj.*

heap (hēp) *n., v.* pile (defs. 1, 2, 8, 9).

hear (hēr) *v.,* **heard** (hûrd), **hearing. 1.** perceive by ear. **2.** listen. **3.** receive report.

hear′say′, *n.* gossip; indirect report.

hearse (hûrs) *n.* vehicle used to carry coffin.

heart (härt) *n.* **1.** muscular organ keeping blood in circulation. **2.** seat of life or emotion. **3.** compassion. **4.** vital part. **5.** (*pl.*) suit of playing cards. —**heart′less,** *adj.*

heart′ache′, *n.* grief.

heart attack, sudden insufficiency of oxygen supply to heart that results in heart muscle damage.

heart′break′, *n.* great sorrow or anguish. —**heart′bro′ken,** *adj.*

heart′burn′, *n.* burning sensation in stomach and esophagus, sometimes caused by rising stomach acid.

heart′en, *v.* encourage.

heart′felt′, *adj.* deeply felt.

hearth (härth) *n.* place for fires.

heart′-rend′ing, *adj.* causing intense grief.

heart′sick′, *adj.* extremely sad.

heart′-to-heart′, *adj.* sincere and intimate.

heart′y, *adj.,* **-ier, -iest. 1.** cordial. **2.** genuine. **3.** vigorous. **4.** substantial. —**heart′i·ly,** *adv.*

heat (hēt) *n.* **1.** warmth. **2.** form of energy raising temperature. **3.** intensity of emotion. **4.** sexual receptiveness in animals. —*v.* **5.** make or become hot. **6.** excite. —**heat′er,** *n.*

heat′ed, *adj.* **1.** supplied with heat. **2.** emotionally charged.

heath (hēth) *n.* **1.** Also, **heath′er.** low evergreen shrub. **2.** uncultivated land overgrown with shrubs.

hea′then (hē′thən) *n., adj.* pagan.

heat′stroke′, *n.* headache, fever, etc., caused by too much heat.

heave (hēv) *v.,* **heaved, heaving,** *n.* —*v.* **1.** raise with effort. **2.** lift and throw. **3.** *Slang.* vomit. **4.** rise and fall. —*n.* **5.** act of heaving.

heav′en (hev′ən) *n.* **1.** abode of God, angels, and spirits of righteous dead. **2.** (*often pl.*) sky. **3.** bliss.

heav′y (hev′ē) *adj.,* **-ier, -iest. 1.** of great weight. **2.** substantial. **3.** clumsy; indelicate. —**heav′i·ly,** *adv.*

heav′y-du′ty, *adj.* made for hard use.

heav′y-hand′ed, *adj.* tactless; clumsy.

heav′y-heart′ed, *adj.* preoccupied with sorrow or worry.

heav′y-set′, *adj.* large in body.

He′brew (hē′brōō) *n.* **1.** member of people of ancient Palestine. **2.** their language, now the national language of Israel. —**He′brew,** *adj.*

heck′le (hek′əl) v., **-led, -ling.** harass with comments or questions.

hec′tare (hek′tār) n. 10,000 square meters (2.47 acres).

hec′tic (-tik) adj. marked by excitement, passion, etc.

hec′tor (-tər) v. bully.

hedge (hej) n., v., **hedged, hedging.** —n. **1.** fence of bushes or small trees. —v. **2.** surround with hedge. **3.** offset (risk, bet, etc.).

hedge′hog′, n. spiny mammal.

he′don·ist (hēd′n ist) n. person living for pleasure.

heed (hēd) v. **1.** notice. **2.** pay serious attention to. **—heed,** n. **—heed′ful,** adj. **—heed′less,** adj.

heel (hēl) n. **1.** back of foot below ankle. **2.** part of shoe, etc., covering this. —v. **3.** furnish with heels. **4.** lean to one side.

heft (heft) n. **1.** heaviness. **2.** significance. —v. **3.** weigh by lifting.

hef′ty, adj., **-tier, -tiest. 1.** heavy. **2.** sturdy. **3.** substantial.

he·gem′o·ny (hi jem′ə nē, hej′ə-mō′-) n., pl. **-nies.** domination or leadership.

heif′er (hef′ər) n. young cow that has not calved.

height (hīt) n. **1.** state of being high. **2.** altitude. **3.** apex. **—height′en,** v.

Heim′lich maneuver (hīm′lik) procedure to aid choking person by applying pressure to upper abdomen.

hei′nous (hā′nəs) adj. hateful.

heir (âr) n. inheritor. **—heir′ess,** n. fem.

heir′loom′, n. possession long kept in family.

heist (hīst) Slang. —n. **1.** robbery. —v. **2.** rob.

hel′i·cop′ter (hel′i kop′tər, hē′li-) n. aircraft lifted by rotating blades.

he′li·um (hē′lē əm) n. light, gaseous element.

he′lix (hē′liks) n., pl. **hel′i·ces** (hel′ə-sēz′), **helixes.** spiral.

hell (hel) n. abode of condemned spirits. **—hell′ish,** adj.

Hel·len′ic (he len′ik, -lē′nik) adj. Greek.

hel·lo′ (he lō′, hə-, hel′ō) interj. (exclamation of greeting.)

helm (helm) n. **1.** control of rudder. **2.** steering apparatus.

hel′met (hel′mit) n. protective head covering.

help (help) v. **1.** aid. **2.** save. **3.** relieve. **4.** avoid. —n. **5.** aid; relief. **6.** helping person or thing. **—help′er,** n. **—help′ful,** adj.

help′ing, n. portion of food served.

help′less, adj. unable to act for oneself. **—help′less·ly,** adv.

help′mate′, n. companion and helper. Also, **help′meet′.**

hel′ter-skel′ter (hel′tər skel′tər) adv. in a disorderly way.

hem (hem) v., **hemmed, hemming,** n. —v. **1.** confine. **2.** fold and sew down edge of cloth. **3.** make throat-clearing sound. —n. **4.** hemmed border.

hem′i·sphere (hem′i sfēr′) n. **1.** half the earth or sky. **2.** half sphere.

hem′lock (hem′lok′) n. **1.** coniferous tree. **2.** poisonous plant.

he′mo·glo′bin (hē′mə glō′bin, hem′ə-) n. oxygen-carrying compound in red blood cells.

he′mo·phil′i·a (hē′mə fil′ē ə) n. genetic disorder marked by excessive bleeding. **—he′mo·phil′i·ac′,** n.

hem′or·rhage (hem′ər ij) n. discharge of blood.

hem′or·rhoid′ (hem′ə roid′) n. (usu-ally pl.) painful dilation of blood vessels in anus.

hemp (hemp) n. **1.** herb fiber used for rope. **2.** intoxicating drug made from hemp plant.

hen (hen) n. **1.** female domestic fowl **2.** female bird.

hence (hens) adv. **1.** therefore. **2.** from now on. **3.** from this place.

hence′forth′ (hens′fôrth′, hens′-fôrth′) adv. from now on.

hench′man (hench′mən) n., pl. **-men. 1.** associate in wrongdoing. **2.** trusted attendant.

hen′na (hen′ə) n. red dye.

hen′pecked′, adj. nagged or controlled by one's wife.

hep′a·ti′tis (hep′ə tī′tis) n. inflammation of the liver.

her (hûr; unstressed hər, ər) pron. **1.** objective case of **she.** —adj. **2.** of or belonging to female.

her′ald (her′əld) n. **1.** messenger or forerunner. **2.** proclaimer. —v. **3.** proclaim. **4.** give promise of.

her′ald·ry, n. art of devising and describing coats of arms, tracing genealogies, etc. **—he·ral′dic** (he ral′dik, hə-) adj.

herb (ûrb; esp. Brit. hûrb) n. flowering plant with nonwoody stem. **—her·ba·ceous** (hûr bā′shəs, ûr-) adj. **—herb·al** (ûr′bəl, hûr′-) adj.

herb′i·cide′ (hûr′bə sīd′, ûr′-) n. substance for killing plants, esp. weeds. **—her′bi·cid′al,** adj.

her·biv′o·rous (hûr biv′ər əs, ûr-) adj. feeding on plants. **—her′bi·vore′** (hûr′bə vôr′, ûr′-) n.

her·cu·le·an (hûr′kyə lē′ən, hûr-kyo̅o̅′lē-) adj. requiring extraordinary strength or effort.

herd (hûrd) n. **1.** animals feeding or moving together. —v. **2.** go in herd. **3.** tend herd.

here (hēr) adv. **1.** in or to this place. **2.** present.

here′a·bout′ adv. in this vicinity. Also, **here′a·bouts′.**

here·af′ter, adv. **1.** in the future. —n. **2.** future life.

here·by′, adv. by this.

he·red′i·tar′y (hə red′i ter′ē) adj. **1.** passing from parents to offspring. **2.** of heredity. **3.** by inheritance.

he·red′i·ty, n. transmission of traits from parents to offspring.

here·in′, adv. in this place.

her′e·sy (her′ə sē) n., pl. **-sies.** unorthodox opinion or doctrine. **—her′e·tic** (her′i tik) n.

here·to·fore′, adv. before now.

here·with′, adv. along with this.

her′it·a·ble (her′i tə bəl) adj. capable of being inherited.

her′it·age (her′i tij) n. **1.** inheritance. **2.** traditions and history.

her·maph′ro·dite′ (hûr maf′rə dīt′) n. animal or plant with reproductive organs of both sexes.

her·met′ic (hûr met′ik) adj. airtight. Also, **hermet′i·cal.**

her′mit (hûr′mit) n. recluse.

her′mit·age (-mi tij) n. hermit's abode.

her′ni·a (hûr′nē ə) n. rupture in abdominal wall, etc.

he′ro (hēr′ō) n., pl. **-roes. 1.** man admired for bravery. **2.** main male character in story. **—her′oine** (her′ō in) n. fem. **—he·ro′ic** (hi rō′ik) adj. **—her′o·ism′** (her′ō iz′əm) n.

her′o·in (her′ō in) n. illegal morphinelike drug.

her′on (her′ən) n. long-legged wading bird.

he′ro sandwich, large sandwich of cold cuts, etc., in long roll.

her′pes (hûr′pēz) n. viral disease characterized by blisters on skin or mucous membranes.

her′ring (her′ing) n. north Atlantic food fish.

her′ring·bone′, n. **1.** pattern of slanting lines in vertical rows. **2.** fabric of this.

hers (hûrz) pron. **1.** possessive form of **she,** used predicatively. **2.** her belongings or family.

her·self′, pron. emphatic or reflexive form of **her.**

hertz (hûrts) n., pl. **hertz.** radio frequency of one cycle per second.

hes′i·tate′ (hez′i tāt′) v., **-tated, -tating. 1.** hold back in doubt. **2.** pause. **3.** stammer. **—hes′i·tant** (-tənt) adj. **—hes′i·ta′tion, hes′i·tan·cy,** n.

het′er·o·dox′ (het′ər ə doks′) adj. unorthodox. **—het′er·o·dox′y,** n.

het′er·o·ge′ne·ous (-jē′nē əs) adj. **1.** unlike. **2.** varied.

het′er·o·sex′u·al, adj. sexually attracted to opposite sex.

hew (hyo̅o̅; often yo̅o̅) v., **hewed, hewed** or **hewn, hewing. 1.** chop or cut. **2.** cut down. **—hew′er,** n.

hex (heks) v. **1.** cast spell on. **2.** bring bad luck to. —n. **3.** jinx.

hex′a·gon′ (hek′sə gon′, -gən) n. six-sided polygon. **—hex·ag′o·nal** (hek sag′ə nl) adj.

hey′day′ (hā′dā′) n. time of greatest success, popularity, etc.

hgt., height.

hgwy., highway.

HI, Hawaii.

hi·a′tus (hī ā′təs) n., pl. **-tuses, -tus.** break or interruption in a series, action, etc.

hi·ba′chi (hi bä′chē) n. small charcoal brazier covered with a grill.

hi′ber·nate′ (hī′bər nāt′) v., **-nated, -nating.** spend winter in dormant state. **—hi′ber·na′tion,** n.

hi·bis′cus (hī bis′kəs, hi-) n. plant with large flowers.

hic′cup (hik′up, -əp) n. **1.** sudden involuntary drawing in of breath. —v. **2.** have hiccups. Also, **hic′cough** (hik′-up).

hick (hik) n. provincial, unsophisticated person.

hick′o·ry (hik′ə rē) n., pl. **-ries.** tree bearing edible nut.

hide (hīd) v., **hid** (hid), **hidden** or **hid, hiding,** n. —v. **1.** conceal or be concealed. —n. **2.** animal's skin.

hide′a·way, n. private retreat.

hide′bound′, adj. narrow and rigid in opinion.

hid′e·ous (hid′ē əs) adj. **1.** very ugly. **2.** revolting.

hide′-out′, n. safe place to hide, esp. from the law.

hi′er·ar′chy (hī′ə rär′kē) n., pl. **-chies.** graded system of officials.

hi′er·o·glyph′ic (hī′ər ə glif′ik, hī′-rə-) adj. **1.** of picture writing, as among ancient Egyptians. —n. **2.** hieroglyphic symbol.

hi′-fi′ (hī′fī′) adj. of high fidelity. **—hi′-fi′,** n.

high (hī) adj. **1.** tall. **2.** lofty. **3.** expensive. **4.** shrill. **5.** Informal. exuberant with drink or drugs. **6.** greater than normal. **7.** elevated in pitch. —adv. **8.** at or high place, rank, etc.

high′ball′, n. drink of whiskey mixed with club soda or ginger ale.

high′brow′, n. **1.** cultured person. —adj. **2.** typical of a highbrow.

high fidelity, reproduction of sound without distortion.

high′-flown′, *adj.* **1.** pretentious. **2.** bombastic.

high frequency, radio frequency between 3 and 30 megahertz.

high′-hand′ed, *adj.* overbearing.

high′lands (-landz) *n.* elevated part of country.

high′light′, *v.* **1.** emphasize. —*n.* **2.** important event, scene, etc. **3.** area of strong reflected light.

high′ly, *adv.* very; extremely.

high′-mind′ed, *adj.* noble in feelings or principles.

high′ness (-nis) *n.* **1.** high state. **2.** (*cap.*) title of royalty.

high′-pres′sure, *adj., v.,* **high-pressured, high-pressuring.** —*adj.* **1.** stressful. —*v.* **2.** persuade aggressively.

high′rise′, *n.* high building. —**high′-rise′,** *adj.*

high′road′, *n.* highway.

high′ school′, *n.* school for grades 9 through 12.

high seas, open ocean, esp. beyond territorial waters.

high′-spir′it•ed, *adj.* lively.

high′-strung′, *adj.* nervous.

high′-tech′, *n.* **1.** technology using highly sophisticated and advanced equipment and techniques. —*adj.* **2.** using or suggesting high-tech.

high′-ten′sion, *adj.* of relatively high voltage.

high′way′, *n.* main road.

high′way′man, *n., pl.* **-men.** highway robber.

hi′jack′ (hī′jak′) *v.* seize (plane, truck, etc.) by force.

hike (hīk) *v.,* **hiked, hiking,** *n.* —*v.* **1.** walk long distance. —*n.* **2.** long walk. —**hik′er,** *n.*

hi•lar′i•ous (hi lâr′ē əs, -lar′-) *adj.* **1.** very funny. **2.** very cheerful. —**hi•lar′i•ty,** *n.*

hill (hil) *n.* high piece of land. —**hill′y,** *adj.*

hill/bil/ly (-bil′ē) *n., pl.* **-lies.** *Sometimes Offensive.* someone from a backwoods area.

hill′ock (-ək) *n.* little hill.

hilt (hilt) *n.* sword handle.

him (him) *pron.* objective case of **he.**

him•self′ (him self′; *medially often* im-) *pron.* reflexive or emphatic form of **him.**

hind (hīnd) *adj.* **1.** rear. —*n.* **2.** female red deer.

hin′der (hin′dər) *v.* **1.** retard. **2.** stop. —**hin′drance,** *n.*

hind′most′ (hīnd′-) *adj.* last.

hind′sight′, *n.* keen awareness of how one should have avoided past mistakes.

Hin′du (hin′dōō) *n.* adherent of Hinduism. —**Hindu,** *adj.*

Hin′du•ism, *n.* major religion in India.

hinge (hinj) *n., v.,* **hinged, hinging.** —*n.* **1.** joint on which door, lid, etc., turns. —*v.* **2.** depend. **3.** furnish with hinges.

hint (hint) *n.* **1.** indirect suggestion. —*v.* **2.** give hint.

hin′ter•land′ (hin′tər land′) *n.* area remote from cities.

hip (hip) *n.* **1.** projecting part of each side of body below waist. —*adj. Slang.* **2.** familiar with the latest styles or ideas.

hip′-hop′, *n. Slang.* popular subculture as characterized by rap music.

hip′pie (hip′ē) *n.* person of 1960s who rejected conventional cultural and moral values.

hip′po (hip′ō) *n., pl.* **-pos.** hippopotamus.

hip′po•drome′ (hip′ə drōm′) *n.* arena, esp. for horse events.

hip′po•pot′a•mus (hip′ə pot′ə məs) *n., pl.* **-muses, -mi** (-mī′). large African water mammal.

hire (hīᵊr) *v.,* **hired, hiring,** *n.* —*v.* **1.** purchase services or use of. —*n.* **2.** payment for services or use.

hire′ling (-ling) *n.* person whose loyalty can be bought.

hir′sute′ (hûr′sōōt, hûr sōōt′) *adj.* hairy. —**hir′sute•ness,** *n.*

his (hiz; *unstressed* iz) *pron.* **1.** possessive form of **he. 2.** his belongings.

His•pan′ic (hi span′ik) *n.* person of Spanish or Latin-American descent. —**Hispanic,** *adj.*

hiss (his) *v.* **1.** make prolonged *s* sound. **2.** express disapproval in this way. —*n.* **3.** hissing sound.

his•tor′ic (hi stôr′ik) *adj.* **1.** Also, **his•tor′i•cal.** of history. **2.** important in or surviving from the past.

his′to•ry (his′tə rē, -trē) *n., pl.* **-ries. 1.** knowledge, study, or record of past events. **2.** pattern of events determining future. —**his•to′ri•an** (hi stôr′ē-ən) *n.*

his′tri•on′ics (his′trē on′iks) *n.pl.* exaggerated, esp. melodramatic, behavior. —**his′tri•on′ic,** *adj.*

hit (hit) *v.,* **hit, hitting,** *n.* —*v.* **1.** strike. **2.** collide with. **3.** meet. **4.** guess. —*n.* **5.** collision. **6.** blow. **7.** success. **8.** *Slang.* murder.

hitch (hich) *v.* **1.** fasten. **2.** harness to cart, etc. **3.** raise or move jerkily. —*n.* **4.** fastening or knot. **5.** obstruction or problem. **6.** jerk.

hitch′hike′, *v.,* **-hiked, -hiking.** beg a ride from a stranger.

hith′er (hith′ər) *adv.* to this place.

hith′er•to′, *adv.* until now.

HIV, human immunodeficiency virus, the cause of AIDS.

hive (hīv) *n.* shelter for bees.

hives (hīvz) *n.pl.* eruptive skin condition.

HMO, *pl.* **HMOs, HMO's.** health maintenance organization: health-care plan that provides comprehensive services to subscribers.

H.M.S., Her (or His) Majesty's Ship.

hoa′gie (hō′gē) *n.* hero sandwich. Also, **hoa′gy.**

hoard (hôrd) *n.* **1.** accumulation for future use. —*v.* **2.** accumulate as hoard. —**hoard′er,** *n.*

hoar′frost′ (hôr′frôst′) *n.* frost (def. 2).

hoarse (hôrs) *adj.* gruff in tone.

hoar′y (hôr′ē) *adj.* white with age.

hoax (hōks) *n.* **1.** mischievous deception. —*v.* **2.** deceive; trick.

hob′ble (hob′əl) *v.,* **-bled, -bling.** **1.** limp. **2.** fasten legs to prevent free movement.

hob′by (hob′ē) *n., pl.* **-bies.** favorite activity or pastime.

hob′by•horse′, *n.* **1.** rocking toy for riding. **2.** favorite subject for discussion.

hob′gob′lin, *n.* something causing superstitious fear.

hob′nob′ (-nob′) *v.,* **-nobbed, -nobbing.** associate socially.

ho′bo (hō′bō) *n., pl.* **-bos, -boes.** tramp; vagrant.

hock (hok) *n.* **1.** joint in hind leg of horse, etc. —*v.* **2.** pawn.

hock′ey (hok′ē) *n.* game played with bent clubs (**hockey sticks**) and ball or disk.

hock′shop′, *n.* pawnshop.

ho′cus-po′cus (hō′kəs pō′kəs) *n.* **1.** sleight of hand. **2.** trickery.

hod (hod) *n.* **1.** trough for carrying mortar, bricks, etc. **2.** coal scuttle.

hodge′podge′ (hoj′poj′) *n.* mixture; jumble.

hoe (hō) *n., v.,* **hoed, hoeing.** —*n.* **1.** tool for breaking ground, etc. —*v.* **2.** use hoe on.

hog (hôg) *n., v.,* **hogged, hogging.** —*n.* **1.** domesticated swine. **2.** greedy or filthy person. —*v.* **3.** take greedily. —**hog′gish,** *adj.*

hogs′head′, *n.* large cask.

hog′wash′, *n.* nonsense; bunk.

hog′-wild′, *adj.* wildly enthusiastic.

hoi′ pol•loi′ (hoi′ pə loi′) common people; the masses.

hoist (hoist) *v.* **1.** lift, esp. by machine. —*n.* **2.** hoisting apparatus. **3.** act of lifting.

hok′ey (hō′kē) *adj.,* **hokier, hokiest. 1.** mawkish. **2.** obviously contrived. —**hok′i•ness,** *n.*

hold (hōld) *v.,* **held** (held), **holding,** *n.* —*v.* **1.** have in hand. **2.** possess. **3.** sustain. **4.** adhere. **5.** celebrate. **6.** restrain or detain. **7.** believe. **8.** consider. —*n.* **9.** grasp. **10.** influence. **11.** cargo space below ship's deck. —**hold′er,** *n.*

hold′ing, *n.* **1.** leased land, esp. for farming. **2.** (*pl.*) legally owned property, esp. securities.

hold′out′, *n.* one who refuses to take part, give in, etc.

hold′up′, *n.* **1.** delay. **2.** robbery at gunpoint.

hole (hōl) *n., v.,* **holed, holing.** —*n.* **1.** opening. **2.** cavity. **3.** burrow. **4.** in golf, one of the cups into which the ball is driven. —*v.* **5.** drive into hole. **6.** make a hole in.

hol′i•day′ (hol′i dā′) *n.* **1.** day or period without work. —*adj.* **2.** festive.

ho′li•ness (hō′lē nis) *n.* holy state or character.

ho•lis′tic (hō lis′tik) *adj.* of or using therapies that consider the body and the mind as an integrated whole.

hol′low (hol′ō) *adj.* **1.** empty within. **2.** sunken. **3.** dull. **4.** unreal. —*n.* **5.** cavity. —*v.* **6.** make hollow.

hol′ly (hol′ē) *n., pl.* **-lies.** shrub with glossy leaves and bright red berries.

hol′ly•hock′ (-hok′, -hôk′) *n.* tall flowering plant.

hol′o•caust′ (hol′ə kôst′, hō′lə-) *n.* **1.** great destruction, esp. by fire. **2.** (*cap.*) Nazi killing of Jews during World War II.

ho′lo•gram′ (hol′ə gram′, hō′lə-) *n.* three-dimensional image made by a laser.

ho•log′ra•phy (hə log′rə fē) *n.* process of making holograms.

hol′ster (hōl′stər) *n.* case for pistol.

ho′ly (hō′lē) *adj.,* **-lier, -liest. 1.** sacred. **2.** dedicated to God.

Holy Ghost, third member of Trinity. Also, **Holy Spirit.**

hom′age (hom′ij, om′-) *n.* reverence or respect.

home (hōm) *n.* **1.** residence. **2.** native place or country. —*adv.* **3.** to or at home. —**home′land′,** *n.* —**home′ward,** *adv., adj.* —**home′less,** *adj.* —**home′made′,** *adj.*

home′ly, *adj.,* **-lier, -liest. 1.** plain; not beautiful. **2.** simple.

home′mak′er, *n.* person who manages a home.

ho′me•op′a•thy (hō′mē op′ə thē) *n.* method of treating disease with small doses of drugs that in a healthy person would cause symptoms like those of the disease. —**ho′me•o•path′ic** (-ə-path′ik) *adj.*

home′sick′, *adj.* longing for home.

home′spun′, *adj.* **1.** spun at home. **2.** unpretentious. —*n.* **3.** cloth made at home.

home′stead (-sted, -stid) *n.* dwelling with its land and buildings.

home′stretch′, *n.* last part of race-track, endeavor, etc.

hom′ey (hō′mē) *adj.,* **-ier, -iest.** cozy.

hom′i•cide′ (hom′ə sīd′, hō′mə-) *n.* killing of one person by another. —**hom′i•cid′al,** *adj.*

hom′i•ly (hom′ə lē) *n., pl.* **-lies.** sermon. —**hom′i•let′ic** (-let′ik) *adj.*

hom′i•ny (hom′ə nē) *n.* **1.** hulled corn. **2.** coarse flour from corn.

homo-, prefix meaning same or identical, as *homogeneous.*

ho′mo•ge′ne•ous (hō′mə jē′nē əs) *adj.* **1.** unvaried in content. **2.** alike. —**ho′mo•ge•ne′i•ty** (-ji nē′ə tē) *n.*

ho•mog′e•nize′ (hə moj′ə nīz′, hō-) *v.,* **-nized, -nizing.** form by mixing and emulsifying.

hom′o•graph′ (hom′ə graf′, hō′mə-) *n.* word spelled the same as another but having a different meaning.

hom′o•nym (hom′ə nim) *n.* word like another in sound, but not in meaning.

ho′mo•pho′bi•a (hō′mə fō′bē ə) *n.* unreasoning hatred of homosexuals.

Ho′mo sa′pi•ens (hō′mō sā′pē ənz) human being.

ho′mo•sex′u•al (hō′mə sek′shōo əl) *adj.* **1.** sexually attracted to same sex. —*n.* **2.** homosexual person. —**ho′mo•sex′u•al′i•ty** (-al′i tē) *n.*

Hon., 1. Honorable. **2.** Honorary.

hon′cho (hon′chō) *n., pl.* **-chos.** *Slang.* leader or important person.

hone (hōn) *n., v.,* **honed, honing.** —*n.* **1.** fine whetstone. —*v.* **2.** sharpen to fine edge.

hon′est (on′ist) *adj.* **1.** trustworthy. **2.** sincere. **3.** virtuous. —**hon′est•ly,** *adv.* —**hon′es•ty,** *n.*

hon′ey (hun′ē) *n.* sweet fluid produced by bees (**hon′ey•bees′**).

hon′ey•comb′, *n.* wax structure built by bees to store honey.

hon′ey•dew′ melon, sweet muskmelon.

hon′ey•moon′, *n.* vacation taken by newly married couple.

hon′ey•suck′le, *n.* shrub bearing tubular flowers.

honk (hongk) *n.* **1.** sound of automobile horn, goose, etc. —*v.* **2.** make such sound.

hon′or (on′ər) *n.* **1.** public or official esteem. **2.** something as token of this. **3.** good reputation. **4.** high ethical character. **5.** chastity. —*v.* **6.** revere. **7.** confer honor. **8.** show regard for. **9.** accept as valid.

hon′or•a•ble, *adj.* **1.** worthy of honor. **2.** of high principles.

hon′or•ar′y (-rer′ē) *adj.* conferred as honor.

hood (hŏŏd) *n.* **1.** covering for head and neck. **2.** automobile engine cover. **3.** hoodlum. —**hood′ed,** *adj.*

hood′lum (hōōd′ləm, hŏŏd′-) *n.* violent petty criminal.

hood′wink′ (hŏŏd′wingk′) *v.* deceive.

hoof (hŏŏf, hōōf) *n., pl.* **hoofs, hooves** (hŏŏvz, hōōvz). horny covering of animal foot. —**hoofed,** *adj.*

hook (hŏŏk) *n.* **1.** curved piece of metal for catching, etc. **2.** fishhook. **3.** sharp curve. —*v.* **4.** seize, etc., with hook.

hook′er, *n. Slang.* prostitute, esp. one who solicits on the street.

hook′up′, *n.* connection of parts or apparatus into circuit, network, machine, or system.

hoo′li•gan (hōō′li gən) *n.* noisy, violent person.

hoop (hōōp, hŏŏp) *n.* circular band.

hoop′la (hōōp′lä) *n. Informal.* **1.** commotion. **2.** sensational publicity.

hoo•ray′ (hŏŏ rā′) *interj., n.* (hurrah.)

hoot (hōōt) *v.* **1.** shout in derision. **2.** (of owl) utter cry. —*n.* **3.** owl's cry. **4.** shout of derision.

hop (hop) *v.,* **hopped, hopping,** *n.* —*v.* **1.** leap, esp. on one foot. —*n.* **2.** such a leap. **3.** plant bearing cones used in brewing. **4.** (*pl.*) the cones of this plant.

hope (hōp) *n., v.,* **hoped, hoping.** —*n.* **1.** feeling that something desired is possible. **2.** object of this. **3.** confidence. —*v.* **4.** look forward to with hope. —**hope′ful,** *adj.*

Ho′pi (hō′pē) *n., pl.* **-pi, -pis.** member of an American Indian people of the southwest.

hop′per (hop′ər) *n.* funnel-shaped trough for grain, etc.

horde (hôrd) *n.* **1.** multitude. **2.** nomadic group.

ho•ri′zon (hə rī′zən) *n.* apparent line between earth and sky.

hor′i•zon′tal (hôr′ə zon′tl) *adj.* **1.** at right angles to vertical. **2.** level. —*n.* **3.** horizontal line, etc.

hor′mone (hôr′mōn) *n.* endocrine gland secretion that activates specific organ, mechanism, etc.

horn (hôrn) *n.* **1.** hard growth on heads of cattle, goats, etc. **2.** hornlike part. **3.** brass wind instrument.

hor′net (hôr′nit) *n.* large wasp.

horn′pipe′, *n.* lively dance.

hor′o•scope′ (hôr′ə skōp′) *n.* chart of heavens used in astrology.

hor•ren′dous (hə ren′dəs) *adj.* dreadful; horrible.

hor′ri•ble (hôr′ə bəl) *adj.* dreadful.

hor′rid (-id) *adj.* abominable.

hor′ror (hôr′ər) *n.* intense fear or repugnance. —**hor′ri•fy′,** *v.,* **-fied, -fying.**

hors-d'oeuvre′ (ôr dûrv′) *n., pl.* **hors-d'oeuvres** (ôr dûrv′, -dûrvz′). tidbit served before meal.

horse (hôrs) *n.* **1.** large domesticated quadruped. **2.** cavalry. **3.** frame with legs for bearing work, etc. —**horse′back′,** *n., adv.* —**horse′man,** *n.* —**horse′wo′man,** *n.fem.*

horse′play′, *n.* boisterous play.

horse′pow′er, *n.* unit of power, equal to 550 foot-pounds per second.

horse′rad′ish, *n.* cultivated plant with pungent root.

horse sense, common sense.

horse′shoe′, *n.* **1.** U-shaped iron plate nailed to horse's hoof. **2.** arrangement in which horseshoes are tossed. **3.** (*pl.*) game in which horseshoes are tossed.

hors′y, *adj.,* **-ier, -iest.** of or like a horse.

hor′ti•cul′ture (hôr′ti kul′chər) *n.* cultivation of gardens.

ho•san′na (hō zan′ə) *interj.* (praise the Lord!)

hose (hōz) *n.* **1.** stockings. **2.** flexible tube for water, etc.

ho′sier•y (hō′zhə rē) *n.* stockings.

hos′pice (hos′pis) *n.* **1.** shelter for pilgrims, strangers, etc. **2.** facility for supportive care of dying persons.

hos′pi•ta•ble (hos′pi tə bəl, ho spit′ə-) *adj.* showing hospitality.

hos′pi•tal (hos′pi tl) *n.* institution for

treatment of sick and injured. —**hos′-pi•tal•i•za′tion,** *n.* —**hos′pi•tal•ize′,** *v.,* **-ized, -izing.**

hos′pi•tal′i•ty (-tal′i tē) *n., pl.* **-ties.** warm reception of guests, etc.

host (hōst) *n.* **1.** entertainer of guests. **2.** great number. **3.** (*cap.*) bread consecrated in Eucharist. —**host′ess,** *n.fem.*

hos′tage (hos′tij) *n.* person given or held as security.

hos′tel (hos′tl) *n.* inexpensive transient lodging.

hos′tile (hos′tl; *esp. Brit.* -tīl) *adj.* **1.** opposed; unfriendly. **2.** of enemies. —**hos•til′i•ty** (ho stil′i tē) *n.*

hot (hot) *adj.,* **hotter, hottest. 1.** of high temperature. **2.** feeling great heat. **3.** sharp-tasting. **4.** ardent. **5.** fresh or new. **6.** *Informal.* currently popular. **7.** *Informal.* performing very well. **8.** *Slang.* recently stolen.

hot′bed′, *n.* **1.** covered and heated bed of earth for growing plants. **2.** place where something thrives and spreads.

hot′-blood′ed, *adj.* excitable.

hot cake, pancake.

hot dog, 1. frankfurter. **2.** *Slang.* show-off.

ho•tel′ (hō tel′) *n.* building offering food, lodging, etc.

hot flash, sudden, brief feeling of heat experienced by some menopausal women.

hot′head′, *n.* impetuous or rash person. —**hot′head′ed,** *adj.*

hot′house′ *n.* greenhouse.

hot line, system for instantaneous communications of major importance.

hot plate, portable electrical appliance for cooking.

hot potato, *Informal.* unpleasant or risky situation or issue.

hot rod, *Slang.* car with speeded-up engine. —**hot rodder.**

hot′shot′, *n. Slang.* skillful and often vain person.

hot tub, large tub of hot water big enough for several persons.

hot water, *Informal.* trouble.

hound (hound) *n.* **1.** any of several breeds of hunting dog. —*v.* **2.** hunt or track.

hour (ou³r, ou′ər) *n.* period of 60 minutes. —**hour′ly,** *adj., adv.*

hour′glass′, *n.* timepiece operating by visible fall of sand.

house *n., v.,* **housed, housing.** —*n.* (hous) **1.** building, esp. for residence, rest, etc. **2.** family. **3.** legislative or deliberative body. **4.** commercial firm. —*v.* (houz) **5.** provide with a house.

house′break′er, *n.* person who breaks into another's house to steal.

house′bro′ken, *adj.* trained to excrete outdoors or to behave appropriately indoors.

house′fly′, *n., pl.* **-flies.** common insect.

house′hold′, *n.* **1.** people of house. —*adj.* **2.** domestic.

house′hold′er, *n.* **1.** person who owns house. **2.** head of household.

house′hus′band, *n.* married man who stays at home to manage the household.

house′keep′er, *n.* person who manages a house.

house′plant′, *n.* ornamental plant grown indoors.

house′warm′ing, *n.* party to celebrate a new home.

house′wife′, *n., pl.* **-wives.** woman in charge of the home.

house′work′, *n.* work done in housekeeping.

hous'ing (hou'zing) *n.* **1.** dwellings collectively. **2.** container.

hov'el (huv'əl, hov'-) *n.* small mean dwelling.

hov'er (huv'ər, hov'-) *v.* **1.** stay suspended in air. **2.** linger about.

Hov'er·craft', *n. Trademark.* vehicle that can skim over water on cushion of air.

how (hou) *adv.* **1.** in what way. **2.** to, at, or in what extent, price, or condition. **3.** why.

how·ev'er, *conj.* **1.** nevertheless. —*adj.* **2.** to whatever extent.

how'itz·er (hou'it sər) *n.* short-barreled cannon.

howl (houl) *v.* **1.** utter loud long cry. **2.** wail. —*n.* **3.** cry of wolf, etc. **4.** wail.

how'so·ev'er, *adv.* however.

hoy'den (hoid'n) *n.* tomboy.

HP, horsepower.

HQ, headquarters.

hr., hour.

H.R., House of Representatives.

H.S., High School.

ht., height.

hub (hub) *n.* central part of wheel.

hub'bub (hub'ub) *n.* confused noise.

hu'bris (hyoō'bris, hoō'-) *n.* excessive pride or self-confidence.

huck'le·ber'ry (huk'əl ber'ē) *n., pl.* **-ries.** edible berry of heath shrub.

huck'ster (huk'stər) *n.* peddler.

HUD (hud) Department of Housing and Urban Development.

hud'dle (hud'l) *v.,* **-dled, -dling,** *n.* —*v.* **1.** crowd together. —*n.* **2.** confused heap or crowd.

hue (hyoō) *n.* **1.** color. **2.** outcry.

huff (huf) *n.* fit of anger.

hug (hug) *v.,* **hugged, hugging,** *n.* —*v.* **1.** clasp in arms. **2.** stay close to. —*n.* **3.** tight clasp.

huge (hyoōj; *often* yoōj) *adj.,* **huger, hugest.** very large in size or extent.

hu'la (hoō'lə) *n.* Hawaiian dance.

hulk (hulk) *n.* hull remaining from old ship.

hulk'ing, *adj.* bulky. Also, **hulk'y.**

hull (hul) *n.* **1.** outer covering of seed or fruit. **2.** body of ship. —*v.* **3.** remove hull of.

hul'la·ba·loo' (hul'ə bə loō') *n., pl.* **-loos.** *Informal.* uproar.

hum (hum) *v.,* **hummed, humming,** *n.* —*v.* **1.** make low droning sound. **2.** sing with closed lips. **3.** be busy or active. —*n.* **4.** indistinct murmur.

hu'man (hyoō'mən) *adj.* **1.** of or like people or their species. —*n.* **2.** Also, **human being.** a person.

hu·mane' (-mān') *adj.* tender; compassionate. —**hu·mane'ly,** *adv.*

hu'man·ism, *n.* system of thought focusing on human interests, values, and dignity. —**hu'man·ist,** *n., adj.*

hu·man·i·tar'i·an (-man'i târ'ē ən) *adj.* **1.** philanthropic. —*n.* **2.** philanthropist.

hu·man'i·ty, *n., pl.* **-ties. 1.** humankind. **2.** human state or quality. **3.** kindness. **4.** (*pl.*) literature, philosophy, etc., as distinguished from the sciences.

hu'man·ize' (-mə nīz') *v.,* **-ized, -izing.** make or become human or humane. —**hu'man·i·za'tion,** *n.*

hu'man·kind', *n.* people collectively.

hu'man·ly, *adv.* by human means.

hum'ble (hum'bəl, um'-) *adj.,* **-bler, -blest,** *v.,* **-bled, -bling.** —*adj.* **1.** low in rank, etc. **2.** meek. —*v.* **3.** abase. —**hum'bly,** *adv.*

hum'bug (hum'bug') *n.* **1.** hoax. **2.** falseness.

hum'drum' (hum'drum') *adj.* dull.

hu'mid (hyoō'mid) *adj.* (of air) moist. —**hu·mid'i·fi'er,** *n.* —**hu·mid'i·fy',** *v.,* **-fied, -fying.** —**hu·mid'i·ty,** *n.*

hu'mi·dor' (-mi dôr') *n.* humid box or chamber.

hu·mil'i·ate' (hyoō mil'ē āt') *v.,* **-ated, -ating.** harm the pride or self-respect of. —**hu·mil'i·a'tion,** *n.*

hu·mil'i·ty, *n.* humbleness.

hum'ming·bird', *n.* very small American bird.

hum'mock (hum'ək) *n.* hillock.

hu·mon'gous (hyoō mung'gəs, -mong'-) *adj. Slang.* extraordinarily large.

hu'mor (hyoō'mər) *n.* **1.** funniness. **2.** mental disposition. **3.** whim. —*v.* **4.** indulge mood or whim of. —**hu'mor·ist,** *n.* —**hu'mor·ous,** *adj.*

hump (hump) *n.* **1.** rounded protuberance. —*v.* **2.** raise in hump.

hump'back', *n.* **1.** back with hump. **2.** person with such a back. Also, **hunch'back'.**

hu'mus (hyoō'məs) *n.* dark organic material in soils, produced by decomposing matter.

hunch (hunch) *v.* **1.** push out or up in a hump. —*n.* **2.** hump. **3.** guess.

hun'dred (hun'drid) *n., adj.* ten times ten. —**hun'dredth,** *adj., n.*

Hun·gar'i·an (hung gâr'ē ən) *n.* native or language of Hungary. —**Hun·gar'ian,** *adj.*

hun'ger (hung'gər) *n.* **1.** feeling caused by need of food. **2.** strong desire. —*v.* **3.** be hungry.

hun'gry, *adj.,* **-grier, -griest. 1.** craving food. **2.** desirous.

hunk (hungk) *n.* **1.** large piece. **2.** *Slang.* handsome, muscular man.

hun'ker (hung'kər) *v.* squat down.

hunt (hunt) *v.* **1.** chase to catch or kill. **2.** search for. —*n.* **3.** act of hunting. **4.** search. —**hunt'er,** *n.* —**hunt'ress,** *n. fem.*

hur'dle (hûr'dl) *n., v.,* **-dled, -dling.** —*n.* **1.** barrier in race track. —*v.* **2.** leap over.

hurl (hûrl) *v.* throw with great force. —**hurl'er,** *n.*

hurl'y-burl'y (hûr'lē bûr'lē) *n.* noisy disorder and confusion.

hur·rah' (hə rä', -rô') *interj.,* *n.* (exclamation of joy, triumph, etc.)

hur'ri·cane' (hûr'i kān', hur'-) *n.* violent storm.

hur'ry (hûr'ē, hur'ē) *v.,* **-ried, -rying,** *n., pl.* **-ries.** —*v.* **1.** move or act with haste. —*n.* **2.** need for haste. **3.** haste. —**hur'ried·ly,** *adv.*

hurt (hûrt) *v.,* **hurt, hurting,** *n.* —*v.* **1.** injure or pain. **2.** harm. **3.** offend. —*n.* **4.** injury or damage.

hur'tle (hûr'tl) *v.,* **-tled, -tling.** strike or rush violently.

hus'band (huz'bənd) *n.* **1.** man of married pair. —*v.* **2.** manage prudently.

hus'band·ry, *n.* farming and raising of livestock.

hush (hush) *interj.* **1.** (command to be silent.) —*n.* **2.** silence.

husk (husk) *n.* **1.** dry covering of seeds. —*v.* **2.** remove husk.

husk'y, *adj.,* **-ier, -iest,** *n., pl.* **-ies.** —*adj.* **1.** big and strong. **2.** hoarse. —*n.* **3.** (*sometimes cap.*) sturdy sled dog of arctic regions.

hus'sy (hus'ē, huz'ē) *n., pl.* **-sies. 1.** ill-behaved girl. **2.** lewd woman.

hus'tle (hus'əl) *v.,* **-tled, -tling,** *n.* —*v.* **1.** work energetically. —*n.* **2.** energetic activity.

hus'tler, *n. Slang.* **1.** person eager for success. **2.** swindler. **3.** prostitute.

hut (hut) *n.* small humble dwelling.

hutch (huch) *n.* **1.** pen for small animals. **2.** chestlike cabinet with open shelves above.

hwy., highway.

hy'a·cinth (hī'ə sinth) *n.* bulbous flowering plant.

hy'brid (hī'brid) *n.* offspring of organisms of different breeds, species, etc.

hy'brid·ize, *v.,* **-ized, -izing.** produce or cause to produce hybrids.

hy·dran'gea (hī drān'jə) *n.* flowering shrub.

hy'drant (hī'drənt) *n.* water pipe with outlet.

hy·drau'lic (hī drô'lik) *adj.* **1.** of or operated by liquid. **2.** of hydraulics.

hy·drau'lics, *n.* science of moving liquids.

hydro-, prefix meaning: **1.** water. **2.** hydrogen.

hy'dro·car'bon (hī'drə kär'bən) *n.* compound containing only hydrogen and carbon.

hy'dro·e·lec'tric (hī'drō-) *adj.* of electricity generated by hydraulic energy. —**hy'dro·e·lec·tric'i·ty,** *n.*

hy'dro·foil' (hī'drə foil') *n.* powered vessel that can skim on water.

hy'dro·gen (-jən) *n.* inflammable gas, lightest of elements.

hy'dro·gen·ate' (hī'drə jə nāt', hī·droj'ə-) *v.,* **-ated, -ating.** combine with or treat with hydrogen.

hydrogen bomb, powerful bomb utilizing thermonuclear fusion.

hydrogen peroxide, liquid used as antiseptic and bleach.

hy'dro·pho'bi·a (hī'drə fō'bē ə) *n.* **1.** rabies. **2.** fear of water.

hy'dro·plane', *n.* **1.** airplane that lands on water. **2.** light, high-speed motorboat.

hy'dro·ther'a·py, *n.* use of water externally to treat disease or injury.

hy·e'na (hī ē'nə) *n.* carnivorous African mammal.

hy'giene (hī'jēn) *n.* **1.** the application of scientific knowledge to the preservation of health. **2.** a condition or practice conducive to health, as cleanliness. —**hy·gi·en'ic** (-jē en'ik, -jen'-, -jē'nik) *adj.*

hy·grom'e·ter (hī grom'i tər) *n.* instrument for measuring humidity.

hy'men (hī'mən) *n.* fold of mucous membrane partly enclosing the vagina in a virgin.

hymn (him) *n.* song of praise.

hym'nal (him'nl) *n.* book of hymns. Also, **hymn'book'.**

hype (hīp) *v.,* **hyped, hyping,** *n. Informal.* —*v.* **1.** create interest in by flamboyant methods. —*n.* **2.** exaggerated promotion.

hyper-, prefix meaning over, above, or excessive, as *hyperactive.*

hy·per·ac'tive (hī'pər-) *adj.* abnormally active.

hy·per'bo·le (hī pûr'bə lē) *n.* exaggeration for rhetorical effect.

hy·per·crit'i·cal (hī'pər-) *adj.* excessively critical.

hy'per·gly·ce'mi·a (-glī sē'mē ə) *n.* abnormally high level of glucose in the blood.

hy'per·ten'sion, *n.* abnormally high blood pressure.

hy'per·ven'ti·la'tion, *n.* prolonged rapid or deep breathing. —**hy'per·ven'ti·late',** *v.*

hy'phen (hī'fən) *n.* short line (-) connecting parts or syllables of a word. —**hy'phen·ate',** *v.*

hyp·no'sis (hip nō'sis) *n., pl.* **-ses** (-sēz). artificially produced sleeplike

state. —**hyp·not′ic** (-not′ik) *adj.*
—**hyp′no·tism′** (-nə tiz′əm) *n.*
—**hyp′no·tist,** *n.* —**hyp′no·tize′,** *v.*

hy′po (hī′pō) *n., pl.* **-pos.** hypodermic needle or injection.

hy′po·al′ler·gen′ic, *adj.* designed to minimize the chance of an allergic reaction.

hy′po·chon′dri·a (hī′pə kon′drē ə) *n.* morbid preoccupation with one's health. —**hy′po·chon′dri·ac′,** *n., adj.*

hy·poc′ri·sy (hi pok′rə sē) *n., pl.* **-sies.** pretense of virtue, piety, etc.

hyp′o·crite (hip′ə krit) *n.* person given to hypocrisy. —**hyp′o·crit′i·cal,** *adj.*

hy′po·der′mic (hī′pə dûr′mik) *adj.* **1.** introduced under the skin, as needle. —*n.* **2.** syringe and needle for hypodermic injections.

hy′po·gly·ce′mi·a (hī′pō glī sē′mē ə) *n.* abnormally low level of glucose in the blood.

hy·pot′e·nuse (hī pot′n ōōs′, -yōōs′) *n.* side of right triangle opposite right angle.

hy′po·ther′mi·a (hī′pə thûr′mē ə) *n.* body temperature below normal.

hy·poth′e·sis (hī poth′ə sis, hi′-) *n., pl.* **-ses** (-sēz′). **1.** proposed explanation. **2.** guess. —**hy′po·thet′i·cal** (-pə thet′i kəl) *adj.*

hys′ter·ec′to·my (his′tə rek′tə mē) *n., pl.* **-mies.** removal of uterus.

hys·te′ri·a (hi ster′ē ə, -stēr′-) *n.* **1.** uncontrollable emotion. **2.** psychological disorder. —**hys·ter′i·cal** (-ster′-) *adj.* —**hys·ter′i·cal·ly,** *adv.*

hys·ter′ics (-ster′iks) *n.pl.* fit of hysteria.

Hz, hertz.

I

I, i (ī) *n.* ninth letter of English alphabet.

I (ī) *pron.* subject form of first pers. sing. pronoun.

IA, Iowa. Also, **Ia.**

-iatrics, suffix meaning medical care or treatment, as *geriatrics.*

-iatry, suffix meaning healing or medical practice, as *psychiatry.*

i′bex (ī′beks) *n., pl.* **i′bex·es, ib′i·ces′** (ib′ə sēz′, ī′bə-), **ibex.** wild goat with backward-curving horns.

ibid. (ib′id) in the same book, chapter, etc., previously cited.

i′bis (ī′bis) *n.* wading bird.

-ible, variant of *-able.*

i′bu·pro′fen (ī′byōō prō′fən) *n.* anti-inflammatory drug.

-ic, 1. adjective suffix meaning: of or pertaining to, as *prophetic;* like or characteristic of, as *idyllic;* containing or made of, as *alcoholic;* produced by or suggestive of, as *Homeric.* **2.** noun suffix meaning: person having, as *arthritic;* agent or drug, as *cosmetic;* follower, as *Socratic.*

ICC, Interstate Commerce Commission.

ice (īs) *n., v.,* **iced, icing.** —*n.* **1.** water frozen solid. **2.** frozen dessert. —*v.* **3.** cover with ice or icing. **4.** cool with ice. —**iced,** *adj.* —**i′ci·ly,** *adv.* —**i′ci·ness,** *n.* —**i′cy,** *adj.*

ice′berg′ (-bûrg) *n.* mass of ice floating at sea.

ice′box′, *n.* food chest cooled by ice.

ice cream, frozen dessert made with cream and flavorings.

ice skate, shoe with metal blade for skating on ice. —**ice-skate,** *v.*

ich′thy·ol′o·gy (ik′thē ol′ə jē) *n.* study of fishes.

i′ci·cle (ī′si kəl) *n.* hanging tapering mass of ice.

ic′ing, *n.* cake covering.

i′con (ī′kon) *n.* sacred image.

i·con′o·clast′ (-ə klast′) *n.* attacker of cherished beliefs. —**i·con′o·clas′tic,** *adj.*

-ics, suffix meaning: **1.** art, science, or field, as *physics.* **2.** activities or practices of a certain kind, as *acrobatics.*

ICU, intensive care unit.

id (id) *n.* unconscious, instinctive part of the psyche.

ID (ī′dē′) *pl.* **IDs, ID's.** document, card, or other means of identification.

ID, Idaho. Also, **Id., Ida.**

i·de′a (ī dē′ə, ī dē′′) *n.* conception in mind; thought.

i·de′al (ī dē′əl, ī dēl′) *n.* **1.** conception or standard of perfection. —*adj.* **2.** being an ideal. **3.** not real. —**i·de′al·ize′,** *v.,* **-ized, -izing.**

i·de′al·ism′, *n.* belief in or behavior according to ideals. —**i·de′al·ist,** *n.*

i·den′ti·cal (ī den′ti kəl, i den′-) *adj.* same. —**i·den′ti·cal·ly,** *adv.*

i·den′ti·fy′, *v.,* **-fied, -fying. 1.** recognize as particular person or thing. **2.** associate. —**i·den′ti·fi·ca′tion,** *n.*

i·den′ti·ty (-tē) *n., pl.* **-ties. 1.** fact of being same. **2.** self.

i′de·ol′o·gy (ī′dē ol′ə jē, id′ē-) *n., pl.* **-gies.** beliefs of group, esp. political. —**i′de·o·log′i·cal,** *adj.*

id′i·om (id′ē əm) *n.* **1.** expression peculiar to a language. **2.** dialect.

id′i·o·syn′cra·sy (-sing′krə sē, -sin′-) *n., pl.* **-sies.** unusual individual trait. —**id′i·o·syn·crat′ic,** *adj.*

id′i·ot (id′ē ət) *n.* foolish person. —**id′i·ot′ic** (-ot′ik) *adj.* —**id′i·ot′i·cal·ly,** *adv.* —**id′i·o·cy,** *n.*

i′dle (īd′l) *adj., v.,* **idled, idling.** —*adj.* **1.** not working. **2.** worthless. **3.** lazy. —*v.* **4.** do nothing. —**i′dler,** *n.* —**i′dly,** *adv.*

i′dol (īd′l) *n.* object worshiped or adored. —**i′dol·ize′,** *v.*

i·dol′a·try (ī dol′ə trē) *n., pl.* **-tries.** worship of idols. —**i·dol′a·ter,** *n.*

i′dyll (īd′l) *n.* composition describing pastoral scene. Also, **i′dyl.** —**i·dyl′lic** (ī dil′ik) *adj.*

i.e., that is.

if (if) *conj.* **1.** in case that. **2.** whether. **3.** though.

if′fy, *adj.,* **-fier, -fiest.** *Informal.* not resolved; indefinite.

ig′loo (ig′lōō) *n., pl.* **-loos.** snow hut.

ig′ne·ous (ig′nē əs) *adj.* **1.** produced by great heat. **2.** of fire.

ig·nite′ (ig nīt′) *v.,* **-nited, -niting.** set on or catch fire. —**ig·ni′tion** (-nish′ən) *n.*

ig·no′ble (ig nō′bəl) *adj.* **1.** dishonorable. **2.** humble.

ig′no·min′i·ous (ig′nə min′ē əs) *adj.* **1.** humiliating. **2.** contemptible.

ig′no·ra′mus (-rā′məs, -ram′əs) *n.* ignorant person.

ig′no·rant (ig′nər ənt) *adj.* **1.** lacking knowledge. **2.** unaware. —**ig′no·rance,** *n.*

ig·nore′ (ig nôr′) *v.,* **-nored, -noring.** disregard.

i·gua′na (i gwä′nə) *n.* large tropical lizard.

IL, Illinois.

il-, prefix equivalent to *in-,* as *illogical.*

ilk (ilk) *n.* family or kind.

ill (il) *adj.* **1.** sick. **2.** evil. **3.** unfavorable. —*n.* **4.** harm. **5.** ailment. —*adv.* **6.** badly. **7.** with difficulty.

Ill., Illinois.

ill′-bred′, *adj.* rude.

il·le′gal (i lē′gəl) *adj.* unlawful.

il·leg′i·ble, *adj.* hard to read.

il′le·git′i·mate (il′i jit′ə mit) *adj.* **1.** unlawful. **2.** born to unmarried parents. —**il′le·git′i·ma·cy** (-mə sē) *n.*

ill′-fat′ed, *adj.* doomed.

il·lib′er·al, *adj.* **1.** not generous. **2.** narrow in attitudes or beliefs.

il·lic′it, *adj.* unlawful; not allowed.

il·lim′it·a·ble (i lim′i tə bəl) *adj.* boundless.

il·lit′er·ate (i lit′ər it) *adj.* **1.** unable to read and write. —*n.* **2.** illiterate person. —**il·lit′er·a·cy,** *n.*

ill′-man′nered, *adj.* having bad manners.

ill′ness, *n.* **1.** state of being ill. **2.** particular ailment; sickness.

il·log′i·cal (i loj′i kəl) *adj.* not logical. —**il·log′i·cal·ly,** *adv.*

ill′-starred′, *adj.* unlucky; ill-fated.

ill′-treat′, *v.* abuse. —**ill′-treat′ment,** *n.*

il·lu′mi·nate′ (i lōō′mə nāt′) *v.,* **-nated, -nating.** supply with light. —**il·lu′mi·na′tion,** *n.*

illus., **1.** illustrated. **2.** illustration.

ill′-use′ *v.,* ill-used, ill-using. *n.* —*v.* (il′yōōz′) **1.** treat badly or unjustly. —*n.* (-yōōs′) **2.** bad or unjust treatment.

il·lu′sion (i lōō′zhən) *n.* false impression or appearance. —**il·lu′so·ry** (-sə rē, -zə-) *adj.*

il′lus·trate′ (il′ə strāt′, i lus′trāt) *v.,* **-trated, -trating. 1.** explain with examples, etc. **2.** furnish with pictures. —**il′lus·tra′tion,** *n.* —**il′lus·tra′tor,** *n.*

il·lus′tri·ous (i lus′trē əs) *adj.* **1.** famous. **2.** glorious.

ill will, hostile feeling.

im-, suffix equivalent to *in-,* as *immature.*

im′age (im′ij) *n.* **1.** likeness. **2.** picture in the mind. **3.** conception of one's character. —*v.* **4.** mirror.

im′age·ry, *n., pl.* **-ries. 1.** mental images collectively. **2.** use of figures of speech.

im·ag′ine (i maj′in) *v.,* **-ined, -ining. 1.** form mental images. **2.** think; guess. —**im·ag′i·na′tion** (-nā′shən) *n.* —**im·ag′i·na·tive** (-nə tiv) *adj.* —**im·ag′i·nar′y** (-ner′ē) *adj.* —**im·ag′i·na·ble,** *adj.*

i·mam′ (i mäm′) *n.* Muslim religious leader.

im·bal′ance (im bal′əns) *n.* lack of balance.

im′be·cile (im′bə sil) *n.* a foolish person. —**im′be·cil′i·ty** (-sil′i tē) *n.*

im·bibe′ (im bīb′) *v.,* **-bibed, -bibing.** drink. —**im·bib′er,** *n.*

im·bro′glio (im brōl′yō) *n., pl.* **-glios.** complicated affair.

im·bue′ (im byōō′) *v.,* **-bued, -buing. 1.** inspire. **2.** saturate.

im′i·tate′ (im′i tāt′) *v.,* **-tated, -tating. 1.** copy. **2.** counterfeit. —**im′i·ta′tive,** *adj.* —**im′i·ta′tion,** *n.*

im·mac′u·late (i mak′yə lit) *adj.* **1.** spotlessly clean. **2.** pure.

im′ma·nent (im′ə nənt) *adj.* being within. —**im′ma·nence,** *n.*

im′ma·te′ri·al (im′ə tēr′ē əl) *adj.* **1.** unimportant. **2.** spiritual.

im′ma·ture′, *adj.* not mature.

im·meas′ur·a·ble, *adj.* limitless.

im·me′di·ate (i mē′dē it) *adj.* **1.** without delay. **2.** nearest. **3.** present. —**im·me′di·a·cy** (-ə sē) *n.*

im′me·mo′ri·al, *adj.* beyond memory or record.

im·mense′ (i mens′) *adj.* vast. —**im·men′si·ty,** *n.*

im•merse′ (i mûrs′) *v.,* **-mersed, -mersing. 1.** plunge into liquid. **2.** absorb. —**im•mer′sion,** *n.*

im′mi•grant (im′i grənt) *n.* person who immigrates.

im′mi•grate′ (-grāt′) *v.,* **-grated, -grating.** come to new country. —**im′mi•gra′tion,** *n.*

im′mi•nent (im′ə nənt) *adj.* about to happen. —**im′mi•nence,** *n.*

im•mo′bile (i mō′bəl, -bēl) *adj.* not moving. —**im′mo•bil′i•ty,** *n.* —**im•mo′bi•lize′,** *v.*

im•mod′er•ate (-it) *adj.* excessive.

im•mod′est, *adj.* not modest.

im′mo•late′ (im′ə lāt′) *v.,* **-lated, -lating. 1.** sacrifice. **2.** destroy by fire. —**im′mo•la′tion,** *n.*

im•mor′al, *adj.* not moral. —**im′mo•ral′i•ty,** *n.*

im•mor′tal, *adj.* **1.** not subject to death or oblivion. —*n.* **2.** immortal being. —**im′mor•tal′i•ty,** *n.* —**im•mor′tal•ize′,** *v.*

im•mov′a•ble (i mōō′və bəl) *adj.* **1.** fixed. **2.** unchanging.

im•mune′ (i myōōn′) *adj.* **1.** protected from disease. **2.** exempt. —**im•mu′ni•ty,** *n.* —**im′mu•ni•za′tion,** *n.* —**im′mu•nize′,** *v.*

immune system, network of cells and tissues that protects the body from pathogens.

im′mu•nol′o•gy (-nol′ə jē) *n.* branch of science dealing with the immune system.

im•mure′ (i myōōr′) *v.,* **-mured, -muring.** confine within walls.

im•mu′ta•ble, *adj.* unchangeable.

imp (imp) *n.* **1.** little demon. **2.** mischievous child. —**imp′ish,** *adj.*

im′pact *n.* (im′pakt) **1.** collision. **2.** influence; effect. —*v.* (im pakt′) **3.** collide with. **4.** have effect.

im•pact′ed, *adj.* (of a tooth) wedged too tightly in its socket to erupt properly.

im•pair′ (im pâr′) *v.* damage; weaken. —**im•pair′ment,** *n.*

im•pale′ (im pāl′) *v.,* **-paled, -paling.** fix upon sharp stake, etc.

im•pal′pa•ble, *adj.* that cannot be felt or understood.

im•pan′el, *v.,* **-eled, -eling.** list for jury duty.

im•part′, *v.* **1.** tell. **2.** give.

im•par′tial, *adj.* unbiased. —**im′par•ti•al′i•ty** (-shē al′i tē) *n.*

im•pas′sa•ble, *adj.* not able to be passed through or along.

im′passe (im′pas, im pas′) *n.* deadlock.

im•pas′sioned, *adj.* full of passion.

im•pas′sive, *adj.* **1.** emotionless. **2.** calm. —**im•pas′sive•ly,** *adv.*

im•pa′tience, *n.* lack of patience. —**im•pa′tient,** *adj.*

im•peach′ (im pēch′) *v.* charge with misconduct in office. —**im•peach′ment,** *n.*

im•pec′ca•ble (im pek′ə bəl) *adj.* faultless. —**im•pec′ca•bly,** *adv.*

im′pe•cu′ni•ous (im′pi kyōō′nē əs) *adj.* having no money.

im•pede′ (im pēd′) *v.,* **-peded, -peding.** hinder.

im•ped′i•ment (im ped′ə mənt) *n.* **1.** hindrance. **2.** speech defect.

im•pel′ (im pel′) *v.,* **-pelled, -pelling.** urge forward.

im•pend′ (im pend′) *v.* be imminent.

im•pen′e•tra•ble, *adj.* that cannot be penetrated. —**im•pen′e•tra•bil′i•ty,** *n.* —**im•pen′e•tra•bly,** *adv.*

im•per′a•tive (im per′ə tiv) *adj.* **1.** necessary. **2.** *Gram.* denoting command.

im•per•cep′ti•ble, *adj.* **1.** very slight. **2.** not perceptible.

im•per′fect, *adj.* **1.** having defect. **2.** not complete. **3.** *Gram.* denoting action in progress. —**im•per•fec′tion,** *n.* —**im•per′fect•ly,** *adv.*

im•pe′ri•al (im pēr′ē əl) *adj.* of an empire or emperor.

im•pe′ri•al•ism′, *n.* policy of extending rule over other peoples. —**im•pe′ri•al•ist,** *n., adj.*

im•per′il, *v.,* **-iled, -iling.** endanger.

im•pe′ri•ous (im pēr′ē əs) *adj.* domineering.

im•per′ish•a•ble, *adj.* immortal; not subject to decay.

im•per′me•a•ble, *adj.* not permitting penetration. —**im•per′me•a•bil′i•ty,** *n.*

im•per′son•al, *adj.* without personal reference or bias.

im•per′son•ate′ (im pûr′sə nāt′) *v.,* **-ated, -ating.** act the part of. —**im•per′son•a′tion,** *n.* —**im•per′son•a′tor,** *n.*

im•per′ti•nence, *n.* **1.** rude presumption. **2.** irrelevance. —**im•per′ti•nent,** *adj.*

im•per•turb′a•ble, *adj.* calm.

im•per′vi•ous (im pûr′vē əs) *adj.* **1.** not allowing penetration. **2.** incapable of being affected.

im•pe•ti′go (im′pi tī′gō) *n.* contagious skin infection.

im•pet′u•ous (im pech′ōō əs) *adj.* rash or hasty. —**im•pet′u•os′i•ty** (-os′i tē) *n.*

im′pe•tus (im′pi təs) *n.* **1.** stimulus. **2.** force of motion.

im•pinge′ (im pinj′) *v.,* **-pinged, -pinging. 1.** strike. **2.** encroach.

im′pi•ous (im′pē əs, im pī′-) *adj.* **1.** irreligious. **2.** disrespectful.

im•pla′ca•ble (im plak′ə bəl, -plā′kə-) *adj.* not to be placated.

im•plant′ *v.* (im plant′) **1.** instill. —*n.* (im′plant′) **2.** device or material used to repair or replace part of the body.

im•plau′si•ble, *adj.* not plausible. —**im•plau•si•bil′i•ty,** *n.*

im′ple•ment (im′plə mənt) **1.** instrument or tool. —*v.* (-ment′, -mənt) **2.** put into effect. —**im′ple•men•ta′tion,** *n.*

im′pli•cate′ (im′pli kāt′) *v.,* **-cated, -cating.** involve as guilty.

im′pli•ca′tion, *n.* **1.** act of implying. **2.** thing implied. **3.** act of implicating.

im•plic′it (im plis′it) *adj.* **1.** unquestioning; complete. **2.** implied.

im•plode′ (im plōd′) *v.,* **-ploded, -ploding.** burst inward. —**im•plo′sion,** *n.*

im•plore′ (im plôr′) *v.,* **-plored, -ploring.** urge or beg.

im•ply′ (im plī′) *v.,* **-plied, -plying. 1.** indicate. **2.** suggest.

im′po•lite′, *adj.* rude.

im•pol′i•tic, *adj.* not wise or prudent.

im•pon′der•a•ble, *adj.* that cannot be weighed, measured or evaluated.

im•port′ *v.* (im pôrt′) **1.** bring in from another country. **2.** matter; signify. —*n.* (im′pôrt) **3.** anything imported. **4.** significance. —**im′por•ta′tion,** *n.* —**im•port′er,** *n.*

im•por′tant (im pôr′tnt) *adj.* **1.** of some consequence. **2.** prominent. —**im•por′tance,** *n.*

im′por•tune′ (im′pôr tōōn′, -tyōōn′, im pôr′chən) *v.,* **-tuned, -tuning.** beg persistently. —**im′por•tu′nate,** *adj.*

im•pose′ (im pōz′) *v.,* **-posed, -posing. 1.** set as obligation. **2.** intrude (oneself). —**im′po•si′tion** (-pə zish′shən) *n.*

im•pos′ing, *adj.* impressive.

im•pos′si•ble, *adj.* that cannot exist or be done. —**im•pos′si•bil′i•ty,** *n.*

im′post (im′pōst) *n.* tax or duty.

im•pos′tor (im pos′tər) *n.* person who deceives under false name. Also, **im•pos′ter.**

im′po•tence (im′pə təns) *n.* **1.** lack of power. **2.** lack of sexual powers. —**im′po•tent,** *adj.*

im•pound′, *v.* seize by law.

im•pov′er•ish (im pov′ər ish, -pov′rish) *v.* make poor.

im•prac′ti•ca•ble (im prak′ti kə bəl) *adj.* incapable of being put into practice or use.

im•prac′ti•cal, *adj.* not usable or useful.

im′pre•ca′tion (-pri kā′shən) *n.* curse. —**im′pre•cate,** *v.*

im•pre•cise′, *adj.* not precise.

im•preg′na•ble (im preg′nə bəl) *adj.* resistant to attack.

im•preg′nate (-nāt) *v.,* **-nated, -nating. 1.** make pregnant. **2.** saturate; infuse. —**im′preg•na′tion,** *n.*

im′pre•sa′ri•o (im′prə sär′ē ō′, -sâr′-) *n.* person who organizes or manages entertainment events.

im•press′ *v.* (im pres′) **1.** affect with respect, etc. **2.** fix in mind. **3.** stamp. **4.** force into public service. —*n.* (im′pres) **5.** act of impressing. —**im•pres′sive,** *adj.*

im•pres′sion (im presh′ən) *n.* **1.** effect on mind or feelings. **2.** notion. **3.** printed or stamped mark.

im•pres′sion•a•ble, *adj.* easily influenced, esp. emotionally.

im•pres′sion•ism, *n.* (*often cap.*) style of 19th-century painting characterized by short brush strokes to represent the effect of light on objects. —**im•pres′sion•ist,** *n., adj.* —**im•pres′sion•is′tic,** *adj.*

im′pri•ma′tur (im′pri mä′tər, -mā′-) *n.* sanction; approval.

im′print (im′print) *n.* mark made by pressure.

im•pris′on, *v.* put in prison. —**im•pris′on•ment,** *n.*

im•prob′a•ble, *adj.* unlikely. —**im•prob′a•bil′i•ty,** *n.*

im•promp′tu (im promp′tōō, -tyōō) *adj., adv.* without preparation.

im•prop′er, *adj.* not right, suitable, or proper. —**im′pro•pri′e•ty** (im′prə pri′i tē) *n.* —**im•prop′er•ly,** *adv.*

im•prove′, *v.,* **-proved, -proving.** make or become better. —**im•prove′ment,** *n.*

im•prov′i•dent, *adj.* not providing for the future. —**im•prov′i•dence,** *n.* —**im•prov′i•dent•ly,** *adv.*

im′pro•vise′ (im′prə vīz′) *v.,* **-vised, -vising.** make, arrange, or perform at short notice. —**im•prov′i•sa′tion** (im•prov′ə zā′shən) *n.*

im•pru′dent, *adj.* not prudent; unwise.

im′pu•dent (im′pyə dənt) *adj.* insolent. —**im′pu•dence,** *n.*

im•pugn′ (im pyōōn′) *v.* cast doubt on.

im′pulse (im′puls) *n.* **1.** inciting influence. **2.** sudden inclination. —**im•pul′sive,** *adj.*

im•pu′ni•ty (im pyōō′ni tē) *n.* exemption from punishment.

im•pure′, *adj.* **1.** not pure. **2.** immoral. —**im•pu′ri•ty,** *n.*

im•pute′ (im pyōōt′) *v.,* **-puted, -puting.** attribute.

in (in) *prep.* **1.** within. **2.** into. **3.** while; during. **4.** into some place. —*adv.* **5.** inside; within.

IN, Indiana.

in-, prefix meaning not or lacking, as *inexperience.*

in., inch.

in ab·sen′tia (in ab sen′shə, -shē ə) *adv. Latin.* in absence.

in·ac′ti·vate′ (in ak′tə vāt′) *v.,* -vated, -vating. make inactive.

in′ad·vert′ent (in′ad vûr′tnt) *adj.* **1.** heedless. **2.** unintentional. —**in′ad·vert′ent·ly,** *adv.*

in·al′ien·a·ble, *adj.* not to be taken away or transferred.

in·am′o·ra′ta (in am′ə rä′tə, in′am-) *n.* female lover.

in·ane′ (i nān′) *adj.* silly; ridiculous. —**in·an′i·ty** (i nan′i tē) *n.*

in·ar′tic′u·late (-lit) *adj.* not clear in expression.

in′as·much′ as, seeing that.

in·au′gu·rate′ (in ô′gyə rāt′) *v.,* -rated, -rating. **1.** induct into office. **2.** begin. —**in·au′gu·ral,** *adj., n.* —**in·au′gu·ra′tion,** *n.*

in′board′, *adj., adv.* inside a hull or aircraft.

in′born′, *adj.* present at birth.

in′breed′, *v.* produce by breeding of related individuals. —**in′breed′ing,** *n.* —**in′bred′,** *adj.*

inc., **1.** incomplete. **2.** incorporated. **3.** increase.

In′ca (ing′kə) *n., pl.* -cas. member of South American Indian people dominant in Peru before the Spanish conquest. —**In′can,** *adj.*

in′can·des′cence (in′kən des′əns) *n.* glow of intense heat. —**in′can·des′cent,** *adj.*

in′can·ta′tion (in′kan tā′shən) *n.* **1.** magic ritual. **2.** spell.

in·ca·pac′i·tate′ (in′kə pas′i tāt′) *v.,* -tated, -tating. make unfit or unable. —**in′ca·pac′i·ty,** *n.*

in·car′cer·ate′ (in kär′sə rāt′) *v.,* -ated, -ating. imprison.

in·car′nate (in kär′nit, -nāt) *adj.* **1.** embodied in flesh. **2.** typified.

in·cen′di·ar′y (in sen′dē er′ē) *adj., n., pl.* -aries. —*adj.* **1.** of or for setting fires. **2.** arousing strife. —*n.* **3.** person who maliciously sets fires.

in·cense′ *v.,* -censed, -censing. —*v.* (in sens′) **1.** enrage. —*n.* (in′sens) **2.** substance burned to give a sweet odor.

in·cen′tive (in sen′tiv) *n.* stimulus.

in·cep′tion (in sep′shən) *n.* beginning.

in·ces′sant (in ses′ənt) *adj.* unceasing. —**in·ces′sant·ly,** *adv.*

in′cest (in′sest) *n.* sexual relations between close relatives. —**in·ces′tu·ous** (-ses′chōō əs) *adj.*

inch (inch) *n.* unit of length, $\frac{1}{12}$ foot.

in·cho′ate (in kō′it) *adj.* just begun; not fully developed.

inch′worm′, *n.* moth larva that moves in looping motion.

in′ci·dence (in′si dəns) *n.* range of occurrence or effect.

in′ci·dent, *n.* **1.** occurrence. **2.** side event. —*adj.* **3.** likely. **4.** dependent. —**in′ci·den′tal** (-den′tl) *adj., n.* —**in′ci·den′tal·ly,** *adv.*

in·cin′er·ate′ (in sin′ə rāt′) *v.,* -ated, -ating. burn to ashes. —**in·cin′er·a·tor,** *n.*

in·cip′i·ent (in sip′ē ənt) *adj.* beginning. —**in·cip′i·ence,** *n.*

in·cise′ (in sīz′) *v.,* -cised, -cising. cut into; engrave. —**in·ci′sion,** *n.*

in·ci′sive (-sī′siv) *adj.* sharp.

in·ci′sor (in sī′zər) *n.* cutting tooth.

in·cite′ (in sīt′) *v.,* -cited, -citing. urge to action. —**in·cite′ment,** *n.*

incl., including.

in·cline′ *v.,* -clined, -clining, *n.* —*v.* (in klīn′) **1.** tend. **2.** slant. **3.** dispose. —*n.* (in′klīn) **4.** slanted surface. —**in′cli·na′tion,** *n.*

in·clude′ (in klōōd′) *v.,* -cluded, -cluding. **1.** contain. **2.** have among others. —**in·clu′sion** (-klōō′zhən) *n.* —**in·clu′sive** (-siv) *adj.*

in·cog′ni·to′ (in′kog nē′tō, in kog′ni tō′) *adj., adv.* using assumed identity.

in′come (in′kum) *n.* money received.

in′com′ing, *adj.* coming in.

in′com·mu′ni·ca′do (in′kə myōō′ni·kä′dō) *adj., adv.* without means of communicating.

in·com′pa·ra·ble, *adj.* unequaled.

in·con′sid′er·ate, *adj.* thoughtless.

in·con′ti·nent, *adj.* **1.** unable to control bodily discharges. **2.** lacking sexual self-restraint. —**in·con′ti·nence,** *n.*

in·cor′po·rate′ (-pə rāt′) *v.,* -rated, -rating. **1.** form a corporation. **2.** include as part.

in′cor·po′re·al, *adj.* not corporeal or material.

in·cor′ri·gi·ble (in kôr′i jə bəl, -kor′-) *adj.* not to be reformed.

in·crease′ *v.,* -creased, -creasing, *n.* —*v.* (in krēs′) **1.** make or become more or greater. —*n.* (in′krēs) **2.** instance of increasing. **3.** growth or addition. —**in·creas′ing·ly,** *adv.*

in·cred′i·ble, *adj.* unbelievable; amazing. —**in·cred′i·bly,** *adv.*

in·cred′u·lous, *adj.* not believing.

in′cre·ment (in′krə mənt, ing′-) *n.* addition; increase. —**in′cre·men′tal** (-men′tl) *adj.*

in·crim′i·nate′ (in krim′ə nāt′) *v.,* -nated, -nating. charge with or involve in a crime. —**in·crim′i·na′tion,** *n.*

in′cu·bate′ (in′kyə bāt′, ing′-) *v.,* -bated, -bating. keep warm, as eggs for hatching. —**in′cu·ba′tion,** *n.*

in′cu·ba′tor, *n.* **1.** heated case for incubating. **2.** apparatus in which premature infants are cared for.

in·cul′cate (in kul′kāt, in′kul kāt′) *v.,* -cated, -cating. teach; instill.

in·cum′bent (in kum′bənt) *adj.* **1.** obligatory. —*n.* **2.** office holder.

in·cur′ (in kûr′) *v.,* -curred, -curring. bring upon oneself.

in·cur′sion (in kûr′zhən, -shən) *n.* raid.

Ind., Indiana.

in·debt′ed, *adj.* obligated by debt.

in′de·ci′pher·a·ble, *adj.* illegible.

in·de·ci′sion, *n.* inability to decide.

in·deed′ (in dēd′) *adv.* **1.** in fact. —*interj.* **2.** (used to express surprise, contempt, etc.)

in′de·fat′i·ga·ble (in′di fat′i gə bəl) *adj.* tireless.

in·del′i·ble (in del′ə bəl) *adj.* uneraseable.

in·dem′ni·fy′ (in dem′nə fī′) *v.,* -fied, -fying. compensate for or insure against loss, etc. —**in·dem′ni·ty,** *n.*

in·dent′ (in dent′) *v.* **1.** notch. **2.** set in from margin.

in·den′ture (in den′chər) *n., v.,* -tured, -turing. —*n.* **1.** contract binding one to service. —*v.* **2.** bind by indenture.

in′de·pend′ent, *adj.* **1.** free. **2.** not influenced by or dependent on others. —**in′de·pend′ence,** *n.*

in′-depth′, *adj.* intensive; thorough.

in′de·struct′i·ble, *adj.* that cannot be destroyed.

in′dex (in′deks) *n., pl.* -dexes, -dices (-də sēz′), *v.* —*n.* **1.** list with page references. **2.** indicator. —*v.* **3.** provide with index.

In′di·an (-dē ən) *n.* **1.** native of India. **2.** Also, **Amer′ican In′dian.** member of the aboriginal peoples of N. and S. America. —**In′dian,** *adj.*

Indian summer, period of mild, dry weather in late fall.

in′di·cate′ (in′di kāt′) *v.,* -cated, -cating. **1.** be a sign of. **2.** point to. —**in′di·ca′tion,** *n.* —**in·dic′a·tive** (-dik′ə tiv) *adj.* —**in′di·ca′tor,** *n.*

in·dict′ (in dīt′) *v.* charge with crime. —**in·dict′ment,** *n.*

in·dif′fer·ent, *adj.* **1.** without interest or concern. **2.** moderate. —**in·dif′fer·ence,** *n.*

in·dig′e·nous (in dij′ə nəs) *adj.* native.

in′di·gent (in′di jənt) *adj.* needy; destitute. —**in′di·gence,** *n.*

in′di·ges′tion, *n.* difficulty in digesting food.

in′dig·na′tion (in′dig nā′shən) *n.* righteous anger. —**in·dig′nant,** *adj.*

in·dig′ni·ty, *n., pl.* -ties. **1.** loss of dignity. **2.** cause of this.

in′di·go′ (in′di gō′) *n., pl.* -gos, -goes. blue dye.

in′dis·crim′i·nate (in′di skrim′ə nit) *adj.* done at random; haphazard

in′dis·posed′, *adj.* **1.** mildly ill. **2.** unwilling. —**in′dis·po·si′tion,** *n.*

in′dis·sol′u·ble (in′di sol′yə bəl) *adj.* that cannot be dissolved, decomposed, undone, or destroyed.

in′di·vid′u·al (in′də vij′ōō əl) *adj.* **1.** single; particular. **2.** of or for one only. —*n.* **3.** single person, animal, or thing. —**in′di·vid′u·al·ly** (-al′i tē) *n.* —**in′di·vid′u·al·ly,** *adv.*

in′di·vid′u·al·ist, *n.* person dependent only on self.

in·doc′tri·nate′ (in dok′trə nāt′) *v.,* -nated, -nating. train to accept doctrine. —**in·doc′tri·na′tion,** *n.*

in′do·lent (in′dl ənt) *adj.* lazy. —**in′do·lence,** *n.*

in·dom′i·ta·ble (in dom′i tə bəl) *adj.* that cannot be dominated.

in′door′, *adj.* inside a building. —**in·doors′,** *adv.*

in·du′bi·ta·ble (in dōō′bi tə bəl, -dyōō′-) *adj.* undoubted.

in·duce′ (in dōōs′, -dyōōs′) *v.,* -duced, -ducing. **1.** persuade; influence. **2.** cause; bring on. —**in·duce′ment,** *n.*

in·duct′ (in dukt′) *v.* bring into office, military service, etc.

in·duc′tion, *n.* **1.** reasoning from particular facts. **2.** act of inducting.

in·dulge′ (in dulj′) *v.,* -dulged, -dulging. **1.** accommodate whims, appetites, etc., of. **2.** yield to. —**in·dul′gence,** *n.* —**in·dul′gent,** *adj.*

in·dus′tri·al·ist (in dus′trē ə list) *n.* owner of industrial plant.

in·dus′tri·al·ize′, *v.,* -ized, -izing. convert to modern industrial methods.

in·dus′tri·ous, *adj.* hard-working.

in′dus·try (in′də strē) *n., pl.* -tries. **1.** trade or manufacture, esp. with machinery. **2.** diligent work. —**in·dus′tri·al,** *adj.*

in·e′bri·ate′ *v.,* -ated, -ating, *n.* —*v.* (in ē′brē āt′) **1.** make drunk. —*n.* (-it) **2.** drunken person.

in·ef′fa·ble (in ef′ə bəl) *adj.* that cannot be described.

in′ef·fec′tu·al, *adj.* futile.

in·ept′ (in ept′, i nept′) *adj.* imcompetent; foolish. —in•ept/i•tude/, n. —in•ept/ly, adv.

in•eq/ui•ty, n., pl. -ties. injustice.

in•ert/ (in ûrt′, i nûrt′) adj. 1. without inherent power to move, resist, or act. 2. slow-moving. —in•er/tia, n.

in•ev/i•ta•ble (in ev′i tə bəl) adj. not to be avoided. —in•ev/i•ta•bil/i•ty, n. —in•ev/i•ta•bly, adv.

in•ex/o•ra•ble (in ek′sər ə bəl) adj. unyielding. —in•ex/o•ra•bly, adv.

in•ex/pert (in eks′pûrt, in′ik spûrt′) adj. unskilled.

in•ex/pli•ca•ble (in ek′spli kə bəl, in′ik splik′ə-) adj. incapable of being explained.

in•ex/tri•ca•ble (in ek′stri kə bəl, in′ik strik′ə-) adj. that cannot be freed or disentangled.

in•fal/li•ble, adj. never failing or making mistakes.

in•fa/my (in′fə mē) n., pl. -mies. evil repute. —in/fa•mous, adj.

in/fant (in′fənt) n. very young baby. —in/fan•cy, n. —in/fan•tile/ (-fəntīl′) adj.

in/fan•try (in′fən trē) n., pl. -tries. soldiers who fight on foot. —in/fan•try•man, n.

in•farct/ (in′ färkt′, in färkt′) n. area of dead or dying tissue, as in the heart. Also, in•farc/tion.

in•fat/u•ate/ (in fach′ōō āt′) v., -ated, -ating. inspire with foolish love. —in•fat/u•a/tion, n.

in•fect/ (in fekt′) v. contaminate, esp. with disease germs. —in•fec/tion, n.

in•fec/tious, adj. spreading readily.

in•fer/ (in fûr′) v., -ferred, -ferring. conclude or deduce. —in/fer•ence, n.

in•fe/ri•or (in fēr′ē ər) adj. 1. less good, important, etc. — n. 2. person inferior to others. —in•fe/ri•or/i•ty (-ôr′i tē) n.

in•fer/nal (in fûr′nl) adj. 1. of hell. 2. Informal. outrageous.

in•fer/no (-nō) n., pl. -nos. hell.

in•fest/ (in fest′) v. overrun; trouble. —in/fes•ta/tion, n.

in/fi•del (in′fi dl, -del′) n. unbeliever.

in/field/, n. 1. area of baseball field inside base lines. 2. players in infield. —in/field•er, n.

in/fight/ing, n. conflict within group.

in•fil/trate (in fil′trāt, in′fil trāt′) v., -trated, -trating. pass in without being noticed. —in/fil•tra/tion, n.

in/fi•nite (in′fə nit) adj. 1. vast; endless. —n. 2. that which is infinite. —in•fin/i•ty (in fin′i tē) n.

in•fin/i•tes/i•mal (in fin′i tes/ə məl) adj. immeasurably small.

in•fin/i•tive (in fin′i tiv) n. simple form of verb.

in•firm/ (-fûrm′) adj. feeble; weak. —in•fir/mi•ty, n.

in•fir/ma•ry (-fûr′mə rē) n., pl. -ries. hospital.

in•flame/, v., -flamed, -flaming. 1. excite. 2. cause bodily reaction marked by redness, pain, etc. —in•flam/ma•ble (-flam′ə bəl) adj. —in•flam/ma•to/ry (-tô′rē) adj. —in/flam•ma/tion (-flə mā′shən) n.

in•flate/ (in flāt′) v., -flated, -flating. 1. swell or expand with air or gas. 2. increase unduly.

in•fla/tion (-shən) n. 1. rise in prices when currency or credit expands faster than available goods or services. 2. act of inflating.

in•flect/ (in flekt′) v. 1. bend. 2. modulate. 3. display forms of a word. —in•flec/tion, n.

in•flict/ (in flikt′) v. impose harmfully. —in•flic/tion, n.

in/flu•ence (in′flōō əns) n., v.,

-enced, -encing. —n. 1. power to affect another. 2. something that does this. —v. 3. affect or alter. —in/flu•en/tial (-en′shəl) adj.

in/flu•en/za (-en′zə) n. contagious disease caused by virus.

in/flux/, n. instance of flowing in.

in/fo•mer/cial (in′fō mûr′shəl) n. program-length television commercial designed to appear to be standard programming rather than an advertisement.

in•form/ (in fôrm′) v. supply with information. —in•form/ant, n. —in•form/er, n. —in•form/a•tive, adj.

in/for•ma/tion (-fər mā′shən) n. factual knowledge. —in/for•ma/tion•al, adj.

information superhighway, large-scale communications network linking computers, television sets, etc.

in/fo•tain/ment (in′fō tān′mənt) n. broadcasting or publishing that treats factual matter in an entertaining way, as by dramatizing real events.

in•frac/tion (in frak′shən) n. violation.

in/fra•red/ (in′frə-) n. part of invisible spectrum.

in/fra•struc/ture, n. 1. basic framework of system or organization. 2. basic facilities, as transportation and communications systems.

in•fringe/ (in frinj′) v., -fringed, -fringing. violate; encroach.

in•fu/ri•ate/ (in fyŏŏr′ē āt′) v., -ated, -ating. enrage.

in•fuse/ (in fyōōz′) v., -fused, -fusing. 1. instill; fortify. 2. steep. —in•fu/sion, n.

in•ge/nious (in jēn′yəs) adj. inventive; clever. —in•ge•nu/i•ty (in′jə-nōō′i tē, -nyōō′-) n.

in/ge•nue/ (an′zhə nōō′) n. innocent young woman in a play.

in•gen/u•ous (in jen′yōō əs) adj. innocent.

in•gest/ (in jest′) v. take into the body, as food or liquid.

in/got (ing′gət) n. cast block of metal.

in•grained/, adj. fixed firmly.

in/grate (in′grāt) n. ungrateful person.

in•gra/ti•ate/ (in grā′shē āt′) v., -ated, -ating. get (oneself) into someone's good graces.

in•gre/di•ent (in grē′dē ənt) n. element or part of mixture.

in/gress (in′gres) n. entrance.

in•hab/it (in hab′it) v. live in. —in•hab/it•ant, n.

in/ha•la/tor (in′hə lā′tər) n. 1. apparatus to help one inhale medicine, etc. 2. respirator.

in•hale/ (in hāl′) v., -haled, -haling. breathe in. —in/ha•la/tion, n.

in•hal/er, n. inhalator.

in•here/ (in hēr′) v., -hered, -hering. be inseparable part or element. —in•her/ent (-hēr′ənt, -her′-) adj.

in•her/it (in her′it) v. become heir to. —in•her/it•ance, n.

in•hib/it (in hib′it) v. restrain or hinder. —in/hi•bi/tion, n.

in/house/ (adj. in′hous′; adv. -hous′) adj., adv. using an organization's own staff or resources.

in•hu/man, adj. 1. brutal; heartless. 2. not human. —in/hu•man/i•ty, n.

in•im/i•cal (i nim′i kəl) adj. 1. adverse. 2. hostile.

in•im/i•ta•ble (i nim′i tə bəl) adj. not to be imitated.

in•iq/ui•ty (i nik′wi tē) n., pl. -ties. 1. wicked injustice. 2. sin.

in•i/tial (i nish′əl) adj., n., v., -tialed,

-tialing. —adj. 1. of or at beginning. —n. 2. first letter of word. —v. 3. sign with initials of one's name. —in•i/tial•ly, adv.

in•i/ti•ate/ (i nish′ē āt′) v., -ated, -ating. 1. begin. 2. admit with ceremony. —in•i/ti•a/tion, n.

in•i/ti•a•tive (i nish′ē ə tiv, i nish′ə-) n. 1. introductory step. 2. readiness to proceed.

in•ject/ (in jekt′) v. force, as into tissue. —in•jec/tion, n.

in•junc/tion (in jungk′shən) n. order or admonition.

in/jure (in′jər) v., -jured, -juring. 1. hurt. 2. do wrong to. —in•ju/ri•ous (-jŏŏr′ē əs) adj. —in/ju•ry, n.

ink (ingk) n. 1. writing fluid. —v. 2. mark with ink. —ink/y, adj.

ink/ling (ingk′ling) n. hint.

in/land (adj. in′lənd; adv., n. -land′, -land) adj. 1. of or in the interior of a region. —adv. 2. of or toward inland area. —n. 3. inland area.

in/-law/ (in lô′, in′lô′) n. relative by marriage.

in/lay/, v., -laid, -laying, n. —v. (in′lā′, in lā′) 1. ornament with design set in surface. —n. (in′lā′) 2. inlaid work.

in/let (-let, -lit) n. narrow bay.

in-line skate, roller skate with four wheels in a straight line.

in/mate/, n. person confined in prison, hospital, etc.

in me•mo/ri•am (in mə môr′ē əm) in memory (of).

in/most/, adj. farthest within. Also, in/ner•most/.

inn (in) n. 1. hotel. 2. tavern.

in/nards (in′ərdz) n.pl. internal parts.

in•nate/ (i nāt′, in′āt) adj. natural; born in one.

in/ner (in′ər) adj. 1. being farther within. 2. spiritual.

inner city, central part of city.

in/ner-di•rect/ed, adj. guided by one's own values.

in/ning (in′ing) n. Baseball. one round of play for both teams.

in/no•cence (in′ə səns) n. 1. freedom from guilt. 2. lack of worldly knowledge. —in/no•cent, adj., n.

in•noc/u•ous (i nok′yōō əs) adj. harmless.

in/no•vate/ (in′ə vāt′) v., -vated, -vating. bring in something new. —in/no•va/tion, n. —in/no•va/tor, adj.

in•nu•en/do (in′yōō en′dō) n., pl. -dos, -does. indirect remark about sex or something bad.

in•nu/mer•a•ble, adj. 1. very numerous. 2. that cannot be counted.

in•oc/u•late/ (i nok′yə lāt′) v., -lated, -lating. immunize. —in•oc/u•la/tion, n.

in•or/di•nate (in ôr′dn it) adj. excessive. —in•or/di•nate•ly, adv.

in/pa/tient, n. patient who stays in hospital while receiving care.

in/put/, n., v., -putted or -put, -putting. —n. 1. power, etc., supplied to machine. 2. information given to computer. —v. 3. enter (data) into computer. —in/put/ter, n.

in/quest, n. legal inquiry.

in•quire/ (in kwīə′r′) v., -quired, -quiring. 1. ask. 2. make investigation. —in•quir/y (in kwīr′ē rē, in′kwə rē) n.

in/qui•si/tion (in′kwə zish′ən, ing′-) n. investigation. —in•quis/i•tor, n.

in•quis/i•tive (-kwiz′i tiv) adj. very curious.

in/road/, n. encroachment.

ins., 1. inches. 2. insurance.

in·sane′ (in sān′) *adj.* mentally deranged. —**in·san′i·ty** (-san′i tē) *n.*

in·sa′ti·a·ble (in sā′shə bəl, -shē ə-) *adj.* impossible to satisfy.

in·scribe′ (in skrīb′) *v.,* **-scribed, -scribing. 1.** write or engrave. **2.** dedicate. —**in·scrip′tion** (-skrip′shən) *n.*

in·scru′ta·ble (in skrōō′tə bəl) *adj.* that cannot be understood. —**in·scru′ta·bil′i·ty,** *n.*

in′sect (in′sekt) *n.* small six-legged animal with body in three parts.

in·sec′ti·cide′ (-sek′tə sīd′) *n.* chemical for killing insects.

in·sem′i·nate′ (in sem′ə nāt′) *v.,* **-nated, -nating. 1.** sow seed in. **2.** impregnate. —**in·sem′i·na′tion,** *n.*

in·sen′si·ble, *adj.* **1.** incapable of feeling or perceiving. **2.** unaware; unconscious. —**in·sen′si·bil′i·ty,** *n.*

in·sert′, *v.* (in sûrt′) **1.** put or set in. —*n.* (in′sûrt) **2.** something inserted. —**in·ser′tion,** *n.*

in′shore′, *adj.* **1.** on or close to the shore. —*adv.* **2.** toward the shore.

in′side′ (in′sīd′, in′sīd′) *prep., adv.* **1.** within. —*n.* **2.** inner part. —*adj.* **3.** inner.

in·sid′er, *n.* person who has influence, esp. because privy to confidential information.

in·sid′i·ous (in sid′ē əs) *adj.* artfully treacherous.

in′sight′, *n.* discernment.

in·sig′ni·a (in sig′nē ə) *n., pl.* **-nia** or **-nias.** badge or other symbol of rank, honor, etc.

in·sin′u·ate′ (in sin′yōō āt′) *v.,* **-ated, -ating. 1.** hint slyly. **2.** put into mind. **3.** make one's way artfully. —**in·sin′u·a′tion,** *n.*

in·sip′id (in sip′id) *adj.* without distinctive qualities; vapid.

in·sist′ (in sist′) *v.* be firm or persistent. —**in·sist′ence,** *n.* —**in·sist′ent,** *adj.*

in′so·far′, *adv.* to such extent.

in′sole′, *n.* inner sole of shoe.

in·so·lent (in′sə lənt) *adj.* boldly rude. —**in′so·lence,** *n.*

in·sol′vent, *adj.* without funds to pay one's debts. —**in·sol′ven·cy,** *n.*

in·som′ni·a (in som′nē ə) *n.* sleeplessness.

in′so·much′, *adv.* **1.** to such a degree (that). **2.** inasmuch (as).

in·sou′ci·ant (in sōō′sē ənt) *adj.* free from concern or anxiety.

in·spect′ (in spekt′) *v.* view critically or officially. —**in·spec′tion,** *n.*

in·spec′tor, *n.* **1.** person with duty to inspect. **2.** minor police official.

in·spire′ (in spī r′) *v.,* **-spired, -spiring. 1.** arouse (emotion, etc.). **2.** prompt to extraordinary actions. **3.** inhale. —**in′spi·ra′tion,** (in′spə rā′shən) *n.* —**in′spi·ra′tion·al,** *adj.*

Inst., *n.* **1.** Institute. **2.** Institution.

in·stall′ (in stôl′) *v.* **1.** put in position for use. **2.** establish. —**in′stal·la′tion,** *n.*

in·stall′ment, *n.* division, as of payment or story. Also, **in·stal′ment.**

installment plan, system for paying in installments.

in′stance (in′stəns) *n., v.,* **-stanced, -stancing.** —*n.* **1.** case; example. —*v.* **2.** cite.

in′stant, *n.* **1.** moment. **2.** point of time now present. —*adj.* **3.** immediate. —**in′stant·ly,** *adv.*

in·stan·ta·ne·ous (-stən tā′nē əs) *adj.* occurring, etc., in an instant.

in·stead′ (in sted′) *adv.* in place of.

in′step′, *n.* upper arch of foot.

in′sti·gate′ (in′sti gāt′) *v.,* **-gated,**

-gating. incite to action. —**in′sti·ga′tion,** *n.* —**in′sti·ga′tor,** *n.*

in·still′ (in stil′) *v.* introduce slowly.

in′stinct (in′stingkt) *n.* natural impulse or talent. —**in·stinc′tive,** *adj.*

in′sti·tute′ (in′sti tōōt′, -tyōōt′) *v.,* **-tuted, -tuting,** *n.* —*v.* **1.** establish. **2.** put into effect. —*n.* **3.** society or organization. **4.** established law, custom, etc.

in′sti·tu′tion, *n.* **1.** organization with public purpose. **2.** established tradition, etc. **3.** act of instituting. —**in′sti·tu′tion·al,** *adj.* —**in′sti·tu′tion·al·ize′,** *v.,* **-ized, -izing.**

in·struct′ (in strukt′) *v.* **1.** order. **2.** teach. —**in·struc′tion,** *n.* —**in·struc′tive,** *adj.* —**in·struc′tor,** *n.*

in′stru·ment (in′strə mənt) *n.* **1.** tool. **2.** device for producing music. **3.** means; agent. **4.** legal document. —**in′stru·men′tal** (-men′tl) *adj.*

in′su·lar (in′sə lar, ins′yə-) *adj.* **1.** of islands. **2.** narrow in viewpoint.

in′su·late′ (-lāt′) *v.,* **-lated, -lating.** cover with material that prevents passage of heat, electricity, or sound. —**in′su·la′tion,** *n.* —**in′su·la′tor,** *n.*

in′su·lin (in′sə lin, ins′yə-) *n.* synthetic hormone used to treat diabetes.

in·sult′ *v.* (in sult′) **1.** treat with open contempt. —*n.* (in′sult) **2.** insulting remark or act.

in·su′per·a·ble (in sōō′pər ə bəl) *adj.* that cannot be overcome.

in·sure′, *v.,* **-sured, -suring. 1.** make certain. **2.** guarantee payment in case of harm to or loss of. —**in·sur′ance,** *n.* —**in·sur′er,** *n.*

in·sur′gent (in sûr′jənt) *n.* **1.** rebel. —*adj.* **2.** rebellious.

in′sur·rec′tion (in′sə rek′shən) *n.* armed revolt.

int., **1.** interest. **2.** interior **3.** interjection. **4.** international. **5.** intransitive.

in·tact′ (in takt′) *adj.* undamaged.

in′take′, *n.* **1.** point at which something is taken in. **2.** what is taken in.

in′te·ger (in′ti jər) *n.* whole number.

in′te·gral (in′ti grəl, in teg′rəl) *adj.* necessary to completeness.

in′te·grate′ (in′ti grāt′) *v.,* **-grated, -grating. 1.** unite. **2.** abolish segregation by race. —**in′te·gra′tion,** *n.*

in·teg′ri·ty (in teg′ri tē) *n.* **1.** soundness of character; honesty. **2.** perfect condition.

in·teg′u·ment (in teg′yə mənt) *n.* skin, rind, etc.

in·tel·lect′ (in′tl ekt′) *n.* **1.** reasoning. **2.** mental capacity.

in′tel·lec′tu·al, *adj.* **1.** of intellect. **2.** devising concepts in dealing with problems. —*n.* **3.** person who pursues intellectual interests.

in·tel′li·gence (in tel′i jəns) *n.* **1.** ability to learn and understand. **2.** news. **3.** gathering of secret information.

in·tel′li·gent, *adj.* having a high mental capacity.

in·tel′li·gi·ble (-jə bəl) *adj.* understandable. —**in·tel′li·gi·bil′i·ty,** *n.*

in·tend′ (in tend′) *v.* plan; design.

in·tend′ed, *n. Informal.* person one plans to marry.

in·tense′ (in tens′) *adj.* **1.** extremely powerful. **2.** emotional. —**in·ten′si·fy′,** *v.,* **-fied, -fying.** —**in·ten′si·ty,** *n.*

in·ten′sive, *adj.* thorough.

in·tent′ (in tent′) *n.* **1.** purpose. —*adj.* **2.** firmly concentrated. **3.** firmly purposeful. —**in·tent′ly,** *adv.*

in·ten′tion, *n.* **1.** purpose. **2.** meaning. —**in·ten′tion·al,** *adj.*

in·ter′ (in tûr′) *v.,* **-terred, -terring.** bury.

inter-, prefix meaning: **1.** between or among, as *interdepartmental.* **2.** reciprocally, as *interdependent.*

in′ter·act′ (in′tər akt′) *v.* act upon one another. —**in′ter·ac′tion,** *n.* —**in′ter·ac′tive,** *adj.*

in′ter·breed′, *v.,* **-bred, -breeding.** crossbreed (plant or animal).

in′ter·cede′ (-sēd′) *v.,* **-ceded, -ceding.** act or plead in behalf. —**in′ter·ces′sion,** *n.*

in′ter·cept′ (-sept′) *v.* stop or check progress.

in′ter·change′, *v.,* **-changed, -changing,** *n.* —*v.* (in′tər chānj′) **1.** exchange. **2.** alternate. —*n.* (in′tər chānj′) **3.** act or place of interchanging.

in′ter·con′ti·nen′tal, *adj.* between or among continents.

in′ter·course′, *n.* **1.** dealings. **2.** sexual relations.

in′ter·de·nom′i·na′tion·al, *adj.* between or involving different religious denominations.

in′ter·de·pend′ent, *adj.* mutually dependent. —**in′ter·de·pend′ence,** *n.*

in′ter·dict′ *n.* (in′tər dikt′) **1.** decree that prohibits. —*v.* (in′tər dikt′) **2.** prohibit. —**in′ter·dic′tion,** *n.*

in′ter·est (in′tər ist, -trist) *n.* **1.** feeling of attention, curiosity, etc. **2.** business or ownership. **3.** benefit. **4.** payment for use of money. —*v.* **5.** excite or hold interest of.

interest group, group acting together because of a common interest, etc.

in′ter·est·ing (-tər ə sting, -trə sting, -tə res′ting) *adj.* engaging the attention or curiosity.

in′ter·face′, *n.,* **-faced, -facing.** —*n.* (in′tər fās′) **1.** common boundary. **2.** computer hardware or software that communicates information between entities, as between computer and user. —*v.* (in′tər fās′, in′tər fās′) **3.** interact or coordinate smoothly.

in′ter·fere′ (-fēr′) *v.,* **-fered, -fering. 1.** hamper. **2.** intervene. **3.** obstruct. —**in′ter·fer′ence,** *n.*

in′ter·im (in′tər əm) *n.* **1.** meantime. —*adj.* **2.** temporary.

in·te′ri·or (in tēr′ē ər) *adj.* **1.** inside. **2.** inland. —*n.* **3.** interior part.

in′ter·ject′ (in′tər jekt′) *v.* add or include abruptly.

in′ter·jec′tion (-jek′shən) *n.* **1.** act of interjecting. **2.** something interjected. **3.** interjected word that forms a complete utterance, as *indeed!*

in′ter·lace′, *v.,* **-laced, -lacing.** weave together; intertwine.

in′ter·lock′, *v.,* lock, join, or fit together closely.

in′ter·loc′u·tor (-lok′yə tər) *n.* participant in conversation.

in′ter·loc′u·to′ry (-tôr′ē) *adj.* **1.** of or in conversation. **2.** *Law.* not final.

in′ter·lop′er (-lō′pər) *n.* intruder.

in′ter·lude′ (-lōōd′) *n.* intervening episode, time, etc.

in′ter·mar′ry, *v.,* **-ried, -rying. 1.** (of groups) become connected by marriage. **2.** marry outside one's religion, ethnic group, etc. —**in′ter·mar′riage,** *n.*

in′ter·me′di·ar′y (-mē′dē er′ē) *adj., n., pl.* **-aries.** —*adj.* **1.** intermediate. —*n.* **2.** negotiator.

in′ter·me′di·ate (-it) *adj.* being or acting between two others.

in·ter′ment (in tûr′mənt) *n.* burial.

in·ter′mi·na·ble (in tûr′mə nə bəl) *adj.* seeming without end; endless. —**in·ter′mi·na·bly,** *adv.*

in′ter·mis′sion (in′tər mish′ən) *n.* interval between acts in drama, etc.

in·ter·mit′tent (-mit′nt) *adj.* alternately ceasing and starting again.

in·tern′ (in tûrn′) *v.* **1.** confine, esp. prisoner of war. —*n.* (tûrn) **2.** Also, **in′terne.** resident assistant physician on hospital staff. —**in·tern′ment**, *n.* —**in′tern·ship′**, *n.*

in·ter′nal (in tûr′nl) *adj.* **1.** interior; inner. **2.** not foreign; domestic.

internal medicine, branch of medicine dealing with diagnosis and nonsurgical treatment of diseases.

in′ter·na′tion·al, *adj.* **1.** among nations. **2.** of many nations.

in′ter·na′tion·al·ism, *n.* principle of international cooperation.

in′ter·na′tion·al·ize′, *v.*, **-ized, -izing. 1.** make international. **2.** bring under international control.

in′ter·ne′cine (-nē′sēn, -sīn, -nes′ēn, -īn) *adj.* **1.** of conflict within a group. **2.** mutually destructive.

In′ter·net′, *n.* large computer network linking smaller networks worldwide.

in′tern·ist (in′tûr nist, in tûr′nist) *n.* doctor specializing in internal medicine.

in′ter·per′son·al, *adj.* between persons.

in′ter·plan′e·tar′y, *adj.* between planets.

in′ter·play′, *n.* reciprocal action.

in·ter′po·late′ (in tûr′pə lāt′) *v.*, **-lated, -lating.** insert to alter or clarify meaning.

in′ter·pose′, *v.*, **-posed, -posing. 1.** place between things. **2.** intervene.

in·ter′pret (in tûr′prit) *v.* **1.** explain. **2.** construe. **3.** translate. —**in·ter′pre·ta′tion**, *n.* —**in·ter′pret·er**, *n.*

in′ter·ra′cial, *adj.* of, for, or between persons of different races.

in′ter·re·lat′ed, *adj.* closely associated.

in·ter′ro·gate′ (in tûr′ə gāt′) *v.*, **-gated, -gating.** question. —**in·ter′ro·ga′tion,** *n.* —**in·ter′rog·a·tive** (in′tə-rog′ə tiv) *adj.* —**in·ter′ro·ga′tor,** *n.*

in′ter·rupt′ (in′tə rupt′) *v.* break in; stop. —**in′ter·rup′tion,** *n.*

in′ter·scho·las′tic, *adj.* existing or occurring between schools.

in′ter·sect′ (-sekt′) *v.* divide by crossing; cross.

in′ter·sec′tion, *n.* **1.** place where roads meet. **2.** act of intersecting.

in′ter·sperse′ (-spûrs′) *v.*, **-spersed, -spersing.** scatter at random.

in′ter·state′, *adj.* involving number of states.

in′ter·stel′lar, *adj.* situated or occurring between the stars.

in·ter′stice (in tûr′stis) *n.* space between.

in′ter·twine′, *v.*, **-twined, -twining.** unite by twining together.

in′ter·ur′ban, *adj.* between cities.

in′ter·val (in′tər val) *n.* **1.** intervening time or space. **2.** difference in musical pitch between two tones.

in′ter·vene′ (-vēn′) *v.*, **-vened, -vening. 1.** come or be between. **2.** mediate. —**in′ter·ven′tion** (-ven′shən) *n.* —**in′ter·ven′tion·ist,** *n.*

in′ter·view′, *n.* **1.** meeting to assess someone or get information. —*v.* **2.** have interview with.

in·tes′tate (in tes′tāt, -tit) *adj.* without having made a will.

in·tes′tine (in tes′tin) *n.* lower part of alimentary canal. —**in·tes′ti·nal,** *adj.*

in′ti·mate, *adj.*, *n.*, *v.*, **-mated, -mating.** —*adj.* (in′tə mit) **1.** close; friendly. **2.** private. **3.** thorough. —*n.* (-mit) **4.** intimate friend. —*v.* (-māt′)

5. imply. —**in′ti·ma·cy** (-mə sē) *n.* —**in′ti·ma′tion,** *n.*

in·tim′i·date′ (in tim′i dāt′) *v.*, **-dated, -dating.** frighten.

in′to (in′tŏŏ; *unstressed* -tŏŏ, -tə) *prep.* to inside of.

in·tone′, *v.*, **-toned, -toning. 1.** use particular spoken tone. **2.** chant.

in·tox′i·cate′ (in tok′si kāt′) *v.*, **-cated, -cating.** make drunk.

in·trac′ta·ble, *adj.* stubborn.

in′tra·mu′ral (in′trə myŏŏr′əl) *adj.* within one school.

in·tran′si·gent (in tran′si jənt) *adj.* uncompromising. —**in·tran′si·gence,** *n.*

in·tran′si·tive (-tiv) *adj.* (of verb) not having a direct object.

in′tra·ve′nous (in′trə vē′nəs) *adj.* within vein.

in·trep′id (in trep′id) *adj.* fearless. —**in′tre·pid′i·ty** (-tre pid′i tē) *n.*

in′tri·cate (in′tri kit) *adj.* complicated. —**in′tri·ca·cy** (-kə sē) *n.*

in·trigue′, *v.*, **-trigued, -triguing,** *n.* —*v.* (in trēg′) **1.** interest by puzzling. **2.** plot. —*n.* (in trēg′, in′trēg) **3.** crafty design or plot.

in·trin′sic (in trin′sik, -zik) *adj.* inherent. —**in·trin′si·cal·ly,** *adv.*

in′tro·duce′ (in′trə dŏŏs′, -dyŏŏs′) *v.*, **-duced, -ducing. 1.** bring to notice, use, etc. **2.** be preliminary to. **3.** make (person) known to another. —**in′tro·duc′tion** (-duk′shən) *n.* —**in′tro·duc′to·ry** (-duk′tə rē) *adj.*

in′tro·spec′tion (in′trə spek′shən) *n.* examination of one's own thoughts and motives. —**in′tro·spec′tive,** *adj.*

in′tro·vert′ (-vûrt′) *n.* person concerned chiefly with inner thoughts or feelings. —**in′tro·ver′sion** (-vûr′zhən) *n.* —**in′tro·vert′ed,** *adj.*

in·trude′ (in trŏŏd′) *v.*, **-truded, -truding.** come or bring in without welcome. —**in·tru′sion** (-trŏŏ′zhən) *n.* —**in·tru′sive** (-siv) *adj.*

in·tu·i′tion (in′tŏŏ ish′ən, -tyŏŏ-) *n.* instinctive perception. —**in·tu′i·tive** (-i tiv) *adj.* —**in·tu′i·tive·ly,** *adv.*

in·un·date′ (in′ən dāt′, -un-) *v.*, **-dated, -dating.** flood. —**in′un·da′tion,** *n.*

in·ure′ (in yŏŏr′, i nŏŏr′) *v.*, **-ured, -uring.** accustom; harden.

in·vade′ (in vād′) *v.*, **-vaded, -vading.** enter as an enemy. —**in·vad′er,** *n.* —**in·va′sion** (-vā′zhən) *n.*

in′va·lid, *n.* **1.** (in′və lid) sick person. —*adj.* **2.** (in′və lid) sick. **3.** (in′və lid) for invalids. **4.** (in val′id) not valid.

in·val′i·date′ (in val′i dāt′) *v.*, **-dated, -dating.** make invalid.

in·val′u·a·ble, *adj.* priceless.

in·vec′tive (in vek′tiv) *n.* abuse.

in·veigh′ (in vā′) *v.* attack violently in words.

in·vei′gle (in vā′gəl, -vē′-) *v.*, **-gled, -gling.** lure into action.

in·vent′ (in vent′) *v.* devise (something new). —**in·ven′tion,** *n.* —**in·ven′tive,** *adj.* —**in·ven′tor,** *n.* —**Usage.** See DISCOVER.

in′ven·to′ry (in′vən tôr′ē) *n.*, *pl.* **-tories.** list or stock of goods.

in·verse′ (in vûrs′, in′vûrs) *adj.* **1.** reversed. **2.** opposite. **3.** inverted.

in·vert′ (-vûrt′) *v.* **1.** turn upside down. **2.** reverse. **3.** make contrary. —**in·ver′sion,** *n.*

in·ver′te·brate, *adj.* **1.** without backbone. —*n.* **2.** invertebrate animal.

in·vest′ (in vest′) *v.* **1.** spend money in hope of profit. **2.** give or devote (time, etc.). **3.** give power or authority to. —**in·vest′ment,** *n.* —**in·ves′tor,** *n.*

in·ves′ti·gate′ (in ves′ti gāt′) *v.*, **-gated, -gating.** examine in detail. —**in·ves′ti·ga′tion,** *n.* —**in·ves′ti·ga′tive,** *adj.* —**in·ves′ti·ga′tor,** *n.*

in·vet′er·ate (in vet′ər it) *adj.* confirmed in habit.

in·vid′i·ous (in vid′ē əs) *adj.* **1.** likely to arouse envy. **2.** unjust.

in·vig′or·ate′ (in vig′ə rāt′) *v.*, **-ated, -ating.** fill with energy.

in·vin′ci·ble (in vin′sə bəl) *adj.* unconquerable. —**in·vin′ci·bil′i·ty,** *n.*

in·vi′o·la·ble (in vī′ə lə bəl) *adj.* that must not or cannot be violated.

in·vi′o·late (-lit, -lāt′) *adj.* **1.** not hurt or desecrated. **2.** undisturbed.

in·vite′ (-vīt′) *v.*, **-vited, -viting. 1.** ask politely. **2.** act so as to make likely. **3.** attract. —**in′vi·ta′tion** (in′-vi tā′shən) *n.*

in·vit′ing, *adj.* attractive or tempting.

in vi′tro (in vē′trō) developed or maintained in a controlled nonliving environment, as a laboratory vessel.

in′vo·ca′tion (in′və kā′shən) *n.* prayer for aid, guidance, etc.

in′voice (in′vois) *n.*, *v.*, **-voiced, -voicing.** —*n.* **1.** bill with prices of goods sent to buyer. —*v.* **2.** list on invoice.

in·voke′ (in vōk′) *v.*, **-voked, -voking. 1.** beg for. **2.** call on in prayer. **3.** cite as authoritative.

in·vol′un·tar′y, *adj.* not done intentionally.

in·volve′ (in volv′) *v.*, **-volved, -volving. 1.** include as necessary. **2.** complicate. **3.** implicate. **4.** engross. —**in·volve′ment,** *n.*

in′ward (in′wərd) *adv.* **1.** Also, **in′wards.** toward the interior. —*adj.* **2.** toward the interior. **3.** inner. —*n.* **4.** inward part. —**in′ward·ly,** *adv.*

in′-your-face′, *adj. Informal.* involving confrontation; defiant; provocative.

Io., Iowa.

I/O, input/output.

i′o·dine′ (ī′ə dīn′, -din; *in Chem. also* -dēn′) *n.* nonmetallic element used in medicine.

i′on (ī′ən, ī′on) *n.* electrically charged particle.

-ion, suffix meaning: action or process (*inspection*); result of action (*creation*); state or condition (*depression*).

i′o·nize′ (ī′ə nīz′) *v.*, **-nized, -nizing. 1.** separate or change into ions. **2.** produce ions in. **3.** become ionized. —**i′on·i·za′tion,** *n.*

i·on′o·sphere (ī on′ə sfēr′) *n.* outermost region of earth's atmosphere, consisting of ionized layers.

i·o′ta (ī ō′tə) *n.* very small quantity.

IOU, written acknowledgment of debt.

ip′so fac′to (ip′sō fak′tō) by the fact itself.

IQ, intelligence quotient.

IRA (*pronounced as initials or* ī′rə) individual retirement account.

I·ra′ni·an (i rā′nē ən, i rä′-) *n.* native of Iran. —**I·ra′ni·an,** *adj.*

I·ra′qi (i räk′ē, i rak′ kē) *n.*, *pl.* **-qis.** native of Iraq. —**I·ra′qi,** *adj.*

i·ras′ci·ble (i ras′ə bəl) *adj.* easily angered.

ire (īr) *n.* anger. —**i′rate** (ī rāt′, ī′rāt) *adj.*

ir′i·des′cence (ir′i des′əns) *n.* play of rainbowlike colors. —**ir′i·des′cent,** *adj.*

i′ris (ī′ris) *n.* **1.** colored part of the eye. **2.** perennial plant with showy flowers.

I′rish (ī′rish) *n.* language or people of Ireland. —**Irish,** *adj.*

irk (ûrk) *v.* annoy. —**irk′some,** *adj.*

i′ron (ī′ərn) *n.* **1.** metallic element. **2.** implement for pressing cloth. **3.** (*pl.*) shackles. —*adj.* **4.** of or like iron. —*v.* **5.** press with iron.

i′ron-clad′, *adj.* **1.** iron-plated, as a ship. **2.** very rigid or exacting.

iron curtain, (formerly) barrier between Communist and non-Communist areas.

i′ro•ny (ī′rə nē, ī′ər-) *n., pl.* **-nies. 1.** figure of speech in which meaning is opposite to what is said. **2.** outcome contrary to expectations. —**i•ron′ic** (ī-ron′ik), *adj.*

Ir′o•quois′ (ir′ə kwoi′, -kwoiz′) *n., pl.* **-quois.** member of a group of North American Indian peoples.

ir•ra′di•ate′ (i rā′dē āt′) *v.,* **-ated, -ating. 1.** illuminate. **2.** expose to radiation. **3.** shine.

ir•ra′tion•al (i rash′ə nl) *adj.* without reason or judgment.

ir•rec′on•cil′a•ble (i rek′ən sī′lə bəl) *adj.* **1.** that cannot be brought into agreement. **2.** bitterly opposed.

ir′re•deem′a•ble (ir′i dē′mə bəl) *adj.* that cannot be redeemed.

ir′re•duc′i•ble (ir′i dōō′sə bəl, -dyōō′-) *adj.* that cannot be reduced.

ir•ref′u•ta•ble (i ref′yə tə bəl) *adj.* impossible to refute.

ir•reg′u•lar (i reg′yə lər) *adj.* **1.** not symmetrical. **2.** not fixed. **3.** not conforming to rule or normality.

ir•rel′e•vant (i rel′ə vənt) *adj.* not relevant. —**ir•rel′e•vance,** *n.*

ir′re•li′gious (ir′i lij′əs) *adj.* **1.** not religious. **2.** hostile to religion.

ir•rep′a•ra•ble (i rep′ər ə bəl) *adj.* that cannot be rectified.

ir′re•press′i•ble (ir′i pres′ə bəl) *adj.* that cannot be repressed.

ir′re•proach′a•ble (ir′i prō′chə bəl) *adj.* blameless.

ir′re•sist′i•ble (ir′i zis′tə bəl) *adj.* not to be withstood.

ir•res′o•lute′ (i rez′ə lōōt′) *adj.* undecided.

ir′re•spec′tive, *adj.* without regard to.

ir′re•spon′si•ble (ir′i spon′sə bəl) *adj.* not concerned with responsibilities. —**ir′re•spon′si•bly,** *adv.*

ir′re•triev′a•ble (ir′i trē′və bəl) *adj.* that cannot be recovered.

ir•rev′er•ent (i rev′ər ənt) *adj.* lacking respect.

ir•rev′o•ca•ble (i rev′ə kə bəl) *adj.* not to be revoked or annulled.

ir′ri•gate′ (ir′i gāt′) *v.,* **-gated, -gating.** supply with water. —**ir′ri•ga′tion,** *n.*

ir′ri•ta•ble (ir′i tə bəl) *adj.* easily angered. —**ir′ri•ta•bil′i•ty,** *n.*

ir′ri•tate′ (-tāt′) *v.,* **-tated, -tating. 1.** anger. **2.** make sore. —**ir′ri•tant** (-tnt) *n.* —**ir′ri•ta′tion,** *n.*

IRS, Internal Revenue Service.

is (iz) *v.* third pers. sing. pres. indic. of **be.**

-ish, suffix meaning: **1.** of or belonging to, as *British.* **2.** like or having characteristics of, as *babyish.* **3.** inclined to, as *bookish.* **4.** near or about, as *fifty-ish.* **5.** somewhat, as *reddish.*

Is•lam′ (is läm′, -lam′, iz′-) *n.* religious faith founded by Muhammad (A.D. 570–632). —**Is•lam′ic,** *adj.*

is′land (ī′lənd) *n.* body of land surrounded by water. —**is′land•er,** *n.*

isle (īl) *n.* small island.

is′let (ī′lit) *n.* tiny island.

ism (iz′əm) *n.* distinctive doctrine, theory, or system.

-ism, suffix meaning: action or practice (*baptism*); state or condition (*barba-*

rism); doctrine or principle (*Marxism*); distinctive feature or usage (*witticism*).

i′so•bar′ (ī′sə bär′) *n.* line on map connecting points at which barometric pressure is the same.

i′so•late′ (ī′sə lāt′) *v.,* **-lated, -lating.** place or keep alone. —**i′so•la′tion,** *n.*

i′so•la′tion•ist, *n.* person opposed to participation in world affairs.

i′so•met′rics, *n.pl.* exercises in which one body part is tensed against another. —**i′so•met′ric,** *adj.*

i•sos′ce•les′ (ī sos′ə lēz′) *adj.* (of triangle) having two sides equal.

i′so•tope′ (ī′sə tōp′) *n.* one of two or more forms of an element that vary in atomic weight.

Is•rae′li (iz rā′lē) *n., pl.* **-lis, -li.** native of Israel. —**Is•rae′li,** *adj.*

is′sue (ish′ōō) *v.,* **-sued, -suing,** *n.* —*v.* **1.** send out. **2.** publish. **3.** distribute. **4.** emit. **5.** emerge. —*n.* **6.** act of issuing. **7.** thing issued. **8.** point in question. **9.** offspring. **10.** result. —**is′su•ance,** *n.*

-ist, suffix meaning: **1.** one who makes or produces, as *novelist.* **2.** one who operates, as *machinist.* **3.** advocate, as *socialist.*

isth′mus (is′məs) *n.* strip of land surrounded by water and connecting two larger bodies.

it (it) *pron.* third pers. sing. neuter pronoun.

ital., italic.

I•tal′ian (i tal′yən) *n.* native or language of Italy. —**I•tal′ian,** *adj.*

—**Pronunciation.** The pronunciation of ITALIAN with the beginning sound (ī), (pronounced like *eye*) is heard primarily from uneducated speakers. This pronunciation is sometimes used as a joke and sometimes as an insult, but is considered offensive in either case.

i•tal′ic (i tal′ik, ī tal′-) *n.* printing type that slopes to right.

itch (ich) *v.* **1.** feel irritation of skin. —*n.* **2.** itching sensation. **3.** restless desire. —**itch′y,** *adj.*

i′tem (ī′təm) *n.* separate article.

i′tem•ize′, *v.,* **-ized, -izing.** state by items; list. —**i′tem•i•za′tion,** *n.*

i•tin′er•ant (ī tin′ər ənt, i tin′-) *adj.* **1.** traveling. —*n.* **2.** person who goes from place to place.

i•tin′er•ar•y (-ə rer′ē) *n., pl.* **-aries. 1.** route. **2.** plan of travel.

-itis, suffix meaning inflammation of a body part, as *tonsillitis.*

its (its) *adj.* possessive form of **it.**

it's (its) contraction of **it is.**

it•self′, *pron.* reflexive form of **it.**

IV (ī′vē′) *n., pl.,* **IVs, IV′s.** apparatus for intravenous delivery of medicines, etc.

I've (īv) contraction of *I have.*

-ive, suffix meaning: tending to (*destructive*); of the nature of (*festive*).

i′vo•ry (ī′və rē, ī′vrē) *n., pl.* **-ries. 1.** hard white substance in tusks. **2.** yellowish white.

ivory tower, remoteness or aloofness from wordly affairs.

i′vy (ī′vē) *n., pl.* **ivies.** climbing evergreen vine —**i′vied,** *adj.*

-ize, suffix meaning: **1.** engage in, as *economize.* **2.** treat in a certain way, as *idolize.* **3.** become or form into, as *unionize.* **4.** make or cause to be, as *civilize.*

J

J, j (jā) *n.* tenth letter of English alphabet.

jab (jab) *v.,* **jabbed, jabbing,** *n.* poke; thrust.

jab′ber (jab′ər) *v.* **1.** talk rapidly or indistinctly. —*n.* **2.** such talk.

jack (jak) *n.* **1.** lifting device. **2.** knave in playing cards. **3.** electrical connecting device. **4.** flag; ensign. —*v.* **5.** raise with jack.

jack′al (jak′əl) *n.* wild dog.

jack′ass′, *n.* **1.** male donkey. **2.** fool.

jack′et (jak′it) *n.* short coat.

Jack Frost, frost personified.

jack′ham′mer, *n.* compressed-air portable drill for rock, etc.

jack′-in-the-box′, *n., pl.* **jack-in-the-boxes.** toy consisting of box from which figure springs up when the lid is opened.

jack′knife′, *n., pl.* **-knives,** *v.,* **-knifed, -knifing.** —*n.* **1.** large folding pocketknife. —*v.* **2.** (of a trailer truck) have or cause to have the cab and trailer swivel into a V.

jack′pot′, *n.* cumulative prize in contest, lottery, etc.

jack rabbit, large rabbit of western America.

Ja•cuz′zi (jə kōō′zē) *n., pl.* **-zis.** *Trademark.* brand name for type of whirlpool bath.

jade (jād) *n.* valuable green stone.

jad′ed, *adj.* weary.

jag (jag) *n. Slang.* drunken spree.

jag′ged, *adj.* sharply notched.

jag′uar (jag′wär) *n.* large South American wildcat.

jai′ a•lai′ (hī′ lī′, hī′ ə lī′) *n.* game played with basketlike rackets.

jail (jāl) *n.* **1.** prison. —*v.* **2.** put in prison. —**jail′er,** *n.*

ja•la•pe′ño (hä′lə pän′yō) *n., pl.* **-ños.** Mexican hot pepper.

ja•lop′y (jə lop′ē) *n., pl.* **-pies.** old, decrepit automobile.

jam (jam) *v.,* **jammed, jamming,** *n.* —*v.* **1.** push or squeeze. **2.** make or become unworkable. —*n.* **3.** people or objects jammed together. **4.** *Informal.* difficult situation. **5.** preserve of entire fruit.

jamb (jam) *n.* side post of door or window.

jam′bo•ree′ (jam′bə rē′) *n.* merry gathering.

Jan., January.

jan′gle (jang′gəl) *v.,* **-gled, -gling,** *n.* —*v.* **1.** sound harshly. —*n.* **2.** harsh sound.

jan′i•tor (jan′i tər) *n.* caretaker of building.

Jan′u•ar′y (jan′yōō er′ē) *n.* first month of year.

Jap′a•nese′ (jap′ə nēz′, -nēs′) *n., pl.* **-nese.** native or language of Japan. —**Japanese,** *adj.*

jar (jär) *n., v.,* **jarred, jarring.** —*n.* **1.** broad-mouthed bottle. **2.** sudden shock or shake. —*v.* **3.** shock or shake. **4.** conflict.

jar′gon (jär′gən, -gon) *n.* language meaningful only to a particular trade, etc.

jas′mine (jaz′min, jas′-) *n.* fragrant shrub.

jas′per (jas′pər) *n.* precious quartz.

jaun′dice (jôn′dis, jän′-) *n.* illness causing yellowed skin, etc.

jaun′diced, *adj.,* **1.** skeptical. **2.** envious.

jaunt (jônt, jänt) *n.* short trip.

jaun′ty (jôn′tē, jän′-) *adj.* **-tier, -tiest.** sprightly. —**jaun′ti•ly,** *adv.*

jave′lin (jav′lin, jav′ə-) *n.* spear.

jaw (jô) *n.* either of two bones forming mouth.

jaw′bone′, *n., v.,* **-boned, -boning.**

—*n.* **1.** bone of the jaw. —*v.* **2.** influence by persuasion.

jay (jā) *n.* noisy colorful bird.

jay′walk′, *v.* cross street improperly. —**jay′walk′er,** *n.*

jazz (jaz) *n.* **1.** popular music of black American origin. **2.** *Slang.* insincere talk.

jazz′y, *adj.,* -ier, -iest. **1.** of or like jazz music. **2.** flashy.

J.D., 1. Doctor of Jurisprudence; Doctor of Law. **2.** Doctor of Laws. **3.** Justice Department.

jeal′ous (jel′əs) *adj.* **1.** resentful of another's success, etc.; envious. **2.** vigilant in guarding something. —**jeal′ous·ly,** *adv.* —**jeal′ous·y,** *n.*

jeans (jēnz) *n.pl.* cotton trousers.

Jeep (jēp) *n. Trademark.* small rugged type of automobile.

jeer (jēr) *v.* **1.** deride. —*n.* **2.** deriding shout.

Je·ho′vah (ji hō′və) *n.* God.

je·june′ (ji jōōn′) *adj.* **1.** insipid. **2.** lacking maturity; childish.

jell (jel) *v.* **1.** become like jelly in consistency. **2.** become clear.

jel′ly (jel′ē) *n., pl.* -lies, *v.,* -lied, -lying. —*n.* **1.** soft, semisolid food, as fruit juice boiled down with sugar. —*v.* **2.** make into jelly.

jel′ly·bean′, *n.* small, bean-shaped, chewy candy.

jel′ly·fish′, *n., pl.* -fish, -fishes. marine animal with soft, jellylike body.

jelly roll, thin cake spread with jelly and rolled up.

jen′ny (jen′ē) *n., pl.* -nies. female donkey, wren, etc.

jeop′ard·ize′ (jep′ər dīz′) *v.,* -ized, -izing. endanger. —**jeop′ard·y,** *n.*

jerk (jûrk) *n.* **1.** quick, sharp pull. **2.** *Slang.* stupid person. —*v.* **3.** pull with a jerk. —**jerk′y,** *adj.*

jer′kin (jûr′kin) *n.* close-fitting, usu. sleeveless jacket.

jerk′wa′ter, *adj.* insignificant and remote.

jer′ry-built′ (jer′ē-) *adj.* flimsily made.

jer′sey (jûr′zē) *n.* **1.** type of shirt. **2.** knitted fabric.

jest (jest) *n., v.* joke; banter. —**jest′er,** *n.*

Je′sus (jē′zəs, -zəz) *n.* founder of Christian religion. Also called **Jesus Christ.**

jet (jet) *n., v.,* jetted, jetting, *adj.* —*n.* **1.** stream under pressure. **2.** Also, **jet plane.** plane operated by jet propulsion. **3.** black stone. —*v.* **4.** spout.

jet lag, fatigue after jet flight to different time zone.

jet′lin′er, *n.* jet plane carrying passengers.

jet propulsion, propulsion of plane, etc., by reactive thrust of jet. —**jet′pro·pelled′,** *adj.*

jet′sam (jet′səm) *n.* goods thrown overboard to lighten distressed ship.

jet′ti·son (jet′ə sən, -zən) *v.* cast (jetsam) out.

jet′ty (jet′ē) *n., pl.* -ties. wharf; pier.

Jew (jōō) *n.* **1.** follower of Judaism. **2.** descendant of Biblical Hebrews. —**Jew′ish,** *adj.*

jew′el (jōō′əl) *n.* precious stone; gem. —**jew′el·er,** *n.* —**jew′el·ry,** *n.*

jib (jib) *n.* triangular sail.

jibe (jīb) *v.,* jibed, jibing. **1.** gibe. **2.** *Informal.* be consistent.

jif′fy (jif′ē) *n., pl.* -fies. short time.

jig (jig) *n., v.,* jigged, jigging. —*n.* **1.** lively folk dance. —*v.* **2.** dance a jig.

jig′ger (jig′ər) *n.* glass measure of 1½ oz. (45 ml) for liquors.

jig′gle, *v.,* -gled, -gling, *n.* —*v.* **1.** move back and forth, etc. —*n.* **2.** act of jiggling.

jig′saw′, *n.* saw with narrow vertical blade for cutting curves, patterns, etc.

jigsaw puzzle, set of irregularly cut flat pieces that form a picture when fitted together.

jilt (jilt) *v.* reject (a previously encouraged suitor).

Jim Crow (jim) *(sometimes l.c.)* policy of discrimination against blacks. —**Jim′-Crow′,** *adj.*

jim′my (jim′ē) *n., pl.* -mies, *v.,* -mied, -mying. —*n.* **1.** short crowbar. —*v.* **2.** force open.

jim′son·weed′ (jim′sən wēd′) *n.* coarse weed with poisonous leaves.

jin′gle (jing′gəl) *v.,* -gled, -gling, *n.* —*v.* **1.** make repeated clinking sound. —*n.* **2.** clink; tinkle. **3.** very simple verse.

jin′go·ism (jing′gō iz′əm) *n.* chauvinism marked by aggressive foreign policy. —**jin′go·is′tic,** *adj.*

jin·rik′i·sha (jin rik′shô, -shä) *n.* rickshaw. Also, **jin·rik′sha.**

jinx (jingks) *n.* **1.** cause of bad luck. —*v.* **2.** cause bad luck.

jit′ters, *n.pl. Informal.* nervousness. —**jit′ter·y,** *adj.*

jive (jīv) *n., v.,* jived, jiving. —*n.* **1.** swing music or early jazz. **2.** deceptive or meaningless talk. —*v.* **3.** *Slang.* fool or kid.

job (job) *n., v.,* jobbed, jobbing. —*n.* **1.** piece of work. **2.** employment. —*v.* **3.** sell wholesale.

job action, work slowdown by employees to win demands.

job′ber, *n.* **1.** wholesaler. **2.** dealer in odd lots of merchandise.

job lot, large assortment of goods sold as a single unit.

jock (jok) *n. Informal.* **1.** athlete. **2.** enthusiast.

jock′ey (jok′ē) *n.* **1.** rider of race horses. —*v.* **2.** maneuver.

jo·cose′ (jō kōs′, jə-) *adj.* merry. Also, **joc′und** (jok′ənd, jō′kənd).

joc′u·lar (jok′yə lər) *adj.* joking. —**joc′u·lar′i·ty** (-lar′i tē) *n.*

jodh′purs (jod′pərz) *n.pl.* riding breeches.

jog (jog) *v.,* jogged, jogging, *n.* —*v.* **1.** nudge. **2.** run at steady pace. —*n.* **3.** nudge. **4.** steady pace. **5.** projection. —**jog′ger,** *n.*

joie de vi′vre (zhwΛd′ vē′vR²) *French.* delight in being alive.

join (join) *v.* **1.** put together. **2.** become member of.

join′er, *n.* assembler of woodwork. —**join′er·y,** *n.*

joint (joint) *n.* **1.** place or part in which things join. **2.** place where two bones join. **3.** cheap, sordid place. **4.** *Slang.* marijuana cigarette. —*adj.* **5.** common. —*v.* **6.** join or divide at joint. —**joint′ly,** *adv.*

joist (joist) *n.* floor beam.

joke (jōk) *n., v.,* joked, joking. —*n.* **1.** amusing remark, story, etc. —*v.* **2.** make or tell joke. **3.** speak only to amuse. —**jok′ing·ly,** *adv.*

jol′ly (jol′ē) *adj.,* -lier, -liest, *v.,* -lied, -lying, *adv.* —*adj.* **1.** merry. —*v.* **2.** try to keep (someone) in good humor. —*adv.* **3.** *Brit. Informal.* very. —**jol′li·ness,** *jol′li·ty, n.*

jolt (jōlt) *n., v.* jar; shake.

jon′quil (jong′kwil, jon′-) *n.* fragrant yellow or white narcissus.

josh (josh) *v. Informal.* tease.

jos′tle (jos′əl) *v.,* -tled, -tling. push or shove.

jot (jot) *n., v.,* jotted, jotting. —*n.* **1.** bit. —*v.* **2.** write.

jounce (jouns) *v.,* jounced, jouncing, *n.* —*v.* **1.** move joltingly. —*n.* **2.** jouncing movement.

jour′nal (jûr′nl) *n.* **1.** daily record. **2.** periodical.

jour′nal·ese′ (-ēz′, -ēs′) *n.* writing style typical of newspapers.

jour′nal·ism (-iz′əm) *n.* newspaper writing. —**jour′nal·ist,** *n.* —**jour′nal·is′tic,** *adj.*

jour′ney (jûr′nē) *n.* **1.** act or course of traveling. —*v.* **2.** travel.

jour′ney·man, *n., pl.* -men. hired skilled worker.

joust (joust) *n.* fight between mounted knights.

jo′vi·al (jō′vē əl) *adj.* hearty and good-humored. —**jo′vi·al′i·ty** (-al′i tē) *n.*

jowl (joul) *n.* jaw or cheek.

joy (joi) *n.* gladness; delight. —**joy′ful, joy′ous,** *adj.*

joy′ride′, *n.* ride for pleasure, esp. in recklessly driven vehicle.

joy′stick′, *n.* **1.** *Informal.* control stick of airplane. **2.** lever for controlling action in computer game.

JP, Justice of the Peace.

Jr., junior. Also, **jr.**

ju′bi·lant (jōō′bə lənt) *adj.* rejoicing. —**ju′bi·la′tion** (-lā′shən) *n.*

ju′bi·lee′ (jōō′bə lē′) *n.* celebration of anniversary.

Ju′da·ism (-dē iz′əm, -də-) *n.* religion of the Jewish people.

judge (juj) *n., v.,* judged, judging. —*n.* **1.** person who decides cases in court of law. **2.** person making authoritative decisions. **3.** discriminating person. —*v.* **4.** decide on.

judg′ment (-mənt) *n.* **1.** decision, as in court of law. **2.** good sense.

judg·men′tal (-men′tl) *adj.* making judgments, esp. on morality.

ju·di′cial (jōō dish′əl) *adj.* of justice, courts of law, or judges.

ju·di′ci·ar′y (-dish′ē er′ē, -dish′ə rē) *n., pl.* -ies, *adj.* —*n.* **1.** legal branch of government. —*adj.* **2.** of judges.

ju·di′cious, *adj.* wise; prudent.

ju′do (jōō′dō) *n.* martial art based on jujitsu.

jug (jug) *n.* **1.** container for liquids. **2.** *Slang.* prison.

jug′ger·naut′ (jug′ər nôt′) *n.* any overpowering, irresistible force.

jug′gle (jug′əl) *v.,* -gled, -gling. perform tricks by tossing and catching objects. —**jug′gler,** *n.*

jug′u·lar (jug′yə lər) *adj.* **1.** of the neck. —*n.* **2.** large vein in neck.

juice (jōōs) *n.* liquid part of plant, fruit, etc. —**juic′y,** *adj.*

juic′er, *n.* **1.** appliance for squeezing fruit and vegetable juice. **2.** *Slang.* heavy drinker.

ju·jit′su (jōō jit′sōō) *n.* Japanese method of wrestling and self-defense.

ju′jube (jōō′jōōb, jōō′jōō bē′) *n.* chewy fruity lozenge.

juke box (jōōk′) coin-operated record player.

Jul., July.

ju′li·enne′ (jōō′lē en′) *adj., v.* (of vegetables) cut into thin strips.

Ju·ly′ (jōō lī′, jə-) *n.* seventh month of year.

jum′ble (jum′bəl) *n., v.,* -bled, -bling. —*n.* **1.** confused mixture. —*v.* **2.** make jumble of.

jum′bo (jum′bō) *adj.* very large.

jump (jump) *v.* **1.** spring up; leap. **2.** rise. —*n.* **3.** spring; leap. **4.** rise. **5.** *Informal.* advantage.

jump′er, *n.* **1.** one that jumps. **2.** sleeveless dress worn over blouse. **3.** electric cable for starting dead car battery.

jump′-start′, *n.* **1.** starting of car engine with jumpers (def. 3). —*v.* **2.** give a jump-start to. **3.** enliven or revive.

jump′suit′, *n.* one-piece suit.

jump′y, *adj.* **-ier, -iest.** nervous.

Jun., June.

junc′tion (jungk′shən) *n.* **1.** union. **2.** place of joining.

junc′ture (-chər) *n.* **1.** point of time. **2.** crisis. **3.** joint.

June (jōōn) *n.* sixth month of year.

jun′gle (jung′gəl) *n.* wildly overgrown tropical land.

jun′ior (jōōn′yər) *adj.* **1.** younger. **2.** lower. —*n.* **3.** third-year high school or college student.

junior college, two-year college.

junior high school, school usu. encompassing grades 7 through 9.

ju′ni·per (jōō′nə pər) *n.* coniferous evergreen shrub or tree.

junk (jungk) *n.* **1.** rubbish. **2.** type of Chinese ship. **3.** *Slang.* narcotics, esp. heroin. —*v.* **4.** discard.

junk′er, *n. Informal.* old vehicle ready to be scrapped.

jun′ket (jung′kit) *n.* **1.** custard. **2.** trip by government official at public expense. —*v.* **3.** entertain.

junk food, high-calorie food of little nutritional value.

junk′ie, *n. Informal.* **1.** drug, esp. heroin, addict. **2.** person who craves or is enthusiastic for something.

junk mail, unsolicited commercial material mailed in bulk.

jun′ta (hōōn′tə, jun′-, hun′-) *n.* military group that seizes power. **—Pronunciation.** When the word JUNTA was borrowed into English from Spanish in the early 17th century, its pronunciation was thoroughly Anglicized to (jun′tə). During the 20th century, esp. in North America, the pronunciation (hōōn′tə), which comes from Spanish (hōōn′tä) has come into frequent use, probably through people's renewed awareness of the word's Spanish origins. A hybrid form, combining English and Spanish influence, (hun′tə) is also heard. Any of these pronunciations is perfectly standard.

Ju′pi·ter (jōō′pi tər) *n.* largest of sun's planets.

ju′ris·dic′tion (jŏŏr′is dik′shən) *n.* authority, range of control, etc., of judge or the like.

ju′ris·pru′dence (-prōōd′ns) *n.* science of law.

ju′rist, *n.* expert in law.

ju′ror (jŏŏr′ər, -ôr) *n.* member of jury. Also, **ju′ry·man,** *fem.* **jur′y·wom′an.**

ju′ry (jŏŏr′ē) *n., pl.* **-ries.** group of persons selected to make decisions, esp. in law court.

just (just) *adj.* **1.** fair; right. **2.** legal. **3.** true. —*adv.* **4.** exactly. **5.** barely. **6.** only. **7.** very recently.

jus′tice (jus′tis) *n.* **1.** fairness; rightness. **2.** administration of law. **3.** high judge.

justice of the peace, local public officer who performs marriages, tries minor cases, etc.

jus′ti·fy′, *v.,* **-fied, -fying. 1.** show to be true, right, etc. **2.** defend. —**jus′ti·fi·ca′tion,** *n.*

jut (jut) *v.,* **jutted, jutting.** project.

jute (jōōt) *n.* East Indian plant whose fibers are used for fabrics.

ju′ve·nile (jōō′və nl, -nīl′) *adj.* **1.** young. —*n.* **2.** young person.

juvenile delinquency, illegal or antisocial behavior by a minor. —**juvenile delinquent.**

jux′ta·pose′ (juk′stə pōz′, juk′stə-pōz′) *v.* **-posed, -posing.** place close for comparison. —**jux′ta·po·si′tion** (-pə zish′ən) *n.*

K

K, k (kā) *n.* eleventh letter of English alphabet.

K, 1. karat. **2.** Kelvin. **3.** kilobyte. **4.** kilometer. **5.** thousand.

k, 1. karat. **2.** kilogram.

ka·bu′ki (kə bōō′kē, kä′bōō kē′) *n.* popular drama of Japan.

kai′ser (kī′zər) *n.* German emperor.

kale (kāl) *n.* type of cabbage.

ka·lei′do·scope′ (kə lī′də skōp′) *n.* optical device in which colored bits change patterns continually.

kan′ga·roo′ (kang′gə rōō′) *n., pl.* **-roos, -roo.** Australian marsupial with long hind legs used for leaping.

kangaroo court, self-appointed tribunal disregarding law or human rights.

Kans., Kansas.

ka′o·lin (kā′ə lin) *n.* fine white clay.

ka′pok (kā′pok) *n.* silky down from seeds of certain trees.

ka·put′ (kä pŏŏt′, -pŏŏt′, kə-) *adj. Informal.* **1.** extinct. **2.** out of order.

ka′ra·o′ke (kar′ē ō′kē) *n.* act of singing along to music in which original vocals have been eliminated.

kar′at (kar′ət) *n.* $\frac{1}{24}$ part: unit for measuring purity of gold.

ka·ra′te (kə rä′tē) *n.* Japanese technique of unarmed combat.

kar′ma (kär′mə) *n.* fate as the result of one's actions in successive incarnations. —**kar′mic,** *adj.*

Kas., Kansas.

ka′ty·did (kā′tē did) *n.* large green grasshopper.

kay′ak (kī′ak) *n.* Eskimo canoe.

ka·zoo′ (kə zōō′) *n.* tubular musical toy that vibrates and buzzes when one hums into it.

KB, kilobyte.

kc, kilocycle.

ke·bab′ (kə bob′) *n.* cubes of marinated meat broiled on a skewer.

keel (kēl) *n.* **1.** central framing member of ship's bottom. —*v.* **2.** fall sideways.

keen (kēn) *adj.* **1.** sharp. **2.** excellent. **3.** intense. **4.** eager. —*v.* **5.** wail; lament. —**keen′ly,** *adv.*

keep (kēp) *v.,* **kept** (kept), **keeping,** *n.* —*v.* **1.** continue. **2.** detain. **3.** support. **4.** maintain. **5.** withhold. **6.** observe. **7.** last. —*n.* **8.** board and lodging. —**keep′er,** *n.*

keep′ing, *n.* **1.** conformity. **2.** care.

keep′sake′, *n.* souvenir.

keg (keg) *n.* small barrel.

kelp (kelp) *n.* large brown seaweed.

Kel′vin (kel′vin) *adj.* of or noting an absolute scale of temperature in which 0° equals −273.16° Celsius.

ken (ken) *n.* knowledge.

Ken., Kentucky.

ken′nel (ken′l) *n.* **1.** doghouse. **2.** establishment where dogs are boarded and cared for.

ker′chief (kûr′chif, -chēf) *n.* cloth head covering.

ker′nel (kûr′nl) *n.* center part of nut.

ker′o·sene′ (ker′ə sēn′) *n.* type of oil.

kes′trel (kes′trəl) *n.* small falcon.

ketch′up (kech′əp, kach′-) *n.* type of thick tomato sauce with spices.

ket′tle (ket′l) *n.* pot for boiling liquids.

ket′tle·drum′, *n.* large drum with round copper bottom.

key (kē) *n.* **1.** metal piece for operating lock. **2.** explanation. **3.** operating lever. **4.** musical tonality. **5.** reef. —*adj.* **6.** chief. —*v.* **7.** excite.

key′board′, *n.* **1.** row of keys on piano, computer, etc. —*v.* **2.** insert (data) into computer. —**key′board′er,** *n.*

key′note′, *n.* **1.** tonic. **2.** theme of meeting, etc.

key′stone′, *n.* stone forming summit of arch.

kg, kilogram.

khak′i (kak′ē, kä′kē) *adj., n.* yellowish brown.

khan (kän, kan) *n.* Asian ruler.

kHz, kilohertz.

KIA, killed in action.

kib·butz′ (ki bŏŏts′, -bōōts′) *n., pl.* **-butzim.** Israeli collective farm.

kib′itz·er (kib′it sər) *n. Informal.* person offering unwanted advice.

kick (kik) *v.* **1.** strike with foot. **2.** recoil. **3.** *Informal.* complain. —*n.* **4.** act of kicking. **5.** *Informal.* thrill.

kick′back′, *n.* portion of an income given, often secretly, to someone who made the income possible.

kick′off′, *n.* **1.** kick that begins play in football or soccer. **2.** beginning of anything.

kick′stand′, *n.* bar for holding cycle upright when not in use.

kid (kid) *n., v.,* **kidded, kidding.** —*n.* **1.** young goat. **2.** leather from its skin. **3.** *Informal.* child. —*v.* **4.** *Informal.* fool; tease. —**kid′der,** *n.*

kid′nap (kid′nap) *v.,* **-napped** or **-naped, -napping** or **-naping.** carry off by force, esp. for ransom; abduct. —**kid′nap·per, kid′nap·er,** *n.*

kid′ney (kid′nē) *n.* **1.** gland that secretes urine. **2.** kind.

kidney bean, plant cultivated for its edible seeds.

kidney stone, abnormal stony mass formed in kidney.

kill (kil) *v.* **1.** murder. **2.** destroy. —*n.* **3.** animal slain.

killer whale, large, predatory, black-and-white dolphin.

kill′ing, *n.* **1.** act of one that kills. **2.** quick, large profit. —*adj.* **3.** fatal. **4.** exhausting.

kill′-joy′, *n.* person who spoils pleasure of others.

kiln (kil, kiln) *n.* large furnace for making bricks, firing pottery, etc.

ki′lo (kē′lō, kil′ō) *n., pl.* **-los. 1.** kilogram. **2.** kilometer.

kilo-, prefix meaning thousand, as *kilo-watt.*

kil′o·byte′ (kil′ə bīt′) *n.* **1.** 1024 bytes. **2.** (loosely) 1000 bytes.

kil′o·gram′, *n.* 1000 grams. Also, **kilo.**

kil′o·hertz′, *n., pl.* **-hertz.** radio frequency of 1000 cycles per second.

kil′o·li′ter (-lē′-) *n.* 1000 liters.

ki·lom′e·ter (ki lom′i tər, kil′ə mē′-) *n.* 1000 meters. **—Pronunciation.** The first pronunciation of KILOMETER is something of a mystery. The usual pronunciation both for *units of measurement* starting with *kilo-* (*kilobyte*) and for *units of length* ending in *-meter* (*centimeter*) gives primary stress to the first syllable and secondary to the third *-me-.* Logically, KILOMETER should follow this pattern, and in fact has been pronounced (kil′ə mē′tər) since the early 1800s. However, another pronunciation of KILOMETER, with stress on the *-om-*, or second syllable, has been around for nearly as long. It is reinforced by words for *instruments* of measurement (rather than *units* of measurement) that also end in *-meter* (*thermometer, barometer*). Although criticized because it does not fit the expected pattern, the pronunciation (ki-lom′i tar) is very common in American English and has gained popularity in Britain. Both pronunciations are used by educated speakers, including scientists.

kil′o•watt′, *n.* 1000 watts.

kilt (kilt) *n.* man's skirt, worn in Scotland.

ki•mo′no (kə mō′nə, -nō) *n., pl.* **-nos.** loose dressing gown.

kin (kin) *n.* relatives. Also, **kins′folk′.** —**kins′man**, *n.* —**kins′wom′an**, *n. fem.*

kind (kīnd) *adj.* **1.** compassionate; friendly. —*n.* **2.** type; group.

kin′der•gar′ten (kin′dər gär′tn, -dn) *n.* school for very young children.

kind′heart′ed (kīnd′-) *adj.* having or showing kindness.

kin′dle (kin′dl) *v.*, **-dled, -dling. 1.** set afire. **2.** rouse.

kin′dling, *n.* material for starting fire.

kind′ly (kīnd′lē) *adj.*, **-lier, -liest**, *adv.* —*adj.* **1.** kind. —*adv.* **2.** in kind manner. **3.** favorably.

kin′dred (kin′drid) *adj.* **1.** related; similar. —*n.* **2.** relatives.

ki•net′ic (ki net′ik, kī-) *adj.* of motion.

king (king) *n.* sovereign male ruler. —**king′ly**, *adj.*

king′dom (-dəm) *n.* government ruled by king or queen.

king′fish′er, *n.* colorful, fish-eating bird.

king′-size′, *adj.* extra large.

kink (kingk) *n.*, *v.* twist; curl. —**kink′y**, *adj.*, **-ier, -iest.**

kin′ship, *n.* **1.** family relationship. **2.** affinity; likeness.

ki•osk′ (kē′osk, kē osk′) *n.* small open structure where newspapers, refreshments, etc., are sold.

kip′per (kip′ər) *n.* salted, dried fish.

kis′met (kiz′mit, -met, kis′-) *n.* fate.

kiss (kis) *v.* **1.** touch with lips in affection, etc. —*n.* **2.** act of kissing.

kit (kit) *n.* set of supplies, tools, etc.

kitch′en (kich′ən) *n.* room for cooking. —**kitch′en•ware′**, *n.*

kite (kīt) *n.* **1.** light, paper-covered frame flown in wind on long string. **2.** type of falcon.

kith and kin (kith) friends and relations.

kitsch (kich) *n.* something tawdry designed to appeal to undiscriminating persons.

kit′ten (kit′n) *n.* young cat.

kit′ten•ish, *adj.* playfully coy or cute.

kit′ty-cor′nered, *adj.* cater-cornered. Also, **kit′ty-cor′ner.**

ki′wi (kē′wē) *n.* **1.** flightless bird of New Zealand. **2.** egg-sized brown fruit with edible green pulp.

KKK, Ku Klux Klan.

Klee′nex (klē′neks) *Trademark.* soft paper tissue.

klep′to•ma′ni•a (klep′tə mā′nē ə) *n.* irresistible desire to steal. —**klep′to•ma′ni•ac′**, *n.*

klutz (kluts) *n. Slang.* clumsy person. —**klutz′y**, *adj.*

km, kilometer.

knack (nak) *n.* special skill.

knack′wurst (näk′wûrst, -wōōrst) *n.* spicy sausage.

knap′sack′ (nap′sak′) *n.* supply bag carried on back.

knave (nāv) *n.* dishonest rascal.

knead (nēd) *v.* work (dough) with the hands.

knee (nē) *n.* middle joint of leg.

knee′cap′, *n.* flat bone at front of knee.

knee′-jerk′, *adj. Informal.* reacting in an automatic, habitual way.

kneel (nēl) *v.*, **knelt** (nelt) or **kneeled, kneeling.** be on one's knees.

knell (nel) *n.* slow, deep sound of bell.

knick′ers (nik′ərz) *n.pl.* type of short breeches.

knick′knack′ (nik′nak′) *n.* trinket.

knife (nīf) *n.*, *pl.* **knives** (nīvz). cutting blade in handle.

knight (nīt) *n.* **1.** chivalrous medieval soldier of noble birth. **2.** holder of honorary rank. **3.** piece in chess. —*v.* **4.** name man a knight. —**knight′hood**, *n.* —**knight′ly**, *adj.*

knit (nit) *v.*, **knitted** or **knit, knitting.** form netlike fabric.

knob (nob) *n.* rounded handle.

knock (nok) *v.* **1.** strike hard. **2.** *Informal.* criticize. —*n.* **3.** hard blow, etc. **4.** *Informal.* criticism.

knock′-knee′, *n.* inward curvature of the legs at the knees.

knock′out′, *n.* **1.** boxing blow that knocks opponent to the canvas. **2.** *Informal.* one that is extremely attractive.

knoll (nōl) *n.* small hill.

knot (not) *n.*, *v.*, **knotted, knotting.** —*n.* **1.** intertwining of cords to bind. **2.** cluster. **3.** lump. **4.** hard mass where branch joins tree trunk. **5.** one nautical mile per hour. —*v.* **6.** tie or tangle. —**knot′ty**, *adj.*

know (nō) *v.*, **knew** (nōō, nyōō), **known, knowing.** —*v.* **1.** understand, remember, or experience. —*n.* **2.** *Informal.* state of knowledge, esp. of secrets. —**know′a•ble**, *adj.*

know′-how′, *n. Informal.* skill.

know′ing, *adj.* **1.** having knowledge. **2.** shrewd. **3.** deliberate.

knowl′edge (nol′ij) *n.* facts, etc., known.

know′ledge•a•ble (-i jə bəl) *adj.* well-informed.

knuck′le (nuk′əl) *n.* **1.** joint of a finger. —*v.* **2. knuckle down,** apply oneself earnestly. **3. knuckle under,** submit; yield.

knuck′le•head′, *n. Informal.* stupid, inept person.

KO (kā′ō′, kā′ō′) knockout.

ko•al′a (kō ä′lə) *n.* gray, tree-dwelling Australian marsupial.

kohl′ra•bi (kōl rä′bē, -rab′ē) *n., pl.* **-bies.** variety of cabbage.

koi (koi) *n., pl.* **kois, koi.** colorful carp.

ko′la (kō′lə) *n.* tropical African tree grown for its nuts, used to flavor soft drinks.

kook (kōōk) *n. Slang.* eccentric. —**kook′y**, *adj.*

Ko•ran′ (kə rän′, -ran′, kô-) *n.* sacred scripture of Islam.

Ko•re′an (kə rē′ən) *n.* native or language of Korea. —**Ko•re′an**, *adj.*

ko′sher (kō′shər) *adj.* permissible to eat according to Jewish law.

kow′tow′ (kou′tou′, -tou′, kō′-) *v.* act obsequiously.

kryp′ton (krip′ton) *n.* inert gas.

KS, Kansas.

ku′dos (kōō′dōz, -dōs, -dos, kyōō′-) *n.* admiration and respect.

kum′quat (kum′kwot) *n.* small citrus fruit.

kung′ fu′ (kung′ fōō′, kōōng′) Chinese technique of unarmed combat.

kvetch (kvech), *Slang.* —*v.* **1.** complain chronically. —*n.* **2.** person who kvetches.

KW, kilowatt. Also, **kw**

KY, Kentucky. Also, **ky.**

L

L, l (el) *n.* twelfth letter of English alphabet.

L., 1. lake. **2.** large. **3.** Latin. **4.** left. **5.** length. **6.** *Brit.* pound. **7.** long.

l., 1. left. **2.** length. **3.** *pl.* **ll.** line. **4.** liter.

LA, Louisiana. Also, **La.**

lab (lab) *n.* laboratory.

la′bel (lā′bəl) *n.*, *v.*, **-beled, -beling.** —*n.* **1.** tag bearing information. —*v.* **2.** put label on.

la′bi•um (lā′bē əm) *n., pl.* **-bia** (-bē-ə). fold of skin bordering the vulva. —**la′bi•al**, *adj.*

la′bor (lā′bər) *n.* **1.** bodily toil; work. **2.** childbirth. **3.** workers as a group. —*v.* **4.** work. Also, *Brit.*, **la′bour.** —**la′bor•er**, *n.*

lab′o•ra•to′ry (lab′rə tôr′ē, lab′ər ə-) *n., pl.* **-ries.** place for scientific work.

la′bored, *adj.* done with difficulty.

la•bo′ri•ous (lə bôr′ē əs) *adj.* involving much effort.

labor union, organization of workers for mutual aid, esp. by collective bargaining.

la•bur′num (lə bûr′nəm) *n.* poisonous tree with drooping yellow flowers.

lab′y•rinth (lab′ə rinth) *n.* maze.

lace (lās) *n.*, *v.*, **laced, lacing.** —*n.* **1.** fancy network of threads. **2.** cord for tying. —*v.* **3.** fasten with lace. —**lac′y**, *adj.*

lac′er•ate′ (las′ə rāt′) *v.*, **-ated, -ating.** tear; mangle.

lach′ry•mal (lak′rə məl) *adj.* of or producing tears.

lach′ry•mose′ (-mōs′) *adj.* tearful.

lack (lak) *n.* **1.** deficiency. —*v.* **2.** be wanting.

lack′a•dai′si•cal (lak′ə dā′zi kəl) *adj.* listless.

lack′ey (lak′ē) *n.* servile follower.

lack′lus′ter, *adj.* uninteresting.

la•con′ic (lə kon′ik) *adj.* using few words. —**la•con′i•cal•ly**, *adv.*

lac′quer (lak′ər) *n.* **1.** kind of varnish. —*v.* **2.** coat with lacquer.

la•crosse′ (lə krôs′) *n.* game of ball played with long rackets.

lac′tate (lak′tāt) *v.*, **-tated, -tating.** secrete milk. —**lac•ta′tion**, *n.*

lac′tose (-tōs) *n.* sweet crystalline substance in milk.

la•cu′na (lə kyōō′nə) *n., pl.* **-nae** (-nē), **-nas. 1.** cavity. **2.** gap.

lad (lad) *n.* boy.

lad′der (lad′ər) *n.* structure of two sidepieces with steps between.

lad′en (lād′n) *adj.* loaded heavily.

lad′ing (lā′ding) *n.* cargo; freight.

la′dle (lād′l) *n.*, *v.*, **-dled, -dling.** —*n.* **1.** large deep-bowled spoon. —*v.* **2.** serve with ladle.

la′dy (lā′dē) *n., pl.* **-dies. 1.** refined woman. **2.** title of noblewoman.

la′dy•bug′, *n.* small spotted beetle. Also, **la′dy•bird′.**

la′dy•fin′ger, *n.* small oblong cake.

la′dy's-slip′per, *n.* orchid with slipper-shaped flower lips.

lag (lag) *v.*, **lagged, lagging**, *n.* —*v.*

1. move slowly or belatedly. —*n.* **2.** instance of lagging. **3.** interval.

la′ger (lä′gər, lô′-) *n.* kind of beer.

lag′gard (lag′ərd) *adj.* **1.** lagging. —*n.* **2.** person who lags.

la·gniappe′ (lan yap′, lan′yap) *n.* **1.** small gift given with a purchase. **2.** gratuity. Also, **la·gnappe′**.

la·goon′ (lə gōōn′) *n.* shallow pond connected with a body of water.

laid′-back′ (lād′-) *adj. Informal.* relaxed; easygoing.

lair (lâr) *n.* den of beast.

lais′sez-faire′ (les′ā fâr′) *adj.* without interfering in trade, etc.

la′i·ty (lā′i tē) *n.* laypersons.

lake (lāk) *n.* large body of water enclosed by land.

La·ko′ta (lə kō′tä) *n., pl.* **-tas** or **-ta.** member of a Plains Indian people.

lam (lam) *n., v.,* **lammed, lamming.** *Slang.* —*n.* **1.** hasty escape. —*v.* **2.** escape; flee. **3. on the lam,** hiding or fleeing from the police.

la′ma (lä′mə) *n.* Tibetan or Mongolian Buddhist priest.

La·maze′ method (lə mäz′) method by which expectant mother is prepared for birth by classes, exercises, etc.

lamb (lam) *n.* young sheep.

lam·baste′ (lam bāst′, -bast′) *v.,* **-basted, -basting.** *Informal.* **1.** beat severely. **2.** reprimand harshly.

lam′bent (lam′bənt) *adj.* flickering or glowing lightly. —**lam′ben·cy,** *n.*

lame (lām) *adj.,* **lamer, lamest,** *v.,* **lamed, laming.** —*adj.* **1.** crippled. **2.** inadequate. —*v.* **3.** make lame.

la·mé′ (la mā′, lä-) *n.* ornamental fabric with metallic threads.

lame duck (lām) elected official completing term after election of successor.

la·ment′ (lə ment′) *v.* **1.** mourn; regret. —*n.* **2.** Also, **lam′en·ta′tion** (lam′ən tā′shən) expression of grief.

lam′i·nate′ *v.,* **-nated, -nating,** *adj.* —*v.* (lam′ə nāt′) **1.** split into thin layers. **2.** cover or form with layers. —*adj.* (-nāt′, -nit) **3.** Also, **lam′i·nat′ed.** made of layers.

lamp (lamp) *n.* light source. —**lamp′shade′, n.** —**lamp′post′,** *n.*

lam·poon′ (lam pōōn′) *n.* **1.** vicious satire. —*v.* **2.** satirize.

lam′prey (lam′prē) *n.* eellike fish.

lance (lans) *n., v.,* **lanced, lancing.** —*n.* **1.** long spear. —*v.* **2.** open with lancet.

lan′cet (lan′sit) *n.* sharp-pointed surgical tool.

land (land) *n.* **1.** part of the earth's surface above water. **2.** country. —*v.* **3.** bring or come to land. **4.** fall to earth or floor.

lan′dau (lan′dô, -dou) *n.* carriage with folding top.

land′ed, *adj.* **1.** owning land. **2.** consisting of land.

land′fall′, *n.* **1.** sighting of land. **2.** land sighted.

land′fill′, *n.* **1.** area of land built up from refuse material. **2.** material deposited on landfill.

land′ing, *n.* **1.** act of one that lands. **2.** place for landing persons and goods. **3.** level part between stairs.

land′locked′, *adj.* **1.** shut in completely or almost completely by land. **2.** having no access to sea.

land′lord′, *n.* person who owns and leases property. —**land′la′dy,** *n.fem.*

land′lub′ber (-lub′ər) *n.* person unused to sea.

land′mark′, *n.* **1.** prominent object serving as a guide. **2.** anything prominent of its kind.

land′mass′, *n.* large area of land.

land′scape′ (-skāp′) *n., v.,* **-scaped, -scaping.** —*n.* **1.** broad view of rural area. —*v.* **2.** arrange trees, shrubs, etc., for effects. —**land′scap′er,** *n.*

land′slide′, *n.* fall of earth or rock.

lane (lān) *n.* narrow road.

lan′guage (lang′gwij) *n.* **1.** speech. **2.** any means of communication.

lan′guid (lang′gwid) *adj.* moving slowly and weakly.

lan′guish (-gwish) *v.* **1.** be or become weak. **2.** pine. —**lan′guor** (-gər) *n.* —**lan′guor·ous,** *adj.*

lank (langk) *adj.* **1.** thin. Also, **lank′y.** **2.** straight and limp.

lan′o·lin (lan′l in) *n.* fat from wool.

lan′tern (lan′tərn) *n.* case for enclosing light.

lantern jaw, long, thin jaw. —**lan′tern-jawed′,** *adj.*

lan′yard (lan′yərd) *n.* short rope.

lap (lap) *v.,* **lapped, lapping,** *n.* —*v.* **1.** lay or lie partly over. **2.** wash against. **3.** take up with tongue. —*n.* **4.** overlapping part. **5.** one circuit of racecourse. **6.** thighs of sitting person.

la·pel′ (lə pel′) *n.* folded-back part on front of a garment.

lap′i·dar′y (lap′i der′ē) *n., pl.* **-ries.** worker in gems.

lap′in (lap′in) *n.* rabbit.

lap′is laz′u·li (lap′is laz′ōō lē, -lī′, laz′yōō-) **1.** deep blue semiprecious gem. **2.** sky-blue color; azure.

lapse (laps) *n., v.,* **lapsed, lapsing.** —*n.* **1.** slight error; negligence. **2.** interval of time. —*v.* **3.** pass slowly. **4.** make error. **5.** slip downward. **6.** become void.

lap′top′, *n.* portable microcomputer that fits on the lap.

lar′ce·ny (lär′sə nē) *n., pl.* **-nies.** theft. —**lar′ce·nist,** *n.*

larch (lärch) *n.* tree of pine family.

lard (lärd) *n.* rendered fat of hogs.

lard′er (lär′dər) *n.* pantry.

large (lärj) *adj.,* **larger, largest. 1.** great in size or number. **2. at large, a.** at liberty. **b.** in general.

large′ly, *adv.* mostly.

large′-scale′, *adj.* extensive.

lar·gess′ (lär jes′, lär′jis) *n.* generosity. Also, **lar·gesse′.**

lar′go (lär′gō) *adj., adv. Music.* slowly.

lar′i·at (lar′ē ət) *n.* long, noosed rope.

lark (lärk) *n.* **1.** songbird. **2.** frolic.

lark′spur′ (-spûr′) *n.* plant with flowers on tall stalks.

lar′va (lär′və) *n., pl.* **-vae** (-vē) young of insect between egg and pupal stages. —**lar′val,** *adj.*

lar′yn·gi′tis (lar′ən jī′tis) *n.* inflammation of larynx.

lar′ynx (lar′ingks) *n., pl.* **larynges** (lə rin′jēz), **larynxes.** cavity at upper end of windpipe. —**la·ryn′ge·al** (lə rin′jē-əl, lar′ən jē′əl) *adj.*

la·sa′gna (lə zän′yə, lä-) [*n.* baked dish of wide strips of pasta layered with cheese, tomato sauce, and usu. meat. Also, **la·sa′gne.**

las·civ′i·ous (lə siv′ē əs) *adj.* lewd.

la′ser (lā′zər) *n.* device for amplifying radiation of frequencies of visible light.

lash (lash) *n.* **1.** blow with whip. **2.** eyelash. —*v.* **3.** strike with or as with lash. **4.** bind.

lass (las) *n.* girl.

las′si·tude′ (las′i tōōd′, -tyōōd′) *n.* weariness.

las′so (las′ō, la sōō′) *n., pl.* **-sos, -soes,** *v.,* **-soed, -soing.** —*n.* **1.** lariat. —*v.* **2.** catch with lasso.

last (last) *adj.* **1.** latest. **2.** final. —*adv.* **3.** most recently. **4.** finally. —*n.* **5.** that which is last. **6.** foot-shaped form on which shoes are made. —*v.* **7.** endure.

last′ing, *adj.* going on or enduring a long time. —**last′ing·ly,** *adv.*

lat., latitude.

latch (lach) *n.* **1.** device for fastening door or gate. —*v.* **2.** fasten with latch.

late (lāt) *adj., adv.,* **later, latest. 1.** after proper time. **2.** being or lasting well along in time. **3.** recent. **4.** deceased.

late′ly, *adv.* recently.

la′tent (lā′tnt) *adj.* hidden.

lat′er·al (lat′ər al) *adj.* on or from the side. —**lat′er·al·ly,** *adv.*

la′tex (lā′teks) *n.* milky plant juice used esp. in making rubber.

lath (lath) *n.* **1.** narrow wood strip. **2.** material for holding plaster. —*v.* **3.** cover with laths.

lathe (lāth) *n.* machine for turning wood, etc., against a shaping tool.

lath′er (lath′ər) *n.* **1.** froth made with soap and water. **2.** froth from sweating. —*v.* **3.** form or cover with lather.

Lat′in (lat′n) *n.* **1.** language of ancient Rome. **2.** member of any people speaking Latin-based language. —**Latin,** *adj.*

Latin America, countries in South and Central America where Spanish or Portuguese is spoken. —**Lat′in-A·mer′i·can,** *adj., n.*

La·ti′no (lə tē′nō, la-) *n.* Hispanic.

lat′i·tude′ (lat′i tōōd′, -tyōōd′) *n.* **1.** distance from equator. **2.** freedom.

la·trine′ (lə trēn′) *n.* toilet, esp. in military installation.

lat′ter (lat′ər) *adj.* **1.** being second of two. **2.** later.

lat′tice (lat′is) *n.* structure of crossed strips. —**lat′tice·work′,** *n.*

laud (lôd) *v.* praise. —**laud′a·ble,** *adj.* —**laud′a·to′ry,** *adj.*

laugh (laf) *v.* **1.** express mirth audibly. —*n.* **2.** act or sound of laughing. —**laugh′ter,** *n.*

laugh′a·ble, *adj.* ridiculous.

laugh′ing·stock′, *n.* object of ridicule.

launch (lônch, länch) *v.* **1.** set afloat or send off. **2.** start. **3.** throw. —*n.* **4.** large open motorboat. —**launch′er,** *n.*

launch pad, platform for launching rockets. Also, **launch′ing pad.**

laun·der (lôn′dər, län′-) *v.* wash and iron.

Laun′dro·mat′ (-drə mat′) *n. Trademark.* self-service laundry with coin-operated machines.

laun′dry, *n., pl.* **-dries. 1.** clothes to be washed. **2.** place where clothes are laundered.

lau′re·ate (lôr′ē it) *n.* person who has been honored.

lau′rel (lôr′əl) *n.* **1.** small glossy evergreen tree. **2.** (*pl.*) honors.

la′va (lä′və, lav′ə) *n.* molten rock from volcano.

lav′a·to′ry (lav′ə tôr′ē) *n., pl.* **-ries. 1.** bathroom. **2.** washbowl.

lave (lāv) *v.,* **laved, laving.** bathe.

lav·en·der (lav′ən dər) *n.* **1.** pale purple. **2.** fragrant shrub yielding oil of lavender.

lav′ish (lav′ish) *adj.* **1.** extravagant. —*v.* **2.** expend or give abundantly.

law (lô) *n.* **1.** rules established by government under which people live. **2.** rule. **3.** legal action. —**law′-a·bid′ing,** *adj.* —**law′break′er,** *n., adj.* —**law′less,** *adj.*

law′ful, *adj.* permitted by law.

lawn (lôn) *n.* **1.** grass-covered land

kept mowed. **2.** thin cotton or linen fabric.

law′suit′, *n.* prosecution of claim in court.

law′yer (lô′yər, loi′ər) *n.* person trained in law.

lax (laks) *adj.* **1.** careless. **2.** slack.

lax′a·tive (lak′sə tiv) *adj.* **1.** purgative. —*n.* **2.** laxative agent.

lay (lā) *v.,* **laid, laying,** *n., adj.* —*v.* **1.** place or put down, esp. in flat position. **2.** produce eggs. **3.** ascribe. **4.** devise. **5.** pt. of **lie.** —*n.* **6.** position. **7.** song. —*adj.* **8.** not clerical or professional. —**lay′man, lay′per·son,** *n.* —**lay′wom·an,** *n.fem.* ——**Usage.** For many speakers, the verbs LAY and LIE are confused because both have the meaning of "in a flat position." LAY means "to put down" or "to place, especially in a flat position." A general rule to remember is that if the word "put" or "place" can be substituted in a sentence, then LAY is the verb to use: *Lay (= put, place) the books on the table. She laid (= put, placed) the baby in the cradle.* But the verb LIE means "to be in a flat position" or "to be situated": *Lie down and rest a moment. The baby is lying down.* For many speakers, the problem comes in the past tense for these two verbs, because the past tense of LIE is *lay,* which looks like, but is not, the present tense of LAY: *The dog will want to lie in the shade; yesterday it lay in the grass.* Note that we can LAY an infant down in a crib; he or she will LIE there until picked up.

lay′a·way plan, method of purchasing in which store reserves item until customer has completed payment.

lay′er, *n.* one thickness.

lay·ette′ (-et′) *n.* outfit for newborn child.

lay′off′, *n.* temporary dismissal of employees.

lay′out′, *n.* arrangement.

laze (lāz) *v.,* **lazed, lazing.** pass (time) lazily.

la′zy (lā′zē) *adj.,* **-zier, -ziest.** unwilling to work. **2.** slow-moving.

lb., *pl.* **lbs., lb.** pound.

l.c., lowercase.

lea (lē, lā) *n.* meadow.

leach (lēch) *v.* **1.** soak through or in. **2.** dissolve by soaking.

lead (lēd for 1–4; led for 5–7) *v.,* **led** (led), **leading,** *n.* —*v.* **1.** guide by going before or with. **2.** influence. **3.** go to. —*n.* **4.** position at front. **5.** heavy malleable metal. **6.** plummet. **7.** graphite used in pencils. —**lead′en,** *adj.* —**lead′er,** *n.* —**lead′er·ship′,** *n.*

leading question (lē′ding) question worded to suggest the desired answer.

lead time (lēd) time between beginning of a process and appearance of results.

leaf (lēf) *n., pl.* **leaves** (lēvz), *v.* —*n.* **1.** flat green part on stem of plant. **2.** thin sheet. —*v.* **3.** thumb through. —**leaf′y,** *adj.*

leaf′let (-lit) *n.* **1.** pamphlet. **2.** small leaf.

league (lēg) *n., v.,* **leagued, leaguing.** —*n.* **1.** alliance; pact. **2.** unit of distance, about three miles. —*v.* **3.** unite in league.

leak (lēk) *n.* **1.** unintended hole. —*v.* **2.** pass or let pass through leak. **3.** allow to be known unofficially. —**leak′age,** *n.* —**leak′y,** *adj.*

lean (lēn) *v.,* **leaned** or **leant, leaning,** *n., adj.* —*v.* **1.** bend. **2.** depend. **3.** incline —*n.* **4.** inclination. **5.** lean flesh. —*adj.* **6.** not fat.

lean′-to′, *n., pl.* **lean-tos.** structure with single-sloped roof abutting a wall.

leap (lēp) *v.,* **leaped** or **leapt** (lept, lēpt), **leaping,** *n.* —*v.* **1.** spring through air; jump. —*n.* **2.** jump.

leap′frog′, *n., v.,* **-frogged, -frogging.** —*n.* **1.** game in which players leap over each other's backs. —*v.* **2.** jump over as in leapfrog.

leap year, year of 366 days.

learn (lûrn) *v.* acquire knowledge or skill. —**learn′er,** *n.* —**learn′ing,** *n.*

learn′ed (lûr′nid) *adj.* scholarly.

learning disability, difficulty in reading, writing, etc., associated with impairment of central nervous system.

lease (lēs) *n., v.,* **leased, leasing.** —*n.* **1.** contract renting property to another for certain time. —*v.* **2.** get by means of lease.

leash (lēsh) *n.* strap for holding dog.

least (lēst) *adj.* **1.** smallest. —*n.* **2.** least amount, etc. —*adv.* **3.** to least extent, etc.

leath′er (le*th*′ər) *n.* prepared skin of animals. —**leath′er·y,** *adj.*

leath′er·neck′, *n. Informal.* U.S. marine.

leave (lēv) *v.,* **left** (left), **leaving,** *n.* —*v.* **1.** depart from. **2.** let remain or be. **3.** have remaining. **4.** bequeath. —*n.* **5.** permission. **6.** farewell. **7.** furlough.

leav′en (lev′ən) *n.* **1.** Also, **leav′en·ing.** fermenting agency to raise dough. —*v.* **2.** produce fermentation.

lech′er·ous (lech′ər əs) *adj.* lustful. —**lech′er·y,** *n.* —**lech′er,** *n.*

lec′tern (lek′tərn) *n.* stand for speaker's papers.

lec′ture (lek′chər) *n., v.,* **-tured, -turing.** —*n.* **1.** instructive speech. —*v.* **2.** give lecture; moralize. —**lec′tur·er,** *n.*

ledge (lej) *n.* narrow shelf.

ledg′er (lej′ər) *n.* account book.

lee (lē) *n.* **1.** shelter. **2.** side away from the wind. **3.** (*pl.*) dregs. —**lee,** *adj.* —**lee′ward,** *adj., adv., n.*

leech (lēch) *n.* bloodsucking worm.

leek (lēk) *n.* plant related to onion.

leer (lēr) *n.* **1.** sly or insinuating glance. —*v.* **2.** look with leer.

leer′y (lēr′ē) *adj.,* **-ier, -iest.** wary.

lee′way′, *n.* **1.** *Naut.* drift due to wind. **2.** extra time, space, etc.

left (left) *adj.* **1.** on side toward west when facing north. **2.** remaining. —*n.* **3.** left side. **4.** political side favoring liberal or radical reform. —**left′-hand′,** *adj.* —**left′-hand′ed,** *adj.* —**left′ist,** *n., adj.*

leg (leg) *n.* **1.** one of limbs supporting a body. **2.** any leglike part.

leg′a·cy (leg′ə sē) *n., pl.* **-cies.** anything bequeathed.

le′gal (lē′gəl) *adj.* of or according to law. —**le·gal′i·ty** (-gal′i tē) *n.* —**le′gal·ize′,** *v.*

le′gal·ese′ (-gə lēz′, -lēs′) *n.* excessive legal jargon.

le·ga′tion (li gā′shən) *n.* **1.** diplomatic minister and staff. **2.** official residence of minister.

le·ga′to (lə gä′tō) *adj., adv. Music.* smooth and connected.

leg′end (lej′ənd) *n.* **1.** story handed down by tradition. **2.** key; inscription. —**leg′end·ar·y,** *adj.*

leg′er·de·main′ (lej′ər də mān′) *n.* sleight of hand.

leg′ging, *n.* covering for leg.

leg′i·ble (lej′ə bəl) *adj.* easily read.

le′gion (lē′jən) *n.* **1.** military unit. **2.** multitude. —*adj.* **3.** very great in number. —**le′gion·naire′,** *n.*

leg′is·late′ (lej′is lāt′) *v.,* **-lated, -lat-**

ing. **1.** make laws. **2.** control by law. —**leg′is·la′tion,** *n.* —**leg′is·la′tive,** *adj.* —**leg′is·la′tor,** *n.*

leg′is·la·ture (-chər) *n.* law-making body.

le·git′i·mate (li jit′ə mit) *adj.* **1.** lawful. **2.** after right or established principles. **3.** born to a married couple. —**le·git′i·ma·cy** (-mə sē) *n.*

le·git′i·mize′, *v.,* **-mized, -mizing.** show to be or treat as legitimate.

leg′ume (leg′yōōm, li gyōōm′) *n.* plant of group including peas and beans. —**le·gu′mi·nous,** *adj.*

lei (lā) *n.* flower wreath for neck.

lei′sure (lē′zhər, lezh′ər) *n.* **1.** free time. —*adj.* **2.** unoccupied; at rest.

lei′sure·ly, *adj.* unhurried.

leit′mo·tif′ (līt′mō tēf′) *n.* **1.** recurring musical phrase in an opera. **2.** dominant theme.

lem′ming (lem′ing) *n.* small rodent noted for periodic mass migrations.

lem′on (lem′ən) *n.* **1.** yellowish fruit of citrus tree. **2.** *Informal.* person or thing that is defective.

lem′on·ade′ (-ə nād′) *n.* beverage of lemon juice and water.

le′mur (lē′mər) *n.* small monkeylike animal.

lend (lend) *v.,* **lent, lending. 1.** give temporary use of. **2.** give. ——**Usage.** See BORROW.

length (lengkth, length, lenth) *n.* size or extent from end to end. —**length′en,** *v.* —**length′wise′,** *adv., adj.* —**length′y,** *adj.*

le′ni·ent (lē′nē ənt, lēn′yənt) *adj.* tolerant; not severe. —**le′ni·en·cy,** *n.*

lens (lenz) *n., pl.* **lenses.** glass for changing convergence of light rays.

Lent (lent) *n.* season of fasting before Easter. —**Lent′en,** *adj.*

len′til (len′til, -tl) *n.* pealike plant.

le′o·nine′ (lē′ə nīn′) *adj.* of or like the lion.

leop′ard (lep′ərd) *n.* large fierce spotted feline.

le′o·tard′ (lē′ə tärd′) *n.* tight, flexible, one-piece garment worn by acrobats, dancers, etc.

lep′er (lep′ər) *n.* person afflicted with leprosy.

lep′re·chaun′ (lep′rə kôn′) *n.* Irish elf.

lep′ro·sy (lep′rə sē) *n.* disease marked by skin ulcerations.

les′bi·an (lez′bē ən) *n.* **1.** female homosexual. —*adj.* **2.** pertaining to female homosexuals.

lese majesty (lēz′) offense against the dignity of a ruler.

le′sion (lē′zhən) *n.* **1.** injury. **2.** morbid change in bodily part.

less (les) *adv.* **1.** to smaller extent. —*adj.* Also, **les′ser. 2.** smaller. **3.** lower in importance. —*n.* **4.** Also, **lesser.** smaller amount, etc. —*prep.* **5.** minus. —**less′en,** *v.* ——**Usage.** FEWER is the comparative form of FEW. It is properly used before plural nouns that refer to individuals or things that can be counted (*fewer words; no fewer than 31 states*). LESS is the comparative form of LITTLE. It should modify only singular mass nouns that refer to things that are abstract or cannot be counted (*less sugar; less doubt*). LESS may be used before plural nouns only when they suggest combination into a unit or group (*less than $50; less than three miles*).

les·see′ (le sē′) *n.* one granted a lease.

les′ser, *adj.* compar. of **little.**

les′son (les′ən) *n.* **1.** something to be

studied. **2.** reproof. **3.** useful experience.

les′sor (les′ôr, le sôr′) *n.* granter of lease.

lest (lest) *conj.* for fear that.

let (let) *v.,* **let, letting,** *n.* —*v.* **1.** permit. **2.** rent out. **3.** cause to. —*n.* **4.** hindrance.

-let, suffix indicating: **1.** small, as *booklet.* **2.** article worn on, as *anklet.*

let′down′, *n.* disappointment.

le′thal (lē′thəl) *adj.* deadly.

leth′ar·gy (leth′ər jē) *n., pl.* **-gies.** drowsy dullness. —**le·thar′gic** (lə-thar′jik) *adj.*

let′ter (let′ər) *n.* **1.** written communication. **2.** written component of word. **3.** actual wording. **4.** (*pl.*) literature. —*v.* **5.** write with letters.

let′tered, *adj.* literate; learned.

let′ter·head′, *n.* **1.** printed information on stationery. **2.** paper with a letterhead.

let′ter-per′fect, *adj.* precise in every detail.

let′tuce (let′is) *n.* plant with large leaves used in salad.

let′up′, *n.* cessation; pause; relief.

leu·ke′mi·a (lōō kē′mē ə) *n.* cancerous disease of blood cells.

leu′ko·cyte (lōō′kə sīt′) *n.* white blood cell.

lev′ee (lev′ē) *n.* embankment.

lev′el (lev′əl) *adj., n., v.,* **-eled, -eling.** —*adj.* **1.** even. **2.** horizontal. **3.** well-balanced. —*n.* **4.** height. **5.** level position. **6.** device for determining horizontal plane. —*v.* **7.** make or become level. **8.** aim.

lev′el·head′ed, *adj.* sensible and judicious.

lev′er (lev′ər, lē′vər) *n.* bar moving on fixed support to exert force.

lev′er·age (-ij) *n.* power or action of lever.

le·vi′a·than (li vī′ə thən) *n.* something of immense size or power.

lev′i·tate (lev′i tāt′) *v.,* **-tated, -tating.** rise or cause to rise into the air, esp. in apparent defiance of gravity. —**lev′i·ta′tion,** *n.*

lev′i·ty (lev′i tē) *n.* lack of seriousness.

lev′y (lev′ē) *v.,* **levied, levying,** *n., pl.* **levies.** —*v.* **1.** raise or collect by authority. **2.** make (war). —*n.* **3.** act of levying. **4.** something levied.

lewd (lōōd) *adj.* obscene.

lex′i·cog′ra·phy (lek′si kog′rə fē) *n.* writing of dictionaries.

lex′i·con′ (-kon′, -kan) *n.* dictionary.

lg., **1.** large. **2.** long.

li′a·bil′i·ty (lī′ə bil′i tē) *n., pl.* **-ties.** **1.** debt. **2.** disadvantage. **3.** state of being liable.

li′a·ble, *adj.* **1.** likely. **2.** subject to obligation or penalty.

li·ai′son (lē ā′zən, lē′ā zôn′) *n.* **1.** contact to ensure cooperation. **2.** intimacy; affair.

li′ar (lī′ər) *n.* person who tells lies.

li′bel (lī′bəl) *n., v.,* **-beled, -beling.** —*n.* **1.** defamation in writing or print. —*v.* **2.** publish libel against. —**li′bel·ous,** *adj.*

lib′er·al (lib′ər əl, lib′rəl) *adj.* **1.** favoring extensive individual liberty. **2.** tolerant. **3.** generous. —*n.* **4.** liberal person. —**lib′er·al·ism,** *n.* —**lib·er·al′i·ty** (-ə ral′i tē) *n.* —**lib′er·al·ize′,** *v.*

liberal arts, college courses comprising the arts, humanities, and natural and social sciences.

lib′er·ate′ (-ə rāt′) *v.,* **-ated, -ating.** set free. —**lib′er·a′tion,** *n.* —**lib′er·a′tor,** *n.*

lib′er·tar′i·an (lib′ər târ′ē ən) *n.* person who advocates liberty in thought or conduct.

lib′er·tine (-tēn′, -tin) *n.* dissolute person.

lib′er·ty, *n., pl.* **-ties.** **1.** freedom; independence. **2.** right to use place. **3.** impertinent freedom.

li·bi′do (li bē′dō) *n., pl.* **-dos. 1.** sexual desire. **2.** instinctual energies and drives derived from the id.

li′brar′y (lī′brer′ē, -brə rē, -brē) *n., pl.* **-ries. 1.** place for collection of books, etc. **2.** collection of books, etc. —**li·brar′i·an,** *n.*

—**Pronunciation.** LIBRARY, with two barely separated *r*-sounds, is particularly vulnerable to the tendency for neighboring sounds that are alike to become different, or for one of them to disappear altogether. This can lead to forms like the pronunciation (lī′ber ē), which is likely to be heard from less educated or very young speakers and is often criticized. However, (lī′brē), the third pronunciation shown above, is considered perfectly standard, even though one of the *r*-sounds has been dropped.

li·bret′to (li bret′ō) *n., pl.* **-brettos, -bretti** (-bret′ē). words of musical drama. —**li·bret′tist,** *n.*

li′cense (lī′sans) *n., v.,* **-censed, -censing.** —*n.* **1.** formal permission. **2.** undue freedom. —*v.* **3.** grant license to. Also, **li′cence.**

li′cen·see′ (-sən sē′) *n.* person to whom a license is granted.

li·cen′tious (-sen′shəs) *adj.* lewd.

li′chen (lī′kən) *n.* crustlike plant on rocks, trees, etc.

lic′it (lis′it) *adj.* lawful.

lick (lik) *v.* **1.** pass tongue over. **2.** *Informal.* beat or defeat. —*n.* **3.** act of licking. **4.** small amount.

lick′e·ty-split′ (lik′i tē-) *adv. Informal.* at great speed.

lick′ing, *n. Informal.* **1.** beating or thrashing. **2.** defeat or setback.

lic′o·rice (lik′ər ish, -ə ris) *n.* plant root used in candy, etc.

lid (lid) *n.* **1.** movable cover. **2.** eyelid. —**lid′ded,** *adj.*

lie (lī) *n., v.,* **lied, lying.** —*n.* **1.** deliberately false statement. —*v.* **2.** tell a lie.

lie (lī) *v.,* **lay** (lā), **lain** (lān), **lying,** *n.* —*v.* **1.** assume or have reclining position. **2.** be or remain. —*n.* **3.** manner of lying. —**Usage.** See LAY.

lie detector, polygraph.

lien (lēn, lē′ən) *n.* right in another's property as payment on claim.

lieu (lōō) *n.* stead.

lieu·ten′ant (lōō ten′ənt; *in Brit. use, except in the navy,* lef ten′ənt) *n.* **1.** commissioned officer in army or navy. **2.** aide.

life (līf) *n., pl.* **lives** (līvz). **1.** quality that distinguishes animals and plants from inanimate things. **2.** period of being alive. **3.** living things. **4.** mode of existence. **5.** animation. —**life′long′,** *adj.* —**life′time′,** *n.* —**life′like′,** *adj.*

life′blood′ *n.* **1.** blood. **2.** vital element.

life′boat′, *n.* boat designed to rescue passengers from sinking ship.

life′guard′, *n.* person employed to protect swimmers, as at a beach.

life preserver, buoyant device to keep a person afloat.

lif′er, *n.* person serving a term of imprisonment for life.

life′sav′er, *n.* person or thing that saves from death or a difficult situation. —**life′sav′ing,** *adj., n.*

life′-size′, *adj.* of the actual size of a person, etc.

life′style′, person's general pattern of living. Also, **life′-style′.**

life′-sup·port′, *adj.* of equipment or techniques that sustain or substitute for essential body functions.

life′work′, *n.* complete or principal work of a lifetime.

lift (lift) *v.* **1.** move or hold upward. **2.** raise or rise. —*n.* **3.** act of lifting. **4.** ride. **5.** *Brit.* elevator.

lift′-off′, *n.* departure from ground by rocket, etc., under own power.

lig′a·ment (lig′ə mənt) *n.* band of tissue holding bones together.

lig′a·ture (lig′ə chər, -chōōr′) *n.* surgical thread or wire for tying blood vessels.

light (līt) *n., adj., v.,* **lighted** or **lit** (lit), **lighting.** —*n.* **1.** something that makes things visible or gives illumination. **2.** daylight. **3.** aspect. **4.** enlightenment. —*adj.* **5.** not dark. **6.** not heavy. **7.** not serious. —*v.* **8.** ignite. **9.** illuminate. **10.** alight; land. **11.** happen (upon).

light′en, *v.* **1.** become or make less dark. **2.** lessen in weight. **3.** mitigate. **4.** cheer.

light′er, *n.* **1.** something that lights. **2.** barge.

light′-fin′gered, *adj.* given to pilfering.

light′-head′ed, *adj.* as if about to faint.

light′-heart′ed, *adj.* cheerful; without worry.

light′house′, *n.* tower displaying light to guide mariners.

light′ning (-ning) *n.* flash of light in sky caused by electrical discharge.

lightning bug, firefly.

lightning rod, metal rod to divert lightning from a structure into the ground.

light′-year′, *n.* distance that light travels in one year.

lig′ne·ous (lig′nē əs) *adj.* of the nature of or resembling wood.

lig′nite (lig′nīt) *n.* kind of coal.

like (līk) *v.,* **liked, liking,** *adj., prep., conj.,* *n.* —*v.* **1.** find agreeable. **2.** wish. —*adj.* **3.** resembling; similar to. —*prep.* **4.** in like manner with. —*conj.* **5.** *Informal.* as; as if. **6.** like person or thing; match. **7.** preference. —**lik′a·ble, like′a·ble,** *adj.*

-like, suffix indicating: like or characteristic of, as *childlike.*

like′ly, *adj.,* **-lier, -liest,** *adv.* —*adj.* **1.** probable. **2.** suitable. —*adv.* **3.** probably. —**like′li·hood′,** *n.*

lik′en, *v.* compare.

like′ness, *n.* **1.** image; picture. **2.** fact of being like.

like′wise′, *adv.* **1.** also. **2.** in like manner.

li′lac (lī′lək, -läk, -lak) *n.* fragrant flowering shrub.

Lil·li·pu′tian (lil′i pyōō′shən) *adj.* **1.** very small. **2.** trivial.

lilt (lilt) *n.* rhythmic cadence.

lil′y (lil′ē) *n., pl.* **-ies.** plant with erect stems and showy flowers.

lil′y-liv′ered (-liv′ərd) *adj.* cowardly.

lily of the valley, *n., pl.* **lilies of the valley.** plant with spike of bell-shaped flowers.

li′ma bean (lī′mə) flat, edible bean.

limb (lim) *n.* **1.** jointed part of an animal body. **2.** branch.

lim′ber (lim′bər) *adj.* **1.** flexible; supple. —*v.* **2.** make or become limber.

lim′bo (lim′bō) *n., pl.* **-bos. 1.** region on border of hell or heaven. **2.** midway state or place. **3.** dance involving bending backward to pass under horizontal bar.

lime (līm) *n.*, *v.*, **limed, liming.** —*n.* **1.** oxide of calcium, used in mortar, etc. **2.** small, greenish, acid fruit of tropical tree. —*v.* **3.** treat with lime.

lime/light/, *n.* public notice; fame.

lim/er·ick (lim/ər ik) *n.* humorous five-line verse.

lime/stone/, *n.* rock consisting chiefly of powdered calcium.

lim/it (lim/it) *n.* **1.** farthest extent; boundary. —*v.* **2.** fix or keep within limits. —**lim/i·ta/tion,** *n.*

lim/it·ed, *adj.* **1.** restricted **2.** (of trains, etc.) making few stops. —*n.* **3.** limited train.

lim/o (lim/ō) *n.*, *pl.* **-os.** *Informal.* limousine.

lim/ou·sine/ (lim/ə zēn/, lim/ə zēn/) *n.* luxurious automobile for several passengers.

limp (limp) *v.* **1.** walk unevenly. —*n.* **2.** lame movement. —*adj.* **3.** not stiff or firm. —**limp/ly,** *adv.*

lim/pet (lim/pit) *n.* small cone-shelled marine animal.

lim/pid (-pid) *adj.* clear. —**lim·pid/i·ty, lim/pid·ness,** *n.*

linch/pin/ (linch/-) *n.* **1.** pin inserted through end of axle to keep wheel on. **2.** something that holds various parts of a structure together.

lin/den (lin/dən) *n.* tree with heart-shaped leaves.

line (līn) *n.*, *v.*, **lined, lining.** —*n.* **1.** long thin mark. **2.** row; series. **3.** course of action, etc. **4.** boundary. **5.** string, cord, etc. **6.** occupation. —*v.* **7.** form line. **8.** mark with line. **9.** cover inner side of.

lin/e·age (lin/ē ij) *n.* ancestry.

lin/e·al (-al) *adj.* **1.** of direct descent. **2.** Also, **lin/e·ar** (-ər). in or of a line.

lin/e·a·ment (-ə mənt) *n.* feature, as of face.

line drive, batted baseball that travels low, fast, and straight.

line/man, *n.*, *pl.* **-men.** worker who repairs telephone, telegraph, etc., wires.

lin/en (lin/ən) *n.* **1.** fabric made from flax. **2.** articles of linen or cotton.

lin/er (lī/nər) *n.* **1.** ship or airplane on regular route. **2.** lining.

line/-up/, *n.* order.

-ling, suffix meaning: **1.** person connected with, as *hireling.* **2.** little, as *duckling.*

lin/ger (ling/gər) *v.* **1.** stay on. **2.** persist. **3.** delay.

lin/ge·rie/ (län/zhə rā/, -jə-, lan/zhə-rē/) *n.* women's undergarments.

lin/go (ling/gō) *n.*, *pl.* **-goes.** *Informal.* language.

lin·gui/ni (-gwē/nē) *n. pl.* pasta in slender flat form.

lin/guist (-gwist) *n.* person skilled in languages.

lin·guis/tics, *n.* science of language. —**lin·guis/tic,** *adj.*

lin/i·ment (lin/ə mənt) *n.* liquid applied to bruises, etc.

lin/ing (lī/ning) *n.* inner covering.

link (lingk) *n.* **1.** section of chain. **2.** bond. —*v.* **3.** unite. —**link/age,** *n.*

links, *n.pl.* golf course.

link/up/, *n.* contact set up between military units.

lin/net (lin/it) *n.* small songbird.

li·no/le·um (li nō/lē əm) *n.* hard, washable floor covering.

lin/seed/ (lin/sēd/) *n.* seed of flax.

lin/sey-wool/sey (lin/zē wŏŏl/zē) *n.* fabric of linen and wool.

lint (lint) *n.* bits of thread.

lin/tel (lin/tl) *n.* beam above door or window.

li/on (lī/ən) *n.* large cat of Africa and Asia. —**li/on·ess,** *n.fem.*

li/on·heart/ed, *adj.* courageous.

li/on·ize/, *v.*, **-ized, -izing.** treat as a celebrity.

lip (lip) *n.* **1.** fleshy margin of the mouth. **2.** projecting edge. **3.** *Slang.* impudent talk.

lip/o·suc/tion (lip/ə suk/shən, lī/pə-) *n.* surgical withdrawal of excess fat from under skin.

lip/read/ing, method of understanding spoken words by interpreting speaker's lip movements. —**lip/read/er,** *n.* —**lip/read/,** *v.*

lip service, insincere profession of friendship, admiration, support, etc.

lip/stick/, *n.* coloring for lips.

liq/ue·fy/ (lik/wə fī/) *v.*, **-fied, -fy-ing.** become liquid. —**liq/ue·fac/tion** (-fak/shən) *n.*

li·queur/ (li kûr/, -kyŏŏr/) *n.* strong sweet alcoholic drink.

liq/uid (lik/wid) *n.* **1.** fluid of molecules remaining together. —*adj.* **2.** of or being a liquid. **3.** in or convertible to cash.

liq/ui·date/ (-wi dāt/) *v.*, **-dated, -dating. 1.** settle, as debts. **2.** convert into cash. **3.** eliminate. —**liq/ui·da/tion,** *n.* —**liq/ui·da/tor,** *n.*

liq/uor (lik/ər) *n.* **1.** alcoholic beverage. **2.** liquid.

lisle (līl) *n.* strong linen or cotton thread.

lisp (lisp) *n.* **1.** pronunciation of *s* and *z* like *th.* —*v.* **2.** speak with lisp. —**lisp/er,** *n.*

lis/some (lis/əm) *adj.* **1.** lithe; lithesome. **2.** nimble. Also, **lis/som.**

list (list) *n.* **1.** series of words, names, etc. **2.** inclination to side. —*v.* **3.** make list. **4.** incline.

lis/ten (lis/ən) *v.* pay attention in order to hear. —**lis/ten·er,** *n.*

list/less (list/lis) *adj.* having no interest in anything.

list price, retail price.

lit., **1.** literally. **2.** literature.

lit/a·ny (lit/n ē) *n.*, *pl.* **-nies. 1.** form of prayer. **2.** tedious account.

li/ter (lē/tər) *n.* metric unit of capacity, = 1.0567 U.S. quarts. Also, *Brit.,* **li/tre.**

lit/er·al (lit/ər əl) *adj.* **1.** in accordance with strict meaning of words. **2.** exactly as written or stated.

lit/er·al-mind/ed, *adj.* interpreting without imagination.

lit/er·ar/y (-ə rer/ē) *adj.* of books and writings.

lit/er·ate (-ər it) *adj.* **1.** able to read and write. **2.** skilled. **3.** educated. —*n.* **4.** literate person. —**lit/er·a·cy** (-ər ə-sē) *n.*

lit/e·ra/ti (-ə rä/tē, -rä/-) *n.pl.* persons of scholarly or literary attainments.

lit/er·a·ture (lit/ər ə chər, -chŏŏr/, li/tra-) *n.* writings, esp. those of notable expression and thought.

lithe (līth) *adj.* limber; supple.

lith/i·um (lith/ē əm) *n.* soft silverwhite metallic element.

lith/o·graph/ (-ə graf/) *n.* print made from prepared stone or plate.

lit/i·gant (lit/i gənt) *n.* person engaged in lawsuit.

lit/i·gate/ (-gāt/) *v.*, **-gated, -gating.** carry on lawsuit. —**lit/i·ga/tion,** *n.*

lit/mus (lit/məs) *n.* blue coloring matter turning red in acid solution.

litmus paper, paper treated with litmus for use as a chemical indicator.

litmus test, use of single issue or factor as basis for judgment.

Litt. D., Doctor of Letters; Doctor of Literature.

lit/ter (lit/ər) *n.* **1.** disordered array. **2.** young from one birth. **3.** stretcher. **4.** bedding for animals. **5.** scattered rubbish, etc. —*v.* **6.** strew in disorder.

lit/ter·bug/, *n.* person who litters public places with trash.

lit/tle (lit/l) *adj.*, **-tler, -tlest. 1.** small. **2.** mean. —*adv.* **3.** not much. —*n.* **4.** small amount.

lit/tor·al (lit/ər əl) *adj.* of the shore of a lake, sea, or ocean.

lit/ur·gy (lit/ər jē) *n.*, *pl.* **-gies.** form of worship. —**li·tur/gi·cal** (li tûr/ji-kəl) *adj.*

liv/able (liv/ə bəl) *adj.* habitable.

live (liv *for 1–5;* līv *for 6–8*), *v.*, **lived, living,** *adj.* —*v.* **1.** be alive. **2.** endure in reputation. **3.** rely for food, etc. **4.** dwell. **5.** pass (life). —*adj.* **6.** alive. **7.** connected to electric power. **8.** not exploded.

live/li·hood/ (līv/lē hŏŏd/) *n.* means of supporting oneself.

live/long/ (liv/-) *adj.* entire; whole.

live/ly (līv/lē) *adj.*, **-lier, -liest.** active; spirited.

liv/er (liv/ər) *n.* abdominal organ that secretes bile.

liv/er·wurst/ (-wûrst/) *n.* liver sausage.

liv/er·y (liv/ə rē, liv/rē) *n.*, *pl.* **-eries. 1.** uniform of male servants. **2.** keeping of horses for hire.

live/stock/ (līv/stok/) *n.* domestic farm animals.

live wire (līv) *Informal.* energetic, vivacious person.

liv/id (liv/id) *adj.* **1.** dull blue. **2.** furious.

liv/ing (liv/ing) *adj.* **1.** live. **2.** sufficient for living. —*n.* **3.** condition of life. **4.** livelihood.

living room, room in home used for leisure activities, entertaining, etc.

living will, document stipulating that no extraordinary measures be taken to prolong signer's life during terminal illness.

liz/ard (liz/ərd) *n.* four-legged reptile.

lla/ma (lä/mə, yä/-) *n.* South American animal.

LL.B., Bachelor of Laws.

LL.D., Doctor of Laws.

load (lōd) *n.* **1.** cargo; anything carried. **2.** charge of firearm. —*v.* **3.** put load on. **4.** oppress. **5.** charge (firearm). —**load/er,** *n.*

loaf (lōf) *n.*, *pl.* **loaves** (lōvz), *v.* —*n.* **1.** shaped mass of bread, etc. —*v.* **2.** idle. —**loaf/er,** *n.*

loam (lōm) *n.* loose fertile soil.

loan (lōn) *n.* **1.** act of lending. **2.** something lent. —*v.* **3.** lend.

loan shark, *Informal.* usurer. —**loan/shark/ing,** *n.*

loan/word/, *n.* word borrowed from another language.

loath (lōth, lōth) *adj.* reluctant.

loathe (lōth) *v.*, **loathed, loathing.** feel disgust at; despise. —**loath/some** (lōth/səm, lōth/-) *adj.*

lob (lob) *v.*, **lobbed, lobbing.** —*v.* **1.** strike or hurl in a high curve. —*n.* **2.** tennis ball so struck.

lob/by, *n.*, *pl.* **-bies,** *v.*, **-bied, -bying.** —*n.* **1.** vestibule or entrance hall. **2.** group that tries to influence legislators. —*v.* **3.** try to influence legislators. —**lob/by·ist,** *n.*

lobe (lōb) *n.* roundish projection.

lo·bot/o·my (la bot/ə mē, lō-) *n.*, *pl.* **-mies.** surgical incision of brain lobe to treat mental disorder. —**lo·bot/o·mize/**, *v.*, **-mized, -mizing.**

lob/ster (lob/stər) *n.* edible marine shellfish.

lo/cal (lō/kəl) *adj.* **1.** of or in particular area. —*n.* **2.** local branch of trade union. **3.** train that makes all stops. —**lo/cal·ly**, *adv.*

lo·cale/ (lō kal/, -käl/) *n.* setting.

lo·cal/i·ty (-kal/i tē) *n.*, *pl.* **-ties.** place; area.

lo/cal·ize/ (-kə līz/) *v.*, **-ized, -izing.** confine to particular place.

lo/cate (lō/kāt, lō kāt/) *v.*, **-cated, -cating.** find or establish place of.

lo·ca/tion *n.* **1.** act or instance of locating. **2.** place where something is.

loc. cit. (lok/ sit/) in the place cited.

lock (lok) *n.* **1.** device for fastening door, lid, etc. **2.** place in canal, etc., for moving vessels from one water level to another. **3.** part of firearm. **4.** tress of hair. —*v.* **5.** secure with lock. **6.** shut in or out. **7.** join firmly.

lock/er, *n.* closet with lock.

lock/et (-it) *n.* small case worn on necklace.

lock/jaw/, *n.* disease in which jaws become tightly locked; tetanus.

lock/out/, *n.* business closure to force acceptance of employer's terms of work.

lock/smith/, *n.* person who makes or repairs locks.

lock/step/, *n.* way of marching in close file.

lock/up/, *n.* jail.

lo/co (lō/kō) *adj. Slang.* crazy.

lo/co·mo/tion (lō/kə mō/shən) *n.* act of moving about.

lo/co·mo/tive, *n.* engine that pulls railroad cars.

lo/co·weed/ (lō/kō-) *n.* plant causing a disease in livestock.

lo/cust (lō/kəst) *n.* **1.** kind of grasshopper. **2.** flowering American tree.

lo·cu/tion (lō kyōō/shən) *n.* phrase.

lode (lōd) *n.* mineral deposit.

lode/star/, *n.* guiding star.

lode/stone/, *n.* magnetic stone.

lodge (loj) *n.*, *v.*, **lodged, lodging.** —*n.* **1.** hut or house. **2.** members or meeting place of fraternal organization. —*v.* **3.** live or house temporarily. **4.** fix or put; become fixed. —**lodg/er**, *n.*

lodg/ing, *n.* **1.** temporary housing. **2.** (*pl.*) rooms.

loft (lôft) *n.* attic or gallery.

loft/y, *adj.*, **-ier, -iest.** **1.** tall. **2.** exalted or elevated. —**loft/i·ly**, *adv.*

log (lôg) *n.*, *v.*, **logged, logging.** —*n.* **1.** section of trunk or limb of felled tree. **2.** Also, **log/book/.** record of events. —*v.* **3.** fell and cut up trees. **4.** record in log. **5.** log in or on, gain access to secured computer system. —**log/ger,** *n.*

lo/gan·ber/ry (lō/gən ber/ē) *n.*, *pl.* **-ries.** dark red acid fruit.

log/a·rithm (lô/gə rith/əm) *n. Math.* symbol of number of times a number must be multiplied by itself to equal a given number.

loge (lōzh) *n.* box in theater.

log/ger·head/ (lô/gər hed/, log/ər-) *n.* **at loggerheads,** disputing.

log/ic (loj/ik) *n.* science of reasoning. —**lo·gi/cian** (lō jish/shən) *n.*

lo·gis/tics (lō jis/tiks, lə-) *n.* management of details of an operation.

log/jam/ (lôg/-) *n.* blockage or impasse.

lo/go (lō/gō) *n.* representation or symbol of company name, trademark, etc. Also, **lo/go·type/.**

log/roll/ing, *n.* exchange of support or favors, esp. in politics.

lo/gy (lō/gē) *adj.*, **-gier, -giest.** heavy; dull.

-logy, suffix meaning science or study of, as *theology.*

loin (loin) *n.* part of body between ribs and hipbone.

loin/cloth/, *n.* cloth worn around the loins or hips.

loi/ter (loi/tər) *v.* linger.

loll (lol) *v.* **1.** recline indolently. **2.** hang loosely.

lol/li·pop/ (lol/ē pop/) *n.* hard candy on stick.

lone (lōn) *adj.* alone.

lone/ly (lōn/lē) *adj.*, **-lier, -liest. 1.** alone. **2.** wishing for company. **3.** isolated. —**lone/li·ness,** *n.*

lon/er, *n.* person who spends much time alone.

lone/some (-səm) *adj.* **1.** depressed by solitude. **2.** lone.

long (lông) *adj.* **1.** of great or specified length. —*adv.* **2.** for long time. —*v.* **3.** yearn.

lon·gev/i·ty (lon jev/i tē) *n.* long life.

long/hand/ (lông/-) *n.* ordinary handwriting.

lon/gi·tude/ (lon/ji tōōd/, -tyōōd/) *n.* distance east and west on earth's surface.

lon/gi·tu/di·nal (-tōōd/n l, -tyōōd/-) *adj.* **1.** of longitude. **2.** lengthwise.

long jump, jump for distance.

long/-lived/ (-līvd/, -livd/) *adj.* having a long life or duration.

long/-range/, *adj.* spanning a long distance or time.

long/shore/man, *n.* person who loads and unloads ships.

long shot, *n.* **1.** racehorse, team, etc., with little chance for winning. **2.** undertaking with little chance for success.

long/-term/, *adj.* involving a long time.

long/-wind/ed (-win/did) *adj.* continuing to speak for too long.

look (lŏŏk) *v.*, **1.** direct the eyes. **2.** seem. **3.** face. **4.** seek. **5.** care for. —*n.* **6.** act of looking. **7.** appearance.

looking glass, mirror.

look/out/, *n.* **1.** watch. **2.** person for keeping watch. **3.** place for keeping watch.

loom (lōōm) *n.* **1.** device for weaving fabric. —*v.* **2.** appear as large and indistinct.

loon (lōōn) *n.* diving bird.

loon/y, *adj.*, **-ier, -iest.** *Informal.* **1.** lunatic; insane. **2.** extremely foolish.

loop (lōōp) *n.* **1.** circular form from length of material or line. —*v.* **2.** form a loop.

loop/hole/, *n.* **1.** small opening in wall, etc. **2.** means of evasion.

loose (lōōs) *adj.*, **looser, loosest,** *v.*, **loosed, loosing.** —*adj.* **1.** free; unconfined. **2.** not firm or tight. **3.** not exact. **4.** dissolute. —*v.* **5.** free. **6.** shoot (missiles). —**loos/en,** *v.*

loot (lōōt) *n.* **1.** spoils. —*v.* **2.** plunder. —**loot/er,** *n.*

lope (lōp) *v.*, **loped, loping,** *n.* —*v.* **1.** move or run with long, easy stride. —*n.* **2.** long, easy stride.

lop/sid/ed, *adj.* uneven.

lo·qua/cious (lō kwā/shəs) *adj.* talkative. —**lo·quac/i·ty** (-kwas/ə tē) *n.*

lord (lôrd) *n.* **1.** master. **2.** British nobleman. **3.** (*cap.*) God. **4.** (*cap.*) Jesus Christ. —*v.* **5.** domineer. —**lord/ly,** *adj.* —**lord/ship,** *n.*

lore (lôr) *n.* learning.

lor/ry (lôr/ē) *n.*, *pl.* **-ries.** *Brit.* truck.

lose (lōōz) *v.*, **lost** (lôst), **losing. 1.** fail to keep. **2.** misplace. **3.** be deprived of. **4.** fail to win.

loss (lôs) *n.* **1.** disadvantage from losing. **2.** thing lost. **3.** waste.

lot (lot) *n.* **1.** object drawn to decide question by chance. **2.** allotted share. **3.** piece of land. **4.** (*often pl.*) *Informal.* a great number or amount. —**Usage.** See ALOT.

lo·thar/i·o (lō thâr/ē ō/) *n.*, *pl.* **-os.** (*often l.c.*) man who obsessively seduces women.

lo/tion (lō/shən) *n.* liquid to rub on skin.

lot/ter·y (lot/ə rē) *n.*, *pl.* **-ies.** sale of tickets on prizes to be awarded by lots.

lot/to (lot/ō) *n.* **1.** game of chance similar to bingo. **2.** lottery in which players choose numbers that are matched against those of the official drawing.

lo/tus (lō/təs) *n.* water lily of Egypt and Asia.

loud (loud) *adj.* **1.** strongly audible. **2.** blatant.

loud/-mouth/ (-mouth/) *n.* a braggart; gossip.

loud/speak/er, *n.* device for increasing volume of sound.

lounge (lounj) *v.*, **lounged, lounging,** *n.* —*v.* **1.** pass time idly. **2.** loll. —*n.* **3.** kind of sofa. **4.** public parlor.

louse (lous) *n.*, *pl.* **lice** (līs). bloodsucking insect.

lous/y (lou/zē) *adj.*, **-ier, -iest. 1.** *Informal.* bad; poor. **2.** troubled with lice. —**lous/i·ness,** *n.*

lout (lout) *n.* boor. —**lout/ish,** *adj.*

lou/ver (lōō/vər) *n.* arrangement of slits for ventilation.

lov/a·ble (luv/ə bal) *adj.* attracting love. Also, **love/a·ble.**

love (luv) *n.*, *v.*, **loved, loving.** —*n.* **1.** strong affection. **2.** sweetheart. —*v.* **3.** have love for. —**lov/er,** *n.* —**lov/ing,** *adj.*

love/lorn/ (-lôrn/) *adj.* deprived of love or a lover.

love/ly (luv/lē) *adj.*, **-lier, -liest.** charming. —**love/li·ness,** *n.*

love/sick/, *adj.* sick from intensity of love.

loving cup, large two-handled drinking cup.

low (lō) *adj.* **1.** not high or tall. **2.** below normal level. **3.** sad. **4.** humble or inferior. **5.** not loud. **6.** base or unfavorable. —*adv.* **7.** in low position. **8.** in quiet tone. —*n.* **9.** thing that is low. **10.** moo. —*v.* **11.** moo.

low/brow/, *n.* **1.** uncultured person. —*adj.* **2.** typical of a lowbrow.

low/-cal/ (lō/kal/, -kal/) *adj.* with fewer calories than usual.

low/down/ *n.* (lō/doun/) **1.** real and unadorned facts. —*adj.* (-doun/) **2.** contemptible; mean.

low/er (lō/ər for 1, 2; lou/ər for 3–5) *v.* **1.** reduce or diminish. **2.** make or become lower. **3.** be threatening. **4.** frown. —*n.* **5.** lowering appearance.

low/er·case/ (lō/ər-) *adj.* **1.** (of a letter) of a form often different from and smaller than its corresponding capital letter. —*n.* **2.** lowercase letter.

low frequency, radio frequency between 30 and 300 kilohertz.

low/-key/, *adj.* understated.

low/life/, *n.*, *pl.* **-lifes.** disreputable or degenerate person.

low/ly, *adj.*, **-lier, -liest.** meek.

low/-mind/ed, *adj.* coarse; vulgar.

low profile, deliberately inconspicuous manner.

lox (loks) *n.* salmon cured in brine.

loy·al (loi'əl) *adj.* faithful; steadfast. —**loy'al·ly,** *adv.* —**loy'al·ty,** *n.*

loz'enge (loz'inj) *n.* **1.** flavored candy, often medicated. **2.** diamond shape.

LPN, licensed practical nurse.

LSD, lysergic acid diethylamide, a powerful psychedelic drug.

Lt., lieutenant.

Ltd., limited.

lub'ber (lub'ər) *n.* clumsy person.

lu'bri·cant (lōō'bri kənt) *n.* lubricating substance.

lu'bri·cate' (-kāt') *v.,* **-cated, -cating.** oil or grease, esp. to diminish friction. —**lu'bri·ca'tor,** *n.*

lu'cid (lōō'sid) *adj.* **1.** bright. **2.** clear in thought or expression. **3.** rational. —**lu·cid'i·ty,** *n.*

Lu'cite (lōō'sīt) *n. Trademark.* transparent plastic.

luck (luk) *n.* **1.** chance. **2.** good fortune. —**luck'less,** *adj.*

luck'y, *adj.,* **-ier, -iest.** having or due to good luck. —**luck'i·ly,** *adv.*

lu'cra·tive (lōō'krə tiv) *adj.* profitable.

lu'cre (lōō'kər) *n.* gain or money.

lu'di·crous (lōō'di krəs) *adj.* ridiculous. —**lu'di·crous·ly,** *adv.*

lug (lug) *v.,* **lugged, lugging,** *n.* —*v.* **1.** pull or carry with effort. **2.** haul. —*n.* **3.** projecting handle. **4.** *Slang.* awkward, clumsy fellow.

luge (lōōzh) *n., v.,* **luged, luging.** —*n.* **1.** small racing sled for one or two persons. —*v.* **2.** race on a luge.

lug'gage (lug'ij) *n.* baggage.

lug nut, large nut, esp. for attaching a wheel to a vehicle.

lu·gu'bri·ous (lōō gōō'brē əs, -gyōō'-) *adj.* excessively mournful.

luke'warm' (lōōk'-) *adj.* slightly warm.

lull (lul) *v.* **1.** soothe, esp. to sleep. —*n.* **2.** brief stillness.

lull'a·by (-ə bī') *n., pl.* **-bies.** song to lull baby.

lum·ba'go (lum bā'gō) *n.* muscular pain in back.

lum'bar (lum'bər, -bär) *adj.* of or close to the loins.

lum'ber (lum'bər) *n.* **1.** timber made into boards, etc. —*v.* **2.** cut and prepare timber. **3.** encumber. **4.** move heavily.

lum'ber·jack', *n.* person who fells trees.

lum'ber·yard', *n.* yard where lumber is stored for sale.

lu'mi·nar'y (lōō'mə ner'ē) *n., pl.* **-ies.** **1.** celestial body. **2.** person who inspires many.

lu'mi·nes'cent (lōō'mə nes'ənt) *adj.* luminous at relatively low temperatures. —**lu'mi·nes'cence,** *n.*

lu'mi·nous (-nəs) *adj.* giving or reflecting light. —**lu'mi·nos'i·ty** (-nos'i tē) *n.*

lum'mox (lum'əks) *n. Informal.* clumsy, stupid person.

lump (lump) *n.* **1.** irregular mass. **2.** swelling. —*adj.* **3.** including many. —*v.* **4.** put together. **5.** endure.

lu'na·cy (lōō'nə sē) *n., pl.* **-cies.** insanity.

lu'nar (-nər) *adj.* **1.** of or according to moon. **2.** crescent-shaped.

lu'na·tic (-tik) *n.* **1.** insane person. —*adj.* **2.** for the insane. **3.** crazy.

lunch (lunch) *n.* **1.** Also, **lunch'eon** (lun'chən). midday meal. —*v.* **2.** eat lunch.

lunch'eon·ette' (lun'chə net') *n.* restaurant for quick, simple lunches.

lung (lung) *n.* respiratory organ.

lunge (lunj) *n., v.,* **lunged, lunging.** —*n.* **1.** sudden forward movement. —*v.* **2.** make lunge.

lu'pine (lōō'pin) *n.* **1.** plant with tall, dense clusters of flowers. —*adj.* **2.** of or resembling the wolf.

lu'pus (lōō'pəs) *n.* any of several diseases characterized by skin eruptions.

lurch (lûrch) *n.* **1.** sudden lean to one side. **2.** helpless plight. —*v.* **3.** make lurch.

lure (lōōr) *n., v.,* **lured, luring.** —*n.* **1.** bait. —*v.* **2.** decoy; entice.

lu'rid (lōōr'id) *adj.* **1.** glaringly lighted. **2.** sensational.

lurk (lûrk) *v.* **1.** loiter furtively. **2.** exist unperceived.

lus'cious (lush'əs) *adj.* delicious.

lush (lush) *adj.* **1.** tender and juicy. **2.** abundant.

lust (lust) *n.* **1.** strong desire. —*v.* **2.** have strong desire. —**lust'ful,** *adj.*

lus'ter (lus'tər) *n.* gloss; radiance. Also, **lus'tre.** —**lus'trous,** *adj.*

lust'y, *adj.,* **-ier, -iest.** vigorous.

lute (lōōt) *n.* stringed musical instrument. —**lut'en·ist,** *n.*

Lu'ther·an (lōō'thər ən) *adj.* of Protestant sect named for Martin Luther. —**Lu'ther·an·ism,** *n.*

lux·u'ri·ant (lug zhōōr'ē ənt, luk-shōōr'-) *adj.* profuse; abundant. —**lux·u'ri·ance,** *n.*

lux·u'ri·ate' (-āt') *v.,* **-ated, -ating.** revel; delight.

lux'u·ry (luk'shə rē, lug'zhə-) *n., pl.* **-ries.** something enjoyable but not necessary. —**lux·u'ri·ous** (lug zhōōr'ē əs, luk shōōr'-) *adj.*

-ly, suffix meaning: in a specified manner, as *loudly;* according to, as *theoretically;* to or from a specified direction, as *inwardly;* like or characteristic of, as *saintly;* every, as *hourly.*

ly·ce'um (lī sē'əm) *n.* hall for lectures, etc.

lye (lī) *n.* alkali solution.

ly'ing-in', *adj.* **1.** of or for childbirth. —*n.* **2.** childbirth.

lymph (limf) *n.* yellowish matter from body tissues. —**lym·phat'ic** (lim fat'ik) *adj.*

lym'pho·cyte' (lim'fə sīt') *n.* white blood cell producing antibodies.

lynch (linch) *v.* put to death without legal authority.

lynx (lingks) *n., pl.* **lynxes, lynx.** kind of wild cat.

lyre (lī∂r) *n.* ancient harplike instrument.

lyr'ic (lir'ik) *adj.* Also, **lyr'i·cal. 1.** (of poetry) musical. **2.** of or writing such poetry. —*n.* **3.** lyric poem. **4.** (*pl.*) words for song. —**lyr'i·cism** (-ə siz'm) *n.* —**lyr'i·cist,** *n.*

M

M, m (em) *n.* thirteenth letter of English alphabet.

ma (mä) *n. Informal.* mother.

MA, Massachusetts.

M.A., Master of Arts.

ma'am (mam, mäm; *unstressed* məm) *n. Informal.* madam.

ma·ca'bre (mə kä'brə, -käb') *adj.* gruesome.

mac·ad'am (mə kad'əm) *n.* roadmaking material containing broken stones. —**mac·ad'am·ize',** *v.,* **-ized, -izing.**

mac'a·ro'ni (mak'ə rō'nē) *n.* tube-shaped food made of wheat.

mac'a·roon' (mak'ə rōōn') *n.* almond or coconut cookie.

ma·caw' (mə kô') *n.* parrot.

mace (mās) *n.* **1.** spiked war club. **2.** staff of office. **3.** spice from part of nutmeg seed. **4.** (*cap.*) *Trademark.* chemical spray for subduing rioters, attackers etc.

mac'er·ate' (mas'ə rāt') *v.,* **-ated, -ating.** soften by steeping in liquid.

ma·che'te (mə shet'ē, -chet'ē) *n.* heavy knife.

Mach'i·a·vel'li·an (mak'ē ə vel'ē-ən) *adj.* unscrupulously wily.

mach'i·na'tion (mak'ə nā'shən) *n.* cunning plan.

ma·chine' (mə shēn') *n.* **1.** apparatus or mechanical device. **2.** group controlling political organization.

machine gun, firearm capable of firing continuous stream of bullets.

ma·chin'er·y, *n., pl.* **-eries.** machines or mechanisms.

ma·chin'ist, *n.* operator of powered tool, ship's engines, etc.

ma·chis'mo (mä chēz'mō) *n.* exaggerated masculinity as basis for code of behavior.

Mach' num'ber (mäk) ratio of speed of object to speed of sound.

ma'cho (mä'chō) *adj.* exaggeratedly virile.

mack'er·el (mak'ər əl) *n.* common food fish.

mack'i·naw' (mak'ə nô') *n.* short, heavy, woolen coat.

mack'in·tosh' (mak'in tosh') *n.* raincoat.

mac'ra·mé' (mak'rə mā') *n.* decorative work of knotted cords.

macro-, prefix meaning large, as *macrocosm.*

mac'ro·bi·ot'ic (mak'rō bi ot'ik) *adj.* of or giving long life.

mac'ro·cosm (mak'rə koz'əm) *n.* universe.

ma'cron (mä'kron, mak'ron) *n.* horizontal line over vowel to show it is long.

mad (mad) *adj.,* **madder, maddest. 1.** insane. **2.** *Informal.* angry. **3.** violent. —**mad'den,** *v.*

mad'am (mad'əm) *n.* **1.** female term of address. **2.** woman in charge of brothel.

mad'cap', *adj.* impulsive; rash.

made, *pt.* of **make.**

mad·e·moi·selle' (mad'ə mə zel', mad'mwə-, mam zel') *n., pl.* **mademoiselles, mesdemoiselles** (mā'də-mə zel', -zelz', mād'mwə-) French term of address for unmarried woman.

mad'man', *n.* man who is or seems mentally ill. —**mad'wo'man,** *n.fem.*

Ma·don'na (mə don'ə) *n.* Virgin Mary.

mad'ras (mad'rəs, mə dras', -dräs') *n.* light cotton fabric.

mad'ri·gal (mad'ri gəl) *n.* song for several voices unaccompanied.

mael'strom (māl'strəm) *n.* **1.** whirlpool. **2.** confusion.

maes'tro (mī'strō) *n., pl.* **-tros.** master, esp. of music.

Ma'fi·a (mä'fē ə, maf'ē ə) *n.* criminal society.

ma'fi·o'so (mä'fē ō'sō) *n., pl.* **-si** (-sē), **-sos.** member of Mafia.

mag'a·zine' (mag'ə zēn') *n.* **1.** periodical publication. **2.** storehouse for ammunition, etc. **3.** cartridge container in repeating weapon.

ma·gen'ta (mə jen'tə) *n.* reddish purple.

mag'got (mag'ət) *n.* larva of fly.

Ma'gi (mā'jī) *n.pl. Bible.* the three wise men.

mag'ic (maj'ik) *n.* **1.** supernatural

power. —*adj.* Also, **mag′i•cal. 2.** sleight of hand. **3.** of magic. **4.** enchanting. —**ma•gi′cian** (mə jish′ən) *n.*

mag′is•te′ri•al (maj′ə stēr′ē əl) *adj.* masterlike; authoritative.

mag′is•trate′ (-strāt′, -strit) *n.* civil public official.

mag′ma (mag′mə) *n.* molten rock.

mag•nan′i•mous (mag nan′ə məs) *adj.* generous; high-minded. —**mag′-na•nim′i•ty** (-nə nim′i tē) *n.*

mag′nate (-nāt, -nit) *n.* business leader.

mag•ne′sia (mag nē′zhə) *n.* magnesium oxide, used as laxative.

mag•ne′si•um (-zē əm, -zhəm) *n.* light, silvery, metallic element.

mag′net (mag′nit) *n.* metal body that attracts iron or steel.

mag•net′ic (-net′ik) *adj.* **1.** of a magnet or magnetism. **2.** attractive.

magnetic field, space near magnet, electric current, moving charged particle in which magnetic force acts.

mag′net•ism (mag′ni tiz′əm) *n.* **1.** characteristic property of magnets. **2.** science of magnets. **3.** great personal charm. —**mag′net•ize′,** *v.* **-ized, -izing.**

mag′net•ite′ (mag′ni tīt′) *n.* common black mineral.

mag•ne′to (mag nē′tō) *n., pl.* **-tos.** small electric generator.

mag•nif′i•cent (mag nif′ə sənt) *adj.* **1.** splendid. **2.** noble.

mag′ni•fy′ (mag′nə fī′) *v.,* **-fied, -fying. 1.** increase apparent size. **2.** enlarge. e —**mag′ni•fi′er,** *n.*

mag′ni•tude′ (-ni tōōd′, -tyōōd′) *n.* size or extent.

mag•no′li•a (mag nōl′yə, -nō′lē ə) *n.* tree with large fragrant flowers.

magnum opus (mag′nəm ō′pəs) chief work.

mag′pie′ (mag′pī′) *n.* black and white bird that steals.

ma′ha•ra′jah (mä′hə rä′jə, -zhə) *n.* (formerly) ruling prince in India. —**ma′ha•ra′nee** (-nē) *n.fem.*

ma•hat′ma (mə hät′mə, -hat′-) *n.* person, esp. in India, held in highest esteem for wisdom and saintliness.

mah′-jongg′ (mä′jông′, -zhông′) *n.* Chinese game.

ma•hog′a•ny (mə hog′ə nē) *n., pl.* **-nies.** tropical American tree or its redbrown wood.

Ma•hom′et (mə hom′it) *n.* Muhammad.

maid (mād) *n.* **1.** unmarried woman. **2.** female servant.

maid′en, *n.* **1.** unmarried woman. —*adj.* **2.** of maidens. **3.** unmarried. **4.** initial. —**maid′en•ly,** *adj.*

maid′en•hair′, *n.* fern with finely divided fronds.

mail (māl) *n.* **1.** material delivered by postal system. **2.** postal system. **3.** armor, usually flexible. —*adj.* **4.** of mail. —*v.* **5.** send by mail. —**mail′box′,** *n.* —**mail carrier,** *n.* —**mail′man′,** *n.*

maim (mām) *v.* cripple; impair.

main (mān) *adj.* **1.** chief; principal. —*n.* **2.** chief pipe or duct. **3.** strength. **4.** ocean. —**main′ly,** *adv.*

main′frame′, *n.* large computer, often the hub of a system serving many users.

main′land′ (-land′, -lənd) *n.* continental land rather than island.

main′stay′, *n.* chief support.

main′stream′, *n.* customary trend of behavior, opinion, etc.

main•tain′ (mān tān′) *v.* **1.** support. **2.** assert. **3.** keep in order or condition. —**main′te•nance** (-tə nəns) *n.*

mai′tre d′hô•tel′ (mā′trə dō tel′) headwaiter. Also, **mai′tre d′** (mā′tər dē′).

maize (māz) *n.* corn.

maj′es•ty (maj′ə stē) *n., pl.* **-ties. 1.** regal grandeur. **2.** sovereign. —**mə•jes′tic** (mə jes′tic) *adj.*

ma•jol′i•ca (mə jol′i kə, mə yol′-) *n.* kind of pottery.

ma′jor (mā′jər) *n.* **1.** army officer above captain. **2.** person of legal age. —*adj.* **3.** larger or more important.

ma′jor-do′mo (-dō′mō) *n.* steward.

ma′jor•ette′ (-jə ret′) *n.* female leader of marchers.

major general, army officer above brigadier general.

ma•jor′i•ty (mə jôr′i tē) *n., pl.* **-ties. 1.** greater number. **2.** full legal age.

make (māk) *v.,* **made** (mād), **making,** *n.* —*v.* **1.** bring into existence. **2.** force. **3.** earn. **4.** accomplish. —*n.* **5.** style. **6.** manufacture.

make′-be•lieve′, *n.* **1.** pretending that fanciful thing is true. —*adj.* **2.** imaginary.

make′shift′, *n., adj.* substitute.

make′up′, *n.* **1.** cosmetics. **2.** organization; composition.

mal-, prefix meaning bad or ill, as *maladjustment.*

mal′a•chite′ (mal′ə kīt′) *n.* green mineral, an ore of copper.

mal′ad•just′ed, *adj.* badly adjusted, esp. to social conditions.

mal′a•droit′ (mal′ə droit′) *adj.* awkward.

mal′a•dy (mal′ə dē) *n., pl.* **-dies.** illness.

ma•laise′ (ma lāz′, -lez′, mə-) *n.* **1.** weakness. **2.** vague uneasiness.

mal′a•mute′ (mal′ə myōōt′) *n.* Alaskan breed of large dogs.

mal′a•prop•ism (mal′ə prop iz′əm) *n.* ludicrous misuse of similar words.

ma•lar′i•a (mə lâr′ē ə) *n.* mosquitoborne disease. —**ma•lar′i•al,** *adj.*

ma•lar′key (mə lär′kē) *n. Informal.* nonsense.

mal′con•tent′ (mal′kən tent′) *n.* dissatisfied person.

mal de mer (mʌl də meʀ′) seasickness.

male (māl) *adj.* **1.** of sex that produces sperm, etc. —*n.* **2.** male person, etc.

mal′e•dic′tion (mal′i dik′shən) *n.* curse.

mal′e•fac′tor (mal′ə fak′tər) *n.* person who does wrong.

ma•lev′o•lent (mə lev′ə lənt) *adj.* wishing evil. —**ma•lev′o•lence,** *n.*

mal•fea′sance (mal fē′zəns) *n.* misconduct in office.

mal•formed′, *adj.* badly formed. —**mal′for•ma′tion,** *n.*

mal′ice (mal′is) *n.* evil intent. —**ma•li′cious** (mə lish′shəs) *adj.*

ma•lign′ (mə līn′) *v.* **1.** speak ill of. —*adj.* **2.** evil.

ma•lig′nan•cy (mə lig′nən sē) *n., pl.* **-cies. 1.** malignant state. **2.** cancerous growth.

ma•lig′nant (-nənt) *adj.* **1.** causing harm or suffering. **2.** deadly.

ma•lig′ni•ty (-ni tē) *n., pl.* **-ties. 1.** state of being malignant. **2.** instance of malignant feeling or behavior.

ma•lin′ger (mə ling′gər) *v.* feign sickness. —**ma•lin′ger•er,** *n.*

mall (môl) *n.* **1.** shaded walk. **2.** covered shopping center.

mal′lard (mal′ərd) *n.* wild duck.

mal′le•a•ble (mal′ē ə bəl) *adj.* **1.** that may be hammered or rolled into shape. **2.** readily influenced.

mal′let (mal′it) *n.* wooden-headed hammer.

mal•nu•tri′tion, *n.* improper nutrition.

mal•o′dor•ous, *adj.* smelling bad.

mal•prac′tice, *n.* improper professional behavior.

malt (môlt) *n.* germinated grain used in liquor-making.

mal•treat′ (mal trēt′) *v.* abuse.

ma′ma (mä′mə, mə mä′) *n. Informal.* mother.

mam′mal (mam′əl) *n.* vertebrate animal whose young are suckled.

mam′ma•ry (mam′ə rē) *adj.* of breasts.

mam′mo•gram′ (mam′ə gram′) *n.* x-ray photograph of a breast, for detection of tumors.

mam′mon (mam′ən) *n.* material wealth, esp. as influence for evil.

mam′moth (mam′əth) *n.* **1.** large extinct kind of elephant. —*adj.* **2.** huge.

mam′my (mam′ē) *n., pl.* **-mies.** *Informal.* mother.

man (man) *n., pl.* **men** (men), *v.,* **manned, manning.** —*n.* **1.** male person. **2.** person. **3.** human race. —*v.* **4.** supply with crew. **5.** operate.

man′a•cle (man′ə kəl) *n., v.,* **-cled, -cling.** handcuff.

man′age (man′ij) *v.,* **-aged, -aging. 1.** take care of. **2.** direct. **3.** cope. —**man′a•ger,** *n.* —**man′a•ge′ri•al** (-i-jēr′ē əl) *adj.*

man′age•ment, *n.* **1.** direction. **2.** persons in charge.

ma•ña′na (mä nyä′nä) *n. Spanish.* tomorrow.

man′a•tee′ (man′ə tē′) *n.* planteating aquatic mammal.

man′da•rin (man′də rin) *n.* **1.** public official in Chinese Empire. **2.** (*cap.*) dialect of Chinese.

man′date (man′dāt) *n.* **1.** authority over territory granted to nation by other nations. **2.** territory under such authority. **3.** command, as to take office. —**man′date,** *v.*

man′da•to′ry (man′də tôr′ē) *adj.* officially required.

man′di•ble (man′də bəl) *n.* bone comprising the lower jaw.

man′do•lin (man′dl in, man′dl in′) *n.* stringed musical instrument.

man′drake (man′drāk, -drik) *n.* narcotic herb.

mane (mān) *n.* long hair at neck of some animals.

ma•neu′ver (mə nōō′vər) *n.* **1.** planned movement, esp. in war. **2.** change position by maneuver. **3.** put in certain situation by intrigue. —**ma•neu′ver•a•ble,** *adj.*

man Friday, *pl.* **men Friday.** reliable male assistant.

man′ful, *adj.* resolute.

man′ga•nese′ (mang′gə nēs′, -nēz′) *n.* hard metallic element.

mange (mānj) *n.* skin disease of animals. —**man′gy,** *adj.*

man′ger (mān′jər) *n.* trough for feeding livestock.

man′gle (mang′gəl) *v.,* **-gled, -gling,** *n.* —*v.* **1.** disfigure, esp. by crushing. **2.** put through mangle. —*n.* **3.** device with rollers for removing water in washing clothes.

man′go (mang′gō) *n., pl.* **-goes.** fruit of tropical tree.

man′grove (mang′grōv, man′-) *n.* kind of tropical tree.

man′han•dle (man′han′dl) *v.,* **-dled, -dling.** handle roughly.

man•hat′tan (man hat′n, mən-) *n.* cocktail of whiskey and vermouth.

man′hole′, *n.* access hole to sewer.

man′hood, *n.* **1.** manly qualities. **2.** state of being a man.

man′-hour′, *n.* ideal amount of work done by a person in an hour.

man′hunt′, *n.* intensive search for fugitive.

ma′ni•a (mā′nē ə) *n.* **1.** great excitement. **2.** violent insanity.

ma′ni•ac′, *n.* lunatic. —**ma•ni′a•cal** (mə nī′ə kəl) *adj.*

man′ic (man′ik) *adj.* irrationally excited or lively.

man′ic-depress′ive, *adj.* suffering from mental disorder in which mania alternates with depression.

man′i•cure′ (man′i kyoor′) *n.* skilled care of fingernails and hands. —**man′i•cure′**, *v.*

man′i•fest′ (man′ə fest′) *adj.* **1.** evident. —*v.* **2.** show plainly. —*n.* **3.** list of cargo and passengers. —**man′i•fes•ta′tion**, *n.*

man′i•fes′to (-fes′tō) *n.*, *pl.* **-toes.** public declaration of intentions.

man′i•fold′ (man′ə fōld′) *adj.* **1.** of many kinds or parts. —*v.* **2.** copy. —*n.* **3.** pipe with many outlets.

man′i•kin (man′i kin) *n.* model of human body.

Ma•nil′a paper (mə nil′ə) strong, light brown or buff paper.

man in the street, ordinary person.

ma•nip′u•late′ (mə nip′yə lāt′) *v.*, **-lated, -lating.** handle with skill or cunning. —**ma•nip′u•la′tor**, *n.*

man′kind′ (man′kīnd′) *n.* human race.

man′ly, *adj.*, **-lier, -liest.** virile.

man′na (man′ə) *n.* divine food given to Israelites.

man′ne•quin (man′i kin) *n.* model for displaying clothes.

man′ner (man′ər) *n.* **1.** way of doing, acting, etc. **2.** (*pl.*) way of acting in society. **3.** sort.

man′ner•ism, *n.* peculiarity of manner.

man′ner•ly, *adj.* polite.

man′nish, *adj.* like a man.

man′-of-war′, *n.*, *pl.* **men-of-war.** warship.

man′or (man′ər) *n.* large estate.

man′pow′er, *n.* available labor force.

man•qué′ (mäng kā′) *adj.* unfulfilled.

man′sard (man′särd) *n.* roof with two slopes of different pitch on all sides.

manse (mans) *n.* house and land of parson.

man′serv′ant, *n.* male servant, as valet.

man′sion (man′shən) *n.* stately house.

man′slaugh′ter, *n.* unlawful killing of person without malice.

man′tel (man′tl) *n.* ornamental structure around fireplace.

man•til′la (man til′ə, -tē′ə) *n.* lace head scarf of Spanish women.

man′tis (man′tis) *n.* kind of carnivorous insect.

man′tle (man′tl) *n.*, *v.*, **-tled, -tling.** —*n.* **1.** loose cloak. —*v.* **2.** envelop.

man′tra (man′trə, mun′-) *n.* Hindu or Buddhist chant for recitation.

man′u•al (man′yōō əl) *adj.* **1.** of or done with hands. —*n.* **2.** small informational book. **3.** hand powered typewriter. —**man′u•al•ly**, *adv.*

man′u•fac′ture (man′yə fak′chər) *n.*, *v.*, **-tured, -turing.** —*n.* **1.** making of things, esp. in great quantity. **2.** thing made. —*v.* **3.** make.

man′u•mit′ (man′yə mit′) *v.*, **-mitted, -mitting.** release from slavery. —**man′u•mis′sion**, *n.*

ma•nure′ (mə nŏŏr′, -nyŏŏr′) *n.* animal dung used as fertilizer.

man′u•script′ (man′yə skript′) *n.* handwritten or typed document.

man′y (men′ē) *adj.* **1.** comprising a large number; numerous. —*n.* **2.** large number.

Mao′ism (mou′iz əm) *n.* policies of Chinese Communist leader Mao Zedong. —**Mao′ist**, *n.*, *adj.*

map (map) *n.*, *v.*, **mapped, mapping.** —*n.* **1.** flat representation of earth, etc. —*v.* **2.** show by map. **3.** plan.

ma′ple (mā′pəl) *n.* northern tree.

mar (mär) *v.*, **marred, marring.** damage.

Mar., March.

ma•ra′ca (mə rä′kə, -rak′ə) *n.* gourd-shaped rattle filled with seeds or pebbles, used as rhythm instrument.

maraschino cherry, (mar′ə skē′nō) cherry preserved in cherry cordial.

mar′a•thon′ (mar′ə thon′, -thən) *n.* long contest, esp. a foot race of 26 miles, 385 yards.

ma•raud′ (mə rôd′) *v.* plunder.

mar′ble (mär′bəl) *n.* **1.** crystalline limestone used in sculpture and building. **2.** small glass ball used in children's game. —*adj.* **3.** of marble.

mar′bling, *n.* intermixture of fat with lean in meat.

march (märch) *v.* **1.** walk with measured tread. **2.** advance. —*n.* **3.** act of marching. **4.** distance covered in march. **5.** music for marching.

March (märch) *n.* third month of year.

mar′chion•ess (mär′shə nis, -nes′) *n.* **1.** wife or widow of marquess. **2.** woman of rank equal to marquess.

Mar′di Gras (mär′dē grä′, grä′) the Tuesday before Lent, often celebrated as a carnival.

mare (mâr) *n.* female horse.

mare′s′-nest′, *n.* complicated situation.

mar′ga•rine (mär′jər in) *n.* butterlike product made from vegetable oils and water or milk.

mar′gin (mär′jin) *n.* **1.** edge. **2.** amount beyond what is necessary.

mar′gin•al, *adj.* **1.** of or at margin. **2.** barely acceptable.

mar′gue•rite′ (mär′gə rēt′) *n.* daisylike chrysanthemum.

mar′i•gold′ (mar′i gōld′) *n.* common, yellow-flowered plant.

ma′ri•jua′na (mar′ə wä′nə) *n.* narcotic plant.

ma•rim′ba (mə rim′bə) *n.* xylophone with chambers for resonance.

ma•ri′na (mə rē′nə) *n.* docking area for small boats.

mar′i•nade′ (mar′ə nād′) *n.* pungent liquid mixture for steeping food.

mar′i•nate′, *v.* -nated, -nating. season by steeping.

ma•rine′ (mə rēn′) *adj.* **1.** of the sea. —*n.* **2.** member of U.S. Marine Corps. **3.** fleet of ships.

Marine Corps, military branch of U.S. Navy.

mar′i•ner (mar′ə nər) *n.* sailor.

mar′i•o•nette′ (mar′ē ə net′) *n.* puppet on strings.

mar′i•tal (mar′i tl) *adj.* of marriage.

mar′i•time′ (mar′i tīm′) *adj.* of sea or shipping.

mar′jo•ram (mär′jər əm) *n.* herb used as seasoning.

mark (märk) *n.* **1.** any visible sign. **2.** object aimed at. **3.** rating; grade. **4.** lasting effect. **5.** German monetary unit. —*v.* **6.** be feature of. **7.** put mark on, as grade or price. **8.** pay attention to. —**mark′er**, *n.*

mark′down′, *n.* price reduction.

marked, *adj.* **1.** conspicuous. **2.** ostentatious. **3.** singled out for revenge. —**mark′ed•ly**, *adv.*

mar′ket (mär′kit) *n.* **1.** place for selling and buying. —*v.* **2.** sell or buy. —**mar′ket•a•ble**, *adj.*

mar′ket•place′, *n.* **1.** open area where market is held. **2.** the world of business, trade, and economics.

marks′man, *n.*, *pl.* **-men.** person who shoots well. —**marks′man•ship′**, *n.* —**marks′wom′an**, *n.fem.*

mark′up′, *n.* price increase by retailer.

mar′lin (mär′lin) *n.* large game fish.

mar′ma•lade′ (mär′mə lād′) *n.* fruit preserve.

mar′mo•set′ (mär′mə zet′, -set′) *n.* small, tropical American monkey.

mar′mot (mär′mət) *n.* bushy-tailed rodent.

ma•roon′ (mə rōōn′) *n.*, *adj.* **1.** dark brownish-red. —*v.* **2.** abandon ashore. **3.** isolate without aid.

mar•quee′ (mär kē′) *n.* **1.** projecting shelter over outer door. **2.** large tent.

mar′que•try (mär′ki trē) *n.* inlaid work forming pattern.

mar′quis (mär′kwis, mär kē′) *n.* rank of nobility below duke. Also, *Brit.* **mar′quess** (-kwis). —**mar•quise′** (-kēz′) *n.fem.*

mar′riage (mar′ij) *n.* **1.** legal union of man and woman. **2.** wedding. —**mar′riage•a•ble**, *adj.*

mar′row (mar′ō) *n.* soft inner tissue of bone.

mar′ry (mar′ē) *v.*, **-ried, -rying.** take, give, or unite in marriage.

Mars (märz) *n.* one of the planets.

marsh (märsh) *n.* low, wet land. —**marsh′y**, *adj.*

mar′shal (mär′shəl) *n.*, *v.*, **-shaled, -shaling.** —*n.* **1.** federal officer. —*v.* **2.** rally; organize.

marsh gas, decomposition product of organic matter.

marsh′mal′low (-mel′ō, -mal′ō) *n.* soft confection made from gelatin.

marsh marigold, yellow-flowered plant of buttercup family.

mar•su′pi•al (mär sōō′pē al) *n.* animal carrying its young in pouch, as the kangaroo. —**mar•su′pi•al**, *adj.*

mart (märt) *n.* market.

mar′ten (mär′tn) *n.* small, American, fur-bearing animal.

mar′tial (mär′shəl) *adj.* warlike; military. —**mar′tial•ly**, *adv.*

martial art, any of various forms of East Asian self-defense or combat.

martial law, law imposed by military forces.

mar′tin (mär′tn) *n.* bird of swallow family.

mar′ti•net′ (mär′tn et′) *n.* disciplinarian.

mar′ti•ni (mär tē′nē) *n.* cocktail of gin and vermouth.

mar′tyr (mär′tər) *n.* **1.** person who willingly dies for a belief. —*v.* **2.** make martyr of. —**mar′tyr•dom**, *n.*

mar′vel (mär′vəl) *n.*, *v.*, **-veled, -veling.** —*n.* **1.** wonderful thing. —*v.* **2.** wonder (at). —**mar′vel•ous**, *adj.*

Marx′ism (märk′siz əm) *n.* doctrine of classless society; communism. —**Marx′ist**, *n.*, *adj.*

mar′zi•pan′ (mär′zə pan′) *n.* confection of almond paste and sugar.

mas•car′a (ma skar′ə) *n.* cosmetic for eyelashes.

mas′cot (mas′kot, -kət) n. person or thing that brings good luck.

mas′cu·line (mas′kyə lin) adj. of or like men. —**mas′cu·lin′i·ty,** n.

ma′ser (mā′zər) n. device for producing electromagnetic waves.

mash (mash) n. **1.** soft pulpy mass. —v. **2.** crush. —**mash′er,** n.

mask (mask) n. **1.** disguise or protection for face. —v. **2.** disguise or cover.

mas′och·ism (mas′ə kiz′əm, maz′-) n. pleasure in suffering.

ma′son (mā′sən) n. builder with stone, brick, etc. —**ma′son·ry,** n.

mas′quer·ade′ (mas′kə rād′) n., v., **-aded, -ading.** —n. **1.** disguise. **2.** party at which guests wear disguise. —v. **3.** wear disguise.

mass (mas) n. **1.** body of coherent matter. **2.** quantity or size. **3.** weight. **4.** (cap.) celebration of the Eucharist. **5. the masses,** common people as a whole. —v. **6.** form into a mass. —adj. **7.** of or affecting the masses. **8.** done on a large scale.

Mass., Massachusetts.

mas′sa·cre (mas′ə kər) n., v., **-cred, -cring.** —n. **1.** killing of many. —v. **2.** slaughter.

mas·sage′ (mə säzh′, -säj′) v., **-saged, -saging.** —v. **1.** treat body by rubbing or kneading. —n. **2.** such treatment. —**mas·seur′** (mə sûr′), n. —**mas·seuse′** (mə sōōs′ -sōōz′) n.fem.

mas′sive (mas′iv) adj. large; heavy.

mass media, means of communication that reaches large numbers of people.

mass noun, noun referring to indefinitely divisible substance or abstract noun.

mass′-produce′, v., **mass-produced, mass-producing.** produce in large quantities. —**mass production.**

mast (mast) n. upright pole.

mas′tec′to·my (ma stek′tə mē) n., pl. **-mies.** surgical removal of a breast.

mas′ter (mas′tər) n. **1.** person in control. **2.** male teacher. **3.** skilled person. —adj. **4.** chief. —v. **5.** conquer. **6.** become expert in.

mas′ter·ful, adj. asserting power.

mas′ter·ly, adj. highly skilled.

mas′ter·mind′, n. **1.** supreme planner. —v. **2.** plan as mastermind.

master of ceremonies, person who conducts events.

mas′ter·piece′, n. work of highest skill.

master′s degree, academic degree awarded to student who has completed at least one year of graduate study.

master sergeant, noncommissioned officer of highest rank.

mas′ter·stroke′, n. extremely skillful action.

mas′ter·y, n., pl. **-teries.** control.

mas′ti·cate′ (mas′ti kāt′) v., **-cated, -cating.** chew. —**mas′ti·ca′tion,** n.

mas′tiff (mas′tif) n. powerful dog.

mas′to·don′ (mas′tə don′) n. large extinct elephantlike mammal.

mas′toid (mas′toid) n. protuberance of bone behind ear.

mas′tur·bate′ (mas′tər bāt′) v., **-bated, -bating.** practice sexual self-gratification. —**mas′tur·ba′tion,** n.

mat (mat) n., v., **matted, matting,** adj. —n. **1.** covering for floor or other surface. **2.** border for picture. **3.** padding. **4.** thick mass. **5.** matte. —v. **6.** cover with mat. **7.** form into mat. —adj. **8.** matte.

mat′a·dor′ (mat′ə dôr′) n. bullfighter.

match (mach) n. **1.** stick chemically tipped to strike fire. **2.** person or thing resembling or equaling another. **3.** game. **4.** marriage. —v. **5.** equal. **6.** fit together. **7.** arrange marriage for.

match′less, adj. unequaled.

match′mak′er, n. arranger of marriages.

mate (māt) n., v., **mated, mating.** —n. **1.** one of pair. **2.** officer of merchant ship. —v. **3.** join; pair. **4.** copulate.

ma·te′ri·al (mə tēr′ē əl) n. **1.** substance of which thing is made. **2.** fabric. —adj. **3.** physical. **4.** pertinent. —**ma·te′ri·al·ly,** adv.

ma·te′ri·al·ism, n. **1.** devotion to material objects or wealth. **2.** belief that all reality is material.

ma·te′ri·al·ize′, v., **-ized, -izing.** give or assume material form.

ma·te′ri·el′ (mə tēr′ē el′) n. supplies, esp. military.

ma·ter′ni·ty (mə tûr′ni tē) n. motherhood. —adj. **3.** physical. —**ma·ter′nal,** adj.

math′e·mat′ics (math′ə mat′iks) n. science of numbers. —**math′e·mat′i·cal,** adj. —**math′e·ma·ti′cian** (-mə tish′ən) n.

mat′i·née′ (mat′n ā′) n. afternoon performance.

mat′ins (mat′nz) n. morning prayer.

ma′tri·arch′ (mā′trē ärk′) n. female ruler. —**ma′tri·ar′chy,** n.

mat′ri·cide′ (ma′tri sīd′, mā′-) n. killing one′s mother.

ma·tric′u·late′ (mə trik′yə lāt′) v., **-lated, -lating.** enroll in school.

mat′ri·mo′ny (ma′trə mō′nē) n., pl. **-nies.** marriage. —**mat′ri·mo′ni·al,** adj.

ma′trix (mā′triks, ma′-) n., pl. **-trices** (-tri sēz′), **-trixes. 1.** place or point where something originates. **2.** mold; model.

ma′tron (mā′trən) n. **1.** dignified married woman. **2.** female institutional officer. —**ma′tron·ly,** adj.

matte (mat) adj. **1.** having a dull surface, without luster. —n. **2.** dull surface or finish. Also, **mat.**

mat′ter (mat′ər) n. **1.** material. **2.** affair or trouble. **3.** pus. **4.** importance. —v. **5.** be of importance.

mat′ter-of-fact′, adj. adhering to fact; straightforward.

mat′ting (mat′ing) n. mat of rushes.

mat′tock (ma′tək) n. digging tool.

mat′tress (ma′tris) n. thick filled case for sleeping on.

ma·ture′ (mə tōōr′, -tyŏōr′, -chōōr′) adj., v., **-turer, -turest,** v., **-tured, -turing.** —adj. **1.** grown or developed. **2.** adult in manner or thought. **3.** payable. —v. **4.** become or make mature. —**ma·tu′ri·ty,** n.

mat′zo (mät′sə) n., pl. **-zos.** unleavened bread.

maud′lin (môd′lin) adj. weakly sentimental.

maul (môl) v. handle roughly.

maun′der (môn′dər) v. **1.** talk meanderingly. **2.** wander.

mau′so·le′um (mô′sə lē′əm, -zə-) n., pl. **-leums, -lea** (-lē′ə). tomb in form of building.

mauve (mōv, môv) n. pale purple.

ma′ven (mā′vən) n. expert.

mav′er·ick (mav′ər ik) n. **1.** unbranded calf. **2.** nonconformist.

maw (mô) n. mouth.

mawk′ish (mô′kish) adj. sickly sentimental. —**mawk′ish·ly,** adv.

max′i (mak′sē) n., pl. **-is.** ankle-length coat or skirt.

max′im (mak′sim) n. general truth.

max′i·mum (mak′sə məm) n. **1.** greatest degree or quantity. —adj. **2.** greatest possible.

may (mā) v., pt. **might** (mīt). (auxiliary verb of possibility or permission.)

May (mā) n. fifth month of year.

may′be, adv. perhaps.

May′day′, n. international radio distress call.

may′flow′er, n. plant that blossoms in May.

may′fly′, n., pl. **-flies.** insect with large transparent forewings.

may′hem (mā′hem, -əm) n. random violence.

may′on·naise′ (mā′ə nāz′) n. salad dressing made chiefly of egg yolks, oil, and vinegar. Also, Informal. **may′o.**

may′or (mā′ər) n. chief officer of city. —**may′or·al,** adj. —**may′or·al·ty,** n.

maze (māz) n. confusing arrangement of paths.

MD, Maryland. Also, **Md.**

M.D., Doctor of Medicine.

me (mē) pers. pronoun. objective case of I.

ME, Maine.

mead (mēd) n. liquor of fermented honey.

mead′ow (med′ō) n. level grassland.

mead′ow·lark′, n. common American songbird.

mea′ger (mē′gər) adj. poor; scanty.

meal (mēl) n. **1.** food served or eaten. **2.** coarse grain.

meal′y-mouthed′, adj. avoiding candid speech.

mean (mēn) v., **meant** (ment), **meaning,** adj., n. —v. **1.** intend (to do or signify). **2.** signify. —adj. **3.** poor; shabby. **4.** hostile; malicious. **5.** middle. —n. **6.** (pl.) method of achieving purpose. **7.** (pl.) money or property. **8.** intermediate quantity. —**mean′ly,** adv.

me·an′der (mē an′dər) v. wander aimlessly.

mean′ing, n. **1.** significance. —adj. **2.** significant. —**mean′ing·ful,** adj.

mean′time′, n. **1.** time between. —adv. Also, **mean′while′. 2.** in time between.

mea′sles (mē′zəlz) n. infectious disease marked by small red spots.

mea′sly (mē′zlē) adj., **-slier, -sliest.** Informal. miserably small.

meas′ure (mezh′ər) v., **-ured, -uring.** n. —v. **1.** ascertain size or extent. —n. **2.** process of measuring. **3.** dimensions. **4.** instrument or system of measuring. **5.** action. —**meas′ure·ment,** n.

meas′ured, adj. careful, deliberate.

meat (mēt) n. **1.** flesh of animals used as food. **2.** edible part of fruit, nut, etc. **3.** essential part; gist.

meat′y, adj., **-ier, -iest. 1.** with much meat. **2.** rewarding attention.

Mec′ca (mek′ə) n. **1.** city in Saudi Arabia, spiritual center of Islam. **2.** (often l.c.) place that attracts many.

me·chan′ic (mə kan′ik) n. skilled worker with machinery.

me·chan′i·cal, adj. of or operated by machinery.

me·chan′ics, n. science of motion and of action of forces on bodies.

mech′a·nism (mek′ə niz′əm) n. **1.** structure of machine. **2.** piece of machinery. —**mech′a·nist,** n.

mech′a·nize′, v., **-nized, -nizing.** adapt to machinery.

med′al (med′l) n. badgelike metal object given for merit.

med′al·ist, n. medal winner.

me·dal′lion (mə dal′yən) n. large medal or medallike ornament.

med'dle (med'l) *v.*, **-dled, -dling.** interfere; tamper. —**med'dler,** *n.* —**med'dle•some,** *adj.*

me•di•a (mē'dē ə) *n.pl.* the means of mass communication.

me'di•an (mē'dē ən) *adj.*, *n.* middle.

me'di•ate' (mē'dē āt') *v.*, **-ated, -ating.** settle (dispute) between parties. —**me'di•a'tor,** *n.*

med'ic (med'ik) *n. Informal.* doctor or medical aide.

Med'i•caid' (med'i kād') *n.* state- and federal-supported medical care for low-income persons.

med'i•cal, *adj.* 1. of medicine. 2. curative. —**med'i•cal•ly,** *adv.*

me•dic'a•ment (mə dik'ə mənt, med'i kə-) *n.* healing substance.

Med'i•care' (med'i kâr') *n.* government-supported medical insurance for those 65 years old or more.

med'i•cate' (-,) *v.*, **-cated, -cating.** treat with medicine. —**med'i•ca'tion,** *n.*

me•dic'i•nal (mə dis'ə nl) *adj.* curative. —**me•dic'i•nal•ly,** *adv.*

med'i•cine (med'ə sin) *n.* 1. substance used in treating disease. 2. art of restoring physical health.

medicine man, among American Indians, person believed to have magical powers.

me'di•e•val (mē'dē ē'vəl, mid ē'-) *adj.* of the Middle Ages. Also, **me'di•ae'val.**

me'di•e•val•ism, *n.* a characteristic of the Middle Ages.

me'di•e•val•ist, *n.* expert in medieval history, etc.

me'di•o'cre (mē'dē ō'kər) *adj.* undistinguished. —**me'di•oc'ri•ty** (-ok'ri tē) *n.*

med'i•tate' (med'i tāt') *v.*, **-tated, -tating.** think intensely. —**med'i•ta'tion,** *n.* —**med'i•ta'tive,** *adj.*

me'di•um (mē'dē əm) *n.*, *pl.* **-diums** for 1–5, **-dia** (-dē ə) for 1–3, 5, *adj.* —*n.* 1. something intermediate or moderate. 2. means of doing. 3. environment. 4. person believed able to communicate with dead. 5. means of mass communication. —*adj.* 6. intermediate.

med'ley (med'lē) *n.* mixture, as of tunes.

meek (mēk) *adj.* submissive.

meer'schaum (mēr'shəm, -shôm) *n.* claylike mineral, used for tobacco pipes.

meet (mēt) *v.*, **met** (met), **meeting,** *n.*, *adj.* —*v.* 1. come into contact with. 2. make acquaintance of. 3. satisfy. —*n.* 4. equal. 5. meeting, esp. for sport. —*adj.* 6. proper.

meet'ing, *n.* 1. a coming together. 2. persons gathered.

mega-, *prefix.* 1. one million. 2. large.

meg'a•hertz' (meg'ə hûrts') *n.*, *pl.* **-hertz.** *Elect.* one million cycles per second.

meg'a•lo•ma'ni•a (meg'ə lō mā'nē ə) *n.* delusion of greatness, riches, etc.

meg'a•phone' (meg'ə fōn') *n.* cone-shaped device for magnifying sound.

meg'a•ton', *n.* one million tons, esp. of TNT, as equivalent in explosive force.

mel'a•mine (mel'ə mēn') *n.* crystalline solid used in manufacturing resins.

mel'an•cho'li•a (mel'ən kō'lē ə) *n.* mental state of severe depression.

mel'an•chol'y (mel'ən kol'ē) *n.*, *pl.* **-cholies.** 1. low spirits; depression. —*adj.* 2. sad.

mé•lange' (mā länzh', -länj') *n.* mixture.

mel'a•nin (mel'ə nin) *n.* pigment accounting for dark color of skin, hair, etc.

mel'a•no'ma (-nō'mə) *n.* darkly pigmented skin tumor.

meld (meld) *v.* display combination of cards for a score.

me'lee (mā'lā) *n.* confused, general fight.

mel'io•rate' (mēl'yə rāt') *v.*, **-rated, -rating.** improve.

mel•lif'lu•ous (mə lif'lōō əs) *adj.* soft and sweet in speech.

mel'low (mel'ō) *adj.* 1. soft and rich. 2. genial. —*v.* 3. make or become mellow.

me•lo'de•on (mə lō'dē ən) *n.* reed organ.

me•lo'di•ous, *adj.* tuneful.

mel'o•dra'ma (mel'ə drä'mə, -dram'ə) *n.* play emphasizing theatrical effects and strong emotions.

mel'o•dra•mat'ic, *adj.* 1. of melodrama. 2. overly emotional.

mel'o•dy (mel'ə dē) *n.*, *pl.* **-dies.** arrangement of musical sounds. —**me•lod'ic** (mə lod'ik) *adj.*

mel'on (mel'ən) *n.* edible fruit of certain annual vines.

melt (melt) *v.*, **melted, melted** or **molten, melting.** 1. make or become liquid, esp. by heat. 2. soften.

melt'down', *n.* melting of nuclear reactor core, causing escape of radiation.

melting pot, place where blending of peoples, races, or cultures takes place.

mem'ber (mem'bər) *n.* 1. part of structure. 2. one belonging to organization. —**mem'ber•ship',** *n.*

mem'brane (mem'brān) *n.* thin film of tissue in animals and plants.

me•men'to (mə men'tō) *n.*, *pl.* **-tos, -toes.** reminder.

mem'oir (mem'wär, -wôr) *n.* 1. autobiography. —*pl.* 2. personal recollection.

mem'o•ra•bil'i•a (-ər ə bil'ē ə, -bil'yə) *n.pl.* souvenirs.

mem'o•ra•ble, *adj.* worth remembering. —**mem'o•ra•bly,** *adv.*

mem'o•ran'dum (mem'ə ran'dəm) *n.*, *pl.* **-dums, -da** (-də). written statement or reminder. Also, **mem'o** (mem'ō).

me•mo'ri•al (mə môr'ē əl) *n.* 1. something honoring memory of a person or event. —*adj.* 2. serving as memorial.

mem'o•rize' (mem'ə rīz') *v.*, **-rized, -rizing.** commit to memory.

mem'o•ry, *n.*, *pl.* **-ries.** 1. faculty of remembering. 2. something that is remembered. 3. length of time of recollection. 4. capacity of computer to store data.

men'ace (men'is) *v.*, **-aced, -acing,** *n.* —*v.* 1. threaten evil to. —*n.* 2. something that threatens.

me•nag'er•ie (mə naj'ə rē, -nazh'-) *n.* collection of animals.

mend (mend) *v.* repair; improve.

men•da'cious (men dā'shəs) *adj.* untruthful. —**men•dac'i•ty** (-das'i tē) *n.*

men'di•cant (men'di kənt) *n.* beggar.

me'ni•al (mē'nē əl) *adj.* 1. humble; servile. —*n.* 2. servant.

me•nin'ges (mi nin'jēz) *n.pl.*, *sing.* **me'ninx** (mē'ningks). three membranes covering brain and spinal cord.

men'in•gi'tis (men'in jī'tis) *n.* inflammation of meninges.

men'o•pause' (men'ə pôz') *n.* cessation of menses, usually between ages of 45 and 50.

me•no'rah (mə nôr'ə) *n.* symbolic candelabrum used by Jews during Hanukkah.

men'stru•a'tion (men'strōō ā'shən) *n.* monthly discharge of blood from uterus. —**men'stru•al,** *adj.* —**men'stru•ate',** *v.*, **-ated, -ating.**

men'sur•a•ble (-shər ə bəl, -sər ə-bəl) *adj.* measurable.

mens'wear', *n.* clothing for men.

-ment, suffix meaning: action or resulting state, as *abridgment*; product, as *fragment*; means, as *ornament*.

men'tal (men'tl) *adj.* of or in the mind. —**men'tal•ly,** *adv.*

men•tal'i•ty (-tal'i tē) *n.*, *pl.* **-ties.** 1. mental ability. 2. characteristic mental attitude.

men'thol (men'thôl, -thol) *n.* colorless alcohol from peppermint oil. —**men'thol•at'ed** (-thə lā'tid) *adj.*

men'tion (men'shən) *v.* 1. speak or write. —*n.* 2. reference.

men'tor (men'tôr, -tər) *n.* adviser.

men'u (men'yōō, mā'nyōō) *n.* list of dishes that can be served.

me•ow' (mē ou', myou) *n.* 1. sound cat makes. —*v.* 2. make such sound.

mer'can•tile' (mûr'kən tēl', -tīl', -til) *adj.* of or engaged in trade.

mer'ce•nar'y (mûr'sə ner'ē) *adj.*, *n.*, *pl.* **-naries.** —*adj.* 1. acting only for profit. —*n.* 2. hired soldier.

mer'chan•dise', *n.*, *v.*, **-dised, -dising.** —*n.* (mûr'chən dīz', -dīs') 1. goods; wares. —*v.* (-dīz') 2. buy and sell.

mer'chant (-chənt) *n.* person who buys and sells goods for profit.

merchant marine, commercial vessels of nation.

mer•cu'ri•al (mər kyŏŏr'ē əl) *adj.* 1. of mercury. 2. unpredictable.

mer'cu•ry (mûr'kyə rē) *n.* 1. heavy metallic element. 2. (*cap.*) one of the planets.

mer'cy (mûr'sē) *n.*, *pl.* **-cies.** 1. pity; compassion. 2. act of compassion. —**mer'ci•ful,** *adj.*

mere (mēr) *adj.* only. —**mere'ly,** *adv.*

merge (mûrj) *v.*, **merged, merging.** combine. —**merg'er,** *n.*

me•rid'i•an (mə rid'ē ən) *n.* circle on earth's surface passing through the poles.

me•ringue' (mə rang') *n.* egg whites and sugar beaten together.

me•ri'no (mə rē'nō) *n.*, *pl.* **-nos.** 1. kind of sheep. 2. soft woolen yarn.

mer'it (mer'it) *n.* 1. excellence or good quality. —*v.* 2. deserve. —**mer'i•to'ri•ous** (-i tôr'ē əs) *adj.*

mer'maid' (mûr'mād') *n.* imaginary sea creature, half woman and half fish. —**mer'man',** *n.masc.*

mer'ry (mer'ē) *adj.*, **-rier, -riest.** gay; joyous. —**mer'ri•ly,** *adv.*

mer'ry-go-round', *n.* revolving amusement ride.

mer'ry•mak'ing, *n.* festivities; hilarity. —**mer'ry•ma'ker,** *n.*

me'sa (mā'sə) *n.* high, steep-walled plateau.

mesh (mesh) *n.* 1. open space of net. 2. net itself. 3. engagement of gears. —*v.* 4. catch in mesh. 5. engage. 6. match or interlock.

mes'mer•ize' (mez'mə rīz') *v.*, **-ized, -izing.** hypnotize; spellbind. —**mes'mer•ism** (-mə riz'əm) *n.*

Mes'o•zo'ic (mez'ə zō'ik) *adj.* pertaining to geologic era occurring between 230 and 65 million years ago.

mes•quite' (me skēt', mes'kēt) *n.* tree of southwest U.S.

mess (mes) *n.* 1. dirty or disorderly condition. 2. group taking meals together regularly. 3. meals so taken.

—v. **4.** make dirty or untidy. **5.** eat in company. —**mess′y,** adj.

mes′sage (mes′ij) n. communication.

mes′sen·ger (mes′ən jər) n. bearer of message.

Mes·si′ah (mi sī′ə) n. **1.** expected deliverer. **2.** (in Christian theology) Jesus Christ.

mes·ti′zo (me stē′zō) n., pl. **-zos, -zoes.** person part-Spanish, part-Indian. Also, **mes·ti′za** (-zə) fem.

meta-, prefix meaning: **1.** after or beyond, as metaphysics. **2.** behind, as metacarpus. **3.** change, as metamorphosis.

me·tab′o·lism (mə tab′ə liz′əm) n. biological processes of converting food into matter and matter into energy. —**met′a·bol′ic** (ə bol′ik) adj.

met′al (met′l) n. **1.** elementary substance such as gold or copper. **2.** mettle. —**me·tal′lic** (mə tal′ik) adj. —**met′al·ware′,** n.

met′al·lur·gy (met′l ûr′jē) n. science of working with metals.

met′a·mor′phose (met′ə môr′fōz, -fōs) v., **-phosed, -phosing.** transform.

met′a·mor′pho·sis (-fə sis) n., pl. **-ses** (-sēz′). change.

met′a·phor (met′ə fôr′, -fər) n. figure of speech using analogy. —**met′a·phor′i·cal,** adj.

met′a·phys′ics, n. branch of philosophy concerned with ultimate nature of reality. —**met′a·phys′ical,** adj. —**met′a·phy·si′cian,** n.

me·tas′ta·size′ (mə tas′tə sīz′) v., **-sized, -sizing.** spread from one to another part of the body. —**me·tas′ta·sis** (-sis) n.

mete (mēt) v., **meted, meting.** allot.

me′te·or (mē′tē ər, -ôr′) n. celestial body passing through earth's atmosphere.

me′te·or′ic (-ôr′ik) adj. **1.** of meteors. **2.** sudden and spectacular.

me′te·or·ite′ (-ə rīt′) n. meteor reaching earth.

me′te·or·ol′o·gy (-ə rol′ə jē) n. science of atmospheric phenomena, esp. weather. —**me′te·or·o·log′i·cal** (-ər ə loj′i kəl) adj. —**me′te·or·ol′o·gist,** n.

me′ter (mē′tər) n. **1.** unit of length in metric system, equal to 39.37 inches. **2.** rhythmic arrangement of words. **3.** device for measuring flow. —v. **4.** measure. Also, Brit., **me′tre.** —**met′ric** (me′trik), **met′ri·cal,** adj.

meth′a·done′ (meth′ə dōn′) n. synthetic narcotic used in treating heroin addiction.

meth′ane (meth′ān) n. colorless, odorless, flammable gas.

meth′a·nol′ (meth′ə nôl′) n. colorless liquid used as solvent, fuel, or antifreeze. Also, **methyl alcohol.**

meth′od (meth′əd) n. system of doing. —**me·thod′i·cal** (mə thod′i kəl), adj. —**meth′od·i·cal·ly,** adv.

meth′od·ol′o·gy (-ə dol′ə jē) n., pl. **-gies.** system of methods and principles.

me·tic′u·lous (mə tik′yə ləs) adj. minutely careful.

mé′tier (mā′tyā) n. field of activity in which one has special ability. Also, **me′tier.**

met′ric (me′trik) adj. of decimal system of weights and measures, based on meter and gram.

met′ro·nome′ (me′trə nōm′) n. device for marking tempo.

me·trop′o·lis (mi trop′ə lis) n. great city.

met′ro·pol′i·tan (me′trə pol′i tn)

adj. **1.** of or in city. **2.** of cities and urban areas.

met′tle (met′l) n. **1.** spirit. **2.** disposition.

met′tle·some (-səm) adj. spirited; courageous.

mew (myōō) n. **1.** cry of a cat. —v. **2.** emit a mew.

mews, n. street with dwellings converted from stables.

Mex′i·can, (mek′si kən) n. native of Mexico. —**Mexican,** adj.

mez′za·nine′ (mez′ə nēn′, mez′ə nēn′) n. low story between two main floors; balcony.

mez′zo-so·pran′o (met′sō-, med′zō-) n. voice, musical part, or singer intermediate in range between soprano and contralto.

M.F.A., Master of Fine Arts.

MI, Michigan.

mi·as′ma (mī az′mə, mē-) n., pl. **-mata** (-mə tə), **-mas.** vapors from decaying organic matter.

mi′ca (mī′kə) n. shiny mineral occurring in thin layers.

Mich., Michigan.

micro-, prefix meaning: **1.** extremely small. **2.** one millionth.

mi′crobe (mī′krōb) n. microorganism, esp. one causing disease.

mi′cro·brew′er·y, n. small brewery usu. producing exotic or high quality beer.

mi′cro·chip′, n. chip (def. 3).

mi′cro·com·put′er, n. compact computer with less capability than minicomputer.

mi′cro·cosm (mī′krə koz′əm) n. world in miniature.

mi′cro·fiche′ (-fēsh′) n. small sheet of microfilm.

mi′cro·film′, n. **1.** very small photograph of book page, etc. —v. **2.** make microfilm of.

mi·crom′e·ter (mī krom′i tər) n. device for measuring minute distances.

mi′cron (mī′kron) n. millionth part of a meter.

mi′cro·or′gan·ism′ (mī′krō-) n. microscopic organism.

mi′cro·phone′ (mī′krə fōn′) n. instrument for changing sound waves into changes in electric current.

mi′cro·proc′es·sor (mī′krō pros′es-ər, -ə sər; esp. Brit. -prō′ses ər, -sə sər) n. computer circuit that performs all functions of CPU.

mi′cro·scope′ (mī′krə skōp′) n. instrument for inspecting minute objects.

mi′cro·scop′ic (-skop′ik) adj. **1.** of microscopes. **2.** extremely small.

mi′cro·sur′ger·y (mī′krō sûr′jə rē) n. surgery performed under magnification.

mi′cro·wave′, n. **1.** short radio wave used in radar, cooking, etc. **2.** oven that uses microwaves to cook food. —v. **3.** cook in microwave oven.

mid (mid) adj. **1.** middle. —prep. **2.** amid.

mid′day′ (-dā′, -dā′) n. noon.

mid′dle (mid′l) adj. **1.** equally distant from given limits. **2.** medium. —n. **3.** middle part.

Middle Ages, period of European history, about A.D. 476 to 1500.

middle class, class of people intermediate between the poor and the wealthy.

Middle East, area including Israel and Arab countries of NE Africa and SW Asia.

Middle English, English language of period c1150–1475.

mid′dle·man′, n. merchant who buys direct from producer.

middle-of-the-road, adj. moderate.

middle school, school encompassing grades 5 or 6 through 8.

mid′dling, adj. **1.** medium. **2.** mediocre.

midge (mij) n. minute fly.

midg′et (mij′it) n. very small person or thing.

mid′land (-lənd) n. interior of country.

mid′night′, n. 12 o'clock at night.

mid′point′, n. point at or near the middle.

mid′riff (-rif) n. part of body between the chest and abdomen.

mid′ship′man, n., pl. **-men.** rank of student at U.S. Naval or Coast Guard academy.

midst (midst) n. middle.

mid′sum′mer (-sum′ər, -sum′-) n. middle of the summer.

mid′term, n. **1.** halfway point of school term. **2.** examination given at midterm.

mid′way′ adj., adv. (mid′wā′) **1.** in or to middle. —n. (-wā′) **2.** area of games and shows at carnival.

mid′wife′, n., pl. **-wives.** woman who assists at childbirth.

mid′win′ter (-win′tər, -win′-) n. middle of winter.

mien (mēn) n. air; bearing.

miff (mif) n. petty quarrel.

miffed (mift), adj. irritated; offended.

might (mīt) v. **1.** pt. of **may.** —n. **2.** strength; power.

might′y, adj., **-ier, -iest,** adv. —adj. **1.** powerful; huge. —adv. **2.** Informal. very. —**might′i·ness,** n.

mi′graine (mī′grān) n. painful headache.

mi′grate (-grāt) v., **-grated, -grating.** go from one region to another. —**mi·gra′tion,** n. —**mi′gra·to′ry** (-grə tôr′-ē) adj. —**mi′grant,** adj., n.

mi·ka′do (mi kä′dō) n., pl. **-dos.** a title of emperor of Japan.

mike (mīk) n. Informal. microphone.

mil (mil) n. one thousandth of inch.

mild (mīld) adj. gentle; temperate.

mil′dew′ (mil′dōō′, -dyōō′) n. **1.** discoloration caused by fungus. —v. **2.** affect with mildew.

mile (mīl) n. unit of distance, equal on land to 5280 ft.

mile′age (mī′lij) n. **1.** miles traveled. **2.** travel allowance.

mile′stone′, n. **1.** marker showing road distance. **2.** important event.

mi·lieu′ (mil yōō′, mēl-; Fr. mē lyœ′) n., pl. **-lieus, -lieux.** environment.

mil′i·tant (mil′i tənt) adj. warlike; aggressive.

mil′i·ta·rism (-tə riz′əm) n. **1.** military spirit. **2.** domination by military. —**mil′i·ta·rist,** n.

mil′i·ta·rize′, v., **-ized, -izing.** equip with military weapons.

mil′i·tar′y (-ter′ē) adj., n., pl. **-taries.** —adj. **1.** of armed forces, esp. on land. —n. **2.** armed forces or soldiers collectively.

military police, soldiers who perform police duties within army.

mil′i·tate′ (-tāt′) v., **-tated, -tating.** act (for or against).

mi·li′tia (mi lish′ə) n. organization for emergency military service. —**mi·li′tia·man,** n.

milk (milk) n. **1.** liquid secreted by female mammals to feed their young. —v. **2.** draw milk from. —**milk′y,** adj. —**milk′maid′,** n.

milk′man′, *n.*, *pl.* -men. man who sells or delivers milk.

milk′weed′, *n.* plant with milky juice.

Milk′y Way′, *Astron.* galaxy containing sun and earth.

mill (mil) *n.* **1.** place where manufacturing is done. **2.** device for grinding. **3.** place where grain is ground. **4.** one tenth of a cent. —*v.* **5.** grind or treat with mill. **6.** groove edges of (coin). **7.** move about in confusion. —**mill′er**, *n.*

mil·len′ni·um (mi len′ē əm) *n.*, *pl.* -niums, -nia (-nē ə). period of a thousand years.

mill′let (-it) *n.* cereal grass.

milli-, prefix meaning thousand or thousandth.

mil′liard (mil′yərd, -yärd) *n.* *Brit.* one billion.

mil′li·gram′ (mil′i gram′) *n.* one thousandth of gram.

mil′li·li·ter, *n.* one thousandth of liter.

mil′li·me·ter, *n.* one thousandth of meter.

mil′li·ner (mil′ə nər) *n.* person who makes or sells women's hats.

mil′li·ner′y (-ner′ē, -nə rē) *n.* **1.** women's hats. **2.** business or trade of a milliner.

mil′lion (mil′yən) *n.*, *adj.* 1000 times 1000. —**mil′lionth**, *adj.*, *n.*

mil′lion·aire′ (mil′yə nâr′) *n.* person having a million dollars or more.

mill′race′, *n.* channel for current of water driving mill wheel.

mill′stone′, *n.* **1.** stone for grinding grain. **2.** heavy mental or emotional burden.

mill′stream′, *n.* stream in millrace.

mime (mīm, mēm) *n.* pantomimist; clown.

mim′e·o·graph′ (mim′ē ə graf′) *n.* **1.** stencil device for duplicating. —*v.* **2.** copy with mimeograph.

mim′ic (mim′ik) *v.*, -icked, -icking, *n.* —*v.* **1.** imitate speech or actions of. —*n.* **2.** person who mimics. —**mim′ic·ry**, *n.*

mi·mo′sa (mi mō′sa, -zə) *n.* semitropical tree or shrub.

min′a·ret′ (min′ə ret′) *n.* tower for calling Muslims to prayer.

mince (mins) *v.*, minced, mincing. **1.** chop fine. **2.** speak, move, or behave with affected elegance.

mince′meat′, *n.* cooked mixture of finely chopped meat, raisins, spices, etc., used in pies.

mind (mīnd) *n.* **1.** thinking part of human or animal. **2.** intellect. **3.** inclination. —*v.* **4.** heed; obey.

mind′-blow′ing, *adj.* **1.** astounding. **2.** producing hallucinogenic effect.

mind′ful, *adj.* careful.

mind′less, *adj.* **1.** heedless. **2.** requiring no intelligence.

mine (mīn) *pron.*, *n.*, *v.*, mined, mining. —*pron.* **1.** possessive form of I. —*n.* **2.** excavation in earth for resources. **3.** stationary explosive device used in war. **4.** abundant source. —*v.* **5.** lay explosive mines. **6.** work in mine. —**min′er**, *n.*

min′er·al (min′ər əl) *n.* **1.** inorganic substance. **2.** substance obtained by mining. —*adj.* **3.** of minerals.

min′er·al·o·gy (-ə rol′ə jē, -ral′ə-) *n.* science of minerals.

mineral water, water containing dissolved mineral salts or gases.

min′e·stro′ne (min′ə strō′nē) *n.* thick vegetable soup.

mine′sweep′er, *n.* ship used to remove explosive mines.

min′gle (ming′gəl) *v.*, -gled, -gling. associate; mix.

min′i (min′ē) *n.* small version.

mini-, prefix meaning: **1.** smaller than others of its kind. **2.** very short.

min′i·a·ture (min′ē ə chər, min′ə-) *n.* **1.** greatly reduced form. **2.** tiny painting. —*adj.* **3.** on small scale.

min′i·a·tur·ize′, *v.*, -ized, -izing. make in or reduce to very small size. —**min′i·a·tur·i·za′tion**, *n.*

min′i·bus′, *n.* small bus.

min′i·com·put′er, *n.* computer with capabilities between those of microcomputer and mainframe.

min′im (min′əm) *n.* smallest unit of liquid measure.

min′i·mal·ism (-mə liz′əm) *n.* style, as in art or music, that is spare and simple.

min′i·mize′ (-mīz′) *v.*, -mized, -mizing. make minimum.

min′i·mum (-məm) *n.* **1.** least possible quantity, degree, etc. —*adj.* **2.** Also, **min′i·mal** (-mal) lowest.

min′ion (min′yən) *n.* servile follower.

min′is·ter (min′ə stər) *n.* **1.** person authorized to conduct worship. **2.** government representative abroad. **3.** head of governmental department. **4.** give care. —**min′is·te′ri·al** (-stēr′ē əl) *adj.* —**min′is·tra′tion**, *n.*

min′is·try (-ə strē) *n.*, *pl.* -tries. **1.** religious calling. **2.** clergy. **3.** duty or office of a department of government. **4.** body of executive officials. **5.** act of ministering.

min′i·van′, *n.* small passenger van.

mink (mingk) *n.* semiaquatic mammal or its soft brown fur.

Minn., Minnesota.

min′now (min′ō) *n.* tiny fish.

mi′nor (mī′nər) *adj.* **1.** lesser in size or importance. **2.** under legal age. —*n.* **3.** person under legal age.

mi·nor′i·ty (mi nôr′i tē, mī-) *n.*, *pl.* -ties. **1.** smaller number or part. **2.** relatively small population group. **3.** state or time of being under legal age.

min′strel (min′strəl) *n.* **1.** musician or singer, esp. in Middle Ages. **2.** white performer with face blacked singing black American songs.

mint (mint) *n.* **1.** aromatic herb. **2.** place where money is coined. **3.** huge sum. —*v.* **4.** make coins.

min′u·et′ (min′yoo et′) *n.* stately dance.

mi′nus (mī′nəs) *prep.* **1.** less. —*adj.* **2.** less than.

mi·nus·cule (min′ə skyool′, mi nus′-kyool) *adj.* tiny.

min′ute *n.* (min′it) **1.** sixty seconds. **2.** (*pl.*) record of proceedings. —*adj.* (mī nōōt′, -nyōōt′) **3.** extremely small. **4.** attentive to detail. —**mi·nute′ly**, *adv.*

mi·nu′ti·ae (mi nōō′shē ē′) *n.pl.* trifling matters.

minx (mingks) *n.* saucy girl.

mir′a·cle (mir′ə kəl) *n.* supernatural act or effect. —**mi·rac′u·lous** (mi-rak′yə ləs) *adj.*

mi·rage′ (mi räzh′) *n.* atmospheric illusion in which images of far-distant objects are seen.

mire (mī°r) *n.*, *v.*, mired, miring. —*n.* **1.** swamp. **2.** deep mud. —*v.* **3.** stick fast in mire. **4.** soil.

mir′ror (mir′ər) *n.* **1.** reflecting surface. —*v.* **2.** reflect.

mirth (mûrth) *n.* gaiety and laughter. —**mirth′less**, *adj.*

mis-, prefix meaning: **1.** wrong, as *misconduct*. **2.** lack of, as *mistrust*.

mis′ad·ven′ture (mis′ad ven′chər) *n.* mishap.

mis′al·li′ance, *n.* incompatible association.

mis′an·thrope′ (mis′ən thrōp′, miz′-) *n.* hater of humanity. —**mis′an·throp′ic** (-throp′ik) *adj.*

mis′ap·ply′, *v.*, -plied, -plying. use wrongly. —**mis′ap·pli·ca′tion**, *n.*

mis′ap·pre·hend′, *v.* misunderstand. —**mis′ap·pre·hen′sion** (-hen′-shən) *n.*

mis′ap·pro′pri·ate′ (-āt′) *v.*, -ated, -ating. use wrongly as one's own.

mis′be·got′ten, *adj.* ill-conceived.

mis′be·have′, *v.*, -haved, -having. behave badly. —**mis′be·hav′ior**, *n.*

misc., miscellaneous.

mis·cal′cu·late′, *v.*, -lated, -lating. judge badly.

mis·call′, *v.* call by a wrong name.

mis·car′riage, *n.* **1.** premature birth resulting in death of fetus. **2.** failure.

mis·car′ry (mis kar′ē; *for 1 also* mis′-kar′ē) *v.*, -ried, -rying. **1.** have miscarriage. **2.** go wrong.

mis·cast′, *v.* cast in unsuitable role.

mis′cel·la′ne·ous (mis′ə lā′nē əs) *adj.* unclassified; various. —**mis′cel·la′ny** (-ə lā′nē) *n.*

mis·chance′, *n.* bad luck.

mis′chief (mis′chif) *n.* **1.** trouble, caused willfully. **2.** tendency to tease. —**mis′chie·vous** (mis′chə vəs), *adj.* —**Pronunciation.** The word MIS-CHIEVOUS is pronounced with three syllables. The pronunciation (mis chē′vē-əs), with four syllables, is usually considered nonstandard. Note that although a spelling *mischievious*, which reflects this nonstandard pronunciation by including an extra *i* after the *v*, was occasionally seen between the 16th and 19th centuries, it is not considered a correct spelling today.

mis′con·ceive′, *v.*, -ceived, -ceiving. misunderstand. —**mis′con·cep′tion**, *n.*

mis·con′duct (-kon′dukt) *n.* improper or illegal conduct.

mis′con·strue′ (mis′kən strōō′) *v.*, -strued, -struing. misinterpret.

mis′cre·ant (mis′krē ənt) *n.* villain.

mis·deed′, *n.* immoral deed.

mis′de·mean′or, *n.* minor offense.

mise-en-scène′ (mē zän sen′) *n.*, *pl.* **mise-en-scènes** (-senz′). **1.** placement of actors, scenery, and properties on stage. **2.** surroundings.

mi′ser (mī′zər) *n.* hoarder of wealth. —**mi′ser·ly**, *adj.*

mis′er·a·ble (miz′ər ə bəl) *adj.* **1.** wretched. **2.** deplorable. **3.** contemptible; despicable.

mis′er·y, *n.*, *pl.* -eries. wretched condition.

mis·fea′sance (mis fē′zəns) *n.* wrongful exercise of lawful authority.

mis·fire′ (mis fī°r′) *v.*, -fired, -firing. fail to fire.

mis·fit′ *n.* **1.** (mis fit′, mis′fit′) poor fit. **2.** (mis′fit′) maladjusted person.

mis·for′tune, *n.* bad luck.

mis·giv′ing, *n.* doubt.

mis·guid′ed, *adj.* mistaken; ill-informed.

mis·han′dle, *v.*, -dled, -dling. **1.** handle roughly. **2.** manage badly.

mis′hap (mis′hap, mis hap′) *n.* unlucky accident.

mish′mash′ (mish′mäsh′, -mash′) *n.* jumble; hodgepodge.

mis′in·form′, *v.* give false information to. —**mis′in·for·ma′tion**, *n.*

mis′in·ter·pret, *v.* interpret wrongly.

mis·judge′, *v.*, -judged, -judging. judge wrongly.

mis·lay′, *v.*, **-laid**, **-laying**. **1.** put in place later forgotten. **2.** misplace.

mis·lead′ (-lēd′) *v.*, **-led**, **-leading**. **1.** lead in wrong direction. **2.** lead into error, as in conduct.

mis·man′age, *v.*, **-aged**, **-aging**. manage badly.

mis·match′ *v.* **1.** (mis mach′) match unsuitably. —*n.* (mis mach′, mis′-mach′) **2.** unsuitable match.

mis·no′mer (mis nō′mər) *n.* misapplied name.

mi·sog′a·my (mi sog′ə mē, mī-) *n.* hatred of marriage.

mi·sog′y·ny (mi soj′ə nē, mī-) *n.* hatred of women. —**mi·sog′y·nist,** *n.*

mis·place′, *v.*, **-placed**, **-placing**. **1.** forget location of. **2.** place unwisely.

mis′print′ (mis′print′, mis print′) *n.* error in printing.

mis′pro·nounce′, *v.*, **-nounced**, **-nouncing**. pronounce wrongly.

mis·quote′, *v.*, **-quoted**, **-quoting**. quote incorrectly.

mis·read′ (-rēd′) *v.*, **-read** (red′), **-reading**. **1.** read wrongly. **2.** misinterpret.

mis′rep·re·sent′, *v.* give wrong idea of.

mis·rule′, *n.* bad or unwise rule. —**mis·rule′**, *v.*

miss (mis) *v.* **1.** fail to hit, catch, meet, do, etc. **2.** feel absence of. —*n.* **3.** (*cap.*) title of respect for unmarried woman. **4.** girl. **5.** failure to hit, catch, etc.

Miss., Mississippi.

mis′sal (mis′əl) *n.* book of prayers, etc., for celebrating Mass.

mis·shap′en, *adj.* deformed.

mis′sile (mis′əl; *esp. Brit.* -īl) *n.* object thrown or shot, as lance or bullet.

mis′sion (mish′ən) *n.* **1.** group sent abroad for specific work. **2.** duty. **3.** air operation against enemy. **4.** missionary post.

mis′sion·ar′y (-ə ner′ē) *n.*, *pl.* **-aries**, *adj.* —*n.* **1.** person sent to propagate religious faith. —*adj.* **2.** of religious missions.

mis′sive (mis′iv) *n.* letter.

mis·spell′, *v.* spell wrongly.

mis·spend′, *v.*, **-spent**, **-spending**. squander.

mis·state′, *v.*, **-stated**, **-stating**. state wrongly.

mis·step′, *n.* error.

mist (mist) *n.* light, thin fog. —**mist′y**, *adj.*

mis·take′ (mi stāk′) *n.*, *v.*, **-took**, **-taken**, **-taking**. —*n.* **1.** error in judgment, action, or belief. —*v.* **2.** take or regard wrongly. **3.** misunderstand. **4.** be in error.

Mis′ter (mis′tər) *n.* title of address for man. *Abbr.*: **Mr.**

mis′tle·toe′ (mis′əl tō′) *n.* parasitic plant with waxy white berries.

mis·treat′, *v.* treat badly. —**mis·treat′ment,** *n.*

mis′tress (mis′tris) *n.* **1.** female in control. **2.** female lover of married man.

mis·tri′al, *n.* trial ended without verdict because of legal error or inability of jury to agree on verdict.

mis·trust′, *n.* lack of trust. —**mis·trust′**, *v.*

mis′un·der·stand′, *v.*, **-stood**, **-standing**. understand wrongly. —**mis′un·der·stand′ing,** *n.*

mis·use′ *n.*, *v.*, **-used**, **-using**. —*n.* (-yōōs′) **1.** improper use. —*v.* (-yōōz′) **2.** use badly or wrongly. **3.** abuse.

mite (mīt) *n.* **1.** tiny parasitic insect. **2.** small thing or bit.

mi′ter (mī′tər) *v.* **1.** join two pieces on diagonal. —*n.* **2.** such joint. **3.** tall cap worn by bishops. Also, *Brit.*, **mi′tre.**

mit′i·gate′ (mit′i gāt′) *v.*, **-gated**, **-gating**. make less severe.

mi·to′sis (mī tō′sis) *n.* method of cell division.

mitt (mit) *n.* thick glove.

mit′ten (mit′n) *n.* fingerless glove.

mix (miks) *v.*, *n.* —*v.* **1.** put together; combine. **2.** associate. **3.** confuse. —*n.* **4.** mixture. **5.** mess.

mixed number, number consisting of whole number and fraction or decimal.

mix′ture (-chər) *n.* act or product of mixing.

mix′-up′, *n.* state of confusion.

ml, milliliter.

mm, millimeter.

MN, Minnesota.

mne·mon′ic (ni mon′ik) *adj.* aiding memory.

MO, **1.** Also, **Mo.** Missouri. **2.** modus operandi.

moan (mōn) *n.* **1.** low groan. —*v.* **2.** utter moans.

moat (mōt) *n.* deep, water-filled ditch around castle.

mob (mob) *n.*, *v.*, **mobbed**, **mobbing**. —*n.* **1.** crowd, esp. disorderly one. —*v.* **2.** attack as a mob.

mo′bile *adj.* (mō′bəl, -bēl) **1.** capable of moving or being moved. —*n.* (-bēl) **2.** suspended artwork with parts that move in the breeze. —**mo·bil′i·ty,** *n.*

mo′bi·lize′ (mō′bə līz′) *v.*, **-lized**, **-lizing**. make ready for war.

mob′ster (mob′stər) *n.* member of criminal mob.

moc′ca·sin (mok′ə sin, -zən) *n.* **1.** soft shoe. **2.** poisonous snake.

mo′cha (mō′kə) *n.* **1.** kind of coffee. **2.** flavoring made from coffee and chocolate.

mock (mok) *v.* **1.** mimic or ridicule. —*adj.* **2.** imitation.

mock′er·y, *n.*, *pl.* **-ies. 1.** derision. **2.** dishonest imitation; travesty.

mock′ing·bird′, *n.* songbird with imitative voice.

mock′-up′, *n.* scale model.

mode (mōd) *n.* prevailing style.

mod′el (mod′l) *n.*, *adj.*, *v.*, **-eled**, **-eling.** —*n.* **1.** standard for imitation. **2.** person who poses, as for artist or photographer. —*adj.* **3.** serving as model. —*v.* **4.** pattern after model. **5.** wear as model. **6.** form.

mo′dem (mō′dəm, -dem) *n.* device enabling transmission of data between computers via telephone lines.

mod′er·ate *adj.*, *n.*, *v.*, **-ated**, **-ating.** —*adj.* (mod′ər it) **1.** not extreme. —*n.* (-ər it) **2.** person having moderate views. —*v.* (-ə rāt′) **3.** make or become less violent or intense. **4.** preside over.

mod′er·a′tor, *n.* director of group discussion.

mod′ern (mod′ərn) *adj.* of recent time. —**mo·der′ni·ty** (-dûr′ni tē) *n.* —**mod′ern·ize′**, *v.*

Modern English, English language since c1475.

mod′ern·ism, *n.* **1.** modern character or tendencies. **2.** modern usage.

mod′est (mod′ist) *adj.* **1.** humble in estimating oneself. **2.** simple; moderate. **3.** decent, moral. —**mod′est·ly,** *adv.* —**mod′es·ty,** *n.*

mod′i·cum (mod′i kəm) *n.* small amount.

mod′i·fy (mod′ə fī′) *v.*, **-fied**, **-fying**. alter or moderate. —**mod′i·fi·ca′tion,** *n.* —**mod′i·fi′er,** *n.*

mod′ish (mō′dish) *adj.* fashionable.

mo·diste′ (mō dēst′) *n.fem.* maker of women's attire.

mod′u·late′ (moj′ə lāt′) *v.*, **-lated**, **-lating. 1.** soften. **2.** *Radio.* alter (electric current) in accordance with sound waves. **3.** alter the pitch or key of. —**mod′u·la′tion,** *n.*

mod′ule (moj′ōōl) *n.* **1.** building unit. **2.** self-contained element of spacecraft. —**mod′u·lar,** *adj.*

mo′dus op′e·ran′di (mō′dəs op′ə-ran′dē, -dī) *n.*, *pl.* **mo′di op′e·ran′di** (mō′dē, -dī). method of operating.

mo′gul (mō′gəl) *n.* powerful or influential person.

mo′hair′ (mō′hâr′) *n.* fabric from fleece of the Angora goat.

Mo·ham′med·an·ism (mōō ham′i-dn iz′əm, mō-) *n.* Islam. —**Mo·ham′med·an,** *n.*, *adj.*

moi·ré′ (mwä rā′, mō-) *n.*, *pl.* **-rés.** fabric with watery appearance.

moist (moist) *adj.* damp. —**mois′ten** (moi′sən) *v.* —**mois′ten·er,** *n.*

mois′ture (-chər) *n.* dampness.

mois′tur·ize′ *v.*, **-ized**, **moisturizing**. add moisture to. —**mois′tur·iz′-er,** *n.*

mo′lar (mō′lər) *n.* broad back tooth.

mo·las′ses (mə las′iz) *n.* thick, dark syrup produced in refining sugar.

mold (mōld) *n.* **1.** form for shaping molten or plastic material. **2.** thing so formed. **3.** fungus growth on animal or vegetable matter. **4.** loose rich earth. —*v.* **5.** shape or form. **6.** become or make covered with mold (def. 3). —**mold′y,** *adj.*

mold′er, *v.* **1.** decay. —*n.* **2.** person who molds.

mold′ing, *n.* decorative strip with special cross section.

mole (mōl) *n.* **1.** small dark spot on skin. **2.** small, furred, underground mammal. **3.** spy who works against government agency he or she is employed by.

mol′e·cule′ (mol′ə kyōōl′) *n.* smallest physical unit of a chemical element or compound. —**mo·lec′u·lar** (mə lek′yə lər) *adj.*

mole′hill′, *n.* **1.** small mound of earth raised by moles. **2.** something small and insignificant.

mole′skin′, *n.* **1.** fur of mole. **2.** heavy cotton fabric.

mo·lest′ (mə lest′) *v.* **1.** annoy or bother. **2.** make indecent sexual advances to. —**mo·lest′er** *n.*

moll (mol) *n. Slang.* female companion of gangster.

mol′li·fy (mol′ə fī′) *v.*, **-fied**, **-fying**. appease in temper.

mol′lusk (mol′əsk) *n.* hard-shelled invertebrate animal. Also, **mol′lusc.**

mol′ly·cod′dle (mol′ē kod′l) *v.*, **-dled**, **-dling**. pamper.

molt (mōlt) *v.* shed skin or feathers.

mol′ten (mōl′tən) *adj.* melted.

mom (mom) *n. Informal.* mother.

mo′ment (mō′mənt) *n.* **1.** short space of time. **2.** importance.

mo′men·tar′y (-mən ter′ē) *adj.* very brief. —**mo′men·tar′i·ly,** *adv.*

mo·men′tous (-men′təs) *adj.* important.

mo·men′tum (-təm) *n.*, *pl.* **-ta** (-tə), **-tums.** force of moving body.

mom′my (mom′ē) *n.*, *pl.* **-mies.** *Informal.* mother.

Mon., Monday.

mon′arch (mon′ərk, -ärk) *n.* hereditary sovereign.

mon′ar·chy, *n.*, *pl.* **-chies. 1.** government by monarch. **2.** country governed by monarch. —**mon′ar•chism,** *n.* —**mon′ar•chist,** *n., adj.*

mon′as•ter′y (mon′ə ster′ē) *n., pl.* **-teries.** residence of monks. —**mo•nas′tic** (mə nas′tik) *adj.* —**mo•nas′ti•cism** (-siz′əm) *n.*

Mon′day (mun′dā, -dē) *n.* second day of week.

mon′e•tar′y (mon′i ter′ē, mun′-) *adj.* of money.

mon′ey (mun′ē) *n., pl.* **moneys, monies. 1.** pieces of metal or certificates used to buy and sell. **2.** wealth.

mon′eyed *adj.* wealthy.

mon′ger (mung′gər, mong′-) *n. Brit.* dealer.

mon′gol•ism (mong′gə liz′əm, mon′-) *n. Offensive.* (earlier term for) Down syndrome.

Mon′gol•oid′ (-loid′) *adj.* designating division of human race including most peoples of eastern Asia.

mon′goose (mong′gōōs′, mon′-) *n., pl.* **-gooses.** carnivorous animal of Asia.

mon′grel (mung′grəl, mong′-) *n.* **1.** animal or plant resulting from crossing of different breeds. —*adj.* **2.** of mixed breeds.

mon′i•ker (mon′i kər) *n. Slang.* name. Also, **mon′ick•er.**

mon′i•tor (mon′i tər) *n.* **1.** pupil who assists teacher. **2.** television or computer screen. —*v.* **3.** check continuously.

monk (mungk) *n.* man who is a member of a religious order.

mon′key (mung′kē) *n.* **1.** mammal strongly resembling a human being. —*v.* **2.** fool. **3.** tamper.

monkey business, mischievous behavior.

monkey wrench, wrench with adjustable jaws.

mono-, prefix meaning one, single, or lone.

mon′o•chrome (mon′ə krōm′) *adj.* of one color.

mon′o•cle (mon′ə kəl) *n.* eyeglass for one eye.

mon′o•cot′y•le•don (mon′ə kot′l-ēd′n) *n.* plant having embryo containing single seed leaf.

mo•noc′u•lar (mə nok′yə lər) *adj.* **1.** having one eye. **2.** for use of only one eye.

mo•nog′a•my (mə nog′ə mē) *n.* marriage of one woman with one man. —**mo•nog′a•mous,** *adj.* —**mo•nog′a•mist,** *n.*

mon′o•gram (mon′ə gram′) *n.* design made of one's initials. —**mon′o•grammed,** *adj.*

mon′o•graph (mon′ə graf′) *n.* treatise on one subject.

mon′o•lith (-lith) *n.* structure of single block of stone. —**mon′o•lith′ic,** *adj.*

mon′o•logue′ (-lôg′) *n.* talk by single speaker. Also, **mon′o•log′.**

mon′o•ma′ni•a, *n.* obsessive zeal for or interest in single thing. —**mon′o•ma′ni•ac,** *n.*

mon′o•nu•cle•o′sis (-nōō′klē ō′sis, -nyōō′-) *n.* infectious disease characterized by fever, swelling of lymph nodes, etc.

mon′o•plane′, *n.* airplane with one wing on each side.

mo•nop′o•ly (mə nop′ə lē) *n., pl.* **-lies. 1.** exclusive control. **2.** thing so controlled. **3.** company having such control. —**mo•nop′o•lize′,** *v.*

mon′o•rail′ (mon′ə rāl′) *n.* **1.** single rail serving as track for wheeled vehicles. **2.** car or train moving on such a rail.

mon′o•so′di•um glu′ta•mate′ (mon′ə sō′dē əm glōō′tə māt′) white crystalline powder used to intensify flavor of foods.

mon′o•syl′la•ble, *n.* word of one syllable. —**mon′o•syl•lab′ic,** *adj.*

mon′o•the•ism, *n.* doctrine or belief that there is only one God.

mon′o•tone′, *n.* single tone of unvarying pitch.

mo•not′o•ny (mə not′n ē) *n.* wearisome uniformity. —**mo•not′o•nous,** *adj.*

mes•sieur′ (mə syœ′) *n., pl.* **mes•sieurs** (me syœ′). French term of address for man.

mon•si′gnor (mon sē′nyər, mon′sē-nyôr′, môn′-) *n., pl.* **-gnors, -gnori** (môn′sē nyôr′ē). title of certain Roman Catholic priests.

mon•soon′ (mon sōōn′) *n.* seasonal wind of Indian Ocean.

mon′ster (mon′stər) *n.* **1.** animal or plant of abnormal form. **2.** wicked creature. **3.** anything huge.

mon•stros′i•ty (mon stros′i tē) *n., pl.* **-ties.** grotesquely abnormal thing.

mon′strous (-strəs) *adj.* **1.** huge. **2.** frightful.

Mont., Montana.

mon•tage′ (mon täzh′; *Fr.* môn-tazh′) *n.* blending of elements from several pictures into one.

month (munth) *n.* any of twelve parts of calendar year.

month′ly, *adj., n., pl.* **-lies,** *adv.* —*adj.* **1.** occurring, appearing, etc., once a month. **2.** lasting for a month. —*n.* **3.** periodical published once a month. —*adv.* **4.** once a month. **5.** by the month.

mon′u•ment (mon′yə mənt) *n.* memorial structure.

mon′u•men′tal (-men′tl) *adj.* **1.** imposing. **2.** serving as monument.

moo (mōō) *n.* **1.** sound cow makes. —*v.* **2.** utter such sound.

mooch (mōōch) *Slang.* —*v.* **1.** try to get without paying. —*n.* **2.** Also, **mooch′er.** person who mooches.

mood (mōōd) *n.* frame of mind.

mood′y, *adj.,* **-ier, -iest.** given to bad moods. —**mood′i•ly,** *adv.*

moon (mōōn) *n.* **1.** body which revolves around earth monthly. **2.** month. —*v.* **3.** gaze dreamily.

moon′light′, *n.* **1.** light from moon. —*v.* **2.** work at second job after principal one.

moon′shine′, *n.* illegally made liquor. —**moon′shin′er,** *n.*

moon′stone′, *n.* pearly gem.

moor (mōōr) *v.* **1.** secure (ship), as at a dock. —*n.* **2.** *Brit.* open peaty wasteland.

moor′ing, *n.* **1.** (*pl.*) cables, etc., by which ship is moored. **2.** place where ship is moored.

moose (mōōs) *n., pl.* **moose.** large animal of deer family.

moot (mōōt) *adj.* debatable.

mop (mop) *n., v.,* **mopped, mopping.** —*n.* **1.** piece of cloth, etc., fastened to stick, for washing or dusting. —*v.* **2.** clean with mop. **3.** *Mil.* **mop up,** destroy final resisting elements.

mope (mōp) *v.,* **moped, moping.** be in low spirits.

mo′ped (mō′ped′) *n.* motorized bicycle.

mop′pet (mop′it) *n.* child.

mor′al (môr′əl) *adj.* **1.** of or concerned with right conduct. **2.** virtuous. —*n.* **3.** (*pl.*) principles of conduct. **4.** moral lesson. —**mor′al•ist,** *n.* —**mor′al•is′tic,** *adj.*

mo•rale′ (mə ral′) *n.* spirits; mood.

mo•ral′i•ty (mə ral′i tē, mô-) *n.* **1.** conformity to rules of right conduct. **2.** moral quality.

mor′al•ize′ (môr′ə līz′) *v.,* **-ized, -izing.** think or pronounce on moral questions.

mor′al•ly, *adv.* **1.** according to morals. **2.** in one's honest belief.

mo•rass′ (mə ras′) *n.* swamp.

mor′a•to′ri•um (môr′ə tôr′ē əm) *n., pl.* **-toria** (tôr′ē ə), **-toriums. 1.** legal permission to delay payment of debts. **2.** any temporary cessation.

mo′ray (môr′ā, mô rā′) *n.* tropical eel.

mor′bid (môr′bid) *adj.* **1.** unwholesome. **2.** of disease. —**mor•bid′i•ty,** *n.* —**mor′bid•ly,** *adv.*

mor′dant (môr′dnt) *adj.* **1.** sarcastic; biting. **2.** burning; corrosive.

more (môr) *adj.* **1.** in greater amount or degree. **2.** additional. —*n.* **3.** additional or greater quantity or degree. —*adv.* **4.** in addition.

mo•rel′ (mə rel′) *n.* edible mushroom.

more•o′ver, *adv.* besides.

mo′res (môr′āz, -ēz) *n.pl.* social and moral customs of group.

morgue (môrg) *n.* place where corpses are taken for identification.

mor′i•bund′ (môr′ə bund′) *adj.* dying.

Mor′mon•ism (môr′mən iz′əm) *n.* religion founded in U.S. in 1830. —**Mor′mon,** *n., adj.*

morn (môrn) *n.* morning.

morn′ing, *n.* **1.** first part of day. —*adj.* **2.** done, or occurring, in the morning.

morn′ing-glo′ry, *n., pl.* **morning-glories.** vine with funnel-shaped flowers.

morning sickness, nausea occurring early in the day during the first months of pregnancy.

mo•roc′co (mə rok′ō) *n.* fine leather.

mo′ron (môr′on) *n.* stupid person. —**mo•ron′ic** (mə ron′ik) *adj.*

mo•rose′ (mə rōs′) *adj.* gloomily ill-humored. —**mo•rose′ly,** *adv.*

mor′pheme (môr′fēm) *n.* minimal grammatical unit.

mor′phine (môr′fēn) *n.* narcotic found in opium.

mor•phol′o•gy (môr fol′ə jē) *n.* **1.** branch of biology dealing with form and structure of organisms. **2.** study of word formation.

Morse code (môrs) *n.* telegraphic code of long and short signals.

mor′sel (môr′səl) *n.* small amount.

mor′tal (môr′tl) *adj.* **1.** liable to death. **2.** causing death. **3.** extreme. —*n.* **4.** human being.

mor•tal′i•ty (môr tal′i tē) *n., pl.* **-ties. 1.** mortal nature. **2.** relative death rate.

mor′tar (môr′tər) *n.* **1.** bowl in which drugs, etc., are pulverized. **2.** short cannon. **3.** material used to bind masonry.

mor′tar•board′, *n.* academic cap with square, flat top and tassel.

mort′gage (môr′gij) *n., v.,* **-gaged, -gaging.** —*n.* **1.** conditional transfer of property as security for debt. —*v.* **2.** put mortgage on.

mor•ti′cian (môr tish′ən) *n.* undertaker.

mor′ti•fy′ (môr′tə fī′) *v.,* **-fied, -fying. 1.** humiliate or shame. **2.** subdue (body) by abstinence or pain.

mor′tise (môr′tis) *n., v.,* **-tised, -tising.** —*n.* **1.** slot in wood for tenon. —*v.* **2.** fasten by mortise.

mor′tu•ar′y (môr′chōō er′ē) *n., pl.*

-aries. place where bodies are prepared for burial.

mo·sa'ic (mō zā'ik) *n.* design made of small colored pieces of stone.

mo'sey (mō'zē) *v. Informal.* stroll.

Mos'lem (moz'ləm, mos'-) *n., adj.* Muslim.

mosque (mosk) *n.* Muslim place of prayer.

mos·qui'to (mə skē'tō) *n., pl.* **-toes, -tos.** common biting insect.

moss (môs) *n.* **1.** small, leafy-stemmed plant growing on rocks, etc. —*v.* **2.** cover with moss.

moss'back', *n. Informal.* person having antiquated ideas.

most (mōst) *adj.* **1.** in greatest amount. **2.** majority of. —*n.* **3.** greatest quantity. —*adv.* **4.** to greatest extent.

most'ly, *adv.* **1.** in most cases. **2.** in greater part.

mote (mōt) *n.* small particle.

mo·tel' (mō tel') *n.* roadside hotel for automobile travelers.

moth (môth) *n.* insect, some of whose larvae eat cloth.

moth'ball', *n.* ball of camphor, etc., for repelling moths.

moth'er (muth'ər) *n.* **1.** female parent. **2.** head of group of nuns. **3.** source. —*adj.* **4.** of, like, or being mother. **5.** native. —*v.* **6.** act as or like mother to. —**moth'er·hood'**, *n.* —**moth'er·ly,** *adj.*

moth'er-in-law', *n., pl.* **mothers-in-law.** mother of one's spouse.

moth'er·land', *n.* **1.** one's native land. **2.** land of one's ancestors.

moth'er-of-pearl', *n.* inner layer of certain shells.

mo·tif' (mō tēf') *n.* recurring subject or theme.

mo'tile (mōt'l, mō'til) *adj. Biology.* capable of moving spontaneously.

mo'tion (mō'shən) *n.* **1.** process of changing position. **2.** action or power of movement. **3.** formal proposal made in meeting. —*v.* **4.** indicate by gesture.

motion picture, series of photographs projected so rapidly that objects seem to be moving.

mo'ti·vate' (mō'tə vāt') *v.,* **-vated, -vating.** give motive to. —**mo'ti·va'tion,** *n.*

mo'tive (-tiv) *n.* **1.** purpose; goal. —*adj.* **2.** of or causing motion.

mot'ley (mot'lē) *adj.* widely, often grotesquely, varied.

mo'to·cross' (mō'tō krôs') *n.* motorcycle race over rough terrain.

mo'tor (mō'tər) *n.* **1.** small, powerful engine. —*adj.* **2.** of or causing motion. **3.** of or operated by motor. —*v.* **4.** travel by automobile.

mo'tor·bike', *n.* small motorcycle.

mo'tor·boat', *n.* boat run by motor.

mo'tor·cade' (-kād') *n.* procession of automobiles.

mo'tor·car', *n.* automobile.

mo'tor·cy'cle, *n.* heavy motor-driven bicycle. —**mo'tor·cy'clist**, *n.*

mo'tor·ist, *n.* automobile driver.

mo'tor·ize', *v.,* **-ized, -izing.** furnish with motors or motor-driven vehicles.

mot'tle (mot'l) *v.,* **-tled, -tling.** mark with spots or blotches.

mot'to (mot'ō) *n., pl.* **-toes, -tos.** phrase expressing one's guiding principle.

moue (mōō) *n., pl.* **moues** (mōō) pouting grimace.

mould (mōld) *n.* mold.

mould'er, *v.* molder.

moult (mōlt) *v., n.* molt.

mound (mound) *n.* heap of earth; hill.

mount (mount) *v.* **1.** go up; get on; rise. **2.** prepare for use or display. **3.** fix in setting. —*n.* **4.** act or manner of mounting. **5.** horse for riding. **6.** Also, **mounting.** support, setting, etc. **7.** hill.

moun'tain (moun'tn) *n.* lofty natural elevation on earth's surface. —**moun'tain·ous,** *adj.*

mountain bike, bicycle designed for off-road use, usu. having smaller frame and wider tires.

moun'tain·eer', *n.* mountain climber. —**moun'tain·eer'ing,** *n.*

mountain lion, cougar.

moun'te·bank' (moun'tə bangk') *n.* charlatan.

mourn (môrn) *v.* grieve; feel or express sorrow (for). —**mourn'er,** *n.* —**mourn'ful,** *adj.* —**mourn'ing,** *n.*

mouse (*n.* mous; *v.* also mouz) *n., pl.* **mice** (mīs), *v.,* **moused, mousing.** —*n.* **1.** small rodent. **2.** palm-sized device used to select items on computer screen. —*v.* (mouz) **3.** hunt for mice.

mousse (mōōs) *n.* **1.** frothy dessert. **2.** foamy preparation used to style hair.

mous·tache' (mus'tash, mə stash') *n.* mustache.

mous'y (mou'sē, -zē) *adj.,* **-ier, -iest.** drably quiet.

mouth *n., pl.* **mouths,** *v.* —*n.* (mouth) **1.** opening through which animal eats. **2.** any opening. —*v.* (mouth) **3.** utter pompously or dishonestly. —**mouth'ful,** *n.*

mouth organ, harmonica.

mouth'piece', *n.* **1.** piece held in or to mouth. **2.** spokesperson.

mouth'wash', *n.* solution for cleaning the mouth.

mouth'-wa'ter·ing, *adj.* appetizing, as in appearance or aroma.

mou'ton (mōō'ton) *n.* processed sheepskin.

move (mōōv) *v.,* **moved, moving,** *n.* —*v.* **1.** change place or position. **2.** change one's abode. **3.** advance. **4.** make formal proposal in meeting. **5.** affect emotionally. —*n.* **6.** act of moving. **7.** purposeful action.

move'ment, *n.* **1.** act or process of moving. **2.** trend in thought. **3.** works of mechanism. **4.** principal division of piece of music.

moving picture, motion picture. Also, **mov'ie.**

mow, *v.,* **mowed, mowed** or **mown, mowing,** *n.* —*v.* (mō) **1.** cut (grass, etc.). **2.** kill indiscriminately. —*n.* (mou) **3.** place in barn where hay, etc., are stored. —**mow'er,** *n.*

moz'za·rel'la (mot'sə rel'ə, mōt'-) *n.* mild, white, semisoft cheese.

MP, 1. a member of Parliament. **2.** Military Police.

mph, miles per hour.

Mr. (mis'tər) *pl.* **Messrs.** (mes'ərz) Mister; title of address for man.

MRI, magnetic resonance imaging: process of producing images of the body using strong magnetic field and low-energy radio waves.

Mrs. (mis'iz, miz'iz) *pl.* **Mmes.** (mā-däm', -dam'). title of address for married woman.

MS, 1. Also, **ms, ms.** manuscript. **2.** Mississippi. **3.** multiple sclerosis.

Ms. (miz) title of address for woman not to be distinguished as married or unmarried.

M.S., Master of Science.

MSG, monosodium glutamate.

MT, Montana.

much (much) *adj.* **1.** in great quantity or degree. —*n.* **2.** great quantity. **3.**

notable thing. —*adv.* **4.** greatly. **5.** generally.

mu'ci·lage (myōō'sə lij) *n.* gummy adhesive.

muck (muk) *n.* **1.** filth. **2.** moist barn refuse. —**muck'y,** *adj.*

muck'rake', *v.,* **-raked, -raking.** expose scandal. —**muck'rak'er,** *n.*

mu'cous (myōō'kəs) *adj.* **1.** secreting mucus. **2.** of or like mucus.

mucous membrane, membrane lining internal surface of organ.

mu'cus (-kəs) *n.* sticky secretion of mucous membrane.

mud (mud) *n.* **1.** wet soft earth. **2.** malicious statements. —**mud'dy,** *adj.,* *v.*

mud'dle (mud'l) *v.,* **-dled, -dling.** —*v.* **1.** mix up; confuse. —*n.* **2.** confusion.

mud'dle·head'ed, *adj.* confused in one's thinking.

mud'sling'ing, *n.* efforts to discredit opponent by malicious remarks.

mu·ez'zin (myōō ez'in, mōō-) *n.* crier who summons Muslims to prayer.

muff (muf) *n.* **1.** tubular covering for hands. —*v.* **2.** bungle. **3.** drop (ball) after catching.

muf'fin (muf'in) *n.* small round bread.

muf'fle (muf'əl) *v.,* **-fled, -fling.** **1.** wrap in scarf, cloak, etc. **2.** deaden (sound).

muf'fler, *n.* **1.** heavy neck scarf. **2.** device for deadening sound.

muf'ti (muf'tē) *n.* civilian dress.

mug (mug) *n., v.,* **mugged, mugging.** —*n.* **1.** drinking cup. **2.** *Slang.* face. —*v.* **3.** assault, usually with intent to rob. —**mug'ger,** *n.*

mug'gy, *adj.,* **-gier, -giest.** hot and humid.

mug shot, photograph of the face of a criminal suspect.

Mu·ham'mad (mōō ham'əd, -hä'-mad) *n.* founder of Islam, A.D. 570-632.

mu·lat'to (mə lat'ō, -lä'tō) *n., pl.* **-toes.** person with mixed black and white ancestry.

mul'ber'ry (mul'ber'ē, -bə rē) *n., pl.* **-ries.** tree, the leaves of some of whose species are used as food by silkworms.

mulch (mulch) *n.* **1.** loose covering of leaves, straw, etc., on plants. —*v.* **2.** surround with mulch.

mulct (mulkt) *v.* **1.** deprive of by trickery. **2.** fine.

mule (myōōl) *n.* **1.** offspring of donkey and mare. **2.** woman's house slipper.

mul'ish (myōō'lish) *adj.* obstinate.

mull (mul) *v.* **1.** study or ruminate (over). **2.** heat and spice.

mul'let (mul'it) *n.* common food fish.

mul'li·gan (mul'i gən) *n.* stew of meat and vegetables.

mul'li·ga·taw'ny (-gə tô'nē) *n.* curry-flavored soup.

mul'lion (mul'yən) *n.* vertical member separating lights of window.

multi-, prefix meaning many.

mul'ti·cul'tur·al·ism (mul'tē kul'-chər ə liz'əm, mul'tī-) *n.* recognition of different cultural identities within unified society.

mul'ti·far'i·ous (mul'tə fâr'ē əs) *adj.* many and varied.

mul'ti·me'di·a (mul'tē-, mul'tī-) *n.* (*used with sing. v.*) combined use of several media or mass media.

mul'ti·na'tion·al, *n.* **1.** corporation with operations in many countries. —*adj.* **2.** pertaining to several nations or multinationals.

mul′ti•ple (mul′tə pəl) *adj.* **1.** consisting of or involving many. —*n.* **2.** number evenly divisible by stated other number.

multiple sclerosis, disease marked by destruction of areas of brain and spinal cord.

mul′ti•plic′i•ty (-plis′i tē) *n., pl.* **-ties.** great number or variety.

mul′ti•ply′ (mul′tə plī′) *v.,* **-plied, -plying. 1.** increase the number of. **2.** add (number) to itself a stated number of times. —**mul′ti•pli′er,** *n.* —**mul′ti•pli•ca′tion,** *n.*

mul′ti•tude′ (mul′ti tōōd′, -tyōōd′) *n.* great number.

mul′ti•tu′di•nous, *adj.* **1.** numerous. **2.** having many parts.

mum (mum) *adj.* silent.

mum′ble (mum′bəl) *v.,* **-bled, -bling,** *n.* —*v.* **1.** speak quietly and unintelligibly. —*n.* **2.** mumbling sound.

mum′ble•ty•peg′ (mum′bəl tē peg′) *n.* game in which pocketknife is flipped so it sticks in ground. Also, **mum′ble-the-peg′** (-thə-).

mum′bo jum′bo (mum′bō jum′bō) senseless language.

mum′mer (mum′ər) *n.* **1.** person in festive disguise. **2.** actor.

mum′my (mum′ē) *n., pl.* **-mies.** dead body treated to prevent decay.

mumps (mumps) *n.pl.* disease marked by swelling of salivary glands.

munch (munch) *v.* chew.

mun•dane′ (mun dān′, mun′dān) *adj.* commonplace.

mu•nic′i•pal (myōō nis′ə pəl) *adj.* of a city.

mu•nic′i•pal′i•ty (-pal′i tē) *n., pl.* **-ties.** self-governing city.

mu•nif′i•cent (myōō nif′ə sənt) *adj.* extremely generous. —**mu•nif′i•cence,** *n.* —**mu•nif′i•cent•ly,** *adv.*

mu•ni′tions (myōō nish′ənz) *n.pl.* weapons and ammunition.

mu′ral (myōōr′əl) *n.* **1.** picture painted on wall. —*adj.* **2.** of walls.

mur′der (mûr′dər) *n.* **1.** unlawful willful killing. —*v.* **2.** commit murder. —**mur′der•er,** *n.* —**mur′der•ess,** *n. fem.* —**mur′der•ous,** *adj.*

murk (mûrk) *n.* darkness.

murk′y, *adj.,* **-ier, -iest.** dark and gloomy. —**murk′i•ness,** *n.*

mur′mur (mûr′mər) *n.* **1.** low, continuous, indistinct sound. **2.** complaint. —*v.* **3.** speak softly or indistinctly. **4.** complain.

mus′ca•dine (mus′kə din, -dīn′) *n.* American grape.

mus′cat (mus′kət, -kat) *n.* sweet grape.

mus′ca•tel′ (mus′kə tel′) *n.* wine made from muscat grapes.

mus′cle (mus′əl) *n., v.,* **-cled, -cling.** —*n.* **1.** bundle of fibers in animal body that contract to produce motion. **2.** brawn. —*v.* **3.** *Informal.* force one's way. —**mus′cu•lar** (-kyə lər) *adj.*

mus′cle-bound′, *adj.* having enlarged and inelastic muscles.

muscular dys′tro•phy (dis′trə fē) hereditary disease characterized by gradual wasting of muscles.

muse (myōōz) *v.,* **mused, musing.** reflect quietly.

Muse (myōōz) *n.* one of nine goddesses of the arts.

mu•se′um (myōō zē′əm) *n.* place for permanent public exhibits.

mush (mush *or, esp. for 2, 3,* mōōsh) *n.* **1.** meal boiled in water until thick, used as food. **2.** anything soft. **3.** *Informal.* maudlin sentiment. —*v.* **4.** travel on foot, esp. with dog team. —**mush′y,** *adj.*

mush′room (mush′rōōm, -rōōm) *n.* **1.** fleshy fungus, usu. umbrella-shaped, sometimes edible. —*v.* **2.** grow quickly.

mu′sic (myōō′zik) *n.* **1.** art of arranging sounds for effect by rhythm, melody, etc. **2.** score of musical composition. —**mu•si′cian** (-zish′ən) *n.*

mus′i•cal, *adj.* **1.** of music. **2.** pleasant-sounding. **3.** sensitive to or skilled in music. —*n.* **4.** Also, **mus′ical com′edy.** a play with music.

mu′si•col′o•gy (-zi kol′ə jē) *n.* scholarly or scientific study of music. —**mu′si•col′o•gist,** *n.*

music video, videotape featuring rendition of pop song.

musk (musk) *n.* fragrant animal secretion, used in perfume. —**musk′y,** *adj.*

mus′ket (mus′kit) *n.* early rifle.

mus′ket•eer′, *n.* soldier armed with musket.

musk′mel′on, *n.* sweet edible melon.

musk′ox′, *n., pl.* **-oxen.** large mammal of arctic regions.

musk′rat′, *n.* large aquatic American rodent.

Mus′lim (muz′lim, mōōz′-, mōōs′-) *n.* **1.** follower of Islam. —*adj.* **2.** of or pertaining to Islam.

mus′lin (muz′lin) *n.* plain-weave cotton fabric.

muss (mus) *Informal.* —*n.* **1.** disorder. —*v.* **2.** rumple. —**muss′y,** *adj.*

mus′sel (mus′əl) *n.* bivalve mollusk, sometimes edible.

must (must) *aux. v.* **1.** be obliged to. **2.** may be assumed to. —*adj.* **3.** necessary. —*n.* **4.** anything necessary. **5.** new wine not yet fermented.

mus′tache (mus′tash, mə stash′) *n.* hair growing on upper lip.

mus′tang (mus′tang) *n.* small wild horse of western U.S.

mus′tard (mus′tərd) *n.* pungent yellow powder made from seeds of mustard plant.

mustard gas, oily liquid with poisonous properties, used in warfare.

mus′ter (mus′tər) *v.* **1.** assemble, as troops; gather. —*n.* **2.** assembly.

mus′ty (mus′tē) *adj.,* **-tier, -tiest. 1.** stale-smelling. **2.** out-dated.

mu′ta•ble (myōō′tə bal) *adj.* subject to change. —**mu′ta•bil′i•ty,** *n.*

mu′tant (myōōt′nt) *n.* **1.** organism resulting from mutation. —*adj.* **2.** resulting from mutation.

mu′tate (myōō′tāt) *v.,* **-tated, -tating.** change or cause to change.

mu•ta′tion, *n.* **1.** sudden change in genetic characteristic. **2.** individual or species characterized by such change. **3.** change.

mute (myōōt) *adj.,* **muter, mutest,** *n., v.,* **muted, muting.** —*adj.* **1.** silent. **2.** incapable of speech. —*n.* **3.** person unable to utter words. **4.** device for muffling musical instrument. —*v.* **5.** deaden sound of.

mu′ti•late′ (myōōt′l āt′) *v.,* **-lated, -lating.** injure by depriving of or damaging part. —**mu′ti•la′tion,** *n.*

mu′ti•ny (myōōt′n ē) *n., pl.* **-nies,** *v.,* **-nied, -nying.** revolt against lawful authority. —**mu′ti•neer′,** *n.* —**mu′ti•nous,** *adj.*

mutt (mut) *n. Slang.* mongrel dog.

mut′ter (mut′ər) *v.* **1.** speak low and indistinctly; grumble. —*n.* **2.** act or sound of muttering.

mut′ton (mut′n) *n.* flesh of sheep, used as food.

mut′ton•chops′, *n.pl.* side whiskers that are narrow at temples and broad and short at jawline.

mu′tu•al (myōō′chōō əl) *adj.* **1.** done,

etc., by two or more in relation to each other. **2.** common.

mutual fund, investment company that invests money of its shareholders.

muz′zle (muz′əl) *n., v.,* **-zled, -zling.** —*n.* **1.** mouth of firearm. **2.** animal's jaws. **3.** cage for this. —*v.* **4.** put muzzle on. **5.** silence.

my (mī) *pron.* possessive form of **I** used before noun.

my•col′o•gy (mī kol′ə jē) *n.* study of fungi. —**my•col′o•gist,** *n.*

my′na (mī′nə) *n.* Asiatic bird sometimes taught to talk.

my•o′pi•a (mī ō′pē ə) *n.* nearsightedness. —**my•op′ic** (-op′ik, -ō′pik) *adj.*

myr′i•ad (mir′ē əd) *n., adj.* very great number.

myrrh (mûr) *n.* aromatic substance from certain plants.

myr′tle (mûr′tl) *n.* **1.** evergreen shrub. **2.** periwinkle (def. 2).

my•self′, *pron., pl.* **ourselves. 1.** intensive form of **I** or **me. 2.** reflexive form of **me.**

mys′ter•y (mis′tə rē) *n., pl.* **-teries. 1.** anything secret, unknown, or unexplained. **2.** obscurity. **3.** secret rite. —**mys•te′ri•ous** (mi stēr′ē əs) *adj.* —**mys•te′ri•ous•ly,** *adv.*

mys′tic (mis′tik) *adj.* Also, **mys′ti•cal. 1.** mysterious or occult. **2.** spiritual. —*n.* **3.** believer in mysticism.

mys′ti•cism (-tə siz′əm) *n.* doctrine of direct spiritual intuition of God, truth, etc.

mys′ti•fy′, *v.,* **-fied, -fying.** bewilder purposely.

mys•tique′ (mi stēk′) *n.* aura of mystery or power.

myth (mith) *n.* **1.** legendary story, person, etc. **2.** false popular belief. —**myth′i•cal,** *adj.*

my•thol′o•gy (mi thol′ə jē) *n., pl.* **-gies.** body of myths. —**myth′o•log′i•cal** (mith′ə loj′i kəl) *adj.*

N

N, n (en) *n.* fourteenth letter of English alphabet.

N, north, northern.

nab (nab) *v.,* **nabbed, nabbing.** *Informal.* seize; arrest.

na′bob (nā′bob) *n.* wealthy, influential, or powerful person.

na′cre (nā′kər) *n.* mother-of-pearl.

na′dir (nā′dər, -dēr) *n.* **1.** lowest point. **2.** point of celestial sphere directly below given point.

nag (nag) *v.,* **nagged, nagging,** *n.* —*v.* **1.** scold constantly. —*n.* **2.** person who nags. **3.** old horse.

nai′ad (nā′ad, -əd, nī′-) *n.* water nymph.

nail (nāl) *n.* **1.** slender piece of metal for holding pieces of wood together. **2.** horny plate at end of finger or toe. —*v.* **3.** fasten with nails. **4.** *Informal.* secure or seize.

na•ive′ (nä ēv′) *adj.* simple; unsophisticated. Also, **na•ïve′.**

na•ive•té′ (nä ēv tā′) *n.* artless simplicity. Also, **na•ïve•té′.**

na′ked (nā′kid) *adj.* **1.** without clothing or covering. **2.** (of eye) unassisted in seeing. **3.** plain.

name (nām) *n., v.,* **named, naming.** —*n.* **1.** word or words by which a person, place, or thing is designated. **2.** reputation. **3.** behalf or authority. —*v.* **4.** give name to. **5.** specify. **6.** appoint.

name′less, *adj.* **1.** having no name. **2.** not referred to by name.

name′ly, *adv.* that is to say.

name′sake′, *n.* one having same name as another.

nan′ny (nan′ē) *n., pl.* **-nies.** child's nursemaid.

nanny goat, female goat.

nan′o·sec′ond (nan′ə sek′ənd, nā′nə-) *n.* one billionth of a second.

nap (nap) *n., v.,* **napped, napping.** —*n.* **1.** short sleep. **2.** short, fuzzy fibers on the surface of cloth. —*v.* **3.** raise fuzz on. **4.** have short sleep.

na′palm (nā′päm) *n.* **1.** highly incendiary jellylike substance used in bombs, etc. —*v.* **2.** bomb or attack with napalm.

nape (nāp, nap) *n.* back of neck.

naph′tha (naf′thə, nap′-) *n.* petroleum derivative.

nap′kin (nap′kin) *n.* piece of cloth or paper used at table to wipe lips or fingers.

na·po′le·on (nə pō′lē ən, -pōl′yən) *n.* flaky pastry with cream filling.

nar′cis·sism (när′sə siz′em) *n.* excessive admiration of oneself. —**nar′cis·sis′tic** (-sis′tik) *adj.*

nar·cis′sus (när sis′əs) *n.* springblooming plant, as daffodil or jonquil.

nar·co′sis (när kō′sis) *n.* stupor.

nar·cot′ic (-kot′ik) *adj.* **1.** sleepinducing. —*n.* **2.** substance that dulls pain, induces sleep, etc. **3.** addictive drug, esp. an illegal one.

nar′rate (nar′āt, na rāt′) *v.,* **-rated, -rating.** tell. —**nar·ra′tion,** *n.* —**nar′ra·tor,** *n.*

nar′ra·tive (-ə tiv) *n.* **1.** story of events. —*adj.* **2.** that narrates. **3.** of narration.

nar′row (nar′ō) *adj.* **1.** not broad or wide. **2.** literal or strict in interpreting rules, etc. **3.** minute. —*v.* **4.** make or become narrow. —*n.* **5.** narrow place, thing, etc.

nar′row-mind′ed, *adj.* unwilling to accept new ideas.

nar′whal (när′wəl) *n.* Arctic whale.

NASA (nas′ə) *n.* National Aeronautics and Space Administration.

na′sal (nā′zəl) *adj.* **1.** of noses. **2.** spoken through nose. —*n.* **3.** nasal sound. —**na′sal·ly,** *adv.*

nas′cent (nas′ənt, nā′sənt) *adj.* beginning to exist or develop.

na·stur′tium (nə stûr′shəm, na-) *n.* garden plant with yellow, orange, or red flowers.

nas′ty (nas′tē) *adj.,* **-tier, -tiest. 1.** disgustingly unclean. **2.** objectionable. —**nas′ti·ly,** *adv.*

na′tal (nāt′l) *adj.* of one's birth.

na′tion (nā′shən) *n.* **1.** people living in one territory under same government. **2.** people related by tradition or ancestry. —**na′tion·al** (nash′ə nl) *adj., n.*

na′tion·al·ism (nash′ə nl iz′əm) *n.* devotion to one's nation. —**na′tion·al·ist,** *n., adj.*

na′tion·al·i·ty (nash′ə nal′i tē) *n., pl.* **-ties. 1.** condition of being member of a nation. **2.** nation.

na′tion·al·ize′, *v.,* **-ized, -izing.** bring under national control.

na′tion·wide′ (nā′shən-) *adj., adv.* across entire nation.

na′tive (nā′tiv) *adj.* **1.** belonging to by birth, nationality, or nature. **2.** of natives. **3.** being the place of origin of a person or thing. —*n.* **4.** person, animal, or plant native to region.

Native American, American Indian.

na·tiv′i·ty (nə tiv′i tē) *n., pl.* **-ties.** birth.

NATO (nā′tō) *n.* North Atlantic Treaty Organization.

nat′ty (nat′ē) *adj.,* **-tier, -tiest.** neat; trim.

nat′u·ral (nach′ər əl) *adj.* **1.** of, existing in, or formed by nature. **2.** to be expected in circumstances. **3.** without affectation. **4.** *Music.* neither sharp nor flat. —**nat′u·ral·ly,** *adv.* —**nat′u·ral·ness,** *n.*

natural childbirth, childbirth without use of drugs.

natural gas, mixture of gaseous hydrocarbons that accumulates in porous sedimentary rocks.

natural history, study of natural objects.

nat′u·ral·ism (-ər ə liz′əm) *n.* artistic or literary style that represents objects or events as they occur in nature or real life. —**nat′u·ral·is′tic,** *adj.*

nat′u·ral·ist, *n.* **1.** student of nature. **2.** adherent of naturalism.

nat′u·ral·ize′, *v.,* **-ized, -izing. 1.** confer citizenship upon. **2.** introduce to region.

natural resource, source of wealth occurring in nature.

natural selection, process by which life forms having traits that enable them to adapt to the environment will survive in greater numbers.

na′ture (nā′chər) *n.* **1.** natural world. **2.** universe. **3.** one's character. **4.** kind or sort.

naught (nôt) *n.* zero.

naugh′ty (nô′tē) *adj.,* **-tier, -tiest. 1.** disobedient; bad. **2.** improper.

nau′sea (nô′zē ə, -zhə, -sē ə, -shə) *n.* **1.** feeling of impending vomiting. **2.** disgust. —**nau′se·ate′** (-zē āt′, -zhē-, -sē-, -shē-) *v.* —**nau′seous** (-shəs, -zē-əs) *adj.*

nau′ti·cal (nô′ti kəl) *adj.* of ships, sailors, or navigation.

nautical mile, unit of distance equal to 1.852 kilometers.

nau′ti·lus (nôt′l əs) *n.* mollusk having pearly shell.

Nav′a·jo′ (nav′ə hō′, nä′və-) *n., pl.* **-jo, -jos, -joes.** member of an American Indian people of the Southwest.

na′val (nā′vəl) *adj.* of ships or navy.

nave (nāv) *n.* main lengthwise part of church.

na′vel (nā′vəl) *n.* pit in center surface of belly.

nav′i·gate′ (nav′i gāt′) *v.,* **-gated, -gating. 1.** traverse (water or air). **2.** direct on a course. —**nav′i·ga′tor,** *n.* —**nav′i·ga·ble,** *adj.*

na′vy (nā′vē) *n., pl.* **-vies.** a nation's warships and crews.

navy blue, dark blue.

nay (nā) *adv., n.* no.

Na′zi (nät′sē, nat′-) *n.* member of the National Socialist party in Germany, headed by Adolf Hitler. —**Na′zism,** *n.*

NB, nota bene.

NC, North Carolina. Also, **N.C.**

NC-17 (en′sē′sev′ən tēn′) *Trademark.* motion-picture rating advising that persons under 17 will not be admitted.

ND, North Dakota. Also, **N.D.**

N.Dak., North Dakota.

NE, 1. Nebraska. **2.** northeast.

neap tide (nēp) tide having lowest high point.

near (nēr) *adv.* **1.** close by. —*adj.* **2.** close. **3.** intimate. —*v.* **4.** approach. —**near′ness,** *n.*

near′by′, *adj., adv.* close by.

near′ly, *adv.* almost.

near′-sight′ed (-sī′tid, -sī′-) *adj.* seeing distinctly only at short distance. —**near′-sight′ed·ness,** *n.*

neat (nēt) *adj.* **1.** orderly. **2.** skillful. **3.** undiluted. —**neat′ly,** *adv.*

neb (neb) *n.* bill or beak.

Nebr., Nebraska.

neb′u·la (neb′yə lə) *n., pl.* **-lae** (-lē′), **-las.** luminous mass of gas or stars. —**neb′u·lar,** *adj.*

neb′u·lous (neb′yə ləs) *adj.* **1.** hazy; vague. **2.** cloudlike.

nec′es·sar′y (nes′ə ser′ē) *adj., n., pl.* **-saries.** —*adj.* **1.** that cannot be dispensed with. **2.** required by facts or reason; unavoidable. —*n.* **3.** something necessary.

ne·ces′si·tate′ (nə ses′i tāt′) *v.,* **-tated, -tating.** make necessary.

ne·ces′si·ty, *n., pl.* **-ties. 1.** something necessary. **2.** fact of being necessary. **3.** poverty.

neck (nek) *n.* **1.** part connecting head and trunk. —*v.* **2.** *Slang.* kiss and embrace amorously.

neck′er·chief (nek′ər chif, -chēf′) *n.* cloth worn around neck.

neck′lace (-lis) *n.* ornament of gems, etc., worn around neck.

neck′tie′, *n.* cloth strip worn under collar and tied in front.

nec′ro·man′cy (nek′rə man′sē) *n.* magic. —**nec′ro·manc′er,** *n.*

ne·cro′sis (nə krō′sis) *n.* death of tissue or of organ.

nec′tar (nek′tər) *n.* **1.** sweet secretion of flower. **2.** drink of gods.

nec′tar·ine′ (nek′tə rēn′) *n.* downless peach.

nee (nā) *adj.* (of woman) born; having as maiden name. Also, **née.**

need (nēd) *n.* **1.** requirement. **2.** condition marked by necessity. —*v.* **3.** depend absolutely or strongly. **4.** be obliged. —**need′less,** *adj.*

nee′dle (nēd′l) *n., v.,* **-dled, -dling.** —*n.* **1.** slender pointed implement for sewing, knitting, etc. **2.** anything similar, as indicator or gauge. **3.** hypodermic syringe. —*v.* **4.** prod.

nee′dle·point′, *n.* embroidery on canvas.

nee′dle·work′, *n.* art or product of working with a needle.

needs (nēdz) *adv.* necessarily.

need′y, *adj.,* **-ier, -iest.** very poor.

ne′er-do-well′ (nâr′-) *n.* person who habitually fails.

ne·far′i·ous (ni fâr′ē əs) *adj.* wicked.

ne·gate′ (ni gāt′, neg′āt) *v.,* **-gated, -gating.** deny; nullify.

neg′a·tive (neg′ə tiv) *adj.* **1.** expressing denial or refusal. **2.** lacking positive attributes. **3.** *Math.* minus. **4.** *Photog.* having light and shade reversed. —*n.* **5.** negative statement, etc. **6.** *Photog.* negative image.

ne·glect′ (ni glekt′) *v.* **1.** disregard; fail to do. —*n.* **2.** disregard; negligence. —**ne·glect′ful,** *adj.*

neg′li·gee′ (neg′li zhā′, neg′li zhā′) *n.* woman's house robe.

neg′li·gent (neg′li jənt) *adj.* neglectful. —**neg′li·gence,** *n.*

neg′li·gi·ble (-jə bəl) *adj.* very small; unimportant.

ne·go′ti·a·ble (ni gō′shē ə bəl, -shə bəl) *adj.* transferable, as securities. —**ne·go′ti·a·bil′i·ty,** *n.*

ne·go′ti·ate′ (-shē āt′) *v.,* **-ated, -ating. 1.** deal with; bargain. **2.** dispose of. —**ne·go′ti·a′tion,** *n.* —**ne·go′ti·a′tor,** *n.*

Ne′gro (nē′grō) *n., pl.* **-groes.** *Sometimes Offensive.* member of racial group having brown to black skin. —**Ne′gro,** *adj.* —**Ne′groid** (-groid) *adj.*

neigh (nā) *n.* **1.** cry of horse; whinny. —*v.* **2.** make cry of horse.

neigh′bor (nā′bər) *n.* **1.** person or thing near another. —*v.* **2.** be near.

neigh′bor·hood, *n.* **1.** surrounding area. **2.** district having separate identity.

nei′ther (nē′thər, nī′-) *conj., adj.* not either. —**Pronunciation.** See EITHER.

nem′e·sis (nem′ə sis) *n., pl.* **-ses.** cause of one's downfall.

neo-, prefix meaning new, recent, or revived.

Ne′o·lith′ic (nē′ə lith′ik) *adj.* of the later Stone Age.

ne·ol′o·gism (nē ol′ə jiz′əm) *n.* new word or phrase.

ne′on (nē′on) *n.* gas used in electrical signs.

ne′o·nate′ (nē′ə nāt′) *n.* newborn child. —**ne′o·na′tal,** *adj.*

ne′o·phyte′ (-fīt′) *n.* beginner.

ne′o·plasm (-plaz′əm) *n.* tumor.

neph′ew (nef′yōō) *n.* son of one's brother or sister.

ne·phri′tis (nə frī′tis) *n.* inflammation of the kidneys.

ne′plus·ul′tra (nē′ plus′ ul′trə, nā′) highest point.

nep′o·tism (nep′ə tiz′əm) *n.* favoritism based on family relationship.

Nep′tune (nep′tōōn, -tyōōn) *n.* planet eighth from the sun.

nerd (nûrd) *n. Slang.* **1.** dull, ineffectual, or unattractive person. **2.** person devoted to nonsocial pursuit.

nerve (nûrv) *n., v.,* **nerved, nerving.** —*n.* **1.** bundle of fiber that conveys impulses between brain and other parts of body. **2.** courage. **3.** *Informal.* presumption. **4.** (*pl.*) anxiety; unease. —*v.* **5.** give courage to.

nerve gas, poison gas that interferes with nerve functions.

nerv′ous, *adj.* **1.** of nerves. **2.** having or caused by disordered nerves. **3.** anxious. —**nerv′ous·ly,** *adv.*

nerv′y, *adj.,* **-ier, -iest.** *Informal.* presumptuous.

-ness, suffix meaning: quality or state, as *goodness.*

nest (nest) *n.* **1.** place used by animal for rearing its young. **2.** group of things fitting tightly together. —*v.* **3.** settle in nest. **4.** fit one within another.

nest egg, money saved for emergencies, retirement, etc.

nes′tle (nes′əl) *v.,* **-tled, -tling.** lie close and snug.

net (net) *adj., n., v.,* **netted, netting.** —*adj.* **1.** exclusive of loss, expense, etc. —*n.* **2.** net profit. **3.** Also, **net′ting.** lacelike fabric of uniform mesh. **4.** bag of such fabric. —*v.* **5.** gain as clear profit. **6.** cover with net. **7.** ensnare.

neth′er (neth′ər) *adj.* lower.

net′tle (net′l) *n., v.,* **-tled, -tling.** —*n.* **1.** plant with stinging hairs. —*v.* **2.** irritate; sting.

net′tle·some (-səm) *adj.* **1.** causing irritation. **2.** easily provoked.

net′work′, *n.* **1.** netlike combination. **2.** group of associated radio or television stations, etc. **3.** any system of interconnected elements. —*v.* **4.** share information informally with others who have common interests.

neu′ral (nōōr′əl, nyōōr′-) *adj.* of nerves or nervous system.

neu·ral′gia (nōō ral′jə, nyōō-) *n.* sharp pain along nerve.

neu·ri′tis (nōō rī′tis, nyōō-) *n.* inflammation of nerve.

neu·rol′o·gy (-rol′ə jē) *n.* study of nerves. —**neu′ro·log′i·cal** (nōōr′ə loj′i kəl) *adj.*

neu′ron (nōōr′on, nyōōr′-) *n.* cell that is basic to nervous system.

neu·ro·sis (nōō rō′sis, nyōō-) *n., pl.* **-ses.** psychoneurosis. —**neu·rot′ic** (-rot′ik) *adj., n.*

neu′ro·sur′ger·y (nōōr′ō sûr′jə rē, nyōōr′-) *n.* surgery of the brain or other nerve tissue.

neu·ro·trans·mit·ter, *n.* chemical substance that transmits nerve impulses across synapse.

neu′ter (nōō′tər, nyōō′-) *adj.* **1.** neither male nor female. —*v.* **2.** spay or castrate. —**neu′ter,** *n.*

neu′tral (nōō′trəl, nyōō′-) *adj.* **1.** taking no side in controversy. **2.** not emphatic or positive. —*n.* **3.** neutral person or state. —**neu·tral′i·ty** (-tral′i tē) *n.* —**neu′tral·ize′,** *v.,* **-ized, -izing.** —**neu′tral·ly,** *adv.*

neu′tron (nōō′tron, nyōō′-) *n.* particle in nucleus of atom.

Nev., Nevada.

nev′er (nev′ər) *adv.* not ever.

nev′er·the·less′, *adv.* in spite of what has been said.

new (nōō, nyōō) *adj.* **1.** of recent origin or existence. **2.** unfamiliar. —*adv.* **3.** recently; freshly.

new′el (nōō′əl, nyōō′-) *n.* post at the head or foot of stair.

New England, group of states in northeast U.S.

new′fan′gled (-fang′gəld) *adj.* of a new kind or fashion.

new′ly, *adv.* **1.** recently. **2.** anew.

new′ly·wed′, *n.* newly married person.

news (nōōz, nyōōz) *n.* report of recent event.

news′cast′, *n.* broadcast of news. —**news′cast′er,** *n.*

news′let′ter, *n.* small informative periodical for specialized group.

news′man′, *n.* journalist. Also, **news′wom′an,** *n.fem.*

news′pa′per (nōōz′-, nyōōz′-) *n.* periodical containing news, etc.

news′print′, *n.* paper on which newspapers are printed.

news′reel′, *n.* motion picture of news events.

news′stand′, *n.* sales booth for periodicals, etc.

news′wor′thy, *adj.* interesting enough to warrant press coverage.

newt (nōōt, nyōōt) *n.* salamander.

New Testament, portion of Christian Bible recording life and teachings of Christ and His disciples.

new′ton (nōōt′n, nyōōt′n) *n.* unit of force.

new wave, movement that breaks with traditional values, etc.

new year, **1.** (*cap.*) first day of year. **2.** year approaching.

next (nekst) *adj.* **1.** nearest after. —*adv.* **2.** in nearest place after. **3.** at first subsequent time.

next′-door′, *adj.* in the next house, apartment, etc.

nex′us (nek′səs) *n., pl.* **nexus.** link or connection.

NH, New Hampshire. Also, **N.H.**

ni′a·cin (nī′ə sin) *n.* nicotinic acid.

nib (nib) *n.* pen point.

nib′ble, *v.,* **-bled, -bling.** —*v.* **1.** bite off in small bits. —*n.* **2.** small morsel.

nice (nīs) *adj.,* **nicer, nicest.** **1.** agreeable. **2.** precise. **3.** fastidious.

ni′ce·ty (nī′si tē) *n., pl.* **-ties.** **1.** subtle point. **2.** refinement.

niche (nich) *n.* **1.** recess in wall. **2.** proper role or vocation.

nick (nik) *n.* **1.** notch or hollow place in surface. **2.** precise or opportune moment. —*v.* **3.** make nick in.

nick′el (nik′əl) *n.* **1.** hard silver-white metal. **2.** five-cent coin.

nick′name′, *n., v.,* **-named, -naming.** —*n.* **1.** name used informally. —*v.* **2.** give nickname to.

nic′o·tine′ (nik′ə tēn′) *n.* alkaloid found in tobacco.

niece (nēs) *n.* daughter of one's brother, sister, brother-in-law, or sister-in-law.

nif′ty (nif′tē) *adj.,* **-tier, -tiest.** *Informal.* smart; fine.

nig′gard·ly (nig′ərd lē) *adj.* stingy.

nig′gling (nig′ling) *adj.* trivial.

nigh (nī) *adv., adj.* near.

night (nīt) *n.* period between sunset and sunrise.

night′cap′, *n.* **1.** alcoholic drink taken before bed. **2.** cap worn while sleeping.

night′club′, *n.* establishment open at night, offering food, drink, and entertainment.

night crawler, earthworm.

night′fall′, *n.* coming of night.

night′gown′, *n.* gown for sleeping.

night′hawk′, *n.* nocturnal American bird.

night′in·gale′ (nīt′n gāl′, nī′ting-) *n.* small European song bird.

night′ly, *adj., adv.* every night.

night′mare′ (-mâr′) *n.* **1.** bad dream. **2.** harrowing event.

night owl, person who often stays up late at night.

night′shade′, *n.* plant sometimes used in medicine.

night′shirt′, *n.* loose shirtlike garment worn in bed.

night stick, club carried by police officers.

ni′hil·ism (nī′ə liz′əm, nē′-) *n.* total disbelief in principles. —**ni′hil·ist,** *n.* —**ni′hil·is′tic,** *adj.*

nil (nil) *n.* nothing.

nim′ble (nim′bəl) *adj.,* **-bler, -blest.** agile; quick. —**nim′bly,** *adv.*

nim′bus (nim′bəs) *n., pl.* **-bi** (-bī) **-buses.** **1.** halo. **2.** rain cloud.

nim′rod (nim′rod) *n.* hunter.

nin′com·poop′ (nin′kəm pōōp′, ning′-) *n.* fool.

nine (nīn) *n., adj.* eight plus one. —**ninth,** *n., adj.*

nine′pins′, *n.pl.* bowling game played with nine wooden pins.

nine′teen′, *n., adj.* ten plus nine. —**nine′teenth′,** *n., adj.*

nine′ty, *n., adj.* ten times nine. —**nine′ti·eth,** *adj., n.*

nin′ny (nin′ē) *n., pl.* **-nies.** fool.

nip (nip) *v.,* **nipped, nipping.** —*v.* **1.** pinch or bite. **2.** check growth of. **3.** affect sharply. **4.** sip. —*n.* **5.** pinch. **6.** biting quality. **7.** sip.

nip′ple, *n.* **1.** milk-discharging protuberance on breast. **2.** nipple-shaped object.

nip′py, *adj.,* **-pier, -piest.** **1.** chilly. **2.** pungent.

nir·va′na (nir vä′nə, -van′ə, nər-) *n.* **1.** (in Buddhism) freedom from all passion. **2.** state of bliss.

nit (nit) *n.* egg of louse.

ni′ter (nī′tər) *n.* white salt used in gunpowder, etc. Also, **ni′tre.**

nit′-pick′, *v. Informal.* argue or find fault pettily.

ni′trate (nī′trāt, -trit) *n.* salt of nitric acid.

ni′tric acid (nī′trik) caustic liquid used in manufacture of explosives, fertilizers, etc.

ni′tro·gen (nī′trə jən) *n.* colorless, odorless, tasteless gas.

ni·tro·glyc′er·in (nī′trə glis′ər in) *n.* colorless, highly explosive oil.

ni′trous (nī′trəs) *adj.* **1.** of niter. **2.** Also, **ni′tric.** containing nitrogen.

nit′ty-grit′ty (nit′ē grit′ē) *n. Slang.* essentials of situation.

nit′wit′, *n.* stupid person.

nix (niks) *adv. Informal.* no.

NJ, New Jersey. Also, **N.J.**

NM, New Mexico.

N. Mex., New Mexico.

no (nō) *adv., n., pl.* **noes,** *adj.* —*adv.* **1.** word used to express dissent, denial or refusal. —*n.* **2.** negative vote. —*adj.* **3.** not any.

no., **1.** north. **2.** number.

no·bil′i·ty (nō bil′i tē) *n., pl.* **-ties. 1.** noble class. **2.** noble quality.

no′ble (nō′bəl) *adj.,* **-bler, -blest,** *n.* —*adj.* **1.** of high rank by birth. **2.** admirable or magnificent. —*n.* **3.** person of noble rank. —**no′ble·man,** *n.* —**no′ble·wom′an,** *n.fem.*

no·blesse′ o·blige′ (nō bles′ ō-blēzh′) moral obligation of the rich to display generous conduct.

no′bod′y (nō′bod′ē, -bud′ē, -bə dē) *n., pl.* **-bodies. 1.** no one. **2.** no one of importance.

no′-brain′er, *n. Informal.* something requiring little thought.

noc·tur′nal (nok tûr′nl) *adj.* **1.** of night. **2.** occurring or active by night.

noc′turne (-tûrn) *n.* dreamy or pensive musical composition.

nod (nod) *v.,* **nodded, nodding,** *n.* —*v.* **1.** incline head briefly. **2.** become sleepy. **3.** sway gently. —*n.* **4.** brief inclination of head, as in assent.

node (nōd) *n.* **1.** protuberance. **2.** joint in plant stem.

nod′ule (noj′ōol) *n.* small knob or lump. —**nod′u·lar,** *adj.*

No·el′ (nō el′) *n.* Christmas.

no′-fault′, *adj.* (of auto accident insurance, divorces, etc.) effective without establishing fault.

nog′gin (nog′ən) *n.* small mug.

noise (noiz) *n., v.,* **noised, noising.** —*n.* **1.** sound, esp. loud or harsh. —*v.* **2.** spread rumors. —**nois′y,** *adj.* —**nois′i·ly,** *adv.*

noi′some (noi′səm) *adj.* offensive.

no′mad (nō′mad) *n.* wanderer. —**no·mad′ic,** *adj.*

no man's land, area between warring armies.

nom de plume (nom′ də plōōm′) name assumed by writer.

no′men·cla′ture (nō′mən klā′chər) *n.* set or system of names.

nom′i·nal (nom′ə nl) *adj.* **1.** in name only; so-called. **2.** trifling.

nom′i·nate′ (-nāt′) *v.,* **-nated, -nating. 1.** propose as candidate. **2.** appoint. —**nom′i·na′tion,** *n.*

nom′i·na·tive (nom′ə nə tiv) *adj.* **1.** denoting noun or pronoun used as the subject of a sentence. —*n.* **2.** nominative case.

nom′i·nee′, *n.* one nominated.

non-, prefix meaning not.

non′age (non′ij, nō′nij) *n.* period of legal minority.

non′a·ge·nar′i·an (non′ə jə nâr′ē-ən, nō′nə-) *n.* person 90 to 99 years old.

non′cha·lant′ (non′shə länt′) *adj.* coolly unconcerned. —**non′cha·lance′,** *n.* —**non′cha·lant′ly,** *adv.*

non′com·bat′ant (non′kəm bat′nt, non kom′bə tnt) *n.* **1.** member of military force who is not a fighter. **2.** civilian in wartime.

non′com·mis′sioned, *adj. Mil.* not commissioned.

non′com·mit′tal, *adj.* not committing oneself.

non′ com/pos men′tis (non′ kom′-pəs men′tis) *Law.* not of sound mind.

non·con·duc′tor, *n.* substance that does not readily conduct heat, electricity, etc.

non′con·form′ist, *n.* person who refuses to conform.

non′de·script′ (non′di skript′) *adj.* of no particular kind.

none (nun) *pron. sing. and pl.* **1.** not one; not any. —*adv.* **2.** in no way.

non·en′ti·ty, *n., pl.* **-ties.** unimportant person or thing.

none′the·less′, *adv.* nevertheless.

no′-no′, *n. Informal.* forbidden thing.

non′pa·reil′ (non′pə rel′) *adj.* **1.** having no equal. —*n.* **2.** person or thing without equal.

non·par′ti·san, *adj.* **1.** not taking sides. **2.** belonging to no party.

non·plus′ (non plus′, non′plus) *v.* confuse.

non·prof′it, *adj.* not profit motivated.

non′rep·re·sen·ta′tion·al, *adj.* not resembling any object in nature.

non′sec·tar′i·an, *adj.* of no one sect. —**nonsectarian,** *n.*

non′sense (non′sens, -səns) *n.* senseless or absurd words or action. —**non·sen′si·cal,** *adj.*

non se′qui·tur (non sek′wi tər, -tōor′) statement unrelated to preceding one.

non′stand′ard, *adj.* not conforming to usage considered acceptable by educated native speakers.

non′stop′, *adj., adv.* without intermediate stops. Also, **non-stop.**

non′sup·port′, *n.* failure to provide financial support.

non·un′ion, *adj.* **1.** not belonging to labor union. **2.** not produced by union workers.

non·vi′o·lence, *n.* policy of refraining from using violence. —**non·vi′o·lent,** *adj.*

noo′dle (nōōd′l) *n.* thin strip of dough, cooked in soup, etc.

nook (nōōk) *n.* corner of room.

noon (nōōn) *n.* 12 o'clock in daytime. —**noon′time′, noon′tide′,** *n.*

no one, not anyone.

noose (nōōs) *n., v.,* **noosed, noosing.** —*n.* **1.** loop with running knot that pulls tight. —*v.* **2.** catch by noose.

nor (nôr; *unstressed* nər) *conj.* or not: used with **neither.**

Nor′dic (nôr′dik) *n.* person marked by tall stature, blond hair, and blue eyes. —**Nor′dic,** *adj.*

norm (nôrm) *n.* standard.

nor′mal (nôr′məl) *adj.* **1.** of standard type; usual. —*n.* **2.** standard; average. —**nor′mal·cy, nor·mal′i·ty** (-mal′i tē) *n.* —**nor′mal·ize′,** *v.,* **-ized, -izing.**

normal school, school for training teachers.

nor′ma·tive (nôr′mə tiv) *adj.* establishing a norm.

Norse (nôrs) *n.* inhabitants or speech of medieval Scandinavia.

north (nôrth) *n.* **1.** cardinal point of compass, on one's right facing the setting sun. **2.** territory in or to north. —*adj., adv.* **3.** toward, in, or from north. —**north′er·ly,** *adj., adv.* —**north′ern,** *adj.* —**north′ern·er,** *n.* —**north′ward,** *adj., adv.*

north′east′, *n.* point or direction midway between north and east. —**north′east′,** *adj., adv.* —**north′-east′ern,** *adj.*

North Star, Polaris.

north′west′, *n.* point or direction midway between north and west. —**north′west′,** *adj., adv.* —**north′west′ern,** *adj.*

nose (nōz) *n., v.,* **nosed, nosing.** —*n.* **1.** part of head containing nostrils. **2.** sense of smell. **3.** projecting part. —*v.* **4.** smell. **5.** pry. **6.** head cautiously.

nose′cone′, *n.* forward section of rocket.

nose′dive′, *n.* **1.** downward plunge. —*v.* **2.** go into a nosedive.

nose′gay′, *n.* small bouquet.

nosh (nosh) *Informal.* —*v.* **1.** snack (on). —*n.* **2.** snack.

no′-show′, *n.* person who neither uses nor cancels reservation.

nos·tal′gia (no stal′jə) *n.* yearning for the past.

nos′tril (nos′trəl) *n.* external opening of nose for breathing.

nos′trum (nos′trəm) *n.* favorite or quack remedy.

nos′y (nō′zē) *adj.,* **-ier, -iest.** *Informal.* unduly inquisitive.

not (not) *adv.* word expressing negation, denial, or refusal.

no′ta be′ne (nō′tə ben′ē) *Latin.* note well.

no′ta·ble (nō′tə bəl) *adj.* **1.** worthy of note; important. —*n.* **2.** prominent person. —**no′ta·bly,** *adv.*

no′ta·rize′ (nō′tə rīz′) *v.,* **-rized, -rizing.** authenticate by notary.

no′ta·ry (nō′tə rē) *n., pl.* **-ries.** official authorized to verify documents. Also, **notary public.**

no·ta′tion (nō tā′shən) *n.* note. —**no·ta′tion·al,** *adj.*

notch (noch) *n.* **1.** angular cut. —*v.* **2.** make notch in.

note (nōt) *n., v.,* **noted, noting.** —*n.* **1.** brief record, comment, etc. **2.** short letter. **3.** importance. **4.** notice. **5.** paper promising payment. **6.** musical sound or written symbols. —*v.* **7.** write down. **8.** notice.

note′book′, *n.* **1.** book with blank pages for writing notes. **2.** laptop computer.

not′ed, *adj.* famous.

note′wor′thy, *adj.* notable.

noth′ing (nuth′ing) *n.* **1.** not anything. **2.** trivial action, thing, etc. —*adv.* **3.** not at all.

noth′ing·ness, *n.* **1.** lack of being. **2.** unconsciousness.

no′tice (nō′tis) *n., v.,* **-ticed, -ticing.** —*n.* **1.** information; warning. **2.** note, etc., that informs or warns. **3.** attention; heed. —*v.* **4.** pay attention to; perceive. **5.** mention.

no′ti·fy′, *v.,* **-fied, -fying.** give notice to. —**no′ti·fi·ca′tion,** *n.*

no′tion (nō′shən) *n.* **1.** idea; conception. **2.** opinion. **3.** whim. **4.** (*pl.*) small items, as pins or trim.

no·to′ri·ous (nō tôr′ē əs, nə-) *adj.* widely known, esp. unfavorably. —**no′to·ri·e·ty** (-tə rī′i tē) *n.*

not′with·stand′ing, *prep.* **1.** in spite of. —*adv.* **2.** nevertheless. —*conj.* **3.** although.

nou′gat (nōō′gət) *n.* pastelike candy with nuts.

nought (nôt) *n.* naught.

noun (noun) *n.* word denoting person, place, or thing.

nour′ish (nûr′ish, nur′-) *v.* sustain with food. —**nour′ish·ment,** *n.*

nou′veau riche′ (nōō′vō rēsh′) *pl.* **nou′veaux riches** (nōō′vō rēsh′). newly rich person.

nou·velle′ cuisine (nōō vel′) cooking that emphasizes fresh ingredients and light sauces.

Nov., November.

no'va (nō'və) *n., pl.* **-vas, -vae** (-vē). star that suddenly becomes much brighter, then gradually fades.

nov'el (nov'əl) *n.* **1.** long fictitious narrative. —*adj.* **2.** new or strange. —**nov'el•ist,** *n.*

nov'el•ty, *n., pl.* **-ties. 1.** unfamiliarity. **2.** new or amusing thing.

No•vem'ber (nō vem'bər) *n.* eleventh month of year.

no•ve'na (nō vē'nə, nə-) *n., pl.* **-nae** (-nē), **-nas.** Roman Catholic devotion occurring on nine consecutive days.

nov'ice (nov'is) *n.* **1.** beginner. **2.** person just received into a religious order.

no•vi'ti•ate (nō vish'ē it, -āt') *n.* period of being novice.

No'vo•caine' (nō'və kān') *n. Trademark.* local anesthetic.

now (nou) *adv.* **1.** at present time. **2.** immediately. —*conj.* **3.** since. —*n.* **4.** the present.

now'a•days' (-ə dāz') *adv.* in these times.

no'where', *adv.* not anywhere.

nox'ious (nok'shəs) *adj.* harmful.

noz'zle (noz'əl) *n.* projecting spout.

nth (enth) *adj.* utmost.

nu'ance (nōō'äns, nyōō'-) *n.* shade of expression, etc.

nub (nub) *n.* gist.

nu'bile (nōō'bil, -bīl, nyōō'-) *adj.* (of a young woman) **1.** marriageable. **2.** sexually attractive.

nu'cle•ar (nōō'klē ər, nyōō'-) *adj.* **1.** of or involving atomic weapons. **2.** of or forming a nucleus.

nuclear energy, energy released by reactions within atomic nuclei, as in nuclear fission or fusion.

nuclear family, social unit composed of father, mother, and children.

nuclear physics, branch of physics dealing with atoms.

nuclear winter, devastation, darkness, and cold that could result from nuclear war.

nu'cle•on (nōō'klē on', nyōō'-) *n.* proton or neutron.

nu'cle•us (-klē əs) *n., pl.* **-cle•i** (-klē-ī), **-cleuses. 1.** central part. **2.** central body of living cell. **3.** core of atom.

nude (nōōd, nyōōd) *adj.* **1.** naked. —*n.* **2.** naked human figure.

nudge (nuj) *v.,* **nudged, nudging,** *n.* —*v.* **1.** push slightly. —*n.* **2.** slight push.

nud'ism (nōō'diz əm, nyōō'-) *n.* practice of going naked. —**nud'ist,** *n.*

nug'get (nug'it) *n.* lump.

nui'sance (nōō'səns, nyōō'-) *n.* annoying thing or person.

nuke (nōōk, nyōōk) *n., v.,* **nuked, nuking.** *Slang.* —*n.* **1.** nuclear weapon or power plant. —*v.* **2.** attack with nuclear weapons.

null (nul) *adj.* of no effect.

null'i•fy', *v.,* **-fied, -fying. 1.** make null. **2.** make legally void.

numb (num) *adj.* **1.** deprived of feeling. —*v.* **2.** make numb.

num'ber (num'bər) *n.* **1.** sum of group of units. **2.** numeral. **3.** one of series or group. **4.** large quantity. —*v.* **5.** mark with number. **6.** count. **7.** amount to in numbers. —**Usage.** See AMOUNT.

num'ber•less, *adj.* too numerous to count.

nu'mer•al (nōō'mər əl, nyōō'-) *n.* **1.** word or sign expressing number. —*adj.* **2.** of numbers.

nu'mer•ate' (-mə rāt') *v.,* **-ated, -ating.** number; count.

nu'mer•a'tor, *n.* part of fraction

written above the line, showing number to be divided.

nu•mer'i•cal (nōō mer'i kəl, nyōō-) *adj.* of, denoting number.

nu'mer•ol'o•gy (nōō'mə rol'ə jē, nyōō'-) *n.* study of numbers to determine supernatural meaning.

nu'mer•ous (-mər əs) *adj.* very many.

nu'mis•mat'ics (nōō'miz mat'iks, -mis-, nyōō'-) *n.* science of coins and medals.

num'skull' (num'skul') *n. Informal.* dunce. Also, **numb'skull'.**

nun (nun) *n.* woman living with religious group under vows.

nun'ner•y (nun'ə rē) *n., pl.* **-neries.** convent.

nup'tial (nup'shəl, -chəl) *adj.* **1.** of marriage. —*n.* **2.** (*pl.*) marriage ceremony.

nurse (nûrs) *n., v.,* **nursed, nursing.** —*n.* **1.** person who cares for sick or children. —*v.* **2.** tend in sickness. **3.** look after carefully. **4.** suckle.

nurs'er•y, *n., pl.* **-eries. 1.** room set apart for young children. **2.** place where young plants are grown.

nursery school, school level below kindergarten age.

nur'ture (nûr'chər) *v.,* **-tured, -turing,** *n.* —*v.* **1.** feed and care for during growth. —*n.* **2.** upbringing. **3.** nourishment.

nut (nut) *n.* **1.** dry fruit consisting of edible kernel in shell. **2.** the kernel. **3.** perforated, threaded metal block used to screw on end of bolt. —**nut'crack'er,** *n.* —**nut'shell',** *n.*

nut'hatch', *n.* small songbird that seeks food along tree trunks.

nut'meg (-meg) *n.* aromatic seed of East Indian tree.

nu'tri•ent (nōō'trē ənt, nyōō'-) *adj.* **1.** nourishing. —*n.* **2.** nutrient substance.

nu'tri•ment (-trə mənt) *n.* nourishment.

nu•tri'tion (-trish'ən) *n.* **1.** process of nourishing or being nourished. **2.** study of dietary requirements. —**nu•tri'tious, nu'tri•tive,** *adj.* —**nu•tri'tion•ist,** *n.*

nuts (nuts) *adj. Informal.* crazy.

nut'ty, *adj.,* **-tier, -tiest. 1.** tasting of or like nuts. **2.** *Informal.* insane; senseless. —**nut'ti•ness,** *n.*

nuz'zle (nuz'əl) *v.,* **-zled, -zling. 1.** rub noses against. **2.** cuddle.

NV, Nevada.

NW, northwest. Also, **N.W.**

NY, New York. Also, **N.Y.**

ny'lon (nī'lon) *n.* **1.** tough, elastic synthetic substance used for yarn, bristles, etc. **2.** (*pl.*) stockings of nylon.

nymph (nimf) *n.* **1.** beautiful goddess. **2.** beautiful girl.

nym'pho•ma'ni•a (nim'fə mā'nē ə) *n.* uncontrollable sexual desire in women. —**nym'pho•ma'ni•ac',** *n.*

O

O, o (ō) *n.* fifteenth letter of English alphabet.

O (ō) *interj.* (expression of surprise, gladness, pain, etc.)

o' (ə, ō) *prep.* shortened form of **of.**

oaf (ōf) *n.* clumsy, rude person. —**oaf'ish,** *adj.*

oak (ōk) *n.* tree having hard wood.

oar (ōr) *n.* **1.** flat-bladed shaft for rowing boat. —*v.* **2.** row. —**oars'man,** *n.*

oar'lock', *n.* support on gunwale for oar.

o•a'sis (ō ā'sis) *n., pl.* **-ses.** fertile place in desert.

oat (ōt) *n.* **1.** cereal grass having edible seed.

oath (ōth) *n.* **1.** solemn affirmation; vow. **2.** curse.

oat'meal', *n.* **1.** meal made from oats. **2.** cooked breakfast food.

ob'du•rate (ob'dōō rit, -dyōō-) *adj.* stubborn; not sorry or penitent. —**ob'du•ra•cy,** *n.*

o•bei'sance (ō bā'səns, ō bē'-) *n.* **1.** bow or curtsy. **2.** homage.

ob'e•lisk (ob'ə lisk) *n.* tapering, four-sided monumental pillar.

o•bese' (ō bēs') *adj.* very fat. —**o•bes'i•ty,** *n.*

o•bey' (ō bā') *v.* **1.** do as ordered by. **2.** respond to, as controls. —**o•be'di•ence** (ō bē'dē əns) *n.* —**o•be'di•ent,** *adj.*

ob•fus'cate (ob'fə skāt', ob fus'kāt) *v.,* **-cated, -cating.** confuse; make unclear. —**ob'fus•ca'tion,** *n.*

ob'i•ter dic'tum (ob'i tər dik'təm) *pl.* **obiter dicta** (-tə) incidental remark.

o•bit'u•ar'y (ō bich'ōō er'ē) *n., pl.* **-aries.** notice of death.

obj., 1. object. **2.** objective.

ob'ject *n.* (ob'jikt, -jekt) **1.** something solid. **2.** thing or person to which attention is directed. **3.** end; motive. **4.** noun or pronoun that represents goal of action. —*v.* (əb jekt') **5.** make protest. —**ob•jec'tor,** *n.*

ob•jec'tion (əb jek'shən) *n.* **1.** argument against. **2.** act of objecting.

ob•jec'tion•a•ble (əb jek'shə nə bəl) *adj.* causing disapproval; offensive.

ob•jec'tive, *n.* **1.** something aimed at. **2.** objective case. —*adj.* **3.** real or factual. **4.** unbiased. **5.** denoting word used as object of sentence. —**ob'jec•tiv'i•ty** (ob'jik tiv'i tē) *n.*

object lesson, practical illustration of principle.

ob•jet d'art (ob'zhä där') *pl.* **objets d'art** (ob'zhä där'). object of artistic worth.

ob'late (ob'lāt, o blāt') *adj.* (of spheroid) flattened at poles.

ob•la'tion (o blā'shən) *n.* offering; sacrifice.

ob'li•gate' (ob'li gāt') *v.,* **-gated, -gating.** bind morally or legally. —**ob'li•ga'tion,** *n.*

ob•lig'a•to'ry (ə blig'ə tôr'ē) *adj.* compulsory.

o•blige' (ə blīj') *v.,* **obliged, obliging. 1.** require. **2.** do a favor for.

o•blig'ing, *adj.* willing to help.

ob•lique' (ə blēk', ō blēk') *adj.* **1.** slanting. **2.** indirect. —**ob•lique'ly,** *adv.* —**ob•lique'ness,** *n.*

ob•lit'er•ate' (ə blit'ə rāt') *v.,* **-ated, -ating.** remove all traces of.

ob•liv'i•on (ə bliv'ē ən) *n.* **1.** state of being forgotten. **2.** forgetfulness. —**ob•liv'i•ous,** *adj.*

ob'long (ob'lông') *adj.* **1.** longer than broad. —*n.* **2.** oblong figure.

ob'lo•quy (ob'lə kwē) *n., pl.* **-quies.** public disgrace.

ob•nox'ious (əb nok'shəs) *adj.* offensive. —**ob•nox'ious•ly,** *adv.*

o'boe (ō'bō) *n.* wind instrument. —**o'bo•ist,** *n.*

obs., obsolete.

ob•scene' (əb sēn') *adj.* offensive to decency. —**ob•scene'ly,** *adv.* —**ob•scen'i•ty,** (-sen'i tē, -sēn'i-) *n.*

ob•scu'rant•ism (əb skyōōr'ən tiz'-əm, ob'skyōō ran'tiz əm) *n.* willful obscuring of something presented to public. —**ob•scu'rant•ist,** *n., adj.*

ob•scure' (əb skyōōr') *adj., v.,*

-scured, -scuring. —*adj.* **1.** not clear. **2.** not prominent. **3.** dark. —*v.* **4.** make obscure. **—ob•scu′ri•ty,** *n.* **—ob•scure′ly,** *adv.*

ob•se′qui•ous (əb sē′kwē əs) *adj.* servilely deferential.

ob′se•quy (ob′si kwē) *n., pl.* **-quies.** funeral rite.

ob•serv′ance (əb zûr′vəns) *n.* **1.** act of observing or conforming. **2.** due celebration of holiday or ritual.

ob•serv′ant, *adj.* quick to notice.

ob•serv′a•to•ry (əb zûr′və tôr′ē) *n., pl.* **-ries.** place equipped for observing stars.

ob•serve′, *v.,* **-served, -serving. 1.** see; notice; watch. **2.** remark. **3.** celebrate duly. **—ob′ser•va′tion** (ob′zər-vā′shən) *n.*

ob•sess′ (əb ses′) *v.* be constantly in the thoughts of. **—ob•ses′sion** (-sesh′-ən) *n.* **—ob•ses′sive,** *adj.*

ob′so•les′cent (ob′sə les′ənt) *adj.* becoming obsolete. **—ob′so•les′cence,** *n.*

ob′so•lete′ (-lēt′) *adj.* no longer in use.

ob′sta•cle (ob′stə kəl) *n.* something in the way.

ob•stet′rics (əb ste′triks) *n.* branch of medicine concerned with childbirth. **—ob′ste•tri′cian** (ob′sti trish′ən) *n.* **—ob•stet′ric,** *adj.*

ob′sti•nate (ob′stə nit) *adj.* **1.** firm; stubborn. **2.** not yielding to treatment. **—ob′sti•na•cy** (-nə sē) *n.* **—ob′sti-nate•ly,** *adv.*

ob•strep′er•ous (əb strep′ər əs) *adj.* unruly.

ob•struct′ (əb strukt′) *v.* block; hinder. **—ob•struc′tion,** *n.* **—ob•struc′tive,** *adj.*

ob•struc′tion•ism (-shə niz′əm) *n.* perverse desire to be obstructive.

ob•tain′ (əb tān′) *v.* **1.** get or acquire. **2.** prevail.

ob•trude′ (əb trōōd′) *v.,* **-truded, -truding.** thrust forward; intrude. **—ob•tru′sive** (-trōō′siv) *adj.*

ob•tuse′ (əb tōōs′, -tyōōs′) *adj.* **1.** blunt. **2.** not perceptive. **3.** (of angle) between 90° and 180°.

ob′verse (n. ob′vûrs) **1.** front. **2.** side of coin having principal design. **3.** counterpart. —*adj.* (ob vûrs′, ob′vûrs) **4.** facing. **5.** corresponding.

ob′vi•ate′ (ob′vē āt′) *v.,* **-ated, -ating.** make unnecessary.

ob′vi•ous (ob′vē əs) *adj.* **1.** readily perceptible. **2.** not subtle. **—ob′vi-ous•ly,** *adv.* **—ob′vi•ous•ness,** *n.*

oc′a•ri′na (ok′ə rē′nə) *n.* egg-shaped wind instrument.

oc•ca′sion (ə kā′zhən) *n.* **1.** particular time. **2.** important time. **3.** opportunity. **4.** reason. —*v.* **5.** give cause for. **—oc•ca′sion•al,** *adj.* **—oc•ca′sion•al•ly,** *adv.*

Oc′ci•dent (ok′si dənt) *n.* West, esp. Europe and Americas. **—Oc′ci•den′tal** (-den′tl) *adj., n.*

oc•cult′ (ə kult′, ok′ult) *adj.* beyond ordinary knowledge. **—n.** **2.** occult matters.

oc′cu•pa′tion (ok′yə pā′shən) *n.* **1.** trade. **2.** possession. **3.** military seizure. **—oc′cu•pa′tion•al,** *adj.*

occupational therapy, therapy utilizing activities for psychological or physical rehabilitation.

oc′cu•py, *v.,* **-pied, -pying. 1.** inhabit or be in. **2.** require as space. **3.** take possession of. **4.** hold attention of. **—oc′cu•pan•cy,** *n.* **—oc′cu•pant,** *n.*

oc•cur′ (ə kûr′) *v.,* **-curred, -curring. 1.** take place. **2.** appear. **3.** come to mind. **—oc•cur′rence,** *n.*

o′cean (ō′shən) *n.* **1.** large body of salt water covering much of earth. **2.** any of its five main parts. **—o′ce•an′-ic** (ō′shē an′ik) *adj.*

o′cea•nog′ra•phy (ō′shə nog′rə fē, ō′shē ə-) *n.* study of oceans.

o′ce•lot′ (os′ə lot′, ō′sə-) *n.* small American wildcat.

o′cher (ō′kər) *n.* yellow-to-red earth used as pigment. Also, **o′chre.**

o′clock′ (ə klok′) *adv.* by the clock.

Oct., October.

oc′ta•gon′ (ok′tə gon′, -gən) *n.* plane figure with eight sides.

oc′tane (ok′tān) *n.* colorless liquid hydrocarbon found in petroleum.

octane number, designation of quality of gasoline.

oc′tave (ok′tiv, -tāv) *n. Music.* **1.** eighth tone from given tone. **2.** interval between such tones.

oc•tet′ (ok tet′) *n.* group of eight, esp. musicians. Also, **oc•tette′.**

Oc•to′ber (ok tō′bər) *n.* tenth month of year.

oc′to•ge•nar′i•an (ok′tə jə när′ē ən) *n.* person 80 to 89 years old.

oc′to•pus (ok′tə pəs) *n., pl.* **-puses, -pi** (-pī). eight-armed sea mollusk.

oc′u•lar (ok′yə lər) *adj.* of eyes.

oc′u•list (-list) *n.* doctor skilled in treatment of eyes.

OD (ō′dē′) *n., pl.* **ODs** or **OD's,** *v.,* **OD'd** or **ODed, OD′ing.** *Slang. —n.* **1.** overdose of a drug, esp. a fatal one. —*v.* **2.** take a drug overdose.

odd (od) *adj.* **1.** eccentric; bizarre. **2.** additional; not part of set. **3.** not evenly divisible by two.

odd′ball′, *n. Informal.* peculiar person or thing.

odd′i•ty, *n., pl.* **-ties. 1.** queerness. **2.** odd thing.

odds (odz) *n.* **1.** chances; probability for or against. **2.** state of disagreement. **3.** odd things.

odds and ends, 1. miscellany. **2.** remnants.

odds′-on′, *adj.* most likely.

ode (ōd) *n.* poem of praise.

o′di•ous (ō′dē əs) *adj.* hateful.

o′di•um (-əm) *n.* **1.** discredit; reproach. **2.** hatred.

o′dor (ō′dər) *n.* quality that affects sense of smell. **—o′dor•ous,** *adj.*

o′dor•if′er•ous (ō′də rif′ər əs) *adj.* having odor, esp. unpleasant.

od′ys•sey (od′ə sē) *n.* long, adventurous journey.

oed′i•pal (ed′ə pəl, ē′də-) *adj.* (*often cap.*) resulting from the Oedipus complex.

Oedipus complex, libidinous feelings of son toward mother.

o′er (ôr) *prep., adv. Poetic.* over.

oeu′vre (*Fr.* œ′vⁿ) *n., pl.* **oeu•vres** (*Fr.* œ′vⁿ). all the works of a writer, painter, etc.

of (uv, ov; *unstressed* əv *or, esp. before consonants,* ə) *prep.* particle indicating: **1.** being from. **2.** belonging to. —*aux. v.* **3.** *Nonstandard.* have. —**Usage.** Because the preposition OF, when unstressed (*a piece of cake*), and the unstressed or contracted auxiliary verb HAVE (*could have gone; could've gone*) are both pronounced (əv) or (ə) in connected speech, inexperienced writers commonly confuse the two words, spelling HAVE as OF (*I would of handed in my book report, but the dog ate it*). Professional writers use this spelling deliberately, especially in fiction, to represent the speech of the uneducated: *If he could of went home, he would of.*

off (ôf) *adv.* **1.** up or away. **2.** deviating. **3.** out of operation or effect.

—*prep.* **4.** up or away from. —*adj.* **5.** not operating or in effect. **6.** in error. **7.** starting on one's way.

of′fal (ô′fəl) *n.* waste parts of butchered animal.

off′beat′, *adj. Informal.* unconventional.

off′-col′or, *adj.* **1.** not having the usual color. **2.** of questionable taste.

of•fend′ (ə fend′) *v.* **1.** err. **2.** annoy greatly.

of•fend′er, *n.* **1.** person who offends. **2.** criminal.

of•fense′ *n.* **1.** (ə fens′) wrong; sin. **2.** (ə fens′) displeasure. **3.** (ə fens′) attack. **4.** (ô′fens) attacking side. Also, **of•fence′.**

of•fen′sive, *adj.* **1.** causing offense. —*n.* **2.** attack.

of′fer (ô′fər) *v.* **1.** present. **2.** propose; suggest. —*n.* **3.** proposal; bid.

of′fer•to•ry (-tôr′ē) *n., pl.* **-ries. 1.** *Rom. Cath. Ch.* offering to God of bread and wine during Mass. **2.** collection at religious service.

off′hand′, *adj.* **1.** Also, **off′hand′ed.** done without previous thought. **2.** curt. **—off′hand′ed•ly,** *adv.*

of′fice (ô′fis) *n.* **1.** place of business. **2.** position of authority. **3.** duty; task. **4.** religious service.

of′fice•hold′er, *n.* public official.

of′fi•cer, *n.* person of rank or authority.

of•fi′cial (ə fish′əl) *n.* **1.** person who holds office. —*adj.* **2.** authorized. **3.** pertaining to public office.

of•fi′ci•ant (ə fish′ē ənt) *n.* cleric at religious service.

of•fi′ci•ate′ (-āt′) *v.,* **-ated, -ating.** perform official duties.

of•fi′cious, *adj.* too forward in offering unwanted help.

off′ing (ô′fing) *n.* future.

off′-key′, *adj.* **1.** not in tune. **2.** somewhat incongruous or abnormal.

off′-lim′its, *adj.* forbidden to be patronized, used, etc.

off′-put′ting, *adj.* provoking uneasiness, annoyance, etc.

off′set′, *v.,* **-set, offsetting.** compensate for.

off′shoot′, *n.* branch.

off′shore′, *adj., adv.* in water and away from shore.

off′spring′, *n.* children or descendants.

off′stage′, *adv., adj.* out of sight of audience.

off′-the-cuff′, *adj.* impromptu.

off′-the-rec′ord, *adj.* not to be quoted.

off′-the-wall′, *adj. Informal.* bizarre.

off year, 1. year without major election. **2.** year marked by reduced production.

oft (ôft) *adv. Poetic.* often.

of′ten (ô′fən, ôf′tən) *adv.* **1.** frequently. **2.** in many cases.

o′gle (ō′gəl) *v.,* **ogled, ogling,** *n.* —*v.* **1.** eye with impertinent familiarity. —*n.* **2.** ogling glance.

o′gre (ō′gər) *n.* **1.** hideous giant who eats human flesh. **2.** cruel person. **—o′gress,** *n.fem.*

oh (ō) *interj.* (exclamation of surprise, etc.).

OH, Ohio.

ohm (ōm) *n.* unit of electrical resistance.

-oid, suffix meaning resembling or like.

oil (oil) *n.* **1.** greasy combustible liquid used for lubricating, heating, etc. —*v.* **2.** supply with oil. —*adj.* **3.** of oil. **—oil′y,** *adj.*

oil/cloth/, *n.* fabric made waterproof with oil.

oil/skin/, *n.* **1.** fabric made waterproof with oil. **2.** (*often pl.*) garment made of this.

oint/ment (oint/mənt) *n.* salve.

OK, Oklahoma.

OK (ō/kā/) *adj., adv., v.,* **OK'd, OK'ing,** *n., pl.* **OK's.** —*adj., adv.* **1.** all right. —*v.* **2.** approve. —*n.* **3.** approval. Also, **O.K., o/kay/.**

Okla., Oklahoma.

o/kra (ō/krə) *n.* leafy vegetable with edible pods.

old (ōld) *adj.* **1.** far advanced in years or time. **2.** of age. **3.** Also, **old/en.** former; ancient. **4.** long-standing. —*n.* **5.** former time.

Old English, English language before c1150.

old/-fash/ioned, *adj.* having style, ideas, etc. of an earlier time.

Old Guard, (*sometimes l.c.*) conservative members of any group.

old hand, person with long experience.

old hat, old-fashioned; dated.

old school, supporters of established custom.

old/ster, *n. Informal.* elderly person.

Old Testament, complete Bible of the Jews, being first division of Christian Bible.

old/-tim/er, *n. Informal.* elderly person.

Old World, Europe, Asia, and Africa. —**old/-world/,** *adj.*

o/le·ag/i·nous (ō/lē aj/ə nəs) *adj.* **1.** oily. **2.** unctuous; fawning.

o/le·an/der (ō/lē an/dər) *n.* poisonous evergreen flowering shrub.

o/le·o·mar/ga·rine (ō/lē ō/-) *n.* margarine. Also, **o/le·o/.**

ol·fac/to·ry (ol fak/tə rē, ōl-) *adj.* pertaining to sense of smell.

ol/i·gar/chy (-gär/kē) *n., pl.* **-chies.** government by small group.

ol/ive (ol/iv) *n.* **1.** evergreen tree valued for its small, oily fruit. **2.** fruit of this tree. **3.** yellowish green.

om/buds·man/ (om/bǎdz mən, om-bŏŏdz/-) *n., pl.* **-men.** official who investigates private individuals' complaints against government. Also, *fem.* **om/buds·wom/an.**

o·me/ga (ō mē/gə, ō meg/ə) *n.* last letter of Greek alphabet.

om/e·let (om/lit, om/ə-) *n.* eggs beaten and fried. Also, **om/e·lette.**

o/men (ō/mən) *n.* sign indicative of future.

om/i·nous (om/ə nəs) *adj.* threatening evil. —**om/i·nous·ly,** *adv.*

o·mit/ (ō mit/) *v.,* **omitted, omitting. 1.** leave out. **2.** fail to do, etc. —**o·mis/sion** (ō mish/ən) *n.*

omni-, prefix meaning all.

om/ni·bus/ (om/nə bus/, -bəs) *n., pl.* **-buses. 1.** bus. **2.** anthology.

om·nip/o·tent (om nip/ə tənt) *adj.* almighty. —**om·nip/o·tence,** *n.*

om/ni·pres/ent (om/nə prez/ənt) *adj.* present everywhere at once.

om·nis/cient (om nish/ənt) *adj.* knowing all things.

om·niv/o·rous (om niv/ər əs) *adj.* eating all kinds of foods.

on (on) *prep.* particle expressing: **1.** position in contact with supporting surface. **2.** support; reliance. **3.** situation or direction. **4.** basis. —*adv.* **5.** onto a thing, place, or person. **6.** forward. **7.** into operation. —*adj.* **8.** in use. —**Usage.** See ABOUT.

once (wuns) *adv.* **1.** formerly. **2.** single time. **3.** at any time. —*conj.* **4.** if ever; whenever.

once/-o/ver, *n. Informal.* quick survey.

on·col/o·gy (-kol/ə jē) *n.* branch of medical science dealing with tumors and cancer. —**on·col/o·gist,** *n.*

on/com/ing, *adj.* approaching.

one (wun) *adj.* **1.** single. **2.** in particular. **3.** common to all. —*n.* **4.** first and lowest whole number. **5.** single person or thing. —*pron.* **6.** person or thing.

one/ness, *n.* unity.

on/er·ous (on/ər əs, ō/nər-) *adj.* burdensome.

one·self/ (wun self/, wunz-) *pron.* person's self. Also, **one's self.**

one/-sid/ed, *adj.* **1.** with all advantage on one side. **2.** biased.

one/-time/, *adj.* former.

one/-track/, *adj. Informal.* obsessed with one subject.

one/-way/, *adj.* moving or allowing movement in one direction only.

on/go/ing, *adj.* in progress.

on/ion (un/yən) *n.* common plant having edible bulb.

on/-line/, *adj.* operating under the direct control of, or connected to, a main computer.

on/look/er, *n.* spectator; witness.

on/ly (ōn/lē) *adv.* **1.** alone; solely. **2.** merely. —*adj.* **3.** sole. —*conj.* **4.** but.

on/o·mat/o·poe/ia (on/ə mat/ə pē/ə, -mä/tə-) *n.* formation of word by imitation of a sound.

on/rush/, *n.* rapid advance.

on/set/, *n.* **1.** beginning. **2.** attack.

on/slaught/ (on/slôt/) *n.* attack.

on/to, *prep.* upon; on.

on·tol/o·gy (on tol/ə jē) *n.* branch of metaphysics studying existence or being.

o/nus (ō/nəs) *n.* burden.

on/ward (-wərd) *adv.* **1.** forward. —*adj.* **2.** moving forward.

on/yx (on/iks, ō/niks) *n.* varicolored quartz.

oo/dles (ōōd/lz) *n.pl. Informal.* large quantity.

ooze (ōōz) *v.,* **oozed, oozing,** *n.* —*v.* **1.** leak out slowly. —*n.* **2.** something that oozes. **3.** soft mud.

o·pac/i·ty (ō pas/i tē) *n., pl.* **-ties.** state of being opaque.

o/pal (ō/pəl) *n.* precious stone, often iridescent.

o/pa·les/cent (ō/pə les/ənt) *adj.* with opallike play of color.

o·paque/ (ō pāk/) *adj.* **1.** not transmitting light. **2.** not shining. **3.** not clear.

op. cit. (op/ sit/) in the work cited.

OPEC (ō/pek) *n.* Organization of Petroleum Exporting Countries.

Op/-Ed/ (op/ed/) *n.* newspaper section devoted to signed articles and letters.

o/pen (ō/pən) *adj.* **1.** not shut. **2.** not enclosed or covered. **3.** available; accessible. **4.** candid. —*v.* **5.** make or become open. **6.** begin. **7.** come apart. —*n.* **8.** any open space.

o/pen-and-shut/, *adj.* easily solved or decided; obvious.

o/pen-end/ed, *adj.* **1.** unrestricted. **2.** having no fixed answer.

o/pen-hand/ed, *adj.* generous.

o/pen·ing, *n.* **1.** unobstructed or unoccupied place. **2.** gap or hole. **3.** beginning. **4.** opportunity.

o/pen-mind/ed, *adj.* without prejudice. —**o/pen-mind/ed·ness,** *n.*

op/er·a (op/ər ə) *n.* sung drama. —**op/er·at/ic** (-ə rat/ik) *adj.*

op/er·a·ble (op/ər ə bəl) *adj.* **1.** able to be operated. **2.** curable by surgery.

opera glasses, small, low-power binoculars.

op/er·ate/ (-ə rāt/) *v.,* **-ated, -ating. 1.** work or run. **2.** exert force or influence. **3.** perform surgery. —**op/er·a/tion,** *n.* —**op/er·a/tor,** *n.*

operating system, software that directs computer's operations.

op/er·a/tion·al, *adj.* **1.** concerning operations. **2.** in operation.

op/er·a·tive (-ər ə tiv, -ə rā/tiv) *n.* **1.** worker. **2.** spy. —*adj.* **3.** in operation.

op/er·et/ta (op/ə ret/ə) *n.* light opera.

oph/thal·mol/o·gy (of/thal mol/ə jē, -thə-, -thal-, op/-) *n.* branch of medicine dealing with eye. —**oph/thal·mol/o·gist,** *n.*

o/pi·ate (ō/pē it, -āt/) *n.* medicine containing opium.

o·pine/ (ō pīn/) *v.,* **-pined, -pining.** express an opinion.

o·pin/ion (ə pin/yən) *n.* belief or judgment.

o·pin/ion·at/ed (-yə nā/tid) *adj.* stubborn in opinions.

o/pi·um (ō/pē əm) *n.* narcotic juice of poppy.

o·pos/sum (ə pos/əm, pos/əm) *n.* pouched mammal of southern U.S.

op·po/nent (ə pō/nənt) *n.* **1.** person on opposite side, as in contest. **2.** person opposed to something.

op/por·tune/ (op/ər tōōn/, -tyōōn/) *adj.* appropriate; timely.

op/por·tun/ism, *n.* unprincipled use of opportunities. —**op/por·tun/ist,** *n.* —**op/por·tun·is/tic,** *adj.*

op/por·tu/ni·ty, *n., pl.* **-ties.** temporary possible advantage.

op·pose/ (ə pōz/) *v.,* **-posed, -posing. 1.** resist or compete with. **2.** hinder. —**op/po·si/tion,** *n.*

op/po·site (op/ə zit, -sit) *adj.* **1.** in corresponding position on other side. **2.** completely different. —*n.* **3.** one that is opposite.

op·press/ (ə pres/) *v.* **1.** weigh down. **2.** treat harshly as a matter of policy. —**op·pres/sion** (ə presh/ən) *n.* —**op·pres/sive,** *adj.* —**op·pres/sor,** *n.*

op·pro/bri·um (ə prō/brē əm) *n.* disgrace and reproach.

opt (opt) *v.* make a choice.

op/tic (op/tik) *adj.* of eyes.

op/ti·cal, *adj.* **1.** made to assist sight. **2.** visual. **3.** of optics.

optical disc, disk on which digital data is stored and read by laser.

optical scanner, device for scanning and digitizing printed material.

op·ti/cian (op tish/ən) *n.* eyeglass maker.

op/tics, *n.* branch of science dealing with light and vision.

op/ti·mal, *adj.* optimum.

op/ti·mism (op/tə miz/əm) *n.* disposition to hope for best. **2.** belief that good will prevail. —**op/ti·mist,** *n.* —**op/ti·mis/tic,** *adj.*

op/ti·mum (-məm) *adj., n.* best.

op/tion (op/shən) *n.* **1.** ability to choose. **2.** choice. —**op/tion·al,** *adj.*

op·tom/e·try (op tom/i trē) *n.* art of testing eyes for eyeglasses. —**op·tom/e·trist,** *n.*

op/u·lent (op/yə lənt) *adj.* wealthy. —**op/u·lence,** *n.*

o/pus (ō/pəs) *n., pl.* **op·er·a** (op/ər ə, ō/prə). work, esp. musical, usually numbered.

or (ôr; *unstressed* ər) *conj.* (used to connect alternatives).

OR, 1. operating room. **2.** Oregon.

-or, suffix meaning: condition or quality, as *pallor*; person or thing that does something, as *orator*.

or•a•cle (ôr'ə kəl) *n.* **1.** one who gave answers from the gods to questions. **2.** wise person.

o'ral (ôr'əl) *adj.* **1.** spoken. **2.** of mouths. —**o'ral•ly,** *adv.*

or'ange (ôr'inj) *n.* **1.** round, reddish-yellow citrus fruit. **2.** reddish yellow.

or'ange•ade' (-ād') *n.* drink with base of orange juice.

o•rang'u•tan' (ô rang'ōō tan', ə rang'-) *n.* large, long-armed ape.

o•ra'tion, *n.* formal speech.

or'a•tor (ôr'ə tər) *n.* eloquent public speaker.

or'a•to'ri•o' (-tôr'ē ō') *n., pl.* **-rios.** religious work for voices and orchestra in dramatic form.

or'a•to'ry, *n., pl.* **-ries. 1.** eloquent speaking. **2.** small room for prayer.

orb (ôrb) *n.* **1.** sphere. **2.** any of heavenly bodies.

or'bit (ôr'bit) *n.* **1.** path of planet, etc., around another body. —*v.* **2.** travel in orbit. —**or'bit•al,** *adj.*

or'chard (ôr'chərd) *n.* plot of fruit trees.

or'ches•tra (ôr'kə strə, -kes trə) *n.* **1.** *Music.* large company of instrumental performers. **2.** main floor of theater. —**or•ches'tral,** *adj.*

or'ches•trate' (ôr'kə strāt') *v.,* **-trated, -trating. 1.** arrange music for orchestra. **2.** arrange elements of. —**or'ches•tra'tion,** *n.*

or'chid (ôr'kid) *n.* tropical plant with oddly shaped blooms.

or•dain' (ôr dān') *v.* **1.** invest as a member of the clergy. **2.** direct.

or•deal' (ôr dēl', ôr'dēl) *n.* severe test.

or'der (ôr'dər) *n.* **1.** authoritative command. **2.** harmonious arrangement. **3.** group bound by common religious rules. **4.** list of items desired. —*v.* **5.** give an order. **6.** arrange.

or'der•ly, *adj., adv., n., pl.* **-lies.** —*adj.* **1.** methodical. **2.** well-behaved. —*adv.* **3.** according to rule. —*n.* **4.** hospital attendant.

or'di•nal (ôr'dn əl) *adj.* **1.** showing position in series, as *first, second,* etc. —*n.* **2.** ordinal number.

or'di•nance (ôr'dn əns) *n.* law.

or'di•nar'y (-dn er'ē) *adj., n., pl.* **-ies.** —*adj.* **1.** normal. —*n.* **2.** ordinary condition, etc. —**or'di•nar'i•ly,** *adv.*

or'di•na'tion (ôr'dn ā'shən) *n.* act or ceremony of ordaining.

ord'nance (ôrd'nəns) *n.* military weapons of all kinds.

or'dure (ôr'jər, -dyŏŏr) *n.* dung.

ore (ôr) *n.* metal-bearing rock.

Ore., Oregon.

o•reg'a•no (ə reg'ə nō') *n.* plant with leaves used as seasoning.

or'gan (ôr'gən) *n.* **1.** large musical keyboard instrument sounded by air forced through pipes, etc. **2.** part of animal or plant with specific function. **3.** periodical. —**or'gan•ist,** *n.*

or'gan•dy (ôr'gən dē) *n., pl.* **-dies.** thin stiff cotton fabric.

or•gan'ic (ôr gan'ik) *adj.* **1.** of carbon compounds. **2.** of living organisms. **3.** raised or grown without synthetic fertilizers, pesticides, etc.

or'gan•ism (-gə niz'əm) *n.* anything living or formerly alive.

or'gan•ize' (-gə nīz) *v.,* **-ized, -izing.** form into coordinated whole; systematize. —**or'gan•i•za'tion,** *n.* —**or'gan•i•za'tion•al,** *adj.*

or•gan'za (ôr gan'zə) *n.* sheer fabric of rayon, nylon, or silk.

or'gasm (ôr'gaz əm) *n.* sexual climax.

or'gy (ôr'jē) *n., pl.* **-gies.** unrestrained indulgence, esp in sexual activities.

o'ri•el (ôr'ē əl) *n.* bay window.

o'ri•ent *n.* (ôr'ē ənt, -ē ent') **1.** (*cap.*) countries of Asia. —*v.* (ôr'ē-ent') **2.** set facing certain way. **3.** inform about one's situation. —**O'ri•en'tal,** *adj.* —**o'ri•en•ta'tion,** *n.*

o'ri•en•teer'ing (-tēr'ing) *n.* sport of navigating unknown terrain.

or'i•fice (ôr'ə fis) *n.* opening.

o'ri•ga'mi (ôr'i gä'mē) *n.* Japanese art of folding paper.

or'i•gin (ôr'i jin) *n.* **1.** source. **2.** beginning. **3.** birth or ancestry.

o•rig'i•nal (ə rij'ə nl) *adj.* **1.** first. **2.** novel. **3.** being new work. **4.** capable of creating something original. —*n.* **5.** primary form. **6.** thing copied. —**o•rig'i•nal'i•ty** (-nal'i tē) *n.*

o•rig'i•nal•ly, *adv.* **1.** at first. **2.** in original manner.

o•rig'i•nate' *v.,* **-nated, -nating. 1.** come to be. **2.** give origin to.

o'ri•ole' (ôr'ē ōl') *n.* bright-colored bird of Europe and America.

or'i•son (ôr'i zən) *n.* prayer.

Or'lon (ôr'lon) *n.* *Trademark.* synthetic fabric resembling nylon.

or'mo•lu' (ôr'mə lōō') *n., pl.* **-lus.** copper-zinc alloy.

or'na•ment *n.* (ôr'nə mənt) **1.** something added to beautify. —*v.* (-mənt', -mənt) **2.** adorn; decorate. —**or'na•men'tal,** *adj.*

or•nate' (ôr nāt') *adj.* lavish. —**or•nate'ly,** *adv.*

or'ner•y (ôr'nə rē) *adj.* *Informal.* ill-tempered.

or'ni•thol'o•gy (ôr'nə thol'ə jē) *n.* study of birds.

o'ro•tund' (ôr'ə tund') *adj.* **1.** rich and clear in voice. **2.** pompous.

or'phan (ôr'fən) *n.* **1.** child whose parents are both dead. —*adj.* **2.** of or for orphans. —*v.* **3.** bereave of parents.

or'phan•age (-fə nij) *n.* home for orphans.

or'tho•don'tics (ôr'thə don'tiks) *n.* branch of dentistry dealing with irregular teeth. —**or'tho•don'tic,** *adj.* —**or'tho•don'tist,** *n.*

or'tho•dox' (ôr'thə doks') *adj.* **1.** sound and correct in doctrine. **2.** conventional. **3.** (*cap.*) of Christian churches of eastern Europe.

or•thog'ra•phy (ôr thog'rə fē) *n., pl.* **-phies.** spelling. —**or'tho•graph'ic** (ôr'thə graf'ik), *adj.*

or'tho•pe'dics (ôr'thə pē'diks) *n.* branch of medicine dealing with the skeletal system.

-ory, suffix meaning: **1.** of, characterized by, or serving to, as *excretory.* **2.** place or instrument for, as *crematory.*

os'cil•late' (os'ə lāt') *v.,* **-lated, -lating.** swing to and fro. —**os'cil•la'tion,** *n.* —**os'cil•la'tor,** *n.*

os•cil'lo•scope' (ə sil'ə skōp') *n.* device that uses cathode-ray tube to display changes in electric quantity.

os'cu•late' (os'kyə lāt') *v.,* **-lated, -lating.** kiss. —**os'cu•la'tion,** *n.*

o'sier (ō'zhər) *n.* tough flexible twig used in wickerwork.

-osis, suffix meaning: **1.** action or condition, as *osmosis.* **2.** abnormal state, as *tuberculosis.*

os•mo'sis (oz mō'sis, os-) *n.* diffusion of liquid through membrane.

os'prey (os'prē, -prā) *n.* large hawk.

os'se•ous (os'ē əs) *adj.* of, like, or containing bone.

os'si•fy' (os'ə fī') *v.,* **-fied, -fying.** make or become bone.

os•ten'si•ble (o sten'sə bəl) *adj.* merely apparent or pretended. —**os•ten'si•bly,** *adv.*

os'ten•ta'tion (os'ten tā'shən, -tən) *n.* pretentious display. —**os'ten•ta'tious,** *adj.*

os'te•o•ar•thri'tis (os'tē ō är thrī'tis) *n.* arthritis marked by decay of cartilage in joints.

os'te•op'a•thy (os'tē op'ə thē) *n.* treatment of disease by manipulating affected part. —**os'te•o•path'** (-ə-path') *n.* —**os'te•o•path'ic,** *adj.*

os'te•o•po•ro'sis (os'tē ō pə rō'sis) *n.* disorder in which bones become increasingly brittle, porous, and prone to fracture.

os'tra•cize' (os'trə sīz') *v.,* **-cized, -cizing.** exclude from society; banish. —**os'tra•cism** (-siz'əm) *n.*

os'trich (ô'strich) *n.* large, swift-footed, flightless bird.

oth'er (uth'ər) *adj.* **1.** additional. **2.** different. **3.** remaining. **4.** former. —*pron.* **5.** other person or thing.

oth'er•wise', *adv.* **1.** in other ways or circumstances. —*adj.* **2.** of other sort.

oth'er•world'ly, *adj.* concerned with spiritual or imaginary world.

ot'ter (ot'ər) *n.* aquatic mammal.

ot'to•man (ot'ə mən) *n.* low, cushioned seat.

ought (ôt) *aux. v.* used to express obligation or advisability. —*n.*

ounce (ouns) *n.* unit of weight equal to $\frac{1}{16}$ lb. avoirdupois or $\frac{1}{12}$ lb. troy.

our (ou^r, ou'ər; *unstressed* är) *pron.* possessive form of **we,** used before noun.

ours, *pron.* possessive form of **we,** used predicatively.

our•selves', *pron.* **1.** reflexive substitute for **us. 2.** intensive with or substitute for **we** or **us.**

-ous, suffix meaning full of or characterized by.

oust (oust) *v.* eject; force out.

oust'er, *n.* ejection.

out (out) *adv.* **1.** away from some place. **2.** so as to emerge or project. **3.** until conclusion. **4.** to depletion. **5.** so as to be extinguished, etc. —*adj.* **6.** away from some place. **7.** extinguished, etc. —*prep.* **8.** out from. **9.** away along. —*n.* **10.** means of evasion.

out-, prefix meaning: **1.** outward, as *outburst.* **2.** outside, as *outbuilding.* **3.** surpass, as *outlast.*

out'age (ou'tij) *n.* interruption or failure in supply of power.

out'-and-out', *adj.* utter; thorough.

out'back', *n.* remote area.

out'board', *adj., adv.* on exterior of ship or boat.

out'break', *n.* **1.** sudden occurrence. **2.** riot.

out'build'ing, *n.* detached building subordinate to main building.

out'burst', *n.* violent outpouring.

out'cast', *n.* exiled person.

out'class', *v.* outdo in style or excellence.

out'come', *n.* consequence.

out'crop', *n.* emerging stratum at earth's surface.

out'cry', *n., pl.* **-cries.** expression of distress or protest.

out•dat'ed, *adj.* obsolete.

out•dis'tance, *v.,* **-tanced, -tancing.** leave behind, as in racing.

out•do', *v.,* **-did, -done, outdoing.** surpass.

out'door', *adj.* done or occurring in open air. —**out'doors',** *adv., n.*

out′er, *adj.* **1.** farther out. **2.** on outside.

out′er•most, *adj.* farthest out.

outer space, space beyond the earth's atmosphere.

out′field′, *n.* part of baseball field beyond diamond. —**out′field′er,** *n.*

out′fit′, *n., v.,* **-fitted, -fitting.** —*n.* **1.** set of articles for any purpose. **2.** set of clothes. **3.** organized group of persons. —*v.* **4.** equip.

out′go′, *n., pl.* **-goes.** expenditure.

out′go′ing *adj.* **1.** (-gō′ing) departing. **2.** (-gō′ing) retiring from a position or office. **3.** (-gō′ing, -gō′-) friendly; sociable.

out′grow′, *v.,* **-grew, -grown, -growing.** grow too large or mature for.

out′growth′, *n.* **1.** natural result. **2.** offshoot.

out′house′, *n.* separate building serving as toilet.

out′ing, *n.* pleasure trip.

out•land′ish (-lan′dish) *adj.* strange.

out′last′, *v.* endure after.

out′law′, *n.* **1.** habitual criminal. **2.** person excluded from protection of law. —*v.* **3.** prohibit by law. **4.** deny protection of law to.

out′lay′, *n.* expenditure.

out′let (-let, -lit) *n.* **1.** opening or passage out. **2.** market for goods.

out′line′, *n., v.,* **-lined, -lining.** —*n.* **1.** line by which object is bounded. **2.** drawing showing only outer contour. **3.** general description. —*v.* **4.** draw or represent in outline.

out′live′ (-liv′) *v.,* **-lived, -living.** live longer than.

out′look′, *n.* **1.** view from place. **2.** mental view. **3.** prospect.

out′ly′ing, *adj.* remote.

out′mod′ed (-mō′did) *adj.* obsolete.

out′num′ber, *v.* be more numerous than.

out′-of-bod′y, characterized by sensation that the mind has left the body.

out′-of-date′, *adj.* obsolete.

out′-of-doors′, *n.* outdoors.

out′-of-the-way′, *adj.* isolated.

out′pa′tient, *n.* patient visiting hospital to receive treatment.

out′place′ment, *n.* assistance in finding new job, provided by company for employee being let go.

out′post′, *n.* **1.** sentinel station away from main army. **2.** place away from main area.

out′put′, *n.* **1.** production. **2.** quantity produced.

out′rage, *n., v.,* **-raged, -raging.** —*n.* **1.** gross violation. **2.** anger. —*v.* **3.** subject to outrage.

out•ra′geous (-rā′jəs) *adj.* very offensive.

ou•tré′ (ōō trā′) *adj.* unconventional; bizarre.

out′reach′ *adj.* concerned with extending services.

out′right′ *adj.* (-rīt′) **1.** utter; thorough. —*adv.* (-rīt′, -rīt′) **2.** at once; completely.

out′run′, *v.,* **-ran, -run, -running. 1.** run faster or farther than. **2.** exceed.

out′sell′, *v.,* **-sold, -selling.** exceed in number of sales.

out′set′, *n.* beginning.

out′shine′, *v.,* **-shone** or **-shined, -shining. 1.** shine more brightly than. **2.** surpass in excellence.

out′side′ *n.* (out′sīd′, out′sīd′) **1.** outer side, aspect, etc. **2.** space beyond enclosure. —*adj.* (out′sīd′, out′-) **3.** being, done, etc., on the outside. **4.** remote. —*adv.* (out′sīd′) **5.** on or to the outside. —*prep.* (out′sīd′, out′sīd′) **6.** at the outside of.

out•sid′er, *n.* person not belonging.

out′skirts′, *n.pl.* outlying districts.

out•smart′, *v.* outwit.

out′spo′ken, *adj.* candid.

out′spread′, *adj.* extended.

out•stand′ing, *adj.* **1.** prominent. **2.** not yet paid.

out′strip′, *v.,* **-stripped, -stripping. 1.** excel. **2.** outdistance.

out′take′, *n.* segment of film edited from published version.

out′ward (-wərd) *adj.* **1.** external. —*adv.* **2.** Also, **out′wards.** toward the outside. —**out′ward•ly,** *adv.*

out′weigh′, *v.* exceed in importance.

out•wit′, *v.,* **-witted, -witting.** get the better of by superior cleverness.

o′va, (ō′və) *n. pl.* of ovum.

o′val (ō′vəl) *adj.* egg-shaped.

o′va•ry (ō′və rē) *n., pl.* **-ries.** female reproductive gland. —**o•var′i•an** (ō-vâr′ē ən) *adj.*

o′vate (ō′vāt) *adj.* egg-shaped.

o•va′tion (ō vā′shən) *n.* enthusiastic applause.

ov′en (uv′ən) *n.* chamber for baking or drying.

o′ver (ō′vər) *prep.* **1.** above in place, authority, etc. **2.** on. **3.** across; through. **4.** in excess of. **5.** concerning. **6.** during. —*adv.* **7.** so as to affect whole surface. **8.** above. **9.** again. —*adj.* **10.** finished. **11.** remaining. **12.** upper.

o′ver•a•chieve′, *v.,* **-chieved, -chieving.** perform better than expected, esp. in school.

o′ver•act′, *v.* perform in an exaggerated manner.

o′ver•age (ō′vər ij) *n.* **1.** surplus. —*adj.* (ō′vər āj′) **2.** beyond desirable age.

o′ver•all′ (ō′vər ôl′) *adj.* **1.** including everything. —*n.* **2.** (*pl.*) loose, stout trousers.

o′ver•awe′, *v.,* **-awed, -awing.** dominate with impressiveness.

o′ver•bear′ing, *adj.* arrogant.

o′ver•bite′, *n.* occlusion in which upper incisor teeth overlap lower ones.

o′ver•blown′, *adj.* pretentious.

o′ver•board′, *adv.* over side of ship into water.

o′ver•cast′ (-kast′, -kast′) *adj.* **1.** cloudy. **2.** gloomy.

o′ver•charge′, *v.,* **-charged, -charging. 1.** charge too high a price. **2.** overload. —*n.* (ō′vər chärj′) **3.** charge exceeding fair price. **4.** excessive load.

o′ver•coat′, *n.* coat worn over ordinary clothing.

o′ver•come′, *v.,* **-came, overcome, overcoming.** defeat; overpower.

o′ver•do′, *v.,* **-did, -done, -doing. 1.** do to excess. **2.** exaggerate.

o′ver•dose′, *n., v.,* **-dosed, -dosing.** —*n.* **1.** excessive dose. —*v.* **2.** take such a dose.

o′ver•draft′, *n.* **1.** act of overdrawing. **2.** amount overdrawn.

o′ver•draw′, *v.,* **-drew, -drawn, -drawing.** draw upon in excess of.

o′ver•drive′, *n.* mechanism that reduces power required to maintain speed by lowering gear ratio.

o′ver•due′, *adj.* due some time before.

o′ver•flow′, *v.,* **-flowed, -flown, -flowing,** *n.* —*v.* (ō′vər flō′) **1.** flow or run over; flood. —*n.* (ō′vər flō′) **2.** instance of flooding. **3.** something that runs over.

o′ver•grow′, *v.,* **-grew, -grown, -growing.** cover with growth.

o′ver•hand′, *adv.* with hand above shoulder.

o′ver•hang′, *v.,* **-hung, -hanging,** *n.* —*v.* (ō′vər hang′) **1.** project over. —*n.* (ō′vər hang′) **2.** projection.

o′ver•haul′ *v.* (ō′vər hôl′, ō′vər hôl′) **1.** investigate thoroughly, as for repair. **2.** overtake. —*n.* (ō′vər hôl′) **3.** complete examination.

o′ver•head′ *adv.* (ō′ver hed′) **1.** aloft. —*n.* (ō′vər hed′) **2.** general business expense.

o′ver•hear′, *v.,* **-heard, -hearing.** hear without speaker's intent.

o′ver•joyed′ (-joid′) *adj.* very happy.

o′ver•kill′, *n.* any greatly excessive amount.

o′ver•land′ (-land′, -lənd) *adv., adj.* across open country.

o′ver•lap′ *v.,* **-lapped, -lapping,** *n.* —*v.* (ō′vər lap′) **1.** extend over and beyond. —*n.* (ō′vər lap′) **2.** overlapping part.

o′ver•lay′, *v.,* **-laid, -laying,** *n.* —*v.* **1.** spread over. —*n.* **2.** something used in overlaying.

o′ver•lie′, *v.* **-lay, -lain, -lying.** lie over or on.

o′ver•look′, *v.* **1.** fail to notice. **2.** afford view over.

o′ver•ly, *adv. Informal.* excessively.

o′ver•night′ *adv.* (-nīt′) **1.** during the night. **2.** suddenly. —*adj.* (-nīt′) **3.** done, made, etc., during the night. **4.** staying for one night.

o′ver•pass′, *n.* bridge crossing other traffic.

o′ver•play′, *v.* exaggerate.

o′ver•pow′er, *v.* **1.** overwhelm in feeling. **2.** subdue.

o′ver•rate′, *v.,* **-rated, -rating.** esteem too highly.

o′ver•reach′, *v.* **1.** extend beyond. **2.** try too hard.

o′ver•re•act′, *v.* react too emotionally. —**o′ver•re•ac′tion,** *n.*

o′ver•ride′, *v.,* **-rode, -ridden, -riding.** prevail over; supersede.

o′ver•rule′, *v.,* **-ruled, -ruling.** rule against.

o′ver•run′, *v.,* **-ran, -run, -running. 1.** swarm over. **2.** overgrow.

o′ver•seas′, *adv.* over or across the sea.

o′ver•see′, *v.,* **-saw, -seen, -seeing.** supervise. —**o′ver•se′er,** *n.*

o′ver•shad′ow, *v.* be more important than.

o′ver•shoe′, *n.* protective shoe worn over another shoe.

o′ver•shoot′, *v.,* **-shot, -shooting.** shoot or go beyond.

o′ver•sight′, *n.* error of neglect.

o′ver•sleep′, *v.,* **-slept, -sleeping.** sleep beyond desired time.

o′ver•state′, *v.,* **-stated, -stating.** exaggerate in describing. —**o′ver•state′ment,** *n.*

o′ver•stay′, *v.,* **-stayed, -staying.** stay too long.

o′ver•step′, *v.,* **-stepped, -stepping.** exceed.

o•vert′ (ō vûrt′, ō′vûrt) *adj.* not concealed.

o′ver•take′, *v.,* **-took, -taken, -taking.** catch up with or pass.

o′ver-the-count′er, *adj.* **1.** not listed on or traded through an organized securities exchange. **2.** sold legally without a prescription.

o′ver•throw′, *v.,* **-threw, -thrown, -throwing,** *n.* —*v.* (ō′vər thrō′) **1.** defeat; put end to. —*n.* (ō′vər thrō′) **2.** act of overthrowing.

o′·ver·time′, *n.* time worked in addition to regular hours. —**o′·ver·time′**, *adv., adj.*

o′·ver·tone′, *n.* **1.** additional meaning. **2.** musical tone added to basic tone.

o′·ver·ture (ō′vər chər, -chŏŏr′) *n.* **1.** offer. **2.** musical prelude.

o′·ver·turn′, *v.* **1.** tip off base. **2.** defeat.

o′·ver·view′, *n.* overall perception or description.

o′·ver·ween′ing (-wē′ning) *adj.* **1.** conceited. **2.** excessive.

o′·ver·weight′, *n.* **1.** excess of weight. —*adj.* (ō′vər wāt′) **2.** weighing more than is normal.

o′·ver·whelm′ (-hwelm′, -welm′) *v.* completely overcome

o′·ver·work′, *v.,* **-worked** or **-wrought, -working,** *n.* —*v.* (ō′ver-wûrk′) **1.** work too hard. —*n.* (ō′vər-wûrk′) **2.** work beyond one's strength.

o′·ver·wrought′ (ō′vər rôt′, ō′vər-) *adj.* highly excited.

o′·vi·duct′ (ō′vi dukt′) *n.* tube through which ova are transported.

o′·void (ō′void) *adj.* egg-shaped.

ov′u·late (ov′yə lāt′, ō′vyə-) *v.,* **-lated, -lating.** produce and discharge eggs (ova) from ovary.

ov′ule (ov′yōōl, ō′vyōōl) *n.* **1.** structure that develops into seed. **2.** small egg.

o′·vum (ō′vəm) *n., pl.* **ova** (ō və). female reproductive cell.

owe (ō) *v.,* **owed, owing.** be obligated to pay or give to another.

owl (oul) *n.* nocturnal bird of prey.

own (ōn) *adj.* **1.** of or belonging to. —*v.* **2.** possess. **3.** acknowledge. —**own′er,** *n.* —**own′er·ship′,** *n.*

ox (oks) *n., pl.* **oxen.** adult castrated male bovine.

ox′blood′, *n.* deep, dull red color.

ox′ford (oks′fərd) *n.* low shoe laced over instep.

ox′i·dant (ok′si dənt) *n.* chemical agent that oxidizes.

ox′ide (ok′sīd, -sid) *n* compound of oxygen and another element.

ox′i·dize′ (ok′si dīz′) *v.,* **-dized, -dizing.** add oxygen to. —**ox′i·di·za′tion, ox′i·da′tion,** *n.*

ox′y·a·cet′y·lene′ (ok′sē ə set′l ēn′, -in) *adj.* denoting a mixture of oxygen and acetylene used for cutting and welding steel.

ox′y·gen (ok′si jən) *n.* colorless, odorless gas necessary to life and fire.

ox′y·gen·ate′ (-jə nāt′) *v.,* **-ated, -ating.** enrich with oxygen.

ox′y·mo′ron (ok′si môr′on) *n., pl.* **-mora.** figure of speech that uses seeming contradictions.

oys′ter (oi′stər) *n.* edible, irregularly shaped mollusk.

oz., ounce.

o′zone (ō′zōn, ō zōn′) *n.* form of oxygen in upper atmosphere.

ozone hole, part of ozone layer depleted by atmospheric pollution.

ozone layer, layer of upper atmosphere where most ozone is concentrated.

P

P, p (pē) *n.* sixteenth letter of English alphabet.

PA, 1. Also, **Pa.** Pennsylvania. **2.** public-address system.

PAC (pak) *n., pl.* **PACs, PAC's.** political action committee.

pace (pās) *n., v.,* **paced, pacing.** —*n.* **1.** rate of movement or progress. **2.** linear measure. **3.** step or gait. —*v.* **4.** set pace for. **5.** step regularly. —**pac′er,** *n.*

pace′mak′er, *n.* **1.** one that sets pace. **2.** electrical device for controlling heartbeat.

pace′set′ter, *n.* leader.

pach′y·derm′ (pak′i dûrm′) *n.* thick-skinned mammal, as the elephant.

pa·cif′ic (pə sif′ik) *adj.* peaceful.

pac′i·fism (pas′ə fiz′əm) *n.* principle of abstention from violence. —**pac′i·fist,** *n.* —**pa′ci·fis′tic,** *adj.*

pac′i·fy′, *v.,* **-fied, -fying. 1.** calm. **2.** appease. —**pac′i·fi·er′,** *n.*

pack (pak) *n.* **1.** bundle. **2.** group or complete set. —*v.* **3.** make into compact mass. **4.** fill with objects. **5.** cram. —**pack′er,** *n.*

pack′age (-ij) *n., v.,* **-aged, -aging.** —*n.* **1.** bundle; parcel. **2.** container. —*v.* **3.** put into package.

pack′et, *n.* **1.** small package. **2.** passenger boat, esp. with fixed route.

pack rat, 1. rat that carries off shiny articles to its nest. **2.** *Informal.* person who saves useless items.

pact (pakt) *n.* agreement.

pad (pad) *n., v.,* **padded, padding.** —*n.* **1.** soft, cushionlike mass. **2.** bound package of writing paper. **3.** dull sound of walking. —*v.* **4.** furnish with padding. **5.** expand with false or useless matter. **6.** walk with dull sound.

pad′ding, *n.* material with which to pad.

pad′dle (pad′l) *n., v.,* **-dled, -dling.** —*n.* **1.** short oar for two hands. —*v.* **2.** propel with paddle. **3.** play in water.

pad′dock (pad′ək) *n.* field for horses.

pad′dy (pad′ē) *n., pl.* **-dies.** rice field.

paddy wagon, van for transporting prisoners.

pad′lock′, *n.* **1.** portable lock. —*v.* **2.** lock with padlock.

pa′dre (pä′drā) *n., pl.* **-dres.** clergyman.

pae′an (pē′ən) *n.* song of praise.

pa′gan (pā′gən) *n.* **1.** worshiper of idols. —*adj.* **2.** idolatrous; heathen. —**pa′gan·ism,** *n.*

page (pāj) *n., v.,* **paged, paging.** —*n.* **1.** written or printed surface. **2.** boy servant. —*v.* **3.** summon by calling name.

pag′eant (paj′ənt) *n.* elaborate spectacle. —**pag′eant·ry,** *n.*

pag′i·nate′ (-ə nāt′) *v.,* **-nated, -nating.** number the pages of (a book, etc.). —**pag′i·na′tion,** *n.*

pa·go′da (pə gō′də) *n.* Far Eastern temple tower, esp. Buddhist.

pail (pāl) *n.* bucket.

pain (pān) *n.* **1.** bodily or mental suffering. **2.** (*pl.*) effort. **3.** penalty. —*v.* **4.** hurt. —**pain′ful,** *adj.*

pain′kil′ler, *n.* something that relieves pain.

pains′tak′ing, *adj.* careful.

paint (pānt) *n.* **1.** liquid coloring matter used as coating. —*v.* **2.** represent in paint. **3.** apply paint to. —**paint′er,** *n.* —**paint′ing,** *n.*

pair (pâr) *n., pl.* **pairs, pair,** *v.* —*n.* **1.** combination of two. —*v.* **2.** arrange in pairs. —**Usage.** See COUPLE.

pais′ley (pāz′lē) *adj.* having a colorful, detailed pattern.

pa·jam′as (pə jä′məz, -jam′əz) *n.pl.* nightclothes.

pal (pal) *n. Informal.* close friend.

pal′ace (pal′is) *n.* official residence of sovereign.

pal′at·a·ble (pal′ə tə bəl) *adj.* agreeable to taste.

pal′ate (-it) *n.* **1.** roof of mouth. **2.** sense of taste. —**pal′a·tal,** *adj.*

pa·la′tial (pə lā′shəl) *adj.* splendidly built or furnished.

pal′a·tine (pal′ə tīn′, -tin) *n.* vassal exercising royal privileges in province. —**pa·lat′i·nate′** (pə lat′n ät′, -it) *n.*

pa·lav′er (pə lav′ər, -lä′vər) *n.* idle talk.

pale (pāl) *adj.,* **paler, palest,** *v.,* **paled, paling,** *n.* —*adj.* **1.** without much color; near-white. **2.** dim. —*v.* **3.** become or make pale. —*n.* **4.** stake. **5.** bounds. **6.** enclosed area.

Pa′le·o·lith′ic (pā′lē ə lith′ik) *adj.* denoting early Stone Age.

pa′le·on·tol′o·gy (pā′lē on tol′ə jē) *n.* science of early life forms, as represented by fossils.

Pa′le·o·zo′ic (-ə zō′ik) *adj.* pertaining to geologic era 570 to 230 million years ago.

pal′ette (pal′it) *n.* board on which painter lays and mixes colors.

pal′i·mo′ny (pal′ə mō′nē) *n.* alimony awarded to member of unmarried couple.

pal′imp·sest′ (pal′imp sest′) *n.* manuscript with text erased to make room for other text.

pal′in·drome′ (pal′in drōm′) *n.* word or verse reading the same backward as forward.

pal′ing (pā′ling) *n.* fence of pales.

pal′i·sade′ (pal′ə sād′) *n.* **1.** fence of pales. **2.** line of tall cliffs.

pall (pôl) *n.* **1.** cloth spread on coffin. **2.** something gloomy. —*v.* **3.** become wearisome or distasteful.

pall′bear′er, *n.* person who carries coffin at funeral.

pal′let (pal′it) *n.* **1.** straw mattress. **2.** portable platform for freight.

pal′li·ate′ (pal′ē āt′) *v.,* **-ated, -ating.** mitigate; excuse.

pal′li·a·tive (-ā′tiv, -ə tiv) *n.* drug that relieves symptoms but does not cure disease.

pal′lid (pal′id) *adj.* pale.

pal′lor (pal′ər) *n.* paleness.

palm (päm) *n.* **1.** inner surface of hand. **2.** tall, unbranched tropical tree. —*v.* **3.** conceal in hand.

pal·met′to (pal met′ō, päl-, pä-) *n., pl.* **-tos, -toes.** species of palm.

palm′is·try (pä′mə strē) *n.* art of telling fortunes from pattern of lines on palms of hands. —**palm′ist,** *n.*

palm′y, *adj.,* **palmier, palmiest.** thriving.

pal′o·mi′no (pal′ə mē′nō) *n., pl.* **-nos.** light-tan horse.

pal′pa·ble (pal′pə bal) *adj.* obvious; tangible. —**pal′pa·bly,** *adv.*

pal′pate (pal′pāt) *v.,* **-pated, -pating.** examine by touch. —**pal·pa′tion,** *n.*

pal′pi·tate′ (pal′pi tāt′) *v.,* **-tated, -tating.** pulsate with unnatural rapidity. —**pal′pi·ta′tion,** *n.*

pal′sy (pôl′zē) *n., pl.* **-sies. 1.** paralysis. **2.** condition with tremors.

pal′try (pôl′trē) *adj.,* **-trier, -triest.** trifling. —**pal′tri·ness,** *n.*

pam′pas (pam′pəz; *attributively* -pəs) *n.* vast South American plains.

pam′per (pam′pər) *v.* indulge; spoil.

pam′phlet (pam′flit) *n.* **1.** thin booklet. **2.** argumentative treatise.

pam′phlet·eer′, *n.* writer of pamphlets.

pan (pan) *n., v.,* **panned, panning.** —*n.* **1.** dish for cooking. —*v.* **2.** wash (gravel, etc.) to search for gold. **3.** *Informal.* criticize harshly. **4.** film panoramically.

Pan, *n.* Greek god of shepherds.

pan-, prefix meaning all.

pan′a·ce′a (pan′ə sē′ə) *n.* cure-all.

pa·nache′ (pə nash′, -näsh′) *n.* grand or flamboyant manner; flair.

pan′cake′, *n.* flat fried batter cake.

pan′cre·as (pan′krē əs, pang′-) *n.* gland near stomach secreting a digestive fluid. **—pan′cre·at′ic,** *adj.*

pan′da (pan′də) *n.* black and white bearlike animal native to Asia.

pan·dem′ic (pan dem′ik) *adj.* epidemic over large area.

pan′de·mo′ni·um (pan′də mō′nē-əm) *n.* uproar.

pan′der (-dər) *n.* **1.** person who caters to base passions of others. **—***v.* **2.** act as pander. **—pan′der·er,** *n.*

pane (pān) *n.* glass section of window.

pan′e·gyr′ic (pan′i jir′ik, -jī′rik) *n.* eulogy.

pan′el (pan′l) *n., v.,* **-eled, -eling.** **—***n.* **1.** bordered section of wall, door, etc. **2.** list of persons called for jury duty. **3.** public discussion group. **—***v.* **4.** arrange in or ornament with panels. **—pan′el·ing,** *n.*

pan′el·ist *n.* member of panel.

pang (pang) *n.* sudden feeling of distress.

pan′han′dle, *v.,* **-dled, -dling.** *Informal.* beg from passersby.

pan′ic (pan′ik) *n.* demoralizing terror. **—pan′ick·y,** *adj.* **—pan′ic-strick′en,** *adj.*

pan′nier (pan′yər, -ē ər) *n.* large basket for carrying goods.

pan′o·ply (pan′ə plē) *n., pl.* **-plies. 1.** impressive display. **2.** suit of armor.

pan′o·ram′a (pan′ə ram′ə, -rä′mə) *n.* **1.** view over wide area. **2.** passing scene. **—pan′o·ram′ic,** *adj.*

pan′sy (pan′zē) *n., pl.* **-sies. 1.** species of violet. **2.** *Brit.* (*Offensive*). homosexual.

pant (pant) *v.* **1.** breathe hard and quickly. **2.** long eagerly.

pan′ta·loons′ (pan′tl ōōnz′) *n.pl. Archaic.* trousers.

pan′the·ism (pan′thē iz′əm) *n.* religious belief or philosophical doctrine that identifies God with the universe. **—pan′the·is′tic,** *adj.*

pan′the·on (pan′thē on′) *n.* **1.** building with tombs or memorials of a nation's illustrious dead. **2.** heroes of a nation, etc., as a group.

pan′ther (pan′thər) *n.* cougar or leopard.

pan′ties (pan′tēz) *n.pl.* women's underpants. Also, **pan′ty.**

pan′to·mime′ (pan′tə mīm′) *n., v.,* **-mimed, -miming. —***n.* **1.** expression by mute gestures. **2.** play in this form. **—***v.* **3.** express in pantomime. **—pan′to·mim′ist,** *n.*

pan′try (pan′trē) *n., pl.* **-tries.** room for kitchen supplies.

pants (pants) *n.pl. Informal.* trousers.

pant′y·hose′, *n.* one-piece stockings plus panties for women.

pant′y·waist, *n.* sissy.

pan′zer (pan′zər) *adj.* **1.** armored. **—***n.* **2.** tank or armored vehicle.

pap (pap) *n.* soft food.

pa′pa (pä′pə, pə pä′) *n. Informal.* father.

pa′pa·cy (pä′pə sē) *n., pl.* **-cies.** office or reign of the pope.

pa′pal (pä′pəl) *adj.* of the pope.

pa·pa′ya (pə pä′yə) *n.* melonlike tropical American fruit.

pa′per (pā′pər) *n.* **1.** thin fibrous sheet for writing, etc. **2.** document. **3.** treatise. **4.** newspaper. **—***v.* **5.** decorate with wallpaper. **—***adj.* **6.** of paper. **—pa′per·y,** *adj.*

pa′per·back′, *n.* book cheaply bound in paper.

paper tiger, person or nation that seems strong but is actually weak.

pa′per·weight′, *n.* small, heavy object placed on papers to keep them from scattering.

pa′pier-mâ·ché′ (pā′pər mə shā′) *n.* molded paper pulp.

pa′pist (pā′pist) *n., adj. Disparaging.* Roman Catholic. **—pa′pism** (-piz′əm) *n.*

pa·poose′ (pa pōōs′) *n.* North American Indian baby.

pap·ri′ka (pa prē′kə) *n.* spice from pepper plant.

Pap test (pap) test for cancer of the cervix.

pa·py′rus (pə pī′rəs) *n., pl.* **-ri.** tall aquatic plant made into paper by ancient Egyptians.

par (pär) *n.* **1.** equality in value or standing. **2.** average amount, etc. **3.** in golf, standard number of strokes.

para- prefix meaning: **1.** beside, as *paradigm.* **2.** beyond, as *parapsychology.* **3.** auxiliary, as *paralegal.*

par′a·ble (par′ə bəl) *n.* moral allegory.

pa·rab′o·la (pə rab′ə lə) *n.* a U-shaped curve, surface, object, etc.

par′a·chute′ (par′ə shōōt′) *n., v.,* **-chuted, -chuting. —***n.* **1.** umbrellalike apparatus used to fall safely through air. **—***v.* **2.** drop or fall by parachute. **—par′a·chut′ist,** *n.*

pa·rade′ (pə rād′) *n., v.,* **-raded, -rading. —***n.* **1.** public procession or assembly for display. **—***v.* **2.** march in display. **3.** display ostentatiously. **—pa·rad′er,** *n.*

par′a·digm′ (par′ə dīm′, -dim) *n.* example or model.

par′a·dise′ (-dīs′, -dīz′) *n.* **1.** heaven. **2.** garden of Eden. **3.** ideal. **—par′a·di·sa′i·cal,** *adj.*

par′a·dox′ (-doks′) *n.* statement that seems self-contradictory. **—par′a·dox′i·cal,** *adj.*

par′af·fin (-fin) *n.* waxy substance from petroleum, used in candles.

par′a·gon′ (-gon′, -gən) *n.* ideal model.

par′a·graph′ (-graf′) *n.* **1.** unit of written or printed matter, begun on new line. **—***v.* **2.** divide into paragraphs.

par′a·keet′ (-kēt′) *n.* small parrot.

par′a·le′gal, *n.* attorney's assistant.

par′al·lax′ (-ə laks′) *n.* apparent displacement of object viewed due to changed position of viewer.

par′al·lel′ (-ə lel′, -ləl) *adj., n., v.,* **-leled, -leling. —***adj.* **1.** having same direction and being same distance apart. **2.** having same characteristics. **—***n.* **3.** parallel line or plane. **4.** anything parallel. **—***v.* **5.** be parallel to. **—par′al·lel·ism,** *n.*

par′al·lel′o·gram (-lel′ə gram′) *n.* a four-sided figure whose opposite sides are parallel.

pa·ral′y·sis (pə ral′ə sis) *n., pl.* **-ses.** loss of voluntary muscular control. **—par′a·lyt′ic** (par′ə lit′ik) *n., adj.* **—par′a·lyze′,** *v.,* **-lyzed, -lizing.**

par′a·med′ic, *n.* person with paramedical duties.

par′a·med′i·cal, *adj.* of supplementary medicine.

pa·ram′e·ter (pə ram′i tər) *n.* determining factor.

par′a·mil′i·ta·ry (par′ə mil′i ter′ē) *adj.* of organizations operating in place of or in addition to a regular military force.

par′a·mount′ (par′ə mount′) *adj.* greatest; utmost.

par′a·mour′ (par′ə mōōr′) *n.* lover of married person.

par′a·noi′a (par′ə noi′ə) *n.* mental disorder marked by systematized delusions ascribing hostile intentions to other persons.

par′a·pet (par′ə pit, -pet′) *n.* wall at edge of roof or terrace.

par′a·pher·nal′ia (-fər näl′yə, -fə-) *n.pl.* **1.** equipment. **2.** belongings.

par′a·phrase′, *v.,* **-phrased, -phrasing,** *n.* **—***v.* **1.** rephrase. **—***n.* **2.** such restatement.

par′a·ple′gi·a (-plē′jē ə, -jə) *n.* paralysis of lower part of body. **—par′a·ple′gic** *n., adj.*

par′a·pro·fes′sion·al, *adj.* engaged in profession in partial or secondary capacity.

par′a·psy·chol′o·gy, *n.* branch of psychology that studies psychic phenomena.

par′a·site′ (par′ə sīt′) *n.* animal or plant that lives on another organism. **—par′a·sit′ic** (-sit′ik) *adj.*

par′a·sol′ (par′ə sôl′) *n.* sun umbrella.

par′a·thy′roid gland, small gland that regulates blood levels of calcium and phosphate.

par′a·troops′, *n.* force of soldiers who reach battle by parachuting from planes.

par′boil′ (pär′boil′) *v.* precook.

par′cel (pär′səl) *n., v.,* **-celed, -celing. —***n.* **1.** goods wrapped together; bundle. **2.** part. **—***v.* **3.** divide.

parch (pärch) *v.* dry by heat.

par·chee′si (pär chē′zē) *n.* game resembling backgammon.

parch′ment (pärch′mənt) *n.* skin of sheep, etc., prepared for writing on.

par′don (pär′dn) *n.* **1.** legal release. **2.** forgiveness. **—***v.* **3.** excuse; forgive. **—par′don·a·ble,** *adj.*

pare (pâr) *v.,* **pared, paring.** cut off outer part of.

par′ent (pâr′ənt, par′-) *n.* father or mother. **—pa·ren′tal** (pə ren′tl) *adj.* **—par′ent·hood′,** *n.*

par′ent·age (-ən tij) *n.* descent.

pa·ren′the·sis (pə ren′thə sis) *n., pl.* **-ses** (-sēz). **1.** upright curves ( ) used to mark off inserted word or phrase. **2.** material so inserted.

par excellence (pär ek′sə läns′) superior.

par·fait′ (pär fā′) *n.* frothy frozen dessert.

pa·ri′ah (pə rī′ə) *n.* outcast.

par′i-mu′tu·el (par′i myōō′chōō əl) *n.* form of betting on races.

par′ish (par′ish) *n.* ecclesiastical district. **—pa·rish′ion·er,** *n.*

par′i·ty (par′i tē) *n.* **1.** equality. **2.** similarity. **3.** guaranteed level of farm prices.

park (pärk) *n.* **1.** tract of land set apart for public. **—***v.* **2.** put vehicle in a place.

par′ka (pär′kə) *n.* hooded garment.

Par′kin·son's disease (pär′kin səns) neurological disease characterized by tremors and shuffling.

park′way′, *n.* broad thoroughfare with dividing strip or side strips planted with trees, etc.

par′lance (pär′ləns) *n.* way of speaking.

par′lay (pär′lā, -lē) *v.* reinvest original amount and its earnings.

par′ley (pär′lē) *n.* **1.** conference between combatants. **—***v.* **2.** hold parley.

par'lia·ment (pär'lə mənt) *n.* legislative body, esp. (*cap.*) of the United Kingdom.

par·lia·men·tar'ian (-men târ'ē ən, -mən-) *n.* expert in parliamentary rules.

par·lia·men'ta·ry (-men'tə rē) *adj.* **1.** of, by, or having a parliament. **2.** in accordance with rules of debate.

par'lor (pär'lər) *n.* room for receiving guests.

Par'me·san' (pär'mə zän', -zən) *n.* hard, dry Italian cheese.

par'mi·gia'na (pär'mə zhä'nə, -zhän') *adj.* cooked with Parmesan cheese.

pa·ro'chi·al (pə rō'kē əl) *adj.* **1.** of a parish. **2.** narrow; provincial.

parochial school, school run by religious organization.

par'o·dy (par'ə dē) *n., pl.* **-dies,** *v.,* **-died, -dying.** —*n.* **1.** humorous imitation. —*v.* **2.** satirize.

pa·role' (pə rōl') *n., v.,* **-roled, -roling.** —*n.* **1.** conditional release from prison. —*v.* **2.** put on parole. —**pa·rol·ee'** (-rō lē') *n.*

par'ox·ysm (par'ək siz'əm) *n.* outburst. —**par'ox·ys'mal,** *adj.*

par·quet' (pär kā') *n.* floor of inlaid design.

par'ri·cide' (par'ə sīd') *n.* crime of killing one's close relative.

par'rot (par'ət) *n.* **1.** hook-billed, bright-colored bird capable of being taught to talk. —*v.* **2.** repeat senselessly.

par'ry (par'ē) *v.,* **-ried, -rying,** *n., pl.* **-ries.** —*v.* **1.** ward off; evade. —*n.* **2.** act of parrying.

parse (pärs) *v.,* **parsed, parsing.** analyze (word or sentence) grammatically.

par'si·mo'ny (pär'sə mō'nē) *n.* excessive frugality. —**par'si·mo'ni·ous,** *adj.*

pars'ley (pär'slē) *n.* garden herb used in seasoning.

pars'nip (pär'snip) *n.* plant with white edible root.

par'son (pär'sən) *n.* member of clergy.

par'son·age (-sə nij) *n.* house provided for parson.

part (pärt) *n.* **1.** portion of a whole. **2.** share. **3.** role. —*v.* **4.** separate.

par·take' (pär tāk') *v.,* **-took, -taken, -taking.** have or take a share.

par·terre' (pär târ') *n.* rear section of theater seats under balcony.

par'the·no·gen'e·sis (pär'thə nō jen'ə sis) *n.* development of egg without fertilization.

par'tial (pär'shəl) *adj.* **1.** being part; incomplete. **2.** biased. **3.** especially fond. —**par·tial'i·ty,** *n.*

par·tic'i·pate' (pär tis'ə pāt') *v.,* **-pated, -pating.** take part; share (in). —**par·tic'i·pant,** *n.* —**par·tic'i·pa'tion,** *n.*

par'ti·ci·ple (pär'tə sip'əl) *n.* adjective derived from verb.

par'ti·cle (pär'ti kəl) *n.* **1.** tiny piece. **2.** functional word.

par·tic'u·lar (pər tik'yə lər, pə-) *adj.* **1.** pertaining to a specific. **2.** noteworthy. **3.** attentive to details. —*n.* **4.** detail.

par·tic'u·lar·ize' *v.,* **-ized, -izing.** give details.

par·tic'u·lar·ly, *adv.* **1.** especially. **2.** specifically.

par·tic'u·late (-lit, -lāt', pär-) *adj.* composed of particles.

part'ing, *n.* departure or separation.

par'ti·san (pär'tə zən, -sən) *n.* **1.** adherent. **2.** guerrilla.

par·ti'tion (pär tish'ən) *n.* **1.** division into portions. **2.** interior wall. —*v.* **3.** divide into parts.

part'ly, *adv.* not wholly.

part'ner (pärt'nər) *n.* **1.** sharer; associate. **2.** joint owner. **3.** spouse or lover. —**part'ner·ship/,** *n.*

par'tridge (pär'trij) *n.* game bird.

part'-song', *n.* song with parts for several voices.

part'-time', *adj.* (-tīm') **1.** involving or working less than the usual or full time. —*adv.* (-tīm') **2.** on a part-time basis.

par'tu·ri'tion (pär'too rish'ən, -tyoo-) *n.* childbirth.

par'ty (pär'tē) *n., pl.* **-ties. 1.** group with common purpose. **2.** social gathering. **3.** person concerned.

party line, 1. guiding policy of political party. **2.** telephone line connecting telephones of several subscribers.

par've·nu' (pär'və nōō', -nyōō') *n., pl.* **-nus.** person with new wealth but not social acceptance.

pass (pas) *v.,* **passed, passed** or **past, passing,** *n.* —*v.* **1.** go past, by, or through. **2.** succeed. **3.** transfer. **4.** approve. **5.** proceed. **6.** go by; elapse. **7.** die. **8.** be accepted. **9.** go unchallenged. —*n.* **10.** narrow route through barrier. **11.** permission or license. **12.** free ticket. **13.** state of affairs. —**pass'er,** *n.*

pas'sa·ble, *adj.* adequate.

pas'sage (pas'ij) *n.* **1.** section of writing, etc. **2.** freedom to pass. **3.** movement; transportation. **4.** corridor. **5.** lapse. **6.** act of passing. —**pas'sage·way',** *n.*

pass'book', *n.* record of depositor's bank balance.

pas·sé' (pa sā') *adj.* out-of-date.

pas'sen·ger (pas'ən jər) *n.* traveler on vehicle or craft.

pass'er·by', *n., pl.* **passersby.** person who passes by.

pass'ing, *adj.* brief; transitory.

pas'sion (pash'ən) *n.* **1.** very strong emotion. **2.** sexual love. **3.** (*cap.*) sufferings of Christ. —**pas'sion·ate,** *adj.* —**pas'sion·ate·ly,** *adv.*

pas'sive (pas'iv) *adj.* **1.** not in action. **2.** acted upon. **3.** submitting without resistance. **4.** designating voice of verbs indicating subject acted upon. —**pas'sive·ly,** *adv.* —**pas'sive·ness, pas·siv'i·ty,** *n.*

passive resistance, nonviolent opposition.

passive smoking, inhaling of others' cigarette, cigar, or pipe smoke.

pass'key', *n.* master key.

Pass'o·ver (pas'ō'vər) *n.* annual Jewish festival.

pass'port, *n.* official document giving permission to travel abroad.

pass'word', *n.* secret word used to gain access.

past (past) *adj.* **1.** gone by, as in time. **2.** of an earlier time. **3.** designating a tense or verb formation showing time gone by. —*n.* **4.** time or events gone by. **5.** past tense. —*adv.* **6.** so as to pass by. —*prep.* **7.** after. **8.** beyond.

pas'ta (pä'stə) *n.* Italian flour-and-egg mixture, as spaghetti.

paste (pāst) *n., v.,* **pasted, pasting.** —*n.* **1.** soft, sticky mixture. **2.** glass used for gems. —*v.* **3.** fasten with paste.

paste'board', *n.* firm board made of layers of paper.

pas·tel' (pa stel') *n.* soft color.

pas'teur·ize' (pas'chə rīz') *v.,* **-ized, -izing.** heat (milk, etc.) to destroy certain bacteria.

pas·tiche' (pa stēsh') *n.* artistic work made up of borrowed details.

pas·tille' (pa stēl') *n.* lozenge.

pas'time' (pas'tīm') *n.* diversion.

past master, expert.

pas'tor (pas'tər) *n.* minister.

pas'to·ral, *adj.* **1.** having rural charm. **2.** of shepherds. **3.** of pastors or spiritual guidance.

pas'to·rale' (-räl') *n.* dreamy musical composition.

pas·tra'mi (pə strä'mē) *n.* seasoned smoked or pickled beef.

pas'try (pā'strē) *n., pl.* **-tries.** food made of rich paste, as pies.

pas'ture, *n., v.,* **-tured, -turing.** —*n.* **1.** grassy ground for grazing. —*v.* **2.** graze on pasture.

past'y (pā'stē) *adj.* like paste in texture or color.

pat (pat) *v.,* **patted, patting,** *n., adj., adv.* —*v.* **1.** strike gently. —*n.* **2.** light stroke. **3.** small mass. —*adj.* **4.** apt; to the point. —*adv.* **5.** perfectly. **6.** unwaveringly.

patch (pach) *n.* **1.** piece of material used to mend or protect. **2.** any small piece. —*v.* **3.** mend, esp. with patches. —**patch'work',** *n.*

patch test, allergy test where patch of material containing allergen is applied to skin.

patch'y, *adj.,* **patchier, patchiest.** irregular in surface or quality.

pate (pāt) *n.* crown of head.

pâ·té' (pä tä', pa-) *n.* paste of puréed or chopped meat, liver, etc.

pa·tel'la (pə tel'ə) *n., pl.* **-tellae** (tel'-ē). kneecap.

pat'ent (pat'nt) *n.* **1.** exclusive right to invention. —*adj.* **2.** protected by patent. **3.** evident. —*v.* **4.** secure patent on.

patent leather, hard, glossy, smooth leather.

patent medicine, drug protected by trademark.

pa·ter'nal (pə tûr'nl) *adj.* **1.** fatherly. **2.** related through father.

pa·ter'nal·ism, *n.* benevolent control. —**pa·ter'nal·is'tic,** *adj.*

pa·ter'ni·ty (-ni tē) *n.* fatherhood.

pa'ter·nos'ter (pä'tər nos'tər) *n.* Lord's Prayer.

path (path) *n.* **1.** Also, **path'way'.** narrow way. **2.** route. **3.** course of action.

pa·thet'ic (pə thet'ik) *adj.* arousing pity. —**pa·thet'i·cal·ly,** *adv.*

path'o·gen (path'ə jən, -jen') *n.* disease-producing agent.

path'o·log'i·cal (-loj'i kəl) *adj.* sick; morbid.

pa·thol'o·gy (pə thol'ə jē) *n.* study of disease. —**pa·thol'o·gist,** *n.*

pa'thos (pā'thos, -thōs) *n.* quality or power of arousing pity.

-pathy, suffix meaning: **1.** feeling, as *antipathy.* **2.** method of treatment, as *osteopathy.*

pa'tient (pā'shənt) *n.* **1.** person under care of a doctor. —*adj.* **2.** enduring calmly. —**pa'tience,** *n.*

pat'i·na (pat'n ə, pə tē'nə) *n.* film on old bronze, etc.

pa'ti·o' (pat'ē ō') *n., pl.* **-tios.** inner open court.

pa'tri·arch' (pā'trē ärk') *n.* **1.** venerable old man. **2.** male head of family. —**pa'tri·ar'chal,** *adj.*

pa'tri·ar'chy (-är'kē) *n., pl.* **-chies.** family group ruled by a father.

pa·tri'cian (pə trish'ən) *n.* **1.** aristocrat. —*adj.* **2.** aristocratic.

pat'ri·cide' (pa'trə sīd') *n.* killing one's father. —**pat'ri·cid'al,** *adj.*

pat·ri·mo·ny (-mō′nē) *n., pl.* **-nies.** inherited estate.

pa·tri·ot (pā′trē ət, -ot′) *n.* person who supports country. —**pa′tri·ot′ic,** *adj.* —**pa′tri·ot·ism** (-ə tiz′əm) *n.* —**pa′tri·ot′i·cal·ly,** *adv.*

pa·trol′ (pə trōl′) *v.,* **-trolled, -trolling,** *n.* —*v.* **1.** pass through or around in guarding. —*n.* **2.** person or group assigned to patrol.

pa·trol′man, *n., pl.* **-men.** police officer who patrols.

pa′tron (pā′trən) *n.* **1.** supporter. **2.** regular customer.

pa′tron·age (pā′trə nij, pa′-) *n.* **1.** support by patron. **2.** political control of appointments to office.

pa′tron·ize′, *v.,* **-ized, -izing. 1.** buy from, esp. regularly. **2.** treat condescendingly.

patron saint, saint regarded as special guardian.

pat′sy (pat′sē) *n., pl.* **-sies.** *Slang.* person easily manipulated.

pat′ter (pat′ər) *v.* **1.** tap lightly and quickly. **2.** speak glibly. —*n.* **3.** pattering sound. **4.** rapid, glib talk.

pat′tern (pat′ərn) *n.* **1.** surface design. **2.** characteristic mode of development, etc. **3.** model for copying. —*v.* **4.** make after pattern.

pat′ty (pat′ē) *n., pl.* **-ties.** flat cake of ground or minced food.

pau′ci·ty (pô′si tē) *n.* scarceness.

paunch (pônch) *n.* belly, esp. when large. —**paunch′y,** *adj.*

pau′per (pô′pər) *n.* poor person.

pause (pôz) *n., v.,* **paused, pausing.** —*n.* **1.** temporary stop. —*v.* **2.** make pause.

pave (pāv) *v.,* **paved, paving. 1.** cover with solid road surface. **2.** prepare. —**pave′ment,** *n.*

pa·vil′ion (pə vil′yən) *n.* **1.** light open shelter. **2.** tent.

paw (pô) *n.* **1.** foot of animal. —*v.* **2.** scrape with paw. **3.** touch clumsily.

pawn (pôn) *v.* **1.** deposit as security for loan. —*n.* **2.** state of being pawned. **3.** piece used in chess. —**pawn′shop′,** *n.*

pawn′bro′ker, *n.* person who lends money on pledged articles.

paw′paw′ (pô′pô′, pə pô′) *n.* small tree bearing purple flowers.

pay (pā) *v.,* **paid, paying.** —*v.* **1.** give money required to. **2.** give as compensation. **3.** yield profit. **4.** let out (rope). —*n.* **5.** wages. **6.** paid employ. —**pay′a·ble,** *adj.* —**pay′ment,** *n.*

pay dirt, 1. profitable soil to mine. **2.** *Informal.* any source of wealth.

pay′load′, *n.* **1.** revenue-producing freight, etc. **2.** explosives, passengers, or cargo carried by an aircraft.

pay′mas′ter, *n.* person in charge of paying out wages.

pay′off′, *n.* **1.** *Informal.* final consequence. **2.** awaited payment.

pay·o′la (pā ō′lə) *n.* bribe.

pay′roll, *n.* **1.** list of employees to be paid. **2.** total of these amounts.

PC, 1. *pl.* **PCs** or **PC's.** personal computer. **2.** politically correct.

PE, physical education.

pea (pē) *n.* round edible seed of legume.

peace (pēs) *n.* freedom from war, trouble, or disturbance. —**peace′mak′er,** *n.* —**peace′time′,** *n.*

peace′ful, *adj.* **1.** at peace. **2.** desiring peace. Also, **peace′a·ble.**

peach (pēch) *n.* sweet juicy pinkish fruit.

pea′cock′ (pē′kok′) *n.* male peafowl, having iridescent tail feathers.

pea′fowl′, *n.* bird of pheasant family.

pea′hen′, *n.* female peafowl.

pea jacket, short heavy coat.

peak (pēk) *n.* **1.** pointed top. **2.** highest point.

peaked, *adj.* **1.** (pēkt) having peak. **2.** (pē′kid) sickly, haggard.

peal (pēl) *n.* **1.** prolonged sound, as of bells or thunder. **2.** set of bells. —*v.* **3.** sound in a peal.

pea′nut′, *n.* pod or edible seed of leguminous plant that ripens underground.

pear (pâr) *n.* elongated edible fruit.

pearl (pûrl) *n.* hard, smooth, nearwhite gem formed within an oyster. —**pearl′y,** *adj.*

peas′ant (pez′ənt) *n.* farm worker.

peat (pēt) *n.* organic soil dried for fuel. —**peat′y,** *adj.*

peb′ble (peb′əl) *n.* small, rounded stone. —**peb′bly,** *adj.*

pe·can′ (pi kän′, -kan′) *n.* smoothshelled nut.

pec′ca·dil′lo (pek′ə dil′ō) *n., pl.* **-loes, -los.** trifling sin.

pec′ca·ry (pek′ə rē) *n., pl.* **-ries.** wild American pig.

peck (pek) *v.* **1.** strike with beak. —*n.* **2.** pecking stroke. **3.** dry measure of eight quarts.

pecking order, hierarchy within group.

pec′tin (pek′tin) *n.* substance in ripe fruit that forms jelly.

pec′to·ral (pek′tər əl) *adj.* **1.** of the chest. —*n.* **2.** pectoral muscle.

pe·cu′liar (pi kyōōl′yər) *adj.* **1.** strange; odd. **2.** uncommon. **3.** exclusive. —**pe·cu′li·ar′i·ty** (-lē ar′i tē) *n.* —**pe·cu′liar·ly,** *adv.*

pe·cu′ni·ar·y (pi kyōō′nē er′ē) *adj.* of money.

ped′a·gogue′ (ped′ə gog′) *n.* teacher. —**ped′a·go′gy** (-gō′jē, -goj′ē) *n.* —**ped′a·gog′ic, ped′a·gog′i·cal,** *adj.*

ped′al (ped′l) *n., v.,* **-aled, -aling.** —*n.* **1.** lever worked by foot. —*v.* **2.** work pedals of. —*adj.* **3.** (pē′dəl) of feet.

ped′ant (ped′nt) *n.* person excessively concerned with details. —**pe·dan′tic,** *adj.* —**ped′ant·ry,** *n.*

ped′dle (ped′l) *v.,* **-dled, -dling.** carry about for sale. —**ped′dler,** *n.*

ped′er·as·ty (ped′ə ras′tē, pē′də-) *n.* sexual relations between a man and a boy. —**ped′er·ast′,** *n.*

ped′es·tal (ped′ə stl) *n.* base for object.

pe·des′tri·an (pə des′trē ən) *n.* **1.** walker. —*adj.* **2.** walking. **3.** prosaic.

pe′di·at′rics (pē′dē a′triks) *n.* study of care and diseases of children. —**pe′di·a·tri′cian** (pē′dē ə trish′ən) *n.* —**pe′di·at′ric,** *adj.*

ped′i·cure′ (ped′i kyŏŏr′) *n.* professional care of the feet.

ped′i·gree′ (ped′i grē′) *n.* **1.** certificate of ancestry. **2.** ancestry.

ped′i·ment (ped′ə mənt) *n.* triangular gablelike architectural feature.

pe·dom′e·ter (pə dom′i tər) *n.* device that measures distance walked.

peek (pēk) *v., n.* peep (defs. 1–3; 5).

peel (pēl) *v.* **1.** remove or lose skin, bark, etc. —*n.* **2.** skin of fruit, etc.

peep (pēp) *v.* **1.** look through small opening. **2.** look furtively. **3.** show slightly. **4.** utter shrill little cry. —*n.* **5.** quick look. **6.** weak sound.

peer (pēr) *n.* **1.** equal. **2.** noble. —*v.* **3.** look closely.

peer′age (-ij) *n.* rank of peer.

peer′less, *adj.* without equal.

peeve (pēv) *n., v.,* **peeved, peeving.** —*n.* **1.** complaint. —*v.* **2.** vex.

peev′ish (pē′vish) *adj.* cross.

pee·wee (pē′wē′) *n.* *Informal.* person or thing that is unusually small.

peg (peg) *n., v.,* **pegged, pegging.** —*n.* **1.** pin of wood, metal, etc. —*v.* **2.** fasten with pegs.

peg leg, wooden leg.

peign·oir′ (pān wär′, pen-) *n.* woman's loose dressing gown.

pe·jo′ra·tive (pi jôr′ə tiv) *adj.* disparaging; negative.

Pe′king·ese′ (pē′kə nēz′, -nēs′) *n., pl.* **Peking-ese.** long-haired Chinese dog with flat muzzle.

pel′i·can (pel′i kən) *n.* large-billed bird.

pel·la′gra (pə lag′rə, -lā′grə, -lä′-) *n.* chronic disease from inadequate diet.

pel′let (pel′it) *n.* little ball.

pell′-mell′ (pel′mel′) *adv.* in disorderly haste.

pel·lu′cid (pə lōō′sid) *adj.* **1.** translucent. **2.** clear.

pelt (pelt) *v.* **1.** throw. **2.** assail. —*n.* **3.** a blow. **4.** skin of beast.

pel′vis (pel′vis) *n.* **1.** cavity in lower body trunk. **2.** bones forming this cavity. —**pel′vic,** *adj.*

pen (pen) *n., v.,* **penned** or (for 4) **pent, penning.** —*n.* **1.** device for writing with ink. **2.** small enclosure. —*v.* **3.** write with pen. **4.** confine in pen.

pe′nal (pēn′l) *adj.* of punishment. —**pe′nal·ize′,** *v.*

pen′al·ty (pen′l tē) *n., pl.* **-ties. 1.** punishment. **2.** disadvantage.

pen′ance (-əns) *n.* punishment as penitence for sin.

pence (pens) *n.* *Brit. pl.* of **penny.**

pen′chant (pen′chənt) *n.* liking.

pen′cil (pen′səl) *n.* enclosed stick of graphite, etc., for marking.

pend (pend) *v.* remain undecided.

pend′ant (pen′dənt) *n.* hanging ornament.

pend′ent (pen′dənt) *adj.* hanging.

pend′ing, *prep.* **1.** until. —*adj.* **2.** undecided.

pen′du·lous (pen′jə ləs, pen′dyə-) *adj.* hanging loosely.

pen′du·lum (-ləm) *n.* hung weight.

pen′e·trate′ (pen′i trāt′) *v.,* **-trated, -trating. 1.** pierce; permeate. **2.** enter. **3.** understand; have insight. —**pen′e·tra′tion,** *n.*

pen′guin (peng′gwin, pen′-) *n.* flightless aquatic bird.

pen′i·cil′lin (pen′ə sil′in) *n.* antibacterial substance produced in certain molds.

pen·in′su·la (pə nin′sə lə) *n.* piece of land nearly surrounded by water. —**pen·in′su·lar,** *adj.*

pe′nis (pē′nis) *n.* male sex organ. —**pe′nile** (pēn′l) *adj.*

pen′i·tent (pen′i tənt) *adj.* **1.** sorry for sin or fault. —*n.* **2.** penitent person. —**pen′i·tence,** *n.*

pen′i·ten′tia·ry (-ten′shə rē) *n., pl.* **-ries.** prison.

pen′knife′, *n.* small pocket knife.

pen′light′, *n.* flashlight shaped like fountain pen.

pen′man, *n., pl.* **-men.** one who writes. —**pen′man·ship′,** *n.*

Penn., Pennsylvania. Also, **Penna.**

pen name, pseudonym.

pen′nant (pen′ənt) *n.* flag, usually tapered. Also, **pen′non.**

pen′ny (pen′ē) *n., pl.* **pennies,** *Brit.* **pence.** small coin, equal to one cent in the U.S. and Canada, and to $\frac{1}{100}$ pound in United Kingdom. —**pen′ni·less,** *adj.*

penny pincher, stingy person. —**pen′ny-pinch′ing,** adj.

pen′ny-weight′, n. (in troy weight) 24 grains, or 1/20 of an ounce.

pen pal, person with whom one exchanges letters.

pen′sion (pen′shən) n. **1.** fixed periodic payment for past service, etc. **2.** (pän sē ōn′) (in France) boarding house or school. —v. **3.** give pension to.

pen′sion•er, n. person receiving pension.

pen′sive (pen′siv) adj. gravely thoughtful. —**pen′sive•ly,** adv.

pent (pent) adj. confined.

penta-, prefix meaning five.

pen′ta•gon′ (pen′tə gon′) n. plane figure having five sides.

pen′ta•gram′ (-gram′) n. five-pointed, star-shaped symbol.

pen•tam′e•ter (pen tam′i tər) n. verse or line of five feet.

Pen′ta•teuch′ (pen′tə tōōk′, -tyōōk′) n. Bible. first five books of the Old Testament.

pen•tath′lon (pen tath′lən, -lon) n. athletic contest of five events.

Pen′te•cost′ (pen′ti kôst′) n. Christian festival; Whitsunday.

Pen′te•cos′tal, adj. of Christian groups that emphasize the Holy Spirit.

pent′house′ (pent′hous′) n. rooftop apartment or dwelling.

pent′-up′, adj. restrained; confined.

pe•nul′ti•mate (pi nul′tə mit) adj. being or occurring next to last.

pe•num′bra (pə num′brə) n., pl. -brae (-brē), -bras. partial shadow outside complete shadow of celestial body in eclipse. —**pe•num′bral,** adj.

pe•nu′ri•ous (pə nōōr′ē əs, -nyōōr′-) adj. **1.** stingy. **2.** very poor.

pen′u•ry (pen′yə rē) n. poverty.

pe′on (pē′ən, -on) n. **1.** unskilled worker. **2.** indentured worker.

pe′o•ny (pē′ə nē) n., pl. -nies. perennial plant with large flowers.

peo′ple (pē′pəl) n., v. -pled, -pling. —n. **1.** body of persons constituting nation or ethnic group. **2.** persons in general. **3.** person's relatives. —v. **4.** populate.

pep (pep) n., v., pepped, pepping. Informal. —n. **1.** vigor. —v. **2.** give vigor to. —**pep′py,** adj.

pep′per (pep′ər) n. **1.** condiment from dried berries. **2.** edible fruit of certain plants. —v. **3.** season with pepper. **4.** pelt with shot. —**pep′per•y,** adj.

pep′per•corn′, n. dried berry of pepper plant.

pepper mill, device for grinding peppercorns.

pep′per•mint′ (-mint′) n. aromatic oil of herb, used as flavoring.

pep•per•o′ni (pep′ə rō′nē) n., pl. -nis. highly seasoned sausage.

pep′sin (pep′sin) n. juice secreted in stomach that digests proteins.

pep′tic (pep′tik) adj. digestive.

per (pûr; unstressed pər) prep. for; by means of.

per•am′bu•late′, v., -lated, -lating. walk about or through.

per•am′bu•la′tor, n. baby carriage.

per an′num (per an′əm) yearly.

per•cale′ (pər kāl′) n. smooth, closely woven cotton fabric.

per cap′i•ta (pər kap′i tə) by or for each person.

per•ceive′ (pər sēv′) v., -ceived, -ceiving. **1.** gain knowledge of by seeing, hearing, etc. **2.** understand. —**perceiv′a•ble,** adj.

per•cent′ (pər sent′) n. number of parts in each hundred.

per•cent′age (-sen′tij) n. proportion or rate per hundred.

per•cen′tile (-tīl, -til) n. value of statistical variable that divides distribution of variable into 100 equal parts.

per•cep′ti•ble (-sep′tə bəl) adj. capable of being perceived.

per•cep′tion, n. **1.** act or faculty of perceiving. **2.** intuition; insight. **3.** result or product of perceiving.

per•cep′tive, adj. **1.** keen. **2.** showing perception.

per•cep′tu•al (-chōō əl) adj. involving perception.

perch (pûrch) n. **1.** place for roosting. **2.** linear measure of 5½ yards. **3.** square rod (30¼ sq. yards). **4.** common food fish. —v. **5.** set or rest on perch.

per•chance′ (pər chans′) adv. Poetic. maybe; by chance.

per′co•late′ (pûr′kə lāt′) v., -lated, -lating. filter through.

per′co•la′tor, n. coffee pot.

per•cus′sion (pər kush′ən) n. **1.** violent impact. —adj. **2.** musical instruments sounded by striking.

per di′em (pər dē′əm) adv. **1.** by the day. —n. **2.** daily pay or allowance for expenses.

per•di′tion (pər dish′ən) n. ruin; hell.

per′e•gri•nate′ (per′i grə nāt′) v., -nated, -nating. travel, esp. on foot. —**per′e•gri•na′tion,** n.

per′e•grine falcon (per′i grin, -grēn′) bird of prey.

per•emp′to•ry (pə remp′tə rē) adj. permitting no denial or refusal. —**per•emp′to•ri•ly,** adv.

per•en′ni•al (pə ren′ē əl) adj. **1.** lasting indefinitely. **2.** living more than two years. —n. **3.** perennial plant. —**per•en′ni•al•ly,** adv.

per′fect (pûr′fikt) adj. **1.** faultless. **2.** designating verb tense indicating action already completed. —n. **3.** Gram. perfect tense. —v. (par fekt′) **4.** make faultless. —**per•fec′tion** (pər fek′shən) n.

per•fec′tion•ism, n. insistence on perfection. —**per•fec′tion•ist,** n.

per′fi•dy (pûr′fi dē) n., pl. -dies. treachery. —**per•fid′i•ous,** adj.

per′fo•rate′ (pûr′fə rāt′) v., -rated, -rating. make holes through. —**per′fo•ra′tion,** n.

per•force′ (pər fôrs′) adv. of necessity.

per•form′ (pər fôrm′) v. **1.** carry out; do. **2.** act, as on stage. —**per•for′mance,** n. —**per•form′er,** n.

performing arts, arts requiring public performance.

per•fume′, n., v., -fumed, -fuming. —n. (pûr′fyōōm, pər fyōōm′) **1.** sweet-smelling liquid. **2.** sweet smell. —v. (pər fyōōm′, pûr′fyōōm) **3.** impart fragrance to. —**per•fum′er•y,** n.

per•func′to•ry (pər fungk′tə rē) adj. done without care or attention. —**per•func′to•ri•ly,** adv.

per•haps′ (pər haps′) adv. maybe.

peri-, prefix meaning around, surrounding, or near.

per′i•car′di•um (per′i kär′dē əm) n. membranous sac enclosing the heart.

per′il (per′əl) n. **1.** danger. —v. **2.** endanger. —**per′il•ous,** adj.

pe•rim′e•ter (pə rim′i tər) n. outer boundary of plane figure.

per′i•ne′um (per′ə nē′əm) n., pl. -nea. area between genitals and anus.

pe′ri•od (pēr′ē əd) n. **1.** portion of time. **2.** mark (.) ending sentence.

pe′ri•od′ic (-od′ik) adj. recurring regularly or intermittently. —**pe′ri•od′i•cal•ly,** adv.

pe′ri•od′i•cal, n. **1.** publication issued at regular intervals. —adj. **2.** periodic.

periodic table, table showing chemical elements in related groups.

per′i•pa•tet′ic (per′ə pə tet′ik) adj. walking or traveling about; itinerant.

pe•riph′er•al (pə rif′ər əl) adj. **1.** located on periphery. **2.** only partly relevant.

pe•riph′er•y, n., pl. -eries. **1.** external boundary. **2.** external surface.

pe•riph′ra•sis (pə rif′rə sis) n., pl. -ses (-sēz′). use of roundabout form of expression.

per′i•scope′ (per′ə skōp′) n. optical instrument consisting of a tube in which mirrors or prisms reflect to give a view from below or behind an obstacle.

per′ish (per′ish) v. **1.** die. **2.** decay. —**per′ish•a•ble,** adj., n.

per′i•stal′sis (per′ə stôl′sis, -stal′-) n., pl. -ses (-sēz). muscle contractions and relaxations that move food along alimentary canal.

per′i•to•ne′um (per′i tn ē′əm, -tō′-) n. lining of abdominal cavity.

per′i•to•ni′tis (-tn ī′tis) n. swelling of peritoneum.

per′i•win′kle (per′i wing′kəl) n. **1.** edible marine snail. **2.** trailing evergreen plant.

per′jure (pûr′jər) v., -jured, -juring. lie under oath. —**per′jur•er,** n.

per′ju•ry (pûr′jə rē) n., pl. -ries. false statement made under oath.

perk (pûrk) v. **1.** move up jauntily. **2.** become lively. —n. **3.** perquisite.

perk′y, adj. cheerful.

per′ma•frost′ (pûr′mə frôst′) n. permanently frozen subsoil.

per′ma•nent (-nənt) adj. **1.** lasting indefinitely. —n. **2.** curl permanently set in hair. —**per′ma•nence,** n. —**per′ma•nent•ly,** adv.

per′me•a•ble (pûr′mē ə bəl) adj. letting fluids through.

per′me•ate′ (-āt′) v., -ated, -ating. penetrate; pervade.

per•mis′sion (-mish′ən) n. authorization. —**per•mis′si•ble,** adj.

per•mis′sive (-mis′iv) adj. **1.** giving permission. **2.** loose or lax in discipline.

per•mit′, v., -mitted, -mitting. —v. (pər mit′) **1.** allow; agree to. **2.** afford opportunity. —n. (pûr′mit, pər mit′) **3.** written order giving permission.

per′mu•ta′tion (pûr′myōō tā′shən) n. alteration, change in order.

per•ni′cious (pər nish′əs) adj. **1.** highly hurtful. **2.** deadly.

per•ox′ide (pə rok′sīd) n. **1.** oxide containing large amount of oxygen. **2.** hydrogen peroxide.

per′pen•dic′u•lar (pûr′pən dik′yə lər) adj. **1.** vertical. **2.** meeting given line at right angles. —n. **3.** perpendicular line or position.

per′pe•trate′ (pûr′pi trāt′) v., -trated, -trating. commit (crime, etc.). —**per′pe•tra′tion,** n. —**per′pe•tra′tor,** n.

per•pet′u•al (pər pech′ōō əl) adj. **1.** lasting forever. **2.** unceasing. —**per•pet′u•ate′,** v.

per′pe•tu′i•ty (pûr′pi tōō′i tē, -tyōō′-) n. forever.

per•plex′ (pər pleks′) v. confuse mentally. —**per•plex′i•ty,** n.

per·qui·site (pûr′kwə zit) *n.* incidental profit.

per se (pûr sā′, sē′, pər) by, of, for, or in itself; intrinsically.

per′se·cute′ (pûr′si kyōōt′) *v.*, **-cuted, -cuting.** oppress persistently, esp. for one's beliefs. —**per′se·cu′tion,** *n.* —**per′se·cu′tor,** *n.*

per·se·vere′ (pûr′sə vēr′) *v.*, **-vered, -vering.** continue steadfastly. —**per′se·ver′ance,** *n.*

per·sim′mon (pər sim′ən) *n.* soft fruit.

per·sist′ (pər sist′, -zist′) *v.* **1.** continue firmly in spite of opposition. **2.** endure. —**per·sist′ence,** *n.* —**per·sist′ent,** *adj.*

per·snick′et·y (pər snik′i tē) *adj. Informal.* fussy.

per′son (pûr′sən) *n.* **1.** human being. **2.** individual personality. **3.** body.

per′son·a·ble, *adj.* attractive in appearance and manner.

per′son·age (-sə nij) *n.* distinguished person.

per′son·al (-sə nl) *adj.* **1.** of, by, or relating to a certain person. **2.** *Gram.* denoting class of pronouns that refer to speaker, person addressed, or thing spoken of. **3.** *Law.* of property that is movable. —**per′son·al·ly,** *adv.*

personal computer, microcomputer designed for individual use.

personal effects, belongings.

per′son·al′i·ty (-sə nal′ə tē) *n., pl.* **-ties. 1.** distinctive personal character. **2.** famous person.

per′son·al·ize′, *v.*, **-ized, -izing. 1.** make personal. **2.** treat as if human.

per·so′na non gra′ta (pər sō′nə non grä′tə) unwelcome.

per·son′i·fy′ (pər son′ə fī′) *v.*, **-fied, -fying. 1.** attribute personal character to. **2.** embody; typify. —**per·son′i·fi·ca′tion,** *n.*

per′son·nel′ (pûr′sə nel′) *n.* employees.

per·spec′tive (pər spek′tiv) *n.* **1.** depiction as to show space relationships. **2.** mental view.

per′spi·ca′cious (pûr′spi kā′shəs) *adj.* mentally keen. —**per′spi·cac′i·ty** (-kas′i tē) *n.*

per·spire′ (pər spī˝r′) *v.*, **-spired, -spiring.** sweat. —**per′spi·ra′tion** (pûr′spə rā′shən) *n.*

per·suade′ (pər swād′) *v.*, **-suaded, -suading. 1.** prevail on to act as suggested. **2.** convince. —**per·sua′sive,** *adj.* —**per·sua′sive·ly,** *adv.*

per·sua′sion (-swā′zhən) *n.* **1.** act or power of persuading. **2.** conviction or belief. **3.** religious system.

pert (pûrt) *adj.* bold; saucy.

per·tain′ (pər tān′) *v.* belong; have reference.

per′ti·nent (-tn ənt) *adj.* relevant. —**per′ti·nence,** *n.* —**per′ti·nent·ly,** *adv.*

per·turb′ (pər tûrb′) *v.* disturb greatly. —**per′tur·ba′tion,** *n.*

pe·ruke′ (pə rōōk′) *n.* man's wig.

pe·ruse′ (pə rōōz′) *v.*, **-rused, -rusing.** read, esp. with care. —**pe·ru′sal,** *n.*

per·vade′ (pər vād′) *v.*, **-vaded, -vading.** be present throughout. —**per·va′sive,** *adj.*

per·verse′ (pər vûrs′) *adj.* stubbornly contrary. —**per·ver′si·ty,** *n.*

per·vert′, *v.* (pər vûrt′) **1.** turn from right or moral course or use. —*n.* (pûr′vûrt) **2.** perverted person. —**per·ver′sion,** *n.*

pe·se′ta (pə sā′tə) *n., pl.* **-tas.** monetary unit of Spain.

pes′ky (pes′kē) *adj.*, **-kier, -kiest.** annoying; troublesome.

pe′so (pā′sō) *n.* monetary unit and coin in Latin America.

pes′si·mism (pes′ə miz′əm) *n.* **1.** disposition to expect worst. **2.** belief that all things tend to evil. —**pes′si·mist,** *n.* —**pes′si·mis′tic,** *adj.* —**pes′si·mis′ti·cal·ly,** *adv.*

pest (pest) *n.* troublesome person, animal, or thing.

pes′ter (pes′tər) *v.* annoy; harass.

pes′ti·cide′ (pes′tə sīd′) *n.* poison used to kill harmful insects or weeds.

pes·tif′er·ous (pe stif′ər əs) *adj.* **1.** bearing disease. **2.** troublesome.

pes′ti·lence (pes′tl əns) *n.* epidemic disease. —**pes′ti·lent,** *adj.*

pes′tle (pes′əl, pes′tl) *n.* instrument for pounding or crushing.

pes′to (pes′tō) *n.* sauce of basil, nuts, garlic, olive oil, and cheese.

pet (pet) *n., adj., v.,* **petted, petting.** —*n.* **1.** tame animal that is cared for affectionately. **2.** favorite. **3.** tantrum. —*adj.* **4.** treated as pet. —*v.* **5.** caress.

pet′al (pet′l) *n.* leaf of blossom.

pe·tard′ (pi tärd′) *n.* explosive device.

pe′ter (pē′tər) *v. Informal.* diminish gradually.

pet′it (pet′ē) *adj. Law.* petty.

pe·tite′ (pə tēt′) *adj.* small.

pe·ti′tion (pə tish′ən) *n.* **1.** request, esp. formal one. —*v.* **2.** present petition. —**pe·ti′tion·er,** *n.*

pet′rel (pe′trəl) *n.* small oceanic bird.

pet′ri·fy′ (pe′trə fī′) *v.*, **-fied, -fying. 1.** turn into stone. **2.** paralyze with fear.

pet′ro·chem′i·cal (pe′trō kem′i kəl) *n.* chemical from petroleum.

pe·tro′le·um (pə trō′lē əm) *n.* oily liquid occurring naturally; source of gasoline, kerosene, paraffin, etc.

pe·trol′o·gy (-trol′ə jē) *n.* study of rocks.

pet′ti·coat′ (pet′ē kōt′) *n.* underskirt.

pet′ti·fog′ (pet′ē fog′) *v.*, **-fogged, -fogging.** quibble over trifles.

pet′tish (pet′ish) *adj.* petulant.

pet′ty (pet′ē) *adj.*, **-tier, -tiest. 1.** small or trivial. **2.** small-minded. —**pet′ti·ness,** *n.*

petty cash, fund for paying minor expenses.

petty jury, jury in civil or criminal trial.

petty officer, noncommissioned officer in navy or coast guard.

pet′u·lant (pech′ə lənt) *adj.* showing impatient irritation. —**pet′u·lance,** *n.*

pe·tu′ni·a (pi tōō′nyə, -tyōō′-) *n.* plant with funnel-shaped flowers.

pew (pyōō) *n.* enclosed bench or seats in church.

pe′wee (pē′wē) *n.* any of certain small birds.

pew′ter (pyōō′tər) *n.* alloy rich in tin.

pf., (of stock) preferred.

PG, motion-picture rating: parental guidance recommended.

PG-13, motion-picture rating: material may be unsuitable for children under 13.

pg., page.

pH, symbol describing acidity or alkalinity of chemical solution.

pha′e·ton (fā′i tn, fā′ə tən) *n.* open carriage or automobile.

pha′lanx (fā′langks, fal′angks) *n., pl.* **phalanxes, phalanges** (fə lan′jēz). **1.** compact body, as of troops, etc. **2.** any bone of fingers or toes.

phal′lus (fal′əs) *n., pl.* **phalli** (fal′ī).

1. penis. **2.** image of penis as symbol of fertility. —**phal′lic,** *adj.*

phan′tasm (fan′taz əm) *n.* apparition.

phan·tas′ma·go′ri·a (-mə gôr′ē ə) *n.* shifting series of illusions.

phan′tom (fan′təm) *n.* **1.** ghostlike image. —*adj.* **2.** unreal.

Phar′aoh (fâr′ō) *n.* title of ancient Egyptian kings.

Phar′i·see′ (far′ə sē′) *n.* **1.** member of ancient Jewish sect. **2.** (*l.c.*) self-righteous person.

phar′ma·ceu′ti·cal (fär′mə sōō′ti-kəl) *adj.* pertaining to pharmacy.

phar′ma·col′o·gy (-kol′ə jē) *n.* study of drugs.

phar′ma·co·poe′ia (-kə pē′ə) *n.* book on medicines.

phar′ma·cy (-sē) *n., pl.* **-cies. 1.** art or practice of preparing medicines. **2.** place for dispensing medicines. —**phar′ma·cist,** *n.*

phar′ynx (far′ingks) *n., pl.* **pharynges** (fə rin′jēz), **pharynxes.** tube connecting mouth and nasal passages with esophagus. —**pha·ryn′ge·al,** *adj.* —**phar′yn·gi′tis** (far′ən jī′tis) *n.*

phase (fāz) *n.* **1.** stage of change. **2.** aspect of changing thing.

phase′out′, *n.* gradual dismissal or termination.

Ph.D., Doctor of Philosophy.

pheas′ant (fez′ənt) *n.* large, long-tailed, brightly colored bird.

phe′no·bar′bi·tal′ (fē′nō bär′bi-tôl′, -tal′) *n.* white powder used as sedative.

phe′nol (fē′nôl) *n.* carbolic acid.

phe·nom′e·non′ (fi nom′ə non′, -nən) *n., pl.* **-ena** (-ə nə). **1.** something observable. **2.** extraordinary thing or person. —**phe·nom′e·nal,** *adj.* —**phe·nom′e·nal·ly,** *adv.*

pher′o·mone′ (fer′ə mōn′) *n.* chemical substance released by animal that influences behavior of other members of species.

phi′al (fī′əl) *n.* vial.

phil-, prefix meaning loving, having affinity for.

phi·lan′der·er (fi lan′dər ər) *n.* a man who has many love affairs. —**phi·lan′der,** *v.*

phi·lan′thro·py (fi lan′thrə pē) *n., pl.* **-pies. 1.** love of humanity. **2.** benevolent act, work, or institution. —**phil′an·throp′ic** (fil′ən throp′ik), *adj.* —**phi·lan′thro·pist,** *n.*

phi·lat′e·ly (fi lat′l ē) *n.* collection and study of postage stamps, etc. —**phi·lat′e·list,** *n.*

-phile, suffix meaning one that loves or has strong enthusiasm for.

phil′har·mon′ic (fil′här mon′ik) *adj.* **1.** music-loving. —*n.* **2.** large orchestra.

phil′is·tine (fil′ə stēn′, -stīn′) *n.* person indifferent to culture.

phil′o·den′dron (fil′ə den′drən) *n., pl.* **-drons, -dra.** tropical climbing plant.

phi·lol′o·gy (fi lol′ə jē) *n.* linguistics. —**phi·lol′o·gist,** *n.*

phi·los′o·pher (fi los′ə fər) *n.* **1.** person versed in philosophy. **2.** person guided by reason.

phi·los′o·phy (-fē) *n., pl.* **-phies. 1.** study of truths underlying being and knowledge. **2.** system of philosophical belief. **3.** principles of particular field of knowledge or action. **4.** calmness. —**phil′o·soph′ic** (fil′ə sof′ik), **phil′o·soph′i·cal,** *adj.* —**phi·los′o·phize′,** *v.*

phle·bi′tis (flə bī′tis) *n.* inflammation of a vein.

phle·bot′o·my (-bot′ə mē) *n., pl.*

-mies. practice of opening a vein to let blood. —**phle·bot′o·mize′,** v. **-mized, -mizing.**

phlegm (flem) n. **1.** thick mucus in the respiratory passages. **2.** apathy.

phleg·mat′ic (fleg mat′ik) adj. unemotional or unenthusiastic.

phlo′em (flō′em) n. tissue in plant through which food passes.

phlox (floks) n. garden plant with showy flowers.

-phobe, suffix meaning one who hates or fears.

pho′bi·a (fō′bē ə) n. morbid fear.

-phobia, suffix meaning fear or dread.

phoe′be (fē′bē) n. small American bird.

phoe′nix (fē′niks) n. mythical bird that burns, then rises from its ashes.

phone (fōn) n., v., **phoned, phoning.** Informal. telephone.

pho′neme (fō′nēm) n. minimal unit of speech sound that distinguishes one word from another.

pho·net′ics (fə net′iks) n. study of speech sounds. —**pho·net′ic,** adj.

phon′ics (fon′iks) n. method of teaching reading and spelling based on phonetics.

phono-, prefix meaning sound.

pho′no·graph′ (fō′nə graf′) n. sound-producing machine using records. —**pho′no·graph′ic,** adj.

pho·nol′o·gy (fə nol′ə jē) n., pl. **-gies.** study of sound changes in language.

pho′ny (fō′nē) adj., **-nier, -niest,** n., pl. **-nies.** Informal. —adj. **1.** false; fraudulent. —n. **2.** something phony. —**pho′ni·ness,** n.

phos′gene (fos′jēn) n. poisonous gas.

phos′phate (fos′fāt) n. **1.** salt of phosphoric acid. **2.** fertilizer containing phosphorus.

phos′phor (fos′fər) n. substance showing luminescence.

phos′pho·res′cent (-fə res′ənt) adj. luminous. —**phos′pho·res′cence,** n.

phos′pho·rus (-fər əs) n. solid nonmetallic element present in all forms of life. —**phos·phor′ic** (-fôr′ik), **phos′pho·rous,** adj.

pho′to (fō′tō) n., pl. **-tos.** Informal. photograph.

photo-, prefix meaning light.

pho′to·cop′y, n., pl. **-copies.** photographic copy. —**pho′to·cop′y,** v.

pho′to·e·lec′tric, adj. of or using electrical effects produced by light.

pho′to·en·grav′ing, n. photographic process of preparing printing plates for printing.

photo finish, finish of race so close as to require scrutiny of photograph to determine winner.

pho′to·gen′ic (fō′tə jen′ik) adj. looking attractive in photos.

pho′to·graph′ (-graf′) n. **1.** picture produced by photography. —v. **2.** take photograph. —**pho·tog′ra·pher** (fə tog′rə fər) n.

pho·tog′ra·phy (fə tog′rə fē) n. process of obtaining images on sensitized surface by action of light. —**pho′to·graph′ic** (fō′tə graf′ik) adj.

pho′ton (fō′ton) n. quantum of electromagnetic radiation.

pho′to·sen′si·tive, adj. sensitive to light.

Pho′to·stat′ (fō′tə stat′) n. **1.** Trademark. camera for photographing documents, etc. **2.** (l.c.) the photograph. —v. **3.** (l.c.) make photostatic copy. —**pho′to·stat′ic,** adj.

pho′to·syn′the·sis, n. conversion by plants of carbon dioxide and water

into carbohydrates, aided by light and chlorophyll.

phrase (frāz) n., v., **phrased, phrasing.** —n. **1.** sequence of words used as unit. **2.** minor division of musical composition. —v. **3.** express in particular way.

phra′se·ol′o·gy (frā′zē ol′ə jē) n. manner of verbal expression.

phre·nol′o·gy (frə nol′ə jē) n. theory that mental powers are shown by shape of skull.

phy·log′e·ny (fī loj′ə nē) n. development of particular group of organisms.

phy′lum (fī′ləm) n., pl. **-la.** primary classification of plants or animals.

phys′ic (fiz′ik) n. medicine, esp. one that purges.

phys′i·cal, adj. **1.** of the body. **2.** of matter. **3.** of physics. —n. **4.** full examination of body.

physical anthropology, study of evolutionary changes in human body structure.

physical science, science that deals with inanimate matter or energy.

physical therapy, treatment of physical disability or pain by techniques such as exercise.

phy·si′cian (fi zish′ən) n. medical doctor.

phys′ics (fiz′iks) n. science of matter, motion, energy, and force. —**phys′i·cist,** n.

phys′i·og′no·my (fiz′ē og′nə mē, -on′ə-) n., pl. **-mies.** face.

phys′i·og′ra·phy (-og′rə fē) n. study of earth's surface.

phys′i·ol′o·gy (-ol′ə jē) n. science dealing with functions of living organisms. —**phys′i·o·log′i·cal** (-ə loj′i·kəl) adj. —**phys′i·ol′o·gist,** n.

phys′i·o·ther′a·py (fiz′ē ō-) n. treatment of disease by massage, exercise, etc.

phy·sique′ (fi zēk′) n. physical structure.

pi (pī) n. the Greek letter, used as symbol for ratio of circumference to diameter.

pi′a·nis′si·mo (pē′ə nis′ə mō′, pyä-) adv. Music. very softly.

pi·an′o (pē an′ō) n., pl. **-anos,** adv. —n. **1.** Also, **pi·an′o·for′te** (-fôr′tā). musical keyboard instrument in which hammers strike upon metal strings. —adv. (pē ä′nō) **2.** Music. softly. —**pi·an′ist** (pē an′ist, pē′ə nist) n.

pi·az′za (pē az′ə, -ät′sə) n. open public square, esp. in Italy.

pi′ca (pī′kə) n. **1.** size of printing type. **2.** unit of measure in printing.

pic′a·resque′ (pik′ə resk′) adj. of a form of fiction that describes adventures of roguish hero.

pic′a·yune′ (pik′ē yōon′, pik′ə-) adj. insignificant; petty.

pic′ca·lil′li (pik′ə lil′ē) n. spiced vegetable relish.

pic′co·lo (pik′ə lō′) n., pl. **-los.** small shrill flute.

pick (pik) v. **1.** choose. **2.** pluck. **3.** dig or break into, esp. with pointed instrument. **4.** nibble listlessly. —n. **5.** choice. **6.** right to choose. **7.** Also, **pick′ax′, pick′axe′.** sharp-pointed tool for breaking rock, etc.

pick′er·el (pik′ər əl) n. small pike.

pick′et (pik′it) n. **1.** pointed stake. **2.** demonstration by labor union in front of workplace. **3.** troops posted to warn of enemy attack. —v. **4.** enclose with pickets. **5.** put pickets in front of.

picket line, line of strikers or other pickets.

pick′le (pik′əl) n., v., **-led, -ling.** —n.

1. cucumber, etc. preserved in spiced vinegar. **2.** predicament. —v. **3.** preserve in vinegar or brine.

pick′pock′et, n. person who steals from others' pockets.

pick′up′, n. **1.** ability to accelerate rapidly. **2.** small open-body truck.

pick′y, adj., **pickier, pickiest.** extremely fussy or finicky.

pic′nic (pik′nik) n., v., **-nicked, -nicking.** —n. **1.** outing and meal in the open. —v. **2.** have picnic. —**pic′nick·er,** n.

pi′cot (pē′kō) n. decorative loop along edge of lace, ribbon, etc.

pic′ture (pik′chər) n., v., **-tured, -turing.** —n. **1.** painting or photograph. **2.** motion picture. —v. **3.** represent in picture. **4.** imagine. —**pic·to′ri·al,** adj.

pic′tur·esque′ (-chə resk′) adj. visually charming or quaint.

pid′dling, adj. trivial; negligible.

pidg′in (pij′ən) n. language developed to allow speakers of two different languages to communicate.

pidgin English, English trade jargon used in other countries.

pie (pī) n. baked dish of fruit, meat, etc., in pastry crust.

pie′bald′ (pī′bôld′) adj. having patches of different colors.

piece (pēs) n., v., **pieced, piecing.** —n. **1.** limited or single portion. **2.** one part of a whole. **3.** artistic work. **4.** rifle or cannon. —v. **5.** make or enlarge by joining pieces.

pièce de ré·sis·tance′ (pyes də Rā zē stäns′) n., pl. **pièces de résistance** (pyes-). **1.** principal dish of meal. **2.** principal item of series.

piece goods, goods sold at retail by linear measure.

piece′meal′, adv. gradually.

piece′work′, n. work done and paid for by the piece.

pie chart, graph in which sectors of circle represent quantities.

pied (pīd) adj. many-colored.

pied′-à-terre′ (pyā′də târ′) n., pl. **pieds-à-terre** (pyā′-). apartment for part-time use.

pie′-eyed′, adj. Slang. drunk.

pier (pēr) n. **1.** structure at which vessels are moored. **2.** masonry support.

pierce (pērs) v., **pierced, piercing. 1.** make hole or way through. **2.** make (hole) in.

pi′e·ty (pī′i tē) n. piousness.

pif′fle (pif′əl) n. Informal. nonsense. —**pif′fling,** adj.

pig (pig) n. **1.** swine. **2.** bar of metal. —**pig′gish,** adj.

pi′geon (pij′ən) n. short-legged bird with compact body.

pi′geon·hole′, n., v., **-holed, -holing.** —n. **1.** small compartment, as in desk, etc. —v. **2.** classify. **3.** put aside and ignore.

pi′geon-toed′, adj. having toes or feet turned inward.

pig′gy·back′, adv. **1.** on the back or shoulders. —adj. **2.** astride the back. **3.** attached to something else.

pig′head′ed, adj. perversely stubborn.

pig iron, crude iron from furnace.

pig′let, n. baby pig.

pig′ment (-mənt) n. coloring matter. —**pig′men·tar′y,** adj.

pig′men·ta′tion, n. coloration.

pig′my (-mē) n., pl. **-mies.** pygmy.

pig′pen′, n. **1.** stall for pigs. **2.** filthy or untidy place. Also, **pig′sty′.**

pig′tail′, n. braid of hair.

pike (pīk) n. **1.** large fresh-water fish. **2.** metal-headed weapon.

pik′er, *n. Slang.* person who does things cheaply or meanly.

pi′laf (pē′läf, pi läf′) *n.* Middle Eastern rice dish.

pi•las′ter (pi las′tər) *n.* shallow decorative feature similar to column.

pil′chard (pil′chərd) *n.* marine fish.

pile (pīl) *n., v.,* **piled, piling.** —*n.* **1.** group of things lying one on another. **2.** large amount of anything. **3.** device for producing energy by nuclear reaction. **4.** Also, **pil′ing.** upright driven into ground as foundation member or to retain earth. **5.** hair; down; wool; fur. **6.** nap (def. 2). **7.** *pl.* hemorrhoids. —*v.* **8.** lay in pile. **9.** accumulate.

pil′fer (pil′fər) *v.* steal, esp. small amounts. —**pil′fer•age,** *n.*

pil′grim (pil′grim, -grəm) *n.* **1.** traveler, esp. to sacred place. **2.** (*cap.*) early Puritan settler in America. —**pil′grim•age,** *n.*

pill (pil) *n.* small mass of medicine to be swallowed.

pil′lage (pil′ij) *v.,* **-laged, -laging,** *n.* plunder.

pil′lar (pil′ər) *n.* upright shaft of masonry.

pill′box′, *n.* **1.** small fort. **2.** box for pills.

pil′lo•ry (pil′ə rē) *n., pl.* **-ries,** *v.,* **-ried, -rying.** —*n.* **1.** wooden framework used to confine and expose offenders. —*v.* **2.** put in pillory. **3.** expose to public contempt.

pil′low (pil′ō) *n.* bag of feathers, etc., used as support for head. —**pil′low•case′,** *n.*

pi′lot (pī′lət) *n.* **1.** operator of aircraft. **2.** expert navigator. —*v.* **3.** steer. —*adj.* **4.** experimental.

pilot light, small flame used to relight main burners.

pi•men′to (pi men′tō) *n., pl.* **-tos.** red fruit of sweet pepper.

pi•mien′to (-myen′tō, -men′-) *n., pl.* **-tos.** pimento.

pimp (pimp) *n., v.* —*n.* **1.** manager of prostitutes. —*v.* **2.** act as pimp.

pim′ple (pim′pəl) *n.* small swelling of skin. —**pim′ply,** *adj.*

pin (pin) *n., v.,* **pinned, pinning.** —*n.* **1.** slender pointed piece of metal, wood, etc., for fastening. —*v.* **2.** fasten with pin. **3.** hold fast.

PIN (pin) personal identification number.

pin′a•fore′ (pin′ə fôr′) *n.* **1.** child's apron. **2.** sleeveless dress.

pin′ball′, *n.* game in which spring-driven ball rolls against pins on sloping board.

pince′-nez′ (pans′nā′, pins′-) *n., pl.* **pince-nez.** eyeglasses supported by pinching the nose.

pin′cers (pin′sərz) *n.pl.* gripping tool with two pivoted limbs.

pinch (pinch) *v.* **1.** squeeze, as between finger and thumb. **2.** cramp or affect sharply. **3.** economize. —*n.* **4.** act of pinching. **5.** tiny amount. **6.** distress; emergency.

pinch′-hit′, *v.,* **-hit, -hitting.** substitute.

pine (pīn) *v.,* **pined, pining,** *n.* —*v.* **1.** long painfully. **2.** fail in health from grief, etc. —*n.* **3.** evergreen tree with needle-shaped leaves.

pine′ap′ple, *n.* tropical fruit.

pin′feath′er, *n.* undeveloped feather.

ping (ping) *v.* **1.** produce sharp sound like bullet striking metal. —*n.* **2.** pinging sound.

Ping′-Pong′ (ping′pong′) *n. Trademark.* table tennis.

pin′head′, *n.* **1.** head of pin. **2.** stupid person.

pin′ion (pin′yən) *n.* **1.** feather or wing. **2.** small cogwheel. —*v.* **3.** bind (the arms).

pink (pingk) *n.* **1.** pale red. **2.** fragrant garden flower. **3.** highest degree. —**pink,** *adj.*

pink′eye′, *n.* contagious inflammation of membrane covering eye.

pinking shears, shears with notched blades.

pin money, small sum set aside.

pin′na•cle (pin′ə kəl) *n.* lofty peak or position.

pin′nate (pin′āt, -it) *adj.* having leaflets on each side of common stalk.

pi′noch′le (pē′nuk əl, -nok-) *n.* game using 48 cards.

pin′point′, *v.* identify.

pin′stripe′, *n.* very thin stripe in fabric. —**pin′striped′,** *adj.*

pint (pīnt) *n.* liquid and dry measure equal to one-half quart.

pin′to (pin′tō, pēn′-) *adj., n., pl.* **-tos.** —*adj.* **1.** piebald. —*n.* **2.** piebald horse.

pinto bean, bean with pinkish mottled seeds.

pin′up′, *n.* large photograph of sexually attractive person.

pin′wheel′, *n.* windmill-like toy that spins on stick.

pin′yin′ (pin′yin′) *n.* system for writing Chinese in Latin alphabet.

pi′o•neer′ (pī′ə nēr′) *n.* **1.** early arrival in new territory. **2.** first one in any effort. —*v.* **3.** act as pioneer.

pi′ous (pī′əs) *adj.* **1.** reverential; devout. **2.** sacred. —**pi′ous•ly,** *adv.*

pip (pip) *n.* **1.** small fruit seed. **2.** spot on playing card, domino, etc. **3.** disease of fowls.

pipe (pīp) *n., v.,* **piped, piping.** —*n.* **1.** tube for conveying fluid. **2.** tube for smoking tobacco. **3.** tube used as musical instrument. —*v.* **4.** play on pipe. **5.** convey by pipe.

pipe dream, unrealistic hope.

pipe′line′, *n.* **1.** linked pipes for transporting oil, water, etc. **2.** route for supplies. **3.** channel of information.

pip′ing, *n.* **1.** pipes. **2.** sound of pipes. **3.** kind of trimming.

pip′pin (pip′in) *n.* kind of apple.

pip′squeak′ (pip′skwēk′) *n. Informal.* small or unimportant person.

pi′quant (pē′kənt, -känt) *adj.* agreeably sharp. —**pi′quan•cy,** *n.*

pique (pēk) *v.,* **piqued, piquing,** *n.* —*v.* **1.** arouse resentment in. **2.** excite (curiosity, etc.). —*n.* **3.** irritated feeling.

pi•qué′ (pi kā′) *n.* corded cotton fabric.

pi′ra•cy (pī′rə sē) *n., pl.* **-cies. 1.** robbery at sea. **2.** illegal use of material. —**pi′rate,** *n., v.*

pi•ra′nha (pi rän′yə, -ran′-, -rä′nə, -ran′ə) *n., pl.* **-nhas, -nha.** small, fiercely predatory fish.

pir′ou•ette′ (pir′ŏŏ et′) *v.,* **-etted, -etting,** *n.* —*v.* **1.** whirl about on the toes. —*n.* **2.** such whirling.

pis•ta′chi•o′ (pi stash′ē ō′) *n., pl.* **-chios.** edible nut.

pis′til (pis′tl) *n.* seed-bearing organ of flower. —**pis′til•late** (-tl it, -āt′) *adj.*

pis′tol (pis′tl) *n.* short hand-held gun.

pis′tol-whip′, *v.,* **pistol-whipped, pistol-whipping.** beat with pistol.

pis′ton (pis′tən) *n.* part moving back and forth in cylinder.

pit (pit) *n., v.,* **pitted, pitting.** —*n.* **1.** hole in ground or other surface. **2.** hollow in body. **3.** part of main floor of

theater. **4.** stone of fruit. —*v.* **5.** mark with pits. **6.** set in enmity or opposition. **7.** remove pit.

pi′ta (pē′tə) *n.* round, flat bread with pocket.

pitch (pich) *v.* **1.** throw. **2.** set at certain point. **3.** fall forward. **4.** drop and rise, as ship. —*n.* **5.** relative point or degree. **6.** musical tone. **7.** slope. **8.** sticky dark substance from coal tar. **9.** sales talk.

pitch′-black′, *adj.* extremely black.

pitch′-dark′, *adj.* very dark.

pitched, *adj.* fought with all available troops.

pitch′er (pich′ər) *n.* **1.** container with spout for liquids. **2.** person who pitches.

pitch′fork′, *n.* sharp-tined fork for handling hay.

pitch pipe, small pipe producing pitches.

pit′e•ous (pit′ē əs) *adj.* pathetic.

pit′fall′, *n.* trap; hazard.

pith (pith) *n.* **1.** spongy plant tissue. **2.** essence. —**pith′y,** *adj.*

pit′i•a•ble (pit′ē ə bəl) *adj.* **1.** deserving pity. **2.** contemptible. —**pit′i•a•bly,** *adv.*

pit′i•ful (-i fəl) *adj.* **1.** deserving pity. **2.** exciting contempt. **3.** full of pity. —**pit′i•ful•ly,** *adv.*

pit′tance (pit′ns) *n.* meager income.

pi•tu′i•tar′y (pi tōō′ə ter′ē, -tyōō-) *adj.* denoting gland at base of brain.

pit′y (pit′ē) *n., pl.* **pities,** *v.,* **pitied, pitying.** —*n.* **1.** sympathetic sorrow. **2.** cause for regret. —*v.* **3.** feel pity for. —**pit′i•less,** *adj.* —**pit′i•less•ly,** *adv.*

piv′ot (piv′ət) *n.* **1.** shaft on which something turns. —*v.* **2.** turn on pivot. —**piv′ot•al,** *adj.*

pix′el (pik′səl, -sel) *n.* smallest element of image in video display system.

pix′y (pik′sē) *n., pl.* **pixies.** fairy. Also, **pix′ie.**

pi•zazz′ (pə zaz′) *n. Informal.* **1.** energy. **2.** dash. Also, **piz•zazz′.**

piz′za (pēt′sə) *n.* dish of cheese, tomato sauce, etc., on baked crust.

piz′zer•i′a (pēt′sə rē′ə) *n.* restaurant serving mainly pizza.

piz′zi•ca′to (pit′si kä′tō) *adj. Music.* played by plucking strings with fingers.

pkg., package.

pkwy., parkway.

pl., 1. place. **2.** plural.

plac′a•ble (plak′ə bəl, plā′kə-) *adj.* forgiving.

plac′ard (plak′ärd, -ərd) *n.* public notice.

pla′cate (plā′kāt, plak′āt) *v.,* **-cated, -cating.** appease. —**pla•ca′tion,** *n.*

place (plās) *n., v.,* **placed, placing.** —*n.* **1.** particular portion of space. **2.** function. **3.** social standing. **4.** stead. —*v.* **5.** put in place. **6.** identify from memory. —**place′ment,** *n.*

pla•ce′bo (plə sē′bō) *n., pl.* **-bos, -boes.** pill, etc., containing no medication, given to reassure patient or as control in testing drug.

pla•cen′ta (plə sen′tə) *n.* organ in uterus which attaches to and nourishes fetus.

plac′id (plas′id) *adj.* serene. —**pla•cid′i•ty,** *n.* —**plac′id•ly,** *adv.*

plack′et (plak′it) *n.* slit at neck, waist, or wrist of garment.

pla′gia•rize′ (plā′jə rīz′) *v.,* **-rized, -rizing.** copy and claim as one's own work. —**pla′gia•rism,** *n.*

plague (plāg) *n., v.,* **plagued, plaguing.** —*n.* **1.** often fatal epidemic disease. **2.** affliction or vexation. —*v.* **3.** trouble; annoy.

plaid (plad) *n.* **1.** fabric woven in many-colored cross bars. —*adj.* **2.** having such pattern.

plain (plān) *adj.* **1.** distinct. **2.** evident. **3.** candid. **4.** ordinary; unpretentious. **5.** bare. **6.** flat. —*adv.* **7.** clearly. **8.** candidly. —*n.* **9.** level area. —**plain/ly,** *adv.*

plain/clothes/man, *n.*, *pl.* -**men.** police officer who wears civilian clothes on duty.

plain/song/, *n.* ancient harmonic music of early Christian Church.

plaint (plānt) *n.* complaint.

plain/tiff (plān/tif) *n.* one who brings suit in court.

plain/tive (plān/tiv) *adj.* melancholy. —**plain/tive•ly,** *adv.*

plait (plāt, plat) *n.*, *v.* **1.** braid. **2.** pleat.

plan (plan) *n.*, *v.*, **planned, planning.** —*n.* **1.** scheme of action or arrangement. **2.** drawing of projected structure. —*v.* **3.** make plan. —**plan/ner,** *n.*

plane (plān) *n.*, *adj.*, *v.*, **planed, planing.** —*n.* **1.** flat surface. **2.** level. **3.** airplane. **4.** tool for smoothing. —*adj.* **5.** flat. —*v.* **6.** glide. **7.** smooth with plane.

plan/et (plan/it) *n.* solid heavenly body revolving about sun. —**plan/e•tar/y,** *adj.*

plan/e•tar/i•um (-i târ/ē əm) *n.*, *pl.* -**iums, -ia.** **1.** optical device that projects a representation of heavens on a dome. **2.** museum with such device.

plane tree, large, spreading shade tree.

plan/gent (plan/jənt) *adj.* resounding loudly.

plank (plangk) *n.* **1.** long flat piece of timber. **2.** point in political platform. —**plank/ing,** *n.*

plank/ton (plangk/tən) *n.* microscopic organisms floating in water.

plant (plant) *n.* **1.** any member of vegetable group. **2.** equipment for business or process; factory. —*v.* **3.** set in ground for growth. **4.** furnish with plants: —**plant/er,** *n.*

plan/tain (plan/tin) *n.* **1.** tropical bananalike plant. **2.** common flat-leaved weed.

plan•ta/tion (plan tā/shən) *n.* large farm, esp. with one crop.

plaque (plak) *n.* **1.** monumental tablet. **2.** sticky, whitish film formed on tooth surfaces.

plas/ma (plaz/mə) *n.* clear liquid part of blood or lymph.

plas/ter (plas/tər) *n.* **1.** pasty mixture for covering walls, etc. **2.** medicinal preparation spread on cloth and applied to body. —*v.* **3.** cover or treat with plaster.

plas/ter•board/, *n.* material for insulating or covering walls.

plaster of Par/is (par/is) form of gypsum in powdery form, used in making plasters and casts.

plas/tic (plas/tik) *adj.* **1.** of or produced by molding. **2.** moldable. **3.** three-dimensional. —*n.* **4.** organic material that is hardened after shaping. —**plas•tic/i•ty** (-tis/ə tē) *n.*

plastic surgery, branch of surgery dealing with repair, replacement, or reshaping of parts of body.

plate (plāt) *n.*, *v.*, **plated, plating.** —*n.* **1.** shallow round dish for food. **2.** gold or silver ware. **3.** sheet of metal used in printing. **4.** shaped holder for false teeth. —*v.* **5.** coat with metal.

pla•teau/ (pla tō/) *n.*, *pl.* -**teaus, -teaux** (-tōz/). raised plain.

plate glass, smooth glass.

plat/en (plat/n) *n.* plate in printing press that presses paper against inked surface.

plat/form (plat/fôrm) *n.* **1.** raised flooring or structure. **2.** set of announced political principles.

plat/i•num (plat/n əm) *n.* precious, malleable metallic element.

plat/i•tude/ (plat/i tōōd/, -tyōōd/) *n.* trite remark.

pla•ton/ic (plə ton/ik) *adj.* without sexual involvement.

pla•toon/ (plə tōōn/) *n.* small military or police unit.

plat/ter (plat/ər) *n.* large serving dish.

plat/y•pus (plat/i pəs) *n.*, *pl.* -**puses, -pi** (-pī/). duckbill.

plau/dit (plô/dit) *n.* (*usu. pl.*) applause.

plau/si•ble (plô/zə bəl) *adj.* apparently true, reasonable, or trustworthy. —**plau/si•bil/i•ty,** *n.*

play (plā) *n.* **1.** dramatic work. **2.** recreation. **3.** fun. **4.** movement. —*v.* **5.** act in a play. **6.** engage in game. **7.** perform on musical instrument. **8.** amuse oneself. **9.** move about lightly. —**play/er,** *n.* —**play/ful,** *adj.* —**play/ful•ly,** *adv.* —**play/go/er,** *n.*

play/back/, *n.* **1.** reproduction of a recording. **2.** apparatus used in producing playbacks.

play/bill/, *n.* program or announcement of play.

play/boy/, *n.* man who pursues life of pleasure without responsibilities or attachments.

play/ground/, *n.* area used, esp. by children, for outdoor recreation.

play/house/, *n.* **1.** theater. **2.** small house for children to play in.

play/mate/, *n.* companion in play.

play/-off/, *n.* extra game played to break a tie.

play on words, pun.

play/pen/, *n.* small enclosure in which baby can play.

play/thing/, *n.* toy.

play/wright/ (-rīt/) *n.* writer of plays.

pla/za (plä/zə, plaz/ə) *n.* **1.** public square, esp. in Spanish-speaking countries. **2.** shopping center.

plea (plē) *n.* **1.** defense; justification. **2.** entreaty.

plea bargain, agreement in which criminal defendant pleads guilty to lesser charge.

plead (plēd) *v.*, **pleaded** or **pled** (pled), **pleading.** **1.** make earnest entreaty. **2.** allege formally in court. **3.** argue (case at law). **4.** allege in justification. —**plead/er,** *n.*

pleas/ant (plez/ənt) *adj.* agreeable; pleasing. —**pleas/ant•ly,** *adv.*

pleas/ant•ry, *n.*, *pl.* -**ries.** good-humored remark.

please (plēz) *v.*, **pleased, pleasing.** give pleasure or satisfaction to.

pleas/ur•a•ble (plezh/ər ə bəl) *adj.* enjoyable.

pleas/ure, *n.* **1.** enjoyment. **2.** person's will or desire.

pleat (plēt) *n.* **1.** double fold of cloth. —*v.* **2.** fold in pleats.

ple•be/ian (pli bē/ən) *adj.* of common people.

pleb/i•scite/ (pleb/ə sīt/) *n.* direct vote by citizens on public question.

plec/trum (plek/trəm) *n.*, *pl.* -**tra** (-trə), -**trums.** object for picking strings of musical instrument.

pledge (plej) *n.*, *v.*, **pledged, pledging.** —*n.* **1.** solemn promise. **2.** property delivered as security on a loan. —*v.* **3.** bind by pledge. **4.** promise. **5.** deliver as pledge.

Pleis/to•cene/ (plī/stə sēn/) *adj.* per-

taining to geologic epoch forming earlier half of Quaternary Period.

ple/na•ry (plē/nə rē, plen/ə-) *adj.* full; complete.

plen/i•po•ten/ti•ar/y (plen/ə pə ten/shē er/ē, -shə rē) *n.*, *pl.* -**aries,** *adj.* —*n.* **1.** diplomat with full authority. —*adj.* **2.** having full authority.

plen/i•tude/ (plen/i tōōd/, -tyōōd/) *n.* abundance.

plen/ty (plen/tē) *n.* **1.** abundant supply. —*adv. Informal.* **2.** very.

pleth/o•ra (pleth/ər ə) *n.* superabundance.

pleu/ri•sy (plŏŏr/ə sē) *n.* inflammation of chest membrane.

Plex/i•glas/ (plek/si glas/) *n. Trademark.* light, durable transparent plastic.

pli/a•ble (plī/ə bəl) *adj.* easily bent or influenced. —**pli/a•bil/i•ty,** *n.*

pli/ant (-ənt) *adj.* pliable.

pli/ers (plī/ərz) *n.pl.* small pincers.

plight (plīt) *n.* **1.** distressing condition. —*v.* **2.** promise.

PLO, Palestine Liberation Organization.

plod (plod) *v.*, **plodded, plodding.** **1.** walk heavily. **2.** work laboriously. —**plod/der,** *n.*

plop (plop) *v.*, **plopped, plopping.** —*v.* **1.** drop with sound like that of object hitting water. **2.** drop with direct impact. —*n.* **3.** plopping sound or fall.

plot (plot) *n.*, *v.*, **plotted, plotting.** —*n.* **1.** secret scheme. **2.** main story of fictional work. **3.** small area of ground. —*v.* **4.** plan secretly. **5.** mark (chart course) on. **6.** divide into plots. —**plot/ter,** *n.*

plov/er (pluv/ər, plō/vər) *n.* shore bird.

plow (plou) *n.* **1.** implement for cutting and turning soil. **2.** similar implement for removing snow. —*v.* **3.** cut or turn with plow. **4.** force way, as through water. Also, **plough.** —**plow/man,** *n.*

plow/share/, *n.* blade of plow.

ploy (ploi) *n.* maneuver; ruse.

pluck (pluk) *v.* **1.** pull out from fixed position. **2.** sound (strings of musical instrument). —*n.* **3.** pull or tug. **4.** courage.

pluck/y, *adj.*, -**ier, -iest.** courageous.

plug (plug) *n.*, *v.*, **plugged, plugging.** —*n.* **1.** object for stopping hole. **2.** device on electrical cord that establishes contact in socket. **3.** *Slang.* advertisement; favorable mention. —*v.* **4.** stop with or insert plug. **5.** *Slang.* mention favorably. **6.** work steadily.

plum (plum) *n.* **1.** oval juicy fruit. **2.** deep purple. **3.** *Informal.* favor widely desired.

plum/age (plōō/mij) *n.* feathers of bird.

plumb (plum) *n.* **1.** plummet. —*adj.* **2.** perpendicular. —*adv.* **3.** vertically. **4.** exactly. **5.** *Informal.* completely. —*v.* **6.** make vertical. **7.** measure depth of.

plumb/ing, *n.* system of water pipes, etc. —**plumb/er,** *n.*

plume (plōōm) *n.*, *v.*, **plumed, pluming.** —*n.* **1.** feather, esp. large one. **2.** ornamental tuft. —*v.* **3.** preen. **4.** adorn with plumes.

plum/met (plum/it) *n.* **1.** weight on line for sounding or establishing verticals. —*v.* **2.** plunge.

plump (plump) *adj.* **1.** somewhat fat or thick. —*v.* **2.** make or become plump. **3.** drop heavily. —*n.* **4.** heavy fall. —*adv.* **5.** directly. **6.** heavily. —**plump/ness,** *n.*

plun/der (plun/dər) *v.* **1.** rob. —*n.* **2.** act of plundering. **3.** loot.

plunge (plunj) *v.*, **plunged, plunging,** *n.* —*v.* **1.** fall abruptly. **2.** rush. **3.** pitch forward. —*n.* **4.** dive.

plung′er, *n.* **1.** pistonlike part moving within the cylinder of certain machines. **2.** device with handle and suction cup, used to unclog drains.

plu′ral (ploŏr′əl) *adj.* **1.** of, being, or containing more than one. —*n.* **2.** plural form. —**plur′al•ize′,** *v.*, **-ized, -izing.**

plu′ral•ism, *n.* condition in which minority groups participate in society, yet maintain their distinctions.

plu•ral′i•ty (ploŏ ral′i tē) *n.*, *pl.* **-ties.** **1.** in election with three or more candidates, the excess of votes given leading candidate over next candidate. **2.** majority.

plus (plus) *prep.* **1.** increased by. —*adj.* **2.** involving addition. **3.** positive. —*n.* **4.** something additional.

plush (plush) *n.* long-piled fabric.

Plu′to (ploŏ′tō) *n.* planet ninth in order from the sun.

plu′to•crat′ (ploŏ′tə krat′) *n.* **1.** wealthy person. **2.** member of wealthy governing class. —**plu•toc′ra•cy** (-tok′rə sē) *n.*

plu•to′ni•um (ploŏ tō′nē əm) *n.* radioactive element.

plu′vi•al (ploŏ′vē əl) *adj.* of rain.

ply (plī) *v.*, **plied, plying,** *n.*, *pl.* **plies.** —*v.* **1.** work with by hand. **2.** carry on, as trade. **3.** supply or offer something repeatedly. **4.** travel regularly. —*n.* **5.** fold; thickness.

ply′wood′, *n.* sheets of wood.

p.m., after noon. Also, **P.M.**

PMS, premenstrual syndrome.

pneu•mat′ic (noŏ mat′ik, nyoŏ-) *adj.* **1.** of gases. **2.** operated by air.

pneu•mo′nia (noŏ mōn′yə, nyoŏ-) *n.* inflammation of lungs.

P.O., post office.

poach (pōch) *v.* **1.** hunt illegally. **2.** cook (eggs, fruit, etc.) in hot water. —**poach′er,** *n.*

pock′et (pok′it) *n.* **1.** small bag sewed into garment. **2.** pouch; cavity. —*adj.* **3.** small. —*v.* **4.** put into one's pocket. **5.** take as profit.

pock′et•book′, *n.* purse.

pock′et•knife′, *n.* small folding knife.

pock′mark′ (pok′märk′) *n.* acne scar.

pod (pod) *n.*, *v.*, seed covering.

po•di•a•try (pə dī′ə trē) *n.* diagnosis and treatment of foot disorders.

po′di•um (pō′dē əm) *n.*, *pl.* **-diums, -dia** (-dē ə). small raised platform.

po′em (pō′əm) *n.* composition in verse. —**po′et** (pō′it) *n.*

po′e•sy (-ə sē) *n.*, *pl.* **-sies.** poetry.

poetic justice, fitting rewards and punishments.

poetic license, liberty taken by writer in deviating from fact to produce desired effect.

po′et•ry (-i trē) *n.* rhythmical composition of words. —**po•et′ic** (pō et′ik), **po•et′i•cal,** *adj.*

po•grom′ (pə grum′, -grom′) *n.* organized massacre, esp. of Jews.

poign′ant (poin′yənt) *adj.* keenly distressing. —**poign′an•cy,** *n.*

poin•set′ti•a (poin set′ē ə, -set′ə) *n.* tropical plant with scarlet flowers.

point (point) *n.* **1.** sharp end. **2.** projecting part. **3.** dot. **4.** definite position or time. **5.** compass direction. **6.** basic reason, purpose, etc. **7.** detail. **8.** unit in accounting, scoring, etc. —*v.* **9.** indicate. **10.** direct.

point′-blank′, *adj.* **1.** direct; plain. —*adv.* **2.** directly.

point′ed, *adj.* **1.** having a point. **2.** sharp. **3.** aimed at a particular person. **4.** emphasized.

point′er, *n.* **1.** one that points. **2.** long stick for pointing. **3.** breed of hunting dog.

poin•til′lism (pwan′tl iz′əm) *n.* technique in painting of using dots of pure color that are optically mixed into resulting hue by viewer.

point′less, *adj.* futile.

poise (poiz) *n.*, *v.*, **poised, poising.** —*n.* **1.** balance. **2.** composure. —*v.* **3.** balance. **4.** be in position for action.

poi′son (poi′zən) *n.* **1.** substance that kills or harms seriously. —*v.* **2.** harm with poison. —**poi′son•er,** *n.* —**poi′son•ous,** *adj.*

poison ivy, 1. vine or shrub having shiny leaves with three leaflets. **2.** rash caused by touching poison ivy.

poke (pōk) *v.*, **poked, poking,** *n.* thrust.

pok′er (pō′kər) *n.* **1.** rod for poking fires. **2.** card game.

pok′er-faced′, *adj.* showing no emotion or intention.

pok′y (pō′kē) *adj.*, **pokier, pokiest.** *Informal.* slow; dull. Also, **poke′y.**

po′lar (pō′lər) *adj.* **1.** arctic or antarctic. **2.** of magnetic poles. —**po•lar′i•ty,** *n.*

polar bear, large white arctic bear.

Po•lar′is (pō lâr′is, -lar′-, pə-) *n.* bright star close to North Pole.

po′lar•i•za′tion (-lər ə zā′shən) *n.* **1.** division of group into opposing factions. **2.** state in which rays of light exhibit different properties in different directions. —**po′lar•ize′,** *v.*, **-ized, -izing.**

pole (pōl) *n.*, *v.*, **poled, poling.** —*n.* **1.** long slender rod. **2.** unit of length equal to 16½ ft.; rod. **3.** square rod, 30¼ sq. yards. **4.** each end of axis. **5.** each end showing strongest opposite force. **6.** (*cap.*) native or citizen of Poland. —*v.* **7.** propel with a pole.

pole′cat′, *n.* small bad-smelling mammal.

po•lem′ics (pə lem′iks) *n.* art or practice of argument. —**po•lem′ic,** *n.*, *adj.* —**po•lem′i•cist,** *n.*

pole vault, athletic event in which vault over horizontal bar is performed with aid of long pole.

po•lice′ (pə lēs′) *n.*, *v.*, **-liced, -licing.** —*n.* **1.** organized civil force for enforcing law. —*v.* **2.** keep in order. —**po•lice′man,** *n.* —**po•lice′wom′an,** *n.*

pol′i•cy (pol′ə sē) *n.*, *pl.* **-cies. 1.** definite course of action. **2.** insurance contract.

pol′i•o•my′e•li′tis (pō′lē ō mī′ə lī′tis) *n.* infantile paralysis. Also, **po′li•o′.**

pol′ish (pol′ish) *v.* **1.** make glossy. —*n.* **2.** polishing substance. **3.** gloss. **4.** refinement.

Pol′ish (pō′lish) *n.* **1.** language or people of Poland. —*adj.* **2.** of Poland.

po•lite′ (pə līt′) *adj.* showing good manners; refined. —**po•lite′ly,** *adv.*

pol′i•tic (pol′i tik) *adj.* **1.** prudent; expedient. **2.** political.

politically correct, marked by progressive attitude on issues of race, gender, etc. —**political correctness,** *n.*

political science, social science dealing with political institutions and government.

po•lit′i•cize′ (pə lit′ə sīz′) *v.*, **-cized, -cizing.** give a political bias to.

pol′i•tick′ing (pol′i tik′ing) *n.* political campaigning.

pol′i•tics (pol′i tiks) *n.* **1.** science or conduct of government. **2.** political

affairs, methods, or principles. —**po•lit′i•cal** (pə lit′i kəl) *adj.* —**pol′i•ti′cian,** *n.*

pol′ka (pōl′kə, pō′kə) *n.* lively dance.

polka dot, pattern of dots.

poll (pōl) *n.* **1.** voting or votes at election. **2.** list of individuals, as for voting. **3.** (*pl.*) place of voting. **4.** analysis of public opinion. —*v.* **5.** receive votes. **6.** vote. **7.** ask opinions of.

pol′len (pol′ən) *n.* powdery fertilizing element of flowers. —**pol′li•nate′,** *v.* —**pol′li•na′tion,** *n.*

pol′li•wog′ (pol′ē wog′) *n.* tadpole.

poll′ster (pōl′stər) *n.* person who takes public-opinion polls.

pol•lute′ (pə loŏt′) *v.*, **-luted, -luting.** contaminate or make foul. —**pol•lu′tion,** *n.* —**pol•lut′ant,** *n.*

po′lo (pō′lō) *n.*, *pl.* **-los.** game played on horseback.

pol′ter•geist′ (pōl′tər gīst′) *n.* boisterous, often destructive ghost.

pol•troon′ (pol troŏn′) *n.* coward.

poly-, prefix meaning many.

pol′y•an′dry (pol′ē an′drē) *n.* practice of having more than one husband at a time.

pol′y•es′ter (pol′ē es′tər) *n.* artificial material for synthetics.

pol′y•eth′yl•ene′ (-eth′ə lēn′) *n.* plastic polymer used esp. for containers and packaging.

po•lyg′a•my (pə lig′ə mē) *n.* practice of having many spouses, esp. wives, at one time. —**po•lyg′a•mist,** *n.* —**po•lyg′a•mous,** *adj.*

pol′y•glot′ (pol′ē glot′) *adj.* able to speak, read, or write several languages.

pol′y•gon′ (pol′ē gon′) *n.* figure having three or more straight sides.

pol′y•graph′ (pol′i graf′) *n.* instrument recording variations in certain body activities, sometimes used to detect lying.

pol′y•he′dron (pol′ē hē′drən) *n.*, *pl.* **-drons, -dra** (-drə). solid figure having four or more sides.

pol′y•math′ (pol′ē math′) *n.* person of great learning in several fields.

pol′y•mer (pol′ə mər) *n.* compound formed by the combination of various molecules with water or alcohol removed. —**pol′y•mer•i•za′tion,** *n.*

pol′y•no′mi•al (pol′ə nō′mē əl) *n.* algebraic expression consisting of two or more terms.

pol′yp (pol′ip) *n.* projecting growth from mucous surface.

po•lyph′o•ny (pə lif′ə nē) *n.* music with two or more melodic lines in equitable juxtaposition. —**pol′y•phon′ic** (pol′ē fon′ik) *adj.*

pol′y•sty′rene (pol′ē stī′rēn, -stēr′ēn) *n.* polymer used in molded objects and as insulator.

pol′y•tech′nic (-tek′nik) *adj.* offering instruction in variety of technical subjects.

pol′y•the′ism, *n.* belief in more than one god.

pol′y•un•sat′u•rat′ed, *adj.* of a class of animal or vegetable fats associated with low cholesterol content.

po•made′ (po mād′, -mäd′) *n.* hair ointment.

pome′gran′ate (pom′gran′it, pom′i-) *n.* red, many-seeded fruit of Asiatic tree.

pom′mel (pum′əl, pom′-) *n.*, *v.*, **-meled, -meling.** —*n.* **1.** knob on sword or saddle. —*v.* **2.** strike; beat.

pomp (pomp) *n.* stately display.

pom′pa•dour′ (pom′pə dôr′, -doŏr′) *n.* arrangement of hair brushed up high from forehead.

pom′pom (pom′pom′) *n.* ornamental tuft.

pomp′ous (pom′pəs) *adj.* affectedly dignified or serious. —**pom•pos′i•ty** (-pos′i tē), *n.* —**pomp′ous•ly,** *adv.*

pon′cho (pon′chō) *n., pl.* **-chos.** blanketlike cloak.

pond (pond) *n.* small lake.

pon′der (pon′dər) *v.* meditate.

pon′der•ous, *adj.* heavy; not graceful.

pon′iard (pon′yərd) *n.* dagger.

pon′tiff (pon′tif) *n.* **1.** pope. **2.** chief priest; bishop. —**pon•tif′i•cal,** *adj.*

pon•tif′i•cate′ (pon tif′i kāt′) *v.,* **-cated, -cating.** speak with affected air of authority.

pon•toon′ (pon tōōn′) *n.* floating support.

po′ny (pō′nē) *n., pl.* **-nies.** small horse.

po′ny•tail′, *n.* hair gathered and fastened at the back of the head so as to hang freely.

poo′dle (pōōd′l) *n.* kind of dog with thick, curly hair.

pool (pōōl) *n.* **1.** body of still water. **2.** group of persons or things available for use. **3.** game resembling billiards. —*v.* **4.** put into common fund.

poop (pōōp) *n.* upper deck on stern of a ship.

poor (pōōr) *adj.* **1.** having little wealth. **2.** wanting. **3.** inferior. **4.** unfortunate. —*n.* **5.** poor persons.

poor′-mouth′, *v. Informal.* complain about poverty, use. as an excuse.

pop (pop) *v.,* **popped, popping,** *n., adv.* —*v.* **1.** make or burst with a short, quick sound. **2.** shoot. —*n.* **3.** short, quick sound. **4.** effervescent soft drink.

pop′corn′, *n.* kind of corn whose kernels burst in dry heat.

pope (pōp) *n. (often cap.)* head of Roman Catholic Church.

pop′in•jay′ (pop′in jā′) *n.* vain, shallow person.

pop′lar (pop′lər) *n.* any of certain fast-growing trees.

pop′lin (pop′lin) *n.* corded fabric.

pop′o′ver, *n.* very light muffin.

pop′py (pop′ē) *n., pl.* **-pies.** showy-flowered herbs, one species of which yields opium.

pop′py•cock′, *n.* nonsense.

pop′u•lace (pop′yə ləs) *n.* population.

pop′u•lar (-lər) *adj.* **1.** generally liked and approved. **2.** of the people. **3.** prevalent. —**pop′u•lar′i•ty** (-lar′i tē) *n.* —**pop′u•lar•ize′,** *v.,* **-ized, -izing.** —**pop′u•lar•ly,** *adv.*

pop′u•late′ (-lāt′) *v.,* **-lated, -lating.** inhabit.

pop′u•la′tion, *n.* **1.** total number of persons inhabiting given area. **2.** body of inhabitants.

pop′u•lism, *n.* political philosophy or movement promoting the interests of the common people. —**pop′u•list,** *n., adj.*

pop′u•lous, *adj.* with many inhabitants.

por′ce•lain (pôr′sə lin, pôrs′lin) *n.* glassy ceramic ware; china.

porch (pôrch) *n.* exterior shelter on building.

por′cu•pine′ (pôr′kyə pīn′) *n.* rodent with stout quills.

pore (pôr) *v.,* **pored, poring,** *n.* —*v.* **1.** ponder or read intently. —*n.* **2.** minute opening in skin.

pork (pôrk) *n.* flesh of hogs as food.

pork barrel, government funds available for popular local improvements.

por•nog′ra•phy (pôr nog′rə fē) *n.* obscene literature or art. —**por′no•graph′ic** (-nə graf′ik) *adj.* —**por•nog′ra•pher,** *n.*

po′rous (pôr′əs) *adj.* permeable by water, air, etc. —**po′rous•ness,** *n.*

por′poise (pôr′pəs) *n.* gregarious aquatic mammal.

por′ridge (pôr′ij, por′-) *n.* boiled cereal.

por′rin•ger (pôr′in jər, por′-) *n.* round dish for soup, etc.

port (pôrt) *n.* **1.** place where ships load and unload. **2.** harbor. **3.** left side of vessel, facing forward. **4.** sweet red wine. —**port,** *adj.*

port′a•ble, *adj.* readily carried.

por′tage (pôr′tij, pôr täzh′) *n.* **1.** overland route between navigable streams. **2.** act of carrying.

por′tal (pôr′tl) *n.* door or gate, esp. a large one.

port•cul′lis (pôrt kul′is) *n.* heavy iron grating at gateway of castle.

por•tend′ (pôr tend′) *v.* indicate beforehand.

por′tent (-tent) *n.* **1.** omen. **2.** ominous significance. —**por•ten′tous,** *adj.*

por′ter (pôr′tər) *n.* **1.** railroad attendant. **2.** baggage carrier. **3.** person who cleans or maintains building, store, etc.

por′ter•house′, *n.* choice cut of beefsteak.

port•fo′li•o′ (pôrt fō′lē ō′) *n., pl.* **-lios. 1.** portable case for papers, etc. **2.** cabinet post.

port′hole′, *n.* opening in ship's side.

por′ti•co′ (pôr′ti kō′) *n., pl.* **-coes, -cos.** roof supported by columns.

por′tion (pôr′shən) *n.* **1.** part of a whole. **2.** share. —*v.* **3.** divide into portions.

port′ly (pôrt′lē) *adj.,* **-lier, -liest. 1.** fat. **2.** stately. —**port′li•ness,** *n.*

port•man′teau (pôrt man′tō) *n., pl.* **-teaus, -teaux** (-tōz, tō). leather trunk.

por′trait (pôr′trit, -trāt) *n.* picture, sculpture, etc., showing specific person. —**por′trai•ture** (-tri chər) *n.*

por′trait•ist, *n.* person who makes portraits.

por•tray′ (pôr trā′) *v.* represent faithfully, as in picture. —**por•tray′al,** *n.*

Por′tu•guese′ (-chə gēz′, -gēs′) *n., pl.* **-guese.** native or language of Portugal. —**Por′tu•guese′,** *adj.*

Portuguese man-of-war, poisonous marine animal.

pose (pōz) *v.,* **posed, posing,** *n.* —*v.* **1.** assume or feign physical position, attitude, or character. **2.** take or give specific position. **3.** ask (question). —*n.* **4.** position or character assumed.

pos′er, *n.* **1.** person who poses, as for artist. **2.** difficult question.

po•seur′ (pō zûr′) *n.* affected person.

posh (posh) *adj.* elegant; luxurious.

pos′it (poz′it) *v.* lay down or assume as a fact or principle.

po•si′tion (pə zish′ən) *n.* **1.** place or attitude. **2.** belief or argument on question. **3.** social or organizational standing. **4.** job. —*v.* **5.** place.

pos′i•tive (poz′i tiv) *adj.* **1.** not denying or questioning. **2.** emphatic. **3.** confident. **4.** showing lights and shades of original. **5.** *Gram.* denoting first degree of comparison. **6.** denoting more than zero. **7.** deficient in electrons. **8.** revealing presence of thing tested for. —*n.* **9.** something positive. **10.** photographic image. —**pos′i•tive•ly,** *adv.*

pos′i•tron′ (poz′i tron′) *n.* particle

with same mass as electron but with positive charge.

pos′se (pos′ē) *n.* body of persons assisting sheriff.

pos•sess′ (pə zes′) *v.* **1.** have under ownership or domination. **2.** have as quality. **3.** obsess. —**pos•ses′sor,** *n.* —**pos•ses′sion** (-zesh′ən) *n.*

pos•sessed′, *adj.* controlled by strong feeling or supernatural.

pos•ses′sive, *adj.* **1.** denoting possession. **2.** obsessed with dominating another.

pos′si•ble (pos′ə bəl) *adj.* that may be, happen, etc. —**pos′si•bil′i•ty,** *n.* —**pos′si•bly,** *adv.*

pos′sum (pos′əm) *n.* opossum.

post (pōst) *n.* **1.** upright support. **2.** position of duty or trust. **3.** station for soldiers or traders. **4.** *Chiefly Brit.* mail. —*v.* **5.** put up. **6.** station at post. **7.** *Chiefly Brit.* mail. **8.** enter in ledger. **9.** hasten. **10.** inform.

post-, prefix meaning after or behind.

post′age (pō′stij) *n.* charge for mailing.

post′al (pōs′tl) *adj.* concerning mail.

post•bel′lum (-bel′əm) *adj.* after war, esp. U.S. Civil War.

post′card′, *n.* small notecard usu. having picture on one side and space for stamp, address, and message on the other.

post•date′ (pōst dāt′, pōst′-) *v.,* **-dated, -dating. 1.** mark with date later than actual date. **2.** follow in time.

post′er (pō′stər) *n.* large public notice.

pos•te′ri•or (po stēr′ē ər, pō-) *adj.* **1.** situated behind. **2.** later. —*n.* **3.** buttocks.

pos•ter′i•ty (po ster′i tē) *n.* descendants.

post•grad′u•ate (pōst graj′ōō it, -āt′) *adj.* **1.** of postgraduates. —*n.* **2.** student taking advanced work after graduation.

post′haste′, *adv.* speedily.

post′hu•mous (pos′chə məs, -chōō-) *adj.* **1.** occurring after one's death. **2.** born after father's death.

post′man, *n.* mail carrier.

post′mark′, *n.* official mark on mail showing place and time of mailing. —**post′mark′,** *v.*

post′mas′ter, *n.* official in charge of post office.

post me•rid′i•em′ (mə rid′ē əm, -em′) afternoon.

post′mis′tress, *n.* woman in charge of post office.

post•mod′ern, *adj.* pertaining to late 20th century artistic movement that developed in reaction to modernism.

post•mor′tem (-môr′təm) —*n.* examination of dead body.

post•na′tal (-nāt′l) *adj.* after childbirth.

post office, government office responsible for postal service.

post′paid′, *adv., adj.* with postage paid in advance.

post•par′tum (-pär′təm) *adj.* following childbirth.

post•pone′ (pōst pōn′, pōs-) *v.,* **-poned, -poning.** delay till later. —**post•pone′ment,** *n.*

post′script′, *n.* note added to letter after signature.

pos′tu•late′, *v.,* **-lated, -lating,** *n.* —*v.* (pos′chə lāt′) **1.** require. **2.** assume. —*n.* (-lit) **3.** something postulated.

pos′ture (pos′chər) *n., v.,* **-tured, -turing.** —*n.* **1.** position of the body.

—v. **2.** place in particular position. **3.** behave affectedly; pose.

post′war′, adj. after a war.

po′sy (pō′zē) n., pl. **-sies.** flower or bouquet.

pot (pot) n., v., **potted, potting.** —n. **1.** round deep container for cooking, etc. **2.** total stakes at cards. **3.** Slang. marijuana. —v. **4.** put into pot.

po′ta·ble (pō′tə bəl) adj. drinkable.

pot′ash′ (pot′ash′) n. potassium carbonate, esp. from wood ashes.

po·tas′si·um (pə tas′ē əm) n. light metallic element.

po·ta′to (pə tā′tō, -tə) n., pl. **-toes.** edible tuber.

pot′bel′ly n., pl. **-lies.** belly that sticks out. —**pot′bel′lied,** adj.

pot′boil′er, n. mediocre work of literature or art produced merely for financial gain.

po′tent (pōt′nt) adj. **1.** powerful. **2.** (of a male) capable of sexual intercourse. —**po′ten·cy,** n.

po′ten·tate′ (-tāt′) n. powerful person, as a sovereign.

po·ten′tial (pə ten′shəl) adj. **1.** possible. **2.** latent. —n. **3.** possibility. —n. —**po·ten′tial·ly,** adv.

poth′er (poth′ər) n., v. fuss.

pot′hole′, n. hole formed in pavement.

po′tion (pō′shən) n. medicinal or magical drink.

pot′luck′, n. **1.** meal to which participants bring food to be shared. **2.** whatever happens to be available.

pot′pour·ri′ (pō′poo rē′) n. **1.** fragrant mixture of dried flowers and spices. **2.** miscellany.

pot′shot′, n. **1.** casual or aimless shot. **2.** random or incidental criticism.

pot′ted, adj. **1.** grown in a pot. **2.** Slang. drunk.

pot′ter (pot′ər) n. **1.** person who makes earthen pots. —v. **2.** putter (def. 1).

pot′ter·y, n., pl. **-teries.** objects made of clay and baked.

pouch (pouch) n. **1.** bag or sack. **2.** baglike sac.

poul′tice (pōl′tis) n. soft moist mass applied as medicine.

poul′try (pōl′trē) n. domestic fowls.

pounce (pouns) v., **pounced, pouncing,** n. —v. **1.** swoop down or spring suddenly. **2.** seize eagerly. —n. **3.** sudden swoop.

pound (pound) n., pl. **pounds, pound,** v. —n. **1.** unit of weight: in U.S., **pound avoirdupois** (16 ounces) and **pound troy** (12 ounces). **2.** British monetary unit. **3.** enclosure for stray animals. —v. **4.** strike repeatedly and heavily. **5.** crush by pounding.

pound cake, rich, sweet cake.

pour (pôr) v. cause to flow; flow.

pout (pout) v. **1.** look sullen. —n. **2.** sullen look or mood.

pov′er·ty (pov′ər tē) n. **1.** poorness. **2.** lack.

POW, pl. **POWs, POW′s.** prisoner of war.

pow′der (pou′dər) n. **1.** solid substance crushed to fine loose particles. —v. **2.** reduce to powder. **3.** apply powder to. —**pow′der·y,** adj.

powder keg, 1. container for gunpowder. **2.** explosive situation.

pow′er (pou′ər) n. **1.** ability to act; strength. **2.** faculty. **3.** authority; control. **4.** person, nation, etc., having great influence. **5.** mechanical energy. **6.** product of repeated multiplications of number by itself. **7.** magnifying capacity of an optical instrument. —**pow′er·ful,** adj.

pow′er·house′, n. **1.** building where electricity is generated. **2.** dynamic person.

power of attorney, written legal authorization for another person to act in one's place.

pow′wow′ (pou′wou′) n. Informal. conference.

pox (poks) n. disease marked by skin eruptions.

pp., 1. pages. **2.** past participle.

ppd., 1. postpaid. **2.** prepaid.

P.P.S., additional postscript. Also, **p.p.s.**

PR, public relations.

prac′ti·ca·ble (prak′ti kə bəl) adj. able to be put into practice; feasible.

prac′ti·cal, adj. **1.** of or from practice. **2.** useful. **3.** level-headed. **4.** concerned with everyday affairs. **5.** virtual. —**prac′ti·cal′i·ty,** n.

prac′ti·cal·ly, adv. **1.** almost. **2.** in a practical way.

prac′tice (-tis) n., v., **-ticed, -ticing.** —n. **1.** habit; custom. **2.** action carried out. **3.** repeated performance in learning. **4.** professional activity. —v. Also, Brit., **prac′tise. 5.** do habitually or as profession. **6.** repeat to acquire skill.

prac·ti′tion·er (-tish′ə nər) n. person engaged in a profession.

prag·mat′ic (prag mat′ik) adj. concerned with practical values and results. —**prag′ma·tism,** n. —**prag′ma·tist,** n.

prai′rie (prâr′ē) n. broad, flat, treeless grassland.

prairie dog, burrowing squirrel of western North America.

praise (prāz) n., v., **praised, praising.** —n. **1.** words of admiration or strong approval. **2.** grateful homage. —v. **3.** give praise to. **4.** worship. —**praise′wor′thy,** adj.

pra·line (prā′lēn, prä′-) n. confection of caramelized nuts and sugar.

pram (pram) n. Brit. Informal. baby carriage.

prance (prans) v., **pranced, prancing,** n. —v. **1.** step about gaily or proudly. —n. **2.** act of prancing.

prank (prangk) n. playful trick. —**prank′ster,** n.

prate (prāt) v., **prated, prating.** talk foolishly.

prat′fall′ (prat′fôl′) n. fall on the buttocks.

prat′tle (prat′l) v., **-tled, -tling,** n. —v. **1.** chatter foolishly or childishly. —n. **2.** chatter.

prawn (prôn) n. large shrimplike shellfish.

pray (prā) v. make prayer.

prayer (prâr) n. **1.** devout petition to or spiritual communication with God. **2.** petition.

pre-, prefix meaning before.

preach (prēch) v. **1.** advocate. **2.** deliver (sermon). —**preach′er,** n. —**preach′y,** adj.

pre·am′ble (prē′am′bəl, prē am′-) n. introductory declaration.

pre·can′cer·ous, adj. showing pathological changes that may be preliminary to malignancy.

pre·car′i·ous (pri kâr′ē əs) adj. uncertain; dangerous.

pre·cau′tion (pri kô′shən) n. prudent advance measure. —**pre·cau′tion·ar′y,** adj.

pre·cede′ (pri sēd′) v., **-ceded, -ceding.** go before.

prec′e·dence (pres′i dens) n. **1.** priority. **2.** something that has gone before.

prec′e·dent (pres′i dənt) n. past case used as example or guide.

pre′cept (prē′sept) n. rule of conduct.

pre·cep′tor (pri sep′tər, prē′sep-) n. teacher.

pre′cinct (prē′singkt) n. bounded or defined area.

pre·ci·os′i·ty (presh′ē os′i tē) n., pl. **-ties.** fastidious refinement.

pre′cious (presh′əs) adj. **1.** valuable. **2.** beloved. **3.** affectedly refined. —**pre′cious·ly,** adv.

prec′i·pice (pres′ə pis) n. sharp cliff.

pre·cip′i·tate′ v., **-tated, -tating,** adj., n. —v. (pri sip′i tāt′) **1.** hasten occurrence of. **2.** separate (solid from solution). **3.** condense (as vapor into rain). **4.** fling down. —adj. (-tit) **5.** rash or impetuous; hasty. —n. (-tit) **6.** substance precipitated. **7.** condensed moisture. —**pre·cip′i·tate·ly,** adv. —**pre·cip′i·ta′tion,** n.

pre·cip′i·tous, adj. **1.** like a precipice. **2.** precipitate.

pré·cis′ (prā sē′, prā′sē) n. summary.

pre·cise′ (pri sīs′) adj. **1.** definite; exact. **2.** distinct. **3.** strict. —**pre·ci′sion** (-sizh′ən), **pre·cise′ness,** n.

pre·clude′ (pri klōōd′) v., **-cluded, -cluding.** prevent. —**pre·clu′sion** (-klōō′zhən) n. —**pre·clu′sive,** adj.

pre·co′cious (pri kō′shəs) adj. forward in development. —**pre·coc′i·ty** (-kos′ə tē) n.

pre·cog·ni′tion (prē′kog nish′ən) n. knowledge of future event through extrasensory means.

pre′-Co·lum′bi·an, adj. of the period before the arrival of Columbus in the Americas.

pre·con·ceive′, v., **-ceived, -ceiving.** form an opinion beforehand. —**pre′con·cep′tion,** n.

pre·con·di′tion, n. something necessary for subsequent result.

pre·cur′sor (pri kûr′sər, prē′kûr-) n. **1.** predecessor. **2.** harbinger.

pred′a·tor (pred′ə tər) n. preying animal.

pred′a·tor′y, adj. **1.** plundering. **2.** feeding on other animals.

pred·e·ces′sor (-ses′ər) n. one who precedes another.

pre·des′ti·na′tion (pri des′tə nā′shən) n. **1.** determination beforehand. **2.** destiny. —**pre·des′tine,** v.

pre′de·ter′mine (prē′di tûr′min) v., **-mined, -mining. 1.** decide in advance. **2.** predestine. —**pre′de·ter′mi·na′tion,** n.

pre·dic′a·ment (pri dik′ə mənt) n. trying or dangerous situation.

pred′i·cate, v., **-cated, -cating,** adj., n. —v. (pred′i kāt′) **1.** declare. **2.** find basis for. —adj. (-kit) **3.** Gram. belonging to predicate. —n. (-kit) **4.** Gram. part of sentence that expresses what is said of subject.

pre·dict′ (pri dikt′) v. tell beforehand. —**pre·dic′tion,** n. —**pre·dict′a·ble,** adj. —**pre·dic′tor,** n.

pre′di·lec′tion (pred′l ek′shən, prēd′-) n. preference.

pre′dis·pose′ (prē′di spōz′) v., **-posed, -posing. 1.** make susceptible. **2.** incline. —**pre′dis·po·si′tion,** n.

pre·dom′i·nate (pri dom′ə nāt′) v., **-nated, -nating. 1.** be more powerful or common. **2.** control. —**pre·dom′i·nance,** n. —**pre·dom′i·nant,** adj.

pre·em′i·nent (prē em′ə nənt) adj. superior; outstanding. —**pre·em′i·nence,** n. —**pre·em′i·nent·ly,** adv.

pre·empt′ (prē empt′) v. **1.** acquire or reserve before others. **2.** occupy to establish prior right to buy. Also, **pre·empt′.** —**pre·emp′tion,** n. —**pre·emp′tive,** adj.

preen (prēn) v. **1.** trim or clean (feathers or fur). **2.** dress (oneself) carefully.

pre·fab'ri·cate', v., -cated, -cating. build in parts for quick assembly. —pre'fab·ri·ca'tion, n. —pre'fab, n. Informal.

pref'ace (pref'is) n., v., -aced, -acing. —n. **1.** preliminary statement. —v. **2.** provide with or serve as preface. —pref'a·to'ry (-ə tôr'ē) adj.

pre'fect (prē'fekt) n. magistrate. —pre'fec·ture (-fek shər) n.

pre·fer' (pri fûr') v., -ferred, -ferring. **1.** like better. **2.** put forward; present (criminal charge, etc.).

pref'er·a·ble (pref'ər ə bəl) adj. more desirable.

pref'er·ence (-əns) n. **1.** liking of one above others. **2.** person or thing preferred. **3.** granting of advantage to one. —pref'er·en'tial (-ə ren'shəl) adj.

pre·fer'ment (pri fûr'mənt) n. promotion.

pre·fig'ure (prē fig'yər) v., -ured, -uring. foreshadow.

pre'fix n. (prē'fiks) **1.** syllable or syllables put before word to qualify its meaning. —v. (also prē fiks') **2.** put before.

preg'nant (preg'nənt) adj. **1.** being with child. **2.** meaningful. —preg'nan·cy, n.

pre·hen'sile (pri hen'sil, -sīl) adj. adapted for grasping.

pre·his·tor'ic, adj. of time before recorded history.

pre·judge', v., -judged, -judging. judge prematurely.

prej'u·dice (prej'ə dis) n., v., -diced, -dicing. —n. **1.** opinion formed without evidence. **2.** disadvantage. —v. **3.** affect with prejudice. —prej'u·di'cial (-dish'əl) adj.

prel'ate (prel'it) n. high church official.

pre·lim'i·nar'y (pri lim'ə ner'ē) adj., n., pl. -naries. —adj. **1.** introductory. —n. **2.** preliminary stage or action.

prel'ude (prel'yōōd, prā'lōōd) n. **1.** Music. **a.** preliminary to a more important work. **b.** brief composition, esp. for piano. **2.** preliminary to major action or event.

pre·mar'i·tal (prē mar'i tl) adj. before marriage.

pre·ma·ture', adj. **1.** born, maturing, or occurring too soon. **2.** overhasty. —pre'ma·ture'ly, adv.

pre·med'i·tate', v., -tated, -tating. plan in advance.

pre·mier' (pri mēr', -myēr') n. **1.** prime minister. —adj. **2.** chief.

pre·miere' (pri mēr', -myâr') n. first public performance.

prem'ise (prem'is) n. **1.** (pl.) building with its grounds. **2.** statement from which a conclusion is drawn.

pre'mi·um (prē'mē əm) n. **1.** great value. **2.** bonus. **3.** periodic insurance payment.

pre'mo·ni'tion (prem'ə nish'ən, prē'mə-) n. foreboding.

pre·na'tal (prē nāt'l) adj. before birth or before giving birth.

pre·oc'cu·py', v., -pied, -pying. engross completely.

pre'or·dain', v. decree in advance.

prep (prep) v., prepped, prepping. get ready; prepare.

prep'ar·a·to'ry school (prep'ər ə·tôr'ē) private secondary school preparing students for college. Also, **prep school.**

pre·pare' (pri pâr') v., -pared, -paring. **1.** make or get ready. **2.** manufacture. —prep'a·ra'tion (prep'ə rā'-

shən) n. —pre·par'a·to'ry, adj. —pre·par'ed·ness, n.

pre·pay' (prē pā') v., -paid, -paying. pay beforehand.

pre·pon'der·ant (pri pon'dər ənt) adj. superior in force or numbers.

prep'o·si'tion (prep'ə zish'ən) n. word placed before noun or adjective to indicate relationship of space, time, means, etc.

pre'pos·sess'ing (prē'-) adj. impressing favorably.

pre·pos'ter·ous (pri pos'tər əs) adj. absurd.

prep'py (prep'ē) n., pl. -pies, adj., -pier, -piest. —n. **1.** student or graduate of a preparatory school. **2.** person who acts or dresses like a preppy. —adj. **3.** of or characteristic of a preppy.

pre'puce (prē'pyōōs) n. skin covering head of penis.

pre'quel (prē'kwəl) n. sequel to film, play, etc., that prefigures the original.

pre·req'ui·site (pri rek'wə zit, prē-) adj. **1.** required in advance. —n. **2.** something prerequisite.

pre·rog'a·tive (pri rog'ə tiv, pə rog'-) n. special right or privilege.

pres., **1.** present. **2.** president.

pres'age (pres'ij) v., -aged, -aging. **1.** portend. **2.** predict.

pres'by·o'pi·a (prez'bē ō'pē ə, pres'-) n. farsightedness.

pres'by·ter (prez'bi tər, pres'-) n. **1.** priest. **2.** elder.

Pres'by·te'ri·an (-bi tēr'ē ən) adj. **1.** (of religious group) governed by presbytery. **2.** (cap.) designating Protestant church so governed. —n. **3.** (cap.) member of Presbyterian Church.

pres'by·ter'y, n., pl. -teries. body of church elders and (in Presbyterian churches) ministers.

pre'school', adj. (prē'skōōl') **1.** of or for children between infancy and kindergarten age. —n. (-skōōl') **2.** nursery for preschool children.

pre'sci·ence (presh'əns, -ē əns) n. foresight. —pre'sci·ent, adj.

pre·scribe' (pri skrīb') v., -scribed, -scribing. **1.** order for use, as medicine. **2.** order. —pre·scrip'tion (-skrip'shən) n. —pre·scrip'tive (-skrip'tiv) adj.

pres'ence (prez'əns) n. **1.** fact of being present. **2.** vicinity. **3.** impressive personal quality.

presence of mind, ability to think clearly and act appropriately, as during a crisis.

pres'ent, adj. (prez'ənt) **1.** being or occurring now. **2.** being at particular place. **3.** Gram. denoting action or state now in progress. —n. (prez'ənt) **4.** present time. **5.** Gram. present tense. **6.** thing bestowed as gift. —v. (pri zent') **7.** give, bring, or offer. **8.** exhibit. —pres'en·ta'tion, n.

pre·sent'a·ble (pri zen'tə bəl) adj. suitable in looks, dress, etc.

pre·sen'ti·ment (-mənt) n. feeling of something impending, esp. evil.

pres'ent·ly (prez'ənt lē) adv. **1.** at present. **2.** soon.

pres'er·va'tion·ist (prez'ər vā'shə-nist) n. one who advocates preservation of wildlife, etc.

pre·serve' (pri zûrv') v., -served, -serving, n. —v. **1.** keep alive. **2.** keep safe. **3.** maintain. **4.** prepare (food) for long keeping. —n. **5.** (pl.) preserved fruit. **6.** place where game is protected. —pres'er·va'tion (prez'ər vā'shən) n. —pre·serv'a·tive, n., adj.

pre·side' (pri zīd') v., -sided, -siding. act as chairman.

pres'i·dent (prez'i dənt) n. **1.** highest executive of republic. **2.** chief officer. —pres'i·den·cy, n.

press (pres) v. **1.** act upon with weight or force. **2.** oppress; harass. **3.** insist upon. **4.** urge to hurry or comply. **5.** smooth with iron. —n. **6.** newspapers, etc., collectively. **7.** device for pressing or printing. **8.** crowd. **9.** urgency. —press'er, n.

press agent, person employed to obtain favorable publicity.

press conference, interview with reporters.

press'ing, adj. urgent.

press release, statement distributed to the press.

pres'sure (presh'ər) n. **1.** exertion of force by one body upon another. **2.** stress. **3.** urgency.

pressure cooker, pot for cooking quickly by steam under pressure.

pressure group, group that tries to influence legislation.

pres'sur·ize', v., -ized, -izing. produce normal air pressure at high altitudes. —pres'sur·i·za'tion, n.

pres'ti·dig'i·ta'tion (pres'ti dij'i-tā'shən) n. sleight of hand.

pres·tige' (pre stēzh', -stēj') n. distinguished reputation. —pres'tig'ious (-stij'əs) adj.

pres'to (pres'tō) adv. Music. quickly.

pre·sume' (pri zōōm') v., -sumed, -suming. **1.** take for granted. **2.** act with unjustified boldness. —pre·sum'a·bly, adv. —pre·sump'tu·ous (-zump'chōō əs) adj.

pre·sump'tion (-zump'shən) n. **1.** presumptuous attitude. **2.** assumption.

pre'sup·pose' (prē'sə pōz') v., -posed, -posing. assume.

pre·teen', n. **1.** child between 10 and 13 years old. —adj. **2.** of or for preteens.

pre·tend' (pri tend') v. **1.** make false appearance or claim. **2.** make believe. **3.** claim, as sovereignty. —pre·tend'er, n. —pre·tense', n.

pre·ten'sion (pri ten'shən) n. **1.** ostentation. **2.** act of pretending.

pre·ten'tious adj. overly self-important. —pre·ten'tious·ly, adv.

pret'er·it (pret'ər it) Gram. —adj. **1.** denoting action in past. —n. **2.** preterit tense.

pre'ter·nat'u·ral (prē'tər nach'ər əl) adj. supernatural.

pre'text (prē'tekst) n. ostensible reason; excuse.

pret'ty (prit'ē) adj., -tier, -tiest, adv. —adj. **1.** pleasingly attractive. —adv. **2.** moderately. **3.** very. —pret'ti·fy', v. —pret'ti·ly, adv.

pret'zel (pret'səl) n. crisp elongated or knotted biscuit.

pre·vail' (pri vāl') v. **1.** be widespread. **2.** exercise persuasion. **3.** gain victory.

pre·vail'ing, adj. **1.** most common. **2.** having superior influence.

prev'a·lent (prev'ə lənt) adj. widespread; general. —prev'a·lence, n.

pre·var'i·cate' (pri var'i kāt') v., -cated, -cating. speak evasively; lie. —pre·var'i·ca'tion, n.

pre·vent' (pri vent') v. hinder; stop. —pre·vent'a·ble. —pre·ven'tion, n. —pre·vent'a·tive, adj., n.

pre'view' (prē'vyōō') n., v. view or show in advance.

pre'vi·ous (prē'vē əs) adj. occurring earlier. —pre'vi·ous·ly, adv.

prey (prā) n. **1.** animal hunted as food by another animal. **2.** victim. **3.**

seize prey. **4.** victimize another. **5.** be obsessive.

price (prīs) *n., v.,* **priced, pricing.** —*n.* **1.** amount for which thing is sold. **2.** value. —*v.* **3.** set price on. **4.** *Informal.* ask the price of.

price′less, *adj.* too valuable to set price on.

pric′ey, *adj.,* **pricier, priciest.** *Informal.* expensive.

prick (prik) *n.* **1.** puncture by pointed object. —*v.* **2.** pierce. **3.** point.

prick′le, *n.* sharp point. —**prick′ly,** *adj.*

prickly heat, rash caused by inflammation of sweat glands.

pride (prīd) *n., v.,* **prided, priding.** —*n.* **1.** high opinion of worth of oneself or that associated with oneself. **2.** self-respect. **3.** that which one is proud of. **4.** group of lions. —*v.* **5.** feel pride. —**pride′ful,** *adj.*

priest (prēst) *n.* person authorized to perform religious rites; member of clergy. —**priest′ess,** *n.fem.* —**priest′hood,** *n.*

prig (prig) *n.* self-righteous person. —**prig′gish,** *adj.*

prim (prim) *adj.* stiffly proper.

pri′ma·cy (prī′mə sē) *n., pl.* **-cies.** supremacy.

pri′ma don′na (prē′mə don′ə, prim′ə) *n.* **1.** principal female opera singer. **2.** temperamental person.

pri′ma fa′ci·e (prī′mə fā′shē ē′, fā′shē) *adj. Law.* sufficient to establish a fact unless rebutted.

pri′mal (prī′məl) *adj.* **1.** first; original. **2.** most important.

pri·ma′ri·ly (prī mâr′ə lē, -mer′-) *adv.* **1.** chiefly. **2.** originally.

pri′ma·ry (prī′mer ē, -mə rē) *adj., n., pl.* **-ries.** —*adj.* **1.** first in importance or in order. **2.** earliest. —*n.* **3.** preliminary election for choosing party candidates.

pri′mate (prī′māt *or, esp. for 1,* -mit) *n.* **1.** high church official. **2.** mammal of order including humans, apes, and monkeys.

prime (prīm) *adj., n., v.,* **primed, priming.** —*adj.* **1.** first in importance or quality. **2.** original. —*n.* **3.** best stage or part. —*v.* **4.** prepare for special purpose or function.

prime meridian, meridian running through Greenwich, England, from which longitude east and west is reckoned.

prime minister, chief minister in some governments.

prim′er (prim′ər; *esp. Brit.* prī′mər) *n.* elementary book, esp. for reading.

prime rate, minimum interest rate charged by banks to best-rated customers.

prime time, hours considered to have largest television audience.

pri·me′val (prī mē′vəl) *adj.* of earliest time.

prim′i·tive (prim′i tiv) *adj.* **1.** earliest. **2.** simple; unrefined.

pri′mo·gen′i·ture (prī′mə jen′i-chər) *n.* state of being firstborn.

pri·mor′di·al (prī môr′dē əl) *adj.* primeval.

primp (primp) *v.* dress fussily.

prim′rose (prim′rōz′) *n.* early-flowering garden perennial.

prince (prins) *n.* high-ranking male member of royalty. —**prin′cess,** *n.fem.*

prince′ly, *adj.* lavish.

prin′ci·pal (prin′sə pəl) *adj.* **1.** chief. —*n.* **2.** chief; leader. **3.** head of school. **4.** person authorizing another to act for him. **5.** capital sum, distinguished from interest.

prin′ci·pal′i·ty (-pal′i tē) *n., pl.* **-ties.** state ruled by prince.

prin′ci·ple (prin′sə pəl) *n.* **1.** rule of conduct or action. **2.** fundamental truth or cause.

print (print) *v.* **1.** reproduce from inked types, plates, etc. **2.** write in letters like those of print. **3.** produce (photograph) from negative. —*n.* **4.** printed state. **5.** (of book) present availability for sale. **6.** print lettering. **7.** anything printed.

print′out′, *n.* printed output of computer.

pri′or (prī′ər) *adj.* **1.** earlier. —*adv.* **2.** previously. —*n.* **3.** officer in religious house. —**pri′or·ess,** *n.fem.* —**pri′o·ry,** *n.*

pri·or′i·tize (prī ôr′i tīz′) *v.,* **-tized, -tizing.** arrange in order of priority.

pri·or′i·ty, *n., pl.* **-ties.** **1.** state of being earlier. **2.** precedence.

prism (priz′əm) *n.* transparent body for dividing light into its spectrum.

pris′on (priz′ən) *n.* building for confinement of criminals. —**pris′on·er,** *n.*

pris′sy (pris′ē) *adj.,* **-sier, -siest.** excessively or affectedly proper.

pris′tine (pris′tēn, pri stēn′) *adj.* original; pure.

pri′vate (prī′vit) *adj.* **1.** belonging to particular person or group. **2.** personal. —*n.* **3.** soldier of lowest rank. —**pri′va·cy,** *n.* —**pri′vate·ly,** *adv.*

pri·va·teer′ (prī′və tēr′) *n.* privately owned vessel commissioned to fight. —**pri′va·teer′ing,** *n.*

private eye, *Informal.* private detective.

pri·va′tion (prī vā′shən) *n.* lack.

priv′et (priv′it) *n.* evergreen shrub.

priv′i·lege (priv′ə lij, priv′lij) *n., v.,* **-leged, -leging.** —*n.* **1.** special advantage. —*v.* **2.** grant privilege to.

priv′y (priv′ē) *adj., n., pl.* **privies.** —*adj.* **1.** sharing secret. **2.** private. —*n.* **3.** outdoor toilet.

privy council, board of personal advisors.

prize (prīz) *n., v.,* **prized, prizing.** —*n.* **1.** reward for victory, superiority, etc. **2.** thing worth striving for. —*v.* **3.** esteem highly.

pro (prō) *n., pl.* **pros,** *adv.* —*n.* **1.** argument in favor of something. **2.** *Informal.* professional. —*adv.* **3.** in favor of a plan, etc.

pro-, prefix meaning: **1.** favoring or supporting, as *prowar.* **2.** before or in front of, as *prognosis.*

prob′a·ble (prob′ə bal) *adj.* **1.** likely to occur, etc. **2.** affording ground for belief. —**prob′a·bil′i·ty,** *n.* —**prob′a·bly,** *adv.*

pro′bate (prō′bāt) *n., adj., v.,* **-bated, -bating.** —*n.* **1.** authentication of will. —*adj.* **2.** of probate. —*v.* **3.** establish will's validity.

pro·ba′tion, *n.* **1.** act of testing. **2.** period of such testing. **3.** conditional release, as from prison.

probe (prōb) *v.,* **probed, probing.** *n.* —*v.* **1.** examine thoroughly. —*n.* **2.** device for exploring wounds, etc. **3.** investigation.

pro′bi·ty (prō′bi tē, prob′i-) *n.* honesty.

prob′lem (prob′ləm) *n.* matter involving uncertainty or difficulty. —**prob′lem·at′ic,** *adj.*

pro·bos′cis (prō bos′is, -kis) *n., pl.* **-cises.** flexible snout.

pro·ced′ure (prə sē′jər) *n.* course of action. —**pro·ced′ur·al,** *adj.*

pro·ceed′ *v.* (prə sēd′) **1.** go forward. **2.** carry on action. **3.** issue forth. —*n.*

(prō′sēd) **4.** (*pl.*). sum derived from sale, etc.

pro·ceed′ing, *n.* **1.** action or conduct. **2.** (*pl.*) **a.** records of society. **b.** legal action.

proc′ess (pros′es; *esp. Brit.* prō′ses) *n.* **1.** series of actions toward given end. **2.** continuous action. **3.** legal summons. **4.** projecting growth. —*v.* **5.** treat by particular process.

pro·ces′sion (prə sesh′ən) *n.* ceremonial movement; parade.

pro·ces′sion·al, *n.* **1.** hymn sung during procession. **2.** hymnal.

pro-choice′ (prō chois′) *adj.* supporting the right to legalized abortion.

pro·claim′ (prō klām′, prə-) *v.* announce publicly. —**proc′la·ma′tion** (prok′lə mā′shən) *n.*

pro·cliv′i·ty (prō kliv′i tē) *n., pl.* **-ties.** natural tendency.

pro·cras′ti·nate′ (prō kras′tə nāt′, prə-) *v.,* **-nated, -nating.** delay. —**pro·cras′ti·na′tion,** *n.*

pro′cre·ate′ (prō′krē āt′) *v.* **-ated, -ating.** produce or have offspring. —**pro′cre·a′tion,** *n.*

proc′tor (prok′tər) *n.* **1.** person who watches over students at examinations. —*v.* **2.** supervise or monitor.

pro·cure′ (prō kyŏŏr′, prə-) *v.* **-cured, -curing.** **1.** get; obtain. **2.** cause. **3.** hire prostitutes. —**pro·cur′a·ble,** *adj.* —**pro·cure′ment,** *n.*

pro·cur′er, *n.* **1.** one that procures. **2.** Also, **pro·cur′ess,** *fem.* person who arranges for prostitution.

prod (prod) *v.,* **prodded, prodding,** *n.* —*v.* **1.** poke. **2.** incite; goad. —*n.* **3.** poke. **4.** goading instrument.

prod′i·gal (prod′i gəl) *adj.* **1.** wastefully extravagant. **2.** lavish. —*n.* **3.** spendthrift.

prod′i·gal′i·ty (-gal′ə tē) *n., pl.* **-ties.** extravagance; lavishness.

pro·di′gious (prə dij′əs) *adj.* huge; wonderful. —**pro·di′gious·ly,** *adv.*

prod′i·gy (prod′i jē) *n., pl.* **-gies.** very gifted person.

pro·duce′ *v.,* **-duced, -ducing,** *n.* —*v.* (prə dōōs′, -dyōōs′) **1.** bring into existence; create. **2.** bear, as young, fruit. **3.** exhibit. —*n.* (prod′ōōs, -yōōs, prō′dōōs, -dyōōs) **4.** product. **5.** agricultural products. —**pro·duc′tion** (prə duk′shən) *n.* —**pro·duc′tive,** *adj.*

prod′uct (prod′əkt) *n.* **1.** thing produced; result. **2.** result obtained by multiplying.

pro′duc·tiv′i·ty (prō′duk tiv′i tē, prod′ək-) *n.* **1.** quality of being productive. **2.** rate at which things are produced.

pro·fane′ (prə fān′, prō-) *adj., v.,* **-faned, -faning.** —*adj.* **1.** irreverent toward sacred things. **2.** secular. —*v.* **3.** defile. **4.** treat (sacred thing) with contempt. —**prof′a·na′tion** (prof′ə-nā′shən) *n.*

pro·fan′i·ty (-fan′i tē) *n., pl.* **-ties.** **1.** profane quality. **2.** blasphemous or vulgar language.

pro·fess′ (prə fes′) *v.* **1.** declare. **2.** affirm faith in. **3.** claim.

pro·fes′sion (prə fesh′ən) *n.* **1.** learned vocation. **2.** declaration; assertion.

pro·fes′sion·al, *adj.* **1.** following occupation for gain. **2.** of or engaged in profession. —*n.* **3.** professional person.

pro·fes′sor (prə fes′ər) *n.* college teacher of highest rank.

prof′fer (prof′ər) *v., n.* offer.

pro·fi′cient (prə fish′ənt) *adj.* expert. —**pro·fi′cien·cy,** *n.*

pro′file (prō′fīl) *n.* **1.** side view. **2.** informal biographical sketch.

prof′it (prof′it) *n.* **1.** pecuniary gain

from business transaction. **2.** net gain after costs. **3.** benefit. —*v.* **4.** gain advantage. **5.** make profit. —**prof'it·a·ble,** *adj.*

prof'it·eer', *n.* **1.** person who makes unfair profit. —*v.* **2.** act as profiteer.

prof'li·gate (prof'li git, -gāt') *adj.* **1.** immoral. **2.** extravagant. —**prof'li·gate,** *n.* —**prof'li·ga·cy,** *n.*

pro for'ma (prō fôr'mə) done as a matter of form or for the sake of form.

pro·found' (prə found') *adj.* **1.** thinking deeply. **2.** intense. **3.** deep. —**pro·fun'di·ty** (-fun'di tē) *n.*

pro·fuse' (-fyōōs') *adj.* extravagant; abundant. —**pro·fuse'ly,** *adv.* —**pro·fu'sion** (-fyōō'zhən) *n.*

pro·gen'i·tor (prō jen'i tər) *n.* ancestor.

prog'e·ny (proj'ə nē) *n.pl.* children.

pro·ges'ter·one (prō jes'tə rōn') *n.* female hormone that prepares uterus for fertilized ovum.

prog·no'sis (prog nō'sis) *n.,* *pl.* **-noses** (-nō'sēz). medical forecast.

prog·nos'ti·cate' (-nos'ti kāt') *v.,* **-cated, -cating.** predict.

pro'gram (prō'gram, -grəm) *n.,* *v.,* **-grammed, -gramming.** —*n.* **1.** plan of things to do. **2.** schedule of entertainments. **3.** television or radio show. **4.** plan for computerized problem solving. —*v.* **5.** make program for or including. —**pro'gram·ma·ble,** *adj.* —**pro'gram·mer,** *n.*

prog'ress, *n.* (prog'res, -rəs; *esp. Brit.* prō'gres) **1.** advancement. **2.** permanent improvement. **3.** growth. —*v.* (prə gres') **4.** make progress.

pro·gres'sion, *n.* **1.** advance. **2.** series.

pro·gres'sive, *adj.* **1.** advancing step by step. **2.** advocating reform.

pro·hib'it (prō hib'it) *v.* forbid; prevent.

pro'hi·bi'tion (prō'ə bish'ən) *n.* **1.** act of prohibiting. **2.** (*cap.*) period, 1920–33, when manufacture and sale of alcoholic drinks was forbidden in U.S. —**pro'hi·bi'tion·ist,** *n.*

pro·hib'i·tive (-hib'ə tiv) *adj.* **1.** serving to prohibit. **2.** too expensive.

proj'ect, *n.* (proj'ekt, -ikt; *esp. Brit.* prō'jekt) **1.** something planned. —*v.* (prə jekt') **2.** plan. **3.** impel forward. **4.** display upon surface, as motion picture or map. **5.** protrude. —**pro·jec'tion,** *n.* —**pro·jec'tor,** *n.*

pro·jec'tile (prə jek'til, -tīl) *n.* object fired with explosive force.

pro·jec'tion·ist (-shə nist) *n.* operator of motion-picture projector.

pro·le·tar'i·at (prō'li târ'ē ət) *n.* working or impoverished class. —**pro'le·tar'i·an,** *adj.,* *n.*

pro-life', *adj.* opposed to legalized abortion.

pro·lif'er·ate' (prə lif'ə rāt') *v.,* **-ated, -ating.** spread rapidly.

pro·lif'ic (-ik) *adj.* productive.

pro·lix' (prō liks', prō'liks) *adj.* tediously long and wordy.

pro'logue (prō'lôg) *n.* introductory part of novel, play, etc.

pro·long' (prə lông') *v.* lengthen. —**pro'lon·ga'tion** (prō'-) *n.*

prom (prom) *n.* formal dance at high school or college.

prom'e·nade' (prom'ə nād', -näd') *n.,* *v.,* **-naded, -nading.** —*n.* **1.** leisurely walk. **2.** space for such walk. —*v.* **3.** stroll.

prom'i·nent (prom'ə nənt) *adj.* **1.** conspicuous. **2.** projecting. **3.** well-known. —**prom'i·nence,** *n.*

pro·mis'cu·ous (prə mis'kyōō əs) *adj.* having numerous sexual partners

on a casual basis. —**prom'is·cu'i·ty,** (prom'i skyōō'i tē) *n.* —**pro·mis'cu·ous·ly,** *adv.*

prom'ise (prom'is) *n.,* *v.,* **-ised, -ising.** —*n.* **1.** assurance that one will act as specified. **2.** indication of future excellence. —*v.* **3.** assure by promise. **4.** afford ground for expectation. —**prom'is·ing,** *adj.*

prom'is·so'ry (prom'ə sôr'ē) *adj.* containing promise of payment.

prom'on·to'ry (prom'ən tôr'ē) *n.,* *pl.* **-ries.** high peak projecting into sea or overlooking low land.

pro·mote' (prə mōt') *v.,* **-moted, -moting. 1.** further progress of. **2.** advance. **3.** organize. —**pro·mot'er,** *n.* —**pro·mo'tion,** *n.*

prompt (prompt) *adj.* **1.** ready to act. **2.** done at once. —*v.* **3.** incite to action. **4.** suggest (action, etc.). —**prompt'ness,** *n.*

prom'ul·gate (prom'əl gāt', prō-mul'gāt) *v.,* **-gated, -gating.** proclaim formally.

prone (prōn) *adj.* **1.** likely; inclined. **2.** lying flat, esp. face downward.

prong (prông) *n.* point.

pro'noun' (prō'noun') *n.* word used as substitute for noun.

pro·nounce' (prə nouns') *v.,* **-nounced, -nouncing. 1.** utter, esp. precisely. **2.** declare to be. **3.** announce. —**pro·nounce'ment,** *n.*

pro·nounced' *adj.* **1.** strongly marked. **2.** decided.

pron'to (pron'tō) *adv.* quickly.

pro·nun'ci·a'tion (prə nun'sē ā'shən) *n.* production of sounds of speech.

proof (prōōf) *n.* **1.** evidence establishing fact. **2.** standard strength, as of liquors. **3.** trial printing. —*adj.* **4.** resisting perfectly.

-proof, suffix meaning resistant.

proof'read' (-rēd') *v.,* **-read** (red'), **proofreading.** read (printers' proofs, etc.) to mark errors. —**proof'read'er,** *n.*

prop (prop) *n.,* *v.,* **propped, propping.** —*n.* **1.** rigid support. **2.** propeller. —*v.* **3.** support with prop.

prop'a·gan'da (prop'ə gan'də) *n.* doctrines disseminated by organization. —**prop'a·gan'dist,** *n.* —**prop'a·gan'dize,** *v.,* **-dized, -dizing.**

prop'a·gate' (prop'ə gāt') *v.,* **-gated, -gating. 1.** reproduce; cause to reproduce. **2.** transmit (doctrine, etc.).

pro'pane (prō'pān) *n.* colorless flammable gas, used esp. as fuel.

pro·pel' (prə pel') *v.,* **-pelled, -pelling.** drive forward. —**pro·pel'lant, pro·pel'lent,** *n.*

pro·pel'ler, *n.* screwlike propelling device.

pro·pen'si·ty (prə pen'si tē) *n.,* *pl.* **-ties.** inclination.

prop'er (prop'ər) *adj.* **1.** suitable; fitting. **2.** correct. **3.** designating particular person, place, or thing.

prop'er·ty, *n.,* *pl.* **-ties. 1.** that which one owns. **2.** attribute.

proph'e·sy (prof'ə sī') *v.,* **-sied, -sying.** predict. —**proph'e·cy** (-sē) *n.*

proph'et (-it) *n.* **1.** person who speaks for God. **2.** inspired leader. **3.** person who predicts. —**pro·phet'ic** (prə fet'ik) *adj.*

pro'phy·lax'is (prō'fə lak'sis) *n.* protection from or prevention of disease. —**pro'phy·lac'tic,** *adj.,* *n.*

pro·pin'qui·ty (prō ping'kwi tē) *n.* nearness.

pro·pi'ti·ate' (prə pish'ē āt') *v.,* **-ated, -ating.** appease.

pro·pi'tious (-pish'əs) *adj.* favorable. —**pro·pi'tious·ly,** *adv.*

pro·po'nent (prə pō'nənt) *n.* advocate; supporter.

pro·por'tion (prə pôr'shən) *n.* **1.** comparative or proper relation of dimensions or quantities. **2.** symmetry. **3.** (*pl.*) dimensions. —*v.* **4.** adjust in proper relation.

pro·por'tion·ate (-shə nit) *adj.* being in due proportion.

pro·pos'al (prə pō'zəl) *n.* **1.** proposition. **2.** offer of marriage.

pro·pose' (prə pōz') *v.,* **-posed, -posing. 1.** suggest. **2.** intend. **3.** offer marriage.

prop'o·si'tion (prop'ə zish'ən) *n.* **1.** proposed plan. **2.** statement that affirms or denies. **3.** proposal of sex. —*v.* **4.** make proposition to.

pro·pound' (prə pound') *v.* offer for consideration.

pro·pri'e·tor (prə prī'ə tər) *n.* owner or manager. —**pro·pri'e·tar'y,** *adj.*

pro·pri'e·ty, *n.,* *pl.* **-ties. 1.** appropriateness. **2.** (*pl.*) morality.

pro·pul'sion (prə pul'shən) *n.* propelling force.

pro·rate' (prō rāt', prō'rāt') *v.,* **-rated, -rating.** divide proportionately.

pro·sa'ic (prō zā'ik) *adj.* commonplace. —**pro·sa'i·cal·ly,** *adv.*

pro·sce'ni·um (prō sē'nē əm, prə-) *n.,* *pl.* **-niums, -nia** (-nē ə). arch separating stage from auditorium. Also, **proscenium arch.**

pro·scribe' (prō skrīb') *v.* **-scribed, -scribing.** prohibit.

prose (prōz) *n.* not verse; ordinary language.

pros'e·cute' (pros'i kyōōt') *v.,* **-cuted, -cuting. 1.** begin legal proceedings against. **2.** go on with (task, etc.) to the end. —**pros'e·cu'tion,** *n.* —**pros'e·cu'tor,** *n.*

pros'e·lyte' (pros'ə līt') *n.,* **-lyted, -lyting.** convert. —**pros'e·lyt·ize'** (-lə tīz') *v.,* **-ized, -izing.**

pros'pect (pros'pekt) *n.* **1.** likelihood of success. **2.** outlook; view. **3.** potential customer. —*v.* **4.** search. —**pro·spec'tive** (prə spek'tiv) *adj.* —**pros'pec·tor,** *n.*

pro·spec'tus (prə spek'təs) *n.* description of new investment or purchase.

pros'per (pros'pər) *v.* be successful. —**pros·per'i·ty** (-per'ə tē) *n.* —**pros'per·ous,** *adj.*

pros'tate (pros'tāt) *n.* gland in males at base of bladder.

pros·the'sis (pros thē'sis) *n.,* *pl.* **-ses** (-sēz). device that substitutes for or supplements missing or defective body part. —**pros·thet'ic** (-thet'ik) *adj.*

pros'ti·tute' (pros'ti tōōt', -tyōōt') *n.,* *v.,* **-tuted, -tuting.** —*n.* **1.** person who engages in sexual intercourse for money. —*v.* **2.** put to base use. —**pros'ti·tu'tion,** *n.*

pros'trate (pros'trāt) *v.,* **-trated, -trating,** *adj.* —*v.* **1.** lay (oneself) face downward, esp. in humility. **2.** exhaust. —*adj.* **3.** lying flat. **4.** helpless. **5.** weak or exhausted.

pro·tag'o·nist (prō tag'ə nist) *n.* main character.

pro'te·an (prō'tē ən, prō tē'-) *adj.* assuming different forms.

pro·tect' (prə tekt') *v.* shield; defend, as from attack. —**pro·tec'tion,** *n.* —**pro·tec'tive,** *adj.*

pro·tec'tion·ism (-shə niz'əm) *n.* practice of protecting domestic industries from foreign competition by imposing import duties.

pro·tec'tor·ate (-tər it) *n.* **1.** relation

by which strong state partly controls weaker state. **2.** such weaker state.

pro•té•gé' (prō'tə zhā') *n.* one under friendly patronage of another. —**pro'té•gée'**, *n.fem.*

pro'tein (prō'tēn, -tē in) *n.* nitrogenous compound.

pro tem•por•e (prō' tem'pə rē', -rā') temporarily.

pro'test, *n.* (prō'test) **1.** objection. —*v.* (prə test', prō'test) **2.** express objection. **3.** declare. —**prot'es•ta'tion,** *n.* —**pro•test'er,** *n.*

Prot'es•tant (prot'ə stənt) *n.* Christian who belongs to a church that began by breaking away from the Roman Catholic Church in the 16th century. —**Prot'es•tant•ism'**, *n.*

proto-, prefix meaning earliest or foremost.

pro'to•col' (prō'tə kôl') *n.* diplomatic etiquette.

pro'ton (prō'ton) *n.* part of atom bearing positive charge.

pro'to•plasm' (prō'tə plaz'əm) *n.* basis of living matter.

pro'to•type', *n.* model; first or typical version. —**pro'to•typ'i•cal,** *adj.*

pro'to•zo'an (-zō'ən) *n., pl.* **-zoans, -zoa** (-zō'ə). one-celled organism that obtains nourishment by ingesting food.

pro•tract' (prō trakt', prə-) *v.* lengthen. —**pro•trac'tion,** *n.*

pro•trac'tor, *n.* instrument for measuring angles.

pro•trude' (prō trōōd', prə-) *v.,* **-truded, -truding.** project; extend. —**pro•tru'sion** (-trōō'zhən) *n.* —**pro•tru'sive** (-trōō'siv) *adj.*

pro•tu'ber•ant (prō tōō'bər ənt) *adj.* bulging out. —**pro•tu'ber•ance,** *n.*

proud (proud) *adj.* **1.** having pride. **2.** arrogant. **3.** magnificent. —**proud'ly,** *adv.*

prove (prōōv) *v.,* **proved, proving. 1.** establish as fact. **2.** test. **3.** be or become ultimately.

prov'e•nance (prov'ə nəns, -näns') *n.* place or source of origin.

prov'en•der (prov'ən dər) *n.* fodder.

prov'erb (prov'ərb) *n.* wise popular saying. —**pro•ver'bi•al** (prə vûr'bē əl) *adj.*

pro•vide' (prə vīd') *v.,* **-vided, -viding. 1.** supply. **2.** yield. **3.** prepare beforehand. —**pro•vid'er,** *n.*

pro•vid'ed, *conj.* if.

prov'i•dence (prov'i dəns) *n.* **1.** God's care. **2.** economy.

prov'i•dent (-dənt) *adj.* showing foresight; prudent.

prov'i•den'tial (-den'shəl) *adj.* coming as godsend.

prov'ince (prov'ins) *n.* **1.** administrative unit of country. **2.** sphere.

pro•vin'cial (prə vin'shəl) *adj.* **1.** of province. **2.** narrow-minded; unsophisticated.

pro•vi'sion (prə vizh'ən) *n.* **1.** something stated as necessary or binding. **2.** act of providing. **3.** what is provided. **4.** arrangement beforehand. **5.** (*pl.*) food supply. —*v.* **6.** supply with provisions.

pro•vi'sion•al, *adj.* temporary.

pro•vi'so (prə vī'zō) *n., pl.* **-sos, -soes.** something required in an agreement; stipulation.

pro•voc'a•tive (prə vok'ə tiv) *adj.* stimulating; exciting.

pro•voke' (-vōk') *v.,* **-voked, -voking. 1.** exasperate. **2.** arouse. —**prov'o•ca'tion** (prov'ə kā'shən) *n.*

pro'vost (prō'vōst) *n.* **1.** superintendent. **2.** high-ranking university administrator.

prow (prou) *n.* front part of ship or aircraft.

prow'ess (prou'is) *n.* **1.** exceptional ability. **2.** bravery.

prowl (proul) *v.* roam or search stealthily. —**prowl'er,** *n.*

prox•im'i•ty (prok sim'i tē) *n.* nearness.

prox'y (prok'sē) *n., pl.* **proxies.** agent.

prude (prōōd) *n.* person overly concerned with proprieties. —**prud'er•y,** *n.* —**prud'ish,** *adj.*

pru'dence, *n.* practical wisdom; caution. —**pru'dent,** *adj.* —**pru'dent•ly,** *adv.*

prune (prōōn) *v.,* **pruned, pruning,** *n.* —*v.* **1.** cut off (branches, etc.). —*n.* **2.** dried plum.

pru'ri•ent (prōōr'ē ənt) *adj.* having lewd thoughts. —**pru'ri•ence,** *n.*

pry (prī) *v.,* **pried, prying,** *n.* —*v.* **1.** look or inquire too curiously. **2.** move with lever. —*n.* **3.** act of prying. **4.** prying person. **5.** lever.

P.S., 1. Also, **p.s.** postscript. **2.** Public School.

psalm (säm) *n.* sacred song.

pseu'do (sōō'dō) *adj.* false.

pseu'do•nym (sōōd'n im) *n.* false name used by writer.

pso•ri'a•sis (sə rī'ə sis) *n.* chronic, inflammatory skin disease.

psych (sīk) *v. Informal.* **1.** intimidate. **2.** prepare psychologically.

psy'che (sī'kē) *n.* human soul or mind.

psy'che•del'ic (sī'ki del'ik) *adj.* noting a mental state of distorted sense perceptions and hallucinations.

psy•chi'a•try (si kī'ə trē, sī-) *n.* science of mental diseases. —**psy'chi•at'ric** (sī'kē ə'trik) *adj.* —**psy•chi'a•trist,** *n.*

psy'chic (sī'kik) *adj.* **1.** of the psyche. **2.** pertaining to an apparently nonphysical force or agency. —*n.* **3.** person sensitive to psychic influences.

psy•cho•ac'tive (sī'kō-) *adj.* affecting mental state.

psy'cho•a•nal'y•sis *n.* **1.** study of conscious and unconscious psychological processes. **2.** treatment according to such study. —**psy'cho•an'a•lyst,** *n.* —**psy'cho•an'a•lyze',** *v.*

psy'cho•gen'ic (sī'kə jen'ik) *adj.* originating in mental process.

psy•chol'o•gy (sī kol'ə jē) *n.* science of mental states and behavior. —**psy'cho•log'i•cal** (-kə loj'i kal) *adj.* —**psy•chol'o•gist,** *n.*

psy'cho•neu•ro'sis (sī'kō nōō rō'sis, -nyōō-) *n., pl.* **-ses.** emotional disorder.

psy'cho•path' (sī'kə path') *n.* —**psy'cho•path'ic,** *adj.*

psy•cho'sis (-kō'sis) *n., pl.* **-ses** (-sēz). severe mental disease. —**psy•chot'ic** (-kot'ik) *adj., n.*

psy'cho•so•mat'ic (-sə mat'ik) *adj.* (of physical disorder) caused by one's emotional state.

psy•cho•ther'a•py, *n., pl.* **-pies.** treatment of mental disorders. —**psy'cho•ther'a•pist,** *n.*

psy'cho•tro'pic (-trō'pik) *adj.* affecting mental activity.

pt., **1.** part. **2.** pint. **3.** point.

ptar'mi•gan (tär'mi gən) *n.* species of mountain grouse.

pter'o•dac'tyl (ter'ə dak'til) *n.* extinct flying reptile.

pto'maine (tō'mān) *n.* substance produced during decay of plant and animal matter.

pub (pub) *n. Brit. Informal.* tavern.

pu'ber•ty (pyōō'bər tē) *n.* sexual maturity. —**pu'ber•tal,** *adj.*

pu•bes'cent (-bes'ənt) *adj.* arriving at puberty. —**pu•bes'cence,** *n.*

pu'bic (pyōō'bik) *adj.* of or near the genitals.

pub'lic (pub'lik) *adj.* **1.** of or for people generally. **2.** open to view or knowledge of all. —*n.* **3.** people.

pub'li•ca'tion, *n.* **1.** publishing of book, etc. **2.** item published.

public defender, lawyer who represents indigent clients at public expense.

public domain, legal status of material not protected by copyright or patent.

pub•lic'i•ty (pu blis'i tē) *n.* **1.** public attention. **2.** material promoting this.

pub'li•cize', *v.,* **-cized, -cizing.** bring to public notice.

public relations, actions of organization in promoting goodwill with the public.

pub'lish (pub'lish) *v.* **1.** issue (book, paper, etc.) for general distribution. **2.** announce publicly. —**pub'lish•er,** *n.*

puck (puk) *n.* black rubber disk hit into goal in hockey.

puck'er (puk'ər) *v., n.* wrinkle.

puck'ish (puk'ish) *adj.* mischievous.

pud'ding (pŏŏd'ing) *n.* soft, creamy dish, usually dessert.

pud'dle (pud'l) *n.* small pool of water.

pudg'y (puj'ē) *adj.,* **-ier, -iest.** short and fat. —**pudg'i•ness,** *n.*

pu'er•ile (pyōō'ər il, -ə rīl') *adj.* childish. —**pu'er•il'i•ty,** *n.*

puff (puf) *n.* **1.** short blast of wind. **2.** inflated part. **3.** anything soft and light. —*v.* **4.** blow with puffs. **5.** breathe hard and fast. **6.** inflate. —**puff'i•ness,** *n.* —**puff'y,** *adj.*

puf'fin (puf'in) *n.* sea bird.

pug (pug) *n.* kind of dog.

pu'gil•ism (pyōō'jə liz'əm) *n.* boxing. —**pu'gil•ist,** *n.*

pug•na'cious (pug nā'shəs) *adj.* always ready to fight. —**pug•nac'i•ty** (-nas'ə tē) *n.*

pug nose, short, broad, somewhat turned-up nose.

puke (pyōōk) *v.,* **puked, puking,** *n. Slang.* vomit.

pul'chri•tude' (pul'kri tōōd', -tyōōd') *n.* beauty.

pule (pyōōl) *v.,* **puled, puling.** whine.

pull (pŏŏl) *v.* **1.** draw; haul. **2.** tear. **3.** move with force. —*n.* **4.** act of pulling. **5.** force. **6.** handle. **7.** *Informal.* influence in politics, etc.

pul'let (pŏŏl'it) *n.* young hen.

pul'ley (pŏŏl'ē) *n.* wheel for guiding rope.

Pull'man (pŏŏl'mən) *n.* sleeping car on railroad.

pull'out', *n.* **1.** withdrawal. **2.** section of publication that can be pulled out.

pull'o'ver, *adj.* **1.** put on by being drawn over the head. —*n.* **2.** pullover garment.

pul'mo•nar'y (pul'mə ner'ē, pŏŏl'-) *adj.* of lungs.

pulp (pulp) *n.* **1.** soft fleshy part, as of fruit or tooth. **2.** any soft mass. —*v.* **3.** make or become pulp.

pul'pit (pŏŏl'pit, pul'-) *n.* platform in church from which service is conducted or sermon is preached.

pul'sar (pul'sär) *n.* source of pulsating radio energy among stars.

pul'sate (pul'sāt) *v.,* **-sated, -sating.** throb. —**pul•sa'tion,** *n.*

pulse (puls) *n., v.,* **pulsed, pulsing.** —*n.* **1.** heartbeat. —*v.* **2.** pulsate.

pul′ver•ize′ (pul′və rīz′) v., **-ized, -izing.** reduce to powder.

pu′ma (pyōō′mə, pōō′-) n. cougar.

pum′ice (pum′is) n. porous volcanic glass used as abrasive.

pum′mel (pum′əl) v., **-meled, -meling.** strike; beat.

pump (pump) n. **1.** apparatus for raising or driving fluids. **2.** women's shoe. —v. **3.** raise or drive with pump. **4.** *Informal.* try to get information from.

pum′per•nick′el (pum′pər nik′əl) n. hard, sour rye bread.

pump′kin (pump′kin *or, commonly,* pung′kin) n. large orange squash of garden vine.

pun (pun) n., v., **punned, punning.** —n. **1.** play with words alike in sound but different in meaning. —v. **2.** make pun. **—pun′ster,** n.

punch (punch) n. **1.** thrusting blow. **2.** tool for piercing material. **3.** sweetened beverage. —v. **4.** hit with thrusting blow. **5.** drive (cattle). **6.** cut or indent with punch.

punch′-drunk′, adj. **1.** showing symptoms of cerebral injury. **2.** dazed.

punch line, climactic phrase in a joke.

punch′y, adj., **punchier, punchiest. 1.** befuddled. **2.** forceful.

punc•til′i•ous (pungk til′ē əs) adj. exact in observance of formalities.

punc′tu•al (pungk′chōō əl) adj. on time. **—punc′tu•al′i•ty,** n.

punc′tu•ate′ (-āt′) v., **-ated, -ating. 1.** mark with punctuation. **2.** interupt periodically.

punc′tu•a′tion, n. use of commas, semicolons, etc.

punc′ture (pungk′chər) n., v., **-tured, -turing.** —n. **1.** perforation. —v. **2.** perforate with pointed object.

pun′dit (pun′dit) n. learned person.

pun′gent (pun′jənt) adj. **1.** sharp in taste. **2.** biting. **—pun′gen•cy,** n.

pun′ish (pun′ish) v. subject to pain, confinement, loss, etc., for offense. **—pun′ish•ment,** n.

pu′ni•tive (pyōō′ni tiv) adj. punishing.

punk (pungk) n. **1.** substance that will smolder, used esp. to light fires. **2.** *Slang.* something or someone worthless or unimportant. **3.** *Slang.* young hoodlum. **4.** Also, **punk rock.** rock music marked by loudness and aggressive lyrics. **5.** style of clothing, etc., suggesting defiance of social norms. —adj. **6.** *Informal.* poor in quality. **7.** of punk rock or punk style.

punt (punt) n. **1.** kick in football. **2.** shallow flat-bottomed boat. —v. **3.** kick (dropped ball) before it touches ground. **4.** propel (boat) with pole.

pu′ny (pyōō′nē) adj., **-nier, -niest.** small and weak.

pup (pup) n. young dog.

pu′pa (pyōō′pə) n., pl. **-pae** (-pē), **-pas.** insect in stage between larva and winged adult. **—pu′pal,** adj.

pu′pil (pyōō′pəl) n. **1.** person being taught. **2.** opening in iris of eye.

pup′pet (pup′it) n. **1.** doll or figure manipulated by hand or strings. **2.** person, government, etc., whose actions are controlled by another. **—pup′pet•ry,** n.

pup′pet•eer′, n. person who manipulates puppets.

pup′py (pup′ē) n., pl. **-pies.** young dog.

pur′chase (pûr′chəs) v., **-chased, -chasing,** n. —v. **1.** buy. —n. **2.** acquisition by payment. **3.** what is bought. **4.** leverage.

pure (pyōōr) adj., **purer, purest. 1.**

free of pollutants. **2.** abstract. **3.** absolute. **4.** chaste. **—pure′ly,** adv.

pure′bred, adj. (pyōōr′bred′) **1.** having ancestors over many generations from a recognized breed. —n. (pyōōr′bred′) **2.** purebred animal.

pu•rée′ (pyōō rā′, -rē′) n., v., **-réed, -réeing.** —n. **1.** cooked food that has been sieved or blended. —v. **2.** make purée of.

pur′ga•to′ry (pûr′gə tôr′ē) n., pl. **-ries. 1.** *Rom. Cath. Theol.* condition or place of purification, after death, from venial sins. **2.** any condition or place of temporary punishment.

purge (pûrj) v., **purged, purging,** n. —v. **1.** cleanse; purify. **2.** rid. **3.** clear by causing evacuation. —n. **4.** act or means of purging. **—pur′ga•tive** (gə-tiv) adj., n.

pu′ri•fy′ (pyōōr′i fī′) v., **-fied, -fying.** make or become pure.

Pu′rim (pōōr′im) n. Jewish commemorative festival.

pur′ism (pyōōr′iz əm) n. insistence on purity in language, style, etc.

Pu′ri•tan (pyōōr′i tn) n. **1.** member of strict Protestant group originating in 16th-century England. **2.** (*l.c.*) person of strict moral views. **—pu′ri•tan′i•cal,** adj.

pu′ri•ty (pyōōr′i tē) n. condition of being pure.

purl (pûrl) v. knit with inverted stitch.

pur′lieu (pûr′lōō, pûrl′yōō) n., pl. **-lieus.** (pl.) neighborhood.

pur•loin′ (pər loin′, pûr′loin) v. steal.

pur′ple (pûr′pəl) n. color blended of red and blue. **—purple,** adj.

pur•port′, v. (pər pôrt′) **1.** claim. **2.** imply. —n. (pûr′pôrt) **3.** meaning.

pur′pose (pûr′pəs) n., v., **-posed, -posing.** —n. **1.** object; aim; intention. —v. **2.** intend. **—pur′pose•ful,** adj. **—pur′pose•less,** adj.

purr (pûr) n. **1.** low continuous sound made by cat. —v. **2.** make this sound.

purse (pûrs) n., v., **pursed, pursing.** —n. **1.** bag for money and small things. **2.** sum of money offered as prize. —v. **3.** pucker.

purs′er, n. financial officer.

pur•su′ant (pər sōō′ənt) adv. according.

pur•sue′, v., **-sued, -suing. 1.** follow to catch. **2.** carry on (studies, etc.).

pur•suit′ (-sōōt′) n. **1.** act of pursuing. **2.** quest. **3.** occupation.

pur•vey′ (pər vā′) v. provide; supply. **—pur•vey′or,** n.

pus (pus) n. liquid matter found in sores, etc.

push (pōōsh) v. **1.** exert force on to send away. **2.** urge. **3.** peddle. —n. **4.** act of pushing. **5.** strong effort.

push′o′ver, n. *Informal.* one easily victimized or overcome.

push′y, adj., **pushier, pushiest.** obnoxiously self-assertive. **—push′i•ness,** n.

pu•sil•lan′i•mous (pyōō′sə lan′ə-məs) adj. cowardly.

puss′y (pōōs′ē) n., pl. **pussies.** cat. Also, **puss.**

puss′y•foot′, v. **1.** go stealthily. **2.** act timidly or irresolutely.

pussy willow, small American willow.

pus′tule (pus′chōōl) n. pimple containing pus.

put (pōōt) v., **put, putting,** n. —v. **1.** move or place. **2.** set, as to task. **3.** express. **4.** apply. **5.** impose. **6.** throw.

pu′ta•tive (pyōō′tə tiv) adj. reputed.

put′-down′, n. *Informal.* snubbing remark.

pu′tre•fy′ (pyōō′trə fī′) v., **-fied, -fying.** rot. **—pu′tre•fac′tion** (-fak′shən) n.

pu•tres′cent (-tres′ənt) adj. becoming putrid. **—pu•tres′cence,** n.

pu′trid (-trid) adj. rotten.

putsch (pōōch) n. sudden political revolt or uprising.

putt (put) v. **1.** strike (golf ball) gently. —n. **2.** such strike.

put′ter (put′ər) v. **1.** busy oneself ineffectively. —n. **2.** club for putting.

put′ty (put′ē) n., v., **-tied, -tying.** —n. **1.** cement of whiting and oil used in windows. —v. **2.** secure with putty.

puz′zle (puz′əl) n., v., **-zled, -zling.** —n. **1.** device or question offering difficulties. —v. **2.** perplex.

Pvt., Private.

PX, post exchange.

pyg′my (pig′mē) n., pl. **-mies.** dwarf.

py′lon (pī′lon) n. tall thin structure.

pyr′a•mid (pir′ə mid) n. **1.** solid with triangular sides meeting in point. —v. **2.** increase gradually. **—py•ram′i•dal** (pə ram′ə dl) adj.

pyre (pīr) n. heap of wood, esp. for burning corpse.

py′rite (pī′rīt) n. common yellow mineral of low value.

py′ro•ma′ni•a (pī′rə mā′nē ə) n. mania for setting fires. **—py′ro•ma′ni•ac′,** n.

py′ro•tech′nics (-tek′niks) n. fireworks. **—py′ro•tech′nic,** adj.

py′thon (pī′thon) n. large snake that kills by constriction.

Q

Q, q (kyōō) n. seventeenth letter of English alphabet.

Q.E.D., which was to be shown or demonstrated.

qt., pl. **qt., qts.** quart.

qty., quantity.

quack (kwak) n. **1.** pretender to medical skill. **2.** sound that duck makes. **—quack′er•y,** n.

quad (kwod) n. **1.** quadrangle. **2.** quadruplet.

quad•ran′gle (-rang′gəl) n. **1.** plane figure with four angles and four sides. **2.** four-sided area surrounded by buildings. **—quad•ran′gu•lar** (kwo drang′gyə lər) adj.

quad′rant (-rənt) n. **1.** arc of 90°. **2.** instrument for measuring altitudes.

quad′ra•phon′ic (-rə fon′ik) adj. of sound reproduced through four recording tracks.

quad′ri•lat′er•al (-lat′ər əl) adj. **1.** four-sided. —n. **2.** four-sided plane figure.

qua•drille′ (kwo dril′, kwə-) n. square dance for four couples.

quad′ri•ple′gi•a (kwod′rə plē′jē ə, -jə) n. paralysis of the entire body below the neck. **—quad′ri•ple′gic,** n., adj.

quad′ru•ped′ (-rōō ped′) n. four-footed animal.

quad•ru′ple (kwo drōō′pəl, -drup′əl) adj., v., **-pled, -pling.** —adj. **1.** of four parts. **2.** four times as great. —n. **3.** number, etc., four times as great as another. —v. **4.** increase fourfold.

quad•ru′plet (-drup′lit, -drōō′plit) n. one of four children born at one birth.

quad•ru′pli•cate (-drōō′pli kit) n. group of four copies.

quaff (kwof, kwaf) v. drink heartily.

quag′mire′ (kwag′mīr′, kwog′-) n. boggy ground.

qua′hog (kwô′hog, kō′-) *n.* edible American clam.

quail (kwāl) *n.*, *pl.* **quails, quail,** *v.* —*n.* **1.** game bird resembling domestic fowls. —*v.* **2.** lose courage; show fear.

quaint (kwānt) *adj.* pleasingly old-fashioned or odd. —**quaint′ly,** *adv.*

quake (kwāk) *v.*, **quaked, quaking,** *n.* —*v.* **1.** tremble. —*n.* **2.** earthquake.

Quak′er (kwā′kər) *n.* member of Society of Friends.

qual′i•fy′ (kwol′ə fī′) *v.*, **-fied, -fy-ing. 1.** make proper or fit. **2.** modify. **3.** mitigate. **4.** show oneself fit. —**qual′i•fi•ca′tion,** *n.*

qual′i•ty, (-i tē) *n.*, *pl.* **-ties. 1.** characteristic. **2.** relative merit. **3.** excellence.

quality time, time devoted exclusively to nurturing cherished person or activity.

qualm (kwäm) *n.* **1.** misgiving; scruple. **2.** feeling of illness.

quan′da•ry (kwon′də rē, -drē) *n.*, *pl.* **-ries.** dilemma.

quan′ti•fy′ (kwon′tə fī′) *v.*, **-fied, -fying.** measure.

quan′ti•ty (-ti tē) *n.*, *pl.* **-ties. 1.** amount; measure. **2.** *Math.* something having magnitude.

quan′tum (-təm) *n.*, *pl.* **-ta,** *adj.* —*n.* **1.** quantity or amount. **2.** *Physics.* very small, indivisible quantity of energy. —*adj.* **3.** sudden and significant.

quar′an•tine′ (kwôr′ən tēn′) *n.*, *v.*, **-tined, -tining.** —*n.* **1.** strict isolation to prevent spread of disease. —*v.* **2.** put in quarantine.

quark (kwôrk, kwärk) *n.* subatomic particle having fractional electric charge and thought to form basis of all matter.

quar′rel (kwôr′əl) *n.*, *v.*, **-reled, -rel-ing.** —*n.* **1.** angry dispute. —*v.* **2.** disagree angrily. —**quar′rel•some,** *adj.*

quar′ry (kwôr′ē) *n.*, *pl.* **-ries,** *v.*, **-ried, -rying.** —*n.* **1.** pit from which stone is taken. **2.** object of pursuit. —*v.* **3.** get from quarry.

quart (kwôrt) *n.* measure of capacity: in liquid measure, ¼ gallon; in dry measure, ⅛ peck.

quar′ter, *n.* **1.** one of four equal parts. **2.** coin worth 25 cents. **3.** (*pl.*) place of residence. **4.** mercy. —*v.* **5.** divide into quarters. **6.** lodge.

quar′ter•back′, *n.* position in football.

quar′ter•ly, *adj.*, *n.*, *pl.* **-lies,** *adv.* —*adj.* **1.** occurring, etc., each quarter year. —*n.* **2.** quarterly publication. —*adv.* **3.** once each quarter year.

quar′ter•mas′ter, *n.* **1.** military officer in charge of supplies, etc. **2.** naval officer in charge of signals.

quar•tet′ (kwôr tet′) *n.* group of four. Also, **quar•tette′.**

quar′to (kwôr′tō) *n.*, *pl.* **-tos.** book page of sheets folded twice.

quartz (kwôrts) *n.* crystalline mineral.

qua′sar (kwā′zär, -zər) *n.* astronomical source of powerful radio energy.

quash (kwosh) *v.* subdue; suppress.

qua′si (kwā′zī, -sī, kwä′sē, -zē) *adj.* resembling; to be regarded as if.

quasi-, prefix meaning somewhat.

Quat′er•nar′y (kwot′ər ner′ē, kwə-tûr′nə rē) *adj.* pertaining to present geologic period forming latter part of Cenozoic Era.

quat′rain (kwo′trān) *n.* four-line stanza.

qua′ver (kwā′vər) *v.* **1.** quiver. **2.** speak tremulously. —*n.* **3.** quavering tone.

quay (kē) *n.* landing beside water.

quea′sy (kwē′zē) *adj.*, **-sier, -siest. 1.** nauseated. **2.** uneasy.

queen (kwēn) *n.* **1.** wife of king. **2.** female sovereign. **3.** fertile female of bees, ants, etc. —*v.* **4.** reign as queen.

queer (kwēr) *adj.* **1.** strange; odd. —*n.* **2.** *Offensive.* homosexual. —*v.* **3.** *Slang.* ruin; impair.

quell (kwel) *v.* suppress.

quench (kwench) *v.* slake or extinguish.

quer′u•lous (kwer′ə ləs, kwer′yə-) *adj.* peevish.

que′ry (kwēr′ē) *n.*, *pl.* **-ries,** *v.*, **-ried, -rying.** question.

quest (kwest) *n.*, *v.* search.

ques′tion (kwes′chən) *n.* **1.** sentence put in a form to elicit information. **2.** problem for discussion or dispute. —*v.* **3.** ask a question. **4.** doubt. —**ques′tion•a•ble,** *adj.* —**ques′tion•er,** *n.*

ques′tion•naire′ (-chə nâr′) *n.* list of questions.

queue (kyōō) *n.*, *v.*, **queued, queu-ing.** —*n.* **1.** line of persons. **2.** braid of hair hanging down the back. —*v.* **3.** form in a line.

quib′ble (kwib′əl) *v.*, **-bled, -bling,** *n.* —*v.* **1.** speak ambiguously in evasion. **2.** make petty objections. —*n.* **3.** act of quibbling.

quiche (kēsh) *n.* pielike dish of cheese, onion, etc.

quick (kwik) *adj.* **1.** prompt; done promptly. **2.** swift. **3.** alert. —*n.* **4.** living persons. **5.** sensitive flesh. —*adv.* **6.** quickly. —**quick′ly,** *adv.*

quick′en, *v.* **1.** hasten. **2.** rouse. **3.** become alive.

quick′ie, *n.* something done or enjoyed in only a short time.

quick′lime′, *n.* untreated lime.

quick′sand′, *n.* soft sand yielding easily to weight.

quick′sil′ver, *n.* mercury.

quid (kwid) *n.* **1.** portion for chewing. **2.** *Brit. Informal.* one pound sterling.

quid pro quo (kwid′ prō kwō′) *pl.* **quid pro quos, quids pro quo.** something given or taken for something else.

qui•es′cent (kwē es′ənt, kwī-) *adj.* inactive. —**qui•es′cence,** *n.*

qui′et (kwī′it) *adj.* **1.** being at rest. **2.** peaceful. **3.** silent. **4.** restrained. —*v.* **5.** make or become quiet. **6.** tranquil. —**qui′et•ly,** *adv.*

quill (kwil) *n.* large feather.

quilt (kwilt) *n.* padded and lined bed covering. —**quilt′ed,** *adj.*

quince (kwins) *n.* yellowish acid fruit.

qui′nine (kwī′nīn) *n.* bitter substance used esp. in treating malaria.

quint (kwint) *n.* quintuplet.

quin•tes′sence (kwin tes′əns) *n.* essential substance. —**quin′tes•sen′tial** (-tə sen′shəl) *adj.*

quin•tet′ (kwin tet′) *n.* group of five. Also, **quin•tette′.**

quin•tu′plet (-tup′lit, -tōō′plit, -tyōō′-) *n.* one of five children born at one birth.

quip (kwip) *n.*, *v.*, **quipped, quipping.** —*n.* **1.** witty or sarcastic remark. —*v.* **2.** make quip.

quire (kwīr) *n.* set of 24 uniform sheets of paper.

quirk (kwûrk) *n.* peculiarity. —**quirk′y,** *adj.*, **-ier, -iest.**

quis′ling (kwiz′ling) *n.* traitor.

quit (kwit) *v.*, **quitted, quitting. 1.** stop. **2.** leave. **3.** relinquish.

quit′claim′, *n.* **1.** transfer of one's interest. —*v.* **2.** give up claim to.

quite (kwīt) *adv.* **1.** completely. **2.** really.

quits (kwits) *adj.* with no further payment or revenge due.

quit′tance (kwit′ns) *n.* **1.** requital. **2.** discharge from debt.

quiv′er (kwiv′ər) *v.* **1.** tremble. —*n.* **2.** trembling. **3.** case for arrows.

quix•ot′ic (kwik sot′ik) *adj.* extravagantly idealistic; impractical.

quiz (kwiz) *v.*, **quizzed, quizzing,** *n.*, *pl.* **quizzes.** —*v.* **1.** question. —*n.* **2.** informal questioning.

quiz′zi•cal, *adj.* **1.** comical. **2.** puzzled. —**quiz′zi•cal•ly,** *adv.*

quoin (koin, kwoin) *n.* **1.** external solid angle. **2.** cornerstone.

quoit (kwoit, koit) *n.* flat ring thrown to encircle peg in game of **quoits.**

quon′dam (kwon′dəm, -dam) *adj.* former.

quo′rum (kwôr′əm) *n.* number of members needed to transact business legally.

quo′ta (kwō′tə) *n.* proportional share due.

quote (kwōt) *v.*, **quoted, quoting,** *n.* —*v.* **1.** repeat verbatim. **2.** cite. **3.** state (price of). —*n.* **4.** *Informal.* quotation. —**quo•ta′tion,** *n.*

quo•tid′i•an (kwō tid′ē ən) *adj.* **1.** daily; everyday. **2.** ordinary.

quo′tient (kwō′shənt) *n.* *Math.* number of times one quantity is contained in another.

R

R, r (är) *n.* eighteenth letter of English alphabet.

R, motion-picture rating: those less than 17 years old must be accompanied by adult.

rab′bi (rab′ī) *n.* Jewish religious leader. —**rab•bin′ic** (rə bin′ik), **rab•bin′i•cal,** *adj.*

rab′bin•ate (rab′ə nit, -nāt′) *n.* **1.** office of a rabbi. **2.** rabbis collectively.

rab′bit (rab′it) *n.* small, long-eared mammal.

rab′ble (rab′əl) *n.* mob.

rab′ble-rous′er (-rou′zər) *n.* demagogue.

rab′id (rab′id) *adj.* **1.** irrationally intense. **2.** violent. **3.** having rabies.

ra′bies (rā′bēz) *n.* fatal disease transmitted by bite of infected animal.

rac•coon′ (ra kōōn′) *n.* small nocturnal carnivorous mammal.

race (rās) *n.*, *v.*, **raced, racing.** —*n.* **1.** contest of speed. **2.** onward course or flow. **3.** group of persons of common origin. **4.** any class or kind. —*v.* **5.** engage in race. **6.** move swiftly. —**rac′er,** *n.* —**ra′cial** (rā′shəl) *adj.*

rac′ism (rā′siz əm) *n.* hatred of or prejudice against another race.

rack (rak) *n.* **1.** structure for storage. **2.** toothed bar engaging with teeth of pinion. **3.** torture device. **4.** destruction. —*v.* **5.** torture. **6.** strain.

rack′et (rak′it) *n.* **1.** noise. **2.** illegal or dishonest business. **3.** Also, **rac′-quet.** netted bat used in tennis, etc.

rack•e•teer′, *n.* criminal engaged in racket.

rac′on•teur′ (rak′on tûr′, -tōōr′, -ən-) *n.* skilled storyteller.

ra•coon′ (ra kōōn′) *n.* raccoon.

rac′quet•ball′, *n.* game similar to handball, played with rackets on four-walled court.

rac′y (rā′sē) *adj.*, **-ier, -iest. 1.** lively. **2.** risqué. —**rac′i•ly,** *adv.*

ra′dar (rā′där) *n.* electronic device capable of locating unseen objects by radio wave.

ra′di•al (-dē əl) *adj.* of rays or radii.

ra′di•ant (-ənt) *adj.* **1.** emitting rays of light. **2.** bright; exultant. **3.** emitted in rays, as heat. —**ra′di•ance,** *n.* —**ra′di•ant•ly,** *adv.*

ra′di•ate′ (-āt′) *v.,* **-ated, -ating. 1.** spread like rays from center. **2.** emit or issue in rays. —**ra′di•a′tion,** *n.*

ra′di•a′tor, *n.* heating device.

rad′i•cal (rad′i kəl) *adj.* **1.** fundamental. **2.** favoring drastic reforms. —*n.* **3.** person with radical ideas. **4.** atom or group of atoms behaving as unit in chemical reaction. —**rad′i•cal•ism,** *n.* —**rad′i•cal•ly,** *adv.*

ra′di•o′ (rā′dē ō′) *n., pl.* **-dios. 1.** way of transmitting sound by electromagnetic waves, without wires. **2.** apparatus for sending or receiving such waves.

ra′di•o•ac′tive, *adj.* emitting radiation from the atomic nucleus. —**ra′di•o•ac•tiv′i•ty,** *n.*

ra′di•ol′o•gy (-ol′ə jē) *n.* use of radiation, as x-rays, for medical diagnosis and treatment.

rad′ish (rad′ish) *n.* crisp root of garden plant, eaten raw.

ra′di•um (rā′dē əm) *n.* radioactive metallic element.

ra′di•us (-əs) *n., pl.* **-dii** (-dē ī), **-diuses. 1.** straight line from center of a circle to circumference. **2.** one of the bones of the forearm.

ra′don (rā′don) *n.* inert gaseous element produced by decay of radium.

RAF, Royal Air Force.

raf′fi•a (raf′ē ə) *n.* fiber made from leafstalks of palm tree.

raff′ish (raf′ish) *adj.* **1.** jaunty; rakish. **2.** gaudily vulgar or cheap.

raf′fle (raf′əl) *n., v.,* **-fled, -fling.** —*n.* **1.** lottery in which chances are sold. —*v.* **2.** dispose of by raffle.

raft (raft) *n.* floating platform of logs.

raft′er (raf′tər) *n.* framing timber of roof.

rag (rag) *n.* worthless bit of cloth. —**rag′ged** (rag′id) *adj.*

ra′ga (rä′gə) *n., pl.* **-gas.** traditional melodic formula of Hindu music.

rag′a•muf′fin (rag′ə muf′in) *n.* ragged child.

rage (rāj) *n., v.,* **raged, raging.** —*n.* **1.** violent anger. **2.** object of popular enthusiasm. —*v.* **3.** be violently angry. **4.** prevail violently.

ra•gout′ (ra gōō′) *n.* stew.

rag′time′, *n.* style of jazz.

rag′weed′, *n.* plant whose pollen causes hay fever.

raid (rād) *n.* **1.** sudden assault or attack. —*v.* **2.** attack suddenly.

rail (rāl) *n.* **1.** horizontal bar used as barrier, support, etc. **2.** one of pair of railroad tracks. **3.** railroad as means of transport. **4.** wading bird. —*v.* **5.** complain bitterly.

rail′ing, *n.* barrier of rails and posts.

rail′ler•y (rā′lə rē) *n.* banter.

rail′road′, *n.* **1.** road with fixed rails on which trains run. —*v.* **2.** transport by means of a railroad. **3.** coerce into hasty action or decision.

rail′way′, *n. Chiefly Brit.* railroad.

rai′ment (rā′mənt) *n.* clothing.

rain (rān) *n.* **1.** water falling from sky in drops. **2.** rainfall. —*v.* **3.** fall or send down as rain. —**rain′y,** *adj.*

rain′bow′ (-bō′) *n.* arc of colors sometimes seen in sky opposite sun during rain.

rain check, 1. postponement of invitation. **2.** ticket for future admission to event postponed by rain.

rain′coat′, *n.* waterproof coat.

rain′fall′, *n.* amount of rain.

rain forest, tropical forest in area of high annual rainfall.

rain′mak′er, *n.* one who induces rain by artificial means.

raise (rāz) *v.,* **raised, raising,** *n.* —*v.* **1.** lift up. **2.** set upright. **3.** cause to appear. **4.** grow. **5.** collect. **6.** rear. **7.** cause (dough) to expand. **8.** end (siege). —*n.* **9.** increase, esp. in pay.

rai′sin (rā′zin) *n.* dried sweet grape.

rai′son d'ê′tre (rā′zōn de′trə) *n., pl.* **raisons d'être.** reason for existence.

ra′jah (rä′jə) *n.* (formerly) Indian king or prince.

rake (rāk) *n., v.,* **raked, raking.** —*n.* **1.** long-handled tool with teeth for gathering or smoothing ground. **2.** dissolute person. **3.** slope. —*v.* **4.** gather or smooth with rake. **5.** fire guns the length of (target).

rake′-off′, *n.* amount received, esp. illicitly.

rak′ish (rā′kish) *adj.* jaunty.

ral′ly (ral′ē) *v.,* **-lied, -lying,** *n., pl.* **-lies.** —*v.* **1.** bring into order again. **2.** call or come together. **3.** revive. **4.** come to aid. —*n.* **5.** sharp rise. **6.** renewal of strength. **7.** mass meeting.

ram (ram) *n., v.,* **rammed, ramming.** —*n.* **1.** male sheep. **2.** device for battering, forcing, etc. —*v.* **3.** strike forcibly.

RAM (ram) *n.* random-access memory: computer memory available for creating, loading, and running programs and temporarily storing data.

ram′ble, *v.,* **-bled, -bling,** —*v.* **1.** stroll idly. **2.** talk vaguely. —*n.* **3.** leisurely stroll. —**ram′bler,** *n.*

ram•bunc′tious (-bungk′shəs) *adj.* difficult to control or handle.

ram′i•fi•ca′tion (ram′ə fi kā′shən) *n.* consequence.

ram′i•fy′ (-ə fī′) *v.,* **-fied, -fying.** divide into branches.

ramp (ramp) *n.* sloping surface between two levels.

ram′page, *n., v.,* **-paged, -paging.** —*n.* (ram′pāj) **1.** violent behavior. —*v.* (ram pāj′) **2.** move furiously about.

ramp′ant (ram′pənt) *adj.* vigorous; unrestrained.

ram′part (-pärt, -pərt) *n.* mound of earth raised for defense.

ram′rod′, *n.* rod for cleaning or loading gun.

ram′shack′le, *adj.* rickety.

ranch (ranch) *n.* large farm, esp. for raising stock. —**ranch′er,** *n.*

ran′cid (ran′sid) *adj.* stale.

ran′cor (rang′kər) *n.* lasting resentment. —**ran′cor•ous,** *adj.*

rand (rand) *n., pl.* **rand.** monetary unit of South Africa.

ran′dom (ran′dəm) *adj.* occurring or done without aim or pattern.

rand′y (ran′dē) *adj.,* **-ier, -iest.** sexually aroused; lustful.

range (rānj) *n., v.,* **ranged, ranging.** —*n.* **1.** limits; extent. **2.** place for target shooting. **3.** distance between gun and target. **4.** row. **5.** mountain chain. **6.** grazing area. **7.** cooking stove. —*v.* **8.** arrange. **9.** pass over (area). **10.** vary.

rang′er (rān′jer) *n.* **1.** warden of forest tract. **2.** civil officer who patrols large area.

rang′y (rān′jē) *adj.,* **-ier, -iest.** slender and long-limbed.

rank (rangk) *n.* **1.** class, group, or standing. **2.** high position. **3.** row. **4.** (*pl.*) enlisted personnel. —*v.* **5.** arrange. **6.** be in particular rank. —*adj.* **7.** growing excessively. **8.** offensively

rank and file, 1. members apart from leaders. **2.** enlisted soldiers.

rank′ing, *adj.* **1.** senior. **2.** renowned.

ran′kle (rang′kəl) *v.,* **-kled, -kling.** irk.

ran′sack (ran′sak) *v.* search thoroughly.

ran′som (ran′səm) *n.* **1.** sum demanded for prisoner. —*v.* **2.** pay ransom for.

rant (rant) *v.* **1.** speak wildly. —*n.* **2.** violent speech. —**rant′er,** *n.*

rap (rap) *v.,* **rapped, rapping,** *n.* —*v.* **1.** strike quickly and sharply. —*n.* **2.** sharp blow. **3.** popular music marked by rhythmical intoning of rhymed verses over repetitive beat. —**rap′per,** *n.*

ra•pa′cious (rə pā′shəs) *adj.* predatory; greedy.

rape (rāp) *n., v.,* **raped, raping.** —*n.* **1.** forcing of sexual intercourse on someone. **2.** abduction or seizure. **3.** plant grown as forage and for its oil. —*v.* **4.** commit rape on. **5.** abduct or seize. —**rap′ist,** *n.*

rap′id (rap′id) *adj.* **1.** swift. —*n.* **2.** (*pl.*) swift-moving part of river. —**ra•pid′i•ty,** *n.* —**rap′id•ly,** *adv.*

ra′pi•er (rā′pē ər) *n.* slender sword.

rap′ine (rap′in) *n.* plunder.

rap•port′ (ra pôr′) *n.* sympathetic relationship.

rap•proche•ment′ (rap′rōsh män′) *n.* establishment of harmonious relations.

rap sheet, *Slang.* record of person's arrests and convictions.

rapt (rapt) *adj.* engrossed.

rap′ture (rap′chər) *n.* ecstatic joy. —**rap′tur•ous,** *adj.*

rare (râr) *adj.,* **rarer, rarest. 1.** unusual. **2.** thin. **3.** (of meat) not thoroughly cooked. —**rar′i•ty,** *n.*

rare′bit (râr′bit) *n.* dish of melted cheese.

rar′e•fy′ (râr′ə fī′) *v.,* **-fied, -fying.** make or become thin, as air.

rar′ing, *adj.* very eager or anxious.

ras′cal (ras′kəl) *n.* dishonest person.

rash (rash) *adj.* **1.** thoughtlessly hasty. —*n.* **2.** skin eruption.

rash′er, *n.* thin slice of bacon.

rasp (rasp) *v.* **1.** scrape, as with file. **2.** irritate. **3.** speak gratingly. —*n.* **4.** coarse file. **5.** rasping sound. —**rasp′y,** *adj.*

rasp′ber′ry (raz′ber′ē, -bə rē) *n., pl.* **-ries.** small juicy red or black fruit.

rat (rat) *n.* rodent larger than a mouse.

ratch′et (rach′it) *n.* wheel or bar with teeth.

rate (rāt) *n., v.,* **rated, rating.** —*n.* **1.** charge in proportion to something that varies. **2.** degree of speed, etc. —*v.* **3.** estimate or fix rate. **4.** consider; judge.

rath′er (rath′ər) *adv.* **1.** somewhat. **2.** in preference. **3.** on the contrary.

raths′kel•ler (rät′skel′ər, rat′-) *n.* restaurant or bar below street level.

rat′i•fy′ (rat′ə fī′) *v.,* **-fied, -fying.** confirm formally.

ra′tio (rā′shō, -shē ō′) *n., pl.* **-tios.** relative number or extent; proportion.

ra′ti•oc′i•na′tion (rash′ē os′ə nā′shən) *n.* reasoning.

ra′tion (rash′ən, rā′shən) *n.* **1.** fixed allowance. —*v.* **2.** apportion. **3.** put on ration.

ra′tion•al (rash′ə nl) *adj.* **1.** sensible. **2.** sane. —**ra′tion•al′i•ty,** *n.*

ra′tion•ale′ (-nal′) *n.* reasonable basis for action.

ra′tion•al•ism, *n.* advocacy of precise reasoning as source of truth. —ra′tion•al•ist, *n.*

ra′tion•al•ize′ (rash′ə nə līz′) *v.,* -ized, -izing. 1. find reason for one's behavior or attitude. 2. make rational.

rat race, exhausting, competitive routine activity.

rat•tan′ (ra tan′, rə-) *n.* hollow stem of climbing palm used for wickerwork.

rat′tle (rat′l) *v.,* -tled, -tling. —*v.* 1. make series of short sharp sounds. 2. chatter. 3. *Informal.* disconcert. —*n.* 4. sound of rattling. 5. child's toy that rattles.

rat′tle•snake′, *n.* venomous American snake.

rat′ty, *adj.,* -tier, -tiest. shabby.

rau′cous (rô′kas) *adj.* 1. hoarse; harsh. 2. rowdy; disorderly.

raun′chy (rôn′chē, rän′-) *adj.* -chier, -chiest. 1. vulgar; smutty. 2. lecherous. 3. dirty; slovenly.

rav′age (rav′ij) *n., v.,* -aged, -aging. ruin. —rav′ag•er, *n.*

rave (rāv) *v.,* raved, raving. talk wildly.

rav′el (rav′əl) *v.* 1. disengage threads. 2. tangle. 3. make clear. —*n.* 4. tangle. 5. disengaged thread.

ra′ven (rā′vən) *n.* large shiny black bird.

rav′en•ing (rav′ə ning) *adj.* greedy for prey.

rav′en•ous, *adj.* very hungry; greedy. —rav′en•ous•ly, *adv.*

ra•vine′ (rə vēn′) *n.* deep, narrow valley.

ra′vi•o′li (rav′ē ō′lē) *n.* small pockets of pasta filled esp. with cheese or meat.

rav′ish (rav′ish) *v.* 1. fill with joy. 2. rape.

rav′ish•ing, *adj.* extremely beautiful.

raw (rô) *adj.* 1. in the natural state. 2. uncooked. 3. open. 4. untrained. —*n.* 5. raw condition or substance.

raw′boned′, *adj.* lean and bony.

raw′hide′, *n.* untanned hide, as of cattle.

ray (rā) *n.* 1. narrow beam of light. 2. trace. 3. line outward from center. 4. flat-bodied deep-sea fish.

ray′on (rā′on) *n.* silklike synthetic fabric.

raze (rāz) *v.,* razed, razing. demolish.

ra′zor (rā′zər) *n.* sharp-edged instrument for shaving.

R.C., Roman Catholic.

rd., road.

re, *n.* (rā) 1. *Music.* second tone of scale. —*prep.* (rē) 2. with reference to.

re-, prefix indicating; 1. repetition, as *reprint, rearm.* 2. withdrawal.

reach (rēch) *v.* 1. come to. 2. be able to touch. 3. extend. —*n.* 4. act of reaching. 5. extent.

re•act′ (rē akt′) *v.* 1. act upon each other. 2. respond.

re•ac′tant (-ak′tənt) *n.* substance that undergoes change in chemical reaction.

re•ac′tion, *n.* 1. extreme political conservatism. 2. responsive action. 3. chemical change. —re•ac′tion•ar′y, *n., adj.*

re•ac′tor, *n.* 1. one that reacts. 2. apparatus for producing useful nuclear energy.

read (rēd) *v.,* read (red), reading. 1. observe and understand (printed matter, etc.). 2. register. 3. utter aloud (something written or printed). 4. obtain and store, as in computer memory. —read′er, *n.* —read′er•ship′, *n.*

read′ing (rē′ding) *n.* 1. something read. 2. interpretation of written or

musical work. 3. data indicated on instrument.

read′-on′ly (rēd) *adj.* noting computer files or memory that can be read but not changed.

read′y (red′ē) *adj.,* readier, readiest, *v.,* readied, readying, *n.* —*adj.* 1. fully prepared. 2. willing. 3. apt. —*v.* 4. make ready. —*n.* 5. state of being ready. —read′i•ly, *adv.* —read′i•ness, *n.*

read′y-made′, *adj.* ready for use when bought.

re•a′gent (rē ā′jənt) *n.* chemical used in analysis and synthesis.

re′al (rē′əl, rēl) *adj.* 1. actual. 2. genuine. 3. denoting immovable property. —re•al′i•ty (-al′i tē), re′al•ness, *n.* —re′al•ly, *adv.*

real estate, land with buildings, etc., on it. Also, re′al•ty.

re′al•ism, *n.* 1. tendency to see things as they really are. 2. representation of things as they really are. —re′al•ist, *n.* —re′al•is′tic, *adj.* —re′al•is′ti•cal•ly, *adv.*

re′al•ize′, *v.,* -ized, -izing. 1. understand clearly. 2. make real. 3. get as profit. —re′al•i•za′tion, *n.*

realm (relm) *n.* 1. kingdom. 2. special field.

ream (rēm) *n.* twenty quires of paper.

reap (rēp) *v.* harvest. —reap′er, *n.*

rear (rēr) *n.* 1. back part. —*adj.* 2. of or at rear. —*v.* 3. care for to maturity. 4. raise; erect. 5. rise on hind legs.

rear admiral, naval officer above captain.

re•arm′ (rē ärm′) *v.* arm again. —re•arm′a•ment, *n.*

rear′most′, *adj.* farthest back.

rear′ward (-wərd) *adv.* 1. Also, rear′wards. toward the rear. —*adj.* 2. located in the rear.

rea′son (rē′zən) *n.* 1. cause for belief, act, etc. 2. sound judgment. 3. sanity. —*v.* 4. think or argue logically. 5. infer. —rea′son•ing, *n.*

rea′son•a•ble (rē′zə nə bəl, rēz′nə-) *adj.* showing sound judgment.

re•as•sure′ (rē′ə shŏor′, -shûr′) *v.,* -sured, -suring. restore confidence of. —re′as•sur′ance, *n.*

re•bate′, *v.,* -bated, -bating. —*v.* (rē′bāt, *also* ri bāt′) 1. return (part of amount paid). —*n.* (rē′bāt) 2. amount rebated.

re•bel′, *v.,* -belled, -belling. —*v.* (ri bel′) 1. rise in arms against one's government. 2. resist any authority. —*n.* (reb′əl) 3. one who rebels. —re•bel′lion, *n.* —re•bel′lious, *adj.* —re•bel′lious•ly, *adv.*

re•bound′, *v.* (ri bound′) 1. bound back after impact. —*n.* (rē′bound′) 2. act of rebounding.

re•buff′ (ri buf′) *n.* 1. blunt check or refusal. —*v.* 2. check; repel.

re•buke′ (ri byŏŏk′) *v.,* -buked, -buking. 1. reprimand.

re′bus (rē′bəs) *n.* puzzle in which pictures and symbols combine to represent a word.

re•but′ (ri but′) *v.,* -butted, -butting. refute. —re•but′tal, *n.*

re•cal′ci•trant (ri kal′si trənt) *adj.* resisting control.

re•call′, *v.* (ri kôl′) 1. remember. 2. call back. 3. withdraw. —*n.* (rē′kôl) 4. act of recalling.

re•cant′ (ri kant′) *v.* retract.

re•cap′ (rē′kap′, *n.,* *v.,* -capped, -capping. —*n.* 1. recapitulation. 2. tire reconditioned by adding strip of new rubber. —*v.* 3. recapitulate. 4. recondition a tire.

re•ca•pit′u•late (rē′kə pich′ə lāt′) *v.,* -lated, -lating. review; sum up.

re•cap′ture, *v.,* -tured, -turing, *n.* —*v.* 1. capture again. 2. experience again. —*n.* 3. recovery by capture.

recd. or rec′d., received.

re•cede′ (ri sēd′) *v.,* -ceded, -ceding. move or appear to move back.

re•ceipt′ (ri sēt′) *n.* 1. written acknowledgment of receiving. 2. (*pl.*) amount received. 3. act of receiving.

re•ceive′, *v.,* -ceived, -ceiving. 1. take (something offered or delivered). 2. experience. 3. welcome (guests). 4. accept.

re•ceiv′er, *n.* 1. one that receives. 2. device that receives electrical signals and converts them. 3. person put in charge of property in litigation. —re•ceiv′er•ship′, *n.*

re′cent (rē′sənt) *adj.* happening, etc., lately. —re′cent•ly, *adv.*

re•cep′ta•cle (ri sep′tə kəl) *n.* container.

re•cep′tion (ri sep′shən) *n.* 1. act of receiving. 2. fact or manner of being received. 3. social function.

re•cep′tion•ist, *n.* person who receives callers in an office.

re•cep′tive (-tiv) *adj.* quick to understand and consider ideas.

re•cep′tor (-tər) *n.* nerve ending that is sensitive to stimuli.

re•cess′ (ri ses′, rē′ses) *n.* 1. temporary cessation of work. 2. alcove. 3. (*pl.*) inner part. —*v.* 4. take or make recess.

re•ces′sion (-sesh′ən) *n.* 1. withdrawal. 2. economic decline.

re•ces′sive (-ses′iv) *adj.* receding.

re•cher′ché (rə shâr′shā, rə shâr′shā′) *adj.* 1. very rare or choice. 2. affectedly refined.

re•cid′i•vism (ri sid′ə viz′əm) repeated or habitual relapse, as into crime. —re•cid′i•vist, *n., adj.*

rec′i•pe (res′ə pē) *n.* formula, esp. in cookery.

re•cip′i•ent (ri sip′ē ənt) *n.* 1. receiver. —*adj.* 2. receiving.

re•cip′ro•cal (ri sip′rə kəl) *adj.* 1. mutual. 2. thing in reciprocal position. —re•cip′ro•cal•ly, *adv.*

re•cip′ro•cate′ (-kāt′) *v.,* -cated, -cating. 1. give, feel, etc., in return. 2. move alternately backward and forward. —re•cip′ro•ca′tion, *n.*

rec′i•proc′i•ty (res′ə pros′i tē) *n.* interchange.

re•cit′al (ri sīt′l) *n.* musical entertainment.

rec′i•ta•tive′ (res′i tə tēv′) *n.* style of vocal music intermediate between speaking and singing.

re•cite′ (ri sīt′) *v.,* -cited, -citing. 1. repeat from memory. 2. narrate. —rec′i•ta′tion (res′i tā′shən) *n.*

reck′less (rek′lis) *adj.* careless.

reck′on (rek′ən) *v.* 1. calculate. 2. regard; as esteem. 3. *Informal.* suppose. 4. deal (with).

reck′on•ing, *n.* 1. settling of accounts. 2. navigational calculation.

re•claim′ (rē klām′) *v.* make usable, as land. —rec′la•ma′tion (rek′-lə mā′shən) *n.*

re•cline′ (ri klīn′) *v.,* -clined, -clining. lean back.

re•clin′er, *n.* chair with adjustable back and footrest.

rec′luse (rek′lōōs, ri klōōs′) *n.* person living in seclusion.

re•cog′ni•zance (ri kog′nə zəns, -kon′ə-) *n.* bond pledging one to do a particular act.

rec′og•nize′ (rek′əg nīz′) *v.,* -nized, -nizing. 1. identify or perceive from previous knowledge. **2.** acknowledge formally. **3.** greet. —**rec′og·ni′tion** (-nish′ən) *n.*

re·coil′ (rē koil′) *v.* **1.** shrink back. **2.** spring back. —*n.* **3.** act of recoiling.

rec′ol·lect′ (rek′ə lekt′) *v.* remember. —**rec′ol·lec′tion,** *n.*

rec′om·mend′ (rek′ə mend′) *v.* **1.** present as worthy. **2.** advise. —**rec′om·men·da′tion,** *n.*

rec′om·pense′ (rek′əm pens′) *v.,* -pensed, -pensing, *n.* —*v.* **1.** repay or reward for services, injury, etc. —*n.* **2.** such compensation.

rec′on·cile′ (rek′ən sīl′) *v.,* -ciled, -ciling. **1.** bring into agreement. **2.** restore to friendliness. —**rec′on·cil′i·a′tion** (-sil′ē ā′shən) *n.*

rec′on·dite (rek′ən dīt′) *adj.* **1.** very profound, difficult, or abstruse. **2.** known by a few; esoteric.

re·con′nais·sance (ri kon′ə səns, -zəns), *n.* survey of enemy territory.

re′con·noi′ter (rē′kə noi′tər, rek′ə-) *v.* search area, esp. for military information.

re·cord′ *v.* (ri kôrd′) **1.** set down in writing. **2.** register for mechanical reproduction. —*n.* (rek′ərd) **3.** what is recorded. **4.** object from which sound is reproduced. **5.** best rate, etc., yet attained. —*adj.* (rek′ərd) **6.** making or being a record. —**re·cord′ing,** *n.*

re·cord′er, *n.* **1.** person who records. **2.** recording device. **3.** flute with eight finger holes.

re·count′ *v.* (rē kount′) **1.** narrate. **2.** count again. —*n.* (rē′kount′) **3.** a second count.

re·coup′ (ri kōōp′) *v.* recover; make up.

re′course (rē′kôrs, ri kôrs′) *n.* resort for help.

re·cov′er (ri kuv′ər) *v.* **1.** get back. **2.** reclaim. **3.** regain health. —**re·cov′er·a·ble,** *adj.* —**recov′er·y,** *n.*

re′-cre·ate′ (rē′krē āt′) *v.,* -created, -creating. create anew.

rec′re·a′tion, *n.* refreshing enjoyment. —**rec′re·a′tion·al,** *adj.*

re·crim′i·nate′ (ri krim′ə nāt′) *v.,* -nated, -nating. accuse in return. —**re·crim′i·na′tion,** *n.*

re·cruit′ (ri krōōt′) *n.* **1.** new member of military or other group. —*v.* **2.** enlist. —**re·cruit′ment,** *n.*

rec′tan·gle (rek′tang′gəl) *n.* parallelogram with four right angles. —**rec·tan′gu·lar** (-tang′gyə lər) *adj.*

rec′ti·fy′ (rek′tə fī′) *v.,* -fied, -fying. correct. —**rec′ti·fi′a·ble,** *adj.* —**rec′ti·fi·ca′tion,** *n.*

rec′ti·lin′e·ar (rek′tl in′ē ər) *adj.* **1.** forming straight line. **2.** formed by straight lines.

rec′ti·tude (rek′ti tōōd′, -tyōōd′) *n.* moral rightness.

rec′tor (rek′tər) *n.* **1.** member of clergy in charge of parish, etc. **2.** head of university, etc.

rec′to·ry, *n., pl.* -ries. parsonage.

rec′tum (rek′təm) *n.* lowest part of intestine. —**rec′tal,** *adj.*

re·cum′bent (ri kum′bənt) *adj.* lying down. —**re·cum′ben·cy,** *n.*

re·cu′per·ate′ (ri kōō′pə rāt′) *v.,* -ated, -ating. regain health. —**re·cu′per·a′tion,** *n.*

re·cur′ (ri kûr′) *v.,* -curred, -curring. **1.** occur again. **2.** return in thought, etc. —**re·cur′rence,** *n.* —**re·cur′rent,** *adj.*

re·cy′cle (rē sī′kəl) *v.,* -cled, -cling. treat (refuse) to extract reusable material.

red (red) *n., adj.,* **redder, reddest.** —*n.* **1.** color of blood. **2.** leftist radical

in politics. —*adj.* **3.** of or like red. **4.** radically to left in politics. —**red′den,** *v.* —**red′dish,** *adj.*

red blood cell, blood cell that contains hemoglobin and carries oxygen to cells and tissues.

red′cap′, *n.* baggage porter.

re·deem′ (ri dēm′) *v.* **1.** pay off. **2.** recover. **3.** fulfill. **4.** deliver from sin by sacrifice. —**re·deem′er,** *n.* —**re·demp′tion** (-demp′shən) *n.*

red′-hand′ed, *adj., adv.* in the act of wrongdoing.

red′head′, *n.* person with red hair. —**red′head′ed,** *adj.*

red herring, something intended to distract attention from the real problem or issue.

red′-hot′, *adj.* **1.** red with heat. **2.** violent; furious. **3.** very fresh or new.

red′-let′ter, *adj.* memorable.

red·lin′ing, *n.* refusal by banks to grant mortgages in specified urban areas.

red′o·lent (red′l ənt) *adj.* **1.** odorous. **2.** suggestive.

re·doubt′ (ri dout′) *n.* small isolated fort.

re·doubt′a·ble, *adj.* evoking fear or respect.

re·dound′ (ri dound′) *v.* occur as result.

re·dress′, *v.* (ri dress′) **1.** set right (a wrong). —*n.* (rē′dres) **2.** act of redressing.

red tape, excessive attention to prescribed procedure.

re·duce′ (ri dōōs′, -dyōōs′) *v.,* -duced, -ducing. **1.** make less in size, rank, etc. **2.** put into simpler form or state. **3.** remove weight. —**re·duc′i·ble,** *adj.* —**re·duc′tion** (-duk′shən) *n.*

re·dun′dant (ri dun′dənt) *adj.* **1.** excessive. **2.** wordy. —**re·dun′dance, re·dun′dan·cy,** *n.*

red′wood′ (red′wŏŏd′) *n.* huge evergreen tree of California.

reed (rēd) *n.* **1.** tall marsh grass. **2.** small piece of cane or metal at mouth of wind instrument. —**reed′y,** *adj.*

reef (rēf) *n.* narrow ridge near the surface of water.

reef′er, *n.* **1.** short heavy coat. **2.** *Slang.* marijuana cigarette.

reek (rēk) *v.* **1.** smell strongly and unpleasantly. —*n.* **2.** such smell.

reel (rēl) *n.* **1.** turning object for wound cord, film, etc. **2.** lively dance. —*v.* **3.** wind on reel. **4.** tell easily and at length. **5.** sway or stagger. **6.** whirl.

re·en′try (rē en′trē) *n., pl.* -tries. **1.** second entry. **2.** return into earth's atmosphere.

ref (ref) *n., v.* referee.

re·fec′to·ry (ri fek′tə rē) *n., pl.* -ries. dining hall.

re·fer′ (ri fûr′) *v.,* -ferred, -ferring. **1.** direct attention. **2.** direct or go for information. **3.** apply. —**re·fer′ral,** *n.*

ref′er·ee′ (ref′ə rē′) *n.* **1.** judge. —*v.* **2.** act as referee.

ref′er·ence (ref′ər əns) *n.* **1.** act or fact of referring. **2.** something referred to. **3.** person from whom one seeks recommendation. **4.** testimonial.

ref′er·en′dum (ref′ə ren′dəm) *n., pl.* -dums, -da. submission to popular vote of law passed by legislature.

re·fill′ *v.* (rē fil′) **1.** fill again. —*n.* (rē′fil′) **2.** second filling.

re·fine′ (ri fīn′) *v.,* -fined, -fining. **1.** free from impurities or error. **2.** teach good manners, taste, etc. —**re·fin′er,** *n.* —**re·fine′ment,** *n.*

re·fin′er·y, *n., pl.* -eries. establishment for refining, esp. petroleum.

re·flect′ (ri flekt′) *v.* **1.** cast back. **2.** show; mirror. **3.** bring (credit or discredit) on one. **4.** think. —**re·flec′tion,** *n.* —**re·flec′tive,** *adj.* —**re·flec′tor,** *n.*

re′flex (rē′fleks) *adj.* **1.** denoting involuntary action. **2.** bent. —*n.* **3.** involuntary movement.

re·flex′ive, *adj.* **1.** (of verb) having same subject and object. **2.** (of pronoun) showing identity with subject.

re·for′est (rē fôr′ist) *v.* replant with forest trees. —**re′for·est·a′tion,** *n.*

re·form′ (rē fôrm′) *n.* **1.** correction of what is wrong. —*v.* **2.** change for better. —**re·form′er,** *n.* —**ref′or·ma′tion** (ref′ər mā′shən) *n.*

re·form′a·to·ry (ri fôr′mə tôr′ē) *n., pl.* -ries. prison for young offenders.

re·frac′tion (ri frak′shən) *n.* change of direction of light or heat rays in passing to another medium. —**re·fract′,** *v.* —**re·frac′tive,** *adj.*

re·frac′to·ry, *adj.* stubborn.

re·frain′ (ri frān′) *v.* **1.** keep oneself (from). —*n.* **2.** recurring passage in song, etc.

re·fresh′ (ri fresh′) *v.* **1.** reinvigorate. **2.** stimulate. —**re·fresh′ment,** *n.* —**re·fresh′ing,** *adj.*

re·frig′er·ate′ (ri frij′ə rāt′) *v.,* -ated, -ating. make or keep cold. —**re·frig′er·ant** (-ə rant) *adj., n.* —**re·frig′er·a′tion,** *n.*

re·frig′er·a′tor, *n.* cabinet for keeping food cold.

ref′uge (ref′yōōj) *n.* shelter from danger.

ref′u·gee′ (ref′yŏŏ jē′) *n.* person who flees for safety.

re·ful′gent (ri ful′jənt) *adj.* shining brightly; radiant. —**re·ful′gence,** *n.*

re·fund′, *v.* (ri fund′) **1.** give back (money). —*n.* (rē′fund) **2.** repayment. —**re·fund′a·ble,** *adj.*

re·fur′bish (rē fûr′bish) *v.* renovate.

re·fuse′, *v.,* -fused, -fusing. —*v.* (ri fyōōz′) **1.** decline to accept. **2.** deny (request). —*n.* (ref′yōōs) **3.** rubbish. —**re·fus′al,** *n.*

re·fute′ (ri fyōōt′) *v.,* -futed, -futing. prove wrong. —**ref′u·ta′tion,** *n.*

re·gain′ (rē gān′) *v.* get again.

re′gal (rē′gəl) *adj.* royal.

re·gale′ (ri gāl′) *v.,* -galed, -galing. **1.** entertain grandly. **2.** feast.

re·ga′lia (-gāl′yə) *n.pl.* emblems of royalty, office, etc.

re·gard′ (-gärd′) *v.* **1.** look upon with particular feeling. **2.** respect. **3.** look at. **4.** concern. —*n.* **5.** reference. **6.** attention. **7.** respect and liking.

re·gard′ing, *prep.* concerning.

re·gard′less, *adv.* **1.** without regard; in spite of. —*adj.* **2.** heedless.

re·gat′ta (ri gat′ə, -gä′tə) *n.* organized series of boat races.

re·gen′er·ate′, *v.,* -ated, -ating, *adj.* —*v.* (ri jen′ə rāt′) **1.** make over for the better. **2.** form anew. —*adj.* (-ər it) **3.** regenerated. —**re·gen′er·a′tion,** *n.* —**re·gen′er·a·tive,** *adj.*

re′gent (rē′jənt) *n.* **1.** person ruling in place of sovereign. **2.** university governor. —**re′gen·cy,** *n.*

reg′gae (reg′ā) *n.* Jamaican music blending blues, calypso, and rock.

reg′i·cide (rej′ə sīd′) *n.* killing of king.

re·gime′ (rə zhēm′, rā-) *n.* system of rule.

reg′i·men (rej′ə mən) *n.* **1.** course of diet, etc., for health. **2.** rule.

reg′i·ment, *n.* (rej′ə mənt) **1.** infantry unit. —*v.* (rej′ə ment′) **2.** subject to strict, uniform discipline. —**reg′i·men′tal,** *adj.*

re′gion (rē′jən) *n.* area; district. —**re′gion·al,** *adj.*

re′gion·al·ism, *n.* feature peculiar to geographical region.

reg′is·ter (rej′ə stər) *n.* **1.** written list; record. **2.** range of voice or instrument. **3.** device for controlling passage of warm air. —*v.* **4.** enter in register. **5.** show. **6.** enter oneself on list of voters. —**reg′is·tra′tion** (-strā′shən) *n.*

reg′is·trar′ (-strär′) *n.* official recorder.

reg′is·try, *n., pl.* **-tries. 1.** registration. **2.** place where register is kept. **3.** register.

re·gress′ (ri gres′) *v.* return to previous, inferior state. —**re·gres′sion,** *n.* —**re·gres′sive,** *adj.*

re·gret′ (ri gret′) *v.,* **-gretted, -gretting,** *n.* —*v.* **1.** feel sorry about. —*n.* **2.** feeling of loss or sorrow. —**re·gret′ta·ble,** *adj.* —**re·gret′ful,** *adj.*

re·group′ (rē grōōp′) *v.* form into new group.

reg′u·lar (reg′yə lər) *adj.* **1.** usual. **2.** symmetrical. **3.** recurring at fixed times. **4.** orderly. **5.** denoting permanent army. —*n.* **6.** regular soldier. —**reg′u·lar′i·ty,** *n.* —**reg′u·lar·ize′,** *v.,* **-ized, -izing.**

reg′u·late′ (-lāt′) *v.,* **-lated, -lating. 1.** control by rule, method, etc. **2.** adjust. —**reg′u·la′tion,** *n.* —**reg′u·la·to′ry** (-lə tôr′ē) *adj.*

reg′u·la′tion, *n.* **1.** act of regulating. **2.** rule.

re·gur′gi·tate′ (ri gûr′ji tāt′) *v.,* **-tated, -tating.** bring back from stomach. —**re·gur′gi·ta′tion,** *n.*

re′ha·bil′i·tate′ (rē′hə bil′i tāt′, rē′ə-) *v.,* **-tated, -tating.** restore to good condition. —**re′ha·bil′i·ta′tion,** *n.*

re·hash′, *v.* (rē hash′) **1.** rework or reuse in new form without significant change. —*n.* (rē′hash′) **2.** act of rehashing. **3.** something rehashed.

re·hearse′ (ri hûrs′) *v.,* **-hearsed, -hearsing. 1.** act or direct in practice for performance. **2.** recount in detail. —**re·hears′al,** *n.*

reign (rān) *n.* **1.** royal rule. —*v.* **2.** have sovereign power or title.

re′im·burse′ (rē′im bûrs′) *v.,* **-bursed, -bursing.** repay, as for expenses. —**re′im·burse′ment,** *n.*

rein (rān) *n.* narrow strap fastened to bridle for controlling animal.

re′in·car·na′tion (rē′in kär nā′shən) *n.* continuation of soul after death in new body.

rein′deer′ (rān′dēr′) *n.* large arctic deer.

re′in·force′ (rē′in fôrs′) *v.,* **-forced, -forcing.** strengthen with support, troops, etc. —**re′in·force′ment,** *n.*

re′in·state′ (rē′in stāt′) *v.,* **-stated, -stating.** put back into former position or state. —**re′in·state′ment,** *n.*

re·it′er·ate′ (rē it′ə rāt′) *v.,* **-ated, -ating.** repeat. —**re·it′er·a′tion,** *n.*

re·ject′, *v.* (ri jekt′) **1.** refuse or discard. —*n.* (rē′jekt) **2.** something rejected. —**re·jec′tion,** *n.*

re·joice′ (ri jois′) *v.,* **-joiced, -joicing.** be or make glad.

re·join′ (-join′) *v.* **1.** answer. **2.** join again.

re·join′der (-dər) *n.* response.

re·ju′ve·nate′ (ri jōō′və nāt′) *v.,* **-nated, -nating.** make young again.

re·lapse′, *v.,* **-lapsed, -lapsing.** —*v.* (ri laps′) **1.** fall back into former state or practice. —*n.* (ri laps′, rē′laps) **2.** act or instance of relapsing.

re·late′ (ri lāt′) *v.,* **-lated, -lating. 1.** tell. **2.** establish or have relation.

re·lat′ed, *adj.* **1.** associated. **2.** connected by blood or marriage.

re·la′tion, *n.* **1.** connection. **2.** relative. **3.** narrative. —**re·la′tion·ship′,** *n.*

rel′a·tive (rel′ə tiv) *n.* **1.** person connected with another by blood or marriage. —*adj.* **2.** comparative. **3.** designating word that introduces subordinate clause.

relative humidity, ratio of water vapor in the air at a given temperature to the amount the air could hold.

rel′a·tiv′i·ty, *n.* principle that time, mass, etc. are relative, not absolute concepts.

re·lax′ (ri laks′) *v.* **1.** make or become less tense, firm, etc. **2.** slacken. —**re′lax·a′tion** (rē′lak sā′shən) *n.*

re′lay (rē′lā) *n.* **1.** fresh supply of persons, etc., to relieve others. —*v.* **2.** carry forward by relays.

re·lease′ (ri lēs′) *v.,* **-leased, -leasing,** *n.* —*v.* **1.** let go; discharge. —*n.* **2.** act or instance of releasing.

rel′e·gate′ (rel′i gāt′) *v.,* **-gated, -gating. 1.** consign to inferior position. **2.** turn over.

re·lent′ (ri lent′) *v.* become more mild or forgiving. —**re·lent′less,** *adj.*

rel′e·vant (rel′ə vənt) *adj.* having to do with matter in question.

re·li′a·ble (ri lī′ə bəl) *adj.* trustworthy. —**re·li′a·bil′i·ty,** *n.*

re·li′ance (-əns) *n.* **1.** trust. **2.** confidence. —**re·li′ant,** *adj.*

rel′ic (rel′ik) *n.* **1.** object surviving from past. **2.** personal memorial of sacred person.

re·lief′ (ri lēf′) *n.* **1.** alleviation of pain, distress, etc. **2.** help. **3.** pleasant change. **4.** projection.

re·lieve′ (ri lēv′) *v.,* **-lieved, -lieving. 1.** ease. **2.** break sameness of. **3.** discharge from duty.

re·li′gion (ri lij′ən) *n.* **1.** spiritual recognition and worship. **2.** particular system of religious belief. —**re·li′gious,** *adj.* —**re·li′gious·ly,** *adv.*

re·lin′quish (ri ling′kwish) *v.* give up; surrender.

rel′i·quar′y (rel′i kwer′ē) *n., pl.* **-ies.** receptacle for religious relics.

rel′ish (rel′ish) *n.* **1.** enjoyment. **2.** chopped pickles, etc. —*v.* **3.** take enjoyment in.

re·live′ (rē liv′) *v.,* **-lived, -living.** experience again.

re·lo′cate (rē lō′kāt) *v.,* **-cated, -cating.** move. —**re·lo·ca′tion,** *n.*

re·luc′tant (ri luk′tənt) *adj.* unwilling. —**re·luc′tance,** *n.*

re·ly′ (ri lī′) *v.,* **-lied, -lying.** put trust in.

REM (rem) *n.* quick, darting movement of eyes during sleep.

re·main′ (ri mān′) *v.* **1.** continue to be. **2.** stay; be left. —*n.pl.* **3.** that which remains. **4.** corpse.

re·main′der (-dər) *n.* that which is left over.

re·mand′ (ri mand′) *v.* send back, as to jail or lower court of law.

re·mark′ (ri märk′) *v.* **1.** say casually. **2.** perceive; observe. —*n.* **3.** casual comment. **4.** notice.

re·mark′a·ble, *adj.* extraordinary.

rem′e·dy (rem′i dē) *n., pl.* **-dies.** —*v.* **-died, -dying. 1.** cure or alleviate. **2.** correct. —*n.* **3.** something that remedies. —**re·me′di·al,** *adj.*

re·mem′ber (ri mem′bər) *v.* **1.** recall to or retain in memory. **2.** mention as sending greetings. —**re·mem′brance** (-brəns) *n.*

re·mind′ (ri mīnd′) *v.* cause to remember. —**re·mind′er,** *n.*

rem′i·nisce′ (rem′ə nis′) *v.,* **-nisced, -niscing.** recall past experiences. —**rem′i·nis′cence,** *n.* —**rem′i·nis′cent,** *adj.*

re·miss′ (ri mis′) *adj.* negligent.

re·mis′sion, *n.* **1.** act of forgiving. **2.** period when symptoms of disease subside.

re·mit′ (-mit′) *v.,* **-mitted, -mitting. 1.** send money. **2.** pardon. **3.** abate.

re·mit′tance, *n.* money, etc., sent.

rem′nant (rem′nənt) *n.* **1.** small remaining part. **2.** trace.

re·mod′el (rē mod′l) *v.,* **-eled, -eling.** alter structure or form.

re·mon′strate (ri mon′strāt) *v.,* **-strated, -strating.** protest; plead in protest.

re·morse′ (ri môrs′) *n.* regret for wrongdoing. —**re·morse′ful,** *adj.* —**re·morse′less,** *adj.*

re·mote′ (ri mōt·) *adj.* **1.** far distant. **2.** faint. —*n.* **3.** remote control (def. 2). —**re·mote′ly,** *adv.*

remote control, 1. control of an apparatus from a distance, as by radio signals. **2.** Also, **remote.** device used for such control.

re·move′ (ri mōōv′) *v.,* **-moved, -moving,** *n.* —*v.* **1.** take away or off. **2.** move to another place. —*n.* **3.** distance of separation. —**re·mov′al,** *n.*

re·mu′ner·ate′ (ri myōō′nə rāt′) *v.,* **-ated, -ating.** pay for work, etc. —**re·mu′ner·a′tion,** *n.*

ren·ais′sance′ (ren′ə säns′) *n.* **1.** revival. **2.** (*cap.*) cultural period of the 14th-17th century marked by interest in culture of antiquity.

re′nal (rēn′l) *adj.* of the kidneys.

rend (rend) *v.* **1.** tear apart. **2.** disturb with noise. **3.** distress.

ren′der, *v.* **1.** cause to be. **2.** do, show, or furnish. **3.** perform. **4.** give back. **5.** melt (fat). —**ren·di′tion** (-dish′ən) *n.*

ren′dez·vous′ (rän′də vōō′, -dā-) *n., pl.* **-vous.** appointment or place to meet.

ren′e·gade′ (ren′i gād′) *n.* deserter.

re·nege′ (ri nig′, -neg′) *v.,* **-neged, -neging.** *Informal.* break promise.

re·new′ (ri nōō′, -nyōō′) *v.* **1.** begin or do again. **2.** make like new; replenish. —**re·new′al,** *n.*

ren′net (ren′it) *n.* **1.** membrane lining stomach of calf or other animal. **2.** preparation of this used in making cheese.

re·nounce′ (ri nouns′) *v.,* **-nounced, -nouncing.** give up voluntarily. —**re·nounce′ment,** *n.*

ren′o·vate′ (ren′ə vāt′) *v.,* **-vated, -vating.** repair; refurbish.

re·nown′ (ri noun′) *n.* fame. —**re·nowned′,** *adj.*

rent (rent) *n.* **1.** Also, **rent′al.** payment for use of property. **2.** tear. —*v.* **3.** grant or use in return for rent.

rent′al, *n.* **1.** amount given or received as rent. **2.** act of renting. **3.** property rented.

re·nun′ci·a′tion (ri nun′sē ā′shən, -shē-) *n.* act of renouncing.

Rep., **1.** Representative. **2.** Republic. **3.** Republican.

re·pair′ (ri pâr′) *v.* **1.** restore to good condition. **2.** go. —*n.* **3.** work of repairing. **4.** good condition.

rep′a·ra′tion (rep′ə rā′shən) *n.* amends for injury.

rep′ar·tee′ (rep′ər tē′, -tā′, -är-) *n.* exchange of wit; banter.

re·past′ (ri past′) *n.* meal.

re·pa·tri·ate (rē pā′trē āt′) v., -ated, -ating. send back to one's native country.

re·pay (ri pā′) v., -paid, -paying. pay back. —**re·pay′ment,** n.

re·peal (ri pēl′) v. **1.** revoke officially. —n. **2.** revocation.

re·peat (ri pēt′) v. **1.** say, tell, or do again. —n. **2.** act of repeating. **3.** musical passage to be repeated.

re·peat′ed, adj. said or done again and again. —**re·peat′ed·ly,** adv.

re·pel′ (ri pel′) v., -pelled, -pelling. **1.** drive back; thrust away. **2.** excite disgust or suspicion. —**re·pel′lent,** adj., n.

re·pent′ (ri pent′) v. feel contrition. —**re·pent′ance,** n. —**re·pent′ant,** adj. —**re·pent′ant·ly,** adv.

re′per·cus′sion (rē′pər kush′ən) n. **1.** indirect result. **2.** echo.

rep′er·toire (rep′ər twär′, -twôr′, rep′ə-) n. group of works that performer or company can perform. Also, **rep′er·to·ry.**

rep′e·ti′tion (rep′ə tish′ən) n. repeated action, utterance, etc. —**rep·e·ti′tious,** adj. —**re·pet′i·tive** (ri pet′ə tiv) adj.

re·pine′ (ri pīn′) v., -pined, -pining. **1.** complain. **2.** yearn.

re·place′ (ri plās′) v., -placed, -placing. **1.** take place of. **2.** provide substitute for. **3.** put back.

re·play′ v., -played, -playing. —v. (rē plā′) **1.** play again. —n. (rē′ plā) **2.** act of replaying. **3.** something replayed.

re·plen′ish (ri plen′ish) v. make full again. —**re·plen′ish·ment,** n.

re·plete′ (ri plēt′) adj. abundantly filled. —**re·ple′tion,** n.

rep′li·ca (rep′li kə) n. copy.

rep′li·cate (-kāt′) v., -cated, -cating. duplicate or reproduce.

re·ply′ (ri plī′) v., -plied, -plying. n., pl. -plies. answer.

re·port′ (ri pôrt′) n. **1.** statement of events or findings. **2.** rumor. **3.** loud noise. —v. **4.** tell of. **5.** present oneself. **6.** inform against. **7.** write about for newspaper. —**re·port′er,** n.

re·pose′ (ri pōz′) n., v., -posed, -posing. —n. **1.** rest or sleep. **2.** tranquillity. —v. **3.** rest or sleep. **4.** put, as trust. —**re·pose′ful,** adj.

re·pos′i·tor′y (ri poz′i tôr′ē) n., pl. -tories. place where things are stored.

re·pos·sess′ (rē′pə zes′) v. take back.

rep′re·hen′si·ble (rep′rə hen′sə bəl) adj. blameworthy.

rep′re·sent′ (rep′ri zent′) v. **1.** express; signify. **2.** act or speak for. **3.** portray. —**rep′re·sen·ta′tion,** n.

rep′re·sent′a·tive (-zen′tə tiv) n. **1.** one that represents another or others. **2.** member of legislative body. —adj. **3.** representing. **4.** typical.

re·press′ (ri pres′) v. **1.** inhibit. **2.** suppress. —**re·pres′sive,** adj. —**re·pres′sion,** n.

re·prieve′ (ri prēv′) v., -prieved, -prieving. n. respite.

rep′ri·mand (rep′rə mand′) n. **1.** severe reproof. —v. **2.** reprove severely.

re·pris′al (ri prī′zəl) n. infliction of injuries in retaliation.

re·proach′ (ri prōch′) v. **1.** blame; upbraid. —n. **2.** blame; discredit. —**re·proach′ful,** adj.

rep′ro·bate′ (rep′rə bāt′) n. **1.** hopelessly bad person. —adj. **2.** depraved. —**rep′ro·ba′tion,** n.

re′pro·duce′ (rē′prə dōōs′, -dyōōs′) v., -duced, -ducing. **1.** copy or duplicate. **2.** produce by propagation. —**re′pro·duc′tion** (-duk′shən) n. —**re′pro·duc′tive,** adj.

re·proof′ (ri prōōf′) n. censure.

re·prove′ (-prōōv′) v., -proved, -proving. blame.

rep′tile (rep′til, -tīl) n. creeping animal, as lizard or snake.

re·pub′lic (ri pub′lik) n. state governed by representatives elected by citizens.

re·pub′li·can, adj. **1.** of or favoring republic. **2.** (cap.) of **Republican Party,** one of two major political parties of U.S. —n. **3.** (cap.) member of Republican Party.

re·pu′di·ate′ (ri pyōō′dē āt′) v., -ated, -ating. reject as worthless, not binding, or false.

re·pug′nant (ri pug′nənt) adj. distasteful. —**re·pug′nance,** n.

re·pulse′ (ri puls′) v., -pulsed, -pulsing. n. —v. **1.** drive back with force. —n. **2.** act of repulsing. **3.** rejection. —**re·pul′sion,** n.

re·pul′sive, adj. disgusting.

rep′u·ta·ble (rep′yə tə bəl) adj. of good reputation.

rep′u·ta′tion (-tā′shən) n. **1.** public estimation of character. **2.** good name.

re·pute′ (ri pyōōt′) n., v., -puted, -puting. —n. **1.** reputation. —v. **2.** give reputation to.

re·quest′ (ri kwest′) v. **1.** ask for. —n. **2.** act of requesting. **3.** what is requested.

Req′ui·em (rek′wē əm) n. Rom. Cath. Ch. mass for dead.

re·quire′ (ri kwīr′) v., -quired, -quiring. **1.** need. **2.** demand. —**re·quire′ment,** n.

req′ui·site (rek′wə zit) adj. **1.** necessary. —n. **2.** necessary thing.

req′ui·si′tion (-zish′ən) n. **1.** formal order or demand. —v. **2.** take for official use.

re·quite′ (ri kwīt′) v., -quited, -quiting. v. give or do in return. —**re·quit′al** (-kwī′tal) n.

re′run′ (rē′run′) n. **1.** showing of motion picture or television program after its initial run. **2.** the program shown.

re·scind′ (ri sind′) v. annul; revoke.

res′cue (res′kyōō) v., -cued, -cuing. n. —v. **1.** free from danger, capture, etc. —n. **2.** act of rescuing.

re·search′ (ri sûrch′, rē′sûrch) n. **1.** diligent investigation. —v. **2.** investigate carefully. —**re·search′er,** n.

re·sem′ble (ri zem′bəl) v., -bled, -bling. be similar to. —**re·sem′blance,** n.

re·sent′ (ri zent′) v. feel indignant or injured at. —**re·sent′ful,** adj. —**re·sent′ment,** n.

res′er·va′tion (rez′ər vā′shən) n. **1.** act of withholding or setting apart. **2.** particular doubt or misgiving. **3.** advance assurance of accommodations. **4.** land for use of an Indian tribe.

re·serve′ (ri zûrv′) v., -served, -serving. n., adj. —v. **1.** keep back. —n. **2.** something reserved. **3.** part of military force held in readiness to support active forces. **4.** reticence. —adj. **5.** kept in reserve.

re·served′, adj. **1.** held for future use. **2.** self-restrained.

re·serv′ist, n. member of military reserves.

res′er·voir′ (rez′ər vwär′, -vwôr′, rez′ə-) n. **1.** place where water is stored for use. **2.** supply.

re·side′ (ri zīd′) v., -sided, -siding. **1.** dwell. **2.** be vested, as powers.

res′i·dence (rez′i dəns) n. **1.** dwelling place. **2.** act or fact of residing.

—res′i·dent, n. **—res′i·den′tial** (-den′shəl) adj.

res′i·den·cy, n., pl. -cies. **1.** residence (def. 2). **2.** period of advanced medical training.

res′i·due (-dōō′, -dyōō′) n. remainder. —**re·sid′u·al** (ri zij′ōō əl) adj.

re·sign′ (ri zīn′) v. **1.** give up (job, office, etc.), esp. formally. **2.** submit, as to fate or force.

re·signed′, adj. acquiescent.

re·sil′i·ent (ri zil′yənt) adj. **1.** springing back. **2.** recovering readily from adversity. —**re·sil′i·ence,** n.

res′in (rez′in) n. exudation from some plants, used in medicines, etc.

re·sist′ (ri zist′) v. withstand; offer opposition to. —**re·sist′ant,** adj.

re·sist′ance, n. **1.** act of resisting. **2.** ability to resist disease. **3.** opposition to electric current.

re·sis′tor, n. device that introduces resistance into electrical circuit.

res′o·lute′ (rez′ə lōōt′) adj. determined on action or result.

res′o·lu′tion, n. **1.** formal expression of group opinion. **2.** determination. **3.** solution of problem.

re·solve′ (ri zolv′) v., -solved, -solving, n. —v. **1.** decide firmly. **2.** state formally. **3.** dispel. **4.** solve. —n. **5.** resolution.

res′o·nant (rez′ə nənt) adj. **1.** resounding. **2.** rich in sound.

res′o·nate (-nāt′) v., -nated, -nating. resound.

re·sort′ (ri zôrt′) v. **1.** apply or turn (to) for use, help, etc. **2.** go often. —n. **3.** place much frequented, esp. for recreation. **4.** recourse.

re·sound′ (ri zound′) v. echo.

re·sound′ing, adj. impressively complete. —**re·sound′ing·ly,** adv.

re′source (rē′sôrs, ri sôrs′) n. **1.** source of aid or supply. **2.** (pl.) wealth.

re·source′ful, adj. clever.

re·spect′ (ri spekt′) n. **1.** detail; point. **2.** reference. **3.** esteem. —v. **4.** hold in esteem. —**re·spect′er,** n.

re·spect′a·ble, adj. **1.** worthy of respect. **2.** decent.

re·spect′ful, adj. showing respect. —**re·spect′ful·ly,** adv.

re·spect′ing, prep. concerning.

re·spec′tive, adj. in order previously named.

res′pi·ra′tor (res′pə rā′tər) n. apparatus to produce artificial breathing.

re·spire′ (ri spīr′) v., -spired, -spiring. breathe. —**res′pi·ra′tion** (res′pə-rā′shən) n. —**res′pi·ra·to′ry,** adj.

res′pite (res′pit) n., v., -pited, -piting. —n. **1.** temporary relief or delay. —v. **2.** relieve or cease temporarily.

re·splend′ent (ri splen′dənt) adj. gleaming. —**re·splend′ence,** n.

re·spond′ (ri spond′) v. answer.

re·spond′ent, n. Law. defendant.

re·sponse′ (-spons′) n. reply.

re·spon′si·bil′i·ty, n., pl. -ties. **1.** state of being responsible. **2.** obligation.

re·spon′si·ble, adj. **1.** causing or allowing things to happen. **2.** capable of rational thought. **3.** reliable.

re·spon′sive, adj. responding readily. —**re·spon′sive·ly,** adv.

rest (rest) n. **1.** quiet or sleep. **2.** cessation from motion, work, etc. **3.** support. **4.** Music. interval of silence. **5.** remainder; others. —v. **6.** be quiet or at ease. **7.** cease from motion. **8.** lie or lay. **9.** be based. **10.** rely. **11.** continue to be. —**rest′ful,** adj. —**rest′ful·ly,** adv.

res·tau·rant (res′tər ənt, -tə ränt′) n. public eating place.

res′tau·ra·teur′ (-tər ə tûr′) n. restaurant owner.

res′ti·tu′tion (res′ti tōō′shən, -tyōō′-) n. 1. reparation. 2. return of rights, etc.

res′tive (res′tiv) adj. restless.

rest′less, adj. 1. lacking rest. 2. uneasy. 3. always moving. —**rest′less·ly,** adv. —**rest′less·ness,** n.

re·store′ (ri stôr′) v., -stored, -storing. 1. bring back, as to use or good condition. 2. give back. —**res′to·ra′tion,** n. —**re·stor′a·tive,** adj., n.

re·strain′ (ri strān′) v. 1. hold back. 2. confine.

re·straint′ (-strānt′) n. 1. restraining influence. 2. confinement. 3. constraint.

re·strict′ (ri strikt′) v. confine; limit. —**re·stric′tion,** n. —**re·stric′tive,** adj.

rest room, room in public building with washbowls and toilets.

re·sult′ (ri zult′) n. 1. outcome; consequence. —v. 2. occur as result. 3. end. —**re·sult′ant,** adj., n.

re·sume′ (ri zōōm′) v., -sumed, -suming. go on with again. —**re·sump′tion** (-zump′shən) n.

ré′su·mé′ (rez′ŏŏ mā′) n. summary, esp. of education and work.

re·sur′face (rē sûr′fis) v., -faced, -facing. 1. give new surface to. 2. come to the surface again.

re·sur′gent (ri sûr′jənt) adj. rising again. —**re·sur′gence,** n.

res′ur·rect′ (rez′ə rekt′) v. bring to life again. —**res′ur·rec′tion,** n.

re·sus′ci·tate′ (ri sus′i tāt′) v. revive. —**re·sus′ci·ta′tion,** n.

re′tail (rē′tāl) n. 1. sale of goods to consumer. —v. 2. sell at retail.

re·tain′ (ri tān′) v. 1. keep or hold. 2. engage. —**re·tain′a·ble,** adj.

re·tain′er, n. 1. fee paid to secure services. 2. old servant.

re·take′ v., -took, retaken, retaking. (rē tāk′) 1. take again. 2. photograph again. —n. (rē′ tāk) 3. picture photographed again.

re·tal′i·ate′ (ri tal′ē āt′) v., -ated, -ating. return like for like, esp. evil. —**re·tal′i·a′tion,** n. —**re·tal′i·a·to′ry** (-ə tôr′ē) adj.

re·tard′ (ri tärd′) v. delay; hinder.

re·tard′ed, adj. slow or weak in mental development.

retch (rech) v. try to vomit.

re·ten′tion (ri ten′shən) n. 1. retaining. 2. power of retaining. 3. memory. —**re·ten′tive,** adj.

ret′i·cent (ret′ə sənt) adj. saying little. —**ret′i·cence,** n.

ret′i·na (ret′n ə) n. coating on back part of eyeball that receives images.

ret′i·nue′ (ret′n ōō′, -yōō′) n. train of attendants.

re·tire′ (ri tī°r′) v., -tired, -tiring. 1. withdraw. 2. go to bed. 3. end working life. 4. put out (a batter, etc.) —**re·tire′ment,** n.

re·tired′, adj. 1. withdrawn from office, occupation, etc. 2. secluded.

re·tir′ee′, n. person who has retired.

re·tir′ing, adj. shy.

re·tort′ (ri tôrt′) v. 1. reply smartly. —n. 2. sharp or witty reply. 3. long-necked vessel used in distilling.

re·touch′ (rē tuch′) v. touch up.

re·trace′ (rē trās′) v., -traced, -tracing. go back over.

re·tract′ (ri trakt′) v. withdraw. —**re·trac′tion,** n. —**re·tract′a·ble,** adj.

re′tread (rē tred′) n. 1. tire that has had new tread added. 2. Informal. person returned to former position or occupation.

re·treat′ (ri trēt′) n. 1. forced withdrawal. 2. private place. —v. 3. make a retreat. 4. withdraw.

re·trench′ (ri trench′) v. reduce expenses. —**re·trench′ment,** n.

ret′ri·bu′tion (re′trə byōō′shən) n. requital according to merits, esp. for evil.

re·trieve′ (ri trēv′) v., -trieved, -trieving, n. —v. 1. regain or restore. 2. locate or access in a computer. 3. recover (killed game). —n. 4. recovery. —**re·triev′er,** n.

ret′ro·ac′tive (re′trō ak′tiv) adj. applying also to past.

ret′ro·fit′, v., -fitted, -fitting. refit with newly developed equipment.

ret′ro·grade′ (re′trə-) adj., v., -graded, -grading. —adj. 1. moving backward. —v. 2. move backward. 3. degenerate.

ret′ro·gress′ (re′trə gres′) v. return to earlier or more primitive condition. —**ret′ro·gres′sion,** n. —**ret′ro·gres′sive,** adj.

ret′ro·spect′ (re′trə spekt′) n. occasion of looking back. —**ret′ro·spec′tive,** adj.

re·turn′ (ri tûrn′) v. 1. go or come back to former place or condition. 2. put or bring back. 3. reply. —n. 4. act or fact of returning. 5. recurrence. 6. requital. 7. reply. 8. (often pl.) profit. 9. report of results.

re·turn·ee′ (ri tûr nē′, -tûr′nē) n., pl. -ees. person who has returned.

re′u·nite′ (rē′yə nīt′) v., -nited, -niting. unite after separation. —**re·un′ion,** n.

rev (rev) n., v., revved, revving. Informal. —n. 1. revolution (in machinery). —v. 2. increase speed of (motor).

Rev., Reverend.

re·vamp′ (rē vamp′) v. renovate.

re·veal′ (ri vēl′) v. disclose.

rev·eil·le (rev′ə lē) n. Mil. signal for awakening.

rev′el (rev′əl) v., -eled, -eling. 1. enjoy greatly. 2. make merry. —n. 3. merry-making. —**rev′el·ry,** n.

rev′e·la′tion, n. disclosure.

re·venge′ (ri venj′) n., v., -venged, -venging. —n. 1. harm in return for harm; retaliation. 2. vindictiveness. —v. 3. take revenge. —**re·venge′ful,** adj. —**re·veng′er,** n.

rev′e·nue′ (rev′ən yōō′, -ə nōō′) n. income, esp. of government or business.

re·ver′ber·ate′ (ri vûr′bə rāt′) v., -ated, -ating. 1. echo back. 2. reflect. —**re·ver′ber·a′tion,** n.

re·vere′ (ri vēr′) v., -vered, -vering. hold in deep respect.

rev′er·ence (rev′ər əns) n., v., -enced, -encing. —n. 1. deep respect and awe. —v. 2. regard with reverence. —**rev′er·ent, rev′er·en′tial** (-ə-ren′shəl) adj.

Rev′er·end, adj. title used with name of member of the clergy.

rev′er·ie (rev′ə rē) n. daydream.

re·verse′ (ri vûrs′) adj., v., -versed, -versing. —adj. 1. opposite in position, action, etc. 2. of or for backward motion. —n. 3. reverse part, position, etc. 4. misfortune. —v. 5. turn in the opposite direction. —**re·ver′sal,** n. —**re·vers′i·ble,** adj.

re·vert′ (-vûrt′) v. go back to earlier state, topic, etc.

re·view′, n. 1. critical article. 2. repeated viewing. 3. inspection. —v. 4. view again. 5. inspect. 6. survey. 7. write a review of. —**re·view′er,** n.

re·vile′ (ri vīl′) v., -viled, -viling. speak abusively to or about.

re·vise′ (ri vīz′) v., -vised, -vising. change or amend content of. —**re·vi′sion,** n. —**re·vis′er,** n.

re·vi′sion·ism (ri vizh′ə niz′əm) n. departure from accepted doctrine. —**re·vi′sion·ist,** n., adj.

re·vi′tal·ize′ (rē vīt′l īz′) v., -ized, -izing. bring new vitality to.

re·viv′al (ri vī′vəl) n. 1. restoration to life, use, etc. 2. religious awakening. —**re·viv′al·ist,** n.

re·vive′, v., -vived, -viving. bring back to life.

re·viv′i·fy′ (ri viv′ə fī′) v., -fied, -fying. bring back to life.

re·voke′ (ri vōk′) v., -voked, -voking. annul or repeal. —**rev′o·ca·ble** (rev′ə ka bəl) adj.

re·volt′ (ri vōlt′) v. 1. rebel. 2. turn away in disgust. 3. fill with disgust. —n. 4. rebellion. —**re·volt′ing,** adj.

rev′o·lu′tion (rev′ə lōō′shən) n. 1. overthrow of government. 2. fundamental change. 3. rotation. —**rev′o·lu′tion·ar′y,** adj., n.

rev′o·lu′tion·ize′, v., -ized, -izing. cause fundamental change in.

re·volve′ (ri volv′) v., -volved, -volving. 1. turn round, as on axis. 2. consider.

re·volv′er, n. pistol with revolving cylinder holding cartridges.

re·vue′ (ri vyōō′) n. theatrical show.

re·vul′sion (ri vul′shən) n. strong feeling of disgust.

re·ward′ (ri wôrd′) n. 1. recompense for merit, service, etc. —v. 2. give reward.

re·ward′ing, adj. giving satisfaction.

re·word′ (rē wûrd′) v. put into other words.

re·write′, v., -wrote, rewritten, -writing. 1. revise. 2. write again.

RFD, rural free delivery.

rhap′so·dize′ (rap′sə dīz′) v., -dized, -dizing. talk with extravagant enthusiasm.

rhap′so·dy (-sə dē) n., pl. -dies. 1. exaggerated expression of enthusiasm. 2. irregular musical composition.

rhe′o·stat′ (rē′ə stat′) n. device for regulating electric current.

rhet′o·ric (ret′ər ik) n. 1. skillful use of language. 2. exaggerated speech.

rhetorical question, question asked for effect, not answer.

rheu′ma·tism (rōō′mə tiz′əm) n. disease affecting joints or muscles. —**rheu·mat′ic** (rōō mat′ik) adj., n.

Rh factor, antigen in blood that may cause severe reaction in individual lacking the substance.

rhine′stone′ (rīn′stōn′) n. artificial diamondlike gem.

rhi·noc′er·os (rī nos′ər əs) n. large thick-skinned mammal with horned snout.

rho′do·den′dron (rō′də den′drən) n. flowering evergreen shrub.

rhom′boid (rom′boid) n. oblique-angled parallelogram with only the opposite sides equal.

rhom′bus (-bəs) n., pl. -buses, -bi (-bī). oblique-angled parallelogram with all sides equal.

rhu′barb (rōō′bärb) n. garden plant with edible leaf stalks.

rhyme (rīm) n., v., rhymed, rhyming. —n. 1. agreement in end sounds of lines or words. 2. verse with such correspondence. —v. 3. make or form rhyme.

rhythm (rith′əm) n. movement with uniformly recurring beat. —**rhyth′mic, rhyth′mi·cal,** adj.

RI, Rhode Island. Also, **R.I.**

rib (rib) *n.*, *v.*, **ribbed, ribbing.** —*n.* **1.** one of the slender curved bones enclosing chest. **2.** riblike part. —*v.* **3.** furnish with ribs. **4.** *Informal.* tease.

rib′ald (rib′əld; *spelling pron.* rī′bəld) *adj.* bawdy in speech. —**rib′ald•ry,** *n.*

rib′bon (rib′ən) *n.* strip of silk, rayon, etc.

ri′bo•fla′vin (rī′bō flā′vin, -bə-) important vitamin in milk, fresh meat, eggs, etc.

rice (rīs) *n.* edible starchy grain.

rich (rich) *adj.* **1.** having great possessions. **2.** abounding. **3.** costly. **4.** containing butter, eggs, cream, etc. **5.** strong; vivid. **6.** mellow. —*n.* **7.** rich people.

rich′es, *n.pl.* wealth.

Rich′ter scale (rik′tər) scale for indicating intensity of earthquake.

rick (rik) *n.* stack of hay, etc.

rick′ets (rik′its) *n.* childhood bone disease caused by lack of vitamin D.

rick′et•y (rik′i tē) *adj.*, **-ier, -iest.** shaky.

rick′shaw (rik′shô, -shä) *n.* two-wheeled passenger vehicle pulled by person.

ric′o•chet′ (rik′ə shā′) *v.*, **-cheted** (-shād′), **-cheting** (-shā′ing), *n.* —*v.* **1.** rebound from a flat surface. —*n.* **2.** such a movement.

ri•cot′ta (ri kot′ə, -kô′tə) *n.* soft Italian cheese.

rid (rid) *v.*, **rid** or **ridded, ridding.** clear or free of. —**rid′dance,** *n.*

rid′dle (rid′l) *n.*, *v.*, **-dled, -dling.** —*n.* **1.** puzzling question or matter. **2.** coarse sieve. —*v.* **3.** speak perplexingly. **4.** pierce with many holes. **5.** put through sieve.

ride (rīd) *v.*, **rode** (rōd), **ridden, riding,** *n.* —*v.* **1.** be carried in traveling. **2.** sit on and manage (horse, etc.). **3.** rest on something. —*n.* **4.** journey on a horse, etc. **5.** vehicle or device in which people ride for amusement.

rid′er, *n.* **1.** person that rides. **2.** clause attached to legislative bill before passage.

ridge (rij) *n.*, *v.*, **ridged, ridging.** —*n.* **1.** long narrow elevation. —*v.* **2.** form with ridge.

rid′i•cule (rid′i kyōōl′) *n.*, *v.*, **-culed, -culing.** —*n.* **1.** derision. —*v.* **2.** deride.

ri•dic′u•lous (ri dik′yə ləs) *adj.* absurd. —**ri•dic′u•lous•ly,** *adv.*

rife (rīf) *adj.* **1.** widespread. **2.** abounding.

riff (rif) *n.* repeated phrase in jazz or rock music.

riff′raff′ (rif′raf′) *n.* rabble.

ri′fle (rī′fəl) *n.*, *v.*, **-fled, -fling.** —*n.* **1.** shoulder firearm with spirally grooved barrel. —*v.* **2.** cut spiral grooves in (gun barrel). **3.** search through to rob.

rift (rift) *n.* split.

rig (rig) *v.*, **rigged, rigging,** *n.* —*v.* **1.** fit with tackle and other parts. **2.** put together as makeshift. **3.** manipulate fraudulently or artificially. —*n.* **4.** arrangement of masts, booms, tackle, etc. **5.** equipment.

rig′ging, *n.* ropes and chains that support and work masts, sails, etc.

right (rīt) *adj.* **1.** just or good. **2.** correct. **3.** in good condition. **4.** on side that is toward the east when one faces north. **5.** straight. —*n.* **6.** that which is right. **7.** right side. **8.** that justly due one. **9.** conservative side in politics. —*adv.* **10.** directly; completely. **11.** set correctly. **12.** in right position. **13.** correct. —**right′ly,** *adv.* —**right′ist,** *adj.*, *n.*

right angle, 90-degree angle.

right′eous (rī′chəs) *adj.* virtuous.

right′ful, *adj.* belonging by or having just claim. —**right′ful•ly,** *adv.*

right′-hand′ed, *adj.* **1.** using the right hand more easily. **2.** for the right hand.

right of way, 1. right of one vehicle to proceed before another. **2.** path that may lawfully be used.

right′-to-life′, *adj.* advocating laws making abortion illegal. —**right′-to-lif′er,** *n.*

right wing, conservative element in organization. —**right′-wing′,** *adj.* —**right′-wing′er,** *n.*

rig′id (rij′id) *adj.* **1.** stiff; inflexible. **2.** rigorous. —**ri•gid′i•ty,** *n.*

rig′ma•role′ (rig′mə rōl′) *n.* **1.** confused talk. **2.** complicated procedure.

rig′or (rig′ər) *n.* **1.** strictness. **2.** hardship. —**rig′or•ous,** *adj.*

ri′gor mor′tis (rig′ər môr′tis) stiffening of body after death.

rile (rīl) *v.*, **riled, riling.** *Informal.* vex.

rill (ril) *n.* small brook.

rim (rim) *n.*, *v.*, **rimmed, rimming.** —*n.* **1.** outer edge. —*v.* **2.** furnish with rim.

rime (rīm) *n.*, *v.*, **rimed, riming.** —*n.* **1.** rhyme. **2.** rough white frost. —*v.* **3.** cover with rime.

rind (rīnd) *n.* firm covering, as of fruit or cheese.

ring (ring) *n.*, *v.*, **rang** (rang), **rung** (rung) (for 11, **ringed**), **ringing.** —*n.* **1.** round band for a finger. **2.** any circular band. **3.** enclosed area. **4.** group cooperating for selfish purpose. **5.** ringing sound. **6.** telephone call. —*v.* **7.** sound clearly and resonantly. **8.** seem; appear. **9.** be filled with sound. **10.** signal by bell. **11.** form ring around.

ring′er, *n.* **1.** person or thing that closely resembles another. **2.** athlete entered in competition in violation of eligibility rules.

ring′lead′er, *n.* leader in mischief.

ring′let (-lit) *n.* long curl of hair.

ring′mas′ter, *n.* person in charge of performances in circus ring.

ring′worm′, *n.* contagious skin disease.

rink (ringk) *n.* floor or sheet of ice for skating on.

rinse (rins) *v.*, **rinsed, rinsing,** *n.* —*v.* **1.** wash lightly. —*n.* **2.** rinsing act. **3.** liquid for rinsing.

ri′ot (rī′ət) *n.* **1.** disturbance by mob. **2.** wild disorder. —*v.* **3.** take part in riot. —**ri′ot•ous,** *adj.*

rip (rip) *v.*, **ripped, ripping,** *n.* tear.

R.I.P., may he, she, or they rest in peace.

rip cord, cord that opens parachute.

ripe (rīp) *adj.*, **riper, ripest. 1.** fully developed; mature. **2.** ready. —**rip′en,** *v.* —**ripe′ness,** *n.*

rip′off′, *n. Slang.* theft or exploitation.

ri•poste′ (ri pōst′) *n.* quick, sharp reply or reaction.

rip′ple (rip′əl) *v.*, **-pled, -pling,** *n.* —*v.* **1.** form small waves. —*n.* **2.** pattern of small waves.

rip′-roar′ing, *adj.* boisterously exciting.

rip′saw′, *n.* saw for cutting wood with the grain.

rip′tide′, *n.* tide that opposes other tides.

rise (rīz) *v.*, **rose** (rōz), **ris•en** (riz′ən), **rising,** *n.* —*v.* **1.** get up. **2.** revolt. **3.** appear. **4.** originate. **5.** move upward.

6. increase. **7.** (of dough) expand. —*n.* **8.** upward movement. **9.** origin. **10.** upward slope. —**ris′er,** *n.*

risk (risk) *n.* **1.** dangerous chance. —*v.* **2.** expose to risk. **3.** take risk of. —**risk′y,** *adj.*

ris•qué′ (ri skā′) *adj.* bawdy.

rite (rīt) *n.* ceremonial act.

rite of passage, event marking passage from one stage of life to another.

rit′u•al (rich′ōō əl) *n.* system of religious or other rites.

ri′val (rī′vəl) *n.*, *adj.*, *v.*, **-valed, -valing.** —*n.* **1.** competitor. **2.** equal. —*adj.* **3.** being a rival. —*v.* **4.** compete with. **5.** match. —**ri′val•ry,** *n.*

riv′er (riv′ər) *n.* large natural stream.

riv′et (riv′it) *n.*, *v.*, **-eted, -eting.** —*n.* **1.** metal bolt hammered after insertion. —*v.* **2.** fasten with rivets.

riv′u•let (riv′yə lit) *n.* small stream.

RN, registered nurse.

roach (rōch) *n.* cockroach.

road (rōd) *n.* open way for travel.

road′block′, *n.* obstruction placed across road to halt traffic.

road′run′ner, *n.* terrestrial cuckoo of western U.S.

roam (rōm) *v.* wander; rove.

roan (rōn) *adj.* **1.** horse with gray or white spots. —*n.* **2.** roan horse.

roar (rôr) *v.* **1.** make loud, deep sound. —*n.* **2.** loud, deep sound.

roast (rōst) *v.* **1.** cook by dry heat. —*n.* **2.** roasted meat. —**roast′er,** *n.*

rob (rob) *v.*, **robbed, robbing.** deprive of unlawfully. —**rob′ber,** *n.* —**rob′ber•y,** *n.*

robe (rōb) *n.*, *v.*, **robed, robing.** —*n.* **1.** long loose garment. **2.** wrap or covering. —*v.* **3.** clothe.

rob′in (rob′in) *n.* red-breasted bird.

ro′bot (rō′bət, -bot) *n.* **1.** humanlike machine that performs tasks. **2.** person who acts mechanically.

ro•bot′ics, *n.* technology of computer-controlled robots.

ro•bust′ (rō bust′, rō′bust) *adj.* healthy.

rock (rok) *n.* **1.** mass of stone. **2.** Also, **rock-′n′-roll.** popular music with steady, insistent rhythm. —*v.* **3.** move back and forth. —**rock′y,** *adj.*

rock bottom, lowest level.

rock′er, *n.* curved support of cradle or rock′ing chair.

rock′et (rok′it) *n.* tube propelled by discharge of gases from it.

rock′et•ry, *n.* science of rocket design.

rock salt, salt occurring in rocklike masses.

ro•co′co (rə kō′kō, rō′kə kō′) *n.* elaborate decorative style of many curves. —**ro•co′co,** *adj.*

rod (rod) *n.* **1.** slender shaft. **2.** linear measure of 5½ yards.

ro′dent (rōd′nt) *n.* small gnawing or nibbling mammal.

ro′de•o′ (rō′dē ō′, rō dā′ō) *n.*, *pl.* **-deos.** exhibition of cowboy skills.

roe (rō) *n.*, *pl.* **roes, roe. 1.** small deer. **2.** fish eggs or spawn.

rog′er (roj′ər) *interj.* (message) received.

rogue (rōg) *n.* rascal. —**ro′guish,** *adj.* —**ro′guer•y,** *n.*

roil (roil) *v.* **1.** make muddy. **2.** vex.

role (rōl) *n.* part of function, as of character in play. Also, **rôle.**

role model, person imitated by others.

roll (rōl) *v.* **1.** move by turning. **2.** rock. **3.** have deep, loud sound. **4.** flatten with roller. **5.** form into roll or ball. —*n.* **6.** list; register. **7.** anything cylindrical. **8.** small cake of bread. **9.** deep long sound.

roll′back′, *n.* return to lower level.

roll call, calling of names for checking attendance.

Roll′er•blade′, *n., v.,* **-bladed, -blading.** —*n.* **1.** *Trademark.* brand of in-line skates. —*v.* **2.** (*often l.c.*) skate on in-line skates.

roller coaster, small railroad that moves along winding route with steep inclines.

roller skate, skate with four wheels. —**roller-skate,** *v.*

rol′lick•ing (rol′i king) *adj.* jolly.

roll′o′ver, *n.* reinvestment of funds.

roll′-top desk, desk with flexible sliding cover.

ro′ly-po′ly (rō′lē pō′lē, -pō′lē) *adj.* short and round.

ROM (rom) *n.* read-only memory: non-modifiable part of computer memory containing instructions to system.

ro•maine′ (rō mān′, rə-) *n.* kind of lettuce.

Ro′man (rō′mən) **1.** native or citizen of Rome or Roman Empire. **2.** (*l.c.*) upright style of printing type. —**Ro′man,** *adj.*

Roman candle, kind of firework.

Roman Catholic Church, Christian Church of which pope (Bishop of Rome) is head. —**Roman Catholic.**

ro•mance′ (rō mans′) *n., v.,* **-manced, -mancing.** —*n.* **1.** colorful, imaginative tale. **2.** colorful, fanciful quality. **3.** love affair. —*v.* **4.** act romantically. **5.** tell fanciful, false story.

Roman numerals, system of numbers using letters as symbols: I = 1, V = 5, X = 10, L = 50, C = 100, D = 500, M = 1,000.

ro•man′tic (rō man′tik) *adj.* **1.** of romance. **2.** impractical or unrealistic. **3.** imbued with idealism. **4.** preoccupied with love. **5.** passionate; fervent. **6.** of a style of art stressing imagination and emotion. —*n.* **7.** romantic person.

ro•man′ti•cism (-tə siz′əm) *n.* (*often cap.*) romantic spirit or artistic style or movement.

ro•man′ti•cize′, *v.,* **-cized, -cizing.** invest with romantic character.

romp (romp) *v., n.* frolic.

romp′ers, *n.pl.* child's loose outer garment.

rood (rōōd) *n.* **1.** crucifix. **2.** one-quarter of an acre.

roof (rōōf, rŏŏf) *n., pl.* **roofs. 1.** upper covering of building. —*v.* **2.** provide with roof. —**roof′er,** *n.*

rook (rŏŏk) *n.* **1.** European crow. **2.** chess piece; castle. —*v.* **3.** cheat.

rook′ie, *n. Slang.* beginner.

room (rōōm, rŏŏm) *n.* **1.** separate space within building. **2.** space. —*v.* **3.** lodge. —**roomer,** *n.* —**room′mate′,** *n.* —**room′y,** *adj.*

roost (rōōst) *n.* **1.** perch where fowls rest. —*v.* **2.** sit on roost.

roost′er, *n.* male chicken.

root (rōōt, rŏŏt) *n.* **1.** part of plant growing underground. **2.** embedded part. **3.** origin. **4.** quantity that, when multiplied by itself so many times, produces given quantity. —*v.* **5.** establish roots. **6.** implant. **7.** root out, exterminate. **8.** dig with snout. **9.** *Informal.* cheer encouragingly. —**root′er,** *n.*

root beer, soft drink flavored with extracts of roots, barks, and herbs.

root canal, root portion of the pulp cavity of a tooth.

rope (rōp) *n., v.,* **roped, roping.** —*n.* **1.** strong twisted cord. —*v.* **2.** fasten or catch with rope.

Roque′fort (rōk′fərt) *n. Trademark.* strong cheese veined with mold, made from sheep's milk.

ro′sa•ry (rō′zə rē) *n., pl.* **-ries.** *Rom. Cath. Ch.* **1.** series of prayers. **2.** string of beads counted in saying rosary.

rose (rōz) *n.* thorny plant having showy, fragrant flowers.

ro•sé (rō zā′) *n.* pink wine.

rose′mar′y (rōz′mâr′ē, -mə rē) *n.* aromatic shrub used for seasoning.

ro•sette′ (rō zet′) *n.* rose-shaped ornament.

ros′ter (ros′tər) *n.* list of persons, groups, events, etc.

ros′trum (ros′trəm) *n., pl.* **-trums, -tra** (-trə). speakers' platform.

ros′y (rō′zē) *adj.,* **-ier, -iest. 1.** pink or pinkish-red. **2.** cheerful; optimistic. **3.** bright. —**ros′i•ly,** *adv.*

rot (rot) *v.,* **rotted, rotting,** *n.* —*v.* **1.** decay. —*n.* **2.** decay. **3.** decay of tissue.

ro′tate (rō′tāt) *v.,* **-tated, -tating.** turn on or as on axis. —**ro′ta•ry** (-tə rē) *adj.* —**ro•ta′tion,** *n.*

ROTC (är′ō tē sē′, rot′sē) Reserve Officers Training Corps.

rote (rōt) *n.* **1.** routine way. **2. by rote,** from memory in mechanical way.

ro•tis′ser•ie (rō tis′ə rē) *n.* rotating machine for roasting.

ro′tor (rō′tər) *n.* rotating part.

ro′to•till′er (rō′tə til′ər) *n.* motorized device with spinning blades for tilling soil.

rot′ten (rot′n) *adj.* **1.** decaying. **2.** corrupt. —**rot′ten•ness,** *n.*

ro•tund′ (rō tund′) *adj.* round.

ro•tun′da (rō tun′də) *n.* round room.

rou•é (rōō ā′) *n.* dissolute man; rake.

rouge (rōōzh) *n., v.,* **rouged, rouging.** —*n.* **1.** red cosmetic for cheeks and lips. —*v.* **2.** color with rouge.

rough (ruf) *adj.* **1.** not smooth. **2.** violent in action or motion. **3.** harsh. **4.** crude. —*v.* **5.** rough thing or part. —*v.* **6.** make rough.

rough′age (-ij) *n.* coarse or fibrous material in food.

rough′en, *v.* make or become rough.

rou•lette′ (rōō let′) *n.* gambling game based on spinning disk.

round (round) *adj.* **1.** circular, curved, or spherical. **2.** complete. **3.** expressed as approximate number. **4.** sonorous. —*n.* **5.** something round. **6.** complete course, series, etc. **7.** cut of beef between rump and leg. **8.** song in which voices enter at intervals. **9.** stage of competition, as in tournament. —*adv.* **10.** in or as in a circle. **11.** in circumference. —*prep.* **12.** around. —*v.* **13.** make round. **14.** travel around. **15.** bring together. —**round′ness,** *n.*

round′a•bout′, *adj.* indirect.

round′house′, *n.* building for servicing locomotives.

round′ly, *adv.* unsparingly.

round trip, trip to and back.

round′up′, *n.* **1.** bringing together. **2.** summary.

rouse (rouz) *v.,* **roused, rousing.** stir up; arouse.

roust′a•bout′ (roust′ə bout′) *n.* laborer.

rout (rout) *n.* **1.** defeat ending in disorderly flight. —*v.* **2.** force to flee in disorder.

route (rōōt, rout) *n., v.,* **routed, routing.** —*n.* **1.** course of travel. —*v.* **2.** send by route.

rou•tine′ (rōō tēn′) *n.* **1.** regular order of action. —*adj.* **2.** like or by routine. **3.** ordinary.

rove (rōv) *v.,* **roved, roving.** wander aimlessly. —**rov′er,** *n.*

row (rō) *v.* **1.** propel by oars. **2.** (rou) dispute noisily. —*n.* **3.** trip in rowboat. **4.** persons or things in line. **5.** (rou) noisy dispute. —**row′boat′,** *n.*

row′dy (rou′dē) *adj.,* **-dier, -diest,** *n., pl.* **-dies.** —*adj.* **1.** rough and disorderly. —*n.* **2.** rowdy person.

roy′al (roi′əl) *adj.* of kings or queens. —**roy′al•ly,** *adv.*

roy′al•ist, *n.* person favoring royal government. —**royalist,** *adj.*

roy′al•ty, *n., pl.* **-ties. 1.** royal persons. **2.** royal power. **3.** share of proceeds, paid to an author, inventor, etc.

rpm, revolutions per minute.

RR, 1. railroad. **2.** rural route.

RSVP, please reply.

rub (rub) *v.,* **rubbed, rubbing,** *n.* —*v.* **1.** apply pressure to in cleaning, smoothing, etc. **2.** press against with friction. —*n.* **3.** act of rubbing. **4.** difficulty.

rub′ber (rub′ər) *n.* **1.** elastic material from a tropical tree. **2.** *pl.* overshoes. —**rub′ber•y,** *adj.*

rubber band, band of rubber used for holding things together.

rubber cement, adhesive.

rub′ber•neck′, *Informal.* —*v.* **1.** stare curiously. —*n.* **2.** curious onlooker. **3.** sightseer.

rubber stamp, stamp with rubber printing surface.

rub′bish (rub′ish) *n.* **1.** waste. **2.** nonsense.

rub′ble (rub′əl) *n.* broken stone.

rub′down′, *n.* massage.

ru•bel′la (rōō bel′ə) *n.* usu. mild viral infection. Also, **German measles.**

ru′ble (rōō′bəl) *n.* monetary unit of Russia and of some former Soviet states.

ru′bric (rōō′brik) *n.* **1.** title or heading. **2.** class or category.

ru′by (rōō′bē) *n., pl.* **-bies.** red gem.

ruck′sack′ (ruk′sak′, rŏŏk′-) *n.* knapsack.

ruck′us (ruk′əs) *n.* noisy commotion.

rud′der (rud′ər) *n.* turning flat piece for steering vessel or aircraft.

rud′dy (rud′ē) *adj.,* **-dier, -diest.** having healthy red color.

rude (rōōd) *adj.,* **ruder, rudest. 1.** discourteous. **2.** unrefined; crude.

ru′di•ment (rōō′də mənt) *n.* basic thing to learn. —**ru′di•men′ta•ry** (-men′tə rē) *adj.*

rue (rōō) *v.,* **rued, ruing,** *n.* regret. —**rue′ful,** *adj.*

ruff (ruf) *n.* deep full collar.

ruf′fi•an (ruf′ē ən) *n.* rough or lawless person.

ruf′fle (ruf′əl) *v.,* **-fled, -fling,** *n.* —*v.* **1.** make uneven. **2.** disturb. **3.** gather in folds. —*n.* **4.** break in evenness. **5.** band of cloth, etc., gathered on one edge.

rug (rug) *n.* floor covering.

Rug′by (rug′bē) *n.* English form of football.

rug′ged (rug′id) *adj.* **1.** roughly irregular. **2.** severe. **3.** strong.

ru′in (rōō′in) *n.* **1.** destruction. **2.** (*pl.*) remains of fallen building, etc. —*v.* **3.** bring or come to ruin or ruins. —**ru′in•a′tion,** *n.* —**ru′in•ous,** *adj.*

rule (rōōl) *n., v.,* **ruled, ruling.** —*n.* **1.** principle; regulation. **2.** control. **3.** ruler (def. 2). —*v.* **4.** control. **5.** decide in the manner of a judge. **6.** mark with ruler. —**rul′ing,** *n., adj.*

rul′er, *n.* **1.** person who rules. **2.**

straight-edged strip for measuring, drawing lines, etc.

rum (rum) *n.* alcoholic liquor.

rum′ba (rum′bə, rōōm′-) *n.* Cuban dance.

rum′ble (rum′bəl) *v.*, **-bled, -bling,** —*v.* **1.** make long, deep, heavy sound. —*n.* **2.** such sound.

ru′mi•nant (rōō′mə nənt) *n.* **1.** cud-chewing mammal, as cows. —*adj.* **2.** cud-chewing.

ru′mi•nate′ (-nāt′) *v.*, **-nated, -nat-ing. 1.** chew cud. **2.** meditate.

rum′mage (rum′ij) *v.*, **-maged, -maging.** search thoroughly.

rum′my (rum′ē) *n., pl.* **-mies.** card game.

ru′mor (rōō′mər) *n.* **1.** unconfirmed but widely repeated story. —*v.* **2.** tell as rumor.

rump (rump) *n.* **1.** hind part of animal's body. **2.** the buttocks.

rum′pus (rum′pəs) *n. Informal.* noise.

run (run) *v.*, **ran** (ran), **run, running,** *n.* —*v.* **1.** advance quickly. **2.** be candidate. **3.** flow; melt. **4.** extend. **5.** operate. **6.** be exposed to. **7.** manage. —*n.* **8.** act or period of running. **9.** raveled line in knitting. **10.** freedom of action. **11.** scoring unit in baseball.

run′a•round′, *n. Informal.* evasive action or response.

run′a•way′, *n.* **1.** fugitive. **2.** something that has broken away from control. —*adj.* **3.** escaped. **4.** uncontrolled.

run′-down′, *adj.* **1.** weary. **2.** fallen into disrepair. **3.** not running because not wound.

run′down′, *n.* short summary.

rung (rung) *n.* **1.** ladder step. **2.** bar between chair legs.

run′-in′, *n.* confrontation.

run′ner, *n.* **1.** one that runs. **2.** messenger. **3.** blade of skate. **4.** strip of fabric, carpet, etc.

run′ner-up′, *n.* competitor finishing in second place.

run′off′, *n.* final contest held to break tie.

run′-of-the-mill′, *adj.* mediocre.

runt (runt) *n.* undersized thing.

run′way′, *n.* strip where airplanes take off and land.

rup′ture (rup′chər) *n., v.*, **-tured, -turing.** —*n.* **1.** break. **2.** hernia. —*v.* **3.** break. **4.** cause breach of.

ru′ral (rōōr′əl) *adj.* of or in the country.

ruse (rōōz) *n.* trick.

rush (rush) *v.* **1.** move with speed or violence. —*n.* **2.** act of rushing. **3.** hostile attack. **4.** grasslike herb growing in marshes. —*adj.* **5.** requiring or marked by haste.

rusk (rusk) *n.* sweet raised bread dried and baked again.

rus′set (rus′it) *n.* reddish brown.

Rus′sian (rush′ən) *n.* native or language of Russia. —**Russian,** *adj.*

rust (rust) *n.* **1.** red-orange coating that forms on iron and steel exposed to air and moisture. —*v.* **2.** make or become rusty. —**rust′y,** *adj.*

rus′tic (rus′tik) *adj.* **1.** rural. **2.** simple. —*n.* **3.** country person.

rus′ti•cate′ (-ti kāt′) *v.*, **-cated, -cat-ing.** go to or live in the country.

rus′tle (rus′əl) *v.*, **-tled, -tling,** *n.* —*v.* **1.** make small soft sounds. **2.** steal (cattle, etc.). —*n.* **3.** rustling sound. —**rus′tler,** *n.*

rut (rut) *n., v.*, **rutted, rutting.** —*n.* **1.** furrow or groove worn in the ground. **2.** period of sexual excitement in male deer, goats, etc. —*v.* **3.** make ruts in. **4.** be in rut.

ru′ta•ba′ga (rōō′tə bā′gə) *n.* yellow turnip.

ruth′less (rōōth′lis) *adj.* without pity or mercy. —**ruth′less•ness,** *n.*

RV, recreational vehicle.

Rx, prescription.

rye (rī) *n.* cereal grass used for flour, feed, and whiskey.

S

S, s (es) *n.* nineteenth letter of English alphabet.

S, south, southern.

Sab′bath (sab′əth) *n.* day of religious observance and rest, observed on Saturday by Jews and on Sunday by most Christians.

sab•bat′i•cal (sə bat′i kəl) *n.* **1.** paid leave of absence for study. —*adj.* **2.** *(cap.)* of the Sabbath.

sa′ber (sā′bər) *n.* one-edged sword. Also, **sa′bre.**

sa′ble (sā′bəl) *n.* small mammal with dark-brown fur.

sab′o•tage′ (sab′ə täzh′) *n., v.*, **-taged, -taging.** —*n.* **1.** willful injury to equipment, etc. —*v.* **2.** attack by sabotage.

sab•o•teur′ (-tûr′) *n.* person who sabotages.

sac (sak) *n.* baglike part.

sac′cha•rin (sak′ər in) *n.* sweet substance used as sugar substitute.

sac′cha•rine (-ər in, -ə rēn′) *adj.* overly sweet.

sa•chet′ (sa shā′) *n.* small bag of perfumed powder.

sack (sak) *n.* **1.** large stout bag. **2.** bag. **3.** *Slang.* dismissal. **4.** plundering. —*v.* **5.** put into a sack. **6.** *Slang.* dismiss. **7.** plunder; loot.

sack′cloth′, *n.* coarse cloth worn for penance or mourning.

sac′ra•ment (sak′rə mənt) *n.* rite in Christian church.

sa′cred (sā′krid) *adj.* **1.** holy. **2.** regarded with reverence.

sac′ri•fice′ (sak′rə fīs′) *n., v.*, **-ficed, -ficing.** —*n.* **1.** offer of life, treasure, etc., to deity. **2.** surrender of something for purpose. —*v.* **3.** give as sacrifice. —**sac′ri•fi′cial** (-fish′əl) *adj.*

sac′ri•lege (-lij) *n.* profanation of anything sacred. —**sac′ri•le′gious** (-lij′-əs, -lē′jəs) *adj.*

sac′ris•tan (sak′ri stən) *n.* sexton.

sac′ris•ty (-ri stē) *n., pl.* **-ties.** room in church, etc., where sacred objects are kept.

sac′ro•il′i•ac′ (sak′rō il′ē ak′, sā′-krō-) *n.* joint in lower back.

sac′ro•sanct′ (sak′rō sangkt′) *adj.* sacred.

sa′crum (sak′rəm, sā′krəm) *n., pl.* **sacra.** bone at rear of pelvis.

sad (sad) *adj.*, **sadder, saddest.** sorrowful. —**sad′den,** *v.*

sad′dle (sad′l) *n., v.*, **-dled, -dling.** —*n.* **1.** seat for rider on horse, etc. **2.** anything resembling saddle. **3.** put saddle on. **4.** burden.

sad′dle•bag′, *n.* pouch laid over back of horse or mounted over rear wheel of bicycle or motorcycle.

sad′ism (sā′diz əm, sad′iz-) *n.* sexual or other enjoyment in causing pain. —**sad′ist,** *n.* —**sa•dis′tic** (sə dis′tik) *adj.*

sa′do•mas′o•chism (sā′dō mas′ə-kiz′əm) *n.* sexual or other enjoyment in causing or experiencing pain. —**sa′-do•mas′o•chist′,** *n.*

sa•fa′ri (sə fär′ē) *n.* (in E. Africa) journey; hunting expedition.

safe (sāf) *adj.*, **safer, safest,** *n.* —*adj.* **1.** secure or free from danger. **2.** dependable. —*n.* **3.** stout box for valuables. —**safe′ty,** *n.* —**safe′ly,** *adv.* —**safe′keep′ing,** *n.*

safe′-con′duct, *n.* document authorizing safe passage.

safe′-de•pos′it, *adj.* providing safekeeping for valuables.

safe′guard′, *n.* **1.** something that ensures safety. —*v.* **2.** protect.

safe sex, sexual activity in which precautions are taken to avoid sexually transmitted diseases.

safety glass, shatter-resistant glass.

safety pin, pin bent back on itself with guard to cover point.

safety razor, razor with blade guard.

saf′flow•er (saf′lou′ər) *n.* thistle-like plant whose seeds yield cooking oil.

saf′fron (saf′rən) *n.* bright yellow seasoning.

sag (sag) *v.*, **sagged, sagging,** *n.* —*v.* **1.** bend, esp. in middle, from weight or pressure. **2.** hang loosely. —*n.* **3.** sagging place.

sa′ga (sä′gə) *n.* heroic tale.

sa•ga′cious (sə gā′shəs) *adj.* shrewd. —**sa•gac′i•ty** (-gas′ə tē) *n.*

sage (sāj) *n., adj.*, **sager, sagest.** —*n.* **1.** wise person. **2.** herb used in seasoning. —*adj.* **3.** wise; prudent.

sage′brush′, *n.* sagelike, bushy plant of dry plains of western U.S.

sa′go (sā′gō) *n.* starchy substance from some palms.

sa′hib (sä′ib) *n.* (in colonial India) term of respect for European.

said (sed) *v.* pt. of SAY. —*adj.* named before.

sail (sāl) *n.* **1.** sheet spread to catch wind to propel vessel or windmill. **2.** trip on sailing vessel. —*v.* **3.** move by action of wind. **4.** travel over water. —**sail′or,** *n.*

sail′cloth′, *n.* fabric used for boat sails or tents.

sail′fish′, *n.* large fish with upright fin.

saint (sānt) *n.* holy person. —**saint′-hood,** *n.* —**saint′ly,** *adj.*

sake (sāk) *n.* **1.** benefit. **2.** purpose. **3.** (sä′kē) rice wine.

sa•laam′ (sə läm′) *n.* **1.** Islamic salutation. **2.** low bow with hand on forehead.

sa•la′cious (sə lā′shəs) *adj.* lewd.

sal′ad (sal′əd) *n.* dish esp. of raw vegetables or fruit.

sal′a•man′der (sal′ə man′dər) *n.* small amphibian.

sa•la′mi (sə lä′mē) *n.* kind of sausage.

sal′a•ry (sal′ə rē) *n., pl.* **-ries.** fixed payment for regular work.

sale (sāl) *n.* **1.** act of selling. **2.** opportunity to sell. **3.** occasion of selling at reduced prices. —**sales′man,** *n.* —**sales′la′dy, sales′wom′an,** *n.fem.* —**sales′per′son,** *n.* —**sales′people,** *n.pl.* —**sales′room′,** *n.*

sales′man•ship′, *n.* skill of selling a product or idea.

sa′li•ent (sā′lē ənt) *adj.* **1.** conspicuous. **2.** projecting. —*n.* **3.** projecting part. —**sa′li•ence,** *n.*

sa′line (sā′lēn, -līn) *adj.* salty.

sa•li′va (sə lī′və) *n.* fluid secreted into mouth by glands. —**sal′i•var′y** (sal′ə ver′ē) *adj.* —**sal′i•vate′** (-vāt′) *v.* —**sal′i•va′tion,** *n.*

sal′low (sal′ō) *adj.* having sickly complexion.

sal′ly (sal′ē) *n., pl.* **-lies,** *v.*, **-lied, -ly-ing.** —*n.* **1.** sudden attack by besieged troops. **2.** witty remark. —*v.* **3.** make sally.

salm'on (sam'ən) *n.* pink-fleshed food fish of northern waters.

sal·mo·nel'la (sal'mə nel'ə) *n., pl.* **-nellae** (-nel'ē), **-nellas.** bacillus that causes various diseases, including food poisoning.

sa·lon' (sə lon'; *Fr.* SA LÔN') *n.* **1.** drawing room. **2.** art gallery.

sa·loon' (sə lōōn') *n.* **1.** place where intoxicating liquors are sold and drunk. **2.** public room.

sal'sa (säl'sə, -sä) *n.* **1.** Latin-American music with elements of jazz, rock, and soul. **2.** sauce, esp. hot sauce containing chilies.

salt (sôlt) *n.* **1.** sodium chloride, occurring as mineral, in sea water, etc. **2.** chemical compound derived from acid and base. **3.** wit. **4.** *Informal.* sailor. —*v.* **5.** season or preserve with salt. —**salt'y,** *adj.*

salt'cel'lar, *n.* shaker or dish for salt.

sal'tine' (sôl tēn') *n.* crisp, salted cracker.

salt lick, place where animals lick salt deposits.

salt of the earth, someone thought to embody the best human qualities.

salt'pe'ter (-pē'tər) *n.* potassium nitrate.

sa·lu'bri·ous (sə lōō'brē əs) *adj.* good for health. —**sa·lu'bri·ty,** *n.*

sal'u·tar'y (sal'yə ter'ē) *adj.* healthful; beneficial.

sal'u·ta'tion (sal'yə tā'shən) *n.* **1.** greeting. **2.** formal opening of letter.

sa·lute' (sə lōōt') *v.,* **-luted, -luting,** *n.* —*v.* **1.** express respect or goodwill, esp. in greeting. —*n.* **2.** act of saluting.

sal'vage (sal'vij) *n., v.,* **-vaged, -vaging.** —*n.* **1.** act of saving ship or cargo at sea. **2.** property saved. —*v.* **3.** save from destruction.

sal·va'tion (-vā'shən) *n.* **1.** deliverance. **2.** deliverance from sin.

salve (sav) *n., v.,* **salved, salving.** —*n.* **1.** ointment for sores. —*v.* **2.** apply salve to.

sal'ver (sal'vər) *n.* tray.

sal'vo (sal'vō) *n., pl.* **-vos, -voes.** discharge of guns, bombs, etc., in rapid series.

sam'ba (sam'bə, säm'-) *n., v.,* **-baed, -baing.** —*n.* **1.** Brazilian dance of African origin. —*v.* **2.** dance the samba.

same (sām) *adj.* **1.** identical or corresponding. **2.** unchanged. **3.** just mentioned. —*n.* **4.** same person or thing. —**same'ness,** *n.*

sam'ple (sam'pəl) *n., adj., v.,* **-pled, -pling.** —*n.* **1.** small amount to show nature or quality. —*adj.* **2.** as sample. —*v.* **3.** test by sample.

sam'pler, *n.* needlework done to show skill.

sam'u·rai' (sam'ŏŏ rī') *n., pl.* **-rai.** member of hereditary warrior class in feudal Japan.

san'a·to'ri·um (san'ə tôr'ē əm) *n., pl.* **-toriums, -toria** (-tôr'ē ə). sanitarium.

sanc'ti·fy' (sangk'tə fī') *v.,* **-fied, -fying. 1.** make holy. **2.** give sanction to. —**sanc'ti·fi·ca'tion,** *n.*

sanc'ti·mo'ni·ous (-mō'nē əs), *adj.* hypocritically devout.

sanc'tion (sangk'shən) *n.* **1.** permission or support. **2.** legal action by one state against another. —*v.* **3.** authorize; approve.

sanc'ti·ty (sangk'ti tē) *n., pl.* **-ties. 1.** holiness. **2.** sacred character.

sanc'tu·ar'y (-chōō er'ē) *n., pl.* **-ies. 1.** holy place. **2.** place of immunity from arrest or harm.

sanc'tum (-təm) *n., pl.* **-tums, -ta.** private place.

sand (sand) *n.* **1.** fine grains of rock. **2.** (*pl.*) sandy region. —*v.* **3.** smooth with sandpaper.

san'dal (san'dl) *n.* shoe consisting of sole and straps.

san'dal·wood', *n.* fragrant wood.

sand'bag', *n.* sand-filled bag used as fortification, ballast, or weapon.

sand'bank', *n.* large mass of sand.

sand bar, bar of sand formed by tidal action.

sand'blast', *v.* clean with blast of air or steam laden with sand.

sand'box', *n.* receptacle holding sand for children to play in.

sand dollar, disklike sea animal.

sand'lot', *n.* **1.** vacant lot used by youngsters for games. —*adj.* **2.** played in a sandlot.

sand'man', *n.* figure in folklore who puts sand in children's eyes to make them sleepy.

sand'pa'per, *n.* **1.** paper coated with sand. —*v.* **2.** smooth with sandpaper.

sand'pip'er (-pī'pər) *n.* small shore bird.

sand'stone', *n.* rock formed chiefly of sand.

sand'storm', *n.* windstorm with clouds of sand.

sand'wich (sand'wich, san'-) *n.* **1.** two slices of bread with filling between. —*v.* **2.** insert.

sane (sān) *adj.,* **saner, sanest.** free from mental disorder; rational.

sang-froid' (*Fr.* sän frwa') *n.* composure.

san·gri'a (sang grē'ə, san-) *n.* iced drink of red wine and fruit.

san'gui·nar'y (sang'gwə ner'ē) *adj.* **1.** bloody. **2.** bloodthirsty.

san'guine (-gwin) *adj.* **1.** hopeful. **2.** red.

san'i·tar'i·um (san'i târ'ē əm) *n., pl.* **-iums, -ia** (-ē ə). place for treatment of invalids and convalescents.

san'i·tar'y (-ter'ē) *adj.* of health.

sanitary napkin, pad worn to absorb menstrual flow.

san'i·ta'tion, *n.* application of sanitary measures.

san'i·tize', *v.,* **-tized, -tizing. 1.** free from dirt. **2.** make less offensive by removing objectionable elements.

san'i·ty, *n.* **1.** soundness of mind. **2.** good judgment.

San'skrit (san'skrit) *n.* extinct language of India.

sap (sap) *n., v.,* **sapped, sapping.** —*n.* **1.** juice of woody plant. **2.** *Slang.* fool. —*v.* **3.** weaken; undermine.

sa'pi·ent (sā'pē ənt) *adj.* wise.

sap'ling (sap'ling) *n.* young tree.

sap'phire (saf'īr) *n.* deep-blue gem.

sar'casm (sär'kaz əm) *n.* **1.** harsh derision. **2.** ironical gibe. —**sar·cas'tic,** *adj.*

sar·co'ma (sär kō'mə) *n., pl.* **-mas, -mata** (-mə tə). type of malignant tumor.

sar·coph'a·gus (sär kof'ə gəs) *n., pl.* **-gi.** stone coffin.

sar'dine' (sär dēn') *n.* small fish.

sar·don'ic (sär don'ik) *adj.* sarcastic. —**sar·don'i·cal·ly,** *adv.*

sa'ri (sär'ē) *n.* length of cloth used as dress in India.

sa·rong' (sə rông') *n.* skirtlike garment.

sar'sa·pa·ril'la (sas'pə ril'ə) *n.* **1.** tropical American plant. **2.** soft drink flavored with roots of this plant.

sar·to'ri·al (sär tôr'ē əl) *adj.* of tailors or tailoring.

SASE, self-addressed stamped envelope.

sash (sash) *n.* **1.** band of cloth usually worn as belt. **2.** framework for panes of window, etc.

sass (sas) *Informal.* —*n.* **1.** impudent back talk. —*v.* **2.** answer back impudently. —**sas'sy,** *adj.*

sas'sa·fras' (sas'ə fras') *n.* American tree with aromatic root bark.

Sa'tan (sāt'n) *n.* chief evil spirit; devil. —**sa·tan'ic** (sə tan'ik) *adj.*

satch'el (sach'əl) *n.* handbag.

sate (sāt) *v.,* **sated, sating.** satisfy.

sat'el·lite' (sat'l īt') *n.* **1.** body that revolves around planet. **2.** subservient follower.

satellite dish, dish-shaped reflector, used esp. for receiving satellite and microwave signals.

sa'ti·ate' (sā'shē āt') *v.,* **-ated, -ating.** surfeit.

sat'in (sat'n) *n.* glossy silk or rayon fabric. —**sat'in·y,** *adj.*

sat'ire (sat'īr) *n.* use of irony or ridicule in exposing vice, folly, etc. —**sa·tir'i·cal** (sə tir'i kəl), **sa·tir'ic,** *adj.* —**sat'i·rist** (sat'ər ist) *n.*

sat'i·rize' (sat'ə rīz') *v.,* **-rized, -rizing.** subject to satire.

sat'is·fac'tory (sat'is fak'tə rē) *adj.* adequate. —**sat'is·fac'to·ri·ly,** *adv.*

sat'is·fy' (-fī') *v.,* **-fied, -fying. 1.** fulfill desire, need, etc. **2.** convince. **3.** pay. —**sat'is·fac'tion** (-fak'shən) *n.*

sat'u·rate' (sach'ə rāt') *v.,* **-rated, -rating.** soak completely.

Sat'ur·day (sat'ər dā', -dē) *n.* seventh day of week.

Sat'urn (-ərn) *n.* sixth planet in order from the sun.

sat'ur·nine' (-ər nīn') *adj.* gloomy.

sa'tyr (sā'tər, sat'ər) *n.* **1.** woodland deity, part man and part goat. **2.** lecherous person.

sauce (sôs) *n.* **1.** liquid or soft relish. **2.** stewed fruit.

sauce'pan', *n.* cooking pan with handle.

sau'cer, *n.* small shallow dish.

sau'cy, *adj.,* **-cier, -ciest.** impertinent. —**sau'ci·ly,** *adv.*

sauer'kraut' (souʳr'krout', souʳər-) *n.* chopped fermented cabbage.

sau'na (sô'nə) *n.* bath heated by steam.

saun'ter (sôn'tər) *v., n.* stroll.

sau'sage (sô'sij) *n.* minced seasoned meat, often in casing.

sau·té' (sō tā', sô-) *v.,* **-téed, -téeing.** cook in a little fat.

sau·terne' (sō tûrn') *n.* sweet white wine.

sav'age (sav'ij) *adj.* **1.** wild; uncivilized. **2.** cruel. —*n.* **3.** uncivilized person. —**sav'age·ly,** *adv.* —**sav'age·ry,** *n.*

sa·van'na (sə van'ə) *n.* grassy plain with scattered trees. Also, **sa·van'nah.**

sa·vant' (sə vänt') *n.* learned person.

save (sāv) *v.,* **saved, saving,** *prep., conj.* —*v.* **1.** rescue or keep safe. **2.** reserve. —*prep., conj.* **3.** except.

sav'ing, *n.* **1.** economy. **2.** (*pl.*) money put by. —*prep.* **3.** except. **4.** respecting.

sav'ior (sāv'yər) *n.* **1.** one who rescues. **2.** (*cap.*) Christ. Also, **sav'iour.**

sa'voir-faire' (sav'wär fâr') *n.* competence in social matters.

sa'vor (sā'vər) *v., n.* taste or smell.

sa'vor·y, *adj., n., pl.,* **-ories.** —*adj.* **1.** pleasing in taste or smell. —*n.* **2.** aromatic plant.

sav'vy (sav'ē) *n.* practical understanding.

saw (sô) *n.* **1.** toothed metal blade.

—v. 2. cut with saw. **—saw′mill,** n. **—saw′yer** (sô′yər) n.

saw′buck′, n. **1.** sawhorse. **2.** Slang. ten-dollar bill.

saw′dust′, n. fine particles of wood produced in sawing.

saw′horse′, n. movable frame for supporting wood while it's being sawed.

sax (saks) n. saxophone.

Sax′on (sak′sən) n. member of Germanic people who invaded Britain in the 5th–6th centuries.

sax′o•phone′ (sak′sə fōn′) n. musical wind instrument.

say (sā) v., **said** (sed), **saying,** n. —v. **1.** speak; declare; utter. **2.** declare as truth. —n. **3.** Informal. right to speak or choose.

say′ing, n. proverb.

say′-so′, n., pl. **say-sos.** Informal. personal assurance; word.

SC, South Carolina. Also, **S.C.**

scab (skab) n., v., **scabbed, scabbing.** —n. **1.** crust forming over sore. **2.** worker who takes striker's place. —v. **3.** form scab. **4.** work as scab. **—scab′by,** adj.

scab′bard (skab′ərd) n. sheath for sword blade, etc.

sca′bies (skā′bēz, -bē ēz′) n. infectious skin disease.

scad (skad) n. (usually pl.) great quantity.

scaf′fold (skaf′əld, -ōld) n. **1.** Also, **scaf′fold•ing.** temporary framework used in construction. **2.** platform on which criminal is executed.

scal′a•wag′ (skal′ə wag′) n. rascal.

scald (skôld) v. **1.** burn with hot liquid or steam. **2.** heat just below boiling. —n. **3.** burn caused by scalding.

scale (skāl) n., v., **scaled, scaling.** —n. **1.** one of flat hard plates covering fish, etc. **2.** flake. **3.** device for weighing. **4.** series of measuring units. **5.** relative measure. **6.** succession of musical tones. —v. **7.** remove or shed scales. **8.** weigh. **9.** climb with effort. **10.** reduce proportionately. **—scal′y,** adj.

scal′lion (skal′yən) n. small green onion.

scal′lop (skol′əp, skal′-) n. **1.** bivalve mollusk. **2.** one of series of curves on a border. —v. **3.** finish with scallops.

scalp (skalp) n. **1.** skin and hair of top of head. —v. **2.** cut scalp from. **3.** buy and resell at inflated price.

scal′pel (skal′pəl) n. small surgical knife.

scam (skam) n., v., **scammed, scamming.** —n. **1.** fraudulent scheme; swindle. —v. **2.** cheat.

scamp (skamp) n. rascal.

scam′per, v. **1.** go quickly. —n. **2.** quick run.

scam′pi (skam′pē, skäm′-) n., pl. **-pi. 1.** large shrimp. **2.** dish of scampi.

scan (skan) v., **scanned, scanning. 1.** examine closely. **2.** glance at. **3.** analyze verse meter.

scan′dal (skan′dl) n. **1.** disgraceful act; disgrace. **2.** malicious gossip. **—scan′dal•ous,** adj. **—scan′dal•mon′ger,** n.

scan′dal•ize′, v., **-ized, -izing.** offend; shock.

scan′ner, n. **1.** person or thing that scans. **2.** device that monitors selected radio frequencies and reproduces any signal detected. **3.** device that optically scans bar codes, etc., and identifies data.

scan′sion (skan′shən) n. metrical analysis of verse.

scant (skant) adj. barely adequate. Also, **scant′y.** **—scant′i•ly,** adv.

scape′goat′ (skāp′gōt′) n. one made to bear blame for others.

scar (skär) n., v., **scarred, scarring.** —n. **1.** mark left by wound, etc. —v. **2.** mark with scar.

scar′ab (skar′əb) n. beetle.

scarce (skârs) adj., **scarcer, scarcest. 1.** insufficient. **2.** rare. **—scar′ci•ty,** **scarce′ness,** n.

scarce′ly, adv. **1.** barely. **2.** definitely not.

scare (skâr) v., **scared, scaring,** n. —v. **1.** frighten. —n. **2.** sudden fright.

scare′crow′, n. object set up to frighten birds away from crops.

scarf (skärf) n., pl. **scarfs, scarves** (skärvz). band of cloth esp. for neck.

scar′i•fy′ (skar′ə fī′) v., **-fied, -fying.** loosen (soil).

scar′let (skär′lit) n. bright red.

scarlet fever, disease marked by fever and rash.

scar′y (skâr′ē) adj. **-ier, -iest.** causing fear.

scat (skat) v., **scatted, scatting.** run off.

scath′ing (skā′thing) adj. bitterly severe.

scat′o•log′i•cal (skat′l oj′i kəl) adj. concerned with excrement or obscenity.

scat′ter (skat′ər) v. throw loosely about.

scat′ter•brain′, n. person incapable of coherent thought.

scav′enge (skav′inj) v., **-enged, -enging.** search for food.

sce•nar′i•o′ (si när′ē ō′, -när′-) n., pl. **-ios.** plot outline.

scene (sēn) n. **1.** location of action. **2.** view. **3.** subdivision of play. **4.** display of emotion. **—sce′nic,** adj.

scen′er•y (sē′nə rē) n. **1.** features of landscape. **2.** stage set.

scent (sent) n. **1.** distinctive odor. **2.** trail marked by this. **3.** sense of smell. —v. **4.** smell. **5.** perfume.

scep′ter (sep′tər) n. rod carried as emblem of royal power. Also, **scep′tre.**

scep′tic (skep′tik) n. skeptic.

sched′ule (skej′ōōl, -ōōl; Brit. shed′-yōōl, shej′ōōl) n., v., **-uled, -uling.** —n. **1.** timetable or list. —v. **2.** enter on schedule.

scheme (skēm) n., v., **schemed, scheming.** —n. **1.** plan; design. **2.** intrigue. —v. **3.** plan or plot. **—sche•mat′ic** (ski mat′ik) adj.

scher′zo (skert′sō) n., pl. **-zos, -zi** (-sē). playful musical movement.

schil′ling (shil′ing) n. monetary unit of Austria.

schism (siz′əm, skiz′-) n. division within church, etc.; disunion.

schiz′oid (skit′soid) adj. having personality disorder marked by depression, withdrawal, etc.

schiz′o•phre′ni•a (skit′sə frē′nē ə) n. kind of mental disorder. **—schiz′o•phren′ic** (-fren′ik) adj., n.

schle•miel′ (shlə mēl′) n. Slang. awkward and unlucky person.

schlep (shlep) v., **schlepped, schlepping,** n. Slang. **1.** carry with great effort. —n. **2.** slow or awkward person. **3.** tedious journey.

schlock (shlok) n. Informal. inferior merchandise. **—schlock′y,** adj.

schmaltz (shmälts, shmôlts) n. Informal. sentimental art, esp. music. **—schmaltz′y,** adj.

schnapps (shnäps, shnaps) n. strong alcoholic liquor.

schol′ar (skol′ər) n. **1.** learned person. **2.** pupil. **—schol′ar•ly,** adj.

schol′ar•ship′, n. **1.** learning. **2.** aid granted to promising student.

scho•las′tic (skə las′tik) adj. of schools or scholars.

school (skōōl) n. **1.** place for instruction. **2.** regular meetings of teacher and pupils. **3.** believers in doctrine or theory. **4.** group of fish, whales, etc. —v. **5.** educate; train. **—school′-teach′er,** n.

schoon′er (skōō′nər) n. kind of sailing vessel.

schwa (shwä) n. vowel sound in certain unstressed syllables, as a in sofa; usually represented by ə.

sci•at′i•ca (sī at′i kə) n. neuralgia in hip and thigh. **—sci•at′ic,** adj.

sci′ence (sī′əns) n. systematic knowledge, esp. of physical world. **—sci′en•tif′ic** (-tif′ik) adj. **—sci′en•tif′i•cal•ly,** adv. **—sci′en•tist,** n.

science fiction, fiction dealing with space travel, robots, etc.

sci-fi (sī′fī′) n., adj. Informal. science fiction.

scim′i•tar (sim′i tər) n. curved sword.

scin•til′la (sin til′ə) n. particle, esp. of evidence.

scin′til•late′ (-tl āt′) v., **-lated, -lating.** sparkle. **—scin′til•la′tion,** n.

sci′on (sī′ən) n. **1.** descendant. **2.** shoot cut for grafting.

scis′sors (siz′ərz) n.pl. cutting instrument with two pivoted blades.

scle•ro′sis (skli rō′sis) n. hardening, as of tissue.

scoff (skôf) v. jeer. **—scoff′er,** n.

scoff′law′, n. person who flouts the law, as by ignoring traffic tickets.

scold (skōld) v. **1.** find fault; reprove. —n. **2.** scolding person.

sconce (skons) n. wall bracket for candles, etc.

scone (skōn, skon) n. small flat cake.

scoop (skōōp) n. **1.** small deep shovel. **2.** bucket of steam shovel, etc. **3.** act of scooping. **4.** quantity taken up. **5.** Informal. earliest news report. —v. **6.** take up with scoop. **7.** Informal. best (competing news media) with scoop (def. 5).

scoot (skōōt) v. go swiftly.

scoot′er, n. low two-wheeled vehicle.

scope (skōp) n. extent.

scorch (skôrch) v. **1.** burn slightly. —n. **2.** superficial burn.

score (skôr) n., pl. **scores,** (for 3) **score,** v., **scored, scoring.** —n. **1.** points made in game, etc. **2.** notch. **3.** group of twenty. **4.** account; reason. **5.** written piece of music. —v. **6.** earn points in game. **7.** notch or cut. **8.** criticize. **—scor′er,** n.

scorn (skôrn) n. **1.** contempt. **2.** mockery. —v. **3.** regard or refuse with scorn. **—scorn′ful,** adj.

scor′pi•on (skôr′pē ən) n. small venomous spiderlike animal.

Scot (skot) n. native or inhabitant of Scotland. **—Scot′tish,** adj., n.pl.

scotch (skoch) v. put an end to.

Scotch, adj. **1.** (loosely) Scottish. —n. **2.** (pl.) (loosely) Scottish people. **3.** whiskey made in Scotland.

scot′-free′, adj. avoiding punishment or obligation.

Scots (skots) n. English spoken in Scotland.

scoun′drel (skoun′drəl) n. rascal.

scour (skou°r) v. **1.** clean by rubbing. **2.** range in searching.

scourge (skûrj) n., v., **scourged, scourging.** —n. **1.** whip. **2.** cause of affliction. —v. **3.** whip.

scout (skout) n. **1.** person sent ahead to examine conditions. —v. **2.** examine as scout.

scowl (skoul) n. **1.** fierce frown. —v. **2.** frown fiercely.

scrab′ble (skrab′əl) v., **-bled, -bling. 1.** scratch with hands, etc. **2.** scrawl.

scrag (skrag) n. scrawny creature.

scrag′gly, adj., **-glier, -gliest.** shaggy.

scram (skram) v., **scrammed, scramming.** Informal. go away quickly.

scram′ble (skram′bəl) v., **-bled, -bling,** n. —v. **1.** move with difficulty, using feet and hands. **2.** mix together. —n. **3.** scrambling progression. **4.** struggle for possession.

scrap (skrap) n., adj., v., **scrapped, scrapping.** —n. **1.** small piece. **2.** discarded material. **3.** Informal. fight. —adj. **4.** discarded. **5.** in scraps or as scraps. —v. **6.** break up; discard. —**scrap′py,** adj.

scrap′book′, n. blank book for clippings, etc.

scrape (skrāp) v., **scraped, scraping,** n. —v. **1.** rub harshly. **2.** remove by scraping. **3.** collect laboriously. —n. **4.** act or sound of scraping. **5.** scraped place. **6.** predicament. —**scrap′er,** n.

scrap′ple (skrap′əl) n. sausagelike food of pork, corn meal, and seasonings.

scratch (skrach) v. **1.** mark, tear, or rub with something sharp. **2.** strike out. —n. **3.** mark from scratching.

scrawl (skrôl) v. **1.** write carelessly or awkwardly. —n. **2.** such handwriting.

scraw′ny (skrô′nē) adj., **-nier, -niest.** thin. —**scraw′ni•ness,** n.

scream (skrēm) n. **1.** loud sharp cry. —v. **2.** utter screams.

screech (skrēch) n. **1.** harsh shrill cry. —v. **2.** utter screeches.

screen (skrēn) n. **1.** covered frame. **2.** anything that shelters or conceals. **3.** wire mesh. **4.** surface for displaying motion pictures. —v. **5.** shelter with screen. **6.** sift through screen. **7.** project on a screen.

screen′play′, n. outline or full script of motion picture.

screw (skrōō) n. **1.** machine part or fastener driving or driven by twisting. **2.** propeller. **3.** coercion. —v. **4.** hold with screw. **5.** turn as screw.

screw′ball′, Slang. —n. **1.** eccentric person. —adj. **2.** eccentric.

screw′driv′er, n. tool for turning screws.

screw′y, adj., **-ier, -iest.** Slang. **1.** crazy. **2.** absurd.

scrib′ble (skrib′əl) v., **-bled, -bling,** n. —v. **1.** write hastily or meaninglessly. —n. **2.** piece of such writing.

scribe (skrīb) n. professional copyist.

scrim′mage (skrim′ij) n., v., **-maged, -maging.** —n. **1.** rough struggle. **2.** play in football. —v. **3.** engage in scrimmage.

scrimp (skrimp) v. economize.

scrip (skrip) n. certificate, paper money, etc.

script (skript) n. **1.** handwriting. **2.** manuscript.

Scrip′ture (skrip′chər) n. **1.** Bible. **2.** (l.c.) sacred or religious writing or book. —**scrip′tur•al,** adj.

scriv′ner (skriv′nər) n. scribe.

scrod (skrod) n. young codfish or haddock.

scrof′u•la (skrof′yə lə) n. tuberculous disease, esp. of lymphatic glands. —**scrof′u•lous,** adj.

scroll (skrōl) n. roll of inscribed paper.

scro′tum (skrō′təm) n., pl. **-ta** (-tə), **-tums.** pouch of skin containing testicles. —**scro′tal,** adj.

scrounge (skrounj) v., **scrounged, scrounging.** Informal. **1.** beg or mooch. **2.** search. —**scroung′er,** n.

scrub (skrub) v., **scrubbed, scrubbing,** n., adj. —v. **1.** clean by rubbing. —n. **2.** low trees or shrubs. **3.** anything small or poor. —adj. **4.** small or poor. —**scrub′by,** adj.

scruff (skruf) n. nape.

scruff′y (skruf′ē) adj., **scruffier, scruffiest.** untidy.

scrump′tious (skrump′shəs) adj. extremely pleasing; delicious.

scru′ple (skrōō′pəl) n. restraint from conscience.

scru′pu•lous (-pyə ləs) adj. **1.** having scruples. **2.** careful.

scru′ti•nize′ (skrōōt′n īz′) v., **-nized, -nizing.** examine closely. —**scru′ti•ny,** n.

scu′ba (skōō′bə) n. self-contained breathing device for swimmers.

scud (skud) v., **scudded, scudding.** move quickly.

scuff (skuf) v. mar by hard use.

scuf′fle, n., v., **-fled, -fling.** —n. **1.** rough, confused fight. —v. **2.** engage in scuffle.

scull (skul) n. **1.** oar used over stern. **2.** light racing boat. —v. **3.** propel with scull.

scul′ler•y (skul′ə rē) n., pl. **-leries.** workroom off kitchen.

scul′lion (-yən) n. kitchen servant.

sculp′ture (skulp′chər) n. **1.** three-dimensional art of wood, marble, etc. **2.** piece of such work. —**sculp′tor** (-tər) n. —**sculp′tress** (-tris) n.fem.

scum (skum) n. **1.** film on top of liquid. **2.** worthless persons.

scup′per (skup′ər) n. opening in ship's side to drain off water.

scurf (skûrf) n. **1.** loose scales of skin. **2.** scaly matter on a surface.

scur′ril•ous (skûr′ə ləs) adj. coarsely abusive or derisive.

scur′ry (skûr′ē, skur′ē) v., **-ried, -rying,** n., pl. **-ries.** hurry.

scur′vy (skûr′vē) n., adj., **-vier, -viest.** —n. **1.** disease from lack of vitamin C. —adj. **2.** contemptible.

scut′tle (skut′l) n., v., **-tled, -tling.** —n. **1.** covered opening, esp. on flat roof. **2.** coal bucket. —v. **3.** sink intentionally. **4.** scurry.

scut′tle•butt′ (-but′) n. Informal. rumor; gossip.

scythe (sīth) n. curved, handled blade for mowing by hand.

SD, South Dakota. Also, **S.D.**

S. Dak., South Dakota.

SE, southeast.

sea (sē) n. **1.** ocean. **2.** body of salt water smaller than ocean. **3.** turbulence of water. —**sea′board′, sea′shore′,** n. —**sea′coast′,** n. —**sea′port′,** n. —**sea′go′ing,** adj.

sea bass (bas) marine food fish.

sea′bed′, n. ocean floor.

sea′far′ing, adj. traveling by or working at sea. —**sea′far′er,** n.

sea′food′, n. edible marine fish or shellfish.

sea gull, gull.

sea horse, small fish with beaked head.

seal (sēl) n., pl. **seals,** (also for 3) **seal,** v. —n. **1.** imprinted device affixed to document. **2.** means of closing. **3.** marine animal with large flippers. —v. **4.** affix seal to. **5.** close by seal. —**seal′ant,** n.

sea legs, ability to adjust balance to motion of ship.

sea level, position of the sea's surface at mean level between low and high tides.

sea lion, large seal.

seam (sēm) n. **1.** line formed in sewing two pieces together. —v. **2.** join with seam.

sea′man, n., pl. **-men.** sailor.

seam′stress (-stris) n. woman who sews.

seam′y, adj., **-ier, -iest.** sordid.

sé′ance (sā′äns) n. meeting to attempt communication with spirits.

sea′plane′, n. airplane equipped with floats.

sea′port′, n. port for seagoing vessels.

sear (sēr) v. **1.** burn. **2.** dry up.

search (sûrch) v. **1.** examine, as in looking for something. **2.** investigate. —n. **3.** examination or investigation. —**search′er,** n.

search′light′, n. device for throwing strong beam of light.

sea′shell′, n. shell of marine mollusk.

sea′sick′ness, n. nausea from motion of ship. —**sea′sick′,** adj.

sea′son (sē′zən) n. **1.** any of four distinct periods of year. **2.** best or usual time. —v. **3.** flavor with salt, spices, etc. —**sea′son•al,** adj.

sea′son•a•ble, adj. appropriate to time of year.

sea′son•ing, n. flavoring, as salt, spices, or herbs.

seat (sēt) n. **1.** place for sitting. **2.** right to sit, as in Congress. **3.** site; location. **4.** established center. —v. **5.** place on seat. **6.** find seats for.

seat belt, strap to keep passenger secure in vehicle.

seat′ing, n. **1.** arrangement of seats. **2.** material for seats.

sea urchin, small, round sea animal with spiny shell.

sea′way′, n. waterway from ocean to inland port.

sea′weed′, n. plant growing in sea.

sea′wor′thy, adj., **-thier, -thiest.** fit for sea travel.

se•ba′ceous (si bā′shəs) adj. secreting a fatty substance.

seb′or•rhe′a (seb′ə rē′ə) n. abnormally heavy discharge from sebaceous glands.

se•cede′ (si sēd′) v., **-ceded, -ceding.** withdraw from nation, alliance, etc. —**se•ces′sion** (-sesh′ən) n.

se•clude′ (si klōōd′) v., **-cluded, -cluding.** locate in solitude. —**se•clu′sion,** n.

sec′ond (sek′ənd) adj. **1.** next after first. **2.** another. —n. **3.** one that is second. **4.** person who aids another. **5.** (pl.) imperfect goods. **6.** sixtieth part of minute of time or degree. —v. **7.** support; further. —adv. **8.** in second place. —**sec′ond•ly,** adv.

sec′ond•ar•y (-an der′ē) adj. **1.** next after first. **2.** of second rank or stage. **3.** less important.

sec′ond-guess′, v. use hindsight in criticizing or correcting.

sec′ond•hand′, adj. not new.

second nature, deeply ingrained habit or tendency.

sec′ond-rate′, adj. of lesser or minor quality or importance.

second string, squad of players available to replace those who start a game.

second wind (wind) energy for renewed effort.

se′cret (sē′krit) adj. **1.** kept from knowledge of others. —n. **2.** something secret. —**se′cre•cy,** n.

sec′re•tar′i•at (sek′ri târ′ē ət) n. group of administrative officials.

sec′re•tar′y (-ter′ē) n., pl. **-taries. 1.** office assistant. **2.** head of department of government. **3.** tall writing desk. —**sec′re•tar′i•al,** adj.

se•crete′ (si krēt′) v., **-creted, -creting. 1.** hide. **2.** discharge or release by secretion.

se•cre′tion (-krē′shən) n. **1.** glandular function of secreting, as bile or milk. **2.** product secreted.

se′cre•tive (sē′kri tiv, si krē′-) adj. **1.** disposed to keep things secret. **2.** secretory. —**se′cre•tive•ly,** adv.

sect (sekt) n. group with common religious faith. —**sec•tar′i•an,** adj., n.

sec′tion (sek′shən) n. **1.** separate or distinct part. —v. **2.** divide.

sec′tor (sek′tər) n. **1.** plane figure bounded by two radii and an arc. **2.** part of combat area.

sec′u•lar (sek′yə lər) adj. worldly; not religious. —**sec′u•lar•ism,** n. —**sec′u•lar•ize′** v., **-ized, -izing.**

se•cure′ (si kyŏŏr′) v., **-cured, -curing.** —adj. **1.** safe. **2.** firmly in place. **3.** certain. —v. **4.** get. **5.** make secure. —**se•cure′ly,** adv.

se•cu′ri•ty (-kyŏŏr′i tē) n., pl. **-ties. 1.** safety. **2.** protection. **3.** pledge given on loan. **4.** certificate of stock, etc.

security blanket, something that gives feeling of security.

se•dan′ (si dan′) n. closed automobile for four or more.

se•date′ (si dāt′) adj. **1.** quiet; sober. —v. **2.** give sedative to. —**se•date′ly,** adv. —**se•da′tion,** n.

sed′a•tive (sed′ə tiv) adj. **1.** soothing. **2.** relieving pain or excitement. —n. **3.** sedative medicine.

sed′en•tar′y (sed′n ter′ē) adj. characterized by sitting.

sedge (sej) n. grasslike marsh plant.

sed′i•ment (sed′ə mənt) n. matter settling to bottom of liquid. —**sed′i•men•ta•ry,** adj.

se•di′tion (si dish′ən) n. incitement to rebellion. —**se•di′tious,** adj.

se•duce′ (si dōōs′, -dyōōs′) v., **-duced, -ducing. 1.** corrupt; tempt. **2.** induce to have sexual intercourse. —**se•duc′er,** n. —**se•duc′tion** (-duk′shən) n. —**se•duc′tive,** adj.

see (sē) v., **saw** (sô), **seen, seeing,** n. —v. **1.** perceive with the eyes. **2.** find out. **3.** make sure. **4.** escort. —n. **5.** jurisdiction of bishop.

seed (sēd) n. **1.** propagating part of plant. **2.** offspring. —v. **3.** sow seed. **4.** remove seed from.

seed′ling, n. plant grown from seed.

seed money, capital for beginning an enterprise.

seed′y, adj., **seedier, seediest. 1.** having many seeds. **2.** shabby.

see′ing, conj. inasmuch as.

seek (sēk) v., **sought, seeking. 1.** search for. **2.** try; attempt.

seem (sēm) v. appear (to be or do).

seem′ing, adj. apparent.

seem′ly, adj., **-lier, -liest.** decorous.

seep (sēp) v. ooze; pass gradually. —**seep′age,** n.

seer (sēr) n. **1.** person who sees. **2.** prophet. —**seer′ess,** n.

seer′suck′er (sēr′suk′ər) n. crinkled cotton fabric.

see′saw′ (sē′sô′) n. **1.** children's sport played on balancing plank. —v. **2.** alternate, waver, etc.

seethe (sēth) v., **seethed, seething.** boil; foam.

see′-through′, adj. transparent.

seg′ment (seg′mənt) n. **1.** part; section. —v. **2.** divide into segments. —**seg′men•ta′tion,** n. —**seg•men′ta•ry** (-men′tə rē) adj.

seg′re•gate′ (seg′ri gāt′) v., **-gated, -gating.** separate from others. —**seg′re•ga′tion,** n.

se′gue (sā′gwā, seg′wā) v., **segued, segueing,** n. —v. **1.** continue at once with the next section, as in piece of music. **2.** make smooth transition. —n. **3.** smooth transition.

seine (sān) n., v., **seined, seining.** —n. **1.** kind of fishing net. —v. **2.** fish with seine.

seis′mic (sīz′mik, sīs′-) adj. of or caused by earthquakes.

seis′mo•graph′ (-mə graf′) n. instrument for recording earthquakes. —**seis•mog′ra•phy,** n.

seis•mol′o•gy (-mol′ə jē) n. science of earthquakes. —**seis′mo•log′i•cal,** adj. —**seis•mol′o•gist,** n.

seize (sēz) v., **seized, seizing. 1.** take by force or authority. **2.** understand.

seiz′ure (sē′zhər) n. **1.** act of seizing. **2.** attack of illness.

sel′dom (sel′dəm) adv. not often.

se•lect′ (si lekt′) v. **1.** choose. —adj. **2.** selected. **3.** choice. —**se•lec′tion,** n. —**se•lec′tive,** adj.

se•lect′man, n., pl. **-men.** town officer in New England.

self (self) n., pl. **selves** (selvz), adj. —n. **1.** person's own nature. **2.** personal advantage or interests. —adj. **3.** identical.

self′-ad•dressed′, adj. addressed for return to sender.

self′-as•ser′tion, n. expression of one's own importance, etc. —**self′-as•ser′tive,** adj.

self′-as•sur′ance, n. confidence in one's ability. —**self′as•sured′,** adj.

self′-cen′tered, adj. interested only in oneself.

self′-con′fi•dence, n. faith in one's own judgment, ability, etc. —**self′-con′fi•dent,** adj.

self′-con′scious, adj. excessively aware of being observed by others; embarrassed or uneasy.

self′-con•tained′, adj. **1.** containing within itself all that is necessary. **2.** reserved in behavior.

self′-con•trol′, n. restraint of one's actions. —**self′-con•trolled′,** adj.

self′-de•fense′, n. **1.** act of defending oneself or one's property. **2.** plea that use of force was necessary in defending one's person.

self′-de•ni′al, n. sacrifice of one's desires.

self′-de•ter′mi•na′tion, n. right or ability to choose government or actions.

self′-ef•fac′ing, adj. keeping oneself in the background.

self′-ev′i•dent, adj. obvious.

self′-im′age, n. conception or evaluation of oneself.

self′-im•por′tant, adj. having or showing exaggerated sense of one's own importance.

self′-in′ter•est, n. one's personal benefit.

self′ish (sel′fish) adj. caring only for oneself. —**self′ish•ly,** adv.

self′less, adj. having little concern for oneself; unselfish.

self′-made′, adj. owing success entirely to one's own efforts.

self′-pos•sessed′, adj. calm; poised.

self′-pres•er•va′tion, n. instinctive desire to guard one's safety.

self′-re•spect′, n. proper esteem for oneself. —**self′-re•spect′ing,** adj.

self′-re•straint′, n. self-control.

self′-right′eous, adj. smugly convinced one is morally right.

self′same′, adj. identical.

self′-sat′is•fied′, adj. complacent.

self′-seek′ing, n. **1.** selfish seeking of one's own interests or ends. —adj. **2.** given to or characterized by self-seeking.

self′-serv′ice, adj. **1.** of a commercial establishment in which customers serve themselves. **2.** designed to be used without the aid of an attendant.

self′-serv′ing, adj. serving to further one's own interests.

self′-styled′, adj. so called only by oneself.

self′-suf•fi′cient, adj. able to supply one's own needs without external assistance.

sell (sel) v., **sold** (sōld), **selling. 1.** part with for payment. **2.** betray. **3.** be for sale. —**sell′er,** n.

sel′vage (sel′vij) n. finished edge on fabric.

se•man′tics (si man′tiks) n. study of meanings of words.

sem′a•phore′ (sem′ə fôr′) n. apparatus for signaling.

sem′blance (sem′bləns) n. **1.** appearance. **2.** copy.

se′men (sē′mən) n. male reproductive fluid.

se•mes′ter (si mes′tər) n. half school year.

semi-, prefix meaning half or partly.

sem′i•cir′cle, n. half circle. —**sem′i•cir′cu•lar,** adj.

sem′i•co′lon, n. mark of punctuation (;) between parts of sentence.

sem′i•con•duc′tor, n. substance, as silicon, with electrical conductivity between that of an insulator and a conductor.

sem′i•fi′nal, adj. **1.** of the next to last round in a tournament. —n. **2.** semifinal round or bout.

sem′i•nal (sem′ə nl) adj. **1.** of or consisting of semen. **2.** influencing future development.

sem′i•nar′ (-när′) n. class of advanced students.

sem′i•nar′y (-ner′ē) n., pl. **-ies.** school, esp. for young women or for divinity students.

Sem′i•nole (-nōl′) n., pl. **-nole, Seminoles.** member of American Indian people of Florida and Oklahoma.

sem′i•pre′cious (sem′ē-, sem′ī-) adj. of moderate value.

Se•mit′ic (sə mit′ik) n. **1.** language family of Africa and Asia, including Hebrew and Arabic. —adj. **2.** of Semitic languages or their speakers.

sem′i•tone′ (sem′ē-, sem′ī-) n. musical pitch halfway between two whole tones.

sem′o•li′na (sem′ə lē′nə) n. ground durum.

sen′ate (sen′it) n. legislative body, esp. (cap.) upper house of legislatures of United States, Canada, etc. —**sen′a•tor** (-i tər) n.

send (send) v., **sent, sending. 1.** cause to go. **2.** have conveyed. **3.** emit. —**send′er,** n.

send′-off′, n. farewell demonstration of good wishes.

se•nile′ (sē′nīl) adj. feeble, esp. because of old age. —**se•nil′i•ty** (si nil′ə tē) n.

sen′ior (sēn′yər) adj. **1.** older. **2.** of higher rank. **3.** denoting last year in school. —n. **4.** senior person.

senior citizen, person 65 years of age or more.

sen•ior′i•ty (sēn yôr′i tē) n., pl. **-ties.** status conferred by length of service.

se•ñor′ (se nyôr′) n., pl. **-ño•res** (-nyôr′es). Spanish. **1.** gentleman. **2.** Mr. or sir. —**se•ño′ra,** n.

se′ño·ri′ta (se′nyō rē′tä) *n. Spanish.*
1. Miss. **2.** young lady.

sen·sa′tion (sen sā′shən) *n.* **1.** operation of senses. **2.** mental condition from such operation. **3.** cause of excited interest.

sen·sa′tion·al, *adj.* **1.** startling; exciting. **2.** of senses or sensation.

sen·sa′tion·al·ism, *n.* use of sensational subject matter.

sense (sens) *n., v.,* **sensed, sensing.**
—n. **1.** faculty for perceiving stimuli (sight, hearing, smell, etc.). **2.** feeling so produced. **3.** (*pl.*) consciousness. **4.** (*often pl.*) rationality; prudence. **5.** meaning. *—v.* **6.** perceive by senses.

sen′si·bil′i·ty (sen′sə bil′i tē) *n., pl.*
-ties. 1. capacity for sensation. **2.** (*often pl.*) sensitive feeling.

sen′si·ble, *adj.* **1.** wise or practical. **2.** aware. *—sen′si·bly, adv.*

sen′si·tive, *adj.* **1.** having sensation. **2.** easily affected.

sen′si·tize′ (-tīz′) *v.,* **-tized, -tizing.** make sensitive.

sen′sor (sen′sôr, -sər) *n.* device sensitive to light, temperature, or radiation level that transmits signal to another instrument.

sen′so·ry (-sə rē) *adj.* of sensation or senses.

sen′su·al (sen′shōō əl) *adj.* **1.** inclined to pleasures of the senses. **2.** lewd. *—sen′su·al′i·ty* (-al′i tē) *n.* *—sen′su·al·ly, adv.*

sen′su·ous, *adj.* **1.** of or affected by senses. **2.** giving or seeking enjoyment through senses.

sen′tence (sen′tns) *n., v.,* **-tenced, -tencing.** *—n.* **1.** group of words expressing complete thought. **2.** judgment; opinion. **3.** assignment of punishment. *—v.* **4.** pronounce sentence upon.

sen·ten′tious (sen ten′shəs) *adj.* using maxims or pompous words.

sen′tient (sen′shənt) *adj.* having feeling. *—sen′tience, n.*

sen′ti·ment (-tə mənt) *n.* **1.** opinion. **2.** emotion. **3.** expression of belief or emotion.

sen′ti·men′tal (-men′tl) *adj.* expressing or showing tender emotion.

sen′ti·nel (sen′tn l, -tə nl) *n.* guard.

sen′try (sen′trē) *n., pl.* **-tries.** soldier on watch.

se′pal (sē′pəl) *n.* leaflike part of flower.

sep′a·rate′, *v.,* **-rated, -rating,** *adj.*
—v. (sep′ə rāt′) **1.** keep, put, or come apart. *—adj.* (-rit) **2.** not connected; being apart. *—sep′a·ra′tion, n. —sep′a·ra·ble, adj.*

sep′a·ra·tist (-ər ə tist, -ə rā′-) *n.* advocate of separation.

sep′a·ra·tor, *n.* apparatus for separating ingredients.

se′pi·a (sē′pē ə) *n.* **1.** brown pigment. **2.** dark brown.

sep′sis (sep′sis) *n.* infection in blood. *—sep′tic* (-tik) *adj.*

Sept., September.

Sep·tem′ber (sep tem′bər) *n.* ninth month of year.

sep·tet′ (sep tet′) *n.* group of seven. Also, **sep·tette′.**

sep′ti·ce′mi·a (sep′tə sē′mē ə) *n.* blood poisoning.

septic tank, tank for decomposition of sewage.

sep′tu·a·ge·nar′i·an (sep′chōō ə jə·nâr′ē ən) *n.* person 70 to 79 years old.

Sep′tu·a·gint (-jint) *n.* oldest Greek version of Old Testament.

sep′ul·cher (sep′əl kər) *n.* burial place. Also, **sep′ul·chre. —se·pul′·chral** (sə pul′krəl) *adj.*

seq., **1.** sequel. **2.** the following.

se′quel (sē′kwəl) *n.* **1.** subsequent event. **2.** literary work, film, etc., continuing earlier one.

se′quence (-kwəns) *n.* **1.** succession; series. **2.** result.

se·ques′ter (si kwes′tər) *v.* **1.** seclude. **2.** seize and hold.

se′quin (sē′kwin) *n.* small spangle.

se·quoi′a (si kwoi′ə) *n.* very large tree of northwest U.S.

se·ra′glio (si ral′yō, -räl′-) *n., pl.* **-glios.** harem.

ser′aph (ser′əf) *n., pl.* **-aphs, -aphim** (-ə fim). angel of highest order. *—se·raph′ic* (sə raf′ik) *adj.*

sere (sēr) *adj.* withered.

ser′e·nade′ (ser′ə nād′) *n., v.,* **-naded, -nading.** *—n.* **1.** music performed as compliment outside at night. *—v.* **2.** compliment with serenade.

ser′en·dip′i·ty (ser′ən dip′i tē) *n.* luck in making accidental discoveries.

se·rene′ (sə rēn′) *adj.* **1.** calm. **2.** fair. *—se·ren′i·ty* (-ren′ə tē) *n.*

serf (sûrf) *n.* **1.** person in feudal servitude. **2.** slave. *—serf′dom, n.*

serge (sûrj) *n.* stout twilled fabric.

ser′geant (sär′jənt) *n.* noncommissioned officer above corporal.

se′ri·al (sēr′ē əl) *n.* **1.** story, etc., appearing in installments. *—adj.* **2.** of serial. **3.** of or in series.

se′ries (sēr′ēz) *n.* things in succession.

ser′if (ser′if) *n.* smaller line used to finish off main stroke of letter.

ser′i·graph′ (ser′i graf′) *n.* silkscreen print.

se′ri·ous (sēr′ē əs) *adj.* **1.** solemn. **2.** important.

ser′mon (sûr′mən) *n.* religious discourse.

ser′pent (sûr′pənt) *n.* snake.

ser′pen·tine′ (-pən tēn′, -tīn′) *adj.* **1.** like a snake. **2.** winding.

ser·rat·ed (ser′ā tid) *adj.* toothed; notched. Also, **ser′rate** (ser′it).

se′rum (sēr′əm) *n., pl.* **serums, sera** (sēr′ə). **1.** pale-yellow liquid in blood. **2.** such liquid from animal immune to certain disease.

serv′ant (sûr′vənt) *n.* person employed at domestic work.

serve (sûrv) *v.,* **served, serving. 1.** act as servant. **2.** help. **3.** do official duty. **4.** suffice. **5.** undergo (imprisonment, etc.). **6.** hand out.

serv′ice (sûr′vis) *n., v.,* **-iced, -icing.** *—n.* **1.** helpful activity. **2.** domestic employment. **3.** armed forces. **4.** act of public worship. **5.** set of dishes, etc. *—v.* **6.** keep in repair.

serv′ice·a·ble, *adj.* usable.

ser′vile (sûr′vil, -vīl) *adj.* slavishly submissive or obsequious. *—ser·vil′i·ty* (-vil′ə tē) *n.*

ser′vi·tor (sûr′vi tər) *n.* servant.

ser′vi·tude′ (-tōōd′, -tyōōd′) *n.* bondage.

ses′a·me (ses′ə mē) *n.* small edible seed of tropical plant.

ses′sion (sesh′ən) *n.* sitting, as of a court or class.

set (set) *v.,* **set, setting,** *n., adj.* *—v.* **1.** put or place. **2.** put (broken bone) in position. **3.** arrange (printing type). **4.** pass below horizon. **5.** become firm. *—n.* **6.** group; complete collection. **7.** radio or television receiver. **8.** represented setting of action in drama. *—adj.* **9.** prearranged. **10.** fixed. **11.** resolved.

set′back′, *n.* return to worse condition.

set·tee′ (se tē′) *n.* small sofa.

set′ter (set′ər) *n.* kind of hunting dog.

set′ting, *n.* **1.** surroundings. **2.** music for certain words.

set′tle (set′l) *v.,* **-tled, -tling. 1.** agree. **2.** pay. **3.** take up residence. **4.** colonize. **5.** quiet. **6.** come to rest. **7.** deposit dregs. *—set′tle·ment, n.* *—set′tler, n.*

set′-to′ (-tōō′) *n., pl.* **set-tos.** brief, sharp fight.

set′up′, *n. Informal.* situation in detail.

sev′en (sev′ən) *n., adj.* six plus one. *—sev′enth, adj., n.*

sev′en·teen′, *n., adj.* sixteen plus one. *—sev′en·teenth′, adj., n.*

seventh heaven, bliss.

sev′en·ty, *n., adj.* ten times seven. *—sev′en·ti′eth, adj., n.*

sev′er (sev′ər) *v.* separate; break off. *—sev′er·ance, n.*

sev′er·al (sev′ər əl) *adj.* **1.** some, but not many. **2.** respective. **3.** various. *—n.* **4.** some.

se·vere′ (sə vēr′) *adj.,* **-verer, -verest. 1.** harsh. **2.** serious. **3.** plain. **4.** violent or hard. *—se·ver′i·ty* (-ver′i·tē) *n.* *—se·vere′ly, adv.*

sew (sō) *v.,* **sewed, sewed** or **sewn, sewing.** join or make with thread and needle. *—sew′er, n.*

sew′age (sōō′ij) *n.* wastes carried by sewers.

sew′er (sōō′ər) *n.* conduit for waste water, refuse, etc.

sex (seks) *n.* **1.** character of being male or female. **2.** sexual intercourse. *—sex′u·al* (sek′shōō əl) *adj.* *—sex′u·al′i·ty, n.*

sex′a·ge·nar′i·an (sek′sə jə nâr′ē·ən) *n.* person 60 to 69 years old.

sex chromosome, chromosome that determines individual's sex.

sex′ism, *n.* bias because of sex, esp. against women. *—sex′ist, n., adj.*

sex′tant (sek′stənt) *n.* astronomical instrument for finding position.

sex·tet′ (seks tet′) *n.* group of six. Also, **sex·tette′.**

sex′ton (sek′stən) *n.* church caretaker.

sexual harassment, unwelcome sexual advances, esp. by a superior.

sexual intercourse, genital contact between individuals, esp. penetration of penis into vagina.

sexually transmitted disease, disease transmitted by sexual contact.

sex′y, *adj.,* **-ier, -iest.** sexually interesting or exciting; erotic.

Sgt., Sergeant.

shab′by (shab′ē) *adj.,* **-bier, -biest. 1.** worn; wearing worn clothes. **2.** mean. *—shab′bi·ly, adv.*

shack (shak) *n.* rough cabin.

shack′le (shak′əl) *n., v.,* **-led, -ling.** *—n.* **1.** iron bond for wrist, ankle, etc. *—v.* **2.** restrain.

shad (shad) *n.* kind of herring.

shade (shād) *n., v.,* **shaded, shading.** *—n.* **1.** slightly dark, cool place. **2.** ghost. **3.** degree of color. **4.** slight amount. *—v.* **5.** protect from light.

shad′ow (shad′ō) *n.* **1.** dark image made by body intercepting light. **2.** shade. **3.** trace. *—v.* **4.** shade. **5.** follow secretly. *—shad′ow·y, adj.*

shad′ow-box′, *v.* go through motions of boxing without an opponent, as in training.

shad′y, *adj.,* **-ier, -iest. 1.** in shade. **2.** arousing suspicion.

shaft (shaft) *n.* **1.** long slender rod. **2.** beam. **3.** revolving bar in engine. **4.** vertical space.

shag (shag) *n.* **1.** matted wool, hair, etc. **2.** napped cloth.

shah (shä) *n.* (formerly) ruler of Persia (now Iran).

shake (shāk) *v.*, **shook** (shŏŏk), **shaken, shaking,** *n.* —*v.* **1.** move with quick irregular motions. **2.** tremble. **3.** agitate. —*n.* **4.** act of shaking. **5.** tremor. —**shak'er,** *n.*

shake'down', *n.* **1.** extortion, as by blackmail. **2.** thorough search.

shake'up', *n. Informal.* organizational reform.

shak'y, *adj.*, **-ier, -iest. 1.** not firm; insecure. **2.** affected by fright.

shale (shāl) *n.* kind of layered rock.

shall (shal; *unstressed* shəl) *v.* **1.** am (is, are) going to. **2.** am (is, are) obliged or commanded to.

shal'lot (shal'ət) *n.* small onionlike plant.

shal·low (shal'ō) *adj.* not deep.

sham (sham) *n. adj.*, *v.*, **shammed, shamming.** —*n.* **1.** pretense or imitation. —*adj.* **2.** pretended. —*v.* **3.** pretend.

sham'ble, *v.*, **-bled, -bling,** *n.* —*v.* **1.** walk awkwardly. —*n.* **2.** shambling gait. **3.** (*pl.*) scene of confusion.

shame (shām) *n.*, *v.*, **shamed, shaming.** —*n.* **1.** distress and guilt over wrong or foolish act. **2.** disgrace. —*v.* **3.** cause to feel shame.

shame'faced' (-fāst') *adj.* **1.** bashful. **2.** showing shame.

sham·poo' (sham pōō') *v.* **1.** wash (hair, rugs, or upholstery). —*n.* **2.** act of shampooing. **3.** soap, etc., for shampooing.

sham'rock (sham'rok) *n.* plant with three-part leaf.

shang'hai (shang'hī) *v.*, **-haied, -haiing.** (formerly) abduct to serve as sailor.

shank (shangk) *n.* part of leg between knee and ankle.

shan'tung' (shan'tung') *n.* silk.

shan'ty (shan'tē) *n.*, *pl.* **-ties.** rough hut.

shape (shāp) *n.*, *v.*, **shaped, shaping.** —*n.* **1.** form. **2.** condition. —*v.* **3.** give form to; take form. **4.** adapt. —**shape'less,** *adj.*

shape'ly, *adj.*, **-lier, -liest.** handsome in shape. —**shape'li·ness,** *n.*

share (shâr) *n.*, *v.*, **shared, sharing.** —*n.* **1.** due individual portion. **2.** portion of corporate stock. —*v.* **3.** distribute. **4.** use, enjoy, etc., jointly. —**share'hold'er,** *n.*

share'crop'per, *n.* tenant farmer who pays as rent part of the crop.

shark (shärk) *n.* marine fish, often ferocious.

sharp (shärp) *adj.* **1.** having thin cutting edge or fine point. **2.** abrupt. **3.** keen. **4.** shrewd. **5.** raised in musical pitch. —*adv.* **6.** punctually. —*n.* **7.** musical tone one half step above given tone. —**sharp'en,** *v.* —**sharp'en·er,** *n.* —**sharp'ly,** *adv.* —**sharp'ness,** *n.*

sharp'shoot'er, *n.* skilled shooter.

shat'ter (shat'ər) *v.* break in pieces.

shat'ter·proof', *adj.* made to resist shattering.

shave (shāv) *v.*, **shaved, shaved or shaven, shaving,** *n.* —*v.* **1.** remove hair with razor. **2.** cut thin slices. —*n.* **3.** act of shaving.

shav'ings, *n.pl.* thin slices of wood.

shawl (shôl) *n.* long covering for head and shoulders.

she (shē) *pron.* **1.** female last mentioned. —*n.* **2.** female.

sheaf (shēf) *n.*, *pl.* **sheaves.** bundle.

shear (shēr) *v.*, **sheared, sheared or shorn, shearing.** clip, as wool.

shears, *n.pl.* large scissors.

sheath (shēth) *n.* **1.** case for sword blade. **2.** any similar covering.

sheathe (shēth) *v.*, **sheathed, sheathing.** put into or enclose in sheath.

she·bang' (shə bang') *n. Informal.* organization or contrivance.

shed (shed) *v.*, **shed, shedding,** *n.* —*v.* **1.** pour forth. **2.** cast (light). **3.** throw off. —*n.* **4.** simple enclosed shelter.

sheen (shēn) *n.* brightness.

sheep (shēp) *n.*, *pl.* **sheep.** mammal valued for wool and meat.

sheep dog, dog trained to herd sheep.

sheep'fold', *n.* enclosure for sheep.

sheep'ish, *adj.* embarrassed or ashamed.

sheer (shēr) *adj.* **1.** very thin. **2.** complete. **3.** steep. —*v.*, *n.* **4.** swerve.

sheet (shēt) *n.* **1.** large piece of cloth used as bedding. **2.** broad thin layer or piece.

sheik (shēk) *n.* (Arab) chief.

shek'el (shek'əl) *n.* ancient Hebrew and modern Israeli monetary unit.

shelf (shelf) *n.*, *pl.* **shelves** (shelvz). **1.** horizontal slab on wall, etc., for holding objects. **2.** ledge.

shelf life, period during which commodity remains fit for use.

shell (shel) *n.* **1.** hard outer covering. **2.** shotgun cartridge. **3.** explosive missile from cannon. **4.** light racing boat. —*v.* **5.** remove shell from. **6.** take from shell. **7.** bombard with shells.

shel·lac' (shə lak') *n.*, *v.*, **-lacked, -lacking.** —*n.* **1.** substance used in varnish. **2.** varnish. —*v.* **3.** coat with shellac.

shell'fish', *n.* aquatic animal having shell.

shell shock, combat fatigue.

shel'ter (shel'tər) *n.* **1.** place of protection. —*v.* **2.** protect.

shelve (shelv) *v.*, **shelved, shelving. 1.** put on shelf. **2.** lay aside. **3.** furnish with shelves. **4.** slope.

she·nan·i·gans (shə nan'i gənz) *n.pl. Informal.* mischief.

shep'herd (shep'ərd) *n.* **1.** person who tends sheep. —*v.* **2.** guide. —**shep'herd·ess,** *n.*

sher'bet (shûr'bit) *n.* frozen fruit-flavored dessert.

sher'iff (sher'if) *n.* county law-enforcement officer.

sher'ry (sher'ē) *n.*, *pl.* **-ries.** fortified wine served as cocktail.

shib'bo·leth (shib'ə lith) *n.* peculiarity of pronunciation or usage that distinguishes a group.

shield (shēld) *n.* **1.** plate of armor carried on arm. —*v.* **2.** protect.

shift (shift) *v.* **1.** move about. **2.** change positions. —*n.* **3.** act of shifting. **4.** period of work.

shift'less, *adj.* resourceless or lazy.

shift'y, *adj.*, **-ier, -iest.** devious.

shill (shil) *n.* person who poses as a customer to lure others.

shil·le·lagh (shə lā'lē, -lə) *n.* rough Irish walking stick or cudgel.

shil'ling (shil'ing) *n.* former British coin, 20th part of pound.

shil'ly-shal'ly (shil'ē shal'ē) *v.*, **shilly-shallied, shilly-shallying.** hesitate or waste time.

shim'mer (shim'ər) *v.* **1.** glow faintly; flicker. —*n.* **2.** faint glow.

shin (shin) *n.* front of leg from knee to ankle.

shin'bone', *n.* tibia.

shin'dig' (shin'dig') *n. Informal.* elaborate and usu. large party.

shine (shīn) *v.*, **shone** (shōn) or (for

4) **shined, shining,** *n.* —*v.* **1.** give forth light. **2.** sparkle. **3.** excel. **4.** polish. —*n.* **5.** radiance. **6.** polish. —**shin'y,** *adj.*

shin'er, *n. Informal.* black eye.

shin'gle (shing'gəl) *n.*, *v.*, **-gled, -gling.** —*n.* **1.** thin slab used in overlapping rows as covering. **2.** (*pl.*) viral skin disease marked by blisters. —*v.* **3.** cover with shingles.

shin splints, painful condition of shins associated with strenuous activity.

Shin'to (shin'tō) *n.* native religion of Japan.

ship (ship) *n.*, *v.*, **shipped, shipping.** —*n.* **1.** vessel for use on water. —*v.* **2.** send as freight. **3.** engage to serve on ship. **4.** send away. —**ship'board',** *n.* —**ship'mate',** *n.* —**ship'ment,** *n.*

-ship, suffix meaning: **1.** state or quality, as *friendship.* **2.** position or rank, as *lordship.* **3.** skill or art, as *horsemanship.*

ship'shape', *adj.*, *adv.* in good order.

ship'wreck', *n.* destruction of ship.

ship'wright', *n.* carpenter in ship repair or construction.

ship'yard', *n.* place where ships are built or repaired.

shire (shīr) *n.* county in Great Britain.

shirk (shûrk) *v.* evade (obligation).

shirr (shûr) *v.* **1.** gather (cloth) on parallel threads. **2.** bake (eggs).

shirt (shûrt) *n.* garment for upper body.

shirt'tail', *n.* part of shirt below waistline.

shirt'waist', *n.* tailored blouse.

shish' ke·bab' (shish' kə bob') cubes of meat broiled on a skewer.

shiv'er (shiv'ər) *v.* **1.** tremble as with cold. **2.** splinter. —*n.* **3.** quiver. **4.** splinter. —**shiv'er·y,** *adj.*

shoal (shōl) *n.* **1.** shallow part of stream. **2.** large number, esp. of fish.

shock (shok) *n.* **1.** violent blow, impact, etc. **2.** anything emotionally upsetting. **3.** state of nervous collapse. **4.** effect of electric charge. **5.** bushy mass of hair, etc. —*v.* **6.** strike with force, horror, etc. **7.** subject to electric shock.

shock absorber, device for damping sudden rapid motion.

shock therapy, treatment for mental disorders using electricity.

shod'dy (shod'ē) *adj.*, **-dier, -diest.** of poor quality. —**shod'di·ly,** *adv.*

shoe (shōō) *n.*, *v.*, **shod** (shod), **shoeing.** —*n.* **1.** external covering for foot. **2.** shoelike machine part. —*v.* **3.** provide with shoes.

shoe'horn', *n.* shaped object to assist in slipping on shoe.

shoe'mak'er, *n.* person who makes or mends shoes.

shoe'string', *n.* very small amount of money.

shoe'tree', *n.* device placed in shoe to hold its shape.

sho'gun (shō'gən) *n.* chief military commander of Japan from 8th to 12th centuries.

shoo (shōō) *v.*, **shooed, shooing.** drive away by shouting "shoo."

shoo'-in', *n.* one regarded as certain to win.

shoot (shōōt) *v.* **1.** hit or kill with bullet. **2.** discharge (firearm, bow, etc.). **3.** pass or send rapidly along. **4.** emit. **5.** grow; come forth. —*n.* **6.** shooting contest. **7.** young twig, etc. —**shoot'er,** *n.*

shooting star, meteor.

shop (shop) *n.*, *v.*, **shopped, shopping.** —*n.* **1.** store. **2.** workshop. —*v.* **3.** look at or purchase goods.

shop′lift′er, *n.* person who steals from shops while posing as customer.

shop′talk′, *n.* conversation about one's work or occupation.

shore (shōr) *v.,* **shored, shoring,** *n.* —*v.* **1.** prop. —*n.* **2.** prop. **3.** land beside water. **4.** land or country.

shorn (shôrn) *v.* pp. of **shear.**

short (shôrt) *adj.* **1.** not long or tall. **2.** rudely brief. **3.** scanty. **4.** inferior. **5.** crumbly, as pastry. —*adv.* **6.** abruptly. —*n.* **7.** anything short. **8.** (pl.) short, loose trousers. **9.** short circuit. —**short′en,** *v.*

short′age (shôr′tij) *n.* scarcity.

short′bread′, *n.* rich butter cookie.

short′cake′, *n.* rich biscuit topped with fruit and cream.

short′change′, *v.,* **-changed, -changing. 1.** give less than the correct change to. **2.** cheat; defraud.

short circuit, *Elect.* abnormal connection between two points in circuit.

short′com′ing, *n.* defect.

short′cut′, *n.* shorter way to goal.

short′en·ing (shôrt′ning) *n.* butter or other fat used to make pastry.

short′hand′, *n.* system of swift handwriting.

short′-hand′ed, *adj.* not having enough workers.

short′-lived′ (-līvd, -livd) *adj.* lasting only a short time.

short′ly, *adv.* in a short time.

short shrift, little attention or consideration.

short′-sight′ed, *adj.* lacking foresight.

short′stop′, *n. Baseball.* player or position between second and third base.

short′-tem′pered, *adj.* irascible.

short′wave′, *n.* radio frequencies used for long-distance transmission.

Sho·sho′ne (shō shō′nē) *n., pl.* **-ne, -nes.** member of an American Indian people.

shot (shot) *n., pl.* **shots** or (for 3), **shot. 1.** discharge of firearm, bow, etc. **2.** range of fire. **3.** (*often pl.*) lead pellets. **4.** act or instance of shooting. **5.** person who shoots. **6.** heavy metal ball.

shot′gun′, *n.* kind of smoothbore gun.

shot put, competition in which heavy metal ball is thrown for distance. —**shot′-put′ter,** *n.*

should (shŏŏd) *v.* pt. of **shall.**

shoul′der (shōl′dər) *n.* **1.** part of body from neck to upper joint of arm or foreleg. —*v.* **2.** push as with shoulder. **3.** take up, as burden.

shout (shout) *v.* **1.** call or speak loudly. —*n.* **2.** loud cry.

shove (shuv) *v.,* **shoved, shoving,** *n.* —*v.* **1.** push hard. —*n.* **2.** hard push.

shov′el, *n., v.,* **-eled, -eling.** —*n.* **1.** implement with broad scoop and handle. —*v.* **2.** dig or clear.

show (shō) *v.,* **showed, shown** or **showed, showing,** *n.* —*v.* **1.** display. **2.** guide. **3.** explain. **4.** prove. **5.** be visible. —*n.* **6.** exhibition. **7.** acted entertainment. **8.** appearance.

show′case′, *n., v.,* **-cased, -casing.** —*n.* **1.** setting for displaying something. —*v.* **2.** exhibit to best advantage.

show′down′, *n.* decisive confrontation.

show′er (shou′ər) *n.* **1.** short fall of rain. **2.** any similar fall. **3.** bath in which water falls from above. —*v.* **4.** rain briefly. **5.** give liberally.

show′-off′ (shō′-) *n.* person who seeks attention.

show′piece′, *n.* something worthy of being exhibited.

show′place′, *n.* place notable for its beauty or historical interest.

show′y, *adj.,* **-ier, -iest.** conspicuous; ostentatious.

shrap′nel (shrap′nl) *n.* shell filled with missiles.

shred (shred) *n., v.,* **shredded** or **shred, shredding.** —*n.* **1.** torn piece or strip. **2.** bit. —*v.* **3.** reduce to shreds.

shrew (shrōō) *n.* **1.** quarrelsome woman. **2.** small mouselike mammal. —**shrew′ish,** *adj.*

shrewd (shrōōd) *adj.* astute.

shriek (shrēk) *n.* **1.** loud shrill cry. —*v.* **2.** utter shrieks.

shrill (shril) *adj.* **1.** high-pitched; piercing. —*v.* **2.** cry shrilly.

shrimp (shrimp) *n.* small long-tailed edible shellfish.

shrine (shrīn) *n.* place for sacred relics.

shrink (shringk) *v.,* **shrank** (shrangk) or **shrunk** (shrungk), **shrunk** or **shrunken, shrinking. 1.** draw back. **2.** become smaller.

shrink′age (shring′kij) *n.* **1.** act of shrinking. **2.** amount of shrinking.

shrinking violet, shy person.

shrink′-wrap′, *v.,* **shrink-wrapped, shrink-wrapping,** *n.* —*v.* **1.** seal in plastic film that when exposed to heat shrinks tightly around object. —*n.* **2.** plastic used to shrink-wrap.

shrive (shrīv) *v.,* **shrove** (shrōv) or **shrived, shriven** (shriv′ən) or **shrived, shriving. 1.** impose penance on. **2.** grant absolution to.

shriv′el (shriv′əl) *v.,* **-eled, -eling.** wrinkle in drying.

shroud (shroud) *n.* **1.** burial gown or cloth. —*v.* **2.** hide from view.

shrub (shrub) *n.* woody perennial plant. —**shrub′ber·y,** *n.*

shrug (shrug) *v.,* **shrugged, shrugging,** *n.* —*v.* **1.** move shoulders to show ignorance, indifference, etc. —*n.* **2.** this movement.

shtick (shtik) *n. Slang.* **1.** showbusiness routine. **2.** special interest, talent, etc. Also, **shtik.**

shuck (shuk) *n.* **1.** husk. **2.** shell. —*v.* **3.** remove shucks from.

shud′der (shud′ər) *v.* **1.** tremble, as from horror. —*n.* **2.** this movement.

shuf′fle (shuf′əl) *v.,* **-fled, -fling,** *n.* —*v.* **1.** drag feet in walking. **2.** mix (playing cards). **3.** shift. —*n.* **4.** shuffling gait. **5.** act of shuffling cards.

shuf′fle·board′, *n.* game played on marked floor surface.

shun (shun) *v.,* **shunned, shunning.** avoid.

shunt (shunt) *v.* divert; sidetrack.

shut (shut) *v.,* **shut, shutting,** *adj.* —*v.* **1.** close. **2.** confine. **3.** exclude. —*adj.* **4.** closed.

shut′out′, *n.* game in which one side does not score.

shut′ter, *n.* **1.** cover for window. **2.** device for opening and closing camera lens.

shut′tle (shut′l) *n., v.,* **-tled, -tling.** —*n.* **1.** device for moving thread back and forth in weaving. **2.** bus, plane, etc., moving between two destinations. —*v.* **3.** move quickly back and forth.

shut′tle·cock′, *n.* feathered object hit back and forth in badminton.

shy (shī) *adj.,* **shyer** or **shier, shyest** or **shiest,** *v.,* **shied, shying,** *n., pl.* **shies.** —*adj.* **1.** bashful. **2.** wary. **3.** short. —*v.* **4.** start aside, as in fear. **5.** throw suddenly. —*n.* **6.** shying movement. **7.** sudden throw.

shy′ster (shī′stər) *n. Informal.* unscrupulous lawyer.

Si′a·mese′ twins (sī′ə mēz′, -mēs′) twins joined together by body part.

sib′i·lant (sib′ə lənt) *adj.* **1.** hissing. —*n.* **2.** hissing sound.

sib′ling (sib′ling) *n.* brother or sister.

sib′yl (sib′əl) *n.* female prophet.

sic (sik) *v.,* **sicked, sicking,** *adv.* —*v.* **1.** urge to attack. —*adv.* **2.** *Latin.* so (it reads).

sick (sik) *adj.* **1.** ill; not well. **2.** of sickness. **3.** nauseated. —*n.pl.* **4.** sick people. —**sick′en,** *v.*

sick′le (sik′əl) *n.* reaping implement with curved blade.

sick′ly, *adj.,* **-lier, -liest,** *adv.* **1.** ailing. **2.** faint; weak.

side (sīd) *n., adj., v.,* **sided, siding.** —*n.* **1.** edge. **2.** surface. **3.** part other than front, back, top, or bottom. **4.** aspect. **5.** region. **6.** faction. —*adj.* **7.** at, from, or toward side. **8.** subordinate. —*v.* **9.** align oneself.

side′bar′, *n.* short news feature highlighting longer story.

side′board′, *n.* dining-room cupboard.

side′burns′, *n.pl.* short whiskers in front of ears.

side effect, *n.* often adverse secondary effect.

side′kick′, *n.* **1.** close friend. **2.** confederate or assistant.

side′light′, *n.* item of incidental information.

side′line′, *n., v.,* **-lines,** *v.,* **-lined, -lining.** —*n.* **1.** business or activity in addition to one's primary business. **2.** additional line of goods. **3.** line defining the side of an athletic field. —*v.* **4.** remove from action.

side′long′, *adj., adv.* to or toward the side.

side′sad′dle, *adv.* with both legs on one side of a saddle.

side′show′, *n.* subordinate event or spectacle.

side′split′ting, *adj.* very funny.

side′step′, *v.,* **-stepped, -stepping.** avoid, as by stepping aside.

side′swipe′, *v.,* **-swiped, -swiping.** strike along side.

side′track′, *v.* divert.

side′walk′, *n.* paved walk along street.

side′ward (-wərd) *adj.* toward one side. —**side′ward, side′wards,** *adv.*

side′ways′, *adj., adv.* **1.** with side foremost. **2.** toward or from a side. Also, **side′wise′.**

sid′ing, *n.* short railroad track for halted cars.

si′dle (sīd′l) *v.,* **-dled, -dling.** move sideways or furtively.

SIDS (sidz) —*n.* sudden infant death syndrome.

siege (sēj) *n.* surrounding of place to force surrender.

si·en′na (sē en′ə) *n.* yellowish- or reddish-brown pigment.

si·er′ra (sē er′ə) *n.* jagged chain of hills or mountains.

si·es′ta (sē es′tə) *n.* midday nap or rest.

sieve (siv) *n., v.,* **sieved, sieving.** —*n.* **1.** meshed implement for separating coarse and fine loose matter. —*v.* **2.** sift.

sift (sift) *v.* separate with sieve.

sigh (sī) *v.* **1.** exhale audibly in grief, weariness, etc. **2.** yearn. —*n.* **3.** act or sound of sighing.

sight (sīt) *n.* **1.** power of seeing. **2.** glimpse; view. **3.** range of vision. **4.** device for guiding aim. **5.** interesting place. —*v.* **6.** get sight of. **7.** aim by sights. —**sight′less,** *adj.*

sight′ed, *adj.* not blind.

sight′read′ (rēd) *v.,* **-read** (-red′), **sightreading.** perform without previous study.

sight′see′ing, *n.* visiting new places and things of interest. —**sight′se′er,** *n.* —**sight′see′,** *v.*

sign (sīn) *n.* **1.** indication. **2.** conventional mark, figure, etc. **3.** advertising board. **4.** trace. **5.** omen. —*v.* **6.** put signature to.

sig′nal (sig′nl) *n., adj., v.,* **-naled, -naling.** —*n.* **1.** symbolic communication. —*adj.* **2.** serving as signal. **3.** notable. —*v.* **4.** communicate by symbols. —**sig′nal•er,** *n.*

sig′nal•ly, *adv.* notably.

sig′na•to′ry (sig′nə tôr′ē) *n., pl.* **-ries.** signer.

sig′na•ture (sig′nə chər) *n.* **1.** person's name in own handwriting. **2.** *Music.* sign indicating key or time of piece.

sig′net (sig′nit) *n.* small seal.

sig•nif′i•cance (sig nif′i kəns) *n.* **1.** importance. **2.** meaning. —**sig•nif′i•cant,** *adj.*

significant other, spouse or cohabiting lover.

sig′ni•fy′, *v.,* **-fied, -fying. 1.** make known. **2.** mean. —**sig′ni•fi•ca′tion,** *n.*

Sikh (sēk) *n.* member of religion of India that rejects Hindu caste system. —**Sikh′ism,** *n.*

si′lage (sī′lij) *n.* fodder preserved in silo.

si′lence (sī′ləns) *n., v.,* **-lenced, -lencing.** —*n.* **1.** absence of sound. **2.** muteness. —*v.* **3.** bring to silence. —**si′lent,** *adj.*

si′lenc•er, *n.* device for deadening report of a firearm.

sil′hou•ette′ (sil′ōō et′) *n., v.,* **-etted, -etting.** —*n.* **1.** filled-in outline. —*v.* **2.** show in silhouette.

sil′i•ca (sil′i kə) *n.* silicon dioxide, appearing as quartz, sand, flint, etc.

sil′i•cate (-kit, -kāt′) *n.* mineral consisting of silicon and oxygen with a metal.

sil′i•con (-kən, -kon′) *n.* abundant nonmetallic element.

sil′i•cone′ (-kōn′) *n.* polymer with silicon and oxygen atoms, used in adhesives, lubricants, etc.

sil′i•co′sis (-kō′sis) *n.* lung disease caused by inhaling silica.

silk (silk) *n.* **1.** fine soft fiber produced by silkworms. **2.** thread or cloth made of it. —*adj.* **3.** Also, **silk′en, silk′y.** of silk.

silk′worm′, *n.* caterpillar that spins silk to make its cocoon.

sill (sil) *n.* horizontal piece beneath window or door.

sil′ly (sil′ē) *adj.,* **-lier, -liest. 1.** stupid. **2.** absurd. —**sil′li•ness,** *n.*

si′lo (sī′lō) *n., pl.* **-los.** airtight structure to hold green fodder.

silt (silt) *n.* **1.** earth, etc., carried and deposited by a stream. —*v.* **2.** fill with silt.

sil′ver (sil′vər) *n.* **1.** valuable white metallic element. **2.** coins, utensils, etc., of silver. **3.** whitish gray. —*adj.* **4.** of or plated with silver. **5.** indicating 25th anniversary.

sil′ver•fish′, *n.* wingless, silvery-gray insect that damages books, etc.

silver lining, prospect of hope or comfort.

silver nitrate, poisonous powder used in photography.

sil′ver-tongued′, *adj.* eloquent.

sil′ver•ware′, *n.* eating and serving utensils of silver or other metal.

sim′i•an (sim′ē ən) *n.* **1.** ape or monkey. —*adj.* **2.** of apes or monkeys.

sim′i•lar (sim′ə lər) *adj.* with general likeness. —**sim′i•lar′i•ty** (-lar′i tē) *n.* —**sim′i•lar•ly,** *adv.*

sim′i•le′ (-ə lē) *n.* phrase comparing two things using "like" or "as."

si•mil′i•tude′ (si mil′i tōōd′, -tyōōd′) *n.* likeness.

sim′mer (sim′ər) *v.* remain or keep near boiling.

si′mo•ny (sī′mə nē) *n.* buying or selling of ecclesiastical preferments.

sim•pa′ti•co′ (sim pä′ti kō′) *adj.* like-minded.

sim′per (sim′pər) *v.* **1.** smile affectedly. —*n.* **2.** affected smile.

sim′ple (sim′pəl) *adj.,* **-pler, -plest. 1.** easy to grasp, use, etc. **2.** not complex. **3.** mentaliy weak. —**sim•plic′i•ty** (-plis′i tē) *n.*

simple interest, interest payable only on the principle.

sim′ple-mind′ed, *adj.* **1.** unsophisticated. **2.** mentally deficient.

sim′ple•ton (-tən) *n.* fool.

sim′pli•fy′ (-plə fī′) *v.,* **-fied, -fying.** make simpler.

sim•plis′tic (-plis′tik) *adj.* foolishly or naïvely simple.

sim′u•late′ (sim′yə lāt′) *v.,* **-lated, -lating.** imitate or feign.

si′mul•cast′ (sī′məl kast′) *n., v.,* **-cast, -casted, -casting.** —*n.* **1.** program broadcast simultaneously on radio and television. —*v.* **2.** broadcast a simulcast.

si′mul•ta′ne•ous (-tā′nē əs) *adj.* occurring at the same time.

sin (sin) *n., v.,* **sinned, sinning.** —*n.* **1.** offense, esp. against divine law. —*v.* **2.** commit sin. —**sin′ner,** *n.* —**sin′ful,** *adj.* —**sin′ful•ly,** *adv.*

since (sins) *adv.* **1.** from then till now. **2.** subsequently. —*conj.* **3.** from time when. **4.** because.

sin•cere′ (sin sēr′) *adj.,* **-cerer, -cerest.** honest; genuine. —**sin•cer′i•ty** (-ser′i tē) *n.* —**sin•cere′ly,** *adv.*

si′ne•cure′ (sī′ni kyōōr′) *n.* job without real responsibilities.

si′ne di′e (sī′nē dī′ē), without fixing a day for future action.

si′ne qua non′ (sin′ā kwä nōn′) indispensable condition or element.

sin′ew (sin′yōō) *n.* **1.** tendon. **2.** strength. —**sin′ew•y,** *adj.*

sing (sing) *v.,* **sang** (sang) or **sung** (sung), **sung, singing. 1.** utter words to music. **2.** make musical sounds. **3.** acclaim. —**sing′er,** *n.*

singe (sinj) *v.,* **singed, singeing,** *n.* scorch.

sin′gle (sing′gəl) *adj., v.,* **-gled, -gling,** *n.* —*adj.* **1.** one only. **2.** unmarried. —*v.* **3.** select. —*n.* **4.** single thing. **5.** unmarried person.

single file, line of persons or things one behind the other.

sin′gle-hand′ed, *adj.* **1.** accomplished by one person. **2.** by one's own effort; unaided. —*adv.* **3.** by one person alone.

sin′gle-mind′ed, *adj.* having or showing a single aim or purpose.

sin′gly, *adv.* **1.** separately. **2.** one at a time. **3.** single-handed.

sing′song′, *adj.* monotonous in rhythm.

sin′gu•lar (sing′gyə lər) *adj.* **1.** extraordinary. **2.** strange. **3.** denoting one person or thing. —*n.* **4.** singular number or form.

sin′is•ter (sin′ə stər) *adj.* threatening evil.

sink (singk) *v.,* **sank** (sangk) or **sunk** (sungk), **sunk** or **sunken, sinking,** *n.* —*v.* **1.** descend or drop. **2.** deteriorate gradually. **3.** submerge. **4.** dig (a hole, etc.). **5.** bury (pipe, etc.). —*n.* **6.** basin connected with drain.

sink′hole′, *n.* hole in rock through which surface water drains into underground passage.

sin′u•ous (sin′yōō əs) *adj.* winding.

si′nus (sī′nəs) *n.* cavity or passage in the skull.

sip (sip) *v.,* **sipped, sipping,** *n.* —*v.* **1.** drink little at a time. —*n.* **2.** act of sipping. **3.** amount taken in sip.

si′phon (sī′fən) *n.* **1.** tube for drawing liquids by gravity and suction to another container. —*v.* **2.** move by siphon.

sir (sûr) *n.* **1.** formal term of address to man. **2.** title of knight or baronet.

sire (sī°r) *n., v.,* **sired, siring.** —*n.* **1.** male parent. —*v.* **2.** beget.

si′ren (sī′rən) *n.* **1.** mythical, alluring sea nymph. **2.** noise-making device used on emergency vehicles.

sir′loin (sûr′loin) *n.* cut of beef from the loin.

si′sal (sī′səl, sis′əl) *n.* fiber used in ropes.

sis′sy (sis′ē) *n., pl.* **-sies.** effeminate or timid boy.

sis′ter (sis′tər) *n.* **1.** daughter of one's parents. **2.** nun. —**sis′ter•hood′,** *n.* —**sis′ter•ly,** *adj.*

sis′ter-in-law′, *n., pl.* **sisters-in-law. 1.** sister of one's spouse. **2.** wife of one's brother.

sit (sit) *v.,* **sat** (sat), **sitting. 1.** rest on buttocks. **2.** be situated. **3.** pose. **4.** be in session. **5.** seat.

si•tar′ (si tär′) *n.* Indian lute.

sit′-down′, *n.* strike in which workers occupy their place of employment and refuse to work.

site (sīt) *n.* position; location.

sit′-in′, *n.* protest by demonstrators who occupy premises.

sitting duck, easy target.

sit′u•ate′ (sich′ōō āt′) *v.,* **-ated, -ating.** locate.

sit′u•a′tion (-ā′shən) *n.* **1.** location. **2.** condition. **3.** job.

six (siks) *n., adj.* five plus one. —**sixth,** *adj., n.*

six′teen′, *n., adj.* ten plus six. —**six•teenth′,** *adj., n.*

sixth sense, power of intuition.

six′ty, *n., adj.* ten times six. —**six′ti•eth,** *adj., n.*

siz′a•ble (sī′zə bəl) *adj.* fairly large. Also, **size′a•ble.**

size (sīz) *n., v.,* **sized, sizing.** —*n.* **1.** dimensions or extent. **2.** great magnitude. **3.** Also, **sizing.** coating for paper, cloth, etc. —*v.* **4.** sort according to size. **5.** treat with sizing.

siz′zle (siz′əl) *v.,* **-zled, -zling,** *n.* —*v.* **1.** make hissing sound, as in frying. —*n.* **2.** sizzling sound.

skate (skāt) *n., pl.* **skates** or (for 3) **skate,** *v.,* **skated, skating.** —*n.* **1.** steel runner fitted to shoe for gliding on ice. **2.** roller skate. **3.** flat-bodied marine fish; ray. —*v.* **4.** glide on skates. —**skat′er,** *n.*

skate′board′, *n.* oblong board on roller-skate wheels.

ske•dad′dle (ski dad′l) *v.,* **-dled, -dling.** *Informal.* run away.

skein (skān) *n.* coil of yarn or thread.

skel′e•ton (skel′i tn) *n.* bony framework of human or animal. —**skel′e•tal,** *adj.*

skeleton key, key that opens various simple locks.

skep′tic (skep′tik) *n.* person who

doubts or questions. —**skep′ti·cal,** *adj.* —**skep′ti·cism** (-siz′əm) *n.*

sketch (skech) *n.* **1.** simple hasty drawing. **2.** rough plan. —*v.* **3.** make sketch (of).

sketch′y, *adj.* -ier, -iest. vague; approximate. —**sketch′i·ly,** *adv.*

skew (skyōō) *v.* turn aside; slant.

skew′er, *n.* **1.** pin for holding meat, etc., while cooking. —*v.* **2.** fasten with skewer.

ski (skē) *n.,* **1.** slender board fastened to shoe for traveling over snow. —*v.* **2.** travel by skis.

skid (skid) *n.,* v., **skidded, skidding.** —*n.* **1.** surface on which to support or slide heavy object. **2.** act of skidding. —*v.* **3.** slide on skids. **4.** slip.

skid row (rō) run-down urban area frequented by vagrants.

skiff (skif) *n.* small boat.

skill (skil) *n.* expertness; dexterity. —**skilled,** *adj.* —**skill′ful,** *adj.*

skil′let (skil′it) *n.* frying pan.

skim (skim) *v.,* **skimmed, skimming. 1.** remove from surface of liquid. **2.** move lightly on surface.

skim milk, milk from which cream has been removed.

skimp (skimp) *v.* scrimp.

skimp′y, *adj.,* -ier, -iest. scant.

skin (skin) *n.,* v., **skinned, skinning.** —*n.* **1.** outer covering, as of body. —*v.* **2.** remove skin.

skin diving, underwater swimming with flippers and face mask, sometimes with scuba gear.

skin′flint′, *n.* stingy person.

skin′ny, *adj.,* -nier, -niest. very thin.

skin′ny-dip′, *v.,* skinny-dipped, skinny-dipping, *n., pl.* skinny-dips. *Informal.* swim in the nude.

skip (skip) *v.,* **skipped, skipping.** —*v.* **1.** spring; leap. **2.** omit; disregard. —*n.* **3.** light jump.

skip′per (skip′ər) *n.* **1.** master of ship. —*v.* **2.** act as skipper of.

skir′mish (skûr′mish) *n.* **1.** brief fight between small forces. —*v.* **2.** engage in skirmish.

skirt (skûrt) *n.* **1.** part of gown, etc., below waist. **2.** woman's garment extending down from waist. **3.** (*pl.*) outskirts. —*v.* **4.** pass around edge of. **5.** border.

skit (skit) *n.* short comedy.

skit′tish, *adj.* apt to shy; restless.

skiv′vy (skiv′ē) *n., pl.* -vies. **1.** man's cotton T-shirt. **2.** (*pl.*) men's underwear consisting of T-shirt and shorts.

skul·dug′ger·y (skul dug′ə rē) *n., pl.* -geries. trickery.

skulk (skulk) *v.* sneak about.

skull (skul) *n.* bony framework around brain.

skull′cap′, *n.* brimless, close-fitting cap.

skunk (skungk) *n.* **1.** small, striped, fur-bearing mammal that sprays acrid fluid to defend itself. **2.** contemptible person.

sky (skī) *n., pl.* **skies.** region well above earth.

sky′cap′, *n.* airport porter.

sky′dive′, *v.,* -dived, -diving. make parachute jump with longest free fall possible. —**sky′div′er,** *n.*

sky′jack′, *v. Informal.* seize (aircraft) while in flight.

sky′light′, (-līt′) *n.* window in roof, ceiling, etc.

sky′line′, *n.* **1.** outline against sky. **2.** apparent horizon.

sky′rock′et, *n.* firework that rises into air before exploding.

sky′scrap′er, *n.* building with many stories.

sky′writ′ing, *n.* writing in sky formed by smoke from airplane.

slab (slab) *n.* broad flat piece of material.

slack (slak) *adj.* **1.** loose. **2.** inactive. —*adv.* **3.** slackly. —*n.* **4.** slack part. **5.** inactive period. —*v.* **6.** slacken. —**slack′ly,** *adv.*

slack′en, *v.* **1.** make or become slack. **2.** weaken.

slack′er, *n.* person who evades work.

slacks, *n.pl.* loose trousers.

slag (slag) *n.* refuse matter from smelting metal from ore.

slake (slāk) *v.,* slaked, slaking. allay (thirst, etc.).

sla′lom (slä′ləm) *n.* downhill ski race over winding course, around numerous barriers.

slam (slam) *v.,* **slammed, slamming,** *n.* —*v.* **1.** shut noisily. —*n.* **2.** this sound.

slam′mer, *n. Slang.* prison.

slan′der (slan′dər) *n.* **1.** false, defamatory spoken statement. —*v.* **2.** utter slander against.

slang (slang) *n.* very informal, colorful language. —**slang′y,** *adj.*

slant (slant) *v.* **1.** slope. —*n.* **2.** slope. **3.** opinion.

slap (slap) *v.,* **slapped, slapping,** *n.* —*v.* **1.** strike, esp. with open hand. —*n.* **2.** such blow.

slap′dash′, *adj.* hasty and careless.

slap′hap′py, *adj.,* -pier, -piest. **1.** befuddled. **2.** agreeably foolish.

slap′stick′, *n.* boisterous comedy with broad farce and horseplay.

slash (slash) *v.* **1.** cut, esp. violently and at random. —*n.* **2.** such cut.

slat (slat) *n.,* v., **slatted, slatting.** —*n.* **1.** thin narrow strip. —*v.* **2.** furnish with slats.

slate (slāt) *n.,* v., **slated, slating.** —*n.* **1.** kind of layered rock. **2.** dark bluish gray. **3.** list of nominees. —*v.* **4.** put in line for appointment.

slat′tern (slat′ərn) *n.* untidy woman. —**slat′tern·ly,** *adj.*

slaugh′ter (slô′tər) *n.* **1.** killing of animals, esp. for food. **2.** brutal killing of people, esp. in great numbers. —*v.* **3.** kill for food. **4.** massacre. —**slaugh′ter·house′,** *n.*

slave (slāv) *n.,* v., **slaved, slaving.** —*n.* **1.** person owned by another. —*v.* **2.** drudge. —**slav′er·y,** *n.*

slav′er (sla′vər) *v.* **1.** let saliva run from mouth. —*n.* **2.** saliva coming from mouth.

Slav′ic (slä′vik, slav′ik) *n.* **1.** language family that includes Russian, Polish, Czech, etc. —*adj.* **2.** of these languages or their speakers.

slav′ish (slā′vish) *adj.* **1.** without originality. **2.** servile.

slaw (slô) *n.* chopped seasoned raw cabbage.

slay (slā) *v.,* slew (slōō), slain, slaying. kill. —**slay′er,** *n.*

slea′zy (slē′zē) *adj.,* -zier, -ziest. shoddy or disreputable.

sled (sled) *n.,* v., **sledded, sledding.** —*n.* **1.** vehicle traveling on snow. —*v.* **2.** ride on sled.

sledge (slej) *n.,* v., **sledged, sledging.** —*n.* **1.** heavy sledlike vehicle. **2.** Also, **sledge′ham′mer.** large heavy hammer. —*v.* **3.** travel by sledge.

sleek (slēk) *adj.* **1.** smooth; glossy. —*v.* **2.** smooth. —**sleek′ly,** *adv.*

sleep (slēp) *v.,* slept (slept), sleeping, *n.* —*v.* **1.** rest during natural suspension of consciousness. —*n.* **2.** state or period of sleeping. —**sleep′less,** *adj.* —**sleep′y,** *adj.*

sleep′er, *n.* **1.** person who sleeps. **2.** railroad car equipped for sleeping. **3.** raillike foundation support. **4.** unexpected success.

sleeping bag, warmly lined bag in which a person can sleep.

sleeping car, railroad car with sleeping accommodations.

sleet (slēt) *n.* hard frozen rain.

sleeve (slēv) *n.* part of garment covering arm. —**sleeve′less,** *adj.*

sleigh (slā) *n.* light sled.

sleight of hand (slīt) skill in conjuring or juggling.

slen′der (slen′dər) *adj.* **1.** small in circumference. **2.** scanty or weak.

sleuth (slōōth) *n.* detective.

slew (slōō) pt. of **slay.**

slice (slīs) *n.,* v., **sliced, slicing.** —*n.* **1.** broad flat piece. —*v.* **2.** cut into slices. —**slic′er,** *n.*

slick (slik) *adj.* **1.** sleek. **2.** sly. **3.** slippery. —*n.* **4.** oil-covered area. —*v.* **5.** smooth. —**slick′ness,** *n.*

slick′er, *n.* raincoat.

slide (slīd) *v.,* slid, sliding, *n.* —*v.* **1.** move easily; glide. —*n.* **2.** act of sliding. **3.** area for sliding. **4.** landslide. **5.** glass plate used in microscope. **6.** transparent picture.

sliding scale, scale, as of prices, that varies with such conditions as the ability of individuals to pay.

slight (slīt) *adj.* **1.** trifling; small. **2.** slim. —*v.* **3.** treat as unimportant. —*n.* **4.** such treatment; snub.

slight′ly, *adv.* barely; partly.

slim (slim) *adj.,* slimmer, slimmest. **1.** slender. **2.** poor. —*v.* **3.** make or become slim. —**slim′ness,** *n.*

slime (slīm) *n.* **1.** thin sticky mud. **2.** sticky secretion. —**slim′y,** *adj.*

sling (sling) *n.,* v., slung (slung), slinging. —*n.* **1.** straplike device for hurling stones. **2.** looped rope, bandage, etc., as support. —*v.* **3.** hurl. **4.** hang loosely.

sling′shot′, *n.* Y-shaped stick with elastic strip between prongs, for shooting small missiles.

slink (slingk) *v.,* slunk (slink), slinking. go furtively. —**slink′y,** *adj.*

slip (slip) *v.,* **slipped, slipping.** —*v.* **1.** move or go easily. **2.** slide accidentally. **3.** escape. **4.** make mistake. —*n.* **5.** act of slipping. **6.** mistake. **7.** undergarment.

slip cover, easily removable cover for piece of furniture.

slip′knot′, *n.* knot that slips easily along cord.

slipped disk, abnormal protrusion of spinal disk between vertebrae.

slip′per, *n.* light shoe.

slip′per·y, *adj.* **1.** causing slipping. **2.** tending to slip.

slip′shod′ (-shod′) *adj.* careless.

slip′-up′, *n.* mistake.

slit (slit) *v.,* slit, slitting, *n.* —*v.* **1.** cut apart or in strips. —*n.* **2.** narrow opening.

slith′er (slith′ər) *v.* slide.

sliv′er (sliv′ər) *n., v.* splinter.

slob (slob) *n.* slovenly or boorish person.

slob′ber, *v., n.* slaver.

sloe (slō) *n.* small sour fruit of blackthorn.

sloe′-eyed′, *adj.* **1.** having very dark eyes. **2.** having slanted eyes.

slog (slog) *v.,* slogged, slogging. **1.** plod heavily. **2.** work hard.

slo′gan (slō′gən) *n.* motto.

sloop (slōōp) *n.* kind of sailing vessel.

slop (slop) *v.*, **slopped, slopping,** *n.*
—*v.* **1.** spill liquid. —*n.* **2.** swill.

slope (slōp) *v.*, **sloped, sloping,** *n.*
—*v.* **1.** incline; slant. —*n.* **2.** amount of inclination. **3.** sloping surface.

slop/py, *adj.* **-pier, -piest. 1.** untidy. **2.** careless. —**slop/pi•ly,** *adv.*

slosh (slosh) *v.* splash.

slot (slot) *n.* narrow opening.

sloth (slôth) *n.* **1.** laziness. **2.** tree-living South American mammal. —**sloth/ful,** *adj.*

slot machine, gambling machine.

slouch (slouch) *v.* **1.** move or rest droopingly. —*n.* **2.** drooping posture. —**slouch/y,** *adj.*

slough, *n.* **1.** (slou) muddy area. **2.** (slŏŏ) marshy pond or inlet. —*v.* (sluf) **3.** be shed. **4.** cast off.

slov/en (sluv'ən) *n.* untidy or careless person. —**slov/en•ly,** *adj.*

slow (slō) *adj.* **1.** not fast. **2.** not intelligent or perceptive. **3.** running behind time. —*adv.* **4.** slowly. —*v.* **5.** make or become slow.

slow burn, *Informal.* gradual build-up of anger.

slow/down/, *n.* slackening of pace or speed.

slow motion, process of projecting or replaying film or television sequence so that action appears to be slowed down.

slow/poke/, *n. Informal.* person who moves, works, or acts very slowly.

slow/-wit/ted, *adj.* slow to understand.

sludge (sluj) *n.* mud.

slue (slōō) *v.*, **slued, sluing.** turn round.

slug (slug) *v.*, **slugged, slugging,** *n.*
—*v.* **1.** hit with fists. —*n.* **2.** slimy, crawling mollusk having no shell. **3.** bullet. **4.** counterfeit coin. **5.** hard blow, esp. with fist. —**slug/ger,** *n.*

slug/gard (slug'ərd) *n.* lazy person.

slug/gish, *adj.* inactive; slow.

sluice (slōōs) *n.* channel with gate to control flow.

slum (slum) *n.* squalid, overcrowded residence or neighborhood.

slum/ber (slum'bər) *v., n.* sleep.

slum/lord/, *n.* landlord of slum dwellings who charges exorbitant rents.

slump (slump) *v.* **1.** drop heavily or suddenly. —*n.* **2.** act of slumping.

slur (slûr) *v.* **slurred, slurring,** *n.* —*v.* **1.** say indistinctly. **2.** disparage. —*n.* **3.** slurred sound. **4.** disparaging remark.

slurp (slûrp) *v.* eat or drink with loud sucking noises.

slush (slush) *n.* partly melted snow.

slush fund, money used for illicit political purposes.

slut (slut) *n.* **1.** slatternly woman. **2.** sexually immoral woman.

sly (slī) *adj.*, **slyer, slyest** or **slier, sliest. 1.** cunning. **2.** stealthy.

smack (smak) *v.* **1.** separate (lips) noisily. **2.** slap. **3.** have taste or trace. —*n.* **4.** smacking of lips. **5.** loud kiss. **6.** slap. **7.** taste. **8.** trace. **9.** small fishing boat. **10.** *Slang.* heroin.

small (smôl) *adj.* **1.** not big. **2.** not great in importance. **3.** ungenerous. —*adv.* **4.** in small pieces. —*n.* **5.** small part, as of back.

small fry, 1. young children. **2.** unimportant people.

small/-mind/ed, *adj.* petty or selfish.

small/pox/, *n.* contagious disease marked by fever and pustules.

small/-scale/, *adj.* **1.** of limited

scope. **2.** being a small version of an original.

small talk, light conversation.

small/-time/, *adj.* not important.

smarm/y (smär'mē) *adj.*, **-ier, -iest.** excessively flattering.

smart (smärt) *v.* **1.** cause or feel sharp superficial pain. —*adj.* **2.** sharp; severe. **3.** clever. **4.** stylish. —*n.* **5.** sharp local pain.

smart al/eck (al'ik) *Informal.* obnoxiously conceited and impertinent person. Also, **smart al/ec.**

smart bomb, air-to-surface missile guided by laser beam.

smart/en, *v.* improve in appearance.

smash (smash) *v.* **1.** break to pieces. —*n.* **2.** act of smashing.

smat/ter•ing (smat'ər ing) *n.* slight knowledge.

smear (smēr) *v.* **1.** rub with dirt, grease, etc. **2.** sully. —*n.* **3.** smeared spot. **4.** slanderous attack.

smell (smel) *v.* **1.** perceive with nose. **2.** have odor. —*n.* **3.** faculty of smelling. **4.** odor. —**smell/y,** *adj.*, **-ier, -iest.**

smelt (smelt) *n., pl.* **smelts, smelt,** *v.* —*n.* **1.** small edible fish. —*v.* **2.** melt (ore or metal). —**smelt/er,** *n.*

smid/gen (smij'ən) *n.* very small amount. Also, **smid/gin, smid/geon.**

smile (smīl) *v.*, **smiled, smiling,** *n.* —*v.* **1.** look pleased, amused, etc. **2.** look favorably. —*n.* **3.** smiling look.

smirch (smûrch) *v.* **1.** soil or sully. —*n.* **2.** stain.

smirk (smûrk) *v.* **1.** smile smugly or affectedly. —*n.* **2.** such a smile.

smite (smīt) *v.*, **smote** (smōt), **smitten** (smit'n) or **smote, smiting. 1.** strike. **2.** charm.

smith (smith) *n.* worker in metal.

smith/er•eens/ (smith'ə rēnz') *n.pl.* fragments.

smith/y (smith'ē, smith'ē) *n., pl.* **smithies.** blacksmith's shop.

smit/ten (smit'n) *adj.* very much in love.

smock (smok) *n.* long, loose overgarment.

smog (smog) *n.* smoke and fog.

smoke (smōk) *n., v.*, **smoked, smoking.** —*n.* **1.** visible vapor from burning. —*v.* **2.** emit smoke. **3.** draw into mouth and puff out tobacco smoke. **4.** treat with smoke. —**smoke/less,** *adj.* —**smok/er,** *n.* —**smok/y,** *adj.*

smoke detector, alarm activated by presence of smoke.

smoke/house/, *n.* building in which meat or fish is cured with smoke.

smoke screen, 1. mass of dense smoke for concealment from enemy. **2.** something intended to deceive.

smoke/stack/, *n.* **1.** pipe for escape of smoke, combustion gases, etc. —*adj.* **2.** engaged in heavy industry, as steelmaking.

smol/der (smōl'dər) *v.* **1.** burn without flame. **2.** continue, but suppressed. Also, **smoul/der.**

smooch (smōōch) *n., v. Informal.* kiss.

smooth (smōōth) *adj.* **1.** even in surface. **2.** easy; tranquil. —*v.* **3.** make smooth. —*n.* **4.** smooth place.

smooth/bore/, *adj.* (of gun) not rifled.

smor/gas•bord/ (smôr'gəs bôrd'; *often* shmôr'-) *n.* buffet meal of assorted foods.

smoth/er (smuth'ər) *v.* suffocate.

smudge (smuj) *n., v.*, **smudged, smudging. 1.** dirty smear. **2.** smoky fire. —*v.* **3.** soil.

smug (smug) *adj.* self-satisfied.

smug/gle, *v.*, **-gled, -gling. 1.** import or export secretly and illegally. **2.** bring or take secretly.

smut (smut) *n.* **1.** soot. **2.** smudge. **3.** obscenity. **4.** fungous disease of plants. —**smut/ty,** *adj.*

snack (snak) *n.* light meal.

snag (snag) *n., v.*, **snagged, snagging.** —*n.* **1.** sharp projection. **2.** obstacle. —*v.* **3.** catch on snag.

snail (snāl) *n.* crawling, spiral-shelled mollusk.

snake (snāk) *n., v.*, **snaked, snaking.** —*n.* **1.** scaly limbless reptile. —*v.* **2.** move like snake. **3.** drag.

snap (snap) *v.*, **snapped, snapping,** *n., adj.* —*v.* **1.** make sudden sharp sound. **2.** break abruptly. **3.** bite (at). **4.** photograph. —*n.* **5.** snapping sound. **6.** kind of fastener. **7.** *Informal.* easy thing. —*adj.* **8.** unconsidered.

snap/drag/on, *n.* plant with spikes of flowers.

snap/pish, *adj.* cross or irritable.

snap/py, *adj.* **-pier, -piest.** *Informal.* **1.** quick. **2.** smart; stylish.

snap/shot/, *n.* unposed photograph.

snare (snâr) *n., v.*, **snared, snaring. 1.** kind of trap. **2.** strand across skin of small drum. —*v.* **3.** entrap.

snarl (snärl) *v., n.* **1.** growl. **2.** tangle.

snatch (snach) *v.* **1.** grab. —*n.* **2.** grabbing motion. **3.** scrap of melody, etc. —**snatch/er,** *n.*

sneak (snēk) *v.* **1.** go or act furtively. —*n.* **2.** person who sneaks.

sneak/er, *n.* rubber-soled shoe.

sneak preview, preview of a motion picture, often shown in addition to an announced film.

sneer (snēr) *v.* **1.** show contempt. —*n.* **2.** contemptuous look.

sneeze (snēz) *v.*, **sneezed, sneezing,** *n.* —*v.* **1.** emit breath suddenly and forcibly from nose. —*n.* **2.** act of sneezing.

snick/er (snik'ər) *n.* derisive, stifled laugh. —**snick/er,** *v.* Also, **snig/ger.**

snide (snīd) *adj.*, **snider, snidest.** derogatory in nasty, insinuating way.

sniff (snif) *v.* **1.** inhale quickly and audibly. —*n.* **2.** such an inhalation. Also, **sniff/le.**

snif/ter (snif'tər) *n.* pear-shaped glass for brandy.

snip (snip) *v.*, **snipped, snipping,** *n.* —*v.* **1.** cut with small, quick strokes. —*n.* **2.** small piece cut off. **3.** cut. **4.** (*pl.*) large scissors.

snipe (snīp) *n., v.*, **sniped, sniping.** —*n.* **1.** shore bird. —*v.* **2.** shoot from hidden position. —**snip/er,** *n.*

snip/pet (snip'it) *n.* small bit, scrap, or fragment.

snip/py, *adj.*, **-pier, -piest.** sharp or curt, esp. in haughty way.

snit (snit) *n.* agitated state.

snitch (snicn) *Informal.* —*v.* **1.** steal; pilfer. **2.** turn informer; tattle. —*n.* **3.** informer.

sniv/el (sniv'əl) *v.* **1.** weep weakly. **2.** have a runny nose.

snob (snob) *n.* person overconcerned with position, wealth, etc. —**snob/bish,** *adj.* —**snob/ber•y,** *n.*

snoop (snōōp) *Informal.* —*v.* **1.** prowl or pry. —*n.* **2.** Also, **snoop/er.** person who snoops.

snoot/y (snōō'tē) *adj.*, **-ier, -iest.** *Informal.* snobbish; condescending.

snooze (snōōz) *v.*, **snoozed, snoozing,** *n. Informal.* nap.

snore (snôr) *v.*, **snored, snoring,** *n.* —*v.* **1.** breathe audibly in sleep. —*n.* **2.** sound of snoring.

snor/kel (snôr'kəl) *n.* **1.** tube through which swimmer can breathe while underwater. **2.** ventilating device for submarines.

snort (snôrt) v. **1.** exhale loudly and harshly. —n. **2.** sound of snorting.

snot (snot) n. *Informal.* **1.** nasal mucus. **2.** impudently disagreeable young person. —**snot′ty,** adj. **-tier, -tiest.**

snout (snout) n. projecting nose and jaw.

snow (snō) n. **1.** white crystalline flakes that fall to earth. —v. **2.** fall as snow. —**snow′drift′,** n. —**snow′-fall′,** n. —**snow′flake′,** n. —**snow′-storm′,** n. —**snow′y,** adj.

snow′ball′, n. **1.** ball of snow. —v. **2.** grow rapidly.

snow′board′, n. board for gliding on snow, resembling a wide ski.

snow′drop′, n. early-blooming plant with white flowers.

snow′man′, n. figure of person made of packed snow.

snow′mo·bile′ (-mə bēl′) n. motor vehicle for travel on snow.

snow′shoe′, n. racketlike shoe for walking on snow.

snow′suit′, n. child's warmly insulated outer garment.

snow tire, tire with deep tread.

snub (snub) v., **snubbed, snubbing,** n., adj. —v. **1.** treat with scorn. **2.** check or stop. —n. **3.** rebuke or slight. —adj. **4.** (of nose) short and turned up.

snuff (snuf) v. **1.** inhale. **2.** smell. **3.** extinguish. —n. **4.** powdered tobacco.

snuf′fle, v., -fled, -fling, n. sniff.

snug (snug) adj., **snugger, snuggest. 1.** cozy. **2.** trim; neat.

snug′gle, v., -gled, -gling. nestle.

so (sō) adv. **1.** in this or that way. **2.** to such degree. **3.** as stated. —conj. **4.** consequently. **5.** in order that.

soak (sōk) v. **1.** wet thoroughly. **2.** absorb. —**soak′er,** n.

so′-and-so′, n., pl. **so-and-sos.** person or thing not definitely named.

soap (sōp) n. **1.** substance used for washing. —v. **2.** rub with soap.

soap′box′, n. improvised platform on which speaker stands.

soap′stone′, n. variety of talc.

soar (sôr) v. fly upward.

sob (sob) v., **sobbed, sobbing,** n. —v. **1.** weep convulsively. —n. **2.** convulsive breath.

so′ber (sō′bər) adj. **1.** not drunk. **2.** grave. —v. **3.** make or become sober. —**so·bri′e·ty** (sə brī′i tē), n.

so′bri·quet′ (sō′bri kā′, -ket′) n. nickname.

so′-called′, adj. called thus.

soc′cer (sok′ər) n. game resembling football.

so′cia·ble (sō′shə bəl) adj. friendly. —**so′cia·bil′i·ty,** n.

so′cial (sō′shəl) adj. **1.** devoted to companionship. **2.** of human society. —**so′cial·ly,** adv.

so′cial·ism (-shə liz′əm) n. theory advocating community ownership of means of production, etc. —**so′cial·ist,** n. —**so′cial·is′tic,** adj.

so′cial·ite′ (-shə līt′) n. socially prominent person.

so′cial·ize′, v., -ized, -izing. **1.** associate with others. **2.** put on socialist basis.

socialized medicine, system to provide nation with complete medical care through government subsidization.

social security, (often caps.) federal program of old age, unemployment, health, disability, and survivors' insurance.

social work, services or activities designed to improve social conditions among poor, sick, or troubled persons.

so·ci′e·ty (sə sī′i tē) n., pl. **-ties. 1.** group of persons with common interests. **2.** human beings generally. **3.** fashionable people.

Society of Friends, Christian sect founded 1650; Quakers.

so′ci·o·ec·o·nom′ic (sō′sē ō-, sō′-shē ō-) adj. pertaining to a combination of social and economic factors.

so′ci·ol′o·gy (sō′sē ol′ə jē, sō′shē-) n. science of social relations and institutions. —**so′ci·ol′o·gist,** n.

sock (sok) n. short stocking.

sock′et (sok′it) n. holelike part for holding another part.

sod (sod) n. grass with its roots.

so′da (sō′də) n. drink made with soda water.

soda cracker, crisp cracker.

soda fountain, counter at which ice cream, sodas, etc., are served.

soda water, water charged with carbon dioxide.

sod′den (sod′n) adj. **1.** soaked. **2.** dull. —**sod′den·ness,** n.

so′di·um (sō′dē əm) n. soft whitish metallic element.

sodium bicarbonate, baking soda.

sodium chloride, salt.

sod′o·my (sod′ə mē) n. anal or oral copulation.

so′fa (sō′fə) n. couch with back and arms.

soft (sôft) adj. **1.** yielding readily. **2.** gentle; pleasant. **3.** not strong. **4.** (of water) free from mineral salts. **5.** without alcohol. —**soft′en,** v.

soft′ball′, n. **1.** form of baseball played with larger, softer ball. **2.** the ball used.

soft′-boiled′, adj. boiled only until the egg's yolk is partially set.

soft′-core′, adj. sexually provocative without being explicit.

soft drink, nonalcoholic drink.

soft′-heart′ed, adj. very sympathetic.

soft′-ped′al, v., **soft-pedaled, soft-pedaling.** make less obvious; play down.

soft sell, quietly persuasive method of selling.

soft soap, persuasive talk.

soft′ware′, n. programs for use with a computer.

sog′gy (sog′ē) adj., -gier, -giest. **1.** soaked. **2.** damp and heavy.

soi·gné′ (swän yā′; Fr. swa nyā′) adj. elegant. Also, **soi·gnée′.**

soil (soil) v. **1.** dirty. —n. **2.** spot or stain. **3.** sewage. **4.** earth; ground.

soi·rée′ (swä rā′) n. evening party.

so′journ v. (sō′jûrn, sō jûrn′) **1.** dwell briefly. —n. (sō′jûrn) **2.** short stay.

sol′ace (sol′is) n., v. comfort in grief.

so′lar (sō′lər) adj. of the sun.

solar cell, cell that converts sunlight into electricity.

so·lar′i·um (sə lâr′ē əm, sō-) n., pl. -iums, -ia (-ē ə). glass-enclosed room for enjoying sunlight.

solar plexus, point on stomach wall just below sternum.

solar system, sun and all the celestial bodies revolving around it.

sol′der (sod′ər) n. **1.** fusible alloy for joining metal. —v. **2.** join with solder.

sol′dier (sōl′jər) n. **1.** member of army. —v. **2.** serve as soldier.

sole (sōl) n., v., **soled, soling,** adj. —n. **1.** bottom of foot or shoe. **2.** edi-

ble flatfish. —v. **3.** put sole on. —adj. **4.** only. —**sole′ly,** adv.

sol′emn (sol′əm) adj. **1.** grave; serious. **2.** sacred. —**so·lem′ni·ty** (sə-lem′ni tē) n. —**sol′emn·ly,** adv.

sol′em·nize′ (-nīz′) v., -nized, -nizing. observe with ceremonies.

so·lic′it (sə lis′it) v. **1.** entreat; request. **2.** lure; entice, as to a prostitute. **3.** solicit trade or sex.

so·lic′i·tor (-i tar) n. **1.** person who solicits. **2.** *Brit.* lawyer.

so·lic′i·tous, adj. anxious; concerned. —**so·lic′i·tude′,** n.

sol′id (sol′id) adj. **1.** having length, breadth, and thickness. **2.** not hollow. **3.** dense. **4.** substantial. **5.** entire. **6.** solid body. —**so·lid′i·fy′,** v. —**so·lid′i·ty,** n.

sol′i·dar′i·ty (-i dar′i tē) n., pl. -ties. unanimity of attitude or purpose.

sol′id·ly, adv. **1.** so as to be solid. **2.** whole-heartedly; fully.

so·lil′o·quy (sə lil′ə kwē) n., pl. -quies. speech when alone. —**so·lil′o·quize′** (-kwīz′) v., -quized, -quizing.

sol′i·taire′ (sol′i târ′) n. **1.** card game for one person. **2.** gem set alone.

sol′i·tar′y (sol′i ter′ē) adj. **1.** alone. **2.** single. **3.** secluded. —**sol′i·tude′,** n.

so′lo (sō′lō) n., pl. -los. performance by one person. —**so′lo·ist,** n.

sol′stice (sol′stis, sōl′-) n. time in summer (June 21) or winter (Dec. 21) when sun is at its farthest from equator.

sol′u·ble (sol′yə bəl) adj. able to be dissolved. —**sol′u·bil′i·ty,** n.

so·lu′tion (sə lōō′shən) n. **1.** explanation or answer. **2.** dispersion of one substance in another. **3.** resulting substance.

solve (solv) v., **solved, solving.** find explanation of.

sol′vent (sol′vənt) adj. **1.** able to pay one's debts. **2.** causing dissolving. —n. **3.** agent that dissolves.

som′ber (som′bər) adj. gloomy; dark. —**som′ber·ly,** adv.

som·bre′ro (som brâr′ō) n., pl. -ros. tall, broad-brimmed hat.

some (sum; unstressed səm) adj. **1.** being an unspecified one or number. **2.** certain. —pron. **3.** unspecified number or amount. —**Usage.** SOME is used in sentences that are affirmative: *I'd like some milk.* ANY is used instead of SOME with negative phrases or in questions: *I don't want any milk. I never see any of my friends these days. Do you have any milk?* But SOME can be used in questions when the answer is expected to be "yes": *Can I have some milk, please?*

some′bod′y (sum′bod′ē, -bud′ē, -bə-dē) pron. some person. Also, **some′one′.**

some′day′, adv. at some distant time.

some′how′, adv. in some way.

som′er·sault′ (sum′ər sôlt′) n. heels-over-head turn of body.

some′thing, n. unspecified thing.

some′time′, adv. **1.** at indefinite time. —adj. **2.** former.

some′times′, adv. at times.

some′what′, adv. to some extent.

some′where′, adv. in, at, or to unspecified place.

som·nam′bu·lism (som nam′byə-liz′əm, səm-) n. sleep-walking.

som′no·lent (som′nə lənt) adj. sleepy. —**som′no·lence,** n.

son (sun) n. male offspring.

so′nar (sō′när) n. method or apparatus for detecting objects in water by means of sound waves.

so•na′ta (sə nä′tə) *n.* instrumental composition.

song (sông) *n.* music or verse for singing. —**song′ster,** *n.* —**song′stress,** *n. fem.*

son′ic (son′ik) *adj.* of sound.

sonic boom, loud noise caused by aircraft moving at supersonic speed.

son′-in-law′, *n., pl.* **sons-in-law.** husband of one's daughter.

son′net (son′it) *n.* fourteen-line poem in fixed form.

so•no′rous (sə nôr′əs, son′ər əs) *adj.* **1.** resonant. **2.** grandiose in expression. —**so•nor′i•ty,** *n.*

soon (sōōn) *adv.* in short time.

soot (sŏŏt, sōōt) *n.* black substance in smoke. —**soot′y,** *adj.*

soothe (sōōth) *v.,* **soothed, soothing.** calm; allay.

sooth′say′er (sōōth′sā′ər) *n.* person who predicts.

sop (sop) *n., v.,* **sopped, sopping.** —*n.* **1.** something given to pacify. —*v.* **2.** soak or dip in liquid.

so•phis′ti•cat′ed (sə fis′ti kā′tid) *adj.* **1.** worldly; not simple. **2.** complex; intricate. —**so•phis′ti•cate** (-kit) *n.* —**so•phis′ti•ca′tion,** *n.*

soph′ist•ry (sof′ə strē) *n., pl.* **-ries.** clever but unsound reasoning.

soph′o•more′ (sof′ə môr′) *n.* second-year high school or college student.

soph•o•mor′ic (-môr′ik) *adj.* intellectually immature.

so′po•rif′ic (sop′ə rif′ik) *adj.* **1.** causing sleep. —*n.* **2.** soporific agent.

sop′py (sop′ē) *adj.,* **-pier, -piest. 1.** drenched. **2.** sentimental.

so•pran′o (sə pran′ō) *n., pl.* **-pranos.** highest singing voice.

sor•bet′ (sôr bā′, sôr′bit) *n.* fruit or vegetable ice.

sor′cer•er (-sər ər) *n.* magician; wizard. Also, *fem.* **sor′cer•ess.** —**sor′cer•y,** *n.*

sor′did (sôr′did) *adj.* **1.** dirty. **2.** morally low.

sore (sôr) *adj.,* **sorer, sorest,** *n.* —*adj.* **1.** painful or tender. **2.** grieved. **3.** causing misery. **4.** *Informal.* annoyed. —*n.* **5.** sore spot.

sore′head′, *n. Informal.* person who is easily annoyed.

sor′ghum (sôr′gəm) *n.* cereal used in making syrup, etc.

so•ror′i•ty (sə rôr′i tē) *n., pl.* **-ties.** club of women or girls.

sor′rel (sôr′əl) *n.* **1.** reddish brown. **2.** sorrel horse. **3.** salad plant.

sor′row (sor′ō) *n.* **1.** grief; regret; misfortune. —*v.* **2.** feel sorrow. —**sor′row•ful,** *adj.*

sor′ry (sor′ē) *adj.* **1.** feeling regret or pity. **2.** wretched.

sort (sôrt) *n.* **1.** kind or class. **2.** character. **3.** manner. —*v.* **4.** separate; classify. —**sort′er,** *n.*

sor′tie (sôr′tē) *n.* **1.** attack by defending troops. **2.** combat mission.

SOS (es′ō′es′) call for help.

so′-so′, *adj.* **1.** neither good nor bad. —*adv.* **2.** tolerably.

sot (sot) *n.* drunkard.

sot′to vo′ce (sot′ō vō′chē) *adv.* in a low voice; softly.

souf•fle′ (sōō flā′) *n.* fluffy baked dish.

sough (sou, suf) *v.* **1.** rustle or murmur, as wind. —*n.* **2.** act of soughing.

sought (sôt) *pt.* and *pp.* of **seek.**

soul (sōl) *n.* **1.** human spiritual quality. **2.** essential quality. **3.** person. **4.**

Also, **soul music.** black popular music drawing on church influences. —*adj.* **5.** of black customs and culture. —**soul′ful,** *adj.*

sound (sound) *n.* **1.** sensation affecting organs of hearing, produced by vibrations (**sound waves**). **2.** special tone. **3.** noise. **4.** inlet or passage of sea. —*v.* **5.** make sound. **6.** say. **7.** give certain impression. **8.** measure depth of. **9.** examine; question. —*adj.* **10.** healthy; strong. **11.** reliable. **12.** valid. —**sound′proof′,** *adj.* —**sound′ly,** *adv.*

sound barrier, abrupt increase in drag experienced by aircraft approaching speed of sound.

sound bite, brief, memorable statement excerpted for broadcast news.

sounding board, 1. thin board placed in musical instrument to enhance resonance. **2.** person whose reactions reveal acceptability of an idea.

sound′proof′, *adj.* **1.** impervious to sound. —*v.* **2.** make soundproof.

sound′track′, *n.* band on motion-picture film on which sound is recorded.

soup (sōōp) *n.* liquid food of meat, vegetables, etc.

soup′y, *adj.,* **-ier, -iest. 1.** resembling soup in consistency. **2.** dense. **3.** overly sentimental.

sour (sou°r) *adj.* **1.** acid in taste; tart. **2.** spoiled. **3.** disagreeable. —*v.* **4.** turn sour. —**sour′ly,** *adv.*

source (sôrs) *n.* origin.

sour grapes, *n.* pretended disdain for something unattainable.

souse (sous) *v.,* **soused, sousing,** *n.* —*v.* **1.** immerse. **2.** pickle. —*n.* **3.** pickled food. **4.** *Slang.* drunkard.

south (south) *n.* **1.** point of compass opposite north. **2.** territory in this direction. —*adj., adv.* **3.** toward, in, or from south. —**south′er•ly** (suth′ər lē) *adj., adv.* —**south′ern** (suth′-) *adj.* —**south′ern•er,** *n.* —**south′ward,** *adj., adv.*

south′east′, *n.,* point or direction midway between south and east. —**south′east′,** *adj., adv.*

south′paw′, *n. Informal.* left-handed person.

south′west′, *n.* point or direction midway between south and west. —**south′west′,** *adj., adv.*

sou′ve•nir′ (sōō′və nēr′) *n.* memento.

sov′er•eign (sov′rin, -ər in) *n.* **1.** monarch. **2.** (formerly) British gold coin worth one pound. —*adj.* **3.** of a sovereign; supreme. —**sov′er•eign•ty,** *n.*

so′vi•et′ (sō′vē et′, -it) *n.* **1.** (in the former USSR) governing body. —*adj.* **2.** (*cap.*) of the former USSR.

sow, *v.* (sō) **1.** plant seed. —*n.* (sou) **2.** female hog. —**sow′er,** *n.*

soy′bean′ (soi′-) *n.* nutritious seed of leguminous plant.

soy sauce, salty sauce made from soybeans.

spa (spä) *n.* resort at mineral spring.

space (spās) *n., v.,* **spaced, spacing.** —*n.* **1.** unlimited expanse. **2.** particular part of this. **3.** linear distance. **4.** interval of time. —*v.* **5.** divide into spaces. **6.** set at intervals.

space′craft′, *n., pl.* **-craft.** vehicle for traveling in outer space.

spaced′-out′, *adj. Slang.* dazed by or as if by drugs.

space heater, device for heating small area.

space′ship′, *n.* rocket vehicle for travel between planets.

space shuttle, reusable spacecraft.

space station, manned spacecraft orbiting the earth and serving as base for research.

spa′cious (spā′shəs) *adj.* roomy.

spade (spād) *n., v.,* **spaded, spading.** —*n.* **1.** tool with blade for digging. **2.** (*pl.*) suit of playing cards. —*v.* **3.** dig with spade.

spa•ghet′ti (spə get′ē) *n.* pasta in form of long strings.

span (span) *n., v.,* **spanned, spanning.** —*n.* **1.** distance between extended thumb and little finger. **2.** space between two supports. **3.** full extent. **4.** team of animals. —*v.* **5.** extend over.

span′dex (span′deks) *n.* elastic synthetic fiber.

span′gle (spang′gəl) *n., v.,* **-gled, -gling.** —*n.* **1.** small bright ornament. —*v.* **2.** decorate with spangles.

span′iel (span′yəl) *n.* kind of dog.

Span′ish (span′ish) *n.* language or people of Spain. —**Spanish,** *adj.*

Spanish fly, preparation of powdered green European beetles once used as aphrodisiac.

spank (spangk) *v.* **1.** strike on buttocks. —*n.* **2.** such a blow.

spank′ing, *adj.* brisk; vigorous.

spar (spär) *n., v.,* **sparred, sparring,** *n.* —*v.* **1.** box. **2.** bandy words. —*n.* **3.** *Naut.* mast, yard, etc. **4.** bright crystalline mineral.

spare (spâr) *v.,* **spared, sparing,** *adj.,* **sparer, sparest.** —*v.* **1.** deal gently with. **2.** part with easily. —*adj.* **3.** kept in reserve. **4.** extra. **5.** lean.

spare′rib′, *n.* cut of pork ribs.

spark (spärk) *n.* **1.** burning particle. **2.** flash of electricity. **3.** trace.

spar′kle, *v.,* **-kled, -kling,** *n.* —*v.* **1.** emit sparks. **2.** glitter. **3.** produce little bubbles. —*n.* **4.** little spark. **5.** brightness.

spark plug, device in internal-combustion engine that ignites fuel.

spar′row (spar′ō) *n.* small, common, hardy bird.

sparse (spärs) *adj.,* **sparser, sparsest.** thinly distributed. —**spar′si•ty,** *n.*

Spar′tan, *adj.* austere.

spasm (spaz′əm) *n.* sudden involuntary muscular contraction.

spas•mod′ic (spaz mod′ik) *adj.* **1.** of spasms. **2.** intermittent.

spas′tic (spas′tik) *adj.* of or marked by spasms.

spat (spat) *n.* petty quarrel.

spate (spāt) *n.* sudden outpouring.

spa′tial (spā′shəl) *adj.* of or in space.

spat′ter (spat′ər) *v., n.* sprinkle in many fine drops.

spat′u•la (spach′ə lə) *n.* broad-bladed implement.

spawn (spôn) *n.* **1.** eggs of fish, mollusks, etc. —*v.* **2.** produce spawn.

spay (spā) *v.* neuter (female dog, cat, etc.).

speak (spēk) *v.,* **spoke** (spōk), **spoken, speaking. 1.** talk. **2.** deliver speech.

speak′eas′y, *n., pl.* **-easies.** place selling alcoholic beverages illegally.

speak′er, *n.* person who speaks.

spear (spēr) *n.* **1.** long staff bearing sharp head. —*v.* **2.** pierce with spear.

spear′head′, *n.* **1.** head of spear. **2.** leader. —*v.* **3.** lead.

spear′mint′, *n.* aromatic herb.

spe′cial (spesh′əl) *adj.* **1.** particular in nature or purpose. **2.** unusual or unique. **3.** exceptional. —*n.* **4.** special thing or person.

spe′cial•ize′, *v.,* **-ized, -izing.** study

of work in special field. **—spe′cial•ist,** *n.* **—spe′cial•i•za′tion,** *n.*

spe′cial•ty, *n., pl.* **-ties.** field of special interest or competence.

spe′cie (spē′shē, -sē) *n.* coined money.

spe′cies (spē′shēz, -sēz) *n.* class of related individuals.

spe•cif′ic (spi sif′ik) *adj.* **1.** definite. **2.** of a particular kind. **3.** peculiar to someone or something. **—spe•cif′i•cal•ly,** *adv.*

spec′i•fi•ca′tion (spes′ə fi kā′shən) *n.* **1.** act of specifying. **2.** detailed requirement.

specific gravity, ratio of density of substance to density of standard substance, water being the standard.

spec′i•fy′, *v.,* **-fied, -fying.** mention or require specifically.

spec′i•men (spes′ə mən) *n.* anything typical of its kind.

spe′cious (spē′shəs) *adj.* plausible but false or incorrect.

speck (spek) *n.* **1.** spot or particle. **—***v.* **2.** spot.

speck′le, *n., v.,* **-led, -ling. —***n.* **1.** small spot. **—***v.* **2.** mark with speckles.

specs (speks) *n.pl. Informal.* **1.** spectacles; eyeglasses. **2.** specifications (def. 2).

spec′ta•cle (spek′tə kəl) *n.* **1.** anything presented to sight. **2.** public display. **3.** (*pl.*) eyeglasses.

spec•tac′u•lar (-tak′yə lər) *adj.* dramatic; thrilling.

spec′ta•tor (spek′tā tər) *n.* observer.

spec′ter (spek′tər) *n.* ghost. Also, **spec′tre. —spec′tral** (-trəl) *adj.*

spec′trum (-trəm) *n., pl.* **-tra** (-trə), **-trums.** band of colors formed when light ray is dispersed.

spec′u•late′ (spek′yə lāt′) *v.,* **-lated, -lating. 1.** think; conjecture. **2.** invest at some risk. **—spec′u•la′tion,** *n.* **—spec′u•la′tive** (-lā′tiv, -lə tiv) *adj.* **—spec′u•la•tor,** *n.*

speech (spēch) *n.* **1.** power of speaking. **2.** utterance. **3.** talk before audience. **4.** language. **—speech′less,** *adj.*

speed (spēd) *n., v.,* **sped** (sped) or **speeded, speeding. —***n.* **1.** swiftness. **2.** rate of motion **—***v.* **3.** increase speed of. **4.** move swiftly. **—speed′y,** *adj.* **—speed′i•ly,** *adv.*

speed•om′e•ter (spē dom′i tər, spi-) *n.* device for indicating speed.

speed′well′, *n.* plant having spikes of small flowers.

spe′le•ol•o•gy (spē′lē ol′ə jē) *n.* exploration and study of caves.

spell (spel) *v.,* **spelled** or **spelt, spelling,** *n.* **—***v.* **1.** give letters of in order. **2.** (of letters) form. **3.** signify. **4.** relieve at work. **—***n.* **5.** enchantment. **6.** brief period.

spell′bound′, *adj.* fascinated.

spe•lunk′er (spi lung′kər) *n.* person who explores caves.

spend (spend) *v.,* **spent, spending. 1.** pay out. **2.** pass (time). **3.** use up. **—spend′er,** *n.*

spend′thrift′, *n.* extravagant spender.

sperm (spûrm) *n.* male reproductive cell. **—sper•mat′ic** (-mat′ik) *adj.*

sper•ma•cet′i (spûr′mə set′ē), *n.* waxy substance from large squareheaded whale (**sperm whale**).

sper•mat′o•zo′on (spûr mat′ə-zō′ən, -on) *n., pl.* **-zoa** (-zō′ə). mature male reproductive cell.

sper′mi•cide′ (-mə sīd′) *n.* spermkilling agent.

spew (spyōō) *v.* **1.** vomit. **2.** gush or pour out.

sphere (sfēr) *n.* **1.** round ball. **2.** particular field of influence or competence. **—spher′i•cal,** *adj.*

sphe′roid (sfēr′oid) *n.* body approximately spherical.

sphinc′ter (sfingk′tər) *n.* muscle closing anus or other body opening.

sphinx (sfingks) *n.* figure of creature with human head and lion's body.

spice (spīs) *n., v.,* **spiced, spicing. —***n.* **1.** aromatic plant substance used as seasoning. **—***v.* **2.** season with spice. **—spic′y,** *adj.*

spick′-and-span′ (spik′ən span′) *adj.* **1.** spotlessly clean. **2.** perfectly new.

spi′der (spī′dər) *n.* web-spinning insectlike animal with eight legs.

spiel (spēl, shpēl) *n. Slang.* highpressure sales talk.

spiff′y (spif′ē) *adj.,* **-ier, -iest.** *Informal.* smart; fine.

spig′ot (spig′ət) *n.* faucet.

spike (spīk) *n., v.,* **spiked, spiking. —***n.* **1.** large strong nail. **2.** stiff, pointed part. **—***v.* **3.** fasten with spikes. **4.** frustrate or stop. **—spik′y,** *adj.,* **-ier, -iest.**

spill (spil) *v.,* **spilled** or **spilt, spilling. 1.** run or let run over. **2.** shed (blood). **—spil′lage,** *n.*

spill′way′, *n.* overflow passage.

spin (spin) *v.,* **spun** (spun), **spinning,** *n.* **—***v.* **1.** make yarn or thread from fiber. **2.** secrete filament. **3.** whirl. **—***n.* **4.** spinning motion. **5.** short ride. **6.** *Slang.* particular viewpoint or bias.

spin′ach (spin′ich) *n.* plant with edible leaves.

spinal column, series of vertebrae forming axis of skeleton.

spinal cord, cord of nerve tissue extending through spinal column.

spin control, *Slang.* attempt to give a bias to news coverage.

spin′dle (spin′dl) *n.* **1.** tapered rod. **2.** any shaft or axis.

spin′dling, *adj.* tall and thin. Also, **spin′dly.**

spin doctor, *Slang.* press agent or spokesperson skilled at spin control.

spine (spīn) *n.* **1.** Also, **spinal column.** connected series of bones down back. **2.** any spinelike part. **3.** stiff bristle or thorn. **—spi′nal,** *adj.* **—spin′y,** *adj.*

spine′less, *adj.* weak in character.

spin′et (spin′it) *n.* small piano.

spinning wheel, device for spinning yarn or thread.

spin′-off′, *n.* by-product or secondary development.

spin′ster (spin′stər) *n. Usually Offensive.* unmarried woman, esp. elderly.

spi′ral (spī′rəl) *n., adj., v.,* **-raled, -raling. —***n.* **1.** curve made by circling a point while approaching or receding from it. **—***adj.* **2.** like or of spiral. **—***v.* **3.** move spirally.

spire (spīr) *n.* tall tapering structure, esp. on tower or roof.

spi•re′a (spī rē′ə) *n.* common garden shrub. Also, **spiraea.**

spir′it (spir′it) *n.* **1.** vital force in humanity; soul. **2.** supernatural being. **3.** feelings. **4.** vigor. **5.** intent. **6.** (*pl.*) alcoholic liquor. **7.** (*cap.*) Holy Ghost. **—***v.* **8.** carry off secretly. **—spir′it•ed,** *adj.*

spir′it•u•al (-chōō əl) *adj.* **1.** of or in spirit; ethereal. **2.** religious. **—***n.* **3.** religious song. **—spir′it•u•al•ly,** *adv.* **—spir′it•u•al′i•ty** (-al′i tē) *n.*

spir′it•u•al•ism, *n.* belief that spirits of dead communicate with living. **—spir′it•u•al•ist,** *n., adj.*

spit (spit) *v.,* **spat** (spat) or **spit** (for 2 **spitted**), **spitting,** *n.* **—***v.* **1.** eject from mouth. **2.** pierce. **—***n.* **3.** saliva. **4.** *Informal.* image. **5.** rod for roasting meat. **6.** point of land.

spite (spīt) *n., v.,* **spited, spiting. —***n.* **1.** malice; grudge. **—***v.* **2.** annoy out of spite. **—spite′ful,** *adj.*

spit′fire′, *n.* person with fiery temper.

spit′tle, *n.* saliva.

spit•toon′ (spi tōōn′) *n.* cuspidor.

splash (splash) *v.* **1.** dash water, etc. **—***n.* **2.** act or sound of splashing. **3.** spot. **—splash′y,** *adj.*

splash′down′, *n.* landing of space vehicle in ocean.

splat (splat) *n.* sound made by splattering.

splat′ter, *v.* splash widely.

splay (splā) *v., adj.* spread out.

spleen (splēn) *n.* **1.** ductless organ near stomach. **2.** ill humor.

splen′did (splen′did) *adj.* gorgeous; superb; fine. **—splen′dor,** *n.*

splice (splīs) *v.,* **spliced, splicing,** *n.* **—***v.* **1.** join, as ropes or boards. **—***n.* **2.** union made by splicing.

splint (splint) *n.* **1.** brace for broken part of body. **2.** strip of wood for weaving. **—***v.* **3.** brace with splints.

splin′ter, *n.* **1.** thin sharp fragment. **—***v.* **2.** break into splinters.

split (split) *v.,* **split, splitting,** *n., adj.* **—***v.* **1.** separate; divide. **2.** burst. **—***n.* **3.** crack or breach. **—***adj.* **4.** cleft; divided.

split′-lev′el, *adj.* **1.** having rooms on levels a half story apart. **—***n.* **2.** splitlevel house.

split pea, dried green pea.

split personality, mental disorder in which person acquires several personalities.

splotch (sploch) *n., v.,* blot; stain.

splurge (splûrj) *v., n.,* **splurged, splurging. —***v.* **1.** big display or expenditure. **—***v.* **2.** be extravagant.

splut′ter (splut′ər) *v.* **1.** talk vehemently and incoherently. **—***n.* **2.** spluttering talk.

spoil (spoil) *v.,* **spoiled** or **spoilt, spoiling,** *v.* **1.** damage; ruin. **2.** become tainted. **—***n.* **3.** (*pl.*) booty. **4.** waste material. **—spoil′age,** *n.*

spoil′sport′, *n.* person who spoils the pleasure of others.

spoils system, practice of filling nonelective public offices with supporters of victorious party.

spoke (spōk) *n.* bar between hub and rim of wheel.

spokes′man, *n., pl.* **-men.** person speaking for others. Also, *fem.,* **spokes′wom′an;** *masc.* or *fem.,* **spokes′per′son.**

sponge (spunj) *n., v.,* **sponged, sponging. —***n.* **1.** marine animal. **2.** its light skeleton or an imitation, used to absorb liquids. **—***v.* **3.** clean with sponge. **4.** impose or live on another. **—spong′er,** *n.*

sponge cake, light cake without shortening.

spon′sor (spon′sər) *n.* **1.** one that recommends or supports. **2.** godparent. **3.** advertiser on radio or television. **—***v.* **4.** act as sponsor for. **—spon′sor•ship,** *n.*

spon•ta′ne•ous (spon tā′nē əs) *adj.* **1.** occurring naturally or without planning. **2.** impulsive. **—spon′ta•ne′i•ty,** *n.*

spontaneous combustion, ignition of a substance without heat from external source.

spoof (spōōf) *n.* **1.** parody. **2.** prank. **—***v.* **3.** make fun of lightly.

spook (spo͞ok) —*n.* **1.** ghost. —*v.* **2.** frighten. —**spook′y,** *adj.*

spool (spo͞ol) *n.* cylinder on which something is wound.

spoon (spo͞on) *n.* **1.** utensil for stirring or taking up food. —*v.* **2.** lift in spoon. —**spoon′ful,** *n.*

spoon′bill′, *n.* large wading bird.

spoon′er·ism (spo͞o′nə riz/əm) *n.* inadvertent transposition of initial sounds of words.

spoon′-feed′, *v.,* spoon-fed, spoon-feeding. **1.** feed with a spoon. **2.** provide information in a simplified way.

spoor (spo͝or) *n.* trail of wild animal.

spo·rad′ic (spə rad′ik) *adj.* occasional; scattered.

spore (spôr) *n.* seed, as of ferns.

sport (spôrt) *n.* **1.** athletic pastime. **2.** diversion. **3.** person who shows sportsmanship. —*adj.* **4.** of or for sport. —*v.* **5.** play. —**sports′man,** *n.* —**sports′wear′,** *n.*

spor′tive, *adj.* playful.

sports car, small, high-powered car.

sports′man·ship′, *n.* ability to win or lose gracefully.

sport-utility vehicle, rugged vehicle with trucklike chassis, designed for occasional off-road use.

sport′y, *adj.,* -ier, -iest. flashy or showy.

spot (spot) *n., v.,* spotted, spotting, *adj.* —*n.* **1.** blot. **2.** locality. —*v.* **3.** stain with spots. **4.** notice. —*adj.* **5.** made, done, etc., at once. —**spot′less,** *adj.* —**spot′ty,** *adj.*

spot check, random sampling or investigation. —**spot′-check′,** *v.*

spot′light′, *n.* **1.** intense light focused on person or thing, as on stage. **2.** intense public attention.

spouse (spous) *n.* husband or wife.

spout (spout) *v.* **1.** discharge (liquid, etc.) with force. **2.** utter insincerely. —*n.* **3.** pipe or lip on container.

sprain (sprān) *v.* **1.** injure by wrenching. —*n.* **2.** such injury.

sprat (sprat) *n.* herringlike fish.

sprawl (sprôl) *v.* **1.** stretch out ungracefully. —*n.* **2.** sprawling position.

spray (sprā) *n.* **1.** liquid in fine particles. **2.** appliance for producing spray. **3.** branch of flowers, etc. —*v.* **4.** scatter as spray. **5.** apply spray to. —**spray′er,** *n.*

spread (spred) *v.,* spread, spreading, *n.* —*v.* **1.** stretch out. **2.** extend. **3.** scatter. —*n.* **4.** extent. **5.** diffusion. **6.** cloth cover. **7.** preparation for eating on bread.

spread′-ea′gle, *adj., v.,* spread-eagled, spread-eagling. —*adj.* **1.** suggesting form of eagle with outstretched wings. —*v.* **2.** stretch out in this position.

spread′sheet′, *n.* **1.** outsize ledger sheet. **2.** such a sheet simulated by computer software.

spree (sprē) *n.* frolic.

sprig (sprig) *n.* twig or shoot.

spright′ly (sprīt′lē) *adj.,* -lier, -liest. lively. —**spright′li·ness,** *n.*

spring (spring) *v.,* sprang (sprang) or sprung (sprung), sprung, springing, *n., adj.* —*v.* **1.** leap. **2.** grow or proceed. **3.** disclose. —*n.* **4.** jump. **5.** natural fountain. **6.** season after winter. **7.** elastic device. —*adj.* **8.** of or for spring (def. 6). —**spring′time′,** *n.* —**spring′y,** *adj.*

spring′board′, *n.* **1.** flexible board used in diving and gymnastics. **2.** starting point.

spring fever, restless feeling associated with spring.

sprin′kle (spring′kəl) *v.,* -kled, -kling,

n. —*v.* **1.** scatter in drops. **2.** rain slightly. —*n.* **3.** instance of sprinkling. **4.** something sprinkled.

sprint (sprint) *v.* **1.** run fast. —*n.* **2.** short fast run. —**sprint′er,** *n.*

sprite (sprīt) *n.* elf; fairy.

sprock′et (sprok′it) *n.* tooth on wheel for engaging with chain.

sprout (sprout) *v.* **1.** begin to grow; bud. —*n.* **2.** plant shoot.

spruce (spro͞os) *adj.,* sprucer, sprucest, *v.,* n. —*adj.* **1.** trim; neat. —*v.* **2.** make spruce. —*n.* **3.** cone-bearing evergreen tree.

spry (sprī) *adj.,* spryer or sprier, spryest or spriest. nimble.

spud (spud) *n.* **1.** spadelike tool. **2.** *Informal.* potato.

spume (spyo͞om) *n.* foam.

spunk (spungk) *n. Informal.* courage; spirit. —**spunk′y,** *adj.*

spur (spûr) *n., v.,* spurred, spurring. —*n.* **1.** sharp device worn on heel to goad horse. **2.** spurlike part. —*v.* **3.** prick with spur. **4.** urge.

spu′ri·ous (spyo͝or′ē əs) *adj.* not genuine. —**spu′ri·ous·ly,** *adv.*

spurn (spûrn) *v.* scorn; reject.

spurt (spûrt) *v.* **1.** gush or eject in jet. **2.** speed up briefly. —*n.* **3.** forceful gush. **4.** brief increase of effort.

sput′ter (sput′ər) *v.* **1.** emit violently in drops. **2.** splutter. —*n.* **3.** act or sound of sputtering.

spu′tum (spyo͞o′təm) *n.* spittle, esp. mixed with mucus.

spy (spī) *n., pl.* spies, *v.,* spied, spying. —*n.* **1.** secret observer, esp. one employed by government. —*v.* **2.** watch secretly. **3.** sight.

spy glass, small telescope.

squab (skwob) *n.* young pigeon.

squab′ble (skwob′əl) *n., v.,* -bled, -bling. —*n.* **1.** petty quarrel. —*v.* **2.** have squabble.

squad (skwod) *n.* small group.

squad car, police car.

squad′ron (-rən) *n.* unit in Navy, Air Force, etc.

squal′id (skwol′id) *adj.* dirty or wretched. —**squal′id·ly,** *adv.*

squall (skwôl) *v.* **1.** strong gust of wind, etc. **2.** loud cry. —*v.* **3.** cry loudly. —**squall′y,** *adj.*

squal′or (skwol′ər) *n.* squalid state.

squan′der (skwon′dər) *v.* use or spend wastefully.

square (skwâr) *n., v.,* squared, squaring, *adj.,* squarer, squarest, *adv.* —*n.* **1.** plane figure with four equal sides and four right angles. **2.** anything square. **3.** tool for checking right angles. **4.** product of number multiplied by itself. **5.** *Slang.* conventional, conservative, unimaginative person. —*v.* **6.** make square. **7.** adjust; agree. **8.** multiply by itself. —*adj.* **9.** being a square. **10.** level. **11.** honest. —*adv.* **12.** directly. —**square′ly,** *adv.*

square dance, dance by sets of four couples arranged in squares.

square root, quantity of which a given quantity is the square.

squash (skwosh) *v.* **1.** crush; suppress. —*n.* **2.** game resembling tennis. **3.** fruit of vinelike plant.

squat (skwot) *v.,* squatted or squat, squatting, *adj.* —*v.* **1.** sit with legs close under body. **2.** settle on land illegally or to acquire title. —*adj.* **3.** Also, **squat′ty.** stocky. —*n.* **4.** squatting position.

squaw (skwô) *n. Often Offensive.* American Indian woman.

squawk (skwôk) *n.* **1.** loud harsh cry. —*v.* **2.** utter squawks.

squeak (skwēk) *n.* **1.** small shrill

sound. —*v.* **2.** emit squeaks. —**squeak′y,** *adj.* —**squeak′er,** *n.*

squeal (skwēl) *n.* **1.** long shrill cry. —*v.* **2.** utter squeals.

squeam′ish (skwē′mish) *adj.* **1.** prudish. **2.** overfastidious.

squee′gee (skwē′jē) *n.* implement for cleaning glass surfaces.

squeeze (skwēz) *v.,* squeezed, squeezing, *n.* —*v.* **1.** press together. **2.** cram. —*n.* **3.** act of squeezing. **4.** hug.

squelch (skwelch) *v.* **1.** make a sucking noise. **2.** silence. —*n.* **3.** crushing retort.

squib (skwib) *n.* **1.** short witty item. **2.** hissing firecracker.

squid (skwid) *n.* marine mollusk.

squig′gle (skwig′əl) *n.* short, irregular curve or twist. —**squig′gly,** *adj.*

squint (skwint) *v.* **1.** look with eyes partly closed. **2.** be cross-eyed. —*n.* **3.** squinting look. **4.** cross-eyed condition.

squire (skwīr) *n., v.,* squired, squiring. —*n.* **1.** country gentleman. **2.** escort. —*v.* **3.** escort.

squirm (skwûrm) *v., n.* wriggle.

squir′rel (skwûr′əl) *n.* bushy-tailed, tree-living rodent.

squirt (skwûrt) *v.* **1.** gush; cause to gush. —*n.* **2.** jet of liquid.

squish (skwish) *v.* **1.** make gushing sound when squeezed. **2.** squash (def. 1). —*n.* **3.** squishing sound.

Sr., **1.** Senior. **2.** Sister.

SRO, **1.** single-room occupancy. **2.** standing room only.

SS, social security.

SST, supersonic transport.

St., **1.** Saint. **2.** Street.

stab (stab) *v.,* stabbed, stabbing, *n.* —*v.* **1.** pierce with pointed weapon. —*n.* **2.** thrust with or wound from pointed weapon.

sta′bi·lize′ (stā′bə līz′) *v.,* -lized, -lizing. make or keep stable.

sta′ble (stā′bəl) *n., v.,* -bled, -bling, *adj.* —*n.* **1.** building for horses, etc. —*v.* **2.** keep in stable. —*adj.* **3.** steady. —**sta·bil′i·ty,** *n.*

stac·ca′to (stə kä′tō) *adj. Music.* disconnected; detached.

stack (stak) *n.* **1.** orderly heap. **2.** (*often pl.*) book storage area. **3.** funnel for smoke. —*v.* **4.** pile in stack.

sta′di·um (stā′dē əm) *n., pl.* -diums, -dia large open structure for games.

staff (staf) *n., pl.* staves (stāvz) or staffs (for 1, 3); staffs (for 2); *n.* —*n.* **1.** stick carried as support, weapon, etc. **2.** body of administrators or assitants. **3.** set of five lines on which music is written. —*v.* **4.** provide with staff.

staff′er, *n.* member of a staff.

stag (stag) *n.* **1.** adult male deer. —*adj.* **2.** for men only. —*adv.* **3.** without a date.

stage (stāj) *n., v.,* staged, staging. —*n.* **1.** single step or degree. **2.** raised platform. **3.** theater. —*v.* **4.** present on stage.

stage′coach′, *n.* horse-drawn public coach that traveled over fixed route.

stage′hand′, *n.* worker in theater who deals with props and scenery.

stage′struck′, *adj.* obsessed with desire to act.

stag′ger (stag′ər) *v.* **1.** move unsteadily. **2.** astonish. **3.** arrange at intervals. —*n.* **4.** staggering movement. **5.** (*pl.*) disease of horses, etc.

stag′ger·ing, *adj.* amazing.

stag′ing (stā′jing) *n.* scaffolding.

stag′nant (stag′nənt) *adj.* **1.** not flowing; foul. **2.** inactive. —**stag′nate**

(-nāt) *v.*, **-nated, -nating.** **—stag•na′-tion,** *n.*

staid (stād) *adj.* sedate.

stain (stān) *n.* **1.** discolored patch. **2.** kind of dye. **—***v.* **3.** mark with stains. **4.** color with stain.

stainless steel, steel allied with chromium to resist rust.

stair (stâr) *n.* series of steps between levels. **—stair′case′, stair′way′,** *n.*

stair′well′, *n.* vertical shaft containing stairs.

stake (stāk) *n.*, *v.*, **staked, staking.** **—***n.* **1.** pointed post. **2.** something wagered. **3.** (*pl.*) prize. **4.** hazard. **—***v.* **5.** mark off with stakes. **6.** wager.

stake′out′, *n.* surveillance by police.

sta•lac′tite (stə lak′tīt) *n.* icicle-shaped formation hanging from cave roof.

sta•lag′mite (stə lag′mīt) *n.* cone-shaped deposit on cave floor.

stale (stāl) *adj.*, **staler, stalest,** *v.*, **staled, staling.** **—***adj.* **1.** not fresh. **—***v.* **2.** make or become stale.

stale′mate′ (-māt′) *n.* deadlocked position, orig. in chess.

stalk (stôk) *v.* **1.** pursue stealthily. **2.** walk in haughty or menacing way. **—***n.* **3.** plant stem. **—stalk′er,** *n.*

stall (stôl) *n.* **1.** compartment for one animal. **2.** sales booth. **3.** (of airplane) loss of air speed. **4.** *Slang.* pretext for delay. **—***v.* **5.** keep in stall. **6.** stop. **7.** lose necessary air speed. **8.** *Slang.* delay.

stal′lion (stal′yən) *n.* male horse.

stal′wart (stôl′wərt) *adj.* **1.** robust. **2.** brave. **—***n.* **3.** stalwart person.

sta′men (stā′mən) *n.* pollen-bearing organ of flower.

stam′i•na (stam′ə nə) *n.* endurance.

stam′mer (stam′ər) *v.* **1.** speak with involuntary breaks or repetitions. **—***n.* **2.** such speech.

stamp (stamp) *v.* **1.** trample. **2.** mark. **3.** put paper stamp on. **—***n.* **4.** act of stamping. **5.** marking device. **6.** adhesive paper affixed to show payment of fees.

stam•pede′ (stam pēd′) *n.*, *v.*, **-peded, -peding.** **—***n.* **1.** panicky flight. **—***v.* **2.** flee in stampede.

stamping ground, favorite haunt.

stance (stans) *n.* way of standing.

stanch (stônch, stanch) *adj.* **1.** staunch. **—***v.* **2.** stop flow, esp. of blood.

stan′chion (stan′shən) *n.* upright post.

stand (stand) *v.*, **stood** (sto͝od), **standing,** *n.* **—***v.* **1.** rise or be upright. **2.** remain firm. **3.** be located. **4.** be candidate. **5.** endure. **—***n.* **6.** firm attitude. **7.** place of standing. **8.** platform. **9.** support for small articles. **10.** outdoor salesplace. **11.** area of trees. **12.** stop.

stand′ard (stan′dərd) *n.* **1.** approved model or rule. **2.** flag. **3.** upright support. **—***adj.* **4.** being model or basis for comparison.

stan′dard-bear′er, *n.* leader of a cause.

stand′ard•ize′, *v.*, **-ized, -izing.** make standard.

standard time, civil time officially adopted for a region.

stand′by′, *n.*, *pl.* **-bys,** *adj.* **—***n.* **1.** chief support. **—***adj.* **2.** substitute.

stand′-in′, *n.* substitute.

stand′ing, *n.* **1.** status or reputation. **2.** duration. **—***adj.* **3.** upright. **4.** stagnant. **5.** lasting; fixed.

stand′off′, *n.* tie or draw; situation in which neither side has advantage.

stand′off′ish, *adj.* tending to be aloof.

stand′out′, *n.* one that is conspicuously superior.

stand′pipe′, *n.* vertical pipe into which water is pumped to obtain required pressure.

stand′point′, *n.* point of view.

stand′still′, *n.* complete halt.

stand′-up′, *adj.* **1.** erect. **2.** performing a comic monologue while standing alone before audience.

stan′za (stan′zə) *n.* division of poem.

sta′ple (stā′pəl) *n.*, *v.*, **-pled, -pling,** *adj.* **—***n.* **1.** bracket-shaped wire fastener. **2.** chief commodity. **—***v.* **3.** fasten with staple. **—***adj.* **4.** basic. **—sta′-pler,** *n.*

star (stär) *n.*, *adj.*, *v.*, **starred, starring.** **—***n.* **1.** heavenly body luminous at night. **2.** figure with five or six points. **3.** asterisk. **4.** principal performer. **5.** famous performer. **—***adj.* **6.** principal. **—***v.* **7.** mark with star. **8.** have leading part. **—star′ry,** *adj.* **—star′dom,** *n.*

star′board′ (-bərd, -bôrd′) *n.* right-hand side of vessel, facing forward. **—star′board′,** *adj.*, *adv.*

starch (stärch) *n.* **1.** white tasteless substance used as food and as a stiffening agent. **2.** preparation from starch. **—***v.* **3.** stiffen with starch.

stare (stâr) *v.*, **stared, staring,** *n.* **—***v.* **1.** gaze fixedly. **—***n.* **2.** fixed look.

star′fish′, *n.* star-shaped marine animal.

star′gaze′, *v.*, **-gazed, -gazing.** **1.** gaze at stars. **2.** daydream.

stark (stärk) *adj.* **1.** utter; sheer. **2.** bleak. **3.** harsh. **—***adv.* **4.** utterly.

star′let (-lit) *n.* young movie actress.

star′light′, *n.* light emanating from the stars. **—star′lit′,** *adj.*

star′ling (-ling) *n.* small bird.

star′ry-eyed′, *adj.* overly romantic or idealistic.

start (stärt) *v.* **1.** begin. **2.** move suddenly. **3.** establish. **—***n.* **4.** beginning. **5.** startled movement. **6.** lead. **—start′er,** *n.*

star′tle, *v.*, **-tled, -tling.** disturb suddenly.

starve (stärv) *v.*, **starved, starving.** **1.** die or suffer severely from hunger. **2.** kill or weaken by hunger. **—star•va′-tion,** *n.*

stash (stash) *v.* **1.** hide away. **—***n.* **2.** something hidden away. **3.** hiding place.

stat (stat) *n.* statistic.

state (stāt) *n.*, *adj.*, *v.*, **stated, stating.** **—***n.* **1.** condition. **2.** pomp. **3.** nation. **4.** commonwealth of a federal union. **5.** civil government. **—***adj.* **6.** ceremonious. **—***v.* **7.** declare. **—state′-hood,** *n.* **—state′house,** *n.*

state′craft′, *n.* art of government.

state′less, *adj.* lacking nationality.

state′ly, *adj.*, **-lier, -liest.** dignified.

state′ment, *n.* **1.** declaration. **2.** report on business account.

state of the art, most advanced stage.

state′room′, *n.* quarters on ship, etc.

states′man, *n.* person skilled in government. **—states′man•ship,** *n.*

stat′ic (stat′ik) *adj.* **1.** fixed; at rest. **—***n.* **2.** atmospheric electricity. **3.** interference caused by it.

sta′tion (stā′shən) *n.* **1.** place of duty. **2.** depot for trains, buses, etc. **3.** status. **4.** place for sending or receiving radio or television broadcasts. **—***v.* **5.** assign place to.

sta′tion•ar′y (-shə ner′ē) *adj.* not moving; not movable; fixed.

sta′tion•er, *n.* dealer in stationery.

sta′tion•er′y (-shə ner′ē) *n.* writing materials.

sta•tis′tics (stə tis′tiks) *n.* science of collecting, classifying, and using numerical facts. **—stat′is•ti′cian** (stat′ə-stish′ən) *n.*

stat′u•ar′y (stach′o͞o er′ē) *n.* statues.

stat′ue (stach′o͞o) *n.* carved, molded, or cast figure.

stat′u•esque′ (-esk′) *adj.* like statue; of imposing figure.

stat′u•ette′ (-et′) *n.* little statue.

stat′ure (-ər) *n.* **1.** height. **2.** status from achievement.

sta′tus (stā′təs, stat′əs) *n.* **1.** social standing. **2.** present condition.

status quo (kwō) existing state.

status symbol, possession believed to indicate high social status.

stat′ute (stach′o͞ot) *n.* law enacted by legislature. **—stat′u•to′ry** (-o͞o tôr′ē) *adj.*

statute of limitations, statute defining period within which legal action may be taken.

staunch (stônch) *adj.* **1.** firm; steadfast; strong. **—***v.* **2.** stanch.

stave (stāv) *n.*, *v.*, **staved** or (for 3) **stove** (stōv), **staving.** **—***n.* **1.** narrow strip of wood. **2.** *Music.* staff. **—***v.* **3.** break hole in. **4.** ward (off).

stay (stā) *v.* **1.** remain; continue. **2.** stop or restrain. **3.** support. **—***n.* **4.** period at one place. **5.** stop; pause. **6.** support.

staying power, endurance.

STD, sexually transmitted disease.

std., standard.

stead (sted) *n.* **1.** place taken by another. **2.** advantage.

stead′fast′, *adj.* **1.** fixed. **2.** loyal.

stead′y, *adj.*, **-ier, -iest,** *v.*, **steadied, steadying.** **—***adj.* **1.** firmly fixed. **2.** uniform; regular. **3.** steadfast. **—***v.* **4.** make or become steady. **—stead′i•ly,** *adv.*

steak (stāk) *n.* slice of meat or fish.

steal (stēl) *v.*, **stole** (stōl), **stolen, stealing.** **1.** take wrongfully. **2.** move very quietly.

stealth (stelth) *n.* secret action. **—stealth′y,** *adj.*

steam (stēm) *n.* **1.** water in form of gas or vapor. **—***v.* **2.** pass off or give off steam. **3.** treat with steam, as in cooking. **—***adj.* **4.** operated by steam. **5.** conducting steam. **—steam′boat′, steam′ship′,** *n.*

steam′er, *n.* **1.** vessel moved by steam. **2.** device for cooking, treating, etc., with steam.

steam′roll′er, *n.* **1.** heavy vehicle with roller used for paving roads. **—***v.* **2.** crush, flatten, or overwhelm as if with steamroller.

steam shovel, machine for excavating.

steed (stēd) *n.* horse, esp. for riding.

steel (stēl) *n.* **1.** iron modified with carbon. **—***adj.* **2.** of or like steel. **—***v.* **3.** make resolute.

steel wool, mass of woven steel, used for scouring and smoothing.

steep (stēp) *adj.* **1.** sloping sharply. **2.** exorbitant. **—***v.* **3.** soak. **4.** absorb. **—steep′ly,** *adv.*

stee′ple (stē′pəl) *n.* **1.** lofty tower on church, etc. **2.** spire.

stee′ple•chase′, *n.* horse race over obstacle course.

stee′ple•jack′, *n.* person who builds or repairs steeples.

steer (stēr) *v.* **1.** guide; direct. **—***n.* **2.** ox.

steer′age (-ij) *n.* part of ship for passengers paying cheapest rate.

steg′o•saur′ (steg′ə sôr′) n. plant-eating dinosaur with bony plates along back.

stein (stīn) n. mug, esp. for beer.

stel′lar (stel′ər) adj. of or like stars.

stem (stem) n., v., **stemmed, stemming.** —n. **1.** supporting stalk of plant. **2.** ancestry. **3.** part of word not changed by inflection. **4.** Naut. bow. —v. **5.** remove stem of. **6.** originate. **7.** stop or check. **8.** make headway against.

stem′ware′, n. glassware with footed stems.

stench (stench) n. bad odor.

sten′cil (sten′səl) n., v., **-ciled, -ciling.** —n. **1.** sheet cut to pass design through when colored over. —v. **2.** print with stencil.

ste•nog′ra•phy (-rə fē) n. writing in shorthand. —**ste•nog′ra•pher,** n.

sten•to′ri•an (sten tôr′ē ən) adj. very loud.

step (step) n., v., **stepped, stepping.** —n. **1.** movement of foot in walking. **2.** distance of such movement. **3.** pace. **4.** footprint. **5.** stage in process. **6.** level on stair or ladder. —v. **7.** move by steps. **8.** press with foot.

step-, prefix showing relation by remarriage of parent. —**step′child,** n. —**step′son′,** n. —**step′daugh′ter,** n. —**step′par′ent,** n. —**step′fath′er,** n. —**step′moth′er,** n. —**step′broth′er,** n. —**step′sis′ter,** n.

step′lad′der, n. ladder with flat treads.

steppe (step) n. vast plain.

-ster, suffix meaning one who is, one who is associated with, or one who makes or does.

ster′e•o (ster′ē ō′, stēr′-) n., pl. **-eos.** stereophonic sound or equipment.

ster′e•o•phon′ic (ster′ē ə fon′ik, stēr′-) adj. (of recorded sound) played through two or more speakers.

ster′e•o•type′, n., v., **-typed, -typing.** —n. **1.** idea, etc., without originality. **2.** simplified image of person, group, etc. —v. **3.** give fixed, trite form to.

ster′ile (ster′il; esp. Brit. -īl) adj. **1.** free from living germs. **2.** unable to produce offspring; barren. —**ste•ril′i•ty** (stə ril′i tē) n.

ster′i•lize′, v., **-lized, -lizing.** make sterile. —**ster′i•li•za′tion,** n. —**ster′i•liz′er,** n.

ster′ling (stûr′ling) adj. **1.** containing 92.5% silver. **2.** of British money. **3.** excellent.

stern (stûrn) adj. **1.** strict; harsh; grim. —n. **2.** hind part of vessel.

ster′num (stûr′nəm) n., pl. **-na, -nums.** flat bone in chest connecting with clavicle and ribs.

ste′roid (stēr′oid, ster′-) n. any of a group of fat-soluble organic compounds.

stet (stet) v., **stetted, stetting. 1.** let it stand (direction to retain material previously deleted). **2.** mark with word "stet."

steth′o•scope′ (steth′ə skōp′) n. medical instrument for listening to sounds in body.

ste′ve•dore′ (stē′vi dôr′) n. person who loads and unloads ships.

stew (stoō, styoō) v. **1.** cook by simmering. —n. **2.** food so cooked.

stew′ard (stoō′ərd, styoō′-) n. **1.** person who manages another's affairs, property, etc. **2.** person in charge of food, supplies, etc., for ship, club, etc. **3.** domestic employee on ship or airplane. —**stew′ard•ship′,** n.

stick (stik) v., **stuck** (stuk), **sticking,**

n. —v. **1.** pierce; stab. **2.** thrust. **3.** cause to adhere. **4.** adhere. **5.** persist. **6.** extend. —n. **7.** small length of wood, etc.

stick′er, n. adhesive label.

stick′-in-the-mud′, n. person who avoids change.

stick′ler n., someone who insists on something difficult.

stick′pin′, n. ornamental pin.

stick shift, manual transmission.

stick′y, adj., **-ier, -iest. 1.** adhering. **2.** humid. —**stick′i•ness,** n.

stiff (stif) adj. **1.** rigid. **2.** not moving easily. **3.** formal. —**stiff′en,** v.

stiff′-necked′, adj. obstinate.

sti′fle (stī′fəl) v., **-fled, -fling. 1.** smother. **2.** repress.

stig′ma (stig′mə) n., pl. **stig•ma•ta** (stig mä′tə, -mə-), **-mas. 1.** mark of disgrace. **2.** pollen-receiving part of pistil. —**stig′ma•tize′,** v.

stile (stīl) n. set of steps over fence, wall, etc.

sti•let′to (sti let′ō) n., pl. **-tos, -toes.** thin-bladed dagger.

still (stil) adj. **1.** motionless. **2.** silent. **3.** tranquil. —adv. **4.** as previously. **5.** until now. **6.** yet. —conj. **7.** nevertheless. —v. **8.** make or become still. —n. **9.** distilling apparatus. —**still′ness,** n.

still′born′, adj. born dead.

still life, picture of inanimate objects.

stilt (stilt) n. one of two poles enabling user to walk above the ground.

stilt′ed, adj. stiffly dignified.

stim′u•lant (stim′yə lənt) n. food, medicine, etc., that stimulates briefly.

stim′u•late′ (-lāt′) v., **-lated, -lating. 1.** rouse to action. **2.** invigorate. —**stim′u•la′tion,** n.

stim′u•lus (-ləs) n., pl. **-li.** something that stimulates.

sting (sting) v., **stung** (stung), **stinging,** n. —v. **1.** wound with pointed organ, as bees do. **2.** pain sharply. **3.** goad. —n. **4.** wound caused by stinging. **5.** sharp-pointed organ. —**sting′er,** n.

stin′gy (stin′jē) adj., **-gier, -giest. 1.** miserly. **2.** scanty.

stink (stingk) v., **stank** (stangk) or **stunk** (stungk), **stunk, stinking,** n. —v. **1.** emit bad odor. —n. **2.** bad odor.

stint (stint) v. **1.** limit. —n. **2.** limitation. **3.** allotted task.

sti′pend (stī′pend) n. regular pay.

stip′ple (stip′əl) v., **-pled, -pling,** n. —v. **1.** paint or cover with tiny dots. —n. **2.** such painting.

stip′u•late′ (stip′yə lāt′) v., **-lated, -lating.** require as condition.

stir (stûr) v., **stirred, stirring,** n. —v. **1.** mix or agitate (liquid, etc.), esp. with circular motion. **2.** move. **3.** rouse; excite. —n. **4.** movement; commotion. **5.** Slang. prison.

stir′-cra′zy, adj. Slang. restless from long confinement.

stir′-fry′, v., **stir-fried, stir-frying.** fry quickly while stirring constantly over high heat.

stir′rup (stûr′əp, stir′-) n. looplike support for foot, suspended from saddle.

stitch (stich) n. **1.** complete movement of needle in sewing, knitting, etc. **2.** sudden pain. —v. **3.** sew.

stock (stok) n. **1.** goods on hand. **2.** livestock. **3.** stem or trunk. **4.** line of descent. **5.** meat broth. **6.** part of gun supporting barrel. **7.** (pl.) framework in which prisoners were publicly confined. **8.** capital or shares of company. —adj. **9.** standard; common. **10.** of stock. —v. **11.** supply. **12.** store.

—**stock′brok′er.** n. —**stock′hold′er,** n.

stock•ade′ (sto kād′) n., v., **-aded, -ading.** —n. **1.** barrier of upright posts. —v. **2.** protect with stockade.

stock company, theatrical company acting repertoire of plays.

stock exchange, place where securities are bought and sold. Also, **stock market.**

stock′ing, n. close-fitting covering for foot and leg.

stocking cap, conical knitted cap with tassel or pompom.

stock′pile′, n., v., **-piled, -piling.** —n. **1.** stock of goods. —v. **2.** accumulate for eventual use.

stock′-still′, adj. motionless.

stock′y, adj., **-ier, -iest.** sturdily built.

stock′yard′, n. enclosure for livestock about to be slaughtered.

stodg′y (stoj′ē) adj., **-ier, -iest.** pompous and uninteresting.

sto′gy (stō′gē) n., pl. **-gies.** long, slender, cheap cigar.

sto′ic (stō′ik) adj. **1.** Also, **sto′i•cal.** not reacting to pain. —n. **2.** person who represses emotion.

stoke (stōk) v., **stoked, stoking.** tend (fire). —**stok′er,** n.

stole (stōl) n. scarf or narrow strip worn over shoulders.

stol′id (stol′id) adj. unemotional; not easily moved. —**sto•lid′i•ty,** n.

stom′ach (stum′ək) n. **1.** organ of food storage and digestion. **2.** appetite; desire. —v. **3.** tolerate.

stomp (stomp) v. tread or tread on heavily.

stone (stōn) n., pl. **stones** or (for 4) **stone,** adj., v., **stoned, stoning,** adv. —n. **1.** hard, nonmetallic mineral substance. **2.** small rock. **3.** gem. **4.** Brit. unit of weight = 14 pounds. **5.** stonelike seed. **6.** concretion formed in body. —adj. **7.** of stone. —v. **8.** throw stones at. **9.** remove stones from. —adv. **10.** entirely. —**ston′y,** adj.

Stone Age, prehistoric period before use of metals.

stoned, adj. Informal. **1.** drunk. **2.** drugged.

stone′wall′, v. be evasive or uncooperative.

stooge (stoōj) n. **1.** assistant to comedian. **2.** person acting in obsequious obedience.

stool (stoōl) n. seat without arms or back.

stool pigeon, Slang. decoy or informer.

stoop (stoōp) v. **1.** bend forward. **2.** condescend. —n. **3.** stooping posture. **4.** small doorway or porch.

stop (stop) v., **stopped, stopping,** n. —v. **1.** cease; halt. **2.** prevent. **3.** close up. **4.** stay. —n. **5.** act, instance, or place of stopping. **6.** hindrance.

stop′gap′, n., adj. makeshift.

stop′o′ver, n. temporary stop on journey.

stop′per, n. **1.** plug. —v. **2.** close with stopper. Also, **stop′ple.**

stop′watch′, n. watch with hand that can be stopped or started instantly.

stor′age (stôr′ij) n. **1.** place for storing. **2.** act of storing. **3.** state of being stored. **4.** fee for storing.

store (stôr) n., v., **stored, storing.** —n. **1.** place where merchandise is kept for sale. **2.** supply. —v. **3.** lay up; accumulate. **4.** put in secure place. —**store′keep′er,** n.

store′front′, n. small, street-level store.

store′house′, *n*. building for storage. —**store′room′**, *n*.

stork (stôrk) *n*. wading bird with long legs and bill.

storm (stôrm) *n*. **1.** heavy rain, snow, etc., with strong winds. **2.** violent assault. —*v*. **3.** blow, rain, etc., strongly. **4.** rage. **5.** attack.

sto′ry (stôr′ē) *n.*, *pl.* **-ries. 1.** fictitious tale. **2.** plot. **3.** newspaper report. **4.** *Informal.* lie. **5.** horizontal section of building.

stoup (stoōp) *n*. basin for holy water.

stout (stout) *adj*. **1.** solidly built. **2.** strong. **3.** firm. —*n*. **4.** dark ale.

stout′-heart′ed, *adj*. brave and resolute.

stove (stōv) *n*. apparatus for giving heat.

stow (stō) *v*. **1.** put away, as cargo. **2.** **stow away**, hide on ship, etc., to get free trip. —**stow′age**, *n*. —**stow′a·way′**, *n*.

strad′dle (strad′l) *v.*, **-dled, -dling,** *n*. —*v*. **1.** have one leg on either side of. —*n*. **2.** straddling stance.

strafe (strāf, sträf) *v.*, **strafed, strafing.** shoot from airplanes.

strag′gle (strag′əl) *v.*, **-gled, -gling.** stray from course; ramble. —**strag′-gler,** *n*.

straight (strāt) *adj*. **1.** direct. **2.** even. **3.** honest. **4.** right. **5.** *Informal.* heterosexual. —*adv*. **6.** directly. **7.** in straight line. **8.** honestly. —*n*. **9.** five-card consecutive sequence in poker. —**straight′en,** *v*.

straight′-arm′, *v*. deflect an opponent by pushing away with the arm held straight.

straight arrow, often righteously conventional person.

straight′a·way′, *adv*. at once. Also, **straight′way′.**

straight′edge′, *n*. bar with straight edge for use in drawing lines.

straight face, expression that conceals feelings, as when keeping a secret.

straight′for′ward, *adj*. direct; frank.

straight man, entertainer who acts as foil for comedian.

strain (strān) *v*. **1.** exert to utmost. **2.** injure by stretching. **3.** sieve; filter. —*n*. **4.** great effort. **5.** injury from straining. **6.** severe pressure. **7.** melody. **8.** descendants. **9.** ancestry. **10.** hereditary trait.

strained, *adj*. not natural.

strait (strāt) *n*. **1.** narrow waterway. **2.** (*pl.*) distress.

strait′en, *v*. **1.** put into financial troubles. **2.** restrict.

strait′jack′et, *n*. **1.** garment of strong material designed to bind arms and restrain violent person. **2.** anything that severely confines or hinders.

strait′-laced′, *adj*. excessively strict in conduct or morality.

strand (strand) *v*. **1.** run aground. **2.** leave helpless —*n*. **3.** shore. **4.** twisted component of rope. **5.** tress. **6.** string, as of beads.

strange (strānj) *adj.*, **stranger, strangest. 1.** unusual; odd. **2.** unfamiliar. —**strange′ly,** *adv*.

stran′ger (strān′jər) *n*. person not known or acquainted.

stran′gle (strang′gəl) *v.*, **-gled, -gling. 1.** kill by choking. **2.** choke. —**stran′gu·la′tion** (-gyə lā′shən) *n*.

stran′gle·hold′, *n*. restrictive force.

stran′gu·late′ (-gyə lāt′) *v.*, **-lated, -lating.** constrict.

strap (strap) *n.*, *v.*, **strapped, strapping.** —*n*. **1.** narrow strip or band. —*v*. **2.** fasten with strap.

strapped, *adj*. needing money.

strat′a·gem (strat′ə jəm) *n*. plan; trick.

strat′e·gy (strat′i jē) *n.*, *pl.* **-gies. 1.** planning and direction of military operations. **2.** plan for achieving goal. —**stra·te′gic** (strə tē′jik) *adj*. —**strat′e·gist,** *n*.

strat′i·fy′ (strat′ə fī′) *v.*, **-fied, -fying.** form in layers. —**strat′i·fi·ca′tion,** *n*.

strat′o·sphere′ (-ə sfēr′) *n*. upper region of atmosphere.

stra′tum (strā′təm, strat′əm) *n.*, *pl.* **-ta** (-tə), **-tums.** layer of material.

straw (strô) *n*. **1.** stalk of cereal grass. **2.** mass of dried stalks. **3.** tube for drinking.

straw′ber′ry (-ber′ē, -bə rē) *n.*, *pl.* **-ries.** fleshy fruit of stemless herb.

straw boss, assistant foreman.

straw vote, unofficial vote taken to determine general trend of opinion.

stray (strā) *v*. **1.** ramble; go from one's course or rightful place. —*adj*. **2.** straying. —*n*. **3.** stray creature.

streak (strēk) *n*. **1.** long mark or smear. **2.** vein; stratum. —*v*. **3.** mark with streaks. **4.** flash rapidly.

stream (strēm) *n*. **1.** flowing body of water. **2.** steady flow. —*v*. **3.** move in stream. **4.** wave.

stream′er, *n*. long narrow flag.

stream′line′, *adj.*, *n.*, *v.*, **-lined, -lining.** —*adj*. **1.** having shape past which fluids move easily. —*n*. **2.** streamline shape. —*v*. **3.** shape with streamline shape. **4.** reorganize efficiently.

street (strēt) *n*. public city road.

street′car′, *n*. public conveyance running on rails.

street smarts, shrewd awareness of how to survive in urban environment. —**street′-smart′,** *adj*.

street′walk′er, *n*. prostitute who solicits on the streets.

street′wise′, *adj*. possessing street smarts.

strength (strengkth, strengʰh, strenth) *n*. **1.** power of body, mind, position, etc. **2.** intensity.

strength′en, *v*. make or grow stronger.

stren′u·ous (stren′yoō əs) *adj*. vigorous; active.

strep throat (strep) acute sore throat caused by streptococci.

strep′to·coc′cus (strep′tə kok′əs) *n.*, *pl.* **-ci** (-sī, -sē). one of group of disease-producing bacteria.

stress (stres) *v*. **1.** emphasize. —*n*. **2.** emphasis. **3.** physical, mental, or emotional strain.

stretch (strech) *v*. **1.** extend; spread. **2.** distend. **3.** draw tight. —*n*. **4.** act of stretching. **5.** extension; expansion. **6.** continuous length.

stretch′er, *n*. **1.** canvas-covered frame for carrying sick, etc. **2.** device for stretching.

strew (stroō) *v*., **strewed, strewed** or **strewn, strewing.** scatter.

stri′at·ed (strī′ā tid) *adj*. furrowed; streaked. —**stri·a′tion** (-ā′shən) *n*.

strick′en (strik′ən) *adj*. **1.** wounded. **2.** afflicted, as by disease or sorrow.

strict (strikt) *adj*. **1.** exacting; severe. **2.** precise. **3.** careful. **4.** absolute. —**strict′ly,** *adv*.

stric′ture (strik′chər) *n*. **1.** adverse criticism. **2.** morbid contraction of body passage.

stride (strīd) *v.*, **strode** (strōd), **stridden** (strid′n), **striding,** *n*. —*v*. **1.** walk with long steps. **2.** straddle. —*n*. **3.** long step. **4.** steady pace.

stri′dent (strīd′nt) *adj*. harsh in sound. —**stri′den·cy,** *n*.

strife (strīf) *n*. conflict or quarrel.

strike (strīk) *v.*, **struck** (struk), **struck** or **strick·en** (strik′ən), **striking,** *n*. —*v*. **1.** deal a blow. **2.** hit forcibly. **3.** cause to ignite. **4.** impress. **5.** efface; mark out. **6.** afflict or affect. **7.** sound by percussion. **8.** discover in ground. **9.** encounter. **10.** (of workers) stop work to compel agreement to demands. **11. strike out,** *Baseball.* put or be put out on three strikes. —*n*. **12.** act of striking. **13.** *Baseball.* failure of batter to hit pitched ball. **14.** *Bowling.* knocking-down of all pins at once.

strik′ing, *adj*. **1.** conspicuously attractive or impressive. **2.** noticeable.

string (string) *n.*, *v.*, **strung** (strung), **stringing.** —*n*. **1.** cord, thread, etc. **2.** series or set. **3.** cord on musical instrument. **4.** plant fiber. —*v*. **5.** supply with strings. **6.** arrange in row. **7.** mount on string. —**stringed,** *adj*. —**string′y,** *adj*.

string bean, bean with edible pod.

strin′gent (strin′jənt) *adj*. very strict. —**strin′gen·cy,** *n*.

string′er (string′-) *n*. **1.** horizontal timber connecting upright posts. **2.** part-time news reporter.

strip (strip) *v.*, **stripped, stripping,** *n*. —*v*. **1.** remove covering or clothing. **2.** rob. **3.** cut into strips. —*n*. **4.** long narrow piece.

stripe (strīp) *n.*, *v.*, **striped, striping.** —*n*. **1.** band of different color, etc. **2.** welt from whipping. —*v*. **3.** mark with stripes.

strip′ling (strip′ling) *n*. youth.

strip mine, mine in open pit. —**strip′-mine′,** *v.*, **strip-mined, strip-mining.**

strip′tease′, *n*. act, as in burlesque, in which performer gradually removes clothing. —**strip′per,** *n*.

strive (strīv) *v.*, **strove** (strōv), **striven** (striv′ən), **striving.** try hard; struggle.

strobe (strōb) *n*. electronic flash producing rapid bursts of light.

stroke (strōk) *v.*, **stroked, stroking,** *n*. —*v*. **1.** rub gently. —*n*. **2.** act of stroking. **3.** blow. **4.** blockage or hemorrhage of blood vessel leading to brain. **5.** one complete movement. **6.** piece of luck, work, etc. **7.** method of swimming.

stroll (strōl) *v*. **1.** walk idly. **2.** roam.

stroll′er, *n*. chairlike carriage in which young children are pushed.

strong (strông) *adj*. **1.** vigorous; powerful; able. **2.** intense; distinct.

strong′-arm′, *adj*. involving physical force. —*v*. **2.** use physical force.

strong′box′, *n*. strongly made box for money.

strong′hold′, *n*. fortress.

stron′ti·um (stron′shē əm, -shəm, -tē əm) *n*. metallic chemical element.

strop (strop) *n.*, *v.*, **stropped, stropping.** —*n*. **1.** flexible strap. —*v*. **2.** sharpen on strop.

struc′ture (struk′chər) *n*. **1.** form of building or arrangement. **2.** something built. —**struc′tur·al,** *adj*.

stru′del (stroōd′l; *Ger.* shtrōōd′l) *n*. fruit-filled pastry.

strug′gle (strug′əl) *v.*, **-gled, -gling,** *n*. —*v*. **1.** contend; strive. —*n*. **2.** strong effort. **3.** combat.

strum (strum) *v.*, **strummed, strumming.** play carelessly on (stringed instrument).

strum′pet (strum′pit) *n*. prostitute.

strut (strut) *v.*, **strutted, strutting,** *n*.

—*v.* **1.** walk in vain, pompous manner. —*n.* **2.** strutting walk. **3.** prop; truss.

strych′nine (strik′nin, -nēn, -nīn) *n.* colorless poison.

stub (stub) *n., v.,* **stubbed, stubbing.** —*n.* **1.** short remaining piece. **2.** stump. —*v.* **3.** strike (one's toe) against something. —**stub′by,** *adj.*

stub′ble (stub′əl) *n.* **1.** short stumps, as of grain stalks. **2.** short growth of beard. —**stub′bly,** *adj.*

stub′born (stub′ərn) *adj.* **1.** unreasonably obstinate. **2.** persistent.

stuc′co (stuk′ō) *n., pl.* **-coes, -cos,** —*v.* **-coed, -coing.** —*n.* **1.** plaster for exteriors. —*v.* **2.** cover with stucco.

stuck′-up′ *adj. Informal.* snobbishly conceited.

stud (stud) *n., v.,* **studded, studding.** —*n.* **1.** projecting knob, pin, etc. **2.** upright prop. **3.** detachable button. **4.** collection of horses or other animals for breeding. **5.** stallion. —*v.* **6.** set or scatter with studs.

stu′dent (stōōd′nt, styōōd′-) *n.* person who studies.

stud′ied (stud′ēd) *adj.* deliberate.

stu′di·o′ (stōō′dē ō′, styōō′-) *n., pl.* **-dios. 1.** artist's workroom. **2.** place equipped for radio or television broadcasting.

stud′y (stud′ē) *n., pl.* **studies,** *v.,* **studied, studying.** —*n.* **1.** effort to learn. **2.** object of study. **3.** deep thought. **4.** room for studying, writing, etc. —*v.* **5.** make study of —**stu′di·ous** (stōō′dē əs, styōō′-) *adj.* —**stu′di·ous·ly,** *adv.*

stuff (stuf) *n.* **1.** material. **2.** worthless matter. —*v.* **3.** cram full; pack.

stuffed shirt, pompous, self-satisfied person.

stuff′ing, *n.* material stuffed in something.

stuff′y, *adj.,* **-ier, -iest. 1.** lacking fresh air. **2.** pompous; pedantic.

stul′ti·fy′ (stul′tə fī′) *v.,* **-fied, -fying. 1.** cause to look foolish **2.** make futile.

stum′ble (stum′bəl) *v.,* **-bled, -bling. 1.** lose balance. **2.** come unexpectedly upon.

stumbling block, obstacle.

stump (stump) *n.* **1.** lower end of tree after top is gone. **2.** any short remaining part. —*v.* **3.** baffle. **4.** campaign politically. **5.** walk heavily.

stun (stun) *v.,* **stunned, stunning. 1.** render unconscious. **2.** amaze.

stun′ning, *adj.* strikingly attractive.

stunt (stunt) *v.* **1.** check growth. **2.** do stunts. —*n.* **3.** performance to show skill, etc.

stu′pe·fy′ (stōō′pə fī′, styōō′-) *v.,* **-fied, -fying. 1.** put into stupor. **2.** stun.

stu·pen′dous (stōō pen′dəs, styōō-) *adj.* **1.** amazing. **2.** immense.

stu′pid (stōō′pid, styōō′-) *adj.* having or showing little intelligence. —**stu·pid′i·ty,** *n.*

stu′por (-pər) *n.* dazed or insensible state.

stur′dy (stûr′dē) *adj.,* **-dier, -diest. 1.** strongly built. **2.** firm.

stur′geon (stûr′jən) *n.* large fish of fresh and salt water.

stut′ter (stut′ər) *v., n.* stammer.

sty (stī) *n., pl.* **sties. 1.** pig pen. **2.** inflamed swelling on eyelid.

style (stīl) *n., v.,* **styled, styling.** —*n.* **1.** particular kind. **2.** mode of fashion. **3.** elegance. **4.** distinct way of writing or speaking. —*v.* **5.** name. —**sty·lis′tic,** *adj.*

styl′ish, *adj.* fashionable.

styl′ist, *n.* person who cultivates distinctive style.

styl′ize (stī′līz) *v.,* **-ized, -izing.** cause to conform to conventionalized style.

sty′lus (stī′ləs) *n.* pointed tool for writing, etc.

sty′mie (stī′mē) *v.,* **-mied, -mying.** hinder or obstruct, as in golf.

styp′tic (stip′tik) *adj.* **1.** checking bleeding. —*n.* **2.** styptic substance.

Sty′ro·foam′ (stī′rə fōm′) *n. Trademark.* lightweight plastic.

suave (swäv) *adj.* polite and agreeable. —**suav′i·ty,** *n.*

sub-, prefix meaning under; below; beneath; less than.

sub′a·tom′ic, *adj.* of particles within an atom.

sub·com·mit′tee, *n.* committee appointed out of main committee.

sub·con′scious, *adj.* existing beneath consciousness. —*n.* **2.** ideas, feelings, etc., of which one is unaware. —**sub·con′scious·ly,** *adv.*

sub·con′ti·nent, *n.* (sub kon′tn ənt, sub′kon′-) *n.* large subdivision of continent.

sub′cul′ture, *n.* group with social, economic, or other traits distinguishing it from others within larger society.

sub·cu·ta′ne·ous, *adj.* beneath the skin.

sub·di·vide′ (sub′di vīd′, sub′di-vīd′) *v.,* **-vided, -viding.** divide into parts. —**sub′di·vi′sion,** *n.*

sub·due′ (sab dōō′, -dyōō′) *v.,* **-dued, -duing. 1.** overcome. **2.** soften.

sub·fam′i·ly (sub fam′ə lē, sub′fam′ə lē) *n., pl.* **-lies. 1.** category of related organisms within a family. **2.** group of related languages within a family.

sub′head′, *n.* **1.** heading of a subdivision. **2.** subordinate division of a title.

sub′ject, *n.* (sub′jikt) **1.** matter of thought, concern, etc. **2.** person under rule of government. **3.** noun or pronoun that performs action of predicate. **4.** one undergoing action, etc. —*adj.* (sub′jikt) **5.** being a subject. **6.** liable; exposed. —*v.* (sab jekt′) **7.** cause to experience. **8.** make liable. —**sub·jec′tion,** *n.*

sub·jec′tive, *adj.* **1.** personal. **2.** from a particular point of view. —**sub′jec·tiv′i·ty,** *n.*

sub·join′ (sab join′) *v.* append.

sub′ju·gate′ (sub′jə gāt′) *v.,* **-gated, -gating.** subdue; conquer. —**sub′ju·ga′tion,** *n.*

sub·junc′tive (sab jungk′tiv) *adj.* **1.** designating verb mode of condition, impression, etc. —*n.* **2.** subjunctive mode.

sub·lease′, *n., v.,* **-leased, -leasing.** —*n.* (sub′lēs′) **1.** lease granted by tenant. —*v.* (sub lēs′) **2.** rent by sublease.

sub·let′ (sub let′, sub′let′) *v.,* **-let, -letting.** (of lessee) let to another person.

sub·li·mate′ (sub′lə māt′) *v.,* **-mated, -mating,** *n.* —*v.* (sub′lə māt′) **1.** deflect (biological energies) to other channels. **2.** sublime. —*n.* (-mit, -māt′) **3.** substance obtained in subliming.

sub·lime′ (sa blīm′) *adj., v.,* **-limed, -liming.** —*adj.* **1.** lofty; noble. —*n.* **2.** that which is sublime. —*v.* **3.** heat (substance) to vapor that condenses to solid on cooling. —**sub·lim′i·ty** (sa blim′i tē) *n.*

sub·lim′i·nal (sub lim′ə nl) *adj.* below threshold of consciousness.

sub′ma·chine′ gun, automatic weapon.

sub′ma·rine′, *n.* (sub′mə rēn′, sub′-mə rēn′) **1.** vessel that can navigate

under water. —*adj.* (sub′mə rēn′) **2.** of submarines. **3.** being under sea.

sub·merge′ (sab mûrj′) *v.,* **-merged, -merging.** plunge under water. —**sub·mer′gence,** *n.*

sub·merse′ (-mûrs′) *v.,* **-mersed, -mersing.** submerge. —**sub·mer′sion,** *n.* —**sub·mers′i·ble,** *adj.*

sub·mis′sive, *adj.* yielding or obeying readily. —**sub·mis′sive·ly,** *adv.*

sub·mit′ (sab mit′) *v.,* **-mitted, -mitting. 1.** yield; surrender. **2.** offer for consideration. —**sub·mis′sion** (-mish′-ən) *n.*

sub·nor′mal (sub nôr′məl) *adj.* of less than normal intelligence.

sub·or′di·nate, *adj., n., v.,* **-nated, -nating.** —*adj.* (sə bôr′dn it) **1.** of lower rank or importance. —*n.* (sə-bôr′dn it) **2.** subordinate person or thing. —*v.* (-dn ät′) **3.** treat as subordinate. —**sub·or′di·na′tion,** *n.*

sub·orn′ (sa bôrn′) *v.* bribe or incite to crime, esp. to perjury.

sub′plot′ (sub′plot′) *n.* secondary plot.

sub·poe′na (sa pē′nə, sab-) *n., v.,* **-naed, -naing.** —*v.* **1.** summons to appear in court. —*v.* **2.** serve with subpoena.

sub ro′sa (sub rō′zə) secretly.

sub·scribe′ (sab skrīb′) *v.,* **-scribed, -scribing. 1.** promise contribution. **2.** agree; sign in agreement. **3.** contract to receive periodical regularly. —**sub·scrip′tion** (-skrip′shən) *n.*

sub′script (sub′skript) *n.* letter, number, etc. written low on line.

sub′se·quent (sub′si kwənt) *adj.* later; following.

sub·ser′vi·ent (sab sûr′vē ənt) *adj.* **1.** servile; submissive. **2.** useful. —**sub·ser′vi·ence,** *n.*

sub·side′ (sab sīd′) *v.,* **-sided, -siding. 1.** sink; settle. **2.** abate. —**sub·sid′ence,** *n.*

sub·sid′i·ar′y (-sid′ē er′ē) *adj., n., pl.* **-aries.** —*adj.* **1.** auxiliary. **2.** subordinate. —*n.* **3.** anything subsidiary.

sub′si·dy (-si dē) *n., pl.* **-dies.** direct pecuniary aid, esp. by government. —**sub′si·dize′,** *v.,* **-dized, -dizing.**

sub·sist′ (sab sist′) *v.* **1.** exist. **2.** live (as on food).

sub′soil′ (sub′soil′) *n.* layer of earth immediately underneath surface soil.

sub·son′ic, *adj.* of a speed below the speed of sound.

sub′stance (sub′stəns) *n.* **1.** matter or material. **2.** density. **3.** meaning. **4.** wealth.

sub·stand′ard, *adj.* below standard; not good enough.

sub·stan′tial (sab stan′shəl) *adj.* **1.** actual. **2.** fairly large. **3.** strong. **4.** of substance. **5.** prosperous.

sub·stan′ti·ate′ (-shē āt′) *v.,* **-ated, -ating.** support with evidence.

sub′stan·tive (sub′stan tiv) *n.* **1.** noun, pronoun, or word used as noun. —*adj.* **2.** of or denoting substantive.

sub′sti·tute′ (sub′sti tōōt′, -tyōōt′) *v.,* **-tuted, -tuting,** *n.* —*v.* **1.** put or serve in place of another. —*n.* **2.** substitute person or thing.

sub′struc′ture (sub′struk′chər) *n.* structure forming a foundation.

sub·sume′ (sab sōōm′) *v.,* **-sumed, -suming.** consider or include as part of something larger.

sub′ter·fuge′ (sub′tər fyōōj′) *n.* means used to evade or conceal.

sub′ter·ra′ne·an (-tə rā′nē ən) *adj.* underground.

sub′text, *n.* underlying or implicit meaning.

sub′ti·tle, *n., v.,* **-tled, -tling.** —*n.* **1.**

secondary or subordinate title, as of book. **2.** text of dialogue, etc., appearing at bottom of motion picture screen, etc. —*v.* **3.** give subtitles to.

sub·tle (sut′l) *adj.*, **-tler, -tlest. 1.** delicate; faint. **2.** discerning. **3.** skillful. —**sub′tle·ty,** *n.*

sub′to·tal (sub′tōt′l, sub tōt′-) *n., v.,* **-totaled, -totaling.** —*n.* **1.** total of part of a group of figures. —*v.* **2.** determine subtotal for.

sub·tract′ (səb trakt′) *v.* take from another; deduct. —**sub·trac′tion,** *n.*

sub·trop′i·cal, *adj.* bordering on tropics.

sub′urb (sub′ûrb) *n.* district just outside city. —**sub·ur′ban,** *adj.*

sub·ur′bi·a (-bē ə) *n.* **1.** suburbs or suburbanites collectively. **2.** life in the suburbs.

sub·vert′ (-vûrt′) *v.* overthrow; destroy. —**sub·ver′sion,** *n.* —**sub·ver′sive,** *adj., n.*

sub′way′ (sub′wā′) *n.* underground electric railway.

sub·ze′ro, *adj.* indicating lower than zero on some scale.

suc·ceed′ (sək sēd′) *v.* **1.** end or accomplish successfully. **2.** follow and replace.

suc·cess′ (-ses′) *n.* **1.** favorable achievement. **2.** good fortune. **3.** successful thing or person. —**suc·cess′ful,** *adj.*

suc·ces′sion (-sesh′ən) *n.* **1.** act of following in sequence. **2.** sequence of persons or things. **3.** right or process of succeeding another. —**suc·ces′sive,** *adj.*

suc·ces′sor, *n.* one that succeeds another.

suc·cinct′ (sak singkt′) *adj.* without useless words; concise.

suc′cor (suk′ər) *n., v.* help; aid.

suc′co·tash′ (suk′ə tash′) *n.* corn and beans cooked together.

suc′cu·lent (suk′yə lənt) *adj.* juicy.

suc·cumb′ (sə kum′) *v.* **1.** yield. **2.** die.

such (such) *adj.* **1.** of that kind, extent, etc. —*n.* **2.** such person or thing.

suck (suk) *v.* **1.** draw in by using lips and tongue. **2.** absorb. **3.** act of sucking.

suck′er, *n.* **1.** one that sucks. **2.** freshwater fish. **3.** *Informal.* lollipop. **4.** shoot from underground stem or root. **5.** *Informal.* gullible person.

suck′le, *v.,* **-led, -ling.** nurse at breast.

suck′ling (-ling) *n.* **1.** infant. **2.** unweaned animal.

su′crose (soo′krōs) *n.* sugar obtained esp. from sugar cane or sugar beet.

suc′tion (suk′shan) *n.* tendency to draw substance into vacuum.

sud′den (sud′n) *adj.* abrupt; quick; unexpected. —**sud′den·ly,** *adv.*

sudden death, overtime period in which tied contest is won after one contestant scores.

suds (sudz) *n.pl.* **1.** lather. **2.** soapy water. —**suds′y,** *adj.*

sue (soo) *v.,* **sued, suing. 1.** take legal action. **2.** appeal.

suede (swād) *n.* soft, napped leather.

su′et (soo′it) *n.* hard fat about kidneys, etc., esp. of cattle.

suf′fer (suf′ər) *v.* **1.** undergo (pain or unpleasantness). **2.** tolerate.

suf′fer·ance (-əns) *n.* **1.** tolerance. **2.** endurance.

suf·fice′ (sə fīs′) *v.,* **-ficed, -ficing.** be enough.

suf·fi′cient (-fish′ənt) *adj.* enough. —**suf·fi′cien·cy,** *n.*

suf′fix (suf′iks) *n.* element added to end of word to form another word.

suf′fo·cate′ (suf′ə kāt′) *v.,* **-cated, -cating.** kill or choke by cutting off air to lungs. —**suf′fo·ca′tion,** *n.*

suf′frage (suf′rij) *n.* right to vote.

suf·fuse′ (sə fyooz′) *v.* overspread.

sug′ar (shoog′ər) *n.* **1.** sweet substance, esp. from sugar cane or sugar beet. —*v.* **2.** sweeten with sugar. —**sug′ar·less,** *adj.* —**sug′ar·y,** *adj.*

sugar beet, beet with white root having high sugar content.

sugar cane, tall grass that is the chief source of sugar.

sug′ar·coat′, *v.* make more pleasant or acceptable.

sugar maple, maple with sweet sap.

sugar plum, candy.

sug·gest′ (səg jest′, sə-) *v.* **1.** offer for consideration or action. **2.** imply. —**sug·ges′tion,** *n.*

sug·gest′i·ble, *adj.* easily led or influenced. —**sug·gest′i·bil′i·ty,** *n.*

sug·ges′tive, *adj.* suggesting, esp. something improper.

su′i·cide′ (soo′ə sīd′) *n.* **1.** intentional killing of oneself. **2.** person who commits suicide. —**su′i·cid′al,** *adj.*

su′i ge′ne·ris (soo′ē jen′ər is, soo′ī) being one of a kind.

suit (soot) *n.* **1.** set of clothes. **2.** legal action. **3.** division of playing cards. **4.** petition. **5.** wooing. —*v.* **6.** clothe. **7.** adapt. **8.** please.

suit′a·ble, *adj.* appropriate; fitting.

suit′case′, *n.* oblong valise.

suite (swēt) *n.* **1.** series or set, as of rooms or furniture. **2.** retinue.

suit′ing (soo′ting) *n.* fabric for making suits.

suit′or (soo′tər) *n.* wooer.

su·ki·ya·ki (soo′kē yä′kē, sook′ē-, skē-) *n.* Japanese dish of meat and vegetables cooked in soy sauce.

sul′fate (-fāt) *n.* salt of sulfuric acid.

sul′fide (-fīd, -fid) *n.* sulfur compound.

sul′fur (-fər) *n.* yellow nonmetallic element.

sul·fur′ic (-fyoor′ik) *adj.* of or containing sulfur. Also, **sul′fur·ous.**

sulfuric acid, corrosive liquid used in chemicals and explosives.

sulk (sulk) *v.* **1.** be sullen and aloof. —*n.* **2.** fit of sulking.

sulk′y, *adj.,* **-ier, -iest,** *n.* —*adj.* **1.** sullen; ill-humored. —*n.* **2.** two-wheeled racing carriage for one person. —**sulk′i·ly,** *adv.*

sul′len (sul′ən) *adj.* **1.** silently ill-humored. **2.** gloomy.

sul′ly (sul′ē) *v.,* **-lied, -lying.** soil; defile.

sul′phur (-fər) *n.* sulfur.

sul′tan (sul′tn) *n.* ruler of Muslim country. —**sul′tan·ate,** *n.*

sul·tan′a (-tan′ə) *n.* raisin.

sul′try (-trē) *adj.,* **-trier, -triest.** hot and close. —**sul′tri·ness,** *n.*

sum (sum) *n., v.,* **summed, summing.** —*n.* **1.** aggregate of two or more numbers, etc. **2.** total amount. **3.** gist. —*v.* **4.** total. **5.** summarize.

su′mac (soo′mak, shoo′-) *n.* small tree with long pinnate leaves.

sum′ma·rize′ (sum′ə rīz′) *v.,* **-rized, -rizing.** make or be summary of.

sum′ma·ry (-rē) *n., pl.* **-ries,** *adj.* —*n.* **1.** concise presentation of main points. —*adj.* **2.** concise. **3.** prompt.

sum·ma′tion (sə mā′shən) *n.* **1.** act of summing up. **2.** total.

sum′mer (sum′ər) *n.* **1.** season between spring and fall. —*adj.* **2.** of, like, or for summer. —*v.* **3.** spend summer. —**sum′mer·y,** *adj.*

sum′mer·house, *n.* structure in garden to provide shade.

sum′mit (sum′it) *n.* highest point.

sum′mon (sum′ən) *v.* order to appear.

sum′mons, *n.* message that summons.

su′mo (soo′mō) *n.* Japanese form of wrestling featuring extremely heavy contestants.

sump (sump) *n.* pit for collecting water, etc.

sump′tu·ous (sump′choo əs) *adj.* revealing great expense; luxurious.

sun (sun) *n., v.,* **sunned, sunning.** —*n.* **1.** heat- and light-giving body of solar system. **2.** sunshine. —*v.* **3.** expose to sunshine.

Sun., Sunday.

sun′bathe′, *v.,* **-bathed, -bathing.** expose body to sunlight.

Sun′belt′, *n. Informal.* southern and southwestern U.S.

sun′block′, *n.* substance that prevents most tanning.

sun′burn′, *n., v.,* **-burned** or **-burnt, -burning.** —*n.* **1.** superficial burn from sun's rays. —*v.* **2.** affect with sunburn.

sun′dae (sun′dā, -dē) *n.* ice cream topped with fruit, etc.

Sun′day (sun′dā, -dē) *n.* first day of week.

sun′der (sun′dər) *v.* separate.

sun′di′al, *n.* outdoor instrument for telling time by shadow.

sun′dry (sun′drē) *adj., n., pl.* **-dries.** —*adj.* **1.** various. —*n.* **2.** (*pl.*) small items of merchandise.

sun′fish′, *n.* fresh-water fish.

sun′flow′er, *n.* tall plant with yellow flowers.

sun′glass′es, *n.pl.* eyeglasses with tinted lenses to permit vision in bright sun.

sun′light′, *n.* light from sun.

sun′lit′, *adj.* lighted by the sun.

sun′ny, *adj.,* **-nier, -niest. 1.** with much sunlight. **2.** cheerful; jolly.

sun′rise′, *n.* ascent of sun above horizon. Also, **sun′up′.**

sun′roof′, *n.* section of automobile roof that can be opened.

sun′screen′, *n.* substance that protects skin from ultraviolet light.

sun′set′, *n.* descent of sun below horizon. Also, **sun′down′.**

sun′shine′, *n.* light of sun.

sun′spot′, *n.* dark spot on sun.

sun′stroke′, *n.* illness from overexposure to sun's rays.

sun′tan′, *n.* darkening of skin caused by exposure to sun.

sup (sup) *v.,* **supped, supping.** eat supper.

su′per (soo′pər) *n.* **1.** superintendent. —*adj.* **2.** very good; first-rate.

super-, prefix meaning above or over; exceeding; larger or more.

su′per·a·bun′dant, *adj.* exceedingly abundant.

su′per·an′nu·at′ed (-an′yoo ā′tid) *adj.* **1.** retired. **2.** antiquated.

su·perb′ (soo pûrb′, sə-) *adj.* very fine. —**su·perb′ly,** *adv.*

su′per·charge′, *v.,* **-charged, -charging. 1.** charge with abundant or excess energy, etc. **2.** supply air to (engine) at high pressure. —**su′per·charg′er,** *n.*

su′per·cil′i·ous (soo′pər sil′ē əs) *adj.* haughtily disdainful.

su′per·con·duc·tiv′i·ty, *n.* disappearance of electrical resistance in certain metals at extremely low temperatures. —**su′per·con′duct′or,** *n.*

su′per·e′go, *n.* part of personality representing conscience.

su·per·fi·cial (-fish'əl) *adj.* **1.** of, on, or near surface. **2.** shallow, obvious, or insignificant. —**su'per·fi'ci·al'i·ty** (-fish'ē al'i tē) *n.*

su·per·flu·ous (soo pûr'floo əs) *adj.* **1.** being more than is necessary. **2.** unnecessary. —**su'per·flu'i·ty** (-floo'i-tē) *n.*

su'per·high'way (soo'pər hī'wā, soo'pər hī'wā') *n.* highway for travel at high speeds.

su'per·hu'man, *adj.* **1.** beyond what is human. **2.** exceeding human strength.

su'per·im·pose', *v.,* -posed, -pos·ing. place over something else.

su'per·in·tend' (soo'pər in tend', soo'prin-) *v.* oversee and direct. —**su'per·in·tend'ent,** *n., adj.*

su·pe'ri·or (sə pēr'ē ər, soo-) *adj.* **1.** above average; better. **2.** upper. **3.** arrogant. —*n.* **4.** superior person. **5.** head of convent, etc. —**su·pe'ri·or'i·ty,** *n.*

su·per·la·tive (sə pûr'lə tiv, soo-) *adj.* **1.** of highest kind; best. **2.** highest in comparison. —*n.* **3.** anything superlative.

su'per·man' (soo'pər-) *n., pl.* -men. person of extraordinary or superhuman powers.

su'per·mar'ket, *n.* self-service food store with large variety.

su'per·nat'u·ral, *adj.* **1.** outside the laws of nature; ghostly. —*n.* **2.** realm of supernatural beings or things.

su'per·no'va, *n., pl.* -vas, -vae (-vē). nova millions of times brighter than the sun.

su'per·nu'mer·ar'y (-noo'mə rer'ē, -nyoo'-) *adj., n., pl.* -aries. —*adj.* **1.** extra. —*n.* **2.** extra person or thing.

su'per·pow'er, *n.* large, powerful nation greatly influencing world affairs.

su'per·script', *n.* letter, number, or symbol written high on line of text.

su'per·sede' (-sēd') *v.,* -seded, -sed·ing. replace in power, use, etc.

su'per·son'ic, *adj.* faster than speed of sound.

su'per·star', *n.* entertainer or sports figure of world renown.

su'per·sti'tion (-stish'ən) *n.* irrational belief in ominous significance of particular thing, event, etc. —**su'per·sti'tious,** *adj.*

su'per·store', *n.* very large store that stocks wide variety of merchandise.

su'per·struc'ture, *n.* upper part of building or vessel.

su'per·vene' (-vēn') *v.,* -vened, -vening. come as something extra. —**su'per·ven'tion** (-ven'shən) *n.*

su'per·vise' (-vīz') *v.,* -vised, -vis·ing. direct and inspect. —**su'per·vi'·sion** (-vizh'ən) *n.* —**su'per·vi'sor,** *n.* —**su'per·vi'so·ry,** *adj.*

su'per·wom'an, *n., pl.* -women. **1.** woman of extraordinary or superhuman powers. **2.** woman who copes successfully with demands of career, marriage, and motherhood.

su·pine' (soo pīn') *adj.* **1.** lying on back. **2.** passive. —**su·pine'ly,** *adv.*

sup'per (sup'ər) *n.* evening meal.

sup·plant' (sə plant') *v.* supersede.

sup'ple (sup'əl) *adj., -pler, -plest.* flexible; limber. —**sup'ple·ly,** *adv.*

sup'ple·ment *n.* (sup'lə mənt) **1.** something added to complete or improve. —*v.* (-ment') **2.** add to or complete. —**sup'ple·men'tal** (-men'tl), **sup'ple·men'ta·ry,** *adj.*

sup'pli·cate (sup'li kāt') *v.,* -cated, -cating. beg humbly. —**sup'pli·ant** (sup'lē ənt), **sup'pli·cant,** *n., adj.*

sup·ply' (sə plī') *v.,* -plied, -plying, *n., pl.* -plies. —*v.* **1.** furnish; provide. **2.** fill (a lack). —*n.* **3.** act of supplying. **4.** that supplied. **5.** stock. —**sup·pli'er,** *n.*

supply'-side', *adj.* of economic theory that reduced taxes will stimulate economic growth.

sup·port' (sə pôrt') *v.* **1.** hold up; bear. **2.** provide living for. **3.** uphold; advocate. **4.** corroborate. —*n.* **5.** act of supporting. **6.** maintenance; livelihood. **7.** thing or person that supports. —**sup·port'a·ble,** *adj.* —**sup·port'·ive,** *adj.*

support group, group of people who meet regularly to support each other by discussing problems.

sup·pose' (sə pōz') *v.,* -posed, -pos·ing. **1.** assume; consider. **2.** take for granted. —**sup·pos'ed·ly** (-pō'zid lē) *adv.* —**sup'po·si'tion** (sup'ə zish'ən) *n.*

sup·pos'i·to·ry (sə poz'i tôr'ē) *n., pl.* -ries. solid mass of medication that melts on insertion into rectum or vagina.

sup·press' (sə pres') *v.* **1.** end forcibly; subdue. **2.** repress. **3.** withhold from circulation. —**sup·pres'sion** (-presh'ən) *n.*

sup'pu·rate (sup'yə rāt') *v.,* -rated, -rating. form or discharge pus. —**sup'pu·ra'tion,** *n.*

su'pra (soo'prə) *adv.* above, esp. in text.

su·prem'a·cist (sə prem'ə sist, soo-) *n.* person who advocates supremacy of particular group.

su·preme' (sə prēm', soo-) *adj.* chief; greatest. —**su·prem'a·cy** (-prem'ə sē) *n.* —**su·preme'ly,** *adv.*

sur'charge', *n., v.,* -charged, -charg·ing. —*n.* (sûr'chärj') **1.** extra or excessive charge, load, etc. —*v.* (sûr-chärj', sûr'chärj') **2.** put surcharge on. **3.** overburden.

sure (shoor, shûr) *adj., surer, surest.* **1.** certain; positive. **2.** reliable. **3.** firm. —**sure'ly,** *adv.*

sure'fire', *adj. Informal.* certain to succeed.

sure'foot'ed, *adj.* not likely to stumble.

sure'ty (shoor'i tē, shoor'tē, shûr'-) *n., pl.* -ties. **1.** security against loss, etc. **2.** person who accepts responsibility for another.

surf (sûrf) *n.* **1.** waves breaking on shore. —*v.* **2.** ride on crest of wave while standing or lying on surfboard. —**surf'er,** *n.*

sur'face (sûr'fis) *n., adj., v.,* -faced, -facing. —*n.* **1.** outer face; outside. —*adj.* **2.** superficial. —*v.* **3.** finish surface of. **4.** come to surface.

surf'board', *n.* board on which person rides in surfing.

sur'feit (sûr'fit) *n.* **1.** excess, esp. of food or drink. **2.** disgust at excess. —*v.* **3.** overeat; satiate.

surge (sûrj) *n., v.,* surged, surging. —*n.* **1.** swelling or rolling movement or body. —*v.* **2.** rise and fall.

surge protector, device to protect computer, etc., from damage by high-voltage electrical surges.

sur'ger·y (-jə rē) *n., pl.* -geries. treatment of disease, etc., by cutting and other manipulations. —**sur'gi·cal** (-ji-kəl) *adj.*

sur'ly (sûr'lē) *adj., -lier, -liest.* rude; churlish. —**sur'li·ness,** *n.*

sur·mise' *v.,* (sər mīz') -mised, -mis·ing, *n.* (sər mīz', sûr'mīz) guess.

sur·mount' (sər mount') *v.* **1.** get over or on top of. **2.** overcome.

sur'name' (sûr'nām') *n.* family name.

sur·pass' (sər pas') *v.* **1.** exceed. **2.** transcend. —**sur·pass'ing,** *adj.*

sur'plice (sûr'plis) *n.* white, loose-fitting robe worn over cassock.

sur'plus (sûr'plus, -pləs) *n.* **1.** amount beyond that needed; excess. —*adj.* **2.** being a surplus.

sur·prise' (sər prīz', sə-) *v.,* -prised, -prising, *n.* —*v.* **1.** come upon unexpectedly; astonish. —*n.* **2.** act of surprising. **3.** something that surprises. **4.** feeling of being surprised.

sur·re'al·ism (sə rē'ə liz'əm) *n.* art attempting to express the subconscious. —**sur·re'al·ist,** *n., adj.*

sur·ren'der (sə ren'dər) *v.* **1.** yield. —*n.* **2.** act of yielding.

sur'rep·ti'tious (sûr'əp tish'əs) *adj.* stealthy; secret.

sur'ro·gate (sûr'ə gāt', -git, sur'-) *n.* **1.** substitute. **2.** judge concerned with wills, estates, etc.

surrogate mother, woman who bears child for another couple.

sur·round' (sə round') *v.* encircle; enclose.

sur·round'ings, *n.pl.* environment.

sur'tax' (sûr'taks') *n.* additional tax, esp. on high incomes.

sur·veil'lance (sər vā'ləns) *n.* close watch.

sur·vey', *v.* (sər vā') **1.** view. **2.** measure or determine dimensions or nature of. —*n.* (sûr'vā) **3.** methodical investigation.

sur·vey'ing, *n.* science of making land surveys. —**sur·vey'or,** *n.*

sur·vive' (sər vīv') *v.,* -vived, -viv·ing. **1.** remain alive. **2.** outlive. —**sur·viv'al,** *n.* —**sur·vi'vor,** *n.*

sus·cep'ti·ble (sə sep'tə bəl) *adj.* apt to be affected. —**sus·cep'ti·bil'i·ty,** *n.*

su'shi (soo'shē) *n.* Japanese dish of rice cakes with raw fish, vegetables, etc.

sus·pect', *v.* (sə spekt') **1.** imagine to be guilty, false, etc. **2.** surmise. —*n.* (sus'pekt) **3.** one suspected. —*adj.* (sus'pekt) **4.** liable to doubt.

sus·pend' (sə spend') *v.* **1.** hang. **2.** keep temporarily inactive. **3.** refuse work to temporarily.

sus·pend'ers, *n.pl.* straps for holding up trousers.

sus·pense' (sə spens') *n.* uncertainty; anxiety.

sus·pen'sion, *n.* **1.** act of suspending. **2.** temporary inactivity. **3.** state in which undissolved particles are dispersed in fluid.

suspension bridge, bridge with deck suspended from cables.

sus·pi'cion (sə spish'ən) *n.* **1.** act or instance of suspecting. **2.** trace.

sus·pi'cious, *adj.* **1.** having suspicions. **2.** causing suspicion.

sus·tain' (sə stān') *v.* support; maintain. —**sus·tain'er,** *n.*

sus'te·nance (sus'tə nəns) *n.* **1.** food. **2.** maintenance.

su'ture (soo'chər) *n., v.,* -tured, -tur·ing. —*n.* **1.** stitch used to close wound. —*v.* **2.** join by suture.

SUV, *pl.* SUVs. sport-utility vehicle.

su'ze·rain·ty (soo'zə rin tē) *n., pl.* -ties. sovereignty of one state over another.

svelte (svelt, sfelt) *adj.* gracefully slender.

SW, southwest.

swab (swob) *n., v.,* swabbed, swab·bing. —*n.* **1.** bit of cloth, etc., esp. on stick. —*v.* **2.** clean with swab.

swaddle

swad'dle (swod'l) *v.*, **-dled, -dling.** bind with strips of cloth.

swag (swag) *n.* something fastened at each end and hanging down in the middle.

swag'ger, *v.* **1.** walk with insolent air. **—***n.* **2.** swaggering gait.

Swa·hi'li (swä hē'lē) *n.* Bantu language of Africa.

swain (swān) *n.* male admirer.

swal'low (swol'ō) *v.* **1.** take into stomach through throat. **2.** assimilate. **3.** suppress. **—***n.* **4.** act of swallowing. **5.** small graceful migratory bird.

swal'low·tail', *n.* kind of butterfly.

swa'mi (swä'mē) *n.* Hindu religious teacher.

swamp (swomp) *n.* **1.** marshy ground. **—***v.* **2.** drench with water. **3.** overwhelm. **—swamp'y,** *adj.*

swan (swon) *n.* large long-necked swimming bird.

swank (swangk) *adj.*, **swanker, swankest. 1.** stylish or elegant. **2.** pretentiously stylish. Also, **swank'y.**

swan song, final act or farewell appearance.

swap (swop) *v.*, **swapped, swapping,** *n.* trade.

swarm (swôrm) *n.* **1.** group of bees. **—***v.* **2.** fly off to start new colony. **3.** cluster; throng.

swarth'y (swôr'thē, -thē) *adj.*, **-ier, -iest.** (esp. of skin) dark.

swash'buck'ler (swosh'buk'lər) *n.* swaggering fellow. **—swash'buck'ling,** *adj.*, *n.*

swas'ti·ka (swos'ti kə) *n.* emblem of Nazi Party.

swat (swot) *v.*, **swatted, swatting,** *n.* *Informal.* **—***v.* **1.** strike. **—***n.* **2.** sharp blow. **—swat'ter,** *n.*

swatch (swoch) *n.* sample of material or finish.

swath (swoth) *n.* long cut made by scythe or mowing machine.

swathe (swoth, swäth) *v.*, **swathed, swathing,** *n.* **—***v.* **1.** wrap closely. **—***n.* **2.** bandage.

sway (swā) *v.* **1.** swing to and fro. **2.** influence or incline. **—***n.* **3.** act of swaying. **4.** rule.

sway'back', *n.* excessive downward curvature of the back, esp. of horses. **—sway'backed',** *adj.*

swear (swâr) *v.*, **swore** (swôr), **sworn, swearing. 1.** affirm on oath; vow. **2.** use profane language. **3.** bind by oath.

sweat (swet) *v.*, **sweat** or **sweated, sweating,** *n.* **—***v.* **1.** excrete moisture through pores. **2.** gather moisture. **—***n.* **3.** secretion of sweat glands. **—sweat'y,** *adj.*

sweat'er, *n.* knitted jacket.

sweat gland, tubular gland in skin that secretes sweat.

sweat'pants', *n.* pants of absorbent fabric.

sweat'shirt', *n.* loose pullover of absorbent fabric.

sweat'shop', *n.* manufacturing establishment employing workers at low wages, for long hours.

Swed'ish (swē'dish) *n.* language or people of Sweden. **—Swedish,** *adj.*

sweep (swēp) *v.*, **swept** (swept), **sweeping,** *n.* **—***v.* **1.** move or clear with broom, etc. **2.** pass or pass over with forceful, rapid movement. **—***n.* **3.** act of sweeping. **4.** extent.

sweep'ing, *adj.* of wide range or scope.

sweep'stakes', *n.* **1.** race for stakes put up by competitors. **2.** lottery.

sweet (swēt) *adj.* **1.** having taste of sugar. **2.** fragrant. **3.** fresh. **4.** pleasant

in sound. **5.** amiable. **—***n.* **6.** anything sweet. **—sweet'en,** *v.*

sweet'bread', *n.* thymus or pancreas, esp. of calf or lamb, used for food.

sweet'bri'er, *n.* fragrant wild rose.

sweet'en·er, *n.* substance, esp. a substitute for sugar, to sweeten food or drink.

sweet'heart', *n.* beloved.

sweet'meat', *n.* confection.

sweet pea, annual vine with fragrant blooms.

sweet pepper, mild-flavored bell-shaped pepper.

sweet potato, plant with sweet edible root.

sweet'-talk', *v.* cajole; flatter.

sweet tooth, liking or craving for sweets.

sweet' wil'liam (wil'yəm) low plant with dense flower clusters.

swell (swel) *v.*, **swelled, swelled** or **swollen, swelling,** *n.*, *adj.* **—***v.* **1.** grow in size, degree, force, etc. **—***n.* **2.** act of swelling. **3.** wave. **—***adj.* **4.** *Informal.* excellent.

swel'ter (swel'tər) *v.* perspire or suffer from heat.

swel'ter·ing, *adj.* **1.** suffering from heat. **2.** oppressively hot.

swerve (swûrv) *v.*, **swerved, swerving,** *n.* **—***v.* **1.** turn aside. **—***n.* **2.** act of swerving.

swift (swift) *adj.* **1.** moving with speed. **2.** prompt or quick. **—***n.* **3.** small bird. **—swift'ly,** *adv.*

swig (swig) *n.*, *v.*, **swigged, swigging.** *Informal.* **—***n.* **1.** deep drink. **—***v.* **2.** drink heartily.

swill (swil) *n.* **1.** moist garbage fed to hogs. **—***v.* **2.** guzzle.

swim (swim) *v.*, **swam** (swam), **swum** (swum), **swimming,** *n.* **—***v.* **1.** move in water by action of limbs, etc. **2.** be immersed. **3.** be dizzy. **—***n.* **4.** act or period of swimming.

swimming hole, place with water deep enough for swimming.

swim'suit', *n.* bathing suit.

swin'dle (swin'dl) *v.*, **-dled, -dling,** *n.* **—***v.* **1.** cheat; defraud. **—***n.* **2.** act of swindling; fraud.

swine (swīn) *n.*, *pl.* **swine.** hog.

swing (swing) *v.*, **swung** (swung), **swinging,** *n.* **—***v.* **1.** move to and fro around point. **2.** brandish. **—***n.* **3.** act, way, or extent of swinging. **4.** progress. **5.** scope. **6.** suspended seat for swinging.

swing'er, *n.* *Slang.* **1.** person with modern attitudes. **2.** sexually uninhibited person.

swing shift, work shift from midafternoon until midnight.

swipe (swīp) *n.*, *v.*, **swiped, swiping.** **—***n.* **1.** sweeping blow. **—***v.* **2.** deal such blow. **3.** *Informal.* steal.

swirl (swûrl) *v.*, *n.* whirl; eddy.

swish (swish) *v.* **1.** rustle. **—***n.* **2.** swishing sound.

Swiss cheese (swis) firm, pale yellow cheese with holes.

switch (swich) *n.* **1.** flexible rod. **2.** device for turning electric current on or off. **3.** change. **—***v.* **4.** whip with switch. **5.** shift; divert. **6.** turn (electric current) on or off.

switch'back', *n.* zigzag highway or railroad track arrangement for climbing steep grade.

switch'blade', *n.* pocketknife with blade released by spring.

switch'board', *n.* panel for controlling electric circuits.

swiv'el (swiv'əl) *n.*, *v.*, **-eled, -eling.**

—*n.* **1.** device permitting rotation of thing mounted on it. **—***v.* **2.** rotate.

swiz'zle stick (swiz'əl) small wand for stirring mixed drinks.

swol'len (swō'lən) pp. of **swell.**

swoon (swōōn) *v.*, *n.* faint.

swoop (swōōp) *v.* **1.** sweep down upon. **—***n.* **2.** sweeping descent.

sword (sôrd) *n.* weapon with blade fixed in hilt or handle.

sword'fish', *n.* marine fish with swordlike upper jaw.

syb'a·rite' (sib'ə rīt') *n.* person devoted to pleasure.

syc'a·more' (sik'ə môr') *n.* plane tree.

syc'o·phant (sik'ə fənt, -fant', sī'kə-) *n.* flatterer; parasite.

syl'lab'i·cate' (si lab'i kāt') *v.*, **-cated, -cating.** divide into syllables. Also, **syl·lab'i·fy'** (-fī').

syl'la·ble (sil'ə bəl) *n.* single unit of speech.

syl'la·bus (sil'ə bəs) *n.*, *pl.* **-buses, -bi** (-bī'). outline of course of study.

syl'lo·gism (sil'ə jiz'əm) *n.* three-part chain of logical reasoning.

sylph (silf) *n.* **1.** graceful woman. **2.** imaginary being supposed to inhabit the air.

syl'van (sil'vən) *adj.* **1.** of forests. **2.** wooded.

sym'bi·o'sis (sim'bē ō'sis, -bī-) *n.*, *pl.* **-ses** (-sēz). living together of two dissimilar organisms. **—sym'bi·ot'ic** (-ot'ik) *adj.*

sym'bol (sim'bəl) *n.* **1.** emblem; token; sign. **2.** thing that represents something else. **—sym·bol'ic** (-bol'ik), **sym·bol'i·cal,** *adj.* **—sym'bol·ize',** *v.*, **-ized, -izing.**

sym'bol·ism, *n.* **1.** representing things by symbols. **2.** symbolic meaning.

sym'me·try (sim'i trē) *n.*, *pl.* **-tries.** pleasing balance or proportion. **—sym·met'ri·cal** (si me'tri kəl) *adj.*

sym'pa·thize' (-thīz') *v.*, **-thized, -thizing. 1.** be in sympathy. **2.** feel or express sympathy.

sym'pa·thy (-thē) *n.*, *pl.* **-thies. 1.** agreement in feeling; accord. **2.** compassion. **—sym'pa·thet'ic** (-thet'ik) *adj.*

sym'pho·ny (sim'fə nē) *n.*, *pl.* **-nies. 1.** composition for orchestra. **2.** harmonious combination. **—sym·phon'ic** (-fon'ik) *adj.*

sym·po'si·um (sim pō'zē əm) *n.*, *pl.* **-siums, -sia** (-zē ə). meeting to present essays on one subject.

symp'tom (simp'təm) *n.* sign or indication, esp. of disease. **—symp'to·r:at'ic** (-mat'ik) *adj.*

syn'a·gogue' (sin'ə gog') *n.* **1.** assembly of Jews for worship. **2.** place of such assembly.

sync (singk) *n.*, *v.*, **synced, syncing.** **—***n.* **1.** synchronization. **2.** harmonious relationship. **—***v.* **3.** synchronize.

syn'chro·nize' (sing'krə nīz') *v.*, **-nized, -nizing. 1.** occur at same time. **2.** show or set to show same time. **—syn'chro·ni·za'tion,** *n.* **—syn'chro·nous,** *adj.*

syn'co·pate' (sing'kə pāt', sin'-) *v.*, **-pated, -pating. 1.** *Music.* play by accenting notes normally unaccented. **2.** *Gram.* omit middle sound in (word). **—syn'co·pa'tion,** *n.*

syn'di·cate, *n.*, *v.*, **-cated, -cating.** **—***n.* (sin'də kit) **1.** combination of persons or companies for large joint enterprise. **2.** agency dealing in news stories, etc. **—***v.* (sin'di kāt') **3.** publish as syndicate.

syn′drome (sin′drōm, -drəm) *n.* characteristic group of symptoms.

syn′er·gism (sin′ər jiz′əm) *n.* joint action of agents so that their combined effect is greater than sum of individual effects.

syn′fu′el (sin′fyōō′əl) *n.* synthetic fuel.

syn′od (sin′əd) *n.* meeting of church delegates.

syn′o·nym (sin′ə nim) *n.* word meaning same as another. —**syn·on′y·mous** (si non′ə məs) *adj.*

syn·op′sis (si nop′sis) *n., pl.* **-ses** (-sēz). brief summary.

syn′tax (sin′taks) *n.* arrangement of words into sentences, etc.

syn′the·sis (sin′thə sis) *n., pl.* **-ses** (-sēz). 1. combination of parts into whole. 2. such whole.

syn′the·size′ (-sīz′) *v.,* **-sized, -sizing.** make by combining parts.

syn′the·siz′er, *n.* electronic, usu. computerized device for creating or modifying musical sounds.

syn·thet′ic (sin thet′ik) *adj.* 1. produced artificially rather than by nature. 2. of synthesis.

syph′i·lis (sif′ə lis) *n.* infectious venereal disease.

syr·inge′ (sə rinj′, sir′inj) *n.* device for drawing in and ejecting fluids.

syr′up (sir′əp, sûr′-) *n.* sweet thick liquid. —**syr′up·y,** *adj.*

sys′tem (sis′təm) *n.* 1. orderly assemblage of facts, parts, etc. 2. plan. 3. organization of body. —**sys′tem·at′ic** (-tə mat′ik) *adj.*

sys′tem·a·tize′ (-tə mə tīz′) *v.,* **-tized, -tizing.** arrange by system.

sys·tem′ic (si stem′ik) *adj.* affecting entire body.

systems analysis, study of data-processing needs of project.

sys′to·le′ (sis′tə lē′) *n.* regular contraction of the heart. —**sys·tol′ic** (si-stol′ik) *adj.*

T

T, t (tē) *n.* twentieth letter of English alphabet.

tab (tab) *n., v.,* **tabbed, tabbing.** —*n.* 1. small flap. 2. tag. —*v.* 3. furnish with tab.

Ta·bas′co (tə bas′kō) *n. Trademark.* pungent condiment sauce.

tab′by (tab′ē) *n., pl.* **-bies,** *adj.* —*n.* 1. striped or brindled cat. 2. silk fabric. —*adj.* 3. striped.

tab′er·nac′le (tab′ər nak′əl) *n.* 1. temporary temple, esp. Jewish. 2. church for large congregation.

ta′ble (tā′bəl) *n., v.,* **-bled, -bling.** —*n.* 1. piece of furniture consisting of level part on legs. 2. food. 3. company at table. 4. compact arrangement of information in parallel columns. —*v.* 5. postpone deliberation on. —**ta′ble·cloth′,** *n.*

tab·leau′ (ta blō′, tab′lō) *n., pl.* **-leaux** (ta blōz′). picture.

ta′ble d′hôte′ (tä′bəl dōt′, tab′əl) meal fixed in courses and price.

ta′ble·land′, *n.* elevated, level region of considerable extent.

ta′ble·spoon′, *n.* 1. large spoon in table service. 2. tablespoonful.

ta′ble·spoon·ful′, *n., pl.* **-fuls.** quantity tablespoon holds, about ½ fluid ounce or 3 teaspoonfuls.

tab′let (tab′lit) *n.* 1. pad of writing paper. 2. small slab. 3. pill.

table tennis, game resembling tennis,

played on table with paddles and small hollow ball.

ta′ble·ware′, *n.* dishes, etc., used at table.

tab′loid (tab′loid) *n.* newspaper about half ordinary size.

ta·boo′ (tə bōō′, ta-) *adj., n., pl.* **-boos,** *v.* —*adj.* 1. forbidden. —*n.* 2. prohibition. —*v.* 3. prohibit.

tab′u·late′ (tab′yə lāt′) *v.,* **-lated, -lating.** arrange in table. —**tab′u·lar,** *adj.* —**tab′u·la′tion,** *n.*

ta·chom′e·ter (ta kom′i tər, tə-) *n.* instrument for measuring velocity.

tach′y·car′di·a (tak′i kär′dē ə) *n.* excessively rapid heartbeat.

tac′it (tas′it) *adj.* 1. silent. 2. implied. 3. unspoken. —**tac′it·ly,** *adv.*

tac′i·turn′ (tas′i tûrn′) *adj.* inclined to silence. —**tac′i·tur′ni·ty,** *n.*

tack (tak) *n.* 1. short nail with flat head. 2. straight windward run of sailing ship. —*v.* 3. fasten by tack. 4. navigate by tacks.

tack′le, *n., v.,* **-led, -ling.** —*n.* 1. fishing equipment. 2. hoisting apparatus. —*v.* 3. undertake to deal with. —**tack′ler,** *n.*

tack′y, *adj.,* **-ier, -iest.** 1. *Informal.* shabby; dowdy. 2. slightly sticky. 3. in poor taste. —**tack′i·ness,** *n.*

ta′co (tä′kō) *n.* fried tortilla folded and filled with chopped meat, cheese, lettuce, etc.

tact (takt) *n.* skill in handling delicate situations. —**tact′ful,** *adj.* —**tact′less,** *adj.*

tac·ti′cian (tak tish′ən) *n.* person versed in tactics.

tac′tics (tak′tiks) *n.* 1. maneuvering of armed forces. 2. methods for attaining success. —**tac′ti·cal,** *adj.*

tac′tile (tak′til, -tīl) *adj.* of sense of touch. —**tac·til′i·ty** (-til′i tē) *n.*

tad (tad) *n. Informal.* 1. small child. 2. small amount or degree.

tad′pole (tad′pōl) *n.* larval form of frogs, toads, etc.

taf′fe·ta (taf′i tə) *n.* lustrous silk or rayon fabric.

taf′fy (taf′ē) *n., pl.* **-fies.** molasses candy.

tag (tag) *n., v.,* **tagged, tagging.** —*n.* 1. small paper, etc., attached as mark or label. 2. game in which players chase and touch each other. —*v.* 3. furnish with tag. 4. touch in playing tag.

t′ai chi ch′uan (tī′ jē′ chwän′, chē′) *n.* Chinese system of meditative exercises. Also, **tai′ chi′.**

tail (tāl) *n.* 1. appendage at rear of animal's body. 2. something resembling this. 3. bottom or end part. —*v.* 4. follow.

tail′gate′, *n., v.,* **-gated, -gating.** —*n.* 1. hinged board at back of vehicle. —*v.* 2. drive too closely behind.

tail′light′, *n.* light at the rear of automobile, train, etc.

tai′lor (tā′lər) *n.* maker or mender of outer garments.

tail′pipe′, *n.* exhaust pipe at rear of motor vehicle.

tail′spin′, *n.* descent of airplane in steep spiral course.

tail′wind′ (-wind′) *n.* wind from directly behind.

taint (tānt) *n.* 1. unfavorable trace. —*v.* 2. contaminate.

take (tāk) *v.,* **took** (tŏŏk), **taken, taking.** 1. seize, catch, or embrace. 2. receive; obtain. 3. select. 4. remove. 5. deduct. 6. conduct. 7. travel by. 8. occupy. 9. assume. 10. require.

take′off′, *n.* 1. leaving of ground in

leaping or flying. 2. *Informal.* piece of mimicry.

take′out′, *adj.* 1. intended to be taken from restaurant and eaten elsewhere. —*n.* 2. food taken out from restaurant.

take′o′ver, *n.* act of seizing authority or control.

talc (talk) *n.* soft mineral, used for lubricants, etc. Also, **tal′cum.**

tal′cum powder (tal′kəm) powder for the skin made of purified talc.

tale (tāl) *n.* story or lie.

tal′ent (tal′ənt) *n.* natural ability.

tal′is·man (tal′is mən, -iz-) *n.* amulet.

talk (tôk) *v.* 1. speak; converse. 2. gossip. —*n.* 3. speech; conversation. 4. conference. 5. gossip. —**talk′a·tive,** *adj.* —**talk′er,** *n.*

talk′ing-to′, *n., pl.* **talking-tos.** scolding.

tall (tôl) *adj.* 1. of great height. 2. of specified height.

tal′low (tal′ō) *n.* 1. suet. 2. hardened fat for soap, etc.

tal′ly (tal′ē) *n., pl.* **-lies,** *v.,* **-lied, -lying.** —*n.* 1. record of amounts. —*v.* 2. record. 3. match.

tal′ly·ho′ (-hō′) *interj.* cry in hunting on catching sight of fox.

Tal′mud (täl′mŏŏd, tal′məd) *n.* collection of Jewish laws. —**Tal·mud′ic,** *adj.*

tal′on (tal′ən) *n.* claw.

tam (tam) *n.* tam-o′-shanter.

ta·ma′le (tə mä′lē) *n.* Mexican dish of cornmeal, meat, red peppers, etc.

tam′a·rack′ (tam′ə rak′) *n.* N American larch.

tam′a·rind (-ə rind) *n.* tropical fruit.

tam′bou·rine′ (-bə rēn′) *n.* small drum with metal disks in frame.

tame (tām) *adj.,* tamer, tamest, *v.,* tamed, taming. —*adj.* 1. not wild; domesticated. 2. uninterestingly conventional. —*v.* 3. domesticate. —**tame′ly,** *adv.* —**tam′er,** *n.*

tam′-o′-shan′ter (tam′ə shan′tər) *n.* cap with flat crown.

tamp (tamp) *v.* force down or in. —**tamp′er,** *n.*

tam′per, *v.* meddle.

tam′pon (tam′pon) *n.* plug of cotton or the like for insertion into wound or body cavity to absorb blood.

tan (tan) *v.,* **tanned, tanning,** *n., adj.* —*v.* 1. convert into leather. 2. make or become brown by exposure to sun. —*n.* 3. light brown. 4. Also, **tan′bark′.** bark used in tanning hides. —*adj.* 5. light brown. —**tan′ner,** *n.* —**tan′ner·y,** *n.*

tan′dem (tan′dəm) *adv.* 1. one behind another. —*adj.* 2. having one following behind another.

tang (tang) *n.* strong flavor.

tan′ge·lo′ (tan′jə lō′) *n., pl.* **-los.** fruit that is a cross between grapefruit and tangerine.

tan′gent (tan′jənt) *adj.* 1. touching. —*n.* 2. tangent line, etc. 3. sudden change of course, thought, etc.

tan·gen′tial (-jen′shəl) *adj.* 1. touching. 2. not relevant.

tan′ge·rine′ (tan′jə rēn′) *n.* loose-skinned fruit similar to orange.

tan′gi·ble (tan′jə bəl) *adj.* 1. discernible by touch. 2. real. 3. definite. —**tan′gi·bil′i·ty,** *n.*

tan′gle (tang′gəl) *v.,* **-gled, -gling,** *n.* —*v.* 1. come or bring together in confused mass. 2. involve. 3. snare. 4. *Informal.* come into conflict. —*n.* 5. tangled state or mass.

tan′go (tang′gō) *n., pl.* **-gos,** *v.,* **-goed, -going.** —*n.* 1. Spanish-

American dance. —*v.* **2.** dance the tango.

tank (tangk) *n.* **1.** large receptacle for liquid or gas. **2.** armored combat vehicle on caterpillar treads.

tank'ard (tang'kərd) *n.* large cup.

tank'er, *n.* ship, truck, or airplane for transporting liquid bulk cargo.

tank top, sleeveless shirt.

tan'nin (tan'in) *n.* astringent compound used in tanning.

tan'ta•lize' (tan'tl īz') *v.,* **-lized, -lizing.** torment by prospect of something desired.

tan'ta•mount' (tan'tə mount') *adj.* equivalent.

tan'trum (tan'trəm) *n.* noisy outburst of bad temper.

tap (tap) *n., v.,* **tapped, tapping.** —*n.* **1.** plug or faucet through which liquid is drawn. **2.** light blow. —*v.* **3.** draw liquid from. **4.** reach or pierce to draw something off. **5.** strike lightly.

tap dance, dance in which rhythm is audibly tapped out by toe or heel. —**tap'-dance',** *v.* —**tap'-danc'er,** *n.*

tape (tāp) *n., v.,* **taped, taping.** —*n.* **1.** narrow strip of flexible material. —*v.* **2.** furnish or tie with tape. **3.** record on tape.

tape deck, audio system component for playing tapes.

tape measure, tape marked for measuring. Also, **tape'line'.**

ta'per (tā'pər) *v.* **1.** make or become narrower toward end. —*n.* **2.** gradual decrease. **3.** small candle.

tape recorder, electrical device for recording or playing back sound recorded on magnetic tape.

tap'es•try (tap'ə strē) *n., pl.* **-tries.** woven, figured fabric for wall hanging, etc.

tape'worm', *n.* parasitic worm in alimentary canal.

tap'i•o'ca (tap'ē ō'kə) *n.* granular food from starch of tuberous plants.

ta'pir (tā'pər, tə pēr') *n.* tropical swinelike animal.

tap'room', *n.* barroom.

tap'root', *n.* main, central root pointing downward and giving off small lateral roots.

tar (tär) *n., v.,* **tarred, tarring.** —*n.* **1.** dark viscid product made from coal, wood, etc. **2.** sailor. —*v.* **3.** cover with tar. —**tar'ry** (tär'ē) *adj.*

tar'an•tel'la (tar'ən tel'ə) *n.* rapid, whirling southern Italian dance.

ta•ran'tu•la (tə ran'chə lə) *n.* large hairy spider.

tar'dy (tär'dē) *adj.,* **-dier, -diest.** late. —**tar'di•ness,** *n.*

tare (tär) *n.* weed.

tar'get (tär'git) *n.* something aimed at.

tar'iff (tar'if) *n.* **1.** list of export or import duties. **2.** one such duty.

tar'nish (tär'nish) *v.* **1.** lose luster. **2.** sully. —*n.* **3.** tarnished coating or state.

ta'ro (tär'ō, târ'ō, tar'ō) *n.* tropical plant cultivated for edible tuber.

ta'rot (tar'ō, ta rō') *n.* any of set of 22 playing cards used for fortunetelling.

tar•pau'lin (tär pô'lin, tär'pə lin) *n.* waterproof covering of canvas, etc.

tar'ra•gon' (tar'ə gon', -gən) *n.* plant with aromatic leaves used as seasoning.

tar'ry (tar'ē) *v.,* **-ried, -rying. 1.** stay. **2.** linger.

tart (tärt) *adj.* **1.** sour; acid. **2.** caustic. —*n.* **3.** pastry shell filled with fruit, etc. —**tart'ly,** *adv.*

tar'tan (tär'tn) *n.* cloth worn by na-

tives of N Scotland, having crisscross pattern.

tar'tar (tär'tər) *n.* **1.** hard deposit on teeth. **2.** savage, intractable person. —**tar•tar'ic** (-tar'ik, -tär'-) *adj.*

tartar sauce, mayonnaise sauce containing chopped pickles, onions, etc.

task (task) *n.* **1.** assigned piece of work. —*v.* **2.** put strain on.

task force, 1. temporary group of armed units for carrying out specific mission. **2.** temporary committee for solving specific problem.

task'mas'ter, *n.* assigner of burdensome tasks.

tas'sel (tas'əl) *n.* fringed ornament hanging from roundish knot.

taste (tāst) *v.,* **tasted, tasting,** *n.* —*v.* **1.** try flavor by taking in mouth. **2.** eat or drink a little of. **3.** perceive flavor. **4.** have particular flavor. —*n.* **5.** act of tasting. **6.** sense by which flavor is perceived. **7.** flavor. **8.** sense of fitness or beauty. —**taste'less,** *adj.*

taste bud, one of numerous small bodies, chiefly in tongue, that are organs for sense of taste.

tast'y, *adj.,* **-ier, -iest. 1.** savory. **2.** tasting good. —**tast'i•ness,** *n.*

tat'ter (tat'ər) *n.* **1.** torn piece. **2.** (*pl.*) ragged clothing.

tat'tle (tat'l) *v.,* **-tled, -tling,** *n.* —*v.* **1.** tell another's secrets. —*n.* **2.** chatter; gossip. —**tat'tler, tat'tle•tale',** *n.*

tat•too' (ta tōō') *n.* **1.** indelible marking on skin by puncturing and dyeing. **2.** design so made. **3.** military signal on drum, bugle, etc., to go to quarters. —*v.* **4.** mark by tattoo.

taunt (tônt, tänt) *v.* **1.** reproach insultingly or sarcastically. —*n.* **2.** insulting or sarcastic gibe.

taupe (tōp) *n.* dark gray usually tinged with brown, purple, yellow, or green.

taut (tôt) *adj.* tight; tense.

tau•tol'o•gy (tô tol'ə jē) *n., pl.* **-gies.** needless repetition. —**tau'to•log'i•cal** (-tl oj'i kal) *adj.*

tav'ern (tav'ərn) *n.* **1.** saloon. **2.** inn.

taw'dry (tô'drē) *adj.,* **-drier, -driest.** gaudy; cheap.

taw'ny (tô'nē) *adj.,* **-nier, -niest,** *n.* —*adj.* **1.** of a dark-yellow or yellowbrown color. —*n.* **2.** tawny color.

tax (taks) *n.* **1.** money regularly paid to government. **2.** burdensome duty, etc. —*v.* **3.** impose tax. **4.** burden. **5.** accuse. —**tax'a•ble,** *adj.* —**tax•a'tion,** *n.*

tax'i (tak'sē) *n., v.,* **taxied, taxiing.** —*n.* **1.** taxicab. —*v.* **2.** go in taxicab. **3.** (of airplane) move on ground under its own power.

tax'i•cab', *n.* automobile carrying paying passengers.

tax'i•der'my (tak'si dûr'mē) *n.* art of preserving and mounting skins of animals. —**tax'i•der'•mist,** *n.*

tax'pay'er, *n.* person who pays tax.

tax shelter, financial arrangement that reduces or eliminates taxes due.

TB, tuberculosis. Also, **T.B.**

tbs., tablespoon. Also, **tbsp.**

T cell, cell involved in regulating immune system's response to infected or malignant cells.

tea (tē) *n.* **1.** dried aromatic leaves of Oriental shrub. **2.** beverage made by infusion of these leaves in hot water. **3.** similar beverage made by steeping leaves or flowers of other plants. **4.** afternoon meal. —**tea'cup',** *n.* —**tea'ket'tle,** *n.* —**tea'pot',** *n.*

teach (tēch) *v.,* **taught, teaching.** impart knowledge to. —**teach'er,** *n.*

teak (tēk) *n.* East Indian tree with hard wood.

teal (tēl) *n.* **1.** any of certain small fresh-water ducks. **2.** greenish blue.

team (tēm) *n.* **1.** persons, etc., associated in joint action. —*v.* **2.** join in team. —**team'mate',** *n.* —**team'work',** *n.*

team'ster (-stər) *n.* driver of team.

tear (târ) *v.,* **tore** (tōr), **torn, tearing,** *n.* —*v.* **1.** pull apart by force. **2.** distress. **3.** divide. **4.** lacerate. **5.** rend. —*n.* **6.** act of tearing. **7.** torn place. **8.** (tēr) Also, **tear'drop'.** drop of fluid secreted by eye duct. —**tear'ful** (tēr'-) *adj.*

tear gas (tēr) gas that makes eyes smart and water.

tear'jerk'er (tēr'jûr'kər) *n. Informal.* sentimental story, etc.

tease (tēz) *v.,* **teased, teasing,** *v.* —*v.* **1.** annoy by raillery. —*n.* **2.** person who teases. —**teas'er,** *n.*

tea'spoon', *n.* small spoon. —**tea'spoon•ful',** *n., pl.* **-fuls.**

teat (tēt, tit) *n.* nipple.

tech'ni•cal (tek'ni kal) *adj.* **1.** pertaining to skilled activity. **2.** considered in strict sense.

tech'ni•cal'i•ty (-kal'i tē) *n., pl.* **-ties. 1.** technical point or detail. **2.** technical character.

Tech'ni•col'or, *n. Trademark.* system of making color motion pictures.

tech•nique' (-nēk') *n.* skilled method. Also, **tech•nic'.**

tech•noc'ra•cy (-nok'rə sē) *n., pl.* **-cies.** government by technological experts.

tech•nol'o•gy (-nol'ə jē) *n., pl.* **-gies. 1.** practical application of science. **2.** technological invention or method. —**tech•no•log'i•cal** (-nə loj'i-kal) *adj.* —**tech•nol'o•gist,** *n.*

tech'no•thrill'er (tek'nō thril'ər) *n.* suspense novel in which sophisticated technology is prominent.

ted'dy bear (ted'ē) stuffed toy bear.

Te De'um (tā dā'əm) hymn of praise and thanksgiving.

te'di•ous (tē'dē əs, tē'jəs) *adj.* long and tiresome. —**te'di•um,** *n.*

tee (tē) *n. Golf.* —*n.* **1.** hard mound of earth at beginning of play for each hole. **2.** object from which ball is driven. —*v.* **3.** place on tee. **4.** strike from tee.

teem (tēm) *v.* abound; swarm.

teens (tēnz) *n.pl.* years (13–19) of ages ending in -teen. —**teen'ag'er, teen,** *n.* —**teen'age', teen'aged',** *adj.*

tee'ter (tē'tər) *Informal.* —*v.* **1.** seesaw. **2.** walk unsteadily. —*n.* **3.** seesaw.

teethe (tēth) *v.,* **teethed, teething.** grow or cut teeth.

tee•to'tal•er (tē tōt'l ər, tē'tōt'-) *n.* person who does not drink alcoholic beverages.

Tef'lon (tef'lon) *n. Trademark.* **1.** polymer with nonsticking properties, used to coat cookware. —*adj.* **2.** impervious to blame or criticisms.

tel., **1.** telegram. **2.** telegraph. **3.** telephone.

tel'e•cast' (tel'i kast') *v.,* **-cast** or **-casted, -casting.** —*v.* **1.** broadcast by television. —*n.* **2.** television broadcast.

tel'e•com•mu'ni•ca'tions, *n.* science and technology of transmitting information in the form of electromagnetic signals.

tel'e•con'fer•ence, *n.* conference of participants in different locations via telecommunications equipment.

tel′e·gen′ic (-jen′ik) *adj.* looking good on television.

tel′e·graph′ (-graf′) *n.* **1.** electrical apparatus or process for sending message (**tel′e·gram′**). —*v.* **2.** send by telegraph. —**te·leg′ra·pher** (tə leg′rə fər) *n.* —**tel′e·graph′ic,** *adj.* —**te·leg′ra·phy** (tə leg′rə fē) *n.*

tel′e·mar′ket·ing, *n.* selling or advertising by telephone.

te·lep′a·thy (tə lep′ə thē) *n.* communication between minds without sensory means. —**tel′e·path′ic** (tel′ə-path′ik) *adj.*

tel′e·phone′ (tel′ə fōn′) *n., v.,* **-phoned, -phoning.** —*n.* **1.** electrical apparatus or process for transmitting speech. —*v.* **2.** communicate by telephone.

tel′e·pho′to, *adj.* of a lens producing large image of small or distant object.

tel′e·scope′, *n., v.,* **-scoped, -scoping.** —*n.* **1.** optical instrument for enlarging image of distant objects. —*v.* **2.** force or slide one object into another. —**tel′e·scop′ic** (-skop′ik) *adj.*

tel′e·thon′ (-thon′) *n.* lengthy television broadcast, usu. to raise money for charity.

tel′e·van′ge·list (tel′i van′jə list) *n.* evangelist who conducts religious services on television. —**tel′e·van′ge·lism** (-liz′əm) *n.*

tel′e·view′, *v.* view with a television receiver. —**tel′e·view′er,** *n.*

tel′e·vise′ (-vīz′) *v.,* **-vised, -vising.** broadcast by television.

tel′e·vi′sion, *n.* radio or electrical transmission of images.

Tel′ex (tel′eks) *n. Trademark.* two-way teletypewriter system.

tell (tel) *v.,* **told** (tōld), **telling. 1.** relate. **2.** communicate. **3.** say positively. **4.** distinguish. **5.** inform. **6.** divulge. **7.** order. **8.** produce marked effect. —**tell′ing,** *adj.*

tell′-all′, *adj.* thoroughly revealing.

tell′er, *n.* bank cashier.

tell′tale′, *n.* **1.** divulger of secrets. —*adj.* **2.** revealing.

te·mer′i·ty (tə mer′i tē) *n.* rash boldness.

temp (temp) *n.* temporary worker.

tem′per, *n.* **1.** state or habit of mind. **2.** heat or passion. **3.** control of one's anger. **4.** state of metal after tempering. —*v.* **5.** moderate. **6.** heat and cool metal to obtain proper hardness, etc.

tem′per·a (tem′pər ə) *n.* technique of painting using media containing egg.

tem′per·a·ment (tem′pər ə mənt, -prə mənt) *n.* mental disposition.

tem′per·a·men′tal (-men′tl) *adj.* **1.** moody or sensitive. **2.** of one's personality.

tem′per·ance (tem′pər əns) *n.* **1.** moderation. **2.** total abstinence from alcohol.

tem′per·ate (-pər it) *adj.* moderate.

Temperate Zone, part of earth's surface lying between either tropic and nearest polar circle.

tem′per·a·ture (-pər ə chər, -prə-) *n.* degree of warmth or coldness.

tem′pest (tem′pist) *n.* violent storm, commotion, or disturbance. —**tem·pes′tu·ous** (-pes′chōŏ əs) *adj.* —**tem·pes′tu·ous·ly,** *adv.*

tem′plate (tem′plit) *n.* pattern, mold, etc., serving as gauge or guide in mechanical work.

tem′ple (tem′pəl) *n.* **1.** place dedicated to worship. **2.** flat area at side of forehead.

tem′po (tem′pō) *n., pl.* **-pos, -pi** (-pē). rate of speed.

tem′po·ral (tem′pər əl) *adj.* **1.** of time. **2.** worldly.

tem′po·rar′y (-pə rer′ē) *adj.* not permanent. —**tem′po·rar′i·ly,** *adv.*

tem′po·rize′ (-rīz′) *v.,* **-rized, -rizing. 1.** delay by evasion or indecision. **2.** compromise.

tempt (tempt) *v.* **1.** entice. **2.** appeal strongly. —**temp·ta′tion,** *n.* —**tempt′er,** *n.* —**tempt′ress,** *n.fem.*

tem·pu′ra (tem pōŏr′ə) *n.* Japanese deep-fried dish of vegetables or seafood.

ten (ten) *n., adj.* nine plus one.

ten′a·ble (ten′ə bəl) *adj.* defensible in argument. —**ten·a·bil′i·ty,** *n.*

te·na′cious (tə nā′shəs) *adj.* **1.** holding fast. **2.** retentive. **3.** obstinate. **4.** sticky. —**te·na′cious·ly,** *adv.* —**te·nac′i·ty** (-nas′i tē) *n.*

ten′an·cy (ten′ən sē) *n., pl.* **-cies.** holding; tenure.

ten′ant (-ənt) *n.* **1.** one renting from landlord. **2.** occupant.

Ten Commandments, precepts delivered to Moses on Mount Sinai.

tend (tend) *v.* **1.** incline in action or effect. **2.** lead. **3.** take care of.

tend′en·cy (ten′dən sē) *n., pl.* **-cies. 1.** disposition to behave or act in certain way. **2.** predisposition.

ten·den′tious (-den′shəs) *adj.* having or showing bias.

ten′der, *adj.* **1.** soft; delicate; weak. **2.** immature. **3.** soft-hearted. **4.** kind. **5.** loving. **6.** sensitive. —*v.* **7.** present formally. **8.** offer. —*n.* **9.** something offered. **10.** person who tends. **11.** auxiliary vehicle or vessel. —**ten′der·ness,** *n.* —**ten′der·ize′,** *v.,* **-ized, -izing.**

ten′der·foot′, *n., pl.* **-foots, -feet.** *Informal.* inexperienced person.

ten′der·heart′ed, *adj.* soft-hearted; sympathetic.

ten′der·loin′, *n.* **1.** tender meat on loin of beef, pork, etc. **2.** brothel district of city.

ten·di·ni′tis (ten′də nī′tis) *n.* inflammation of tendon.

ten′don (-dən) *n.* band of fibrous tissue connecting muscle to bone or part.

ten′dril (-dril) *n.* clinging threadlike organ of climbing plants.

ten′e·ment (-ə mənt) *n.* run-down apartment house.

ten′et (-it) *n.* principle, doctrine, dogma, etc.

Tenn., Tennessee.

ten′nis (-is) *n.* game of ball played with rackets (**tennis rackets**) on rectangular court (**tennis court**).

ten′on (-ən) *n.* projection inserted into cavity (**mortise**) to form joint.

ten′or (-ər) *n.* **1.** continuous course or progress. **2.** perceived meaning or intention. **3.** male voice between bass and alto.

ten′pins′, *n.* bowling game played with ten pins.

tense (tens) *adj.,* **tenser, tensest,** *v.,* **tensed, tensing,** *n.* —*adj.* **1.** taut; rigid. **2.** emotionally strained. —*v.* **3.** make or become tense. —*n.* **4.** verb inflection indicating time of action or state. —**tense′ly,** *adv.*

ten′sile (ten′səl, -sil, -sīl) *adj.* **1.** of tension. **2.** ductile.

ten′sion (-shən) *n.* **1.** stretching or being stretched. **2.** strain. **3.** strained relations.

tent (tent) *n.* portable shelter, usually fabric.

ten′ta·cle (ten′tə kəl) *n.* long, flexible organ of octopuses, etc.

ten′ta·tive (-tə tiv) *adj.* in trial; experimental. —**ten′ta·tive·ly,** *adv.*

ten′ter·hook′ (-tər hŏŏk′) *n.* **on tenterhooks,** in suspense.

tenth (tenth) *adj., n.* next after ninth.

ten′u·ous (ten′yōŏ əs) *adj.* **1.** lacking a sound basis. **2.** thin, slender. **3.** rarefied. —**ten′u·ous·ly,** *adv.*

ten′ure (-yər) *n.* **1.** holding of something. **2.** assurance of permanent work.

te′pee (tē′pē) *n.* American Indian tent.

tep′id (tep′id) *adj.* lukewarm. —**te·pid′i·ty, tep′id·ness,** *n.*

te·qui′la (tə kē′lə) *n.* Mexican liquor.

term (tûrm) *n.* **1.** name for something. **2.** period, as of school instruction. **3.** (*pl.*) conditions of agreement or bargain. —*v.* **4.** name; designate.

ter′mi·nal (-mə nl) *adj.* **1.** at end; concluding. **2.** leading to death. —*n.* **3.** end or extremity. **4.** terminating point for trains, buses, etc. **5.** point of electrical connection. **6.** device for entering information into or receiving information from computer. —**ter′mi·nal·ly,** *adv.*

ter′mi·nate′ (-nāt′) *v.,* **-nated, -nating. 1.** end or cease. **2.** occur at end. —**ter′mi·na′tion,** *n.*

ter′mi·nol′o·gy (-nol′ə jē) *n., pl.* **-gies.** terms of technical subject.

ter′mi·nus (-nəs) *n.* **1.** end. **2.** end of line for buses, trains, etc.

ter′mite (tûr′mīt) *n.* destructive woodeating insect.

tern (tûrn) *n.* gull-like aquatic bird.

ter′race (ter′əs) *n., v.,* **-raced, -racing.** —*n.* **1.** raised level with abrupt drop at front. **2.** flat roof. **3.** open area connected with house. —*v.* **4.** make or furnish as or with terrace.

ter′ra cot′ta (ter′ə kot′ə) **1.** hard, usually unglazed earthenware. **2.** brownish red.

ter′ra fir′ma (fûr′mə) solid land.

ter·rain′ (tə rān′) *n.* area of land of specified nature.

ter′ra·pin (ter′ə pin) *n.* edible North American turtle.

ter·rar′i·um (tə râr′ē əm) *n., pl.* **-iums, -ia** (-ē ə). glass tank for raising plants or land animals.

ter·raz′zo (tə rä′tsō, -raz′ō) *n.* mosaic flooring composed of stone chips and cement.

ter·res′tri·al (tə res′trē əl) *adj.* of or living on earth.

ter′ri·ble (ter′ə bəl) *adj.* **1.** dreadful. **2.** severe. —**ter′ri·bly,** *adv.*

ter′ri·er (ter′ē ər) *n.* hunting dog.

ter·rif′ic (tə rif′ik) *adj.* **1.** excellent. **2.** terrifying. —**ter·rif′i·cal·ly,** *adv.*

ter′ri·fy′ (ter′ə fī′) *v.,* **-fied, -fying.** fill with terror.

ter′ri·to′ry (ter′i tôr′ē) *n., pl.* **-ries. 1.** region. **2.** land and waters of state. **3.** region not a state but having elected legislature and appointed officials. —**ter′ri·to′ri·al,** *adj.*

ter′ror (ter′ər) *n.* intense fear.

ter′ror·ism, *n.* use of violence and threats to obtain political demands. —**ter′ror·ist,** *n., adj.*

ter′ror·ize′, *v.,* **-ized, -izing.** fill with terror. —**ter′ror·i·za′tion,** *n.*

ter′ry (ter′ē) *n., pl.* **-ries.** pile fabric with loops on both sides. Also, **terry cloth.**

terse (tûrs) *adj.* **1.** concise. **2.** curt; brusque. —**terse′ly,** *adv.*

ter′ti·ar′y (tûr′shē er′ē) *adj.* of third rank or stage.

tes′sel·late′ (tes′ə lāt′) *v.,* **-lated, -lating.** form mosaic pattern from small squares.

test (test) *n.* **1.** trial of or substance used to try quality, content, etc. **2.** examination to evaluate student or class. —*v.* **3.** subject to test.

tes•ta•ment (tes′tə mənt) *n.* legal will. —**tes′ta•men′ta•ry** (-men′tə rē) *adj.*

tes′tate (-tāt) *adj.* having left a valid will. —**tes′ta•tor,** *n.*

tes′ti•cle (-ti kəl) *n.* either of two male sex glands located in scrotum. Also, **tes′tis** (tes′tis).

tes′ti•fy′ (-tə fī′) *v.,* **-fied, -fying. 1.** give evidence. **2.** give testimony.

tes′ti•mo′ni•al (-mō′nē əl) *n.* written declaration certifying character, etc.

tes′ti•mo′ny, *n., pl.* **-nies. 1.** statement of witness under oath. **2.** proof.

tes•tos′ter•one (tes tos′tə rōn′) *n.* male sex hormone.

test tube, small cylindrical glass container used in laboratories.

tes′ty (tes′tē) *adj.,* **-tier, -tiest.** irritable. —**tes′ti•ly,** *adv.*

tet′a•nus (tet′n əs) *n.* infectious disease marked by muscular rigidity.

tête′-à-tête′ (tāt′ə tāt′, tet′ə tet′) *n.* private conversation.

teth′er (teth′ər) *n.* **1.** rope, chain, etc., for fastening animal to stake. —*v.* **2.** fasten with tether.

tet′ra (te′trə) *n., pl.* **-ras.** small, brightly colored fish of tropical American waters.

tet′ra•he′dron (-hē′drən) *n., pl.* **-drons, -dra.** solid contained by four plane faces.

Tex., Texas.

text (tekst) *n.* **1.** main body of matter in book or manuscript. **2.** quotation from Scripture, esp. as subject of sermon, etc. —**tex′tu•al** (-chōō əl) *adj.* —**tex′tu•al•ly,** *adv.*

text′book′, *n.* book used by student to study.

tex′tile (teks′tīl, -til) *n.* **1.** woven material. —*adj.* **2.** woven. **3.** of weaving.

tex′ture (teks′chər) *n.* characteristic surface or composition. —**tex′tur•al,** *adj.*

thal′a•mus (thal′ə məs) *n.* part of brain that transmits and integrates sensory impulses.

tha•lid′o•mide′ (thə lid′ə mīd′) *n.* drug formerly used as sedative, found to cause fetal abnormalities.

thal′li•um (thal′ē əm) *n.* rare metallic element.

than (than, then; *unstressed* thən, ən) *conj.* particle introducing second member of comparison.

thank (thangk) *v.* **1.** express gratitude for. —*n.* **2.** (*usually pl.*) expression of gratitude. —**thank′ful,** *adj.* —**thank′less,** *adj.* —**thanks′giv′ing,** *n.*

Thanksgiving Day, festival in acknowledgment of divine favor, celebrated in U.S. on fourth Thursday of November and in Canada on second Monday of October.

that (that; *unstressed* thət) *pron., pl.* **those** (thōz), *adj., adv., conj.* —*pron., adj.* **1.** demonstrative word indicating **a.** the person, thing, etc., more remote. **b.** one of two persons, etc., pointed out or mentioned before (opposed to **this**). **2.** relative pronoun used as: **a.** subject or object of relative clause. **b.** object of preposition. —*adv.* **3.** to that extent. —*conj.* **4.** word used to introduce dependent clause or one expressing reason, result, etc.

thatch (thach) *n.* **1.** rushes, leaves, etc., for covering roofs. —*v.* **2.** cover with thatch.

thaw (thô) *v.* **1.** melt. **2.** remove ice or frost from. —*n.* **3.** act or instance of thawing.

the (*stressed* thē; *unstressed before a consonant* thə, *unstressed before a vowel* thē) *def. article.* **1.** word used, esp. before nouns, with specifying effect. —*adv.* **2.** word used to modify comparative or superlative form of adjective or adverb.

the′a•ter (thē′ə tər, thē′-) *n.* **1.** building for dramatic presentations, etc. **2.** dramatic art. **3.** place of action. Also, **the′a•tre.** —**the•at′ri•cal** (-a′tri-kəl) *adj.*

thee (thē) *pron. Archaic.* you.

theft (theft) *n.* act or instance of stealing.

their (thâr; *unstressed* thər) *pron.* **1.** possessive form of **they** used before noun. **2.** (*pl.*) that which belongs to them.

the′ism (thē′iz əm) *n.* belief in one God. —**the′ist,** *n.*

them (them; *unstressed* thəm, əm) *pron.* objective case of **they.**

theme (thēm) *n.* **1.** subject of discourse, etc. **2.** short essay. **3.** melody. —**the•mat′ic** (-mat′ik) *adj.*

them•selves′ (them selvz′, them′-) *pron.* emphatic or reflexive form of **them.**

then (then) *adv.* **1.** at that time. **2.** soon afterward. **3.** at another time. **4.** besides. **5.** in that case. —*adj.* **6.** being such at that time.

thence (thens) *adv.* **1.** from that place or time. **2.** therefore.

thence′forth′ (thens′fôrth′, thens′-fôrth′) *adv.* from that place or time on. Also, **thence′for′ward.**

the•ol′o•gy (-ol′ə jē) *n.* study of God and of God's relations to the universe. —**the′o•lo′gian** (-ə lō′jən, -jē ən) *n.* —**the′o•log′i•cal** (-loj′i kəl) *adj.*

the′o•rem (thē′ər əm, thēr′əm) *n.* **1.** *Math.* statement embodying something to be proved. **2.** rule or law, esp. one expressed by equation or formula.

the′o•ret′i•cal (thē′ə ret′i kəl) *adj.* **1.** in theory. **2.** not practical. **3.** speculative.

the′o•ry, (thē′ə rē, thēr′ē) *n., pl.* **-ries. 1.** proposition used to explain class of phenomena. **2.** proposed explanation. **3.** principles. —**the′o•rist,** *n.* —**the′o•rize′,** *v.*

ther′a•py (ther′ə pē) *n., pl.* **-pies. 1.** treatment of disease. **2.** psychotherapy. —**ther′a•pist** (-pist) *n.* —**ther′a•peu′tic** (-pyōō′tik) *adj.* —**ther′a•peu′tics,** *n.*

there (thâr; *unstressed* thər) *adv.* **1.** in or at that place, point, matter, respect, etc. **2.** to that place. —**there′a•bouts′,** *adv.* —**there•af′ter,** *adv.* —**there•by′,** *adv.* —**there•in′,** *adv.* —**there•to′,** *adv.* —**there•un′der,** *adv.*

there′fore′, *adv.* consequently.

there•of′, *adv.* of or from that.

there•on′, *adv.* **1.** on that. **2.** immediately after that.

there′up•on′, *adv.* **1.** immediately after that. **2.** because of that. **3.** with reference to that.

there•with′, *adv.* with or in addition to that.

ther′mal (thûr′məl) *adj.* of heat.

ther′mo•dy•nam′ics (thûr′mō dī-nam′iks) *n.* science concerned with relations between heat and mechanical energy or work.

ther•mom′e•ter (thər mom′i tər) *n.* instrument for measuring temperature.

ther′mo•nu′cle•ar (thûr′mō-) *adj.* of nuclear-fusion reactions at extremely high temperatures.

ther′mo•plas′tic (thûr′mə-) *adj.* soft and pliable whenever heated, as some

plastics, without change of inherent properties.

Ther′mos (thûr′məs) *n. Trademark.* container with vacuum between double walls for heat insulation.

ther′mo•sphere′, *n.* region of upper atmosphere in which temperature increases continually with altitude.

ther′mo•stat′ (-mə stat′) *n.* device regulating temperature of heating system, etc. —**ther′mo•stat′ic,** *adj.*

the•sau′rus (thi sôr′əs) *n., pl.* **-sauruses, -sauri** (-sôr′ī). book of synonyms and antonyms.

these (thēz) *pron.* pl. of **this.**

the′sis (thē′sis) *n., pl.* **-ses** (-sēz). **1.** proposition to be proved. **2.** essay based on research.

thes′pi•an (thes′pē ən) *adj.* **1.** of dramatic art. —*n.* **2.** actor or actress.

they (thā) *pron.* nominative plural of **he, she,** and **it.**

thi′a•mine (thī′ə min, -mēn′) *n.* vitamin B1. Also, **thi′a•min.**

thick (thik) *adj.* **1.** not thin. **2.** in depth. **3.** compact. **4.** numerous. **5.** dense. **6.** husky. **7.** slow-witted. —*adv.* **8.** so as to be thick. —*n.* **9.** something thick. —**thick′en,** *v.* —**thick′en•er,** *n.*

thick′et, *n.* thick growth of shrubs, bushes, etc.

thick′set′, *adj.* **1.** set closely; dense. **2.** with heavy or solid body.

thick′-skinned′, *adj.* not sensitive to criticism or contempt.

thief (thēf) *n., pl.* **thieves** (thēvz). person who steals. —**thieve,** *v.,* **thieved, thieving.** —**thiev′er•y** (thē′-və rē) *n.*

thigh (thī) *n.* part of leg between hip and knee.

thigh′bone′, *n.* femur.

thim′ble (thim′bəl) *n.* cap to protect finger while sewing.

thin (thin) *adj.,* **thinner, thinnest,** *v.,* **thinned, thinning.** —*adj.* **1.** having little extent between opposite sides; slender. **2.** lean. **3.** scanty. **4.** rarefied; diluted. **5.** flimsy. **6.** weak. —*v.* **7.** make or become thinner. —**thin•ner,** *n.* —**thin′ly,** *adv.*

thing (thing) *n.* **1.** inanimate object. **2.** entity. **3.** matter. **4.** item.

think (thingk) *v.,* **thought** (thôt), **thinking. 1.** conceive in mind. **2.** meditate. **3.** believe. —**think′er,** *n.*

think tank, research organization employed to analyze problems and plan future developments.

thin′-skinned′, *adj.* sensitive to criticism or contempt.

third (thûrd) *adj.* **1.** next after second. —*n.* **2.** next after the second. **3.** any of three equal parts.

third′-class′, *adj.* of the lowest class or quality.

third degree, use of brutal measures by police (or others) in extorting information or confession.

third dimension, 1. thickness or depth. **2.** aspect that heightens reality.

third party, 1. party to case or quarrel who is incidentally involved. **2.** in two-party political system, usu. temporary party composed of independents.

third′-rate′, *adj.* distinctly inferior.

Third World, developing countries of Asia, Africa, and Latin America.

thirst (thûrst) *n.* **1.** sensation caused by need of drink. —*v.* **2.** be thirsty. —**thirst′y,** *adj.* —**thirst′i•ly,** *adv.*

thir′teen′ (thûr′tēn′) *n., adj.* ten plus three. —**thir•teenth′,** *adj., n.*

thir′ty (thûr′tē) *n., adj.* ten times three. —**thir′ti•eth,** *adj., n.*

this (this) *pron., pl.* **these** (thēz). *adj.,*

adv. **—pron.**, *adj.* **1.** demonstrative word indicating something as just mentioned, present, near, etc. **—adv. 2.** to the indicated extent.

this'tle (this'əl) *n.* prickly plant.

thith'er (thith'ər, thith'-) *adv.* to that place, point, etc.

tho (thō) *conj., adv. Informal.* though.

thong (thông) *n.* **1.** strip of leather. **2.** sandal with strip of leather, etc., passing between first two toes.

tho'rax (thôr'aks) *n., pl.* **thoraxes, thoraces** (thôr'ə sēz'). part of body between neck and abdomen. **—tho·rac'ic** (thô ras'ik) *adj.*

thorn (thôrn) *n.* sharp spine on plant. **—thorn'y**, *adj.*

thor'ough (thûr'ō, thur'ō) *adj.* complete. **—thor'ough·ly**, *adv.*

thor'ough·bred' (-ō bred', -ə bred') *adj.* **1.** of pure breed. **2.** well-bred. **—n. 3.** thoroughbred animal or person.

thor'ough·fare', *n.* road, street, etc., open at both ends.

thor'ough·go·ing, *adj.* doing things thoroughly.

those (thōz) *pron., adj.* pl. of **that**.

thou (thou) *pron.* you (now little used except provincially, archaically, in poetry or elevated prose, in addressing God, and by the Friends).

though (thō) *conj.* **1.** notwithstanding that. **2.** even if. **3.** nevertheless. **—adv. 4.** however.

thought (thôt) *n.* **1.** mental activity. **2.** idea. **3.** purpose. **4.** regard.

thought'ful, *adj.* **1.** meditative. **2.** heedful. **3.** considerate.

thought'less, *adj.* **1.** showing lack of thought. **2.** careless; inconsiderate. **—thought'less·ly**, *adv.*

thou'sand (thou'zand) *n., adj.* ten times one hundred. **—thou'sandth**, *adj., n.*

thrall (thrôl) *n.* **1.** person in bondage; slave. **2.** slavery; bondage.

thrash (thrash) *v.* **1.** beat thoroughly. **2.** toss wildly.

thread (thred) *n.* **1.** fine spun cord of flax, cotton, etc. **2.** filament. **3.** helical ridge of screw. **4.** connected sequence. **—v. 5.** pass end of thread through needle's eye. **6.** fix beads, etc., on thread.

thread'bare', *adj.* shabby.

threat (thret) *n.* expression of intent to harm.

threat'en, *v.* **1.** utter threats. **2.** look ominously close.

three (thrē) *n., adj.* two plus one.

three'-di·men'sion·al, *adj.* having or seeming to have depth as well as width and height.

three'fold', *adj.* **1.** having three parts. **2.** three times as great.

three R's, reading, writing, and arithmetic.

three score, *adj.* sixty.

thresh (thresh) *v.* separate grain or seeds from a plant. **—thresh'er**, *n.*

thresh'old (thresh'ōld, -hōld) *n.* **1.** doorway sill. **2.** entrance. **3.** beginning; border.

thrice (thrīs) *adv.* three times.

thrift (thrift) *n.* frugality.

thrift shop, store that sells second-hand goods.

thrift'y, *adj.*, **-ier, -iest.** saving; frugal.

thrill (thril) *v.* **1.** affect with sudden keen emotion. **2.** vibrate. **—n. 3.** sudden wave of keen emotion or excitement.

thrill'er, *n.* suspenseful play or story.

thrive (thrīv) *v.*, **thrived, thriving.** flourish.

throat (thrōt) *n.* passage from mouth to stomach or lungs.

throat'y, *adj.*, **-ier, -iest.** (of sound) husky; hoarse.

throb (throb) *v.*, **throbbed, throbbing**, *n.* **—v. 1.** beat violently or rapidly. **2.** vibrate. **—n. 3.** act of throbbing.

throe (thrō) *n.* **1.** spasm. **2.** (*pl.*) pangs.

throm·bo'sis (throm bō'sis) *n.* clotting of blood in circulatory system.

throne (thrōn) *n.* official chair of sovereign, bishop, etc.

throng (thrông) *n., v.* crowd.

throt'tle (throt'l) *n., v.*, **-tled, -tling. —n. 1.** device controlling flow of fuel. **—v. 2.** choke. **3.** check.

through (throo) *prep.* **1.** in at one end and out at other. **2.** during all of. **3.** having finished. **4.** by means or reason of. **—adv. 5.** in at one end and out at other. **6.** all the way. **7.** to the end. **8.** finished. **—adj. 9.** passing through.

through·out', *prep.* **1.** in all parts of. **—adv. 2.** in every part, etc.

throw (thrō) *v.*, **threw** (throo), **thrown, throwing**, *n.* **—v. 1.** propel or cast. **2.** fell in wrestling. **3.** host. **4.** confuse. **—n. 5.** act of throwing. **—throw'er**, *n.*

throw'a·way', *adj.* **1.** to be discarded after use. **—n. 2.** notice distributed free.

throw'back', *n.* **1.** setback or check. **2.** reversion to ancestral type.

thru (throo) *prep., adv., adj. Informal.* through.

thrush (thrush) *n.* **1.** migratory singing bird. **2.** fungal disease of mouth.

thrust (thrust) *v.*, **thrust, thrusting**, *n.* **—v. 1.** push; shove. **2.** stab. **—n. 3.** push; lunge. **4.** stab.

thru'way' (throo'wā') *n.* expressway providing direct route between distant areas.

thud (thud) *n., v.*, **thudded, thudding. —n. 1.** dull striking sound. **—v. 2.** make thudding sound.

thug (thug) *n.* violent criminal.

thumb (thum) *n.* **1.** short, thick finger next to the forefinger. **—v. 2.** manipulate with thumb.

thumb'nail', *n.* **1.** nail of thumb. **—adj. 2.** brief and concise.

thumb'screw', *n.* **1.** instrument of torture that compresses thumb. **2.** screw turned by thumb and finger.

thumb'tack', *n.* **1.** tack with large, flat head. **—v. 2.** secure with thumbtack.

thump (thump) *n.* **1.** blow from something thick and heavy. **—v. 2.** pound.

thump'ing, *adj.* **1.** exceptional. **2.** of or like a thump.

thun'der (thun'dər) *n.* **1.** loud noise accompanying lightning. **—v. 2.** give forth thunder. **3.** speak loudly. **—thun'der·ous**, *adj.* **—thun'der·storm'**, *n.*

thun'der·bolt', *n.* flash of lightning with thunder.

thun'der·clap', *n.* crash of thunder.

thun'der·cloud', *n.* electrically charged cloud producing lightning and thunder.

thun'der·head', *n.* mass of cumulus clouds warning of thunderstorms.

thun'der·struck', *adj.* astonished.

Thurs., Thursday.

Thurs'day (thûrz'dā, -dē) *n.* fifth day of week.

thus (thus) *adv.* **1.** in this way. **2.** consequently. **3.** to this extent.

thwack (thwak) *v.* **1.** strike hard with something flat. **—n. 2.** thwacking blow.

thwart (thwôrt) *v.* frustrate.

thy (thī) *adj. Archaic.* your.

thyme (tīm; *spelling pron.* thīm) *n.* plant of mint family.

thy'mus (thī'məs) *n.* gland at base of neck that helps produce T cells.

thy'roid (thī'roid) *adj.* of thyroid gland.

thyroid gland, ductless gland near windpipe, involved in controlling metabolism and growth.

thy·self' (thī self') *pron.* **1.** emphatic appositive to **thou** or **thee**. **2.** substitute for reflexive **thee**.

ti·ar'a (tē ar'ə, -är'ə, -âr'ə) *n.* woman's ornamental coronet.

Ti·bet'an (ti bet'n) *n.* native or language of Tibet. **—Tibetan**, *adj.*

tib'i·a (tib'ē ə) *n., pl.* **-iae** (-ē ē'), **-ias.** bone from knee to ankle.

tic (tik) *n.* sudden twitch.

tick (tik) *n.* **1.** soft, recurring click. **2.** bloodsucking mitelike animal. **3.** cloth case of mattress, pillow, etc. **—v. 4.** produce tick (def. 1).

tick'er, *n.* **1.** one that ticks. **2.** telegraphic instrument that prints stock prices and market reports, etc., on tape (**ticker tape**). **3.** *Slang.* heart.

tick'et, *n.* **1.** slip indicating right to admission, transportation, etc. **2.** tag. **3.** summons for traffic or parking violation. **—v. 4.** attach ticket to.

tick'ing, *n.* cotton fabric for ticks (def. 3).

tick'le, *v.*, **-led, -ling**, *n.* **—v. 1.** touch lightly so as to make tingle or itch. **2.** gratify. **3.** amuse. **—n. 4.** act of tickling. **—tick'lish**, *adj.*

tickler file, file for reminding user at appropriate times of matters needing attention.

tick'-tack-toe' (tik'tak tō') *n.* game for two players, each trying to complete row of three X's or three O's on nine-square grid.

tidal wave, large, destructive ocean wave produced by earthquake.

tid'bit' (tid'bit') *n.* choice bit.

tid'dly·winks' (tid'lē wingks') *n.* game in which small disks are snapped with larger disks into cup.

tide (tīd) *n., v.*, **tided, tiding. —n. 1.** periodic rise and fall of ocean waters. **2.** stream. **—v. 3.** be enough to get over difficult period. **—tid'al**, *adj.*

tide'land', *n.* land alternately exposed and covered by tide.

ti'dings (tī'dingz) *n.pl.* news.

ti'dy (tī'dē) *adj.*, **-dier, -diest**, *v.*, **-died, -dying. —adj. 1.** neat; orderly. **2.** fairly large. **—v. 3.** make tidy. **—ti'di·ly**, *adv.*

tie (tī) *v.*, **tied, tying**, *n.* **—v. 1.** bind with cord, etc. **2.** confine. **3.** equal or be equal. **—n. 4.** something used to tie or join. **5.** necktie. **6.** equality in scores, votes, etc. **7.** contest in which this occurs. **8.** bond of kinship, affection, etc.

tie'dye'ing, *n.* method of dyeing with sections of garment bound so as not to receive dye.

tie'-in', *n.* link, association, or relationship.

tier (tēr) *n.* row or rank.

tie'-up', *n.* **1.** undesired stoppage of business, traffic, etc. **2.** connection.

tiff (tif) *n.* petty quarrel.

ti'ger (tī'gər) *n.* large striped Asian cat. **—ti'gress**, *n.fem.*

tiger lily, lily with flowers of dull-orange color spotted with black.

tight (tīt) *adj.* **1.** firmly in place. **2.** taut. **3.** fitting closely. **4.** impervious to fluids. **5.** stingy. **—tight'en**, *v.* **—tight'ly**, *adv.* **—tight'ness**, *n.*

tight′-fist′ed, *adj.* stingy.

tight′-lipped′, *adj.* reluctant to speak.

tight′rope′, *n.* taut wire or cable on which acrobats perform.

tights, *n.pl.* close-fitting pants, worn esp. by acrobats, etc.

tight′wad′, *n. Slang.* stingy person.

til′de (til′də) *n.* diacritical mark (˜) placed over letter.

tile (tīl) *n., v.,* **tiled, tiling.** —*n.* **1.** thin piece of baked clay, etc., used as covering. —*v.* **2.** cover with tiles.

til′ing, *n.* **1.** operation of covering with tiles. **2.** tiles collectively.

till (til) *prep., conj.* **1.** until. —*v.* **2.** labor on to raise crops. **3.** plow. —*n.* **4.** drawer in back of counter for money. —**till′age,** *n.* —**Usage.** TILL and UNTIL are used interchangeably in speech and writing: *It rained till/until nearly midnight.* TILL is not a shortened form of UNTIL and is not spelled *'till.* 'TIL is usually considered a spelling error, though commonly used in business and advertising: *open 'til ten.*

till′er *n.* **1.** one that tills. **2.** handle on head of rudder.

tilt (tilt) *v.* **1.** lean; slant. **2.** charge or engage in joust. —*n.* **3.** act of tilting. **4.** slant.

tim′ber (tim′bər) *n.* **1.** wood of growing trees. **2.** trees. **3.** wood for building. **4.** wooden beam, etc. —*v.* **5.** furnish or support with timber.

tim′ber•line′, *n.* altitude or latitude at which timber ceases to grow.

timber wolf, large brindled wolf of forested Canada and northern United States.

tim′bre (tam′bər, tim′-) *n.* characteristic quality of a sound.

time (tīm) *n., v.,* **timed, timing.** —*n.* **1.** duration. **2.** period of time. **3.** occasion. **4.** point in time. **5.** appointed or proper time. **6.** meter of music. **7.** rate. —*v.* **8.** determine or record time. —**tim′er,** *n.*

time clock, clock with attachment that records times of arrival and departure of employees.

time′hon′ored, *adj.* long valued or used; traditional.

time′keep′er, *n.* **1.** person who keeps time. **2.** timepiece, esp. as regards time accuracy.

time′less, *adj.* **1.** eternal. **2.** referring to no particular time.

time line, **1.** linear representation of events in the order in which they occurred. **2.** schedule.

time′ly, *adj.,* **-lier, -liest,** *adv.* —*adj.* **1.** opportune. —*adv.* **2.** opportunely.

time′-out′, *n.* brief suspension of activity, as in sports contest.

time′piece′, *n.* clock; watch.

times, *prep.* multiplied by.

time′-shar′ing, *n.* **1.** plan in which several people share cost of vacation home. **2.** system in which users at different terminals simultaneously use a single computer.

time′ta′ble, *n.* schedule of times of departures, work completion, etc.

time′worn′, *adj.* **1.** showing the effects of long use. **2.** trite.

time zone, one of 24 divisions of globe coinciding with meridians at successive hours from observatory at Greenwich, England.

tim′id (tim′id) *adj.* **1.** easily alarmed. **2.** shy. —**ti•mid′i•ty,** *n.*

tim′ing (tī′ming) *n.* control of speed or occasion of an action, event, etc., so that it occurs at the proper moment.

tim′or•ous (tim′ər əs) *adj.* **1.** fearful. **2.** timid. —**tim′or•ous•ly,** *adv.*

tim′pa•ni (tim′pə nē) *n.pl.* kettledrums. —**tim′pa•nist,** *n.*

tin (tin) *n., v.,* **tinned, tinning.** —*n.* **1.** malleable metallic element. —*v.* **2.** cover with tin. —**tin′ny,** *adj.*

tinc′ture (tingk′chər) *n.* medicinal solution in alcohol.

tin′der (tin′dər) *n.* inflammable substance. —**tin′der•box′,** *n.*

tine (tīn) *n.* prong of fork.

tin′foil′, *n.* tin or alloy in thin sheet, used as wrapping.

tinge (tinj) *v.,* **tinged, tingeing** or **tinging,** *n.* —*v.* **1.** impart trace of color, taste, etc., to. —*n.* **2.** slight trace.

tin′gle (ting′gəl) *v.,* **-gled, -gling,** *n.* —*v.* **1.** feel or cause slight stings. —*n.* **2.** tingling sensation.

tink′er (ting′kər) *n.* **1.** mender of pots, kettles, pans, etc. —*v.* **2.** do the work of a tinker. **3.** work or repair unskillfully or clumsily.

tin′kle (ting′kəl) *v.,* **-kled, -kling,** *n.* —*v.* **1.** make light ringing sounds. —*n.* **2.** tinkling sound.

tin plate, thin iron or steel sheet coated with tin.

tin′sel (tin′səl) *n.* **1.** glittering metal in strips, etc. **2.** anything showy and worthless.

tint (tint) *n.* **1.** color or hue. —*v.* **2.** apply tint to.

tin•tin•nab•u•la′tion (tin′ti nab′yə lā′shən) *n.* ringing or sound of bells.

ti′ny (tī′nē) *adj.,* **-nier, -niest.** very small.

-tion, suffix meaning action or process, result of action, or state or condition.

tip (tip) *n., v.,* **tipped, tipping.** —*n.* **1.** small gift of money. **2.** piece of private information. **3.** useful hint. **4.** slender or pointed end. **5.** top. —*v.* **6.** give tip to. **7.** furnish with tip. **8.** tilt. **9.** overturn.

tip′-off′, *n. Slang.* hint or warning.

tip′ple, *v.,* **-pled, -pling.** drink alcoholic liquor. —**tip′pler,** *n.*

tip′ster (-stər) *n.* person who sells tips.

tip′sy, *adj.,* **-sier, -siest.** slightly intoxicated.

tip′toe′, *n., v.,* **-toed, -toeing.** —*n.* **1.** tip of toe. —*v.* **2.** move on tiptoes.

tip′top′ (-top′, -top′) *n.* **1.** extreme top. —*adj.* **2.** situated at very top. **3.** *Informal.* of highest excellence.

ti′rade (tī′rād, tī rād′) *n.* long denunciation or speech.

ti′ra•mi•su (tir′ə mē′sōō) *n.* Italian dessert.

tire (tīªr) *v.,* **tired, tiring,** *n.* —*v.* **1.** exhaust strength, interest, patience, etc. —*n.* **2.** hoop of metal, rubber, etc., around wheel. —**tire′less,** *adj.* —**tire′some,** *adj.*

tired (tīªrd) *adj.* **1.** exhausted; fatigued. **2.** weary. —**tired′ly,** *adv.*

tis′sue (tish′ōō) *n.* **1.** substance composing organism. **2.** light, gauzy fabric.

tissue paper, very thin paper.

ti′tan (tīt′n) *n.* person or thing of great size or power. —**ti•tan′ic** (tī-tan′ik) *adj.*

ti•tan′i•um (tī tā′nē əm) *n.* corrosion-resistant metallic element.

tit for tat (tit′ far tat′) equivalent given in retaliation, repartee, etc.

tithe (tīth) *n.* tenth part, paid to church.

ti′tian (tish′ən) *n., adj.* yellowish or golden brown.

tit′il•late′ (tit′l āt′) *v.,* **-lated, -lating.** **1.** tickle. **2.** excite agreeably.

tit′i•vate′ (-ə vāt′) *v.,* **-vated, -vating.** make smart or spruce.

ti′tle (tīt′l) *n., v.,* **-tled, -tling.** —*n.* **1.** name of book, picture, etc. **2.** caption. **3.** appellation, esp. of rank. **4.** championship. **5.** right to something. **6.** document showing this. —*v.* **7.** furnish with title.

tit′mouse′ (tit′mous′) *n., pl.* **-mice.** small bird with crest and conical bill.

tit′ter (tit′ər) *n.* **1.** restrained laugh. —*v.* **2.** laugh in this way.

tit′tle (tit′l) *n.* very small thing.

tit′u•lar (tich′ə lər, tit′yə-) *adj.* **1.** of or having a title. **2.** being so in title only. —**tit′u•lar•ly,** *adv.*

tiz′zy (tiz′ē) *n., pl.* **-zies.** *Slang.* dither.

TN, Tennessee.

TNT, trinitrotoluene.

to (tōō; *unstressed* tŏŏ, tə) *prep.* **1.** particle specifying point reached. **2.** sign of the infinitive. —*adv.* **3.** toward. **4.** to and fro, to or from place or thing.

toad (tōd) *n.* tailless, froglike amphibian.

toad′stool′, *n.* ˙ungus with umbrellalike cap.

toad′y, *n., pl.* **toadies,** *v.,* **toadied, toadying.** —*n.* **1.** fawning flatterer. —*v.* **2.** be toady.

toast (tōst) *n.* **1.** words said before drinking to a person or event. **2.** sliced bread browned by heat. —*v.* **3.** propose as toast. **4.** make toast.

toast′er, *n.* appliance for toasting bread.

toast′mas′ter, *n.* person who introduces the after-dinner speakers or proposes toasts. —**toast′mis′tress,** *n.fem.*

toast′y, *adj.,* **-ier, -iest.** cozily warm.

to•bac′co (tə bak′ō) *n., pl.* **-cos, -coes.** **1.** plant with leaves prepared for smoking or chewing. **2.** the prepared leaves.

to•bac′co•nist (-bak′ə nist) *n.* dealer in tobacco.

to•bog′gan (tə bog′ən) *n.* **1.** long, narrow, flat-bottomed sled. —*v.* **2.** coast on toboggan.

to•day′ (tə dā′) *n.* **1.** this day, time, or period. —*adv.* **2.** on this day. **3.** at this period.

tod′dle (tod′l) *v.,* **-dled, -dling.** go with short, unsteady steps, like a young child. —**tod′dler,** *n.*

tod′dy (tod′ē) *n., pl.* **-dies.** drink made of alcoholic liquor and hot water, sweetened.

to-do′ (tə dōō′) *n., pl.* **to-dos.** *Informal.* fuss.

toe (tō) *n.* **1.** digit of foot. **2.** part covering toes. —**toe′nail′,** *n.*

toe′hold′, *n.* **1.** small niche that supports the toes. **2.** any slight advantage.

tof′fee (tô′fē) *n.* taffy.

to′fu (tō′fōō) *n.* soft cheeselike food made from curdled soybean milk.

to′ga (tō′gə) *n.* ancient Roman outer garment.

to•geth′er (tə geth′ər) *adv.* **1.** into or in proximity, association, or single mass. **2.** at same time. **3.** in cooperation.

to•geth′er•ness, *n.* warm fellowship.

togs, *n.pl. Informal.* clothes.

toil (toil) *n.* **1.** hard, exhausting work. —*v.* **2.** work hard.

toi′let (toi′lit) *n.* **1.** receptacle for excretion. **2.** bathroom. **3.** Also, **toilette′,** act or process of dressing.

toi′let•ry, *n., pl.* **-ries.** article or preparation used in grooming oneself.

toilet water, scented liquid used as light perfume.

to•kay′ (tō kā′) *n.* **1.** rich, sweet, aromatic wine. **2.** the variety of grape from which it is made.

toke (tōk) *n., v.,* **toked, toking.** *Slang.*

—n. 1. puff on marijuana cigarette. **—v. 2.** puff or smoke (marijuana).

to′ken (tō′kən) n. **1.** thing expressing or representing something else. **2.** metal disk used as ticket, etc. **—adj. 3.** being merely a token; minimal.

to′ken•ism, n. minimal conformity to law or social pressure.

tole (tōl) n. enameled or lacquered metal.

tol′er•a•ble (tol′ər ə bəl) adj. **1.** endurable. **2.** fairly good.

tol′er•ance (-əns) n. fairness toward different opinions, etc. **—tol′er•ant,** adj. **—tol′er•ant•ly,** adv.

tol′er•ate′ (-ə rāt′) v., **-ated, -ating. 1.** allow. **2.** put up with. **—tol′er•a′-tion,** n.

toll (tōl) v. **1.** sound bell slowly and repeatedly. **—n. 2.** payment, as for right to travel. **3.** payment for long-distance telephone call.

toll′booth′, n. booth where toll is collected.

tom (tom) n. male of various animals.

tom′a•hawk′ (tom′ə hôk′) n. light ax used by North American Indians.

to•ma′to (tə mā′tō) n., pl. **-toes.** cultivated plant with pulpy, edible fruit.

tomb (tōōm) n. burial place for dead body; grave. **—tomb′stone′,** n.

tom′boy′ (tom′-) n. boisterous, romping girl. **—tom′boy′ish,** adj.

tom′cat′, n. male cat.

Tom Col′lins (kol′inz) tall iced drink containing gin, lemon or lime juice, and carbonated water.

tome (tōm) n. large book.

tom′fool′er•y (tom′fōō′lə rē) n., pl. **-eries.** foolish or silly behavior.

Tommy gun, type of submachine gun.

tom′my•rot′, n. Slang. nonsense.

to•mor′row (tə môr′ō) n. **1.** day after this day. **—adv. 2.** on day after this day.

tom′-tom′, n. primitive drum.

ton (tun) n. unit of weight, equal to 2000 pounds (**short ton**) in U.S. and 2240 pounds (**long ton**) in Great Britain. **2.** Naut. unit of volume, equal to 100 cubic feet.

to•nal′i•ty (tō nal′i tē) n., pl. **-ties. 1.** relation between tones of musical scales. **2.** the tones.

tone (tōn) n., v., **toned, toning. —n. 1.** sound. **2.** quality of sound. **3.** quality, etc., of voice. **4.** firmness. **5.** expressive quality. **6.** elegance; amenity. **—v. 7.** give proper tone to. **—ton′al,** adj.

tone′-deaf′, adj. unable to distinguish differences in musical pitch.

tongs (tôngz) n.pl. two-armed implement for grasping.

tongue (tung) n. **1.** organ on floor of mouth, used for tasting, etc. **2.** language. **3.** tonguelike thing.

tongue′-lash′ing, n. severe scolding.

tongue′-tied′, adj. unable to speak, as from shyness.

tongue twister, sequence of words difficult to pronounce rapidly.

ton′ic (ton′ik) n. **1.** invigorating medicine. **—adj. 2.** invigorating.

to•night′ (tə nīt′) n. **1.** this night. **—adv. 2.** on this night.

ton′nage (tun′ij) n. **1.** carrying capacity or total volume of vessel. **2.** duty on cargo or tonnage. **3.** ships.

ton′sil (ton′səl) n. oval mass of tissue in throat.

ton′sil•lec′to•my (-sə lek′tə mē) n., pl. **-mies.** removal of tonsils.

ton′sil•li′tis (-lī′tis) n. inflammation of tonsils.

ton•so′ri•al (ton sôr′ē əl) adj. of barbers.

ton′sure (ton′shər) n. shaved part of cleric's head.

to′ny (tō′nē) adj., **-ier, -iest.** swank.

too (tōō) adv. **1.** also. **2.** excessively.

tool (tōōl) n. **1.** mechanical instrument, as hammer or saw. **2.** exploited person; dupe. **—v. 3.** decorate with tool.

toot (tōōt) v. sound horn.

tooth (tōōth) n., pl. **teeth** (tēth). **1.** hard white structure attached to jaw, used in chewing. **2.** projection, as on comb or saw. **—tooth′ache′,** n. **—tooth′brush′,** n. **—tooth′paste′,** n. **—tooth′pick′,** n.

tooth and nail, with all one's resources and energy.

tooth′some (-səm) adj. tasty.

tooth′y (tōō′thē, -thē) adj., **toothier, toothiest.** having or displaying conspicuous teeth.

top (top) n., v., **topped, topping. —n. 1.** highest point, part, rank, etc. **2.** lid. **3.** child's spinning toy. **4.** separable upper part of clothing. **—v. 5.** put top on. **6.** be top of. **7.** surpass.

to′paz (tō′paz) n. colored crystalline gem.

top brass, high-ranking officials.

top′coat′, n. light overcoat.

top′flight′ (top′-) adj. excellent.

top hat, man's tall silk hat.

top′-heav′y, adj. disproportionately heavy at top.

top′ic (top′ik) n. subject of discussion or writing.

top′i•cal, adj. **1.** of or dealing with matters of current interest. **2.** of topics. **3.** applied to local area.

top kick, Mil. Slang. first sergeant.

top′mast′, n. mast next above lower mast on sailing ship.

top′most, adj. highest.

top′-notch′, adj. Informal. first-rate.

to•pog′ra•phy (tə pog′rə fē) n., pl. **-phies.** description of features of geographical area.

top′per, n. **1.** one that tops. **2.** Slang. top hat. **3.** short coat worn by women.

top′ping, n. sauce or garnish placed on food.

top′ple, v., **-pled, -pling.** fall; tumble.

top′-se′cret, adj. extremely secret.

top′soil′, n. fertile upper soil.

top′sy-tur′vy (top′sē tûr′vē) adv., adj. **1.** upside down. **2.** in confusion.

tor (tôr) n. hill.

To′rah (tōr′ə, tôr′ə) n. **1.** five books of Moses; Pentateuch. **2.** (also l.c.) whole Jewish Scripture.

torch (tôrch) n. light carried in hand.

torch′bear′er, n. **1.** person who carries torch. **2.** leader in movement.

tor′e•a•dor′ (tôr′ē ə dôr′) n. bullfighter.

tor•ment′ v. (tôr ment′) **1.** cause great suffering to. **—n.** (tôr′ment) **2.** agony. **—tor•men′tor,** n.

tor•na′do (tôr nā′dō) n., pl. **-does, -dos.** destructive storm.

tor•pe′do (tôr pē′dō) n., pl. **-does,** v., **-doed, -doing. —n. 1.** self-propelled missile launched in water and exploding on impact. **—v. 2.** strike with torpedo.

tor′pid (tôr′pid) adj. **1.** inactive; sluggish. **2.** dull; apathetic; lethargic. **—tor•pid′i•ty,** n.

tor′por (-pər) n. **1.** suspension of physical activity. **2.** apathy.

torque (tôrk) n. rotating force.

tor′rent (tôr′ənt) n. rapid, violent stream. **—tor•ren′tial** (tô ren′shəl, tə-) adj. **—tor•ren′tial•ly,** adv.

tor′rid (tôr′id) adj. **1.** very hot. **2.** passionate.

tor′sion (tôr′shən) n. **1.** act of twisting. **2.** twisting by two opposite torques. **—tor′sion•al,** adj.

tor′so (tôr′sō) n., pl. **-sos, -si.** trunk of body.

tort (tôrt) n. Law. civil wrong (other than breach of contract or trust) for which law requires damages.

torte (tôrt) n., pl. **tortes.** rich cake, made with eggs and nuts.

tor′tel•li′ni (tôr′tl ē′nē) n. (used with sing. or pl. v.) small ring-shaped pieces of pasta filled with meat or cheese.

tor•til′la (tôr tē′ə) n. flat, round bread of Mexico, made from cornmeal or wheat flour.

tor′toise (tôr′təs) n. turtle.

tor′toise-shell′, n. **1.** horny brown and yellow shell of certain turtles, used for making combs, etc. **2.** synthetic tortoiseshell. **—adj. 3.** colored like tortoiseshell.

tor′tu•ous (tôr′chōō əs) adj. **1.** twisting; winding. **2.** indirect.

tor′ture (tôr′chər) n., v., **-tured, -turing. —n. 1.** infliction of great pain. **—v. 2.** subject to torture.

To′ry (tōr′ē) n., pl. **-ries. 1.** (also l.c.) conservative. **2.** American supporter of Great Britain during Revolutionary period. **—To′ry•ism,** n.

toss (tôs) v. **1.** throw or pitch. **2.** pitch about. **3.** throw upward. **—n. 4.** throw or pitch.

toss′up′, n. **1.** tossing of coin to decide something by its fall. **2.** Informal. even chance.

tot (tot) n. small child.

to′tal (tōt′l) adj., n., v., **-taled, -taling. —adj. 1.** entire. **2.** utter; outright. **—n. 3.** total amount. **—v. 4.** add up. **—to•tal′i•ty** (-tal′i tē) n.

to•tal′i•tar′i•an (tō tal′i târ′ē ən) adj. of centralized government under sole control of one party. **—to•tal′i•tar′i•an•ism,** n.

tote (tōt) v., **toted, toting,** n. Informal. **—v. 1.** carry or bear, as burden. **—n. 2.** act or course of toting. **3.** that which is toted. **4.** tote bag.

tote bag, open handbag.

to′tem (tō′təm) n. object in nature assumed as emblem of clan, family, or related group.

totem pole, pole with totemic figures, erected by Indians of northwest coast of North America.

tot′ter (tot′ər) v. **1.** falter. **2.** sway as if about to fall.

tou′can (tōō′kan, -kän) n. large-beaked tropical American bird.

touch (tuch) v. **1.** put hand, finger, etc., in contact with something. **2.** come or be in contact. **3.** reach. **4.** affect with sympathy. **5.** refer to. **—n. 6.** act or instance of touching. **7.** perception of things through contact. **8.** contact. **—touch′ing,** adj.

touch′ and go′, precarious condition.

touch′down′, n. Football. act of player in touching ball down to ground behind opponent's goal line.

tou•ché′ (tōō shā′) interj. (used to acknowledge telling remark or rejoinder).

touched, adj. **1.** moved; stirred. **2.** slightly crazy; unbalanced.

touch′-me-not′, n. yellow-flowered plant whose ripe seed vessels burst open when touched.

touch′stone′, n. **1.** stone used to test purity of gold and silver by color produced when it is rubbed with them. **2.** any criterion.

touch′y, adj., **-ier, -iest. 1.** irritable. **2.** requiring tact. —**touch′i•ness,** n.

tough (tuf) adj. **1.** not easily broken. **2.** difficult to chew. **3.** sturdy. **4.** pugnacious. **5.** trying. —n. **6.** ruffian. —**tough′en,** v.

tou•pee′ (tōō pā′) n. wig or patch of false hair worn to cover bald spot.

tour (tŏŏr) v. **1.** travel or travel through, esp. for pleasure. —n. **2.** trip. **3.** period of duty. —**tour′ist,** n. —**tour′ism,** n.

tour′ de force′ (tŏŏr′ də fôrs′) n., pl. **tours de force.** exceptional achievement.

tour′na•ment (tŏŏr′nə mənt, tûr′-) n. **1.** meeting for contests. **2.** contest between mounted knights. **3.** competition involving number of rounds. Also, **tour′ney.**

tour′ni•quet (tûr′ni kit, tŏŏr′-) n. bandlike device for arresting bleeding by compressing blood vessels.

tou′sle (tou′zəl, -səl) v., **-sled, -sling.** dishevel.

tout (tout) Informal. —v. **1.** solicit (business, votes, etc.) importunately. **2.** advertise. **3.** give tip on (race, etc.). —n. **4.** person who touts.

tow (tō) v. **1.** drag by rope or chain. —n. **2.** act of towing. **3.** thing towed.

to•ward′ (tôrd, twôrd) prep. Also, **to•wards′. 1.** in direction of. **2.** with respect to. **3.** nearly.

tow′boat′, n. boat for pushing barges.

tow′el (tou′əl, toul) n. cloth or paper for wiping.

tow′el•ing, n. fabric of cotton or linen used for towels.

tow′er (tou′ər) n. **1.** tall structure. —v. **2.** rise high.

tow′er•ing, adj. **1.** very high or great. **2.** violent; furious.

tow′head′ (tō′hed′) n. person with light-colored hair.

town (toun) n. **1.** small city. **2.** center of city. —**towns′man,** n. —**towns′wom′an,** n.fem. —**towns′peo′ple, towns′folk′,** n.pl.

town house, one of group of similar houses joined by common side walls.

town meeting, meeting of voters in town.

town′ship, n. **1.** division of county. **2.** (in U.S. surveys) district 6 miles square.

tow′path′ (tō′path′) n. path along bank of canal or river.

tox•e′mi•a (tok sē′mē ə) n. blood poisoning resulting from presence of toxins in blood. —**tox•e′mic,** adj.

tox′ic (tok′sik) adj. **1.** of toxin. **2.** poisonous. —**tox•ic′i•ty,** n.

tox′i•col′o•gy (-si kol′ə jē) n. science of poisons.

toxic shock syndrome, rapidly developing toxemia.

tox′in (tok′sin) n. poisonous product of organism.

toy (toi) n. **1.** plaything. —v. **2.** play.

trace (trās) n., v., **traced, tracing.** —n. **1.** mark or trace left by something. **2.** small amount. —v. **3.** follow trace of. **4.** find out. **5.** draw over lines of.

trac′er•y, n., pl. **-eries.** ornamental pattern of interlacing lines, etc.

tra′che•a (trā′kē ə) n., pl. **-cheae** (-kē ē′). air-conveying tube from larynx to bronchi.

tra′che•ot′o•my (-ot′ə mē) n., pl. **-mies.** operation of cutting into trachea to help person breathe.

track (trak) n. **1.** parallel rails for railroad. **2.** wheel rut. **3.** footprint or other mark left. **4.** path. **5.** course. —v. **6.** follow; pursue.

track′ball′, n. computer input device for controlling pointer on screen by rotating ball set inside case.

track record, record of achievements or performance.

tract (trakt) n. **1.** region. **2.** brief treatise.

trac′ta•ble (trak′tə bəl) adj. easily managed. —**trac′ta•bil′i•ty,** n.

trac′tion (-shən) n. **1.** act or instance of pulling. **2.** adhesive friction.

trac′tor (-tər) n. vehicle for pulling farm machinery, etc.

trade (trād) n., v., **traded, trading.** —n. **1.** buying, selling, or exchange of commodities; commerce. **2.** exchange. **3.** occupation. —v. **4.** buy and sell. **5.** exchange. —**trad′er,** n. —**trades′man,** n.

trade′-in′, n. goods given in whole or part payment for purchase.

trade′mark′, n. name, symbol, etc., identifying brand or source of things for sale.

trade name, word or phrase whereby particular class of goods is designated.

trade′-off′, n. exchange of one thing for another.

trade union, labor union.

trade wind (wind) sea wind blowing toward equator from latitudes up to 30° away.

tra•di′tion (trə dish′ən) n. **1.** handing down of beliefs, customs, etc., through generations. **2.** something so handed down. —**tra•di′tion•al,** adj. —**tra•di′tion•al•ist,** n., adj.

tra•duce′ (trə dōōs′, -dyōōs′) v., **-duced, -ducing.** slander.

traf′fic (traf′ik) n., v., **-ficked, -ficking.** —n. **1.** traveling persons and things. **2.** trade. —v. **3.** trade.

traffic circle, circular roadway at multiple intersection.

traffic light, set of signal lights at intersection.

tra•ge′di•an (trə jē′dē ən) n. actor or writer of tragedy. —**tra•ge′di•enne′,** n.fem.

trag′e•dy (traj′i dē) n., pl. **-dies. 1.** serious drama with unhappy ending. **2.** sad event. —**trag′ic,** adj.

trail (trāl) v. **1.** draw or drag. **2.** be drawn or dragged. **3.** track. —n. **4.** path. **5.** track, scent, etc., left.

trail′blaz′er, n. pioneer.

trail′er, n. van attached to truck for hauling freight, etc. **2.** vehicle attached to car or truck with accommodations for living.

train (trān) n. **1.** railroad locomotive with cars. **2.** moving line of persons, vehicles, etc. **3.** series of events, ideas, etc. **4.** trailing part. —v. **5.** instruct or undergo instruction. **6.** make or get fit. **7.** direct. —**train•ee′,** n. —**train′er,** n.

traipse (trāps) v., **traipsed, traipsing.** Informal. walk aimlessly.

trait (trāt) n. characteristic.

trai′tor (trā′tər) n. **1.** betrayer of trust. **2.** person guilty of treason.

tra•jec′to•ry (trə jek′tə rē) n., pl. **-ries.** curve described by projectile in flight.

tram (tram) n. Brit. streetcar.

tram′mel (tram′əl) n., v. **-meled, -meling.** —n. **1.** impediment to action. —v. **2.** hamper.

tramp (tramp) v. **1.** tread or walk firmly. **2.** march. —n. **3.** firm, heavy tread. **4.** hike. **5.** vagabond.

tram′ple, v., **-pled, -pling.** step roughly on.

tram′po•line′ (tram′pə lēn′, -lin) n.

cloth or rubber sheet attached to frame by springs for tumbling.

trance (trans) n. half-conscious or hypnotic state.

tran′quil (trang′kwil) adj. peaceful; quiet. —**tran′quil•ly,** adv. —**tran•quil′li•ty,** n. —**tran′quil•ize′,** v.

tran′quil•iz′er (-kwi lī′zər) n. drug to reduce tension.

trans-, prefix meaning across; through; on the other side; changing thoroughly; beyond or surpassing.

trans•act′ (tran sakt′, -zakt′) v. carry on business. —**trans•ac′tion,** n.

trans•at•lan′tic (trans′at lan′tik, tranz′-) adj. **1.** passing across Atlantic. **2.** on other side of Atlantic.

trans•ceiv′er (tran sē′vər) n. radio transmitter and receiver combined.

tran•scend′ (tran send′) v. **1.** go or be beyond. **2.** excel.

tran•scend′ent, adj. **1.** extraordinary. **2.** superior; supreme.

tran•scen•den′tal (tran′sen den′tl, -sən-) adj. beyond ordinary human experience.

trans•con•ti•nen′tal (trans′kon tn-en′tl) adj. across a continent.

tran•scribe′ (tran skrīb′) v., **-scribed, -scribing. 1.** copy. **2.** make recording of. —**tran•scrip′tion** (-skrip′shən), **tran′script,** n.

trans•duc′er (trans dōō′sər, -dyōō′, tranz-) n. device that converts signal from one form of energy to another.

tran′sept (tran′sept) n. transverse portion of cross-shaped church.

trans•fer′, v., **-ferred, -ferring,** n. —v. (trans fûr′, trans′far) **1.** convey, hand over, or transport. **2.** be transferred. —n. (trans′far) **3.** means or act of transferring. —**trans•fer′a•ble,** adj. —**trans•fer′al,** n. —**trans•fer′ence,** n.

trans•fig′ure, v., **-ured, -uring. 1.** transform. **2.** glorify.

trans•fix′, v. **1.** pierce. **2.** paralyze with terror, etc.

trans•form′, v. change in form, nature, etc. —**trans′for•ma′tion,** n.

trans•form′er, n. device for converting electrical currents.

trans•fuse′ (-fyōōz′) v., **-fused, -fusing. 1.** transmit, as by pouring. **2.** transfer blood from one person to another. —**trans•fu′sion,** n.

trans•gress′ (trans gres′, tranz-) v. **1.** go beyond limit. **2.** violate law, moral code, etc. —**trans•gres′sion** (-gresh′-ən) n. —**trans•gres′sor,** n.

tran′sient (tran′shənt, -zhənt, -zē-ənt) adj. **1.** lasting or staying only a short time. —n. **2.** transient person.

tran•sis′tor (tran zis′tər) n. small electronic device replacing vacuum tube.

trans′it (tran′sit, -zit) n. passage or conveyance.

tran•si′tion (tran zish′ən, -sish′-) n. passage from one condition, etc., to another. —**tran•si′tion•al,** adj.

tran′si•tive (tran′si tiv, -zi-) adj. (of verb) regularly accompanied by direct object. —**tran′si•tive•ly,** adv.

tran′si•to′ry (tran′si tôr′ē, -zi-) adj. **1.** not enduring. **2.** brief.

trans•late′ (trans lāt′, tranz-, trans′lāt, tranz′-) v., **-lated, -lating.** change from one language into another. —**trans•la′tion,** n. —**trans•lat′a•ble,** adj. —**trans•lat′or,** n.

trans•lit′er•ate′ (-lit′ə rāt′) v., **-ated, -ating.** change into corresponding characters of another alphabet or language.

trans•lu′cent (-lōō′sənt) adj. not transparent but transmitting light diffusely.

trans'mi•gra'tion, *n.* passage of soul into another body.

trans•mis'sion (-mish'ən) *n.* **1.** act or process of transmitting. **2.** something transmitted. **3.** set of gears to transfer force between mechanisms, as in automobile. **4.** broadcast.

trans•mit' (-mit') *v.,* **-mitted, -mitting. 1.** send over or along. **2.** communicate. **3.** hand down. **4.** cause or permit light, heat, etc., to pass through. **5.** emit radio waves. **—trans•mit'ter,** *n.*

trans•mog'ri•fy' (-mog'rə fī') *v.,* **-fied, -fying.** change in appearance or form; transform.

trans•mute' (-myōōt') *v.,* **-muted, -muting.** change from one nature or form to another. **—trans•mut'a•ble,** *adj.* **—trans•mu•ta'tion,** *n.*

trans•na'tion•al, *adj.* going beyond national boundaries or interests.

trans'o•ce•an'ic, *adj.* across or beyond ocean.

tran'som (tran'səm) *n.* window above door.

trans'pa•cif'ic (trans'-) *adj.* passing across Pacific.

trans•par'ent (-pâr'ənt) *adj.* **1.** allowing objects to be seen clearly through it. **2.** frank. **3.** obvious. **—trans•par'en•cy,** *n.*

tran•spire' (tran spīr') *v.,* **-spired, -spiring. 1.** occur. **2.** give off waste matter, etc., from surface.

trans•plant' *v.* (trans plant') **1.** remove and put or plant in another place. **—n. 2.** (trans'plant') act of transplanting. **3.** something transplanted. **—trans'plan•ta'tion,** *n.*

trans•port' *v.* (trans pôrt') **1.** convey from one place to another. **2.** enrapture. **—n.** (trans'pôrt) **3.** something that transports. **—trans'por•ta'tion,** *n.* **—trans•port'er,** *n.*

trans•pose' (-pōz') *v.,* **-posed, -posing.** alter relative position, order, musical key, etc. **—trans'po•si'tion,** *n.*

trans•sex'u•al, *n.* **1.** person with sex surgically altered. **2.** person feeling identity with opposite sex.

trans•ship', *v.,* **-shipped, -shipping.** transfer from one conveyance to another. **—trans•ship'ment,** *n.*

trans'sub•stan'ti•a'tion, *n.* (in the Eucharist) conversion of whole substance of bread and wine into body and blood of Christ.

trans•verse' (trans vûrs', tranz-; trans'vûrs, tranz'-) *adj.* **1.** lying across. **—n. 2.** something transverse. **—trans•verse'ly,** *adv.*

trans•ves'tite (trans ves'tīt, tranz-) *n.* person who dresses like opposite sex.

trap (trap) *n., v.,* **trapped, trapping. —n. 1.** device for catching animals. **2.** scheme for catching a person unawares. **3.** U-shaped section in pipe to prevent escape of air or gases. **—v. 4.** catch in or set traps.

tra•peze' (tra pēz', trə-) *n.* suspended bar used in gymnastics.

trap'e•zoid' (trap'ə zoid') *n.* four-sided figure with two parallel sides.

trap'pings, *n.pl.* equipment or dress.

trap'shoot•ing, *n.* sport of shooting at clay pigeons hurled from trap.

trash (trash) *n.* rubbish. **—trash'y,** *adj.*

trau'ma (trou'mə, trô'-) *n., pl.* **-mata, traumas. 1.** externally produced injury. **2.** experience causing permanent psychological harm. **—trau•mat'ic** (-mat'ik) *adj.*

tra•vail' (trə vāl', trav'āl) *n.* **1.** toil. **2.** labor pains.

trav'el (trav'əl) *v.,* **-eled, -eling,** *n.* **—v. 1.** journey. **2.** move. **—n. 3.** journeying. **—trav'el•er,** *n.*

trav'e•logue' or **-log'** (-lôg', -log'), *n.* lecture or film describing travels.

trav•erse, *v.,* **-ersed, -ersing,** *n.* **—v.** (trə vûrs', trav'ərs) **1.** pass over or through. **—n.** (trav'ərs, trə vûrs') **2.** act of traversing.

trav'es•ty (trav'ə stē) *n., pl.* **-ties,** *v.,* **-tied, -tying. —n. 1.** literary burlesque. **2.** debased likeness. **—v. 3.** make travesty on.

trawl (trôl) *n.* **1.** fishing net dragged on bottom of water. **—v. 2.** fish with trawl. **—trawl'er,** *n.*

tray (trā) *n.* flat, shallow receptacle or container.

treach'er•y (trech'ə rē) *n., pl.* **-eries.** betrayal; treason. **—treach'er•ous,** *adj.*

trea•cle (trē'kəl), *n.* something very sweet or sentimental.

tread (tred) *v.,* **trod** (trod), **trodden** or **trod, treading,** *n.* **—v. 1.** step, walk, or trample. **2.** crush. **—n. 3.** manner of walking. **4.** surface meeting road or rail. **5.** horizontal surface of step. **—tread'er,** *n.*

trea'dle (tred'l) *n.* lever, etc., worked by foot to drive machine.

tread'mill', *n.* apparatus worked by treading on moving steps, as for exercise.

trea'son (trē'zən) *n.* violation of allegiance to sovereign or state.

treas'ure (trezh'ər) *n., v.,* **-ured, -uring. —n. 1.** accumulated wealth. **2.** thing greatly valued. **—v. 3.** prize. **4.** put away for future use.

treas'ure-trove' (-trōv') *n.* **1.** anything valuable that one finds. **2.** treasure of unknown ownership, found hidden.

treas'ur•y, *n., pl.* **-uries. 1.** place for keeping public or private funds. **2.** the funds. **3.** (*cap.*) government department that handles funds. **—treas'ur•er,** *n.*

treat (trēt) *v.* **1.** behave toward. **2.** deal with. **3.** relieve or cure. **4.** discuss. **5.** entertain. **—n. 6.** entertainment. **7.** something special and enjoyable. **—treat'ment,** *n.*

trea'tise (trē'tis) *n.* writing on particular subject.

trea'ty (trē'tē) *n., pl.* **-ties.** formal agreement between states.

tre'ble (treb'əl) *adj., n., v.,* **-bled, -bling. —adj. 1.** triple. **2.** of highest pitch or range. **—n. 3.** treble part in music. **—v. 4.** triple.

tree (trē) *n., v.,* **treed, treeing. —n. 1.** plant with permanent, woody, usually branched trunk. **—v. 2.** drive up tree.

tre'foil (trē'foil, tref'oil) *n.* herb with leaf divided in three parts.

trek (trek) *v.,* **trekked, trekking,** *n.* journey.

trel'lis (trel'is) *n.* lattice.

trem'ble (trem'bəl) *v.,* **-bled, -bling,** *n.* **—v. 1.** quiver. **—n. 2.** act or state of trembling.

tre•men'dous (tri men'dəs) *adj.* extraordinarily great.

trem'o•lo (trem'ə lō') *n., pl.* **-los.** vibrating effect on instrument or in voice.

trem'or (trem'ər, trē'mər) *n.* **1.** involuntary shaking. **2.** vibration.

trem'u•lous (trem'yə ləs) *adj.* **1.** trembling. **2.** fearful.

trench (trench) *n.* ditch or cut.

trench'ant (tren'chənt) *adj.* **1.** incisive. **2.** vigorous.

trench coat, belted raincoat with epaulets.

trench'er, *n.* flat piece of wood on which meat is served or carved.

trench'er•man, *n., pl.* **-men.** person with hearty appetite.

trench foot, disease of feet due to prolonged exposure to cold and wet.

trench mouth, acute ulcerating infection of gums and teeth.

trend (trend) *n.* **1.** tendency. **2.** increasingly popular fashion.

trend'y, *adj.,* **-ier, -iest.** *Informal.* following current fads.

trep'i•da'tion (trep'i dā'shən) *n.* fearful anxiety.

tres'pass (tres'pəs, -pas) *v.* **1.** enter property illicitly. **2.** sin. **—n. 3.** act of trespassing. **—tres'pass•er,** *n.*

tress (tres) *n.* braid of hair.

tres'tle (tres'əl) *n.* supporting frame or framework.

tri-, prefix meaning three.

tri'ad (trī'ad, -əd) *n.* group of three.

tri•age' (trē äzh') *n.* sorting victims to determine priority of medical treatment.

tri'al (trī'əl) *n.* **1.** examination before judicial tribunal. **2.** test. **3.** attempt. **4.** state of being tested. **5.** source of suffering.

tri'an•gle (trī'ang'gəl) *n.* figure with three straight sides and three angles. **—tri•an'gu•lar,** *adj.*

Tri•as'sic (trī as'ik) *adj.* pertaining to period of Mesozoic Era.

tribe (trīb) *n.* people united by common descent, etc. **—trib'al,** *adj.*

tribes'man, *n., pl.* **-men.** man belonging to tribe. **—tribes'wom'an,** *n. fem.*

trib'u•la'tion (trib'yə lā'shən) *n.* **1.** trouble. **2.** affliction.

tri•bu'nal (trī byōōn'l, tri-) *n.* **1.** court of justice. **2.** place of judgment.

trib'une (trib'yōōn, tri byōōn') *n.* **1.** person who defends rights of the people. **2.** rostrum.

trib'u•tar'y (trib'yə ter'ē) *n., pl.* **-taries,** *adj.* **—n. 1.** stream flowing into larger body of water. **—adj. 2.** flowing as tributary.

trib'ute (trib'yōōt) *n.* **1.** speech or gift expressing gratitude or respect. **2.** tax paid to acknowledge subjugation.

trice (trīs) *n.* instant.

tri'cen•ten'ni•al (trī'sen ten'ē əl) *n.* tercentennial.

tri'ceps (trī'seps) *n.* muscle at back of upper arm.

trick (trik) *n.* **1.** artifice or stratagem. **2.** prank. **3.** knack. **4.** cards won in one round. **—v. 5.** deceive or cheat by tricks. **—trick'er•y,** *n.* **—trick'ster,** *n.* **—trick'y,** *adj.*

trick'le (trik'əl) *v.,* **-led, -ling,** *n.* **—v. 1.** flow in small amounts. **—n. 2.** trickling flow.

tri'col'or (trī'kul'ər) *adj.* **1.** of three colors. **—n. 2.** three-colored flag, esp. of France.

tri•cus'pid, *adj.* having three cusps or points, as tooth.

tri'cy•cle (trī'si kəl, -sik'əl) *n.* child's vehicle with large front wheel and two smaller rear wheels.

tri'dent (trīd'nt) *n.* three-pronged spear.

tried (trīd) *adj.* tested; proved.

tri•en'ni•al (trī en'ē əl) *adj.* **1.** lasting three years. **2.** occurring every three years. **—n. 3.** period of three years. **4.** third anniversary.

tri'fle (trī'fəl) *n., v.,* **-fled, -fling. —n. 1.** article of small value. **2.** trivial matter or amount. **—v. 3.** deal without due respect. **4.** act idly or frivolously. **—tri'fling,** *adj.*

trig'ger (trig'ər) *n.* **1.** projecting

tongue pressed to fire gun. **2.** device to release spring. —*v.* **3.** precipitate.

tri•go•nom•e•try (trig′ə nom′i trē) *n.* mathematical study of relations between sides and angles of triangles.

trill (tril) *v.* **1.** sing or play with vibratory effect. —*n.* **2.** act or sound of trilling.

tril/lion (tril′yən) *n., adj.* 1 followed by 12 zeroes.

tril/o•gy (tril′ə jē) *n., pl.* **-gies.** group of three plays, operas, etc., on related theme.

trim (trim) *v.,* **trimmed, trimming,** *n., adj.,* **trimmer, trimmest.** —*v.* **1.** make neat by clipping, paring, etc. **2.** adjust (sails or yards). **3.** dress or ornament. —*n.* **4.** proper condition. **5.** adjustment of sails, etc. **6.** dress or equipment. **7.** trimming. —*adj.* **8.** neat. **9.** in good condition. —**trim′ly,** *adv.* —**trim′mer,** *n.*

tri•ma•ran/ (trī′mə ran′) *n.* boat with three hulls.

tri•mes/ter (trī mes′tər, trī′mes-) *n.* **1.** period of three months. **2.** one of three divisions of academic year.

trim/ming (trim′ing) *n.* something used to decorate.

tri•ni/tro•tol/u•ene/ (trī nī′trō tol′yōō ēn′) *n.* high explosive, known as TNT.

Trin/i•ty (trin′i tē) *n.* unity of Father, Son, and Holy Ghost.

trin/ket (tring′kit) *n.* **1.** bit of jewelry, etc. **2.** trifle.

tri/o (trē′ō) *n., pl.* **trios.** group of three.

trip (trip) *n., v.,* **tripped, tripping.** —*n.* **1.** journey. **2.** stumble. **3.** *Slang.* drug-induced event. —*v.* **4.** stumble or cause to stumble. **5.** slip. **6.** tread quickly. —**trip′per,** *n.*

tri•par/tite (trī pär′tīt) *adj.* **1.** divided into or consisting of three parts. **2.** participated in by three parties.

tripe (trīp) *n.* **1.** ruminant's stomach, used as food. **2.** *Slang.* worthless statements or writing.

tri/ple (trip′əl) *adj., n., v.,* **-pled, -pling.** —*adj.* **1.** of three parts. **2.** three times as great. —*n.* **3.** *Baseball.* hit allowing batter to reach third base. —*v.* **4.** make or become triple. —**tri′ply,** *adv.*

tri/plet (trip′lit) *n.* one of three children born at a single birth.

trip•li•cate (-li kit, -kāt′) *adj.* **1.** triple. —*n.* **2.** set of three copies.

tri/pod (trī′pod) *n.* three-legged stool, support, etc.

trip/tych (trip′tik) *n.* set of three panels side by side, with pictures or carvings.

trite (trīt) *adj.,* **triter, tritest.** commonplace; hackneyed.

trit/u•rate/ (trich′ə rāt′) *v.,* **-rated, -rating,** *n.* —*v.* (trich′ə rāt′) **1.** to reduce to fine particles or powder; pulverize. —*n.* (-ər it) **2.** triturated substance.

tri/umph (trī′əmf, -umf) *n.* **1.** victory. **2.** joy over victory. —*v.* **3.** be victorious or successful. **4.** rejoice over this. —**tri•um/phal,** *adj.* —**tri•um/phant,** *adj.*

tri•um/vir (trī um′vər) *n., pl.* **-virs, -viri** (-və rī′). *Rom. Hist.* any of three magistrates exercising same public function.

tri•um/vi•rate (-vər it, -və rāt′) *n.* **1.** *Rom. Hist.* the office of triumvir. **2.** government of three joint magistrates. **3.** association of three, as in office.

triv/et (triv′it) *n.* device protecting table top from hot objects.

triv/i•a (triv′ē ə) *n.* things that are very unimportant.

triv/i•al, *adj.* trifling. —**triv/i•al/i•ty,** *n.* —**triv/i•al•ly,** *adv.*

tro/chee (trō′kē) *n.* verse foot of two syllables, long followed by short. —**tro•cha/ic** (-kā′ik) *adj.*

trog/lo•dyte/ (trog′lə dīt′) *n.* **1.** cave dweller. **2.** hermit.

troi/ka (troi′ka) *n.* **1.** Russian vehicle drawn by three horses. **2.** ruling group of three.

troll (trōl) *v.* **1.** sing in rolling voice. **2.** sing as round. **3.** fish with moving line. —*n.* **4.** *Music.* round. **5.** underground monster.

trol/ley (trol′ē) *n.* **1.** trolley car. **2.** pulley on overhead track or wire.

trolley bus, bus drawing power from overhead wires.

trolley car, electric streetcar receiving current from a trolley.

trol/lop (trol′əp) *n.* **1.** untidy or slovenly woman. **2.** prostitute.

trom•bone/ (trom bōn′, trom′bōn) *n.* brass wind instrument with long bent tube. —**trom•bon/ist,** *n.*

troop (trōōp) *n.* **1.** assemblage. **2.** cavalry unit. **3.** body of police, etc. —*v.* **4.** gather or move in numbers. **5.** walk, as if in a march.

troop/ship/, *n.* ship for conveyance of military troops; transport.

tro/phy (trō′fē) *n., pl.* **-phies.** **1.** memento taken in hunting, war, etc. **2.** silver cup, etc., given as prize.

trop/ic (trop′ik) *n.* **1.** either of two latitudes (**tropic of Cancer** and **tropic of Capricorn**) bounding torrid zone. **2.** (*pl.*) region between these latitudes. —**trop/i•cal,** *adj.*

trop/o•sphere/ (trop′ə sfēr′, trō′pə-) *n.* lowest layer of atmosphere.

trot (trot) *v.,* **trotted, trotting,** *n.* —*v.* **1.** go at gait between walk and run. **2.** go briskly. **3.** ride at trot. —*n.* **4.** trotting gait. —**trot/ter,** *n.*

troth (trôth, trōth) *n.* **1.** fidelity. **2.** promise.

trou/ba•dour/ (trōō′bə dôr′) *n.* medieval lyric poet of W Mediterranean area who wrote on love and gallantry.

trou/ble (trub′əl) *v.,* **-bled, -bling,** *n.* —*v.* **1.** distress. **2.** put to or cause inconvenience. **3.** bother. —*n.* **4.** annoyance or difficulty. **5.** disturbance. **6.** inconvenience. —**trou/ble•some,** *adj.*

trou/bled, *adj.* **1.** emotionally or mentally distressed. **2.** economically or socially distressed.

trou/ble•mak/er, *n.* person who causes trouble.

troub/le•shoot/er, *n.* expert in eliminating causes of trouble.

trough (trôf) *n.* **1.** open boxlike container. **2.** long hollow or channel.

trounce (trouns) *v.,* **trounced, trouncing.** beat severely.

troupe (trōōp) *n.* company of performers. —**troup/er,** *n.*

trou/sers (trou′zərz) *n.pl.* outer garment divided into two separate leg coverings.

trous/seau (trōō′sō, trōō sō′) *n., pl.* **-seaux, -seaus** (-sōz). bride's outfit.

trout (trout) *n.* freshwater game fish.

trow/el (trou′əl) *n.* **1.** tool for spreading or smoothing. **2.** small digging tool.

troy (troi) *adj.* expressed in troy weight.

troy weight, system of weights for precious metals and gems.

tru/ant (trōō′ənt) *n.* **1.** student absent from school without leave. —*adj.* **2.** absent from school without leave. —**tru/an•cy,** *n.*

truce (trōōs) *n.* suspension of military hostilities.

truck (truk) *n.* **1.** hand or motor vehicle for carrying heavy loads. —*v.* **2.** transport by or drive a truck. **3.** trade. —**truck/er,** *n.*

truck/le (truk′əl) *v.,* **-led, -ling.** submit humbly.

truckle bed, trundle bed.

truc/u•lent (truk′yə lənt, trōō′kyə-) *adj.* aggressive. —**truc/u•lence,** *n.*

trudge (truj) *v.,* **trudged, trudging,** *n.* —*v.* **1.** walk, esp. wearily. —*n.* **2.** tiring walk.

true (trōō) *adj.,* **truer, truest.** **1.** conforming to fact. **2.** real. **3.** sincere. **4.** loyal. **5.** correct. —**tru/ly,** *adv.* —**true/ness,** *n.*

true/-blue/, *adj.* staunch; true.

truf/fle (truf′əl) *n.* **1.** edible fungus. **2.** chocolate confection resembling truffle.

tru/ism (trōō′iz əm) *n.* obvious truth.

trump (trump) *n.* **1.** playing card of suit outranking other suits. **2.** the suit itself. —*v.* **3.** take with or play trump. **4.** fabricate.

trump/er•y, *n., adj.* **-eries.** nonsense; twaddle.

trum/pet (trum′pit) *n.* **1.** brass wind instrument with powerful, penetrating tone. —*v.* **2.** blow trumpet. **3.** proclaim. —**trum/pet•er,** *n.*

trun/cate (trung′kāt) *v.,* **-cated, -cating.** shorten by cutting.

trun/cheon (trun′chən) *n.* club.

trun/dle (trun′dl) *v.,* **-dled, -dling,** *n.* —*v.* **1.** roll, as on wheels. —*n.* **2.** small roller, wheel, etc.

trundle bed, low bed on casters, usually pushed under another bed when not in use. Also, **truckle bed.**

trunk (trungk) *n.* **1.** main stem of tree. **2.** box for clothes, etc. **3.** body of person or animal, excepting head and limbs. **4.** storage space in car. **5.** elephant's long flexible nasal appendage. **6.** *pl.* shorts.

trunk line, **1.** major long-distance transportation line. **2.** telephone line between two switching devices.

truss (trus) *v.* **1.** bind or fasten. **2.** furnish or support with a truss. —*n.* **3.** rigid supporting framework. **4.** apparatus for confining hernia.

trust (trust) *n.* **1.** reliance on person's integrity, justice, etc. **2.** confident hope. **3.** credit. **4.** responsibility. **5.** care. **6.** something entrusted. **7.** holding of legal title for another's benefit. **8.** combination of companies, often monopolistic, controlled by central board. —*v.* **9.** place confidence in. **10.** rely on. **11.** hope. **12.** believe. **13.** give credit. —**trust/wor/thy,** *adj.*

trus•tee/, *n.* **1.** administrator of company, etc. **2.** holder of trust (def. 7).

trus•tee/ship, *n.* **1.** office of trustee. **2.** control of territory granted by United Nations. **3.** the territory.

trust fund, money, etc., held in trust.

trust territory, territory which United Nations has placed under administrative control of a country.

trust/y, *adj.,* **-ier, -iest,** *n., pl.* **trust-ies.** —*adj.* **1.** reliable. —*n.* **2.** trusted one. **3.** trustworthy convict given special privileges.

truth (trōōth) *n.* **1.** true facts. **2.** conformity with fact. **3.** established fact, principle, etc. —**truth/ful,** *adj.*

try (trī) *v.,* **tried, trying.** **1.** attempt. **2.** test. **3.** examine judicially. **4.** strain endurance, patience, etc., of.

try/ing, *adj.* annoying; irksome.

try/out/, *n. Informal.* trial or test to ascertain fitness for some purpose.

tryst (trist, trīst) *n.* **1.** appointment, as

of lovers, to meet. **2.** the meeting. **3.** place of meeting. —*v.* **4.** meet.

tsar (zär, tsär) *n.* czar.

tset/se fly (tset/sē, tsē/tsē) African fly transmitting disease.

T/-shirt/, *n.* short-sleeved knitted undershirt. Also, **tee/-shirt/.**

tsp., teaspoon.

T square, T-shaped ruler used in mechanical drawing.

tsu·na·mi (tsŏŏ nä/mē) *n., pl.* **-mis.** large sea wave caused by undersea earthquake.

tub (tub) *n.* **1.** bathtub. **2.** deep, open-topped container.

tu/ba (tŏŏ/bə, tyŏŏ/-) *n.* low-pitched brass wind instrument.

tub/by (tub/ē) *adj.* **-bier, -biest.** short and fat.

tube (tŏŏb, tyŏŏb) *n.* **1.** hollow pipe for fluids, etc. **2.** compressible container for toothpaste, etc. **3.** railroad or vehicular tunnel. —**tu/bu·lar** (-byə-lər) *adj.* —**tub/ing,** *n.*

tu/ber (tŏŏ/bər, tyŏŏ/-) *n.* fleshy thickening of underground stem or shoot. —**tu/ber·ous,** *adj.*

tu/ber·cle (-kəl) *n.* small roundish projection, nodule, or swelling.

tu·ber/cu·lo/sis (-lō/sis) *n.* infectious disease marked by formation of tubercles. —**tu·ber/cu·lar, tu·ber/cu·lous,** *adj.*

tube/rose/ (tŏŏb/-, tyŏŏb/-) *n.* cultivated flowering plant.

tu/bule (-byŏŏl) *n.* small tube.

tuck (tuk) *v.* **1.** thrust into narrow space or retainer. **2.** cover snugly. **3.** draw up in folds. —*n.* **4.** tucked piece or part.

tuck/er, *n.* **1.** piece of cloth formerly worn by women about neck and shoulders. —*v.* **2.** *Informal.* tire; exhaust.

Tues., Tuesday. Also, **Tue.**

Tues/day (tŏŏz/dā, -dē, tyŏŏz/-) *n.* third day of week.

tuft (tuft) *n.* **1.** bunch of feathers, hairs, etc., fixed at base. **2.** clump of grasses, etc. —*v.* **3.** arrange in or form tufts. —**tuft/ed,** *adj.*

tug (tug) *v.*, **tugged, tugging,** *n.* —*v.* **1.** drag; haul. —*n.* **2.** act of tugging. **3.** tugboat.

tug/boat/, *n.* powerful vessel used for towing.

tug of war, 1. contest between teams pulling opposite ends of rope. **2.** struggle for supremacy.

tu·i/tion (tŏŏ ish/ən, tyŏŏ-) *n.* charge for instruction.

tu/lip (tŏŏ/lip, tyŏŏ/-) *n.* plant bearing showy, cup-shaped flowers.

tulle (tŏŏl) *n.* thin silk or rayon net.

tum/ble (tum/bəl) *v.*, **-bled, -bling,** *n.* —*v.* **1.** fall over or down. **2.** perform gymnastic feats. **3.** roll about; toss. —*n.* **4.** act of tumbling.

tum/ble-down/, *adj.* dilapidated.

tum/bler, *n.* **1.** drinking glass. **2.** performer of tumbling feats.

tum/ble-weed/, *n.* plant whose upper part becomes detached and is driven about by wind.

tum/brel (tum/brəl) *n.* farmer's cart that can be tilted to discharge its load. Also, **tum/bril.**

tu·mes·cent (tŏŏ mes/ənt, tyŏŏ-), *adj.* swelling; tumid. —**tu·mes/cence,** *n.*

tu/mid (tŏŏ/mid, tyŏŏ-) *adj.* **1.** swollen. **2.** turgid; bombastic.

tum/my (tum/ē) *n., pl.* **-mies.** *Informal.* stomach or abdomen.

tu/mor (tŏŏ/mər, tyŏŏ/-) *n.* abnormal swelling of cells in part of body. —**tu/mor·ous,** *adj.*

tu/mult (tŏŏ/mult, -məlt, tyŏŏ/-) *n.*

disturbance, commotion, or uproar. —**tu·mul/tu·ous** (-mul/chŏŏ əs) *adj.*

tun (tun) *n.* large cask.

tu/na (tŏŏ/nə, tyŏŏ/-) *n.* large oceanic fish.

tun/dra (tun/drə, tŏŏn/-) *n.* vast, treeless, arctic plain.

tune (tŏŏn, tyŏŏn) *n., v.*, **tuned, tuning.** —*n.* **1.** melody. **2.** state of proper pitch, frequency, or condition. **3.** harmony. —*v.* **4.** adjust to correct pitch. **5.** adjust to receive radio or television signals. —**tune/ful,** *adj.* —**tune/less,** *adj.* —**tun/er,** *n.*

tune/-up/, *n.* adjustment, as of motor, to improve working condition.

tung/sten (tung/stən) *n.* metallic element used for electric-lamp filaments, etc.

tu/nic (tŏŏ/nik, tyŏŏ/-) *n.* **1.** coat of uniform. **2.** ancient Greek and Roman garment. **3.** woman's upper garment.

tun/ing fork, steel instrument struck to produce pure tone of constant pitch.

tun/nel (tun/l) *n., v.*, **-neled, -neling.** —*n.* **1.** underground passage. —*v.* **2.** make tunnel.

tur/ban (tûr/bən) *n.* head covering made of scarf wound round head.

tur/bid (tûr/bid) *adj.* **1.** muddy. **2.** dense. **3.** confused.

tur/bine (tûr/bin, -bīn) *n.* motor producing torque by pressure of fluid.

tur/bo·jet/ (tûr/bō-) *n.* **1.** jet engine that compresses air by turbine. **2.** airplane with such engines.

tur/bo·prop/ (-prop/) *n.* **1.** turbojet with turbine-driven propeller. **2.** airplane with such engines.

tur/bot (tûr/bət) *n.* flatfish.

tur/bu·lent (tûr/byə lənt) *adj.* **1.** disorderly. **2.** tumultuous.

tu·reen/ (tŏŏ rēn/, tyŏŏ-) *n.* large covered dish for soup, etc.

turf (tûrf) *n.* **1.** covering of grass and roots. **2.** familiar area, as of residence or expertise.

tur/gid (tûr/jid) *adj.* **1.** swollen. **2.** pompous or bombastic. —**tur·gid/i·ty,** *n.* —**tur/gid·ly,** *adv.*

tur/key (tûr/kē) *n.* large, edible American bird.

turkey vulture, blackish brown New World vulture.

tur/mer·ic (tûr/mər ik) *n.* aromatic spice from Asian plant.

tur/moil (tûr/moil) *n.* tumult.

turn (tûrn) *v.* **1.** rotate. **2.** reverse. **3.** divert. **4.** depend. **5.** sour. **6.** nauseate. **7.** alter. **8.** become. **9.** use. **10.** pass. **11.** direct. **12.** curve. —*n.* **13.** rotation. **14.** change or point of change. **15.** one's due time or opportunity. **16.** trend. **17.** short walk, ride, etc. **18.** inclination or aptitude. **19.** service or disservice.

turn/a·bout/, *n.* change of opinion, loyalty, etc.

turn/coat/, *n.* renegade.

turning point, point at which decisive change takes place.

tur/nip (tûr/nip) *n.* fleshy, edible root of cabbagelike plant.

turn/off/, *n.* small road that branches off from larger one.

turn/out/, *n.* **1.** attendance at meeting, show, etc. **2.** output.

turn/o/ver, *n.* **1.** rate of replacement, investment, trade, etc. **2.** small pastry with filling.

turn/pike/ (-pīk/) *n.* **1.** barrier across road (**turnpike road**) where toll is paid. **2.** turnpike road.

turn/stile/, *n.* gate with revolving arms to allow people through one by one.

turn/ta/ble, *n.* rotating platform.

tur/pen·tine/ (tûr/pən tīn/) *n.* oil from resin from coniferous trees.

tur/pi·tude/ (tûr/pi tŏŏd/, -tyŏŏd/) *n.* depravity.

tur/quoise (tûr/koiz, -kwoiz) *n.* **1.** greenish-blue mineral used in jewelry. **2.** bluish green.

tur/ret (tûr/it, tur/-) *n.* **1.** small tower. **2.** towerlike gun shelter.

tur/tle (tûr/tl) *n.* marine reptile with shell-encased body.

tur/tle·dove/ (-duv/) *n.* small Old World dove.

tur/tle·neck/, *n.* **1.** high, close-fitting collar. **2.** garment with turtleneck.

tusk (tusk) *n.* very long tooth, as of elephant or walrus.

tus/sle (tus/əl) *v., n.*, **-sled, -sling.** fight; scuffle.

tus/sock (tus/ək) *n.* tuft of growing grass.

tu/te·lage (tŏŏt/l ij, tyŏŏt/-) *n.* **1.** guardianship. **2.** instruction.

tu/tor (tŏŏ/tər, tyŏŏ/-) *n.* **1.** private instructor. **2.** college teacher (below instructor). —*v.* **3.** teach. —**tu·to/ri·al** (-tôr/ē al) *adj.*

tut/ti-frut/ti (tŏŏ/tē frŏŏ/tē) *n.* ice cream, flavored with variety of fruits.

tu/tu/ (tŏŏ/tŏŏ/) *n.* short, full skirt worn by ballerina.

tux (tuks) *n. Informal.* tuxedo.

tux·e/do (tuk sē/dō) *n., pl.* **-dos.** semiformal jacket or suit for men.

TV, television.

twad/dle (twod/l) *n.* nonsense.

twain (twān) *adj., n. Archaic.* two.

twang (twang) *v.* **1.** sound sharply and ringingly. **2.** have nasal tone. —*n.* **3.** twanging sound.

tweak (twēk) *v.* **1.** seize and pull or twist. **2.** make minor adjustment to. —*n.* **3.** sharp pull and twist.

tweed (twēd) *n.* coarse, colored wool cloth.

tweet (twēt) *n.* **1.** chirping sound. —*v.* **2.** chirp.

tweez/ers (twē/zərz) *n.pl.* small pincers.

twelve (twelv) *n., adj.* ten plus two. —**twelfth,** *adj., n.*

Twelve Step, of or based on program for recovery from addiction that provides 12 progressive levels toward attainment.

twen/ty (twen/tē) *n., adj.* ten times two. —**twen/ti·eth,** *adj., n.*

twerp (twûrp) *n. Slang.* insignificant or despicable person.

twice (twīs) *adv.* **1.** two times. **2.** doubly.

twid/dle (twid/l) *v.*, **-dled, -dling. 1.** turn round and round, esp. with the fingers. **2.** twirl (one's fingers) about each other.

twig (twig) *n.* slender branch on tree.

twi/light/ (twī/līt/) *n.* **1.** light from sky when sun is down. **2.** waning period after success.

twill (twil) *n.* fabric woven in parallel diagonal lines.

twin (twin) *n.* either of two children born at single birth.

twine (twīn) *n., v.*, **twined, twining.** —*n.* **1.** strong thread of twisted strands. —*v.* **2.** twist or become twisted together. **3.** encircle.

twinge (twinj) *n., v.*, **twinged, twinging.** —*n.* **1.** sudden, sharp pain. —*v.* **2.** give or have twinge.

twin/kle (twing/kəl) *v.*, **-kled, -kling,** *n.* —*v.* **1.** shine with light, quick gleams. —*n.* **2.** sly, humorous look. **3.** act of twinkling.

twin/kling, *n.* instant.

twirl (twûrl) *v.* **1.** spin; whirl. —*n.* **2.** a twirling.

twist (twist) *v.* **1.** combine by winding together. **2.** distort. **3.** combine in coil, etc. **4.** wind about. **5.** writhe. **6.** turn. —*n.* **7.** curve or turn. **8.** spin. **9.** wrench. **10.** spiral.

twist'er, *n. Informal.* tornado.

twit (twit) *v.,* **twitted, twitting,** —*v.* **1.** taunt; tease. —*n.* **2.** *Informal.* fool.

twitch (twich) *v.* jerk. —*n.* **2.** quick jerky movement.

twit'ter (twit'ər) *v.* **1.** utter small, tremulous sounds, as bird. **2.** tremble with excitement. —*n.* **3.** twittering sound. **4.** state of excitement.

two (tōō) *n., adj.* one plus one.

two'-bit', *adj. Informal.* inferior or unimportant.

two bits, *Informal.* 25 cents.

two'-faced', *adj.* deceitful or hypocritical.

two'-fist'ed, *adj.* strong and vigorous.

two'fold' *adj.* (-fōld') **1.** having two parts. **2.** twice as great. —*adv.* (fōld') **3.** in two-fold measure.

two'-ply', *adj.* consisting of two layers strands, etc.

two'some (-səm) *n.* pair.

two'-time', *v.,* **two-timed, two-timing.** *Informal.* be unfaithful to.

two'-way', *adj.* **1.** allowing movement in two directions. **2.** involving two participants.

twp., township.

TX, Texas.

-ty, suffix meaning state or condition, as *certainty.*

ty·coon' (tī kōōn') *n.* businessperson having great wealth and power.

tyke (tīk) *n.* small child.

tympanic membrane, membrane separating middle from external ear.

tym'pa·num (tim'pə nəm) *n.* **1.** middle ear. **2.** tympanic membrane.

type (tīp) *n., v.,* **typed, typing.** —*n.* **1.** kind or class. **2.** representative specimen. **3.** piece used in printing. **4.** such pieces collectively. —*v.* **5.** typewrite. —**typ'ist,** *n.*

type'cast', *n.,* **-cast, -casting.** cast (actor) exclusively in same kind of role.

type'script', *n.* typewritten matter.

type'set'ter, *n.* **1.** person who sets type. **2.** machine for setting type. —**type'set',** *v.* **-set, -setting.**

type'writ'er, *n.* machine for writing mechanically.

ty'phoid (tī'foid) *n.* infectious disease marked by intestinal disorder. Also, **typhoid fever.**

ty·phoon' (tī fōōn') *n.* cyclone or hurricane of western Pacific.

ty'phus (tī'fəs) *n.* infectious disease transmitted by lice and fleas.

typ'i·cal (tip'i kəl) *adj.* **1.** serving as a representative specimen. **2.** conforming to the characteristics of a particular group.

typ'i·fy', *v.,* **-fied, -fying.** serve as typical example of.

ty'po (tī'pō) *n., pl.* **-pos.** error in typography or typing.

ty·pog'ra·phy (tī pog'rə fē) *n.* **1.** art or process of printing. **2.** general character of printed matter.

ty·ran'no·saur' (ti ran'ə sôr', tī-) *n.* large dinosaur that walked upright.

tyr'an·ny (tir'ə nē) *n., pl.* **-nies.** **1.** despotic abuse of authority. **2.** government or rule by tyrant. —**ty·ran'ni·cal** (ti ran'i kəl, tī-) *adj.* —**tyr'an·nize',** *v.,* **-nized, -nizing.**

ty'rant (tī'rənt) *n.* oppressive, unjust, or absolute ruler.

ty'ro (tī'rō) *n., pl.* **-ros.** novice.

tzar (zär, tsär) *n.* czar.

U

U, u (yōō) *n.* twenty-first letter of English alphabet.

u·biq'ui·tous (yōō bik'wi təs) *adj.* simultaneously present everywhere.

ud'der (ud'ər) *n.* mammary gland, esp. of cow.

UFO (yōō'ef'ō'; *sometimes* yōō'fō) unidentified flying object.

ug'ly (ug'lē) *adj.,* **-lier, -liest. 1.** repulsive. **2.** dangerous.

u·ku·le·le (yōō'kə lā'lē) *n.* small guitar.

ul'cer (ul'sar) *n.* open sore, as on stomach lining. —**ul'cer·ous,** *adj.* —**ul'cer·ate',** *v.,* **-ated, -ating.**

ul'na (ul'nə) *n.* larger bone of forearm. —**ul'nar,** *adj.*

ul·te'ri·or (ul tēr'ē ər) *adj.* **1.** not acknowledged; concealed. **2.** later.

ul'ti·mate (-mit) *adj.* **1.** final; highest. **2.** basic. —**ul'ti·mate·ly,** *adv.*

ul'ti·ma'tum (-mā'təm, -mä'-) *n., pl.* **-tums, -ta** (-tə). final demand.

ultra-, prefix meaning beyond; on the far side of; extremely.

ul'tra·con·serv'a·tive (ul'trə kənsûr'və tiv) *adj.* extremely conservative, esp. in politics.

ul'tra·fiche' (-fēsh') *n.* form of microfiche with images greatly reduced in size.

ul'tra·high' frequency (ul'trə hī') radio frequency between 300 and 3000 megahertz.

ul'tra·ma·rine', *n.* deep blue.

ul'tra·sound', *n.* application of sound above human hearing to medical diagnosis and therapy.

ul'tra·vi'o·let, *adj.* of invisible rays beyond violet in spectrum.

um'ber (um'bər) *n.* **1.** reddish brown. —*adj.* **2.** of or like umber.

umbilical cord (um bil'i kəl) cordlike structure connecting fetus with placenta, conveying nourishment and removing wastes.

um·bil'i·cus (-kəs) *n., pl.* **-ci** (-sī). navel. —**um·bil'i·cal,** *adj.*

um'brage (um'brij) *n.* resentment.

um·brel'la (um brel'ə) *n.* cloth-covered framework carried for protection from rain, etc.

um'laut (ōōm'lout) *n.* **1.** (in Germanic languages) assimilation in which vowel is influenced by following vowel. **2.** diacritical mark (¨) used over vowel to indicate umlaut.

ump (ump) *n., v.* umpire.

um'pire (um'pī°r) *n., v.,* **-pired, -piring.** —*n.* **1.** judge or arbitrator. —*v.* **2.** be umpire in.

ump'teen' (ump'tēn') *adj. Informal.* innumerable. —**ump'teenth',** *adj.*

UN, United Nations.

un-, prefix indicating negative or opposite sense, as in *unfair, unwanted,* and *unfasten.*

un·a'ble (un ā'bəl) *adj.* lacking necessary power, skill, or resources.

un'ac·count'a·ble, *adj.* **1.** inexplicable. **2.** not responsible.

un'af·fect'ed, *adj.* **1.** without affectation. **2.** not concerned or involved.

u·nan'i·mous (yōō nan'ə məs) *adj.* completely agreed. —**u'na·nim'i·ty** (-nə nim'i tē) *n.*

un'as·sum'ing (un'-) *adj.* modest; without vanity.

un'at·tached', *adj.* **1.** not attached. **2.** not engaged or married.

un·a·vail'ing, *adj.* not effective.

un'a·wares', *adv.* not knowingly.

un·bal'anced, *adj.* **1.** out of balance. **2.** irrational; deranged.

un·bear'a·ble, *adj.* unendurable.

un·be·com'ing, *adj.* unattractive or unseemly.

un·bend', *v.,* **-bent, -bending. 1.** straighten. **2.** act in genial, relaxed manner.

un·bend'ing, *adj.* rigidly formal or unyielding.

un·bid'den, *adj.* **1.** not commanded. **2.** not asked.

un·blush'ing, *adj.* showing no remorse; shameless.

un·bos'om, *v.* disclose (secrets, etc.).

un·bowed' (-boud') *adj.* **1.** not bent. **2.** not subjugated

un·brid'led, *adj.* unrestrained.

un·bro'ken, *adj.* **1.** not broken. **2.** undisturbed. **3.** not tamed.

un·bur'den, *v.* **1.** free from burden. **2.** relieve one's mind, conscience, etc., by confessing.

un·called'-for', *adj.* not warranted.

un·can'ny, *adj.* unnaturally strange or good.

un·cer'e·mo'ni·ous, *adj.* **1.** informal. **2.** rudely abrupt.

un·chart'ed, *adj.* not shown on map; unexplored.

un·clad', *adj.* naked.

un'cle (ung'kəl) *n.* **1.** brother of one's father or mother. **2.** husband of one's aunt.

Uncle Sam (sam) United States government.

un·com'pro·mis'ing, *adj.* refusing to compromise; rigid.

un'con·cern', *n.* lack of concern; indifference.

un'con·di'tion·al, *adj.* absolute; without conditions or reservations.

un'con·scion·a·ble (-shən-) *adj.* not reasonable or honest.

un·con'scious, *adj.* **1.** lacking awareness, sensation, or cognition. **2.** not perceived at level of awareness. **3.** done without intent. —*n.* **4. the unconscious,** part of psyche rarely accessible to awareness but influencing behavior.

un·couth' (un kōōth') *adj.* rude; boorish.

unc'tion (ungk'shən) *n.* **1.** anointment with oil. **2.** soothing manner of speech.

unc'tu·ous (-chōō əs) *adj.* **1.** oily. **2.** overly suave.

un·cut' (un-) *adj.* **1.** not shortened; unabridged. **2.** not yet given shape, as a gemstone.

un·daunt'ed, *adj.* not discouraged.

un'de·mon'stra·tive, *adj.* reserved.

un'der (un'dər) *prep., adj., adv.* **1.** beneath; below. **2.** less than. **3.** lower.

under-, prefix meaning: **1.** below or beneath, as *underbrush.* **2.** lower in grade, as *understudy.* **3.** of lesser degree or amount, as *underestimate.*

un'der·a·chieve', *v.,* **-achieved, -achieving.** perform below one's intellectual potential.

un'der·age', *adj.* being below legal or required age.

un'der·bel'ly, *n., pl.* **-ies. 1.** lower abdomen. **2.** vulnerable area.

un'der·brush', *n.* low shrubs, etc., in forest.

un'der·car'riage, *n.* supporting framework underneath vehicle.

un·der·clothes′, *n.pl.* underwear.

un·der·cov′er, *adj.* secret.

un·der·cur′rent, *n.* hidden tendency or feeling.

un·der·cut′, *v.*, -cut, -cutting. sell at lower price than.

un·der·de·vel′oped, *adj.* 1. insufficiently developed. 2. having relatively low living standards and industrial development.

un·der·dog′, *n.* 1. weaker contestant, etc. 2. victim of injustice.

un·der·done′, *adj.* not cooked enough.

un·der·es′ti·mate′ (-māt′) *v.*, -mated, -mating. estimate too low.

un·der·ex·pose′, *v.*, -posed, -posing. expose (film) to insufficient light or for too short a period.

un·der·gar′ment, *n.* item of underwear.

un·der·go′, *v.*, -went, -gone, -going. experience; endure.

un·der·grad′u·ate (-it) *n.* college student before receiving first degree.

un·der·ground′ *adv.* (un′dər-ground′), *adj.* (-ground′). 1. under the ground. 2. secret. —*n.* (-ground′) 3. secret resistance army.

un·der·growth′, *n.* underbrush.

un·der·hand′, *adj.* sly; secret.

un·der·line′, *v.*, -lined, -lining. 1. draw line under. 2. stress.

un·der·ling′ (-ling) *n.* subordinate.

un·der·mine′ (un′dər mīn′, un′dər-mīn′) *v.*, -mined, -mining. weaken or destroy; stop secretly.

un·der·neath′ (-nēth′, -nēth′) *prep.*, *adv.* beneath.

un·der·pass′, *n.* passage running underneath.

un·der·pin′ning, *n.* 1. system of supports. 2. foundation; basis.

un·der·priv′i·leged, *adj.* denied normal privileges of society.

un·der·score′, *v.*, -scored, -scoring. underline; stress.

un·der·sec′re·tar′y, *n., pl.* -taries. government official subordinate to principal secretary.

un·der·signed′, *n.* the undersigned, person signing document.

un·der·staffed′, *adj.* having not enough workers.

un·der·stand′, *v.*, -stood, -standing. 1. know meaning of. 2. accept as part of agreement. 3. sympathize. —*un′der·stand′ing*, *n.*

un·der·state′, *v.*, -stated, -stating. 1. state less strongly than facts warrant. 2. set forth in restrained terms. —*un′der·state′ment*, *n.*

un·der·stud′y, *n., pl.* -studies. substitute for performer.

un·der·take′, *v.*, -took, -taken, -taking. 1. attempt. 2. promise. 3. arrange funerals.

un·der·tak′er, *n.* funeral director; mortician.

un·der·tak′ing (un′dər tā′king, un′dər tā′-) *n.* enterprise; task.

un·der-the-coun′ter, *adj.* illegal; unauthorized.

un·der·tone′, *n.* 1. low tone. 2. underlying quality. 3. subdued color.

un·der·tow′ (-tō′) *n.* strong subsurface current moving opposite surface current.

un·der·wear′, *n.* garments worn next to skin, under other clothing.

un·der·world′, *n.* 1. criminal element. 2. land of the dead.

un·der·write′ (un′dər rīt′, un′dər-rīt′) *v.*, -wrote, -written, -writing. guarantee, esp. expense.

un·do′ (un dōō′) *v.*, -did, -done, -do-

ing. 1. return to original state. 2. untie. 3. destroy.

un·do′ing, *n.* 1. reversing. 2. ruin. 3. cause of ruin.

un·du·late′ (un′jə lāt′, -dyə-) *v.*, -lated, -lating. have wavy motion or form. —*un′du·la′tion*, *n.*

un·dy′ing, *adj.* eternal; unending.

un·earned′, *adj.* 1. not earned by service. 2. not deserved. 3. (of income) derived from investments.

un·earth′, *v.* discover.

un·earth′ly, *adj.* supernatural; weird.

un·eas′y, *adj.*, -ier, -iest. anxious.

un′e·quiv′o·cal, *adj.* not ambiguous.

un·e·vent′ful, *adj.* routine.

un′ex·cep′tion·al, *adj.* ordinary.

un·feel′ing, *adj.* lacking sympathy. —*un·feel′ing·ly*, *adv.*

un·flap′pa·ble (un flap′ə bəl) *adj.* not easily upset or panicked.

un·fledged′ (-flejd′) *adj.* 1. lacking sufficient feathers for flight. 2. immature.

un·found′ed, *adj.* not supported by evidence.

un·frock′, *v.* deprive of ecclesiastical rank, authority, and function.

un·gain′ly (-gān′lē) *adj.* clumsy.

un′guent (ung′gwənt) *n.* salve.

un·hand′, *v.* release from grasp.

un·hinge′, *v.*, -hinged, -hinging. 1. take off hinges. 2. make mentally unstable; unbalance.

uni-, prefix meaning one.

u′ni·corn′ (yōō′ni kôrn′) *n.* mythical horselike animal with one horn.

u′ni·form′ (yōō′nə fôrm′) *adj.* 1. exactly alike. 2. constant. —*n.* 3. distinctive clothing of specific group. —*v.* 4. put in uniform. —*u′ni·form′i·ty*, *n.*

u′ni·fy′ (-fī′) *v.*, -fied, -fying. make into one. —*u′ni·fi·ca′tion*, *n.*

u′ni·lat′er·al, *adj.* one-sided.

un′im·peach′a·ble (un′im pē′chə-bəl) *adj.* above reproach.

un′in·hib′it·ed, *adj.* unrestrained by convention.

un·in′ter·est·ed, *adj.* not interested; indifferent. —**Usage.** See DISINTERESTED.

un′ion (yōōn′yən) *n.* 1. uniting; combination. 2. labor group for mutual aid on wages, etc. —*un′ion·ist*, *n.*, *adj.* —*un′ion·ize′*, *v.*

Union Jack, British flag.

u·nique′ (yōō nēk′) *adj.* 1. only. 2. most unusual or rare. —**Usage.** UNIQUE is an adjective representing an absolute state that cannot exist in degrees. Therefore, it cannot be sensibly used with a limiting or comparative adverb such as "very," "most," or "extremely": *She has a unique* (not "*very unique*" or "*most unique*") *style of singing.*

u′ni·sex′ (yōō′ni seks′) *adj.* of type or style used by both sexes.

u′ni·son (-sən, -zən) *n.* agreement.

u′nit (yōō′nit) *n.* 1. single entity. 2. one of a number of identical or similar parts within whole.

U′ni·tar′i·an (yōō′ni târ′ē ən) *n.* 1. member of Christian denomination asserting unity of God. —*adj.* 2. concerning Unitarians or their beliefs.

u·nite′ (yōō nīt′) *v.*, -united, uniting. join, make, etc., into one.

United Nations, organization of nations to preserve peace and promote human welfare.

u′ni·ty (yōō′ni tē) *n., pl.* -ties. 1. state of being one. 2. agreement.

u′ni·ver′sal (yōō′nə vûr′səl) *adj.* 1. of all; general. 2. applicable or existing

everywhere. —*u′ni·ver·sal′i·ty* (-sal′-i tē) *n.*

Universal Product Code, standardized bar code.

u′ni·verse′ (-vûrs′) *n.* all things that exist, including heavenly bodies.

u′ni·ver′si·ty (-vûr′si tē) *n., pl.* -ties. institution composed of various specialized colleges.

un·kempt′ (un kempt′) *adj.* untidy.

un·lead′ed (-led′id) *adj.* (of gasoline) free of pollution-causing lead.

un·less′ (un les′, ən-) *conj., prep.* except that.

un·let′tered, *adj.* illiterate.

un·mit′i·gat′ed, *adj.* 1. not lessened. 2. absolute.

un·nerve′, *v.*, -nerved, -nerving. deprive of courage, strength, or determination.

un·par′al·leled′, *adj.* without equal.

un·plumbed′, *adj.* not explored in depth.

un·prin′ci·pled, *adj.* without principles or ethics.

un·print′a·ble, *adj.* unfit for print, esp. because obscene.

un·rav′el, *v.*, -eled, -eling. 1. disentangle. 2. solve.

un′re·con·struct′ed, *adj.* stubbornly maintaining beliefs considered out of date.

un·re·mit′ting, *adj.* not abating.

un·rest′, *n.* 1. restless state. 2. strong, almost rebellious, dissatisfaction.

un·ruf′fled, *adj.* calm.

un·ru′ly (un rōō′lē) *adj.*, -lier, -liest. lawless.

un·sa′vo·ry, *adj.* morally objectionable.

un·sea′son·a·ble, *adj.* 1. being out of season. 2. inopportune.

un·seat′, *v.* 1. dislodge from seat. 2. remove from political office.

un·seem′ly, *adj.*, -lier, -liest. improper.

un·set′tle, *v.*, -tled, -tling. 1. cause to be unstable; disturb. 2. agitate mind or emotions of.

un·sound′, *adj.* 1. unhealthy. 2. not solid. 3. not valid. 4. not secure.

un·spar′ing, *adj.* 1. profuse. 2. unmerciful.

un·speak′a·ble, *adj.* 1. exceeding the power of speech. 2. inexpressibly bad.

un·sta′ble, *adj.* 1. unsteady. 2. changeable. 3. emotionally unsettled.

un·strung′, *adj.* nervously upset; unnerved.

un·sung′, *adj.* not celebrated, as in song; unappreciated.

un·ten′a·ble, *adj.* not defensible as true.

un·think′a·ble, *adj.* not to be imagined; impossible.

un·ti′dy, *adj.*, -dier, -diest. not tidy or neat. —*un·tid′i·ly*, *adv.*

un·tie′, *v.*, -tied, -tying. loosen or open (something tied).

un·til′ (un til′) *conj., prep.* 1. up to time when. 2. before. —**Usage.** See TILL.

un′to (un′tōō; *unstressed* -tə) *prep.* Archaic. to.

un·told′, *adj.* countless.

un·touch′a·ble, *adj.* 1. beyond control or criticism. 2. too vile to touch. —*un·touch′a·ble*, *n.*

un·to·ward′, *adj.* unfavorable or unfortunate.

un·well′, *adj.* ill or ailing.

un·wield′y, *adj.*, -ier, -iest. awkward to handle.

un·wit′ting, *adj.* not aware.

un·wont'ed (un wôn'tid, -wōn'-, -wun'-) *adj.* not habitual or usual.

up (up) *adv., prep., n., v.,* **upped, up·ping.** —*adv.* **1.** to higher place, etc. **2.** erectly. **3.** out of bed. **4.** at. —*prep.* **5.** to, on, or in a higher place, etc. —*n.* **6.** rise. —*v.* **7.** increase.

up'-and-com'ing, *adj.* likely to succeed; promising.

up'beat', *adj.* optimistic; happy.

up·braid' (up brād') *v.* chide.

up'bring'ing, *n.* care and training of children.

UPC, Universal Product Code.

up'com'ing, *adj.* about to take place or appear.

up'coun'try, *adj., adv.* of, toward, or situated in the interior of a region.

up·date' (up'dāt', up'dāt') *v.,* **-dated, -dating.** modernize, esp. in details.

up·end', *v.* set on end.

up'-front', *adj.* **1.** invested or paid in advance. **2.** honest; candid.

up·grade' *n., v.,* **-graded, -grading.** —*n.* (up'grād') **1.** upward incline. **2.** increase, rise, or improvement. —*v.* (up grād', up'grād') **3.** raise in position, quality, or value.

up·heav'al (up hē'vəl) *n.* sudden and great movement or change.

up'hill', *adv.* up a slope or incline.

up·hold', *v.,* **-held, -holding.** support. —**up·hold'er,** *n.*

up·hol'ster (up hōl'stər, ə pōl'-) *v.* provide (furniture) with coverings, etc. —**up·hol'ster·er,** *n.* —**up·hol'ster·y,** *n.*

up'keep', *n.* maintenance.

up'land (up'lənd, -land') *n.* elevated region.

up·lift' *v.* (up lift') **1.** improve; exalt. —*n.* (up'lift') **2.** improvement.

up·on' (ə pon', ə pôn') *prep.* on.

up'per, *adj.* higher.

up'per·case', *adj.* **1.** (of a letter) capital. —*n.* **2.** capital letter.

upper hand, controlling position; advantage.

up'pi·ty (up'i tē) *adj. Informal.* haughty, snobbish, or arrogant.

up'right' (up'rīt', up rīt') *adj.* **1.** erect. **2.** righteous.

up'ris'ing (up'rī'zing, up rī'-) *n.* revolt.

up'roar', *n.* tumult; noise; din. —**up·roar'i·ous,** *adj.*

up·root', *v.* tear up by roots.

up'scale', *adj.* of or for people at upper end of economic scale.

up·set' *v.,* **-set, -setting,** *n., adj.* —*v.* (up set') **1.** turn over. **2.** distress emotionally. **3.** defeat. —*n.* (up'set') **4.** overturn. **5.** defeat. (up set') **6.** disorderly. **7.** distressed.

up'shot', *n.* final result.

upside down, with upper part undermost. **2.** in or into complete disorder. —**up'side-down',** *adj.*

up'stage', *adv., v.,* **-staged, -staging.** —*adv.* **1.** at or toward back of stage. —*v.* **2.** outdo professionally or socially.

up'stairs', *adv., adj.* on or to upper floor.

up'start', *n.* person newly risen to wealth or importance.

up'-to-date', *adj.* **1.** until present time; current. **2.** modern; latest.

up'ward (up'wərd) *adv.* to higher place. Also, **up'wards.** —**up'ward,** *adj.*

u·ra'ni·um (yŏŏ rā'nē əm) *n.* white, radioactive metallic element, important in development of atomic energy.

U·ra·nus (yŏŏr'ə nəs, yŏŏ rā'-) *n.* planet seventh in order from the sun.

ur·ban (ûr'bən) *adj.* of or like a city.

ur·bane' (ûr bān') *adj.* polite or suave. —**ur·ban'i·ty** (-ban'i tē) *n.*

ur'chin (ûr'chin) *n.* ragged child.

u·re'a (yŏŏ rē'ə, yŏŏr'ē ə) *n.* compound occurring in body fluids, esp. urine.

u·re'ter (yŏŏ rē'tər) *n.* duct that conveys urine from kidney to bladder.

u·re'thra (yŏŏ rē'thrə) *n., pl.* **-thrae** (-thrē), **-thras.** duct that conveys urine and, in males, semen.

urge (ûrj) *v.,* **urged, urging,** *n.* —*v.* **1.** force, incite, or advocate. **2.** entreat. **3.** desire; impulse.

ur'gent (ûr'jənt) *adj.* vital; pressing. —**ur'gen·cy,** *n.*

u·ri·nal (yŏŏr'ə nl) *n.* wall fixture used by men for urinating.

u'ri·nar'y (-ner'ē) *adj.* **1.** of urine. **2.** of organs that secrete and discharge urine.

u'ri·nate' (-nāt') *v.,* **-nated, -nating.** pass urine. —**u'ri·na'tion,** *n.*

u'rine (yŏŏr'in) *n.* secretion of kidneys. —**u'ric** (yŏŏr'ik) *adj.*

urn (ûrn) *n.* vase or pot.

u·rol'o·gy (yŏŏ rol'ə jē) *n.* medical study of urinary or genitourinary tract. —**u·rol'o·gist,** *n.*

us (us) *pron.* objective case of **we.**

us·age (yŏŏ'sij, -zij) *n.* **1.** custom. **2.** treatment.

use, *v.,* **used, using,** *n.* —*v.* (yŏŏz or, *for pt. form of 5,* yŏŏst) **1.** do something with aid of. **2.** expend. **3.** make practice of. **4.** treat. **5.** accustom. —*n.* (yŏŏs) **6.** act or way of using. **7.** service or value. —**use'ful,** *adj.* —**use'less,** *adj.* —**us'er,** *n.*

us'er-friend'ly, *adj.* easy to operate or understand.

ush'er (ush'ər) *n.* person who escorts people to seats, as in theater.

u'su·al (yŏŏ'zhŏŏ əl) *adj.* **1.** customary. **2.** common. —**u'su·al·ly,** *adv.*

u·surp' (yŏŏ sûrp', -zûrp') *v.* seize without right. —**u·surp'er,** *n.*

u'su·ry (yŏŏ'zhə rē) *n.* lending money at exorbitant rates of interest. —**u'sur·er,** *n.*

UT, Utah. Also, **Ut.**

u·ten'sil (yŏŏ ten'səl) *n.* device, container, etc., esp. for kitchen.

u'ter·us (yŏŏ'tər əs) *n., pl.* **-teri** (-tə-rī') part of woman's body in which fertilized ovum develops. —**u'ter·ine** (-in) *adj.*

u·til'i·tar'i·an (yŏŏ til'i târ'ē ən) *adj.* of practical use.

u·til'i·ty, *n., pl.* **-ties. 1.** usefulness. **2.** public service.

u'ti·lize' (yŏŏt'l īz') *v.,* **-lized, -lizing.** use. —**u'ti·li·za'tion,** *n.*

ut'most (ut'mōst') *adj.* **1.** greatest. **2.** furthest.

U·to'pi·an (yŏŏ tō'pē ən) *adj.* impossibly perfect.

ut'ter (ut'ər) *v.* **1.** speak; say. —*adj.* **2.** complete; total.

ut'ter·ly, *adv.* completely; absolutely.

u'vu·la (yŏŏ'vyə lə) *n., pl.* **-las, -lae.** small, fleshy part on soft palate.

V

V, v (vē) *n.* twenty-second letter of English alphabet.

VA, Virginia. Also, **Va.**

va'can·cy (vā'kən sē) *n., pl.* **-cies. 1.** state of being vacant. **2.** vacant space or position.

va'cant (-kənt) *adj.* **1.** empty. **2.** devoid. **3.** unintelligent.

va'cate (vā'kāt) *v.,* **-cated, -cating. 1.** empty. **2.** annul.

va·ca'tion (vā kā'shən, və-) *n.* **1.** freedom from duty, business, etc. **2.** holiday. —*v.* **3.** take a vacation.

vac'ci·nate' (vak'sə nāt') *v.,* **-nated, -nating.** inoculate against disease. —**vac'ci·na'tion,** *n.*

vac·cine' (vak sēn') *n.* substance injected into bloodstream to give immunity.

vac'il·late' (vas'ə lāt') *v.,* **-lated, -lating. 1.** waver; fluctuate. **2.** be irresolute. —**vac'il·la'tion,** *n.*

va·cu'i·ty (va kyōō'i tē, va-) *n., pl.* **-ties. 1.** emptiness. **2.** lack of intelligence. —**vac'u·ous** (vak'yōō əs) *adj.* —**vac'u·ous·ly,** *adv.*

vac'u·um (vak'yōōm, -yōō əm, -yəm) *n.* space from which all matter has been removed.

vacuum bottle, bottle with double wall enclosing vacuum to retard heat transfer.

vacuum cleaner, apparatus for cleaning by suction.

vac'uum-packed', *adj.* packed with as much air as possible evacuated before sealing.

vacuum tube, sealed bulb, formerly used in radio and electronics.

vag'a·bond' (vag'ə bond') *adj.* **1.** wandering. —*n.* **2.** vagrant.

va·gar'y (və gâr'ē, vā'gə rē) *n., pl.* **-garies.** capricious act or idea.

va·gi'na (və jī'nə) *n., pl.* **-nas, -nae.** passage from uterus to vulva. —**vag'i·nal** (vaj'ə nl) *adj.*

va'grant (vā'grənt) *n.* **1.** homeless person with no job. —*adj.* **2.** wandering. —**va'gran·cy,** *n.*

vague (vāg) *adj.,* **vaguer, vaguest. 1.** not definite. **2.** indistinct.

vain (vān) *adj.* **1.** futile. **2.** conceited. —**vain'ly,** *adv.*

vain'glo'ry, *n.* boastful pride. —**vain·glo'ri·ous,** *adj.*

val'ance (val'əns, vā'ləns) *n.* drapery across top of window.

vale (vāl) *n.* valley.

val'e·dic'to'ri·an (val'i dik tôr'ē ən) *n.* graduating student who delivers valedictory.

val'e·dic'to·ry (-tə rē) *n., pl.* **-ries.** farewell address, esp. one delivered at commencement.

va'lence (vā'ləns) *n.* combining capacity of atom or radical.

val'en·tine' (val'ən tīn') *n.* **1.** affectionate card or gift sent on February 14 (**Saint Valentine's Day**). **2.** sweetheart chosen on that day.

val'et (va lā', val'it, val'ā) *n.* personal manservant.

val'iant (val'yənt) *adj.* brave.

val'id (val'id) *adj.* **1.** sound; logical. **2.** legally binding. —**va·lid'i·ty** (və lid'i tē) *n.*

va·lise' (və lēs') *n.* traveling bag.

val'ley (val'ē) *n.* long depression between uplands or mountains.

val'or (val'ər) *n.* bravery, esp. in battle.

val'u·a·ble (-yŏŏ ə bəl, -yə bəl) *adj.* **1.** of much worth, importance, etc. —*n.* **2.** (*usually pl.*) valuable articles. —**val'u·a·bly,** *adv.*

val'u·a'tion (-yŏŏ ā'shən) *n.* estimation or estimated value.

val'ue, *n., v.,* **-ued, -uing.** —*n.* **1.** worth or importance. **2.** equivalent or estimated worth. **3.** conception of what is good. —*v.* **4.** estimate worth of. **5.** esteem. —**val'ue·less,** *adj.*

valve (valv) *n.* device controlling flow of liquids, etc.

va•moose' (va mōōs') *v.*, **-moosed**, **-moosing.** *Slang.* leave hurriedly.

vamp (vamp) *n.* **1.** *Slang.* seductive woman. —*v.* **2.** improvise.

vam'pire (vam'pīr) *n.* **1.** corpse supposed to be reanimated and to suck blood of living persons. **2.** extortionist. **3.** Also, **vampire bat.** South and Central American bat.

van (van) *n.* **1.** vanguard. **2.** covered truck for moving furniture, etc. **3.** small closed trucklike vehicle.

van'dal (van'dl) *n.* person who willfully damages or destroys property. —**van'dal•ism,** *n.* —**van'dal•ize'**, *v.*, **-ized, -izing.**

Van•dyke' (van dīk') *n.* short, pointed beard.

vane (vān) *n.* **1.** weathervane. **2.** one of set of blades set diagonally on a rotor to move or be moved by fluid.

van'guard' (van'-) *n.* **1.** foremost part. **2.** leaders of a movement.

va•nil'la (va nil'ə; *often* -nel'ə) *n.* **1.** tropical orchid, whose fruit (**vanilla bean**) yields flavoring extract. **2.** the flavoring.

van'ish (van'ish) *v.* disappear.

van'i•ty (van'i tē) *n.*, *pl.* **-ties. 1.** vainness. **2.** makeup table. **3.** compact (def. 4).

van'quish (vang'kwish, van'-) *v.* conquer; defeat. —**van'quish•er,** *n.*

van'tage (van'tij) *n.* superior position or situation.

vap'id (vap'id) *adj.* insipid; dull.

va'por (vā'pər) *n.* **1.** exhalation, as fog or mist. **2.** gas.

va'por•ize', *v.*, **-ized, -izing.** change into vapor. —**va'por•i•za'tion,** *n.* —**va'por•iz'er,** *n.*

var'i•a•ble (vâr'ē ə bəl) *adj.* **1.** changeable. **2.** inconstant. **3.** something variable. —**var'i•a•bil'i•ty,** *n.* —**var'i•a•bly,** *adv.*

var'i•ance (-əns) *n.* **1.** divergence or discrepancy. **2.** disagreement.

var'i•ant, *adj.* **1.** varying. **2.** altered in form. —*n.* **3.** variant form, etc.

var'i•a'tion (-ā'shən) *n.* **1.** change. **2.** amount of change. **3.** variant. **4.** transformation of melody with changes in harmony, etc.

var'i•col'ored (vâr'i kul'ərd) *adj.* having various colors.

var'i•cose' (var'i kōs') *adj.* abnormally swollen, as veins.

var'i•e•gate' (vâr'ē i gāt', vâr'i-) *v.*, **-gated, -gating. 1.** mark with different colors, etc. **2.** vary.

va•ri'e•ty (va rī'i tē) *n.*, *pl.* **-ties. 1.** diversity. **2.** number of different things. **3.** kind; category. **4.** variant.

var'i•ous (vâr'ē əs) *adj.* **1.** of different sorts. **2.** several.

var'mint (vär'mənt) *n.* **1.** undesirable, usu. verminous animal. **2.** obnoxious person.

var'nish (vär'nish) *n.* **1.** resinous solution drying in hard, glossy coat. **2.** gloss. —*v.* **3.** lay varnish on.

var'y (vâr'ē) *v.*, **varied, varying. 1.** change; differ. **2.** cause to be different. **3.** deviate; diverge.

vas'cu•lar (vas'kyə lər) *adj.* of vessels that convey fluids, as blood or sap.

vase (vās, vāz, väz) *n.* tall container, esp. for flowers.

vas•ec'to•my (va sek'tə mē, və-) *n.*, *pl.* **-mies.** surgery for male sterilization.

vas'sal (vas'əl) *n.* **1.** feudal holder of land who renders service to lord. **2.** subject, follower, or slave.

vast (vast) *adj.* immense; huge.

vat (vat) *n.* large container for liquids.

vaude'ville (vôd'vil, vōd'-, vô'də-) *n.* theatrical entertainment made up of separate acts.

vault (vôlt) *n.* **1.** arched ceiling or roof. **2.** arched space, chamber, etc. **3.** room for safekeeping of valuables. —*v.* **4.** build or cover with vault. **5.** leap. —**vault'ed,** *adj.*

vault'ing, *adj.* **1.** leaping. **2.** excessive.

vaunt (vônt, vänt) *v.* **1.** boast of. —*n.* **2.** boast.

VCR, videocassette recorder.

VD, venereal disease.

V'-Day', *n.* day of military victory.

VDT, video display terminal.

veal (vēl) *n.* flesh of calf as used for food.

vec'tor (vek'tər) *n.* **1.** quantity possessing both magnitude and direction. **2.** person or animal that transmits disease-causing organism.

veep (vēp) *n. Informal.* vice president, esp. of U.S.

veer (vēr) *v.* change direction.

veg'e•ta•ble (vej'tə bəl, vej'i tə-) *n.* **1.** plant used for food. **2.** any plant.

veg'e•tar'i•an (vej'i târ'ē ən) *n.* **1.** person who eats only vegetable food on principle (**vegetarianism**). —*adj.* **2.** of or advocating vegetarianism. **3.** suitable for vegetarians.

veg'e•tate' (-tāt') *v.*, **-tated, -tating. 1.** grow as plants do. **2.** live dull, inactive life. —**veg'e•ta'tive,** *adj.*

veg'e•ta'tion (-ā'shən) *n.* **1.** plants collectively. **2.** act or process of vegetating.

ve'he•ment (vē'ə mənt) *adj.* **1.** impetuous or impassioned. **2.** violent. —**ve'he•mence,** **ve'he•men•cy,** *n.*

ve'hi•cle (vē'i kəl) *n.* means of transport, etc. —**ve•hic'u•lar** (-hik'yə lər) *adj.*

veil (vāl) *n.* **1.** material concealing face. **2.** part of headdress, as of nun or bride. **3.** cover; screen. **4.** pretense. —*v.* **5.** cover with veil.

vein (vān) *n.* **1.** vessel conveying blood from body to heart. **2.** tubular riblike thickening, as in leaf or insect wing. **3.** stratum of ore, coal, etc. **4.** mood. —*v.* **5.** furnish or mark with veins.

Vel'cro (vel'krō) *n. Trademark.* fastening tape with opposing pieces of nylon that interlock.

veld (velt, felt) *n.* open grassy country in South Africa. Also, **veldt.**

vel'lum (vel'əm) *n.* parchment.

ve•loc'i•ty (va los'i tē) *n.*, *pl.* **-ties.** speed.

ve•lour' (va lŏŏr') *n.* velvetlike fabric used for clothing and upholstery.

vel'vet (vel'vit) *n.* fabric with thick, soft pile. —**vel'vet•y,** *adj.*

vel'vet•een' (-vi tēn') *n.* cotton fabric resembling velvet.

ve'nal (vēn'l) *adj.* corrupt.

vend (vend) *v.* sell. —**ven'dor,** *n.*

ven•det'ta (ven det'ə) *n.* long, bitter feud.

vending machine, coin-operated machine for selling small articles.

ve•neer' (va nēr') *v.* **1.** overlay with thin sheets of fine wood, etc. —*n.* **2.** veneered layer of wood. **3.** superficial appearance.

ven'er•a•ble (ven'ər ə bəl) *adj.* worthy of reverence.

ven'er•ate' (-ə rāt') *v.*, **-ated, -ating.** revere. —**ven'er•a'tion,** *n.*

ve•ne're•al (va nēr'ē əl) *adj.* relating to or caused by sexual intercourse.

ve•ne'tian blind (va nē'shən) window blind with horizontal slats.

venge'ance (ven'jəns) *n.* revenge.

venge'ful, *adj.* seeking vengeance.

ve'ni•al (vē'nē əl, vēn'yəl) *n.* pardonable.

ven'i•son (ven'ə sən, -zən) *n.* flesh of deer used for food.

ven'om (ven'əm) *n.* **1.** poisonous fluid secreted by some snakes, spiders, etc. **2.** spite; malice. —**ven'om•ous,** *adj.*

ve'nous (vē'nəs) *adj.* **1.** of or having veins. **2.** of or being blood carried back to heart by veins.

vent (vent) *n.* **1.** outlet, as for fluid. **2.** expression. **3.** slit in garment. —*v.* **4.** express freely.

ven'ti•late' (ven'tl āt') *v.*, **-lated, -lating. 1.** provide with fresh air. **2.** submit to discussion. —**ven'ti•la'tion,** *n.* —**ven'ti•la'tor,** *n.*

ven'tral (ven'trəl) *adj.* of or near belly; abdominal.

ven'tri•cle (ven'tri kəl) *n.* either of two lower cavities of heart.

ven•tril'o•quism' (ven tril'ə kwiz'əm) *n.* art of speaking so that voice seems to come from another source. —**ven•tril'o•quist,** *n.*

ven'ture (ven'chər) *n.*, *v.*, **-tured, -turing.** —*n.* **1.** hazardous undertaking. —*v.* **2.** risk; dare. **3.** enter daringly. —**ven'ture•some** (-səm), **ven'tur•ous,** *adj.*

ven'ue (ven'yōō) *n.* scene or locale of action or event.

Ve'nus (vē'nəs) *n.* second planet from sun.

Ven'us's-fly'trap', *n.* plant with hinged leaves that trap insects.

ve•rac'i•ty (va ras'ə tē) *n.* truthfulness or accuracy. —**ve•ra'cious** (-rā'shəs) *adj.*

ve•ran'da (-ran'də) *n.* open porch. Also, **ve•ran'dah.**

verb (vûrb) *n.* part of speech expressing action, occurrence, existence, etc., as "saw" in the sentence "I saw Tom."

ver'bal (vûr'bəl) *adj.* **1.** of or in form of words. **2.** oral. **3.** of verbs.

ver'bal•ize', *v.*, **-ized, -izing.** express in words.

ver•ba'tim (vər bā'tim) *adv.* word for word.

ver•be'na (vər bē'nə) *n.* plant with long spikes of flowers.

ver'bi•age (vûr'bē ij) *n.* **1.** wordiness. **2.** manner of verbal expression.

ver•bose' (vər bōs') *adj.* wordy. —**ver•bos'i•ty** (-bos'i tē) *n.*

ver•bo'ten (vər bōt'n, fər-) *adj.* forbidden.

ver'dant (vûr'dnt) *adj.* green with vegetation. —**ver'dan•cy,** *n.*

ver'dict (vûr'dikt) *n.* decision.

ver'di•gris' (vûr'di grēs', -gris) *n.* green or bluish patina on some metals.

ver'dure (vûr'jər) *n.* **1.** greenness. **2.** green vegetation.

verge (vûrj) *n.*, *v.*, **verged, verging.** —*n.* **1.** edge or margin. —*v.* **2.** border. **3.** incline; tend.

ver'i•fy' (ver'ə fī') *v.*, **-fied, -fying. 1.** prove to be true. **2.** ascertain correctness of. —**ver'i•fi•a•ble,** *adj.* —**ver'i•fi•ca'tion,** *n.*

ver'i•ly (-lē) *adv. Archaic.* truly.

ver'i•si•mil'i•tude' (-si mil'i tōōd', -tyōōd') *n.* appearance of truth.

ver'i•ta•ble (-tə bəl) *adj.* genuine.

ver'i•ty (-tē) *n.*, *pl.* **-ties.** truth.

ver'mi•cel'li (vûr'mi chel'ē, -sel'ē) *n.* pasta in long threads.

ver•mil'ion (vər mil'yən) *n.* **1.** bright red. —*adj.* **2.** of or like vermilion.

ver'min (vûr'min) *n.pl. or sing.* small, troublesome animals collectively. —**ver'min·ous,** *adj.*

ver·mouth' (vər mōōth') *n.* white wine flavored with herbs.

ver·nac'u·lar (vər nak'yə lər, və-nak'-) *adj.* **1.** (of language) used locally or in everyday speech. —*n.* **2.** native speech. **3.** language of particular group.

ver'nal (vûr'nl) *adj.* of spring.

ver'sa·tile (vûr'sə tl; *esp. Brit.* -tīl') *adj.* doing variety of things well. —**ver'sa·til'i·ty,** *n.*

verse (vûrs) *n.* **1.** line of poem. **2.** type of metrical line, etc. **3.** poem. **4.** poetry. **5.** division of Biblical chapter.

versed, *adj.* expert; skilled.

ver'si·fy' (vûr'sə fī') *v.,* **-fied, -fying. 1.** treat in or turn into verse. **2.** compose verses.

ver'sion (vûr'zhən, -shən) *n.* **1.** translation. **2.** account. **3.** particular form.

ver'sus (vûr'səs, -səz) *prep.* in opposition or contrast to.

ver'te·bra (vûr'tə brə) *n., pl.* **-brae, -bras.** bone or segment of spinal column. —**ver'te·bral,** *adj.*

ver'te·brate' (-brit, -brāt') *adj.* **1.** having vertebrae. —*n.* **2.** vertebrate animal.

ver'tex (vûr'teks) *n., pl.* **-texes, -tices** (-tə sēz'). highest point.

ver'ti·cal (vûr'ti kəl) *adj.* **1.** perpendicular to plane of horizon. —*n.* **2.** something vertical.

ver·tig'i·nous (vər tij'ə nəs) *adj.* **1.** whirling. **2.** affected with or liable to cause vertigo.

ver'ti·go' (vûr'ti gō') *n., pl.* **-goes.** dizziness.

verve (vûrv) *n.* vivaciousness, energy, or enthusiasm.

ver'y (ver'ē) *adv., adj.,* **-ier, -iest.** —*adv.* **1.** extremely. —*adj.* **2.** identical. **3.** mere. **4.** actual. **5.** true.

ves'i·cle (ves'i kəl) *n.* small sac in body.

ves'pers (ves'pərz) *n.* evening service.

ves'sel (ves'əl) *n.* **1.** ship or boat. **2.** container. **3.** tube, as for blood.

vest (vest) *n.* **1.** sleeveless garment worn under jacket. —*v.* **2.** clothe or robe. **3.** endow with powers, etc.

ves'tal (ves'tl) *adj.* chaste.

vest'ed, *adj.* held completely and permanently.

vested interest, special interest in system, arrangement, or institution for personal reasons.

ves'ti·bule (ves'tə byōōl') *n.* small room between entrance and main room.

ves'tige (ves'tij) *n.* **1.** trace of something extinct. **2.** slight trace of something. —**ves·tig'i·al** (ve stij'ē əl, -stij'əl) *adj.*

vest'ing, *n.* the granting to an employee of the right to pension benefits despite early retirement.

vest'ment, *n.* ceremonial garment.

vest'-pock'et, *adj.* conveniently small.

ves'try (ves'trē) *n., pl.* **-tries. 1.** room in church for vestments or for meetings, etc. **2.** church committee managing temporal affairs.

vet (vet) *n. Informal.* **1.** veterinarian. **2.** veteran.

vetch (vech) *n.* plant used for forage and soil improvement.

vet'er·an (vet'ər ən) *n.* **1.** person who has served in armed forces. **2.** experienced person. —*adj.* **3.** experienced.

vet'er·i·nar'i·an (-ə när'ē ən) *n.* veterinary practitioner.

vet'er·i·nar'y (-ner'ē) *n., pl.* **-naries.** *adj.* —*n.* **1.** veterinarian. —*adj.* **2.** of medical and surgical treatment of animals.

ve'to (vē'tō) *n., pl.* **-toes,** *v.,* **-toed, -toing.** —*n.* **1.** power or right to reject or prohibit. **2.** prohibition. —*v.* **3.** reject by veto.

vex (veks) *v.* **1.** irritate. **2.** worry. —**vex·a'tion,** *n.* —**vex·a'tious,** *adj.* —**vexed,** *adj.*

vi'a (vī'ə, vē'ə) *prep.* by way of.

vi'a·ble (vī'ə bəl) *adj.* **1.** capable of living. **2.** practicable; workable.

vi'a·duct' (vī'ə dukt') *n.* long highway or railroad bridge.

vi'al (vī'əl, vīl) *n.* small glass container.

vi'and (vī'ənd) *n.* **1.** article of food. **2.** (*pl.*) dishes of food.

vibes (vībz) *n.pl.* **1.** *Slang.* something, esp. an emotional aura, emitted as if by vibration. **2.** vibraphone.

vi'brant (vī'brənt) *adj.* **1.** resonant. **2.** energetic; vital. —**vi'bran·cy,** *n.*

vi'bra·phone (vī'brə fōn') *n.* instrument like metal xylophone, with electrically enhanced resonance.

vi'brate (vī'brāt) *v.,* **-brated, -brating. 1.** move very rapidly to and fro; oscillate. **2.** tremble. **3.** resound. **4.** thrill. —**vi·bra'tion,** *n.* —**vi'bra·tor,** *n.*

vi·bra'to (vi brä'tō) *n., pl.* **-tos.** pulsating effect produced by rapid but slight alterations in pitch.

vi·bur'num (vī bûr'nəm) *n.* shrub bearing white flower clusters.

vic'ar (vik'ər) *n.* **1.** parish priest. **2.** representative of bishop.

vic'ar·age (-ij) *n.* residence or position of vicar.

vi·car'i·ous (vī kâr'ē əs, vi-) *adj.* **1.** done or suffered in place of another. **2.** substitute. —**vi·car'i·ous·ly,** *adv.*

vice (vīs) *n.* **1.** evil habit or fault. **2.** immoral conduct. **3.** vise. —*prep.* **4.** instead of.

vice-, prefix meaning deputy.

vice'-ad'mi·ral (vīs') *n.* commissioned officer ranking above rear admiral.

vice·ge'rent (-jēr'ənt) *n.* deputy to sovereign or magistrate.

vice president, officer next in rank to president. —**vice' pres'i·den·cy,** *n.*

vice'roy (vīs'roi) *n.* ruler of country or province as deputy of sovereign.

vi'ce ver'sa (vī'sə vûr'sə, vīs', vī'sē) in opposite way.

vi'chys·soise' (vish'ē swäz', vē'shē-) *n.* cold cream soup of potatoes and leeks.

vi·cin'i·ty (vi sin'i tē) *n., pl.* **-ties.** neighborhood; nearby area.

vi'cious (vish'əs) *adj.* **1.** immoral; depraved. **2.** evil. **3.** malicious.

vi·cis'si·tude' (vi sis'i tōōd', -tyōōd') *n.* change, esp. in condition.

vic'tim (vik'təm) *n.* **1.** sufferer from action or event. **2.** dupe. **3.** sacrifice. —**vic'tim·ize',** *v.,* **-ized, -izing.**

vic'tor (vik'tər) *n.* winner. —**vic·to'ri·ous** (-tôr'ē əs) *adj.*

vic'to·ry (-tə rē) *n., pl.* **-ries.** success in contest.

vict'ual (vit'l) *n.* **1.** (*pl.*) food. —*v.* **2.** supply with victuals. —**vict'ual·er,** *n.*

vid'e·o' (vid'ē ō') *adj.* **1.** of television. —*n.* **2.** videotape or videocassette.

vid'e·o·cas·sette', *n.* cassette containing videotape.

videocassette recorder, electronic device for recording and playing videocassettes.

vid'e·o·disc', disc on which pictures and sound are recorded for playback on TV set.

video game, electronic game played on screen or television set.

vid'e·o·tape', *n., v.,* **-taped, -taping.** —*n.* **1.** magnetic tape on which TV program, motion picture, etc., can be recorded. —*v.* **2.** record on this.

vie (vī) *v.,* **vied, vying.** contend for superiority.

view (vyōō) *n.* **1.** seeing or beholding. **2.** range of vision. **3.** landscape, etc., within one's sight. **4.** aspect. **5.** mental survey. **6.** purpose. **7.** notion; opinion. —*v.* **8.** see; look at. **9.** regard. —**view'er,** *n.*

view'find'er, *n.* camera part for viewing what will appear in picture.

view'point', *n.* **1.** place from which view is seen. **2.** attitude toward something.

vig'il (vij'əl) *n.* period of staying awake, esp. as watch.

vig'i·lant (-lənt) *adj.* **1.** wary. **2.** alert. —**vig'i·lance,** *n.*

vig'i·lan'te (-lan'tē) *n.* person who takes law into own hands.

vi·gnette' (vin yet') *n., v.,* **-gnetted, -gnetting.** —*n.* **1.** literary sketch. —*v.* **2.** make vignette of.

vig'or (vig'ər) *n.* **1.** active strength. **2.** energy. —**vig'or·ous,** *adj.*

Vik'ing (vī'king) *n.* medieval Scandinavian raider.

vile (vīl) *adj.,* **viler, vilest. 1.** very bad. **2.** offensive. **3.** evil. —**vile'ly,** *adv.* —**vile'ness,** *n.*

vil'i·fy' (vil'ə fī') *v.,* **-fied, -fying.** defame. —**vil'i·fi·ca'tion,** *n.*

vil'la (vil'ə) *n.* luxurious country residence.

vil'lage (vil'ij) *n.* small town. —**vil'lag·er,** *n.*

vil'lain (vil'ən) *n.* wicked person. —**vil'lain·ous,** *adj.* —**vil'lain·y,** *n.*

vil'lein (vil'ən, -ān) *n.* feudal serf.

vim (vim) *n.* vigor.

vin'ai·grette' (vin'ə gret') *n.* dressing, esp. for salad, of oil and vinegar, usu. with herbs.

vin'di·cate' (vin'di kāt') *v.,* **-cated, -cating. 1.** clear, as from suspicion. **2.** uphold or justify. —**vin'di·ca'tion,** *n.* —**vin'di·ca·tor,** *n.*

vin·dic'tive (vin dik'tiv) *adj.* holding grudge; vengeful.

vine (vīn) *n.* creeping or climbing plant with slender stem.

vin'e·gar (vin'i gər) *n.* sour liquid obtained by fermentation. —**vin'e·gar·y,** *adj.*

vine'yard (vin'yərd) *n.* plantation of grapevines.

vin'tage (vin'tij) *n.* **1.** wine from one harvest. **2.** grape harvest.

vint'ner (vint'nər) *n.* person who makes wine.

vi'nyl (vīn'l) *n.* type of plastic.

vi·o'la (vē ō'lə) *n.* stringed instrument resembling violin but slightly larger.

vi'o·late' (-lāt') *v.,* **-lated, -lating. 1.** break or transgress. **2.** break through or into. **3.** desecrate. **4.** rape. —**vi'o·la'tion,** *n.* —**vi'o·la'tor,** *n.*

vi'o·lent, *adj.* **1.** uncontrolled, strong, or rough. **2.** of destructive force. **3.** intense; severe. —**vi'o·lence,** *n.* —**vi'o·lent·ly,** *adv.*

vi'o·let (vī'ə lit) *n.* **1.** low herb bearing flowers, usually purple or blue. **2.** bluish purple.

vi'o·lin' (vī'ə lin') *n.* stringed instrument played with bow. —**vi′o•lin′ist**, *n.*

vi′o•lon•cel′lo (vē′ə lən chel′ō, vī′-) *n., pl.* **-los.** cello.

VIP (vē′ī′pē′) *Informal.* very important person.

vi′per (vī′pər) *n.* **1.** Old World venomous snake. **2.** malicious or treacherous person. —**vi′per•ous,** *adj.*

vi•ra′go (vi rä′gō, -rä′-) *n., pl.* **-goes, -gos.** shrewish woman.

vi′ral (vī′rəl) *adj.* of or caused by virus.

vir′gin (vûr′jin) *n.* **1.** person who has not had sexual intercourse. —*adj.* **2.** being, or like virgin. **3.** untried; unused. —**vir′gin•al,** *adj.* —**vir•gin′i•ty,** *n.*

vir′gule (vûr′gyōol) *n.* oblique stroke (/) used as dividing line.

vir′ile (vir′əl) *adj.* **1.** manly. **2.** vigorous. **3.** capable of procreation. —**vi•ril′i•ty,** *n.*

vi•rol′o•gy (vī rol′ə jē, vi-) *n.* study of viruses. —**vi•rol′o•gist,** *n.*

vir′tu•al (vûr′chōō əl) *adj.* **1.** such in effect, though not actually. **2.** simulated by computer.

virtual reality, realistic simulation by computer system.

vir′tue (vûr′chōō) *n.* **1.** moral excellence. **2.** chastity. **3.** merit. —**vir′tu•ous,** *adj.* —**vir′tu•ous•ly,** *adv.*

vir•tu•o′so (vûr′chōō ō′sō) *n., pl.* **-sos, -si.** person of special skill, esp. in music. —**vir′tu•os′i•ty** (-os′i tē) *n.*

vir′u•lent (vir′yə lənt, vir′ə-) *adj.* **1.** poisonous; malignant. **2.** hostile. —**vir′u•lence,** *n.*

vi′rus (vī′rəs) *n.* **1.** infective agent. **2.** corrupting influence. **3.** segment of self-replicating code planted illegally in computer program.

vi′sa (vē′zə) *n.* passport endorsement permitting foreign entry or immigration.

vis′age (viz′ij) *n.* **1.** face. **2.** aspect.

vis′-à-vis′ (vē′zə vē′) *prep.* **1.** in relation to. **2.** opposite.

vis′cer•a (vis′ər ə) *n.pl.* **1.** soft interior organs of body. **2.** intestines.

vis′count (vī′kount′) *n.* nobleman ranking below earl or count. —**vis′count•ess,** *n.fem.*

vis′cous (vis′kəs), *adj.* sticky; gluey. Also, **vis′cid** (vis′id).

vise (vīs) *n.* device, usually with two jaws, for holding object firmly.

vis′i•ble (viz′ə bəl) *adj.* **1.** capable of being seen. **2.** perceptible or manifest. —**vis′i•bil′i•ty,** *n.*

vi′sion (vizh′ən) *n.* **1.** power or sense of sight. **2.** imagination or unusually keen perception. **3.** mental image of something imaginary.

vi′sion•ar′y (vizh′ə ner′ē) *adj., n., pl.* **-ies.** —*adj.* **1.** fanciful. **2.** seen in vision. **3.** unreal. —*n.* **4.** seer of visions. **5.** bold or impractical schemer.

vis′it (viz′it) *v.* **1.** go to for purposes of talking, staying, etc. **2.** afflict. —*n.* **3.** act of visiting. **4.** stay as guest. —**vis′i•tor, vis′i•tant,** *n.*

vis′it•a′tion (-i tā′shən) *n.* **1.** visit. **2.** bringing of good or evil, as by supernatural force.

vi′sor (vī′zər) *n.* front piece, as of helmet or cap.

vis′ta (vis′tə) *n.* extended view in one direction.

vis′u•al (vizh′ōō əl) *adj.* **1.** of or by means of sight. **2.** visible.

vis′u•al•ize′, *v.,* **-ized, -izing. 1.** make visual. **2.** form mental image of. —**vis′u•al•i•za′tion,** *n.*

vi′tal (vīt′l) *adj.* **1.** of life. **2.** living;

energetic; vivid. **3.** giving or necessary to life. **4.** essential.

vi•tal′i•ty (-tal′i tē) *n., pl.* **-ties. 1.** vital force. **2.** physical or mental vigor. **3.** power of continued existence.

vital signs, essential body functions, comprising pulse rate, body temperature, and respiration.

vital statistics, statistics concerning deaths, births, and marriages.

vi′ta•min (vī′tə min) *n.* food element essential in small quantities to maintain life. —**vi′ta•min′ic,** *adj.*

vi′ti•ate′ (vish′ē āt′) *v.,* **-ated, -ating. 1.** impair. **2.** invalidate.

vit′i•cul′ture (vit′i kul′chər, vī′ti-) *n.* cultivation of grapes.

vit′re•ous (vi′trē əs) *adj.* of or like glass.

vitreous humor, transparent gelatinous substance that fills eyeball.

vit′ri•fy′, *v.,* **-fied, -fying.** change to glass.

vit′rine′ (vi trēn′) *n.* glass cabinet.

vit′ri•ol (vi′trē əl) *n.* **1.** glassy metallic compound. **2.** sulfuric acid. **3.** caustic criticism, etc. —**vit′ri•ol′ic** (-ol′ik) *adj.*

vi•tu′per•ate′ (vī tōō′pə rāt′, -tyōō′-, vi-) *v.,* **-ated, -ating.** criticize harshly. —**vi•tu′per•a′tion,** *n.*

vi•va′cious (vi vā′shəs, vī-) *adj.* lively; animated. —**vi•vac′i•ty** (-vas′i tē) *n.*

viv′id (viv′id) *adj.* **1.** bright, as color or light. **2.** full of life. **3.** intense; striking. —**viv′id•ly,** *adv.*

viv′i•fy′, *v.,* **-fied, -fying.** give life to.

viv′i•sec′tion (viv′ə sek′shən) *n.* dissection of live animal.

vix′en (vik′sən) *n.* **1.** female fox. **2.** ill-tempered woman.

vi•zier′ (vi zēr′, viz′yər) *n.* high official in certain Muslim countries.

vo•cab′u•lar′y (vō kab′yə ler′ē) *n., pl.* **-laries. 1.** words used by people, class, or person. **2.** collection of defined words, usually in alphabetical order.

vo′cal (vō′kəl) *adj.* **1.** of the voice. **2.** of or for singing. **3.** articulate or talkative. —*n.* **4.** vocal composition or performance. —**vo′cal•ize′,** *v.,* **-ized, -izing.** —**vo′cal•i•za′tion,** *n.*

vocal cords, membranes in larynx producing sound by vibration.

vo′cal•ist (-kə list) *n.* singer.

vo•ca′tion (vō kā′shən) *n.* occupation, business, or profession. —**vo•ca′tion•al,** *adj.*

voc′a•tive (vok′ə tiv) *adj.* of or being grammatical case used to indicate one being addressed.

vo•cif′er•ate′ (vō sif′ə rāt′) *v.,* **-ated, -ating.** cry noisily; shout. —**vo•cif′er•ous,** *adj.*

vod′ka (vod′kə) *n.* colorless distilled liquor.

vogue (vōg) *n.* **1.** fashion. **2.** popular favor.

voice (vois) *n., v.,* **voiced, voicing.** —*n.* **1.** sound uttered through mouth. **2.** speaking or singing voice. **3.** expression. **4.** choice. **5.** right to express opinion. **6.** verb inflection indicating whether subject is acting or acted upon. —*v.* **7.** express or declare. —**voice′less,** *adj.*

voice box, larynx.

voice mail, electronic system that routes voice messages to appropriate recipients.

voice′-o′ver, *n.* voice of off-screen narrator or announcer.

void (void) *adj.* **1.** without legal force. **2.** useless. **3.** empty. —*n.* **4.** empty

space. —*v.* **5.** invalidate. **6.** empty out. —**void′a•ble,** *adj.*

voile (voil) *n.* lightweight, semisheer fabric.

vol., volume.

vol′a•tile (vol′ə tl) *adj.* **1.** evaporating rapidly. **2.** explosive. **3.** rapidly changeable in emotion.

vol•ca′no (vol kā′nō) *n., pl.* **-noes, -nos. 1.** vent in earth from which lava, steam, etc., are expelled. **2.** mountain with such vent. —**vol•can′ic** (-kan′ik) *adj.*

vole (vōl) *n.* short-tailed stocky rodent.

vo•li′tion (vō lish′ən, və-) *n.* act or power of willing.

vol′ley (vol′ē) *n.* **1.** discharge of many missiles together. **2.** returning of ball before it hits ground. —*v.* **3.** hit or fire volley.

vol′ley•ball′, *n.* **1.** game in which large ball is volleyed back and forth over net. **2.** ball used in this game.

volt (vōlt) *n.* unit of electromotive force. —**volt′age,** *n.* —**volt′me′ter,** *n.*

vol′u•ble (vol′yə bəl) *adj.* glibly fluent. —**vol′u•bil′i•ty,** *n.*

vol′ume (vol′yōom, -yəm) *n.* **1.** book. **2.** size in three dimensions. **3.** mass or quantity. **4.** loudness or fullness of sound.

vo•lu′mi•nous (və lōō′mə nəs) *adj.* **1.** filling many volumes. **2.** ample.

vol′un•tar′y (vol′ən ter′ē) *adj.* **1.** done, made, etc., by free choice. **2.** controlled by will. —**vol′un•tar′i•ly,** *adv.*

vol′un•teer′, *n.* **1.** person who offers self, as for military duty. **2.** worker forgoing pay. —*v.* **3.** offer for some duty or purpose.

vo•lup′tu•ous (və lup′chōō əs) *adj.* **1.** luxurious; sensuous. **2.** full and shapely. —**vo•lup′tu•ous•ly,** *adv.*

vo•lute′ (və lōot′) *n.* spiral object.

vom′it (vom′it) *v.* **1.** eject from stomach through mouth. **2.** eject with force. —*n.* **3.** vomited matter.

voo′doo (vōo′dōo) *n.* polytheistic religion deriving chiefly from African cults.

vo•ra′cious (vô rā′shəs) *adj.* greedy; ravenous. —**vo•ra′cious•ly,** *adv.* —**vo•rac′i•ty** (-ras′i tē) *n.*

vor′tex (vôr′teks) *n., pl.* **-texes, -tices** (-tə sēz′). whirling movement or mass.

vo′ta•ry (vō′tə rē) *n., pl.* **-ries.** worshiper; devotee.

vote (vōt) *n., v.,* **voted, voting.** —*n.* **1.** formal expression of wish or choice, as by ballot. **2.** right to this. **3.** votes collectively. —*v.* **4.** cast one's vote. **5.** cause to go or occur by vote. —**vot′er,** *n.*

vouch (vouch) *v.* **1.** answer for. **2.** give assurance, as surety or sponsor.

vouch′er, *n.* document, receipt, etc., proving expenditure.

vouch•safe′, *v.,* **-safed, -safing.** grant or permit.

vow (vou) *n.* **1.** solemn promise, pledge, or personal engagement. —*v.* **2.** make vow.

vow′el (vou′əl) *n.* **1.** speech sound made with clear channel through middle of mouth. **2.** letter representing vowel.

voy′age (voi′ij) *n., v.,* **-aged, -aging.** —*n.* **1.** journey, esp. by water. —*v.* **2.** make voyage.

vo•yeur′ (vwä yûr′, voi ûr′) *n.* person who obtains sexual gratification by looking at sexual objects or acts. —**vo•yeur′ism,** *n.*

V.P., Vice President. Also, **VP.**

vs., versus.

VT, Vermont. Also, **Vt.**

vul′can•ize′ (vul′kə nīz′) *v.,* **-ized, -izing.** treat rubber with sulfur and heat. —**vul′can•i•za′tion,** *n.*

vul′gar (vul′gər) *adj.* **1.** lacking good breeding or taste. **2.** obscene. **3.** plebeian. **4.** vernacular. —**vul•gar′i•ty** (-gar/i tē) *n.*

vul′ner•a•ble (vul′nər ə bəl) *adj.* **1.** liable to physical or emotional hurt. **2.** open to attack.

vul′ture (vul′chər) *n.* large, carrion-eating bird.

vul′va (vul′və) *n., pl.* **-vae, -vas.** external female genitals.

vy′ing (vī′ing) *adj.* competing.

W

W, w (dub′əl yōō′, -yōō) *n.* twenty-third letter of English alphabet.

W, west, western.

WA, Washington.

wack′y (wak′ē) *adj.,* **-ier, -iest.** *Slang.* odd or irrational.

wad (wod) *n., v.,* **wadded, wadding.** —*n.* **1.** small soft mass. —*v.* **2.** form into wad. **3.** stuff.

wad′dle (wod′l) *v.,* **-dled, -dling.** —*v.* **1.** sway in walking, as duck. —*n.* **2.** waddling gait.

wade (wād) *v.,* **waded, wading.** —*v.* **1.** walk through water, sand, etc. —*n.* **2.** act of wading.

wa′fer (wā′fər) *n.* **1.** thin crisp biscuit. **2.** small disk of bread used in Eucharist.

waf′fle (wof′əl) *n., v.,* **-fled, -fling.** —*n.* **1.** batter cake baked in a double griddle (**waffle iron**). —*v.* **2.** speak or write evasively.

waft (wäft, waft) *v.* **1.** float through air or over water. —*n.* **2.** sound, odor, etc., wafted.

wag (wag) *v.,* **wagged, wagging,** *n.* —*v.* **1.** move rapidly back and forth. —*n.* **2.** act of wagging. **3.** joker. —**wag′gish** *adj.*

wage (wāj) *n., v.,* **waged, waging.** —*n.* **1.** pay; salary. **2.** recompense. —*v.* **3.** carry on (war, etc.).

wa′ger (wā′jər) *v., n.* bet.

wag′gle (wag′əl) *v.,* **-gled, -gling,** *n.* wag.

wag′on (wag′ən) *n.* four-wheeled vehicle for drawing heavy loads.

wagon train, train of wagons and horses.

waif (wāf) *n.* homeless child.

wail (wāl) *n.* **1.** long mournful cry. **2.** sound like this. —*v.* **3.** utter wails. —**wail′er,** *n.*

wain′scot (wān′skət, -skot, -skōt) *n.* woodwork lining wall.

waist (wāst) *n.* part of body between ribs and hips. —**waist′band′,** *n.* —**waist′line′,** *n.*

waist′coat′ (wes′kət, wāst′kōt′) *n. Brit.* vest.

wait (wāt) *v.* **1.** stay in expectation. **2.** be ready. **3.** await. **4.** wait on; serve. —*n.* **5.** act of waiting. **6.** delay. **7.** ambush.

wait′er, *n.* man who waits on table. —**wait′ress,** *n.fem.*

waiting list, list of persons waiting, as for reservations or admission.

waive (wāv) *v.,* **waived, waiving.** give up; forgo.

waiv′er, *n.* statement of relinquishment.

wake (wāk) *v.,* **waked** or **woke** (wōk), **waked, waking,** *n.* —*v.* **1.** stop sleeping; rouse from sleep. —*n.* **2.**

vigil, esp. beside corpse. **3.** track or path, esp. of vessel.

wake′ful, *adj.* awake; alert.

wak′en, *v.* wake.

wale (wāl) *n., v.,* **waled, waling.** —*n.* **1.** mark left on skin by rod or whip. **2.** vertical rib or cord in fabric. —*v.* **3.** mark with wales.

walk (wôk) *v.* **1.** go or traverse on foot. **2.** cause to walk. —*n.* **3.** act, course, or manner of walking. **4.** distance walked. **5.** branch of activity. **6.** sidewalk or path.

walk′a•way′, *n.* easy victory.

walk′ie-talk′ie (wô′kē tô′kē) *n.* portable radio transmitter and receiver.

walking stick, 1. stick used for support in walking. **2.** insect with long twiglike body.

walk′out′, *n.* strike in which workers leave place of work.

wall (wôl) *n.* **1.** upright structure that divides, encloses, etc. —*v.* **2.** enclose, divide, etc., with wall.

wall′board′, *n.* artificial material used to make or cover walls, etc.

wal′let (wol′it) *n.* small flat case for paper money, etc.

wall′eye′ (wôl′-) *n.* **1.** condition in which eye or eyes are turned outward. **2.** N American freshwater food fish. Also, **walleyed pike.**

wall′flow′er, *n.* **1.** person who, because of shyness, remains at the side at a party. **2.** perennial plant with fragrant flowers.

wal′lop (wol′əp) *Informal.* —*v.* **1.** thrash or defeat. —*n.* **2.** blow.

wal′lop•ing, *adj. Informal.* **1.** very large. **2.** impressive.

wal′low (wol′ō) *v.* lie or roll in mud, etc.

wall′pa′per, *n.* decorative paper for covering walls and ceilings.

wal′nut′ (wôl′nut′, -nat) *n.* northern tree valued for edible nut.

wal′rus (wôl′rəs) *n.* large tusked mammal of Arctic seas.

waltz (wôlts) *n.* **1.** dance in triple rhythm. —*v.* **2.** dance a waltz.

wam′pum (wom′pəm) *n.* shell beads, formerly used by North American Indians as money.

wan (won) *adj.,* **wanner, wannest.** pale; worn-looking. —**wan′ly,** *adv.*

wand (wond) *n.* slender rod or shoot.

wan′der (won′dər) *v.* move aimlessly; stray. —**wan′der•er,** *n.*

wan′der•lust′, *n.* desire to travel.

wane (wān) *v.,* **waned, waning,** *n.* —*v.* **1.** (of moon) decrease periodically. **2.** decline or decrease. —*n.* **3.** decline or decrease.

wan′gle (wang′gəl) *v.,* **-gled, -gling.** bring out or obtain by scheming or underhand methods.

wan′na•be′ (won′ə bē′) *n. Informal.* one who aspires, often vainly, to emulate another's success or status.

want (wont) *v.* **1.** feel need or desire for. **2.** lack; be deficient in. —*n.* **3.** desire or need. **4.** lack. **5.** poverty.

want′ing, *adj., prep.* lacking.

wan′ton (won′tn) *adj.* **1.** malicious; unjustifiable. **2.** lewd. —*n.* **3.** lascivious person.

war (wôr) *n., v.,* **warred, warring.** —*n.* **1.** armed conflict. —*v.* **2.** carry on war.

war′ble (wôr′bəl) *v.,* **-bled, -bling.** —*v.* **1.** sing with trills, etc., as birds. —*n.* **2.** warbled song.

war′bler, *n.* small songbird.

ward (wôrd) *n.* **1.** division of city. **2.** division of hospital. **3.** person under legal care of guardian or court. **4.** custody. —*v.* **5. ward off,** repel or avert.

ward′en (wôr′dn) *n.* **1.** keeper. **2.** administrative head of prison.

ward′er, *n.* guard.

ward heeler, minor politician who does chores for political machine.

ward′robe′, *n.* **1.** stock of clothes. **2.** clothes closet.

ware (wâr) *n.* **1.** (*pl.*) goods. **2.** pottery. **3.** vessels for domestic use.

ware′house′, *n., v.,* **-housed, -housing.** —*n.* (wâr′hous′) **1.** storehouse for goods. —*v.* (-houz′, -hous′) **2.** store in warehouse.

war′fare′, *n.* waging of war.

war′head′, *n.* section of missile containing explosive or payload.

war′-horse′, *n. Informal.* veteran of many conflicts.

war′like′, *adj.* waging or prepared for war.

war′lock′, *n.* male witch.

warm (wôrm) *adj.* **1.** having, giving, or feeling moderate heat. **2.** cordial. **3.** lively. **4.** kind; affectionate. —*v.* **5.** make or become warm. —**warmth,** *n.*

warm′-blood′ed, *adj.* having relatively constant body temperature that is independent of environment.

warmed′-o′ver, *adj.* **1.** reheated. **2.** stale; not new.

warm′heart′ed, *adj.* having emotional warmth.

war′mon′ger, *n.* person who advocates or incites war.

warn (wôrn) *v.* **1.** give notice of danger, evil, etc. **2.** caution. —**warn′ing,** *n.*

warp (wôrp) *v.* **1.** bend out of shape; distort. —*n.* **2.** bend or twist. **3.** lengthwise threads in loom.

war′rant (wôr′ənt) *n.* **1.** justification. **2.** guarantee. **3.** document authorizing something. —*v.* **4.** authorize or justify. **5.** guarantee.

warrant officer, military officer between enlisted and commissioned grades.

war′ran•ty, *n., pl.* **-ties.** guarantee.

war′ren (wôr′ən) *n.* place where rabbits live.

war′ri•or (wôr′ē ər) *n.* soldier.

war′ship′, *n.* ship for combat.

wart (wôrt) *n.* small hard elevation on skin. —**wart′y,** *adj.*

war′y (wâr′ē) *adj.,* **warier, wariest.** careful. —**war′i•ly,** *adv.*

was (wuz, woz; *unstressed* wəz) *v.* first and third pers. sing., past indicative of **be.**

wash (wosh) *v.* **1.** cleanse in or with water. **2.** flow over. **3.** carry in flowing. **4.** cover thinly. —*n.* **5.** act of washing. **6.** Also, **wash′ing.** clothes, etc., to be washed. **7.** liquid covering. **8.** rough water or air behind moving ship or plane. —**wash′a•ble,** *adj.* —**wash′bowl′,** *n.* —**wash′cloth′,** *n.*

Wash., Washington.

wash′board′, *n.* board to scrub clothes on.

washed′-out′, *adj.* **1.** faded. **2.** *Informal.* weary or tired-looking.

washed′-up′, *adj. Informal.* done for; having failed.

wash′er, *n.* **1.** machine for washing. **2.** flat ring of rubber, metal, etc., to give tightness.

wash′out′, *n.* **1.** destruction from action of water. **2.** *Slang.* failure.

wash′room′, *n.* public room with toilets.

wasn′t (wuz′ənt, woz′-) contraction of **was not.**

wasp (wosp) *n.* **1.** stinging insect. **2.** *Slang.* (*cap. or caps.*) white Anglo-Saxon Protestant.

wasp′ish, *adj.* irritable; snappish.

was′sail (wos′əl, wo säl′) *n.* drinking party.

waste (wāst) *v.,* **wasted, wasting,** *n., adj.* —*v.* **1.** squander. **2.** fail to use. **3.** destroy gradually. **4.** become wasted. —*n.* **5.** useless expenditure. **6.** neglect. **7.** gradual decay. **8.** devastation. **9.** anything left over. —*adj.* **10.** not used. **11.** left over or worthless. —**waste′- ful,** *adj.*

waste′land′, *n.* barren land.

wast′rel (wā′stral) *n.* **1.** spendthrift. **2.** idler.

watch (woch) *v.* **1.** look attentively. **2.** be careful. **3.** guard. —*n.* **4.** close, constant observation. **5.** guard. **6.** period of watching. **7.** small timepiece. —**watch′band′,** *n.* —**watch′ful,** *adj.*

watch′dog′, *n.* **1.** dog that guards property. **2.** guardian, as against illegal conduct.

watch′man, *n.* person who keeps watch.

watch′tow′er, *n.* tower for guard.

watch′word′, *n.* **1.** password. **2.** slogan.

wa′ter (wô′tər) *n.* **1.** transparent liquid forming rivers, seas, lakes, rain, etc. **2.** liquid solution. **3.** liquid organic secretion. —*v.* **4.** moisten or supply with water. **5.** dilute. **6.** discharge water. —*adj.* **7.** of, for, or powered by water.

wa′ter•bed′, *n.* water-filled plastic bag used as bed.

water buffalo, domesticated Asian buffalo with curved horns.

water chestnut, aquatic plant with edible, nutlike fruit.

water closet, room containing flush toilet.

wa′ter•col′or, *n.* **1.** pigment mixed with water. **2.** painting using such pigments.

wa′ter•course′, *n.* **1.** stream of water. **2.** bed of stream.

wa′ter•cress′, *n.* plant that grows in streams and bears pungent leaves used in salad.

wa′ter•fall′, *n.* steep fall of water.

wa′ter•fowl′, *n., pl.* **-fowl, -fowls.** aquatic bird.

wa′ter•front′, *n.* part of city or town on edge of body of water.

water gap, transverse gap in mountain ridge.

wa′ter•ing place, resort by water or having mineral springs.

water lily, aquatic plant with showy flowers.

water line, one of series of lines on ship's hull indicating level to which it is immersed.

wa′ter•logged′, *adj.* filled or soaked with water.

wa′ter•mark′, *n.* **1.** mark showing height reached by river, etc. **2.** manufacturer's design impressed in paper. —*v.* **3.** put watermark in (paper).

wa′ter•mel′on, *n.* large sweet juicy fruit of a vine.

water moccasin, cottonmouth.

wa′ter•proof′, *adj.* **1.** impervious to water. —*v.* **2.** make waterproof.

water rat, aquatic rodent.

wa′ter•repel′lent, *adj.* repelling water but not entirely waterproof.

wa′ter•shed′, *n.* **1.** area drained by river, etc. **2.** high land dividing such areas. **3.** important point of division or transition.

water ski, short, broad ski for gliding over water behind boat. —**wa′- ter-ski′,** *v.,* **water-skied, water- skiing.** —**wa′ter•ski′er,** *n.*

wa′ter•spout′, *n.* tornadolike storm over lake or ocean.

water table, underground level beneath which soil and rock are saturated with water.

wa′ter•tight′, *adj.* **1.** constructed or fitted to be impervious to water. **2.** allowing no doubt.

wa′ter•way′, *n.* body of water as route of travel.

water wheel, wheel turned by water to provide power.

wa′ter•works′, *n.pl.* apparatus for collecting and distributing water, as for city.

wa′ter•y, *adj.* of, like, or full of water. —**wa′ter•i•ness,** *n.*

watt (wot) *n.* unit of electric power.

wat′tle (wot′l) *n.* **1.** flesh hanging from throat or chin. **2.** interwoven rods and twigs.

wave (wāv) *n., v.,* **waved, waving.** —*n.* **1.** ridge on surface of liquid. **2.** surge; rush. **3.** curve. **4.** vibration, as in transmission of sound, etc. **5.** sign with moving hand, flag, etc. —*v.* **6.** move with waves. **7.** curve. **8.** signal by wave. —**wav′y,** *adj.*

wave′length′, *n.* distance between two successive points in wave.

wa′ver (wā′vər) *v.* **1.** sway. **2.** hesitate. **3.** fluctuate.

wax (waks) *n.* **1.** yellowish substance secreted by bees. **2.** any similar substance. —*v.* **3.** rub with wax. **4.** (esp. of moon) increase. **5.** become. —**wax′en,** *adj.* —**wax′y,** *adj.*

wax museum, museum displaying wax effigies of famous persons.

wax myrtle, bayberry of southeastern U.S.

wax paper, paper made moisture-resistant by paraffin coating.

wax′wing′, *n.* small crested bird.

way (wā) *n.* **1.** manner; fashion. **2.** plan; means. **3.** direction. **4.** road or route. **5.** custom.

way′bill′, *n.* list of goods with shipping directions.

way′far′er, *n.* rover.

way′lay′ (wā′lā′, wā lā′) *v.* ambush.

way′-out′, *adj. Informal.* very unconventional.

ways and means, methods of raising revenue.

way′side′, *n.* **1.** side of road. —*adj.* **2.** beside road.

way′ward (-ward) *adj.* capricious.

we (wē) *pron.* nominative plural of **I.**

weak (wēk) *adj.* **1.** not strong; frail. **2.** deficient. —**weak′en,** *v.* —**weak′- ness,** *n.*

weak′-kneed′, *adj.* yielding readily to opposition, pressure, or intimidation.

weak′ling (-ling) *n.* weak creature.

weak′ly, *adj.,* **-lier, -liest,** *adv.* —*adj.* **1.** sickly. —*adv.* **2.** in weak manner.

weal (wēl) *n. Archaic.* well-being.

wealth (welth) *n.* **1.** great possessions or riches. **2.** profusion. —**wealth′y,** *adj.*

wean (wēn) *v.* **1.** accustom to food other than mother's milk. **2.** detach from obsession or vice.

weap′on (wep′ən) *n.* instrument for use in fighting.

weap′on•ry, *n.* weapons collectively.

wear (wâr) *v.,* **wore** (wôr), **worn, wearing,** *n.* —*v.* **1.** have on body for covering or ornament. **2.** impair or diminish gradually. **3.** weary. **4.** undergo wear. **5.** last under use. —*n.* **6.** use of garment. **7.** clothing. **8.** gradual impairment or diminution. —**wear′a- ble,** *adj.*

wea′ri•some (wēr′ē səm) *adj.* **1.** tiring. **2.** tedious.

wea′ry, *adj.,* **-rier, -riest,** *v.,* **-ried, -rying.** —*adj.* **1.** tired. **2.** tedious. —*v.* **3.** tire. —**wea′ri•ly,** *adv.*

wea′sel (wē′zəl) *n.* small carnivorous animal.

weath′er (weth′ər) *n.* **1.** state of atmosphere as to moisture, temperature, etc. —*v.* **2.** expose to weather. **3.** withstand. —*adj.* **4.** of or on windward side.

weath′er-beat′en, *adj.* worn or marked by weather.

weath′er•ing, *n.* action of wind and water on exposed rock.

weath′er•ize′, *v.,* **-ized, -izing.** make secure against cold weather.

weath′er•proof′, *adj.* **1.** able to withstand all kinds of weather. —*v.* **2.** make weatherproof.

weath′er•vane′, *n.* device to show direction of wind.

weave (wēv) *v.,* **wove** (wōv), **woven** or **wove, weaving,** *n.* —*v.* **1.** interlace, as tc form cloth. **2.** take winding course. —*n.* **3.** pattern or method of weaving. —**weav′er,** *n.*

web (web) *n., v.,* **webbed, webbing.** —*n.* **1.** something woven. **2.** fabric spun by spiders. **3.** membrane between toes in ducks, etc. **4. the Web,** World Wide Web. —*v.* **5.** cover with web.

web′foot′, *n.* foot with webbed toes. —**web′foot′ed,** *adj.*

Web′ster (web′stər) *n. Informal.* a dictionary of the English language. Also, **Web′ster's.**

wed (wed) *v.,* **wedded, wedded** or **wed, wedding. 1.** bind or join in marriage. **2.** attach firmly.

Wed., Wednesday.

wed′ding, *n.* marriage ceremony.

wedge (wej) *n., v.,* **wedged, wedging.** —*n.* **1.** angled object for splitting. —*v.* **2.** split with wedge. **3.** thrust or force like wedge.

wed′lock, *n.* matrimony.

Wednes′day (wenz′dā, -dē) *n.* fourth day of week.

wee (wē) *adj.* tiny.

weed (wēd) *n.* **1.** useless plant growing in cultivated ground. —*v.* **2.** free from weeds. **3.** remove as undesirable. —**weed′y,** *adj.*

weeds (wēdz) *n.pl.* black clothes for mourning.

week (wēk) *n.* **1.** seven successive days. **2.** working part of week.

week′day′, *n.* any day except Sunday, or, often, Saturday and Sunday.

week′end′ (-end′, -end′) *n.* **1.** Saturday and Sunday. —*adj.* **2.** of or for weekend.

week′ly, *adj., adv., n., pl.* **-lies.** —*adj.* **1.** happening, appearing, etc., once a week. **2.** lasting a week. —*adv.* **3.** once a week. **4.** by the week. —*n.* **5.** weekly periodical.

weep (wēp) *v.,* **wept** (wept), **weeping. 1.** shed tears. **2.** mourn.

wee′vil (wē′vəl) *n.* beetle destructive to grain, fruit, etc.

weft (weft) *n.* threads interlacing with warp.

weigh (wā) *v.* **1.** measure heaviness of. **2.** burden. **3.** consider. **4.** lift. **5.** have heaviness. —**weigh′er,** *n.*

weight (wāt) *n.* **1.** amount of heaviness. **2.** system of units for expressing weight. **3.** heavy mass. **4.** pressure. **5.** burden. **6.** importance. —*v.* **7.** add weight to. —**weight′y,** *adj.* —**weight′less,** *adj.*

weir (wēr) *n.* **1.** dam in a stream. **2.** fence set in stream to catch fish.

weird (wērd) *adj.* **1.** supernatural. **2.** uncannily strange.

weird′o (wēr′dō) *n. Slang.* odd, eccentric, or abnormal person.

wel′come (wel′kəm) *n., v.,* **-comed, -coming,** *adj.* —*n.* **1.** friendly reception. —*v.* **2.** receive or greet with pleasure. —*adj.* **3.** gladly received. **4.** given permission or consent.

weld (weld) *v.* **1.** unite, esp. by heating and pressing. —*n.* **2.** welded joint. —**weld′er,** *n.*

wel′fare′ (wel′fâr′) *n.* **1.** well-being. **2.** provision of benefits to poor.

well (wel) *adv., compar.* **better,** *superl.* **best,** *adj., n., v.* —*adv.* **1.** excellently; properly. **2.** thoroughly. —*adj.* **3.** in good health. **4.** good. —*n.* **5.** hole made in earth to reach water, oil, etc. **6.** source. **7.** vertical shaft. —*v.* **8.** rise or gush.

well′-advised′, *adj.* prudent.

well′-appoint′ed, *adj.* attractively furnished.

well′-be′ing, *n.* good or prosperous condition.

well′born′, *adj.* of good family.

well′-bred′, *adj.* showing good manners.

well′-dis•posed′, *adj.* feeling favorable, sympathetic, or kind.

well′-done′, *adj.* **1.** performed accurately and skillfully. **2.** thoroughly cooked.

well′-found′ed, *adj.* having or based on good reasons, sound information, etc.

well′-ground′ed, *adj.* having good basic knowledge of a subject.

well′-heeled′, *adj.* prosperous.

well′-informed′, *adj.* having extensive knowledge.

well′man′nered, *adj.* polite.

well′-mean′ing, *adj.* intending good. —**well′-meant′,** *adj.*

well′-nigh′, *adv.* nearly.

well′-off′, *adj.* **1.** in good or favorable condition. **2.** prosperous.

well′-round′ed, *adj.* desirably varied.

well′spring′, *n.* source.

well′-to-do′, *adj.* prosperous.

well′-worn′, *adj.* **1.** showing effects of extensive use. **2.** trite.

Welsh (welsh, welch) *n.* people or language of Wales.

welt (welt) *n.* **1.** wale from lash. **2.** strip around edge of shoe. **3.** narrow border along seam. —*v.* **4.** put welt on.

wel′ter (wel′tər) *v.* **1.** roll, as waves. **2.** wallow.

wen (wen) *n.* small cyst.

wench (wench) *n.* girl or young woman.

wend (wend) *v.,* **wended, wending.** *Archaic.* go.

went (went) *v.* pt. of **go.**

were (wûr; *unstressed* wər) *v.* past plural and pres. subjunctive of **be.**

weren′t (wûrnt, wûr′ənt) contraction of **were not.**

were′wolf′ (wâr′woŏlf, wēr′-, wûr′-) *n., pl.* **-wolves.** (in folklore) human turned into wolf.

west (west) *n.* **1.** point of compass opposite east. **2.** territory in this direction. —*adj. adv.* **3.** toward or from west. —**west′er•ly,** *adj., adv.* —**west′ern,** *adj.* —**west′ern•er,** *n.*

west′ern•ize′ (wes′tər nīz′) *v.,* **-ized, -izing.** influence with or convert to western ideas and customs.

west′ward (-wərd) *adj.* **1.** moving or facing west. —*adv.* **2.** Also, **west′-**

wards. toward west. —*n.* **3.** westward part. —**west′ward•ly,** *adj., adv.*

wet (wet) *adj.,* **wetter, wettest,** *n., v.,* **wet** or **wetted, wetting.** —*adj.* **1.** covered or soaked with water. **2.** rainy. —*n.* **3.** moisture. —*v.* **4.** make or become wet.

wet blanket, one that dampens enthusiasm.

wet nurse, woman hired to suckle another's infant.

wet suit, close-fitting rubber suit worn for body warmth, as by scuba divers.

whack (hwak, wak) *Informal. v.* **1.** strike sharply. —*n.* **2.** smart blow.

whale (hwāl, wāl) *n., pl.* **whales** or **whale,** *v.,* **whaled, whaling.** —*n.* **1.** large fishlike marine mammal. —*v.* **2.** hunt and kill whales.

whale′bone′, *n.* elastic horny substance in upper jaw of some whales.

wharf (hwôrf, wôrf) *n., pl.* **wharves.** structure for mooring vessels.

wharf′age, *n.* **1.** use of wharf. **2.** charge for such use.

what (hwut, wut) *pron., pl.* **what,** *adv.* —*pron.* **1.** which one? **2.** that which. **3.** such. —*adv.* **4.** how much. **5.** partly.

what•ev′er, *pron.* **1.** anything that. **2.** no matter what. —*adj.* **3.** no matter what.

what′not′, *n.* small open cupboard, esp. for knickknacks.

what′so•ev′er, *pron., adj.* whatever.

wheat (hwēt, wēt) *n.* grain of common cereal grass, used esp. for flour.

whee′dle (hwēd′l, wēd′l) *v.,* **-dled, -dling.** influence by flattery.

wheel (hwēl, wēl) *n.* **1.** round object turning on axis. —*v.* **2.** turn on axis. **3.** move on wheels. **4.** turn.

wheel′bar′row, *n.* one-wheeled cart lifted at one end.

wheel′base′, *n. Auto.* distance between centers of front and rear wheel hubs.

wheel′chair′, *n.* chair mounted on wheels for use by persons who cannot walk.

wheeze (hwēz, wēz) *v.,* **wheezed, wheezing,** *n.* —*v.* **1.** whistle in breathing. —*n.* **2.** wheezing breath.

whelp (hwelp, welp) *n.* **1.** young of dog, wolf, bear, etc. —*v.* **2.** bring forth whelps.

when (hwen, wen; *unstressed* hwən, wən) *adv.* **1.** at what time. —*conj.* **2.** at that time. **3.** and then.

whence (hwens, wens) *adv., conj.* from what place.

when•ev′er, *adv.* at whatever time.

where (hwâr, wâr) *adv.* **1.** in, at, or to what place? **2.** in what respect? —*conj.* **3.** in, at, or to what place. **4.** and there.

where′a•bouts′, *adv.* **1.** where. —*n.* **2.** location.

where′as′, *conj.* **1.** while on the contrary. **2.** considering that.

where′by′, *conj.* by what or which; under the terms of which.

where′fore′, *adv., conj.* **1.** why; for what. —*n.* **2.** reason.

where•in′, *conj.* **1.** in what or in which. —*adv.* **2.** in what way or respect?

where′of′, *adv., conj.* of what.

where′up•on′, *conj.* **1.** upon which. **2.** at or after which.

wher•ev′er, *conj.* at or to whatever place.

where′with•al′ (-with ôl′, -with-) *n.* means.

whet (hwet, wet) *v.,* **whetted, whetting.** sharpen. —**whet′stone′,** *n.*

wheth′er (hweth′ər, weth′-) *conj.* (word introducing alternative.)

whey (hwā, wā) *n.* watery part that separates out when milk curdles.

which (hwich, wich) *pron.* **1.** what one? **2.** the one that. —*adj.* **3.** what one of (those mentioned).

which•ev′er, *pron.* any that.

whiff (hwif, wif) *n.* **1.** slight puff or trace. —*v.* **2.** blow in whiffs.

while (hwīl, wīl) *n., conj., v.,* **whiled, whiling.** —*n.* **1.** time. —*conj.* **2.** in time that. —*v.* **3.** pass (time) pleasantly.

whim (hwim, wim) *n.* irrational or fanciful decision or idea.

whim′per (hwim′pər, wim′-) *v.* **1.** cry softly and plaintively. —*n.* **2.** whimpering cry. —**whim′per•er,** *n.*

whim′sy (hwim′zē, wim′-) *n., pl.* **-sies.** fanciful idea; whim. —**whim′si•cal,** *adj.*

whine (hwīn, wīn) *n., v.,* **whined, whining.** —*n.* **1.** low complaining sound. —*v.* **2.** utter whines.

whin′ny (hwin′ē, win′ē) *v.,* **-nied, -nying,** *n., pl.* **-nies.** neigh.

whip (hwip, wip) *v.,* **whipped, whipping,** *n.* —*v.* **1.** strike repeatedly; flog. **2.** jerk; seize. **3.** cover with thread; overcast. **4.** beat (cream, etc.). **5.** move quickly; lash about. —*n.* **6.** instrument with lash and handle for striking. **7.** party manager in legislature.

whip′cord′, *n.* fabric with diagonal ribs.

whip′lash′, *n.* **1.** lash of whip. **2.** neck injury caused by sudden jerking of the head.

whip′per•snap′per (hwip′ər snap′ər, wip′-) *n.* insignificant, presumptuous person, esp. young one.

whip′pet (hwip′it, wip′-) *n.* type of slender swift dog.

whip′poor•will′ (hwip′ər wil′, wip′-) *n.* nocturnal American bird.

whir (hwûr, wûr) *v.,* **whirred, whirring,** *n.* —*v.* **1.** move with buzzing sound. —*n.* **2.** such sound.

whirl (hwûrl, wûrl) *v.* **1.** spin or turn rapidly. **2.** move quickly. —*n.* **3.** whirling movement. **4.** round of events, etc. —**whirl′er,** *n.*

whirl′i•gig′ (hwûr′li gig′, wûr′-) *n.* toy revolving in wind.

whirl′pool′, *n.* whirling current in water.

whirl′wind′ (-wind′) *n.* whirling mass of air.

whisk (hwisk, wisk) *v.* **1.** sweep up. **2.** move or carry lightly. **3.** beat. —*n.* **4.** act of whisking. **5.** kitchen tool for beating.

whisk′er, *n.* **1.** (*pl.*) hair on man's face. **2.** bristle on face of cat, etc.

whis′key (hwis′kē, wis′-) *n.* distilled alcoholic liquor made from grain or corn. Also, **whis′ky.**

whis′per (hwis′pər, wis′pər) *v.* **1.** speak very softly. —*n.* **2.** sound of whispering. **3.** something whispered. —**whis′per•er,** *n.*

whist (hwist, wist) *n.* card game.

whis′tle (hwis′əl, wis′-) *v.,* **-tled, -tling,** *n.* —*v.* **1.** make clear shrill sound with breath, air, or steam. —*n.* **2.** device for making such sounds. **3.** sound of whistling.

whis′tle-blow′er, *n.* person who publicly discloses corruption or wrongdoing.

whistle stop, 1. small town. **2.** short talk from rear platform of train during political campaign.

whit (hwit, wit) *n.* particle; bit.

white (hwīt, wīt) *adj.* **1.** of color of

snow. **2.** having light skin. **3.** pale. —*n.* **4.** color without hue, opposite to black. **5.** Caucasian. **6.** white or light part. —**whit′en,** *v.*

white blood cell, nearly colorless blood cell of immune system.

white′-bread′, *adj.* bland; conventional.

white′-col′lar, *adj.* of professional or office workers whose jobs usu. do not involve manual labor.

white elephant, useless, expensive possession.

white′fish′, *n.* small food fish.

white gold, gold alloy colored white esp. by presence of nickel.

white goods, household linens.

white lie, harmless lie; fib.

white′wash′, *n.* **1.** substance for whitening walls, etc. —*v.* **2.** cover with whitewash. **3.** cover up faults or errors of.

white water, frothy water, as in rapids.

whith′er (hwith′ər, with′-) *adv., conj. Archaic.* to what place.

whit′ing (hwīt′ing, wī′-) *n.* small Atlantic food fish.

whit′low (hwit′lō, wit′-) *n.* inflammation on finger or toe.

Whit′sun·day (hwit′sun′dā, -dē, -sən dā′, wit′-) *n.* seventh Sunday after Easter.

whit′tle (hwit′l, wit′l) *v.,* **-tled, -tling. 1.** cut bit by bit with knife. **2.** reduce. —**whit′tler,** *n.*

whiz (hwiz, wiz) *v.,* **whizzed, whizzing,** *n.* —*v.* **1.** move with hum or hiss. —*n.* **2.** whizzing sound. **3.** person who is very good at something. Also, **whizz.**

who (hōō) *pron.* **1.** what person? **2.** the person that.

whoa (hwō, wō) *interj.* (stop!)

who·dun′it (-dun′it) *n.* detective story.

who·ev′er, *pron.* anyone that.

whole (hōl) *adj.* **1.** entire; undivided. **2.** undamaged. **3.** *Math.* not fractional. —*n.* **4.** entire amount or extent. **5.** complete thing. —**whol′ly,** *adv.* —**whole′ness,** *n.*

whole′-heart′ed, *adj.* sincere.

whole′sale′, *n., adj., v.,* **-saled, -saling.** —*n.* **1.** sale of goods in quantity, as to retailers. —*adj.* **2.** of or engaged in wholesale. —*v.* **3.** sell by wholesale. —**whole′sal′er,** *n.*

whole′some (-səm) *adj.* beneficial; healthful. —**whole′some·ly,** *adv.*

whole′-wheat′, *adj.* prepared with complete wheat kernel.

whom (hōōm) *pron.* objective case of **who.**

whom·ev′er, *pron.* objective case of **whoever.**

whoop (hwōōp, hwŏŏp, wōōp, wŏŏp; *esp. for 2* hōōp, hŏŏp) *n.* **1.** loud shout or cry. **2.** gasping sound characteristic of whooping cough. —*v.* **3.** utter whoops.

whoop′ing cough (hōō′ping, hŏŏp′ing) infectious disease characterized by short, convulsive coughs followed by whoops.

whop′per (hwop′ər, wop′-) *n. Informal.* **1.** something uncommonly large. **2.** big lie.

whop′ping, *adj. Informal.* uncommonly large.

whore (hôr; *often* hŏŏr) *n., v.,* **whored, whoring.** —*n.* **1.** prostitute. —*v.* **2.** consort with whores.

whorl (hwûrl, hwôrl, wûrl, wôrl) *n.* circular arrangement; spiral.

whose (hōōz) *pron.* possessive case of **who.**

who′so·ev′er, *pron.* whoever.

why (hwī, wī) *adv., n., pl.* **whys.** —*adv.* **1.** for what reason. —*n.* **2.** cause or reason.

WI, Wisconsin.

wick (wik) *n.* soft threads that absorb fuel and burn in candle, etc.

wick′ed (wik′id) *adj.* **1.** evil; sinful. **2.** naughty. —**wick′ed·ly,** *adv.*

wick′er, *n.* **1.** slender pliant twig. —*adj.* **2.** made of wicker. —**wick′er·work′,** *n.*

wick′et (wik′it) *n.* **1.** small gate. **2.** framework in cricket.

wide (wīd) *adj.* **1.** wider, widest,** *adv.* —*adj.* **1.** broad. **2.** extensive. **3.** expanded. **4.** far. —*adv.* **5.** far. **6.** to farthest extent. —**wid′en,** *v.*

wide′-awake′, *adj.* **1.** fully awake. **2.** alert or observant.

wide′-eyed′, *adj.* with eyes open wide, in amazement or innocence.

wide′spread′, *adj.* occurring widely.

wid′ow (wid′ō) *n.* **1.** woman whose husband has died. —*v.* **2.** make widow of. —**wid′ow·er,** *n.masc.* —**wid′ow·hood,** *n.*

width (width, witth) *n.* **1.** breadth. **2.** piece of full wideness.

wield (wēld) *v.* **1.** exercise (power, etc.). **2.** brandish.

wie′ner (wē′nər) *n.* small sausage; frankfurter.

wife (wīf) *n., pl.* **wives** (wīvz). married woman. —**wife′ly,** *adj.*

wig (wig) *n.* artificial covering of hair for head.

wig′gle (wig′əl) *v.,* **-gled, -gling,** *n.* —*v.* **1.** twist to and fro; wriggle. —*n.* **2.** wiggling movement. —**wig′gly,** *adj.* —**wig′gler,** *n.*

wig′wag′ (wig′wag′) *v.,* **-wagged, -wagging,** *n.* —*v.* **1.** signal in code with flags, etc. —*n.* **2.** such signaling. **3.** message so sent.

wig′wam (-wom) *n.* American Indian dwelling.

wild (wīld) *adj.* **1.** not cultivated. **2.** uncivilized. **3.** violent. **4.** uninhabited. **5.** disorderly. —*adv.* **6.** wildly. —*n.* **7.** wilderness. —**wild′ly,** *adv.*

wild′cat′, *n., v.,* **-catted, -catting.** —*n.* **1.** large North American feline. —*v.* **2.** prospect independently. —*adj.* **3.** not called or sanctioned by labor union.

wil′de·beest (wil′də bēst′, vil′-) *n.* gnu.

wil′der·ness (wil′dər nis) *n.* wild or desolate region.

wild′-eyed′, *adj.* **1.** having a wild expression in the eyes. **2.** extreme or radical.

wild′fire′, *n.* outdoor fire that spreads rapidly and is hard to extinguish.

wild′flow′er, *n.* flower of plant that grows wild.

wild′-goose′ chase′, senseless search for something unobtainable.

wild′life′, *n.* animals living in nature.

wile (wīl) *n.* trick to fool or trap.

will (wil) *n.* **1.** power of conscious action or choice. **2.** wish; pleasure. **3.** attitude, either hostile or friendly. **4.** declaration of wishes for disposition of property after death. —*v.* **5.** decide to influence by act of will. **6.** consent to. **7.** give by will. —*auxiliary verb.* **8.** am (is, are) about to. **9.** am (is, are) willing to.

will′ful, *adj.* **1.** intentional. **2.** headstrong. Also, **wil′ful.**

wil′lies (wil′ēz) *n.pl.* nervousness.

will′ing, *adj.* **1.** consenting. **2.** cheerfully done, given, etc. —**will′ing·ly,** *adv.* —**will′ing·ness,** *n.*

will′-o′-the-wisp′ (wil′ə thə wisp′) *n.* **1.** flitting, elusive light. **2.** something that fascinates and deludes.

wil′low (wil′ō) *n.* slender tree or shrub with tough, pliant branches.

wil′low·y, *adj.,* **-lowier, -lowiest.** tall and slender.

wil′ly-nil′ly (wil′ē nil′ē) *adv.* willingly or unwillingly.

wilt (wilt) *v.* **1.** wither or droop. —*n.* **2.** wilted state.

wil′y (wī′lē) *adj.,* **wilier, wiliest.** crafty.

wimp (wimp) *n. Informal.* weak, ineffectual person. —**wimp′y,** *adj.*

win (win) *v.,* **won** (wun), **winning,** *n.* —*v.* **1.** succeed or get by effort. **2.** gain (victory). **3.** persuade. —*n.* **4.** victory.

wince (wins) *v.,* **winced, wincing,** *n.* —*v.* **1.** shrink, as from pain or blow. —*n.* **2.** wincing movement.

winch (winch) *n.* **1.** windlass. **2.** crank.

wind (wind for 1–5; wīnd for 6–8), *n., v.,* **winded** (for 5) or **wound** (wound) (for 6–8), **winding.** —*n.* **1.** air in motion. **2.** gas in stomach or bowels. **3.** animal odor. **4.** breath. —*v.* **5.** make short of breath. **6.** meander. **7.** roll into cylinder or ball. **8.** turn (handle, etc.). —**wind′y** (win′dē) *adj.*

wind′bag′ (wind′-) *n.* pompous talker.

wind′break′ (wind′-) *n.* shelter from wind.

wind′chill factor (wind′chil′) apparent temperature felt on exposed skin owing to combination of temperature and wind speed.

wind′ed (win′did) *adj.* breathless.

wind′fall′ (wind′-) *n.* **1.** something blown down. **2.** unexpected luck.

winding sheet (wīn′ding) shroud.

wind instrument (wind) musical instrument sounded by breath.

wind′lass (wind′ləs) *n.* drum mechanism for hoisting.

wind′mill′ (wind′-) *n.* mill operated by wind acting on vanes.

win′dow (win′dō) *n.* opening for air and light, usually fitted with glass in frame.

window dressing, 1. art, act, or technique of decorating store display windows. **2.** something done solely to create favorable impression.

win′dow·pane′, *n.* pane of glass for window.

win′dow-shop′, *v.,* **windowshopped, window-shopping.** look at articles in store windows without making purchases. —**window shopper.**

wind′pipe′ (wind′-) *n.* trachea.

wind′shield′ (wind′-, win′-) *n.* glass shield above automobile, etc., dashboard.

wind′sock′ (wind′-) *n.* mounted cloth cone that catches wind to indicate wind direction.

wind′storm′ (wind′-) *n.* storm with heavy wind but little or no precipitation.

wind′surf′ing (wind′-) *n.* sport of riding on surfboard mounted with a sail. —**wind′surf′,** *v.* —**wind′surf′er,** *n.*

wind′-swept′ (wind′-) *adj.* exposed to or blown by wind.

wind′up′ (wīnd′-) *n.* close; end.

wind′ward (wind′wərd) *n.* **1.** direction from which wind blows. —*adj.* **2.** of, in, or to windward.

wine (wīn) *n., v.,* **wined, wining.** —*n.* **1.** fermented juice, esp. of grape. **2.** dark purplish red. —*v.* **3.** entertain with wine. —**win′y,** *adj.*

win′er·y, *n., pl.* **-eries.** place for making wine.

wing (wing) *n.* **1.** organ of flight in birds, insects, and bats. **2.** winglike or projecting structure. **3.** flight. **4.** supporting surface of airplane. —*v.* **5.** travel on wings. **6.** wound in wing or arm. —**wing′ed,** *adj.*

wing′ding′, *n. Slang.* noisy, exciting party.

wink (wingk) *v.* **1.** close and open (eye) quickly. **2.** signal by winking. **3.** twinkle. —*n.* **4.** winking movement.

win′ner (win′ər) *n.* one that wins.

win′ning, *n.* **1.** (*pl.*) that which is won. —*adj.* **2.** charming.

win′now (win′ō) *v.* **1.** free from chaff by wind. **2.** separate.

wi′no (wī′nō) *n., pl.* **winos.** person addicted to wine.

win′some (win′səm) *adj.* sweetly or innocently charming.

win′ter (win′tər) *n.* **1.** last season of year. —*adj.* **2.** of, like, or for winter. —*v.* **3.** pass winter. **4.** keep during winter. —**win′try,** *adj.*

win′ter·green′, *n.* creeping aromatic shrub.

wipe (wīp) *v.,* **wiped, wiping,** *n.* —*v.* **1.** rub lightly. **2.** remove or blot. —*n.* **3.** act of wiping. —**wip′er,** *n.*

wire (wī°r) *n., adj., v.,* **wired, wiring.** —*n.* **1.** slender, flexible piece of metal. **2.** telegram or telegraph. —*adj.* **3.** made of wires. —*v.* **4.** bind with wire. **5.** *Elect.* install system of wires in. **6.** telegraph.

wire′less, *adj.* **1.** activated by electromagnetic waves rather than wires. —*n.* **2.** *Brit.* radio.

wire service, agency that sends syndicated news by wire to its subscribers.

wire′tap′, *v.,* **-tapped, -tapping,** *n.* —*v.* **1.** connect secretly into telephone. —*n.* **2.** act of wiretapping.

wir′ing, *n.* system of electric wires.

wir′y, *adj.,* wirier, wiriest. like wire; lean and strong. —**wir′i·ness,** *n.*

Wis., Wisconsin. Also, **Wisc.**

wis′dom (wiz′dəm) *n.* **1.** knowledge and judgment. **2.** wise sayings.

wisdom tooth, last tooth to erupt.

wise (wīz) *adj.* **1.** having knowledge and judgment. **2.** prudent. **3.** informed. —*n.* **4.** way; respect.

wise′a·cre (-ā′kər) *n.* conceited, often insolent person.

wise′crack′, *n.* **1.** smart or facetious remark. —*v.* **2.** make or say as a wisecrack.

wish (wish) *v.* **1.** want; desire. **2.** bid. —*n.* **3.** desire. **4.** that desired. —**wish′ful,** *adj.* —**wish′ful·ly,** *adv.*

wish′bone′, *n.* forked bone in front of breastbone in most birds.

wish′y-wash′y (wish′ē wosh′ē) *adj.* thin or weak.

wisp (wisp) *n.* small tuft. —**wisp′y,** *adj.*

wis·te′ri·a (wi stēr′ē ə) *n.* climbing shrub with purple flowers.

wist′ful (wist′fəl) *adj.* **1.** pensive. **2.** longing. —**wist′ful·ly,** *adv.*

wit (wit) *n.* **1.** power of combining perception with clever expression. **2.** person having this. **3.** (*pl.*) intelligence. —*v.* **4.** *Archaic.* know. **5. to wit,** namely.

witch (wich) *n.* **1.** woman thought to practice magic. **2.** ugly or mean old woman. —**witch′craft′,** *n.*

witch doctor, person in some cultures who uses magic esp. to cure illness.

witch′er·y, *n., pl.* **-eries. 1.** magic. **2.** charm.

witch ha′zel (hā′zəl) preparation for bruises, etc.

with (with, *with*) *prep.* **1.** accompanied by. **2.** using. **3.** against.

with·draw′ (*with* drô′, with-) *v.,* **-drew, -drawn, -drawing. 1.** draw back. **2.** retract. —**with·draw′al,** *n.*

with′er (*with*′ər) *v.* shrivel; fade.

with′ers, *n.pl.* part of animal's back just behind neck.

with·hold′ (*with* hōld′, with-) *v.,* **-held, -holding.** hold or keep back.

withholding tax, that part of employee's tax liability withheld by employer from wages.

with·in′ (*with* in′, with-) *adv.* **1.** inside; inwardly. —*prep.* **2.** in; inside of. **3.** at point not beyond.

with·out′, *prep.* **1.** lacking. **2.** beyond. —*adv.* **3.** outside. **4.** outwardly. **5.** lacking.

with·stand′ (*with* stand′, with-) *v.,* **-stood, -standing.** resist.

wit′less, *adj.* stupid.

wit′ness (wit′nis) *v.* **1.** see. **2.** testify. **3.** attest by signature. —*n.* **4.** person who witnesses. **5.** testimony.

wit′ti·cism′ (wit′ə siz′əm) *n.* witty remark.

wit′ting, *adj.* knowing; aware.

wit′ty, *adj.,* **-tier, -tiest.** showing wit. —**wit′ti·ly,** *adv.*

wiz′ard (wiz′ərd) *n.* magician. —**wiz′ard·ry,** *n.*

wiz′ened (wiz′ənd, wē′zənd) *adj.* shriveled.

wk., week.

w/o, without.

wob′ble (wob′əl) *v.,* **-bled, -bling.** move unsteadily from side to side. —**wob′bly,** *adj.*

woe (wō) *n.* grief or affliction. —**woe′ful,** *adj.* —**woe′ful·ly,** *adv.*

woe′be·gone′ (-bi gôn′) *adj.* showing woe.

wok (wok) *n.* Chinese cooking pan.

wolf (wŏŏlf) *n., pl.* **wolves** (wŏŏlvz), *v.* —*n.* **1.** wild carnivorous animal of dog family. —*v.* **2.** *Informal.* eat ravenously. —**wolf′ish,** *adj.*

wolf′hound′, *n.* kind of hound.

wolfs′bane′, *n.* poisonous plant.

wol·ver·ine′ (wŏŏl′və rēn′) *n.* North American mammal of weasel family.

wom′an (wŏŏm′ən) *n., pl.* **women** (wim′in). adult female human being. —**wom′an·hood′,** *n.* —**wom′an·ly,** *adj.*

womb (wŏŏm) *n.* uterus.

wom′bat (wom′bat) *n.* burrowing, herbivorous Australian marsupial.

won′der (wun′dər) *v.* **1.** be curious about. **2.** marvel. —*n.* **3.** something strange. **4.** Also, **won′der·ment.** amazement.

won′der·ful, *adj.* **1.** exciting wonder. **2.** excellent.

won′drous, *adj.* **1.** wonderful. —*adv.* **2.** remarkably.

wont (wônt, wōnt, wunt) *adj.* **1.** accustomed. —*n.* **2.** habit. —**wont′ed,** *adj.*

won't (wōnt) contraction of will not.

woo (wŏŏ) *v.* seek to win, esp. in marriage. —**woo′er,** *n.*

wood (wŏŏd) *n.* **1.** hard substance under bark of trees. **2.** timber or firewood. **3.** (*often pl.*) forest. —*adj.* **4.** made of wood. **5.** living in woods. —*v.* **6.** plant with trees. —**wood′craft′,** *n.* —**wood′y,** *adj.*

wood′bine′ (-bīn′) *n.* any of various vines, as the honeysuckle.

wood′chuck′, *n.* bushy-tailed burrowing rodent. Also called **ground′hog′.**

wood′cut′, *n.* print made from a carved block of wood.

wood′ed, *adj.* covered with trees.

wood′en, *adj.* **1.** made of wood. **2.** without feeling or expression.

wood′land′ (-land′, -lənd) *n.* forest.

wood′peck′er, *n.* bird with hard bill for boring.

wood′pile′, *n.* stack of firewood.

wood′ruff (-rəf, -ruf′) *n.* fragrant plant with small white flowers.

wood′shed′, *n.* shed for storing firewood.

woods′man, *n.* person who works in woods.

woods′y, *adj.,* **-ier, -iest.** of or resembling woods.

wood′wind′ (-wind′) *n.* musical instrument of group including flute, clarinet, oboe, and bassoon.

wood′work′, *n.* wooden fittings inside building. —**wood′work·er,** *n.*

woof (wŏŏf, wŏŏf) *n.* **1.** yarns from side to side in loom. **2.** bark.

woof′er (wŏŏf′ər) *n.* loudspeaker to reproduce low-frequency sounds.

wool (wŏŏl) *n.* **1.** soft curly hair, esp. of sheep. **2.** garment, yarn, or fabric of wool. **3.** curly, fine-stranded substance. —**wool′en** or (*esp. Brit.*) **wool′len,** *adj., n.*

wool′gath′er·ing, *n.* daydreaming.

wool′ly, *adj.* **1.** of or resembling wool. **2.** confused or disorganized.

woolly bear, caterpillar with woolly hairs.

word (wûrd) *n.* **1.** group of letters or sounds that represents concept. **2.** talk or conversation. **3.** promise. **4.** tidings. **5.** (*pl.*) quarrel. —*v.* **6.** express in words. —**word′less,** *adj.*

word′age (wûr′dij) *n.* **1.** words collectively. **2.** number of words.

word′ing, *n.* way of expressing.

word of mouth, oral communication.

word′play′, *n.* witty repartee.

word processing, production of documents using computers.

word processor, computer program or system for word processing.

word′y, *adj.,* **-ier, -iest.** using too many words. —**word′i·ness,** *n.*

work (wûrk) *n.* **1.** exertion; labor. **2.** task. **3.** employment. **4.** place of employment. **5.** materials on which one works. **6.** result of work. **7.** (*pl.*) industrial plant. —*adj.* **8.** of or for work. —*v.* **9.** do work. **10.** operate successfully. **11.** move or give. **12.** solve. **13.** excite. **14.** ferment. —**work′a·ble,** *adj.* —**work′er,** *n.*

work′a·day′ (wûr′kə dā′) *adj.* commonplace; uneventful.

work′a·hol′ic (-hô′lik) *n.* person who works compulsively.

work′horse′, *n.* **1.** horse used for heavy labor. **2.** person who works tirelessly.

work′house′, *n.* penal institution for minor offenders.

working class, social or economic class composed of workers.

work′load′, *n.* amount of work that machine or employee is expected to perform.

work′man, *n., pl.* **-men.** laborer.

work′man·like′, *adj.* skillful.

work′man·ship′, *n.* **1.** skill of workman. **2.** quality of work done.

work′out′, *n.* **1.** practice or test to maintain or determine physical ability or endurance. **2.** structured regime of physical exercise.

work′shop′, *n.* **1.** place where work is done. **2.** seminar.

work′sta′tion, *n.* **1.** work area for one person, as in office, usu. with electronic equipment. **2.** powerful small computer used for graphics-intensive processing.

work′up′, *n.* thorough medical diagnostic examination.

world (wûrld) *n.* **1.** earth; globe. **2.** particular part of earth. **3.** milieu. **4.** humanity. **5.** universe. **6.** great quantity.

world′-class′, *adj.* of the highest caliber.

world′ly, *adj.,* **-lier, -liest. 1.** secular or earthly. **2.** devoted to affairs of this world; sophisticated; shrewd. **3.** of this world. —**world′li•ness,** *n.*

world′ly-wise′, *adj.* wise as to the affairs of this world.

world′-wea′ry, *adj.* blasé.

World Wide Web, system of extensively interlinked documents: branch of the Internet.

worm (wûrm) *n.* **1.** small slender creeping animal. **2.** (*pl.*) intestinal disorder. —*v.* **3.** move like worm. **4.** extract (secret) craftily. **5.** free from worms.

worm′wood′, *n.* bitter aromatic herb.

worn (wôrn) *adj.* exhausted; spent.

worn′-out′, *adj.* **1.** exhausted. **2.** destroyed by wear.

wor′ry (wûr′ē) *v.,* **-ried, -rying,** *n., pl.* **-ries.** —*v.* **1.** make or feel anxious. **2.** seize with teeth and shake. —*n.* **3.** anxiety. **4.** cause of anxiety. —**wor′ri•some,** *adj.*

worse (wûrs) *adj.* **1.** less good; less favorable. —*n.* **2.** that which is worse. —*adv.* **3.** in worse way. —**wors′en,** *v.*

wor′ship (wûr′ship) *n., v.,* **-shiped, -shiping** or **-shipped, -shipping.** —*n.* **1.** homage paid to God. **2.** rendering of such homage. —*v.* **3.** render religious reverence to. —**wor′ship•er,** *n.* —**wor′ship•ful,** *adj.*

worst (wûrst) *adj.* **1.** least satisfactory; least well. —*n.* **2.** that which is worst. —*adv.* **3.** in the worst way. —*v.* **4.** defeat.

wor′sted (wŏŏs′tid, wûr′stid) *n.* **1.** firmly twisted wool yarn or thread. **2.** fabric made of it.

worth (wûrth) *adj.* **1.** good enough to justify. **2.** having value of. —*n.* **3.** excellence; importance. **4.** quantity of specified value. —**worth′less,** *adj.* —**worth′less•ness,** *n.*

worth′while′, *adj.* repaying time and effort spent.

wor′thy (wûr′thē) *adj.,* **-thier, -thiest,** *n., pl.* **-thies.** —*adj.* **1.** of adequate worth. **2.** deserving. —*n.* **3.** person of merit. —**wor′thi•ly,** *adv.*

would (wŏŏd; *unstressed* wəd) *v.* past of **will** (defs. 8, 9).

would′-be′, *adj.* wishing, pretending, or intended to be.

wound (wŏŏnd) *n.* **1.** injury from external violence. —*v.* **2.** inflict wound. **3.** grieve with insult or reproach.

wrack (rak) *n.* ruin.

wraith (rāth) *n.* ghost.

wran′gle (rang′gəl) *v.,* **-gled, -gling,** *n.* dispute. —**wran′gler,** *n.*

wrap (rap) *v.,* **wrapped** or **wrapt, wrapping,** *n.* —*v.* **1.** enclose; envelop. **2.** wind or fold about. —*n.* **3.** shawl.

wrap′per, *n.* **1.** one that wraps. **2.** Also, **wrapping.** outer cover. **3.** long loose garment.

wrath (rath) *n.* **1.** stern or fierce anger. **2.** vengeance.

wreak (rēk) *v.* inflict.

wreath (rēth) *n.* circular band of leaves, etc.

wreathe (rēth) *v.,* **wreathed, wreathing.** encircle with wreath.

wreck (rek) *n.* **1.** anything reduced to

ruins. **2.** destruction. **3.** person in poor state. —*v.* **4.** damage.

wreck′age, *n.* ruin or damage.

wreck′er, *n.* **1.** vehicle for towing wrecked automobiles. **2.** one that demolishes buildings.

wren (ren) *n.* small active bird.

wrench (rench) *v.* **1.** twist forcibly. **2.** injure by wrenching. —*n.* **3.** wrenching movement. **4.** tool for turning bolts, etc.

wrest (rest) *v.* **1.** twist violently. **2.** get by effort. —*n.* **3.** twist; wrench.

wres′tle (res′əl) *v.,* **-tled, -tling,** *n.* —*v.* **1.** contend with by trying to force other person down. —*n.* **2.** this sport. **3.** struggle. —**wres′tler,** *n.* —**wres′tling,** *n.*

wretch (rech) *n.* pitiable person.

wretch′ed, *adj.* **1.** pitiable. **2.** despicable. **3.** pitiful.

wrig′gle (rig′əl) *v.,* **-gled, -gling,** *n.* wiggle; squirm. —**wrig′gly,** *adj.*

wring (ring) *v.,* **wrung** (rung), **wringing,** *n.* —*v.* **1.** twist or compress. **2.** expel by wringing. **3.** clasp tightly. —*n.* **4.** twist or squeeze. —**wring′er,** *n.*

wrin′kle (ring′kəl) *n., v.,* **-kled, -kling.** —*n.* **1.** ridge or furrow. —*v.* **2.** form wrinkles in. —**wrin′kly,** *adj.*

wrist (rist) *n.* joint between hand and arm.

writ (rit) *n.* **1.** formal legal order. **2.** writing.

write (rīt) *v.,* **wrote** (rōt), **written** (rit′n), **writing. 1.** form (letters, etc.) by hand. **2.** express in writing. **3.** produce, as author or composer. —**writ′er,** *n.*

write′-in′, *n.* candidate or vote for candidate not listed on ballot but written in by voter.

write′-off′, *n.* something cancelled, as a debt.

writhe (rīth) *v.,* **writhed, writhing,** *n.* —*v.* **1.** twist, as in pain. —*n.* **2.** writhing movement. —**writh′er,** *n.*

wrong (rông) *adj.* **1.** not right or good. **2.** deviating from truth or fact. **3.** not suitable. **4.** under or inner (side). —*n.* **5.** evil; injury; error. —*v.* **6.** do wrong to. **7.** misjudge. —**wrong′do′er,** *n.* —**wrong′do′ing,** *n.* —**wrong′ful,** *adj.* —**wrong′ly,** *adv.*

wrong′head′ed, *adj.* misguided and stubborn.

wrought (rôt) *adj.* **1.** worked. **2.** shaped by beating.

wrought′-up′, *adj.* perturbed.

wry (rī) *adj.,* **wrier, wriest. 1.** twisted; distorted. **2.** ironic. —**wry′ly,** *adv.* —**wry′ness,** *n.*

WV, West Virginia. Also, **W. Va.**

WWW, World Wide Web.

WY, Wyoming. Also, **Wyo.**

WYSIWYG (wiz′ē wig′) *adj.* of or being computer display screen that shows text exactly as it will appear when printed.

X, x (eks) *n.* twenty-fourth letter of English alphabet.

X, motion-picture rating applied to sexually explicit films.

X chromosome, sex chromosome that determines femaleness when paired with another X chromosome.

xen′o•pho′bi•a (zen′ə fō′bē ə, zē′nə-) *n.* fear or hatred of foreigners. —**xen′o•pho′bic,** *adj.*

xe•rog′ra•phy (zi rog′rə fē) *n.* copy-

ing process in which resins are fused to paper electrically.

Xe′rox (zēr′oks) *n.* **1.** *Trademark.* brand name for copying machine using xerography. **2.** (*l.c.*) copy made on Xerox. —*v.* **3.** (*l.c.*) print or reproduce by Xerox.

Xmas (kris′məs; *often* eks′məs) *n.* Christmas.

X-rat•ed (eks′rā′tid), *adj.* sexually explicit; obscene.

x′-ray′, *n.* **1.** highly penetrating type of electromagnetic ray, used esp. in medicine. —*v.* **2.** photograph or treat with x-rays.

xy′lo•phone′ (zī′lə fōn′) *n.* musical instrument of wooden bars, played with small hammers. —**xy′lo•phon′ist,** *n.*

Y

Y, y (wī) *n.* twenty-fifth letter of English alphabet.

-y, suffix meaning: **1.** full of or like, as *cloudy.* **2.** inclined to, as *squeaky.* **3.** dear or little, as *kitty.* **4.** action of, as *inquiry.* **5.** quality or state, as *victory.*

yacht (yot) *n.* **1.** pleasure ship. —*v.* **2.** sail in yacht. —**yacht′ing,** *n.* —**yachts′man,** *n.*

ya′hoo (yä′hōō) *n.* coarse stupid person.

yak (yak) *n., v.,* **yakked, yakking.** —*n.* **1.** long-haired Tibetan ox. **2.** *Slang.* incessant idle or gossipy talk. —*v.* **3.** *Slang.* gab; chatter.

yam (yam) *n.* edible potatolike root.

yam′mer (yam′ər) *v. Informal.* whine or chatter.

yank (yangk) *v.* **1.** pull suddenly; jerk. —*n.* **2.** sudden pull; jerk.

Yan′kee (yang′kē) *n.* native or inhabitant of the United States, northern U.S., or New England.

yap (yap) *v.,* **yapped, yapping,** *n.* **1.** yelp. **2.** chatter.

yard (yärd) *n.* **1.** linear unit (3 feet). **2.** long spar. **3.** enclosed outdoor area, used as a lawn, etc.

yard′age (yär′dij) *n.* amount in yards.

yard′arm′, *n.* either of the yards of square sail.

yard′stick′, *n.* **1.** measuring stick one yard long. **2.** criterion.

yar′mul•ke (yär′məl kə, -mə-, yä′-) *n.* cap worn by Jewish males during prayer.

yarn (yärn) *n.* **1.** many-stranded thread. **2.** story.

yar′row (yar′ō) *n.* plant with flat-topped clusters of white-to-yellow flowers.

yaw (yô) *v.* **1.** deviate. —*n.* **2.** deviation.

yawl (yôl) *n.* small sailboat.

yawn (yôn) *v.* **1.** open mouth wide involuntarily, as from sleepiness or boredom. —*n.* **2.** act of yawning.

Y chromosome, sex chromosome present only in males and paired with X chromosome.

ye (yē) *pron. Archaic.* **1.** you. **2.** the.

yea (yā) *adv., n.* yes.

year (yēr) *n.* period of 365 or 366 days. —**year′ly,** *adv., adj.*

year′book′, *n.* **1.** book published annually with information on past year. **2.** commemorative book published as by graduating class.

year′ling (-ling) *n.* animal in its second year.

yearn (yûrn) *v.* desire strongly.

year′-round′, *adj.* **1.** continuing,

available, or used throughout the year. —*adv.* **2.** throughout the year.

yeast (yēst) *n.* yellowish substance, used to leaven bread.

yell (yel) *v.* shout loudly.

yel'low (yel'ō) *n.* **1.** color of butter, lemons, etc. —*adj.* **2.** of or like yellow. **3.** *Slang.* cowardly.

yellow fever, infectious tropical disease transmitted by mosquitoes.

yelp (yelp) *v.* **1.** give sharp, shrill cry. —*n.* **2.** such a cry.

yen (yen) *n. Informal.* desire.

yeo'man (yō'mən) *n.* **1.** petty officer in navy. **2.** independent farmer.

yes (yes) *adv., n.* expression of affirmation or assent.

ye•shi'va (yə shē'və) *n.* Orthodox Jewish school.

yes'-man', *n., pl.* **yes-men.** person who always agrees with superiors.

yes'ter•day (yes'tər dā', -dē) *adv., n.* day before today.

yet (yet) *adv.* **1.** so far; up to this (or that) time. **2.** moreover. **3.** still. **4.** nevertheless. —*conj.* **5.** but.

yew (yōō) *n.* evergreen coniferous tree.

Yid'dish (yid'ish) *n.* German-based Jewish language.

yield (yēld) *v.* **1.** produce; give. **2.** surrender. **3.** give way. —*n.* **4.** that which is yielded; product.

yip (yip) *v.,* **yipped, yipping.** *Informal.* bark sharply.

yo'del (yōd'l) *v.,* **-deled, -deling. 1.** sing with quick changes to and from falsetto. —*n.* **2.** song yodeled.

yo'ga (yō'gə) *n.* Hindu series of postures and breathing exercises practiced to attain physical and mental control and tranquillity.

yo'gi (yō'gē) *n.* Hindu who practices yoga.

yo'gurt (yō'gərt) *n.* custardlike food made from milk fermented by bacteria. Also, **yo'ghurt.**

yoke (yōk) *n., v.,* **yoked, yoking.** —*n.* **1.** piece put across necks of oxen pulling cart, etc. **2.** pair. —*v.* **3.** couple with, or place in, yoke.

yo'kel (yō'kəl) *n.* rustic.

yolk (yōk) *n.* yellow part of egg.

yon'der (yon'dər) *adj., adv. Archaic.* over there. Also, **yon.**

yore (yôr) *n.* time past.

you (yōō; *unstressed* yŏŏ, yə) *pron.* person or persons addressed.

young (yung) *adj.* **1.** in early stages of life, operation, etc. **2.** of youth. —*n.* **3.** young persons. **4.** young offspring. —**young'ish,** *adj.*

young'ster (-stər) *n.* child.

your (yŏŏr, yôr; *unstressed* yər) *pron., adj.* possessive of **you;** (without noun following) **yours.** —**Usage.** Do not confuse YOUR and YOU'RE. YOUR is the possessive form of "you": *Your book is*

overdue at the library. YOU'RE is the contraction of "you are": *You're just the person we need for this job.*

you're (yŏŏr; *unstressed* yər) contraction of **you are.** —**Usage.** See YOUR.

your•self', *pron.* emphatic or reflexive form of **you.**

youth (yōōth) *n.* **1.** young state. **2.** early life. **3.** young persons. **4.** young man. —**youth'ful,** *adj.*

yowl (youl) *v., n.* howl.

yo'-yo (yō'yō) *n., pl.* **yo-yos,** *v.,* **yo-yoed, yo-yoing.** —*n.* **1.** spoollike toy spun out and reeled in by string looped on finger. —*v.* **2.** move up and down or back and forth.

yr., year.

yuc'ca (yuk'ə) *n.* tropical American plant.

yuck (yuk) *interj. Slang.* (exclamation of disgust or repugnance). —**yuck'y,** *adj.*

yule (yōōl) *n.* Christmas.

yule'tide', *n.* Christmas season.

yum'my (yum'ē) *adj.,* **-mier, -miest.** very pleasing, esp. to taste.

yup'pie (yup'ē) *n.* young, ambitious, and affluent professional who lives in or near a city.

Z

Z, z (zē; *esp. Brit.* zed) *n.* twenty-sixth letter of English alphabet.

zaf'tig (zäf'tik, -tig) *adj. Slang.* (of a woman) pleasantly plump.

za'ny (zā'nē) *n., pl.* **-nies,** *adj.* **-nier, -niest.** —*n.* **1.** clown. **2.** fool. —*adj.* **3.** silly. —**za'ni•ness,** *n.*

zap (zap) *v.,* **zapped, zapping.** *Slang.* kill or defeat.

zeal (zēl) *n.* intense ardor or eagerness. —**zeal'ous** (zel'əs) *adj.*

zeal'ot (zel'ət) *n.* excessively zealous person; fanatic. —**zeal'ot•ry,** *n.*

ze'bra (zē'brə) *n.* wild, striped horselike animal.

Zen (zen) *n.* Buddhist movement emphasizing enlightenment by meditation and direct, intuitive insight. Also, **Zen Buddhism.**

ze'nith (zē'nith) *n.* highest point.

zeph'yr (zef'ər) *n.* mild breeze.

zep'pe•lin (zep'ə lin) *n.* large dirigible of early 20th century.

ze'ro (zēr'ō) *n., pl.* **-ros, -roes. 1.** symbol (0) indicating nonquantity. **2.** nothing. **3.** starting point of a scale.

zero hour, starting time.

zero population growth, condition in which population remains constant because of equal number of births and deaths.

zest (zest) *n.* something adding flavor, interest, etc. —**zest'ful,** *adj.*

zig'zag' (zig'zag') *n., adj., adv., v.,*

-**zagged, -zagging.** —*n.* **1.** line going sharply from side to side. —*adj., adv.* **2.** with sharp turns back and forth. —*v.* **3.** go in zigzag.

zilch (zilch) *n. Slang.* zero; nothing.

zil'lion (zil'yən) *n. Informal.* extremely large, indeterminate number.

zinc (zingk) *n.* bluish metallic element.

zinc oxide, salve made of zinc and oxygen.

zing (zing) *n.* **1.** sharp singing sound. —*v.* **2.** make such sound. —*interj.* **3.** (descriptive of such sound.)

zin'ni•a (zin'ē ə) *n.* bright, fullflowered plant.

Zi'on (zī'ən) *n.* **1.** Jewish people. **2.** Palestine as Jewish homeland. **3.** heaven as final gathering place of true believers.

Zi'on•ism, *n.* advocacy of Jewish establishment of state of Israel. —**Zi'on•ist,** *n., adj.*

zip (zip) *v.,* **zipped, zipping,** *n. Informal.* —*v.* **1.** go very speedily. —*n.* **2.** energy.

ZIP code (zip) code numbers used with address to expedite mail.

zip'per, *n.* fastener with interlocking edges.

zip'py, *adj.,* **-pier, -piest.** *Informal.* lively; smart.

zir'con (zûr'kon) *n.* mineral used as gem when transparent.

zir•co'ni•um (zûr kō'nē əm) *n.* metallic element used in metallurgy and ceramics.

zit (zit) *n. Slang.* pimple.

zith'er (zith'ər, zith'-) *n.* stringed musical instrument. Also, **zith'ern.**

zo'di•ac' (zō'dē ak') *n.* imaginary belt of heavens containing paths of all major planets, divided into twelve constellations.

zom'bie (zom'bē) *n.* reanimated corpse.

zone (zōn) *n., v.,* **zoned, zoning.** —*n.* **1.** special area. —*v.* **2.** mark into zones. —**zon'al,** *adj.*

zonked (zongkt) *adj. Slang.* stupefied from or as if from alcohol or drugs.

zoo (zōō) *n.* place where live animals are exhibited.

zo•ol'o•gy (zō ol'ə jē) *n.* scientific study of animals. —**zo'o•log'i•cal** (-ə loj'i kal) *adj.* —**zo•ol'o•gist,** *n.*

zoom (zōōm) *v.* speed sharply.

zoom lens, camera lens allowing continual change of magnification without loss of focus.

zo'o•phyte' (-fīt') *n.* plantlike animal, as coral.

zuc•chi'ni (zōō kē'nē) *n.* cucumbershaped squash.

zwie'back' (zwī'bak', -bäk', swē'-) *n.* biscuit of dried, twice-baked bread.

zy'gote (zī'gōt) *n.* cell produced by union of two gametes. —**zy•got'ic** (-got'ik) *adj.*

Concise Thesaurus

A

abandon, v. **1.** go away from, depart from, leave, forsake, jilt, walk out on, desert, relinquish, evacuate, drop, discard, cast off, quit, vacate. **2.** resign, retire, quit, abjure, forswear, withdraw, forgo. **3.** drop, discontinue, abstain from, abdicate, waive, give up, yield, surrender, resign, cede, renounce, repudiate. —**Ant.** keep, maintain; pursue.

abandoned, adj. **1.** forsaken, left, left alone, forlorn, forsaken, neglected, deserted, relinquished, dropped, discarded, cast off, cast aside, cast out, cast off, shunned, jilted, dropped, rejected, demitted, sent down. **2.** unrestrained, uninhibited, loose, wanton, wild, reckless, intemperate. **3.** bad, evil, wicked, depraved, unprincipled, sinful, corrupt, licentious, amoral, profligate, vicious, dissolute, shameless, shameful, immoral, incorrigible, impenitent, irreclaimable, reprobate, demoralized, vice-ridden, debauched, dissipated, lewd, lascivious, wanton, unregenerate, degenerate. —**Ant.** virtuous, honest, good, righteous.

abase, v. lower, reduce, humble, degrade, downgrade, demote; disgrace, dishonor, debase, take down a peg, humiliate, mortify, shame. —**Ant.** elevate, exalt, honor.

abash, v. shame, embarrass, mortify, disconcert, discompose, confound, confuse; cow, humble, humiliate, discountenance, affront.

abate, v. lessen, diminish, reduce, discount, decrease, lower, slow, subside, decline, sink, wane, ebb, slack off, slacken, fade, fade out, fade away. —**Ant.** increase, intensify.

abatement, n. **1.** alleviation, mitigation, lessening, let-up, diminution, decrease, slackening. **2.** suppression, termination, ending, end, cessation. **3.** subsidence, decline, sinking, ebb, slack, fade-out, fading. —**Ant.** intensification, increase.

abbreviate, v. shorten, abridge, reduce, curtail, cut, contract, compress; crop, dock, pare down, trim, prune, truncate; condense, digest, epitomize, summarize, abstract. —**Ant.** lengthen, expand.

abbreviation, n. shortening, abridgment, reduction, curtailment, cut, contraction, compression; truncation; condensation, digest, epitome, brief, essence, heart, core, soul. —**Ant.** lengthening, expansion.

ABC's, n. essentials, rudiments, basics, fundamentals, principles, grammar, elements.

abdicate, v. renounce, disclaim, disavow, disown, repudiate; resign, retire, quit, relinquish, abandon, surrender, cede, give up, yield, waive. —**Ant.** retain.

abdication, n. renunciation, disclaimer, disavowal, repudiation, resignation, retirement, quittance; abandonment, surrender, cession, waiver. —**Ant.** commitment.

abdomen, n. stomach, belly, visceral cavity, viscera; paunch, pot, guts, gut, potbelly, tummy, bay window, breadbasket, spare tire, beer belly.

abduct, v. kidnap, carry off, bear off, capture, carry away, ravish, steal away, run away or off with, seize, snatch, grab.

abduction, n. kidnapping, capture, ravishment, seizure.

aberrant, adj. **1.** straying, stray, deviating, deviate, wandering, errant, erring, devious, erratic, rambling, diverging, divergent. **2.** abnormal, irregular, unusual, odd, eccentric, peculiar, exceptional, weird, queer, curious, singular, strange; unconforming, nonconforming, anomalous. —**Ant.** direct; normal.

aberration, n. **1.** wandering, straying, deviation, rambling, divergence, departure. **2.** strangeness, abnormality, abnormity, oddness, anomaly, irregularity, eccentricity; peculiarity, curiosity, oddity. **3.** unsoundness, illusion, hallucination, delusion.

abet, v. aid, assist, help, support, back, succor, sustain; countenance, sanction, uphold, second, condone, approve, favor; encourage, incite, instigate, urge, provoke, egg on, prod, goad, promote, conduce, advocate, advance, further, subsidize. —**Ant.** hinder.

abeyance, n. suspension, suspense, inactivity, hiatus, recess, deferral, intermission, interregnum, dormancy, quiescence, adjournment, postponement. —**Ant.** operation, action.

abhor, v. hate, detest, loathe, abominate, despise, regard with repugnance or loathing or disgust, execrate, view with horror, shrink from, shudder at, bear malice or spleen, recoil from, be aghast at. —**Ant.** love.

abhorrence, n. hate, hatred, loathing, execration, odium, abomination, aversion, repugnance, revulsion, disgust, horror, antipathy, detestation, animosity, enmity. —**Ant.** love, attraction.

abhorrent, adj. **1.** hating, loathing, loathsome, execrating, execratory, antipathetic, detesting, detestable. **2.** horrible, horrifying, shocking, disgusting, revolting, sickening, nauseating, obnoxious, repellant, offensive, repugnant, repulsive, odious; hateful, detestable, abominable, invidious, contemptible, loathsome, horrid, heinous, execrable. **3.** remote, far, distant, removed. —**Ant.** amiable, lovable.

abide, v. **1.** remain, stay, wait, wait for, tarry, continue, linger, rest, sojourn. **2.** dwell, reside, live, inhabit, tenant, stay. **3.** remain, continue, endure, last, persist, persevere, remain steadfast or faithful or constant, go on, keep on. **4.** stand by, support, second; await or accept the consequences of. **5.** await, attend, wait for for. **6.** stand one's ground against, await or sustain defiantly. **7.** put up with, stand, suffer, brook, allow, tolerate, bear, endure, submit to, accept.

ability, n. **1.** power, proficiency, expertness, dexterity, capacity, ableness, adeptness, know-how, mastery, capability, knack, facility, competency, competence, enablement; puissance, prepotency. **2.** faculty, talent, aptitude, skill, skillfulness, aptness, ingenuity, facility, knack, cleverness, wit, gift, genius. —**Ant.** inability.

abject, adj. **1.** humiliating, disheartening, debasing, degrading. **2.** contemptible, despicable, scurvy, hateful; base, mean, low, vile, groveling, corrupt; faithless, treacherous, perfidious, dishonorable, inglorious, dishonest, false, fraudulent; disgraceful, ignominious, discreditable. —**Ant.** exalted.

able, adj. **1.** qualified, fit, fitted, competent, capable, apt. **2.** talented, accomplished, gifted, endowed, superior; skilled, clever, adroit, expert, ingenious, skillful, masterful, masterly, adept, proficient, versed. —**Ant.** unable, incompetent, inept.

able-bodied, adj. well-knit, brawny, burly, sturdy, strapping, strong, powerful, vigorous, red-blooded, robust, vital, lusty.

abnormal, adj. nonconforming, nonconformant, unconventional, irregular, erratic, anomalous, unusual, unnatural, queer, odd, peculiar, aberrant, eccentric, weird, curious, strange, singular, idiosyncratic, freakish, extraordinary, bizarre, perverse, deviant, deviating, off-beat, kinky. —**Ant.** normal, regular.

abnormality, n. unusualness, eccentricity, abnormity, irregularity, unconformity, anomaly, peculiarity, aberrance, aberration, deviation, idiosyncrasy, singularity, curiosity; malformation, monstrosity, freakishness, deformity, distortion, defect. —**Ant.** regularity, normality.

abolish, v. suppress, end, put an end to, cease, void, annul, invalidate, nullify, cancel, revoke, rescind, repeal, eradicate, stamp out, annihilate, extirpate, destroy, do away with, abrogate, obliterate, delete, expunge, extirpate, erase, extinguish, put out, eliminate, terminate, demolish, liquidate, quash. —**Ant.** establish.

abolition, n. end, termination, destruction, annihilation, extirpation, abrogation, obliteration, eradication, elimination, extinction; annulment, nullification, invalidation, cancellation, revocation, repeal, repudiation. —**Ant.** establishment.

abominable, adj. detestable, hateful, loathsome, abhorrent, odious, contemptible, despicable, vile, monstrous, execrable, base, horrid, deplorable, scurvy; horrible, horrifying, disgusting, nauseating, sickening, revolting, repugnant, obnoxious, foul, noxious, offensive, repulsive, terrible, awful, distasteful, frightful. —**Ant.** likable, admirable, delightful.

abominate, v. abhor, regard with aversion, detest, hate, loathe, execrate, contemn, despise, regard with repugnance, view with horror, shrink from, shudder at, bear malice. —**Ant.** like, love, enjoy.

abomination, n. **1.** hatred, loathing, abhorrence, detestation, revulsion, loathsomeness, odiousness, odium; aversion. **2.** vice, sin, impurity, corruption, wickedness, evil, viciousness, depravity, immorality, amorality, profligacy, defilement, pollution, filth.

abortive, adj. **1.** failing, unsuccessful, miscarrying, immature, premature. **2.** undeveloped, underdeveloped, rudimentary, primitive. —**Ant.** consummate, complete, successful.

abound, v. prevail, teem, swarm, be very prevalent, thrive, flourish, proliferate, throng, flow, overflow with, be filled with, be rich in, bristle with, rain, pour, stream, shower. —**Ant.** lack, be scarce.

about, prep. **1.** of, concerning, regarding, in the matter of, apropos, in regard to, respecting, with regard or respect or reference to, relating or relative to, touching, involving, involved with. **2.** connected with, in connection with, relating or relative to. **3.** near, around, round, not far from, close to. **4.** near, close to, approximately, almost. **5.** around, circling, encircling, inclosing, enclosing, on every side, surrounding. **6.** on one's person, having in one's possession. **7.** on the point of, ready, prepared. **8.** here and there, in, on, hither and yon, to and fro, back and forth, hither and thither. —adv. **9.** near, approximately, nearly, almost, well-nigh. **10.** nearby, close, not far, around. **11.** on every side, in every direction, all around, everywhere, every place, all over. **12.** half round, reversed, backwards, opposite direction. **13.** to and fro, back and forth, hither and thither, hither and yon, here and there. **14.** in succession, alternately, in rotation.

about-face, *n.* 180° turn, reversal, turnabout, reverse, changeabout, reversion, volte-face.

above, *adv.* **1.** overhead, aloft, on high, atop, on top of. **2.** higher, beyond, over, superior, surpassing. **3.** before, prior, earlier, sooner, previous, first. **4.** in heaven, on high, *in excelsis.* —*prep.* **5.** over, in a higher place than, higher than, superior to. **6.** more, greater than, more than, exceeding. **7.** superior to, beyond, surpassing. —*adj.* **8.** supra, said, written, mentioned previously, foregoing, preceding.

aboveboard, *adv.* **1.** in open sight, without tricks, without disguise, openly, overtly, candidly, honestly, frankly, sincerely, guilelessly, unequivocally, unequivocatingly. —*adj.* **2.** open, candid, overt, honest, frank, sincere, guileless, unequivocal, unequivocating. —**Ant.** underhand, treacherous, seditious.

abrade, *v.* wear off, wear down, scrape off; erode, wear away, rub off.

abrasion, *n.* **1.** sore, scrape, cut, scratch. **2.** friction, abrading, rubbing, erosion, wearing down, rubbing off.

abreast, *adv., adj.* side by side, alongside, equal, aligned, in alignment.

abridge, *v.* **1.** condense, digest, scale down, reduce, epitomize, abstract. **2.** curtail, reduce, lessen, diminish, contract. **3.** deprive, cut off, dispossess, divest. —**Ant.** expand, extend.

abridgment, *n.* **1.** condensation, shortening, digest, epitome, curtailment, reduction, abbreviation, contraction, retrenchment, compression; compendium, synopsis, abstract, abstraction, summary, syllabus, brief, outline, précis. **2.** dispossession, limitation. —**Ant.** expansion, extension, enlargement.

abroad, *adv.* **1.** overseas, beyond the sea, away. **2.** out-of-doors, outside, out of the house. **3.** astir, in circulation, bruited about. **4.** broadly, widely, expansively, at large, everywhere, ubiquitously, in all directions. **5.** untrue, wide of the truth. —**Ant.** here, domestically.

abrogate, *v.* abolish, cancel, annul, repeal, disannul, revoke, rescind, nullify, void, invalidate. —**Ant.** ratify, establish.

abrogation, *n.* abolition, cancellation, annulment, repeal, disannulment, revocation, rescission, nullification, invalidation. —**Ant.** establishment.

abrupt, *adj.* **1.** sudden, unceremonious, short, precipitous, hasty, blunt, curt, brusque, uncomplaisant; rude, rough, discourteous, inconsiderate, boorish. **2.** discontinuous, spasmodic, uneven. **3.** steep, precipitous, acclivitous, craggy. —**Ant.** gradual, slow, deliberate.

abscond, *v.* depart suddenly, depart secretly, steal away, sneak off *or* out, decamp, run away, run off, escape, flee, fly, bolt. —**Ant.** remain.

absence, *n.* **1.** want, lack, need, deficiency, defect. **2.** nonappearance. —**Ant.** presence.

absent, *adj.* **1.** away, out, not in, not present, off. **2.** lacking, missing, not present, away. —*v.* **3.** stay away, keep away. —**Ant.** present.

absent-minded, *adj.* forgetful, preoc-

cupied, abstracted, oblivious, inattentive, wandering, withdrawn; musing, in a brown study, dreaming, daydreaming. —**Ant.** attentive.

absolute, *adj.* **1.** complete, whole, entire, perfect, free from imperfection, ideal. **2.** pure, unmixed, unadulterated, sheer, unqualified. **3.** unqualified, utter, total, entire, unconditional, unrestricted, unlimited, unbound, unbounded. **4.** arbitrary, despotic, autocratic, dictatorial, tyrannous, tyrannical, imperious, Nazi, Fascist, Fascistic. **5.** uncompared, categorical, certain, unquestionable, unequivocal. **6.** positive, affirmative, unquestionable, indubitable, certain, sure, unequivocal, unequivocating, firm, definite. —**Ant.** mixed; relative.

absolutely, *adv.* **1.** completely, wholly, entirely, unqualifiedly, definitely, unconditionally. **2.** positively, affirmatively, unquestionably, definitely, unequivocally, indubitably, really, without doubt, beyond doubt.

absolve, *v.* **1.** acquit, exonerate, free from blame, exculpate, excuse, forgive, pardon, clear, release, liberate, set free, free, disentangle, discharge, loose, rid. **2.** set free, loose, release, liberate, exempt. **3.** pardon, excuse, forgive. —**Ant.** blame, censure.

absorb, *v.* **1.** swallow, consume, assimilate, amalgamate, devour, engulf, ingurgitate; destroy. **2.** engross, occupy.

abstemious, *adj.* temperate, continent, sober, abstinent, self-denying, ascetic, sparing, austere, stinting, frugal. —**Ant.** greedy, gluttonous, grasping.

abstinence, *n.* **1.** abstemiousness, sobriety, soberness, teetotalism, moderation, temperance. **2.** self-restraint, forbearance, avoidance, self-denial, nonindulgence. —**Ant.** indulgence.

abstract, *adj.* **1.** apart, special, unrelated, separate, isolated. **2.** theoretical, unpractical. **3.** abstruse, difficult, deep, complex, complicated. **4.** *(art)* nonrepresentational, unrealistic, unphotographic. —*n.* **5.** summary, digest, epitome, abridgment, synopsis, compendium, condensation, brief; syllabus, outline, précis; gist, substance. **6.** essence, distillation, condensation, substance; core, heart, idea. —*v.* **7.** draw away, take away, remove, distill; separate, fractionate. **8.** divert, disengage. **9.** steal, purloin, rob, pilfer, shoplift, hijack. **10.** separate, consider apart, isolate, dissociate; disjoin, disunite. **11.** summarize, epitomize, distill, abridge, abbreviate, outline, condense, edit, digest. —**Ant.** concrete; interpolate.

abstruse, *adj.* esoteric, recondite, profound, deep, difficult, knotty, complex, involved, secret, hermetic, orphic. —**Ant.** open, straightforward, obvious.

absurd, *adj.* ridiculous, silly, nonsensical, senseless, outlandish, farcical, mad, idiotic, imbecile, imbecilic, moronic, childish, laughable, ludicrous, risible, crazy, nutty, nuts, preposterous, foolish, inane, asinine, stupid, unwise, false, unreasonable, irrational, illogical, unreasoned, unsound, meaningless, paradoxical, incongruous, self-contradictory. —**Ant.** sensible, rational.

abundance, *n.* overflow, plenty, fullness, copiousness, fertility, profusion, superfluity, superabundance, excess, surplus, glut, satiety, oversufficiency, plentifulness, plenitude, plenteousness, prodigality, extravagance, oversupply, flood, wealth, bountifulness, inex-

haustibility. —**Ant.** lack, need, paucity.

abundant, *adj.* abounding, teeming, thick, plentiful, plenteous, flowing, copious, profuse, overflowing, rich, replete, ample, oversufficient, superabundant, excess, excessive, inexhaustible, bountiful, bounteous, abounding in, rich in, luxuriant, lavish. —**Ant.** sparse, scarce, poor.

abuse, *v.* **1.** misuse, misapply, mistreat, misemploy, misappropriate; desecrate, profane, pervert, exploit, prostitute; deceive, betray, seduce, subvert. **2.** maltreat, ill-use, injure, harm, hurt, wrong, mistreat, manhandle, ill-treat, damage. **3.** revile, malign, vilify, vituperate, berate, rate, rail at, upbraid, scold, carp at, censure, assail, lambaste, rebuke, bawl out, inveigh against, reproach; traduce, slander, defame, denounce, criticize, insult, swear at, curse, libel, decry, deprecate, find fault with, fault, asperse, calumniate, disparage; satirize, lampoon. —*n.* **4.** misuse, misapplication, mistreatment, misemployment, misappropriation; desecration, profanation, prostitution; deception, betrayal, seduction, subversion. **5.** censure, adverse criticism, blame, condemnation, hostile condemnation; denunciation, vilification, malignment, vituperation, tonguelashing, calumny, obloquy, imprecation, scurrility, billingsgate, scolding, censoriousness, insult, invective, slander, defamation, aspersion, calumniation, curse, disparagement; contumely, scorn, reproach, opprobrium. —**Ant.** esteem; praise, acclaim.

abyss, *n.* chasm, gulf, bottomless pit, abysm, depths, pit, crater, crevasse, shaft, well, hollow, cavity, void, deep, hell.

academic, *adj.* **1.** scholarly, scholastic, lettered, literary, humanistic, erudite, learned, cultured, scientific, pedagogical, pedagogic, educational, highminded, instructive, instructional, didactic, tutorial, intellectual, professorial, donnish, collegiate. **2.** theoretical, hypothetical, speculative, conjectural, abstract, ivory-tower, idealistic, visionary, unrealistic, impractical, nonpragmatic, sophistic. **3.** conventional, formal, dry, standard, traditional, unoriginal, orthodox, commonplace, formulaic, pro forma, trite, conformist, prosaic, stale, uninspired, boring, tiresome. —**Ant.** illiterate, informal.

accept, *v.* **1.** receive, take, allow, permit. **2.** admit, agree to, accede to, acquiesce in, assent to, approve, allow, concede, acknowledge. **3.** resign oneself to, reconcile oneself to, suffer, undergo, stand, withstand, stomach, bear, endure, brook, take, tolerate, accommodate oneself to, yield, consent. **4.** believe, acknowledge. —**Ant.** reject.

access, *n.* **1.** entry, entrance, doorway, ingress, entrée, passage, adit, right of entry, admittance, way, way in, route, approach. —*v.* **2.** reach, approach, contact, get, communicate with, go into, enter.

accident, *n.* **1.** blunder, mistake, mischance, misfortune, disaster, calamity, catastrophe, casualty, mishap, misadventure, contingency. **2.** fortuity, chance, fortune, luck, fluke, serendipity. —**Ant.** design, premeditation.

accidental, *adj.* **1.** casual, fortuitous, chance, lucky, unlucky, unfortunate, serendipitous, unpremeditated, unintentional, unwitting, inadvertent, unexpected, unanticipated, random, unforeseen, undesigned, unplanned, contingent. **2.** nonessential, incidental, subsidiary, secondary, dispensable, expendable, adventitious. —**Ant.** planned, designed, essential.

acclaimed, *adj.* notable, distinguished, great, major, famous, honored, famed, renowned, celebrated, prominent, world-renowned, world-famous, stellar, world-class, outstanding, preeminent, premier.

accolade, *n.* honor, praise, tribute, award, distinction, decoration, laurels, kudos.

accommodate, *v.* **1.** oblige, serve; aid, assist, help, abet. **2.** provide, equip, supply, furnish, minister to. **3.** furnish room for, board, show hospitality, house, entertain. **4.** make suitable, suit, fit, adapt, adjust, modify, customize, tailor. **5.** bring into harmony, adjust, reconcile, compose, harmonize. **6.** contain, hold. **7.** conform, agree, concur, assent. —**Ant.** inconvenience, incommode.

accompany, *v.* **1.** go along, attend, join, escort, convoy, wait on, chaperone, squire, usher, come with. **2.** coexist with, consort with; belong with, associate with, consider together with, couple with. —**Ant.** desert, abandon, forsake.

accomplice, *n.* associate, partner, confederate, accessory, ally, colleague, collaborator, coconspirator, cohort, partner in crime, abettor, henchman.

accomplish, *v.* **1.** fulfill, complete, achieve, execute, do, carry out, perform, finish, attain, consummate, culminate, conclude, gain, dispatch, effect, effectuate, perfect, realize. **2.** succeed in, be successful with *or* in, triumph over, win over. —**Ant.** fail.

accomplishment, *n.* **1.** fulfillment, completion, effecting, realization, conclusion, culmination, execution. **2.** achievement, success, consummation, triumph, coup, feat, tour de force. **3.** attainment, acquirement, acquisition, proficiency. **4.** talent, skill, ability, gift, aptitude, faculty, capability, forte, strength, expertise. —**Ant.** failure.

accord, *v.* **1.** agree, assent, concur, correspond, coincide, conform, go together, be at one, be harmonious *or* in harmony, harmonize. **2.** adapt, accommodate, reconcile, suit, fit. **3.** grant, concede, yield, give up *or* in, allow, deign, vouchsafe. —**Ant.** conflict, disagree.

accordingly, *adv.* **1.** correspondingly, appropriately, suitably, in conformance, in compliance, compliantly, agreeably. **2.** in due course, consequently, hence, therefore, thus, so, wherefore.

account, *n.* **1.** narrative, narration, recital, report, history, chronicle, journal, anecdote, description, story, exposé, tale. **2.** explanation, elucidation. **3.** explication, clearing up, exposition. **4.** reason, consideration, motive, excuse, purpose. **5.** consequence, importance, value, consideration, worth, distinction, repute, reputation. **6.** estimation, judgment, consideration, regard. **7.** profit, advantage, benefit. **8.** statement, ledger, inventory, register, score, book, books. **9.** record, ledger; balance. —*v.* **10.** give an explanation for, explain, elucidate. **11.** make excuses for, give reasons for, answer, reply. **12.** explain, explicate. **13.** count, reckon, estimate, consider, regard, judge, deem, rate, assess, hold, see, view, look upon.

accurate, *adj.* correct, exact, precise, true, unerring, error-free, on target, on the money, verified, valid, real, factual, scientific,; meticulous, scrupu-

lous, careful, conscientious. —**Ant.** inaccurate.

accuse, *v.* **1.** arraign, indict, charge, incriminate, impeach. **2.** blame, inculpate, charge, involve, point to, censure, hold responsible, denounce, cite, point the finger at. —**Ant.** exonerate.

accustomed, *adj.* **1.** customary, habitual, usual, characteristic, familiar, common, traditional, normal, regular, routine, ordinary, set, typical. **2.** wont, used to, in the habit of. —**Ant.** unused, unaccustomed.

acerbic, *adj.* **1.** sour, tart, acid, acidy, acidulous, acetose. **2.** sarcastic, mordant, sardonic, ironic, wry, satiric, caustic, biting, scathing. —**Ant.** sweet, dulcet, generous, upbeat, Pollyannaish, goody-goody.

ache, *v.* **1.** suffer, hurt, suffer pain, throb, smart, sting, pound, be sore, have pangs, feel distress. **2.** long, yearn, crave, hunger, hanker, pine, yen. —*n.* **3.** pain, continued *or* dull pain, agony, pang, soreness, smarting, throbbing.

achieve, *v.* **1.** carry through, accomplish, consummate, complete, effect, execute, do, perform, realize, reach. **2.** gain, obtain, acquire, procure, secure, get, attain, realize, win. —**Ant.** fail.

achievement, *n.* **1.** exploit, feat, deed, victory, triumph. **2.** accomplishment, realization, attainment, consummation, acquisition, acquirement, fulfillment, completion. —**Ant.** failure.

acid, *adj.* **1.** acerbic, sour, tart, vinegary. **2.** acerbic, caustic, scathing, biting, ill-natured, ill-tempered, sarcastic, sardonic, scornful, wry, mordant. —**Ant.** sweet, mild.

acknowledge, *v.* **1.** admit, confess, own, declare, grant, concede, give in, allow, agree. **2.** realize, recognize. **3.** accept, receive, allow. **4.** appreciate, be grateful for, express gratitude for. **5.** reply to, answer, react to, respond to.

acquaintance, *n.* **1.** associate, companion, friend. **2.** personal knowledge, familiarity, understanding, awareness; experience.

acquiesce, *v.* assent, accede, comply, agree, concur, consent, bow, submit, yield, resign *or* reconcile oneself, rest, be satisfied *or* content (with). —**Ant.** protest, object.

acquire, *v.* **1.** appropriate, gain, win, earn, attain; take over, take possession of, procure, secure, obtain, get. **2.** accomplish, achieve. —**Ant.** forfeit, lose.

acquit, *v.* **1.** absolve, exonerate, exculpate, pardon, excuse, forgive. **2.** release *or* discharge, liberate, set free. **3.** settle, pay, fulfill. —**Ant.** convict, condemn.

acrimonious, *adj.* harsh, bitter, biting, sharp, rancorous, angry, contentious, disputatious, antagonistic, hostile, vitriolic. —**Ant.** peaceful, pacific, irenic, tactful, diplomatic.

act, *n.* **1.** feat, exploit, achievement, transaction, accomplishment, performance. **2.** deed, performance. **3.** decree, edict, law, statute, judgment, award. **4.** record, deed, enactment, ordinance. **5.** turn, routine, performance, stint. —*v.* **6.** exert energy *or* force, operate, function, perform, do, work. **7.** function, be active, substitute for. **8.** produce an effect, operate, be efficient *or* effective *or* efficacious. **9.** behave, perform, conduct *or* deport *or* comport oneself. **10.** pretend, sham, dissemble, feign, fake, do imitations, dissimulate, play. **11.** play parts, do imitations *or* impersonations. **12.** represent, imper-

sonate, imitate, play the part of. **13.** feign, counterfeit, fake, imitate. **14.** behave as, play the part of.

action, *n.* **1.** movement, work, performance, moving, working, performing, operation. **2.** deed, act. **3.** *(plural)* conduct, behavior, deportment, demeanor, ways, manner, manners. **4.** energetic activity. **5.** exertion, energy, effort. **6.** gesture. **7.** skirmish, brush, affair, encounter, meeting, engagement, conflict, combat, fight, battle, clash, sortie. —**Ant.** lethargy, inactivity.

active, *adj.* **1.** acting, moving, working, operative, effective, functioning, potent. **2.** busy, dynamic, lively, brisk, bustling, energetic, strenuous, vigorous, animated, enterprising, efficient, fervent, earnest, eager, diligent, industrious; engaged, on the go, occupied, consumed with. **3.** nimble, sprightly, agile, alert, smart, quick, animated, spry, spirited, supple, lively. **4.** practical, working, applicable, applied. —**Ant.** inactive, lazy.

actual, *adj.* **1.** true, genuine, real, veritable, factual, verifiable, authentic, verified, manifest, realistic, solid, hard, palpable, tangible, certain, positive, absolute, sure, categorical, decided, definite, determinate, substantial. **2.** current, existent, physical, now existing, present, here and now. —**Ant.** unreal, untrue, fake.

acute, *adj.* **1.** pointed, cuspidate, narrows, aciform, acicular, acuminate, sharp, sharpened. **2.** intense, poignant, touching; severe, fierce, violent, distressing, crucial, critical, dangerous, grave, serious; excruciating, keen, sudden, piercing, penetrating. **3.** sharp, penetrating, perceptive, keen, astute, incisive, insightful, sensitive, discriminating, discerning, intelligent, perspicacious, sharp-witted, shrewd, clever, knowing, wise, sage, sagacious, sapient; smart, bright, ingenious, alert, aware, on the qui vive. —**Ant.** blunt.

adapt, *v.* suit, adjust, modify, alter, change, remodel, customize, tailor, reshape, shape, fashion, fit, reconcile, accommodate, prepare, conform, make conformable *or* suitable, qualify, compose; accustom, acclimate, habituate, get used to.

add, *v.* **1.** unite, annex, connect, affix, join; append, attach, supplement, increase, make an addition to, augment, adjoin, tack on. **2.** total, sum up, combine, count up, tote up, reckon, sum, aggregate. —**Ant.** subtract, deduct.

addict, *n.* **1.** substance abuser, user, drug abuser, doper, freakhead, dope fiend, dopehead, pothead, tea head, hophead, junkie, shmecker, A-head, speed freak, pillhead, pill popper, crackhead, acidhead, acid freak, tripper, mainliner, skin-popper, toker. **2.** fan, enthusiast, admirer, aficionado, devotee, disciple, follower, buff, hound, fiend, groupie, freak, maniac, bug, nut.

addiction, *n.* dependency, compulsive need, obsession, fixation, habit, craving, appetite, itch, lust, passion, monkey on one's back, jones, substance abuse.

addition, *n.* **1.** uniting, adding, joining. **2.** summing up, totaling, summation, counting up, reckoning. **3.** increase, increment, enlargement, aggrandizement, augmentation, extension, accession; supplement, appendix, accessory, adjunct, attachment, addendum, appendage. —**Ant.** deduction, subtraction.

address, *n.* **1.** discourse, lecture, speech, oration, talk, sermon. **2.** location, whereabouts, post office. **3.** residence, domicile, abode, habitation, lodging, dwelling, home quarters, house. —*v.* **4.** talk to, deliver *or* give a speech to, lecture, direct (speech *or* writing to), speak to. **5.** greet, hail, approach, accost. **6.** invoke, appeal to, apply to.

adequate, *adj.* commensurate, equal, suitable, suited, fit for, fitted, capable, proper, qualified, competent, good enough, satisfactory; sufficient, enough, ample, plenty; acceptable, passable, average, fair, fair to middling, tolerable, all right, O.K., okay, not bad, so-so, up to snuff, up to the mark. —**Ant.** inadequate, insufficient.

adhere, *v.* **1.** stick fast, cleave, cling to, stick, hold, cohere. **2.** be devoted, identify, be attached, be a follower, be faithful, be true. **3.** hold closely *or* firmly to. —**Ant.** separate.

adherent, *n.* **1.** supporter, follower, partisan, disciple; devotee, enthusiast, maven, groupie, fan, aficionado. —*adj.* **2.** clinging, adhering, sticking, cleaving. —**Ant.** recreant, deserter.

adjacent, *adj.* near, close, contiguous, adjoining, juxtaposed, abutting, neighboring, nearby, touching. —**Ant.** distant.

adjoining, *adj.* bordering, neighboring, abutting, contiguous, adjacent, near *or* close *or* next to, touching.

adjourn, *v.* suspend, postpone, interrupt, procrastinate, put off, defer, delay, prorogue. —**Ant.** convene, begin.

adjunct, *n.* **1.** addition, appendix, supplement, attachment. **2.** aide, attaché, subordinate, accessory.

adjust, *v.* **1.** fit, make correspondent *or* conformable to, adapt, accommodate, suit. **2.** regulate, set, repair, fix; change, modify, alter. **3.** arrange, rectify, reconcile, settle, redress, harmonize, get right, put to rights, correct, patch up. **4.** adapt oneself, make oneself suitable *or* suited for, acclimate, accustom.

ad-lib, *v.* **1.** improvise, extemporize, make up, invent, throw away, wing it. —*n.* **2.** improvisation, extemporization, invention, throwaway. —*adj.* **3.** improvised, extemporized, extemporaneous, made up, extempore, impromptu, unrehearsed, unpremeditated, spontaneous, offhand, off the cuff, spur of the moment, ad hoc.

administer, *v.* **1.** manage, conduct, control, execute; rule, govern; direct, superintend, oversee, supervise. **2.** dispense, distribute, supply, job, furnish, contribute. **3.** give, dispense, apply, dose, deal out, dole out.

admirable, *adj.* estimable, praiseworthy, fine, rare, excellent, wonderful, awe-inspiring, splendid, marvelous, superior, great, brilliant, first-rate, worldclass. —**Ant.** abhorrent.

admiration, *n.* wonder, awe, pleasure, approbation, delight, esteem, appreciation, reverence, veneration; liking, affection, regard. —**Ant.** abhorrence, disgust, hatred.

admire, *v.* esteem; revere, worship, respect, regard highly, look up to, idolize, venerate; like, delight in. —**Ant.** detest, hate.

admission, *n.* **1.** entrance, introduction, access, admittance, entry, entrée, ticket, pass, Annie Oakley, key, shibboleth. **2.** confession, acknowledgment, allowance, concession, profession, declaration, divulgence, revelation. —**Ant.** rejection; denial.

admit, *v.* **1.** allow to enter, grant *or* afford *or* permit entrance to, let in, give

or afford access to, receive. **2.** permit, allow, agree to, concede, bear. **3.** acknowledge, own, avow, confess. —**Ant.** reject; deny.

admonish, *v.* **1.** caution, advise, warn, counsel. **2.** rebuke, censure, reprove. **3.** recall to duty, remind, notify, make aware, apprise, acquaint, inform.

ado, *n.* fuss, stir, flurry, dither, pother, commotion, disturbance, hubbub, upset, uproar, upheaval, turmoil, hurly-burly, ruckus, brouhaha, foofaraw. —**Ant.** calm, serenity, tranquillity.

adolescent, *adj.* **1.** immature, puerile, juvenile; maturing, pubescent, teenaged, youthful, young. —*n.* **2.** youth, teenager, teen, teenybopper, juvenile, minor. —**Ant.** adult.

adore, *v.* idolize, worship, love, have a crush on, dote on; respect, honor, esteem, reverence, revere, venerate, idolize, admire, exalt, hallow. —**Ant.** abhor, detest, abominate, hate.

adorn, *v.* **1.** embellish, add luster to. **2.** decorate, enhance, beautify, deck, bedeck, ornament, trim, array. —**Ant.** disfigure, deface.

adroit, *adj.* expert, ingenious, skillful, dexterous, clever, resourceful, ready, quick, apt, adept, agile, nimble, cunning, astute, shrewd, knowing, talented, gifted, able, capable. —**Ant.** clumsy, maladroit.

adult, *adj.* mature, grown up, full-grown, ripe, of age. —*n.* **2.** grown-up, man, woman. —**Ant.** immature, adolescent.

advance, *v.* **1.** move *or* set *or* push *or* bring forward, further, forward. **2.** propose, bring to view *or* notice, adduce, propound, offer, allege. **3.** improve, further, forward, promote, strengthen. **4.** promote, elevate, dignify, exalt. **5.** increase, raise the price of, augment. **6.** update, accelerate, quicken, hasten, speed up, bring forward. **7.** furnish *or* supply on credit, lend, loan. **8.** move *or* go forward, proceed, move on. **9.** improve, progress, make progress, grow, increase, flourish, rise, thrive. **10.** rise, increase, appreciate. —*n.* **11.** moving forward, progress, procedure, way; march, procession. **12.** advancement, promotion, improvement, advance, rise. **13.** overture, proposal, proposition, tender, offer, proffer, offering. —*adj.* **14.** going before, preceding, precedent. **15.** beyond, ahead, before. —**Ant.** retreat.

advantage, *n.* **1.** favorable opportunity *or* state *or* circumstance *or* means *or* situation, vantage point, superiority, superior condition. **2.** benefit, interest, avail, gain, profit, value; return, dividend; utility, usefulness, expediency, use, service. **3.** superiority, ascendancy, preeminence, upper hand, dominance, edge, head start. **4.** behalf, vantage; privilege, prerogative, convenience, accommodation. —**Ant.** disadvantage.

adventurous, *adj.* daring, bold, intrepid, brave, temerarious, heroic, fearless, audacious, courageous, venturous, venturesome, enterprising, dashing, risk-taking, cutting-edge, daredevil, brash, rash, foolhardy, reckless, devil-may-care, hazardous, risky, dangerous, perilous. —**Ant.** timid, tame, docile, cautious, unadventurous.

adversary, *n.* antagonist, opponent, enemy, foe, competitor, rival; snake in the grass. —**Ant.** ally, compatriot, friend.

adverse, *adj.* **1.** antagonistic, contrary, opposite, conflicting, opposed, hostile, against, con, contra, inimical, unfriendly. **2.** unfavorable, unlucky, un-

fortunate; calamitous, disastrous, catastrophic. —**Ant.** favorable, beneficial.

adversity, *n.* calamity, distress, catastrophe, disaster; bad luck, misfortune, misery, trouble, affliction, wretchedness. —**Ant.** happiness, wealth.

advice, *n.* **1.** admonition, warning, caution; counsel, opinion, recommendation, guidance, suggestion, persuasion, urging, exhortation. **2.** communication, information, news, report, intelligence, tidings, word, notice, notification.

advisable, *adj.* expedient, advantageous, politic, proper, fit, suitable, desirable, correct, prudent, practical, sound, seemly, wise, intelligent, smart, sensible, commonsense, judicious.

advise, *v.* **1.** give counsel to, counsel, admonish, caution, warn, recommend to, suggest, guide, commend, admonish, urge, encourage, confer *or* consult with, put one's two cents in. **2.** tell, announce, make known, inform, notify, apprise, acquaint.

advocate, *v.* **1.** plead in favor of, support, urge, argue for, speak for, recommend, champion, back, endorse, uphold, stand behind, second, favor. —*n.* **2.** lawyer, attorney, counselor, counselor-at-law, counsel; intercessor. **3.** defender, vindicator, espouser, upholder, supporter, maintainer, promoter, patron, friend, champion, backer, exponent, proponent, apologist. —**Ant.** oppose; opponent.

aesthete, *n.* art lover, dilettante, connoisseur, virtuoso, expert, collector, tastemaker, maven.

affable, *adj.* courteous, urbane, debonair, suave, civil, approachable, polite, friendly, cordial, pleasant, amiable, obliging, gracious; benign, mild, easy, casual, social. —**Ant.** discourteous, boorish, reserved.

affect, *v.* **1.** effect, exert influence on, accomplish, bring about, influence, sway, act on; modify, alter, transform, change. **2.** move, strike, impress, touch, stir, overcome. **3.** pretend, feign, fake, assume, adopt.

affectation, *n.* pretension, pretentiousness, posturing, pomposity, airs, mannerisms, pose, artificiality, pretense, affectedness, unnaturalness, insincerity. —**Ant.** sincerity.

affected, *adj.* **1.** unnatural, artificial, contrived, stilted, studied, stiff, mannered, awkward, specious, spurious. **2.** assumed, pretended, feigned, simulated, hollow, false, fake, insincere, counterfeit, bogus, sham, phony. **3.** pretentious, pompous, posturing, mincing, highfalutin, la-di-da. **4.** afflicted, attacked, seized, moved, stirred, touched, struck, influenced, gripped, impressed, distressed, upset, troubled, hurt, stricken. —**Ant.** sincere, genuine.

affecting, *adj.* touching, pathetic, piteous, moving, impressive.

affection, *n.* **1.** attachment, liking, friendliness, amity, fondness, devotion, friendship, tenderness, endearment, heart, love, goodwill, regard, warmth, kindliness, sympathy. **2.** feeling, inclination, partiality, proclivity, disposition, predisposition, bent, bias. —**Ant.** abhorrence.

affectionate, *adj.* tender, loving, fond, attentive, attached, devoted, warm, kind, sympathetic, caring, doting, passionate.

affectless, *adj.* unemotional, unfeeling, remote, numb, dead, distant, passionless, dispassionate, detached, disinterested, indifferent, lukewarm, impersonal, cold, cool, cold-blooded, self-absorbed, impassive, untouchable. —**Ant.** emotional, animated, passionate, excitable.

affirm, *v.* **1.** state, assert, aver, maintain, declare, depose, testify, say, pronounce. **2.** establish, confirm, ratify, approve, endorse. —**Ant.** deny.

affliction, *n.* **1.** pain, distress, grief, adversity, misfortune, hardship, ordeal, torment, trial, mishap, trouble, tribulation, calamity, catastrophe, disaster. **2.** sickness, loss, calamity, persecution, suffering, misery, woe, depression, wretchedness, heartbreak; curse, disease, plague, scourge, epidemic. —**Ant.** relief.

affront, *n.* **1.** offense, slight, disrespect, insult, impertinence, contumely, scorn, indignity, abuse, outrage, injury. **2.** shame, disgrace, degradation. —*v.* **3.** offend, insult, slight, abuse, outrage. **4.** shame, disgrace, discountenance, confuse, confound, disconcert, abash. —**Ant.** compliment.

afraid, *adj.* scared, fearful, alarmed, frightened, agitated, hesitant, suspicious, having qualms, aflutter, intimidated, lily-livered, panic-stricken, weak-kneed, fainthearted, nervous, anxious, jittery, on edge, shaky, edgy, jumpy, craven, yellow, horrified, horror-stricken, dismayed, in dread, awestruck, bullied, terrorized, petrified, unmanned, aghast, diffident, mistrustful, full of misgivings, perturbed, shaking in one's boots, trembling, aquiver, having palpitations, sick at heart, disheartened, unsure, consternated, distrustful, dreading, faltering, cowering, wincing, flinching, shrinking from, shuddering, quailing, startled, appalled, daunted, cowed, overawed, abashed, deterred, discouraged, browbeaten, threatened, bulldozed, tremulous, irresolute, dispirited, downcast, lacking confidence or backbone, spineless, pessimistic, hopeless, desperate, despairing, insecure, gun-shy, shellshocked, traumatized, terrified, disquieted, shocked, apprehensive, timid, cowardly, pusillanimous, timorous, shy, cautious, overcautious. —**Ant.** bold, sanguine, confident.

age, *n.* **1.** lifetime, lifespan, stage, period, life, duration. **2.** maturity, majority, adulthood, years of discretion. **3.** old age, decline, twilight of life, dotage. **4.** era, epoch, time, date, period. —*v.* **5.** grow old, mature, ripen. —**Ant.** youth.

aged, *adj.* old, ancient, decrepit, elderly, superannuated, gray, venerable, long-lived, past one's prime, full of years. —**Ant.** young.

aggravate, *v.* worsen, make severe, intensify, heighten, increase, make serious or grave, exacerbate, magnify, inflame. —**Ant.** assuage, improve, better.

aggregate, *adj.* **1.** added, combined, total, complete. —*n.* **2.** sum, mass, assemblage, total, gross, body, amount. —*v.* **3.** bring together, assemble, collect, amass, accumulate, gather. **4.** amount to, add up to. **5.** combine into a mass, form a collection. —**Ant.** particular.

aggressive, *adj.* **1.** belligerent, hostile, unfriendly, quarrelsome, combative, warlike, martial, bellicose, disputatious, pugnacious, attacking, offensive, assaulting, militant, assailing. **2.** energetic, vigorous, pushing, enterprising, assertive, determined, forward, forceful, bold, pushy. —**Ant.** retiring, bashful, shy.

aghast, *adj.* dismayed, horrified, appalled, horror-struck, undone, stricken, stunned, shocked, agape, dumb-

founded, thunderstruck, overwhelmed, jolted, jarred, shaken up, shook up.

agile, *adj.* quick, light, nimble, sprightly, active, lively, brisk, swift, lithe, limber, supple, flexible, animated; ready, smart, alert, keen, sharp, dextrous, resourceful, acute, adroit. —**Ant.** awkward, clumsy, maladroit.

agitate, *v.* **1.** shake or move briskly, disturb, toss, jar; move to and fro. **2.** disturb, ruffle, stir or work up, perturb, excite, fluster, disquiet, rattle, disconcert, unsettle, upset, unnerve, rock, shake up. **3.** discuss, debate, controvert, campaign or argue for, dispute, promote, protest. **4.** arouse public interest, ferment, disturb, rouse. —**Ant.** tranquilize.

agitation, *n.* **1.** agitating, shaking, jarring, disturbing, churning, stirring. **2.** turbulence, arousal, commotion, ferment, stimulation, overstimulation, provocation, incitement, rabble-rousing, disturbance, excitement, turmoil, tumult, storm; unrest, disquiet, ado, to-do. **3.** urging, persistence; debate, discussion, dispute, argument, campaign. —**Ant.** serenity, calm, tranquility.

agony, *n.* **1.** pain, distress, anguish, grief, angst, trouble, misery, woe, wretchedness, affliction, suffering, torment, torture, rack; throe, paroxysm, spasm, seizure, pang; ache. **2.** excitement, suspense, anticipation, apprehension, tension, nervousness, anxiety, insecurity, doubt, uncertainty, irresolution. —**Ant.** comfort.

agree, *v.* **1.** assent, yield, consent, accede, settle, concede, acquiesce, allow, comply. **2.** harmonize, concur, unite, accord, combine. **3.** come to an agreement or arrangement or understanding, compromise, arrive at a settlement, see eye to eye. **4.** accord, correspond, compare favorably, coincide, conform, tally, match, stand up, suit. **5.** be applicable or appropriate or similar, resemble. **6.** make or write a contract or bargain, contract, stipulate, bargain. **7.** concede, grant, allow, let, permit, approve. —**Ant.** disagree.

agreement, *n.* **1.** bargain, contract, covenant, treaty, pact, settlement, accord, word, compact, understanding, arrangement, deal. **2.** unanimity, harmony, concord, conformity, unity, uniformity, compatibility, concurrence. —**Ant.** disagreement.

aid, *v.* **1.** support, help, succor, assist, serve, abet, back, second; spell, relieve. **2.** promote, facilitate, ease, simplify. **3.** be of help, give help or assistance. —*n.* **4.** help, support, succor, assistance, service, furtherance; relief, charity. **5.** assistant, helper, supporter, servant, aide, aide-de-camp, right hand, cohort, ally, comrade. —**Ant.** hinder, obstruct; obstacle, obstruction.

ailing, *adj.* sickly, sick, ill, unwell, not well, failing, weak, flagging, languishing, abed, indisposed, infirm, diseased, queasy, unhealthy, troubled, afflicted, suffering, in distress, distressed, in pain, hurting, bothered, disabled, under the weather, feeling poorly, in poor health, prostrate, infected, laid up, bedridden, confined to one's bed, hospitalized, on the sick list, out of commission, out of sorts, laid low, listless. —**Ant.** healthy, well.

ailment, *n.* disorder, infirmity, affliction, indisposition, malaise, malady, disease, sickness, complaint, ill, debility, disability, handicap, defect.

aim, *v.* **1.** direct, point, give direction to. **2.** strive, seek, try, purpose. —*n.* **3.**

direction, sighting. **4.** target, purpose, end, object, goal, intent, intention, reason, design, scheme, ambition, desire, aspiration, objective, plan, point.

air, *n.* **1.** atmosphere, ambience, aura, climate, mood, sense, feeling, quality. **2.** breeze, breath, zephyr, wind. **3.** character, complexion, appearance, impression, aspect, look, mien; manner, demeanor, attitude, conduct, carriage, behavior, deportment, bearing. **4.** (*plural*) pretension, pretense, show, hauteur, arrogance, superiority, superciliousness, affectation, haughtiness. —*v.* **5.** ventilate. **6.** expose, display, show off, parade, exhibit, reveal, disclose, divulge; broadcast, publish, circulate, make public or known, tell, express, declare.

alarm, *n.* **1.** fear, apprehension, fright, consternation, terror, panic, dismay, trepidation, dread, anxiety, distress, uneasiness, excitement. **2.** warning, alert, danger or distress signal, notification, tocsin, siren. —*v.* **3.** terrify, frighten, scare, startle, appall, shock, dismay, daunt, unnerve, panic. —**Ant.** calm, comfort.

alert, *adj.* **1.** attentive, vigilant, watchful, aware, wide-awake, on guard, on one's toes, wary, observant, circumspect, heedful, cautious, on the lookout, on the qui vive. **2.** nimble, brisk, lively, quick, active, agile, sprightly, spirited. —*v.* **3.** prepare for action, warn, alarm, signal, notify, advise, caution. —**Ant.** asleep, listless.

alien, *n.* **1.** stranger, foreigner, immigrant, outsider, *Auslander*, nonnative, newcomer; extraterrestrial, E.T. —*adj.* **2.** strange, foreign; exotic, outlandish, unfamiliar, unaccustomed. **3.** adverse, hostile, opposed, unfriendly, differing, unallied, unconnected, separate. —**Ant.** native; friendly.

alive, *adj.* **1.** existing, living, breathing, quick, among the living, in the land of the living. **2.** unextinguished, operative, functioning. **3.** lively, active, alert, vivacious, animated, spirited, spry, sprightly, energetic, vigorous. **4.** swarming, thronged, aswarm, crowded, ahum, humming, buzzing, jumping, astir, packed, bustling. —**Ant.** dead.

all-around, *adj.* all-round, adaptable, versatile, many-sided, many-talented, flexible, elastic, well-rounded, Renaissance. —**Ant.** narrow, restricted, limited.

allay, *v.* quiet, appease, moderate, soothe, soften, assuage, alleviate, lighten, lessen, mitigate, mollify, temper, relieve, ease. —**Ant.** aggravate.

allege, *v.* declare, affirm, attest, state, assert, aver, charge, avow, say, depose, claim, purport, accuse. —**Ant.** deny.

allegiance, *n.* duty, obligation, faithfulness, loyalty, fealty, fidelity; homage. —**Ant.** treason, treachery.

alleviate, *v.* ease, lessen, diminish, quell, abate, mitigate, lighten, relieve, assuage, allay, mollify. —**Ant.** aggravate, intensify.

alliance, *n.* **1.** association, coalition, combination, bloc, partnership, affiliation, connection, federation, confederacy, confederation, league, union, treaty, pact, compact, bond. **2.** marriage, intermarriage, relation, relationship. **3.** affinity, unity.

allot, *v.* **1.** divide, distribute, parcel out, apportion, assign, share, deal out, dole out, mete out, deal, dispense, measure out. **2.** appropriate, allocate, set apart, appoint, earmark.

allow, *v.* **1.** let, permit, grant. **2.** grant,

yield, cede, relinquish, give, consent to, agree to, authorize. **3.** admit, acknowledge, concede, own, confess. **4.** set apart, take into consideration, make concessions for; add; deduct. **5.** bear, suffer, tolerate, put up with, stand for, brook, sanction, permit, countenance. —**Ant.** forbid, prohibit; refuse.

allowance, *n.* **1.** allotment, stipend, pin *or* pocket money, ration, allocation, dole, quota. **2.** deduction, discount, rebate, reduction, credit. **3.** acceptance, admission, concession, acknowledgment. **4.** sanction, tolerance, leave, permission, license, permit, authorization, authority, approval, approbation, imprimatur, sufferance.

ally, *v.* **1.** unite, unify, join, confederate, combine, connect, league, associate, affiliate, collaborate, band together, team up, marry, wed. —*n.* **2.** comrade, collaborator, coconspirator, associate, partner, friend, confederate, aide, accomplice, accessory, assistant, abettor; colleague, coadjutor, auxiliary. —**Ant.** enemy, foe, adversary.

almost, *adv.* nearly, well-nigh, somewhat, toward, about, approximately, practically, virtually, bordering on, on the brink *or* verge of, little short of; barely, hardly, scarcely, not quite, all but, close to, closing in on.

alone, *adj.* apart, lone, lonely, lonesome, single, solitary, desolate, isolated, enisled, unaccompanied, solo, unescorted, by oneself, unattended, unassisted, abandoned, on one's own, singlehanded, individual, singular, unique, odd. —**Ant.** together, accompanied.

also, *adv.* in addition, too, further, likewise, besides, moreover, furthermore.

alter, *v.* modify, change, permute, vary, revise, transform; adjust, adapt, convert, redo. —**Ant.** preserve, keep.

alternate, *v.* **1.** take turns, rotate, change, exchange, interchange; succeed. —*n.* **2.** substitute, stand-in, variant, alternative, second choice, deputy, backup, understudy, pinch hitter, surrogate.

alternative, *n.* **1.** choice, option, selection, other, alternate, variant, possibility, substitute, surrogate. —*adj.* **2.** mutually exclusive, different, variant, another, additional, substitute.

always, *adv.* **1.** all the time, uninterruptedly, perpetually, in perpetuity, unendingly, ever after, till the end of time, everlastingly, eternally, forever, continually, ever, evermore, forevermore, unceasingly. **2.** every time, each time, at all times, again and again, without exception; often, usually, as a rule. —**Ant.** never.

amateur, *n.* lay person, dabbler, beginner, abecedarian, nonexpert, dilettante, tyro, novice, nonprofessional, neophyte, greenhorn; bungler, second-rater, mediocrity. —**Ant.** professional, expert.

amaze, *v.* astound, surprise, astonish, stagger, stupefy, bewilder, confuse, perplex, daze, dumbfound, awe, stun, floor, take aback, dazzle, nonplus, confound, flabbergast, throw for a loop, take one's breath away, boggle one's imagination, knock one's socks off, make one gasp.

ambiguous, *adj.* **1.** equivocal, doubtful, dubious, unclear, uncertain, vague, indistinct, indeterminate; inconclusive, undefined, questionable, indefinite, misty, foggy; misleading, deceptive. **2.** difficult, obscure, unclassifiable, anomalous. **3.** puzzling, enigmatic, problematic, cryptic, myste-

rious, confusing. —**Ant.** explicit, clear.

ambition, *n.* **1.** goal, object, aim, hope, desire, dream, wish, objective, purpose; hunger, thirst, appetite, craving, aspiration, enterprise, yearning, longing. **2.** energy, initiative, drive, enterprise, enthusiasm, zeal, avidity, get up and go, passion. —**Ant.** satisfaction; sloth, laziness.

ambitious, *adj.* **1.** aspiring, enterprising, hopeful, enthusiastic, energetic, vigorous, zealous, eager, desirous. **2.** showy, pretentious, ostentatious, overweening, pushy. —**Ant.** apathetic; humble.

ambivalent, *adj.* undecided, uncertain, equivocal, contradictory, unresolved, dubious, mutable, vacillating, irresolute, hesitant, on the fence.

ameliorate, *v.* improve, better, amend, raise, elevate, promote, reform. —**Ant.** aggravate.

amiable, *adj.* gracious, agreeable, kindhearted, well-disposed, warm, genial, congenial, winning, affable, pleasant, obliging, approachable, good-natured, affectionate, kind, friendly, amicable. —**Ant.** hostile.

amid, *prep.* among, in the middle *or* center of, surrounded by, in the thick of.

among, *prep.* amid, between, surrounded by.

amorous, *adj.* **1.** loving, amatory, tender. **2.** enamored, in love, fond of, ardent, tender, passionate, impassioned, erotic, filled with desire, lustful, libidinous, lecherous, on the make, horny, hot. —**Ant.** indifferent, cold.

ample, *adj.* **1.** large, spacious, expansive, wide-ranging, extensive, vast, great, capacious, roomy, broad, wide. **2.** liberal, generous, free, abundant, copious, abounding, unrestricted, rich, lavish, inexhaustible, plenteous, plentiful, overflowing, full, bountiful, exuberant, substantial. —**Ant.** insufficient, meager, scanty, sparse.

amplify, *v.* **1.** enlarge, extend, greaten, expand, widen, broaden, develop, augment, increase, supplement, expatiate on, detail, lengthen, dilate, magnify. **2.** exaggerate, overstate, blow up, magnify, stretch, embellish, embroider, elaborate on. —**Ant.** abridge, abbreviate.

amuse, *v.* entertain, divert, please, occupy, interest, beguile, charm, cheer, enliven, tickle. —**Ant.** bore.

amusing, *adj.* **1.** entertaining, diverting, pleasing, charming, cheering, lively. **2.** comical, comic, droll, risible, laughable, delightful, mirth-provoking, funny, farcical, ludicrous, ridiculous, absurd. —**Ant.** boring, tedious.

ancestral, *adj.* hereditary, inherited, patrimonial.

ancestry, *n.* **1.** pedigree, descent, stock, genealogy, heritage. **2.** family, house, race, line, lineage, forebears, forefathers. —**Ant.** posterity, descendants.

ancient, *adj.* old, primeval, primordial, stone-age, Neanderthal, neolithic; aged, antique, antiquated, archaic, quaint, old-fashioned, obsolescent, obsolete, archaic, timeworn, venerable, hoary, superannuated, fossilized, passé, bygone, dead as a dodo *or* dinosaur, extinct, outmoded, unfashionable, out-of-date; antediluvian, prehistoric, of yore. —**Ant.** new, modern.

anger, *n.* **1.** displeasure, resentment, exasperation, wrath, pique, ire, fury, indignation, rage, choler, bile, spleen, irritation, vexation, annoyance, irritability, outrage. —*v.* **2.** displease, vex,

irritate, arouse, nettle, exasperate, infuriate, enrage, incense, madden, pique, annoy, rile, gall, provoke, outrage, make one's blood boil. —**Ant.** patience, delight; calm, gladden, cheer.

angry, *adj.* indignant, resentful, irate, incensed, enraged, wrathful, resentful, splenetic, fuming, livid, up in arms, steamed up, infuriated, furious, mad, passionate, inflamed; provoked, irritated, nettled, galled, chafed, piqued, annoyed, irascible, indignant, exasperated, aggravated. —**Ant.** patient, calm.

anguish, *n.* **1.** pain, pang, suffering, distress, misery, grief, woe, anxiety, angst, agony, torment, torture, rack. —*v.* **2.** agonize, distress, torture, disturb, upset, afflict, trouble, beset, torment. —**Ant.** comfort.

animal, *n.* **1.** creature, being, organism, mammal. **2.** beast, brute, monster, savage, ogre, Neanderthal. —*adj.* **3.** living, sentient. **4.** carnal, fleshly, sensual, crude, unspiritual, physical; beastly, brutal, bestial, subhuman.

animate, *v.* **1.** revitalize, activate, breathe life into, vivify, enliven, vitalize, quicken. **2.** invigorate, encourage, inspire, inspirit, hearten, energize, fortify, stimulate, motivate, spur, rouse, arouse, waken. **3.** refresh, exhilarate, buoy up, excite, fire, heat, urge, provoke, incite, kindle, prompt. —**Ant.** thwart, discourage, dishearten.

animation, *n.* liveliness, vivacity, spirit, life, vigor, vitality, verve, pep, energy; enthusiasm, ardor, exhilaration, cheerfulness, sprightliness, buoyancy, dash, élan, zest, fervor, fire, intensity, dynamism, excitement, airiness. —**Ant.** sluggishness, torpor.

announce, *v.* proclaim, publish, declare, report, set forth, promulgate, publicize, advertise, broadcast, air, make public *or* known, herald, circulate; tell, reveal, divulge, propound, express publicly, go public with; signal, state, aver, assert, notify, confirm, pronounce, present. —**Ant.** suppress.

annoy, *v.* molest, harry, hector, badger, tease, irk, pester, harass, bother, worry, trouble, irritate, chafe, fret, disturb, disquiet, vex, nettle, exasperate, aggravate, provoke, incense, rile, madden, nag, plague, bedevil, needle, hassle, bug, get up someone's nose, get in someone's face, ride, pick on. —**Ant.** comfort, soothe.

answer, *n.* **1.** reply, response, retort, riposte, rejoinder. **2.** solution. **3.** defense, plea. —*v.* **4.** reply, make reply *or* response, respond, rejoin. **5.** be responsible *or* liable *or* accountable. **6.** pass, serve, do, suit; suffice, be sufficient. **7.** reply to, respond to. **8.** serve, suit, satisfy, fulfill. **9.** atone for, make amends for. —**Ant.** ask, question; differ.

antagonist, *n.* opponent, adversary, rival, competitor, contestant, contender, competition, opposition, enemy, foe. —**Ant.** ally, friend.

anticipate, *v.* **1.** foresee, expect, foretaste, forecast, foretell, prophesy, prophesize, predict, tell the future, augur. **2.** expect, look forward to, prepare for, count on, await, wait for. **3.** preclude, obviate, prevent, forestall, intercept, nullify.

antipathy, *n.* **1.** repugnance, dislike, aversion, disgust, abhorrence, hatred, detestation, hate, loathing, horror. **2.** contrariety, opposition. —**Ant.** attraction, sympathy, love.

antique, *adj.* **1.** ancient, old, archaic, bygone, of yore, venerable, hoary; antediluvian, aboriginal, medieval, Neanderthal, primitive, extinct, dead as a dodo, primeval. **2.** antiquated, old-fashioned, out-of-date, obsolescent, obsolete, passé, outmoded, old hat, quaint, nostalgic, dated, out of fashion, unfashionable, out of vogue, stale, of other times, of the old school, old world, timeworn, secondhand, trite, stale. —*n.* **3.** heirloom, collectible, collector's item, antiquity, museum piece, classic, work of art, artwork, article of virtu, bric-a-brac, showpiece, objet d'art, bibelot, curio, rarity. —**Ant.** modern, new.

antisocial, *adj.* unfriendly, asocial, unsociable, standoffish, aloof, distant, unapproachable, solitary, reclusive, hermitlike, eremitic, eremitical, withdrawn, misanthropic, sociopathic. —**Ant.** social, sociable, friendly, gregarious.

anxiety, *n.* **1.** apprehension, fear, dread, angst, nervousness, foreboding; worry, distress, uneasiness, disquietude, disquiet; trouble, pain. **2.** solicitous desire, eagerness, solicitude, concern, longing, ache. —**Ant.** security, calmness, equanimity.

anxious, *adj.* concerned, worried, apprehensive, uneasy, troubled, disquieted, uncertain, apprehensive, tense, distressed, disturbed, nervous, fretful, edgy, on edge, perturbed, restless, upset, wary, cautious, watchful. —**Ant.** secure, certain, sure, confident.

apathetic, *adj.* unfeeling, passionless, emotionless, indifferent, unconcerned, impassive, stoical, cool, cold, uninterested, phlegmatic, dull, lifeless, flaccid, obtuse, sluggish, torpid, callous, cold-blooded, insensible, soulless. —**Ant.** alert, emotional, passionate, ardent, animated.

ape, *v.* imitate, mimic, counterfeit, copy, affect, emulate, follow, mirror.

apex, *n.* tip, point, vertex, summit, top, pinnacle, zenith; acme, climax.

apology, *n.* **1.** excuse, plea, explanation, reparation. **2.** defense, espousal, justification, vindication. **3.** poor substitute, makeshift.

appall, *v.* frighten, horrify, terrify, dismay, alarm, startle, discomfit, unnerve, repel, disgust, daunt, shock, petrify. —**Ant.** reassure, comfort.

apparel, *n.* clothes, clothing, togs, duds, gear, threads, glad rags, dress, garb, attire, costume, garments, vesture, vestments, robes, rig, accouterments, trappings, outfit, equipment.

apparent, *adj.* **1.** plain, clear, open, evident, obvious, marked, conspicuous, patent, unquestionable, unmistakable, manifest. **2.** seeming, ostensible, unreal, specious, illusory, outward, superficial, external. **3.** visible, open, in sight, perceptible, detectable, discernible. —**Ant.** concealed, obscure; real.

apparition, *n.* **1.** specter, vision, illusion, phantom, wraith, spirit, sprite, ghost, phantasm, shade, chimera. **2.** appearance, appearing, manifestation, phenomenon.

appeal, *n.* **1.** entreaty, request, petition, prayer, call, supplication, invocation. **2.** application, suit, solicitation. **3.** attraction, lure, allurement, charm, fascination, interest. —*v.* **4.** entreat, supplicate, petition, ask, request, solicit, plead, apply, sue, beseech, beg, implore, pray.

appear, *v.* **1.** become visible, come into sight *or* view, emerge, crop up, materialize, enter the picture, manifest, show up, arise, turn up, see the light. **2.** have an appearance, seem, look, show, have the appearance. **3.** be obvious *or* manifest *or* clear. —**Ant.** disappear.

appearance, *n.* **1.** form, being, apparition; arrival, coming, advent. **2.** aspect, mien, guise, air, expression, look; manner, demeanor, presence. **3.** show, seeming, semblance, face, pretense, pretext, colors.

appease, *v.* **1.** pacify, quiet, soothe, calm, placate, tranquilize, mollify, alleviate, mitigate, temper, allay, assuage, ease, abate, lessen; still, hush, lull; keep down, quell, subdue. **2.** satisfy, fulfill, propitiate. **3.** conciliate, propitiate, win over, make amends, accede to the demands of, make favorable. —**Ant.** aggravate, perturb; dissatisfy.

appetite, *n.* hunger, desire, longing, craving, thirst; demand; propensity, liking, relish, gusto, zest, zeal, passion, predilection, inclination, proclivity, tendency, preference, enthusiasm, bent, keenness, hankering, longing, yearning. —**Ant.** renunciation, apathy.

applause, *n.* hand-clapping, cheering, cheers, shouting; approval, acclamation, approbation, acclaim, plaudits; laurels, éclat, commendation, praise, kudos. —**Ant.** disapproval, condemnation.

apple-polish, *v.* fawn, toady, flatter, kowtow, truckle, blandish, cajole, honey, sweet-talk, butter up, bootlick, suck up to, brown-nose.

applicable, *adj.* fit, suitable, suited, relevant, apt, fitting, befitting, proper, apropos, germane, pertinent, pointed, appropriate, relevant, apposite, right, seemly. —**Ant.** inept.

application, *n.* **1.** applying, appliance, utilization, use, practice, employment, operation, exercise. **2.** usability, utility, relevance, aptness, aptitude, suitability, pertinence. **3.** request, petition, solicitation, appeal, claim. **4.** attention, effort, assiduity, industry, persistence, perseverance, diligence, devotion, dedication, commitment. —**Ant.** inattention, laziness.

apply, *v.* **1.** lay on, place on *or* upon. **2.** use, employ, put to use, effect, utilize. **3.** devote, dedicate, commit, focus, concentrate, address, pay attention; credit, assign, appropriate, allot. **4.** have a bearing, refer, be pertinent, hold true *or* good, be appropriate, impinge. **5.** ask, petition, sue, entreat, solicit, appeal, request.

appoint, *v.* **1.** nominate, assign, name, elect, select, choose, set apart, designate, point out, allot, destine. **2.** constitute, ordain, establish, prescribe, direct, require, command, order, decree, impose *or* insist on. **3.** fix, settle, determine, agree on *or* upon. **4.** equip, rig, outfit, accouter, furnish, supply; decorate. —**Ant.** dismiss; strip.

appointment, *n.* **1.** nomination, election, selection, assignment, appointing, designating, designation, place, installation. **2.** office, post, station, sinecure, position, job, situation, place, assignment, berth. **3.** engagement, agreement, arrangement, assignation, rendezvous, tryst, meeting, date.

apportion, *v.* divide, allot, distribute, assign, allocate, appoint, partition, measure, mete, dole out, deal, dispense, parcel out.

appreciate, *v.* **1.** esteem, prize, value, estimate *or* rate highly, cherish, enjoy, admire, treasure, respect, honor. **2.** be aware *or* conscious of, detect, understand, comprehend, recognize, perceive, know. **3.** rise *or* increase in value *or* worth. —**Ant.** disparage; scorn.

apprehension, *n.* **1.** anticipation, anxiety, misgiving, dread, fear, angst, alarm; worry, uneasiness, suspicion, distrust, mistrust, suspense, expectation. **2.** understanding, intelligence, reason. **3.** view, opinion, idea, belief, sentiment. **4.** arrest, seizure, capture. —**Ant.** confidence, composure; release.

apprise, *v.* inform, tell, advise, give notice to, notify, warn, acquaint, disclose to.

appropriate, *adj.* **1.** fitting, fit, right, suitable, suited, apt, befitting, meet, felicitous, proper, opportune, apropos, seemly, due, becoming, seemly, happy, germane, pertinent, to the point. —*v.* **2.** set apart, direct, assign, apportion, allocate, devote, earmark, allot; seize, expropriate, annex, usurp, steal, pilfer, adopt, take as one's own, arrogate, impound, make off with. —**Ant.** inappropriate, inept.

approve, *v.* **1.** commend, praise, recommend, appreciate, value, esteem, prize. **2.** sanction, authorize, confirm, endorse, ratify, validate, uphold, support, sustain; countenance, condone, permit, allow, accept, assent to, tolerate. —**Ant.** disapprove.

apt, *adj.* **1.** inclined, disposed, prone, liable. **2.** likely. **3.** clever, bright, intelligent, brilliant, ingenious; adroit, handy, dexterous, skillful, expert. **4.** appropriate, suited, pertinent, relevant, fit, fitting, apt, befitting, meet, germane, applicable, apropos, felicitous, happy, seemly. —**Ant.** inapt, indisposed, malapropos.

aptitude, *n.* **1.** tendency, propensity, predilection, disposition, proclivity, inclination, bent; gift, ability, capability, facility, capacity, skillfulness, flair, genius, talent, knack, faculty. **2.** readiness, intelligence, cleverness, talent; understanding, ability, aptness. **3.** fitness, suitability, applicability, relevance, appropriateness.

arbitrary, *adj.* **1.** discretionary. **2.** capricious, uncertain, unreasonable, willful, fanciful, whimsical; varying, erratic, inconsistent, unpredictable, irrational, chance, random, subjective. **3.** uncontrolled, unlimited, unrestrained; absolute, despotic, dictatorial, totalitarian, tyrannical, imperious, overbearing, peremptory, domineering; authoritarian, summary, autocratic, dogmatic, highhanded, inconsiderate. —**Ant.** systematic, rational, fair, certain.

archaic, *adj.* old, ancient, antiquated, antique, old-fashioned, out of date, passé, outmoded, obsolete, obsolescent, old-timey, superseded, superannuated, antediluvian, dated, discarded, dead, old hat, démodé. —**Ant.** modern, up to date.

archetype, *n.* model, form, pattern, prototype, example, type, paragon, ideal, standard, epitome, quintessence, exemplar, embodiment, personification, paradigm, nonpareil.

ardent, *adj.* passionate, glowing, fervent, fervid, fierce, keen, avid, intense, eager, sanguine, enthusiastic, zealous; vehement, forceful, impassioned, strenuous, hot, burning, fiery, warm, glowing. —**Ant.** cool, apathetic.

ardor, *n.* **1.** warmth, fervor, fervency, eagerness, zeal, passion, enthusiasm, desire, keenness, intensity, vehemence, forcefulness. **2.** fire, burning, heat, warmth, glow. —**Ant.** indifference.

arduous, *adj.* **1.** laborious, hard, difficult, tough, backbreaking, toilsome, onerous, burdensome, wearisome, exhausting, herculean. **2.** energetic, strenuous; vigorous; tiring, exhausting, formidable, taxing, grueling, tiring, fatiguing. **3.** severe, unendurable, harsh, daunting. —**Ant.** easy.

argue, *v.* **1.** debate, discuss, reason, wrangle. **2.** contend, dispute, bicker, quarrel, squabble, remonstrate, spar, fight, disagree. **3.** contest, controvert, debate, discuss, dispute. **4.** maintain, say, assert, hold, claim, insist, contend. **5.** demonstrate, establish, suggest, signify, show, indicate, prove, imply, infer, betoken, evince, denote. —**Ant.** agree.

argument, *n.* **1.** controversy, dispute, debate, discussion, disagreement, quarrel, polemic, altercation, conflict. **2.** reasoning, reason, proof, point, position, logic, plea, claim, assertion, contention, defense, ground, evidence. **3.** fact, statement; theme, thesis, topic, subject, matter. —**Ant.** agreement.

arid, *adj.* **1.** dry, sere, moistureless, desert, parched; barren, infertile. **2.** dull, lifeless, uninteresting, dry, empty, jejune. —**Ant.** wet, damp.

aroma, *n.* **1.** perfume, odor, scent, fragrance, bouquet, redolence, smell, savor. **2.** subtle quality, spirit, essence, characteristic, character, aura, atmosphere, air; suggestion, hint, flavor. —**Ant.** stench.

arouse, *v.* **1.** animate, stir, rouse, awaken; inspirit, inspire, excite, incite, provoke, instigate, stimulate, warm, kindle, fire, spark, summon up, turn on, foment, encourage, quicken, stir up, call forth. **2.** awaken, get up, arise, rouse, revive, stir, wake up. —**Ant.** calm, mitigate.

arrange, *v.* **1.** order, place, adjust, array, group, sort, dispose, organize, systematize, line up, align, form, position, classify, class, rank, distribute. **2.** settle, determine, establish, adjust. **3.** prepare, plan, contrive, devise, concoct, organize. **4.** orchestrate, score, interpret, adapt, adjust. **5.** settle, agree, come to terms. **6.** prepare, adjust, adapt, make preparations *or* plans. —**Ant.** disarrange, disorder, disturb.

array, *v.* **1.** arrange, order, range, marshal, rank, place, dispose, draw up. **2.** clothe, apparel, dress, attire, equip, accouter, rig, outfit; deck, bedeck, ornament, trim, decorate, garnish, adorn. —*n.* **3.** order, arrangement, disposition; allotment. **4.** display, show, exhibit, exhibition, showing, demonstration. —**Ant.** disarray.

arrest, *v.* **1.** seize, apprehend, capture, detain, catch, take, trap, take into custody, take prisoner. **2.** catch, fix, secure, rivet, engage, capture, occupy, attract. **3.** stop, check, bring to a standstill, stay, slow, retard, hinder, deter, obstruct, delay, interrupt, restrain, hold, withhold. —*n.* **4.** detention, custody, imprisonment, apprehension, capture, seizure, restraint, collar, bust. **5.** stoppage, halt, stay, staying, check, hindrance, obstruction, deterrent, detention, restraint, delay, interruption. —**Ant.** release; activate, animate; continue.

arrival, *n.* **1.** advent, coming, appearance. **2.** reaching, attainment, success. **3.** newcomer; passenger, traveler, tourist. —**Ant.** departure.

arrive, *v.* come, make an appearance, appear, turn up, show up; reach a point, attain, attain a position of success, prosper, get ahead, make the grade, make it. —**Ant.** depart; fail.

arrogance, *n.* haughtiness, pride, insolence, disdain, effrontery, superciliousness, scorn, contumely, self-confidence, self-importance, self-aggrandizement, self-glorification, self-applause, self-assertion, impertinence, presumption, presumptuousness,

nerve, gall, loftiness, hubris, pomposity, pompousness, pretension, pretentiousness, braggadocio, bluster, swagger, snobbery, snobbishness, snobbism, brazenness, overbearing manner, imperiousness, highhandedness, contemptuousness, uppitiness, superiority, airs, vainglory, ostentation, bombast, bumptiousness, cheek, impudence, audacity, immodesty, conceit, egotism, hauteur. —**Ant.** humility.

arrogant, *adj.* presumptuous, haughty, imperious, supercilious, assuming, proud, insolent, scornful, contumelious, overbearing, dictatorial, highhanded, lordly, immodest, pompous, brazen, cavalier, disdainful, contemptuous, self-important, vainglorious, vain, snobbish, high and mighty, (Brit.) toffee-nosed, swell-headed, on one's high horse, swollen, puffed up, bumptious, magisterial, strutting, cocky, high-flown, ostentatious, inflated, highfalutin, gloating, saucy, audacious, overweening, conceited, egotistic, egotistical. —**Ant.** humble, self-effacing.

art, *n.* **1.** trade, craft; skill, adroitness, dexterity, talent, expertise, know-how, aptitude, ingenuity, knack, cleverness. **2.** cunning, guile, deceit, duplicity, wiliness, dishonesty, artfulness, trickery, craftiness, slyness.

artifice, *n.* **1.** ruse, device, subterfuge, wile, machination, expedient, trick, stratagem. **2.** craft, trickery, guile, deception, deceit, art, cunning, artfulness, fraud, duplicity, double-dealing. **3.** skillful, apt, *or* artful contrivance.

artificial, *adj.* **1.** unreal, inauthentic, fabricated, manmade, unnatural, synthetic, manufactured, imitation, plastic, made-up, concocted, phony, phony-baloney, fashioned, mock, false, fake, imitation, spurious, ersatz, pretend, counterfeit, simulated, sham, bogus. **2.** affected, put-on, insincere, pretentious, assumed, feigned, deceitful, disingenuous, forced, pretended, contrived, factitious, meretricious, faked. —**Ant.** real, genuine, authentic.

artless, *adj.* ingenuous, naive, unsophisticated, natural, simple, guileless, open, frank, plain, unaffected, candid, honest, sincere, innocent, genuine, direct, straightforward, aboveboard, uncomplicated, unpretentious, unassuming, humble, ordinary, true, truthful, trusting, trustful, unsuspicious, unsuspecting; unskillful, rude, crude, inexpert, primitive, incompetent, clumsy, bungling, awkward. —**Ant.** cunning, sly, crafty.

ascend, *v.* **1.** mount, rise, climb *or* go upward, soar, climb, arise. **2.** climb, mount, scale, go *or* get up. —**Ant.** descend; fall.

ascertain, *v.* determine, establish, define, pinpoint, fix, certify, settle, verify; learn, find out, discover, uncover, get at. —**Ant.** guess, assume.

ascribe, *v.* attribute, impute, refer, assign, charge.

ashamed, *adj.* abashed, humiliated, mortified, shame-faced, embarrassed, red-faced, chagrined, blushing, sheepish, struck dumb, crushed, sorry, penitent, humbled, abased, dashed, bowed down, crestfallen. —**Ant.** proud.

ask, *v.* **1.** put a question to, interrogate, question, inquire of, interview, quiz. **2.** inquire, seek information. **3.** request, solicit, petition, sue, appeal, seek, beseech, implore, beg, supplicate, entreat. **4.** demand, expect, require, exact, call for. **5.** request, petition, sue, appeal, pray, beg. —**Ant.** answer.

askance, *adv.* **1.** sideways, sidewise,

obliquely, crookedly, at an angle. **2.** suspiciously, dubiously, doubtfully, skeptically, mistrustfully, critically.

aspect, *n.* **1.** feature, attribute, characteristic, facet, element, side, detail, quality, angle, circumstance, manifestation. **2.** countenance, expression, mien, visage; air. **3.** view, viewpoint, point of view, attitude; outlook, prospect, direction, bearing, exposure, orientation.

aspire, *v.* desire, long, yearn, covet, pine for, hanker after, be eager for, aim for, hope, wish, aim, dream of, have ambitions, be ambitious, strive for, expect, promise oneself, be set upon, set one's heart *or* mind on.

assail, *v.* assault, set *or* fall upon, attack; abuse, impugn, maltreat, asperse, malign.

assassinate, *v.* murder, kill, slay, destroy, dispatch, do in, immolate, butcher, slaughter, bring *or* take down, do away with, put to death, execute, take *or* put out a contract on, put a hit on, deliver the coup de grace, massacre, make a martyr of, martyr, commit homicide, deal a mortal *or* fatal *or* lethal blow, take out, hire a hit man, extinguish, take *or* end someone's life, shed someone's blood, mark for death, shoot down, finish off, put an end to, eliminate, rub out, conspire against, attack, make an attempt on someone's life; waste.

assault, *n.* **1.** assailing, attack, onslaught, onset, combat, invasion, aggression, charge, offensive, blitzkrieg, strike, raid, incursion, sortie; beating, battering, violation, molestation, abuse. —*v.* **2.** attack, assail, storm, charge, invade, beset, rush, harm, hit, strike, batter, maul, modest, abuse.

assemble, *v.* **1.** bring together, gather, congregate, collect, convene, convoke, summon, muster, marshal, rally, call, call together. **2.** put together, manufacture, construct, erect, fabricate, make, piece together, connect, set up. **3.** meet, convene, congregate, gather, gather together, come together, unite, amass. —**Ant.** disperse.

assembly, *n.* **1.** company, assemblage, throng, mob, gathering, convention, congress, convocation, meeting, group, body, congregation, flock, crowd, multitude, host, horde. **2.** congress, legislature, parliament, lower house, conclave, synod, council, diet.

assent, *v.* **1.** acquiesce, accede, concur, agree, fall in, consent, admit, yield, allow. —*n.* **2.** agreement, concurrence, acquiescence, consent, allowance, approval, concord, accord, approbation. —**Ant.** refuse, deny, dissent.

assert, *v.* **1.** declare, affirm, maintain, aver, say, pronounce, allege, avow. **2.** maintain, defend, uphold, support, vindicate, claim, emphasize. **3.** press, make felt, emphasize. —**Ant.** controvert, contradict, deny.

assertion, *n.* allegation, statement, contention, pronouncement, pronunciamento, insistence, proclamation, avowal, declaration, claim, affirmation, predication, vindication, defense. —**Ant.** denial, contradiction.

assiduous, *adj.* constant, unremitting, continuous, applied; industrious, untiring, tireless, persistent, persisting, devoted, zealous, perseverant, dedicated, committed, studious, attentive, diligent, sedulous. —**Ant.** dilatory; lazy.

assign, *v.* **1.** distribute, allot, apportion, allocate, measure, apportion, consign, grant, give out, appropriate. **2.** appoint, designate, order, nominate, elect, select, choose, specify; fix, determine, pinpoint. **3.** ascribe, attribute, refer, adduce, allege, advance, show, offer, bring up *or* forward.

assist, *v.* help, support, aid, sustain, patronize, befriend, further, facilitate, benefit, second, abet, back, speed, promote, serve, succor, relieve, spell, reinforce. **—Ant.** impede, obstruct, hinder.

associate, *v.* **1.** connect, link. **2.** join, affiliate, team up with. **3.** unite, combine, couple. **4.** fraternize, consort, keep company. **—***n.* **5.** acquaintance, consort, comrade, fellow, companion, friend, mate, peer, equal; confederate, accomplice, ally, partner, colleague, right hand, henchman. **—Ant.** dissociate, alienate; adversary, opponent.

association, *n.* **1.** organization, alliance, union, guild, group, confraternity, sodality, sisterhood, brotherhood, team, society, club, fraternity, sorority, lodge; company, corporation, firm, partnership; set, coterie, clique, band. **2.** companionship, relationship, camraderie, intimacy, fellowship, friendship. **3.** connection, combination, link, affiliation, conjunction, bond, tie, pairing, relationship, linkage.

assume, *v.* **1.** presume, believe, fancy, expect, think, surmise, guess, suppose, presuppose, take for granted, infer. **2.** accept, adopt, arrogate, appropriate, acquire, undertake, take on, take upon oneself. **3.** pretend, feign, affect, simulate, counterfeit, put on, sham, fake. **4.** appropriate, arrogate, usurp.

assumption, *n.* supposition, presupposition, assuming, presumption, taking for granted; hypothesis, conjecture, guess, surmise, belief, fancy, expectation, postulate, theory.

assurance, *n.* **1.** declaration, avowal, averment, deposition. **2.** pledge, promise, guarantee, commitment, vow, word of honor, warranty, surety, guaranty, oath. **3.** certainty, certitude, security, confidence, firmness, trust. **4.** courage, bravery, self-reliance, self-confidence, intrepidity, sang-froid. **5.** boldness, impudence, presumption, arrogance, effrontery, rudeness, impertinence, nerve, cheek, audacity, insolence, brazenness. **—Ant.** denial; distrust, uncertainty; cowardice, diffidence.

astonish, *v.* amaze, strike with wonder, surprise, astound, shock, dumbfound, bowl over, floor, flabbergast, fill with awe, awe, startle; daze, stun, stupefy, confound, stagger, overwhelm.

astringent, *adj.* stern, severe, austere, sharp, harsh, rigorous, hard, unrelenting.

astute, *adj.* keen, shrewd, cunning, artful, crafty, sly, wily, penetrating, eagle-eyed, sharp, quick, perspicacious, ingenious, intelligent, sagacious, discerning, subtle, clever, adroit, calculating, canny, arch, foxy, perceptive, observant, alert, quick-witted, wise, insightful, knowledgeable. **—Ant.** ingenuous, naive, candid, unsophisticated; dull.

asylum, *n.* **1.** hospital, institute, retreat, sanitarium. **2.** refuge, haven, preserve, reserve, sanctuary, shelter, retreat, safe house, harbor.

atheist, *n.* agnostic, disbeliever, nonbeliever, infidel, skeptic, doubter, heathen, pagan, gentile. **—Ant.** believer.

atom, *n.* iota, jot, dot, whit, tittle, scintilla, mote; indivisible particle.

atrocious, *adj.* **1.** wicked, cruel, iniquitous, villainous, fiendish, execrable, abominable, inhuman, savage, barbaric, brutal, barbarous, ruthless, hei-

nous, flagitious, monstrous, felonious, flagrant, dreadful, gruesome, grisly, ghastly, unspeakable, horrifying, horrible, dreadful, awful, infamous, grievous, outrageous, diabolical, devilish, infernal, satanic, Mephistophelean, hellish. **2.** bad, tasteless, execrable, detestable, abominable, awful, terrible, rotten, horrid, appalling, horrendous, frightful, lousy, third-rate. **—Ant.** kind, benevolent; tasteful, praiseworthy.

attach, *v.* **1.** fasten to, affix, join, cement, connect, subjoin, append, secure, pin, rivet, add, tack on, annex. **2.** go with, accompany. **3.** associate, attribute, assign, ascribe, pin, apply, put, place, fix, affix. **4.** attract, charm, endear, enamour, captivate, engage, bind. **5.** adhere, pertain, belong, obtain, cleave, stick to. **—Ant.** detach, separate; repel.

attachment, *n.* **1.** affection, friendship, regard, admiration, fondness, liking, love, devotion; fidelity, faithfulness, affinity, partiality, assiduity, bent, predilection. **2.** tie, fastening, junction, connection, link, bond. **—Ant.** detachment, separation.

attack, *v.* **1.** assail, assault, molest, threaten, interfere with, storm, charge, oppugn, engage in battle, set upon. **2.** criticize, impugn, censure, blame, abuse, berate, revile, inveigh against, denounce, condemn, malign, vilify, denigrate, disparage, deprecate, slander. **—***n.* **3.** onslaught, assault, offense, onset, encounter, aggression, invasion. **—Ant.** defend; defense.

attain, *v.* reach, achieve, accomplish, effect, secure, gain, procure, acquire, get, obtain, win; arrive at, reach. **—Ant.** lose.

attempt, *v.* **1.** try, undertake, seek, make an effort, essay, endeavor, strive, venture, take on, take a shot *or* crack at, have a go at. **—***n.* **2.** trial, essay, effort, endeavor, enterprise, bid, undertaking. **3.** attack, assault. **—Ant.** accomplish, attain.

attend, *v.* **1.** be present at, haunt, frequent. **2.** accompany, go with, escort, squire, usher, follow. **3.** minister to, serve, wait on. **4.** tend, take charge of. **5.** heed, listen to, pay attention to, respect.

attendant, *n.* **1.** escort, companion, comrade, follower; servant, waiter, valet, footman, lackey, flunky, menial, slave. **2.** attender, frequenter. **3.** concomitant, accompaniment, consequence. **—***adj.* **4.** present, in attendance, accompanying, concomitant, consequent.

attention, *n.* **1.** concentration, care, consideration, observation, heed, regard, mindfulness, notice, watchfulness, alertness. **2.** civility, courtesy, homage, deference, respect, politeness, regard. **3.** (*plural*) regard, court, courtship, suit, devotion, wooing. **4.** notice, acclaim, notoriety, publicity, press, prominence, distinction, limelight. **—Ant.** inattention.

attentive, *adj.* **1.** observant, intent, regardful, mindful, heedful, thoughtful, alive, alert, awake, on the qui vive; wary, circumspect, watchful, careful. **2.** polite, courteous, gallant, gracious, accommodating, considerate, solicitous, civil, respectful, deferential, assiduous. **—Ant.** inattentive, unwary; discourteous.

attitude, *n.* **1.** position, disposition, manner, bearing, stance, carriage, demeanor, mien, pose. **2.** position, posture, opinion, feeling, viewpoint, point of view, approach, thought, inclination, tendency, bent, orientation.

attract, *v.* cause to approach, magnetize; draw, pull, invite, allure, win, engage, captivate, endear, enamor, charm, absorb, transfix, enthrall, engross, preoccupy, absorb, enrapture, cast a spell over, beguile, fascinate, hypnotize, mesmerize, entrance, bewitch, intrigue, entice, lure, appeal to, fascinate, please, seduce, interest, be irresistible to, hold one's attention, take one's fancy. **—Ant.** repel, repulse.

attribute, *v.* **1.** ascribe, impute, assign, charge, credit, trace to. **—***n.* **2.** quality, character, characteristic, property, quiddity, feature, trait, virtue, mark; peculiarity, quirk, eccentricity, idiosyncrasy, singularity, uniqueness.

audacious, *adj.* **1.** bold, daring, spirited, adventurous, fearless, intrepid, brave, courageous, dauntless, venturesome, undaunted, valiant, confident, reckless, rash, foolhardy, daredevil, devil-may-care, doughty, mettlesome. **2.** bold, impudent, presumptuous, assuming, unabashed, unashamed, shameless, flagrant, insolent, impertinent, brazen, forward, pert, saucy, defiant, rude, disrespectful, cheeky. **—Ant.** cowardly, feckless; shy, retiring, humble, subservient, craven, timid, timorous, abject, servile.

aura, *n.* atmosphere, mood, feeling, feel, air, ambiance, climate, character, quality, spirit, overtone, sense, undertone, odor, aroma, emanation.

austere, *adj.* **1.** harsh, hard, stern, strict, forbidding, severe, formal, stiff, inflexible, rigorous, uncompromising, relentless, stringent, restrictive. **2.** grave, sober, serious. **3.** simple, severe, without ornament, plain, Spartan, spare, down-home. **4.** rough, harsh, sour, astringent, acerbic, bitter. **—Ant.** soothing, flexible; kind; sweet.

austerity, *n.* severity, harshness, strictness, asceticism, rigor, rigidity, rigorousness, stiffness, inflexibility. **—Ant.** lenience, flexibility.

authentic, *adj.* **1.** reliable, trustworthy, veritable, true, accurate, actual, factual, legitimate, undisputed, verifiable, authoritative. **2.** genuine, real, true, bona fide, unadulterated, pure, uncorrupted. **—Ant.** unreliable, inaccurate; sham, fraudulent, corrupt.

authoritative, *adj.* **1.** official, conclusive, unquestioned, authentic, valid, documented, certified, validated, legitimate, sanctioned. **2.** sound, verifiable, accurate, factual, dependable, true, trustworthy, truthful, reliable; scholarly, learned. **3.** impressive, positive; peremptory, dogmatic, authoritarian, dictatorial, imperious, autocratic. **—Ant.** unofficial; unreliable; conciliatory.

authority, *n.* **1.** control, influence, command, rule, jurisdiction, dominion, right, prerogative, hegemony, sway, power, supremacy. **2.** expert, specialist, scholar, sage, arbiter, judge, sovereign. **3.** statute, law, rule, ruling. **4.** warrant, justification, permit, permission, sanction, liberty, authorization. **5.** testimony, witness, word.

authorize, *v.* **1.** empower, commission, allow, permit, let. **2.** sanction, approve, countenance, endorse, license, entitle, okay, give one's imprimatur. **3.** establish, entrench. **4.** warrant, justify, legalize, support, back. **—Ant.** forbid, prohibit.

automatic, *adj.* **1.** self-moving, self-acting, mechanical, robotic, automated. **2.** involuntary, uncontrollable, reflex, unconscious, instinctive, instinctual, natural, spontaneous, impulsive, knee-jerk, unavoidable. —**Ant.** manual; deliberate, intentional.

auxiliary, *adj.* **1.** supporting, helping, helpful, accessory, supplementary, aiding, assisting, abetting. **2.** subsidiary, subordinate, secondary, ancillary, extra, reserve, additional. —*n.* **3.** helper, aide, ally, assistant, confederate, deputy, amanuencis, supporter, alter ego, man *or* girl Friday. —**Ant.** chief, main.

available, *adj.* **1.** accessible, ready, at one's disposal, present, obtainable, nearby, on tap, within reach, at hand, handy, usable, of use *or* service, serviceable; suitable, fit, appropriate, fitting, befitting. **2.** valid, efficacious, profitable, advantageous. —**Ant.** unavailable; unbecoming; invalid, unprofitable.

avenge, *v.* revenge, vindicate, take vengeance, exact satisfaction for, get even, settle the score, punish, exact reprisals. —**Ant.** forgive, pardon.

average, *n.* **1.** mean, norm, standard, usual, median. —*adj.* **2.** common, usual, customary, general, typical, regular, mean, medial, normal, intermediate, middle; mediocre, middling, ordinary, passable, tolerable, satisfactory, run-of-the-mill, commonplace, undistinguished, unexceptional, so-so, mezzo-mezzo, indifferent, fair, fair to middling, not bad, decent.

averse, *adj.* disinclined, reluctant, unwilling, loath, opposed, resistant, indisposed, anti, against, contrary, hostile, adverse. —**Ant.** inclined, disposed.

aversion, *n.* repugnance, disgust, antipathy, antagonism, animosity, hostility, odium, horror, loathing, detestation, hate, hatred, abhorrence; dislike, distaste, objection, disinclination, unwillingness, reluctance. —**Ant.** predilection, liking; favor.

avoid, *v.* keep away from *or* clear of, shun, evade, escape, elude, fight shy of, eschew, leave alone, steer clear of, refrain from, dodge, circumvent, sidestep, fly from, retreat, abstain, shrink from, hang back, flee from, run away, bolt, abscond. —**Ant.** confront, face.

await, *v.* **1.** wait for, look for, expect. **2.** attend, be in store for, be ready for.

aware, *adj.* cognizant *or* conscious (of), informed, mindful, apprised, knowledgeable, knowing, in the know, enlightened, *au courant*, hip to, wise to, acquaint with, privy to, undeceived, in on. —**Ant.** unaware, oblivious.

awe, *n.* **1.** reverence, respect, veneration; dread, fear, terror. —*v.* **2.** solemnize; daunt, cow, frighten, intimidate. —**Ant.** contempt, irreverence; scorn.

awkward, *adj.* **1.** clumsy, bungling, unskillful, inexpert, gauche, inept, maladroit, all thumbs, blundering, ham-handed, oafish. **2.** inelegant, ungraceful, ungainly, unwieldy, unmanageable, coarse, rude, crude, wooden, stiff, constrained, gawky, unrefined, unpolished, rough. **3.** hazardous, dangerous, perilous, risky, precarious. **4.** trying, embarrassing, touchy, sensitive, uncomfortable, delicate, unpleasant, ticklish, sticky. —**Ant.** deft, adroit, adept; graceful, refined, polished.

B

babble, *v.* **1.** gibber, blabber, gabble, jabber, bibble-babble, blather, prate, prattle. **2.** talk, chat, gossip, chatter, natter, palaver, gab, jaw, schmooze.

—*n.* **3.** nonsense, gibberish, twaddle, prattle, mumbo jumbo, drivel, blather, rubbish, garbage, junk.

back, *n.* **1.** rear, posterior, end. —*v.* **2.** support, sustain, second, uphold, promote, encourage, sponsor, underwrite, bankroll, invest in, bet on, aid, abet, favor, assist; countenance, allow, side with, endorse, stand by. —**Ant.** front, fore, face.

backward, *adv.* **1.** rearward, in reverse, regressively, back foremost, retrogressively, behind. —*adj.* **2.** reversed, returning. **3.** behind, late, slow, tardy, behindhand. **4.** shy, reticent, diffident, retiring, coy, unwilling, loath, chary, averse, reluctant, hesitant, bashful, wavering, disinclined, timid. **5.** slow, retarded, undeveloped, underdeveloped; ignorant, dimwitted, dull, stupid, slowwitted, feebleminded. —**Ant.** forward; precocious.

backwater, *n.* back country, hinterland, outback, backwoods, Podunk, bush, up-country, sticks, boondocks, boonies, middle of nowhere.

bad, *adj.* **1.** evil, wicked, ill, corrupt, base, depraved, unprincipled, vicious, vile, wrong, unspeakable, nefarious, debauched, amoral, immoral; disingenuous, rascally, mischievous, naughty, unruly, ill-behaved, rowdy, misbehaving, disobedient, wild, disorderly; sinful, criminal, dishonest, villainous; baneful, deleterious, pernicious, harmful, hurtful, noxious, poisonous, ruinous, injurious, detrimental. **2.** defective, worthless, poor, inferior, imperfect; wretched, miserable, egregious, execrable, substandard, incompetent, ill-qualified, inadequate. **3.** incorrect, faulty. **4.** invalid, unsound. **5.** sick, ill. **6.** regretful, sorry, apologetic, rueful, sad, conscience-stricken, remorseful, contrite, wretched, upset. **7.** unfavorable, unfortunate, adverse, unpropitious, inauspicious, troubled, grim, distressing, unlucky, unhappy. **8.** offensive, disagreeable, mean, abominable. **9.** vile, wretched, shabby, scurvy. **10.** severe, serious, distressing, grave, terrible, awful, painful. **11.** rotten, decayed, putrid, contaminated, spoiled, tainted. —**Ant.** good.

bag, *n.* **1.** container, case, receptacle, pouch, sack, sac, poke, reticule, packet, pocket; lunchpail, lunchbox, lunchbag, moneybag, shopping bag, paper bag. **2.** luggage, baggage, suitcase, duffel, duffel bag, carry-on, overnight bag, overnighter, backpack, knapsack, rucksack, haversack, satchel, saddlebag, valise, grip, carryall, traveling bag, portmanteau, carpetbag, dittybag, gym bag, pullman case, bandbox, Gladstone bag. **3.** purse, handbag, pocketbook, shoulder bag, clutch purse, change purse, wallet, evening bag, minaudiére, briefcase, tote bag, portfolio, schoolbag, attache case, cosmetic bag, kit, bag kit, fanny pack, flight bag, garment bag, handbill, book bag. —*v.* **4.** catch, net, trap, entrap, kill, ensnare, snare, capture, land, shoot.

bailiwick, *n.* domain, field, sphere, purview, territory, province, department, jurisdiction, realm, terrain, precinct.

balance, *n.* **1.** equilibrium, equilibration, symmetry, harmony, proportion, equipoise, equality. **2.** poise, composure, self-control, equilibrium, equipoise, self-possession. —*v.* **3.** weigh, compare, equilibrate, estimate, assay. **4.** counterpoise, counterbalance, offset, counteract, neutralize, countervail, compensate, allow for, make up for. **5.** proportion, equalize, square, adjust.

ball, *n.* **1.** sphere, globe, orb. **2.** dance, assembly, dancing party.

ban, *v.* **1.** prohibit, interdict, outlaw, forbid, proscribe, taboo, bar, disallow, debar, embargo. —*n.* **2.** prohibition, interdiction, interdict, taboo, proscription. —**Ant.** permit, allow; permission, blessing.

band, *n.* **1.** company, party, troop, crew, gang, group, platoon, corps, horde, pack, bunch, team, ensemble, assemblage, body; clique, coterie, set, society, association, sodality, horde, host, assembly. —*v.* **2.** unite, affiliate, merge, join together, team up, confederate.

banish, *v.* exile, expel, expatriate, deport, ostracize, outlaw, extradite, transport, eject, oust; reject, cast out, send *or* drive *or* put away, exclude, dismiss, dispel. —**Ant.** admit, receive.

bankrupt, *v.* **1.** impoverish, pauperize, ruin, deplete, exhaust, drain dry, bleed. —*adj.* **2.** impoverished, pauperized, insolvent, indigent, impecunious, destitute, broke, stone-broke, flat broke, in receivership, in Chapter 11, on the ropes *or* rocks, wiped out, in the red, tapped out. **3.** ruined, worn out, jejune, exhausted, spent, broken, wasted.

banter, *n.* **1.** badinage, raillery, repartee, kidding (around), ribbing, joking, jesting, pleasantry, persiflage; mockery, ridicule, derision. —*v.* **2.** tease, twit, make fun of; ridicule, deride, mock, jeer, chaff.

bar, *n.* **1.** obstruction, hindrance, deterrent, stop, impediment, obstacle, barrier, barricade. **2.** ridge, shoal, reef, sand-bunk, bank, sandbar, shallow. **3.** counter, zinc; canteen, cantina, gin mill, brasserie, roadhouse, pub, saloon, café, bistro, nightclub, cocktail lounge. —*v.* **4.** hinder, obstruct, deter, stop, impede, barricade, prevent, prohibit, restrain, forbid, forestall, hamper, retard, ban, embargo. **5.** exclude, shut out, eliminate, block, except. —**Ant.** suffer, allow, permit.

barbarian, *n.* **1.** savage, philistine, alien, brute, boor, ruffian, yahoo, vulgarian, Neanderthal, redneck, lowbrow, lout, oaf, ignoramus, hooligan, vandal, ruffian, tough, skinhead. —*adj.* **2.** rude, uncivilized, savage, primitive, barbaric, barbarous, rough, crude, coarse, untutored, ignorant, uncultivated, unlettered, philistine, heathen, insensitive, uncivil, ill-mannered, impolite, boorish, loutish. **3.** cruel, ferocious, wild, feral, inhuman, brutal, harsh. —**Ant.** cosmopolite; refined, civilized, cultivated; humane.

bare, *adj.* **1.** naked, nude, uncovered, unclothed, undressed; exposed, unprotected, unsheltered, unshielded, open. **2.** unfurnished, undecorated, plain, stark, Spartan, monastic, ascetic, mean, poor, meager, unadorned, bald, empty, barren. **3.** basic, literal, straightforward, direct, unvarnished, cold, hard, plain, simple, sheer, mere, sole, just. **4.** unconcealed, undisguised, unreserved, conspicuous, obvious, glaring, evident, palpable. —*v.* **5.** disclose, denude, lay open, expose, unfold, unmask, divulge, reveal, uncover. —**Ant.** covered, dressed.

bargain, *n.* **1.** compact, agreement, stipulation, arrangement, contract, convention, concord, understanding, covenant, pact, settlement, deal, concordat, treaty, stipulation, transaction. **2.** good purchase, buy. —*v.* **3.** contract, agree, stipulate, covenant, transact. **4.** trade, sell, transfer. **5.** haggle, negotiate, barter, dicker, wrangle.

barren, *adj.* **1.** sterile, unprolific, childless, infecund, traitless, dry, unfruitful, infertile, unproductive, poor, bare. **2.** uninteresting, jejune, dull, stupid; uninstructive, unsuggestive, ineffectual, ineffective. —**Ant.** fertile; interesting, effectual.

barrier, *n.* bar, obstruction, hindrance, barricade, block, stop, impediment, obstacle, restraint; fence, railing, stockade, palisade, wall; limit, boundary.

base, *n.* **1.** bottom, stand, rest, pedestal, understructure, substructure, foot, basis, foundation, ground, groundwork; principle. **2.** fundamental part, ingredient, element. **3.** station, goal, starting-point, point of departure. —*adj.* **4.** low, despicable, contemptible, meanspirited, mean, degraded, degrading, selfish, cowardly. **5.** degraded, inferior, unworthy, groveling, servile, subservient, scurry, downtrodden, undignified, miserable, vile, scurrilous, lowly, slavish, menial, beggarly, abject, sordid, ignoble. **6.** mean, sorry, tacky, shoddy, common, poor, inferior, cheap, tawdry, worthless; debased, counterfeit, fake, spurious, shabby, coarse. **7.** unrefined, plebeian, vulgar, lowly, humble, unknown, baseborn; impure, corrupted, corrupt, vile, venal. **8.** scandalous, shameful, ignominous, disreputable, disgraceful, discreditable, dishonorable, infamous, notorious. —*v.* **9.** found, rest, establish, ground, secure, build, anchor, fix, hinge, form; position, post, place. —**Ant.** top, peak; moral, virtuous; good, valuable; refined, pure; honorable.

bashful, *adj.* diffident, shy, abashed, timid, timorous, coy, sheepish, retiring, meek, nervous, self-conscious, reticent, awkward, modest, self-effacing; embarrassed, shamefaced, ashamed. —**Ant.** arrogant, immodest, forward, brazen.

basics, *n.* fundamentals, essentials, rudiments, principles, grammar, rules, guidelines, ABC's.

basis, *n.* bottom, base, foundation, ground, principle, underpinning, infrastructure, heart, core, footing.

batter, *v.* **1.** hit, strike, clout, pummel, bash, thrash, clobber, beat, pound, belabor, smite, pelt; bruise, wound; break, shatter, shiver, smash, destroy, demolish, ruin. **2.** attack, assault, bombard. **3.** abuse, mistreat, maltreat, violate, harm, maul, bruise, mangle, disfigure.

battle, *n.* **1.** action, skirmish, campaign, contest, conflict, engagement, military engagement *or* encounter. **2.** warfare, combat, war, fight. —*v.* **3.** strive, struggle, fight, combat, war, contest, conflict, contend with.

beach, *n.* **1.** coast, seashore, littoral, shore, strand, sands, margin, rim. —*v.* **2.** put ashore, strand, run aground.

beam, *n.* **1.** ray, pencil, streak, gleam, suggestion, hint, glimmer. —*v.* **2.** shine, gleam, glisten, glitter, radiate. **3.** smile, grin, brighten.

bear, *v.* **1.** support, hold up, uphold, sustain. **2.** carry, transport, convey, waft; conduct, guide, take. **3.** thrust, drive, force, push, press. **4.** render, give, yield, afford, produce. **5.** transmit, utter, spread, broadcast, advertise, exhibit, show, demonstrate. **6.** sustain, endure, suffer, undergo, tolerate, brook, abide, put up with, stand, stand for, submit to; allow, admit, permit, admit of, hold up under, be capable of. **7.** maintain, keep up, carry on. **8.** entertain, harbor, cherish. **9.** give birth to, bring forth.

bearing, *n.* **1.** carriage, posture, manner, mien, deportment, stance, atti-

tude, presence, demeanor, behavior, conduct, air. **2.** relation, connection, relationship, correlation, pertinence, relevance, significance, dependency, reference, application.

beastly, *adj.* **1.** bestial, animalistic, animal, brutish, brutal, primitive, barbaric, base, inhuman. **2.** unkind, cruel, uncivil, mean, ruthless, merciless, pitiless. **3.** inclement, stormy, severe, disagreeable, miserable, abominable, execrable, horrid, ghastly, foul, vile, nasty, rotten.

beat, *v.* **1.** hit, pound, strike, thrash, belabor, batter, knock, thump, drub, maul, baste, pummel, thwack, whack, punch, scourge, bludgeon, club, bash, pelt, clout, manhandle, cudgel, cane, whip, flog, lash, buffet. **2.** conquer, subdue, overcome, vanquish, overpower, defeat, checkmate. **3.** excel, outdo, surpass. **4.** throb, pulsate, palpitate, pound, thump. **5.** win, conquer. —*n.* **6.** stroke, blow. **7.** pulsation, throb, tattoo, rhythm.

beautiful, *adj.* handsome, comely, seemly, attractive, lovely, charming, alluring, appealing, radiant, gorgeous, exquisite, good-looking, shapely, stunning, aesthetically pleasing, arresting, enchanting, dazzling, pretty, fair, fine, elegant, beauteous, graceful, pulchritudinous. —**Ant.** ugly; inelegant, ungraceful.

beautify, *v.* embellish, adorn, ornament, decorate, elaborate, garnish, bedeck, deck, deck out, dress up, enhance, prettify, glamorize, titivate, cosmeticize. —**Ant.** uglify, despoil, mar, deface, vandalize.

beauty, *n.* **1.** loveliness, pulchritude, elegance, grace, gracefulness, symmetry, bloom, charm, style, good looks, allure, comeliness, seemliness, fairness, attractiveness. **2.** belle, knockout, stunner, siren, dream, dish. **3.** grace, charm, excellence, attraction, elegance, refinement. —**Ant.** ugliness; gracelessness.

becoming, *adj.* attractive, comely, neat, pretty, graceful, fetching, chic, stylish, fashionable, tasteful. **2.** fit, proper, apt, suitable, appropriate, meet, right, correct, decorous, congruous, fitting, seemly. —**Ant.** unbecoming, ugly, inappropriate, indecorous.

bedlam, *n.* hubbub, din, confusion, racket, noise, clamor, chaos, agitation, riot, pandemonium, babel, tumult, uproar, hullabaloo, ruckus, rumpus, commotion, turmoil, furor, madhouse. —**Ant.** calm, tranquility, peace, serenity.

befitting, *adj.* fitting, proper, suitable, seemly, appropriate, becoming, fit, apt, due, apropos. —**Ant.** unbecoming, improper, unsuitable, inappropriate.

beg, *v.* ask for, entreat, pray, crave, implore, beseech, importune, plead with, wheedle, cajole, whine, petition, sue, request, supplicate, sue for; solicit, sponge, cadge, scrounge, panhandle.

begin, *v.* **1.** commence, start, initiate, inaugurate, institute, enter upon, set about. **2.** originate, open, launch, establish, found, set up, create; arise. —**Ant.** end, conclude, die.

beginner, *n.* amateur, tyro, neophyte, greenhorn, novice, novitiate, pupil, student, newcomer, learner, new arrival, raw recruit, abecedarian, tenderfoot.

beginning, *n.* **1.** initiation, inauguration, inception, dawning, birth, genesis, opening, origin, creation, day one, start, commencement, outset, rise, onset, arising, emergence. **2.** source,

birth, origin, rise, first cause, wellspring, fountainhead, origination.

begrudge, *v.* envy, grudge, covet, resent, be spiteful.

beguile, *v.* **1.** mislead, swindle, dupe, hoodwink, bamboozle, take in, con, trick, hoax, defraud, lead up the garden path, pull the wool over (someone's) eyes, delude, cheat, deceive, fool. **2.** divert, charm, amuse; entertain, cheer, solace, please, distract, engage; fascinate, mesmerize, enchant, entrance, allure, seduce, bewitch, enrapture.

behave, *v.* conduct oneself, act, deport *or* comport oneself, demean oneself, acquit oneself; act properly, be obedient *or* good. —**Ant.** misbehave.

behavior, *n.* demeanor, conduct, manners, deportment, bearing, carriage, mien, air, comportment. —**Ant.** misbehavior.

belief, *n.* **1.** opinion, view, tenet, doctrine, dogma, creed, idea, conviction, principle, persuasion. **2.** certainty, conviction, security, dependence, faith, assurance, confidence, believing, trust, reliance. **3.** credence, credit, acceptance, assent.

bend, *v.* **1.** curve, crook, bow, deflect, draw, flex. **2.** cause to yield, subdue, persuade, influence, mold, dispose, bias, incline, direct, turn. **3.** yield, submit, bow, stoop, kneel, give way, acquiesce, agree. **4.** crook, deflect, deviate, swerve, diverge, incline. —*n.* **5.** curve, crook, bow, rib, elbow, turn, angle, curvature, turning.

beneficial, *adj.* healthful, healthy, salubrious, salutary, wholesome; favorable, supportive, good, serviceable, useful, helpful, profitable, advantageous. —**Ant.** unwholesome, unfavorable, disadvantageous.

benevolent, *adj.* kind, kindly, well-disposed, kindhearted, gracious, humane, humanitarian, sympathetic, compassionate, thoughtful, considerate, tender, tenderhearted; unselfish, generous, liberal, obliging, benign, benignant, charitable, philanthropic, altruistic, magnanimous, open-handed; beneficial, helpful, salutary. —**Ant.** cruel, selfish, egotistical.

bent, *adj.* **1.** curved, crooked, hooked, bowed, flexed, deflected. **2.** determined, set on, decided, intent, resolute, resolved, fixed on. —*n.* **3.** inclination, leaning, bias, tendency, propensity, proclivity, disposition, turn, penchant, predilection, partiality, liking, fondness, proneness; ability, aptitude, talent, gift, flair, knack. —**Ant.** straight; undecided; disinclination.

bequeath, *v.* leave, will, pass on, pass along, devise, legate, hand down, transmit, make over.

beseech, *v.* **1.** implore, beg, entreat, pray, petition, obsecrate, obtest, supplicate, importune, adjure. **2.** solicit, ask, entreat, beg, implore, importune, crave.

beset, *v.* assail, harass, surround, encompass, encircle, enclose, besiege, beleaguer.

besides, *adv.* **1.** moreover, in addition, furthermore, else, otherwise, too, also, yet, further. —*prep.* **2.** over and above, in addition to, except, other than, save, distinct from.

best, *adj.* **1.** finest, first, paramount, superlative, preeminent, unexcelled, unsurpassed, unrivaled, superb, excellent, A-one, first-rate, top, foremost, choicest, most suitable. **2.** kindest, nicest, most, beneficent *or* benevolent. —*v.* **3.** beat, conquer, win out over, surpass, overpower, get the better of, defeat, vanquish, trounce, rout, crush, outdo, overwhelm, overcome, outwit, master, subdue.

bet, v. gamble, wager, risk, stake, hazard, play, take chance or flier, venture, speculate, try one's luck, game, put money on; count on, rely on.

betray, v. **1.** deliver, expose, give up, uncover, reveal, divulge, impart. **2.** be unfaithful to, be a traitor to, deceive, be disloyal to, disappoint, let down, cheat on, stab in the back, sell down the river. **3.** show, exhibit, display, manifest, indicate, imply, betoken, evince, expose, uncover, reveal. —Ant. protect, safeguard.

better, adj. **1.** superior; more useful, more valuable, more suitable, more appropriate, more fit, more applicable. **2.** larger, greater, bigger. —v. **3.** improve, amend, ameliorate, meliorate, emend; advance, promote; reform, correct, rectify. **4.** improve upon, surpass, exceed, outdo, outstrip, excel. —Ant. worse; worsen.

bewilder, v. confuse, perplex, puzzle, mystify; confound, nonplus, astonish, daze, stagger, befog, muddle, befuddle, baffle, bemuse, flabbergast, floor, throw for a loop.

bewitch, v. cast a spell over, charm, enchant, captivate, spellbind, entrance, beguile, intrigue, transfix, transport, enrapture, fascinate, hypnotize, mesmerize, seduce.

bias, n. **1.** prejudice, inclination, preconception, predilection, prepossession, proclivity, propensity, proneness, partiality, predisposition, bent, leaning, tendency. —v. **2.** prejudice, warp, predispose, bend, influence, incline, dispose, sway, color, taint, distort, jaundice. —Ant. justness, impartiality.

bid, v. **1.** command, order, direct, charge, require, enjoin, summon, demand, tell, dictate, instruct. **2.** offer, propose, tender, proffer. —n. **3.** offer, proposal. —Ant. forbid, prohibit, enjoin.

big, adj. **1.** large, great, huge, bulky, massive, immense, colossal, Brobdingian, jumbo, humongous, gargantuan, elephantine, enormous, monstrous, outsized, tremendous, capacious, gigantic, extensive. **2.** important, significant, outstanding, weighty, major, momentous, grave, notable, consequential; haughty, proud, arrogant, pompous, swollen, inflated, tumid, self-important, conceited, self-sufficient, bombastic, boastful. **3.** generous, bighearted, kindly, munificent, charitable, philanthropic, magnanimous, unselfish. —Ant. small; trivial, nugatory.

bigoted, adj. intolerant, narrow-minded, closed-minded, narrow, one-sided, partial, jaundiced, small-minded, illiberal, hidebound, parochial, biased, prejudiced, know-nothing, meanspirited. —Ant. tolerant, broad-minded, open-minded, generous.

bill, n. **1.** account, reckoning, score, charge, invoice, statement. **2.** bulletin, handbill, notice, advertisement, broadside, poster, placard, announcement, throwaway, circular.

billow, v. swell, expand, distend, inflate, bloat, balloon, belly, fill out, puff up, mushroom. —Ant. contract, shrink.

bind, v. **1.** band, bond, tie, make fast, fasten, secure, gird, attach. **2.** encircle, border; confine, restrain, restrict. **3.** engage, obligate, oblige. —Ant. untie, unbind.

birth, n. **1.** act of bearing, bringing forth, delivery, parturition. **2.** lineage, heritage, patrimony, nativity, extraction, parentage, descent, ancestry, line, blood, family, race. **3.** origin, beginning, rise, creation, emergence, start, origination. —Ant. death, end.

bit, n. particle, speck, grain, mite, crumb, iota, jot, atom, trace, touch, hint, suggestion, suspicion, scintilla, tittle, whit, fragment, morsel, piece, scrap, shred.

bitter, adj. **1.** harsh, acrid, biting, acerbic, sharp, caustic, mordant. **2.** grievous, distasteful, painful, miserable, dispiriting, unwelcome, distressing, intense, sore, poignant, sorrowful, calamitous. **3.** piercing, stinging, biting, nipping, sharp, keen, cutting, severe, cold, freezing, wintry. **4.** harsh, sarcastic, caustic, cutting, reproachful, vicious, acrimonious, acerbate, severe, stern, sardonic, scornful, sneering. **5.** fierce, cruel, savage, mean, merciless, ruthless, relentless, virulent, dire. —Ant. sweet.

black, adj. **1.** dark, dusky, sooty, inky, jet-black, raven, ebony, sable, swarthy. **2.** soiled, dirty, dingy, dusky, stained. **3.** gloomy, sad, dismal, sullen, hopeless, dark, depressing, doleful, funereal, somber, mournful, forbidding, disastrous, calamitous. **4.** amoral, evil, wicked, sinful, fiendish, inhuman, devilish, diabolic, infernal, monstrous, atrocious, horrible, outrageous, heinous, flagitious, nefarious, treacherous, traitorous, infamous, villainous. —Ant. white; clean, pure, undefiled; happy; good, upright.

blame, v. **1.** reproach, reprove, reprehend, censure, condemn, find fault, criticize, disapprove, upbraid, rebuke, scold, chide, take to task, chew out. —n. **2.** censure, reprehension, condemnation, stricture, disapproval, disapprobation, reproach, reproof, animadversion. **3.** guilt, culpability, fault, wrong, misdeed, misdoing, shortcoming, sin, defect, reproach. —Ant. credit, honor.

blameless, adj. irreproachable, guiltless, unimpeachable, faultless, innocent, nonculpable, inculpable, not guilty, undefiled, unsullied, spotless, unblemished, clean, immaculate, virginal. —Ant. guilty, culpable; sullied, besmirched.

blanch, v. whiten, bleach, etiolate, pale, fade, lose color, turn white, go pale, be aghast,. —Ant. darken; blush.

bland, adj. **1.** gentle, agreeable, affable, friendly, kindly, mild, amiable;, mild-mannered; complaisant, self-satisfied. **2.** soft, mild, balmy, soothing, nonirritating. **3.** dull, flavorless, insipid, boring, uninteresting, jejune, tasteless. —Ant. cruel, unfriendly; boorish, crude; irritable, irksome.

blank, adj. **1.** unmarked, void, empty, unadorned, plain, bare, undistinguished. **2.** spacey, passive, impassive, emotionless, expressionless, vacant, vacuous, mindless, unexpressive. **3.** amazed, astonished, nonplussed, astounded, confused, dumbfounded, disconcerted. **4.** complete, utter, pure, simple, unadulterated, unmixed; perfect, entire, absolute, unrelieved, stark, sheer, utter, pure, unqualified, unmitigated, unabated, mere. —n. **5.** space, line, area; form; void, vacancy, emptiness. —Ant. distinguished, marked; blasé; impure; significant.

blarney, n. **1.** flattery, blandishment, cajolery, honey, sweet talk, soft soap. **2.** nonsense, rubbish, blather, humbug, claptrap, flummery.

blasé, adj. **1.** worldly-wise, sophisticated, jaded, knowing, worldly, disillusioned, world-weary. **2.** unconcerned, indifferent, uninterested, unsurprised, nonchalant, cool, superior, supercilious, emotionless, unimpressed, bored, phlegmatic, apathetic, insouciant, carefree, lighthearted, casual.

blasphemy, n. profanity, cursing, iniquity, irreverence, oath, impiety, imprecation, execration, abuse, swearing, impiousness, sacrilege. —Ant. reverence, piety.

blast, n. **1.** wind, squall, gust, gale, blow, storm. **2.** blare, sound, noise, roar, din, racket, bedlam, boom. **3.** explosion, eruption, detonation, outburst, burst, outbreak, discharge. —v. **4.** blow, toot, blare. **5.** wither, blight, kill, shrivel. **6.** defame, discredit, denounce, criticize, attack; devastate, ruin, destroy, annihilate. **7.** explode, burst, blow up, dynamite.

blaze, n. **1.** fire, flame, holocaust, inferno; glow, gleam, brightness; outburst. —v. **2.** burn, shine, flame, flare up, flicker.

bleach, v. whiten, blanch, etiolate, pale, lose color. —n. —Ant. darken, dye.

blemish, v. **1.** stain, sully, spot, taint, injure, tarnish; mar, damage, scar, disfigure, deface, impair. —n. **2.** stain, defect, blot, spot, speck, disfigurement, flaw, taint, fault, imperfection, scar, mark, impairment. —Ant. purify; purity, immaculateness.

blend, v. **1.** mingle, combine, coalesce, mix, meld, intermingle, commingle, amalgamate, unite, compound. —n. **2.** mixture, combination, amalgamation, mix, mingling, melding, compound, alloy. —Ant. separate.

blind, adj. **1.** sightless, stone-blind, purblind, unsighted, eyeless, myopic, short-sighted, nearsighted. **2.** ignorant, imperceptive, obtuse, insensitive, naive, ingenuous, undiscerning, unenlightened, benighted. **3.** irrational, uncritical, indiscriminate, headlong, rash, heedless, careless, mindless, senseless, unthinking, delusional, thoughtless, unreasoning, inconsiderate. **4.** hidden, concealed, eclipsed, overshadowed, obscure, remote, dim, confused, dark. **5.** closed, dead-end, shut. —Ant. discerning, enlightened; rational, discriminating; open.

bliss, n. blitheness, happiness, gladness, joy, delight, felicity, glee, enjoyment, pleasure, gaiety, exhilaration, transport, rapture, ecstasy, nirvana. —Ant. misery, unhappiness, dejection.

blithe, adj. **1.** joyous, merry, gay, glad, cheerful, happy, mirthful, blissful, delighted, jubilant, sprightly, lighthearted, buoyant, lively, animated, elated, vivacious, joyful, blithesome. **2.** carefree, unconcerned, happy-go-lucky, insouciant, blase, casual, indifferent, detached, nonchalant, uncaring, careless. —Ant. unhappy, miserable, cheerless.

block, n. **1.** obstacle, hindrance, impediment, blocking, blockade, obstruction, deterrent, bar, stumbling block, barrier, stoppage, blockage, jam. —v. **2.** prevent, barricade, bar, hamper, balk, frustrate, obstruct, close, hinder, deter, arrest, stop, blockade, impede, check. —Ant. encourage, advance, continue.

bloody, adj. **1.** bloodstained, sanguinary, gory. **2.** murderous, cruel, bloodthirsty, savage, barbarous, ferocious, fierce, remorseless, homicidal, inhuman, ruthless.

bloom, n. **1.** flower, blossom, efflorescence. **2.** freshness, glow, flush, vigor, prime. —*v.* **3.** flourish, thrive, effloresce; glow.

blot, *n.* **1.** spot, stain, inkstain, erasure, blotting, blotch, splotch, obliteration, blur. **2.** blemish, reproach, stain, taint, dishonor, disgrace, spot. —*v.* **3.** spot, stain, bespatter; sully, disfigure, deface. **4.** darken, dim, obscure, eclipse, hide, overshadow.

blow, *n.* **1.** stroke, buffet, thump, thwack, rap, slap, cuff, box, beat, knock. **2.** shock, surprise, bombshell, jolt, revelation; calamity, reverse, disaster, misfortune, affliction. **3.** blast, wind, gale, gust. **4.** blossom, flower, bloom. —*v.* **5.** pant, puff, wheeze, breathe, exhale.

blowhard, *n.* braggart, bragger, boaster, braggadocio, miles gloriosus, blusterer, self-advertiser, self-promoter, blower, vaunter, swagger, showoff, bigmouth, loudmouth, windbag, gasbag. —**Ant.** introvert, milquetoast, shrinking violet.

blue, *n.* **1.** prude, censor, pedant. —*adj.* **2.** depressed, dismal, unhappy, morose, gloomy, downhearted, down in the mouth *or* dumps, doleful, melancholy, dispiriting, dispirited, dejected, sad, glum, downcast, crestfallen, despondent. **3.** prudish, moral, rigid, unbending, righteous, puritanical, self-righteous, severe. **4.** obscene, lewd, lascivious, licentious, indecent, risqué, ribald, adult, X-rated, pornographic, vulgar, smutty, bawdy, erotic, offensive, improper, titillating, sexy, coarse, indelicate, scurrilous, suggestive, immoral, amoral. —**Ant.** happy, mirthful; open minded; moral; clean, proper.

blueprint, *n.* plan, outline, scheme, design, schema, master plan, ground plan, diagram, program, model, paradigm, pattern, original, game plan, strategy.

bluff, *adj.* **1.** abrupt, unconventional, blunt, direct, frank, open, honest, hearty, rough, crude. **2.** steep, precipitous, abrupt. —*n.* **3.** fraud, deceit, lie, dissembling. —*v.* **4.** mislead, defraud, deceive, lie, dissemble, fake. —**Ant.** suave, diplomatic, tactful; gradual; plain.

blunder, *n.* **1.** mistake, error, faux pas, gaffe, lapse, slip, misstep, slipup, miscue, misjudgment, impropriety, solecism, indiscretion, indecorum, bungle, misdoing, boner, howler, blooper, goof, boo-boo. —*v.* **2.** bungle, botch, bobble, err, make an error, bumble, muff, flub, fluff, mess up, goof up, louse up, screw up.

blunt, *adj.* **1.** rounded, worn, not sharp, dull. **2.** abrupt, bluff, brusque, curt, short, obtuse, difficult, gruff, uncourtly, uncivil, rough, plainspoken, direct, candid, frank, undiplomatic, straightforward, unceremonious, outspoken, brash, indelicate, thoughtless, harsh, discourteous, rude, impolite. **3.** slow, dull, dimwitted, dull-witted, stupid, thick, stolid. —*v.* **4.** soften, mitigate, mollify, soothe, weaken, dim, blur, obscure. **5.** numb, paralyze, deaden, stupefy, make insensible. —**Ant.** sharp, acute; courteous, civil, polite; quick, alert.

boast, *v.* **1.** exaggerate, brag, vaunt, swagger, crow, bluster, shoot off one's mouth, blow one's own horn, talk big, gloat, strut, lay it on thick. —*n.* **2.** bluster, bragging, rodomontade, swaggering, braggadocio, hot air, gas. —**Ant.** deprecate, belittle.

body, *n.* **1.** carcass, corpse, remains, cadaver. **2.** trunk, torso; substance, essence, core, heart, matter; bulk, main

part. **3.** collection, group; company, party, band, coterie, society, clique, set; association, corporation. **4.** consistency, density, substance, thickness, richness, viscosity, firmness, solidity. —**Ant.** spirit, soul.

bogus, *adj.* false, sham, counterfeit, inauthentic, bastard, mock, phony, spurious, brummagem, pinchbeck, pseudo, imitation, fraudulent, fictitious, specious, fake, ersatz. —**Ant.** genuine, real, true, authentic.

bohemian, *adj.* **1.** free-living, freespirited, casual, unconventional, unconstrained, unorthodox, free and easy, offbeat, eccentric, artistic, arty. —*n.* **2.** nonconformist, free spirit, maverick, eccentric, social dropout, beatnik, hippie. —**Ant.** conformist, conservative, straight arrow.

boil, *v.* **1.** bubble, seethe, foam, froth, churn, stew, simmer, rage.

boisterous, *adj.* rough, noisy, loud, clamorous, roaring, unrestrained, wild, tumultuous, turbulent, violent, impetuous, stormy, tempestuous, uproarious, obstreperous, roistering, vociferous, rambunctious, rowdy, unruly, chaotic, undisciplined, lively, high-spirited. —**Ant.** calm, serene, pacific.

bold, *adj.* **1.** fearless, courageous, brave, intrepid, daring, dauntless, valorous, valiant, heroic, manly, doughty, undaunted, hardy, spirited, mettlesome, gallant, stouthearted, resolute. **2.** forward, brazen, brassy, presumptuous, shameless, insolent, impudent, immodest, defiant, overconfident, saucy, pushing. **3.** pronounced, outstanding, striking, vigorous, clear, vivid, distinct, conspicuous, prominent, obvious, evident. —**Ant.** cowardly, timorous, timid; backward, shy; inconspicuous.

bond, *n.* **1.** binder, fastener, fastening, band, cord, ligature, ligament, link, rope. **2.** tie, connection, link, attraction, attachment, union. **3.** agreement, pact, covenant, security, promise; obligation, contract, compact. **4.** *(plural)* chains, fetters, captivity, constraint, restriction, bondage; prison, imprisonment.

bondage, *n.* slavery, indenture, servitude, serfdom, thralldom, subjection, subjugation, enslavement, captivity, imprisonment, confinement. —**Ant.** freedom.

bonhomie, *n.* good humor, goodhumoredness, affability, cordiality, geniality, hospitality, warmth, graciousness, heartiness, good nature, amiability, neighborliness, friendliness, congeniality, sociability. —**Ant.** unfriendliness, surliness, enmity.

bonus, *n.* bounty, premium, reward, honorarium, gift, subsidy, extra, tip, emolument, dividend, perquisite, perk.

border, *n.* **1.** side, edge, margin; periphery, circumference, lip, brim, verge, brink. **2.** frontier, limit, confine, boundary. —*v.* **3.** bound, limit, confine; adjoin, abut, touch, neighbor, be adjacent.

bore, *v.* weary, fatigue, tire, annoy, wear out, exhaust, jade, leave cold. —**Ant.** amuse.

bother, *v.* **1.** annoy, pester, worry, trouble, plague, tease, harass, irritate, hector, hound, dog, nag, pick on, needle, nettle, hassle, bully, abuse, burden, vex, harry; molest, disturb. **2.** bewilder, confuse, perplex, puzzle, perturb, upset, disconcert, discomfit. —**Ant.** solace, comfort.

bottom, *n.* **1.** base, foot. **2.** underside. **3.** foundation, base, basis, substructure, underpinning, groundwork. **4.**

seat, buttocks, rear end, derriere, rump, posterior, hindquarters, behind, fundament, backside, butt, buns, duff, tush, keister, fanny, can, gluteus maximus. —*adj.* **5.** fundamental, basic, elementary; undermost, lowest. —**Ant.** top; superficial, superfluous.

bounty, *n.* **1.** generosity, munificence, charity, liberality, philanthropy, unselfishness, goodness, kindness, beneficence. **2.** gift, award, present, benefaction. **3.** reward, premium, bonus, award, gratuity.

bow, *v.* **1.** stoop, bend, buckle, give way. **2.** yield, submit, defer, capitulate, bend, give in. **3.** weigh down, burden, overload, subdue, crush, depress, cast down.

brag, *v.* boast, rodomontade, bluster, crow, strut, talk big, swagger, bluster, vaunt, gloat, exaggerate, trumpet. —**Ant.** depreciate, be modest.

brains, *n.* understanding, intelligence, mind, intellect, sense, thought, imagination, perspicacity, perceptiveness, perception, reason, capacity, wisdom, sagacity, wit, acumen, discernment, knowledge. —**Ant.** stupidity.

branch, *n.* **1.** bough, limb, arm, shoot, offshoot, stem, shoot, sprig, twig, ramification. **2.** section, subdivision, department; member, portion, part; article. —*v.* **3.** divide, subdivide, diverge, ramify.

bravado, *n.* boasting, swaggering, braggadocio, pretense, brag, boldness, self-assurance, machismo, arrogance, pretension, prentiousness, pride, pridefulness, bluster, bombast, rodomontade. —**Ant.** shame, modesty.

brave, *adj.* **1.** courageous, fearless, gallant, confident, cool, cool under fire, spirited, spunky, plucky, audacious, valorous, spirited, chivalrous, impetuous, dashing, intrepid, daring, dauntless, doughty, bold, valiant, heroic, manly, hard, mettlesome, stouthearted. —*v.* **2.** face, defy, challenge, dare, meet, confront, withstand, prepare for, steel oneself, oppose, pit oneself against; endure, bear, disregard, suffer, tolerate. —**Ant.** cowardly, fearful; craven, pusillanimous.

bravery, *n.* boldness, courage, intrepidity, daring, prowess, heroism, pluck, gallantry, spirit, audacity, nerve, mettle, fearlessness, spunk, valor, fortitude, determination, staunchness, stoutheartedness, firmness, resoluteness, resolution, indomitability, stalwartness, manfulness, manliness, machismo, true grit. —**Ant.** cowardice.

brawl, *n.* **1.** quarrel, squabble, argument, spat, wrangle, feud, disagreement, dispute, fracas, disturbance, disorder, row, tumult, clamor, rumpus, fray, fight, affray, altercation, melee, riot. —*v.* **2.** quarrel, squabble, argue, wrangle, feud, disagree, dispute, fight, bicker.

brazen, *adj.* **1.** brassy, barefaced, brash, outspoken, immodest, audacious, candid, open, unabashed, shameless. **2.** bold, forward, impudent, insolent, defiant, rude, saucy, pert, fresh, cheeky. —**Ant.** shy, diffident, modest.

breach, *n.* **1.** break, rupture, fracture, crack, gap, hole, split, fissure, rift, rent, opening, chasm. **2.** infraction, violation, infringement. **3.** alienation, disaffection, falling out, misunderstanding; split, rift, schism, severance, separation; dissension, disagreement, difference, variance, quarrel, dispute. —**Ant.** observance.

break, *v.* **1.** fracture, rupture, fragment, crack, crush, shatter, splinter, shiver; smash, defeat, run, batter, demolish, destroy. **2.** contravene, transgress, disobey, violate, defy, infringe, ignore, disregard, flout, fail to observe. **3.** dissolve, annul, negate, dismiss. **4.** lacerate, wound, cut, injure, harm, hurt. **5.** interrupt, suspend, disrupt, stop; abbreviate, curtail. **6.** exceed, outdo, surpass, beat. **7.** reveal, announce, tell, make public, disclose, open, unfold, divulge. **8.** ruin, bankrupt, make bankrupt. **9.** impair, weaken, enfeeble, enervate; dispirit. **10.** tame, make obedient. **11.** discharge, degrade, cashier, demote. **12.** dissolve, separate, split. —*n.* **13.** disruption, separation, rent, tear, rip, rift, schism, severance, split; breach, gap, fissure, crack, chasm, rupture, fracture. **14.** suspension, stoppage, stop, caesura, hiatus, interruption, lacuna, pause, discontinuity, hesitation, gap, irregularity. —**Ant.** repair.

breed, *v.* **1.** beget, bear, bring forth, conceive, give birth to, produce, engender, father, mother. **2.** propagate, procreate, originate, create, beget, occasion, generate. **3.** raise, rear, bring up, nurture; train, educate, discipline, instruct, teach, school. **4.** grow, develop, flourish, arise, rise. —*n.* **5.** race, lineage, strain, family, pedigree, line, extraction, stock, progeny. **6.** sort, kind, species, class, denomination, order, rank, character, nature, description, type, variety.

breeze, *n.* wind, air, blow, zephyr, breath, puff, draft, gust. —**Ant.** calm.

brevity, *n.* shortness, briefness; conciseness, compactness, condensation, succinctness, pithiness; terseness, curtness, economy. —**Ant.** lengthiness.

brief, *adj.* **1.** short, short-lived, fleeting, momentary, passing, evanescent, fugitive, transitory, ephemeral, transient, temporary. **2.** concise, succinct, pithy, condensed, compact, laconic; curt, short, terse, abrupt. —*n.* **3.** outline, précis, synopsis, summary, epitome, syllabus, abstract, abridgment, digest, resume, condensation, extract, conspectus, compendium, breviary. —*v.* **4.** advise, inform, coach, instruct, enlighten, fill in, run down, explain. —**Ant.** long, lengthiness.

bright, *adj.* **1.** radiant, radiating, refulgent, resplendent, effulgent, lucent, lustrous, glowing, beaming, lambent, splendid, brilliant, shining, irradiant, gleaming, luminous; scintillating, sparkling, twinkling, glistening, glistering, shimmering, coruscating, glittering; flashing, flaming, blazing; shiny, sheeny, glossy, burnished; vivid, light, sunny, fulgid, fulgent. **2.** clear, transparent, pellucid, translucent, lucid, limpid, unclouded, crystal, cloudless, lambent. **3.** illustrious, distinguished, glorious, famous, celebrated, noted, eminent, prominent, renowned. **4.** quick-witted, intelligent, keen, discerning, acute, gifted, bright, talented, expert, ingenious, creative, shrewd, cunning, artful, sharp, clever. **5.** lively, animated, cheerful, merry, happy, sprightly, lighthearted, gay, vivacious, genial, pleasant. **6.** favorable, auspicious, propitious, promising, encouraging, inspiriting, inspiring, enlivening, exhilarating. —**Ant.** dull; opaque, dense; undistinguished, ignominious; slow, stupid; laconic, doleful, melancholy; unfavorable, discouraging.

brilliance, *n.* **1.** brightness, shine, splendor, luster, refulgence, effulgence, radiance, brilliancy; sparkle, glitter, glister, gleam. **2.** excellence, distinction, eminence, renown, prominence, preeminence, singularity, fame, illustri-

ousness. —**Ant.** dullness; notoriety, oblivion.

brim, *n.* rim, edge, border, margin, periphery, circumference, bound, brink, lip. —**Ant.** center.

bring, *v.* **1.** take along, conduct, convey, lead; fetch; guide, convoy, escort, invite, accompany, transport, carry. **2.** lead, induce, prevail upon, draw. —**Ant.** remove, withdraw.

brisk, *adj.* **1.** active, lively, energetic, busy, vigorous; animated, sprightly, pert, quick, nimble, agile, alert, spry, on the qui vive, spirited, bright, vivacious. **2.** sharp, invigorating, refreshing, bracing, keen, crisp, stimulating, acute. —**Ant.** slow, lethargic; dull.

brittle, *adj.* fragile, frail, breakable, frangible, stiff, hard; weak, delicate, sensitive, insecure. —**Ant.** supple, flexible, elastic.

broad, *adj.* **1.** wide. **2.** large, extensive, expansive, vast, spacious, ample. **3.** diffused, diffuse, open, full. **4.** liberal, large, big, tolerant, open-minded, hospitable. **5.** main, general, rough, approximate, sweeping, unspecific. **6.** plain, clear, bold, obvious, evident, explicit, pronounced, undisguised, unsubtle; plainspoken, open, unconfined, free, unrestrained. **7.** rough, coarse, countrified, unrefined, vulgar, indecent, indelicate, gross. —**Ant.** narrow; stingy; refined, cultivated, decent.

broad-minded, *adj.* tolerant, open, open-minded, liberal, large-minded, progressive, generous, charitable, forbearing, tolerant, easygoing, lenient, live-and-let-live, unbigoted, unparochial, ecumenical. —**Ant.** narrow-minded, bigoted, close-minded.

brood, *n.* **1.** offspring, litter, young, progeny, issue, babies, children. **2.** breed, kind, sort, line, lineage, stock, family, strain, species, class, order. —*v.* **3.** incubate, sit, hatch, set. **4.** dwell on, ponder, ruminate over, meditate on, revolve in one's mind, reflect, weigh, study, think about, have morbid thoughts, sulk, be pensive, contemplate, suffer, obsess, anguish over, be in a brown study, muse, mope, pout, pine, eat one's heart out, fret, worry, agonize, despair, be sullen.

brook, *n.* **1.** stream, rivulet, run, runnel, runlet, streamlet, rill, burn, branch. —*v.* **2.** bear, suffer, tolerate, allow, stand, endure, abide, put up with, submit to, brave, withstand, countenance.

brother, *n.* fellow man, countryman, kinsman, associate, bro, friend, sibling.

brownie, *n.* fairy, elf, pixie, leprechaun, nix, nixie, sprite, imp.

brush, *n.* **1.** grazing, touch; encounter, brief encounter, meeting; engagement, affair, contest, collision, action, fight, battle, skirmish, struggle, conflict. **2.** undergrowth, brambles, underbrush, grove, bushes, scrub, thicket, copse, shrubs, bracken, brake.

brusque, *adj.* abrupt, blunt, rough, unceremonious, bluff, gruff, overbearing, ill-mannered, churlish, terse, brash, candid, frank, undiplomatic, tactless, outspoken, ungracious, uncivil, discourteous, impolite, rude, crude, curt. —**Ant.** courteous, courtly, polished, refined, gentle.

brutal, *adj.* **1.** savage, cruel, inhuman, ruthless, pitiless, unfeeling, barbarous, barbarian, uncivilized, ferocious, brutish, barbaric, truculent. **2.** crude, coarse, gross, harsh, rude, rough, uncivil, ungracious, impolite, unmannerly, ungentlemanly, brusque. **3.** irrational, unreasoning, brute, unthinking. **4.** bestial, beastly, animal, carnal.

—**Ant.** kind, sensitive; artistic; gracious, rational, sensible; human.

brute, *n.* **1.** beast, quadruped, animal. **2.** barbarian, savage, heathen, Neanderthal, lout, red neck, yahoo, lout, boor, oaf, ogre. —*adj.* **3.** animal, brutish, irrational, unreasoning. **4.** savage, cruel, brutal. **5.** sensual, carnal, physical. —**Ant.** human; kind; spiritual.

bubbly, *adj.* **1.** frothy, foamy, effervescent, sparkling, spumescent, carbonated. **2.** high-spirited, vivacious, animated, lively, bouncy, effusive, energetic, sprightly, effervescent, sparky, perky, pert, peppy, frisky, merry, rollicking, blithe, bright, jaunty, cheery, cheerful, excited, ebullient, buoyant. —**Ant.** flat, colorless.

building, *n.* edifice, structure, construction, erection.

bulk, *n.* **1.** size, magnitude, mass, volume, dimensions. **2.** greater part, majority, most; body, mass. —*v.* **3.** grow, swell, bulge, expand, enlarge, aggrandize.

bulky, *adj.* massive, ponderous, large, voluminous, ungainly, awkward, unwieldy, clumsy, cumbersome; great, big, large, huge, vast. —**Ant.** small, delicate.

bunch, *n.* cluster; bundle, batch, clump, crowd, knot, gathering, duster, assortment, mass, group, lot, bundle, batch, collection.

burden, *n.* **1.** load, weight. **2.** encumbrance, impediment, trouble, grievance, trial, strain, pressure, onus, albatross, millstone, cross. **3.** substance, core, point, essence, epitome, central idea, tenor, drift. —*v.* **4.** load, overload, oppress, weigh down, tax, encumber, saddle with. —**Ant.** unload, lighten, help.

burn, *v.* **1.** flame, blaze, flare, smolder, ignite, be on fire. **2.** tingle, be hot, glow. **3.** consume, scorch, sear, overcook, blacken, singe, char, toast. **4.** desire, long, yearn, pine, itch, ache.

burst, *v.* **1.** explode, crack, blow up, split, rupture, shatter. **2.** rend, tear, break. —*n.* **3.** explosion. **4.** spurt, outpouring, gust. —**Ant.** implode.

bury, *v.* **1.** inter, entomb, inhume, lay to rest. **2.** sink, submerge, plunge, inundate. **3.** cover, hide, conceal, secrete, shroud, enshroud, obscure. —**Ant.** disinter; rise; uncover.

business, *n.* **1.** occupation, trade, craft, metier, profession, calling, employment, vocation, pursuit, work, province, area, subject, topic, concern, obligation. **2.** company, concern, enterprise, corporation, firm, partnership. **3.** affair, matter, concern, transaction. **4.** commerce, trade, traffic. **5.** function, duty, office, position, role, responsibility, charge, obligation.

busy, *adj.* **1.** engaged, occupied, diligent, industrious, employed, engrossed, rapt, preoccupied, working, assiduous, sedulous, hardworking. **2.** active, brisk, bustling, hectic, lively, hustling, energetic, buzzing, ahum, abuzz, rushing, pressured. —**Ant.** indolent, unoccupied, lazy.

but, *conj.* **1.** however, nevertheless, yet, further, moreover, still. **2.** excepting, save, except. —*prep.* **3.** excepting, except, save, excluding. —*adv.* **4.** only, just, no more than.

butcher, *n.* **1.** murderer, slayer, killer, assassin, cutthroat, thug, hit man, ripper, serial killer, executioner. —*v.* **2.** kill, slaughter, exterminate, liquidate, dismember, disembowel, massacre, murder, assassinate. **3.** bungle, botch, fail in, foul up, screw up, make a mess or hash of.

buy, v. **1.** purchase, acquire, obtain, get, come by, procure, secure. **2.** hire, bribe, corrupt, suborn, pay off. —**Ant.** sell.

byword, n. slogan, motto, catch phrase, password, shibboleth, proverb, maxim, apothegm, aphorism, saw, adage, saying, parable, catchword, epithet.

C

cabin, n. hut, shanty, shack, lean-to, bungalow, lodge, chalet, cottage, shed, hovel.

cadaverous, adj. **1.** deathly pale, deathly, ghastly, ghostly, ghostlike, spectral, corpselike, pallid, livid. **2.** gaunt, haggard, drawn, withered, shriveled, emaciated, skeletal, wasted, hollow-eyed, scrawny, peaked, wizened. —**Ant.** robust, hearty, healthy.

cagey, adj. cunning, clever, shrewd, wily, calculating, conniving, scheming, designing, Machiavellian, manipulative, astute, smart, wise, artful, canny, crafty, foxy, ingenious, sharp, slick, nimble-witted, quick-thinking, quick-witted, sharp-witted, savvy, hip.

cajole, v. wheedle, coax, beguile, entice, inveigle, flatter, soft-soap, sweet-talk, blandish, seduce, persuade, butter up.

calamity, n. affliction, adversity, ill fortune, misery, wretchedness, bad luck, distress, trouble, evil, hardship, trial, reverse, mischance, misadventure, mishap, blow, misfortune, disaster, catastrophe, cataclysm, destruction, ruin, devastation, tragedy, desolation, reversal. —**Ant.** fortune, blessing, boon.

calculate, v. count, figure, reckon, cast, estimate, weigh, assess, evaluate, gauge, determine, ascertain, workout, appraise, deliberate, compute, rate. —**Ant.** assume, guess.

calculation, n. **1.** computation, figuring, reckoning, counting, determining, assessment, appraisal, estimate, estimation. **2.** estimate, forecast, expectation, prospect, prediction, deliberation, anticipation. **3.** forethought, planning, circumspection, caution, wariness, foresight, cautiousness, discretion, prudence, deliberation. —**Ant.** guess, assumption.

call, v. **1.** cry out, shout, yell, roar, bellow, hail. **2.** announce, proclaim. **3.** awaken, waken, rouse, wake up, arouse. **4.** summon, invite, send for, bid, gather, collect, rally. **5.** convoke, convene, call together, assemble, muster. **6.** name, give a name to, label, term, designate, style, dub, christen, baptize, identify, title, entitle, nominate, denominate. **7.** shout, cry, voice. **8.** visit, stop. —n. **9.** shout, cry, yell, whoop, outcry. **10.** summons, signal; invitation, bidding; appointment. **11.** need, occasion; demand, claim, requisition.

callous, adj. hard, hardened, inured, indurated; thick-skinned, heartless, hardhearted, hard-bitten, tough, cold, unfeeling, insensible, blunt, apathetic, unimpressible, phlegmatic, affectless, unsympathetic, uncaring, hardboiled, hardnosed, emotionless, unemotional, diffident, indifferent, unsusceptible, obtuse. —**Ant.** soft; sensitive.

calm, adj. **1.** still, quiet, smooth, motionless, balmy, halcyon, even, placid, pacific, tranquil, unruffled, mild,

peaceful. **2.** serene, self-possessed, cool, collected, dispassionate, staid, impassive, coolheaded, stoical, unruffled, composed, undisturbed, sedate, aloof. —n. **3.** stillness, serenity, calmness, quiet, smoothness, tranquility, peacefulness, aloofness, self-possession, composure, repose, equanimity. —v. **4.** still, quiet, tranquilize, pacify, hush, lull, sedate, smooth, appease, compose; allay, assuage, mollify, soothe, soften, placate. —**Ant.** perturbed; tempestuous; excite, agitate.

cancel, v. **1.** cross out, delete, erase, expunge, obliterate, blot out, efface, rub out. **2.** void, nullify, annul, countermand, revoke, rescind, counterbalance, compensate for, allow for. —**Ant.** ratify.

candid, adj. **1.** frank, open, outspoken, sincere, ingenuous, naive, artless, honest, plain, guileless, straightforward, aboveboard, truthful, forthright, direct, unequivocal, plain-speaking, blunt, uncalculating, unpremeditated, uncontrived, honorable. **2.** impartial, honest, just, fair, unprejudiced, objective, evenhanded, judicious, unbigoted, unbiased. —**Ant.** concealed, hidden, wily, deceitful; biased, prejudiced.

candor, n. frankness, honesty, forthrightness, directness, candidness, ingenuousness, simplicity, naivete, straightforwardness, truthfulness, sincerity, openness, outspokenness, bluntness, brusqueness, plain speaking. —**Ant.** evasiveness, deceitfulness.

cantankerous, adj. ill-natured, irritable, irascible, quarrelsome, fractious, cross, crotchety, captious, choleric, foul-tempered, mean-tempered, grumpy, ornery, testy, touchy, peevish, surly, vinegary, vinegarish, petulant, snappish, waspish, perverse, crusty, bearish, contrary, grouchy, bilious, splenetic, curmudgeonly, crabby. —**Ant.** sweet-natured, kindly, gracious.

capable, adj. **1.** able, competent, efficient, proficient, qualified, talented, skilled, adept, expert, masterful, intelligent, clever, skillful, ingenious, sagacious, gifted, accomplished. **2.** fitted, adapted, suited, qualified. —**Ant.** incompetent, bungling, amateurish.

capacious, adj. spacious, roomy, ample, large, broad, comprehensive, wide, voluminous. —**Ant.** confining, narrow.

capacity, n. **1.** ability, power, aptitude, potential, brains, acumen, sense, understanding, power, faculty, wit, genius, aptness, bent, forte, leaning, propensity, ableness, talent, discernment; caliber, cleverness, skill, skillfulness, competency, competence, readiness, capability. **2.** position, condition, character, place, role, job, relation, function, realm, bailiwick, sphere, area, province; office, post, charge, responsibility, duty. —**Ant.** incapacity, incompetence.

caper, v. **1.** skip, leap, spring, hop, gambol, frolic, frisk, play, romp, cavort, rollick. —n. **2.** escapade, prank, frolic, lark, antic, adventure, bit of mischief, stunt, high jinks, shenanigan.

capital, n. **1.** metropolis, seat of power, major city, stronghold. **2.** wealth, principal, investment, worth, resources, assets, stock. —adj. **3.** principal, first, main, central, paramount, preeminent, foremost, important, chief, prime, primary, major, leading, cardinal, essential, vital. **4.** excellent, first-rate, splendid, fine, first-class, superior, matchless, peerless, choice, select, outstanding, superb, extraordinary,

great, super. **5.** fatal, serious. —**Ant.** trivial, unimportant.

capricious, adj. wayward, arbitrary, whimsical, whimsied, crotchety, quirky, unreliable, fanciful, wanton, inconstant, changeable, impulsive, unpredictable, fickle, temperamental, mercurial, volatile, unstable, erratic, chimerical, eccentric, flighty, unsteady, variable. —**Ant.** predictable, stable, steady.

capsize, v. overturn, upset, go topsy-turvy, turn turtle, flip over, turn over, go arsey-versey, go head over heels, go tail over teakettle, keel over, heel over, keel. —**Ant.** right.

captivate, v. charm, enthrall, enchant, fascinate, hypnotize, mesmerize, steal one's heart, dazzle, enrapture, seduce, allure, entice, ensorcel, cast a spell over, put a spell on, thrill, entrance, obsess, ensnare, trap, transfix, haunt, beguile, bewitch, enamor, win, catch. —**Ant.** repel, repulse.

captivity, n. bondage, servitude, enslavement, slavery, thralldom, serfdom, subjugation, subjection; imprisonment, confinement, incarceration, detention, arrest. —**Ant.** freedom.

capture, v. **1.** seize, take prisoner, catch, arrest, snare, apprehend, collar, nick, place behind bars, trap, impound, grab, nab; imprison, incarcerate. —n. **2.** arrest, seizure, apprehension; imprisonment, incarceration, detention, captivity. —**Ant.** release.

care, n. **1.** worry, anxiety, concern, solicitude, trouble, anguish, angst, distress, grief, suffering, misery, tribulation, woe. **2.** heed, caution, pains, anxiety, regard, attention, vigilance, carefulness, meticulousness, pountiliousness, mindfulness, solicitude, circumspection, alertness, watchfulness, wakefulness. **3.** charge, responsibility, protection, custody, safekeeping, guardianship, supervision. —v. **4.** have concern or regard, be solicitous or anxious, worry, be troubled, fret, mind. **5.** like, be inclined or disposed, or interested, fancy, be keen on.

careen, v. sway, lurch, lean, heel over, swing, roll, rock, wobble, reel, weave, waver, tip, veer, swerve, keel over.

careful, adj. **1.** cautious, circumspect, watchful, wakeful, vigilant, guarded, chary, discreet, wary, suspicious, prudent, tactful; trustworthy. **2.** painstaking, meticulous, discerning, exact, thorough, concerned, scrupulous, finical, conscientious, attentive, assiduous, sedulous, heedful, thoughtful. —**Ant.** careless.

caregiver, n. protector, keeper, guardian, caretaker, attendant, custodian, warden, nurse, matron, fiduciary, nanny, au pair, babysitter, healthcare worker or aide.

careless, adj. **1.** inattentive, incautious, unwary, unthoughtful, forgetful, remiss, negligent, neglectful, casual, indifferent, irresponsible, imprudent, absentminded, unmindful, heedless, reckless, indiscreet, thoughtless, unconcerned. **2.** negligent, remiss, reckless, slapdash, rash, cursory, lackadaisical, perfunctory; inaccurate, inexact, imprecise, wrong, error-ridden, sloppy. —**Ant.** careful.

careworn, adj. drawn, worn, pinched, worn-down, strained, bedraggled, rundown, decrepit, haggard, hollow-eyed, ravaged, woebegone.

caricature, n. **1.** burlesque, exaggeration, travesty, takeoff, parody, farce, satire, lampoon, cartoon, pasquinade, spoof, sendup. —v. **2.** burlesque, exaggerate, travesty, parody, take off, satirize, lampoon, ridicule, mock, distort, send up.

carnal, *adj.* **1.** human, temporal, worldly, mundane, earthly, unregenerate, natural, unspiritual. **2.** sensual, fleshly, bodily, animal, physical, sexual, corporal, voluptuous. **3.** lustful, impure, gross, lecherous, lascivious, salacious, libidinous, concupiscent, lewd, lubricious, wanton, lubricous, sexual, erotic, licentious, prurient, goatish, dirty. —**Ant.** spiritual, moral, intellectual.

carriage, *n.* **1.** vehicle, cart, wagon, conveyance; dogcart, brougham, hansom, victoria, calash, buckboard, carryall, shay, sulky, surrey. **2.** bearing, posture, comportment, manner, mien, deportment, behavior, conduct, demeanor.

carry, *v.* **1.** move, bear, transport, convey, haul, lug, drag, cart, tote, schlep; take, bring, transfer, transmit, lead, conduct; communicate, broadcast. **2.** wear, hold, have around one, keep, bear, maintain, contain. **3.** support, maintain; bear, stand, sustain, suffer. **4.** lead, impel, drive, conduct, urge. **5.** effect, accomplish, gain, secure, win, capture.

cascade, *n.* **1.** waterfall, falls, cataract, Niagara, downpour, shower, torrent, deluge. —*v.* **2.** spill, spill over, overflow, fall, flow over, brim over, overbrim, pour, pour down, plummet, shower, rain, tumble down.

case, *n.* **1.** instance, example, event, happening, occasion, illustration, occurrence. **2.** state, circumstance, situation, condition, contingency; plight, predicament. **3.** patient, victim, invalid. **4.** dispute, action, suit, lawsuit, cause, process, trial. **5.** receptacle, box, container, chest; folder, envelope, sheath.

cast, *v.* **1.** throw, fling, hurl, deposit, propel, put, toss, pitch, sling, pitch. **2.** throw off, shed, slough, put off, lay aside. **3.** throw out, send forth, hurl, toss. **4.** set aside, throw aside, discard, reject, dismiss, disband. **5.** emit, eject, vomit, spew forth, puke. **6.** bestow, confer. **7.** arrange, plan out, allot, apportion, appoint, assign. **8.** mold, form, found. **9.** compute, calculate, reckon; forecast, foretell. —*n.* **10.** throw, fling, toss. **11.** appearance, form, shape, mien, demeanor. **12.** sort, kind, style. **13.** tendency, inclination, turn, bent, trend, air. **14.** tinge, tint, hue, shade, touch; dash, trace, hint, suggestion.

caste, *n.* rank, class, status, social level, social stratum, order, level, standing, place, station, position, estate, echelon, grade.

castle, *n.* **1.** fortress, citadel, stronghold. **2.** palace, chateau, mansion, palazzo, hall, manor.

casual, *adj.* **1.** unexpected, fortuitous, unforeseen, chance, accidental, serendipitous, unpremeditated, unintentional. **2.** careless, negligent, unconcerned, indifferent, nonchalant, offhand, apathetic, cool, uninterested, dispassionate, insouciant, blase, relaxed, lackadaisical, informal. **3.** random, uncertain, erratic, unsure, haphazard, sporadic, unsystematic, irregular, occasional. **4.** easygoing, natural, easy, relaxed, offhand, happy-go-lucky, devil-may-care, laid-back. —**Ant.** premeditated, deliberate, calculated; careful; regular, routine.

cataclysm, *n.* disaster, calamity, catastrophe, debacle, crash, collapse, convulsion, meltdown; flood, deluge, inundation.

catalogue, *n.* list, roll, roster, register, record, inventory.

catastrophe, *n.* disaster, mishap, cataclysm, calamity, misfortune, mischance, bad luck, tragedy, accident, fiasco, failure. —**Ant.** triumph, good luck.

catch, *v.* **1.** seize, capture, restrain, stop, check, curb, intercept, snatch, arrest, apprehend, grab, get hold of grip, grasp, hold, take prisoner, nab, nick collar, pinch. **2.** trap, snare, net, ensnare, entrap, bag, net, round up. **3.** surprise, discover, detect, take unawares, find. **4.** captivate, attract, draw, charm, enchant, fascinate, win, bewitch, seduce, entice, allure, enthrall. —*n.* **5.** capture, seizure, arrest, apprehension, take, bag, prize, trophy, acquisition, conquest. **6.** fastener, clasp, pin, hook, clip, bolt. —**Ant.** release, let go.

catchword, *n.* slogan, catchphrase, byword, password, shibboleth, motto, watchword, maxim, household word, tag line, battle cry, rallying cry.

cause, *n.* **1.** occasion, origin, source, root, agent, genesis, wellspring, prime mover, creator, producer, reason, ground, grounds, basis; motive, determinant, incitement, inducement, justification. **2.** purpose, object, aim, end. —*v.* **3.** bring about, effect, determine, make, produce, create, induce, generate, provoke, promote, originate, occasion, give rise to, result in, precipitate, engender, motivate, compel.

caustic, *adj.* corrosive, cutting, scathing, stinging, slashing, mordant, incisive, keen, acid, trenchant, sharp, ironic, satiric, sarcastic, sardonic, mordacious, burning, destructive, astringent, biting, acrimonious, bitter, critical, harsh. —**Ant.** bland, harmless, innocuous.

caution, *n.* **1.** prudence, discretion, circumspectness, watchfulness, circumspection, heed, care, wariness, heedfulness, vigilance, alertness, discretion, forethought, providence. **2.** warning, admonition, advice, caveat, notice, forewarning, tip, tip-off, word to the wise, injunction, counsel. —*v.* **3.** warn, admonish, advise, enjoin, counsel, forewarn, tip off. —**Ant.** carelessness, imprudence.

cautious, *adj.* prudent, careful, heedful, watchful, discreet, wary, apprehensive, suspicious, vigilant, alert, provident, chary, circumspect, guarded. —**Ant.** careless, heedless, indiscreet.

caveat, *n.* warning, caution, forewarning, notice, notification, admonition, recommendation, suggestion, word to the wise, tip, tipoff.

cavity, *n.* hollow, hole, void, pit, opening, space, gap, crater.

cease, *v.* stop, desist, stay; terminate, end, finish, leave off, halt, break off; discontinue. —**Ant.** start, begin; continue, persist.

cede, *v.* yield, resign, surrender, relinquish, abandon, renounce, abdicate, give up; turn over, grant, transfer, convey, give, hand over. —**Ant.** persist, maintain.

celebrate, *v.* **1.** commemorate, keep, honor, observe. **2.** proclaim, announce. **3.** praise, extol, laud, glorify, honor, applaud, exalt, eulogize, lionize, commend. **4.** solemnize, ritualize, sanctify, consecrate, hallow, dedicate. **5.** have *or* give *or* throw a party, party, revel, rejoice, make merry, entertain, paint the town red, whoop *or* live it up, kill the fatted calf, enjoy oneself, frolic, carouse, have a rave, cut loose, go on a spree, have a ball.

celebrated, *adj.* famous, renowned, well-known, distinguished, illustrious, eminent, famed, prominent, noted, noteworthy, renowned, acclaimed. —**Ant.** obscure, unknown.

celebrity, *n.* **1.** fame, renown, celebrityhood, stardom, superstardom, name, acclaim, acclamation, recognition, eminence, prominence, prestige, popularity, notability, distinction, illustriousness, reputation, repute, éclat; notoriety. **2.** notable, big name, personage, star, superstar, luminary, VIP, dignitary, personality, toast of the town, name, somebody, nabob, big shot, biggie, megastar, hot shot, big enchilada. —**Ant.** nobody, nonentity, has-been, wannabe.

celestial, *adj.* heavenly, ethereal, empyreal, empyrean, elysian, spiritual, godly, sublime, immortal, supernatural, otherworldly, transcendental, unearthly, divine, paradisial, paradisaic, supernal. —**Ant.** earthly, mundane, terrestrial.

censure, *n.* **1.** condemnation, reproof, disapproval, disapprobation, blaming, criticism, blame, reproach, reprehension, rebuke, reprimand, stricture, animadversion. —*v.* **2.** criticize, disapprove, condemn, find fault with. **3.** reprove, rebuke, reprimand, reprehend, chide, blame, reproach, upbraid. —**Ant.** praise, commend.

center, *n.* middle, midst, heart, core, midpoint, focus, nucleus, focal point; pivot, hub, point, axis. —**Ant.** brim, edge, periphery.

ceremony, *n.* rite, ritual, formality, observance, solemnity, service, celebration, consecration, sanctification, hallowing. —**Ant.** informality.

certain, *adj.* **1.** confident, sure, assured, convinced, satisfied, indubitable, indisputable, unquestionable, undeniable, incontestable, irrefutable, unquestioned, incontrovertible, absolute, positive, plain, patent, obvious, clear. **2.** sure, inevitable, infallible, unfailing. **3.** fixed, agreed upon, settled, prescribed, determined, determinate, constant, stated, given. **4.** definite, particular, special, especial. **5.** unfailing, reliable, trustworthy, dependable, trusty. —**Ant.** uncertain, unclear, unsure; unsettled; indefinite; fallible, unreliable.

certainty, *n.* **1.** unquestionableness, inevitability, certitude, assurance, confidence, conviction. **2.** fact, truth, reality, actuality. —**Ant.** doubt, uncertainty.

challenge, *v.* **1.** question, dispute, defy, contest, object to, call into doubt *or* question, impugn; dare, provoke, confront. —*n.* **2.** question, dispute, doubt. **3.** dare, provocation, confrontation, defiance, ultimatum. **4.** trial, test, problem, demand, stimulation.

champion, *n.* **1.** winner, victor, hero. **2.** defender, protector, vindicator, backer, advocate, guardian, supporter. **3.** fighter, warrior. —*v.* **4.** defend, support, maintain, fight for, advocate, protect, guard, back, stand up for, sustain, uphold, espouse. —**Ant.** loser; oppose.

chance, *n.* **1.** fortune, fate, luck, accident, fortuity, serendipity. **2.** possibility, predictability, odds, prospect, likelihood, contingency, probability. **3.** opportunity, opening, occasion, time, turn. **4.** risk, hazard, peril, danger, jeopardy. —*v.* **5.** happen, occur, befall, take place. —*adj.* **6.** casual, accidental, fortuitous, unexpected, unpremeditated, unforeseen, serendipitous, unplanned, incidental, unintentional, inadvertant. —**Ant.** necessity, inevitability; surety.

change, v. **1.** alter, make different, turn, transmute, transform, vary, modify. **2.** exchange, substitute, convert, shift, replace; barter, trade, commute. —n. **3.** variation, alteration, modification, deviation, transformation, transmutation, mutation, conversion, transition. **4.** substitution, exchange. **5.** variety, novelty, innovation, vicissitude. —**Ant.** remain, endure; immutability.

chaotic, adj. confused, upset, tumultuous, turbulent, disordered, unruly, disorderly, anarchic, scattered, disarrayed, higgledy-piggledy, jumbled, helter-skelter, topsy-turvy, noisy, clamorous, uproarious, wild, frenzied, hectic, in pandemonium, at sixes and sevens.

character, n. **1.** individual, personality, person, personage. **2.** feature, trait, characteristic, quality, distinction, attribute, nature, disposition, mien, cast, mark, idiosyncrasy, peculiarity, singularity. **3.** name, reputation, repute, standing, status. **4.** morality, integrity, respectability, rectitude, honesty, goodness, honor, courage **5.** symbol, mark, letter, figure, emblem, sign, label, rune, heiroglyph

characteristic, adj. **1.** typical, distinctive, discrete, special, peculiar, singular, representative, emblematic, symbolic, idiosyncratic, symptomatic. —n. **2.** feature, quality, trait, peculiarity, mark, attribute, property, idiosyncrasy, earmark, quiddity.

charge, v. **1.** command, enjoin, exhort, order, urge, bid, require. **2.** blame, accuse, indict, arraign, impeach, inculpate, incriminate, involve, inform against, betray. **3.** attack, assault, set on. —n. **4.** duty, responsibility, commission, office, trust, employment. **5.** care, custody, superintendence, ward, management. **6.** command, injunction, exhortation, order, direction, mandate, instruction, precept. **7.** accusation, indictment, imputation, allegation, crimination, incrimination. **8.** price, fee, cost; tax, lien, expense, encumberance, outlay, expenditure, liability, debt. **9.** onset, attack, onslaught, assault, encounter.

charismatic, adj. alluring, attractive, fascinating, hypnotic, mesmerising, magnetic, captivating, spellbinding, beguiling, glamorous, entrancing, riveting, bewitching, prepossessing, unforgettable, irresistable, charming, seductive, magical.

charitable, adj. **1.** generous, openhanded, liberal, philanthropic, giving, altruistic, public-spirited, munificent, unselfish, big hearted, magnanimous, unsparing, beneficent, benign, kind, benignant, benevolent, bountiful, lavish. **2.** understanding, forgiving, merciful, forbearing, compassionate, well-disposed, kind, tolerant, good, indulgent, compassionate, humane, sympathetic, broad-minded, liberal, lenient, considerate, mild, kindly. —**Ant.** mean, stingy; narrow-minded, inconsiderate.

charm, n. **1.** attractiveness, allurement, fascination, enchantment, appeal, allure, magnetism, charisma, desirability, elegance, urbanity, grace, sophistication, refinement; culture; bewitchment, spell, witchery, magic, sorcery. **2.** trinket, bauble, jewelry; amulet, talisman, fetish. —v. **3.** enchant, fascinate, captivate, catch, entrance, enrapture, transport, delight, please; attract, allure, enamor, bewitch; influ-

ence, control, subdue. —**Ant.** revulsion; disgust.

chary, adj. **1.** careful, wary, discreet, guarded, prudent, cautious, circumspect. **2.** shy, bashful, modest, reticent, coy, reserved, private, self-effacing. **3.** fastidious, choosy, particular, finicky, fussy, meticulous, punctilious. **4.** sparing, stingy, frugal, economical, stinting, parsimonious. —**Ant.** careless, indiscreet, imprudent, unreserved, lavish.

chaste, adj. virtuous, pure, moral, decent, undefiled, modest, celibate, abstinent, stainless, wholesome, virgin, virginal, intact, faithful, continent; clean, elevated, unsullied; unaffected, simple, subdued, austere, restrained, unadorned, severe, neat, straight, honest. —**Ant.** sinful, impure, immodest; unrefined, coarse, inelegant.

chasten, v. discipline, punish, chastise, restrain, subdue, humble, scold, chide, admonish, upbraid, correct, castigate. —**Ant.** indulge, reward.

cheap, adj. **1.** inexpensive, low-priced, bargain, discounted, on sale, reasonable, economy, budget. **2.** paltry, common, mean, low, lowly, poor, inferior, base, shoddy, shabby, tawdry, seedy, sleazy, tacky, trashy, second-rate, worthless, chintzy, cheapjack. **3.** stingy, miserly, frugal, penny-pinching, niggardly, tightfisted, cheeseparing, parsimonious. —**Ant.** dear, expensive, costly; exceptional, extraordinary, elegant.

cheat, n. **1.** fraud, swindle, deception, trick, imposture, wile, deceit, artifice, chicanery, stratagem, hoax, imposition, snare, trap, pitfall, catch. **2.** swindler, imposter, trickster, sharper, cheater, dodger, charlatan, fraud, fake, phony, mountebank, rogue, con man, knave. —v. **3.** deceive, defraud, trick, victimize, mislead, dupe, gudgeon, cog, gull, cozen, outwit, bamboozle, delude, hoodwink, beguile, inveigle, swindle, con; entrap, hoax, ensnare, fool, cajole; dissemble.

check, v. **1.** stop, halt, delay, arrest. **2.** curb, restrain, block, limit, retard, hamper, impede, thwart, control, repress, chain, bridle, hinder, hobble, obstruct, curtail. **3.** investigate, verify, assess, test, measure, examine, compare, authenticate, confirm, substantiate, validate, corroborate, inspect, monitor, study, scrutinize. **4.** agree, coincide, jibe, tally, conform, fit, mesh, correspond. **5.** pause, stop. —n. **6.** restraint, curb, bridle, bit, hindrance, obstacle, obstruction, impediment, control, bar, barrier, restriction, damper, interference, repression, repulse, halt. **7.** rebuff, arrest, stoppage, cessation, repulse, halt. **8.** bill, reckoning, tariff, tab, charge; ticket, receipt, coupon, tag, stub. —**Ant.** continue, advance, foster, support.

cheer, n. **1.** encouragement, comfort, solace, consolation. **2.** gladness, gaiety, happiness, buoyancy, liveliness, elation, blitheness, levity, animation, joy, mirth, glee, merriment, cheerfulness. —v. **3.** gladden, enliven, inspirit, exhilarate, animate, encourage. **4.** shout, applaud, acclaim, salute. —**Ant.** derision; misery; discourage, deride; boo, hiss.

cheerful, adj. **1.** cheery, gay, blithe, happy, lively, lighthearted, all smiles, ebullient, glad, exuberant, merry, spirited, sprightly, joyful, joyous, mirthful, buoyant, gleeful, sunny, jolly. **2.** pleasant, bright, gay, winsome, gladdening, cheery, cheering, inspiring, animating. —**Ant.** miserable; unpleasant.

cherish, v. **1.** foster, harbor, entertain,

humor, encourage, indulge. **2.** nurse, nurture, nourish, tend, cuiltvate, preserve, support, sustain, comfort. **3.** treasure, cling to, hold dear, prize, value. —**Ant.** abandon, scorn, disdain.

chief, n. **1.** head, leader, ruler, chieftain, commander, principal, superior, supervisor, boss, manager, ringleader, kingpin, head honcho, number one, numero uno, big cheese. —adj. **2.** principal, most important, prime, first, supreme, leading, paramount, key, foremost, primary, main, superior, premier, otstanding, greatest, great, grand, cardinal, master; vital, essential. —**Ant.** follower, disciple; unimportant, trivial, trifling; secondary.

chiefly, adv. mostly, principally, mainly, especially, particularly, above all, most of all, primarily, predominantly, largely, by and large, on the whole, generally, in general, usually, as a rule, preeminently, eminently. —**Ant.** last, lastly.

childish, adj. childlike, puerile, infantile, babyish, juvenile, immature, naive, jejune, inexperienced, adolescent, undeveloped, backward, retarded, young, tender; weak, silly, simple, ingenuous, guileless, trusting, sophmoric. —**Ant.** adult, sophisticated.

chill, n. **1.** cold, coldness, frigidity, sharpness, nippiness, nip in the air, cold snap, coolness, rawness, artic air, iciness, frost. **2.** shivering, ague, cold, flu, influenza, grippe, sniffles. **3.** coolness, iciness, aloofness, unfriendliness, hostility, chilliness. —adj. **4.** chilly, cold, cool, numbing, raw, penetrating, icy, frigid, wintery, frosty, arctic, polar, glacial. **5.** indifferent, unsympathetic, cold blooded, cold, unfriendly, hostile, aloof; depressing, bleak, discouraging, standoffish, apathetic. —v. **6.** cool, freeze, refrigerate, ice. **7.** dampen, dispirit, discourage, dishearten, depress, deject, distress. —**Ant.** warm; friendly; heartening.

chivalrous, adj. courteous, gallant, noble, courtly, gracious, helpful, thoughtful, considerate, unselfish, attentive, generous, giving, magnanimous, greathearted, benevolent, altruistic, kindhearted, kindly, polite. —**Ant.** ill-bred, rude, selfish, self-centered, ungenerous.

choice, n. **1.** selection, choosing, election, option, alternative, preference. —adj. **2.** worthy, excellent, superior, fine, select, rare, uncommon, valuable, precious.

choose, v. select, elect, prefer, pick, cull, decide, determine, judge, opt, settle on.

chop, v. cut, cut up, mince, hack, dice, cube, hash, hew, lop off, crop, sever, cleave, dissever, whack, disjoin, separate, sunder, subdivide, saw, snip, split, splinter, chip, rive, rend, break up, slash, slice into pieces, carve up, quarter, dissect, dismember, anatomize, disconnect, take apart, divide, atomize, chew up, butcher, fragment, mangle, mutilate, shred.

chronic, adj. **1.** inveterate, constant, habitual, confirmed, hardened, dyed in the wool. **2.** perpetual, continuous, continuing, unending, never-ending, everlasting, long = standing, lingering, lasting, long-lived. —**Ant.** fleeting, temporary.

chuckle, v., n. laugh, giggle, titter, chortle, crow, snigger. —**Ant.** cry, sob.

chutzpah, n. audacity, pluck, self-confidence, self-assertiveness, brashness, boldness, temerity, temerariousness, aggressiveness, effrontery, presumption, presumptuousness, brazenness, impudence, impertinence, insolence, nerve, cheek, gall, face, crust, brass. **—Ant.** timidity, modesty, self-effacement.

circle, n. **1.** ring, periphery, circumference, perimeter. **2.** ring, circlet, crown. **3.** compass, area, sphere, province, field, region, bounds, circuit. **4.** cycle, period, series. **5.** coterie, set, clique, society, club, company, class, fraternity. **6.** sphere, orb, globe, ball. **—**v. **7.** surround, encircle, encompass, round, bound, include. **8.** orbit, circuit, revolve, circumnavigate, go around, tour.

circuit, n. **1.** course, tour, journey, circle, round, ambit, lap, revolution, orbit. **2.** circumference, perimeter, periphery, girth, border, edge, limit, ambit, margin, outline, confines, pale, bound, boundary, compass.

circuitous, adj. indirect, roundabout, circular, wandering, meandering, crooked, devious, deviant, tortuous, serpentine, twisting, vagrant, oblique, errant, circumambulatory, circumlocutory. **—Ant.** straight, straightforward, blunt.

circumstance, n. **1.** event, happening, occurence, incident, episode, affair, occasion. **2.** situation, state, state of affairs, condition, case.

civil, adj. polite, courteous, courtly, gracious, complaisant, cordial, formal, respectful, deferential, obliging; affable, urbane, debonair, chivalrous, gallant, suave; refined, well-mannered, well-bred, civilized, proper, polished. **—Ant.** uncivil, discourteous; rude; ill-mannered, unrefined.

claim, v. **1.** demand, require, ask, call for, challenge, seek, exact, insist, command, be entitled to. **2.** assert, declare, allege, state, affirm, contend, maintain, uphold. **—**n. **3.** demand, request, requirement, requisition, call. **4.** right, title, privilege, pretension.

clannish, adj. exclusive, exclusionary, exclusory, select, selective, restricted, restrictive, cliquish, cliquey, snobbish, snobby, elite, elect, ethnocentric. **—Ant.** open, unrestricted, all-embracing.

clash, v. **1.** clang, crash, clap, dash, clatter, clank. **2.** fight, battle, differ, argue, dispute, quarrel, squabble, feud, contend, conflict, struggle, disagree, interfere. **—**n. **3.** conflict, opposition, disagreement, interference, struggle, engagement, fight, battle, difference, argument, dispute, altercation, quarrel, squabble, contradiction. **—Ant.** harmony, agreement.

clasp, n. **1.** brooch, pin, clip, hook, fastening, catch, hasp. **2.** hold, old in one's arms, clutch, enfold, grip, embrace, hug, grasp. **—**v. **3.** clip, fasten secure, close, hold, hook, pin, clamp. **4.** grasp, grip, clutch. **5.** embrace, hug, clutch, grasp, fold, envelop.

class, n. **1.** rank, level, grade, order, stratum; status, caste, pedigree, birth, descent, extraction, stock. **2.** group, category, division, classification, genre, domain, realm; kind, type, sort. **3.** breeding, refinement, taste, savoir-faire, prestige, elegance, distinction, discernment, merit, excellence, importance. **—**v. **4.** rank, grade, rate, order, categorize, classify, arrange, sort, group, type.

clean, adj. **1.** unsoiled, unstained, clear, unblemished, pure, flawless, spotless, unsullied, neat, immaculate. **2.** pure, purified, unmixed, unadulterated, clarified. **3.** unsullied, undefiled, moral, decent, virtuous, respectable, good, blameless, innocent, upright,

honorable, chaste. **4.** neat, trim, clean-cut, simple, definite, smooth, even, straight, tidy. **5.** complete, perfect, entire, whole, unabated, unimpaired. **—**adv. **6.** cleanly, neatly. **7.** wholly, completely, perfectly, entirely, altogether, fully, thoroughly, in all respects, out and out. **—**v. **8.** scour, launder, neaten, tidy up, straighten up, scrub, sweep, brush, wipe, mop, dust, wash, rinse, lave, cleanse, shower, sponge, vacuum, polish, bathe, disinfect, sanitize, purify, clear; decontaminate. **—Ant.** dirty, soiled, impure, contaminated; immoral.

clear, adj. **1.** unclouded, light, bright, pellucid, limpid, diaphanous, crystalline, transparent, luminous. **2.** bright, shining, lucent. **3.** perceptible, understood, distinct, intelligible, orotund, comprehensible, lucid, plain, perspicuous, conspicuous, obvious. **4.** distinct, evident, plain, obvious, apparent, manifest, palpable, patent, unmistakable, unequivocal, unambiguous, indisputable, undeniable, unquestionable. **5.** innocent, pure, not guilty, unsullied, irreproachable, unblemished, clean, unspotted, unadulterated, moral, undefiled, virtuous, immaculate, spotless. **6.** serene, calm, untroubled, fair, cloudless, sunny. **7.** unobstructed, open, free, unimpeded, unhindered, unhampered, unencumbered, unentangled. **8.** smooth, clean, even, regular, unblemished. **9.** emptied, empty, free, rid. **10.** limitless, unlimited, unqualified, unequivocal, boundless, free, open. **—**v. **11.** clarify, purify, refine, clean, cleanse. **12.** acquit, absolve, exonerate, vindicate, excuse, justify. **13.** extricate, disentangle, disabuse, rid, disencumber, disengage. **14.** liberate, free, emancipate, set free, disenthrall, loose, unchain, unfetter, let go. **—Ant.** cloudy, dim, obscure; indistinct, unclear; guilty, culpable; troubled, disturbed, perturbed, obstructed; limited, confined.

clearly, adv. definitely, distinctly, evidently, plainly, understandably, obviously, certainly, surely, assuredly, entirely, completely, totally, apparently, manifestly, positively, without doubt, unequivocally, unquestionably, incontestably, undoubtedly, indubitably, demonstrably, absolutely, utterly. **—Ant.** confusedly, indefinitely; partly.

clever, adj. **1.** bright, quick, able, apt, smart, intelligent, expert, gifted, talented, ingenious, quick-witted, perceptive, discerning, wise, sage, sagacious, original, resourceful, inventive, creative, sharp, imaginative, shrewd, cunning, artful, crafty, sly, foxy, wily. **2.** skillful, adroit, dextrous, nimble, agile, handy, deft, adept. **—Ant.** dull, slow, dimwitted; clumsy, awkward, maladroit.

climb, v. **1.** mount, ascend, scale, surmount. **2.** rise, arise. **—**n. **3.** ascent, climbing, scaling, rise. **—Ant.** descend; descent.

close, v. **1.** stop, obstruct, shut, block, bar, stop up, clog, choke. **2.** enclose, cover in, shut in. **3.** end, terminate, finish, conclude, cease, complete. **4.** terminate, conclude, cease, end. **—**adj. **5.** shut, tight, closed, fast, confined. **6.** enclosed, shut in. **7.** heavy, unventilated, muggy, oppressive, uncomfortable, dense, thick. **8.** secretive, reticent, taciturn, close-mouthed, silent, uncommunicative, incommunicative, reserved, withdrawn. **9.** parsimonious, stingy, tight, closefisted, penurious, niggardly, miserly, mean. **10.** compact, condensed, dense, thick, solid, compressed, firm. **11.** near, nearby, adjoin-

ing, adjacent, neighboring, immediate. **12.** intimate, confidential, attached, dear, devoted. **13.** strict, searching, minute, scrupulous, exact, exacting, accurate, precise, faithful, nice. **14.** intent, fixed, assiduous, intense, concentrated, earnest, constant, unremitting, relentless, unrelenting. **—**n. **15.** end, termination, conclusion, finish, completion cessation, culmination. **—Ant.** open.

clothes, n. clothing, attire, apparel, wear, ensemble, dress, garments, habit, costume, garb, vestments, habiliments, accouterment, outfit, rags, glad rags, wardrobe.

cloud, n. **—**v. becloud, bedim, shadow, confuse, blut, befog, muddle, muddy, overshadow, obscure, shade. **—Ant.** clarify.

cloudy, adj. **1.** overcast, shadowy, clouded, murky, lowering, gloomy, cloudy, dismal, depressing, sullen. **2.** obscure, indistinct, dim, blurred, blurry, unclear, befogged, muddled, confused, dark, turbid, muddy, opaque. **—Ant.** clear; distinct.

club, n. **1.** stick, cudgel, bludgeon, blackjack, billy, bat, mace, truncheon, baton, staff. **2.** society, organization, association, circle, set, coterie, clique, fraternity, sorority, sodality, brotherhood, sisterhood, alliance, union, league, confederation, federation, order, group.

clumsy, adj. **1.** awkward, unskillful, ungainly, gawky, gauche, lumbering, ungraceful, lubberly. **2.** unhandy, maladroit, unskillful, inexpert, bungling, ponderous, heavy, heavy-handed, inept bumbling, cloddish, uncoordinated, oafish, butterfingers, ham-handed, ham-fisted, all thumbs.. **—Ant.** adroit, clever, dexterous.

coarse, adj. **1.** low-quality, second-rate, shoddy, tawdry, trashy, kitschy, common, inferior, faulty, crude, rude, rough. **2.** indelicate, unpolished, uncivil, impolite, gruff, bluff, rude, loutish, uncouth, unrefined, impolite, boorish, churlish. **3.** gross, broad, indecent, vulgar, crass, ribald, lewd, lascivious, amoral, immoral, dirty, improper, obscene, smutty, filthy, foul, offensive, scurrilous, foulmouthed. **—Ant.** pure, refined; civil, civilized, cultivated; decent, decorous.

coast, n. shore, seashore, strand, beach, seaside, seacoast, littoral, coastline, seaboard.

coax, v. wheedle, cajole, beguile, inveigle, persuade, flatter, urge, charm, manipulate. **—Ant.** force, bully; deter.

coherence, n. cohesion, union, connection, congruity, consistency, correspondence, harmony, harmoniousness, orderliness, organization, agreement, unity, rationality, logic. **—Ant.** incoherence, disorder.

cold, adj. **1.** chilly, chill, cool, frigid, gelid, frozen, freezing. **2.** unemotional, unenthusiastic, passionless, apathetic, unresponsive, unsympathetic, unaffected, stoical, affectless, dispassionate, phlegmatic, unfeeling, unsusceptible, unimpressible, unimpressed, cool, sluggish, torpid, indifferent, cold-blooded, unconcerned, heartless, unperturbed, imperturbable. **3.** polite, formal, standoffish, aloof, distant, unapproachable, stonyhearted, reserved, unresponsive, unfriendly, inimical, hostile. **4.** calm, deliberate, depressing, dispiriting, disheartening, uninspiring, spiritless, unaffecting, dull. **5.** bleak, raw, cutting, keen, bitter, biting, numbing, glacial, Siberian, nippy, nipping, arctic, polar, frosty, icy, wintry, chill, chilly. —*n*. **6.** chill, shivers, ague, sniffles, grippe, flu. —**Ant.** warm, hot.

collect, *v.* gather, assemble, amass, accumulate, aggregate, scrape together, compile, pile up, heap up, get together, rack up, hoard. —**Ant.** strew, broadcast, spread.

collection, *n.* set, accumulation, mass, heap, pile, hoard, store, gathering, assemblage, assembly, compilation, aggregation.

color, *n.* **1.** hue, tint, shade, tone, cast, tinge, tincture, pigmentation; pigment, dye, stain, paint. —*v.* **2.** affect, influence, distort, falsify, taint, twist, warp, bias, slant, twist; misrepresent, disguise, mask, conceal. **3.** blush, redden, flush, turn red.

colorless, **1.** pale, pallid, white, wan, ashen, sallow, sickly, washed out, blanched, bleached, etiolated, haggard. **2.** lifeless, boring, bland, dull, drab, insipid, uninteresting, vacuous, vapid, tedious, spiritless, dry, dreary, namby-pamby, lackluster, uninspired, monotonous, humdrum, run-of-the-mill, jejune, wearisome, tiresome. —**Ant.** flushed; exciting, colorful.

combat, *v.* **1.** fight, contend, battle, oppose, struggle, contest, war, clash, duel, spar, strive against, defy, wrestle with, resist, withstand. —*n.* **2.** fight, skirmish, contest, battle, struggle, fracus, fray, affray, melee, donnybrook, brawl, conflict, war, brush, affair, encounter, engagement, duel, warfare, strife; altercation, feud, quarrel, dispute, row. —**Ant.** support, defend.

combination, *n.* **1.** conjunction, association, union, grouping, set, array, connection, coalescence, blending. **2.** composite, compound, mixture, amalgamation, amalgam, alloy, aggregate, blend, emulsion, mix. **3.** alliance, confederacy, federation, union, league, organization, cartel, bloc, trust, syndication, consortium, coalition, association, society, club; cartel, combine, monopoly; conspiracy, cabal.

combine, *v.* unite, join, conjoin, associate, coalesce, blend, mix, incorporate, involve, compound, amalgamate, unify, connect, link, band, ally, mingle, commingle, consolidate, fuse, synthesize, bind, bond, put together, relate. —**Ant.** dissociate, separate.

comfort, *v.* **1.** soothe, console, relieve, ease, cheer, pacify, calm, cheer, hearten, encourage, reassure, assuage, solace, gladden, refresh. —*n.* **2.** relief, consolation, solace, encouragement. **3.** luxury, ease, abundance, opulence, plenty; security. —**Ant.** agitate, discommode, incommode; discomfort, discouragement.

comical, *adj.* amusing, humorous, funny, comic, laugh-provoking, hilarious, mirthful, sidesplitting, jocular, silly, droll, risible, playful, clownish, ludic; laughable, ridiculous, ludicrous, absurd, foolish.

command, *v.* **1.** order, direct, bid, demand, charge, instruct, enjoin, require. **2.** govern, control, oversee, manage, rule, lead, preside over; dominate, overlook. **3.** exact, compel, secure, demand, require, claim. —*n.* **4.** order, direction, bidding, injunction, charge, mandate, behest, commandment, requisition, requirement, instruction, dictum. **5.** control, mastery, disposal, ascendancy, rule, sway, superintendence, power, management, domination. —**Ant.** obey.

commence, *v.* begin, open, start, initiate, launch, establish, originate, inau-

gurate, enter upon *or* into. —**Ant.** end, finish, terminate.

commendation, *n.* **1.** recommendation, praise, approval, approbation, applause; medal. **2.** eulogy, encomium, panegyric, praise. —**Ant.** censure, blame.

comment, *n.* **1.** explanation, elucidation, expansion, criticism, critique, opinion, remark, view, reaction, observation, clarification, note, addendum, annotation, exposition, commentary. **2.** remark, observation, criticism. —*v.* **3.** remark, explain, annotate, criticize.

commerce, *n.* marketing, merchandising, interchange, traffic, trade, dealing, exchange, business.

common, *adj.* **1.** mutual, reciprocal, shared, joint. **2.** public, communal, community, general, collective, nonprivate, universal. **3.** notorious. **4.** widespread, general, ordinary, universal, prevalent, popular. **5.** familiar, usual, customary, frequent, habitual, run-of-the mill, stock, regular, conventional, standard, garden-variety, workaday, average, everyday. **6.** hackneyed, trite, stale, commonplace, overused, tired, banal, stereotyped, cliché. **7.** mean, low, base, mediocre, inferior. **8.** coarse, vulgar, ordinary, undistinguished, ill-bred, low-class, plebeian, unrefined. —**Ant.** exceptional, singular, extraordinary, separate; unfamiliar, strange.

commotion, *n.* **1.** tumult, disturbance, perturbation, agitation, disorder, bustle, ado, turmoil, turbulence, riot, violence. **2.** sedition, insurrection, uprising, revolution. —**Ant.** peace, calm, serenity.

communicate, *v.* **1.** impart, convey, transfer, transmit; give, bestow. **2.** divulge, announce, declare, disclose, reveal, make known, tell, spread, promulgate, publicize, broadcast, air. —**Ant.** withhold, conceal.

community, *n.* **1.** hamlet, town, village, city. **2.** public, commonwealth, society. **3.** agreement, identity, similarity, likeness. —*adj.* **4.** common, joint, cooperative.

compact, *adj.* **1.** dense, solid, firm, tightly packed, condensed. **2.** concise, pithy, terse, laconic, short, sententious, succinct, brief, pointed, meaningful. —*v.* **3.** condense, consolidate, compress. **4.** stabilize, solidify. —*n.* **5.** covenant, pact, contract, treaty, agreement, bargain, entente, arrangement, convention, concordat. —**Ant.** diverse, dispersed.

companion, *n.* **1.** associate, comrade, confederate, partner, fellow, mate, colleague, confrere, pal, buddy, intimate. **2.** assistant; nurse, governess, escort.

company, *n.* **1.** group, band, party, troop, assemblage, body, unit. **2.** companionship, fellowship, association, society. **3.** assembly, throng, group, ensemble, troop, flock, gathering, concourse, crowd, circle, set, coterie, retinue, entourage, followers, congregation. **4.** firm, partnership, corporation, concern, house, syndicate, association, business, establishment, enterprise, institution.

compare, *v.* **1.** liken, contrast, associate, make an analogy with, refer, analogize. **2.** Resemble, equal, correspond, match, parallel, approximate, rival, compete, be a match for, be on par with, vie with. **3.** contrast, measure against, weigh, juxtapose, relate, correlate.

comparison *n.* contrast, juxtaposition, balance, weighing; match, similarity, resemblance, likeness, relationship, commensurability, kinship.

compartment, *n.* division, section, apartment, cabin, roomette, room, berth, slot, cubby.

compassion, *n.* sorrow, pity, sympathy, feeling, mercy, commiseration, kindness, kindliness, tenderness, heart, tenderheartedness, clemency, empathy, solicitousness, solicitude, caring, consideration, concern, fellow feeling. —**Ant.** mercilessness, indifference.

compassionate, *adj.* pitying, sympathetic, tender, kind, merciful, tenderhearted, kindly, clement, gracious, benignant, gentle, empathetic, understanding, caring, solicitous, comforting, consoling, supportive, responsive, considerate. —**Ant.** merciless, pitiless, harsh, cruel, mean.

compel, *v.* **1.** force, drive, coerce, constrain, oblige, commit, impel, motivate, necessitate. **2.** subdue, subject, bend, bow, overpower. —**Ant.** restrain.

compensate, *v.* **1.** counterbalance, counterpoise, offset, equalize, neutralize, square, even up, countervail, make up for. **2.** remunerate, reward, pay, recompense, reimburse. **3.** atone, make amends, expiate.

compensation, *n.* **1.** recompense, remuneration, payment, amends, reparation, indemnity, reward. **2.** atonement, requital, satisfaction, indemnification.

compete, *v.* contend, vie, contest, rival, emulate, oppose, dispute, conflict, fight, battle, clash, strive, cope, struggle. —**Ant.** support.

competent, *adj.* fitting, suitable, sufficient, convenient, satisfactory, acceptable, O.K., all right, adequate; qualified, fit, apt, capable, proficient. —**Ant.** incompetent, inapt.

competitor, *n.* opponent, contestant, rival, antagonist, foe, enemy, competition, opposition, adversary, contender. —**Ant.** ally, friend.

complain, *v.* grumble, growl, murmur, mutter, whine, moan, wail, lament, bemoan, groan, grouse, carp, whimper, cry, gripe, squak, kick, beef.

complement, *v.* **1.** complete, supplement, add to, round out, perfect, flesh out, top off, enhance. —*n.* **2.** supplement, completion, perfection, consummation, finishing touch.n

complete, *adj.* **1.** whole, entire, full, intact, unbroken, unimpaired, undivided, one, perfect, developed, unabated, undiminished, fulfilled. **2.** finished, ended, concluded, consummated, done, consummate, perfect, thorough; through-and-through, dyed-in-the-wool, rank, total, unqualified, unmitigated. —*v.* **3.** finish, end, conclude, consummate, perfect, accomplish, do, fulfill, achieve, effect, terminate, close, wrap up. —**Ant.** incomplete; unfinished; begin, commence, initiate.

complex, *adj.* **1.** compound, composite, complicated, mixed, mingled. **2.** involved, complicated, intricate, perplexing, tangled. —*n.* **3.** net, network, complication, web, tangle. —**Ant.** simple; simplex.

compliment, *n.* **1.** praise, commendation, admiration, tribute, honor, eulogy, encomium, panegyric. **2.** regard, respect, civility; flattery. —*v.* **3.** commend, praise, honor, flatter, pay homage to *or* tribute to, laud. **4.** congratulate, felicitate. —**Ant.** insult, injury; decry, disparage.

comply, *v.* acquiesce, obey, yield, conform, consent, assent, agree, accede, concede, concur, submit. —**Ant.** refuse.

composed, *adj.* calm, tranquil, serene, undisturbed, collected, peaceful, cool, placid, pacific, unruffled, sedate, unperturbed, self-possessed, controlled, imperturbable, quiet, cool, unflappable, relaxed. —**Ant.** upset, perturbed, disturbed, disquieted.

composure, *n.* serenity, calm, calmness, tranquility, equability, peacefulness, quiet, coolness, equanimity, self-possession. —**Ant.** agitation.

comprehend, *v.* **1.** understand, conceive, know, grasp, see, discern, imagine, perceive, apprehend, realize, fathom, absorb, assimilate, appreciate. **2.** include, comprise, embrace, take in, embody, contain.

comprehensive, *adj.* exhaustive, thorough, full, inclusive, broad, wide, large, extensive, sweeping, encyclopedic. —**Ant.** limited.

comprise, *v.* include, comprehend, contain, embrace, embody; consist *or* be composed of. —**Ant.** exclude.

compulsory, *adj.* **1.** compelling, coercive, constraining. **2.** compelled, forced, obligatory, arbitrary, binding, necessary, unavoidable, inescapable, ineluctable. —**Ant.** free, unrestrained, unrestricted.

compute, *v.* reckon, calculate, estimate, count, figure, determine, ascertain.

comrade, *n.* associate, companion, intimate, friend, fellow, partner, mate, colleague, confrere, cohort, compeer, crony, ally, sidekick, chum, buddy, pal, coworker, brother, bro, homeboy, homey.

conceal, *v.* **1.** hide, secrete, cover, put away, bury, screen, camouflage. **2.** keep secret, hide, disguise, dissemble. —**Ant.** reveal.

conceit, *n.* **1.** arrogance, hubris, cockiness, narcissism, pride, vainglory, self-esteem, vanity, amour-propre, egotism, complacency. **2.** fancy, imagination, whim, notion, vagary; thought, idea, belief, conception; metaphor, trope, figure, theme, image. —**Ant.** humility, modesty.

conceited, *adj.* vain, proud, egotistical, self-important, self-centered, egocentric, self-satisfied, smug, complacent, self-sufficient, swell-headed, narcissistic, immodest, full of oneself, cocky, cocksure, snotty, arrogant, preening, in love with oneself, vainglorious, inflated, blind to one's own faults, stuck on oneself, stuck-up, supercilious, haughty, high and mighty, smug, superior. —**Ant.** humble, modest, shy, retiring.

conceive, *v.* **1.** imagine, speculate, perceive, see, understand, realize, comprehend, envision, conjure up, hypothesize, postulate, posit, suppose, create, ideate, think. **2.** understand, apprehend, comprehend.

concentrate, *v.* **1.** focus, direct, center, consolidate. **2.** intensify, purify, clarify, reduce to an essence, reduce condense, boil down, distill. **3.** think, focus one's thoughts, apply oneself. —**Ant.** dissipate, disperse.

concern, *v.* **1.** affect, touch, interest, relate to, engage, involve, include. **2.** disquiet, trouble, disturb, worry, bother, perturb, unsettle, upset. —*n.* **3.** business, affair, problem, involvement, responsibility, interest, matter. **4.** solicitude, anxiety, care, worry, burden, responsibility. **5.** relation, bearing, appropriateness, consequence. **6.** firm, company, business, establishment, enterprise, organization, corporation, partnership, house. —**Ant.** exclude; calm; unconcern, indifference.

conciseness, *n.* brevity, laconicism,

summary, terseness, pithiness, directness, succinctness, cogency, compression, sententiousness, compactness, trenchancy. —**Ant.** diversity.

conclusion, *n.* **1.** end, close, termination, finish, completion, ending, finale. **2.** summing up, summation. **3.** result, issue, outcome, aftermath, denouement. **4.** settlement, arrangement, wind-up. **5.** decision, judgment, determination. **6.** deduction, inference. —**Ant.** beginning, commencement.

concur, *v.* **1.** agree, consent, coincide, harmonize. **2.** cooperate, combine, help, conspire, contribute. —**Ant.** disagree.

condemn, *v.* **1.** blame, censure, disapprove, denounce, disparage, rebuke, scold, reprimand, upbraid, reprove, reproach, sit in judgment, judge, criticize. **2.** doom, find guilty, sentence, damn, convict. —**Ant.** liberate, release, exonerate.

condense, *v.* compress, concentrate, consolidate, contract; abridge, epitomize, digest, shorten, abbreviate, abstract, reduce, diminish, curtail. —**Ant.** expand.

condescend, *v.* deign, stoop, descend, humble *or* demean *or* degrade oneself, lower oneself, show noblesse oblige, come down off one's high horse.

condition, *n.* **1.** state, case, situation, circumstance, conjuncture, circumstances. **2.** requisite, prerequisite, requirement, contingency, consideration, proviso, provision, stipulation, sine qua non.

conduct, *n.* **1.** behavior, demeanor, action, actions, deportment, comportment, attitude, posture, bearing, carriage, mien, manners. **2.** direction, management, execution, guidance, leadership, administration, supervision, control, regulation, government. —*v.* **3.** behave, deport, act, bear, comport, acquit. **4.** direct, manage, carry on, supervise, regulate, administrate, administer, execute, guide, lead. **5.** lead, guide, escort, convoy, usher.

confederation, *n.* alliance, confederacy, league, fedcration, union, unity, society, state, ur.ified group, association, combine, combination, coalition.

confer, *v.* **1.** bestow, give, donate, grant, award, present, vouchsafe, allow, promise. **2.** consult together, discuss, deliberate, discourse, parley, converse, advise, talk, meet, come to a decision.

conference, *n.* meeting, interview, parley, colloquy, convention, consultation, congress, council, seminar, forum, colloquium, symposium, gathering, assembly.

confess, *v.* acknowledge, avow, own, admit, disclose, divulge, tell the truth, make a confession, confide in, spill one's guts, testify, share one's secrets, accept responsibility, unburden oneself, reveal, come clean, grant, concede; declare, aver, confirm.

confidence, *n.* **1.** trust, belief, faith, reliance, dependence. **2.** self-reliance, assurance, boldness, intrepidity, self-confidence, courage, poise, aplomb, conviction, coolness. —**Ant.** distrust, mistrust; modesty.

confident, *adj.* sure, bold, believing, assured, self-assured, secure, certain, positive, convinced; brave, intrepid, dauntless, cocksure, fearless. —**Ant.** shy, modest, diffident.

confidential, *adj.* **1.** secret, restricted, private, classified, intimate, hush-hush. **2.** familiar, trusted, trusty, trustworthy, faithful, honorable, honest.

confine, *v.* **1.** enclose, bound, circum-

scribe, circle, encircle, limit, bind, restrict. **2.** immure, imprison, incarcerate, lock-up, pen, jail, shut-up, coop up. —*n.* **3.** (*usually plural*) bounds, boundary, perimeter, periphery, limits; frontiers, borders.

confirm, *v.* **1.** make certain *or* sure, assure, corroborate, verify, substantiate, authenticate. **2.** make valid *or* binding, ratify, sanction, approve, validate, bind. **3.** make firm, strengthen, settle, establish, fix, assure.

conflict, *v.* **1.** collide, clash, antagonize, oppose, vary with, interfere. **2.** contend, fight, combat, battle. —*n.* **3.** battle, struggle, encounter, contest, collision, fight, fray, war, combat, engagement, fracas, brawl, donnybrook, siege, strife; contention, controversy, opposition, variance, dispute, argument, wrangle, altercation, disagreement, feud, quarrel, row, squabble, tiff, spat, dust-up. **4.** interference, discord, disunity, disharmony, inconsistency, antagonism, clash. —**Ant.** harmony, peace, friendliness.

conform, *v.* **1.** comply, yield, agree, assent, harmonize. **2.** tally, match, agree, correspond, square. **3.** adapt, adjust, accommodate. —**Ant.** disagree, dissent.

confuse, *v.* **1.** jumble, disorder, disarrange, disturb, disarray. **2.** confound, mix, mix up, intermingle, mingle. **3.** perplex, mystify, nonplus, bewilder, astonish, surprise, disarm, shock, disconcert, embarrass, disturb. **4.** disconcert, abash, mortify, shame, confound, throw for a loop. —**Ant.** enlighten.

confusion, *n.* **1.** perplexity, embarrassment, surprise, astonishment, shock, bewilderment, distraction. **2.** disorder, disarray, disarrangement, jumble, mess, turmoil, chaos, tumult, furor, commotion, ferment, agitation, stir. **3.** embarrassment, abashment, shamefacedness, shame, mortification. —**Ant.** enlightenment; clarity.

congenial, *adj.* sympathetic, kindred, similar, friendly, amiable, amicable, *gemutleicheit*, propitious, favorable, genial, agreeable, pleasing, pleasant, complaisant, suited, adapted, well-suited, suitable, apt, proper. —**Ant.** unsympathetic, disagreeable; unsuitable.

congress, *n.* meeting, assembly, conference, council, convention.

conjecture, *n.* **1.** hypothesis, theory, guess, surmise, opinion, supposition, inference, deduction. —*v.* **2.** conclude, suppose, assume, presume, suspect, surmise, hypothesize, theorize, guess. —**Ant.** determine, ascertain.

connect, *v.* join, unite, link, conjoin, couple, associate, network, affiliate, relate, tie, bind, attach, combine; cohere. —**Ant.** disconnect, disjoin.

connection, *n.* **1.** junction, conjunction, union, joining, association, alliance, dependence, interdependence. **2.** link, yoke, connective, bond, tie, coupling. **3.** association, relationship, affiliation, affinity. **4.** circle, set, coterie, acquaintanceship, network. **5.** relation, family members, relative, kinswoman, kinsman, kin, kith. —**Ant.** disjunction, dissociation.

conquer, *v.* **1.** win, gain, be victorious, triumph. **2.** overcome, subdue, vanquish, overpower, overthrow, subjugate, defeat, master, subject, beat, rout, overrun, quash, gain the upper hand, crush, reduce. **3.** surmount, overcome, overwhelm. —**Ant.** surrender, submit, give up, yield.

conquest, *n.* **1.** captivation, seduction, enchantment. **2.** vanquishment, victory, triumph, win. **3.** subjugation, overthrow, defeat, mastery, subjection, rout. —**Ant.** surrender.

conscientious, *adj.* just, upright, honest, principled, fair, moral, ethical, righteous, right-minded, upright, honorable, straightforward, incorruptible, faithful; careful, particular, painstaking, scrupulous, assiduous, sedulous, diligent, persevering, meticulous, punctilious, rigorous, thorough, attentive, serious, exacting, demanding; devoted, dedicated. —**Ant.** dishonest, corrupt, unscrupulous.

conscious, *adj.* **1.** awake, aware, sentient, alert, knowing, cognizant, percipient, intelligent. **2.** sensible, sensitive, felt; rational, reasoning. **3.** deliberate, intentional, purposeful, willful, studied. —**Ant.** unconscious.

consecrate, *v.* **1.** sanctify, hallow, venerate, elevate. **2.** devote, dedicate. —**Ant.** desecrate.

consecutive, *adj.* successive, continuous, regular, uninterrupted, one after another, succeeding, following. —**Ant.** alternate, random.

consent, *v.* **1.** agree, assent, permit, allow, let, concur, yield, give in, submit, cede, concede, comply, accede, acquiesce. —*n.* **2.** assent, acquiescence, permission, compliance, concurrence, agreement. **3.** accord, concord, agreement, consensus. —**Ant.** refuse, disagree; dissent.

consequence, *n.* **1.** effect, result, outcome, issue, upshot, sequel, aftermath, denouncement, event, end. **2.** importance, significance, moment, weight, concern, interest. **3.** distinction, importance, singularity, weight.

conservative, *n.* **1.** reactionary, right-winger, rightist, tory, fundamentalist, old fogey, traditionalist, conformist, Neanderthal. —*adj.* **2.** reactionary, right, nonprogressive, tory, right-wing; unprogressive, backward, orthodox, traditional, hidebound, conventional, standard, fundamentalist, dyed-in-the-wool; prudent, stable, staid, sober, old-world, cautious, temperate, old-fashioned, sober-sided.

consider, *v.* **1.** contemplate, meditate, reflect, ruminate, ponder, muse on, brood over, deliberate, weigh, revolve, study, think about. **2.** think, suppose, assume, presume. **3.** regard, respect, honor. —**Ant.** ignore.

considerate, *adj.* thoughtful, kind, charitable, patient, concerned, helpful, friendly, neighborly, gracious, obliging, accommodating, generous, unselfish, sympathetic, compassionate, solicitous, well-disposed, respectful, civil, polite, well-bred, chivalrous, genteel. —**Ant.** inconsiderate.

consideration, *n.* **1.** thought, meditation, reflection, cogitation, study, examination, rumination, deliberation, contemplation, attention, advisement, regard. **2.** recompense, payment, remuneration, fee, reward, honorarium, emolument, tip, gratuity, compensation, pay. **3.** thoughtfulness, sympathy, solicitude, respect, caring, regard, attentiveness, kindness, kindliness, patience, concern. **4.** importance, consequence, weight, significance, moment, interest.

consistent, *adj.* **1.** agreeing, concordant, compatible, congruous, consonant, harmonious, suitable, apt, conformable, conforming. **2.** constant, faithful, assiduous, unwavering, stable, devoted, perseverant, sedulous, immutable, persistent. —**Ant.** inconsistent.

consolation, *n.* comfort, solace, relief, encouragement, reward. —**Ant.** discomfort, discouragement.

console, *v.* comfort, solace, cheer, encourage, soothe, relieve, calm. —**Ant.** aggravate, agitate, disturb.

consonant, *n.* —*adj.* in agreement, concordant, consistent, harmonious, compatible, congruous, conformant, suitable, fitting, predictable. —**Ant.** discordant, inconsistent.

conspicuous, *adj.* **1.** visible, manifest, noticeable, clear, marked, salient, discernible, perceptible, plain, open, apparent, ostentatious, showy, evident, public. **2.** prominent, outstanding, obvious, striking, noteworthy, attractive, eminent, distinguished, noted, celebrated, illustrious, notorious, renowned, well-known. —**Ant.** unclear, imperceptible; undistinguished, trifling.

conspire, *v.* **1.** plot, intrigue, cabal, contrive, devise. **2.** combine, concur, cooperate, agree.

constancy, *n.* firmness, fortitude, resolution, determination, inflexibility, decision, tenacity, steadfastness, faithfulness, fidelity, fealty, devotion, loyalty; regularity, stability, immutability, uniformity, permanence, sameness. —**Ant.** randomness, faithlessness, irregularity, instability.

constant, *adj.* **1.** invariable, uniform, stable, unchanging, fixed, immutable, invariable, unvarying, permanent. **2.** perpetual, unremitting, uninterrupted, continual, recurrent, assiduous, unwavering, unfailing, persistent, persevering, determined. **3.** steadfast, faithful, loyal, dependable, staunch, true, tried and true, true-blue, trusty, devoted, steady, resolute, firm, unshaking, unshakable, unwavering, unswerving, determined. —**Ant.** inconstant, variable, random, unstable, changeable; sporadic; unsteady, wavering.

consternation, *n.* amazement, dread, dismay, bewilderment, awe, alarm, terror, fear, panic, fright, horror. —**Ant.** composure, equanimity.

constrain, *v.* **1.** force, compel, oblige, coerce. **2.** confine, check, bind, restrain, curb. —**Ant.** liberate, free.

constrict, *v.* compress, contract, shrink, cramp, squeeze, bind, tighten. —**Ant.** unbind, untie.

construct, *v.* build, frame, form, devise, erect, make, fabricate, raise, assemble, fashion, shape, forge, invent, put together. —**Ant.** raze.

consult, *v.* confer, deliberate, discuss with, interview, seek the opinion of, take the advice of, meet with, counsel, converse, come to a mutual decision, offer advice, advise, talk over with, question, look up.

consume, *v.* **1.** destroy, expend, use up, use, exhaust, spend, waste, deplete, drain, dissipate, squander, eat up, devour. **2.** absorb, engross, occupy one's attention, obsess, preoccupy, distract, keep one busy.

consummate, *v.* **1.** complete, perfect, fulfill, accomplish, achieve, climax, attain, end, realize, finish, effect, execute, do. —*adj.* **2.** complete, perfect, done, finished, effected, fulfilled, excellent, supreme. —**Ant.** imperfect, unfinished, base.

contain, *v.* hold, accommodate, include, embody, embrace, bear, carry, have inside, admit, encompass.

contaminate, *v.* defile, pollute, sully, stain, soil, tarnish, taint, corrupt, befoul, besmirch, infect, poison, vitiate, rot, infect, spoil, debase, adulterate.

contemplate, *v.* **1.** look at, view, observe, regard, survey, behold, scrutinize, inspect. **2.** consider, reflect on, meditate on, study, ponder, deliberate, think about, revolve in one's mind,

muse, ruminate, mull over, cogitate, brood over, chew on, study, examine. **3.** intend, mean, purpose, design, plan.

contempt, *n.* **1.** scorn, disdain, derision, contumely, disgust; loathing, abhorrence, odium, hatred, hate. **2.** dishonor, disgrace, shame. —**Ant.** respect, reverence; honor.

contemptible, *adj.* despicable, mean, low, miserable, base, vile, scurvy, inferior, abject, shabby, shameful, nefarious, infamous, villianous. —**Ant.** splendid, admirable.

contemptuous, *adj.* disdainful, scornful, sneering, insolent, arrogant, supercilious, haughty, derisive, insulting, snide. —**Ant.** humble, respectful.

contend, *v.* **1.** struggle, strive, fight, battle, combat, vie, compete, rival. **2.** debate, dispute, argue, wrangle. **3.** assert, maintain, claim, aver, theorize, argue, postulate.

content, *adj.* **1.** satisfied, contented, sanguine, happy, comfortable, sated, pleased with the status quo, appeased, gratified, uncomplaining, O.K., blasé, blithe, unambitious, smug, self-satisfied. **2.** assenting, acceding, resigned, willing, agreeable. —*v.* **3.** appease, gratify, satisfy. —**Ant.** dissatisfied, malcontent, miserable.

contention, *n.* **1.** struggling, struggle, strife, discord, dissension, quarrel, disagreement, squabble, feud; rupture, break, falling out; opposition, combat, conflict, competition, rivalry, contest. **2.** disagreement, dissension, debate, wrangle, altercation, dispute, argument, controversy. —**Ant.** agreement.

contentment, *n.* happiness, satisfaction, content, ease, satiety, comfort, pleasure, gratification, tranquility, serenity, peace. —**Ant.** misery.

contest, *n.* **1.** struggle, conflict, battle, combat, war, fight, encounter. **2.** competition, contention, rivalry, match, tournament, tourney, rivalry, meet, game. **3.** strife, dispute, controversy, debate, argument, altercation, quarrel, contention. —*v.* **4.** struggle, fight, compete, contend, vie, combat, battle. **5.** argue against, dispute, controvert, counter, confute, object to, refute, litigate, debate, oppose, contend against. **6.** doubt, question, challenge, dispute. **7.** rival, strive, compete, vie, contend for.

continual, *adj.* unceasing, incessant, ceaseless, uninterrupted, unremitting, constant, continuous, unbroken, successive, perpetual, unending, habitual, permanent, everlasting, eternal; recurrent, recurring, frequentative, repeated, repetitious, repetitive. —**Ant.** periodic, sporadic.

continue, *v.* **1.** keep on, go onward or forward, persist, persevere, pursue, proceed with. **2.** last, endure, remain, persist. **3.** remain, abide, tarry, stay, rest. **4.** persist in, extend, perpetuate, prolong, carry on, maintain, retain; carry over, postpone, adjourn. —**Ant.** cease, interrupt.

contract, *n.* **1.** agreement, compact, bargain, covenant, understanding, deal, commitment, obligation, arrangement, pact, convention, concordat, treaty, stipulation. —*v.* **2.** draw together, compress, concentrate, condense, reduce, lessen, diminish, squeeze, constrict, decrease, shorten, narrow, shrivel, shrink. —**Ant.** disperse, spread.

contradict, *v.* deny, gainsay, dispute, controvert, impugn, challenge, assail, oppose, argue against, defy. —**Ant.** corroborate, support.

contradictory, *adj.* contrary, opposed, opposite, opposing, antagonistic, incongruous, conflicting, incompatible, discrepant, irreconcilable, paradoxical, inconsistent, contrary. —**Ant.** corroborative.

contrary, *adj.* **1.** opposite, opposed, contradictory, conflicting, discordant, counter, opposing. **2.** untoward, unfavorable, adverse, unfriendly, hostile, oppugnant, antagonistic, disagreeable, irreconcilable. **3.** perverse, self-willed, intractable, obstinate, refractory, headstrong, stubborn, pigheaded, contumacious. —**Ant.** obliging, compliant, tractable.

contrast, *v.* **1.** oppose, compare, differentiate, juxtapose, discriminate, distinguish, set off. —*n.* **2.** opposition, comparison, differentiation, difference, discrimination, contrariety, juxtaposition.

contrive, *v.* plan, devise, invent, design, hatch, brew, concoct, form, make; plot, complot, conspire, scheme; manage, effect.

control, *v.* **1.** dominate, command, manage, govern, rule, direct, reign over. **2.** check, curb, hinder, restrain, bridle, constrain. —*n.* **3.** regulation, domination, command, management, direction, government, rule, reign, sovereignty, mastery, superintendence.

controversy, *n.* dispute, contention, debate, disputation, disagreement, confrontation, questioning, altercation; quarrel, wrangle, argument, squabble, spat. —**Ant.** concord, agreement, accord.

convene, *v.* **1.** assemble, meet, congregate, collect, gather. **2.** convoke, summon, call to order. —**Ant.** disperse, adjourn.

convenient, *adj.* **1.** suitable, opportune, expedient, suited, fit, appropriate, suitable, adapted, serviceable, well-suited, favorable, easy, comfortable, agreeable, helpful, advantageous, useful. **2.** at hand, accessible, handy, nearby, within reach, at one's fingertips, close at hand, available, ready. —**Ant.** inconvenient.

convention, *n.* **1.** assembly, conference, convocation, meeting. **2.** agreement, consent. **3.** custom, precedent.

conventional, *adj.* accepted, usual, habitual, customary, regular, common, traditional, normal, standard, orthodox, established, ordinary, everyday, old-fashioned, formal, stuffy, stodgy, old hat. —**Ant.** unconventional, unusual.

conversant, *adj.* **1.** familiar, versed, learned, skilled, practiced, well-informed, proficient. **2.** acquainted, associating. —**Ant.** unfamiliar, ignorant.

converse, *v.* **1.** talk, chat, speak, discuss, confabulate, hold a dialogue. —*n.* **2.** discourse, talk, conversation, discussion, colloquy. **3.** opposite, reverse, transformation.

convert, *v.* **1.** change, transmute, transform, modify, alter, mutate, metamorphose, remodel, switch, change over, redo, remake; proselyte, proselytize. —*n.* **2.** proselyte, neophyte, disciple. —**Ant.** renegade, recreant.

convey, *v.* **1.** carry, transport, bear, bring, transmit, lead, conduct. **2.** communicate, impart.

convince, *v.* persuade, satisfy, sway, influence, win over, talk into.

convulsion, *n.* seizure, frenzy, paroxysm, fit, spasm, attack, outburst, outbreak, irruption, upheaval, eruption, storm, tumult, furor.

cool, *adj.* **1.** chilly, unheated, cold, refreshing. **2.** calm, unexcited, serene,

levelheaded, unflappable, relaxed, under control, imperturbable, phlegmatic, unmoved, deliberate, composed, collected, self-possessed, unruffled, sedate, undisturbed, placid, quiet, dispassionate, unimpassioned. **3.** frigid, distant, aloof, standoffish, snobbish, stuck-up, frosty, superior, chilling, freezing, apathetic, repellent. **4.** indifferent, lukewarm, tepid, unconcerned, cold-blooded. **5.** audacious, impudent, bold, brazen, overconfident, presumptuous, impertinent, insolent, shameless. —*v.* **6.** allay, calm, moderate, quiet, temper, assuage, abate, dampen. —**Ant.** warm, tepid, lukewarm, hot.

copy, *n.* **1.** reproduction, replica, likeness, double, twin, transcript, imitation, carbon, duplicate, facsimile, fax, Xerox, photocopy. **2.** original, manuscript, pattern, model, archetype. —*v.* **3.** imitate, ape, mimic, follow in someone's footsteps, mime, impersonate, emulate, parrot, echo; duplicate, transcribe. —**Ant.** original.

core, *n.* **1.** center, middle, heart, nucleus, inside, focus. **2.** heart, pith, gist, essence, marrow, quintessence. **3.** pit, seed.

corpse, *n.* body, remains, carcass, cadaver, stiff.

correct, *v.* **1.** set right, rectify, amend, emend, reform, remedy, repair, fix, cure. **2.** admonish, warn, rebuke, discipline, chasten, berate, scold, punish, castigate. —*adj.* **3.** factual, truthful, accurate, proper, precise, exact, faultless, perfect, right, true, valid, fitting, apt, suitable, appropriate, unimpeachable. —**Ant.** ruin, spoil; incorrect, wrong.

correspond, *v.* **1.** conform, agree, harmonize, accord, match, tally, concur, coincide, fit, suit. **2.** communicate, write, be in touch, keep in contact. —**Ant.** differ, diverge.

corrupt, *adj.* **1.** dishonest, venal, false, untrustworthy, bribable, degenerate, degraded. **2.** debased, depraved, base, perverted, wicked, sinful, evil, dissolute, profligate, abandoned, reprobate. **3.** putrid, impure, putrescent, rotten, contaminated, adulterated, tainted, corrupted, spoiled, infected. —*v.* **4.** bribe, lure, entice, suborn, buy off, lead astray. **5.** pervert, deprave, debase, vitiate, debauch. **6.** infect, taint, pollute, contaminate, adulterate, spoil, defile, putrefy, poison. —**Ant.** honest; honorable; pure, unspoiled, unadulterated; purify.

corruption, *n.* **1.** perversion, depravity, abandon, dissolution, sinfulness, evil, immorality, wickedness, profligacy, debauchery, degradation. **2.** dishonesty, baseness, bribery. **3.** decay, rot, putrefaction, putrescence, foulness, pollution, defilement, contamination, adulteration. —**Ant.** righteousness; honesty; purity.

cosmetic, *n.* **1.** makeup, greasepaint, cover-up, paint, rouge, foundation, pancake, war paint. —*adj.* **2.** beautifying, decorative, enhancing, improving, corrective. **3.** superficial, surface, shallow, cursory, passing, slapdash, skin-deep, lick and a promise, once over lightly.

cost, *n.* **1.** price, charge, expense, expenditure, outlay. **2.** sacrifice, loss, penalty, damage, detriment, suffering, pain.

costly, *adj.* valuable, dear, high-priced, high, exorbitant, outrageous, overpriced, top-dollar, at a premium; exclusive, sumptuous, expensive, precious, rich, splendid. —**Ant.** cheap.

coterie, *n.* society, association, set, circle, clique, club, brotherhood, fraternity, sisterhood, sorority, in crowd.

cottage, *n.* cabin, lodge, hut, shack, shanty, chalet, bungalow, lean-to, snuggery, retreat. —**Ant.** palace, castle.

counsel, *n.* **1.** advice, opinion, judgment, guidance, exhortation, direction, instruction, suggestion, recommendation, caution, warning, admonition. **2.** consultation, deliberation, discussion, consideration, forethought. **3.** purpose, plan, design, scheme. **4.** lawyer, solicitor, barrister, advocate, counselor, adviser, guide.

countenance, *n.* **1.** aspect, appearance, look, expression, mien. **2.** face, visage, physiognomy. **3.** favor, encouragement, aid, assistance, support, patronage, sanction, approval, approbation. —*v.* **4.** favor, encourage, support, aid, abet, patronize, sanction, approve. —**Ant.** condemn, prohibit.

counteract, *v.* neutralize, counterbalance, annul, countervail, offset, contravene, thwart, oppose, resist, hinder, check, frustrate, defeat. —**Ant.** cooperate, promote.

counterfeit, *adj.* **1.** spurious, false, fraudulent, forged, fake, imitation, bogus, phony, funny. **2.** sham, pretended, feigned, simulated, fraudulent, false, mock, fake, unreal, ersatz, make-believe, pretend, insincere, artificial, meretricious, pseudo, factitious, synthetic. —*n.* **3.** imitation, forgery, falsification, sham. —*v.* **4.** imitate, forge, copy, fake, falsify. **5.** resemble, simulate, feign, sham, pretend, dissemble. —**Ant.** genuine.

couple, *n.* **1.** pair, twosome, duo, duet; yoke, brace, two, span. —*v.* **2.** fasten, link, join, unite, associate, pair, conjoin, connect, combine, wed. —**Ant.** separate, disjoin.

courage, *n.* fearlessness, dauntlessness, intrepidity, fortitude, pluck, spirit, heroism, daring, audacity, bravery, mettle, valor, hardihood, bravado, gallantry, chivalry, boldness, dauntlessness, nerve, grit, guts, spunk, moxie. —**Ant.** cowardice.

course, *n.* **1.** advance, tack, direction, bearing. **2.** path, way, run, orbit, route, channel, way, road, track, passage. **3.** progress, passage, process. **4.** process, career, race. **5.** conduct, behavior, deportment. **6.** method, mode, procedure. **7.** sequence, succession, order, turn, regularity.

courteous, *adj.* civil, polite, well-mannered, well-bred, urbane, debonair, affable, gracious, courtly, respectful, obliging, well-behaved, formal, ceremonious, tactful, polished, urbane, civilized, proper, decorous, considerate, diplomatic, gentlemanly, ladylike, chivalrous, considerate. —**Ant.** discourteous, rude, curt, brusque.

cover, *v.* **1.** overlay, overspread, envelop, enwrap, clothe. **2.** shelter, protect, shield, guard, defend. **3.** hide, screen, cloak, disguise, secrete, veil, shroud, mask, enshroud. **4.** include, comprise, provide for, take in, embrace, contain, embody, comprehend. **5.** suffice, defray, offset, compensate for, counterbalance. —*n.* **6.** lid, top, case, covering, integument. **7.** protection, shelter, asylum, refuge, concealment, guard, defense. **8.** veil, screen, disguise, mask, cloak. —**Ant.** uncover; exposure.

coward, *n.* sissy, mouse, baby, spineless, jellyfish, invertebrate, milksop, mama's boy, Scaramouche, chicken, yellowbelly, milquetoast, Caspar Milquetoast, candyass, crybaby, shirker, scaredy cat, recreant, quitter, yellowbellied sapsucker, sneak, cur, girlie-man, shrinking violet, slacker, milksop, mollycoddle, weak sister, weakling, wuss, wimp, pantywaist, gutless wonder, doormat.

cowardice, n. fearfulness, baseness, cold feet, yellow streak, spinelessness, cravenness, faint-heartedness, cowardliness, pusillanimity, timidity. **—Ant.** boldness, bravery, temerity.

cowardly, adj. shy, spineless, frightened, namby-pamby, craven, pusillanimous, recreant, timid, timorous, faint-hearted, white-livered, lily-livered, chicken-hearted, yellow, fearful, afraid, scared. **—Ant.** brave, bold, valiant.

coy, adj. retiring, diffident, shy, self-effacing, bashful, modest, self-conscious, sheepish, unassuming, unpretentious, reserved, shrinking, timid, demure; evasive, reluctant, recalcitrant. **—Ant.** bold, pert, brazen, arch.

cozy, adj. comfortable, snug, secure, safe, warm, easeful, comforting, intimate, close, homespun, homelike, homey, soft, comfy, gemütlickeit, down-home, restful, relaxing, easy. **—Ant.** cold, unwelcoming.

crack, v. 1. break, snap, fracture, rupture, shiver, shatter, smash, split; crackle, craze. —n. 2. snap, report. 3. break, flaw, split, fissure, cleft, chink, breach, crevice, fracture, rift, gap, slit, rupture, breach, cranny, interstice.

crackpot, n. 1. eccentric, crank, character, oddity, odd duck, oddball, queer fish, crackbrain, screwball, nut case. 2. fanatic, zealot, maniac, faddist, believer, true believer. —adj. 3. impractical, crazy, lunatic, visionary, quixotic.

craft, n. 1. skill, ingenuity, dexterity, talent, deftness, cleverness, mastery, know-how, expertise, flair, genius, ability, aptitude, expertness. 2. skill, art, artfulness, craftiness, subtlety, artifice; cunning, deceit, guile, shrewdness, deceitfulness, deception, fraud, trickery, duplicity, foxiness, craftiness. 3. handicraft, trade, art, vocation, metier, calling, occupation, profession, work.

crafty, adj. skillful, sly, cunning, deceitful, artful, wily, insidious, treacherous, two-faced, duplicitous, tricky, designing, scheming, plotting, arch, shrewd, foxy, clever, canny, calculating, sneaky, shifty, dodgy. **—Ant.** gullible, naive.

cram, v. stuff, crowd, pack, compress, squeeze, overcrowd, gorge, jam, fill, glut, press.

cranky, adj. 1. ill-tempered, cross, crotchety, cantankerous, testy, tetchy, touchy, grouchy, crabby, surly, gruff, choleric, peevish, contentious, petulant, querulous, splenetic, churkish, curmudgeonly, waspish, perverse. 2. eccentric, queer, odd, strange, peculiar, curious. **—Ant.** amiable, good-natured; rational.

crave, v. 1. long for, desire, want, yearn or hunger for. 2. require, need. 3. beg for, beseech, entreat, implore, solicit, supplicate. **—Ant.** relinquish, renounce.

crazy, adj. 1. demented, insane, mad, deranged, lunatic, cracked, unbalanced, non compos mentis, certifiable, crackers, gaga, goofy, loony, off one's rocker, screwy, batty, bats, bonkers, out of one's gourd, screwy, nuts, nutty as a fruitcake, loco, bananas, out to lunch, meshuga, psycho, schizzy, schizoid, mental, out of one's mind, cuckoo, crackers, ditzy, crackbrained, a few bricks shy of a load, not playing with a full deck, off one's nut, flipped out, have a screw loose, have bats in one's belfry, mad as a hatter, unhinged, gone round the bend, wild-eyed, queer in the head, addled, ber-

serk, not all there, wacky, off one's rocker, not having all one's marbles. 2. silly, stupid, absurd, moronic, foolish, nonsensical, inane, preposterous, ridiculous, laughable, ludicrous, asinine, moronic, idiotic, harebrained, crackpot, screwball, crackbrain, cockamamie, fatuous, daffy, cockeyed. 3. ill-considered, impractical, imprudent, unsound, pointless, irrational, rash, reckless, quixotic, wild, visionary. 4. avid, zealous, excited, keen, eager, enthusiastic. 5. infatuated, stuck on, wild or mad about, nuts, nutty, ape, besotted, sweet on, enamored, gaga for. **—Ant.** sane, well-balanced; firm; strong.

create, v. make, form, bring into being, conceive, engender, generate, think up, frame, forge, fashion, fabricate, develop, manufacture, design, contrive, devise, initiate, start, dream up, begin, give birth to, produce, originate, invent, cause, occasion.

credible, adj. believable, trustworthy, reliable, satisfactory; probable, possible.

credit, n. 1. belief, trust, confidence, faith, reliance, credence. 2. influence, authority, power. 3. trustworthiness, credibility, reliability, reputability. 4. repute, estimation, character; reputation, name, esteem, regard, standing, position, rank, condition; notoriety. 5. commendation, honor, merit. 6. acknowledgment, ascription. —v. 7. believe, trust, confide in, have faith in, rely upon. **—Ant.** discredit.

credulous, adj. believing, trusting, trustful, unsuspecting, gullible, trustful, simple, silly, superstitious, impressionable, wide-eyed, easily fooled, naive, innocent. **—Ant.** incredulous, cautious, wary.

crime, n. offense, wrong, sin; infraction, violation, breach, misdemeanor, tort, felony: trespassing, breaking and entering, theft, robbery, assault, battery, statutory rape, rape, embezzlement, slander, libel, treason, manslaughter, murder.

criminal, adj. 1. felonious, unlawful, illegal, lawless, illicit, dishonest, crooked; evil, bad, corrupt, vile, black, immoral, amoral, villainous, depraved, disgraceful, reprehensible, nefarious, flagitious, iniquitous, wicked, sinful, wrong. —n. 2. convict, malefactor, evildoer, wrongdoer, lawbreaker, outlaw, miscreant, villain, desperado, mafioso, transgressor, sinner, culprit, delinquent, offender, felon; crook, hoodlum, gangster, thug, tough, mobster, hood.

cripple, v. disable, maim, weaken, impair, break down, ruin, destroy, lame, handicap, damage, debilitate.

crisis, n. climax, juncture, exigency, strait, pinch, emergency, disaster, catastrophe, calamity, danger.

criterion, n. standard, rule, principle, measure, parameter, touchstone, test, proof, sine qua non.

critic, n. 1. reviewer, appraiser, commentator, censor, judge, connoisseur, maven, expert. 2. censurer, carper, faultfinder, caviler.

critical, adj. 1. captious, carping, censorious, faultfinding, caviling, severe. 2. discriminating, tasteful, judicial, fastidious, nice, exact, precise. 3. decisive, climacteric, crucial, determining, momentous, important. 4. dangerous, perilous, risky, suspenseful, hazardous, precarious, ticklish. **—Ant.** unimportant, superficial, trivial.

criticism, n. 1. censure, disparagement, disapproval, condemnation, faultfinding, stricture, animadversion,

reflection. 2. review, critique, comment, judgment, appraisal, analysis, assessment, evaluation.

crooked, adj. 1. bent, curved, winding, devious, sinuous, tortuous, serpentine. 2. deformed, misshapen, disfigured, twisted, awry, askew, crippled. 3. criminal, dishonest, illicit, wrong, unscrupulous, knavish, tricky, fraudulent, dishonorable, unlawful, illegal, deceitful, insidious, crafty, treacherous. **—Ant.** straight; honest, upright.

cross, n. 1. trouble, misfortune, misery, burden. —v. 2. oppose, thwart, frustrate, baffle, contradict, foil. 3. interbreed, cross-breed, hybridize, blend, combine, mongrelize. —adj. 4. irate, piqued, annoyed, surly, choleric, grouchy, splenetic, huffy, pettish, in a pet, grumpy, crusty, querulous, short-tempered, petulant, fractious, irascible, waspish, crabbed, cranky, curmudgeonly, churlish, sulky, cantankerous, ill-natured, peevish, sullen, ill-tempered, intemperate, impatient, complaining, snappish, irritable, fretful, moody, touchy, testy, unpleasant, unkind, mean, angry, spiteful, resentful, gloomy, glowering, morose, sour, vexed. **—Ant.** aid, support; complaisant, amenable, agreeable, sweet.

crowd, n. 1. throng, multitude, mass, mob, flock, swarm, company, host, horde, herd. 2. masses, proletariat, plebians, rabble, mob, people, populace, hoi polloi, plebs, proles, citizenry. —v. 3. assemble, throng, swarm, flock together, herd. 4. push, shove, cram, pack, press, squeeze, cramp, force.

crude, adj. 1. unrefined, natural, unprocessed, original, unfinished, unprepared, coarse, raw. 2. rudimentary, primitive, unripe, immature, undeveloped, unpolished, unfinished, incomplete. 3. rustic, coarse, boorish, uncouth, rough, rude, clumsy, awkward. 4. undisguised, blunt, bare, rough, direct. **—Ant.** refined; aged, mature, ripe; complete, perfect; indirect, subtle.

cruel, adj. 1. barbarous, bloodthirsty, sanguinary, ferocious, fell, hard-hearted, harsh, heartless, callous, beastly, vicious, sadistic, fiendish, satanic, atrocious, barbaric, remorseless, uncaring, conscienceless, unsympathetic, merciless, unmerciful, relentless, implacable, pitiless, ruthless, truculent, brutal, savage, inhuman, brutish, barbarian, unmoved, unfeeling, unrelenting. 2. severe, hard, bitter. **—Ant.** kind, benevolent, beneficial.

crush, v. 1. squeeze, press, bruise, crumple, rumple, wrinkle, compress. 2. break, shatter, pulverize, granulate, powder, mash, smash, crumble, disintegrate. 3. put down, quell, overpower, subdue, overwhelm, overcome, quash, conquer, oppress.

cry, v. 1. lament, grieve, weep, bawl, sorrow, sob, shed tears, bewail, bemoan, squall, blubber, whimper, keen, snivel, moan, groan, mewl, pule, wail. 2. call, shout, yell, yowl, scream, exclaim, ejaculate, clamor, roar, shriek, howl, bellow, vociferate. 3. yelp, bark, bellow, hoot. —n. 4. shout, scream, wail, shriek, screech, yell, yowl, roar, whoop, bellow, clamor. 5. exclamation, outcry, clamor, ejaculation. 6. weeping, lament, lamentation, tears. **—Ant.** laugh.

crying, adj. 1. weeping, wailing, in tears, shedding tears, bawling, sobbing, blubbering. 2. flagrant, notorious, demanding, urgent, important, great, enormous. —**Ant.** laughing; nugatory, trifling.

cunning, n. **1.** ability, skill, adroitness, expertness, expertise, cleverness, genius, talent, art, aptitude, deftness, handiness, skillfulness, finesse. **2.** craftiness, shrewdness, artfulness, wiliness, trickery, intrigue, artifice, guile, craft, deceit, deceitfulness, slyness, deception. —adj. **3.** ingenious, skillful, expert, apt, deft, adroit, talented, able, handy. **4.** artful, wily, tricky, foxy, crafty, sly, intriguing, duplicitous, double-dealing. —**Ant.** stupidity, inability; dullness; naive, gullible, dull.

curb, n. **1.** restraint, check, control, bridle, rein. —v. **2.** control, restrain, check, bridle, repress, suppress, contain, subdue, reduce, diminish, hold down. —**Ant.** encourage, further, foster.

cure, n. **1.** course of treatment, therapy, medication, medicine, drug, prescription, remedy, restorative, specific, antidote. —v. **2.** remedy, restore, heal, make well or whole, mend, repair, correct, rectify, fix.

cure-all, n. remedy, cure, relief, nostrum, elixir, panacea, sovereign remedy, universal remedy, theriac, catholicon.

curious, adj. **1.** inquisitive, inquiring, prying, spying, peeping, snooping, interfering, intrusive, nosy, meddlesome, interested. **2.** strange, novel, unusual, singular, rare, foreign, exotic, queer, extraordinary, unique, odd, peculiar, eccentric, outré, offbeat, weird, bizarre, freakish, erratic, pixilated, quaint, outlandish, grotesque, abnormal, kinky. —**Ant.** blasé; common, commonplace, usual, customary.

current, adj. **1.** contemporary, contemporaneous, ongoing, known, in circulation, in the air, present-day, present, prevailing, prevalent, general, common, circulating, widespread, popular, rife. **2.** accepted, stylish, modish, latest, up-to-date, trendy, chic, voguish, in vogue, à la mode, fashionable. —n. **3.** stream, river, tide, flow, undercurrent; course, progress, progression, drift, mainstream, trend. —**Ant.** outmoded, uncommon, unpopular.

curse, n. **1.** imprecation, execration, fulmination, blasphemy, profanity, damnation, malediction, oath, denunciation, anathema, ban. **2.** evil, misfortune, calamity, trouble, vexation, annoyance, affliction, torment, bane, thorn, harm, cross to bear, hex, disaster, trial, plague, scourge. —v. **3.** blaspheme, swear, imprecate, execrate, fulminate, damn, denunciate, accurse, maledict, anathematize, condemn, profane, excommunicate. **4.** doom, destroy, plague, scourge, afflict, trouble, vex, annoy, burden, saddle, handicap. —**Ant.** blessing, benediction.

curt, adj. **1.** short, shortened, brief, abbreviated, concise, laconic, blunt, terse. **2.** rude, snappish, abrupt, dry, brusque, gruff. —**Ant.** long, drawn-out, lengthy; courteous, courtly.

curtail, v. lessen, diminish, decrease, dock, shorten, abbreviate, blunt, abridge, reduce, cut. —**Ant.** extend, expand.

cushion, v. absorb, insulate, lessen, diminish, check, slow, alleviate, meliorate, soften, mitigate, buffer, mollify.

custody, n. **1.** keeping, guardianship, care, custodianship, charge, safekeeping, watch, preserving, protection, preservation; possession, ownership, mastery, holding. **2.** imprisonment, confinement, detention, incarceration.

custom, n. habit, practice, usage, procedure, rule, convention, form, observance, formality.

customary, adj. usual, habitual, wonted, accustomed, conventional, common, regular, normal, routine, everyday, ordinary. —**Ant.** unusual, rare, uncommon, irregular.

cut, v. **1.** gash, slash, slit, lance, pierce, penetrate, incise, wound. **2.** wound, hurt, move, touch, slight, insult. **3.** divide, sever, carve, cleave, sunder, bisect, chop, hack, hew, fell, saw, lop off, crop. **4.** reap, mow, harvest. **5.** clip, shear, pare, prune. **6.** abridge, edit, shorten, abbreviate, curtail. **7.** lower, lessen, reduce, diminish. **8.** dissolve, dilute, thin, water, water down. —n. **9.** incision, wound, slash, gash, slit; channel, passage, strait. **10.** style, fashion, mode, kind, sort.

cutting, adj. **1.** sharp, keen, incisive, trenchant, piercing. **2.** mordant, mordacious, caustic, biting, acid, wounding, sarcastic, sardonic, bitter, severe. —**Ant.** dull; kind.

cynical, adj. distrustful, pessimistic, sarcastic, sardonic, satirical, unbelieving, disbelieving, sneering, contemptuous, derisive, cutting, scornful, ridiculing, censorious, captious, waspish, world-weary, jaded, supercilious, misanthropic, withering, biting, trenchant, hypercritical, ill-tempered, ill-natured, crusty, cantankerous, curmudgeonly. —**Ant.** innocent, trustful, credulous, naive, optimistic, hopeful; good-natured, pleasant.

D

dabbler, adj. **1.** nonprofessional, amateur, dilettante, putterer, tinkerer, Sunday painter. **2.** beginner, tyro, starter, novice, neophyte, abecedarian, tenderfoot, greenhorn, raw recruit. —**Ant.** professional, expert, adept.

dainty, adj. **1.** delicate, beautiful, charming, exquisite, fine, elegant, graceful, neat. **2.** choice, appetizing, tasty, toothsome, delicious, savory, palatable, tender, juicy, delectable, luscious. **3.** particular, fastidious, scrupulous, sensitive, overrefined, mincing, genteel, finicky, squeamish, finical, overnice. —**Ant.** clumsy, inelegant; disgusting, distasteful; sloppy.

damage, n. **1.** injury, harm, hurt, detriment, mischief, impairment, mutilation, destruction, devastation, vandalism, loss. —v. **2.** injure, harm, hurt, impair, mar, wound, mutilate, disfigure, deface, ruin, spoil, wreck. —**Ant.** improvement; improve, better.

damn, v. **1.** doom, condemn, sentence, excommunicate, consign to hell, banish, expel. **2.** condemn, attack, denounce, castigate, blast, blame, find fault with, criticize, upbraid, berate, reprove, reprimand, censure, repudiate. **3.** curse at, swear at, execrate, imprecate, vituperate, anathematize, fulminate, thunder against, blaspheme against.

damp, adj. **1.** moist, humid, dank, steamy, wet, clammy. —n. **2.** moisture, humidity, dankness, wet, wetness, dampness, fog, vapor, steam, clamminess. **3.** dejection, depression, dispiritedness, chill, discouragement. —**Ant.** dry, arid.

danger, n. hazard, risk, peril, threat, insecurity, imperilment, endangerment, uncertainty, jeopardy, liability, exposure; injury, evil. —**Ant.** security, safety.

dappled, adj. multicolored, multihued, varicolored, mottled, motley, spotted, polka-dot, flecked, maculate, freckled, freckly, pied, brindled, bespeckled, stippled, shadowed, shadowy.

dare, v. venture, hazard, risk, brave, challenge, defy, endanger, provoke, gamble, make bold, imperil, stake, try.

daredevil, adj. daring, rash, adventurous, risk-taking, reckless, heedless, foolhardy, wild, devil-may-care, venturesome, nervy, temerarious, gutsy, death-defying, impulsive, impetuous, madcap, audacious, intrepid, brave, imprudent, bold, fearless.

daring, n. **1.** courage, adventurousness, boldness, bravery, derring-do, pluck, mettle, spunk, guts, valor, grit, audacity, intrepidity, heroism. —adj. **2.** courageous, venturesome, adventurous, bold, brave, audacious, dauntless, undaunted, intrepid, fearless, valiant, valorous, gallant, chivalrous, doughty, hardy, rash, reckless, unafraid, plucky, gutsy, heroic. —**Ant.** cowardice; timid, cowardly, pusillanimous, fearful.

dark, adj. **1.** dim, gloomy, murky, umbrageous, shadowy, tenebrous, penumbral, dusky, unilluminated, unlit, sunless, shady, black, stygian, inky, jet-black, pitch-dark, pitchy, Cimmerian. **2.** gloomy, cheerless, dismal, dreary, dull, drab, bleak, mournful, dour, somber, grim, sad, morose, morbid, disheartening, discouraging. **3.** sullen, frowning, sulky, morose, dour, funereal, grim, somber, brooding, glum, moody, lugubrious, sour, depressed, grumpy, dyspeptic, glaring, threatening. **4.** unenlightened, ignorant, untaught, untutored, uneducated, unlettered, benighted, in the dark. **5.** obscure, recondite, abstruse, dim, deep, profound, cryptic, incomprehensible, unintelligible, occult, cabalistic, mysterious, puzzling, enigmatic, enigmatical, mystic, mystical. **6.** hidden, secret, concealed. **7.** infernal, wicked, sinful, nefarious, flagitious, foul, infamous, hellish, devilish, evil, bad, satanic, vile, base, iniquitous, sinister, villainous. —**Ant.** light, fair; cheerful; pleasant; intelligent, educated; clear, intelligible; open, revealed; heavenly, godly.

dash, v. **1.** strike, break; throw, thrust; splash, splatter. **2.** rush, dart, bolt, fly. —n. **3.** pinch, bit, suggestion, soupçon, hint, touch, tinge, smack, sprinkle, sprinkling. **4.** vigor, spirit, élan, flourish, éclat, bravado.

daunt, v. **1.** intimidate, overawe, subdue, dismay, frighten, appall. **2.** discourage, dispirit, dishearten, thwart, frustrate. —**Ant.** encourage, actuate.

dauntless, adj. fearless, bold, undaunted, intrepid, brave, courageous, daring, indomitable, unconquerable, valiant, valorous, unafraid, unflinching, stalwart, audacious, gallant, stouthearted, plucky, heroic, chivalrous, doughty, undismayed. —**Ant.** fearful, cowardly, timid, timorous.

dawdle, v. idle, linger, loiter, tarry, lag, poke along, dally, dilly-dally, loll, laze, lollygag, take one's time, procrastinate, temporize, put off, straggle, lie about, waste time. —**Ant.** hasten, hurry.

dawn, n. **1.** daybreak, sunrise, sunup, break of day, first light, crack of dawn, cockcrow, dawning. —v. **2.** appear, open, begin, break, arise, emerge, unfold, begin, originate. —**Ant.** sunset; disappear.

daydream, v. **1.** imagine, fantasize, dream, muse, pipe-dream, woolgather, build castles in the air. —n. **2.** reverie, dream, fantasy, imagining, woolgathering, fancy, musing, castle in Spain.

daze, v. **1.** stun, stupefy, blind, dazzle, bedazzle, shock, stagger, startle, astonish, astound, amaze, surprise, overcome, overpower, dumbfound, benumb, paralyze, floor, flabbergast, bowl over, blow one's mind. **2.** confuse, bewilder, befuddle, puzzle, mystify, baffle, perplex, nonplus. —n. **3.** confusion, flurry, whirl, spin, perplexity, bemusement, bewilderment, fog, state of shock, shell-shock, paralysis, spaciness, cloud, stupefaction.

dazzle, v. **1.** bedazzle, blind, daze, bedaze. **2.** astonish, amaze, stun, stupefy, overwhelm, astound, confound, flabbergast.

dead, adj. **1.** deceased, lifeless, extinct, inanimate, defunct, departed. **2.** insensible, numb, unfeeling, indifferent, cool, cold, callous, obtuse, frigid, affectless, phlegmatic, unemotional, unsympathetic, apathetic, lukewarm. **3.** infertile, barren, sterile. **4.** still, motionless, inert, inoperative, useless, dull, inactive, unemployed. **5.** smothered, extinguished, out. **6.** complete, absolute, utter, entire, total. **7.** straight, direct, unerring, exact, precise, sure. —**Ant.** alive, live, animate; fervid, eager, warm, animated; fertile; partial; crooked, indirect, devious.

deadly, adj. **1.** fatal, lethal, mortal. **2.** implacable, truculent, sanguinary, murderous, bloodthirsty, remorseless, ruthless.

deal, v. **1.** act, behave. **2.** trade, do business, traffic. **3.** distribute, dole, mete, dispense, apportion, allot, give, assign. —n. **4.** bargain, arrangement, pact, contract, transaction, negotiation, understanding. —**Ant.** gather, collect.

dear, adj. **1.** beloved, loved, precious, darling, esteemed, adored, cherished, prized, valued, pet, treasured, favorite, admired, honored. **2.** expensive, highpriced, costly, valuable, high; exorbitant, overpriced, outrageous. —**Ant.** hateful; cheap.

death, n. **1.** decease, demise, passing, dying, end, departure. **2.** stop, cessation, termination, extinction, obliteration, annihilation, destruction, decimation, finish, surcease, end, finale. —**Ant.** life.

debase, v. **1.** adulterate, corrupt, vitiate, contaminate, pollute, taint, mar, spoil, poison, defile, foul, befoul. **2.** lower, depress, reduce, impair, deteriorate, degrade, abase, demean, devalue, depreciate, demote, belittle, diminish. —**Ant.** purify; elevate, raise, exalt.

debate, n. **1.** discussion, argument, controversy, disputation, wrangle, polemic, one-on-one, dispute, contention. **2.** deliberation, consideration, reflection, cogitation, thought. —v. **3.** discuss, dispute, argue, contend, hold. **4.** deliberate, consider, discuss, argue. —**Ant.** agreement.

debt, n. liability, obligation, duty, due, debit, responsibility, encumbrance.

debut, n. **1.** introduction, appearance, arrival, coming out, introduction, inauguration, induction, initiation, unveiling, launching, installation, premiere. —v. **2.** come out, appear, arrive, enter, launch, premiere, make a debut.

decadence, n. decline, degeneration, retrogression, decay, fall, deterioration; corruption, dissolution, immorality, debauchery, dissipation, degeneracy, indulgence. —**Ant.** flourishing, progress; morality, improvement.

decay, n. **1.** deteriorate, decline, retrogress, degenerate, fall, fall away, wither, perish. **2.** decompose, putrefy,

rot, disintegrate. —n. **3.** decline, deterioration, degeneration, decadence, weakening, wasting, atrophy, collapse, downfall, impairment, dilapidation. **4.** decomposition, putrefaction, rotting, rot. —**Ant.** flourish, grow; progress.

deceit, n. **1.** deceiving, concealment, fraud, fraudulence, dishonesty, dissimulation, duplicity, deception, cheating, guile, hypocrisy, craftiness, slyness, insincerity, disingenuousness. **2.** trick, stratagem, artifice, wile, trickery, subterfuge, ploy, ruse, maneuver, hoax, double-cross, con, sham, chicanery, device, cozenage. **3.** falseness, duplicity, treachery, perfidy. —**Ant.** honesty, forthrightness.

deceitful, adj. **1.** dishonest, underhanded, lying, crafty, sly, cunning, duplicitous, hypocritical, scheming, insincere, disingenuous, false, hollow, empty, deceiving, fraudulent, designing, tricky, wily, two-faced. **2.** misleading, fraudulent, deceptive, counterfeit, illusory, fallacious, crooked, phony. —**Ant.** sincere, honest, forthright; genuine.

deceive, v. mislead, delude, cheat, cozen, dupe, gull, fool, hoax, cheat, swindle, betray, con, two-time, take for a ride, bamboozle, hoodwink, trick, double-cross, defraud, outwit; entrap, ensnare, betray.

decent, adj. **1.** fitting, appropriate, suited, suitable, apt, proper, fit, seemly, becoming. **2.** tasteful, modest, seemly, proper, decorous, respectable, clean, polite, dignified. —**Ant.** indecent, indecorous, improper, unfit, unsuitable.

deception, n. **1.** deceiving, gulling, fraudulence, dupery, dissimulation, hanky-panky, dishonesty, chicanery, trickery, double-dealing, underhandedness, duplicity, deceit, intrigue, hypocrisy, sophistry. **2.** artifice, sham, cheat, imposture, treachery, subterfuge, stratagem, ruse, hoax, fraud, trick, wile, maneuver, imposture, pretense.

deceptive, adj. deceiving, misleading, delusive, fallacious, specious, false, deceitful, illusory, unreliable. —**Ant.** genuine, authentic.

decide, v. determine, settle, resolve, purpose, conclude, arbitrate, judge, make up one's mind. —**Ant.** waver, hesitate, vacillate.

decided, adj. **1.** unambiguous, unquestionable, definite, unmistakable, undeniable, indeniable, indisputable, indubitable, certain, sure, emphatic, pronounced, absolute, unequivocal, categorical, incontrovertible. **2.** fixed, firm, adamant, stony, assertive, resolute, determined, resolved, unwavering, unhesitating, unfaltering. —**Ant.** undecided, ambiguous, indefinite; irresolute, hesitant.

decipher, v. decode, decrypt, unravel, break, crack, solve, figure out, translate, unriddle, work out, dope out, puzzle out, explain, elucidate, analyze, interpret, resolve. —**Ant.** encode, encipher, obscure, hide.

decisive, adj. incontrovertible, firm, resolute, determined, conclusive, final, finishing, irreversible, critical, crucial, mortal. —**Ant.** indecisive, irresolute, vacillating, wavering.

declaim, v. orate, perorate, hold forth, elocute, lecture, preach, sermonize, harangue, speechify, rant, rave, thunder, trumpet, shout, tub-thump, mouth off. —**Ant.** mumble, mutter.

declare, v. **1.** announce, proclaim, pronounce, decree, rule, proclaim, promulgate, trumpet. **2.** affirm, assert, say, proclaim, avow, aver, protest, make known, state, utter. **3.** manifest,

reveal, disclose, publish. —**Ant.** deny, controvert; suppress.

decline, v. **1.** refuse, avoid, reject, deny. **2.** stoop, condescend, lower oneself, abase, debase. **3.** fail, weaken, deteriorate, pale, diminish, degenerate, decay, languish. —n. **4.** failing, loss, enfeeblement, deterioration, degeneration, enervation, weakening, decay, diminution, lessening, retrogression. —**Ant.** agree; rise; improve, increase; strengthening.

decorate, v. adorn, bedeck, beautify, ornament, embellish, deck, deck out, dress, dress up, trim, spruce up, smarten, appoint, garnish, pretty up, titivate, accouter, furbish, dandify, prettify, doll up, gussy up. —**Ant.** simplify, streamline, strip.

decorous, adj. proper, decent, seemly, becoming, sedate, conventional, fitting, fit, suitable, seemly, dignified, correct, mannerly, refined, elegant, polite, genteel, demure. —**Ant.** indecorous, indecent, unseemly, unbecoming, unfit.

decorum, n. etiquette, gentility, good form, courtliness, punctilio, correctness, protocol, politeness, politesse, manners, manner, behavior, comportment, deportment, decency, propriety, dignity. —**Ant.** indecency, impropriety.

decrease, v. **1.** diminish, lessen, abate, fall off, decline, contract, dwindle, shrink, wane, ebb, subside. —n. **2.** abatement, diminution, reduction, decline, wane, subsidence, falling off, contraction, shrinking, dwindling, lessening, ebb, ebbing. —**Ant.** increase.

decree, n. **1.** order, directive, edict, command, commandment, dictum, injunction, mandate, proclamation, declaration, directive, instruction, prescription, prescript, ruling, fiat, ukase, pronunciamento. —v. **2.** order, direct, command, dictate, rule, require, prescribe, direct, enjoin, bid, mandate, instruct, pronounce, ordain.

decrepit, adj. weak, feeble, enfeebled, infirm, aged, superannuated, effete, broken down, falling apart, frail, wornout, wasted away, unfit, debilitated, enervated, disabled, crippled, doddering, dilapidated, deteriorating, crumbling, decaying, antiquated, tumbledown, ramshackle, rickety, derelict, creaky, run-down. —**Ant.** sturdy, strong, trim, in good shape, new.

decry, v. disparage, censure, belittle, discredit, deprecate, condemn, put down, criticize, attack, denounce, impugn, blast, lambaste, repudiate, reject, oppugn. —**Ant.** praise, laud, commend.

deduce, v. conclude, infer, reason, gather, assume, presume, judge, make out, dope out, conjecture, speculate, guess, reckon, suppose, surmise, think, understand.

deed, n. act, performance, exploit, achievement, action, feat, accomplishment.

deem, v. judge, regard, think, consider, hold, believe, account, count, suppose.

deep, adj. **1.** recondite, abstruse, abstract, difficult, profound, arcane, esoteric, inscrutable, occult, weighty; mysterious, obscure, unfathomable. **2.** grave, serious, grievous, intense, poignant, heartfelt, profound. **3.** absorbing, absorbed, involved, intense, heartfelt, great, extreme. **4.** penetrating, intelligent, bright, cunning, sagacious, wise, learned, erudite, knowledgeable, knowing, perspicacious, insightful, sharp-witted, acute, discerning, astute, shrewd, artful. —**Ant.** shallow.

deface, v. mar, disfigure, vandalize, mutilate, blemish, deform, spoil, soil, injure, harm; blot out, efface, obliterate, erase, eliminate. —Ant. beautify.

defeat, v. 1. overcome, conquer, overwhelm, vanquish, beat, subdue, trounce, whip, crush, best, do in, thrash, overthrow, subjugate, suppress, rout, check. 2. frustrate, thwart, foil, baffle, disconcert, unnerve, balk, foil, check, end, finish. —n. 3. overthrow, vanquishment, downfall, rout, setback, Waterloo. 4. frustration, bafflement. —Ant. yield, surrender, submit.

defect, n. 1. blemish, flaw, fault, shortcoming, imperfection, mar, blotch, scar, blot, foible, weakness. 2. deficiency, want, lack. —v. 3. desert, abandon, revolt, rebel, betray, go over to the other side. —Ant. sufficiency, perfection; support.

defective, adj. imperfect, incomplete, faulty, deficient, insufficient, flawed, broken, out of order, on the blink, on the fritz, inadequate. —Ant. perfect, complete, adequate.

defend, v. 1. guard, garrison, fortify, shield, shelter, screen, preserve, protect, keep watch over, safeguard, secure. 2. uphold, champion, argue for, back, support, maintain, assert, justify, plead, espouse, vindicate, stick up for, go to bat for. —Ant. attack.

defer, v. delay, postpone, put off, prevent, adjourn; procrastinate. —Ant. speed, expedite.

deference, n. 1. homage, honor, veneration, reverence, obeisance, tribute, respect, esteem, appreciation, admiration. 2. submission, subjection, submissiveness, compliance, acquiescence. —Ant. disrespect, insolence.

defiant, adj. antagonistic, insubordinate, contumacious, obstinate, unruly, headstrong, disobedient, stubborn, refractory, recalcitrant, rebellious, insolent, resistant; daring, courageous, brave, bold, audacious. —Ant. friendly, amiable; cowardly.

definite, adj. 1. defined, determined, specific, particular, exact, explicit, pronounced, fixed, precise, determinate. 2. certain, clear, express, sure, positive, assured, fixed, settled, confirmed. —Ant. indefinite, undetermined, indeterminate; uncertain, unclear.

deformed, adj. malformed, misshapen, crippled, lame, disfigured, distorted, twisted, grotesque, contorted, abnormal, warped, bent, perverted.

defy, v. challenge, resist, dare, brave, flout, face, confront, stand up to, thumb one's nose at, scorn, despise. —Ant. encourage, support, help.

degradation, n. humiliation, disgrace, debasement, dishonor, disrepute, discredit, shame, ignominy, abasement; degeneration, decline, decadence, degeneracy, perversity, depravity, turpitude, immorality, deterioration, corruption, baseness, debauchery, profligacy, prodigality. —Ant. exaltation.

degrade, v. 1. demote, depose, downgrade, lower, break, cashier, bust. 2. debase, deprave, lower, abase, vitiate, deteriorate. 3. humiliate, dishonor, disgrace, discredit, humble, shame, mortify, belittle, deprecate, cheapen, reduce, lower. —Ant. exalt.

dejected, adj. depressed, dispirited, disheartened, pouting, dour, low-spirited, discouraged, despondent, downhearted, sad, unhappy, miserable, lugubrious, glum, gloomy, grim, wretched, sullen, brooding, sulky, downcast, down, low, crestfallen, mel-

ancholy, blue, forlorn, disconsolate, sorrowful, morose, heartbroken, down in the dumps or mouth. —Ant. happy, cheerful, lighthearted.

delay, v. 1. put off, defer, postpone, procrastinate, defer, suspend, shelve, put on hold, put on ice, put on the back burner, table. 2. impede, slow, retard, hinder, detain, stop, arrest. 3. linger, loiter, tarry, wait, hesitate, lag behind, dawdle, stall, dally, mark time, drag one's feet, shilly-shally, dilly-dally. —n. 4. wait, holdup, delaying, procrastination, loitering, tarrying, dawdling, stay, setback, stop. 5. deferment, postponement, respite, deferring, interlude, hiatus, lull, interruption, suspension, stoppage, gap, lacuna. —Ant. expedite, hasten, speed.

delegate, n. 1. representative, deputy, envoy, ambassador, legate, agent. —v. 2. depute, entrust, commission, appoint, designate, name, assign, nominate, empower, authorize, accredit, mandate.

delete, v. cancel, strike or take out, erase, expunge, eradicate, remove, efface, blot out, obliterate.

deliberate, adj. 1. weighed, considered, studied, intentional, purposive, purposeful, premeditated, voluntary, willful, planned, calculated, conscious, prearranged, preconceived, cold-blooded. 2. careful, slow, unhurried, leisurely, methodical, thoughtful, circumspect, cautious, wary, measured, regular, even, sure, steady, unhesitating, unfaltering. —v. 3. weigh, consider, ponder over, reflect, study, think, ruminate, meditate. 4. consult, confer. —Ant. haphazard, unintentional; careless, unwary, incautious.

delicacy, n. 1. tenderness, sensitivity, tact, diplomacy, feeling, sensibility, consideration, thoughtfulness, solicitude, solicitousness. 2. refinement, finesse, dexterity, skill, deftness, facility, artistry, artfulness, adroitness, grace. 3. frailty, unhealthiness, fragility, feebleness, weakness, debility, valetudinarianism. 4. treat, rare treat, tidbit, morsel, choice morsel, dainty, goody, luxury, savory.

delicate, adj. 1. fine, dainty, exquisite, nice, fragile, graceful, elegant, choice. 2. faint, gradual, nice, precise, muted, soft, subdued, slight, subtle. 3. tender, fragile, frail, dainty, slight, weak, slender, sensitive, frangible. 4. critical, precarious, dangerous, ticklish, sensitive, sticky, tricky, touchy, hairy. 5. scrupulous, careful, painstaking, exact, exacting, precise, accurate; discriminating, fastidious, demanding. —Ant. rude, crude; blunt; rough, insensitive, unbreakable; careless.

delicious, adj. pleasing, luscious, palatable, savory, dainty, delicate, delectable, ambrosial, mouthwatering, toothsome, choice, flavorful, tasty, appetizing, scrumptious, yummy. —Ant. unpleasant, bitter, acrid, unpalatable.

delight, n. 1. enjoyment, pleasure, transport, delectation, gratification, bliss, joy, rapture, ecstasy. —v. 2. please, satisfy, transport, enrapture, enchant, charm, ravish, gratify, gladden, cheer, tickle, amuse, entertain, excite, thrill, captivate, entrance, fascinate. —Ant. disgust, revulsion, displeasure; displease.

delightful, adj. pleasing, pleasant, pleasurable, enjoyable, charming, enchanting, agreeable, delectable, rapturous, joyful, lovely, amusing, entertaining, diverting, exciting, thrilling; attractive, winning, winsome, engag-

ing, fascinating, captivating, ravishing, congenial, compatible. —Ant. unpleasant, disagreeable, revolting, repellent.

deliver, v. 1. give up, surrender, hand over, transfer, give over, yield, resign, cede, grant, relinquish. 2. give forth, emit, cast, direct, deal, discharge. 3. utter, pronounce, announce, proclaim, declare, communicate, publish, impart, promulgate, advance. 4. set free, liberate, release, free, emancipate. 5. redeem, rescue, save, release, extricate, disentangle. —Ant. limit, confine.

delude, v. mislead, deceive, beguile, cozen, cheat, dupe, gull, defraud, trick, con, lead down the garden path, take in, fool. —Ant. enlighten.

deluge, n. inundation, flood, downpour, rainstorm, torrent, monsoon, overflow, cataclysm, catastrophe.

delusion, n. deception, trick, stratagem, artifice, ruse, pretense; illusion, misconception, fancy, fallacy, error, mistake, hallucination.

demand, v. 1. claim, require, exact, ask for, call for, challenge, clamor for, need, want, necessitate, cry out for, insist on. 2. ask, inquire. —n. 3. claim, requisition, requirement, bid, behest, order, insistence, outcry, want, need, desire. 4. inquiry, question, asking, interrogation. —Ant. waive, relinquish.

demolish, v. ruin, destroy, put an end to, lay waste, raze, level, smash, topple, devastate, annihilate, crush, quash, dispose of. —Ant. construct, build, create.

demonstrate, v. 1. show, explain, explicate, expound, spell out, illustrate, make clear, make plain, make evident, prove, establish, show and tell. 2. exhibit, manifest, display, evidence, evince, present, disclose, divulge, expose. 3. protest, object, march, rally, boycott, strike, picket, parade.

demure, adj. 1. prudish, prim, overmodest, priggish, fastidious, dainty, delicate, squeamish, proper, Victorian, puritanical. 2. sober, modest, serious, sedate, decorous, coy. —Ant. licentious, immodest; indecorous.

denounce, v. 1. condemn, assail, censure, attack, stigmatize, decry, repudiate, oppose, oppugn, reject, criticize, impugn, revile, vilify, shame, pillory, slur, scorn, blame, brand, label. 2. inform against, accuse, denunciate, give away, betray, report, reveal, incriminate, implicate, complain about, charge. —Ant. commend, exonerate.

dense, adj. 1. thick, solid, heavy, close, compact, condensed, composed, impenetrable. 2. crowded, tight, packed, impassable. 3. stupid, foolish, dim, dim-witted, slow, slow-witted, dull, obtuse, stolid, cloddish, thick, dumb, oafish, cloddish.

deny, v. 1. dispute, controvert, oppose, refute, negate, gainsay, contradict. 2. turn down, forbid, decline, disallow, reject, renounce, abjure, disavow. 3. refuse, repudiate, disown, disavow, renounce, disclaim, forswear. —Ant. concede, agree, concur; accept; receive.

depart, v. 1. go away, start, set out, leave, quit, retire, withdraw, absent, go, retreat, exit, decamp, abscond, flee, skip, cut and run, disappear, vanish, evaporate, shove off, hit the road, split. 2. turn aside, diverge, deviate, vary, change, abandon, stray, veer. 3. die, pass on or away. —Ant. arrive; converge.

depict, v. 1. represent, portray, paint, limn, delineate, design, outline, sketch, reproduce, draw. 2. describe, characterize, give an account of, recount, relate, bring to life, tell tales of, reveal.

deplore, v. grieve, regret, lament, bemoan, bewail, mourn. —**Ant.** boast.

deposit, v. **1.** place, put, lay down, lay. **2.** throw down, drop, precipitate. **3.** entrust, leave, lodge, consign, keep, place, put; bank, save, store, hoard; secure. —n. **4.** sediment, deposition, precipitate; silt, mud, slime, sand, alluvium. **5.** coating; lode, vein, ore.

depraved, adj. corrupt, perverted, corrupted, immoral, wicked, evil, sinful, iniquitous, profligate, debased, dissolute, reprobate, indecent, unprincipled, unscrupulous, unregenerate, debauched, dirty, low, shameless, loose, wanton, libertine, lecherous, libidinous, lustful, carnal, concupiscient, degenerate, licentious, lascivious, lewd. —**Ant.** upright, honest; honorable, decorous, modest.

depress, v. **1.** dispirit, deject, oppress, dishearten, grieve, cast a pall over, burden, weigh down, discourage, dampen, chill, sadden. **2.** reduce, weaken, dull, debilitate, enervate, sap; diminish, reduce, bring down, lower. **3.** devalue, cheapen, depreciate, reduce, devaluate. **4.** humble, humiliate, abase, debase, degrade, abash, shame, bring low. —**Ant.** inspirit, encourage; elevate; gladden.

depressed, adj. dejected, downcast, sad, unhappy, miserable, morose, saddened, blue, despondent, melancholy, gloomy, morbid, in despair, desperate, hopeless, grieving, angst-ridden, moody, somber, in poor or low spirits, sullen, brooding, funereal, lugubrious, dour, grim, sulky, down, low, singing the blues, wretched, down in the mouth, discouraged, disheartened, melancholic, anguished, distraught, despairing, down in the dumps, disconsolate, desolate, glum, woebegone, forlorn, heartbroken, crestfallen, downhearted, dispirited, in low spirits, heavy-hearted. —**Ant.** happy, cheerful.

deprive, v. dispossess, bereave, strip, divest, disallow, deny, withhold, refuse, withdraw, remove, expropriate, take away. —**Ant.** endow.

deprived, adj. poor, impoverished, destitute, poverty-stricken, badly off, needy, in need, in want, wanting, underprivileged, disadvantaged, impecunious, low-born, pauperized, insolvent, indigent, penniless, poor as a church mouse, in straitened circumstances, pinched, down and out, broke, stony broke, hard up, born on the wrong side of the tracks.

depth, n. **1.** deepness, extent, measure, profoundness, profundity. **2.** obscurity, abstruseness, reconditeness, intricacy, complexity **3.** profundity, wisdom, sagacity, understanding, perception, perspicacity, acuteness, acuity, astuteness, insight, acumen, penetration. **4.** intensity, profundity, strength, vividness, brilliance, richness. **5.** deep, chasm, abyss, pit, bottomless pit, nadir.

derelict, adj. **1.** deserted, abandoned, neglected; ruined, run-down, tumbledown, dilapidated. **2.** neglectful, negligent, remiss, delinquent, careless, heedless, lax, slack, irresponsible, slipshod, sloppy, slovenly. —n. **3.** tramp, vagrant, outcast, pariah, loafer, good-for-nothing, vagabond, slacker, hobo, bum, street person, homeless person, parasite on society, ne'er-do-well, panhandler.

derogatory, adj. disparaging, belittling, demeaning, derogative, depreciatory, deprecatory, depreciative, slight-

ing, uncomplimentary, insulting, disdainful, scornful, contemptuous, spiteful, abusive, pejorative, defamatory, malicious, maligning, critical, censorious, negative, abasing, debasing, lowering, minimizing, denigrating, diminishing, detracting, offensive. —**Ant.** flattering, complimentary.

descent, n. **1.** falling, fall, sinking, descending. **2.** inclination, declination, slope, slant, dip, drop, plunge, plummet, declivity, grade, decline. **3.** extraction, lineage, derivation, parentage, genealogy. —**Ant.** ascent, rise.

describe, v. narrate, account, recount, recite, report, chronicle, tell, relate; delineate, portray, characterize, limn, represent, depict, identify, label, style.

desert, n. **1.** waste, wilderness, Sahara, barrens, infertile land, heath, tundra, wild, dust bowl. —adj. **2.** desolate, barren, forsaken, wild, uninhabited, lonely, arid, bare, vacant, empty, uncultivated. —v. **3.** abandon, forsake, leave behind, give up, relinquish, leave, quit, renounce, maroon, strand, abscond.

design, v. **1.** plan, devise, project, contrive, invent, create, conceive, originate, think up, develop, form, organize, frame, fashion, forge, mold, make. **2.** intend, purpose, mean, propose. **3.** sketch, draw, delineate. —n. **4.** plan, scheme, proposal, proposition, project, conception, study, undertaking, enterprise. **5.** sketch, plan, drawings, blueprint, outline, draft, pattern, layout, diagram, map, model, prototype. **6.** end, intention, purpose, intent, aim, object, goal, point, target. —**Ant.** achieve, execute, accomplish; execution; accident, fortuity, chance.

designing, adj. contriving, scheming, sly, artful, cunning, tricky, wily, crafty, deceitful, treacherous, arch, Machiavellian, astute, unscrupulous. —**Ant.** open, candid, frank, honest, guileless, artless, naive.

desire, v. **1.** wish or long for, crave, want, wish, covet, fancy. **2.** ask, importune, request, solicit. —n. **3.** longing, hankering, yen, ache, craving, yearning, wish, need, hunger, appetite, thirst. **4.** request, wish, aspiration. **5.** lust, libido, sex drive, lasciviousness, concupiscence, sexual appetite, sexuality, sensuality, prurience, libidinousness, lustfulness, horniness, randiness, the hots, hot pants. —**Ant.** abominate, loathe, abhor.

desolate, adj. **1.** barren, laid waste, devastated, ravaged, scorched, destroyed. **2.** deserted, empty, bleak, remote, uninhabited, desert, lonely, alone, lone, solitary, forsaken, lonesome. **3.** miserable, wretched, unhappy, sad, woeful, woebegone, disconsolate, inconsolable, forlorn, lost, cheerless, joyless, comfortless, down, sorrowful, mournful, gloomy, dejected, downcast, depressed, hopeless, dreary, dismal. —v. **4.** lay waste, devastate, ravage, ruin, sack, destroy, despoil. **5.** depopulate. **6.** sadden, depress, dismay, dishearten, daunt, dispirit, discourage. **7.** forsake, abandon, desert. —**Ant.** fertile, populous, crowded; happy, delighted; cultivated; build, create; cheer.

despair, n. hopelessness, desperation, despondency, discouragement, gloom, disheartenment, misery, melancholy, woe, anguish, grief, distress. —**Ant.** encouragement, hope, optimism.

desperate, adj. **1.** reckless, foolhardy, impetuous, wild, mad, rash, headlong, frantic. **2.** urgent, pressing, compelling, acute, critical, serious, grave; precarious, perilous, life-threatening, haz-

ardous, tenuous, dangerous. **3.** wretched, forlorn, hopeless, desolate, frantic, at one's wit's end, at the end of one's rope or tether. **4.** extreme, excessive, great, heroic, prodigious. —**Ant.** careful; hopeful.

despicable, adj. contemptible, vile, base, worthless, detestable, scurvy, sordid, wretched, miserable, ignoble, ignominious, shabby, shameful, reprehensible, mean, abject, low, pitiful. —**Ant.** lovable, likable, worth.

despise, v. scorn, disdain, spurn, sneer at, look down on, be contemptuous of; hate, detest, abhor, loathe. —**Ant.** love, like, admire.

despite, prep. notwithstanding, in spite of, undeterred by, regardless of, without considering, ignoring, without regard for.

despondency, n. depression, dejection, discouragement, melancholy, gloom, desperation, despair, sadness, blues, grief, anguish, sorrow, misery, low spirits, blue meanies. —**Ant.** elation, joy, happiness.

despondent, adj. depressed, dejected, discouraged, dour, wretched, heartbroken, spiritless, moody, somber, morose, sorrowful, unhappy, down, downcast, miserable, gloomy, grim, sullen, brooding, sulking, desolate, forlorn, disconsolate, disheartened, downhearted, melancholy, sad, blue, dispirited, hopeless, low-spirited, low, down in the mouth, down in the dumps. —**Ant.** elated, joyful, happy.

destiny, n. fate, karma, kismet, lot, fortune, future, doom, destination, end, outcome, disposition.

destitute, adj. needy, poor, indigent, penniless, impoverished, in want, insolvent, down-and-out, hard up, broke, stony broke, poverty-stricken, bankrupt, down on one's luck, down at the heels, on one's uppers, badly off. —**Ant.** affluent, rich, opulent.

destroy, v. **1.** smash, demolish, raze, spoil, consume, level, wreck, crush, wipe out, tear down, break up, trash, ruin, waste, ravage, devastate, desolate, lay waste. **2.** end, terminate, finish, do away with, bring to an end, exterminate, extinguish, extirpate, annihilate, eradicate, slay, kill, uproot. **3.** nullify, invalidate, counteract, neutralize, cancel, reverse, annul, stop. —**Ant.** create; originate, start.

destruction, n. **1.** extinction, extermination, desolation, havoc, laying waste, rack and ruin, devastation, ruin, eradication. **2.** killing, liquidation, assassination, slaying, holocaust, annihilation, murder, slaughter, death, massacre, genocide. **3.** plague, pandemic, deluge, catastrophe, calamity. —**Ant.** birth, origin; creation.

destructive, adj. ruinous, harmful, injurious, baneful, poisonous, unwholesome, damaging, detrimental, dangerous, hurtful, toxic, noxious, baleful, pernicious, mischievous, deleterious, fatal, deadly, lethal; extirpative, eradicative. —**Ant.** salutary; creative.

detain, v. **1.** delay, arrest, retard, stop, slow, stay, check, keep. **2.** impound, lock up, put away, hold, restrain, confine, arrest. **3.** keep back, withhold, retain. —**Ant.** promote, encourage; advance.

detect, v. discover, catch, expose, find, find out, ascertain, uncover, locate, determine, dig up, unearth, learn, hear of, hear; note, notice, spot, observe, perceive, identify, discern, feel, catch, scent, smell.

deter, v. discourage, restrain, dissuade, hinder, prevent, stop, inhibit, intimidate, daunt, obstruct, check, impede, frighten off. —Ant. encourage, further, continue.

determine, *v.* **1.** settle, decide, conclude, judge. **2.** conclude, infer, learn, find out, discover, ascertain, verify, check, certify. **3.** affect, act on, shape, govern, regulate, dictate, fix, decide, establish, condition, influence, resolve. **4.** impel, induce, lead, incline.

determined, *adj.* staunch, resolute, unflinching, firm, inflexible, rigid, rigorous, unfaltering, unwavering, dogged, strong-willed, tenacious, intent, fixed, persistent, persevering, steady, stubborn, obstinate, adamant, single-minded, unflinching, unhesitating, unyielding. —Ant. irresolute, vacillating, wavering, faltering, flexible.

detest, *v.* abhor, hate, loathe, abominate, execrate, despise, scorn, hold in contempt, revile, disdain, sneer at, look down on. —Ant. love, like.

detestable, *adj.* abominable, hateful, execrable, loathsome, vile, odious, abhorred, abhorrent, despicable, contemptible, beneath contempt, sordid, miserable, scurvy, vile, shabby, ignoble, mean, base, low, reprehensible, ignominious, shameful. —Ant. lovable, likable.

detriment, *n.* loss, damage, injury, hurt, harm, ill, impairment, disadvantage, prejudice, drawback, liability. —Ant. advantage, profit.

devastate, *v.* ravage, lay waste, desolate, destroy, strip, pillage, plunder, sack, spoil, despoil, raze, ruin, wreck, demolish, obliterate. —Ant. build, erect, create.

development, *n.* **1.** expansion, growth, elaboration, progress, increase, enlargement, increment, advance, improvement. **2.** opening, disclosure, developing, unfolding, maturing, maturation, evolution, maturity. —Ant. deterioration, decadence, degeneration.

deviate, *v.* depart, swerve, digress, diverge, part, wander, veer, err, stray, drift, turn aside *or* away. —Ant. converge.

device, *n.* **1.** invention, contrivance, gadget, mechanism, machine, implement, utensil, apparatus, instrument, appliance, tool, contraption, widget. **2.** plan, scheme, project, design, expedient. **3.** wile, ruse, artifice, shift, trick, stratagem, evasion, maneuver. **4.** design, figure, emblem, trademark, badge, logotype, colophon, symbol, crest, seal; motto, slogan, legend.

devilish, *adj.* satanic, diabolic, diabolical, demonic, demoniac, infernal, Mephistophelian, fiendish, hellish, villainous, sinister, wicked, evil, sinful, heinous, malign, malevolent, cruel; impish, naughty, mischievous, prankish. —Ant. good, fine, upstanding, righteous, godly.

devise, *v.* order, arrange, plan, think out, contrive, invent, prepare, concoct, scheme, project, design, make up, conceive, dream up, formulate, create, frame. —Ant. disorder, disarrange.

devote, *v.* assign, apply, consign, give up, commit, allocate, set aside, appropriate, pledge, dedicate, consecrate. —Ant. resign, relinquish.

devotion, *n.* **1.** dedication, consecration. **2.** attachment, fondness, loyalty, allegiance, affection, love. **3.** devotedness, zeal, fervor, intensity, fanaticism, enthusiasm, willingness, ardor, eagerness, earnestness. **4.** religion, religiousness, piety, faith, devoutness, sanctity, saintliness, godliness, reverence, holiness, spirituality.

devout, *adj.* **1.** churchgoing, staunch, dedicated, faithful, reverent, pious, devoted, religious, worshipful, holy, saintly. **2.** earnest, sincere, hearty, serious, honest, genuine, heartfelt, zealous. —Ant. atheistic, agnostic; insincere, scornful.

dexterous, *adj.* skillful, supple, lithe, agile, adroit, deft, handy, nimble, clever, expert, apt, ready, quick, able, keen, sharp, artful. —Ant. clumsy, awkward, maladroit, unapt.

dialect, *n.* **1.** provincialism, idiom, localism, jargon, patois, variant, vernacular, cant, slang, argot. **2.** language, tongue, speech.

diction, *n.* phraseology, wording, expression, terminology, word choice, vocabulary, style, usage, grammar, language; distinctness, enunciation, pronunciation.

die, *v.* **1.** decease, pass away *or* on, perish, expire, depart. **2.** cease, stop, end, vanish, disappear. **3.** weaken, fail, subside, fade, sink, faint, decline, wither, decay.

difference, *n.* discrepancy, disparity, dissimilarity, inconsistency, unlikeness, variation, diversity, imbalance, disagreement, inequality, dissimilitude, divergence, contrast, contrariety; discrimination, distinction. —Ant. similarity; agreement.

different, *adj.* **1.** differing, unlike, diverse, discrete, conflicting, dissimilar, disparate, distinct, opposite, separate, distinguishable, divergent, altered, changed, contrary, contrasted, deviant, deviating, variant. **2.** sundry, divers, miscellaneous, various, manifold, assorted, multifarious, numerous, abundant, varied, many, several. **3.** unusual, peculiar, unique, odd, singular, distinctive, extraordinary, special, remarkable, bizarre, strange, weird, rare, unconventional, original, new, novel, out of the ordinary, exceptional. —Ant. similar, like; uniform, identical.

differentiate, *v.* **1.** modify, specialize, transform, convert, adapt, adjust, alter, change. **2.** distinguish, oppose, set off, tell apart, discriminate, separate, contrast. —Ant. group together.

difficult, *adj.* **1.** hard, arduous, tough, strenuous, onerous, laborious, burdensome, toilsome. **2.** obscure, complex, intricate, puzzling, enigmatic, thorny, baffling, profound, abstruse, perplexing. **3.** intractable, recalcitrant, contrary, refractory, stubborn, obstinate, unmanageable, austere, rigid, reserved, forbidding, unaccommodating. **4.** fastidious, particular, fussy, demanding, finicky, nitpicking, critical, troublesome. —Ant. easy, simple; clear, plain; accommodating; careless, sloppy.

difficulty, *n.* **1.** dilemma, predicament, quandary, fix, exigency, hardship, obstacle, distress, pitfall, snag, hindrance, strain, tribulation, emergency, trouble, problem. **2.** reluctance, unwillingness, obstinacy, stubbornness. —Ant. ease; willingness.

diffident, *adj.* shy, self-conscious, self-effacing, bashful, abashed, embarrassed, timid, sheepish, modest. —Ant. forward, bold, unabashed.

digest, *v.* **1.** understand, assimilate, study, ponder, consider, comprehend, take in, grasp, study, think over, meditate on, contemplate, ruminate over, reflect on. **2.** arrange, systematize, classify, codify. —*n.* **3.** summary, epitome, abstract, synopsis, abridgment, brief, conspectus, condensation, précis, resume, abbreviation. —Ant. expand.

dignify, *v.* ennoble, exalt, uplift, glorify, honor, elevate, grace, build up, raise, promote, magnify, distinguish, enhance, improve, better, upgrade. —Ant. demean, humble.

digress, *v.* deviate, diverge, wander, maunder, expatiate, go off on a tangent, detour, ramble, stray.

dilate, *v.* expand, spread out, enlarge, engross, widen, extend, swell, distend. —Ant. shrink, constrict.

dilemma, *n.* predicament, problem, question, quandary, difficulty, strait, plight, trouble; double bind, catch-22, impasse, deadlock, stalemate, bind, fix, jam, spot, pickle.

dilettante, *n.* **1.** amateur, dabbler, Sunday painter, trifler, nonprofessional, tyro, putterer. **2.** connoisseur, aesthete, expert, authority, specialist, collector, maven.

diligence, *n.* persistence, effort, application, industry, assiduity, industriousness, steadiness, steadfastness, focus, concentration, perseverance, assiduousness, sedulousness, constancy, devotion, earnestness, conscientiousness, constancy, thoroughness, scrupulousness, meticulousness, punctilio. —Ant. carelessness, laziness.

diligent, *adj.* industrious, assiduous, sedulous, occupied, busy, intent, steady, steadfast, focused, concentrating, constant, attentive, persistent, painstaking, persevering, indefatigable, untiring, tireless, unremitting, hardworking, thorough, meticulous, scrupulous, punctilious. —Ant. lazy, careless; remiss.

dim, *adj.* **1.** obscure, dark, shadowy, fuzzy, tenebrous, gloomy, dusky, nebulous, hazy, cloudy, foggy, misty, murky, crepuscular. **2.** indistinct, unclear, ill-defined, blurred, vague, faint, imperceptible, weak, indiscernible, confused, indefinite. **3.** dull, slow, stupid, obtuse, doltish, foolish, dense, thick, dumb. —*v.* **4.** darken, cloud, obscure, dull. **5.** blur, dull, fade. —Ant. clear, bright, distinct; definite.

diminish, *v.* lessen, reduce, decrease, subside, ebb, dwindle, shrink, decline, lower, curtail, cut down, truncate, abbreviate, shorten, abridge, compress, condense, make smaller *or* shorter, abate, contract, shrivel up. —Ant. increase.

diminutive, *adj.* little, small, tiny, dwarf, dwarflike, dwarfish, minute, microscopic, submicroscopic, miniature, petite, minuscule, undersized, pygmy, midget, Lilliputian, teenyweeny, itsy-bitsy. —Ant. large, immense.

dip, *v.* **1.** plunge, immerse, dive, duck, submerge, douse, bathe, dunk. **2.** sink, drop, incline, decline, slope downward, fall, go down, descend, sag, subside, slump, lower. —Ant. rise.

diplomatic, *adj.* politic, tactful, artful, discreet, prudent, wise, considerate, sensitive, courteous, polite, thoughtful, discerning, perceptive, perspicacious, shrewd, knowing. —Ant. tactless, rude.

direct, *v.* **1.** guide, advise, regulate, conduct, manage, control, handle, run, administer, supervise, operate, dispose, lead, govern, rule. **2.** order, command, instruct, require, tell, charge, dictate, enjoin. **3.** point, focus, train, level, aim. —*adj.* **4.** straight, undeviating. **5.** immediate, personal, unbroken, simple, evident. **6.** straightforward, downright, plain, categorical, unequivocal, unambiguous, express, open, sincere, outspoken, plain-spoken, candid, honest, blunt, uninhibited, unreserved, frank, earnest, ingenuous, obvious, naive. —**Ant.** divert, mislead; crooked; devious; ambiguous, sly.

dirty, *adj.* **1.** soiled, foul, unclean, filthy, squalid, defiled, grimy, dingy. **2.** dirtying, soiling, befouling, besmirching. **3.** vile, mean, base, vulgar, low, groveling, scurvy, shabby, contemptible, despicable. **4.** indecent, obscene, nasty, lascivious, lewd, lecherous, licentious, immoral, amoral, risqué, off-color, prurient, salacious, coarse, blue, lubricious, bawdy, earthy, libidinous, smutty, ribald, scabrous, X-rated, pornographic, adult. —**Ant.** clean; elevated, exalted; decent, moral.

disability, *n.* handicap, impairment, defect, infirmity; incapacity, disqualification, inability, incompetence, impotence, incapability, unfitness, helplessness. —**Ant.** ability, capacity, capability.

disable, *v.* weaken, damage, ruin, impair, harm, hurt, destroy, cripple, incapacitate, enfeeble, paralyze; disqualify, incapacitate, eliminate. —**Ant.** strengthen; qualify; include.

disadvantage, *n.* **1.** drawback, inconvenience, hindrance, deprivation, flaw, defect, handicap, liability, shortcoming, weakness, weak spot, fault. **2.** detriment, hurt, harm, damage, injury, loss, disservice. —**Ant.** advantage.

disappear, *v.* vanish, fade, cease, pass away, end, evaporate, vaporize, evanesce, become extinct, perish, die. —**Ant.** appear.

disappointment, *n.* **1.** setback, loss, blow, fiasco, calamity, disaster, dissatisfaction, fizzle, washout, failure, defeat, frustration, unfulfillment. **2.** dejection, depression, discouragement, distress, regret, disenchantment, sorrow, letdown, mortification, frustration, chagrin. —**Ant.** fulfillment, victory; consummation.

disapprove, *v.* object to, criticize, condemn, censure, decry, put down, deplore, deprecate, belittle, look down on, frown on, knock, look down one's nose at, reproach, take exception to, find disfavor with, disdain, scorn, repudiate, oppugn, oppose.

disaster, *n.* misfortune, calamity, mischance, mishap, accident, misadventure, blow, debacle, cataclysm, trouble, act of God, catastrophe, adversity, affliction. —**Ant.** luck, fortune.

disband, *v.* break up, disorganize, demobilize, dissolve, disperse, dismiss, scatter, separate, retire. —**Ant.** organize, unite.

discern, *v.* **1.** perceive, see, recognize, notice, apprehend, discover, descry, espy, come upon, behold. **2.** discriminate, distinguish, differentiate, judge.

discharge, *v.* **1.** unload, disburden, relieve, unburden. **2.** remove, send forth, get rid of, expel, eject, emit. **3.** fire, shoot, set off, detonate. **4.** relieve, release, absolve, exonerate, clear, acquit, liberate, set free, free. **5.** fulfill, perform, execute, observe. **6.** dismiss, cashier, fire, remove, expel, break. **7.** pay, honor, disburse, make good on, liquidate, dissolve, settle. —*n.* **8.** emission, ejection, expulsion, removal, evacuation, voiding. **9.** detonation, firing, shooting. **10.** fulfillment, execution, performance, observance. —**Ant.** load, burden.

disciple, *n.* follower, adherent, apostle, devotee, votary; partisan, fan, aficionado, supporter; pupil, student, scholar, apprentice, proselyte, learner. —**Ant.** leader; rebel.

discipline, *n.* **1.** training, drill, exercise, instruction, practice, regimen, inculcation, indoctrination, schooling. **2.** penalty, punishment, chastisement, castigation, correction. **3.** subjection, direction, rule, order, control, regulation, subjugation, government. **4.** rules, regulations. —*v.* **5.** train, exercise, drill, practice, instruct, teach, condition, coach, break in, indoctrinate, educate. **6.** punish, correct, chastise, castigate, reprove, reprimand, rebuke, scold.

disclose, *v.* **1.** reveal, make known, make public, publicize, impart, report, inform, divulge, show, tell, unveil, communicate. **2.** uncover, lay open, expose, bare, bring to light; muckrake. —**Ant.** conceal, hide; cover.

disconcert, *v.* disturb, confuse, perturb, ruffle, discompose, discomfort, make uneasy, put off, fluster, agitate, upset, unsettle, baffle, puzzle, rattle, shake up, discombobulate, perplex, bewilder, frustrate, embarrass, abash; disarrange, disorder. —**Ant.** calm; order, arrange.

disconsolate, *adj.* inconsolable, unhappy, desolate, forlorn, heart-broken, sad, melancholy, dejected, gloomy, miserable, cheerless, sorrowful, depressed, blue, wretched, downhearted, in low spirits, morose, dour, sullen, brooding, anxious, hopeless. —**Ant.** happy, cheerful, delighted.

discontent, *n.* discontentment, dissatisfaction, uneasiness, inquietude, restlessness, unhappiness, distaste, malaise, agitation, restiveness, displeasure. —**Ant.** contentment; satisfaction, pleasure, ease, restfulness.

discontinue, *v.* put an end to, interrupt, stop, cease, quit, desist, drop, suspend, break off, give up, terminate. —**Ant.** continue, further.

discourage, *v.* **1.** dishearten, dispirit, daunt, depress, deject, overawe, cow, awe, subdue, abash, embarrass, dismay, intimidate, frighten. **2.** dissuade, deter, hinder, prevent, obstruct, throw cold water on, inhibit, suppress, stop, hamper, oppose, prevent. —**Ant.** encourage, hearten, embolden.

discouragement, *n.* **1.** depression, dejection, hopelessness, despair, frustration, dismay, disappointment, disenchantment, chagrin, intimidation. **2.** deterrent, damper, wet blanket, cold water, impediment, obstacle, obstruction, setback, barrier, opposition, hindrance. —**Ant.** encouragement.

discover, *v.* **1.** learn of, ascertain, unearth, determine, track down, identify, locate, smoke out, ferret out, dig up; find out, detect, espy, descry, discern, see, notice. **2.** originate, bring to light, invent, conceive of, devise, contrive, pioneer, stumble on. —**Ant.** conceal.

discreet, *adj.* wise, judicious, prudent, circumspect, tactful, sensitive, thoughtful, politic, artful, diplomatic, cautious, careful, heedful, considerate, wary, guarded, watchful. —**Ant.** indiscreet, careless, imprudent; incautious, inconsiderate.

discrepancy, *n.* gap, disparity, lacuna, dissimilarity, deviation, divergence, incompatibility, difference, inconsistency, incongruity, disagreement, discordance, contrariety, variance, variation. —**Ant.** similarity, congruity, consistency, concord, accord, agreement.

discriminate, *v.* **1.** distinguish, separate, discern, make out, differentiate. **2.** favor, disfavor, segregate, set apart, show prejudice, be biased, be intolerant. —**Ant.** group, unite; indiscriminate, undistinguished.

discuss, *v.* examine, reason, deliberate, argue, debate, talk over, sift, consider, converse about, chat, review, consult on, thrash out.

disdain, *v.* **1.** sneer, mock, jeer at, snub, deride, insult, taunt, ridicule, lord it over, look down one's nose at, ignore, repudiate, reject, abhor, loathe, execrate, despise, scorn, spurn. —*n.* **2.** contempt, derision, superiority, mockery, dismissal, ridicule, rejection, repudiation, scorn, contumely, contemptuousness, haughtiness, arrogance, superciliousness, hauteur. —**Ant.** accept, like, love; love, admiration, regard.

disdainful, *adj.* contemptuous, scornful, haughty, arrogant, derisive, sneering, superior, pompous, proud, snobbish, lordly, jeering, mocking, insolent, insulting, hoity-toity, stuck-up, highfalutin, high and mighty, swaggering, aloof, standoffish, supercilious, contumelious. —**Ant.** friendly, amiable, considerate, attentive.

disease, *n.* morbidity, illness, sickness, ailment, complaint, affection, disorder, malady, abnormality, derangement, distemper, indisposition, infirmity, affliction, infection, cancer, plague. —**Ant.** health, salubriety.

disfigure, *v.* mar, deface, injure, deform, spoil, ruin, blemish, damage, scar, mutilate, impair, distorted. —**Ant.** beautify.

disgrace, *n.* **1.** ignominy, shame, dishonor, infamy, disfavor, humiliation, embarrassment, degradation, debasement, discredit, vilification, mortification, disapproval, disapprobation, disparagement, stain, taint, notoriety, baseness. **2.** odium, obloquy, degradation, opprobrium, scandal, blemish, aspersion, slur, stigma, smirch, black mark. —*v.* **3.** shame, dishonor, defame, disfavor, humiliate, disapprove, discredit, degrade, debase, stain, sully, taint, tarnish, reproach.

disgust, *v.* **1.** sicken, nauseate, turn one's stomach. **2.** offend, displease, repel, repulse, revolt. —*n.* **3.** distaste, nausea, loathing, hatred, abhorrence, disrelish. **4.** dislike, detestation, repugnance, aversion, dissatisfaction, antipathy, contempt, hatred, odium, animus, animosity, enmity, antagonism. —**Ant.** please, delight, attract; relish, liking, love; satisfaction.

disgusting, *adj.* offensive, offending, loathsome, sickening, nauseous, nauseating, sick-making, fulsome, off-putting, repellant, obnoxious, gross, vile, nasty, repulsive, revolting, odious, hateful, repugnant, foul, abominable, abhorrent, distasteful, detestable. —**Ant.** delightful, delectable, attractive, beautiful.

dishonest, *adj.* unprincipled, immoral, duplicitous, unreliable, untrustworthy, underhanded, dishonorable, unfair, cheating, lying, double-dealing, unprincipled, hypocritical, crooked, shady, unscrupulous, conniving, corrupt, knavish, thievish, deceitful, treacherous, perfidious; false, fraudulent, counterfeit, fake, bogus, artificial, phony. —**Ant.** honest, upright.

dishonorable, *adj.* **1.** ignoble, base, depraved, debased, inglorious, degrading, disgraceful, shameful, shameless, false, fraudulent. **2.** infamous, notorious, unscrupulous, unprincipled, corrupt, traitorous, perfidious, dishonest, two-faced, duplicitous, despicable, reprehensible, heinous, villainous, low, mean, scurvy, vile, disreputable, disgraceful, scandalous, ignominious, discreditable, flagitious, contemptible, unchivalrous. —**Ant.** honorable.

disintegrate, v. reduce to particles or fragments, break up, decay, rot, fall apart, separate, shatter, crumble, decompose, molder. —Ant. integrate.

disinterested, adj. objective, neutral, just, detached, unbiased, unprejudiced, unselfish, impartial, fair, generous, liberal, open-minded, equitable, dispassionate, evenhanded, impersonal, altruistic. —Ant. biased, prejudiced, illiberal, bigoted, selfish, partial.

dislike, v. disrelish, disgust, distaste, repugnance, antipathy, loathing, aversion, antagonism, displeasure, disfavor, disaffection, hatred, animus, animosity, enmity, detestation, contempt, ill will, hostility. —Ant. like; relish, delight, delectation.

disloyal, adj. unfaithful, faithless, untrue, untrustworthy, deceitful, double-dealing, two-faced, cheating, unreliable, fickle, false, perfidious, treacherous, traitorous, treasonable, subversive, disaffected, unpatriotic. —Ant. loyal, faithful, true, honest.

dismay, v. **1.** discourage, dishearten, daunt, appall, terrify, horrify, frighten, scare, intimidate, disconcert, put out, alarm, paralyze. —n. **2.** consternation, terror, horror, panic, fear, alarm. —Ant. encourage, hearten, embolden; security, confidence.

dismiss, v. release, let go, discharge, discard, reject, set or put aside; fire, depose, replace, remove, give the old heave-ho, show someone the door, oust, give the boot, cashier, pink-slip, can, sack, down-size. —Ant. hire, employ.

disobedient, adj. insubordinate, naughty, mischievous, bad, ill-behaved, obstreperous, unmanageable, fractious, wayward, intractable, undutiful, contrary, perverse, willful, headstrong, recalcitrant, mutinous, mulish, pigheaded, contumacious, defiant, refractory, unruly, rebellious, obstinate, stubborn, unsubmissive, uncompliant. —Ant. obedient.

disobey, v. transgress, violate, disregard, defy, infringe, flout, ignore, resist, oppose, violate, overstep, break, contravene, be insubordinate, thumb one's nose at, be unruly, rebel, refuse to comply, be fractious, act up. —Ant. obey.

disorder, n. **1.** disorderliness, disarray, jumble, mess, litter, clutter, chaos, untidiness, muddle, jumble, shambles, hodgepodge, disarrangement, confusion, irregularity, disorganization, derangement. **2.** disturbance, tumult, brawl, uproar, fight, unrest, quarrel, bustle, clamor, riot, turbulence, pandemonium, upheaval, ferment, fuss, hubbub, hullabaloo, commotion, turmoil, bedlam, rumpus, free-for-all, fracas, donnybrook, scuffle, melee, breach of the peace. **3.** ailment, malady, derangement, illness, complaint, sickness, disease, indisposition. —v. **4.** disarrange, disarray, mess up, disorganize, unsettle, disturb, derange, discompose, upset, confuse, confound. —Ant. order.

disparity, n. dissimilarity, inequality, difference, distinction, dissimilitude, gap, discrepancy, imbalance, incongruity, contrast, unevenness, inconsistency. —Ant. similarity, equality, similitude.

dispense, v. deal, distribute, apportion, allot, dole, mete out, furnish, supply, provide, parcel, disburse, issue, assign.

disperse, v. **1.** scatter, dissipate, separate. **2.** spread, diffuse, disseminate, broadcast, sow, scatter; dispel. **3.** van-

ish, disappear, evanesce. —Ant. unite, combine; appear.

displace, v. **1.** misplace, move, dislocate, transfer, shift, relocate, disturb, disarrange, disorder, unsettle. **2.** replace, remove, depose, oust, dismiss, expel, unseat, eject, evict, exile, banish, discharge, fire, sack, kick out.

display, v. **1.** show, exhibit, demonstrate, make visible, evince, manifest. **2.** reveal, uncover, betray, unveil, disclose, demonstrate. **3.** unfold, open out, spread out. **4.** show, flourish, flaunt, parade, show off. —n. **5.** show, exhibition, manifestation. **6.** parade, ostentation, flourish, flaunting, spectacle, show, pageantry, pomp, splash, éclat. —Ant. conceal, hide; cover.

displeasure, n. dissatisfaction, annoyance, disapprobation, disapproval, distaste, dislike; anger, ire, wrath, indignation, annoyance, irritation, chagrin, exasperation, vexation; offense. —Ant. pleasure, satisfaction, approval, delight; calm, peace.

disposition, n. **1.** temper, temperament, nature, character, humor, attitude, personality, makeup, spirit, frame of mind. **2.** inclination, willingness, bent, tendency, proneness, bias, predisposition, proclivity. **3.** arrangement, order, grouping, location, placement. **4.** settlement, outcome, finale, result, fate, end, upshot, aftermath, consequence, issue, dispensation. **5.** regulation, appointment, management, control, direction. —Ant. indisposition, unwillingness.

dispute, v. **1.** argue, discuss, debate, agitate. **2.** wrangle, contest, quarrel, bicker, spat, squabble, spar, brawl. **3.** oppose, decry, gainsay, controvert, contradict, deny, impugn. —n. **4.** argumentation, argument, disagreement, conflict, discord, strife, feud, contention, debate, controversy, disputation, altercation, quarrel, wrangle, bickering, spat, squabble, tiff, row. —Ant. agree, concur; agreement, concurrence.

disregard, v. **1.** ignore, neglect, overlook, disobey, pay no attention or heed or regard to, take no notice of. **2.** slight, insult, snub, disparage, disdain, cut, give the cold shoulder, reject, spurn, high-hat. —n. **3.** neglect, inattention, inattentiveness, oversight. **4.** disrespect, slight, indifference, contempt, disdain, aloofness. —Ant. regard, view, notice, note; attention; respect.

disrespectful, adj. discourteous, impolite, rude, crude, uncivil, insulting, flippant, outspoken, offensive, naughty, impudent, impertinent, irreverent, ill-mannered, insolent, pert, indecorous, saucy, forward, fresh, cheeky. —Ant. respectful, courteous, polite, civil, reverent.

dissatisfaction, n. discontent, displeasure, dislike, disappointment, disapproval, disapprobation, uneasiness, unhappiness, frustration, discomfort, disquiet, malaise. —Ant. satisfaction, approval, approbation.

dissent, n. difference, dissidence, disagreement, dissatisfaction, opposition, nonconformity, separation, friction, discord, contention, strife, conflict. —Ant. agreement, concurrence, satisfaction, unity.

dissipate, v. **1.** scatter, disperse, dispel, disintegrate. **2.** waste, squander, run through, exhaust, throw away, fritter away. **3.** scatter, disappear, vanish, disintegrate. **4.** debauch, revel, carouse, party, sow wild oats, go on a spree, burn the candle at both ends. —Ant. integrate, unite; appear; join.

dissolve, v. **1.** sever, loose, loosen,

free, disunite, break up; dismiss, disperse, adjourn. **2.** destroy, dispel, ruin, disintegrate, break down, terminate, end; perish, crumble, die, expire. —Ant. solidify; unite; meet; integrate; originate.

distaste, n. dislike, disinclination, disfavor, antipathy, revulsion, nausea, horror, aversion, repugnance, disgust, displeasure, dissatisfaction, disrelish. —Ant. taste, delectation, liking, love, satisfaction; relish.

distasteful, adj. **1.** disagreeable, displeasing, offensive, repugnant, repulsive, obnoxious, off-putting, objectionable, nasty, foul, unpleasant. **2.** unpalatable, unsavory, nauseating, loathsome, revolting, sick-making, fulsome, vile, disgusting, sickening. —Ant. tasteful, agreeable, pleasant, inoffensive; attractive, delightful.

distinct, adj. **1.** distinguished, distinguishable, different, individual, separate, detached, discrete, sui generis, singular, various, varied, dissimilar. **2.** definite, well-defined, sharp, perceptible, understandable, vivid, precise, exact, noticeable, recognizable, obvious, unambiguous, clear-cut, explicit, marked, evident, apparent, unequivocal, clear, plain, unmistakable, unconfused. —Ant. indistinct, blurred, same; similar; indefinite, unclear, confused.

distinction, n. **1.** difference, contrast, separation, distinctiveness, differentiation, discrimination. **2.** honor, credit, prominence, greatness, uniqueness, excellence, merit, quality, worth, prestige, consequence, glory, reputation, repute, name, fame, celebrity, renown, importance, note, account, eminence, superiority. —Ant. indifference; similarity; disrepute, dishonor.

distinguish, v. **1.** mark, characterize, identify, indicate, separate, set apart. **2.** discriminate, differentiate, separate, divide, classify, categorize. **3.** discern, recognize, perceive, know, tell. **4.** make prominent or conspicuous or eminent.

distinguished, adj. **1.** conspicuous, marked, extraordinary. **2.** noted, eminent, famed, famous, celebrated, renowned, illustrious, respected, noteworthy, preeminent, prominent, honored. —Ant. undistinguished, common; infamous; unknown; unrefined, coarse.

distress, n. **1.** pain, anxiety, sorrow, grief, agony, anguish, misery, adversity, hardship, trial, tribulation, suffering, trouble, affliction, sorrow, woe, ache, torment, angst, chagrin. **2.** need, necessity, want, privation, deprivation, destitution, poverty, indigence. —v. **3.** trouble, worry, disturb, perturb, upset, vex, harass, harry, oppress, afflict, bother, grieve, pain, make miserable or unhappy. —Ant. comfort; fulfillment, opulence; console, mitigate, delight.

distribute, v. **1.** deal out, deal, allot, apportion, assign, mete, dole, dispense, give. **2.** disperse, spread, scatter, strew, diffuse, disseminate. **3.** divide, separate, classify, categorize, dispose, sort, arrange, group, order. —Ant. collect, keep; unite.

distrust, v. **1.** doubt, suspect, mistrust, question, be skeptical of, be wary of, discredit, disbelieve, be leery of, smell a rat. —n. **2.** doubt, suspicion, mistrust, misgiving, doubtfulness, uncertainty, skepticism, disbelief, incredulity, hesitation, wariness, qualm. —Ant. trust, depend.

disturbance, n. **1.** perturbation, agitation, commotion, disorder, disruption, disarray, upheaval, upset, confusion, derangement. **2.** disorder, tumult, riot, uproar, violence, trouble, outburst, turmoil, turbulence, brouhaha, brawl, melee, fray, fracas, donnybrook. —**Ant.** order, organization; calm, serenity.

diverge, v. **1.** branch off, separate, fork, bifurcate, divide, split, radiate, ramify, spread apart. **2.** differ, deviate, disagree, vary. —**Ant.** converge, unite; agree, concur.

diverse, adj. **1.** unlike, dissimilar, separate, different, disagreeing. **2.** various, varied, multiform, manifold, variant, divergent, assorted, mixed, miscellaneous, heterogeneous. —**Ant.** similar, like.

divert, v. **1.** turn aside, deflect, switch, redirect, change, alter, avert, shift, sidetrack. **2.** draw aside or away, turn aside, distract. **3.** distract, entertain, amuse, delight, gratify, exhilarate, beguile, interest, engage, occupy. —**Ant.** fix; weary, bore, tire.

divest, v. **1.** strip, unclothe, denude, disrobe, undress. **2.** strip, dispossess, deprive, relieve, rid, get rid, disencumber. —**Ant.** invest.

divide, v. **1.** separate, sunder, cut off, sever, shear, cleave, part. **2.** apportion, share, deal out, partition, distribute, portion. **3.** set at odds, sow dissension among, split, disaffect, alienate, disunite, cause to disagree, estrange. **4.** classify, sort, arrange, distribute, categorize, grade, group, order, rank, organize, assort, arrange. —**Ant.** unite; keep, retain; disarrange.

division, n. **1.** partition, dividing, separation, apportionment, allotment, distribution, sharing. **2.** mark, boundary, partition, demarcation. **3.** section, part, compartment, partition, segment. **4.** disagreement, dissension, difference, variance, rupture, disunion, strife, upset, conflict, discord, breach, rift, estrangement, alienation, feud. —**Ant.** agreement, union, accord.

do, v. **1.** perform, act. **2.** execute, finish, carry out, conclude, end, terminate, complete. **3.** accomplish, finish, achieve, attain, effect, bring about, execute, carry out. **4.** exert, put forth. **5.** behave, proceed, act, fare, manage.

doctrine, n. tenet, dogma, theory, precept, belief, canon, conviction, creed, credo, opinion, idea, concept, proposition, thesis, postulate, article of faith, principle; teachings.

dodge, v. equivocate, quibble, evade, be evasive, elude, sidestep, duck, hedge, double-talk, waffle.

dominant, adj. ruling, governing, controlling, most influential, prevailing, prevalent, common, principal, predominant, leading, reigning, supreme, superior, paramount, preeminent, outstanding, important, first, chief, main, primary, ascendant. —**Ant.** secondary.

donation, n. gift, contribution, offering, grant, benefaction, boon, award, bequest, bestowal, alms, giving, largess, present, gratuity.

doom, n. **1.** fate, destiny, lot, karma, kismet, fortune. **2.** ruin, death, downfall, destruction, extinction, annihilation, end. **3.** judgment, decision, sentence, condemnation. —v. **4.** destine, predestine, foreordain, decree. **5.** condemn, sentence, ordain.

dormant, adj. **1.** asleep, inactive, torpid, quiescent, slumbering, at rest, quiet, still, comatose, torpid, hibernating, somnolent, lethargic, dull, sluggish. **2.** quiescent, inoperative, in abeyance, latent, potential, inert, suspended, hidden, unexpressed, con-

cealed. —**Ant.** awake, active; operative; kinetic.

doubt, v. **1.** distrust, mistrust, suspect, question, disbelieve, discredit, have misgivings. **2.** hesitate, waver, vacillate, fluctuate, scruple, be uncertain, have doubts or reservations. —n. **3.** undecidedness, indecision, uncertainty, faltering, irresolution, hesitation, hesitancy, vacillation, misgiving, suspense; mistrust, distrust, suspicion, reservations, qualms, anxiety, worry. —**Ant.** trust; decision, certainty, conviction.

doubtful, adj. **1.** uncertain, unsure, ambiguous, equivocal, indeterminate, undecided, fifty-fifty. **2.** undetermined, unsettled, indecisive, dubious, enigmatic, problematic, puzzled. **3.** hesitating, hesitant, wavering, irresolute, vacillating, dubious, skeptical, incredulous. —**Ant.** certain, sure, unambiguous, decided; settled; unhesitating, resolute.

dowdy, adj. badly dressed, frumpy, shabby, old-fashioned, chintzy, frowzy, seedy, slovenly, sloppy, messy, drab, dull, unbecoming, unfashionable, tacky, cheapjack. —**Ant.** fashionable, chic, modish, à la mode.

downhearted, adj. dejected, discouraged, depressed, downcast, despondent, disheartened, sad, sorrowful, unhappy, dispirited, crestfallen, blue, low-spirited, wretched, woebegone. —**Ant.** happy, elated.

downright, adj. utter, absolute, complete, outright, positive, perfect, arrant, out-and-out, thoroughgoing, flat-out, unqualified, unmitigated, direct, straightforward, plain, frank, open, candid, blunt, brash, unambiguous, outright, categorical, unequivocal, explicit.

drag, v. **1.** draw, pull, haul, trail, tug. **2.** trail, linger, loiter, dawdle, lag, straggle, poke along. —**Ant.** drive, push; speed, expedite.

draw, v. **1.** drag, haul, pull, tug, tow, lead. **2.** attract, lure, elicit, magnetize. **3.** delineate, sketch, depict, trace. **4.** frame, formulate, compose, write, draw up, prepare, form. **5.** get, derive, deduce, infer, understand. **6.** produce, bring in, bear. **7.** draw or pull out, attenuate; extend, stretch, lengthen. —**Ant.** drive, push.

dread, n. **1.** terror, fear, apprehension, angst, fright, trepidation, uneasiness, anticipation, alarm, nervousness, dismay, worry, anxiety, consternation, distress, perturbation, disquiet, aversion, horror, panic, cold feet, butterflies, heebie-jeebies. **2.** awe, reverence, veneration. —adj. **3.** frightful, dire, terrible, dreadful, horrible, feared, terrifying. —**Ant.** intrepidity; bravery; pleasant, delightful.

dreary, adj. **1.** gloomy, dismal, drear, cheerless, chilling, chill, depressing, comfortless, somber, bleak, doleful, wretched, funereal, glum, morose. **2.** monotonous, tedious, wearisome, dull, boring, uninteresting, tiresome, lifeless, colorless, drab, arid, dry, dead, prosaic, humdrum, ordinary, vapid, run-of-the-mill, unexciting. —**Ant.** cheerful, comforting; interesting, engaging.

drench, v. steep, wet, soak, ret, saturate, flood, drown, inundate. —**Ant.** dry.

dress, n. **1.** costume, frock, gown; clothing, garb, attire, apparel, garments, vestments, clothes, suit, habit, habiliment; regalia, array, panoply. —v. **2.** attire, robe, garb, clothe, array, accouter, apparel, rig, deck out. **3.** trim, ornament, adorn, decorate. —**Ant.** undress.

drive, v. **1.** push, force, impel, propel, send. **2.** overwork, overtask, overburden, overtax. **3.** urge, constrain, impel, compel, force. **4.** go, travel, ride. —n. **5.** vigor, pressure, effort, energy, impetus, vim, spunk, enterprise, ambition, determination, industry, initiative, zeal, enthusiasm, get-up-and-go, pep, zip, push, hustle. —**Ant.** curb, restrain.

droll, adj. queer, odd, risible, eccentric, ridiculous, diverting, amusing, comical, waggish, witty, funny. —**Ant.** serious.

droop, v. sink, bend, hang down, dangle, flag, languish, fail, weaken, decline, faint, wilt, wither, fade, slump, sag. —**Ant.** rise.

drunk, adj. **1.** drunken, intoxicated, inebriated, besotted, tipsy, crapulent, crapulous, under the influence, under the weather, in one's cups, soused, pickled, high as a kite, boozy, boozed up, tight, lit, three sheets to the wind, under the table, loaded, stoned, stewed to the gills, bombed out of one's mind, plastered, crocked, sloshed, smashed, blotto, befuddled, tanked, polluted, stinko, soused, juiced up, on a bender or jag. **2.** delirious, excited, exhilarated, exuberant, animated, ecstatic, flushed, fevered, inflamed, in high spirits. —**Ant.** sober; sedate.

drunkard, n. toper, sot, tippler, drinker, inebriate, dipsomaniac, alcoholic, problem drinker, wino, boozer, lush, souse, alky, rummy, juicer, juicehead. —**Ant.** teetotaler, dry.

dry, adj. **1.** arid, parched, dehydrated, desiccated, waterless, barren, bare, sere, moistureless, thirsty. **2.** plain, bald, unadorned, unembellished. **3.** dull, uninteresting, dreary, tiresome, boring, tedious, jejune, barren, monotonous, prosaic, stale, commonplace, uninspired, wearisome, vapid. **4.** sarcastic, biting, sardonic, keen, sharp, pointed, sly, witty, droll, wry, cynical, cutting, keen, ironic. —**Ant.** wet, drenched; interesting, fascinating.

dubious, adj. **1.** doubtful, undecided, indeterminate, uncertain, unsure, inconclusive, dubitable, fluctuating, wavering. **2.** questionable, equivocal, ambiguous, obscure, unclear, misleading, vague, cryptic, mysterious, enigmatical. —**Ant.** definite, incisive, certain; unquestionable, unequivocal, clear.

dull, adj. **1.** slow, obtuse, stupid, blunted, unimaginative, sluggish, dense, bovine, cloddish, backward, dumb, dim, unintelligent, stolid. **2.** insensible, unfeeling, insensate, apathetic, numb, unresponsive, hard, inured, phlegmatic, unimpassioned, lifeless, callous, dead. **3.** listless, spiritless, torpid, inactive, lifeless, inert, inanimate. **4.** boring, depressing, monotonous, uninspired, unoriginal, humdrum, tedious, uninteresting, tiresome, dreary, vapid, wearisome, dry, jejune. —v. **5.** blunt, deaden, desensitize, narcotize, stupefy, paralyze, obtund, benumb. **6.** depress, dishearten, discourage, dispirit, sadden, deject. —**Ant.** bright, imaginative, quick; sensitive; spirited, active, animated; interesting; encourage, inspirit, hearten.

dumb, adj. **1.** mute, speechless, silent, voiceless, quiet, taciturn, mum, wordless; inarticulate. **2.** stupid, dull. —**Ant.** voluble, talkative, loquacious.

duplicate, adj. **1.** double, twofold; identical, twin, matching. —n. **2.** facsimile copy, replica, clone, dead ringer, Xerox copy, photocopy, fax, reproduction, transcript. —v. **3.** copy, replicate, reproduce, repeat, double, imitate, photocopy, clone, match, Xerox. **—Ant.** original.

duplicity, n. deceitfulness, deceit, double-dealing, deception, guile, cheating, delusion, cunning, hoax, victimization, trickery, hypocrisy, dissimulation, chicanery, artifice, fraud, dishonesty, perfidy, treachery, flimflam. **—Ant.** naiveté, honesty, openness, simplicity.

durable, adj. lasting, enduring, stable, constant, permanent, heavy-duty, indestructible, substantial, tough, stout, strong, sound, dependable, reliable, long-wearing. **—Ant.** unstable, temporary, temporal.

dusky, adj. dim, shadowy, murky, cloudy, dark, shady, obscure, clouded, penumbral, unilluminated, unlit, gloomy, tenebrous, crepuscular. **—Ant.** fair, blond, light; clear, unclouded.

dutiful, adj. respectful, docile, submissive, deferential, reverential, polite, considerate, yielding, obedient; compliant, willing, obliging, faithful, reliable, responsible, diligent, conscientious. **—Ant.** disrespectful, disobedient, irreverent.

duty, n. **1.** obligation, responsibility, burden, onus, task, assignment, job, occupation, calling, function, role, part, bit, charge. **2.** office, function, responsibility, service, business. **3.** homage, respect, deference, reverence; loyalty, fidelity, faithfulness, allegiance.

dwarf, n. **1.** homunculus, manikin, pygmy, midget, Lilliputian, runt. **—adj. 2.** diminutive, tiny, small, little, Lilliputian, stunted, dwarfed, undersized. **—v. 3.** stunt; overshadow, diminish, dominate, minimize. **—Ant.** giant, colossus; huge, gigantic, immense, colossal.

dwell, v. **1.** abide, reside, lodge, remain, rest, have quarters, stay, live, inhabit. **2.** continue, perpetuate. **—Ant.** leave, depart; cease, end, terminate, stop.

dwindle, v. diminish, lessen, decline, decrease, wane, shrink, waste away, reduce, fade, peter out, ebb, taper off, shrivel away, degenerate, sink, decay. **—Ant.** increase, grow, wax.

E

eager, adj. avid, ardent, enthusiastic, zealous, keen, hot, hungry, passionate, energetic, excited, itchy, breathless, impatient, anxious, atingle, champing at the bit, raring to go. **—Ant.** reluctant, disinclined, hesitant.

earn, v. **1.** gain, acquire, win, get, obtain, secure, procure, collect, make, receive, reap. **2.** merit, deserve, warrant, rate, qualify for, be worthy of.

earnest, adj. **1.** sincere, zealous, ardent, eager, fervent, resolute, serious, fervid, determined, purposeful. **2.** deep, firm, stable, intent, steady, faithful, true. **—Ant.** insincere, apathetic; faithless, unfaithful, wavering.

earth, n. **1.** globe, world, planet, terra firma. **2.** ground, soil, turf, sod, dirt, loam. **—Ant.** heaven; sky.

earthly, adj. **1.** terrestrial, worldly, mundane, physical, material, earthy. **2.** possible, conceivable, imaginable, feasible. **—Ant.** spiritual; impossible, inconceivable.

earthy, adj. **1.** plain, simple, unadorned, down-to-earth, unpretentious, matter-of-fact, unsophisticated, uncomplicated, direct, practical, pragmatic,

clear-eyed. **2.** unrefined, impolite, rude, crude, vulgar, scatological, obscene, blue, gross, risqué, dirty, wanton, ribald, bawdy, coarse, shameless, uninhibited, abandoned, lusty, rough, indecent. **—Ant.** refined, elevated, delicate.

ease, n. **1.** comfort, relaxation, rest, repose, well-being, leisure, effortlessness, contentment, happiness. **2.** tranquility, serenity, calmness, quiet, quietude, peace. **3.** informality, unaffectedness, naturalness, lightness, flexibility, freedom. **—v. 4.** comfort, relieve, disburden, relax, soothe, tranquilize, pacify, calm, still. **5.** tranquilize, soothe, allay, alleviate, mitigate, abate, assuage, lighten, lessen, reduce. **6.** facilitate, expedite, simplify, smooth, further, clear, assist, aid, help, advance, forward, oil the works. **—Ant.** discomfort, effort; disturbance, perturbation; affectation; burden; increase.

easy, adj. **1.** facile, light, unstrained, unhurried, leisurely, gentle, moderate. **2.** tranquil, untroubled, comfortable, contented, satisfied, quiet, at rest. **3.** easygoing, compliant, submissive, complying, accommodating, agreeable, yielding, docile, pliant, tractable, amenable, soft. **4.** lenient, light, undemanding, flexible, indulgent, tolerant. **5.** informal, unrestrained, unconstrained, unembarrassed, smooth, down-to-earth, unceremonious. **—Ant.** difficult, hard, immoderate; troubled, disturbed, uncomfortable, disagreeable, unyielding; restrained, embarrassed.

easygoing, adj. relaxed, placid, calm, serene, tranquil, even-tempered, permissive, tolerant, casual, mellow, carefree, poised, composed, collected, easy, unruffled, self-possessed, imperturbable, nonchalant, insouciant, laidback, cool. **—Ant.** tense, rigid, demanding.

ebb, n. **1.** reflux, regression, regress, retrogression. **2.** decline, decay, deterioration, degeneration, wane. **—v. 3.** subside, abate, recede, retire. **4.** decline, sink, wane, decrease, decay, waste or fade away. **—Ant.** flow, neap; wax; increase, swell, well; rise.

eccentric, adj. **1.** off-center, uncentered, off-balance, unbalanced. **2.** odd, unusual, peculiar, unconventional, strange, curious, bizarre, sui generis, idiosyncratic, unorthodox, unique, quirky, far-out, kinky, queer, aberrant, weird, freakish, offbeat, off-the-wall, oddball, bizzarro. **—n. 3.** character, oddity, original, strange one, crank, individualist, nonconformist, crackpot, freak, oddball, odd duck, card, weirdo, loner.

economical, adj. saving, provident, sparing, thrifty, frugal; stingy, tight, penurious, parsimonious, cheap, miserly, tightfisted, mean, penny-pinching, scrimping. **—Ant.** lavish, spendthrift.

economy, n. **1.** frugality, thriftiness, thrift, saving, conservatism, restraint, control. **2.** briefness, brevity, succinctness, terseness, conciseness, concision, compactness, curtness. **—Ant.** lavishness.

ecstatic, adj. overjoyed, joyful, elated, bursting, rapturous, exhilarated, thrilled, blissful, euphoric, rhapsodic, excited, delighted, gleeful, happy, glad, orgasmic, delirious, exultant, jubilant, transported, on cloud nine, in seventh heaven, beside oneself, happy as a lark. **—Ant.** glum, dispirited, downhearted.

edge, n. **1.** border, rim, lip, margin,

boundary, verge, brink, side, brim, fringe, limit, perimeter, periphery. **—v. 2.** inch, sidle, crawl, creep, steal, worm, work one's way. **—Ant.** center.

edify, v. enlighten, educate, illuminate, improve, better, transform, uplift, raise, boost, lift, elevate.

educate, v. teach, instruct, school, drill, indoctrinate, edify, tutor, inform, enlighten, coach, prepare, ready, rear, cultivate, civilize, train, discipline.

education, n. **1.** teaching, schooling, cultivation, upbringing, drilling, instruction, tuition, training. **2.** learning, knowledge, enlightenment, culture, lore, erudition. **—Ant.** illiteracy.

eerie, adj. fearful, awesome, weird, uncanny, strange, ghostly, spectral, unearthly, mysterious, scary, creepy, spooky. **—Ant.** common, ordinary.

effect, n. **1.** result, consequence, upshot, aftermath, end, outcome, issue. **2.** power, efficacy, force, validity, weight. **3.** operation, execution; accomplishment, fulfillment. **4.** purport, intent, tenor, significance, signification, meaning, import. **—v. 5.** bring about, accomplish, cause, make happen, achieve, do, perform, complete, consummate, realize, secure, obtain, execute, produce, create. **—Ant.** cause.

effective, adj. **1.** capable, competent, efficient, efficacious, productive, useful, serviceable, able, functional, effectual. **2.** operative, in force, active, functioning, real, actual, basic, essential. **—Ant.** ineffective, incompetent, inefficient, ineffectual; inactive, inoperative.

effort, n. application, endeavor, exertion, attempt, struggle, strain, labor, pains, energy, toil, trouble, work, elbow grease, striving. **—Ant.** ease.

effusive, adj. demonstrative, extravagant, gushing, profuse, enthusiastic, emotional, exuberant, rhapsodic, ebullient, lavish, voluble, outgoing, unrestrained, unrepressed, expansive, unreticent, talkative. **—Ant.** taciturn, laconic.

egocentric, adj. self-centered, self-referencing, conceited, egotistic, egotistical, egomaniacal, selfish, spoiled, narcissistic, self-loving, self-absorbed, vain, vainglorious, stuck-up, stuck on oneself. **—Ant.** modest, self-effacing, humble.

egotism, n. self-love, egoism, selfishness, conceit, narcissism, solipsism, self-importance, self-indulgence, egocentricity, self-absorption, pride, vainglory, braggadocio, swellheadedness, egomania, amour-propre. **—Ant.** altruism, modesty.

elaborate, adj. **1.** meticulous, thourough, complete, exhaustive, minute, precise, exact, painstaking, labored, studied; fancy, extravagant, showy, Byzantine, decorated, baroque, rococo, detailed, ornate, intricate, complicated, complex. **—v. 2.** ornament, decorate, embellish, complicate, adorn; develop, cultivate, enhance, enrich, improve, enlarge, expand, refine. **—Ant.** simple; simplify.

elate, v. cheer, cheer up, excite, exhilarate, inspirit, exalt, lift, uplift, elevate, delight, overjoy, thrill, transport, tickle. **—Ant.** depress, discourage.

elect, v. **1.** select, choose, prefer, pick, vote, determine, designate, name, usher in. **—v. 2.** select, chosen, choice, first-rate, superior, elite, of the first water. **—Ant.** refuse, reject; second-rate.

elegant, adj. tasteful, fine, luxurious,

sumptuous, grand, opulent, swank, fancy, ritzy, plush; refined, polished, cultivated, debonair, polished, suave, soigné, to the manner born, well-bred, aristocratic, chic, fashionable, grand, posh, dignified, artistic, genteel, courtly, graceful; choice, nice, superior; excellent. **—Ant.** inelegant, distasteful; unrefined, disgraceful; inferior.

element, *n.* **1.** component, constituent, ingredient, unit, part, essential, fundamental, segment, piece, feature, factor, detail. **2.** rudiment, principle, basis, basic. **3.** habitat, environment, medium, milieu, atmosphere, locale, sphere, domain. **—Ant.** whole, nonessential; compound.

elementary, *adj.* primary, rudimentary, basic, fundamental, rudimental; easy, straightforward, clear, understandable, plain, simple, uncomplicated. **—Ant.** advanced, secondary; complex, complicated.

elevate, *v.* raise, lift up, exalt, hallow, sanctify, heighten, increase, intensify, promote, advance, improve, enhance, dignify, refine; animate, cheer, elate, liven, inspirit, uplift. **—Ant.** lower, debase, decrease; depress.

elevation, *n.* loftiness, grandeur, dignity, nobility, nobleness, refinement, exaltation, sublimity. **—Ant.** valley; depths.

eligible, *adj.* suitable, qualified, acceptable, fitted, fit, worthy, admissible, desirable, proper, appropriate. **—Ant.** unsuitable, ineligible.

eliminate, *v.* get rid of, expel, remove, exclude, reject, omit, ignore, cut, delete, erase, dismiss, elide, take away, kick out, kill, destroy, excommunicate, banish, scorn, repudiate, disdain, drop, dispose of, cancel, terminate, dispose of, annihilate, eradicate, expunge, obliterate, bury, waste. **—Ant.** include, accept.

elude, *v.* **1.** avoid, escape, evade, slip away from, shun, dodge. **2.** puzzle, bewilder stump, baffle, confound, foil, thwart, confuse, frustrate, disconcert. **—Ant.** grasp.

emanate, *v.* emerge, issue, proceed, come forth, originate, arise, spring, flow, ooze, exude, radiate, emit.

embarrass, *v.* disconcert, abash, make uncomfortable, confuse, upset, shame, mortify, humble, humiliate, fluster, discombobulate, disgrace, distress, discomfit, discompose, chagrin. **—Ant.** comfort, console.

embarrassment, *n.* **1.** bashfulness, awkwardness, clumsiness, uneasiness, disconcertment, abashment, perplexity, confusion, discomposure, discomfort, mortification, chagrin. **2.** trouble, annoyance, vexation, distress, harassment, hindrance, deterrent, difficulty, mess, predicament, dilemma, problem. **—Ant.** comfort, composure; encouragement.

embellish, *v.* **1.** beautify, ornament, adorn, decorate, garnish, bedeck, improve, trick out, enrich, gild, embroider. **2.** enhance, embroider, exaggerate about, elaborate, overdo, dress up. **—Ant.** strip down, simplify.

emblem, *n.* token, sign, symbol, figure, image, badge, device, representation, insigne, seal, crest, trademark, mark.

embrace, *v.* **1.** clasp, hug, grasp, hold, enfold, cuddle. **2.** accept, adopt, espouse, welcome, receive, seize. **3.** encircle, surround, enclose, contain. **4.** include, contain, comprise, comprehend, cover, embody, incorporate, encompass. **—Ant.** exclude, reject.

emerge, *v.* come forth, emanate, issue, spread, stream; appear, surface, develop, transpire, happen, evolve. **—Ant.** hide.

emergency, *n.* crisis, straits, urgency, turning point, exigency, necessity, extremity, pinch, dilemma, quandary, danger, predicament, difficulty.

eminence, *n.* repute, distinction, prominence, celebrity, renown, importance, preeminence, superiority, greatness, conspicuousness, note, fame, rank, position, esteem, exaltation, respect, reverence, illustriousness. **—Ant.** disrepute, obscurity.

eminent, *adj.* distinguished, signal, notable, noteworthy, noted, esteemed, respected, revered, honored, dignified, important, preeminent, great, superior, famous, celebrated, well-known, prominent, celebrated, renowned, outstanding, illustrious, conspicuous, exalted. **—Ant.** disreputable, commonplace, ordinary; low, debased; inconspicuous.

emit, *v.* send *or* give forth, discharge, eject, vent, exhale, exude, emanate, issue, radiate, send out, put forth, give off, expel. **—Ant.** inspire, inhale, accept.

emotion, *n.* feeling, passion, sentiment, sensation, fervor; compassion, sympathy, empathy. **—Ant.** apathy.

empathy, *n.* compassion, understanding, responsiveness, concern, consideration, tender-heartedness, caring, sensitivity, identification, involvement, sharing, fellow feeling, perceptiveness, perceptivity, sympathy. **—Ant.** callousness, indifference.

emphasize, *v.* stress, accent, accentuate, italicize, bring out, underline, underscore, play up, highlight, feature, mark, spotlight, single out, punctuate, point up, call attention to. **—Ant.** deemphasize, play down, underplay, ignore.

emphatic, *adj.* significant, marked, striking, positive, energetic, express, insistent, categorical, resolute, explicit, assertive, intense, forcible, forceful, pronounced, strong, decided, unequivocal, definite, dynamic. **—Ant.** insignificant, uncertain, unsure.

employ, *v.* **1.** use, engage, hire, retain, occupy, enlist, recruit, enroll, sign up, take on, commission. **2.** use, apply, make use of.

employee, *n.* worker, servant, agent, clerk, wage earner, staff member, hand, underling, minion, helper, aide, assistant. **—Ant.** employer, boss.

empower, *v.* **1.** enable, enfranchise, inspire, actualize, self-actualize. **2.** authorize, sanction, entitle, warrant, license. **—Ant.** disenfranchise, marginalize.

empty, *adj.* **1.** void, hollow, unfilled, bare, barren, blank; vacant, unoccupied, uninhabited. **2.** unsatisfactory, meaningless, superficial, trivial, insincere, worthless, valueless, idle, hollow, delusive, vain, ineffectual, ineffective, unsatisfying. **3.** frivolous, foolish, vacuous, inane, stupid. —*v.* **4.** clear, remove, eject, vacate; unload, unburden, pour out, evacuate, drain, discharge, exhaust, drain. **—Ant.** full, replete; occupied, inhabited; satisfactory, effectual; serious.

enchant, *v.* fascinate, cast a spell over, spellbind, mesmerize, hypnotize, beguile, enthrall, entrance, attract, allure, captivate, charm, enrapture, transport, bewitch, delight, seduce, entice. **—Ant.** bore.

encircle, *v.* surround, ring, confine, hem in, wreathe, circle, compass, encompass, environ, gird, enfold, enclose.

enclose, *v.* surround, encircle, encompass, circumscribe, shut in, pen, confine, bound, envelop, wall in, immure. **—Ant.** set free.

encounter, *v.* **1.** meet, confront, face, experience. **2.** contend against, engage with, attack, cope with, compete with. —*n.* **3.** meeting. **4.** battle, combat, conflict, confrontation, engagement, contest, competition, brush, struggle, fight, clash, skirmish, altercation, dispute, duel, quarrel, disagreement, quarrel.

encourage, *v.* **1.** inspirit, embolden, hearten, stimulate, incite; reassure, assure, console, comfort. **2.** urge, abet, second, support, favor, countenance, advance, foster, promote, aid, help, foment. **—Ant.** discourage, dispirit.

encumber, *v.* **1.** impede, hamper, retard, embarrass, obstruct, complicate, involve, entangle, handicap, hinder, inconvenience, trammel, slow down. **2.** load, oppress, overload, burden, weigh down, strain, saddle, tax. **—Ant.** disencumber; unload, unburden.

end, *n.* **1.** extremity, extreme. **2.** limit, bound, boundary, termination, tip, terminus. **3.** close, termination, conclusion, finish, outcome, issue, consequence, result, completion, attainment. **4.** finale, conclusion, peroration. **5.** purpose, aim, object, objective, goal, intention, design, intent, drift. —*v.* **6.** terminate, conclude, wind up, finish, complete, close. **7.** stop, cease, discontinue, conclude. **—Ant.** beginning, start; begin, commence, open; continue.

endeavor, *v.* **1.** attempt, essay, try, make an effort, strive, struggle, labor; seek, aim. —*n.* **2.** effort, pains, undertaking, enterprise, exertion, struggle, essay, attempt, trial.

endless, *adj.* limitless, unlimited, vast, illimitable, immeasurable, unending, boundless, infinite, interminable, incessant, unceasing, eternal, continuous, perpetual, everlasting, nonstop. **—Ant.** limited, finite.

endow, *v.* equip, invest, enrich; confer, bestow, give, grant, present. **—Ant.** divest.

endowment, *n.* gift, grant, bequest, largess, bounty, present; capacity, talent, faculties, quality, power, ability, aptitude, capability, genius. **—Ant.** incapacity.

endure, *v.* **1.** sustain, hold out against, undergo, bear, support, suffer, experience. **2.** experience, stand, tolerate, bear, brook, allow, permit, submit. **3.** continue, last, persist, remain. **—Ant.** fail, subside; refuse; die, perish, fail.

enemy, *n.* foe, adversary, opponent, antagonist, rival, competitor, contestant, contender, the opposition, the other side. **—Ant.** friend, ally.

energetic, *adj.* **1.** lively, dynamic, animated, spirited, tireless, indefatigable, sprightly, spry, vital, high-powered, peppy, zippy, full of beans, forcible, vigorous, active. **2.** powerful, effective, effectual, strong, efficacious, potent. **—Ant.** lazy, inactive; ineffective, impotent, weak.

energy, *n.* **1.** activity, exertion, power, force, operation, dynamism, vigor, potency, zeal, push, spirit, animation, life, vitality, vivacity, liveliness, spirit, drive, verve, dash, élan, pep, zip, zing, get-up-and-go. **2.** force, power, might, efficacy, strength, intensity. **—Ant.** inertia, inactivity; weakness.

engender, *v.* **1.** produce, cause, give

rise to, originate, beget, create, occasion, excite, stir up, incite, generate, breed. **2.** procreate, beget, create, generate, breed. —**Ant.** terminate; kill.

enigma, *n.* puzzle, riddle, problem, question, conundrum, mystery, poser.

enjoyment, *n.* delight, delectation, pleasure, gratification, happiness, joy, relish, zest, recreation, entertainment, diversion. —**Ant.** detestation, abhorrence, displeasure, boredom.

enlarge, *v.* extend, augment, amplify, dilate, increase, aggrandize, magnify, expand, greaten, swell, spread, wax, widen, stretch, inflate, broaden, lengthen. —**Ant.** limit, decrease, lessen, abate.

enlighten, *v.* illumine, edify, teach, inform, instruct, educate, inform, apprise, advise, counsel, make aware. —**Ant.** confuse.

enliven, *v.* **1.** invigorate, animate, inspirit, vivify, stimulate, pep up, energize, vitalize, inspire, rouse, kindle, spark off, quicken. **2.** exhilarate, gladden, cheer, brighten, inspire, delight, buoy up, uplift. —**Ant.** dispirit, slow; depress.

enormous, *adj.* **1.** huge, immense, vast, colossal, mammoth, gigantic, prodigious, elephantine, gargantuan, titanic, tremendous, Brobdingnagian, massive, monstrous. **2.** outrageous, atrocious, flagitious, depraved, wicked, flagrant, scandalous, egregious. —**Ant.** small, diminutive, tiny; honorable.

enrage, *v.* infuriate, anger, incense, inflame, provoke, madden, exasperate, aggravate, inflame, make someone's blood boil, tick someone off, make someone see red. —**Ant.** tranquilize, calm, assuage.

entangle, *v.* **1.** complicate, ensnare, enmesh, tangle, knot, mat. **2.** mix up, embarrass, confuse, perplex, bewilder, involve, ensnare, embroil. —**Ant.** simplify.

enterprise, *n.* **1.** project, plan, undertaking, venture, adventure, effort, scheme, program. **2.** boldness, daring, mettle, audacity, zeal, drive, vigor, ambition, readiness, spirit, energy, resolve, purpose, gumption, guts.

enterprising, *adj.* ambitious, ready, resourceful, adventurous, venturesome, dashing, bold, energetic, spirited, eager, zealous, resolute, determined, hard-working, industrious, purposeful, goal-oriented, diligent, assiduous, persevering, tireless, indefatigable, aggressive. —**Ant.** phlegmatic, lazy.

entertain, *v.* **1.** divert, amuse, please. **2.** receive, consider, admit. **3.** harbor, cherish, hold, tolerate, allow, maintain, sustain, support. —**Ant.** bore; refuse, reject; expel.

enthusiasm, *n.* eagerness, earnestness, sincerity, interest, warmth, avidity, gusto, relish, exuberance, excitement, keenness, fervor, zeal, ardor, passion, devotion. —**Ant.** coolness.

enthusiast, *n.* zealot, devotee, fan, aficionado, admirer, supporter, promoter, champion, adherent, disciple, booster.

enthusiastic, *adj.* ardent, zealous, eager, fervent, passionate, vehement, fervid, burning, impassioned, keen, hearty, avid, energetic, vigorous, devoted, exuberant, fanatical. —**Ant.** blasé, dispassionate, cool, unenthusiastic.

entice, *v.* allure, inveigle, excite, lure, attract, decoy, tempt, seduce, coax, cajole, wheedle, persuade, draw, beguile,

blandish, wheedle. —**Ant.** discourage, deter, dissuade.

entire, *adj.* **1.** whole, complete, unbroken, perfect, unimpaired, intact, undiminished, undivided, continuous. **2.** full, complete, thorough, unqualified, unrestricted, unmitigated. —**Ant.** partial, imperfect, divided; restricted, incomplete.

entitle, *v.* **1.** empower, qualify, allow, permit, make eligible, authorize, fit, enfranchise. **2.** name, designate, call, title, dub, label, term. —**Ant.** disqualify.

entrance, *n.* **1.** entry, ingress, access, entree. **2.** entry, door, portal, gate, doorway, passage, inlet. **3.** admission, entry, admittance. —*v.* **4.** fascinate, captivate, bewitch, beguile, spellbind, enthrall, overpower, mesmerize, hypnotize, enrapture, enchant, charm, delight, transport. —**Ant.** exit; disenchant.

entreat, *v.* appeal, implore, beg, beseech, supplicate, crave, solicit, pray, importune, petition, sue.

enumerate, *v.* count, name, list, itemize, specify, detail, spell out, catalogue, take stock of, quote, recite, relate, narrate, recount, recapitulate, rehearse, cite.

envelop, *v.* wrap, cover, enfold, hide, conceal, surround, enclose, encompass, shroud, swathe, swaddle, embrace.

envy, *n.* **1.** jealousy, enviousness, grudge, covetousness. —*v.* **2.** covet, begrudge, resent. —**Ant.** generosity.

epicure, *n.* gastronome, gourmet, epicurean, voluptuary, sensualist, glutton, gourmand, hedonist, sybarite, bon vivant, Lucullus.

episode, *n.* occurrence, event, incident, happening, experience.

equable, *adj.* even, uniform, tranquil, steady, regular, even-tempered, temperate, easygoing, serene, calm, placid, composed, cool, unruffled, levelheaded, unflappable. —**Ant.** uneven, irregular, turbulent, intemperate.

equal, *adj.* **1.** proportionate, commensurate, balanced, coordinate, correspondent, equivalent, tantamount, like, alike. **2.** uniform, even, regular, unvarying, invariant. **3.** adequate, sufficient, competent, suitable, fit. —*n.* **4.** peer, match, mate, fellow. —*v.* **5.** match, meet, even, square with, correspond to, parallel, rival, be commensurate with. —**Ant.** unequal, disproportionate, incommensurate, dissimilar; uneven, irregular, variable; inadequate, insufficient, unsuitable.

equip, *v.* furnish, provide, supply, stock, attire, dress, deck out, fit out, outfit, rig, array, accouter.

equipment, *n.* apparatus, paraphernalia, gear, accouterments.

equivocal, *adj.* **1.** ambiguous, uncertain, vague, hazy, indefinite, unclear, indistinct, doubtful, questionable, dubious, indeterminate. **2.** evasive, misleading, roundabout, hedging, oblique, circumlocutory, ambivalent, waffling, wishy-washy. —**Ant.** unequivocal, certain; definite, unquestionable.

eradicate, *v.* remove, destroy, extirpate, abolish, obliterate, uproot, exterminate, annihilate. —**Ant.** insert, add; originate, create.

erase, *v.* efface, expunge, cancel, obliterate, delete, scratch, wipe out. —**Ant.** create.

erect, *adj.* **1.** upright, standing, vertical, perpendicular, plumb. —*v.* **2.** build, raise, construct, upraise. **3.** set up, found, establish, institute. —**Ant.**

horizontal; raze, destroy; dissolve, liquidate.

erroneous, *adj.* mistaken, incorrect, inaccurate, false, wrong, untrue, invalid, fallacious, faulty, flawed, botched. —**Ant.** correct, accurate, true.

error, *n.* **1.** mistake, inaccuracy, fault, flaw, gaffe, goof, foul-up, boner, blunder, slip, oversight. **2.** offense, wrongdoing, fault, sin, transgression, trespass, misdeed, iniquity.

escape, *v.* **1.** flee, abscond, decamp, fly, steal away, run away. **2.** shun, fly, elude, evade, avoid. —*n.* **3.** flight; getaway, departure, decampment, bolt, breakout.

escort, *n.* **1.** convoy, guard, guide, protection, safeguard, guidance. —*v.* **2.** conduct, usher, guard, guide, convoy, accompany, attend, shepherd, squire, conduct, watch over.

especially, *adv.* particularly, chiefly, principally, unusually, specifically, conspicuously, uniquely, notably, strikingly, noticeably, mainly, predominantly, primarily, first of all, above all, significantly, prominently, signally, specially, markedly.

essential, *adj.* **1.** indispensable, necessary, vital, requisite, required, imperative, quintessential, elemental, principal, primary, key, main, leading, chief, fundamental, rudimentary, elementary, basic, inherent, intrinsic, important. —*n.* **2.** necessity, basic, element. —**Ant.** dispensable, unnecessary, unimportant.

establish, *v.* **1.** set up, found, institute, form, organize, create, fix, settle, install. **2.** verify, substantiate, prove, confirm, certify, affirm, show, authenticate, validate, support, demonstrate, substantiate, back up. **3.** appoint, ordain, fix, enact, decree. —**Ant.** liquidate, dissolve; disprove.

esteem, *v.* **1.** prize, value, honor, revere, respect, appreciate, treasure, cherish, hold dear, admire, look up to, venerate, estimate, regard. —*n.* **2.** respect, regard, favor, admiration, honor, reverence, veneration. **3.** estimation, valuation, estimate, appreciation, opinion. —**Ant.** disregard; disrespect, disfavor; deprecation.

estimable, *adj.* respectable, reputable, worthy, deserving, meritorious, good, excellent, honored, praiseworthy, laudable. —**Ant.** disreputable, unworthy, bad, inferior.

estimate, *v.* **1.** judge, compute, reckon, gauge, count, assess, approximate, determine, guess, calculate, conjecture, value, evaluate, appraise. —*n.* **2.** judgment, calculation, valuation, estimation, opinion, computation, approximation, assessment, appraisal, viewpoint.

estimation, *n.* judgment, opinion, appreciation, regard, honor, veneration, esteem, respect, reverence.

eternal, *adj.* **1.** endless, everlasting, infinite, unending, never-ending, interminable, unceasing, perpetual, ceaseless, incessant, constant, nonstop, relentless, permanent. **2.** timeless, immortal, deathless, undying, imperishable, indestructible. —**Ant.** transitory, ephemeral; perishable, mortal.

ethical, *adj.* moral, virtuous, principled, high-principled, honest, law-abiding, licit, legitimate, civilized, upright, decent, honorable, conscientious, righteous, right-minded, right-thinking, upstanding, just, scrupulous, proper, open, fair, good, straightforward, noble. —**Ant.** unethical, immoral.

etiquette, *n.* decorum, propriety, code of behavior, convention, form, ceremony, formalities, protocol, rules, customs, politeness, courtesy, good manners, seemliness, civility. —**Ant.** impropriety, indignity.

eulogize, *v.* praise, extol, laud, commend, panegyrize, applaud, honor, flatter, compliment. —**Ant.** criticize, condemn.

evade, *v.* **1.** escape, elude, escape from, circumvent, shirk, avoid, shun, sidestep, dodge. **2.** baffle, foil, elude. **3.** prevaricate, equivocate, quibble, fence, hedge, maneuver, fudge, waffle, cop out. —**Ant.** face, confront.

evaporate, *v.* **1.** vaporize, dehydrate, dry. **2.** disappear, fade, vanish, evanesce, melt away, dissolve, disperse. —**Ant.** condense, sublimate.

evasion, *n.* **1.** avoidance, dodging, escape. **2.** prevarication, equivocation, quibbling, subterfuge, sophistry, deception, deceit, chicanery, artifice, trickery, excuse, fudging, waffling, double-talk.

even, *adj.* **1.** level, flat, smooth, plane. **2.** parallel, flush, level. **3.** regular, equable, uniform, steady, well-balanced, in equilibrium, conforming, standard. **4.** commensurate, equal; square, balanced. **5.** calm, placid, tranquil, even-tempered, temperate, composed, sedate, peaceful. **6.** fair, just, equitable, impartial. —*adv.* **7.** still, yet; just; fully, quite, completely; indeed. —*v.* **8.** level, smooth; balance, equilibrate, counterpoise. —**Ant.** uneven, irregular; unsteady; unequal, incommensurate; agitated, intemperate; unfair, unjust, prejudiced, biased.

evening, *n.* eventide, dusk, twilight, gloaming, nightfall, eve, even, sundown, sunset, p.m. —**Ant.** dawn, sunrise.

event, *n.* **1.** occurrence, happening, affair, case, occasion, experience, circumstance, episode, incident. **2.** result, issue, consequence, outcome, upshot, end.

ever, *adv.* **1.** continuously, eternally, perpetually, constantly, always, forever, yet, still, at all times, endlessly, forever and a day, till the end of time, till the cows come home. **2.** by any chance, at all, at any time. —**Ant.** never.

evidence, *n.* **1.** ground, grounds, proof, testimony. **2.** indication, sign, signal. **3.** information, deposition, affidavit, exhibit, testimony, proof. —*v.* **4.** make clear, show, manifest, demonstrate.

evident, *adj.* plain, clear, obvious, manifest, palpable, patent, unmistakable, apparent, discernible, noticeable, conspicuous. —**Ant.** concealed, hidden.

evil, *adj.* **1.** wicked, bad, immoral, amoral, sinful, iniquitous, flagitious, depraved, vicious, corrupt, perverse, wrong, base, vile, nefarious, malicious, malignant, malevolent. **2.** harmful, injurious, wrong, bad, pernicious, destructive, mischievous. **3.** unfortunate, disastrous, miserable, unlucky, inauspicious, dire, ominous. —*n.* **4.** wickedness, depravity, iniquity, unrighteousness, sin, corruption, baseness, badness. **5.** harm, mischief, misfortune, disaster, calamity, misery, pain, woe, suffering, sorrow. —**Ant.** good.

exact, *adj.* **1.** accurate, correct, precise, literal, faithful, close. **2.** strict, rigorous, rigid, unbending, exacting, demanding, severe, scrupulous. **3.** methodical, careful, punctilious, accurate, critical, nice, regular, precise, orderly. —*v.* **4.** call for, demand, require, force, compel. **5.** extort, wrest, wring, ex-

tract. —**Ant.** inexact, inaccurate, imprecise, unfaithful, free; disorderly.

exalt, *v.* **1.** elevate, promote, dignify, raise, ennoble. **2.** praise, extol, glorify, bless, honor, idolize, dignify, revere, venerate, celebrate. **3.** elate, make proud, please. —**Ant.** lower, debase; damn, condemn; displease.

examination, *n.* **1.** inspection, inquiry, observation, investigation, study, analysis, probe, search, exploration, research, survey, appraisal, assessment, scrutiny, scanning, inquisition. **2.** test, trial, quiz, exam.

examine, *v.* **1.** inspect, scrutinize, search, probe, explore, study, investigate, test. **2.** catechize, quiz, interrogate, question, test, cross-examine, grill, pump.

example, *n.* sample, specimen, representative, illustration, case, pattern, model, instance, prototype, standard, archetype, exemplar, pattern, norm, criterion, benchmark.

exasperate, *v.* irritate, annoy, vex, infuriate, exacerbate, anger, incense, provoke, nettle, needle enrage, inflame, rile, embitter, irk, bother, harass, pique, gall, rankle, torment, badger, bug, peeve, get under someone's skin, get someone's goat, rub someone the wrong way. —**Ant.** calm, assuage, tranquilize.

exceed, *v.* overstep, transcend, surpass, cap, top, outdo, excel, outstrip, beat, overtake, be superior to, go beyond, overwhelm, better, outdistance, pass, eclipse, overextend.

excel, *v.* surpass, outdo, exceed, transcend, outstrip, eclipse, beat, win over, cap, top, dominate, outrank, overshadow, eclipse; shine, be preeminent.

excellence, *n.* superiority, eminence, preeminence, transcendence, supremacy, prominence, greatness, finesse, distinction; merit, virtue, purity, goodness, uprightness. —**Ant.** baseness; inferiority.

excellent, *adj.* superb, outstanding, exceptional, matchless, peerless, nonpareil, supreme, superlative, capital, first-class, select, distinguished, noteworthy, splendid, remarkable, marvelous, extraordinary, great, super, terrific, good, choice, worthy, fine, first-rate, estimable, superior, better, admirable, prime. —**Ant.** bad, inferior, base.

except, *prep.* but, save, excepting, excluding, barring, not counting, apart from, other than, saving. —**Ant.** including.

exceptional, *adj.* unusual, extraordinary, special, uncommon, irregular, peculiar, rare; strange, unnatural, anomalous, abnormal, aberrant. —**Ant.** customary, common, usual, normal, regular, natural.

excess, *n.* **1.** superfluity, superabundance, nimiety, redundancy, overflow, surfeit, glut, overabundance, overkill. **2.** surplus, remainder. **3.** immoderation, intemperance, overindulgence, dissipation, prodigality, extravagance, dissolution, debauchery. —**Ant.** lack, need, want.

excessive, *adj.* immoderate, extravagant, extreme, exorbitant, inordinate, outrageous, unreasonable, disproportionate, undue, extortionate, unjustifiable, enormous. —**Ant.** reasonable, proportionate.

excitable, *adj.* emotional, passionate, fiery, quick-tempered, volatile, jumpy, nervous, restive, restless, fidgety, edgy, touchy, high-strung, mercurial, testy, hot-blooded, feverish, hysterical, hot-tempered, hasty, irascible, irritable,

choleric. —**Ant.** unemotional, cool, calm, serene, tranquil.

excite, *v.* **1.** stir, arouse, rouse, awaken, stimulate, animate, kindle, spur, move, motivate, animate, galvanize, electrify, spark, light a fire under, inflame, incite. **2.** stir up, provoke, disturb, agitate, irritate, discompose. —**Ant.** pacify, calm, soothe.

excited, *adj.* ruffled, discomposed, stormy, perturbed, aroused, disturbed, upset, worked up, overwrought, nervous, edgy, uneasy, flustered, frantic, frenetic, beside oneself, jittery, impassioned, stimulated, brisk, agitated, stirred up, agog, eager, enthusiastic, passionate, animated, lively, spirited, fervent. —**Ant.** calm, unruffled, composed, pacific.

excitement, *n.* agitation, commotion, ado, to-do, perturbation, upset, restlessness, disquiet, tension, unrest, malaise, stir, disturbance, activity, ferment, furor, turmoil, tumult, hubbub, brouhaha. —**Ant.** serenity, peace.

exclamation, *n.* outcry, ejaculation, interjection, cry, complaint, call, utterance, yell, bellow, protest, vociferation, shout, clamor.

exclude, *v.* **1.** bar, restrain, keep out, shut out. **2.** debar, eliminate, expel, eject, reject, prohibit, withhold, except, omit, preclude; proscribe, prevent. —**Ant.** include; accept.

exclusive, *adj.* **1.** incompatible, inimical, excluding, barring, restricted, limited. **2.** restrictive, closed, private, cliquish, snobbish, fastidious, select, narrow, clannish, snobbish, selfish, illiberal, narrow, narrow-minded, uncharitable; fashionable, chic, aristocratic, choice, upper-class, elegant, stylish, trendy. —**Ant.** inclusive, including; liberal; poor.

excursion, *n.* journey, tour, trip, jaunt, junket, outing, cruise, airing, expedition, voyage, ramble, stroll, walk, hike, trek, drive, ride, sail.

excuse, *v.* **1.** forgive, pardon, overlook, acquit, absolve, exonerate, exculpate. **2.** apologize for, exonerate, exculpate, clear, vindicate. **3.** condone, allow, permit, warrant, mitigate, extenuate, palliate, justify. **4.** release, disoblige, free, liberate, disencumber. —*n.* **5.** plea, apology, absolution, justification, explanation, story, reason, defense, vindication. **6.** pretext, pretense, subterfuge, evasion, makeshift, loophole. —**Ant.** condemn; oblige, shackle.

execute, *v.* **1.** carry out, accomplish, do, perform, implement, achieve, effect, consummate, finish, complete. **2.** kill, put to death, garrote, remove, murder, butcher, slay. **3.** enforce, effectuate, administer; sign, seal, and deliver.

exemption, *n.* immunity, impunity, privilege, freedom, exception. —**Ant.** culpability.

exercise, *n.* **1.** exertion, labor, toil, work, action, activity. **2.** drill, calisthenics, workout, practice, training, schooling, discipline. **3.** practice, use, application, employment, performance, operation. **4.** ceremony, ritual, procedure, observance, service. —*v.* **5.** discipline, drill, train, school. **6.** practice, use, apply, employ, effect, exert. **7.** discharge, perform. **8.** harass, irritate, vex, harry, distress, agitate, worry, annoy, make uneasy, try, burden, trouble, pain, afflict. —**Ant.** laziness, sloth.

exertion, *n.* effort, action, activity, endeavor, struggle, attempt, strain, trial, striving, work, toil, drive, industry.

exhaust, v. **1.** empty, drain, void. **2.** use up, expend, consume, waste, squander, dissipate, spend, fritter away. **3.** enervate, tire, prostrate, wear out, fatigue, weaken, cripple, debilitate. —**Ant.** fill; use; innervate, invigorate, strengthen.

exhaustion, n. tiredness, debilitation, enervation, weariness, lassitude, weakness, fatigue. —**Ant.** energy, exhilaration, strength.

exhibit, v. **1.** expose, present, display, show, demonstrate, offer. **2.** manifest, display, show, betray, reveal, express, disclose, indicate, evince. —n. **3.** exhibition, showing, show, display, demonstration, offering, exposition, manifestation. —**Ant.** conceal, hide.

exhilarate, v. make cheerful or merry, cheer, gladden, enliven, inspirit, animate, inspire, elate, excite, transport, enrapture. —**Ant.** depress, sadden, deject.

exorbitant, adj. extraordinary, outrageous, immoderate, extortionate, extreme, disproportionate, preposterous, undue, unjustifiable, excessive, inordinate, extravagant, unreasonable, unconscionable, enormous. —**Ant.** reasonable, inexpensive.

expand, v. increase, extend, swell, enlarge, dilate, distend, inflate, bloat, aggrandize, spread or stretch out, unfold, develop. —**Ant.** contract, shrink.

expect, v. look forward to, anticipate, await, hope for, wait for, count on, rely on, envision, foresee, contemplate.

expectation, n. confidence, watchfulness, apprehension, suspense, expectancy, anticipation, hope, trust, prospect.

expedient, adj. **1.** advantageous, fit, suitable, profitable, advisable, proper, right, correct, pertinent, applicable, fitting, apropos, appropriate, desirable. —n. **2.** device, contrivance, means, resource, shift, resort. —**Ant.** unsuitable, inapt, undesirable.

expedite, v. speed up, hasten, quicken, speed, step up, push, accelerate, hurry, precipitate; dispatch. —**Ant.** slow.

expedition, n. **1.** excursion, journey, voyage, mission, exploration, field trip, trek, trip, junket, safari. **2.** promptness, speed, haste, quickness, dispatch, alacrity, swiftness, dispatch. —**Ant.** sloth.

expel, v. drive or force away, drive or force out, discharge, eject; dismiss, oust, banish, exile, expatriate, deport. —**Ant.** accept, invite.

expend, v. **1.** use, employ, consume, spend, exhaust, use up. **2.** pay, disburse, spend, lay out. —**Ant.** save, husband, conserve.

expense, n. **1.** cost, charge, price, outlay, expenditure. **2.** loss, injury, harm, debit, detriment, sacrifice, impairment, ruin, destruction.

expensive, adj. costly, dear, high-priced, up-market, valuable, precious, priceless, extravagant, at a premium. —**Ant.** inexpensive, cheap, tawdry.

experience, n. **1.** incident, event, happening, affair, episode, occurrence, circumstance, adventure, encounter. **2.** knowledge, know-how, sophistication, skill, judgment, common sense, wisdom, sagacity. —v. **3.** meet with, undergo, feel, encounter, live through, know, observe; endure; suffer. —**Ant.** inexperience, naiveté.

experienced, adj. skilled, expert, veteran, practiced, accomplished, proficient, knowledgeable, knowing, wise, sage, versed, qualified, adroit, adept, shrewd, prepared, masterly, professional, competent, efficient, capable, au fait. —**Ant.** inexperienced, inexpert, naive, artless, unqualified.

experiment, n. **1.** test, trial, examination, proof, assay, procedure, experimentation, research, investigation. —v. **2.** try, test, examine, prove, assay.

expert, n. **1.** specialist, authority, connoisseur, master, scholar, pundit, maven, virtuoso, wizard, champion. —adj. **2.** trained, skilled, skillful, experienced, practiced, knowledgeable, learned, qualified, adept, polished, capable, masterly, superior, first-rate, adept, au fait, accomplished, excellent, superb, wonderful, proficient, dexterous, adroit, clever, apt, quick. —**Ant.** butcher, shoemaker, dolt; untrained, inexperienced, maladroit.

explain, v. **1.** elucidate, expound, explicate, interpret, clarify, throw light on, make plain or manifest. **2.** account for, justify, excuse, rationalize, legitimize, extenuate. —**Ant.** confuse.

explanation, n. **1.** clarification, elucidation, explication, exposition, definition, interpretation, description. **2.** meaning, interpretation, solution, key, answer, definition, account, justification.

explicit, adj. **1.** clear, unequivocal, express, unambiguous, precise, definite, exact, categorical, determinate. **2.** open, outspoken, candid, frank, direct, forthright, straightforward, definite, unashamed, unabashed. —**Ant.** unclear, equivocal, ambiguous, indefinite; clandestine, concealed.

exploit, n. **1.** deed, feat, attainment, accomplishment, achievement. —v. **2.** use, profit from, capitalize on, manipulate, utilize, take advantage of.

expose, v. **1.** lay open, subject, risk, endanger, imperil, jeopardize. **2.** bare, uncover; exhibit, display. **3.** make known, betray, uncover, unveil, disclose, reveal, unmask, bring to light; muckrake. —**Ant.** conceal, hide.

exposition, n. **1.** exhibit, exhibition, show, demonstration, display. **2.** explanation, elucidation, commentary, treatise, critique, interpretation, exegesis, explication.

exposure, n. **1.** disclosure, unmasking, presentation, display, divulgement, revelation, exposé. **2.** aspect, orientation, view, outlook, setting, location. —**Ant.** hiding, concealment.

express, v. **1.** utter, declare, state, word, speak, assert, articulate, verbalize, phrase, voice, say, tell, communicate. **2.** show, manifest, reveal, expose, indicate, exhibit, represent. **3.** indicate, signify, designate, denote, show, demonstrate, reveal, betoken, convey. **4.** press or squeeze out, expel, extract, wring out. —adj. **5.** clear, distinct, definite, explicit, plain, obvious, positive, unambiguous, categorical; unsubtle. **6.** special, particular, singular, signal. **7.** quick, speedy, prompt, immediate, swift, direct, fast, rapid, nonstop. —**Ant.** conceal.

expression, n. **1.** utterance, verbalization, announcements, declaration, assertion, statement. **2.** phrase, term, idiom. **3.** language, diction, phraseology, wording, phrasing, presentation. **4.** manifestation, sign, indication, token, symbol, representation. **5.** look, countenance, aspect, air, mien, intonation, tone. —**Ant.** silence.

expressive, adj. **1.** meaning, allusive, eloquent, revealing, significant, suggestive, meaningful, indicative. **2.** striking, telling, lively, vivid, strong, emphatic. —**Ant.** expressionless, meaningless.

exquisite, adj. **1.** dainty, beautiful, elegant, rare, delicate, appealing, charming. **2.** fine, admirable, consummate, perfect, matchless, complete, valuable, precious. **3.** intense, acute, keen, poignant. **4.** sensitive, responsive. **5.** rare, select, choice, excellent, precious, valuable, priceless; vintage. **6.** refined, elegant, delicate, discriminating, polished, debonair. —**Ant.** ugly, hideous; imperfect, valueless, worthless; dull; vacuous, vapid; common, ordinary; poor, inferior; boorish.

extemporaneous, adj. unstudied, spontaneous, unrehearsed, unplanned, unscripted, ad-lib, extempore, impromptu, improvised, unpremeditated, offhand, off the cuff. —**Ant.** prepared, premeditated.

extend, v. **1.** stretch or draw out, attenuate. **2.** lengthen, prolong, protract, continue. **3.** expand, spread out, dilate, enlarge, widen, diffuse, fill out. **4.** hold forth, offer, bestow, grant, give, impart, yield. —**Ant.** shorten, abbreviate; discontinue; shrink, curtail.

extensive, adj. **1.** wide, broad, large, extended, spacious, ample, vast. **2.** far-reaching, comprehensive, thorough; inclusive.

extent, n. space, degree, magnitude, measure, amount, scope, compass, range, expanse, stretch, reach, size; length, area, volume.

exterior, adj. **1.** outer, outside, outward, external, surface, superficial. **2.** outlying, extraneous, foreign, extrinsic. —n. **3.** outside, face, facing, surface, covering, coating, front, skin, shell, facade. **4.** appearance, mien, aspect, face. —**Ant.** interior, inner; important; interior, inside.

exterminate, v. extirpate, annihilate, destroy, eradicate, abolish, eliminate, obliterate, wipe out, root out, deracinate. —**Ant.** create, generate, originate.

extinct, adj. **1.** extinguished, quenched, out, put out. **2.** obsolete, dated, outmoded, old-fashioned, antiquated, passé, out-of-date, antediluvian, ancient, old hat, archaic. **3.** ended, terminated, over, dead, gone, vanished. —**Ant.** extant; modern; begun, initiated.

extol, v. praise, laud, eulogize, commend, glorify, exalt, celebrate, applaud, panegyrize, acclaim, pay tribute or homage to. —**Ant.** condemn, damn.

extract, v. **1.** draw forth or out, get, pull or pry out. **2.** deduce, divine, understand. **3.** extort, exact, evoke, educe, draw out, elicit, wrest, wring, bleed. **4.** derive, withdraw, distill. —n. **5.** excerpt, quotation, citation, selection. **6.** decoction, distillate, solution.

extraneous, adj. external, extrinsic, foreign, alien, strange, out of place, off or beside the point, adventitious; inappropriate, not germane, not pertinent, nonessential, superfluous, peripheral, incidental, irrelevant, inappropriate, needless. —**Ant.** internal, intrinsic; appropriate, pertinent, essential, vital.

extraordinary, adj. exceptional, special, inordinate, uncommon, singular, signal, rare, phenomenal, unique, curious, peculiar, odd, bizarre, strange, abnormal, nonpareil, amazing, marvelous, fantastic, incredible, fabulous, miraculous, far-out, unreal, remarkable, unusual, egregious, unheard of. —**Ant.** ordinary, common, usual, customary.

extravagant, adj. **1.** imprudent, wasteful, lavish, profligate, reckless, spendthrift, prodigal, immoderate, excessive, inordinate, exorbitant. **2.** unreasonable, fantastic, wild, foolish, absurd, outrageous, preposterous. —**Ant.** prudent, thrifty, moderate; reasonable, thoughtful, sensible.

extreme, *adj.* **1.** utmost, greatest, rarest, highest; superlative. **2.** outermost, endmost, ultimate, last, uttermost, remotest. **3.** extravagant, immoderate, excessive, fanatical, uncompromising, radical, outré, unreasonable. **4.** unusual, exceptional, uncommon, outstanding, notable, noteworthy, abnormal, extraordinary. —*n.* **5.** farthest, furthest, remotest. **6.** acme, limit, end; extremity. —**Ant.** reasonable.

extremity, *n.* **1.** terminal, limit, end, termination, extreme, verge, limit, edge, margin, periphery, frontier, border, boundary, bounds. **2.** utmost, extreme, maximum, limits.

exuberance, *n.* cheerfulness, joy, exhilaration, buoyancy, animation, liveliness, spirit, enthusiasm, excitement, zest, energy, vigor, superabundance, excess, copiousness, profusion, luxuriance, lavishness, superfluity, redundancy, overflow. —**Ant.** dejection, somberness, melancholy, lassitude; paucity, lack, need, want.

F

fable, *n.* **1.** legend, tale, parable, allegory, myth, story, romance, fancy, tradition, saga, epic, folktale, fairy tale. **2.** lie, untruth, falsehood, fib, fiction, invention, fabrication, tall tale, cock-and-bull story, whopper. —**Ant.** truth, gospel.

fabricate, *v.* **1.** construct, build, frame, erect, make, manufacture, raise, fashion, form, produce, assemble, put together. **2.** devise, invent, coin, create, originate, concoct, imagine, hatch, design, think up. **3.** forge, fake, falsify, counterfeit, feign, trump up, cook up. —**Ant.** destroy, raze.

fabulous, *adj.* **1.** unbelievable, incredible, amazing, astonishing, fantastic, marvelous, wonderful, miraculous, phenomenal, astounding. **2.** untrue, unreal, unrealistic, invented, fabled, fictional, fictitious, fabricated, coined, made up, imaginary, mythical, legendary, storied, fanciful, storybook, fairytale. —**Ant.** commonplace; real, natural.

face, *n.* **1.** countenance, visage, front, features, look, expression, physiognomy, look, appearance, aspect, mien; sight, presence. **2.** show, pretense, pretext, exterior. —*v.* **3.** meet face to face, confront, encounter, meet, meet with, brave, deal *or* cope with. —**Ant.** back; interior.

facet, *n.* aspect, side, angle, position, posture, phase, view, viewpoint, feature, light, slant, particular, detail.

facile, *adj.* **1.** effortless, easy, adroit, deft, dexterous, fluent, flowing, smooth, graceful, elegant. **2.** superficial, glib, slick, surface, shallow, slight. —**Ant.** labored, laborious, profound.

faction, *n.* side, bloc, camp, cabal, cadre, splinter group, circle, clique, set, pressure group, junta, ring, gang, group, party, sect, interest, division, wing, denomination, order, school, society, body.

factory, *n.* manufactory, mill, workshop, plant, works.

factual, *adj.* actual, real, true, demonstrable, provable, evidential, evidentiary, verifiable, de facto, genuine, certain, undoubted, unquestioned, valid,

authentic, bona fide. —**Ant.** imaginary, groundless, illusory.

faculty, *n.* ability, capacity, aptitude, capability, knack, turn, talent, skill, potential, flair, gift, genius, cleverness, dexterity. —**Ant.** inability, incapacity.

fade, *v.* **1.** wither, droop, languish, decline, decay, die out, perish, ebb, wane, wilt, waste away, languish, deteriorate, shrivel, peter out. **2.** blanch, etiolate, bleach, pale. **3.** disappear, vanish, die out, pass away, evanesce. —**Ant.** flourish; flush; appear.

fail, *v.* **1.** come short, fall short, disappoint, miscarry, misfire, falter, abort, founder, run aground, come to nothing, go wrong, flop, fizzle. **2.** fall off, dwindle, pass *or* die away, decline, fade, weaken, sink, wane, give out, cease, disappear. **3.** desert, forsake, disappoint, let down, abandon. —**Ant.** succeed.

failing, *n.* shortcoming, weakness, foible, deficiency, defect, frailty, imperfection, fault, flaw, blemish, blind spot. —**Ant.** success, sufficiency; strength.

failure, *n.* **1.** unsuccessfulness, miscarriage, abortion, failing. **2.** neglect, omission, dereliction, nonperformance, deficiency, insufficiency, defectiveness. **3.** loser, nonstarter, incompetent, nonentity, also-ran, flop, dud, lemon, washout, dead duck. **4.** decline, decay, deterioration, loss. **5.** bankruptcy, insolvency, failing, bust, downfall, ruin. —**Ant.** success; adequacy, sufficiency; effectiveness.

faint, *adj.* **1.** indistinct, ill-defined, dim, faded, dull. **2.** feeble, halfhearted, faltering, irresolute, weak, languid, drooping. **3.** giddy, vertiginous, unsteady, woozy, lightheaded, dizzy, swooning. **4.** cowardly, timorous, pusillanimous, fearful, timid, dastardly, fainthearted. —*v.* **5.** swoon, pass out, black out. —*n.* **6.** swoon, unconsciousness, blackout, collapse. —**Ant.** strong; distinct; brave, bold.

fair, *adj.* **1.** unbiased, equitable, just, honest, impartial, disinterested, unprejudiced. **2.** reasonable, passable, tolerable, average, middling. **3.** bright, sunny, cloudless; fine. **4.** unobstructed, open, clear, distinct, unencumbered, plain. **5.** clean, spotless, pure, untarnished, unsullied, unspotted, unblemished, unstained. **6.** beautiful, lovely, comely, pretty, attractive, pleasing, handsome. **7.** courteous, civil, polite, gracious. —*n.* **8.** exhibit, exhibition, festival, kermis, bazaar, show. —**Ant.** unfair.

fairy, *n.* fay, pixy, pixie, leprechaun, nix, nixie, brownie, elf, sprite.

faith, *n.* **1.** sureness, certitude, conviction, confidence, trust, reliance, credit, credence, assurance. **2.** belief, doctrine, tenet, creed, dogma, religion, persuasion. —**Ant.** discredit, distrust.

faithful, *adj.* **1.** strict, thorough, true, devoted. **2.** true, reliable, trustworthy, trusty. **3.** stable, dependable, steadfast, staunch, loyal, constant. **4.** credible, creditable, believable, trustworthy, reliable. **5.** strict, rigid, accurate, precise, exact, conscientious, close. —**Ant.** unfaithful, faithless.

faithless, *adj.* **1.** disloyal, false, inconstant, fickle, perfidious, treacherous. **2.** unreliable, untrustworthy, untrue. **3.** untrusting; unbelieving, doubting. **4.** skeptical, freethinking, atheistic, agnostic, heathen, infidel. —**Ant.** faithful.

fake, *adj.* **1.** fraudulent, false, unreal, forged, fabricated, counterfeit, bogus, phony, sham, spurious, pretend, pinchbeck. —*n.* **2.** fraud, hoax, impos-

ture, deception, counterfeit, forgery, imitation, sham, phony. —*v.* **3.** pretend, feign, affect, counterfeit, sham, simulate, act, make-believe, affect.

false, *adj.* **1.** erroneous, incorrect, amiss, faulty, flawed, unfactual, imprecise, inexact, inaccurate, invalid, unsound, unreal, imaginary, spurious, mistaken, wrong, untrue, improper. **2.** untruthful, lying, mendacious, untrue, concocted, meretricious, fallacious, fabricated, fictitious. **3.** deceitful, treacherous, faithless, insincere, hypocritical, disingenuous, disloyal, unfaithful, two-faced, inconstant, recreant, perfidious, traitorous. **4.** deceptive, deceiving, misleading, fallacious. **5.** spurious, artificial, bogus, phony, forged, sham, counterfeit, ersatz, unreal, fake, feigned, imitation, fraudulent, factitious, make-believe, synthetic, mock, unnatural. **6.** substitute, ersatz, supplementary, stand-in. —**Ant.** true; genuine.

falsehood, *n.* lie, fib, untruth, distortion, fabrication, fiction, misstatement, prevarication, distortion, cock-and-bull story. —**Ant.** truth.

fame, *n.* reputation, acclaim, prominence, cachet, brilliance, repute, renown, eminence, celebrity, honor, illustriousness, superiority, preeminence, stardom, name, glory; notoriety. —**Ant.** infamy, disrepute.

familiar, *adj.* **1.** common, well-known, frequent, everyday, ordinary, current, usual, routine, customary, habitual, traditional. **2.** well-acquainted, conversant, well-versed. **3.** easy, informal, unceremonious, unconstrained, free. **4.** intimate, close, friendly, affable, social, sociable, relaxed, free-and-easy, amicable. **5.** presuming, presumptive, unreserved, disrespectful, bold, forward, insolent, impudent. —**Ant.** unfamiliar, unknown.

familiarity, *n.* **1.** acquaintance, grasp, experience, knowledge, understanding. **2.** intimacy, friendliness, affability, sociability, ease, informality, closeness, naturalness. **3.** disrespect, boldness, presumption, impudence, insolence, impertinence, impropriety. —**Ant.** unfamiliarity.

famous, *adj.* celebrated, renowned, popular, noted, prominent, public, well-known, famed, notable, eminent, distinguished, illustrious, honored, venerable, lionized. —**Ant.** unknown, undistinguished.

fanatical, *adj.* zealous, enthusiastic, visionary, frenzied, rabid, extreme, maniacal, mad, frenzied, frantic, frenetic, fervent, obsessive, compulsive, monomaniacal, passionate, agog, immoderate, excessive, fiendish, hysterical, single-minded, hot-headed, quixotic.

fancy, *n.* **1.** imagination, fantasy, hallucination, illusion, dream, pipe dream, mirage, phantasm, phantom, figment. **2.** image, conception, idea, thought, notion, impression. **3.** caprice, whim, vagary, quirk, humor, crotchet. **4.** preference, liking, inclination, fondness. —*adj.* **5.** fine, elegant, choice. **6.** ornamental, decorated, ornate. **7.** fanciful, capricious, whimsical, irregular, extravagant. —*v.* **8.** picture, envision, conceive, imagine. **9.** like, be pleased with, take a fancy to, favor, prefer, be attracted to, want, have an appetite for. —**Ant.** plain; regular, ordinary; dislike, abhor.

fascinate, *v.* bewitch, charm, enchant, entrance, enrapture, spellbind, intrigue, beguile, transfix, engross, absorb, enthrall, hypnotize, mesmerize, attract, seduce, cast a spell over, entice, captivate, allure, infatuate, enamor. —**Ant.** repel, disgust.

fashion, *n.* **1.** custom, style, vogue, mode, trend, look, taste, fad, rage, craze. **2.** custom, style, conventionality, conformity. **3.** haut monde, beau monde, in crowd, jet set, high society, society. **4.** manner, way, mode, method, attitude, approach. **5.** make, form, figure, shape, stamp, mold, pattern, model, cast. **6.** kind, sort. —*v.* **7.** make, shape, frame, construct, model, style, create, work, manufacture, mold, form. **8.** accommodate, adapt, suit, fit, adjust.

fashionable, *adj.* stylish, chic, in vogue, in fashion, in style, smart, trendy, voguish, exclusive, inside, swank, tony, au courant, à la mode, soigné, soignée, all the rage, hip, with it, in. —**Ant.** unfashionable, dowdy.

fast, *adj.* **1.** quick, swift, rapid, fleet. **2.** energetic, active, alert, quick. **3.** dissolute, dissipated, profligate, unmoral, wild, reckless, extravagant, prodigal. **4.** strong, resistant, impregnable. **5.** immovable, fixed, secure, steadfast, staunch, firm. **6.** tied, knotted, fastened, fixed, tight, close. **7.** permanent, lasting, enduring, eternal. **8.** loyal, faithful, steadfast. —*adv.* **9.** tightly, fixedly, firmly, securely, tenaciously. **10.** quickly, swiftly, rapidly, speedily. **11.** energetically, recklessly, extravagantly, wildly, prodigally. —**Ant.** slow, lethargic; upright, moral; weak, defenseless; feeble; temporary; disloyal, faithless.

fasten, *v.* make fast, fix, secure, anchor, attach, pin, rivet, bond, bind, stick, affix, tie, connect, link, hook, clasp, clinch, clamp, tether. —**Ant.** loosen, loose, untie.

fat, *adj.* **1.** bulky, overfed, overweight, heavy, rotund, tubby, flabby, fleshy, plump, corpulent, obese, adipose, stout, portly, chubby, pudgy, potbellied, beefy, broad in the beam, big-boned, paunchy. **2.** oily, fatty, unctuous, greasy, pinguid. **3.** rich, profitable, remunerative, lucrative. **4.** fertile, rich, fruitful, productive. **5.** plentiful, copious, abundant. —**Ant.** thin, skinny, cadaverous; poor; scarce, scanty; barren.

fatal, *adj.* **1.** deadly, mortal, toxic, terminal, lethal; destructive, disastrous, ruinous, pernicious, calamitous, catastrophic. **2.** fateful, inevitable, doomed, predestined, foreordained, damned, decreed, inescapable. —**Ant.** lifegiving, constructive; indeterminate.

fate, *n.* **1.** fortune, luck, lot, chance, destiny, karma, kismet, providence, doom. **2.** death, destruction, ruin, doom, downfall, undoing, disaster, collapse, nemesis, end, finish. —*v.* **3.** predetermine, destine, predestine, foreordain, preordain.

fatherly, *adj.* paternal, parental, protecting, protective; kind, tender, benign.

fault, *n.* **1.** defect, imperfection, blemish, flaw, failing, frailty, foible, deficiency, peccadillo, weakness, shortcoming, vice. **2.** error, mistake, slip, thunder, lapse, failure, oversight, gaffe, offense. **3.** misdeed, sin, transgression, trespass, misdemeanor, offense, wrong, delinquency, indiscretion, culpability. —**Ant.** strength.

faulty, *adj.* incomplete, flawed, unsound, damaged, impaired, broken, defective, imperfect, bad. —**Ant.** perfect, complete, consummate.

favor, *n.* **1.** courtesy, gesture, service, good turn, kindness, goodwill, benefit, good deed. **2.** partiality, bias, patron-

age, prejudice. **3.** gift, present. —*v.* **4.** prefer, encourage, patronize, approve, countenance, allow. **5.** facilitate, ease; propitiate, conciliate, appease. **6.** encourage, benefit, help, aid, help, support, assist. —**Ant.** cruelty; disfavor; disapprove, disallow, discourage.

favorite, *adj.* **1.** preferred, chosen, pet, best-liked, best-loved, fair-haired, popular, beloved, loved, prized, treasured, dearest, precious, adored, esteemed, dearly beloved. —*n.* **2.** preference, pet, darling, chosen one, apple of one's eye, fair-haired one, ideal, flavor of the month.

fear, *n.* **1.** apprehension, consternation, dismay, alarm, qualms, timidity, cowardice, second thoughts, trepidation, dread, terror, fright, horror, panic. **2.** anxiety, solicitude, angst, foreboding, distress, misgiving, worry, unease, concern. **3.** awe, respect, reverence, veneration. —*v.* **4.** be afraid of, shudder at, quiver, tremble at, shrink from, apprehend, dread. **5.** revere, venerate, reverence, respect. —**Ant.** boldness, bravery, intrepidity; security, confidence.

fearless, *adj.* brave, intrepid, bold, courageous, heroic, valorous, valiant, dauntless, plucky, gallant, daring, reckless. —**Ant.** cowardly.

feasible, *adj.* **1.** practicable, workable, viable, doable, applicable, possible. **2.** suitable, suited, usable, practical, practicable. **3.** likely, probable, realistic. —**Ant.** unfeasible, impractical, impossible; unsuitable, unsuited; unlikely, improbable.

feast, *n.* **1.** celebration, anniversary, commemoration, ceremony, banquet, fête, entertainment, carousal, revelry, sumptuous repast, spread, blowout. —*v.* **2.** eat, gourmandize, glut *or* stuff *or* gorge oneself, wine and dine, overindulge. **3.** gratify, delight, please, cheer, gladden.

feat, *n.* achievement, accomplishment, deed, action, act, exploit, attainment, tour de force.

feature, *n.* characteristic, peculiarity, trait, property, mark, attribute, hallmark, quality, aspect, facet, quirk, peculiarity, idiosyncrasy.

feeble, *adj.* **1.** weak, feckless, ineffective, ineffectual. **2.** infirm, sickly, debilitated, enervated, declining, frail. **3.** faint, dim, weak, obscure, imperceptible, indistinct. —**Ant.** strong, effective, effectual; healthy; clear.

feed, *v.* **1.** nourish, sustain, purvey, provision, cater, supply, maintain, nurture. **2.** satisfy, minister to, gratify, please. —**Ant.** starve.

feeling, *n.* **1.** consciousness, perception, impression; emotion, passion, sentiment, sensibility; sympathy, empathy, compassion. **2.** tenderness, sensitivity, sentiment, sentimentality, susceptibility, pity. **3.** intuition, idea, notion, inkling, suspicion, sense, belief, hunch, theory, presentiment, tenor. —*adj.* **4.** sentient, emotional, sensitive, tender; sympathetic. **5.** emotional, impassioned, passionate. —**Ant.** apathy, coolness; unemotional, insensitive, unsympathetic; cool.

feign, *v.* **1.** invent, concoct, devise, fabricate, forge, counterfeit. **2.** simulate, pretend, counterfeit, affect; emulate, imitate, mimic. **3.** make believe, pretend, imagine.

female, *n.* **1.** woman, girl. —*adj.* **2.** feminine, delicate, womanly, soft, gentle, maternal, nurturing. —**Ant.** male; masculine, manly.

ferocious, *adj.* fierce, savage, wild,

cruel, violent, ravenous, vicious, feral, brutal, bestial, merciless, ruthless, pitiless, inhuman, barbaric, bloodthirsty, predatory, fiendish, monstrous, rapacious. —**Ant.** mild, tame, calm.

fertile, *adj.* productive, prolific, fecund, fruitful, rich, teeming, bounteous, abundant, copious, plenteous, luxuriant. —**Ant.** sterile, barren.

fervent, *adj.* fervid, ardent, earnest, warm, heated, hot, burning, glowing, fiery, inflamed, eager, zealous, vehement, impassioned, passionate, enthusiastic, intense, fanatical, excited, frantic, frenzied, emotional, heartfelt, ecstatic. —**Ant.** cool, apathetic.

fervor, *n.* ardor, intensity, earnestness, eagerness, enthusiasm, fervency, warmth, zeal, gusto, ebullience, spirit, verve, passion, fire, heat, vehemence. —**Ant.** coolness, apathy.

feud, *n.* hostility, quarrel, argument, difference, falling out, dispute, conflict, vendetta, strife, enmity, animosity, antagonism, rivalry, discord, grudge, bad blood, hard feelings, dissension.

fiction, *n.* **1.** novel, fantasy, story, fable, tale, legend, myth. **2.** fabrication, figment, unreality, lie, falsehood, prevarication, invention, falsity. —**Ant.** nonfiction, fact; reality.

fictitious, *adj.* **1.** imaginary, illusory, fanciful, fancied, invented, created, concocted, made-up, dreamed up, unreal, visionary, chimerical, mythical. **2.** artificial, bogus, fake, mock, ungenuine, deceptive, counterfeit, factitious, synthetic. —**Ant.** real, genuine.

fidelity, *n.* **1.** loyalty, faithfulness, devotion, fealty, dependability, resolve, allegiance, trustworthiness, reliability, constancy, steadfastness, staunchness, firmness, steadiness, stability, dedication. **2.** accuracy, precision, faithfulness, exactness, closeness. —**Ant.** disloyalty, unfaithfulness; inaccuracy.

fierce, *adj.* **1.** ferocious, wild, vehement, violent, savage, cruel, fell, feral, bestial, inhuman, sanguinary, dangerous, brutal, bloodthirsty, murderous, homicidal. **2.** truculent, barbarous, intractable, angry, hostile, aggressive, stormy, violent, tempestuous, tumultuous, raging, merciless, remorseless, ruthless, uncontrollable, frenzied, untamed, furious, passionate, turbulent, impetuous. —**Ant.** tame, domesticated; calm; civilized; cool, temperate.

fiery, *adj.* **1.** hot, flaming, heated, fervent, fervid, burning, afire, glowing. **2.** fervent, fervid, vehement, inflamed, impassioned, spirited, ardent, impetuous, passionate, fierce, zealous, excited, eager, hot-headed. —**Ant.** cool, cold; dispassionate.

fight, *n.* **1.** battle, war, combat, encounter, conflict, contest, scrimmage, bout, clash, hostilities, duel, brawl, donnybrook, fracas, riot, engagement, fray, affray, action, skirmish, affair, struggle. **2.** melee, struggle, scuffle, tussle, riot, row, fray. —*v.* **3.** contend, strive, battle, combat, conflict, contest, engage, struggle, clash, feud, take up arms, joust, confront, oppose, encounter, make war, brawl, strive against, cross swords, exchange blows, grapple, wrestle; dispute, defy, resist; protest, withstand, oppugn; argue, quarrel, wrangle, squabble, disagree.

filthy, *adj.* **1.** dirty, foul, unclean, defiled, squalid, nasty, vile, scummy, slimy, grungy, shabby, sordid, soiled, grimy, unkempt, slovenly. **2.** obscene, vile, dirty, pornographic, licentious, lascivious, indecent, impure, smutty, X-rated, gross, offensive, bawdy, ribald, blue, foul-mouthed, immoral, taboo. **—Ant.** clean, spotless, immaculate.

final, *adj.* **1.** last, latest, ultimate, ending, concluding, terminal, closing. **2.** conclusive, decisive, definitive. **—Ant.** prime, primary.

fine, *adj.* **1.** superior, high-grade, choice, excellent, admirable, elegant, superb, magnificent, exceptional, first-rate, quality, marvelous, prime, choice, great, supreme, peachy, exquisite, finished, consummate, perfect, refined, select, delicate. **2.** powdered, pulverized, minute, small, little. **3.** keen, sharp, acute. **4.** outstanding, masterly, masterful, virtuoso, skilled, accomplished, brilliant. **—Ant.** inferior, poor, bad, unfinished; dull; unskilled, maladroit.

finish, *v.* **1.** bring to an end, end, cease, stop, terminate, conclude, close. **2.** use up, complete, consume. **3.** complete, perfect, consummate, polish. **4.** accomplish, achieve, execute, complete, perform, do. —*n.* **5.** end, conclusion, termination, close. **6.** polish, elegance, refinement. **—Ant.** begin, start, commence; originate, create; beginning.

finished, *adj.* **1.** ended, completed, consummated, over, done, done with; complete, consummate, perfect. **2.** polished, refined, elegant, perfected; trained, experienced, practiced, qualified, accomplished, proficient, skilled, gifted, talented. **—Ant.** begun; incomplete, imperfect; unrefined, inelegant; inexperienced, unqualified, unskilled, maladroit.

firm, *adj.* **1.** hard, solid, stiff, rigid, inelastic, compact, condensed, compressed, dense. **2.** steady, unshakable, rooted, fast, fixed, stable, secure, immovable. **3.** fixed, settled, unalterable, established, confirmed. **4.** steadfast, unwavering, determined, immovable, resolute, staunch, constant, steady, reliable. —*n.* **5.** company, partnership, association, business, concern, house, corporation. **—Ant.** flabby, flaccid, elastic, soft; unsteady, unstable; wavering, irresolute, inconstant, unreliable.

fitness, *n.* **1.** condition, physical condition, conditioning, tone, vigor, well-being, shape, fettle, health, healthfulness, trim, repair, order, salubrity, salubriousness. **2.** appropriateness, suitability, applicability, aptness, cogency, propriety, competence, pertinence, seemliness, adequacy.

fix, *v.* **1.** make fast, fasten, pin, attach, tie, secure, stabilize, establish, set, plant, implant. **2.** settle, determine, establish, define, limit. **3.** repair, mend, correct, emend, remedy, rectify, doctor, straighten out. —*n.* **4.** difficulty, quandry, straits, corner, predicament, dilemma, plight, spot, double bind, pickle, jam, bind, pinch. **—Ant.** loosen, loose, detach; unsettle; break.

flame, *n.* **1.** blaze, conflagration, holocaust, inferno, fire. **2.** heat, ardor, zeal, passion, fervor, warmth, enthusiasm. —*v.* **3.** burn, blaze. **4.** glow, burn, warm; shine, flash. **5.** inflame, fire.

flash, *n.* **1.** flame, outburst, flare, gleam, glare. **2.** instant, split second, moment, twinkling, wink. **3.** ostentation, display. —*v.* **4.** glance, glint, glitter, scintillate, gleam.

flat, *adj.* **1.** horizontal, level, even, equal, plane, smooth. **2.** low, recumbent, outstretched, reclining, supine, prone, prostrate. **3.** unqualified, downright, positive, outright, peremptory, absolute. **4.** uninteresting, dull, tedious, lifeless, boring, spiritless, prosaic,

unanimated; insipid, vapid, tasteless, stale, dead, unsavory. **—Ant.** vertical, upright, perpendicular; doubtful, dubious; spirited, animated; tasteful, savory; pointed.

flatter, *v.* apple-polish, fawn, toady, kowtow, truckle, blandish, praise, compliment, court, play up to, curry favor with, cajole, wheedle, coax, beguile, entice, inveigle, flatter, soft-soap, honey, sweet-talk, butter up, bootlick, suck up to, brown-nose. **—Ant.** insult, affront, offend.

flavor, *n.* **1.** taste, savor, tang, piquancy, zest. **2.** seasoning, extract, flavoring. **3.** characteristic, essence, quality, spirit, soul, nature, quality, property, style, mark, feel, feeling. **4.** smell, odor, aroma, perfume, fragrance.

flaw, *n.* defect, imperfection, blot, blemish, spot, fault; crack, crevice, breach, break, cleft, fissure, rift, fracture.

fleet, *adj.* swift, fast, quick, rapid, speedy, expeditious, fleet-footed, nimble-footed, hasty, express, snappy. **—Ant.** slow, sluggish.

flexible, *adj.* **1.** pliable, pliant, flexile, limber, plastic, elastic, supple. **2.** adaptable, tractable, compliant, yielding, gentle. **—Ant.** inflexible, rigid, solid, firm; intractable, unyielding.

flock, *n.* bevy, covey, flight, gaggle; brood, hatch, litter; shoal, school; swarm; pride; drove, herd, pack; group, company, body, band, pack, bunch, troop, assembly, congregation, collection, mass, mob, throng, gang, host, horde, crowd.

flood, *n.* **1.** deluge, inundation, overflow, flash flood, freshet, tidal wave, tide, torrent, stream. **2.** abundance, surge, rush, flow, gut, surfeit, profusion, plethora, excess, superfluity. —*v.* **3.** inundate, submerge, overflow, swamp, immerse, drown. **4.** overwhelm, glut, saturate, choke; swarm, surge, rush, crowd, pour; permeate, fill, engulf, cover.

flourish, *v.* **1.** thrive, prosper, be successful, grow, increase, develop, bloom, blossom, thrive, burgeon, boom, succeed. **2.** brandish, wave, parade, flaunt, display, show off, be ostentatious, boast, brag, vaunt. —*n.* **3.** parade, fanfare, display, ostentation, show, display, dash. **4.** decoration, ornament, adornment, embellishment, elaboration, frill, floweriness, floridness. **—Ant.** decline, die, fail; disfigure, mar.

flow, *v.* **1.** gush, spout, stream, spurt, jet, discharge. **2.** proceed, run, pour, roll on. **3.** overflow, abound, teem, pour. —*n.* **4.** current, flood, stream. **5.** stream, river, rivulet, rill, streamlet. **6.** outpouring, discharge, overflowing.

fluctuate, *v.* waver, vacillate, change, vary, alternate, seesaw, swing, waver, shift, undulate, oscillate.

fluent, *adj.* flowing, articulate, eloquent, well-spoken, facile, easy, graceful, natural, effortless, ready, polished, slick, expressive, glib, voluble, copious, smooth. **—Ant.** terse, curt, silent.

fly, *v.* **1.** take wing, soar, hover, flutter, flit, wing, flap. **2.** hasten, hurry, run, race, dash, sprint, scoot. **3.** elapse, pass, glide, slip by, expire.

foe, *n.* enemy, opponent, adversary, antagonist, competition, opposition, contestant. **—Ant.** friend, ally, associate.

fog, *n.* **1.** cloud, mist, haze, pea soup; soup; smog. **2.** cloud, confusion, obfuscation, dimming, blurring, darken-

ing. —*v.* **3.** befog, becloud, obfuscate, dim, blur, darken. **4.** daze, bewilder, befuddle, muddle. **—Ant.** clarity; clear, brighten; clarify.

foible, *n.* weakness, fault, failing, frailty, defect, imperfection, infirmity, shortcoming, flaw, peculiarity, idiosyncrasy, quirk. **—Ant.** strength, perfection.

follow, *v.* **1.** succeed, ensue. **2.** conform, obey, heed, comply, observe. **3.** accompany, attend. **4.** pursue, chase, trail, track, trace. **5.** ensue, succeed, result, come next, arise, proceed. **—Ant.** lead; order.

follower, *n.* **1.** adherent, partisan, disciple, protégé, student, pupil. **2.** attendant, servant; supporter, retainer, companion, associate. **3.** supporter, devotee, fan, aficionado, promoter, enthusiast, advocate, proponent, booster, rooter, groupie. **—Ant.** leader, teacher; enemy, foe.

food, *n.* provisions; rations, nutrition, nutriment, nourishment, aliment, bread, sustenance, victuals; meat, viands; diet, regimen, fare, menu.

fool, *n.* **1.** simpleton, dolt, dunce, blockhead, nincompoop, ninny, numbskull, ignoramus, booby, sap, idiot, ass, jackass, silly, featherbrain, loon, goose, dimwit, nitwit, halfwit, imbecile, moron, clod, oaf, birdbrain, dumbbell, fathead, chump, schmuck, nit, twit, twerp, jerk, dope, retard, space cadet, mental midget. **2.** jester, buffoon, harlequin, zany, clown, merry-andrew. —*v.* **3.** impose on, trick, deceive, delude, hoodwink, cozen, cheat, gull, gudgeon, hoax, dupe. **4.** joke, jest, play, toy, trifle, dally, idle, banter, tease, twit, kid, fiddle, monkey. **—Ant.** genius.

foolish, *adj.* **1.** silly, senseless, fatuous, stupid, inane, dull, vacant, vapid, slow, asinine, simple, witless. **2.** ill-considered, unwise, thoughtless, irrational, imprudent, unreasonable, absurd, ridiculous, nonsensical, preposterous, foolhardy. **—Ant.** bright, brilliant, clever, intelligent; wise, sage, sagacious.

forbid, *v.* outlaw, proscribe, disallow, inhibit, prohibit, taboo, interdict, prevent, preclude, stop, obviate, deter, discourage, ban, hinder, veto, debar. **—Ant.** allow, permit, encourage.

forbidding, *adj.* hostile, stern, harsh, unfriendly, ugly, bad, ominous, dangerous, offensive, unpleasant, unappealing, dismaying, grim, disagreeable, rebarbative, off-putting, menacing, threatening, minatory. **—Ant.** attractive, appealing.

force, *n.* **1.** strength, power, impetus, intensity, might, vigor, energy. **2.** coercion, violence, compulsion, constraint, enforcement, pressure. **3.** efficacy, effectiveness, effect, efficiency, validity, potency, potential. —*v.* **4.** compel, constrain, oblige, coerce, necessitate. **5.** drive, propel, impel. **6.** overcome, overpower, violate, ravish, rape. **—Ant.** weakness, frailty; ineffectiveness, inefficiency.

forecast, *v.* **1.** predict, augur, foretell, foresee, anticipate, prophesize, be prescient, see the future, read tea leaves. **2.** prearrange, plan, contrive, project. **3.** conjecture, guess, estimate. —*n.* **4.** prediction, augury, conjecture, guess, estimate, foresight, prophecy, prevision, anticipation, forethought, prescience.

foreigner, *n.* alien, stranger, nonnative, outsider, outlander, immigrant, newcomer, new arrival, *Auslander.* **—Ant.** native.

foresight, *n.* **1.** prudence, forethought, prevision, care, anticipation, insight, circumspection, perspicacity, precaution; forecast. **2.** prescience, prevision, foreknowledge, prospect, expectation, perception.

forgive, v. pardon, excuse, allow, indulge, overlook, ignore, disregard; clear, acquit, absolve, exonerate, exculpate, spare, let off; cancel, waive, abolish, void, nullify, erase. **—Ant.** blame, condemn, censure.

forlorn, adj. **1.** abandoned, deserted, forsaken, desolate, alone, neglected, outcast, shunned, friendless, bereft, lonesome, lost, solitary. **2.** desolate, dreary, unhappy, miserable, wretched, pitiable, pitiful, helpless, woebegone, disconsolate, comfortless, pathetic, woeful, melancholy, glum, depressed, dejected, mournful, inconsolable, lugubrious. **—Ant.** accompanied; happy, cheerful.

form, n. **1.** shape, figure, outline, mold, appearance, cast, cut, configuration. **2.** mold, model, pattern. **3.** manner, style, arrangement, sort, kind, order, type. **4.** figure, body, shape, build, physique, anatomy. **5.** ceremony, ritual, formula, formality, conformity, rule, convention. **6.** document, paper, application, business form, blank. **7.** method, procedure, system, mode, practice, formula, approach. **—**v. **8.** construct, frame, shape, model, mold, fashion, outline, cast. **9.** fabricate, forge, shape, fashion, turn out, manufacture, make, produce. **10.** compose, make up, serve for, constitute. **11.** order, arrange, organize, systematize, dispose, combine. **12.** frame, invent, contrive, devise, conceive, contrive, create, originate, dream up, compose, formulate, concoct, coin, imagine.

formal, adj. **1.** standard, customary, established, prescribed, proper, academic, conventional, conformal, conforming, conformist. **2.** ceremonial, ceremonious, ritual, conventional. **3.** ceremonious, stiff, prim, precise, punctilious, starched, dignified, stuffy, strait-laced, stodgy. **4.** perfunctory, external. **5.** official, express, explicit, strict, rigid, definite, authorized, spelled-out, formalized, legal, rigorous. **6.** rigorous, methodical, regular, set, fixed, rigid, stiff, exacting, strict, formulaic, unbending, systematic, orderly.

formidable, adj. dreadful, appalling, threatening, menacing, fearful, terrible, frightful, horrible, alarming, awesome, intimidating, daunting; mind-boggling, incredible, prodigious, impressive; arduous, staggering, overwhelming, difficult, challenging, onerous. **—Ant.** pleasant, friendly, amiable.

forsake, v. **1.** quit, leave, desert, abandon. **2.** give up, renounce, forswear, relinquish, recant, drop, forgo, yield, repudiate, surrender, resign, abdicate, deny, turn one's back on.

fortunate, adj. lucky, happy, propitious, favorable, advantageous, providential, opportune, well-timed, timely, auspicious; successful, prosperous, blessed, fortuitous, favored. **—Ant.** unlucky, unfortunate.

forward, adv. **1.** onward, ahead, up ahead, in advance, frontward. **2.** out, forth, to the fore, into view, into the open. **—**adj. **3.** well-advanced, up front, ahead. **4.** ready, prompt, eager, willing, sincere, earnest, zealous. **5.** pert, bold, presumptuous, assuming, confident, impertinent, impudent, brazen, flippant, disrespectful, cheeky, saucy, pushy, fresh. **6.** radical, extreme, unconventional, progressive. **—Ant.** backward.

foster, v. **1.** promote, encourage, further, favor, patronize, forward, advance, stimulate, cultivate, back, help, assist. **2.** bring up, rear, breed, nurse, nourish, sustain, support; care for, cherish. **—Ant.** discourage.

foul, adj. **1.** offensive, gross, disgusting, loathsome, repulsive, repellent, noisome, fetid, putrid, stinking. **2.** filthy, dirty, unclean, squalid, polluted, sullied, soiled, tarnished, stained, tainted, impure. **3.** stormy, unfavorable, rainy, tempestuous. **4.** abominable, wicked, vile, base, shameful, infamous, sinful, scandalous. **5.** scurrilous, obscene, smutty, profane, vulgar, low, coarse. **6.** unfair, dishonorable, underhanded, cheating. **—**v. **7.** soil, defile, sully, stain, dirty, besmirch, smut, taint, pollute, poison. **8.** defile, dishonor, disgrace, shame, taint, blacken, denigrate, debase, degrade, demean, defame, devaluate, belittle, discredit. **—Ant.** delightful, attractive, pleasant; pure; saintly, angelic; fair, honorable; clean, purify; clear; honor.

foundation, n. **1.** base, basis, substructure, underpinning, fundamental, principle, grounds, groundwork, rationale, footing. **2.** establishment, founding, institution, creation, inauguration, setting up, origination, organization, organizing, settlement; endowment. **—Ant.** superstructure.

fragrant, adj. perfumed, odorous, redolent, sweet-smelling, sweet-scented, aromatic, odoriferous, balmy. **—Ant.** noxious.

frail, adj. brittle, fragile, breakable, frangible; delicate, weak, dainty, thin, slight; infirm, feeble, decrepit, sickly, puny, scrawny; ailing, unwell, ill, poorly, wasting away, consumptive. **—Ant.** strong, pliant, elastic, unbreakable, healthy.

frank, adj. **1.** open, unreserved, unrestrained, unrestricted, nonrestrictive, outspoken, candid, sincere, free, bold, truthful, uninhibited. **2.** artless, ingenuous, guileless, innocent, on the level, naive. **3.** undisguised, avowed, downright, outright, direct. **—Ant.** secretive, restrained, restricted; sly, artful, dissembling.

fraud, n. deceit, trickery, duplicity, treachery, swindling, double-dealing, chicanery, fraudulence; breach of confidence, trick, deception, guile, artifice, ruse, stratagem, wile, hoax, humbug, scam, flimflam, gyp, rip-off. **—Ant.** honesty.

free, adj. **1.** unfettered, independent, at liberty, unrestrained, unrestricted; self-governing, autonomous, democratic, sovereign. **2.** unregulated, unrestricted, unimpeded, open, unobstructed. **3.** clear, immune, exempt, uncontrolled, decontrolled. **4.** easy, firm, swift, unimpeded, unencumbered. **5.** loose, unattached, unfastened, untied, lax. **6.** frank, open, unconstrained, unceremonious, familiar, informal, easy, relaxed, casual, natural. **7.** loose, licentious, ribald, lewd, immoral, libertine. **8.** liberal, lavish, generous, bountiful, unstinted, munificent, charitable, unsparing, openhanded. **—**v. **9.** liberate, set free, release, unchain, rescue, redeem, emancipate, manumit, deliver, disenthrall. **10.** rid, relieve, disengage, clear, unburden, disencumber. **—Ant.** dependent, restrained, restricted; close, obstructed; difficult; unfamiliar; moral, upright; stingy, niggardly; confine, enthrall.

freedom, n. **1.** liberty, independence, self-determination, autonomy, self-government. **2.** release, deliverance,

liberation, emancipation, exemption, relief, immunity, franchise, privilege. **3.** range, latitude, scope, play, noninterference, margin; ease, license, facility, permission, right, privilege, authority, authorization, carte blanche. **4.** frankness, honesty, candor, naturalness, unrestraint, openness, ingenuousness. **5.** familiarity, license, looseness, laxity; boldness, audacity, brass, nerve, gall. **—Ant.** dependence; restriction; difficulty; secrecy; unfamiliarity, restraint.

frenzy, n. agitation, excitement, paroxysm, enthusiasm, turmoil, passion, distraction, seizure, outburst, bout, fit; rage, fury, raving, mania, insanity, delirium, derangement, aberration, lunacy, madness, fever, furor, transport. **—Ant.** calm, coolness; sanity, judgment.

frequently, adv. often, many times, repeatedly, regularly, continually, over and over, time and again, habitually, commonly, usually, customarily, ordinarily, generally. **—Ant.** seldom.

fresh, adj. **1.** new, recent, novel, modern, up-to-date, original, unconventional, different, alternative, unorthodox. **2.** youthful, healthy, robust, vigorous, well, hearty, hardy, strong. **3.** refreshing, pure, cool, unadulterated, sweet, invigorating. **4.** inexperienced, artless, untrained, immature, raw, green, uncultivated, unskilled, unsophisticated, untested, naive, wet behind the ears. **—Ant.** stale, old; impure, contaminated; experienced, skilled.

fret, v. **1.** worry, fume, rage, agonize, lose sleep, grieve, brood, whine, fuss, complain, whimper, stew, be upset or anxious. **2.** torment, worry, harass, annoy, irritate, vex, taunt, goad, tease, nettle, needle.

fretful, adj. irritable, peevish, petulant, querulous, touchy, testy, tetchy, temperamental, vexed, edgy, cross, irascible, choleric, crabby, moody, grumpy, sulky, disagreeable, impatient, abrupt, cranky, waspish, pettish, splenetic, captious, snappish, short-tempered, ill-tempered. **—Ant.** calm, even-tempered, temperate, easy-going.

friction, n. discord, disaccord, disharmony, conflict, dissension, disagreement, contention, dispute, controversy, dissent, bickering, argument, wrangling, ill will, bad blood, animosity, rivalry, hostility, strife, antagonism, strain, incompatibility, contentiousness, enmity. **—Ant.** friendliness, amity, cooperation.

friend, n. **1.** companion, crony, chum, acquaintance, intimate, partner, comrade, alter ego, ally, playmate, pal, chum, confidant. **2.** well-wisher, patron, supporter, backer, encourager, advocate, defender. **3.** ally, associate, confrère, confederate, fellow, colleague, coworker, cohort. **—Ant.** enemy, foe, adversary.

friendly, adj. **1.** kind, kindly, amicable, fraternal, amiable, cordial, sociable, congenial, convivial, simpatico, neighborly, genial, well-disposed, benevolent, affectionate, kindhearted, demonstrative, affable, approachable, familiar, chummy. **2.** helpful, favorable, advantageous, propitious. **—Ant.** unfriendly, inimical; unfavorable.

fright, n. dismay, consternation, terror, fear, alarm, panic, dread, horror, trepidation, shock, apprehension. **—Ant.** bravery, boldness.

frighten, v. scare, terrify, alarm, appall, shock, dismay, intimidate, panic, startle, petrify, unnerve, distress, daunt, cow, scare out of one's wits, make one's hair stand on end.

frightful, *adj.* dreadful, terrible, alarming, terrific, fearful, awful, shocking, dread, dire, horrid, horrible, hideous, ghastly, gruesome, atrocious, abhorrent, loathsome, grisly, lurid, macabre, horrifying, horrendous, unspeakable, vile, repugnant. **—Ant.** delightful, attractive, beautiful.

frivolous, *adj.* **1.** unimportant, trifling, petty, paltry, trivial, flimsy, inconsequential, nugatory, insignificant, minor, niggling, superficial, worthless, two-bit, penny-ante. **2.** silly, foolish, childish, puerile, scatterbrained, birdbrained, irresponsible, flighty, giddy, airy-fairy. **—Ant.** important, vital; mature, adult, sensible.

frugal, *adj.* prudent provident, saving, conservative, moderate, economical, thrifty, chary, provident, saving, sparing, careful; parsimonious, stingy, penurious, mean, miserly. **—Ant.** lavish, wasteful.

fruitful, *adj.* prolific, fertile, fecund, productive, profitable; plentiful, abundant, rich, copious, bountiful, luxurious, flourishing. **—Ant.** barren, scarce, scanty, unprofitable, fruitless.

fruitless, *adj.* **1.** useless, worthless, bootless, pointless, unrewarding, to no avail, unavailing, profitless, ineffectual, unprofitable, vain, idle, futile, abortive. **2.** barren, sterile, unfruitful, unproductive, infecund, unprolific. **—Ant.** fruitful, useful, profitable, effectual; abundant, fertile.

frustrate, *v.* defeat, nullify, baffle, disconcert, foil, balk, check, thwart, stymie, block, counter, forestall, prevent, stop, halt, hamper, hinder, cripple, impede; upset, exasperate, discourage, disappoint. **—Ant.** encourage, foster.

fulfill, *v.* **1.** carry out, consummate, execute, discharge, accomplish, achieve, complete, effect, realize, perfect. **2.** perform, do, obey, observe, discharge. **3.** satisfy, meet, anwer, fill, comply with. **4.** complete, end, terminate, bring to an end, finish, conclude. **—Ant.** fail; dissatisfy; create, originate.

full *adj.* **1.** filled, replete, primming, jampacked, loaded, bursting, chockfull, jammed, crammed, crowded, stuffed; gorged, saturated, satiated, sated. **2.** complete, thorough, total, comprehensive, broad, extensive, exhaustive. **3.** complete, entire, whole, uncut, intact, unshortened. **4.** wide, broad, ample, generous, copious. **5.** utmost, greatest, maximum, top, extreme, highest.

fume, *n.* **1.** smoke, vapor, exhalation, gas. **2.** rage, fury, agitation, storm. **—v. 3.** smoke, vaporize. **4.** seethe, smolder, rant, explode, get steamed up, chafe, fret, rage, rave, flare up, bluster, storm, fly off the handle, blow a gasket.

fun, *n.* merriment, enjoyment, pleasure, amusement, divertissement, glee, jollity, mirth, cheer, high spirits, delight, frolic, recreation, entertainment, pastime, joy, sport, diversion, joking, jesting, playfulness, gaiety, frolic. **—Ant.** misery, melancholy.

fundamental, *adj.* **1.** basic, underlying, principal, main, central, rudimentary, prime, cardinal, quintessential, inherent, intrinsic, important, crucial, critical, chief, essential, primary, elementary, necessary, indispensable. **2.** original, first. **—n. 3.** principle, rule, basic law, essence, essential. **—Ant.** superficial, superfluous, dispensable; last, common; nonessential.

funny, *adj.* amusing, diverting, comical, farcical, absurd, ridiculous, comic, risible, waggish, sidesplitting, hilarious, uproarious, jocular, merry, slapstick, zany, entertaining, hysterical, droll, witty, facetious, humorous, laughable, ludicrous, incongruous, foolish; peculiar, odd, unusual, curious, strange, queer, mysterious, weird, bizarre, eccentric, off the wall. **—Ant.** sad, melancholy, humorless.

furnish, *v.* **1.** provide, supply; purvey, cater. **2.** appoint, equip, fit up, rig, deck out, decorate, outfit, fit out.

fury, *n.* **1.** passion, furor, frenzy, rage, ire, anger, choler, rancor, wrath. **2.** violence, turbulence, fierceness, impetuousness, impetuosity, vehemence. **3.** shrew, virago, termagant, vixen, nag, hag, maenad; spitfire, hellcat, she-devil, witch, bitch. **—Ant.** calm, serenity.

fuss, *n.* activity, ado, bustle, bother, dither, flurry, fret, excitement, furor, agitation, unrest, trouble, disquiet, stir, uproar, hubbub, brouhaha, flap, stink, hoopla, to-do, stir, commotion. **—Ant.** inactivity, quiet, serenity.

futile, *adj.* **1.** ineffectual, useless, unsuccessful, vain, unavailing, idle, profitless, unprofitable, bootless, worthless, valueless, fruitless, unproductive. **2.** trivial, frivolous, minor, nugatory, unimportant, trifling. **—Ant.** effective, effectual, successful; profitable, worthy; basic, important, principal, major.

G

gadget, *n.* device, tool, appliance, implement, instrument, utensil, mechanism, contrivance, contraption, invention, creation, doohickey, dingus, thingumabob, gizmo, thingamajig, doodad, widget, whatchamacallit.

gaiety, *n.* **1.** merriment, mirth, glee, jollity, joyousness, liveliness, levity, exhilaration, elation, bouyancy, blitheness, delight, exultation, mirthfulness, jubilation, high spirits, happiness, felicity, pleasure, joie de vivre, sportiveness, hilarity, vivacity, life, cheerfulness, joviality, animation, spirit. **2.** showiness, finery, gaudiness, brilliance, glitter, flashiness, flash, cheeriness, brightness, garishness. **—Ant.** sadness, melancholy, misery.

gain, *v.* **1.** obtain, secure, procure, get, acquire, attain, earn, win, achieve, capture, net, reap, glean, garner, collect. **2.** reach, get to, arrive at, attain. **3.** improve, better, progress, advance, forward; near, approach. **—n. 4.** profit, increase, yield, return, benefit, income, advantage, advance; profits, winnings, earnings, proceeds, revenue. **—Ant.** lose; worsen; retreat; losses.

gall, *v.* **1.** irritate, annoy, irk, vex, nettle, peeve, provoke, bother, harass, plague, goad, nag, needle, rankle, aggravate, exasperate, get one's goat. **—n. 2.** overconfidence, impertinence, forwardness, temerity, effrontery, brazenness, brashness, impudence, insolence, nerve, cheek, crust, brass, guts, chutzpah, moxie.

gallant, *adj.* **1.** brave, high-spirited, valorous, valiant, chivalrous, courageous, bold, intrepid, fearless, daring. **2.** majestic, stately, grand, imposing, glorious, magnificent, splendid, fine. **3.** polite, courtly, chivalrous, noble, attentive, thoughtful, considerate, well-bred, courteous. **—Ant.** cowardly, fearful; tawdry; impolite, discourteous.

game, *n.* **1.** amusement, pastime, di-

version, divertissement, play, fun, sport, contest, competition. **2.** scheme, artifice, strategy, stratagem, plan, plot, undertaking, venture, adventure. **—adj. 3.** plucky, brave, bold, spirited, daring, devil-may-care, unflinching, gutsy, resolute, intrepid, dauntless, valorous, fearless, heroic, gallant.

gang, *n.* band, group, crew, crowd, company, party, set, clique, coterie, horde, pack, mob, ring; squad, shift, team.

garb, *n.* **1.** fashion, mode, style, cut. **2.** clothes, clothing, dress, costume, attire, apparel, habiliments, habit, garments, raiment, vesture. **—v. 3.** dress, clothe, attire, array, apparel.

garish, *adj.* glaring, loud, showy, tawdry, gaudy, flashy, cheap, florid, vulgar, harsh, meretricious, tasteless, trashy, glitzy. **—Ant.** elegant.

garnish, *v.* **1.** adorn, decorate, ornament, embellish, grace, enhance, beautify, trim, bedeck, bedizen, set off. **—n. 2.** decoration, ornamentation, ornament, adornment, garniture, garnishment. **—Ant.** strip.

garrulous, *adj.* talkative, loquacious, prating, prattling, wordy, diffuse, babbling, verbose, prolix. **—Ant.** taciturn, silent, reticent.

gasp, *v.* pant, puff, blow, snort, huff, gulp for air, wheeze.

gather, *v.* **1.** get together, collect, aggregate, assemble, muster, marshal, bring or draw together. **2.** learn, infer, understand, deduce, assume, conclude. **3.** accumulate, amass, garner, hoard. **4.** pluck, garner, reap, harvest, glean, cull, crop. **5.** grow, increase, accrete, collect, thicken, condense. **—Ant.** separate, disperse; decrease.

gathering, *n.* assembly, meeting, mob, flock, swarm, multitude, assemblage, crowd, convocation, congregation, company, throng, horde, host, group, body, association, conclave.

gaudy, *adj.* showy, tawdry, garish, brilliant, loud, flashy, conspicuous, obvious, vulgar, unsubtle, ostentatious, tinselly, trashy, tatty, crude, tasteless, shoddy, honky-tonk, tacky, chintzy, glitzy. **—Ant.** elegant, refined, subtle.

gaunt, *adj.* thin, emaciated, haggard, lean, spare, skinny, scrawny, bony, skeletal, wasted, starved, cadaverous, pinched, underweight, hollow-cheeked, spindly, lanky, lank, angular, rawboned, meager. **—Ant.** obese, fat.

gay, *adj.* **1.** joyous, gleeful, jovial, glad, happy, lighthearted, lively, convivial, vivacious, animated, frolicsome, sportive, hilarious, jolly, carefree, debonair, jubilant, high-spirited, bubbly, effervescent, sparkling, in high spirits, joyful, merry, good-humored, expansive, cheerful, sprightly, blithe, airy. **2.** bright, showy, fine, brilliant. **—Ant.** unhappy, miserable; dull.

general, *adj.* **1.** popular, public, widespread, shared, extensive, global, worldwide, inclusive, comprehensive, overall, catholic, universal. **2.** normal, common, usual, prevalent, customary, regular, ordinary, popular, habitual, everyday, familiar, accustomed, run-of-the-mill, nonexclusive, widespread, prevailing. **3.** miscellaneous, unrestricted, mixed, assorted, heterogeneous, diversified, encyclopedic, blanket, sweeping, across-the-board, sweeping, unspecialized, nonspecific. **4.** vague, lax, indefinite, ill-defined, inexact, imprecise, broad, loose, approximate. **—Ant.** special, partial; uncommon, unusual, extraordinary; specific; definite, exact, precise.

generally, *adv.* usually, commonly,

ordinarily, often, in general, normally, typically, on average, as a rule, by and large, mostly, mainly, for the most part, on the whole, roughly, broadly, loosely, largely, in the main, principally. **—Ant.** rarely.

generosity, *n.* kindness, liberality, lavishness, benevolence, philanthropy, unselfishness, good nature, beneficence, humanity, big-heartedness, largesse, munificence, charity, bounteousness, magnanimity. **—Ant.** stinginess, niggardliness, parsimony.

generous, *adj.* **1.** munificent, bountiful, unselfish, unstinting, liberal, charitable, openhanded, beneficent. **2.** noble, high-minded, magnanimous; large, big. **3.** ample, plentiful, abundant, flowing, overflowing, copious, lavish, handsome, full. **—Ant.** stingy, tightfisted, selfish, niggardly; small, parsimonious; scarce, scanty, barren.

genial, *adj.* **1.** affable, amiable, warm, congenial, good-natured, neighborly, sociable, hospitable, easygoing, convivial, cheerful, sympathetic, cordial, friendly, pleasant, agreeable, kindly, well-disposed, hearty, encouraging. **2.** enlivening, lively, warm, mild, conducive, gentle. **—Ant.** unsympathetic, unpleasant, discouraging; cool.

genius, *n.* **1.** intelligence, brilliance, ingenuity, wit, brains, judgment, acumen, insight, capacity, ability, talent, gift, aptitude, faculty, bent. **2.** intellect, mastermind, master, virtuoso, maestro, expert, adept, brain, brainiac, Einstein, brain surgeon, rocket scientist, whiz kid, wunderkind, prodigy, walking encyclopedia. **—Ant.** inability, incapacity.

gentle, *adj.* **1.** soft, bland, peaceful, clement, moderate, pacific, soothing, kind, tender, humane, lenient, merciful, meek, mild, kindly, amiable, submissive, gentle-hearted, kindhearted. **2.** gradual, moderate, temperate, tempered, light, mild. **3.** wellborn, noble, highborn. **4.** honorable, respectable, refined, cultivated, polished, well-bred, polite, elegant, courteous, courtly. **5.** manageable, tractable, tame, docile, trained, peaceable, quiet. **—Ant.** immoderate, turbulent, unkind, cruel, heartless; sudden, abrupt; unrefined, unpolished, impolite; intractable, wild, noisy.

genuine, *adj.* authentic, real, true, bona fide, verifiable, veritable, legitimate, proper, original, *echt*, factual, provable, honest-to-God, the real McCoy. **—Ant.** false, counterfeit.

get, *v.* **1.** obtain, acquire, procure, secure, gain. **2.** earn, win, gain. **3.** learn, understand, fathom, see, perceive, follow, comprehend, appreciate, take in, work out, apprehend, grasp. **4.** capture, seize, arrest, apprehend, pick up, bag, nab, pinch. **5.** prevail on *or* upon, persuade, induce, influence, coax, cajole, wheedle, sway, cause, dispose. **—Ant.** lose.

ghastly, *adj.* **1.** dreadful, horrible, frightful, hideous, grisly, dismal, awful, horrid, gruesome, terrifying, grim, loathsome, ugly, terrible, shocking. **2.** pale, deathly, white, wan, cadaverous, haggard, pallid, drawn, livid, pastyfaced, ashen. **—Ant.** lovely, attractive, beautiful; ruddy, robust, healthy.

ghost, *n.* **1.** apparition, phantom, spirit, phantasm, wraith, revenant, shade, spook, specter, supernatural being, illusion, banshee, ghoul, hallucination, vision, haint, poltergeist, doppelganger, zombie. **2.** shadow, hint, suggestion, trace, scintilla, glimmer, soupçon.

giant, *adj.* **1.** oversize, outsize, huge,

enormous, great, grand, king-size, gigantic, mammoth, jumbo, colossal, gargantuan, immense, massive, monstrous, monster, vast, Brobdingnagian, Bunyanesque, elephantine, humongous. **—n. 2.** superhuman, ogre, Cyclops, leviathan, whale, gorilla, King Kong, mammoth, colossus, titan, Atlas, Goliath, amazon, behemoth, monster. **—Ant.** lilliputian, tiny.

giddy, *adj.* **1.** lightheaded, light, dizzy, faint, vertiginous, swimming, reeling, spacey, seeing double, groggy, confused. **2.** silly, frivolous, lighthearted, merry, playful, whimsical, pixilated, foolish, goofy, wacky. **3.** emptyheaded, flighty, featherbrained, witless, spacey, scatterbrained, capricious, irresponsible, fickle, volatile, mercurical, reckless, whimsical. **4.** high, tipsy, tiddly, pixilated, intoxicated, inebriated, addled, muddled, befuddled, stupefied. **—Ant.** sober.

gift, *n.* **1.** donation, present, contribution, offering, boon, alms, favor, handout, honorarium, giveaway, bonus, charity, gratuity, tip, benefaction, grant, largess, subsidy, allowance, endowment, bequest, legacy, dowry, inheritance, bounty. **2.** talent, strength, endowment, power, faculty, ability, capacity, forte, capability, genius, bent, aptitude, flair, knack, facility, power.

gigantic, *adj.* huge, enormous, tremendous, colossal, mammoth, massive, giant, stupendous, towering, staggering, gargantuan, Brobdingnagian, jumbo, super-duper, monstrous, elephantine, immense, prodigious, herculean, titanic, cyclopean, vast, extensive, infinite, humongous. **—Ant.** small, tiny, infinitesimal, microscopic.

gingerly, *adj.* **1.** cautious, careful, circumspect, mindful, heedful, wary, chary, fastidious, dainty, squeamish, tentative, nervous, canny, timid, shy, prudent, discreet, guarded, politic. **—adv. 2.** cautiously, carefully, heedfully, warily, charily, delicately, daintily, tentatively.

give, *v.* **1.** deliver, bestow, hand over, offer, vouchsafe, impart, accord, furnish, provide, supply, donate, contribute, afford, spare, accommodate with, confer, grant, cede, relinquish, yield, turn over, assign, present, award. **2.** set forth, issue, show, present, offer. **3.** afford, yield, produce. **4.** issue, put forth, emit, publish, utter, give out (with), pronounce, render. **5.** communicate, impart, divulge. **6.** draw back, recede, retire, relax, cede, yield, give over, give away, sink, give up. **—Ant.** receive.

glad, *adj.* **1.** delighted, pleased, elated, inspirited, jubilant, triumphant, exhilarated, gratified, contented. **2.** cheerful, joyous, joyful, happy, merry, cheery, animated, lighthearted, blithe, exuberant, on cloud nine, in high spirits. **—Ant.** miserable, unhappy, sad.

glamour, *n.* allure, allurement, attraction, seductiveness, appeal, charm, charisma, fascination, magnetism, exoticism, star quality, sophistication, urbanity, elegance. **—Ant.** ordinariness, dowdiness.

glance, *v.* **1.** reflect, glint, shimmer, twinkle, sparkle, flicker, glitter, flash, glimpse, gleam, glisten, scintillate, shine. **2.** glimpse, look, peek, peep, scan. **—n. 3.** glitter, gleam; glimpse, look, gander.

glare, *n.* **1.** dazzle, flare, glitter, luster, brilliance, sparkle, flash. **2.** showiness, ostentation, garishness, gaudiness, flashiness. **3.** frown, stare, dirty look, black look, scowl, glower. **—v. 4.**

shine, dazzle, gleam. **5.** glower, scowl, look daggers at, frown.

gleam, *n.* **1.** ray, flash, beam, glimmer, glimmering. **—v. 2.** shine, glimmer, flash, glitter, sparkle, beam.

glee, *n.* joy, exultation, delight, exuberance, cheer, exhilaration, elation, joy, rapture, enjoyment, high spirits, jubilation, merriment, jollity, hilarity, mirth, joviality, gaiety, liveliness, verve, life. **—Ant.** misery, sadness, melancholy.

glib, *adj.* **1.** fluent, voluble, talkative, garrulous, ready. **2.** slippery, smooth, facile, artful, slick, unctuous, fasttalking, superficial. **—Ant.** taciturn, silent, quiet; artless, guileless.

glide, *v.* slide, slip, flow, coast, skate, sail, stream, float, soar. **—Ant.** stick.

glisten, *v.* reflect, glint, twinkle, wink, blink, glow, glimmer, shimmer, sparkle, shine, gleam, glitter.

gloom, *n.* **1.** darkness, dimness, shadow, shade, obscurity, gloominess, murkiness, dusk, cloudiness, blackness, dullness. **2.** melancholy, sadness, depression, dejection, despondency, doldrums, moroseness, woe, desolation, blues. **—Ant.** brightness, effulgence; joy, glee, happiness.

gloomy, *adj.* **1.** dark, shaded, obscure, shadowy, dim, dusky; dismal, lowering. **2.** depressed, dejected, sad, melancholy, despondent, downcast, crestfallen, downhearted, glum, dispirited, disheartened, morose, lugubrious, dismal, moody, doleful, forlorn, sullen, dreary, blue, saturnine, in the dumps. **—Ant.** bright, effulgent, dazzling; happy, delighted, gleeful.

glorious, *adj.* **1.** admirable, delightful, superb, splendid, brilliant, superior, excellent. **2.** famous, renowned, noted, celebrated, famed, eminent, distinguished, illustrious. **—Ant.** horrible; unknown; notorious.

glory, *n.* **1.** praise, honor, distinction, renown, fame, prestige, repute, eminence, celebrity. **2.** resplendence, splendor, magnificence, grandeur, pomp, brilliance, effulgence. **—v. 3.** revel, relish, delight, pride oneself, crow, gloat, exult, rejoice, triumph. **—Ant.** infamy, dishonor; gloom.

gloss, *n.* **1.** luster, sheen, polish, glaze, shine. **2.** show, mask, front, mien, appearance, pretext, facade, surface, veneer, disguise, camouflage, pretense. **3.** explanation, exegesis, critique, comment, note, interpretation, analysis, annotation, commentary. **—v. 4.** polish, shine, glaze, varnish. annotate, explain, interpret, analyze.

glossy, *adj.* **1.** lustrous, shiny, shining, glazed, smooth, sleek. **2.** slick, artificial, simulated, feigned, pseudo, false, unreal, imitation, fraudulent, counterfeit, specious, plausible.

gluttonous, *adj.* greedy, devouring, voracious, ravenous, grasping, insatiable, ravening, hoggish, piggish, piggy, avid, rapacious. **—Ant.** abstinent, abstemious, restrained.

godly, *adj.* God-fearing, moral, pure, reverent, pietistic, blessed, pious, saintly, devout, religious, holy, righteous, good. **—Ant.** sinful, heathen, atheistic.

good, *adj.* **1.** moral, righteous, religious, pious, pure, virtuous, conscientious, meritorious, worthy, exemplary, upright, upstanding, right-thinking, principled, ethical, godly, law-abiding. **2.** commendable, adroit, efficient, proficient, able, skillful, expert, ready, dexterous, clever, capable, qualified, fit, suited, suitable, convenient. **3.** satisfactory, excellent, exceptional, valuable, precious, capital, admirable, commendable. **4.** well-behaved, dutiful respectful, submissive, acquiescent, tractable, obedient, heedful. **5.** kind, beneficent, friendly, kindly, benevolent, humane, favorable, well-disposed, gracious, obliging. **6.** honorable, worthy, deserving, fair, unsullied, immaculate, unblemished, innocent, unimpeached. **7.** reliable, safe, trustworthy, honest, competent. **8.** genuine, sound, valid. **9.** agreeable, pleasant, genial, cheering. **10.** satisfactory, advantageous, favorable, auspicious, propitious, fortunate, profitable, useful, serviceable, beneficial. —*n.* **11.** profit, worth, advantage, benefit, usefulness, utility, gain. **12.** excellence, merit, righteousness, kindness, virtue. **13.** (*plural*) property, belongings, effects, chattel, furniture. **14.** (*plural*) wares, merchandise, stock, commodities. —**Ant.** bad.

goodness, *n.* **1.** virtue, morality, integrity, honesty, uprightness, godliness, honor, rectitude, decency, nobility, ethicality, high-mindedness, piety, purity, innocence, character, respectability, trustworthiness, probity, righteousness, good. **2.** kindness, benevolence, charity, unselfishness, graciousness, goodwill, compassion, beneficence, warmth, tolerance, patience, mercy, justice, generosity, kindliness, benignity, humanity. **3.** excellence, worth, value, quality, merit, superiority, distinction. —**Ant.** evil.

gorgeous, *adj.* sumptuous, magnificent, splendid, rich, grand, glorious, exquisite, beautiful, breathtaking, radiant, showy, colorful, marvelous, regal, elegant, lustrous, resplendent, brilliant, glittering, dazzling, superb, bodacious. —**Ant.** poor; ugly.

gossip, *n.* **1.** scandal, small talk, hearsay, palaver, idle talk, tittle-tattle, rumor, information, word, chit chat, grapevine, inside dope, scuttlebutt, dish, newsmongering. **2.** chatterer, babbler, gabber, Nosy Parker, scandalmonger, busybody, tattletale, telltale, yenta, quidnunc, bigmouth, chatterbox, blabbermouth. —*v.* **3.** chatter, prattle, prate, palaver, tattle, whisper behind someone's back, spread rumors, blab.

govern, *v.* **1.** rule, reign, hold sway, control, command, sway, influence, have control, lead, sit on the throne, wield the scepter, run the show, be in power, exercise *or* wield power, be in the driver's seat. **2.** direct, guide, restrain, check, conduct, manage, supervise, superintend, oversee, command, look after. —**Ant.** obey; follow.

grace, *n.* **1.** attractiveness, charm, gracefulness, comeliness, ease, elegance, symmetry, beauty; polish, refinement. **2.** favor, kindness, kindliness, love, goodwill, benignity, benevolence, friendliness. **3.** mercy, clemency, pardon, leniency, forgiveness. **4.** sanctity, holiness, devoutness, devotion, piety, piousness, blessedness. —*v.* **5.** adorn, embellish, beautify, enhance, deck, decorate, ornament; honor, dignify. —**Ant.** ugliness; disfavor; condemnation; hate, abhorrence; dishonor, disgrace.

graceful, *adj.* **1.** flowing, fluid, facile, smooth, willowy, supple, limber, lithe, lissome, nimble, athletic, agile, pliant, sprightly, airy, dextrous, deft, light, spry; adroit, skillful, adept, artful, accomplished, gifted, proficient, talented. **2.** elegant, refined, tasteful, artistic, urbane, exquisite, debonair, soigné, dapper, polished, suave, savvy, well-mannered, polite, courteous, man-

nerly, tactful, diplomatic. —**Ant.** clumsy, maladroit; oafish, loutish, boorish, tasteless.

gracious, *adj.* **1.** kind, kindly, benevolent, benign, courteous, chivalrous, well-mannered, mannerly, polite, courtly, friendly, well-disposed, favorable. **2.** compassionate, tender, merciful, lenient, clement, mild, gentle. **3.** indulgent, beneficent, accommodating, considerate, thoughtful, forbearing, welcoming, affable, sociable, amiable, agreeable, cordial, tolerant, accepting, patient, lenient, understanding, obliging. —**Ant.** ungracious, unkind, impolite; cool, cruel.

gradual, *adj.* slow, by degrees, little by little, step by step, moderate, gentle, easy, even, regular, steady, piecemeal. —**Ant.** sudden, precipitous, abrupt, immoderate.

grand, *adj.* **1.** imposing, stately, august, majestic, dignified, exalted, elevated, eminent, princely, regal, kingly, royal, great, illustrious. **2.** lofty, magnificent, great, large, palatial, splendid, brilliant, superb, glorious, sublime, noble, fine. **3.** main, principal, chief, head, leading, foremost, highest. **4.** complete, comprehensive, inclusive, all-inclusive, total, sum. —**Ant.** base, undignified; ignoble; secondary; incomplete.

grandeur, *n.* magnificence, splendor, grandness, resplendence, magnitude, sweep, amplitude, scope, loftiness, nobility, stateliness, majesty, sublimity, luxuriousness, pomp. —**Ant.** insignificance, nullity.

grant, *v.* **1.** bestow, confer, award, bequeath, give. **2.** agree *or* accede to, admit, allow, concede, accept, cede, yield. —*n.* **3.** gift, present, endowment, bequest, subsidy; award, donation, contribution, allowance, aid. —**Ant.** receive.

graphic, *adj.* **1.** distinct, well-defined, detailed, explicit, clear, lucid, plain, unmistakable, precise, photographic, descriptive, realistic, true-to-life, lifelike, vivid, picturesque, striking, telling. **2.** diagrammatic, well-delineated, delineated.

grasp, *v.* **1.** seize, hold, clasp, grip, clutch, grab, catch. **2.** lay hold of, seize upon, fasten on; concentrate on, comprehend, understand. —*n.* **3.** grip, hold, clutches. **4.** hold, possession, mastery. **5.** reach, comprehension, compass, scope. —**Ant.** loose, loosen; misunderstand.

grateful, *adj.* **1.** appreciative, thankful, obliged, indebted. **2.** pleasing, agreeable, welcome, refreshing, pleasant, gratifying, satisfying, satisfactory. —**Ant.** ungrateful; unpleasant, disagreeable, unsatisfactory.

gratify, *v.* please, indulge, humor, satisfy, refresh, fulfill, delight, reward, cheer, gladden, sate, satiate. —**Ant.** displease, dissatisfy.

grave, *n.* **1.** crypt, vault, mausoleum, burial ground, cemetary plot, final resting place, eternal rest, place of interment, tomb, sepulcher, pit, excavation. —*adj.* **2.** sober, solemn, serious, dignified, sedate, earnest, staid, thoughtful, unsmiling, somber, dour, gloomy, grim. **3.** weighty, momentous, important, serious, consequential, critical, vital, urgent, pressing, pivotal, perilous. —**Ant.** undignified, thoughtless; unimportant, trivial, trifling.

great, *adj.* **1.** immense, enormous, huge, gigantic, vast, ample, grand, large, big. **2.** numerous, countless. **3.** considerable, important, momentous, serious, weighty. **4.** notable, remarkable, noteworthy. **5.** distinguished, fa-

mous, famed, eminent, noted, prominent, celebrated, illustrious, grand, renowned. **6.** consequential, important, vital, critical. **7.** chief, principal, main, grand, leading. **8.** noble, lofty, grand, exalted, elevated, dignified, majestic, august. —**Ant.** small; insignificant; paltry; infamous, notorious; trivial; secondary.

greed, *n.* desire, avidity, avarice, cupidity, covetousness, greediness, voracity, ravenousness, rapacity, selfishness, gluttony, insatiability. —**Ant.** generosity.

greedy, *adj.* **1.** grasping, rapacious, selfish, avaricious, acquisitive, materialistic, money-hungry. **2.** gluttonous, voracious, ravenous, starved, insatiable, piggish, hoggish. **3.** desirous, covetous, eager, anxious. —**Ant.** generous, unselfish.

greet, *v.* address, welcome, receive, usher in, meet; hail, accost, salute, address.

grief, *n.* suffering, distress, sorrow, regret, anguish, heartache, agony, torment, desolation, heartbreak, remorse, tribulation, ordeal, bitterness, curse, dejection, trauma, affliction, wretchedness, woe, misery, sadness, melancholy, moroseness. —**Ant.** joy, happiness, glee, delight.

grieve, *v.* **1.** lament, weep, mourn, sorrow, suffer, bewail, regret, rue, deplore, mope, eat one's heart out, bemoan. **2.** distress, sadden, depress, agonize, break one's heart, pain. —**Ant.** delight in.

grievous, *adj.* **1.** distressing, sad, sorrowful, painful, lamentable, regrettable. **2.** deplorable, lamentable, calamitous, heinous, egregious, awful, monstrous, appalling, shocking, intolerable, shameful, unbearable, outrageous, flagrant, atrocious, flagitious, dreadful, gross, iniquitous. **3.** severe, heavy, painful, grave, serious, acute, distressing, damaging, hurtful, wounding. —**Ant.** delighted, happy, joyful; delightful, pleasant, favorable.

grim, *adj.* **1.** stern, unrelenting, merciless, uncompromising, harsh, unyielding. **2.** sinister, ghastly, repellent, frightful, horrible, dire, appalling, horrid, grisly, gruesome, hideous, dreadful. **3.** severe, hard, fierce, forbidding, ferocious, cruel, savage, ruthless. —**Ant.** merciful, lenient, sympathetic; wonderful, delightful, pleasant; amenable, genial, congenial, amiable.

grit, *n.* spirit, pluck, fortitude, courage, valor, bravery, resolve, toughness, mettle, nerve, backbone, gameness, dauntlessness, tenacity, determination, hardihood, staunchness, stalwartness, doughtiness, guts, gutsiness, spunk, chutzpah, moxie, stick-to-itiveness, resolution.

groggy, *adj.* confused, muddled, dazed, addled, befuddled, stupefied, stunned, reeling, in a stupor, unsteady, shaky, wobbly, weak-kneed, numb, faint, punch-drunk, spacey, foggy, befogged, muzzy, dopey, woozy, punchy, slap-happy. —**Ant.** clearheaded, alert.

gross, *adj.* **1.** whole, entire, total, overall, aggregate. **2.** glaring, flagrant, outrageous, shameful, heinous, grievous. **3.** coarse, indelicate, indecent, low, animal, sensual, vulgar, broad, lewd. **4.** fat, obese, corpulent, overweight, heavy, ponderous, large, big, bulky, massive, great. **5.** disgusting, repulsive, repellent, revolting, nauseating, sickening, gruesome, lurid. —**Ant.** partial, incomplete; delicate, decent; small, dainty, slim.

grouchy, *adj.* cantankerous, irritable,

irascible, fractious, cross, crabby, crotchety, choleric, foul-tempered, mean-tempered, grumpy, ornery, curmudgeonly, splenetic, bilious, tetchy, testy, touchy, peevish, surly, vinegary. **—Ant.** even-tempered, gracious.

ground, *n.* **1.** land, earth, soil, mold, turf, sod, terra firma, loam, dirt. **2.** (*often plural*) foundation, basis, base, premise, motive, reason, cause, consideration, factor, account. *—v.* **3.** found, fix, settle, establish, base, set. **4.** instruct, prepare, train, teach, coach, tutor, inform, initiate.

grow, *v.* **1.** increase, swell, enlarge, dilate, greaten, expand, extend, flourish, develop, thicken, spread, thrive, prosper. **2.** sprout, germinate; arise, issue, stem, spring up, originate. **3.** swell, wax, extend, mature, ripen, advance, improve. **4.** raise, cultivate, produce, propagate, plant, sow, breed. **—Ant.** decrease, shrink; wane, deteriorate.

growth, *n.* **1.** development, evolution, cultivation, nurturing, extension, proliferation, flowering, advance, success, progress, increase, augmentation, expansion. **2.** product, outgrowth, result; produce. **—Ant.** failure, stagnation.

grudge, *n.* **1.** malice, ill will, spite, resentment, bitterness, rancor, hard feelings, grievance, pique, aversion, venom, vendetta, vengefulness, animosity, animus, odium, vindictiveness, malevolence, enmity, hatred. *—v.* **2.** begrudge, envy, resent, mind, covet. **—Ant.** good will, amiability.

grudging, *adj.* reluctant, unenthusiastic, unwilling, begrudging; apathetic, indifferent, perfunctory, lukewarm, tepid; ungenerous, mean-spirited, resentful, bitter, rancorous. **—Ant.** enthusiastic, generous.

guarantee, *n.* **1.** guaranty, warrant, pledge, assurance, promise, surety, security, bond, obligation, word of honor. *—v.* **2.** guaranty, secure, ensure, insure, warrant, promise.

guard, *v.* **1.** protect, keep safe, preserve, save, watch over, shield, defend, shelter. **2.** hold, check, watch, be careful. *—n.* **3.** protector, guardian, sentry, watchman, defender, sentinel. **4.** defense, protection, shield, bulwark, security, aegis, safety. **—Ant.** attack, assault; ignore; danger.

guardian, *n.* **1.** guard, protector, defender, champion, paladin. **2.** trustee, warden, keeper, custodian. **—Ant.** assailant.

guess, *v.* **1.** conjecture, hazard, suppose, fancy, believe, imagine, think. **2.** estimate, solve, answer, penetrate. *—n.* **3.** notion, judgment, conclusion, conjecture, surmise, supposition, estimate, hypothesis, speculation, assumption, feeling, suspicion, postulate, theory, shot in the dark. **—Ant.** know.

guide, *v.* **1.** lead, pilot, steer, conduct, direct, show *or* point the way, escort, instruct, induce, influence, regulate, manage, govern, rule. *—n.* **2.** leader, counselor, adviser, guru, mentor, teacher, master, director, conductor. **3.** model, criterion, exemplar, standard, ideal, example, illustration. **4.** beacon, light, landmark, lodestar, mark, sign, signal, indication, key, clue. **—Ant.** follow.

guile, *n.* cunning, treachery, deceit, artifice, duplicity, deception, trickery, fraud, craft, artfulness, chicanery, shrewdness. **—Ant.** ingenuousness, honesty.

guileless, *adj.* artless, honest, sincere, open, candid, frank, truthful, ingenuous, naive, unsophisticated, simpleminded. **—Ant.** cunning, sly, deceitful, artful, treacherous.

guilt, *n.* guiltiness, culpability, criminality, blame, responsibility, crime, sinfulness, misconduct, wrongdoing, reproach, shamefulness, condemnation. **—Ant.** exoneration, innocence.

guiltless, *adj.* innocent, spotless, blameless, immaculate, pure, unsullied, unpolluted, untarnished, sinless. **—Ant.** culpable, guilty.

guilty, *adj.* **1.** wrong, culpable, responsible, at fault, blameworthy, sinful, answerable, criminal, malfeasant, delinquent, offending, reprehensible. **2.** sorry, regretful, remorseful, contrite, apologetic, repentant, rueful, penitent, conscience-stricken; ashamed, embarrassed, sheepish, mortified, red-faced. **—Ant.** innocent, blameless; unrepentant; proud.

guise, *n.* appearance, aspect, semblance, look, image, likeness, mien, air, disguise, front, facade, pretense; behavior, bearing, demeanor; form, shape, fashion, mode, manner.

guru, *n.* teacher, guide, instructor, tutor, coach, trainer, handler, preceptor, master, docent, expert, mentor, Svengali. **—Ant.** student, acolyte, follower.

gush, *v.* **1.** pour, stream, spurt, flow, spout, flood, cascade, rush, spurt, jet, burst, run. **2.** bubble over, overflow, effervesce, be effusive, prate, babble, jabber, blather, chatter, make a fuss, run off at the mouth, run one's mouth.

H

habit, *n.* **1.** disposition, tendency, bent, wont, inclination, predisposition, second nature, attitude, penchant, proclivity, frame of mind. **2.** custom, practice, routine, convention, policy, pattern, mode, rule, way, usage, wont, manner.

habitat, *n.* home, locality, haunt, environment, turf, locale, site, domain, baiwick, realm, terrain, element, sphere of activity, neighborhood, precincts, range, territory, surroundings, environs, vicinity, stamping ground, home ground, milieu.

habitual, *adj.* confirmed, inveterate, accustomed, customary, established, chronic, hardened, ingrained, persistent, constant; usual, common, regular, familiar, ordinary, set, standard, routine, normal, natural, traditional, fixed, settled, ritual. **—Ant.** rare, unaccustomed, unusual, uncommon, irregular.

habituate, *v.* accustom, familiarize, acclimate, acclimatize, train, inure, harden, make used (to).

hack, *v.* **1.** cut, notch, chop, hew, mangle, lacerate, gash, slash, butcher, mutilate, damage. *—n.* **2.** cut, notch, gash. *—adj.* **3.** hackneyed, trite, clichéd, overdone, old, banal, used, worn out, commonplace, stale, stereotyped; old-hat. **—Ant.** novel, new.

hackneyed, *adj.* trite, clichéd, stale, timeworn, overused, tired, routine, stereotyped, tedious, mediocre, humdrum, moldy, run-of-the-mill, well-worn, unoriginal, bromidic, platitudinous, commonplace, pedestrian, worn-out, banal, cornball, bathetic, stock, set, old-hat, warmed-over, moth-eaten, threadbare, corny. **—Ant.** original, inventive.

haggard, *adj.* careworn, gaunt, emaciated, drawn, anemic, weak, feeble, spent, exhausted, ghastly, cadaverous, run-down, weary, withered, hollow-cheeked, hollow-eyed, meager, spare,

worn, wasted. **—Ant.** hale, hearty, robust.

haggle, *v.* bargain, negotiate, bicker, deal, squabble, dicker, disagree, wrangle, dispute, cavil, argue.

hale, *adj.* robust, healthy, vigorous, sound, strong, hearty, fit as a fiddle, able-bodied, hardy, wholesome, flourishing, in fine fettle, in the pink. **—Ant.** haggard, weak, feeble.

halfhearted, *adj.* unenthusiastic, indifferent, uninterested, cold, cool, lukewarm, nonchalant, phlegmatic, lackadaisical, insouciant, uncaring, perfunctory, curt, abrupt, discouraging. **—Ant.** enthusiastic, eager, encouraging.

hallowed, *adj.* sacred, consecrated, holy, blessed, sacrosanct, inviolable; honored, revered. **—Ant.** profane; despised.

hallucination, *n.* illusion, delusion, aberration, phantasm, vision, fantasy, mirage, daydream, dream, chimera, phantom, figment of the imagination, apparition, specter, ghost, doppelganger, wraith, haint. **—Ant.** reality.

halt, *v.* hold, stop, cease, desist, quit, end, terminate, check, curb, stem, discontinue, conclude, shut down, come to a standstill. **—Ant.** continue, persist.

hamper, *v.* impede, hinder, hold back, encumber, prevent, obstruct, restrain, clog, slow, balk, delay, retard, inhibit, block, interfere with, frustrate, restrict, curb, limit, handicap, trammel, bar, curtail, lessen, diminish, reduce. **—Ant.** promote, further, encourage, speed.

handsome, *adj.* **1.** comely, fine, admirable, good-looking, hunky, dishy, attractive, well-made. **2.** liberal, considerable, ample, large, generous, magnanimous, sizable, substantial. **—Ant.** ugly, unattractive.

handy, *adj.* **1.** convenient, useful, practical, functional, serviceable. **2.** near, nearby, at hand, close, adjacent, convenient, close by, near at hand, close at hand. **3.** adept, dexterous, skilled, skillful, artful, adroit, deft, clever, proficient.

hang, *v.* **1.** suspend, dangle, hover, swing. **2.** execute, lynch, string up, kill, garrote. **3.** drape, decorate, adorn, furnish. **4.** depend, rely, rest; hold fast, cling, adhere. **5.** be doubtful *or* undecided, waver, hesitate, demur, halt. **6.** loiter, linger, hover, float. **7.** impend, be imminent.

happen, *v.* come to pass, take place, occur, develop, materialize, transpire, prove, chance; befall, betide.

happiness, *n.* good fortune, pleasure, contentment, gladness, bliss, content, contentedness, beatitude, blessedness, delight, joy, enjoyment, gratification, satisfaction, felicity, jubilation, cheerfulness, cheeriness, elation, exuberance, exhilaration, high spirits, ecstasy, rapture. **—Ant.** misery, dissatisfaction.

happy, *adj.* **1.** joyous, joyful, glad, blithe, merry, cheerful, contented, gay, blissful, delighted, satisfied, pleased, gladdened, elated, ecstatic, euphoric, exultant, overjoyed, jubilant. **2.** favored, lucky, fortunate, propitious, advantageous, successful, prosperous. **3.** appropriate, fitting, apt, felicitous, opportune, befitting, pertinent. **—Ant.** unhappy, sad, cheerless, melancholy; unlucky, luckless, unfortunate; inappropriate, inapt.

harangue, *n.* **1.** diatribe, tirade, oration, declamation, philippic, screed, exhortation, vituperation, rodomontade, address, speech, bombast. —v. 2. preach, lecture, sermonize, pontificate, vituperate, rant and rave, rant, declaim, address.

harass, v. trouble, harry, raid, molest, disturb, distress; plague, vex, worry, badger, pester, annoy, torment, torture.

harbor, n. 1. haven, port. 2. shelter, refuge, asylum, protection, cover, sanctuary, retreat. —v. 3. shelter, protect, lodge. 4. conceal, hide, secrete. 5. entertain, indulge, foster, cherish.

hard, adj. 1. solid, firm, inflexible, rigid, unyielding, resistant, resisting, adamantine, flinty, impenetrable, compact. 2. difficult, toilsome, burdensome, wearisome, exhausting, laborious, arduous, onerous, fatiguing, wearying. 3. difficult, complex, intricate, complicated, perplexing, tough, puzzling. 4. vigorous, severe, violent, stormy, tempestuous, inclement. 5. oppressive, harsh, rough, cruel, severe, unmerciful, grinding, unsparing, unrelenting. 6. severe, harsh, stern, austere, strict, exacting, callous, unfeeling, unsympathetic, impassionate, insensible, unimpressible, insensitive, indifferent, unpitying, inflexible, relentless, unyielding, cruel, obdurate, adamant, hardhearted. 7. unfriendly, unkind; harsh, unpleasant. 8. unsympathetic, unsentimental, shrewd, hardheaded, callous. —adv. 9. energetically, vigorously, violently. 10. earnestly, intently, incessantly. 11. harshly, severely, gallingly, with difficulty. —Ant. soft; easy; fair; merciful; sympathetic; kind.

harden, v. 1. solidify, indurate, ossify, petrify. 2. strengthen, confirm, fortify, steel, brace, nerve, toughen, inure; habituate, accustom, season, train, discipline.

hardship, n. want, deprivation, misery, distress, adversity, unhappiness, bad luck, difficulty, trial, oppression, privation, need, austerity, trouble, affliction, burden, suffering, misfortune, grievance.

hardy, adj. 1. vigorous, hearty, sturdy, hale, robust, stout, strong, sound, healthy, rugged, tough, durable, stalwart, red-blooded. 2. bold, daring, courageous, brave, intrepid. —Ant. weak, feeble, unsound, unhealthy; cowardly, pusillanimous.

harm, n. 1. injury, damage, hurt, abuse, misfortune, wound, molestation, ill-treatment, mischief, detriment. 2. wrong, evil, wickedness, wrongdoing, iniquity. —n. 3. injure, hurt, damage; maltreat, molest, abuse, wound. —Ant. good.

harmful, adj. injurious, detrimental, hurtful, deleterious, pernicious, mischievous, destructive, damaging, dangerous; unhealthy, noisome, noxious, toxic, poisonous, venomous. —Ant. beneficial.

harmonious, adj. 1. amicable, congenial, sympathetic, agreeable, compatible, in accord, simpatico. 2. consonant, congruous, concordant, consistent, correspondent, symmetrical. 3. melodious, tuneful, agreeable, concordant, sweet-sounding. —Ant. unsympathetic; discordant, incongruous, asymmetrical; cacophonous, noisy.

harmony, n. 1. agreement, concord, unity, unanimity, rapport, peace, amity, friendship, accord, unison. 2. balance, orderliness, closeness, togetherness, parallelism, congruity, consonance, conformity, correspondence, consistency, congruence, fitness, suitability. 3. melody, melodiousness, concord, euphony, tunefulness.

—Ant. discord, disagreement; nonconformity, unfitness; cacophony, noise.

harrowing, adj. trying, stressful, distressing, painful, agonizing, vexing, alarming, unnerving, heart-rending, traumatic, nerve-wracking, disquieting, dismaying, horrible, torturous, frightening, excruciating, harsh, hairy. —Ant. pleasant, relaxing.

harry, v. 1. harass, torment, worry, molest, plague, trouble, vex, hector, gall, fret, disturb, harrow, chafe, annoy, pester. 2. ravage, devastate, plunder, strip, rob, pillage. —Ant. help, support, succor.

harsh, adj. 1. unpleasant, severe, austere, bleak, dour, spartan; stringent, Draconian, tyrannical, abusive, punishing, punitive, inhuman, merciless, ruthless, pitiless; disagreeable, impolite, discourteous, uncivil, rude, nasty, curt, abrupt, bluff, gruff, curmudgeonly, brusque, rough, hard, unfeeling, unkind, brutal, cruel, stern, acrimonious, bad-tempered, ill-natured, crabbed, choleric, splenetic, surly, sullen, irascible, churlish, peevish, grouchy, bilious, cross, sarcastic, acerbic. 2. jarring, unaesthetic, inartistic, discordant, dissonant, unharmonious. —Ant. gentle, pleasant, kind, good-natured; aesthetic, harmonious.

haste, n. 1. swiftness, quickness, urgency, briskness, celerity, alacrity, quickness, rapidity, dispatch, speed, expedition, promptitude. 2. need, hurry, flurry, hustle, bustle, ado, precipitancy, precipitation, rush, rashness, recklessness. —Ant. sloth.

hasten, v. hurry, accelerate, urge, press, expedite, quicken, speed, precipitate, dispatch; rush, fly, sprint, race, bolt, dash, scurry, scamper.

hasty, adj. 1. speedy, quick, hurried, swift, rapid, fast, fleet, brisk, prompt, immediate, instantaneous. 2. precipitate, rash, foolhardy, reckless, indiscreet, thoughtless, impetuous, careless, headlong, unthinking. —Ant. slow, deliberate; discreet, thoughtful.

hatch, v. 1. incubate, breed, brood. 2. contrive, devise, plan, plot, formulate, originate, invent, dream up, cook up, fabricate, produce, concoct, design, scheme, project.

hate, v. 1. dislike, detest, abhor, loathe, despise, scorn, recoil from, execrate, abominate. —n. 2. hatred, abhorrence, loathing, odium, animosity, antipathy, animus, aversion, hostility, antagonism, malice, detestation, enmity, malevolence, spite, scorn, vindictiveness, contempt. —Ant. like, love.

hateful, adj. detestable, odious, abominable, execrable, loathsome, abhorrent, repugnant, invidious, obnoxious, offensive, disgusting, nauseating, revolting, vile, repulsive, horrid, horrible, despicable, scurvy, heinous, foul, contemptible; malignant, malevolent, malicious, evil, spiteful, contemptuous, mean, nasty, ugly. —Ant. lovable, appealing, attractive, likable.

hatred, n. aversion, animosity, hate, detestation, loathing, abomination, odium, horror, repugnance, revulsion. —Ant. attraction, love, favor.

haughty, adj. disdainful, proud, arrogant, supercilious, snobbish, lordly, contemptuous, superior, self-important, smug, self-satisfied, complacent, pretentious, conceited, egotistical, overbearing, overweening, patronizing, vain, condescending, disdainful, scornful, highfalutin, hoity-toity, stuck-up, swell-headed, high and mighty, on one's high horse, la-di-da,

snooty, uppity. —Ant. humble, shy, self-effacing.

have, v. 1. hold, occupy, possess, own, keep, contain. 2. get, receive, take, obtain, acquire, gain, secure, procure. 3. experience, enjoy, suffer, undergo. 4. permit, allow.

havoc, n. devastation, ruin, destruction, desolation, waste, damage.

hazard, n. 1. danger, peril, jeopardy, risk. 2. chance, accident, luck, fortuity, fortuitousness, uncertainty. —v. 3. venture, dare, gamble, stake, risk, jeopardize, endanger, imperil, threaten. —Ant. safety, security; certainty, surety.

haze, n. 1. vapor, dust, mist, cloud, fog, smog. 2. obscurity, dimness, cloud, vagueness, blur, nebulousness, fuzziness, muddle. —Ant. clearness, clarity.

head, n. 1. command, authority. 2. commander, director, chief, chieftain, leader, principal, commander in chief, master. 3. top, summit, acme. 4. culmination, crisis, conclusion. 5. source, origin, rise, fountainhead, wellspring, font, beginning, headwaters. —adj. 6. front, leading, topmost, chief, principal, main, cardinal, foremost, first. —v. 7. lead, direct, supervise, oversee, control, guide, manage, administer, command, rule, govern.

headlong, adj. rushed, precipitate, precipitous, hasty, abrupt, hurried, impetuous, sudden, impulsive, reckless.

headstrong, adj. willful, stubborn, obstinate, intractable, self-willed, dogged, pigheaded, tenacious, contrary, mulish. —Ant. amenable, tractable, genial, agreeable.

heal, v. 1. cure, remedy, restore, repair, renew, revitalize, rejuvenate; mend, recover, recuperate, improve. 2. amend, settle, harmonize, compose, soothe, reconcile, patch up, put right, set straight. —Ant. discompose; soil, pollute, infect.

healthy, adj. 1. healthful, hale, sound, hearty, well, robust, vigorous, strong. 2. nutritious, nourishing, salubrious, salutary, hygienic, invigorating, bracing, wholesome, beneficial, tonic. —Ant. unhealthy, ill, sick, weak; unwholesome, enervating.

heap, n. 1. mass, stack, pile, mound, stack, hoard, store, mountain, stockpile, supply, accumulation, collection. —v. 2. pile or heap up, amass, accumulate. 3. bestow, confer, cast, shower.

hear, v. 1. listen to, perceive, attend to, pay attention to, understand, catch, heed, harken to 2. understand, learn, find out, discover, gather, get wind of, pick up on, ascertain, be told or advised or informed.

heat, n. 1. warmth, fever, fire, fieriness, torridness, hotness. 2. warmth, intensity, ardor, fervor, zeal, flush, fever, excitement, impetuosity, vehemence, violence. —v. 3. stimulate, warm, stir, animate, arouse, excite, rouse, intensify, impassion, inflame, kindle, ignite, quicken, awaken, activate, hot up. —Ant. coolness; phlegm; cool, discourage.

heathen, n. 1. gentile, pagan, barbarian, savage, Philistine, nonbeliever, infidel, idolater, atheist, skeptic, heretic. —adj. 2. gentile, pagan, heathenish, irreligious, unenlightened, barbarous, savage, Philistine. —Ant. civilized, religious.

heave, v. 1. raise, lift, hoist, elevate. 2. pant, exhale, breathe. 3. vomit, retch. 4. rise, swell, dilate, bulge, expand.

heavenly, *adj.* **1.** blissful, beautiful, divine, seraphic, cherubic, angelic, saintly, sainted, holy, beatific, blessed, beatified, glorified. **2.** celestial, unearthly, extraterrestrial, otherworldly, ultramundane. —**Ant.** hellish, satanic, diabolical, devilish.

heavy, *adj.* **1.** weighty, ponderous, massive. **2.** burdensome, harsh, oppressive, depressing, onerous, distressing, severe, grievous, cumbersome. **3.** broad, thick, coarse, blunt. **4.** serious, intense, momentous, weighty, important, pithy, concentrated. **5.** trying, difficult. **6.** downhearted. **7.** ponderous, dull, tedious, tiresome, wearisome, burdensome, boring, lifeless. **8.** dense. —**Ant.** light.

hectic, *adj.* **1.** frantic, busy, rushed, overactive, bustling, furious, frenzied, frenetic, perfervid, hysterical, hyper. **2.** feverish, fevered, febrile, hot, heated, burning, flushed. —**Ant.** calm. cool.

heed, *v.* **1.** pay *or* give attention to, consider, regard, notice, mark, follow, listen to, observe, obey. —*n.* **2.** attention, notice, observation, consideration, care, caution, heedfulness, watchfulness, vigilance. —**Ant.** disregard, ignore.

height, *n.* **1.** altitude, stature, elevation, tallness. **2.** hill, peak, crag, tor, cliff, bluff, promontory, headland, prominence, mountain. **3.** top, peak, pinnacle, apex, eminence, acme, summit, zenith, culmination. —**Ant.** depth, abyss.

hell, *n.* **1.** Gehenna, Tartarus, inferno, Abaddon, Avernus, Hades, Erebus, pandemonium, abyss, limbo, underworld, infernal regions, nether regions, bottomless pit, lower world. **2.** damnation, perdition, ruin, downfall, destruction; punishment, misery, wretchedness, torture. —**Ant.** heaven.

help, *v.* **1.** cooperate, aid, assist, encourage, befriend, support, second, uphold, back, abet, succor, save. **2.** further, facilitate, promote, ease, foster. **3.** relieve, ameliorate, alleviate, remedy, cure, heal, restore, improve, better. **4.** refrain from, avoid, forbear. —*n.* **5.** support, backing, aid, assistance, relief, succor. —**Ant.** discourage, attack, undermine.

helper, *n.* aid, assistant, supporter, auxiliary, ally, colleague, amanuensis, right hand, henchman, sidekick, cohort, partner, deputy, subordinate, underling, employee.

helpful, *adj.* useful, convenient, beneficial, advantageous, serviceable, practical, pragmatic, utilitarian, valuable, constructive, supportive, sensible, profitable. —**Ant.** useless, inconvenient, disadvantageous, uncooperative.

herd, *n.* **1.** drove, flock, clutch, crowd, group, pack, bunch, cluster, multitude, host, horde, throng, mass, swarm, press, crush, gathering. —*v.* **2.** flock, assemble, associate, keep company, gather, congregate, collect.

heritage, *n.* inheritance, estate, patrimony, birthright, legacy, bequest.

heroic, *adj.* intrepid, dauntless, gallant, valorous, brave, courageous, bold, daring, fearless, valiant, noble, plucky, stouthearted, chivalrous, audacious, honorable, virtuous, steadfast, staunch, stalwart. —**Ant.** cowardly, fearful.

hesitate, *v.* **1.** waver, vacillate, falter, equivocate, dither, fluctuate, alternate, yo-yo, shilly-shally, fumble, tergiversate, waffle, falter, stumble, hem and haw, blow hot and cold, change one's mind. **2.** demur, delay, pause, wait, hang back, dilly-dally, temporize, think

twice, balk, boggle at, shrink from, stall. —**Ant.** resolve, decide.

hew, *v.* **1.** cut, chop, hack. **2.** make, shape, fashion, form. **3.** sever, cut down, fell.

hide, *v.* conceal, secrete, screen, mask, cloak, veil, shroud, cover, disguise, withhold, suppress, cache, squirrel away, camouflage, keep secret, obscure, repress, hush up, silence, eclipse, blot out, block. —**Ant.** open, reveal.

hideous, *adj.* horrible, frightful, ugly, grotesque, lurid, grisly, grim, revolting, repellent, repulsive, nauseating, detestable, odious, monstrous, dreadful, appalling, terrifying, terrible, ghastly, macabre, shocking. —**Ant.** beautiful, lovely, attractive.

high, *adj.* **1.** lofty, tall, elevated, towering, skyscraping. **2.** intensified, energetic, intense, strong. **3.** expensive, costly, dear, high-priced. **4.** exalted, elevated, eminent, prominent, preeminent, distinguished. **5.** shrill, sharp, acute, high-pitched, strident. **6.** chief, main, principal, head. **7.** consequential, important, grave, serious, capital, extreme. **8.** lofty, haughty, arrogant, snobbish, proud, lordly, supercilious. **9.** elated, merry, hilarious, happy; giddy, pixilated, intoxicated, inebriated. —**Ant.** low.

hilarity, *n.* laughter, gaiety, joviality, exuberance, cheerfulness, boisterousness, jubilation, elation, revelry, vivacity, conviviality, exhilaration, high spirits, glee, mirth, merriment, levity, jollity, hilariousness, hysterics, joy, jocularity.

hill, *n.* elevation, prominence, eminence, mound, rise, highland, knoll, hillock, foothill, mount, hummock, height, butte. —**Ant.** valley, dale, glen, hollow, depth.

hinder, *v.* **1.** interrupt, check, retard, impede, encumber, delay, hamper, obstruct, trammel. **2.** block, thwart, prevent, obstruct. —**Ant.** encourage, disencumber.

hindrance, *n.* impediment, deterrent, hitch, encumbrance, obstruction, check, restraint, hobble, obstacle, snag, barrier, drawback, stumbling block, curb, limitation. —**Ant.** help, aid, support.

hint, *n.* **1.** suggestion, implication, intimation, allusion, insinuation, innuendo, reminder, inkling. —*v.* **2.** imply, intimate, insinuate, suggest, mention.

hire, *v.* **1.** engage, employ; let, lease, rent, charter. —*n.* **2.** rent, rental; pay, stipend, salary, wages, remuneration.

history, *n.* record, chronicle, account, annals, story, relation, narrative, description, depiction, portrayal, representation, recital, narration.

hit, *v.* **1.** strike, knock, smack, whack, bash, bang, thump, punch, buffet, slap, swat, beat, pummel, batter, whip, sock. **2.** reach, attain, gain, win, accomplish, achieve. **3.** touch, suit, fit, befit, affect. **4.** find, come upon, meet with, discover, happen upon. **5.** collide, strike, clash. —*n.* **6.** blow, stroke; success.

hitch, *v.* **1.** couple, join, link, fix, make fast, fasten, connect, hook, tether, attach, tie, unite, harness, yoke. —*n.* **2.** halt, obstruction, hindrance, catch, impediment, snag, difficulty, trouble, problem, handicap, mishap. —**Ant.** loose, loosen, untie.

hoarse, *adj.* husky, throaty, guttural, gruff, harsh, grating, raucous, rough.

hold, *v.* **1.** have, keep, retain, possess, own, occupy. **2.** bear, sustain, hold up, support, maintain, keep (up), con-

tinue, carry on. **3.** engage in, observe, celebrate, preside over, carry on, pursue. **4.** hinder, restrain, keep back; confine, detain, imprison, impound, incarcerate, coop up. **5.** contain, admit, accomodate, include, comprise. **6.** think, believe, embrace, espouse, entertain, have, regard, consider, esteem, judge, deem. **7.** continue, persist, last, endure, remain. **8.** adhere, cling, remain, stick. —*n.* **9.** grasp, grip. **10.** control, influence.

hole, *n.* **1.** aperture, opening, cavity, excavation, pit, hollow, crater, depression, breach, fissure, orifice, slit, slot, crack, concavity. **2.** burrow, lair, den, retreat, cave.

holy, *adj.* **1.** blessed, sacred, consecrated, hallowed, dedicated, sacrosanct, inviolable, religious, sanctified, venerated, heavenly, celestial. **2.** saintly, godly, divine, pious, devout, spiritual, pure, virtuous, pietistic, religious, God-fearing, blessed, incorruptible, chaste, unsullied, sinless, immaculate, reverent, reverential, faithful. —**Ant.** unholy, desecrated, impious, piacular, sinful, impure, corrupt.

homage, *n.* **1.** respect, reverence, deference, obeisance, honor, tribute. **2.** fealty, allegiance, faithfulness, fidelity, loyalty, devotion. **3.** devotion, worship, adoration. —**Ant.** disrespect, irreverence, dishonor; faithlessness, disloyalty.

home, *n.* **1.** house, apartment, residence, household, abode, dwelling, domicile, habitation. **2.** refuge, retreat, institution, asylum, hospice, shelter. **3.** hearth, fireside, family; rightful place.

homely, *adj.* plain, simple, unpretentious, modest, unassuming, informal, homespun, familiar, friendly, gemütlichkeit, congenial, folksy, down-home; unattractive, coarse, inelegant, uncomely, ugly, ill-favored. —**Ant.** beautiful.

honest, *adj.* **1.** honorable, upright, fair, just, incorruptible, trusty, lawabiding, ethical, principled, reputable, aboveboard, straight, fair, just, on the level, decent, reliable, creditable, proper, trustworthy, truthful, virtuous, moral. **2.** open, sincere, candid, straightforward, frank, unreserved, ingenuous. —**Ant.** dishonest; corrupt, disingenuous, untrustworthy, secretive.

honesty, *n.* **1.** uprightness, probity, integrity, justice, fairness, trustworthiness, virtue, virtuousness, morality, righteousness, character, reliability, propriety, rectitude, honor. **2.** truthfulness, sincerity, candor, frankness, truth, veracity, earnestness, openness, guilelessness. —**Ant.** dishonesty, inequity; deceit, insincerity.

honor, *n.* **1.** esteem, fame, glory, repute, reputation, credit. **2.** credit, distinction, dignity. **3.** respect, deference, homage, reverence, veneration, consideration, distinction. **4.** privilege, favor, distinction, joy, pleasure, delight. **5.** character, principle, probity, uprightness, honesty, integrity, nobleness. **6.** purity, chastity, virginity, virtue, innocence. —*v.* **7.** revere, esteem, venerate, respect, adore, worship, hallow. —**Ant.** dishonor, disrepute, discredit; indignity; disfavor; indecency; execrate, abominate.

honorable, *adj.* **1.** upright, honest, noble, highminded, just, fair, trusty, trustworthy, true, virtuous. **2.** dignified, distinguished, noble, illustrious, great. **3.** creditable, reputable, estimable, right, proper, equitable. —**Ant.** ignoble, untrustworthy, corrupt; undignified; disreputable.

hope, *n.* **1.** expectation, wish, yearning, hankering, craving, dream, fancy, ambition, longing, desire. **2.** confidence, prospect, promise, anticipation, assumption, conviction, belief, trust, reliance, faith. —*v.* **3.** trust, expect, anticipate, await, wish, want, desire, long for, pray, dream, set one's sights on, hold one's breath, wait with bated breath, cross one's fingers. —**Ant.** hopelessness.

hopeful, *adj.* **1.** expectant, sanguine, optimistic, confident, assured. **2.** encouraging, bright, rosy, promising, heartening, auspicious, propitious. —**Ant.** hopeless.

hopeless, *adj.* **1.** desperate, despairing, despondent, forlorn, gloomy, disconsolate. **2.** irremediable, remediless, incurable, irreparable, beyond saving *or* repair. **3.** futile, vain, pointless, worthless, unavailing, useless, bootless. —**Ant.** hopeful.

horrendous, *adj.* terrible, overwhelming, frightful, fearful, horrific, gruesome, lurid, macabre, awful, grotesque, dreadful, ghastly, terrifying, stupefying, dire, atrocious.

horrible, *adj.* **1.** horrendous, terrible, horrid, dreadful, awful, appalling, frightful, hideous, grim, ghastly, shocking, revolting, repulsive, repellent, dire, formidable, horrifying, harrowing. **2.** appalling, disgraceful, foul, abhorrent, unspeakable, monstrous, scandalous, outrageous, loathsome, deplorable, shocking, abominable, odious. —**Ant.** attractive, delightful, beautiful; welcome, fine.

horror, *n.* **1.** fear, abhorrence, terror, dread, dismay, consternation, panic, alarm. **2.** aversion, repugnance, loathing, antipathy, detestation, revulsion, distaste, aversion, antipathy, animosity, hatred, abomination. —**Ant.** calm, serenity; attraction, delight, love.

hostile, *adj.* opposed, adverse, averse, unfriendly, inimical, antagonistic, contrary, warlike, oppugnant, antipathetic. —**Ant.** friendly, amiable, amicable.

hostility, *n.* **1.** enmity, antagonism, animosity, animus, ill will, unfriendliness, antipathy, malevolence, malice, opposition, hatred. **2.** (*plural*) war, warfare, fighting, conflict, combat, bloodshed. —**Ant.** friendliness, good will, love; peace, truce.

hot, *adj.* **1.** heated, torrid, sultry, burning, fiery, white-hot, red-hot, piping hot, blistering, scorching, sizzling, searing, scalding, boiling, sweltering. **2.** pungent, piquant, sharp, acrid, spicy, peppery, biting, blistering. **3.** ardent, fervent, fervid, angry, furious, vehement, intense, excited, excitable, irascible, animated, violent, passionate, impetuous. —**Ant.** cold.

hotheaded, *adj.* reckless, rash, incautious, headstrong, impetuous, emotional, hot-tempered, passionate, fiery, headlong, volatile, hasty, wild, foolhardy, heedless, daredevil, devil-may-care, madcap, thoughtless. —**Ant.** cool, serene, phlegmatic.

house, *n.* **1.** domicile, dwelling, residence, home, abode, homestead, household. **2.** firm, company, partnership, business, establishment. —*v.* **3.** accommodate, board, put up, take in, lodge, harbor, shelter, reside, dwell.

household, *n.* **1.** family, ménage, people, brood, folks, occupants, dwellers, home, homestead, hearth, fireside, hearth and home. —*adj.* **2.** domestic, family, home, domiciliary, residential. **3.** simple, ordinary, common, commonplace, plain, prosaic, everyday, garden-variety, homespun, plain-Jane. **4.** familiar, well-known, public, famous, unmistakable, notorious.

hubbub, *n.* noise, tumult, uproar, clamor, din, racket, disorder, confusion, disturbance, riot, hurly-burly, excitement, whirl, activity, ferment, agitation, ado, rumpus, commotion, bedlam, fracas, pandemonium, ruckus. —**Ant.** serenity, calm.

huge, *adj.* large, extensive, mammoth, vast, gigantic, colossal, stupendous, bulky, enormous, immense, tremendous, humongous, oversized, outsized, great, massive, gargantuan, prodigious, monumental, titanic, elephantine, leviathan, jumbo, Brobdingnagian, Cyclopean. —**Ant.** tiny, small, infinitesimal, microscopic.

humane, *adj.* **1.** merciful, kind, kindly, kindhearted, tender, human, benevolent, sympathetic, compassionate, gentle, accommodating, understanding, sensitive, magnanimous, philantropic, tolerant, patient, forbearing, just, beneficent, humanitarian, benignant, charitable. **2.** refining, polite, cultivating, elevating, humanizing, spiritual. —**Ant.** inhumane, cruel, ruthless, merciless; boorish, degrading.

humble, *adj.* **1.** low, lowly, lowborn, inferior, mean, ignoble, ordinary, plebeian, simple, obscure, unprepossessing, unimportant, plain, common, poor; meek, modest, submissive, self-effacing, servile, obsequious, subservient, unassuming, unpresuming, unpretending, unpretentious. **2.** respectful, reserved, deferential, polite, courteous, courtly. —*v.* **3.** lower, abase, debase, chasten, demean, lose face, chagrin, degrade, humiliate, reduce, mortify, shame, subdue, abash, crush, break, make (someone) eat humble pie, take (someone) down a peg. —**Ant.** haughty, immodest, snobbish, conceited, pretentious; impolite, discourteous; raise, elevate.

humbug, *n.* **1.** trick, hoax, fraud, imposture, deception, con game, swindle, imposition. **2.** falseness, deception, sham, pretense, hypocrisy, charlatanism. **3.** cheat, impostor, swindler, charlatan, pretender, confidence man, deceiver, quack.

humid, *adj.* damp, dank, wet, moist, muggy, clammy, sticky, steamy, sultry, soggy. —**Ant.** dry.

humiliate, *v.* mortify, degrade, debase, dishonor, disgrace, abash, abase, chasten, demean, lower, chagrin, embarrass, discredit, shame, humble, crush, break, put down, subdue. —**Ant.** honor, elevate, exalt.

humiliation, *n.* mortification, shame, abasement, degradation, chagrin, disgrace, ignominy, indignity, discredit, embarrassment, humbling, dishonoring, belittling, depreciation, disparagement, derogation, obloquy. —**Ant.** honor, elevation.

humility, *n.* lowliness, meekness, humbleness, submissiveness, modesty, shyness, timidity, bashfulness, mildness, diffidence, servility, self-effacement, self-abasement, unpretentiousness. —**Ant.** haughtiness.

humor, *n.* **1.** wit, fun, facetiousness, pleasantry, comedy, drollery, waggishness, raillery, banter, jokes, jests. **2.** disposition, tendency, temperament, temper, nature, spirits, frame of mind, mood; whim, caprice, fancy, vagary. —*v.* **3.** indulge, gratify, placate, soothe, please, mollify, appease, baby, spoil.

humorous, *adj.* amusing, funny, jocose, jocular, droll, comic, comical, witty, facetious, waggish, sportive, ludicrous, laughable, risible, farcical, sidesplitting, hilarious, whimsical, playful. —**Ant.** serious, sad, melancholy.

hunch, *n.* feeling, impression, presentiment, suspicion, premonition, intimation, gut sense, instinct, foreboding, funny feeling, intuition, guess.

hungry, *adj.* ravenous, famished, starved, starving, voracious, empty, hollow. —**Ant.** sated.

hunt, *v.* **1.** chase, pursue, track, dog, hound, trail, trace, stalk, prey upon. **2.** search for, seek, scour, quest after, ransack, investigate, explore, examine, check out. —*n.* **3.** chase, pursuit, hunting; search.

hurry, *v.* **1.** rush, haste, hasten, be quick, move swiftly *or* quickly, speed, race, dash, hustle, scurry, tear, run, fly, scoot, shake a leg, step on it, get a move on, hotfoot it, skedaddle, get cracking. **2.** hasten, urge, forward, accelerate, quicken, expedite, hustle, dispatch. —*n.* **3.** bustle, haste, dispatch, celerity, speed, rush, urgency, eagerness, quickness, alacrity, promptitude, expedition. **4.** bustle, ado, precipitation, flurry, flutter, confusion, perturbation, dither, furor, frenzy, agitation, upset, fuss, to-do, turmoil. —**Ant.** delay, slow.

hurt, *v.* **1.** injure, harm, damage, mar, maim, disable, handicap, impair. **2.** pain, ache, smart, sting, torment, throb, gripe, distress, bother, grieve, afflict, wound. —*n.* **3.** injury, harm, damage, detriment, disadvantage; bruise, wound; pang, distress, suffering, torment, agony, torture, anguish.

hut, *n.* cottage, cabin, shed, hovel, shack, shanty, lean-to, hole in the wall.

hypocrite, *n.* deceiver, pretender, dissembler, pharisee, double-dealer, two-face, Tartuffe, faker, phony, con artist, imposter, pretender, charlatan, liar, humbug, wolf in sheep's clothing.

hypocritical, *adj.* sanctimonious, pharisaical, Pecksniffian; insincere, deceiving, dissembling, pretending, false, hollow, empty, deceptive, misleading, deceitful, double-dealing, untrustworthy, underhand, perfidious, treacherous. —**Ant.** honest, direct, forthright, sincere.

I

icon, *n.* picture, image, symbol, idol, representation, sign.

iconoclast, *n.* unbeliever, disbeliever, doubter, questioner, challenger, heretic, nonconformist, rebel, trail-blazer. —**Ant.** believer, supporter.

idea, *n.* **1.** thought, conception, concept, construct, scheme, perception, mental image, notion; impression, apprehension, fancy. **2.** opinion, view, belief, sentiment, judgment, supposition. **3.** intention, plan, object, objective, aim, design.

ideal, *n.* **1.** example, model, conception, epitome, standard, pattern, paragon, paradigm, nonpareil, nonesuch. **2.** aim, object, intention, objective. —*adj.* **3.** perfect, consummate, complete. **4.** unreal, unpractical, impractical, imaginary, visionary, fanciful, fantastic, illusory, chimerical.

identical, *adj.* same, alike, twin, indistinguishable, exact, equal, selfsame, undifferentiated, duplicated, reduplicated, clonal, cloned, one and the same, same-old same-old. —**Ant.** unique, nonpareil.

ideology, *n.* philosophy, belief, belief system, credo, creed, ethos, ethic, convictions, tenets, principles, dogma, doctrine, teachings, view, outlook, faith, religion, school, cult, weltan-schauung. —**Ant.** nihilism.

idiosyncrasy, n. mannerism, quirk, tic, trait, habit, trick, peculiarity, characteristic, attribute, property, mark, hallmark, token, singularity, trademark, affectation.

idle, adj. **1.** unemployed, unoccupied, inactive. **2.** indolent, slothful, listless, lethargic, loafing, shiftless, lackadaisical, lazy, sluggish. **3.** worthless, unimportant, trivial, trifling, insignificant, useless, fruitless, vain, ineffective, unavailing, ineffectual, abortive, baseless, groundless. **4.** frivolous, vain, wasteful. —v. **5.** waste, fritter away, while away, kill time, laze about, loiter, loaf, lounge, mess around, putter, waste time, goof off, goldbrick. —**Ant.** employed, occupied; active, energetic; worthy, important; thrifty.

idol, n. **1.** image, icon, symbol, statue, effigy, fetish, false god, pagan deity. **2.** hero, heroine, superstar, celebrity, luminary; favorite, fair-haired boy or girl, darling, pet.

if, conj. in case, provided, providing, granting, supposing, even though, though; whether, whether or not.

iffy, adj. uncertain, unsure, doubtful, problematic, chancy, unsettled, ambiguous, conjectural, speculative, unpredictable, incalculable, unforeseeable, dicey. —**Ant.** certain, sure.

ignoble, adj. **1.** mean, base, ignominious, degraded, dishonorable, contemptible, vulgar, low. **2.** inferior, base, mean, insignificant. **3.** lowly, humble, obscure, plebeian, peasant. —**Ant.** noble, honorable; superior, significant; haughty.

ignominious, adj. discreditable, humiliating, degrading, disgraceful, dishonorable, shameful, infamous, disreputable, opprobrious, despicable, scandalous, contemptible. —**Ant.** creditable, honorable, reputable.

ignominy, n. disgrace, dishonor, disrepute, contempt, discredit, humiliation, indignity, stigma, shame, infamy, obloquy, opprobrium, scandal, odium, abasement, debasement, degradation, notoriety. —**Ant.** credit, honor, repute, fame, distinction.

ignorant, adj. illiterate, unlettered, uneducated, unlearned, uninstructed, untutored, untaught, unenlightened; benighted, oblivious, unaware, unknowing, in the dark, uninformed. —**Ant.** literate, lettered, educated.

ignore, v. overlook, slight, disregard, neglect, turn one's back on, brush off, pass over, be blind to. —**Ant.** notice, note, regard, mark.

ill, adj. **1.** unwell, sick, indisposed, unhealthy, ailing, diseased, unsound, indisposed, infirm, out of commission, under the weather, out of sorts, not up to snuff, afflicted. **2.** evil, wicked, bad, wrong, iniquitous, naughty. **3.** objectionable, unsatisfactory, poor, faulty. **4.** hostile, belligerent, malevolent, malicious, harsh, cruel, unkindly, unkind, unfavorable, adverse. —n. **5.** evil, wickedness, depravity, badness. **6.** harm, injury, hurt, pain, affliction, misery, trouble, misfortune, calamity. **7.** disease, ailment, illness, affliction, indisposition, infirmity. —**Ant.** well, hale, healthy; good.

illegal, adj. unauthorized, unlawful, illegitimate, illicit, unlicensed, criminal, felonious, prohibited, forbidden, taboo, wrongful, proscribed. —**Ant.** legal, licit, authorized.

ill-mannered, adj. impolite, uncivil, discourteous, rude, coarse, uncouth, unpolished, crude, rough, ill-bred, dis-

respectful, ungracious, insulting, boorish, loutish.

ill-natured, adj. cross, cranky, petulant, testy, snappish, unkindly, unpleasant, sulky, ill-tempered, crabbed, morose, sullen, dour, gloomy, sour, crusty, perverse, bitter, contrary, temperamental, crotchety, cantankerous, curmudgeonly. —**Ant.** good-natured, kindly, pleasant, amiable, friendly.

illusion, n. delusion, hallucination, deception, fantasy, chimera, fancy, false impression, misconception, misapprehension, daydream, phantasm, phantom, phantasmagoria, mirage, vision, figment of the imagination, specter, will o' the wisp, ghost. —**Ant.** fact, reality.

illusory, adj. deceptive, misleading, unreal, fictional, untrue, fallacious, false, mistaken, fancied, fanciful, visionary, imaginary, misleading, delusional, chimerical. —**Ant.** real, concrete.

illustration, n. comparison, example, case, instance, sample, specimen, exemplar, representation, elucidation, explanation, explication.

image, n. **1.** icon, idol, representation, statue, effigy, picture, simulacrum, fetish. **2.** reflection, likeness, effigy, figure, representation. **3.** idea, conception, notion, mental picture. **4.** form, appearance, semblance, guise, aspect, mold. **5.** counterpart, epitome, duplicate, replica, clone, twin, dead ringer, facsimile, copy. —**Ant.** original.

imagery, n. picture, pictures, pictorialization, illustration, visualization, iconography, representation, portrayal, depiction, rendering, rendition.

imaginary, adj. fanciful, unreal, visionary, baseless, chimerical, hypothetical, conjectural, fictitious, make-believe, made-up, mythical, notional, abstract, fantastic, oneiric, delusional, phantasmagoric, shadowy, fancied, illusory, imagined. —**Ant.** real.

imagine, v. conceive, image, picture, conceive of, realize, envisage, visualize, create, concoct, contemplate, ponder, think, believe, fancy, assume, suppose, guess, conjecture, hypothesize, presume, infer, gather, surmise, suspect, judge.

imitate, v. follow, mimic, ape, mock, impersonate, copy, parrot, emulate, echo, duplicate, reproduce, simulate, counterfeit.

immediate, adj. **1.** instant, without delay, present, instantaneous, abrupt, sudden, swift; spontaneous, instinctive, automatic, knee-jerk. **2.** present, next, near, close, proximate. **3.** pressing, urgent, actual, present, existing, current. —**Ant.** later.

immediately, adv. **1.** instantly, at once, promptly, right away, right now, without hesitation, straightaway, without delay, presently, directly, instantaneously, forthwith. **2.** directly, closely, without intervention. —**Ant.** later, anon.

immense, adj. huge, great, vast, extensive, large, elephantine, gargantuan, impressive, imposing, enormous, gigantic, voluminous, massive, staggering, mammoth, colossal, titanic, jumbo, humongous. —**Ant.** small, tiny, submicroscopic.

immerse, v. **1.** plunge, dip, sink, duck, douse, submerge, inundate. **2.** embed, bury; involve, absorb, engage, engross, involve, occupy. —**Ant.** withdraw; disinter.

imminent, adj. impending, near, at hand, threatening, menacing, looming,

approaching, forthcoming, close, nigh. —**Ant.** delayed, far off.

immoderate, adj. excessive, extreme, exorbitant, unreasonable, inordinate, extravagant, intemperate. —**Ant.** moderate, reasonable, temperate.

immoral, adj. debauched, indecent, wanton, libertine, lecherous, unregenerate, reprobate, nefarious, unethical, abandoned, depraved, self-indulgent, dissipated, licentious, dissolute, profligate, unprincipled, vicious, sinful, corrupt, amoral, wicked, bad, wrong, evil, iniquitous, vile, degenerate, villainous, dishonest. —**Ant.** moral, pious, good.

immortal, adj. undying, eternal, everlasting, deathless, enduring, imperishable, indestructible, endless, unending, perpetual, perdurable, permanent, never-ending, constant, timeless. —**Ant.** passing, ephemeral.

impair, v. weaken, cripple, damage, harm, mar, spoil, ruin, injure; worsen, diminish, deteriorate, lessen. —**Ant.** repair.

impart, v. **1.** communicate, disclose, divulge, reveal, intimate, confide, make known, tell, relate. **2.** give, bestow, grant, cede, confer. —**Ant.** conceal, hide.

impartial, adj. unbiased, just, fair, unprejudiced, disinterested, equitable, objective, neutral, evenhanded, judicious. —**Ant.** partial.

impatient, adj. **1.** uneasy, restless, unquiet, nervous, fidgety, agitated, fretful, eager, chafing, itchy, antsy. **2.** hasty, impetuous, rash, headlong, vehement, precipitate, sudden, curt, brusque, abrupt. **3.** irritable, testy, fretful, violent, hot, snappish, short, querulous. —**Ant.** patient, restful, quiet; gradual, slow; calm, unperturbed.

impeach, v. attack, challenge, question, discredit, impugn, deprecate, decry, criticize, castigate, slander, censure, accuse, blame, reproach; charge, indict, arraign, incriminate, inculpate. —**Ant.** praise; exculpate, vindicate.

impede, v. retard, slow, delay, hinder, hamper, prevent, encumber, obstruct, check, stop, block, thwart, interrupt, restrain. —**Ant.** aid, encourage.

impediment, n. bar, barrier, block, restraint, restriction, hindrance, obstacle, obstruction, encumbrance, check, holdup, snag, bottleneck. —**Ant.** help, support, spur, stimulus.

impel, v. compel, drive, urge, press on, incite, constrain, force, push. —**Ant.** restrain.

imperfect, adj. **1.** defective, faulty, deficient, flawed, patchy, spotty, blemished, incomplete. **2.** rudimentary, undeveloped, underdeveloped, incomplete; immature.

impertinent, adj. intrusive, presumptuous, impudent, insolent, uncivil, discourteous, forward, disrespectful, impolite, brassy, rude, fresh, bold, arrogant, insulting, officious, saucy, pert, brazen. —**Ant.** polite, courteous, respectful.

impetuous, adj. impulsive, rash, precipitate, spontaneous, violent, abrupt, reckless, headstrong, devil-may-care, daredevil, sudden, quick, hasty, furious, unpremeditated, offhand, spur-of-the-moment, unthinking, hot-headed. —**Ant.** planned, careful.

implacable, adj. unappeasable, inexorable, inflexible, intractable, uncompromising, unrelenting, remorseless, unbending, relentless, rancorous, merciless, ruthless, cruel, unforgiving, pitiless, unsympathetic, hard. —**Ant.** flexible, merciful.

implicate, v. involve, concern, entangle, include, associate, embroil, ensnare, entrap, enmesh, connect, point to, incriminate. —**Ant**. exonerate.

implore, v. call upon, supplicate, beseech, entreat, crave, beg, solicit, importune.

impolite, adj. uncivil, rude, discourteous, disrespectful, insolent, ungracious, indelicate, ill-bred, coarse, insulting, offensive, unpolished, unrefined, boorish, ill-mannered, rough, savage, churlish, crude, indecorous, vulgar. —**Ant**. polite.

importance, n. consequence, weight, moment, significance, value, worth, substance, account, concern, matter, import, momentousness, weightiness. —**Ant**. unimportance, insignificance.

impostor, n. pretender, deceiver, imitator, wolf in sheep's clothing, humbug, dissembler, impersonator, swindler, shark, phony, fourflusher, faker, cheat, confidence man, con man, trickster, hypocrite, charlatan, mountebank.

impotent, adj. powerless, helpless, enfeebled, weak, frail, feeble, enervated, effete, debilitated; inept, incompetent, crippled, paralyzed, disabled, incapacitated, ineffectual, ineffective, uninfluential, lightweight, wimpish, wimpy, nebbishy, shooting blanks. —**Ant**. powerful, strong.

impregnable, adj. unassailable, invincible, invulnerable, impenetrable, inviolable, indomitable, safe, secure, mighty. —**Ant**. vulnerable.

improper, adj. **1**. inapplicable, unsuited, unfit, inappropriate, unsuitable. **2**. indecent, unbecoming, unseemly, indecorous, unfitting, untoward, immodest, impolite; suggestive, off-color, bawdy, ribald, obscene, scurrilous, scabrous, lewd, dirty, immoral, vulgar, lascivious, licentious, foul, vile, pornographic. **3**. abnormal, irregular, faulty, mistaken, wrong, imprecise, inexact. —**Ant**. proper.

impropriety, n. **1**. misbehavior, misconduct, indecorousness, indecorum, unseemliness, naughtiness, vulgarity, disorderliness. **2**. error, indiscretion, faux pas, solecism, gaffe, vulgarism, indecency.

improve, v. **1**. ameliorate, better, amend, emend, upgrade, enhance, fix up, reform, repair, rehabilitate, correct, right, rectify. **2**. mend, gain, get better, convalesce, recuperate, recover, rally, revive. —**Ant**. worsen, impair; fail, sink.

improvident, adj. **1**. incautious, unwary, thoughtless, neglectful, careless, imprudent, heedless, without or lacking foresight. **2**. thriftless, wanton, profligate, spendthrift, extravagant, lavish, shiftless, wasteful, prodigal, shortsighted. —**Ant**. provident, cautious; thrifty.

improvised, adj. extemporaneous, impromptu, unpremeditated, ad hoc, offhand, off the cuff, spur-of-the-moment, throwaway, unrehearsed, spontaneous. —**Ant**. premeditated, rehearsed, studied.

impudence, n. impertinence, effrontery, insolence, rudeness, brass, disrespect, audacity, cockiness, arrogance, brazenness, lip, boldness, presumption, presumptiveness, sauciness, pertness, flippancy, nerve, gall, chutzpah, back talk, sass. —**Ant**. politeness, courtesy, respectfulness.

impudent, adj. bold, brazen, brassy, presumptuous, shameless, forward, cocky, cocksure, arrogant, disrespectful, audacious, offensive, insolent, impertinent, insulting, rude, presumptive,

saucy, pert, flippant, fresh, sassy, smart-mouthed. —**Ant**. polite, courteous, well-behaved.

impulsive, adj. emotional, impetuous, rash, unpredictable, extemporaneous, offhand, instinctive, sudden, snap, headlong, reckless, foolhardy, madcap, imprudent, quick, hasty, unpremeditated. —**Ant**. cool, cold, unemotional, premeditated.

impute, v. attribute, charge, ascribe, refer, assign, credit; insinuate, imply, suggest, hint at.

inability, n. incapability, incapacity, disqualification, paralysis, impotence, incompetence, ineptness, unfitness. —**Ant**. ability.

inaccuracy, n. **1**. incorrectness, imprecision, erroneousness, inexactness, inexactitude. **2**. error, blunder, mistake, slip, gaffe, fault, flaw, boner. —**Ant**. accuracy.

inaccurate, adj. inexact, imprecise, off base, flawed, imperfect, loose, general, unspecific; incorrect, wrong, erroneous, mistaken, false, fallacious, illogical, unsound, faulty, improper, full of hot air. —**Ant**. accurate.

inactive, adj. inert, dormant, inanimate, unmoving, immobile, nonfunctional, inoperative; indolent, lazy, sluggish, torpid, passive, idle, slothful, dilatory. —**Ant**. active, energetic, dynamic, busy.

inadequate, adj. inapt, incompetent, insufficient, incommensurate, defective, imperfect, incomplete; deficient, scarce, meager, scanty, sparse, skimpy. —**Ant**. adequate.

inadvertent, adj. **1**. unintentional, accidental, unwitting, chance. **2**. heedless, inattentive, unintentional, thoughtless, careless, negligent, unobservant. —**Ant**. intentional, purposive, purposeful.

inanimate, adj. **1**. lifeless, inorganic, abiotic, inert, inactive, dormant, nonliving, motionless, immobile. **2**. indolent, dull, passive, torpid, unresponsive, listless, stagnant, slow, insensible, unconscious, lifeless, sluggish, inert, spiritless; dead, defunct. —**Ant**. animate, alive; spirited.

inborn, adj. innate, inbred, native, natural, congenital, inherent, instinctive, inherited, hereditary, constitutional, deep-seated, ingrained. —**Ant**. acquired, learned, conditioned, environmental.

incapable, adj. unable, incompetent, inefficient, impotent, unqualified. —**Ant**. capable, competent, efficient, potent, qualified.

incentive, n. motive, inducement, incitement, enticement, stimulus, spur, impulse, goad, encouragement, prod, reward, perk. —**Ant**. discouragement, disincentive.

incessant, adj. uninterrupted, unceasing, ceaseless, continual, continuous, constant, unending, never-ending, relentless, unrelenting, unremitting, perpetual, eternal, everlasting. —**Ant**. interrupted, spasmodic, sporadic; temporary.

incident, n. event, occurrence, happening, circumstance, accident, occasion, proceeding, fact, experience, episode.

incidental, adj. fortuitous, chance, accidental, casual, contingent, random, haphazard, serendipitous, aleatory, adventitious, unplanned, fluky. —**Ant**. fundamental.

incisive, adj. **1**. penetrating, trenchant, biting, acute, cutting, caustic, tart, acerbic, cynical, critical, stinging, sarcastic, sardonic, satirical, acid, severe,

cruel. **2**. sharp, keen, acute, piercing, perceptive, trenchant, canny, shrewd, perspicacious. —**Ant**. superficial, dull.

incite, v. urge on, stimulate, encourage, back, prod, push, spur, inspire, prompt, move, stir up, exhort, foment, egg on, goad, instigate, provoke, arouse, fire; induce, persuade, cause. —**Ant**. discourage.

inclination, n. bent, leaning, tendency, set, propensity, liking, preference, predilection, predisposition, proclivity, bias, proneness, prejudice, penchant, leaning, tendency. —**Ant**. dislike, antipathy.

include, v. contain, embrace, comprise, comprehend, embody, incorporate, cover, encompass, subsume, take in. —**Ant**. exclude, preclude.

income, n. return, returns, receipts, revenue, profits, salary, wages, proceeds, take, gross, net, bottom line, fees, pay, stipend, interest, annuity, gain, earnings. —**Ant**. expense, expenditure.

incompatible, adj. **1**. inconsistent, incongruous, unsuitable, unsuited, contradictory, irreconcilable. **2**. mismatched, unsuited, clashing, jarring, conflicting, discordant, contrary, opposed, difficult, contradictory, inharmonious. —**Ant**. compatible, consistent, appropriate; harmonious.

incompetent, adj. unqualified, unable, incapable, inadequate, unskillful, inept, maladroit, inexpert, awkward, bungling, gauche, useless, inefficient, floundering, oafish, not up to snuff, clumsy, unfit, insufficient. —**Ant**. competent, efficient, able, capable, adequate, fit.

incongruous, adj. **1**. unbecoming, inappropriate, incompatible, out of keeping, discrepant, absurd. **2**. inconsonant, dissonant, inharmonious, discordant. **3**. inconsistent, incoherent, illogical, unfitting, contrary, contradictory, paradoxical. —**Ant**. congruous, becoming, appropriate, proper; harmonious; logical, consistent, coherent, sensible.

inconsistent, adj. incompatible, inharmonious, incongruous, unsuitable, irreconcilable, incoherent, discrepant, out of keeping, inappropriate. —**Ant**. consistent, coherent, harmonious, suitable.

inconstant, adj. changeable, fickle, inconsistent, variable, moody, fluctuating, erratic, flighty, fitful, vague, capricious, vacillating, wavering, mercurial, volatile, unsettled, unstable, mutable, uncertain, unsteady, irresolute, unreliable, undependable. —**Ant**. constant, steady, invariant, settled, staid.

incontrovertible, adj. undeniable, indisputable, incontestable, unquestionable, irrefutable, indubitable, sure, certain, definite, absolute, positive. —**Ant**. deniable, controvertible, disputable, questionable.

inconvenient, adj. burdensome, unwieldly, onerous, difficult, cumbersome, awkward, inopportune, disadvantageous, troublesome, annoying, vexatious, irritating, irksome, disturbing, upsetting, untimely, incommodious. —**Ant**. convenient, opportune, advantageous.

incorrect, adj. wrong, not valid, untrue, false, erroneous, mistaken, fallacious, specious, imprecise, spurious, illogical, faulty, improper, inexact, inaccurate. —**Ant**. correct.

increase, v. **1**. augment, add to, enlarge, extend, prolong, advance, further, better, improve. **2**. grow, dilate, swell, wax, develop, distend, inflate, burgeon, spread, proliferate, snowball, heighten, broaden, widen, expand, enlarge, multiply. —*n.* **3.** growth, augmentation, enlargement, expansion, addition, extension, spread. —**Ant.** decrease.

incredulous, *adj.* unbelieving, skeptical, doubtful, dubious, unconvinced, wary, mistrustful, suspicious; amazed, astonished. —**Ant.** credulous, trusting, susceptible.

indecent, *adj.* offensive, distasteful, improper, unbecoming, unseemly, inappropriate, repulsive, repellent, shameful, in bad taste, outrageous, vulgar, indelicate, coarse, rude, gross, immodest, unrefined, indecorous; obscene, filthy, lewd, licentious, lascivious, pornographic, bawdy, ribald, X-rated, prurient, smutty, degenerate, debauched. —**Ant.** decent.

indefinite, *adj.* **1.** unlimited, unconfined, unrestrained, undefined, undetermined, indistinct, confused. **2.** vague, obscure, confusing, equivocal, dim, unspecific, doubtful, unsettled, uncertain. —**Ant.** definite.

independence, *n.* freedom, liberty, emancipation, desenthrallment, autonomy, self-determination, self-government, self-rule, sovereignty; self-sufficiency, self-reliance. —**Ant.** dependence, reliance.

indifference, *n.* **1.** unconcern, listlessness, apathy, insensibility, nonchalance, insouciance, aloofness, detachment, phlegm, coolness, insensitiveness, inattention. **2.** unimportance, triviality, insignificance. **3.** mediocrity, inferiority, averageness, ordinariness. —**Ant.** concern, warmth, sensibility; importance, significance; superiority.

indignation, *n.* consternation, irritation, annoyance, vexation, pique, resentment, exasperation, wrath, anger, ire, fury, rage, choler, shirtiness. —**Ant.** calm, serenity, composure.

indignity, *n.* injury, slight, contempt, offenses, humiliation, affront, insult, outrage, scorn, obloquy, contumely, reproach, abuse, opprobrium, dishonor, disrespect, snub, slap, discourtesy. —**Ant.** dignity; honor, respect.

indiscriminate, *adj.* **1.** unselective, careless, random, promiscuous, uncritical, undiscriminating. **2.** confused, undistinguishable, mixed, haphazard, choatic, jumbled, unsystematic, casual, unmethodical, wholesale, erratic, higgledy-piggledy. —**Ant.** discriminating; systematic, methodical.

indispensable, *adj.* crucial, vital, urgent, imperative, important, compelling, necessary, requisite, essential, needed, basic. —**Ant.** dispensable, disposable, unnecessary, nonessential.

indisposed, *adj.* **1.** sick, ill, unwell, ailing, out of sorts, under the weather, out of commission. **2.** disinclined, unwilling, reluctant, averse, loath, hesitant, resistant. —**Ant.** well, healthy, hardy, hale; eager, willing.

indisputable, *adj.* incontrovertible, incontestable, unquestionable, undeniable, indubitable; evident, apparent, obvious, certain, manifest, sure, absolute, definitive, definite, positive. —**Ant.** questionable, dubitable, dubious; uncertain.

indolent, *adj.* idle, lazy, slothful, slow, inactive, sluggish, torpid, listless, inert, lethargic, shiftless, languid, stagnant. —**Ant.** energetic, active, industrious.

indomitable, *adj.* resolute, steadfast, staunch, tireless, unflagging, brave,

dauntless, fearless, intrepid, plucky, mettlesome; invincible, unconquerable, unyielding, unbeatable. —**Ant.** yielding, weak, feeble.

induce, *v.* **1.** persuade, influence, cause, stimulate, move, actuate, prompt, instigate, goad, incite, urge, impel, spur, prevail upon. **2.** bring about, produce, cause, effect, bring on. —**Ant.** dissuade.

inducement, *n.* attraction, lure, bait, encouragement, provocation, impetus, incentive, motive, cause, stimulus, spur, incitement, carrot, come-on, perk. —**Ant.** discouragement.

indulge, *v.* yield to, satisfy, gratify, humor, pamper, give way to, favor; suffer, foster, permit, allow; coddle, pamper, spoil. —**Ant.** deny, forbid; discipline, punish.

industrious, *adj.* busy, hard-working, diligent, assiduous, intense, conscientious, energetic, tireless, dogged, tenacious, sedulous, persistent, persevering, perseverant. —**Ant.** lazy, indolent.

ineffectual, *adj.* **1.** useless, unavailing, futile, nugatory, ineffective, unsuccessful, sterile, barren, unproductive, fruitless, pointless, abortive, purposeless. **2.** powerless, impotent, feeble, weak, effete, tame, lame. —**Ant.** effectual, efficacious, efficient.

inefficient, *adj.* incapable, ineffective, feeble, weak, incompetent, inexpert, unskillful, slipshod, inept, deficient. —**Ant.** efficient, effectual, efficacious.

inept, *adj.* **1.** inapt, unfitted, unfitting, unsuitable, unsuited, unseemly, improper, imprudent, unwise, misguided, ill-advised, inappropriate, out of place, anomalous. **2.** absurd, foolish, stupid, pointless, inane, ridiculous. **3.** clumsy, awkward, bungling, maladroit, ungainly, gauche, bumbling, incompetent, unskillful, oafish, inexpert. —**Ant.** fit, suitable, apt, appropriate.

inert, *adj.* inactive, immobile, unmoving, lifeless, insensible, dead, passive, motionless, unresponsive, inanimate, still, quiescent, static; slow dull, idle, leaden, slack, dormant, supine, otiose, listless. —**Ant.** active, kinetic.

inexorable, *adj.* unyielding, unalterable, inflexible, unbending, firm, solid, steadfast; severe, relentless, unrelenting, implacable, merciless, cruel, pitiless, ruthless, remorseless; imminent, unavoidable, inevitable. —**Ant.** flexible, yielding; merciful.

inexpensive, *adj.* cheap, low-priced, economical, reasonable, budget, thrifty, discount, bargain-basement. —**Ant.** expensive.

inexperienced, *adj.* immature, innocent, naive, callow, unsophisticated, unworldly, fledgling, unseasoned, raw, green, unpracticed, unschooled, untutored, uninformed, uninitiated, wet behind the ears, born yesterday. —**Ant.** experienced, skilled, practiced.

infallible, *adj.* trustworthy, sure, certain, reliable, unfailing, foolproof, dependable; unerring, faultless, perfect, oracular. —**Ant.** fallible, unreliable, uncertain.

infamous, *adj.* **1.** disreputable, illfamed, notorious, scandalous, discreditable, dishonorable, stigmatized. **2.** detestable, shameful, bad, nefarious, odious, wicked, outrageous, shocking, vile, base, ignominious, evil, iniquitous, abominable, despicable, loathsome, foul, low, rotten, dark, heinous, villainous. —**Ant.** reputable, famed; honorable, good.

infamy, *n.* notoriety, disgrace, dishonor, discredit, shame, disrepute, ob-

loquy, odium, opprobrium, scandal, debasement, abasement, ignominy, ill repute, stigma. —**Ant.** honor, credit, repute.

infantile, *adj.* babyish, childish, puerile, immature, weak, juvenile, jejune. —**Ant.** mature, adult.

inflame, *v.* kindle, excite, rouse, arouse, incite, fire, stimulate, touch off, ignite, provoke, excite, incense, anger, enrage, rile, animate, motivate, prod, goad, urge, move. —**Ant.** discourage.

inflate, *v.* distend, swell, swell out, dilate, expand, puff up *or* out, bloat, blow up, balloon, dilate, enlarge, pump up; exaggerate, embellish, embroider. —**Ant.** deflate.

inflexible, *adj.* rigid, stiff, inelastic, unbending, undeviating, unyielding, rigorous, implacable, stern, relentless, unrelenting, inexorable, unremitting, immovable, resolute, steadfast, firm, stony, solid, persevering, stubborn, dogged, pigheaded, mulish, steely, stony, obstinate, refractory, willful, headstrong, intractable, obdurate, adamant, dyed in the wool. —**Ant.** flexible, easygoing, malleable.

influence, *n.* **1.** sway, rule, authority, power, pressure, weight, impact, force, effect, leverage, hold, mastery, ascendancy, pull, clout, control, predominance. —*v.* **2.** modify, affect, sway, impress, bias, direct, control. **3.** move, impel, actuate, activate, incite, rouse, arouse, instigate, induce, persuade.

inform, *v.* **1.** communicate, enlightened, brief, impart, disclose, divulge, report, reveal, tip off, apprise, make known, advise, notify, tell, acquaint. **2.** animate, inspire, quicken, enliven, inspirit. —**Ant.** conceal, hide.

informal, *adj.* irregular, unusual, anomalous, unconventional, natural, easy, unceremonious, casual, unstilted, familiar, ordinary, everyday, relaxed, free, unaffected, unassuming, unpretentious. —**Ant.** formal, regular, customary, conventional.

information, *n.* knowledge, news, data, facts, circumstances, situation, intelligence, advice, report, word, message, lowdown, dish, inside story.

infringe, *v.* **1.** violate, transgress, breach, break, overstep, disobey. **2.** trespass, encroach, invade, intrude, impinge. —**Ant.** obey.

infuriate, *v.* enrage, anger, incense, madden, provoke, inflame, rile, vex, irritate, irk, chafe, peeve, pique, gall, outrage, nettle, raise (someone's) hackles, make (someone's) blood boil, miff, peeve, bug. —**Ant.** calm, pacify.

ingenious, *adj.* clever, skillful, adroit, bright, gifted, able, resourceful, inventive, shrewd, cunning, smart, talented, deft, handy, creative, imaginative, original, sharp-witted, crafty, on the ball. —**Ant.** unskillful, maladroit.

ingenuous, *adj.* unreserved, unrestrained, frank, candid, free; simple, innocent, unsophisticated, childlike, trusting, open, guileless, artless, innocent, naive, straightforward, sincere, honest, aboveboard, unaffected. —**Ant.** reserved, restrained, secretive, sly, insincere.

ingredient, *n.* constituent, element, component, part, factor, making. —**Ant.** whole.

inherent, *adj.* innate, inherited, native, natural, inborn, inbred, essential, intrinsic, basic, engrained, congenital, hereditary, indigenous, immanent, built-in, part and parcel. —**Ant.** acquired.

inheritance, *n.* heritage, patrimony, legacy, bequest, birthright.

inhibit, *v.* 1. restrain, hinder, arrest, check, repress, obstruct, stop; discourage. 2. prohibit, forbid, interdict, prevent. —**Ant.** encourage, support, abet, promote.

initiate, *v.* 1. begin, originate, set going, start, commence, introduce, inaugurate, open, launch, trigger, activate, instigate, institute. 2. teach, instruct, indoctrinate, train. —*n.* 3. new member, pledge, tyro, beginner, learner, amateur, freshman, novice, greenhorn, rookie, neophyte, newcomer, tenderfoot, fledgling, apprentice, recruit, novitiate, abecedarian. —**Ant.** terminate, conclude, finish.

injure, *v.* 1. damage, impair, harm, hurt, spoil, ruin, break, mar, disable, handicap, wound. 2. wrong, maltreat, mistreat, abuse, offend, wound, outrage, affront.

injurious, *adj.* 1. harmful, hurtful, damaging, ruinous, detrimental, pernicious, deleterious, baneful, destructive, mischievous. 2. unjust, wrongful, prejudicial, biased, inequitable, iniquitous. 3. offensive, insulting, abusive, derogatory, defamatory, slanderous, libelous, contumelious, scornful, deprecatory. —**Ant.** beneficial; just, right; complimentary.

injury, *n.* 1. harm, damage, ruin, detriment, wound, impairment, mischief, hurt, abuse, mistreatment, offense, outrage, mayhem. 2. wrong, injustice, mistreatment, malfeasance.

innocent, *adj.* 1. pure, untainted, sinless, virtuous, virginal, blameless, faultless, impeccable, spotless, immaculate, chaste, pristine, spotless, undefiled, unsullied, uncorrupted, sweet. 2. honest, in the clear, unimpeachable, irreproachable, above suspicion, faultless, guiltless, blameless. 3. upright, honest, forthright. 4. naive, simple, trusting, gullible, credulous, childlike, green, inexperienced, unworldly, unaffected, sincere, earnest, born yesterday, uninitiated, unsophisticated, artless, guileless, ingenuous. —**Ant.** impure, tainted, sinful; guilty, culpable; dishonest; disingenuous, sophisticated, artful.

innocuous, *adj.* 1. harmless, inoffensive, innocent, unhurtful, benign. 2. well-meaning, unthreatening; insipid, neutral, dull, banal, toothless, ineffective, weak, anemic, pointless.

inquire, *v.* ask, question, query, investigate, examine, search, probe, research, inspect, study, explore, scrutinize, survey. —**Ant.** answer, reply.

inquiry, *n.* 1. investigation, examination, study, scrutiny, probe, search, inspection, survey, inquest, analysis, exploration, research. 2. inquiring, questioning, cross-examination, inquisition, interview, interrogation; query, question. —**Ant.** answer, reply.

inquisitive, *adj.* inquiring, prying, nosy, curious, scrutinizing, questioning, interested, analytical, investigative, probing, exploratory.

insane, *adj.* deranged, demented, lunatic, crazed, crazy, maniacal, unbalanced, unhinged, mental, not all there, non compos mentis, of unsound mind, mad; paranoiac, schizophrenic, delirious; foolish, senseless, stupid, thoughtless, asinine, idiotic, irrational, absurd, fatuous, moronic, harebrained. —**Ant.** sane.

insanity, *n.* 1. derangement, dementia, lunacy, madness, mental illness *or* disorder, hysteria, abnormality, craziness, mania, aberration; schizophrenia, paranoia, psychosis, neurosis. 2.

senselessness, foolhardiness, folly, foolishness, fatuity, fatuousness, lunacy, nonsense, inanity, absurdity, stupidity, idiocy, imbecility, asininity, irrationality, irresponsibility, craziness, madness, bootlessness, ridiculousness, risibility, ludicrousness, laughability. —**Ant.** sanity, probity.

inscrutable, *adj.* impenetrable, mysterious, hidden, secretive, recondite, obscure, abstruse, arcane, enigmatic, incomprehensible, inexplicable, unexplainable, unfathomable, unknowable, baffling. —**Ant.** clear, comprehensible, understandable.

insecure, *adj.* 1. unsafe, exposed, unprotected, dangerous, vulnerable, defenseless, open, pregnable. 2. uncertain, unsure, risky, precarious, shaky, unreliable, worrisome. —**Ant.** secure, safe; certain, sure.

insidious, *adj.* treacherous, stealthy, deceitful, artful, cunning, sly, wily, intriguing, subtle, crafty, tricky, arch, crooked, foxy, Machiavellian, scheming. —**Ant.** upright, forthright; artless, ingenuous.

insinuate, *v.* 1. hint, suggest, intimate, impute; imply, whisper, indicate. 2. instill, infuse, introduce, inject, inculcate.

insolent, *adj.* bold, rude, disrespectful, impudent, pert, saucy, bold, presumptuous, offensive, crude, insubordinate, fresh, cheeky, contumelious, sassy, impertinent, brazen, brassy, abusive, overbearing, contemptuous, insulting. —**Ant.** polite, courteous, retiring; complimentary.

inspection, *n.* examination, investigation, scrutiny, study, survey, scan, check, perusal, vetting.

instance, *n.* case, example, illustration, exemplification, exemplar, precedent; event, occurrence, episode, experience.

instant, *n.* moment, minute, second, twinkling, flash, jiffy, trice.

instruct, *v.* 1. direct, command, order, prescribe, bid, require, tell, enjoin, charge, importune. 2. teach, train, educate, tutor, coach, drill, discipline, indoctrinate, school, inform, enlighten, apprise, guide, edify, prepare, inculcate. —**Ant.** mislead.

instruction, *n.* 1. education, tutoring, coaching, training, drill, exercise, tuition, guidance, preparation, lessons, classes, tutorial, tutelage, edification, indoctrination, schooling, teaching. 2. order, direction, mandate, command, advice, directive, recommendation.

instructor, *n.* teacher, trainer, coach, mentor, adviser, educator, scholastic, academician, lecturer, professor, master, guru, tutor, pedagogue, schoolmaster, preceptor. —**Ant.** student, pupil.

instrument, *n.* tool, implement, utensil, device, gadget, apparatus, gizmo.

insult, *v.* 1. affront, offend, scorn, injure, slander, abuse. —*n.* 2. affront, indignity, offense, contumely, scorn, outrage. —**Ant.** compliment, dignify; dignity.

intact, *adj.* perfect, solid, all in one piece, uncut, together, uninjured, unaltered, sound, whole, unimpaired, complete, undiminished, unbroken, entire. —**Ant.** impaired, unsound, incomplete.

integrity, *n.* 1. uprightness, honesty, honor, morality, ethics, rectitude, right, righteousness, probity, principle, virtue, goodness. 2. wholeness, entirety, completeness, unity, totality, coherence, soundness. —**Ant.** dishonesty, disrepute; part.

intellect, *n.* mind, understanding, rea-

son, sense, common sense, brains, rationality, judgment, cleverness, wit. —**Ant.** inanity.

intellectual, *adj.* 1. mental, cerebral; rational, reasoning, intelligent. 2. literate, erudite, cultivated, cultured, highbrow, academic, scholarly, bookish, thoughtful, thought-provoking, brainy, witty. —*n.* 3. thinker, intellect, genius, highbrow, mastermind, wit, connoisseur, savant, brain, egghead, professor, mental giant, longhair, brainiac, scholar, academician, sage, wise man *or* woman, guru, pundit, polymath, expert, authority, critic, bluestocking, member of the intelligentsia. —**Ant.** illiterate, untutored, ignorant, unenlightened, loutish; ignoramus, lowbrow, yahoo, know-nothing.

intelligence, *n.* 1. intellect, capacity, brainpower, cleverness, astuteness, quickness, wit, sense, insight, perspicacity, perception, discernment, wisdom, sagacity, mind, understanding, discernment, reason, acumen, aptitude, penetration. 2. knowledge, news, information, tidings, word, message, scoop, lowdown, inside story. —**Ant.** stupidity.

intelligent, *adj.* 1. understanding, rational, gifted, knowledgeable, erudite, intellectual. 2. astute, clever, quick, alert, bright, apt, discerning, shrewd, smart, perspicacious, insightful, percipient, wise, sage, sagacious, enlightened, knowing, brainy, perceptive, sharp, canny, aware, keen-witted, savvy, quick-witted, keen, gifted, sensible, aware, au fait. —**Ant.** stupid, unintelligent, slow; dull.

intend, *v.* have in mind, mean, design, propose, contemplate, expect, meditate, project, aim for *or* at, purpose, plan, determine.

intensify, *v.* aggravate, deepen, quicken, strengthen; concentrate, focus, sharpen, whet, reinforce, emphasize. —**Ant.** alleviate, lessen, weaken, dilute.

intent, *n.* 1. intention, design, purpose, meaning, plan, plot, aim, goal, end, focus, objective, object, mark. —*adj.* 2. fixed, steadfast, bent, resolute, set, concentrated, unshakable, eager, focused, steady, intense. —**Ant.** irresolute, apathetic.

intentional, *adj.* deliberate, purposeful, premeditated, designed, planned, intended, meant, willful, studied, preconceived. —**Ant.** unintentional, purposeless, unpremeditated; involuntary.

interesting, *adj.* pleasing, attractive, gratifying, engaging, absorbing, exciting, fulfilling, entertaining, gripping, riveting, engrossing, compelling, inviting, intriguing, provocative, stimulating, fascinating, enchanting, spellbinding, captivating. —**Ant.** uninteresting, dull, prosaic.

interpret, *v.* 1. explain, explicate, elucidate, shed *or* cast light on, define, translate, decipher, decode. 2. construe, understand, take to mean, read, figure out, unravel.

interrupt, *v.* 1. discontinue, suspend, cut short, disrupt, hold up, terminate. 2. stop, cease, break off, disturb, hinder, interfere with, butt in. —**Ant.** continue.

intimate, *adj.* 1. close, closely associated, familiar, dear, confidential, warm, affectionate, loving, cherished, bosom. 2. private, personal, confidential, hidden, privy, secret. 3. detailed, deep, cogent, exacting, exact, precise. 4. inmost, deep within; intrinsic, inner, deep-rooted, deep-seated. —*n.* 5. friend, associate, confidant, comrade, companion, alter ego, sidekick, chum.

pal, buddy, bro, homey, crony, familiar. —*v.* **6.** hint, suggest, insinuate, allude to, imply, indicate, communicate, tip off. —**Ant.** open, public, known, blatant; enemy, foe; announce, proclaim.

intimidate, *v.* overawe, cow, subdue, dismay, frighten, daunt, abash, appall, browbeat, terrorize, tyrannize, alarm; discourage, dissuade. —**Ant.** encourage, hearten.

intolerable, *adj.* unbearable, unendurable, insufferable, insupportable, unacceptable, excessive, outrageous. —**Ant.** tolerable, bearable.

intolerant, *adj.* bigoted, illiberal, narrow, proscriptive, prejudiced, discriminatory, partial, close-minded, parochial, one-sided, opinionated, chauvinistic, xenophobic, jingoistic, biased, dictatorial, fascistic, totalitarian, fanatical. —**Ant.** tolerant, liberal, unprejudiced.

intractable, *adj.* stubborn, obstinate, unmanageable, perverse, fractious, refractory, headstrong, pigheaded, dogged, unbending, inflexible, obdurate, adamant, stony, willful, unyielding, contumacious. —**Ant.** tractable, amiable, amenable, easygoing, flexible.

intrinsic, *adj.* essential, native, innate, inborn, inbred, natural, inherent, basic, fundamental, elemental, organic, congenital, hereditary, immanent, underlying, constitutional; true, real, genuine. —**Ant.** extrinsic.

introduce, *v.* **1.** present, announce, make known, acquaint. **2.** broach, suggest, offer, mention, propose, bring up, advance, set forth, put forward. **3.** originate, start, begin, establish, set up, launch, initiate, institute, pioneer, set up, organize. **4.** add, insert, put in, interpose, inject, interpolate.

intrude, *v.* trespass, obtrude, encroach, violate, infringe, interfere, interrupt, intervene, butt in, barge in, horn in.

inundate, *v.* flood, deluge, overflow, overspread, overwhelm, glut.

invaluable, *adj.* priceless, precious, valuable, inestimable, incalculable, irreplaceable, treasured, incomparable. —**Ant.** worthless.

invariable, *adj.* unalterable, unchanging, uniform, steady, stable, regular, set, rigid, unwavering, constant, invariant, changeless, unvarying; unchangeable, immutable, permanent, fixed. —**Ant.** variable, changing, varying, mutable.

invent, *v.* **1.** devise, contrive, originate, discover, create, conceive, imagine, formulate, improvise, coin. **2.** produce, create, imagine, fancy, conceive, fabricate, concoct, make up, cook up.

inventory, *n.* roll, list, roster, listing, record, account, catalogue, register.

investigation, *n.* examination, inspection, inquiry, scrutiny, study, review, quest, search, probe, analysis, inquest, interrogation, inquisition, research, exploration.

invigorate, *v.* animate, inspirit, enliven, strengthen, fortify, energize, quicken, vitalize, stimulate, restore, exhilarate, rejuvenate, be tonic, refresh, freshen. —**Ant.** enervate, enfeeble, weaken, devitalize.

invincible, *adj.* unbeatable, mighty, unstoppable, superhuman, unrivaled, unsurpassed, supreme, dominant, inexorable, matchless, undefeated, unconquerable, insuperable, impregnable, impenetrable, indomitable. —**Ant.** weak, beatable, third-rate.

invite, *v.* **1.** call, request, ask, bid, summon, solicit. **2.** attract, appeal, engage, capture, captivate, allure, lure, tempt, entice, draw, induce, beckon.

involuntary, *adj.* **1.** unintentional, reluctant, accidental, unpremeditated, unwitting, unconscious, impulsive, unplanned, unwanted. **2.** automatic, reflex, unwilled, instinctive, uncontrolled. —**Ant.** voluntary, intentional, willed.

involve, *v.* **1.** include, embrace, contain, comprehend, comprise, entail, imply. **2.** entangle, implicate, connect, tie, bind. —**Ant.** exclude, preclude.

irate, *adj.* angry, enraged, furious, infuriated, wrathful, livid, steaming, inflamed, incensed, mad as a wet hen, irked, aggravated, worked up, fuming, nettled, annoyed, exasperated, seeing red, splenetic, hopping *or* boiling mad, upset, livid, up in arms, hot under the collar, on the warpath, burned up, piqued, provoked, irritated, vexed. —**Ant.** pleased, calm.

irregular, *adj.* sporadic, uneven, random, unequal, fitful, haphazard, uncertain, occasional, casual, unmethodical, unsystematic, disorderly, capricious, erratic; eccentric, lawless, aberrant, devious, unconforming, nonconformist, unusual, abnormal, anomalous, extraordinary, unnatural, peculiar, queer, odd, weird, bizarre, strange, singular, exceptional, offbeat, uncommon, freakish, freaky. —**Ant.** regular.

irrepressible, *adj.* unrestrained, unconstrained, enthusiastic, effervescent, vivacious, uninhibited, exuberant, high-spirited, ebullient, buoyant, boisterous, unstoppable. —**Ant.** gloomy, depressive.

irritate, *v.* vex, annoy, chafe, fret, gall, nettle, ruffle, pique, incense, irk, anger, enrage, infuriate, exasperate, provoke, pester, bother, hector, harass, harry, nag, plague, worry, fluster, trouble, pick on, needle, hassle, peeve, get on (someone's) nerves, drive (someone) up the wall, get up (someone's) nose, burn (someone) up. —**Ant.** please, delight.

isolation, *n.* solitude, loneliness; separation, disconnection, segregation, detachment, ostracism, exclusion, quarantine, excommunication.

issue, *n.* **1.** delivery, emission, sending, promulgation. **2.** point, crux; problem, question. **3.** product, effect, result, consequence, event, outcome, upshot, denouement, conclusion, end, consummation. —*v.* **4.** put out, deliver, circulate, publish, distribute. **5.** send out, discharge, emit. **6.** come forth, emerge, flow out. **7.** come, proceed, emanate, flow, arise, spring, originate, ensue.

J

jabber, *v.* prattle, chatter, babble, prate, run on, natter, palaver, gabble, blather, tittle-tattle, gibber, drivel, gab, gas, yap. —**Ant.** discourse, orate.

jaded, *adj.* **1.** world-weary, bored, blasé, spoiled, sated, satiated, glutted, burned out. **2.** tired, weary, spent, exhausted, worn out, fatigued, enervated, spent, dead, bushed, pooped. —**Ant.** fresh, bright-eyed, eager.

jam, *v.* **1.** push, stuff, press, shove, wedge, pack, crowd, ram, force, squeeze, bruise, crush, cram. —*n.* **2.** dilemma, quandary, predicament, trouble, difficulty, bind, fix, pickle, hot water, scrape, tight spot.

jargon, *n.* **1.** idiom, vocabulary, phraseology, language, vernacular, argot, patois, patter, lingo, cant, slang. **2.** mumbo-jumbo, nonsense, double-talk, gibberish, rubbish, hogwash, claptrap.

jaunty, *adj.* **1.** spirited, lively, frisky, blithe, jovial, jubilant, merry, gay, sprightly, cheerful, lighthearted, upbeat, buoyant, perky, carefree, breezy. **2.** chic, stylish, debonair, elegant, flashy, colorful, sporty, dashing, smart, natty, spruce, dapper. —**Ant.** dull, drab.

jealous, *adj.* **1.** envious, resentful, bitter, grudging, covetous, green with envy. **2.** suspicious, distrustful, mistrustful; anxious, insecure, threatened, vulnerable. —**Ant.** generous, open, trusting.

jeer, *v.* **1.** deride, scoff, gibe, mock, humiliate, taunt, sneer at, ridicule, twit, rag. —*n.* **2.** sneer, scoff, gibe, derision, ridicule, taunt, aspersion, hoot, hiss, boo, catcall, obloquy.

jeopardy, *n.* hazard, risk, danger, peril, threat, menace, risk, hazard, vulnerability, uncertainty, exposure. —**Ant.** security.

job, *n.* position, situation, post, employment, work, livelihood; assignment, duty, task, concern, responsibility, chore, function, role, mission, undertaking, province, project, activity, business. —**Ant.** unemployment.

join, *v.* **1.** link, couple, fasten, attach, conjoin, combine, confederate, associate, consolidate, amalgamate, connect, unite, bring together. **2.** adjoin, abut, touch, be adjacent to, border, meet, verge on. —**Ant.** separate, divide.

joke, *n.* witticism, quip, jest, trick, raillery, prank, bon mot, laugh, pun, story, anecdote, gag, wisecrack, crack, one-liner, routine, shtick.

jolly, *adj.* gay, glad, happy, spirited, jovial, merry, sportive, playful, cheerful, convivial, festive, joyous, mirthful, jocund, frolicsome, frisky, animated, exuberant, jaunty, buoyant, blithe, expansive, in a good humor *or* mood, gleeful, lively. —**Ant.** serious, morose, mirthless.

journey, *n.* **1.** excursion, trip, jaunt, tour, expedition, pilgrimage, voyage, outing, junket, cruise, odyssey, trek, travel. —*v.* **2.** travel, tour, peregrinate, roam, rove, voyage, go abroad, trek, wander, gad about, gallivant; go, proceed, fare.

jovial, *adj.* merry, jolly, convivial, expansive, sportive, hilarious, gay, jocose, jocular, jocund, joyous, joyful, blithe, happy, glad, mirthful, lighthearted, in high spirits. —**Ant.** serious, mirthless, cheerless, unhappy.

joy, *n.* satisfaction, exultation, gladness, delight, rapture, buoyancy, gratification, happiness, contentment, enjoyment, elation, exhilaration, gaiety, glee, cheerfulness, jubilation, lightheartedness, felicity, bliss, pleasure, ecstasy, transport. —**Ant.** dissatisfaction, misery; unhappiness.

joyful, *adj.* glad, delighted, joyous, happy, blithe, buoyant, elated, cheerful, gleeful, pleased, gratified, ecstatic, exultant, overjoyed, jubilant, gay, merry, jocund, blithesome, jolly, jovial, on cloud nine, in seventh heaven, tickled pink. —**Ant.** sad, unhappy, melancholy, depressed.

joyless, *adj.* sad, cheerless, unhappy, gloomy, dismal, miserable, mournful, melancholy, wretched, inconsolable, depressed, dejected, doleful, grief-stricken, morose, heartsick, woeful, woebegone, dreary, lugubrious, desolate, grim, austere, dour. —**Ant.** joyous.

judge, *n.* **1.** justice, magistrate; arbiter, arbitrator, umpire, referee, adjudicator, mediator, moderator; critic, authority, expert, specialist. —*v.* **2.** try, pass sentence upon. **3.** estimate, consider, regard, esteem, appreciate, reckon, deem. **4.** decide, determine, conclude, form an opinion, pass judgment, rule, decree, find.

judgment, *n.* **1.** ruling, finding, order, verdict, decree, decision, determination, conclusion, opinion, estimate, appraisal, critique, review, aperçu. **2.** understanding, discrimination, discernment, perspicacity, sagacity, wisdom, intelligence, prudence, eye, brains, taste, penetration, discretion, common sense, judiciousness, wit, clearheadedness, acumen, levelheadedness, perspicuity, shrewdness, acuity, acuteness, insight, expertise, keenness, astuteness, practicality, circumspection, tact, diplomacy, sensibility, rationality, reasonableness.

judicial, *adj.* critical, analytical, keen, sharp, perceptive, perspicacious, discriminating, judicious; juridical, forensic.

judicious, *adj.* **1.** practical, expedient, discreet, prudent, politic, tactful, diplomatic, careful, circumspect. **2.** wise, sensible, well-advised, rational, reasonable, sober, sound, intelligent, aware, sage, thoughtful, reasonable, sane, logical, astute, perceptive, discerning, well-informed, enlightened, sagacious, considered, common-sense. —**Ant.** impractical, indiscreet, imprudent; silly, nonsensical, unsound, unreasonable.

jumble, *v.* **1.** disarrange, disorganize, confound, shuffle, muddle, mix, confuse, mix up. —*n.* **2.** medley, mixture, hodgepodge, muddle, mess, farrago, chaos, disorder, confusion, gallimaufry, potpourri, clutter, tangle, disarray. —**Ant.** separate, isolate; order.

jump, *n.* leap, bound, spring, caper, vault, hop, skip, hurdle, pounce.

junction, *n.* combination, union, joining, meeting, confluence, conjunction, intersection, connection, linking, coupling, juncture; seam, welt, joint.

just, *adj.* **1.** unbiased, neutral, objective, reasonable, equitable, fair, impartial, evenhanded, right, lawful. **2.** true, correct, accurate, exact, proper, regular, normal. **3.** rightful, legitimate, lawful, legal; deserved, merited, appropriate, condign, suited, suitable, apt, due. **4.** righteous, blameless, honest, upright, pure, conscientious, good, uncorrupt, virtuous, honorable, straightforward, ethical, moral, principled, decent, law-abiding. —**Ant.** unjust.

justify, *v.* vindicate, exonerate, exculpate, absolve, acquit, defend, warrant, excuse, explain, rationalize. —**Ant.** inculpate, convict, indict, accuse, condemn.

K

keen, *adj.* **1.** sharp, acute, honed, razor-sharp. **2.** sharp, cutting, biting, severe, bitter, poignant, caustic, acrimonious. **3.** piercing, penetrating, discerning, astute, sagacious, sharp-witted, quick, shrewd, clever, keen-eyed, keen-sighted, clear-sighted, clearheaded. **4.** ardent, eager, zealous, earnest, fervid, enthusiastic, avid, devoted, passionate, intense, anxious. —**Ant.** dull.

keep, *v.* **1.** retain, hold, hang on to, preserve, conserve, have, save, maintain control. **2.** tend, care for, look af-

ter, take charge of, guard, protect, safeguard, feed, nourish, nurture, provide for, board. **3.** amass, accumulate, hoard, save up, retain, preserve, store, put away. **4.** continue, persist, persevere, carry on, sustain, prolong. **5.** follow, obey, mind, regard, heed, abide by, adhere to, pay attention to, observe, defer to, agree to. —**Ant.** lose, donate; cease.

keeping, *n.* **1.** congruity, harmony, conformity, consistency, agreement. **2.** custody, protection, care, charge, guardianship, trust. —**Ant.** incongruity, nonconformity, inconsistency.

kibitz, *v.* **1.** meddle, interfere, second-guess, Monday-morning quarterback, pry, snoop. **2.** advise, counsel, coach, direct.

kill, *v.* **1.** slaughter, slay, assassinate, massacre, butcher, execute, liquidate, dispatch, silence, butcher, snuff out, waste, ice, murder; hang, electrocute, behead, guillotine, strangle, garrote. **2.** extinguish, exterminate, eradicate, obliterate, annihilate, destroy, do away with. —**Ant.** create, originate.

killjoy, *n.* doomsayer, Cassandra, pessimist, damper, crepehanger, worrywart, grump, malcontent, cynic, prophet of doom, spoilsport, wet blanket, grouch, sourpuss, grinch, drag, party pooper, gloomy Gus, dog in the manger. —**Ant.** optimist, positivist, enthusiast.

kind, *adj.* **1.** gracious, kindhearted, kindly, good, genial, amiable, cordial, pleasant, liberal, decent, gracious, hospitable, mild, benign, benevolent, benignant, beneficent, friendly, humane, generous, bounteous, charitable, humanitarian, giving, unselfish, tolerant, indulgent, forbearing, forgiving, patient, helpful, accommodating; gentle, affectionate, loving, sweet, caring, thoughtful, considerate, understanding, solicitous, feeling, warm, tender, compassionate, sympathetic, tenderhearted, softhearted, good-natured. —*n.* **2.** sort, nature, character, manner, persuasion, stripe, description; genus, species, breed, set, class, type, variety, style, genre, race. —**Ant.** unkind, malevolent, unsympathetic, cruel, selfish, apathetic.

kindle, *v.* **1.** set fire to, ignite, inflame, fire, light. **2.** rouse, arouse, awaken, bestir, inflame, provoke, incite, stimulate, animate, foment, prompt, prick, goad, excite, agitate, jolt, inspire, energize, galvanize. —**Ant.** extinguish, quench.

kindness, *n.* **1.** service, favor, good turn. **2.** friendliness, graciousness, goodness, goodwill, humaneness, decency, gentleness, understanding, thoughtfulness, consideration, cordiality, hospitality, warmth, geniality, indulgence, tolerance, patience, good nature, benevolence, beneficence, humanity, benignity, generosity, philanthropy, charity, sympathy, compassion, tenderness, amiability. —**Ant.** unkindness, malevolence.

kingdom, *n.* monarchy, realm, sovereignty, dominion, empire, domain, principality, province, sphere of influence.

kinship, *n.* relationship, affinity, connection, bearing, correspondence, similarity, association, alliance, agreement, parallelism; consanguinity, blood tie, family tie, lineage, common descent, flesh and blood.

knack, *n.* aptitude, aptness, facility, dexterity, skill, adroitness, dexterousness, skillfulness, expertness, genius, intuition, gift, talent, bent, ability, flair, capacity, proficiency.

knot, *n.* **1.** group, company, cluster, clique, collection, assembly, aggregation, congregation, bunch, gathering, band, throng, crew, gang, squad, crowd. **2.** difficulty, perplexity, puzzle, conundrum, rebus; snarl, tangle.

knotty, *adj.* complicated, complex, involved, intricate, difficult, hard, tough, thorny, perplexing. —**Ant.** easy, straightforward, uncomplicated.

know, *v.* **1.** perceive, understand, apprehend, comprehend, grasp, be familiar with, be acquainted with. **2.** recognize, identify, remember, recall, recollect. **3.** distinguish, discriminate, discern, differentiate, separate.

knowledge, *n.* **1.** enlightenment, erudition, wisdom, science, information, learning, scholarship, lore. **2.** understanding, discernment, perception, apprehension, comprehension, judgment, awareness, cognition, grasp, consciousness, insight.

kvetch, *v.* **1.** complain, whine, find fault, grouse, gripe, bellyache. —*n.* **2.** complainer, whiner, faultfinder, nitpicker, smell fungus.

L

labor, *n.* **1.** toil, work, exertion, drudgery, travail, moil, sweat, effort, strain, pains, industry, slavery, donkey-work, grind, elbow grease. —*v.* **2.** work, toil, strive, drudge, moil, sweat, strain, struggle, slave, grind. —**Ant.** idleness, indolence, sloth.

labored, *adj.* overdone, overworked, overwrought, ornate, unnatural, excessive, contrived, artificial, affected.

laborious, *adj.* **1.** toilsome, arduous, onerous, burdensome, difficult, tiresome, wearisome, fatiguing, grueling, backbreaking, herculean, exhausting, taxing, tough, hard, uphill, stiff, strenuous, tiring. **2.** diligent, hard-working, assiduous, industrious, sedulous, painstaking, detailed, careful, thorough, scrupulous, dogged. —**Ant.** easy, simple.

lacerate, *v.* **1.** tear, mangle, gash, cut, slash, rip, maim, rend, claw. **2.** hurt, injure, harm, wound, damage.

lack, *n.* **1.** deficiency, need, want, dearth, scarcity, paucity, shortcoming, absence, shortage, shortfall, deficit, scantiness, insufficiency, defectiveness. —*v.* **2.** want, need, require, be deficient in, fall short of. —**Ant.** sufficiency, copiousness, abundance.

lackadaisical, *adj.* listless, indolent, enervated, blasé, indifferent, languid, languorous, lazy, unconcerned, uninvolved, apathetic, nonchalant, lethargic, sluggish, limp, bovine, numb. —**Ant.** peppy, alert, industrious, energetic.

lackluster, *adj.* dull, ordinary, plain, pedestrian, routine, unexceptional, banal, colorless, prosaic, commonplace, everyday, mediocre, so-so, wishywashy, drab, lifeless, flat, leaden, blah. —**Ant.** brilliant, extraordinary, distinctive.

lag, *v.* **1.** fall behind *or* back, loiter, linger, delay, straggle, dawdle, trail, dally, hang back. **2.** decrease, diminish, slow, falter, slacken, abate, ebb, wane, fall off, lighten —*n.* **3.** retardation, slowing, slowdown, decrease, dimination, abatement, ebb. —**Ant.** speed, quicken, expedite; expedition.

laggard, *n.* lingerer, dawdler, slowpoke, plodder, foot-dragger, straggler, idler, loiterer, slouch, sluggard, loafer, snail.

laid-back, *adj.* relaxed, easygoing, at ease, casual, offhand, free and easy, dégagé, undemanding, loose, lax, nonchalant, blasé, flexible. **—Ant.** rigid, strict, severe.

lament, *v.* **1.** bewail, bemoan, deplore, grieve, weep, mourn *or* sorrow over *or* for. **—***n.* **2.** lamentation, moan, wail, wailing, moaning. **3.** dirge, elegy, monody, threnody, knell, requiem. **—Ant.** rejoice.

language, *n.* **1.** speech, communication, tongue. **1.** dialect, jargon, idiom, terminology, vernacular; lingo, lingua franca. **3.** speech, phraseology, jargon, style, expression, diction.

large, *adj.* **1.** big, huge, enormous, immense, gigantic, colossal, massive, vast, great, extensive, broad, sizeable, grand, spacious, ample, monumental, mammoth, gargantuan, elephantine, Brobdinngagian, monstrous, staggering, stupendous, wide, substantial, capacious, jumbo, humongous. **2.** multitudinous; abundant, copious, ample, liberal, plentiful, lavish, bountiful, prolific. **—Ant.** small, tiny; scanty, sparse, scarce, rare.

last, *adj.* **1.** final, ultimate, latest; concluding, conclusive, decisive, definitive, utmost, extreme, terminal, hindmost. **—***v.* **2.** go on, continue, endure, perpetuate, remain, survive, persist, stay, abide, go the distance. **—Ant.** first; fail, die.

late, *adj.* **1.** tardy, slow, dilatory, delayed, belated, overdue, behindhand, unpunctual, past due. **2.** continued, lasting, protracted. **3.** recent, modern, advanced. **4.** former, past, recent, previous, old, preceeding; deceased, departed, dead. **—Ant.** early, fast.

latent, *adj.* hidden, concealed, covert, veiled; potential. **—Ant.** kinetic; open.

latitude, *n.* range, scope, extent, liberty, freedom, indulgence.

laud, *v.* praise, extol, applaud, celebrate, esteem, honor, commend, acclaim, glorify, exalt, recommend, promote. **—Ant.** censure, condemn, criticize.

laugh, *v.* **1.** chortle, cackle, cachinnate, chuckle, hawhaw, guffaw, hoot, roar; giggle, snicker, snigger, titter. **—***n.* **2.** chuckle, grin, smile; laughter, cachinnation, horse laugh. **—Ant.** cry, mourn, wail.

laughable, *adj.* funny, amusing, humorous, droll, comical; ludicrous, farcical, ridiculous, risible, absurd, foolish, asinine. **—Ant.** sad, serious.

lavish, *adj.* **1.** unstinted, extravagant, excessive, prodigal, profuse, abundant, liberal, bountiful, effusive, opulent, free, unstinting, unsparing, unselfish, generous, overspending; wasteful, improvident. **—***v.* **2.** expend, shower, thrust, heap, pour, bestow, endow; waste, dissipate, squander, spend, sink. **—Ant.** stingy, niggardly; provident; save.

law, *n.* **1.** rule, regulation, statute, act, measure, ordinance, decree, edict, order, command, directive, injunction, commandment, mandate, canon, ukase **2.** principle, theory, theorem, axiom, proposition, deduction, formula, corollary, postulate, conclusion, inference.

lawful, *adj.* **1.** legal, legitimate, valid, just, rightful, proper, licit, de jure, constitutional. **2.** sanctioned, allowed, permitted, permissible, justifiable, authorized. **—Ant.** illegal, illicit, illegitimate; forbidden.

lawless, *adj.* **1.** unlawful, illegal, illicit, criminal, dishonest, felonious, larcenous, venal, corrupt, crooked. **2.** an-

archic, chaotic, unruly, disorderly, unregulated, undisciplined, mutinous, rebellious, turbulent, wild, violent, rowdy, fractious. **3.** wicked, sinful, villainous, iniquitous, nefarious, treacherous, depraved, dissolute, immoral, unprincipled, godless, diabolical, satanic, fiendish, debased, unrepentant, rascally, incorrigible, unregenerate. **—Ant.** legal, honest; law-abiding, orderly, disciplined; principled, moral.

lax, *adj.* **1.** loose, relaxed, slack, casual, easygoing, flexible, laid-back, nonchalant, blasé. **2.** negligent, careless, remiss, neglectful, unrigorous, heedless, slipshod, slovenly, permissive, weak, indulgent. **—Ant.** rigorous, responsible.

lay, *v.* **1.** place, put, deposit, set, position, locate. **2.** present, offer, submit, set forth, advance, put forward. **3.** wager, bet, stake, risk. **4.** impute, ascribe, impute, direct, lodge, prefer, aim, attribute, charge. **5.** burden, penalize, assess, impose. **—***n.* **6.** position, lie, site. **7.** song, lyric, musical poem, poem, ode, ballad, air, rhyme, refrain, melody. **—***adj.* **8.** secular, nonecclesiastical, unclerical, laic, laical. **9.** unprofessional, amateur, nonspecialist, inexpert.

lazy, *adj.* idle, indolent, slothful, slow-moving, sluggish, inert, lethargic, dilatory, shiftless, slack, easygoing, languid, languorous, inactive, torpid, listless, lax, laid-back. **—Ant.** industrious, quick.

lead, *v.* **1.** conduct, go before, precede, guide, direct, usher, steer, show the way, escort. **2.** guide, influence, induce, persuade, convince, draw, entice, lure, allure, seduce, lead on. **3.** excel, outstrip, surpass, exceed, precede, outrun, outdo. **—***n.* **4.** precedence, advance, vanguard, head. **5.** advantage, edge, supremacy, margin, preeminence. **6.** example, model, direction, guidance, pattern, precedent. **—Ant.** follow.

leading, *adj.* chief; principal, most important, foremost, major, influential, prime, cardinal, paramount, primary; capital, ruling, governing; best, outstanding, preeminent, supreme, peerless, matchless, unrivaled, unequaled. **—Ant.** secondary, minor.

league, *n.* **1.** association, guild, society, band, fellowship, club, covenant, compact, alliance, confederation, combination, coalition, confederacy, union.

lean, *v.* **1.** incline, slant, tilt, tip, tend toward, bend, slope. **2.** repose, rest, rely, depend, trust, confide. **—***adj.* **3.** skinny, thin, gaunt, emaciated, slim, slender, spare, wiry, bony, angular, gangling, gangly, spare, skeletal, scrawny, haggard, pinched, lanky, lank, meager. **4.** sparse, barren, unfruitful, inadequate, deficient, jejune. **—Ant.** fat, obese; fertile, fruitful, adequate.

leap, *v., n.* jump, bound, spring, vault, hop, hurdle, skip.

learn, *v.* ascertain, detect, discover, hear, find out, understand, gather, determine, uncover; be taught, master, become proficient, acquire knowledge, memorize, commit to memory, study.

learning, *n.* erudition, lore, knowledge, scholarship, store of information, culture, wisdom, education, schooling.

leave, *v.* **1.** quit, vacate, abandon, forsake, desert, depart from, retire from, withdraw *or* escape from, relinquish, renounce. **2.** desist from, stop, forbear, cease, abandon, let alone. **3.** bequeath, will, devise, transmit. **—***n.* **4.** permission, allowance, freedom, liberty, li-

cense, consent, authorization, sanction. **—Ant.** arrive, gain.

legend, *n.* **1.** epic, saga, folk tale, romance, narrative, tradition, fiction, fairy tale, tall tale, fantasy, fable, myth, story, fiction. **2.** celebrity, luminary, personage, phenomenon, wonder, somebody, genius, immortal, eminence, notable. **—Ant.** fact, history.

legitimate, *adj.* **1.** legal, lawful, licit, statutory, authorized, permitted, sanctioned. **2.** reasonable, logical, sensible, common-sense, valid, warranted, called-for, correct, proper, acceptable, justifiable, just, fair. **—***v.* **3.** authorize, justify, legalize, sanction, warrant, validate, certify. **—Ant.** illegitimate; unreasonable, incorrect, improper.

leisurely, *adj.* deliberate, slow, relaxed, idle, lax, languid, sluggish, lazy, laid-back, premeditated, unhurried, easygoing. **—Ant.** unpremeditated, quick, hurried, hasty.

lengthen, *v.* extend, stretch, prolong, protract, attenuate, elongate, draw out, continue, increase, drag out. **—Ant.** shorten, abbreviate.

lenient, *adj.* mild, clement, kind, kindly, sparing, humane, indulgent, patient, permissive, compassionate, forgiving, easygoing, magnanimous, generous, tolerant, understanding, merciful, easy, gentle, soothing, tender, forbearing, long-suffering, charitable, big-hearted. **—Ant.** harsh, cruel, brutal, merciless.

lessen, *v.* **1.** diminish, decrease, abate, dwindle, fade, shrink. **2.** diminish, decrease, depreciate, disparage, reduce, lower, degrade. **3.** decrease, diminish, abate, abridge, reduce. **—Ant.** increase; raise; lengthen, enlarge.

let, *v.* **1.** allow, permit, sanction, authorize, license, give leave, enable, suffer, grant. **2.** lease, rent, sublet, hire, charter, contract to. **—Ant.** prevent, disallow.

level, *adj.* **1.** even, flat, smooth, uniform, plain, flush. **2.** horizontal. **3.** equal, on a par, equivalent. **4.** even, equable, uniform. **—***v.* **5.** even, equalize, smooth, flatten. **6.** raze, demolish, destroy. **—Ant.** uneven; vertical; unequal.

liable, *adj.* **1.** subject, exposed, likely, open, susceptible, vulnerable; disposed, apt, prone, inclined. **2.** obliged, responsible, answerable, accountable, obligated, blameworthy. **—Ant.** protected, secure.

liberal, *adj.* **1.** progressive, reform. **2.** tolerant, unbigoted, broadminded, lenient, disinterested, impartial, dispassionate, fair, unbigoted, unopinionated, unjaundiced, unprejudiced, magnanimous, generous, honorable. **3.** generous, bountiful, beneficent, free, charitable, openhanded, munificent; abundant, ample, bounteous, unstinting, lavish, plentiful, handsome, copious, large. **—Ant.** illiberal; intolerant, prejudiced; stingy, parsimonious, niggardly.

liberate, *v.* set free, release, emancipate, free, disengage, unfetter, manumit, disenthrall, deliver, set loose, loose, let out, discharge, ransom. **—Ant.** imprison, incarcerate; enthrall, enslave.

libertine, *n.* **1.** rake, roué, debauchee, lecher, sensualist, profligate, reprobate, womanizer, adulterer, whoremonger, philanderer, Don Juan, Casanova, wolf, lady-killer, old goat, satyr, dirty old man, skirt-chaser. **—***adj.* **2.** amoral, licentious, lascivious, lewd, dissolute, depraved, corrupt, perverted, immoral, sensual, lecherous, decadent, prurient, salacious, carnal, bestial. **—Ant.** prude; puritanical, prim, priggish.

liberty, *n.* freedom, liberation, independence; franchise, right, prerogative, authorization, carte blanche, sanction, permission, leave, license, privilege, immunity.

lie, *n.* **1.** falsehood, prevarication, mendacity, untruth, fiction, invention, misrepresentation, tall tale, whopper, story, falsification, fib. **2.** place, position, location, lay, site. **—v. 3.** falsify, fabricate, misrepresent, perjure, invent, tell tales, prevaricate, fib. **4.** recline, stretch out, rest, repose, be prostrate *or* recumbent. **—Ant.** truth.

life, *n.* **1.** animation, vigor, vivacity, vitality, sprightliness, verve, dazzle, dash, élan, zest, pungency, brio, flair, vim, exuberance, effervescence, sparkle, spirit, activity, energy, pep, zing, get-up-and-go. **2.** existence, being, sentience, viability, survival.

lifeless, *adj.* **1.** inanimate, unconscious, insensate, inert, unmoving, insensible, dead. **2.** dead, defunct, extinct. **3.** dull, inactive, inert, passive, sluggish, torpid, spiritless; boring, tiresome, lackluster, tedious, flat, stale, vapid, wooden. **—Ant.** alive, animate, live, organic; alive, extant; active, animated, spirited; lively, exciting.

lift, *v.* raise, elevate, hold up, boost, hoist, heave up; exalt, uplift, promote, advance, improve, better, enhance; cheer up, stimulate, encourage, inspire, inspirit. **—Ant.** lower; debase; dispirit, depress.

light, *n.* **1.** illumination, radiance, daylight; dawn, sunrise, daybreak. **2.** aspect, viewpoint, point of view, angle, approach. **—adj. 3.** pale, whitish, blanched. **4.** undemanding, effortless, moderate, bearable, endurable, easy. **5.** shallow, humorous, slight, trivial, trifling, inconsiderable, unsubstantial, flimsy, insubstantial, gossamer, airy, flighty. **6.** airy, sprightly, spry, active, swift, nimble, agile, alert. **7.** carefree, gay, cheery, cheerful, happy, sunny, buoyant, merry, joyful, jovial, jolly, easygoing, lighthearted. **8.** frivolous, lightheaded, volatile, flighty, giddy, dizzy, silly, vacuous, superficial, inane. **—v. 9.** alight, get *or* come down, descend, land, disembark. **10.** kindle, set fire to, ignite, set afire, fire, burn, touch off. **—Ant.** darkness, sunset; difficult; deep, considerable, substantial; cheerless, sad; serious; board, embark, mount; quench.

lighten, *v.* **1.** illuminate, brighten, shine, gleam, illume. **2.** mitigate, relieve, alleviate, reduce, lessen, disencumber, disburden, unburden, ease. **3.** cheer, gladden, brighten. **—Ant.** darken, adumbrate; intensify, aggravate; sadden.

lighthearted, *adj.* carefree, cheerful, easygoing, buoyant, laid-back, jolly, sunny, bright, gay, cheery, joyous, joyful, blithe, glad, happy, merry, jovial. **—Ant.** heavy-hearted, cheerless, morose, sad, gloomy, melancholy.

like, *v.* **1.** value, esteem, enjoy, cherish, admire, respect, treasure, prize, rate highly, find worthwhile, be inclined toward, appreciate, delight in, take pleasure in, be fond of, approve of, have a fondness *or* affinity *or* taste *or* appetite *or* soft spot for, be partial to, take to, find agreeable *or* congenial, be attracted to, relish, love, adore, worship, go for, prefer, have a penchant *or* predilection for, be sweet on, get a kick *or* charge *or* bang out of, take a shine to, dig, fancy. **—adv. 2.** similar, comparable, equivalent, equal,

identical, analogous, akin, allied, parallel, corresponding, homolgous, of a piece, much the same as, along the same lines. **—Ant.** despise, dislike; different, dissimilar.

likely, *adj.* apt, liable, probable, possible, expected; fitting, seemly, right, proper, qualified, acceptable, able, suitable, appropriate. **—Ant.** unlikely, improbable; unseemly, improper.

likeness, *n.* **1.** resemblance, similarity, agreement, correspondence, analogy, parallelism, approximation, equivalence, congruity, comparability, conformity, accord, coincidence, comparison, match, sameness. **2.** copy, replica, duplicate, reproduction, model, facsimile, representation, portrait, image, simulacrum, icon, figure. **—Ant.** difference.

liking, *n.* preference, inclination favor, disposition, bent, bias, leaning, propensity, capacity, proclivity, proneness, predilection, predisposition, tendency; partiality, fondness, affection, affinity, penchant; eye, appetite, weakness, soft spot, taste. **—Ant.** dislike, disfavor, disinclination.

limber, *adj.* pliant, flexible, supple, pliable, lithe, willowy, elastic, springy, resilient, nimble, lissome, graceful, athletic. **—Ant.** rigid, unbending, unyielding, stiff.

limelight, *n.* public eye *or* notice *or* stage *or* attention, cynosure, fame, celebrity, renown, stardom, glory, prominence, eminence, notoriety, exposure, publicity, réclame, acclaim, repute. **—Ant.** reclusiveness, seclusion.

limit, *n.* **1.** bound, extent, boundary, confine, edge, perimeter, frontier, termination. **2.** restraint, restriction, constraint, check, hindrance. **—v. 3.** restrain, restrict, confine, check, hinder, bound, circumscribe, define, narrow, curb, bridle.

linger, *v.* remain, stay on, persist, endure, hang around, pause, lag, idle, tarry, delay, dawdle, loiter.

link, *n.* **1.** bond, tie, connection, connective, copula, vinculum. **—v. 2.** bond, join, unite, connect, league, conjoin, fasten, pin, bind, tie, couple, associate, wed, relate. **—Ant.** separation; separate, split, rive.

list, *n.* **1.** catalogue, inventory, roll, roster, directory, index, record, slate, file, laundry list, shopping list, schedule, series, register. **2.** leaning, tilt, tilting, careening. **—v. 3.** register, catalogue, enlist, enroll, record, index, note, itemize, enumerate, tabulate, chronicle, book, enter, schedule. **4.** careen, incline, lean.

listen, *v.* hearken, hear, hark, attend, give ear, lend an ear, obey, heed, mind.

listless, *adj.* lethargic, weary, weak, enervated, tired, languid, lifeless, phlegmatic, unemotional, inert, passive, impassive; unenthusiastic, indifferent, apathetic, lukewarm, tepid, insouciant, uncaring, inattentive, heedless. **—Ant.** energetic, dynamic, active, lively; enthusiastic, eager.

listlessness, *n.* indifference, inattention, inattentiveness, heedlessness; lethargy, languor, insouciance, apathy.

litter, *n.* **1.** rubbish, debris, detritus, refuse, waste, trash, junk, shreds, fragments. **2.** untidiness, disorder, confusion, clutter, mess, disarray. **—v. 3.** strew, scatter, derange, mess up, disarrange, disorder.

little, *adj.* **1.** small, diminutive, miniature, undersized, short, slight, mini, baby, dwarf, pygmy, midget, toy, ban-

tam, petite, miniscule, Lilliputian, teeny-weeny, itsy-bitsy, microscopic, undersized, picayune, minute, tiny, infinitesimal, wee. **2.** short, brief. **3.** weak, feeble, slight, inconsiderable, trivial, paltry, insignificant, unimportant, petty, scanty. **4.** mean, narrow, illiberal, paltry, stingy, selfish, small, niggardly. **—adv. 5.** slightly, barely, just, hardly, scarcely. **—Ant.** large, immense, huge; important; liberal, generous.

livelihood, *n.* maintenance, living, sustenance, support, subsistence, survival, keep, upkeep, daily bread.

lively, *adj.* **1.** energetic, active, vigorous, brisk, spry, frisky, perky, bouncy, peppy, vivacious, alert, nimble, agile, quick. **2.** animated, spirited, vivacious, bubbly, effervescent, sprightly, gay, blithe, blithesome, buoyant, gleeful. **3.** eventful, stirring, moving. **4.** strong, keen, distinct, vigorous, forceful, clear, piquant. **5.** striking, telling, effective. **6.** vivid, bright, brilliant, fresh, clear, glowing, sparkling, gorgeous, rich. **—Ant.** inactive, torpid; leaden; uneventful; weak, dull, unclear; ineffective; dim, stale.

living, *adj.* **1.** alive, live, quick, existing; extant, surviving. **2.** active, lively, strong, vigorous, quickening. **—n. 3.** livelihood, maintenance, sustenance, subsistence, support, upkeep, keep. **—Ant.** dead.

load, *n.* **1.** burden, onus, weight, encumbrance, incubus, pressure, millstone, cross, albatross, responsibility, care, trouble, worry, anxiety. **—v. 2.** weight, weigh down, burden, encumber, freight, oppress, saddle with, overwhelm. **—Ant.** unload, lighten, disencumber.

loath, *adj.* reluctant, averse, unwilling, disinclined, indisposed; hesitant, wary, leery, cautious, chary, careful. **—Ant.** eager, anxious, willing.

loathe, *v.* abominate, detest, hate, abhor, despise, execrate, shrink *or* recoil from, shudder at. **—Ant.** adore, love.

loathing, *n.* disgust, dislike, aversion, abhorrence, hatred, hate, odium, detestation, repugnance, revulsion, horror, antipathy; animus, animosity, hostility. **—Ant.** liking, love; friendship, regard.

loathsome, *adj.* disgusting, nauseating, sickening, repulsive, offensive, repellent, revolting, detestable, abhorrent, hateful, odious, base, despicable, repugnant, abominable, execrable, contemptible, noisome, nasty, vile. **—Ant.** attractive, delightful, lovable.

locale, *n.* place, location, site, spot, locality, setting, situation, neighborhood, venue.

lodge, *n.* **1.** shelter, habitation, cabin, hut, cottage, chalet. **2.** club, association, society. **—v. 3.** shelter, harbor, house, quarter, accomodate, board, put up, billet. **4.** place, put, set, plant, infix, deposit, lay, settle.

lofty, *adj.* **1.** high, elevated, towering, tall. **2.** exalted, elevated, majestic, noble, regal, imposing, august, stately, honorable, superior, illustrious, immortal, sublime. **3.** haughty, proud, arrogant, prideful, grandiose, condescending. **—Ant.** lowly; debased; humble.

loiter, *v.* linger, dally, dawdle, idle, loaf, delay, tarry, lag, lounge about, laze, lollygag.

lone, *adj.* **1.** alone, unaccompanied, solitary, lonely, secluded, apart, separate, separated, deserted, uninhabited, unoccupied, unpopulated, empty. **2.** isolated, solitary, sole, unique, lonely.

—Ant. accompanied, together; inhabited, occupied.

lonely, adj. lone, solitary, lonesome; sequestered, remote, dreary, desolate, deserted; friendless, outcast, forsaken, reclusive, secluded, withdrawn, unsocial, hermitlike, solo. —Ant. crowded, populous.

lonesome, adj. lonely, alone, unpopular, unwelcome, outcast, deserted, estranged; secluded; desolate, isolated.

long, adj. **1.** lengthy, extensive, drawn out, attenuated, protracted, stretched, prolonged, extended. **2.** overlong, long-winded, tedious, boring, wordy, prolix. —v. **3.** crave, desire, yearn for, pine for, hanker for or after, wish, want, hunger, covet, dream of, eat one's heart out. —Ant. short, abbreviated; interesting; forgo.

longing, n. craving, desire, hankering, yearning, aspiration, wish, hunger, fancy, yen, itch, lust. —Ant. disinterest, apathy, satisfaction.

look, v. **1.** see, observe, consider, contemplate, view, regard, survey, scan, study, examine, read, inspect, scrutinize, notice, watch, witness, pay attention, check out, stare, gaze, glance. —n. **2.** appearance, manner, looks, air, aspect, demeanor, behavior, mien, expression, face, countenance.

loose, adj. **1.** free, unfettered, unbound, untied, unrestrained, unrestricted, released, unattached, unfastened, unconfined, at liberty, at large, on the loose. **2.** disordered, unbound, disorganized, messy, scattered, uncombined. **3.** lax, slack, careless, negligent, heedless, sloppy, relaxed. **4.** wanton, libertine, unchaste, immoral, dissolute, licentious, debauched, promiscuous, abandoned, fast, profligate. **5.** general, vague, indefinite, inexact, imprecise, ill-defined, indeterminate, broad, casual, careless, sloppy, slapdash, nonspecific, indistinct. —v. **6.** loosen, free, set free, unfasten, undo, unlock, unbind, untie, unloose, release, liberate. **7.** relax, slacken, ease, loosen. —Ant. bound, fettered; combined; tight, taut; moral, chaste; definite, specific; bind, commit; tighten.

loot, n. **1.** spoils, plunder, booty, prize, haul, boodle, swag. —v. **2.** plunder, rob, sack, rifle, raid, despoil, ransack, pillage, rape, ravage.

lordly, adj. **1.** grand, magnificent, majestic, royal, regal, kingly, aristocratic, dignified, noble, lofty. **2.** arrogant, lofty, imperious, domineering, overbearing, despotic, dictatorial, tyrannical. —Ant. menial, servile; humble, obedient, meek.

lore, n. **1.** learning, knowledge, erudition, culture, tradition, mythos, ethos. **2.** wisdom, counsel, advice, teaching, doctrine, lesson.

loss, n. **1.** detriment, disadvantage, damage, injury, harm, hurt, destruction. **2.** privation, deprivation, denial, sacrifice, forfeiture, bereavement. —Ant. gain.

lost, adj. **1.** forfeited, vanished, departed, gone, missing, missed. **2.** bewildered, nonplussed, at sea, confused, perplexed, puzzled. **3.** wasted, misspent, squandered, dissipated. **4.** defeated, vanquished. **5.** destroyed, ruined, wrecked, demolished, devastated, unsalvageable. **6.** depraved, abandoned, dissolute, corrupt, reprobate, profligate, licentious, shameless, hardened, irredeemable, irreclaimable. —Ant. found; pure, honorable, chaste.

loud, adj. **1.** earsplitting, blaring, thunderous, sonorous, fortissimo, noisy, clamorous, resounding, deafening,

stentorian, boisterous, tumultuous. **2.** gaudy, flashy, showy, obtrusive, vulgar, obvious, blatant, tawdry, garish, tasteless, ostentatious, extravagant, splashy, jazzy, glitzy, coarse, rude, crude, cheap. —Ant. soft, quiet; sedate, tasteful.

loutish, adj. boorish, unrefined, uncouth, ill-bred, rough, oafish, cloddish, clumsy, crass, churlish, coarse, crude, brutish, beastly. —Ant. refined, gracious, graceful.

love, n. **1.** affection, predilection, liking, inclination, regard, friendliness, kindness, fondness, devotion, warmth, attachment, attraction, admiration, adulation, ardor, fervor, rapture, infatuation, partiality, crush, passion, adoration. —v. **2.** like, delight in, enjoy, relish, take pleasure in, be partial to, appreciate, value, rate highly, have a taste or appetite or passion for, prefer, be taken with, get a kick or bang or charge out of, be captivated or fascinated by, dig. **3.** have affection for, be enamored of, be in love with, adore, adulate, worship, lose one's heart to, idolize, dote on, cherish, admire, treasure, esteem, be infatuated with, be sweet on, hold dear, think the world of, be hung up on, have a crush on, be crazy or nuts or mad or wild about, be attracted to, be bewitched by, be under (someone's) spell, be stuck on. —Ant. hatred, dislike; detest, abhor, abominate, hate.

lovely, adj. beautiful, good-looking, pretty, handsome, attractive, comely, fair, fetching, engaging, captivating, alluring, betwitching, gorgeous, ravishing, pulchritudinous, elegant, eyecatching, charming, exquisite, enchanting, winning, dishy. —Ant. ugly, unattractive, homely.

low, adj. **1.** short, squat, little, small, stubby, stunted. **2.** limited, sparse, scanty, inadequate, deficient. **3.** feeble, weak, exhausted, sinking, dying, expiring. **4.** depressed, dejected, dispirited, unhappy, sad, miserable. **5.** undignified, infra dig, lowly, dishonorable, disreputable, unbecoming, disgraceful. **6.** groveling, abject, sordid, mean, base, lowly, degraded, menial, servile, ignoble, vile. **7.** humble, lowly, meek, lowborn, poor, plain, plebeian, vulgar, base. **8.** coarse, vulgar, rude, crude. **9.** hushed, muted, muffled, indistinct, whispered, soft, subdued, gentle, quiet. —Ant. high, upright.

lower, v. **1.** reduce, decrease, diminish, lessen. **2.** soften, modulate, turn down, quiet down. **3.** degrade, humble, abase, humiliate, disgrace, debase. **4.** let down, drop, depress, take down, sink. **5.** darken, loom, menace, threaten; glower, frown, scowl; sulk, mope, pout. —Ant. raise, increase; elevate, honor; brighten.

loyal, adj. faithful, true, patriotic, devoted, constant, dependable, trustworthy, steadfast, staunch, stable, reliable, dedicated, unswerving, unwavering, true-blue. —Ant. faithless, disloyal, treacherous.

loyalty, n. faithfulness, allegiance, fealty, devotion, dedication, constancy, patriotism, fidelity, dependability, reliability, resolve. —Ant. faithlessness, disloyalty.

lucid, adj. **1.** shining, bright, lucent, radiant, brilliant, resplendent, luminous. **2.** clear, transparent, pellucid, limpid, crystalline; intelligible, plain, unmistakable, obvious, distinct, evident, understandable; rational, sane, sober, sound, reasonable. —Ant. dull; unclear, dull; unreasonable.

lucky, adj. fortunate, fortuitous,

happy, favored, charmed, blessed; providential, timely, opportune, advantageous, convenient, auspicious, propitious, favorable, prosperous. —Ant. unfortunate, unlucky.

ludicrous, adj. laughable, ridiculous, amusing, comical, funny, facetious, waggish, jocular, jocose, witty, droll; absurd, farcical, nonsensical, preposterous, incongruous, asinine, foolish, silly, zany, risible, crazy. —Ant. miserable, serious, tragic.

lukewarm, adj. **1.** tepid, warmish, moderately warm, room-temperature. **2.** halfhearted, unenthusiastic, so-so, unimpassioned, nonchalant, blasé, lackadaisical, insouciant, apathetic, phlegmatic, laid-back, unresponsive, unmoved, indifferent, unsympathetic, laodicean. —Ant. dedicated, enthusiastic.

luminous, adj. **1.** bright, shining, luminescent, glowing, lucid, lucent, radiant, brilliant, lustrous, gleaming, shimmering, dazzling, sparkling, effulgent, resplendent. **2.** lighted, lit, illuminated. **3.** brilliant, bright, intelligent, smart, clever, enlightening. **4.** clear, intelligible, penetrating, discerning, explicit, incisive, understandable, perspicacious, plain, lucid. —Ant. dull; dark; stupid; unclear, unintelligible.

lunacy, n. **1.** madness, craziness, insanity, derangement, mental disorder, psychosis, mania, dementia, dementedness. **2.** folly, foolishness, foolhardiness, absurdity, fatuity, silliness, illogicality, irrationality, poor judgment, stupidity, nuttiness. —Ant. sanity, normalcy, sobriety.

lure, n. **1.** enticement, decoy, attraction, allurement, temptation, inducement, magnet, siren song, charm, come-on, bait. —v. **2.** allure, decoy, entice, draw, attract, tempt, seduce, induce, coax, inveigle, beguile, persuade, catch.

lurid, adj. **1.** vivid, glaring, sensational; shocking, startling, melodramatic, graphic; gory, grisly, gruesome, macabre, revolting, disgusting, appalling, frightful, terrible, horrid, horrifying; shining, fiery, red, intense, fierce, terrible, unrestrained, passionate. **2.** wan, pale, pallid, sallow, ghastly; gloomy, murky, dismal, lowering. —Ant. mild, controlled; cheery.

lurk, v. skulk, sneak, prowl, slink, steal; lie in wait, lie in ambush, lie low, lie hidden or concealed, hide, lush.

luscious, adj. delicious, juicy, delectable, palatable, savory, mouthwatering, tasty, appetizing, rich, sweet, epicurean, ambrosial, succulent, scrumptious, yummy. —Ant. unpalatable, disgusting, nauseating.

lush, adj. tender, juicy, succulent, luxuriant, fresh, moist, ripe; luxurious, sumptuous, opulent, palatial, deluxe, fancy, rich, resplendent, splendid, grand, extravagant, magnificent. —Ant. dry, tasteless; stringent, Spartan.

lust, n. **1.** desire, passion, appetite, craving, eagerness, cupidity. **2.** libido, libinousness, sex drive, horniness, desire, randiness, sexuality, sensuality, wantonness, sexual appetite, prepotency, goatishness, lechery, concupiscence, carnality, lubricity, salaciousness, licentiousness, appears twice, lasciviousness, libertinism, license. —v. **3.** crave, desire, need, want, demand, hunger for, itch, ache.

luster, n. **1.** gleam, glow, luminosity, radiance, effulgence, brilliance, shine, shimmer, sparkle, glitter, glisten, sheen, gloss. **2.** brilliance, brightness, radiance, luminosity, resplendence. **3.** illustriousness, excellence, merit, distinction, glory, honor, repute, renown, eminence, celebrity, dash, élan, éclat. **—Ant.** dullness, tarnish; disrepute, dishonor.

lusty, *adj.* **1.** hearty, vigorous, strong, healthy, robust, energetic, lively, sturdy, stout, husky, powerful. **2.** lecherous, amorous, libidinous, sexual, sensual, carnal, consupiscent, randy, horny, on the make. **—Ant.** weak, frail, unhealthy.

luxurious, *adj.* **1.** splendid, grand, extravagant, magnificent, lavish, deluxe, fancy, elegant, palatial, royal, rich, sumptuous, ornate, delicate, opulent, well-appointed, swanky, ritzy, plush, posh. **2.** voluptuous, sensual, self-indulgent, epicurean, sybaritic, hedonistic, pampered. **—Ant.** poor, squalid. mean, Spartan.

lyrical, *adj.* melodic, musical, sweet, mellow, lilting, airy, graceful, light-hearted, buoyant, sunny; exuberant, rhapsodic, ecstatic, rapturous, effusive, emotional, impassioned. **—Ant.** sorrowful, elegiac.

M

macabre, *adj.* gruesome, horrible, grim, ghastly, morbid, weird, grisly, gory, ghoulish, dreadful, eerie, frightful, dire, terrifying, terrible, fearsome, deathly, cadaverous. **—Ant.** delightful.

Machiavellian, *adj.* crafty, deceitful, cunning, wily, astute, unscrupulous, clever, artful, designing, insidious, sly, shrewd, subtle, arch, expedient, foxy, scheming, treacherous, nefarious, hypocritical, two-faced, sneaky, underhanded, tricky, intriguing, double-dealing, equivocal. **—Ant.** ingenuous, honest, straightforward.

machination, *n.* manipulation, maneuver, stratagem, ploy, artifice, tactic, wile, device, trick, plot, cabal, intrigue, scheme, conspiracy, ruse, move, gambit.

machismo, *n.* manliness, supermanliness, virility, potency, boldness, courageousness, dominance, prepotency, primacy, arrogance, braggadocio, swagger, cockiness, pride.

mad, *adj.* **1.** insane, lunatic, deranged, raving, distracted, crazy, crazed, maniacal, demented, unhinged, delirious, out of one's mind, psychotic, non compos menti, of unsound mind, mentally, unbalanced, mentally ill, touched, screwy, cuckoo, certifiable, not all there, cracked, nutty, nuts, loony, loopy, batty, loco, wacky, meshuga, off one's rocker, bananas, crazy as a bedbug or coot, crackers, bonkers. **2.** furious, exasperated, angry, enraged, raging, incensed, provoked, wrathful, irate, infuriated, fuming, berserk, irritated, exasperated. **3.** excited, frantic, frenzied, wild, rabid. **4.** violent, furious, stormy. **5.** senseless, foolish, imprudent, impractical, ill-advised, excessive, reckless, unsound, unsafe, harmful, dangerous, perilous, unwise, rash, ill-advised, ill-considered, foolhardy. **6.** silly, childish, immature, puerile, nonsensical, madcap, heedless, absurd, indiscreet, extravagant, irrational, fatuous. **7.** infatuated, wild about, desirous, ardent, passionate, enthusiastic, eager, avid, zealous, fervent, fervid, fanatical, keen, hooked. **—Ant.** sane; calm; serene; sensible, wise.

madden, *v.* infuriate, irritate, provoke,

vex, annoy, enrage, anger, inflame, exasperate, incense, irk, pique, torment, plague; bedevil, rile, hassle. **—Ant.** calm, mollify.

magic, *n.* enchantment, sorcery, necromancy, occultism, mysticism, spell, shamanism, wizardry, voodoo, vodun, conjuration, divination, black art, deviltry, thaumaturgy, miracle working, witchcraft; legerdemain, conjuring, sleight of hand, prestidigitation, hocus-pocus.

magician, *n.* sorcerer, necromancer, enchanter, conjuror, illusionist, wizard, magus, Merlin, Circe, Houdini, witch, warlock, thaumaturge, miracle worker, shaman.

magisterial, *adj.* **1.** dictatorial, dominating, dogmatic, doctrinaire, imperious, authoritarian, lordly. **2.** masterful, masterly, authoritative, commanding, expert.

magnificence, *n.* splendor, grandeur, impressiveness, sumptuousness, pomp, state, majesty, luxury, luxuriousness, éclat, brilliance, nobility, opulence, elegance, lavishness, augustness, sublimity, superiority, distinction. **—Ant.** squalor, poverty, meanness.

magnificent, *adj.* **1.** splendid, fine, superb, august, stately, majestic, imposing, sumptuous, rich, royal, resplendent, opulent, lavish, luxurious, grand, gorgeous, beautiful, princely, impressive, glorious, awe-inspiring, commanding, dazzling, brilliant, radiant, excellent, exquisite, elegant, superior, extraordinary; showy, pretentious, flamboyant, flashy, ostentatious. **2.** noble, sublime, dignified, great, regal, distinguished, exalted, awesome. **—Ant.** squalid, poor; base.

magnify, *v.* **1.** enlarge, augment, increase, add to, amplify, expand, inflate, heighten, boost, exacerbate, aggravate. **2.** exaggerate, overstate, dramatize, make a mountain out of a molehill, embellish, elaborate, stretch, embroider, lay it on thick. **—Ant.** decrease, understate.

maim, *v.* mutilate, cripple, lacerate, mangle, injure, disable, lame, incapacitate, put out of commission, wound, deface, mar, impair, injure, damage.

main, *adj.* **1.** chief, cardinal, prime, paramount, primary, principal, first, foremost, preeminent, predominant, major, leading, capital. **2.** pure, sheer, utmost, direct, brute, utter, out-and-out, absolute, mere, plain. **—Ant.** secondary, unimportant.

mainstay, *n.* support, backbone, spine, sine qua non, supporter, anchor, bulwark, buttress, linchpin, backer, champion, upholder, sustainer, pillar, brace, standby, prop, crutch.

maintain, *v.* **1.** keep, continue, preserve, retain, keep up, uphold, persevere, perpetuate, prolong, sustain, support. **2.** affirm, assert, aver, state, hold, allege, declare. **3.** contend, hold, claim, defend, vindicate, justify, advocate, champion, plead for, back, make a case for. **4.** provide for, support, sustain, keep up, nuture. **—Ant.** discontinue.

maintenance, *n.* upkeep, care, preservation, conservation, support; subsistence, livelihood, living, allowance, sustenance, stipend, contribution, keep, daily bread. **—Ant.** desuetude.

majestic, *adj.* regal, royal, princely, kingly, queenly, elevated, exalted, glorious, monumental, striking, awesome, impressive, marvelous, imperial, noble, lofty, stately, grand, august, dignified, imposing, splendid, magnificent, sublime. **—Ant.** base, squalid, unprepossessing, plebeian.

major, *adj.* greater, larger, main, chief, important; vital, critical, crucial, principal, foremost, paramount, primary, prime, notable, noteworthy, significant, outstanding, dominant. **—Ant.** minor.

make, *v.* **1.** form, build, assemble, produce, fabricate, create, contrive, design, construct, manufacture, fashion, mold, shape. **2.** cause, render, generate, create, produce. **3.** transform, convert, change, turn, alter, modify, metamorphose, transmute. **4.** give rise to, prompt, occasion. **5.** get, gain, acquire, obtain, secure, procure, earn, win. **6.** do, effect, bring about, perform, execute, accomplish, practice, act. **7.** cause, require, oblige, persuade, coerce, provoke, induce, compel, force, order. **—n. 8.** style, form, build, shape, brand, kind, sort, type, trade, name; construction, structure, constitution. **—Ant.** destroy.

makeshift, *adj.* improvised, stopgap, provisional, expedient, emergency, tentative, standby, slapdash, surrogate, stand-in, temporary, substitute, reserve, spare, make-do, jerry-built.

malady, *n.* disease, illness, sickness, affliction, disorder, complaint, ailment, indisposition.

male, *adj.* masculine, manly, virile, manful, macho. **—Ant.** female.

malevolence, *n.* ill will, rancor, malignity, resentment, malice, maliciousness, spite, spitefulness, odium, hostility, meanness, evil, animosity, animus, bitterness, invidiousness, envy, vindictiveness, treachery, deceit, grudge, hate, hatred, venom. **—Ant.** benevolence, good will.

malevolent, *adj.* malicious, malignant, resentful, spiteful, begrudging, hateful, venomous, vicious, hostile, ill-natured, evil-minded, punitive, retributive, vengeful, insidious, rancorous, envious, blackhearted. **—Ant.** benevolent, friendly, amiable.

malice, *n.* evil, cruelty, villainy, viciousness, hostility, odiumy, wickedness, beastliness, vileness, perversity, ill will, spite, spitefulness, animosity, animus, enmity, malevolence, grudge, venom, hate, hatred, bitterness, rancor. **—Ant.** good will, benevolence.

malign, *v.* **1.** slander, libel, revile, abuse, slur, smear, decry, calumniate, defame, disparage, vilify, criticize, belittle, depreciate, denigrate, insult, deregate. **—adj. 2.** evil, pernicious, baleful, injurious, unfavorable, baneful, malevolent. **—Ant.** compliment, praise; good, favorable, benevolent.

malignant, *adj.* **1.** malicious, spiteful, malevolent, rancorous, bitter, malign, evil, vicious, invidious, hateful, venomous. **2.** dangerous, perilous, harmful, hurtful, virulent, pernicious, lethal, deadly, fatal, life-threatening, toxic, poisonous. **—Ant.** benevolent; benign.

malinger, *v.* shirk, slack, slack off, dodge, duck duty, get out of, gold-brick, goof off, loaf, vegetate.

malleable, *adj.* adaptable, plastic, shapeable, bendable, ductile, moldable, pliant, pliable, supple, flexible, elastic, compliant. **—Ant.** rigid, refractory.

maltreat, *v.* mistreat, abuse, injure, ill-treat, ill-use, misuse, damage, manhandle, harm, hurt, molest, maul, brutalize, rough up. **—Ant.** honor, respect.

manage, *v.* **1.** bring about, succeed, accomplish, arrange, contrive. **2.** conduct, handle, direct, govern, control, guide, regulate, engineer, rule, administer, supervise, superintend. **3.** handle, wield, manipulate, control. **4.** dominate, influence; train, educate, handle. —**Ant.** mismanage, bungle.

management, *n.* handling, direction, control, regulation, conduct, charge, supervision, manipulation, government, governance, operation, running, stewardship, command, administration, superintendence, care, guidance, disposal, treatment, oversight, surveillance. —**Ant.** mismanagement.

manager, *n.* administrator, executive, superintendent, supervisor, boss, director, overseer, governor, head, proprietor, chief. —**Ant.** employee, underling.

mandate, *n.* command, order, fiat, decree, ukase, injunction, edict, ruling, commission, requirement, precept, requisite, prerequisite.

maneuver, *n.* **1.** procedure, move; scheme, tactic, gambit, ploy, subterfuge, wile, machination, intrigue, plot, plan, design, stratagem, ruse, artifice, trick. —*v.* **2.** manipulate, handle, intrigue, trick, scheme, plot, plan, design, finesse, contrive, machinate, engineer, devise, finagle, wangle.

mangle, *v.* cut, lacerate, crush, slash; disfigure, maim, ruin, spoil, butcher, deform, wreck, mar, deface, mutilate, destroy.

mania, *n.* **1.** excitement, enthusiasm, furor, craze, fad, rage, passion, fascination, preoccupation, obsession. **2.** insanity, madness, aberration, derangement, dementia, frenzy, lunacy, hysteria. —**Ant.** phobia; rationality.

manifest, *adj.* **1.** evident, obvious, apparent, plain, clear, distinct, blatant, explicit, discernible, definite, patent, open, palpable, visible, unmistakable, conspicuous. —*v.* **2.** show, display, reveal, disclose, open, exhibit, evince, evidence, appear, expose, present, indicate, betray, demonstrate, declare, express, make known. —**Ant.** latent, hidden, inconspicuous; conceal.

manifold, *adj.* **1.** various, many, numerous, multitudinous. **2.** varied, various, multifarious, multifaceted, diverse, diversified, assorted, miscellaneous, sundry. —**Ant.** simple, singular.

manly, *adj.* **1.** manful, mannish, masculine, male, virile. **2.** strong, brave, honorable, courageous, bold, valiant, intrepid, undaunted, brave, valorous, plucky, daring, dauntless, fearless, chivalrous, gallant, noble, heroic. —**Ant.** feminine; weak, cowardly.

manner, *n.* **1.** mode, fashion, style, way, habit, custom, method, technique, procedure, means, approach, form. **2.** demeanor, deportment, air, bearing, behavior, carriage, conduct, comportment, attitude, mien, aspect, look, appearance. **3.** kind, sort.

manufacture, *v.* assemble, fabricate, make, construct, build, compose, create, produce, originate, concoct, contrive, invent, cook up. —**Ant.** destroy.

many, *adj.* numerous, multifarious, abundant, myriad, innumerable, manifold, sundry, various, varied, multitudinous, profuse, diverse, assorted. —**Ant.** few.

mar, *v.* damage, impair, ruin, spoil, injure, blot, deface, disfigure, mutilate, scar, wreck, blight, harm, hurt, taint, deform, distort, maim.

margin, *n.* border, edge, rim, limit, confine, bound, marge, verge, brink, perimeter, periphery, lip, side, boundary, frontier. —**Ant.** center.

mark, *n.* **1.** spot, blemish, smear,

stain, smudge, streak, nick, scratch, splotch, trace, impression, line, cut, dent, bruise. **2.** badge, brand, sign, symbol, token, insigne, stamp, characteristic, hallmark, label, feature, attribute, trait, quality, property, identification, indication. **3.** note, importance, distinction, eminence, consequence. —*v.* **4.** label, tag. **5.** signify, specify, distinguish, indicate, designate, point out, brand, identify, imprint, impress, characterize. **6.** note, pay attention to, heed, notice, observe, regard, eye, spot, watch, see; respect, mind, obey.

marriage, *n.* **1.** wedding, nuptials; wedlock, matrimony. **2.** union, alliance, association, confederation, affiliation, connection, coupling, merger, amalgamation. —**Ant.** divorce; separation.

marshal, *v.* arrange, array, order, rank, dispose; gather, convoke. —**Ant.** disorder; scatter.

marvelous, *adj.* wonderful, wondrous, extraordinary, amazing, astonishing, astounding, miraculous, remarkable, sensational, phenomenal, splendid, superb, glorious, spectacular, breathtaking, mind-boggling, improbable, incredible, unbelievable, surprising, terrific, fantastic, fabulous, smashing, out of this world. —**Ant.** terrible, ordinary, commonplace.

mask, *n.* **1.** face covering, veil, false face. **2.** disguise, concealment, pretense, guise, camouflage, show, semblance, cover-up, cloak, facade, veil; pretext, ruse, trick, subterfuge, evasion. —*v.* **3.** disguise, conceal, hide, veil, screen, cloak, shroud, cover, camouflage.

mass, *n.* **1.** load, stack, mound, mountain, bunch, bundle, lot, batch, hoard, store, assortment, miscellany, abundance, profusion, multitude, horde, host, crowd, throng, drove, swarm, aggregate, aggregation, assemblage, heap, congeries, collection, accumulation, conglomeration, pile, quantity.. **2.** main body, bulk, majority. **3.** size, bulk, massiveness, magnitude, dimension. —*v.* **4.** assemble; collect, gather, marshal, amass, convoke; heap *or* pile up, aggregate.

massacre, *n.* **1.** killing, slaughter, carnage, extermination, annihilation, butchery, murder, genocide, blood bath, mass murder, liquidation, pogrom. —*v.* **2.** kill, butcher, slaughter, murder, slay, obliterate, eradicate, decimate, mow down.

massive, *adj.* **1.** bulky, heavy, large, immense, huge, tremendous, mountainous, hulking, mammoth, prodigious, colossal, oversized, enormous, gigantic, towering, vast, titanic, mighty, weighty, whopping, elephantine, humongous. **2.** solid, substantial, great, imposing, ponderous. —**Ant.** diminutive; flimsy.

master, *n.* **1.** adept, expert, authority, mastermind, maestro, maven, past master, old hand, professional, pro, ace, genius, virtuoso, cracker jack, wizard. **2.** owner, head, leader, chief, commander, lord, governor, director, controller, employer, boss, overseer, supervisor, taskmaster, ruler, slave driver, high muck-a-muck, kingpin, skipper, Pooh-Bah, the man, big wheel, big cheese, Mr. Big, head honcho, big enchilada. **3.** teacher, instructor, guide, leader, tutor, mentor, guru, swami. —*adj.* **4.** chief, principal, head, leading, cardinal, primary, prime, main. **5.** dominating, predominant. **6.** skilled, adept, expert, skillful. —*v.* **7.** conquer, subdue, subject, subjugate, overcome, overpower. **8.** rule, direct,

govern, manage, superintend, oversee. —**Ant.** amateur, incompetent; slave, underling, minion; pupil, beginner, initiate.

matchless, *adj.* unique, original, beyond compare, peerless, unrivaled, unequaled, inimitable, unparalleled, incomparable, unmatched, consummate. —**Ant.** unimportant, unimpressive.

material, *n.* **1.** substance, matter, stuff, fabric. **2.** element, component, constituent. —*adj.* **3.** tangible, concrete, solid, real, substantive, palpable, physical, corporeal. **4.** important, essential, vital, consequent, momentous, serious, significant. —**Ant.** spiritual; immaterial.

matter, *n.* **1.** substance, material, stuff. **2.** situation, issue, question, condition, fact, concern, occurrence, thing, affair, business, question, subject, topic. **3.** consequence, importance, essence, import, significance, moment. **4.** trouble, difficulty, problem, complication, worry, upset, dilemma, quandry. **5.** ground, reason, cause. —*v.* **6.** signify, be of importance, count, make a difference, be of consequence. —**Ant.** insignificance; ease.

mature, *adj.* **1.** ripe, aged, complete, grown, adult, full-grown, fully-developed, maturated. **2.** polished, refined, developed, consummated, completed, perfected, elaborated, ready, prepared. —*v.* **3.** ripen, age, develop, mellow, season. **4.** perfect, complete. —**Ant.** immature, childish, adolescent.

maxim, *n.* proverb, aphorism, saying, adage, apothegm, axiom, byword, saw, epigram, motto, slogan, witticism, truism, catchphrase.

meager, *adj.* scanty, paltry, skimpy, spare, bare, puny, trifling, pathetic, deficient, sparse, mean, insignificant; thin, lean, emaciated, spare, gaunt, skinny, lank, scrawny, bony, undernourished, half-starved. —**Ant.** abundant.

mealymouthed, *adj.* devious, hypocritical, false, deceitful, duplicitous, two-faced, insincere, smarmy, slick, oily, roundabout, vague, ambiguous, indirect, equivocal, circumlocutory, periphrastic. —**Ant.** straightforward, candid.

mean, *v.* **1.** plan, intend, purpose, contemplate, destine, foreordain, predestine, design. **2.** signify, indicate, denote, imply, express. —*adj.* **3.** inferior, base, abject, modest, humble, common, servile. **4.** common, humble, low, undignified, ignoble, plebeian, coarse, rude, vulgar. **5.** unimportant, unessential, nonessential, inconsequent, dispensable, insignificant, petty, paltry, little, poor, wretched, despicable, contemptible, low, base, vile, foul, disgusting, repulsive, repellent, depraved, immoral; small-minded. **6.** unimposing, shabby, sordid, unclean, run-down, seedy, wretched, dismal, dreary, abysmal, sorry, squalid, poor. **7.** penurious, parsimonious, illiberal, cheap, stinting, penny-pinching, money-grubbing, measly, stingy, miserly, tight, niggardly, selfish, narrow, mercenary. **8.** intermediate, middle, medium, average, moderate. —*n.plural.* **9.** agency, instrumentality, method, approach, mode, way. **10.** resources, backing, support. **11.** revenue, income, substance, wherewithal, property, wealth. **12.** (*sing.*) average, median, middle, midpoint, center, norm. —**Ant.** exalted, dignified; important, essential; imposing, splendid, rich, generous; superior.

meander, *v.* wander, stroll, amble,

rove, mosey; ramble, zigzag, snake, twist, wind, turn.

meandering, *adj.* wandering, erratic, rambling, roundabout, circuitous, winding, serpentine, tortuous, indirect, oblique, convoluted, labyrinthine, curvy, crooked, zigzag, twisting, twisted; circumlocutory, periphrastic. —**Ant.** straight, direct; concise, terse.

meaning, *n.* **1.** tenor, gist, trend, idea, purport, significance, signification, sense, import, denotation, connotation, interpretation, content, message, substance. **2.** intent, intention, aim, object, purpose, design, drift, spirit, implication.

measureless, *adj.* limitless, boundless, immeasurable, immense, prodigious, vast, endless, infinite, unending, never-ending, unlimited, inexhaustible, incalculable, indeterminate. —**Ant.** limited, finite.

meddlesome, *adj.* prying, curious, interfering, intrusive, officious, nosy, inquisitive, eavesdropping, spying.

mediate, *v.* intercede, interpose, arbitrate, reconcile, settle.

medicine, *n.* medication, medicament, remedy, drug, prescription, pharmaceutical, cure, nostrum, dose, relief.

mediocre, *adj.* indifferent, ordinary, common, commonplace, everyday, garden-variety, run-of-the-mill, pedestrian, uninspired, unimaginative, tolerable, second-rate, third-rate, inferior, so-so, unexceptional, fair, medium, average, middling, passable, mean. —**Ant.** superior.

meditate, *v.* **1.** contemplate, plan, reflect on, devise, scheme, plot, concoct, contrive, think over, dwell on. **2.** reflect, ruminate, contemplate, ponder, muse, cogitate, think, study.

meditative, *adj.* pensive, thoughtful, reflecting, abstracted, engrossed, rapt, brooding, lost in thought, contemplative; studious. —**Ant.** thoughtless.

medium, *n.* **1.** mean, average, mean proportion, mean average. **2.** means, agency, method, mode, approach, mechanism, technique, way, route, device, contrivance, expedient, course, instrumentality, instrument. **3.** environment, atmosphere, ether, air, temper, conditions, influences. —*adj.* **4.** average, mean, normal, standard, everyday, ordinary, middling; mediocre.

meek, *adj.* humble, patient, submissive, spiritless, tame, yielding, forbearing, docile, unassuming, unpretentious, deferential, shy, retiring, lowly, timid, weak, compliant, tractable, subdued, unaggressive, nonmilitant, acquiescent, manageable, mild, peaceful, pacific, calm, soft, gentle, modest. —**Ant.** forward, unyielding, immodest.

meet, *v.* **1.** join, connect, intersect, cross, converge, come together, unite. **2.** encounter, stumble *or* bump into, see, rendezvous, get together, come upon. **3.** encounter, compete with, battle, fight, confront, face, oppose. **4.** settle, discharge, fulfill, satisfy, gratify, answer, comply with. **5.** gather, assemble, congregate, convene, collect, muster. **6.** concur, agree, see eye to eye, unite, conjoin. —*n.* **7.** meeting, contest, competition, match. —**Ant.** diverge; dissatisfy; scatter; disagree.

melancholy, *n.* **1.** sorrow, misery, woe, anguish, unhappiness, gloom, depression, sadness, dejection, despondency, gloominess, blues, hypochondria. **2.** pensiveness, thoughtfulness, sobriety, seriousness. —*adj.* **3.** sad, depressed, dejected, gloomy, despondent, blue, dispirited, sorrowful, unhappy,

disconsolate, inconsolable, miserable, dismal, doleful, low, dour, lugubrious, moody, glum, down in the mouth, downhearted, downcast, low-spirited. **4.** sober, serious, thoughtful, pensive. —**Ant.** cheer, happiness; cheerful, happy.

mellow, *adj.* **1.** ripe, full-flavored, soft, sweet, aged, mature,. **2.** softened, subtle, muted, toned down, improved. **3.** soft, rich, mellifluous, dulcet, melodious, tuneful, sweet, smooth. **4.** genial, jovial, good-humored, good-natured, laid-back, casual, easygoing, gentle, cordial, warm, amiable, agreeable, pleasant. —*v.* **5.** soften, ripen, develop, mature, improve, perfect, age, season, sweeten. —**Ant.** immature.

melody, *n.* tune, song, air, descant, theme, strain, refrain.

melt, *v.* **1.** liquefy, fuse, dissolve, thaw. **2.** pass, dwindle, fade, fade out, blend. **3.** soften, gentle, mollify, relax, assuage, touch, move. —**Ant.** freeze.

memento, *n.* keepsake, remembrance, souvenir, token, reminder, relic, memorial, trophy, monument, favor, commemoration, testimonial, memento mori.

memorable, *adj.* notable, noteworthy, newsworthy, impressive, significant, remarkable, marked, signal, unforgettable, outstanding, standout, extraordinary, exceptional, indelible, haunting. —**Ant.** forgettable, unimpressive, fleeting.

menace, *n.* **1.** threat, danger, peril, hazard, risk; intimidation, scare, warning. —*v.* **2.** threaten, intimidate, daunt, terrorize, terrify, frighten, scare, alarm, cow, bully, browbeat, bare one's teeth.

mend, *v.* **1.** darn, patch, repair, renew, fix, restore, retouch. **2.** correct, rectify, make better, amend, emend, ameliorate, meliorate, improve, set right. **3.** heal, recover, regain one's health, improve, become better. —**Ant.** ruin, destroy; die, languish.

menial, *adj.* **1.** servile, mean, base, low, humble, subservient, slavish, demeaning, ignoble, degrading. **2.** fawning, groveling, toadying, sycophantic, obsequious, cringing, bootlicking. —*n.* **3.** servant, domestic, attendant, footman, butler, valet, maid, maidservant, waiter; flunky, slave, underling, hireling, serf, minion, lackey. —**Ant.** noble, dignified; master.

mental, *adj.* **1.** intellectual, cerebral, intellective, theoretical, abstract, rational, reasoning, cognitive, psychological, psychic. **2.** neurotic, delusional, irrational, lunatic, mad, demented, unstable, deranged, disturbed, nutty, loony, bonkers, crackers, bananas, crazy, insane, psychotic, batty.

mention, *v.* **1.** refer to, allude to, name, specify, cite, speak of, make known, impart, disclose, divulge, communicate, declare, state, tell, aver. —*n.* **2.** reference, indirect reference, allusion, note, citation, naming.

mercenary, *adj.* venal, grasping, sordid, acquisitive, avaricious, covetous, greedy, penny-pinching, predatory, money-grubbing, materialistic, covetous, stingy, tight, miserly, mean, niggardly, selfish. —**Ant.** generous, unselfish, charitable, giving.

merciful, *adj.* compassionate, kind, clement, lenient, forgiving, magnanimous, charitable, considerate, indulgent, mild, gracious, benignant, beneficent, generous, big, large; tender, humane, kindhearted, tenderhearted, softhearted, sympathetic, forbearing, liberal, tolerant. —**Ant.** merciless, cruel, heartless, callous, unsympathetic, pitiless.

merciless, *adj.* pitiless, cruel, hard, hardhearted, severe, ruthless, heartless, brutal, savage, barbarous, barbaric, harsh, tough, callous, tyrannical, malevolent, inflexible, relentless, unrelenting, fell, unsympathetic, uncompassionate, unfeeling, inexorable. —**Ant.** merciful, lenient, kind, compassionate.

mercurial, *adj.* **1.** sprightly, active, spirited, lively, animated, vivacious, dynamic, excited, ebullient, buoyant, frisky, energetic. **2.** flighty, fickle, changeable, volatile, moody, inconstant, woody, temperamental, fidgety, unquiet, capricious, whimsical, erratic, restless, unstable. —**Ant.** inactive, dispirited, phlegmatic; constant, steady.

mercy, *n.* compassion, pity, benevolence, consideration, generosity, quarter, forgiveness, indulgence, clemency, lenience, tolerance, magnaminity, beneficence, tenderheartedness, softheartedness, leniency, forbearance, quarter, favor, kindness, tenderness, mildness, gentleness, tolerance, sympathy, favor, humanity, liberality, charity, thoughtfulness. —**Ant.** cruelty, pitilessness, harshness.

mere, *adj.* bare, scant, simple, pure, sheer, unmixed, entire, basic, stark, absolute, only, just, nothing but, unmitigated. —**Ant.** considerable.

merit, *n.* **1.** worth, excellence, value, quality, virtue, good, goodness; desert, entitlement, due, credit. —*v.* **2.** deserve, be worthy of, earn, be entitled to, warrant, rate.

merriment, *n.* gaiety, mirth, hilarity, laughter, revelry, high spirits, joyfulness, jubilation, festivity, glee, fun, hilarity, enjoyment, frolicking, levity, lightheartedness, cheerfulness, conviviality, vivacity, jollity, joviality, jocularity. —**Ant.** misery, melancholy.

merry, *adj.* jolly, gay, happy, jovial, joyful, joyous, mirthful, hilarious, gleeful, blithe, blithesome, frolicsome, cheery, cheerful, glad, festive, convivial, carefree, lighthearted, buoyant, rejoicing, jubilant, vivacious, delightful, exhilarating. —**Ant.** sad, unhappy.

mess, *n.* **1.** dirtiness, untidiness, disarray, muss, clutter, filth, pig sty, dump, sloppiness, litter, debris, upset. **2.** chaos, disorder, disarray, disorganization, shambles, clutter, tangle, mare's nest, mishmash, confusion, muddle, medley, farrago, hodgepodge, jumble; mixture, miscellany, mélange, salmagundi. **3.** unpleasantness, difficulty, predicament, plight, muddle, pickle, pinch, trouble, dilemma, quandry, imbroglio, fine kettle of fish, jam, foul-up, screw-up, snafu. —*v.* **4.** muddle, confuse, mix, mix-up. —**Ant.** tidiness; order, system; arrange.

metamorphosis, *n.* change, transformation, transmutation, mutation, alteration, modification, transfiguration, conversion, transmogrification. —**Ant.** stasis.

mete, *v.* distribute, apportion, parcel out, dole, allot, dispense, share, ration, assign, allocate, deal, measure.

method, *n.* **1.** mode, procedure, way, means, manner, fashion, technique, approach, route, avenue, routine, practice, process, course. **2.** order, system, arrangement, disposition, rule, structure, organization, design, pattern.

meticulous, *adj.* careful, finical, finicky, solicitous, exact, precise, accurate, fastidious, scrupulous, thorough, particular, painstaking, punctilious, fussy, strict, critical, demanding. —**Ant.** careless, inexact, imprecise.

middle, *adj.* **1.** central, equidistant,

halfway, medial. **2.** intermediate, intervening. —*n.* **3.** center, midpoint, midst, heart, bull's-eye. —**Ant.** end, final, initial.

midst, *n.* middle, center stage, arena, center, thick, heart, core. —**Ant.** rim, edge.

might, *n.* power, ability, force, energy, muscle, potency, puissance, strength, efficacy. —**Ant.** weakness, inability.

mighty, *adj.* **1.** powerful, strong, vigorous, robust, sturdy, muscular, puissant, potent. **2.** sizable, huge, immense, enormous, vast, tremendous, bulky, massive, prodigious, monumental, towering. —**Ant.** feeble, weak, impotent; small, negligible.

migrate, *v.* voyage, journey, go, travel, settle, relocate, expatriate, immigrate, emigrate, move, resettle. —**Ant.** remain, stay.

mild, *adj.* **1.** amiable, gentle, temperate, kind, compassionate, indulgent, clement, soft, pleasant, equable, easygoing, conciliatory, lenient, mellow, affable. **2.** placid, peaceful, tranquil, pacific, calm. **3.** bland, emollient, mollifying, soothing, calming. —**Ant.** intemperate, unkind, unpleasant; stormy, turbulent; piquant, biting, bitter.

milieu, *n.* environment, medium, situation, locality, background, class, sphere, surroundings, element, climate, environs, ambiance, setting, context, atmosphere.

mind, *n.* **1.** intellect, intelligence, wit, wits, mentality, brainpower, wisdom, insight, shrewdness, understanding, reason, sense. **2.** brain, brains. **3.** sanity, reason, mental balance. **4.** disposition, temper, inclination, bent, intention, leaning, proclivity, bias. **5.** opinion, sentiments, belief, contemplation, judgment, consideration. **6.** purpose, intention, intent, will, wish, liking, desire, wont. **7.** remembrance, recollection, recall, memory. —*v.* **8.** pay attention, heed, obey, attend, attend to, mark, regard, notice, note. **9.** tend, take care of, watch, look after. **10.** be careful *or* cautious *or* wary. **11.** care, object, resent, dislike, disapprove of.

mindless, *adj.* **1.** asinine, thickheaded, obtuse, idiotic, imbecile, moronic, witless, senseless, brainless, feebleminded, fatuous, addlebrained, featherbrained, inane, simple, unthinking, undemanding, silly, purposeless, unpurposeful, aimless, pointless, stupid, no-brain. **2.** heedless, careless, unmindful, thoughtless, inattentive, unthinking, unaware. —**Ant.** aware; dutiful.

mingle, *v.* **1.** mix, blend, unite, commingle, intermix, join, conjoin, combine, intermingle, amalgamate, merge, marry, compound. **2.** participate, associate, socialize, circulate, hobnob, consort.

minor, *adj.* lesser, smaller, inferior, secondary, subordinate, petty, inconsiderable, unimportant, small, insignificant, obscure, inconsequential, trifling, trivial, negligible, slight, paltry, small-time, penny-ante, picayune, two-bit, minor-league, bush-league. —**Ant.** major.

minute, *n.* **1.** moment, instant, split second, flash, trice, blink of an eye, two shakes, jiffy, second. **2.** (*plural*) note, log, summary, memorandum, record, proceedings. —*adj.* **3.** small, tiny, little, infinitesimal, minuscule, diminutive, miniature, wee, microscopic, baby, Lilliputian, itty-bitty. **4.** detailed, exact, precise, thorough. —**Ant.** tre-

mendous, huge, large; general, inexact, rough.

miraculous, *adj.* **1.** marvelous, wonderful, wondrous, extraordinary, incredible, unbelievable, inexplicable, spectacular, amazing, astounding, astonishing, mind-boggling, phenomenal, remarkable, fantastic, fabulous, out of this world. **2.** supernatural, preternatural, magical, superhuman. —**Ant.** prosaic, commonplace; natural.

mirth, *n.* joy, joyousness, gaiety, jollity, glee, merriment, amusement, frolicking, revelry, high spirits, buoyancy, exuberance, joviality, laughter, hilarity, levity, high spirits, exhilaration, delight. —**Ant.** sadness, misery.

misadventure, *n.* mischance, mishap, ill fortune, ill luck, misfortune, accident, disaster, calamity, catastrophe. —**Ant.** luck, fortune.

miscellaneous, *adj.* indiscriminate, promiscuous, mixed, diverse, motley, sundry, assorted, multifarious, manifold, heterogeneous, diversified, varied, various, mingled, confused. —**Ant.** specific, special, homogeneous.

mischief, *n.* **1.** harm, trouble, injury, damage, hurt, detriment, wrong, difficulty, disruption, destruction, disadvantage. **2.** evil, malice, malicious mischief, vandalism; misfortune, trouble. **3.** misbehavior, naughtiness, impishness, roguishness, rascality, deviltry, mischievousness, playfulness, monkey business, monkeyshines, shenanigans. —**Ant.** good, advantage.

miser, *n.* skinflint, tightwad, pinchpenny, hoarder, penny pincher, cheeseparer, Scrooge, cheapskate, money-grubber. —**Ant.** philanthropist.

miserable, *adj.* **1.** wretched, unhappy, uneasy, uncomfortable, distressed, disconsolate, doleful, forlorn, depressed, woeful, woebegone, sad, dejected, despondent, mournful, desolate, desperate, despairing, melancholy, glum, gloomy, dismal, tearful, distraught, afflicted, anguished, suffering, angst-ridden, brokenhearted, heartbroken. **2.** poverty-stricken, poor, needy, destitute, penniless. **3.** contemptible, bad, wretched, mean, despicable, low, abject, worthless. **4.** deplorable, pitiable, lamentable, unfortunate, unlucky, ill-starred, starcrossed, luckless; calamitous, catastrophic, disastrous, cursed. —**Ant.** happy; wealthy; good; fortunate, lucky.

miserly, *adj.* penurious, niggardly, cheap, stingy, parsimonious, tightfisted, mercenary, avaricious, covetous, greedy, penny-pinching, close, mean, money-grubbing, chintzy, mingy. —**Ant.** generous, unselfish.

misery, *n.* **1.** wretchedness, distress, tribulation, woe, trial, hardship, calamity, disaster, curse, misfortune, ordeal, trouble, adversity, burden, affliction, suffering, agony, anguish, torture. **2.** grief, anguish, woe, unhappiness, sorrow, torment, desolation, heartache, angst, anxiety, discomfort, wretchedness, despair, depression, despondency, dejection. —**Ant.** happiness, joy; delight.

misfortune, *n.* **1.** ill luck, bad luck, ill fortune, hard luck, adversity, loss. **2.** accident, disaster, calamity, catastrophe, reverse, affliction, mishap, mischance, adversity, distress, hardship, trouble, blow, disaster, contretemps, tragedy, shock, reversal, bad news. —**Ant.** luck, fortune.

misgiving, *n.* apprehension, doubt, distrust, suspicion, mistrust, worry,

concern, anxiety, qualm, scruple, disquiet, hesitation, question, uncertainty, uneasiness, discomfort, dread, premonition, foreboding, funny feeling. —**Ant.** trust.

mislead, *v.* misguide, lead astray, delude, deceive, misinform, fool, outwit, hoodwink, trick, bamboozle, dupe, gull, misdirect, pull the wool over (someone's) eyes, give (someone) a bum steer, con, lead up the garden path. —**Ant.** lead, conduct.

misshapen, *adj.* distorted, deformed, malformed, grotesque, awry, gnarled, crippled, monstrous, contorted, warped, misproportioned, disproportionate, ill-formed, crooked, twisted, irregular. —**Ant.** shapely, well-formed.

mist, *n.* cloud, fog, fogbank, haze, smog, soup, drizzle, vapor. —**Ant.** clarity.

mistake, *n.* **1.** error, blunder, slip, inaccuracy, erratum, typo, misprint, fault, oversight, fumble, gaffe, faux pas, botch, misstep, flub, blooper, goof, boo-boo. **2.** misapprehension, misconception, misunderstanding. —*v.* **3.** misapprehend, misconceive, misunderstand, misjudge, err, get wrong, misread. —**Ant.** accuracy; understanding.

mistaken, *adj.* erroneous, wrong, incorrect, misconceived, inaccurate, amiss, in error, wide of the mark, on the wrong track; faulty, false, fallacious, misinformed, flawed, warped, misguided, cockeyed. —**Ant.** correct, accurate.

misunderstanding, *n.* **1.** mistake, misapprehension, error, misconception, misreading, misjudgment, false impression, wrong idea, misinterpretation. **2.** disagreement, dissension, discord, difference, difficulty, quarrel, dispute, argument, controversy, rift, falling out. —**Ant.** understanding; agreement, concord.

mix, *v.* **1.** blend, combine, mingle, commingle, confuse, jumble, unite, compound, amalgamate, homogenize. **2.** consort, mingle, associate, join. —*n.* **3.** mixture, concoction, alloy, blend, amalgam. —**Ant.** separate; dissociate.

mixture, *n.* **1.** blend, combination, compound, amalgamation, association, synthesis, merger, fusion, alloy. **2.** hodgepodge, gallimaufry, conglomeration, jumble, medley, melange, olio, potpourri, miscellany, farrago, salmagundi; variety, diversity. —**Ant.** element, constituent.

moan, *n.* **1.** complaint, grievance, grumbling, groan, wail, lament, lamentation. —*v.* **2.** complain, grouse, whine, whimper, gripe, beef, bemoan, bewail, grieve, lament, mourn, deplore. **3.** sigh, mourn, weep, cry, keen, grieve, sob, snivel.

mock, *v.* **1.** ridicule, deride, taunt, flout, gibe, scorn, abuse, sneer at, rag, rib, tease, jeer, chaff, scoff, banter, make sport of; mimic, ape, satirize, imitate, caricature, lampoon, parody, burlesque, spoof, send up, roast. **2.** defy, challenge, dare, face, confront, thumb one's nose at. **3.** deceive, delude, disappoint, cheat, dupe, fool, defeat, mislead. —*n.* **4.** mockery, derision, ridicule, banter, sport, sneer. —*adj.* **5.** substitute, artificial, simulated, synthetic, imitation, ersatz, make-believe, bogus, pseudo, phony, feigned, pretended, counterfeit, sham, false, spurious, fake. —**Ant.** praise, honor.

mockery, *n.* **1.** ridicule, derision, disdain, taunting, disparagement, contempt, abuse, scorn, contumely. **2.** impersonation, imitation, show, mimicry, caricature, parody, burlesque, lampoon, satire, spoof, takeoff, sendup. **3.** travesty, pretense, pretext, sham, farce.

mode, *n.* **1.** method, way, manner, style, fashion. **2.** form, variety, degree, modification.

model, *n.* **1.** standard, paragon, prototype, ideal, pattern, example, archetype, mold, guide, nonpareil, nonesuch, paradigm, exemplar, blueprint, criterion, classic example, original. **2.** representation, facsimile, copy, image, imitation. —*v.* **3.** form, plan, pattern, mold, shape, fashion, design.

moderate, *adj.* **1.** reasonable, temperate, judicious, just, fair, deliberate, mild, cool, steady, calm, peaceful. **2.** medium, average, usual. **3.** mediocre, fair. **4.** middle-of-the-road, conservative, temperate. —*n.* **5.** mugwump, middle-of-the-roader, conservative. —*v.* **6.** allay, meliorate, pacify, calm, assuage, sober, mitigate, soften, mollify, temper, qualify, appease, abate, lessen, diminish, reduce. —**Ant.** immoderate; unusual; radical; disturb, increase, intensify.

modern, *adj.* recent, up-to-date, current, contemporary, today's, brandnew, up-to-the-minute, present-day, latest, newfangled, present, new, novel, fresh; chic, fashionable, stylish, modish, in vogue, trendy, hip, hot. —**Ant.** old, archaic, ancient, obsolete.

modest, *adj.* **1.** moderate, humble, unpretentious, simple, plain, ordinary, homely, inconspicuous, decent, becoming, proper. **2.** inextravagant, unostentatious, retiring, unassuming, unobtrusive. **3.** decent, demure, prudish, chaste, pure, virtuous. —**Ant.** immodest, immoderate, improper; extravagant.

modesty, *n.* **1.** unobtrusiveness, humility, diffidence, reticence, reluctance, meekness. **2.** moderation, decency, propriety, simplicity, purity, chastity, prudery, prudishness, shame, bashfulness, coyness; demureness, virtue. —**Ant.** indecency; licentiousness.

modify, *v.* **1.** change, alter, vary, qualify, temper, adjust, restrict, adapt, transform, revise, amend, revamp, refashion, redo, limit, shape, reform. **2.** reduce, qualify, moderate, temper, soften, abate, tone down, modulate, limit, restrict.

moist, *adj.* damp, humid, dank, wet, dewy, dank, clammy, muggy, steamy, misty, foggy, rainy, soggy, moisture-laden. —**Ant.** dry, arid.

molest, *v.* attack, assail; harass, harry, disturb, trouble, annoy, badger, needle, nettle, gall, chafe, beleaguer, vex, plague, tease, pester, torment, torture, irritate, fret, hector, inconvenience, discommode, worry, bother.

moment, *n.* **1.** minute, instant, second, jiffy, trice, flash, twinkling, blink of an aye, trice. **2.** importance, consequence, significance, weight, gravity, seriousness, prominence, concern, note, interest, import, consideration. **3.** momentum, force, power, impetus, drive. —**Ant.** insignificance; inertia.

momentous, *adj.* important, consequential, vital, weighty, serious, grave, decisive, crucial, critical, vital, pivotal, portentous, charged. —**Ant.** unimportant, trivial, trifling.

monetary, *adj.* pecuniary, financial, fiscal, capital, cash, money, economic.

money, *n.* **1.** coin, cash, currency, specie, change, coin of the realm, legal tender, bills, banknotes. **2.** funds, capital, assets, property, wealth, riches. **3.**

mazuma, long green, lettuce, dough, loot, bread, moolah, greenbacks, bucks, scratch, gelt, kale, cabbage.

mongrel, *n.* cross, hybrid, mutt, half-breed, cur, mixed breed, crossbreed. —**Ant.** purebred, thoroughbred.

monopolize, *v.* consume, possess, corner, control, dominate, appropriate, co-opt, engross, usurp, arrogate, preempt, take over, gobble up, grab, hog, preoccupy. —**Ant.** share.

monotonous, *adj.* tedious, humdrum, tiresome, uniform, boring, soporific, wearisome, prosaic, banal, dry, dreary, colorless, routine, mechanical, run-of-the-mill, ordinary, commonplace, uneventful, ho-hum, dull, unvaried, unvarying. —**Ant.** interesting, amusing, diverting.

monster, *n.* **1.** ogre, giant, dragon, troll, bogeyman, Cyclops, griffin, gargoyle, sphinx, centaur, hippogriff. **2.** mooncalf, monstrosity, mutant, mutation, freak, deformity, eyesore. **3.** fiend, brute, miscreant, wretch, beast, villain, demon, devil.

monstrous, *adj.* **1.** huge, great, large, tremendous, gigantic, monster, prodigious, enormous, immense, vast, stupendous, colossal. **2.** frightful, hideous, revolting, shocking, repulsive, horrible, nightmarish, grotesque, gruesome, ghoulish, freakish, atrocious, terrible, dreadful, horrendous, loathsome, heinous, fiendish, barbaric, savage, inhuman, brutal, brutish, beastly. —**Ant.** small, tiny; delightful, attractive.

mooch, *v.* beg, scrounge, cadge, panhandle, hit up, bum, sponge off.

mood, *n.* disposition, frame of mind, humor, temper, vein, attitude, inclination, nature, spirit, atmosphere, sense, feeling.

moody, *adj.* gloomy, sullen, ill-humored, perverse, sulky, waspish, crotchety, abrupt, curt, crabby, crusty, cantankerous, huffy, curmudgeonly, cranky, petulant, temperamental, touchy, mercurial, volatile, unstable, fitful, erratic, mercurial, fussy, fidgety, changeable, flighty, fickle, restless, unquiet, agitated, anxious, snappish, pettish, testy, tetchy, crabby, surly, short-tempered, irritable, irascible, captious, peevish, fretful, spenetic, spiteful, morose, intractable, stubborn. —**Ant.** amiable, temperate, tractable.

moot, *adj.* doubtful, debatable, disputable, disputed, unsettled, arguable, controversial, questionable, unresolved, undecided, at issue, problematical, up in the air. —**Ant.** indubitable, indisputable.

moral, *adj.* **1.** ethical, upright, honest, straightforward, righteous, open, just, good, virtuous, honorable, idealistic, humane, high-minded, principled, scrupulous, incorruptible, noble. —*n.* **2.** (*plural*) ethics, integrity, standards, morality, scruples, ideals, principles, probity, rectitude. —**Ant.** immoral, amoral.

morbid, *adj.* **1.** gloomy, lugubrious, glum, morose, somber, melancholy, depressed, sensitive, extreme. **2.** unwholesome, diseased, pathological, pathogenic, unhealthy, sick, sickly, tainted, corrupted, vitiated. —**Ant.** cheerful; wholesome, salubrious.

moreover, *adv.* besides, further, furthermore, and, also, too, likewise, to boot, into the bargain, as well, what is more.

morose, *adj.* sullen, gloomy, depressed, despondent, despairing, melancholy, sad, dour, doleful, grim, funereal, cheerless, bleak, moody, sour,

sulky, churlish, splenetic, surly, ill-humored, ill-natured, perverse, petulant. —**Ant.** cheerful, happy, good-natured.

mortal, *adj.* **1.** human; transitory, fleeting, temporal, transient, ephemeral; physical, bodily, corporeal, fleshy, worldly, perishable. **2.** fatal, final, lethal, deadly, terminal, disastrous. —*n.* **3.** human being, man, woman, person, soul, individual, creature, earthling. —**Ant.** immortal, god.

mortify, *v.* **1.** shame, humiliate, humble, embarrass, abash, abase, subdue, restrain. **2.** punish, castigate, discipline, control, subdue, subjugate. —**Ant.** honor.

mostly, *adv.* in the main, generally, chiefly, especially, particularly, for the most part, customarily. —**Ant.** seldom.

motion, *n.* **1.** movement, move, action, change, shift, traveling, progress, passage, transit; stir, turbulence, agitation. **2.** gait, deportment, carriage, bearing, air. **3.** gesture, gesticulation, signal, sign, movement, move. —**Ant.** stasis.

motionless, *adj.* stable, fixed, unmoving, still, transfixed, quiescent, stationary, immobile, quiet, stock-still, inactive. —**Ant.** mobile.

motive, *n.* motivation, inducement, incentive, incitement, stimulus, spur, influence, occasion, reason, ground, cause, purpose.

mount, *v.* **1.** go up, ascend, climb, scale, get up on. **2.** raise, put into position, fix on. **3.** prepare, produce, make ready, ready. —**Ant.** descend.

mourn, *v.* grieve, lament, bewail, bemoan, sorrow for, regret, rue, deplore. —**Ant.** laugh, rejoice.

move, *v.* **1.** stir, advance, budge, progress, make progress, proceed, move on, remove. **2.** turn, revolve, spin, gyrate, rotate, operate. **3.** act, bestir oneself, take action. **4.** stir, shake, agitate, excite, arouse, rouse; shift, transfer, propel. **5.** prompt, actuate, induce, influence, impel, activate, incite, rouse, instigate. **6.** affect, touch, stir, upset, agitate, disquiet, disturb, strike, ruffle, make an impression, have an effect, shake up.

movement, *n.* **1.** move, motion, change, repositioning, relocation, shift, transfer. **2.** motion, progress, development, advance, increase, activity, eventfulness. —**Ant.** inertia, stasis.

multifarious, *adj.* numerous, various, many, abundant, multitudinous, manifold, diverse, sundry, multifold, legion, myriad, various and sundry. —**Ant.** singular, unique.

multitude, *n.* host, crowd, throng, mass, army, swarm, collection, horde, mob, drove, herd, legion, scores.

mundane, *adj.* **1.** worldly, earthly, terrestrial, terraqueous, secular, temporal. **2.** common, ordinary, banal. —**Ant.** unearthly, extraordinary.

murder, *n.* **1.** killing, assassination, homicide, manslaughter, slaying, slaughter, butchery, bloodshed, carnage, liquidation. —*v.* **2.** kill, slay, assassinate, destroy, put an end to, put to death, wipe out, exterminate, eradicate, eliminate, bump off, knock off, blow away, do in, rub out, waste, ice, snuff out, take for a ride, hit. **3.** spoil, mar, ruin, abuse, destroy, wreck, mangle, butcher, mutilate.

murky, *adj.* dark, gloomy, cheerless, obscure, dim, cloudy, dusky, lowering, overcast, misty, hazy, threatening, gray, dismal, dreary, bleak, grim, funereal, shady, shadowy. —**Ant.** bright, light, clear.

murmur, *n.* **1.** grumble, susurration, susurrus, drone, hum, whispering, mumble, complaint, plaint, whimper, mutter. —*v.* **2.** mumble, mutter, whisper. **3.** complain, grumble, grouse, moan, lament, wail.

muscular, *adj.* brawny, sinewy, well-muscled, well-built, well-knit, rugged, robust, athletic, broad-shouldered, beefy, sturdy, burly, husky, hunky, strong, powerful, mighty, Bunyanesque, buff, pumped up, well-developed. —**Ant.** weak, feeble, underdeveloped.

muse, *v.* reflect, meditate, ponder, contemplate, think of *or* about, consider, chew over, weigh, evaluate, study, mull over, cogitate, deliberate, ruminate, think, brood; dream.

muster, *v.* call together, mobilize, rally, round up, assemble, gather, summon, convoke, collect, marshal, convene, congregate. —**Ant.** scatter, separate.

mutable, *adj.* **1.** changeable, alterable, variable, protean. **2.** fickle, changing, inconstant, unstable, vacillating, unsettled, wavering, unsteady, uneven, unpredictable, erratic, volatile, undependable, unreliable, mercurial, capricious. —**Ant.** immutable, invariable; stable, settled, motionless.

mute, *adj.* silent, dumb, speechless, still, voiceless, wordless, tightlipped, taciturn, reserved, quiet, hushed, stifled, mum. —**Ant.** loquacious, voluble, talkative.

mutilate, *v.* injure, disfigure, maim, damage, mar, cripple, mangle, lame, butcher, disable, spoil, ruin, deface, destroy, vandalize.

mutinous, *adj.* **1.** seditious, insurrectionary, revolutionary, insurgent. **2.** rebellious, refractory, insubordinate, unruly, racalcitrant, obstinate, defiant, disobedient, insubordinate, contumacious, turbulent, riotous. —**Ant.** patriotic; obedient.

mutiny, *n.* **1.** revolt, rebellion, insurrection, revolution, uprising, insurgency, subversiveness, sedition. —*v.* **2.** revolt, rebel, rise up, strike; disobey, subvert, agitate against. —**Ant.** obedience.

mutual, *adj.* reciprocal, balanced, correlative, complementary, requited, common, interchangeable, communal, joint, shared. —**Ant.** single, singular.

mysterious, *adj.* secret, arcane, furtive, unclear, esoteric, occult, cryptic, inscrutable, mystical, obscure, puzzling, inexplicable, baffling, bewildering, confounding, confusing, perplexing, mystifying, weird, bizarre, strange, uncanny, curious, unexplainable, unintelligible, incomprehensible, enigmatic, impenetrable, recondite, hidden, concealed, dark, abstruse, cabalistic, unfathomable. —**Ant.** clear.

myth, *n.* legend, story, fiction, fable, allegory, parable, saga, folktale, fiction, history, tradition, epic, tale, tall tale.

N

nag, *v.* **1.** criticize, ride, scold, carp at, upbraid, henpeck, pick at *or* on, berate, find fault with, bully, provoke, nettle, plague, torment, pester, harass, harry, hector, importune, irritate, annoy, vex. —*n.* **2.** scold, harpy, fishwife, shrew, virago, pest, termagant, maenad.

naive, *adj.* unsophisticated, ingenuous, innocent, credulous, childlike, born yesterday, gullible, inexperienced, green, unworldly, trusting, simpleminded, simple, unaffected, natural, unsuspecting, artless, guileless, candid, open, plain. —**Ant.** sophisticated, disingenuous, artful, sly.

naked, *adj.* **1.** nude, bare, undressed, stripped, exposed, unclothed. **2.** bare, stripped, destitute, desert, denuded. **3.** unsheathed, exposed, bare. **4.** defenseless, unprotected, unguarded, exposed, unarmed, open. **5.** simple, plain, manifest, evident, unembellished, stark, overt, patent, obvious, conspicuous, palpable, unvarnished, unmitigated, blatant, barefaced, glaring, flagrant, pure, unalloyed, blunt, undeniable, undisguised, unadorned, mere, bare, sheer. **6.** plainspoken, blunt, direct, outspoken, unvarnished, uncolored, unexaggerated, plain. —**Ant.** covered, dressed; protected; exaggerated, embellished.

namby-pamby, *adj.* **1.** insipid, bland, wishy-washy, insubstantial, overrefined, overnice, precious, jejune, goody-goody. **2.** weak, spineless, indecisive, wavering, wimpish, wimpy. —**Ant.** strong, forthright, decisive.

name, *n.* **1.** appellation, title, label, tag, designation, epithet. **2.** reputation, repute, character, credit. **3.** fame, repute, note, distinction, renown, eminence, honor, praise. —*v.* **4.** call, title, entitle, dub, denominate. **5.** specify, mention, indicate, designate, identify, nominate.

nameless, *adj.* **1.** anonymous, unknown, obscure, undistinguished, unremarked, unnamed, untitled, unspecified, incognito. **2.** ineffable, unnamable, indescribable, inexpressible, unutterable, unspeakable.

narrate, *v.* recount, relate, tell, report, rehearse, repeat, review, unfold, chronicle, reveal, retail, describe, detail, recite.

narrative, *n.* story, account, recital, history, chronicle, tale, description, revelation, portrayal, report, record, statement, anecdote.

narrow-minded, *adj.* prejudiced, biased, bigoted, intolerant, illiberal, partial, opinionated, one-sided, reactionary, parochial, stiff-necked, conventional, hidebound, meanspirited, petty, puritanical, ultraconservative, old-fogyish, strait-laced, stuffy, square. —**Ant.** liberal, broadminded, tolerant, unprejudiced.

nasty, *adj.* **1.** filthy, dirty, disgusting, unclean, foul, impure, loathsome, polluted, defiled, offensive, vile, odious, onbnoxious, sick-making, fetid, noisome, rank, rancid, malodorous, noxious. **2.** nauseous, nauseating, disgusting, sickening, offensive, repulsive, repellent, objectionable. **3.** obscene, smutty, pornographic, lewd, licentious, lascivious, indecent, ribald, gross, indelicate, blue vulgar, sordid, coarse, crude, bawdy, risqué, off-color, suggestive, X-rated, raunchy. **4.** vicious, spiteful, ugly, bad-tempered, disagreeable, surly, abusive, irascible, cruel, inconsiderate, rude, churlish, obnoxious, crotchety, crabby, cranky, cantankerous, curmudgeonly, mean. —**Ant.** clean, pure, unpolluted; delightful; decent, honorable; amiable, agreeable.

nation, *n.* **1.** race, stock, ethnic group, population, clan, people, tribe. **2.** state, country, commonwealth, kingdom, realm, domain, land, political entity.

native, *adj.* **1.** inborn, inherent, inherited, natural, innate, inbred, heredity,

in the blood, intrinsic, constitutional, congenital. **2.** indigenous, autochthonous, aboriginal, natural, domestic, local, homegrown. **3.** unadorned, natural, real, genuine, original. —*n.* **4.** inhabitant, aborigine, resident, citizen. —**Ant.** acquired; imported; decorated; foreigner, alien.

nature, *n.* **1.** character, quality, attributes, properties, features, makeup, personality, identity, temperament. **2.** kind, variety, description, class, category, genre, sort, character, type, species, quality. **3.** universe, world, earth, cosmos, creation, environment, macrocosm.

naughty, *adj.* **1.** ill-behaved, misbehaved, bad, disobedient, mischievous, roguish, devilish, unruly, obstreperous, rambunctious, undisciplined, fractious, wayward, defiant. **2.** risqué, improper, off-color, ribald, profane, dirty, vulgar, smutty.

nauseate, *v.* **1.** sicken, revolt, disgust. **2.** loathe, abhor, abominate, detest, reject. —**Ant.** delight, enchant, attract; like, love, adore.

nauseous, *adj.* **1.** sickening, revolting, nasty, repellent, disgusting, repugnant, repulsive, foul, sick-making, stomachturning, loathsome, abhorrent, detestable, despicable, nauseating, offensive. **2.** ill, sick to one's stomach, green around the gills, queasy, squeamish. —**Ant.** attractive, lovable; well.

near, *adj.* **1.** close, nigh, at hand, nearby, adjacent, contiguous, touching, adjoining, bordering, abutting. **2.** imminent, impending, approaching, forthcoming, at hand. **3.** related, connected, intimate, familiar, allied, attached. **4.** faithful, close, accurate, literal. —**Ant.** far.

nearly, *adv.* **1.** almost, approximately, well-nigh, about, not quite, all but, virtually, practically, as good as. **2.** intimately, identically, exactly, precisely, closely.

neat, *adj.* **1.** orderly, ordered, trim, tidy, spruce, smart, nice, clean, uncluttered, fastidious, spick-and-span, shipshape, organized, systematic, neat as a pin. **2.** clever, effective, adroit, finished, well-planned, dexterous, apt. —**Ant.** disorderly, sloppy; maladroit, ineffective.

necessary, *adj.* **1.** essential, indispensable, required, compulsory, imperative, obligatory, of the essense, urgent, exigent, top priority, compelling, life-and-death, of the utmost importance, requisite, needed, needful, vital, unavoidable. **2.** sure, certain, predestined, fated, inexorable, predetermined. —**Ant.** unnecessary, dispensable.

necessity, *n.* **1.** needfulness, indispensability, need, indispensableness. **2.** requirement, requisite, demand, necessary, sine qua non, essential, prerequisite. **3.** compulsion, fate, destiny, kismet, karma, inevitability, inevitableness, unavoidability, unavoidableness, irresistibility. **4.** poverty, neediness, indigence, necessitousness, need, want, destitution, penury, straits, difficulty, pauperism. —**Ant.** dispensability; wealth.

need, *n.* **1.** requirement, want, necessity, exigency, emergency, urgency. **2.** want, necessity, lack, demand. **3.** destitution, poverty, neediness, want, deprivation, necessity, indigence, penury, distress, privation. —*v.* **4.** require, want, lack, miss, demand. —**Ant.** wealth, opulence.

neglect, *v.* **1.** disregard, ignore, slight, overlook, spurn, rebuff, scorn, disdain, cold-shoulder; omit, be remiss. —*n.* **2.** disregard, dereliction, negligence, remissness, carelessness, failure, omission, default, inattention, heedlessness. —**Ant.** regard, attend; regard, attention, care.

neglectful, *adj.* disregardful, remiss, careless, negligent, inattentive, indifferent, heedless, thoughtless. —**Ant.** regardful, careful, thoughtful.

negligible, *adj.* minor, unimportant, trivial, trifling, inconsequential, paltry, piddling, inappreciable, nugatory, worthless, petty, niggling, insignificant, slight, marginal, small, slender, slim, minuscule, outside, off. —**Ant.** significant, important.

negotiate, *v.* **1.** arrange, arrange for, organize, orchestrate, conduct, handle, maneuver, manage, engineer, accomplish, execute, effect, complete, pull off, settle. **2.** bargain, deal, haggle, discuss, debate, transact, mediate, consult, come to terms.

nerve, *n.* **1.** strength, vigor, energy, power, force, might. **2.** courage, coolness, boldness, bravery, determination, pluck, mettle, spirit, will, tenacity, valor, daring, staunchness, firmness, steadfastness, intrepidity, fortitude, resolution, resoluteness, endurance. **3.** brashness, presumption, temerity, brass, brazenness, gall, effrontery, impertinence, impudence, insolence, audacity, chutzpah, crust. —**Ant.** weakness, frailty, cowardice.

nervous, *adj.* excitable, uneasy, apprehensive, fearful, timid, timorous; high-strung, tense, agitated, overwrought, upset, edgy, on edge, fidgety, fretful, shaky, skittish, jumpy, jittery, in a dither, in a sweat, uptight, on pins and needles, rattled, strung out. —**Ant.** confident, bold, intrepid.

new, *adj.* **1.** original, unique, unusual, different, latest, contemporary, advanced, trendy, fashionable, experimental, creative, recent, modern, up-to-date, novel, fresh. **2.** further, additional, fresh. **3.** unaccustomed, unused, fresh. —**Ant.** old, stale.

nice, *adj.* **1.** pleasing, pleasant, agreeable, delightful, worthy, worthwhile, satisfactory, good. **2.** kind, amiable, pleasant, cordial, warm, gracious, genial, charming, outgoing, polite, courteous, refined, winsome, attractive, likable, friendly. **3.** accurate, precise, skilled, delicate, fastidious, exact, exacting, critical, rigorous, strict, demanding, scrupulous. **4.** tactful, careful, delicate, discriminating, discerning, particular. **5.** minute, fine, subtle, refined. **6.** refined, well-mannered, well-spoken. **7.** suitable, proper, polite. **8.** neat, trim, fastidious, finical, finicky, dainty, squeamish, fussy. —**Ant.** unpleasant; unkind; inaccurate; tactless, careless; unrefined; improper, impolite; sloppy.

nickname, *n.* sobriquet, epithet, handle, nom de guerre, appellation, pet name, assumed name, alias, stage name, pen name, nom de plume, pseudonym.

nimble, *adj.* agile, quick, lively, active, brisk, spry, lithe, limber, sprightly, energetic, adroit, deft, dextrous; ready, alert, swift, awake, acute, quick-witted, intelligent, keen, sharp, brilliant, on the qui vive. —**Ant.** slow, clumsy, awkward.

noble, *adj.* **1.** highborn, aristocratic, high-class, upper-class, high-ranking, titled, lordly, patrician, blueblooded, to the manor born. **2.** high-minded, upright, righteous, virtuous, honest, incorruptible, principled, moral, decent, self-sacrificing, altruistic, staunch, steadfast, true, loyal, faithful, trustworthy, magnanimous, superior, elevated,

exalted, worthy, lofty, honorable, great, large, generous. **3.** admirable, dignified, imposing, stately, exquisite, sublime, superb, elegant, rich, sumptuous, luxurious, magnificent, impressive, grand, lordly, splendid. —*n.* **4.** nobleman, noblewoman, patrician, blueblood, peer, aristocrat, lord, lady. —**Ant.** lowborn; base; undignified; serf, slave.

noise, *n.* clamor, din, hubbub, racket, clatter, rattle, blare, uproar, outcry, crash, thunder, rumble, hullabaloo, caterwauling, cacophony, rumpus, bawling, babel; commotion, bedlam, fracas, pandemonium, tumult, ado. —**Ant.** quiet, peace.

noiseless, *adj.* silent, quiet, still, inaudible, soundless, mute, soft, hushed, muffled, deadened, dampened, stifled. —**Ant.** noisy, clamorous, tumultuous.

noisy, *adj.* loud, deafening, earsplitting, jarring, harsh, piercing, shrill, resounding, cacophonous, thunderous, blaring, blasting, stentorian, clamorous, boisterous, tumultuous, riotous, vociferous, obstreperous, blustering, uproarious. —**Ant.** quiet, silent, peaceful.

nominal, *adj.* titular, so-called, formal, in name only, self-styled, so-disant, purported, supposed, would-be, pretended.

nonchalant, *adj.* unconcerned, indifferent, cool, apathetic, unexcited, calm, casual, imperturbable, unflappable, dispassionate, detached, insouciant, aloof, blasé, offhand, unenthusiastic, relaxed, collected, composed, easygoing, happy-go-lucky, laid-back. —**Ant.** passionate, enthusiastic.

nondescript, *adj.* **1.** undistinguished, dull, ordinary, commonplace, unremarkable, bland, blah, everyday, colorless, drab, insipid, characterless, unexceptional. **2.** unclassifiable, amorphous, indescribable. —**Ant.** marvelous, exciting, unusual.

nonsense, *n.* twaddle, balderdash, senselessness, moonshine, absurdity, folly, trash, silliness, idiocy, asininity, stupidity, screwiness, nuttiness, craziness, madness, rubbish, drivel, gobbledygook, gibberish, blather, bunk, poppycock, double-talk, mumbo jumbo, rot, hogwash, malarky, bilge, baloney, claptrap, hot air, applesauce, horsefeathers, garbage, tripe, bull, hooey, a crock, horse hockey, fiddlesticks, hokum, bushwa.

normal, *adj.* usual, ordinary, standard, regular, routine, average, conventional, common, general, typical, customary, natural, conformist, orthodox, run-of-the-mill, garden-variety, commonplace, everyday, traditional, habitual, accustomed, set, humdrum, simple, plain, unpretentious, unremarkable, expected, established, accepted, prevalent, universal. —**Ant.** abnormal, unusual, extraordinary, atypical, unnatural, rare, unorthodox, remarkable, unexpected.

notable, *adj.* **1.** noteworthy, noted, noticeable, remarkable, signal, different, distinctive, singular, peerless, striking, unparalleled, outstanding, distinguished, unusual, uncommon, extraordinary, great, conspicuous, memorable. **2.** prominent, important, eminent, distinguished, famed, famous, well-known, conspicuous, notorious. **3.** celebrity, personage, dignitary, luminary, VIP, name, big shot, legend, eminence. —**Ant.** common, ordinary; unimportant, undistinguished.

note, *n.* **1.** message, letter, communication, correspondence, postcard,

word, line; memo, memorandum, record, minute. **2.** comment, remark, commentary, observation, explanation, exegesis, gloss, criticism, critique, assessment, annotation, footnote. **3.** eminence, distinction, mark, consequence, substance, weight, merit, prestige, high-standing, repute, celebrity, fame, renown, reputation, name. **4.** notice, heed, observation; consideration, regard. —*v.* **5.** mark down, jot down, record, make a note of, register. **6.** mention, designate, refer to, indicate, denote. **7.** notice, see, perceive, spot, remark, observe, regard, look at, mark, consider, contemplate, pay attention to, study.

noted, *adj.* famous, celebrated, distinguished, famed, notable, renowned, eminent, illustrious, well-known, prominent, popular; notorious; respected, distinguished, esteemed, acclaimed. —**Ant.** unknown, undistinguished; notorious, infamous.

noteworthy, *adj.* notable, significant, remarkable, newsworthy, impressive, signal, outstanding, standout, extraordinary, exceptional, great, major, unusual, rare, uncommon, singular, unique, different, important. —**Ant.** insignificant, unremarkable.

notice, *n.* **1.** information, intelligence, advice, news bulletin, notification, mention, announcement. **2.** intimation, warning, signal, sign, indication, admonition, threat, tip, word, advice, caveat. **3.** sign, placard, poster, billboard, advertisement. **4.** observation, perception, attention, heed, note, cognizance. **5.** comment, mention, account, criticism, critique, review. —*v.* **6.** discern, perceive, see, become aware of, pay attention to, distinguish, discriminate, recognize, understand, regard, heed, note, observe, mark, remark.

notify, *v.* give notice to, inform, apprise, acquaint, make known to, advise, alert, tell, warn.

notion, *n.* **1.** conception, idea, concept, thought, image, impression, mental picture, inkling, intuition. **2.** opinion, view, belief, sentiment, impression, judgment. **3.** whim, caprice, fancy, crotchet, whimsy, impulse, vagary, inclination, conceit, quirk, kink.

nourish, *v.* **1.** feed, maintain, keep, provide for, look after, care for, nurture, nurse, sustain, support, tend, attend. **2.** foster, cherish, harbor, strengthen, fortify, stimulate, cultivate, advance, promote, promulgate, foment, succor, aid, help, encourage. —**Ant.** neglect.

novelty, *n.* **1.** originality, newness, innovation, uniqueness, freshness, inventiveness. **2.** fad, rage, wrinkle, craze. **3.** knickknack, curio, gimmick, bauble, toy, plaything, ornament, kickshaw, trinket, trifle, bibelot, whatnot, gewgaw, gimcrack, tchotchke.

now, *adv.* **1.** today, nowadays, currently, these days, at the moment, at present, in these times, in this day and age, under the circumstances, in the present climate, things being what they are, under these conditions, at this juncture, on this occasion, any longer or more; for the time being. **2.** immediately, instantly, without delay, at once, right away, promptly, straightaway, as soon as possible, ASAP, in a jiffy, posthaste, forthwith, directly, without hesitation, pronto, instantaneously, in a second or minute, tout de suite, at the drop of a hat, before one can say "Jack Robinson."

noxious, *adj.* **1.** harmful, hurtful, unhealthy, unwholesome, injurious, mephitic, miasmatic, nocuous, noisome, detrimental, baneful, deleterious, pestilential, poisonous, destructive, deadly. **2.** corrupting, immoral, pernicious. —**Ant.** harmless, wholesome, beneficial; moral.

nucleus, *n.* center, kernel, core, heart, pith, focus, hub.

nude, *adj.* uncovered, undressed, unclothed, undraped, naked, bare, exposed, denuded, stark-naked, au naturel, in the altogether, in the buff, in one's birthday suit. —**Ant.** covered, dressed.

nullify, *v.* invalidate, negate, annul, abrogate, quash, undo, cancel out, vitiate. —**Ant.** confirm, establish.

number, *n.* **1.** sum, total, count, aggregate, collection. **2.** numeral, integer, digit, figure. **3.** quantity, collection, company, multitude, crowd, slew, gang, bunch, party, bevy, platoon, swarm, legion, mob, host, mass, handful, few, several, loads, tons, horde, many. —*v.* **4.** count, enumerate, calculate, compute, reckon, tally, figure, add up, sum up, total, tot up; account; include, consist of.

numberless, *adj.* innumerable, numerous, myriad, countless, uncounted, untold, infinite, incalculable, immeasurable. —**Ant.** finite.

numerous, *adj.* many, numberless, copious, ample, plentiful, plenteous, plenty, abundant, swarming, thronging, surplus, multitudinous, myriad, profuse, innumerable, uncountable; diverse, multifarious, various, varied, assorted, sundry. —**Ant.** few.

nurse, *v.* **1.** tend, take care of, minister to, look after, treat, attend. **2.** foster, cherish, preserve, develop, succor, promote, foment, encourage, aid, abet, help. **3.** nourish, nurture, feed, rear, raise, cultivate; coddle, baby, pamper, spoil. **4.** suckle, feed, give suck to, breast-feed, wet-nurse. —**Ant.** neglect.

nutrition, *n.* food, nutriment, aliment, nourishment, sustenance, subsistence.

nutritious, *adj.* healthful, healthy, wholesome, nutritive, nourishing, beneficial, salutary, alimentary, life-giving.

O

oaf, *n.* **1.** simpleton, blockhead, dunce, dolt, fool, nincompoop, ninny, jackass, half-wit, numbskull, bonehead, pinhead, ignoramus, dimwit, nitwit, booby, fathead, knucklehead, sap, dope, idiot, imbecile, moron. **2.** lout, bungler, clumsy person, yahoo, bumpkin, clod, clodhopper, yokel, buffoon, boor, redneck, lummox, jerk, galoot, clown, hick, goose, goon. —**Ant.** genius.

oath, *n.* **1.** promise, vow, pledge, affirmation, word of honor. **2.** profanity, curse, blasphemy, malediction, imprecation, expletive, obscenity, swear word, dirty word, four-letter word.

obedient, *adj.* submissive, compliant, docile, tractable, yielding, agreeable, amenable, acquiescent, pliant, adherent, deferential, respectful, dutiful, subservient, passive, timid. —**Ant.** disobedient, recalcitrant, refractory.

obese, *adj.* fat, stout, plump, pudgy, corpulent, portly, gross, fleshy, chubby, big, big-boned, huge, enormous, overweight, heavy, tubby, paunchy, rotund, pot-bellied, broad in the beam. —**Ant.** thin, skinny, slender, slim.

object, *n.* **1.** thing, reality, fact, manifestation, phenomenon, tangible, item, entity. **2.** focus, butt, quarry, target, objective, goal, end, destination, aim. **3.** purpose, reason, idea, basis, base, target, goal, end, motive, intent, intention. —*v.* **4.** protest, disapprove, be averse, refuse, interfere, argue, oppose, complain, remonstrate, draw the line, take exception. —**Ant.** approve.

objective, *n.* **1.** end, termination, object, destination, aim, target, goal, purpose, intent, intention, ambition, aspiration, design, desire, hope. —*adj.* **2.** unprejudiced, unbiased, impartial, fair, impersonal, just, judicious, neutral, equitable, disinterested, dispassionate, evenhanded, open-minded, detached. —**Ant.** subjective, biased.

obligation, *n.* **1.** requirement, duty, responsibility, charge, burden, onus, demand, compulsion, liability, accountability, accountableness. **2.** agreement, contract, covenant, bond, stipulation, promise, pledge, requirement, constraint.

oblige, *v.* **1.** require, constrain, compel, force, necessitate, bind, coerce, obligate. **2.** indulge, cater to, gratify, favor, accommodate, serve, please, benefit. —**Ant.** disoblige, liberate, free; unfetter.

obliging, *adj.* helpful, accommodating, willing, indulgent, gracious, civil, polite, agreeable, amenable, supportive, neighborly, kind, generous, chivalrous, amiable, friendly, outgoing, considerate, courteous, thoughtful, solicitous. —**Ant.** unhelpful, selfish.

obliterate, *v.* erase, efface, do away with, expunge, rub out, delete, blot out, eradicate, wipe out, conceal, eliminate; destroy, annihilate, kill, exterminate, extirpate. —**Ant.** construct, create, originate; restore.

oblivious, *adj.* **1.** unaware, unconscious, insensitive, unconcerned, distant, detached, removed, abstracted, forgetful, absent-minded. **2.** heedless, disregardful, neglectful, careless, negligent. —**Ant.** heedful, regardful, careful.

obnoxious, *adj.* revolting, repulsive, disgusting, nauseating, noisome, vile, repellent, repugnant, sickening, sickmaking, foul, noxious, execrable, abominable, loathsome, scurvy, despicable, awful, terrible, nasty, distasteful, objectionable, offensive, odious, hateful. —**Ant.** delightful, favorable.

obscene, *adj.* immodest, indecent, lewd, pornographic, coarse, ribald, smutty, offensive, filthy, immoral, indelicate, impure, unchaste, gross, disgusting, lubricious, off-color, risqué, vulgar, degenerate, dissolute, debauched, wanton, libertine, bawdy, blue, scabrous, erotic, sensual, carnal, dirty, libidinous, licentious, lecherous, lustful, lascivious, salacious, prurient, foul-mouthed, scurrilous, scatalogical, X-rated, adult. —**Ant.** modest, decent, moral, pure, chaste.

obscure, *adj.* **1.** unclear, uncertain, doubtful, dubious, ambiguous, vague, hazy, enigmatic, perplexing, baffling, confusing; cryptic, esoteric, arcane, recondite, abstruse, complex, intricate, unfamiliar, mysterious. **2.** inconspicuous, unnoticeable, unnoticed, unknown, undistinguished, undistinguishable, unnoted. **3.** remote, retired, secluded. **4.** indistinct, blurred, blurry, imperfect, dim, veiled. **5.** dark, murky, dim, clouded, cloudy, gloomy, dusky, somber, shadowy, lurid, unilluminated, dismal. —**Ant.** clear, certain, unambiguous, conspicuous, noted; distinct; bright.

observant, *adj.* **1.** attentive, watchful, heedful, mindful, vigilant, aware. **2.** perceptive, quick, alert, on the qui vive, keen-eyed, eagle-eyed, sharp, shrewd. **3.** careful, obedient, respectful. —**Ant.** inattentive, careless; dull; disobedient.

observation, *n.* **1.** examination, inspection, survey, scrutiny, surveillance, noticing, perceiving, watching, regarding, attending. **2.** notice, observance, awareness, discovery, attention. **3.** information, record, memorandum. **4.** remark, comment, aside, note, reflection, opinion, sentiment, impression, declaration, pronunciamento, pronouncement, proclamation, word, utterance.

observe, *v.* **1.** perceive, notice, see, discover, detect. **2.** regard, witness, mark, watch, note, view. **3.** remark, comment, mention; utter, say. **4.** obey, comply, conform, follow, fulfill. **5.** solemnize, celebrate, keep, commemorate, mark, keep holy, recognize. —**Ant.** ignore.

obsession, *n.* fixed idea, idée fixe, fixation, compulsion, mania, passion, hang-up, preoccupation, domination, prepossession.

obsolete, *adj.* out of date, outdated, outmoded, passé, dead, antediluvian, extinct, old hat, superannuated, dated, discarded, superseded, antiquated, old-fashioned, ancient, old, archaic. —**Ant.** modern, new, up-to-date.

obstacle, *n.* obstruction, hindrance, impediment, interference, check, block, barrier, hurdle, snag, hitch, catch, Catch-22. —**Ant.** aid, support; license, franchise, permission.

obstinate, *adj.* mulish, obdurate, unyielding, recusant, stubborn, perverse, unbending, contumacious, inflexible, willful, headstrong, refractory, firm, intractable, resolute, pertinacious, persistent, dogged, tenacious, perverse, pigheaded, single-minded, contrary, fixed, recalcitrant, uncooperative, intransigent, adamant, set in one's ways, inexorable, steadfast, staunch, stiff, rigid. —**Ant.** submissive, flexible, tractable, irresolute.

obstruct, *v.* block, stop, close, occlude, choke, clog, bar, hinder, barricade, dam up; arrest, halt, prohibit, forbid, preclude, debar, impede, prevent; retard, slow, check, arrest, interrupt, hamper, stall, delay, interfere with. —**Ant.** encourage, help, support, further.

obstruction, *n.* **1.** obstacle, hindrance, barrier, occlusion, impediment, bar, check, stumbling block, hurdle, snag, bottleneck, limitation, constraint, restriction. **2.** stopping, cessation, proscription, check. —**Ant.** encouragement, furtherance; continuation.

obtain, *v.* get, acquire, procure, secure, gain, achieve, earn, win, attain, come by, grasp, capture, seize, take possession of, get one's hands on. —**Ant.** lose, forgo.

obtrusive, *adj.* **1.** meddlesome, meddling, intrusive, interfering, impertinent, importunate, forceful, invasive, interruptive, disruptive, presumptuous, officious, forward, prying, pushy, nosy. **2.** protruding, projecting; prominent, pronounced, noticeable, conspicuous, blatant, ostentatious, showy, flashy, loud. —**Ant.** reticent, circumspect.

obvious, *adj.* plain, manifest, evident, clear, open, apparent, patent, palpable, perceptible, distinct, unmistakable, self-evident, barefaced, clear-cut, conspicuous, visible, overt, ostensible, prominent, glaring, undeniable, sim-

occasion, *n.* **1.** occurrence, event, time, incident, moment, circumstance. **2.** opportunity, advantage, chance, convenience, opening. **3.** ground, reason, cause, motive, call, justification, provocation, impulse, stimulus, inducement, influence. —*v.* **4.** bring about, cause, motivate, originate, create, move, give rise to, produce, effect, prompt, provoke, evoke, induce, generate, engender, impel. —**Ant.** suppress.

occult, *adj.* **1.** mysterious, hidden, concealed, secret, undisclosed, unrevealed, unknown; dark, private, obscure, abstruse, shadowy, mysterious, esoteric, arcane, weird, strange, fantastic, mystical, recondite, cabalistic, veiled, shrouded. **2.** supernatural, metaphysical, preternatural, transcendental, alchemical, magical, unnatural. —**Ant.** natural.

occupation, *n.* **1.** job, position, post, situation, appointment, line, field, career, work, calling, trade, business, profession, métier, vocation, employment, pursuit, craft. **2.** possession, tenure, use, control, rule, subjugation, oppression, bondage, occupancy. **3.** seizure, invasion, capture, conquest, takeover, appropriation.

occupy, *v.* **1.** take up, use, engage, employ, busy, absorb, monopolize, catch, grip, involve, engross, interest. **2.** possess, capture, seize, keep, take hold of, conquer, invade, overrun, take over.

occur, *v.* **1.** come to pass, take place, happen, befall, arise, chance, develop, materialize, surface, transpire. **2.** appear, be met with, be found, arise, offer, meet the eye.

occurrence, *n.* event, incident, circumstance, affair, proceeding, transaction, happening, phenomenon, matter, experience, instance, development, manifestation, materialization, appearance.

odd, *adj.* **1.** different, extraordinary, unusual, strange, weird, unexpected, atypical, exotic, anomalous, idiosyncratic, deviant, outlandish, uncanny, abnormal, freakish, offbeat, peculiar, singular, unique, queer, quaint, eccentric, uncommon, rare, fantastic, bizarre, whimsical. **2.** occasional, casual, irregular, sporadic, random, part-time, varied, miscellaneous, incidental, sundry. —**Ant.** ordinary, common, unexceptional, usual.

odious, *adj.* **1.** hateful, despicable, detestable, execrable, abominable, invidious. **2.** obnoxious, offensive, disgusting, loathsome, repellent, repulsive, forbidding, noisome, vile, base, nasty, distasteful. —**Ant.** attractive, lovable; inviting.

odor, *n.* smell, aroma, fragrance, redolence, scent, perfume, bouquet; stench, stink, fetor.

offbeat, *adj.* unusual, unconventional, uncommon, unexpected, strange, bizarre, weird, peculiar, odd, queer, unorthodox, idiosyncratic, Bohemian, outre, outlandish, deviant, novel, innovative, original, fresh, different, extraordinary, out of the ordinary, out of the way, rare, special, eccentric, unique, far-out, off the wall, freaky, kinky. —**Ant.** commonplace, conventional.

offend, *v.* **1.** irritate, annoy, vex, chafe, provoke, nettle, mortify, pique, needle, rankle, ruffle, outrage, rile, anger, rattle, miff, gall, fret; displease, affront, insult, hurt, slight, snub, give offense, pain, chagrin, disgruntle, embarrass, humiliate. **2.** sin, transgress, err, stumble. —**Ant.** please, delight, compliment.

offense, *n.* **1.** transgression, wrong, sin, trespass, misdemeanor, crime, fault, felony, violation, breach, infraction, wrongdoing, peccadillo, misdeed, infringement, dereliction, lapse, slip, error. **2.** displeasure, unpleasantness, umbrage, resentment, wrath, indignation, anger, ire, annoyance, irritation, pique. **3.** attack, assault, onset, aggression. —**Ant.** delight, pleasure; defense.

offensive, *adj.* **1.** displeasing, irritating, annoying, vexing, vexatious, unpleasant, disrespectful, uncivil, discourteous, impolite, objectionable, impertinent, rude, insolent, hateful, detestable, opprobrious, insulting, abusive. **2.** disagreeable, distasteful, disgusting, repulsive, obnoxious, unsavory, foul, vile, fetid, rank, rancid, putrid, putrescent, rotten, unpalatable, unpleasant, revolting, repellent, nauseating, nauseous, sickening, loathsome. **3.** repugnant, insulting, execrable, abominable, shocking, revolting. **4.** antagonistic, hostile, contentious, quarrelsome, combative, warlike, martial, bellicose, belligerent, provocative, threatening, aggressive, assailant, invading, attacking. —**Ant.** pleasing, pleasant, polite, courteous; agreeable, tasteful, attractive; delightful; defensive.

offer, *v.* **1.** present, proffer, tender, bid. **2.** propose, give, move, put forward, tender. **3.** volunteer, sacrifice, immolate, present. —*n.* **4.** presentation, proposal, proposition, overture; bid. —**Ant.** refuse; refusal, denial.

offhand, *adj.* **1.** casual, nonchalant, informal, unceremonious, relaxed, easygoing, unstudied, laid-back, blasé, insouciant, lighthearted, superficial, cursory, cavalier. **2.** unpremeditated, spontaneous, impromptu, improvisatory, extemporaneous, impulsive, ad lib, spur of the moment, off the cuff, ad hoc. —**Ant.** studied, formal.

office, *n.* **1.** business, department, firm, company, establishment, house, corporation, organization. **2.** position, post, station, berth, situation. **3.** responsibility, charge, appointment, trust, obligation, commission, employment, occupation, assignment, chore, job, place, role, function, purpose, bit, service, task, work, duty.

officious, *adj.* forward, obtrusive, forceful, direct, interfering, meddlesome, meddling, bold, aggressive, insistent, persistent, demanding, importunate, intrusive, dictatorial. —**Ant.** retiring, discreet, aloof.

often, *adv.* regularly, many times, habitually, commonly, ordinarily, continually, continuously, again and again, over and over, time and again, time after time, day in and day out, most of the time, mostly, frequently, generally, usually, repeatedly, customarily. —**Ant.** seldom.

ointment, *n.* unguent, emollient, salve, balm, lotion, cream, demulcent.

old, *adj.* **1.** aged, elderly, aging, senior, advanced in years, gray, past one's prime, over the hill, superannuated. **2.** familiar, known. **3.** former, past, ancient, primeval, olden, primitive, antediluvian, antiquated, passé, antique, old-fashioned. **4.** deteriorated, dilapidated, worn, decayed. **5.** experienced, practiced, skilled, adroit, veteran, proficient, adept. —**Ant.** new, modern; inexperienced, green.

old-fashioned, *adj.* outmoded, outdated, stale, tired, unfashionable, dead, superseded, obsolescent, stuffy, obsolete, antique, passé, antiquated, old, ancient, archaic, old-hat, timeworn, out. —**Ant.** modern.

omen, *n.* sign, augury, foreboding, portent, token, indication, harbinger, premonition, foreshadowing, warning, forewarning, handwriting on the wall, presage, prognostication.

ominous, *adj.* **1.** foreboding, fateful, dark, black, gloomy, lowering, menacing, sinister, threatening; unfavorable, ill-omened, ill-starred, inauspicious, unpropitious. **2.** significant, foreboding, portentous, prophetic, oracular, meaningful, indicative. —**Ant.** favorable, propitious; insignificant, meaningless.

only, *adv.* **1.** alone, solely, just, exclusively. **2.** merely, barely, simply, but, just, no more than. **3.** singly, uniquely. —*adj.* **4.** sole, single, unique, solitary, lone. **5.** distinct, exclusive, alone. —*conj.* **6.** but, excepting *or* except that, however, on the other hand, on the contrary.

ooze, *v.* **1.** percolate, exude, seep, drip, drop, weep, secrete, bleed, leak, drain, trickle. —*n.* **2.** mire, slime, mud, muck, sludge, slush, goo, gunk, glop. —**Ant.** pour, flood.

open, *adj.* **1.** unclosed, uncovered, unenclosed. **2.** accessible, available, public, unrestricted, free. **3.** unfilled, unoccupied, vacant, untaken, available, free, clear. **4.** undecided, unsettled, undetermined, debatable, disputable, arguable, moot, up in the air. **5.** liable, subject to, unprotected, bare, undefended, exposed. **6.** unreserved, candid, frank, ingenuous, artless, guileless, unconcealed, undisguised; sincere, honest, fair, aboveboard. **7.** expanded, extended, spread out, unclosed. **8.** generous, liberal, free, bounteous, bountiful, munificent, magnanimous, open-handed. **9.** obvious, evident, clear, apparent, plain. —*v.* **10.** unclose, unlock, unfasten, uncover, untie, undo, pull out. **11.** uncover, lay bare, bare, expose, reveal, divulge, disclose. **12.** expand, extend, spread out. **13.** begin, start, commence, initiate, inaugurate, launch, activate, kick off, establish, get the show on the road *or* the ball rolling. —**Ant.** closed; close.

opening, *n.* **1.** gap, hole, aperture, orifice, perforation; slit, slot, break, crack, crevice, fissure, split, separation, chink, cranny, breach, rift, chasm, cleft, fissure, rent. **2.** beginning, start, birth; origin, outset, onset, launch, debut, presentation, commencement, initiation, dawn. **3.** vacancy, chance, opportunity, occasion, foothold, break, foot in the door. —**Ant.** closing.

operate, *v.* **1.** work, run, use, act, function, perform, go, serve. **2.** manage, carry on, run, direct, conduct, control, handle, manipulate, drive. —**Ant.** fail, break.

operation, *n.* **1.** action, process, procedure, manipulation, performance, proceeding. **2.** efficacy, influence, virtue, effect, force, action. **3.** undertaking, enterprise, project, venture, procedure, deal, course, transaction, business, affair, maneuver. —**Ant.** failure.

operative, *adj.* operating, exerting, influencing, influential; effective, efficacious, efficient, effectual, serviceable. —**Ant.** inoperative; ineffectual, inefficient.

opiate, *n.* narcotic, drug, anodyne, sedative, sedation, soporific, dope, downer. —**Ant.** stimulant.

opinion, *n.* sentiment, point of view, conclusion, persuasion, belief, judgment, notion, conception, idea, impression, estimation, thought, conviction, perception, theory, way of thinking, viewpoint.

opinionated, *adj.* obstinate, stubborn, conceited, dogmatic, pigheaded, doctrinaire, inflexible, cocksure, obdurate, dictatorial, dogged, mulish, overbearing; one-sided, partial, partisan, prejudiced, biased, bigoted. —**Ant.** liberal, open-minded, unprejudiced.

opponent, *n.* adversary, antagonist, competitor, rival, disputant, contender, competition, contestant; enemy, foe, the opposition, the other side. —**Ant.** ally, friend, associate.

opportune, *adj.* 1. appropriate, favorable, advantageous, suitable, apt, suited, fit, fitting, fitted, fortunate, propitious, auspicious, felicitous, beneficial, helpful, profitable, lucky. 2. convenient, timely, well-timed, lucky, felicitous, seasonable, germane. —**Ant.** inopportune, inappropriate; inconvenient.

opportunity, *n.* chance, occasion, time, opportune moment, moment, opening, possibility, break.

oppose, *v.* 1. resist, counter, object to, defy, take a stand against, resist, contest, attack, counterattack, fight, grapple with, contend against, combat, withstand, thwart, confront, contravene, interfere with, oppugn. 2. hinder, obstruct, prevent, check, bar, block, impede, stop, restrain, inhibit, restrict, obviate, thwart, foil, frustrate. 3. offset, contrast, counterbalance, match, play off against, pit against. 3. contradict, gainsay, deny, refuse. —**Ant.** support, aid, help.

opposite, *adj.* 1. facing, fronting, vis-à-vis. 2. contrary, reverse, incompatible, irreconcilable, inconsistent, unlike, contradictory, antithetical, divergent, diverse, differing, different. 3. opposed, adverse, refractory, hostile, antagonistic, inimical. —**Ant.** compatible, consistent, like, same; friendly, amiable.

opposition, *n.* 1. antagonism, hostility, resistance, counteraction, disapproval, objection, conflict, defiance, antipathy, adversity. 2. competition, enemy, foe, opponent, adversary, antagonist. 3. offset, antithesis, contrast. 4. contrariety, inconsistency, incompatibility, difference. —**Ant.** help, support, furtherance; consistency, compatibility.

oppress, *v.* 1. depress, weigh down, burden, afflict, trouble, overload, encumber, weary, overwhelm, pressure. 2. maltreat, harass, abuse, harry, persecute, wrong. 3. overwhelm, crush, overpower, subdue, suppress, repress, subjugate, tyrannize, enslave, trample, ride roughshod over. —**Ant.** delight; liberate.

oppression, *n.* 1. repression, suppression, subjection, subjugation, enslavement, maltreatment, abuse, injury, pain, cruelty, injustice, tyranny, despotism, persecution, severity. 2. hardship, affliction, wretchedness, woe, misery, suffering, calamity. 3. depression, sadness, misery, torment, torture, anguish, angst, gloom. —**Ant.** kindness, justice; happiness, joy.

optimistic, *adj.* hopeful, upbeat, sanguine, full of hope, expectant, confident, sunny, rosy, cheerful, positive, buoyant, bright, trustful, secure, bullish, idealistic, quixotic, Pollyannaish, Panglossian. —**Ant.** pessimistic, discouraged, doubtful, hopeless.

option, *n.* choice, selection, preference, alternative, opportunity, recourse, way out, privilege.

opulent, *adj.* 1. wealthy, rich, affluent, moneyed, prosperous, well-off, well-to-do, comfortable, well-heeled, flush, loaded, in the chips; lavish, deluxe, splendid, fancy, magnificent, grand, swanky, posh, ritzy, plush, sumptuous, luxurious. 2. abundant, copious, plentiful, bountiful, prolific, profuse. —**Ant.** poor, squalid; scarce.

oral, *adj.* verbal, spoken, mouthed, uttered, said, vocal, voiced, enunciated, articulated, word-of-mouth, viva voce. —**Ant.** tacit, silent, taciturn.

oration, *n.* speech, address, lecture, discourse, declamation, harangue, declaration, recitation, monologue, sermon, spiel.

orbit, *n.* 1. circuit, revolution, track, circle, round, cycle, ellipse, path, course. —*v.* 2. revolve, go around, encircle, circle, circumvent.

ordain, *v.* 1. appoint, call, nominate, elect, select, destine. 2. decree, order, enact, prescribe, determine. 3. predestine, predetermine, destine, fate.

ordeal, *n.* trial, test, tribulation, hardship, affliction, trouble, distress, misery, suffering, anguish, angst, grief, misfortune, disaster, calamity, adversity, tragedy, difficulty, ill fortune, judgment.

order, *n.* 1. direction, injunction, mandate, law, ukase, dictate, edict, fiat, directive, command, instruction, rule, canon, prescription. 2. succession, sequence. 3. method, arrangement, harmony, regularity, symmetry. 4. disposition, array, arrangement. 5. category, caste, level, group, order, hierarchy, scale, class, kind, sort, genus, subclass; tribe, family. 6. rank, status, importance, standing, position, grade, class, degree. 7. fraternity, sorority, fellowship, association, guild, company, society, brotherhood, sisterhood, association, community. 8. peace, calm, serenity, quiet, tranquility, discipline, lawfulness, peacefulness. —*v.* 9. direct, command, instruct, bid, require; ordain. 10. regulate, conduct, manage, run, operate, adjust, arrange, systematize, organize, classify, categorize, sort out, codify.

orderly, *adj.* 1. regular, systematic, methodical, harmonious, symmetrical, uniform, neat, tidy, shipshape. 2. well-regulated, neat, trim, organized, well-organized. 3. well-disciplined, well-trained, well-behaved, disciplined, law-abiding, peaceable, civilized, civil, decorous, well-mannered, polite, tranquil, nonviolent. —**Ant.** irregular, unsystematic; sloppy, unregulated; undisciplined.

ordinary, *adj.* 1. common, usual, customary, regular, normal, expected, general, routine, standard, conventional, orthodox, traditional, typical, everyday, familiar, set, established, bourgeois, modest, plain, simple, accustomed, habitual, frequent. 2. inferior, second-rate, mean, midding, prosaic, commonplace, run-of-the-mill, average, workaday, passable, so-so, fair, undistinguished, pedestrian, bland, insipid, garden-variety, humdrum, mediocre, indifferent. 3. plain, homely, common-looking, commonplace. —**Ant.** uncommon, extraordinary, unusual; superior; beautiful.

organic, *adj.* 1. systematic, systematized, organized, coherent, integrated, consistent, orderly, structured. 2. constitutional, structural, inherent, fundamental, essential, vital, radical, integral, basic, elementary, innate, native, visceral. —**Ant.** inorganic.

organize, *v.* 1. coordinate, harmonize, unite, structure, standardize, arrange, classify, codify, catalogue, construct, form, dispose, constitute, make, shape, frame, systematize, order. 2. establish, found, form, institute, create, originate, initiate, build, develop, put together, set up. —**Ant.** destroy, ruin; disorder.

origin, *n.* 1. source, rise, fountainhead, derivation, beginning, root, basis, base, wellspring, fount, creation, genesis, dawn, origination, start, commencement, inception, outset, launching, cradle, foundation, birthplace. 2. parentage, birth, extraction, lineage, heritage, descent, ancestry, pedigree, genealogy, stock. —**Ant.** end; posterity.

original, *adj.* 1. primary, initial, first, earliest, basic, beginning; native, indigenous, primordial, primeval, primitive, aboriginal. 2. new, fresh, novel, inventive, creative, innovative, unique, imaginative, unusual, ingenious. —*n.* 3. archetype, pattern, prototype, model, source, master. —**Ant.** secondary; old, old-fashioned.

originate, *v.* 1. arise, spring, rise, begin, emanate, flow, proceed, stem, issue, emerge, emanate, develop, derive, result. 2. initiate, invent, discover, create, author, engender, conceive, introduce, coin, devise, pioneer, design, concoct, mastermind, compose, organize, formulate, generate, produce, develop. —**Ant.** terminate; follow.

ornament, *n.* 1. accessory, detail, embellishment, adornment, enhancement, trimming, gingerbread, garnish, frill, embroidery, beautification, frippery, bauble, trinket, decoration, ornamentation, design. —*v.* 2. decorate, adorn, embellish, beautify, trim, garnish, grace, bedeck, enhance, embroider, elaborate, accessorize, dress up. —**Ant.** essential, necessity.

ornate, *adj.* elaborate, adorned, embellished, showy, splendid, flamboyant, highfalutin, intricate, sumptuous, elegant, decorated, florid, flowery, overdone, rococo, baroque, fancy, lavish, rich, busy, fussy, frilly, gaudy, garish. —**Ant.** simple, plain.

orthodox, *adj.* conventional, regular, customary, expected, accepted, recognized, approved, sanctioned, canonical, received, authoritative, doctrinaire, official, prevailing, prevalent, doctrinal, traditional, standard, conformable, conformist, conforming, correct, common, ordinary, popular, kosher, conservative, reactionary, die-hard, hidebound, pedantic. —**Ant.** freethinking, unconventional, rebellious.

ostensible, *adj.* apparent, outward, external, superficial, patent, evident, clear, plain, manifest, conspicuous, obvious, prominent, noticeable; professed, pretended, plausible. —**Ant.** concealed, hidden, implausible.

ostentation, *n.* pretension, pretentiousness, semblance, exhibition, exhibitionism, flaunting, flashiness, show, showiness, pretense, pretext, display, pageantry, pomp, pompousness, flourish, flamboyance, window dressing.

ostracize, *v.* banish, exile, expatriate, disenfranchise, excommunicate, expel, blackball, blacklist, boycott, isolate, segregate, exclude, avoid, shun, snub, cut, cold-shoulder. —**Ant.** accept, welcome.

outcome, *n.* end, result, consequence, issue, aftereffect, effect, upshot, development, aftermath, outgrowth, product, wake, pay off, bottom line.

outdo, *v.* surpass, excel, exceed, beat, outstrip, outdistance, overcome, defeat, transcend, outshine, top, cap, trump.

outgoing, adj. friendly, sociable, approachable, open, gregarious, genial, amiable, cordial, warm, affable, familiar, informal, amicable, accessible, easygoing, communicative, talkative, extroverted, demonstrative, expansive, effusive. **—Ant.** restrained, shy, reserved.

outlaw, n. **1.** criminal, gangster, desperado, fugitive, renegade, pirate, mugger, mobster, mafioso, con artist, highwayman, holdup man, robber, thief, bandit, brigand. —v. **2.** forbid, ban, disallow, bar, exclude, interdict, proscribe, prohibit.

outline, n. **1.** contour, silhouette. **2.** plan, draft, drawing, rough, sketch, cartoon. —v. **3.** delineate, draft, draw, sketch, trace, profile, rough out, define, lay out.

outrage, n. **1.** violence, violation. **2.** affront, insult, offense, abuse, indignity. —v. **3.** shock, abuse, maltreat, injure, offend, ravish, rape.

outspoken, adj. frank, open, unreserved, candid, straightforward, plainspeaking, specific, unequivocal, direct, forthright, explicit, blunt, brusque, tactless, crude. **—Ant.** reserved, taciturn.

outstanding, adj. **1.** renowned, famous, memorable, celebrated, distinguished, special, noteworthy, important, exceptional, first-rate, superb, remarkable, extraordinary, sensational, super, prominent, eminent, conspicuous, striking. **2.** unsettled, unpaid, owing, due, unresolved, ongoing, leftover. **—Ant.** inconspicuous; paid, settled.

overbearing, adj. domineering, dictatorial, repressive, dogmatic, bullying, officious, highhanded, overweening, magisterial, despotic, autocratic, peremptory, arbitrary, cavalier, pretentious, pushy, haughty, arrogant, imperious, supercilious. **—Ant.** humble, servile.

overcome, v. **1.** conquer, defeat, beat, triumph over, subjugate, suppress, subdue, vanquish, rout, crush. **2.** surmount. **3.** overpower, overwhelm, discomfit.

overlook, v. **1.** omit, slip upon, pass over, forget, fail to notice, slight, disregard, miss, neglect, ignore. **2.** excuse, forgive, pardon, permit, allow, condone, write off, gloss over. **—Ant.** regard, attend.

overpower, v. overcome, overwhelm, vanquish, subjugate, subdue, conquer, master, rout, crush, defeat, beat, quell, prevail.

overrule, v. disallow, rescind, revoke, repeal, recall, repudiate, set aside, nullify, cancel, annul. **—Ant.** allow, permit, approve.

oversee, v. supervise, direct, manage, superintend, survey, watch, overlook, administer, operate, run, control, handle.

oversight, n. **1.** mistake, blunder, slip, error, erratum, omission, lapse, neglect, inadvertence, laxity, failure, dereliction, carelessness, fault, inattention. **2.** management, direction, control, superintendence, supervision, charge, surveillance, care, guidance, administration; protection, auspices, care, keeping, custody, hands. **—Ant.** attention.

overt, adj. evident, clear, obvious, clear-cut, patent, visible, open, plain, manifest, showing, apparent, public. **—Ant.** private, concealed, clandestine, secret.

overthrow, v. **1.** cast down, over-

come, defeat, vanquish, beat, rout, depose, overwhelm, conquer, master, oust, unseat, topple, overturn, dethrone, thrash, overpower, subjugate, crush. **2.** upset, overturn. **3.** knock down, demolish, destroy, raze, level. **4.** subvert, ruin, destroy. —n. **5.** deposition, fall, displacement. **6.** defeat, destruction, ruin, rout, downfall, end, fall, collapse, ouster, suppression, dispersion, demolition. **—Ant.** support.

overture, n. **1.** approach, advance, tender, opening, proposal, proposition, offer. **2.** prelude, introduction; prologue. **—Ant.** finale, termination, close, end, epilogue.

overturn, v. **1.** bring down, depose, dethrone, unseat, oust, eject, topple, ruin, defeat, overcome, overpower, overthrow, destroy, vanquish, conquer, upset. **2.** upset, capsize, founder, invert, upend, tip over, turn turtle.

overwhelm, v. **1.** overpower, crush, overcome, overtax, devastate, stagger, destroy, subdue, suppress, quash, quell, conquer, beat, oppress, weigh down, subdue, defeat, vanquish. **2.** overload, overburden, cover, bury, sink, drown, inundate, engulf, submerge, flood, deluge, swamp, immerse. **3.** stagger, astound, astonish, bewilder, dumbfound, stun, shock, nonplus, confound, bowl over, knock one's socks off, blow one's mind, surprise, discombobulate.

own, v. **1.** have, hold, possess. **2.** acknowledge, admit, allow, confess, concede, avow; recognize.

pace, n. **1.** step, tempo, speed, velocity, clip, rate; gait. **2.** step, stride, walk, trot, jog, singlefoot, amble, rack, canter, gallop, run. —v. **3.** step, plod, trudge, walk, move, go, stride, tread, traverse.

pacific, adj. **1.** conciliatory, appeasing. **2.** peaceable, peaceful, calm, tranquil, at peace, quiet, unruffled, gentle, serene, still, smooth, soothing. **—Ant.** hostile; agitated, perturbed.

pacify, v. **1.** quiet, calm, tranquilize, assuage, still, smooth, moderate, soften, ameliorate, mollify, meliorate, better, soothe. **2.** appease, conciliate. **—Ant.** agitate, perturb, aggravate, worsen; anger, provoke.

pack, n. **1.** package, bundle, parcel, packet; knapsack, backpack, rucksack, duffel bag. **2.** set, gang, collection, crowd, throng, horde, mass, flock, herd, lots, loads, party, drove, mob, swarm, bevy, gathering, congregation, group, band, company, crew, squad. —v. **3.** stow, compress, compact, jam, stuff, fill, squeeze, ram, press, wedge, tamp, cram. **4.** load, burden, lade.

package, n. bundle, parcel, packet, pack, bale, container, case, crate, carton, box.

pact, n. agreement, compact, contract, deal, arrangement, treaty, entente, understanding, deal, concord, bond, covenant, league, union, concordat, alliance, bargain.

pagan, n. **1.** heathen, idolater, gentile, unbeliever, polytheist, infidel, barbarian. —adj. **2.** heathen, heathenish, gentile, irreligious, idolatrous, infidel, polytheistic. **—Ant.** believer; pious, religious.

pageant, n. **1.** spectacle, extravaganza, show, masque, tableau, ritual, ceremony, formality, event, affair,

gala, presentation. **2.** display, show, procession, parade.

pain, n. **1.** suffering, distress, hurt, discomfort, soreness, smarting, spasm, cramp, affliction, woe, grief, wretchedness, tribulation, trial, discomposure, ordeal, torture, misery, anguish, agony, torment, throe, pang, ache, twinge, stitch. **2.** (plural) care, efforts, trouble, exertion, toil, labor. —v. **3.** afflict, torture, torment, distress, hurt, harm, injure, trouble, grieve, aggrieve, disquiet, discommode, incommode, inconvenience, displease, worry, tease, irritate, vex, annoy, wound, cut to the quick. **—Ant.** joy, delight, pleasure; ease; please.

painful, adj. **1.** distressing, torturous, agonizing, tormenting, stinging, throbbing, burning, piercing, stabbing, raw, bitter, excruciating. **2.** laborious, difficult, arduous, severe, rigorous, careful, painstaking. **—Ant.** pleasant, soothing; easy, simple.

painstaking, adj. careful, assiduous, sedulous, strenuous, industrious, meticulous, diligent, conscientious, thorough, exacting, earnest, detailed, demanding, rigorous, arduous. **—Ant.** careless, frivolous.

pair, n. **1.** twosome, matched set, duo, twins, double, dyad, couple, brace, span, yoke, two, tandem, team. —v. **2.** match, mate, couple, marry, join, pair off, partner, unite, yoke, twin, team, double.

palatable, adj. agreeable, savory, sapid, tasty, gustatory, luscious, delicious, delectable, flavorsome, edible, yummy. **—Ant.** unpalatable, distasteful, tasteless, flavorless.

palatial, adj. magnificent, grand, imposing, noble, stately, majestic, splendid, splendiferous, sumptuous, luxurious, deluxe, opulent, elegant, lavish, impressive, extravagant, swank, posh, ritzy, classy. **—Ant.** humble, simple.

pale, adj. **1.** pallid, wan, white, ashy, ashen, colorless, faded, washed out, sallow, pasty-faced, whey-faced, haggard, ghastly, ghostly, bloodless, anemic, drained. **2.** dim, faint, feeble, obscure, weak, ineffective, inadequate, puny, insignificant, lame, poor, halfhearted, tame, lifeless, empty, spiritless, uninspired, sterile. **—Ant.** ruddy, hale, hearty; robust.

pall, n. **1.** shroud, blanket, cover, covering, veil. —v. **2.** glut, satiate, fill, cloy, sate, surfeit, overstuff, gorge. **3.** weary, tire, fatigue, wear on, jade, bore, irk, irritate, sicken.

palliate, v. **1.** moderate, abate, relieve, alleviate, ease, modify, reduce, diminish, lessen, mitigate, soften, cushion. **2.** qualify, hedge, temper, season, excuse, sugarcoat, gloss over, prettify, whitewash, varnish, camouflage. **—Ant.** intensify, worsen.

pallid, adj. **1.** pale, faded, washed out, colorless, white, whitish, ashen, sallow, wan, pasty, ghastly, whey-faced. **2.** dull, colorless, insipid, anemic, unexciting, flat, lifeless, bland, weak, feeble, nondescript, jejune, monotonous, humdrum. **—Ant.** robust.

palpable, adj. **1.** obvious, evident, manifest, plain, unmistakable. **2.** tangible, material, real, bodily, substantial, objective, somatic, solid, tactile, corporeal, fleshy, physical, concrete. **—Ant.** obscure, unclear; intangible, spiritual.

paltry, adj. trifling, petty, minor, trashy, mean, worthless, contemptible, insignificant, unimportant, trivial, inconsiderable, slight, small, pitiful, pathetic, pitiable, puny, sorry, wretched, miserable, inconsequential, meager, beggarly, base, low, contemptible, piddling, penny-ante, Mickey Mouse. **—Ant.** important, major, significant, considerable, essential.

pamper, *v.* indulge, gratify, humor, coddle, baby, cater to, spoil, pet. **—Ant.** discipline.

pan, *v.* criticize, find fault, deprecate, censure, put down, fault, disparage, denigrate, disdain, despise, excoriate, reject, ridicule, knock, rap, flame, flay, roast, trash. **—Ant.** praise, extol.

panache, *n.* sophistication, savoir-faire, cultivation, taste, smartness, swagger, spirit, brio, gusto, zest, energy, cachet, éclat, showiness, dash, flair, style, flamboyance, dazzle, showmanship, élan, verve, bravura, brilliance, virtuosity.

pang, *n.* **1.** pain, stab, stitch, twinge, prick, throe. **2.** qualm, scruple, compunction, scrupulousness, hesitation, misgiving, remorse, regret, contrition, guilt, mortification, anguish, malaise, discomfort.

panic, *n.* **1.** terror, fright, alarm, fear, dread, horror, hysteria, consternation, anxiety, nervousness, apprehension. **—***v.* **2.** terrorize, frighten, alarm, unnerve. **—Ant.** security; soothe, calm.

pant, *v.* **1.** gasp, breathe heavily, puff, huff, heave, wheeze, blow. **2.** long, yearn, thirst, crave, hanker after, yearn for, ache for, want, covet, pine for, long for, be dying for, have one's heart set on, give one's eyeteeth for, sigh for, hunger, desire.

paradigm, *n.* model, ideal, guide, archetype, example, exemplar, standard, pattern, blueprint, criterion, classic example, locus classicus.

paragon, *n.* epitome, archetype, prototype, quintessence, standard, exemplar, criterion, model, ideal, pattern, nonesuch, masterpiece.

parallel, *adj.* **1.** corresponding, similar, analogous, like, resembling, correspondent. **—***n.* **2.** match, counterpart, analogue, equivalent, equal, complement. **3.** correspondence, analogy, similarity, resemblance, likeness. **—***v.* **4.** match, resemble, repeat, echo, duplicate, correspond to, imitate. **5.** equal, be equivalent to. **—Ant.** unique, unlike, singular, unusual; dissimilarity; differ.

paralyze, *v.* stun, shock, benumb, unnerve, deaden, stop in one's tracks, stiffen, immobilize, freeze, disable, cripple, incapacitate, deactivate, transfix.

paramount, *adj.* supreme, dominant, main, predominant, first, prime, primary, cardinal, essential, basic, requisite, vital, superior, preeminent, chief, principal. **—Ant.** base, inferior, unimportant.

paraphernalia, *n.* belongings, effects; equipment, apparatus, accessories, gear, chattels, baggage, impediments, appointments, appurtenances, accouterments, trappings, rig, equipage, stuff, junk.

paraphrase, *n.* **1.** rendering, version, translation, rewrite, rehash, rendition, rephrase. **—***v.* **2.** restate, approximate, rephrase, reword, render, translate; explain, explicate, interpret.

parasite, *n.* yes-man, sycophant, leech, hanger-on, bloodsucker, toady, flatterer, flunky, freeloader, sponge, cadger, scrounger, jackal, hyena.

parcel, *n.* **1.** package, bundle, pack, packet. **2.** quantity, lot, group, batch, collection. **3.** lot, plot, tract, acreage, portion, land. **—***v.* **4.** divide, distribute, mete out, apportion, deal out, allot, dole out, hand out, share, divvy up.

pardon, *n.* **1.** indulgence, allowance, excuse, forgiveness; remission, amnesty, absolution. **—***v.* **2.** forgive, absolve, remit, indulge, allow, let off, condone, excuse, overlook; acquit, clear, release, exonerate, exculpate. **—Ant.** censure, blame.

pare, *v.* **1.** peel; clip, cut, trim, shuck, shave. **2.** diminish, lessen, clip, reduce, decrease, curtail, slash, lower. **—Ant.** increase.

parentage, *n.* birth, descent, lineage, ancestry, origin, extraction, heritage, patrimony, genealogy, family tree, line, derivation, pedigree, family, stock, strain, bloodline, roots.

pariah, *n.* outcast, undesirable, untouchable, castaway, castoff, Ishmael, persona non grata, leper, outsider, excommunicate.

parity, *n.* equality, equivalence, correspondence, similarity, analogy, parallelism, likeness, sameness, uniformity, par, congruity, similitude, congruence, conformity. **—Ant.** in equality, dissimilarity, difference.

parley, *n.* **1.** conference, discussion, talk, conversation, discourse, dialogue, palaver, deliberation, meeting, colloquy, powwow, huddle. **—***v.* **2.** confer, discuss, speak, converse, talk, discourse, negotiate, deal.

parody, *n.* travesty, burlesque, imitation, caricature, lampoon, satire, mockery, mimicry, spoof, take-off, sendup, distortion, roast.

paroxysm, *n.* fit, spasm, attack, access, seizure, throe, convulsion, spell, fugue, outburst, eruption, irruption, explosion, storm, flare-up.

parsimonious, *adj.* sparing, frugal, stingy, tight, tightfisted, close, niggardly, miserly, illiberal, mean, closefisted, cheap, economical, thrifty, penurious. **—Ant.** generous, openhanded, unsparing.

part, *n.* **1.** portion, division, piece, fragment, fraction, section, allotment, share, percentage, scrap, shard, factor, constituent, component, ingredient, element, member, organ. **2.** allotment, share, apportionment, portion, lot, dividend, concern, participation, interest, stock. **3.** (*usually plural*) region, quarter, neighborhood, area, corner, vicinity, neck of the woods, district, section. **4.** duty, function, role, office, responsibility, charge. **—***v.* **5.** divide, break, cleave, separate, sever, sunder, disunite, dissociate, dissever, disconnect, disjoin, detach. **6.** share, allot, portion, parcel out, apportion, distribute, deal out, mete out. **7.** depart, leave, go, quit; pass on *or* away, die, go to Glory, go to meet one's Maker. **—Ant.** all, none, nothing, everything.

partial, *adj.* **1.** incomplete, unfinished, fragmentary, imperfect, limited. **2.** biased, prejudiced, one-sided, unfair, unjust, influenced, partisan, discriminatory, inclined. **—Ant.** complete, perfect; unbiased, unprejudiced, liberal, just, fair.

partiality, *n.* bias, favor, prejudice, one-sidedness, injustice, unfairness, favoritism, predisposition, leaning. **2.** fondness, liking, preference, bent, leaning, tendency, predilection, inclination, taste, relish, appreciation, fancy, love, weakness, soft spot, penchant. **—Ant.** justice, fairness; dislike, disfavor.

particle, *n.* mite, whit, jot, iota, tittle, bit, mote, grain, ace, scrap, scintilla, spark, suggestion, hint, suspicion, gleam, crumb, dot, spot, morsel, shred, sliver, smidgen, speck, molecule, atom.

particular, *adj.* **1.** special, specific, certain, peculiar, singular, isolated, individual, distinct, definite, precise, express. **2.** one, individual, single, separate, distinct, discrete. **3.** noteworthy, marked, unusual, notable, extraordinary; peculiar, singular, strange, odd, uncommon. **4.** exceptional, especial, characteristic, distinctive. **5.** certain, personal, special. **6.** detailed, descriptive, minute, circumstantial, critical, scrupulous, strict, careful, exact, precise. **7.** demanding, fussing, meticulous, selective, hypercritical, critical, finical, finicky, discriminating, dainty, nice, fastidious, scrupulous. **—***n.* **8.** point, detail, circumstance, item, feature, particularity, specific, element, fact, information. **—Ant.** general, overall; common, ordinary; inexact, imprecise; undiscriminating, indiscriminate.

particularly, *adv.* **1.** exceptionally, especially, specially. **2.** specially, especially, individually, characteristically, uniquely, separately, discretely, un

partisan, *n.* **1.** adherent, supporter, follower, disciple, devotee, backer, champion, enthusiast, fan, zealot, booster. **—***adj.* **2.** biased, partial, one-sided, sectarian, opinionated, prejudiced, parochial, myopic, shortsighted, narrowminded, limited. **—Ant.** leader; unbiased, impartial.

partition, *n.* **1.** division, distribution, portion, share, allotment, apportionment. **2.** separation, division, split-up, partitioning, breakup, segmentation. **3.** part, section, division, segment, piece. **4.** barrier, wall, dividing wall, screen. **—***v.* **5.** divide, separate, apportion, portion, parcel out, deal out, mete out, share. **—Ant.** unity; unite.

partner, *n.* **1.** sharer, partaker, associate, accessory, accomplice, comrade, ally, companion, participant, colleague. **2.** husband, wife, spouse, lover, consort, companion, helpmate, helpmeet.

party, *n.* **1.** celebration, fete, gathering, function, reception, soirée, festivities, frolic, spree, romp, carousal, debauchery, orgy, get-together, bash, shindig, blowout, wingding, rave. **2.** group, gathering, assembly, assemblage, company. **3.** body, faction, circle, coterie, clique, set, combination, ring, league, alliance.

pass, *v.* **1.** go, move, proceed. **2.** disregard, pass over, skim over, skim, ignore. **3.** transcend, exceed, surpass, excel. **4.** spend; circulate. **5.** convey, transfer, transmit, send, deliver. **6.** sanction, approve, okay, enact. **7.** leave, go away, depart. **8.** end, terminate, expire, cease. **9.** go on, happen, take place, occur. **10.** vanish, fade, die, disappear. **—***n.* **11.** notch, defile, ravine, gorge, gulch, canyon, channel. **12.** permission, license, ticket, passport, visa. **13.** stage, state, juncture, situation, condition. **—Ant.** attend, regard, note, notice; disapprove; arrive, come; initiate, begin, start; appear.

passage, *n.* **1.** paragraph, verse, line, section, clause, text, extract, excerpt, selection, part, portion, sentence, phrase, citation, quotation. **2.** way, route, avenue, channel, road, path, byway, lane, street, thoroughfare. **3.** movement, transit, transition, passing. **4.** voyage, trip, tour, excursion, journey. **5.** progress, course, advance, elapse, flow, march. **6.** passing, ratification, adoption, legitimization, legalization, enactment.

passion, *n.* **1.** feeling, emotion, enthusiasm, zeal, ardor, ardency, eagerness, intensity, frenzy, fire, burning, fervor,

penniless

transport, rapture, excitement; hope, fear, joy, grief, anger, love, attachment, affection, fondness, warmth. **2.** anger, ire, resentment, fury, wrath, rage, vehemence, indignation, high dudgeon. **—Ant.** coolness, apathy.

passionate, *adj.* **1.** impassioned, emotional, ardent, vehement, excited, excitable, impulsive, fervent, fervid, zealous, warm, enthusiastic, earnest, glowing, burning, fiery; animated, impestuous, violent. **2.** quick-tempered, irascible, short-tempered, cross, quarrelsome, pugnacious, belligerent, temperamental, testy, touchy, choleric, hasty, hotheaded, fiery, peppery. **3.** sexual, erotic, sensual, amorous, lustful, lecherous, lusty, aroused, hot, randy, horny, on the make. **—Ant.** dispassionate, cool, cold; calm, collected.

passive, *adj.* **1.** inactive, quiescent, inert, receptive, prone, nonaggressive, motionless, placid, phlegmatic, apathetic, listless, imperturbable, unreceptive, indifferent, out of it. **2.** suffering, receiving, submitting, submissive, patient, unresisting, repressed, deferential, yielding, compliant, gentle, meek, forbearing, tolerant, resigned, longsuffering. **—Ant.** active, energetic; hostile, resisting.

password, *n.* watchword, shibboleth, countersign, open sesame.

pastime, *n.* diversion, amusement, sport, entertainment, recreation, hobby, avocation, distraction, relaxation, leisure, play.

patch, *v.* mend, repair, restore, fix, correct, emend; settle, smooth. **—Ant.** break, crack, ruin, spoil.

patent, *adj.* open, manifest, evident, plain, clear, apparent, transparent, manifest, self-evident, unequivocal, explicit, tangible, physical, flagrant, prominent, blatant, solid, concrete, obvious, palpable, unmistakable, conspicuous, unconcealed. **—Ant.** concealed, hidden, unclear, dim.

path, *n.* way, walk, lane, trail, footpath, pathway, route, course, track, passage, road, avenue.

pathetic, *adj.* pitiable, touching, moving, affecting, tender, stirring, poignant, tragic, heartbreaking, wretched, sad, mournful, sorrowful, doleful, woeful, lamentable, pitiful, plangent, plaintive.

patience, *n.* **1.** calmness, composure, endurance, fortitude, stoicism, stability, courage, self-possession, inner strength, submissiveness, submission, sufferance, resignation. **2.** perseverance, diligence, assiduity, sedulousness, indefatigability, indefatigableness, persistence, doggedness, tenacity, assiduousness, steadfastness, staunchness, constancy, determination. **—Ant.** impatience.

patient, *adj.* persevering, diligent, persistent, sedulous, assiduous, indefatigable, untiring; long-suffering, philosophical, unaggressive, acquiescent, submissive, resigned, passive, unrepining; quiet, calm, serene, unruffled, unexcited, self-possessed, stoical, composed; forbearing, tolerant, lenient, forgiving, accommodating. **—Ant.** hostile, agitated; excited, perturbed.

pattern, *n.* **1.** model, original, prototype, archetype, ideal, standard. **2.** design, motif, figure, decoration, ornament, device. **3.** system, arrangement, order, plan, theme; repetition, regularity. **4.** plan, layout, diagram, blueprint, guide, mold, matrix, template. **5.** example, instance, sample, specimen, representation. **6.** figure, formation, configuration, composition, layout.

—v. 7. imitate, copy, mimic, model on, follow, emulate, simulate.

pause, *n.* **1.** rest, wait, hesitation, suspension, lacuna, hiatus, interruption, delay, intermission, moratorium, lull, lapse, holdup, abeyance, breather, breathing space, break; stop, halt, cessation, stoppage. **—v. 2.** hesitate, waver, deliberate, wait, rest, interrupt, tarry, delay, mark time, suspend, hold up, falter. **3.** cease, stop, arrest, halt, desist, forbear. **—Ant.** continuity, continuousness.

pay, *v.* **1.** settle, liquidate, discharge, honor meet. **2.** satisfy, compensate, reimburse, remunerate, recompense; reward; indemnify. **3.** yield, be profitable to, repay, requite. **4.** punish, repay, retaliate, requite, revenge. **5.** make amends, suffer, be punished, make compensation. **—n. 6.** payment, compensation, recompense, settlement, return, reward, gain, profit, consideration, wages, salary, income, stipend, remuneration, emolument, fee, allowance. **7.** requital, reward, punishment, just deserts.

payment, *n.* pay; expenditure, outlay, expense, contribution, disbursement, charge.

peace, *n.* **1.** agreement, treaty, armistice, truce, pact, accord, entente, entente cordiale, amity, harmony, concord. **2.** order, security. **3.** calm, quiet, tranquility, peacefulness, calmness, serenity. **—Ant.** insecurity; agitation, disturbance.

peaceable, *adj.* pacific, peaceful, amicable, friendly, amiable, mild, inoffensive, dovish, nonviolent, temperate, compatible, congenial, genial, civil, cordial, gentle; calm, tranquil, serene, quiet, placid, quiescent. **—Ant.** hostile, unfriendly; noisy.

peaceful, *adj.* tranquil, placid, serene, unruffled, calm, complacent; composed, dignified, gracious, mellow; unexcited, unagitated, pacific. **—Ant.** perturbed, disturbed.

peak, *n.* point, top, crest, summit, acme, pinnacle, apex, culmination, apogee, zenith, crown, consummation, climax. **—Ant.** base, bottom, abyss.

peaked, *adj.* pale, sickly, wan, drawn, haggard, pinched, emaciated, unhealthy, infirm, wasted, hollow-eyed, anemic, pallid, pasty, sallow, whey-faced, washed out, drained, gaunt, weak, feeble, sickly, unwell, ailing, waxen. **—Ant.** hale, hearty, robust.

pearly, *adj.* opalescent, opaline, nacreous, lustrous, iridescent, mother-of-pearl, pale, whitish, light, snowy, dove-gray, pearl-gray.

peccadillo, *n.* petty sin *or* offense, slight crime, trifling fault, indiscretion, transgression, trespass, infraction, misdeed, violation, lapse, mistake, gaffe, blunder, faux pas, slip, error, misstep, botch, stumble, goof, fault, misdemeanor, shortcoming, weakness.

peculiar, *adj.* **1.** strange, odd, curious, weird, queer, eccentric, bizarre, uncommon, unusual, extraordinary, singular, exceptional, abnormal, anomalous, aberrant, deviant, outlandish, offbeat, unorthodox, quaint, sui generis, quirky, funny, freakish. **2.** characteristic, appropriate, proper, individual, particular, select, especial, special, specific, unique, exclusive, distinctive. **—Ant.** usual, common, ordinary; general, unspecific.

peculiarity, *n.* **1.** idiosyncrasy, abnormality, irregularity, quirk, kink, crotchet, caprice. **2.** singularity, oddity, rarity, eccentricity. **3.** distinction, feature, characteristic, property, quality,

trait, attribute, earmark, hallmark, specialty.

pedestrian, *n.* **1.** walker, stroller. **—adj. 2.** on foot, walking, afoot. **3.** commonplace, prosaic, dull, boring, banal, tiresome, mundane, tedious, monotonous, run-of-the-mill, dry, humdrum, insipid, flat, colorless, dreary, vapid, stale, trite, lifeless, dead, dull as dishwater, jejune. **—Ant.** interesting, fascinating, engaging.

pedigree, *n.* genealogy, descent, family tree, family, heritage, ancestry, lineage, line, race, derivation, patrimony, birth, origin, extraction, strain, stock, blood, bloodline, parentage, roots.

peek, *v.* peep, peer, pry, glimpse, look, squint at, have a gander at.

peel, *v.* **1.** strip, skin, decorticate, pare, flay, flake off, shuck, hull, scale. **—n. 2.** skin, rind, bark, coating, peeling. **—Ant.** cover.

peerless, *adj.* matchless, unequaled, unsurpassed, unique, incomparable, unparalleled, nonpareil, consummate, preeminent, paramount, supreme, inimitable, ne plus ultra, superlative, unmatched, unrivaled, superior, the best.

peevish, *adj.* cross, querulous, fretful, vexatious, vexed, captious, discontented, petulant, testy, irritable, crusty, snappish, waspish, touchy, crabby, churlish, carping, curmudgeonly, crotchety, grumpy, cantankerous, pettish, caviling, cranky, bilious, acrimonious, splenetic, short-tempered, ill-tempered, ill-natured, unpleasant, disagreeable, nasty, out of sorts. **—Ant.** good-natured, friendly, pleasant, amiable, agreeable.

pell-mell, *adv.* headlong, hurriedly, recklessly, agitatedly, frantically, frenziedly, wildly, higgledy-piggledy, helter-skelter, slapdash, rashly, feverishly, chaotically, impulsively, impetuously, hastily, precipitously, spontaneously.

pelt, *v.* **1.** strike, bombard, shower, bomb, pepper, strafe, shell, attack, assail, assault, pound, clobber, pummel, wallop, work over, beat, belabor, batter. **—n. 2.** blow, whack, hit, smack, slap, bang, thump, wallop, stroke. **3.** skin, hide, coat, fur, fleece.

penchant, *n.* liking, leaning, inclination, taste, fondness, bent, propensity, proclivity, affinity, preference, predilection, disposition, predisposition, prejudice, bias, partiality, soft spot, tendency.

penetrate, *v.* **1.** pierce, bore, probe, stab, puncture, enter; permeate, sink in, diffuse, suffuse, pervade. **2.** reach, get to, hit, strike, affect *or* impress deeply, touch. **3.** understand, discern, comprehend, fathom, sense, discover, grasp, unravel, perceive, figure out.

penetrating, *adj.* **1.** piercing, sharp, acute; shrill, strident, earsplitting, pervasive; pungent, harsh, biting, stinging. **2.** acute, discerning, critical, keen, shrewd, sharp, sharp-witted, intelligent, wise, sagacious, incisive, trenchant, searching, deep, perceptive, quick, discriminating, sensitive, clever, smart. **—Ant.** blunt; uncritical, silly, stupid, undiscriminating.

penitent, *adj.* sorry, contrite, repentant, atoning, remorseful, regretful, sorrowful, rueful, griefstricken, sad, apologetic, conscience-stricken, shamefaced.

penniless, *adj.* poor, indigent, poverty-stricken, destitute, needy, impoverished, straitened, pinched, down and out, broke, hard-up, impecunious, necessitous, bankrupt, ruined, insolvent, wiped out, financially embarrassed, in reduced circumstances. **—Ant.** rich, wealthy.

pensive, *adj.* serious, sober, grave, thoughtful, meditative, reflective, musing, cogitative, brooding, preoccupied, in a trance *or* reverie, dreamy, wistful, contemplative, thinking. **—Ant.** frivolous, silly, unthinking, thoughtless, vapid.

penurious, *adj.* mean, parsimonious, stingy, tight, tightfisted, pennypinching, cheap, ungenerous, thrifty, grudging, skinflinty, close-fisted, close, miserly, niggardly, chintzy. **—Ant.** generous.

people, *n.* **1.** community, tribe, race, nation, clan, family, population, society. **2.** persons, human beings, humans, men and women, living souls, bodies, individuals, creatures, folks. **3.** populace, commonalty, public. **—v. 4.** populate, colonize, settle, occupy.

perceive, *v.* **1.** see, discern, notice, note, discover, observe, descry, espy, distinguish, make out, catch sight of, glimpse, spot, mark, remark, detect, identify, take in. **2.** apprehend, understand, see, discern, appreciate, grasp, feel, sense, gather, comprehend, deduce, infer, conclude, determine, ascertain, figure out, decipher. **—Ant.** ignore.

perceptible, *adj.* noticeable, detectable, solid, concrete, appreciable, understandable, discernible, apparent, perceivable, evident, obvious, notable, manifest, plain, clear, prominent, palpable, patent, unmistakable, recognizable. **—Ant.** undiscernible, concealed.

perception, *n.* **1.** appreciation, grasp, comprehension, knowledge, perspective, cognition, recognition, perceiving, view, opinion, apprehension, understanding, discernment. **2.** intuition, insight, instinct, feeling, impression, idea, notion. **—Ant.** misapprehension, misunderstanding.

perceptive, *adj.* astute, discerning, sensitive, responsive, keen, sharp, quick-witted, intelligent, acute, sensible, observant, bright, insightful, perspicacious, understanding, appreciative, sagacious, judicious, alert, attentive, on the ball. **—Ant.** obtuse, insensitive.

perennial, *adj.* timeless, endless, unfailing, ceaseless, enduring, perpetual, perdurable, everlasting, permanent, imperishable, undying, deathless, eternal, immortal, lasting, durable, stable, lifelong, persistent, chronic, constant, incessant, continual, uninterrupted, unceasing. **—Ant.** evanescent, temporary, flimsy, mortal; inconstant; sporadic.

perfect, *adj.* **1.** complete, finished, absolute, fulfilled, pure, entire, whole, ideal, completed, full, consummate. **2.** faultless, spotless, unblemished, excellent, exquisite. **3.** skilled, adept, adroit, expert, accomplished. **4.** typical, exact; thorough, sound, unqualified, pure, unmixed, unadulterated. **—v. 5.** complete, finish, realize, fulfill, achieve, effect, execute, carry out, bring to perfection, consummate, accomplish. **—Ant.** incomplete, unfinished; imperfect; maladroit; mixed, impure.

perform, *v.* **1.** carry out, execute, do, discharge, transact. **2.** fulfill, accomplish, achieve, effect. **—Ant.** fail.

perfume, *n.* **1.** essence, attar, scent, extract, fragrance, cologne, toilet water; incense. **2.** redolence, scent, odor, smell, aroma, fragrance, bouquet, nose. **—Ant.** stench, stink, noxiousness.

perfunctory, *adj.* routine, automatic,

businesslike, robotic, unspontaneous, formal, apathetic, removed, distant, offhand, cursory, fleeting, rushed, hasty, hurried, mechanical, indifferent, careless, superficial; negligent, slovenly, heedless, reckless, uninterested, thoughtless. **—Ant.** careful, diligent, thoughtful.

peril, *n.* risk, jeopardy, danger, hazard, threat, exposure, vulnerability, susceptibility, uncertainty, insecurity. **—Ant.** safety, security.

period, *n.* interval, time, term, span, duration, spell, space, stretch, while; days, eon, years, age, era, epoch; course, cycle.

periphery, *n.* **1.** boundary, border, edge, rim, bound, margin, brim, ambit, circumference, perimeter. **2.** surface, outside, edge. **—Ant.** center; inside.

perish, *v.* **1.** die, pass away, pass on, expire, decease. **2.** decay, age, wither, shrivel, rot, molder, disappear, vanish, evanesce. **—Ant.** survive.

perky, *adj.* jaunty, pert, brisk, lively, cheerful, cheery, bouncy, bright, peppy, spirited, frisky, animated, vivacious, effervescent, bubbly, buoyant, gay, vigorous, invigorated, bright-eyed and bushy-tailed. **—Ant.** flaccid, retiring.

permanent, *adj.* lasting, unchanging, unchanged, changeless, unchangeable, fixed, persistent, unaltered, stable, immutable, invariant, invariable, constant; enduring, durable, abiding, perpetual, everlasting, remaining, perdurable, eternal, unending, endless, undying, indestructible, abiding, perennial, long-lived. **—Ant.** unstable, temporary, variable, inconstant; temporal.

permeate, *v.* pass through, penetrate, pervade, diffuse through, osmose, saturate, sink in, imbue, infiltrate, enter, seep through, soak through, percolate through, spread throughout.

permission, *n.* liberty, license, enfranchisement, franchise, leave, permit, freedom, allowance, consent, assent, acquiescence, sufferance, tolerance, laxity, lenience, sanction, acceptance, authorization, approval, indulgence, approbation, countenance. **—Ant.** refusal.

permit, *v.* **1.** allow, let, tolerate, agree to, endure, suffer, consent to, authorize, sanction, give leave, brook, admit, grant, enable, empower, enfranchise. **—n. 2.** license, franchise, permission, authority, authorization, warrant. **—Ant.** refuse, disallow.

pernicious, *adj.* **1.** ruinous, harmful, hurtful, detrimental, deleterious, injurious, destructive, damaging, baneful, noxious. **2.** virulent, toxic, poisonous, life-threatening, deadly, fatal, lethal. **3.** evil, wicked, malevolent, malicious, bad, iniquitous, villainous, nefarious, vicious, invidious, venomous, spiteful. **—Ant.** beneficial, salubrious, healthful; good.

perpendicular, *adj.* vertical, upright, standing, erect, plumb, straight up and down, at right angles to, at ninety degrees to. **—Ant.** horizontal, parallel.

perpetrate, *v.* do, cause, effect, effectuate, commit, bring about, bring off, perform, carry out, pull off, accomplish, execute, be responsible for, practice.

perpetual, *adj.* everlasting, permanent, continuing, continuous, nonstop, recurrent, repetitive, enduring, constant, eternal, ceaseless, unceasing, incessant, never-ending, long-lived, timeless, immutable, unending, endless, uninterrupted, interminable, infinite.

—Ant. temporary, finite, impermanent; discontinuous.

perplex, *v.* **1.** confuse, puzzle, bewilder, mystify, confound, distract, baffle, befuddle, disconcert, stump, stymie, nonplus, stupefy, stun, daze, dumbfound, flabbergast, throw for a loop. **2.** complicate, confuse, tangle, snarl, entangle. **—Ant.** clarify.

persecute, *v.* **1.** oppress, harass, badger, molest, vex, afflict, irritate, trouble, annoy. **2.** punish, discriminate against, suppress, subjugate, abuse, outrage, victimize, tyrannize, torture, torment. **3.** importune, annoy, tease, bother, pester, harass, harry, plague, bully, hound, irritate.

perseverance, *n.* persistence, tenacity, pertinacity, resolution, resolve, staying power, stamina, grit, pluck, patience, endurance, diligence, devotion, decisiveness, firmness, purposefulness, stubbornness, doggedness, determination, steadfastness, indefatigability. **—Ant.** irresolution, impatience.

persevere, *v.* persist, continue, keep on, last, stick it out, hold on, endure, sustain, resolve, decide, pursue doggedly, cling to. **—Ant.** fail, cease, desist.

persist, *v.* **1.** persevere, continue, last, linger, stay, endure, remain. **2.** insist, stand fast *or* firm, be staunch *or* steadfast, strive, toil, labor, work hard at. **—Ant.** stop, discontinue.

persistent, *adj.* **1.** persisting, persevering, enduring, indefatigable, pertinacious, tenacious, stubborn, pigheaded, immovable, obstinate, obdurate, inflexible, rigid, firm, fast, fixed, staunch, resolute, resolved, determined, unfaltering, unswerving, unflagging, tireless, dogged, unwavering, steadfast. **2.** continued, continual, continuous, continuing, unending, intermirnable, unrelenting, perpetual, incessant, unceasing, nonstop, repeated, constant, steady, repetitive, regular. **—Ant.** amenable, obedient; inconstant, sporadic.

person, *n.* human being, human, man *or* woman *or* child, living soul, mortal, body, somebody, individual, personage, onep; character.

personality, *n.* character, nature, temperament, disposition, makeup, psyche, persona, constitution, essence, features, attribute, temper, spirit, frame of mind, self, personal identity.

persuade, *v.* **1.** prevail on, induce, urge, influence, exhort, importune, dispose, actuate, move, entice, impel, incline, prompt, sway, press, force, compel, seduce. **2.** win over, convince, satisfy, convert, talk into. **—Ant.** dissuade, discourage.

pert, *adj.* bold, forward, impertinent, saucy, presumptuous, impudent, flippant, brash, brazen, cheeky, insolent, disrespectful, rude, impolite, fresh, out of line, brassy, big-mouthed, smart, wise. **—Ant.** retiring, shy, bashful; polite, courteous.

pertinent, *adj.* pertaining, relating, relevant, apt, germane, appropriate, apposite, fit, fitting, fitted, suited, suitable, applicable, proper. **—Ant.** irrelevant, inappropriate, unsuited, unsuitable, improper.

perturb, *v.* **1.** disturb, upset, fluster, ruffle, unsettle, disconcert, vex, worry, alarm, shake up, discompose, unnerve, discomfit, disquiet, agitate, stir up, trouble. **2.** disturb, derange, disorder, confuse, addle, muddle, disorganize. **—Ant.** pacify, calm, tranquilize; clarify.

peruse, *v.* study, read, scrutinize, examine, survey, pore over, inspect, review, vet, scan, browse, run through, eyeball. —Ant. skim.

pervade, v. permeate, diffuse, fill, soak, sink in, penetrate, pass through.

perverse, adj. **1.** wrongheaded, contradictory, improper, irregular, unfair, contrary, contumacious, disobedient, wayward, cantankerous, obstreperous, captious, fractious, irascible, sullen, surly, quarrelsome, churlish, curmudgeonly, bad-tempered, testy, cross, contentious, crabby, irritable, grouchy, cranky. **2.** willful, persistent, obstinate, stubborn, headstrong, pigheaded, dogged, intractable, unyielding, refractory. **3.** wicked, evil, bad, sinful, piacular, perverted, distorted. —Ant. amiable, obedient; amenable, tractable; good.

perverted, adj. deviant, deviate, abnormal, unnatural, warped, twisted, misguided, misapplied, distorted, wicked, amoral, immoral, profligate, dissolute, degraded, degenerate, debauched, evil, malign, malicious, malevolent, sinful, iniquitous, bad, base, foul, corrupt, corrupted, unprincipled, outrageous, perverse. —Ant. straight, good, moral, incorruptible, righteous, upstanding, noble, blameless, principled.

pessimistic, adj. cynical, gloomy, dark, foreboding, negative, hopeless, glum, despairing, depressed, dejected, despondent, melancholy, downhearted, heavy-hearted, defeatist, sad, sorrowful, blue, joyless, bleak, forlorn. —Ant. optimistic, rosy, sanguine, positive, buoyant, cheerful, lighthearted, joyous.

pest, n. **1.** nuisance, annoyance, bother, vexation, irritant, nag, trial, gadfly, heckler, curse, thorn in one's side, pain in the neck, nudge. **2.** pestilence, plague, scourge, bane; epidemic, pandemic.

pester, v. harass, annoy, vex, torment, torture, molest, harry, hector, tease, trouble, plague, nettle, disturb, provoke, bother, worry, gall, badger, irritate, chafe, nag, irk, fret, heckle, needle, peeve, pique, exasperate, get on (someone's) nerves, try (someone's) patience, persecute, hassle, bug, drive (someone) up the wall, give (someone) a hard time. —Ant. please, delight, entertain, divert.

pet, n. **1.** favorite, idol, apple of one's eye, fair-haired girl or boy, darling; lapdog. **2.** peevishness, sulk, bad temper, pique, bad mood, irascibility, huff, petulance, cantankerousness, moodiness. —v. **3.** fondle, indulge, baby, caress, stroke, pat, cuddle, pamper, humor, dote on, molly-coddle, spoil. **4.** sulk, be peevish, fume.

petition, n. **1.** request, supplication, suit, prayer, plea, entreaty, solicitation, appeal, application. —v. **2.** entreat, supplicate, beg, pray, request, ask, plead, appeal, solicit, sue, beseech, implore, importune.

petty, adj. **1.** unimportant, trifling, paltry, nugatory, trivial, minor, inferior, niggling, puny, piddling, measly, small-time, of no account, no big deal, inconsequential, unimportant, lesser, little, small, insignificant, negligible, inconsiderable, slight, diminutive. **2.** narrow, narrowminded, small. **3.** mean, ungenerous, stingy, miserly, grudging, cheap, tightfisted, niggardly, parsimonious. —Ant. important, considerable, significant; broadminded; generous.

petulance, n. irritability, peevishness, fretfulness, impatience, bad mood, ill temper, irascibility, churlishness, chol-

era, spleen, moodiness, sourness, huff, crabbiness, crossness, perversity, grouchiness, grumpiness, captiousness, pettishness, testiness, waspishness. —Ant. calm, good humor.

petulant, adj. irritable, peevish, fretful, vexatious, waspish, snappish, testy, short-tempered, hotheaded, hot-tempered, peppery, bilious, splenetic, choleric, moody, crabby, huffy, perverse, grumpy, pettish, touchy, irascible, cross, snarling, captious, acrimonious, impatient, sour, testy, cantankerous, curmudgeonly, crotchety. —Ant. even-tempered, temperate, pleasant.

phantom, n. **1.** phantasm, apparition, specter, ghost, spirit, shade, wraith, vision, spook; illusion, delusion, figment of the imagination, chimera, hallucination, fancy, mirage. —adj. **2.** unreal, illusive, spectral, illusory, phantasmal, imaginary, hallucinatory. —Ant. real, flesh-and-blood, material.

phenomenon, n. **1.** fact, occurrence, event, occasion, experience, happening, incident, circumstance. **2.** prodigy, marvel, wonder, miracle, curiosity, spectacle, sight, sensation, rarity, exception.

philander, v. flirt, trifle, dally, cheat, commit adultery, fool around, deceive, sleep around, play the field, traduce, betray.

philanderer n. playboy, lover, flirt, roué, rake, lady-killer, skirt-chaser, Casanova, Lothario, Romeo, Don Juan, womanizer, wolf, stud, macho man, adulterer, cheat, deceiver.

phlegm, n. **1.** sluggishness, stoicism, apathy, lethargy, torpor, stolidness, listlessness, indolence, indifference. **2.** coolness, calm, self-possession, coldness, impassivity, impassiveness. —Ant. concern; interest, warmth.

phobia, n. dread, fear, horror, terror, apprehension, qualm, loathing, revulsion, repugnance, distaste, antipathy, aversion, hatred. —Ant. like, attraction, love.

phony, adj. **1.** false, sham, counterfeit, inauthentic, bastard, mock, pretend, make-believe, synthetic, artificial, fraudulent, imitation, bogus, ersatz, unreal, factitious, trumped-up, pretend, spurious, brummagem, pinchbeck, pseudo. —n. **2.** impostor, faker, mountebank, charlatan, pretender, fraud, humbug, bluffer, fourflusher, trickster, double-dealer, quack, deceiver, hypocrite, crook. —Ant. genuine, authentic.

physical, adj. **1.** bodily, corporeal, corporal, mortal, fleshly, incarnate, carnal, earthly, natural, somatic; tangible, sensible. **2.** material, real, natural, palpable, concrete, actual, true, solid, manifest. —Ant. mental, spiritual; unnatural, unreal.

pick, v. **1.** choose, select, cull. **2.** criticize, find fault with. **3.** steal, rob, pilfer. **4.** pierce, indent, dig into, break up, peck. **5.** pluck, harvest, garner, gather, reap, collect, get, acquire. —n. **6.** choice, option, preference, election, selection; choicest part, best.

picture, n. **1.** painting, drawing, photograph, representation, portrait, depiction, illustration, sketch, portrayal, artwork. **2.** image, representation, similitude, semblance, likeness. **3.** description, account, representation. —v. **4.** imagine; depict, describe, delineate, portray, show, illustrate, display, paint, draw, represent.

picturesque, adj. **1.** striking, interesting, colorful, intriguing, unusual, unique, original, charming, idyllic, pretty, lovely, eye-catching, delightful,

pleasing, scenic, beautiful. **2.** graphic, vivid, impressive; intense, lively. —Ant. uninteresting, dull, colorless.

piece, n. **1.** portion, share, fraction, part, division, proportion, quantity, segment, section; bit, morsel, chunk, hunk, sliver, lump, particle, shard, remnant, scrap, shred, fragment. **2.** thing, example, instance, specimen. **3.** short story, story, article, essay, composition, paper, theme, novella; poem, ode, sonnet; play. —Ant. all, everything; none, nothing.

piecemeal, adv. **1.** gradually, bit by bit, inchmeal, inchwise, slowly, by degrees. **2.** separately, fractionally, disjointedly, spasmodically.

pierce, v. **1.** penetrate, enter, run through or into, perforate, stab, puncture, bore, drill, skewer, impale, thrust or poke into, lance, spear, spit, fix, transfix. **2.** affect, touch, move, rouse, strike, thrill, excite, melt, stir, pain, wound, cut to the quick.

piety, n. **1.** reverence, deference, dedication, dutifulness, loyalty, affection, regard, respect. **2.** godliness, devoutness, devotion, sanctity, grace, holiness, piousness, religiousness, veneration. —Ant. irreverence, disrespect.

pile, n. **1.** assemblage, mound, stack, stockpile, supply, deposit, batch, hoard, aggregation, congeries, assortment, conglomeration, collection, mass, heap, accumulation. **2.** hair, down; wool, fur, pelage; nap. —v. **3.** heap up, accumulate, assemble, amass, collect, stack, mound, hoard, aggregate, stockpile.

pilfer, v. steal, rob, thieve, plunder, embezzle, palm, snatch, grab, misappropriate, appropriate, take, purloin, pinch, filch, lift, nick, pocket, swipe, rifle, shoplift, rip off, hook, snitch.

pilgrimage, n. journey, trip, excursion, tour, voyage, expedition, trek.

pillage, v. **1.** rob, plunder, rape, despoil, sack, spoil. —n. **2.** booty, plunder, spoils. **3.** rapine, depredation, devastation, spoliation.

pillar, n. shaft, column, stele, post, upright, piling, pile, pilaster, obelisk, support, pier, prop.

pillory, v. mock, ridicule, deride, scorn, revile, sneer at, vilify, slur, stigmatize, brand, besmirch, smear, tarnish, blacken, skewer, crucify, tar and feather. —Ant. praise, esteem.

pin, n. **1.** peg, fastening, bolt. **2.** brooch, clip. —v. **3.** fasten, fix, affix, attach, secure, tack, staple, clip, immobilize, tie down.

pine, v. **1.** yearn, long, ache, hunger, thirst, crave, itch, sigh. **2.** languish, fade, dwindle, wilt, droop, pine away.

pinnacle, n. peak, eminence, culmination, tower, tip, crest, cap, crown, summit, apex, acme, zenith, top, climax, maximum, consummation, utmost, extreme. —Ant. base.

pioneer, v. **1.** lead, precede, blaze a trail, break new ground, open up, kick off, guide, forerun. **2.** initiate, introduce, originate, institute, trigger, launch, develop, inaugurate, found, invent, create, dream up. —n. **3.** frontiersman, explorer, colonist, early settler; groundbreaker, predecessor, innovator, leader, trendsetter, pacesetter, forerunner, precursor, pathfinder, trailblazer, vanguard, bellwether, point man, point woman, point person. —adj. **4.** first, earliest, advance, original, maiden, initial, avant-garde, trailblazing, cutting-edge.

pious, adj. **1.** devout, reverent, worshipful, reverential, dutiful, God-fearing, faithful, moral, spiritual, virtuous, saintly, angelic, seraphic, Christ-like, godly, religious, holy. **2.** sanctimonious, hypocritical, self-righteous, mealy-mouthed, pharisaical, unctuous, goody-goody, oily, smarmy. —Ant. impious, irreligious, unholy.

piquant, *adj.* **1.** pungent, sharp, flavorsome, tart, spicy. **2.** stimulating, interesting, attractive, sparkling. **3.** smart, racy, sharp, clever. —Ant. insipid; uninteresting, unattractive; dull.

pique, *v.* **1.** offend, nettle, sting, irritate, chafe, vex; affront, wound, displease. **2.** interest, stimulate, excite, incite, stir; spur, prick, goad. —Ant. please, delight; compliment.

pit, *n.* **1.** hole, cavity, burrow, hollow. **2.** excavation, shaft, mine, ditch, trench, trough, well; pitfall, trap. **3.** hollow, depression, dent, indentation. **4.** stone, pip, seed, core.

piteous, *adj.* pathetic, pitiable, tearful, deplorable, wretched, miserable; affecting, distressing, moving, pitiful, lamentable, woeful, plaintive, grievous, heartbreaking, sorrowful, sad, mournful, morose, doleful, heart-rending, poignant, deplorable, regrettable, emotional. —Ant. pleasant, cheerful.

pithy, *adj.* terse, concise, brief, short, compact, epigrammatic, compressed, condensed, aphoristic, sententious, distilled, crisp, abridged, abbreviated, concentrated, succinct, compendious, laconic, summary, to the point, short and sweet. —Ant. expansive, lengthy, prolix, verbose.

pitiful, *adj.* **1.** pitiable, pathetic, piteous. **2.** small, insignificant, trifling, unimportant, beggarly, sorry, contemptible, deplorable, mean. —Ant. superior, delightful.

pitiless, *adj.* merciless, cruel, mean, unmerciful, ruthless, savage, brutal, harsh, tyrannical, stonyhearted, harsh, severe, cold, implacable, relentless, inexorable, hardhearted, heartless, inhumane, callous, malevolent, unsympathetic, indifferent, thoughtless. —Ant. merciful, softhearted, kind, kindly.

pity, *n.* **1.** sympathy, compassion, commiseration, condolence, empathy, sorrow, kindness, tenderness, mercy. —*v.* **2.** commiserate, be *or* feel sorry for, sympathize with, empathize, bleed for, weep for, feel for. —Ant. apathy, cruelty, ruthlessness.

place, *n.* **1.** space, plot, spot, location, locale, locality, site, position, point, locus, area, scene, setting. **2.** condition, position, situation, circumstances. **3.** job, post, office, function, duty, berth, appointment, livelihood, charge, responsibility, employment, rank. **4.** region, area, section, sector. **5.** residence, dwelling, house, home, domicile, apartment, quarters, lodgings, digs, abode. **6.** stead, lien. **7.** opportunity, occasion, reason, ground, cause. —*v.* **8.** position, range, order, dispose, arrange, situate, put, set, locate, station, deposit, lay, seat, fix, establish. **9.** class, classify, sort, order, arrange, rank, group, categorize, regard, view, see, consider. —Ant. misplace, displace.

placid, *adj.* calm, peaceful, unruffled, tranquil, serene, quiet, undisturbed, pacific, still, sedate, temperate, composed, poised, self-possessed, unexcitable, easygoing, unflappable. —Ant. turbulent, tumultuous, perturbed.

plague, *n.* **1.** epidemic, pestilence, disease, Black Death, pandemic, holocaust, scourge. **2.** affliction, calamity, evil, curse, bane, blight, visitation, torment, torture. **3.** trouble, vexation, an-

noyance, nuisance, torment. —*v.* **4.** trouble, anguish, distress, torment, torture, molest, bother, incommode, discommode. **5.** vex, harry, hector, harass, fret, worry, pester, badger, annoy, tease, irritate, disturb, hound, nag, needle, exasperate, gall, irk, bug.

plain, *adj.* **1.** clear, distinct, lucid, unambiguous, unequivocal, intelligible, understandable, perspicuous, evident, manifest, simple, vivid, transparent, graphic, direct, crystal-clear, obvious, unmistakable, patent, apparent. **2.** downright, sheer, direct, transparent. **3.** unambiguous, candid, outspoken, blunt, direct, straightforward, forthright, sincere, frank, guileless, artless, ingenuous, open, unreserved, honest, open-hearted. **4.** homely, unpretentious, homey, simple, basic, austere, stark, colorless, drab, bare, Spartan, unvarnished, undecorated, unembellished, unadorned, frugal. **5.** ugly, homely, unattractive. **6.** ordinary, common, commonplace, unostentatious. **7.** flat, level, plane, featureless, smooth, even. —*n.* **8.** grassland, pasture, meadowland, veldt, steppe, tundra, heath, moor, flatland, down, mesa, plateau, savanna, prairie, pampas. —Ant. un

plan, *n.* **1.** scheme, plot, arrangement, program, pattern, layout, procedure, project, formula, method, system, design, contrivance. **2.** drawing, sketch, floorplan, blueprint, draft, map, chart, diagram, representation. —*v.* **3.** arrange, outline, organize, map out, delineate, develop, scheme, plot, design, devise, contrive, invent, concoct, hatch.

platform, *n.* **1.** stage, dais, rostrum, pulpit; landing. **2.** principles, beliefs, tenets, policy, program, plank, party line.

platitude, *n.* cliché, commonplace, banality, bromide, truism, generalization, prosaicism, old saw, chestnut. —Ant. witticism, mot.

plausible, *adj.* likely, believable, reasonable, credible, conceivable, probable, sound, sensible, rational, logical, acceptable. —Ant. implausible.

play, *n.* **1.** drama, piece, show; comedy, tragedy, melodrama, farce. **2.** amusement, recreation, game, sport, diversion, pastime. **3.** fun, jest, trifling, frolic. **4.** action, activity, movement, exercise, operation, motion. **5.** freedom, liberty, scope, elbow room. —*v.* **6.** act, perform, enact, characterize, impersonate, personate. **7.** compete, contend with *or* against, engage. **8.** stake, bet, wager. **9.** represent, imitate, emulate, mimic. **10.** do, perform, bring about, execute. **11.** toy, trifle, sport, dally, caper, romp, disport, frolic, gambol, skip, revel, frisk, cavort, fool around. —Ant. work.

playful, *adj.* high-spirited, cheerful, fun-loving, mischievous, devilish, frisky, coltish, antic, frolicsome, sportive, sprightly, prankish, puckish, impish, puppyish, kittenish, whimsical, larky. —Ant. somber, sober.

plead, *v.* **1.** entreat, appeal, beg, supplicate, request, petition, implore, beseech, solicit, importune, apply to. **2.** argue, persuade, reason. **3.** assert, maintain, declare, affirm, avow, swear, offer, allege, cite, make a plea, apologize, answer, make excuse.

pleasant, *adj.* **1.** pleasing, agreeable, enjoyable, pleasurable, acceptable, welcome, gratifying. **2.** companionable, sociable, engaging, winning, outgoing, welcoming, hospitable, gracious, charming, genteel, suave, debonair, well-bred, urbane, culti-

vated, delightful, congenial, polite, courteous, friendly, personable, amiable. **3.** fair, sunny, clear bright, cloudless, balmy, nice, fine. **4.** gay, sprightly, merry, cheery, cheerful, lively, sportive, vivacious. **5.** jocular, facetious, playful, humorous, witty, amusing, clever, jocose. —Ant. unpleasant, displeasing.

pleasing, *adj.* agreeable, pleasant, acceptable, pleasurable, charming, delightful, amusing, diverting, entertaining, enjoyable, delectable, interesting, engaging, attractive, winning, winsome. —Ant. disagreeable, unpleasant, unacceptable.

pleasure, *n.* **1.** happiness, gladness, delectation, enjoyment, delight, joy, well-being, satisfaction, gratification, fulfillment, contentment, comfort; amusement, diversion, entertainment, recreation, pastime, leisure. **2.** luxury, sensuality, voluptuousness. **3.** will, desire, choice, preference, purpose, wish, mind, inclination, predilection, option, fancy, discretion. —Ant. displeasure, unhappiness; disinclination.

plentiful, *adj.* bountiful, profuse, bounteous, lavish, generous, unstinted, ample, plenteous, copious, abundant, full, rich; fertile, fruitful, productive, exuberant, luxuriant, thriving, prolific, bumper. —Ant. sparse, scanty, barren, fruitless.

plenty, *n.* fullness, abundance, copiousness, plenteousness, plentifulness, profusion, wealth, bountifulness, lavishness, fertility, luxuriance, exuberance, affluence, overflow, extravagance, prodigality; superabundance, overfullness, plethora, excess. —Ant. paucity, scarcity.

pliant, *adj.* pliable, ductile, plastic, clastic, malleable, workable, bendable; supple, flexible, lithe, limber; compliant, easily influenced, yielding, adaptable, manageable, tractable, facile, docile, impressionable, susceptible, responsive, receptive, easily led. —Ant. inflexible; unyielding, rigid, intractable.

plight, *n.* condition, state, situation, predicament, circumstances, difficulty, quandry, straits, trouble, extremity, case, dilemma, hole, jam, pickle, fix, spot, scrape, hot water, fine kettle of fish, mess.

plod, *v.* **1.** tramp, slog, drag, tread, lumber, stomp, galumph, walk heavily, pace, trudge. **2.** toil, moil, labor, drudge, sweat, work, slave, grind, grub, plug away.

plot, *n.* **1.** plan, scheme, intrigue, conspiracy, cabal, stratagem, machination. **2.** story, theme, thread, story line, chain of events, denouement, outline, scenario, skeleton. —*v.* **3.** devise, contrive, concoct, brew, hatch, frame, design, arrange, organize, dream up, cook up, calculate. **4.** conspire, scheme, contrive, plan, intrigue, machinate, collude.

ploy, *n.* stratagem, strategy, tactic, trick, maneuver, artifice, tactic, scheme, gimmick, dodge, wile, device, feint, gambit, ruse.

pluck, *v.* **1.** pull, jerk, yank, snatch, tug, tear, rip, grab, catch, clutch; pick, remove, withdraw, extract, draw out. —*n.* **2.** courage, grit, backbone, gameness, hardiness, fortitude, stouthearted-ness, doughtiness, intrepidity, steadfastness, resolve, resolution, spirit, bravery, boldness, determination, mettle, nerve, guts, moxie, chutzpah, spunk.

plump, *adj.* fleshy, fat, chubby, stout, portly, corpulent, obese, zaftig, pudgy, full-figured, Rubenesque, curvaceous, buxom, voluptuous, pneumatic, over-weight, roly-poly, ample, full-bodied, tubby, rotund, squat, chunky, beefy, busty, broad in the beam, hippy, well-upholstered, round. —**Ant.** thin, slender, skinny.

plunder, *v.* **1.** rob, despoil, fleece, pillage, loot, ransack, rifle, ravage, rape, sack, vandalize, maraud, desolate, devastate, strip, lay waste. —*n.* **2.** pillage, rapine, spoliation, robbery, looting, depredation, vandalism, sack, theft, plundering. **3.** loot, booty, spoils, prizes, boodle.

plunge, *v.* **1.** immerse, submerge, dip. **2.** dive; rush, hasten; descend, drop, hurtle over. —*n.* **3.** leap, dive, rush, dash, dip, plummet, drop, descent, fall, pitch, nosedive.

poetry, *n.* verse, versification, rhyme, metrics, meter, rhythm.

poignant, *adj.* **1.** distressing, heartfelt, serious, intense, severe, bitter, tragic, heartbreaking, excruciating, pathetic, piteous, upsetting, moving, touching, emotional, dramatic, stirring, profound, deep, earnest, sincere. **2.** keen, strong, biting, mordant, caustic, acid, pointed. **3.** pungent, piquant, sharp, biting, acrid, stinging. —**Ant.** superfluous, trivial; mild.

pointed, *adj.* **1.** sharp, piercing, acute, barbed, penetrating, epigrammatic, succinct, stinging, piquant, biting, mordant, sarcastic, caustic, severe, keen, incisive, pungent, telling, trenchant. **2.** directed, aimed, explicit, marked, personal. **3.** marked, emphasized, accented, accentuated. —**Ant.** blunt, dull, mild.

poise, *n.* **1.** balance, equilibrium, equipoise, counterpoise. **2.** composure, self-possession, steadiness, stability, aplomb, assurance, dignity, equanimity, sang-froid, coolness, presence of mind, reserve, serenity, coolheadedness, self-control, control. **3.** carriage, mien, demeanor, savoir-faire, sophistication, grace, polish, urbanity, breeding, behavior. —**Ant.** instability, awkwardness.

poison, *n.* **1.** toxin, venom. —*v.* **2.** envenom, infect. **3.** defile, adulterate, debase, pervert, subvert, warp, corrupt, ruin, vitiate, contaminate, pollute, taint, canker.

policy, *n.* course *of action,* expediency, tactic, approach, game plan, design, scheme, program, method, system, conduct, behavior, strategy, tactics, principles, protocol, way, regulation, custom, practice, procedure, rule, management, administration, handling.

polish, *v.* **1.** brighten, smooth, burnish, shine, buff, rub, gloss, clean. **2.** finish, refine, improve, perfect, cultivate, enhance, ameliorate, fix, civilize, make elegant. —*n.* **3.** smoothness, gloss, shine, sheen, luster, glaze, sparkle, gleam, glow, radiance, brightness, brilliance. **4.** refinement, elegance, poise, grace, graciousness, savoir-faire, cultivation, suaveness, breeding, good manners, chivalrousness, gentility, culture, politeness, politesse, propriety, dignity, smoothness, good taste, tastefulness, sophistication, urbanity, diplomacy, tactfulness, courteousness, civility. —**Ant.** dullness.

polished, *adj.* **1.** smooth, glossy, burnished, shining, shiny, shined, lustrous, brilliant. **2.** refined, debonair, cultivated, graceful, sophisticated, urbane, soigné, courtly, genteel, civilized, well-bred, polite, cultured, finished, elegant, poised. **3.** accomplished, expert, proficient, skillful, adept, gifted, masterful, virtuoso,

superlative, superb, superior; faultless, impeccable, flawless, excellent, perfect. —**Ant.** dull, dim; unrefined, impolite; inelegant; clumsy, amateurish, imperfect.

polite, *adj.* respectful, deferential, diplomatic, tactful, formal, proper, well-mannered, courteous, civil, well-bred, gracious, genteel, urbane, polished, poised, courtly, cultivated, refined, finished, elegant, chivalrous. —**Ant.** impolite, rude, discourteous, uncivil.

politic, *adj.* **1.** sagacious, prudent, wise, tactful, diplomatic, discreet, judicious, provident, astute, wary. **2.** shrewd, artful, sly, cunning, underhanded, tricky, foxy, clever, subtle, Machiavellian, wily, intriguing, scheming, crafty, unscrupulous, strategic. **3.** expedient, judicious, political. —**Ant.** imprudent, indiscreet, improvident; artless, ingenuous, direct, open, honest.

pollute, *v.* **1.** befoul, dirty, defile, adulterate, poison, blight, sully, soil, taint, tarnish, stain, contaminate, vitiate, corrupt, debase, deprave. **2.** desecrate, profane, violate, dishonor, defile. —**Ant.** purify; honor, revere, respect.

ponder, *v.* consider, meditate, reflect, cogitate, deliberate, ruminate, brood, mull over, chew over, muse, think, study; weigh, contemplate, examine. —**Ant.** forget, ignore.

ponderous, *adj.* **1.** heavy, massive, unwieldy, huge, awkward, clumsy, cumbersome, weighty, bulky. **2.** important, momentous, weighty, significant, consequential, grave, serious, critical, crucial. —**Ant.** light, weightless; unimportant.

poor, *adj.* **1.** needy, indigent, necessitous, straitened, insolvent, ruined, bankrupt, destitute, penniless, poverty-stricken, impecunious, impoverished, hard up, distressed, in want, badly off, pinched, down and out, broke, short, financially embarrassed, in reduced circumstances. **2.** deficient, insufficient, meager, lacking, incomplete. **3.** faulty, inferior, unsatisfactory, substandard, shabby, jerry-built, seedy, worthless, valueless. **4.** sterile, barren, unfertile, fruitless, unproductive. **5.** lean, emaciated, thin, skinny, meager, hungry, underfed, lank, gaunt, shrunk. **6.** cowardly, abject, mean, base. **7.** scanty, paltry, meager, insufficient, inadequate. **8.** humble, unpretentious, unassuming, modest, inconsequential. **9.** unfortunate, hapless, unlucky, star-crossed, doomed, luckless, miserable, unhappy, pitiable, piteous, pathetic, wretched, sad, jinxed. —**Ant.** rich, wealthy; sufficient, adequate, complete; superior; fertile; well-fed; bold, brave; bold, pretentious; fortunate, lucky.

popular, *adj.* **1.** favorite, approved, accepted, received, liked. **2.** common, prevailing, current, general, prevalent, in vogue, faddish, dominant, predominant, customary, habitual, universal. —**Ant.** unpopular; uncommon, rare, unusual.

populous, *adj.* crowded, filled, over-crowded, packed, jam-packed, crammed, teeming, swarming, bristling, crawling, alive.

port, *n.* harbor, haven, refuge, anchorage, mooring; asylum.

portent, *n.* indication, omen, augury, sign, warning, presage.

portion, *n.* **1.** part, section, segment, division, subdivision, parcel, hunk, chunk, lump, wedge, slice, sliver, fraction, piece, bit, scrap, morsel, fragment. **2.** share, allotment, quota, dole,

dividend, division, apportionment, lot. **3.** serving, helping, ration, plate, platter. —*v.* **4.** divide, distribute, allot, apportion, deal *or* parcel out, mete, share. —**Ant.** all, everything; none, nothing.

portray, *v.* picture, delineate, limn, depict, paint, represent, sketch, show, render, characterize, describe; impersonate, pose as.

pose, *v.* **1.** sit, model; attitudinize. **2.** state, assert, propound. —*n.* **3.** attitude, posture, bearing, mien, stance, position; affectation, pretense, act, facade, show, ostentation.

position, *n.* **1.** station, place, locality, spot, location, site, locale, placement, whereabouts, situation, post. **2.** situation, condition, state, circumstances. **3.** class, caste, station, importance, status, standing, rank, place. **4.** post, job, situation, place, employment. **5.** placement, disposition, array, arrangement. **6.** stance, bearing, mien, posture, attitude, pose. **7.** proposition, thesis, contention, principle, dictum, predication, assertion, doctrine. —*v.* **8.** put, place, site, settle, dispose, arrange, fix, set, situate. **9.** locate, fix, discover, establish, determine.

positive, *adj.* **1.** explicit, express, sure, certain, definite, precise, clear, unequivocal, categorical, unmistakable, direct. **2.** arbitrary, enacted, decided, determined, decisive, unconditional. **3.** incontrovertible, substantial, indisputable, indubitable. **4.** stated, expressed, emphatic. **5.** confident, self-confident, self-assured, assured, convinced, unquestioning, overconfident, stubborn, peremptory, obstinate, dogmatic, overbearing. —**Ant.** unsure, indefinite, unclear, equivocal; conditional; doubtful; tacit; tractable, self-effacing.

possess, *v.* **1.** have, hold, own, enjoy, be blessed *or* endowed with. **2.** occupy, hold, have, control, dominate; preoccupy, obsess, charm, captivate, enchant, enthrall. —**Ant.** lose.

possession, *n.* **1.** custody, occupation, tenure. **2.** ownership, title, control, keeping, care, protection, guardianship, proprietorship. —**Ant.** loss.

possible, *adj.* feasible, practicable, likely, viable, workable, doable, attainable, potential; plausible, imaginable, conceivable, credible, thinkable, tenable, reasonable. —**Ant.** impossible, impractical, unlikely.

post, *n.* **1.** column, pillar, pole, support, upright, stake, pale, picket, strut, prop, brace, pier, piling, pylon, leg, prop. **2.** position, office, situation, job, duty, role, function, employment, work, task, chore, assignment, appointment. **3.** station, round, beat, position. —*v.* **4.** announce, advertise, publicize, publish, proclaim, promulgate, propagate; affix, tack up. **5.** station, place, set.

postpone, *v.* put off, defer, delay, procrastinate, adjourn, suspend, shelve, put on ice, table, put on the back burner.

posture, *n.* **1.** position, pose, attitude. **2.** position, condition, state, situation, disposition.

potent, *adj.* **1.** powerful, mighty, strong, vigorous, forceful, formidable, authoritative. **2.** cogent, influential, efficacious, effective, convincing, persuasive, compelling, sound, valid, impressive. —**Ant.** weak, impotent, powerless, feeble, frail; ineffectual.

potential, *adj.* **1.** possible, likely, implicit, implied, imminent, budding, embryonic, dormant, hidden, concealed, latent, passive, future. **2.** capable,

able, latent. —*n.* **3.** possibility, potentiality, capacity, capability, aptitude, what it takes, the right stuff. —**Ant.** kinetic, impossible; incapable, unable; impossibility.

pound, *v.* **1.** strike, beat, thrash, batter, pelt, hammer, pummel, bludgeon, maul, clobber, lambaste.

poverty, *n.* **1.** destitution, need, lack, want, privation, insolvency, pennilessness, bankruptcy, financial ruin, impoverishment, necessity, neediness, indigence, penury, distress. **2.** deficiency, sterility, barrenness, unfruitfulness. **3.** scantiness, jejuneness, sparingness, meagerness, scarcity, scarceness, lack, insufficiency, shortage, dearth, paucity, inadequacy. —**Ant.** wealth; abundance, fertility, fruitfulness.

power, *n.* **1.** ability, capability, capacity, faculty, competence, competency, might, strength, puissance. **2.** strength, might, muscle, brawn, vigor, force, energy. **3.** control, command, dominion, authority, sway, rule, ascendancy, influence, sovereignty, suzerainty, prerogative. —**Ant.** inability, incapacity, incompetence.

powerful, *adj.* **1.** mighty, potent, forceful, strong, vigorous, robust, energetic, sturdy, stalwart, tough, resilient, dynamic. **2.** cogent, influential, convincing, effective, efficacious, effectual, strong, compelling, forceful, substantial, weighty, authoritative, important, impressive, persuasive, formidable, telling. —**Ant.** weak, frail, feeble; ineffective, ineffectual.

practicable, *adj.* possible, feasible, workable, performable, doable, achievable, attainable, viable, realizable, practical. —**Ant.** impracticable, impossible, unattainable.

practical, *adj.* **1.** sensible, businesslike, pragmatic, efficient, useful, functional, realistic, reasonable, sound, utilitarian, applicable, serviceable, empirical. **2.** judicious, discreet, sensible, discriminating, balanced, reasoned, sound, shrewd, hard-nosed, expedient, down-to-earth. —**Ant.** impractical, inefficient; indiscreet, unsound.

practice, *n.* **1.** custom, habit, wont, routine, convention, tradition, procedure, rule, way, style, mode. **2.** exercise, drill, experience, discipline, repetition, rehearsal, training, workout, application, study. **3.** performance, operation, action, process. —*v.* **4.** carry out, perform, do, drill, exercise, follow, observe. —**Ant.** inexperience.

praise, *n.* **1.** praising, commendation, acclamation, plaudit, compliment, acclaim, tribute, ovation, honor, homage, exultation, laudation, approval, approbation, applause, kudos; encomium, eulogy, panegyric. —*v.* **2.** laud, approve, commend, admire, extol, celebrate, eulogize, panegyrize. **3.** glorify, magnify, exalt, worship, bless, adore, honor, revere, venerate, hallow. —**Ant.** condemnation, disapprobation, disapproval, criticism.

pray, *v.* importune, entreat, supplicate, beg, beseech, implore, sue, petition, invoke, appeal to, plead with, solicit, request, ask.

precarious, *adj.* **1.** uncertain, unstable, unsure, insecure, dependent, unsteady. **2.** delicate, ticklish, sensitive, slippery, touch-and-go, questionable, doubtful, dubious, unreliable, undependable, risky, perilous, hazardous, dangerous. **3.** groundless, unfounded, baseless. —**Ant.** certain, stable, sure, secure, independent, reliable, dependable; well-founded.

precaution, *n.* foresight, prudence,

providence, wariness, forethought, vigilance, apprehension, circumspection, anticipation.

precious, *adj.* **1.** expensive, prized, irreplaceable, high-priced, valuable, costly, dear, invaluable, priceless. **2.** esteemed, choice, idolized, adored, valued, revered, venerable, dear, beloved, darling, cherished. **3.** choice, fine, delicate, select, pretty, exquisite, chichi, dainty. —**Ant.** inexpensive, cheap; worthless; ugly, unattractive.

precipitate, *v.* **1.** hasten, accelerate, hurry, speed up, expedite, speed, rush, quicken, advance, dispatch, trigger, provoke, instigate, incite, facilitate, press, further. **2.** cast down, hurl *or* fling down, plunge. —*adj.* **3.** headlong, hasty, rash, reckless, indiscreet, impetuous, volatile, hotheaded, foolhardy. **4.** sudden, abrupt, violent, unexpected. —**Ant.** slow, retard; considered.

precipitous, *adj.* steep, abrupt, sheer, perpendicular, bluff. —**Ant.** gradual, sloping.

precise, *adj.* **1.** definite, exact, defined, fixed, correct, strict, explicit, literal, specific, unerring, error-free, accurate. **2.** meticulous, scrupulous, careful, conscientious, rigorous, unbending, inflexible, severe, prim, absolute, fastidious, particular, finicky, fussy, exacting, critical, rigid, puritanical, demanding, crucial. —**Ant.** indefinite, incorrect, inexact, lenient; flexible, tractable.

predatory, *adj.* predacious, plundering, ravaging, pillaging, rapacious, voracious, ravenous, greedy, larcenous, thieving.

predicament, *n.* dilemma, plight, difficulty, trial, emergency, crisis, impasse, imbroglio, quandary; situation, state, condition, position, case.

predict, *v.* foretell, prophesy, foresee, forecast, presage, augur, prognosticate, foretoken, portend, divine, forewarn, forebode.

prediction, *n.* prophecy, forecast, augury, prognostication, foretoken, portent, divination, soothsaying, presage.

predilection, *n.* prepossession, favoring, partiality, predisposition, disposition, inclination, bent, preference, leaning, bias, prejudice, proclivity, fondness. —**Ant.** disfavor, disinclination, dislike.

predominant, *adj.* ascendant, prevailing, prevalent, dominant, controlling, ruling, preeminent, superior, supreme, leading, paramount, main, chief, transcendant, important, primary, sovereign, telling, influential. —**Ant.** rare, retrograde.

predominate, *v.* preponderate, prevail, outweigh, overrule, surpass, dominate, control, rule, reign, overshadow, hold sway, lord it over.

preeminent, *adj.* eminent, surpassing, dominant, superior, over, above, distinguished, excellent, peerless, unequaled, inimitable, matchless, outstanding, unique, unrivaled, paramount, consummate, predominant, supreme, superb. —**Ant.** undistinguished, inferior.

preface, *n.* introduction, foreword, preamble, prologue, prelude, preliminary, prolegomena. —**Ant.** appendix, epilogue.

prefer, *v.* like better, favor, choose, elect, select, pick out, pick, incline *or* lean toward, opt for, embrace, espouse, esteem, approve, single out, fix upon, fancy. —**Ant.** exclude, dislike.

preference, *n.* choice, selection, pick, predilection, favorite, desire, option, partiality, proclivity, fancy, predispo-

tion, bent, inclination, leaning, prejudice, favoritism. —**Ant.** exclusion.

prejudice, *n.* **1.** preconception, bias, partiality, prejudgment, leaning, preconceived notion, jaundiced eye, predilection, predisposition, disposition, bigotry, unfairness, partisanship, favoritism, racism, discrimination, intolerance, apartheid, Jim Crow, sexism, male chauvinism, ageism. —*v.* **2.** bias, influence, warp, twist, poison, slant, distort. —**Ant.** judgment, decision.

preliminary, *adj.* **1.** advance, initial, opening, antecedent, premonitory, preceding, introductory, preparatory, prefatory, precursive, prior. —*n.* **2.** introduction, prelude, preface, prolegomena, preparation, groundwork, opening, beginning, overture. —**Ant.** resulting, concluding; conclusion, end, appendix, epilogue.

premeditate, *v.* consider, plan, deliberate, predetermine, prearrange.

premium, *n.* **1.** prize, door prize, bounty. **2.** bonus, gift, reward, recompense, extra, dividend, award, perquisite, perk; incentive, inducement, incitement, lure, bait, stimulus, goad, spur, come-on, freebie.

preoccupied, *adj.* absorbed, engrossed, meditating, meditative, rapt, thoughtful, pensive, brooding, reflective, ruminative, pondering, musing, concentrating, inattentive, in a brown study, lost in thought, abstracted, faraway, oblivious, absent-minded, wrapped up, distracted, vague, out of it, in a spell, spacey. —**Ant.** unthinking, thoughtless.

prepare, *v.* **1.** contrive, devise, plan, plan for, anticipate, get *or* make ready, provide, arrange, order. **2.** manufacture, make, compound, fix, compose, fabricate, produce, fashion, forge, mold, build, construct, assemble. —**Ant.** destroy, ruin.

preposterous, *adj.* absurd, senseless, foolish, inane, asinine, ludicrous, laughable, risable, nonsensical, fatuous, mindless, crack-brained, mad, idiotic, incredible, outrageous, exorbitant, outlandish, outré, weird, bizarre, unreasonable, ridiculous, excessive, extravagant, irrational. —**Ant.** rational, reasonable, sensible.

prerogative, *n.* right, privilege, precedence, license, franchise, immunity, freedom, liberty, power, due, advantage, claim, sanction, authority.

presage, *n.* **1.** presentiment, foreboding, foreshadowing, indication, premonition, foreknowledge. **2.** portent, omen, sign, token, augury, warning, signal, prognostic. **3.** forecast, prediction, prophecy, prognostication, divination. —*v.* **4.** portend, foreshadow, forecast, predict.

prescribe, *v.* lay down, predetermine, appoint, ordain, order, rule, enjoin, direct, dictate, decree, establish, hand down, institute, demand, require, stipulate, command, instruct, define, specify.

presence, *n.* **1.** attendance, company. **2.** nearness, vicinity, neighborhood, proximity, vicinage, closeness. **3.** personality, aura, air, magnetism, charisma, attractiveness, bearing, carriage, mien, aspect, impression, appearance, poise, self-assurance, confidence, comportment, deportment, aplomb, sophistication. —**Ant.** absence.

present, *adj.* **1.** current, contemporary, present-day, existing, extant; here, at hand, near, immediate, closest, adjacent, proximate, close, remaining, nearby. —*n.* **2.** now, nowadays, today, these days, the time being, this juncture, our times, the moment, the hour. **3.** gift, donation, offering, bounty, contribution, endowment, bonus, benefaction, largess, grant, gratuity, boon, tip. —*v.* **4.** give, endow, bestow, grant, confer, donate. **5.** afford, furnish, yield, offer, proffer. **6.** show, exhibit; introduce. —**Ant.** absent; then; receive.

presently, *adv.* by and by, in a little while, in due course, after a time, before long, in a minute, after a while, in a jiffy, at once, immediately, directly, right away, without delay, shortly, forthwith, soon. —**Ant.** later.

preserve, *v.* **1.** keep, retain, conserve. **2.** guard, safeguard, shelter, shield, protect, defend, save. **3.** keep up, maintain, continue, uphold, sustain. —**Ant.** forgo; lose.

prestige, *n.* reputation, influence, weight, importance, distinction, status, standing, rank, stature, significance, eminence, esteem, preeminence, prominence, predominance, primacy, superiority, supremacy, ascendancy, renown, fame, cachet, celebrity, glamour, stardom, charisma. —**Ant.** disrepute, notoriety.

presume, *v.* **1.** assume, presuppose, suppose, take for granted, believe, surmise, gather, imagine, suspect, fancy, conjecture, guess. **2.** venture, undertake, dare, take the liberty, make bold.

presumptuous, *adj.* bold, impertinent, forward, arrogant, insolent, saucy, impudent, impertinent, forward, immodest, egotistical, audacious, rude, fresh, proud, brazen, brash, overweening. —**Ant.** modest, polite.

pretend, *v.* feign, affect, put on, assume, falsify, simulate, fake, sham, counterfeit, allege, profess; lie, make believe.

pretense, *n.* **1.** pretending, feigning, shamming, make-believe; subterfuge, fabrication, pretext, excuse. **2.** show, cover, cover-up, semblance, dissembling, mask, cloak, veil; pretension.

pretentious, *adj.* pompous, arrogant, exaggerated, grandiose, inflated, high-flown, vain, vainglorious, affected, ostentatious, showy, la-di-da, posy, high-falutin, mannered, precious, hoity-toity. —**Ant.** earthy, plain.

pretty, *adj.* **1.** good-looking, appealing, lovely, cute, fetching, winsome, charming, fair, attractive, comely, pleasing, beautiful. **2.** fine, pleasant, excellent, splendid. —*adv.* **3.** moderately, fairly, somewhat, to some extent. **4.** very, quite. —**Ant.** ugly; unpleasant; completely.

prevail, *v.* **1.** predominate, preponderate. **2.** win, succeed, triumph. —**Ant.** lose.

prevailing, *adj.* **1.** prevalent, predominant, preponderating, dominant, preponderant. **2.** current, general, common. **3.** superior, influential, effectual, effective, efficacious, successful. —**Ant.** rare, uncommon; inferior, ineffectual, ineffective, unsuccessful.

prevalent, *adj.* universal, catholic, frequent, ubiquitous, pervasive, omnipresent, usual, customary, commonplace, ascendant, established, widespread, current, common, prevailing, extensive, predominant, predominating, accepted, used, general. —**Ant.** rare, unusual, uncommon.

prevent, *v.* hinder, stop, obstruct, hamper, impede, forestall, thwart, intercept, preclude, obviate, interrupt, avert, avoid, prohibit, ban, bar, forbid, enjoin, proscribe, foil, frustrate, abort, nip in the bud, check, block, balk, ward off, fend off, stave off, arrest,

curb, restrain, inhibit, delay, retard, slow, mitigate, control. —**Ant.** encourage, aid, help, abet, support, continue.

previous, *adj.* prior, earlier, former, preceding, foregoing, past, erstwhile, one-time, sometime. —**Ant.** later, following.

price, *n.* charge, cost, expense, outlay, expenditure, payment, amount, figure, fee; penalty, toll, sacrifice.

pride, *n.* conceit, self-esteem, egotism, hubris, overconfidence, self-love, vanity, arrogance, vainglory, self-importance; insolence, haughtiness, snobbishness, superciliousness, hauteur, presumption, smugness, snobbery. —**Ant.** modesty; humility.

prim, *adj.* stiff, starched, formal, strait-laced, precise, proper; coy, demure, prudish, prissy, modest, puritanical, rigid, blue, priggish. —**Ant.** flexible, informal; lewd, licentious, profligate.

primary, *adj.* **1.** first, highest, chief, principal, main, prime, leading, cardinal, preeminent, predominant. **2.** first, earliest, initial, primordial, embryonic, germinal, ultimate, primitive, original, primeval, aboriginal. **3.** elementary, essential, underlying, elemental, rudimentary, beginning, opening, fundamental, basic, ordinate. —**Ant.** last, final, ultimate; secondary.

primitive, *adj.* **1.** prehistoric, primal, primeval, prime, primary, primordial, original, aboriginal, pristine, first, antediluvian. **2.** uncivilized, uncultured, simple, unsophisticated, unrefined, raw, barbaric, barbarian, uncouth, savage, quaint, crude, rude, coarse, rough. —**Ant.** secondary; civilized, sophisticated, cultured.

principal, *adj.* first, highest, prime, paramount, capital, chief, primary, ranking, predominant, starring, prevailing, foremost, main, leading, cardinal, preeminent. —**Ant.** ancillary, secondary.

principally, *adv.* especially, chiefly, mainly, primarily, firstly, above all, in the main, mostly, for the most part, largely, predominantly, particularly, on the whole, in essence, essentially, basically. —**Ant.** lastly.

principle, *n.* **1.** truth, given, precept, tenet, dictum, canon, rule, standard, test, parameter. **2.** theorem, assumption, truism, axiom, postulate, maxim, law, proposition. **3.** doctrine, tenet, credo, creed, ethic, dogma, idea, sentiment, belief, opinion. **4.** integrity, honesty, probity, righteousness, uprightness, rectitude, virtue, incorruptibility, goodness, trustworthiness, honor, morals, morality, conscience.

private, *adj.* **1.** individual, personal, singular, especial, special, particular, peculiar. **2.** confidential, secret, clandestine, hidden, concealed, covert, surreptitious, off the record, hush-hush, not for publication, top secret, eyes only. **3.** alone, secluded, cloistered, sequestered, solitary, retired, retiring, reclusive, withdrawn, reticent, antisocial, hermitic, reserved. —**Ant.** public, general; known; open.

privation, *n.* hardship, deprivation, loss; destitution, want, need, necessity, distress, lack, indigence, poverty, penury, straits, misery. —**Ant.** ease, wealth.

privilege, *n.* right, benefit, advantage, allowance, indulgence, consent, sanction, authority, immunity, leave, prerogative, advantage, license, freedom, liberty, permission, franchise, carte blanche.

prize, *n.* **1.** reward, premium, award,

trophy, honor, accolade; winnings, jackpot, windfall, purse, receipts, haul, take. —*v.* **2.** value, esteem, treasure, cherish, appreciate, hold dear.

probe, *v.* examine, explore, question, investigate, scrutinize, go into, search, sift, prove, test, study, delve into, plumb, dig into. —**Ant.** overlook, ignore.

problem, *n.* question, doubt, uncertainty, puzzle, riddle, enigma, rebus, conundrum, poser; dilemma, quandary, difficulty, trouble, imbroglio. —**Ant.** certainty, certitude, surety.

procedure, *n.* **1.** proceeding, conduct, management, operation, way, action, method, system, approach, strategy, scheme, policy, routine, tradition, practice, wont, modus operandi, methodology, course, process. **2.** act, deed, transaction, maneuver, goings on.

proceed, *v.* advance, go on, progress, move on, continue, make headway, forge ahead, press onward, pass on. **2.** go *or* come forth, issue, emanate, spring, arise, result, ensue, originate, stem, develop, derive, emerge. —**Ant.** retreat.

process, *n.* course, procedure, operation, proceeding, system, approach, method, technique; activity, function, development.

proclaim, *v.* announce, declare, advertise, promulgate, publish, trumpet, circulate, broadcast, pronounce, make known, herald.

procrastinate, *v.* temporize, play for time, stall, shelve, table, evade, delay, postpone, put off, defer, adjourn, prolong. —**Ant.** speed, expedite.

procure, *v.* **1.** acquire, gain, get, secure, win, obtain, appropriate. **2.** bring about, effect, cause, contrive. —**Ant.** lose.

prod, *v.* poke, jab, nudge, elbow; spur, urge, impel, egg on, push, thrust, stir, prompt, motivate, provoke, encourage, stimulate, needle, pester, harass, badger, nag, hound, carp at, goad, rouse, incite.

prodigal, *adj.* **1.** reckless, profligate, extravagant, lavish, wasteful, immoderate, intemperate, improvident, wanton. **2.** abundant, profuse, plenteous, copious, plentiful, bounteous, bountiful. —*n.* **3.** spendthrift, waster, wastrel, squanderer, carouser, playboy, profligate, big spender. —**Ant.** cautious, provident, thrifty; scarce, scanty.

prodigious, *adj.* **1.** enormous, immense, huge, gigantic, tremendous, vast, immeasurable, colossal, mammoth, extensive, titanic. **2.** wonderful, marvelous, amazing, stupendous, astonishing, astounding, phenomenal, staggering, striking, mind-boggling, extraordinary, miraculous, wondrous, uncommon, unusual, strange. **3.** abnormal, monstrous, anomalous. —**Ant.** small, tiny, infinitesimal; negligible; common; normal, usual.

produce, *v.* **1.** give rise to, cause, generate, occasion, originate, create, effect, make, manufacture, bring about. **2.** bear, bring forth, yield, furnish, supply, afford, give. **3.** exhibit, show, demonstrate, bring forward. —*n.* **4.** yield, product, crops, fruits, production. —**Ant.** destroy, ruin; subdue, squelch; hide, conceal.

productive, *adj.* generative, creative; imaginative, inventive, resourceful, ingenious; rich, fecund, prolific, fertile, fruitful. —**Ant.** barren, sterile, unproductive.

profane, *adj.* **1.** irreverent, irreligious, blasphemous, sacrilegious, idolatrous, infidel, disrespectful, atheistic, sinful, piacular, wicked, impious, ungodly, godless, unredeemed, unredeemable. **2.** unconsecrated, secular, temporal. **3.** unholy, heathen, pagan, unhallowed, impure, polluted. **4.** common, low, mean, base, vulgar. —*v.* **5.** debase, misuse, defile, desecrate, violate, pollute, contaminate, degrade, pervert, corrupt. **—Ant.** sacred, spiritual; pure, hallowed, holy; elevated, exalted.

profession, *n.* **1.** vocation, calling, occupation, trade, craft, business, employment, specialty, line, sphere, field, work, métier. **2.** confession, statement, affirmation, acknowledgement, admission, professing, avowal, declaration, assertion.

proffer, *v.* offer, tender, volunteer, propose, suggest, hint. **—Ant.** refuse.

proficient, *adj.* skilled, adept, talented, gifted, expert, veteran, skillful, competent, practiced, experienced, qualified, trained, conversant, accomplished, finished, able, apt, capable, dextrous, polished, ace, topnotch, whiz-bang. **—Ant.** unskilled, maladroit, awkward, clumsy, untrained, unable, inept.

profit, *n.* **1.** gain, return, yield. **2.** returns, proceeds, revenue, dividend. **3.** advantage, benefit, gain, good, welfare, improvement, advancement. —*v.* **4.** gain, improve, advance, better, further, benefit, promote, aid, help, serve, avail, be advantageous. **—Ant.** loss; lose.

profound, *adj.* deep, intense, extreme, wise, learned, erudite, astute, analytical, penetrating, sagacious; abstruse, recondite arcane, esoteric, intricate, knotty, inscrutable, unfathomable, obscure, subtle, occult, secret, cabalistic, cryptic, enigmatic, puzzling, mysterious, mystifying. **—Ant.** shallow, superficial.

profuse, *adj.* extravagant, abundant, copious, ample, plentiful, lavish, bountiful, prolific, luxuriant, exuberant, lush, thick, rich, productive, fruitful, fecund, generous, liberal, unsparing, unstinting. **—Ant.** scarce, scanty.

profusion, *n.* abundance, plenty, copiousness, bounty, quantity, superabundance, wealth, glut, surplus, surfeit, plethora, superfluity, host, hoard, multitude, prodigality, profligacy, excess. **—Ant.** scarcity, need, want.

progress, *n.* **1.** proceeding, advancement, advance, progression, headway. **2.** growth, development, improvement, increase, betterment. —*v.* **3.** advance, proceed; develop, improve, grow, increase, expand, evolve, mature, ripen, burgeon, spread, extend, upgrade. **—Ant.** retrogression; recession; recede, decrease, diminish.

prohibit, *v.* **1.** forbid, interdict, disallow, bar, ban, outlaw, proscribe, taboo. **2.** prevent, hinder, preclude, obstruct, block, impede, hamper, inhibit, frustrate, foil, thwart, check, restrain. **—Ant.** allow, permit; encourage, foster, further.

prohibition, *n.* interdiction, prevention, embargo, ban, restriction, taboo, proscription, injunction. **—Ant.** permission.

project, *n.* **1.** plan, scheme, design, layout, proposal. **2.** activity, lesson, enterprise, assignment, obligation, undertaking, program, venture, commitment, engagement, occupation, job, work. —*v.* **3.** propose, contemplate, plan, contrive, scheme, plot, devise, concoct, brew, frame. **4.** throw, cast, toss, hurl, fling, launch, propel, shoot. **5.** extend, protrude, obtrude, bulge, jut out, stick out.

prolific, *adj.* **1.** fruitful, fertile, productive, teeming. **2.** abundant, copious, bountiful, profuse, plentiful, rich, lush, rife, fecund. **—Ant.** fruitless, unfruitful, barren, sterile; scarce.

prolong, *v.* lengthen, extend, protract, elongate, stretch, drag out, keep up, string out. **—Ant.** abbreviate, shorten, curtail.

prominent, *adj.* **1.** conspicuous, noticeable, outstanding, manifest, obvious, evident, pronounced, eye-catching, striking, glaring, salient, flagrant, egregious, patent, unmistakable, discernible, principal, chief, important, main. **2.** projecting, jutting out, protuberant. **3.** important, leading, well-known, eminent, celebrated, famed, famous, distinguished, illustrious, renowned, acclaimed, honored, prestigious, notable, noteworthy, respected. **—Ant.** inconspicuous, unimportant; recessed; negligible, unknown.

promiscuous, *adj.* **1.** miscellaneous, hodgepodge, heterogeneous, random, chaotic, motley, scrambled, disorganized, disorderly, indiscriminate, confused, mixed, intermixed, intermingled, mingled, jumbled, garbled. **2.** nonselective, indiscriminate, careless, heedless, haphazard, uncritical, unfussy, slipshod, irresponsible, thoughtless. **—Ant.** pure, unmixed; selective, careful.

promise, *n.* **1.** word, pledge, assurance, vow, oath, bond, commitment, agreement, contract, covenant, compact. —*v.* **2.** pledge, agree, engage, assure, swear, vow, guarantee, take an oath.

promote, *v.* **1.** further, advance, encourage, forward, assist, aid, back, sanction, abet, boost, foster, develop, strengthen, stimulate, inspirit, help, support. **2.** elevate, raise, exalt, upgrade, kick upstairs. **—Ant.** discourage, obstruct; lower, debase.

prone, *adj.* **1.** inclined, disposed, liable, tending, bent, apt, likely, predisposed, of a mind, given, leaning. **2.** prostrate, recumbent, reclining, face down, horizontal. **—Ant.** averse; upright.

proof, *n.* **1.** evidence, testimony, certification, confirmation, verification, corroboration, validation, authentication, documentation, demonstration. **2.** test, trial, examination, measure, standard, touchstone, criterion.

propensity, *n.* inclination, bent, leaning, tendency, disposition, likelihood, proneness, bias, predisposition. **—Ant.** disinclination, aversion, distaste.

proper, *adj.* **1.** appropriate, fit, suitable, suited, apropos, convenient, fitting, befitting, correct, right, becoming, meet. **2.** correct, dignified, genteel, seemly, refined, punctilious, decorous, decent, respectable, polite, well-mannered. **3.** special, own, separate, distinct, particular, respective, distinctive, unique, specific, individual, peculiar. **4.** strict, accurate, precise, exact, just, formal, correct, orthodox, expected, accepted, normal, established, usual. **—Ant.** improper.

property, *n.* **1.** possession, possessions, goods, effects, chattels, paraphernalia, gear, assets, means, resources, holdings, estate, belongings. **2.** land, real estate, acreage. **3.** ownership, right. **4.** attribute, quality, characteristic, feature, trait, mark, hallmark, oddity, idiosyncrasy, peculiarity, quirk.

prophesy, *v.* foretell, predict, forecast, forewarn, augur, prognosticate, divine;

presage, foreshadow, portend, bode, harbinger, herald, promise.

proportion, *n.* **1.** relation, ratio, arrangement; comparison, analogy. **2.** size, extent, dimensions. **3.** percentage, division, quota, allotment, ration, portion, part, piece, share. **4.** symmetry, concord, suitableness, congruity, correspondence, correlation, harmony, agreement, balance, distribution, arrangement. —*v.* **5.** adjust, regulate, redistribute, arrange, balance, harmonize, modify, modulate, shape, fit, match, conform. **—Ant.** disproportion.

proposal, *n.* plan, scheme, offer, bid, recommendation, outline, draft, suggestion, design, overture, approach, proposition, program, project, outline.

propose, *v.* **1.** offer, proffer, tender, suggest, recommend, present. **2.** nominate, name, suggest, introduce, submit, advance, put forward. **3.** plan, intend, design, mean, purpose. **4.** state, present, propound, pose, posit. **—Ant.** refuse.

propriety, *n.* **1.** decorum, etiquette, protocol, good behavior, courtesy, punctili, dignity, gentility, decency, modesty. **2.** suitability, appropriateness, aptness, fitness, suitableness, seemliness. **3.** rightness, justness, correctness, accuracy. **—Ant.** impropriety, immodesty, indecency; unseemliness, ineptitude; inaccuracy.

prosaic, *adj.* stale, banal, clichéd, stereotyped, pedestrian, hackneyed, flat, stock, routine, ordinary, workaday, mediocre, bland, trite, threadbare, tired, dead, lifeless, jejune, boring, unpoetic, insipid, monotonous, ho-hum, run of the mill, commonplace, dull, matter-of-fact, unimaginative, vapid, humdrum, tedious, tiresome, wearisome, uninteresting. **—Ant.** interesting, fascinating, beguiling.

prospect, *n.* **1.** anticipation, expectation, expectance, likelihood, intention, contemplation. **2.** view, scene, outlook, panorama, landscape, seascape, sight, spectacle, aspect, survey, vista, perspective. —*v.* **3.** search, explore, look for.

prosper, *v.* succeed, thrive, flourish, progress, develop, grow rich, make good, make one's fortune, make it. **—Ant.** fail, die.

prosperous, *adj.* **1.** fortunate, successful, flourishing, thriving. **2.** affluent, wealthy, rich, well-to-do, well-off. **3.** favorable, propitious, fortunate, lucky, auspicious, golden, bright. **—Ant.** unfortunate, unsuccessful; poor, impoverished; unfavorable.

prostitute, *n.* **1.** harlot, whore, strumpet, call girl, trollop, chippy, fallen or loose woman, hooker, lady of the night, ho, tart, hustler, streetwalker, courtesan. —*v.* **2.** degrade, demean, debase, lower, cheapen, defile, pervert, sell out, misapply, misuse, abuse.

protect, *v.* defend, guard, shield, cover, screen, shelter, save, harbor, house, secure, safeguard, preserve, conserve, tend. **—Ant.** attack, assail.

protection, *n.* **1.** preservation, guard, defense, shelter, screen, cover, security, refuge, safety, shield, barrier, immunity, bulwark, haven, sanctuary. **2.** aegis, patronage, sponsorship, care, custody, charge, safekeeping, keeping. **—Ant.** attack.

protest, *n.* **1.** objection, disapproval, protestation, opposition, complaint, grievance, dissent, disagreement, demurral, disclaimer, denial, scruple, qualm, compunction, squawk, beef. —*v.* **2.** remonstrate, dissent, take exception, take issue with, demure, op-

pose, grumble, disapprove, disagree, scruple, kick, gripe, grouse, beef, complain, object. **3.** declare, affirm, assert, avow, aver, testify, attest, confirm, announce, insist on, profess. **—Ant.** approval; approve.

prototype, *n.* model, pattern, example, exemplar, original, archetype, first, precedent, mold, standard, paragon, epitome.

protract, *v.* draw out, lengthen, extend, prolong, continue, stretch, drag out. **—Ant.** curtail, abbreviate, discontinue.

proud, *adj.* **1.** narcissistic, complacent, self-centered, boastful, bragging, self-satisfied, egotistical, vain, conceited. **2.** arrogant, overweening, haughty, overbearing, self-important, cocky, cocksure, high and mighty, snobbish, overconfident, disdainful, supercilious, snooty, imperious, presumptuous. **3.** honorable, creditable, estimable, illustrious, distinguished, eminent, reputable. **4.** stately, majestic, magnificent, noble, imposing, splendid, lofty, dignified, respected, august, grand. **—Ant.** discontented, dissatisfied; humble, self-effacing; dishonorable; ignoble, base.

prove, *v.* **1.** demonstrate, show, confirm, authenticate, corroborate, validate, certify, affirm, manifest, establish, evince, evidence, substantiate, verify, justify, ascertain, determine. **2.** try, test, examine, assay, check, analyze. **—Ant.** disprove.

proverb, *n.* maxim, saying, adage, epigram, precept, truth, saw, axiom, aphorism, byword, apothegm; platitude, bromide, truism, cliché, commonplace, chestnut.

provide, *v.* **1.** furnish, supply, afford, yield, produce, contribute, equip, outfit, accommodate, provision, purvey, give. **2.** prepare, get ready, procure, provide for, make provision for, arrange for, anticipate, forearm. **—Ant.** deprive.

provoke, *v.* **1.** anger, enrage, exasperate, irk, vex, irritate, incense, gall, rile, distress, upset, disturb, perturb, outrage, offend, insult, pique, madden, get on one's nerves, annoy, chafe, aggravate, exacerbate, infuriate, ire, nettle, affront. **2.** stir up, arouse, call forth, incite, stimulate, excite, fire, rouse, inflame, animate, inspirit, motivate, induce, encourage, goad, spur, impel, egg on. **3.** give rise to, induce, bring about, promote, foment, kindle, instigate. **—Ant.** assuage, calm, propitiate.

prowl, *v.* lurk, sneak, skulk, slink; scour, scavenge, patrol, cruise, cover, rove, roam, wander; prey, plunder, pillage, steal, stalk, seek, hunt, track.

prudence, *n.* **1.** calculation, foresight, forethought, judgment, discretion, common sense, circumspection, caution, wisdom. **2.** providence, care, economy, frugality, carefulness, thrift. **—Ant.** carelessness, imprudence, incaution.

prudent, *adj.* **1.** wise, judicious, cautious, discreet, tactful, sensible, discerning, politic, discriminating, reasonable, canny, shrewd, vigilant, guarded, sagacious, circumspect, careful, wary, provident. **2.** provident, frugal, sparing, economical, thrifty, saving, careful. **—Ant.** imprudent, indiscreet; tactless, careless; improvident, prodigal.

prudish, *adj.* priggish, puritanical, prissy, prim, squeamish, fussy, strait-laced, stiff, rigid, overnice, formal, decorous, modest, proper, demure, pure, coy, reserved. **—Ant.** immodest, indecent.

prying, *adj.* curious, inquisitive, peeping, peering, peeking; nosy, meddlesome, interfering. **—Ant.** unconcerned, uninterested, discreet.

pseudo, *adj.* sham, counterfeit, false, spurious, pretended, fake, phony, bogus, fraudulent, ersatz, make-believe, unreal, inauthentic, artificial, imitation, mock, dishonest, deceitful, hypocritical, forged. **—Ant.** genuine, real.

publish, *v.* make public, put out, broadcast, air, announce, proclaim, promulgate, declare, disclose, divulge, reveal, impart, advertise, publicize, spread, makeknown, report, break the news, inform. **—Ant.** conceal, hide.

puerile, *adj.* **1.** immature, babyish, jejune, infantile, sophomoric, juvenile, childish, youthful. **2.** foolish, irrational, trivial, nugatory, silly, ridiculous, asinine, shallow, inconsequential, insignificant, irresponsible, idle. **—Ant.** mature, rational.

pulsate, *v.* beat, palpitate, pulse, pound, drum, thump, reverberate, hammer, throb; vibrate, quiver, oscillate.

pungent, *adj.* **1.** spicy, strong, penetrating, aromatic, highly seasoned, tangy, tasty, flavorful, biting, acrid, hot, peppery, piquant, sharp. **2.** poignant, distressing, upsetting, hurtful, piercing, intense, severe, acute, agonizing, oppressive, excruciating, consuming, racking, smart. **3.** caustic, biting, sarcastic, sardonic, mordant, penetrating, piercing, trenchant, cutting, severe, acrimonious, bitter, waspish. **4.** stimulating, acute, keen, sharp. **—Ant.** mild, bland; painless; dull.

punish, *v.* correct, discipline, penalize, reprove, rebuke, take to task, dress down, admonish, teach a lesson, throw the book at, call onto the carpet, castigate, scold, berate, chastise, chasten, thrash, beat, spank; flog, whip, lash, scourge. **—Ant.** praise, laud; forgive.

pupil, *n.* disciple, scholar, student, learner, schoolchild, apprentice; tyro, greenhorn, neophyte, novice, beginner, abecedarian, rookie. **—Ant.** teacher, expert.

purchase, *v.* **1.** buy, acquire, get, obtain, procure. **—n.** **2.** buying, acquisition, procurement, obtaining, securing. **—Ant.** sell, lose; sale.

pure, *adj.* **1.** unmixed, unadulterated, uncontaminated, unalloyed, clean, unsullied, untainted, unstained, undefiled, spotless, untarnished, immaculate, unpolluted, uncorrupted. **2.** unmodified, simple, homogeneous, genuine, faultless, perfect. **3.** thoroughbred, purebred, pedigreed. **4.** utter, sheer, unqualified, absolute. **5.** virginal, virgin, intact, guileless, moral, decent, decorous, sinless, innocent, chaste, undefiled, unsullied, modest, virtuous. **6.** honorable, principled, righteous, pious, worthy, ethical, above reproach, guiltless, innocent, true, honest, upright, sincere. **—Ant.** impure.

purge, *v.* purify, cleanse, clear, clean, clarify, scour, wash out. **—Ant.** pollute.

puritan, *n.* **1.** moralist, pietist, fanatic, purist, prude, zealot, stuffed shirt, killjoy, bluenose. **—adj.** **2.** prim, proper, prudish, strait-laced, rigid, inflexible, stern, uncompromising, hard-line, moralistic, pietistic, stuffy, stiff, strict, severe, narrow-minded, narrow, austere, ascetic, Spartan, intolerant, hard-nosed, blue, uptight. **—Ant.** libertine, immoralist, heathen; debauched, immoral, wanton, broad-minded, free-thinking, loose.

purport, *v.* **1.** profess, claim, mean, intend, signify. **2.** express, imply. **—n.** **3.** tenor, import, meaning, intention, claim, design, significance, signification, implication, drift, suggestion, gist, spirit. **—Ant.** understand, see; infer; insignificance, meaninglessness.

purpose, *n.* **1.** object, intent, intention, determination, aim, end, design, view, goal, ambition, objective, target, point, rationale, reason. **2.** result, effect, advantage, consequence. **—v.** **3.** propose, design, intend, mean, contemplate, plan, aim, aspire, have in mind, consider. **—Ant.** purposelessness.

push, *v.* **1.** shove, shoulder, thrust, drive, move, slide. **2.** press, urge, persuade, drive, impel. **—n.** **3.** attack, effort, onset.

put, *v.* **1.** place, lay, set, deposit, position, situate, station, stand, rest, settle, locate. **2.** set, levy, impose, inflict. **3.** express, state, utter, word, phrase, write.

puzzle, *n.* **1.** riddle, enigma, problem, rebus, paradox, conundrum, mystery, brainteaser, cipher, poser, maze, question. **—v.** **2.** bewilder, perplex, confound, mystify, confuse, baffle, nonplus, stymie, stump, flummox, throw for a loop.

Q

quagmire, *n.* **1.** swamp, marsh, fen, bog, mire, morass, slough. **2.** predicament, difficulty, dilemma, pickle, tight spot, fix, jam, corner, box, quandary.

quaint, *adj.* **1.** strange, odd, curious, bizarre, peculiar, queer, singular, eccentric, unorthodox, whimsical, offbeat, fanciful, outlandish, unconventional, fantastic, weird, unusual, extraordinary, unique, uncommon. **2.** picturesque, charming, old-fashioned, antiquated, antique, archaic, outdated, passé. **—Ant.** common, usual, ordinary; modern.

quake, *v.* **1.** shake, shudder, tremble, shiver, vibrate, stagger, quaver, quiver. **—n.** **2.** temblor, earthquake, tremor, seismic activity.

qualify, *v.* **1.** fit, suit, adapt, prepare, equip, ready, condition, certify, make eligible. **2.** characterize, call, name, designate, label, signify. **3.** modify, limit, mitigate, restrain, narrow, restrict. **4.** moderate, mitigate, meliorate, soften, ameliorate, mollify, soothe, ease, assuage, temper, reduce, diminish.

quality, *n.* **1.** characteristic, attribute, property, character, feature, mark, distinction, trait. **2.** nature, grade, kind, sort, description, status, rank, condition. **3.** excellence, superiority, standing. **4.** accomplishment, deed, feat, attainment. **—Ant.** inferiority, baseness; failure.

qualm, *n.* uneasiness, second thoughts, doubt, uncertainty, hesitation, reluctance, disinclination, queasiness, apprehensiveness, compunction, scruple, twinge, remorse, misgiving, pang, worry, concern, sinking feeling. **—Ant.** self-assurance, confidence, certainty.

quandary, *n.* dilemma, predicament, strait, uncertainty, doubt, plight, difficulty. **—Ant.** ease, comfort.

quarrel, *n.* **1.** dispute, altercation, disagreement, argument, contention, controversy, dissension, feud, breach, break, rupture, debate, discord, row, squabble, scuffle, fracas, melee, donnybrook, difference, spat, tiff, fight, misunderstanding, wrangle, brawl, tumult. —v. **2.** squabble, fall out, disagree with, differ, disagree, be at odds, feud, battle, scrap, bicker, dispute, argue, wrangle, spar, brawl, clash, jar, fight.

quarrelsome, adj. argumentative, disputatious, cantankerous, disagreeable, fractious, querulous, choleric, contrary, dyspeptic, hostile, dissident, contentious, testy, petulant, irascible, irritable, peevish, cross, curmudgeonly, cranky, grouchy, combative, belligerent, bellicose, truculent, pugnacious, antagonistic. —**Ant.** peaceable, amicable.

queasy, adj. **1.** squeamish, fastidious, overfastidious, delicate, finicky, finical, picky, particular. **2.** nauseated, nauseous, qualmish, sickish, seasick, airsick, carsick, queer, queerish, puky, barfy, green around the gills, woozy, bilious. **3.** uncomfortable, uneasy, nervous, apprehensive, worried, troubled, ill at ease, doubtful, hesitant.

queer, adj. strange, unconventional, odd, singular, curious, fantastic, uncommon, weird, peculiar, extraordinary, eccentric, freakish, anomalous, bizarre, uncanny, exotic, fey, outlandish, outré, unnatural, unorthodox, atypical, offbeat. —**Ant.** conventional, ordinary, common.

quell, v. **1.** suppress, stifle, extinguish, put an end to, crush, quash, subdue, overpower, overcome. **2.** vanquish, put down, defeat, conquer. **3.** quiet, allay, calm, pacify, compose, lull, hush. —**Ant.** encourage, foster; defend, lose; agitate, disturb, perturb.

querulous, adj. complaining, petulant, peevish, snappish, abrupt, irritable, irascible, fractious, perverse, ill-natured, crotchety, cantankerous, curmudgeonly, choleric, dyspeptic, cross, testy, sour, crabby, quarrelsome, fretful, whining, touchy, waspish; caviling, carping, discontented, faultfinding, hypercritical, censorious, fussy, finicky, overparticular, annoyed, piqued. —Ant. calm, equable; pleased, contented.

question, n. **1.** inquiry, query, interrogation. **2.** dispute, controversy. —v. **3.** interrogate; ask, inquire, query, examine, quiz, test, interview, sound out, grill, pump. **4.** doubt, mistrust, distrust, suspect. **5.** dispute, challenge. —**Ant.** answer, reply; agree, concur.

questionable, adj. doubtful, uncertain, dubitable, dubious, debatable, disputable, controvertible, moot, borderline, suspect, suspicious, shady, problematical, unreliable, unsure, ambiguous. —**Ant.** certain, sure, positive.

quibble, n. **1.** evasion, prevarication, equivocation, sophistry, sophism, hairsplitting, nitpicking, subterfuge, cavil. —v. **2.** evade, prevaricate, equivocate, cavil, shuffle, trifle, split hairs, be evasive, pettifog, nitpick.

quick, adj. **1.** prompt, immediate, rapid, fast, swift, speedy, instantaneous, fleet, hasty, hurried, expeditious. **2.** impatient, hasty, abrupt, curt, short, precipitate, sharp, unceremonious, testy, waspish, snappish, irritable, peppery, irascible, petulant, touchy. **3.** lively, keen, acute, sensitive, alert, sharp, shrewd, intelligent, discerning. **4.** vigorous, energetic, active, nimble, animated, agile, lively, alert, brisk. —**Ant.** slow; patient, deliberate; calm; dull, stupid; lethargic, lazy.

quiet, n. **1.** tranquility, rest, repose, calm, stillness, quietude, serenity, peace, calmness, silence. —adj. **2.**

peaceable, peaceful, pacific, calm, tranquil, serene, silent. **3.** motionless, still, unmoving, unmoved, fixed, stationary, at rest, inactive, composed, unexcited. **4.** inconspicuous, subdued; repressed, unstrained, unobtrusive. —v. **5.** still, hush, silence. **6.** tranquilize, pacify, calm, compose, lull, soothe. —**Ant.** disturbance, perturbation; war; warlike, noisy, clamorous, conspicuous, obvious, blatant; disturb, perturb.

quip, v. **1.** joke, banter, jest, gibe, wisecrack, josh, crack wise. —n. **2.** witticism, joke, jest, ad lib, barb, aphorism, epigram, pun, double entendre, one-liner, crack, wheeze, chestnut, smart remark, jape, gibe, wisecrack, gag, bon mot, sally.

quit, v. **1.** stop, cease, discontinue, desist. **2.** depart from, leave, go, withdraw or retire from, exit, decamp, desert, flee, forsake, abandon, take off, skip. **3.** give up, let go, relinquish, release, resign, surrender. —adj. **4.** released, free, clear, liberated, rid, absolved, acquitted, discharged, exempt. —**Ant.** start; initiate, originate; continue; arrive, enter; chained, confined.

quiver, v. **1.** shake, tremble, vibrate, quake, shudder, shiver. —n. **2.** tremble, tremor, shudder, shiver, trembling, shake, spasm, quaver.

quixotic, adj. idealistic, impractical, unrealistic, fantastic, chimerical, fanciful, dreamy, starry-eyed, optimistic, Pollyannaish, rash, absurd, mad, foolhardy, preposterous, ridiculous, visionary, impracticable, romantic, imaginary, wild. —**Ant.** realistic, practicable, practical.

quizzical, adj. **1.** questioning, curious, puzzled, inquisitive, inquiring, interrogatory. **2.** skeptical, suspicious, dubious, doubting, wary, distrustful, incredulous, unbelieving. **3.** queer, odd, funny, curious, peculiar, strange, weird.

R

rabid, adj. **1.** overwrought, violent, berserk, hysterical, frantic, frenzied, frenetic, furious, raging, wild, mad, maniacal. **2.** extreme, extremist, radical, fanatic, fanatical, fervent, perfervid, overzealous, irrational, wild-eyed, over the top. —**Ant.** calm, composed, reasonable.

race, n. **1.** competition, contest. **2.** course, stream. **3.** nation, people, clan, family, tribe; generation, stock, line, lineage, breed, kin, kindred, progeny, descendants, offspring, children. **4.** humankind. —v. **5.** run, speed, hurry, hasten, hie, dash, sprint, fly, rush, scramble, step on it, get a move on.

rack, n. **1.** torment, anguish, torture, pain, agony. —v. **2.** torture, distress, torment, agonize, excruciate. **3.** strain, force, wrest, stretch, wrench, batter, beat, tear at.

racket, n. **1.** din, uproar, noise, clamor, fuss, tumult, hubbub, outcry, disturbance, row, rumpus, hullabaloo, ado, commotion, brouhaha, pandemonium, to-do, hue and cry. —**Ant.** quiet, tranquility, peace.

racy, adj. **1.** vigorous, lively, animated, spirited. **2.** sprightly, piquant, pungent, strong, flavorful. **3.** suggestive, risqué, ribald, bawdy, off-color, smutty, salacious, vulgar, pornographic, obscene, naughty, earthy, lewd, gross, blue, indecent, adult. —**Ant.** dispirited, dejected; mild, bland.

radiant, adj. shining, bright, brilliant,

beaming, effulgent, resplendent, sparkling, splendid, glittering, luminous, shimmering, scintillating, dazzling, twinkling, incandescent, lustrous, gleaming, glossy, glowing. —**Ant.** dull.

radiate, v. **1.** shine, beam, glow, gleam, burn, luminesce, incandesce, twinkle, glimmer, sparkle, flash, glare, dazzle, blaze, shimmer, glisten, glitter, coruscate, scintillate. **2.** diffuse, disperse, emit, spread, propagate, scatter, emanate, throw off, give off.

radical, adj. **1.** fundamental, basic, original, constitutional, elementary, inherent, cardinal, principal, primary, deep-seated, profound, underlying, organic, natural, rudimentary, essential, innate, ingrained. **2.** thoroughgoing, extreme, complete, entire, total, exhaustive, comprehensive, drastic, severe, revolutionary, unqualified, thorough, fanatical, excessive, immoderate, extravagant, violent. —n. **3.** extremist, revolutionary, rebel, nonconformist, iconoclast, nihilist, pioneer, trailblazer, progressive, zealot, fanatic, immoderate, militant, anarchist, Jacobin, terrorist. —**Ant.** superfluous; incomplete, moderate.

rage, n. **1.** anger, ire, fury, frenzy, passion, vehemence, wrath, exasperation, madness, raving. **2.** fury, violence, turbulence, tumultuousness, storm. **3.** ardor, fervor, enthusiasm, eagerness, desire, passion, frenzy, vehemence. **4.** mode, fashion, fad, craze, vogue, mania. —v. **5.** rave, fume, storm, chafe, fret, rant, run amok, go berserk, explode, boil, seethe, smolder, fulminate, blow up, hit the roof or ceiling, go ape, have a fit. —**Ant.** calm, equanimity.

ragged, adj. **1.** tattered, torn, shredded, rent, ripped, frayed, threadbare, patched. **2.** shabby, poor, mean, seedy, tacky, grungy. —**Ant.** neat, whole.

raid, n. **1.** onset, attack, seizure, onslaught, blitz, expedition, bust. **2.** invasion, inroad, incursion. —**Ant.** defense.

raillery, n. banter, kidding, kidding around, teasing, joshing, frivolity, repartee, joking, jesting, ridicule, ribbing, ragging, twitting, fooling around, badinage, persiflage, give-and-take, back-and-forth.

raise, v. **1.** lift, lift up, elevate, heave, hoist, loft. **2.** rouse, arouse, awake, awaken, call forth, evoke, stir up, excite. **3.** build, erect, construct, rear, set up. **4.** cause, promote, cultivate, grow, propagate. **5.** originate, engender, give rise to, bring up or about, produce, effect, cause. **6.** invigorate, animate, inspirit, heighten, intensify. **7.** advance, elevate, promote, exalt. **8.** gather, collect, muster, marshal, assemble, bring together. **9.** increase, intensify, heighten, aggravate, amplify, augment, enhance, enlarge. —**Ant.** lower; pacify; destroy, raze; kill; weaken, dispirit; debase, dishonor; scatter, disperse, broadcast.

ramble, v. **1.** stroll, amble, walk, wander, saunter, stray, roam, travel, drift, hike, trek, meander, rove, range, straggle. —n. **2.** walk, stroll, amble, excursion, tour, promenade, constitutional, tramp, hike, trek.

rambling, adj. **1.** wandering, aimless, irregular, straggling, straying, meandering, maundering, labyrinthine, muddled, scrambled, discursive, roundabout, circuitous, tortuous, disjointed, illogical, circumlocutory, incoherent, periphrastic, interminable. —**Ant.** direct, pointed.

rambunctious, adj. boisterous, high-spirited, exuberant, roisterous, rollicking, unrestrained, uninhibited, irrepressible, untamed, knockabout, uproarious, wild, rowdy; unruly, disobedient, riotous, obstreperous, disorderly, fractious. —**Ant.** docile.

rampage, n. **1.** spree, tear, binge, outburst, orgy, riot, furor, tumult, uproar, frenzy, rage, turmoil, fury, convulsion. —v. **2.** rage, storm, rave, rant, tear, tear around, riot, go berserk, run amok.

ramshackle, adj. shaky, rickety, flimsy, dilapidated, broken down, tumbledown, crumbling, decrepit, unsteady, tottering, ruined, run-down, neglected, derelict, jerry-built. —**Ant.** luxurious, sumptuous, palatial.

rancor, n. resentment, antipathy, antagonism, hostility, vindictiveness, vengefulness, spleen, acrimony, animus, bad feeling, bad blood, bitterness, ill will, hatred, malice, spite, venom, malevolence, animosity, enmity. —**Ant.** amiability, goodwill, benevolence.

random, adj. haphazard, chance, fortuitous, accidental, serendipitous, arbitrary, nonspecific, unplanned, unsystematic, unpremeditated, incidental, hit or miss, casual, stray, aimless. —**Ant.** specific, particular.

range, n. **1.** extent, limits, scope, sweep, latitude, reach, span, radius, sphere, orbit, area, compass. **2.** rank, class, order, kind, sort. **3.** row, line, series, tier, file. **4.** area, trace, region. —v. **5.** align, rank, classify, class, order, arrange, array, dispose. **6.** vary, fluctuate, spread, run the gamut, course. **7.** extend, stretch out, run, go, lie. **8.** roam, rove, wander, stroll, straggle. **9.** extend, be found, occupy, lie, run, cover.

rank, n. **1.** position, standing, station, order, class, level, status, grade, echelon, division. **2.** row, line, tier, series, range. **3.** weight, authority, ascendancy, superiority, influence, power, prestige, distinction, eminence, dignity. **4.** order, arrangement, array, alignment. —v. **5.** arrange, line up, align, array, range. **6.** classify, dispose, sort, class, arrange. —adj. **7.** tall, vigorous, luxuriant, abundant, overabundant, exuberant. **8.** strong, gamy, pungent, offensive, noxious, fetid, rancid, putrid. **9.** utter, absolute, complete, entire, sheer, gross, extravagant, excessive. **10.** offensive, disgusting, repulsive, repellent, miasmatic, mephitic. **11.** coarse, indecent, foul, gross, vulgar, lurid, vile, obscene.

rankle, v. irritate, annoy, vex, distress, plague, nettle, fester, gall, inflame, incense, embitter, rile, aggravate, chafe, grate, torment, pain, provoke, anger, exasperate, irk. —**Ant.** placate, please.

ransom, n. **1.** redemption, rescue, emancipation, deliverance, liberation, release. —v. **2.** redeem, release, restore, deliver, deliver up, rescue.

rapid, adj. speedy, fast, quick, swift, fleet, high-speed, brisk, prompt, express, lightning-fast, hurried, hasty, precipitate, impetuous, immediate, instantaneous, instant, sudden. —**Ant.** slow.

rapidity, n. swiftness, speed, fleetness, quickness, haste, velocity, alacrity, celerity, promptness, dispatch, briskness, expeditiousness. —**Ant.** lethargy, slowness.

rapport, n. relationship, interrelationship, affinity, attraction, bond, sympathy, empathy, closeness, understanding, like-mindedness, accord, concord, harmony, compatibility, goodwill, fel-

low feeling, fellowship, kinship, oneness, unity, camaraderie. —**Ant.** enmity, incompatibility.

rapt, adj. **1.** engrossed, preoccupied, occupied, absorbed, abstracted, thoughtful, bemused, faraway, single-minded, concentrated, fixed, fixated. **2.** enraptured, rapturous, transported, ecstatic, transfigured, enthralled, fascinated, enchanted, gripped, held, riveted, spellbound, entranced, bewitched, captivated, mesmerized, hypnotized, delighted, under a spell. —**Ant.** distracted.

rapture, n. ecstasy, joy, delight, transport, bliss, beatitude, exultation, exaltation, elation, euphoria, thrill, enchantment, pleasure. —**Ant.** misery, disgust, revulsion.

rare, adj. **1.** scarce, uncommon, exceptional, atypical, unusual, sparse, infrequent, extraordinary, singular, phenomenal, recherché, unique, one of a kind, limited, few and far between, unparalleled. **2.** excellent, admirable, fine, choice, exquisite, incomparable, inimitable. —**Ant.** common, usual, frequent, ordinary; base, inferior.

rarefied, adj. **1.** thin, attenuated, tenuous, ethereal, vaporous, insubstantial, airy, gaseous, diffuse, diluted, dilute, adulterated, weak, watered down, porous. **2.** refined, esoteric, special, secret, recondite, inside, privileged.

rascal, n. imp, devil, mischief-maker, cad, villain, blackguard, good-for-nothing, wastrel, wretch, knave, rogue, scamp, scoundrel, miscreant, scapegrace.

rash, adj. hasty, impetuous, reckless, headlong, precipitate, impulsive, thoughtless, heedless, indiscreet, incautious, unwary, injudicious, imprudent, wild, madcap, hare-brained, hotheaded, adventurous, quixotic, bold, brash, daring, devil-may-care, foolhardy, audacious. —**Ant.** thoughtful, considered, discreet, cautious.

ratify, v. confirm, corroborate, consent to, agree to, approve, sanction, substantiate, validate, establish, endorse, support, uphold, sustain, verify, authenticate, certify, affirm, clinch, settle. —**Ant.** refute, veto, disapprove.

ration, n. **1.** allowance, portion, share, quota, allotment, helping, part, provision, percentage, dole, amount. —v. **2.** apportion, distribute, mete, dole, deal, parcel out.

rational, adj. **1.** reasonable, sensible, well-balanced, sane, sound, normal, logical, clearheaded, cleareyed, sober, of sound mind. **2.** intelligent, wise; judicious, discreet, sagacious, enlightened. **3.** sane, lucid, sound, sober, common-sense, practical, pragmatic, down-to-earth, acceptable. —**Ant.** irrational, unreasonable; unintelligent, stupid, unwise, indiscreet; unsound.

rationalize, v. **1.** explain, clarify, elucidate, explicate, illuminate. **2.** justify, excuse, alibi, exculpate, extenuate, explain away, vindicate, whitewash, gloss over.

raucous, adj. **1.** noisy, discordant, strident, harsh, dissonant, earsplitting, thunderous, rackety, cacophonous, stridulant, shrill, grating, piercing, jarring, screechy, shrieky, squawky. **2.** obstreperous, riotous, disorderly, boisterous, unruly, rowdy, rambunctious, uproarious, irrepressible, wild, tumultuous, rollicking, turbulent, fractious. —**Ant.** melodious, sweet-sounding.

ravage, n. **1.** devastation, destruction, ruin, waste, desolation, damage, havoc, despoilment, plunder, pillage. —v. **2.** damage, demolish, raze, wreck, mar, ruin, devastate, destroy, lay

waste; despoil, plunder, pillage, sack, ransack, loot. —**Ant.** construction, creation; build; repair.

ravenous, adj. ravening, voracious, greedy, swinish, piggish, hoggish, starved, hungry, famished, insatiable, gluttonous, devouring; rapacious, raptorial, predacious, predatory. —**Ant.** sated, satisfied.

raw, adj. **1.** unprepared, unfinished, unrefined, unmade, crude, rude, rough, makeshift. **2.** uncooked, unprepared, fresh, natural. **3.** ignorant, inexperienced, new, unseasoned, immature, untrained, undisciplined, green, unskilled, untried, unpracticed. **4.** damp, chilly, cold, wet, windy, frigid, freezing, nippy, biting, penetrating. —**Ant.** prepared, finished, refined, done, polished; cooked; done; intelligent, disciplined, skilled; dry, warm, arid.

reach, v. **1.** get to, attain, arrive at, come to. **2.** touch, seize, outstretch, extend, hold out. **3.** stretch, extend. —n. **4.** extent, distance, range, compass, area, sphere, influence, stretch, scope, grasp. —**Ant.** fail.

reactionary, n. conservative, ultraconservative, rightist, right-winger, enemy of progress, establishmentarian, nonprogressive, hard-liner, royalist, moderate, orthodox, traditionalist, tory, mossback, fundamentalist, throwback, old fogy, puritan, fuddy-duddy, stuffed shirt, bluenose, anachronism, stick-in-the-mud, fossil, square, back number. —**Ant.** radical.

ready, adj. **1.** prepared, set, fitted, fit. **2.** equipped, geared, completed, adjusted, arranged. **3.** willing, agreeable, cheerful, disposed, inclined. **4.** prompt, quick, alert, acute, sharp, keen, adroit, facile, clever, skillful, nimble. —v. **5.** make ready, prepare, equip, organize, set, fit out, get ready. —**Ant.** unprepared, unfit; unwilling, indisposed, disinclined; slow, deliberate, unskillful.

real, adj. true, actual, faithful, factual, authentic, legitimate, verifiable, right, bonafide, official, valid, genuine; sincere, unfeigned, heartfelt, honest, unaffected. —**Ant.** false, fake, counterfeit, fraudulent; insincere.

realistic, adj. practical, hardheaded, cleareyed, clear-sighted, clearheaded, down-to-earth, common sense, sensible, reasonable, levelheaded, sane, rational, no-nonsense, hard-nosed, business-like, sober, blunt, factual, pragmatic, tough-minded, undeceived, ungullible, unsentimental, unromantic. —**Ant.** impractical, flighty.

realize, v. **1.** grasp, understand, comprehend, appreciate, recognize, perceive, see, conceive. **2.** accomplish, effect, effectuate, perform, produce, achieve, fulfill.

realm, n. kingdom, empire, sovereignty, sphere, domain, province, department; area, territory, responsibility, jurisdiction, bailiwick.

rear, n. **1.** back, background. —v. **2.** bring up, nurture, raise, nurse. **3.** raise, elevate, lift, loft, lift up, hold up; build, put up, erect, construct. —**Ant.** front; face.

reason, n. **1.** ground, cause, motive, purpose, end, design, raison d'être, objective, aim, object. **2.** justification, explanation, excuse, rationale, ratiocination, rationalization. **3.** judgment, common sense, understanding, intellect, intelligence, mind. **4.** sanity, rationality, reasonability, mind. —v. **5.** argue, ratiocinate, justify; rationalize. **6.** conclude, infer. **7.** persuade, convince, influence.

reasonable, *adj.* **1.** rational, logical, sensible, intelligent, wise, judicious, right, fair, equitable. **2.** moderate, tolerable, adequate, satisfactory, acceptable, equitable, fair, conservative. **3.** sane, rational, sober, sound, sensible, judicious, level-headed. —**Ant.** unreasonable, illogical, irrational; immoderate, intolerable; unsound, insane.

reassure, *v.* encourage, hearten, embolden, buoy up, cheer, uplift, brace, support, bolster, comfort, inspirit, put (someone's) mind at rest. —**Ant.** disconcert, unnerve, dishearten, discourage.

rebel, *n.* **1.** insurgent, insurrectionist, mutineer, revolutionary, resister, freedom fighter; nonconformist, heretic, dissenter, apostate, schismatic. —*adj.* **2.** insurgent, mutinous, rebellious, insubordinate. —*v.* **3.** revolt, mutiny, rise up, take up arms; dissent, disobey, defy, challenge, resist, flout. —**Ant.** patriot; loyal, obedient.

rebellion, *n.* resistance, defiance, insurrection, mutiny, sedition, revolution, revolt; insubordination, disobedience, contumacy.

rebellious, *adj.* defiant, insubordinate, mutinous, rebel, seditious, insurgent; refractory, disobedient, contumacious, incorrigible, unruly, difficult, unmanageable, obstinate, obstreperous, recalcitrant, fractious, rambunctious. —**Ant.** subordinate, obedient, patriotic.

rebuff, *v.* **1.** reject, snub, slight, spurn, cut, dismiss, drop, repulse, repel, brush off, high-hat, kiss off. —*n.* **2.** rejection, snub, dismissal, repulsion, brushoff, kissoff, repudiation, slight, refusal. —**Ant.** welcome, embrace.

rebuke, *v.* **1.** reprove, reprimand, censure, upbraid, chide, reproach, reprehend, lecture, berate, castigate, criticize, take to task, revile, chew out, give (someone) a piece of one's mind, bawl out, admonish, scold, remonstrate with. —*n.* **2.** reproof, reprimand, censure, reproach, reprehension, chiding, scolding, remonstration, expostulation, tongue-lashing. —**Ant.** praise.

recalcitrant, *adj.* stubborn, obstinate, disobedient, uncompliant, refractory, rebellious, contumacious, opposing, willful, defiant, headstrong, perverse, contrary, fractious, unruly, insubordinate, intractable, adamant, inflexible, immovable, uncontrollable, wayward. —**Ant.** obedient, compliant.

recall, *v.* **1.** recollect, think back to, reminisce, call to mind, remember. **2.** call back, revoke, rescind, retract, withdraw, recant, repeal, annul, countermand, nullify. —*n.* **3.** memory, recollection. **4.** revocation, retraction, repeal, cancellation, annulment, disavowal, denial, withdrawal, recantation, nullification; impeachment. —**Ant.** forget; enforce; ratify; sanction.

recent, *adj.* late, modern, up-to-date, fresh, new, novel, just out, brand-new, current, late-model. —**Ant.** early, old, ancient.

receptive, *adj.* responsive, open, open-minded, hospitable, welcoming, sympathetic, impressionable, susceptible, amenable, reachable, teachable, educable, swayable, persuadible, suggestible, tractable, flexible, pliant, interested, willing, responsive. —**Ant.** resistant, recalcitrant.

recherché, *adj.* **1.** unusual, exotic, rare, novel, uncommon, unfamiliar, strange, foreign, unheard of, mysterious. **2.** quaint, choice, exquisite, precious, special, superior, select, peerless, superlative. **3.** affected,

overrefined, unnatural, artificial, put-on, stagy, theatrical. —**Ant.** down-to-earth, everyday.

recital, *n.* account, narrative, description, recitation, rehearsal, relation, history, story, report, narration, telling, recounting, rendition, version, repetition, recap.

recite, *v.* repeat, relate, narrate, recount, describe, quote, present, report, detail, chronicle, list, share, recapitulate, tell, recap.

reckless, *adj.* careless, rash, heedless, incautious, negligent, foolhardy, injudicious, impulsive, irresponsible, foolish, unwise, thoughtless, imprudent, improvident, remiss, inattentive, indifferent, regardless, unconcerned, daredevil, breakneck, madcap, harebrained, mad, wild. —**Ant.** careful, heedful, cautious, thoughtful, provident.

reckon, *v.* **1.** count, compute, calculate, enumerate. **2.** suppose, assume, presume, venture, imagine, conclude, daresay, esteem, consider, regard, account, deem, estimate, judge, evaluate.

reclaim, *v.* recover, bring or get back, regain, restore, rescue, redeem, salvage, retrieve, rejuvenate, save.

recognize, *v.* **1.** identify, place, recall, recollect, remember, detect. **2.** acknowledge, perceive, understand, realize, accept, allow, see, admit, concede, appreciate, grant, respect, be aware of. **3.** approve, sanction, accept, endorse, ratify, validate, acknowledge. **4.** honor, reward, pay respect, pay homage, give recognition to, salute, show appreciation, acknowledge, show one's gratitude. —**Ant.** forget; deny; reject; ignore.

recoil, *v.* **1.** draw or shrink back, falter, flinch, quail. **2.** rebound, spring or fly back, react, reverberate. —**Ant.** advance.

recommend, *v.* **1.** commend, approve, condone, endorse, praise, push, favor, support, promote, second, vouch for, back, plug. **2.** advise, counsel, guide, urge, exhort, suggest, propose, advocate, propound, persuade. —**Ant.** condemn, disapprove.

recompense, *v.* **1.** repay, remunerate, reward, requite, compensate for. —*n.* **2.** compensation, payment, reward, requital, remuneration, repayment, amends, indemnification, satisfaction, retribution, reparation, atonement, redress, restitution.

reconcile, *v.* **1.** content, win over, convince, persuade. **2.** pacify, conciliate, placate, propitiate, appease. **3.** compose, settle, adjust, make up, harmonize, make compatible or consistent. —**Ant.** dissuade; anger, arouse, disturb.

record, *v.* **1.** set down, enter, register, enroll, transcribe, document, note, log, chronicle, report, itemize, list, enumerate, catalog. —*n.* **2.** account, chronicle, history, note, register, memorandum, report, document, log, journal, archive, annal, diary, list, catalog.

recount, *v.* relate, narrate, tell, recite, describe, enumerate, report, communicate, impart, reveal, review, detail, specify.

recourse, *n.* resource, resort, refuge, hope, expedient, means, device, help, strength, last resort, backup, reserve, alternative, remedy, place to turn.

recover, *v.* **1.** regain, get again, reclaim, retrieve, restore, recoup, repossess, recapture, redeem, win or take back. **2.** heal, mend, recuperate, rally, convalesce, improve, revive, pull

through, get back on one's feet, regain one's strength.

rectify, *v.* **1.** set right, correct, remedy, mend, emend, amend, revise, improve, redress, cure, repair, fix, square, better, ameliorate. **2.** adjust, regulate, put right, straighten. —**Ant.** worsen, ruin.

redeem, *v.* **1.** buy or pay off, ransom, recover, reclaim, repossess, retrieve, buy back, repurchase. **2.** ransom, free, liberate, rescue, save, deliver, emancipate, release.

redress, *n.* **1.** reparation, restitution, amends, indemnification, compensation, satisfaction, indemnity, restoration, remedy, relief, atonement. —*v.* **2.** remedy, repair, correct, amend, mend, emend, right, rectify, adjust, relieve, ease. —**Ant.** blame, punishment; damage.

reduce, *v.* **1.** diminish, decrease, shorten, abridge, curtail, retrench, abate, lessen, attenuate, contract. **2.** subdue, suppress, subject, subjugate, conquer, vanquish, overcome, overpower, overthrow, depose. **3.** debase, depress, lower, degrade. —**Ant.** increase; defend; honor, exalt, elevate.

refer, *v.* **1.** direct, commit, deliver, consign. **2.** assign, attribute, ascribe, impute. **3.** relate, apply, obtain, pertain, belong, respect. **4.** advert, allude, hint at, mention, indicate, quote, cite, note.

reference, *n.* **1.** naming, remark, indication, hint, intimation, innuendo, insinuation, specification, notation, quotation, direction, allusion, referral, mention, citation. **2.** witness; testimonial, endorsement, relation, regard, respect, concern, connection, relevance, pertinence.

refined, *adj.* **1.** cultivated, polished, genteel, elegant, polite, courteous, courtly, civilized, well-bred. **2.** purified, clarified, distilled, strained. **3.** subtle, discriminating, sensitive, fastidious, nice, sophisticated. **4.** minute, precise, exact, exquisite. —**Ant.** unrefined, inelegant, impolite, discourteous; polluted, contaminated; obvious, direct; general, inexact.

reflect, *v.* **1.** mirror, cast or throw back, rebound. **2.** reproduce, demonstrate, exhibit, illustrate, reveal, expose, suggest, show, manifest, espouse. **3.** meditate, think, ponder, ruminate, cogitate, muse, deliberate, study, contemplate, consider.

reflection, *n.* **1.** image, representation, counterpart. **2.** consideration, thought, deliberation, cogitation, rumination, meditation, study, contemplation, thinking, musing. **3.** imputation, aspersion, reproach, censure. —**Ant.** original; thoughtlessness; praise.

reflective, *adj.* pensive, meditative, contemplative, musing, thoughtful, pondering, deliberating, reflecting, reasoning, cogitating. —**Ant.** thoughtless, inconsiderate, unthinking.

reform, *n.* **1.** improvement, amendment, correction, reformation, change, modification, rectification, rehabilitation, recovery, reorganization, renovation, betterment, amelioration. —*v.* **2.** better, rectify, correct, amend, emend, ameliorate, mend, improve, repair, restore. —**Ant.** deterioration; worsen, deteriorate.

reformation, *n.* improvement, betterment, correction, reform, amendment, reorganization, rehabilitation, renovation, rectification, modification, change, transformation, melioration.

refrain, *v.* restrain, cease, abstain, desist, forbear, keep from, eschew, avoid, renounce, leave off, curb oneself, hold oneself back, withhold. —**Ant.** continue, persist.

refresh, *v.* **1.** reinvigorate, revive, stimulate, freshen, resuscitate, vitalize, energize, fortify, exhilarate, brace, cheer, enliven, reanimate. **2.** restore, repair, renovate, renew, retouch. —**Ant.** dispirit, discourage.

refuge, *n.* shelter, protection, cover, security, safety; asylum, retreat, sanctuary, hiding place, haven, harbor, stronghold, cloister, safehouse, citadel, hideaway, hideout.

refurbish, *v.* renovate, refurnish, redecorate, brighten, restore, polish, renew, spruce up, remodel, overhaul, repair, recondition, revamp.

refuse, *v.* **1.** decline, reject, spurn, turn down, deny, rebuff, repudiate. —*n.* **2.** rubbish, trash, waste, litter, dirt, debris, detritus, castoffs, junk, sweepings, garbage; slag, lees, dregs, scum, sediment, dross. —**Ant.** allow, permit, sanction, approve.

regain, *v.* recover, recapture, repossess, retrieve, get back. —**Ant.** lose, miss.

regal, *adj.* royal, kingly, queenly, magisterial, majestic, noble, sovereign, imperial, exalted, stately, princely, splendid. —**Ant.** servile.

regale, *v.* amuse, divert, entertain, beguile, refresh, please, delight, indulge, gratify, captivate, fascinate, entrance, enchant, charm, gladden, titillate, tickle.

regard, *v.* **1.** look upon, think of, consider, esteem, account, judge, deem, hold, suppose, estimate. **2.** respect, esteem, honor, revere, reverence, value. **3.** look at, observe, notice, note, see, remark, mark. **4.** relate to, concern, refer to, respect. —*n.* **5.** reference, relevance, association, bearing, connection, relation. **6.** point, particular, detail, matter, consideration. **7.** thought, concern, attention. **8.** look, gaze, view. **9.** respect, deference, concern, esteem, estimation, consideration, reverence. **10.** liking, affection, interest, love. —**Ant.** disregard; disrespect, dishonor; inattention; dislike.

region, *n.* part, area, division, district, section, portion, quarter, district, zone, locality, sector, dominion, precinct, province, territory, locale, site, sphere, vicinity, vicinage, space, tract, domain, field, jurisdiction, bailiwick.

register, *n.* **1.** record, catalogue, account book, ledger, archive. **2.** roll, roster, catalogue, list, record, chronicle, schedule, annals. **3.** registry, entry, registration, enrollment. —*v.* **4.** enroll, list, record, catalogue, chronicle, enter. **5.** demonstrate, show, evince, display, express, indicate, reveal, betray, divulge, reflect.

regret, *v.* **1.** deplore, lament, feel sorry about, grieve at, bemoan, bewail, rue, mourn for, repent. —*n.* **2.** sorrow, lamentation, woe, mournfulness, grief. **3.** remorse, penitence, contrition, repentance, compunction, guilt, conscience, qualm, self-reproach, self-condemnation, second thoughts. —**Ant.** rejoice; joy; unregeneracy.

regular, *adj.* **1.** usual, normal, customary, routine, ordinary, common, commonplace, traditional, time-honored, conventional, typical, habitual, familiar, standard, predictable, scheduled, fixed, invariable, methodical. **2.** conforming, symmetrical, uniform, even, systematic, formal, fixed, orderly, invariant, harmonious, classic, well-proportioned, unvarying, methodical, constant. **3.** recurrent, periodic, habitual, established, fixed, steady,

systematic, rhythmic, dependable, orderly, uniform, automatic. —**Ant.** irregular.

regulate, *v.* control, direct, manage, rule, order, adjust, modify, modulate, balance, fix, govern, organize, maintain, monitor, handle, run, operate, administer, oversee, arrange, set, systematize, dispose, conduct, guide.

regulation, *n.* **1.** rule, order, direction, law, precept, ruling, code, bylaw, edict, ordinance, statute, decree, dictate. **2.** direction, control, management, arrangement, ordering, disposition, disposal, adjustment, balance, organization. —**Ant.** misdirection, mismanagement.

rehearse, *v.* **1.** recite, act, practice, drill, train, exercise, study, repeat. **2.** relate, enumerate, recount, delineate, describe, portray, narrate, recapitulate, repeat, review, report, recap. —**Ant.** extemporize.

reign, *n.* **1.** rule, sway, dominion, sovereignty, ascendancy, hegemony, command, leadership, jurisdiction, control, domination, governance, government, mastery, power, influence. —*v.* **2.** rule, govern, prevail, predominate, hold sway, influence, command, dominate, control, run the show, manage. —**Ant.** obey.

reject, *v.* **1.** refuse, repudiate, decline, disallow, spurn, veto, shun, spurn, dismiss, turn thumbs down, brush off, brush aside, turn down, deny, rebuff, repel, renounce. **2.** discard, throw away, exclude, eliminate, jettison, scrap, junk, scratch, disown. —**Ant.** accept.

relate, *v.* **1.** tell, recite, narrate, recount, rehearse, report, describe, delineate, detail, repeat, communicate, present, divulge, impart, reveal, make known. **2.** associate, connect, ally, couple, link. —**Ant.** dissociate, disconnect, separate, alienate.

relation, *n.* **1.** connection, relationship, association, alliance, dependence. **2.** reference, regard, respect. **3.** narration, recitation, recital, description, rehearsal, relating, telling; narrative, account, report, story, chronicle, tale, history. —**Ant.** independence.

relationship, *n.* relation, connection, association, affiliation, bearing, link, tie, interconnection, reference, pertinence. **2.** kinship, affinity, family tie, consanguinity, blood tie. —**Ant.** dissociation.

relax, *v.* **1.** loosen, slacken, moderate, release, relieve, reduce, ease up on. **2.** diminish, ebb, wane, mitigate, weaken, lessen, reduce, remit, abate, debilitate, enfeeble, enervate. **3.** ease, unbend, relent, soften. —**Ant.** tighten; intensify, increase; harden.

release, *v.* **1.** free, liberate, set free, loose, unloose, unfasten, set at liberty, discharge, deliver, dismiss. **2.** disengage, loose, extricate. —*n.* **3.** liberation, deliverance, emancipation, discharge, freedom, rescue, salvation. —**Ant.** fasten, fetter, imprison; engage, involve; incarceration, imprisonment.

relentless, *adj.* unrelenting, inflexible, rigid, stern, severe, unbending, unforgiving, unappeasable, implacable, merciless, ruthless, unmerciful, stubborn, perseverent, dogged, intransigent, determined, steely, tough, stiff-necked, pitiless, hard, obdurate, adamant, unyielding, remorseless, inexorable. —**Ant.** flexible, soft, pliant, merciful.

relevant, *adj.* pertinent, applicable, germane, apposite, appropriate, suitable, fitting, apt, proper, suited, related,

relative, significant, akin, allied, to the point. —**Ant.** irrelevant.

reliable, *adj.* trustworthy, trusty, dependable, infallible, unfailing, honest, principled, conscientious, punctilious, honorable, safe, sure, certain, secure, sound, responsible, predictable, stable, reputable. —**Ant.** unreliable, untrustworthy, undependable.

relief, *n.* **1.** deliverance, alleviation, ease, assuagement, mitigation, abatement, release, remission, liberation, amelioration, comfort. **2.** help, assistance, aid, succor, redress, remedy. —**Ant.** intensity, intensification.

relieve, *v.* **1.** ease, alleviate, assuage, mitigate, allay, lighten, reduce, abate, lift, raise, palliate, soften, comfort, soothe, lessen, diminish. **2.** unburden, disburden, free, liberate, disencumber, rescue, release, save, ease. **3.** aid, help, assist, succor, remedy, support, sustain. —**Ant.** intensify, increase; burden.

religious, *adj.* **1.** pious, holy, devout, faithful, reverent, godly, churchgoing, God-fearing, spiritual. **2.** conscientious, scrupulous, exacting, punctilious, strict, rigid, rigorous, fastidious, meticulous, sedulous, assiduous, demanding. —**Ant.** irreligious, impious, unfaithful, irreverent; flexible, lenient.

relinquish, *v.* renounce, surrender, give up, resign, yield, cede, waive, forswear, forgo, abdicate, leave, forsake, desert, renounce, quit, abandon, let go, resign, drop, vacate, retire from. —**Ant.** demand, require.

relish, *n.* **1.** liking, taste, enjoyment, appreciation, gusto, zest, avidity, anticipation, appetite, fondness, pleasure, propensity, proclivity, inclination, bent, partiality, predilection, preference. **2.** taste, flavor, savor. —*v.* **3.** like, enjoy, appreciate, prefer, delight in, take pleasure in, be partial to, fancy, savor, anticipate. —**Ant.** distaste, aversion.

reluctant, *adj.* unwilling, disinclined, hesitant, loath, averse, indisposed, unenthusiastic, opposed; cautious, chary, leery, circumspect, careful. —**Ant.** willing, agreeable, amenable, unhesitating, eager, avid.

remain, *v.* **1.** continue, stay, last, abide, endure. **2.** wait, tarry, linger, loiter, dally, stop over, delay, stay, rest. —*n.* **3.** (*plural*) remnants, scraps, remainder, refuse, leavings, crumbs, orts, residue, relics, detritus, leftovers, rest. —**Ant.** leave, depart.

remainder, *n.* residuum, remnant, excess, residue, rest, balance, surplus, others, leftovers.

remark, *v.* **1.** say, observe, note, perceive, heed, regard, notice; comment, state. —*n.* **2.** notice, regard, observation, heed, attention, consideration. **3.** comment, utterance, note, observation, declaration, assertion, statement. —**Ant.** disregard, ignore; inattention.

remarkable, *adj.* notable, conspicuous, unusual, extraordinary, exceptional, impressive, phenomenal, astonishing, astounding, incredible, noteworthy, striking, wonderful, uncommon, strange, rare, distinguished, prominent, singular, signal, special, marvelous, unique, outstanding, memorable, unforgettable. —**Ant.** common, usual, ordinary.

remedy, *n.* **1.** cure, relief, medicine, treatment, restorative, therapy, prescription, drug, cure-all, nostrum, medicament, medication, ointment, balm. **2.** antidote, corrective, antitoxin, counteraction, countermeasure, relief, redress, answer, solution. —*v.* **3.** cure, heal, put *or* set right, restore, recondition, repair, redress. **4.** counteract, remove, correct, right, improve, rectify, ameliorate, straighten out, repair. —**Ant.** sicken, worsen.

remember, v. **1.** recall, recollect, reminisce, think or look back; call to mind, turn one's mind or thoughts back, hark back, return. **2.** retain, memorize, keep or bear in mind. —**Ant.** forget.

remembrance, n. reminder, keepsake, memento, souvenir, trophy, token, memorial, memento mori.

remiss, adj. **1.** negligent, careless, thoughtless, lax, slack, forgetful, unmindful, neglectful, inattentive, heedless. **2.** languid, sluggish, dilatory, slothful, slow, tardy, lax, delinquent. —**Ant.** careful, thoughtful, attentive; energetic, quick.

remission, n. **1.** pardon, forgiveness, absolution, indulgence, exoneration, discharge, deliverance, amnesty, reprieve, release, exemption, acquittal. **2.** abatement, diminution, lessening, relaxation, moderation, mitigation. **3.** release, relinquishment. **4.** decrease, subsidence, respite, stoppage, pause, interruption, relief, hiatus, suspense, suspension, abatement. —**Ant.** blame, censure, conviction; increase, intensification; increase.

remnant, n. remainder, remains, residue, residuum, rest; trace, vestige, leftover, relic, fragment, scrap, shred, end, bit.

remorse, n. regret, compunction, penitence, contrition, repentance, ruefulness, sorrow, woe, guilt, bad conscience, humiliation, self-reproach, mortification, shame, bitterness. —**Ant.** conviction.

remorseful, adj. regretful, penitent, contrite, repentant, rueful, sorry, apologetic, conscience-stricken, guilt-ridden, humiliated, mortified, shamefaced, ashamed, humbled, bitter. —**Ant.** impenitent.

remorseless, adj. relentless, pitiless, uncompassionate, unrelenting, merciless, unmerciful, ruthless, cruel, savage, implacable, inexorable, callous, heartless, hardhearted, inhumane, barbarous. —**Ant.** merciful, compassionate.

remote, adj. **1.** distant, far apart, far-off, outlying, inaccessible, removed; alien, foreign; outside, irrelevant, unrelated, unconnected. **2.** slight, faint, inconsiderable. **3.** abstracted, aloof, detached, withdrawn, reserved, standoffish. —**Ant.** close, near; connected, related; considerable, substantial.

remove, v. **1.** replace, displace, dislodge, transfer, transport, carry. **2.** take, withdraw, separate, extract, eliminate. **3.** kill, assassinate, do away with, destroy, murder, dispose of, purge.

rend, v. tear apart, wrench, mangle, shred, split, divide, rip, rive, sunder, sever, cleave, chop, fracture, tear, dissever, crack, snap, lacerate, rupture.

render, v. **1.** make, cause to be, cause to become. **2.** do, perform, play. **3.** deliver, hand in, present, offer, provide, tender, furnish, supply, give, contribute, afford. **4.** exhibit, show, demonstrate; depict, represent, portray, execute, achieve. **5.** present, give, assign. **6.** deliver, return. **7.** translate, interpret, decode, decipher, convert, explain, restate, rephrase. **8.** give back, restore, return, give up, surrender, cede, yield, relinquish, resign, provide.

renew, v. **1.** restore, replenish, restock. **2.** re-create, rejuvenate, regenerate, restore, reinstate, renovate, repair,

mend. **3.** revive, reestablish, ressurect, resume, reopen, recommence.

renounce, v. **1.** give up, put aside, forsake, forgo, relinquish, abandon, forswear, leave, quit resign, abdicate. **2.** repudiate, disown, disclaim, reject, disavow, deny, recant. —**Ant.** claim, accept, desire.

renovate, v. redecorate, remodel, modernize, refurbish, refurnish, refit, restore, revamp, repair, overhaul, fix up.

renown, n. repute, fame, celebrity, glory, prominence, mark, luster, stardom, distinction, note, eminence, reputation, name, honor, esteem, acclaim, prestige, éclat. —**Ant.** disrepute, infamy; oblivion.

rent, n. **1.** rental, return, payment, hire, lease, fee. **2.** tear, split, fissure, slit, crack, crevice, cleft, rift, gap, opening, rip, rupture, breach, break, fracture, laceration. **3.** schism, separation, disunion, breach. —v. **4.** lease, let, hire, charter, farm out.

repair, v. **1.** restore, mend, remodel, renew, renovate, patch, revamp, adjust, amend, fix. **2.** make good, make up for, remedy, retrieve. **3.** make amends for, atone for, redress. —**Ant.** break, destroy, ruin.

repay, v. pay back, return, reimburse, indemnify, refund; recompense, compensate, requite, reciprocate, reward, return the favor, settle up, square with.

repeat, v. **1.** reiterate, recapitulate, iterate, recite, rehearse, relate, restate, retell, quote, recount, recap. **2.** reproduce, echo, reecho, redo. —n. **3.** repetition, iteration; duplicate, copy, reproduction, replica, encore, reprise.

repel, v. **1.** repulse, parry, ward off. **2.** resist, withstand, rebuff, oppose, confront. **3.** reject, decline, refuse, discourage. **4.** offend, disgust, sicken, nauseate, revolt, turn one's stomach, make one's skin crawl, give one the creeps, turn one off. —**Ant.** attract; approve, accept.

repent, v. regret, atone, be contrite, be sorry, rue, feel remorse, be penitent, lament, bemoan, apologize, be ashamed.

repentance, n. compunction, contrition, contriteness, penitence, remorse, sorrow, regret, shame, atonement, embarrassment, humiliation, mortification. —**Ant.** impenitence.

replace, v. **1.** supersede, supplant, substitute, succeed. **2.** restore, return, make good, refund, repay; replenish.

reply, v. **1.** answer, respond, echo, rejoin. —n. **2.** answer, rejoinder, retort, comeback, reaction, rise, riposte, replication, response, feedback.

represent, v. **1.** designate, stand for, denote, symbolize, exemplify, typify, embody, epitomize, illustrate, image, depict, express, portray, personate, delineate, figure, present. **2.** set forth, describe, state, delineate, characterize, report, assert, define, outline, sketch, depict, picture, portray, paint; pretend.

repress, v. **1.** check, suppress, subdue, put down, quell, quash, reduce, crush. **2.** check, restrain, curb, bridle, control, stifle, squelch, contain, constrain, inhibit, hamper, hinder, frustrate, discourage. —**Ant.** foster, support, help, aid.

reprisal, n. retaliation, revenge, vengeance, redress, vendetta, retribution, requital, vindication, repayment, recompense, getting even.

reproach, v. chide, abuse, reprimand, condemn, criticize, rebuke, scold, reprove, call to account, cen-

sure, blame, remonstrate with, castigate, find fault with, shame, abash, discredit, reprehend, upbraid. —n. **2.** blame, censure, upbraiding, reproof, abuse, vilification, discredit, reprehension, rebuke, criticism, remonstrance, condemnation, expostulation, disapproval, disapprobation. **3.** disgrace, dishonor, shame, disrepute, odium, scandal, obloquy, opprobrium, ignominy, indignity, infamy, insult, scorn, offense. —**Ant.** praise, honor.

reproduce, v. **1.** copy, duplicate, repeat, imitate, represent, replicate, recreate, simulate, match. **2.** generate, propagate, beget, give birth, breed, multiply, procreate, spawn, foal. —**Ant.** initiate, originate.

repudiate, v. **1.** reject, disclaim, disavow, disown, scorn, retract, rescind, reverse, abandon, abrogate, forswear, forgo, deny, discard, renounce. **2.** condemn, disapprove. —**Ant.** accept; approve, commend.

repugnance, n. distaste, aversion, dislike, repulsion, abhorrence, disgust, abomination, execration, nausea, hatred, hostility, antipathy. —**Ant.** attraction, liking, sympathy.

repugnant, adj. **1.** repulsive, offputting, repellant, revolting, vile, abominable, loathsome, foul, unpalatable, unsavory, intolerable, noisome, obnoxious, nauseating, sick-making, unpleasant, horrid, distasteful, objectionable, offensive. **2.** opposing, objecting, protesting, averse, unfavorable, antagonistic, inimical, adverse, contrary, hostile, opposed. —**Ant.** attractive, tasteful; favorable, amiable.

reputation, n. **1.** estimation, regard, repute, standing, stature, status, position, name, character. **2.** credit, esteem, honor, fame, celebrity, distinction, renown, name, notoriety, acclaim, repute. —**Ant.** dishonor, infamy.

repute, n. **1.** estimation, reputation. **2.** name, reputation, distinction, credit, honor. —v. **3.** consider, esteem, account, regard, hold, deem, reckon.

request, n. **1.** solicitation, petition, suit, entreaty, plea, application, supplication, prayer, demand. —v. **2.** ask for, sue, petition, entreat, beg, supplicate, solicit, beseech, require, plead for, importune, seek.

require, v. **1.** need, demand, command, press for, instruct, coerce, force, insist, call for, request, order, enjoin, direct, ask. **2.** obligate, necessitate, want, need, call for, lack, desire. —**Ant.** forgo.

requirement, n. **1.** requisite, need, claim, requisition, prerequisite, demand, precondition, condition, stipulation, criterion, sine qua non, provision, proviso, necessity, essential, desideratum, musto. **2.** mandate, order, command, directive, injunction, ukase, charge, claim, precept.

requisite, adj. **1.** required, necessary, essential, indispensable, needed, needful. —n. **2.** necessity, requirement, criterion, sine qua non. —**Ant.** dispensable, unnecessary; luxury, superfluity.

requite, v. **1.** repay, remunerate, reimburse, recompense, pay, satisfy, compensate. **2.** retaliate, avenge, revenge, punish. —**Ant.** dissatisfy; forgive.

rescue, v. **1.** save, deliver, liberate, set free, emancipate, manumit, release, redeem, ransom, extricate; recover, preserve. —n. **2.** liberation, release, redemption, ransom, recovery, deliverance, salvation, emancipation. —**Ant.** incarceration, imprisonment.

research, n. **1.** inquiry, investigation,

examination, scrutiny, study, exploration, delving, digging, fact-finding, inspection, probe, analysis, experimentation, checking. —*v.* **2.** investigate, study, inquire, examine, scrutinize.

resemblance, *n.* **1.** similarity, likeness, analogy, semblance, similitude, correspondence, congruity, equivalence, comparability, agreement. **2.** appearance, representation, semblance, image. —**Ant.** dissimilarity; misrepresentation.

resentful, *adj.* bitter, embittered, envious, spiteful, jealous, begrudging, vindictive, indignant, disgruntled, acrimonious, peeved, irritated, riled, piqued, irate, annoyed, provoked, furious, incensed, agitated, upset, worked up, antagonistic, hostile, hateful, rancorous, malevolent. —**Ant.** grateful, benevolent, friendly.

reserve, *v.* **1.** keep back, save, retain, husband, withhold, conserve, preserve, keep, hold, store up. **2.** set apart, set aside, bank. —*n.* **3.** reservation, qualification, exception. **4.** store, stock, supply. **5.** self-restraint, restraint, reticence, silence, taciturnity, constraint, coldness, coolness, aplomb, detachment, formality, aloofness, cool. —**Ant.** splurge, squander, waste; prodigality; warmth, enthusiasm.

reside, *v.* **1.** dwell, abide, live, sojourn, stay, lodge, inhabit, remain. **2.** abide, lie, be present, inhere, exist.

residence, *n.* **1.** dwelling, house, home, habitation, domicile, abode, place, living quarters. **2.** tenancy, visit, residency, stay, sojourn.

resign, *v.* give up, submit, yield, cede, surrender, abdicate, relinquish, forgo, abandon, forsake, quit, leave, renounce, withdraw, vacate, retire, release.

resignation, *n.* **1.** abdication, abandonment, surrender, relinquishment. **2.** submission, meekness, patience, acquiescence, endurance, compliance, forbearance, sufferance, acceptance, capitulation, passivity, reconciliation. —**Ant.** application; boldness, rebelliousness.

resilient, *adj.* ductile, elastic, flexible, springy, supple, recoiling; buoyant, cheerful, bouncy. —**Ant.** rigid, inflexible, inelastic.

resist, *v.* **1.** withstand, strive against, oppose, confront, thwart, impede, block, obstruct, combat, battle, oppugn, countervail, defy, weather, stand up to, hold at bay, hold the line against, fight, assail, attack, counteract, rebuff. **2.** refrain *or* abstain from, refuse, forgo, turn down, deny. —**Ant.** defend; accept.

resolute, *adj.* resolved, firm, steadfast, determined, set, adamant, staunch, dogged, single-minded, indefatigable, tireless, unflagging, unswerving, perseverant, persistent, tenacious, deliberate, immutable, opinionated, purposeful, earnest, sincere, fixed, unflinching, unwavering, inflexible, hardy, unshaken, bold, undaunted, pertinacious. —**Ant.** weak, feeble, frail, flexible, lenient.

resolve, *v.* **1.** fix *or* settle on, determine, decide, confirm, establish, agree, undertake, fix. **2.** work out, figure out, clear up, answer, explain, explicate, solve. —*n.* **3.** resolution, determination, decision, purpose, intention, obstinacy, dedication, devotion, perseverance, doggedness, tenacity, constancy, indefatigability. —**Ant.** indecision.

respect, *n.* **1.** particular, detail, point, regard, feature, matter, aspect, quality, trait, characteristic, attribute, element, property. **2.** relation, reference, connection, regard. **3.** esteem, deference, regard, estimation, veneration, reverence, homage, honor, admiration, approbation, approval, affection, feeling. —*v.* **4.** honor, revere, reverence, esteem, venerate, regard, consider, defer to, admire, adulate, adore, love. **5.** regard, heed, attend to, pay attention to, obey, notice, consider. —**Ant.** disregard.

respectable, *adj.* **1.** estimable, worthy, honorable, upright, honest, respected, reputable, unimpeachable, aboveboard. **2.** proper, decent, presentable, moral, modest, chaste, innocent, pure, clean. **3.** fair, fairly good, moderate, middling, passable, tolerable, considerable, large, appreciable, sizable, substantial, significant, satisfactory, tidy. —**Ant.** unworthy, dishonorable; improper; poor, small, insignificant.

respectful, *adj.* courteous, polite, well-mannered, cordial, gracious, obliging, considerate, thoughtful, well-bred, decorous, civil, deferential. —**Ant.** disrespectful, discourteous, impolite.

respite, *n.* **1.** relief, delay, hiatus, cessation, postponement, intermission, break, interruption, breather, holiday, interval, rest, recess. **2.** stay, reprieve, suspension, postponement, pause. —**Ant.** continuation.

response, *n.* answer, reply, rejoinder, riposte, retort, reaction, return, comeback, feedback.

responsible, *adj.* **1.** accountable, answerable, liable. **2.** chargeable, guilty, at fault, culpable to, blame, accountable, blamable, censurable. **3.** capable, able, reliable, solvent, trustworthy, trusty, dutiful, honest, dependable, stable, creditable, ethical. —**Ant.** innocent; incapable, unreliable.

rest, *n.* **1.** sleep, nap, doze, slumber, repose, siesta, snooze, shuteye. **2.** relaxation, intermission, break, interval, recess, breather, holiday, respite, interlude, time off, cessation, vacation. **3.** leisure, ease, indolence, relaxation, idleness, loafing, inactivity. **4.** remainder, balance, remains, remnants, leftovers, others, excess, surplus, overage. —*v.* **5.** lie down, recline, relax, repose, unwind, loll about, loaf, laze about, take one's ease, put up one's feet, take it easy, nap, lounge, snooze, sleep, doze, catch forty winks, sack out, hit the hay. **6.** lie, be placed *or* situated, reside, be found, remain, stay. **7.** place, position, put, lay, set, lean, prop.

restful, *adj.* calm, tranquil, peaceful, undisturbed, serene, pacific; relaxing, soothing, sedative, comforting, soporific, hypnotic. —**Ant.** perturbed, disturbed, agitated; upsetting.

restitution, *n.* reparation, redress, indemnification, restoration, recompense, amends, compensation, remuneration, requital, satisfaction, repayment.

restive, *adj.* **1.** uneasy, restless, nervous, impatient, ill at ease, edgy, fidgety, jumpy, skittish, high-strung, fretful, apprehensive, anxious, agitated, jittery, uptight, hyper, excitable, unquiet. **2.** refractory, disobedient, obstinate, mulish, stubborn, pigheaded, intractable, fractious. —**Ant.** restful, patient, quiet, serene; obedient.

restore, *v.* **1.** reestablish, replace, reinstate, renew. **2.** renew, refurbish, rehabilitate, fix, touch up, revive, rejuvenate, renovate, repair, mend. **3.** return, give back, make restitution; replace, reimburse, return, repay. **4.** reproduce, reconstruct, rebuild. —**Ant.** disestab-

lish, destroy; break, ruin; accept, receive; raze.

restrain, *v.* **1.** check, keep down, repress, curb, bridle, suppress, hold, keep, constrain. **2.** restrict, circumscribe, confine, hinder, abridge, hamper, limit, inhibit, curtail, stifle, interfere with, handicap. —**Ant.** unbridle; broaden, widen.

restrict, *v.* confine, limit, restrain, abridge, curb, circumscribe, bound, impede, regulate, demarcate. —**Ant.** free, broaden, disencumber.

result, *n.* **1.** outcome, consequence, effect, conclusion, issue, event, end, termination, product, fruit, upshot, development, sequel, followup, denouement. —*v.* **2.** spring, arise, proceed, follow, flow, come, issue, ensue, rise, originate. **3.** terminate, end, resolve, eventuate, end, conclude, culminate. —**Ant.** cause.

retain, *v.* **1.** keep, hold, withhold, preserve, detain, reserve. **2.** recollect, memorize, remember, recall. **3.** hire, engage, employ, commission, take on. —**Ant.** loose, lose; forget; disengage, fire.

retaliate, *v.* avenge, requite, return, repay, revenge, counter, reciprocate, settle a score, give as good as one gets, give (someone) a taste of his *or* her own medicine, wreak vengeance, strike back, get even. —**Ant.** forgive, pardon.

retard, *v.* slow, delay, hinder, hamper, impede, decelerate, clog, obstruct, check, stall, thwart, balk, restrict, frustrate, interfere with. —**Ant.** speed, expedite, accelerate.

reticent, *adj.* taciturn, silent, reserved, quiet, uncommunicative, quiet, shy, timid, retiring, unresponsive, laconic, tightlipped. —**Ant.** voluble, communicative.

retire, *v.* withdraw, leave, depart, go away, retreat, seclude oneself, fall back, recede; retract. —**Ant.** advance, attack.

retired, *adj.* withdrawn, secluded, sequestered, cloistered, isolated, removed, apart, solitary, abstracted. —**Ant.** advanced.

retort, *v.* **1.** counter, fling back, rebut, come back with, reply, respond, return, answer, retaliate, rejoin. —*n.* **2.** reply, response, answer, riposte, rejoinder, rebuttal, comeback.

retreat, *n.* **1.** departure, withdrawal, retirement, seclusion, privacy, solitude. **2.** sanctuary, den, haven, hideaway, hideout, sanctum sanctorum, shelter, refuge, asylum. —*v.* **3.** retire, withdraw, leave, depart, draw back, turn tail, decamp, evacuate, flee, take flight. —**Ant.** advance.

retribution, *n.* requital, revenge, vengeance, retaliation, reprisal, redress, quid pro quo, satisfaction, punishment, justice, just deserts, repayment, reward, recompense, compensation. —**Ant.** forgiveness, pardon.

retrieve, *v.* recover, regain, restore, save, rescue, recoup, reclaim.

reveal, *v.* make known, communicate, disclose, divulge, unveil, uncover, discover, publish, impart, tell, announce, proclaim, expose, display, give vent to, air, ventilate, leak. —**Ant.** conceal, hide, veil, cover.

revenge, *n.* **1.** vengeance, retaliation, requital, reprisal, retribution. **2.** vindictiveness, revengefulness, vengefulness, spitefulness. —*v.* **3.** avenge, retaliate, requite, vindicate, exact revenge. —**Ant.** forgiveness, pardon.

revengeful, *adj.* vindictive, spiteful,

malevolent, resentful, malicious, malignant, implacable, grudging, bitter, invidious. —**Ant.** forgiving, benevolent.

reverence, *n*. **1.** worship, honor, esteem, admiration, glorification, beatification, sanctification, idolization, adulation, adoration, fealty, deference, obeisance, veneration, respect, homage, awe. —*v*. **2.** venerate, revere, honor, adore, adulate, worship, idolize, respect, enshrine, sanctify, beatify, glorify, esteem, admire. —**Ant.** disrespect; despise.

reverse, *n*. **1.** opposite, antithesis, contrary, converse, counterpart. **2.** check, misfortune, defeat, mishap, misadventure, affliction. —*v*. **3.** overturn, upend, turn topsy-turvy, transpose, invert. **4.** alter, change, modify; renounce, recant, take back. **5.** revoke, annul, repeal, veto, rescind, overthrow, countermand, quash, override, nullify, invalidate, undo, negate, upset. —**Ant.** same.

review, *n*. **1.** critique, criticism, evaluation, commentary, notice, opinion, judgment, survey. **2.** rereading, rehash, postmortem, reassessment, study, reconsideration, reexamination. **3.** inspection, examination, investigation. —*v*. **4.** survey, inspect, criticize, examine, study, weigh, scrutinize, consider.

revive, *v*. **1.** reactivate, revitalize, reanimate, resuscitate, revivify, reinvigorate, reinspirit. **2.** bring back, quicken, renew, refresh, rouse. **3.** recover, reawake, come around, regain consciousness. —**Ant.** kill; languish, die.

revoke, *v*. take back, withdraw, annul, cancel, reverse, rescind, repudiate, renounce, recant, repeal, retract, deny, invalidate, void, nullify, negate, quash, veto, abrogate, abolish.

revolt, *v*. **1.** rebel, mutiny, rise. **2.** disgust, repel, shock, nauseate, offend, horrify, repulse, sicken. —*n*. **3.** insurrection, rebellion, mutiny, revolution, uprising, overthrow, sedition, coup d'état, putsch, takeover. —**Ant.** attract, delight.

revolution, *n*. **1.** overthrow, sea change, revolt, rebellion, mutiny, coup, uprising, insurgency, insurrection, upheaval. **2.** cycle, rotation, circuit, turn, round, orbit, spin, lap, circle, gyration.

revolve, *v*. **1.** rotate, spin, circulate, turn, roll. **2.** orbit, circle. **3.** consider, think about, ruminate on, ponder, reflect on, brood over, study, weigh, contemplate, meditate on, chew over.

reward, *n*. **1.** recompense, prize, desert, compensation, pay, award, favor, return, tribute, honor, remuneration, requital, merit. **2.** bounty, premium, bonus. —*v*. **3.** recompense, requite, compensate, pay, remunerate, redress.

ribald, *adj*. scurrilous, offensive, coarse, wanton, irreverent, loose, indecent, low, obscene, pornographic, blue, indelicate, naughty, shameless, lusty, gross, filthy, dirty, vulgar, bawdy, earthy, lubricious, lewd, licentious, racy, lascivious, smutty, rude. —**Ant.** pure, inoffensive, refined, polished, elegant.

rich, *adj*. **1.** well-to-do, wealthy, moneyed, opulent, affluent, prosperous, well-off, flush, well-heeled, well-fixed, loaded. **2.** abounding, abundant, bounteous, bountiful, fertile, plenteous, plentiful, copious, ample, luxuriant, productive, fruitful, prolific. **3.** valuable, valued, precious, costly, estimable, sumptuous, elegant. **4.** deep, strong, vivid, intense, vibrant, lus-

trous, lively, bright, gay. —**Ant.** poor, impoverished; scarce, barren, sterile; weak; dull.

riddle, *n*. conundrum, puzzle, enigma, poser, question, problem, mystery, brainteaser.

ridicule, *n*. **1.** derision, mockery, gibes, jeers, taunts, raillery, satire, sendup, burlesque, sarcasm, sneer, banter, wit, irony. —*v*. **2.** deride, tease, chaff, twit, mock, taunt, make fun of, sneer at, burlesque, satirize, rail at, lampoon, jeer *or* scoff at, rib, roast, send up. —**Ant.** praise, honor; respect.

ridiculous, *adj*. absurd, preposterous, laughable, nonsensical, inane, asinine, funny, ludicrous, droll, comical, farcical, hilarious, sidesplitting, risible, outlandish, bizarre, grotesque, zany, wild, far-out. —**Ant.** sensible.

rife, *adj*. **1.** common, prevalent, widespread, prevailing. **2.** abundant, plentiful, numerous, plenteous, abounding, copious, ubiquitous, multitudinous. —**Ant.** rare, unusual; scarce, scanty.

right, *adj*. **1.** just, good, equitable, fair, upright, honest, lawful, licit, legal, moral, proper, correct, righteous, virtuous, ethical, fair, true, honorable, principled, aboveboard, legitimate. **2.** correct, proper, suitable, fit, appropriate, becoming, *de rigueur*, befitting, seemly, *comme il faut*. **3.** correct, true, exact, precise, perfect, factual, sound, valid, accurate. —*n*. **4.** claim, title, due, ownership. **5.** virtue, justice, fairness, integrity, equity, equitableness, uprightness, rectitude, goodness, lawfulness. —**Ant.** wrong.

righteous, *adj*. moral, upright, holy, God-fearing, virtuous, good, honest, fair, right, equitable, law-abiding, just, upstanding, ethical, honorable, reputable, trustworthy. —**Ant.** immoral, bad, dishonest, unfair.

rigid, *adj*. **1.** stiff, unyielding, unbending, firm, hard, inelastic, inflexible. **2.** unmoving, immovable, static, stationary. **3.** inflexible, strict, severe, stern, rigorous, austere, unbending, harsh, stringent, puritanical, hard and fast, hard-nosed, hard-line, adamant, straitlaced, abdurate, resolute, relentless, inexorable. —**Ant.** flexible, soft; compliant, elastic, lenient.

rigorous, *adj*. **1.** rigid, severe, harsh, stern, austere, strict, hard, inflexible, stiff, unyielding, stringent. **2.** exact, demanding, finical, punctilious, precise, literal, meticulous. —**Ant.** flexible, soft; inaccurate.

rim, *n*. **1.** edge, border, lip, margin, brim, boundary, verge, skirt, confine. —*v*. **2.** edge, border, bound, margin, confine. —**Ant.** center, inside.

ring, *n*. **1.** circlet, loop, hoop; annulus. **2.** arena, enclosure, rink, circle. **3.** circle, organization, band, pack, team, crew, confederation, cartel, bloc, clan, society, cabal, faction, group, alliance, federation, coalition, union, affiliation, clique, coterie, set, combination, confederacy, league; gang, mob, syndicate. —*v*. **4.** surround, encircle, circle. **5.** peal, resonate, vibrate, reverberate, resound, reecho, tinkle, jingle, jangle, chime, toll, knell, ding-dong, clang, gong.

riot, *n*. **1.** outbreak, disorder, brawl, uproar, tumult, disturbance, commotion, fray, melee, altercation, rumpus, turbulence, fracas, pandemonium, donnybrook, unrest, row, strife, imbroglio, anarchy, disruption, violence, rampage, storm, ruckus, confusion. **2.** revelry, festivity. —*v*. **3.** revolt, rebel, take to the streets, mount the barricades, protest, go on a rampage, run

riot, storm, create a disorder, disturb the peace, create a disturbance, brawl, fight. **4.** carouse, revel.

rip, *v*. **1.** cut, tear, tear apart, slash, slit, rend. —*n*. **2.** rent, tear, laceration, cut, split, gash, slash, rift, rupture, cleft.

ripe, *adj*. **1.** mature, mellow, grown, aged. **2.** full, complete, consummate, perfect, finished. **3.** developed, ready, prepared, set, enthusiastic, eager, fit. —**Ant.** immature; imperfect, unfinished; undeveloped, unprepared.

ripen, *v*. mature, age, grow, develop, mellow, grow up, maturate, evolve, blossom, flower, come into season.

rise, *v*. **1.** get up, arise, stand, stand up. **2.** revolt, rebel, mutiny, oppose, resist. **3.** spring up, grow. **4.** come into existence, appear, come forth. **5.** occur, happen. **6.** originate, issue, arise, come up, be derived, proceed. **7.** move upward, ascend, mount, arise. **8.** succeed, be promoted, advance. **9.** swell, puff up, enlarge, increase. —*n*. **10.** rising, ascent, mounting. **11.** advance, elevation, promotion. **12.** increase, augmentation, enlargement, swelling. **13.** source, origin, beginning, commencement, birth, fountainhead, wellspring. —**Ant.** sink; support; die; fail; decrease, deflate; open.

risible, *adj*. funny, amusing, comic, comical, laugh-provoking, laughable, droll, humorous, hilarious, rich, ludicrous, absurd, ridiculous, farcical, priceless, hysterical, sidesplitting. —**Ant.** sober, solemn.

risk, *n*. **1.** hazard, chance, danger, dangerous chance, venture, chance, gamble, peril, jeopardy, exposure. —*v*. **2.** hazard, take a chance, endanger, imperil; jeopardize. **3.** venture upon, dare.

rite, *n*. ceremony, procedure, practice, observance, form, usage, ritual, formality, custom, routine, solemnity, sacrament, solemnization.

ritual, *n*. **1.** ceremony, rite, formality, routine, practice, convention, custom, protocol. —*adj*. **2.** ceremonial, formal, sacramental, ceremonious. —**Ant.** unceremonious, informal.

rival, *n*. **1.** competitor, contestant, challenger, adversary, contender, antagonist, opponent. —*adj*. **2.** competing, competitive, opposed, emulating, opposing. —*v*. **3.** compete *or* contend with, oppose, challenge, contest, combat, vie with, struggle against. **4.** match, equal, emulate, measure up to, compare with. —**Ant.** ally, friend.

roam, *v*. walk, go, travel, ramble, wander, peregrinate, rove, stray, meander, amble, perambulate, drift, saunter, dawdle, dally, stroll, range, prowl, traipse, cruise, gallivant, jaunt, mosey, loiter.

roar, *v*. **1.** cry, bellow, bawl, shout, yell, vociferate. **2.** laugh, guffaw, howl, hoot. **3.** resound, boom, thunder, peal.

rob, *v*. **1.** rifle, sack, steal, deprive, plunder, pillage, pilfer, pinch, burgle, loot, ransack, hijack, burglarize, mug, hold up, roll, shoplift. **2.** defraud, cheat, deprive, rook, rip off, prey upon, swindle, fleece, bilk, victimize.

robber, *n*. thief, second-story man, kleptomaniac, shoplifter, pilferer, brigand, bandit, marauder, freebooter, pirate, pickpocket, burgler, cat burglar, sneak thief, mugger, holdup man, ripoff artist, hijacker, carjacker.

robust, *adj*. sturdy, healthy, strong, hardy, vigorous, stalwart, hale, powerful, firm, sound, athletic, brawny, muscular, sinewy, fit, hearty, stout, tough, able-bodied, strapping, rugged, lusty, well-knit, husky, buff, pumped up. —**Ant.** weak, feeble, unhealthy.

rogue, *n.* rascal, scamp, mischiefmaker, wastrel, good-for-nothing, miscreant, outlaw, desperado, villain, scoundrel, trickster, swindler, cheat, mountebank, quack, sharper, charlatan, louse, rat, creep, stinker, bum, SOB.

roil, *v.* **1.** muddy, foul, dirty, pollute, befoul, contaminate. **2.** disturb, agitate, perturbate, stir, stir up, churn, whip, whip up. **3.** rile, anger, irritate, irk, vex, peeve, provoke, gripe. —**Ant.** clarify, calm.

roll, *v.* **1.** turn, revolve, rotate, wheel, gyrate, spin, cycle, tumble, somersault, whirl, bowl. **2.** billow, rise and fall, wave, undulate. **3.** sway, rock, swing, list, tilt. —*n.* **4.** register, list, record, directory, slate, docket, index, schedule, annals, inventory, catalogue, roster. **5.** cylinder, roller, spindle.

romance, *n.* **1.** novel, tale, story, fiction. **2.** fancy, fabrication, extravagance, exaggeration; falsehood, fable, fiction, lie. **3.** love affair, amour, liaison, relationship, dalliance, intrigue. **4.** sentiment, mystery, nostalgia, adventure, glamour, fascination, exoticism, intrigue, fantasy, imaginativeness, colorfulness, color.

romantic, *adj.* **1.** fanciful, unpractical, quixotic, extravagant, exaggerated, wild, imaginative, unrealistic, fantastic. **2.** improbable, imaginary, fantastic, chimerical, fictitious, fabulous, unreal. **3.** picturesque, exotic, glamorous, sentimental, emotional, nostalgic, sweet. **4.** amorous, aroused, ardent, affectionate, lustful, passionate, impassioned, overfriendly, loving, lovey-dovey, fresh, on the make. —**Ant.** practical, realistic; probable.

romp, *v.* **1.** play, frolic, gambol, frisk, cavort, caper, rollick, revel, roister, lark about, kick up one's heels. —*n.* **2.** gambol, frolic, caper, revel, escapade. **3.** triumph, easy victory, runaway, pushover.

rosy, *adj.* **1.** cherry, cerise, rose-red, ruby, pink, reddish, roseate. **2.** red, rubicund, glowing, blushing, florid, apple-cheeked, flushed, blooming, ruddy, healthy. **3.** bright, promising, cheerful, optimistic, favorable, auspicious, sunny, hopeful, encouraging, sanguine. —**Ant.** dark, dim, cheerless, pessimistic.

rot, *v.* **1.** decompose, decay, mold, molder, putrefy, spoil, corrupt. **2.** waste *or* wither away, languish, die, decline, atrophy, deteriorate, degenerate. —*n.* **3.** decay, putrefaction, decomposition, corruption, mold, blight, disintegration, deterioration. —**Ant.** purify.

rotate, *v.* turn, spin, revolve, gyrate, pirouette, go round, wheel, whirl, twirl, pivot, reel.

rotten, *adj.* **1.** decomposed, decayed, putrefied, putrescent, putrid, tainted, foul, miasmatic, noxious, ill-smelling, fetid, rank. **2.** corrupt, offensive, amoral, immoral, venal, degenerate, villainous, iniquitous, evil, wicked, vile, base, perverted, depraved, unscrupulous, unprincipled, warped. **3.** contemptible, disgusting, unwholesome, treacherous, dishonest, deceitful, corrupt, heinous, despicable, miserable, wretched, nasty, filthy, low, mean, lousy, stinking, lowdown, terrible, awful, horrible. —**Ant.** pure; moral; wholesome, honest.

rough, *adj.* **1.** uneven, bumpy, irregular, rugged, jagged, coarse, craggy. **2.** violent, disorderly, wild, boisterous,

turbulent, riotous; sharp, severe, harsh. **3.** turbulent, choppy, roiled, storm-tossed, disturbed, stormy, agitated, tempestuous, inclement. **4.** harsh, grating, jarring, noisy, cacophonous, inharmonious, discordant, flat, raucous. **5.** uncultured, indelicate, unrefined, impolite, uncivil, unpolished, rude, inconvenient, uncomfortable, crude, coarse. **6.** rudimentary, crude, raw, rough-hewn, formless, unshaped, plain, imperfect, unpolished, uncorrected, unfinished, unwrought, undressed, unprepared, unset, uncut. **7.** general, approximate, cursory, quick, hasty, sketchy, ballpark, vague, inexact, incomplete. —**Ant.** even, regular; orderly; fair; harmonious; cultured, refined; finished, polished; precise, exact.

round, *adj.* **1.** circular, disklike; ringshaped, hooplike, annular; curved, arched; cylindrical; spherical, globular, rotund, orbed. **2.** full, complete, entire, whole, unbroken. —*n.* **3.** circle, ring, curve; cylinder. **4.** course, cycle, revolution, period, series, succession. —**Ant.** angular, square, rectangular, polygonal.

rouse, *v.* **1.** stir, excite, animate, kindle, fire, inflame, stimulate, awaken, provoke, electrify, galvanize, prompt, goad, prod, move, spur. **2.** anger, provoke, incite, ire, fire up. —**Ant.** calm; pacify.

row, *n.* **1.** argument, disagreement, quarrel, dispute, altercation, tiff, squabble, fight, set-to, donnybrook, scrap, knock-down-drag-out. —*v.* **2.** argue, quarrel, squabble, fight, dispute, disagree, wrangle, cross swords, have words, bicker, have a tiff, scrap, fall out.

rowdy, *adj.* **1.** boisterous, noisy, raucous, rackety, rambunctious, disorderly, unruly, brawling, roistering, obstreperous, rip-roaring, riotous, ruffian, rough and tumble. —*n.* **2.** mischiefmaker, ruffian, hooligan, brawler, streetfighter, tough, street tough, hood, hoodlum, hooligan, thug, bullyboy, bully, yahoo, lout, skinhead.

royal, *adj.* regal, majestic, kingly, queenly, sovereign, stately, august, imperative, imposing, imperial, princely. —**Ant.** servile.

ruckus, *n.* commotion, disturbance, fuss, row, to-do, hubbub, rumpus, uproar, racket, turmoil, brouhaha.

rude, *adj.* **1.** discourteous, unmannerly, ill-mannered, impolite, ungallant, ungracious, ill-bred, oafish, loutish, unrefined, uncivil, coarse; curt, brusque, saucy, pert, impertinent, impudent, insolent, offensive, disrespectful, flippant, gruff, tactless, undiplomatic, fresh. **2.** unlearned, untutored, uneducated, untaught, ignorant, uncultured, unrefined, untrained, uncivilized, philistine, oafish, loutish, coarse, uncouth, vulgar, boorish. **3.** rough, harsh, ungentle, coarse, rugged, crude. **4.** unwrought, raw, crude, rough, shapeless, amorphous. **5.** inartistic, inelegant, primitive, rustic, artless, clumsy, bumbling, makeshift, homespun, basic, bare, simple, unadorned, unpolished, undecorated. —**Ant.** courteous, mannerly; learned; gentle; artistic, elegant.

rudimentary, *adj.* **1.** basic, essential, introductory, abecedarian, formative, first, primal, seminal, elementary, fundamental, primary, initial. **2.** undeveloped, embryonic, elementary, imperfect, crude, coarse, primitive, immature, vestigial, primordial. —**Ant.** advanced; mature, perfect.

ruffle, *v.* **1.** disarrange, rearrange, dis-

order, rumple, wrinkle, dishevel, mix up, tousle, tangle, muss up, damage, derange. **2.** disturb, discompose, irritate, vex, annoy, upset, agitate, trouble, torment, plague, harry, harass, worry, molest, disconcert, confuse, perturb, disorient, unnerve, fluster, affect, bother, intimidate, rattle, throw, shake up. —*n.* **3.** disturbance, perturbation, annoyance, vexation, confusion, commotion, flurry, tumult, bustle, agitation, ripple, stir, wrinkle. —**Ant.** arrange, order; compose; composure, peace.

rugged, *adj.* **1.** broken, uneven, rocky, hilly, craggy, irregular. **2.** rough, harsh, stern, severe, hard, austere. **3.** severe, hard, trying, difficult, arduous, Spartan, rigorous, onerous, demanding, burdensome. **4.** harsh, grating, inharmonious, cacophonous, scabrous. **5.** rude, uncultivated, unrefined, unpolished, crude. **6.** hardy, durable, strong, sturdy, robust, tough, stalwart; independent, self-reliant, individualistic, bold, self-sufficient. —**Ant.** even, smooth, regular; easy, flexible; fair; harmonious; cultivated, refined; weak wimpy.

ruin, *n.* **1.** decay, dilapidation, ruination, perdition, destruction, dissolution, degradation, corruption, failure, collapse, debacle, havoc, damage, disintegration, devastation, spoliation. **2.** downfall, destruction, fall, overthrow, defeat, undoing, subversion, wreck. —*v.* **3.** spoil, demolish, destroy, damage, devastate, annihilate, dissolve, wipe out, overthrow, raze, shatter, wreck, crush, flatten, pulverize, smash, wreak havoc on, reduce to ruin; corrupt, dishonest, defile, debase. —**Ant.** construction; creation; create, build.

rule, *n.* **1.** principle, regulation, standard, law, canon, ruling, ordnance, decree, statute, direction, guideline, guide, precept, order. **2.** control, government, dominion, command, domination, mastery, sway, authority, direction. —*v.* **3.** administer, command, govern, manage, control, handle, lead, direct, guide, conduct. **4.** decree, decide, deem, judge, settle, establish, order, demand.

rumor, *n.* story, talk, gossip, hearsay, information, scoop, tidings, chat, chitchat, leak, disclosure, revelation, inside story, bruit, news, report, tittletattle, scandal, item, whisper, *on dit,* calumny, obloquy, buzz, dish, talk of the town, scuttlebutt, grapevine, jungle telegraph, lowdown, info, poop, dirt.

run, *v.* **1.** race, hasten, hurry, sprint, scurry, dart, bolt, dash, tear, scoot, scuttle, zip, gallop, jog, trot, lope, rush, scramble, hustle, step on it, step lively, hotfoot it, get the lead out, get cracking, scud, speed, scamper. **2.** flow, diffuse, flood, gush, spill, dribble, spurt, trickle, spout, cascade, seep, pour, stream; go, move, proceed. **3.** flee, escape, take flight, abscond, take to one's heels, bolt, decamp, clear out, retreat, retire, make a getaway, scram, skedaddle, skip out, fly the coop, head for the hills, vamoose. **5.** operate, function, perform, work, go, continue. **6.** extend, stretch, reach, spread. **7.** contend, compete, challenge. **8.** pursue, hunt, chase. **9.** convey, transport, ferry, drive, carry. **10.** operate, carry on, conduct, manage, direct, control, oversee, supervise, head, lead, administer, coordinate. —*n.* **11.** period, spell, interval. **12.** series, set, course, passage, motion, extent, progress.

rupture, *n.* **1.** breaking; bursting;

breach, fracture, break, split, burst, disruption, breakup, schism, disunity, severance, division, separation. —v. 2. break, fracture, split, burst, disrupt, separate, cleave, divide, breach, part, sunder. —**Ant.** seam, union; unite, organize.

rural, adj. 1. country, pastoral, sylvan, bucolic, rustic, Arcadian, exurban, agrarian, agricultural. 2. peasant, plain, simple, homespun, down-home, countrified, hillbilly, backwoods, awkward, cloddish, gawky, uncultured, unrefined, guileless, artless, ingenuous, oafish, bumptious, hay seed, hick, backwater, naive, unsophisticated, rugged, rough; crude, boorish, loutish. —**Ant.** urban.

rush, v. 1. hurry, hasten, run, race, make haste, speed, dash, sprint, hustle, bustle, scurry, scamper, scramble, scoot, scuttle, move it, hotfoot it, skedaddle, make it snappy, step on it, hightail it, shake a leg, dart, bolt, tear, zip, step lively, get the lead out, get cracking, fly, get a wiggle on. —n. 2. hurry, haste, speed, quickness, immediacy, hustle, bustle, dash, busyness, turmoil, flurry, commotion, ferment, fluster, ado, to-do, excitement, harum-scarum, activity, urgency, exigency. —adj. 3. urgent, top-priority, emergency, exigent, hurry-up. —**Ant.** delay, retard; sloth, lethargy, sluggishness; low-priority.

ruthless, adj. pitiless, merciless, unpitying, unmerciful, cruel, hard, harsh, severe, hardhearted, uncompassionate, unrelenting, adamant, relentless, inexorable, fell, truculent, inhuman, ferocious, savage, barbarous, unsympathetic, fierce, remorseless, vicious, callous, unfeeling, tough, heartless, brutal, brutish, mean. —**Ant.** merciful, compassionate, humane.

S

sabotage, n. 1. subversion, subversiveness, damage, destruction, impairment, injury, undermining, weakening, treachery, betrayal, traitorousness. —v. 2. undermine, subvert, damage, hurt, disable, weaken, incapacitate, wreck, disrupt, spoil, ruin, cripple, disable, monkey with.

saccharine, adj. 1. oversweet, sickly sweet, cloying, treacly, sugary. 2. mawkish, oversentimental, maudlin, bathetic, sticky, treacly, cloying, mushy, soppy, sappy, icky. 3. ingratiating, fawning, obsequious, insinuating, silken, silky, suave, sycophantic. —**Ant.** astringent, bracing.

sack, n. 1. bag, pouch. 2. pillaging, looting, plundering, pillage, destruction, devastation, desolation, spoliation, ruin, ruination, waste, ravage, rapine. —v. 3. pillage, loot, rob, spoil, despoil, ruin, lay waste, plunder, devastate, demolish, destroy, ravage, rape.

sacred, adj. 1. consecrated, holy, blessed, sanctified, awe-inspiring, sainted, venerable, hallowed, divine, worshipful. 2. dedicated, consecrated, revered. 3. secure, protected, sacrosanct, immune, inviolate, inviolable, untouchable. 4. religious, spiritual, ceremonial, churchly, priestly, ecclesiastical, ritual, solemn, sacramental, liturgical, hieratic. —**Ant.** blasphemous.

sacrifice, v. 1. give up, forgo, forfeit, forsake, relinquish, surrender, lose, yield, renounce, forswear; forbear, desist, cease, stop, refrain from, deny oneself, waive, swear off, eschew.

—n. 2. forfeiture, loss, relinquishment, renunciation, surrender, forswearing, deprivation, privation, denial, self-denial, abdication, abrogation, yielding, forbearance, waiver, abjuration, abstention, eschewal. —**Ant.** indulge in; continue, persist; reward, indulgence.

sacrilege, n. blasphemy, impiety, irreverence, profanity, desecration, profanation, heresy, sin, offense, abomination, violation, crime, infamy, disgrace, scandal, debasement, defilement, contamination, perversion, outrage, secularization.

sad, adj. 1. sorrowful, mournful, unhappy, despondent, disconsolate, depressed, dejected, melancholy, discouraged, gloomy, morose, low, glum, lugubrious, heartsick, crestfallen, disheartened, blue, heartbroken, woebegone, wretched, miserable, down in the dumps, singing the blues, tearful, downcast, downhearted. 2. somber, dark, dull, dismal, dreary, bleak, funereal, dispiriting, depressing. 3. grievous, deplorable, disastrous, dire, calamitous, unfortunate, lamentable, sorry, pathetic, lousy, rotten, awful, terrible. —**Ant.** happy.

safe, adj. 1. secure, protected, sheltered, shielded, guarded. 2. dependable, sound, risk-free, solid, bona fide, tried and true, conservative, trustworthy, sure, reliable. 3. cautious, wary, careful. —**Ant.** unsafe.

safeguard, n. 1. defense, guard, protection, precaution, bulwark, shield, aegis, armor, armament, cushion, security, insurance. —v. 2. defend, guard, protect, shield, secure, bulwark, preserve, shelter, conserve, save, keep, care for, look after.

saga, n. edda, epic, tale, tradition, legend, history, story, adventure, narrative, chronicle, romance.

sagacious, adj. wise, sage, shrewd, discerning, clever, intelligent, judicious, rational, acute, sharp, keen, perspicacious, sharp-witted. —**Ant.** unwise, irrational.

sage, n. 1. wise man, philosopher, savant, expert, elder, guru, pundit, oracle, authority. —adj. 2. prudent, sagacious, sensible, profound, discerning, reasonable, logical, common-sense, thoughtful, circumspect, wary, careful, insightful, sapient, astute, knowledgeable, learned, enlightened, erudite, knowing. —**Ant.** dolt; imprudent.

sailor, n. mariner, salt, tar, seaman, seafarer, seafaring man or woman, seadog, skipper, swabbie, gob, yachtsman, yachtswoman, deck hand. —**Ant.** landlubber.

sake, n. 1. cause, account, interest, score, regard, consideration, benefit, welfare, advantage, behalf, respect, reason. 2. purpose, end, reason, objective.

salacious, adj. lusty, lecherous, rakish, lewd, carnal, wanton, lascivious, libidinous, concupiscent; obscene, pornographic, prurient. —**Ant.** modest, prudish.

salient, adj. prominent, conspicuous, important, remarkable, outstanding, pronounced, noticeable, significant, important, marked, striking, impressive, distinctive, unique, principal, chief, primary, noteworthy, notable, eminent. —**Ant.** inconspicuous; unimportant.

sallow, adj. pallid, washed out, wan, waxen, sickly, bloodless, anemic, pasty, pasty-faced, whey-faced, greenish, green around the gills, yellowish, jaundiced.

salvage, v. rescue, redeem, deliver, save, recover, regain, retrieve, recoup, ransom, recycle, reclaim. —**Ant.** discard.

same, adj. 1. identical; similar, like, corresponding, interchangeable, equal. 2. unvarying; unchanging, constant, uniform, unvarying, verbatim, monotonous. —**Ant.** different; disagreeing.

sample, n. specimen, example, illustration, pattern, model, representation, cross section, exemplar; taste, nibble, bite.

sanctify, v. bless, consecrate, dedicate, hallow, purify, beatify, enshrine, glorify, exalt, canonize. —**Ant.** desecrate.

sanctimonious, adj. hypocritical, unctuous, pious, canting, mealy-mouthed, smarmy, two-faced, pretentious, dissembling, feigning, insincere, self-satisfied, complacent, pietistic, pharisaical, holier than thou, smug, Tartuffian, Pecksniffian, simon-pure, self-righteous, goody-goody, goody-two-shoes. —**Ant.** sincere.

sanction, n. 1. authority, permission, countenance, approval, confirmation, legalization, legitimation, validation, license, certification, imprimatur, seal of approval, support, ratification, solemnification, authorization. —v. 2. authorize, countenance, approve, confirm, ratify, support, allow, bind. —**Ant.** disapproval; disallow, disapprove.

sanctuary, n. church, temple, shrine, altar, sanctum, chapel, synagogue, mosque, house of worship or God; asylum, refuge, retreat, shelter, safety, protection.

sane, adj. rational, reasoning, reasonable, lucid, clearheaded, clear-thinking, lucid, sound, normal, all there, compos mentis, wise, judicious, sapient, sagacious, sage, prudent, sensible. —**Ant.** insane, foolish.

sanitary, adj. hygienic, unpolluted, clean, aseptic, disinfected, sterile, antiseptic, germ-free; healthy, salutary, wholesome, salubrious, healthful. —**Ant.** polluted; unhealthy, unwholesome.

sarcasm, n. scorn, contumely, acrimony, acerbity, harshness, asperity, venom, poison, virulence, spite, spitefulness, malice, malevolence, satire, cynicism, disdain, irony, derision, bitterness, ridicule; taunt, gibe, jeer.

sarcastic, adj. cynical, biting, cutting, mordant, bitter, derisive, ironical, sardonic, satirical, scornful, contumelious, nasty, trenchant, incisive, acrimonious, acerbic, acid, acidic, acidulous, acrid, harsh, aspersive, venomous, virulent, poisonous, spiteful, disdainful, mocking, contemptuous, critical, censorious, captious, caviling, scathing, caustic, sneering, malignant, malicious, malefic, malevolent.

satanic, adj. evil, wicked, diabolical, devilish, infernal, hellish, malicious, fiendish, immoral, amoral, dark, black, demonic, ghoulish, sinister, iniquitous, depraved, perverted, perverse, godless, ungodly, impious, unholy. —**Ant.** godly, angelic, benevolent.

satiate, v. cloy, glut, stuff, gorge, sate, surfeit; gall, disgust, bore, tire, weary.

satire, n. irony, sarcasm, ridicule, lampoon, pasquinade, burlesque, exposure, denunciation, mockery, spoof, sendup, takeoff.

satirical, adj. mocking, spoofing, irreverent, derisive, disparaging, abusive, scornful, flippant, ridiculing, chaffing, trenchant, cynical, sarcastic, sardonic, ironical, taunting, biting, keen, sharp, cutting, severe, mordant, mordacious, bitter, acid.

satisfaction, *n.* **1.** gratification, enjoyment, pleasure, contentment, ease, comfort. **2.** reparation, restitution, amends, expiation, atonement, damages, compensation, indemnification, remuneration, recompense, requital. **3.** payment, discharge, repayment. —**Ant.** dissatisfaction, displeasure, discomfort.

satisfy, *v.* **1.** gratify, meet, appease, pacify, content, please. **2.** fulfill, fill, satiate, sate, suffice, surfeit. **3.** assure, convince, persuade, reassure, content. —**Ant.** dissatisfy, displease.

saturate, *v.* soak, impregnate, imbue, wet, drench, waterlog, steep. —**Ant.** dry.

saucy, *adj.* impudent, disrespectful, audacious, brassy, bold, pert, cheeky, flippant, irrepressible, forward, impertinent, cocky, sassy, fresh, flip, insolent, brazen.

savage, *adj.* **1.** wild, rugged, uncultivated, sylvan, rough. **2.** barbarous, uncivilized, rude, unpolished, wild. **3.** fierce, ferocious, wild, untamed, feral, ravenous. **4.** enraged, furious, angry, irate, infuriated. **5.** cruel, brutal, beastly; inhuman, fell, merciless, unmerciful, pitiless, ruthless, bloodthirsty, truculent, sanguinary. —**Ant.** cultivated, cultured; tame; calm; merciful.

savant, *n.* scholar, sage, intellectual, polymath, expert, authority, pundit, egghead, wonk, brain, rocket scientist, maven, Einstein, wizard, whiz, genius, guru, connoisseur.

save, *v.* **1.** rescue, salvage, preserve, deliver, retrieve, free, redeem, liberate. **2.** safeguard, keep, protect, secure, shelter, shield, guard, preserve. **3.** set apart, reserve, lay by, economize, hoard, store up, husband, put away *or* aside, retain, preserve, conserve, scrimp, scrape.

savior, *n.* rescuer, deliverer, saver, lifesaver, safekeeper, preserver, liberator, redeemer, emancipator, salvation, champion, friend in need, Good Samaritan, knight in shining armor, paladin.

savor, *n.* **1.** taste, flavor, relish; odor, scent, fragrance. —*v.* **2.** taste, sample, perceive, detect, sense; enjoy, relish, indulge in, appreciate, delight in, value, cherish.

say, *v.* **1.** utter, pronounce, speak, remark, affirm, allege. **2.** express, state, word, declare, tell, argue. **3.** recite, repeat, iterate, reiterate, rehearse. **4.** report, allege, maintain, hold, assert, mention, rumor, suggest, hint, whisper.

scamp, *n.* rascal, imp, mischief-maker, cutup, rogue, little devil, scalawag, urchin, brat, slyboots, sly dog, smooth operator. —**Ant.** goody-two-shoes.

scandal, *n.* **1.** disgrace, damage, discredit, dishonor, offense, embarrassment, sin, outrage, infamy, degradation, shame, disrepute, opprobrium, odium, ignominy. **2.** defamation, rumor, hearsay, whisper, talk, bruit, *on dit*, scuttlebutt, gossip, slander, character assassination, aspersion, detraction, calumny, obloquy, libel, innuendo, insinuation, abuse, dirt, slur, smear, stigma, smirch, spot, taint, blemish, black mark, dish, talk of the town. —**Ant.** honor, repute; praise, kudos.

scanty, *adj.* meager, sparse, insufficient, inadequate, deficient, scarce, minimal, measly, skimpy, thin, spare, small, paltry, poor, stinted, lean. —**Ant.** abundant, adequate.

scapegoat, *n.* patsy, goat, fall guy, whipping boy, sacrifice, offering, victim, target, stooge, front, dupe, gull, cat's-paw, straw man, sucker.

scarce, *adj.* rare, insufficient, deficient, scanty, scant, inadequate, wanting, lacking, meager, rare, unusual, in short supply, hard to come by, at a premium, uncommon, infrequent. —**Ant.** abundant, sufficient.

scare, *v.* **1.** terrify, alarm, startle, frighten, shock, intimidate, dismay, daunt, appall, terrorize, threaten, menace, cow, intimidate, horrify, spook, make one's hair stand on end, make one's flesh crawl *or* creep, give one goosebumps. —*n.* **2.** fright, terror, alarm, panic, shock, surprise, start.

scatter, *v.* **1.** sprinkle, broadcast, strew, spread, diffuse, shower, litter, distribute, sow, disseminate. **2.** dispel, disperse, dissipate, separate, drive away, break up, disband. —**Ant.** gather.

scene, *n.* **1.** location, site, place, area, locale, spot, locality, sphere, milieu, whereabouts, backdrop, background. **2.** view, scenery, sight, panorama, vista, picture, prospect, landscape. **3.** incident, episode, situation; commotion, upset, row, disturbance, brouhaha, furor, tantrum. **4.** exhibition, demonstration, spectacle, show, display.

scent, *n.* **1.** odor, aroma, fragrance, bouquet, whiff, trace, smell, savor, redolence, perfume. **2.** track, trail, spoor. —*v.* **3.** detect, perceive, smell, determine, discern, sense, sniff out, get wind of, recognize.

schedule, *n.* **1.** roll, catalogue, table, list, inventory, register; timetable. —*v.* **2.** enter, register, list, enroll, tabulate, classify, program, organize, plan, outline, arrange, book, assign, earmark.

scheme, *n.* **1.** plan, design, program, project, system, plot, course of action, outline, method, technique, approach, game plan, scenario. **2.** plot, intrigue, stratagem, cabal, conspiracy, contrivance, machination, ploy, subterfuge, ruse, maneuver, tactic, trick, dodge, racket. **3.** system, pattern, diagram, schema, arrangement. —*v.* **4.** plan, plot, contrive, project, devise, design, intrigue, hatch, conspire, machinate, connive, concoct, maneuver, formulate, organize.

scholar, *n.* **1.** academic, professor, researcher, teacher, pedagogue, authority, expert, pundit, man *or* woman of letters, bookman, bluestocking, intellectual, highbrow, bookworm, brain, egghead, longhair, wonk, connoisseur, savant, wise man, sage. **2.** student, pupil, disciple, learner, undergraduate, schoolchild. —**Ant.** ignoramus, dropout.

scholarship, *n.* learning, knowledge, erudition, information, science, wisdom, lore, expertise, know-how; study, research, investigation, academic inquiry. —**Ant.** ignorance.

schooling, *n.* education, training, teaching, guidance, instruction, tuition, tutelage, learning, preparation, indoctrination, edification, enlightenment.

scientific, *adj.* orderly, methodical, systematic, meticulous, thorough, precise, detailed, painstaking, well-organized, rational.

scoff, *n.*, *v.* mock, scorn, jeer, gibe, sneer, disdain, despise, flout, taunt, ridicule, deride, belittle, disparage, dismiss, make light *or* fun of, spoof, lampoon, tease, rib, kid, rag. —**Ant.** envy, praise, exalt.

scold, *v.* **1.** chide, reprove, reproach,

berate, censure, rail at, reprimand, blame, rebuke, admonish, criticize, tonguelash, rate, revile, vituperate, upbraid, find fault with, lecture, castigate, bawl out, dress down, give (someone) a piece of one's mind, chew out, give (someone) a tonguelashing *or* talking-to, rake (someone) over the coals, haul (someone) on the carpet. —*n.* **2.** nag, shrew, fishwife, hellcat, fury, tigress, old battle-ax, Xanthippe, virago, termagant, maenad, bacchante. —**Ant.** praise, honor.

scope, *n.* range, extent, space, reach, area, compass, expanse, breadth, sphere, orbit, span, sweep, gamut, radius, ken, purview, horizon; leeway, space, spread, elbowroom, freedom, capacity, stretch, opportunity, margin, room, latitude, liberty; tract, area, length.

scorch, *v.* sear, blacken, roast, broil, sizzle, burn, singe, char, blister, parch, shrivel, wither.

score, *n.* **1.** record, account, reckoning, register, tally, number, count, amount, sum, total. **2.** notch, scratch, stroke, line, nick, groove, cut, mark. **3.** account, reason, rationale, basis, cause, provocation, ground, consideration, motive, purpose. —*v.* **4.** record, reckon, tabulate, count. **5.** notch, mark, scratch, incise, groove, nick, cut. **6.** gain, win, succeed, triumph, have an impact, make an impression *or* hit.

scorn, *n.* **1.** contempt, contemptuousness, deprecation, abuse, dismissal, rejection, disdain, contumely, superciliousness, insolence. **2.** mockery, derision, derisiveness, ridicule, sneering, scoffing, taunting. —*v.* **3.** disdain, reject, rebuff, disown, disavow, disregard, ignore, shun, snub, flout, hold in contempt, spurn, put down, look down one's nose at, disparage, high-hat, despise, detest. —**Ant.** affection, pleasure.

scoundrel, *n.* villain, knave, rogue, evildoer, mischief-maker, devil, demon, brute, fiend, beast, monster, blackguard, bounder, wretch, scamp, cad, rascal, fox, cur, hound, dog, miscreant, trickster, sharper, cheat, fake, charlatan, mountebank, good-for-nothing, heel, louse, con artist, smooth operator, sly dog, stinker. —**Ant.** hero.

scourge, *n.* **1.** curse, misfortune, evil, bane, adversity, torment, torture, misery, woe, affliction, calamity, plague, pest, nuisance. —*v.* **2.** flog, beat, horsewhip, whale, belt, flagellate, lash, whip. **3.** punish, chastise, chasten, correct, discipline, castigate, afflict, torment.

scramble, *v.* **1.** hasten, rush, scurry, hurry, run, race, scoot, dash, skedaddle, hightail it, hotfoot it, scamper, scuttle, bustle, hustle. **2.** clamber, creep, scrabble, claw, climb, struggle, crawl, go on all fours. **3.** vie, compete, contend, jostle, struggle, strive. **4.** mix, intermix, blend, mix up, mingle, jumble. **5.** confuse, mix up, muddle, garble. —*n.* **6.** bustle, rush, hurry, flurry, flutter, commotion. **7.** clutter, jumble, mix, mishmash. **8.** struggle, tussle, competition, contest, disorder, riot, pandemonium, free-for-all, hassle.

scrap, *n.* **1.** fragment, piece, portion, particle, mite, sliver, snippet, whit, iota, speck, molecule, atom, dab, trace, hint, scintilla, suggestion; morsel, crumb, bit, bite. —*adj.* **2.** fragmentary, piecemeal; waste. —*v.* **3.** break up, demolish, dismantle, destroy, pull to pieces, wreck, smash, ruin. **4.** throw away, discard, reject, abandon, forsake, forget, get rid of, discard, dispose of, consign to the scrapheap, trash, junk, dispense with, shed, slough. —Ant. whole.

scream, *v.* **1.** shriek, screech, cry, squeal, yowl, wail, caterwaul, howl. —*n.* **2.** outcry, cry, shriek, screech, squeal, yowl, wail, caterwaul, howl, yell, bellow, roar, shout.

screen, *n.* **1.** partition, divider, wall; shelter, cover, protection, guard, shield, defense. —*v.* **2.** shelter, protect, veil, defend, shield, conceal, guard, camouflage, hide, cover, cloak, mask, shroud.

scruple, *n.* **1.** hesitation, hesitancy, reluctance, misgiving, second thoughts, doubt, uncertainty, apprehension, uneasiness, discomfort, squeamishness, pang of conscience, restraint, compunction, demurral, suspicion, mistrust, qualm. —*v.* **2.** hesitate, waver, pause, falter, vacillate, demur, be loath to, balk at, shrink from, have doubts *or* compunctions about, have misgivings *or* qualms, think twice, be reluctant.

scrupulous, *adj.* **1.** conscientious, reluctant, hesitant, cautious, wary, careful, circumspect. **2.** punctilious, meticulous, overnice, strict, fastidious, particular, fussy, finicky, painstaking, religious, minute, careful, exacting, exact, accurate, precise, demanding, rigorous. **3.** honorable, righteous, upstanding, principled, high-minded, ethical, moral, just, honest. —**Ant.** remiss, careless, sloppy; unprincipled, dishonest, shifty.

scrutinize, *v.* examine, investigate, analyze, probe, inspect, check, survey, observe, assess, evaluate, critique, criticize, review, eyeball, peruse, scan, audit, ponder, consider, view, contemplate, weigh, research, anatomize, dissect, study, sift. —**Ant.** neglect, overlook.

scrutiny, *n.* examination, investigation, dissection, study, analysis, probe, exploration, sifting, check, observation, evaluation, critique, once-over, perusal, research, inquiry, inspection, inquisition, search.

scurrilous, *adj.* **1.** foulmouthed, profane, scabrous, nasty, derogatory, defamatory, disparaging, calumnious, malign, aspersive, vile, low, derisive, abusive, opprobrious, vituperative, reproachful, insolent, insulting, offensive, contumelious. **2.** coarse, ribald, licentious, gross, indecent, dirty, smutty, off-color, prurient, salacious, lewd, lascivious, pornographic, foul, filthy, vulgar, obscene. —**Ant.** decent, polite; proper.

seamless, *adj.* smooth, continuous, unvarying, integrated, indivisible, unbroken, uninterrupted, connected, uniform, homogeneous. —**Ant.** disjointed, fragmented.

seamy, *adj.* sordid, nasty, dark, disreputable, shameful, unwholesome, unsavory, distasteful, squalid, depraved, degenerate, debased, low, degraded, foul, vile, odious, abhorrent, ugly, repulsive, repellent, contemptible, despicable, shabby, base, miserable, rotten, ignoble, mean.

search, *v.* **1.** look for, seek, explore, investigate, examine, scrutinize, inspect, check, comb through, scour, scout out, hunt *or* rummage through, probe; pierce, penetrate. —*n.* **2.** exploration, examination, investigation, inspection, scrutiny, research, analysis, probe, study, perusal, searching, inquiry, inquisition; pursuit, quest, hunt.

seasonable, *adj.* suitable, timely, apt, fitting, providential, propitious, well-timed, proper, welcome, fortunate, auspicious, lucky, favorable, advantageous, happy, felicitous, gratifying, opportune, fit, convenient, appropriate. —**Ant.** unseasonable, unsuitable, untimely, inopportune.

seasoned, *adj.* experienced, knowledgeable, proficient, accomplished, adept, practiced, well-versed, skilled, prepared, established, veteran, longstanding, proven, professional, habituated, acclimated, accustomed, familiar, tempered, hardened, strengthened, toughened, grizzled, aged, well-developed, mature. —**Ant.** inexperienced, immature, green, new, unproven, unaccustomed.

seasoning, *n.* **1.** flavoring, flavor, tang, piquancy, zest, relish, sauce, essence, extract, condiment, spice, herb. **2.** experience, practice, exercise, training, discipline, maturation, development, mellowing, tempering, aging, hardening, strengthening, toughening, acclimitization, habituation, familiarization.

seat, *n.* **1.** place, chair, bench, banquette, sofa, couch, settee, easy chair, throne, stool. **2.** bottom, base, fundament. **3.** site, situation, location, locality, locale; residence, home, domicile, abode, estate, realm, sphere.

secede, *v.* abdicate, withdraw, retire, abandon, forsake, apostasize, break away from, quit, drop out, separate, resign, turn one's back on, wash one's hands of, defect, split off. —**Ant.** join.

secluded, *adj.* withdrawn, isolated, separate, lonely, alone, solitary, detached, desolate, deserted, retired, sequestered, cloistered, monastic, hermetic, eremitic, reclusive, private. —**Ant.** public, open, sociable.

secrecy, *n.* mystery, privacy, stealth, surreptitiousness, concealment, furtiveness, covertness, sneakiness, confidentiality, secretiveness, clandestineness, inscrutability, slyness.

secret, *adj.* **1.** clandestine, hidden, shrouded, undisclosed, stealthy, surreptitious, furtive, underhand, concealed, secreted, screened, buried, masked, disguised, covert, private, confidential, quiet, undercover, hush-hush, off the record, backstair, dissembling, cloak-and-dagger, unrevealed, mysterious, unknown. **2.** reticent, close-mouthed, secretive. **3.** retired, withdrawn, reclusive, monastic, solitary, secluded, private. **4.** occult, obscure, cryptic, arcane, incomprehensible, esoteric, cabalistic, inscrutable, mysterious, latent, abstruse, recondite, puzzling, perplexing, mystifying. —**Ant.** open, manifest, obvious, apparent.

secrete, *v.* hide, conceal, cover, cache, bury, camouflage, cloak, mask, stash, screen, ensconce, shroud, disguise. —**Ant.** reveal, expose, uncover.

secular, *adj.* worldly, temporal, terrestrial, mundane, earthly, earthy, lay, nonclerical, nonecclesiastical, nonreligious, civil, state, material, unspiritual, profane. —**Ant.** religious, spiritual, ecclesiastical.

secure, *adj.* **1.** safe, protected, sheltered, shielded, guarded, defended; invincible, invulnerable, impregnable, unassailable, unthreatened, immune, unimperiled, snug, cozy. **2.** steady, firm, moored, anchored, sound, solid, sturdy, fixed, stable, fast, locked, fastened, riveted, atttached, affixed. **3.** sure, definite, established, inevitable, probable, evident, easy, positive, certain, confident, assured, guaranteed. —*v.* **4.** obtain, procure, get, acquire, gain, win, earn. **5.** protect, guard, safeguard, shelter, shield, defend. **6.** make certain, ensure, assure, guarantee. **7.** make firm, fasten, affix, attach, anchor, rivet, moor. —**Ant.** insecure; unstable; unsure; lose; unloose, loosen.

sedate, *adj.* **1.** calm, quiet, composed, peaceful, even-tempered, sober, undisturbed, unexcited, staid, cool, collected, serene, placid, tranquil, unruffled, unperturbed, imperturbable, detached, unflappable, controlled, solemn, earnest, serious, settled, demure, grave, thoughtful, contemplative. **2.** proper, formal, decorous, dignified, refined, old-fashioned, conventional, staid, strait-laced, fussy, prim, prudish. —**Ant.** agitated, perturbed, excited, nervous; wanton, improper, undignified, abandoned, unrestrained, indecorous.

sedative, *n.* **1.** sleeping pill, depressant, soporific, tranquilizer, opiate, drug, narcotic, calmative, barbiturate, antispasmodic, hypnotic, quieter, quietener, soother, pacifier, anodyne, downer, knockout drops, Mickey Finn. —*adj.* **2.** soothing, relaxing, calming, depressing, hypnotic, sleep-inducing, tranquilizing, narcotic, calmative, somniferous, soporific, palliative. —**Ant.** stimulant.

sediment, *n.* lees, dregs, grounds, precipitate, deposit, remains, residue, detritus.

sedition, *n.* agitation, rabble-rousing, fomentation, instigation, incitement to riot, whipping *or* stirring *or* firing up; insurgency, insurgence, treachery, treason, subversion, dissidence, Putsch, disaffection, insubordination, mutiny, rebellion, revolt, revolution, riot, insurrection, uprising. —**Ant.** pacification; fidelity, loyalty, fealty, allegiance, patriotism.

seduce, *v.* tempt, lead astray, debauch, deprave, pervert, corrupt, entice, beguile, inveigle, decoy, attract, tantalize, enchant, entrance, bewitch, allure, lure, delude, deceive, mislead, charm, captivate, fascinate, entrap, ensnare, sweet-talk. —**Ant.** repel; reform.

seductive, *adj.* tempting, captivating, alluring, enticing, appealing, tantalizing, inviting, enchanting, entrancing, bewitching, fascinating, flirtatious, coquettish, on the make, provocative, irresistible, winning, prepossessing, unctuous, attractive, beguiling; deceptive. —**Ant.** unattractive, repellent, abhorrent, dull, insipid, prudish.

see, *v.* **1.** perceive, look at, spy, espy, mark, spot, witness, recognize, catch sight of, glimpse, note, notice, discern, behold, regard, gaze, gape, stare, glare. **2.** view, visit, watch, attend, take in, survey. **3.** perceive, discern, penetrate, understand, comprehend, remark, apprehend, appreciate, fathom, grasp, realize, know, take in, be conscious *or* aware of, get the drift of. **4.** learn, ascertain, find out, determine, investigate, discover, learn. **5.** experience, endure, survive, live through, know, feel, meet with, suffer, undergo. **6.** receive, entertain, visit with. **7.** go out with, date, socialize with, consort *or* associate with; attend, escort, accompany, show, lead, usher, conduct, take, bring. **8.** consider, think, deliberate, make up one's mind, mull over, contemplate, decide, ruminate, reflect, brood over.

seedy, *adj.* shabby, run-down, dilapidated, worn, decayed, deteriorated, mangy, grubby, squalid, sleazy, ramshackle, ragged, shoddy, shopworn, scruffy, tatty, ratty, down-at-heel, fly-blown, motheaten. —**Ant.** spruce, trim, smart.

seek, v. **1.** search for, look for, hunt for, quest after, pursue, follow, solicit, go after. **2.** ask for, request, inquire after, beg, solicit, demand, invite. **3.** aspire, aim, undertake, try, endeavor, essay.

seem, v. appear, look; pretend, assume, makebelieve, play, play-act.

seemly, adj. fitting, becoming, suited, well-suited, suitable, appropriate, proper, apt, comme il faut, apposite, apropos, characteristic, reasonable, congruous, compatible, consonant, congenial, befitting, meet; decent, decorous, right, demure, sedate, dignified, genteel, prudent, discreet, diplomatic, politic. —**Ant.** unsuitable, inappropriate; indecorous, improper.

seethe, v. **1.** fume, smolder, burn, rage, rant, rave, be angry or incensed, get red in the face or hot under the collar, blow up. **2.** boil, stew, simmer, bubble, surge, foam, froth.

segregate, v. isolate, separate, set apart, dissociate, segment, partition, seclude, sequester, exclude, ostracize, discriminate against, practice apartheid or Jim Crow. —**Ant.** unite, associate, blend; desegregate.

seize, v. **1.** grasp, grab, clutch, grip, snatch, take hold of. **2.** capture, take into custody, arrest, apprehend, entrap, trap, catch, take, pick up, nab, collar, cop, snare, pinch. **3.** confiscate, appropriate, commandeer, liberate, capture, impound, annex, usurp, take possession of, arrogate. —**Ant.** loose.

select, v. **1.** choose, prefer, pick, hand pick, pick out, opt for, single out, settle on, elect, decide on, cull. —adj. **2.** selected, chosen, preferred, choice, special, preferable, favorite, exceptional, first-rate, world-class, superior, prime, valuable, excellent. **3.** exclusive, selective, limited, restrictive, eclectic, privileged, elite, closed, private, rarefied, hoity-toity, discriminatory. —**Ant.** reject.

selective, adj. discriminating, choosy, scrupulous, particular, demanding, exacting, discerning, eclectic, fastidious, picky, fussy, finicky. —**Ant.** undiscriminating.

self-conscious, adj. shy, modest, retiring, unsure, embarrassed, sheepish, shamefaced, coy, diffident, self-effacing, shrinking, apprehensive, insecure, reserved, timid, backward, awkward, gauche, uncomfortable, uneasy, hesitant, nervous, halting, stammering, faltering, ill at ease, bashful, reticent, reluctant, chary, meek, abashed, confused, unassuming, demure. —**Ant.** self-confident, self-assured; poised.

self-evident, adj. evident, obvious, patent, incontrovertible, definite, express, distinct, clear-cut, apparent, undeniable, unmistakable, palpable, tangible, true, axiomatic, self-explanatory, clear. —**Ant.** mysterious.

selfish, adj. greedy, covetous, grasping, avaricious, acquisitive, materialistic, self-indulgent, self-aggrandizing, self-centered, self-absorbed, self-serving, monomaniacal, self-interested, self-seeking, egoistic, egotistical; mercenary, tightfisted, miserly, niggardly, pennypinching, cheeseparing, grudging, uncharitable, possessive, thoughtless, inconsiderate, illiberal, parsimonious, stingy, mean. —**Ant.** unselfish, generous, liberal, charitable, noble, self-sacrificing.

self-satisfied, adj. content, complacent, smug, satisfied, sanctimonious,

holier-than-thou, priggish, overconfident, conceited, self-important, vain, pompous, swellheaded, arrogant, overweening, overbearing. —**Ant.** modest, unassuming.

sell, v. trade, barter, vend, exchange, transfer, convey, dispose of; market, merchandise, offer, peddle, hawk, handle, traffic in, retail, stock, furnish, supply, push, promote, auction, consign, deal in. —**Ant.** buy.

semblance, n. **1.** appearance, aspect, form, show, exterior, image, figure, look, mask, facade, front, face, veneer, form, shape, mien, bearing, air, likeness, similarity, similitude, analogy, congruousness, affinity, resemblance. **2.** guise, pretense, simulation, impression, affectation, pose, air. —**Ant.** dissimilarity, difference.

seminal, adj. original, progenitive, creative, primary, primal, basic, fundamental, basal, founding, formative, innovative, imaginative, unprecedented, precedent-setting, landmark, influential; germinal, germinative, generative, embryonic, incipient, potential, latent, undeveloped, in utero. —**Ant.** derivative, imitative.

send, v. **1.** transmit, dispatch, forward, convey, deliver, assign, remit, ship, mail. **2.** impel, throw, cast, hurl, toss, propel, fling, project, release, discharge, shoot, fire, let fly. —**Ant.** receive.

senile, adj. senescent, decrepit, weak, infirm, feeble, geriatric, doddering, doddery, declining, failing, in one's dotage, superannuated, old, aged, elderly, rickety, fogyish, old-fogyish, forgetful, absentminded, oblivious, simple-minded, childish, in one's second childhood, over the hill, out of it. —**Ant.** youthful, alert.

sensation, n. **1.** sense, percept, image, sensibility, feeling, perception, impression; foreboding, awareness, consciousness, sneaking suspicion, presentiment, prescience. **2.** excitement, stimulation, animation; agitation, commotion, perturbation, stir, thrill, furor, tumult, uproar, disturbance, to-do, brouhaha, fuss.

sensational, adj. startling, thrilling, exciting, stimulating, electrifying, galvanizing, shocking, stirring, staggering, spine-tingling, hair-raising, show-stopping, breathtaking, astounding, astonishing, amazing, mind-boggling, mind-blowing, incredible, unbelievable, spectacular, out of this world, fantastic, extravagant, marvelous, wonderful, matchless, superb, peerless, phenomenal, extraordinary, fabulous, stupendous. —**Ant.** prosaic, dull.

sense, n. **1.** feeling, perception, impression, sensation. **2.** awareness, recognition, realization, apprehension, appreciation, understanding, cognizance, consciousness. **3.** perception, estimation, appreciation, discernment, discrimination, penetration, insight, acumen. **4.** meaning, signification, signficance, import, interpretation, denotation, connotation, intelligibility, coherence, drift, gist, nuance, message, substance. **5.** opinion, judgment, feeling, idea, notion, sentiment. —v. **6.** perceive, feel, detect, intuit, divine, suspect, have a hunch or feeling, realize, pick up on, apprehend, become aware or conscious of, discern, appreciate, recognize.

senseless, adj. **1.** insensate, unconscious, insensible, inert, stunned, comatose, dead to the world, anesthetized, numb, knocked out cold. **2.** unperceiving, undiscerning, unappreciative, unfeeling, apathetic, uninterested. **3.** stu-

pid, foolish, silly, idiotic, dizzy, moronic, fatuous, imbecilic, brainless, mindless, half-witted, birdbrained, harebrained, empty-headed, simple, weak-minded, witless; nonsensical, pointless, illogical, irrational, absurd, ridiculous, ludicrous, inane, meaningless, asinine; crazy, demented, insane, wild, mad, wacky, screwball, screwy, nutty, batty. —**Ant.** sensitive; intelligent; rational; sane.

sensibility, n. **1.** responsiveness, sensitiveness, perceptiveness, alertness, awareness, susceptibility. **2.** quickness, intelligence, judgment, judiciousness, keen-wittedness, penetration, discernment, insight, perception, keenness, acumen, acuity, acuteness, sensitivity, sensitiveness. **3.** consciousness, appreciation, awareness, perception, intuition, feeling, sentience, understanding. **4.** delicacy, tenderness, concern, sympathy, warmth, sentiment, sentimentalism, sentimentality. —**Ant.** insensibility; dullness; callousness.

sensible, adj. **1.** commonsensical, common-sense, rational, reasonable, logical, realistic, practical, pragmatic, expedient, sound, sane, wise, sagacious, sage, judicious, discreet, politic, intelligent, down-to-earth, sober, clear-headed, cleareyed, efficient, hardheaded, tactful, tactical, well-thought-out, well-considered, appropriate, advisable, circumspect, cautious, careful. **2.** cognizant, aware, conscious, acquainted with, sensitive to, mindful of, in touch with, alert, awake, wise to, perceptive, alive, understanding, observant. **3.** appreciable, considerable, significant, substantial, substantive, noticeable, perceptible. **4.** perceptible, discernible, detectable, evident, recognizable, manifest, palpable, tangible, material, physical, substantive, corporeal, visible, observable, phenomenal, objective, identifiable. —**Ant.** insensible, irrational, unsound; unaware; trifling.

sensitive, adj. **1.** impressionable, susceptible, easily affected, touchy, emotional, vulnerable, thin-skinned, high-strung, hypersensitive, volatile, excitable, temperamental; irritable, testy, irascible, petulant, quick-tempered. **2.** tender, sore, feeling, susceptible, sensate. **3.** delicate, responsive, subtle, acute, reactive, finely tuned. —**Ant.** insensitive; phlegmatic, thick-skinned, unemotional; numb, insenate; non-responsive.

sensual, adj. **1.** voluptuous, sensuous, luxurious; sumptuous, rich, sybariticc, hedonistic, epicurean, physical, carnal, bodily, fleshly, animal, animalistic. **2.** libidinous, lustful, lusty, sexual, erotic, lecherous, goatish, abandoned, wanton, profligate, debauched, dissipated, lubricious, salacious, prurient, loose, dirty, lewd, unchaste, gross, licentious, lascivious, dissolute. —**Ant.** modest, prudish.

sensuous, adj. sentient, feeling, sensible, perceptible, sensory; sybaritic, hedonistic, epicurean, sumptuous, rich, luxurious, voluptuous, luscious, delectable, delightful, aesthetic; physical, carnal, fleshly, animal. —**Ant.** Spartan, austere.

sentient, adj. aware, alive, conscious, awake, cognizant, sensitive, sensible, witting, susceptible, susceptive, feeling, perceptive, responsive, receptive, impressionable, sensate, reactive, discriminative, discriminatory. —**Ant.** dulled, numb, insensate.

sentiment, n. **1.** attitude, disposition, opinion, feeling, judgment, view, outlook, position, belief, notion, ideal, conviction, persuasion, thought. **2.** emotion, sentimentality, feeling, susceptibility, nostalgia, sentimentalism, mawkishness, bathos; sensitiveness, sensibility, tenderness, tenderheartedness, affection, passion. —**Ant.** coolness, apathy, pragmatism, rationality.

sentimental, *adj*. **1.** emotional, compassionate, tenderhearted, tender, sympathetic, warmhearted, heart-felt, poignant, affecting, touching, moving, stirring. **2.** romantic, maudlin, mawkish, emotional, nostalgic, tearful, teary-eyed, tear-jerking, weepy, simpering, sweet, oversweet, saccharine, mushy, soppy, corny, schmaltzy, icky-sweet, yucky.

sentimentality, *n*. emotionalism, romanticism, nostalgia, pathos, bathos, mawkishness, tenderness, teariness, tearfulness, mush, soppiness, schmaltz, corn, kitschiness. —**Ant.** reason.

separate, *v*. **1.** keep apart, divide, partition, divorce, detach, unhook, rend, part, put apart, disjoin, disconnect, dissever, sever, disunite, sunder, disengage, dissociate, split, break up, disassemble, disentangle, unravel. **2.** withdraw, cleave, part company *or* ways, disband, divorce, secede, diverge. —*adj*. **3.** separated, disjoined, disunited, disconnected, disassociated, unattached, apart, divided, severed, detached, distinct, discrete; apart, withdrawn, solitary, removed, cloistered, secluded, shut away, locked up, segregated, free, independent, sequestered, alone, isolated. **4.** independent, individual, particular, different, unrelated, other, unique, sole, lone, single, solitary. —**Ant.** unite, connect; together, whole; social, sociable; integral, same, identical, general.

separation *n*. **1.** splitup, split, breakup, break, rift, estrangement, divorce, disunion. **2.** division, split, schism, partition, disassociation, independence, dissociation, severance, detachment, removal. **3.** fracture, fragmentation, disintegration, shattering, rupture, disjunction, split, breakup, dismemberment, segregation, division, sundering.

sequence, *n*. **1.** succession, order, arrangement, series, progression, set, run, concatenation, system, chain, string, train, course, cycle, organization, suit, suite. **2.** outcome, sequel, consequence, result, followup, upshot, issue, development.

serendipity, *n*. luck, chance, happenstance, accident, break, fortuity, fortuitousness, adventitiousness, randomness, fortune, fluke, flukiness, dumb luck. —**Ant.** premeditation, fate, predestination, logic.

serene, *adj*. **1.** calm, peaceful, tranquil, quiet, still, noiseless, silent, pacific, peaceable, halcyon, restful, idyllic, pastoral, bucolic; unruffled, undisturbed, imperturbable, unperturbed, untroubled; poised, self-possessed, even-tempered, temperate, nonchalant, easygoing, laid-back, placid, composed, sedate, staid, collected, cool. **2.** fair, clear, unclouded, bright. —**Ant.** agitated, disturbed, excitable, mercurial, irritable, self-conscious, nervous; cloudy, inclement.

serenity, *n*. calmness, composure, self-possession, poise, aplomb, nonchalance, unflappability; tranquility, peacefulness, calm, sereneness, peace, quiet, restfulness, stillness. —**Ant.** perturbation, disturbance, agitation, pandemonium, uproar, hurly-burly.

series, *n*. sequence, succession, set, progression, run, cycle, string, train,

concatenation, suit, suite, line; order, arrangement, organization, system.

serious, *adj*. **1.** thoughtful, reflective, contemplative, meditative, deep, profound, grave, unsmiling, poker-faced, pensive, humorless, somber, grim, dour, severe, austere, stern, ascetic, solemn, sober, sedate, staid, earnest. **2.** weighty, important, momentous, vital, significant, consequential, grave, urgent, pressing, crucial, dangerous, life-or-death, deep, profound, grave, critical. —**Ant.** lighthearted, jocular, trivial.

sermonize, *v*. preach, evangelize, homilize, preachify, prelect, lecture, hold forth, discourse, dilate, expatiate, dogmatize, moralize.

servant, *n*. domestic, help, helper, employee, menial, factotum, lackey, dogsbody; housekeeper, maid, handyman, valet, butler, cleaning woman *or* man, nanny, au pair, cook, chef. —**Ant.** employer.

serve, *v*. **1.** wait on, attend, minister to, look after, be at (someone's) beck and call. **2.** assist, help, aid, succor, accommodate, oblige, gratify, be of assistance. **3.** function, answer, do, suffice, be useful, fill the bill, suit, be adequate *or* suitable. **4.** promote, contribute, forward, advance, assist. **5.** provide, cater, satisfy, purvey, distribute, supply, offer, make available, dish *or* dole *or* deal out, pass around *or* out, handle.

serviceable, *adj*. **1.** working, workable, functional, operating, operative; helpful, useful, handy, utile, aidful, employable, utilitarian, advantageous, profitable, convenient, available, effective, valuable; durable, tough, long-lasting, wear-resistant. **2.** adequate, tolerable, passable, fair, fairish, unexceptional, middling, so-so, decent, respectable, acceptable, satisfactory.

servile, *adj*. submissive, obsequious, compliant, sheepish, docile, obedient, passive, subservient, craven, acquiescent, deferential, ingratiating, toadying, truckling, wheedling, flattering, unctuous, timeserving, apple-polishing, bootlicking, smarmy, brown-nosing, menial, slavish, cringing, cowering, low, fawning, abject, ignoble, inferior, mean, base, sycophantic, groveling. —**Ant.** proud, noble, masterful, independent, dignified, disobedient, mutinous, insolent, disrespectful.

set, *v*. **1.** put, place, position, pose, locate, situate, post, appoint, station, site, stanel, lay, install, lodge, mount, deposit, drop, park, plant. **2.** fix, appoint, ordain, settle, establish, determine, fasten on, prescribe, assign, define, predetermine. **3.** adjust, arrange, order, dispose, place. **4.** turn, synchronize, fix, calibrate, coordinate, regulate. **5.** decline, sink, subside, fall, wane, go down. **6.** solidify, congeal, jell, freeze, stiffen, coagulate, clot, thicken, harden. —*n*. **7.** assortment, outfit, group, combination, number, selection, arrangement, grouping, collection, series. **8.** group, clique, coterie, company, circle, class, ring, crowd, gang, faction, sect. **9.** direction, bent, inclination, disposition, attitude. **10.** bearing, carriage, mien, posture, appearance, aspect. **11.** stage, scene, mounting, *mise en scéne*, scenery, decor, backdrop, setting. —*adj*. **12.** fixed, established, prearranged, decided, determined, settled, prefixed, predetermined. **13.** prescribed, foreordained. **14.** customary, normal, regular, habitual, traditional, conventional, scheduled, routine, standard, unvarying, unchanging, wonted, usual. **15.** fixed,

rigid, immovable. **16.** resolved, determined, stubborn, fixed, obstinate, stiff, unyielding. —**Ant.** displace, abolish; rise; soften, melt.

settle, *v*. **1.** fix, agree upon, decide, appoint, confirm, affirm, conclude, make sure of, determine, choose, select, set, establish. **2.** pay, discharge, repay, satisfy, clear, quit, defray, liquidate. **3.** locate in, emigrate, put down roots, relocate, take up residence, stay, dwell, reside, make one's home, abide, inhabit, live, set up housekeeping; populate, pioneer, people, colonize. **4.** quiet, tranquilize, calm, compose, still, pacify. **5.** stabilize, establish, decide, arrange, agree, order, dispose, organize, straighten out, compose, put to rights, reconcile, resolve, conclude, put an end to, adjust, calm down, subside, quiet down, become tranquil, rest, sink down, decline, sink, fall, gravitate. —**Ant.** unsettle.

sever, *v*. separate, divide, cut apart, part, cut, cleave, lop, chop, hack, hew, slice, shear, dock, rend, split, sunder, break off, disunite, disjoin, detach, disengage, disconnect; dissolve, terminate, suspend, abandon, discontinue. —**Ant.** unite.

severe, *adj*. **1.** harsh, extreme, fierce, trenchant, biting, acerb, bitter, caustic, satirical, keen, stinging, mordant, mordacious, sharp, cutting. **2.** serious, grave, stern, forbidding, glowering, dour, grim, stiff, sober, unsmiling, cold, frigid, aloof, austere, rigid, rigorous, strict, strait-laced, sedate; unfeeling, unsympathetic, cruel, harsh, brutal, stonyhearted, flinty, ironhanded, oppressive, obdurate, pitiless, merciless, punitive, ruthless, despotic, dictatorial, authoritative, autocratic, relentless, hard, unrelenting, inexorable, abrupt, peremptory, curt, short. **3.** restrained, modest, spare, plain, simple, unadorned, stark, bare, austere, ascetic, monastic, Spartan, crude, undecorated, unembellished, unembroidered, unornamented, chaste. **4.** uncomfortable, distressing, unpleasant, acute, afflictive, violent, intense, dangerous, critical, dreadful, awful, life-threatening, dire; mortal, fatal, terminal. **5.** rigid, strict, painstaking, fastidious, exigent, taxing, exact, critical, demanding, accurate, methodical, systematic, exacting. —**Ant.** mild; gradual; flexible; comfortable; inaccurate.

sexy *adj*. **1.** erotic, exciting, seductive, suggestive, arousing, sensual, sensuous, carnal, fleshly, voluptuous, earthy, lustful, animal, provocative, inviting, alluring, flirtatious, coquettish, appealing, attractive, fascinating, captivating, stunning, bedroom, come-hither. **2.** pornographic, explicit, X-rated, obscene, smutty, lewd, gross, libidinous, lascivious, lubricious, licentious, indecent, dirty, filthy, vulgar, coarse, off-color, ribald, risqué, bawdy, titillating, indelicate, suggestive, shameless, raunchy.

shabby, *adj*. **1.** threadbare, worn, ragged, bedraggled, shopworn, moth-eaten, tattered, scruffy, tatty, out at the elbows. **2.** shoddy, ramshackle, run-down, neglected, decrepit, seedy, squalid, sordid, slummy, wretched. **3.** mean, mean-spirited, base, contemptible, deplorable, egregious, scurvy. **4.** disreputable, discreditable, dishonorable, shameful, ignominious, shady. **5.** unfair, inequitable, unjust, unsporting, unsportsmanlike, discriminatory.

shack, *n*. shanty, hut, shed, hutch, hovel, cabin, crib, outbuilding, outhouse, lean-to, dump.

shackle, *n.* **1.** fetter, chain, anklet, iron, ball and chain, restraint, cuff, bracelet, handcuff, manacle, hobble. **2.** restriction, restraint, deterrent, check, barrier, hindrance, bar, impediment, obstacle, obstruction, encumbrance. —*v.* **3.** confine, bind, tie, secure, truss, tether, trammel, restrain, restrict, fetter, chain, manacle, handcuff, hobble, hog-tie. **4.** restrict, trammel, impede, encumber, obstruct, block, restrain, hold back, deter, hinder, discourage, handicap, curb, control, inhibit, limit, rein, bridle, check, circumscribe, confine, slow, stultify, dull. —**Ant.** disencumber, extricate, release, liberate, free.

shade, *n.* **1.** darkness, dimness, shadiness, murkiness, shadow, obscurity, gloom, gloominess, dusk, umbrage, penumbra. **2.** specter, ghost, apparition, spirit, phantom, phantasm, wraith, vision, banshee, spook, revenant, haunting. **3.** variation, amount, degree, hair, trace, hint, intimation, tinge, modicum, soup

shake, *v.* **1.** sway, vibrate, fluctuate, oscillate, pulsate, gyrate, swing, wiggle, wriggle, squirm, shimmy, twitch, jiggle, waggle, roll, bump, grind; quake, wobble, dither, teeter, quiver, waver, tremble, agitate, rock, convulse, shudder, shiver, totter. **2.** brandish, wave, display, show off, exhibit, flap, flutter, parade, flourish. **3.** agitate, disturb, move, intimidate, frighten, daunt, upset, disconcert, discombobulate, unnerve, discomfort, worry, fluster, disquiet, confound, confuse, perplex, rattle, throw for a loop. **4.** unsettle, undermine, impair, harm, damage, discourage, weaken, enfeeble. —*n.* **5.** tremor, blow, disturbance, shock.

shaky, *adj.* **1.** unsteady, unstable, rickety, dilapidated, ramshackle, decrepit, on its last legs, feeble, unbalanced, teetery, teetering, tottery, tottering, wobbly, doddering, fragile, spindly. **2.** tremulous, aflutter, faint, shuddering, unsteady, dizzy, vertiginous, shivering, quivering, apprehensive, fidgety, flustered, edgy, fretful, agitated, upset, uneasy, anxious, nervous, jittery, jumpy, skittish. **3.** unstable, unsound, flimsy, tenuous, questionable, unsubstantiated, untrustworthy, undependable, unreliable, uncertain, unsure, doubtful, dubious, precarious, problematic, risky, ticklish, dicey, iffy. —**Ant.** steady, solid, stable; confident; certain, reliable, proven, safe.

shallow *adj.* superficial, skin-deep, surface, outward, external, slight, trivial, insignificant, unimportant, frivolous, trifling, thin, slim, slender, flimsy, foolish, idle, cursory, uncritical, insubstantial, meaningless, cosmetic, nominal, passing, nonessential, petty, paltry, empty, hollow, idle, vain.

sham, *n.* **1.** imitation, pretense, fake, fraud, hoax, humbug, forgery, counterfeit, phony, copy, imposture, cheat, deception, simulacrum. —*adj.* **2.** pretended, counterfeit, false, fake, fraudulent, paste, simulated, make-believe, fictitious, ersatz, bogus, artificial, synthetic, phony, pseudo, spurious, mock. —*v.* **3.** pretend, simulate, counterfeit, assume, affect, imitate, deceive, feign, defraud, impose, make believe, hoax, con. —**Ant.** genuine, authentic, bona fide, real.

shame, *n.* **1.** humiliation, mortification, remorsefulness, embarrassment, loss of face, abashment, chagrin. **2.** disgrace, derision, ignominy, dishonor, disrepute, degradation, vilification, calumny, abasement, reproach, obloquy,

opprobrium, odium, infamy, contempt. **3.** scandal, stigma, denigration, defamation, descredit, derogation, disparagement. **4.** modesty, humility, decorum, decency, propriety, respectability, shyness, coyness, diffidence, timidity, prudishness, bashfulness, meekness. —*v.* **5.** abash, humiliate, mortify, embarrass, chagrin, put down, chasten, take (someone) down a peg, humble, confuse, disconcert. **6.** disgrace, reproach, dishonor, calumniate, degrade, defame, discredit, stigmatize, scandalize, debase, tarnish, stain, taint, smear, blacken, besmirch, sully, soil. **7.** force, bully, coerce, drive, push, impel, compel, intimidate, pressure. —**Ant.** honor.

shameful, *adj.* disgraceful, blameworthy, scandalous, mortifying, humiliating, dishonorable, ignominious, disreputable, degrading, indecent, inglorious, deplorable, corrupt, unprincipled, unethical, immoral, outrageous, infamous, vicious, villainous, iniquitous, vile, base, mean, evil, wicked, horrid, shocking, indecorous, unseemly, low. —**Ant.** honorable.

shameless, *adj.* **1.** immodest, wild, flagrant, unrestrained, wanton, uncontrolled, barefaced, audacious, unblushing, brazen, indecent, indecorous, brash, rude, improper, forward, impudent, bold, insolent, indelicate, unabashed, unashamed, shocking, outrageous. **2.** corrupt, impure, indecent, dishonorable, sinful, unprincipled, depraved, profligate, abandoned, wanton, dissolute, reprobate, vicious, hard, hardened, callous, incorrigible, lost. —**Ant.** shy, diffident, bashful, modest; proper, pure, chaste, decent, principled, honorable, righteous, upstanding, incorruptible.

shape, *n.* **1.** outline, lines, contours, profile, silhouette; build, body, physique, form, figure; appearance, aspect. **2.** guise, disguise, likeness, image, form, appearance. **3.** arrangement, order, configuration, pattern. **4.** condition, situation, state, status, trim, order. **5.** mold, cast, pattern, form, structure. —*v.* **6.** make, fabricate, manufacture, forge, form, fashion, mold, model, cast, sculpt; carve, trim, hew, hack. **7.** word, express, term, formulate, put, pose, embody in words. **8.** adjust, adapt, frame, fit, accommodate, change, modify, remodel.

shapeless *adj.* **1.** formless, unformed, amorphous, unstructured, indefinite, undefined, vague, nebulous, uncertain, hazy, fuzzy, rough, rude, crude, chaotic, inchoate. **2.** deformed, misshapen, lumpy, distorted, twisted, battered, bent, malformed, contorted, warped, gnarled, grotesque, abnormal, monstrous, ill-formed, badly proportioned, ungraceful.

share, *n.* **1.** portion, part, allotment, division, allocation, allowance, due, ration, apportionment, contribution, quota, lot, proportion, cut, piece, stake, slice. —*v.* **2.** divide, distribute, dispense, apportion, allot, portion, parcel out, allocate, ration, split, partition, deal out, dole, mete out. **3.** partake, participate, join in, engage in, take part, receive, enter into.

sharp, *adj.* **1.** keen, acute, edged, pointed, knifelike, peaked. **2.** abrupt, precipitous, sheer, marked, vertical, sudden. **3.** distinct, marked, clear. **4.** pungent, biting, acrid, spicy, burning, hot, mordacious, bitter, piquant, tangy, harsh, acid, tart, sour. **5.** shrill, piercing, loud, high, high-pitched, penetrating, piercing, strident, loud, earsplitting. **6.** cold, piercing, freezing,

nipping, cutting, severe, fierce, biting. **7.** painful, distressing, intense, severe, extreme, acute, piercing, fierce, excruciating, agonizing. **8.** harsh, merciless, unmerciful, severe, acute, cutting, incisive, caustic, trenchant, scathing, malicious, nasty, malevolent, malignant, acid, sarcastic, sardonic, acrimonious, mordant, mordacious, piercing, probing, penetrating, pointed, biting, unkind, spiteful, virulent, venomous, poisonous. **9.** fierce, violent, intense. **10.** vigilant, alert, awake, on the qui vive, attentive. **11.** acute, shrewd, keenwitted, smart, agile, astute, clever, penetrating, discerning, perspicacious, ingenious, discriminating, ready, smart, cunning, intelligent, bright, quick, sensitive, alert, observant, incisive, vigorous, understanding, active, reasoning. **12.** dishonest, shady, unlawful, deceitful, artful, crafty, foxy, sly, cunning, calculating, unscrupulous, corrupt, treacherous, deceptive, sneaky, cheating. —**Ant.** dull, blunt; unclear; mild; soft; warm; merciful; stupid, dim; honest, aboveboard.

shatter, *v.* break, crush, shiver, disintegrate, burst, pulverize, smash, splinter, fragment, fracture, rupture, crash, split, crack; explode, implode, destroy, ruin, wreck, demolish, devastate, blast, undermine, blow to bits *or* smithereens, reduce to rubble; overcome, overwhelm, paralyze, confound, confuse, stupefy, stun, knock for a loop.

sheer, *adj.* **1.** transparent, diaphanous, thin, clear, revealing, see-through, filmy, gauzy, gossamer, translucent, light, peekaboo. **2.** absolute, unmitigated, out-and-out, unalloyed, plain, total, rank, complete, arrant, thoroughgoing, outright, unmixed, mere, simple, pure, downright, unadulterated, unqualified, utter. **3.** steep, precipitous, abrupt, perpendicular, bluff, vertical. —**Ant.** opaque; gradual.

shelter, *n.* **1.** protection, safeguard, refuge, retreat, asylum, cover, screen, safety, security, defense, concealment, bastion, safe house, bulwark, sanctuary, shield, haven, port, ark, harbor. —*v.* **2.** protect, guard, cover, safeguard, screen, keep, secure, defend, shield, hide, shroud, house, harbor, receive, accept, admit, lodge, board, entertain. —**Ant.** exposure; betray, expose, abandon, evict.

shiftless, *adj.* **1.** lazy, indolent, slothful, unambitious, slack, dilatory, uninspired, unmotivated, unenterprising, idle, lackadaisical, irresponsible, aimless, time-wasting, clock-watching, goldbricking, good-for-nothing. **2.** improvident, inefficient, unresourceful. —**Ant.** ambitious, energetic, enterprising, sedulous, hard-working.

shimmer, *v., n.* glisten, shine, flash, glance, sparkle, glitter, scintillate, coruscate, twinkle, glister, spark, gleam, glimmer, glow, flicker, glint.

shine, *v.* **1.** beam, glare, gleam, glisten, glimmer, shimmer, sparkle, flare, glitter, coruscate, twinkle, scintillate, glint, flicker, flash, glow, radiate. —*n.* **2.** radiance, light, brightness, gleam, glow, shimmer. **3.** polish, luster, gloss, brilliance, twinkle, scintillation, glow, sheen, patina, brightness, sparkle, shimmer, glitter, gleam, radiance.

shining, *adj.* **1.** radiant, gleaming, glowing, shimmering, glossy, glassy, beaming, glittering, twinkling, dazzling, coruscating, sparkling, scintillating, flickering, lambent, fulgent, bright, brilliant, resplendent, glistening, effulgent, lustrous. **2.** conspicuous, fine, outstanding, distinguished, eminent, prime, splendid, choice, excellent, select.

shirk, *v.* evade, avoid, dodge, shun, get out of, shrink from, duck, elude, escape, sidestep, malinger, goldbrick, slack off, goof off, waste time, lollygag.

shiver, *v.* **1.** tremble, quake, quaver, totter, wobble, shimmy, teeter, shudder, shake, quiver; vibrate, rattle. **2.** shake, quake, tremble, shudder, quiver, thrill, frisson, tremor, flutter; goosebumps, chill.

shock, *n.* **1.** blow, impact, collision, encounter, concussion, clash, tingle, jolt, jar. **2.** surprise, thunderbolt, bombshell, revelation, eye-opener, jolt; disturbance, commotion, agitation; trauma, stupor, paralysis, collapse, breakdown, prostration. —*v.* **3.** startle, stagger, surprise, stun, jar, jolt, shake up, numb, daze, appall, astonish, flabbergast, astound, paralyze, stupefy, bewilder, dumbfound. **4.** frighten, petrify, traumatize, repel, upset, horrify, disgust, outrage, nauseate, offend, sicken, revolt.

shoddy *adj.* shabby, second-rate, imperfect, poor, inferior, bad, cheap, cheapjack, meretricious, tacky, chintzy, Drummagem, pinchbeck, tawdry, tinselly, artificial, plastic, trashy, junky, ratty, mangy, low-quality, mediocre, substandard, low-grade, gimcrack, crummy, lousy, tasteless, tinny, rundown, seedy, insubstantial, flimsy. —**Ant.** first-rate, superior, well-made, quality, perfect.

shore, *n.* **1.** beach, coast, bank, seashore, riverbank, margin, strand. **2.** support, prop, brace, buttress, stay, post, beam, strut.

short, *adj.* **1.** little, small, tiny, diminutive, wee, slight, petite, dwarfish, squat, runty, stunted, stubby, pintsized, sawn-off, knee-high to a grasshopper. **2.** concise, pithy, epigrammatic, brief, terse, succinct, laconic, condensed, compendious, compressed, abbreviated, abridged, curt, sententious. **3.** abrupt, curt, sharp, blunt, bluff, brusque, gruff, drabby, waspish, snappish, discourteous, impolite, curmudgeonly, petulant, short-tempered, testy, uncivil, rude. **4.** scanty, poor, insufficient, deficient, inadequate, wanting, lacking, needful, shy of, low on. **5.** substandard, inferior, unacceptable, below par. —*adv.* **6.** suddenly, abruptly, peremptorily, instantly, unexpectedly, hurriedly, hastily, out of the blue, without notice *or* warning. —**Ant.** tall, long.

shortage *n.* lack, scarcity, scarceness, want, shortfall, need, deficiency, deficit, dearth, paucity, insufficiency, inadequacy, scantiness, meagerness.

shortcoming *n.* imperfection, blemish, flaw, weak spot, handicap, liability, drawback, weakness, frailty, defect, failure, failing, deficiency, inadequacy, foible, fault, Achilles' heel, lack, blind spot, vice.

shorten, *v.* **1.** curtail, abbreviate, cut, trim, prune, compress, truncate, summarize, contract, shrink, abstract, digest, epitomize, abridge, condense, lessen, limit, restrict, reduce, retrench. **2.** take in, reduce, decrease, diminish, lessen, contract. —**Ant.** lengthen, elongate, extend.

short-lived, *adj.* temporary, fleeting, passing, brief, transitory, transient, ephemeral, evanescent, impermanent, momentary, fugitive, fly-by-night, quick, hasty, not long for this world. —**Ant.** permanent, enduring, lasting, everlasting, stable, perpetual, eternal, constant, abiding.

shortsighted, *adj.* **1.** myopic, dim-sighted, near-sighted. **2.** unthinking, unimaginative, unprogressive; improvident, injudicious, careless, heedless, reckless, thoughtless, imprudent, impulsive, brash, rash, unwary, blind, foolhardy, irresponsible; wasteful, profligate, prodigal, spendthrift, happy-go-lucky. —**Ant.** presbyopic, far-sighted; visionary, thoughtful, prudent.

shout, *v.* cry out, hoot, exclaim, vociferate, yell, scream, bawl, bellow, howl, roar, hoot, clamor, call out, yelp. —**Ant.** whisper.

shove, *v.* **1.** push, propel, impel, thrust, drive, force, move, press on, set in motion, jar, jolt, launch, start; constrain, compel, oblige, coerce. **2.** jostle, elbow, shoulder, nudge, bump, knock, jab, push aside, jar, strike, hit, butt into.

show, *v.* **1.** exhibit, display, present, expose, manifest, evidence, evince, offer, tender, parade, flaunt, demonstrate. **2.** point out, indicate. **3.** guide, accompany, lead, usher, escort, direct, lead, conduct. **4.** interpret, make clear *or* known, clarify, elucidate, explain, express, discover, reveal, disclose, divulge, publish, proclaim. **5.** prove, confirm, argue, prove, substantiate, corroborate, verify, certify, authenticate, demonstrate, evidence. **6.** accord, grant, bestow, confer. **7.** look, appear, seem, be visible. —*n.* **8.** display, ostentation, pomp, pretension, pretentiousness, affectation, exhibition, flourish, dash, pageantry, ceremony. **9.** showing, spectacle, exhibition, production, presentation, exhibit, exposition, fair, appearance. **10.** deception, pretense, pretext, simulation, illusion. —**Ant.** hide, conceal.

showy, *adj.* ostentatious, pompous, flamboyant, conspicuous, pretentious, florid, bravura, opulent, resplendent, sumptuous, gorgeous, luxurious, flashy, tawdry, gaudy, meretricious, garish, loud; fancy, elaborate, fussy, ornate, overdone, excessive, intricate, baroque, rococo, Byzantine. —**Ant.** subtle, discreet, austere, plain, simple, modest, unassuming.

shrewd, *adj.* astute, sharp, acute, clever, smart, cunning, canny, foxy, sly, crafty, artful, wily, manipulative, calculating, knowing, diplomatic, politic, smooth, suave, quick, discerning, discriminating, perceptive, perspicuous, perspicacious, keen, intelligent, penetrating, ingenious, sagacious, wise, sage, ingenious, inventful, resourceful, prudent, sensible, judicious. —**Ant.** dull, unworldly, naive, guileless, stupid, imperceptive.

shriek, *n.*, *v.* cry, scream, screech, yell, scream, squawk, squall, yelp.

shrink, *v.* **1.** retreat, recede, withdraw, draw back, back away, cower, cringe, wince, shy away, balk at, quail, boggle, scruple, demur, avoid, recoil, flinch, retire. **2.** contract, constrict, compress, condense, deflate, reduce, wither, shrivel, lessen, diminish, decrease, dwindle, wane, peter out; shorten, condense, abbreviate, cut, curtail, abridge. —**Ant.** advance, attack; swell, expand, amplify, distend, inflate, dilate, increase.

shrivel, *v.* wither, wrinkle, wizen, dry up, desiccate, dehydrate, parch, scorch, sear; decrease, pucker up, curl up, contract, shrink. —**Ant.** blossom, expand.

shroud, *v.* cover, veil, cloak, shield, screen, mask, disguise, camouflage, blanket, shade, protect, swathe, envelop, wrap, surround, curtain, hide, conceal, obscure, cloud, becloud. —**Ant.** reveal, expose.

shudder, *n.* shiver, quaver, quake, quiver, shake, twitch, tremble, convulsion, paroxysm, spasm, fit; rattle, vibration.

shun, *v.* elude, avoid, evade, eschew, sidestep, skirt, circumvent, dodge, steer clear of, shrink from, flee *or* escape from; rebuff, refuse, spurn, disdain, reject, cold-shoulder, repudiate, scorn, brush off. —**Ant.** confront, pursue, seek.

shut, *v.* **1.** close, fasten, secure, shut, lock, bolt, seal, slam. **2.** confine, enclose, jail, imprison. **3.** bar, exclude, prohibit, preclude. —*adj.* **4.** closed, fastened, sealed, locked, bolted. —**Ant.** open.

shy, *adj.* **1.** bashful, diffident, retiring, timid, coy, withdrawn, reserved, private, meek, mild, modest, sheepish, self-conscious, introverted, apprehensive, nervous. **2.** suspicious, distrustful, wary, heedful, cautious, careful, chary, reluctant, leery, guarded, afraid, fearful, anxious, worried, distrustful, cowardly, craven, timid. **3.** short, missing, lacking, deficient. —*v.* **4.** recoil, draw back, shrink, flinch, balk. —**Ant.** self-confident, aggressive, obtrusive, forward; trusting; incautious, careless; advance, attack.

sick, *adj.* **1.** ill, unwell, ailing, infirm, unhealthy, diseased, afflicted, under the weather, out of sorts, laid up, not up to snuff, indisposed. **2.** nauseous, vomiting, nauseated, queasy, squeamish, green around the gills. **3.** pale, wan, ashen, pasty, whey-faced, haggard, woebegone, weak, drawn, peaked, pallid, white, sickly. **4.** affected, troubled, stricken, wretched, miserable, woeful. —**Ant.** well, hale, healthy.

sickly, *adj.* **1.** unhealthy, ailing, sick, unwell, puny, weak, frail, feeble, delicate, wan, anemic, infirm. **2.** weak, mawkish, mushy, maudlin, cloying, insipid, schmaltzy, sentimental, faint. —**Ant.** strong, healthy.

sidekick, *n.* partner, associate, colleague, partner in crime, ally, comrade, comrade in arms, companion, confederate, cohort, henchman, subordinate, stooge, assistant, right hand, man Friday, girl Friday, factotum. —**Ant.** enemy, foe, adversary, opponent.

sign, *n.* **1.** token, signal, notice, indication, trace, evidence, clue, symptom, manifestation, betokening, vestige, hint, suggestion. **2.** mark, device, representation, emblem, brand, stamp, insigne, badge, character, note, symbol. **3.** omen, presage, portent, augury, foreboding, warning, forewarning, indi..ation, prophecy, prognostication, foreshadowing, handwriting on the wall. —*v.* **4.** signify, betoken, indicate, mean, signal. **5.** affix a signature to, autograph, inscribe, witness, mark, sign on the dotted line.

significance, *n.* **1.** import, importance, consequence, moment, weight, weightiness, relevance, value, worth, excellence, merit, prestige, authority, influence. **2.** import, meaning, sense, purport, message, idea, point, implication, pith, essence, gist, implication, drift, vein, impression, connotation, signification. —**Ant.** triviality.

significant, *adj.* **1.** important, consequential, momentous, weighty, substantial, substantive, noteworthy, notable, valued, valuable, meretorious, relevant, signal, outstanding, impressive, critical, crucial, vital. **2.** meaningful, expressive, eloquent, pithy, pregnant, informative, sententious, cogent, telling, convincing, signifying, indicative or suggestive of. —**Ant.** insignificant.

signify, v. **1.** signal, make known, express, indicate, communicate. **2.** convey, symbolize, betoken, represent, mean, connote, suggest, portend, denote, indicate, purport, imply. **3.** matter, count, carry weight, be consequential or important, impress, stand out, merit consideration.

silent, adj. **1.** quiet, still, noiseless, hushed, tranquil, peaceful, calm, soundless. **2.** speechless, dumb, mute; closemouthed, taciturn, uncommunicative, tightlipped, mum, reticent, reserved, secretive, private, discreet, restrained, inhibited, prudent. **3.** inactive, dormant, quiescent, hidden. **4.** unspoken, tacit, implicit, understood, implied, unexpressed. —**Ant.** noisy, clamorous; voluble, talkative; spoken, stated.

silly, adj. **1.** foolish, stupid, idiotic, foolhardy, irresponsible, simple, dopey, vacuous, simpering, birdbrained, dullwitted, dimwitted, witless, childish, puerile, jejune, juvenile, sophomoric, fatuous, unwise, imbecilic, moronic. **2.** absurd, ridiculous, inane, asinine, senseless, ludicrous, laughable, risible, macaronic, frivolous, trivial, nonsensical, preposterous, mad, crazy, insane, irrational, illogical, pointless, idiotic, wishy-washy, insipid. —**Ant.** sensible, mature, sane, rational, serious.

similar, adj. like, alike, identical, akin, analagous, comparable, parallel, homogeneous, equivalent, equal, correspondent, complementary, resembling. —**Ant.** dissimilar, different, opposite, contradictory, contrary, antithetical.

similarity, n. likeness, resemblance, congruity, equivalence, comparability, sameness, analogy, affinity, agreement, correspondence, accordance, harmony, similitude, correspondence, parallelism. —**Ant.** difference, dissimilarity.

simple, adj. **1.** clear, intelligible, uncomplicated, plain, comprehensible, clear, straightforward, easy, elementary, basic, facile, light, effortless, understandable, unmistakable, lucid. **2.** plain, modest, clean, undecorated, unostentatious, unpretentious, uncluttered, stark, classic, severe, austere, homey, Spartan, unadorned, natural, unaffected, unembellished, neat. **3.** unaffected, unassuming, homely, unpretentious. **4.** mere, bare, pure, sheer, absolute, elementary, simplex, uncomplicated. **5.** sincere, frank, candid, open, unaffected, uncomplicated, unpretentious, above board, straightforward, direct, forthright, upright, righteous, honest; undesigning, green, childlike, innocent, natural, artless, naive, guileless, ingenuous, unsophisticated. **6.** humble, lowly. **7.** unimportant, insignificant, trifling, trivial, nonessential, unnecessary, immaterial, inconsequential. **8.** common, ordinary, usual, customary. **9.** unlearned, ignorant, uneducated, untutored, dullwittted, half-witted, slow-witted, simple-minded, feebleminded, thick, bovine, obtuse, dumb, dull, backward, witless, brainless, stupid, dense, silly, naive, foolish, credulous, shallow. —**Ant.** complicated, complex; fancy, ornate, ostentatious; pretentious; compound; pompous; grand, magisterial; important; unusual; erudite, learned, profound.

simulate, v. imitate, mimic, pretend, feign, parrot, ape, copy, assume, affect, counterfeit, act, fake, sham, playact, put on, dissemble, disguise, cloak, mask.

sin, n. **1.** transgression, trespass, violation, crime, infraction, dereliction, misdemeanor, infringement, breach, misdeed, impiety, fault, profanation, desecration, iniquity, evil, sacrilege, desecration, peccadillo, foible, failing, frailty, offense, wrong; wickedness, vice, corruption, ungodliness, evil, immorality, depravity, irreverence, guilt. —v. **2.** transgress, trespass, do wrong, offend, fall from grace, stray, lapse, go astray, err. —**Ant.** virtue.

sincere, adj. candid, honest, open, truthful, above board, straightforward; direct, frank, upfront, on the level, honorable, conscientious, scrupulous, upright, forthright, earnest, guileless, artless, plain, simple; veracious, heartfelt, unequivocal, serious, deep, fervent, hearty, wholehearted, genuine, true, unaffected, real, unfeigned. —**Ant.** insincere.

sincerity, n. honesty, candor, frankness, truthfulness, openness, straightforwardness, forthrightness, seriousness, earnestness, artlessness, veracity, uprightness, trustworthiness, integrity, probity, genuineness, artlessness, ingenuousness, guilelessness. —**Ant.** insincerity.

sinful, adj. wicked, iniquitous, depraved, evil, immoral, amoral, corrupt, wrongful, vile, base, profligate, criminal, ungodly, unholy, sacrilegious, irreligious, impious, irreverent, demonic, profane, diabolical, satanic, fiendish, shameful, dissolute, heinous, debased, degenerate, perverted, unrepentant, unregenerate, bad, mischievous, piacular. —**Ant.** virtuous.

sing, v. trill, croon, vocalize, carol, lilt, give voice, descant, chant, intone, pipe, belt, warble.

single, adj. **1.** separate, only, individual, sole, distinct, particular, singular, solitary, one, lone, unique. **2.** alone, solitary, isolated. **3.** unmarried, unwed, unattached, free. **4.** simple, unmixed, pure, uncompounded, unadulterated. —n. **5.** one, individual, monad, singleton. —**Ant.** accompanied; multiple, together; married, wed, conjugal; adulterated, mixed.

singleminded, adj. resolute, firm, resolved, determined, dedicated, devoted, uncompromising, unswerving, unfaltering, persistent, relentless, purposeful, persevering, unwavering, tireless, committed, obstinate, dogged, tenacious. —**Ant.** undecided, distracted, dilatory.

singular, adj. **1.** extraordinary, remarkable, unusual, uncommon, rare, different, abnormal, aberrant, atypical, special, outlandish, offbeat, outré, far-out, strange, peculiar, odd, bizarre, fantastic, peculiar, unusual, eccentric, queer, curious, unaccountable. **2.** outstanding, noteworthy, significant, important, conspicuous, notable, signal, superior, prominent, preeminent, eminent, exceptional, unparalleled, unprecedented. **3.** unique, separate, individual, single, lone, isolated, rare, distinct, unique, one of a kind. —**Ant.** common, ordinary; mediocre, second-rate; imitative, duplicate.

sinister, adj. **1.** threatening, menacing, fateful, foreboding, dark, gloomy, portentous, ominous, inauspicious, unlucky, unfavorable, unpropitious, baleful, malign, malefic, unfortunate, disastrous. **2.** bad, evil, base, wicked, malevolent, malignant, malign, harmful, pernicious, treacherous, nefarious, diabolical, demonic, satanic, sinful, piacular, depraved, corrupt, perverse, spiteful, dishonest, crooked, baleful, villainous, insidious, sneaky, furtive,

underhanded. —**Ant.** benign, favorable, fortunate; good, honest.

sip, v. **1.** drink; sample, savor, taste. —n. **2.** drink, taste, sample, soupçon, drop, bit, swallow, nip, dram, swig, spoonful, thimbleful, mouthful, shot.

sit, v. **1.** be seated, roost, perch, settle down, take a seat, take a load off; rest, relax. **2.** be situated, dwell, settle, lie, rest, remain, abide, repose, stay. **3.** meet, assemble, gather, get together, be in session, convene. —**Ant.** stand, lie.

situation, n. **1.** location, position, setting, site, place, locality, locale, spot. **2.** condition, case, instance, quandry, dilemma, plight, state, status, status quo, state of affairs, lay of the land, juncture, pass, circumstances, predicament. **3.** position, post, job, employment, place, office, berth, appointment, capacity.

size, n. **1.** dimensions, proportions, measurements, expanse, range, scope, area, square footage, spread, stretch, amplitude, magnitude, extent; volume, bulk, weight, mass. **2.** immensity, vastness, enormousness, hugeness, greatness.

skeptic, n. doubter, questioner, scoffer, cynic, doubting Thomas, disbeliever, agnostic, atheist, infidel, heathen, nullifidian. —**Ant.** believer, theist.

skeptical, adj. skeptic, doubtful, dubious, doubting, questioning, disbelieving, unbelieving, incredulous, mistrustful, distrustful, scoffing, cynical, agnostic. —**Ant.** trusting, gullible, credulous.

sketch, n. **1.** drawing, outline, draft, diagram, tracing, blueprint, plan, schematic, design, delineation. **2.** skit, play, act, routine, stint. —v. **3.** depict, draw, diagram, trace, plan, outline, design, rough out, delineate, portray, represent.

sketchy, adj. hasty, hurried, imperfect, slight, cursory, incomplete, unfinished, patchy, skimpy, rough, vague, crude, fuzzy, indistinct, ill-defined, unrefined, unpolished, rough-hewn, perfunctory, once-over, slipshod, superficial. —**Ant.** finished, well-defined, polished.

skill, n. **1.** ability, aptitude, talent, expertise, expertness, facility, artistry, art, mastery, handiness, knack, technique, cleverness, adeptness, adroitness, dexterity, ingenuity, proficiency, deftness, quickness, cunning, craft, artifice, efficiency, effectiveness, readiness, facility, ease. **2.** capability, strength, gift, faculty, know-how, accomplishment, forte. —**Ant.** clumsiness, inability; weakness, failure.

skillful, adj. skilled, expert, ready, able, talented, capable, adroit, deft, adept, proficient, efficient, effective, dexterous, competent, qualified, practiced, masterly, masterful, gifted, accomplished, apt, clever, ingenious, resourceful, creative, knowledgeable, professional, trained, experienced, conversant, versed. —**Ant.** unskillful, inexpert, maladroit, awkward, inept, unqualified.

skin, n. **1.** hide, pelt, fur, fleece, epidermis, derma, integument. **2.** covering, peel, rind, hull, bark, shell, husk, crust, coat, coating, outside, incrustation, pellicle, veneer, lamina, overlay, outer layer, film, membrane. —v. **3.** flay, peel, hull, shell, pare, strip, husk, excoriate, decorticate.

skinny, adj. thin, bony, underweight, slim, slender, lean, slight, narrow, lanky, lank, gaunt, gangling, gangly, rawboned, scraggy, spare, anemic, emaciated, starved, half-starved, anorexic, anorectic, undernourished, pinched, hollow-cheeked, haggard, wasted, shrunken, angular, skeletal, scrawny, wiry; cadaverous, all skin and bones. —**Ant.** fleshy, fat, obese, corpulent, zaftig.

skip, v. **1.** spring, jump, gambol, cavort, frisk, prance, romp, dance, leap, bound, caper, hop. **2.** omit, overlook, avoid, ignore, cut, steer clear of, disregard, skip over, skim over, leave out, pass by. —n. **3.** leap, cavort, gambol, frisk, prance, romp, jump, spring, bound, caper, hop, dance.

skirmish, n. encounter, brush, action, battle, fight, engagement, confrontation, showdown, struggle, set-to, contest, conflict, combat, brush, fray, clash, fracas, melee, scrap, tussle, dust-up.

skittish, adj. **1.** uneasy, restless, restive, impatient, unquiet, hectic, feverish, sensitive, nervous, tense, agitated, flustered, ruffled, jittery, fretful, uptight, shaky, on pins and needles, in a dither or tizzy, anxious, jumpy, quivery, flighty, fidgety, edgy, fluttery, excitable, high-strung. **2.** unconfident, self-conscious, cowardly, craven, shy, timid, bashful, timorous, coy. **3.** frisky, lively, giddy, frivolous, whimsical, capricious. **4.** unpredictable, uncertain, variable, fickle, erratic, fitful, volatile, mercurial, unreliable, fluctuating, unstable. **5.** cautious, guarded, suspicious, apprehensive, leery, wary, chary, hesitant. —**Ant.** down-to-earth, stable, calm, confident, resolute, determined.

skulk, v. lurk, slink, sneak, hide, prowl, steal, lie low, creep, slip, tiptoe, pussyfoot, lie in wait. —**Ant.** emerge, appear.

slack, adj. **1.** loose, relaxed, limp, droopy, sagging, flaccid, floppy, soft, baggy. **2.** indolent, slothful, negligent, lazy, remiss, careless, lax, neglectful, delinquent, inattentive. **3.** slow, sluggish, dilatory, tardy, late, lingering, laggard, easygoing, slothful, sluggish, lethargic, shiftless. **4.** dull, inactive, blunted, idle, quiet. —n. **5.** decrease, decline, lull, pause, cutback, lessening, reduction, abatement, downturn, dwindling, lag, slowing, loosening; relaxation, indolence, negligence, laziness, remissness, laxness, inattentiveness, delinquency, lethargy, sloth. —v. **6.** shirk, neglect, goldbrick, malinger, loaf, idle, goof off, lollygag. **7.** relax, ease up, let up on, decline, decrease, diminish, weaken, abate, reduce, slacken, moderate, mitigate. —**Ant.** tight, tense, taut; diligent, industrious, busy, expeditious, quick.

slacken, v. **1.** loosen, relax, relieve, abate, mitigate, moderate, temper, qualify, remit, lessen, diminish. **2.** restrain, inhibit, delay, retard, slow, detain, check, curb, bridle, repress, subdue, control. —**Ant.** quicken.

slant, v. **1.** slope, lean, incline, tilt, angle, pitch, cant, bend, list, tip. —n. **2.** tilt, ramp, gradient, deflection, leaning, lean, angle, cant, incline, inclination, pitch, slope, obliquity, obliqueness. **3.** bent, leaning, prejudice, bias, inclination, partiality, turn, one-sidedness. **4.** viewpoint, angle, attitude, approach, standpoint, aspect, idea, twist.

slapdash, adj. careless, slipshod, sketchy, perfunctory, rough, crude, patchy, skimpy, sloppy, haphazard, any which way, hit or miss, hurried, hasty, superficial, cursory, lick and a promise, quick and dirty, once over lightly. —**Ant.** careful, meticulous.

slash, v. **1.** cut, slit, slice, gash, hack, score, knife, lacerate, scar, wound, pierce, enter, penetrate. **2.** cut, reduce, decrease, drop, lower, trim, alter, abridge, abbreviate. —n. **3.** stroke, cut, wound, gash, slit, incision, slice, gouge, tear, rip, laceration, piercing, penetration, opening, slit, hole.

slaughter, n. **1.** killing, butchering, butchery, massacre, carnage, homicide, murder, manslaughter, slaying, execution, sacrifice, bloodshed, genocide, bloodletting, blood bath, extermination, liquidation, pogrom. —v. **2.** butcher, execute, exterminate, liquidate, destroy, put to death, persecute, massacre, murder, slay, kill, wipe out, devastate, decimate.

slave, n. lackey, peon, drudge, workhorse, laborer, toiler, grind, hack, dogsbody, gofer; scullion, odalisque, helot, bondswoman, bondsman, bondservant, esne, thrall, villein, serf, vassal. —**Ant.** master.

slavery, n. **1.** enslavement, bondage, servitude, serfdom, vassalage, thralldom, subjection, captivity, yoke, enthrallment. **2.** toil, drudgery, exertion, pains, chores, travail, grind, strain, sweat, hard labor, laboriousness, labor, donkey work, hack work, scut work.

slavish, adj. **1.** submissive, abject, passive, sheepish, docile, obedient, subservient, craven, deferential, toadying, servile, groveling, menial, drudging, obsequious, fawning, sycophantic, cringing. **2.** base, mean, ignoble, sordid, low, inferior, slimy, unctuous, smarmy. —**Ant.** independent; elevated, exalted.

sleek, adj. smooth, slick, glossy, polished, lustrous, shiny, silky, silken, velvety, velvet, satiny, satin, glabrous; bright, lustrous, brilliant, even, polished; suave, urbane, well-groomed, elegant, trim, graceful, streamlined, svelte.

sleep, v. **1.** rest, repose, slumber, catnap, nap, drowse, doze, drop off, snore, snooze, catch forty winks, catch some Z's. —n. **2.** dormancy, inactivity; slumber, rest, repose, nap, catnap, doze, siesta, forty winks, beauty sleep.

slender, adj. **1.** slight, slim, thin, lean, willowy, sylphlike, svelte, lissome, lithe, graceful, lanky, spare, narrow. **2.** slim, slight, little, scanty, small, trivial, meager, trifling, insignificant, inadequate, insufficient. **3.** thin, weak, slim, narrow, slight, poor, unlikely, remote, small, meager, puny, feeble, flimsy. —**Ant.** large, fat, obese, corpulent; substantial; likely, certain.

slide, v. slip, slither, glide, coast, skim, skate, escapade, skid, sled, toboggan, creep, slink; drop, fall, decline, decrease.

slight, adj. **1.** small, insignificant, superficial, shallow, trivial, nugatory, negligible, minor, unlikely, inconsequential, tenuous, paltry, unimportant. **2.** slender, slim, petite, delicate, diminutive, tiny, short, miniature, wee, bantam, pint-sized. **3.** unstable, insubstantial, insecure, inadequate, rickety, precarious, dainty, frail, flimsy, weak, feeble, delicate, fragile. **4.** unsubstantial, inconsiderable, infinitesimal, trifling, minute, tiny, slender. —v. **5.** ignore, disregard, omit, forget, reject, neglect, disdain, overlook, shun, snub, rebuff, cut, cold-shoulder, despise, flout, scoff at, scorn, dis. —n. **6.** neglect, disregard, disdain, indifference, snub, coldness, rebuff, rejection, scorn, contumely, contempt, inattention. **7.** affront, insult, disrespect, slur, offense, indignity, outrage. —**Ant.**

considerable; compliment, welcome, honor.

slim, adj. **1.** slender, thin, slight, lean, spare, scrawny, bony, skinny, svelte, lithe, lanky, lissome, graceful, willowy, sylphlike. **2.** small, poor, slight, insignificant, trifling, trivial, nugatory, unimportant, paltry, meager, inadequate, remote, negligible, minor, feeble, flimsy, tenuous, inconsiderable, scanty, weak, thin, unsubstantial. —**Ant.** fat; considerable, substantial.

slip, v. **1.** slide, skid, slither, glide. **2.** be mistaken, err, blunder, make a mistake, miscalculate, go astray or wrong, transgress, sin, mess up. —n. **3.** mistake, error, blunder, fault, inadvertance, blooper, lapse, boner, carelessness, negligence, oversight; faux pas, indiscretion, gaffe, impropriety, transgression, sin, peccadillo, backsliding.

slippery, adj. **1.** slick, smooth, lubricious, slithery, oily, lubricated, glassy, sleek, icy, slimy, greased. **2.** risky, precarious, dangerous, hazardous, unsafe, ticklish. **3.** changeable, volatile, mutable, unstable, shifting, uncertain. **4.** untrustworthy, shifty, tricky, unreliable, undependable, treacherous, perfidious, disloyal, dishonest, deceitful, devious, evasive, wily, slick, crafty, sly, foxy, cunning, sneaky, shady, slimy, smarmy, cagey.

slope, v., n. slant, incline, decline, rise, fall, dip, sink, drop, angle, pitch, tip, tilt.

sloppy, adj. slovenly, slatternly, frowzy, blowzy, untidy, messy, dirty, grungy, disorderly, careless, loose, bedraggled, disheveled, unkempt, dowdy, frumpy, shabby, scruffy, unwashed, unclean, disorganized, cluttered, haphazard, topsy-turvy, in disarray, unorganized, lax, hit or miss, slipshod, slapdash, negligent, slack, remiss, indifferent, unconcerned. —**Ant.** careful, fastidious, tidy, neat, well-groomed, organized, methodical, meticulous.

slothful, adj. idle, sluggardly, indolent, dilatory, shirking, dronish, goldbricking, lethargic, apathetic, phlegmatic, lazy, sluggish, inactive, inert, indifferent, lax, shiftless, do-nothing, slow, laggard, languorous, languid, lackadaisical, layabout, torpid, slack, supine. —**Ant.** industrious, busy, diligent, active, energetic.

slow, adj. **1.** deliberate, gradual, progressive, measurable, perceptible, by degrees, moderate. **2.** lazy, sluggish, sluggardly, dilatory, indolent, lazy, slothful, laggard, torpid, dawdling, leaden, ponderous, plodding, snaillike, tortoiselike, creeping, crawling; unhurried, leisurely, easy, relaxed, restful, lackadaisical. **3.** dull, dense, stupid, unintelligent, thick, dumb, simple, simple-minded, obtuse, backward, dimwitted, bovine, unresponsive, cloddish, doltish, unimaginative, stolid, slow on the uptake, not too swift. **4.** slack, inactive, quiet, unproductive, sluggish. **5.** dragging, late, unpunctual, delayed, dilatory, lagging, tardy, behindhand. **6.** tiresome, wearisome, monotonous, tame, uneventful, dead, dry, ennuyant, soporific, sleepy, somnolent, uninteresting, tedious, humdrum, dull, boring. —v. **7.** retard, hinder, impede, obstruct; slack off, hold back, take it easy, ease up, relax. —**Ant.** fast; energetic, industrious; hurried, rapid, swift; quick, quick-witted; busy; punctual; lively, eventful, exciting, invigorating; advance, promote; hurry, race.

sluggish, adj. inactive, slow, lazy, lethargic, languid, languorous, laggard, lax, sluggardly, dilatory, shiftless, slack, do-nothing, lackadaisical, slothful, indolent, dull, inert, torpid, dronish, stuporous, comatose, phlegmatic, indifferent, apathetic, soporific, sleepy, somnolent, lifeless, limp, tired, drowsy. **—Ant.** quick, active, energetic.

slur, v. **1.** slight, disregard, pass over, gloss over, give short shrift, ignore, overlook. **2.** affront, smear, insult, offend, brand, stigmatize, slight, calumniate, disparage, slander, depreciate, asperse. **—n. 3.** smear, calumny, aspersion, discredit, insinuation, imputation, putdown, slander, libel, disparagement, slight, innuendo, insult, affront, blot, stain, stigma, brand, black mark, disgrace. **—Ant.** compliment, praise.

sly, adj. **1.** cunning, wily, artful, foxy, crafty, clever, guileful, astute, scheming, designing, conniving, tricky, shrewd, deceitful, disingenuous. **2.** stealthy, surreptitious, furtive, insidious, secret, underhanded, crooked, devious, covert, sneaky, shady, shifty, subtle, clandestine. **3.** naughty, impish, devilish, arch, waggish, puckish, mischievous, roguish. **—Ant.** direct, straightforward, guileless, ingenuous.

small, adj. **1.** little, tiny, diminutive, short, petite, mignonne, miniature, minute, minuscule, midget, mini, elfin, Lilliputian, baby, bantam, undersized, pint-sized, peewee. **2.** slender, slim, petite, skinny, thin, slight, narrow. **3.** unimportant, trivial, minor, slight, secondary, lesser, trifling, trivial, nugatory, inconsequential, petty, paltry, insignificant, puny, negligible; limited, diminished, reduced. **4.** uninspired, shallow, unoriginal, unimaginative, flat, commonplace, mundane, everyday. **5.** mean-spirited, mean, stingy, ungenerous, parsimonious, niggardly, selfish, tight, illiberal, narrow, skimpy, uncharitable, scanty, meager, cheap, petty, stinting, grudging, miserly, tightfisted, tight, close. **6.** foolish, humiliated, embarrassed, chagrined, disconcerted, uncomfortable, ashamed, mortified, abashed. **—Ant.** large.

small-minded, adj. **1.** narrowminded, narrow, small, illiberal, selfish, stingy, grudging, ungenerous, uncharitable, mean, petty, closeminded, bigoted, hidebound, rigid, puritanical, shortsighted, myopic, unimaginative, intolerant. **2.** provincial, parochial, insular, limited, confined. **—Ant.** liberal, broadminded, tolerant, flexible, freethinking, imaginative, urbane.

smarmy, adj. **1.** insincere, false, sly, deceitful, guileful, disingenuous, hypocritical, mealymouthed, sanctimonious. **2.** suave, sleek, smug, insinuating, unctuous, slimy, fulsome, oily. **3.** obsequious, servile, toadying, brownnosing, bootlicking, craven, wheedling, flattering, sycophantic, ingratiating.

smart, v. **1.** pain, hurt, sting, pinch, ache, throb, burn, prickle, tingle, stab, pierce. **2.** hurt, wound, insult, affront. **—adj. 3.** quick, swift, sharp, keen, stinging, poignant, penetrating, painful, severe. **4.** brisk, vigorous, active, energetic, effective, animated, spirited, perky, breezy, lively. **5.** quick, prompt, nimble, agile, alert, active. **6.** intelligent, astute, brilliant, adept, quickwitted, acute, ingenious, capable, apt, bright, sharp, clever, expert, adroit. **7.** canny, perceptive, discerning, witty, trenchant, knowledgeable, erudite, aware, shrewd, cunning, streetwise, savvy, hip, with it. **8.** neat, trim, dashing, spruce, jaunty. **9.** elegant, chic, fashionable, voguish, à la mode, mod-

ish, stylish, soignée, well-groomed, dapper. **—Ant.** mild, gentle; sluggish, slow; dull, stupid, slow-witted; witless, imperceptive; unfashionable, dowdy, frumpy.

smell, n. odor, scent, aroma, fragrance, perfume, bouquet, whiff; stink, stench, reek, fetor, fetidness, effluvium, noxiousness.

smitten, adj. enamored, captivated, enthralled, enchanted, enraptured, charmed, infatuated, bewitched, beguiled, lovestruck, moonstruck, besotted, doting, gaga, swept off one's feet, bowled over, on cloud nine. **—Ant.** repelled, antipathetic.

smooth, adj. **1.** level, even, plain, regular, flush, plane, flat. **2.** bald, hairless, naked, bare, cleanshaven, depilated. **3.** flat, unruffled, calm, undisturbed, calm, peaceful, tranquil, pacific, peaceable. **4.** elegant, polished, fluent, facile, honey-tongued, syrupy, eloquent, diplomatic, glib, voluble, soft-spoken, slippery, slick, slimy, suave, unctuous. **5.** pleasant, agreeable, polite, courtly, courteous. **—v. 6.** sands, plane, stroke, polish, buff, refine, burnish, scrape; level, press, flatten, iron, roll, even out. **7.** tranquilize, ameliorate, allay, minimize, mitigate, lessen, reduce, temper, calm, soothe, assuage, mollify, better. **8.** gloss over, palliate, soften, appease. **—Ant.** rough, uneven, irregular; hairy; wrinkled, rumpled, disturbed; bluff, brusque.

smug, adj. complacent, self-satisfied, hypocritical, pharisaical, holier than thou, sanctimonious, arrogant, haughty, conceited, self-centered, egotistical, self-important, overconfident, condescending, self-righteous, overweening, opinionated, superior, cavalier, pompous, highhanded. **—Ant.** humble, modest.

snare, n. **1.** trap, noose, net, seine, springe, pitfall, boobytrap, ambush, lure, bait, decoy; trick, ruse, wile, stratagem, subterfuge, deception, chicanery. **—v. 2.** trap, entrap, entangle, catch, seize, capture, net, bag; lure, entice, decoy, inveigle, seduce, tempt, captivate.

sneak, v. **1.** slink, lurk, skulk, steal, creep, cower, prowl, sidle, pussyfoot. **—n. 2.** sneaker, prowler, lurker, informer, rat, tattletale, nark, stoolpigeon, stoolie, snitch, fink.

sneaky, adj. underhanded, devious, sly, cunning, wily, secretive, unscrupulous, shifty, slippery, slimy, furtive, disingenuousness, deceitful, dishonest, clandestine, covert, undercover, insidious, artful, untrustworthy, misleading, insincere, guileful, crafty, scheming, duplicitous, lying, cheating, doubledealing. **—Ant.** forthright, aboveboard, trustworthy, sincere.

sneer, v. **1.** smirk, curl one's lip, sniff; scorn, jeer, gibe, scoff, despise, mock, flout, disdain, deride, ridicule, criticize, underrate. **—n. 2.** scorn, contempt, mockery, ridicule, scoff, gibe, jeer, derision, disdain.

snide, adj. derogatory, nasty, mean, deprecatory, denigrating, disparaging, belittling, demeaning, offensive, insulting, hurtful, spiteful, abusive, churlish, surly, cruel, insinuating, vicious, slanderous, libelous. **—Ant.** complimentary, favorable.

snobbish, adj. pretentious, affected, pompous, self-important, self-satisfied, haughty, supercilious, lordly, conceited, vain, arrogant, self-centered, egotistical, smug, superior, lofty, condescending, patronizing, disdainful, scornful, contemptuous, presumptu-

ous, snooty, snotty, uppity, highfalutin, high and mighty, hoity-toity, stuck-up, high-hat, social-climbing, overweening, putting on airs.

snub, v. **1.** disdain, humiliate, humble, slight, scorn, shun, ignore, avoid, coldshoulder, high-hat, rebuff, cut, disregard, overlook, deny, spurn, refuse, dismiss, repudiate, brush off, reject, put down, freeze (someone) out. **—n. 2.** rebuke, rebuff, rejection, denial, refusal, dismissal, repudiation, putdown, brush off, cut, cold shoulder, slight, affront, insult. **—Ant.** accept, welcome.

soak, v. **1.** steep, drench, wet, sop, immerse, douse, bathe, inundate, waterlog, saturate. **2.** permeate, osmose, penetrate, impregnate. **—Ant.** dry.

soar, v. **1.** fly, glide, rise, hover, float, hang. **2.** tower, rise, rocket, surge, levitate, dart, shoot, ascend, mount; increase, climb, escalate, spiral, upward, skyrocket, shoot up.

sober, adj. **1.** unintoxicated; temperate, continent, abstinent, abstemious, dry, on the wagon, teetotaling, nonindulgent. **2.** serious, grave, solemn, quiet, sedate, somber, plain, simple, repressed, dreary, gloomy, subdued, staid. **3.** calm, serene, tranquil, peaceful, cool, moderate, dignified, cool, composed, unexcited, unimpassioned, unruffled, collected, dispassionate, unconcerned, reasonable, rational, earnest, steady, levelheaded, balanced, practical, realistic, controlled, sane, sound. **4.** somber, drab, colorless, dreary, dull, neutral, dark. **—Ant.** drunk; frivolous, flippant, wild; immoderate.

sociable, adj. social, friendly, affable, approachable, gregarious, outgoing, extroverted, amiable, amicable, congenial, convivial, cordial, neighborly, chummy. **—Ant.** unsociable, unfriendly.

social, adj. sociable, friendly, amiable, companionable, genial, affable, accessible, cooperative, convivial, hospitable, familiar. **—Ant.** antisocial, unfriendly.

society, n. **1.** organization, association, circle, fellowship, club, league, institute, alliance, academy, guild, union, group, order, fraternity, brotherhood, sorority, sisterhood, sodality, company, partnership, corporation. **2.** community, culture, civilization, world; organization, system; humankind, people, the public. **3.** companionship, company, fellowship, sodality, camaraderie, friendship.

soft, adj. **1.** yielding, cushiony, spongy, squeezable, plushy, compressible, flexible, pliant, supple, pliable, plastic, moldable, malleable, impressible. **2.** smooth, agreeable, delicate. **3.** muted, quiet, mellow, faint, soothing, smooth, gentle, low, subdued, melodious, mellifluous, dulcet, sweet, pleasing, pleasant, flowing. **4.** gentle, mild, balmy, moderate, halcyon, summary, springlike, restful, relaxing, lazy, genial. **5.** gentle, mild, lenient, easygoing, tolerant, kind, merciful, indulgent, permissive, liberal, lax, easy, benign, compassionate, tender, sympathetic. **6.** smooth, soothing, ingratiating, mollifying. **7.** impressionable, yielding, compliant, flexible, irresolute, submissive, deferential, tame, undecided, weak, delicate, sensitive. **8.** weak, feeble, frail, effect, delicate, puny, flabby, poor, wishy-washy. **—Ant.** hard, inflexible, unyielding, harsh, rough.

soften, v. **1.** melt, affect, mollify, mellow, soothe, relax, appease, palliate, tenderize. **2.** appease, assuage, mollify, moderate, mitigate, modify, soothe, alleviate, diminish, reduce, cushion, lessen, relieve, calm, quell, still, quiet, ease, allay, lighten, abate, qualify, temper, blunt, dull. —**Ant.** harden.

solace, *n.* **1.** comfort, alleviation, condolence, succor, support, help, reassurance, cheer, consolation, relief. —*v.* **2.** comfort, console, cheer, soothe, condole, support, soccor, reassure, hearten; gladden, delight, please, gratify. **3.** relieve, alleviate, soothe, mitigate, ameliorate, alleviate, lighten, assuage, allay, soften. —**Ant.** aggrieve, aggravate.

sole, *adj.* only, single, solitary, alone, lone, singular, personal, exclusive, select, individual, unattended, unique, separate, particular.

solemn, *adj.* **1.** grave, sober, reserved, earnest, sedate, staid, taciturn, mirthless, unsmiling, morose, morbid, gloomy, grim, solemn, glum, serious. **2.** impressive, awe-inspiring, awesome, momentous, moving, sublime, superb, august, imposing, venerable, grand, majestic, pompous, stately. **3.** formal, stately, conventional, plenary, dignified, serious, ceremonious, ritual, ceremonial. **4.** religious, holy, divine, sacramental, liturgical, ecclesiastical, hallowed, reverential, devotional, sacred, ritualistic. —**Ant.** jovial; unimpressive; informal; profane.

solicit, *v.* seek, entreat, ask for, request, apply for, beseech, pray, beg, importune, urge, implore, crave, supplicate, sue, petition, appeal to.

solid, *adj.* **1.** three-dimensional, cubic. **2.** dense, compact, firm, hard, stable, concrete, concentrated, consolidated, compacted. **3.** unbroken, continuous, undivided, unrelieved, complete, whole, entire, uniform. **4.** firm, cohesive, compact. **5.** dense, thick, tough, sturdy, firm, durable, rugged, heavy, substantial, sound, stable, dependable, well-made, stout. **6.** real, genuine, complete, sound, good. **7.** soberminded, sober, cogent, weighty, valid, reasonable, authoritative, incontrovertible, irrefutable, powerful, forceful, convincing, persuasive, sensible. **8.** thorough, vigorous, dynamic, telling, powerful, effective, forceful, mighty, intensive, downright, firm, strong, great, stout. **9.** united, consolidated, unanimous. **10.** successful, solvent, wealthy, rich; reliable, honorable, law-abiding, steady, stable, stalwart, steadfast, upstanding, upright, estimable, dependable, sober, well-established, sound, trustworthy, honest, sure, safe. —**Ant.** flat, two-dimensional; fluid, liquid; loose; divided; sparse; counterfeit; weak; separate; unsuccessful.

solitary, *adj.* **1.** unaccompanied, solo, unattended, alone, friendless, single, sole, individual, unsocial, lonesome, forlorn, lone, lonely. **2.** isolated, retired, reclusive, hermetic, withdrawn, distant, desolate, out-of-the-way, forsaken, abandoned, lonely, deserted, unfrequented, remote, secluded.

solitude, *n.* **1.** seclusion, isolation, solitariness, aloneness, withdrawal, retreat, remoteness, loneliness, retirement, privacy, refuge, asylum. **2.** desert, waste, wilderness, emptiness.

somber, *adj.* **1.** gloomy, dark, foreboding, bleak, leaden, dreary, overcast, shadowy, dim, unlighted, dusky, murky, cloudy, dull, sunless, dismal. **2.** depressing, depressed, morose, sad, cheerless, joyless, unsmiling, grave, gloomy, grim-faced, long-faced, saturnine, dismal, lugubrious, mournful, dolorous, doleful, funereal, melancholy. —**Ant.** cheerful.

soothe, *v.* **1.** tranquilize, pacify, sol-

ace, calm, relieve, comfort, refresh. **2.** allay, mitigate, assuage, alleviate, appease, mollify, soften, lull, quell, quiet, ease, lighten, palliate. —**Ant.** upset, disturb.

sophisticated, *adj.* **1.** cosmopolitan, urbane, suave, polished, elegant, refined, cultured, cultivated, experienced, knowledgeable, knowing, soigné, blasé, worldly-wise, savvy, knowing, worldly. **2.** advanced, complex, multifaceted, highly developed, complicated, intricate, elaborate, fancy, subtle, high-tech, modern, contemporary, sleek, streamlined, improved, cutting-edge, fashionable, trendy, voguish, modish, in style, hot, deluxe, posh, elegant, high-class, superior, chic, smart, up-to-date, up-to-the-minute, exclusive. —**Ant.** unsophisticated.

sorcery, *n.* magic, wizardry, witchery, enchantment, witchcraft, spell, necromancy, divination, charm, alchemy, shamanism, black art, satanism.

sordid, *adj.* **1.** dirty, filthy, soiled, unclean, foul, squalid, unsanitary, polluted, fetid, maggoty, flyblown, putrid, slimy, slummy, seamy, seedy, mean, wretched, sleazy. **2.** mean, abject, ignoble, amoral, degraded, depraved, corrupt, vile, debased, ignominious, shameful, dishonorable, despicable, disreputable, shabby, scurvy, rotten, scurvy, low, base. **3.** selfish, self-seeking, mercenary, avaricious, stingy, tight, close, close-fisted, greedy, grasping, swinish, rapacious, money-grubbing, materialistic, venal, cheap, miserly, niggardly. —**Ant.** clean; honorable; generous.

sore, *adj.* **1.** painful, sensitive, tender, raw, inflamed, smarting, chafed, burning, hurting, throbbing, irritated. **2.** grieved, distressed, upset, irritated, irked, agitated, disturbed, perturbed, ruffled, aggrieved, sorrowful, hurt, pained, depressed, vexed. **3.** grievous, distressing, painful, depressing, severe, sharp, troublesome, harrowing, agonizing, bitter, onerous, heavy, burdensome, fierce, oppressive. —*n.* **4.** injury, damage, swelling, rawness, inflammation, bruise, abrasion, cut, laceration, scrape, burn, infection, abscess, wound, ulcer, pustule, boil, cancer, canker. —**Ant.** tough.

sorrow, *n.* **1.** heartache, heartbreak, torment, agony, dolor, unhappiness, desolation, mourning, grieving, sadness, depression, dejection, melancholy, distress, anxiety, anguish, grief, sadness, woe, suffering, misery, wretchedness, regret. **2.** affliction, adversity, trouble, trial, tribulation, hardship, hard luck, cares, strain, misfortune. —*v.* **3.** grieve, mourn, bemoan, regret, agonize, moan, suffer, cry, weep, wail, sob, groan, bewail, lament. —**Ant.** joy, gladness, delight.

sorrowful, *adj.* **1.** grief-stricken, grieved, sad, unhappy, melancholy, gloomy, downcast, blue, dispirited, heartsick, broken-hearted, heavy-hearted, disconsolate, inconsolable, depressed, dejected, aggrieved, afflicted, mournful, regretful, sorry, crestfallen, wretched, rueful, woeful, tearful, plaintive. **2.** distressing, grievous, lamentable, dismal, dreary, doleful, unfortunate, bitter, unlucky, hapless, sorry. —**Ant.** happy; lucky.

sorry, *adj.* **1.** regretful, penitent, repentant, apologetic, remorseful, contrite, guilt-ridden, conscience-stricken. **2.** pitiable, miserable, deplorable, abject, depressing, wretched, pathetic, dismal, sordid, grim, star-crossed, unfortunate, sad, grievous, painful. **3.**

sorrowful, grieved, sad, unhappy, melancholy, depressed. **4.** wretched, poor, mean, pitiful, base, ignoble, sordid, low, vile, abject; contemptible, bad, scurvy, despicable; paltry, worthless, shabby, petty, trifling, trivial. —**Ant.** happy.

sort, *n.* **1.** kind, species, classification, category, brand, make, mark, stamp, mold, stripe, ilk, variety, class, group, family, description, order, race, rank, character, description, nature, type. **2.** character, quality, nature. **3.** example, pattern, sample, exemplar. **4.** manner, fashion, way, method, means, style. —*v.* **5.** arrange, assort, organize, systematic, catalogue, group, pigeonhole, order, classify, class, file, order, rank, grade, categorize, combine, merge, alphabetize, separate, divide, distribute.

soul, *n.* spirit, anima, breath, vital force, being, inner *or* true self, essence, psyche, heart, mind, intellect, reason, brain, brains, intelligence, wit, wits, powers, faculties, emotions, vitality, animation, life, consciousness. —**Ant.** body.

sound, *n.* **1.** noise, tone, din, cacophony, ring. —*v.* **2.** resound, echo, reverberate, resonate. **3.** utter, articulate, voice, vocalize, enunciate, pronounce, express. **4.** plumb, test, check, question, probe, examine, inspect, survey, investigate, fathom, ascertain, determine. —*adj.* **5.** undamaged, intact, in good shape, unscathed, uninjured, unharmed, unbroken, whole, entire, complete, intact, perfect, unimpaired. **6.** healthy, hale, hearty, robust, hardy, vigorous. **7.** solvent, secure, well-established, safe, conservative, non-speculative, riskless. **8.** reliable, dependable, trustworthy, responsible, right-minded, upstanding, solid, loyal, virtuous, honest, honorable. **9.** true, truthful, just, fair, judicious, reasonable, rational, sane, sensible, balanced, lucid, logical, practical, prudent, wise, common-sense. **10.** enduring, substantial, firm, solid, strong, sturdy, tough, rugged, durable, reliable, dependable, well-constructed. **11.** correct, orthodox, right, proper. **12.** unbroken, deep, profound, uninterrupted, untroubled, peaceful, fast, undisturbed. —**Ant.** silence; damaged; unhealthy; unreliable; risky; irrational; unstable, flimsy, jerry-built; improper; fitful, troubled, disturbed.

sour, *adj.* **1.** acid, acidic, vinegary, lemony, acerbic, bitter, astringent, tart. **2.** fermented, turned, spoiled, curdled, rancid, bad, gone off. **3.** distasteful, disagreeable, unpleasant, nasty, bad, terrible, regrettable, unhappy, bitter. **4.** harsh, embittered, bitter, churlish, curmudgeonly, grouchy, curt, caustic, brusque, gloomy, edgy, sullen, glum, dour, saturnine, vexatious, spiteful, ill-tempered, bad-tempered, austere, severe, morose, peevish, testy, short-tempered, hot-tempered, touchy, acrimonious, cross, petulant, crabbed, snappish, waspish, uncivil, rude, crude, rough. —**Ant.** sweet, pleasant, delightful; good-natured, cheerful.

sovereign, *n.* **1.** monarch, king, queen, emperor, empress, prince, princess, chief, head, master, mistress, lady, lord, ruler, potentate. —*adj.* **2.** regal, royal, majestic, princely, imperial, noble, lordly, aristocrat, monarchical, queenly, kingly. **3.** supreme, chief, highest, foremost, ranking, leading, commanding, directing, superior, ruling, preponderant, preeminent, reigning, governing, absolute, omnipotent, all-powerful, transcendent, surpassing, ultimate, paramount, principal, predominant. **4.** utmost, extreme, greatest. **5.** potent, effective, efficacious, effectual. **—Ant.** dependent.

spacious, *adj.* **1.** ample, large, enormous, commodious, sizable, voluminous, outsize, oversize, capacious, roomy, wide. **2.** extensive, vast, huge, extended, tremendous, broad, great, immense, enormous, broad, wide, deep. **—Ant.** small, cramped, restricted, claustrophobic.

span, *n.* **1.** distance, amount, piece, length, extent. **2.** extension, reach, extent, stretch, period, course, interval, time, term, spell. **—v. 3.** bridge, extend over, reach, pass over, stretch across, cross, compass.

spare, *v.* **1.** forgo, sacrifice, avoid, dispense with, manage, without, surrender. **2.** save, rescue, redeem, deliver, pardon; release, liberate, free, let go, have mercy on, let off, forgive, acquit, excuse, grant, amnesty. **—adj. 3.** extra, reserve, superfluous, surplus, additional, auxilliary, supplementary; leftover, unused, idle, free, leisure, unspoken for, available, unoccupied. **4.** economical, temperate, moderate, careful, restricted, meager, frugal, sparing, scanty, parsimonious. **5.** lean, thin, slender, slight, gaunt, scrawny, cadaverous, gangling, wiry, slim, underweight, sinewy, lank, skinny, rawboned, emaciated, anorexic, skin and bones, angular, skeletal. **—Ant.** splurge, condemn; inadequate; corpulent, fat, plump; profuse, profligate.

sparkle, *v.* **1.** glisten, glitter, shine, shimmer, glint, flicker, blink, twinkle, glimmer, flash, spark, twinkle, gleam, coruscate, scintillate. **2.** effervesce, fizz, bubble. **—n. 3.** luster, dazzle, spark, gleam, brilliance, radiance, brightness, éclat, spark, scintillation, glister, glitter, twinkle, twinkling, coruscation. **4.** vivacity, fire, wittiness, effervescence, ebullience, animation, brilliance, liveliness, spirit, vigor, energy, élan, gaiety, joy, cheerfulness, gusto, glow, piquancy, pizzazz, oomph.

sparse, *adj.* **1.** thin, scattered, dispersed, spotty, scarce, few and far between, sporadic, occasional, infrequent, uncommon, here and there. **2.** little, scanty, meager, spare, insignificant, inappreciable, limited, restricted. **—Ant.** abundant.

speak, *v.* utter, talk, voice, converse, discourse, remark, observe, declare, assert, aver, mention, discuss, give voice to, orate, air, communicate, disclose, reveal, enunciate, pronounce, say, articulate, express, address, state, tell, comment, lecture, expatiate, descant.

special, *adj.* distinct, distinctive, distinguished, different, particular, rare, unorthodox, unconventional, unique, specialized, remarkable, inimitable, idiosyncratic, curious, odd, strange, bizarre, weird, notable, noteworthy, especial, peculiar, characteristic, singular, specific, certain, individual, single, unusual, uncommon, extraordinary, exceptional. **—Ant.** common, ordinary, familiar, usual, customary, conventional.

specific, *adj.* particular, definite, precise, exact, express, explicit, definitive, distinct, set, fixed, determined, predetermined, indicated, spelled out, established, unambiguous, specified, restricted, limited, clear cut, unequivocal, individual, peculiar, certain. **—Ant.** generic, vague.

specimen, *n.* type, example, sample, model, pattern, instance, exemplar, representive, illustration, case in point.

specter, *n.* ghost, phantom, spirit, wraith, vision, revenant, doppelgänger, chimera, illusion, apparition, shade, shadow, hallucination, image, spook, bogeyman, undead, zombie. **—Ant.** reality.

speculation, *n.* **1.** thinking, meditation, reflection, deliberation, evaluation, rumination, cogitation, cerebration, pondering, wondering, ratiocination, analysis, pensiveness, study, musing, contemplation, consideration. **2.** conclusion, supposition, conjecture, surmise, view, hypothesis, theory, guesswork, guess, postulation, opinion, analysis, idea, notion.

speech, *n.* **1.** statement, utterance, remark, observation, declaration, assertion, asseveration, averral, comment, mention, talk. **2.** talk, oration, address, lecture, disquisition, sermon, homily, discourse; tirade, phillipic, filibuster, harangue. **3.** language, words, lingo, tongue, dialect, patois, idiom, jargon, tongue, parlance, slang. **4.** conversation, parley, discussion, discourse, communication.

speechless, *adj.* **1.** dumbfounded, shocked, dazed, paralyzed, nonplussed, stunned, flummoxed, dumbstruck, wordless, tonguetied, thunderstruck, inarticulate. **2.** silent, inarticulate, voiceless, dumb, mute. **—Ant.** loquacious, voluble, talkative.

speed, *n.* **1.** rapidity, alacrity, celerity, quickness, fleetness, velocity, speediness, briskness, promptness, timeliness, swiftness, dispatch, expedition, haste, hurry, momentum, pace, headway, impetus, drive. **—v. 2.** promote, facilitate, boost, accelerate, help, assist, aid, drive, impel, advance, further, forward, expedite, favor; accelerate, quicken, hasten, hurry, precipitate. **3.** rush, hurry, hasten, run, race, dart, bolt, sprint, hustle, tear, fly, scurry, zip, zoom, skedaddle, make tracks, burn rubber, high tail it, step on the gas, go like greased lightning, put the pedal to the metal, go like a bat out of hell, fly like the wind. **—Ant.** sloth.

spend, *v.* **1.** disburse, expend, pay *or* lay out, dispose of; squander, throw away, fritter away, go through, splurge, be prodigal, waste, lavish, dissipate. **2.** exhaust, use up, consume. **3.** employ, use, allot, assign, invest, put in, pass, apply, devote. **—Ant.** earn, save.

sphere, *n.* **1.** ball, orb; globe, earth; planet, star. **2.** field, environment, orbit, area, place, province, territory, bailiwick, jurisdiction, reach, scope, compass, circle, compass, coterie, set, realm, domain, quarter. **3.** stratum, walk of life, rank, class, caste, level, rank, station, position.

spin, *v.* **1.** draw out, twist, wind. **2.** circle, wheel, swirl, eddy, revolve, twist, pivot, reel, pirouette, twirl, whirl, turn, rotate, gyrate. **3.** invent, concoct, make up, devise, produce, fabricate, evolve, develop. **4.** tell, narrate, relate, weave, recount, unfold. **5.** draw out, extend, protract, prolong, lengthen, perpetuate, continue, extend keep going.

spineless, *adj.* limp, weak, feeble, flabby, weak-willed, indecisive, irresolute, ineffectual, ineffective, powerless, impotent; cowardly, fearful, timid, lily-livered, craven, chicken, yellow, wimpy, nebbishy. **—Ant.** strong, decisive, brave.

spirit, *n.* **1.** animation, vitality, soul, psyche, self, heart, breath, anima, being, power, essence, life, mind, consciousness. **2.** goblin, sprite, elf, fairy,

hobgoblin; angel, genius, demon, *prāna*. **3.** ghost, specter, apparition, phantom, phantasm, revenant, wraith, spook, reincarnation, shade, shadow. **4.** courage, fortitude, resolution, tenacity, pluck, grit, backbone, strength, might, power, forcefulness, spunk, mettle, zest, panache, élan, gusto, passion, eagerness, avidity, vigor, liveliness, enthusiasm, energy, zeal, zealousness, ardor, fervor, fire, vivacity, enterprise, ambition, resourcefulness. **5.** character, temperament, temper, disposition, attitude, mood, bent, inclination, humor, sorts, frame of mind. **6.** character, nature, drift, tenor, gist, sense, complexion, quintessence, essence. **7.** meaning, intent, intention, significance, purport, heart, meat, pith, marrow, substance.

spirited, *adj.* excited, animated, sprightly, sparkling, dynamic, bouyant, ebullient, effervescent, vivacious, ardent, active, energetic, enthusiastic, eager, avid, keen, passionate, ardent, fervent, lively, vigorous, courageous, intrepid, audacious, valiant, brave, impetuous, bold. **—Ant.** dispirited, inactive, indolent.

spite, *n.* **1.** spitefulness, vindictiveness, vengefulness, vengeance, ill will, malevolence, maliciousness, malice, rancor, gall, malignity, poison, venom, spleen, animosity, resentment, hostility, bitterness, antagonism, animus, antipathy, grudge, hate, pique, hatred. **—v. 2.** annoy, irritate, vex, upset, disconcert, offend, provoke, pique, thwart, injure, hurt, harm, wound, needle. **—Ant.** forgiveness, benevolence.

spiteful, *adj.* malicious, venomous, malevolent, revengeful, vengeful, vindictive, bitter, acrimonious, invidious, hostile, antagonistic, mean, cruel, hateful, rancorous, splenetic, unforgiving, retaliatory, retributive, punitive. **—Ant.** benevolent, friendly.

splendid, *adj.* **1.** splendorous, gorgeous, magnificent, sumptuous, luxurious, superb, resplendent, showy, marvelous, spectacular, lavish, ornate, majestic, brilliant, extraordinary, awe-inspiring, awesome, lush, plush, rich, supreme, sublime, t anscendent, dazzling, imposing, grand, beautiful, impressive. **2.** glorious, renowned, famed, famous, illustrious, eminent, conspicuous, distinguished, prominent, superior, noteworthy, exemplary, admirable, sublime, outstanding, successful, remarkable, celebrated, brilliant, noble. **3.** marvelous, exceptional, extraordinary, superior, excellent, fabulous, fantastic, incredible, first-class, peerless, unrivaled, matchless, nonpareil, capital, superlative, laudable, praiseworthy, fine, striking, admirable. **—Ant.** sordid, squalid; ignoble.

splendor, *n.* **1.** magnificence, radiance, resplendence, sumptuousness, stateliness, majesty, panoply, spectacle, glory, luxury, lavishness, brilliance, grandeur, pomp, show, display, dash, élan, éclat. **2.** distinction, glory, brillance, fame, eminence, renown, celebrity. **3.** brightness, brilliance, light, luster, dazzle, refulgence. **—Ant.** squalor, anonymity.

spoil, *v.* **1.** damage, impair, ruin, wreck, disfigure, destroy, demolish, upset, undermine, injure, hurt, corrupt, vitiate, mar, harm. **2.** baby, pamper, coddle, mollycoddle, indulge, pet, dote on, suffocate, cater to, overindulge, favor, gratify, treat, cosset. **3.** decay, molder, decompose, turn, go off, ferment, sour, rot, putrefy, disintegrate, crumble. **—n. 4.** (*often plural*) booty, plunder, loot, pillage, prizes, pickings, swag, take, boodle. —**Ant.** preserve, conserve, save; abuse, discipline, punish; sweeten.

spontaneous, *adj.* impulsive, instinctive, automatic, unpremeditated, unannounced, unplanned, impromptu, extemporaneous, extempore, impromptu, improvised, off the cuff, ad hoc, adlibbed, offhand, spur-of-the-moment, natural, unexpected, unrehearsed, unprepared, unconstrained, voluntary, gratuitous, free, unselfish. —**Ant.** premeditated, rehearsed, stilted, unnatural, stiff.

sport, *n.* **1.** pastime, game, athletics, distraction, relaxation, pleasure, enjoyment, merriment, jollity, mirth, glee, hilarity, amusement, diversion, fun, entertainment, frolic, gambol, rollicking, romp, jest, recreation, play. **2.** derision, jesting, ridicule, mockery, taunting, teasing, ribbing, kidding, twitting, bullying, raillery. —*v.* **3.** play, frolic, gambol, romp, caper, cavort, lark, roister, rollick, fool around, be frisky. **4.** ridicule, make fun, make a monkey of, chaff, mock, deride, bully, laugh at, roast, taunt, jibe, twit, rib, kid, jeer, rail, razz, josh, make a laughingstock of, send up, caricature, lampoon, needle.

spot, *n.* **1.** mark, stain, blot, speck, blotch, patch, fleck, particle, mote. **2.** blemish, flaw, stain, taint, stigma, smudge, discoloration, splotch. **3.** place, location, locality, locale, scene, setting, section, neighborhood, area, site, situation. —*v.* **4.** stain, mark, blot, speckle, fleck, spray, splash, spatter, soil, sully, dirty, taint, smudge, besmirch, blemish, stigmatize, tarnish.

spread, *v.* **1.** unroll, unfold, open, display, extend, lay out, fan out, unfurl, expand, stretch out, draw out. **2.** extend, protract, prolong, drag out, disperse, distribute, stretch, expand, dilate. **3.** dispose, distribute, diffuse, disseminate, broadcast, strew, sow, dissipate, shed, scatter, disperse. **4.** overlay, smear, apply, smooth, rub, layer, plaster, overspread, cloak, blanket, cover, coat. **5.** emit, scatter, diffuse, radiate. **6.** publicize, make known, air, announce, make public, herald, disseminate, broadcast, publish, circulate, divulge, promulgate, propagate, disperse. —*n.* **7.** expansion, development, increase, proliferation, growth, mushrooming, extension, enlargement, broadening, dispersion, dissemination, distribution, dispensing, diffusion. **8.** extent, reach, area, span, sweep, vastness, range, limits, bounds, size, dimensions, breadth, depth, compass; stretch, scope, span, amplitude, magnitude, expanse.

spring, *v.* **1.** leap, jump, bound, hop, dart, fly, bounce, vault. **2.** arise, appear, grow, emerge, loom, sprout, shoot up, burst forth; start, originate, commence, begin, evolve, rise, issue, emanate, flow, proceed from, stem from, derive from, develop from. **3.** grow, develop, increase, wax, thrive. —*n.* **4.** leap, jump, hop, bounce, skip, bound, vault. **5.** elasticity, bounciness, bounce, flexibility, sprightliness, airiness, springiness, suppleness, resilience, resiliency, buoyancy, vigor. **6.** source, origin, mouth, fountainhead, fount, wellspring, beginning, root, inception, cause, head.

spry, *adj.* active, nimble, agile, brisk, flexible, light, vigorous, strenuous, robust, sound, hale, hearty, lively, energetic, animated, quick, smart, alert, ready, prompt. —**Ant.** doddering.

spur, *n.* **1.** goad, prick, prod, urging, prompting, pressure, encouragement, whip, goad, incitement, stimulus, stimulation, motive, motivation, impetus, incentive, inducement, cause, provocation, impulse, instigation. —*v.* **2.** urge, prod, egg on, impel, prompt, press, push, drive, pressure, goad, prick, whip, incite, provoke, encourage, animate, excite, motivate, stimulate, induce, instigate. —**Ant.** discourage.

spurn, *v.* reject, disdain, scorn, despise, refuse, decline, repudiate, rebuff, snub, sneer at, scoff at, brush off, cold-shoulder, turn down, turn one's nose up, sneeze at. —**Ant.** accept.

spurt, *v.* **1.** gush, spout, flow, issue, spew, squirt, shoot, erupt, burst, surge, stream, jet, well, spring. —*n.* **2.** spate, outbreak, effort, rise, increase, jet, spout. —**Ant.** drip, ooze.

squalid, *adj.* **1.** sordid, slummy, seamy, seedy, shabby, sleazy, mean, vile, fetid, neglected, slovenly, unkempt, sloppy, slipshod, frowzy, foul, repulsive, unclean, dirty, filthy, nasty. **2.** sordid, wretched, miserable, degraded, debased, ignoble, scurvy, rotten, deplorable, sorry, pathetic, pitiful, abject, awful, shameful. —**Ant.** splendid, palatial.

squeamish, *adj.* **1.** moral, proper, puritanical, prim, staid, rigid, modest, prudish; blue. **2.** particular, scrupulous, fastidious, finical, finicky, punctilious, demanding, critical, exacting, difficult, fussy, fastidious, meticulous, painstaking, persnickety, dainty, delicate, hypercritical, faultfinding, caviling, carping, captious, nice. —**Ant.** liberal, loose, lackadaisical.

stab, *v.* **1.** pierce, wound, gore, stick, puncture, prick, jab, impale, knife, skewer, spit, slash, spear, penetrate, pin, transfix; poke, plunge, thrust, insert. **2.** attempt, try, essay; guess, conjecture, estimate, guesstimate. —*n.* **3.** thrust, blow; wound, puncture, jab, laceration, incision, slash.

stability, *n.* permanence, constancy, steadiness, balance, poise, security, safety, evenness, regularity, firmness, continuance, solidity, soundness, sturdiness, durability, staunchness, steadfastness, dependability, reliability, tenacity, perseverance, persistence, perdurability, endurance, faithfulness, fixedness, strength, immovability, fixedness. —**Ant.** instability.

stable, *adj.* **1.** firm, steady, fixed, strong, sturdy, established, set, regular, safe, secure, durable, immovable, permanent, invariable, unvarying, steadfast, staunch, resolute, unchangeable, unchanging. **2.** enduring, permanent, constant, persisting, persistent, perdurable, lasting, abiding, secure, fast, perpetual, eternal, everlasting. **3.** unwavering, steadfast, staunch, constant, reliable, steady, solid. —**Ant.** unstable, changeable, rocky, shaky, inconstant, fluctuating, volatile; shortlived, temporary; dilatory.

stagger, *v.* **1.** sway, reel, totter, lurch, teeter, wobble, rock, pitch. **2.** waver, falter, vacillate, hesitate, doubt. **3.** shock, astound, astonish, stun, perplex, overwhelm, overcome, stupefy, bewilder, flabbergast, flummox, floor, startle, jolt, tax, burden, bowl over, confound, amaze, nonplus, dumbfound, surprise. **4.** alternate, zigzag, rearrange, reorder, overlap, vary, space out.

staid, *adj.* sedate, settled, sober, serious, proper, decent, demure, seemly, smug, priggish, complacent, decorous, correct, rigid, stiff, prim, dignified, restrained, cool, collected, quiet, com-

posed, serene, calm, solemn, grave. —**Ant.** wild, indecorous.

stain, *n.* **1.** discoloration, spot, blemish, defect, flaw, mark, imperfection, smirch, blot. **2.** stigma, disgrace, dishonor, taint, black eye, brand, blot, tarnish. **3.** dye, reagent, tint, coloring, tinge, pigment, tincture. —*v.* **4.** discolor, taint, spot, streak, soil, dirty, blemish, blot. **5.** blemish, sully, spot, taint, soil, tarnish, disgrace, dishonor, stigmatize, corrupt, spoil, ruin, besmirch, shame, disgrace, debase, defile, contaminate, pollute. **6.** tint, dye, tinge, color.

stake, *n.* **1.** wager, bet, ante, pot; risk, jeopardy, chance, peril, hazard. —*v.* **2.** risk, hazard, put money on, chance, gamble, take a chance, chance, jeopardize, wager, venture, bet, imperil, put at risk, run a risk.

stale, *adj.* **1.** vapid, flat, dry, hardened, hard, tasteless, sour, insipid, spoiled rotten, turned, gone off. **2.** old, banal, overused, antiquated, old-fashioned, clichéd, threadbare, uninteresting, hackneyed, trite, unoriginal, tired, boring, tiresome, warmed over, shopworn, familiar, stock, stereotyped, old-hat, common, commonplace. —**Ant.** fresh, modern.

stalemate, *n.* impasse, deadlock, standstill, standoff, tie, Mexican standoff.

stalwart, *adj.* **1.** strong, stout, well-developed, robust, sturdy, brawny, mighty, powerful, rugged, lusty, solid, able-bodied, fit, hearty, hale, husky, beefy, sinewy, muscular, athletic, strapping, vigorous, pumped up, buff. **2.** strong, brave, valiant, redoubtable, undaunted, courageous, heroic, stouthearted, audacious, plucky, lionhearted, spirited, red-blooded, bold, valorous, intrepid, daring, fearless, firm, resolute, indomitable, gallant. **3.** firm, steadfast, resolute, determined, tenacious, unyielding, unwavering, unfaltering, unflinching, unflagging, indefatigable, tireless, relentless, uncompromising, redoubtable, formidable. —**Ant.** weak, feeble; fearful; infirm, unsteady.

stamina, *n.* strength, vigor, energy, endurance, ruggedness, indefatigability, resistance, staying power, mettle, might, staunchness, steadfastness, health, robustness, hardiness, fortitude, stick-to-itiveness, grit, guts. —**Ant.** weakness.

stammer, *v.* stutter, pause, hesitate, stumble, hem and haw, falter.

stamp, *v.* **1.** strike, beat, trample, tramp, tread, step, stomp, crush, pound. **2.** eliminate, abolish, annihilate, kill, exterminate, terminate, destroy, extinguish, extirpate, quell, subdue, suppress, repress, squelch, squash, quash, eradicate. **3.** tag, term, name, style, characterize, designate, identify, classify, categorize, denominate, mark, label, brand. **4.** impress, imprint, print, mark, record, register, inscribe, engrave, emboss. —*n.* **5.** impression, design, pattern, brand, mark, print, seal. **6.** character, kind, type, sort, description, cut, style, cast, mold, fashion, grade, genre, class, level, classification, description, variety, form, make.

stand, *v.* **1.** halt, stop, pause. **2.** remain, continue, persist, stay, abide, prevail, obtain, apply, exist, be firm or resolute or steadfast or steady. **3.** set, erect, place, put, fix. **4.** face, meet, encounter, resist, oppose. **5.** endure, undergo, submit to, survive, tolerate, brook, countenance, face, confront, withstand, experience, cope with, brave, stand for, handle, bear, sustain, weather, outlast, abide, stomach, suffer, admit, allow. —*n.* **6.** halt, stop, stopover, rest, stay. **7.** position, stance, posture, policy, standpoint, viewpoint, opinion, belief, philosophy, sentiment, feeling, line, attitude. **8.** resistance, defense, effort, opposition, defiance, fight.

standard, *n.* **1.** criterion, measure, benchmark, archetype, touchstone, yardstick, paradigm, paragon, type, ideal, requirement, precept, principle, law, canon, axiom, fundamental, gauge, test, model, example, exemplar, sample, basis, pattern, guide, rule. **2.** average, norm, par, mean, rating, level. —*adj.* **3.** recognized, usual, accepted, customary, habitual, orthodox, set, approved, definitive, established, traditional, classic, conventional, prevalent, regular, familiar, ordinary, stock, typical, normal, staple, universal, prescribed, defined, authoritative, official, required, textbook, basic, exemplary, guiding, sample.

standing, *n.* **1.** position, status, station, place, grade, order, level, stratum, rank, condition; reputation, repute, eminence, prominence. **2.** existence, continuation, duration, residence, membership, experience. —*adj.* **3.** still, static, stationary, stagnant, unmoving, motionless. **4.** continuing, continuous, fixed, ongoing, perpetual, unceasing, constant, permanent, unchanging, steady, lasting, durable. **5.** operative, in force, effective, in effect, established, settled.

stare, *v.* gaze, gape, goggle, watch, gawk, rubberneck, glare, peer, glower, scowl.

stark, *adj.* **1.** sheer, utter, downright, complete, perfect, thoroughgoing, unmitigated, unconditional, unqualified, flagrant, patent, gross, rank; arrant, simple, mere, pure, absolute, entire, unmistakable. **2.** severe, austere, spartan, bare, plain, simple, cold, harsh, grim, bald, blunt, unadorned. **3.** harsh, grim, desolate, dreary, severe, bleak, austere, barren, depressing, empty, vacant. —*adv.* **4.** utterly, absolutely, wholly, entirely, totally, fully, completely, quite, irrevocable, certifiably, plainly, obviously, clearly.

start, *v.* **1.** begin, be on one's way, set out *or* forth, go, leave, hit the road, move, get going, get under way, commence, depart. **2.** issue, emerge, crop up, develop, get under way, begin, originate, spring up, come up, come, arise. **3.** jump, jerk, flinch, quail, shy, recoil, wince, shrink, draw back, twitch, spring back. **4.** set up, begin, commence, originate, open, activate, get off the ground, embark on, open, set in motion, kick off, create, inaugurate, conceive, invent, start up, organize, establish, found, institute, initiate. —*n.* **5.** beginning, opening, outset, initiation, commencement, creation, origin, birth, genesis, inception, startup, emergence, rise, onset, inauguration, kickoff, founding, foundation, establishment. **6.** jerk, recoil, wince, flinch, balk, shy, cringe, spasm, fit, twitch, jump. —**Ant.** end, terminate.

startle, *v.* disturb, shock, agitate, surprise, unsettle, upset, disconcert, jolt, jar, dismay, perturb, stun, discombobulate, shake up, nonplus, terrify, electrify, thrill, alarm, amaze, astound, astonish, scare, frighten. —**Ant.** calm, pacify.

state, *n.* **1.** condition, case, circumstances, juncture, predicament, state of affairs, shape, position, posture, mode, pass, plight, emergency, crisis, exigency, quandry, dilemma, situation, status, estate, surroundings, environment, rank, position, standing, stage. **2.** constitution, structure, form, phase, shape, stage. **3.** estate, station, rank, position, standing. **4.** dignity, pomp, display, grandeur, style, splendor, brilliance, glory, magnificence. **5.** nation, country, land, sovereign state, government, federation, commonwealth, community, territory. —*adj.* **6.** public, national, government, federal. **7.** formal, solemn, official, ceremonial, ceremonious, pompous, stately, imposing, sumptuous, dignified. —*v.* **8.** declare, aver, assert, report, articulate, voice, delineate, claim, maintain, allege, submit, confirm, testify, say, relate, recount, narrate, describe, expound, explain, elucidate, interpret, set forth, express, affirm, specify.

stately, *adj.* imposing, grand, august, solemn, distinguished, impressive, striking, awesome, lofty, elevated, noble, imperial, grandiose, dignified, majestic, elegant, magnificent, regal, royal, splendid, glorious, sublime, superb, luxurious, opulent, sumptuous. —**Ant.** humble, mundane.

statement, *n.* declaration, communication, report, announcement, proclamation, description, explanation, excuse, position, assertion, allegation, expression, account, claim, affirmation, averral, utterance, disclosure, communiqué, manifesto, testimony, affidavit, press release.

station, *n.* **1.** position, post, place, spot, site, situation, location. **2.** depot, train station, bus station, terminal, way station, whistle stop. **3.** position, place, status, caste, level, class, office, standing, rank. —*v.* **4.** assign, spot, site, appoint, install, garrison, billet, place, post, position, locate, establish, set, fix.

status, *n.* **1.** condition, state, circumstance, situation, state of affairs, shape, position. **2.** condition, position, standing, rank, station, place, grade, level, order, stratum. **3.** importance, stature, eminence, preeminence, prominence, significance, reputation, repute.

staunch, *adj.* **1.** firm, steadfast, stable, unflinching, unshrinking, unswerving, unfaltering, undeviating, unwavering, steady, constant, resolute, true, faithful, principled, loyal, dependable, reliable, devoted, true-blue, trusty, trusted. **2.** solid, sturdy, well-built, substantial, tough, rugged, long-lasting, strong, sound, stout. —**Ant.** unsteady, disloyal.

stay, *v.* **1.** remain, dwell, reside, live, visit, wait, linger, put up, abide, sojourn, tarry, stop, rest, lodge. **2.** continue, remain, stop, halt, wait, stand, freeze. **3.** pause, wait, loiter, tarry, stop, delay, linger, procrastinate, lag. **4.** arrest, stop, thwart, prevent, halt, interrupt, block, hold back, detain, restrain, obstruct, arrest, check, hinder, delay, postpone, discontinue, put off, defer, suspend, adjourn, hold, curb, retard, slow, impede, foil, hamper, discourage, deter, suppress, quell, prevent. **5.** sustain, bolster, strengthen, uphold. —*n.* **6.** stop, stoppage, arrest, setback, check, prevention, discontinuation, halt, pause, delay, standstill; interruption, blockage, postponement, delay, deferral, deferment, reprieve, suspension, adjournment, break, hiatus, lacuna. **7.** stop, stopover, visit, layover, sojourn, rest, repose. **8.** prop, buttress, brace, support; crutch. —**Ant.** leave.

steadfast, *adj.* **1.** fixed, immovable, enduring, constant, deep-rooted, regular, set, fast, firm, established, perdurable, lasting, abiding, stable. **2.** staunch, determined, resolved, single-minded, dedicated, steady, sure, dependable, trustworthy, trusty, reliable, resolute, constant, strong, firm, loyal, regular, purposeful, persevering, indefatigable, persistent, tireless, true, faithful, unwavering, unflinching, unfaltering. —**Ant.** unsteady; weak; sporadic, unfaithful.

steady, *adj.* **1.** firm, fixed, steadfast, stable, even, equable, poised, balanced, regular, uniform, habitual, direct. **2.** undeviating, invariable, unvarying, unwavering, changeless, regular, constant, unchanging, uninterrupted, uniform, unremitting, continuous, perpetual, nonstop, persistent, unbroken, uninterrupted, endless, relentless. **3.** solid, substantial, strong, sound, stout, firm, stable. **4.** firm, devoted, staunch, faithful, loyal, inveterate, confirmed, longstanding, consistent, persistent, unwavering, steadfast. **5.** settled, dignified, poised, sensible, serious, level-headed, practical, down-to-earth, reliable, dependable, trustworthy, staid, sedate, sober. —*v.* **6.** stabilize, hold fast, support, brace, secure, strengthen. —**Ant.** unsteady.

steal, *v.* **1.** take, pilfer, rifle, thieve, burglarize, purloin, filch, appropriate, shoplift, walk *or* make off with, liberate, misappropriate, usurp, rob, cheat, overcharge, fleece, defraud, pocket, pirate, abscond with, loot, plunder, strip, despoil, pillage, defalcate, embezzle, swindle, lift, pinch, boost, borrow, hijack, nick, swipe, rip off, snitch, cop. **2.** win, gain, draw, lure, allure. —**Ant.** provide, donate.

stealthy, *adj.* furtive, surreptitious, secretive, sneaking, slinking, skulking, secret, clandestine, cunning, crafty, tricky, artful, wily, sly, sneaky, skulking, covert, sub rosa, undercover, underhanded, backstairs, closet, hidden, private, confidential. —**Ant.** obvious, open, manifest.

stem, *v.* **1.** rise, arise, originate, develop, derive, issue, generate, flow, spring, sprout, emanate, descend, proceed, result. **2.** stop, check, dam up, stanch, halt, arrest, curb, control, quell, suppress, obstruct, hinder, stay, retard, diminish, reduce, lessen, tamp, plug, tighten.

stereotyped, *adj.* stock, routine, clichéd, set, standard, customary, familiar, fixed, settled, conventional, hackneyed, overused, run-of-the-mill, overdone, overworked, commonplace, trite, banal, dull, ordinary, lifeless, uninteresting, stale, jejune, tiresome, tired, old, tedious, platitudinous, bromidic, dreary, boring, worn, pointless, insipid, dead, deadly, unimaginative, old-hat, moldy, mediocre, unoriginal, humdrum, moth-eaten. —**Ant.** original, unique, one-of-a-kind, imaginative, rare, uncommon, unusual, interesting, fresh.

sterile, *adj.* **1.** pure, aseptic, sanitary, germ-free, sterilized, uninfected, uncontaminated, unpolluted, uncorrupted, antiseptic. **2.** infertile, impotent, childless, gelded, fixed, spayed, barren, unproductive, fruitless, unfruitful, bare, dry, unprofitable, poor, infecund. —**Ant.** septic, contaminated; fertile, prolific.

stern, *adj.* **1.** firm, strict, adamant, austere, stringent, demanding, critical, rigid, rigorous, flinty, steely, authoritarian, tough, uncompromising, Spartan, ascetic, disciplined, severe, harsh, hard, inflexible, unremitting, obdurate, hardhearted, unsparing, unforgiving, merciless, unyielding, unrelenting, steadfast, implacable, forbidding, unsympathetic, rough, cruel, unfeeling. **2.** unsmiling, frowning, serious, somber, saturine, sour, grim, grave, gloomy, funereal, lugubrious, dour, gruff, crabby, churlish. —**Ant.** soft, lenient, flexible.

stew, v. **1.** simmer, boil, seethe, bubble, scald, cook, parboil; agonize, fret, brood, chafe, smolder, worry, get upset, get hot under the collar. —n. **2.** ragout, goulash, salmagundi, mixture, mishmash, hash, olla podrida, gallimaufry, potage, hotpot, pot au feu, chowder, bouillabaisse.

stick, n. **1.** stake, twig, branch, shoot, switch, rod, staff, pole, cane, wand, baton, club, cudgel, bat. —v. **2.** poke, thrust, impale, spike, skewer, spit, run through, jab, prick, perforate, drill, bore, riddle, pierce, puncture, stab, penetrate, spear, transfix, pin, gore. **3.** fasten, infix, implant, attach, glue, affix, nail pin, weld, solder, bond, tie, unite, join, cement, paste. **4.** adhere, cohere, cling, cleave, hold. **5.** hold, last, endure, dwell, continue, persevere, remain, stay, persist, abide. **6.** balk, shy, scruple, demur, boggle, object, kick, protest, vacillate, falter, hesitate, waver, doubt. —**Ant.** sever, separate; detach, disengage.

stiff, adj. **1.** rigid, firm, solid, unflexible, unbendable, unbending, unyielding, inelastic, brittle, starchy, starched, hard, tough, solidified, congealed, thick, dense, compact. **2.** violent, strong, steady, powerful, brisk, forceful, gutsy, howling, unremitting, fresh. **3.** firm, purposive, energetic, staunch, dogged, tenacious, indomitable, relentless, strong, stout, unrelenting, unyielding, resolved, obstinate, stubborn, pertinacious. **4.** graceless, awkward, maladroit, gauche, clumsy, inelegant, crude, abrupt. **5.** formal, ceremonious, punctilious, constrained, starched, frigid, cool, haughty, wooden, stuffy, aloof, tense, unrelaxed, pompous, stilted, mannered, snobbish, reserved, standoffish, chilly, unfriendly, uptight, forced, artificial, labored, pedantic, turgid, prim, priggish. **6.** laborious, difficult, excruciating, rough, intense, arduous, tiring, exhausting, harrowing, challenge, tough. **7.** harsh, punitive, hurtful, punishing, abusive, drastic, distressing, severe, rigorous, straitlaced, austere, strict, dogmatic, uncompromising, positive, absolute, inexorable, overwhelming, unbearable, merciless, cruel. **8.** excessive, steep, exorbitant, dear, expensive, great, high. **9.** taut, tight, tense. —n. **10.** prude, prig, stuffed shirt, puritan, blue nose, reactionary, conservative, stick-in-the-mud, old fogey, wallflower, bore, fuddy-duddy, square, fossil, anachronism; skinflint, miser, cheapskate, tightwad, piker. —**Ant.** flexible.

stifle, v. **1.** smother, suffocate, strangle, garrote, choke, throttle, asphyxiate. **2.** keep or choke back, repress, check, stop, suppress, withhold, restrain, control, prevent, cover up, hold in. **3.** crush, stop, halt, obviate, prevent, preclude, put down, destroy, suppress, demolish, extinguish, kill, eliminate, stamp out, quash, silence, check, curb, decimate. —**Ant.** encourage, further, foster.

stigma, n. mark, stain, reproach, smirch, demerit, blemish, scar, taint, blot, spot, brand, defilement, sullying, tarnish, disgrace, infamy, defamation, deprecation, calumny, condemnation,

disparagment, disrepute, ignominy, scandal, pillory, dishonor, opprobrium, odium, shame, blot on the escutcheon. —**Ant.** laurels, honor.

still, adj. **1.** in place, at rest, motionless, stationary, unmoving, inert, even, flat, smooth, undisturbed, unruffled, restful, comfortable, quiescent. **2.** soundless, quiet, hushed, noiseless, silent, mute. **3.** tranquil, calm, peaceful, peaceable, pacific, placid, serene. —v. **4.** silence, lull, hush, quiet, mute, stifle, muffle, smother. **5.** calm, appease, allay, assuage, alleviate, relieve, mollify, subdue, suppress, repress, soothe, compose, pacify, smooth, tranquilize. —n. **6.** stillness, quiet, silence, tranquility, serenity, peace, noiselessness, hush, calm. —**Ant.** stirring, mobile, moving; noisy, clamorous; agitated, disturbed; noise.

stimulate, v. **1.** rouse, arouse, stir, rally, waken, awaken, activate, incite, animate, excite, quicken, pique, galvanize, energize, vitalize, enliven, vivify, invigorate, urge, provoke, instigate, goad, spur, prod, prick, inflame, fire, inspire, encourage, fuel, nourish, jolt, whip up. **2.** invigorate. —**Ant.** discourage, unnerve, deaden.

stimulus, n. incentive, incitement, spur, goad, prompt, urge, fillip, impetus, drive, impulse, push, motivation, inspiration, encouragement, enticement, stimulation, motive, provocation; stimulant. —**Ant.** discouragement; wet blanket; soporific.

stingy, adj. niggardly, penurious, pennypinching, cheeseparing, economical, skimpy, sparing, frugal, tightfisted, mercenary, greedy, covetous, moneygrubbing, cheap, uncharitable, selfish, closefisted, stinting, petty, meanspirited, measly, unaccommodating, small-minded, petty, grudging, grasping, illiberal, venal, skinflinty, extortionate, usurous, shabby, near, churlish, sordid, parsimonious, miserly, mean, close, tight, avaricious. —**Ant.** generous.

stint, v. **1.** limit, restrict, control, curb, confine, restrain; pinch, straiten, starve, famish, skimp, scrimp, begrudge, economize, cut corners, withhold. —n. **2.** limit, limitation, restriction, restraint, constraint, control, curb, check, condition, reservation, qualification. **3.** share, rate, allotment, portion, quota, bit, assignment, stretch, term, shift, time, turn, duty, responsibility, charge, obligation, job, task, chore. —**Ant.** liberate, free.

stir, v. **1.** move, trouble, perturb, affect, upset, activate, agitate, disturb, mix, merge, blend, scramble, amalgamate, beat, whip up, shake. **2.** incite, instigate, prompt, motivate, encourage, hearten, inspire, inspirit, excite, move, drive, impel, rouse, foment, arouse, provoke, stimulate, animate, urge, goad, spur, prod, induce, persuade, convince, awaken, waken, rally, quicken, galvanize, energize. **3.** affect, touch, impress, strike, hit hard, have a profound effect on, alter one's feelings, excite, move. —n. **4.** movement, bustle, ado, to-do, agitation, commotion, disorder, uproar, tumult, activity, action, flurry, confusion, fuss, disturbance, excitement, hubbub, din, uproar, pandemonium, babel.

stock, n. **1.** store, goods, inventory, stockpile, armanentarium, cache, selection, goods, wares, reservoir, assortment, selection, variety, range, supplies, supply, provision, reserve, hoard. **2.** race, bloodline, dynasty, genealogy, extraction, roots, breeding, heritage, family tree, lineage, family,

descent, pedigree, ancestry, line, parentage, house, tribe. —adj. **3.** staple, standard, standing, customary, ordinary, regular, routine, permanent. **4.** common, commonplace, ordinary, usual, routine, banal, clichéd, stereotypical, stale, hackneyed, everyday, standard, traditional, orthodox, conventional, trite, worn-out, old, tired, tiresome, run-of-the-mill, boring, corny. —v. **5.** supply, store, fill, handle, market, inventory, furnish, provide, offer, keep.

stocky, adj. thickset, squat, chunky, stubby, stumpy, dumpy, chunky, solid, burly, beefy, heavyset, portly, memomorphic, short, thick, solid.

stoop, v. **1.** bend, lean, bow, crouch, duck, hunch, hunker, slouch. **2.** descend, condescend, sinks, deign, lower or abase or degrade or humble or humiliate oneself. **3.** stoop down, descend.

stop, v. **1.** cease, leave off, break off, bring to a close, give up, quit, halt, termination, end, finish, conclude, abandon, discontinue, desist or refrain from. **2.** interrupt, suspend, stay, postpone, defer, arrest, check, halt, restrain, intermit, terminate, end. **3.** cut off, intercept, withhold, thwart, interrupt, obstruct, impede, hinder, prevent, thwart, frustrate, foil, balk, preclude, delay, restrain, repress, suppress. **4.** block, obstruct, close, jam, plug, clog, choke off, seal off, blockade. **5.** cease, pause, break, interrupt, take a breather, rest, quit. —n. **6.** halt, cessation, arrest, ban, prohibition, close, standstill, conclusion, finish, end, termination, check. **7.** stay, visit, break, rest, layover, sojourn, stopover. **8.** station, depot, terminal. **9.** block, blockage, obstruction, obstacle, hindrance, impediment. —**Ant.** start, commence, initiate.

storm, n. **1.** turbulence, roaring, inclement, weather, tempest; gale, hurricane, tornado, cyclone, duststorm, squall, noreaster, rainstorm, whirlwind, hailstorm, snowstorm, ice storm, blizzard, thunderstorm. **2.** upheaval, agitation, stir, rumpus, furor, turmoil, disorder, disruption, ferment, tumult, perturbation, hurly burly, chaos, riot, uproar, brouhaha, melee, violence, commotion, disturbance, strife. **3.** outburst, outcry, eruption, furor, explosion, uproar, outbreak. —v. **4.** blow; rain, snow, sleet, squall, howl, hail, thunder and lightning. **5.** rage, rave, bluster, thunder, explode, blow one's top or stack, have a temper tantrum, act up, roar, rant, fume, complain. **6.** rush, attack, assault, besiege, assail, raid, blitz, bombard, shell, bomb.

story, n. **1.** narrative, tale, legend, recounting, yarn, account, recital, fairy, story, myth, epic, saga, fable, romance, anecdote, allegory, parable, record, history, chronicle. **2.** lie, fib, confabulation, falsehood, untruth, alibi, excuse, tall tale,. **3.** article, item, report, news, feature, information, scoop, lowdown, copy, dispatch, release, file. **4.** contention, testimony, assertion, version, representation, report, account, description, statement, allegation.

stout, adj. **1.** rotund, obese, tubby, overweight, heavyset, big, burly, heavy, plump, bulky, thickset, fat, corpulent, plump, portly, fleshy. **2.** bold, hardy, undaunted, dauntless, brave, gutsy, gritty, plucky, valorous, valiant, gallant, intrepid, fearless, staunch, resolute, doughty, invincible, indomitable, courageous. **3.** firm, stubborn, obstinate, determined, intent, contumacious, resolute. **4.** strong, stalwart, sturdy, brawny, healthy, robust, strapping, lusty, hulking, beefy, husky, sinewy, athletic, brawny, muscular, hefty, vigorous, energetic, dynamic, able-bodied. **5.** strong, substantial, sturdy, durable, tough, solid, heavy-duty, reinforced. —**Ant.** slim, slender, thin; fearful; weak; light.

straight, *adj.* **1.** candid, frank, open, honest, direct, straightforward, explicit, blunt, unequivocal, unambiguous. **2.** honorable, honest, virtuous, upright, erect, just, fair, equitable, impartial, aboveboard, respectable, decent, trustworthy, dependable, reliable, upfront, straight-shooting, principled, moral, ethical, on the up-and-up, truthful, straightforward. —**Ant.** devious, crooked, dishonest.

straightforward, *adj.* **1.** direct, straight, undeviating, unwavering, unswerving, to the point. **2.** honest, truthful, above board, upright, plain-spoken, on the level, on the up and up, honorable, just, fair. —**Ant.** devious; dishonest.

strain, *v.* **1.** stretch, tighten, tauten; force, overtax, burden, overwork, push; surpass, exceed. **2.** try hard, make an effort, struggle, strive, push, labor, toil, exert oneself. **3.** sprain, impair, injure, hurt, harm, damage, tax, pull, weaken, wrench, twist, tear, overexert. **4.** filter, sift, sieve, drain, filtrate, purify, percolate, ooze, seep through. —*n.* **5.** force, stress, tension, burden, anxiety, worry, obligation, demand, pressure, effort, exertion. **6.** sprain, damage, harm, impairment, weakness, injury, wrench. **7.** family, stock, descent, race, pedigree, lineage, ancestry, extraction. **8.** tenor, tone, drift, quality, spirit, complexion, vein, theme, mood, humor, cast, thread, impression, character, tendency, trait. **9.** streak, trace, vein, suspicion, touch, soupçon, dash, tinge, smack, dash, hint, suggestion, scintilla, iota, jot, bit.

strait, *n.* difficulty, distress, need, vicissitude, rigor, fix, quandry, emergency, exigency, crisis, pinch, dilemma, predicament, plight, trouble, mess, bind, pickle, jam, scrape, tight spot, hot water. —**Ant.** ease.

straitlaced, *adj.* prim, stuffy, hidebound, prudish, moralistic, rigid, proper, staid, strict, narrowminded, overscrupulous, conservative, old-fashioned, stiff, goody-goody, goody two-shoes, priggish, puritanical, bluenosed, finicky, finial, fuddy-duddy, fussy, prissy, Victorian. —**Ant.** liberal, free-thinking, bohemian, loose, free and easy, relaxed.

strange, *adj.* **1.** unusual, atypical, aberrant, extraordinary, curious, bizarre, odd, queer, eerie, wierd, uncommon, funny, quaint, fantastic, singular, peculiar, unfamiliar, inexplicable, unexplained, irregular, unconventional, rare, mysterious, mystifying, eccentric, abnormal, out of the ordinary, grotesque, remarkable, surprising, amazing, astounding, astonishing, flabbergasting, anomalous, exceptional. **2.** alien, foreign, exotic, outlandish, unfamiliar, unheard of, unknown. **3.** unacquainted, unaccustomed, unfamiliar, unknown, unexperienced. **4.** distant, reserved, aloof, detached, indifferent, standoffish, haughty, snobbish, formal, remote, withdrawn, reticent, unfriendly, unsociable, frigid, chilly, cold, supercilious, superior. —**Ant.** usual, commonplace.

stranger, *n.* alien, foreigner, outlander, *Auslander,* immigrant, emigré,

outsider, visitor, newcomer, unknown quantity. —**Ant.** friend, relative, ally.

strangle, *v.* garrote; choke, stifle, suffocate, smother, throttle, asphyxiate, wring (someone's) neck.

stratagem, *n.* plan, scheme, trick, ruse, deception, artifice, wile, feint, expedient, intrigue, device, maneuver, contrivance, machination, dodge, subterfuge, lure, plan, plot, ploy, tactic, conspiracy.

strategy, *n.* tactics, plan, design, scheme, policy, procedure, blueprint, scenario, gameplan, master plan; skillful management.

stream, *n.* **1.** current, rivulet, rill, brook, tributary, freshet, run, waterway, channel, kill, branch, creek, streamlet, run, river. **2.** flow, current, outpouring, effusion, rush, spurt, spout, fountain, flood, deluge, cataract, cascade, course, tide. **3.** flow, succession, torrent, rush, succession, series, barrage, line, chain, string. —*v.* **4.** pour, flow, run, issue, emit, course, rush, surge, pour, gush, flood, spurt, shoot.

street, *n.* way, road, roadway, avenue, boulevard, concourse, lane, thoroughfare, drive, passage, byway, thruway, highway; path, footpath, alley, alleyway.

strength, *n.* **1.** power, force, vigor, muscle, sinew, intensity, focus, toughness, health, might, potency, energy, resources, assets, means, ability, capacity. **2.** firmness, courage, backbone, stamina, tenacity, willpower, perseverance, persistence, nerve, determination, gameness, grit, pluck, fortitude, resolution. **3.** effectiveness, efficacy, potency, cogency, soundness, weight, incisiveness, persuasiveness, validity. **4.** intensity, brightness, loudness, vividness, pungency. —**Ant.** weakness.

strenuous, *adj.* **1.** difficult, hard, tough, arduous, laborious, toilsome, tiring, exhausting, taxing, demanding, uphill. **2.** vigorous, energetic, active, enthusiastic, dynamic, intense, indefatigable, tireless, persistent, dogged, tenacious, animated, spirited, eager, zealous, ardent, resolute, determined, forceful, earnest. —**Ant.** easy.

stress, *n.* **1.** anxiety, worry, distress, pain, suffering, grief, anguish, pressure, tension, tenseness, overwork, exhaustion, troubles, misery, woes, overexertion, burden, upset, pressure, strain. **2.** importance, significance, emphasis, weight, insistence, urgency, accent, force. —*v.* **3.** underscore, underline, highlight, mark, note, bring home, make a point of, spotlight, feature, emphasize, press, focus on, accent. —**Ant.** ease; insignificance; overlook.

stretch, *v.* **1.** draw out, extend, distend, dilate, expand, widen, enlarge, broaden, lengthen, elongate. **2.** hold out, reach forth, reach, extend, stretch forth, spread. **3.** tighten, tauten, strain, exaggerate. —*n.* **4.** length, span, spread, sweep, area, tract, distance, expanse, extent, extension, range, reach, compass. **5.** elasticity, give, resilience, stretchiness. —**Ant.** curtail, abbreviate.

strict, *adj.* **1.** rigid, rigorous, narrow, constrictive, restrictive, stringent, inflexible, stiff, severe, firm, hard, tough, unbending, unyielding, exacting, demanding, stern, narrow, illiberal, uncompromising, harsh, austere, authoritarian, tyrannical, repressive, autocratic, ironfisted, coldblooded, ruthless, merciless, pitiless, unsympathetic, straitlaced. **2.** exact, precise, accurate, scrupulous, meticulous, com-

pulsive, punctilious, finicky, attentive, conscientious, particular. **3.** close, careful, minute, precise, exact, faithful, critical. **4.** absolute, perfect, thorough, complete. —**Ant.** flexible.

strife, *n.* **1.** conflict, discord, disharmony, rivalry, competition, dispute, dissension, bickering, quarreling, squabbling, arguing, variance, difference, disagreement, contrariety, opposition. **2.** quarrel, struggle, clash, fight, conflict; animosity, antagonism, friction, hostility, hatred, enmity, ill will, bad blood. —**Ant.** peace.

strike, *v.* **1.** thrust, hit, smite, knock, smack, batter, pummel, thrash, punch, hammer, batter, belabor, pelt, bludgeon, horsewhip, flog, slap, slug, whack, wallop, whack, sock, belt, bash, lambaste, bop, beat, pound, cuff, buffet. **2.** catch, arrest, impress. **3.** come across, meet with, meet, encounter, discover, find, stumble upon, chance upon, hit upon. **4.** affect, overwhelm, impress, influence, afflict, hit.

strip, *v.* **1.** uncover, peel, decorticate, skin, bare, denude. **2.** remove, confiscate, seize, expropriate. **3.** withhold, deprive, divest, dispossess, dismantle. **4.** rob, plunder, despoil, pillage, ransack, loot, spoliate, ravage, rifle, sack, devastate, spoil, desolate, lay waste. —**Ant.** cover; furnish; invest.

strive, *v.* **1.** endeavor, try, attempt, strain, make every effort, work at, exert oneself, essay, struggle, toil. **2.** contend, battle, wrestle, compete, fight, struggle.

stroke, *n.* **1.** striking, blow, hitting, smack, whack, swipe, slam, wallop, strike, beating, beat, knock, rap, tap, pat, thump. **2.** apoplexy, paralysis, seizure, fit, spasm, embolism, aneurysm, cerebrovascular accident, shock, attack. **3.** feat, achievement, action, act, work, example, accomplishment. —*v.* **4.** caress, rub gently, massage, pet, pat, touch.

stroll, *v.* **1.** ramble, saunter, meander, perambulate, promenade, amble, walk, wander, roam, rove, stray. —*n.* **2.** ramble, saunter, promenade, amble, walk, wander, constitutional.

strong, *adj.* **1.** powerful, vigorous, hale, hearty, healthy, robust, mighty, sturdy, brawny, w'ry, athletic, sinewy, strapping, sturdy, burly, stout, beefy, hefty, husky, buff, pumped up, hardy, muscular, stout, stalwart, herculean. **2.** powerful, able, competent, talented, skilled, experienced, qualified, trained, knowledgeable, potent, capable, puissant, efficient. **3.** firm, courageous, valiant, brave, valorous, bold, intrepid, fearless. **4.** influential, resourceful, persuasive, convincing, compelling, trenchant, profound, formidable, telling, cogent, impressive. **5.** clear, firm, loud. **6.** well-supplied, rich, substantial. **7.** cogent, forceful, forcible, effective, efficacious, conclusive, irrefutable, substantial, potent, powerful. **8.** resistive, resistant, solid, firm, secure, compact, impregnable, impenetrable. **9.** firm, determined, staunch, unswerving, committed, devoted, unfaltering, tenacious, unwavering, resolute, solid, tough, stout. **10.** intoxicating, alcoholic, potent, spiritous, hard. **11.** intense, brilliant, glaring, vivid, dazzling. **12.** distinct, marked, sharp, stark. **13.** strenuous, energetic, forceful, active, dynamic, unflagging, tireless, diligent, indefatigable, steadfast, rabid, staunch, fervent, vehement, incompromising, assiduous, sedulous, hard-working, vigorous, zealous, eager, earnest, ardent. **14.** hearty, fervent, fervid, thoroughgoing, vehement, stubborn, dogged, obstinate, pertinacious, perseverant, persistent. **15.** pungent, redolent, intense, concentrated, heady, penetrating, fragrant, aromatic, odoriferous; sharp, acrid, piquant, spicy, hot, biting. **16.** smelly, rank, noisome, stinky, foul, rotten, putrid, putrescent, odoriferous. —**Ant.** weak.

structure, *n.* **1.** construction, organization, anatomy, skeleton, system, arrangement, form, makeup, framework, order, design, nature, character, composition, organism, scheme, complex, configuration, shape. **2.** building, edifice, house, construction, pile.

struggle, *v.* **1.** strain, expend energy, exert oneself, make an effort, cope, endeavor, try, attempt; contend, strive, oppose, contest, fight, vie, rival, wrestle, battle, conflict. —*n.* **2.** contention, competition, contest, rivalry, dust up, brush, clash, tusssle, match, fray, melee, encounter, skirmish, fight, battle, conflict, strife. **3.** effort, strife, strain, endeavor, exertion, labor, toil, work, travail, drudgery, pains.

strut, *v.* swagger, parade, flaunt, show off, bristle, display oneself, act like a peacock, promenade, prance, vaunt, brag, boast, crow, gasconade.

stubborn, *adj.* obstinate, perverse, contrary, dogged, persistent, tenacious, pertinacious, determined, stiff-necked, intractable, refractory, inflexible, intransigent, unrelenting, uncompromising, recalcitrant, unyielding, unbending, rigid, stiff, contumacious, headstrong, pigheaded, mulish, bullheaded, adamant, wayward, willful, singleminded, obdurate, fixed, set, opinionated, resolute, persevering, hard, tough, stiff, strong, stony. —**Ant.** tractable, amenable, adaptable, pliable, pliant, flexible; irresolute.

student, *n.* pupil, learner, disciple, undergraduate, schoolchild, trainee, apprentice, beginner, tyro, abecedarian, scholar; observer, commentator, critic, admirer, follower, devotee, fan, maven. —**Ant.** teacher.

studied, *adj.* deliberate, premeditated, calculated, planned, intentional, voluntary, conscious, contrived, feigned, labored, forced, wooden, artificial, designed, overwrought, stale, predetermined, willful, considered, elaborate. —**Ant.** unpremeditated, spontaneous, extempore, ad-libbed, ad hoc, impulsive, instinctive.

study, *n.* **1.** attention, application, exploration, scrutiny, learning, lessons, bookwork, cramming, concentration, investigation, inquiry, research, reading, reflection, meditation, cogitation, thought, consideration, contemplation. **2.** field, area, subject, topic, sphere, theme, bailiwick, specialty, major. **3.** zealousness, endeavor, effort, assiduity, enterprise, sedulousness, assiduousness. **4.** overview, presentation, article, paper, analysis, review, discussion, survey, results, research, thesis, results, opinion. **5.** library, den, office, haunt, studio, retreat, sanctum sanctorum. —*v.* **6.** read, investigate, memorize, rehearse, analyze, scrutinize, survey, inspect, scan, review, look into, observe, practice. **7.** think, reflect, consider, muse, deliberate, meditate, ponder, weigh, estimate, examine, contemplate, scrutinize, turn over, ruminate, chew on.

stuff, *n.* **1.** material, substance, matter, fabric, ingredients, essentials, makings, building blocks, fundamentals, essence, basics, elements, makeup, components, constituents, parts, units, pieces, segments, factors, features, details, items, specifics,

particulars, rudiments, principles. **2.** character, qualities, temperament, attitude, spirit, substance, grit, talent, abilities, background, attributes, experience, professionalism, capabilities. **3.** rubbish, trash, waste, nonsense, twaddle, balderdash, humbug, rot, garbage, tripe, poppycock, malarkey, hogwash, bunk, swill, eyewash, baloney, claptrap, piffle, bull, inanity, absurdity. —*v.* **4.** fill, cram, pack, jam, ram, crowd, compress, squeeze, squash, shove, force, press, stow. **5.** stop up, clog, block up, choke, plug, obstruct.

stun, *v.* **1.** knock out, shock, dizzy, daze, traumatize, numb, benumb, strike, hit, smack. **2.** startle, astound, stupefy, daze, dazzle, overpower, boggle the mind, disarm, astonish, amaze, overcome, bewilder, paralyze, stagger, jar, jolt, shake up, bowl over, excite, overwhelm, confound, confuse, perplex, nonplus, dumbfound, flabbergast, discombobulate.

stupid, *adj.* **1.** unintelligent, obtuse, dense, simple, simpleminded, subnormal, feebleminded, fatuous, fatheaded, bovine, dull, dullwitted, lumpish, doltish, moronic, cretinous, idiotic, imbecilic, weakminded, thick, thickheaded, thickwitted, witless, brainless, mindless, emptyheaded, birdbrained, boneheaded, addled, slow, slowwitted, dumb, dopey, sluggish, stolid, impassive, slow on the pickup, dead between the ears, shallow, mentally deficient *or* incompetent, vacant, nobody home, driveling, cloddish, intellectually challenged, unteachable. **2.** foolish, foolhardy, trifling, trivial, silly, frivolous, harebrained, crazy, insane, mad, crackbrained, scatterbrained, screwball, screwy, absurd, ludicrous, idiotic, risible, laughable, ridiculous, nonsensical, bootless, irrational, half-baked, cuckoo, inane, asinine, senseless, simple, half-witted, witless, dumb. **3.** dull, vapid, pointless, prosaic, tedious, uninteresting, stale, monotonous, unimaginative, vacuous, boring, insipid, flat, humdrum, tiresome, heavy. —**Ant.** bright, intelligent, clever, shrewd.

sturdy, *adj.* **1.** well-built, strong, energetic, vigorous, healthy, solid, tough, lusty, robust, stalwart, hardy, muscular, rugged, substantial, strapping, burly, athletic, husky, hefty, brawny, sinewy, stout, powerful. **2.** stalwart, formidable, staunch, steadfast, firm, stout, indomitable, unbeatable, unconquerable, persevering, resolute, vigorous, determined, uncompromising, unyielding, enduring, pertinacious, dogged. —**Ant.** weak, decrepit.

style, *n.* **1.** kind, sort, type, variety, category, class, make, brand, genre, design, look, fashion, pattern, cut, shape, line, form, appearance, character. **2.** mode, manner, method, approach, system. **3.** sophistication, refinement, polish, savvy, savoir-faire, fashion, elegance, smartness, chic, stylishness, taste, flair, dash, panache, cachet, vogue, class, élan, éclat, pizzazz, swankiness, spiffiness, trendiness. **4.** touch, characteristic, mark. —*v.* **5.** call, denominate, name, designate, address, entitle, title, christen, dub, label, tag, brand, characterize, term.

suave, *adj.* smooth, polished, cultivated, cosmopolitan, debonair, gracious, nonchalant, civilized, courteous, charming, diplomatic, disarming, smooth-talking, persuasive, winning, knowing, savvy, fashionable, politic, genteel, fulsome, sleek, slick, unctuous, sociable, cordial, genial, congen-

ial, affable, ingratiating, agreeable, polite, urbane, sophisticated, worldly, mundane. —**Ant.** bluff, self-conscious, clumsy, gauche, unsophisticated, naive, country.

subdue, *v.* **1.** conquer, defeat, suppress, overthrow, rout, beat, lick, quell, quash, crush, control, master, dominate, gain the upper hand, get the best of, put down, punish, subjugate, vanquish, overcome, overpower, subject. **2.** repress, reduce, overcome. **3.** tame, break, discipline, domesticate. **4.** tone down, soften, mollify, moderate, temper, hush, mellow, soft-pedal, curb, check. —**Ant.** liberate; awaken; intensify.

subject, *n.* **1.** theme, topic, argument, text, leitmotif, conception, point, thesis, issue, angle, gist, substance, business, affair, object, subject matter. **2.** ground, motive, reason, basis, source, excuse, rationale, cause. **3.** minion, underling, vassal, inferior, menial, dependent, subordinate. —*adj.* **4.** subordinate, subservient, submissive, controlled, inferior, answerable, dependent, secondary, collateral, subjected, inferior. **5.** obedient, tractable, docile, complaint, biddable, amenable, submissive. **6.** open, exposed, prone, vulnerable, susceptible, sensitive, apt, likely, liable. **7.** dependent, relative, conditional, contingent. —*v.* **8.** dominate, control, influence, conquer, subjugate, subdue, enslave, humble, crush, vanquish, master, put down. **9.** make liable, lay open, expose, submit, put through, impose on, cause to undergo. —**Ant.** sovereign, dominant; exempt.

subjective, *adj.* **1.** mental, inner, unreal, visionary, notional, abstract, chimerical, theoretical, imaginary, illusory, fancied, imagined. **2.** personal, individual, idiosyncratic. **3.** introspective, contemplative, introverted, meditative, ruminative, thoughtful, pensive. **4.** substantial, essential, inherent. —**Ant.** objective.

submerge, *v.* submerse, dip, sink, inundate, wash, soak, drench, saturate, douse, souse, wet, dunk, plunge, immerse, duck, dive, flood, swamp, engulf, drown, overwhelm. —**Ant.** surface.

submissive, *adj.* **1.** unresisting, yielding, acquiescent, deferential, accomodating, flexible, manageable, biddable, humble, obedient, tractable, compliant, pliant, yielding, amenable, agreeable. **2.** menial, mean, lowly, abject, degraded, debased, obsequious, servile, subservient, subject, submissive, slavish, ingratiating, sycophantic, toadying, truckling, bootlicking, brown-nosing, passive, resigned, patient, docile, tame, long-suffering, subdued, meek, timid, uncomplaining. —**Ant.** rebellious, intractable, refractory, fractious, unruly, disobedient, proud.

submit, *v.* yield, surrender, bow, capitulate, cave in, concede, consent, accede, defer, succumb, bend, knuckle under, resign oneself, accept, acquiesce, put up with, comply, obey, agree. —**Ant.** resist, disobey, disagree.

subordinate, *adj.* **1.** lower, inferior, below, beneath, under. **2.** secondary, unimportant, ancillary, minor. **3.** subservient; dependent, accessory, secondary, subject, ancillary, tributary, auxiliary, contributory. —*n.* **4.** inferior, subject, underling, minion, menial, drudge, stooge, aide, assistant, factotum, juror, hireling, lackey, servant, slave. —*v.* **5.** lower, subject, reduce, make secondary. —**Ant.** superior; primary, chief, leading, dominant.

subside, v. **1.** sink, lower, decline, drop, recede, precipitate, descend, settle. **2.** quiet, abate, calm, moderate, let up, die down, wear off, decrease, diminish, lessen, wane, ebb. —**Ant.** rise; increase.

substance, n. **1.** matter, material, fabric, composition, make up, stuff. **2.** essence, subject matter, quintessence, quiddity, gravamen, theme, subject. **3.** meaning, gist, nub, crux, heart, core, kernel, meat, sum total, significance, import, pith, essence, purport, point.

substantial, adj. **1.** real, actual, physical, worldly, mundane, palpable, valid, true, hard, solid, material, corporeal. **2.** ample, generous, abundant, goodly, tidy, healthy, major, large, massive, bulky, monumental, considerable, sizable. **3.** solid, stout, firm, well-built, durable, sturdy, strong, stable, sound. **4.** wealthy, well-heeled, affluent, rich, well-to-do, successful, prosperous, propertied, influential, responsible, reliable, consequential, powerful, significant, worthy, estimable. **5.** worthy, valuable, consummate, worthwhile, profitable, rewarding. —**Ant.** airy, ethereal, insubstantial, immaterial; trivial; unstable, unsound; poor; unworthy.

substitute, n. **1.** surrogate, makeshift, stopgap, stand-in, replacement, alternative, relief, standby, stand-in, understudy, proxy, alternative, representative, deputy, agent, temporary, relief, expedient, duplicate, copy, reproduction, contrivance, pinch hitter, double. —v. **2.** replace, displace, relieve, exchange places, make do, stand in, supplant, switch, take the place of, double for, cover for, pinch-hit-for. —**Ant.** original, starter, regular.

succeed, v. **1.** flourish, prosper, win, triumph, achieve, make good, progress, advance, get ahead, make it, arrive, get to the top, thrive, do well, make a hit, go swimmingly, prevail. **2.** follow, replace, ensue, come after, supervene; displace, supplant, replace, supersede. —**Ant.** fail; precede.

succession, n. **1.** order, sequence, progression, set, suit, suite, chain, train, string, concatenation, flow, procession, course, series. **2.** descent, transmission, lineage, race, dynasty, birthright, descendants, bloodline, ancestry.

successive, adj. consecutive, following, sequential, ordered, sequent, serial; uninterrupted, continuous, unbroken, continual, succeeding.

sudden, adj. unexpected, abrupt, unannounced, precipitate, immediate, rapid, accelerated, expeditious, hurried, fast, swift, brisk, unplanned, unlooked for, unforeseen, quick, unanticipated; hasty, headlong, impetuous, rash, impulsive; unwonted, surprising, startling. —**Ant.** deliberate, premeditated, foreseen.

suffer, v. **1.** undergo, experience, endure, live through, brook, face, confront, withstand, sustain, submit to, take, abide, accept, receive, bow, bear, tolerate, allow, permit, humor, indulge, stomach, stand, meet with, feel. **2.** agonize, hurt, smart, ache, throb, sweat, grieve, sorrow, anguish, moan, shed, tears, mourn, weep, cry, complain.

sufficient, adj. enough, adequate, ample, satisfactory, competent, suitable, requisite, fitting, passable, acceptable, middling, so-so, fair, tolerable, not bad. —**Ant.** insufficient.

suggest, v. propose, recommend, indi-

cate, hint, insinuate, intimate, advance, urge, advocate, support, offer, present, mention, introduce, prompt, advise, counsel; adumbrate, shadow. —**Ant.** express.

suggestion, **1.** recommendation, proposition, proposal, advice, counsel, plan, scheme, opinion, idea, notion, view, guidance, warning, admonition, hint, caveat. **2.** touch, suspicion, hint, indication, trace, whisper, insinuation, innuendo, intimation, implication, soupçon, breath, tinge, tincture, shade, dash, vein, streak, strain, smack, iota, jot.

suggestive, adj. evocative, indicative, reminiscent, provocative, representative, symbolic.

sullen, adj. **1.** silent, reserved, sulky, taciturn, melancholy, depressed, dejected, brooding, pouting, temperamental, glum, dour, lugubrious, somber, sober, saturnine, pessimistic, cynical, cynical, despondent, down-hearted, desolate, lugubrious, morose, moody. **2.** ill-humored, sour, resentful, aloof, surly, cross, churlish, grumpy, petulant, perverse, crotchety, choleric, crabby, irritable, glowering, spiteful, malevolent, malign, acrimonious, vexatious, splenetic, bad-tempered. **3.** gloomy, dismal, cheerless, clouded, overcast, somber, mournful, depressing, funeral, dispiriting, dreary, lowering, shadowy, tenebrous, murky, black, sunless, gray, obscure, dusky, subfuse, dark.

sully, v. **1.** soil, stain, tarnish, taint, blemish, disgrace, dishonor. **2.** dirty, contaminate, corrupt, pollute.

summary, n. **1.** summarization, recapitulation, encapsulation, condensation, shortening, consolidation, review, distillation, digest, extract, abstract, brief, synopsis, compendium, epitome, epitomization, essence, outline, précis, résumé, quintessence, skeleton, heart, core, kernel, nub, abridgment. —adj. **2.** brief, comprehensive, concise, short, condensed, compendious, concentrated, compact, succinct, pithy. **3.** curt, abrupt, quick, short, perfunctory, terse, peremptory, laconic.

summit, n. top, peak, apex, pinnacle, acme, vertex, culmination, crown, climax, apogee, zenith. —**Ant.** base, bottom.

summon, v. **1.** call, invite, command, order, enjoin, ask, send for, bid; convene, assemble, gather together, convoke. **2.** call forth, rouse, mobilize, muster, invoke, gather, evoke, elicit, arouse, activate, incite.

superb, adj. wonderful, marvelous, superior, glorious, divine, outstanding, sensational, unequaled, noteworthy, peerless, unrivaled, matchless, first-rate, superlative, perfect, classic, exceptional, extraordinary, striking, dazzling, brilliant, marvelous, fantastic, miraculous, incredible, unbelievable, fabulous, stupendous, staggering, mind-boggling, breathtaking, smashing, super, terrific, magic, mind-blowing, far-out, unreal, stately, majestic, grand, magnificent, admirable, fine, excellent, exquisite, elegant, splendid, sumptuous, rich, luxurious, gorgeous. —**Ant.** inferior.

superficial, adj. shallow, external, outward, exterior, slight, skin-deep, surface, outside, cursory, uncritical, cosmetic, perfunctory, slapdash, sloppy, once-over, light, insubstantial, minor, hasty, hurried, summary, passing, rushed, mechanical, careless, spotty, patchy, sketchy, nominal, meaningless. —**Ant.** basic, profound, radical.

superfluous, adj. unnecessary, extra, gratuitous, dispensable, uncalled-for, unneedful, needless, de trop, redundant, excessive, superabundant, surplus, supernumerary, spare, overabundant, supererogatory. —**Ant.** essential.

superior, adj. **1.** first-rate, excellent, outstanding, exceptional, consummate, glorious, sublime, superb, high-ranking, high-level, high-class, upper-class, lofty, noble, better, classy, elevated, distinguished, preferred, choice, select, elite, superlative, matchless, unequaled, peerless, unrivaled, nonpareil, supreme, notable, noteworthy, worthy, estimable, transcendent, surpassing. **2.** supercilious, lordly, lofty, pretentious, highfalutin, haughty, arrogant, condescending, snobbish, snooty, disdainful, patronizing, overweening, overbearing, scornful, pompous, high and mighty, stuffy, hoity-toity, uppity, stuck-up, la-di-da. —**Ant.** inferior, second-rate, worse, lower-class, undistinguished; humble.

superiority, n. **1.** lead, dominance, preeminence, ascendancy, supremacy, dominance, leadership, primacy, predominance, hegemony. **2.** prominence, eminence, importance, distinction, prestige, renown, excellence, greatness, magnificence, inimitability, worthiness, fame, notability, illustriousness, brilliance, éclat, power, influence, consequence, accomplishment, esteem. —**Ant.** inferiority.

supernatural, adj. **1.** unnatural, superhuman, miraculous, preternatural, phantasmagorical, occult, ghostly, spectral, metaphysical, unearthly, otherworldly, mystic, paranormal, psychic, uncanny, weird, eerie, mysterious, arcane, unreal, magical, dark. **2.** extraordinary, abnormal, unusual, odd, exceptional, remarkable, out of the ordinary, fabulous, rare, fantastic, inexplicable.

supersede, v. **1.** replace, displace, oust, substitute for, take the place of, supplant, succeed, remove. **2.** void, overrule, annul, neutralize, revoke, nullify, cancel, suspend, stay, rescind.

supplant, v. displace, supersede, oust, turn out, eject, dismiss, unseat, substitute, exchange, replace, succeed, remove.

supple, adj. flexible, bendable, elastic, pliant, pliable; lithe, limber, lissome, willowy, nimble, graceful, athletic, bouncy. —**Ant.** rigid, inflexible.

supplement, n. **1.** reinforcement, appendage, adjunct, accessory, codicil, insert, sequel, extension, addition, complement, addendum, appendix, epilogue, postscript. —v. **2.** add to, extend, augment, lengthen, expatiate on, expand, amplify, enhance, magnify, develop, flesh out, elaborate on, enlarge on, append, attach, complement.

supply, v. **1.** furnish, provide, give, endow, purvey, present, deliver, accommodate, provision, replenish, stock, fill. **2.** make up, make up for, satisfy, fulfill, replenish. **3.** fill, substitute for, occupy. —n. **4.** stock, store, stockpile, quantity, inventory, hoard, reserve, reservoir, cache, accumulation, fund.

support, v. **1.** bear, hold up, sustain, uphold. **2.** undergo, endure, suffer, sustain, withstand, weather, brook, abide, countenance, face, submit to, tolerate, bear, stand, stomach, go through, put up with. **3.** sustain, keep up, maintain, pay for, fund, finance, sponsor, underwrite, bankroll, provide for, nourish, nurture. **4.** back, bolster, strengthen, fortify, boost, champion, promote, advance, stand up for, brace, buttress, sanction, uphold, second, further, advocate, endorse, forward, defend, protect, shield. **5.** aid, reassure, sumpathize with, maintain, help, assist, advocate, succor, abet, relieve, patronize. **6.** corroborate, confirm, verify, authenticate, certify, substantiate, affirm, endorse, attest to, vouch for, validate, ratify, bear out. —*n.* **7.** maintenance, sustenance, living, expenses, upkeep, funding, resources, finances, budget, bread, livelihood, subsistence, keep. **8.** help, aid, succor, assistance, relief, backing, backup, reinforcement, bolstering, encouragement. —**Ant.** fail, abandon, deny, undermine.

suppose, *v.* **1.** assume, presume, surmise, infer, presuppose, take for granted. **2.** believe, think, consider, judge, deem, conclude, fancy, imagine. **3.** hypothesize, theorize, postulate, posit, assume, propose.

supposed, *adj.* **1.** reputed, putative, conjectural, alleged, assumed, presumed, imagined, suppositious, hypothetical, theoretical, postulated, speculative, soi-disant, self-styled. **2.** expected, obliged, required; intended, meant.

sure, *adj.* **1.** undoubted, indubitable, indisputable. **2.** confident, certain, definite, persuaded, cocksure, satisfied, positive, assured, convinced. **3.** reliable, dependable, steadfast, unshakable, undeviating, unfaltering, certain, trusty, trustworthy, honest, infallible, unfailing. **4.** firm, established, stable, solid, safe, secure, steady. **5.** unerring, accurate, precise, certain, foolproof, effective, sure-fire, unfailing, infallible. **6.** inevitable, unavoidable, guaranteed, inexorable, ineluctable, inescapable, foreordained, destined. —**Ant.** unsure, uncertain.

surface, *n.* **1.** outside, exterior, covering, skin, integument, top, façade, face, boundary, interface. —*v.* **2.** materialize, appear, show up, emerge, arise, rise, come up, pop up, crop up. —**Ant.** inside, interior; disappear, vanish.

surpass, *v.* exceed, excel, transcend, best, worst, better, top, cap, leave behind, prevail over, outdo, beat, outstrip, outdistance, outperform, outclass, outshine, overshadow, eclipse.

surplus, *n.* remainder, excess, overage, leftover, oversupply, overdose, glut, extra, spare, surfeit, superfluity, overabundance, redundance, superabundance, residue. —**Ant.** insufficiency, inadequacy.

surprise, *v.* astonish, amaze, shock, take aback, nonplus, dumbfound, dazzle, stun, stagger, strike, hit, awe, floor, flabbergast, bowl over, knock out, dizzy, flabbergast, discombobulate, catch unawares, stupefy, open (someone's) eyes, astound, take unawares, startle, disconcert, bewilder, confuse.

surrender, *v.* **1.** yield, give *or* deliver up, cede, abandon, deliver, hand over, forsake, sacrifice, eschew, relinquish, renounce, resign, waive, forgo. **2.** submit, yield, capitulate, quit, cry uncle, succumb, submit, acquiesce, comply, concede, crumble, give up, throw in the towel, raise the white flag. —*n.* **3.** resignation, submission, renunciation, transferal, concession, conveyance, capitulation, relinquishment.

surveillance, *n.* watch, vigil, stakeout, oversight, inspection, examination, care, control, management, supervision, superintendence, observation, scrutiny, reconaissance.

survey, *v.* **1.** view, scan, observe, watch, inspect, examine, scrutinize, appraise, evaluate, study, measure, assess, investigate, review, criticize, look into, size up, contemplate, ponder. —*n.* **2.** examination, inspection, critique, appraisal, study, evaluation, measure, scan, scrutiny, inquiry, investigation, review, poll, questionnaire, research.

survive, *v.* continue, persist, live, remain, succeed, outlive, subsist, last, endure, persist, pull through. —**Ant.** languish, die, fail.

suspect, *v.* **1.** distrust, mistrust, disbelieve, be suspicious, have suspicions, doubt. **2.** imagine, believe, surmise, feel, think, sense, fancy, imagine, theorize, hypothesize, postulate, have a funny *or* queer feeling, feel in one's bones *or* gut, have a hunch, consider, suppose, guess, conjecture. —*adj.* **3.** suspected, suspicious, questionable, dubious, doubtful, shady, shifty. —**Ant.** trust.

suspend, *v.* **1.** hang, attach, dangle, swing, fasten. **2.** defer, postpone, delay, withhold, shelve, table, keep in abeyance. **3.** stop, cease, desist, hold up, hold off, discontinue, intermit, interrupt, arrest, debar.

suspense, *n.* **1.** uncertainty, doubt, indefiniteness, insecurity, irresolution, expectancy, unsureness, incertitude, indetermination. **2.** indecision, vacillation, hesitation, hesitancy, wavering, second thoughts, scruple, misgiving. **3.** anxiety, tension, apprehension, nervousness, anticipation, agitation, anxiousness, expectancy, expectation, fearfulness, dread, angst, uneasiness, disquiet, foreboding, stress, strain, edginess, jumpiness. —**Ant.** certainty; decision.

suspicion, *n.* **1.** doubt, mistrust, misgiving, distrust, dubiousness, skepticism, qualm, wariness, apprehensiveness, apprehension, cautiousness, hesitation, uncertainty, leeriness, second thoughts, funny feeling. **2.** imagination, hunch, notion, idea, supposition, conjecture, guess. **3.** trace, hint, suggestion, shade, strain, inkling, soupçon, touch, shadow, tinge, taste, scintilla, jot, iota, dash, glimmer, flavor, streak, bit. —**Ant.** trust.

sustain, *v.* **1.** hold *or* bear up, bear, maintain, continue, keep up, preserve, prolong, persist in, carry, support, uphold. **2.** undergo, stand, withstand, experience, tolerate, weather, brave, support, suffer, endure, bear. **3.** maintain, support, provide subsistence for, nourish, nurture. **4.** purvey, supply, cater, furnish, support, aid, countenance, help. **5.** uphold, confirm, establish, recognize, allow, approve. **6.** confirm, ratify, approve, sanction, authorize, endorse, validate, corroborate, justify. —**Ant.** fail; disapprove.

swagger, *v.* **1.** strut, parade, prance, sashay, promenade, vaunt, show off, strut like a peacock. **2.** boast, brag, trumpet, crow, gasconade, talk big, lay it on thick, exaggerate, go on about, toot one's own horn, bluster, blow. —*n.* **3.** boasting, bragging, arrogance, display, ostentation, posturing, cockiness, conceit, machismo, boastfulness, virility, pomposity, bluster, insolence, pride, affectation, braggadocio.

swallow, *v.* **1.** eat, consume, devour, dispatch, ingest, taste, savor, take in, gorge, gulp, engorge, imbibe, drink, gulp, guzzle, swill, put away. **2.** consume, assimilate, absorb, engulf, devour. **3.** accept, receive, believe, credit, take on faith, buy, fall for. —*n.* **4.** mouthful, bite, morsel, nibble, guzzle, swig, gulp, drink, sip, taste.

swarm, *n.* **1.** horde, bevy, crowd, multitude, throng, mass, host, flock, cloud, army, mass, drove, flood, pack, bunch, stream. —*v.* **2.** crowd, throng, mass, congregate, gather, flock, stream, flow, abound, teem.

sway, *v.* **1.** swing, wave, brandish, flourish, display. **2.** incline, lean, bend, tend. **3.** fluctuate, vacillate, oscillate, rock, undulate, waver, totter. **4.** rule, reign, govern, lead, prevail. **5.** direct, dominate, control, persuade, convince, impress, bring around, incline, influence. —*n.* **6.** rule, dominion, control, leadership, power, sovereignty, government, authority, mastery, predominance, ascendency. **7.** influence, control, command, grip, hegemony, power, authority, bias.

swear, *v.* **1.** declare, affirm, avow, aver, vouchsafe, warrant, depose, state, vow, testify. **2.** promise, vow, take a solemn oath, guarantee, assure, give one's word, pledge, agree. **3.** curse, imprecate, blaspheme, execrate, use profanity, utter profanities, use four-letter words.

sweeping, *adj.* **1.** broad, wide, extensive, comprehensive, wholesale, all-inclusive, general, universal, widespread, blanket, umbrella, catholic, exhaustive, radical, thorough, across the board, vast. **2.** exaggerated, overstated, extravagant, unqualified, hasty. —**Ant.** narrow; qualified.

sweet, *adj.* **1.** sugary, honeyed, syrupy, saccharine; cloying, sentimental, treacly, precious, gushy, sticky, soppy, sloppy, icky, maudlin, schmaltzy, sickening. **2.** fresh, pure, clean, new. **3.** musical, melodious, euphonious, euphonic, lyrical, golden, silvery, mellifluous, harmonious, tuneful, in tune, dulcet, tuneful, mellow. **4.** fragrant, redolent, aromatic, perfumed, ambrosial, balmy, scented. **5.** pleasing, pleasant, agreeable, pleasurable, enjoyable, delightful, charming, lovable, kind, amiable, genial, warm, unassuming, easygoing, gracious, engaging, winning, winsome, attractive, gentle. **6.** dear, beloved, precious, treasured, prized. **7.** considerate, attentive, thoughtful, kindhearted, generous, solicitous, compassionate, sympathetic, gracious, accommodating. —**Ant.** sour, bitter.

swell, *v.* **1.** inflate, dilate, distend, increase, enlarge, dilate, wax, mushroom, balloon, bloat, grow, expand, blow up. **2.** bulge, protrude. **3.** grow, increase, augment, enlarge. **4.** arise, grow, well up, glow, warm, thrill, heave, expand. —*n.* **5.** bulkiness, distention, inflation, swelling. **6.** bulge, protuberance, augmentation, growth. —*adj.* **7.** stylish, elegant, fashionable, posh, ritzy, classy, luxurious, smart, chic, chi-chi, swanky, deluxe, grand. **8.** grand, fine, firstrate, marvelous, superb, splendid, spectacular, thrilling, super, terrific, wonderful, dandy, brilliant. —**Ant.** decrease, diminish.

swift, *adj.* **1.** speedy, quick, fleet, hasty, lively, rapid, fast, expeditious; brisk, sudden, abrupt. **2.** quick, prompt, ready, eager, alert, zealous. —**Ant.** slow, slothful.

swindle, *v.* **1.** cheat, cozen, defraud, dupe, trick, gull, victimize, deceive, inveigle, bilk, hoodwink, fleece, fool, exploit, sucker, gyp, buffalo, sting, screw, bamboozle, diddle, rook, rip off, con. —*n.* **2.** fraud, trickery, confidence game, gyp, three-card monte, shell game, chicanery, hoax, flimflam, cheating, racket, rip off, scam, deception.

swindler, *n.* confidence man, con artist, scoundrel, villain, fraud, four-flusher, cheat, deceiver, charlatan, mountebank, flimflam, bunco artist, schemer, rip off artist, scam artist, rogue, rascal, knave, sharper, trickster, impostor, embezzler.

swing, *v.* **1.** sway, oscillate, rock, fluctuate, wave, vibrate. **2.** suspend, hang, dangle, flap, waggle. —*n.* **3.** sway, vibration, oscillation, fluctuation. **4.** freedom, margin, range, scope, trend, play, sweep.

symmetry, *n.* balance, proportion, evenness, orderliness, uniformity, congruity, correspondence, agreement, consistency, equality, uniformity, symmetricalness, equilibrium, order, regularity, harmony. —**Ant.** disorder, lopsidedness, imbalance, disequilibrium.

sympathetic, *adj.* **1.** sympathizing, comforting, consoling, soothing, solacing, sensitive, compassionate, commiserating, kind, understanding, comprehending, supportive, caring, concerned, thoughtful, solicitous, responsive, well-meaning, considerate, empathetic, empathic, warmhearted, kindhearted, benign, benevolent, tender, affectionate. **2.** compatible, consonant, agreeable, pleasant, likeminded, simpatico, in tune with, on the same wavelength, attractive, congenial, attached, affected *or* touched by. —**Ant.** unsympathetic, apathetic, insensitive, uncaring; incompatible.

sympathy, *n.* **1.** compassion, pity, empathy, commiseration, tenderness, understanding, warmth, warmheartedness, solicitousness, consolation, caring, solace, sensitivity, thoughtfulness, responsiveness, consideration, fellow feeling, concern, support. **2.** compatibility, affinity, rapport, concord, agreement, harmony, camaraderie, fellowship, closeness, congeniality, unity. —**Ant.** antipathy, apathy; enmity.

system, *n.* **1.** organization, arrangement, classification, order, network, nexus, pattern, setup, set, structure, organism, economy, assemblage, combination, complex, correlation. **2.** plan, method, approach, modus operandi, process, technique, scheme, procedure, practice, routine, way, methodology, fashion, project, arrangement, classification.

systematic, *adj.* orderly, well-ordered, organized, well-organized, methodical, standard, standardized, routine, planned, businesslike, regular. —**Ant.** slapdash, messy, sloppy, disorderly, disorganized.

T

taboo, *adj.* **1.** forbidden, interdicted, out of bounds, sinful, wrong, anathema, off limits, prohibited, banned, sacred, unclean, dirty, traif, verboten, restricted, unspeakable, untouchable, unacceptable, rude, impolite, indecent, outlawed, illegal, unlawful. —*n.* **2.** prohibition, interdiction, outlawing, ban, proscription, anathema, restriction, forbidden fruit, exclusion, ostracism. —**Ant.** allowed, sanctioned, approved; permission, approval.

tacit, *adj.* silent, unexpressed, undeclared, unstated, unvoiced, unspoken, unsaid, implied, implicit, understood, inferred. —**Ant.** expressed, overt.

tacky, *adj.* **1.** inferior, tinny, junky, tinselly, secondhand, shoddy, broken-down, shabby, rundown, ramshackle, decrepit, shopworn, seedy, tatty, threadbare. **2.** unfashionable, unstylish, dowdy, frumpy, frumpish, frowzy,

drab, stale, old-fashioned, outmoded, stodgy, colorless. **3.** tasteless, gaudy, vulgar, chintzy, cheap, tawdry, cheesy, brummagem, glitzy, sleazy, loud, garish, low-class, low-rent. —**Ant.** elegant, classy.

tactful, *adj.* diplomatic, discreet, prudent, judicious, delicate, dexterous, discerning, knowing, politic, poised, savvy, polite, courteous, urbane, gallant, adroit, skillful, careful, acute, clever, perceptive, sensitive, considerate, thoughtful, understanding. —**Ant.** tactless, maladroit.

tactic, *n.* strategy, move, ploy, plan, ruse, devise, scheme, design, campaign, operation, master plan, blueprint, maneuver, procedure.

take, *v.* **1.** get, acquire, procure, win, lay hold of, lay one hands on, gain possession of, gain, obtain, secure. **2.** seize, catch, capture, clasp, snatch, clutch, grab, grasp, grip, embrace. **3.** pick, select, choose, opt for, settle on, decide on, fasten on, elect. **4.** subtract, deduct, discard, remove, take away *or* off *or* from. **5.** carry, bear, transport, bring, haul, ferry, deliver, cart, convey, transfer. **6.** conduct, escort, convey, guide, accompany, lead. **7.** obtain, exact, demand. **8.** occupy, use up, consume. **9.** attract, hold, draw. **10.** captivate, enthrall, capture, lure, seduce, charm, delight, attract, interest, engage, bewitch, fascinate, allure, enchant. **11.** assume, adopt, accept, bear, undertake, arrogate, acknowledge. **12.** ascertain, determine, fix. **13.** experience, feel, perceive. **14.** regard, view, accept, assess, believe, think, judge, deem, feel, consider, suppose, assume, presume, hold. **15.** perform, discharge, assume, adopt, appropriate. **16.** grasp, gather, conclude, deduce, infer, apprehend, comprehend, understand. **17.** suffer, brave, abide, undergo, swallow, stomach, brook, countenance, undergo, experience, bear, stand, tolerate, submit to, endure. **18.** employ, establish, put in place, effect, apply, adopt, resort to, use, make use of. **19.** require, need, necessitate, call for, demand. **20.** deceive, cheat, trick, fool, impose upon, dupe, hoodwink, swindle, con, bamboozle, bilk, hoax, humbug, gull, lead down the garden path, pull the wool over (someone's) eyes, swindle, defraud. **21.** catch, engage, fix. —**Ant.** give.

tale, *n.* **1.** story, narrative, narration, report, record, chronicle, history, anecdote, story, fable, account, fiction, memoir, novel, novella, legend, myth. **2.** lie, fib, falsehood, fabrication, untruth, exaggeration, cock-and-bull story, prevarication, tall tale. **3.** rumor, gossip, scandal, slander, allegation, dish, whispering, scuttlebutt.

talent, *n.* ability, aptitude, capacity, power, flair, facility, knack, ingenuity, endowment, strength, proclivity, capability, gift, genius, faculty, forte. —**Ant.** inability, incapability, weakness.

talk, *v.* **1.** speak, converse, discourse, communicate, express oneself. **2.** consult, confer, discuss; parley, chat, confabulate, rap, gossip. **3.** chatter, prattle, jabber, blather, babble, gibber, cackle, rattle on, run off at the mouth, jaw, beat one's gums, prate. **4.** orate, lecture, speak, sermonize, give an address *or* speech, speechify, harangue, discourse. **5.** utter, speak, mention. —*n.* **6.** speech, talking, conversation, discussion, meeting, consultation, palaver, chat, tête-à-tête, colloquy, discourse, dialogue, chat, communication, parley, conference, confabulation, one-

on-one, pow wow, rap session. **7.** report, rumor, gossip, tittle-tattle, tattle, gab, blabbing, hearsay, information, news, dope, dish, lowdown, inside story, bruit. **8.** prattle, empty words, words, clap trap, verbage, hot air, nonsense, chatter, rubbish, poppycock, malarky, applesauce, hooey, baloney, horse hockey, hogwash, bull, horse feathers. **9.** language, dialect, lingo, idiom, speech, jargon, parlance, argot, cant, patois.

talkative, *adj.* garrulous, loquacious, wordy, verbose, prolix, longwinded, voluble, chatty, effusive, loggorheic, big-mouthed, chatty, gabby, longdrawn. —**Ant.** taciturn, silent, laconic, terse.

tall, *adj.* high, elevated, towering, big, soaring, giant, gigantic, monumental, colossal, sky-scrapping, lofty, long-legged, leggy, lanky, gangling, rangy, huge, gigantic, large. —**Ant.** short.

tame, *adj.* **1.** domesticated, housebroken, broken, trained, obedient, disciplined, subdued, submissive, defanged, docile, gentle. **2.** mild, gentle, fearless, unafraid. **3.** tractable, pliant, compliant, amenable, biddable, obedient, docile, submissive, meek, subdued, crushed, suppressed, under (someone's) thumb, passive, unassertive, ineffective. **4.** dull, insipid, unanimated, spiritless, flat, empty, vapid, vacuous, jejune, tiresome, bland, lifeless, prosaic, humdrum, dead, prosaic, boring, uninteresting, uninspired, uninspiring, run-of-the-mill, ordinary, commonplace, toothless, tedious. **5.** spiritless, cowardly, pusillanimous, timid, timorous, fainthearted, lily-livered, yellow, chicken, wimpy. —*v.* **6.** domesticate, break, subdue, train, house-train, master, discipline, make tractable. **7.** soften, tone down, temper, moderate, mute, mitigate, subdue, mollify, pacify, defang, calm, tranquilize, control, curb, repress, subjugate, enslave. —**Ant.** feral, savage, wild, fearful; refractory, disobedient; exciting, spirited; brave, intrepid, valiant.

tamper, *v.* **1.** meddle, interfere, intrude, tinker, monkey around, intervene; damage, misuse, alter. **2.** bribe, suborn, seduce, lead astray, corrupt.

tangible, *adj.* **1.** physical, tactile, solid, concrete, sensible, appreciable, visible, objective, touchable, discernible, material, substantial, palpable, corporeal. **2.** real, actual, genuine, manifest, ostensive, patent, certain, open, plain, positive, obvious, evident, in evidence, perceptible. **3.** definite, certain, specific, ineluctable, inescapable. —**Ant.** intangible; unreal, imperceptible.

tantalize, *v.* torment, tease, torture, taunt, tempt, bait, frustrate, plague, harass, harry, irritate, vex, provoke, annoy, bother, try, afflict, pester.

tardy, *adj.* **1.** late, behindhand, unpunctual, overdue, behind schedule, delayed, detained, retarded, slack, dilatory, slow, backward. **2.** slow, dilatory, belated, slack, retarded, sluggish, reluctant, indolent, lackadaisical, listless, phlegmatic, slothful, lethargic, languid, languorous, lazy, lainback, laggard. —**Ant.** early, punctual, prompt.

tart, *adj.* **1.** sour, sourish, acidic, acidulous, dry, lemony, vinegary, tangy, astringent, acerbic, sharp, piquant, acrid, harsh, pungent, bitter. **2.** bitter, acid, corrosive, mordant, astringent, acerbic, incisive, keen, barbed, nasty, sardonic, vicious, cynical, trenchant, caustic, sarcastic, acrimonious, cutting, biting, stinging. —**Ant.** sweet, mellow.

task, *n.* **1.** duty, job, assignment, business, charge, stint, mission, undertaking, employment, occupation, métier, profession, function, work, labor, drudgery, toil. **2.** struggle, strain, effort, test, trial, exertion, travail, striving, strife, pains, trouble.

taste, *v.* **1.** try, sip, savor, nibble; sample, examine, assess, judge, rate. **2.** undergo, experience, feel, sample, know, encounter, come up against, meet with. **3.** smack, savor. —*n.* **4.** sensation, flavor, savor, scent. **5.** morsel, bit, sip, bite, nip, morsel, swig, swallow, mouthful, sample. **6.** relish, palate, penchant, fancy, appetite, stomach, tolerance, gusto, zest, liking, fondness, predilection, disposition, partiality, preference, predisposition. **7.** discernment, perception, discrimination, cultivation, refinement, polish, elegance, stylishness, sense, judgment, appreciation, understanding, penetration, insight, acumen, connoisseurship. **8.** manner, style, mode, fashion, form, design, motif, character.

tasteful, *adj.* proper, decorous, fitting, fit, approprioate, refined, cultivated, cultured, finished, polite, polished, restrained, correct, tactful, discreet, discriminating, *comme il faut*, harmonious, aesthetic, fastidious, elegant, graceful, charming.

tasteless, *adj.* **1.** flavorless, insipid, bland, dull, savorless, flat, watery, uninteresting, wishy-washy, vapid, unsavory, blah. **2.** inappropriate, unseemly, wrong, unsuitable, inapt, improper, ill-chosen, infelicitous. **3.** distasteful, unsavory, gross, base, low, indelicate, offensive, indecorous, uncouth, uncultured, gauche, boorish, maladroit, objectionable, coarse, crass, crude, garish, gaudy, meretricious, cheap, flashy, unaesthetic, tacky, vulgar. —**Ant.** tasteful.

tasty, *adj.* delicious, flavorful, delectable, luscious, ambrosial, scrumptious, savory, palatable, appetizing, toothsome, mouthwatering, yummy. —**Ant.** bland.

taunt, *v.* **1.** reproach, insult, censure, deride, blame, twit, chide, reprove, berate, scorn, upbraid, sneer at, flout, revile. **2.** ridicule, tease, torment, annoy, razz, ride, insult, burlesque, lampoon, poke fun at, kid, rib, roast, put down, rag, hassle, bug, get on (someone's) case, mock, jeer, scoff at, make fun of, twit, provoke. —*n.* **3.** gibe, jeer, derision, sneer, raspberry, Bronx cheer, dig, sarcasm, scorn, contumely, reproach, challenge, scoff, derision, insult, reproach, censure, ridicule.

taut, *adj.* tense, stretched, rigid, unrelaxed, inelastic, tight, drawn, stiff, strained. —**Ant.** loose, relaxed.

tawdry, *adj.* cheap, gaudy, showy, garish, loud, tatty, tinselly, tacky, tinny, shabby, cheapjack, ostentatious, flashy, meretricious, plastic. —**Ant.** tasteful, elegant.

teach, *v.* instruct, educate, inform, guide, coach, edify, mentor, counsel, advise, impart, develop, communicate, enlighten, discipline, train, drill, practice, exercise, tutor, school, indoctrinate, implant, instill, inculcate, demonstrate, show, familiarize, acquaint, give lessons to, drum into (someone's) head. —**Ant.** learn.

teacher, *n.* instructor, tutor, lecturer, professor, don, guide, coach, mentor, guru, educator, trainer, counselor, adviser, schoolteacher. —**Ant.** student, pupil.

tear, *n.* **1.** (*plural*) grief, sorrow, woe,

lamentation, regret, remorse, sadness, anguish, suffering, weeping, sobbing, weepiness, whimpering, blubbering, regret, affliction, misery. **2.** rip, rent, rupture, hole, split, slash, gore, cut, slit, gash, rift, laceration, fissure. **3.** rage, passion, flurry, outburst. —*v.* **4.** pull apart, rend, rip, rive, rupture, shred, mutilate, mangle, claw, sunder, sever. **5.** distress, shatter, afflict, upset, disturb, disconcert, affect. **6.** rend, split, divide, rip, cleave, slit, slash, cut, separate. **7.** cut, lacerate, wound, injure, mangle, damage, impair.

tease, *adj.* irritate, bother, bait, taunt, torment, beleaguer, bedevil, needle, worry, pester, goad, provoke, badger, twit, tantalize, frustrate, aggravate, rag, pick on, rib, kid, roast, give (someone) a hard time, inflame, importune, fret, gall, trouble, provoke, disturb, annoy, rail at, vex, plague, molest, harry, harass, chafe, chaff, hector. —**Ant.** calm, assuage, mollify.

technique, *n.* method, system, approach, tack, line, process, apparatus, procedure, practice, mechanism, routine, modus operandi, way, manner, fashion, style, mode.

tedious, *adj.* long, prolonged, overlong, endless, long-winded, wordy, tiresome, irksome, jading, wearying, wearisome, prolix, labored, laborious, repetitive, repetitious, mechanical, wearing, exhausting, tiring, fatiguing, monotonous, dull, boring, dreary, dry, drab, colorless, vapid, insipid, flat, banal, unexciting, prosaic, soporific, sleep-inducing, humdrum, routine, two-dimensional. —**Ant.** interesting.

tell, *v.* **1.** narrate, relate, give an account of, recount, describe, report, recite. **2.** communicate, make known, apprise, acquaint, inform, teach, impart, explain. **3.** announce, proclaim, make known, air, broadcast, impart, release, break, advertise, trumpet, herald, publish, publicize. **4.** utter, express, word, mouth, mention, speak. **5.** reveal, divulge, disclose, 'intimate, leak, betray, declare; acknowledge, own, confess, admit, unbosom, get off one's chest, blab, tattle, let the cat out of the bag, spill the beans, spill one's guts, squeal, rat, blow the whistle. **6.** say, make plain. **7.** discern, identify, describe, distinguish, discover, make out. **8.** bid, order, command, urge, require, charge, direct, dictate, instruct. **9.** mention, cite, enumerate, count, reckon, number, compute, calculate. **10.** operate, have force or effect, carry weight, be influential.

temper, *n.* **1.** temperament, constitution, character, personality, individuality, complexion, makeup, nature. **2.** state or frame of mind, vein, disposition, mood, humor. **3.** passion, tantrum, fit of pique, fury, rage, frenzy, irritation, anger, resentment. **4.** calmness, self-control, self-possession, sang-froid, balance, restraint, aloofness, moderation, coolness, equanimity, tranquility, composure. —*v.* **5.** modify, qualify, adjust, regulate, fix, lighten, palliate, reduce, relax, slacken, appease, moderate, mitigate, assuage, mollify, alleviate, relieve, tone down, mute, mellow, soften, soothe, calm, pacify, tranquilize, restrain. **6.** suit, adapt, fit, accommodate, adjust.

temperament, *n.* disposition, humor, frame of mind, mood, vein, complexion, composition, makeup, temper, constitution, nature, attitude, personality, individuality.

temperamental, *adj.* moody, irascible, petulant, impatient, waspish, peevish, snappish, irritable, sensitive, hy-

persensitive, volatile, mercurial, excitable, explosive, capricious, erratic, changeable, thin-skinned, difficult, touchy, testy, hot-tempered, bad-tempered, short-tempered, cantankerous, hotheaded, hot-blooded, curmudgeonly; crabby, grumpy, huffy, crotchety, cranky, grouchy, cross, tetchy. —**Ant.** serene, composed.

temperate, *adj.* moderate, reasonable, disciplined, forbearing, controlled, sensible, sane, rational, abstinent, economical, thrifty, judicious, sparing, discreet, cautious, restrained, continent; composed, steady, stable, equable, sober-sided, sober, calm, cool, reserved, detached, dispassionate, imperturbable, self-possessed, quiet, serene, placid. —**Ant.** intemperate, immoderate.

temporary, *adj.* transient, transitory, impermanent, makeshift, stopgap, standby, provisional, substitute, acting, part-time, occasional, discontinuous, fleeting, passing, momentary, fly-by-night, unstable, brief, changeable, fugitive, evanescent, short-lived, ephemeral. —**Ant.** permanent, lasting, perdurable, infinite.

tempt, *v.* **1.** induce, persuade, entice, allure, seduce, attract, lead astray, invite, inveigle, decoy, lure, whet one's appetite, seduce, captivate, coax, cajole. **2.** tantalize, frustrate, dare, provoke, test, try, prove.

tempting, *adj.* enticing, inviting, persuasive, seductive, attractive, alluring, tantalizing, captivating, appealing, irrestible, titillating, fetching, winsome, appetizing, mouthwatering. —**Ant.** repulsive, repellent.

tenacious, *adj.* **1.** dogged, determined, resolute, diligent, steadfast, stalwart, staunch, strong-willed, single-minded, uncompromising, unyielding, obdurate, mulish, pigheaded, adamant, refractory, immovable, firm, unfaltering, unsweeping, unwavering, strong, sturdy, solid. **2.** pertinacious, persistent, stubborn, obstinate, opinionated, sure, positive, certain. —**Ant.** dilatory, irresolute, lackadaisical, uncertain.

tenacity, *n.* perseverance, persistency, pertinacity, obstinacy, grit, purposefulness, stamina, assiduity, strength, diligence, sudulousness, stick-to-itiveness, unshakeability, toughness, resilience, fortitude, determination, backbone. —**Ant.** weakness, irresolution, dilatoriness.

tendency, *n.* direction, trend, disposition, predisposition, proneness, propensity, predilection, susceptibility, readiness, partiality, affinity, fondness, li²ing, turn, tenor, current, penchant, proclivity, inclination, leaning, bias, prejudice, drift, bent, movement. —**Ant.** stasis, disinclination.

tender, *adj.* **1.** soft, delicate, gentle, light, soothing. **2.** weak, delicate, feeble, frail, infirm, unstable, shaky, unsound, sickly, ailing. **3.** young, immature, youthful, inexperience, callow, raw, tenderfooted, green, impressionable, vulnerable, undeveloped, uninitiated, juvenile. **4.** gentle, delicate, soft, lenient, mild. **5.** softhearted, responsive, sensitive, considerate, caring, solicitous, humane, benevolent, charitable, generous, altruistic, good-natured, feeling, thoughtful, sympathetic, tenderhearted, compassionate, pitiful, kind, merciful, affectionate. **6.** affectionate, loving, sentimental, fond, romantic, adoring, amorous, amatory. **7.** considerate, careful, chary, reluctant. **8.** acute, raw, inflamed, hurting, aching, painful, sore, sensitive. **9.** fragile, breakable, frangible, friable. **10.** touchy, tricky, difficult, troublesome, precarious, ticklish, delicate, sensitive. —*v.* **11.** offer, proffer, propose, extend, submit, advance, put forth, present. —*n.* **12.** offer, bid, presentation, proposition, offering, proposal, proffer. —**Ant.** coarse, rough; healthy, sound, strong; mature, experienced, adult; merciless, ruthless; apathetic; inconsiderate; tough; accept.

tenet, *n.* belief, principle, doctrine, fundamental, axiom, article of faith, ideology, precept, dogma, opinion, notion, position, conviction, idea, axiom, canon, credo, creed, teaching, persuasion, view.

tense, *adj.* **1.** tight, taut, stretched, inelastic, inflexible, unbendable, wooden, stiff, rigid, strained. **2.** nervous, neurotic, jittery, unquiet, uneasy, apprehensive, fearful, expectant, holding one's breath, on edge, edgy, on pins and needles, agitated, perturbed, upset, alarmed, excited, strained. —**Ant.** loosed, limp, flaccid, lax; relaxed, expansive.

tentative, *adj.* experimental, trial, provisional, impermanent, undecided, undetermined, temporary, acting, probationary, indefinite. —**Ant.** definite, confirmed, definitive.

tenuous, *adj.* **1.** thin, slender, small, slim, slight, attenuated, minute. **2.** rare, thin, airy, rarefied. **3.** unimportant, insignificant, negligible, inconsequential, trivial, trifling, nugatory, unsubstantial. —**Ant.** thick, dense, substantial, significant.

terminate, *v.* **1.** end, finish, stop, cease, discontinue, abolish, extinguish, conclude, close, complete. **2.** bound, restrict, abate, limit. **3.** issue, result, turn out, eventuate, prove. —**Ant.** begin, open.

terrible, *adj.* **1.** dreadful, awful, fearful, frightful, appalling, dire, horrific, horrible, horrifying, terrifying, terrific, horrendous, horrid, gruesome, hideous, monstrous. **2.** distressing, shocking, appalling, severe, extreme, excessive. —**Ant.** delightful, pleasant; moderate.

terrify, *v.* frighten, scare, alarm, terrorize, shock, horrify, paralyze, stun, petrify, startle, panic, dismay, apall, upset, agitate, perturb, daunt, cow, intimate, browbeat, bully, make one's blood run cold, make one's hair stand on end, fill with dread. —**Ant.** pacify, soothe, calm.

terror, *n.* horror, fear, panic, fright, apprensiveness, fearfulness, agitation, perturbation, disquiet, upset, discomposure, alarm, dismay, consternation. —**Ant.** security, calm.

terrorize, *v.* dominate, coerce, terrify, frighten, alarm, dismay, scare, taunt, disconcert, make uneasy, cow, bulldoze, browbeat, compel, impel, push around, bully, force, persecute, intimidate. —**Ant.** befriend, hearten.

terse, *adj.* brief, concise, pithy, neat, laconic, precise, short, crisp, clear-cut, exact, compact, succinct, curt, sententious, condensed, abbreviated, abstracted, summary, concentrated. —**Ant.** wordy, diffuse, garrulous.

test, *n.* **1.** trial, proof, assay, evaluation, checkup, investigation, study, analysis. **2.** examination, quiz, exam. —*v.* **3.** try, check, evaluate, assess, probe, investigate, essay, prove, examine; refine, assay.

testimony, *n.* evidence, deposition, avowal, statement, affidavit, claim, assertion, witnessing, attestation, declaration, confirmation, verification, au-

thentication, affirmation, corroboration.

testy, *adj.* temperamental, thin-skinned, querulous, quarrelsome, disagreeable, irritable, impatient, touchy, tetchy, petulant, edgy, on edge, short-tempered, peevish, vexatious, fractious, contentious, choleric, snappish, waspish, splenetic, crusty, grumpy, grouchy, bearish, cross, cranky, irascible, fretful, crotchety, crabby, cantankerous, captious, carping, faultfinding. —**Ant.** even-tempered, imperturbable, cool, composed, calm.

thankful, *adj.* grateful, appreciative, pleased, glad, satisfied, content, indebted, beholden, obligated, obliged. —**Ant.** thankless, ungrateful.

theatrical, *adj.* dramatic, histrionic, melodramatic, stagy, operatic, exaggerated, forced, unnatural, showy, pretentious, pompous, ostentatious, sensational, artificial, mannered, affected, overdone, overwrought, hyperbolic, camp, campy, ham, hammy, phony, false, fake, unrealistic. —**Ant.** modest, low-key.

theft, *n.* robbery, larceny, burglary, stealing, pilfering, thievery, appropriation, filching, purloining, lifting, shoplifting, embezzlement, hijacking, pinching, pocketing, liberation, swiping, ripoff, heist.

theme, *n.* **1.** subject, topic, thesis, idea, notion, concept, keynote, gist, essence, core, substance, argument, point, text. **2.** composition, essay, review, study, article, piece, exercise, dissertation, treatise, tract, disquisition, monograph, paper. **3.** motif, leitmotif, thread, tenor, ideas; pattern, trend.

theory, *n.* **1.** assumption, presumption, supposition, presupposition, law, hypothesis, rationale, explanation, system, conjecture, guess, speculation, proposition, postulate, inference, plan, scheme, proposal. **2.** view, contemplation, notion, opinion, judgement, conclusion, conception.

therapeutic, *adj.* healing, curative, remedial, corrective, restorative, healthy, salubrious, medicinal, medical, adjuvant, alleviative, palliative, helpful, beneficial, salutary. —**Ant.** harmful, toxic.

thick, *adj.* **1.** broad, wide, solid, bulky, substantial, ample, close, massive; thickset, stocky, squat, stout, plump, portly, chunky, dumpy. **2.** dense, close, concentrated, condensed, compact, compressed, impenetrable, opaque, obscure, hazy, choking; full, filled, deep, clotted, chock-full, teeming, swarming, crawling, crammed, brimming, alive, crowded, jam-packed, bursting. **3.** inarticulate, indistinct, distorted, hoarse, gruff, rough, guttural, husky, raspy, gravelly. **4.** pronounced, marked, strong, distinct, obvious, decided, typical. **5.** heavy, dense, viscous, gelatinous, coagulated, clotted, jelled, congealed, stiff, firm, rigid, solid. **6.** friendly, close, intimate, inseparable, devoted, familiar, confidential, chummy, on good terms, palsy-walsy. **7.** stupid, slow, slow-witted, dense, stolid, obtuse, thickheaded, dull, dull-witted, half-witted, dim-witted, dopey, slow on the pickup, doltish, imbecilic, moronic, obtuse, bovine, simple, brainless; insensitive, thick-skinned.

thick-skinned, *adj.* insensate, numb, apathetic, unfeeling, hard, hard-hearted, unsympathetic, unaffected, affectless, pachydermatous; insensitive, dull, obtuse, callous, invulnerable, stoical, steely, hardened, toughened,

tough, inured, insusceptible, impervious, hard-boiled. —**Ant.** sensitive, vulnerable.

thief, *n.* **1.** robber; pickpocket, purse snatcher, mugger. **2.** burglar, pirate, swindler, con artist, embezzler, looter, pilferer, bandit, thug, purloiner, shoplifter, hijacker, cheat, charlatan, trickster, flimflam man, crook, ruffian, outlaw, desperado; kleptomaniac.

thin, *adj.* **1.** slim, slender, lean, spare, slight, lanky, spindly, gangling, underweight, undernourished, underfed, skinny, gaunt, scrawny, skeletal, cadaverous, puny, starved, anorexic, anemic, pinched, wasted, haggard, hollow-cheeked, emaciated. **2.** unplentiful, sparse, scanty, slimpy, paltry, piddling, meager. **3.** unsubstantial, slight, flimsy. **4.** transparent, translucent, see-through, filmy, gauzy, gossamer, sheer, light, silky, delicate, diaphanous, weak. **5.** faint, slight, poor, feeble. —*v.* **6.** rarefy, dilute, reduce, attenuate, decrease, water down, weaken, diminish. —**Ant.** thick, fat, overweight, obese; abundant; substantial; increase, thicken, strengthen.

think, *v.* **1.** conceive, imagine, fancy, realize, envision, invert, concoct, picture. **2.** consider, regard, suppose, look upon, judge, infer, deduce, conclude, evaluate, reckon, deem, esteem, count, characterize. **3.** bear in mind, call to mind, recollect, recall, remember. **4.** intend, mean, design, propose, entertain the idea *or* notion of, purpose. **5.** believe, suppose, imagine, dream, fantasize. **6.** anticipate, expect. **7.** cogitate, meditate, reason, speculate, deliberate, mull over, consider, reflect, muse, ponder, ruminate, contemplate.

thirst, *n.* desire, wish, craving, eagerness, yen, longing, pining, hankering, yearning, hunger, appetite, rapacity, greed, cupidity, covetousness, avidity, voracity, voraciousness, ravenousness, lust, passion, enthusiasm, fancy, itch. —**Ant.** distaste, repugnance, abhorrence, apathy.

thorough, *adj.* complete, entire, thoroughgoing, unqualified, perfect, downright, out-and-out, sheer, utter, absolute, unmitigated, unalloyed; painstaking, methodical, exhaustive, careful, scrupulous, conscientious, extensive, detailed, comprehensive, total, encyclopedic, all-out. —**Ant.** incomplete, partial.

thought, *n.* **1.** concept, conception, opinion, view, sentiment, persuasion, judgment, belief, idea, notion, tenet, conviction, speculation, brainstorm, observation, impression. **2.** consideration, contemplation, meditation, reflection, musing, brooding, pondering, rumination, deliberation, mental activity, cerebration, brown study, cogitation, thinking. **3.** intention, design, plan, scheme, purpose, intent. **4.** anticipation, expectation, hope, prospect, dream, vision, fancy. **5.** consideration, attention, thoughtfullness, kindliness, kindheartedness, concern, compassion, solicitude, sympathy, tenderness, care, regard.

thoughtful, *adj.* **1.** contemplative, speculative, musing, pondering, ruminative, deliberation, mental activity, cerebration, brown study, meditative, reflective, pensive, deliberative, serious, grave, earnest, abstracted, engrossed, preoccupied, rapt, intent, absorbed, introspective, sober, woolgathering, daydreaming. **2.** careful, heedful, mindful, regardful, considerate, attentive, discreet, prudent, wary, circumspect. **3.** considerate, attentive, concerned, solicitous, compassionate, sensitive, kind, kind-hearted, tender, sympathetic, charitable, helpful, courteous, polite, gallant, chivalrous, gracious, tactful. —**Ant.** thoughtless.

thoughtless, *adj.* **1.** unthinking, unreflective, absentminded, forgetful, careless, heedless, inattentive, inadvertent, indifferent, unconcerned, ill-considered, imprudent, negligent, neglectful, lax, remiss, unmindful, unobservant, unwatchful, reckless, rash, foolhardy, foolish, stupid, silly, flighty, scatterbrained. **2.** inconsiderate, rude, impolite, tactless, insensitive, ill-mannered, unthinking, discourteous, unchivalrous, ungracious, unkind, clumsy, awkward, gauche. —**Ant.** thoughtful.

threaten, *v.* **1.** menace, endanger, jeopardize, imperil, terrorize, bully, browbeat, daunt, cow, **2.** loom, indicate, presage, impend, portend, augur, forebode, foreshadow, prognosticate. —**Ant.** protect, defend.

threatening, *v.* daunting, fearsome, dire, intimidating, menacing, ominous, looming, sinister, foreboding, portentous, inauspicious, imminent, impending

thrifty, *adj.* frugal, provident, economical, sparing, saving, prudent, foresighted, careful, parsimonious, scrimping, skimping, tightfisted, penurious, penny-pinching, niggardly, stingy, cheap, on a tight budget. —**Ant.** wasteful, prodigal, improvident.

thrill, *v.* excite, stimulate, arouse, stir, rouse, quicken, rally, animate, galvanize, electrify, enliven, move, titillate, touch, strike, grip, rivet, give (someone) a kick *or* bang *or* charge, inspire, turn on, energize, stir up, inflame, impassion, inspirit, intoxicate, exhilarate. —**Ant.** disappoint, bore, deaden, depress.

thrive, *v.* prosper, succeed, flourish, grow, boom, bloom, wax, develop, burgeon, ripen, increase, advance, luxuriate. —**Ant.** languish, die.

throng, *n.* multitude, crowd, congregation, gathering, assembly, assemblage, swarm, horde, host, mass, crush, bevy, herd, flock, press, jam, pack. —*v.* **2.** swarm, assemble, crowd, press, fill, pack, cram, crush, jam, flock, mass, congregate, jostle, herd.

throw, *v.* project, propel, cast, hurl, pitch, toss, fling, launch, send, sling, clash, let fly.

thrust, *v.* **1.** push, force, shove, impel, ram, propel, prod, press, drive. **2.** stab, pierce, enter, plunge, stick, jab, poke, puncture, penetrate. —*n.* **3.** lunge, stab, push, drive, tilt, shove, poke, prod, puncture, penetration.

thwart, *v.* frustrate, baffle, oppose, prevent, hinder, obstruct, check, curb, arrest, impede, stymie, foil, stop, stump, balk, block, nagate, nullify, circumvent, outwit, bar, overcome, surmount, restrain, forestall, anticipate, defeat. —**Ant.** favor, encourage, support, help.

tidy, *adj.* clean, neat, trim, shipshape, spruce, spick-and-span, well-kept, snug; orderly, systematic, meticulous, fastidious, scrupulous, well-organized, methodical. —**Ant.** unkempt, messy, sloppy, untidy, slovenly, slipshod.

tie, *v.* **1.** bind, fasten, knot. **2.** lash, secure, attach, couple, moor, tether, rivet, anchor, join, unite, connect, link, knit, yoke, lock. **3.** confine, restrict, limit, obligate, constrain, curtail, hamper, hinder, curb, cramp. **4.** equal. —*n.* **5.** lace, throng, line, leash, ribbon, cord, string, rope, band, ligature. **6.**

draw, deadlock, stalemate, equality, dead heat. **7.** link, connection, bond, relationship, affiliation, involvement, entanglement, liaison. —**Ant.** untie, loosen, release.

tight, *adj.* **1.** secure, fixed, firm, fast, sealed, close-fitting, impervious, impenetrable, impermeable, snug, airtight, leakproof, waterproof. **2.** taut, tense, stretched, constricting, shrunken, contracted, compressed, condensed. **3.** strict, stringent, restrictive, tough, severe, rigorous, stern, harsh, austere, uncompromising, inflexible, unyielding, hard and fast, autocratic, despotic, tyrannical. —**Ant.** loose.

time, *n.* **1.** duration, stretch, patch, period, interval, term, spell, span, space. **2.** epoch, era, period, season, age, date, day, heyday, lifetime. **3.** opportunity, occasion, chance, break; juncture, pass, contingency. —*v.* **4.** regulate, gauge, measure, schedule, set, control, organize, fix, adjust.

timely, *adj.* seasonable, opportune, fortunate, lucky, providential, propitious, favorable, auspicious, appropriate, fit, seemly, proper, convenient, well-timed, prompt, punctual. —**Ant.** untimely, inappropriate, inopportune.

timid, *adj.* fearful, shy, diffident, sheepish, apprehensive, afraid, nervous, anxious, modest, mousy, wary, chary, circumspect, bashful, retiring, coy, blushing, shrinking, timorous, fainthearted, tremulous, cowardly, yellow, lily-livered, chicken, chicken-hearted, gutless, pusillanimous. —**Ant.** bold, fearless, intrepid, valiant.

tinny, *adj.* **1.** unresonant, harsh, metallic, twangy, reedy, thin, hollow, weak, feeble. **2.** inferior, cheap, low-grade, insubstantial, shoddy, tacky, tatty, tinselly, shabby, tawdry, flimsy, cheapjack. —**Ant.** resonant; well-made, superior, substantial.

tint, *n.* **1.** color, hue, tinge, dye, wash, cast, touch, hint, trace, suggestion, shade, stain, tincture, rinse. —*v.* **2.** color, tinge, stain, dye, rinse, touch up.

tiny, *adj.* small, little, minute, microscopic, wee, teeny, miniature, diminutive, minuscule, mini, micro, infinitesimal, midget, petite, slight, delicate, dainty, elfin, pygmy, lilliputian, bantam, pint-sized, puny, inconsequential, insignificant, negligible, trifling, paltry, itty-bitty, itsy-bitsy.

tirade, *n.* denunciation, outburst, diatribe, phillipic, jeremiad, screed, invective, harangue, declamation.

tire, *v.* **1.** exhaust, weary, fatigue, tucker out, weaken, drain, sap, enervate, debilitate, frazzle, deplete, wear out, jade. **2.** exasperate, bore, weary, irk, annoy, pester, bother, irritate, vex, tax, needle, hassle, get up (someone's) nose.

tired, *adj.* exhausted, fatigued, sleepy, worn out, spent, drained, sapped, weary, wearied, enervated, bushed, pooped, all in, wiped out, beat, ready to drop, bone-tired, dead on one's feet. —**Ant.** energetic, fiery, tireless.

tireless, *adj.* untiring, indefatigable, vital, vigorous, dynamic, lively, spirited, strenuous, energetic, active, industrious, enterprising, hard-working, unfaltering, unflagging, dogged, persistent, steadfast, determined, resolute, diligent, persevering, perseverant, assiduous, staunch, unwavering, tenacious. —**Ant.** tired, slothful.

tiresome, *adj.* **1.** wearisome, tedious, boring, monotonous, flat, insipid, bland, soporific, dry, prosaic, dreary, unexciting, uninteresting, drab, vapid,

dull, fatiguing, humdrum. **2.** annoying, vexatious, vexing, irritating, irksome, bothersome, burdensome, trying, exasperating, oppressive, disagreeable, troublesome, onerous, arduous. —**Ant.** interesting, enchanting.

title, *n.* **1.** name, designation, epithet, appellation, denomination, cognomen. **2.** championship, crown. **3.** right, interest, privilige, ownership, deed, prerogative, birthright, claim. —*v.* **4.** designate, entitle, denominate, term, call, style, name, label, christen, baptize.

toil, *n.* **1.** work, labor, effort, drudgery, exertion, travail, pains, sweat of one's brow, grind, trouble. —*v.* **2.** labor, work, strive, sweat, grind, exert oneself, struggle, drudge. —**Ant.** indolence, sloth.

tolerance, *n.* **1.** toleration, patience, leniency, indulgence, long-suffering, sufferance, forbearance, endurance, resistance, imperviousness. **2.** liberality, catholicity, impartiality, permissiveness, generosity, evenhandedness, fairness, charity, magnanimity, broadmindedness, openmindedness. **3.** play, clearance, allowance, variation. —**Ant.** intolerance.

tool, *n.* instrument, implement, utensil, contrivance, device, gadget, apparatus, appliance, aid, mechanism, contraption, gizmo.

top, *n.* **1.** apex, zenith, acme, peak, crest, head, crown, height, high point, apogee, meridian, summit, pinnacle, vertex, culmination. —*adj.* **2.** highest, topmost, uppermost, upper. **3.** best, greatest, leading, preeminent, first, finest, choicest, foremost, chief, principal. —*v.* **4.** surpass, excel, outdo, better, outstrip, exceed, beat, trancend, overshadow. —**Ant.** bottom, foot; lowest; worst.

topic, *n.* subject, theme, thesis, argument, text, issue, question, point, area of study *or* inquiry, keynote, gist, substance, thread, angle, subject matter.

torment, *v.* **1.** afflict, pain, rack, grill, try, torture, abuse, mistreat, maltreat, harrow, harass, harry, hector, bait, badger, bully, vex, annoy, irritate, agonize, distress, excruciate, crucify. **2.** plague, worry, annoy, pester, tease, provoke, needle, nettle, bedevil, nag, persecute, irk, exasperate, aggravate, beleaguer, trouble, tantalize, fret, hassle. —*n.* **3.** agony, wretchedness, suffering, affliction, torture, misery, distress, anguish, woe, travail, affliction, pain, curse, hell, horror. —**Ant.** please; delight; soothe, mollify; joy, pleasure, amelioration.

torrent, *n.* stream, flow, downpour, flood, deluge, rush, effusion, gush, outpouring, inundation, overflow, tide, cascade, outburst, spate. —**Ant.** drop, drip, dribble.

torrid, *adj.* **1.** hot, humid, muggy, steamy, tropical, burning, sultry, stifling, sweltering, sizzling, boiling, blistering, arid, scorching, fiery, parching. **2.** ardent, lustful, amorous, erotic, sexy, hot, inflamed, impassioned, passionate, fervent, intense. —**Ant.** arctic, frigid, cold; dispassionate, cool.

torture, *v.* torment, afflict, try, rack, grill, abuse, mistreat, maltreat, maim, mutilate, mangle, trouble, distress, wrong, oppress, persecute, agonize, worry, annoy, harass, bully, badger, bait.

toss, *v.* throw, cast, fling, hurl, pitch, lob, send, launch, lash, heave, sling, propel, thrust, catapult, let fly, chuck.

total, *adj.* **1.** whole, entire, complete, gross, overall, comprehensive, finished, final, full; absolute, utter, unalloyed, unmitigated, thorough, perfect, outright, out-and-out, all-out, down-right, unconditional, unqualified. —*n.* **2.** sum, whole, amount, total number, quantity, entirety, totality, aggregate, gross.

totality, *n.* total, all, sum total, aggregate, whole, grand total, everything, entirety, all and sundry, kit and caboodle, whole nine yards, whole bit, whole schmear, whole shebang, whole shooting match, the lot, beginning and end, be-all and end-all, alpha and omega.

touch, *v.* **1.** handle, feel, palpate, stroke. **2.** tap, pat, brush against, caress, rub, pet, strike, hit. **3.** come up to, attain, reach, arrive at. **4.** approach, rival, match, equal, compare with, hold a candle to, stack up against, be on a par with, be in the same league *or* class with. **5.** affect, impress, sway, quicken, influence, disturb, arouse, excite, impassion, stimulate, move, strike, stir, melt, soften. **6.** pertain *or* relate to, concern, regard, affect. —*n.* **7.** stroke, pat, hit, stroke, brush, caress, tap, blow. **8.** hint, trace, suggestion, dash, intimation, soupçon, tinge, suspicion, streak, bit, whiff, speck.

touchy, *adj.* **1.** sensitive, hypersensitive, thin-skinned, temperamental, excitable, explosive, mercurial, changeable, unstable, tense, high-strung, volatile. **2.** irritable, irascible, cranky, crabby, crotchety, grouchy, querulous, quarrelsome, captious, petulant, peevish, choleric, dyspeptic, splenetic, argumentative, disputatious, snappish, bearish, waspish, short-tempered, curmudgeonly, faultfinding, cross, cantankerous, testy, tetchy. **3.** delicate, ticklish, difficult, tricky, sticky, precarious, perilous, parlous, dangerous, critical, touch-and-go, sensitive, risky, chancy, hazardous, uncertain, hair-raising, nerve-racking, terrifying, slippery. —Ant. imperturbable.

tough, *adj.* **1.** firm, strong, hard, long lasting, substantial, stout, rugged, sound, well-built, hardy, sturdy, hardy, durable. **2.** difficult, hard, demanding, taxing, troublesome, exacting, strenuous; baffling, perplexing, thorny, knotty, irksome, puzzling, mystifying. **3.** hardened, incorrigible, troublesome, stubborn, obstinate, obdurate, refractory, adamant, callous, hard-boiled, hard-nosed, intractable, unsentimental, cold, stony, unbending, inflexible, rigid. —Ant. weak, feeble, sickly; flexible, soft.

tour, *n.* excursion, trip, journey, expedition, visit, travel, voyage, pilgrimage, junket, jaunt, outing, peregrination, safari, drive, cruise, trek.

towering, *adj.* tall, lofty, high, soaring, outstanding, sky-high, imposing, impressive, huge, gigantic, superior, paramount, supreme, unparalleled, unsurpassed, unrivaled, overwhelming, colossal, enormous, great, elevated. —Ant. short, low.

toxic, *adj.* harmful, injurious, hazardous, dangerous, damaging, deleterious, poisonous, venomous, virulent, malignant, deadly, lethal, pestilent, pestilential. —Ant. beneficial, healthful.

trace, *n.* **1.** vestige, mark, sign, remnant, track, spoor, scent, footprint, trail, record. **2.** mark, sign, token, clue, hint, indication, evidence. **3.** hint, suggestion, touch, taste, intimation, whiff, suspicion, tinge, dash, spot, bit, speck, soupçon. —*v.* **4.** track, follow, trail, dog, pursue, stalk, shadow, tail. **5.** ascertain, find out, discover, investigate, determine, detect, seek, search for, hunt down, un-

earth. **6.** draw, map, chart, sketch, reproduce, draft, plot, copy, delineate, outline, diagram. —Ant. abundance, plethora.

tract, *n.* **1.** stretch, extent, district, area, zone, belt, expanse, spread, vicinity, locality, section, sector, patch, quarter, parcel, plot, portion, lot, territory, region. **2.** treatise, pamphlet, booklet, brochure, leaflet, broadside, essay, sermon, thesis, text, monograph, article, paper, critique, homily, dissertation, disquisition, phillipic, jeremiad, diatribe, screed.

trade, *n.* **1.** commerce, traffic, business, dealing, exchange, barter, industry, buying and selling, merchandising, marketing. **2.** purchase, sale, exchange, swap. **3.** occupation, vocation, métier, livelihood, living, employment, pursuit, work, job, career, position, place, situation, business, profession, craft, calling. —*v.* **4.** barter, exchange, swap, return, switch, interchange. **5.** barter, transact *or* do business, merchandise, market, bargain, traffic *or* deal in.

tragic, *adj.* mournful, melancholy, sad, depressing, lamentable, funereal, forlorn, dolorous, grievous, dismal, lugubrious, unhappy, cheerless, miserable, pathetic, distressing, pitiful, piteous, pitiable, appalling, wretched, shocking, upsetting, unfortunate, ill-fated, star-crossed, ill-starred, inauspicious, unlucky, calamitous, sorrowful, disastrous, fatal, dire, awful, horrible, terrible, deplorable, catastrophic, crushing, dreadful. —Ant. comic, happy, fortunate, auspicious.

trail, *v.* **1.** drag, draw, tow, haul, pull, tag along, trawl. **2.** track, trace, hunt down, follow, pursue, dog, shadow, stalk, chase, tail. —*n.* **3.** path, track, route, way, course; scent, spoor, smell, trace.

train, *v.* discipline, teach, instruct, drill, coach, prepare, exercise, tutor, guide, indoctrinate, raise, rear, bring up.

trance, *n.* daze, daydream, reverie, spell, transport, exaltation, brown study, stupor, coma, swoon, hypnotic *or* cataleptic state, semi-consciousness, rapture, ecstasy, fugue, stupefaction, absorption, paralysis.

tranquil, *adj.* calm, peaceful, serene, placid, halcyon, quiet, silent, still, unruffled, noiseless, relaxed, sedate, unperturbed, undisturbed, even, cool, self-possessed, composed, collected, mild, gentle, restful. —Ant. troubled, perturbed, raucous.

transact, *v.* carry on, enact, conclude, settle, perform, manage, negotiate, conduct, handle, administer, discharge, perform, complete, finish.

transform, *v.* change, alter, metamorphose, metamorphosize, modify, transmogrify, mutate, vary, evolve, develop, mature, convert, transfigure, transmute. —Ant. retain.

transient, *adj.* transitory, temporary, fleeting, passing, flitting, flying, ephemeral, short-lived, momentary, evanescent, short-term, impermanent, fly-by-night, brief, fugitive. —Ant. permanent, perpetual, lasting, stable, durable, perdurable.

translation, *n.* paraphrase, version, transliteration, conversion, gloss, rewording, interpretation, rendition, rendering, treatment.

translucent, *adj.* semitransparent, see-through, pellucid, sheer, diaphanous, filmy, lucid, limpid, clear, translucid. —Ant. opaque, dense, solid.

transparent, *adj.* **1.** diaphanous,

clear, pellucid, lucid, limpid, crystalline, translucent. **2.** direct, unambiguous, unequivocal, straightforward, forthright, aboveboard, plain-spoken, artless, guileless, ingenuous, open, frank, candid. **3.** plain, apparent, evident, undisguised, recognizable, patent, unmistakable, crystal clear, manifest, obvious. —Ant. opaque; clandestine, secretive; concealed.

transport; *v.* **1.** carry, convey, bear, remove, transfer, ship, haul, transmit, forward, shift, send, move, deliver, dispatch. **2.** banish, exile, deport, send away, expatriate, ostracize, expel, oust, eject. —*n.* **3.** conveyance, carrier, shipment, transfer, transportation. **4.** joy, bliss, rapture, ecstasy, happiness, exaltation, exultation, delight, bliss, exhilaration, elation, euphoria, nirvana, seventh heaven, paradise, cloud nine, beatitude, felicity, enthusiasm, passion, fervor, ardor, fury, frenzy.

trap, *n.* **1.** pitfall, snare, springe, lure, bait, decoy. **2.** ambush, pitfall, artifice, maneuver, wile, machination, ruse, plot, conspiracy, subterfuge, device, deception, deceit, con game, hoax, sham, pretense, scam, flimflam, stratagem, trick. —*v.* **3.** snare, ensnare, entrap, bag, catch, capture, nab, cop, net, seize, ambush. **4.** trick, fool, deceive, dupe, con, inveigle, beguile, mislead, cajole, bamboozle, delude, betray, hoax, lead on.

traumatic, *adj.* injurious, harmful, hurtful, damaging, wounding, acute, upsetting, wrenching, painful, disturbing, distressing, dreadful, troubling, shattering, shocking, stunning, devastating, excruciating, agonizing, torturous, racking.

travesty, *n.* burlesque, parody, mockery, farce, lampoon, caricature, take-off, sendup.

treacherous, *adj.* **1.** traitorous, turncoat, renegade, seditious, unfaithful, faithless, untrustworthy, treasonable, treasonous, perfidious, disloyal. **2.** deceptive, unreliable, insidious, recreant, deceitful, false, double-crossing, betraying, deceiving, misleading, two-faced, hypocritical, underhanded, Machiavellian, conspiratorial. **3.** dangerous, perilous, hazardous, unsound, parlous, tricky, ticklish, touchy, uncertain, unstable, insecure. —Ant. faithful, trustworthy, loyal; reliable; stable, secure.

treachery, *n.* betrayal, treason, apostasy, recreance, recreancy, defection, abandonment, desertion, disloyalty, faithlessness, double-dealing, duplicity, guile, underhandedness, double-cross, perfidy, sabotage, subversion, deceit, chicanery, knavery, villainy, iniquity. —Ant. loyalty, fealty.

treason, *n.* sedition, disloyalty, sell out, betrayal, perfidy, subversiveness, deception, double-crossing, treachery, disaffection, lese majesty, mutiny, insurrection, incitement to riot, rebellion. —Ant. loyalty, allegiance.

treasure, *n.* **1.** wealth, riches, fortune, money, cash, cache, hoard, funds; valuables, jewels. —*v.* **2.** prize, cherish, love, hold dear, value, appreciate, esteem, respect, admire, regard highly, adore.

treat, *v.* **1.** act *or* behave toward. **2.** look upon, consider, regard, deal with. **3.** discuss, deal with, handle, manage, study, examine, consider, touch on, investigate, explore, scrutinize, analyze, review, criticize. **4.** entertain, take out, wine and dine, pay for, host, regale, feast. **5.** negotiate, settle, bargain, come to terms, confer, consult, advise. —*n.* **6.** favor, gift, present, bonus, freebie, perk; feast, fête, entertainment, banquet.

tremble, *v.* **1.** shake, quiver, quaver, quake, shiver, shudder. **2.** vibrate, wobble, teeter, shimmy, oscillate, totter.

tremendous, *adj.* **1.** huge, gigantic, stupendous, monumental, prodigious, monstrous, enormous, immense, vast, gargantuan, outsize, oversized, towering, colossal. **2.** dreadful, awful, horrid, alarming, startling, frightening, staggering, stunning, dire, horrendous, terrible, terrifying, horrifying, appalling. **3.** amazing, astounding, astonishing, dazzling, stunning, staggering, awesome, flabbergasting, wonderful, remarkable, fabulous, extraordinary, marvelous, terrific —**Ant.** small, tiny, microscopic.

tremor, *n.* **1.** trembling, shaking, shuddering, vibration, oscillation, shivering, quivering, quaking. **2.** quake, earthquake, temblor, seismic activity, tectonic shift.

trend, *n.* **1.** course, drift, tendency, tenor, current, disposition, predisposition, leaning, bias, bent, proneness, propensity, direction, inclination. **2.** fashion, style, vogue, rage, fad, mode, look, craze. —*v.* **3.** tend, veer, extend, stretch, run, incline, lean, bend, drift, swing, shift, head.

trespass, *n.* **1.** invasion, encroachment, intrusion, infringement. **2.** offense, sin, wrong, transgression, violation, infraction, breach, contravention, vice, crime, misdemeanor, misdeed, error, fault. —*v.* **3.** encroach, infringe, intrude, invade, butt in, interfere, intervene. **4.** transgress, offend, err, do wrong, sin.

trial, *n.* **1.** test, proof, experiment, tryout, trial run, checking, dry run, demonstration, inspection, experience, scrutiny, examination, testing. **2.** attempt, effort, endeavor, struggle, try, venture, shot, stab, fling, whirl, essay. **3.** test, assay, criterion, proof, touchstone, standard. **4.** affliction, suffering, tribulation, difficulty, distress, sorrow, grief, trouble, misery, agony, anguish, adversity, misfortune, vicissitude, cross, rigor, woe, hardship, hard luck, hard times. —**Ant.** consolation.

trick, *n.* **1.** device, expedient, artifice, maneuver, humbug, fraud, imposture, hoax, subterfuge, intrigue, wile, stratagem, ruse, deception, fraud, trickery, cheating, deceit, duplicity, machination, conspiracy, con. **2.** prank, joke, practical joke, antic, horseplay, tomfoolery, caper, mischief, gag, shenanigans. **3.** jugglery, sleight of hand, legerdemain, prestidigitation, magic, stunt, illusion, hocus-pocus. —*v.* **4.** cheat, swindle, beguile, gull, hoax, hoodwink, bamboozle, mislead, outwit, circumvent, outmaneuver, bilk, rook, outfox, dupe, fool, deceive, defraud, delude.

trickery, *n.* artifice, trick, stratagem, dissimulation, guile, cunning, wiles, wiliness, duplicity, fraud, deception, deceit, chicanery, double-dealing, subterfuge, imposture, cheating, fraud, humbug, knavery, shrewdness, slyness, craftiness, craft, evasiveness, hanky-panky, skulduggery, hocus-pocus. —**Ant.** honesty, sincerity, trustworthiness, guilelessness.

trifling, *adj.* **1.** trivial, insignificant, unimportant, petty, paltry, negligible, puny, measly, picayune, minor, inconsequential, nugatory, slight, worthless, piddling, immaterial. **2.** frivolous, shallow, inane, jejune, banal, vapid, insipid, superficial, lightweight, light,

empty. —**Ant.** important, significant, substantial, major; profound, serious.

trim, *v.* **1.** shorten, abbreviate, crop, snip, dock, reduce, pare, clip, prune, shave, shear, cut, lop, curtail. **2.** modify, adjust, prepare, arrange. **3.** dress up, array, deck, bedeck, ornament, beautify, decorate, adorn, embellish, garnish, embroider, trick out. —*n.* **4.** condition, order, form, health, fitness, repair, shape, situation, state. **5.** dress, array, equipment, gear, trappings, trimmings. **6.** trimming, edging, embroidery, border, frill, fringe, ornamentation, adornment, embellishment, decoration; cutting, clipping, priming, reduction. —*adj.* **7.** neat, smart; well-groomed, well-kempt, crisp, dapper, spick-and-span, shipshape, spruce, tidy, well-ordered, orderly, ordered. —**Ant.** augment, increase.

trip, *n.* **1.** journey, voyage, excursion, pilgrimage, travel, tour, jaunt, junket, outing, expedition, trek, peregrination, cruise, drive, safari. **2.** stumble, misstep, fall, faltering. **3.** slip, mistake, error, blunder, erratum, faux pas, indiscretion, lapse, oversight, miss. —*v.* **4.** stumble, misstep, fall down, tumble, lurch, flounder, topple, sprawl, plunge, falter, stagger. **5.** bungle, blunder, err, slip, miss, overlook. **6.** tip, tilt.

trite, *adj.* commonplace, ordinary, common, hackneyed, threadbare, shopworn, stereotyped, old-hat, hackneyed, clichéd, bromidic, antiquated, archaic, obsolete, banal, flat, insipid, jejune, vapid, stale. —**Ant.** original, fresh, uncommon, unusual, extraordinary.

triumph, *n.* **1.** victory, conquest, subjugation, routing, overthrow, success, achievement, accomplishment, attainment, coup. **2.** joy, exultation, ecstasy, rejoicing, elation, rapture, glory, delight, exhilaration, jubilation, celebration. —*v.* **3.** win, succeed, prevail, dominate, defeat, vanquish, conquer, beat, rout, overcome, overwhelm, subdue. **4.** rejoice, exult, celebrate, glory, be elated *or* glad, delight, rejoice. —**Ant.** defeat, loss.

trivial, *adj.* trifling, petty, unimportant, insignificant, nugatory, futile, vain, fruitless, bootless, meaningless, inconsequential, nonessential, minimal, minor, paltry, puny, measly, picayune, lightweight, slight, immaterial, frivolous, small. —**Ant.** important, significant, weighty, momentous.

trophy, *n.* **1.** token, remembrance, record, reminder, memento, souvenir, keepsake, commemoration, memorial. **2.** prize, award, reward, laurels, garland, loving cup, wreath, medal, citation, palm, booty, spoils.

trouble, *v.* **1.** disturb, distress, ail, undermine, try, anguish, alarm, worry, concern, agitate, upset, discompose, disquiet, perturb, grieve, disorder, disarrange, distract, perplex, puzzle, baffle, discombobulate, confuse, derange, embarrass, disconcert, abash. **2.** inconvenience, put out, burden, encumber, discommode, incommode. **3.** annoy, vex, bother, afflict, provoke, needle, nettle, exasperate, aggravate, gall, beleaguer, irritate, irk, pester, plague, fret, torment, torture, harry, hector, harass, nag, bully, pick at *or* on, badger, molest, get on one's nerves *or* under one's skin, give (someone) a hard time. —*n.* **4.** molestation, harassment, annoyance, bother, irritation, nuisance, vexation, difficulty, embarrassment. **5.** misery, distress, affliction, concern, worry, grief, agitation, care, agony, anguish, torment, torture, cross, catastrophe, suffering, calamity,

dolor, adversity, bad luck, hard times, strife, vicissitude, tribulation, trial, misfortune, woe, pain, sorrow. **6.** disturbance, agitation, row, turbulence, unrest, discord, turmoil, tumult, fighting, uprising, skirmish, revolt, rebellion, outbreak, disorder. **7.** inconvenience, exertion, fuss, ado, stir, flurry, pains, effort. —**Ant.** calm, mollify; support, accommodate; happiness, joy, celebration; peace, serenity, tranquility.

troublesome, *adj.* **1.** annoying, worrisome, worrying, irksome, irritating, exasperating, bothersome, pestiferous, pesky, vexatious, confusing, baffling, perplexing, galling, nagging, harassing. **2.** laborious, difficult, arduous, strenuous, tiring, tiresome, rigorous, excruciating, taxing, hard, burdensome, wearisome. —**Ant.** simple, easy, trouble-free.

true, *adj.* **1.** factual, actual, real, bona fide, authentic, genuine, veracious, truthful, realistic, valid, verified, verifiable, veritable. **2.** sincere, earnest, wholehearted, honest, honorable, just, faithful, equitable, fair. **3.** loyal, faithful, trusty, trustworthy, devoted, dedicated, fast, firm, stable, dependable, reliable, resolute, true blue, staunch, constant, steady, steadfast, unswerving, unwavering, unfaltering. **4.** accurate, exact, faithful, correct, literal, unvarnished, unadulterated, precise; agreeing. **5.** right, proper, legitimate, rightful. **6.** reliable, sure, unfailing, persisting, certain, persevering. —**Ant.** untrue, false.

trust, *n.* **1.** reliance, confidence, dependence, sureness, positiveness, assurance, security, conviction, certitude, certainty, belief, faith, credence, credit. **2.** expectation, hope, faith. **3.** credit, reliability, dependability, trustworthiness, credibility. **4.** obligation, responsibility, charge. **5.** commitment, office, duty, charge. —*v.* **6.** rely on, confide in, count on, bank on, reckon on, have confidence in, depend upon. **7.** believe, credit. **8.** expect, hope, look for, have faith. **9.** entrust, commit, consign, delegate, empower, assign, sign *or* hand over. —**Ant.** mistrust, distrust.

trustworthy, *adj.* reliable, true, dependable, trusty, tried, safe, secure, constant, stable, honest, honorable, faithful, staunch, loyal, steadfast, steady, straightforward, honest, upright, scrupulous. —**Ant.** deceitful, dubious

truth, *n.* **1.** fact, reality, verity, veracity. **2.** genuineness, reality, authenticity, actuality. **3.** honesty, uprightness, integrity, sincerity, candor, frankness, openness, ingenuousness, probity, fidelity, virtue. **4.** accuracy, correctness, rightness, precision, exactness, nicety. —**Ant.** lie, fiction, fabrication, untruth; fraudulence; dishonesty; inaccuracy.

try, *v.* **1.** attempt, essay, endeavor, struggle, undertake, venture, seek, take a shot *or* crack *or* stab at, strive, make an effort. **2.** test, prove, demonstrate, inspect, scrutinize, analyze, evaluate, check out, sample, appraise, assess, judge, examine, investigate.

tumult, *n.* **1.** commotion, disturbance, disorder, turbulence, uproar, upset, disquiet, bedlam, chaos, brouhaha, stir, ado, pandemonium, hullabaloo, brawl, donnybrook, furor, row, turmoil, frenzy, rage, rumpus, ruckus, hubbub, fracas, agitation, affray, melee; riot, outbreak, uprising, revolt, insurrection, rampage, revolution, mutiny. **2.** agitation, perturbation, confusion, excitement, ferment. —**Ant.** peace, order; calm, serenity.

tumultuous, *adj.* **1.** uproarious, chaotic, frenzied, furious, hectic, wild, savage, frantic, hysterical, tempestuous, stormy, fierce, turbulent, riotous, violent. **2.** noisy, disorderly, irregular, boisterous, clamorous, rowdy, unruly, obstreperous. **3.** disturbed, agitated, excited, perturbed, confused, unquiet, restive, restless, nervous, uneasy. —**Ant.** calm, peaceful, pacific; regular, orderly; quiet, restful.

tuneful, *adj.* musical, melodious, melodic, euphonious, mellifluent, mellow, smooth, harmonic, harmonious, dulcet, sweet, rich, rhythmic. —**Ant.** discordant, sour, flat.

turmoil, *n.* commotion, disturbance, tumult, agitation, disquiet, upset, chaos, confusion, ferment, frenzy, violence, fury, turbulence, stir, ado, brouhaha, hysteria, disorder, bustle, trouble, uproar. —**Ant.** quiet, serenity, order, peace.

turn, *v.* **1.** rotate, spin, revolve, roll, reel, pivot, swivel, gyrate, circle, whirl, twirl, wheel, swirl, pirouette, eddy. **2.** change, reverse, divert, deflect, avert, sheer, veer, swerve, deviate, diverge, shift, digress, depart, transfer. **3.** change, alter, metamorphose, transmute, transform, adapt, reorganize, modify, shape, reform, convert. **4.** direct, point, aim. **5.** shape, form, create, concoct, formulate, construct, cast, coin, fashion, mold. **6.** curve, bend, twist, wind, loop, arc, meander, snake, zigzag, coil. **7.** go bad, spoil, curdle, rot, decay, molder, putrefy, become rancid, sour, ferment. —*n.* **8.** rotation, spin, cycle, circuit, round, spin, whirl, twirl, gyration, revolution. **9.** change, reversal, alteration, shift. **10.** direction, drift, trend. **11.** change, deviation, twist, bend, turning, vicissitude, variation. **12.** shape, style, mode, form, mold, cast, fashion, manner. **13.** inclination, bent, tendency, disposition, predisposition, bias, leaning, penchant, prejudice, proneness, predilection, aptitude, talent, proclivity, propensity. **14.** need, exigency, requirement, necessity.

tutor *v.* teach, instruct, educate, train, enlighten, advise, guide, prepare, direct, ground, mentor, coach, drill, indoctrinate, school.

twilight, *n.* **1.** evening, dusk, eventide, gloaming, sunset, sundown, half-light, dimness, obscurity, shadows, nightfall, crepuscule. **2.** decline, diminution, waning, ebb, weakening, close, end, ending, finish, conclusion, downturn, slump, decay. —**Ant.** dawn; waxing.

twist, *v.* **1.** intertwine, braid, plait, weave, entwine, interlace, interweave; combine, associate. **2.** contort, distort, change, alter, pervert, warp, bias, color, falsify, misrepresent, misconstrue, garble. **3.** wind, snake, meander, turn, zigzag, coil, curve, bend, roll. **4.** writhe, squirm, wriggle. **5.** turn, spin, rotate, revolve. —*n.* **6.** curve, bend, turn. **7.** turning, turn, rotation, rotating, spin. **8.** spiral, helix, coil.

twit, *v.* **1.** taunt, gibe, banter, ridicule, mock, pick on, scoff, jeer, tweak, make fun of, razz, ride, rib, roast, kid, rag, tease. **2.** deride, reproach, upbraid, chide, reprove, censure, blame, berate, scorn, revile, sneer at.

tycoon, *n.* magnate, leader, captain of industry, top executive, baron, czar, personage, mogul, CEO, chairman of the board, business leader, financier, millionaire, billionaire, panjandrum,

nabob, VIP, worthy, big shot, wheel, wheeler-dealer, big cheese, big wheel, bigwig, brass hat, big-time operator, big enchilada, top dog. —**Ant.** nobody, nonentity, cipher; underling, subordinate, lackey, flunky.

type, *n.* **1.** kind, sort, class, category, genre, order, variety, species, breed, strain, ilk, classification, group, family, genus, phylum, form, stamp. **2.** sample, specimen, example, representative, prototype, paradigm, epitome, personification, standard, quintessence, pattern, model, exemplar, original, archetype. **3.** form, character, stamp. **4.** image, figure, device, sign, symbol, emblem, mark, token.

typical *adj.* **1.** normal, standard, ordinary, regular, natural, general, generic, common, universal, representative, characteristic, specific. **2.** conventional, usual, commonplace, common, ordinary, run-of-the-mill, orthodox, classic, in keeping, in character, to be expected. —**Ant.** atypical, distinctive, unusual, unexpected, unorthodox.

tyrannical, *adj.* arbitary, despotic, authoritarian, fascistic, autocratic, bullying, totalitarian, dictatorial, cruel, harsh, severe, oppressive, unjust, overbearing, highhanded, ironfisted, absolute, magisterial, imperious, domineering, dominating, inhuman. —**Ant.** judicious, liberal, just, humane, democratic, egalitarian.

tyrant, *n.* despot, autocrat, dictator, authoritarian, overlord, slave driver, bully, Hitler, czar, martinet, fascist, Nazi, supremacist, absolute ruler *or* monarch, totalitarian, oppressor. —**Ant.** democrat, egalitarian, liberator.

U

ugly, *adj.* **1.** repulsive, offensive, hideous, grotesque, ghastly, gruesome, monstrous, displeasing, ill-favored, hard-featured, unlovely, unattractive, unprepossessing, unsightly, homely. **2.** revolting, terrible, base, sordid, evil, foul, perverted, depraved, degenerate, abominable, execrable, despicable, odious, vile, monstrous, corrupt, heinous, amoral. **3.** disagreeable, unpleasant, offensive, nasty, loathsome, repugnant, repulsive, nauseating, disgusting, sickening, revolting, obnoxious, objectionable. **4.** troublesome, disadvantageous, uncomfortable, awkward, hazardous, perilous, touch, ticklish, precarious, threatening, dangerous, ominous. **5.** surly, spiteful, ill-natured, quarrelsome, argumentative, peevish, irritable, cross, crabby, querulous, curmudgeonly, rude, irascible, churlish, disagreeable, hostile, nasty, cantankerous, crotchety, mean, temperamental, obnoxious, obstreperous, peevish, testy, tetchy, rancorous, malicious, vicious, bad-tempered. —**Ant.** beautiful.

ulterior, *adj.* unacknowledged, underlying, surreptitious, underhanded, unavowed, unexpressed, hidden, concealed, covert, secret, private, personal, confidential, latent, obscure, ambiguous, cryptic, enigmatic. —**Ant.** open, explicit.

ultimate, *adj.* final, decisive, last, latest, terminal, concluding, conclusive, eventual, supreme, utmost, absolute, categorical, extreme, furthest, farthest, remotest. —**Ant.** prime, primary.

ultimatum, *n.* warning, notice, threat, demand, requirement, condition, stipulation, insistence, final offer.

unabashed, *adj.* **1.** bold, brazen, undaunted, fearless, doughty, confident, sure. **2.** shameless, brazen-faced, forward, immodest, unblushing. —**Ant.** timid, retiring; modest, prim.

unable *adj.* **1.** not able, unfit, unqualified, powerless, impotent, incapable, helpless, incompetent, ineffective, ineffectual. **2.** disabled, incapacitated, crippled, paralyzed, debilitated, weak, feeble. —**Ant.** able.

unaccountable, *adj.* **1.** not answerable, not responsible, independent, autonomous, sovereign. **2.** inexplicable, inscrutable, strange, mysterious, puzzling, baffling, odd, peculiar, weird, uncanny, unfathomable, unexplainable, incomprehensible, unintelligible. —**Ant.** accountable.

unaccustomed, *adj.* unusual, unfamiliar, uncommon, unexpected, unprecedented, peculiar, curious, rare, new. —**Ant.** common, typical, familiar.

unaffected, *adj.* **1.** sincere, genuine, honest, real, unfeigned, natural, unpretentious, unassuming, unstudied, unartificial, down to earth, plain, naive, simple, guileless, artless. **2.** unmoved, untouched, unimpressed, unstirred. —**Ant.** affected.

unanimity, *n.* accord, agreement, unanimousness, harmony, unity, unison, concert, uniformity, concurrence, consensus, concord, concordance, solidarity, likemindedness. —**Ant.** discord, disagreement, dissension.

unassuming, *adj.* modest, unpretentious, humble, simple, approachable, friendly, warm, accessible, unaffected, down to earth, self-effacing, unostentatious. —**Ant.** immodest, pretentious, pompous, self-important.

unbearable, *adj.* unendurable, intolerable, insufferable, insupportable, unacceptable, outrageous, unreasonable, inhuman, unthinkable, unspeakable, appalling, offensive. —**Ant.** bearable, tolerable.

unbecoming, *adj.* **1.** inappropriate, ill-suited, unsuited, unapt, unsuitable, unfitted, unfitting, unfit, out of place *or* character. **2.** unseemly, improper, indecent, indelicate, indecorous, clumsy, awkward, gauche, maladroit, tasteless, rude, impolite, offensive, objectionable. —**Ant.** becoming, appropriate; seemly, proper.

unbelievable, *adj.* incredible, beyond belief, doubtful, dubious, unimaginable, inconceivable, implausible, unlikely, improbable, unthinkable, far-fetched, unrealistic, preposterous, absurd, ridiculous, mind-boggling, flabbergasting.

unbiased, *adj.* fair, equitable, impartial, tolerant, unprejudiced, even-handed, just, reasonable, fair-minded, objective, judicious, dispassionate, detached, unbigoted, aloof, uncolored, nonpartisan, undogmatic, liberal, neutral, disinterested. —**Ant.** biased, prejudiced.

uncalled-for, *adj.* unnecessary, needless, unprovoked, unsolicited, unwelcome, unjustified, unfounded, unjustifiable, improper, out of line *or* order, impertinent, intrusive, officious, unwarranted, gratuitous, wanton, supererogatory. —**Ant.** necessary, essential, proper.

uncanny, *adj.* strange, preternatural, supernatural, weird, odd, eerie, singular, erratic, eccentric, queer, mysterious, inexplicable, unfathomable, inscrutable, extraordinary, ghostly, unearthly, spooky, creepy. —**Ant.** common, usual, natural.

uncertain, *adj.* **1.** insecure, precarious, unsure, doubtful, dubious, unpredictable, problematical, touchy, ticklish, touch-and-go, explosive, unstable, unreliable, unsafe, fallible, perilous, dangerous, hazardous, risky. **2.** unsure, undecided, indeterminate, undetermined, unfixed, unsettled, indefinite, ambiguous, questionable, dubious, up in the air, conjectural, speculative, debatable, touch and go. **3.** doubtful, vague, hazy, indefinite, fuzzy, obscure, ambiguous, indistinct. **4.** undependable, unreliable, changeable, variable, capricious, unsteady, irregular, fitful, desultory, chance, fickle, erratic, wavering, sporadic, occasional. —**Ant.** certain.

uncivil, *adj.* **1.** uncivilized, illmannered, unmannerly, rude, impolite, discourteous, ungracious, unchivalrous, ill-bred, vulgar, disrespectful, uncouth, boorish, loutish, churlish, crusty, besmirched, sullied, stained, brusque, curt, impudent. **2.** uncivilized. —**Ant.** civil.

uncivilized, *adj.* ill-mannered, uncultured, unrefined, uneducated, unpolished, unsophisticated, inelegant, uncouth, boorish, loutish, coarse, crude, gross, philistine, provincial, rough, rude, gauche, maladroit, clumsy, awkward, vulgar, tasteless, unenlightened, lowbrow, crass.

unclean, *adj.* **1.** dirty, soiled, filthy, grimy, unwashed, untidy, slovenly, squalid, smudged, bedraggled, slatternly, besmirched, sullied, stained, nasty, foul. **2.** evil, vile, base, impure, unvirtuous, unchaste, sinful, corrupt, polluted. —**Ant.** clean.

uncomfortable, *adj.* **1.** disquieting, embarrassing, disconcerting, upsetting, unnerving, unsettling, disturbing, bewildering, discomforting. **2.** uneasy, ill at ease, embarrassed, queasy, flustered, agitated, upset, shaken, unsettled, perturbed, rattled, troubled, disturbed, unhappy, miserable, cheerless. —**Ant.** comfortable.

uncommon, *adj.* unusual, rare, scarce, infrequent, unexpected, occasional, sporadic, unique, atypical, different, odd, singular, strange, peculiar, remarkable, queer, extraordinary, exceptional. —**Ant.** common.

uncommunicative, *adj.* reserved, taciturn, tight-lipped, closemouthed, reticent, inexpressive, silent, mute, secretive. —**Ant.** communicative, talkative, voluble, outgoing.

uncompromising, *adj.* unyielding, unwavering, staunch, loyal, committed, devoted, tried and true, dependable, faithful, unfaltering, resolute, determined, single-minded, immovable, inflexible, rigid, firm, steadfast, obstinate, subborn, adamant. —**Ant.** irresolute, half-hearted, flexible.

unconditional, *adj.* unrestricted, absolute, complete, total, utter, sheer, unqualified, unconditioned, unreserved, categorical. —**Ant.** conditional, restricted, qualified.

unconscionable, *adj.* **1.** unscrupulous, unprincipled, unethical, immoral, amoral, conscienceless, evil, wicked, criminal, unjust, unfair, contemptible, despicable, base, ignoble, shady, dishonest, unlawful. **2.** inexcusable, unacceptable, unforgivable, unpardonable, indefensible, unreasonable, excessive, extravagant, outrageous, extortionate, egregious, inordinate, immoderate, exorbitant. —**Ant.** scrupulous; reasonable.

uncouth, *adj.* awkward, clumsy, gauche, maladroit, boorish, loutish,

oafish, uncivilized, lowbrow, base, vulgar, crude, gross, crass, barbaric, coarse, insensitive, ignorant, unmannerly, discourteous, rude, illmannered, uncivil, ucivilized. —**Ant.** courteous, urbane, well-bred.

uncover, *v.* lay bare, disclose, dig up, unveil, show, unearth, excavate, discover, dredge up, turn up, reveal, expose, open, strip. —**Ant.** conceal, bury.

undeniable, *adj.* irrefutable, indisputable, indubitable, incontrovertible, incontestable, unquestionable; obvious, evident, clear, certain, sure, unimpeachable, unassailable. —**Ant.** doubtful, dubitable, questionable.

undergo, *v.* experience, suffer, bear, weather, stand, withstand, submit to, survive, countenance, face, tolerate, sustain, endure. —**Ant.** avoid.

underground, *adj.* **1.** subterranean, subterrestrial, subsurface, belowground, underearth, buried, sunken, covered. **2.** secret, clandestine, hidden, concealed, covert, stealthy, shrouded, furtive, sneaky, subversive, underhanded, backstairs, undercover, cabalistic, surreptitious. **3.** avant-garde, experimental, antiestablishment, revolutionary, radical, subversive, altetrnative, nonconformist, guerrilla.

underhanded, *adj.* secret, stealthy, covert, furtive, backstairs, sneaky, devious, tricky, wily, sly, crafty, dishonorable, deceitful, dishonest, cunning, clandestine, surreptitious. —**Ant.** straightforward, aboveboard, forthright, open, candid.

understand, *v.* **1.** perceive, grasp, realize, comprehend, interpret, conceive, know, see, apprehend, discern, envision, appreciate, recognize, get the drift of, be conversant with, catch on to. **2.** learn, hear, gather, get wind of, take it, be advised. —**Ant.** misunderstand.

understanding, *n.* **1.** comprehension, awareness, grasp, knowledge, mastery, acquaintance, familiarity, deftness, adroitness, skill, competence, proficiency, expertise, know-how. **2.** interpretation, opinion, apprehension, opinion, reading, view, judgement, perception, estimation, viewpoint. **3.** intelligence, wisdom, intellect, mind, brain, reason, sense; discernment, insight, intuition, discrimination, penetration, sensitivity, sympathy, enlightenment, sagacity, savvy. **4.** agreement, contract, bargain, settlement, pact, covenant, accord, treaty, reconciliation, settlement, arrangement, alliance.

undine, *n.* sprite, water nymph, sylph.

undying, *adj.* immortal, deathless, endless, unceasing, interminable, infinite, perpetual, continuous, imperishable, timeless, constant, indestructible, sempiternal, perdurable, lasting, unending, eternal, everlasting, permanent. —**Ant.** mortal, temporary, short-lived, evanescent, ephemeral.

unearthly, *adj.* otherworldly, extraterrestrial, extrasensory, supernatural, preternatural, ghostly, spectral, unnatural, inexplicable, weird, unreal, uncanny, spooky, creepy, strange, eerie, bizarre; sublime, celestial, heavenly, empyreal. —**Ant.** earthly, terrestrial.

uneasy, *adj.* disquieted, upset, ill at ease, unquiet, nervous, restless, restive, impatient, jittery, jumpy, skittish, fidgety, hectic, agitated, disturbed, perturbed, anxious, worried, concerned, apprehensive, on edge, edgy, uncomfortable, flustered, discombobulated, troubled, angst-ridden, fretful, uncertain.

uneducated, *adj.* untutored, un-

schooled, unenlightened, benighted, uninstructed, unread, uncultured, uncultivated, untaught, uninformed, unlettered, illiterate, ignorant. —**Ant.** cultivated, cultured, literate.

unemployed, *adj.* unoccupied, idle, out of work, inactive, twiddling one's thumbs, at leisure, at liberty, jobless, between engagements. —**Ant.** employed, working, on the job, busy.

unequaled, *adj.* unparalleled, nonpariel, transcendant, sublime, surpassing, supreme, superlative, superior, outstanding, extraordinary, superb, unique, original, sui generis, matchless, unmatched, unsurpassed, unrivaled, peerless, inimitable, incomparable, beyond compare. —**Ant.** ordinary, run-of-the-mill, mediocre.

unexpected, *adj.* unforeseen, unlooked-for, unannounced, undreamt-of, unanticipated, precipitate, sudden, abrupt; surprising, shocking, stunning, startling, fortuitous, chance. —**Ant.** expected, foreseen, anticipated, gradual.

unfair, *adj.* **1.** biased, partial, prejudiced, jaundiced, unjust, inequitable, unreasonable. **2.** unscrupulous, dishonest, underhanded, dishonorable, crooked, untrustworthy, corrupt, base, heinous, iniquitous, wrongful, cheating, sneaky, shifty, wily. —**Ant.** fair.

unfaithful, *adj.* **1.** false, disloyal, perfidious, faithless, treacherous, treasonous, seditious, traitorous, deceitful, recreant, untrustworthy, unreliable, undependable. **2.** fickle, untrue, inconstant; philandering, cheating, adulterous. —**Ant.** faithful, steadfast, loyal, true, constant.

unfavorable, *adj.* disadvantageous, unpropitious, inauspicious, inopportune, unfortunate, ominous, disastrous, adverse, inimical. —**Ant.** favorable.

unfeeling, *adj.* insensible, insensate, numb; callous, unsympathetic, inured, hardened, tough, stolid, unresponsive, cold, heartless, affectless, unaffected, insensitive, stony-hearted, uncompassionate, thick-skinned, hard-boiled, hard-nosed, apathetic, uncaring, indifferent, hard, hardhearted. —**Ant.** feeling, sympathetic.

unfortunate, *adj.* **1.** unlucky, unhappy, luckless, unsuccessful, jinxed, cursed, woebegone, pathetic, doomed, ill-fated, pitiable, pitiful, wretched, miserable, sorry, hopeless, hapless, star-crossed, ill-starred, born under a bad sign. **2.** inauspicious, unpropitious, ominous, sinister, portentous. —**Ant.** fortunate.

unfriendly, *adj.* inimical, antagonistic, contrary, unsympatethic, inhospitable, cold, remote, aloof, distant, haughty, standoffish, formal, unsociable, unapproachable, rancorous, adversarial, contentious, hateful, malevolent, hostile, unkind. —**Ant.** friendly.

ungodly, *adj.* irreligious, impious, godless, antireligious, heathen, accursed, blasphemous, heretical, iconoclastic, atheistic, sacrilegious, demonic, diabolical, satanic, feindish, infernal, hellish, damnable, damned, sinful, piacular, profane; wicked, depraved, dissolute, iniquitous, beastly, degenerate, unrepentant, filthy, indecent, polluted, corrupted, base, immoral, heinous, dissolute, blackhearted, perverted, lawless, execrable, vile, evil. —**Ant.** godly.

unguarded, *adj.* **1.** unprotected, undefended, open, naked, uncovered, exposed, vulnerable, helpless, assailable, in jeopardy, at risk, defenseless. **2.** incautious, inattentive, heedless, unthinking, indiscreet, unwise, hasty, imprudent, thoughtless, careless. —Ant. guarded, protected; cautious, careful.

unhappy, adj. **1.** sad, miserable, wretched, sorrowful, depressed, dejected, melancholy, gloomy, glum, dolorous, dispirited, troubled, crestfallen, chapfallen, down in the dumps or mouth, despondent, woeful, woebegone, downcast, cheerless, disconsolate, inconsolable, distressed, afflicted. **2.** unlucky, unfortunate, hapless, hopeless, woebegone, pitiable, pitiful, doomed, cursed, jinxed, ill-starred, star-crossed, unsuccessful. **3.** unfavorable, disastrous, ill-omened, calamitous, inauspicious, unpropitious. **4.** infelicitous, inappropriate, inapt, unapt, inexpedient, ill-advised. —Ant. happy.

unhealthy, adj. **1.** sick, sickly, delicate, frail, weak, feeble, enfeebled, ill, ailing, under the weather, off one's feed, not up to snuff, unwell, debilitated, unsound, indisposed, bedridden, invalid, out of commission, diseased, afflicted. **2.** unwholesome, unhealthful, unsanitary, unhygienic, insalubrious, deleterious, poisonous, harmful, detrimental, injurious, malign, toxic, noxious. —Ant. healthy.

uniform, adj. **1.** homogeneous, consistent, unaltered, invariable, unchanging, unwavering, unvarying, unvaried, unchanged, constant, steady, stable, regular. **2.** undiversified, unvariegated, dun, solid, plain. **3.** regular, even, unbroken, smooth. **4.** agreeing, alike, similar, parallel, identical, analogous, comparable, akin. —Ant. heterogeneous; variegated; uneven; dissimilar.

unimportant, adj. trivial, trifling, paltry, nugatory, secondary, insignificant, petty, slight, unimposing, puny, insubstantial, nonsubstantive, negligible, minor, irrelevant, obscure, inconsequential, small-time, second-rate, niggling, piddling, picayune, inappreciable, worthless, not worth mentioning, silly, frivolous, of no account or concern, immaterial, unimpressive, low-level, bush-league, minor-league, penny-ante, small potatoes, not worth shaking a stick at, not worth one's time. —Ant. important.

union, n. **1.** junction, combination, conjunction, amalgamation, fusion, synthesis, mixture, unification, solidarity, integration, concatenation, unity, coalition. **2.** society, association, organization, club, circle, fellowship, syndicate, coalition, federation, fraternity, sorority, brotherhood, sisterhood, team, gang, party, bloc, league, confederacy, alliance. **3.** marriage, matrimony, wedlock. **4.** agreement, harmony, congruity, coherence, compatibility, consonance, accord. —Ant. separation, sundering; divorce; disharmony, incongruity.

unique, adj. **1.** sole, only, single, lone, solitary, separate, particular. **2.** unequaled, unexcelled, unparalleled, unrivaled, incomparable, beyond compare, second to none, unsurpassed, inimitable, matchless, peerless. **3.** rare, unusual, singular, odd, eccentric, erratic, queer, quaint, outlandish, curious, peculiar, strange, uncommon, once in a lifetime, exceptional, infrequent. —Ant. common, usual.

unite, v. **1.** join, combine, unify, merge, intermix, relate, integrate, bring together, incorporate, connect, couple, link, yoke, associate. **2.** combine, amalgamate, compound, blend, coalesce, bond, alloy, bind, glue, fasten, fuse, weld, consolidate. **3.** marry, wed,

join together, link, connect, merge. —Ant. separate, part, sever.

unity, n. **1.** oneness, union, singleness, singularity, individuality, integrity, congruity, uniformity, homogeneity, identity, similarity, sameness, likeness. **2.** concord, harmony, agreement, unison, concert, unanimity, uniformity, consistency, constancy, consensus, solidarity, compatibility, concurrence, continuity, rapport, sympathy, likemindedness. —Ant. difference; disagreement.

universal, adj. general, generic, prevalent, widespread, ubiquitous, omnipresent, catholic, common, worldwide, wide-ranging, encompassing, all-encompassing, cosmic. —Ant. particular.

unjust, adj. **1.** inequitable, partial, unfair, prejudiced, biased, unreasonable, jaundiced. **2.** undeserved, unjustified, unjustifiable, unmerited, unfounded, illegitimate, wrongful, improper, unlawful, indefensible, unwarranted, inexcusable. —Ant. just, evenhanded, objective, impartial; condign, fitting, well-deserved.

unkind, adj. harsh, cruel, unmerciful, unfeeling, unsympathetic, insensitive, uncaring, heartless, thoughtless, unthoughtful, inconsiderate, callous, tough, stern, severe, mean, distressing. —Ant. kind.

unlawful, adj. illegal, illicit, illegitimate, criminal, felonious, lawless, outlawed, banned, forbidden, taboo, prohibited, proscribed, interdicted, disallowed, unauthorized, unsanctioned. —Ant. lawful, legal.

unlike, adj. different, dissimilar, diverse, distinct, opposite, contrasting, divergent, separate, incompatible, incongruous, unequal, disparate, variant, heterogeneous. —Ant. like.

unlikely adj. improbable, implausible, doubtful, dubious, unrealistic, farfetched, remote, hard to imagine, unimaginable, unexpected, unthinkable, inconceivable, unanticipated, unpredictable, questionable, surprising, startling, odd, peculiar, strange, weird, unsuitable, inappropriate. —Ant. likely.

unlimited, adj. unrestricted, unconstrained, unrestrained, unqualified, unconditional, full, absolute; endless, immense, immeasurable, innumerable, myriad, boundless, unfettered, limitless, unbounded, vast, extensive, infinite, inexhaustible, interminable, never-ending. —Ant. limited.

unlucky, adj. **1.** luckless, unfortunate, hapless, hopeless, doomed, cursed, wretched, miserable, pathetic, unhappy, star-crossed, ill-fated, unsuccessful, ill-omened. **2.** sinister, portentous, ominous, menacing, inauspicious, unpropitious, unpromising, fateful, baneful, malign, adverse. —Ant. lucky.

unmindful, adj. heedless, indifferent, lax, remiss, derelict, slack, inadvertent, regardless, careless, inattentive, neglectful, negligent, unobservant, forgetful, oblivious. —Ant. mindful, solicitous, careful, concerned, attentive.

unmistakable, adj. clear, plain, manifest, unambiguous, unequivocal, explicit, indisputable, unquestionable, definite, evident, obvious, palpable, patent. —Ant. unclear, dim.

unmitigated, adj. unqualified, absolute, categorical, sheer, total, perfect, plain, utter, unalloyed, relentless, out-and-out, thoroughgoing, complete, consummate. —Ant. softened, lessened.

unnatural, adj. **1.** affected, forced,

strained, theatrical, artificial, contrived, labored, stilted, self-conscious, mannered, insincere, feigned, false. **2.** unusual, strange, abnormal, irregular, anomalous, aberrant, odd, peculiar, queer, unexpected, uncharacteristic, out of character, atypical. **3.** bizarre, weird, uncanny, freakish, outlandish, preternatural, supernatural, queer, grotesque, spooky, strange, extraordinary, monstrous, prodigious, fantastic, abnormal. —Ant. natural.

unnecessary, adj. needless, superfluous, extra, dispensable, expendable, disposable, surplus, inessential, supererogatory, de trop. —Ant. necessary.

unnerve, v. weaken, enfeeble, sap, undermine, undo, discourage, enervate, disarm, agitate, perturb, ruffle, rattle, dismay, faze, shake, fluster, disconcert, upset, nonplus, throw for a loop, intimidate, bewilder, distract, confound, stupefy, stun, discombobulate. —Ant. steel, encourage.

unparalleled, adj. matchless, unmatched, unequaled, unrivaled, peerless, incomparable, inimitable, superlative, singular, unique, rare, one of a kind, exceptional, consummate. —Ant. typical, ordinary, mediocre.

unpleasant, adj. unpleasing, disagreeable, objectionable, uncomfortable, unsavory, unpalatable, unappetizing, offensive, obnoxious, noisome, repulsive, repellent, revolting, nauseating, odious, abominable, noxious. —Ant. pleasant.

unpretentious, adj. modest, unassuming, unpresuming, simple, plain, homely, ordinary, unexceptional, shy, abashed, bashful, self-effacing, humble, demure, diffident, reticent, unostentatious, inconspicuous, understated, moderate, reserved, retiring, unobtrusive, down to earth. —Ant. pretentious.

unprincipled, adj. unscrupulous, unethical, immoral, amoral, lawless, ungodly, dishonest, dishonorable, corrupt, perverse, perverted, base, calculating, conniving, tricky, shrewd, cagey, crafty, scheming, canny, wily, guileful, sneaky, duplicitous, deceptive, perfidious, treacherous, double-dealing, underhanded, conscienceless, criminal, unjust, untrustworthy, disreputable, louche, crooked, fiendish, diabolical, iniquitous, indecent, depraved, dissolute, wicked, bad, evil, vile, selfish, Machiavellian. —Ant. principled, scrupulous.

unqualified, adj. **1.** unfit, incompetent, ineligible, unsuited, untrained, unprepared, ill-suited, unsuitable. **2.** absolute, unmitigated, out-and-out, thorough, complete, direct, unrestricted, unreserved, unconditional, categorical, consummate, perfect, sheer, outright, downright. —Ant. qualified, competent, capable, able.

unquestionable, adj. indisputable, indubitable, incontrovertible, undeniable, irrefutable, incontestable, unequivocal, unmistakable, unambiguous, unimpeachable, positive, certain, sure, definite, patent, clear, obvious, conclusive. —Ant. questionable, dubious, uncertain.

unquiet, adj. restless, restive, impatient, troubled, anxious, worried, concerned, hectic, feverish, fevered, disordered, unsettled, turbulent, tumultuous, disturbed, agitated, upset, vexed, dismayed, alarmed, apprehensive, ill at ease, uneasy, nervous, perturbed, fidgety, jittery, skittish, jumpy, edgy, on edge, on pins and needles, on tenterhooks, discombobulated. —Ant. quiet.

unreal, *adj.* **1.** imaginary, fantastic, phantasmagorical, fanciful, fancied, fictitious, illusory, supernatural, chimerical, spectral, nonexistent, make-believe, made-up, mythical, pretend. **2.** synthetic, mock, counterfeit, fake, phony, bogus, falsified, false, unnatural, simulated, imitation, artificial, sham, spurious. **3.** unrealistic, visionary, idealistic, unworkable, speculative, hypothetical, conjectural, suppositional, pie in the sky, abstract, academic, theoretical, impractical. —**Ant.** real.

unreasonable, *adj.* **1.** irrational, illogical, brainless, senseless, foolish, silly, preposterous, ridiculous, ludicrous, laughable, insane, crazy, far-fetched, absurd, stupid, nonsensical, idiotic, fatuous, asinine, myopic, blind. **2.** immoderate, exorbitant, excessive, inordinate, outrageous, unwarranted, unjustifiable, extortionate, unjust, unfair, extravagant. —**Ant.** reasonable.

unrefined, *adj.* **1.** unpurified, impure, raw, natural, unprocessed, coarse, harsh, crude. **2.** unpolished, uncultivated, unsophisticated, plebeian, ill-bred, inelegant, callow, uncultured, rude, boorish, loutish, uncouth, gauche, bumbling, awkward, provincial, primitive, ignorant, barbaric, brutish, vulgar, gross. —**Ant.** refined.

unrelenting, *adj.* unabating, relentless, continual, unremitting, implacable, inexorable, merciless, ruthless, remorseless, pitiless, grim, obdurate, adamant, inflexible, rigid, severe, cruel, hard, bitter, harsh, stern, austere. —**Ant.** forbearing.

unruffled, *adj.* smooth, calm, placid, unperturbed, tranquil, serene, collected, imperturbable, cool, sedate, steady, even, untroubled, self-possessed, relaxed, laid-back, dispassionate, composed, peaceful, self-controlled, undisturbed. —**Ant.** ruffled, agitated, turbulent.

unruly, *adj.* ungovernable, undisciplined, uncooperative, defiant, wayward, disobedient, insubordinate, unmanageable, uncontrollable, refractory, fractious, adamantine, stubborn, obstreperous, recalcitrant, intractable, willful, headstrong, rebellious, contumacious, perverse, contrary; lawless, turbulent, tumultuous, mutinous, violent, tempestuous, rowdy, boisterous, wild, disorderly, riotous. —**Ant.** obedient, tractable, docile.

unsatisfactory, *adj.* disappointing, deficient, wanting, lacking, failing, losing, incomplete, inadequate, insufficient, imperfect, faulty, defective, flawed, inferior, mediocre, unacceptable, weak, below par, substandard, displeasing, unfulfilling, intolerable. —**Ant.** satisfactory.

unsavory, *adj.* tasteless, unpleasant, offensive, obnoxious, disagreeable, objectionable, unappetizing, unpalatable, disgusting, repellent, nauseating, revolting, sickening, rotten, distasteful. —**Ant.** savory, tasteful.

unscrupulous, *adj.* conscienceless, unprincipled, dishonorable, dishonest, unethical, immoral, amoral, wicked, evil, lawless, antisocial, corrupt, untrustworthy, treacherous, iniquitous, insidious, sly, cunning, shifty, slippery, sneaky, crooked, vile, depraved, dissolute, unregenerate, reprobate, nefarious, base, villainous, Machiavellian, double-dealing, deceptive, deceitful. —**Ant.** scrupulous, principled, moral, ethical.

unseemly, *adj.* in poor or bad taste, out of place, undignified, unfitting, unbecoming, improper, indecorous, inde-

cent, naughty, offensive, objectionable, coarse, rude, indelicate, unbefitting, shameful, disreputable, unsuitable, discreditable, inappropriate. —**Ant.** seemly, fitting, proper, appropriate.

unselfish *adj.* generous, giving, magnanimous, kind, kindly, openhanded, goodhearted, bighearted, beneficent, benevolent, charitable, lavish, unstinting, ungrudging, unsparing, liberal, altruistic, selfless, high-minded, self-sacrificing, self-abnegating, humane, humanitarian, philanthropic, obliging, considerate, thoughtful, compassionate, solicitous, gracious, caring, loving. —**Ant.** selfish, grasping, self-indulgent, mean.

unsettled, *adj.* unstable, unsteady, shaky, undependable, unsure, unfixed, undetermined, indeterminate, changeable, variable, inconstant, unpredictable, fluctuating, wavering, vacillating, fickle, faltering, irresolute. —**Ant.** settled, stable, steady.

unsightly, *adj.* unpleasant, unprepossessing, homely, plain, ill-favored, unattractive, ugly, disagreeable, hideous, frightful, awful, monstrous, grotesque, repulsive. —**Ant.** beautiful.

unskillful, *adj.* untrained, inexpert, unaccomplished, untalented, inept, incompetent, unqualified, unprofessional, bumbling, all thumbs, awkward, bungling, clumsy, maladroit. —**Ant.** skillful.

unsophisticated, *adj.* simple, inexperienced, childlike, unworldly, innocent, green, callow, artless, ingenuous, guileless, naive, provincial, downhome, natural, unrefined, unpolished, uncultured, uncultivated, inelegant. —**Ant.** sophisticated.

unsound, *adj.* **1.** diseased, debilitated, feeble, afflicted, impaired, sickly, sick, ill, ailing, delicate, injured, wounded, infirm, unhealthy, unwholesome. **2.** fallacious, unfounded, invalid, false, erroneous, untenable, illogical, flawed, specious, meretricious, spurious, faulty. **3.** frail, rickety, shaky, swobbly, defective, decayed, rotten, fragile, breakable, frangible. **4.** insane, mad, crazy, unbalanced, unstable, deranged, demented. —**Ant.** sound; healthy; valid; sturdy; sane.

unstable, *adj.* **1.** unsteady, shaky, insecure, unfixed, unmoored, unattached, loose, precarious. **2.** changeable, variable, unpredictable, unreliable, erratic, volatile, fluctuating, indefinite, mutable, unsteadfast, inconstant, fickle, capricious, mercurial, flighty, wavering, vacillating, undecided, unsettled. —**Ant.** stable, secure, fixed, firm; constant, invariable, predictable.

unsteady, *adj.* **1.** unstable, infirm, wobbly, tottering, off-balance, swaying, rocky, shaky, stumbling, trembling, staggering, teetering, unbalanced, lurching, listing, floundering, foundering, faltering. **2.** fluctuating, wavering, flickering, moving, inconstant, vacillating, fickle, changeable, unstable, irregular, uneven, erratic, variable. **3.** irregular, uneven, stop-and-go, halting, sporadic, fitful, intermittent, periodic, spasmodic. —**Ant.** steady; upright, stable; constant, even; regular, uniform, consistent.

unsuccessful, *adj.* **1.** ineffective, inefficient, ineffectual, unproductive, unprofitable, worthless, vain, unavailing, useless, fruitless, bootless, abortive, sterile, luckless, pointless, futile, losing, purposeless. **2.** defeated, beaten, foiled, confounded, stumped, hindered, frustrated, balked, checked, stopped, blocked, stymied, overcome, down and out, crushed, finished, whipped,

thwarted, disappointed, met one's Waterloo, ruined, checkmated, on the ropes or skids, KOed, knocked out, flummoxed, bankrupt, thrown in the towel, down for the count —**Ant.** successful.

unsuitable, *adj.* **1.** unseemly, improper, infelicitous, indecent, indecorous, inappropriate, unfitting, unbefitting, unbecoming. **2.** unqualified, inapt, wrong, unfit, ill-equipped, incorrect, incongruous. —**Ant.** suitable, fitting, appropriate.

unsympathetic, *adj.* uncaring, unfeeling, callous, indifferent, impassive, stolid, apathetic, stony, pitiless, ruthless, aloof, hardhearted, antipathetic, averse, unmoved, unaffected, untouched, unresponsive, cold. —**Ant.** sympathetic, compassionate, empathetic, understanding.

unthinkable, *adj.* **1.** inconceivable, incredible, beyond belief, unimaginable, incomprehensible, mind-boggling. **2.** unacceptable, impossible, out of the question, preposterous, absurd, illogical, ludicrous, laughable, unlikely. —**Ant.** credible; plausible, possible.

untidy, *adj.* slovenly, disordered, sloppy, messy, disheveled, unkempt, dirty, littered, cluttered, chaotic. —**Ant.** tidy.

untimely, *adj.* unpropitious, unseasonable, inappropriate, inopportune, premature, early, advanced, precocious. —**Ant.** timely, well-timed.

untruth, *n.* falsehood, fib, lie, fiction, story, tale, tall tale, fabrication, fable, forgery, invention, misrepresentation, prevarication, equivocation, deceit, mendacity, dishonesty, distortion, duplicity. —**Ant.** truth, veracity.

unusual, *adj.* uncommon, irregular, atypical, different, unconventional, unorthodox, infrequent, extraordinary, exceptional, rare, strange, remarkable, singular, curious, queer, peculiar, bizarre, freakish, unique, weird, odd. —**Ant.** usual, typical, common, ordinary.

unwary, *adj.* incautious, unguarded, imprudent, unwise, indiscreet, hasty, careless, rash, heedless, precipitous, impetuous, foolhardy, reckless, thoughtless, headlong. —**Ant.** wary, careful, prudent.

unwholesome, *adj.* unhealthy, unhygienic, unhealthful, deleterious, detrimental, harmful, injurious, noxious, noisome, poisonous, toxic, baneful, pernicious. —**Ant.** wholesome.

unwieldy, *adj.* bulky, unmanageable, clumsy, awkward, cumbersome, ungainly, oversized, ponderous, heavy. —**Ant.** manageable, light.

upbraid, *v.* reproach, chide, reprove, reprimand, scold, rebuke, berate, chastise, castigate, blame, censure, take to task, rake (someone) over the coals, call (someone) on the carpet, bawl out, chew out. —**Ant.** praise.

uphold, *v.* **1.** support, sustain, maintain, approve, sanction, embrace, back, defend, protect, justify, aid, vindicate, promote, preserve, espouse, endorse, advocate, champion. **2.** raise, elevate. —**Ant.** attack, subvert.

uplifting, *adj.* spiritual, civilizing, elevating, exalting, inspiriting, inspiring, edifying, improving, bettering, educational, instructive, enlightening. —**Ant.** debasing, degrading.

uppity, *adj.* arrogant, haughty, impertinent, insolent, pompous, pretentious, overwhelming, high and mighty, affected, disdainful, scornful, presumptuous, cocky, sassy, saucy, supercilious, snobbish, snobby, stuck-up, snooty, hifalutin, hoity-toity, on one's high horse. —**Ant.** modest, unassuming, down to earth.

upright, *adj.* honest, just, fair, conscientious, scrupulous, principled, moral, ethical, righteous, honorable, straight, straightforward, aboveboard, virtuous, true, good, pure, high-minded, upstanding, decent, trustworthy, unimpeachable, incorruptible. —**Ant.** dishonest, conniving.

uprising, *n.* insurrection, revolt, revolution, rebellion, mutiny, riot, coup d' état, dissension, conflict, strife, violence. —**Ant.** pacification.

uproar, *n.* disturbance, tumult, disorder, turbulence, commotion, hubbub, furor, din, clamor, noise; outcry, babel, bedlam, pandemonium, strife, discord, brouhaha, racket, rumpus, brawl, donnybrook, fracas, melee, riot. —**Ant.** peace, quiet.

upset, *v.* **1.** overturn, capsize, upend, invert, spill, topple, turn, topsy-turvy, reverse. **2.** overthrow, defeat, depose, displace, thrash, rout, overcome, vanquish, beat, triumph over. **3.** disturb, distress, trouble, ruffle, dismay, worry, bother, unsettle, frighten, derange, unnerve, disconcert, agitate, perturb, fluster. —*n.* **4.** overturn, overthrow, defeat, conquest, triumph, victory, rout. —*adj.* **5.** disordered, muddled, confused, chaotic, untidy, messy; sloppy. **6.** worried, troubled, unnerved, distracted, dismayed, apprehensive, nervous, anxious, angstridden, frightened, fearful, on edge, distressed, deranged, off balance, flustered, queasy, uneasy, sick at heart, disheartened, bewildered, rattled, fazed, discombulated, concerned, disconcerted, agitated, disturbed, perturbed, irritated, vexed, bothered, in a state, freaked out, beside oneself. —**Ant.** steady, stable.

urbane, *adj.* sophisticated, knowing, diplomatic, tactful, civil, poised, cultured, cultivated, well-bred, courteous, polite, refined, elegant, polished, smooth, savvy, suave. —**Ant.** unsophisticated, unrefined, boorish, discourteous, impolite.

urge, *v.* **1.** push, force, impel, drive. **2.** press, push, hasten, accelerate, speed, hurry, rush, hustle. **3.** impel, constrain, move, activate, animate, incite, instigate, goad, stimulate, spur, egg on, prompt, exhort. **4.** induce, persuade, solicit, beg, beseech, importune, entreat, implore. **5.** insist upon, allege, assert, aver, argue, demand, affirm, hold, declare. **6.** recommend, suggest, counsel, persuade, advocate, advise. —*n.* **7.** impulse, pressure, impetus, desire, compulsion, itch, yen, hunger, drive, longing, yearning, thirst, craving, lust, appetite, passion. —**Ant.** deter, discourage.

urgent, *adj.* **1.** pressing, compelling, vital, life-and-death, exigent, emergency, rush, imperative, immediate, top priority, requisite, necessary. **2.** insistent, earnest, eager, energetic, tenacious, firm, forceful. —**Ant.** unimportant.

use, *v.* **1.** employ, utilize, make use of, apply, avail oneself of, exercise, resort to, have recourse to. **2.** expend, deplete, run through, consume, use up, waste, exhaust. —*n.* **3.** employment, usage, utilization, application, exercise. **4.** utility, function, account, usefulness, service, advantage, profit, benefit, avail. **5.** help, profit, good, purpose, point, object, reason, end, advantage. **6.** custom, practice, usage, habit, routine. convention, tradition. **7.** treatment, management, operation,

manipulation, wielding, handling. —**Ant.** disuse.

useful, *adj.* **1.** serviceable, advantageous, profitable, helpful, expedient, valuable, fruitful, productive, worthwhile, effectual, effective, efficacious, beneficial, salutary. **2.** practical, practicable, workable, functional, utilitarian, usable. —**Ant.** useless.

useless, *adj.* **1.** unavailing, futile, fruitless, vain, ineffectual, ineffective, abortive, impractical, pointless, idle, unsuccessful, profitless, bootless, valueless, worthless, hopeless. **2.** unserviceable, unusable, inept, hopeless, incompetent, inefficient, unproductive. —**Ant.** useful.

usual, *adj.* habitual, accustomed, same, customary; common, ordinary, familiar, prevailing, prevalent, everyday, conventional, stock, workaday, normal, routine, typical, general, frequent, regular, expected, predictable, settled, constant, fixed, well-known, established, traditional, set, stereotypical, unexceptional, unremarkable, unoriginal. —**Ant.** unusual.

usually, *adv.* as a rule, for the most part, generally, typically, almost always, predominantly, chiefly, in the main, mainly, by and large, mostly, normally, commonly, regularly, predominantly.

utensil, *n.* instrument, tool, vessel, gadget, household item, implement, appliance, device, contrivance, contraption, invention.

utilitarian, *adj.* useful, practical, serviceable, helpful, functional, pragmatical, workaday, handy, convenient, effective, valuable, advantageous. —**Ant.** impractical, useless.

utter, *v.* **1.** express, speak, enunciate, articulate, pronounce, say, voice, vent, air, broach. **2.** publish, declare, proclaim, announce, promulgate. —*adj.* **3.** complete, total, sheer, thorough, thoroughgoing, unreserved, out-and-out, downright, categorical, absolute, unconditional, unqualified, entire. —**Ant.** partial, incomplete, relative.

V

vacant, *adj.* **1.** empty, void, hollow, devoid or destitute of, lacking, wanting. **2.** untenanted, unoccupied, empty, uninhabited, deserted, abandoned. **3.** free, unoccupied, unemployed, spare, extra, unfilled, unengaged, unspoken-for, leisure, unencumbered. **4.** unthinking, thoughtless, abstracted, vacuous, blank, expressionless, deadpan, dull, absentminded, uncomprehending, inane, fatuous. —**Ant.** full; occupied; busy; thoughtful.

vacate, *v.* quit, abandon, leave, depart, abandon, evacuate, desert, forsake, withdraw from, relinquish, clear or move out. —**Ant.** occupy.

vacillate, *v.* fluctuate, waver, hesitate, falter, demur, scruple, vary, seesaw, shift, change.

vacuous, *adj.* vacant, empty, hollow, void, blank, insipid, vapid, fatuous, foolish, silly, asinine, inane, spacey, abstracted, absentminded, oblivious, uncomprehending, emptyheaded, airheaded, vapid, bubblebrained, out to lunch, nobody home. —**Ant.** serious, attentive, alert, on the qui vive, intelligent.

vague, *adj.* **1.** indefinite, unspecific, general, ill-defined, hazy, fuzzy, blurred, misty, foggy, shadowy, un-

clear, inexact, inchoate, shapeless, amorphous, imprecise, obscure, dim, indistinct. **2.** unclear, indeterminate, ambiguous, equivocal, nonspecific, unspecified, inexact, in doubt, uncertain, unknown, unfixed, lax, loose. —**Ant.** definite, specific, lucid.

vain, *adj.* **1.** useless, hollow, idle, unsuccessful, empty, abortive, unproductive, worthless, unimportant, nugatory, otiose, empty, puny, paltry, petty, trifling, trivial, ineffective, ineffectual, unavailing, pointless, profitless, bootless, unfruitful, futile. **2.** conceited, haughty, boastful, bragging, cocky, self-centered, self-important, swellheaded, narcissistic, egotistical, complacent, self-satisfied, smug, proud, arrogant, overweening, preening, pompous, inflated, stuck-up, stuck on oneself. —**Ant.** useful, productive, successful, effective; modest, down to earth, meek, diffident, humble.

valiant, *adj.* brave, bold, courageous, stouthearted, intrepid, heroic, gallant, dauntless, undaunted, daring, audacious, fearless, staunch, stalwart, tough, strong, gutsy, plucky, spunky, spirited, determined, resolute, tenacious, indomitable. —**Ant.** timid, cowardly.

valid, *adj.* just, well-founded, sound, convincing, telling, conclusive, definitive, decisive, substantial, logical, analytical, subtle, cogent, authoritative, forceful, effective, binding, legal, lawful, licit. —**Ant.** invalid, fallacious, deceptive, misleading.

valor, *n.* courage, boldness, heroism, prowess, gallantry, daring, audacity, mettle, tenacity, resolution, determination, fortitude, strength, invincibility, bravery, intrepidity, spirit, fearlessness, backbone, pluck, spunk, guts. —**Ant.** timidity, cowardice, faintheartedness.

valuable, *adj.* **1.** costly, expensive, rare, precious, dear, invaluable, priceless. **2.** prized, treasured, valued, appreciated, esteemed, admired, respected, worthy, estimable. **3.** useful, desirable, excellent, important, beneficial, advantageous, profitable, helpful, fruitful, productive, effective, worthwhile, significant, consequential, vital, substantial. —**Ant.** worthless, meretricious.

value, *n.* **1.** worth, merit, desirability, usefulness, utility, importance, significance, benefit. **2.** expense, charge, cost, price. **3.** valuation, evaluation, assessment, appraisal, estimation. **4.** importance, consequence, weight, significance. —*v.* **5.** estimate, rate, price, evaluate, assay, assess, appraise. **6.** regard, esteem, appreciate, prize, treasure, cherish, admire, respect.

vanish, *v.* **1.** disappear, evanesce, fade, melt away, evaporate, vaporize, dissolve, deliquesce, dwindle, disperse, dissipate, disintegrate, decompose, diminish, become invisible. **2.** end, come to an end, stop, finish, conclude, terminate, die out, perish, become extinct, peter out, expire, cease, fade. —**Ant.** appear; begin.

vanity, *n.* **1.** pride, conceit, arrogance, cockiness, haughtiness, hauteur, amour-propre, self-esteem, egotism, immodesty, narcissism, smugness, complacency, self-satisfaction, self-aggrandizement, self-importance, swellheadedness, high opinion of oneself. **2.** ostentation, pretentiousness, pretension, pomposity, pompousness, pomp, exhibitionism, flamboyance, flashiness, flash, flaunting, showiness, showing off, affectation, airs, posturing, grandi-

vanquish

osity, preening. **—Ant.** humility, modesty, diffidence.

vanquish, *v.* conquer, defeat, eliminate, overthrow, overwhelm, overcome, overpower, destroy, triumph *or* prevail over, be victorious over, get the better of, win out over, subjugate, suppress, subdue, crush, quell, rout, reduce, surmount, foil, outwit, beat, best, lick, trounce, thrash, whip, shatter. **—Ant.** lose, surrender, capitulate.

variable, *adj.* **1.** changeable, alterable, adjustable, adaptable, mutable, protean, chameleon-like, versatile, flexible. **2.** inconstant, fickle, flighty, mercurial, capricious, volatile, unpredictable, erratic, inconsistent, indecisive, irresolute, indefinite, unstable, uncertain, unreliable, undependable. **3.** changing, irregular, unfixed, vacillating, wavering, fluctuating, unsteady. **—Ant.** invariable; constant.

variance, *n.* **1.** variation, disparity, disagreement, deviation, divergence, discrepancy, diversity, disparateness, incongruity, inconsistency, unlikeness, difference. **2.** disagreement, contention, conflict, misunderstanding, argument, debate, schism, rift, difference of opinion, dispute, quarrel, controversy, dissension, discord, strife. **—Ant.** similitude, sameness, agreement.

variation, *n.* **1.** change, mutation, permutation, modulation, transformation, metamorphosis, morphing, conversion, alteration, modification, vicissitude. **2.** variance, deviation, divergence, difference, dissimilarity, unlikeness, incongruity, disparateness, discrepancy; variety, diversity. **—Ant.** sameness.

variety, *n.* **1.** variation. **2.** diversity, multiplicity, multifariousness, diversification, heterogeneity, miscellaneousness, miscellany. **3.** assortment, mixture, mix, choice, selection, range, choice, collection, group. **4.** kind, sort, type, category, brand, make, breed, order, genre, strain, class, species. **—Ant.** sameness, monotony.

various, *adj.* **1.** differing, different, distinct, separate, individual. **2.** several, many, multiple, numerous, manifold, multifarious, miscellaneous, diverse, sundry, varied. **—Ant.** uniform, identical, same, similar.

vary, *v.* **1.** change, alter, diversify, reorganize, modulate, modify. **2.** transform, metamorphose, convert, transmute, change. **3.** differ, deviate, depart, diverge, digress. **4.** alternate, switch, fluctuate, vacillate, shift, seesaw.

vast, *adj.* extensive, voluminous, capacious, massive, immense, huge, enormous, gigantic, colossal, tremendous, great, prodigious, stupendous, colossal, titanic, monumental, mammouth, elephantine, Brobdingnagian, behemouth; measureless, immeasurable, unbounded, boundless, unlimited, limitless, infinite, interminable, endless, never-ending, incalcuable, indeterminate, inexhaustible. **—Ant.** limited, small.

vehement, *adj.* **1.** impassioned, passionate, ardent, zealous, fervent, fervid, burning, fiery, afire, ablaze. **2.** angry, rancorous, truculent, ferocious, furious, wrathful, incensed, infuriated, fuming, all steamed up, hot under the collar, on the warpath. **3.** intense, fierce, powerful, potent, energetic, vigorous, violent, forceful. **—Ant.** mild, subdued, cool, dispassionate.

veneration, *n.* respect, reverence, worship, adoration, deference, homage, esteem, honoring, obeisance, regard, devotion, admiration, idolization, piety, adulation, deification, awe. **—Ant.** disrespect, irreverence.

vengeance, *n.* avenging, revenge, retribution, requital, retaliation, reprisal, recompense, punishment, castigation, chastisement, punitive measure. **—Ant.** forgiveness, pardon, forbearance.

venial, *adj.* excusable, forgivable, pardonable, trifling, trivial, tolerable, petty, minor, insignificant, unimportant, inconsequential. **—Ant.** inexcusable, unforgivable, mortal, heinous.

venom, *n.* **1.** poison, toxin, bane, snakebite. **2.** malice, malignity, maliciousness, animosity, hostility, enmity, antagonism, rancor, spite, spitefulness, acrimony, bitterness, acerbity, malevolence, gall, spleen, poisonousness, virulence, viciousness, meanness, jealousy, hatred, hate, contempt.

venture, *n.* **1.** hazard, danger, chance, jeopardy, risk, peril. **2.** speculation, bet, gamble, experiment, plunge, fling, wager, undertaking, enterprise. **—***v.* **3.** endanger, imperil, risk, jeopardize, hazard; gamble, bet, wager. **4.** dare, presume, make bold, volunteer, hazard, broach, offer, put forward.

verbal, *adj.* worded, linguistic, oral, vocal, enunciated, articulated, expressed, viva voce, aloud, spoken, word-of-mouth, conversational, colloquial; unwritten. **—Ant.** unarticulated, unspoken, silent, tacit; written.

verbose, *adj.* wordy, prolix, diffuse, redundant, loquacious, talkative, voluble, garrulous, grandiloquent, bombastic, flowery. **—Ant.** laconic, terse, succinct.

verge, *n.* **1.** edge, rim, margin, brim, lip, border, brink, limit. **2.** bound, end, confine, perimeter, circumference, compass, belt, strip. **—***v.* **3.** border, approach, come close to. **4.** tend, lean, incline, slope, sink, extend, stretch.

vernacular, *adj.* **1.** colloquial, informal, conversational, spoken, nonliterary, nonacademic, vulgate, vulgar, demotic, general, popular, everyday, familiar, ordinary, commonplace. **2.** local, native, regional, indigenous, autochthonous. **—***n.* **3.** vocabulary, terminology, phraseology, language, nomenclature, lexicon; tongue, speech, talk, idiom, argot, patois, patter, slang, cant, jargon, dialect, lingo.

versatile, *adj.* adaptable, flexible, adjustable, changeable, multipurpose, multifaceted, many-sided, all-round, all-purpose, general, diversified, encyclopedic, protean, resourceful, handy, inventive, creative, imaginative, ingenious, gifted, talented, multitalented, Renaissance, polymathic, polyhistoric. **—Ant.** one-sided, one-note, limited, rigid, specialized.

versed, *adj.* conversant, acquainted, informed, familiar, intimate, grounded, competent, accomplished, proficient, knowledgeable, expert, experienced, practiced, skilled, well-read, learned, lettered, cultured, cultivated. **—Ant.** uninformed, ignorant, inexpert, incompetent.

version, *n.* **1.** account, story, rendition, rendering, view, side, report, chronicle, telling, description, interpretation. **2.** variant, form, rendition, model, style, adaption, variation, variety, type, portrayal, idea, notion, concept, conception.

verve, *n.* spirit, buoyance, dash, style, stylishness, animation, life, liveliness, sparkle, energy, vigor, exuberance, effervescence, joie de vivre, brio, élan, gusto, panache, flair, enthusiasm, ardor, zeal, passion, fire, esprit, vivacity,

vivaciousness, vitality, zest, oomph, zing, pizazz, flash.

vestige, *n.* **1.** remnant, residue, relic, remains, reminder, memorial, fragment, shard, shred, scrap. **2.** trace, hint, suggestion, mark, evidence, token, glimmer, inkling, taste, sign, suspicion, soupçon.

vet, *v.* examine, inspect, check out, look over, scan, scrutinize, review, investigate, size up; appraise, verify, check, authenticate, validate, certify, corroborate, substantiate, vouch for, guarantee, warrant, back up.

vex, *v.* **1.** irritate, annoy, pester, bother, exasperate, chafe, gall, peeve, badger, plague, harass, provoke, anger, irk, fret, nettle, hassle, get on (someone's) nerves, get up (someone's) nose, get in (someone's) face. **2.** torment, trouble, distress, dismay, perturb, upset, worry, agonize. **—Ant.** delight.

viable, *adj.* tenable, sustainable, supportable, operable; workable, doable, achievable, feasible, reason, sensible, possible, practical, practicable. **—Ant.** tenuous, precarious; dubious, doubtful, impractical, unworkable.

vibrate, *v.* **1.** oscillate; swing, sway, waver, fluctuate, undulate; shake, tremble, wobble, jiggle, shudder, rock, quake, quaver, quiver, shiver, pulsate, pulse, beat, throb, palpitate. **2.** resound, echo, reverberate, resonate, ring.

vice, *n.* **1.** sin, offense, crime, scandal, transgression, trespass, infraction, breach, immorality, depravity, iniquity, sinfulness, degeneracy, evil, venality, profligacy, wickedness, corruption. **2.** shortcoming, foible, fault, failing, fraility, weakness, infirmity; flaw, blemish, blot, imperfection, defect, deficiency. **—Ant.** virtue.

vicinity, *n.* area, neighborhood, locale, locality, territory, environs, precincts, district, surroundings, environment, milieu.

vicious, *adj.* **1.** immoral, depraved, evil, villainous, nefarious, degenerate, debauched, perverted, debased, dissolute, reprobate, iniquitous, vile, profligate, sinful, corrupt, abandoned, wanton, lecherous, libidinous, lewd. **2.** spiteful, malign, malignant, malicious, malevolent, mean, nasty, venomous, rancorous, vindictive, hateful, bitter, acrimonious, defamatory, slanderous. **3.** savage, ferocious, fierce, violent, wild, untamed, brutal, bestial, ravening, feral, fiendish, unruly, illtempered, bad-tempered, refractory. **—Ant.** moral; virtuous; benign, benevolent, kindly; tame, gentle, docile, sweet.

victim, *n.* prey, quarry; martyr, sufferer, casualty, injured party, sacrificial lamb, scapegoat; dupe, fool, butt, fall guy, patsy, sap, sucker, schlemiel, schnook.

victimize, *v.* **1.** persecute, prey on, bully, harass, pursue, pick on, vex, exploit, take advantage of, use, maltreat, abuse, molest, afflict, torment, torture, oppress, tyrannize. **2.** dupe, swindle, cheat, bilk, take in, take for a ride, get the better of, set up, beguile, deceive, trick, defraud, fool, con, gull, outwit, outsmart, outfox, bamboozle, snooker, rook, flimflam, hoodwink, sucker, shaft, screw.

victory, *n.* conquest, triumph, win, ascendancy, supremacy, superiority, mastery, championship, vanquishment, upper hand, domination, defeat, subjugation, rout, success, coup. **—Ant.** defeat.

vie, *v.* compete, rival, oppose, contend,

struggle, strive, endeavor, fight, challenge, confront, battle, combat, joust.

view, *n.* **1.** sight, look, glimpse, glance, peek, peep. **2.** prospect, outlook, aspect, perspective, panorama, spectacle, landscape, picture, scene, vista. **3.** aspect, perspective, angle, position, slant, appearance. **4.** scrutiny, observation, vision, sight, study, scanning, contemplation, examination, survey, inspection. **5.** aim, intention, expectation, hope, dream, vision, prospect, purpose, reason, end, design, intent, objective, object. **6.** version, story, side, interpretation, rendition, rendering, telling, report, account, description. **7.** point of view, approach, position, conviction, standpoint, conception, idea, notion, opinion, theory, belief, judgment, estimation, assessment, understanding, feeling, sentiment, impression. —*v.* **8.** see, behold, witness, contemplate, regard, watch, observe, scrutinize, take in, look at, survey, inspect, examine, consider, assess, gauge.

vigilant, *adj.* watchful, attentive, wary, alert, observant, wide-awake, sharp, eagle-eyed, on the lookout, on the qui vive, on one's toes, on one's guard, guarded, circumspect, cautious, careful, chary. —**Ant.** inattentive, unmindful, negligent, lax, slack.

vigorous, *adj.* energetic, strenuous, dynamic, active, powerful, forceful, spirited, vital, lively, lusty, virile, hardy, hearty, stalwart, fit, athletic, tough, strong, robust, sturdy, sound, healthy, spry, peppy, full of beans. —**Ant.** weak, inactive, lethargic, languorous.

vile, *adj.* **1.** immoral, wicked, sinful, base, low, vicious, evil, depraved, corrupted, perverted, debauched, debased, dissolute, reprobate, despicable, execrable, shameless, fiendish, iniquitous. **2.** offensive, noxious, obnoxious, unpleasant, loathsome, distasteful, unsavory, objectionable, repulsive, disgusting, revolting, repellent, nauseating, repugnant, sickening, foul, filthy, nasty, dirty. **3.** vulgar, obscene, coarse, gross, lewd, licentious, salacious, scabrous, crass, smutty, rude. **4.** mean, menial, degrading, lowly, low, ignominious, ignoble, servile, demeaning, slavish, abject, sordid, shameful, beneath contempt, contemptible. **5.** valueless, paltry, miserable, wretched, petty, mean, inferior, second-rate, sorry, puny, pitiful, pathetic, worthless, cheap, tawdry, trashy, shabby, shoddy, sleazy, seedy, tacky, two-bit, chintzy, lousy, cheapjack, cheesy, crappy. —**Ant.** virtuous, moral; pleasant, delightful, tasteful; refined, genteel, elevated; noble, dignified, prestigious; valuable, first-rate.

villain, *n.* antagonist, scoundrel, criminal, traitor, turncoat, quisling, Judas, Benedict Arnold, blackguard, knave, rascal, rogue, wretch, malefactor, miscreant, reprobate, evildoer, fiend, demon, devil, archfiend, ogre, monster, brute, beast, dog, cur, hound, rat, viper, reptile, snake in the grass, heel, degenerate, pervert, bad guy, villain, worm, cur, swine, good-for-nothing, rat, stinker, louse, creep, bum, bastard, black hat, SOB, fink. —**Ant.** hero, protagonist.

vindicate, *v.* **1.** clear, exonerate, exculpate, absolve, acquit, excuse, dispel, suspicion. **2.** uphold, justify, maintain, defend, assert, support, argue for, advocate, make a case for, show evidence for. —**Ant.** convict, indict.

vindictive, *adj.* revengeful, vengeful,

spiteful, acrimonious, bitter, grim, unforgiving, rancorous, malign, malicious, vicious, venomous, mean, nasty, unrelenting, relentless, merciless, implacable. —**Ant.** forgiving, merciful.

violation, *n.* **1.** breach, disturbance, infringement, infraction, trespass, offense, sin, crime, vice, transgression. **2.** desecration, profanation, sacrilege, blasphemy, disrespect, irreverence, defilement. **3.** rape, defloration, deflowering, outrage, attack, defilement, assault, molestation, harassment, abuse, victimization. —**Ant.** respect, reverence, honoring.

violence, *n.* **1.** injury, wrong, harm, damage, wounding, outrage, injustice. **2.** force, compulsion, coercion, duress, constraint. **3.** vehemence, force, ferocity, fierceness, virulence, immoderation, roughness, fury, intensity, severity, might, power, strength, energy, vigor, acuteness. **4.** brutality, savagery, bestiality, bloodthirstiness, murderousness, wildness, frenzy, passion, cruelty, barbarousness.

virgin *adj.* **1.** pure, stainless, unsullied, undefiled, unblemished, wholesome, clean, chaste, decent, modest, virtuous, moral, good, continent, abstinent, intact. **2.** untouched, untried, unused, inexperienced, untested, unfledged, untrained, unripe, immature, budding, fresh, new, raw, green; first, initial, inaugural, maiden. —**Ant.** impure, unchaste; experienced, mature, seasoned.

virile, *adj.* masculine, manly, male, manful; dynamic, forceful, spirited, vital, lively, lusty, vigorous, potent, powerful, strong, robust, fit, hardy, stalwart, tough, athletic. —**Ant.** effeminate; impotent.

virtue, *n.* **1.** goodness, uprightness, righteousness, fairness, nobility, good conduct, morality, probity, rectitude, integrity, honor, honesty, decency, high-mindedness, character, respectability. **2.** chastity, virginity, purity, honor, innocence, abstinence, continence, self-restraint, incorruptibility. **3.** justice, prudence, temperance, fortitude; faith, hope, charity. **4.** excellence, worth, value, credit, strength, good point, merit, quality, asset. **5.** effectiveness, efficacy, force, power, potency, strength, might. —**Ant.** vice.

virtuous, *adj.* **1.** right, upright, moral, ethical, noble, just, honorable, honest, high-principled, upstanding, respectable, righteous, just, fair, high-minded, scrupulous, trustworthy, reliable, uncorrupted, uncorruptible, good. **2.** innocent, decent, proper, unsullied, virginal, chaste, pure. —**Ant.** immoral, evil.

virulent, *adj.* **1.** venomous, poisonous, toxic, pernicious, septic, miasmic, lethal, life-threatening, fatal, noxious, baneful, deleteriuos, harmful, pestilential, unhealthy, unwholesome, destructive, malignant, deadly. **2.** hostile, antagonistic, hateful, malicious, splenetic, bitter, acrimonious, spiteful, vicious, acerbic, acid, mordant, trenchant, caustic, nasty, trenchant, sarcastic. —**Ant.** harmless.

visible, *adj.* **1.** perceptible, discernible, detectable, noticeable, obvious, unmistakable, plain, clear, open. **2.** apparent, manifest, obvious, evident, open, clear, patent, palpable, conspicuous, observable, prominent, distinct, identifiable, unmistakable. —**Ant.** invisible.

vision, *n.* **1.** sight, eyesight, perception, acuity. **2.** perception, discernment, farsightedness, foresight, insight,

imagination, understanding. **3.** view, perspective, image, conception, idea, notion, dream, plan, scheme, expectation. **4.** apparition, specter, shade, wraith, revenant, unrealistic, idealistic, ghost, phantom, phantasm, illusion, chimera, fantasy, fancy, delusion, mirage, hallucination, daydream, dream, nightmare; revelation, prophecy.

visionary, *adj.* fanciful, fantastic, chimerical, quixotic, dreamy, wishful, unrealizable, unpractical, impractical, impracticable, fancied, unreal, unrealistic, idealistic, ideal, transcendent, abstract, imaginary, speculative, illusory, chimerical, romantic, sentiment, utopian, ambitious, pretentious. —**Ant.** practical, practicable.

vital, *adj.* indispensable, imperative, fundamental, cardinal, requisite, required, mandatory, compulsive, crucial, basic, central, pivotal, essential, necessary, needful, significant, consequential, momentous, weighty, important, critical. —**Ant.** unnecessary, optional, dispensable, secondary, unimportant.

vivacious, *adj.* lively, animated, effervescent, bubbly, gay, buoyant, merry, blithe, playful, jaunty, sprightly, spirited, brisk, energetic, ebullient, cheerful, sunny. —**Ant.** dull, inactive, languid, lethargic.

vivid, *adj.* **1.** bright, brilliant, intense, clear, lucid, strong, fresh, dazzling, rich, colorful, glowing, lively. **2.** picturesque, graphic, pictorial, true to life, lifelike, realistic, detailed. **3.** clear, sharp, keen, acute, lucid, powerful. **4.** strong, distinct, striking, dramatic, memorable. —**Ant.** dull, obscure, vague.

vocation, *n.* business, occupation, career, profession, calling, trade, métier, employment, pursuit, job, line of work.

vogue, *n.* **1.** fashion, style, trend, craze, look, taste, fad, latest thing, last word, *dernier cri.* **2.** popularity, preference, prevalence, fashionableness, currency, acceptance, favor, usage, custom, practice.

void, *adj.* **1.** invalid, not binding, unenforceable, inoperative, unavailing, futile, idle, pointless, useless, ineffectual, vain, ineffective, nugatory. **2.** empty, deserted, vacant. **3.** unoccupied, vacated, unfilled, unused, blank, clear. —*n.* **4.** emptiness, nothingness, vacantness, blankness, barrenness, desolation, vacuity, black hole, outer space, vacuum. **5.** gap, opening, space, vacancy, place, slot, niche, emptiness. —*v.* **6.** invalidate, nullify, annul, cancel, delete, vacate, quash, reverse, rescind, abrogate. **7.** empty, drain, purge, clear, discharge, evacuate, vacate, emit. —**Ant.** valid, full, occupied; validate; fill.

voluble, *adj.* fluent, glib, eloquent, articulate, vocal, facile; talkative, garrulous, chatty, windy, longwinded, wordy, bombastic, loquacious. —**Ant.** stammering, hesitant; curt, terse, taciturn.

volume, *n.* **1.** size, extent, dimensions, area, capacity, measure, amount, magnitude. **2.** bulk, mass, quantity, amount, supply, aggregate, abundance.

voluntary, *adj.* **1.** deliberate, considered, purposeful, remediated, volitional, willful, intentional, intended, designed, planned. **2.** spontaneous, free, elective, willing, unsolicited, gratuitous, unforced, natural, unconstrained. —**Ant.** involuntary.

voluptuous, *adj.* **1.** sensual, sensuous, carnal, sybaritic, opulent, sumptuous, indulgent, libidinous, hedonistic, pleasure-loving, gratifying, luxurious, epicurean. **2.** seductive, alluring, ravishing, enticing, luscious, shapely, buxom, full-figured, well-endowed, zaftig, sexy, curvaceous, stacked, dishy. —**Ant.** ascetic; skinny.

voracious, adj. ravenous, gorging, gluttonous, insatiable, avaricious, prodigious, grasping, acquisitive, covetous, predacious, greedy, rapacious. —**Ant.** temperate, forbearing, abstemious.

vow, v. pledge, promise, swear, give one's word, take an oath, assure, declare, guarantee.

voyage, n. trip, pilgrimage, journey, expedition, excursion, tour, trek, flight, cruise, sailing.

vulgar, adj. **1.** coarse, gross, obscene, indelicate, indecent, indecorous, tasteless, improper, dirty, off-color, lewd, smutty, filthy, pornographic, raunchy, ribald, crude, rude, low, base, vile. **2.** low-class, unrefined, boorish, uncouth, oafish, uncultivated, uncultured, gauche, base-born, ill-bred, inelegant, tasteless, common, mean, ignoble, plebeian. **3.** commonplace, common, ordinary, undistinctive, unaesthetic, banal, pedestrian. —**Ant.** decent, proper, refined; distinctive.

vulnerable, adj. **1.** defenseless, exposed, naked, open, unfortified, unprotected, unguarded, helpless, at risk, in jeopardy, assailable, at (someone's) mercy. **2.** open, susceptible, sensitive, ingenuous, naive, unwary, easily led, credulous, weak-minded, childlike, unworldly, unsuspecting, gullible, guileless, trusting, receptive, persuadable, pliant, impressionable, suggestible, liable, predisposed. —**Ant.** invulnerable, impregnable, invincible, impervious; wary, hardened, insusceptible.

W

wacky, adj. eccentric, irrational, whimsical, knockabout, clownish, slapstick, comical, hilarious, nonsensical, absurd, ludicrous, inane, lunatic, preposterous, wild, zany, madcap, foolish, silly, crazy, screwball, goofy, oddball, nuts, nutty, loony, crackpot, cracked, cuckoo, screwy, bonkers, meshuga, flaky. —**Ant.** serious, sobersided.

waffle, v. vacillate, dither, equivocate, double-talk, sidestep, skirt, evade, dodge, mislead, deceive, hedge, quibble, be undecided, shift, waver, seesaw, fluctuate, hem and haw, shilly-shally, beat around the bush, yo-yo.

wage, n. **1.** (usually plural) money, fee, payment, pay, salary, stipend, earnings, emolument, compensation, remuneration, income, allowance; recompense, return, reward, comeuppance. —v. **2.** carry on, undertake, pursue, conduct, practice, proceed with, engage in.

wait, v. **1.** stay, rest, remain, be inactive, repose, linger, abide, tarry, pause, delay, postpone, loiter, bide one's time, mark or waste time, sit tight, shilly-shally, hang fire. —n. **2.** delay, stay, holdup, postponement, lull, interruption, discontinuation, halt, pause, stop, break, rest, interval, gap, hiatus, intermission, recess, breather, abeyance, lapse, rest period. —**Ant.** go, depart, leave, proceed.

waive, v. **1.** relinquish, forgo, resign, abdicate, forsake, cede, abandon, yield, forbear, sacrifice, surrender, renounce, give up, remit. **2.** defer, put

off or aside, postpone, overlook, disregard, ignore. —**Ant.** require, demand, claim.

wake, v. **1.** awake, stir, come to, regain consciousness, rise, arise, get up. **2.** rouse, waken, arouse, stir, rally, awaken. **3.** stimulate, activate, animate, inspire, bring to life, vitalize, kindle, provoke, motivate, excite, quicken, galvanize, inflame, fire, impel, drive. —n. —**Ant.** sleep; lull; subdue, pacify.

walk, v. **1.** step, stride, stroll, pace, trot, amble, stride, ramble, shamble, pad, shuffle, saunter, sashay, flounce, mince, trip, sidle, tiptoe, waddle, perambulate, promenade, parade, swagger, strut, prance, stamp, march, tramp, hike, trudge, slog, trek, plod, traipse, trek, trundle, tread, go by shanks' mare. —n. **2.** stroll, promenade, trek, slog, amble, saunter, ramble, march, tramp, hike, constitutional.

wan, adj. washed out, pale, pallid, sickly, ashen, white, livid, pasty, bloodless, sallow, colorless, ghastly, drawn, haggard, worn, cadaverous, fatigued, tired, anemic, weak, feeble. —**Ant.** ruddy, robust.

wander, v. **1.** ramble, rove, roam, stray, range, stroll, meander, saunter, prowl, gad about, traipse, gallivant, drift, cruise. **2.** ramble, curve, wind, meander, zigzag, bend, twist, snake. **3.** deviate, err, go astray, digress, drift, lapse. **4.** rave, be delirious or incoherent, babble, ramble, gibber, maunder.

wane, v. decrease, decline, dwindle, lessen, abate, subside, ebb, fade, diminish, fail, sink. —n. —**Ant.** wax.

wangle, v. manipulate, maneuver, engineer, manage, fix, fiddle, finagle, connive, machinate, scheme, plot, intrigue, connive, con, talk into, pull off, angle, swing.

want, v. **1.** desire, wish, long for, pine for, hope for, crave, covet, lust after, hunger or thirst for, have an itch or yen for, yearn for, aspire to, aim for, pant after; need, miss, demand, necessitate, require, lack. —n. **2.** necessity, need, exigency, requirement, desideratum. **3.** lack, absence, privation, shortage, dearth, scarcity, scarceness, inadequacy, insufficiency, scantiness, paucity, meagerness, deficiency, defect, defectiveness. **4.** destitution, poverty, need, homelessness, pinch, bankruptcy, insolvency, privation, penury, indigence, straits. —**Ant.** reject; plenty, abundance, plethora, superfluity; wealth, affluence.

wanton, adj. **1.** immoral, evil, wicked, vicious, cruel, violent, malicious, malevolent, merciless, inhumane, spiteful, perverse, contrary. **2.** deliberate, calculated, willful, unprovoked, groundless, arbitrary, gratuitous, unjustifiable, supererogatory, unwarranted, uncalled for. **3.** unruly, wayward, ungovernable, intractable, daring, heedless, foolhardy, uninhibited, unrestrained, unbridled, wild, reckless. **4.** unchaste, abandoned, dissipated, debauched, degenerate, depraved, hedonistic, loose, lascivious, lewd, licentious, dissolute, lustful, prurient, libertine, lecherous, salacious, incontinent, concupiscent, libidinous. **5.** extravagant, excessive, profligate, lavish, wasteful, extreme, outrageous, profuse, immoderate, intemperate, improvident, undue, unwarranted, unconscionable, incontinent. —**Ant.** moral, virtuous; justifiable, restrained, sober, inhibited; chaste, pure; moderate, temperate.

war, n. **1.** fighting, warfare, military action, military operations, military expedition, military campaign, clash of

arms, armed conflict, combat, struggle, conflict, hostilities, aggression, strife, battle, pitched battle, encounter, engagement, clash, fray, confrontation, attack, counterattack, assault, skirmish, encroachment, invasion, offensive, offense, onslaught, slaughter, bloodshed, blood feud, blitzkrieg, Armageddon, holocaust. **2.** belligerence, bellicosity, discord, competition, conflict, disagreement, dissension, dispute, antagonism, rivalry, contest, contention, fracas, match, debate, wrangle, altercation, controversy, feud, quarrel, squabble, row, tiff, breach of the peace, scrap, bickering, standoff, showdown. —v. **3.** fight, battle, contend, combat, oppose, struggle, strive, resist, withstand, attack, assault, campaign against, stand up to, take up arms, cross swords, joust, fence. —**Ant.** peace.

warlike, adj. martial, military, militaristic, hawkish, war-mongering, jingoistic; bellicose, belligerent, hostile, inimical, pugnacious, contentious, combative, aggressive, unfriendly, bloodthirsty. —**Ant.** peaceful, peaceable.

warm, adj. **1.** heated, lukewarm, tepid, moderate, comfortable. **2.** hearty, enthusiastic, earnest, sincere, passionate, heartfelt, wholehearted, fervent, ardent, eager. **3.** amiable, genial, hospitable, welcoming, friendly, neighborly, kind, warmhearted, responsive, cordial, hearty. **4.** attached, friendly, amiable, amicable, affectionate, tender, sympathetic, compassionate, loving, amorous, close, inimate. **5.** heated, irritated, annoyed, testy, touchy, irascible, vexed, angry, irate, furious. **6.** animated, spirited, lively, brisk, vigorous, vehement. —v. **7.** cheer, please, delight, move, animate, stir, rouse, arouse. —**Ant.** cool.

warn, v. caution, admonish, forewarn, advise, counsel, exhort, urge, notify, apprise, inform, alert, tip off, signal, sound an alarm.

warning, n. **1.** caution, admonition, threat, caveat, tip, notification, signal, counsel, advice. **2.** omen, sign, signal, indication, forewarning, foreshadowing, prophecy, augury, portent.

warrant, n. **1.** authorization, sanction, justification, approval, certification. **2.** pledge, guarantee, assurance, security, surety, warranty. **3.** certificate, affidavit, document, credential, license, permit, voucher, writ, order, mandate, decree. —v. **4.** authorize, sanction, approve, justify, vindicate, endorse, guarantee, vouch for. **5.** assure, certify, uphold, back up, stand behind, promise, guarantee, secure, affirm, vouch for, attest.

wary, adj. alert, cautious, vigilant, chary, fearful, apprehensive, suspicious, on edge, on guard, careful, circumspect, watchful, discreet, prudent, observant, foresighted. —**Ant.** foolhardy, careless.

wash, v. **1.** cleanse, clean, launder, scrub, mop, swab, rub, scour, soak, rinse, flush. **2.** bathe, shower, shampoo, soap up, lather, sponge off.

washout, n. **1.** failure, total loss, disaster, disappointment, debacle, rout, calamity, catastrophe, farce, setback, misfire, shellacking, flop, fiasco, botch, fizzle, clinker, lead balloon, lemon, bomb, bummer. **2.** failure, flop, nonstarter, loser, misfit, nebbish, schlemiel, schnook, sad sack, dud, bust, dead duck, turkey, also-ran. —**Ant.** success.

waste, v. **1.** consume, misuse, burn up, fritter away, spend, throw away, expend, squander, misspend, splurge, dissipate. **2.** destroy, consume, wear away, erode, eat away, reduce, wear down, exhaust, disable, debilitate, emaciate, enfeeble. **3.** destroy, demolish, wreck, decimate, lay waste, devastate, desolate, ruin, ravage, pillage, plunder, sack, loot, despoil. **4.** diminish, dwindle, deteriorate, decline, wither, shrink, ebb, wane, decay. —*n.* **5.** consumption, misuse, dissipation, diminution, decline, loss, destruction, decay, impairment. **6.** extravagance, prodigality, improvidence, squandering, overindulgence, lavishness. **7.** desert, tundra, wilderness, wild, badlands, wasteland, emptiness. **8.** refuse, rubbish, trash, garbage, detritus, scrap, litter, junk, debris. —*adj.* **9.** unused, useless, superfluous, worthless, leftover, surplus, extra, *de trop.* **10.** rejected, unproductive, unsalvageable, unrecycleable, useless, worthless, purposeless, unusable. —**Ant.** preserve.

watch, *v.* **1.** look, see, observe, note, notice, pay attention to, follow, scrutinize, examine, inspect. **2.** contemplate, regard, mark, view, gaze at, stare at, take in, behold, eye, survey, observe, look at *or* upon. **3.** wait for, await, expect, anticipate, be watchful *or* vigilant, be prepared *or* ready. **4.** guard, protect, tend, mind, supervise, look after, keep an eye on, keep safe, take care of, chaperone, baby-sit. —*n.* **5.** observation, inspection, attention, vigil, watchfulness, alertness, surveillance, lookout.

watchful, *adj.* vigilant, alert, observant, attentive, heedful, careful, circumspect, cautious, wary, wakeful, wide-awake, awake. —**Ant.** careless, heedless, inattentive.

wave, *n.* **1.** ridge, swell, undulation, whitecap, billow, heave, comber, ripple, breaker, surf, sea; surge, upsurge, tide, current, flood. —*v.* **2.** undulate, billow, ripple, fluctuate, oscillate. **3.** flutter, swing, flap, quiver, wag, shake, wiggle, float, sway, rock. —**Ant.** hollow.

waver, *v.* **1.** wave, sway, flutter, flicker, hover, flit, flitter, float. **2.** shake, rock, tremble, quiver, quaver, shudder, shiver. **3.** vacillate, fluctuate, waffle, dither, equivocate, seesaw, yo-yo, falter, balk, boggle, demur, shy, hedge, shilly-shally, vary, alternate, hesitate.

wax, *v.* increase, intensify, extend, grow, expand, magnify, amplify, swell, spread, distend, lengthen, elongate, widen, broaden, stretch, enlarge, dilate, augment, snowball, develop, burgeon, flourish, proliferate. —**Ant.** wane.

way, *n.* **1.** manner, mode, fashion, means, technique, procedure, system, approach, method, modus operandi. **2.** manner, character, nature, behavior, style, pattern, conduct, habit, custom, usage, practice, approach, spirit, feeling, sense, disposition, temperament, personality. **3.** means, course, plan, method, scheme, device. **4.** respect, aspect, sense, feature, point, particular detail, part. **5.** direction; passage, progression, advance, headway. **6.** distance, space, interval. **7.** path, street, trail, course, road, route, track, avenue.

wayward, *adj.* **1.** contrary, headstrong, stubborn, balky, insubordinate, contumacious, rebellious, recalcitrant, obstinate, disobedient, unruly, refractory, intractable, willful, perverse. **2.** capricious, unstable, unpredictable, volatile, flighty, whimsical, fickle, mercurial, erratic, variable, inconstant,

changeable. —**Ant.** agreeable, amenable, obedient, tractable; constant, stable.

weak, *adj.* **1.** fragile, frail, breakable, delicate, frangible, flimsy, shaky, rickety, unsound, unsteady, unstable. **2.** feeble, senile, anile, doddering, doting, infirm, decrepit, weakly, sickly, unhealthy, unwell, debilitated, enervated, anemic, exhausted, wan, haggard, vitiated, effete, invalid. **3.** impotent, ineffectual, ineffective, inefficient, inadequate, inefficacious, useless, worthless. **4.** unconvincing, inconclusive, lame, unpersuasive, empty, hollow, pathetic, pitiful, half-baked, puny, unbelievable, illogical, unsatisfactory, vague. **5.** unintelligent, simple, foolish, stupid, senseless, silly. **6.** unassertive, retiring, spineless, feckless, irresolute, weak-kneed, namby-pamby, wishy-washy, meek, timid, cowardly. **7.** faint, slight, feeble, dim, inconsiderable, flimsy, poor, meager, paltry, puny. **8.** deficient, inadequate, unsatisfactory, faulty, imperfect, inferior, flawed, defective, insufficient. —**Ant.** strong.

weaken, *v.* worsen, enfeeble, debilitate, enervate, emasculate, unnerve, undermine, sap, cripple, disable, injure, damage, impair, handicap, exhaust, deplete, diminish, lessen, lower, impoverish, vitiate, degrade, reduce, mitigate, moderate, minimize, dilute, thin, attenuate, extenuate, adulterate, contaminate. —**Ant.** strengthen.

weakling, *n.* coward, born victim, born loser, pushover, lightweight, second-rate, washout, mouse, milksop, namby-pamby, creampuff, softie, baby, doormat, yes-man, milquetoast, jellyfish, weak sister, empty suit, invertebrate, wuss, wimp, schnook, schlemiel, nerd, twerp, turkey, drip, dweeb, crybaby, mama's boy, pantywaist, sissy, nebbish, gutless wonder, chicken, quitter, nervous Nellie, yellow-belly, pansy, patsy, sucker, lame.

weakness, *n.* **1.** feebleness, fragility, frailty, delicacy, vulnerability, infirmity. **2.** flaw, defect, fault, shortcoming, foible, failing, imperfection, liability, blemish, deficiency. **3.** fondness, preference, affection, appreciation, tenderness, liking, inclination, bent, leaning, proclivity, propensity, partiality, appetite, taste, soft spot. —**Ant.** strength.

wealth, *n.* **1.** property, riches, assets, holdings, capital, funds, cash, valuables, bankroll. **2.** abundance, profusion, fullness, plethora, bounty, store, plenitude, plenty, copiousness, richness, amplitude. **3.** assets, possessions, goods, property. **4.** prosperity, affluence, opulence, fortune, treasure, wherewithal, resources, means. —**Ant.** poverty, indigence.

wealthy, *adj.* rich, affluent, opulent, prosperous, well-to-do, well-off, comfortable, flush, well-heeled, loaded, fat, moneyed, upper-class, privileged, to the manor born, noveau riche, rolling in dough, rich as Croesus *or* Rockefeller, well-fixed, well-provided-for. —**Ant.** poor, poverty-stricken; indigent.

wearisome, *adj.* **1.** fatiguing, tiring, exhausting, debilitating, vitiating, wearing, taxing. **2.** tiresome, boring, tedious, soporific, monotonous, humdrum, dull, bland, insipid, vapid, jejune, prosaic, vexatious, trying, irritating, irksome, exasperating, bothersome, annoying. —**Ant.** vitalizing, energizing, interesting, exciting.

weary, *adj.* **1.** exhausted, tired, wearied, enervated, debilitated, fatigued, spent, drained, sapped, knocked out,

bone-tired, finished, all in, frazzled, tuckered out, dead on one's feet, pooped, zonked, shot. **2.** impatient, bored, indignant, sick and tired, fed up, dissatisfied. —*v.* **3.** fatigue, tire, exhaust, tire or wear out, jade, drain, tax, enervate, debilitate, sap, weaken. **4.** annoy, bother, irritate, burden, vex, exasperate, irk. —**Ant.** energetic; forbearing, patient; invigorating; enliven, energize; delight.

weep, *v.* shed tears, cry, sob, wail, whimper, blubber, moan, sigh, groan, bawl, whine, snivel, mewl, pule, murmur, mope, lament, sorrow, suffer, grieve, complain, deplore, bewail, bemoan, turn on the waterworks. —**Ant.** laugh, rejoice, celebrate.

weigh, *v.* consider, balance, ponder, contemplate, study, revolve, meditate, muse, reflect, think over, mull over, ruminate, chew over, brood, examine, review, pore over, judge, assess, evaluate.

weight, *n.* influence, authority, prestige, credit, importance, substance, force, impact, value, worth, seriousness, gravity, moment, import, consequence, significance, efficacy, effectiveness, power.

weighty, *adj.* **1.** heavy, ponderous, massive, bulky, cumbersome, hefty. **2.** burdensome, irksome, troublesome, wearisome, oppressive, distressing, onerous. **3.** important, momentous, significant, serious, crucial, grave, consequential. **4.** influential, powerful, important, forceful, authoritative, prestigious, prominent. —**Ant.** light; unimportant, insignificant.

weird, *adj.* eerie, strange, uncanny, mysterious, unnatural, unearthly, supernatural, preternatural, fearsome, dreadful, awful, odd, peculiar, queer, curious, fantastic, bizarre, grotesque, outlandish, freakish, freaky, spooky, creepy. —**Ant.** natural.

welfare, *n.* well-being, commonweal, prosperity, good fortune, good health, success, happiness, benefit, good, profit, advantage, interest.

well, *adv.* **1.** satisfactorily, favorably, adequately, agreeably, nicely, advantageously, fortunately, happily. **2.** commendably, meritoriously, excellently, successfully, superbly, splendidly, admirably. **3.** properly, correctly, skillfully, efficiently, accurately. **4.** justly, reasonably, easily, in fairness, with propriety, properly. **5.** adequately, sufficiently, satisfactorily. **6.** thoroughly, soundly, carefully, abundantly, amply, fully. **7.** considerably, rather, quite, fairly. **8.** personally, intimately, closely, thoroughly, profoundly, deeply, entirely. —*adj.* **9.** sound, healthy, hale, hearty, robust, fit, vigorous, wholesome, strong, in good shape, in fine fettle. **10.** satisfactory, good, fine, pleasing, agreeable, all right. **11.** proper, fitting, gratifying, suitable, befitting, appropriate. **12.** fortunate, successful, well-off, happy. —**Ant.** poorly, badly; unwell, infirm, weak, ill, sick.

well-built, *adj.* **1.** well-endowed, well-knit, well-proportioned, sinewy, hunky, luscious, alluring, appealing, desirable, stunning, gorgeous, muscular, powerful, strapping, rugged, robust, sturdy, broad-shouldered, athletic, brawny, burly, stacked, curvaceous, shapely, comely, graceful, lissome, svelte, slender, slim, voluptuous, zaftig, buxom, sexy, dishy, eye-popping, an eyeful, eye candy, built. **2.** sturdy, strong, durable, solid, rugged, sound, stout, substantial, enduring, heavy-duty, long-wearing, dependable, well-constructed. **—Ant.** scrawny, frail; unsound, rickety.

wet, *adj.* **1.** soaked, drenched, sopping, soppy, saturated, dripping, sodden, damp, waterlogged, flooded, moist, dampened, moistened. **2.** damp, moist, dank, humid, dewy, foggy, misty, drizzling, rainy. **—Ant.** dry.

wherewithal, *n.* means, resources, wealth, riches, supplies, means, fortune, money, cash, funds, capital, bankroll, finances, holdings, assets, property, credit.

whim, *n.* fancy, fantasy, vision, dream, idea, notion, caprice, whimsy, humor, vagary, quirk, inclination, playfulness, impulse, impetuosity, crotchet. **—Ant.** plan.

whimsical, *adj.* **1.** capricious, mercurial, volatile, erratic, flighty, fickle, unpredictable, inconsistent, impetuous, changeable. **2.** crotchety, freakish, fanciful, odd, peculiar, curious, singular, queer, quaint, eccentric, fey, playful. **—Ant.** deliberate, serious, sober.

whine, *v.* complain, grouse, mutter, wail, carp, gripe, squack, grouch, beef, kick, cavil, fret, grumble; moan, lament, groan, wail, whimper, howl, sob, snivel, pule, mewl, cry.

whip, *v.* lash, beat, flog, thrash, horsewhip, cane, spank, strap, scourge, beat, switch, flagellate; chastise, castigate, punish, discipline.

whirl, *v.* gyrate, pirouette, spin, swirl, turn, circle, eddy, rotate, revolve, twirl, wheel.

whitewash, *v.* **1.** gloss over, cover up, hide, conceal, disguise, camouflage, paper over, mask, mislead, cloak, dissemble, sugarcoat, prevaricate, stonewall. **2.** justify, condone, equivocate, excuse, exculpate, extenuate, qualify, minimize, downplay, rationalize, explain away, vindicate. **—Ant.** confess, reveal.

whole, *adj.* **1.** entire, full, total, all, gross; together, undiminished, undivided, integral, complete, uncut, unbroken, unimpaired, perfect, uninjured, faultless, undamaged, unharmed, unscathed, in one piece, solid, inviolate, sound, intact. **—**n. **2.** totality, total, sum, entirety, aggregate, sum total, everything. **—Ant.** partial; part.

wholesome, *adj.* salutary, beneficial, helpful, healthful, salubrious, nourishing, nutritious, healthy, invigorating, tonic, bracing, life-giving, restorative. **—Ant.** unwholesome.

wicked, *adj.* evil, bad, immoral, amoral, lawless, unrepentant, unprincipled, sinful, piacular, unrighteous, ungodly, godless, sacrilegious, satanic, demonic, fiendish, ghoulish, hellish, impious, profane, blasphemous; profligate, corrupt, depraved, dissolute, blackhearted, beastly, base, low, debased, degenerate, perverse, perverted, foul, offensive, abominable, shameful, disgraceful, shameless, unregenerate, criminal, heinous, vicious, vile, iniquitous, abandoned, flagitious, nefarious, treacherous, villainous, atrocious. **—Ant.** good, virtuous.

wide, *adj.* broad, extensive, roomy, vast, spacious, ample; comprehensive, large, expanded, distended, encyclopedic, inclusive, wide-ranging, far-reaching, widespread. **—Ant.** narrow.

wild, *adj.* **1.** untamed, undomesticated, feral, savage, vicious, unbroken, ferocious. **2.** uncultivated, uninhabited, desolate, empty, barren, deserted, waste, virgin, unpopulated. **3.** uncivilized, barbarous, savage, primitive, backward, fierce, barbarian. **4.** violent,

furious, boisterous, tempestuous, stormy, disorderly, frenzied, turbulent, impetuous. **5.** frantic, mad, distracted, distraught, hysterical, frenzied, unhinged, berserk, manic, rabid, crazy, insane. **6.** enthusiastic, eager, anxious, agog, fervent, impatient, excited. **7.** ardent, passionate, exciting, romantic, tempestuous, intense, chaotic, crazy, madcap. **8.** undisciplined, willful, unruly, obstreperous, fractious, disobedient, refractory, intractable, boisterous, rowdy, lively, uproarious, freewheeling, unconventional, lawless, turbulent, headstrong, self-willed, ungoverned, unrestrained, riotous, wayward. **9.** unrestrained, unrestricted, unchecked, unbridled, uncontrolled, untrammeled. **10.** absurd, irrational, imprudent, foolhardy, reckless, rash, extravagant, unworkable, impractical, impracticable. **11.** queer, grotesque, bizarre, strange, fantastic, far-out, freakish, imaginary, fanciful, visionary. **12.** disorderly, disheveled, unkempt, messy, sloppy, tousled, windblown. **—**n. **13.** waste, wilderness, tundra, desert, heath, wasteland, emptiness. **—Ant.** tame, domesticated.

wild-eyed, *adj.* **1.** wild, manic, maniacal, rabid, frantic, frenzied, raving, mad, crazy, berserk. **2.** visionary, quixotic, unrealistic, extreme, fanatical, fanatic, far-out, off the wall, harebrained. **—Ant.** calm, composed; sensible, practical.

wile, *n.* **1.** trick, artifice, stratagem, feint, subterfuge, plot, conspiracy, dodge, trap, snare, ruse, deception, move, gambit, maneuver. **2.** deceit, cunning, duplicity, guile, slyness, foxiness, craftiness, artfulness, trickery, chicanery, fraud, cheating, defrauding, imposture, imposition.

will, *n.* **1.** determination, commitment, resolve, resolution, resoluteness, decision, forcefulness. **2.** volition, choice, election, preference. **3.** wish, desire, longing, liking, pleasure, disposition, inclination. **4.** intention, intent, purpose, determination. **5.** order, direction, command, behest, bidding. **—**v. **6.** decide, decree, determine, direct, command, bid, order, ordain, require.

willful, *adj.* **1.** willed, willing, deliberate, conscious, premeditated, purposeful, voluntary, intentional, volitional. **2.** self-willed, headstrong, perverse, obstinate, recalcitrant, immovable, dogged, determined, uncompromising, pertinacious, intractable, wayward, stubborn, intransigent, contrary, contumacious, perverse, refractory, disagreeable, pigheaded, cantankerous, unruly, inflexible, obdurate, adamant. **—Ant.** unintentional, involuntary; tractable, docile, obedient.

wily, *adj.* crafty, cunning, artful, sly, shrewd, astute, sneaky, shifty, disingenuous, sharp, smooth, slick, oily, unctuous, slippery, cagey, foxy, tricky, intriguing, arch, designing, calculating, perfidious, deceitful, treacherous, crooked, Machiavellian, duplicitous, double-dealing, underhanded. **—Ant.** guileless, ingenuous.

win, *v.* **1.** succeed, advance, win out, triumph, progress, overcome, conquer, prevail, be victorious, take first prize, carry the day. **2.** obtain, gain, procure, secure, earn, acquire, achieve, attain, reach, collect, receive, realize, net, bag. **3.** win over, persuade, convince, induce, prevail upon, influence, sway, charm, bring around. **—Ant.** lose.

wince, *v.* recoil, shrink, quail, shy, falter, stagger, blanch, cower, balk, demur, cringe, flinch, draw back, squirm, writhe.

wind, *n.* **1.** air, whiff, puff, breath, current, blast, draft, zephyr, breeze, gust, blow, gale, hurricane, whirlwind, cyclone, tornado, twister, typhoon, waterspout. **2.** noise, bombast, bluster, boasting, braggadocio, blather, maundering, yammering, windiness, flatulence, emptiness, idle talk, nonsense, humbug, hot air, clap trap, hooey, rot, hogwash, baloney, bull. **—**v. **3.** change direction, bend, turn, meander, curve, twist, snake, zigzag, ramble, veer, coil, sheer, swerve, deviate, spiral, angle, dogleg, skew, be tortuous *or* sinuous *or* circuitous *or* indirect. **4.** coil, twine, twist, encircle, spiral, curl, wrap, wreathe.

winning, *adj.* engaging, endearing, prepossessing, fetching, enchanting, bewitching, charming, captivating, attractive, alluring, charismatic, magnetic, magical, entrancing, seductive, winsome, persuasive, convincing, dynamic, compelling. **—Ant.** repellent, obnoxious.

wisdom, *n.* **1.** discretion, judgment, judiciousness, perspicacity, perception, foresight, discernment, sense, common sense, reason, penetration, acumen, acuity, intelligence, sagacity, insight, understanding, prudence, savvy. **2.** knowledge, information, lore, scholarship, learning, erudition, enlightenment. **—Ant.** foolishness; ignorance.

wise, *adj.* **1.** discerning, judicious, discreet, sage, sensible, penetrating, sagacious, intelligent, perspicacious, perceptive, insightful, intelligent, acute, astute, brilliant, clever, bright, quickwitted, profound, rational, prudent, reasonable. **2.** learned, erudite, schooled, scholarly, enlightened, knowing, well-read, cultivated, cultured, versed, knowledgeable, informed. **3.** advisable, sensible, judicious, discreet, expedient, tactful, strategic, diplomatic, prudent, politic, proper, appropriate, fitting. **—Ant.** unwise.

wish, *v.* **1.** want, crave, desire, have an appetite for, thirst for, yearn, hope, long for; need, lack. **2.** bid, require, request, demand, direct, command, order. **—**n. **3.** desire, passion, whim, keenness, longing, craving, yearning, thirst, appetite, hunger, urge, fondness, want, preference, predisposition, inclination.

wit, *n.* **1.** drollery, facetiousness, repartee, waggishness, raillery, levity, joking, jocularity, pungency, piquancy, sarcasm, irony, wisecrack, humor. **2.** understanding, judgment, discernment, insight, intelligence, sagacity, wisdom, intellect, mind, brains, cleverness, brilliance, acuity, sense.

withdraw, *v.* **1.** draw back *or* away, recoil, shrink, shy, wince, quail, demur, flinch; take back, subtract, remove, retract, cancel, void, annul, recall, disavow, recant, revoke, rescind. **2.** depart, retire, retreat, repair, absent oneself, quit, clear out, abscond, decamp, escape, fly, flee, scramble, scram. **—Ant.** advance, arrive.

wither, *v.* shrivel, fade, decay, wrinkle, wizen, contract, constrict, shrink, dry, parch, desiccate, shrivel, wilt, languish, droop, waste away. **—Ant.** flourish, thrive.

withhold, *v.* hold back, restrain, retain, reserve, control, curb, bridle, inhibit, check, keep back, suppress, repress, hide, conceal. **—Ant.** grant, concede, unleash, reveal.

withstand, *v.* resist, oppose, combat, defy, stand up to, confront, face, face up to, hold out against; bear, endure, countenance, brook, undergo, experience, weather, tolerate, suffer. —Ant. submit, yield, surrender.

witness, *v.* **1.** see, perceive, observe, view, behold, spot, watch, look at, mark, notice, note. **2.** testify, affirm, swear, certify, vouch for, verify, confirm, prove, show, bear witness. —*n.* **3.** observer, onlooker, bystander, beholder, spectator, eyewitness. **4.** testimony, evidence, deposition, corroboration, statement.

witty, *adj.* facetious, droll, humorous, funny, amusing, entertaining, diverting, clever, original, ingenious, subtle, piquant, pungent, penetrating, astute, insightful, trenchant, mordant, waggish, wisecracking, sparkling, scintillating, brilliant, jocose, jocular. —Ant. silly, stupid.

wizard, *n.* **1.** enchanter, magician, sorcerer, alchemist, shaman, magus, Merlin, mystic, necromancer, conjurer, charmer, diviner, seer, soothsayer. **2.** expert, adept, virtuoso, artist, marvel, miracle worker, genius, master, past master, whiz.

woe, *n.* distress, affliction, trouble, sorrow, grief, misery, anguish, hardship, adversity, calamity, misfortune, tribulation, trial, agony, wretchedness, heartache, regret, suffering, lamentation, gloom, depression, melancholy. —Ant. joy, happiness, bliss, exultation.

woman, *n.* female, lady. —Ant. man.

womanly, *adj.* womanlike, womanish; feminine, female; attractive, mature, motherly, fully developed, ripe, nurturing.

wonder, *v.* **1.** think, speculate, muse, theorize, puzzle, be curious, mull over, conjecture, meditate, ponder, question, inquire. **2.** marvel, be astonished *or* thunderstruck *or* awed *or* dumbstruck *or* dumbfounded *or* astounded; gape, stare. —*n.* **3.** surprise, stupefaction, fascination, astonishment, amazement, awe, bewilderment, perplexity, mystification, puzzlement; admiration.

wonderful, *adj.* marvelous, extraordinary, remarkable, awesome, startling, wondrous, miraculous, spectacular, stunning, fascinating, surprising, prodigious, astonishing, amazing, astounding, phenomenal, unique, curious, strange, odd, peculiar. —Ant. usual, ordinary, common.

word, *n.* **1.** expression, utterance; assertion, affirmation, declaration, statement. **2.** guarantee, vow, oath, assurance, promise, pledge. **3.** intelligence, tidings, news, report, facts, data, bulletin, message, communiqué, account, advice, information, inside story, lowdown, scuttlebutt, gossip, dish, dope. **4.** signal, order, instruction, high sign, command. —*v.* **5.** express, style, phrase, say, put into words, couch, utter, term, state, set forth.

wordy, *adj.* prolix, redundant, repetitious, diffuse, inflated, turgid, windy, flatulent, bombastic, rambling, longwinded, talky, loquacious, garrulous, verbose, superfluous, long-drawn, grandiloquent, magniloquent, endless, interminable, overlong. —Ant. terse, concise, succinct.

work, *n.* **1.** exertion, labor, toil, trouble, pains, travail, industriousness, sweat of one's brow, drudgery, effort. **2.** undertaking, task, duty, assignment, chore, enterprise, project, responsibility. **3.** employment, industry, occupation, job, position, situation, business, profession, trade, craft, calling, career, line, livelihood, pursuit, vocation, metier. **4.** deed, performance, fruit, frui-

tion, feat, creation, accomplishment, opus, output, artifact, production, handiwork, piece, composition, masterpiece, achievement. —*v.* **5.** labor, toil, drudge, sweat, slave, exert oneself, take pains. **6.** act, operate, function, go. **7.** operate, use, manipulate, manage, handle. **8.** bring about, perform, produce, cause, do, execute, finish, effect, originate, accomplish, achieve. **9.** mold, create, shape, construct, make, fashion, execute, finish. —Ant. leisure, indolence, idleness, sloth.

worldly, *adj.* **1.** nonspiritual, secular, earthly, mundane, temporal, terrestrial, material, physical, corporeal, fleshly, human, mortal, profane. **2.** worldlywise, sophisticated, experienced, savvy, knowledgeable, refined, polished, cultured, cultivated, soigné, blasé, poised, stylish, in the know, knowing, urbane, cosmopolitan, suave. —Ant. celestial, heavenly, sacred, spiritual; naive.

world-weary, *adj.* apathetic, anomic, jaded, indifferent, bored, dull, suffering from ennui, dégagé, blasé, impassive, detached, melancholic, listless, burned out, pessimistic, cynical. —Ant. optimistic, enthusiastic, cheerful, hopeful.

worry, *v.* **1.** fret, torment oneself, agonize, be anxious *or* fearful *or* concerned *or* nervous, be upset *or* distressed, chafe, be troubled *or* vexed, fidget, stew, brood, sweat bullets, despair, mope, pine, eat one's heart out, imagine the worst, dread, feel edgy *or* jumpy, lose sleep, tear one's hair out. **2.** upset, agitate, perturb, trouble, try, torture, torment, annoy, plague, pester, bother, vex, tease, harry, hector, harass, tease, tantalize, molest, persecute, badger, irritate, disquiet, disturb, distress, irritate, rankle. —*n.* **3.** uneasiness, anxiety, misgiving, nervousness, distress, agitation, perturbation, apprehension, foreboding, solicitude, concern, disquiet, misgiving, anguish, woe, heartache, uncertainty, doubt. —Ant. comfort, solace; sang-froid, equanimity.

worsen, *v.* **1.** increase, intensify, heighten, deepen, magnify, exacerbate, aggravate, inflame. **2.** weaken, decline, dwindle, fade, give way, degrade, disintegrate, deteriorate, degenerate, slip, slide, backslide, fall apart, crumble, erode, fail, decay, go from bad to worse, go downhill, got to pot, go to the dogs. —Ant. abate; improve.

worship, *n.* **1.** reverence, homage, veneration, devotion, respect, esteem, exaltation, adoration, honor, praise, admiration, adulation, glorification, magnification, regard, idolizing, idolatry, deification. —*v.* **2.** revere, respect, venerate, reverence, honor, glorify, adore, extol, exalt, praise, admire, glorify, regard highly, adulate, idolize, deify, love, dote on, put on a pedestal, bow down before. —Ant. detest, execrate, scorn.

worth, —*n.* usefulness, value, benefit, advantage, significance, importance, merit, worthiness, profit, credit, virtue, perfection, indispensability, excellence, quality. —Ant. worthlessness.

worthy, *adj.* commendable, meritorious, worthwhile, deserving, qualified, creditable, estimable, praiseworthy, excellent, exemplary, distinguished, firstrate, righteous, upright, honest. —Ant. unworthy.

wound, *n.* **1.** injury, hurt, damage, handicap, trauma; cut, gash, puncture, bruise, slit, burn, contusion, laceration, lesion. **2.** harm, slight, blow, dis-

tress, torment, torture, offense, wrong, insult, pain, grief, anguish. —*v.* **3.** injure, hurt, harm, damage, maim, disable, handicap, traumatize; cut, stab, lacerate, shoot, burn.

wrath, *n.* anger, ire, rage, resentment, indignation, irritation, fury, spleen, vexation, annoyance, outrage, temper, displeasure, exasperation. —Ant. forbearance, mercy, toleration.

wrathful, *adj.* angry, irate, vexed, outraged, mad, acrimonious, infuriated, furious, choleric, livid, splenetic, fuming, enraged, raging, incensed, provoked, exasperated, indignant, on a rampage, hot under the collar, on the warpath, at the end of one's patience, in high dudgeon, ticked off, POed, having a fit. —Ant. lenient, understanding, indulgent.

wreck, *n.* **1.** ruin, destruction, demolition, decimation, annihilation, spoliation, obliteration, leveling, devastation, desolation. —*v.* **2.** spoil, destroy, demolish, raze, decimate, smash, crush, annihilate, wipe out, devastate, ruin, shatter, lay waste to, flatten, pulverize, ravage, eradicate, trash. —Ant. create.

wretched, *adj.* **1.** miserable, pitiable, dejected, dismal, despondent, distressed, woeful, afflicted, woebegone, forlorn, unhappy, despairing, hopeless, melancholy, heartbroken, heartsick, inconsolable, crestfallen, desolate, depressed. **2.** sorry, miserable, despicable, mean, base, vile, bad, contemptible, poor, pitiful, worthless, sordid, squalid, abject, shameful, inferior. —Ant. happy.

wrong, *adj.* **1.** bad, evil, wicked, sinful, immoral, corrupt, iniquitous, reprehensible, unjust, unfair, unethical, illegal, illicit, illegitimate, unlawful, criminal, crooked, dishonest, disgraceful, dishonorable, blameworthy, opprobrious, shameful. **2.** erroneous, inaccurate, incorrect, false, untrue, fallacious, misleading, deceptive, in error, mistaken. **3.** improper, inappropriate, unfit, infelicitous, out of place, wrongheaded, imprudent, misguided, illconsidered, unsuitable. **4.** awry, amiss, askew, astray, flawed, defective, unsound, not working, out of order. —*n.* **5.** evil, wickedness, misdoing, evil deed, misdeed, sin, vice, immorality, iniquity, trespass, transgression, offense, infraction, violation, crime, felony, misdemeanor, breach of the law, peccadillo, mistake, lapse in judgment, personal failing. —*v.* **6.** injure, harm, maltreat, mistreat, misuse, abuse, oppress, cheat, defraud, dishonor, discredit, malign, calumniate, take advantage of, violate, offend, insult, wound, victimize. —Ant. right.

wrongheaded, *adj.* perverse, misguided, injudicious, unwise, erroneous, deluded, opinionated, contrary, ornery, mulish, balky, bullheaded, wayward, obstinate, unreasonable, difficult, barking up the wrong tree. —Ant. reasonable, compliant.

wry, *adj.* witty, waggish, wisecracking, droll, humorous, biting, trenchant, mordant, pungent, piquant, pointed, ironic, sardonic, sarcastic.

X

xenophobic, *adj.* chauvinistic, insular, separatist, segregationist, discriminatory, intolerant, biased, bigoted, racist, ethnocentric, restrictive, exclusive, exclusionary, closed-door, selective, restricted, restrictive. **—Ant.** inclusive, welcoming.

X-rated, *adj.* erotic, sexually explicit, sexy, sexual, adult, salacious, lewd, racy, coarse, licentious, lubricious, lascivious, scabrous, risqué, foul-mouthed, prurient, offensive, taboo, obscene, pornographic, smutty, blue, off-color, dirty, filthy, indecent, vulgar, crude, raw, foul, gross, raunchy. **—Ant.** clean, wholesome, innocuous.

Y

yahoo, *adj.* **1.** boor, vulgarian, oaf, philistine, lowbrow, lout, barbarian, know-nothing, ignoramus, illiterate, redneck, ruffian, hooligan, Neanderthal, subhuman, slob. **2.** country bumpkin, provincial, peasant, back-woodsman, hillbilly, clodhopper, rube, yokel, hayseed, hick. **3.** nincompoop, ass, jackass, pinhead, clod, clot, idiot, nit, nitwit, moron, bird brain, jerk, sap, imbecile, dope, dunce, halfwit, fool, lummox, galoot, dolt, dimwit, bozo, boob, retard, butthead.

yearn long, hanker, pine, yen, ache, itch, thirst, lust, crave, hunger, covet, pant, desire, want, wish, fancy, prefer, aspire, aim.

yearning, *n.* longing, craving, desire, hankering, pining, itch, thirst, hunger, appetite, yen, wish, urge, passion, lust, aspiration, aim.

yell, *v.* cry out, shout, scream, bellow, howl, roar, yap, bark, bawl, vociferate, yelp, caterwaul, squall, shriek, wail, whoop, cheer, screech, squeal, hoot, thunder, bay, clamor, boom, rumble, snarl, growl. **—Ant.** whisper.

yes-man, *n.* flatterer, sycophant, hanger-on, doormat, jackal, lickspittle, toady, apple-polisher, stooge, bootlicker, flunky, lackey, rubber stamp; menial, underling, hireling, inferior, minion, slave, dogsbody, gofer.

yield, *v.* **1.** give forth, produce, furnish, supply, render, bear, impart, afford, bestow, turn out, generate, engender, breed, propagate. **2.** give up, cede, surrender, submit, give way, concede, knuckle under, capitulate, succumb, throw in the towel, collapse; relinquish, abandon, abdicate, resign, waive, forgo. **—***n.* **3.** produce, harvest, fruit, crop, output, production; reward, profit, gain, earnings, proceeds, take.

young, *adj.* **1.** youthful, juvenile, teen-

age, adolescent, pubescent, prepubescent, underage, minor, junior, underaged, in one's prime, at a tender age, blooming, in the flower of one's life, immature, jejune, puerile, boyish, girlish, childish, childlike, babyish, virgin, inexperienced, undeveloped, unfledged, unsophisticated, innocent, naive, callow, green, wet behind the ears. **2.** fresh, vigorous, robust, fit, strong, healthy, strapping, spry, lively, energetic. **—***n.* **3.** offspring, children, spawn, issue, babies, progeny, brood, litter, rug rats, kids. **—Ant.** aged, old, ancient; mature, grown-up, full-fledged, experienced, progenitors, parents.

youth, *n.* **1.** youngness, youthfulness, prime, bloom, childhood, salad days, schooldays, younger generation, springtime of life, heyday, minority, adolescence, teens, puberty, pubescence, early years, boyhood, girlhood, infancy, babyhood, immaturity, puerility, callowness, naiveté, innocence, virginity. **2.** young man, youngster, teen-ager, adolescent stripling, lad, boy, girl, juvenile, minor, virgin, innocent, naif. **—Ant.** maturity; man, woman, adult.

yo-yo, *v.* vacillate, fluctuate, vary, be undecided, hedge, quibble, shift, dither, equivocate, waffle, hesitate, waver, seesaw, fluctuate, hem and haw, shilly-shally. **—Ant.** decide.

yucky, *adj.* unappetizing, unpalatable, unsavory, disgusting, sickening, nauseating, repugnant, repellent, repulsive, revolting, sick-making, distasteful, off-putting, noisome, fulsome, stomach-turning, foul, gross, vile, rotten, objectionable, execrable, horrid, horrible, abhorrent, offensive, loathsome, intolerable. **—Ant.** appealing, agreeable, yummy.

yummy, *adj.* delicious, savory, luscious, delectable, delightful, appetizing, tasty, appealing, juicy, tempting, succulent, toothsome, enjoyable, gratifying, pleasing, satisfying, rich, mouth-watering, sensuous, luxurious, voluptuous, sumptuous, splendid, opulent, lavish, lush, velvety, creamy, ambrosial, piquant, redolent. **—Ant.** sickening, unappetizing, yucky.

Z

zaftig, *adj.* rounded, Rubenesque,

chubby, well-fed, full-figured, plump, pleasingly plump, curvaceous, curvy, buxom, busty, voluptuous, pneumatic, built for comfort, well-built, well-upholstered, broad in the beam. **—Ant.** skinny, emaciated.

zany, *adj.* **1.** comic, comical, farcical, clownish, amusing, wise-cracking, witty, merry, funny, droll, whimsical, waggish, playful, gay, madcap, eccentric, antic, prankish, lunatic, ludicrous, absurd, nonsensical, inane, silly, foolish, hilarious, crazy, kooky, off-the-wall, loopy, nutty, goofy, wacky, loony, crackpot. **—***n.* **2.** comic, clown, comedian, joker, jokester, jester, fool, wag, wit, eccentric, stooge, cutup, merry, prankster, merry-andrew, madcap, buffoon, kook, nut, weirdo, laughingstock, screwball.

zap, *v.* attack, hit, strike, defeat, destroy, kill, slaughter, murder, liquidate, eliminate, annihilate, terminate, take out, waste, jolt, bombard, nuke, cancel, stop, undo, do in, finish off, rub out, polish off, snuff out, ice, knock out, abort, scrub, censor, skip over, edit out, delete, erase.

zeal, *n.* ardor, enthusiasm, diligence, industriousness, indefatigability, eagerness, fervor, desire, endeavor, fervency, warmth, earnestness, seriousness, vehemence, energy, forcefulness, intensity, passion, spirit. **—Ant.** apathy, stolidness, impassivity.

zealot, *n.* enthusiast, partisan, adherent, disciple, follower, devotee; fanatic, maniac, extremist, radical, militant, terrorist, bigot, skinhead.

zealous, *adj.* ardent, enthusiastic, devoted, diligent, industrious, eager, earnest, fervid, fervent, intense, vehement, forceful, energetic, lively, passionate, spirited. **—Ant.** apathetic, uninterested, dispassionate, cool.

zero, *n.* cipher, nothing, nil, naught, aught, zip, nada, nix, goose egg, diddly, diddly-squat, squat, zilch.

zest, *n.* taste, flavor, relish, gusto, pungency, piquancy, edge, bite, zip, zing, pizazz, spiciness, spice, tang; enjoyment, delight, pleasure; zeal, ardor, enthusiasm, passion, spiritedness. **—Ant.** dullness.

zone, *n.* belt, tract, area, region, quarter, sector, sphere, territory, province, department, district, section, party, segment, precinct, locale, locality, domain, realm, bailiwick.

PART THREE

Ready Reference Guide

Nations of the World

Nation	Population	Area (sq. mi.)	Area (sq. km)	Capital
Afghanistan	23,738,085	252,000	652,680	Kabul
Albania	3,293,252	10,632	27,536	Tirana
Algeria	29,830,370	919,352	2,381,121	Algiers
Angola	10,623,994	481,226	1,246,375	Luanda
Argentina	35,797,536	1,084,120	2,807,870	Buenos Aires
Armenia	3,465,611	11,490	29,759	Yerevan
Australia	18,438,824	2,974,581	7,704,164	Canberra
Austria	8,054,078	32,381	83,866	Vienna
Azerbaijan	7,735,918	33,430	86,583	Baku
Bahamas	262,034	5,353	13,864	Nassau
Bahrain	603,318	266	688	Manama
Bangladesh	125,340,261	54,501	141,157	Dhaka
Barbados	257,731	166	429	Bridgetown
Belarus	10,439,916	80,154	207,598	Minsk
Belgium	10,203,683	11,800	30,562	Brussels
Belize	224,663	8,866	22,962	Belmopan
Benin	4,440,000	44,290	114,711	Porto Novo
Bhutan	1,865,191	19,300	49,987	Thimphu
Bolivia	7,669,868	404,388	1,047,364	La Paz
Bosnia and Herzegovina	2,607,734	19,741	51,129	Sarajevo
Botswana	1,500,765	275,000	712,250	Gaborone
Brazil	164,511,366	3,286,170	8,511,180	Brasilia
Brunei	307,616	2,226	5,765	Bandar Seri Begawa
Bulgaria	8,652,745	42,800	110,852	Sofia
Burkina Faso	10,891,159	106,111	274,827	Ouagadougou
Burundi	6,052,614	10,747	27,834	Bujumbura
Cambodia	11,163,861	69,866	180,952	Phnom Penh
Cameroon	14,677,510	179,558	465,055	Yaoundé
Canada	29,123,194	3,690,410	9,558,161	Ottawa
Cape Verde	393,843	1,557	4,032	Praia
Central African Republic	3,342,051	238,000	616,420	Bangui
Chad	7,166,023	501,000	1,297,590	N'Djamena
Chile	14,508,168	286,396	741,765	Santiago
China	1,221,591,778	3,691,502	9,560,990	Beijing
Colombia	37,418,290	439,828	1,139,154	Bogotá
Comoros	589,797	719	1,862	Moreni
Congo, Democratic Republic of	32,560,000	905,063	2,344,113	Kinshasa
Congo, People's Republic of	2,583,198	132,000	341,880	Brazzaville
Costa Rica	3,534,174	19,238	49,826	San José
Croatia	5,026,995	21,835	56,552	Zagreb

Nation	Population	Area (sq. mi.)	Area (sq. km)	Capital
Cuba	10,999,041	44,200	114,478	Havana
Cyprus	752,808	3,572	9,251	Nicosia
Czech Republic	10,318,958	30,449	78,862	Prague
Denmark	5,268,775	16,576	42,931	Copenhagen
Djibouti	434,116	8,960	23,206	Djibouti
Dominica	83,226	290	751	Roseau
Dominican Republic	8,228,151	19,129	49,544	Santo Domingo
Ecuador	11,690,535	109,483	283,560	Quito
Egypt	64,791,891	386,198	1,000,252	Cairo
El Salvador	5,661,827	13,176	34,125	San Salvador
Equatorial Guinea	442,516	10,824	28,034	Malabo
Eritrea	3,589,687	47,076	121,926	Asmara
Estonia	1,444,721	17,413	45,099	Tallinn
Ethiopia	58,732,577	424,724	1,100,035	Addis Ababa
Fiji	792,441	7,078	18,332	Suva
Finland	5,109,148	130,119	337,008	Helsinki
France	58,470,421	212,736	550,986	Paris
Gabon	1,190,159	102,290	264,931	Libreville
Gambia	1,248,085	4,003	10,367	Banjul
Georgia	5,174,642	26,872	69,598	Tbilisi
Germany	84,068,216	137,852	357,036	Berlin
Ghana	18,100,703	91,843	237,873	Accra
Greece	10,583,126	50,147	129,880	Athens
Grenada	95,537	133	344	St. George's
Guatemala	11,558,407	42,042	108,888	Guatemala City
Guinea	7,405,375	96,900	250,971	Conakry
Guinea-Bissau	1,178,584	13,948	36,125	Bissau
Guyana	706,116	82,978	214,913	Georgetown
Haiti	6,611,407	10,714	27,749	Port-au-Prince
Honduras	5,751,384	43,277	112,087	Tegucigalpa
Hungary	9,935,774	35,926	93,048	Budapest
Iceland	272,550	39,709	102,846	Reykjavik
India	967,612,804	1,246,880	3,229,419	New Delhi
Indonesia	209,774,138	741,100	1,919,449	Jakarta
Iran	67,540,002	635,000	1,644,650	Tehran
Iraq	22,219,289	172,000	445,480	Baghdad
Ireland	3,555,500	27,136	70,282	Dublin
Israel	5,534,672	7,984	20,678	Jerusalem
Italy	57,534,088	116,294	301,201	Rome
Ivory Coast	14,986,218	127,520	330,276	Abidjan
Jamaica	2,615,582	4,413	11,429	Kingston
Japan	125,716,637	141,529	366,560	Tokyo
Jordan	4,540,185	37,264	96,513	Amman
Kazakhstan	16,898,572	1,049,155	2,717,311	Akmola
Kenya	28,803,085	223,478	578,808	Nairobi
Kuwait	2,076,805	8,000	20,720	Kuwait
Kyrgyzstan	4,540,185	76,460	198,031	Bishkek
Laos	5,116,959	91,500	236,985	Vientiane
Latvia	2,437,649	25,395	65,773	Riga

Nation	Population	Area (sq. mi.)	Area (sq. km)	Capital
Lebanon	3,858,736	3,927	10,170	Beirut
Lesotho	2,007,814	11,716	30,344	Maseru
Liberia	2,602,068	43,000	111,370	Monrovia
Libya	5,648,359	679,400	1,759,646	Tripoli
Liechtenstein	31,416	65	168	Vaduz
Lithuania	3,635,932	25,174	65,200	Vilnius
Luxembourg	422,474	999	2,587	Luxembourg
Macedonia	2,113,866	9,928	25,713	Skopje
Madagascar	14,061,627	226,657	587,041	Antananarivo
Malawi	9,609,081	49,177	127,368	Lilongwe
Malaysia	20,376,235	127,317	329,751	Kuala Lumpur
Maldives	280,391	115	297	Malé
Mali	9,945,383	478,841	1,240,198	Bamako
Malta	379,365	122	315	Valletta
Marshall Islands	60,652	70	181	Majuro
Mauritania	2,411,317	398,000	1,030,820	Nouakchott
Mauritius	1,154,272	788	2,040	Port Louis
Mexico	97,563,374	756,198	1,966,322	Mexico City
Micronesia	127,616	271	701	Kolonia
Moldova	4,475,232	13,100	33,929	Kishinev
Monaco	31,892	1/2	1.29	Monaco
Mongolia	2,538,211	600,000	1,554,000	Ulan Bator
Morocco	30,391,423	172,104	445,749	Rabat
Mozambique	18,165,476	297,731	771,123	Maputo
Myanmar (Burma)	46,821,943	261,789	678,033	Yangon
Nepal	22,641,061	54,000	139,860	Katmandu
Netherlands	15,653,091	16,163	41,862	Amsterdam
New Zealand	3,587,275	103,416	267,847	Wellington
Nicaragua	4,386,399	57,143	148,000	Managua
Niger	9,388,859	458,976	1,188,747	Niamey
Nigeria	107,129,469	356,669	923,772	Abuja
North Korea	24,317,004	50,000	12,950	Pyongyang
Norway	4,404,456	124,555	322,597	Oslo
Oman	2,264,590	82,800	214,452	Muscat
Pakistan	132,185,299	310,403	803,943	Islamabad
Panama	2,693,417	28,575	74,009	Panama City
Papua New Guinea	4,496,221	178,260	461,693	Port Moresby
Paraguay	5,651,634	157,047	406,751	Asunción
Peru	24,949,512	496,222	1,285,214	Lima
Philippines	76,103,564	114,830	297,409	Manila
Poland	38,700,291	121,000	313,390	Warsaw
Portugal	9,867,654	35,414	91,722	Lisbon
Qatar	665,485	8,500	22,015	Doha
Romania	21,399,114	91,654	237,383	Bucharest
Russian Federation	147,987,101	6,593,000	17,075,870	Moscow
Rwanda	7,737,537	10,169	26,337	Kigali
St. Kitts-Nevis	41,803	104	269	Basseterre
St. Lucia	159,639	238	616	Castries

Nation	Population	Area (sq. mi.)	Area (sq. km)	Capital
St. Vincent and the Grenadines	119,092	150	388	Kingstown
San Marino	24,714	24	62	San Marino
São Tomé and Principe	147,865	387	1,002	São Tomé
Saudi Arabia	20,087,965	830,000	2,149,700	Riyadh
Senegal	9,403,546	76,084	197,057	Dakar
Seychelles	78,142	175	453	Victoria
Sierra Leone	4,891,546	27,925	72,325	Freetown
Singapore	3,461,929	240	621	Singapore
Slovakia	5,393,016	18,932	49,033	Bratislava
Slovenia	1,945,998	7,819	20,251	Ljubljana
Solomon Islands	426,855	11,458	29,676	Honiara
Somalia	9,940,232	246,198	637,652	Mogadishu
South Africa	42,327,458	472,000	1,222,480	Pretoria & Cape Town
South Korea	45,948,811	38,232	99,020	Seoul
Spain	39,244,195	194,988	505,018	Madrid
Sri Lanka	18,762,075	25,332	65,609	Colombo
Sudan	32,594,128	967,500	2,505,825	Khartoum
Suriname	443,446	63,251	163,820	Paramaribo
Swaziland	1,031,600	6,704	17,363	Mbabane
Sweden	8,946,193	173,394	449,090	Stockholm
Switzerland	7,248,984	15,944	41,294	Bern
Syria	16,137,899	71,227	184,477	Damascus
Tajikistan	6,013,855	55,240	143,071	Dushanbe
Tanzania	29,460,753	363,950	942,630	Dodoma
Thailand	59,450,818	198,242	513,446	Bangkok
Togo	4,735,610	21,830	56,539	Lomé
Trinidad and Tobago	1,273,141	1,980	5,128	Port-of-Spain
Tunisia	9,183,097	48,330	125,174	Tunis
Turkey	63,528,225	300,948	779,455	Ankara
Turkmenistan	4,255,351	188,417	488,000	Ashgabat
Uganda	20,604,874	91,343	236,578	Kampala
Ukraine	50,684,635	233,090	603,703	Kiev
United Arab Emirates	2,262,309	32,300	83,657	Abu Dhabi
United Kingdom	58,610,182	94,242	244,086	London
United States	267,954,767	3,615,122	9,363,165	Washington, D.C.
Uruguay	3,261,707	172,172	445,925	Montevideo
Uzbekistan	23,860,452	172,741	447,399	Tashkent
Vanuatu	181,358	5,700	14,763	Vila
Venezuela	22,396,407	352,143	912,050	Caracas
Vietnam	75,123,880	126,104	326,609	Hanoi
Western Samoa	219,509	1,133	2,934	Apia
Yemen	13,972,477	207,000	536,130	Sanaa
Yugoslavia	10,392,000	39,449	102,172	Belgrade
Zambia	9,349,975	290,585	752,615	Lusaka
Zimbabwe	11,423,175	150,804	390,582	Harare

Continents

Name	Area in Sq. Mi.	Population
Asia	17,000,000	3,069,000,000
Africa	11,700,000	600,000,000
North America	9,400,000	400,000,000
South America	6,900,000	287,000,000
Antarctica	5,100,000	—
Europe	4,063,000	702,300,000
Australia	2,966,000	16,250,000

Great Oceans and Seas of the World

Ocean or Sea	Area sq. mi.	Area sq. km	Location
Pacific Ocean	70,000,000	181,300,000	Bounded by N and S America, Asia, and Australia
Atlantic Ocean	31,530,000	81,663,000	Bounded by N and S America, Europe, and Africa
Indian Ocean	28,357,000	73,444,630	S of Asia, E of Africa, and W of Australia
Arctic Ocean	5,540,000	14,350,000	N of North America, Asia, and the Arctic Circle
Mediterranean Sea	1,145,000	2,965,550	Between Europe, Africa, and Asia
South China Sea	895,000	2,318,050	Part of N Pacific, off coast of SE Asia
Bering Sea	878,000	2,274,000	Part of N Pacific, between N America and N Asia
Caribbean Sea	750,000	1,943,000	Between Central America, West Indies, and S America
Gulf of Mexico	700,000	1,813,000	Arm of N Atlantic, off SE coast of North America
Sea of Okhotsk	582,000	1,507,380	Arm of N Pacific, off E coast of Asia
East China Sea	480,000	1,243,200	Part of N Pacific, off E coast of Asia
Yellow Sea	480,000	1,243,200	Part of N Pacific, off E coast of Asia
Sea of Japan	405,000	1,048,950	Arm of N Pacific, between Asia mainland and Japanese Isles
Hudson Bay	400,000	1,036,000	N North America
Andaman Sea	300,000	777,000	Part of Bay of Bengal (Indian Ocean), off S coast of Asia
North Sea	201,000	520,600	Arm of N Atlantic, off coast of NW Europe
Red Sea	170,000	440,300	Arm of Indian Ocean, between N Africa and Arabian Peninsula

Great Oceans and Seas of the World *(Continued)*

Ocean or Sea	Area sq. mi.	sq. km	Location
Black Sea	164,000	424,760	SE Europe-SW Asia
Baltic Sea	160,000	414,000	N Europe
Persian Gulf	92,200	238,800	Between Iran and Arabian Peninsula
Gulf of St. Lawrence	92,000	238,280	Arm of N Atlantic, between mainland of SE Canada and Newfoundland
Gulf of California	62,600	162,100	Arm of N Pacific, between W coast of Mexico and peninsula of Lower California

Notable Mountain Peaks of the World

Name	Country or Region	Altitude ft.	m
Mt. Everest	Nepal-Tibet	29,028	8,848
K2	Kashmir	28,250	8,611
Kanchenjunga	Nepal-Sikkim	28,146	8,579
Makalu	Nepal-Tibet	27,790	8,470
Dhaulagiri	Nepal	26,826	8,180
Nanga Parbat	Kashmir	26,660	8,125
Annapurna	Nepal	26,503	8,078
Gasherbrum	Kashmir	26,470	8,068
Gosainthan	Tibet	26,291	8,013
Nanda Devi	India	25,661	7,820
Tirich Mir	Pakistan	25,230	7,690
Muztagh Ata	China	24,757	7,546
Communism Peak	Tajikistan	24,590	7,495
Pobeda Peak	Kyrgyzstan-China	24,406	7,439
Lenin Peak	Kyrgyzstan-Tajikistan	23,382	7,127
Aconcagua	Argentina	22,834	6,960
Huascarán	Peru	22,205	6,768
Illimani	Bolivia	21,188	6,458
Chimborazo	Ecuador	20,702	6,310
Mt. McKinley	United States (Alaska)	20,320	6,194
Mt. Logan	Canada (Yukon)	19,850	6,050
Cotopaxi	Ecuador	19,498	5,943
Kilimanjaro	Tanzania	19,321	5,889
El Misti	Peru	19,200	5,880
Demavend	Iran	18,606	5,671
Orizaba (Citlaltepetl)	Mexico	18,546	5,653
Mt. Elbrus	Russian Federation	18,465	5,628
Popocatépetl	Mexico	17,887	5,450
Ixtaccíhuatl	Mexico	17,342	5,286
Mt. Kenya	Kenya	17,040	5,194

Name	Country or Region	Altitude ft.	m
Ararat	Turkey	16,945	5,165
Mt. Ngaliema (Mt. Stanley)	Zaire-Uganda	16,790	5,119
Mont Blanc	France	15,781	4,810
Mt. Wilhelm	Papua New Guinea	15,400	4,694
Monte Rosa	Italy-Switzerland	15,217	4,638
Mt. Kirkpatrick	Antarctica	14,855	4,528
Weisshorn	Switzerland	14,804	4,512
Matterhorn	Switzerland	14,780	4,505
Mt. Whitney	United States (California)	14,495	4,418
Mt. Elbert	United States (Colorado)	14,431	4,399
Mt. Rainier	United States (Washington)	14,408	4,392
Longs Peak	United States (Colorado)	14,255	4,345
Mt. Shasta	United States (California)	14,161	4,315
Pikes Peak	United States (Colorado)	14,108	4,300
Mauna Kea	United States (Hawaii)	13,784	4,201
Grand Teton	United States (Wyoming)	13,766	4,196
Mauna Loa	United States (Hawaii)	13,680	4,170
Jungfrau	Switzerland	13,668	4,166
Mt. Victoria	Papua New Guinea	13,240	4,036
Mt. Erebus	Antarctica	13,202	4,024
Eiger	Switzerland	13,025	3,970
Mt. Robson	Canada (B.C.)	12,972	3,954
Mt. Fuji	Japan	12,395	3,778
Mt. Cook	New Zealand	12,349	3,764
Mt. Hood	United States (Oregon)	11,253	3,430
Mt. Etna	Italy	10,758	3,280
Lassen Peak	United States (California)	10,465	3,190
Haleakala	United States (Hawaii)	10,032	3,058
Mt. Olympus	Greece	9,730	2,966
Mt. Kosciusko	Australia	7,316	2,230

World Time Differences[†]

Amsterdam	6:00 P.M.	London	5:00 P.M.
Athens	7:00 P.M.	Madrid	6:00 P.M.
Bangkok	12:00 Mid.	Manila	1:00 A.M.*
Berlin	6:00 P.M.	Mexico City	6:00 P.M.
Bombay	10:30 P.M.	Montreal	12:00 Noon
Brussels	6:00 P.M.	Moscow	8:00 P.M.
Buenos Aires	2:00 P.M.	Paris	6:00 P.M.
Cape Town	7:00 P.M.	Prague	6:00 P.M.
Dublin	5:00 P.M.	Rio de Janeiro	2:00 P.M.
Havana	12:00 Noon	Rome	6:00 P.M.
Istanbul	7:00 P.M.	Shanghai	1:00 P.M.*
Lima	12:00 Noon	Stockholm	6:00 P.M.

[†]at 12:00 noon Eastern Standard Time
*morning of the following day

World Time Differences *(Continued)*

Sydney (N.S.W.)	3:00 A.M.*	Warsaw	6:00 P.M.
Tokyo	2:00 A.M.*	Zurich	6:00 P.M.
Vienna	6:00 P.M.		

U. S. Time Differences†

Atlanta	12:00 Noon	Los Angeles	9:00 A.M.
Baltimore	12:00 Noon	Memphis	11:00 A.M.
Boston	12:00 Noon	Miami	12:00 Noon
Buffalo	12:00 Noon	Milwaukee	11:00 A.M.
Chicago	11:00 A.M.	Minneapolis	11:00 A.M.
Cincinnati	12:00 Noon	Nashville	11:00 A.M.
Cleveland	12:00 Noon	New York	12:00 Noon
Columbus	12:00 Noon	New Orleans	11:00 A.M.
Dallas	11:00 A.M.	Omaha	11:00 A.M.
Denver	10:00 A.M.	Philadelphia	12:00 Noon
Des Moines	11:00 A.M.	Phoenix	10:00 A.M.
Detroit	12:00 Noon	Pittsburgh	12:00 Noon
El Paso	10:00 A.M.	Salt Lake City	10:00 A.M.
Honolulu	7:00 A.M.	San Diego	9:00 A.M.
Houston	11:00 A.M.	San Francisco	9:00 A.M.
Indianapolis	12:00 Noon	Seattle	9:00 A.M.
Juneau	8:00 A.M.	St. Louis	11:00 A.M.
Kansas City	11:00 A.M.	Washington, D.C.	12:00 Noon

Facts About the United States

State	*Population (1990)*	*Area (sq. mi.)*	*Capital*
Alabama	4,040,587	51,609	Montgomery
Alaska	550,403	586,400	Juneau
Arizona	3,665,228	113,909	Phoenix
Arkansas	2,350,725	53,103	Little Rock
California	29,760,021	158,693	Sacramento
Colorado	3,294,394	104,247	Denver
Connecticut	3,287,116	5,009	Hartford
Delaware	666,168	2,057	Dover
Florida	12,937,926	58,560	Tallahassee
Georgia	6,478,216	58,876	Atlanta
Hawaii	1,108,229	6,424	Honolulu
Idaho	1,006,749	83,557	Boise
Illinois	11,430,602	56,400	Springfield
Indiana	5,544,159	36,291	Indianapolis
Iowa	2,776,755	56,290	Des Moines
Kansas	2,477,574	82,276	Topeka
Kentucky	3,685,296	40,395	Frankfort
Louisiana	4,219,973	48,522	Baton Rouge

†at 12:00 noon Eastern Standard time

State	Population (1990)	Area (sq. mi.)	Capital
Maine	1,227,928	33,215	Augusta
Maryland	4,781,468	10,577	Annapolis
Massachusetts	6,016,425	8,257	Boston
Michigan	9,295,297	58,216	Lansing
Minnesota	4,375,099	84,068	St. Paul
Mississippi	2,573,216	47,716	Jackson
Missouri	5,117,073	69,674	Jefferson City
Montana	799,065	147,138	Helena
Nebraska	1,578,385	77,237	Lincoln
Nevada	1,201,833	110,540	Carson City
New Hampshire	1,109,252	9,304	Concord
New Jersey	7,730,188	7,836	Trenton
New Mexico	1,515,069	121,666	Santa Fe
New York	17,990,455	49,576	Albany
North Carolina	6,628,637	52,586	Raleigh
North Dakota	638,800	70,665	Bismarck
Ohio	10,847,115	41,222	Columbus
Oklahoma	3,145,585	69,919	Oklahoma City
Oregon	2,842,321	96,981	Salem
Pennsylvania	11,881,643	45,333	Harrisburg
Rhode Island	1,003,464	1,214	Providence
South Carolina	3,486,703	31,055	Columbia
South Dakota	696,004	77,047	Pierre
Tennessee	4,877,185	42,246	Nashville
Texas	16,986,510	267,339	Austin
Utah	1,722,850	84,916	Salt Lake City
Vermont	562,758	9,609	Montpelier
Virginia	6,187,358	40,815	Richmond
Washington	4,866,692	68,192	Olympia
West Virginia	1,793,477	24,181	Charleston
Wisconsin	4,891,769	56,154	Madison
Wyoming	453,588	97,914	Cheyenne
Washington, D.C.	606,900	63	—
Total U.S.	248,709,873		

Major U.S. Cities

Rank	City, State	Population	Rank	City, State	Population
1.	New York, N.Y.	7,333,253	11.	San Jose, Calif.	816,884
2.	Los Angeles, Calif.	3,448,613	12.	Indianapolis, Ind.	752,279
3.	Chicago, Ill.	2,731,743	13.	San Francisco, Calif.	734,676
4.	Houston, Tex.	1,702,086	14.	Baltimore, Md.	702,979
5.	Philadelphia, Pa.	1,524,249	15.	Jacksonville, Fla.	665,070
6.	San Diego, Calif.	1,151,977	16.	Columbus, Ohio	635,913
7.	Phoenix, Ariz.	1,048,949	17.	Milwaukee, Wis.	617,044
8.	Dallas, Tex.	1,022,830	18.	Memphis, Tenn.	614,289
9.	San Antonio, Tex.	998,905	19.	El Paso, Tex.	579,307
10.	Detroit, Mich.	992,038	20.	Washington, D.C.	567,094

Major U.S. Cities *(Continued)*

Rank	City, State	Population	Rank	City, State	Population
21.	Boston, Mass.	547,725	61.	Birmingham, Ala.	264,527
22.	Seattle, Wash.	520,947	62.	St. Paul, Minn.	262,071
23.	Austin, Tex.	514,013	63.	Newark, N.J.	258,751
24.	Nashville-Davidson,		64.	Anchorage, Alaska	253,649
	Tenn.	504,505	65.	Aurora, Colo.	250,717
25.	Denver, Colo.	493,559	66.	Riverside, Calif.	241,644
26.	Cleveland, Ohio	492,901	67.	Norfolk, Va.	241,426
27.	New Orleans, La.	484,149	68.	St. Petersburg, Fla.	238,585
28.	Oklahoma City, Okla.	463,201	69.	Lexington-Fayette, Ky.	237,612
29.	Fort Worth, Tex.	451,814	70.	Raleigh, N.C.	236,707
30.	Portland, Oreg.	450,777	71.	Rochester, N.Y.	231,170
31.	Kansas City, Mo.	443,878	72.	Baton Rouge, La.	227,482
32.	Charlotte, N.C.	437,797	73.	Jersey City, N.J.	226,022
33.	Tucson, Ariz.	434,726	74.	Stockton, Calif.	222,633
34.	Long Beach, Calif.	433,852	75.	Akron, Ohio	221,886
35.	Virginia Beach, Va.	430,295	76.	Mobile, Ala.	204,490
36.	Albuquerque, N. Mex.	411,994	77.	Lincoln, Nebr.	203,076
37.	Atlanta, Ga.	396,052	78.	Richmond, Va.	201,108
38.	Fresno, Calif.	386,551	79.	Shreveport, La.	196,982
39.	Honolulu, Hawaii	385,881	80.	Greensboro, N.C.	196,167
40.	Tulsa, Okla.	374,851	81.	Montgomery, Ala.	195,471
41.	Sacramento, Calif.	373,964	82.	Madison, Wis.	194,586
42.	Miami, Fla.	373,024	83.	Lubbock, Tex.	194,467
43.	St. Louis, Mo.	368,215	84.	Garland, Tex.	194,218
44.	Oakland, Calif.	366,926	85.	Hialeah, Fla.	194,120
45.	Pittsburgh, Pa.	358,883	86.	Des Moines, Iowa	193,965
46.	Cincinnati, Ohio	358,170	87.	Jackson, Miss.	193,097
47.	Minneapolis, Minn.	354,590	88.	Spokane, Wash.	192,781
48.	Omaha, Nebr.	345,033	89.	Bakersfield, Calif.	191,060
49.	Las Vegas, Nev.	327,878	90.	Grand Rapids, Mich.	190,395
50.	Toledo, Ohio	322,550	91.	Huntington Beach,	
51.	Colorado Springs, Colo.	316,480		Calif.	189,220
52.	Mesa, Ariz.	313,649	92.	Columbus, Ga.	186,470
53.	Buffalo, N.Y.	312,965	93.	Fremont, Calif.	183,575
54.	Wichita, Kans.	310,236	94.	Yonkers, N.Y.	183,490
55.	Santa Ana, Calif.	290,827	95.	Fort Wayne, Ind.	183,359
56.	Arlington, Tex.	286,922	96.	Tacoma, Wash.	183,060
57.	Tampa, Fla.	285,523	97.	San Bernardino, Calif.	181,718
58.	Anaheim, Calif.	282,133	98.	Chesapeake, Va.	180,577
59.	Corpus Christi, Tex.	275,419	99.	Newport News, Va.	179,127
60.	Louisville, Ky.	270,308	100.	Dayton, Ohio	178,540

Distances Between U.S. Cities

	Atlanta	Chicago	Dallas	Denver	Los Angeles	New York	St. Louis	Seattle
Atlanta	—	592	738	1,421	1,981	762	516	2,354
Boston	946	879	1,565	1,786	2,739	184	1118	2,831
Chicago	592	—	857	909	1,860	724	251	1,748
Cincinnati	377	255	870	1,102	1,910	613	550	2,003
Cleveland	587	307	1,080	1,216	2,054	458	558	2,259
Dallas	738	857	—	683	1,243	1,391	547	2,199
Denver	1,421	909	683	—	838	1,633	781	1,074
Detroit	619	247	1,045	1,156	2,052	486	463	1,947
El Paso	1,293	1,249	543	554	702	1,902	1,033	1,373
Kansas City	745	405	452	552	1,360	1,117	229	1,626
Los Angeles	1,981	1,860	1,243	838	—	2,624	1,589	956
Miami	614	1,199	1,405	1,911	2,611	1,106	1,123	2,947
Minneapolis	942	350	860	840	1,768	1,020	492	1,398
New Orleans	427	860	437	1,120	1,680	1,186	609	2,608
New York	762	724	1,381	1,633	2,624	—	888	2,418
Omaha	1,016	424	617	485	1,323	1,148	394	1,533
Philadelphia	667	671	1,303	1,578	2,467	95	841	2,647
Pittsburgh	536	461	1,318	1,349	2,157	320	568	2,168
St. Louis	516	251	547	781	1,589	888	—	1,890
San Francisco	2,308	1,856	1,570	956	327	2,580	1,916	687
Seattle	2,354	1,748	2,199	1,074	956	2,418	1,890	—
Washington, D.C.	547	600	1,183	1,519	2,426	215	719	2,562

Major American Holidays

New Year's Day	January 1	Labor Day	First Monday in September
Martin Luther King Day	January 15[1]	Columbus Day	October 12[4]
Inauguration Day	January 20	Veterans Day	November 11
Lincoln's Birthday	February 12[2]	Election Day	Tuesday after first Monday in November
Washington's Birthday	February 22[2]		
Good Friday	Friday before Easter	Thanksgiving Day	Fourth Thursday in November
Memorial Day	May 30[3]		
Independence Day	July 4	Christmas Day	December 25

[1]officially observed on 3rd Monday in January
[2]officially observed as President's Day on 3rd Monday in February
[3]officially observed on last Monday in May
[4]officially observed on 2nd Monday in October

Presidents of the United States

Name (and party)	State of birth	Born	Term	Died
George Washington (F)	Va.	1732	1789–1797	1799
John Adams (F)	Mass.	1735	1797–1801	1826
Thomas Jefferson (D-R)	Va.	1743	1801–1809	1826
James Madison (D-R)	Va.	1751	1809–1817	1836
James Monroe (D-R)	Va.	1758	1817–1825	1831
John Quincy Adams (D-R)	Mass.	1767	1825–1829	1848
Andrew Jackson (D)	S.C.	1767	1829–1837	1845
Martin Van Buren (D)	N.Y.	1782	1837–1841	1862
William Henry Harrison (W)	Va.	1773	1841–1841	1841
John Tyler (W)	Va.	1790	1841–1845	1862
James Knox Polk (D)	N.C.	1795	1845–1849	1849
Zachary Taylor (W)	Va.	1784	1849–1850	1850
Millard Fillmore (W)	N.Y.	1800	1850–1853	1874
Franklin Pierce (D)	N.H.	1804	1853–1857	1869
James Buchanan (D)	Pa.	1791	1857–1861	1868
Abraham Lincoln (R)	Ky.	1809	1861–1865	1865
Andrew Johnson (R)	N.C.	1808	1865–1869	1875
Ulysses Simpson Grant (R)	Ohio	1822	1869–1877	1885
Rutherford Birchard Hayes (R)	Ohio	1822	1877–1881	1893
James Abram Garfield (R)	Ohio	1831	1881–1881	1881
Chester Alan Arthur (R)	Vt.	1830	1881–1885	1886
Grover Cleveland (D)	N.J.	1837	1885–1889	1908
Benjamin Harrison (R)	Ohio	1833	1889–1893	1901
Grover Cleveland (D)	N.J.	1837	1893–1897	1908
William McKinley (R)	Ohio	1843	1897–1901	1901
Theodore Roosevelt (R)	N.Y.	1858	1901–1909	1919
William Howard Taft (R)	Ohio	1857	1909–1913	1930
Woodrow Wilson (D)	Va.	1856	1913–1921	1924
Warren Gamaliel Harding (R)	Ohio	1865	1921–1923	1923
Calvin Coolidge (R)	Vt.	1872	1923–1929	1933
Herbert Clark Hoover (R)	Iowa	1874	1929–1933	1964
Franklin Delano Roosevelt (D)	N.Y.	1882	1933–1945	1945
Harry S. Truman (D)	Mo.	1884	1945–1953	1972
Dwight D. Eisenhower (R)	Tex.	1890	1953–1961	1969
John Fitzgerald Kennedy (D)	Mass.	1917	1961–1963	1963
Lyndon Baines Johnson (D)	Tex.	1908	1963–1969	1973
Richard Milhous Nixon (R)	Cal.	1913	1969–1974	1994
Gerald R. Ford (R)	Neb.	1913	1974–1977	
James Earl Carter, Jr. (D)	Ga.	1924	1977–1981	
Ronald Wilson Reagan (R)	Ill.	1911	1981–1989	2004
George H. W. Bush (R)	Mass.	1924	1989–1993	
William J. Clinton (D)	Ark.	1946	1993–2001	
George W. Bush (R)	Conn.	1946	2001–	

F-Federalist; D-Democrat; R-Republican; W-Whig.

Forms of Address

The forms of address shown below cover most of the commonly encountered problems in correspondence. Although there are many alternative forms, the ones given here are generally preferred in conventional usage.

As a complimentary close, use "Sincerely yours," but, when particular formality is preferred, use "Very truly yours."

Government (United States)

President
Address: The President
The White House
Washington, D.C. 20500
Salutation: Dear Mr. *or* Madam
President:

Vice President
Address: The Vice President
United States Senate
Washington, D.C. 20510
Salutation: Dear Mr. *or* Madam Vice
President:

Cabinet Member
Address: The Honorable *(full
name)*
Secretary of *(name of
Department)*
Washington, D.C. *(zip
code)*
Salutation: Dear Mr. *or* Madam
Secretary:

Attorney General
Address: The Honorable *(full
name)*
Attorney General
Washington, D.C. 20530
Salutation: Dear Mr. or Madam
Attorney General:

Senator
Address: The Honorable *(full
name)*
United States Senate
Washington, D.C. 20510
Salutation: Dear Senator *(surname):*

Representative
Address: The Honorable *(full
name)*
House of Representatives
Washington, D.C. 20515
Salutation: Dear Mr. *or* Madam
(surname):

Chief Justice
Address: The Chief Justice of the
United States
The Supreme Court of
the United States
Washington, D.C. 20543
Salutation: Dear Mr. *or* Madam Chief
Justice:

Associate Justice
Address: Mr. *or* Madam Justice
(surname)
The Supreme Court of
the United States
Washington, D.C.
20543
Salutation: Dear Mr. *or* Madam
Justice:

Judge of a Federal Court
Address: The Honorable *(full
name)*
Judge of the *(name of
court; if a district court,
give district)*
(Local address)
Salutation: Dear Judge *(surname):*

Religious Leaders

Minister, Pastor, or Rector
Address: The Reverend *(full
name)*
*(Title), (name of
church)*
(Local address)
Salutation: Dear (Mr., Ms., Miss, *or*
Mrs.) *(surname):*

Rabbi
Address: Rabbi *(full name)*
(Local address)
Salutation: Dear Rabbi *(surname):*

Catholic Cardinal
Address: His Eminence *(Christian
name)* Cardinal
(surname)
Archbishop of *(province)*
(Local address)
Salutation: *Formal:* Your Eminence:
Informal: Dear Cardinal
(surname):

Forms of Address *(Continued)*

Catholic Archbishop
Address: The Most Reverend *(full name)*
Archbishop of *(province)*
(Local address)
Salutation: *Formal:* Your Excellency:
Informal: Dear
Archbishop *(surname):*

Catholic Bishop
Address: The Most Reverend *(full name)*
Bishop of *(province)*
(Local address)
Salutation: *Formal:* Your Excellency:
Informal: Dear Bishop
(surname):

Catholic Monsignor
Address: The Right Reverend
Monsignor *(full name)*
(Local address)
Salutation: *Formal:* Right Reverend
Monsignor:
Informal: Dear
Monsignor *(surname):*

Catholic Priest
Address: The Reverend *(full name), (initials of order, if any)*
(Local address)
Salutation: *Formal:* Reverend Sir:
Informal: Dear Father
(surname):

Catholic Sister
Address: Sister *(full name)*
(Name of organization)
(Local address)
Salutation: Dear Sister *(full name):*

Catholic Brother
Address: Brother *(full name)*
(Name of organization)
(Local address)
Salutation: Dear Brother *(given name):*

Protestant Episcopal Bishop
Address: The Right Reverend *(full name)*
Bishop of *(name)*
(Local address)
Salutation: *Formal:* Right Reverend
Sir *or* Madam
Informal: Dear Bishop
(surname):

Protestant Episcopal Dean
Address: The Very Reverend *(full name)*
Dean of *(church)*
(Local address)
Salutation: *Formal:* Very Reverend
Sir *or* Madam
Informal: Dear Dean
(surname):

Methodist Bishop
Address: The Reverend *(full name)*
Methodist Bishop
(Local address)
Salutation: *Formal:* Reverend Sir or
Madam:
Informal: Dear Bishop
(surname):

Mormon Bishop
Address: Bishop *(full name)*
Church of Jesus Christ of
Latter-day Saints
(Local address)
Salutation: *Formal:* Sir:
Informal: Dear Bishop
(surname):

Miscellaneous

President of a university or college
Address: (Dr., Mr., Ms., Miss, *or* Mrs.) *(full name)*
President, *(name of institution)*
(Local address)
Salutation: Dear (Dr., Mr., Ms., Miss, *or* Mrs.) *(surname):*

Dean of a college or school

  Address: Dean *(full name)*
           School of *(name)*
           (Name of institution)
           (Local address)
  Salutation: Dear Dean *(surname):*

Professor

  Address: Professor *(full name)*
           Department of *(name)*
           (Name of institution)
           (Local address)
  Salutation: Dear Professor
                 (surname):

Planets of the Solar System

	Mean Distance from Sun in Miles	*Diameter in Miles*	*Number of Satellites*
Mercury	36,000,000	3,000	0
Venus	67,000,000	7,600	0
Earth	93,000,000	7,900	1
Mars	141,000,000	4,200	2
Jupiter	489,000,000	87,000	16
Saturn	886,000,000	72,000	15
Uranus	1,782,000,000	31,000	5
Neptune	2,793,000,000	33,000	2
Pluto	3,670,000,000	1,900	1

First-Magnitude Stars (In Order of Brightness)

	*Distance in Light-Years**		*Distance in Light-Years**
Sirius	8.6	Altair	16
Canopus	700?	Betelgeuse	200
Alpha Centauri	4.3	Aldebaran	60
Vega	26	Spica	200
Capella	50	Pollux	32
Arcturus	40	Antares	400
Rigel	600?	Fomalhaut	24
Procyon	10.4	Deneb	700?
Achernar	70	Regulus	60
Beta Centauri	300	Alpha Crucis	200

*Light-year = 5,880,000,000,000 miles

Alphabetical List of the Elements

Name	Symbol	Atomic No.	Atomic Mass*	Name	Symbol	Atomic No.	Atomic Mass*
Actinium	Ac	89	(227)	Neodymium	Nd	60	144.24
Aluminum	Al	13	26.98154	Neon	Ne	10	20.18
Americium	Am	95	(243)	Neptunium	Np	93	(237)
Antimony	Sb	51	121.75	Nickel	Ni	28	58.71
Argon	Ar	18	39.948	Niobium	Nb	41	92.9064
Arsenic	As	33	74.9216	Nitrogen	N	7	14.0067
Astatine	At	85	(210)	Nobelium	No	102	(256)
Barium	Ba	56	137.34	Osmium	Os	76	190.2
Berkelium	Bk	97	(247)	Oxygen	O	8	15.999
Beryllium	Be	4	9.01218	Palladium	Pd	46	106.4
Bismuth	Bi	83	208.9808	Phosphorus	P	15	30.97376
Boron	B	5	10.81	Platinum	Pt	78	195.09
Bromine	Br	35	79.904	Plutonium	Pu	94	(242)
Cadmium	Cd	48	112.41	Polonium	Po	84	(210)
Calcium	Ca	20	40.08	Potassium	K	19	39.098
Californium	Cf	98	(249)	Praseodymium	Pr	59	140.907
Carbon	C	6	12.011	Promethium	Pm	61	(147)
Cerium	Ce	58	140.12	Protactinium	Pa	91	(231)
Cesium	Cs	55	132.9054	Radium	Ra	88	(226)
Chlorine	Cl	17	35.453	Radon	Rn	86	(222)
Chromium	Cr	24	51.996	Rhenium	Re	75	186.2
Cobalt	Co	27	58.9332	Rhodium	Rh	45	102.9055
Copper	Cu	29	63.546	Rubidium	Rb	37	85.468
Curium	Cm	96	(247)	Ruthenium	Ru	44	101.07
Dysprosium	Dy	66	162.50	Samarium	Sm	62	150.4
Einsteinium	Es	99	(254)	Scandium	Sc	21	44.9559
Erbium	Er	68	167.26	Selenium	Se	34	78.96
Europium	Eu	63	151.96	Silicon	Si	14	28.086
Fermium	Fm	100	(253)	Silver	Ag	47	107.87
Fluorine	F	9	18.99840	Sodium	Na	11	22.9898
Francium	Fr	87	(223)	Strontium	Sr	38	87.62
Gadolinium	Gd	64	157.25	Sulfur	S	16	32.06
Gallium	Ga	31	69.72	Tantalum	Ta	73	180.948
Germanium	Ge	32	72.59	Technetium	Tc	43	(99)
Gold	Au	79	196.967	Tellurium	Te	52	127.60
Hafnium	Hf	72	178.49	Terbium	Tb	65	158.9254
Helium	He	2	4.00260	Thallium	Tl	81	204.32
Holmium	Ho	67	164.9304	Thorium	Th	90	232.0381
Hydrogen	H	1	1.0079	Thulium	Tm	69	168.9342
Indium	In	49	114.82	Tin	Sn	50	118.69
Iodine	I	53	126.9045	Titanium	Ti	22	47.9
Iridium	Ir	77	192.2	Tungsten	W	74	183.85
Iron	Fe	26	55.847	Unnilhexium	Unh	106	(263)
Krypton	Kr	36	83.80	Unnilpentium	Unp	105	(260)
Lanthanum	La	57	138.91	Unnilquadium	Unq	104	(257)
Lawrencium	Lr	103	(257)	Unnilseptium	Uns	107	(262)
Lead	Pb	82	207.2	Uranium	U	92	238.03
Lithium	Li	3	6.94	Vanadium	V	23	50.941
Luletium	Lu	71	174.97	Xenon	Xe	54	131.30
Magnesium	Mg	12	24.305	Ytterbium	Yb	70	173.04
Manganese	Mn	25	54.9380	Yttrium	Y	39	88.9059
Mendelevium	Md	101	(256)	Zinc	Zn	30	65.38
Mercury	Hg	50	200.59	Zirconium	Zr	40	91.22
Molybdenum	Mo	42	95.94				

*Approx. values for radioactive elements given in parentheses.

PERIODIC TABLE OF THE ELEMENTS

Legend:

1A	
1	← Group
H	← Atomic number
1.00797	← Symbol
	← Atomic mass (Approx. values in parentheses)

1A	2A	3B	4B	5B	6B	7B	8B	8B	8B	1B	2B	3A	4A	5A	6A	7A	8A
1 H 1.00797																	2 He 4.0026
3 Li 6.939	4 Be 9.0122											5 B 10.811	6 C 12.011	7 N 14.0067	8 O 15.9994	9 F 18.9984	10 Ne 20.183
11 Na 22.9898	12 Mg 24.312											13 Al 26.9815	14 Si 28.086	15 P 30.9738	16 S 32.064	17 Cl 35.453	18 Ar 39.948
19 K 39.102	20 Ca 40.08	21 Sc 44.956	22 Ti 47.90	23 V 50.942	24 Cr 51.996	25 Mn 54.938	26 Fe 55.847	27 Co 58.933	28 Ni 58.71	29 Cu 63.54	30 Zn 65.37	31 Ga 69.72	32 Ge 72.59	33 As 74.922	34 Se 78.96	35 Br 79.909	36 Kr 83.80
37 Rb 85.47	38 Sr 87.62	39 Y 88.905	40 Zr 91.22	41 Nb 92.906	42 Mo 95.94	43 Tc (98)	44 Ru 101.07	45 Rh 102.905	46 Pd 106.4	47 Ag 107.870	48 Cd 112.40	49 In 114.82	50 Sn 118.69	51 Sb 121.75	52 Te 127.60	53 I 126.904	54 Xe 131.30
55 Cs 132.905	56 Ba 137.34	57 La 138.91	72 Hf 178.49	73 Ta 180.948	74 W 183.85	75 Re 186.2	76 Os 190.2	77 Ir 192.2	78 Pt 195.09	79 Au 196.967	80 Hg 200.59	81 Tl 204.37	82 Pb 207.19	83 Bi 208.980	84 Po (210)	85 A (210)	86 Rn (222)
87 Fr (223)	88 Ra (226)	89 Ac (227)	104 Unq (257)	105 Unp (260)	106 Unh (263)	107 Uns (262)											

Lanthanide series:

58 Ce 140.12	59 Pr 140.907	60 Nd 144.24	61 Pm (147)	62 Sm 150.35	63 Eu 151.96	64 Gd 157.25	65 Tb 158.924	66 Dy 162.50	67 Ho 164.930	68 Er 167.26	69 Tm 168.934	70 Yb 173.04	71 Lu 174.97
90 Th 232.038	91 Pa (231)	92 U 238.03	93 Np (237)	94 Pu (242)	95 Am (243)	96 Cm (247)	97 Bk (247)	98 Cf (249)	99 Es (254)	100 Fm (253)	101 Md (256)	102 No (254)	103 Lw (257)

Weights and Measures

Troy Weight
24 grains = 1 pennyweight
20 pennyweights = 1 ounce
12 ounces = 1 pound

Avoirdupois Weight
27 11/32 grains = 1 dram
16 drams = 1 ounce
16 ounces = 1 pound
100 pounds = 1 short cwt.
20 short cwt. = 1 short ton

Apothecaries' Weight
20 grains = 1 scruple
3 scruples = 1 dram
8 drams = 1 ounce
12 ounces = 1 pound

Linear Measure
12 inches = 1 foot
3 feet = 1 yard
5 1/2 yards = 1 rod
40 rods = 1 furlong
8 furlongs
(5,280 feet) = 1 statute mile

Mariners' Measure
6 feet = 1 fathom
1,000 fathoms (approx.) = 1 nautical mile
3 nautical miles = 1 league

Apothecaries' Fluid Measure
60 minims = 1 fluid dram
8 fluid drams = 1 fluid ounce
16 fluid ounces = 1 pint
2 pints = 1 quart
4 quarts = 1 gallon

Square Measure
144 square inches = 1 square foot
9 square feet = 1 square yard
30 1/4 square yards = 1 square rod
160 square rods = 1 acre
640 acres = 1 square mile

Cubic Measure
1,728 cubic inches = 1 cubic foot
27 cubic feet = 1 cubic yard

Surveyors' Measure
7.92 inches = 1 link
100 links = 1 chain

Liquid Measure
4 gills = 1 pint
2 pints = 1 quart
4 quarts = 1 gallon
31 1/2 gallons = 1 barrel
2 barrels = 1 hogshead

Dry Measure
2 pints = 1 quart
8 quarts = 1 peck
4 pecks = 1 bushel

Wood Measure
16 cubic feet = 1 cord foot
8 cord feet = 1 cord

Angular and Circular Measure
60 seconds = 1 minute
60 minutes = 1 degree
90 degrees = 1 right angle
180 degrees = 1 straight angle
360 degrees = 1 circle

Metric System

The metric system is a decimal system of weights and measures, adopted first in France, but now widespread over the world. It is universally used in science, mandatory for use for all purposes in a large number of countries, and permitted for use in most (as in U.S. and Great Britain).

The basic units are the *meter* (39.37 inches) for length, and the *gram* (15.432 grains) for mass or weight.

Derived units are the *liter* (0.908 U.S. dry quart, or 1.0567 U.S.

liquid quart) for capacity, being the volume of 1,000 grams of water under specified conditions, the *are* (119.6 square yards) for area, being the area of a square 10 meters on a side, and the *stere* (35.315 cubic feet) for volume, being the volume of a cube 1 meter on a side, the term stere being, however, usually restricted to measuring fire wood.

Names for units larger and smaller than the above are formed from the above names by the use of the following prefixes:

kilo   1,000 deka 10   centi 0.01
hecto 100   deci   0.1   milli 0.001

To these are often added mega = 1,000,000, myria = 10,000, and micro = 0.000 001. Not all of the possible units are in common use.

In many countries names of old units are applied to roughly similar metric units.

Linear Measure
10 millimeters = 1 centimeter
10 centimeters = 1 decimeter
10 decimeters = 1 meter
10 meters = 1 dekameter
10 dekameters = 1 hectometer
10 hectometers = 1 kilometer

Liquid Measure
10 milliliters = 1 centiliter
10 centiliters = 1 deciliter
10 deciliters = 1 liter
10 liters = 1 dekaliter
10 dekaliters = 1 hectoliter
10 hectoliters = 1 kiloliter

Square Measure
100 sq. millimeters = 1 sq. centimeter
100 sq. centimeters = 1 sq. decimeter
100 sq. decimeters = 1 sq. meter
100 sq. meters = 1 sq. dekameter
100 sq. dekameters = 1 sq. hectometer
100 sq. hectometers = 1 sq. kilometer

Weights
10 milligrams = 1 centigram
10 centigrams = 1 decigram
10 decigrams = 1 gram
10 grams = 1 dekagram
10 dekagrams = 1 hectogram
10 hectograms = 1 kilogram
100 kilograms = 1 quintal
10 quintals = 1 ton

Cubic Measure
1,000 cu. millimeters = 1 cu. centimeter
1,000 cu. centimeters = 1 cu. decimeter
1,000 cu. decimeters = 1 cu. meter

Foreign Alphabets

ARABIC			GREEK				HEBREW			RUSSIAN		
Letter	Name	Transliteration	Letter		Name	Transliteration	Letter	Name	Transliteration	Letter		Transliteration
ا	alif	'[1], a	A	α	alpha	a	א	aleph	- or '	А	а	a
ب	bā	b	B	β	beta	b	ב	beth	b, bh, v	Б	б	b
ت	tā	t	Γ	γ	gamma	g				В	в	v
ث	thā	th					ג	gimel	g, gh	Г	г	g
ج	jim	j	Δ	δ	delta	d	ד	daleth	d, dh	Д	д	d
ح	hā	ḥ[2]	E	ε	epsilon	e				Е	е	e, ye
خ	khā	kh	Z	ζ	zeta	z	ה	he	h	Ж	ж	zh, ż
د	dāl	d	H	η	eta	e (or ē)	ו	vav	v, w	З	з	z
ذ	dhāl	dh	Θ	θ	theta	th	ז	zayin	z	И	и	i
ر	rā	r					ח	cheth	ḥ	Й	й	ī, y, j, i
ز	zā	z	I	ι	iota	i	ט	teth	ṭ	К	к	k
س	sin	s	K	κ	kappa	k	י	yod	y, j, i	Л	л	l
ش	shin	sh	Λ	λ	lambda	l	כ ך[1]	kaph	k, kh	М	м	m
ص	ṣād	ṣ	M	μ	mu	m	ל	lamed	l	Н	н	n
ض	ḍād	ḍ	N	ν	nu	n	מ ם[1]	mem	m	О	о	o
ط	tā	ṭ	Ξ	ξ	xi	x	נ ן[1]	nun	n	П	п	p
ظ	ẓā	ẓ	O	o	omicron	o	ס	samekh	s	Р	р	r
ع	'ain	'[3]	Π	π	pi	p	ע	ayin	'	С	с	s
غ	ghain	gh	P	ρ	rho	r	פ ף[1]	pe	p, ph, f	Т	т	t
ف	fā	f	Σ	σ, ς[1]	sigma	s	צ ץ[1]	sadhe	ṣ	У	у	u
ق	qāf	q[4]	T	τ	tau	t	ק	koph	q	Ф	ф	f
ك	kāf	k	Y	υ	upsilon	y	ר	resh	r	Х	х	kh, x
ل	lām	l	Φ	φ	phi	ph	שׁ	shin	sh, ś	Ц	ц	ts, c
م	mim	m	X	χ	chi	ch, kh	שׂ	sin	ś	Ч	ч	ch, č
ن	nūn	n	Ψ	ψ	psi	ps	ת	tav	t	Ш	ш	sh, ś
ه	hā	h	Ω	ω	omega	o (or ō)				Щ	щ	shch, šč
و	wāw	w, ū								Ъ	ъ[1]	"
ي	yā	y, i								Ы	ы	y, i
										Ь	ь[2]	'
										Э	э	ė, eh, e
										Ю	ю	yu, ju
										Я	я	ya, ja

[1]Glottal stop.
[2]A voiceless pharyngeal fricative.
[3]A voiced pharyngeal fricative.
[4]A voiceless uvular stop.

[1]At end of word.

[1]At end of word.

[1]At end of word.

[1]Represents the sound (y) between an unpalatalized consonant and a vowel.
[2]Indicates that the preceding consonant is palatalized, or represents (y) between a palatalized consonant and a vowel.

Signs And Symbols

Astrology

Signs of the Zodiac

♈ Aries, the Ram
♉ Taurus, the Bull
♊ Gemini, the Twins
♋ Cancer, the Crab
♌ Leo, the Lion
♍ Virgo, the Virgin
♎ Libra, the Scales
♏ Scorpio, the Scorpion
♐ Sagittarius, the Archer
♑ Capricorn, the Goat
♒ Aquarius, the Water Bearer
♓ Pisces, the Fishes

Astronomy

Astronomical Bodies

☉ 1. the sun. 2. Sunday.
☽☾● 1. the moon. 2. Monday.
●● new moon.
☽☽☾● the moon, first quarter.
○☽ full moon.
☾☾☾● the moon, last quarter.
☿ 1. Mercury. 2. Wednesday.
♀ 1. Venus. 2. Friday.
⊕♁⊖ Earth
♂ 1. Mars. 2. Tuesday.
♃ 1. Jupiter. 2. Thursday.
♄ 1. Saturn. 2. Saturday.
♅⛢♅ Uranus.
♆ Neptune.
♇ Pluto.
✳✳ star.
☄ comet.

Biology

♂ male; a male organism, organ, or cell; a staminate flower or plant.
♀ female; a female organism, organ, or cell; a pistillate flower or plant.
▢ a male.
○ a female.
× crossed with; denoting a sexual hybrid.

Business

@ at; as in: eggs @ 99¢ per dozen.
a/c account.
B/E bill of exchange.
B/L bill of lading.
B/P bills payable.
B/R bills receivable.
B/S bill of sale.
c&f. cost and freight.
c/o care of.
L/C letter of credit.
O/S out of stock.
P&L profit and loss.
w/ with.
w/o without.
1. (before a figure or figures) number; numbered; as in: #40 thread. 2. (after a figure or figures) pound(s); as in: 20#.

Mathematics

Arithmetic and Algebra

+ 1. plus; add. 2. positive; positive value; as: +64. 3. denoting underestimated approximate accuracy, with some figures omitted at the end; as in: $\pi = 3.14159+$.
− 1. minus; subtract. 2. negative; negative value; as: −64. 3. denoting overestimated approximate accuracy, with some figures omitted at the end; as in: $\pi = 3.1416-$.
± 1. plus or minus; add or subtract; as in: $4 \pm 2 = 6$ or 2. 2. positive or negative; as in: $\sqrt{a^2} = \pm a$. 3. denoting the probable error associated with a figure derived by experiment and observation, approximate calculation, etc.
× · times; multiplied by; as in: $2 \times 4 = 2 \cdot 4$.
÷/− divided by; as in: $8 \div 2 = 8/2 = {}^8/_2 = 4$.
:/− denoting the ratio of (in proportion).
= equals; is equal to.
∷ equals; is equal to (in proportion); as in: $6 : 3 :: 8 : 4$.
≠≢ is not equal to.
≡ is identical with.
≢≢ is not identical with.
≈ is approximately equal to.
~ 1. is equivalent to. 2. is similar to.
> is greater than.
≫ is much greater than.
< is less than.
≪ is much less than.
≯ is not greater than.

≮	is not less than.
≥ ≧	is equal to or greater than.
≤ ≦	is equal to or less than.
χ	varies directly as; is directly proportional to; as in: α.
√ ⁻√	the radical sign, indicating the square root of; as in: $\sqrt{81} = 9$.
( )	parentheses; as in: $2(a + b)$.
[ ]	brackets; as in: $4 + 3 \, [a(a + b)]$.
{ }	braces; as in: $5 + b\{(a + b) \, [2 - a(a + b)] - 3\}$.

Note: Parentheses, brackets, and braces are used with quantities consisting of more than one member or term, to group them and show they are to be considered together.

∞	infinity.
%	percent; per hundred.
′ ″ ‴	prime, double prime, triple prime,
etc.	etc., used to indicate: *a.* constants, as distinguished from the variable denoted by a letter alone. *b.* a variable under different conditions, at different times, etc.
∪	union.
∩	intersection.
⊂	is a subset of.
⊃	contains as a subset.
⊄	is not a subset of.
⊅	does not contain as a subset.
Ø∧○	set containing no numbers; empty set.
∈	is a member of.
∉	is not a member of.

Geometry

∠	angle (*pl.* ∢); as in: $\angle ABC$.
⊥	1. a perpendicular (*pl.* ⊥s). 2. is perpendicular to; as in: AB ⊥ CD.
‖	1. a parallel (*pl.* ‖s). 2. is parallel to; as in: AB‖CD.
△	triangle (*pl.* ▲); as in: $\triangle ABC$.
▭	rectangle; as in: ▭ABCD.
□	square: as in: □ABCD.
▱	parallelogram; as in: ▱ABCD.
○	circle (*pl.* ⑤).
≅ ≡	is congruent to; as in: $\triangle ABD \equiv \triangle CEF$.
∼	is similar to; as in: △ACE ∼CEF.
∴	therefore; hence.
∵	since, because.
π	the Greek letter pi, representing

the ratio (3.14159+) of the circumference of a circle to its diameter.

⌢	(over a group of letters) indicating an arc of a circle; as: ⌢GH, the arc between points G and H.
°	degree(s) of arc; as in: 90°.
′	minute(s) of arc; as in: 90°30′.
″	second(s) of arc; as in: 90°30′15″.

Miscellaneous

&	the ampersand, meaning and.
&c.	et cetera; and others; and so forth; and so on.
′	foot; feet; as in: 6′ = six feet.
″	inch; inches; as in: 6′2″ = six feet, two inches.
×	1. by: used in stating dimensions; as in: 2′ × 4′ × 1′; a 2″ × 4″ board. 2. a sign (the cross) made in place of a signature by a person who cannot write; as in:

his

George × Walsh

mark.

†	1. dagger. 2. died.
‡	double dagger.
©	copyright; copyrighted.
®	registered; registered trademark.
*	1. asterisk. 2. born.
/	slash; diagonal.
¶	paragraph mark.
§	section mark.
″	ditto; indicating the same as the aforesaid: used in lists, etc.
. . .	ellipsis: used to show the omission of words, letters, etc.
˜	tilde.
ˆ	circumflex.
¸	cedilla; as in: ç.
´	acute accent.
`	grave accent.
¨	1. dieresis. 2. umlaut.
¯	macron.
˘	breve.
℞	take (L *recipe*).
°	degree(s) of temperature; as in: 99°F, 36°C.

Monetary

$	1. dollar(s), in the United States, Canada, Liberia, etc. 2.

peso(s), in Colombia, Mexico, etc. 3. cruzeiro(s), in Brazil. 4. escudo(s), in Portugal.

¢   cent(s), in the United States, Canada, etc.

£   pound(s), in United Kingdom, Ireland, etc.

p   new penny (new pence), in United Kingdom, Ireland, etc.

/s.   (formerly) shilling(s), in United Kingdom, Ireland, etc.

d.   (formerly) penny (pence), in United Kingdom, Ireland, etc.

¥   yen (*pl.* yen) in Japan.

Index